# BRADFORD'S CROSSWORD SOLVER'S DICTIONARY

# BRADFORD'S CROSSWORD SOLVER'S DICTIONARY

ANNE R. BRADFORD

Collins

Published by Collins
An imprint of HarperCollins Publishers
Westerhill Road
Bishopbriggs
Glasgow G64 2QT

Eleventh Edition 2018

10 9 8 7 6 5 4 3 2 1



First edition published by Longman; second, third and fourth editions published by Peter Collin Publishing Ltd

ISBN 978-0-00-829814-2



www.collinsdictionary.com

Typeset by Davidson Publishing Solutions, Glasgow

Printed by Thomson Press (India) Ltd



A catalogue record for this book is available from the British Library.

If you would like to comment on any aspect of this book, please contact us at the given address or online.
E-mail: dictionaries@harpercollins.co.uk
facebook.com/collinsdictionary
@collinsdict

MIX
Paper from responsible sources
FSC™ C007454

This book is produced from independently certified FSC™ paper to ensure responsible forest management.

For more information visit: www.harpercollins.co.uk/green

# Contents

# Author's Preface

Word puzzles have existed nearly as long as words themselves with examples being found during archaeological excavations. In his book, *The Anatomy of the Crossword*, D.St.P. Barnard describes letter patterns in triangular or diamantine form and an ingenious word square discovered at a Roman site at Cirencester.

Word puzzles are a source of pleasure even to quite young children. I myself remember playing a game where we each had a square grid - 5×5 or 6×6 - and we took turns choosing a letter to insert in it until all the squares were occupied, scoring points for any proper words that appeared either across the grid or down.

The Victorians were fond of acrostics, usually in verse form with the initial letters of each line giving the solution. Double acrostics went a step further with both the initial and last letters of each line being employed. At first these tended to be tributes of a sort. They became quite difficult puzzles when the initial verse was turned into a definition of the answer, and the subsequent lines became clues to the acrostic part.

We shun the light and fly by night (BAT (initial letter) OWL (final))

1. An interjection that may make you start — BoO
2. A feathered foe may pierce you to the heart — ArroW
3. A tax oft levied on a horse and cart — ToLL

Many years later we were playing a simpler version (BAT is the only answer),

My first is in cable, but not in wire,
My second in arson, but not in fire
My last is in lettuce, though not in bean
My whole in daylight is rarely seen.

Spoken word games were equally popular before the age of electronics. 'I-spy' is still with us and repetitive round games are very good for the memory. For example, 'I love my love with an A because she is - adorable', to be repeated by the next player who adds 'I love my love with a B because she is - beautiful' and on through the alphabet, but ignoring X and Z for the most part.

Acrostics were followed by the earliest form of the crossword as we know it, consisting of simple grids which allowed for both across and down answers, hence 'cross' words. The USA was the first country to provide this exercise in regular print when the *New York World* introduced it in 1913. More than a decade passed before such puzzles appeared in Britain, with *The Sunday Times* being the first to publish one, in 1925.

My mother and at least one of her sisters loved crosswords, so I was introduced to them at an early age. She had taught me to read and write long before I started school – entry in those days being after the 5th birthday – but although I had a passion for words I did no regular crossword puzzles until my late teens, and it was a few years more before I really took them seriously. I struggled with the weekly Ximenes puzzle in the weekend paper, learning many new words. He was particularly fond of 'lat' a form of pillar, so I started to write down a sort of memorandum. It was then that the idea came to me of a 'reverse dictionary' where headword and definition would change place. Full of enthusiasm, and by this time staying at home raising a family, I wrote to several leading dictionary publishers, none of whom were interested – possibly rightly so because when I pressed ahead with the project regardless, it was over 20 years before I had anything like enough material for a book. I analysed each crossword I completed (as I do still), selecting synonyms, cross references, familiar adjectives and also anagram indicators. These were entered into alphabetical files and each week I worked out the percentage already included, having a target of 70% in mind in order to make a book worthy of publication. It was quite a few years before I converted to an alphabetical main file, my back up ones being indexed by page numbers. Besides analysing puzzles I was also working my way through English dictionaries and other word books in search of further material, and barely arriving at the end of one before a new edition of another reached the market.

It was about 25 years before my labours bore fruit with the eventual appearance of *Longman's Crossword Solver's Dictionary* in 1986, but the firm was taken over by Penguin around 1990 and the reference section closed down, so I was once again seeking a publisher. A year or so later I was lucky to find Peter Collin, who published only reference works. The name *Collin's Crossword Solver's Dictionary* was unsuitable for obvious reasons, and so it became Bradford's, but might well have been Collins when this company took it on in 2002. Now, with the publication of the 11th edition of the dictionary, I am surprised to find myself still here; perhaps crosswords do keep the brain ticking over. I am certainly glad that they show no sign of disappearing under the weight of all the new types of puzzles trying to take over. I am pleased to say that my eldest daughter, Gillian, has inherited my love of crosswords and has agreed to take over editing the dictionary when the time comes.

Although I don't get involved in crossword events these days, I keep a 'finger in the pie' via *Crossword* magazine, and send sincere greetings to friends made many years ago.

Anne R. Bradford *2018*

# Solving Crossword Clues

Crossword puzzles tend to be basically 'quick' or 'cryptic'. A 'quick' crossword usually relies on a one- or two-word clue which is a simple definition of the answer required. Many words have different meanings, so that the clue 'ball' could equally well lead to the answer 'sphere', 'orb', or 'dance'. The way to solve 'quick' crosswords is to press on until probable answers begin to interlink, which is a good sign that you are on the right track.

'Cryptic' crosswords are another matter. Here the clue usually consists of a basic definition, given at either the beginning or end of the clue, together with one or more definitions of parts of the answer. Here are some examples taken from all-time favourites recorded over the years:

1. *'Tradesman who bursts into tears'* (**Stationer**)

   *Tradesman* is a definition of stationer. *Bursts* is cleverly used as an indication of an anagram, which *into tears* is of stationer.

2. *'Sunday school tune'* (**Strain**)

   Here *Sunday* is used to define its abbreviation S, *school* is a synonym for train, and put together they give strain, which is a synonym of *tune*.

3. *'Result for everyone when head gets at bottom'* (**Ache**)
   (used as a 'down' clue)

   This is what is known as an '& lit' clue, meaning that the setter has hit on a happy composition which could literally be true. *Everyone* here is a synonym for each, move the *head* (first letter) of the word to the *bottom*, and the answer is revealed, the whole clue being the definition of the answer in this case.

4. *'Tin out East'* (**Sen**)

   In this example, *tin*, implying 'money', requires its chemical symbol Sn to go *out*(side) *East*, or its abbreviation, E, the whole clue being a definition of a currency (sen) used in the East.

5. *'Information given to communist in return for sex'* (**Gender**)

   *Information* can be defined as gen; *communist* is almost always red, *in return* indicates 'reversed', leading to gen-der, a synonym for *sex*.

6. *'Row about no enclosure of this with sardines'* (**Tin-opener**)

   *Row* is a synonym for tier, *about* indicates 'surrounding', *no enclosure* can be no pen, leading to ti-no pen-er, and another '& lit' clue.

7. *'Cake-sandwiches-meat, at Uncle Sam's party'* (**Clambake**)

   *Meat* here is lamb, *sandwiches* is used as a verb, so we have C-lamb-ake, which is a kind of party in America. *Uncle Sam* or US is often used to indicate America.

8. *'Initially passionate meeting of boy and girl could result in it'* (**Pregnancy**)

   *Initially* is usually a sign of a first letter, in this case 'p' for *passionate* + Reg (a *boy*) and Nancy (a *girl*), and another clever '& lit'.

With 'cryptic' clues the solver needs to try to analyse the parts to see what he or she is looking for – which word or words can be the straight definition, and which refer to the parts or hint at anagrams or other subterfuges. Whilst it would be unrealistic to claim total infallibility, practice has shown that in most crosswords some 90% of the answers are to be found in this work.

Anne R. Bradford

# How to use the Dictionary

This dictionary is the result of sixty years' analysis of over 500,000 crossword clues, ranging from plain 'quick' crosswords requiring only synonyms to the different level of cryptic puzzles. Therefore the words listed at each entry may be connected to the keyword in various ways, such as:

- a straightforward synonym
- a commonly-associated adjective
- an associated or proper noun
- a pun or other devious play on words

Keywords are listed alphabetically; in cases where the heading consists of more than one word, the first of these words is taken to be the keyword, and in cases where the end of a word is bracketed, the material up to the opening bracket is taken to be the keyword. Keywords marked with the symbol ▸ refer the user to other entries where additional information may be found. Keywords marked with the symbol ▹ give leads to anagrams and other ploys used by crossword setters. If the keywords found in the clue do not lead directly to the required answer, the solver should look under words given as cross-references to other entries. These are indicated by the symbol →, with the cross-referenced word shown in capitals.

Some additional entries have been divided into two parts - a general entry similar to the standard entries which appear elsewhere, and a panel entry which contains a list of more specific or encyclopedic material. So, for example, the entry 'Artist(e), Artistic' includes not only a list of general words connected with 'Artist', 'Artiste', or 'Artistic' in some way, such as 'Bohemian', 'Cubist', 'Fine', and 'Virtuoso', but also a panel with the heading 'Artists' containing a list of the names of specific artists, such as 'Bellini', 'Constable', and 'Rembrandt'. For added help, the words in these panels are arranged by length, with all three-letter words grouped together in alphabetical order, then all four-letter words, then all five-letter words, and so on.

**Publisher's Note**
All words included in this publication have been sourced from crossword puzzles published in the last sixty years, and no word is excluded on the grounds of religion, gender, or race. The presence of any word does not in any way represent the views of the author or the Publisher, HarperCollins.

# The Crossword Club

If you are interested in crosswords, you might like to consider joining the Crossword Club. Membership is open to all who enjoy tackling challenging crosswords and who appreciate the finer points of clue-writing and grid-construction. The Club's magazine, *Crossword*, contains two prize puzzles each month. A sample issue and full details are available on request.

The Crossword Club
Coombe Farm
Awbridge
Romsey, Hants.
SO51 0HN
UK

email: bh@thecrosswordclub.co.uk
website address: www.thecrosswordclub.co.uk

# About the Author

Anne Bradford's love of words began to make itself evident even in her schooldays, when, as Head Girl of her school, she instituted a novel punishment – instead of making rulebreakers write lines, she had them write out pages from a dictionary, on the grounds that this was a more useful exercise. Little did she know this was soon to be her own daily routine!

As Anne tells in her preface to this edition, she conceived the idea for the dictionary pretty well along with her first child. Over the space of 25 years, Anne continued to build on her collection of solutions, analysing every crossword clue as she solved it and adding it to her steadily growing bank of entries. This unique body of material eventually reached such proportions that she had the idea of offering it to her fellow crossword solvers as a reference book, and since then, the book has gone from strength to strength, providing valuable help to countless cruciverbalists over a number of editions.

Anne Bradford continues to devote time each day to solving crosswords, averaging some 20 a week – both quick and cryptic – and still avidly collects new solutions for her *Crossword Solver's Dictionary* at a rate of around 150 a week, compiling each solution by hand (without the use of a computer!). This latest edition therefore includes much new material, gleaned by a true crossword lover who not only solves crosswords but, as an active member of the Crossword Club, can offer the user an insight into the mind of a cunning crossword compiler.

# Aa

**A, An** Ack, Adult, Ae, Alpha, Angstrom, Are, Argon, D, Ein, Her, If, L, One, Per, They
**A1** Tiptop
**AA** Milne
**Aardvark** Ant-bear, Ant-eater, Earth-hog, Ground-hog
**Aaron's Rod** Hagtaper
**Aba, Abba** Patriarch
**Abacus** Counter, Soroban
**Abaft** Astern, Sternson
**Abalone** Ormer, Paua, Perlemoen
**Abandon(ed), Abandonment** Abdicate, Abnegate, Abort, Adrift, Aguna(h), Amoral, Apostasy, Back down, Cade, Cancel, Castaway, Cast off, Chuck, Corrupt, Decommission, Defect, Derelict, → DESERT, Desolate, Desuetude, Dice, Discard, Disown, Dissolute, Disuse, Ditch, Drop, Dump, Elan, Evacuate, Expose, Flagrant, Forhoo(ie), Forhow, Forlend, Forsake, Gomorra, Gretel, Hansel, Homeless, Immoral, Jack(-in), Jettison, Jilt, Leave, Licentious, Lonely, Loose, Louche, Mad, Maroon, Old, Orgiastic, Profligate, Quit, Rakish, Rat, Relinquish, Renounce, Reprobate, Resign, Scrap, Scrub, Shed, Shelve, Sink, Strand, Vacate, Waive, Wanton, Wild, Yield
**Abase** Degrade, Demean, Disgrace, Eat crow, Embrute, Grovel, → HUMBLE, Kowtow, Lessen
**Abash(ed)** Daunt, Discountenance, Mortify, Shame-faced
**Abate(ment)** Allay, Appal, Decrescent, Deduction, Defervescence, Diminish, Ending, Let up, Lyse, Lysis, Moderate, Reduce, Remit, → SUBSIDE
▷**Abate** *may indicate* a contention
**Abattoir** Knackery, Slaughterhouse
**Abbey** Abbacy, Ampleforth, Bath, Buckfast, Cloister, Downside, Fonthill, Fountains, Glastonbury, Györ, Je(r)vaulx, Medmenham, Melrose, Minster, Nightmare, Northanger, Priory, Rievaulx, Tintern, Westminster, Whitby, Woburn
**Abbot** Aelfric, Archimandrite, Brother, Eutyches, Friar
**Abbreviate, Abbreviation** Abridge, Ampersand, Compendium, Condense, Curtail, → SHORTEN, Sigla
**ABC** Absey
**Abdicate, Abdication** Cede, Demission, Disclaim, Disown, Resign
**Abdomen** Belly, C(o)eliac, Epigastrium, Gaster, Hypochondrium, Opisthosoma, Paunch, Pleon, → STOMACH, Tummy, Venter, Ventral
**Abduct(ed), Abduction** Asport, Enlèvement, Kidnap, Rapt, Ravish, Shanghai, Steal
**Aberdeen** Granite City
**Aberrant, Aberration** Abnormal, Aye-aye, Boss, Chromatic, Deviant, Idolon, Perverse, Spherical
**Abet(tor)** Aid, Back, Candle-holder, Second
**Abeyance, Abeyant** Dormant, Shelved, Sleeping, Store
**Abhor(rent)** → DETEST, Dissent, Execrable, → HATE, Loathe, Odious, Shun
**Abide (by)** Accept, Adhere, Dwell, Inhere, → LAST, Lie, Live, Observe, Remain, Stand, Tarry
**Abigail** Maid, Masham
**Ability** Acumen, Aptitude, Calibre, Capacity, Cocum, → COMPETENCE, Efficacy, ESP, Facility, Faculty, Ingine, Initiative, Instinct, Lights, Potential, Power, Prowess, Savey, Savoir-faire, Savv(e)y, Skill, Talent, Tenacity
**Abject** Base, Craven, Grovel, Humble, Servile, Slave

**Abjure** Eschew, Forswear, Recant, Renege, Reny
**Ablaze** Afire, Alow, Ardent
**Able** Ablins, Accomplished, →ADEPT, Aiblins, Apt, Can, Capable, →COMPETENT, Fere, Fit, Idiot savant, Literate, Proficient, Seaman, Streetwise, Yibbles
**Abnegate** Disown
**Abnormal(ity)** Anomalous, Aplasia, Atypical, Autism, →DEVIANT, Dysfunction, Ectopic, Erratic, Etypical, Exceptional, Freakish, Hare-lip, Malocclusion, Odd, Peloria, Phenocopy, Preternatural, →QUEER, Sport, Teras, Trisome, Unconventional, Unnatural, Varus
**Aboard** On
**Abode** Domicile, Dwelling, Habitat, →HOME, In(n), Lain, Libken, Lien, Limbo, Midgard, Remain, Seat
**Abolish, Abolition(ist)** Abrogate, Annihilate, Annul, Axe, →BAN, D, Delete, Destroy, Eradicate, Erase, Extirpate, John Brown, Nullify, Remove, Repeal, Rescind, Scrap, Tubman, Wilberforce
**Abomasum** Read
**Abominable, Abominate, Abomination** Anathema, Bane, Cursed, →HATE, Nefandous, Nefast, Revolting, Snowman, Vile, Yeti
**Aboriginal, Aborigine** Adivasi, Ainu, Aranda, Autochthon, Awakabal, Black-fellow, Buck, Bushman, Carib, Devil's Marbles, Dharuk, Dhurga, Dieri, Diyari, Evolué, Fringe-dweller, Gurindji, Indigenous, Inuit, Kamilaroi, Kipper, Koori, Maori, Motu, Myall, Nisga'a, Nyunga(r), Pintubi, Pitjant(jat)jara, Pre-Dravidian, Sakai, San, Sican, Truganini, Vedda(h), Warlpiri, Wemba, Weniba, Wergaia, Wiradhuri, Wiradjuri, Yagara, Yupik
**Abort(ion), Abortive** Apiol, Back-street, Cancel, Chlamydial, Contagious, Ecbolic, Foeticide, Induced, Misbirth, Miscarry, Moon-calf, Slip, Sooterkin, Spontaneous, Teras, Termination
**Abound(ing)** Bristle, Copious, Enorm, Flush, Overflow, Rich, Rife, Swarm, Teem
**About** A, Almost, Anent, Around, C, Ca, Cir(c), Circa, Circiter, Concerning, Encompass, Environs, Going, Near, Of, On, Over, Re, Regarding, Round, Soon at, Upon
▷**About** *may indicate* one word around another
**Above** Abune, Aforementioned, Aloft, Over, Overhead, Overtop, Owre, Sopra, Superior, Supra-, Suspicion, Ubi supra, Upon, Us
**Abracadabra** Cantrip, Heypass
**Abrade, Abrasive** Alumina, Carbanado, Carborundum®, Chafe, Emery, Erode, File, Garnet paper, →GRATE, Ground glass, Rub, Sand(paper), Scrape, Scrat, Scuff
**Abraham** Father of the faithful, Lincoln, Patriarch, Urite
**Abreast** Afront, Alongside, Au courant, Au fait, Beside, Level, Up
**Abridge(ment)** Audley, Compress, Condense, Contract, Cut, Digest, Dock, Edit, Epitome, Pot, Shorten, Trim
**Abroad** Afield, Away, Distant, Elsewhere, Forth, Offshore, Out, Overseas
▷**Abroad** *may indicate* an anagram
**Abrogate** Abolish, Repeal, Replace, Rescind
**Abrupt(ly)** Bold, Brusque, Curt, Gruff, Jerky, Offhand, Premorse, Prerupt, Sharp, Short, Staccato, Terse
▷**Abrupt** *may indicate* a shortened word
**Abscess** Gumboil, Impost(h)ume, Ulcer, Warble
**Abscond** Absquatulate, Bolt, Decamp, Desert, Elope, Escape, Flee, Jump ship, Leg-bail, Levant, Run away, Truant, Welch, Welsh
**Abseil(ing)** Dulfer, Rappel, Roping-down
**Absence, Absent(ee), Absent-minded(ness)** A, Abs, Abstracted, Away, AWOL, Distant, Distracted, Distrait, Dreamy, Drought, Exeat, Exile, Gone, Hookey, Lack, Malingerer, Missing, Mitch, No show, Oblivious, Sabbatical, Scatty, Skip, Truant, Vacuity, Vague, Void, Wanting, Wool-gathering
**Absinthe** Wormwood
**Absolute(ly)** Arrant, Bang, Complete, Dead, Deep-dyed, Downright, Fairly, Flat, Heartily, Implicit, Indeed, Ipso facto, Just, Literally, Meer, Mere, Mondo, Nominative, Not half, Okey-doke(y), Outright, Plenary, Plumb, Quite, Real, Sheer, Simply, Thorough, Total, Truly,

Unadulterated, Unbounded, Unconditional, Unmitigated, Unqualified, Utter, Veritable, Very, Yeah

**Absolve, Absolution** Acquit, Assoil, Assoilzie, Clear, Exculpate, Excuse, Exonerate, Pardon, Redeem, Shrift, Shrive

**Absorb(ed), Absorbent, Absorbing, Absorption** Assimilate, Autism, Blot, Consume, Desiccant, Devour, Digest, Dope, Drink, Eat, → ENGROSS, Enrapt, Imbibe, Immerse, Ingest, Inhaust, Intent, Merge(r), Occlude, Occupy, Osmosis, Permeable, Porous, Preoccupation, Preoccupied, Rapt, Sorbefacient, Spongy, Subsume, Unputdownable, Yrapt

**Absquatulate** Skedaddle

**Abstain(er), Abstemious, Abstention, Abstinence, Abstinent** Band of Hope, Celibacy, Chastity, Continent, Desist, Eschew, Fast, Forbear, Forgo, Maigre, Nazarite, Nephalism, Pioneer, Rechab(ite), Refrain, Resist, Sober, Teetotaller, Temperate, TT, Virtue

**Abstract(ed), Abstraction** Abrege, Abridge, Academic, Appropriate, Brief, Compendium, Deduct, Digest, Discrete, Distrait, Dreamy, Epitome, Essence, Inconscient, Metaphysical, Musing, Notional, Précis, Preoccupied, Prepossessed, Prescind, Remove, Résumé, Reverie, Scatty, Stable, Steal, Subduct, Summary, Syllabus, Tachism

**Abstruse** Arcane, Cryptic, Deep, Esoteric, Impenetrable, Metaphysical, Obscure, Recondite, Subtle, Unclear

**Absurd(ity)** Alician, Apagoge, Charade, Cockeyed, Fantastic, Farcical, Folly, Gonzo, Inept, Irrational, Laputan, Ludicrous, Madness, Nonsense, Paradox, Preposterous, Priceless, Ridiculous, Risible, Silly, Solecism, Stupid, Surreal, Toshy, Whim-wham

**Abundance, Abundant** Abounding, A-gogo, Ample, Aplenty, Bounty, Copious, Corn in Egypt, Cornucopia, Cosmic, Excess, Flood, Flush, Fouth, Fowth, Fruitful, Galore, Lashings, Lavish, Liberal, Lots, Lush, Luxuriance, Manifold, Mickle, Mine, Mint, Muckle, Natural, Oodles, Oodlins, Opulent, Over, Plenitude, Plenteous, → PLENTIFUL, Plenty, Pleroma, Plethora, Plurisie, Profusion, Prolific, Relative, Replete, Rich, Rife, Rock and manger, Routh, Rowth, Sonce, Sonse, Store, Stouth and routh, Superabound, Surfeit, Tallents, Teeming, Tons, Uberous

**Abuse(r), Abusive** Assail, Becall, Billingsgate, Blackguard, Brutalise, Chemical, Clapperclaver, Contumely, Cruelty, Diatribe, Disparage, Drug, Ear-bashing, Elder, Exploit, Flak, Fustilarian, Fustil(l)irian, Hail, Hate mail, Ill-treat, Ill-use, Injury, Insolent, Insult, Invective, Jobbery, Limehouse, Malpractice, Maltreat, Miscall, → MISTREAT, Misuse, Mofo, Molest, Mud, Obloquy, Oppress, Opprobrium, Philippic, Rail, Rampallian, Rate, Rayle, Revile, Ritual, Satanic, Satire, Scarab(ee), Scurrilous, Serve, Sexual, Slang, Slate, Sledging, Snash, Solvent, Stick, Strap, Substance, Thersitical, Tirade, Torture, Traduce, Verbal, Vilify, Violate, Vituperation, Wosbird

**Abut** Adjoin, Border, Touch

**Abysm(al), Abyss** Avernus, Barathrum, Barranca, Chasm, Deep, Gulf, Swallet, Tartarean, Tartarus

**Abyssinia** Ethiopia

**AC** Current, Erk

**Acacia** Bablah, Boree, Brigalow, Eumong, Eumung, Fever tree, Gidgee, Gidjee, Koa, Mimosa, Mulga, Myall, Sallee, Shittim, Wattle

**Academic(ian)** A, Acca, Acker, Chair, Dean, Della-Cruscan, Don, Fellow, Hypothetic(al), Immortals, Lector, Literati, Master, Pedantic, PRA, Prof(essor), RA, Reader, Rector, Scholar

**Academy, Academic** A, Athenaeum, Bookish, City, Dollar, Donnish, Erudite, Forty, French, Hypothetic(al), Learned, Loretto, Lyceum, Manege, Military, Moot, Naval, Oxbridge, Plantilla, RA, RADA, Royal, St Cyr, Sandhurst, School, Seminary, Studious, The Shop, West Point

**Acanthus** Brankursine, Ruellia

**Accede** Defer

**Accelerate, Acceleration, Accelerator** Angular, Antedate, Betatron, Bevatron, Collider, Cosmotron, Cyclotron, Festinate, G, Gal, Grav, Gun, Hasten, Increase, Linac, Linear, Particle, Rev, Signatron, Speed, Step up, Stringendo, Supercollider, Synchrotron, Throttle

**Accent(ed), Accentuate** Acute, Beat, Breve, Brogue, Bur(r), Circumflex, Cut-glass, Doric, Drawl, Emphasise, Enclitic, Enhance, Gammat, Grave, Hacek, Intonation, Kelvinside, Lilt,

Long, Macron, Marcato, Martelé, Mockney, Morningside, Mummerset, Nasal, Orthotone, Oxford, Oxytone, Paroxytone, Perispomenon, Pitch, Primary, Proparoxytone, Rhotic, Rhythm, Rinforzando, Secondary, Sforzando, Stress, Tittle, Tone, Tonic, Twang

**Accentor** Dunnock

**Accept(able), Acceptance, Accepted, Accepting** A, Accede, Adequate, Admit, Adopt, Agree, Allow, Alright, Approbate, Bar, Believe, Buy, Can-do, Common, Compliant, Conform, Consent, Cool, Cosher, Decent, Done, Eligible, Embrace, Epenthesis, Face, Fatalism, Freeload, Going, Grant, Idee recue, Include, Kosher, Meet, Nod, Obey, On, Orthodox, Pass muster, Pocket, Proper, Putative, Realise, Receive, Recognise, Resipiscence, Respectable, Satisfactory, Settle, Stand, Stomach, Street cred, Suppose, Swallow, Take (on board), Tolerate, U, Uptake, Valid, Wear, Welcome, Widespread

**Access(ible), Accessibility, Accession** Aisle, A portee, Arrival, Avenue, Blue-jacking, Card, Come-at-able, Conditional, Credit, Direct, Door, Entrée, → ENTRY, Fit, Gangway, Gateway, Get-at-able, Hack, Hatchway, Ingo, Key, Log in, Log on, Manhole, Near, Open, Passe-partout, Passkey, Password, Phreaking, Ping, Random, Recourse, Remote, Sequential, Slip road, Sociable, Spasm, Superuser, Tap into, Telnet, To hand, Unrestricted, User name, Wayleave

**Accessory, Accessories** Abettor, Addition, Aide, Ally, Ancillary, Appendage, Appurtenance, Attachment, Attribute, Bandanna, Bells and whistles, Belt, Cribellum, Cuff-links, Extra, Findings, Fitment, Nicety, Scarf, Staffage, Trappings, Trimming, Umbrella

**Accident(al)** Adventitious, Arbitrary, Bechance, Blowdown, Blunder, Calamity, Casualty, → CHANCE, Circumstance, Contingency, Contretemps, Crash, Criticality, Dent, Disaster, Double flat, Fall, Fluke, Fortuitous, Hap, Hit and run, Inadvertent, Meltdown, Mischance, Mishap, Note, Pile up, Prang, Promiscuous, Random, Rear-ender, Serendipity, Shunt, Smash, Smash-up, Spill, Stramash, Unintentional, Unmeant, Wreck

**Accidie** Acedia, Sloth, Torpor

**Acclaim** Accolade, Applaud, Brava, Bravo, Cheer, Clap, Credit, Eclat, Encomium, Fame, Fanfare, Hail, Honour, Kudos, Ovation, Praise, Salute, Toast, Zindabad

**Acclimatise** Adapt, Attune

**Accolade** Award, Brace, Dubbing, Honour, Palm, Token, Tribute

**Accommodate, Accommodating, Accommodation** Accustom, Adapt, Almshouse, Amenable, B and B, Bedsit, Berth, Billet, Board, Botel, Bunkhouse, Camp, Chalet, Chambers, Compromise, Crashpad, Digs, Flotel, Gaff, Gite, Grace and favour, Hall, Homestay, Hostel, Hotel, House, Houseboat, Humour, Lend, Loan, Lodge, Lodgement, Minshuku, Motel, → OBLIGE, Parador, Pension, Penthouse, Pew, Pied a terre, Pliant, Prefab, Quarters, Rapprochement, Recurve, Room, Sheltered, Single-end, Sorehon, Stabling, Stateroom, Steerage, Storage, Tent, Timeshare, Wharepuni, Xenodochium, Youth hostel

▷**Accommodating** *may indicate* one word inside another

**Accompany(ing), Accompanied (by), Accompaniment, Accompanist** Accessory, Alberti, And, Attach, Attend, Backing, Chaperone, Chum, Concomitant, Consort, Continuo, Descant, Duenna, Enclose, → ESCORT, Fixings, Harmonise, Herewith, Obbligato, Obligate, Obligato, Repetiteur, Side-dish, Side-order, Soundtrack, Tag along, Trimmings, Vamp, Wag, Wasabi

**Accomplice** Abettor, Aide, → ALLY, Bagman, Bonnet, Collaborator, Confederate, Cope(s)-mate, Federarie, Federary, Partner, Shill, Stale, Swagsman

**Accomplish(ed), Accomplishment** Able, → ACHIEVE, Arch, Attain, Char(e), Clever, Complete, Consummate, Deed, Done, Doss, Effect, Expedite, Exploit, Fulfil, Galant, Master, Over, Perform, Polished, Prowess, Put through, Realise, Ripe, Savant, Skill, Success, Tour de force

**Accord, According(ly), According to** After, Agree, Ala, Allow, As per, Attune, Befit, Chime, Comply, Congree, Consensus, Give, Grant, Harmony, Jibe, Meech Lake, Meet, One, Per, So, Sort, Thus, Unison

**According to nature** SN

**Accordion** Bandoneary, Bandoneon, Button, Concertina, Flutina, Piano, Squeeze-box

**Accost** Abord, Approach, Collar, Greet, Hail, Importune, Molest, Solicit, Tackle, Waylay

**Account(s)** AC, Anecdote, Answer, Appropriation, Audit, Bank, Battels, Behalf, Bill, Books,

Budget, Cause, Charge, Checking, Chequing, Chronicle, Control, Credit, Current, Debit, Deposit, Description, Detailed, Discretionary, Drawing, Due, Enarration, Expense, Explain, Explanation, Exposition, Interim, ISA, Joint, Lawin, Ledger, Log, Long, Memoir, Narration, Nominal, Nostro, Numbered, Overdue, Procès-verbal, Real, Reason, Recital, Record, Regest, Register, Relation, →REPORT, Repute, Résumé, Sake, Savings, Short, Statement, Suspense, Swindlesheet, Tab, Tale, TESSA, The estimated, Thesis, Trust, Version, Viable, Vostro

**Accountable** Responsible

**Accountancy, Accountant** Auditor, Bean counter, Bookkeeper, CA, Certified, Cost, Double entry, Forensic, Hyde, Liquidator, Purser, Reckoner, Single entry, Vestry-clerk

**Accoutrement** Frontlet

**Accredit** Attribute

**Accrue** Earn, Grow

**Accumulate, Accumulation** Accrue, Adsorb, Aggregate, →AMASS, Augment, Backlog, Build, Collect, Drift, Drusen, Fortune, Gather, Hoard, Laitance, Lodg(e)ment, Multiply, Oedema, Pile, Pool, Rack up, Rollover, Run up, Save, Stack, Stockpile, Uplay

**Accuracy, Accurate(ly)** Bang-on, Cocker, →CORRECT, Dead-on, Exact, Fair, Faultless, Fidelity, Griff, Minute, Precise, Realistic, Right, Split second, Spot-on, To scale, True, Unerring, Veracious, Word-perfect

**Accursed** Argued, Blest, Blist, Damned, Sacred

**Accusation, Accuse(d)** Allege, Arraign, Asperse, Attaint, Bill, Blame, Calumny, Censure, Challenge, Charge, Criminate, Denounce, Dite, Gravamen, Impeach, Impute, Incriminate, Indictment, Information, Libel, Name, Panel, Plaint, Prosecute, Recrimination, Suspect, Tax, Threap, Threep, Traduce, Wight, Wite, Wyte

**Accustom(ed)** Acclimatise, Acquaint, Adjust, Attune, Enure, Familiar, General, Habituate, Harden, Inure, Seasoned, Teach, Wont, Woon

**Ace(s)** Aviator, Basto, Blackjack, Crabs, Crack, Demon, Dinger, →EXPERT, Jot, Master, Mega, Mournival, One, Quatorze, Smashing, Spadille, Spadill(i)o, Spot, Tib, Virtuoso, Whizz, Wonderful

**Acerbate, Acerbic(ity)** Astringent, Intensify, Sarcasm, Trenchant

**Acetylene** Carbide, Ethyne

**Ache, Aching** Aitch, Die, Hunger, Long, Mulligrubs, Nag, Otalgia, Pain, Sore, Stitch, Stound, Stownd, Throb, Work, Yearn, Yen

**Achieve(ment)** Accomplish, Acquisition, Attain, Big League, Come, Compass, Coup, Cum laude, →EFFECT, Enacture, Exploit, Feat, Fulfil, Gain, Hatchment, Height, Masterpiece, Realise, Res gestae, Satisfice, Satisfy, Stroke, Succeed, Threepeat, Triumph, Trock, Troke, Truck

**Achilles** Heel, Tendon

**Achromatic** Piperic

**Acid(ity)** Acrimony, Biting, Corrosive, Drop, Etchant, Hydroxy, Reaction, Ribosomal, Ribozyme, Sharp, Solvent, Sour, Tart, Vinegar, Vitriol

---

**ACIDS**

*2 letters:*
PH

*3 letters:*
DNA
EPA
GLA
HCL
LSD
Oxo
RNA

*4 letters:*
Acyl
Dopa
PABA
Pyro
Uric
Wood

*5 letters:*
Algin
Amide
Amino
Auric
Boric
Caro's
Eisel
Fatty
Folic
Iodic
L-dopa
Lewis
Malic
Mucic
Oleic
Orcin
Osmic
Trona

*6 letters:*
Acetic
Adipic
Bromic
Capric
Cholic
Citric
Cyanic
Domoic
Erucic
Formic
Gallic
Lactic
Lauric
Leucin
Lipoic

Lysine
Maleic
Marine
Niacin
Nitric
Oxalic
Oxygen
Pectic
Phenol
Picric
Quinic
Serine
Sialic
Sorbic
Tannic
Tiglic
Toluic
Valine

***7 letters:***
Abietic
Acrylic
Alanine
Alginic
Benzoic
Butyric
Caproic
Cerotic
Chloric
Chromic
Creatin
Cystine
Ellagic
Eugenic
Ferulic
Folacin
Fumaric
Fusidic
Glycine
Guanine
Leucine
Malonic
Meconic
Melanic
Muramic
Nitrous
Nucleic
Orcinol
Peracid
Plumbic
Proline
Prussic
Pteroic
Pyruvic
Racemic
Sebacic
Selenic
Silicic
Stannic
Stearic
Suberic
Terebic
Titanic
Valeric
Vanadic
Xanthic
Xylonic

***8 letters:***
Abscisic
Adenylic
Arginine
Ascorbic
Aspartic
Butanoic
Caprylic
Carbamic
Carbolic
Carbonic
Chlorous
Cinnamic
Creatine
Cresylic
Crotonic
Cyclamic
Cysteine
Decanoic
Ethanoic
Fulminic
Glutamic
Glyceric
Glycolic
Guanylic
Hippuric
Hydracid
Iopanoic
Itaconic
Linoleic
Lysergic
Manganic
Margaric
Molybdic
Muriatic
Myristic
Nonanoic
Palmitic
Periodic
Phthalic
Retinoic
Rhodanic
Succinic
Sulfonic
Tantalic
Tartaric
Telluric
Tungstic
Tyrosine
Uridylic
Valproic

***9 letters:***
Aqua-regia
Carnitine
Cevitamic
Citydylic
Dichromic
Glutamine
Histidine
Hydrazoic
Hydriodic
Isocyanic
Linolenic
Mefenanic
Methanoic
Nalidixic
Nicotinic
Ornithine
Panthenic
Pectolite
Pentanoic
Polybasic
Propanoic
Propenoic
Propionic
Saccharic
Salicylic
Sassolite
Selenious
Sulphonic
Sulphuric
Tellurous
Threonine

***10 letters:***
Aquafortis
Asparagine
Barbituric
Carboxylic
Citrulline
Dithionous
Dodecanoic
Glucuronic
Glutamatic
Glutaminic
Hyaluronic
Isoleucine
Margaritic
Methionine
Neuraminic
Omega fatty
Orthoboric
Pelargonic
Perchloric
Phosphonic
Phosphoric
Proprionic
Pyrogallic
Ricinoleic
Thiocyanic
Thymidylic
Trans-fatty
Tryptophan

***11 letters:***
Arachidonic
Butanedioic
Decanedioic
Ethanedioic
Ferricyanic
Ferrocyanic
Gibberellic
Hydnocarpic
Hydrobromic
Hydrocyanic
Hyponitrous
Methacrylic
Octanedioic
Pantothenic
Permanganic
Phosphorous
Ribonucleic
Sarcolactic
Taurocholic
Tryptophane

***12 letters:***
Dicraboxylic
Hydrochloric
Hydrofluoric
Hypochlorous
Indoleacetic
Orthosilicic
Persulphuric
Phenylalanin
Polyadenalic
Propanedioic
Prostacyclin
Pyroligneous
Terephthalic

***13 letters:***
Galactosamine
Heptadecanoic
Indolebutyric

Phenylalanine
Prostaglandin
Pyrosulphuric
Thiosulphuric
Transbutadoic

*14 letters:*
Hypophosphorus
Hyposulphurous
Metaphosphoric
Peptide nucleic
Polyphosphoric
Pyrophosphoric

*15 letters:*
Orthophosphoric
Paramenobenzone
Pteroylglutamic
Trichloroacetic

*16 letters:*
Deoxyribonucleic
Triiodothyronine

---

**Acknowledge(ment)** Accept, Acclaim, Admit, Agnise, Allow, Answer, Apologise, Avow, Cognovit, Con, Concede, Confess, Credit, Grant, Greet, Mea culpa, Nod, Own, Profess, React, Receipt, Recognise, Reply, Resipiscence, Respect, Righto, Roger, Salute, Ta, Thank you, Touché, Wilco, Yo

**Acme** Apex, Apogee, Climax, Comble, Crest, Peak, Summit, Top, Zenith

**Acne** Blemish, Spots

**Acolyte** Chela, Minion, Nethinim, Novice, Server, Thurifer

**Acorn(s), Acorn-shell** Balanus, Glans, Mast, Rac(c)ahout, Valonia

**Acoustic(s)** Harmonics, Phenocamptics, Phonics, Sonics

**Acquaint(ance), Acquainted** Advise, Au fait, Bowing, Cognisant, Contact, Enlighten, Familiar, → **INFORM**, Knowledge, Nodding, Notify, Slight, Tell, Versed

**Acquiesce(nce), Acquiescent** Accede, Accept, Amenable, Bow, Comply, Conform, Resigned, Righto, Roger, Wilco, Yield

**Acquire, Acquisition, Acquisitive** Acquest, Adopt, Adsorb, Come by, Consume, Cop, Earn, Ern, Gain, → **GET**, Glom, Grasping, Greedy, Inherit, Irredentist, Land, Learn, Obtain, Procure, Purchase, Rapacity, Secure, Steal, Take-over, Target, Usucap(t)ion, Wangle

**Acquit(tal)** Absolve, Assoil, Cleanse, Clear, Exonerate, Free, Loose, Loste, Pardon, Vindicate

**Acre(s)** A, Area, Bigha, Hide, Rival, Rood

**Acrid, Acrimonious, Acrimony** Acid, Bitter(ness), Empyreuma, Mordant, Pungent, Resentment, Rough, Sour, Spleen, Surly, Virulent, Vitriolic

**Acrobat(s), Acrobatics** Equilibrist, Gymnast, Hot dog, Jerry-come-tumble, Ropedancer, Rope-walker, Speeler, Splits, Trampoline, Trick cyclist, Tumbler, Wing-walker

**Acropolis** Citadel, Parthenon

**Across** A, Ac, Athwart, Betwixt, O'ed, Opposite, Over, Through, Transit

**Act(ing), Action, Active, Acts** A, Actus reus, Affirmative, Afoot, Amdram, Antic, Assist, Assumpsit, Atonement, Auto, Barnstorm, Barrier, Battle, Behave, Bit, Blitz, Business, Byplay, Camp, Campaign, Capillary, Caretaker, Case, Caster, Catastasis, Cause, Charade, Class, Come, Conduct, Consolation, Consolidation, COPPA, Coup, Daff, Deal, Declaratory, → **DEED**, Delaying, Deputise, Detinue, Dido, Direct, Do, DORA, Double, Enabling, Enclosure, Epitasis, Evasive, Excitement, Exert, Exploit, Factory, Feat, Feign, Forthcoming, Forth-putting, Function, Go slow, Habeas corpus, Histrionic, Homestead, Houdini, Identic, Impersonate, Impro(visation), Improbation, Incident, Industrial, Interim, Juristic, Lance-jack, Law, Lawsuit, Litigate, Local, Lock-out, Locutionary, Maino(u)r, Manner, Masterstroke, Measure, Method, Mime, Movement, Mum, Mutiny, Navigation, Onstage, Outtake, Overt, Partypiece, Pas, Perform(ance), Perlocutionary, Personate, Play, Positive, Pp, Practice, Pretence, Private, Procedure, Process, Public, Qua, Quia timet, Qui tam, Quiver, Rearguard, Reflex, Reform bill, Replevin, Represent, Reprobator, Riot, Rising, Roleplay, Routine, Sasine, Scenery, Secondary, Septennial, Serve, Settlement, Sham, Showdown, Shtick, Sick-out, Simulate, Speech, Sprightly, Stamp, Stanislavski, Statute, Steps, Strike, Stunt, Suit, Supporting, Synergy, Tactic, Terminer, Test, Theatricise, Thellusson, Thing, Transitory, Treat, Trover, Truck, Turn, Twig, Uniformity, Union, Vicegerent, Walk-out, War, Windlass

**Actinium** Ac

**Actinon** An

**Activate** Arm, Energise, Engage, Goad, Spark, Spur, Stur, Styre, Trigger

**Active, Activist, Activity** A, Aerobic, Agile, Agitator, Alert, Alive (and kicking), Animated, Astir, At, Athletic, Biko, Brisk, Business, Bustle, Busy, Cadre, Campaigner, Deedy, DIY, Do(ing), Dynamited, Dynamo, Ecowarrior, Effectual, Energetic, Energic, Erupting, Exercise, Extra-curricular, Floruit, Fluster, Game, Go-go, Goings-on, Hum, Hustle, Hyper, In play, Leish, Licht, Live, Mobile, Motile, Niche Market, Nightlife, Nimble, Nippy, Ongo, On the go,

Op, Operant, Optical, Overdrive, Play, Rambunctious, Residual, Shenanigan, Sideline, Spree, Sprightly, Springe, Spry, Sthenic, Stir, Strenuous, Surge, Third house, Vacuum, Voice, Wick, Wimble, Working, Ya(u)ld, Zionist

**Actor(s), Actor-like** Agent, Alleyn, Artist, Ashe, Barnstormer, Benson, Betterton, Bit player, Borgnine, Brando, Burbage, Cast, Character, Comique, Company, Co-star, Diseur, Donat, Equity, Gable, Garrick, Gielgud, Guiser, Ham, Hamfatter, Heavy, Histrio(n), Impersonator, Jay, Juve(nile), Kean, Keaton, Luvvie, MacReady, Mime(ster), Morley, Mummer, Olivier, O'Toole, Pantomimist, Performer, Player, Playfair, Protagonist, RADA, Roscian, Roscius, Savoyard, Scofield, Sim, Spear-carrier, Stager, Strolling, Super, Theatrical, Thespian, Tragedian, Tree, Tritagonist, Trouper, Understudy, Ustinov, Utility man, Wolfit

**Actress** Bankhead, Bow, Buffa, Dietrich, Duse, Figurant, Garbo, Harlow, Ingenue, Loren, Pierrette, Siddons, Soubrette, Starlet, Swanson, Terry, West

**Actual(ity), Actually** De facto, Entelechy, Literal, Live, Material, Physical, Real, Real-life, Tangible, True, Very

**Actuate, Actuator** Suppository

**Acumen, Acuity** Insight, Nous, Sense, Shrewdness

**Acupressure** Jin shin do, Shiatsu

**Acupuncture** Moxa, Stylostixis

**Acute** Astute, Dire, Fitché, Incisive, → INTENSE, Keen, Quick-witted, Sharp

▸**Ad** *see* ADVERT(ISE)

**Adage** Aphorism, Byword, Gnome, Maxim, Motto, Paroemia, Proverb, Saw, Saying, Truism

**Adam** Bede, Delved, Jailer, Motherless

**Adamant** Firm, Inexorable, Insistent, Obdurate, Rigid, Unbending

**Adam's ale** Water

**Adapt(er), Adaptable, Adaptation, Adaptor** Acclimatise, Adjust, Arrange, Bushing, Coevolution, Convert, Ecad, Elastic, Evolve, Flexible, Modify, Naturalise, Persona, Pliant, Refashion, Rehabilitate, Reorient, Resilient, Tailor, Timeserver, Transform, Versatile, Version

**Add(ed), Addendum, Adder, Adding** Accrue, Adscititious, Affix, Annex, → APPENDIX, Attach, Cast, Contribute, Coopt, Count, Death, Dub, Ech(e), Eik, Eke, Elaborate, Embroider, Enhance, Enlarge, Forthgoing, Fortify, Gain, Insert, Lace, More, Plus, Puff, Ramp up, Reckon, Reinforce, Retrofit, Score, Spike, Sum, Summate, Tack on, Top up, Tot(e), Total, Viper

**Addict(ion), Addicted, Addictive** Abuser, Acid freak, Acidhead, A colt's tooth, Alcoholic, Base head, Blunthead, Buff, Chocoholic, Cokehead, Couch potato, Dependency, Devotee, Dope-fiend, Dopehead, Drug, Etheromaniac, Fan, Fiend, Freak, Given, Glue-sniffing, Habit-forming, Hophead, Hound, Hype, Jones, Joypopper, Junkie, Lover, Mainliner, Mania, Moreish, Narcotist, Need, Opiate, Opioid, Opium, Pillhead, Pillpopper, Pothead, Shooter, Shopaholic, Slave, Smackhead, Snowbird, Space-cadet, Speedfreak, Stoner, Sybaritism, Theism, User, Vinolent, Wino, Workaholic

**Addison** Spectator

**Addition(al), Additive** Accession, Accompaniment, Addend, Additive, Adipate, Adjunct, Adscititious, Adulterant, Advene, Also, And, Annexure, Antiknock, Appendage, (As an) in, Bolt-on, Booster, Braata, Carrag(h)anin, Carrageenan, Codicil, Corollary, Cyclamate, Dextran, Eik, Eke, Encore, E-number, Epexegesis, Epithesis, Etc, Excess, Extender, Extension, → EXTRA, Extramural, Extraneous, Footnote, Further, Implant, → IN ADDITION, Increment, Mae, Makeweight, Mo, Monkey, New, Odd, On, On top, Other, Padding, Paragog(u)e, Parergon, Plus, Preservative, PS, Rider, Ripieno, Spare, Spice, Suffect, Suffix, Supplementary, Surcharge, Thereto, Top-up, Verandah, Wing

**Address, Address system** Accommodation, Accost, Adroit, Allocution, Apostrophe, Apostrophise, Appellation, Art, → ATLAS, Ave, Bach, Bub, Buster, Call, Cariad, Chuck, Compellation, Cousin, Dedication, Delivery, Den, Diatribe, Direction, Discourse, Effendi, Election, Epilogue, Epirrhema, Esquire, Gettysburg, Gospodin, Hail, Home, Homily, Inaugural, Invocation, IP, Jimmy, Kiddo, Lala, Lecture, Letterhead, Lincoln, Mac, Mester, Milord, Mister, Mush, My Lord, Mynheer, Nkosi, Ode, Orate, Parabasis, Past master, Pastoral, Peptalk, Poste-restante, Prelection, Relative, Rig, Salute, Sermon, Sir(ree), Sirrah, Speech, Squire, Stance, Tact, Tannoy®, Telegraphic, → TITLE, Towkay, Tuan, URL, Valedictory, Wambenger, Web(site), Wus, Y'all, You-all

**Adduce** Cite
**Adelphic** Adam
**Adept** Able, Adroit, Buff, Dab, Deacon, Don, → EXPERT, Fit, Handy, Mahatma, Master, Past master
**Adequate** Condign, Does, Due, Egal, Equal, Ere-now, Passable, Proper, → SUFFICIENT, Tolerable, Valid
**Adhere(nt), Adherence, Adhesive** Allegiance, Ally, Araldite®, Believer, Blutack®, Bond, Burr, Cement, Child, Cling, Conform, Cow Gum®, Dextrin, Disciple, Emplastic, Epoxy, Fidelity, Follower, Glair, Glue, Goldsize, Guebre, Gum, Hot-melt, Impact, Isinglass, Jain(a), Leech, Loyalist, Mixtion, Moonie, Mucilage, Nomism, Partisan, Paste, Resin, Sealant, Sectator, Servitor, Stand pat, Sticker, Superglue, Supporter, Synechia, Votary, Waterglass
**Adjacent, Adjoining** Bordering, Conterminous, Contiguous, Handy, Neighbouring, Nigh
**Adjective** Adnoun, Attribution, Epithet, Gerundive
**Adjourn(ment)** Abeyance, Defer, Delay, Moratoria, → POSTPONE, Prorogate, Recess, Rise, Suspend
**Adjudicate, Adjudication, Adjudicator** Arbiter, Decide, Judge, Jury, Referee, Try, Umpire
**Adjunct** Addition, Aid, Ancillary, Rider
**Adjure** Obtest
**Adjust(able), Adjustment, Adjuster** Acclimatise, Accommodate, Adapt, Attune, Calibrate, Coapt, Confirm, Dress, Ease, Fine-tune, Fit, Focus, Gang, Gauge, Gear, Gerrymander, Handicap, J'adoube, Modify, Modulate, Orientate, Prepare, Preset, Primp, Redo, Redress, Reduce, Regulate, Reorientate, Reset, Resize, Retrofit, Scantle, Scotopia, Set, Sliding, Sort, Suit, Tailor, Temper, Toe-in, Tram, Trim, True, Tune, Tweak, Twiddle, Vernier
▷**Adjust** *may indicate* an anagram
**Adjutant** Aide, Argala, Officer, Stork
**Adler** Irene
**Ad-lib** Ex tempore, Extemporise, Improv(ise), Wing it
**Administer, Administrate, Administration, Administrator** Adhibit, Anele, Apply, Arrondissement, Bairiki, Bureaucrat, Control, Corridors of power, Curia, → DIRECT, Dispence, Dispense, Executive, Front office, Governor, Intendant, Intinction, Leadership, → MANAGE, MBA, Penpusher, Pepys, Provost, Raj, Regime, Registrar, Run, Secretariat, Soke, Steward, Sysop, Trustee, Whitehall
**Admirable, Admiration, Admire(d), Admirer** Adulation, Aesthete, Beau, Bee's knees, Clinker, Clipper, Conquest, Crichton, Envy, Esteem, Estimable, → EXCELLENT, Fine, Flame, Fureur, Gaze, Gem, Ho, Iconise, Idolater, Laudable, Lionise, Partisan, Popularity, Rate, Regard, Respect, Revere(nce), Ripping, Rocking, Splendid, Stotter, Suitor, Swain, Toast, Tribute, Venerate, Wonder, Worthy, Wow
**Admiral** Adm, AF, Anson, Beatty, Beaufort, Benbow, Blake, Bligh, Boscawen, Butterfly, Byng, Byrd, Capitan, Drake, Effingham, Fisher, High, Hood, Hornblower, Howard, Jellicoe, Keyes, Marrowfat, Mountbatten, Navarch, Nelson, Old Grog, Port, Raeder, Rear, Red, Rodney, Spee, Sturdee, Togo, Vanessa, Van Nieman, Van Tromp, Vice, White
**Admiralty** Sea-board
**Admission, Admit(ter), Admit(ting), Admitted, Admittance** Accept, Access, Acknowledge, Agree, Allow, Avow, Cognovit, Concede, → CONFESS, Enter, Entrée, Entry, Estoppel, Gateman, Give, Grant, Induct, Ingress, Initiate, Intromit, Mea culpa, Ordain, Ordination, Owe, Own (up), Privy, Recognise, Shrift, Take, Tho(ugh), Turnstile, Yield
**Admonish, Admonition** Advice, Caution, Chide, Lecture, Moralise, Pi-jaw, Rebuke, Reprimand, → SCOLD, Tip, Upbraid, Warn
**Ado** Bother, Bustle, Fuss, Lather
**Adolescence, Adolescent** Bobbysoxer, Bodgie, Developer, Grower, Halflin, Immature, Juvenile, Neanic, Puberty, Teenager, Tweenager, Veal, Widgie, Youth
**Adonais** Keats
**Adonis** Pheasant's Eye
**Adopt(ed)** Accept, Affect, Affiliate, Allonym, Assume, Catch on, Dalt, Embrace, Espouse, Father, Foster, Latch on, Mother, Take up

**Adoration, Adore(r), Adoring** Doat, Dote, Goo-goo, Homage, Idolise, Latria, Love, Pooja(h), Puja, Revere, Venerate, Worship, Zoolater

**Adorn(ed), Adornment** Antefix, Aplustre, Attrap, Banderol, Bedeck, Bedight, Begem, Bejewel, Caparison, Clinquant, Deck, Dight, Drape, Embellish, Emblaze, Emblazon, Embroider, Enchase, Equip, Festoon, Flourish, Furnish, Garland, Garnish, Grace, Graste, Jewellery, Ornament, Ornate, Riband, Story, Tassel, Tattoo, Tatu, Tinsel, Trappings

**Adrenaline** Epinephrin(e)

**Adrift** Aimless

**Adroit(ness)** Address, Adept, Clever, Dextrous, Expert, Neat, Skilful, Slick

**Adulate, Adulation** Flatter(y), Praise, → **WORSHIP**

**Adullam** Cave

**Adult** Amadoda, Consenting, Grown-up, Imago, Man, Mature, Upgrown, X

**Adulterant, Adulterate** Cut, Debase, Impurify, Lime, Load, Mix, Multum, → **POLLUTE**, Sophisticate, Weaken

**Adulterer, Adulterous, Adultery** Avoutery, Co-respondent, Cuckold, Extra-marital, Fornication, Francesca, Lenocinium, Two-timer, Unfaithful

**Adumbrate** Outline

**Advance(d), Advancement** A, Abord, Accelerate, Ahead, Anabasis, Ante, Approach, Ascend, Assert, Better(ment), Breakthrough, Bring on, Charge, Come, Develop, Early, Edge, Elevation, Evolué, Extreme, Far, Fast-forward, Fore, Forge, Forrit, Forward, Further, Gain, Get on, Grubstake, Haut(e), Hi-tec(h), Impress, Imprest, Incede, Late, Lend, → **LOAN**, March, Mortgage, On(ward), Onrush, Outcome, Overture, Pass, Piaffe, Posit, Postulate, Precocious, Predestination, Prefer, Prepayment, Prepone, Prest, Process, Progress, → **PROMOTE**, Propose, Propound, Push, Retainer, Ripe, Rise, Scoop, Step, Sub, Submit, Tiptoe, Top end, Ultramodern, Upfront, Upgang, Voorskot

**Advantage(ous)** Accrual, Ad, Aid, → **ASSET**, Avail, Batten, Benefit, Bisque, Boon, Boot, Bright, Edge, Emolument, Expedient, Exploit, Favour, Forehand, Fruit, Gain, Grouter, Handicap, Handle, Head-start, Help, Impose, Inside (track), Interess, Interest, Key, Lever(age), Mechanical, Mess of pottage, Nonmonetary, Obvention, Odds, One-up, Oneupmanship, Oyster, Pecuniary, Percentage, Plus, Privilege, Prize, Pro, Pull, Purchase, Sake, Salutary, Serviceable, Start, Stead, Strength, Toe-hold, Trade, Trump card, Upper-hand, Upside, Upstage, Use, Van, Whiphand, Whipsaw

**Advent(ist)** Coming, Shaker

**Adventure(r), Adventuress, Adventurous** Argonaut, Assay, Aunter, Bandeirante, Bold, Buccaneer, Casanova, Condottiere, Conquistador, Dareful, Daring, Emprise, Enterprise, Escapade, → **EXPLOIT**, Filibuster, Gallant, Gest, Lark, Mata Hari, Mercenary, Merchant, Picaresque, Picaro, Picaroon, Risk, Routier, Rutter, Swashbuckler, Vamp, Viking, Voyage

**Adversary** Antagonist, Anti, Arch-enemy, Cope(s)mate, Enemy, Foe, Nemesis, Opponent

**Adverse, Adversity** Calamity, Cross, Down, Downside, Hardship, Harrow, Misery, Reversal, Setback, Unfavourable, Untoward, Woe

**Advert(ise), Advertisement, Advertiser, Advertising** Above the line, Ad, Air, Allude, Attack, Banner, Bark, Bill, Blipvert, Blurb, Circular, Classified, Coign(e), Coin, Commercial, Copy, Corporate, Direct mail, Display, Dodger, Earpiece, Flier, Flyer, Flyposting, Flysheet, Hard sell, Hype, Infomercial, Jingle, Knocking copy, Madison Avenue, Mailshot, Market, Niche, Noise, → **NOTICE**, Out, Packshot, Parade, Personnel, Placard, Playbill, Plug, → **POSTER**, Proclaim, Promo, Promote, Promulgate, Prospectus, Puff, Quoin, Refer, Sandwich board, Semisolus, Shoutline, Showbill, Signwrite, Skyscraper, Sky-write, Splash, Sponsor, Spot, Stunt, Subliminal, Teaser, Tele-, Throwaway, Tout, Trailer, Trawl, Want(s) (ad), Wrap around

**Advice** Careers, Conseil, Counsel, → **GUIDANCE**, Guideline, Helpline, Information, Invoice, Opinion, Pointer, Read, Recommendation, Re(e)de, Reed, Tip (off)

**Advise(d), Adviser, Advisable** Acquaint, Aide, Apprise, Assessor, Avise(ment), Back-seat driver, Brains trust, CAB, Cabal, Camarilla, Consigliere, Consultant, Cornerman, Counsel, Egeria, Enjoin, Enlighten, Exhort, Expedient, Forewarn, Genro, Indicate, Induna, Inform, Instruct, Mentor, Monitor, Notify, Oracle, Peritus, Politic, Prudent, Ralph, → **RECOMMEND**, Starets, Staretz, Tutor, Urge, Warn, Weld, Wise

**Advocacy** Encouragement
**Advocate(d)** Agent, Argue, Attorney, Back, Barrister, Campaigner, Counsel, Devil's, Endorse, Exponent, Gospel, Intercede, Lawyer, Move, Paraclete, Peat, Peddle, Pleader, Pragmatist, Preach, Proponent, Protagonist, Silk, Statist, Suffragette, Syndic, Urge
**Aeon** Hadean, Phanerozoic
**Aerate** Ventilate
**Aerial** Aeolian, Aery, Antenna, Beam, Clover, Clover leaf, Communal, Dipole, Directional, Dish, Ethereal, Ferrite-rod, Folded dipole, Frame, Ground-plane, Lead-in, Long-wire, Loop, Minidish, Parabolic, Rhombic, Satellite dish, Slot, Squarial, Yagi
**Aerobatics** Stunt
**Aerobic(s)** Pilates, Step, Zumba®
**Aerodrome** →**AIRPORT**, Landing field, Rotor-station
**Aerodynamics** Slipstream, Spoiler
**Aerofoil** Spoiler, Tab, Tailplane, Trimtab
▸**Aeroplane** *see* **AIRCRAFT**
**Aerosol** Atomiser, Flyspray, Ioniser, Mace®
**Aesir** Loki
**Aesthete, Aesthetic** Arty, Beautiful, Essene, Poseur, Tasteful
**Affable, Affability** Amiable, Avuncular, Benign, Bonhomie, Cordial, Gracious, Hearty, Pleasant, Suave, Urbane
**Affair(s)** Amour, Business, Carry on, Cerne, Concern, Current, Dalliance, Dreyfus, Effeir, Effere, Event, External, Extra-marital, Fight, Fling, Foreign, Go, Indaba, Internal, Intrigue, Liaison, Matter, Pash, Pidgin, Pi(d)geon, Ploy, Relationship, Res, Romance, Shebang, Situation, Subject, Thing
**Affect(ed), Affectation, Affection(ate), Affecting** Air, Airtsy-mairtsy, Alter, Artificial, Arty, Assume, Breast, Camp, Chi-chi, Childerowing, Concern, Cordial, Crachach, Crazy, Distress, Effete, Emotive, Endearment, Euphuism, Foppery, Frappant, Genteel, Grip, Haw-haw, Heart, Heartstrings, High-camp, High-sounding, Hit, Impress, Intimate, Ladida, Ladyism, Lah-di-dah, Lovebirds, Lovey-dovey, Mannered, Mimic, Mimmick, Minauderie, Mincing, Minnick, Minnock, Mouth-made, Mwah, Phoney, Play at, →**POSE**, Poseur, Precieuse, Preciosity, Pretence, Pretentious, Prick-me-dainty, Prosy, Side, Smitten, Spoilt, Stag(e)y, Stir, Storge, Stricken, Strike, Supervene, Susceptible, Sway, Sympathetic, Synthetic, Tender, Topophilia, Touched, Touchy-feely, Tushery, Twee, Unction, Unnatural, Upend, Vain, Warm, Yah
**Affiliate(d), Affiliation** Adopt, Align, Associate, Cognate, Merge, Unite
**Affinity** Bro, Intimacy, Kin(ship), Penchant, Rapport, Tie
**Affirm(ative), Affirmation** Assert, Attest, Avow, Maintain, Positive, Predicate, Profess, Protestation, State, Uh-huh, →**VERIFY**, Yebo
**Affix(ed)** Append, Ascribe, →**ATTACH**, Connect, Fasten, On
**Afflict(ed), Affliction** Aggrieve, Ail, Asthma, Cross, Cup, Curse, Dead leg, Disease, Furnace, Harass, Hay fever, Hurt, Lacerate, Lumbago, Molest, Nosology, Oppress, Palsy, Persecute, Pester, Plague, Scourge, Smit, Sore, →**SORROW**, Stricken, Teen, Tene, Tic, Tine, Tribulation, →**TROUBLE**, Try, Unweal, Visitation, Woe
**Affluence, Affluent** Abundance, Dinky, Ease, Fortune, Grey panther, Inflow, Moneyed, Opulence, Upmarket, Wealth
**Afford** Allow, Bear, Give, Manage, Offer, Provide, Run to, Spare, Yield
**Affray** Brawl, Fight, Fracas, Free-for-all, Mêlée, Scuffle, Skirmish
**Affront(ed)** Assault, Defy, Facer, Indignant, →**INSULT**, →**OFFEND**, Outrage, Scandal, Slight, Slur, Snub
**Afghan(istan)** Bactria, Dard, Hound, Kaf(f)ir, Pakhto, Pakhtu, Pashto, Pashtu, Pathan, Pushto(o), Pushtu, Taliban
**Afloat** Aboard, Abroach, Adrift, Buoyant, Natant
**Afoot** Astir, Up
**Aforesaid** Above, Same
**Afraid** Adrad, Alarmed, Chicken, Fearful, Funk, Insecure, Nesh, Rad, Regretful, Scared, Timorous, Windy, Yellow

**Afresh** De novo

**Africa(n)** Abyssinian, Adamawa, Akan, Algerian, Angolan, Ashanti, Baganda, Bambara, Bantu, Barbary, Barotse, Basotho, Basuto, Bechuana, Beento, Bemba, Beninese, Berber, Biafran, Bintu, Black, Boer, Botswana(n), Burundu, Bushman, Cairene, Carthaginian, Chewa, Chichewa, Ciskei, Congo(l)ese, Cushitic, Dagomba, Damara, Dark continent, Dinka, Duala, Dyula, Efik, Eritrean, Ethiopian, Eve, Fang, Fantee, Fanti, Fingo, Flytaal, Fula(h), Gabonese, Galla, Gambian, Ganda, Gazankulu, Grikwa, Griqua, Guinean, Gullah, Hamite, Hausa, Herero, Hutu, Ibibio, Ibo, Igbo, Impi, Ivorian, Kabyle, Kenyan, Khoikhoi, Khoisan, Kikuyu, Kongo, Kushite, Lango, Lesotho, Liberian, Libyan, Lowveld, Lozi, Luba, Luo, Maghreb, Maghrib, Malagasy, Malawi, Malian, Malinke, Mande, Mandingo, Mandinka, Masai, Mashona, Matabele, Mende, Moor, Moroccan, Mosotho, Mossi, Mozambican, Mswahili, Munt(u), Mzee, Nama(qua), Namibian, Ndebele, Negrillo, → NEGRO, Ngoni, Nguni, Nilot(e), Nubian, Nuer, Numidian, Nyanja, Oromo, Ovambo, Pedi, Pied noir, Pondo, Pygmy, Qwaqwa, Rastafarian, Rhodesian, Rwandan, Sahelian, San, Senegalese, Shilluk, Shluh, Shona, Somali, Songhai, Songhay, Sotho, Soweto, Sudanese, Susu, Swahili, Swazi, Tanzanian, Temne, Tiv, Togolese, Tonga, Transkei, Transvaal, Tshi, Tsonga, Tswana, Tuareg, Tunisian, Tutsi, Twi, Ugandan, Uhuru, Venda, Voltaic, Waswahili, Watu(t)si, Wolof, X(h)osa, Yoruban, Zairean, Zulu

**Afrikaan(s), Afrikaner** Cape Dutch, Mynheer, Taal, Volk, Voortrekker

**After(wards)** About, A la, At, Behind, Belated, Beyond, Eft, Epi-, → LATER, Next, On, Once, Past, Post hoc, Rear, Since, Sine, Subsequent, Syne

**Afterbirth** Secundines, Sooterkin

**Afterimage** Photogene

▷**After injury** *may indicate* an anagram

**Afterlife** Other world, The Great Beyond, Valhalla

**Aftermath** Consequence, Debris, Fall out, Legacy, Mow(ing), Rawing, Rawn, Rowan, Rowen, Rowing, Sequel(a), Wake

**Afternoon** A, Arvo, Ex-am, PM, Postmeridian, Undern

**Afterpiece, Afterthought** Addendum, Codicil, Epimetheus, Exode, Footnote, Note, PS, Supplement

**Aftertaste** T(w)ang

**Afterword** Postlude

**Again** Afresh, Agen, Ancora, Anew, Back, Bis, De novo, Ditto, Do, Eft, Eftsoons, Encore, Iterum, Mair, More, Moreover, O(v)er, Re-, Recurrence, Reprise, Than, Then

**Against** A, Anent, Anti, Beside, Con, Counter, For, Gainsayer, Hostile, Into, Nigh, On, One-to-one, Opposing, To, V, Versus

**Agape** Feast, Hiant, Ringent, Yawning

**Agar** Blood

**Agate** Chalcedonyx, Moss, Murr(h)a, Onyx, Ruin

**Agave** Aloe, Century plant, Henequen, Lily, Maenad, Maguey, Sisal

**Age(d), Ages, Aging** Absolute, Achievement, Ae, Aeon, Aet, Alcheringa, Anno domini, Antique, Archaise, Atomic, Augustan, Azilian, Bronze, Calpa, Century, Chair-days, Chellean, Coon's, Copper, Cycle, Dark, Date, Day, Discretion, Distress, Doddery, Eld, Elizabethan, Eon, Epact, Epoch(a), Era, Eternity, Generation, Gerontic, Golden, Grey, Heroic, Hoar, Hore, Ice, Information, Iron, Jazz, Jurassic, Kaliyuga, Kalpa, La Tene, Lias, Magdalenian, Maglemosian, Mature, Mental, Mesolithic, Middle, Millennium, Neolithic, New, New Stone, Of, Old, Oligocene, Paleolithic, Passé, Periclean, Period, Phanerozoic, Pre-Cambrian, Progeria, Radiometric, Reason, Reindeer, Saros, Season, S(a)eculum, Senescence, Senility, Silver, Solera, Space, Steam, Stone, Teens, Third, Time, Troisieme, Villanovan, Wear, Wrinkly, Yellow, Yonks, Yug(a)

**Ageless** Classic, Evergreen

**Agency, Agent** Advertising, Agitator, Alkylating, Ambassador, Antistatic, Art, Autolysin, Bailiff, Baking soda, Bargaining, Barm, Bicarb(onate), Bond, Botex, Broker, BSI, Bureau, Buyer, Catalyse, Catalyst, Cat's paw, Cause, Chelating, Chemical, Child support, CIA, Commis, Commission, Complexone, Comprador(e), Confidential, Consul, Consular, Counter, Countryside, Crown, Customs, Dating, Defoaming, Del credere, Developing, Dicumaral,

Disclosing, Distributor, Doer, Double, Emissary, Emulsifier, Emulsifying, Environment, Envoy, Enzyme, -er, Escort, Estate, Exciseman, Executant, Executor, Express, Factor, FBI, Fed, Federal, Finger, Flack, Forwarding, Free, Galactagogue, G-man, Go-between, Good offices, Hand, Hirudin, House, Implement, Indian, Influence, Institorial, Instrument, Intermediary, Isinglass, Itar Tass, Kinase, Land, Law, Leavening, Legate, Literary, Magic bullet, Man, Masking, Mata Hari, Means, Medium, Melanin, Mercantile, Mitogen, Mole, Moral, Mouthwash, Mutagen, Narc, Narco, Nerve, Ninja, Nucleating, OO, Operation, -or, Orange, Order paper, Oxidizing, Parliamentaire, Parliamentary, Patent, Pathogen, Pawn, Peace corps, Penetration, Pinkerton, Press, Procurator, Provocateur, Proxy, Publicist, Realtor, Reducing, Rep(resentative), Resident, Reuters, Riot, Road, Runner, Salesman, Secret (service), Setter, Shipping, Ship's husband, SIS, Sleeper, Solvent, Soman, Spook, Spy, Steward, Stock(broker), Surfactant, Syndic, Tass, Teratogen, Third party, Ticket, Tiger team, Tool, Training, Travel, UNESCO, Vakeel, Vakil, Virino, Voice, Welfare, Wetting, Wire service, Yeast

**Agenda** Business, Hidden, Order paper, Programme, Remit, Schedule

**Aggie** Agnes, Ines, Nessa, Nesta

**Aggravate** Annoy, Compound, Exacerbate, Exasperate, Harass, Inflame, Irk, Needle, Nettle, Provoke, Rankle, Try, Vex

**Aggregate, Aggregation** Ballast, Congeries, Corporation, Detritus, Etaerio, Eumerism, Granulite, Gravel, Group, Hard core, Manifold, Number, Omnium, Ore, Ped, Sum, Total

**Aggression, Aggressive(ly), Aggressor, Aggro** Anti-Imperialism, Arsey, Assertive, Attack, Bad ass, Ballbreaker, Bare-knuckle, Battleaxe, Bellicose, Belligerent, Biffo, Bovver, Bullish, Butch, Combative, Defiant, Enemy, Feisty, Foe, Go-getter, Growl, Gungho, Hard-hitting, Hawk, Hysterical, Imbrocate, Invader, In-your-face, Kick-ass, Laddish, Lairy, Macho, Militant, Nasty, On-setter, Pushing, Rambo, Rampant, Road rage, Sabre-rattling, Self-assertive, Shirty, Tooth and nail, Truculent, Violent, Wild

**Aggrieve(d)** Miff, Sore

**Agile** Acrobatic, Deft, Lissom(e), Nifty, Nimble, Quick, Sprightly, Spry, Supple, Swank, Twinkletoes, Wiry

**Agitate(d), Agitation, Agitator** Acathisia, Activist, Ado, Aflutter, Agitprop, Akathisia, Alarm, Arouse, Betoss, Boil, Bolshie, Bother, Bristling, Chartist, Churn, Commotion, Commove, Convulse, Delirium, Demagogue, Discompose, Dismay, Distraught, → **DISTURB**, Doodah, Ebullient, Emotion, Euoi, Euouae, Evovae, Excite, Extremist, Fan, Fantad, Fanteeg, Fantigue, Fantod, Ferment, Firebrand, Flap, Flurry, Fluster, Flutter, Fraught, Frenzy, Fuss, Fusspot, Goad, Heat, Hectic, Het (up), Impatience, Jabble, Jumpy, Kerfuffle, Khilafat, Lather, Militant, Overwrought, Panicky, Pedetic, Perturb, Poss, Pother, Protest, Rabble-rouser, Rattle, Restless, Rouse, Ruffle, Seethed, Shake, Sod, Stew, Stir(-up), Swivet, Tailspin, Taking, Tempest(uous), Tenterhooks, Tew, Thermal, Tizzy, Toss, Tremor, Trepidation, Trouble, Turbulent, Turmoil, Tweak, Twitchy, Twittery, Unrest, Upset, Welter, Whisk, Wrought up, Young Italy, Ytost

▷**Agitate** *may indicate* an anagram

**Agley** Awry, Unevenly

**Aglow** Alight, Fervid, Tipsy

▶**Agnes** *see* **AGGIE**

**Agnostic** Laodicean

**Ago** Bygone, Lang syne, Of yore, → **SINCE**

**Agog** Astir, Athirst, Eager, Excited, Keen, Pop-eyed

**Agonise, Agony** Ache, Anguish, Brood, Dead thraw, Dread, Ecstasy, Heartache, → **PAIN**, Throe(s), Torment, Torture

**Agree(ing), Agreed, Agreement** Accede, Accept, Accord, Acquiescence, Adhere, Agt, Align, Aline, Allow, Amen, Analog(ue), Analogy, Apply, Articles, As one, Assent, Assort, Atone, Ausgleich, Aye, Bilateral, Bipartite, Bond, Cahoots, Camp David, Cartel, Champerty, Charterparty, Chime, Closing, Coincide, Collective, Comart, Community, Compact, Comply, Comport, Concensus, Concert, Concord(at), Concordance, Concur, Condone, Conform, Congree, Congruent, Consension, Consensus, → **CONSENT**, Consentience, Consist, Consonant, Contract, Contrahent, Contrat, Convention, Correspond, Cotton,

Covenant, Covin, Covyne, Cushty, Dayton Accords, Deal, Deffo, Deign, Determine, Done, Embrace, Entente, Equate, Escrow, Fadge, Finalise, Gatt, Gentleman's, Handfast, Harmony, Homologous, Identity, Indenture, Jibe, Knock-for-knock, League, Like-minded, Mercosur, Munich, National, Net Book, Nod, Non-con, Nudum pactum, Okay, On, Pact(um), Pair, Placet, Plant, Plea bargaining, Predetermine, Prenuptial, Procedural, Productivity, Protocol, Rabat(te), Recognise, Reconcile, Repo, Repurchase, Rhyme, Right(o), Right on, Roger, Sanction, Schengen, Service, Settlement, Side, Sort(ance), Specialty, Sponsion, Square, Standstill, Substantive, Suit, Sweetheart, Sympathy, Synastry, Sync(hronise), Synesis, Syntony, Tally, Technology, Test-ban, Threshold, Trade, Treaty, Trucial, Uh-huh, Unanimous, Union, Unison, Unity, Unspoken, Wilco, Wukkas, Yah, Yalta, Yea, Yea-say, Yes

**Agreeable** Amene, Comfy, Harmonious, Kind, Melodic, Obliging, Palatable, Pleasant, Sapid, Sweet, Well-disposed, Willing, Winsome

**Agriculture, Agricultural(ist)** Arval, Ceres, Farming, Geoponic, Georgic, Inari, Moshav, Permaculture, Slash and burn, Smallholding, Tull

**Aground** Ashore, Beached, Sew, Stranded

**Ague** Dumb, Exies

▷**Ague(ish)** *may indicate* an anagram

**Ah** Ach, Ay

**Ahead** Anterior, Before, Fast, Foreship, Forward, Frontwards, In store, Onward, Precocious, Trendsetting, Up

**Aiblins** Perhap, Perhaps, Yibbles

**Aid(s), Aide** Accessory, ADC, Adjutant, Adviser, Artificial, Assist, Audiovisual, Audiphone, Baby-walker, Caliper, Crampon, Crutch, Decca, → DEPUTY, Ear-trumpet, First, Foreign, Fresh-card, Galloper, Gift, Grant, Hearing, Help(line), Key, Legal, Lend-lease, Lifebelt, Life-saver, Mnemonic, Monitor, Monocle, Optophone, Orthosis, PA, Paralegal, Realia, Red Crescent, Red Cross, Relief, Satnav, Seamark, Second, Serve, Sex, Sherpa, Stepping-stone, Subsidy, Subvention, Succour, Support, Teaching, Visual, Yeoman('s) service, Zimmer®

**AIDS** Slim

**Ail(ment), Ail(ing)** Affect, Afflict(ion), Complaint, Croup, Disease, Disorder, Enteritis, Gout, Malady, Misorder, Narks, Occupational, Pink-eye, Pip, Queasy, Sickness, Suffer, TB, Unwell

**Aim** Approach, Aspire, Bead, Bend, End, Ettle, Eye, Goal, Hub, Intent, Level, Mark, Mint, Mission, Object, Peg, Plan, Plank, Point, Point blank, Purpose, Quest, Reason, Sake, Seek, Sight(s), Target, Tee, Telos, Train, Try, View, Visie, Vizy, Vizzie, Zero-in

**Aimless** Adrift, Drifting, Erratic, Haphazard, Random, Unmotivated

**Air(s), Airer, Air-space, Airy** Aerate, Aerial, Aero, Affectation, Allure, Ambiance, Ambience, Anthem, Appearance, Aquarius, Arietta, Arioso, Atmosphere, Attitude, Aura, Bearing, Breath, Calypso, Canzona, Canzone, Cavatina, Clothes horse, Compressed, Dead, Demaine, Descant, Ditty, Draught, Dry, Emphysema, Ether(eal), Expose, Fan, Filmy, Fixed, Flimsy, Front, Gemini, Greensleeves, Heat-island, Heaven, Horse, Hot, Inflate, Libra, Lift, Light, Liquid, Look, Lullaby, Madrigal, Maiden, Manner, Melody, Microburst, Mien, Night, Nitre, Oat, Open, Oxygen, Ozone, Parade, Periptery, Pneumatic, Poseur, Radio, Screen, Scuba, Serenade, Serenata, Serene, Shanty, Side, Sinus, Sky, Slipstream, Solo, Song, Strain, Swank, Thin, Tidal, Trigon, → TUNE, Vent, Ventilate, Vital, Wake, Wind

**Airbed** Lilo®

**Airborne** Ab, Uprisen

**Air Chief Marshal** Dowding

**Air-conditioning** Plenum system

**Aircraft, Airship** Aerodyne, Aerostat, Angels, AST, Auster, Autoflare, Autogiro, Autogyro, Aviette, Avion, Battleplane, Biplane, Blimp, Boeing, Brabazon, Bronco, Broomstick, Camel, Canard, Canberra, Cessna, Chaser, Chopper, Coleopter, Comet, Concorde, Convertiplane, Corsair, Crate, Cropduster, Cyclogiro, Delta-wing, Dirigible, Dive-bomber, Doodlebug, Dornier, Drone, Eagle, Enola Gay, Eurofighter, F, Ferret, Fixed-wing, Flivver, Flying fortress, Flying wing, Fokker, Freedom-fighter, Freighter, Galaxy, Glider, Gotha, Gyrodyne, Gyroplane, Hang-glider, Harrier, Hawkeeze, Heinkel, Helicopter, Helo, Hercules, Hindenburg, Hunter, Hurricane, Hypersonic, Interceptor, Intruder, Jet star, Jumbo, Jump-jet, Kite, Lancaster,

Liberator, Lifting-body, Liner, Link trainer, Lysander, Messerschmitt, Microjet, Microlight, Microlite, MIG, Mirage, Monoplane, Mosquito, Moth, Multiplane, Nacelle, Nightfighter, Nightfinder, Nimrod, Oerlikon, Orion, Ornithopter, Orthopter, Parasol, Penguin, Phantom, → PLANE, Provider, Prowler, Pusher, Ramjet, Red Arrows, Rigid, Rotaplane, Runabout, Scout, Scramjet, Semi-rigid, Shackleton, Skiplane, Skyhawk, Skytrain, Sopwith, Sopwith Camel, Spaceship, Spitfire, SST, Stack, Starfighter, Starlifter, Stealth bomber, STOL, Stratocruiser, Stratotanker, Stuka, Super Sabre, Sweptwing, Swing-wing, Tankbuster, Taube, Taxiplane, Thunderbolt, Thunderchief, Tomcat, Tornado, Torpedo bomber, Towplane, Tracker, Trident, Tri-jet, Triplane, Tube, Turbofan, Turbo-jet, Turbo-prop, Turboramjet, Variable geometry, Vertical takeoff, Vessel, Vigilante, Viking, Viscount, Vomit comet, Voodoo, VTOL, War bird, Widebody, Wild weasel, Zeppelin

**Aircraftsman, Airman** AC, Aeronaut, AR, Bleriot, Co-pilot, Erk, FL, Fokker, Kiwi, LAC, Loadmaster, Observer, RAF, Red Arrows

**Aircraftswoman** Penguin, Pinguin

▸**Airfield** *see* AIRPORT

**Air force** Luftwaffe

**Airless** Close, Stuffy

**Airlift** Thermal

**Airline, Airway** Aeroflot, Anthem, BAC, BEA, Bronchus, Carrier, Duct, Easy Jet, El Al, Iberia, JAL, KLM, Larynx, Lot, Lyric, Purple, Qantas, Ryanair, SAS, S(ch)norkel, Trochea, TWA, Upcast, Vent, Weasand(-pipe), Windpipe

▸**Airman** *see* AIRCRAFTSMAN, FLIER(S)

**Airmen** Red Arrows

**Airport** Chiang Kai Shek, Drome, Dulles, Dyce, Entebbe, Faro, Gander, Gatwick, Greenham Common, Heliport, Idlewild, John Lennon, Kennedy, La Guardia, Landing strip, Le Bourget, Lod, Luton, Lydda, Lympne, Malev, Miami, O'Hare, Orly, Pearson, Prestwick, Ronaldsway, Runway, Shannon, Stansted, Stolport, Tegal, Terminal, Vertiport, Wick

**Air-raid** Blitz, Mission

**Air-tight** Hermetic, Indisputable, Sealed

**Aisle** Catwalk, Cross, Gangway

**Aitch** Ache, Aspirate, H

**Ajar** Agee

**Ajax** Lav, Loo

**Aka** Alias

**Akimbo** Spread

**Akin** Alike, Cognate, Congener, Kindred, Related, Sib

**Alabaster** Oriental

**Alacrity** Readiness

**Alarm(ed), Alarming, Alarmist** Affear, Affright, Agitation, Alert, Arouse, Bell, Bleep, Bugaboo, Caution, Clock, Concern, Dismay, Eek, False, Fire, Flap, Fricht, Fright, Frit, Ghast, Hairy, Larum, Panic, Perturb, Radio, Rock, Rouse, Scaremonger, Siren, Smoke, Startle, Tirrit, Tocsin, Trepidation, Tripwire, Unease, Unnerve, Warn, Worry, Yike(s)

**Alas** Ah, Alack, Ay, Eheu, Ha, Haro, Harrow, Io, Lackadaisy, Lackaday, O, Oh, Ohone, O me, Ou, Sadly, Waesucks, Waly, Wel(l)away, Well-a-day, Wellanear, Woe

**Alaskan** AK, Aleut, Che(e)chako, Sourdough, Tlingit, Yupik

**Alb** Sticharion

**Alban** Berg

**Albanian** Arna(o)ut

**Albatross** Alcatras, Black-footed, Golf, Gooney(-bird), Millstone, Omen, Onus, Quaker-bird, Wandering

**Albeit** Tho(ugh)

**Albert** Chain, Chevalier, Consort, Hall, Herring, Slang

**Albion** Perfidious

**Album** Autograph, Looseleaf, LP, Photo, Record, Stamp

**Albumen, Albumin** Chalaza, Glair, Leucosin, Mucin, Myogen, Protein, Ricin, Serum, Treadle, Treddle, White

**Alchemic, Alchemist, Alchemy** Adept, Arch-chimic, Brimstone, Cagliostro, Faust(us), Hermetic(s), Multiplier, Orpiment, Paracelsus, Quicksilver, Sal ammoniac, Sorcery, Spagyric, Spagyrist, Witchcraft

**Alcides** Hercules

**Alcohol(ic)** Absolute, Acrolein, Aldehyde, Amyl, Bibulous, Blue ruin, Booze, Borneol, Butyl, Catechol, Cetyl, Chaptalise, Cholesterol, Choline, Citronellol, Cresol, Denatured, Diethyl, Diol, Dipsomaniac, Drinker, Ethal, Ethanol, Ethyl, Farnesol, Feni, Fenny, Firewater, Fusel-oil, Geraniol, Glycerin(e), Grain, Grog, Gut-rot, Hard, Hard stuff, High-proof, Inebriate, Inositol, Isopropyl, Jakey, Jungle juice, Lauryl, Linalool, Lush, Mahua, Mahwa, Malt, Manniferous, Mannite, Mannitol, Mercaptan, Mescal, Mescalin(e), Methanol, Meths, Methyl, Moonshine, Mow(r)a, Nerol, Phytol, Pisco, Plonko, Polyol, Potato spirit, Propyl, Pyroligneous, Rotgut, Rubbing, Rubby, Scrumpy, Secondary, Snake juice, Sorbitol, Sphingosine, Spirits, Spirits of wine, Spirituous, Sterol, Taplash, Terpineol, Thiol, Tincture, Tocopherol, Toper, Triol, Wash, White lightning, Wino, Witblits, Wood, Xylitol

**Alcove** Apse, Bay, Bole, Carrel(l), Dinette, Ingleneuk, Inglenook, Lunette, Niche, Nook, Recess, Reveal, Tokonoma

**Alcyonarian** Sea-feather

**Aldehyde** Acrolein, Aldol, Citronella, Piperonal, Vanillin

**Alder** Fothergilla

**Alderman** Bail(l)ie, CA

**Alderney** CI, Cow

**Ale, Alehouse** Audit, Barleybree, Barley-broo, Barley-broth, Barley wine, Beer, Brown, Bummock, CAMRA, Church, Draught, Feast, Four, Heather, Humming, Humpty-dumpty, Keg, Lager, Lamb's wool, Light, Mild, Morocco, Nappy, Nog, Nogg, October, Pale, Plain, Porter, Purl, Real, Small, Stout, Swats, Sweet, Tiddleywink, Tipper, White, Whitsun, Wort, Yard, Yill, Yorkshire stingo

**Alert** Agog, Alive, Amber, Arrect, Astir, Astute, Attentive, Awake, Aware, Bleep, Clear-headed, Conscious, Full, Gleg, Gogo, Intelligent, Observant, Open-eyed, Presential, Qui vive, Receptive, Red, Ring-tone, Scramble, Security, Sharp, Sharp-witted, Sprack, Sprag, Stand-to, Tentie, Up and coming, Vigilant, Volable, Warm, Wary, Watchful, Wide-awake, Yellow

**Alewife** Barkeeper, Gaspereau

**Alexander, Alexandrine** Alex, Arius, Macedonian, Pope, Sandy, Sasha, Sawn(e)y, Selkirk, Senarius

**Alfalfa** Lucern(e), Luzern

**Alfred** Dreyfus, Garnet, Jingle

**Alfresco** Barbecue, Plein-air

**Alga(e)** Anabaena, Blanketweed, Chlorella, Chlorophyte, Conferva, Desmid, Diatom, Dulse, Green, Heterocontae, Isokont, Jelly, Nostoc, Periphyton, Phycology, Pleuston, Pond scum, Prokaryon, Protococcus, Red, Rhodophyte, Scum, Sea-lace, Seaweed, Spirogyra, Star-jelly, Stonewort, Ulothrix, Ulotrichales, Valonia, Volvox, Witches' butter, Yellow-green, Zooxanthella

**Algebra** Boolean, Linear, Quadratics

**Algeria(n)** .dz, Kabyle, Nimidian, Pied noir

**Algonquin** Innu, Wampanoag

**Alias** Aka, Byname, Epithet, Moni(c)ker, Nick(name), Pen-name, Pseudonym

**Alibi** Airtight, Excuse, Watertight

**Alien(ate), Alienation** A-effect, Amortise, Antagonise, Devest, Disaffect, Drop-out, Ecstasy, Embitter, Erotic, Estrange, ET, Exotic, External, Foreign, Forinsecal, Fremd, Hostile, Invader, Little green man, Martian, Metic, Outlandish, Outsider, Philistine, Repugnant, Strange(r), Vulcan

**Alight** Aflame, Alowe, Avail(e), Avale, Detrain, Disembark, Dismount, Flambe, In, Lambent, Land, Lit, Perch, Pitch, Rest, Settle

**Align** Arrange, Associate, Collimate, Dress, Juxtapose, Marshal, Orient, Side, Straighten, Synchronize

▸**Alike** *see* LIKE(NESS)

**Alimentary** Oesophagus, Pharynx
**Aliquot** Submultiple
**Alive** Alert, Animated, Breathing, Extant, Quick, Teeming
**Alkali(ne), Alkaloid** Antacid, Apomorphine, Atropine, Base, Bebeerine, Berberine, Betaine, Bile, Borax, Brak, Brucine, Caffein(e), Capsaicin, Chaconine, Choline, Cinchon(id)ine, Codeine, Colchicine, Corydaline, Curarine, Emetin(e), Ephedrine, Ergotamine, Gelsemin(in)e, Guanidine, Harmalin(e), Harmin(e), Hydrastine, Hyoscine, Hyoscyamine, Ibogaine, Kali, Limewater, Lixivium, Lobeline, Lye, Mescalin, Mineral, Narceen, Narceine, Nicotine, Papaverine, Physostigmine, Pilocarpin(e), Piperine, Potash, Potass, Pyrralidine, Quinine, Reserpine, Rhoeadine, Scopaline, Scopolamine, Soda, Solanine, Sparteine, Stramonium, Thebaine, Theine, Theobromine, Theophylline, Totaquine, Tropine, Tubocurarine, Veratridine, Veratrin(e), Vinblastine, Vinca, Vincristine, Volatile, White, Yohimbine
**Alkane** Hexane
**All** A, En bloc, → ENTIRE, Entity, Every man Jack, Finis, Omni, Pan, Quite, Sum, → TOTAL, Toto, Tutti, Whole
**Allah** Bismillah, God
**All at once** Holus-bolus, Per saltum, Suddenly
**Allay** Alleviate, Appease, Calm, Disarm, Lessen, Quieten, Reassure, Relieve, Solace, Soothe
**Allegation, Allege(d)** Accuse, Assert, Aver, Claim, Declare, Mud, Obtend, Plead, Purport, Represent, Smear, So-called
**Allegiance** Faith, Foy, Loyalty, Tribalism
**Allegory, Allegorical** Apologue, Decameron, Fable, Mystic, Myth, Parable
**All-embracing** Eclectic, Exhaustive
**Allergy** Atopy, Aversion, Bagassosis, Hay fever, Hives
**Alleviate** Allay, Alleg(g)e, Calm, Ease, Mitigate, Mollify, Palliate, → RELIEVE, Temper
**Alley** Aisle, Blind, Bonce, Bowling, Corridor, Ennog, Ginnel, Lane, Laura, Marble, Passage, Rope-walk, Silicon, Skittle, Tin Pan, Twitten, Vennel, Walk, Wynd
**Alliance** Agnation, Axis, Bloc, Cartel, Coalition, Combine, Compact, Confederation, Dreibund, Dual, Entente, Federacy, → LEAGUE, Marriage, NATO, Quadruple, Syndicate, Triple, Union
**Alligator** Al(l)igarta, Avocado, Caiman, Cayman
**Alliteration** Cynghanedd, Head-rhyme
**Allocate, Allocation** Allot, Apportion(ment), Assign, Cast, Designate, Distribute, Earmark, Placement, Priorate, Quota, Ration, Share, Soum, Zone
**Allot(ment), Allow(ance), Allowed, Allowing** Abear, Admit, Affect, Alimony, Allocation, Although, Aret(t), Assign, Attendance, Authorise, Award, Batta, Bestow, Beteem(e), Borrow, Brook, Budget, Bug, Cap, Cater, Charter, Child, Cloff, Confess, Cor(r)ody, Countenance, Diet, Discount, Dole, Down, Draft, Elasticity, Empower, Enable, Entitle, Excuse, Expenses, Feod, Field, Fya, Give, Grant, House-bote, Husbandage, Indulge, Jobseekers', Latitude, Legit(imate), Let, License, Licit, Luit(en), Machining, Mag, Maintenance, Mete, Mobility, Okay, Palimony, Parcel, Pension, Percentage, → PERMIT, Personal, Pin-money, Pittance, Plot, Portion, Prebend, Privy purse, Provide, Quarterage, Quota, Ratio, Ration, Rebate, Rood, Salt-money, Sanction, Separate, Separation, Sequel, Share(-out), Shrinkage, Sizings, Stint, Stipend, Subsistence, Suffer, Table money, Tare, Tax, Teene, Though, Tolerance, Tolerate, Tret, Viaticum, Vouchsafe, Weighting, Whack, Yield
**Allotment-holder** Cleruch
**Allotropic** Graphite
▸**Allow(ance)** *see* ALLOT(MENT)
**Alloy** Albata, Alnico®, Amalgam, Babbitt, Bell-metal, Billon, Blend, Brass, Britannia metal, Bronze, Cermet, Chrome(l), Compound, Constantan, Cupronickel, Duralumin®, Dutch leaf, Electron, Electrum, Eureka, Eutectoid, Ferrochrome, Ferrosilicon, Gunmetal, Invar®, Iridosmine, Kamacite, Latten, Magnalium, Magnox, Manganin®, Marmem, Mischmetal, Mix, Monel®, Nichrome®, Nickel-silver, Nicrosilal, Nimonic, Nitinol, Occamy, Oreide, Oricalche, Orichalc, Ormolu, Oroide, Osmiridium, Paktong, Pewter, Pinchbeck, Platinoid, Porous, Potin, Pot metal, Prince's metal, Shakudo, Shibuichi, Similor, Solder, Speculum, Spelter, Steel, Stellite®, Tambac, Terne, Tombac, Tombak, Tutenag, White metal, Y, Zircal(l)oy, Zircoloy
▹**Alloy** *may indicate* an anagram

**All right** A1, Assuredly, Fit, Hale, Hunky(-dory), Jake, OK, Safe, Tickety-boo, Well
**All-round(er)** Generalist, Overhead, Versatile
**All-seeing** Panoptic
**Allspice** Jamaica pepper, Pim(i)ento
**All the same** Even so, Nath(e)less, Nevertheless
**Allude, Allusion** Cite, Enchantment, Glance, Hint, Imply, Innuendo, Mention, Refer, Reference, Suggest
**Allure, Alluring** Agaçant(e), Charm, Circe, Come-hither, Decoy, Delilah, Desirable, Enchantment, Entice, Femme fatale, Glam, Glamour, Houri, Inviting, It, Magnet(ic), Provocative, SA, Seduce, Seductive, Sexy, Siren, Tempt, Trap, Trepan, Vamp
**Alluvium** Carse, Deposit
**Ally, Allied** Accomplice, Agnate, Aide, Alley, Alliance, Ami, Backer, Belamy, Co-belligerent, Cognate, Colleague, Compadre, Dual, Foederatus, German(e), Holy, Marble, Marmoreal, Pal, Partner, Plonker, Related, Taw, Unholy, Unite
**Almanac** Calendar, Clog, Ephemeris, Morrison, Nautical, Nostradamus, Whitaker's, Wisden, Zadkiel
**Almighty** Creator, Deity, Dollar, God, Jehovah, Omnipotent
**Almond** Amygdal, Burnt, Emulsion, Jordan, Marchpane, Marzipan, Orgeat, Praline, Ratafia, Sugared, Valencia
**Almost** Anear, Anigh, Barely, Close on, Most, Near(ly), Nigh(ly), Practically, Ripe, Une(a)th, Virtually, Well-nigh, Welly
**Alms, Alms-giving** Awmous, Charity, Dole, Eleemosynary, Handout, Zakat
**Aloe** Agave, Pita
**Aloft** Aheight, Airborne
**Alone** Dernful, Eremite, Hat, Hermit, Jack, Lee-lane, Onely, Pat, Secco, Separate, Single, Singly, Sola, Solo, Solus, Tod, Unaccompanied, Unaided, Unattended, Unholpen
**Along, Alongside** Abeam, Aboard, Abreast, Adjacent, Apposed, Beside, By, Parallel, Synchronous
**Aloof** Abeigh, Apart, Asocial, Chilly, Cool, Detached, Distant, Frosty, Hou inch, Ice maiden, Indrawn, Insular, Mugwump, Offish, Remote, Reserved, Reticent, Skeigh, Snooty, Stand-offish, Taciturn, Toffee-nosed, Unapproachable
**Alopecia** Baldness
**Alpaca** Paco
**Alpha** A, Male
**Alphabet(ical)** ABC, Absey, Augmented Roman, Black-out, Brahmi, Braille, Chalcidian, Christcross, Cyrillic, Deaf, Devanagari, Estrang(h)elo, Finger, Futhark, Futhorc, Futhork, Glagol, Glagolitic, Glossic, Grantha, Hangul, Horn-book, Index, International, IPA, ITA, Kana, Kanji, Katakana, Kufic, Latin, Manual, Nagari, Og(h)am, Pangram, Phonetic, Pinyin, Romaji, Roman, Runic, Signary, Slavonic, Syllabary
**Alpine, Alps** Australian, Bernese, Cottian, Dinaric, Eiger, Gentian, Graian, Julian, Laburnum, Lepontine, Maritime, Matterhorn, Ortles, Pennine, Rhaetian, Rock plant, Savoy, Southern, Transylvanian, Tyrol, Western
**Also** Add, And, But and, Eke, Frore, Item, Likewise, Moreover, Plus, Too, Und, Withal
**Also-ran** Loser
**Altar, Altar-cloth, Altarpiece** Butsudan, Diptych, Dossal, Dossel, Family, High, Polyptych, Retable, Shrine, Tabula, Triptych
**Alter, Alteration** Adapt, Adjust, Airbrush, Become, Bushel, Change, Changeover, Chop and change, Convert, Cook, Correct, Customise, Distort, Evolve, Falsify, Lib, Material, Modify, Modulate, Munge, Mutate, Paraphonia, Recast, Refashion, Revise, Rework, Temper, Transient, Transmogrify, Transpose, Tweak, Up-end, Variance, → **VARY**
▷**Alter(native)** *may indicate* an anagram
**Altercation** Affray, Barney, Brawl, Fracas, Quarrel, Row, Words, Wrangle
**Alternate, Alternating, Alternation, Alternative** Aka, Boustrophedon, Bypass, Different, Either, Exchange, Fallback, In lieu, Instead, Intercut, Metagenesis, → **OPTION**, Or else, Ossia, Other, Rotate, Second best, Second string, Seesaw, Solidus, Staggered, Stop-go, Systaltic, Tertian, Variant, Vicissitude

▹**Alternately** *may indicate* every other letter
**Althaea** Mallow, Malva
**Although** Admitting, Albe(e), All-be, But, Even, Howsoever, Howsomever, Whereas, While, Whilst
**Altitude** Cabin, Elevation, Height, Meridian, Pressure, Rated, Snowline
**Alto** Countertenor
**Altogether** Algate(s), All-to-one, Bare, Completely, En bloc, Entirely, Holus-bolus, Idea, In all, Lock, stock and barrel, Naked, Nuddy, Nude, Nudity, Outright, Overall, Purely, Slick, Starkers, Tout (ensemble), Uncut, Wholly
▹**Altogether** *may indicate* words to be joined
**Altruistic, Altruism** Heroic, Humane, Philanthropic, Self-denial, Selfless(ness), Unselfish
**Alum** Potash
**Aluminium, Alumino-silicate** Al, Allanite, Bauxite, Cryolite, Euclase, Gibbsite, Sillimanite, Stilbite, Tinfoil
**Alumnus** Graduate, OB
**Alveolus** Air-sac
**Always** Algate(s), Ay(e), Constant, E'er, Eternal, Ever(more), Forever, For keeps, I, Immer, Semper, Sempre, Still
**Amalgam(ate)** Blend, Coalesce, Consolidate, Fuse, Merge, Mix, Unify, Unite
**Amalthea** Cornucopia
**Amanuensis** Tironian
**Amarylli(d)s** Leocojum, Lily, Polianthes
**Amass** Accrue, Accumulate, Assemble, Collect, Gather, Heap, Hoard, Pile (up), Rake-in, Upheap
**Amateur(s)** A, AA, Armchair, Beginner, Corinthian, Dabbler, Dilettante, DIY, Enthusiast, Grand, Hacker, Ham, Inexpert, L, Laic, Lay(man), Neophyte, Newbie, Novice, Prosumer, Sunday painter, Tiro, Tyro
**Amatory** Eros, Erotic, Fervent
**Amaze(d), Amazement, Amazing** Agape, Agog, Astonish, Astound, Awe, Awhape, Bewilder, Boggle, Cor, Criv(v)ens, Double take, Dum(b)found, Far out, Flabbergast, Gasser, Gee-whiz, Gobsmack, Goodnow, Grace, Humdinger, Incredible, Jesus wept, Magical, Monumental, O, Open-eyed, Open-mouthed, Perplex, Phenomenal, Poleaxe, Pop-eyed, Prodigious, Sensational, Spellbind, Stagger, Strewth, Stupefaction, Stupendous, Thunderstruck, Unreal, Wow
**Amazon(ian)** Ant, ATS, Brimstone, Britannia, Dragon, Hippolyta, Hoyden, Jivaro, Orellana, Penthesilea, Pirai, Shield-maid, Shield-may, Thalestris, Tupi, Virago
**Ambassador** At-large, Diplomat, Elchee, Elchi, Eltchi, Envoy, Extraordinary, Fetial, HE, Internuncio, Leaguer, Ledger, Legate, Leidger, Leiger, Lieger, Minister, Nuncio, Plenipo, Plenipotentiary, Pronuncio
**Amber** Colophony, Electric, Lammer, Ligure, Resin, Retinite, Succinite, Succinum
**Ambergris** Gris-amber
**Ambience** Atmosphere, Aura, Milieu, Setting
**Ambiguous, Ambiguity** Amphibology, Cryptic, Delphic, Double, Double entendre, Elusive, Enigmatic, Epicene, Equivocal, Gnomic, Inexactness, Loophole, Oracular, Unclear, Weasel words
**Ambit** Scope
**Ambition, Ambitious** Adventurer, Aim, Arrivisme, Aspiring, Careerism, Dream, Drive, Emulate, End, Go-ahead, Goal, Go-getter, Gold-digger, Grail, High-flier, Holy Grail, Hope, Keen, Naked, Office-hunter, Purpose, Pushy, Rome-runner, Spiralist, Thrusting, Type A, Wannabe
**Amble** Dawdle, Meander, Mosey, Pace, Poddle, Pootle, Saunter, Single-foot, Stroll, Traipse
**Ambrose** Emrys
**Ambrosia(l)** Amreeta, Amrita, Beebread, Fragrant, Odorant, Ragweed, Savoury
**Ambulance, Ambulanceman** Air, Badger, Blood-wagon, Field, Meat wagon, Pannier, Paramedic, Van, Yellow-flag, Zambu(c)k

**Ambulatory** Stoa
**Ambush(ed)** Ambuscade, Belay, Bushwhack, Emboscata, Embusque, Forelay, Forestall, Jump, Latitant, Lie in wait, Lurch, Perdu(e), Trap, Watch, Waylay
**Amelia** Bloomer
**Ameliorate** Amend, Ease, Emend, Improve, Lenify, Remedy
**Amen** Ammon, Approval, Inshallah, Verify
**Amenable** Putty
**Amend(ment)** Alter, Change, Correct, Edit, Expiate, Expurgate, Fifth, Insertion, Modify, Protocol, Redeem, Redress, Reform, Repair, Restore, → **REVISE**, Satisfy
▷**Amend** *may indicate* an anagram
**Amenity** Facility
**Ament** Catkin, Idiot
**America(n)** A, Algonki(a)n, Algonqu(i)an, Am, Angeleno, Basket Maker, Caddo, Cajun, Canadian, Carib, Chicano, Chickasaw, Chinook, Digger, Doughface, Down-easter, Federalist, Flathead, Fox, Gringo, Gullah, Guyanese, Huron, Interior, Joe, Jonathan, Latino, Miskito, Mission Indian, Mistec, Mixtec, Mound builder, Native, New Englander, New World, Norteno, → **NORTH AMERICAN (INDIAN)**, Olmec, Paisano, Paleface, Redneck, Salish, Sannup, Stateside, Statesman, Statist, Tar-heel, Tico, Toltec, Tupi, Uncle Sam, US(A), WASP, Yankee (Doodle), Yanqui
**Americium** Am
**Amethyst** Oriental
**Amiable, Amicable** Friendly, Genial, Gentle, Inquiline, Mungo, Peaceful, Sweet, Warm
**Amid(st)** Among, Atween, Between, Inter, Twixt
**Amide** Asparagine
**Amine** Putrescine, Spermine, Toluidine, Tyramine
**Amino-acid** Dopa, Tyrosine, Valine
**Amiss** Awry, Ill, Up, Wrong
**Amity** Concord, Peatship
**Ammeter** Tong-test
**Ammonia(c), Ammonium** Amide, Amine, Caustic, Choline, Ethylamine, Hartshorn, Imide, Mindererus spirit, Oshac, Sal alembroth, Sal ammoniac, Sal volatile
**Ammonite** Serpent-stone
**Ammunition** Ammo, Bandoleer, Bandolier, Birdshot, Buckshot, Bullets, Cartridge, Chain-shot, Dum-dum, Firepower, Grape(shot), Grenade, Mud, Pellet, Round, Shot, Slug, Tracer
**Amnesia** Anterograde, Fugal, Fugue, Lethe, Retrograde
**Amnesty** Oblivion, Pardon
**Amoeba** Melboean, Rhizopoda
**Amok** Rampaging
**Among** Amid(st), In, Inter al, Within
**Amorous(ly)** Casanova, Erotic, Fervent, Flirty, Lustful, Nutty, Romantic, Sheep's eyes, Smickly, Spoony, Warm
**Amorphous** Formless, Guanine, Nuclein, Shapeless, Vague
**Amount** Capacity, Come, Degree, Dose, Element, Figure, Glob, Gobbet, Handful, Lashings, Levy, Lot, Measure, Nip, Number, Ocean, Offset, Outage, Plethora, Pot(s), Premium, Price, Quantity, Quantum, Quota, Shedload, Slew, Span, Stack, Stint, Sum, Throughput, Trace, Volume, Whale, Wheel
**Amour** Affair(e), Intrigue, Love
**Ampersand** Tironian sign
**Amphetamine** Benny, Benzedrine, Speed
**Amphibian(s), Amphibious** Amb(l)ystoma, Amtrack, Anura, Axolotl, Batrachian, Caecilia, Caecilian, Desman, Eft, Frog, Guana, Hassar, Herpetology, Hillbender, Horned toad, Labyrinthodont, Mermaid, Mudpuppy, Newt, Olm, Ophiomorph, Proteus, Rana, Salamander, Salientia, Seal, Siren, Tadpole, Toad, Tree frog, Urodela(n), Urodele, Weasel
**Amphipod** Sand-screw, Shrimp
**Amphitheatre** Arena, Bowl, Circus Maximus, Coliseum, Colosseum, Ring, Stage

**Ample, Amplitude** Bellyful, Copious, Enough, Generous, Good, Large, Much, Opulent, Plethora, Profuse, Rich, Roomy, Round, Sawtooth, Spacious, Uberous, Voluminous
**Amplifier, Amplify** Booster, Double, Eke, Enlarge, Hailer, Laser, Loud hailer, Loudspeaker, Maser, Megaphone, Multiply, Push-pull, Solion, Soundboard, Tannoy®, Transistor, Treble
**Amputate** Sever, Transfix
**Amulet** Abraxas, Charm, Churinga, Fetish, Greegree, Grigri, Grisgris, Haemon, Pentacle, Periapt, Phylactery, Sea-bean, Talisman, Telesm, Tiki, Toadstone, Token
**Amuse(ment), Amusing(ly)** Account, Beguile, Caution, Cottabus, Disport, Diversion, Divert, Divertimento, Divertissement, Dodgems, Drole, Droll, Entertain, Fruit machine, Fun, Game, Gas, Giocoso, Glee, Hoke, Hoot, Jocular, Killing, Laughter, Levity, Light, Occupy, Pantheon, Pleasure, Popjoy, Priceless, Recreation, Regale, Rich, Riot, Scream, Slay, Solace, → **SPORT**, Tickle, Titillate, Trifle, Wacky
**Amy** Johnson, Robsart
▸**An** *see* **A**
**Ana(s)** Story, Teal
**Anabaptist** Abecedarian, Dipper, Dopper, Hutterite, Knipperdolling
**Anableps** Four-eyes
**Anachronism, Anachronistic** Archaism, Solecism, Unhistorical
**Anaconda** Water boa
**Anacreon** Te(i)an
**Anaemia, Anaemic** Aplastic, Cooley's, Diamond-blackfan, Exsanguinous, Fanconi's, Favism, Haemolytic, Megaloblastic, Miner's, Pallid, Pernicious, Sallow, Sickle-cell, Sicklemia, Thalassaemia
**Anaesthetic, Anaesthetise(d), Anaesthetist** Analgesic, Apgar, Avertin®, Basal, Benzocaine, Bupivacaine, Caudal, Chloralose, Chloroform, Cocaine, Endotracheal, Epidural, Ether, Eucain(e), Fluothane, Freeze, Gas, General, Halothane, Hibernation, Infiltrate, Intravenous, Jabber, Ketamine, Lidocaine, Lignocaine, Local, Metopryl, Morphia, Novocaine, Number, Opium, Orthocaine, Pentothal, Phenacaine, Phencyclidine, Procaine, Rhigolene, Special K, Spinal, Stovaine, Topical, Trike, Twilight sleep, Under, Urethan(e)
**Anagram** Jumble
**Anal, Anus** Back passage, Jacksie, Jacksy, Poepol, Proctal, Ring, Tewel
**Analgesic** Aspirin, Bute, Co-codamol, Codeine, Diclofenac, Disprin, Endorphin, Fentanyl, Ketamine, Menthol, Meperidine, Methadone, Morphia, Moxa, Opium, Oxycodone, Painkiller, Paracetamol, Pethidine, Phenacetin, Phencyclidine, Quina, Relief, Salicin(e), Sedative
**Analogous, Analogy** Akin, Comparison, Corresponding, Like, Parallel, Similar
**Analogue** Guanazolo
**Analyse(r), Analysis, Analytic(al)** Alligate, Anagoge, Anatomy, Assay, Assess, Blot, Breakdown, Combinatorial, Conformational, Construe, Cost-benefit, Critique, Diagnosis, Diaphantine, Dimensional, Discourse, Dissect, Emic, E-nose, Esda, Eudiometer, Examine, Explication, Factor, Force-field, Fourier, Gap, Gravimetric, Harmonic, Input-output, Job, Kicksorter, Lexical, Linguistic, Logical, Miscue, Numerical, Parse, Pollen, Post-mortem, Process, Psych out, Qualitative, Quant, Quantitative, Reductionism, Resolution, Review, Risk, Rundown, Sabermetrics, Scan(sion), Scientific, Semantics, Sift, Spectral, Spectroscopic, Spectrum, Statistician, Swot, Systems, Test, Titrate, Transactional, Unpick, Volumetric
▹**Analysis** *may indicate* an anagram
**Analyst** Alienist, Investment, Jung, Lay, Psychiatrist, Quant(ative), Researcher, Shrink, Systems, Trick cyclist
**Anarchist, Anarchy** Bakunin, Black Bloc(k), Black Hand, Bolshevist, Chaos, Kropotkin, Lawless, Nihilism, Provo, Punk, Rebel, Revolutionary, Riotous, Trotskyite, Unrule
**Anathema** Ban, Curse, Execration, Maranatha, Oath, Warling
**Anatole, Anatolia(n)** Asia minor, France, Hittite, Ionian, Turk
**Anatomy, Anatomist** Bones, Cuvier, De Graaf, Dubois, Fallopio, Framework, Henle, Herophilus, Histology, Hunter, Malpighi, Meibom, Morbid, Osteology, Pacini, Prosector, Puccini, Schneider, Spiegel, Topology, Worm
**Ancestor, Ancestral, Ancestry** Adam, Avital, Dawn man, Descent, Elder, Extraction,

For(e)bear, Forefather, Gastraea, Grandsire, Hereditary, Humanoid, Kachina, Lin(e)age, Parent, Parentage, Pedigree, Predecessor, Primogenitor, Proband, Profectitious, Progenitor, Propositus, Roots, Sire, Tipuna, Tree, Tupina

**Anchor(age)** Atrip, Berth, Bower, Cell, Deadman, Drag, Drift, Drogue, Eremite, Grapnel, Hawse, Hermit, Host, Kedge, Kedger, Killick, Killock, Laura, Moor, Mud-hook, Mushroom, Nail, Presenter, Ride, Roads(tead), Rode, Root, Scapa Flow, Sea, Sheet, Spithead, Stock, Stream, Toehold, Waist, Weather

**Anchorite** Recluse

**Anchorman** Emcee, Newsman

**Anchovy** Fish, Pear

**Ancient** Antediluvian, Archaic, Auld-warld, Bygone, Early, Gonfanoner, Historic, Hoary, Iago, Immemorial, Lights, Neanderthal, Neolithic, Ogygian, →OLD(ER), Old-world, Prehistoric, Primeval, Primitive, Pristine, Ur, Veteran

**Ancient city** Carthage, Ur

**Ancillary** Adjunct, Secondary, Subservient

**And** Als(o), Ampassy, Ampersand, Amperzand, Ampussyand, Besides, Et, Furthermore, Item, 'n', Plus, Tironian sign, Und

**Andalusite** Macle

**Andiron** Chenet, Dog, Firedog

**Andrew(es)** Aguecheek, Lancelot, Merry

**Androgynous** Epicene

**Android** Automaton, Golem, Replicant, Robot

**Anecdote(s)** Ana, Exemplum, Personalia, Story, Tale, Yarn

**Anemometer** Wind-sleeve, Windsock

**Anemone** Actinia, Pasque-flower, Windflower

**Aneurin** Thiamine

**Anew** De integro, De novo

**Angel(s), Angelic** Abdiel, Adramelech, Apollyon, Archangel, Ariel, Arioch, Asmadai, Avenging, Azrael, Backer, Banker, Beelzebub, Belial, Benefactor, Cake, Cherub, Clare, Destroying, Deva, Dominion, Dust, Eblis, Ethereal, Fallen, Falls, Gabriel, Guardian, Heavenly host, Hierarchy, Host, Iblis, Investor, Israfel, Ithuriel, Lucifer, Michael, Nurse, Power, Principality, Raphael, Recording, Rimmon, Saint, St, Seraph, Spirit, Throne, Uriel, Uzziel, Virtue, Watcher, Zadkiel, Zephiel

**Angela** Brazil

**Angelica** Archangel

**Angel's wings** Begonia

**Anger, Angry** →ANNOY, Apeshit, Ballistic, Bate, Berserk, Bile, Black, Boiling, Bristle, Choler(ic), Conniption, Cross, Dander, Disgruntled, Displeased, Dudgeon, Enrage, Exasperation, Face, Fiery, Fired up, Fuff, Fury, Gnar, Gram, Hacked off, Heat, Het up, Horn-mad, Huff, Incense, Inflame, Infuriate, Iracund, Irascible, Ire, Kippage, Livid, Mad, Monkey, Moody, Nettle, Pique, Provoke, Radge, Rage, Rampant, Ratty, Renfierst, Rile, Road rage, Roil, Rouse, Sore, Spewy, Spleen, Steam, Stroppy, Tamping, Tantrum, Tarnation, Teed off, Teen(e), Temper, Tene, Tirade, Tooshie, Uptight, Vex, Vies, Warm, Waspish, Waxy, Worked-up, Wound up, Wrath, Wroth, Yond

**Angina** Sternalgia, Vincent's

**Angle(d), Angler, Angular, Angles, Angling** Acute, Aglee, Argument, Aspect, Attitude, Axil, Azimuthal, Baiter, Boxy, Canthus, Cast, Catch, Central, Chiliagon, Coign, Complementary, Conjugate, Contrapposto, Corner, Cos, Critical, Diedral, Diedre, Dihedral, Elbow, Elevation, Ell, Exterior, Facial, Fish, Fish-hook, Fork, Geometry, Gonion, Hade, Haversine, Hip, Hour, Hyzer, In, Incidence, Interior, L, Laggen, Laggin, Latitude, Loft, Longitude, Mitre, Mung, Negative, Nook, Oblique, Obtuse, Parallax, Pediculate, Perigon, Peterman, Phase, Piend, Piscator, Pitch, Pitch-cone, Plan, Plane, Polyhedral, Position, Positive, Quoin, Radian, Rake, Re-entrant, Reflex, Right, Rod(ster), Rod(s)man, Round, Salient, Sally, Saltchucker, Sine, Sinical, Slant, Slip, Solid, Spherical, Stalling, Standpoint, Steeve, Steradian, Straight, Supplementary, Sweepback, The gentle craft, Tilt, Trigonometry, Trotline, Vertical, Viewpoint, Visual, Walton, Waltonian, Washin, Weather, Wide-gab

**Anglesey** Mona
**Anglican(s)** CE-men, Conformist, Episcopal
**Anglo-Catholic** High-church, Spike
**Anglo-Indian** Qui-hi, Qui-hye, Topi-wallah
**Anglo-Saxon** Hereward
**Angora** Goat, Mohair, Rabbit
**Angostura** Cusparia bark
**Angst** Dread
**Anguish(ed)** Agony, Distress, Gip, Grief, Gyp, Hag-ridden, Heartache, Misery, →PAIN, Pang, Sorrow, Throes, →TORMENT, Torture, Woe
**Angus** Aberdeen
**Animal(s)** Acrita, Anoa, Armadillo, Atoc, Bag, Bandog, Barbastel, Beast, Bestial, Brute, Cariacou, Carnal, Chalicothere, Chameleon, Cleanskin, Coati, Creature, Criollo, Critter, Ethology, Fauna, Felis, Feral, Gerbil, Guanaco, Herd, Huanaco, Ichneumon, Jacchus, Jerboa, Kinkajou, Klipdas, Livestock, Mammal, Marmoset, Marmot, Meiofauna, Menagerie, Mesozoa, Metazoa, Moose, Morken, Musquash, Noctule, Oribi, Pack, Packhorse, Parazoon, Party, Pet, Political, Protozoa, Pudu, Pygarg, Quadruped, Quagga, Rac(c)oon, Rhesus, Rotifer, Sensual, Sloth, Stud, Symphile, Tarsier, Teledu, Urson, Waler, Wheel, Xenurus, Yale, Yapock, Zerda, Zoo
**Animal-catcher** Utricularia
**Animate(d), Animatedly, Animation** Activate, Actuate, Alive, Arouse, Biophor, Cartoon, Claymation, Con spirito, Ensoul, Excite, Fire, Frankenstein, Frisky, Heat, Hortatory, Hot, Incite, Inspire, Lit, Live, Morph, Mosso, Perky, Pixil(l)ation, Rouse, Spark, Spiritoso, Spritely, Stop-motion, Suspended, Toon, Verve, Vivacity, Vivify
**Animosity** Antagonism, Dislike, Enmity, Friction, Hostility, Ill-will, Malevolence, Malice, Pique, Rancour, Spleen, Strife
**Aniseed** Pernod, Sambuca
**Ankle** Coot, Cuit, Cute, Hock, Hucklebone, Knee, Malleolus, Talus
**Ankle(t), Ankle covering** Cootikin, Cuitikin, Cutikin, Gaiter, Jess
**Anna, Anne, Annie** Boleyn, Hathaway, Laurie, Oakley, Page, Pavlova, Pice, Sewell, Sister
**Annabergite** Nickel-bloom, Nickel-ochre
**Annal(s), Annalist** Acta, Archives, Chronicles, History, Recorder, Register, Tacitus
**Annatto** Roucou
**Annex(e)** Acquire, Add, Affiliate, Attach, Codicil, Extension, Lean-to, Subjoin
**Annie** Laurie, Orphan
**Annihilate** Abolish, Destroy, Erase, Exterminate, Obliterate, Slay, Unbe
**Anniversary** Birthday, Feast, Jubilee, Obit, Triennial, Wedding, Yahrzeit
**Annotate, Annotator** Comment, Interpret, Note, Postil, Scholiast
**Announce(r), Announcement** Banns, Bellman, Bill(ing), Blazon, Bulletin, Communiqué, Continuity, Crier, Declare, Decree, Disclose, Divulgate, Flash, Gazette, Herald, Hermes, Impart, Inform, Intimate, Lutine bell, Meld, Name and shame, Newsflash, Noise, Notice, Oracle, Post, Preconise, Presenter, Press release, Proclaim, Profess, Promulgate, Pronunciamente, Publish, Release, →REPORT, Rescript, Speaker(ine), State, Statement, Tannoy, Toastmaster, Town crier, Trumpet
**Annoy(ance), Annoyed, Annoying** Aggravate, Aggrieve, Anger, Antagonise, Badger, Bane, Beset, Bind, Blight, Bother, Bug(ger), Bugbear, Chafe, Chagrin, Choleric, Contrary, Cross, Deuce(d), Displeasance, Displeasure, Disturb, Doggone, Doh, Drag, Drat, Fash, Fleabite, Frab, Fumed, Gall, Gatvol, Get, Gordon Bennett, Grate, Hack off, Hang, Harass, Hassle, Hatter, Hector, Hip, Hoots, Huff, Hump, Humph, Incense, Irk, →IRRITATE, Madden, Mickey-taking, Miff, Mischief, Molest, Moryah, Nag, Nark, Needle, Nettle, Niggle, Noisome, Noy(ance), Peeve, Perisher, Pesky, Pester, Pipsqueak, Pique, Plague, Provoke, Rankle, Rats, Ratty, Resentful, Ride, Rile, Roil, Rub, Shirty, Spite, Sting, Sturt, Testy, Tiresome, Tracasserie, Troublesome, Try, Vex, Wazzock
**Annual, Annuity** Almanac, Bedder, Book, Consolidated, Contingent, Deferred, Etesian, →FLOWER, Half-hardy, Hardy, Immediate, Life, Pension, Perpetuity, →PLANT, Rente, Tontine, Yearbook, Yearly

**Annul(ment)** Abolish, Abrogate, Cashier, Cassation, Dissolution, Invalidate, Irritate, Negate, Quash, Recision, Repeal, Rescind, Reversal, Revoke, Vacate, Vacatur, Vacuate, →**VOID**

**Annular** Toric

▶**Annunciation** *see* **ANNOUNCE(R)**

**Anodyne** Balm, Narcotic, Paregoric, Sedative

**Anoint(ing)** Anele, Cerate, Chris(o)m, Consecrate, Embrocate, Grease, Hallow, Nard, Smear

**Anomaly, Anomalous** Aberration, Eccentric, Gravity, Magnetic, Mean, Odd(ity), True

▷**Anomaly** *may indicate* an anagram

**Anon** Again, Anew, Erelong, Later, Soon

**Anonymous** Adespota, Anon, A.N.Other, Faceless, Grey, Impersonal, Nameless, Somebody, Unknown, Unnamed, Valentine

**Anorak** Cagoule, Geek, Nerd, Parka, Trainspotter, Wonk

**Another** Extra, Fresh, Per pro

**Answer(ing), Answer(s)** A, Account, Acknowledge, Amoebaean, Ans, Antiphon, Because, Comeback, Crib (sheet), Defence, Dusty, Echo, Key, Lemon, Light, No, Oracle, Quotient, Rebuttal, Rebutter, Rein, Rejoin(der), Repartee, Reply, Rescript, Respond, Response, Responsum, Retort, Return, Riposte, Serve, Sol, Solution, Solve, Verdict, Yes

**Ant(s), Anthill** Amazon, Army, Bull(dog), Carpenter, Colony, Driver, Dulosis, Emmet, Ergataner, Ergates, Ergatogyne, Ergatomorph, Fire, Formic, Formicary, Kelep, Leafcutter, Legionary, Myrmecoid, Myrmidon, Nasute, Neuter, Pharaoh, Pismire, Red, Sauba, Slave, Slave-maker, Soldier, Termite, Thief, Umbrella, Velvet, White, Wood

**Antacid** Limewater, Magnesia, Peptic

**Antagonist(ic), Antagonise, Antagonism** Adverse, Alienate, Antibiosis, Enemy, Estrange, Hostile, Oppugnant, Peare, Peer

**Antarctica** Adelie Land, Byrd Land, Graham Land, Marie Byrd Land, Wilkes Land

**Antbear** Aardvark, Tamanoir

**Ante** Bet, Punt, Stake

**Ant-eater** Aardvark, Banded, Echidna, Edental, Giant, Manis, Numbat, Pangolin, Scaly, S(e)ladang, Spiny, Tamandu, Tamandua, Tapir

**Antelope** Addax, Antilope, Blackbuck, Blaubok, Blesbok, Bloubok, Bluebuck, Bongo, Bontebok, Bubal(is), Bushbuck, Cabric, Chamois, Chikara, Chiru, Dikdik, Duiker, Duyker, Dzeren, Eland, Elk, Gazelle, Gemsbok, Gerenuk, Gnu, Goa, Goat, Goral, Grysbok, Harnessed, Hartbees, Hartebeest, Impala, Inyala, Izard, Kaama, Kid, Klipspringer, Kob, Kongoni, Koodoo, Kudu, Lechwe, Madoqua, Marshbuck, Mhorr, Mohr, Nagor, Nilgai, Nilgau, Nyala, Nylghau, Oribi, Oryx, Ourebi, Ox, Pale-buck, Pallah, Prongbuck, Pronghorn, Pronk, Puku, Pygarg, Reebok, Reedbuck, Rhebok, Roebuck, Sable, Saiga, Sasin, Sassaby, Serow, Sitatunga, Situtunga, Springbok, Steenbok, Steinbock, Stemback, Stembok, Suni, Takin, Thar, Topi, Tragelaph, Tsessebe, Waterbuck, Wildebeest

**Antenatal** Labour

**Antenna** Aerial, Dipole, Dish, Feeler, Horn, Rabbit's ears, Sensillum, Squarial, TVRO

**Anterior** Anticous, Earlier, Front, Prior

**Anteroom** Foyer, Voiding-lobby

**Anthelmintic** Worm

**Anthem** Chant, Die Stem, Hymn, Introit, Isodica, Marseillaise, Motet(t), National, Offertory, Psalm, Red Flag, Responsory, Song, Star Spangled Banner, Stem, Theme, Tract, Troparion

**Anthology** Album, Ana, Chrestomathy, Digest, Divan, Florilegium, Garland, Omnibus, Pick, Spicilege

**Anthony** Absolute, Adverse, Runt, Trollope

**Anthracite** Blind-coal, Glance coal

**Anthrax** Sang, Splenic fever, Woolsorter's disease

**Anthropo(i)d** Onychophora, Peripatus, Sivapithecus

**Anthropologist, Anthropology** Ethnography, Ethnologist, Heyerdahl, Levi-Strauss, Mead, Somatology, Strathern, Strehlow, Verchow

**Anti** Against, Agin, Averse, Con, Gainst, Hostile

**Anti-abortion** Right to life

**Anti-aircraft** AA, Ack-ack
**Anti-bacterial, Antibiotic** Aclarubicin, Actinomycin, Allicin, Amoxicillin, Ampicillin, Aureomycin®, Avoparcin, Bacitracin, Bacteriostat, Carbenicillin, Cecropin, Cephalosporin, Cipro®, Ciprofloxacin, Cloxacillin, Colistin, Cortisone, Co-trimoxazole, Cycloserine, Doxorubicin, Doxycycline, Drug, Erythromycin, Gentamicin, Gramicidin, Griseofulvin, Interferon, Interleukin, Kanamycin, Lincomycin, Macrolide, Magainin, Methicillin, Mitomycin, Neomycin, Nystatin, Opsonin, Oxacillin, Oxytetracycline, Penicillin, Polymyxin, Puromycin, Quinolone, Rifampicin, Rifamycin, Spectinomycin, Streptokinase, Streptomycin, Streptothricin, Terramycin®, Tetracycline, Tyrocidine, Tyrothricin, Vancomycin, Virginiamycin, Wide-spectrum
**Antibody** Agglutinin, Alemtuzumab, Amboceptor, Antitoxin, Blocker, Catuximab, H(a)emolysin, Hybroid, IgA/E/G/M/O, Infliximab, Isoagglutinin, Lysin, Monoclonal, Opsonin, Precipitin, Reagin, Rituximab, Trastuzumab
**Anti-British** Khilafat
**Antic(s)** Caper, Dido, Frolic, Gambado, Hay, Prank, Shenanigan, Stunt
**Anti-carlist** Queenite
**Antichrist** The Beast, The Man of Sin
**Anticipate, Anticipation** Against, Antedate, Apprehend, Augur, Await, Dread, Drool, Envisage, → EXPECT, Forecast, Foresee, Foresight, Forestall, Foretaste, Foretell, Forethought, Hope, Intuition, Pre-empt, Preparation, Prevenancy, Prolepsis, Prospect, Schedule, Second-guess, Type
**Anticlimax** Bathos, Comedown, Damp squib, Deflation, Disappointment, Letdown, Non-event
**Anticline** Upwrap
**Anticlockwise** Dextrorse, Laevorotatory, Widdershins, Withershins
**Anticoagulant** C(o)umarin, Heparin, Hirudin, Prostacyclin, Warfarin
**Anticommunist** John Birch(er), McCarthyism
**Anticyclone** High
**Antidepressant** Prozac
**Antidote** Adder's wort, Alexipharmic, Angelica, Antivenin, Arrowroot, Bezoar, Contrayerva, Cure, Dimercaprol, Emetic, Guaco, Interleukin, Mithridate, Nostrum, Orvietan, Picrotoxin, Remedy, Ribavirin, Senega, Theriac(a), (Venice-)Treacle
**Anti-feminist** Traditional
**Anti-freeze** Glycerol, Lagging
**Anti-fur** PETA
**Antigen** Agglutinogen, Hapten(e)
**Antihistamine** Dimenhydrinate, Quercetin
**Anti-imperialist** Guelf, Guelph
**Antimacassar** Tidy
**Anti-monarchist** Republican
**Antimonopoly** Trust buster
**Antimony** Kohl, Sb, Speiss, Stibium, Tartar emetic
**Antinuclear** CND
**Antioxidant** Glutathione, Lycopene
**Anti-parliamentarian** Poujadist
**Antiparticle** Antiquark
**Antipasto** Caponata
**Antipathy** Allergy, Animosity, Aversion, Detest, → DISLIKE, Dyspathy, Enmity, Intolerance, Repugnance
**Anti-perfectionist** Cobden
**Antiphon** The Reproaches
**Antipodean** Antarctic, Antichthon, Aussie, Enzed, Underworld
**Antipope** Novatian(us)
**Anti-protectionist** Cobden
**Antiquated, Antique, Antiquarian** Ancient, Archaic, A(u)stringer, Bibelot, Curio, Dryasdust, Egyptian, Egyptologist, FAS, Fogram(ite), Fog(e)y, Fossil, Moth-eaten, Old-fangled, Ostreger, Passe, Relic

**Anti-reformer** Obscurant
**Anti-revolutionary** Vendean, White
**Anti-Roman** Ghibel(l)ine
**Anti-royalist** Puritan, Whig
**Anti-Semitic** Pamyat
**Antiseptic** Acriflavine, Borax, Carbolic, Cassareep, Creosote, Cresol, Crystal violet, Dettol®, Disinfectant, Eupad, Eusol, Formaldehyde, Formalin, Formol, Gentian violet, Germicide, Guaiacol, Iodine, Lister, Lysol®, Merbromin, Mouthwash, Phenol, Sterile, Tar, Thymol, Tutty
**Anti-slavery** Free-soil, Wilberforce
**Anti-smoker** ASH, Misocapnic
**Antisocial** Aggro, Hoodie, Hostile, Ishmaelitish, Litterbug, Litter-lout, Loner, Misanthropic, Oik, Psychopath, Sociopath, Standoffish, Yobbish
**Antithesis** Contrary, Converse, Inverse, Opposite
**Anti-three** Noetian
**Antitoxin** Antibody, Antivenin, Guaco, Serum, Vaccine
**Anti-Trinitarian** Patripassian
**Anti-union** Secesher
**Antivenom** Guaco
**Antiviral** Rebavirin
**Antivitamin** Pyrithiamine
**Antler(s)** Bay, Bosset, Crown, Hartshorn, Horn, Palm, Rights, Staghorn, Surroyal, Tine
**Ant-proof** Bilian
▸**Anus** *see* **ANAL**
**Anvil** Bick-iron, Block, Incus, Stiddie, Stithy
**Anxiety, Anxious** Abdabs, Afraid, Angst, Brood, Care(ful), Cark, Concern, Disquiet, Disturbed, Dreading, Dysthymia, Eager, Edgy, Fanteeg, Fantigue, Fantod, Fear, Fraught, Fretting, Grave, Habdabs, Heebie-jeebies, Hinky, Hung-up, Hypochondria, Impatient, Inquietude, Itching, Jimjams, Jitters, Jumpy, Keen, Nerviness, Panic, Reck, Restless, Scruple, Separation, Shpilkes, Solicitous, Stewing, Stress, Suspense, Sweat, Tension, Toey, Trepidation, Tribulation, Twitchy, Unease, Unquiet, Upset, Uptight, White-knuckle, Willies, Worriment, Worryguts, Worrywort
**Any** Arrow, Ary, Some
**Anybody, Anyone** Everyman, One, Whoso, You
**Anyhow, Anyway** Anyroad(s), At least, However, Leastways, Leastwise, Nonetheless, Regardless
**Anything** Aught, Diddly-squat, Oucht, Ought, Owt, Whatnot
▹**Anyway** *may indicate* an anagram
**Apace** Posthaste
**Apache** Arizona, AZ, Geronimo
**Apart** Aloof, Aside, Asunder, Atwain, Beside, Poles, Separate
**Apartheid** Racism, Segregation, Verkrampte
**Apartment** Atrium, Ben, Condo(minium), Cubicle, Digs, Duplex, Efficiency, Flat, Insula, Mansion, Pad, Paradise, Penthouse, Pied-a-terre, Quarters, Room, Simplex, Solitude, State, Suite, Tenement, Unit, Walk-up
**Apathetic, Apathy** Accidie, Acedia, Incurious, Indifferent, Inertia, Languid, Lethargic, Listless, Lobotomized, Lukewarm, Mopish, Pococurante, Spiritless, Stoical, Torpid, Unenthusiastic
**Ape(-like), Apeman** Anthropoid, Barbary, Big-foot, Bonobo, Catarrhine, Copy, Dryopithecine, Gelada, Gibbon, Gorilla, Great, → **IMITATE**, Impersonate, Magot, Mimic, → **MONKEY**, Naked, Night, Orang, Paranthropus, Parrot, Pithecoid, Pongid, Pongo, → **PRIMATE**, Proconsul, Replicate, Sacred, Shrewdness, Simian, Simulate, Troglodyte, Yowie
**Aperient** Cascara, Laxative, Senna
**Aperitif** Campari, → **DRINK**, Pastis, Pernod®, Sherry
**Aperture** Balistraria, Chink, Fenestella, Hole, Keyhole, Opening, Orifice, Osculum, Peephole, Pinhole, Porta, Punctum, Relative, Spiracle, Swallow, Window
**Apex** Acme, Culmen, Gonion, Keystone, Knoll, Knowe, Solar, Summit, Vertex

**Aphid** Ant-cow, Blackfly, Dolphin-fly, Greenfly, Phylloxera
**Aphorism** Adage, Epigram, Gnome, Maxim, Pensée, Proverb, Sutra
**Aphrodisiac, Aphrodite** Cytherean, Erotic, Idalian, Paphian, Philter, Philtre, Spanish fly, Urania, Yohimbine
**Aplomb** Assurance, Cool, Equanimity, Poise, Sangfroid, Serenity
**Apocryphal** Spurious, Tobit
**Apogee** Top
**Apograph** Roneo®
**Apollo** Belvedere, Moonshot, Pythian, Sun
**Apologetic, Apologist, Apology** Advocate, Ashamed, Cut up, Excuse, Humble pie, Justifier, Mockery, My bad, Oops, Pardon, Scuse, Sir-reverence
**Apoplexy** Stroke
**Apostate** Citer, → HERETIC, Pervert, Rat, Recreant, Renegade, Reneguer, Runagate, Turncoat
**Apostle, Apostolic** Cuthbert, → DISCIPLE, Evangelist, Johannine, Jude, Mark, Matthew, papal, Pauline, Philip, Spoon, Thad(d)eus, Thomas, Twelve
**Apostrophe, Apostrophise** Elision, Greengrocer's, O(h), Soliloquy, Tuism
**Apothecary** Chemist, Dispenser, Druggist, LSA, Pharmacist, Pottingar
**Apothegm** Dictum, Maxim, Motto
**Apotheosis(e)** Deify
**Appal(ling)** Abhorrent, Abysmal, Affear(e), Aghast, Dire, Dismay, Egregious, Execrable, Frighten, Horrify, Piacular, Shock, Tragic
▷**Appallingly** *may indicate* an anagram
**Apparatus** Absorptiometer, Aerator, Alembic, Alkalimeter, Appliance, Aqualung, Aristotle's lantern, ASDIC, Aspirator, Atom smasher, Autoclave, Bascule, Block and tackle, Breeches buoy, Bridgerama, Caisson, Calorimeter, Chemostat, Churn, Cider press, Clinostat, Codec, Coherer, Colorimeter, Commutator, Condenser, Convector, Converter, Convertor, Cosmotron, Critical, Cryostat, Cyclotron, Davis, Decoy, Defibrillator, Desiccator, → DEVICE, Digester, Ebullioscope, Effusiometer, Egg, Electrograph, Electrophorus, Electroscope, Elutriator, Enlarger, Eprouvette, Equipment, Eudiometer, Exciter, Fixings, Gadget, Gasogene, Gazogene, Gearbox, Generator, Giant('s) stride, Golgi, Graith, Gyroscope, Gyrostat, Hang-glider, Heater, Heliograph, Helioscope, Hemocytometer, Hodoscope, Holophote, Horse, Hydrophone, Hygrostat, Incubator, Inhalator, Injector, Inspirator, Installation, Instrument, Ionizer, Iron lung, Isotron, Jacquard, Kipp's, Kymograph, Langmuir-trough, Lease-rod, Life-preserver, Loom, Masora(h), Microreader, Mimeograph, Mine-detector, Multi-gym, Nephoscope, Nitrometer, Oscillator, Oscillograph, Osmometer, Oxygenator, Paper-feeder, Pasteuriser, Peat-seeker, Percolator, Phon(o)meter, Photophone, Photostat®, Phytotron, Plate-warmer, Plethysmograph, Plumber's snake, Pommel horse, Potometer, Projector, Proto®, Pulmotor®, Push-pull, Radiator, Radiosonde, Rattlebag, Rattletrap, Rectifier, Replenisher, Resistor, Respirator, Respirometer, Resuscitator, Retort, Rotisserie, Rounce, Sailboard, Scintiscanner, Scrubber, Scuba, Searchlight, Seeder, Semaphore, Set, Skimmer, Slide rest, Smoker, Snake, Sniffer, Snorkel, Snowbox, Soundboard, Spectrometer, Sphygmograph, Spirophore, Starter, Steamer, Stellarator, Steriliser, Still, Substage, Switchboard, Switchgear, Tackle, Tackling, Talk-you-down, Telecine, Teleprinter, Teleseme, Tellurian, Thermopile, Tokamak, Transformer, Transmitter, Tribometer, Tromp(e), Tuner, Ventouse, Wheatstone's bridge, Whip-and-derry, ZETA
**Apparel** Attire, Besee, → COSTUME, Garb, Raiment, Wardrobe, Wardrop, Wear
**Apparent(ly)** Ap, Clear, Detectable, Evident, Manifest, Open, Ostensible, Outward, Overt, Palpable, Plain, Prima facie, Seeming, Semblance, Visible
▷**Apparent** *may indicate* a hidden word
**Apparition** Avatar, Dream, Eidolon, Fetch, Ghost, Gytrash, Hallucination, → ILLUSION, Phantom, Shade, Spectre, Vision, Visitant, Wraith
**Appeal(ing)** Ad, Attract, Beg, Cachet, Call, Catchpenny, Charisma, Charm, Cri de coeur, Cry, Dreamy, Entreat, Entreaty, Epirrhema, Exhort, Eye-catching, Fetching, Glamorous, Howzat, Intil, Invocation, It, Mediagenic, Miserere, O, Oath, Oomph, Plead, Popular, SA, Screeve, Sex(iness), Solicit, SOS, Suit, Yummy

**Appear(ance), Appearing** Advent, Air, Apport, Arise, Arrival, Aspect, Broo, Brow, Burst, Cameo, Cast, Coax, Colour, Compear, Crop up, Debut, Dishy, Effeir, Effere, Emerge, Enter, Entrance, Exterior, Eye, Facade, Face, Fa(s)cia, Facies, Far(r)and, Farrant, Feature, Figure, Format, Garb, Guise, Habitus, How's that, Hue, Image, Implore, Kithe, Kythe, Looks, Loom, Manifestation, → MANNER, Materialise, Mien, Occur, Ostensibly, Ostent, Outward, Person, Phase, Phenomenon, Physiognomy, Pop-up, Presence, Prettiness, Prosopon, Represent, Rig, Rise, Scenery, Seem, Semblance, Show, Species, Spectre, Spring, Superficies, Theophany, Veneer, View, Visage, Visitation, Vraisemblance, Whistle-stop, Winning, Wraith

**Appease(ment)** Allay, Alleviate, Atone, Calm, Conciliation, Danegeld, Mitigate, → MOLLIFY, Munichism, Pacation, Pacify, Placate, Propitiate, Relieve, Sate, Satisfy, Soothe, Sop, Sweeten

**Appellant, Appellation** Nomen, Roe

**Append(age)** Addition, Adjunct, Affix, Aglet, Allantois, Annex, Antennule, Aril, Arista, Attach, Cercus, Chelicera, Codpiece, Ctene, Fang, Flagellum, Gnathite, Hanger-on, Limb, Lobe, Lug, Nose-leaf, Palp(us), Paraglossa, Parapodium, Pedipalp, Pendicle, Postfix, Proboscis, Stipel, Stipule, Suffix, Swimmeret, Tab, Tail, Tailpiece, Tentacle, Ugly, Uropod, Uvula

**Appendix** Addendum, Apocrypha, Codicil, Grumbling, Label, Pendant, Pendent, Rider, Schedule, Vermiform

**Appertain** Belong

**Appetite, Appetitive, Appetise(r), Appetising, Appetize(r)** Amuse-bouche, Amuse-gueule, Angels on horseback, Antepast, Antipasto, Aperitif, Appestat, Bhagee, Bhajee, Bulimia, Bulimy, Canapé, Canine, Concupiscence, Concupy, Crudités, Desire, Dim-sum, Entremes(se), Entremets, Flesh, Hunger, Inner man, Limosis, Malacia, Meze, Mezze, Mouth-watering, Nacho, Orectic, Orexis, Palatable, Passion, Pica, Polyphagia, Relish, Savoury, Tapa(s), Titillate, Twist, Ventripotent, Voracious, Whet, Yerd-hunger, Yird-hunger

**Applaud, Applause** Acclaim, Bravo, → CHEER, Clap, Claque, Crack-up, Eclat, Encore, Extol, Hand, Hum, Kentish fire, Olé, Ovation, Praise, Root, Ruff, Tribute

**Apple** Adam's, Alligator, Bad, Baldwin, Balsam, Biffin, Blenheim orange, Braeburn, Bramley, Candy, Cashew, Charlotte, Codlin(g), Cooker, Costard, Crab, Custard, Dead Sea, Discord, Eater, Golden Delicious, Granny Smith, Greening, Jenneting, John, Jonathan, Kangaroo, Leather-coat, Love, Mammee, May, McIntosh (red), Medlar, Nonpareil, Oak, Pacific Rose, Pearmain, Pippin, Pomace, Pome(roy), Pomroy, Pom(e)water, Potato, Punic, Pupil, Pyrus, Quarantine, Quarenden, Quar(r)ender, Quarrington, Queening, Quodlin, Redstreak, Reinette, Rennet, Ribston(e), Ripstone, Rotten, Royal gala, Ruddock, Russet, Sage, Seek-no-further, Snow, Sops-in-wine, Sorb, Star, Sturmer (Pippin), Sugar, Sweeting, Thorn, Toffee, Windfall, Winesap

**Apple juice** Malic

**Apple-picker** Atalanta

**Applicant** Candidate, Ordinand, Postulant

**Application, Applicable, Apply, Appliance(s)** Address, Adhibit, Aftershave, Appeal, Appose, Assiduity, Astringent, Barrage, Blender, Brace, Concentration, Dab, Dedicate, Devote, Diligence, Dispose, Dressing, Drier, Exercise, Exert, Foment, Fridge, Gadget, Germane, Give, Implement, Impress, Inlay, Juicer, Kettle, Lay, Liniment, Liquidiser, Lotion, Machine, Mixer, Mod con, Ointment, Opodeldoc, Pertain, Pertinent, Petition, Plaster, Poultice, Put, Request, Resort, Respirator, Rub, Sinapism, Stupe, Talon, Toggle, Truss, Usage, → USE, Vice, Water-softener, White goods

**Appliqué** Hawaiian

**Appoint(ee), Appointment** Advowson, Assign, Berth, Co-opt, Date, Delegate, Depute, Designate, Dew, Due, Executor, Induction, Installation, Make, Name, → NOMINATE, Nominee, Office, Ordain, Ordinate, Place, Position, Post, Posting, Rendezvous, Room, Set, Tryst

▷**Appointed** *may indicate* an anagram

**Apportion(ment)** Allocate, Allot, Cede, Distribute, Entail, Mete, Parcel, Ration, Share, Weigh

**Apposite** Apt, Cogent, Germane, Pat, Pertinent, Relevant, Suitable

**Appraise, Appraisal** Analyse, → EVALUATE, Eye-up, Gauge, Guesstimate, Judge, Once-over, Review, Tape, Valuate, → VALUE, Vet

**Appreciate, Appreciation** Accrue, Acknowledgement, Admire, Aesthetics, Cherish, Clap, Comprehensible, Dig, Empathy, Endear, Esteem, Feel, Grasp, Gratefulness, Gratitude, Increase, Phwoar, Prize, Realise, Recognise, Regard, Relish, Rise, Savour, Sense, Stock, Taste, Thank you, Treasure, → VALUE, Welcome

**Apprehend(ing), Apprehension** Afears, Alarm, Anticipate, Arrest, Attuent, Awestruck, → CATCH, Collar, Fear, Foreboding, Grasp, Insecure, Insight, Intuit, Noesis, Perceive, Presentiment, Quailing, See, Suspense, Take, Trepidation, Uh-oh, Unease, Uptake

**Apprehensive** Jumpy, Nervous, Toey, Uneasy, Worried

**Apprentice(ship)** Article, Commis, Cub, Devil, Garzone, Improver, Indent(ure), Jockey, L, Learner, Lehrjahre, Novice, Noviciate, Novitiate, Printer's devil, Pupillage, Snob, Tiro, Trainee, Turnover, Tyro(ne)

**Apprise** Enlighten

**Approach(ing), Approachable** Abord, Access, Accost, Advance, Affable, Anear, Angle, Anigh, Appropinquate, Appulse, Asymptotic, Avenue, Border, Close, Coast, Come, Converge, Cost(e), Draw nigh, Drive, Driveway, Fairway, Feeler, Final, Friendly, Gate, Imminent, Ingoing, Line, Near, Nie, Open, Overture, Pitch, Procedure, Road, Run-in, Run-up, Slip road, Stealth, Strategy, Towards, Upcoming, Verge, Warm

**Appropriate(ly), Appropriateness** Abduct, Abstract, Annex, Applicable, Apposite, Apt, Aright, Arrogate, Asport, Assign, Bag, Befitting, Borrow, Collar, Commandeer, Commensurate, Condign, Confiscate, Congruous, Convenient, Decent, Due, Element, Eligible, Embezzle, Expedient, Fit, Germane, Good, Happy, Hijack, Hog, Impound, In keeping, In order, Jump, Just, Meet, Nick, OK, Pertinent, Pilfer, Plagiarise, Pocket, Pre-empt, Proper, Propriety, Purloin, Relevant, Right, Seemly, Seise, Seize, Sequester, Sink, Snaffle, Snatch, Steal, Suit(ed), Swipe, Take, Timely, Toward, Trouser, Usurp

**Approval, Approve(d), Approbation** Accolade, Accredit, Admire, Adopt, Agree, Allow, Amen, Applaud, Assent, Attaboy, Aye, Blessing, Bravo, Brownie points, Change, Cheer, Clap, Command, → COUNTENANCE, Credit, Cushty, Dig, Eclat, Endorse, Favour, For, Green light, Handclap, Hear hear, Homologate, Hubba-hubba, Hurra(h), Imprimatur, Initial, Kitemark, Know, Kudos, Laud, Mandate, Nod, Official, Okay, Olé, Orthodox, Pass, Plaudit, Praise, Rah, Ratify, Recognise, Recommend, Right-on, Rubber-stamp, Sanction, Stotter, Thumbs-up, Tick, Tribute, Vivat, Voice, Warm to, Yay, Yes, Zindabad

**Approximate(ly), Approximation** Almost, Around, Ballpark, Bordering, Circa, Close, Coarse, Estimate, Guess, Imprecise, Near, Rough and ready, Roughly

**Apricot** Mebos

**April, April fool** Apr, Huntiegowk, Hunt-the-gowk

**Apron** Airside, Barm-cloth, Bib, Blacktop, Brat, Bunt, Canvas, Dick(e)y, Ephod, Fig-leaf, Gremial, Ice, Napron, Pinafore, Pinner, Pinny, Placket, Rim, Stage, Tablier, Tier, Waist

**Apse** Concha, Exedra, Niche, Recess, Tribune

**Apt(ly)** Apposite, Appropriate, Apropos, Ben trovato, Capable, Evincive, Fit, Gleg, Happy, Inclined, Liable, Pat, Prone, Relevant, Suitable, Tends, True, Well-timed

**Aptitude** Ability, Bent, Ear, Eye, Faculty, Feel, Flair, Gift, Knack, Know-how, Nose, Penchant, Skill, Sprachgefuhl, Talent, Taste, Tendency, Touch, Viability

**Aqua(tic)** Euglena, Flustra, Lentic, Lotic, Regia, Rotifera, Zizania

**Aqualung** Rebreather, Scuba

**Aquamarine** Bice, Madagascar

**Aquarium** Fish tank, Oceanarium

**Aqueduct** Canal, Channel, Conduit, Hadrome, Xylem

**Aquiline** Hooked

**Arab(ian), Arabia, Arabic** Abdul, Adeni, Adnan, Algorism, Ali (Baba), Baathist, Bahraini, Bahrein, Bedouin, Bedu, Druse, Druz(e), Effendi, Fedayee(n), Gamin, Geber, Hani, Hashemite, Hassaniya, Himyarite, Horse, Iraqi, Jawi, Kuwaiti, Lawrence, Moor, Mudlark, Nabat(a)ean, Nas(s)eem, Nes(h)ki, Omani, Omar, PLO, Qatari, Rag(head), Saba, Sab(a)ean, Saracen, Saudi, Seleucid, Semitic, Sheikh, Shriner, Street, Syrian, UAR, Urchin, Yemen(i)

**Arabis** Cress

**Arachnid** Mite, Podogona, Ricinulei, Scorpion, Solpuga, →SPIDER
**Arbitrary** Despotic, Freakish, Haphazard, Peculiar, Random, Thetic, Wanton, Whim
**Arbitrate, Arbitration, Arbitrator, Arbiter** ACAS, Birlieman, Byrlawman, Censor, Daysman, Judge, Negotiator, Ombudsman, Pendulum, Prud'homme, Ref(eree), Umpire
**Arboreal, Arbour** Bower, Dendroid, Pergola, Trellis
**Arc** Azimuth, Bow, Carbon, →CURVE, Dink, Electric, Flashover, Fogbow, Foil, Halo, Hance, Haunch, Island, Limb, Mercury, Octant, Quadrant, Rainbow, Reflex, Seadog, Semicircle, Trajectory, White rainbow
**Arcade** Amusement, Burlington, Cloister, Galleria, Gallery, Loggia, Mall, Penny, Triforium, Video
**Arcadia(n)** Idyllic, Nemoral, Sylvan
**Arcane** Esoteric, Mystic, Obscure, Occult, Orphism, Recherché, Rune, Secret
**Arch(ed), Arching, Archway** Acute, Admiralty, Alveolar, Arblaster, Arcade, Arcature, Archivolt, Arcuate, Camber, Chief, Coom, Counterfort, Crafty, Cross-rib, Crown-green, Ctesiphon, →CUNNING, Curve, Discharging, Elfin, Embow, Espiegle, Eyebrow, Fallen, Flying buttress, Fog-bow, Fornicate, Fornix, Gill, Gothic, Hance, Haunch, Hog, Horseshoe, Instep, Intrados, Inverted, Keel, Keystone, Knowing, Lancet, Leery, Lierne, Limb-girdle, Manteltree, Marble, Neural, Norman, Ogee, Ogive, Opistholomos, Order, Parthian, Pectoral, Pelvic, Pergola, Plantar, Pointed, Portal, Proscenium, Recessed, Relieving, Roach, Roguish, Roman, Saddlebow, Safety, Saucy, Segmental, Shouldered, Skew, Sly, Soffit, Span, Squinch, Stilted, Subarcuate, Trajan, Trilith, Triumphal, Vault, Zygoma
**Archaeological, Archaeologist, Archaeology** Bell, Carter, Childe, Dater, Dig, Evans, Industrial, Layard, Leakey, Mallowan, Mycenae, Petrie, Pothunter, Qumran, Schliemann, Sutton Hoo, Type-site, Wheeler, Winckelmann, Woolley
**Archaic** Ancient, Dated
**Archangel** Azrael, Gabriel, Israfeel, Israfel, Israfil, Jerahmeel, Lucifer, Michael, Raguel, Raphael, Sariel, Satan, Uriel, Yellow
**Arch-binder** Voussoir
**Archbishop** Anselm, Athanasius, Augustine, Becket, Cosmo, Cranmer, Davidson, Dunstan, Ebor, Elector, Hatto, Hume, Lambeth, Lanfranc, Lang, Langton, Laud, Metropolitan, Morton, Primate, Runcie, Scroop, Temple, Trench, Tutu, Whitgift
**Archdeacon** Rev, Ven(erable)
**Archduke** Trio
**Archer(y)** Acestes, Bow-boy, →BOWMAN, Cupid, Eros, Hood, Petticoat, Philoctetes, Sagittary, Tell, Toxophilite
**Archetype, Archetypal** Avatar, Classic, Form, Model, Pattern
**Archibald, Archie, Archy** Ack-ack, Cockroach, Oerlikon, Rice, Roach
**Archilochian** Epode
**Archimandrite** Eutyches
**Archimedes** Screw
**Archipelago** Alexander, Antarctic, Azores, Bismarck, Camaguey, Dhivehi, East Indian, Fiji, Franz Josef Land, Gran Canaria, Gulag, Japan, Kerguelen, Malay, Maldives, Marquesas, Mergui, Nicobar Islands, Novaya Zemlya, Orkney, Palmer, Paumotu, St Pierre and Miquelon, Scilly Isles, Severnaya Zemlya, Spitsbergen, Sulu, Svalbard, Tierra del Fuego, Tonga, Tuamoto, West Indies
**Architect(ure), Architectural** Arcology, Baroque, Bauhaus, Beaux arts, Bricolage, Brutalism, Byzantine, Cartouche, Churrigueresque, Community, Composite, Computer, Corinthian, Creator, Crossette, Data-flow, Decorated, Decorated style, Designer, Domestic, Doric, Early English, Elizabethan, English Gothic, Entablature, Fantail, Federation, Flamboyant, Founder, Georgian, Gothic, Greek Revival, International model, International style, Ionic, Italian, Jacobean, Landscape, Listed, Lombard, Maker, Mission, Moderne, Moorish, Moresque, Mudejar, Naval, Neoclassical, Neo-gothic, Norman, Palladian, Pelasgian, Perpendicular, Picnostyle, Planner, Plateresque, Prostyle, Queen Anne, Romanesque, Saracenic, Saxon, Spandrel, Spandril, Tectonic, Tudor, Tudorbethan, Tuscan, Vitruvian

## ARCHITECTS

*3 letters:*
Cox
Pei

*4 letters:*
Adam
Kent
Loos
Nash
Shaw
Webb
Wood
Wren

*5 letters:*
Aalto
Barry
Gaudi
Hooke
Horta
Inigo
Nervi
Pugin
Scott
Soane
Speer
Utzon
Wyatt

*6 letters:*
Breuer
Casson
Foster
Lasdun
Nissen
Repton
Romano
Spence
Street
Voysey
Wright

*7 letters:*
Agrippa
Alberti
Behrens
Bernini
Blacket
Columbo
De Lorme
Erskine
Griffin
Gropius
Lutyens
Neumann
Percier
Seidler
Venturi
Vignola

*8 letters:*
Bramante
Chalgrin
Fontaine
Greenway
Niemeyer
Palladio
Piranesi
Saarinen
Stirling
Vanbrugh

*9 letters:*
Borromini
Hawksmoor
Mackmurdo
Macquarie
Vitruvius

*10 letters:*
Inigo Jones
Mackintosh
Tange Kenzo
Trophonius
Van der Rohe
Waterhouse

*11 letters:*
Abercrombie
Butterfield
Churrighera
Le Corbusier

*12 letters:*
Brunelleschi

*15 letters:*
Vitruvius Pollio

---

**Architrave** Epistyle, Platband
**Archive(s)** Backfile, Morgue, Muniment, PRO, Records, Register
**Archon** Draco
**Arch-villain** Ringleader
**Arctic** Estotiland, Frigid, Hyperborean, In(n)uit, Inupiat, Polar, Tundra
**Ardent, Ardour** Aflame, Aglow, Boil, Broiling, Burning, Eager, Elan, Enthusiasm, Fervent, Fervid, Fiery, Fire, Flagrant, Flaming, Gusto, Heat, Het, → HOT, Hot-brained, Impassioned, In, Mettled, Mettlesome, Passion(ate), Perfervid, Rage, Spiritous, Vehement, Warm-blooded, Zealous, Zeloso
**Arduous** Laborious, Schlap, Steep, Toilsome, Trying, Uphill
**Are** A, Exist, 're
**Area** Acre, Aleolar, Apron, Arctogaea, Are, Assisted, Bailiwick, Beachhead, Beat, Belgravia, Belt, Biscay, Bovate, Broca's, Built-up, Carucate, Catchment, Centare, Centiare, Centre, Chill-out, Clearing, Concourse, Conservation, Conurbation, Courtyard, Craton, Curtilage, Dec(i)are, Dedans, Depressed, Dessiatine, Development, Diocese, Disaster, District, Docklands, Domain, Downtown, Enclave, Endemic, Eruv, Estate, Extent, Exurb, Farthingland, Field, Forecourt, Gau, Ghetto, Goal, Grey, Growth, Heartland, Hectare, Henge, Hide, Hinterland, Hotspot, Husbandland, Imperium, Input, Karst, Landmass, Lathe, Latitude, Lek, Locale, Locality, Lodg(e)ment, Manor, Metroplex, Milieu, Mofussil, Morgen, Motor, Mush, Neogaea, Niche, Nidderdale, No-go, No-man's-land, Notogaea, Orb(it), Oxgang, Oxgate, Oxland, Pale, Parish, Patch, Penalty, Place, Pleasance, Plot, Precinct, Province, Purlieu, Quad, Quadrat, Quarter (section), Rain-forest, Range, Redevelopment, Refugium, → REGION, Remit, Renosterveld, Res(ervation), Reserve, Rest, Restricted, Retrochoir, Riding, Rood, Rule, Sector, Service, Shire, Site, Slurb, Space, Special, Staging, Sterling, Subdistrict, Subtopia, Suburb, Sun belt, Support, Surface, Tableland, Target, Tartary, Technical, Terra, Terrain, Territory, Theatre, Tie, Tract, Tundra, Tye, Uptown, Urban, Ure, Vicinity, Weald, White, Wilderness, Work station, Yard, Zone
**Areca** Betel

**Arena** Battleground, Bullring, Centre court, Circus, Cockpit, Dohyo, Field, Lists, Maidan, Olympia, → RING, Rink, Snowdome, Stadium, Tiltyard, Velodrome, Venue
**Argal** Ergo
**Argent** Ag, Silver
**Argentina** RA
**Argon** Ar
**Argonaut** Acastus, Jason, Lynceus, Meleager, Nautilus, Paper nautilus, Paper-sailor
**Argot** Flash, Idiom, Jargon, Lingo, Scamto, Shelta
**Argue, Argument(ative)** Altercation, Antistrophon, Argie-bargie, Argle-bargle, Argy-bargy, Bandy, Barney, Beef, Bicker, Blue, Brush, Cangle, Case, Casuism, Cavil, Choplogic, Conflict, Contend, Contention, Contest, Contra, Cosmological, Debate, Deprecate, Diallage, Difference, Dilemma, Ding-dong, Dispute, Dissent, Elenchus, Elenctic, Enthusiasm, Enthymeme, Eristic, Exchange, Expostulate, Forensic, Fray, Free-for-all, Generalisation, Hysteron proteron, Logic, Logomachy, Mexican standoff, Moot, Niggle, Ob and soller, Object, Odds, Ontological, Paralogism, Patter, Pettifog, Plead, Polemic, Polylemma, Premiss, Propound, Pros and cons, Quarrel, Quibble, Quodlibet, Rammy, Ratiocinate, → REASON, Rebut, Remonstrate, Row, Run-in, Scene, Sequacious, Socratise, Sophism, Sophistry, Sorites, Spar, Spat, Split hairs, Squabble, Stickle, Straw man, Stroppy, Stushie, Summation, Syllogism, Teleological, Theme, Thetic, Third man, Tiff, Transcendental, Trilemma, Truculence, Verbal, Vociferate, Words, Wrangle, Wrestle, Yike
**Argyle** Argathelian, Gravy-boat, Sock
**Aria** Ballad, Cabaletta, Cantata, Cavatina, Melody, Nessun dorma, Song
**Arid** Dry, Parched, Sere, Siccity
**Ariel** Pen
**Aris** Arse, → BOTTOM, Can
**Arise** Appear, Be, Develop, Emanate, Emerge, Stem, Upgo, Wax
**Aristocracy, Aristocrat(ic)** Blood, Blue blood, Boyar, Buckeen, Classy, Debrett, Duc, Elite, Eupatrid, Gentle, Gentry, Grandee, High-hat, Junker, Milord, Nob, Noble, Optimate, Passage, Patrician, Thane, Thegn, Titled, Toff, Tony, Top drawer, U-men, Upper-crust, Viscount, Well-born
**Aristotle** Peripatetic, Stagirite, Stagyrite
**Arithmetic(ian)** Algorism, Algorith, Arsmetrick, Cocker, Euclid, Logistic, Modular, Quadrivium, Sums
**Ark(wright)** Chest, Noah, Zoo
**Arly** Thicket
**Arm(ed), Arms** Akimbo, Arsenal, Bayonet, Bearing, Brachial, Branch, Bundooks, Canting, Cove, Crest, Cross bow, Division, Embattle, Equip, Escutcheon, Estoc, Fin, Firth, Frith, Gnomon, Halbert, Hatchment, Heel, Heraldic, Inlet, Jib, Krupp, Limb, Loch, Long, Machete, Member, Munitions, Musket, Olecranon, Pick-up, Present, Quillon, Radius, Rail, Ramous, Rocker, Rotor, SAA, Sail, Secular, Shield, Shotgun, Side, Small(-bore), Smooth-bore, Spiral, Sten-gun, Tappet, Taser®, Tentacle, Timer, Tone, Tooled-up, Transept, Tremolo, Ulnar, Water pistol, → WEAPON, Whip, Winchester
▷**Arm** *may indicate* an army regiment, etc.
**Armada** Fleet, Spanish
**Armadillo** Dasypod, Dasypus, Fairy, Giant, Pangolin, Peba, Pichiciego, Tatou(ay), Xenurus
**Armature** Keeper, Shuttle
**Armband** Torc, Torque
**Armchair** Bergere, Carver
**Armenian** Haikh, Yezedi
**Armhole** Scye
**Armistice** Still-stand, Truce, VE Day, VJ Day
**Armless** Inermous
**Armour(ed), Armoury** Ailette, Armature, Armet, Barbette, Battledress, Beaver, Besagew, Bevor, Body, Brasset, Breastplate, Brigandine, Buckler, Byrnie, Camail, Cannon, Casemate, Casspir, Cataphract, Chaffron, Chain, Chamfrain, Chamfron, Character, Chausses, Coat, Corium, Cors(e)let, Couter, Cuirass, Cuish, Cuisse, Culet, Curat, Curiet, Cush, Defence,

Fauld, Garderobe, Garniture, Gear, Genouillère, Gere, Gorget, Greave, Habergeon, Hauberk, Hoplology, Jack, Jambe, Jambeau, Jazerant, Jesserant, Lamboys, Loricate, Mail, Male, Mentonnière, Mesail, Mezail, Nasal, Nosepiece, Palette, Panoply, Panzer, Pauldron, Pectoral, Petta, Placcat, Placket, Plastron, Plate, Poitrel, Poleyn, Pouldron, Puldron, Rerebrace, Rest, Roundel, Sabaton, Scale, Secret, → SHIELD, Solleret, Spaudler, Splint, Stand, Tace, Tank, Taslet, Tasse(t), Thorax, Tonlet, Tuille, Vambrace, Vantbrass, Ventail(e), Ventayle, Visor, Voider, Weed

**Armpit** Axilla, Oxter

**Armstrong** Astronaut, Louis, Neil, Satchmo, Trumpeter

**Army** Arrière-ban, Arrière-garde, BEF, Blue Ribbon, Church, Colours, Confederate, Crowd, Federal, Field, Fyrd, Golden (Horde), Horde, Host, IRA, Junior Service, Land, Landwehr, Lashkar, Legion, Line, Military, Militia, Mobile Command, Multitude, New Model, Para-military, Red, SA, Sabaoth, Sally, Salvation, SAS, Sena, Service, Soldiers, Squad, Standing, Stratonic, Swarm, TA, Tartan, Terracotta, Territorial, Thin red line, Volunteer, War, Wehrmacht

▷**Army** *may indicate* having arms

**Aroma(tic)** Allspice, Aniseed, Aryl, Balmy, Camphor, Coriander, Fenugreek, Fragrant, Nose, Odorous, Pomander, Redolent, Spicy, Stilbene, Vanillin, Wintergreen

**Around** About, Ambient, Circa, Near, Peri-, Skirt, Tour

▷**Around** *may indicate* one word around another

**Arouse(d), Arousal** Alarm, Attract, Cold pig, Displease, Elicit, Evoke, → EXCITE, Fan, Fire, Goad, Incite, Incur, Indignant, Inflame, Inspire, Kindle, Must(h), Needle, Provoke, Stimulate, Stole, Suscitate, Touch up, Urolagnia, Waken, Whet

**Arpad** ELO

**Arrange(r), Arrangement** Adjust, Array, Attune, Ausgleich, Bandobast, Bank, Bundobust, Cartel, Cohabitation, Collate, Concert, Concinnity, Configuration, Coordinate, Design, Display, Dispose, Do, Drape, Dress, Echelon, Edit, Engineer, File, Finger, Fix, Foreordain, Format, Formation, Formwork, Geometry, Grade, Ikebana, Jig, Layout, Lend-lease, Lineation, Marshal, Modus vivendi, Neaten, Orchestrate, Orchestration, Ordain, → ORDER, Ordonnance, Organise, Pack, Pattern, Perm, Permutation, Plan, Position, Prepare, Prepense, Quincunx, Redactor, Regulate, Run, Rustle up, Schedule, Schema, Scheme, Score, Set(ting) (up), Settle, Sort, Spacing, Stack, Stage-manage, Stereoisomerism, Stow, Straighten, Structure, Style, Syntax, System, Tabulate, Tactic, Taxis, Tidy, Timeshare, Transcribe, Vertical, Wangle

▷**Arrange** *may indicate* an anagram

**Arrant** Utter

**Arras** Tapestry

**Array(ed)** Attire, Bedight, Caparison, Deck, Herse, Logic, Marshal, Matrice, Matrix, Muster, Panoply, Phased, Seismic, Ula

**Arrear(s)** Aft, Ahint, Backlog, Behind, Debt, Owing

**Arrest(ed), Arresting** Abort, Alguacil, Alguazil, Ament, Apprehend, Attach, Attract, Blin, Book, Bust, Caption, Capture, Cardiac, Catch, Cessation, Check, Citizen's, Collar, Cop, Detain, False, Furthcoming, Hold, House, Infangthief, Knock, Lag, Lift, Lightning, Nab, Nail, Nick, Nip, Nobble, Pinch, Pull in, Restrain, Retard, Riveting, Round-up, Run-in, Salient, Sease, Seize, Snaffle, Snatch, Spellbind, Stasis, Staunch, Stop, Sus(s), Turn in

**Arris** Groin

**Arrival, Arrive, Arriving, Arriviste** Accede, Advent, Attain, Come, Destination, End up, Entrance, Get, Happen, Hit, Inbound, Influx, Johnny-come-lately, Land, Latecomer, Natal, Nativity, Newcomer, Parvenu, Pitch up, Reach, Roll up, Show, Strike

**Arrogance, Arrogant** Assumption, Boastful, Bold, Bravado, Bumptious, Cavalier, Cocksure, Cocky, Contemptuous, Disdain, Dogmatic, Effrontery, Haughty, Haut(eur), High, High and mighty, High-handed, High-hat, High-minded, Hogen-mogen, Hoity-toity, Hubris, Imperious, Jumped up, Lordly, Morgue, Overweening, Pompous, Presumption, Pretentious, Proud, Proud-stomached, Prussianism, Side, Snobbish, Snooty, Stuck-up, Surquedry, Surquedy, Toploftical, Topping, Turkeycock, Uppish, Uppity, Upstart, Yuppy

**Arrogate** Appropriate, Assume, Claim, Impute, Usurp

**Arrow, Arrow-head** Acestes, Any, Ary, Blunt, Bolt, Broad(head), Cloth-yard shaft, Cursor, Dart, Dogbolt, Filter, Flechette, Flight, Greygoose, Greyquill, Greyshaft, Greywing, Missile, Pheon, Pointer, Quarrel, Reed, Sagittate, Shaft, Sheaf, Straight

**Arrow-maker** Fletcher

**Arrowroot** Kuzu, Maranta, Pia, Portland

**Arse** → BOTTOM, Khyber (pass)

**Arsenal** Ammo, Armo(u)ry, Depot, Fire-arms, Magazine, Side, Toulon, Weaponry

**Arsenate, Arsenic(al), Arsenide** As, Erythrite, Realgar, Resalgar, Rosaker, Salvarsan, Scorodite, Skutterudite, Smaltite, Speiss, White, Zarnich

**Arson(ist)** Firebug, Pyromania, Torching

**Art(s), Arty, Art movement, Art school, Art style** Abstract, Alla prima, American, Applied, Ars, Arte Povera, Bauhaus, Black, Bloomsbury, Body, Bohemian, Bonsai, Britart, Brut, Chiaroscuro, Clair-obscure, Clare-obscure, Click, Clip, Cobra, Collage, Commercial, Conceptual, Concrete, Constructivism, Contrapposto, Craft, Cubism, Culture vulture, Cunning, Curious, Dada, Daedal(e), Deco, Decorative, Dedal, De Stijl, Die Brucke, Diptych, Divisionism, Earth, Ekphrasis, Enamel(ling), Environmental, Es, Expressionism, Fauvism, Feat, Fine, Finesse, Flemish, Folk, Fugue, Futurism, Genre, Gothic, Graphic, Grisaille, Guile, High Renaissance, Humanities, Ikebana, Impressionist, Jugendstil, Kakemono, Kano, Ka pai, Kinetic, Kirigami, Kitsch, Knack, Lacquerware, Land, Liberal, Mandorla, Mannerism, Martial, Masterwork, Mehndi, Minimal, Modern(e), Montage, Motivated, Music, Mystery, Nabis, Nazarene, Neoclassical, Neo-impressionism, New Wave, Nihonga, Noli-me-tangere, Norwich, Nouveau, Objets trouves, Optical, Orchesis, Origami, Orphic Cubism, Orphism, Outsider, Pastiche, Performance, Performing, Perigordian, Photomontage, Plastic, Pointillism, Pop, Postimpressionism, Postmodern, Practical, Pre-Raphaelite, Primitive, Psychedelic, Public, Purism, Quadratura, Quadrivium, Rangoli, Relievo, Repousse, Scraperboard, Sienese, → SKILL, Social realism, Stained glass, Still-life, Suprematism, Surrealism, Synchronism, Tachism(e), Tactics, Tatum, Tenebrism, Tessera, Toreutics, Trecento, Triptych, Trivium, Trompe l'oeil, Trouvé, Tsutsumu, Ukiyo-e, Useful, Verism, Virtu, Visual, Vorticism

▷**Art** *may indicate* an -est ending

**Artefact(s)** Neolith, Palaeolith, Tartanalia, Tartanry, Xoanon

▷**Artefact** *may indicate* an anagram

**Artemis** Selene

**Artemus** Ward

**Artery** Aorta, Brachial, Carotid, Coronary, Duct, Femoral, Frontal, Iliac, Innominate, M1, Maxillary, Phrenic, Pulmonary, Radial, Route, Spermatic, Temporal

**Artful** Cute, Dodger, Foxy, Ingenious, Quirky, Shifty, Sly, Subtle, Tactician, Wily

**Arthropod** Insecta, Limulus, Myriapod, Myriopod, Peripatus, Prototracheata, Sea-slater, Tardigrade, Tick, Trilobite, Water-bear

**Artichoke** Cardoon, Jerusalem

**Article(s)** A, An, Apprentice, Artefact, Association, City, Clause, Column, Commodity, Cutting, Death, Definite, Doctrine, Faith, Feature, Feuilleton, Five, Gadget, Genuine, Great, Indefinite, Indenture, Item, Leader, Leading, Object, Op-ed, Paper, Paraphernalia, Part, Piece, Pot-boiler, Rag-out, Report, Shipping, Sidebar, Specify, Tenet, The, Thing, Thinkpiece, Thirty-nine, Treatise, Turnover, Utensil, War, Ware

**Articulation, Articulate(d)** Clear, Coherent, Coudé, Diarthrosis, Distinct, Eloquent, Enounce, Express, Fluent, Fortis, Gimmal, Gomphosis, Hinged, Intonate, Jointed, Jymold, Lenis, Limbed, Lisp, Pretty-spoken, Pronounce, Schindylesis, Single-tongue, Tipping, Tonguing, Trapezial, Utter, Verbalise, Vertebrae, Vocal, Voice, Wrist

**Artifice(r), Artificial** Android, Astroturf, Bogus, Chouse, Contrived, Davenport-trick, Dodge, Ersatz, Factitious, False, Feint, Finesse, Golem, Guile, Hoax, Inauthentic, In vitro, Logodaedaly, Made, Man-made, Mannered, Mock, Opificer, Phoney, Postiche, Pretence, Prosthetic, Pseudo, Reach, Ruse, Sell, Set, Sham, Spurious, Stratagem, → STRATEGY, Synroc, Synthetic, Theatric, → TRICK, Unnatural, Wile, Wright

**Artificial respiration** Kiss of life, Schafer's method

**Artillery(man)** Battery, Cannon(ier), Cohorn(e), Drumfire, Field (piece), Fougade, Fougasse,

Guns, Mortar, Ordnance, Pyroballogy, RA, Rafale, Ramose, Ramus, Train

**Artiodactyl** Camel, Chevrotain, Deerlet

**Artisan** Craftsman, Decorator, Joiner, Journeyman, Mechanic, Peon, Pioneer, Pioner, Pyoner, Shipwright, Weaver, Workman

**Artist(e), Artistic** Aesthetic, Animator, Ballerina, Blaue Reiter, Bohemian, Cartoonist, Colourist, Cubist, Cultural, Dadaist, Daedal(e), Deccie, Decorator, Die Brucke, Enameller, Escape, Etcher, Fauve, Fine, Foley, Gentle, Gilder, Graffiti, ICA, Illustrator, Impressionist, Landscapist, Left Bank, Limner, Linear, Maestro, Make-up, Master, Mime, Miniaturist, → **MUSICIAN**, Nabis, Nazarene, Oeuvre, Orphism, → **PAINTER**, Pastellist, Pavement, Paysagist, Perspectivist, Piss, Player, Plein-airist, Pre-Raphaelite, Primitive, Quick-change, RA, Rap, Screever, → **SCULPTOR**, Sideman, Sien(n)ese, Stripper, Surrealist, Tachisme, Tagger, Tap dancer, Touch, Trapeze, Trecentist, Virtuose, Virtuoso, Water-colourist

---

## ARTISTS

*3 letters:*
Arp
Cox
Dix
Dou
Dow
Ono

*4 letters:*
Bell
Chia
Cole
Cuyp
Dadd
Dali
Done
Doré
Douw
Dufy
Emin
Etty
Goya
Gris
Hals
John
Klee
Lely
Long
Marc
Miró
Nash
Opie
Phiz
Rees
West

*5 letters:*
Aiken
Appel
Bacon
Bakst
Balla
Blake
Bosch
Brown
Buren
Burra
Corot
Crane
Crome
Danby
David
Degas
Dulac
Dürer
Ensor
Ernst
Gelée
Ghika
Grosz
Herge
Hirst
Hoare
Homer
Hooch
Johns
Klimt
Kline
Leech
Léger
Lippi
Lotto
Lowry
Makar
Manet
Monet
Moses
Munch
Nolan
Olley
Olsen
Orpen
Poons
Redon
Riley
Rodin
Seago
Steen
Steer
Tatum
Watts

*6 letters:*
Albers
Boudin
Braque
Bratby
Brucke
Calder
Callot
Claude
Clouet
Cotman
Derain
De Wint
Dobell
D'Orsay
Eakins
Escher
Fabrio
Fuseli
Gilles
Giotto
Greuze
Guardi
Haydon
Herman
Hopper
Ingres
Knight
Larkin
Le Nain
Man Ray
Massys
Millet
Moreau
Morris
Newman
Oliver
Renoir
Ribera
Rivera
Romano
Romney
Rothko
Rubens
Sendak
Seurat
Signac
Sisley
Strang
Stubbs
Tissot
Titian
Turner
Vasari
Warhol
Zeuxis

*7 letters:*
Acconci
Allston
Apelles
Attwell
Audubon
Bellini
Bernini
Bonnard
Borduas
Boucher
Bruegel
Cassall
Cellini
Cézanne

Chagall
Chardin
Chirico
Christo
Cimabue
Collier
Courbet
Cranach
Daumier
Da Vinci
Duchamp
El Greco
Epstein
Gauguin
Hobbema
Hockney
Hogarth
Hokusai
Holbein
Hoppner
Kneller
Lepicie
Lorrain
Martens
Martini
Matisse
Meldrum
Memling
Millais
Morisot
Morland
Murillo
Nattier
O'Keeffe
Parrish
Picabia
Picasso
Pollock
Popover
Poussin
Preston
Prudhon
Pucelle
Rackham
Raeburn
Raphael
Rouault
Russolo
Sargent
Schiele
Sickert
Spencer
Tiepolo
Uccello
Utamaro
Utrillo
Van Dyke
Van Eyck
Van Gogh
Vermeer
Watteau
Zeuxian
Zoffany

***8 letters:***
Annigoni
Auerbach
Barbizon
Baselitz
Beckmann
Boccioni
Bronzino
Carracci
Clemente
Daguerre
Daubigny
Drysdale
Eastlake
Giordana
Kauffman
Kaufmann
Kirchner
Landseer
Leonardo
Magritte
Malevich
Mantegna
Masaccio
Mondrian
Munnings
Nevinson
Passmore
Perceval
Perugino
Piranesi
Pissarro
Pontormo
Reynolds
Rockwell
Rossetti
Rousseau
Severini
Thorburn
Topolski
Veronese
Whistler
Whiteley

***9 letters:***
Beardsley
Bonington
Canaletto
Carpaccio
Constable
Correggio
De Chirico
De Kooning
Delacroix
Delaroche
Delauncey
Donatello
Fragonard
Francesca
Friedrich
Gericault
Giorgione
Grunewald
Hiroshige
Kandinsky
Kokoschka
Le Lorrain
Mitsunobo
Nicholson
Oldenburg
Rembrandt
Thornhill
Velasquez

***10 letters:***
Alma-Tadema
Botticelli
Burne-Jones
Caravaggio
Fiorentino
Giacometti
Guillaumin
Holman Hunt
Madox Brown
Modigliani
Motherwell
Rowlandson
Schwitters
Signorelli
Sutherland
Tintoretto
Van der Goes
Van der Meer
Waterhouse

***11 letters:***
Fairweather
Fra Angelico
Gentileschi

***12 letters:***
Fantin-Latour
Gainsborough
Lichtenstein
Michelangelo
Rauschenberg
Winterhalter

***14 letters:***
Jackson Pollock

***15 letters:***
Hieronymus Bosch
Toulouse-Lautrec

---

**Artless(ness)** Candid, Candour, Homespun, Ingenuous, Innocent, Naive, Natural, Open, Seely, Simple
**Art nouveau** Jugendstil
**Arturo** Toscanini
**Arum** Acorus, Green-dragon, Lily, Lords and ladies, Taro, Titan
**As** Aesir, Als, Arsenic, Coin, Eg, Forasmuch, Kame, Qua, Ridge, 's, Since, So, Thus, Ut, While
**As above** US, Ut supra
**Asafoetida** Hing
**As before** Anew, Ditto, Do, Stet
**Asbestos** Amiant(h)us, Amosite, Chrysolite, Crocidolite, Earthflax, Fireproof, Rockwood

**Ascend(ant), Ascent, Ascension** Anabasis, Climb, Dominant, Escalate, Gradient, Lift, Pull, Ramp, Right, Rise, Sclim, Sklim, Slope, Up, Upgang, Uphill, Uprise, Zoom
**Ascertain** Determine, Discover, →ESTABLISH, Prove
**Ascetic** Puritanical, Whirling dervish
**Ascetic(ism)** Agapetae, Anchor(et), Anchorite, Ancress, Ashramite, Austere, Dervish, Diogenes, Encratite, Eremital, Essene, Fakir, Faquir, Gymnosophist, Hermit, Jain(ite), Monk, Nazarite, Nazirite, Nun's flesh, Sad(d)hu, Self-denial, Simeon Stylites, Stylite, Sufic, Therapeutae, Yogi(n)
**Ascidian** Chordate, Urochordate
**Asclepiad** Stapelia
**Ascribe** Assign, →ATTRIBUTE, Blame, Credit, Imply, Impute
**Asdic** Sonar
**As far as** Quoad
**As good as** Equal, Tantamount
**Ash(es), Ashen, Ashy** Aesc, Aizle, Bone, Breeze, Cinders, Cinereal, Clinker(s), Easle, Embers, Fly, Fraxinas, Griseous, Hoop, Kali, Lahar, Pallor, Pearl, Pozz(u)olana, Prickly, Rowan, Ruins, Soda, Sorb, Spodo-, Stinking, Tephra, Urn, Varec, Volcanic, Wednesday, Weeping, White, Witchen, Yg(g)drasil(l)
**Ashamed** Abashed, Embarrassed, Hangdog, Mortified, Repentant, Sheepish, Shent
**Ashore** Aland, Beached, Coast, Grounded, Stranded
**Ash-pan** Backet
**Ashram** Haven
**Asia(n), Asiatic** Afghan, Altaic, Angaraland, Armenian, Azari, Azerbaijani, Balinese, Bangladeshi, Bengali, Bithynia, Cambodian, Cantonese, Desi, E, Evenki, Ewenki, Filipino, Gook, Harijan, Harsha, Hun, Hyksos, Indian, Indonesian, Jordanian, Karen(ni), Kashmir, Kazakh, Kirghiz, Korean, Kurd, Kyrgyz, Lao(tian), Lydian, Malay, Medea, Media, Mongol, Naga, Negrito, Nepalese, Pasht(o)um, Pathan, Phrygian, Punjabi, Pushtu, Samo(y)ed, Saudi, Shan, Siamese, Sindi, Sogdian, Sri Lankan, Taiwanese, Tamil, Tartar, Tatar, Tibetan, Tocharian, Tokharian, Turanian, Turk(o)man, Uzbeg, Uzbek, Vietnamese
**Asia Minor** Anatolia, Ionic
**Aside** Apart, By(-speech), Despite, Private, Separate, Shelved, Sotto voce, Stage whisper
**Asinine** Crass, Dull, Idiotic, Puerile, Stupid
**Ask** Bed, Beg, Beseech, Bid, Cadge, Charge, Demand, Desire, Eft, Enquire, Entreat, Evet, Implore, Intreat, Invite, Lobby, Newt, Petition, Pray, Prithee, Pump, Query, Quiz, Request, Require, Rogation, Seek, Solicit, Speer, Speir, Touch
**Askance** Asconce, Askew, Oblique, Sideways
**Askew** Agee, Aglee, Agley, Ajee, Aslant, Awry, Crooked, Oblique, Skivie
**Aslant** Skew
**Asleep** Dormant, Dove, Inactive, Napping
**As needed** Ad hoc
**As often as** Toties quoties
**Asparagus** Asperge, Sparrow-grass, Spear, Sprew, Sprue, Yard-long bean
**Aspect** Angle, Bearing, Brow, Face, Facet, Facies, Factor, Feature, Guise, Hue, Look, Mien, Nature, Outlook, Panorama, Perfective, Perspective, Phase, Print, Scene, Sextile, Side, →VIEW, Visage, Vista
**Aspen** Trembling poplar
**Aspersion, Asperse** Calumny, Defame, Innuendo, Libel, Slander, Slur, Smear, Traduce
**Asphalt** Bitumen, Blacktop, Gilsonite®, Pitch, Pitch Lake, Uinta(h)ite
**Asphyxia, Asphyxiate** Apn(o)ea, Choke
**Aspirant, Aspirate, Aspiration, Aspire** Aim, Ambition, Breath, Buckeen, Challenger, Desire, Dream, Endeavour, Ettle, Goal, H, Hope(ful), Pretend, Pursue, Rough, Spiritus, Wannabe(e), Would be, Yearn, Yuppie
**Ass(es)** Buridan's, Burnell, Burro, Cardophagus, Chigetai, Clot, Couscous, Cuddie, Dawcock, Denarius, Dick(e)y, Donkey, Dziggetai, Funnel, Golden, Hemione, Hemionus, Hinny, Jack, Jenny, Jerusalem pony, Kiang, Kourbash, Kourmiss, Kouskous, K(o)ulan, Kumiss, Kurbash, Kyang, Liripipe, Liripoop, Moke, Neddy, Nitwit, Onager, Quagga, Sesterce, Simp, →STUPID PERSON

**Assail(ant)** Afflict, Assault, Attack, Batter, Bego, Belabour, Bepelt, Beset, Besiege, Bombard, Foe, Harry, Impugn, Mugger, Onsetter, Oppugn, Pillory, Ply, Revile

**Assassin(ate), Assassination** Attentat, Booth, Brave, Bravo, Brutus, Casca, Cassius, Character, Corday, Cut-throat, Dallas, Frag, Gar(r)otte, Gunman, Highbinder, Hitman, Hit squad, Killer, Ninja, Oswald, Sword, Sworder, Thuggee, Triggerman, Tyrannicide

**Assault** ABH, Assail, Assay, Attack, Battery, Bombard, GBH, Hamesucken, Head-butt, Indecent, Invasion, Knee, Maul, Molest, Mug, Push, → **RAID**, Scalade, Stoor, Storm, Stour, Stowre, Work over

**Assay(ing)** Cupel, Docimasy, Examine, Proof, Radio, Test, Wet

**As seen** Voetstoots

**Assemble(d), Assembly** Aggregate, Agora, Amass, Audience, Ball, Band, Bevy, Bottom-hole, Brood, Bundestag, Chapter, Chatuaqua, Cho(u)ltry, Church, Clutch, Co, Collation, → **COLLECTION**, Comitia, Company, Conclave, Concourse, Congeries, Congregate, Congress, Consistory, Constituent, Convene, Conventicle, Convention, Convocation, Convoke, Corroboree, Cortes, Council, Court (baron), Covey, Curia, Dail Eireann, Dewain, Diet (of Worms), Dietine, Divan, Donnybrook, D(o)uma, Ecclesia, Eisteddfod, Erect, Feis(eanna), Fit, Flotilla, Folkmoot, Folkmote, Force, Forgather, Fuel, Gather(ing), Gemot(e), General, Gorsedd, Group, Headstock, Hoi polloi, House, Interjoin, Jirga, Kgotla, Knesset, Landtag, Legislative, Lekgotla, Levee, Loya jirga, Majlis, Make, Mass, Meet, → **MEETING**, Mejlis, Moot, Murder, Muster, National, Nide, Oireachtas, Panegyry, Panoply, Parishad, Parliament, Patron, Pattern, Plenum, Pnyx, Powwow, Prefabrication, Presence, Primary, Quorum, Rally, Rallying-point, Rechate, Recheate, Reichstag, Relie, Repair, Resort, Riksdag, Rodeo, Roll up, Round-up, Sanghat, Sanhedrin, Sanhedron, School, Scratch, Sedge, Sejm, Senate, Senedd, Sheaf, Skupshtina, Sobranje, Soc, Society, Squadron, Stort(h)ing, String, Student, Synagogue, Synedrion, Synod, T(h)ing, Tribunal, Troop, Troupe, Turn out, Unlawful, Vidhan Sabha, Volksraad, Wapens(c)haw, Wapins(c)haw, Wappens(c)haw, Wardmote, Weapon-s(c)haw, Witan, Witenagemot, Zemstvo

**Assent** Accede, Acquiesce, Agree, Amen, Aye, Comply, Concur, Jokol, Nod, Placet, Royal, Sanction, Viceregal, Yea, Yield

**Assert(ing), Assertion, Assertive** Affirm, Allege, Bumptious, Claim, Constate, Contend, → **DECLARE**, Dogmatic, Forceful, Ipse-dixit, → **MAINTAIN**, Pose, Predicate, Proclaim, Pronounce, Protest, Pushing, Pushy, Rumour, Swear (blind), Thetical, Vouch

**Assess(ment), Assessor** Actuary, Affeer, Appraise, Audition, Cense, Church-rate, Claims, Consider, Critique, Eleven-plus, Estimate, Evaluate, Exam, Formative, Gauge, Guesstimate, Inspect, → **JUDGE**, Levy, Means test, Measure, Perspective, Rating, Referee, Report, Risk, Scot and lot, Size up, Special, Stent, Stocktake, Summative, Tax, Value, Weigh

**Asset(s)** Advantage, Capital, Chargeable, Chattel, Collateral, Current, Equity, Fixed, Floating, Goodwill, Intangible, Inventory, Liquid, Net, Plant, Property, Resource, Seed corn, Talent, Tangible, Virtue, Wasting

**Assiduous** Attentive, Busy, Constant, Diligent, Studious, Thorough

**Assign(ation), Assignment** Allocate, → **ALLOT**, Apply, Appoint, Aret, Ascribe, Attentat, Attribute, Award, Base, Date, Dedicate, Deploy, Depute, Detach, Detail, Duty, Entrust, Errand, Fix, Give, Grant, Impute, Mission, Ordain, Placement, Point, Quota, Refer, Sort, Tak(e), Tryst

**Assimilate(d)** Absorb, Blend, Digest, Esculent, Fuse, Imbibe, Incorporate, Merge, Osmose

**Assist(ance), Assistant** Acolyte, Adjoint, Adjunct, Adviser, Aid(e), Aide-de-camp, Ally, Alms, Attaché, Attend, Au pair, Batman, Befriend, Best boy, Busboy, Cad, Chainman, Clerk, Collaborate, Counterhand, Counter-jumper, Deputy, Dresser, Ex parte, Facilitate, Factotum, Famulus, Feldschar, Felds(c)her, Girl Friday, Gofer, Grant-in-aid, → **HAND**, Handlanger, Help, Henchman, Legal aid, Leg-up, Matross, McKenzie friend, Medicaid, Mentor, National, Nipper, Number two, Offsider, Omnibus, Orderly, Paralegal, Paramedic, Proproctor, Public, Reinforce, Relief, Running-mate, Second, Secretary, Server, Service, Servitor, Shill, Sidekick, Sidesman, Smallboy, Social, Stead, Subeditor, Subsidiary, Subsidy, Suffragan, Supernumerary, → **SUPPORT**, Tawny Owl, Underling, Usher, Whipper-in

**Assize** Botley, Circuit, Court, Maiden, Oyer

**Associate(d), Association** Accessory, Accomplice, Affiliate, Alliance, Amphictyony, Ass,

Attach, Bedfellow, Brotherhood, Camp-follower, Cartel, Chapel, Chum, Clang, Club, Cohort, Colleague, Combine, Comecon, Community, Company, Compeer, Complice, Comrade, Concomitant, Confrère, → CONNECT, Connotation, Consort(ium), Contact, Co-partner, Correlate, Crony, Enclisis, Familiar, Fellow, Fraternise, Fraternity, Free, Gesellschaft, Goose club, Guild, Hobnob, Housing, Identify, Inquiline, Intime, Involvement, Join, Kabele, Kebele, Kindred, League, Liaison, Link, Lloyds, Mell, Member, MENSA, Mess, Mix, Moshav, Oddfellows, Pal, Parent teacher, Partner(ship), Phoresy, Press, Probus, Professional, Relate, Residents', Ring, Round Table, Samit(h)i, Sangh(at), Sidekick, Sodality, Stablemate, Staff, Symbiosis, Syndicate, Synonymous, Tenants', Toc H, Toenadering, Trade, UN(A), Union, Verein, Whiteboy, Wiener Werkstatte, Word, Yoke-fellow, Yoke-mate

**Assort(ed), Assortment** Choice, Congeries, Etc, Medley, Miscellaneous, Motley, Olio, Paraphernalia, Pick-'n'-mix, Ragbag, Range, Various

▷**Assorted** *may indicate* an anagram

**Assuage** Allay, Appease, Beet, Calm, Ease, Mease, Mitigate, Mollify, Relieve, Slake, Soften, Soothe, Temper

**As such** Qua

**Assume(d), Assuming, Assumption** Adopt, Affect, Arrogate, Artificial, Attire, Axiom, Believe, Deem, Don, Donné(e), Feign, Gather, Hypothesis, Lemma, Occam's Razor, Pose, Posit, Postulate, Preconception, Premise, Premiss, Presuppose, Pretend, Pretentious, Principle, Putative, Put on, Saltus, Say, Shoulder, Side, Simulate, Suppose, Surmise, Take, Uppity, Usurp

▷**Assumption** *may indicate* 'attire'

**Assure(d), Assurance** Aplomb, Aver, Avouch, Belief, Calm, → CERTAIN, Comfort, Confidence, Confirm, Earnest, Gall, Guarantee, Knowing, Life, Pledge, Poise, Promise, Secure, Self-confidence, Term, Thoughten, Warranty

**Assuredly** Indeed, Perdie, Verily, Yea

**Assyrian** Sennacherib

**Astatine** At

**Aster** Starwort

**Astern** Abaft, Apoop, Rear

**Asteroid** Achilles, Ceres, Eros, Eros 433, Hermes, Hygiea, Icarus, Juno, Minor planet, Pallas, Phaethon, Pholus, Planetoid, Sea-star, Star, Starfish, Trojan, Vesta

**Astir** Afoot, Agate, Agog, Buzz

**Astonish(ed), Astonishing, Astonishment, Astound(ing)** Abash, Admiraunce, Amaze, Banjax, Bewilder, Bowl over, Breathtaking, Confound, Corker, Crikey, Daze, Donnert, Dumbstruck, Dum(b)found, Eye-popping, Flabbergast, Gobsmack, Heavens, Mindblowing, Mind-boggling, Miracle, Open-eyed, Open-mouthed, Phew, Pop-eyed, Prodigious, Rouse, Shake, Singular, Stagger, Startle, Stun, Stupefaction, Stupefy, Stupendous, Surprise, Thunderstruck, Wide-eyed, Wow

**Astray** Abord, Amiss, Errant, Lost, Will, Wull

**Astride** Athwart, En cavalier, Spanning, Straddle-back

**Astringent** Acerbic, Alum, Catechu, Dhak, Gambi(e)r, Harsh, Kino, Krameria, Myrobalan, Obstruent, Puckery, Rhatany, Sept-foil, Severe, Sour, Stypsis, Styptic, Tormentil, Witch-hazel

**Astrologer, Astrology, Astrological** Archgenethliac, Chaldean, Culpeper, Faust, Figure-caster, Genethliac, Judicial, Lilly, Magus, Midheaven, Moore, Nostradamus, Soothsayer, Starmonger, Zadkiel

**Astronaut** Aldrin, Cosmonaut, Gagarin, Glenn, Lunarnaut, Spaceman, Spacer, Spacewalker, Taikonaut

**Astronomer, Astronomy, Astronomical** Airy, Almagest, Aristarchus, Azimuth, Barnard, Bessel, Bliss, Bradley, Brahe, Callipic, Cassegrain, Cassini, Celsius, Christie, Coal sack, Copernicus, Dyson, Eddington, Encke, Eratosthenes, Eudoxus, Flamsteed, Galileo, Gamma-ray, Graham-Smith, Hale, Halley, Herschel, Hertzsprung, Hewish, Hipparchus, Hoyle, Hubble, Huggins, Idris, Infra red, Jeans, Kepler, Lagrange, Laplace, Leverrier, Lockyer, Lovell, Maskelyne, Meton, Moore, Neutrino, Observer, Olbers, Omar Khayyam, Oort, Physical, Planetesimal, Planetology, Pond, Ptolemy, Quadrivium, Radar, Radio, Reber, Rees, Roche, Roemer, Russell, Ryle, Schwarzschild, Selenography, Selenology, Seyfert, Sosigenes,

Spencer-Jones, Stargazer, Star read, Telescopy, Tycho Brahe, Ultraviolet, Urania, Uranic, Uranography, Wolfendale, Woolley, X-ray, Zwicky

**Astrophel** Penthia

**Astrophysicist** Seifert

**Astute** Acute, Canny, Crafty, Cunning, Downy, Perspicacious, Shrewd, Subtle, Wide, Wily

**As usual** Solito

**As well** Additionally, Also, Both, Eke, Even, Forby, Likewise, To boot, Too

**Asylum** Bedlam, Bin, Bughouse, Frithsoken, Funny-farm, Girth, Grith, Haven, Institution, Loony bin, Lunatic, Madhouse, Magdalene, Nuthouse, Political, Rathouse, Refuge, Retreat, Sanctuary, Shelter, Snake-pit

**Asylum-seeker** Refugee

**Asymmetric(al), Assymetry** Contrapposto, Imbalance, Lopsided, Skew

**At** Astatine, In, Kip, To, Up-bye

**Atahualpa** Inca

**At all** Ava, Ever, Oughtlings

**At all events** Algate

**Atavistic** Reversion, Throw-back

**At first** Erst

**Atheist** Doubter, Godless, Infidel, Irreligious, Sceptic

**Athenian, Athene** Attic, Cleruch, Pallas, Pericles, Solon, Timon

**Athlete, Athletic(s)** Agile, Agonist, Blue, Bolt, Coe, Discobolus, Field, Gymnast, Hammer throw, Hop, skip and jump, Hurdler, Jock, Leish, Miler, Milo, Nurmi, Olympian, Owens, Pacemaker, Pole vault, Quarter-miler, Runner, Sexual, Shamateur, Shot-putter, Sportsman, Sporty, Sprinter, Track, Track and field, Triple jump, Weightlifter

**Athodyd** Ram-jet

**Athwart** Across, Awry, Oblique, Traverse

**Atingle** Thriling

**Atlantic** Herring pond, Millpond, Pond

**Atlas** Dialect, Linguistic, Maps, Range, Silk, Telamon

▹**At last** *may indicate* a cobbler

**ATM** Cash dispenser, Hole-in-the-wall

**Atmosphere** Aeropause, Aerospace, Afterdamp, Air, Ambience, Aura, Chemosphere, Climate, E-layer, Elements, Epedaphic, E-region, Ether, Exosphere, F-layer, Fug, Geocorona, Ionosphere, Lid, Magnetosphere, Mesophere, Meteorology, Miasma, Mood, Ozone, Standard, Stratosphere, Substratosphere, Thermosphere, Tropopause, Troposphere, Upper, Vibe(s), Vibrations

**At most** Al piu

**Atoll** Bikini, Enewetak, Eniwetok, Funafuti, Kwajalein, Male, Motu, Tarawa

**Atom(ic), Atoms, Atomism** Bose-Einstein condensate, Boson, Chromophore, Dimer, Electron, Excimer, Free, Fusion, Gram, Ion, Iota, Isobare, Isotone, Isotope, Labelled, Ligand, Logical, Mesic, Mesonic, Molecule, Monad, Monovalent, Muonic, Nematic, Nuclide, Odoriphore, Particle, Pile, Primeval, Radionuclide, Recoil, Sellafield, Side-chain, Species, Steric, Stripped, Substituent, Tagged, Windscale, Xylyl

**Atomiser** Airbrush, Nebuliser

**At once** Directly, Ek dum, Holus-bolus, Immediate, Instanter, Presto, Statim, Straight away, Swith, Tight, Tit(e), Titely, Tout de suite, Tyte

**At one** Agreed

**Atone(ment)** Aby(e), Acceptilation, Appease, Assoil, Expiate, Penance, Purge, Redeem, Redemption, Yom Kippur

**Atop** Upon

▹**At random** *may indicate* an anagram

**Atrium** Auricle

**Atrocious, Atrocity** Abominable, Abysmal, Brutal, Diabolical, Enorm, Flagitious, Heinous, Horrible, Massacre, Monstrous, Outrage, Piacular, Terrible, Vile

**Atrophy** Degeneration, Disuse, Marasmus, Sudeck's, Sweeny, Wasting

▹**At sea** *may indicate* an anagram

**Attach(ed), Attachment** Accessory, Accrete, Addition, Adhesion, Adhibition, Adnate, Adnation, Adscript, Affix, Allonge, Annexe, Appendage, Bolt, Bro, Byssus, Cleat, Covermount, Curtilage, Devotement, Devotion, Diffus, Distrain, Dobby, Extra, Eyehook, Feller, Fixation, Fob, Frog, Garnish, Glom, Glue, Harness, →JOIN, Latch, Menge, Moor, Netsuke, Obconic, Piggyback, Pin, Prunt, Reticle, Sew, Sidecar, Snell, Stick, Tack on, Tendon, Tendril, Tie, Weld

**Attack(ing), Attacker** Access, Affect, Aggression, Airstrike, Alert, Ambuscade, Ambush, Anti, Apoplexy, Asperse, Assail, Assault, Assiege, At, Banzai, Barrage, Batter, Bego, Belabour, Beset, Besiege, Bestorm, Blitz(krieg), Bodrag(ing), Bombard, Bordraging, Bout, Broadside, Brutalise, Bushwhack, Calumny, Camisade, Camisado, Campaign, Cannonade, Carte, Charge, Clobber, Club, Counteroffensive, Coup de main, Denounce, Depredation, Descent, Diatribe, Discomfit, Dive-bomb, Excoriate, Feint, Fire-bomb, Fit, Flèche, Fly at, Foray, Fork, Forward, Gas, Get, Glass, Handbag, Happy-slapping, Harangue, Harry, Hatchet job, Headbutt, Heart, Heckle, Iconoclast, Ictus, Impingement, Impugn, Incursion, Infestation, Inroad, Invade, Invective, Inveigh, Jump, Knee, Lampoon, Lash out, Lese-majesty, Let fly, Lunge, Maraud, Molest, Mug, Offence, Offensive, Onding, Onfall, Onrush, Onset, Onslaught, Oppugn, Outflank, Panic, Philippic, Pillage, Pillory, Pin, Poke, Polemic, Pounce, Predacious, Pre-emptive, Push, Quart(e), Raid, Rally, Roll, Rough, Sail, Sandbag, Savage, Second strike, Seizure, Sic(k), Siege, Skitch, Slam, Snipe, Sortie, Spasm, Storm, Strafe, Straff, Strike, Swoop, Thrust, Tilt, Tirade, Vilify, Vituperate, Wage, Warison, Warray, Wolf-pack, Zap

**Attain(ment)** Accomplish, Achieve, Arrive, Earn, Fruition, Get, Land, Peak, Reach

**Attempt** Attentat, Bash, Bid, Burl, Crack, Debut, Effort, Egma, Endeavour, Essay, Go, Mint, Nisus, Offer, Potshot, Pursuit, Seek, Shot, Show, Shy, Spell baker, Stab, Strive, Tackle, Trial, →TRY, Venture, Whack, Whirl

**Attend(ance), Attendant, Attendee, Attender, Attending** Accompany, Acolyte, Address, Aide, Appearance, Apple-squire, Await, Batman, Bearer, Be at, Behold, Bell-hop, Best man, Bower woman, Bridesmaid, Bulldog, Caddy, Cavass, Chaperone, Chasseur, Checker, Cloakroom, Commissionaire, Corybant, Courtier, Cuadrilla, Cupbearer, Custrel, Delegate, Doula, Dresser, Entourage, Equerry, Escort, Esquire, Famulus, Footman, Gate(-keeper), G(h)illie, Gilly, Hand-maiden, Harken, Hear, →HEED, Hello, Holla, Iras, Jack, Janitor, Kavass, Keeper, Led captain, Lifeguard, →LISTEN, Loblolly-boy, Maenad, Marshal, Minister, Mute, Note, Observe, Orderly, Outrider, Outrunner, Page, Panisc, Panisk, Paranymph, People, Pew-opener, Presence, Pursuivant, Racegoer, Respect, Roll-up, Satellite, Second, Server, S(a)ice, Sort, Sowar, Squire, Steward, Syce, Therapeutic, There, Trainbearer, Trolleydolly, Turn-out, Up at, Usher, Valet, Varlet(to), Visit, Wait, Waiter, Watch, Whiffler, Yeoman, Zambuck

**Attention, Attentive** Achtung, Alert, Assiduity, Care(ful), Concentration, Court, Coverage, Dutiful, Ear, Eye, Focus, Gallant, Gaum, Gorm, Hark, Heed, Interest, Mind, Note, Notice, Observant, Present, Ps(s)t, Punctilious, Qui vive, →REGARD, Respect, Selective, Solicitous, Spellbound, Spotlight, Tentie, Tenty, Thorough, Thought, TLC, Uxorious, Voila

**Attenuate, Attenuation** Lessen, Neper, Rarefy, Thin, Weaken

**Attest** Affirm, Certify, Depose, Guarantee, Notarise, Swear, →WITNESS

**Attic** Athenian, Bee-bird, Cockloft, Garret, Greek, Koine, Loft, Mansard, Muse, Salt, Sky parlour, Solar, Soler, Sollar, Soller, Tallat, Tallet, Tallot

**Attila** Etzel, Hun

**Attire** Accoutre, Adorn, Apparel, Clobber, Clothe, Clothing, →DRESS, Garb, Get up, Habit, Slacks, Wet suit

**Attitude** Air, Aspect, Behaviour, Demeanour, Hauteur, Light, →MANNER, Mindset, Nimby, Outlook, Phase, Pose, Position, Possie, Posture, Propositional, Scalogram, Sense, Song, Spirit, Stance, Standpoint, Tone, Uppity, Viewpoint

**Attorney** Advocate, Counsellor, Crown, DA, District, Lawyer, Private, Proctor, Prosecutor, Public

**Attract(ion), Attractive(ness), Attractor** Adorable, Attrahent, Bait, Barrie, Beauté du diable, Becoming, Bedworthy, Bewitch, Bimbo, Bonnie, Bonny, Bootylicious, Catchy, Charisma, →CHARM, Cheesecake, Clou, Comely, Crowd puller, Cute, Cynosure, Dinky, Dipolar, Dish(y), Dolly, Draught, →DRAW, Dreamboat, Duende, Engaging, Entice, Epigamic,

Eye candy, Eye-catching, Eyeful, Fanciable, Fascinate, Feature, Fetching, Fox(y), Goodly, Gravity, Great, Groovy, Heartthrob, Himbo, Honeypot, Hot, Hot stuff, Hotty, Hunky, Inducement, Inviting, Irresistible, It, Jolie laide, Loadstone, Lodestone, Looker, Lovable, Lovely, Lure, Luscious, Magnes, Magnet(ism), Mecca, Mediagenic, Meretricious, Nubile, Ornamental, Pack in, Personable, Pheromone, Photogenic, Picture postcard, Picturesque, Plum, Popsy, Prepossessing, Pretty, Pull, Seduce, Sematic, Sexpot, Shagtastic, Sideshow, Sightly, Slick, Smasher, Snazzy, Soote, Speciosity, Spunk, Stotter, Striking, Studmuffin, Stunner, Taking, Taky, Tasteful, Tasty, Tempt, Theme-park, Toothsome, Tottie, Totty, Triff(ic), Va-va-voom, Viewly, Weber, Winning, Winsome, Zaftig, Zoftig, Zoophilia

**Attribute, Attribution** Accredit, Allot, Ap(p)anage, Ascribe, Asset, Attach, By, Credit, Gift, Impute, Lay, Metonym, Owe, Property, Proprium, Quality, Refer, Resource, Shtick, Strength, Toast, Trait

**Attune** Accord, Adapt, Temper

**Atypical** Aberrant, Anomalous, Singular, Uncommon, Unwonted

**Aubergine** Brinjal, Brown jolly, Egg-apple, Egg-plant, Mad-apple

**Aubrey** Beardsley

**Auburn** Abram, Chestnut, Copper, Titian, Vill(age)

**Auction(eer)** Barter, Bridge, Cant, Dutch, E-bay, Hammer, Knock out, Outcry, Outro(o)per, Roup, Sale, Subhastation, Tattersall, Trade sale, Vendue, Warrant sale

**Audacious, Audacity** Bald-headed, Bold, Brash, Cheek, Chutspah, Chutzpah, Cool, Daring, Der-doing, Devil-may-care, Effrontery, Face, Gall, Hardihead, Hardihood, Indiscreet, Insolence, Intrepid, Neck, Nerve, Rash, Sauce

**Audible** Out loud

**Audience, Auditorium** Assembly, Captive, Court, Durbar, Gate, Hearing, House, Interview, Pit, Ratings, Sphendone, Theatre, Tribunal

**Audiovisual** AV

**Audit(or)** Accountant, Check, Ear, Eardrum, Environmental, Examine, Green, Inspect, Listener, Medical, Position, Vet

**Audition** Apply, Cattle-call, Hearing, Screen-test

**Auditory** Acoustic, Oral

**Audrey** Hoyden

**Au fait** Up-to-date

**Auger** Miser

**Aught** Anything

**Augment(ed)** Accrue, Boost, Eche, Eke, Grow, Ich, Increase, Pad, Supplement, Swell, Tritone

**Augur(y)** Bode, Divination, Ornithoscopy, Portend

**August** Awe-inspiring, Exalted, Grand, Grandiose, Imperial, Imposing, Lammas, Majestic, Noble, Royal, Solemn, Stately, Stern, Strindberg

**Augustine, Augustus** Austin, Hippo, John

**Auk** Guillemot, Ice-bird, Puffin, Roch, Rotch(e)

**Aunt(ie)** Agony, Augusta, BBC, Beeb, Giddy, Maiden, Naunt, Sainted, Tia, Welsh

**Aura** Air, Aroma, Emanation, Halo, Mystique, Nimbus, Odour, Vibe(s), Vibrations

**Aureole** Coronary, Halo, Nimbus

**Auricle** Ear, Otic

**Aurora** Australis, Borealis, Eos, Leigh, Matutinal, Merry dancers, Northern lights, Southern (lights)

**Auspice(s)** Aegis, Patronage

**Auspicious** Favourable, Red-letter

**Auster** S-wind

**Austere, Austerity** Ascetic, Astringent, Bleak, Cutback, Dantean, Dervish, Dour, Hard, → **HARSH**, Killjoy, Moral, Plain, Rigour, Self-disciplined, Severe, Spartan, Stark, Stern, Stoic, Stoor, Strict, Stringent, Vaudois, Waldensian

**Austin** Friar

**Australia(n)** A, Alf, Antichthone, Antipodean, .au, Aussie, Balt, Banana-bender, Bananalander, Billjim, Bodgie, Canecutter, Cobber, Currency, Current, Darwinian, Digger,

Godzone, Gumsucker, Gurindji, Koori, Larrikin, Lucky Country, Murree, Murri, Myall, Norm, Ocker, Ossie, Outbacker, Oz(zie), Pintupi, Roy, Sandgroper, Strine, Sydneysider, Wallaby, Yarra-yabbies

**Austrian** Cisleithan, Tyrolean

**Authentic(ate), Authentication** Certify, Des(h)i, Echt, Genuine, Honest, Notarise, Official, Probate, Pukka, Ratify, Real, Sign, Simon-pure, Test, True, Validate

**Author(ess)** Agent, Anarch, Architect, Auctorial, Biographer, Cause, Chronicler, Creator, Hand, Inventor, Me, Memoirist, Parent, Penman, Playwright, Rhymer, Satirist, Scenarist, Source, Volumist, Wordsmith, → WRITER

▷**Author** *may refer to* author of puzzle

**Authorise(d), Authorisation** Accredit, Allow, Assigning, Carte blanche, Chit, Clearance, Command, Consent, Countersign, Credentials, Delegate, Depute, Empower, Enable, Entitle, Exequatur, Franchise, ID card, Imprimatur, Initial, Legal(ise), Legit, → LICENCE, Licit, Mandate, Official, OK, Passport, → PERMIT, Plenipotentiary, Prescribe, Proxy, Ratify, Retainer, Rubber-stamp, Sanction, Say-so, Seal, Sign, Signature, Stamp, Undersign, Warrant

**Authority, Authoritarian, Authoritative** Ascetic, Bossy, Canon, Chair, Charter, Circar, Cocker, Commission, Commune, Crisp, Curule, Definitive, Domination, Domineering, Dominion, Establishment, Ex cathedra, Executive, Expert, Fascist, Free hand, Gravitas, Hegemony, Hoyle, Inquirendo, Jackboot, Leadership, Licence, License, Light, Local, Magisterial, Mana, Mandate, Mantle, Mastery, Municipal, Name, Officious, Omnipotence, Oracle, Permit, PLA, Potency, → POWER, Prefect, Prestige, Pundit, Regime, Remit, Right, Rod, Savant, Say-so, Sceptre, Sircar, Sirkar, Source, Stern, Supremacy, Supremo, Sway, Top-brass, Tyrannous, Unitary, Warrant

**Autobiography** Memoir

**Autochthonous** Aboriginal

**Autocrat(ic)** Absolute, Bossy, Caesar, Cham, Despot, Dictator, Khan, Neronian, Overbearing, Repressive, Tenno, Tsar, Tyrant

**Autocue** Teleprompter

**Autogenous** Self-made

**Autograph** Signature

**Autolycus** Scrapman

**Automatic, Automaton** Android, Aut, Browning, Deskill, Droid, Instinctive, Knee-jerk, Machine, Mechanical, Pistol, Quarter-boy, Quarter-jack, Reflex, Robot, RUR, Zombi(e)

**Autonomous** Independent, Self-governing

**Auto-pilot** George

**Autopsy** Necropsy

**Auto-suggestion** Coueism, Hypnosis

**Autumn(al)** Fall, Filemot, Leaf-fall, Libra, Philamot

**Auxiliary** Adjunct, Adjuvant, Adminicle, Aide, Ancillary, Be, Feldsher, Foederatus, Have, Helper, Ido, Modal, Reservist, Subsidiary

**Avail(able)** Abounded, Benefit, Dow, Eligible, Going, Handy, In season, Off-the-shelf, On, On call, On hand, On tap, Open, Out, Pickings, Potluck, → READY, Serve, To hand, Up for grabs, Use, Utilise, Worth

**Avalanche** Bergfall, Deluge, Icefall, Landfall, Landslide, Landslip, Lauwine, Rockfall, Slide, Slip, Snowdrop

**Avant-garde** Advanced, Modernistic, Progressive, Spearhead, Ultramodern

**Avarice, Avaricious** Cupidity, Gimmes, Golddigger, Greed, Miserly, Money-grubbing, Pleonexia, Predatory, Shylock, Sordid

**Avatar** Epiphany, Incarnation, Rama

**Avaunt** Away, Go

**Avenge(r)** Alecta, Eriny(e)s, Eumenides, Goel, Kurdaitcha, Megaera, Nemesis, Nightrider, Punish, Redress, Requite, → REVENGE, Steed, Tisiphone, Wreak

**Avenue** Allee, Alley, Approach, Arcade, Boulevard, Channel, Corso, Cradle-walk, Hall, Madison, Mall, Midway, Passage, Vista, Way, Xyst(us)

**Aver** Affirm, Assert, Asseverate, Declare, Depose, State, Swear, Vouch

**Average** Adjustment, Av, Batting, Dow Jones, Everyman, Fair, Mean, Medial, Mediocre,

Middle-brow, Middling, Moderate, Moving, Norm, Par, Particular, Passable, Run, Run-of-the-mill, Soso, Standard, Usual, Weighted

**Averse, Aversion, Avert** Against, Allergy, Antipathy, Apositia, Counter, Disgust, Dislike, Distaste, Hatred, Horror, Indisposed, Obviate, Opposed, Pet, Phengephobia, Phobic, Photophobia, Revulsion, Risk, Scunner, Sit(i)ophobia, Stave off

**Avert** Avoid, → DEFLECT, Forfend, Parry, Ward

**Aviary** Volary, Volery

**Aviation** Civil

**Aviator** Airman, Alcock, Bleriot, Brown, Byrd, Co-pilot, De Havilland, Earhart, Flier, Hinkler, Icarus, Johnson, Lindbergh, Pilot, Red Baron, Richthofen, Yeager

**Avid** Agog, Athirst, → EAGER, Greedy, Keen

**Avifauna** Ornis

**Avignon** Pont

**Avocado** Aguacate, Alligator pear, Guac(h)amole, Pear

**Avocet** Scooper

**Avoid(er), Avoidable, Avoidance** Abstain, Ba(u)lk, Boycott, Buck, Bypass, Circumvent, Cop-out, Cut, Dodge, Duck, Elude, Escape, Eschew, Evade, Evitable, Evitate, Evite, Fly, Forbear, Fudge, Gallio, Hedge, Miss, Needless, Obviate, Parry, Prevaricate, Save, Scape, Scutage, Secede, Shelve, Shirk, Shun, Sidestep, Skirt, Skive, Spare, Spurn, Steer clear, Tergiversate, Waive

**Avoirdupois** Size, Weight

**Avow(ed)** Acknowledged, Affirm, Declare, Own, Swear

**Await(ed)** Abide, Bide, Expect, Godot, Stand by, Tarry

**Awake(ning), Awaken** Alert, Aware, Conscious, Conversion, Evoke, Fly, Rouse, Vigilant

**Award** Academy, Accolade, Acquisitive, Addeem, Addoom, Allot, Alpha, Apple, Arbitrament, Aret(t), Bafta, Bar, Bestow, Blue riband, Bursary, Cap, Charter Mark, Clasp, Clio, Compensation, Crown, Decoration, Degree, Dunmow flitch, Edgar, Emmy, Exhibition, Genie, Gold disc, Golden handshake, Golden Raspberry, Golden Starfish, Grammy, Grant, Honours, Juno, Logie, Lourie, Medal, Meed, Mete, MOBO, Oscar, Padma Shri, Palatinate, Palme d'Or, Premium, Present(ation), Prix Goncourt, → PRIZE, Purse, Queen's, Razzie, Rosette, Scholarship, Tony, Trophy, Vir Chakra, Yuko

**Aware(ness)** Alert, Apperception, Aware, C(o)enesthesis, Coconscious, Cognisant, Conscious, Conversant, Enlightenment, ESP, Est, Hep, Hip, Informed, Knowing, Liminal, Mindshare, Onto, Open-eyed, Panaesthesia, Perception, Prajna, Presentiment, Privy, Realisation, Samadhi, Scienter, Sensible, Sensile, Sensitive, Sentience, Streetwise, Switched on, Vigilant, Weet, Wit, Wot

**Away** Abaxial, Absent, Afield, Apage, Aroint, Avaunt, Beyond, By, For-, Forth, Fro(m), Go, Hence, Off, Out, Past

▷**Away** *may indicate* a word to be omitted

**Awe(d)** Dread, D(o)ulia, Fear, Intimidate, Loch, Overcome, Popeyed, Regard, Respect, Reverent, Scare, Solemn, Wonderment

**Awe-inspiring, Awesome** Breathtaking, Mega, Numinous, Terrific

**Awful(ly)** Alas, Appalling, Deare, Dere, Dire, Fearful, Horrendous, Lamentable, Lousy, Nasty, O so, Piacular, Rotten, Terrible, Third rate, Turkey, Unspeakable

▷**Awfully** *may indicate* an anagram

**Awkward(ness)** All thumbs, Angular, Blate, Bolshy, Bumpkin, Cack-handed, Clumble-fisted, Clumsy, Complicated, Contrary, Corner, Crabby, Cubbish, Cumbersome, Cussed, Disconcerting, Dub, Embarrassing, Farouche, Fiddly, Fix, Gangly, Gauche, Gawky, Geeky, Graceless, Ham-fisted, Handless, Hobbledehoy, Hot potato, Howdy-do, Inconvenient, Inelegant, Inept, Jam(pot), Kittle-cattle, Knotty, Lanky, Left-handed, Loutish, Lurdan(e), Lurden, Maladdress, Maladroit, Mauther, Mawr, Naff, Nasty, Nonconformist, Ornery, Perverse, Refractory, Slouch, Slummock, So-and-so, Spot, Sticky, Stiff, Stroppy, Stubborn, Stumblebum, Swainish, Thorny, Ticklish, Tricky, Twiddley, Uncoordinated, Uncouth, Uneasy, Ungainly, Ungraceful, Unhandy, Unskilful, Unwieldy, Wooden, Wry

**Awl(-shaped)** Brog, Els(h)in, Nail, Stob, Subulate

**Awn(ing)** Barb, Beard, Canopy, Ear, Shade, Shamiana(h), Sunblind, Sunshade, Velarium

**Awry** Agley, Amiss, Askent, Askew, Athwart, Cam, Haywire, Kam(me), Pear-shaped, Skew, Wonky

**Axe(s)** Abolish, Adz(e), Bardiche, Bill, Celt, Chop(per), Cleaver, Curtal, Ditch, Eatche, Gisarme, Gurlet, Halberd, Halbert, Hatchet, Hew, Holing, Ice, Jeddart staff, Jethart-staff, Labrys, Lochaber, Mattock, Meat, Palstaff, Palstave, Partisan, Piolet, Retrench, Sax, Scrap, Scrub, Slate, Sparth(e), Sperthe, Spontoon, Stone, Thunderbolt, Tomahawk, Twibill, X, Y, Z

**Axeman** Bassist, Guitarist, Hendrix

**Axe-shaped** Securiform

**Axilla** Armpit

**Axiom** Adage, Motto, Peano's, Proverb, Saw, Saying

**Axis** Alliance, Anorthic, Anticous, Axle, Caulome, Chital, Cob, Columella, Deer, Epaxial, Henge, Hinge, Major, Minor, Modiolus, Myelon, Neutral, Optic, Pivot, Polar, Precess, Principal, Rachis, Radical, Spindle, Stem, Sympodium, Visual, X, Y, Z, Zone

**Axle, Axle-shoulder** Arbor, Axis, Driving, Fulcrum, Hurter, Journal, Live, Mandrel, Mandril, Pivot, Spindle, Stub

**Ay** Ever, I, Indeed

**Aye** Always, Eer, Ever, Yea, Yes

**Ayers Rock** Uluru

**Ayesha** She

**Azo-dye** Para-red

**Aztec** Nahuatl

# Bb

**B** Bachelor, Black, Book, Born, Boron, Bowled, Bravo, Flipside

**Babble(r), Babbling** Blather, Brook, Chatter, Gibber, Haver, Hubbub, Jabber, Lallation, Lalling, Lurry, Prate, Prattle, Psycho, Runnel, Tonguester, Tonguework, Twattle, Waffle, Witer

**Babe** → BABY, Cutie

**Babel** Charivari, Confusion, Din, Dovercourt, Medley

**Baboon** Ape, Bobbejaan, Chacma, Cynocephalus, Dog-ape, Drill, Gelada, Hamadryas, Mandrill, Sphinx

**Baby** Bairn, Band-Aid®, Battered, Blue, Bub, Bunting, Changeling, Coddle, Cub, Designer, Duck, Fledgling, Grand, Indulge, Infant, Jelly, Litter, Miniature, Neonate, Newborn, Nursling, Pamper, Papoose, Plunket, Preverbal, Rhesus, Rugrat, Ruth, Sis, Small, Sook, Spoil, Sprog, Suckling, Tar, Test tube, Thalidomide, Tot, War, Wean

**Babylonian** Mandaean, Mandaites, Nasorean, Sabian, Semiramis, Sumerian

**Baby-sitter** Minder

**Bacchanalian, Bacchus** Drunken, Ivied, Upsee, Ups(e)y

**Bacchantes** Maenads

**Bachelor** Alumnus, BA, Bach, Benedict, Budge, Celibate, En garçon, Knight, Pantagamy, Parti, Seal, Single, Stag, Wifeless

**Bacillus** Comma, Germ, Klebs-Loffler, Micrococcus, Tubercle, Virus

**Back(er), Backing, Back out, Back up, Backward** Abet, Accompany, Addorse, Aft, Again, Ago, Aid, Angel, Anticlockwise, Antimacassar, Arear, Arrear, Arrière, Assist, Auxiliary, Baccare, Backare, Bankroll, Behind, Buckram, Champion, Chorus, Consent, Countenance, Croup, Cry off, Culet, Defender, Donor, Dorsal, Dorse, Dorsum, Dos, Ebb, Empatron, Encourage, Endorse, Fakie, Finance, Frae, Fro, Full, Fund(er), Gaff, Grubstake, Half, Help, Hind, Historic, Incremental, La-la, Late, Lining, Notaeum, Notal, Notum, On, Partisan, Patronise, Pendu, Poop, Pro, Pronotum, Punt, Rear(most), Rearwards, Reinforce, Reinforcement, Reticent, Retral, Retro(grade), Retrogress, Retrorse, Retrospective, Return, Rev, Reverse, Ridge, Root, Running, Scenery, Shy, Spinal, Sponsor, Standby, Stern, Sternboard, Sternway, → SUPPORT, Sweeper, Syndicate, Tail, Telson, Tergum, Third, Thrae, Three-quarter, Tonneau, Ulu, Uphold, Verso, Vie, Vo, Wager, Watteau

▷**Back(ing)** *may indicate* a word spelt backwards

**Back and forth** Boustrophedon

**Backbiter, Backbiting** Catty, Defame, Detract, Libel, Molar, Slander, Tooth

**Backbone** Atlas, Chine, Coccyx, Grit, Guts, Mettle, Spina, Spine, Spirit

**Backbreaking** Gruelling, Last straw

**Backchat** Lip, Mouth, Sass

**Backcloth, Backdrop** Cyclorama, Scenery

**Back comb** Tease

**Backer** Angel, Benefactor, Funder, Patron, Punter, Seconder, Sponsor

**Backfire, Backlash** Billabong, Boomerang, Own goal, Reaction

**Backgammon** Acey-deucy, Blot, Lurch, Tick-tack, Trick-track, Tric-trac, Verquere

**Background** Antecedence, Chromakey, Context, Cyclorama, Field, Fond, History, Horizon, Microwave, Muzak®, Natural, Retrally, Setting, Ulterior

**Backhander** Bribe, Palm grease, Payola, Reverso, Sweetener

**Back number** Has-been

**Backpack(er)** Hike(r)

**Back problem** Kyphosis, Lumbago, Osteoporosis, Scolioma, Scoliosis
**Backroom** Boffin, Boy, Moor
**Backside** Bum, Tush
**Backslide(r), Backsliding** Apostate, Lapse, Regress, Relapse, Revert
**Back-stabber** Epidural
**Back-to-back** Consecutive
**Backwash** Rift, Wake
**Backwater** Bogan, Ebb, Logan, Retreat, Slough, Wake
**Backwoods(man)** Boondocks, Boonies, Hinterland, Rowdy
**Backyard** Court, Patio
**Bacon** Bard, Canadian, Collar, Danish, Essayist, Flitch, Forehock, Francis, Gammon, Green, Lardo(o)n, Pancetta, Pig(meat), Pork, Rasher, Roger, Smoked, Spec(k), Streaky, Verulam
**Bacteria(l), Bacteriologist, Bacterium** Acidophilus, Actinomycete, Aerobe, Amphitricha, Bacilli, Bacteriological, Baregine, Botulinum, → BUG, Campylobacter, Chlamydia, Clostridia, Cocci, Coliform, Corynebacterium, Culture, Detritivore, Diplococcus, E-coli, Enterococcus, Escherichia, Foul-brood, → GERM, Gonococcus, Gram-negative, Gram-positive, Hib, Intestinal flora, Klebsiella, Koch, Legionella, Listeria, Lysogen, Meningococcus, Microbe, Micrococcus, Microphyte, Mother, MRSA, Mycoplasma, Nitrifying, Nitrite, Nitrous, Nostoc, Operon, Packet, Pasteur, Pasteurella, Pathogen, Peritrich(a), Petri, Pneumococcus, Probiotic, Prokaryote, Proteus, Pseudomonas, Pus, Ray-fungus, Rhizobium, Rickettsia, Salmonella, Schizomycete, Sepsis, Septic, Serogroup, Serotype, Serum, Shigella, Spirilla, Spirochaete, Spirulina, Spore, Staph, Staphylococcus, Strep(tococcus), Streptobacillus, Streptomyces, Sulphur, Superbug, Thermophil(e), Treponemata, Vibrio, Vincent's angina, Vinegar-plant, Yersinia, Zoogloea
**Bad(die), Badness** Abysmal, Addled, Atrocious, Chronic, Crook, Defective, Degenerate, Diabolic, Drastic, Dud, Duff, Dystopia, Egregious, Evildoer, Execrable, Faulty, Fearful, Fourth-rate, God-awful, Half-pie, Heinous, Humongous, Humungous, Ill (timed), Immoral, Infamous, Inferior, Injurious, Lither, Lulu, Mal(vu), Nasty, Naughty, Nefandrous, Nefarious, Nice, Notorious, Off, Ominous, Oncus, Onkus, Outlaw, Parlous, Piacular, Poor, Rancid, Rank, Reprobate, Ropy, Scampish, Scoundrel, Shocking, Sinful, Spoiled, The pits, Turpitude, Undesirable, Unhealthy, Unspeakable, Unwholesome, Useless, Wack, Wick, → WICKED
▷**Bad(ly)** *may indicate* an anagram
**Badge** Armband, Brassard, Brooch, Button, Chevron, Cockade, Cockleshell, Comm, Cordon, Crest, Eagle, Emblem, Ensign, Epaulet, Episemon, Fáinne, Film, Flash, Garter, Gorget, ID, Insigne, Insignia, Kikumon, Mark, Medal, Mon, Numerals, Orange, Pilgrim's sign, Pin, Rondel, Rosette, Scallop(-shell), Shield, Shouldermark, → SIGN, Symbol, Tiger, Token, Totem, Vernicle, Vine branch, Vine-rod, Wings
**Badger** → ANNOY, Bait, Bedevil, Beset, Brock, Browbeat, Bug, Bullyrag, Cete, Dassi(e), Ferret, Gray, Grey, Grill, → HARASS, Harry, Hassle, Heckle, Hog, Honey, Hound, Nag, Pester, Plague, Provoke, Ratel, Ride, Roil, Sand, Sow, Stinking, Teledu, Wisconsin
**Bad habit** Cacoethes, Vice
**Badinage** Banter, Chaff, Raillery
**Bad luck** Ambs-ace, Ames-ace, Deuce-ace, Hard cheese, Hard lines, Hoodoo, Jinx, Jonah, Shame, Voodoo
**Badminton** Shuttlecock
**Bad-tempered** Cantankerous, Carnaptious, Crabby, Curmudgeon, Curnaptious, Curst, Grouchy, Grum(py), Irritable, Marabunta, Moody, Nowty, Patch, Scratchy, Shirty, Sour, Splenetic, Stroppy
**Bad woman** Harridan, Loose, Mort
**Baffle(d), Baffling** Anan, Balk, Befog, Bemuse, Bewilder, Confound, Confuse, Elude, Evade, Floor, Flummox, Foil, Fox, Get, Hush-kit, Mate, Muse, Mystify, Nark, Nonplus, Perplex, Pose, Puzzle, Stump, Throw, Thwart
**Bag(gage), Bags** Acquire, Air, Albatross, Alforja, Allantois, Amaut, Amowt, Ascus, Ballonet, Bean, Bedroll, Besom, Bin-liner, Bladder, Blue, Body, Bounty, Briefcase, Bulse, Bum, Buoyancy, Caba(s), Cachet, Caecum, Callet, Capture, Carpet, Carrier, Carryall, Case, Cecum, Claim, Clutch, Cly, Cod, Coffee, Colostomy, Cool(er), Corduroy, Crone, Crumenal, Cyst,

Daypack, Dilli, Dilly, Dime, Diplomatic, Ditty, Doggy, Dorothy, Douche, Duffel, Dunnage, Earth, → EFFECTS, Emery, Excess, Fanny pack, Faradel, Fishwife, Flannels, Flotation, Follicle, Galligaskins, Game, → GEAR, Gladstone, Golf, Goody, Grab, Green, Grip, Gripsack, Grow, Haversack, Holdall, Ice, Impedimenta, Jelly, Jiffy®, Kill, Knapsack, Ladies' companion, Lavender, Lithocyst, Loose, Lucky, Mail, Marsupium, Materiel, Meal-poke, Messenger, Minx, Mixed, Money, Monkey, Moon, Mummy, Musette, Musk, Muzzle, Mystery, Nap, Necessaire, Net, Nunny, Organiser, Overnight, Overnighter, Oxford, Packsack, Pantaloons, Plastic, Plus fours, Pochette, Pock(et), Pocketbook, Pockmanky, Pockmantie, Poke, Politzer's, Poly(thene), Port(manteau), Portmantle, Portmantua, Post, Pot, Pouch, Pounce, Pudding, Punch, Purse, Rake, Red, Reticule, Ridicule, Rucksack, Sabretache, Sac(cule), Sachet, Sack, Saddle, Sag, Satchel, Scent, School, Scrip, Scrotum, Sea, Shapeless, Shopper, Shoulder, Sick, Slattern, Sleeping, Snood, Specialty, Sponge, Sporran, Stacks, Steal, Strossers, Sugar, Survival, Tea, Toilet, Tool, Tote, → TRAP, Trews, Trollop, Trouse(r), Tucker (box), Udder, Unmentionables, Utricle, Valise, Vanity, Viaticals, Waist, Wallet, Wash, Water, Weekend, Win, Woolpack, Work, Wrap, Wrapping, Ziplock

**Bagatelle** Bauble, Fico, Trifle, Trinket

**Bagpipe(r)** Biniou, Chanter, Chorus, Cornemuse, Drone, Gaita, Musette, Pibroch, Piffero, Pipe major, Skirl, Sourdeline, Uillean, Zampogna

**Bahama(s), Bahamian** BS, Conch

**Bail(er), Bailment** Bond, Ladle, Mainpernor, Mainprise, Mutuum, Remand, Replevin, Replevy, Scoop

**Bailey** Bridge, Castle wall, Ward

**Bailiff** Adam, Bandog, Beagle, Bum, Factor, Foud, Grieve, Huissier, Hundreder, Hundredor, Land-agent, Nuthook, Philistine, Reeve, Shoulder-clapper, Shoulder-knot, Steward, Tipstaff, Water

**Bairn** Baby, → CHILD, Infant, Wean

**Bait** Angleworm, Badger, Bait, Berley, Brandling, Burley, Capelin, Chum, Dap, Decoy, Entice, Gentle, Gudgeon, Harass, Hellgram(m)ite, Incentive, Lobworm, Lug(worm), Lure, Mawk, → RAG, Ragworm, Sandworm, Sledge, Teagle, Tease, Tempt, Tole, Toll

**Bake(r), Baked, Baking** Alaska, Batch, Baxter, Coctile, → COOK, Cottar, Fire, Icer, Kiln-dry, Mr Bun, Oven, Pieman, Roast, Scorch, Shir(r)

**Baker's daughter** Own

**Baker Street** Irregular

**Bakery** Patisserie

**Balance(d)** Account, Aileron, Bank, Beam, Compensation, Counterpoise, Countervail, Counterweight, Equalise, Equate, Equilibrium, Equipoise, Equiponderate, Even, Fixed, Funambulate, Gyroscope, Gyrostat, Horn, Hydrostatic, Invisible, Isostasy, Launce, Level-headed, Libra, Librate, Meet, Offset, Otocyst, Otolith, Pease, Peise, Perch, Peyse, Poise, → REMAINDER, Remnant, Residual, Rest, Running, Scale, Sea-legs, Sober, Spring, Stability, Stand, Steady, Steelyard, Symmetry, Together, Torsion, → TOTAL, Trade, Trial, Trim, Tron(e), Unicycle, Visible

**Balcony** Circle, Gallery, Loggia, Mirador, Moucharaby, Pew, Porch, Quarter-gallery, Sundeck, Tarras, Terrace, Veranda(h)

**Bald, Baldness** Alopecia, Apterium, Awnless, Barren, Calvities, Coot, Crude, Egghead, Fox-evil, Glabrous, Hairless, Madarosis, Open, Peelgarlic, Pilgarlic(k), Pollard, Psilosis, Slaphead, Smoothpate, Stark, Tonsured

**Balderdash** Claptrap, Drivel, Flapdoodle, Nonsense, Poppycock, Rot, Twaddle

**Baldmoney** Emeu, Meu, Spignel

**Bale** Bl, Bundle, Evil, Lave, Pack, Sero(o)n, Truss

**Baleful** Evil, Malefic, Malignant

▸**Balk** *see* BAULK

**Balkan** Albanian, Bosnian, Bulgarian, Croat, Macedon, Rumanian, Serb, Slavonic, Thrace, Vlach

**Ball(s)** Aelopile, Aelopyle, Aeolipile, Aeolipyle, Agglomerate, Alley, Ally, Ammo, Aniseed, Apple, Bal pare, Beach, Bead, Beamer, Bearings, Bhaji, Birthing, Bobble, Boll, Bolus, Bosey, Bosie, Bouncer, Bowl, Break, Buckshot, Buzzer, Caltrap, Caltrop, Camphor, Cap, Cheese, Cherry, Chin, Chinaman, Chopper, Clew, Clue, Condylar, Condyle, Cotill(i)on, Cramp,

Creeper, Croquette, Crystal, Cue, Curve, Daisy-cutter, → DANCE, Delivery, Dink, Dodge, Dollydrop, Doosra, Dot, Dribbler, Dumpling, Eight, Ensphere, Eolipile, Eolipyle, Eolopile, Eolopyle, Falafel, Felafel, Full-pitch, Full-toss, Fungo, Fur, Gazunder, → GLOBE, Glomerate, Gobstopper, Googly, Goolies, Gool(e)ys, Grounder, Grub(ber), Grubhunter, Gutta, Gutter, Gutty, Hank, Hop, Hummer, Hunt, Inswinger, Ivory, Jinglet, Jump, Knob, Knur(r), Leather, Leg-break, Leg-cutter, Lob, Long-hop, Marble, Masked, Masque(rade), Matzo, Meat, Medicine, Minié, Mirror, Moth, Musk, Nur(r), O, Object, Off-break, Off-cutter, Off-spin, Orb, Outswinger, Over, Overarm, Pakora, Parrel truck, Pea, Pellet, Pill, Poi, Pomander, Pompom, Pompon, Prom, Puck, Punch, Quenelle, Rabbit, Race, Rissole, Root, Round, Rover, Rundle, Seamer, Shooter, Shot, Skier, Skittle, Sliotar, Sneak, Sphere, Spinner, Stress, Strike, Swinger, Swiss, Taw, Tea, Testes, Thenar, Three, Tice, Time, Track(er), Witches, Wood, Wrecker's, Wrecking, Yorker, Zorb®

**Ballad** Bab, Bothy, Broadside, Bush, Calypso, Carol, Fanzone, Folk-song, Forebitter, Lay, Lillibullero, Lilliburlero, Mento, Reading Gaol, Singsong, → SONG, Torch-song

**Ballast** Kentledge, Makeweight, Road bed, Stabiliser, Trim, Weight

**Ball-boy** Dry-bob

**Ballerina** Coryphee, Dancer, Pavlova, Prima, Rambert

**Ballet, Ballet movement, Ballet-system** Anastasia, Arabesque, Assemblé, Balancé, Ballon, Battement, Bharat Natyam, Bolshoi, Brisé, Cabriole, Cambré, Chainé, Changement, Checkmate, Cinderella, Daphnis and Chloe, Développé, Don Pasquale, Écarté, Echappé, Enchainement, Entrechat, Firebird, Fouetté, Giselle, Jeté, Kirov, Laban, Labanotation, Leg business, Mayerling, Nutcracker, Pas de basque, Pas de bourrée, Pas de chat, Petit battement, Petrushka, Pirouette, Plastique, Plie, Pointe, Pointer, Port de bras, Relevé, Saut, Swan Lake

**Ballet-interlude** Divertimento

**Ballista** Scorpion

**Ballistic** Wildfire

**Balloon(ist)** Aeronaut, Aerostat, Airship, Bag, Barrage, Billow, Blimp, Bloat, Dirigible, Distend, Dumont, Enlarge, Fire, Fumetto, Glass, Hot air, Inflate, Kite, Lead, Montgolfier, Piccard, Pilot, Rawinsonde, Sonde, Swell, Trial, Weather, Zeppelin

**Ballot** Butterfly, Election, Mulligan, → POLL, Postal, Referendum, Second, Secret, Suffrage, Ticket, Vote

**Ballot-box** Urn

**Ballpoint** Bic®, Biro®

**Ballyhoo** Ado, Hype, Racket

**Balm(y)** Anetic, Arnica, Balsam, Calamint, Emollient, Fragrant, Garjan, Gilead, Gurjun, Lemon, Lenitive, Lotion, → MILD, Mirbane, Myrbane, Nard, Oil, Opobalsam, Ottar, Redolent, Remedy, Soothe, Spikenard, Tiger, Tolu, Unguent

**Balmoral** Bonnet, Cap, Castle

**Baloney** Bunk, Hooey, Nonsense

**Balsam** Canada, Copaiba, Copaiva, Friar's, Nard, Noli-me-tangere, Peruvian, Resin, Spikenard, Tamanu, Tolu(ic), Touch-me-not, Tous-les-mois, Turpentine, Wood oil

**Balt** Esth, Lett

**Baltic** Estonian, Lettic

**Balustrade** Spindle

**Bamboo** Cane, Grass, Kendo, Split cane, Tabasheer, Whangee

**Bamboozle(d)** Cheat, Dupe, Flummox, Hoodwink, Horn-swoggle, Mystify, Nose-led, Perplex, Trick

**Ban(ned)** Abolish, Accurse, Anathema, Black(ing), Censor, Curfew, Debar, D-notice, Driving, Embargo, Estop, Exclude, Excommunicate, Forbid, For(e)say, For(e)speak, Gag, Gate, Green, Hosepipe, Moratorium, No, Outlaw, Prohibit, Proscribe, Suppress, Taboo, Tabu, Test, Verboten, Veto

**Banal** Anorak, Corny, Dreary, Flat, Hackneyed, Jejune, Mundane, Ordinary, Platitudinous, Stale, → TRITE, Trivial

**Banana(s)** Abaca, Hand, Loco, → MAD, Maranta, Matoke, Musa, Plantain, Raving, Scitamineae, Split, Strelitzia, Top, Zany

**Band(ed), Bands** Absorption, Alice, Amalgamate, Ambulacrum, Anadem, Ankle-strap, Anklet, Annulet, Armlet, Barrulet, Belt, Border, Braid, Brake, Brass, Brassard, Brassart, Caravan, CB, Channel, Chevron, Chinstrap, Chromosome, Cingulum, Circlet, Citizens', Clarain, Closet, Cohort, Collar, Collet, Combo, Company, Conduction, Corslet, Coterie, Crape, Crepe, Crew, Deely boppers, Dog collar, Elastic, ELO, Endorse, Energy, Enomoty, Facia, Falling, Fascia, Fasciole, Ferret, Ferrule, Fess, Filament, Fillet, Fourchette, Fraternity, Frequency, Frieze, Frog, Frontlet, Galloon, Gamelan, → GANG, Garage, Garland, Garter, Gasket, Gaskin, Gastric, Geneva, German, Gird, Girr, Girth, Group, Guard, → HOOP, Hope, Iron, Jazz, Jug, Kara, Kitchen, Label, Laticlave, Led Zeppelin, Line, Lytta, Macnamara's, Manacle, Maniple, Mariachi, Massed, Military, Mourning, Myrmidon, Noise, Oasis, Obi, One-man, Orchestra, Orchestrina, Pack, Parral, Parrel, Parsal, Parsel, Pass, Patte, Pipe, Plinth, Property, Purfle, Puttee, Retinaculum, Rib, Ribbon, Ridge, Rigwiddie, Rigwoodie, Rim, Ring, Robbers, Round, Rubber, Rymme, Sash, Scarf, Screed, Scrunchie, Scrunchy, Sect, Shadow, Shallal, Shash, Sheet, Shoe, Side, Snood, Space, Speckled, Spectrum, Steel, Strake, Strand, Strap, Stratum, String, Stripe, Succinctory, Suspender, Swath(e), Sweat, Tambu-bambu, Tape, Tendon, Thecla, Thoroughbrace, Throat-latch, Tie, Tippet, Torques, Tourniquet, Trabecula, Train, Trangle, Tribute, Troop, Troupe, Tumpline, Turm, Tyre, Unite, Valence, Vinculum, Virl, Vitrain, Vitta, Wanty, Wedding, Weed, Weeper, Welt, Wings, With(e), Wristlet, Zona, Zone, Zonule

**Bandage** Bind, Blindfold, Capeline, Dressing, Fillet, Gauze, Ligature, Lint, Living, Pledget, Roller, Scapular, Sling, Spica, Suspensor, Swaddle, Swathe, T, Tape, Truss, Tubigrip®, Wadding

**Bandicoot** Bilby, Pig-rat

**Bandit** Apache, Bravo, Brigand, Desperado, Fruit-machine, Gunslinger, Ishmael, Klepht, Moss-trooper, Outlaw, Pirate, Rapparee, → ROBBER, Slot machine, Squeegee, Turpin

**Bandsman, Band-leader** Alexander, Bugler, Conductor, Drum-major, Maestro, Miller, Wait

**Bandstand** Kiosk, Stage

**Bandy** Bow, Bow-legged, Club, Curved, Exchange, Revie, Toss, Vie

**Bane** Bugbear, Curse, Dioxin, Evil, Harm, Nemesis, Poison

**Bang(er)** Amorce, Andouillette, Beat, Big, Cap, Chipolata, Clap, Cracker, Crate, Crock, Explode, Firecracker, Flivver, Fringe, Haircut, Heap, Implode, Jalopy, Jammy, Maroon, Pep(p)eroni, Rattletrap, Report, Sausage, Sizzler, Slam, Sonic, Thrill, TNT, Wham, Wurst

**Bangladesh** .bd

**Bangle** Anklet, Armlet, Bracelet, Kara

**Banish(ment)** Ban, Debar, Deport, Depose, Dispel, Excommunicate, Exile, Expatriate, Expel, Extradition, Forsay, Maroon, Ostracise, → OUTLAW, Relegate, Rusticate

**Banjo** Ukulele

**Bank(ing), Bank on** An(n)icut, Asar, Backs, Bar, Bay, Beneficiary, Bet, Bk, Blood, Bluff, Bottle, Brae, Brim, Bund, Camber, Cay, Central, Chesil, Clearing (house), Cloud, Commercial, Cooperative, Data, Depend, Deposit, Dogger, Down, Drawee, Drift, Dune, Dyke, Earthwork, Escarp, Fog, Food, Gene, Giro, Glacis, Gradient, Gradin(e), Hack, Hele, Hill(side), Home, Incline, Investment, Jodrell, Joint-stock, Kaim, Kame, Land, Left, Lender, Levee, Link, Lombard Street, Memory, Merchant, Mound, Nap, National, Needle, Nore, Overslaugh, Oyster, Parapet, Penny, Piggy, Pot, Private, Rake, Ramp, Rampart, RBS, Recycle, Reef, → RELY, Reserve, Retail, Ridge, Rivage, Riverside, Rodham, Row, Sandbar, Savings, Seed, Shallow, Shelf, Side, Slope, Soil, Sperm, Spit, Spoil, Staithe, State, Sunk, Telephone, Terrace, Terreplein, Tier, Treasury, Trust, Vault, Wells Fargo, West, World

**Banker** Agent, Aileron, Baring, Cert(ainty), Financial, Financier, Fugger, Gnome, Lender, Lombard, Medici, → RIVER, Rothschild, Shroff, Teller

▷**Banker** *may indicate* a river

**Banknote(s)** Flimsy, Greenback, Snuff-paper, Wad

**Bankrupt(cy)** Break, Broke, Bung, Bust, Cadaver, Carey Street, Chapter-eleven, Crash, Debtor, Deplete, Duck, Dyvour, Fail, Fold, Fraudulent, Impoverish, Insolvent, Lame duck, Notour, Penniless, Receivership, Ruin, Rump, Scat, Sequestration, Skatt, Smash

▷**Bankrupt** *may indicate* 'red' around another word

**Bank system** Giro

**Bann(s)** Out-ask
**Banner** Banderol(e), Bandrol, Bannerol, Blue blanket, Censor, → FLAG, Gumphion, Labarum, Masthead, Oriflamme, Sign, Standard, Star-spangled, Streamer
**Banquet** Beanfeast, Dine, Feast, Junket, Nosh-up, Running, Spread
**Banquette** Firestep
**Bant** Diet, Reduce
**Bantam** Dandy-cock, Dandy-hen
**Banter** Backchat, Badinage, Borak, Borax, Chaff, Dicacity, Dieter, Flirtation, Jest, → JOKE, Josh, Persiflage, Picong, Rag, → RAILLERY, Rally, Repartee, Ribaldry, Roast, Rot, Tease
**Bantu** Basotho, Gazankulu, Herero, Hutu, Lebowa, Qwaqwa, Shangaan, Sotho, Swahili, Transkei, Tswana, Tutsi, X(h)osa
**Bap** Bread, Roll, Tommy
**Baptise(d), Baptism, Baptist** Affusion, Amrit, Christen, Clinical, Conditional, Dip, Dipper, Dopper, Dunker, Hypothetical, Illuminati, Immersion, Insufflation, John, Mandaean, Mersion, Palingenesis, Private, Sabbatarian, Sprinkle, Tinker
**Bar(s)** Address, Angle-iron, Anti-roll, Apartheid, Astragal, Asymmetric, Axletree, Bail, Ban, Barrelhouse, Bass, Baulk, Beam, Bierkeller, Bilboes, Billet, Bistro, Blackball, Blacklist, Block(ade), Bloom, Bolt, Boom, Bottega, Brasserie, Breakfast, Buffet, Bull, Bullion, Bumper, But, Buvette, Café(-chantant), Café-concert, → CAGE, Cake, Came, Candy, Cantina, Capo, Capstan, Channel, Chocolate, Clasp, Clip joint, Cocktail, Coffee, Colour, Counter, Cramp(on), Cross(head), Crow, Crush, Currency, Dive, Doggery, Double, Double-tree, Dram, Draw, Drift, Dumbbell, Efficiency, Element, Espresso, Estaminet, Estop(pel), Except, Exchange, Exclude, Fern, Fid, Fire, Flinders, Fonda, Forbid, Foreclose, Forestall, Fret, Gad, Gastropub, Gemel, Gin palace, Glazing, Grate, Grid, Grog-shop, Gunshop, Hame, Handrail, Handspike, Heck, Hershey, → HINDRANCE, Horizontal, Hound, Hyphen, Impediment, Ingoes, Ingot, Ingowes, Inn, Inner, Judder, Juice, Karaoke, Keeper, Kickstand, Knuckleduster, Latch, Let, Lever, Limbo, Line, Lingot, Local, Lock out, Lounge, Luncheon, Macron, Magnet, Mandrel, Mandril, Measure, Menu, Merchant, Milk, Mousing, Muesli, Mullion, Nail, Nanaimo, Navigation, Nineteenth hole, No-go, Norman, Obstacle, Obstruct, Omerta, Onely, Orgue, Outer, Overslaugh, Oxygen, Parallel, Perch, Pile, Pinch, Pole, Posada, Prescription, Prevent, Prison, Private, Prohibit, Pub, Public, Putlog, Rack, Raddle, Rail, Ramrod, Rance, Randle-balk, Randle-perch, Randle-tree, Raw, Reach, Restrict, Rib, Risp, Rod, Roll, Roo, Rung, Saddle, Salad, Saloon, Sand, Sans, Save, Saving, Scroll, Semantron, Shaft, Shanty, Shet, Shop, Shut, Side, Singles, Skewer, Slice, Slot, Snack, Snug, Soap, Spacer, Spar, Speakeasy, Sperre, Spina, Spit, Splinter, Spoke, Sprag, Stancher, Stanchion, Status, Stave, Stemmer, Sternson, Stick, Stirre, Stretcher, Stripe, Strut, Suspend, Sway, Swee, T, Tael, Tap(-room), Tapas, Taphouse, Task, Tavern(a), Temple, Tiki, Title, Toll, Tombolo, Tommy, Tool, Torsion, Tow, Trace, Trangle, Transom, Trapeze, Treadle, Trellis, Triblet, Trundle, Type, U-bolt, Vinculum, Wall, Ward, Wet, Whisker, Window, Wine, Wire, Wrecking, Z, Zed, Zygon
**Barabbas** Robber
**Barb(ed)** Bur(r), Cutter, Fluke, Harl, Herl, → HOOK, Jag(g), Jibe, Pheon, Prickle, Ramus, Spike, Tang, Thorn, Vexillum
**Barbados, Barbadian** Bajan, Bim(m)
**Barbara** Allen, Major
**Barbarian, Barbaric** Boor, Crude, Fifteen, Foreigner, Goth, Heathen, Hun, Inhuman, Lowbrow, Merciless, Outlandish, Philistine, Rude, Savage, Tartar, Tatar(ic), Vandal, Visigoth
**Barbary** Ape, Roan
**Barbecue** BBQ, Braai(vleis), Chargrill, Cook-out, Flame-grill, Grill, Hangi, Hibachi, Roast, Spit
**Barbel** Beard
**Barber** Epilate, Figaro, Hair, Scrape(r), Shaver, Strap, Sweeney Todd, Tonsor, Trimmer
**Barbiturate** Goofball
**Bard(ic)** Ariosto, Druid, Gorsedd, Griot, Heine, Meat, Minstrel, Muse, Ossian, Ovate, Scald, Scop, Skald, Taliesin
**Bare, Bare-headed** Adamic, Aphyllous, Bald, Barren, Blank, Bodkin, Cere, Décolleté, Denude, Hush, Lewd, Marginal, Mere, Moon, → NAKED, Nude, Open, Plain, Scablands, Scant, Sear, Stark(ers), Strip, Timber line, Topless, Uncase, Uncover, Unfurnished, Unpainted, Unveil

**Bareback** Godiva

**Barefoot** Discalced, Unshod

**Barely** At a pinch, At a stretch, Hand-to-mouth, Hardly, Just, Merely, Scarcely, Scrimp

**Bargain(ing)** Agreement, Bargoon, Barter, Basement, Bon marche, Braata, Chaffer, Champerty, → CHEAP, Cheapo, Collective, Compact, Compromise, Contract, Coup, Deal, Dicker, Distributive, Effort, Find, Go, Haggle, Hard, Higgle, Horse-trade, Huckster, Indent, Integrative, Negotiate, Option, → PACT, Plea, Productivity, Scoop, Snip, Steal, Supersaver, Time, Trade, Trock, Troke, Truck, Wanworth, Wheeler-dealing

**Barge** Birlinn, Bucentaur, Budgero(w), Butty, Casco, Elbow, Gabbard, Gabbart, Galley-foist, Gloriana, Hopper, Intrude, Jostle, Keel, Lighter, Nudge, Obtrude, Pra(a)m, Ram, Scow, → SHIP, Thrust, Trow, Wherry

▷**Barge** *may indicate* an anagram

**Bargee, Bargeman** Hobbler, Keeler, Keelman, Legger, Lighterman, Ram, Trow

**Barium** Ba, Witherite

**Bark** Angostura, Ayelp, Azedarach, Bass, Bast, Bay, Bowwow, Bull's wool, Calisaya, Cambium, Canella, Caribbee, Cascara, Cascara sagrada, Cascarilla, Cassia, China, Cinchona, Cinnamon, Cork, Cortex, Crown, Cusparia, Hack, Honduras, Jamaica, Jesuits', Kina, Kinakina, Latration, Liber, Mezereon, Mezereum, Myrica, Parchment, Peel, Pereira, Peruvian, Phloem, Quebracho, Quest, Quill, Quillai, Quina, Quinquina, Red, Rind, Sagrada, Salian, Sassafras, Scrape, Scurf, Shag, → SHIP, Skin, Slippery elm, Tan, Tap(p)a, Totaquine, Waff, Waugh, Winter's, Woof, Wow, Yaff, → YAP, Yellow, Yelp, Yip

**Bar-keep(er), Barmaid, Barman, Bartender** Advocate, Ale-wife, Barista, Bencher, Curate, Hebe, Luckie, Lucky, Portia, Tapster, Underskinker

**Barley (water)** Awn, Bear, Bere, Bigg, Hordeum, Malt, Orgeat, Pearl, Pot, Scotch, Truce, Tsamba

**Barm(y)** Yeast

**Barmecide, Barmecidal** Imaginary

**Barn** Bank, Byre, Cowshed, Dutch, Farm, Grange, Mow, Perchery, Skipper, Tithe

**Barnaby** Long, Rudge

**Barnacle** Acorn, Cirriped(e), Cypris, Goose(neck), Limpet, Sticker

**Barnet** Hair-do

**Barometer** Aneroid, Glass, Orometer, Pierglass, Statoscope, Sympiesometer, Torricellian tube, Weatherglass

**Baron** B, Corvo, Drug, Magnate, Munchausen, Noble, Press, Red, Robber, Thyssen, Tycoon

**Baronet** Bart

**Baronne Dudevant** Sand

**Baroque** Fancy, Gothic, Ornate, Rococo

▷**Baroque** *may indicate* an anagram

**Barrack(s), Barracking** Asteism, Boo, Cantonment, Casern(e), Cat-call, Deepcut, Garrison, Glasshouse, Heckle, Irony, Jeer, Quarters

**Barrage** Balloon, Boom, Broadside, Fusillade, Heat, Salvo, Shellfire

**Barred** Banned, Edh, Trabeculated

**Barrel** Bbl, Bl, Bran-tub, Butt, Cade, Capstan, Cascabel, Cask, Chase, Clavie, Cracker, Croze, Cylinder, Drum, Hogshead, Keg, Kibble, Morris-tube, Oak, Oildrum, Organ, Pièce, Pork, Run(d)let, Tan-vat, Thrall, Tierce, Tun, Vat, Water, Wood

**Barrel-organ** Apollonicon, Hurdy-gurdy, Serinette, Street piano

**Barren** Addle, Arid, Badlands, Bleak, Blind, Blunt, Clear, Dry, Eild, → EMPTY, Farrow, Fruitless, Hardscrabble, Hi(r)stie, Jejune, Sterile, Unbearing, Unfruitful, Waste, Wasteland, Wilderness, Yeld, Yell

**Barricade** Road-block, Sandbag

**Barrier** Baffle, Bail, Barbed wire, Barrage, Barricade, Bayle, Block, Boom, Breakwater, Cauld, Checkrail, Cheval de frise, Chicane, Cordon (sanitaire), Crash, Crush, → DAM, Defence, Deterrent, Door, Drawgate, Dyke, Fence, Firewall, Floodgate, Fraise, Gate, Guard rail, Ha-ha, Handicap, Heat, Hedge, Hindrance, Hurdle, Levee, Mach, Obstacle, Obstruct, Pain, Paling, Potential, Rail(-fence), Rampart, Restraint, Revetment, Ring fence, Roadblock, Rope,

Sandbag, Sand break, Screen, Skreen, Sonic, Sound, Spina, Stockade, Thames, Thermal, Tollgate, Trade, Transonic, Traverse, Turnpike, Turnstile, Vapour, → WALL

**Barrister** Advocate, Attorney, Brief, Counsel, Devil, Lawyer, Recorder, Revising, Rumpole, Sergeant (at law), Serjeant(-at-law), Silk, SL, Templar, Utter

**Barrow** Applecart, Clyde, Dolly, Drill, Handcart, Henge, How, Hurley, Kurgan, Molehill, Mound, Pushcart, Tram, Trolley, Truck, Tumulus

**Barrow-boy** Coster, Trader

**Bar-tail** Scamel, Staniel, Stannel

**Barter** Chaffer, Chop, Coup, Dicker, → EXCHANGE, Haggle, Hawk, Niffer, Permutate, Sco(u)rse, Swap, → TRADE, Traffic, Truck

**Bartolomew** Black

**Baryon** Hyperon

**Barytes** Gauk, Gawk

**Basalt** Diabase, Melaphyre, Tachylite, Tephrite, Toadstone, Trap(pean), Traprock, Wacke

**Base** Adenine, Aggregate, Air, Airhead, Alkali, Bag, Bed, Beggarly, Billon, Board, Bottom, Brest, Caitiff, Camp, Choline, Cloud, Codon, Cytosine, Degenerate, Degraded, Diethyl, Dog, Down, E, Erinite, → ESTABLISH, Figure, First, Floor, Fond, Foot, Foothold, Footstall, Fort Knox, Found, Foundation, Fundus, Garrison, Guanine, Harlot, Headquarters, Histamine, Home, Hydroxide, Ignoble, Ignominious, Imidazole, Indamine, Infamous, Iniquitous, Install, Knowledge, La Spezia, Leuco, Lewis, Litmus, → LOW, → MEAN, Nefarious, Nook, Oasis®, Octal, Pararosaniline, Parasaniline, Partite, Patten, Platform, Plinth, Podium, Predella, Premise, Prisoner's, Ptomaine, Purin(e), Pyrimidine, Pyrrolidine, Raca, Radix, Raft, Rascally, Ratty, Rests, Ribald, Root, Rosaniline, Roux, Rude, Scapa Flow, Schiff, Servile, Shameful, Shand, Sheeny, Sinister, Snide, Socle, Soda, Sordid, Spaceport, Springing, Staddle, → STAND, Station, Stylopodium, Substrate, Ten, Tetracid, Thymine, Torus, Triacid, Turpitude, Unworthy, Uracil, Vile

**Baseball(er)** Apple, Nine, Red Sox, Twi-night, Yankees

**Baseless** Idle, Invalid, Unfounded, Ungrounded

**Base-line** Datum

**Basement** Bargain, Below stairs, Cellar, Crypt

**Bash** Attempt, Belt, Bonk, Clout, Dint, Go, Hit, Rave, Shot, Slog, Strike, Swat, Swipe

**Bashful** Awed, Blate, Coy, Diffident, Dwarf, Modest, Prudish, Retiring, Shame-faced, Shamefast, Sheep-faced, Sheepish, → SHY

**Basic(s), Basically, Basis** ABC, Abcee, Abecedarian, Alkaline, Aquamanale, Aquamanile, At bottom, At heart, Bare, Bedrock, Brass tacks, Cardinal, Clipboard, Crude, Elemental, → ESSENTIAL, Fiducial, Fond, Foundation, Fundamental, Grass roots, Ground(work), Gut, In essence, Integral, Intrinsic, Logic, Meat and potatoes, Need-to-know, Nitty-gritty, No-frills, No-nonsense, Nuts and bolts, One-horse, Ontology, Origin, Pou sto, Presumption, Primal, Primitive, Primordial, Principle, Protoplasm, Radical, Rudimentary, Spit-and-sawdust, Standard, Staple, Substance, Substratum, Underlying, Unsophisticated, Uracil

**Basil** Holy, Pot-herb

**Basilica** St Peter's

**Basilisk** Cannon, Lizard

**Basin** Aquamanale, Aquamanile, Artesian, Aspergillum, Aspersorium, Benitier, Bidet, Bowl, Brazil, Canning, Catch, Catchment, Chott, Cirque, Corrie, Cwm, Dish, Dock, Doline, Donets, Drainage, Font, Foxe, Geosyncline, Great, Impluvium, Kuzbass, Kuznetsk, Lavabo, Laver, Minas, Monteith, Ocean, Okavango, Pan, Park, Pelviform, Piscina, Playa, Porringer, Pudding, Reservoir, River, Salt pan, Scapa Flow, Sink, Slop(-bowl), Stoop, Stoup, Sugar, Tank, Tarim, Tidal, Washhand

**Bask** Apricate, Revel, Sun, Sunbathe, → WALLOW

**Basket, Basket-work** Baalam, Bass, Bassinet, Bread, Buck, Cabas, Calathus, Canasta, Canephorus, Car, Cesta, Chip, Clothes, Cob, Coop, Corbeil(le), Corbicula, Corf, Creel, Cresset, Dosser, Fan, Flasket, Flax kit, Frail, Gabion, Goal, Hamper, Hanging, Hask, Junket, Kago, Kajawah, Kipe, Kit, Kite, Leap, Linen, Litter, Luncheon, Maund, Mocock, Mocuck, Moses, Murlain, Murlan, Murlin, Osiery, Pannier, Ped, Petara, Pitara(h), Plate, Pollen, Pottle, Punnet, Raffia, Rip, Round file, Scull, Scuttle, Seed-lip, Skep, Skull, Trolley, Trout, Trug,

Van, Wagger-pagger(-bagger), Waste(-paper), Wattlework, Whisket, Wicker(-work), Will(e), Wisket, Work

**Basketball** Tip-off

**Basket-bearer** Canephor(a), Canephore, Canephorus

**Basket-maker** Alfa, Cane, Halfa, Wicker

**Basque** Biscayan, Bodice, Euskarian, Jacket

**Bass** Alberti, Ale, Alfie, B, Black, Bourdon, Continuo, Deep, Double, El-a-mi, Figured, Fish, Ground, Largemouth, Low, Ostinato, Serran, Smallmouth, String, Thorough, Walking

**Bassoon** Fagotto, Sausage

**Bast** Liber

**Bastard, Bastard-wing** Alula, Base, Basket, By-blow, Filius nullius, Git, Haram(za)da, Illegitimate, Mamzer, Misborn, Momzer, Mongrel, Sassaby, Side-slip, Slink, Sod, Spuriae, Spurious, Whoreson

▹**Bastard** *may indicate* an anagram

**Baste** Enlard, Sew, Stitch, Tack

**Bastion** Citadel, Lunette, Moineau

**Bat(sman), Bats, Bat's wing, Batter, Batting, Batty** Aliped, Ames, Assail, Barbastelle, Baton, Belfry, Blink, Buzz-bait, Certifiable, Chiroptera, Close, Club, Cosh, Crackers, Crease, Cudgel, Dad, Die Fledermaus, Eyelid, False vampire, Flittermouse, Flutter, Flying fox, Fruit, Fungo, Grace, Hammerhead, Hatter, Haywire, Hit, Hobbs, Hook, Horseshoe, In, Ink mouse, Innings, Insectivorous, Kalong, Knock, Language, Lara, Leisler, Live, Man, Mastiff, Maul, May, Mormops, Mouse-eared, Myopic, Nictate, Nictitate, Night, Nightwatchman, Noctilio, Nora, Nurdle, Opener, Paddle, Patagium, Pinch-hit, Pipistrel(le), Poke, Pummel, Rabbit, Racket, Racquet, Ram, Rearmouse, Reremice, Reremouse, Roussette, Ruin, Sauch, Saugh, Scorer, Scotch hand, Serotine, Sledge, Spectre, Stick, Stonewall, Straight, Striker, Swat, Switch hitter, Tail(ender), Trap-stick, Trunnion, Vampire, Vespertilionid, Viv, Whacky, Willow, Wood

**Batch** Bake, Bunch, Caboodle, Clutch, Crop, Job lot, Tranche

**Bath(room), Bath-house** Aerotone, Aeson's, Aquae sulis, Bagnio, Bain-marie, Balneotherapy, Banya, Bed, Bidet, Bird, Blanket, Blood, Bubble, Caldarium, Cor, Dip, Dust, Earth, En suite, Epha, Eye, Foam, Hammam, Hip, Hot tub, Hummaum, Hummum, Jacuzzi®, Lav, Laver, Mik vah, Mud, Mustard, Oil, Oliver, Piscina, Plunge, Salt, San, Sauna, Shower, Sitz, Slipper, Soak, Spa, Sponge, Steam, Stew, Stop, Sudarium, Tepidarium, Therm, Tub, Turkish, Tye, Vapour, Whirlpool, Wife

**Bathe(r), Bathing** Archimedes, Balneal, Balneation, Balneology, Balneotherapy, Bay(e), Beath, Bogey, Bogie, Dip, Dook, Douk, Embay, Foment, Immerse, Lave, Lip, Skinny-dip, Souse, Splash, Stupe, → **SWIM**, Tub, → **WASH**

**Bathos** Anticlimax

**Bathrobe** Peignoir

**Batman** Valet

**Baton** Mace, Rod, Sceptre, Staff, Stick, Truncheon, Wand

**Baton-bearer** Majorette

**Batrachian** Frog, Toad

▹**Bats, Batting** *may indicate* an anagram

**Battalion** Bn, Corps, Troop

**Batten** Bar, Dropper, Fasten, Lath, Tie

**Batter(ed)** Bombard, Bruise, Buffet, Decrepit, Eyelash, Eyelid, Fritter, Marmelise, Pound, Slugger, Thump

**Battery** Accumulator, Acid, Artillery, Button-cell, Cannonade, Cross, Drycell, Electric, Field, Floating, Galvanic, Heliac, Henhouse, Li(thium)-ion, Magnetic, Masked, Nicad, Nickel cadmium, NIMH, Penlight, Pra(a)m, Primary, Solar, Storage, Transducer, Troop, Voltaic, Waffle, Water

**Battle(s), Battleground** Action, Affair, Ben, Campaign, Clash, Cockfight, Cockpit, Combat, → **CONFLICT**, Crossfire, Darraign, Deraign, Encounter, Engagement, Field, → **FIGHT**, Fray, Front, Hosting, Joust, Maiden, Martian, Paoli, Pitched, Royal, Running, Sarah, Sciamachy, Shoot-out, Skiamachy, Skirmish, Spurs, Stoor, Stour, Stowre, Strife, Theatre, Theomachy, Tussle, Wage, → **WAR**, Wargame

## BATTLES

***3 letters:***
Kut
Ulm

***4 letters:***
Alma
Chad
Ivry
Jena
Laon
Lodi
Loos
Mons
Nile
Zama

***5 letters:***
Accra
Alamo
Allia
Arcot
Arras
Boyne
Bulge
Crecy
Ipsus
Issus
Lewes
Lissa
Marne
Mylae
Nancy
Parma
Pavia
Pydna
Sedan
Somme
Tours
Valmy
Ypres

***6 letters:***
Actium
Arbela
Arcola
Argyle
Arnhem
Barnet
Camlan
Cannae
Cressy
Crimea
Imphal
Kosovo
Lutzen
Maldon
Midway
Mohacs
Mycale
Naseby
Sadowa
Senlac
Shiloh
Tobruk
Towton
Varese
Verdun
Vigrid
Wagram
Wipers

***7 letters:***
Aboukir
Alamein
Almanza
Argonne
Bautzen
Beaches
Britain
Bull Run
Cambrai
Carrhae
Chalons
Colenso
Coronel
Corunna
Deorham
Dunkirk
Evesham
Flodden
Flowers
Glencoe
Iwo Jima
Jericho
Jutland
Legnano
Lepanto
Leuctra
Magenta
Marengo
Nations
Newbury
Nineveh
Okinawa
Orleans
Panipat
Picardy
Plassey
Plataea
Poltava
Pultowa
Salamis
Sempach
Vimelro
Vitoria
Warburg

***8 letters:***
Antietam
Ardennes
Ayacucho
Blenheim
Borodino
Bosworth
Chioggia
Clontarf
Culloden
Custozza
Edgehill
Erzurium
Flanders
Fontenay
Hastings
Hydaspes
Inkerman
Jemappes
Kulikova
Le Cateau
Lechfeld
Manassas
Marathon
Mehawand
Metaurus
Montreal
Naumachy
Navarino
Normandy
Omdurman
Palo Alto
Philippi
Poitiers
Ragnarok
Rossbach
Saratoga
Solomons
Spion Kop
St Albans
Syracuse
Talavera
Toulouse
Waterloo
Yorktown

***9 letters:***
Agincourt
Balaclava
Caporetto
Castilion
Chaeronea
El Alamein
Gallipoli
Ladysmith
Moerkirch
Nicopolis
Otterburn
Oudenarde
Pharsalus
Princeton
Ramillies
Sedgemoor
Solferino
St Vincent
The Saints
Trafalgar
Vercellae
Wandewash
Worcester

***10 letters:***
Adrianople
Armageddon
Austerlitz
Beneventum
Bennington
Brunanburh
Bunker Hill
Camperdown
Ferhbellin
Gettysburg
Lundy's Lane
Majuba Hill
Malplaquet
Mount Badon
Petersburg
Quatre Bras
River Plate
Shipka Pass
Stalingrad
Steenkerke
Tannenberg
Tewkesbury

***11 letters:***
Aegospotami
Aljubarrota
Armentières
Aubers Ridge
Bannockburn
Belleau Wood
Bismarck Sea
Chapultepec
Chattanooga
Hohenlinden
Marston Moor
Philiphaugh
Prestonpans
Rorke's Drift
Thermopylae
Wounded Knee

***12 letters:***
Flodden Field
Mons Graupius
Monte Cassino
Roncesvalles

***13 letters:***
Alcazar-Quivir
Bosworth Field
Little Bighorn
Neuve-Chapelle
Neville's Cross
Passchendaele
Spanish Armada

***14 letters:***
Castlebar Races
Stamford Bridge

***15 letters:***
Missionary Ridge
Plains of Abraham
Teutoberger Wald

***16 letters:***
Las Navas de Tolosa

**Battle-axe** Amazon, Bill, Gorgon, Halberd, Ogress, Sparth(e), Termagant, Termagent, Turmagant, Turmagent

**Battlement** Barmkin, Crenellate, Merlon, Rampart

**Battle-order** Phalanx

**Battleship** Carrier, Destroyer, Dreadnought, Gunboat, Man-o'-war, Pocket, Potemkin, Repulse

**Bauble** Bagatelle, Gaud, Gewgaw, Trifle, Trinket

**Bauhaus** Gropius

**Baulk** Demur, Gib, Hen, Impede, Jib, Reest, Reist, Shy, Thwart

**Bavardage** Fadaise

**Bawd(y)** Earthy, Hare, Racy, Raunchy, Risque, Sculdudd(e)ry, Skulduddery, Smutty

**Bawl** Bellow, Gollar, Howl, Weep

**Bay** Ab(o)ukir, Aere, Alum, Arm, Baffin, Bantry, Bark, Bell, Bengal, Bez, Bight, Biscay, Bonny, Botany, Broken, Brown, Byron, Cape Cod, Capri, Cardigan, Chesapeake, Cienfuegos, Classis, Cleveland, Colwyn, Corpus Christi, Cove, Covelet, Creek, Cubicle, Daphne, Delagoa, Delaware, Discovery, Dublin, Dundalk, Dvina, False, Famagusta, Fleet, Freshwater, Frobisher, Fundy, Galway, Gdansk, Georgian, Gibraltar, Glace, Golden, Great Australian Bight, Green, Guanabara, Guantanamo, Gulf, Hangzhou, Harbour, Hawke's, Herne, Hervey, Horse, → **HOWL**, Hudson, Inhambane, Inlet, Ise, Islands, James, Jervis, Jiazhou, Kavalla, Kuskokwim, Laura, Laurel, Layby, Loading, Lobito, Loblolly, Lutzow-Holm, MA, Magdalena, Manila, Massachusetts, Montego, Moreton, Narragansett, New York, Niche, Oleander, Omaha, Oriel, Passamaquoddy, Pegasus, Pigs, Plenty, Plymouth, Port Phillip, Poverty, Recess, Red, Roan, St Austell, St Michel, San Francisco, San Pedro, Santiago, Scene, Setubal, Shark, Sick, Sligo, Stall, Suvla, Swansea, Table, Tampa, Tasman, The Wash, Thunder, Tiger, Tor, Toyama, Tralee, Trincomalee, Ungava, Vae, Vigo, Vlore, Voe, Vyborg, Waff, Walfish, Walvis, Wash, Whitley, Wick, Yowl

**Bayonet** Jab, Skewer, Spanish, Stab, Sword

**Bazaar** Alcaiceria, Emporium, Fair, Fete, Market, Pantechnicon, Sale, Sook, Souk

**BBC** Auntie, Beeb

**Be** Exist, Live, Occur

**Beach(head)** Aground, Anzio, Bikini, Bondi, Chesil, Coast, Daytona, Foreshore, Ground, Hard, Lido, Littoral, Machair, Miami, Myrtle, Omaha, Palm, Plage, Raised, Sand, Sea-coast, Seashore, Seaside, Shingle, Shore(line), Storm, Strand, Waikiki

**Beachcomber** Arenaria, Layabout

**Beachwear** Bikini, Thong

**Beacon** Belisha, Bonfire, Brecon, Fanal, Floating, Ivinghoe, Landing, Lantern, Lighthouse, Lightship, Need-fire, Pharos, Racon, Radar, Radio, Robot, Signal

**Bead(s), Beaded** Adderstone, Aggri, Aggry, Astragal, Baily's, Ballotini, Bauble, Blob, Bugle, Cabling, Chaplet, Crab's-eyes, Crab-stones, Dewdrop, Drop, Droplet, Gadroon, Gaud, Globule, Job's tears, Kumbaloi, Love, Mala, Moniliform, Nurl, Ojime, Passament, Passement, Paternoster, Poppet, Poppit, Prayer, Rosary, Sabha, St Cuthbert's, Se(a)wan, Spacer, Spacer plate, Strand, Subha, Sweat, Taktite, Tasbih, Tear, Wampum(peag), Worry

**Beadle** Apparitor, Bederal, Bedral, Bumble, Herald, Paritor, Shammash, Shammes, Verger

**Beagle** Snoopy, Spy

**Beak** AMA, Bailie, Bill, Cad, Cere, Coracoid, Coronoid, Egg-tooth, Gar, JP, Kip(p), Magistrate, Master, Metagnathous, Mittimus, Nasute, Neb, Nib, Nose, Pecker, Prow, Ram, Rectal, Rostellum, Rostrum, Shovel

**Beaker** Bell, Cup, Goblet, Mug

**Beakless** Erostrate

**Beak-shaped** Coracoid

**Beam(ing)** Arbor, Architrave, Balance, Ba(u)lk, Bar, Binder, Boom, Bowstring, Box, Breastsummer, Bressummer, Broadcast, Bum(p)kin, Cantilever, Carline, Carling, Cathead, Collar, Crossbar, Crosshead, Crosspiece, Deck, Effulge, Electron, Full, Girder, Grin, Hammer, Hatch, Herisson, Holophote, I, Irradiate, Joist, Ke(e)lson, Landing, Laser, Lee, Lentel, Lintel, Manteltree, Maser, Molecular, Moonlight, Needle, Outrigger, Particle, Pencil, Port, Principal, Proton, Purlin, Putlock, Putlog, Radiant, Radio, → **RAFTER**, → **RAY**, Rayon, Refulgent,

Rident, Ridgepole, Rood, Roof-tree, Sandwich, Scale, Scantling, Sealed, Searchlight, Shaft, Shine, Shore, Sleeper, Smile, Soffit, Solive, Spar, Stanchion, Starboard, Stemson, Sternpost, Sternson, Straining, Streamer, Stringer, Stringpiece, Summer, Sunlight, Support, Tailing, Tie, Timber, Trabeate, Trabecula, Transom, Trave, Trimmer, Truss, Universal, Viga, Walking, Weather, Weigh-bauk, Yard, Yardarm

**Beamish** Galumphing, Nephew

**Bean(s)** Abrus, Adsuki, Aduki, Adzuki, Arabica, Asparagus pea, Bag, Baked, Berry, Black, Black-eye, Borlotti, Broad, Bush, Butter, Cacao, Calabar, Can(n)ellini, Castor, Cherry, Cluster, Cocoa, Coffee, Cow-pea, Dwarf, Edamame, Fabaceous, Fava, Flageolet, French, Frijol(e), Garbanzo, Goa, Gram, Green, Haricot, Harmala, Head, Horse, Hyacinth, Jack, Jelly, Jequirity, Jumping, Kachang putch, Kidney, Lablab, Legume, Lentil, Lima, Locust, Molucca, Moong, Moth, Mung, Nelumbo, Nib, Noddle, Ordeal, Pichurim, Pinto, Pole, Pulse, Runner, St Ignatius's, Sassafras nut, Scarlet, Scarlet runner, Shell, Silverskin, Snap, Snuffbox, Soy(a), String, Sugar, Sword, Tepary, Tofu, Tonga, Tonka, Tonquin, Urd, Wax, Winged, Yard-long

**Beanfeast** → PARTY, Spree, Wayzgoose

**Beanpole** Thin

**Bear(er), Bear lover** Abide, Abrooke, Andean, Arctic, Arctophile, Aurora, Baloo, Balu, Barley, Beer, Bigg, Breed, Brook, Brown, Bruin, Brunt, → CARRY, Cave, Churl, Cinnamon, Coati-mondi, Coati-mundi, Cub, Demean, Dree, Ean, → ENDURE, Engender, Exert, Fur-seal, Gest(e), Gonfalonier, Great, Grizzly, Hack, Ham(m)al, Harbinger, Have, Hod, Hold, Honey, Humf, Hump(h), Jampanee, Jampani, Keb, Kinkajou, Koala, Kodiak, Koolah, Lioncel(le), Lionel, Little, Lug, Meet, Mother, Nandi, Nanook, Owe, Paddington, Panda, Pertain, Polar, Pooh, Produce, Rac(c)oon, Roller, Rupert, Russia, Sackerson, Seller, Shoulder, Sit, Sloth, Spawn, Spectacled, Stand, Stay, Stomach, → SUFFER, Sun, Sunbear, Sustain, Targeteer, Teddy, Teem, Thole, Throw, Tolerate, Tote, Transport, Undergo, Upstay, Ursine, Water, Whelp, White, Wield, Withstand, Wombat, Woolly, Yean, Yield, Yogi

**Bearberry** Manzanita, Uva-ursi

**Beard(ed)** Aaron, Alfalfa, Anchor, Arista, Assyrian, Aureole, Awn, Balaclava, Barb, Barbiche, Beaver, Belgrave, Cadiz, Cathedral, Charley, Charlie, Confront, Defy, Ducktail, Escort, Excrement, Face, Five o'clock shadow, Forked, Fungus, Goatee, Hair(ie), Hairy, Hear(ie), Hirsute, Imperial, Jewish, Kesh, Lincolnesque, Mephistopheles, Newgate frill, Newgate fringe, Old Dutch, Olympian, Outface, Peak, Pencil, Raleigh, Rivet, Roman T, Screw, Shenandoah, Spade, Stibble, Stiletto, Stubble, Swallowtail, Tackle, Tile, Trojan, Tuft, Uncle Sam, Vandyke, Whiskerando, Whiskery, Ziff

**Beardless** Callow, Clean, Tahr, Tehr

▷**Bearhug** *may indicate* Teddy or similar around a word

**Bearing(s)** Air, Allure, Amenaunce, Armorial, Aspect, Azimuth, Babbitt, Ball, Behaviour, Billet, Bush, Carriage, Deportment, Dignity, Direction, E, Endurance, Gait, Germane, Gest, Gudgeon, Hatchment, Haviour, Heading, → HERALDIC, Hugger-mugger, Lioncel(le), Lionel, Manner, Martlet, Mascle, Middy, Mien, N, Needle, Nor, Pall, Pheon, Port, Presence, Reference, Relevant, Roller, S, Seme(e), Subordinary, Teeming, Tenue, Thrust, W, Yielding

▷**Bearing** *may indicate* compass points

**Beast(ly)** → ANIMAL, Arna, Behemoth, Blond, Brute, Caliban, Caribou, Chimera, → CREATURE, Dieb, Dragon, Dzeren, Fatstock, Gargoyle, Gayal, Genet, Godzilla, Grampus, Hippogriff, Hodog, Hog, Hydra, Hy(a)ena, Jumart, Kinkajou, Lion, Mammoth, Marmot, Mastodon, Meerkat, Mhorr, Monoceros, Narwhal, Ogre, Oliphant, Opinicus, Oryx, Panda, Peccary, Potto, Quagga, Queen's, Rac(c)oon, Rhytina, Rother, Rumptifusel, Sassaby, Steer, Sumpter, Swinish, Tarand, Teg, Theroid, Triceratops, Triton, Wart-hog, Whangam, Yahoo, Yak, Yale, Zizel

**Beat(ing), Beaten, Beater** Anoint, Arsis, Assault, Athrob, Bandy, Bang, Baste, Bastinado, Batter, Battue, Battuta, Beetle, Belabour, Belt, Bepat, Best, Blatter, Bless, Bo Diddley, Bubble, Cadence, Cane, Cat, Chastise, Clobber, Club, Clump, Cob, Conquer, Cream, Cudgel, Cuff, Curry, Debel, → DEFEAT, Ding, Donder, Dress, Drub, Drum, Duff up, Dunt, Elude, Excel, Fatigue, Faze, Feague, Feeze, Fibbed, Firk, Flagellate, Flail, Flam, Flap, Float, Flog, Floor, Flush, Fly, Fustigate, Hammer, Hiding, Hipster, Hollow, Horsewhip, Ictus, Inteneration, Jole, Joll, Joule, Jowl, Knock, Knubble, Lace, Laidy, Laldie, Lambast(e), Larrup, Lash, Lather, Latin,

Laveer, Lay, Leather, Lick, Lilt, Lounder, Mall, Malleate, Manor, Mell, Mersey, Mullah, Muller, Nubble, Onceover, Outclass, Outdo, Outflank, Outshine, Outstrip, Outstroke, Overcome, Overwhelm, Paik, Palpitate, Pandy, Panel, Paradiddle, Pash, Paste, Pelt, Pip, Ploat, Pommel, Pound, Prat, Pug, Pulsate, Pulsatile, Pulse, Pulsedge, Pummel, Pun, Quop, Raddle, Ram, Ratten, Resolve, Retreat, Rhythm, Ribroast, Rope's end, Round, Rout, Rowstow, Ruff(le), Scourge, Scutch, Slat, Slipper, Smight, Smite, Soak, Sock, Sort, Strap, Strap-oil, Strike, Surpass, Swinge, Swingle, Syncopation, Systole, Taber, Tabor, Tabrere, Tachycardia, Tact, Tala, Tan, Tattoo, Tempo, Thesis, Thrash, Thresh, Throb, Thud, Thump, Thwack, Tick, Time, Tired, Top, Torture, Tricrotic, Trounce, Tuck, Tund, Verberate, Vibrate, Wallop, Wappend, Weary, Welt, Wham, Whip, Whisk, Whitewash, Whop, Whup, Worst, Wraught, Ybet, Yerk, Yirk

▹**Beaten-up** *may indicate* an anagram

**Beat it** Skedaddle, Vamo(o)se

**Beatitude** Macarism

**Beau** Admirer, Blade, Brummel, Cat, Damoiseau, Dandy, Flame, Geste, Lair, Lover, Masher, Nash, Spark, Suitor, Tibbs

**Beaufort** Scale, Windscale

**Beaut(y), Beautiful, Beautify** Adorn, Advantage, Angelic, Aphrodite, Astrid, Bathing, Belle, Bellibone, Bombshell, Bonny, Bright, Camberwell, Charmer, Colleen, Comeliness, Comely, Corker, Cracker, Dish, Doll, Embellish, Enhance, Exquisite, Eye candy, Eyeful, Fair, Fairness, Fine, Glamorise, Glamour (puss), Glorious, Glory, Gorgeous, Grace, Helen, Houri, Hyperion, Junoesque, Kanta, Lana, Looks, Monism, Ornament, Peri, Picture, Pink, Prettiness, Pride, Pulchritude, Purler, Radiant, Scenic, Sheen, Smasher(oo), Smicker, Specious, Stunner, Sublime, To kalon

**Beautician** Glamoriser

**Beauty spot** Patch, Tempe, Tika

**Beaver** Beard, Castor, Eager, Grind, Kit, Mountain, Oregon, Rodent, Sewellel

**Becalm(ed)** Doldrums

**Because (of)** As, Forasmuch, Forwhy, Hence, In (that), Inasmuch, Ipso facto, Sens, Since, Why

**Beckon** Gesture, Nod, Summons, Waft, Wave, Wheft

**Become, Becoming** Apt, Besort, Decent, Decorous, Dignified, End up, Enter, Fall, Fit, Flatter, Get, Go, Grow, Happen, Occur, Seemly, Suit, Wax, Worth

**Bed(s), Bedcover, Bedding, Bedstead** Air, Allotment, Amenity, Apple-pie, Arroyo, Bacteria, Bark, Base, Bassinet, → BEDCOVER, Berth, Border, Bottom, Bottomset, Box, Brancard, Bundle, Bunk, Caliche, Camp, Capillary, Carrycot, Channel, Charpoy, Cill, Cot(t), Couch(ette), Counterpane, Couvade, Coverlet, Cradle, Crib, Cross, Cul(t)ch, Day, Divan, Doona, Doss, Duvet, Erf, False, Feather, Field, Filter, Flock, Flower, Fluidized, Flying, Form, Four-poster, Futon, Gault, Greensand, Hammock, Hospital, Hover, Inlay, Kago, Kang, Kingsize, Kip, Knot, Knot garden, Lay(er), Lazy, Lilo®, Linen, Litter, Marriage, Mat, Matrix, Mattress, Mosquito net, Mudflat, Murphy, Naked, Nap, Nest, Nookie, Oyster, Pad, Paillasse, Pallet, Palliasse, Pan, Parterre, Passage, Patch, Pavement, Pay, Pig, Pit, Plank, Plant, Plot, Private, Procrustean, Puff, Queensize, Quilt, Reed, Retire, River, Rollaway, Roost, Rota, Sack, Sand, Scalp, Settle, Shakedown, Sick, Sill, Sitter, Sleep, Sofa, Spawning, Standing, Stratum, Stretcher, Substratum, Sun, T(h)alweg, Tanning, Test, The downy, Thill, Trough, Truckle, Trundle, Twin, Wadi, Wady, Ware, Water, Wealden, Wedding

**Bedaub** Cake, Deck, Smear

**Bed-bug** B, B flat, Chinch, Flea, Louse, Vermin

**Bedchamber, Bedroom** Boudoir, Bower, Br, Chamber, Cubicle, Dorm(itory), Dormer, Dorter, Ruelle, Ward

**Bedcover** Palampore, Palempore, Puff

**Bedeck** Adonise, Adorn, Array, Festoon

▹**Bedevilled** *may indicate* an anagram

**Bedfellow** Ally

**Bedjacket** Nightingale

**Bedlam** Asylum, Chaos, Furore, Madness, Mayhem, Nuthouse, Tumult, Uproar

**Bedraggled** Scruffy
**Bed-rest** Dutch-wife
**Bedridden** Infirm
**Bedrock** Costean
**Bedsit** Pad
**Bedwetting** Enuresis
**Bee** Afrikanised, Athenia, Bike, Bumble, Carpenter, Cuckoo, Deborah, Debra, Deseret, Dog, Drone, Drumbledor, Dumbledore, Group, Hiver, Honey, Humble, Husking, Killer, King, Lapidary, Leaf-cutter, Mason, Melissa, Mining, Nurse, Pollinator, Queen, Quilting, Raising, Solitary, Spell, Spell-down, Spelling, Swarm, Trixie, Worker, Working
**Beech** Antarctic, Copper, Fagus, Hornbeam, Mast, Taw(h)ai, Tree
**Bee-eater** Merops, Rainbow-bird
**Beef(y)** Aitchbone, Baron, Bleat, Brawny, Bresaola, Brisket, Bull(y), Bullock, Carp, Carpaccio, Charqui, Chateaubriand, Chuck, Clod, Complain, Corned, Entrecote, Filet mignon, Flank, Grievance, Gripe, Groan, Grouch, Ground, Grouse, Grump, Hefty, Hough, Hung, Jerk, Keema, Kobe, Liebig, Mart, Mice, Minced, Moan, Mousepiece, Muscle(-bound), Neat, Ox, Pastrami, Peeve, Plate, Porterhouse, Ribeye, Roast, Rother, Salt-horse, Salt-junk, Sauerbraten, Sey, Shin, Silverside, Sirloin, Stolid, Stroganoff, Topside, Tournedos, Tranche, Undercut, Vaccine, Wagyu, Wellington, Whine
**Beefeater** Billman, Exon, Gin, Oxpecker, Warder, Yeoman
**Bee-glue** Propolis
**Beehive** Alveary, Apiary, Ball, Dioptric, Gum, Skep, Utah
**Beekeeping** Apiculture
**Beelzebub** Devil
**Been** Bin
**Beer** Ale, Alegar, Amber fluid, Amber liquid, Bantu, Barley sandwich, Bitter, Black, Bock, Budweiser, Chaser, Cobra, Coldie, Draught, Drink, Dry, Entire, Export, Gill, Ginger, Granny, Grog, Guest, Heavy, Herb, Home-brew, Keg, Kvass, Lager, Lambic, Lite, Lush, Malt, March, Middy, Mild, Milk stout, Mum, Near, Nog, October, Pils(e)ner, Pint, Pony, Porter, Real, Real ale, Rice, Root, Round, Saki, Scoobs, Sherbet, Six-pack, Skeechan, Slip, Small, Spruce, Stingo, Stout, Stubby, Suds, Swankie, Swanky, Swats, Swipes, Switchel, Table, Taplash, Tinnie, Tipper, Tshwala, Tube, Turps, Wallop, Wheat, Zythum
**Beer-drinker** Froth-blower
**Beer garden** Brasserie
**Bee's nest** Bink
**Beet** Blite, Chard, Fat-hen, Goosefoot, Mangel(wurzel), Seakale, Silver, Spinach, Sugar
**Beethoven** WoO
**Beetle** Ambrosia, Anobiid, Argus tortoise, Asiatic, Bacon, Bark, Batler, Bee, Black, Blister, Bloody-nosed, Boll weevil, Bombardier, Bruchid, Bug, Bum-clock, Buprestidae, Buprestis, Burying, Bustle, Buzzard-clock, Cabinet, Cadelle, Cane, Cantharis, Carabid, Cardinal, Carpet, Carrion, Chafer, Christmas, Churchyard, Cicindela, Click, Clock, Cockchafer, Cockroach, Coleoptera, Coleopterous, Colorado, Coprophagan, Curculio, Darkling, Deathwatch, Dermestid, Devil's coach-horse, Diamond, Diving, Dor(r), Dor-fly, Dumbledore, Dung, Dyticus, Dytiscus, Earwig, Elater, Elmbark, Elytron, Elytrum, Firefly, Flea, Flit, Furniture, Glow-worm, Gold(smith), Goliath, Gregor, Ground, Grub, Hammer, Hangover, Hercules, Hop-flea, Hornbug, House longhorn, Huhu, Humbuzz, Impend, Japanese, Jewel, June bug, Khapra, Ladybird, Ladybug, Lamellicorn, Larder, Leaf, Leather, Longhorned, Longicorn, Mall(et), Maul, May-bug, Meloid, Minotaur, Museum, Musk, Oakpruner, Oil, Overhang, Pill, Pinchbuck, Pine, Pine-chafer, Potato, Project, Protrude, Race(-bug), Rhinoceros, Rhynchophora, Roach, Rosechafer, Rove, Sacred, Saw palmetto, Scamper, Scarab(ee), Scavenger, Scolytus, Scurry, Sexton, Shard, Skelter, Sledge(-hammer), Snapping, Snout, Soldier, Spanish fly, Spider, Spring, Squirr, Stag, Tenebrio, Tiger, Toktokkie, Tortoise, Tumble-bug, Tumble-dung, Turnip-flea, Typographer, Vedalia, VW, Water, Weevil, Whew, Whirligig, Wireworm, Woodborer, Wood-engraver
**Beetle-crushers** Cops
**Befall** Happen, Occur

**Befit(ting)** Seemly, Suit

**Before(hand)** A, Advance, Already, An, Ante, Avant, By, Coram, Earlier, Early, Ere, Erst(while), First, → FORMER, Or (e'er), Parava(u)nt, Pre, Previously, Prior, Pro, Sooner, Till, To, Until, Van, Zeroth

**Before food** Ac

**Befriend** Assist, Cotton, Fraternise, Support

**Befuddle(ment)** Bemuse, Confuse, Dwaal, Inebriate, Stupefy

**Beg(gar), Beggarly, Begging** Abr(ah)am-man, Ask, Badgeman, Belief, Beseech, Besognio, Bey, Bezonian, Blighter, Blue-gown, Cadge, Calendar, Cap in hand, Clapper-dudgeon, Crave, Down and outer, → ENTREAT, Exoration, Flagitate, Fleech, Gaberlunzie, Gangrel, Hallan-shaker, Implore, Impoverish, Irus, Jarkman, Lackall, Lazar(us), Lazzarone, Limitary, Lumpenproletariat, Maund, Mendicant, Montem, Mooch, Mouch, Mump, Niggardly, Obtest, Palliard, Panhandle, Pauper, Penelophon, Penniless, → PLEAD, Pled, Pray, Prig, Procreate, Prog, Ptochocracy, Rag, Randie, Randy, Ruffler, Ruin(ate), Sadhu, Schnorr(er), Screeve, Scrounge, Shool(e), Skelder, Skell, Solicit, Standpad, Sue, Suppliant, Supplicate, Thig(ger), Toe-rag, Touch, Undo, Uprightman, Whipjack

**Beget** Create, Engender, Gender, Kind, Procreate, Sire

**Beggar rule** Ptochocracy

**Begging bowl** Clackdish, Clapdish

**Begin(ner), Beginning** Ab initio, Ab ovo, Alpha, Alphabetarian, Author, B, Babyhood, Basic, Black, Cause, Che(e)chako, Clapdash, Commence, Curtain-raiser, Daw, Dawn, Deb, Debut, Embryo, Enter, Exordium, Fall-to, Fledgling, Found, Fountainhead, Genesis, Germ, Get at, Go, Greenhorn, Inaugural, Inception, Inchoate, Incipient, Incipit, Initial, Initiate, Intro, Johnny-raw, L, Launch, Lead, Learn, Learner, Logos, Nascent, Neophyte, Noob, → NOVICE, Oncome, Onset, Ope(n), Ord, → ORIGIN, Outbreak, Outset, Pose, Prelim(inary), Presidium, Primer, Rookie, Seed, Set, Set forth, Shoot, → START, Startup, Strike up, Takeoff, Tenderfoot, Threshold, Tiro, To-fall, Tyro(ne), Yearn

**Begone** Aroint, Aroynt, Avaunt, Scram, Shoo, Vamo(o)se

**Begonia** Elephant's-ear(s)

**Begorrah** Bedad, Musha

**Begrudge** Envy, Resent

**Beguile(r), Beguiled** Amuse, Bewitch, Charm, Coax, Distract, Divert, Enchant, Ensnare, Entice, Eprise, Flatter, Gull, Intrigue, Jack-a-lantern, Tice, Trick, Wile

**Behalf** Ex parte, For, Part, Sake

**Behave(d), Behaviour, Behaving** Abear, Accepted, Acquired, Act, Appeasement, Attitude, Carriage, Conduct, Consummatory, Convenance, Decorum, Demean, Deportment, Do, Effrontery, Ensocial, Epimeletic, Etepimeletic, Ethics, Ethology, Etiquette, Form, Freak out, Goings-on, Guise, Horme, Life style, → MANNER, Meme, Nature, Netiquette, Noblesse oblige, Obey, Orientation, Practice, Praxeology, Quit, React, Response, Ruly, Satisficing, Strong meat, Treat, Tribalism, Unreasonable

**Behead** Decapitate, Decollate, Guillotine

**Behind(hand)** Abaft, Aft(er), Ahent, Ahind, Ahint, Apoop, Arear, Arere, Arrear, Arse, Astern, Backside, Beneath, Bottom, Bum, Buttocks, Can, Croup, Derrière, Fud, Fundus, Late, Overdue, Post, Prat, → REAR, Rump, Slow, Tardy, Tushie

**Behold(en)** Affine, Ecce, Eye, Grateful, Here's, Indebted, La, Lo, Look, Observe, See, View, Voilà

**Beige** Buff, Greige, Neutral, Oatmeal, Sandy, Suede, Tan

**Being** Cratur, Creature, Critter, Ens, Entia, Entity, Esse, Essence, Existence, Human, Man, Metaphysics, Mode, Nature, Omneity, Ontology, Organism, → PERSON, Saul, Soul, Subsistent, Substance, Supreme, Ubiety, Wight

**Bejabers** Arrah

**Bejewel** Enchase, Stud

**Belated** Hindsight

**Belch** Boak, Boke, Brash, Burp, Emit, Eruct, Erupt, Rift, Spew, Toby, Yex

**Belcher** Foulard, Handkerchief, Hanky, Toby

**Beldam(e)** Crone, Hag, Harridan, Scold

**Beleaguer** Besiege
**Belfry** Campanile, Tower
**Belgian** Flemish, Walloon
**Belief, Believable, Believe, Believed, Believer, Believing** Accept, Accredit, Adam and Eve, Anata, Animism, Ativism, Bahaism, Bigot, Buy, Capernaite, Catechism, Chiliasm, Christian, Confidence, Conviction, Convulsionist, Creationism, Credence, Credit, Credulity, Creed, Cult, Culture, Deem, De fide, Deist, Di(o)physite, Doctrine, Dogma, Doxastic, Doxy, Dukkha, Dyophysite, Evangelical, Faith, Formulism, Gnostic, Guess, Heresy, Heterodoxy, Hold, Holist, Idea, Ideology, Idolater, Imagine, Islam, Ism, Latitudinarian, Lore, Ludism, Manichaeism, Mechanist, Meme, Messianist, Methink, Mithraism, Monotheist, Mysticism, Neo-vitalist, Notion, One-worldism, Opine, → OPINION, Orthopraxy, Ovist, Pacifism, Pantheism, Pelagianism, Persuasion, Physicism, Pluralism, Postmillenarian, Presumption, Rasta, Reckon, Religion, Reputed, Revelationist, S(h)aivism, Second Coming, Secularism, Seeing, Shema, Solfidian, Solipsism, Superstition, Suppose, Supremacist, Suspect, Swallow, Tenet, Test, Tetratheism, Thanatism, Theist, Theosophy, Think, Threap, Threep, Traducianism, Transcendentalism, Trinitarian, Triphysite, Trow, Trust, Ubiquitarianism, Umma(h), Unitarian, Universalism, Wear, Ween, Wis(t), Zooism
**Belittle** Abase, Cheapen, Cry down, Decry, Demean, Deprecate, Depreciate, Derogate, Detract, Diminish, Discredit, Disparage, Do-down, Downgrade, Downplay, Humble, Pooh-pooh, Sell short, Slight
**Bell(s), Bell-shaped** Acton, Agogo, Alarm, Angelus, Ben, Big Ben, Bob, Bow, Bronte, Cachecope, Campana, Canterbury, Carillon, Chime, Chinese pavilion, Clanger, Crotal, Curfew, Currer, Daisy, Death, Diving, Division, Ellis, Gong, Grandsire, Inventor, Jar, Knell, Liberty, Low, Lutine, Market, Mass, Minute, Mort, Muffin, Night, Pancake, Passing, Pavilion, Peal, Peter, Pinger, Pudding, Ring, Roar, Sacring, Sanctus, Shark, Sleigh, Tailor, Tantony, Tenor, Tent, Tintinnabulum, Tocsin, Toll, Tom, Triple, Tubular, Vair, Vaire, Verr(e)y, Vesper, Wind
**Belladonna** Nightshade
**Bell-bird** Arapunga, Campanero
**Belle** Bathing, Beauty, Brighton, Starr, Toast, Venus
**Bell-founder** Belleter
**Bellicose, Belligerence, Belligerent** Aggressive, Chippy, Combatant, Gung-ho, Hostile, Ire, Jingoist, Martial, Militant, Pugnacious, Truculent, Warmonger
**Bellow(s)** Buller, Holla, Holler, Moo, Rant, Rave, Roar, Rout, Saul, Thunder, Troat, Tromp(e), Trumpet, Windbag
**Bell-ringer, Bell-ringing** Bob, Campanology, Changes, Clapper, Course, Grandsire, Handstroke, Hunting, Maximus, Quasimodo, Rope, Sally, Tintinnabulation, Tocsin, Toller
**Belly** Abdomen, Alvine, Bag, Beer, Beer-gut, Boep, Bow window, Bunt, Calipee, Celiac, Coeliac, Delhi, Gut, Kite, Kyte, Paunch, Pod, → STOMACH, Swell, Tum(my), Venter, Wame, Weamb, Wem(b), Womb
**Bellyache** Grouch, Whine
**Belong, Belonging(s)** Appertain, Apply, Appurtenant, Chattels, Effects, Incident, Inhere, Intrinsic, Membership, Our, Paraphernalia, Pertain, → PROPERTY, Relate, Roots, Things, Traps
**Beloved** Acushla, Alder-lief(est), Amy, Boyfriend, David, Dear, Doy, Esme, Inamorata, Joy, Leve, Lief, Loor, Morna, Pet, Popular, Precious
**Below** Beneath, Inf(erior), Infra, Nether, Sub, Subjacent, Under, Unneath
**Belt(ed)** Baldric(k), Band, Bandoleer, Bandolier, Baudric(k), Bible, Black, Brown, Carousel, Cartridge, Chastity, Cholera, Clitellum, Clobber, Clock, Clout, Commuter, Conveyor, Copper, Cotton, Crios, Demolition, Equator, Fan, Flog, Fold and thrust, Galvanic, Garter, Gird(le), Girt, Great, Green, Hip, Hydraulic, Ice, Inertial, Judoka, Kuiper, Lap, Larrup, Life, Lonsdale, Mitre, Money, Muesli, Orion's, Orogenic, Polt, Pound, Radiation, Roller, Roll-on, Rust, Safety, Sahel, Sam Browne, Sanitary, Sash, Seat, Slug, Speed, Stockbroker, Storm, Strap, Stratosphere, Sun, Surcingle, Suspender, Swipe, Sword, Taiga, Tawse, Tear, Thump, Tore, Tract, Van Allen, Wampum, Wanty, Webbing, Wing, Zodiac, Zone, Zonulet, Zoster
**Belt up** Sh

**Belvedere** Gazebo, Mirador
**Bemoan** → LAMENT, Mourn, Rue, Sigh, Wail
**Bemuse** Infatuate, Stonn(e), Stun, Stupefy, Throw
**Ben** Battle, Craig, Hur, Jonson, Mountain, Nevis, Spence
**Benbow** Admiral
**Bench** Back, Banc, Banker, Bink, Bleachers, Church, Common, Counter, Court, Cross, Exedra, Form, Front, Government, King's, Knifeboard, Magistrates, Opposition, Optical, Penalty, Pew, Queen's, Rout seat, Rusbank, → SEAT, Settle, Siege, Stillage, Thoft, Thwart, Treasury, Trestle, Widow's
**Benchmark** Criteria, Standard, Yardstick
**Bend(er), Bending, Bends** Adapt, Angle, Arc, Arch, Articular, Becket, Bight, Binge, Bow, Buck(le), Bust, Camber, Carrick, Chicane, Circumflect, Contort, Corner, Crank(le), Crimp, Cringe, → CROOK, Crouch, Curl, Curve, Diffraction, Dog-leg, Double up, Elbow, Engouled, Epinasty, Es(s), Expansion, Falcate, Fawn, Flex(ural), Flexion, Flexure, Fold, Geller, Geniculate, Genu, Genuflect, Grecian, Hairpin, Hinge, Hook, Horseshoe, Hunch, Incline, Inflect, Jag, Kink, Knee(cap), Kneel, Knot, Kowtow, Meander, Mould, Nutant, Orgy, Ox-bow, Pitch, Plash, Pliant, Plié, Ply, Recline, Reflex, Retorsion, Retortion, Retroflex, Riband, S, Sag, Scarp, Sheet, Souse, Spree, Spring, Stave, Stoop, Swan-neck, Sway, Trend, Twist, U, Ups(e)y, Uri, Wale, Warp, → YIELD, Z, Zigzag
▷**Bendy** *may indicate* an anagram
**Beneath** Below, Infra dig, Nether, Sub, Under, Unworthy
**Benedict(ine)** Black Monk, Cluniac, Cluny, Dom, Eggs, Maurist, Olivetan, OSB, Tironensian, Tyronensian
**Benediction** Apostolic, Ben(t)sh, Blessing, God-speed
**Benefactor, Benefactress** Angel, Backer, Barmecide, Carnegie, Donor, Fairy Godmother, Maecenas, → PATRON, Philanthropist, Promoter, Rockefeller
**Beneficial, Beneficiary, Benefit, Benefice, Beneficent** Advantage, → AID, Alms, Ameliorate, Asset, Avail, Behalf, Behoof, Behove, Bespeak, Bonus, Boon, Boot, Charity, Child, Collature, Commendam, Commensal, Conferee, Cost, Devisee, Disablement, Dole, Donee, Edifying, Endorsee, Enjoy, Enure, Exploit, Family allowance, FIS, For, Fringe, Fund-raiser, Gain, Giro, Grandisonian, Grantee, Healthful, Housing, Incapacity, Incumbent, Inheritor, Injury, Interest, Inure, Invalidity, Jobseeker's allowance, Legal aid, Living, Manna, Maternity, Ménage, Mileage, Neckverse, Pay, Perk, Perquisite, Philanthropy, Plenarty, Plus, Portioner, Postulate, Prebend, Profit, Sake, Salutary, Sanative, Serve, Service, Sickness, Sinecure, Soft, Spin-off, Stipend, Supplementary, Symbiotic, Therapeutic, Trickle down, UB40, Unalist, Unemployment, Use, Usufruct, Va(u)ntage, Well-being, Wholesome, Wonderful, Workfare
**Benevolence, Benevolent** Charitable, Clement, Dobbie, Dobby, Goodwill, Humanitarian, Kind, Liberal, Nis(se), Pecksniffian, Philanthropy, Pickwickian, Sprite
**Bengali** Oriya
**Benighted** Ignorant
**Benign** Affable, Altruistic, Gracious, Innocuous, Kindly, Trinal
**Benin** DY
**Benito** Duce, Mussolini
**Benjamin** Franklin
**Bennett** Alan, Phil
**Bent** Akimbo, Bowed, Brae, Concave, Coudé, Counterfeit, Courb, Criminal, Crooked, Curb, Determined, Diptrap, Dorsiflex, Falcate, Fiorin, Flair, Geniculate, Habit, Heath, Inclination, Ingenium, Intent, Inverted, Leant, Out, Peccant, Penchant, Ply, Predisposition, Propensity, Reclinate, Redtop, Round-shouldered, Scoliotic, Stooped, Swayed, Talent, Taste, Tendency, Twisted
▷**Bent** *may indicate* an anagram
**Bent grass** Fiorin, Redtop
**Bentham** Utilitarian
**Benzine** Kinone, Phene, Toluene, Toluol
**Bequeath, Bequest** Bestow, Chantr(e)y, Demise, Endow, Gift, Heirloom, → LEAVE, Legacy, Mortification, Pass down, Pittance, Testament, Transmit, Will

**Berate(d)** Censure, Chastise, Chide, Harangue, Jaw, Reproach, Scold, Shent, Slate, Vilify
**Berber** Almoravide, Kabyle, Moor, Rif(i), Riff, Shluh, Tuareg
**Bereave(d), Bereavement** Deprive, Loss, Mourning, Orb, Sorrow, Strip, Widow
**Beret** Green
**Berg** Alban, Floe, Kopje
**Berk** Clot
**Berlin** Irving
**Bermuda** Shorts
**Bernard** Levin, Shaw
**Bernini** Baroque
**Berry** Acai, Allspice, Bacca, Blackcurrant, Coffee, Coral, Cow, Cubeb, Curlew, French, Fruit, Goji, Goosegog, Haw, Hound's, Indian, Konini, Miracle, Mistletoe, Pea, Pepo, Peppercorn, Persian, Pigeon, Pimento, Poke, Pottage, Quinsy, Raccoon, Rhein, Rhine, Rowan, Sal(l)al, Salmonberry, Slae, Sloe, Snow, Sop, Sun, Tay, Tomatillo, Winter, Wolf
**Berserk** Amok, Ape-shit, Baresark, Frantic, Freak, Frenzy, Gungho, Rage
**Berth** Anchorage, Bunk, Cabin, Couchette, Dock, Marina, Moor, Seat, Sick, Sleeping, Space
**Beryl** Aquamarine, Emerald, Heliodor, Morganite, Silica
**Beryllium** Be
**Beseech** Beg, Crave, Entreat, Implore, Invoke, Obsecrate, Pray
**Beset** Amidst, Assail, Assiege, Badger, Bego, Embattled, Environ, Harry, Infest, Obsess, Perplex, Scabrid, Siege
**Beside(s)** Adjacent, Again, Along, And, Apart from, At, Au reste, By, Else, Forby(e), Further(more), Moreover, Next, On, To, Withal, Yet
**Besiege(d)** Beset, Best(ed), Blockade, Gherao, Girt, Invest, Obsess, Plague, Poliorcetic, Surround
▹**Besiege** *may indicate* one word around another
**Besmear** Dribble
**Besmirch(ed)** Bloody, Bludie, Smear, Soil, Spoil, Sully
**Besom** Cow, Kow
**Besot(ted)** Dotard, Infatuate, Intoxicate, Lovesick, Smitten, Stupefy
**Bespangle** Adorn, Gem
**Bespatter** Daub
**Bespeak, Bespoken** Address, Bee, Beta, Engage, Hint
**Best** A1, Ace, All-time, Aristocrat, Beat, Bonzer, Cap, Cat's whiskers, Champ(ion), Choice, Conquer, Cream, Creme, Crown, Damnedest, Defeat, Deluxe, Elite, Every, Eximious, Finest, First, Flagship, Flower, Foremost, Greatest, Highlight, Ideal, Nicest, Optima, Outdo, Outfox, Outplay, Outwit, Overcome, Peak, Peerless, Pick, Pièce de résistance, Pink, Plum, Purler, Quintessence, Ream, Sunday, Super, Supreme, The, The tops, Tiptop, Top dog, Top (flight), Top drawer, Topper, Transcend, Ultimate, Utopian, Vanquish, Wale, World-class
**Bestial** Animalistic, Atrocious
**Bestiality** Zoophalia
**Bestiary** Physiologus
**Best man** Paranymph
**Bestow(al)** Accord, Award, Bequeath, Confer, Convey, Donate, Endow, →GIVE, Grant, Impart, Investiture, Present
**Bestride** Cross, Straddle
**Bet(ting), Betting System** Accumulator, A cheval, Ante, Antepost, Back, Banco, Banker, Chance, Daily double, Dice, Double, Each way, Fixed odds, Flutter, Gaff, Gamble, Go, Hedge, Impone, Lay (odds), Long shot, Martingale, Mise, Note, Pari-mutuel, Parlay, Perfecta, Pip, Place, Pot, Predict, Punt, Quadrella, Quinella, Ring, Risk, Roll up, Roulette, Saver, Set, Side, SP, Spec, Sport, Spread, Stake, Superfecta, Take, Tattersalls, Tatts, Totalisator, Totalise, Tote, Treble, Treble chance, Triella, Trifecta, →WAGER, Win, Yankee
**Betel** Areca, Catechu, Paan, Pan, Pawn, Siri(h)
**Betimes** Anon, Early, Soon
**Betise** Solecism
**Betoken** Portend

**Betray(al), Betrayed, Betrayer** Abandon, Abuse, Belewe, Bewray, Breach, Cornuto, Cuckold, Desert, Disclose, Divulge, Dob, Dobbin, Double-cross, Gethsemane, Giveaway, Grass, Judas, Peach, Proditor, Renegade, Renege, Rumble, Sell, Sellout, Shop, Sing, Sinon, Snitch, Split on, Stab, Telltale, Traditor, Trahison, Traitor, Treachery, Treason, Turncoat

**Betroth(ed), Betrothal** Affiance, Affy, Assure, Engage, Ensure, Espouse, Fiancé(e), Handfasting, Pledge, Promise, Sponsalia, Subarr(h)ation, Trothplight

**Better** Abler, Ameliorate, Amend, Apter, Bigger, Buck, Cap, Comparative, Convalescent, Cured, Edify, Enrich, Fairer, Finer, Gambler, Gamester, Imponent, Improve, Layer, Master, Meliorate, Mend, Mitigate, Outdo, Outpeer, Outpoint, Outshine, Outsmart, Outstrip, Outwit, Piker, Preponderate, Punter, Race-goer, Reform, Revise, Score off, Superior, Surpass, Throw, Top, Turfite, Upgrade, Work, Worst

**Between** Amid, Bet, Betwixt, Inter, Interjacent, Linking, Mesne, Twixt

**Bevel** Angle, Cant, Chamfer, Oblique, Slope, Splay

**Beverage** Alcopop, Ale, Cocoa, Coffee, Cordial, Cup, → **DRINK**, Eggcream, Hydromel, Lambswool, Mobbie, Mobby, Nectar, Refreshment, Tea

**Bevy** Flock, Group, Herd, Host

**Bewail** Lament

**Beware** Cave, Fore, Heed, Look out, Mind, Mistrust, Pas op, Tut

**Bewilder(ed), Bewildering, Bewilderment** Amaze, Astound, At sea, Baffle, Bemuse, Buffalo, Confound, Confuse, Consternation, Daze, Disorient, Distract, Egarement, Floor, Flummox, Mate, Maze, Mind-boggling, Mizmaze, Muddle, Mystify, Obfuscate, Perplex, Stump, Stun, Taivert, Tutulbay, Wander, Will, Wull

**Bewitch(ed), Bewitching** Charm, Delight, Elf-shot, Enchant, Ensorcell, Enthral, Glam(orous), Hex, Hoodoo, Hypnotise, Jinx, Obeah, Obiah, Sirenise, Spellbound, Strike

**Beyond** Above, Ayont, Besides, Farther, Meta-, Outwith, Over, Past, Thule, Trans, Ulterior, Ultra

**Bezique** Royal marriage

**Bhang** Benj

**Bias(ed)** Angle, Aslant, Bent, Chauvinism, Colour, Discriminatory, Forward, Grid, Imbalance, Loaded, Nepotism, One-sided, Partial, Parti pris, Partisan, Penchant, Preconception, Predilection, → **PREJUDICE**, Prepossess, Proneness, Set, Sexism, Skew, Slant, Slope, Spin, Subjective, Tendency, Unfair, Unjust, Warp

**Bib, Bibulous** Apron, Beery, Feeder, Napkin, Pout, Tope, Tucker

**Bibelot** Objet d'art

**Bible, Biblical** Adulterous, Alcoran, Alkoran, Antilegomena, Apocrypha, ASV, Authority, AV, Avesta, Bamberg, Book, Breeches, Bug, Coverdale, Cranmer, Cromwell, Douai, Douay, Family, Ferrara, Fool, Forgotten sins, Gemara, Geneva, Gideon, Good book, Goose, Gospel, Gutenberg, Haggada, Hagiographa, Helachah, Heptateuch, Hermeneutic, Hexapla, Hexateuch, Holy, Holybook, Holywrit, Idle, Isagogic, Itala, Italic, King James (version), Leda, Matthew Parker, Mazarin(e), Midrash, Missal, Murderer, New English, NT, Omasum, Ostrog, OT, Pentateuch, Peshito, Peshitta, Peshitto, Polyglot, Psalter, Revised Version, RSV, RV, Scriptures, Septuagint, Stomach, Talmud, Tanach, Tantra, Targum, Taverner, Taverners, Text, Thirty-six-line, Torah, Treacle, Tyndale, Unrighteous, Vinegar, Vulgate, Whig, Wicked, Wife-hater, Wyclif(fe), Zurich

**Biblical scholar** Rechabite, USPG, Wycliffe

**Bibliophagist, Bibliophile** Bookworm

**Bicarb** Saleratus

**Bicker(ing)** Argue, Bowl, Brawl, Coggie, Dispute, Spat, Tiff, Wrangle

**Bi-coloured** Dichroism

**Bicycle, Bike(r)** All-terrain, Bambi, Bee, Bone-shaker, Chopper, Coaster, Crog(gy), Dandy-horse, Dirt, Draisene, Draisine, Exercise, Fixed-wheel, Hell's Angels, Hobby, Hobbyhorse, Kangaroo, Mixte, Moped, Mount, Mountain, Multicycle, Ordinary, Pedal, Penny-farthing, Quad, Racer, Raleigh®, Recumbent, Roadster, Rocker, Safety, Scooter, Ski-bob, Solo, Spin, Stationary, Swarm, Tandem, Trail, Tree, UCI, Velocipede

**Bid(der), Bidding (system)** Abundance, Acol, Apply, Blackwood, Call, Canape, Command, Contract, Cue, Declare, Double, Forcing, Gone, Hostile, INT, Invite, Jump, Misère, Nod, NT,

→ **OFFER**, Order, Pass, Pre-empt(ive), Proposal, Psychic, Puffer, Redouble, Rescue, Shut-out, Summon, Take-out, Take-over, Tell, Tender, Try on, Vied, White bonnet

**Biddy** Crone, Gammer, Hen

**Biennial** Trieteric

**Bier** Hearse, Litter

**Bifurcate** Fork

**Big** Altruistic, Beamy, Bulky, Bumper, Burly, Capacious, Cob, Corpulent, Enormous, Fat, Ginormous, Global, Gross, → **LARGE**, Loud, Mansize, Massive, Mighty, Obese, Roomy, Skookum, Slockdoliger, Slockdologer, Soc(k)dologer, Sogdolager, Sogdoliger, Spectacular, Stonker, Strapping, Substantial, Swopper, Thumping, Tidy, Titanic, Vast, Whacker, Whopper, XL

**Bigamy, Bigamist, Bigamous** Bluebeard, Diandrous

**Bigfoot** Sasquatch, Yeti

**Bighead(ed)** Besserwisser, Ego, Uppity

**Bight** Canterbury, Great Australian, Heligoland, Karamea, Loop, South Taranaki

**Bigmouth** Boaster

**Bigot(ed)** Chauvinist, Dogmatist, Fanatic, Hide-bound, Intolerant, Narrow-minded, Racialist, Racist, Redneck, Sectarian, Sexist, Wowser, Zealot

**Bigshot, Bigwig** Cheese, Grandee, Law lord, Nib, Nob, Oner, Oneyer, Oneyre, Swell, Titan, Toff, → **VIP**

**Bijou** Doll-like

▸**Bike** *see* **BICYCLE**

**Bikini** Atoll, Tanga

**Bile, Bilious(ness)** Cholaemia, Choler, Gall, Icteric, Melancholy, Scholaemia, Venom, Yellow

**Bilge** Leak, Pump, Rhubarb, Rot, Waste

**Bilingual** Diglot

**Bilious** Irascible

**Bilk** Default

**Bill(ed), Billy** Ac(c), Accommodation, Accompt, Account, Act, Ad, Addition, Allonge, Appropriation, Barnacle, Beak, Bearer, Becke, Budd, Buffalo, Bunter, Can, Caress, Carte, Charge, Cheque, Chit(ty), Cody, Coo, Cop, Coronoid, Cross(-bencher), Debt, Demand, Dixy, Docket, Double, Due, Egg-tooth, Enabling, Exactment, Fee, Fin, Finance, Foreign, Gates, Goat, Hybrid, Inland, Invoice, IOU, Kaiser, → **LAW**, Lawin(g), Legislation, Liam, Liar, Line-up, List, Measure, Menu, Nail, Neb, Ness, Nib, → **NOTE**, Notice, Paper, Pay, Petition, Platypus, Police, Pork barrel, Portland, Poster, Private, Private member's, Programme, Pruning, Public, Puffing, Reckoning, Reform, Remanet, Rhamphotheca, Rostral, Rostrum, Score, Selsey, Short, Shot, Show, Sickle, Silly, Sparth(e), Sperthe, Spoon, Sticker, Tab, Tariff, Tenner, Tenuirostral, Time, Tomium, Trade, Treasury, True, Twin, Victualling, Watch, Willy

**Billet** Berth, Casern, Cess, Chit, Coupon, Note, Quarter

**Billet doux** Capon, Mash note, Valentine

**Billiards, Billiards player, Billiards stroke** Bar, Cannon-game, Cueist, Jenny, Lagging, Long jenny, Massé, Nursery cannon, Pills, Pocket, Pool, Potter, Pyramids, Short jenny, Snooker, String, Whitechapel

**Billion** Gillion, Milliard, Tera

**Bill of sale** Bs

**Billow** Roil, Roller, Rule, Surge, Swell, Wave

▸**Billy** *see* **BILL(ED)**

**Billygoat** Gruff

**Bimbo** Twinkle

**Bin** Bing, Box, Bread, Chilly, Container, Crib, Crock, Discard, Dump, Hell, Litter, Loony, Orderly, Pedal, Receptacle, Sin, Snake-pit, Stall, Throw away, Wagger-pagger, Wheelie, Wheely

**Binary** ASCII, Contact, Semidetached

**Bind(er), Binding** Adherent, Adhesive, Akedah, Alligate, Apprentice, Astrict, Astringent, Bale, Bandage, Bandeau, Bandster, Bias, Bibliopegist, Boyer, Brail, Burst, Calf, Cement,

Cerlox®, Chain, Cinch, Circuit, Clamp, Colligate, Complain, Cord, Cover, Cramp-iron, Cummerbund, Dam, Deligation, Desmasomal, De Vigneaud, Drag, Edge, Embale, Enchain, Engage, Enslave, Enwind, → **FASTEN**, Fetter, Final, Galloon, Gird, Girdle, Grolier, Half-calf, Half-leather, Haworth, Hay-wire, Hold, Hole, Hopkins, Incumbent, Indenture, Iron, Keckle, Krebs, Lace, Lash(er), Law-calf, Leash, Ligament, Ligature, Mail, Marl, Marry, Martin, Meyerhof, Morocco, Muslin, Obi, Objure, Obligate, Oblige, Oop, Organdie, Oup, Parpen, Paste grain, Perfect, Pinion, Porter, Quarter, Raffia, Red Tape, Restrict, Ring, → **ROPE**, Roxburghe, Seize, Sheaf, Spiral, Strap, Stringent, Stygian, Swathe, Syndesis, Tape, Tether, Thirl, Thong, Three-quarter, Tie, Tree-calf, Truss, Twine, Unsewn, Valid, Whip, Withe, Yapp, Yerk, Yoke

**Bindweed** Bearbine, Convolvulus, With(y)wind

**Bing** Crosby, Go, Heap

**Binge, Binging** Bat, Beano, Bend(er), Blind, Carouse, Dipsomania, → **DRINK**, Drinking-bout, Engorge, Gorge, Overdo, Party, Pig out, Riot, Soak, Souse, Splore, Spree, Toot, Tout

**Bingo** Beano, Housey-housey, Keno, Lotto, Tombola

**Binocular(s)** Glasses, Jumelle, OO, Stereoscope

**Biochemical, Biochemist(ry)** Ames, Boyer, Chain, Dam, De Vigneaud, DNA, Haworth, Hopkins, Krebs, Martin, Meyerhof, Porter, Proteomics, Todd

**Biofuel** Ethanol

**Biographer, Biography** Boswell, CV, Hagiography, History, Life story, Memoir, Plutarch, Potted, Profile, Prosopography, Strachey, Suetonius, Vita

**Biology, Biologist** Algology, Berg, Bordet, Carrel, Cladistics, Cohen, Dawkins, Delbruck, Genetics, Haller, Kendrew, Kinsey, Mendel, Molecular, Morphology, Phenetics, Photodynamics, Shatten, Somatology, Stoechiology, Stoich(e)iology, Taxonomy, Teratology, Transgenics, Weismann

**Bionomics** Ecology

**Bioscope** Kinema

**Biped** Man, Yahoo

**Birch** Alder, Betula, Birk, Cane, Cow, Flog, Hazel, Kow, Larch, Larrup, Reis, Rice, Rod, Silver, Swish, Thrash, Twig, Weeping, Whip, White, Withe

**Bird(s)** Al(l)erion, Altricial, Aves, Avian, Bertram, Brood, Damsel, Dawn chorus, Doll, Early, Flier, Fowl, Gal, → **GIRL**, Grip, Hen, Jail, Layer, Left, Limicoline, Nestling, Ornis, Ornithology, Pecker, Pen, Perching, Poultry, Praecoces, Prison, Quod, Raptor, Rare, Roaster, Sentence, Sis, Skirt, Stretch, Time, Visitant, Warbler

---

## BIRDS

*2 letters:*
Ka
Ox

*3 letters:*
Ani
Auk
Boo
Cob
Emu
Fum
Jay
Kae
Kea
Mag
Maw
Mew
Moa
Nun
Owl
Pea
Pie
Ree
Roc
Ruc
Tit
Tui

*4 letters:*
Barb
Chat
Cirl
Cobb
Cock
Coly
Coot
Crax
Crow
Dodo
Dove
→ **DUCK**
Emeu
Erne
Eyas
Fung
Gled
Gnow
Guan
Guga
Gull
Hawk
Hern
Huia
Huma
Ibis
Iynx
Jynx
Kagu
Kaka
Kite
Kiwi
Knot
Koel
Kora
Lark
Loom
Loon
Lory
Mina
Monk
Myna
Nene
Otis
Pavo
Pawn
Pern
Piet
Pink
Pown
Pyat
Pyot
Rail
Rhea
Roch
Rook
Ruff
Ruru
Rype
Shag
Skua

Smee
Sora
Swan
Taha
Tara
Teal
Tern
Tick
Tody
Tuli
Weka
Wren
Xema
Yale
Yite

***5 letters:***
Agami
Ardea
Ariel
Bennu
Booby
Bosun
Buteo
Cahow
Capon
Colin
Colly
Crake
Crane
Diver
Eagle
Egret
Eider
Finch
Fleet
Flute
Friar
Galah
Glede
Goose
Goura
Grebe
Heron
Hobby
Homer
Isaac
Junco
Kawau
Kight
Liver
Lowan
Macaw
Madge
Manch
Mavis
Merle
Mimus
Mohua
Monal
Murre
Mynah
Nandu
Nelly
Noddy
Ousel
Ox-eye
Peggy
Pekan
Pewit
Picus
Pilot
Piper
Pipit
Pitta
Poaka
Poker
Potoo
Prion
Quail
Quest
Quist
Raven
Reeve
Rifle
Robin
Rotch
Ryper
Saker
Satin
Scape
Scart
Scaup
Scops
Scray
Scrub
Serin
Shama
Sitta
Skart
Snipe
Solan
Soree
Spink
Sprug
Squab
Stare
Stilt
Stint
Stork
Swift
Sylph
Terek
Tewit
Topaz
Twite
Umber
Umbre
Urubu
Veery
Vireo
Wader
Whaup
Widow
Wonga
Yaffa

***6 letters:***
Aquila
Avocet
Avoset
Bantam
Barbet
Bishop
Bittor
Bittur
Boiler
Bonxie
Boubou
Brolga
Budgie
Bulbul
Caille
Canary
Chough
Chukar
Condor
Corbie
Coucal
Cuckoo
Curlew
Cushat
Darter
Dikkop
Dipper
Drongo
Duiker
Dunlin
Duyker
Elanet
Evejar
Falcon
Fulmar
Gambet
Gander
Gannet
Garuda
Gentle
Gentoo
Go-away
Godwit
Gooney
Goslet
Grakle
Grouse
Hagden
Hagdon
Haglet
Hermit
Hoopoe
Houdan
Jabiru
Jacana
Jaeger
Jubjub
Kakapo
Kotare
Kotuku
Lanner
Leipoa
Linnet
Lintie
Locust
Loerie
Loriot
Lourie
Lungie
Magpie
Martin
Matata
Menura
Merlin
Merops
Missel
Mistle
Monaul
Mopoke
Mossie
Motmot
Mudhen
Musket
Mutton
Nandoo
Nhandu
Oriole
Oscine
Osprey
Oxbird
Parrot
Parson
Pavone
Peahen
Peeper
Peewee
Peewit
Pernis
Petrel
Phoebe
Pigeon
Piopio
Plover
Pouter
Progne
Puffin
Pukeko
Pullet
Queest
Quelea
Quoist
Redcap
Redleg
Reeler
Roller
Rotche
Scamel
Scarth
Scaury
Scoter
Scraye
Sea-cob
Sea-mew
Seapie
Shrike
Simara
Simorg
Simurg
Siskin
Skarth
Smeath
Smeeth
Soland
Sorage
Strich
Sultan
Sylvia
Tailor
Takahe
Tarcel
Tassel
Tewhit
Thrush
Tom-tit
Toucan
Towhee
Trogon
Turaco
Turbit
Turkey
Tyrant
Tystie

Verdin
Walker
Waxeye
Weaver
Whidah
Whydah
Willet
Woosel
Yaffle
Ynambu
Yucker
Zoozoo

***7 letters:***
Amokura
Anhinga
Antbird
Ant-pita
Apteryx
Axebird
Babbler
Bécasse
Bee-kite
Bittern
Bittour
Bluecap
Blue-eye
Blue jay
Bluetit
Boobook
Bullbat
Bunting
Buphaga
Bush-tit
Bustard
Buzzard
Cacique
Cariama
Cheeper
Chewink
Chicken
Coal-tit
Cole-tit
Colibri
Corella
Cotinga
Courlan
Courser
Cow-bird
Creeper
Crombec
Cropper
Diamond
Dinorus
Dottrel
Dovekie
Dragoon
Dunnock
Emu-wren
Estrich
Fantail
Fern-owl
Figbird
Finfoot
Flicker
Frigate
Gleerie
Gobbler
Goburra
Gorcrow
Goshawk
Grackle
Grallae
Grey jay
Hacklet
Hadedah
Hagbolt
Hagdown
Halcyon
Harrier
Hemipod
Hoatzin
Horn owl
Humming
Ice-bird
Jacamar
Jackdaw
Kahawai
Kamichi
Kestrel
Killdee
Kinglet
Koekoea
Lapwing
Leghorn
Limpkin
Manakin
Marabou
Martlet
Mesites
Minivet
Moorhen
Mudlark
Oilbird
Ortolan
Oscines
Ostrich
Oven-tit
Pandion
Peacock
Peafowl
Pelican
Penguin
Phoenix
Pickmaw
Piculet
Pinnock
Pintado
Pintail
Pochard
Pockard
Poe-bird
Poussin
Poy-bird
Quetzal
Rainbow
Rasores
Ratitae
Redpoll
Redwing
Regulus
Rooster
Rosella
Rotchie
Ruddock
Sakeret
Sawbill
Scooper
Scourie
Sea-dove
Seaduck
Seagull
Sea-lark
Sea-mell
Seriema
Simurgh
Sirgang
Sitella
Skimmer
Skylark
Snow-cap
Spadger
Sparrow
Squacco
Staniel
Stinker
Sturnus
Sunbird
Swallow
Tanager
Tanagra
Tarrock
Tattler
Teacher
Teuchat
Tiercel
Tinamou
Titanis
Titlark
Titling
Tokahea
Totanus
Touraco
Tumbler
Tweeter
Vulture
Vulturn
Wagtail
Waxbill
Waxwing
Whooper
Widgeon
Wimbrel
Witwall
Wood-owl
Woosell
Wren-tit
Wrybill
Wryneck
Yang-win

***8 letters:***
Aasvogel
Accentor
Adjutant
Aigrette
Alcatras
Altrices
Amadavat
Aquiline
Araponga
Arapunga
Arenaria
Avadavat
Barnacle
Bateleur
Bee-eater
Bellbird
Blackcap
Bluebird
Blue-wing
Boatbill
Boattail
Bobolink
Bob-white
Buln-buln
Caracara
Cardinal
Cargoose
Cheewink
Chirn-owl
Cockatoo
Cockerel
Coquette

Curassow
Dabchick
Didapper
Dip-chick
Dobchick
Dotterel
Eagle-owl
Estridge
Fauvette
Fernbird
Firebird
Fish-hawk
Flamingo
Gambetta
Gang-gang
Garefowl
Garganey
Gnatwren
Great-tit
Greenlet
Grisette
Grosbeak
Guacharo
Hackbolt
Hangbird
Hangnest
Hawfinch
Hazelhen
Heath-hen
Hemipode
Hernshaw
Hickwall
Hoactzin
Hornbill
Killdeer
Kingbird
King crow
Kiskadee
Landrail
Lanneret
Laverock
Longspur
Lorikeet
Lyrebird
Macaroni
Magotpie
Man-of-war
Marabout
Marsh-tit
Megapode
Mire-drum
Miromiro
Moorcock
Moorfowl
Morepork
Murrelet
Nightjar
Notornis
Nuthatch
Ovenbird
Oxpecker
Paradise
Parakeet
Peesweep
Peetweet
Percolin
Petchary
Phaethon
Pheasant
Philomel
Piciform
Pihoihoi
Podargus
Poorwill
Prunella
Puffbird
Quarrian
Quarrion
Rainbird
Rallidae
Redshank
Redstart
Reedling
Reed-wren
Rice-bird
Rifleman
Ring-dove
Ringtail
Riroriro
Rocketer
Rock-lark
Rose-comb
Sand-bark
Sandlark
Sandpeep
Scolopar
Screamer
Sea-eagle
Shake-bag
Shelduck
Shoebill
Shoveler
Silktail
Sittella
Skua-gull
Snowbird
Snowy owl
Stanniel
Starling
Struthio
Surfbird
Swiftlet
Tantalus
Tapacolo
Tapaculo
Teru-tero
Thrasher
Thresher
Throstle
Tickbird
Ticklace
Titmouse
Tom-noddy
Toucanet
Tragopan
Trembler
Troopial
Troupial
Tubenose
Umbrella
Umbrette
Waldropp
Water-hen
Wheatear
Whimbrel
Whinchat
Whipbird
Whitecap
White-eye
Wildfowl
Wirebird
Woodchat
Woodcock
Wood ibis
Woodlark
Woodwale
Wood wren
Xanthura
Yoldring
Zopilote

***9 letters:***
Accipiter
Aepyornis
Albatross
Ant-thrush
Aylesbury
Bald eagle
Baldicoot
Baltimore
Beccaccia
Beccafico
Beefeater
Bergander
Blackbird
Blackhead
Blackpoll
Blood bird
Bower-bird
Brambling
Broadbill
Bullfinch
Campanero
Cassowary
Chaffinch
Chatterer
Chickadee
Coachwhip
Cockatiel
Cormorant
Corncrake
Crocodile
Cross-bill
Currawong
Dove prion
Dowitcher
Eider duck
Estreldid
Fairy-wren
Fieldfare
Field lark
Fig-pecker
Firecrest
Fish-eagle
Fledgling
Francolin
Friarbird
Frogmouth
Gallinule
Gerfalcon
Gier-eagle
Goldcrest
Goldeneye
Goldfinch
Goldspink
Goldstone
Goosander
Grassbird
Grassquit
Grenadier
Guillemot
Hammerkop
Happy Jack
Helldiver
Heronshaw
Hornywink
Icteridae
Impundulu
Jack-snipe
Kittiwake
Lintwhite
Little auk
Little owl
Mallemuck

Merganser
Mistletoe
Mollymawk
Moundbird
Mousebird
Nightcrow
Night-hawk
Nutjobber
Nutpecker
Olive-back
Organ-bird
Ossifraga
Ossifrage
Ouzel-cock
Owl-parrot
Paddy bird
Pardalote
Partridge
Passerine
Peaseweep
Peregrine
Phalarope
Pictarnie
Pine finch
Porphyrio
Ptarmigan
Razorbill
Redbreast
Red siskin
Riflebird
Rosy-finch
Sabrewing
Salangane
Sandpiper
Sapsucker
Satinbird
Scansores
Sea-turtle
Secretary
Sedge-wren
Seedeater
Sheldrake
Shoveller
Silver eye
Skunk-bird
Solitaire
Sooty tern
Spoonbill
Standgale
Stonechat
Stormbird
Storm-cock
Sugarbird
Swart-back
Sword-bill
Talegalla
Thickhead
Thick-knee
Thornbill
Tiercelet
Trochilus
Trumpeter
Turnstone
Volucrine
Water cock
Waterfowl
Water-rail
Willowtit
Wind-hover
Woodshock
Woodspite
Xanthoura

***10 letters:***

Aberdevine
Arctic tern
Bananaquit
Bearded tit
Bishopbird
Bluebreast
Bluethroat
Brain-fever
Bubbly-jock
Budgerigar
Bush-shrike
Butter-bump
Cape pigeon
Chiff-chaff
Crested tit
Demoiselle
Dickcissel
Didunculus
Dive-dapper
Dollarbird
Dung-hunter
Ember-goose
Eyas-musket
Fallow-chat
Fly-catcher
Four o'clock
Fringillid
Goatsucker
Gobemouche
Gooney-bird
Grassfinch
Greenfinch
Greenshank
Guinea fowl
Hen-harrier
Herald-duck
Honey-eater
Honey guide
Hooded crow
Kingfisher
Kookaburra
Locust-bird
Magpie lark
Mallee fowl
Marsh-robin
Meadowlark
Night-churr
Night heron
Noisy miner
Nutcracker
Peckerwood
Pettichaps
Pettychaps
Pick-cheese
Pine-marten
Pratincole
Quaker-bird
Racket-tail
Rafter-bird
Rain-plover
Ramphastos
Reed-thrush
Regent-bird
Rhinoceros
Roadrunner
Ruby-throat
Saddleback
Saddlebill
Sanderling
Sandgrouse
Sand-martin
Screech-owl
Sea swallow
Shearwater
Sheathbill
Sicklebill
Silverbill
Silver gull
Snowy egret
Spatchcock
Stone-snipe
Sun bittern
Tailorbird
Tanagridae
Tropicbird
Turtledove
Wattlebird
Weasel coot
Weaver bird
Whisky-jack
Whisky-john
Wonga-wonga
Woodgrouse
Woodpecker
Woodpigeon
Wood shrike
Wood thrush
Yaffingale
Yellowbird
Yellowhead
Yellowlegs
Yellowyite

***11 letters:***

Apostlebird
Bokmakierie
Bristlebird
Buffalo-bird
Butcherbird
Canada goose
Cape sparrow
Carrion crow
Cooper's hawk
Coppersmith
Corn-bunting
Fallow-finch
Fringilline
Gnatcatcher
Gobe-mouches
Golden eagle
Grallatores
Green linnet
Happy-family
Herring gull
Honey-sucker
House martin
Humming-bird
Ichthyornis
Java sparrow
Leatherhead
Little grebe
Meadow pipit
Mockingbird
Moor-buzzard
Moss-bluiter
Moss-cheeper
Nightingale
Pied wagtail
Plantcutter
Purple finch
Pyrrhuloxia
Reed bunting
Reed-sparrow
Reed-warbler
Scissorbill
Scissortail
Screech-hawk
Snowbunting
Sparrow-hawk
Stilt-plover

Stone-curlew
Stone plover
Stormpetrel
Stymphalian
Swallowtail
Thunderbird
Tree-creeper
Tree-sparrow
Wall creeper
Water-thrush
Weaver-finch
Whitethroat
Wishtonwish
Woodcreeper
Woodswallow
Woodwarbler
Yellow-ammer

*12 letters:*
Bramblefinch
Bronze-pigeon
Chimney-swift
Collared dove
Cow-blackbird
Cuckoo-shrike
Drongo-cuckoo
Drongo-shrike
Flowerpecker
Golden plover
Hedgesparrow
Hedge-warbler
Hermit thrush
Honey creeper
Marsh-warbler
Missel-thrush
Mosquito-hawk
Mound-builder
Painted snipe
Peppershrike
Ring-dotterel
Ringed plover
Sage-thrasher
Sandwich tern
Sedge-warbler
Serpent-eater
Spotted crake
Standard-wing
Stonechatter
Stormy petrel
Tangle-picker
Throstle-cock
Water-wagtail
Whippoorwill
Willy wagtail
Yellow-hammer
Yellowthroat
Yellow-yowley

*13 letters:*
Archaeopteryx
Babblingbrook
Bermuda petrel
Boatswain-bird
Cetti's warbler
Chaparral cock
Cock-of-the-rock
Indigo bunting
Mocking thrush
Owlet nightjar
Oyster-catcher
Pintado petrel
Pipiwharauroa
Plantain-eater
Sandy-laverock
Screech-martin
Screechthrush
Turkey buzzard
Whistling duck
Willow-wagtail
Willow warbler
Wilson's petrel

*14 letters:*
Chimney-swallow
Glossy-starling
Manx shearwater
Pied Flycatcher
Savanna-sparrow
Skunk blackbird
Tawny frogmouth
Welcome swallow
Woodchat shrike

*15 letters:*
Baltimore oriole
Chipping sparrow
Chuck-will's-widow
Green woodpecker
Montagu's harrier
Purple gallinule
Rainbow lorikeet
Rough-legged hawk

*16 letters:*
Loggerhead shrike
Roseate spoonbill
Tyrant flycatcher
White-fronted tern

*17 letters:*
Pectoral sandpiper
Spotted flycatcher

*18 letters:*
Grasshopper-warbler
Paradise flycatcher
Rough-legged buzzard

*19 letters:*
White-crowned sparrow

*20 letters:*
Mother Carey's chickens
Rose-breasted grosbeak

---

▷**Bird** *may indicate* a prison sentence
**Bird-catcher** Avicularia, Fowler, Papageno
**Bird-like** Hirundine, Sturnine
**Bird's nest(ing)** Caliology, Monotropa, Soup
**Birdsong** Cheep, Chirp, Trill, Twitter
**Bird-watcher** Augur, Twitcher
**Birkenhead** F.E.Smith
**Birmingham** Brum(magem)
**Birth** Breech, Burden, Congenital, Crowning, Dawn, Delivery, Drop, Extraction, Genesis, Geniture, Happy event, Jataka, Lineage, Multiple, Nativity, Natural, Origin, Parage, Parity, Parthenogenesis, Parturition, Virgin, Water, Whelp(ing), Year
**Birth-control** Contraception, Contragestion
**Birthday** Anniversary, Genethliac, Official, Prophet's
**Birthmark** Blemish, Mole, Mother-spot, Naevus, Port wine stain, Stigmata, Strawberry
**Birthright** Heritage, Mess, Patrimony
**Birthwort** Aristolochia
**Bis** Again, Anew
**Biscuit** Abernethy, Amaretto, Bake, Bath-oliver, Biscotto, Bourbon, Brandysnap, Brown George, Butter, Butterbake, Captain's, Charcoal, Cookie, Cracker, Cracknel, Crispbread, Custard cream, Dandyfunk, Digestive, Dog, Dunderfunk, Fairing, Fig roll, Flapjack, Florentine, Fly cemetery, Fortune cookie, Four-by-two, Garibaldi, Ginger nut, Gingersnap, Hardtack, Jammy dodger, Jumbal, Kiss, Krumbak, Langue de chat, Lavash, Lebkuchen, Macaroon, Marie, Mattress, Matza(h), Matzo(h), Nut, Oatcake, Oliver, Oreo, Osborne, Parkin,

Perkin, Petit four, Petticoat tail, Pig's ear, Pilot, Poppadom, Poppadum, Pretzel, Puff, Ratafia, Rice, Rusk, Rye-roll, Sea, Ship's, Shortbread, Snap, Soda, Sponge finger, Sweetmeal, Tack, Tan, Tararua, Tea, Teiglach, Tollhouse cookie, Wafer, Water, Wine, Zwieback

**Bisexual** AC/DC, Freemartin, Switch-hitter

**Bishop(ric)** Aaronic, Abba, Aberdeen, Aidan, Ambrose, Apollinaris, B, Bench, Berkeley, Boy, Bp, Cambrensis, Cantuar, Chad, Chorepiscopal, Coadjutor, Coverdale, Cranmer, Diocesan, Dunelm, Ebor, Ely, Eparch, Episcopate, Eusebian, Exarch, Exon, Golias, Hatto, Henson, Jansen, Latimer, Lord, Magpie, Man, Metropolitan, Missionary, Norvic, Odo, Ordainer, Patriarch, Peter, Petriburg, Piece, Polycarp, Pontiff, Prelate, Priest, Primate, Primus, Proudie, Ridley, Roffen, RR, St Swithin, Sarum, See, Sleeve, Sodor and Man, Suffragan, The purple, Titular, Tulchan, Weaver, Weed, Winton, Wrexham

**Bismarck** Otto

**Bismuth** Bi

**Bison** Bonas(s)us, Buffalo, Gaur, Indian, Ox, Wisent

**Bistro** Caff

**Bit** Ate, Baud, Byte, Cannon, Cantle(t), Centre, Chad, Cheesecake, Chip, Chunk, Coin, Crumb, Curb, Curn, Dash, Degree, Drib, Drill, Excerpt, Feature, Fleck, Flibbert, Fraction, Fraise, Gag, Haet, Hait, Hate, Ion, Iota, Jaw, Jot, Leptum, Mite, Modicum, Morsel, Mote, Mu, Nit, Ort, Ounce, Pelham, Peni, Penny, → PIECE, Pinch, Port, Rap, Rare, Ratherish, Ring, Rowel, Scintilla, Scrap, Section, Shaving, Shiver, Shrapnel, Shred, Smattering, Smidge(n), Smidgeon, Smidgin, Snaffle, Snatch, Snippet, Some, Soupcon, Spale, Speck(le), Splinter, Spot, Spudding, Stop, Suspicion, Tad, Tait, Tate, Threepenny, Trace, Unce, Vestige, What, Whit

**Bite(r), Biting, Bitten** Astringent, Begnaw, Canapé, Caustic, Champ, Chelicera, Chew, Cold, Eat, Engouled, Erose, Etch, Gnash, Gnat, Gnaw, Hickey, Hickie, Incisor, Knap, Masticate, Midge, Molar, Mordacious, Mordant, Morsel, Morsure, Nacho, Nibble, Nip(py), Occlude, Peck, Pium, Pointed, Premorse, Rabid, Raw, Sarcastic, Sharp, Shrewd, Snack, Snap, Sound, Spammie, Tang, Tart, Teeth

**Bitter(ness), Bitters** Absinth, Acerb, Acid, Acrid, Acrimonious, Ale, Aloe, Angostura, Animosity, Astringent, Barbed, Beer, Bile, Cassareep, Caustic, Eager, Edge, Envenomed, Ers, Fell, Gall, Heated, Jaundiced, Jealousy, Keen, Keg, Marah, Maror, Myrrh, Picamar, Pique, Quinine, Radicchio, Rancorous, Rankle, Resentful, Sarcastic, Sardonic, Snell, Sore, Sour, Spleen, Tannin, Tart(aric), Venom, Verjuice, Virulent, Vitriolic, Wersh, Wormwood, Wry

**Bitter end** At outrance

**Bittern** Boomer, Bull-of the-bog, Butterbump, Heron, Mossbluiter, Sedge, Siege

**Bittersweet** Dulcamara, Poignant, Staff-tree

**Bitumen** Albertite, Asphalt, Blacktop, Elaterite, Gilsonite®, Maltha, Mineral tar, Pissasphalt, Pitch, Slime, Tar, Tarseal, Uintaite

**Bivalve** Arkshell, Calamari, Clam, Cockle, Lamellibranch, Mollusc, Muscle, Mussel, Oyster, Pelecypod, Piddock, Razorshell, Scallop, Tuatua, Whelk

**Bivouac** Camp

**Bizarre** Antic, Atypical, Curious, Eccentric, Exotic, Fantastic, Far-out, Freaky, Gonzo, Grotesque, Kafkaesque, Left field, Odd, Offbeat, Off-the-wall, Outlandish, Outré, Pythonesque, Queer, Rum, Strange, Surreal, Weird

▷**Bizarre** *may indicate* an anagram

**Blab(ber), Blabbermouth** Babble, Gossip, Prate, Sing, Squeal, Telltale

**Black(en), Blackness, Black-out** Afro-American, Amadoda, Asperse, Atramental, B, Ban, BB, Bess, Blae, Boycott, Cape Coloured, Carbon, Char, Charcoal, Cilla, Coal, Coloured, Cypress, Death, Debar, Demonise, Denigrate, Dinge, Dwale, Ebon(y), Eclipse, Ethiop, Evil, Gladwellise, Graphite, Grime, Heben, Hole, Ink(y), Ivory, Japan, Jeat, Jet, Jim Crow, Kohl, Lepidomelane, Macabre, Malign, Market, Melanic, Melano, Moor, Muntu, Myall, Negritude, Negro, Niello, Niger, Nigrescent, Nigritude, Obliterate, Obscure, Outage, Oxford, Piceous, Pitch, Platinum, Pongo, Prince, Profit, Pudding, Puke, Raven, Sable, Scab, School, Scorch, Sericon, Sheep, Slae, Sloe, Sodium, Solvent, Sombre, Soot, Sooterkin, Soul brother, Soul sister, Starless, Stygian, Swart(y), Swarth(y), Tar, Tarnish, Uncle Tom, Weeds

**Black art** Necromancy, Nigromancy

**Blackball** Ban, Debar, Exclude, Ostracise, Pill, Pip, Reject

**Blackberry** Acini, Bramble, Mooch, Mouch
**Blackbird** Collybird, Crow, Jackdaw, Merl(e), Ousel, Raven, Woosel
**Blackboard** Slate
**Blackcurrant** Cassis, Quinsy-berry
**Black eye(d)** Half-mourning, Keeker, Mouse, Shiner, Susan
**Blackguard** Evildoer, Heel, Leg, Nithing, Raff, Revile, Rotter, Scoundrel, Sweep
**Blackhead** Comedo
**Black hole** Collapsar
**Blackjack** Billie, Billy, Bombard, Cosh, Flag, Sphalerite, Tankard, Truncheon, Vingt(-et)-un
**Blackleg** Fink, Rat, Scab, Snob
**Black-letter** Gothic
**Black magic** Goety
**Blackmail(er)** Bleed, Chantage, Chout, Exact, Extort, Greenmail, Honey-trap, Ransom, Shakedown, Strike, Vampire
**Black Maria** Paddywagon
**Blackout** ARP, Eclipse, Faint, Power cut, Shallow water, Swoon, Syncope
**Black Sea** Pontic, Pontus Euxinus
**Black sheep** Neer-do-well, Reprobate
**Blacksmith** Brontes, Burn-the-wind, Farrier, Forger, Harmonious, Plater, Shoer, Vulcan
**Blackthorn** Sloe
**Bladder(wort)** Air, Balloon, Blister, Cholecyst, Cyst, Gall, Hydatid, Isinglass, Popweed, Sac, Sound, Swim, Urinary, Utricle, Varec(h), Vesica, Vesicle
**Blade(s)** Acrospire, Andrew Ferrara, Bilbo, Brand, Brown Bill, Catling, Claymore, Cleaver, Co(u)lter, Cutlass, Dandy, Espada, Faible, Fin, Flick knife, Foible, Forte, Froe, Gallant, Gleave, Gouge, Guillotine, Hydrofoil, Knife, Kris, Lance, Lawnmower, Leaf, Man, Mouldboard, Oar, Omoplate, Paddle, Palmetto, Peel, Propeller, Rachilla, Rapier, Razor, Rip, Rotor, Scalpel, Scapula, Scimitar, Scissor, Scull, Scythe, Share, Skate, Spade-, Spatula, Spatule, Spear, Spoon, Stiletto, Stock, Strigil, Sweep, Switch, → **SWORD**, Symitar, Toledo, Turbine, Vane, Vorpal, Wash, Web
**Blair** Eric, Lionel, Orwell, Tony
**Blame(worthy)** Accuse, Censure, Condemn, Confound, Culpable, Decry, Dirdam, Dirdum, Discommend, Dispraise, Fault, Guilt, Incriminate, Inculpate, Odium, Rap, Reprehensible, Reproach, Reprove, Stick, Thank, Twit, Wight, Wite, Wyte
**Blameless** Exculpable, Innocent, Irreproachable, Lily-white, Unimpeachable
**Blanch** Bleach, Etiolate, Scaud, Whiten
**Blancmange** Carrageen, Flummery, Mould, Shape, Timbale
**Bland** Anodyne, Antiseptic, Dull, Flavourless, Glop, Insipid, Mild, Neutral, Pabulum, Pigling, Sleek, Smooth, Spammy, Suave, Tame, Tasteless, Unctuous, Vapid
**Blandish(ment)** Agremens, Agrement, Cajole, → **COAX**, Flatter, Soft soap, Treacle, Wheedle
**Blank** Burr, Cartridge, Deadpan, Empty, Erase, Flan, Flyleaf, Ignore, Lacuna, Mistigris, Planchet, Shot, Space, Tabula rasa, → **VACANT**, Vacuous
**Blanket** Across the board, Afghan, All-over, Bluey, Chilkat, Comprehensive, Counterpane, Cover, Electric, Envelop, Fire, General (purpose), Hudson's Bay, Kaross, Mackinaw, Manta, Obscure, Overall, Overlay, Poncho, Quilt, Rug, Saddle, Sarape, Security, Serape, Shabrack, Smog, Snow(fall), Space, Stroud, Swaddle, Umbrella, Wagga, Wet, Whittle
**Blare** Horn, Trumpet
**Blarney** Cajolery, Flattery, Nonsense, Sawder, Sleeveen, Soft soap, Taffy
**Blasé** Bored, Worldly
**Blaspheme, Blasphemous, Blasphemy** Abuse, → **CURSE**, Defame, Profanity, Revile, Sacrilege
**Blast(ed), Blasting** Blare, Blight, Blore, Blow, Bombard, Dang, Darn, Dee, Drat, Dynamite, Expletive, Explode, Fanfare, Flaming, Flurry, Fo(e)hn, Gale, Grit, Gust, Hell, Noser, Oath, Pan, Parp, Planet-struck, Pryse, Rats, Ruddy, Scarth, Scath(e), Sere, Shot, Sideration, Skarth, Sneeze, Stormer, Tantara, Toot, Tout, Tromp(e), Trump(et), Tucket, Volley
**Blatant** Bare-faced, Conspicuous, Flagrant, Hard-core, Noticeable, Open, Overt, Strident, Unashamed, Unsubtle, Vulgar

**Blather** Baloney, Gabble, Gibber, Waffle
**Blaze(r), Blazing** Afire, Beacon, Bonfire, Burn, Bushfire, Cannel, Conflagration, Firestorm, → FLAME, Flare, Glare, Inferno, Jacket, Low(e), Lunt, Palatinate, Race, Ratch, Sati, Star, Sun, Tead(e), Trail
**Bleach(er)** Agene, Blanch, Chemic, Chloride, Decolorate, Etiolate, Fade, Frost, Janola®, Keir, Kier, Ozone, Perborate, Peroxide, Whiten, Whitster
**Bleak** Ablet, Abysmal, Bare, Barren, Blay, Bley, Cheerless, Desolate, Dour, Dreary, Dreich, Gaunt, Midwinter, Raw, Soulless, Stark, Wintry
**Bleary** Blurred, Smudged
**Bleat** Baa, Blat, Bluster, Maa
**Bleed(er), Bleeding** Breakthrough, Cup, Diapedesis, Ecchymosis, Emulge, Epistaxis, Extort, Extravasate, Fleam, Haemorrhage, Leech, Menorrhagia, Menorrh(o)ea, Metrorrhagia, Milk, Purpura, Rhinorrhagia, Root-pressure, Sap
**Bleep** Earcon, Pager, Ping
**Blefuscudian** Big-endian, Little-endian
**Blemish** Birthmark, Blot, Blotch, Blur, Botch, Defect, Disfigurement, Eyesore, Flaw, Imperfection, Lepra, Mackle, Mar, Mark, Milium, Mote, Naevus, Scar, Smirch, Smudge, Speck, Spot, Stain, Sully, Taint, Tash, Verruca, Vice, Wart, Wen
**Blench** Flinch, Recoil, Wince
**Blend(er), Blending** Amalgam, Chameleon, Coalesce, Combine, Commix, Contemper, Contrapuntal, Counterpoint, Electrum, Fit, Fuse, Fusion, Go, Harmonize, Hydrate, Interfuse, Interlace, Intermingle, Intermix, Liquidise, Meld, Melt, → MERGE, Mingle, Mix, Osmose, Portmanteau, Puree, Scumble, Sfumato, Sourmash, Stir, Synalepha
▷**Blend** *may indicate* an anagram
**Blenny** Eel-pout, Gunnel, Shanny
**Bless(ing), Blessed(ness)** Amen, Anoint, Approval, Asset, Beatify, Beatitude, Benedicite, Benediction, Benison, Benitier, Bensh, Bismillah, Bonus, Boon, Brachah, Brocho, Charmed, Consecrate, Cup, Damosel, Darshan, Elysium, Ethereal, Favour, Felicity, Fortunate, Gesundheit, Giver, God-gifted, Godsend, Grace, Gwyneth, Hallow, Holy (dam), Informal, Kiddush, Luck, Macarise, Mercy, Mitzvah, Mixed, Sain, Saint, Sanctify, Sanctity, Sheva Brachoth, Sheva Brochos, Sneeze, Toronto, Urbi et orbi, Xenium
**Bless me** Lawk(s)
**Blight** Afflict, Ague, American, Apple, Bespot, Blast, Canker, Destroy, Early, Eyesore, Fire, Late, Mar, Planning, Potato, Rot, → RUIN, Rust, Sandy, Shadow, Viticide, Waldersterben, Wither
**Blighter** Cuss, Perisher, Varment, Varmint
**Blimey** Coo, Cor, Crimini, Crumbs, O'Riley, Strewth
**Blimp** Airship, Colonel
**Blind(ness), Blind spot** Amaurosis, Amblyopia, Artifice, Austrian, Awning, Bedazzle, Beesome, Beetle-eyed, Binge, Bisson, Blend, Blotto, Camouflage, Carousal, Cecity, Chi(c)k, Cog, Colour, Concealed, Dazzle, Drop serene, Drunk, Eyeless, Feint, Festoon, Flash, Gravel, Hemeralopia, Hemianopsia, Homer, Hood, Invisible, Jalousie, Legless, Meropia, Mole, Night, Nyctalopia, Onchocerciasis, Persian, Persiennes, Pew, Pickled, Prestriction, Rash, River, Roller, Roman, Sand, Scotoma, Seel, Shade, Shutter, Sightless, Slat, Snow, Stimie, Stimy, Stymie, Sun, Swear, Teichopsia, Typhlology, Venetian, Visually challenged, Window, Word, Yblent
**Blindfish** Amblyopsis
**Blindfold** Bandage, Hood, Hoodwink, Muffle, Seal, Wimple
**Blindworm** Anguis
**Bling** Tsatske
**Blink, Blinker(s), Blinkered, Blinking** Bat, Blepharism, Blinders, Bluff, Broken, Eye-flap, Flash, Haw, Idiot, Insular, Nictate, Owl-eyed, Owly, Twink, Wapper, Water, Wink
**Bliss(ful)** Beatitude, Bouyan, Cheer, Composer, Delight, → ECSTASY, Eden, Elysium, Glee, Happy, Heaven, Idyll, Ignorance, Joy, Married, Millenium, Nirvana, Paradise, Rapture, Seventh heaven, Sion, Tir-na-nog, Utopia, Valhalla, Walhalla, Wedded
**Blister(ed), Blistering** Blab, Blain, Bleb, Blood, Bubble, Bullate, Cantharidine, Cold sore,

Epispastic, Fever, Herpes, Hot, Measle, Overgall, Pemphigus, Phlyct(a)ena, Scorching, Tetter, Vesicant, Vesicle, Visicate, Water

**Blitz** Attack, Bombard, Onslaught, Raid

**Blizzard** Buran, Gale, Snowstorm, Whiteout

**Bloat(ed), Bloater** Buckling, Gross, Oedema, Puff, Strout, Swell, Swollen, Tumefy, Tumid, Turgid, Two-eyed steak, Yarmouth

**Blob** Bead, Bioblast, Dollop, Drop, Globule, O, Pick, Spatter, Spot, Tear

**Bloc** Alliance, Cabal, Cartel, Eastern, Party

**Block(er), Blockage, Blocked, Blocking** Altar, Anvil, Ashlar, Atresia, → BAR, Barber's, Barracks, Barricade, Barrier, Battle-axe, Brake, Breeze, Brick, Briquet(te), Building, Bung, Bunt, Cake, Capital, Catasta, Cavity, Chinese, Choke, Chunk, Cinder, Cleat, Clint, Clog, Clot, Cloy, Compass, Condo(minium), Congest, Constipated, Cube, Cut-off, Cyclopean, Cylinder, Dado, → DAM, Dead-eye, Debar, Defect, Delete, Dentel, Dentil, Die, Dit, Domino, Ear-plug, Eclipse, Electrotint, Embargo, Embolism, Emphractic, Encompass, Erratic, Euphroe, Fiddle, Filibuster, Fill, Fipple, Frog, Gypsum, Hack-log, Head off, Heart, High-rise, Hunk, Ice, Ileus, Impasse, Impede, Impost, Ingot, Input, Insula, Interclude, Interrupt, Investment, Ischaemia, Jack, Jam, Licence, Lifestyle, Limitation, Line, Lingot, Lodgment, Log-jam, Lump, Measuring, Mental, Ministroke, Mitre, Monkey, Mounting, Mutule, Nerve, Nifedipine, Nog, Notepad, Oasis®, Obstacle, → OBSTRUCT, Obturate, Occlude, Office, Opossum, Oppilate, Pad, Page, Parry, Perched, Pile-cap, Pile-up, Pillow, Planer, Plinth, Plummer, Power, Pre-empt, Prevent, Process, Psychological, Quad, Ram, Saddle, Scotch, Seal, Sett, Siege, Slab, Snatch, Snooker, Stalemate, Stap, Starting, Stenosis, Stimie, Stimy, Stone, Stonewall, Stop, Stumbling, Stymie, Sun(screen), Swage, Tamp, Tenement, Tetrapod, Thwart, Tint, Tower, Tranche, Trig, Triglyph, Truck, Uphroe, Upping-stock, Veto, Vibropac®, Wedge, Wig, Wood(cut), Wrest, Writer's, Zinco, Zugzwang

**Blockbuster** Epic

**Blockhead** Jolterhead, Mome, Nitwit, Noodle, Pig sconce, Stupid

**Blockhouse** Igloo

**Blog** Twitter

**Bloke** Beggar, Chap, Codger, Cove, Fellow, Geezer, Gent, Man, Oik

**Blond(e)** Ash, Bombshell, Bottle, Cendré, Fair, Flaxen, Goldilocks, Nordic, Peroxide, Platinised, Platinum, Strawberry, Tallent, Tow-haired, Towhead

**Blood(y), Blood-letter, Blood-letting** A, Ancestry, B, Bad, Bally, Blue, Bluggy, Blut, Buck, Butchery, Claret, Clot, Cold, Cruor, Cup, Dutch pink, Ecchymosis, Ensanguine, Epigons, Factor, Family, First, Fresh, Full, Globin, → GORE, Haematoma, Haemoglobin, Haemorrhage, H(a)emal, Ichor, Internecine, Introduce, Kin, Kinship, Knut, Leech, Life, Menses, Microcyte, New, Nut, O, Opsonin, Parentage, Penny dreadful, Persue, Phlebotomist, Pigeon's, Plasma, Platelet, Plurry, Properdin, Pup, Purple, Race, Rare, Red, Rh negative, Rh positive, Ruby, Sang, Sangrado, Schistosoma, Serum, Show, Stroma, Thrombin, Toff, Type, Venisection, Welter, Whole, Young

**Blood disease, Blood disorder, Blood-poisoning** Acidosis, Agranulocytosis, Cachaemia, Haematuria, Haemophilia, Hyperaemia, Hypinosis, Hypoglycaemia, Hypokalaemia, Hypomagnesaemia, Isch(a)emia, Leukemia, Lipaemia, Melanaemia, Oligaemia, Oligocythaemia, Purpura, Pyaemia, Sapraemia, Septicemia, Spanaemia, Thalassemia, Thrombocytopenia, Toxaemia, Uraemia

**Bloodhound** Lime, Lyam, Lym, Rach(e), Ratch, Sleuth, Spartan, Tracker

**Bloodless** Anaemic, Isch(a)emic, Wan, White

**Blood money** Eric

▸**Blood-poisoning** *see* BLOOD DISEASE

**Blood-pressure** Hypertension, Hypotension, Normotensive

**Bloodshot** Red-eyed

**Blood-sport** Hunting, Shooting, Venery

**Blood-sucker** Anoplura, Asp, Bed bug, Dracula, Flea, Gnat, Horseleech, Ked, Lamia, Leech, Louse, Midge, Mosquito, Parasite, Reduviid, Soucouyant, Sponger, Tick, Vampire(-bat)

**Bloodthirsty** Gory, Lurid, Murderous, Tiger

**Blood vessel** Artery, Vein, Venule

**Bloom(er), Blooming** Anthesis, Bally, Blossom, Blow, Blush, Boner, Bread, Clanger, Cobalt, Dew, Dratted, Effloresce, Error, Film, Flipping, Floral, Florence, Florescent, Flourish, Flowery, Flush, Full-blown, Gaffe, Glaucous, Heyday, Howler, Knickers, Loaf, Miscalculation, Nickel, Out, Peach, → **PLANT**, Pruina, Rationals, Reh, Remontant, Rosy, Ruddy, Thrive, Underwear

▷**Bloomer** *may indicate* a flower

**Bloop(er)** Outtake

**Blossom** Blow, Burgeon, Catkin, Develop, Efflorescence, Festoon, Flourish, Flower, Marybud, May, Orange, Pip, Springtime, Thrive

**Blot (out)** Atomy, Blob, Cartel, Delete, Disgrace, Dry, Eclipse, Eyesore, Obliterate, Obscure, Pad, Smear, Smudge, Southern, Splodge, Splotch

**Blotch(y)** Blemish, Giraffe, Monk, Mottle(d), Spot, Stain

**Blotto** Legless

**Blouse** Choli, Garibaldi, Gimp, Guimpe, Kabaya, Kerbaya, Middy, Pneumonia, Sailor, Shell, Shirtwaist, Smock, Tunic, Waist(er), Windjammer

**Blow(er), Blown** Appel, Bang, Bash, Bat, Bellows, Biff, Billow, Blip, Bloom, Bluster, Body, Box, Brag, Breeze, Buckhorse, Buffet, Bump, Burst, Buster, Calamity, Chop, Clap, Clat, Claut, Clip, Clout, Clump, Conk, Coup, Crosswind, Cuff, Dad, Daud, Dawd, Dev(v)el, Dinnyhayser, Dint, Dod, Double whammy, Douse, Dowse, Dry, Estramacon, Etesian, Exsufflate, Facer, Fan, Fillip, Finisher, Fisticuffs, Fuse, Gale, Grampus, Gust, Hammer, Hander, Haymaker, Headwind, Hit, Hook, Hurricane, Ictus, Impact, Insufflate, Karate, Kibosh, Knuckle sandwich, KO, Lame, Lander, Left-hander, Lick, Lounder, Montant(o), Muff, Muzzler, Neck-herring, Northerly, Noser, Oner, One-two, Paddywhack, Paik, Pash, Peise, Peyse, Phone, Piledriver, Plague, Plug, Plump(er), Polt, Pow, Puff, Punch, Purler, Raft, Rats, Rattler, Rib-roaster, Roundhouse, Sas(s)arara, Scat, Scud, Settler, Shake, Short, Sideswipe, Side-winder, Sis(s)erary, Skatt, Skiff, Skite, Skyte, Slap, Slat, Slog, Slug, Smack, Snell, Snot, Sock, Sockdolager, Sockdologer, Southwester, Spanking, Spat, Spout, Squall, Squander, Squelcher, Stripe, Stroke, Strooke, Stunning, Sufflate, Supercharger, Swash, Swat, Swinger, Swipe, Tap, Telephone, Thump, Thwack, Tingler, Tootle, Triple whammy, Trump(et), Tuck, Twister, Undercut, Upper-cut, Waft, Wallop, Wap, Waste, Welt, Whammy, Whample, Whang, Whap, Wheeze, Wherret, Whiffle, Whirret, Whistle, → **WIND**, Winder, Windswept, Wipe, Wuther, Zonk

**Blowfly** Bluebottle

**Blowhole** spout hole

**Blown-up** Elated, Enlarged, Exploded

**Blow-out** Binge, Bloat, Blowhole, Exhale, Feast, Feed, Flat, Fulminate, Lava, Nosh-up, Snuff, Spiracle, → **SPREAD**

**Blowpipe** Hod, Peashooter, Sarbacane, Sumpit(an)

**Blub(ber)** Cry, Fat, Nettlefish, Snotter, Sob, Speck, → **WEEP**, Whimper

**Bludge** Sinecure

**Bludgeon** Bulldoze, Bully, Club, Cosh, Cudgel, Life-preserver, Sap

**Blue(s), Bluesman** Abattu, Accablé, Adult, Anil, Aqua, Aquamarine, Azure, Azurn, Beard, Berlin, Bice, Bleuâtre, Blow, Boogie, Bottle, Butterfly, C, Caesious, Cafard, Cambridge, Cantab, Celeste, Cerulean, City, Clair de lune, Classic, Cobalt, Coomassie, Copenhagen, Cornflower, Country, Coventry, Cyan, Danish, Danube, Dejected, Dirty, Disconsolate, Doldrums, → **DOWN**, Duck-egg, Eatanswill, Eggshell, Electric, Erotica, Facetiae, Firmament, Fritter, Gentian, Germander, Glaucous, Glum, Hauyne, Heliotrope, Hump, Ice, Indecent, Indigo, Indol(e), Iron, Isatin(e), Kingfisher, Lapis lazuli, Lavender, Leadbelly, Lewd, Lionel, Low, Mazarine, Melancholic, Methylene, Midnight, Monastral®, Mope, Morose, Murder, Nattier, Naughty, Navy, Nile, Obscene, Ocean, Off-colour, Oxford, Peacock, Periwinkle, Perse, Petrol, Phycocyan, Porn, Powder, Prussian, Rabbi, Racy, Ribald, Riband, Right, Ripe, Robin's egg, Royal, Sad, Sapphire, Saxe, Saxon(y), Scurrilous, → **SEA**, Shocking, → **SKY-TINCTURED**, Slate, Smalt(o), Smutty, Sordid, Spirit, Splurge, Squander, Stafford, Steel, Stocking, Teal, Thenard's, Tony, Top shelf, Tory, Trist, True, Trypan, Turnbull's, Turquoise, Ultramarine, Unhappy, Urban, Verditer, Washing, Watchet, Wedgwood®, Welkin, Woad, Zaffer, Zaffre

▷**Blue** *may indicate* an anagram

**Bluebell** Blawort, Blewart, Campanula, Harebell, Hyacinth

**Bluebottle** Blawort, Blewart, Blowfly, Blowie, Brommer, Brummer, Cop, Cornflower, Fly, Officer, Policeman

▶**Blue-legged** *see* BLUESTOCKING

**Blueprint** Cyanotype, Design, DNA, Draft, Drawing, Format, Plan, Recipe, Scheme, Template

**Bluestocking, Blue-legged** Basbleu, Carter, Erudite, Femme savante, Hamburg(h), Mrs Montagu, Précieuse, Sheba

**Bluff(ing)** Blunt, Cle(e)ve, Cliff, Clift, Crag, Double, Escarpment, Fake, Flannel, Four-flush, Frank, Hal, Headland, Height, Hoodwink, Kidology, Pose, Precipice, Scarp, Steep, Trick

**Blunder(er), Blundering** Barry (Crocker), Betise, Bévue, Bish, Bloomer, Blooper, Boner, Boob, Break, Bull, Bumble, Bungle, Clanger, Clinker, Cock-up, Crass, Err, Etourderie, Fault, Faux pas, Floater, Flub, Fluff, Gaff(e), Goof, Howler, Inexactitude, Inexpert, Josser, Malapropism, Misstep, → MISTAKE, Muddle, Mumpsimus, OG, Oversight, Ricket, Slip, Slip up, Solecism, Stumble, Trip

**Blunt(ed), Bluntly** Abrupt, Alleviate, Bald, Bate, Bayt, Brash, Brusque, Candid, Deaden, Disedge, Downright, Dull, Explicit, Forthright, Frank, Hebetate, Home truth, Mole, Morned, Obtund, Obtuse, Outspoken, Plainspoken, Pointblank, Pointless, Rebate, Retund, Retuse, Roundly, Snub, Straight-out, Stubby, Unsubtle

**Blur(red), Blurring, Blurry** Cloud, Confuse, Daze, Fog, Fuzz, Halation, Hazy, Indistinct, Mackle, Macule, Mudge, Muzzy, Pixilation, → SMUDGE, Stump, Tortillon, Unfocussed, Vague

**Blurb** Ad, Puff

**Blush(ing)** Colour, Cramoisy, Crimson, Erubescent, Erythema, Incarnadine, Mantle, → REDDEN, Rosy, Rouge, Rubescent, Ruby, Rufescent, Rutilant

**Bluster(ing), Blusterer, Blustery** Arrogance, Bellow, Blore, Brag, Bravado, Fanfaronade, Gusty, Hector, Huff-cap, Rage, Rant, Rodomontade, Roister, Sabre-rattler, Squally, Squash, Swagger, Swashbuckler, Vapour, Windbag, Wuthering

**BMW** Beemer

**Boa** Feather, Fur, Ophidian

**Boadicea** Charioteer

**Boar** Barrow, Calydonian, Erymanthian, Hog, Pentheus, Sanglier, Sounder, Tusker, Wild

**Board(s), Boarding** Abat-voix, Admiralty, Aquaplane, Baffle, Banker, Barge, Bd, Beaver, Billet, Body, Bristol, Building, Bulletin, Catchment, Centre, Cheese, Chess, Chevron, Chimney, Circuit, Clip, Collegium, Committee, Contignation, Control, Counter, Cribbage, Dagger, Dam, Dart, Daughter, Deal, Deck, Directors, Diving, Draft, Draining, Draught, Drawing, Duck, Embark, Embus, Emery, Emplane, Enter, Entrain, Expansion, Fa(s)cia, Fare, Farm out, Featheredge, Fibre, Fibro, Fibrolite®, Flannelgraph, Flash, Food, Full, Gangplank, Gib(raltar), Groaning, Gunwale, Gutter, Hack, Half, Half-royal, Hawk, Hoarding, Idiot, Instrument, Insulating, Ironing, Kennels, Kip, Lag, Lap, Leader, Ledger, Lee, Lodge, Log(-chip), Magnetic, Malibu, Management, Marketing, Masonite®, Match, Message, Mill, Monkey, Mortar, Mother, Moulding, Muft(i)at, Notch, Notice, Otter, Ouija, Paddle, Palette, Pallet, Panel, Paper, Parochial, Particle, Paste, Patch, Pedal, Peg(board), Pension, Planch(ette), Plank, Plaster, Plug, Ply(wood), Printed circuit, Punch, Quango, Ribbon-strip, Roof, Running, Sandwich, Sarking, Scale, Scaleboard, School, Score, Scraper, Scratch, Screed, Sheathing, Shelf, Shifting, Shingle, Shooting, Side-table, Sign, Skim, Skirting, Sleeve, SMART®, Smoke, Snow, Sounding, Splasher, Spring, Stage, Stretcher, Strickle, Stringboard, Supervisory, Surf, Switch, → TABLE, Teeter(-totter), Telegraph, Thatch, Theatre, Timber, Tourist, Trade, Tray, Trencher, Tribunal, Verge, Wainscot, Wobble, Wokka, Wood chip

▷**Board** *may refer to* chess or draughts

**Boarder** Interne, Pensioner, PG, Roomer

**Boarding house** Digs, Kip, Lodgings, Pension

**Boast(er), Boastful, Boasting** Bigmouth, Big-note, Blew, Blow, Blowhard, Bluster, Bobadil, Bounce, Brag, Braggadocio, Bravado, Breeze, Bull, Cock-a-hoop, Crake, Crow, Fanfaronade, Gas, Gascon(nade), Gloat, Glory, Hot air, Immodest, Jact(it)ation, Line, Loudmouth, Ostent(atious), Prate, Rodomontade, Scaramouch, Self-glorious, Show-off, Skite, Spread-eagle, Swagger, Swank, Tall, Thrasonic, Vainglory, Vapour, Vaunt, Yelp

**Boat(s)** Ark, Barge, Bark, Cat, Flagship, Fly(ing), Fore-and-after, Goldie, Isis, Keel, Kit, Lugger, Privateer, She, → SHIP, → VESSEL

---

**BOATS**

*1 letter:*
Q

*2 letters:*
PT

*3 letters:*
Hoy

*4 letters:*
Cock
Cott
Four
Junk
Lake
Long
Mail
Pont
Proa
Saic
Sail
Scow
Tilt
Trow
Yawl
Zulu

*5 letters:*
Canal
Coble
Eight
Ferry
Funny
Gravy
Gulet
Hatch
Jolly
Kaiak
Kayak
Motor
Power
Pucan
Sauce
Skiff
Sloop
Smack
Stake
Swing
Track
Wager
Waist
Whiff

*6 letters:*
Advice
Bawley
Caique
Cobble
Codder
Cutter
Dragon
Dugout
Galiot
Galley
Hooker
Howker
Launch
Monkey
Narrow
Packet
Pedalo
Puffer
Pulwar
Sailer
Sandal
Sea Dog®
Tanker
Tender
Torpid
Trek-ox
Wangan
Wangun
Wherry

*7 letters:*
Assault
Coaster
Coracle
Cruiser
Curragh
Dredger
Drifter
Four-oar
Foyboat
Galliot
Gondola
Liberty
Lighter
Lymphad
Pair-oar
Passage
Pearler
Scooter
Sculler
Shallop
Sharpie
Slogger
Sounder
Vedette
Vidette
Wanigan

*8 letters:*
Billyboy
Corecore
Corecoro
Corvette
Faltboat
Flatboat
Foldboat
Gallivat
Johnboat
Mackinaw
Monohull
Mosquito
Pleasure
Shrimper
Skipjack
Surfboat

*9 letters:*
Destroyer
Firefloat
Hydrofoil
Lapstrake
Lap streak
Outrigger
Oysterman
Vaporetto
Weekender
Whaleback
Whaleboat

*10 letters:*
Hydroplane
Purse seine
Track-scout
Trekschuit

*11 letters:*
Cockleshell
Double scull
Salmon coble
Sidewheeler

*12 letters:*
Clinker-built
Sternwheeler
Tangle-netter

*13 letters:*
Black skipjack
Paddle steamer
Revenue cutter

---

**Boater** Bargeman, → HAT, Punter, Straw
**Boatman** Bargee, Charon, Cockswain, Coxswain, George, Gondolier, Harris, Hoveller, Legger, Noah, Phaon, Punter, Voyageur, Waterman, Wet-bob
**Boat population** Tank(i)a
**Boat-shaped** Carina, Scaphoid
**Boatswain** Bosun, Serang, Smee
**Bob** Acres, Beck, Bounce, Clip, Curtsey, Deaner, Dip, Dock, Dop, Duck, Dylan, Eton crop, Float, Haircut, Hairdo, Hod, Hog, Jerk, Major, Maximus, Minor, Nod, Page-boy, Peal, Plain,

Plumb, Plummet, Popple, Rob, Royal, S, Shingle, Short cut, Skeleton, Skip, Sled(ge), Sleigh, Tester, Wiggle

**Bobbin** Pirn, Quill, Reel, Shuttle, Spindle, Spool

**Bobble** Pompom

**Bobby** Bluebottle, Busy, Copper, Flatfoot, Patrolman, Peeler, Pig, → POLICEMAN, Rosser, Wolly

**Bobby-dazzler** Dinger, Stunner

**Bobsleigh** Lauf

**Bock** Stein

**Bode** Augur

**Bodgie** Aussie, Ted

**Bodice** Basque, Bolero, Bustier, Chemise, Chemisette, Choli, Corsage, Gilet, Halter, Jirkinet, Liberty, Plastron, Polonie, Polony, Spencer, Tucker, Waist, Watteau

**Bodkin** Eyeleteer, Needle, Poniard, Stilet(to)

**Body, Bodies, Bodily** Administration, Amount, Anatomic, Astral, Barr, Board, Bouk, Buik, Buke, Bulk, Cadaver, Cadre, Carcase, Carcass, Carnal, Caucus, Centrosome, Chapel, Chapter, Chassis, Chondriosome, Ciliary, Clay, Coachwork, Coccolite, Cohort, Column, Comet, Committee, Contingent, Cormus, Corpora, Corpor(e)al, Corps, Corpse, Corpus, Corse, Cytode, Detail, Dog's, Earth, Elaiosome, Electorate, Establishment, Flesh, Food, Form, Frame, Fuselage, Gate, Gazo(o)n, Golgi, Goner, Grey, → GROUP, Heavenly, Hull, Immune, Incarnate, Inclusion, Kenning, Ketone, Lewy, Lich, Lifting, Like, Lithites, Malpighian, → MASS, Militia, Mitochondrion, Moit, Mote, Mummy, Nacelle, Nave, Nucleole, Nucleolus, Olivary, Orb, Order, Pack, Personal, Phalanx, Physique, Pineal, Plant, Platelet, Platoon, Polar, Politic, Posse, Purview, Quango, Quasar, Relic(t), Remains, Review, Ruck, Satellite, Sect, Senate, Shaft, Solid, Soma(tic), Soredium, Sound, Sound-box, Soyle, Spinar, Spore, Squad(ron), Square, Staff, Statoblast, Stiff, Strobila, Syndicate, Synod, Systemic, Tagma, Testis, Thallus, Torse, Torso, Trunk, Turm, Ulema, Uvula, Vase, Vitreous, Wolffian, X

▷**Body** *may indicate* an anagram

**Body builder** Atlas, Expander, He-man, Muscleman, Steroid

**Bodyguard** Amulet, Beefeater, → ESCORT, Gentleman-at-arms, House-carl, Lifeguard, Minder, Praetorian, Protector, Retinue, Schutzstaffel, → SHIELD, SS, Sun cream, Switzer, Triggerman, Varangian, Yeomen

**Body map** Scintiscan

**Body segment** Arthromere, Genome, Metamere

**Bodysnatcher** Burke, Hare

**Boer** Afrikaner, Kruger, Van der Merwe

**Boffin** Brain, Egghead, Expert

**Bog(gy)** Allen, Blanket, Can, Carr, Clabber, Fen, Gents, Glaur, Hag, Lair, Latrine, Lerna, Lerne, Letch, Loo, Machair, Marish, Marsh, Merse, Mire, Moory, Morass, Moss(-flow), Moss-hag, Mud, Muskeg, Peat, Petary, Quag, Raised, Salt marsh, Serbonian, Slack, Slade, Slough, Spew, Spouty, Stodge, Sump, Swampland, Urinal, Vlei, Washroom, WC, Yarfa, Yarpha

**Boggle** Astonish, Bungle, Demur, Hesitate, Perplex, Shy

**Bogie** Trolley

**Bog-trotter** Tory

**Bogus** Assumed, Counterfeit, Ersatz, Fake, False, Faux, Histrionic, Phoney, → SHAM, Snide, Snobbish, Spoof, Spurious

**Bog(e)y, Bogeyman** Boggart, Bug(aboo), Bugbear, Chimera, Colonel, Eagle, Gremlin, Mumbo jumbo, Nis(se), Ogre, Par, Poker, Rawhead, Scarer, Siege, Spectre, Troll

**Bohemian** Arty, Beatnik, Boho, Calixtin(e), Demi-monde, Gypsy, Hippy, Hussite, Mimi, Offbeat, Taborite, Trustafarian, Zingara, Zingaro

**Boil(er), Boiled, Boiling (point)** Aleppo, Angry, Anthrax, Blain, Blanch, Botch, Brew, Bubble, C, Carbuncle, Coction, Cook, Copper, Cree, Dartre, Decoct, Ebullient, Foam, Furuncle, Gas-fired, Gathering, Hen, Herpes, Hijinks, Kettle, Laddish, Leep, Ligroin, Phlegmon, Pimple, Pinswell, Poach, Poule, Rage, Reflux, Rowdy, Samovar, Seethe, Set pot, Simmer, Sod, Sore, Steam, Stew, Stye, Tea-kettle, Water tube

**Boisterous(ly), Boisterousness** Ariot, Gilp(e)y, Goustrous, Gusty, Hoo, Hurly-burly, Knockabout, Ladette, Lively, Noisy, Rambunctious, Randy, Riotous, Rollicking, Rorty, Rough, Rounceval, Rowdy, Slap-happy, Slapstick, Splurge, Stormy, Strepitoso, Tearer, Termagant, Tomboy, Turbulent, Wild, Zoo

**Bold(ly), Boldness** Assertive, Assumptive, Audacious, Brash, Brass, Bravado, Bravery, Bravura, Brazen, Brussen, Caleb, Confident, Crust, Daredevil, Dauntless, Defiant, Derring-do, Diastaltic, Enterprising, Familiar, Foolhardy, Forward, Free, Gallus, Gutsy, Hard-edge, Hardihood, Heroics, High-spirited, Impudent, Intrepid, Malapert, Manful, Mature, Mettle, Minx, Outspoken, Parrhesia, Pert, Plucky, Presumptive, Rash, Risoluto, Sassy, Stout, Temerity, Unabashed, Unshrinking, Upfront, Valiant

**Bole** Niche, Stem, Trunk

**Bolivar** Liberator

**Bollard** Cone, Kevel

**Bolshevik, Bolshie** Agitator, Anarchist, Communist, Maximalist, Mutinous, Rebel, Soviet, Stroppy

**Bolster** Cushion, Dutch wife, Pillow, → PROP, Reinforce, Support

**Bolt** Arrow, Captive, Carriage, Coach, Cuphead, Dash, Dead, Do a runner, Eat, Elope, Expansion, Explosive, Fasten, Fish, Flee, Gobble, Gollop, Gorge, Gulp, Hurtle, Latch, Levant, Levin, Lightning, Lock, Machine, Missile, Panic, Pig, Pintle, Ragbolt, Ring, Rivet, Roll, Scoff, Screw, Slot, Snib, Sperre, Stay, Stud, Tap, Through, Thunder, Toggle, U, Wing, Wolf, Wring

**Bolus** Ball

**Bomb(ed), Bomber, Bombing, Bombshell** Atom, Attack, B, Benny, Blast, Blitz, Blockbuster, Blonde, Borer, Bunkerbuster, Buzz, Candle, Car, Carpet, Cluster, Cobalt, Daisycutter, Depth charge, Deterrent, Dirty, Dive, Doodlebug, Drogue, Egg, Enola Gay, Fission, Flop, Flying, Flying Fortress, Fragmentation, Fusion, Glide, Greek fire, Grenade, H, Hand grenade, Harris, Homicide, Hydrogen, Lancaster, Land-mine, Letter, Liberator, Loft, Logic, Mail, Megaton, Millennium, Mills, Minnie, Mint, Molotov cocktail, Mortar, Nail, Napalm, Necklace, Neutron, Nuclear, Nuke, Packet, Parcel, Petar, Petard, Petrol, Pineapple, Pipe, Plaster, Plastic, Prang, Precision, Radium, Ransom, Robot, Sex, Shell, Skip, Smart, Smash, Smoke, Sneak-raid, Stealth, Stick, Stink, Stratofortress, Stuka, Suicide, Tactical, Tank, Terrorist, Thermonuclear, Thunderbolt, Time, Torpedo, Turkey, UXB, V1, Volcanic, Vulcan, Walleye

**Bombard(ment)** Attack, Barrage, Battery, Besiege, Blitz, Cannonade, Crossfire, Drum-fire, Mortar, Pelt, Shell(fire), Shower, Stone, Stonk, Strafe, Straff

**Bombardon** Tuba

**Bombast(ic)** Ampullosity, Euphuism, Fustian, Grandiloquent, Grandiose, Hot air, Magniloquence, Mouthy, Orotund, Pomp, Rant, Swol(le)n, Timid, Tumid, Turgent

**Bombay** Nasik

**Bombay duck** Bum(m)alo

▸**Bomber** *see* BOMB(ED)

**Bona fide** Authentic, Echt, Genuine

**Bonanza** Luck, Windfall

**Bonaparte** Boney, → NAPOLEON, Plon-plon

**Bond(s), Bondage, Bonding, Bondsman** Adhesive, Affinity, Afrikander, Agent, Assignat, Baby, Bail, Bearer, Cedula, Cement, Chain, Chemical, Compact, Connect, Consolidate, Consols, Coordinate, Copula, Corporate, Covalent, Covenant, Daimyo, Dative, Debenture, Deep-discount, Double, Duty, Electrovalent, English, Enslave, Ernie, Escrow, Esne, Fetter, Fleming, Flemish, Geasa, Gilt, Glue, Granny, Heart, Herringbone, Hydrogen, Hyphen, Income, Investment, Ionic, James, Junk, Knot, Liaise, Ligament, Ligature, Link(age), Long, Manacle, Managed, Metallic, Mortar, Multicentre, Municipal, Nexus, Noose, Obligation, Pair, Peptide, Performance, → PLEDGE, Post-obit, Premium, Property, Rapport, Recognisance, Relationship, Revenue, Ridge, Running, Samurai, Savings, Security, Semipolar, Serf, Servitude, Shackle, Shogun, Single, Singlet, Sinter, Slave, Solder, Stacked, Starr, Subjection, Superglue, Surety, Thete, Thral(l)dom, Three-per-cent, → TIE, Tiger, TIGR, Treasury, Triple, Trivalent, Tusking, Valence, Valency, Vassal, Vinculum, Yearling, Yoke, Zebra

**Bone(s), Bony** Acromion, Anableps, Angular, Antler, Anvil, Apatite, Astragalus, Atlas, Axis, Baculum, Baleen, Busk, Calcaneus, Caluarium, Cannon, Capitate, Capitellum, Carcass, Carina, Carpal, Carpus, Cartilage, Catacomb, Centrum, Chine, Chordate, Clavicle, Cly, Coccyx, Coffin, Columella, Concha, Condyle, Coracoid, Coral, Costa, Coxa, Crane, Cranium, Cuboid, Cuneiform, Cuttlefish, Dentary, Diaphysis, Dib, Dice, Diploe, Doctor, Dolos, Endosteal, Ethmoid, Femur, Fetter, Fibula, Fillet, Fossil, Frontal, Funny, Ganoid, Gaunt, Hamate, Hammer, Haunch, Hause-bane, Hip, Horn, Huckle, Humerus, Hyoid, Ilium, Incus, Innominate, Interclavicle, Involucrum, Ischium, Ivory, Jugal, Kneecap, Knuckle, Lacrimal, Lamella, Long, Luez, Lunate, Luz, Malar, Malleolus, Malleus, Mandible, Manubrium, Marrow, Mastoid, Maxilla, Medulla, Membrane, Merrythought, Metacarpal, Metatarsal, Napier's, Nasal, Navicular, Occipital, Odontolite, Olecranon, Omoplate, Orthopaedics, Os, Ossicle, Osteo-, Palatine, Parasphenoid, Parietal, Patella, Pecten, Pectoral, Pedal, Pelvis, Pen, Percoid, Perone, Petrous, Phalanx, Pigeon-breasted, Pisiform, Ploughshare, Premaxilla, Prenasal, Pterygoid, Pubis, Pygostyle, Quadrate, Rack, Radiale, Radialia, Radius, Relic, Rib, Ring, Rump-post, Sacrum, Scaphoid, Scapula, Sclere, Scrawny, Sepium, Sequestrum, Sesamoid, Share, Shin, Skeleton, Skull, Spade, Sphenoid, Splint, Splinter, Spur, Squamosal, Stapes, → STEAL, Sternebra, Sternum, Stifle, Stirrup, Suboperculum, Synchondrosis, T, Talus, Tarsometatarsus, Tarsus, Temporal, Tibia, Tibiotarsus, Tot, Trapezium, Triquetral, Trochanter, Trochlea, True-rib, Turbinate, Tympanic, Ulna, Vertebrae, Vomer, Whirl, Wish, Wormian, Zygomatic

**Bone disease** Ehrlichiosis

**Bonehead(ed)** Capitellum, Capitulum, Obtuse

**Bonehouse** Charnel house, Ossuary

**Boneshaker** Dandy-horse, Draisene, Draisine, Velocipede

**Bonfire** Bale-fire, Beltane, Blaze, Chumping, Clavie, Feu de joie, Pyre

**Boniface** Inn-keeper, Landlord, Taverner

**Bonne-bouche** Cate

**Bonnet** Balmoral, Bongrace, Cap, Cornette, Cowl, Easter, Feather, Glengarry, Hood, Hummel, Hummle, Kiss-me(-quick), Mobcap, Mutch, Poke, Scotch, Sun, Tam(my), Toorie, Tourie, War

**Bonny** Blithe, Gay, Merry, Sonsy, Weelfar'd

**Bonsai** Saikei

**Bonus** Bisque, Bounty, Braata, Bye, Christmas box, Danger money, Dividend, Easter egg, Escalator, Extra, Hand-out, Icing, Lagniappe, No-claim, Plus, → PREMIUM, Reversionary, Reward, Scrip, Signing, Spin-off, Windfall

**Boo** Barrack, Explode, Jeer

**Boob** Gaffe, Nork, Simpleton, Stumer

**Booby** Dunce, Gremial, Hick, Patch, Patchcocke, Patchoke, → STUPID, Wooden spoon

**Booby trap** Infernal machine

**Boojum** Snark

**Book(s), Bookish, Bookwork** Abcee, Absey, Academic, Address, Adversaria, Album, Antilegomena, Antiphonary, Appointment, Audio, B, Backlist, Bank(pass), Bedside, Bestiary, Bestseller, Birthday, Black, Block, Blockbuster, Blook, Blotter, Blue, Cash, Catalogue, Chick, Chrestomathy, Classic, Closed, Codex, Coffee-table, Day, Diary, Digest, Directory, Diurnal, Eightvo, Ench(e)iridion, Engage(ment), Enter, Erudite, Exercise, Facetiae, Field, Folio, Fortune, Garland, Good, Gradual, Gradus, Guard, Guest, Guide, Hardback, Hardcover, Herd, Hymnal, Imprint, Index, Issue, Lectionary, Ledger, Lib, Liber, Literary, Livraison, Manual, Memorandum, Missal, Monograph, Muster, Octavo, Octodecimo, Office, Open, Order, Page-turner, Paperback, Pass, Pedantic, Peerage, Pension, Phrase, Pica, Picture, Plug, Polyglot, Potboiler, Pseudepigrapha, Publication, Puzzle prize, Quair, Quarto, Quire, Rare, Rate, Read, → RESERVE, Road, Roman-a-clef, Scrap, Script, Sealed, Sext, Sexto, Sextodecimo, Sixmo, Sixteenmo, Sketch, Softback, Source, Spelling, Spine-chiller, Statute, Studious, Study, Style, Swatch, Symbolical, Table, Tablet, Talking, Tall copy, Te igitur, Text(ual), Thirty-twomo, Thriller, Title, Titule, Tome, Trade, Transfer, Twelvemo, Twenty-fourmo, Unputdownable, Visiting, Visitor's, Vol(ume), Waste, White, Whodunit, Work, Year

## BOOKS

***2 letters:***
Ex
NT
OT

***3 letters:***
Dan
Eph
Gal
Hab
Hag
Jud
Lam
Log
Rag
Red
Rom
Sir
Sus
Tit

***4 letters:***
Acts
Amos
Blad
Edda
Ezek
Ezra
Joel
John
Jude
Luke
Macc
Mark
Mook
Obad
Ruth
Veda

***5 letters:***
Atlas
Bible
Chron
Hosea
James
Kells
Kings
Manga
Micah
Nahum
Pop-up
Snobs
Sutra
Titus
To-bit

***6 letters:***
Aeneid
Baruch
Caxton
Course
Daniel
Eccles
Esdras
Esther
Exeter
Exodus
Haggai
Herbal
I Ching
Isaiah
Jashar
Jasher
Joshua
Judges
Prayer
Primer
Prompt
Psalms
Ration
Reader
Romans
Scroll
Tanach
Tanack

***7 letters:***
Chumash
Cookery
Ezekiel
Genesis
Grolier
Hebrews
Malachi
Martyrs
Matthew
Numbers
Obadiah
Octapla
Omnibus
Orarium
Ordinal
Psalter
Susanna
Timothy

***8 letters:***
Breviary
Clarissa
Domesday
Doomsday
Georgics
Grimoire
Habakkuk
Haggadah
Haggadoh
Hermetic
Libretto
Megillah
Nehemiah
Ordinary
Philemon
Porteous
Portesse
Prophets
Proverbs
Sama-Veda
Triodion
Vercelli
Vesperal

***9 letters:***
Apocrypha
Decameron
Ephesians
Formulary
Galatians
Gazetteer
Hexateuch
Kama Sutra
Leviticus
Maccabees
Portolano
Reference
Remainder
Satyricon
Sibylline
Sybilline
Telephone
Tripitaka
Vade-mecum
Zephadiah

***10 letters:***
Apocalypse
Chronicles
Colossians
Compendium
Cyclopedia
Dictionary
Heptameron
Heptateuch
Hitopadesa
Incunabula
Passionary
Persuasion
Teratology

***11 letters:***
Blaue Reiter
Commonplace
Concordance
Corinthians
Deuteronomy
Evangeliary
Hagiographa
Nomenclator
Philippians
Revelations

***12 letters:***
Bodice-ripper
Ecclesiastes
Encyclopedia
Lamentations
Panchatantra
Paralipomena
Processional
Responsorial
Twelve Tables

***13 letters:***
Penny dreadful
Pharmacopoeia
Thessalonians

***14 letters:***
Ecclesiasticus

---

**Bookbinder, Bookbinding** Fanfare, Grolier, Mutton-thumper, Organdie, Yapp
**Book-case** Breakfront, Credenza, Press, Satchel
**Bookie(s), Bookmaker(s)** Binder, John, Layer, Librettist, Luke, Mark, Matthew, Printer,

Ringman, Roget, The ring, To-bit, Turf accountant
**Booking** Gig, Reservation, Ticket
**Bookkeeper, Bookkeeping** Clerk, Double entry, Librarian, Posting, Recorder, Satchel, Single-entry
**Booklet** B, Brochure, Folder, Inlay, Pamphlet
**Book-like** Solander
**Book-lover** Incunabulist
**Bookmark, Bookplate** Ex libris, Flag, Tassel
**Book-scorpion** Chelifer
**Bookseller, Bookshop** Bibliopole, Colporteur, Conger, Librair(i)e, Sibyl, Stallman
**Bookworm** Reader, Sap, Scholar
**Boom(ing)** Baby, Beam, Boost, Bowsprit, Bump, Fishpole, Gaff, Increase, Jib, Loud, Orotund, Plangent, Prosper, Resonance, Resound, Roar, Sonic, Spar, Supersonic, Swinging, Tail, Thrive, Thunder, Torpedo, Wishbone
**Boomer** Bittern, Bull-of the-bog, Butter-bump, Kangaroo, Mire-drum
**Boomerang** Backfire, Kiley, Kyley, Kylie, Rebound, Recoil, Ricochet, Throwstick, Woomera
**Boon** Asset, Bene, Benefit, Blessing, Bounty, Cumshaw, Gift, Godsend, Mills, Mitzvah, Prayer, Windfall
**Boor(ish)** Borel, Bosthoon, Bumpkin, Chav, Chuffy, Churl, Clodhopper, Coarse, Crass, Curmudgeon, Goth, Grobian, Hog, Ill-bred, Jack, Jungli, Keelie, Kern(e), Kernish, Kill-courtesy, Lob, Lout, Lumpen, Lumpkin, Ocker, Oik, Peasant, Philistine, Pleb, Rude, Trog, Uncouth, Unmannerly, Yahoo, Yob, Yokel
**Boost(er)** Adrenalin, Afterburner, Amplify, Augment, Bolster, Ego, Eik, Eke, Elevate, Encourage, Fillip, Headstart, Help, Hoist, Hype, Impetus, Increase, Injection, Invigorate, Lift, Perk up, Promote, Propel, Raise, Rap, Reheat, Reinforce, Reinvigorate, Spike, Steal, Step up, Steroid, Supercharge, Tailwind, Thrust, Tonic, Upturn, Wrap
**Boot(s)** Addition, Adelaide, Ankle-jack, Avail, Balmoral, Beetle-crushers, Benefit, Blucher, Bottine, Bovver, Brogan, Brogue, Buskin, Cerne, Chelsea, Chukka, Clodhopper, Cockers, Cold, Combat, Concern, Cothurn(us), Cowboy, Cracowe, Crowboot, Daisy roots, Denver, Derby, Desert, Dismiss, Field, Finn(e)sko, Finsko, Fire, Football, Galage, Galosh, Gambado, Go-go, Granny, Gum, Heave-ho, Hessian, High shoe, Hip, Jack, Jemima, Jodhpur, Kamik, Kick-start, Kinky, Kletterschuh, Lace-up, Larrigan, Last, Mitten, Moon, Muchie, Muc(k)luc(k), Mukluk, Pac, Para, Profit, Riding, Rock, Russian, Sabot, → **SACK**, Seven league, → **SHOE**, Shoepac(k), Skivvy, Smarty, Snow, Stogy, Surgical, Tackety, Thigh, Toe, Tonneau, Top, Trunk, Ugg, Vamp, Vibram®, Vibs, Wader, Walking, Warm, Weller, Wellie, Wellington, Welly
**Booth** Assassin, Crame, Cubicle, Kiosk, Polling, Sideshow, Stall, Stand, Telephone, Toll, Tolsel, Tolsey, Voting
**Bootleg(ger)** Cooper, Coper, Hooch, Illicit, Pirate, Runner
**Bootless** Futile, Idle, Unprofitable, Vain
**Bootlicker** Yesman
**Booty** Creach, Creagh, Haul, Loot, Pelf, Pillage, Prey, Prize, Rump, Spoil(s), Spolia optima, Swag
**Booze(r)** Alkie, → **DRINK**, Inn, Lager lout, Liquor, Local, Pub, Sot, Spree, Tipple, Tope
**Bora** Rite, Wind
**Borage** Bugloss, Comfrey, Cool-tankard, Gromwell, Myosote, Viper's gloss
**Borax** Tincal
**Bordeaux** Claret
**Bordello** Stew
**Border(s), Bordering, Borderland, Borderline** Abut, Adjoin, Apron, Bed, Bind, Bound, Boundary, Braid, Brim, Brush, Checkpoint, Circumjacent, Coast, Cot(t)ise, Dado, Demarcation, Dentelle, → **EDGE**, Enclose, Engrail, Extremity, Fimbria, Frieze, Fringe, Frontier, Furbelow, Guilloche, Head-rig, Hedgerow, Hem, Herbaceous, Impale, Kerb, Lambrequin, Limb, Limbate, Limbo, Limen, Limes, Limit, Limitrophe, Line, Lip, List, March, Marchland, → **MARGIN**, Mat, Mattoid, Meith, Mete, Mount, Neighbour, Orle, Outskirts, Pale, Pand, Pelmet, Penumbra, Perimeter, Purfle, Purlieu, Rand, Rim, Rio Grande, Roadside, Roon, Royne, Rubicon, Rund, Rymme, Scottish, Screed, Selvage, Selvedge, Side,

Skirt, Skirting, Splenium, Strand, Strip, Surround, Swage, T(h)alweg, The Marches, Trench, Tressure, Valance, Valence, →**VERGE**, Wayside

▷**Borders** *may indicate* first and last letters

**Bore(d), Boredom, Borer, Boring** Aiguille, Airshaft, Anobium, Anorak, Apathy, Aspergillum, Aspergillus, Aspersoir, Auger, Awl, Beetle, Bind, Bit, Blasé, Bought, Broach, Brog, Bromide, Calibre, Cataclysm, Chamber, Chokebore, Deadly, Def(fed), Drag, →**DRILL**, Drudgery, Dry, Dullsville, Dusty, Dweeb, Eager, Eagre, Eat, Eger, Elshin, Elsin, Endured, Ennui, Ennuye, Fag, Flat, Foozle, Gasbag, Gim(b)let, Gouge, Gribble, Grind, Had, Heigh-ho, Ho-hum, Irk, Jack, Jaded, Jumper, Land, Listless, Longicorn, Longueur, Meh, Menial, Mind-numbing, Miser, Mole, Mopoke, Motormouth, Nerd, Noyance, Nudni(c)k, Nuisance, Nyaff, Oilwell, Operose, Pain, Pall, Penetrate, Perforate, Pest, Pholas, Pierce, Pill, Platitude, Possessed, Probe, Prosaic, Prosy, Punch, Ream(ingbit), Rifle, Rime, Saddo, Sat, Schmoe, Scolytus, Screw, Severn, Shothole, Smooth, Snooze, Snore, Sondage, Spleen, Spod, Spudding-un, Square, Sting, Stob, Stupid, Tediosity, Tedious, Tedisome, Tedium, Tedy, Terebra, Teredo, Termes, Termite, Thirl, Tidal wave, Tire, Tonnell, Trepan, Trocar, Tunnel, Turn-off, Underwent, Uninterested, Vapid, →**WEARY**, Well, Wimble, Windbag, Wonk, Woodworm, Workaday, Worldweary, Xylophaga, Yawn

**Borgia** Cesare, Lucretia

**Boric** Sassolin, Sassolite

**Born** B, Begun, Free, Great, Nascent, Nat(us), Né(e)

**Borneo** Dyak, Kalimantan, Sabahan

**Boron** B

**Borough** Borgo, Brooklyn, Close, County, Manhattan, Pocket, Port, Quarter, Queens, Rotten, The Bronx, Township, Wick

**Borrow(ed), Borrowing** Adopt, Appropriate, Cadge, Copy, Derivative, Eclectic, George, Hum, Leverage, Scrounge, Scunge, Stooze, Straunge, →**TAKE**, Touch

**Borsch** Beetroot

**Bosh** Humbug, Nonsense, Rot

**Bosom** Abraham's, Breast, Bristols, Bust, Close, Gremial, Heart, Inarm, Intimate, Poitrine

**Boson** Gauge, Squark

**Boss(ed), Bossy** Alder(man), Big White Chief, Blooper, Burr, Cacique, Capo, Cazique, Cow, Dictate, Director, Dominate, Domineer, Don, Gadroon, Gaffer, Governor, Guv, Headman, Honcho, Hugo, Hump, Inian, Inion, Jewel, Kingpin, Knob, Knop, Knot, Leader, Maestro, →**MANAGER**, Massa, Master, MD, →**MISTAKE**, Mistress, Mr Big, Netsuke, Noop, Nose-led, Omphalos, Oubaas, Overlord, Overseer, Owner, Padrone, Pannikin, Pellet, Protuberance, Rivet, Ruler, Run, Sherang, Straw, Stud, Superintendent, Superior, Supervisor, Supremo, Taskmaster, Top banana, Topdog, Umbo(nate)

**Boston** Hub

**Bot** Oestrus

**Botany, Botanist** Banks, Bryology, Candolle, Carpology, Cockayne, Darwin, Dendrologist, Field, Frees, Fuchs, Garden, Godet, Graminology, Herbist, Hessayon, Jungermann, Linnaeus, Marchant, Mendel, Mycology, Phytogenesis, Phytology, Pteridology, Tradescant, Weigel

**Botch(ed)** Bungle, Clamper, Cock-up, Flub, Fudge, Mismanage, Mux, Pig's ear, Quat, Spoil, Tink

**Both** Couple, Mutual, Together, Two

**Bother(some)** Ado, Aggro, Annoy, Brush, Care, Darn, Deave, Deeve, Disturb, Drat, Fash, Fluster, Fracas, Fuss, Get, Harassment, Harry, Hassle, Hector, Hoot-toot, Incommode, Irk, Irritate, Moither, Molest, Nag, Nark, Nonplus, Nuisance, Palaver, Perturb, Pesky, Pest(er), Pickle, Reke, Rile, S(c)htook, S(c)htuck, Todo, →**TROUBLE**, Vex

**Bottle(s)** Ampul(la), Bacbuc, Balthasar, Balthazar, Beer, Belshazzar, Blackjack, Borachio, Bravado, Bundle, Canteen, Carafe, Carboy, Case, Cellar, Chapine, Cock, Cork, Costrel, Courage, Cruet, Cruse, Cucurbital, Cutter, Dead-man, Decanter, Demijohn, Fearlessness, Feeding, Fiasco, Filette, Flacket, Flacon, Flagon, Flask, Gas, Glass can, Goatskin, Gourd, Grit, Guts, Half-jack, Hen, Hotty, Hot-water, Imperial, Ink, Jeroboam, Junk, Klein, Lachrymal, Lagena, Magnetic, Magnum, Marie-Jeanne, Matrass, Medicine, Melchior, Methuselah, Mettle, Mickey, Middy, Nansen, Nebuchadnezzar, →**NERVE**, Nursing, Phial, Pig, Pilgrim,

Pitcher, Pluck, Pooter, Pycnometer, Rehoboam, Repress, Resource, Retort, Salmanaser, Salmanazar, Scent, Screwtop, Siphon, Smelling, Split, Squeeze, Squeezy, Stubby, Sucking, Suppress, Tear, Tube, Twenty-sixer, Vial, Vinaigret(te), Wad, Wallop, Water, Water bouget, Weighing, Winchester, Wine, Woulfe

▹**Bottle(d)** *may indicate* an anagram or a hidden word

**Bottleneck** Stoppage

**Bottom** Anus, Aris, Arse, Ass, Backside, Base, Batty, Beauty, Bed, Benthos, Bilge, Booty, Breech, Builder's, Bum, Butt, Buttocks, Coit, Copper, Croup(e), Croupon, Demersal, Derrière, Doup, Dowp, Duff, End, Fanny, Floor, Foot, Foundation, Fud, Fundus, Ground, Haunches, Hunkers, Hurdies, Jacksy, Keel(son), Kick, Lumbar, Minimus, Nadir, Nates, Planing, Podex, Posterior, Pottle-deep, Prat, Pyramus, Quark, Rear, Rock, Root, Rump, Seat, Ship, Sill, Sole, Staddle, Stamina, Tail, Tush, Twerk, Weaver

**Bottom drawer** Glory box

**Bottomless** Subjacent

**Botulism** Limberneck

**Boudoir** Bower, Room

**Bouffant** Pouf

**Bough** Branch, Limb, Roughie, Roughy

**Bought** Coft

**Boulder** Erratic, Gibber, Rock, Sarsen, → **STONE**

**Boule** Senate

**Bounce(r), Bouncing, Bouncy** Ananias, Ball, Balloon, Bang, Blague, Bound, Bumper, Caper, Convention, Dandle, Dap, Dead-cat, Doorman, Dop, Dud, Eject, Elastic, Evict, Fib, Jounce, Keepy-uppy, Kite, Liar, Lie, Lilt, Lollop, Muscleman, Quest, Resilient, Ricochet, Spiccato, Spring, Stot, Tale, Tamp, Tigger, Trampoline, Valve, Verve, Vitality, Yorker, Yump

▹**Bouncing** *may indicate* an anagram

**Bound(er), Boundary** Adipose, Ambit, Apprenticed, Articled, Bad, Barrier, Baseline, Beholden, Border, Bourn(e), Bubalis, Buck, Cad, Cavort, Certain, Circumference, Curvet, Cusp, Dart, Decreed, Demarcation, Demarkation, Divide, Dool, Dule, Duty, End, Engirt, Entrechat, Erub, Eruv, Event horizon, Exciton, Extent, Fence, Finite, Four, Frape, Frontier, Galumph, Gambado, Gambol, Girt, Goal, Harestane, Hedge, Hedgerow, Heel, Held, Hoarstone, Hops, Hourstone, Ibex, Interface, Izard, Jump, Kangaroo, K/T, → **LEAP**, Leapfrog, Liable, Limes, Limit, Linch, Lollop, Lope, March-stone, Mason-Dixon line, Meare, Meer, Meith, Mere, Merestone, Mete, Milestone, Moho, Muscle, Obliged, Ourebi, Outedge, Outfield, Outward, Pale, Parameter, Perimeter, Periphery, Plate, Prance, Precinct, Prometheus, Purlieu, Quickset, Redound, Ring-fence, Roller, Roo, Roped, Roue, Rubicon, Scoundrel, Scoup, Scowp, Serf, Side, Sideline, Six(er), Skelp, Skip, Spang, Spring, Sten(d), Stoit, Stylolite, Sure, T(h)alweg, Terminator, Tide, Tied, Touchline, Tramline, Upstart, Vault, Verge, Wallaby, Wound

**Boundless** Illimited, Unlimited, Vast

▹**Bounds** *may indicate* outside letters

**Bounty, Bountiful** Aid, Bligh, Boon, Bumper, Christian, Generosity, → **GIFT**, Goodness, Grant, Head money, Honorarium, King's, Largess(e), Lavish, Philanthropy, Queen Anne's, Queen's, Reward

**Bouquet** Aroma, Attar, Aura, Compliment, Congratulations, Corsage, Fragrancy, Garni, Nose, Nosegay, Odour, Perfume, Plaudit, Posy, Pot pourri, Scent, Spiritual, Spray

**Bourbon** Alfonso, Biscuit

**Bourgeois(ie)** Biedermeier, Common, Middle class, Pleb(eian), Pooter(ish)

**Bout** Bender, Binge, Bust, Contest, Dose, Drinking, Episode, Go, Jag, Match, Spell, Spree, Turn, Venery, Venewe, Venue

**Boutique** Shop

**Bovine** Stolid

**Bow(ing), Bower, Bowman** Accede, Alcove, Arbour, Arc, Arch, → **ARCHER**, Arco, Arson, Bandy, Beck, Bend, Bluff, Boudoir, Bow-boy, Bowyer, Buckle, Butterfly, Capitulate, Cellist, Clara, Congé(e), Crescent, Crook, Cupid, → **CURVE**, Defer, Dicky, Drail, Droop, Duck, East end, Echelles, Eros, Eugh, Eyes, Fiddle(r), Fiddlestick, Foredeck, Halse, Hawse, Headgear,

Honour, Incline, Inswing(er), Jook, Jouk, Kneel, Knuckle, Kotow, Laval(l)ière, Lean, Londoner, Long, Loof, Lout, Lowt, Luff, Martellato, Menuhin, Moulinet, Namaste, Nameste, Nock, Nod, Nutate, Oar, Obeisance, Obtemper, Outswing, Paganini, Pergola, Port, Prore, Prow, Quarrel, Reverence, Saddle, Salaam, Seamer, Shelter, Slope, Sound, Spiccato, Staccato, Starboard, Stick, → **SUBMIT**, Swing, Throw, Tie, Torrent, Tureen, Weather, Yew, Yield

**Bowdler(ize)** Comstockery, Edit(or), Expurgate, Water

**Bowels** Entrails, Guts, Innards, Melaena, Viscera

▷**Bower** *may indicate* using a bow

**Bowl(ing), Bowler, Bowl over, Bowls** B, Basin, Begging, Bicker, Bocce, Bocci(a), Boccie, Bodyline, Bool, Bosey, Boules, Bouncer, Cage-cup, Calabash, Caldera, Candlepins, Cap, Carpet, Caup, Chalice, Cheese, Chinaman, Christie, Christy, Cog(g)ie, Cog(g)le, Concave, Coolamon, Crater, Cup, Deliver, Derby, → **DISH**, Dismiss, Dome, Doosra, Drake, Dumbfound, Dust, Ecuelle, End, Finger, Fivepin, Font, Goblet, Goldfish, Googly, Grail, Grub, Headgear, Hog, Hoop, Human, Inswing(er), Jack, Jeroboam, Jorum, Kegler, Krater, Lavabo, Laver, Leg-spin, Lightweight, Lob, Locke, Mazer, Monteith, Night, Offbreak, Off-cutter, Old, Outswing, Over-arm, Overpitch, Pace(man), Pan, Pétanque, Piggin, Pitch, Porringer, Pot-hat, Pottinger, Punch, Raku, Rice, Rink, Roll, Rose, Roundarm, Salad, Seam(er), Skip, Skittle(s), Slep, Spare, Speed, Spinner, Spofforth, Stadium, Stagger, Strike, Stummel, Sucrier, Super, Swing, Ten-pin, Throw, Tom, Tureen, Underarm, Underhand, Underwood, Voce, Washbasin, Wassail, Wood, York(er)

**Box(ing)** ABA, Alert, Ark, Baignoire, Ballot, Bandbox, Bareknuckle, Bento, Bijou, Bimble, Binnacle, Black, Blow, Blue, Bonk, Booth, Buist, Bunk, Bush, Caddy, Call, Camera, Canister, Cardboard, Carton, Case, Cash, Casket, Cassette, Cassolette, Chest, Chinese, Chocolate, Christmas, Ciborium, Clog, Coach, Coffer, Coffin, Coffret, Coin, Commentary, Compartment, Confessional, Cool, Coupling, Crash, Crate, Cuff, Dabba, Dead-letter, Deed, Dialog(ue), Dispatch, Ditty, Dog, Drawer, Dredging, Driving, Earpiece, Egg, Encase, Enclose, Etui, → **FIGHT**, File, Fist, Fund, Fuse, Fuzz, Gear, Glory, Glove, Go-kart, Grass, Hat, Hay, Hedge, Hive, Honesty, Horse, Hover, Humidor, Hunting, Hutch, Ice, Idiot, Inherce, Inro, Inter, Jewel, Journal, Juke, Junction, Jury, Keister, Kick, Kiosk, Kite, Knevell, Knife, Knowledge, Ladle, Letter, Light, Live, Locker, Lodge, Loge, Loose, Lug, Lunch, Mail, Match, Message, Mill, Mitre, Mocock, Mocuck, Money, Music(al), Nest(ing), Noble art, Noble science, Omnibus, Orgone, Ottoman, Out, Package, Packing, Paddle, Paint, Pandora's, Papeterie, Patch, Pattress, Peepshow, Peg, Pen, Penalty (area), Petara, Pew, Phylactery, Piggybank, Pill, Pillar, Pitara, Pix, Poor, Post, Pounce(t), Powder, Press, Prize fight, Prompt, Protector, Puff, Pugilism, Punnet, Pyxis, Red, Register, Resonance, Ring, Rope-a-dope, Royal, Safe-deposit, Saggar(d), Sagger, Salt, Sand, Savate, Scent, Scrap, Scrine, Seggar, Selection, Sentry, Set-top, Shadow, Shoe, Shooting, Side, Signal, Skinner, Skip(pet), Slipcase, Smudge, Sneeshin-mull, Sneeze, Soap, Solander, Sound, Sound body, → **SPAR**, Spice, Spit, Spring, Squawk, Squeeze, Stock, Strong, Stuffing, Swell, Tabernacle, Tar, Tee, Tefillin, Telephone, Telly, Thai, Tick, Tin, Tinder, Tivo, Tool, Touch, Trunk, Tube, Tuck, TV, Urn, Vanity, Vasculum, Vinaigrette, Voice, Weather, Window, Wine, Witness, Yakhdan

**Boxer(s)** Ali, Amycus, Babyweight, Bantamweight, Bruiser, Bruno, Canine, Carnera, Carpentier, Carthorse, Chinaman, Cooper, Corbett, Crater, Cruiserweight, Darcy, Dempsey, Dog, Eryx, Farr, Featherweight, Flyweight, Foreman, Hamed, Hearns, Heavyweight, Lightweight, Liston, McCoy, Middleweight, Mosquito-weight, Pandora, Patterson, Pollux, Pug, Pugil(ist), Rebellion, Rocky, Shadow, Shorts, Southpaw, Sparrer, Strawweight, Sugar Ray Leonard, Sugar Ray Robinson, Tyson, Welterweight, Wilde

**Boxing-glove** Hurlbat, Muffle, Whirlbat, Whorlbat

**Boy(s)** Altar, Amoretto, Anchor, Apprentice, Ball, Barrow, Beach, Bevin, Blue-eyed, Bovver, Bub(by), Cabin, Callant, Catamite, Champagne, Chiel(d), → **CHILD**, Chokra, Chummy, Cub, Cupid, Dandiprat, Draw, Errand, Galopin, Garçon, Gorsoon, Gossoon, Green Mountain, Groom, Grummet, Ha, Hansel, I say, Jack, Kid, Klonkie, Knave, Knave-bairn, Kwedien, Lackbeard, → **LAD**, Lilywhite, Loblolly, Loon(ie), Message, Minstrel, Nibs, Nipper, Office, Page, Poster, Pot, Prentice, Principal, Putto, Rent, Roaring, Rude, Shaver, Ship's, Son, Spalpeen, Sprig, Stripling, Swain, Tad, Tar, Ted(dy), Tiger, Toxic, Toy, Urchin, Whipping, Wide, → **YOUTH**

▹**Boy** *may indicate* an abbreviated name

**Boycott** Avoid, Ban, Bat, Black, Blacklist, Exclude, Geoff(rey), Hartal, Isolate, Ostracise, Shun, Swadeshi

**Boyfriend** Beau, Date, Fella, Fellow, Squeeze, Steady

**Boyle** Juno

**Bp** Bishop, DD, RR

**Brace(s), Bracing** Accolade, Clamp, Couple, Crosstree, Fortify, Gallace, Gallows, Gallus(es), Gird, Hound, Invigorate, Ozone, Pair, Pr, Rear-arch, Rere-arch, Sea air, Skeg, Spider, Splint, Stage, Steady, Stiffener, Strut, →**SUPPORT**, Suspenders, Tauten, Tense, Thorough, Tone, Tonic, Two(-hander)

**Bracelet** Armil(la), Armillary, Armlet, Bangle, Charm, Cuff, Darbies, Handcuff, Identity, Manacle, Manilla, Wristband

**Brachiopod** Ecardines, Lamp-shell, Spirifer

**Bracken** Brake, Fern, Pteridium, Tara

**Bracket** Ancon, Angle-iron, Bibb, Brace, Cantilever, Console, Corbel, Couple, Cripple, Gusset, Hanger, Lance rest, Misericord(e), Modillion, Mutule, Parenthesis, Potence, Pylon, Rigger, Round, Sconce, Square, Straddle, Strata, →**STRUT**, Trivet, Truss

**Brackish** Stagnant

**Bract** Glume(lla), Hypsophyll, Involucel, Involucre, Job's tears, Leaf, Lemma, Palea, Palet, Phyllary, Spathe

**Brad** Nail, Pin, Rivet, Sprig

**Brae** Hillside

**Brag(gart), Bragging** Basilisco, Birkie, Bluster, Boast, Bobadil, Boister, Bombastic, Braggadocio, Bull, Cockalorum, Crow, Falstaff, Fanfaronade, Gab, Gascon, Hot-air, Loudmouth, Mouth off, Parolles, Puckfist, Puff, Rodomontader, Scaramouch(e), Skite, Slam, Swagger, Thrason, Thrasonic, Tongue-doubtie, Tongue-doughty, Upstart, Vainglorious, Vapour, Vaunt

**Brahma(n)** San(n)yasi(n)

**Braid** A(i)glet, Aiguillette, Enlace, Fishbone, French, Frog, Galloon, Lacet, Pigtail, Plait, Plat, Rickrack, Ricrac, Scrambled eggs, Seaming-lace, Sennet, Sennit, Sinnet, Soutache, Tress, Trim, Twist, Weave

**Braille (system)** Moon

**Brain(box), Brain disease, Brain-power, Brain problem, Brains, Brainstorm, Brainy** Amygdala, Appestat, Bean, Boffin, Bright, Brilliant, Broca's area, Cerebellum, Cerebrum, Contravene, Cortex, Crane, Cranium, Diencephalon, Dura mater, Egghead, Einstein, Encephalon, Epencephalon, Fornix, Genius, Gliosis, Grey matter, Gyrus, Harn(s), Head, Headpiece, Hippocampus, Hydrocephalus, Hypothalamus, Inspiration, Insula, Intellect, Intelligence, IQ, Kuru, Left, Limbic, Loaf, Lobe, Lobule, Mastermind, Mater, Medulla, Medulla oblongata, Metencephalon, Mind, Noddle, Noesis, Nous, Peduncle, Pericranium, Pia mater, Pons, Pontile, Prosencephalon, Quick, Rhinencephalon, Rhombencephalon, Ringleader, Sconce, Sense, Sensorium, Smarty pants, Striatum, Subcortex, Sulcus, Tapagnosia, Tectum, Telencephalon, Thalamencephalon, Thalamus, Upper stor(e)y, Vermis, Vortex, Wetware

▹**Brain(s)** *may indicate* an anagram

**Brainless** Anencephaly, Bimbo, Stupid, Thick

**Brainwash(ing)** Indoctrinate, Menticide, Persuade, Programme, Propaganda

**Brake, Braking** ABS, Adiantum, Aerodynamic, Air, Anchors, Antilock, Bracken, Centrifugal, Copse, Curb, Disc, Dive, Drag, Drum, Estate car, Fern, Fly, Foot, Grove, Hand, Hub, Hydraulic, Nemoral, Overrun, Ratchet, Rein, Rim, Shoe, Shooting, →**SLOW**, Spinney, Sprag, Tara, Thicket, Vacuum, Westinghouse

**Bramble, Brambly** Batology, Blackberry, Boysenberry, Brier, Cloudberry, Rubus, Thorn, Wait-a-bit, Youngberry

**Bran** Cereal, Chesil, Chisel, Oats, Pollard

**Branch(ed), Branches, Branching, Branch office** Affiliate, Antler, Arm, BO, Bough, Chapel, Cladode, Cow, Dendron, Department, Dept, Diverge, Diversify, Diverticulum, Divide, Filiate, Fork, Grain, Jump, Kow, Lateral, Leaf-trace, Limb, Lobe, Lobus, Loop, Lye, Lylum,

Offshoot, Olive, Osier, Patulous, Phylloclade, Prong, Rachilla, Raguly, Ramate, Ramulus, Reis, Rice, Shroud, Side-line, Special, Spray(ey), Sprig, Spur, Stirpes, Tributary, Turning, Turn-off, Twig, Wattle, Whip, Yard

**Branch-rib** Lierne

**Brand(ing)** Broadsword, Buist, Burn, Cauterise, Chop, Class, Dealer, Denounce, Earmark, Ember, Excalibur, Falchion, Faulchin, Faulchion, Flambeau, Givenchy, Home, Idiograph, Ilk, Inust, Iron, Label, Line, → **MARK**, Marque, Name, Neckverse, Own, Power, Sear, Sere, Stigma, Sweard, Sword, Torch, Trade name, Wipe

**Brandish** Bless, Flaunt, Flourish, Hurtle, Waffle, Wampish, Wave

**Brandy** Aguardiente, Applejack, Apricot, Aqua vitae, Armagnac, Ball of fire, Bingo, Calvados, Cape smoke, Cherry bounce, Cognac, Cold without, Dop, Eau de vie, Fine, Fine champagne, Framboise, Grappa, Kirsch, Mampoer, Marc, Mirabelle, Mobbie, Mobby, Nantes, Nantz, Napoleon, Palinka, Peach, Quetsch, Slivovic(a), Slivovitz, Smoke, VSOP

**Bras** Arms

**Brash** Cheeky, Cocky, Flashy, Hollywood, Impudent, Jack-the-lad, Jumped-up, Pushy, Rain, Rash, Uppity

**Brass(y), Brassware** Alpha-beta, Althorn, Benares, Brazen, Bugle, Cheek, Club, Corinthian, Cornet, Corni, Cornopean, Dinanderie, Effrontery, Face, Front, Harsh, High, Horn, Horse, Latten, Lip, Lolly, Loot, Lota(h), Loud, Matrix, → **MONEY**, Moola(h), Oof, Oricalche, Orichalc, Ormolu, Palimpsest, Pyrites, Sass, Snash, Sopranino, Talus, Top, Trombone, Trumpet, Tuba, White, Wood, Yellow metal

**Brassard** Armlet

**Brass hat** Brig

**Brassica** Brussels (sprout), → **CABBAGE**, Colza, Turnip

**Brassière** Gay deceiver

**Brat** Ankle-biter, Bairn, Bantling, Bra(t)chet, Enfant terrible, Gait(t), Gamin, Geit, Get, Git, Gyte, Hellion, Horror, Imp, Lad, Perisher, Terror, Tyke, Urchin

**Braun** Eva

**Bravado, Brave(ry)** Amerind, Apache, Bold, Conan, Confront, Corragio, Courage, Creek, Dare, → **DEFY**, Derring-do, Doughty, Dress, Face, Fearless, Gallant, Game, Gamy, Gutsy, Hardy, Heroism, Hiawatha, Impavid, Indian, Intrepid, → **LION**, Lion-hearted, Lionly, Manful, Manly, → **MEXICAN**, Nannup, → **NORTH AMERICAN**, Plucky, Prow(ess), Russian roulette, Sannup, Skookum, → **SOUTH AMERICAN**, Spunk, Stalwart, Stout, Uncas, Valiant, Valour, Venturesome, Wight, Withstand, Yeoman

**Bravo** Acclaim, B, Bandit, Bully, Desperado, Euge, Murderer, Olé, Shabash, Spadassin, Villain

**Brawl(er)** Affray, Bagarre, Bicker, Brabble, Donnybrook, Dust, Dust-up, Fight, Flite, Flyte, Fracas, Fratch, Fray, Free-for-all, Melee, Prawl, Punch up, Rammy, Roarer, Roughhouse, Row, Ruck, Scold, Scrap, Scuffle, Set-to, Shindig, Slugfest, Spar, Stoush, Tar, Troublesome, Tussle, Wrangle

**Brawn** Beef, Burliness, Headcheese, He-man, Might, Muscle, Power, Rillettes, Sinew

**Bray** Cry, Heehaw, Stamp, Vicar, Whinny

**Braze** Solder

**Brazen** Blatant, Bold, Brash, Brassy, Flagrant, Forward, Impudent, Shameless, Unabashed

**Brazier** Brasero, Fire, Hibachi, Mangal, Scaldino

**Brazil(ian)** Caboclo, Carioca, Cream-nut, Para, Yanomami, Yanomamo

**Breach** Affray, Alienation, Assault, Break, Chasm, Cleft, Coupure, Foul, Gap(e), Great schism, Gulf, Infraction, Redan, Rift, Rupture, Saltus, Schism, Solecism, Solution, Trespass, Violate

**Bread, Bread crumbs** Afikomen, Azym(e), Bagel, Baguette, Bannock, Bap, Barmbrack, Barm cake, Barn brith, Batch, Baton, Black, Bloomer, Brewis, Brioche, Brown, Brownie, Bun, Cash, Chal(l)ah, Chametz, Chapati, Cheat, Ciabatta, Cob, Coburg, Compone, Corn (pone), Corsned, Croissant, Crostini, Croute, Crouton, Crumpet, Crust, Currant, Currency, Damper, Dibs, Dika, Doorstep, Dosh, Dough, Elephant's-foot, Eucharist, Eulogia, Fancy, Flatbread, Focaccia, Fougasse, French (stick), Funds, Garlic, Gluten, Graham, Granary, Grissini, Guarana, Hallah, Hametz, Hometz, Horse, Host, Indian, Injera, Jannock, Johnny-cake, Lavash, Laver, Leavened, Loaf, Long tin, Manchet, Maori, Matzo, Milk loaf, Milk-sop,

→ MONEY, Monkey, Na(a)n, Pain, Panada, Panary, Pane, Paneity, Panettone, Panini, Panko, Paratha, Pay, Petit pain, Pikelet, Pit(t)a, Pone, Poori, Popover, Poppadom, Poultice, Prozymite, Pumpernickel, Puree, Puri, Quick, Raspings, Ravel, Roll, Rooty, Roti, Round, Rusk, Rye, St John's, Sally Lunn, Schnecken, Shewbread, Shive, Simnel, Sippet, Smor(re)brod, Soda, Soft-tommy, Sop, Sourdough, Split tin, Staff of life, Standard, Stollen, Stottie, Sugar, Sweet, Tartine, Tea, Tommy, Tortoise-plant, Twist, Wastel, White, Wholemeal, Wrap, Zakuski, Zwieback

**Breadfruit** Ja(c)k

**Breadth** Amplitude, Expanse, Scope

**Breadwinner** Earner, Pa

**Break, Breakaway, Break-down, Break down, Breaker, Break-in, Break-up, Break up, Broken** Adjourn, Analyse, Apn(o)ea, Aposiopesis, Bait, Biodegrade, Breach, Bread, Breather, Burst, Bust, Caesura, Caesure, Cantle, Career, Cark, Cesure, Chance, Chinaman, Chip, Cleave, Coffee, Comb, Comma, Commercial, Comminute, Compost, Compurgatory, Conk, Contravene, Crack, Crock, Crumble, Dash, Deave, Debacle, Decompose, Deeve, Degrade, Demob, Destroy, Detach, Diaresis, Diffract, Disband, Disintegrate, Disperse, Disrupt, Dissect, Duvet day, Elevenses, Entracte, Erumpent, Erupt, Exeat, Fast, Fault, Flaw, Four, → FRACTURE, Fragment, Fritter, Frush, Gaffe, Gap, Gap year, Give, Greenstick, Haematolysis, Half-term, Half-time, Harm, Hernia, Hiatus, Holiday, Hydrolyse, Infringe, Interim, Interlude, Intermission, Interrupt, Interspace, → INTERVAL, Irrupt, Kark, Knap, Knickpoint, Lacuna, Lapse, Layover, Leave, Lull, Lysis, Moratorium, Natural, Nickpoint, Nooner, Outage, Parse, Part, Pause, Phreak, Pick-axe, Playtime, Poach, Polarise, Price, Reave, Recess, Recrudescent, Relief, Rend, Resolve, Resorption, Respite, Rest, Rift, Rise, Ruin, Rupture, Sabbatical, Saltus, Schism(a), Secede, Service, Shatter, Shear, Shiver, Smash, Smokeho, Smoko, Snap, Splinter, Split, Start, Stave, Stop, Stop-over, Stove, Sunder, Take five, Take ten, Tame, Tea-ho, Tear, Tenderise, Time-out, Torn, Transgress, Truce, Twist, Vacation, Violate, Watergate, Weekend

**Breakable** Brittle, Delicate, Fissile, Fragile, Frail, Friable

**Breakdown** Abruption, Analyse, Autolysis, Cataclasm, Collapse, Conk, Crack-up, Glitch, Glycolosis, Glycolysis, Haematolysis, Histolysis, Hydrolysis, Lyse, Lysis, Malfunction, Nervous, Ruination

**Breaker** Billow, Circuit, Comber, Ice, Roller, Smasher, Surf

**Breakfast** B, Brunch, Chota-hazri, Continental, Deskfast, Disjune, English, Kipper, Petit déjeuner, Power, Wedding

**Breakneck** Headlong

**Breakthrough** Discovery, Quantum leap

**Breakwater** Groyne, Jetty, Mole, Pier, Tetrapod

**Bream** Fish, Porgy, Sar(gus), Sea, Silver, Tai, White

**Breast(s), Breastbone, Breastwork** Bazuma, Boob, Bosom, Brave, Brisket, Bristols, Bust, Chimney, Clean, Counter, Diddy, Duddy, Dug, Falsies, Garbonza, Gazunga, Heart-spoon, Jubbies, Jugs, Knockers, Norg, Nork, Pigeon, Rampart, Redan, Sangar, Stem, Sternum, Stroke, Sungar, Supreme, Tit, Xiphisternum

**Breastplate** Armour, Byrnie, Curat, Curiet, Pectoral, Plastron, Rational, Rest, Shield, Thorax, Xiphiplastron

**Breath(e), Breathing, Breather** Aerobe, Air-sac, Apneusis, Aqualung, Aspirate, Bated, Blow, Branchia, Buteyko method, Caesural, Cheyne-Stokes, Circular, Cypress-knee, Eupnoea, Exhalation, Expiration, Flatus, Gasp, Gill, H, Halitosis, Hauriant, Haurient, Hobday, Hypernoea, Hyperventilation, Hypopnoea, Inhale, Inspiration, Insufflation, Interval, Knee, Lenticellate, Lung, Nares, Nostril, Orthopnoea, Oxygenator, Pant, Pause, Plosion, Pneuma, Prana, Pulmo, Rale, Respire, Respite, Rest, Rhonchus, Rough, Scuba, Sigh, Smooth, Sniff, Snore, Snorkel, Snortmast, Snotter, Snuffle, Souffle, Spiracle, Spirit, Spiritus, Stertor, Stridor, Suspire, Tachypnoea, Trachea, Vent, Wheeze, Whiff, Whift, Whisper, Whist, Wind, Windpipe

**Breathalyser** Windbag

**Breathless(ness)** Anhelation, Apnoea, Asthma, Dyspnoea, Emphysema, Orthopnoea, Puffed-out, Purfled, Tachypnoea, Wheezing

**Breathtaking** Amazing, Asphyxia, Awesome, Superb, Throttling

**Breech(es)** Bible, Buckskin, Chaps, Chausses, Flog, Galligaskins, Hose, Jodhpurs, Kneecords, Knickerbockers, Pantaloons, Petticoat, Plushes, Riding, Smallclothes, Smalls, Trews, Trouse(rs), Trunk hose, Trusses

**Breed(er), Breeding(-place)** Bear, Beget, Blood, Cleck, Digoneutic, Endogamous, Engender, Engend(r)ure, Eugenics, Fancier, Fast, Generation, Gentilesse, Gentility, Gentrice, Hetero, Hotbed, In-and-in, Line, Lineage, → MANNERS, Origin, Panmixia, Procreate, Propagate, Pullulate, Race, Raise, Rear, Savoir vivre, Seminary, Sire, Species, Stirpiculture, Stock, Strain, Stud, Telegony, Thremmatology, Tribe, Voltinism

**Breeze, Breezy** Air, Breath, Brisk, Cakewalk, Catspaw, Chipper, Crosswind, Doctor, Draught, Fresh, Gentle, Gust, Land, Light, Mackerel, Moderate, Piece of cake, Pushover, Sea, Slant, Sniffler, Snifter, Strong, Tiff, Zephyr

**Brethren** Bohemian, Close, Darbyite, Elder, Exclusive, Herrnhuter, Ignorantine, Kin, Open, Plymouth, Trinity

**Breton** Armoric, Brezonek

**Breve** Minim, Note, O

**Breviary** Porteous, Portesse

▸**Brevity** *see* BRIEF(S)

**Brew(ery), Brewer, Brewing** Afoot, Ale, Billycan, Boutique, Brose, Browst, Bummock, → CONCOCT, Contrive, Dictionary, Distillery, Elixir, Ferment, Infusion, Liquor, Malt, Oast house, Percolate, Perk, Potion, Scald, Steep, Teapot, Witches', Yeast, Yill, Zymurgy

**Briar** Bramble, Canker, Lawyer

**Bribe(ry)** Backhander, Barratry, Barretry, Bonus, Boodle, Bung, Buy, Carrot, Dash, Douceur, Embracery, Get at, Gift, Graft, Grease, Hamper, Hush-money, Insult, Kickback, Lubricate, Oil, Palm, Palm-grease, Palm-oil, Payola, Schmear, Slush, Soap, Sop, Square, Straightener, Suborn, Sweeten(er), Tamper, Tempt, Tenderloin, Vail, Vales

**Bric-a-brac** Bibelot, Curio, Rattle-trap, Smytrie, Tatt, Victoriana, Virtu

**Brick(s), Brickwork** Adobe, Air, Bat, Bath, Bonder, Bondstone, Boob, Breeze(-block), Bristol, Bullnose, Bur(r), Clanger, Clay, Clinker, Closer, Course, Dutch clinker, Fire, Fletton, Gaffe, Gault, Gold, Good egg, Hard stocks, Header, Ingot, Klinker, Lateritious, Lego®, Malm, Nog(ging), Opus latericium, Red, Rubber, Rubble, Soldier, Spawn, Sport, Stalwart, Stretcher, Terra-cotta, Testaceous, Tile, Trojan, Trump

**Brickbat** Flak, Missile

**Bricklayer** Churchill

**Bride(s)** Bartered, Danaides, Ellen, Hen, Mail-order, Newlywed, Spouse, War, Wife, Ximena

**Bridesmaid** Paranymph

**Bridge(head), Bridge player** Acol, Air, Al Sirat, Aqueduct, Assess, Auction, Australian, Avignon, Ba(u)ck, Bailey, Balance, Barre, Bascule, Bestride, Bifrost, Biritch, Board, Bridle-chord, Brig, Brooklyn, Cable-stayed, Cantilever, Capo, Capodastro, Capotasto, Catwalk, Chevalet, Chicago, Chicane, Clapper, Clifton, Contract, Counterpoise, Cross, Cut-throat, Deck, Declarer, Drawbridge, Duplicate, Floating, Flying, Flyover, Foot, Forth, Four-deal, Gangplank, Gangway, Gantry, Girder, Golden Gate, Hog's back, Humber, Humpback, Humpbacked, Ice, Irish, Jigger, Land, Lattice, Leaf, Lifting, Ligger, Link, London, Menai, Millau, Millennium, Murray, Nasion, Overpass, Pivot, Plafond, Ponceau, Pons, Ponticello, Pontifice, Pont levis, Pontoon, Raft, Rainbow, Rialto, Road, Rubber, Severn, Sighs, Sinvat, Skew, Snow, → SPAN, Spanner, Stamford, Straddle, Suspension, Swing, Tay, Temper, Tête-de-pont, Through, Tide over, Toll, Tower, Transporter, Traversing, Trestle, Truss, Turn, Vertical lift, Viaduct, Vint, Waterloo, Weigh, Wheatstone, Wire

**Bridge pair** EW, NS, SN, WE

**Bridge protector** Ice-apron

**Bridge system** Acol

**Bridie** Onion

**Bridle** Bit, Branks, Bridoon, Bristle, Browband, Crownpiece, Curb, Double, Hackamore, Halter, Headstall, Musrol, Noseband, Pelham, Rein, Scold's

**Bridle path** Orbit, Track

**Brief(s), Briefing, Briefly, Brevity** Acquaint, Advocate, Aphoristic, Attorney, Awhile,

Barristerial, Bluette, Brachyology, Breviate, Cameo, Cape, Compact, → CONCISE, Conspectus, Counsel, Crisp, Curt, Dossier, Enlighten, Ephemeral, Fill in, Fleeting, In a word, Inform, Instruct, King's, Laconic, Lawyer, Legal eagle, Momentary, Nearly, Nutshell, Pants, Papal, Pennorth, Pithy, Precise, Prime, Scant, → SHORT(EN), Short-term, Short-winded, Sitrep, Skimpy, Sparse, Succinct, Summing, Tanga, Terse, Transient, Undershorts, Undies, Update, Watching

**Brig** Br, Hermaphrodite, Jail, Nancy Bell, → SHIP, Snow

**Brigade** Anchor Boys, Boys', Corps, Fire, Fur, Girls', Green-ink, International, Naval, Red, Troop

**Brigand** Bandit, Bandolero, Cateran, Haidu(c)k, Heiduc, Heyduck, Klepht, Pillager, Pirate, → ROBBER, Rob Roy, Trailbaston

**Bright(ness), Brighten** Afterglow, Alert, Ashine, Barnaby, Bertha, Brainbox, Brainy, Breezy, Brilliant, Brisk, Cheery, Chiarezza, Chipper, Clara, Cla(i)re, Clear, Clever, Cuthbert, Danio, Day-glo, Effulgent, Eileen, Elaine, Ellie, Facula, Fair, Floodlit, Florid, Garish, Gay, Glad, Glary, Glow, Helen, Hono(u)r, Hubert, Illuminate, Light, Lit, Loud, Lucent, Lucid, Luculent, Luminous, Lurid, Lustre, Net(t), Nit, Nitid, Perk up, Radiant, Roarie, Rorie, Ro(a)ry, Rosy, Ruddy, Scintillating, Sematic, Sharp, Sheeny, Sheer, Shere, Skyre, Smart, Spark(y), Splendour, Starry, Stilb, Sunlit, Sunny, Vive, Vivid, White, Zara

**Bright spot** Facula

**Brilliant, Brilliance** Ace, Aine, Blaze, Brainy, Bravura, Bright, Def, Eclat, Effulgent, Eurian, Fantastic, Five-star, Flaming, Flashy, Galaxy, Gay, Gemmy, Genius, Gifted, Glare, Glitter, Glossy, High flyer, Humdinger, Inspired, Irradiance, Lambent, Leam, Lucent, Lustre, Magnificent, Masterstroke, Mega-, Meteoric, Nitid, Pear, → RADIANT, Refulgent, Resplendent, Shiny, Spangle, Splendid, Splendour, Star, Superb, Virtuoso, → VIVID, Water

**Brim(ming)** Awash, Edge, Lip, Rim, Snap, Ugly

**Brimstone** Hellfire, S, Sulphur

**Brindisi** Skolion, Toast

**Brindled** Piebald, Tabby, Tawny

**Brine** Muriatic, Ozone, Pickle, Saline, Salt

**Bring** Afferent, Bear, Carry, Cause, Conduct, Convey, Deploy, Earn, Evoke, Fet, Fetch, Foist, Get, Hatch, Induce, Land, Precipitate, Produce, Wreak, Yield

**Bring up** Breed, Educate, Exhume, Foster, Nurture, Raise, → REAR

**Brink** → EDGE, Eve, Lip, Rim, Shore, → VERGE

**Brio** Elan, Panache

**Brisk(ly), Briskness** Abrupt, Active, Alacrity, Alert, Allegro, Breezy, Busy, Cant, Chipper, Con moto, Crank, Crisp, Crouse, Fresh, Gaillard, Galliard, Jaunty, Kedge, Kedgy, Kidge, Lively, Nippy, Peart, Perk, Pert, Rattling, Roaring, Scherzo, Sharp, Skelp, Smacking, Smart, Snappy, Spanking, Spirited, Sprightly, Vivace, Yare, Zippy

**Bristle(s), Bristling, Bristly** Aciculum, Arista, Awn, Barb, Beard, Bewhiskered, Birse, Bridle, Campodeiform, Chaeta, En brosse, Flurry, Fraught, Frenulum, Glochidium, Gooseflesh, Hackles, Hair, Hérissé, Hispid, Horrent, Horripilation, Nereid, Polychaete, Seta, Setose, Striga, Strigose, Stubble, Styloid, Vibraculum, Villus, Whisker

**Bristle-tail** Campodea

**Brit(ish), Briton(s)** All-red, Anglo, Herring, Iceni, Insular, Isles, Kipper, Limey, Pict, Pom, Rooinek, Rosbif, Saxon, Silt, Silurian, UK

**Britain** Alban(y), Albion, GB, Old Dart

**Britannia (metal)** Tutania

**Brittany** Armorica

**Brittle** Bruckle, Crackly, Crimp, Crisp, Delicate, Edgy, → FRAGILE, Frangible, Froughy, Frowy, Frush, Hot-short, Redsear, Red-share, Red-shire, Redshort, Shivery, Spall, Spalt

▹**Brittle** *may indicate* an anagram

**Broach** Approach, Open, Raise, Spit, Suggest, Tap, Widen

**Broad(ly)** Beamy, Catholic, Cheesy, Crumpet, Dame, Doll, Doxy, Drab, Eclectic, Gaping, General, Generic, Hippy, Largo, Latitudinous, Liberal, Loose, Outspoken, Ovate, Pro, Roomy, Spatulate, Squat, Tart, Thick, Tolerant, Wide, Woman

**Broadband** On line

**Broad-beaked** Latirostrate

**Broadcast(er), Broadcasting** Ad(vertise), Air, Announce, Beam, Blaze, Breaker, Broadband, CB, Diffuse, Disclose, Disperse, Disseminate, DJ, Downlink, Emission, Ham, IBA, Joyce, Live, Long wave, Monophonic, Multicast, Narrowband, Network, Newscast, OB, On, Outside, Pirate, Programme, Promulgate, Public address, Put out, Radiate, Radio, Radio ham, Recording, Reith, Relay, Road show, RTE, Run, Satellite, → **SCATTER**, Scattershot, Screen(ed), SECAM, Seed, Send, Shortwave, Simulcast, Sky, Sow, Sperse, Sportscast, Spread, Sprinkle, Stereophonic, Talk radio, Telebridge, Telethon, Tokyo Rose, Transmission, Veejay, Vent, Ventilate, Wavelength, Wireless

**Broadminded** Tolerant

**Broad-nosed** Platyrrhine

**Broadsheet** Newspaper

**Broadside** Barrage, Criticism, Harangue, Salvo, Tire

**Broadway** Boulevard, Esplanade, Great White Way, Motorway

**Brocade** Arrasene, Baldachin, Baldaquin, Baudekin, Bawdkin, Kincob, Zari

**Brochette** Skewer

**Brochure** Booklet, Catalogue, Leaflet, Pamphlet, Programme, Prospectus, Throwaway, Tract, Travelogue

**Brogue** Accent, → **SHOE**

**Broke(n)** Badly off, Bankrupt, Boracic, Bust(ed), Crocked, Duff, Dysfunctional, Evans, Fragmentary, Fritz, Impoverished, Insolvent, Kaput, On the rocks, Penniless, Puckeroo, Shattered, Skint, Stony, Stove, Strapped

▷**Broken** *may indicate* an anagram

**Broken off** Prerupt

**Broker** Agent, Banian, Banyan, Discount, Go-between, Government, Insurer, Jobber, Kerbstone, Marriage, Mediator, → **MERCHANT**, Power, Shadchan, Uncle

**Bromide** Halide, Haloid, Platitude, Truism

**Bromine** Br

**Bronchitis, Bronchitic** Chesty, Husk

**Bronte(s)** Bell, Cyclops

**Brontosaurus** Apatosaurus

**Bronze(d), Bronze age** Aeneous, Aluminium, Bell, Bras(s), Brown, Corinthian, Eugubine, Gunmetal, Hallstatt(ian), Helladic, Kamakura, Manganese, Minoan, Mycenean, Ormolu, Phosphor, Schillerspar, Sextans, Suntanned, Talos, Tan, Third, Torso

**Brooch** Breastpin, Cameo, Clasp, Fibula, Luckenbooth, Ouch, Owche, Pin, Plaque, Preen, Prop, Spang, Sunburst

**Brood(y)** Clecking, Clock, Clucky, Clutch, Cogitate, Contemplate, Cour, Cover, Covey, Dwell (on), Eyas, Eye, Eyrie, Hatch, Hover, Incubate, Introspect, Kindle, Litter, Meditate, Mill, Mope, Mull, Nest, Nid, Nyas, Perch, Pet, → **PONDER**, Repine, Roost, Sit, Spawn, Sulk, Team

**Brook** Abide, Babbling, Becher's, Beck, Branch, Burn, Countenance, Creek, Endure, Ghyll, Gill, Kerith, Kill, Pirl, Purl, Rill(et), River, Rivulet, Runlet, Runnel, Springlet, Stand, Stomach, Stream, Suffer, Thole, Tolerate, Wear

**Brooklime** Water purple

**Broom** Besom, Brush, Butcher's, Cow, Cytisus, Genista, Gorse, Greenweed, Hog, Knee-holly, Kow, New, Orobranche, Plantagenet, Retama, Spanish, Spart, Sweeper, Whisk

**Brose** Atholl, Pease

**Broth** Bouillon, Bree, Brew(is), Court bouillon, Cullis, Dashi, Gruel, Kail, Kale, Muslin-kale, Pot liquor, Pottage, Ramen, Scotch, Skilly, → **SOUP**, Stock

**Brothel** Bagnio, Bawdy-house, Bordel(lo), Call house, Cathouse, Corinth, Crib, Den, Flash-house, Honkytonk, Hothouse, Ken, Kip, Knocking shop, Leaping-house, Red-light, Seraglio, Sporting house, Stew, Vaulting-house

**Brother(s), Brotherhood** Ally, Bhai, Billie, Billy, Blood, Boet, Brer, Brethren, Bro, Bud, Comrade, Confraternity, Confrerie, Félibre, Felibrige, Fellow, Fra, Freemason, Grimm, Guild, Lay, Marx, → **MONK**, Moose, My, Plymouth, Pre-Raphaelite, Sib(ling), Theatine, Trappist, Worker

**Brought (back)** Redux

**Brow** Beaten Eye, Crest, Forehead, Glabella, High, Knitted, Ridge, Sinciput, Superciliary, Tump-line
**Browbeat(en)** Badger, Bully, Butt, Cow, Hangdog, Hector, Nut
**Brown(ed)** Abram, Adust, Amber, Apricate, Auburn, Au gratin, Bay, Biscuit, Bisque, Bister, Bistre, Bole, Br, Braise, Brindle, Bronzed, Brunette, Bruno, Burnet, Burnt umber, Camel, Capability, Caramel, Caromel, Centennial, Chamois, Chocolate, Cinnamon, Cocoa, Cook, Coromandel, Drab, Dun, Duncan, Fallow, Fawn, Filemot, Fulvous, Fusc(ous), Grill, Hazel, Infuscate, Ivor, John, Khaki, Liver, March, Meadow, Mocha, Mousy, Mushroom, Nut, Oatmeal, Ochre, Olive, Oxblood, Philamot, Pygmalion, Rufous, Rugbeian, Russet, Rust, Sallow, Sand, Scorch, Seal, Sepia, Sienna, Snuff, Soare, Sore, Sorrel, Spadiceous, Sunburnt, Tan, Taupe, Tawny, Tenné, Tenny, Terracotta, Testaceous, Toast, Tom, Umber, Vandyke, Wallflower, Walnut, Wholemeal, Windsor
**Browne** Sam
**Brownian movement** Agitation, Pedesis
**Brownie** Dobbie, Dobby, Dobie, Goblin, Hob, Kobold, Leprechaun, Nis(se), Rosebud, Sprite
**Browse(r), Browsing** Eland, Giraffe, Gopher, Graze, Mouch, Netscape®, Pasture, Read, Scan, Stall-read, Surf, Tapir, Window-shopper
**Bruce** Robert
**Bruise** Black eye, Clour, Contund, Contuse, Crush, Damage, Ding, Ecchymosis, Frush, Golp(e), Haematoma, Hurt, Intuse, Livedo, Lividity, Mark, Mouse, Pound, Purpure, Rainbow, Shiner, Ston(n), Stun, Surbate, Vibex
**Brummagem** Tatty
**Brunette** Dark, Latin
**Brush (off), Brushed, Brushwood** Bavin, Boot, Bottle, Brake, Broom, Carbon, Caudate, Chaparral, Clash, Clothes, Dandy, Dismiss, Dust, Encounter, Fan, Filbert, Filecard, Firth, Fitch, Flesh, Foxtail, Frith, Grainer, Hag, Hagg, Hair, Hair-pencil, Hog, Kindling, Kiss, Liner, Lip, Loofa(h), Mop, Ovenwood, Paint, Pallet, Pig, Pope's head, Pun in, Putois, Rebuff, Rice, Rigger, Sable, Scrap, Scratch, Scrub, Scuff, Shaving, Shoe, Shrug(-off), Skim, Skirmish, Spat, Striper, Sweep, Tail, Tar, Thicket, Tooth, Touch, Undergrowth, Whisk, Wipe, Wire
**Brush-shaped** Penicillate
**Brusque** Abrupt, Blunt, Brief, Curt, Downright, Gruff, Offhand, Pithy, Short
**Brussels** Carpet, Lace
**Brutal(ity), Brute** Animal, Atrocity, Barbaric, Beast, Bestial, Bête, Caesar, Caliban, Cruel, Down and dirty, Gorilla, Hun, Iguanodon, Inhuman, Nazi, Nero, Ostrogoth, Pitiless, Quagga, Rambo, Rottweiler, Roughshod, Ruffian, Stupid, Thresher-whale, Thug, Torture, Yahoo
**Brutus** Wig
**Bryophyte** Moss, Musci, Tree-moss
**Bubble(s), Bubbly** Aeration, Air-bell, Air-lock, Air pocket, Barmy, Bead(ed), Bell, Bleb, Blister, Boil, Bright, Buller, Cavitate, Champagne, Champers, Cissing, Ebullition, Effervesce, Embolus, Enthuse, Espumoso, Fizz, Foam, → **FROTH**, Gassy, Globule, Gloop, Gurgle, Head, Iridescent, Magnetic, Magnum, Mantle, Mississippi, Moët, Perrier, Popple, Rale, Reputation, Roundel, Rowndell, Seed, Seethe, Simmer, Soap, South Sea, Vesicle, Widow
**Bubble and squeak** Colcannon
**Buccaneer** Corsair, Dampier, Drake, Freebooter, Morgan, Picaroon, Pirate
**Buck (up)** Bongo, Brace, Cheer, Dandy, Deer, Dollar, Elate, Encheer, Fast, Hart, Jerk, Leash, Male, Ourebi, Pitch, Pricket, Ram, Rusa, Sore, Sorel(l), Sorrel, Spade, Spay(a)d, → **STAG**, Staggard, Stud, Water, Wheel
**Buckaroo** Cowboy, Cowpoke
**Bucket(s)** Bail, Bale, Clamshell, Dipper, Fire, Ice, Jacob's ladder, Kibble, Ladle, Noria, Pail, Pelt, Piggin, Rain, Rust, Scuttle, Situla, Slop, Spittoon, Stoop(e), Stope, Stoup, Tub
**Buckeye** Ohio
**Buckle** Artois, Bend, Clasp, Contort, Crumple, Deform, Dent, Distort, Fasten, Give, Warp
▹**Buckle** *may indicate* an anagram
**Buckle-beggar** Patrico
**Buckler** Ancile, Rondache, → **SHIELD**, Targe
▹**Bucks** *may indicate* an anagram

**Buck's fizz** Mimosa
**Buckshee** Free
**Buckthorn** Cascara, Rhineberry, Wahoo
**Buckwheat** Brank, Polygonium, Sarrasin, Sarrazin
**Bucolic** Aeglogue, Eglogue, Idyllic, Pastoral, Rural, Rustic
**Bud(ding), Buddy** Botoné, Bottony, Bulbil, Burgeon, Cacotopia, Caper, Clove, Cobber, Deb, Eye, Gem(ma), Germinate, Hibernaculum, Holly, Knop, Knosp, Knot, Nascent, Pal, Scion, Serial, Shoot, Sprout, Statoblast, Taste, Turion, Would-be
**Buddha, Buddhism, Buddhist** Abhidhamma, Ahimsa, Amitabha, Anata, Anatta, Anicca, Arhat, Asoka, Bardo, Bodhisattva, Dalai Lama, Dukkha, Esoteric, Foism, Gautama, Hinayana, Jain, Jataka, Jodo, Kagyu, Mahatma, Mahayana, Maitreya, Maya, Nichiren, Pali, Pitaka, Pure Land, Rinzai, Ryobu, Sakya-muni, Sangha, Satori, Shinto, Siddhartha Gautama, Sila, Sima, Soka Gakkai, Soto, Sutra, Tantric, Theravada, Tripitaka, Triratna, Vajrayana, Zen(o)
**Budge** Dislodge, Jee, Move, Shift, Stir, Submit
**Budgerigar** Shell parrakeet, Shell parrot
**Budget(ary)** Allocation, Allot, Cheap, Cut-price, Estimate, Fiscal, Operating, Plan, Programme, Rudder, Save, Shoestring
**Buff** Altogether, Beige, Birthday suit, Blind man's, Cineaste, Cognoscenti, Eatanswill, Expert, Fan, Fawn, Ham, Maven, Mavin, Nankeen, Natural, Nude, Nut, Polish, → RUB, Streak
**Buffalo** African, Anoa, Arna, Asiatic, Bison, Bonasus, Bugle, Cap, Cape, Carabao, Indian, Obstinacy, Ox, Perplex, Takin, Tamarao, Tamarau, Timarau, Water, Zamouse
**Buffer** Bootblack, Cofferdam, Cushion, Cutwater, Fender, Sleek-stone
**Buffet** Bang, Blow, Box, Carvery, Counter, Cuff, Finger-food, Fork luncheon, Fork-supper, Hit, Lam, Maltreat, Meal, Perpendicular, Running, Shove, Sideboard, Smorgasborg, Strike, Strook(e), Thwack
**Buffoon(ery)** Antic, Clown, Comedian, Droll, Fool, Goliard, Harlequin, Horseplay, Iniquity, Jack pudding, Japer, Jester, Mime(r), Mome, Mountebank, Mummer, Nutter, Oaf, Pantagruel, Pantaloon(ery), Pickle-herring, Pierrot, Punchinello, Scaramouch, Schmoe, Scogan, Scoggin, Scurril(e), Slouch, Tomfool, Vice, Wag, Zany
**Bug(s)** Ambush, Annoy, Anoplura, Antagonise, Arthropod, Assassin, Bacteria, Bedevil, Beetle, Berry, Bishop's mitre, Bunny, Cabbage, Capsid, Chinch, Cicada, Cimex, Coccidae, Cockchafer, Coffee, Corixid, Creepy-crawly, Croton, Damsel, Debris, Defect, Demon, Dictograph®, Eavesdrop, E-coli, Entomology, Error, Exasperate, Flea, Gastroenteritis, Germ, Get at, Gold, Gremlin, Ground, Harlequin, Harvest, Hassle, Hemiptera, → INSECT, Irritate, Jitter, June, Kissing, Lace, Lightning, Listeria, Maori, May, Mealy, Micrococcus, Microphone, Midge, Mike, Milkweed, Millennium, Mite, Nark, Nettle, Peeve, Pest(er), Pill, Rankle, Reduviid, Rhododendron, Rile, Salmonella, Shield, Skeeter, Sow, Squash, Tap, Termite, Vex, Virus, Water-measurer, Weevil, Wheel, Wiretap
**Bugbear** Anathema, Bargest, Bête noire, Bogey, Bogle, Bogy, Eten, Ettin, Poker, Rawhead
**Buggy** Baby, Beach, Car, Cart, Inside-car, Pushchair, Shay, Tipcart, Trap
**Bughouse** Fleapit, Loco
**Bugle, Bugle call** Boots and saddles, Chamade, Clarion, Cornet, Flugelhorn, Hallali, Kent, Keyed, Last post, Ox, Reveille, Taps, → TRUMPET, Urus
**Build (up), Building(s), Building site, Build-up** Abbey, Accrue, Aggrade, Anabolism, Ar(a)eostyle, Assemble, Backlog, Barn, Basilica, Bathhouse, Bhavan, Big, Boathouse, Brick-laying, Bricks and mortar, Capitol, Chapterhouse, Cob, Colosseum, Commons, Construction, Containment, Cookhouse, Corncrib, Cot, → CREATE, Cruck, Curia, Days' house, Develop, Dipteros, Dome, Draft, Drystone, Duplex, Ectomorph, Edifice, Edify, Egg box, Embassy, Endomorph, Erect, Exchange, Fabric, Fleapit, Folly, Gain, Gatehouse, Gazebo, Granary, Guardhouse, Guildhall, Hangar, Heapstead, High-rise, Hotel, Hut, Infill, Insula, Kaaba, Ken, Linhay, Listed, Lodge, Low-rise, Lyceum, Malting, Mansion, Mesomorph, Minaret, Monopteron, Mosque, Motel, Mould, Observatory, Odeon, Odeum, Outhouse, Palace, Palazzo, Pataka, Pavilion, Pentagon, Pentastyle, Phalanstery, Phalanx, Physique, Pile, Planetarium, Plaque, Portakabin®, Post Office, Premises, Proliferation, Prytaneum, Quonset®, Raise, Rectory, Ribbon, Rondavel, Rotunda, Shard, Shippen, Skyscraper,

Somatotype, Squat, Stance, Statehouse, Stature, Stockpile, Structure, Summerhouse, Suspension, Synthesis, System, Systyle, Tectonic, Telecottage, Temple, Tenement, Terminal, Terrapin®, Tholus, Toolshed, Tower, Tower block, Town hall, Triplex®, Whata, Wheelhouse

**Builder** Bob, Body, Brick(layer), Brickie, Cheops, Constructor, Cowboy, Developer, Engineer, Entrepreneur, Mason, Millwright, Scaffolder, Spiderman, Stonemason, Waller

▷**Building** *may indicate* an anagram

**Built-up** Urban

**Bulb** Camas(h), Camass, Chive, Cive, Corm, Flash, Garlic, Globe, Halogen, Lamp, Light, Olfactory, Pearl, Rupert's drop, Scallion, Set, Shallot, Squill

**Bulgaria** BG

**Bulge, Bulging** Astrut, Bag, Bias, Biconvex, Bug, Bulbous, Bunchy, Chockfull, Cockle, Distend, Entasis, Expand, Exsert, Hump, Inion, Node, Prolate, Protrude, Protuberant, Relievo, Rotund, Shoulder, Strout, Strut, → **SWELL**, Torose, Tumid

**Bulimia** Hyperphagia

**Bulk(y)** Aggregate, Ample, Big, Body, Bouk, Coerce, Corpulent, Density, Domineer, Eche, Edict, Eke, Extent, Gross, Hull, Immensity, Lofty, Mass(ive), Obese, Peak, Pester, Preponderance, Roughage, Scalar, → **SIZE**, Stout, Threaten, Vol(ume), Voluminous, Weight

**Bulkhead** Collision

**Bull(s), Bullock, Bully(ing)** Abuser, Anoa, Apis, Bakha, Beef, Blarney, Bludgeon, Bluster, Bouncer, Bovine, Brag, Brave, Browbeat, Buchis, Bucko, Centre, Cuttle, Despot, Domineer, Dragoon, Drawcansir, Encierro, Englishman, Eretrian, Fancyman, Farnese, Flashman, Flatter, Friesian, Gold, Gosh, Hapi, Harass, Harridan, Hawcubite, Haze(r), Hector, Hibernicism, Hogwash, Hoodlum, Huff, Intimidate, Investor, Iricism, Irish(ism), John, Killcow, Lambast, Maltreat, Menace, Merwer, Mick(e)(y), Mistake, Mithraism, Mohock, Nandi, Neat, Oppressor, Ox, Pamplona, Papal, Pennalism, Pick on, Piker, Pistol, Placet, Poler, Pussy-whip, Railroad, Rhodian, Roarer, Rot, Ruffian, Sitting, Souteneur, Spit and polish, Stag, Stale, Strong-arm, Swash-buckler, Taradiddle, Taurine, Taurus, Threaten, Toitoi, Tommy-rot, Torment, Tosh, Trash, Tripe, Twaddle, Tyran(ne), Tyrannise, Tyrant, Unigenitus, Victimise, Winged, Zo(bo)

**Bulldog** British, Marshal, Tenacious

**Bulldoze(r)** Angledozer, Coerce, Earthmover, Flatten, Leveller, Overturn, Raze

**Bullet(s)** Ammo, Balata, Ball, Baton round, Biscayan, Blank, Dumdum, Fusillade, Lead towel, Magazine, Magic, Minié, Minié ball, Missile, Pellet, Percussion, Plastic, Round, Rubber, Shot, Slug, Soft-nosed, Tracer

**Bulletin** All points, Memo, Message, Newscast, Newsflash, Newsletter, News sheet, Noticeboard, Report, Summary, Update

**Bulletproof** Flakjacket, Kevlar

**Bull-fight(er), Bull-fighting** Banderillero, Banderillo, Capework, Corrida, Cuadrilla, Encierro, Escamillo, Faena, Mano a mano, Matador, Picador, Rejoneador, Tauromachy, Toreador, Torero

**Bullfinch** Bellowing, Monk

**Bull-head** Cottoid, Father-lasher, Pogge, Sea-poacher

**Bull-rider** Europa

**Bull-roarer** Rhombos, Tu(r)ndun

**Bull's eye** Carton, Focus, Gold, Humbug, Prick, Target

**Bullshit** BS

▶**Bully** *see* **BULL(S)**

**Bulrush** Pandanaceous, Raupo, Reed, Reed-mace, Tule

**Bulwark** Bastion, Defence, Rampart, Resistor

**Bum** Ass, Beach, Beg, Beggar, Cadge, Deadbeat, Prat, Scrounge, Sponge, Thumb, Tramp, Vagabond

**Bumble, Bumbling** Beadle, Bedel(l), Inept

▷**Bumble** *may indicate* an anagram

**Bumboat woman** Buttercup

**Bumf** Spam

**Bump(er), Bumps, Bumpy** Barge, Big, Blow, Bouncer, Bradyseism, Bucket, Bustle,

Cannon, Clour, Collide, Dodgem, Dunch, Encephalocele, Fender, Goose, Hillock, Immense, Impact, Inian, Inion, Jo(u)le, Joll, Jolt, Jostle, Jounce, Jowl, Keltie, Kelty, Knar, Knock, Large, Mamilla, Mogul, Nudge, Organ, Overrider®, Phrenology, Ratchet, Reveille, Rouse, Speed, Supernaculum, Thump, Twitter, Uneven

**Bumph** Loo-roll

**Bumpkin** Bucolic, Bushwhacker, Clodhopper, Hawbuck, Hayseed, Hick, Jock, Lout, Oaf, Peasant, Put(t), Rube, Rustic, Yokel, Zany

**Bumptious** Arrogant, Brash, Cocky, Crass, Randie, Randy, Uppity

**Bun** Barmbrack, Bath, Black, Chelsea, Chignon, Chou, Cookie, Currant, Devonshire split, Hot-cross, Huffkin, Mosbolletjie, Muffin, Roll, Teacake, Toorie, Topknot, Wad

**Bunch(ed)** Acinus, Anthology, Bob, Botryoid, Boughpot, Bouquet, Bundle, Cluster, Conglomerate, Fascicle, Finial, Flock, Gang, → GROUP, Hand, Handful, Ilk, Knot, Lot, Lump, Nosegay, Panicle, Posy, Raceme, Spray, Sprig, Staphyline, Tassel, Tee, Truss, Tuft, Tussie-mussie, Tussock

**Bundle(d)** Axoneme, Bale, Bavin, Bluey, Bottle, Byssus, Daftar, Desmoid, Dorlach, Dossie, Drum, Fag(g)ot, Fascicle, Fasciculate, Fascine, Fibre, Fibrovascular, Kemple, Knitch, Lemniscus, Matilda, → PACK(AGE), Packet, Parcel, Sack, Sheaf, Shiralee, Shock, Shook, Stela, Stook, Swag, Tie, Top, Trousseau, Truss, Vascular, Wad, Wadge, Wap, Yalm, Ye(a)lm

**Bung** Chive, Clog, Cork, Dook, Obturate, Plug, Stopgap, Stopper, Stopple

**Bungalow** Chalet, Dak

**Bungle(r), Bungled, Bungling** Awkward, Blunder, Blunk, Bodge, Boob, Boss shot, Botch, Bumble, Bummle, Dub, Duff, Fluff, Foozle, Foul, Foul up, Fumble, Goof, Gum up, Ineptitude, Maladroit, Mash, Mess, Mis(h)guggle, Muddle, Muff, Mull, Prat, Screw, Spoil, Tinker

**Bunk(er), Bunk off, Bunkum** Abscond, Absquatulate, Balderdash, Baloney, Berth, Blah, Bolt, Casemate, Claptrap, Clio, Coal, Couchette, Decamp, Entrap, Flat, Flit, Guff, Guy, Hazard, History, Hogwash, Hokum, Hooey, Humbug, Malarky, Moonlight flit, Moonshine, Nonsense, Rot, Sandtrap, Scuttle, Skive, Stokehold, Tommy-rot, Tosh, Trap, Tripe, Truant, Twaddle, Wind

**Bunter** Billy, Owl

**Bunthorne** Aesthete, Poet

**Bunting** Bird, Cirl, Flag, Fringilline, Ortolan, Pennant, Snow, Streamer, Tanager, Towhee, Yellow-hammer, Yowley

**Buoy (up)** Anchor, Bell, Breeches, Can, Dan, Daymark, Dolphin, Float, Gas, Life, Marker, Nun, Raft, Reassure, Ring, Seamark, Sonar, Sonobuoy, Spar, Sustain, Wreck

**Buoyancy, Buoyant** Afloat, Blithe, Cork, Floaty, Mae West, Resilient

**Burble** Blat, Gibber, Waffle

**Burbot** Eel-pout

**Burden** Albatross, Backpack, Beare, Bob, Brunt, Cargo, Cark, Chant, Chorus, Cross, Cumber, Deadweight, Drone, Droore, Encumber, Encumbrance, Fa-la, Fardel, Folderol, Fraught, Freight, Gist, Handicap, Hardship, Hum, Imposition, Lade, → LOAD, Lumber, Millstone, Monkey, Oercome, Onus, Oppress, Overtax, Payload, Put-upon, Refrain, Rumbelow, Saddle, Servitude, Shanty, Substance, Task, Tax, Tenor, Theme, Torch, Tote, Trouble, Weight, White man's, Woe, Workload, Yoke

**Burdensome** Deere, Irksome, Onerous, Oppressive, Weighty

**Burdock** Clote(-bar), Clothur, Cockle-bar, Gobo, Hardoke, Weed

**Bureau** Agency, Agitprop, Breakfront, Cominform, Davenport, Desk, Federal, Interpol, Kominform, Marriage, → OFFICE, Volunteer, Weather

**Bureaucracy, Bureaucrat(ic)** Apparatchik, Bean-counter, Bumbledom, CS, Functionary, Impersonal, Jack-in-office, Mandarin, Red tape, Tapist, Technocrat, Wallah

**Burgeon(ing)** Asprout, Blossom, Bud, Grow, Sprout, Swell

**Burger** Grillsteak

**Burgess, Burgher** Citizen, Freeman, Portman

**Burgh** Burrowstown, Parliamentary, Police, Royal

**Burglar(y), Burgle** Aggravated, Area-sneak, Break-in, Cat, Crack(sman), House-breaker, Intruder, Larcenist, Peterman, Picklock, Raffles, Robber, Safebreaker, Screw, Thief, Yegg

**Burgundy** Macon, Vin
**Burial (place)** Catacomb, Charnel, Committal, Crypt, Cubiculum, Darga(h), Funeral, God's acre, Golgotha, Grave, Green, Interment, Kurgan, Lair, Last rites, Pyramid, Sepulchre, Sepulture, Speos, Sutton Hoo, Tholos, Tomb, Tumulus, Vault, Vivisepulture, Zoothapsis
**Burin** Graver
**Burlesque** Caricatura, Caricature, Comedy, Farce, Heroicomical, Hudibrastic(s), Hurlo-thrumbo, Lampoon, Macaronic, Parody, Satire, Skimmington, Skit, Spoof, Travesty
**Burlington** RA
**Burly** Bluff, Brawny, Stout, Strapping
**Burma, Burmese** Karen(ni), Mon(-Khmer), Myanmar, Naga, Shan
**Burn(ed), Burner, Burning, Burnt** Ablaze, Adust, Afire, Alow(e), Ardent, Argand, Arson, Ash, Auto-da-fé, Back, Bake, Bats-wing, Beck, Bishop, Blaze, Blister, Blowlamp, Blowtorch, Blush, Bonfire, Brand, Brazier, Bren(ne), Brent, Brook(let), Bunsen, Causalgia, Caustic, Cauterise, Char, Chark, Chinese, Cinder, Clavie, Coal, Coke, Combust, Conflagration, Cremate, Crozzled, Crucial, Deflagrate, Destruct, Effigy, Eilding, Ember, Emboil, Empyreuma, Fervid, Fircone, → **FIRE**, First degree, Fishtail, Flagrant, Flambe, Flare, Flash, Flicker, Frazzle, Fresh(et), Gleed, Glow, Gut, Holocaust, Ignite, In, Incendiary, Incense, Incinerate, Intense, Inure, Inust(ion), Itch, Kill, Lean, Lit, Live, Lunt, Moorburn, Muirburn, Offering, On, Oxidise, Oxyacetylene, Phlogiston, Pilot, Plo(a)t, Powder, Pyric, Pyromania, Raster, Rill, Runnel, Sati, Scald, Scaud, Scorch, Scouther, Scowder, Scowther, Sear, Second degree, Sienna, Sike, Singe, Sizzle, Smart, Smoulder, Sore, Stake, Suttee, Swale, Third-degree, Thurible, Torch, Umber, Urent, Ustion, Ustulation, Weeke, Welsbach, Wick, Ybrent
**Burning bush** Wahoo
**Burp** Belch, Eruct
**Burr(ing), Burrs** Beggar's lice, Beggar's ticks, Brei, Brey, Clote, Croup, Dialect, Knob, Rhotacism
**Burrow(er), Burrowing** Biscacha, Dig, Earth, Earthworm, Fossorial, Gopher, Groundhog, Hole, Holt, How, Howk, Mine, Mole, Nuzzle, Root, Sand-screw, Sett, Terricole, Tunnel, Viscacha, Warren, Wombat, Worm
**Bursar(y)** Camerlengo, Camerlingo, Coffers, Grant, Purser, Scholarship, Tertiary, Treasurer
**Bursitis** Beat
**Burst(ing), Bursts** Agog, Blowout, Bout, Brast, Break, Dehisce, Disrupt, Dissilient, Ebullient, Erumpent, Erupt, → **EXPLODE**, Fits and starts, Flare-up, Flurry, Fly, Gust, Implode, Pop, Rhexus, Rupture, Salvo, Sforzato, Shatter, Spasm, Spirt, Split, Sprint, Spurt, Stave, Tetterous
**Burundi** RU
**Bury** Conceal, Cover, Eard, Earth, Embowel, Engrave, Engulf, Enhearse, Entomb, Graff, Graft, Imbed, Inearth, Inhearse, Inherce, Inhume, Inter, Inurn, Landfill, Repress, Sepulture, Sink, Ye(a)rd, Yird
**Bus** Address, Aero, Bandwagon, Battle, Bendy, Car, Charabanc, Coach, Crew, Double-decker, Greyhound, Highway, Hondey, Hopper, ISA, Jitney, Mammy-wagon, Purdah, Rattletrap, Single-decker, Tramcar, Trolley, Trunk, Walking
**Bus conductor** Cad, Clippy
**Bush(es), Bush-man, Bushy** Aloe, Arbutus, Bitou, Bramble, Brier, Bullace, Busket, Butterfly, Calico, Clump, Cotton, Creosote, Dumose, Elder, Firethorn, Furze, Glib, Greasewood, Hawthorn, Hedge, Hibiscus, Ivy-tod, Jaborandi, Kapok, Kiekie, Mallee, Matagouri, Mimosa, Mulberry, Outback, Pachysandra, Poinsettia, Poly-poly, President, Prostanthera, Rag, Sallee, San, Scrog, Shepherd, Shrub, Sloe, Sloethorn, Sugar, Thicket, Tire, Tod(de), Tumatakuru
**Bush-baby** Durukuli, Galago, Nagapie, Night-ape
**Bushel** Ardeb, Bu, Co(o)mb, Cor, Ephah, Fou, Homer, Peck, Weight, Wey
**Bushwalker** Hoon
**Business** Affair, Agency, Agenda, Biz, Bricks and clicks, Brokerage, Bus, Cahoot, Cartel, Cerne, Chaebol(s), Co, Commerce, Company, Concern, Conglomerate, Corporate, Craft, Custom, Dealership, Dot-com, Duty, Enterprise, Ergon, Establishment, Exchange, Fasti, Field, Firm, Funny, Game, Gear, Goings on, Hong, Industry, Kaizen, Keiretsu, Lifestyle,

Line, Métier, Monkey, Office, Palaver, Partnership, Pidgin, Pi(d)geon, Practice, Professional, Racket, Shebang, Shop, Show, Thick, To-do, Trade, Traffic, Transaction, Tread, Turnover, Unincorporated, Vocation, Wall Street, Zaibatsu, Zaikai

**Businesslike** Orderly

**Businessman** Babbitt, Baron, Capitalist, City, Dealer, Entrepreneur, Fat-cat, Financier, Magnate, Realtor, Taipan, Trader, Tycoon

**Busk(er)** Bodice, Corset, Entertainer, German-band

**Buskin(s)** Brod(e)kin, Cothurn(us), Shoe

**Buss** Kiss, Osculate, Smack

**Bussu** Troelie, Troely, Troolie

**Bust** Beano, Boob, Bosom, Brast, Break, Chest, Dollarless, Falsies, Figurehead, Fold, Herm(a), Insolvent, Kaput, Mamma, Penurious, Portrait, Raid, Rupture, Sculp, Shatter(ed), Skint, Spree, Statue, Swoop, Term(inus), To-tear, To-torne, Ups(e)y

▷**Bust** *may indicate* an anagram

**Bustard** Bird, Otis, Turkey

**Buster** Keaton

**Bustle** Ado, Beetle, Do, Dress-improver, Flap, Fuss, Pad, Scurry, → STIR, Swarm, To-do, Tournure, Whew

**Busy** Active, At (it), Bee, Deedy, → DETECTIVE, Dick, Doing, Eident, Employ, Engaged, Ergate, Eventful, Eye, Fuss, Goer, Hectic, Hive, Hot spot, Humming, Manic, Occupied, Operose, Ornate, Prodnose, Stir, Stirabout, Tec, Throng, Worksome

**Busybody** Bee, Bustler, Meddler, Noser, Pantopragmatic, Pragmatic, Snooper, Trout, Yenta

**But** Aber, Algates, Bar, Except, However, Keg, Merely, Nay, Only, Save, Sed, Simply, Tun, Without, Yet

**Butch** He-man, Macho

**Butcher(s), Butchery** Cumberland, Decko, Dekko, Eyeful, Flesher, Gander, Glimpse, Ice, Kill, Killcow, Look, Looksee, Mangle, Massacre, Mow down, Ovicide, Peek, Sever, Shambles, Shochet, Shufti, Slaughter, Slay, Slink

**Butler** Bedivere, Bread-chipper, Crichton, Jeeves, Khansama(h), Major-domo, RAB, Rhett, Samuel, Servant, Sewer, Sommelier, Steward

**Butt (in)** April fool, Aris, Arse, Ass, Barrel, Bumper, Buns, Bunt, Clara, Dimp, Dout, Dowt, Dunch, Enter, Geck, Glasgow kiss, Goat, Header, Horn, Interject, Jesting-stock, Laughing-stock, Mark, Nut, Outspeckle, Pantaloon, Pipe, Push, Rainwater, Ram, Roach, Scapegoat, Snipe, Stompie, → STOOGE, Straight man, Stub, Stump, Target, Tun, Ups

**Butter** Adulation, Apple, Beurre, Billy, Blandish, Brandy, Butyric, Cacao, Cocoa, Coconut, Drawn, Flatter, Galam, Garcinia, Ghee, Ghi, Goa, Goat, Illipi, Illupi, Kokum, Mahua, Mahwa, Maitre d'hotel, Mow(r)a, Nut, Nutter, Palm, Pat, Peanut, Print, Ram, Rum, Scrape, Shea, Spread, Vegetable

▷**Butter** *may indicate* a goat or such

**Buttercup** Bumboat woman, Crowfoot, Crow-toe, Goldilocks, Meadow rue, Ranunculus, Reate, Thalictrum

**Butterfingers** Muff

**Butterfish** Nine-eyes

**Butterflies, Butterfly** Apollo, Argus, Birdwing, Blue, Brimstone, Brown, Cabbage white, Camberwell beauty, Cardinal, Chequered skipper, Chrysalis, Cleopatra, Clouded yellow, Collywobbles, Comma, Common blue, Copper, Dilettante, Eclosion, Elfin, Emperor, Fritillary, Gate-keeper, Gatemen, Grayling, Hair-streak, Heath, Hesperid, Imaginal, Kaleidoscope, Kallima, Large copper, Large white, Leaf, Lycaena, Marbled-white, Meadow brown, Metalmark, Milk-weed, Monarch, Morpho, Mountain ringlet, Mourning-cloak, Nerves, Nymphalid, Nymphean, Orange-tip, Owl, Painted lady, Papilionidae, Peacock, Pieris, Psyche, Purple emperor, Red admiral, Rhopalocera, Ringlet, Satyr(idae), Satyrinae, Scotch argus, Silverspot, Skipper, Small white, Snake's head, Speckled wood, Stamper, Stroke, Sulphur, Swallow-tail, Thecla, Thistle, Tiger swallowtail, Tortoiseshell, Two-tailed pasha, Umber, Vanessa, Wall brown, White admiral

**Buttermilk** Bland, Lassi

**Butternut** Souari

**Butter-tree** Mahua, Mahwa, Mow(r)a

**Buttocks** Aristotle, Arse, Ass, Bahookie, Booty, Bottom, Buns, Callipygous, Can, Cheeks, Coit, Derrière, Doup, Duff, Fanny, Fud, Fundament, Gluteus maximus, Haunch, Heinie, Hinder-end, Hinderlan(d)s, Hunkers, Hurdies, Jacksie, Jacksy, Keester, Keister, Mooning, Nache, Nates, Posterior, Prat, Quatch, Quoit, Rump, Seat, Tail, Tush

**Button(s)** Barrel, Bellboy, Buzzer, Eject, Fastener, Frog, Hash, Hold, Hot, Key, Knob, Mescal, Mouse, Mute, Netsuke, Olivet, Page(boy), Panic, Pause, Pearl, Press, Push, Snooze, Stud, Switch, Toggle, Toolbar

**Buttonhole** Accost, Boutonniere, Carnation, Detain, Doorstep, Eye, Flower, Slit

**Buttress** Brace, Counterfort, Flying, Hanging, Pier, Prop, Reinforce, Stay, Support, Tambour

**Butty** Chum, Oppo

**Buxom** Bonnie, Busty, Plump, Rolypoly, Sonsy, Well-endowed, Wench

**Buy(ing), Buyer, Buy off** Accept, Believe, Bid, Bribe, Bulk, Coemption, Coff, Corner, Customer, Emption, Engross, Impulse, Monopsonist, Munich, Oligopsony, Panic, Purchase, Redeem, Regrate, Shop, Shout, Spend, Subscribe, Take, Trade, Treat, Vendee

▷**Buyer** *may indicate* money

**Buzz(er)** Bee, Birr, Bombilate, Bombinate, Button, Drone, Fly, Hornet, Hum, Kazoo, Kick, Ring, Rumour, Scram, Thrum, Wasp, Whirr, Whisper, Zed, Zing, Zoom

**Buzzard** Bee-kite, Bird, Buteo, Hawk, Honey, Pern, Puttock, Turkey, Vulture

**By** Alongside, At, Beside, Gin, Gone, In, Near, Neighbouring, Nigh, Of, On, Past, Per, Through, With, X

**Bye** Au revoir, Extra

**Bye-bye** Adieu, Farewell, Tata

**By far** Out and away

**Bygone** B.C., Dead, Departed, Past, Yore

**By Jove** Egad

**Bypass** Avoid, Beltway, Circuit, Coronary artery, → DETOUR, Dodge, Evade, Hot-wire, Ignore, Omit, Ring-road, Shunt, Skirt

**By-product** Epiphenomenon, Spill-over, Spin-off

**Byre** Cowshed, Manger, Stable, Trough

**By so much** The

**Bystander** Looker-on, Observer

**Byte** Nybble

**By the way** Apropos, Incidentally, Ob(iter)

**Byway** Alley, Lane, Path

**Byword** Adage, Ayword, Nayword, Phrase, Proverb, Slogan

**Byzantine** Catapan, Comnenus, Complex, Complicated, Exarch, Intricate, Intrince, Theme

▷**Byzantine** *may indicate* an anagram

# Cc

**C** Around, Caught, Celsius, Cent, Centigrade, Charlie, Conservative, San
**Cab** Boneshaker, Crawler, Drosky, Fiacre, Four-wheeler, Growler, Gurney, Hackney, Hansom, Mini, Noddy, Taxi, Vettura
**Cabal(ler)** Arlington, Ashley, Bloc, Buckingham, Clifford, Clique, Conspiracy, Coterie, Faction, Junto, Lauderdale, Party, Plot
**Cab(b)alistic** Abraxis, Gematria, Mystic, Notarikon, Occult
**Cabaret** Burlesque, Floorshow, Moulin Rouge
**Cabbage(-head), Cabbage soup** Black, Bok choy, Borecole, Brassica, Castock, Cauliflower, Cavolo nero, Chinese (leaf), Chinese leaves, Chou, Choucroute, Cole, Collard, Crout, Custock, Drumhead, Gobi, Kerguelen, Kohlrabi, Kraut, Loaf, Loave, Mibuna, Mizuna, Pak-choi, Pamphrey, Pe-tsai, Red, St Patrick's, Sauerkraut, Savoy, Sea-kale, Shchi, Shtchi, Skunk, Thieve, Turnip, Wild, Wort
**Caber** Fir, Janker, Log, Sting
**Cabin** Berth, Bibby, Bothy, Box, Cabana, Caboose, Camboose, Coach, Cottage, Crannog, Crib, Cuddy, Den, Gondola, Hovel, Hut, Izba, Lodge, Log, Loghouse, Long-house, Pod, Pressure, Room, Roundhouse, Saloon, Shack, Shanty, Signal box, Stateroom, Trunk
**Cabin-boy** Grummet
**Cabinet** Armoire, Bahut, Cabale, Case, Cellaret, Chiffonier, Chill(er), Closet, Commode, Console, Cupboard, Display, Dresser, Encoignure, Filing, Kitchen, Locker, Medicine, Ministry, Nest, Official family, Repository, Secretaire, Shadow, Shrinal, Unit, Vitrine
**Cabinet maker** Banting, Chippendale, Ebeniste, Garret-master, Hepplewhite, Joiner, PM
**Cable(way), Cable-car** Arrester, Choucroute, Coax(ial), Extension, Flex, Halser, Hawser, Jumper, Jump leads, Junk, Kissagram, Landline, Lead, Lead-in, Lifeline, Log line, Null-modern, Oil-filled, Outhaul, Outhauler, Rope, Shroud, Slatch, Snake, Téléférique, → **TELEGRAM**, Telegraph, Telepherique, Telpher(age), Topping lift, Towrope, Trunking, Vine, Wire, Yoke
**Cache** Deposit, Hidlin(g)s, → **HOARD**, Inter, Stash, Store, Treasure
**Cachet** Prestige
**Cack-handed** Awkward, Ham-fisted
**Cackle** Cluck, Gaggle, Gas, Haw, Horse laugh, Snicker, Titter
**Cacography** Scrawl
**Cacophony** Babel, Caterwaul, Charivari, Discord, Hubbub, Jangle
**Cactus, Cactus-like** Alhagi, Barel, Cereus, Cholla, Christmas, Dildo, Easter, Echino-, Echinopsis, Hedgehog, Jointed, Jojoba, Maguey, Mescal, Mistletoe, Nopal, Ocotillo, Ombrophobe, Opuntia, Organ-pipe, Peyote, Pita(ha)ya, Prickly pear, Retama, Saguaro, Schlumbergera, Stapelia, Star, Strawberry, Torch-thistle, Tuna, Xerophytic
**Cad** Base, Boor, Bounder, Churl, Cocoa, Heel, Oik, Rascal, Rat, Rotter, Skunk, Varlet
**Cadaver(ous)** Body, Corpse, Deathly, Emaciated, Ghastly, Goner, Haggard, Stiff
**Caddy** Porter, Tea, Teapoy
**Cadence** Authentic, Beat, Close, Deceptive, Euouae, Evovae, Fa-do, Flow, Imperfect, Interrupted, Lilt, Meter, Perfect, Plagal, Rhythm
**Cadenza** Fireworks
**Cadet(s)** Junior, OTC, Plebe, Recruit, Rookie, Scion, Snooker, Space, Syen, Trainee, Westpoint, Younger
**Cadge(r)** Beg, Bludge, Bot, Bum, Freeload, Impose, Mutch, Ponce, → **SCROUNGE**, Sponge
**Cadmium** Cd
**Caesar** Despot, Imperator, Julian, Nero

**Caesium** Cs

**Café, Cafeteria** Automat, Bistro, Brasserie, Buvette, Canteen, Carvery, Commissary, Cybercafe, Diner, Dinette, Donko, Eatery, Estaminet, Filtré, Greasy spoon, Hashhouse, Internet, Juke joint, Milk bar, Netcafé, Noshery, Pizzeria, Pull-in, Snackbar, Tearoom, Tea-shop, Transport, Truckstop

**Cage** Aviary, Bar, Battery, Box, Cavie, Confine, Coop, Corf, Dray, Drey, Enmew, Faraday, Fold, Frame, Fruit, Grate, Hutch, Keavie, Mew, Mortsafe, Pen, → **PRISON**, Rib, Roll, Safety, Squirrel, Trave

**Cag(e)y** Chary, Close, Evasive

**Cahoots** Collusion, Hugger-mugger

**Cairn** Barp, Burial, Clearance, Dog, Horned, Man, Mound, Raise

**Caisson** Bends

**Caitiff** Meanie

**Cajole(ry)** Beflum, Beguile, Blandish, Blarney, Carn(e)y, → **COAX**, Cuittle, Entice, Humbug, Inveigle, Jolly, Persuade, Wheedle, Whillywha(w), Wiles

**Cake(s)** Agnus dei, Angel, Baba, Babka, Baklava, Banbury, Bannock, Bara brith, Barm(brack), Battenberg, Bhaji, Biffin, Birthday, Black bun, Block, Brandy snap, Brioche, Brownie, Buckwheat, Bun, Carcake, Carrot, Cattle, Chapat(t)i, Chillada, Chupati, Chupattie, Chupatty, Clapbread, Clot, Coburg, Cookie, Corn dodger, Cotton, Cream horn, Cream puff, Croquante, Croquette, Cruller, Crumpet, Cup, Currant, Dainty, Devil's food, Donut, Doughnut, Drizzle, Dundee, Eccles, Eclair, Fairy, Falafel, Fancy, Farl(e), Filter, Fish, Flapjack, Frangipane, Frangipani, Fritter, Galette, Gateaux, Genoa, Gingerbread, Girdle, Griddle, → **HARDEN**, Hockey, Hoe, Hot, Idli, Jaffa, Jannock, Johnny, Jumbal, Jumbles, Koeksister, Kruller, Kuchen, Kueh, Lady's finger, Lamington, Lardy, Latke, Layer, Linseed, Macaroon, Madeira, Madeleine, Maid of honour, Marble, Meringue, Millefeuille, Moon, Mooncake, Mud, Muffin, Napoleon, Nut, Oatmeal, Oil, Pan, Panettone, Paratha, Parkin, Parliament, Pastry, Pat, Patty, Pavlova, Pepper, Petit four, Pikelet, → **PLASTER**, Pomfret, Pone, Pontefract, Poonac, Poori, Popover, Potato, Pound, Profiterole, Puff, Puftaloon(a), Puri, Queencake, Ratafia, Ready-mix, Religieuse, Rice, Rock, Rosti, Roti, Rout, Rum baba, Rusk, Sachertorte, Saffron, Sally Lunn, Salt, Sandwich, Savarin, Scone, Seed, Set, Simnel, Singing-hinny, Slab, Slapjack, Soap, Soul, Spawn, Spice, Sponge, Stollen, Stottie, Sushi, Swiss roll, Tablet, Tansy, Tea(bread), Tipsy, Torte, Tortilla, Traybake, Twelfth, Upside down, Vetkoek, Wad, Wafer, Waffle, Wedding, Wonder, Yeast, Yule log

▷**Cake** *may indicate* an anagram

**Cake-shaped** Placentiform

**Cakestand** Curate

**Cakewalk** Doddle, Romp

**Calaboose** Jail, Loghouse

**Calamari** Squid

**Calamine** Electric, Hemimorphite

**Calamitous, Calamity** Blow, Catastrophe, Dire, → **DISASTER**, Distress, Fatal, Ill, Jane, Ruth, Storm, Tragic, Unlucky, Visitation, Woe

**Calcareous** Ganoin, Lithite

**Calcium** Ca, Colemanite, Dogger, Dripstone, Flowstone, Otolith, Quicklime, Scawtite, Whewellite, Wollastonite

**Calculate(d), Calculation, Calculator** Abacus, Actuary, Arithmetic, Assess, Cast, Comptometer, Compute(r), Cost, Design, Estimate, Extrapolate, Four-function, Log, Napier's bones, Number-crunch, Prorate, Quip(p)u, Rate, → **RECKON**, Slide-rule, Sofar, Soroban, Tactical, Tell, Work out

**Calculus** Cholelith, Differential, Functional, Infinitesimal, Integral, Lambda, Lith, Lithiasis, Predicate, Propositional, Science, Sentential, Sialolith, Stone, Tartar, Urolith

**Caldera** Crater

**Caledonian** Kanak

**Calendar** Advent, Agenda, Almanac, Chinese, Diary, Dies fasti, Fasti, Gregorian, Hebrew, Intercalary, Jewish, Journal, Julian, Luach, Lunisolar, Menology, Newgate, New Style, Ordo, Perpetual, Planner, Revolutionary, Roman, Sothic, Year planner

**Calender(ing)** Dervish, Mangle, Swissing
**Calf** Ass, Bobby, Boss(y), Box, Cf, Deacon, Divinity, Dogie, Dogy, Fatted, Freemartin, Golden, Law, Leg, Maverick, Mottled, Poddy, Sleeper, Slink, Smooth, Stirk, Sural, Tollie, Tolly, Tree, Veal(er), Vitular
**Caliban** Moon-calf
**Calibrate, Calibre** Bore, Capacity, Graduate, Mark, → QUALITY, Set, Text
**California(n)** Fresno, Golden State
**Californium** Cf
**Caliph** Abbasid(e), Omar, Vathek
**Call(ed), Call (for), Calling, Call on, Calls, Call up** Adhan, Ahoy, Alarm, Alew, Appeal, Arraign, Art, Awaken, Azan, Banco, Bawl, Beck(on), Behote, Bevy, Bid, Bird, Boots and saddles, Bugle, Business, Buzz, Career, Chamade, Cite, Claim, Clang, Clarion, Cleep, Clepe, Close, Cold, Conference, Conscript, Convene, Convoke, Coo, Cooee, Cry, Curtain, Denominate, Dial, Drift, Dub, Duty, Effectual, Emergency, Encore, Entail, Evoke, First post, Game, Go, Hail, Hallali, Halloa, Halloo, Haro, Heads, Heave-ho, Hech, Heckle, Hete, Hey, Hight, Ho, Holla, Hot(e), House, Howzat, Huddup, Hurra(h), Invocation, Job, Junk, Last (post), Levy, Line, Local, Look in, Margin, Métier, Misère, Mobilise, Mot, Name, Nap, Need, Nemn, Nempt, Niche, Nominate, No trumps, Nuisance, Olé, Oyez, Page, Party, Peter, Phone, Photo, Pop in, Post, Profession, Prompt, Proo, Pruh, Pursuit, Rechate, Recheat, Retreat, Reveille, Ring, Roll, Rort, Round, Rouse, Route, Sa-sa, Scream, See, Sennet, → SHOUT, Shut-out, Slam, Slander, Slogan, Soho, Sola, SOS, STD, Style, Subpoena, Summon(s), Tails, Tally ho, Tantivy, Taps, Telephone, Term, Toho, Toll, Trumpet, Trunk, Turn, Tweet, Visit, Vocation, Waken, Wake-up, War cry, Whoa-ho-ho, Wo ha ho, Yclept, Yeehaw, Yell, Yo, Yodel, Yodle, Yo-ho(-ho), Yoicks, Yoo-hoo
**Calla(s)** Aroid, Lily, Maria
**Caller** Fresh, Guest, Herring, Inspector, Muezzin, Rep, Traveller, → VISITOR
**Calligraphy** Grass style, Kakemono
**Callipers** Odd legs
**Callisthenics** T'ai chi (ch'uan)
**Call off** Abort
**Callosity, Call(o)us** Bunion, Case-hardened, Cold(-hearted), Corn, Hard, Horny, Obtuse, Porosis, Ringbone, Seg, Thylose, Tough, Tylosis, Unfeeling
**Callow** Crude, Green, Immature, Jejune
**Calm(ing)** Abate, Alegge, Aleye, Allay, Allege, Appease, Assuage, Ataraxy, Composed, Cool, Dead-wind, Dispassionate, Doldrums, Easy, Easygoing, Easy-osy, Eevn, Emollient, Equable, Equanimity, Even, Eye, Flat, Glassy, Halcyon, Level, Loun(d), Lown(d), Lull, Mellow, Mild, Milden, Millpond, Mollify, Nerveless, Nonchalant, Pacify, Palliate, Patient, Peaceable, Peaceful, Philosophical, Phlegmatic, Placate, Placid, Quell, Quiet, Raise, Relax(ed), Repose, Restful, Restrained, Salve, Sedate, Self-possessed, Seraphic, Serena, Serene, Settle, Simmer down, Sleek, Sober, → SOOTHE, Sopite, Steady, Still(ness), Stilly, Subdue, Subside, Supercool, Tame, Tranquil(lise), Unfazed, Unruffled, Unturbid, Windless
**Calorie** Gram, Kilogram
**Calumniate, Calumny** Abuse, Aspersion, Backbite, Defame, Libel, Malign, Sclaunder, Slander, Slur
**Calvary** Golgotha
**Calvin(ist), Calvinism** Accusative, Coolidge, Genevan, Hopkins, Huguenot, Infralapsarian, Perseverance of saints, Predestination, Sublapsarian, Supralapsarian
**Calydonian** Boar
**Calypso** Ogygia, Siren, Soca, Sokah, → SONG
**Cam** Cog, Dwell, River, Snail, Tappet
**Camaraderie** Fellowship, Rapport, Team spirit
**Camber** Hog, Slope
**Cambium** Phellogen
**Cambodia(n)** K, Kampuchean, Khmer (Rouge), Montagnard, Pol Pot
**Cambria(n)** Menevian, Wales
**Cambric** Lawn

**Cambridge** Blue, Cantab, Squat, Uni
**Came** Arrived
**Camel, Camel train** Aeroplane, Arabian, Artiodactyla, Bactrian, Beige, Caisson, Colt, Dromedary, Kafila, Llama, Oont, Sopwith, Tulu
**Camelopard** Giraffe
**Cameo** Anaglyph, Camaieu, Carving
**Camera, Camera man** All-round, Box, Brownie®, Camcorder, Candid, Chambers, Cine, Compact, Digicam, Digital, Disc, Dolly, Electron, Flash, Gamma, Gatso®, Grip(s), Iconoscope, Image orthicon, Imager, Instant, Kinetograph, Kodak®, Lucida, Miniature, Minicam, Movie, Nannycam, Nikon®, Obscura, Orthicon, Palmcorder, Panoramic, Pantoscope, Periphery, Phone-cam, Pinhole, Point and shoot, Polaroid®, Process, Programmed, Projectionist, Reflex, Retina, Schmidt, Shutterbug, SLR, Somascope, Speed, Spycam, Steadicam®, Stop-frame, Subminiature, Swing-back, Video, Vidicon, Viewfinder, Webcam
**Cameraderie** Fellowship
**Camouflage(d)** Battledress, Cloak, Conceal, → **DISGUISE**, Mark, Maskirovka, Secret, Unnoticeable, War-dress
▷**Camouflaged** *may indicate* an anagram
**Camp(er), Camping** Affectation, Aldershot, Auschwitz, Banal, Base, Belsen, Bivouac, Boma, Boot, Buchenwald, Caerleon, Cantonment, Castral, Colditz, Concentration, Coterie, Dachau, David, Death, Depot, D(o)uar, Dumdum, Epicene, Everestpack, Faction, Fat, Flaunt, Flying, Garrison, Gay, Gulag, Happy, Health, High, Holiday, Labour, Laer, La(a)ger, Laogai, Lashkar, Leaguer, Low, Lumber, Manyat(t)a, Motor, Nudist, Oflag, Outlie, Outpact, Party, Peace, Prison, Sect, Side, Site, Stagey, Stalag, Stative, Summer, Swagman, Tent, Theatrical, Transit, Treblinka, Valley Forge, Work, Zare(e)ba, Zariba, Zereba, Zeriba
**Campaign(er)** Activist, Agitate, Appeal, Barnstorm, Battle, Blitz, Blitzkrieg, Canvass, Contend, Crusade, Dardanelles, Doorknock, Drive, Ecologist, Electioneer, Enterprise, Field, Gallipoli, Hustings, Jihad, Lobby, Mission, Offensive, Pankhurst, Promotion, Real Ale, Roadshow, Run, Satyagraha, Smear, Stint, Stopes, Strategist, Suffragette, The stump, Tree-hugger, Vendetta, Venture, Veteran, War, War horse, Warray, Warrey, Whispering, Whistle-stop, Wilberforce, Witchhunt, Women's Lib
**Campanula** Rampion
**Campeador** Chief, Cid
**Camp-follower** Lascar, Leaguer-lady, Leaguer-lass, Sutler
**Camphor** Carvacrol, Cineol(e), Menthol
**Campion** Catchfly, Flower of Jove, Knap-bottle, Lychnis, Ragged robin, Silene
▷**Camptown** *may indicate* de-
**Campus** Dorm
**Can(s), Canned** Able, Aerosol, Billy, Bin, Bog, Capable, Chimney, Churn, Cooler, Dow, Dyke, Gaol, Garbage, Gents, Headphones, Is able, Jail, Jerry, John, Jug, Karsy, Kazi, Latrine, Lav(atory), Loo, May, Nick, Pail, Petrol, Pie-eyed, Pitcher, Pot, Preserve, → **PRISON**, Privy, Six-pack, Stir, Tank, Tin, Trash, Tube, Watering
**Canada, Canadian** Abenaki, Acadian, Bella Bella, Bella Coola, Beothuk, Bois-brûlé, .ca, Canuck, Che(e)chako, Comox, Coureur de bois, Dakotan, Dene, Dogrib, Habitans, Hare, Heiltsuk, Herring choker, Inuit, Johnny Canuck, Joual, Maliseet, Manitoban, Metis, Micmac, Montagnais, Naskapi, Nuxalk, Péquiste, Quebeccer, Quebecker, Québecois, Salishan, Salteaux, Saulteaux, Slavey, Stoney, Tsimshian, Ungava, Yukon
**Canal** Alimentary, Ampul, Anal, Birth, Caledonian, Channel, Conduit, Corinth, Cruiseway, Da Yunhe, Duct, Duodenum, Ea, Ear, Enteron, Erie, Food, Foss(e), Gota, Grand (Trunk), Grande Terre, Grand Union, Groove, Gut, Haversian, Houston Ship, Kiel, Klong, Labyrinth, Lode, Manchester Ship, Meatus, Midi, Mittelland, Moscow, Navigation, New York State Barge, Oesophagus, Panama, Pharynx, Pipe, Pound, Regent's, Resin, Rhine-Herne, Ring, Root, Sault Sainte Marie, Scala, Schlemm's, Semi-circular, Ship, Shipway, Soo, Spinal, Stone, Suez, Suo, Urethra, Vagina, Venice, Vertebral, Waterway, Welland, Zanja
**Canal-boat** Barge, Fly-boat, Gondola, Vaporetto
**Canapé** Cate, Chesterfield, Crostini, Snack, → **SOFA**, Titbit
**Canary** Bird, Grass, Prisoner, Roller, Serin, Singer, Yellow

**Cancel(led), Cancellation** Abandon, Abort, Abrogate, Adeem, Annul, Attainder, Axe, Counteract, Countermand, Cross, Delete, Destroy, Erase, Invalidate, Kill, Negate, Nix, Nullify, Obliterate, Override, Rained off, Red line, Remit, Repeal, Rescind, Retract, Retrait, Revoke, Scrap, Scratch, Scrub, Undo, Unmake, Void, Wipe, Write off

**Cancer(ian), Cancerous** Big C, Breast, Carcinoma, Crab, Curse, Hepatoma, Kaposi's sarcoma, Leukaemia, Liver, Lymphoma, Marek's disease, Moon child, Oat-cell, Oncogenic, Tropic, Tumour, Wolf

**Candela** Cd

▸**Candelabra** *see* CANDLE(STICK)

**Candid, Candour** Albedo, Blunt, Camera, Direct, Forthright, Franchise, Frank, Honesty, Ingenuous, Man-to-man, Open, Outspoken, Plain(-spoken), Round, Straight, Upfront

**Candida** Fungus

**Candidate(s)** Agrege, Applicant, Aspirant, Contestant, Entrant, Field, Literate, Maybe, Nomenklatura, Nominee, Office-seeker, Ordinand, Plainant, Postulant, Prospect, Running mate, Short list, Slate, Spoiler, Stalking-horse, Testee

**Candied, Candy** Angelica, Caramel, Cotton, Eryngo, Eye, Fondant, Glace, Maple, Rock, Snow, Succade, Sucket, Sugar, → SWEET

**Candle(stick), Candelabra, Candles** Amandine, Bougie, C(i)erge, Chanukiah, Corpse, Dip, Fetch, Girandole, Hanukiah, International, Jesse, Lampadary, Light, Long-sixes, Menorah, Mould, New, Padella, Paschal, Pricket, Roman, Rushlight, Sconce, Serge, Shammash, Shammes, Shammosim, Shortsix, Slut, Sperm, Standard, Tace, Tallow, Tallow-dip, Taper, Tea-light, Torchère, Tricerion, Vigil light, Wax, Waxlight

**Candlefish** Eulachon, Oolakon, Oulachon, Oulakon, Ulic(h)an, Ulic(h)on, Ulikon

▸**Candy** *see* CANDIED

**Cane, Caning** Arrow, Baculine, Bamboo, Baste, Beat, Birk, Crabstick, Dari, Dhurra, Doura, Dur(r)a, Ferula, Ferule, Goor, Gur, Jambee, Malacca, Narthex, Penang-lawyer, Pointer, Raspberry, Rat(t)an, Rod, Six of the best, Split, Stick, Sugar, Swagger-stick, Swish, Switch, Sword, Swordstick, Tan, Tickler, Vare, Wand, Whangee, Wicker(-work)

**Canine** Biter, C, Dhole, Dog, Eye-tooth

**Canker** Corrosion, Curse, Lesion, Ulcer

**Cannabis** Benj, Bhang, Bifter, Blow, Boneset, Durban poison, Ganja, Ganny, Grass, Hash, Hemp, Henry, Louie, Number, Pot, Skunk, Wacky baccy, Zol

**Cannibal** Anthropophagus, Heathen, Laestrygones, Long pig, Man-eater, Ogre, Thyestean, Wendigo

**Cannon** Amusette, Barrage, Basilisk, Bombard, Breechloader, Carom, Carronade, Cascabel, Chaser, Collide, Criterion, Culverin, Demi-culverin, Drake, Drop, Falcon, Fieldpiece, Gun, Howitzer, Kiss, Long-tom, Loose, Monkey, Mons Meg, Mortar, Nursery, Oerlikon, Saker, Stern-chaser, Trunnion, Water, Zamboorak, Zomboruk, Zumbooru(c)k

**Cannot** Canna, Cant, Downa(e), Downay

**Canny** Astute, Careful, Fly, Frugal, Prudent, Scot, Shrewd, Slee, Sly, Thrifty, Wice, Wily, Wise

**Canoe(ist)** Bidarka, Bidarkee, Canader, Canadian, Dugout, Faltboat, Kayak, Log, Mokoro, Monoxylon, Montaria, Oomiack, Paddler, Peterborough, Piragua, Pirogue, Rob Roy, Surf, Waka, Woodskin

**Canon(ise)** Augustinian, Austin, Besaint, Brocard, Camera, Cancrizens, Chapter, Chasuble, Code, Crab, Criterion, Decree, Honorary, Infinite, Isidorian, → LAW, Line, Mathurin(e), Minor, Nocturn, Norbertine, Nursery, Pitaka, Polyphony, Prebendary, Precentor, Precept, Premonstrant, Premonstratensian, Regular, Residential, Retrograde, Rota, Round, Rule, Secular, Square, Squier, Squire, Standard, Tenet, Unity, Vice-dean, White

**Canoodle** Neck

**Canopy** Awning, Baldachin, Baldaquin, Chuppah, Ciborium, Clamshell, Dais, Gable, Gore, He(a)rse, Huppah, Majesty, Marquee, Marquise, Parachute, Parapente, Pavilion, Shamiana(h), Sky, State, Tabernacle, Tent, Tester, Treetop, Umbrella, Veranda(h), Virando

**Cant** Argot, Bevel, Doublespeak, Heel, Incline, Jargon, Mummery, Outrope, Patois, Patter, Rogue's Latin, Shelta, Slang, Slope, Snivel, Snuffle, Tip

**Cantankerous** Cussed, Disputative, Fire-eater, Ornery, Perverse, Querulous, Testy, Tetchy

**Cantata** Kinderspiel, Motet, Tobacco

**Canteen** Chuck-wagon, Cutlery, Dry, Mess, Munga, Naafi, Soup kitchen, Wet
**Canter** Amble, Hypocrite, Jog, Lope, Run, Tit(t)up, Tripple
**Canticle** Benedictus, Carol, Nunc dimittis
**Canto** Air, Duan, Fit(te), Fitt, Fytte, Melody, Passus, Verse
**Canton(ese)** Aargau, Appenzell, Basil, Basle, District, Eyalet, Fribourg, Glarus, Graubunden, Jura, Lucerne, Neuchatel, Quarter, St Gall, Schaffhausen, Schwyz, Solothurn, Tanka, Thurgau, Ticino, Unterwalden, Uri, Valais, Vaud, Zug, Zurich
**Cantor** Haz(z)an
**Cantred** Commot(e)
**Canvas** Awning, Big top, Binca®, Burlap, Drab(b)ler, Fly-sheet, Found, Lug-sail, Mainsail, Maintopsail, Marquee, Oil-cloth, Paint, Raven's-duck, Reef, → SAIL, Sportsail, Square-sail, Staysail, Stuns(ai)l, Tarp(aulin), Tent(age), Trysail, Wigan, Woolpack
**Canvass(er), Canvassing** Agent, Doorstep, Drum, Electioneer, Mainstreeting, Poll, Press flesh, Solicit
▹**Canvasser** *may indicate* a painter or a camper
**Canyon** Arroyo, Box, Canada, Coprates, Defile, Gorge, Grand, Grand Coulee, Kings, Nal(l)a, Nallah, Ravine, Submarine
**Cap(ped)** Abacot, Amorce, Balaclava, Balmoral, Barret, Baseball, Bathing, Bearskin, Bellhop, Bendigo, Ber(r)et, Better, Biggin, Biretta, Bishop's, Black, Blakey, Blue, Blue-bonnet, Bonnet-rouge, Bycoket, Call, Calotte, Calpac(k), Calyptrate, Capeline, Caul, Chaco, Chape, Chapeau, Chaperon, Chapka, Charge, Chechia, Cheese-cutter, Cloth, Cockernony, Coif, College, Coonskin, Cope, Cornet, Cowl, Cradle, Crest, → CROWN, Czapka, Davy Crockett, Deerstalker, Dunce's, Dutch, Excel, Fatigue, Ferrule, Filler, Flat, Fool's, Forage, Friar's, Gandhi, Garrison, Gimme, Glengarry, Gorblim(e)y, Grannie, Granny, → HAT, Havelock, Headgear, Hub, Hummel bonnet, Hunting, Iceberg, International, Jockey, Juliet, Kalpak, Kepi, Kilmarnock (cowl), Kippa, Kippoth, Kipput, Kiss-me(-quick), Knee, Legal, Liberty, Lid, Limit, Maintenance, Mob, Monmouth, Monteer, Montero, Mor(r)ion, Mortar-board, Muffin, Mutch, Newsboy, Night, Old wife, Outdo, Pagri, Patella(r), Percussion, Perplex, Petrol, Phrygian, Pile, Pileus, Pinner, Polar, Puggaree, Quoif, Rate, Root, Schapska, Screw, Shacko, Shako, Shower, Skullcap, Split, Square, Squirrel-tail, Statute, Stocking, Summit, → SURPASS, Taj, Tam(-o'-shanter), Thimble, Thinking, Thrum, Toe, Toorie, Top, Toque, Toy, Trenchard, Trencher, Truck, Tuque, Turk's, Watch, Wishing, Yarmulka, Yarmulke, Zuchetto
**Capable, Capability** Able, Brown, Capacity, Competent, Deft, Effectual, Efficient, Firepower, Intelligent, Qualified, Reach, Skilled, Susceptible, Up to, Viable
**Capacitance, Capacious, Capacity** Ability, Ample, Aptitude, C, Cab, Calibre, Carrying, Co(o)mb, Competence, Condenser, Content, Cor, Cubic, Endowment, Excess, Field, Full, Function, Gift, Legal, Limit, Log, Mneme, Potency, Potential, Power, Prowess, Qua, Rated, Receipt, Roomy, Scope, Size, Skinful, Space, Tankage, Thermal, Tonnage, Valence, Vital, Volume
**Caparison** Robe, Trap(pings)
**Cape(s)** Agulhas, Almuce, Athlete, Beachy Head, Blanc(o), Bon, Burnouse, Byron, C, Calimere Point, Canaveral, Canso, Cardinal, Chelyuskin, Cloak, Cod, Comorin, Delgado, Dezhnev, Domino, Dungeness, East(ern), Fairweather, Faldetta, Fanion, Fanon, Farewell, Fear, Fichu, Finisterre, Flattery, Gallinas Point, Good Hope, Guardafui, Harp, Hatteras, Head(land), Helles, Hoe, Hogh, Hook of Holland, Horn, Inverness, Kennedy, Leeuwin, Lindesnes, Lizard, Manteel, Mantilla, Mantle, Mant(e)let, Mantua, Matapan, May, Miseno, Moz(z)etta, Muleta, Naze, Ness, Nordkyn, North, Northern, Ortegal, Palatine, Palliser, Parry, Pelerine, Peninsula, Point, Poncho, Promontory, Race, Ras, Ray, Reinga, Roca, Ruana, Runaway, Sable, St Vincent, Sandy, Scaw, Serape, Skagen, Skaw, Sontag, Southwest, Talma, Tippet, Trafalgar, Ushant, Verde, Vert, Waterproof, Western, Wrath, York
**Cape of Good Hope** Stellenbosch
**Caper(ing)** Antic, Bean, Boer, Capparis, Capriole, Cavort, Dance, Dido, Escapade, Flisk, Frisk, Frolic, Gambado, Gambol, Harmala, Harmalin(e), Harmel, Harmin(e), Jaunce, Jaunse, Pigeon-wing, Prance, Prank, Romp, Saltant, Sault, Scoup, Scowp, Skip, Tit(t)up
**Capet** Marie Antoinette
**Cape Town** SA

**Capital(s)** A1, Assets, Block, Boodle, Bravo, Bully, Cap, Chapiter, Chaptrel, Circulating, Doric, Equity, Euge, Excellent, Fixed, Flight, Float, Floating, Fonds, Great, Helix, Human, Initial, Ionic, Lethal, Lulu, Metropolis, Party, Principal, Refugee, Risk, Rustic, Seat, Seed money, Share, Social, Splendid, Sport, Stellar, Stock, Super, Topping, UC, Upper case, Venture, Wealth, Working

---

## CAPITALS

***3 letters:***
Fes
Fez
Gap
Jos
Ray
Rio
Ude
Ufa
Van
Zug

***4 letters:***
Aden
Agra
Albi
Apia
Auch
Baki
Baku
Bari
Bern
Bida
Boac
Bonn
Brno
Caen
Cali
Chur
Cluj
Cork
Dili
Doha
Faro
Graz
Head
Homs
Hums
Ipoh
Jaen
Jolo
Kiel
Kiev
Kobe
Laon
Laos
Leon
Lima
Linz
Lomé
Male
Metz
Nara
Nuuk
Oslo
Pegu
Pune
Riga
Rome
Safi
San'a
Sian
Sion
Susa
Suva
Vila
Xian

***5 letters:***
Aarau
Abiya
Abuja
Adana
Agana
Aijal
Akita
Akure
Amman
Aosta
Arlon
Assen
Batum
Beira
Belém
Berne
Bisho
Blois
Boise
Bonne
Bourg
Braga
Cairo
Chiba
Colon
Cuzco
Cuzev
Dacca
Dakar
Delhi
Dhaka
Dijon
Dilli
Dover
Dutse
Emisa
Enugu
Goias
Gotha
Guaco
Hanoi
Harar
Hefei
Hofei
Hsian
Ikeja
Jambi
Jammu
Jinan
Kabul
Kandy
Karor
Kazan
Kizyl
Konia
Konya
Koror
Kyoto
Lagos
Lassa
Laval
Le Paz
Le Puy
Lhasa
Liege
Lille
Lyons
Macao
Melun
Meroe
Minna
Minsk
Monza
Namur
Nancy
Natal
Nimes
Nukus
Oskub
Palma
Paris
Parma
Patna
Pella
Perth
Petra
Pinsk
Poona
Praha
Praia
Quito
Rabat
Rouen
Salem
Sanaa
Scone
Segou
Seoul
Siena
Simla
Sofia
Stans
Sucré
Tepic
Terni
Tokyo
Trier
Tunis
Turin
Turku
Uxmal
Vaasa
Vadso
Vaduz
Wuhan
Yanan
Yenan
Zomba

***6 letters:***
Abakan
Albany
Almaty
Andros
Angkor
Ankara
Annecy
Anyang
Asmara
Astana
Athens
Austin
Bagdad
Baguio
Bamako
Bangui
Banjul
Bassau
Bastia
Batumi
Bauchi
Beirut
Berlin
Bhopal
Bogota
Bruges
Brunei
Cahors
Canton
Chonju
Colima
Colmar
Cracow
Cucuta
Cuenca
Cuiaba
Darwin
Denver
Dessau
Dispur
Dodoma
Dublin
Edessa
Erfurt
Fuchou
Geneva
Giyani
Gondar
Grozny
Habana
Haikou

Harare
Harbin
Havana
Helena
Hobart
Hohhot
Ibadan
Iloilo
Ilorin
Imphal
Jaffna
Jaipur
Jalapa
Johore
Juneau
Kaduna
Kaunas
Kerman
Kigali
Kisumu
Kohima
Kuwait
Lahore
Lisbon
Loanda
Lokoja
London
Luanda
Lusaka
Macapá
Maceió
Madrid
Maikop
Majuro
Malabo
Manama
Manaus
Manila
Maputo
Marsan
Maseru
Mekele
Merano
Merida
Moroni
Moscow
Mumbai
Munich
Murcia
Muscat
Mutare
Nagpur
Nakuru
Namibe
Nassau
Nevers
Niamey
Nouméa
Oaxaca
Orense
Ottawa
Oviedo
Owerri
Palmas
Panaji
Panjim
Peking
Pierre
Prague
Puebla
Punaka
Quebec
Quetta
Ranchi
Recife
Regina
Rennes
Riyadh
Roseau
Ryazan
Saigon
Sardes
Sardis
Sarnen
Sendai
Skopje
Sokoto
Sparta
St Gall
St Paul
Sydney
Tabora
Taipei
Tallin
Tarawa
Tarbes
Tarsus
Tehran
Tetuan
Thebes
Thimbu
Tirana
Tobruk
Toledo
Toluca
Topeka
Ulundi
Umtata
Urumqi
Vesoul
Vienna
Warsaw
Xanadu
Xining
Yangon
Yaunde
Zagreb
Zurich
Zwolle

***7 letters:***
Abidjan
Ajaccio
Alençon
Algiers
Alma Ata
Altdorf
Antioch
Atlanta
Augusta
Auxerre
Baghdad
Bangkok
Barnaul
Begawan
Beijing
Belfast
Belfort
Bien Hoa
Bijapur
Bikaner
Bishkek
Bobigny
Bologna
Calabar
Caracas
Cardiff
Cayenne
Cesenza
Cetinje
Chengdu
Chennai
Coblenz
Coimbra
Colombo
Conakry
Concord
Cordoba
Cotonou
Cremona
Cuttack
Douglas
Durango
Foochow
Funchal
Gangtok
Goiania
Guiyang
Haarlem
Halifax
Hanover
Hassett
Herisau
Honiara
Huhehot
Iqaluit
Iquique
Isfahan
Izhevsk
Jackson
Jakarta
Kaesong
Kaifeng
Kampala
Karachi
Kashmir
Katsina
Kayseri
Kharkov
Khartum
Koblenz
Konakri
Kuching
Kunming
Kwangju
Lansing
Lanzhou
Lashkar
Legaspi
Lerwick
Liestal
Limoges
Lincoln
Louvain
Lucerne
Lucknow
Madison
Malacca
Managua
Masbate
Mathura
Mbabane
Memphis
Messene
Morelia
Munster
Nairobi
Nalchik
Nanjing
Nanking
Nanning
Nicosia
Nineveh
Novi Sad
Olomouc
Orleans
Oshogbo
Pachuca
Palermo
Palikit
Papeete
Perugia
Phoenix
Pishpek
Plovdiv
Potenza
Potsdam
Punakha
Quimper
Raleigh
Rangoon
San José
San Juan
Santa Fe
Sao Tomé
Sapporo
Saransk
Segovia
Seville
Stanley
St John's
Taiyuan
Tallinn
Tangier
Tbilisi
Teheran
Tel Aviv
Thimphu
Tiemcen
Toronto
Trenton
Trieste
Tripoli
Umuahia
Urumshi
Valetta
Vicenza
Vilnius
Vilnyus
Vitoria
Xanthus
Yakutsk
Yaounde
Yerevan

***8 letters:***
Abeokuta
Abu Dhabi
Adelaide
Agartala

Ashgabet
Asuncion
Auckland
Bar-le-Duc
Belgrade
Belmopan
Besancon
Beyrouth
Boa Vista
Brasilia
Brisbane
Brussels
Budapest
Cagliari
Calcutta
Campeche
Canberra
Cape Town
Castries
Chambéry
Changsha
Chaumont
Cheyenne
Chisinau
Coahuila
Columbia
Columbus
Culiacan
Curitiba
Damascus
Debrecen
Dehra Dun
Denpasar
Djibouti
Dushanbe
Ecbatana
Edmonton
Eraklion
Florence
Freetown
Fribourg
Funafuti
Gaborone
Godthaab
Golconda
Hamilton
Hangzhou
Hannover
Hargeisa
Hartford
Helsinki
Honolulu
Istanbul
Jayapura
Kandahar
Katmandu
Khartoum
Kilkenny
Kinshasa
Kirkwall
Kishinev
La Spezia
Lausanne
Liaoyand
Lilongwe
Luneburg
Mandalay
Mechelen
Mexicali
Monrovia
Monterey
Nanchang
Nanching
Nanterre
Narbonne
Ndjamena
New Delhi
Pago Pago
Pamplona
Pergamum
Peshawar
Pnom-Penh
Port Said
Port-Vila
Pretoria
Pristina
Roskilde
Saltillo
Salvador
Salzburg
Santiago
Sao Paulo
Sarajevo
Seremban
Shah Alam
Shanghai
Shenyang
Shillong
Silvassa
Srinagar
Sterling
St Helier
Szczecin
Tashkent
The Hague
Thonburi
Tiaxcala
Torshavn
Toulouse
Usumbura
Valencia
Valletta
Victoria
Vladimir
Warangai
Windhoek
Winnipeg
Yinchuan
Zaragoza

***9 letters:***

Amsterdam
Annapolis
Ashkhabad
Ayutthaya
Banda Aceh
Bandar Ser
Bangalore
Benin City
Birobijan
Bucharest
Bujumbura
Cartagena
Changchun
Changshar
Chengchow
Cherkessk
Chihuahua
Darmstadt
Des Moines
Edinburgh
Fongafale
Fortaleza
Frankfort
Grand Turk
Guangzhou
Heraklion
Hyderabad
Innsbruck
Islamabad
Jalalabad
Jerusalem
Karlsruhe
Kathmandu
Kingstown
Kisangani
Knoxville
Kuch Bihar
Lamberene
Leningrad
Ljubljana
Magdeburg
Maiduguri
Marrakesh
Melbourne
Mogadishu
Montauban
Monterrey
Nashville
Nelspriut
Nuku'alofa
Perigueux
Perpignan
Phnom Penh
Podgorica
Polokwane
Port Blair
Port Louis
Porto Novo
Port Royal
Putrajaya
Pyongyang
Resources
Reykjavik
Rio Branco
Samarkand
San Merino
Singapore
Solothurn
St George's
Stockholm
Stuttgart
Thorshavn
Trebizond
Trondheim
Ulan Bator
Vientiane
Wad Medani
Wiesbaden
Zhengzhou

***10 letters:***

Addis Ababa
Basse-terre
Baton Rouge
Bellinzona
Birobidzan
Bratislava
Bridgetown
Campobosso
Carson City
Chandigarh
Charleston
Cienfuegos
Cochabamba
Concepcion
Cooch Behar
Copenhagen
Cuernavaca
Diyarbakir
Eisenstadt
Frauenfeld
Georgetown
Harrisburg

Heidelberg
Hermosillo
Joao Pessoa
Klagenfurt
Kota Baharu
Kragujevac
Launceston
Leeuwarden
Libreville
Little Rock
Maastricht
Mexico City
Middelburg
Mogadiscio
Montevideo
Montgomery
Montpelier
Nouakchott
Panama City
Paramaribo
Persepolis
Podgoritsa
Porto Velho
Providence
Rawalpindi
Sacramento
Trivandrum
Tskhinvali
Valladolid
Valparaiso
Washington
Wellington
Whitehorse
Willemstad
Winchester
Yashkar-Ola

***11 letters:***
Bhubaneswar
Brazzaville
Buenos Aires
Campo Grande
Carcassonne
Charlestown
Dares Salaam
Fredericton
Gandhinagar
Guadalajara
Hermoupolis
Johore Bahru
Kuala Lumpur
Montbeliard
Nakhichevan
Ouagadougou
Pandemonium
Pondicherry
Port Moresby
Porto Alegre
Port of Spain
Rio Gallegas
Saarbrucken
San Salvador
Springfield
St Peter Port
Tallahassee
Tegucigalpa
Thohoyandou
Ulaanbaatar
Vatican City
Vladikavkaz
Yellowknife

***12 letters:***
Antananarivo
Anuradhapura
Barquisimeto
Barranquilla
Bloemfontein
Chilpancingo
Fort-de-France
Indianapolis
Johannesburg
Kota Kinabalu
Mont-de-Marsan
Muzzafarabad
Pandaemonium
Petrozavodsk
Ponta Delgada
Port-au-Prince
Port Harcourt
Rio de Janeiro
Salt Lake City
San Cristobal
Santo Domingo
Schaffhausen
Schoemansdal
Seringapatam
Shijiazhuang
Sidi-bel-Abbes
Tenochtitian
Ujungpandang
Villahermosa
Williamsburg
Yamoussoukro

***13 letters:***
Belo Horizonte
Charlottetown
Florianopolis
Funafuti Atoll
Guatemala City
Hertogenbosch
Jefferson City
Udjung Pandang
Yaren District

***14 letters:***
Andorra la Vella
Constantinople
Kuala Trengganu
Oaxaca de Juarez
Puerto Princesa
's-Hertogenbosch

***15 letters:***
Chalons-sur-Marne
Charlotte Amalie
Clermont-Ferrand
Sekondi-Takoradi

***16 letters:***
Pietermaritzburg
Trixtia Gutiérrez

---

**Capitalise** Carpe diem
**Capitalist** Bloated, Financier, Moneyer, Sloane
▷**Capitalist** *may indicate* a citizen of a capital
**Capitulate** Acquiesce, Comply, Defer, Fall, →SURRENDER, Yield
**Capless** Bare
▷**Capless** *may indicate* first letter missing
**Capo** Barre
**Capone** Al, Scarface
▷**Capriccioso** *may indicate* an anagram
**Caprice, Capricious** Arbitrary, Boutade, Capernoitie, Cap(p)ernoity, Conceit, Desultory, Devious, Eccentric, Elf(in), Erratic, Facile, Fancy, Fickle, Fitful, Freak, Humoresk, Humoresque, Irony, Megrim, Migraine, Mood, Notion, Perverse, Quirk, Vagary, Wayward, Whim(sy)
**Capricorn** Goat
**Capsize** Crank, Keel, Overbalance, Overturn, Purl, Tip, Turn turtle, Upset, Whemmle, Whomble
▷**Capsized** *may indicate* a word upside down
**Capstan** Sprocket, Windlass
**Capsule** Amp(o)ule, Boll, Bowman's, Cachet, Habitat, Internal, Nidamentum, Ootheca, Orbiter, Ovisac, Pill, Pyxidium, Space, Spacecraft, Spansule, Spermatophore, Suppository, Time, Urn

**Captain** Ahab, Bligh, Bobadil, Bones, Bossyboots, Brassbound, Capt, Channel, Chief, Cid, Commander, Condottiere, Cook, Copper, Cuttle, Flint, Group, Hardy, Hook, Hornblower, Kettle, Kidd, Kirk, Leader, Macheath, Magnate, Master, Nelson, Nemo, Oates, Old man, Owner, Patron, Patroon, Post, Privateer, Protospatharius, Pugwash, Rittmaster, Shipmaster, Skip(per), Standish, Subah(dar), Subedar, Swing, Trierarch
**Caption** Cutline, Heading, Headline, Inscription, Masthead, Roller, Sub-title, Title
**Captious** Critical, Peevish
**Captivate(d), Captivating** Beguile, Bewitch, Charm, Enamour, Enchant, Enthrall, Epris(e), Rapt, Take, Winsome
**Captive, Captivity** Babylonish, Bonds, Chains, Duress, Hostage, POW, Prisoner, Slave, Thrall
**Capture** Abduct, Annex, Bag, Carbon, Catch, Collar, Cop, Data, Electron, Enchain, Ensnare, Enthral(l), Entrance, Grab, Land, Motion, Nail, Net, Prize, Rush, Seize, Snabble, Snaffle, Snare, Storm, → TAKE, Trap
**Capuchin** Cebus, Monkey, Sajou
**Capybara** River-hog
**Car(s)** Alvis, Aston Martin, Astra, Audi, Austin, Auto(matic), Banger, Beemer, Beetle, Bentley, Benz, Berlin, Biza, BL, Bluebird, BMW, Bomb, Boneshaker, Brake, Bubble, Buffet, Bugatti, Buick, Bumper, Bus, Cab(riolet), Cable, Caddie, Cadillac, Catafalco, Catafalque, Chariot, Chelsea-tractor, Chevrolet, Chorrie, Citroen, Classic, Clunker, Coach, Compact, Company, Concept, Convertible, Cortina, Coupé, Courtesy, Crate, Daimler, Diesel, Diner, Dodgem®, Drag(ster), Drophead, Dual control, Dune buggy, Dunger, Elf, Estate, E-type, Fastback, Ferrari, Fiat, Fleet, Flivver, Ford, Formula, Freight, Friday, Gas guzzler, Getaway, Ghost, Gondola, Gran turismo, Griddle, GT, Gyrocar, Hardtop, Hatchback, Heap, Hearse, Hillman, Honda, Horseless carriage, Hot hatch, Hot-rod, Imp, Indy, Irish, Jag(uar), Jalop(p)y, Jamjar, Jammy, Jam sandwich, Jaunting, Jim Crow, Kart, Kia, Kit, Knockabout, Lada, Lagonda, Lancia, Landaulet, Landrover, Lexus, Lift-back, Limo, Limousine, Lincoln, Lotus, Merc(edes), MG, Mini, Minicab, Model T, Morgan, Morris, Motor, Muscle, Nacelle, Notchback, Observation, Opel, Outside, Pace, Palace, Panda, Parlo(u)r, Patrol, Pimpmobile, Polo, Popemobile, Popular, Production, Prowl, Pullman, Racer, Ragtop, Railroad, Rattletrap, Reliant Robin, Restaurant, Roadster, Roller, Rolls (Royce), Rover, RR, Runabout, Runaround, Rust bucket, Saab, Saloon, Scout, Seat, Sedan, Service, Shooting-brake, Side, Skoda, Sleeper, Sleeping, Soft-top, Speedster, Sports, Squad, Standard, Station wagon, Steam, Stock, Stretch-limo, Subcompact, Sunbeam, Supermini, SUV, Tank, Taxi, Telepherique, Telpher, Three-wheeler, Tin Lizzie, Tonneau, Tourer, Touring, Tram, Triumph, Trolley, Tumble, Turbo, Two-seater, Uno, Vehicle, Veteran, Vintage, Voiture, Volvo, VW, Wheeler, Wheels
**Carafe** Flask
**Caramel** Brûlé
**Carapace** Turtleback
**Carat** K, Point
**Caravan(ner)** Caf(f)ila, Convoy, Fleet, Kafila, Motor home, Romany, Safari, Trailer, Trailer trash, Winnebago®
**Caravanserai** Choltry, Choutry, Inn, Khan
**Caraway** Aj(o)wan, Carvy, Seed
**Car-back** Boot, Dick(e)y, Tonneau
**Carbamide** Urea
**Carbide** Silicon
**Carbine** Escopette, Gun, Musket
**Carbohydrate** Agar, Agarose, Callose, Carrageenan, Cellulose, Chitin, Dextran, Disaccharide, Glycogen, Heptose, Hexose, Inulin, Ketose, Laminarin, Mannan, Mucilage, Pectin, Pectose, Pentene, Pentosan(e), Pentose, Pentylene, Polysaccharide, Saccharese, Saccharide, Sorbitol, Starch, Sucrose, Sugar
**Carbolic** Orcin
**Carbon(ate), Carbonated** Activated, Ankerite, Austenite, Buckminsterfullerene, Buckyball, C, Charcoal, Chessylite, Coke, Dialogite, Diamond, Drice, Dry ice, Flame, Flimsy, Fullerene, Gas black, Gassy, Graphite, Lampblack, Martensite, Natron, Petroleum coke, Scawtite, Siderite, Soot, Spode, Spodium, Urao, Witherite, Zaratite

**Carbon deficiency** Acapnia
**Carbon dioxide** Drice, Dry ice
**Carboy** Demijohn
**Carbuncle** Anthrax, Eyesore, Ruby
**Carcase, Carcass** Body, Cadaver, Carrion, Corpse, Cutter, Krang, Kreng, Morkin, Mor(t)ling
**Carcinogen** Alar
**Card(s), Cardboard, Carding** Accelerator, Access, Ace, Affinity, Amex®, Arcana, Baccarat, Basto, Bill, Birthday, Blister, Blue Peter, Boarding, Bower, Business, Calling, Canasta, Cartes, Cash, Caution, Charge, Cheque, Chicane, Cigarette, Clock, Club, Coat, Comb, Communion, Community, Compass, Cooling, Court(esy), Credit, Cue, Curse of Scotland, Dance, Debit, Deck, Deuce, Devil's (picture) books, Diamond, Doffer, Donor, Drawing, Ecarté, Eccentric, Euchre, Expansion, Face, False, Flash, Flaught, Flop, Flush, Fourchette, → GAME, Get-well, Gold, Goulash, Graphics, Green, Greetings, Guide, Hand, Hard, Health, Heart, Hole, Honour, Humorist, ID, Identification, Identity, Idiot, Intelligent, Jack, Jambone, Jamboree, Joker, Kanban, Key, King, Knowing, Laser, Leading, Letter, Loo, Loyalty, Magnetic, Manille, Master, Matador, Maximum, Meishi, Meld, Memory, Menu, Mise, Mistigris, Mogul, Mournival, Natural, Notelet, Oddity, Ombre, Original, Oyster, Pack, Past, Pasteboard, Payment, PC, Phone, Picture, Piquet, Placard, Place, Plastic, Playing, Postal, Proximity, Punch(ed), Quatorze, Quatre, Queen, Queer, Quiz, Race, Rail, Ration, Red, Rippler, Rove, Royal marriage, Score, Scraperboard, Scratch, Scream, Screwball, Scribble, Shade, Show, SIM, Singleton, Smart, Soda, Solo, Sound, Spade, Spadille, Squeezer, Stiffener, Store, Strawboard, Sure, Swab, Swipe, Swish, Switch, Swob, Swot, Talon, Tarok, Tarot, Tease(r), Tenace, Test, Thaumatrope, Ticket, Tiddy, Time, Top-up, Tose, Toze, Trading, Trey, Trump, Two-spot, Union, Valentine, Visa, Visiting, Wag, Warrant, Weirdie, Whitechapel, Wild, Wit, Woolpack, Yellow, Zener
**Cardigan** Ballet-wrap, Jacket, Lumber jacket, Wampus, Wam(m)us, Woolly
**Cardinal** Apostolic vicar, Camerlingo, Chief, College, Eight, Eminence, Eminent, Grosbeak, Hat, HE, Hume, Legate, Manning, Mazarin, Medici, Monseigneur, Newman, Nine, Number, Pivotal, Polar, Prefect, Prelate, Radical, Red, Red-hat, Richelieu, Sacred college, Seven, Sin, Spellman, Ten, Virtue, Vital, Wolsey, Ximenes
**Card-player** Dealer, Pone
**Care(r), Caring** Attention, Befriend, Burden, Cark, Caution, Cerne, Charge, Cherish, Community, → CONCERN, Cosset, Custody, Doula, Elder, Empathy, Exactitude, Grief, Guard, Heed, Hoot, Husbandry, Intensive, Kaugh, Keep, Kiaugh, Maternal, Mind, Mother, Pains, Palliative, Parabolanus, Primary, Providence, Reck(e), Regard, Reke, Residential, Respite, Retch, Rought, Shared, Sitter, Solicitude, Stewardship, → TEND, Tenty, Thought, Treatment, Trouble, Trust, Ts(o)uris, Ward, Warm, Worry
**Careen(ing)** Parliament-heel
**Career(ist)** Course, Hie, Hurtle, Life, Line, Profession, Run, Rush, Scorch, Speed, Start, Tear, Vocation, Yuppie
▷**Career** *may indicate* an anagram
**Carefree** Blithe, → CARELESS, Dozy, Footloose, Happy-go-lucky, Irresponsible, → NEGLIGENT, Oops, Perfunctory, Rollicking, Salad days, Sans souci, Thoughtless, Tinker's cuss, Tinker's damn
**Careful(ly)** Assiduous, Canny, Cautious, Chary, Circumspect, Delicate, Diligent, Discreet, Easy, Gentle, Heedy, Hooly, Leery, Meticulous, Mindful, Painstaking, Penny-pinching, Penny-wise, Pernickety, Provident, Prudent, Scrimp, Scrupulous, Softly-softly, Studious, Tentie, Tenty, Thorough, Thrifty, Vigilant, Ware, Wary
**Careless(ness), Carelessly** Airy, Anyhow, Blithe, Casual, Cavalier, Cheery, Debonair, Easy, Free-minded, Gallio, Improvident, Imprudent, Inadvertent, Inattention, Inconsiderate, Insouciance, Irresponsible, Lax, Lighthearted, Neglect, Négligé, → NEGLIGENT, Nonchalant, Oops, Oversight, Perfunctory, Raffish, Rash, Reckless, Remiss, Resigned, Riley, Rollicking, Slam-bang, Slapdash, Slaphappy, Slipshod, Sloppy, Sloven(ly), Slubber, Taupie, Tawpie, Thoughtless, Unguarded, Unmindful, Untenty, Unwary
▷**Carelessly** *may indicate* an anagram

**Caress** Bill, Coy, Embrace, Feel, Fondle, Kiss, Lallygag, Lollygag, Noursle, Nursle, Pet, Straik, Stroke, Touch

**Caretaker** Acting, Charge d'affaires, Concierge, Curator, Custodian, Dvornik, Granthi, Guardian, Interim, Janitor, Nightwatchman, Porter, Sexton, Shammash, Shammes, Superintendent, Verger, Warden

**Careworn** Haggard, Lined, Tired, Weary

**Cargo** Boatload, Bulk, Burden, Deck(load), Fraught, Freight(age), Hold, Lading, Last, → LOAD, Navicert, Payload, Shipload, Shipment, Tonnage

**Caribbean** Bajun, Belonger, Cuban, Puerto Rican, Soca, Sokah, Spanish Main, Taino, WI

**Caribou** Tuktoo, Tuktu

**Caricature, Caricaturist** Ape, Beerbohm, Burlesque, Caran d'Ache, Cartoon, Cruikshank, Doyle, Farce, Gillray, Mimicry, Rowlandson, Scarfe, Skit, Spy, Take off, Tenniel, Toon, Travesty

**Carlin** Pug

**Carmelite** Barefoot, White (Friar)

**Carmen** AA, BL, Chai, RAC

**Carnage** Bloodshed, Butchery, Massacre, Slaughter

**Carnal** Bestial, Lewd, Outward, Sensual, Sexual, Worldly

**Carnation** Buttonhole, Clove pink, Dianthus, Gillyflower, Malmaison, Picotee, Pink

**Carnival** Fair, Fasching, Festival, Fete, Fiesta, Mardi Gras, Mas, Moomba, Rag, Revelry, Surf

**Carnivore, Carnivorous** Allosaur, Cacomistle, Cacomixl, Civet, Coati, Creodont, Ermelin, Fennec, Fo(u)ssa, Genet, Geophagus, Glutton, Grison, Hyena, Meerkat, Mink, Otter, Ratel, Stoat, Sundew, Suricate, Viverridae, Weasel, Wolverine, Zoophagan

**Carob** Algar(r)oba, Locust (tree), St John's bread

**Carol(ler)** Noel, Sing, Song, Wait, Wassail, Yodel

**Carousal, Carouse** Bend, Birl(e), Bouse, Bride-ale, Compotation, Drink, Mallemaroking, Mollie, Orge, Orgy, → REVEL, Roist, Screed, Spree, Upsee, Upsey, Upsy, Wassail

**Carp(er)** Beef, Cavil, Censure, Complain, Crab, Critic, Crucian, Crusian, Fault, Gibel, Goldfish, Gripe, Id(e), Koi, Kvetch, Mirror, Mome, Nag, Nibble, Niggle, Nitpick, Prussian, Roach, Roundfish, Scold, Snipe, Twitch, Whine, Yerk, Yirk

**Carpenter** Beveller, Bush, Cabinet-maker, Carfindo, Chippy, Chips, Fitter, Joiner, Joseph, Menuisier, Quince, Sawyer, Shipwright, Tenoner, Woodworker, Wright

▷**Carpenter** *may indicate* an anagram

**Carpet(ing)** Admonish, Aubusson, Axminster, Beetle, Berate, Bessarabian, Body, Broadloom, Brussels, Castigate, Chide, Dhurrie, Drugget, Durrie, Dutch, Excoriation, Kali, Kelim, Khilim, Kidderminster, Kilim, Kirman, Lecture, Lino, Magic, Mat(ting), Moquette, Persian, Rate, Red, Reprimand, Reproach, Reprove, Roast, Rug, Runner, Shagpile, Shark, Shiraz, Stair, Turkey, Wall-to-wall, What for, Wig, Wilton

**Carrageen** Sea-moss

**Carriage** Air, Ar(a)ba, Aroba, Baby buggy, Bandy, Barouche, Bearing, Berlin(e), Bier, Brake, Brit(sch)ka, Britska, Britzka, Brougham, Buckboard, Buggy, Cab, Cabriolet, Calash, Calèche, Car, Cariole, Caroche, Carriole, Carryall, Cartage, Chaise, Charabanc, Charet, Chariot, Chassis, Chay, Clarence, Coach, Coch, Composite, Conveyance, Corridor, Coupé, Curricle, Demeanour, Dennet, Deportment, Désobligeante, Diner, Dormeuse, Dormitory-car, Dos-a-dos, Do-si-do, Drag, Dros(h)ky, Ekka, Equipage, Fiacre, Fly, Four-in-hand, Freight, Gait, Gig, Gladstone, Go-cart, Growler, Gun, Haulage, Hearse, Herdic, Horseless, Howdah, Hurley-hacket, Jampan, Job, Landau(let), Landing, Limber, Mien, Non-smoker, Norimon, Observation-car, Perambulator, Phaeton, Pick-a-back, Pochaise, Pochay, Poise, Pony, Port(age), Portance, Postage, Postchaise, Posture, Poyse, Pram, Pullman, Purdah, Railcar, Railway, Randem, Rath(a), Remise, Ricksha(w), Rig, Rockaway, Saloon, Set-up, Shay, Sled, Sleeper, Smoker, Sociable, Spider, Spider phaeton, Spring, Stanhope, Sulky, Surrey, Tarantas(s), Taxi, T-cart, Tender, Tenue, Tilbury, Tim-whiskey, Tonga, Trail, Transit, Trap, Van, Vetture, Victoria, Voiture, Wagonette, Waterage, Whirligig, Whisk(e)y, Whisky gig

**Carriageway** Dual

**Carrier** Aircraft, Airline, Arm, Backpack, Baldric, Barkis, Barrow, Bomb-ketch, Briefcase, Bulk, Cacolet, Caddie, Caddy, Cadge, Camel, Charon, Coaster, Common, Conveyor, Donkey,

Escort, Fomes, Fomites, Frog, Grid, Hamper, Haul, Haversack, Hawker, Hearse, Hod, Janker, Jill, Majority, Minority, Nosebag, Noyade, Obo, Omnibus, Packhorse, Pap(p)oose, People, Personnel, Pigeon, Porter, Rucksack, Satchel, Schistosoma, Semantide, Sling, Sound, Spore, Straddle, Stretcher(-bearer), Tiffin, Tranter, →TRAY, Troop, Trug, TWA, Vector, Wave

**Carrion** Cadaver, Carcase, Carcass, Flesh, Ket, Morkin, Stapelia

**Carrot(s)** Bribe, Lure, Redhead, Seseli, Titian

**Carry(ing), Carry over** Asport, Bear, Chair, Convey, Enlevé, Escort, Ferry, Frogmarch, Hawk, Hent, Humf, Hump, Humph, Kurvey, Land, Move, Pack, Pickaback, Port, Reappropriate, Stock, Sustain, Tide over, Tote, →TRANSPORT, Trant, Waft, Wage, With, Yank

**Carryall** Tote bag

**Carry on** Continue, Create, Wage

**Carry out** Execute, Implement, Mastermind, Perform, Pursue, Transact

**Cart(er)** Apple, Bandy, Barrow, Bogey, Buck, Buggy, Caddie, Cape, Car(r)iole, Chapel, Dandy, Democrat, Democrat wagon, Dog, Dolly, Dray, Egyptologist, Float, Furphy, Gambo, Gill, Golf, Governess, Gurney, Hackery, Hock, Jag, Jill, Lead, Mail(-gig), Night, Pie, Pram, Push, Rickshaw, Scot, Scotch, Shandry, T, Tax(ed), Telega, Trolley, Tumbrel, Tumbril, Village, Wag(g)on, Wain, Water, Wheelbarrow, Whitechapel

**Carte** Menu

**Carte blanche** Free rein

**Cartel** Duopoly, Firms, OPEC, Ring, Syndicate, Zaibatsu

**Carthaginian** Punic

**Carthorse** Aver, Shire

**Carthusian** Bruno, DOM

**Cartilage** Antitragus, Arytenoid, Chondral, Chondrin, Chondrus, Cricoid, Darwin's tubercle, Disc, Ensiform, Epiglottis, Gristle, Hyaline, Lytta, Meniscus, Semilunar, Tendrons, Thyroid, Tragus, Worm, Xiphoid

**Cartload** Fother, Seam

**Cartographer** Cabot, Chartist, Kremer, Mercator, OS, Speed

**Carton** Box, Case, Crate, Shoebox, Sydney, Tub

**Cartoon(ist)** Addams, Andy Capp, Animated, Bairnsfather, Bateman, Caricature, Comic, Comic strip, Disney, Drawn, Emmet, Fougasse, Fumetto, Garland, Goldberg, Heath Robinson, Lancaster, Leech, Low, Manga, Mel, Partridge, Popeye, Robinson, Scarfe, Schulz, Short, Shrek, Spy, Strip, Superman, Tenniel, Thurber, Tidy, Tintin, Trog

**Cartridge** Ball, Blank, Bullet, Cartouche, Cassette, Crystal, Doppie, Live, Magazine, Magnetic, Magnum, QIC, Rim-free, Shell, Spent

**Cart-track** Rut

**Cartwheel** Handspring

**Caruncle** Aril, Carnosity, Strophiole

**Carve(d), Carver, Carving** Abated, Alcimedon, Apsaras, Armchair, Bas relief, Camaieu, Cameo, Chair, Chip, Chisel, Cilery, Crocket, Cut, Dismember, Doone, Emboss, Enchase, Engrave, Entail, Entayle, Fiddlehead, Gargoyle, Gibbons, Glyphic, Glyptic, Hew, Incise, Inscribe, Insculp, Intaglio, Knotwork, Netsuke, Nick, Petroglyph, Relievo, Scrimshaw, Sculp(t), Slice, Tondo, Trophy, Truncheon, Tympanum, Whakairo, Whittle

**Caryatid** Column, Telamon

**Caryocar** Butternut

**Casanova** Heartbreaker, Leman, Philanderer, Playboy, Seducer, Womaniser

**Cascade** Cataract, Fall, Lin(n), Stream, Waterfall

**Cascara** Amarga, Buckthorn, Honduras bark, Rhamnus, Sagrada, Wahoo

**Case(s), Casing** Abessive, Ablative, Accusative, Action, Adessive, Allative, Altered, Appeal, Aril, Ascus, Assumpsit, Attaché, Basket, Beer, Bere, Bin, Binnacle, Bittacle, Blimp, Boll, Box, Brief, Bundwall, Burr, Burse, C, Ca, Cabinet, Cachet, Calyx, Canister, Canterbury, Capsule, Cartouch(e), Cartridge, Cask(et), Cause célèbre, Cellaret, Chase, Chitin, Chrysalis, Cocoon, Coffin, Comitative, Compact, Crate, Croustade, Crust, Cyst, Dative, Declension, Detinue, Digi-pack, Dihedron, Dispatch, Display, Dossier, Dressing, Elative, Elytron, Enallage, Enclose, Ensheath, Ergative, Essive, Etui, Etwee, Event, Example, Flan, Flapjack,

Flask, Frame, Gearbox, Genitive, Glass, Grip, Hanaper, Hard, Hatbox, Helmet, Hold-all, Holster, Housewife, Hull, Humidor, Husk, Illative, Imperial, → IN CASE, Index, Indusium, Inessive, Instance, Kalamdan, Keg, Keister, Locative, Locket, Lorica, Manche, Matchbox, Matter, Mermaid's purse, Mezuzah, Music, Nacelle, Nominative, Non-suit, Nutshell, Objective, Oblique, Ochrea, Ocrea, Outpatient, Packing, Pair, Papeterie, Patient, Peapod, Pencil, Penner, Phylactery, Pipe, Plight, Plummer-block, Pod, Port, Portfolio, Possessive, Prima facie, Puparium, Queer fish, Quiver, Recce, Reconnoitre, Red box, Sabretache, Sad, Satchel, Scabbard, Scissor, Seashell, Sheath(e), Shell, Situation, Six-pack, Sleeve, Sporocyst, Sporran, Stead, Sted, Straitjacket, Subjective, Suit, Tantalus, Tea-chest, Telium, Test, Theca, Tichborne, Toolbox, Trial, Trunk, Type, Valise, Vanity bag, Vasculum, Vitrine, Vocative, Volva, Walise, Walking, Wallet, Wardian, Wing, Worst, Writing

**Case-harden** Nitrode

**Casein** Curd

**Casement** Frame, Roger, Sash, Window

**Cash** Blunt, Bonus, Bounty, Bread, Change, Coin, Digital, Dosh, Dot, Float, Funds, Hard (currency), Idle money, Imprest, Liquid, Lolly, → MONEY, Needful, Ochre, Oof, Oscar, Pence, Petty, Ready, Realise, Redeem, Rhino, Spondulicks, Spot, Sterling, Stumpy, Tender, Tin, Wampum, Wherewithal

**Cashew** Hog-plum

**Cashier, Cash machine** Annul, ATM, Break, Depose, Disbar, Dismiss, Displace, Oust, Teller, Treasurer

**Cashmere** Circassienne

**Casino** Monte Carlo

**Cask(et)** Armet, Barrel, Barrico, Bas(i)net, Box, Breaker, Butt, Cade, Casque, Cassette, Chest, Coffer, Coffin, Drum, Firkin, Galeate, Harness, Heaume, Hogshead, Keg, Leaguer, Octave, Pin, Pipe, Puncheon, Pyxis, Run(d)let, Salade, Sallet, Sarcophagus, Scuttlebutt, Shook, Shrine, Solera, Tierce, Tun, Wine

**Cask-stand** Stillion

**Cassava** Manioc, Tapioca, Yuc(c)a

**Casserole** Boeuf bourguignon, Diable, Hotpot, Navarin, Osso bucco, Pot, Ratatouille, Salmi, Stockpot, Terrine, Tzimmes

**Cassette** Cartridge, Tape, Video

**Cassia** Cleanser, Senna

**Cassio** Lieutenant

**Cassiterite** Needle-tin, Tinstone

**Cassock** Gown, Soutane, Subucula

**Cast (down, off, out), Casting** Abattu, Actors, Add, Angle, Appearance, Bung, Cavel, Cire perdue, Dash, Death mask, Die, Discard, Ecdysis, Ectype, Eject, Emit, Endocranial, Exorcise, Exuviae, Exuvial, Fling, Form, Found, Fusil, Grape, Hawk, Heave, Hob, Horoscope, Hue, Hurl, Impression, Ingo(w)es, Keb, Look, Lose, Lost wax, Mew, Mo(u)lt, Moulage, Mould, Moult, Performers, Pick, Plaster(stone), Plastisol®, Players, Print, Put, Reject, Sand, Sculptured, Sent, Shed, Shoot, Shy, Sling, Slive, Slough, Spoil, Stamp, Stookie, Swarm, Tailstock, Terracotta, → THROW, Toss, Tot, Warp, Wax, Worm, Ytost

▷**Cast** *may indicate* an anagram or a piece of a word missing

**Castanet** Crotal(um), Knackers

**Castaway** Adrift, Crusoe, Gunn, Left, Man Friday, Outcast, Robinson, Selkirk, Shipwrecked, Stranded, Weft

▷**Cast by** *may indicate* surrounded by

**Caste** Brahmin, Burakumin, Class, Dalit, Group, Harijan, Hova, Kshatriya, Rajpoot, Rajpout, Rajput, Rank, Scheduled, Sect, Shudra, Sudra, Untouchable, Vaisya, Varna

**Caster** Truckle

**Castigate** Berate, Chasten, Chastise, Criticise, Denounce, Flay, Keelhaul, Lash, Punish, Rate, Scold

**Cast-iron** Spiegeleisen

**Castle(d)** Barbara, Bouncy, Broch, C, Casbah, Chateau, Citadel, Fastness, Fort, Kasba(h), Maiden, Man, Mot(t)e, Motte and bailey, Move, Palace, Rook, Stronghold, Villa

## CASTLES

*4 letters:*
Drum
Keep
Sand
Trim

*5 letters:*
Blair
Blois
Conwy
Corfe
Hever
Leeds
Spain
Upnor

*6 letters:*
Cawdor
Forfar
Glamis
Howard
Ludlow
Raglan
Wemyss

*7 letters:*
Adamant
Alnwick
Amboise
Arundel
Beeston
Belvoir
Blarney
Braemar
Calzean
Camelot
Canossa
Chillon
Colditz
Cooling
Culzean
Despair
Harlech
Kremlin
Lincoln
Otranto
Schloss
Skipton
Sudeley
Warwick
Windsor

*8 letters:*
Balmoral
Bamburgh
Bastille
Berkeley
Carbonek
Chepstow
Crotchet
Doubting
Egremont
Elephant
Elsinore
Inverary
Kronberg
Malperdy
Pembroke
Perilous
Rackrent
Reculver
Rhuddlan
Richmond
Stirling
Stokesay
Stormont
Tintagel
Urquhart
Wartburg

*9 letters:*
Dangerous
Dunsinane
Edinburgh
Lancaster
Restormel
Rochester
Sherborne
Trausnitz

*10 letters:*
Caerphilly
Kenilworth
Pontefract

*11 letters:*
Carisbrooke
Chateauroux
Eilean Donan
Gormenghast

*12 letters:*
Fotheringhay
Herstmonceux
Sissinghurst

*13 letters:*
Carrickfergus

---

**Castor** Muffineer, Wheel
**Castor-oil** Ricinus
**Castrate(d), Castrato** Alter, Cut, Doctor, Emasculate, Eunuch, Evirate, Farinelli, Geld, Glib, Lib, Manzuoli, Moreschi, Mutilate, Neuter, Senesino, Spado, Spay, Staig, Steer, Swig, Wethers
**Castro** Fidel
**Casual(ly), Casuals** Accidental, Adventitious, Airy(-fairy), Blasé, Blithe, Chance, Chav(ette), Flippant, Grass, Haphazard, Idle, Incidental, Informal, Jaunty, Lackadaisical, Leisurewear, Nonchalant, Odd(ment), Odd-jobber, Offhand, Off-the-cuff, Orra, Overly, Passing, Promiscuous, Random, Scratch, Shoe, Slaphappy, Slipshod, Sporadic, Stray, Temp, Throwaway, Trendy
**Casualty** Blue on blue, Caduac, Chance-medley, ER, → VICTIM
**Casuist** Jesuit
**Cat** Ailuro-, Barf, Big, Boat, Boke, Bush, Catamount, Dandy, Domestic, Egurgitate, Fat, Felid, Feline, Flog, Foss, Garfield, Glaring, Gossip, Grimalkin, Gus, Hipster, Jazzer, Lair, Lash, Mewer, Mog, Native, Neuter, Nib, Oriental, Painter, Palm, Pardal, Practical, Puss, Queen, Regurgitate, Sacred, Scourge, Sick, Singed, Spew, Spue, Swinger, Top, Vomit, Whip

---

## CATS

*3 letters:*
Gib
Kit
Rex
Tom

*4 letters:*
Eyra
Lion
Lynx
Manx
Musk
Pard
Puma

*5 letters:*
Alley
Civet
Felix
Fossa
Genet
Hodge
Korat
Liger

Manul
Ounce
Quoll
Rasse
Rumpy
Tabby
Tiger
Tigon
Zibet

*6 letters:*
Angora
Birman
Bobcat
Cougar
Foussa
Jaguar
La Perm
Malkin
Margay
Mouser
Musang
Ocelot
Ocicat
Serval
Somali
Sphynx
Tibert
Tybalt
Weasel
Zibeth

*7 letters:*
Burmese
Caracal
Cheetah
Clowder
Dasyure
Foumart
Genette
Leopard
Linsang
Lioncel
Maltese
Nandine
Pallas's
Panther
Persian
Pharaoh
Polecat
Ragdoll
Siamese
Tiffany
Tigress
Viverra

*8 letters:*
Balinese
Baudrons
Cacomixl
Cheshire
Devon Rex
Kilkenny
Long-hair
Mountain
Munchkin
Ringtail
Snowshoe
Tiffanie

*9 letters:*
Asparagus
Binturong
Bluepoint
Chantilly
Chartreux
Delundung
Himalayan
Lioncelle
Maine Coon
Marmalade
Mehitabel
Niebelung
Sealpoint
Shorthair
Tobermory
Tonkinese

*10 letters:*
Abyssinian
Cacomistle
Cornish Rex
Jaguarondi
Jaguarundi
Ring-tailed
Selkirk Rex
Turkish Van

*11 letters:*
Bengal tiger
Colourpoint
Egyptian Mau
Havana Brown
Russian Blue
Tongkingese

*12 letters:*
American Curl
Scottish Fold

*13 letters:*
Tortoise-shell
Turkish Angora

*14 letters:*
Asian Shorthair
Australian Mist
Siberian Forest

*15 letters:*
Norwegian Forest

*16 letters:*
American Wirehair

*17 letters:*
American Shorthair

*19 letters:*
Californian Spangled

---

**Cataclysm(ic)** Apocalypse, Dire
**Catacomb** Cemetery, Crypt, Hypogeum, Vault
**Catalepsy, Catalepsis, Cataleptic** Catatony, Comatose, Trance
**Catalogue(r)** Categorise, Cattle dog, Dewey, Dictionary, Durchkomponi(e)rt, File, Index, Inventory, Itemise, Jane's, K(ochel), List, Litany, Magalog, MARC, Messier, Ragman, Ragment, Raisonné, Record, Register, Roll, Shelf, Specialogue, Star, Subject, Table, Tabulate, Thematic, Union
**Catalyst** Accelerator, Agent, Aldol, Chemical, Enzyme, Erepsin, Impetus, Influence, Kryptonite, Stereospecific, Unicase, Ziegler
**Catamite** Ganymede, Gunsel, Ingle, Pathic
**Cataplasm** Poultice
**Catapult** Ballista, Ging, Launch, Mangon(el), Perrier, Petrary, Propel, Scorpion, Shanghai, Sling, Slingshot, Stone-bow, Tormentum, Trebuchet, Wye, Y
**Cataract** Cascade, Film, Overfall, Pearl, Pearl-eye, Torrent, Waterfall, Web and pin
**Catarrh(al)** Coryza, Nasal, Rheum
**Catastrophe, Catastrophic** Act of God, Apocalypse, Calamity, Crisis, Damoclean, →DISASTER, Doom, Epitasis, Fiasco, Meltdown, Ruinous, Tragedy
**Catatonia** Stupor
**Cat-call** Boo, Jeer, Mew, Miaow, Miaul, Razz, Wawl, Whistle, Wrawl
**Catch(y), Catcher, Catching, Caught** Air, Apprehend, Arrest, Attract, Backstop, Bag, Benet, Bone, C, Capture, Chape, Clasp, Cog, Collar, Conquest, Contagious, Contract, Cop, Corner, Cotton on, Ct, Deprehend, Detent, Dolly, Engage, Enmesh, Ensnare, Entoil, Entrap,

Fang, Fastener, Field, Fish, Fumble, Gaper, Get, Glee(some), Grasp, Had, Hank, Hasp, Haud, Haul, Hear, Hitch, Hold, Hook, Inmesh, Keddah, Keight, Kep(pit), Kheda, Kill, Land, Lapse, Lasso, Latch, Lazo, Lime, Lock, Morse, Nab, Nail, Net, Nick, Nim, Nobble, Noose, Overhear, Overhent, Overtake, Parti, Paul, Pawl, Rap, Release, Rope, Round, Rub, Safety, Save, Sean, Sear, See(n), Seize, Sitter, Skier, → **SNAG**, Snap, Snare, Snarl, Sneck, Snib, Snig(gle), → **SONG**, Stop, Surprise, Swindle, Tack, Taen, Take, Tallow, Tane, Tickle, Trammel, Trap, Trawl, Trick, Tripwire, Troll, Twenty two, Twig, Understand, Window, Wrestle

**Catchword** Motto, Shibboleth, Slogan, Tag

**Catechism** Carritch, Shorter, Test

**Categorise, Categories, Category** Assort, → **CLASS**, Classify, Etic, Genera, Genre, Genus, Grade, Infraclass, Infraorder, Label, Order, Pigeonhole, Range, Rubric, Specie, Stereotype, Taxon, Triage, Type

**Cater(er)** Acatour, Cellarer, Feed, Manciple, → **PROVIDE**, Purveyor, Serve, Steward, Supply, Victualler, Vivandière

**Caterpillar** Army worm, Aweto, Boll worm, Cabbageworm, Cotton-worm, Cutworm, Eruciform, Geometer, Gooseberry, Grub, Hop-dog, Hornworm, Inchworm, Larva, Looper, Measuring worm, Osmeterium, Palmer, Silkworm, Tent, Webworm, Woolly-bear

**Caterwaul** Meow, Wrawl

**Catfish** Hassar, Woof

**Cathartic** Black draught, Turbeth

**Cathedral** Amiens, Basilica, Birmingham, Burgos, Chartres, Chester, Chichester, → **CHURCH**, Cologne, Cortona, Dome, Duomo, Durham, Ely, Evreux, Exeter, Gloucester, Guildford, Hereford, Hertford, Huesca, Kirkwall, Lateran, Lichfield, Lincoln, Lugo, Minster, Mullingar, Norwich, Notre Dame, Rheims, Ripon, Rochester, St Albans, St Davids, St Paul's, Salisbury, Santiago de Compostela, Sens, Teruel, Up(p)sala, Viseu, Wakefield, Wells, Westminster, Winchester, Worcester, York

**Catherine** Braganza, Parr

**Catherine-wheel** Girandole

**Catheter** Balloon

**Cathode** Electrode, Filament, Ray

**Catholic** Assumptionist, Broad, Christian Socialism, Comprehensive, Defenders, Doolan, Eclectic, Ecumenical, General, German, Irvingism, Jebusite, Jesuit, Latin, Lazarist, Left-footer, Liberal, Marian, Old, Opus Dei, Ostiary, Papalist, Papaprelatist, Passionist, Recusant, Redemptionist, Roman, Romish, Salesian, Spike, Theatine, Thomist, Tike, Tory, Tridentine, Tyke, Uniat, Universal, Ursuline, Waldenses, Wide

**Catkin** Amentum, Chat, Lamb's tail, Pussy-willow, Salicaceous

**Cat-lover** Ailurophile

**Catmint** Nep, Nepeta, Nip

**Catnap** Kip

**Cato** Porcian, Uticensis

**Cats-eye** Chatoyant, Cymophane

**Catsmeat** Lights

**Catspaw** Pawn, Property, Tool

**Cat's tail** Reed-mace, Typha

**Cat's whiskers** Vibrissa

**Cattle(pen)** Aberdeen Angus, Africander, Ankole, Aver, Ayrshire, Beef, Beefalo, Belgian Blue, Belted Galloway, Bestial, Black, Bovine, Brahman, British White, Buffalo, Carabao, Charbray, Charolais, Chillingham, Dairy, Dexter, Drove, Durham, Fee, Friesian, Friesland, Galloway, Gaur, Gayal, Guernsey, Gyal, Heard, Herd, Hereford, Highland, Holstein (Friesian), Illawarra, Jersey, Kerry, Kine, Kittle, Kouprey, Kraal, Ky(e), Kyloe, Lairage, Limousin, Lincoln, Longhorn, Luing, Neat, Nout, Nowt, Owsen, Oxen, Piemontese, Rabble, Redpoll, Rother, Santa Gertrudis, Shorthorn, Simment(h)al, Soum, South Devon, Sowm, Steer, Stock, Store, Stot, Sussex, Tamarao, Tamarau, Teeswater, Wagyu, Welsh Black

**Cattle disease** Actinobacillosis, Actinomycosis, Anthrax, Black water, Dry-bible, Footrot, Gallsickness, Heart-water, Hoove, Johne's, Listeriosis, Lumpy jaw, Mange, Mastitis, Milk lameness, Moorill, New Forest, Quarter-ill, Red-water, Rinderpest, Scours, Scrapie, Texas fever, Wire-heel, Woody-tongue

**Cattle food** Fodder, Poonac, Silage

**Cattleman** Cowboy, Herder, Maverick, Puncher, Rancher, Ringer, Stock-rider

**Catty** Kin, Spiteful

**Catwalk** Runway

**Caucasian** Aryan, Azabaijani, Azeri, Cherkess, European, Georgian, Iberian, Kabardian, Melanochroi, Paleface, Semite, Shemite, White, Yezdi, Yezidee, Zezidee

**Caucus** Assembly, Cabal, Cell, Gathering, Race

▸**Caught** *see* **CATCH(Y)**

**Caul** Baby-hood, Kell, Membrane, Sillyhow

**Cauldron** Kettle, Pot

**Cauliflower** Curd, Ear, Floret, Gobi

**Caulk** Fill, Pay, Pitch, Snooze

**Causation, Cause(d), Causes** Aetiology, Agent, Bandwagon, Beget, Breed, Bring, Case, Célèbre, Common, Compel, Create, Crusade, Determinant, Due, Effect, Efficient, Encheason, Engender, Entail, Evoke, Expedite, Factor, Final, First, Flag-day, Formal, Gar(re), Generate, Ideal, Incur, Induce, Inspire, Lead, Lost, Make, Material, Motive, Movement, Natural, → **OCCASION**, Parent, Pathogen, Precipitate, Probable, Promote, Prompt, Provoke, Proximate, Reason, Root, Sake, Secondary, Show, Source, Teleology, Topic, Trigger, Ultimate, Wreak

**Causeway** Giant's, Mole, Tombolo

**Caustic** Acid, Acrimonious, Alkaline, Bleach, Burning, Common, Erodent, Escharotic, Lime, Lunar, Lye, Moxa, Potash, Pungent, Sarcastic, Scathing, Seare, Soda, Tart, Vitriol, Waspish, Withering

**Cauterise, Cauterisation** Brand, Burn, Disinfect, Inustion, Moxibustion, Sear

**Caution, Cautiously, Cautious (person)** Achitophel, Admonish, Ahithophel, Alert, Amber, Awarn, Beware, Book, Cagey, Card, Care, Cave, Caveat, Chary, Circumspect, Credence, Cure, Defensive, Deliberate, Discretion, Fabian, Forewarn, Gingerly, Guard(ed), Hedger, Heedful, Leery, Prudent, Pussyfoot, Rum, Scream, Skite, Tentative, Thrift, Timorous, Vigilant, Ware, → **WARN**, Wary, Yellow card

**Cavalcade** Pageant, Parade, Procession, Sowarree, Sowarry

**Cavalier** Brusque, Careless, Cicisbeo, Devil-may-care, Gallant, Lively, Malignant, Monarchist, Offhand, Peart, Rider, Royalist

▹**Cavalier** *may indicate* an anagram

**Cavalry(man)** Blues, Car(a)bineer, Car(a)binier, Cornet, Cossack, Dragoon, Equites, Heavies, Horse, Horse Guards, Household, Hussar, Ironsides, Knights, Lancers, Life Guards, Light-horse, Plunger, Ressaldar, Risaldar, Rough-rider, Rutter, Sabres, Sabreur, Silladar, Spahee, Spahi, Trooper, Uhlan, Yeomanry

**Cave(rn), Caves, Cave-dwelling, Cave in, Cavernous** Acherusia, Aladdin's, Alert, Altamira, Antar, Antre, Beware, Bone, Capitulate, Cellar, Cheddar, Collapse, Corycian, Deep, Den, Domdaniel, Erebus, Fingal's, Fore, Grot(to), Hollow, Jenolan, Lascaux, Look-out, Lupercal, Mammoth, Mind out, Nix, Pot-hole, Proteus, Sepulchre, Snow, Spel(a)ean, Speleology, Spelunker, Speos, Tassili, Trophonian, Vault, Waitomo, Ware, Weem, Wookey Hole

**Cave-dweller** Pict, Troglodyte, Troll

**Caveman** Adullam, Aladdin, Fingal, Neanderthal, Primitive, Troglodyte, Troll

**Cavendish** Tobacco

**Caviar(e)** Beluga, Osietra, Raun, Roe, Sevruga, Sturgeon

**Cavil** Carp, Haggle, Quibble, Split hairs

**Cavity** Acetabulum, Amygdale, Amygdule, Androclinium, Antrum, Archenteron, Atrial, Atrium, Body, Camera, Camouflet, Celom, Chamber, Cisterna, Clinandrium, Coelenteron, Coelom(e), Conceptacle, Concha, Countermark, Crater, Crypt, Cyst, Dent, Domatium, Druse, Enteron, Follicle, Foss, Gap, Geode, Glenoid, Gloryhole, Hold, Hole, Honeycomb, Lacuna, Locule, Mediastinum, Mialoritic, Orbita, Orifice, Pelvis, Pharynx, Pleural, Pocket, Pothole, Pulp, Resonant, Sac, Segmentation, Sinus, Splanchnocele, Stomod(a)eum, Tartarus, Tear,

Thunderegg, Tympanum, Vacuole, Vein, Ventricle, Vesicle, Vitta, Vomica, Vug, Vugg, Vugh, Well

**Cavort(ing)** Dance, Frolic, Gambol, Jag, Rollick, Romp, Scamper

**Cavy** Agouti, Capybara, Hograt, Musk, Paca

**Cayman Islands** Tax haven

**Cease(fire)** Abate, Blin, Cut, Desist, Devall, Die, Disappear, Halt, Ho, Intermit, Leese, Lin, Lose, Pass, Quit, Refrain, Remit, Sessa, → **STOP**, Truce

**Ceaseless** Eternal, Incessant, Non-stop, Perpetual

**Cecil** Rhodes

**Cedar(wood)** Arolla, Atlas, Barbados, Cryptomeria, Deodar, Incense, Jamaica, Japanese, Toon

**Cede** Grant, Yield

**Ceiling** Absolute, Barrel, Cap, Cloud, Coffered, Cove, Cupola, Dome, Glass, Lacunar, Laquearia, Limit, Plafond, Roof, Service, Silver, Soffit, Stained glass

**Celebrate(d), Celebration, Celebrity** Ale, A-list, All-star, Beanfeast, Beano, Besung, Big name, Bigwig, Binge, B-list, Brat-packer, Brilliant, Carnival, Cel, Chant, Commemorate, Crowd-puller, Distinguished, Do, Eclat, Emblazon, Encaenia, Epithalamion, Epithalamium, Fabulous, Fame, Feast, Feis, Fest(al), Festivity, Fete, Fiesta, First-footing, Gala, Gaudeamus, Gaudy, Glitterati, Glorify, Goings on, Grog-up, Guest star, Harvest home, Headliner, Hen-night, Hogmanay, Hold, Holiday, Honour, Hoop-la, Jamboree, Jol, Jollifications, Jollities, Joncanoe, Jubilee, Junkanoo, Keep, Large it, Laud, Legend, Limelight, Lion, Loosing, Lowsening, Luminary, Maffick, Mardi Gras, Mass, Mawlid al-Nabi, Megastar, Monstre sacre, Name, Noted, Nuptials, Observe, Occasion, Orgy, Panathenaea, Party, Personage, Personality, Pinata, Praise, Randan, Rave-up, Record, Rejoice, Renown, Repute, Revel, Rite, Roister, Sangeet, Saturnalia, See in, Sex symbol, Shindig, Sing, Sleb, Slugfest, Spree, Stag-night, Star, Storied, Sung, Supermodel, Superstar, Tet, Treat, Triumph, Wassail, Wet, Whoopee, World famous

**Celerity** Dispatch, Haste, Speed, Velocity

**Celery** Alexanders, Smallage, Stick

**Celestial** Asteroid, Chinese, Cosmic, Divine, Ethereal, Heavenly, Seraph, Stellar, Supernal, Uranic

**Celibate, Celibacy** Bachelor, Chaste, Nun, Paterin(e), Priest, Rappist, Rappite, Shakers, Single, Spinster

**Cell(s), Cellular** Alveolus, Amyloidal, Anuploid, Battery, Black hole, Blood, Bullpen, Cadre, Chamber, Chapel, Condemned, Crypt, Cubicle, Cytoplasm, Death, Dendritic, Dungeon, Ectoblast, Group, Laura, Lock up, Oosphere, Padded, Peter, Priesthole, → **PRISON**, Prokaryon, Proviral, Safety, Strip, Tank, Unit

---

**CELLS**

*1 letter:*
T

*3 letters:*
Dry
Egg
Pec
Sex
Wet

*4 letters:*
Axon
Comb
Cone
Cyte
Fuel
Germ
Hair
HeLa
Mast
Oxum
Soma
Stem
Zeta

*5 letters:*
Ascus
Basal
Canal
Clark
Cyton
Flame
Giant
Gland
Guard
Islet
Linin
Lymph
Nerve
Nicad
Solar
Sperm
Spore
Stone
Swarm
Water
White
X-body

*6 letters:*
Button
Censor
Collar
Cybrid
Cytoid
Diaxon
Gamete
Goblet
Hadley
Helper
Killer
Morula
Mother
Neuron
Oocyte
Plasma
Sensor
Sickle

Somite
Target
Thread
Zygote

*7 letters:*
Bimorph
Cadmium
Cambium
Cathode
Conical
Daniell
Energid
Euploid
Gemmule
Gravity
Helper T
Initial
Lithite
Myotome
Myotube
Neurite
Neurone
Neutron
Plastid
Primary
Purinje
Schwann
Sertoli
Sleeper
Somatic
Spindle
Spireme
Sporule
Storage
Tapetum
Vesicle
Voltaic

*8 letters:*
Akaryote
Auxocyte
Basidium
Basophil
Blasteme
Blastula
Congenic
Cytology
Daughter
Defensin
Ectomere
Endoderm
Endosarc
Ependyma
Epiblast
Eukaryon
Galvanic
Gonidium
Gonocyte
Hapteron
Hemocyte
Meiocyte
Meristem
Monocyte
Myoblast
Neoblast
Palisade
Parietal
Platelet
Purkinje
Receptor
Retinula
Schizont
Selenium
Seredium
Squamous
Standard
Sweatbox
Symplast
Synergid
Tracheid
Unipolar
Zoosperm
Zoospore

*9 letters:*
Adipocyte
Antipodal
Astrocyte
Athrocyte
Auxospore
Basophile
Coenocyte
Companion
Corpuscle
Desmosome
Ectoplasm
Embryo-sac
Fibrocyte
Haemocyte
Honeycomb
Hybridoma
Idioblast
Internode
Iridocyte
Karyology
Laticifer
Leclanché
Leucocyte
Leukocyte
Macromere
Merozoite
Microcyte
Micromere
Myelocyte
Myofibril
Notochord
Organelle
Periplasm
Periplast
Phagocyte
Phellogen
Proembryo
Satellite
Secondary
Spermatid
Sporocyte
Suspensor
Syncytium
Synkaryon
Thymocyte
Trabecula
Tracheide

*10 letters:*
Ameloblast
Archespore
Blastoderm
Blastomere
Centrosome
Choanocyte
Chromaffin
Chromosome
Cnidoblast
Eosinophil
Epithelium
Fibroblast
Gametocyte
Histiocyte
Leucoblast
Leukoblast
Lymphocyte
Macrophage
Melanocyte
Mesenchyme
Microphage
Multipolar
Myeloblast
Neuroblast
Neutrophil
Normoblast
Osteoblast
Osteoclast
Perikaryon
Phelloderm
Protoplast
Spermatium
Spherocyte
Suppressor
Totipotent
White-blood

*11 letters:*
Aplanospore
Arthrospore
Calyptrogen
Endothelium
Erythrocyte
Granulocyte
Interneuron
Kinetoplast
Lymphoblast
Megaloblast
Melanoblast
Microgamete
Microvillus
Motor neuron
Odontoblast
Poikilocyte
Propoceptor
Schistocyte
Spheroplast
Suppressor T
Trophoblast

*12 letters:*
Aplanogamete
Chondroblast
Cytogenetics
Electrolytic
Erythroblast
Gametrangium
Haematoblast
Interstitial
Paraphysisis
Photovoltaic
Reticulocyte
Spermatocyte
Spermatozoid
Spermatozoon
Spongioblast

*13 letters:*
Chromatophore
Mitochondroin
Photoelectric
Photoreceptor
Sustentacular

*14 letters:*
Spermatogonium
Weston standard

**Cellar** Basement, Bodega, Coalhole, Dunny, Hypogeum, Night, Ratskeller, Salt, Shaker, Storm, Vault, Vaultage, Vaut, Wine

**Cell division** Amitosis

**Cellist, Cello** Casals, Du Pré, Hermit, Prisoner, Tortelier

**Celluloid, Cellulose** Acetate, Cel, Film, Viscose, Xylonite

**Celt(ic)** Archdruid, Belgic, Breton, Brython, Cornish, Druid, Gadhel, Gael(dom), Goidel, Helvetii, Kelt, La Tène, Manx, P, Q, Taffy, Welsh

**Cement** Araldite®, Asbestos, Blast-furnace, Ciment fondu, Compo, Concrete, Fix, Flaunch, Glue, Granolithic, Grout, Gunite, High-alumina, Hydraulic, Lute, Luting, Maltha, Mastic, Mastich, Mortar, Paste, Pointing, Porcelain, Portland, Putty, Rice-glue, Roman, Rubber, Screed, Setter, Slurry, → STICK, Trass, Water

**Cemetery** Aceldama, Arenarium, Arlington, Boneyard, Boot Hill, Campo santo, Catacomb, Churchyard, God's Acre, Golgotha, Graveyard, Musall, Necropolis, Père Lachaise, Potter's field, Saqqara, Urnfield

**Cenotaph** Monument

**Censer** Cassolette, Navicula, Thurible

**Censor(ious), Censorship, Censure** Abridge, Accuse, Admonition, AD notice, Airbrush, Animadvert, Appeach, Ban, Banner, Berate, Blame, Blue-pencil, Bowdler, Braid, Carpet, Castigate, Cato, Chasten, Comstockery, → CONDEMN, Counter-intelligence, Critical, Criticise, Cut, Damn, Dang, Decry, Denounce, Dispraise, Edit, Excommunicate, Excoriate, Expurgate, Gag, Obloquy, Opprobrium, Rap, Rebuke, Redact, Repress, Reprimand, Reproach, Reprobate, Reprove, Satirise, Scold, Scrub, Slam, Slate, Stricture, Strop, Suppress, Tax, Tear into, Tirade, Traduce, Wig

**Census, Census taker** Count, Head-count, Numerator, Poll

**Cent(s)** Bean, Coin, Ct, Penny, Red, Zack

**Centaur** Ch(e)iron, Horseman, Nessus, Sagittary, Therianthropic

**Centenary, Centennial** Anniversary, Colorado

**Centipede** Chilopoda, Earwig, Pauropod, Polypod, Scolopendra, Scutiger, Thousand-legs

**Central(ly), Centre** Active, Amid, Arts, Assessment, Attendance, Axis, Battlebus, Bosom, Broca's, Bunt, Call, Cardinal, Chakra, Civic, Community, Contact, Core, Cost, Crisis, Day, Daycare, Dead, Design, Detention, Detoxification, Deuteron, Deuton, Downtown, Drop-in, Epergne, Eye, Field, Focus, Foyer, Frontal, Garden, Health, Heart, Heartland, Heritage, Hotbed, Hothouse, Hub, Incident, Inmost, Inner, Internal, Interpretive, Job, Juvenile, Juvie, Kernel, Kingpin, Law, Leisure, Lincoln, Live, Main, Mark-white, Mecca, Median, Medulla, Mid(st), Midfield, Midpoint, Midway, Mission, Music, Nave, Navel, Nerve, Nub, Nucleus, Omphalus, Pompidou, Profit, Property, Reception, Rehabilitation, Remand, Respiratory, Rest, Service, Shopping, Social Education, Storm, Teachers', Theme park, Trauma, Visitor, Waist, Weather, Youth custody

**Central American** Mangue, Mayan, Miskito, Olmec, Otomi, Pueblo, Totomac, Zapotec

**Central heating** Cen, CH

▷**Centre** *may indicate* middle letters

**Centrepiece** Epergne

**Century** Age, C, Eon, Era, Le Grand Siecle, Magdeburg, Maiden, Period, Siècle, Ton

**Cephalopod** Ammonite, Calamary, Cuttle, Loligo, Nautilus, Octopus, Sepia, Squid

**Ceramic(s)** Agateware, Arcanist, Cermet, China, Earthen, Ferrite, Ferronneries, Porcelain, Pottery, Sialon, Syalon®, Tiles

**Cerberus** Hellhound

**Cereal** Amelcorn, Awn, Barley, Blé, Bran, Bread-basket, Buckwheat, Bulgar, Bulg(h)ur, Cassava, Corn, Cornflakes, Couscous, Emmer, Farina, Gnocchi, Grain, Granola, Groats, Hominy, Maize, Mandioc(a), Mandiocca, Manihot, Mani(h)oc, Mealie, Millet, Muesli, Oats, Paddy, Popcorn, Proso, Rye(corn), Sago, Samp, Sarassin, Seed, Semolina, Sorghum, Spelt, Sweetcorn, Tapioca, Tef(f), Triticale, Triticum, Wheat, Zea

**Cerebral** Sensoria

**Cerebrate, Cerebration** Pore, Thought

**Ceremonial, Ceremony** Aarti, Amrit, Asperges, Baptism, Barmitzvah, Chado, Chanoyu, Commemoration, Common Riding, Coronation, Dedication, Doseh, Durbar, Encaenia,

Enthronement, Etiquette, Eucharist, Firewalk, Flypast, Form(al), Formality, Function, Gongyo, Habdalah, Havdalah, Havdoloh, Heraldry, Investiture, Koto(w), Last rites, Mass, Matsuri, Maundy, Mummery, Nipter, Observance, Occasion, Official, Ordination, Pageantry, Parade, Pomp, Powwow, Protocol, Rite, Rite of passage, Ritual, Sacrament, Sado, Seder, Service, State, Sun dance, Tea, Topping-out, Trooping (the Colour), Unveiling, Usage

**Cerium** Ce

**Cert(ain), Certainty** Absolute, Actual, Assured, Banker, Bound, Cast-iron, Cinch, Cocksure, Confident, Conviction, Convinced, Decided, Definite, Destined, Doubtless, Exact, Fact, Fate, Foolproof, Indubitable, Inevitable, Infallible, Keen, Lock, Monte, Moral, Nap, Needly, One, Positive, Poz, Precise, Racing, Real, Red-hot, Shoo-in, Siccar, Sicker, Snip, Some, Stiff, → SURE, Sure-fire, Truth, Type, Unerring, Yes

**Certainly** Agreed, And how, Ay, Aye-aye, Betcha, Certes, Fegs, Forsooth, Indeed, Iwis, Jokol, Of course, OK, Oke, Pardi(e), Pardy, Perdie, Siccar, Sicker, → SURE, Truly, Verily, Well, Yea, Yes, Yokul, Ywis

**Certificate, Certified, Certify** Accredit, Affirm, Assure, Attest, Bene decessit, Birth, Bond, Chit, Cocket, Confirm, Credential, Death, Debenture, Depose, Diploma, Docket, Document, End-user, Enseal, Gold, Guarantee, Landscrip, Licence, Lines, Marriage, Medical, MOT, Notarise, Paper, Patent, Proven, Savings, School, Scrip, Scripophily, Security, Share, Smart-ticket, Stamp note, Stock, Sworn, Talon, Testamur, Testimonial, Treasury, U, Unruly, Voucher, Warrant

**Cesare** Borgia

**Cessation** Abeyance

**Cesspit** Bog, Dungmere, Jawhole, Sinkhole, Slurry

**Cetacean** Dolphin, Porpoise, Whale

**Cete(acean)** Badger

**Ceylon(ese)** Serendip, Vedda(h)

**Chad** Dimpled, Swinging

**Chafe(r), Chafing** Champ, Chunter, Fray, Fret, Gall, Harass, Intertrigo, Irritate, Pan, Rankle, → RUB, Scratch, Scuff, Seethe, Worry

**Chaff(y)** Badinage, Banter, Bran, Chip, Cornhusk, Dross, Have on, Hay, Husk, Rag, Raillery, Rally, Ramentum, Refuse, Roast, Rot, Tease, Twit

**Chaffer(ing)** Bandy, Bargain, Haggle, Higgle, Hucksterage, Traffic

**Chaffinch** Wheatbird, Whitewing

**Chagrin** Annoyance, Envy, Mortify, Spite, Vexation

**Chain(s), Chained** Acre's-breadth, Albert, Anklet, Band, Bicycle, Bind, Bond, Bracelet, Branched, Bucket, Cable, Catena, Chatelaine, Check, Choke, Cistron, Closed, Cordillera, Cyclic, Daisy, Decca, Dixie, Drive, Duplex, Dynasty, Engineer's, Esses, Fanfarona, Festoon, Fetter, Fob, Food, Furlong, Gleipnir, Golden, Grand, Gunter's, Gyve, Heavy, Human, Learner's, Light, Line, Link, Lockaway, Manacle, Markov, Mayor, Micella(r), Micelle, → MOUNTAIN, Network, Noria, Open, Paper, Pennine, Pitch, Range, Rockies, Rode, Roller, Safety, Seal, → SERIES, Shackle, Side, Sierra, Slang, Snigging, Snow, Span, Sprocket, Straight, String, Strobila, Supply, Surveyor's, Suspensor, Team, Tether, Tiller, Trace, Tug, Tyre, Voluntary, Watch

**Chain-gang** Coffle

**Chair** Balloon-back, Basket, Bath, Beanbag, Bench, Bentwood, Berbice, Bergère, Birthing, Bosun's, Butterfly, Camp, Cane, Captain's, Carver, Club, Commode, Cromwellian, Curule, Deck, Dining, Director's, Easy, Elbow, Electric, Emeritus, Estate, Fauteuil, Fiddle-back, Folding, Frithstool, Garden, Gestatorial, Guérite, High, Jampan, Jampanee, Jampani, Ladder-back, Lounger, Love-seat, Lug, Merlin, Morris, Musical, Nursing, Personal, Pew, Potty, Preside, Professorate, Reader, Recliner, Rocker, Ruckseat, Rush-bottomed, → SEAT, Sedan, Settee, Sledge, Steamer, Stool, Straight, Sugan, Swivel, Throne, Wainscot, Wheel, Windsor, Wing

**Chair-back** Ladder, Splat

**Chairman** Convener, Emeritus, Humph, Landammann, Mao, MC, Pr(a)eses, Prof, Prolocutor, Sheraton, Speaker

**Chalaza** Albumen, Treadle, Treddle

**Chalcedony** Agate, Enhydros
**Chaldean** Babylonian, Ur
**Chalet** Cabana, Cot, Lodge, Skio
**Chalice** Calyx, Grail, Mixed, Poisoned
**Chalk(y)** Black, Calcareous, Cauk, Cawk, Crayon, Credit, Cretaceous, Dentin, French, Pastel, Senonian, Soapstone, Spanish, Steatite, Tailor's, White(n), Whit(en)ing
**Challenge(r), Challenging** Accost, Acock, Appeal, Assay, Call, Cartel, Champion, Charge, Claim, Confront, Contest, Contradict, Cross-examine, Dare, Daur, Defy, Dispute, Face, Gage, Gainsay, Gauntlet, Glove, Haka, Hazard, Hen(ner), Iconoclasm, Impugn, Insubordinate, Opponent, Oppose, Oppugn, Provoke, Query, Question, Recuse, Remonstrate, Rival, Sconce, Shuttle, Tackle, Taker, Tall order, Tank, Threat, Tongue-twister, Vie, Wero, Whynot
**Chamber(s)** Airlock, Anteroom, Apartment, Atrium, Auricle, Bladder, Bubble, Camarilla, Camera, Camera obscura, Casemate, Cavern, Cavitation, Cavity, Cell(a), Chanty, Close-stool, Cloud, Cofferdam, Columbarian, Combustion, Commons, Compartment, Cubicle, Cylinder, Decompression, Dene-hole, Dolmen, Echo, Firebox, Float, Fogou, Fumatorium, Fume, Gas, Gazunder, Gilded, Hall, Hopper, Horrors, Hyperbaric, Hypogea, Inspection, Ionization, Jerry, Jordan, Kiva, Lavatory, Lethal, Locule, Lok Sabha, Lower, Magma, Manhole, Manifold, Mattamore, Mesoscaphe, Naos, Plenum, Po(t), Presence, Priest('s)-hole, Privy, Reaction, Resonance-box, Room, Roum, Second, Serdab, Sick, Silo, Spark, Star, Stateroom, Steam-chest, Swell-box, Syndical, Synod, Thalamus, Undercroft, Upper, Utricle, Vault, Ventricle, Wilson cloud, Zeta
**Chamberlain** Camerlengo, Camerlingo, Censor
**Chameleon** Adaptor, American, Anole, Ethiopian, Floating voter, Lizard, Tarand
**Chamfer** Bevel, Groove
**Chamois** Ibex, Izard, Shammy
**Champ(er), Champers** Bite, Chafe, Chew, Chomp, Eat, Fume, Gnash, Gnaw, Hero, Ivories, Mash, Morsure, Munch
**Champagne** Black velvet, Boy, Brut, Bubbly, Buck's fizz, Charlie, Fizz, Gigglewater, Krug, Mumm, Pink, Pop, Sillery, Simkin, Simpkin, Stillery, Troyes, Widow
**Champion(s)** Ace, Adopt, Advocate, Ali, Apologist, Apostle, Artegal, Assert, Back, Belt, Brill(iant), Campeador, Ch, Cid, Cock, Crusader, Cupholder, Defend, Don Quixote, Doucepere, Douzeper, Dymoke, Endorse, Enoch, Espouse, Gladiator, Gun, Harry, → **HERO**, Herodotus, Horse, Kemp, Kemper(yman), King, Knight, Maestro, Maintain, Matchless, Messiah, Messias, Neil, Paladin, Palmerin, Partisan, Patronise, Peerless, Perseus, Promachos, Proponent, Protagonist, Roland, St Anthony, St David, St Denis, St George, St James, St Patrick, Seven, Spiffing, Spokesman, Star, Support, Tiro, Title-holder, Torch-bearer, Tribune, Upholder, Victor, Wardog, → **WINNER**, World-beater, Yokozuna
**Championship** Five Nations, Open, Seven, Six Nations, Super Bowl, Title, Tri-nations
**Chance (upon), Chancy** Accident, Adventitious, Aleatory, Aunter, Bet, Break, Buckley's, Cast, Casual, Cavel, Coincidence, Contingent, Dice, Earthly, Encounter, Even, Fat, → **FATE**, Fighting, First refusal, Fluke, Fortuitous, Fortuity, Fortune, → **GAMBLE**, Game, Hap, Happenstance, Hit and miss, Hobnob, Iffy, Inadvertent, Incidental, Kevel, Light, Loaves and fishes, Look-in, Lot, → **LOTTERY**, Luck, Main, Meet, Mercy, Occasion, Occur, Odds, Odds-on, Opening, Opportunity, Outside, Peradventure, Posse, Potluck, Prayer, Probability, Prospect, Random, Rise, Risk, Run into, Russian roulette, Serendipity, Shot, Shout, Slant, Snip, Spec, Sporting, Stake, Stochastic, Stray, Sweep, Toss-up, Treble, Turn, Tychism, Unlooked for, Ventre, Venture, Wager, Wild card
**Chancel** Adytum, Bema, Nave
**Chancellor** Adolf, Bismarck, Brandt, Dollfuss, Kohl, Logothete, Minister, More, Schmidt, Vicar-general, Wolsey
**Chancery** Court, Hanaper
**Chandelier** Candlestick, Corona, Drop, Electrolier, Gasolier, Girandole, Lustre, Pendant
**Chandler** Acater, Acatour, Raymond, Tallow
**Chanel** Coco
**Chaney** Lon
**Change(able), Changes, Changing** About-face, Adapt, Adjust, Agio, Aleatoric, → **ALTER**,

Amendment, Amoeba, Attorn, Backtrack, Barter, Become, Bob-major, Budge, Capricious, Cash, Catalysis, Cent, Chameleon, Channel-hop, Chop, Chump, Climacteric, Climate, Cline, Codicil, Commute, Convert, Cool, Coppers, Covary, Cut, Denature, Departure, Development, Diachrony, Differentiate, Dissolve, Disturb, Diversion, Eclipse, Ectopia, Edit, Embellish, Emend, Enallage, Esterify, Eustatic, Evolution, Evolve, Exchange, Fickle, Find, Flighty, Float, Fluctuate, Fluid, Flux, Gradate, Grandsire, Guard, Gybe, Histogen, Holiday, Inconstant, Inflect, Innovate, Instead, Inversion, Kaleidoscope, Kembla, Killcrop, Labile, Loose, Make-over, Menopause, Mercurial, Metabolic, Metabolise, Metamorphose, Metamorphosis, Metathesise, Mew, Mobile, Modify, Modulate, Morph, Mutable, Mutalis mutandis, Mutanda, Mutation, Ontogeny, Parallax, Paraphrase, Peal, Pejoration, Peripet(e)ia, Permute, Port, Primp, Prisere, Prophase, Protean, Quantum leap, Quarter, Rat, Realise, Recant, Reconstruct, Rectify, Redact, Redo, Refine, Reform, Refraction, Regeneration, Regime, Rejig, Relapse, Reschedule, Reset, Reshuffle, Resipiscence, Rest, Restyle, Reverse, Revise, Revolutionise, Rework, Sandhi, Scourse, Sd, Sea, Seasonal, Seesaw, Sere, Sex, Shake-out, Shake-up, Shift, Shrapnel, Shuffle, Silver, Small, Sublimation, Substitute, Supervene, Swap, Sweeping, Swing, Switch, Tempolabile, Toggle, Tolsel, Tolsey, Tolzey, Transfer, Transfiguration, Transform, Transition, Translate, Transmew, Transmogrify, Transmute, Transpose, Transubstantial, Triple, Turn (about), Tweak, Uncertain, Unpredictable, Unsettled, Unstable, Upheaval, U-turn, Vagary, Variant, Variation, Vary, Veer, Versatile, Vicissitude, Volatile, Volte-face, Wankle, Washers, Waver, Weathercock, Wheel, Wow

▷**Change(d)** *may indicate* an anagram

**Changeling** Auf, Killcrop, Oaf, Turncoat

**Changing room(s)** Cubicle, Pavilion

**Channel** Access, Aflaj, Airwave, Al Jazeera, Aqueduct, Artery, Beagle, Bed, Billabong, Binaural, Bristol, Canal, Canaliculus, Chimb, Chime, Chine, Chute, Conduit, Course, Creek, Culvert, Cut, Cutting, Datagram, Distribution, Ditch, Drain, Duct, Dyke, Ea, Eau, English, Estuary, Euripus, Fairway, Falaj, Feeder, Floodway, Flume, Foss, Funnel, Furrow, Gat, Gate, Geo, Gio, Glyph, Groove, Grough, Gully, Gut, Gutter, Head-race, Ingate, Ion, ITV, Katabothron, Katavothron, Khor, Kill, Kos, Kyle, Lake, La Manche, Lane, Latch, Leat, Lee-lane, Leet, Limber, Major, Meatus, Medium, Menai Strait, Minch, Moat, Mozambique, Multiplex, Narrows, News, North, Nulla(h), Offtake, Penstock, Pentland Firth, Pescadores, Pipeline, Qanat, Race, Raceway, Rean, Rebate, Rigol(l), Rigolets, Rivulet, Run, St George's, Sea-gate, Seaway, Sewer, Shatt-el-Arab, Shunt, Side, Sinus, Sky, Sloot, Sluice, Sluit, Sny(e), Solent, Solway Firth, Sound, Source, Sow, Spillway, Sprue, Strait, Suez, Sure, Swash, Tailrace, Tideway, Tracheole, Trough, Ureter, Vallecula, Vein, Wasteweir, Watercourse, Waterspout, Wheel race, Wireway, Yucatan

**Channel swimmer** Webb

**Chant** Anglican, Anthem, Antiphon, Canticle, Cantillate, Cantus, Chaunt, Daimoku, Decantate, Euouae, Evovae, Gregorian, Haka, Harambee, Hare Krishna, Hymn, Incantation, Intone, Introit, Karanga, Mantra(m), Motet, Pennillion-singing, Plainsong, Proper, Psalm, Sing, Slogan, Te Deum, The Reproaches, Yell

**Chantilly** Cream, Lace

**Chaos, Chaotic** Abyss, Anarchy, Confusion, Disorder, Disorganised, Fitna, Fractal, Havoc, Helter-skelter, Hun-tun, Jumble, Maelstrom, Mare's nest, Mayhem, Mess, Mixter-maxter, Muddle, Muss, Pandemonium, Shambles, Shambolic, Snafu, Tohu bohu, Turmoil

▷**Chaotic** *may indicate* an anagram

**Chap(s)** Beezer, Bloke, Bo, Bod, Bor, Buffer, Cat, Chafe, Cheek, Chilblain, Chop, Cleft, Cod, Codger, Cove, Crack, Customer, Dog, Fella, Feller, Fellow, Flews, Genal, Gent, Gink, Guy, Hack, Johnnie, Joll, Jowl, Kibe, Lad, → MAN, Maxilla, Mouth, Mum, Ocker, Person, Rent, Rime, Spray, Spreathe, Spreaze, Spreethe, Spreeze, Wang

**Chapel** Alamo, Bead-house, Bethel, Bethesda, Beulah, Cha(u)ntry, Chevet, Crypt, Ebenezer, Feretory, Galilee, Lady, Oratory, Parabema, Proprietary, Prothesis, Sacellum, Sistine

**Chaperon(e)** Beard, Cap, Cicerone, Duenna, Escort, Gooseberry, Griffin, Griffon, Gryphon, Muffin

**Chaplain(cy)** CF, Ordinary, Padre, Priest, Scarf, Skypilot, Slope

**Chaplet** Anadem, Coronet, Fillet, Garland, Wreath

▹**Chaps** *may indicate* an anagram

**Chapter** Accidents, C, Canon, Cap, Capitular, Cathedral, Ch, Chap, Cr, Division, Episode, Lodge, Phase, Section, Social, Sura(h), Verse

**Char(woman)** Adust, Barbecue, Burn, Cleaner, Coal, Daily, Duster, Mop(p), Mrs Mop(p), Rosie Lee, Scorch, Sear, Singe, Smoulder, Toast, Togue, Torgoch

**Charabanc** Bus, Chara, Coach

**Character(s)** Aesc, Agma, Alphabet, Ampersand, Ampussyand, Antihero, Atmosphere, Aura, Backbone, Backslash, Brand, Calibre, Case, Cipher, Clef, Cliff, Climate, Coloration, Complexion, Contour, Credit, Delimiter, Deuteragonist, Devanagari, Digamma, Digit, Domino, Dramatis personae, Emoticon, Ess, Essence, Eta, Ethos, → FEATURE, Fibre, Fish, Fist, Form, Grain, Graphics, Grass, Grit, Hair, Heart, Her, Hieroglyphic, Him, Homophone, Hue, Ideogram, Ideograph, Italic, Kanji, Kern, Kind, La(m)bda, Letter, Logogram, Make-up, Mark, Mettle, Mu, Nagari, → NATURE, Non-person, Nu, Ogam, Ogham, Pahlavi, Pantaloon, Part, Pehlevi, Person(a), Personage, → PERSONALITY, Phonogram, Physiognomy, Pi, Polyphone, Protagonist, Psi, Raisonneur, Reference, Reference-mark, Repute, Rho, Role, Rune, Runic, Sampi, San, Script, Sel(f), Sigma, Sign, Sirvente, Slash, Sonancy, Sort, Space, Sphenogram, Stamp, Subscript, Superhero, Superscript(ion), Swung dash, Syllabary, Symbol, Tab, Temperament, Testimonial, Ton(e), Trait, Uncial, Unit, Vav, Vee, Waw, Wen, Wild card, Wyn(n), Yogh, Zeta

**Characterise(d), Characterism, Characteristic(s)** Acquired, Archetypal, Aspect, Attribute, Aura, Cast, Cedilla, Colour, Control, Depict, Distinctive, Earmark, Escape, Ethos, Example, Facies, Feature, Hair, Hallmark, Has, Headmark, Identity, Idiomatic, Idiosyncrasy, Jizz, Keystroke, Lineament, Mark, Metamorphism, Mien, Nature, Notate, Note, Obelisk, Peculiar, Persona, Phenotype, Point, Property, Quality, Signature, Stamp, Stigma, Strangeness, Streak, Style, Trademark, → TRAIT, Transfer, Typical, Vein, Way

**Characterless** Anon, Impersonal, Inane, Wet

**Charade** Enigma, Pretence, Riddle

**Charcoal** Activated, Carbon, Coke, Fusain, Sugar

**Chard** Beet

**Charge(s), Charged, Charger** Access, Accusal, Accuse, Aerate, Agist, Allege, Anchorage, Animate, Anion, Annulet, Arraign, Ascribe, Assault, Baton, Battery, Bear, Behest, Blame, Book, Brassage, Brush, Buckshot, Bum rap, Burden, Care, Carriage, Carrying, Cathexis, Cellarage, Command, Commission, Community, Complaint, Congestion, Corkage, Cost, Count, Cover, Criminate, Damage, Debit, Delate, Delf, Delph, Demurrage, Depth, Depute, Directive, Dittay, Dockage, Due, Duty, Dynamise, Electric, Electron(ic), Entrust, Entry, Exit, Expense, Extraordinary, Fare, Fee, Fill, Fixed, Flag fall, Fleur-de-lis, Floating, Flock, Freight, Fullage, Fuse, Fusil, Fuze, Gazump, Giron, Gravamen, Gyron, → HERALDIC, Horse, Hot, Hypothec, Impeach, Impute, Incriminate, Indict, Inescutcheon, Inform, Instinct, Ion, Isoelectric, Laid, Last, Let, Levy, Lien, Lioncel(le), Lionel, Live, Load, Lozenge, Mandate, Metage, Mine, Mob, Mount, Mulct, Nominal, Nuclear, Objure, Obtest, Onrush, Onslaught, Onus, Ordinary, Orle, Overhead, Pastoral, Pervade, Pew-rent, Plaint, Positive, Postage, Premium, Prime, Prix fixe, Q, Quayage, Rack-rent, Rampage, Rap, Rate, Recrimination, Red-dog, Rent, Report, Reprise, Reverse, Roundel, Run, → RUSH, Saddle, Service, Sortie, Space, Specific, Stampede, Steed, Storm, Supplement, Tariff, Task, Tax(ation), Tear, Terms, Tilt, Toll, Tonnage, → TRAY, Tressure, Trickle, Trust, Tutorage, Upfill, Vaire, Vairy, Verdoy, Vigorish, Ward, Warhead, Warhorse, Wharfage, Yardage

**Chariot(eer)** Auriga, Automedon, Biga, Cart, Charet, Curricle, Ekka, Hur, Phaethon, Quadriga, Rath(a), Vimana, Wagon, Wain

**Charisma(tic)** Oomph, Pentecostal, Personality, Stardust

**Charitable, Charity** Agape, Aid, Alms, Alms-deed, Awmous, Barnardo's, Benevolent, Benign, Breadline, Caritas, Cause, Chugger, Dole, Dorcas, Eleemosynary, Glove money, Goodwill, Good works, Kiwanis, Lady Bountiful, Largesse, Leniency, Liberal, Lion, Love, Mercy, Oddfellow, Openhanded, Outreach, Oxfam, Pelican, Philanthropic, Red Cross, Rotarian, Samaritan, SCOPE, Zakat

**Charivari** Rough music, Uproar

**Charlatan** Cheat, Crocus, Empiric, Escroc, Faker, Fraud, Imposter, Katerfelto, Mountebank, Poseur, Quack(salver), Saltimbanco, Sham
**Charlemagne** Carlovingian
**Charles, Charley, Charlie(s)** Beard, C, Car, Champagne, Chan, Chaplin, Checkpoint, Chuck, Darwin, Dimwit, Elia, Fox, Half-wit, Lamb, Mug, (Old) Rowley, Pretender, Ray, Reynard, Rug-gown, Sap, Schmoe, Snow, Tail-end, Twit, Watchman
**Charles de Gaulle** Airport
**Charlock** Runch
**Charlotte** Bronte, Russe, Yonge
**Charm(er), Charmed, Charming** Abracadabra, Abrasax, Abraxas, Agacerie, Allure, Amulet, Appeal, Aroma, Attraction, Bangle, Beguile, Bewitch, Bracelet, Breloque, Captivate, Charisma, Chocolate box, Circe, Comether, Cramp-bone, Cute, Cutie, Debonair, Delectable, Delight(ful), Disarming, Emerods, Enamour, Enchant, Endear, Engaging, Ensorcell, → **ENTRANCE**, Fascinate, Fay, Fetching, Fetish, Grace, Greegree, Gri(s)gris, Hand of glory, Horseshoe, Houri, Incantation, Juju, Lucky, Magical, Magnetic, Mascot, Mojo, Nice, Obeah, Obi(a), Periapt, Personal, Phylactery, Porte-bonheur, Pretty, Prince, Pull, Purty, Quaint, Quark, Ravish, Seduce, Siren, Smoothie, Spellbind, Suave, Sweetness, Taking, Talisman, Tefillah, Telesm, Temptress, Tephillah, Tiki, Trinket, Unction, Voodoo, Winning, Winsome
▷**Charming** *may indicate* an anagram
**Chart(ed), Charting, Charts** Abac, Alignment, Atlas, Bar, Bar-graph, Bottle, Breakeven, Card, Control, Diagram, Draw, Eye, Feast movement, Flip, Flow, Gantt, Graph, Histogram, Histograph, Horoscope, Hydrography, Isogram, Isopleth, List, Log, Magna Carta, → **MAP**, Mappemond, Movement, Nomogram, Organisation, Pedigree, Pie, Plane, Plot, Portulano, Rating, Ringelmann, Run, Snellen, Social, Sociogram, Table, Test, Timetable, Tree, Venn, Waggoner, Wall, Weather, Z, Zodiac
**Charta, Charter** Atlantic, Book, Citizen's, Covenant, Freedom, Hire, Lease, Let, Novodamus, Rent, Social (Chapter), Tenants', Time, Voyage
**Chary** Cagey, Careful, Cautious, Frugal, Shy, Wary
**Charybdis** Maelstrom, Whirlpool
**Chase(d), Chaser, Chasing** Cannock, Chace, Chevy, Chivy, Ciseleur, Ciselure, Course, Cranbome, Decorate, Drink, Game, Harass, Hound, → **HUNT**, Inlaid, Inscribe, Jumper, Oxo, Progress, Pursuit, Race, Scorse, Sic(k), Snag, Steeple, Sue, Suit, Toreutic, Venery, Wild-goose
**Chasm** Abyss, Crevasse, Fissure, Gap, Gorge, Gulf, Hiatus, Ravine, Rent, Schism, Yawn
**Chaste, Chastity** Aggie, Agnes, Attic, Celibate, Classic, Clean, Continent, Fatima, Florimell, Ines, Innocent, Modesty, Nessa, Nunlike, Platonic, → **PURE**, Vestal, Virginal, Virtue
**Chasten(ed), Chastise(d), Chastisement** Beat, Castigate, Contrite, Correct, Deflate, Discipline, Disple, Lash, Punish, Rib-roast, Rollicking, Scold, Scourge, Shame-faced, Spank, Strap, Whip
**Chat, Chatter(box), Chatterer** Babble, Bavardage, Bird, Blab(ber), Blatherskite, Blether, Campanero, Causerie, Chelp, Chew the fat, Chinwag, Clack, Clishmaclaver, Confab(ulate), Converse, Cosher, Coze, Crack, Dialogue, Fireside, Froth, Gab(ble), Gas, Gasbag, Gibber, Gibble-gabble, Gossip, Gup, Hobnob, Jabber, Jargon, Jaw, Kilfud, Liaise, Madge, Mag(pie), Nashgab, Natter, Patter, Pie, Pourparler, Prate, Prattle, Rabbit, Rabble, Rap, Rattle, Schmooze, Scuttlebutt, Shmoose, Shoot the breeze, Stone, Talk, Talkee-talkee, Talky-talky, Tattle, Tongue-work, Twattle, Waffle, Whin, Windbag, Witter, Wongi, Yacketyyak, Yad(d)a-yad(d)a-yad(d)a, Yak, Yap, Yarn, Yatter, Yellow-breasted, Yoking
**Chateau** Castle, Cru, Fontainebleau, Malmaison, Rambouillet, Schloss
**Chateaubriand** René
**Chattel** Asset, Chose, Deodand, Effects
**Chaucer(ian)** Dan, OE
**Chauffeur** Cabby, Coachy, Driver, Sice, Syce
**Chauvinist** Alf, Bigot, Jingo, MCP, Partisan, Patriot, Racist, Sexist
**Cheap(en)** A bon marché, Bargain, Base, Budget, Catchpenny, Cheesy, Chintzy, Cut-price, Debase, Downmarket, Flashy, Gimcrack, Giveaway, Ignoble, Jitney, Kitsch, Knockdown, Low, Off-peak, Poor, Rubbishy, Sacrifice, Shoddy, Steerage, Stingy, Tacky, Tarty, Tatty, Tawdry,

Ticky-tacky, Tinhorn, Tinpot, Tinselly, Trashy, Trivial, Tuppenny, Two-bit, Twopenny, Twopenny-halfpenny, Undear, Vile

▷**Cheap** *may indicate* a d- or p- start to a word

**Cheapside** Bow

**Cheapskate** Piker

**Cheat(ers), Cheating** Adultery, Bam, Bamboozle, Bedswerver, Beguile, Bilk, Bite(r), Bob, Bonnet, Bubble, Bucket, Bullock, Bunce, Burn, Cabbage, Cardsharp(er), Charlatan, Chiaus, Chicane(ry), Chisel, Chouse, Clip, Cod, Cog(ger), Colt, Con, Cony-catcher, Cozen, Crib, Cross, Cross-bite(r), Cuckold, Cully, Defraud, Delude, Diddle, Dingo, Dish, Do, Do down, Doublecross, Double-dealer, Duckshove, Dupe, Escroc, Faitor, Fiddle, Finagle, Fix, Flam, Flanker, Fleece, Fob, Foister, Fox, Fraud, Gaff, Gamesmanship, Gazump, Gip, Glasses, Grifter, Gudgeon, Gull(-catcher), Gum, Gyp, Hoax, Hocus, Hoodwink, Hornswoggle, Horse, Intake, Jockey, Leg, Magsman, Mulct, Mump, Nick, Nobble, Pasteboard, Picaro(on), Plagiarist, Poop, Queer, Revoke, Rib, Rig, Rip off, Rogue, Rook, Rush, Scam, Screw, Screw over, Sell, Shaft, Sharper, Sharpie, Sharp practice, Short-change, Slur, Smouch, Snap, Specs, Stack, Stiff, Sting, Swindle, Take-in, Thimble-rigging, Trepan, Trick(ster), Trim, Twister, Two-time, Welch, Welsh, Wheedle

**Check(ed)** Abort, Anchor, Arrest, Audit, Ba(u)lk, Bauk, Bill, Block, Body, Bridle, Case, Certified, Collate, Compesce, Confirm, Control, Count, Counteract, Counterroll, Countertally, Cramp, Cross-index, Curb, Dam, Damp, Detain, Detent, Diligence, Discovered, Ditch, Dogs-tooth, Encumber, Examine, Foil, Forestall, Frisk, Frustrate, Gingham, Halt, Hamper, Hinder, Hobble, Houndstooth, Inhibit, Inspect, Jerk, Jerque, Let, Limit(ation), Mate, Measure, Medical, Meter, Monitor, MOT, Nip, Observe, Obstacle, Overhaul, Parity, Perpetual, Plumb, Prevent, Proof(read), Rain, Reality, Rebuff, Rebuke, Rein, Repress, Reprime, Repulse, Reread, Resist, →**RESTRAIN**, Retard, Revoke, Road test, Saccade, Scan, Screen, Security, Service, Setback, Shepherd's, Shorten, Sit-upon, Sneap, Sneb, Snib, Snub, Sound, Spongebag, Spot, Standard, Std, →**STEM**, Stent, Stint, Stocktake, Stop(-go), Stunt, Style, Subdue, Suppress, Tab, Tally, Tartan, Tattersall, Test, Thwart, Tick, Trash, Verify, Vet

**Checkers** Chinese, Piece

**Check-out** Till

**Cheddar** Cheese, Gorge

**Cheek(y)** Alforja, Audacity, Backchat, Brash, Brass-neck, Buccal, Buttock, Chap, Chit, Chollers, Chutzpah, Cool, Crust, Cub, Effrontery, Flippant, Fresh, Gall, Gena(l), Gobby, Gum, Hard-faced, Hussy, Impertinent, Impudent, Insult, Irreverent, Jackanapes, Joll, Jowl, Lip, Malapert, Malar, Masseter, Neck, Nerve, Noma, Pert, Presumption, Quean, Sass, Sauce, Sideburns, Tyke, Uppity, Upstart, Wang, Whippersnapper, Yankie, Zygoma

**Cheep** Chirp, Chirrup, Peep

**Cheer(s), Cheerful(ness), Cheering** Acclaim, Agrin, Applaud, Arrivederci, Banzai, Barrack, Blithe, Bonnie, Bravo, Bright, Bronx, Bubbly, Buck, Buoy(ant), Cadgy, Canty, Carefree, Cheery, Chin-chin, Chipper, Chirpy, Chirrupy, →**COMFORT**, Consolate, Console, Convivial, Crouse, Debonair, Drink, Ease, Elate, Elevate, Encourage, Enliven, Euge, Exhilarate, Exuberant, Festive, Genial, Gladden, Goodbye, Happy-go-lucky, Hearten, Hilarity, Holiday, Hooch, Hoorah, Hooroo, Hurra(h), Huzzah, Insouciance, Insport, Joco, Jocose, Jocund, Jolly, Jovial, Kia-ora, L'allegro, Light-hearted, Lightsome, Lively, Liven, Meal, Nash, Olé, Optimistic, Ovate, Peart, Perky, Plaudit, Please, Praise, Prosit, Rah, Riant, Rivo, Roar, Root, Rosy, Rumbustious, Shout, Sko(a)l, Slainte, Smiley, Sonsie, Sunny, Ta, Tata, Thanks, Three, Tiger, Tiggerish, Toodle-oo, Up, Upbeat, Uplift, Vivacious, Warm, Winsome, Yell

**Cheerless** Bleak, Dismal, Drab, Drear, Gloomy, Glum, Sober, Wint(e)ry

**Cheese, Cheesy** American, Amsterdam, Appenzell, Asiago, Au gratin, Bel Paese, Blue, Blue vein, Boc(c)oncini, Boursin, Brie, Caboc, Caerphilly, Cambazola, Cambozola, Camembert, Cantal, Casein, Caseous, Cauliflower, Cheddar, Cheshire, Chessel, Chèvre, Churnton, Colby, Comte, Cottage, Coulommiers, Cream, Crowdie, Curd, Damson, Danish blue, Derby, Dolcelatte, Double Gloucester, Dunlop, Dutch, Edam, Emmental(er), Emmenthal(er), Ermite, Esrom, Ewe, Fet(a), Fondue, Fontina, Fromage frais, Fynbo, Gloucester, Goat, Gorgonzola, Gouda, Grana Padano, Grand Panjandrum, Green, Gruyère, Halloumi, Hard, Havarti, Huntsman, Ilchester, Islay, Jarlsberg®, Junket, Kebbock, Kebbuck, Kenno, Killarney,

Lancashire, Leicester, Lemon, Limburg(er), Lymeswold®, Macaroni, Manchego, Mascarpone, Monterey Jack, Mousetrap, Mozzarella, Mu(e)nster, Mycella, Neufchatel, Numero uno, Oka, Orkney, Paneer, Parmesan, Pecorino, Pont l'Eveque, Port Salut, Pot, Provolone, Quark, Raclette, Rarebit, Reblochon, Red Leicester, Rennet, Ricotta, Romano, Roquefort, Sage Derby, Samso, Sapsago, Skyr, Stilton®, Stone, Stracchino, Swiss, Taleggio, Tilsit, Tofu, Truckle, Vacherin, VIP, Wensleydale, Whey, Yarg

**Cheesecake** Pin-up, Talmouse

**Cheese-scoop** Pale

**Cheetah** Coalition, Hunting-cat

**Chef** Blanc, Commis, Escoffier, Oliver, Ramsay, Roux, Stein

**Chekhov** Anton

**Chelsea** Bun, Pensioner, Tractor

**Chemical(s)** Acanthin, Acid, Acrolein, Adrenalin®, Agent Orange, Alar, Aldehyde, Alkali, Alkyd, Allomone, Alum(ina), Amide, Amino-group, Ammonia, Anabolic, Avertin, Barilla, Benzene, Bicarb(onate), Bradykinin, Bromic, Bute, Camphene, Camphor, Carbide, Carnallite, Caseose, Catalyst, Cephalin, Cerebroside, Coal tar, Co-factor, Depside, Developer, Dioxide, Dopamine, Encephalin, Enkephalin(e), Enol, Ethanal, Ethoxy, Ethyl, Fine, Fixer, Fluoride, Formyl, Freon, Fungicide, Furosemide, Gamone, Gibbsite, Glutamine, Glycol, Halide, Halon, Harmin, Heavy, Hecogenin, Heptane, Hexylene, Hexylresorcinol, Histamine, Hormone, Hypo, ICI, Imine, Imipramine, Indican, Inositol, Insecticide, Interleukin, Larvicide, Lewisite, Limonene, Lipid, Masking-agent, Massicot, Morphactin, Naioxone, Napalm, Naphtha, Natron, Neurotransmitter, Nitre, Nitroluene, Nonylphenol, Oestrogen, Olefin, Olein, Oxide, Oxysalt, Paraben, Pentane, Pentene, Pentyl, Peptide, Periclase, Phenol, Phenyl, Pheromone, Potash, Potassa, Psoralen, Ptomaine, Reagent, Resorcin, Resorcinol, Restrainer, Sequestrant, Serotonin, Soman, Soup, Stearate, Steroid, Strontia, Styrene, Sulphide, Terpene, Thio-salt, Toluol, Toner, Trimer, Tritide, Trona, Trotyl, Urethane, Weedicide, Weedkiller, Xanthene, Xylol

**Chemise** Cymar, Sark, Serk, Shift, Shirt, Simar(re), Smock, Symar

**Chemist** Analyst, Apothecary, Dispenser, Druggist, Drugstore, FPS, Pharmacist, Pothecary

---

## CHEMISTS

*3 letters:*
FCS
LSA
MPS
RIC

*4 letters:*
Bohn
Curl
Davy
Gahn
Hahn
Todd
Urey

*5 letters:*
Curie
Debye
Dewar
Haber
Kroto
Nobel
Prout
Soddy

*6 letters:*
Baeyer
Bunsen
Hevesy
Liebig
Muller
Nernst
Proust
Sanger
Schiff
Wohler

*7 letters:*
Buchner
Faraday
Fischer
Helmont
Hodgkin
Macadam
Pasteur
Pauling
Smalley
Ziegler

*8 letters:*
Lipscomb
Mulliken
Newlands
Sabatier
Smithson
Weizmann
Welsbach

*9 letters:*
Arrhenius
Backeland
Berzelius
Butenandt
Cavendish
Lavoisier
Leclanche
Pelletier
Priestley
Strassman

*10 letters:*
Mendeleyev
Paracelsus

*11 letters:*
Hinshelwood
Le Chatelier

---

**Chemistry** Alchemy, Alchymy, Analytical, Chemurgy, Iatrochemistry, Inorganic, Nuclear, Organic, Physical, Radiation, Spageric, Spagiric, Spagyric, Stinks, Stoecheometry, Stoechiometry, Stoich(e)iometry, Technical, Zymurgy

**Cheops** Khufu
**Cheque** Bank, Blank, Bouncer, Crossed, Giro, Gregory, Open, Rubber, Stumer, Tab, Traveller's
**Chequer** Dice
**Cherish(ed)** Dear, Dote, Enshrine, Entertain, Esteem, Foment, Foster, Harbour, Inshrine, Nestle, Nurse, Nurture, Pamper, Pet, Precious, Prize, Refocillate, Treasure
**Cheroot** Cigar, Manil(l)a
**Cherry (tree)** Amarelle, Amazon, Ball, Barbados, Bigaroon, Bigarreau, Bird, Blackheart, Bladder, Cerise, Choke, Cornelian, Gean, Ground, Hagberry, Heart, Jerusalem, Kearton, Kermes, Kermesite, Malpighia, Marasca, Maraschino, May-duke, Maz(z)ard, Merry, Morel(lo), Prunus, Red, Sweet, Whiteheart
**Cherry-pie** Heliotrope
**Cherub** Angel, Putto, Seraph
**Chervil** Cow-parsley
**Chess (move), Chess player, Chess term** Andersson, Black, Blindfold, Castling, Cleat, Endgame, En passant, Euwe, Fianchetto, FIDE, Fischer, Fool's mate, Grandmaster, Hexagonal, J'adoube, Karpov, Kasparov, Lightning, Mate, Miranda, Patzer, Pin, Plank, Rapid transit, Shogi, Short, Spassky, Speed, Staunton, White, Zugzwang, Zwischenzug
**Chessman** Bishop, Black, Castle, Cheque, Horse, King, Knight, Pawn, Pin, Queen, Rook, White
**Chest(y)** Ark, Bahut, Bosom, Box, Breast, Buist, Bunker, Bureau, Bust, Caisson, Cap-case, Case, Cassone, Chapel, Charter, Chiffonier, Coffer, Coffin, Coffret, Commode, Community, Crate, Cub, Dresser, Girnel, Hope, Hutch, Inro, Kist, Larnax, Locker, Lowboy, Meal-ark, Medicine, Ottoman, Pectoral, Pereion, Pigeon, Pleural, Ribcage, Safe, Scrine, Scryne, Sea, Shrine, Slop, Steam, Sternum, Tallboy, Tea, Thorax, Toolbox, Treasure, Trunk, Wangan, Wangun, Wanigan, War, Wind
**Chester** Deva
**Chestnut** Aesculus, Auburn, Badious, Bay, Castanea, Castanospermum, Ch, Chincapin, Chinese, Chinkapin, Chinquapin, Cliché, Conker, Dwarf, Favel(l), Hoary, Horn-nut, Horse, Marron, Marron glacé, Moreton Bay, Old hat, Roan, Russet, Saligot, Soare, Sorrel, Spanish, Sweet, Water
**Chest protector** →ARMOUR, Bib
**Chevalier** Bayard, Knight, Pretender
**Chevron** Dancette, Stripe, V-shape
**Chew(ing)** Bite, Champ, Chaw, Chomp, Crunch, Cud, Eat, Fletcherism, Gnaw, Gum, Manducate, Masticate, Maul, Meditate, Moop, Mou(p), Munch, Ruminate, Siri(h), Spearmint
**Chewink** Ground-robin
**Chiastolite** Macle
**Chic** Dapper, Debonair, Elegant, Fashionable, Heroin, In, Kick, Modish, Posh, Radical, Smart, Soigné, Stylish, Swish, Tonish, Trim
**Chicago** Windy City
**Chicane(ry)** Artifice, Deception, Fraud, Wile
**Chichester** Yachtsman
**Chichi** Precious
**Chick(en)** Australorp, Battery, Biddy, Boiler, Broiler, Capon, Cheeper, Chittagong, Chuckie, Clutch, Cochin(-China), Corn-fed, Coronation, Coward, Cowherd, Craven, Drumstick, Eirack, Gutless, Hen, Howtowdie, Kiev, Layer, Maran, Marengo, Minorca, Mother Carey's, Niderling, Parson's nose, Pavid, Poltroon, Poot, Pope's nose, Poult, Pout, Prairie, Precocial, Pullus, Quitter, Roaster, Rooster, Scaredy-cat, Spatchcock, Spring, Squab, Supreme, Sussex, Timorous, Unheroic, Unmanly, Wimp, Windy, Wishbone, Wyandotte, Yellow
**Chickenfeed** Maize, Peanuts, Pittance
**Chickenpox** Varicella
**Chickpea** Chana, Falafel, Felafel, Garbanzo
**Chickweed** Snow-in-summer
**Chicory** Endive, Radiccio, Succory, Witloof
**Chide** Admonish, Berate, Dress, Objurgate, Rate, Rebuke, Reprove, Row, Scold, Tick off, Twit, Upbraid

**Chief(tain)** Ag(h)a, Arch, Ardrigh, Ariki, Boss, Caboceer, Cacique, Calif, Caliph, Capital, Capitan, Capitayn, Capo, Caractacus, Caradoc, Cardinal, Cazique, Ch, Chagan, Cock of the loft, Coriolanus, Dat(t)o, DG, Dominant, Duke, Eleutherarch, Emir, Figurehead, Finn (MacCool), First, Foremost, Geronimo, Governor, Grand, Haggis, → **HEAD**, Hereward, Jarl, Kaid, Keystone, King, Leader, MacDuff, → **MAIN**, Mass, Mocuddum, Mokaddam, Mugwump, Muqaddam, Nawab, Nizam, Nkosi, Oba, Overlord, Paramount, Pendragon, Predominant, Premier, Primal, Prime, Principal, Provost-marshal, Quanah, Raja(h), Rajpramukh, Rangatira, Rangatiratanga, Ratoo, Ratu, Sachem, Sagamore, Sardar, Sarpanch, Sea-king, Sheikh, Sirdar, Staple, Sudder, Supreme, Tanist, Tank, Taxiarch, Thane, Top

**Chiffonier** Cabinet, Commode

**Chilblain** Kibe

**Child(ren), Childhood, Childish** Aerie, Alannah, Ankle biter, Auf, Babe, Baby, Bach(ch)a, Badger, Bairn, Bambino, Bantling, Boy, Brat, Brood, Butter-print, Ch, Changeling, Cherub, Chick, Chickabiddy, Chit, Collop, Cub, Descendants, Dream, Duddie weans, Elfin, Eyas, Feral, Foster, Foundling, Gait, Gangrel, Ge(i)t, Girl, Guttersnipe, Gyte, Heir, Hellion, Hurcheon, Imp, Infancy, Infant, Inner, Issue, It, Jailbait, Jejune, Juvenile, Kid, Kiddie(wink), Kiddy, Kidult, Kinder, Lad, Lambkin, Latchkey, Limb, Litter, Littlie, Littling, Love, Mamzer, Mardy, Minion, Minor, Mite, Moppet, Munchkin, Naive, Nipper, Nursling, Offspring, Pantywaist, Papoose, P(a)ediatric, Petty, Piccanin(ny), Pickin, Pickle, Pre-school, Problem, Progeny, Puerile, Puss, Putto, Ragamuffin, Rip, Romper, Rug rat, Scion, Second, Seed, Siblings, Small fry, Smout, Smowt, Sprog, Street arab, Subteen, Tacker, Ted, Teeny-bopper, Tike, Toddle(r), Tot(tie), Totty, Trot, Tweenager, Tweenie, Tyke, Urchin, Waif, Wean, Weanel, Weanling, Weeny-bopper, Whelp, Young, Youngster, Younker, Youth

**Childbearing, Childbirth** Couvade, Dystocia, Intrapartum, Lamaze, Natural, Obstetrics, Parity, Parturient, Parturition, Puerperal, Tocology, Tokology

**Child-eater, Child-killer** Herod, Thyestes

**Childless** Atocous, Atokous, Barren, Nullipara, Sine prole, Sp

**Childlike** Superwaif

**Chile(an)** CH, Mapuche

**Chill(er), Chilly** Bleak, Cauldrife, → **COLD**, Cold snap, Cool, Cryogen, Flu, Frappé, Freeze, Freon®, Frigid, Frosty, Gelid, Ice, Iciness, Laze, Mimi, Nippy, Oorie, Ourie, Owrie, Parky, Raw, Refrigerate, Relax, Rigor, Scare, Wind

**Chilli** Bird's eye, Cayenne, Dorset gust, → **PEPPER**, Pimentón, Scoville

**Chime(s)** Agree, Bell, Clam, Cymar, Jingle, Peal, Rhime, Ring, Semantron, Tink, → **TOLL**, Wind

**Chimera** Geep, Graft, Griffin, Illusion

**Chimney (pot), Chimney corner** Can, Cow(l), Femerall, Flare stack, Flue, Funnel, Lamp, Lug, Lum, Smokestack, Stack, Stalk, Steeplejack, Stovepipe, Tallboy, Tunnel

**Chimney-sweep** Chummy, Snowball

**Chimp(anzee)** Ape, Bonobo, Jocko, Pygmy

**Chin, Chinwag** Chitchat, Double, Genial, Hill-man, Jaw, Jowl, Mentum

**China(man), Chinese** Ami, Amigo, Amoy, Bone, Boxer, Bud(dy), Cameoware, Cantonese, Catayan, Cathay, Celestial, Ceramic, Ch, Chelsea, Chink(y), Chow, Coalport, Cochin, Cock, Colleague, Communist, Confucius, Crackle, Crockery, Cully, Delft, Derby, Dresden, Eggshell, Etrurian, Flowery land, Friend, Fukien, Google, Googly, Goss, Hakka, Han, Hard paste, Hizen, Hmong, Imari, Ironstone, Kanji, Kaolin, Kuo-yu, Limoges, Macanese, Manchu, Manchurian, Mandarin, Mangi, Maoist, Mate, Meissen, Middle kingdom, Min, Ming, Minton, National, Oppo, Pal, Pareoean, Pekingese, Pe-tsai, Pinyin, Porcelain, → **POTTERY**, Putonghua, Queensware, Quina, Red, Rockingham, Royal Worcester, Rusticware, Saxe(-blue), Semiporcelain, Seric, Sèvres, Shanghai, Sinaean, Sinic, Sino-, Soft paste, Spode®, Sun Yat-sen, Tai-ping, Taiwanese, Taoist, Teng, Tocharian, Tungus, Uigur, Wal(l)y, Ware, Wedgwood®, Whiteware, Willow pattern, Willowware, Worcester, Wu, Yao, Yellow peril

**Chindit** Wingate

**Chine** Chink, Chynd, Ridge

**Chink(y)** Chinaman, Chop, Cleft, Clink, Cloff, Crack, Cranny, Crevice, Gap, Rent, Rift, Rima, Rimose, Sinic, Window

**Chintz** Kalamkari

**Chip(s), Chippy** Bargaining, Blitter, Blue, Bo(a)st, Buffalo, Carpenter, Chocolate, Counter, Cut, Deep-fried, EPROM, EROM, Fish, Flake, Fragment, French fry, Game, Hack, Ill-tempered, Knap, Log, Micro, Microchip, Nacho(s), Neural, Nick, Pentium®, Pin, Potato, Shaving, Silicon, Sliver, Spale, Spall, Span, Splinter, Tease, Teraflop, Tortilla, Transputer, Virus, Wood

▷**Chip** *may indicate* an anagram

**Chipmunk** Gopher, Hackee, Suslik, Zizel

**Chippendale** Chinese

**Chipper** Jaunty, Spry, Wedge

**Chiron** Centaur

**Chiropody** Pedicure, Podiatry

**Chiropractic** McTimoney

**Chirp(y), Chirrup** Cheep, Cherup, Chirm, Chirr, Cicada, Peep, Pip, Pipe, Pitter, Sing, Stridulate, Trill, Tweet, Twitter, Warble

**Chisel(ler), Chisel-like** Bam, Boaster, Bolster, Bur, Burin, Carve, Cheat, Clip, Cold, Drove, Firmer, Gad, →**GOUGE**, Half-round, Mason, Paring, Scalpriform, Scauper, Scorper, Sculpt, Slick, Socket, Sting

**Chit** Docket, Girl, Memo, Note, Voucher

**Chivalry, Chivalrous** Brave, Bushido, Courtly, Datin, Gallant, Gent, Grandisonian, Knightly, Quixotic

**Chivvy** Badger, Harass, Pursue

**Chloride, Chlorine** Calomel, Carnallite, Muriate

**Chlorophyll** Granum, Leaf-green

**Chock** Trig

**Chocolate** Aero, Brown, Cacao, Carob, Cocoa, Dragee, Ganache, Milk, Neapolitan, Noisette, Pinole, Plain, Praline, Rolo®, Theobroma, Truffle, Vegelate, Vermicelli

**Choice, Choose, Choosy, Chosen** Adopt, Anthology, Appoint, Aryan, Ballot, Capped, Cherry-pick, Cull, Dainty, Decide, Delicacy, Druthers, Eclectic, Elect, Elite, Esnecy, Fine, Fork, Free will, Hercules, Hobson's, Leet, Leve, Liberty, Lief, List, Multiple, Nap, Opt, Option, Or, Ossian, Peach, Peacherino, Peculiar, →**PICK**, Picking, Plum(p), Precious, Predilect, Prefer, Proairesis, Rare, Recherché, →**SELECT**, Single out, Superb, Try(e), Via media, Volition, Wale, Will

**Choiceless** Beggar

**Choir, Choral, Chorister, Chorus** Antiphony, Antistrophe, Anvil, Apse, Bass, Burden, Chant, Choragus, Choregus, Chorister, Choryphaeus, Dawn, Decani, Faburden, Fauxbourdon, Glee, Glee club, Group, Hallelujah, Harmony, Hymeneal, Motet, Ninth, Parabasis, Precentor, Quirister, →**REFRAIN**, Reprise, Ritual, Schola cantorum, Serenata, Singing, Stop, Strophe, Treble, Triad, →**UNISON**

**Choir-master** Choragus, Choregus, Precentor

**Choke(r)** Accloy, Block, Clog, Die, Gag, Garotte, Glut, Silence, Smoor, Smore, Smother, Stap, Stifle, Stop, Strangle(hold), Strangulate, →**THROTTLE**, Warp

**Choky** Can, Prison

**Choler** Irascibility, Yellow bile

**Cholera** Asiatic, British, Hog

**Cholesterol** Spinacene, Squalene

**Choliamb** Scazon

**Chomp** Bite, Chew

▶**Choose** *see* **CHOICE**

**Chop, Chops, Chopper(s), Choppy** Adze, Air tax, Ax(e), Cakehole, Celt, Charge, Cheek, Chump, Cleave, Copter, Côtelette, Cuff, Curtail, Cutlet, Dice, Dismissal, False teeth, Fell(er), Flew, Hack, Hash, Helicopter, Hew, Ivory, Karate, Lop, Machete, Mince, Mouth, Mutton, Rotaplane, Rough, Split, Standing, Suey, Teeth, To-rend, Underhand, Wang

**Chopin** Pantoufle, Shoe

**Chopstick(s)** Waribashi

**Chord(s)** Altered, Arpeggio, Barré, Broken, Common, Diameter, Eleventh, Harmony,

Intonator, Latus rectum, Neapolitan sixth, Nerve, Ninth, Picardy third, Riff, Seventh, Sixth, Submediant, Thirteenth, Triad, Vocal

**Chore** Darg, Duty, Fag, Grind, Task

**Chorea** Sydenham's

**Choreographer** Arranger, Ashton, Balanchine, Bourne, Cecchetti, Cranko, Cunningham, Dolin, Fokine, Laban, Lifar, Massine, Murphy, Tetley, Tharp

▸**Chorus** *see* **CHOIR**

**Chosen** Elite, Korea

**Chough** Chewet

**Chow** Nosh

**Chowder** Bouillabaisse, Clam, Skink, Soup

**Christ** Ecce homo, Lamb of God, Logos, Messiah, Pantocrator, Paschal Lamb, Prince of Peace, Saviour, Son (of God), Son of Man, The Good Shepherd, The Redeemer, X, Xt

**Christ Church** The House

**Christen(ing)** Baptise, Dub, Launch, Name-day

**Christian(ity)** Abcee, Abecedarian, Absey, Adventist, Albigenses, Anabaptist, Antioch, Baptist, Beghard, Believer, Cathar(ist), Charismatic, Colossian, Coptic, Dior, Donatist, D(o)ukhobor, Ebionite, Eucharistic, Fletcher, Galilean, Gentile, Giaour, Gilbertine, Gnostic, Godsquad, Goy, Heteroousian, Holy roller, Homo(i)ousian, Hutterite, Jehovah's Witness, Lutheran, Maronite, Marrano, Melchite, Melkite, Methodist, Molinism, Monarchian, Monophysite, Monotheist, Moral, Mozarab, Muscular, Mutineer, Nazarene, Nestorian, Phalange, Pilgrim, Presbyterian, Protestant, Quaker, Quartodeciman, RC, Sabotier, Scientist, SCM, Shambe, Solifidian, Traditor, Uniat(e), Unitarian, Valdenses, Waldensian, Wesleyan, Xian, Zwinglian

**Christian Scientist** Eddy

**Christmas(time)** Advent, Beetle, Box, Cactus, Card, Carol, Chrissie, C(h)rimbo, Day, Dec, Island, Nativity, Noel, Nowel(l), Pudding, Stocking, Xmas, Yuletide

**Christopher** Kit, Robin, Sly, Wren

**Chromatin** Karyotin

**Chromatology** Size-exclusion

**Chromium** Cr

**Chromosome** Aneuploid, Autosome, Barr body, Centromere, Cistron, Euchromatin, Flow-sorted, Gene, Genome, Haploid, Homologous, Id(ant), Karyotype, Lampbrush, Operon, Philadelphia, Ploid(y), Polytene, Prophage, Satellite, Sex, Telocentric, Telomere, Trisomy, X, Y

**Chronic** Long

**Chronicle(r)** Anglo-Saxon, Annal, Brut, Calendar, Diary, Froissart, Hall, Historian, Historiographer, History, Holinshed, Logographer, Moblog, Narrative, Paralipomena, Parian, Paris, → **RECORD**, Register, Saga, Stow

**Chrysalis** Nymph, Pupa

**Chrysanthemum** Corn-marigold, Feverfew, Korean

**Chrysolite** Olivine, Peridot

**Chub** Chavender, Cheven, Chevin, Fish

**Chubby** Butterball, Dumpy, Plump, Rotund

**Chuck (out)** Berry, Bin, Bung, Buzz, Chook(ie), Discard, Eject, Fling, Food, Four-jaw, Grub, Independent-jaw, Jettison, Lob, Magnetic, Pat, Pitch, Scroll, Shy, Sling, Three-jaw, Toss, Turf

**Chuckle** Chortle, Giggle, Gurgle, Laugh, Titter

**Chuffed** Glad

**Chukka** Polo

**Chum(my)** Ally, Associate, Boet, Buddy, China, Cobber, Cock, Companion, Comrade, Crony, Cully, Mate, Pal, Playmate, Sociable, Sodality

**Chump** Cretin, Fool, Mug(gins), Noddle, Sap, → **STUPID PERSON**

**Chunk(y)** Boxy, Chubby, Gob, Nub, Nugget, Piece, Slab, Squat, Wad, Wedge, Wodge

**Church** Abbey, Apostolic, Armenian, Auld Licht, Autocephalous, Basilica, Bethel, Bethesda, Broad, Brood, Byzantine, → **CATHEDRAL**, Catholic, CE, Ch, Chapel, Chevet, Christendom, Classis, Clergy, Collegiate, Congregational, Coptic, Decanal, Delubrum, Duomo, Easter (Orthodox), Eastern, EC, Ecumenical, Episcopal, Episcopalian, Established, Faith, Fold,

Free, Greek, High, House, Institutional, Kirk, Lateran, Latin, Low, Lutheran, Maronite, Melchite, Methodist, Minster, Moonie, Moravian, Mormon, Mother, National, Nazarene, Nestorian, New, New Jerusalem, Notre Dame, Old Light, Oratory, Orthodox, Parish, Peculiar, Pentecostal, Preaching-house, Prebendal, Presbyterian, Ratana, RC, Reformed, Relief, Rome, Russian Orthodox, Sagrada familia, St Bride's, Schism house, Schism shop, Secession, Shrine, Smyrna, Station, Stave, Steeple, Steeplehouse, Tabernacle, Temple, Title, Titular, Transept, Triumphant, Unification, Unitarian, United Free, United Reformed, Visible, Wee Free, Western, Wool

**Churchgoer, Churchman, Churchwarden** Acolyte, Anglican, Antiburgher, Auld Licht, Azymite, Baptist, Barnabite, Believer, Bluenose, Cameronian, Cantor, Classis, Clay, Cleric, Clerk, Congregation, Deacon, Dom, Dopper, Elder, Evangelist, Hatto, High, Ignorantine, Incumbent, Invisible, Knox, Lay-reader, Lector, Lutheran, Marrowman, Methodist, Metropolitan, Militant, Moderator, Moonie, Mormon, MU, Newman, Old Light, Oncer, Parson, PE, Pew-opener, Pipe, Pontiff, Prebendary, Precentor, Predicant, Predikant, Prelate, Presbyterian, Priest, Protestant, Puritan, Racovian, Rector, Romanist, Ruridecanal, Sacrist(an), Sidesman, Sim, Simeonite, Socinian, Spike, Subchanter, Subdeacon, Succentor, Swedenborgian, Tantivy, Triumphant, Ubiquitarian, Unitarian, Verger, Vestryman, Visible, Wesleyan, Worshipper, Wren

**Church house** Deanery, Manse, Parsonage, Presbytery, Rectory, Vicarage

**Churchill** Tank, Winston

**Churchyard** God's acre, Stoke Poges

**Churl(ish)** Attercop, Boor, Crabby, Curmudgeonly, Cynical, Ethercap, Ettercap, Gruff, Ill-natured, Nabal, Peasant, Rustic, Serf, Surly, Unsportsmanlike

**Churn** Agitate, Bubble, Kirn, Seethe, Sicken

**Chute** Flume, Runway

**Ciao** Adieu, Adios, Aloha

**CIC** Shogun, Sirdar

**Cicada** Greengrocer, Locust, Periodical, Tettix

**Cicatrix** Scar

**Cicely** Myrrh, Seseli, Sweet

**Cicero** Cic, Orator, Tully

**Cicerone** Guide

**CID** Sûreté

**Cid** Campeador, Chief, Hero

**Cider** Drink, Hard, Perry, Scrumpy, Sweet

**Ci-devant** Ex

**Cigar(ette), Cigarette cards** Beedi(e), Bidi, Biftah, Bifter, Blunt, Bumper, Burn, Camberwell carrot, Cancer stick, Caporal, Cartophily, Cheroot, Cigarillo, Claro, Coffin nail, Conch, Concha, Corona, Dog-end, Doob, Durry, Fag, Filter-tip, Gasper, Giggle(-stick), Havana, Joint, Locofoco, Long-nine, Loosies, Low-tar, Maduro, Manilla, Marijuana, Number, Panatella, Paper-cigar, Perfecto, Puritano, Reefer, Regalia, Roach, Roll-up, Segar, Smeek, Smoke, Snout, Splif(f), Stogie, Stog(e)y, Stompie, Stub, Tab, Twist, Weed, Whiff, Woodbine, Zol

**C-in-C** Supremo

**Cinch** Belt, Certainty, Doddle, Duck soup, Easy, Girth, Stroll

**Cinchona** Kina, Quina

**Cinder(s)** Ash, Breeze, Clinker, Dander, Embers, Slag, Tap

**Cinderella** Drudge, Stepdaughter

**Cinema(s)** Art house, Big screen, Biograph, Bioscope, Bughouse, Circuit, Drive-in, Films, Fleapit, Flicks, Grindhouse, Home, IMAX®, Megaplex, Movies, Multiplex, Multiscreen, Mutoscope, New Wave, Nickelodeon, Nouvelle Vague, Odeon, Picture palace, Pictures, Plaza, Scope, Silver-screen, Theatre, Tivoli

**Cinnabar** Vermilion

**Cinnamon, Cinnamon stone** Canella, Cassia (bark), Essonite, Hessonite, Saigon, Spice

**Cipher** Chi-rho, Code, Cryptogram, Enigma, Nihil, Nobody, Nonentity, → **NOTHING**, Number, O, Steganogram, Zero

**Circadian** Diurnal

**Circle** Almacantar, Almucantar, Annulet, Antarctic, Arctic, Circassian, Co, Colure, Company, Compass, Concentric, Cordon, Corn, Corolla, Corona, Coterie, Cromlech, Crop, Cycloid, Cyclolith, Dip, Director, Disc, Dress, Druidical, Eccentric, Ecliptic, Eddy, Embail, Enclose, Engird, Epicyclic, Equant, Equator, Equinoctial, Euler's, Fairy ring, Family, Fraternity, Full, Galactic, Girdle, Gloriole, Great, Gyrate, Gyre, Halo, Henge, Hoop, Horizon, Hour, Hut, Inner, Inorb, Lap, Longitude, Loop (the loop), Magic, Malebolge, Mandala, Meridian, Mohr's, Mural, Nimbus, O, Orb, Orbit, Outer, Parhelic, Parquet, Parterre, Penannular, Peristalith, Pitch, Polar, Quality, Red-line, Rigol, → RING, Ring-cross, Rondure, Rotate, Roundel, Roundlet, Seahenge, Sentencing, Set, Setting, Small, Sphear, Sphere, Stemme, Stone, Stonehenge, Striking, Surround, Tinchel, Tondino, Traffic, Transit, Tropic, Turning, Umbel, Upper, Vertical, Vicious, Vienna, Virtuous, Volt, Wheel, Whorl

**Circlet** Diadem, Wreath

**Circuit(-board), Circuitous** Ambit, AND, Autodyne, Bridge, Bus, Bypass, Chipset, Closed, Comparator, Daughterboard, Detour, Diocese, Discriminator, Dolby®, Electrics, Equivalent, Eyre, Feedback, Gate, Gyrator, Half-adder, Highway, Home, IC, Indirect, Integrated, Interface, Lap, Le Mans, Limiter, Live, Logic, Loop, Microchip, Microprocessor, Monza, Motherboard, NAND, NOR, NOT, Open, OR, Orbital, Perimeter, Phantom, Phase, Preamp, Printed, Push-pull, Quadripole, Racetrack, Reactance, Ring main, Round, Roundure, Rubber-chicken, Scaler, Series, Short, Silverstone, Smoothing, Sound card, Spa, Squelch, Stage, Three-phase, Tour, Trunk, Windlass, XNOR, XOR

**Circuit-breaker** Air gap, Fuse

**Circular** Annular, Brochure, Court, Disc(al), Endless, Flysheet, Folder, Leaflet, Mailshot, Newsletter, Orbital, Orby, Round, Spiral, Unending, Vertical, Wheely

**Circulate, Circulation, Circulatory** Ambient, Astir, Bandy, Bloodstream, Cyclosis, Disseminate, Eddy, Flow, Gross, Gyre, Issue, Mingle, Mix, Orbit, Out and about, Pass, Publish, Report, Revolve, Rotate, Scope, Send round, Spread, Stir, Treadmill, Troll, Utter

▷**Circulating** *may indicate* an anagram

**Circumcise(r), Circumcision** Bris, Brith, Brit milah, Infibulate, Milah, Mohel, Pharaonic, Sandek

**Circumference** Boundary, Girth, Perimeter, Size

**Circumflex** Perispomenon

**Circumlocution** Bafflegab, Periphrasis, Tautology

**Circumnavigation** Periplus

**Circumscribe(d)** Define, Demarcate, Enclose, Eruv, Limit, Restrain, Restrict

**Circumspect** Cagey, Canny, Chary, Discreet, Guarded, Prudential, Wary, Watchful

**Circumstance(s), Circumstantial** Case, Concept, Detail, Event, Fact, Formal, → INCIDENT, Mitigating, Precise, Shebang, Situation, Stede

**Circumvent** Bypass, Dish, Dodge, Evade, Negotiate, Outflank, Outwit, Usurp

**Circus, Circus boy** Arena, Big top, Eros, Flea, Flying, Harrier, Hippodrome, Marquee, Maximus, Media, Monty Python, Oxford, Piccadilly, Ring, Sanger, Slang, Three-ring

**Cissy** Nelly

**Cist** Cistvaen, Kistvaen

**Cistercian** Trappist

**Cistern** Feed-head, Flush-box, Sump, Tank, Tub, Vat

**Citadel** Acropolis, Alhambra, Castle, Fort(ress), Kasbah, Keep, Kremlin, Sea-girt

**Citation, Cite** Adduce, Allegation, Instance, Mensh, Mention, Name, Quote, Recall, Reference, Repeat, Sist, Summon

**Citizen(s), Citizenry, Citizenship** Burgess, Burgher, Civism, Cleruch, Cosmopolitan, Denizen, Dicast, Ephebe, Franchise, Freeman, Jus sanguinis, Jus soli, Kane, Keelie, Militia, National, Oppidan, Patrial, People, Proletarian, Propr(a)etor, Quirites, Resident, Roman, Second-class, Senior, Snob, Subject, Townspeople, Trainband, Trierarch, Venireman, Vigilante, Voter

**Citroen** DS

**Citron, Citrous** Bergamot

**Citrus** Acid, Calamondin, Cedrate, Hesperidium, Lemon, Lime, Mandarin, Min(n)eola, Orange, Pomelo, Satsuma, Tangerine, Ugli

**City** Agra, Astrakhan, Athens, Atlantis, Babylon, Bishopric, Brum, Burgh, Cardboard, Carthage, Cosmopolis, Ctesiphon, Dodge, EC, Empire, Eternal, Forbidden, Free, Garden, Gath, Heavenly, Hilversum, Holy, Imperial, Inner, Jericho, LA, Leonine, Medina, Megalopolis, Metropolis, Micropolis, Mother, Municipal, Mycenae, Nineveh, NY, Persepolis, Petra, Pompeii, Rhodes, Salem, See, Smoke, Sparta, Square mile, Tech, Teheran, The Big Smoke, Town, Ur, Urban(e), Vatican, Weltstadt, Wen, Yonkers

**Civet** Binturong, Cat, Fo(u)ssa, Genet(te), Herpestes, Linsang, Musang, Nandine, Palm, Paradoxine, Paradoxure, Rasse, Suricate, Toddy-cat, Viverra, Zibet

**Civil(ian), Civilisation, Civilised, Civility** Amenity, Amicable, Christian, Cit, Citizen, Civ(vy), Comity, Courtesy, Culture, Fertile crescent, Humane, Humanised, Indus Valley, Kultur, Maya, Mesopotamia, Minoan, Mufti, Municipal, Nok, Non-combatant, Paramilitary, Plain clothes, Polite, Politesse, Push-button, Respectful, Secular, Temporal, Urbane

**Civil Defence** ARP, CD

**Civil Service** CS

**Clacker** Crotalum

**Clad(ding)** Sarking, Weatherboard

**Clag(gy)** Stickjaw

**Claim(s)** Allege, Appeal, Arrogate, Assert, Asseverate, Bag, Challenge, Charge, Crave, Darraign(e), Darrain(e), Darrayn, Demand, Deraign, Droit, Encumbrance, Exact, Haro, Harrow, Insist, Lien, List, Maintain, Nochel, Plea, Pose, Posit, Postulate, Predicate, Pretence, Pretend, Profess, Pulture, Purport, Puture, Rank, Repossess, Revendicate, Right, Set-off, Small, Sue, Title

**Claimant** Irredentist, Petitioner, Pot-waller, Pretender, Prospector, Tichborne, Titler, Usurper

**Clairvoyance, Clairvoyancy, Clairvoyant** ESP, Extrasensory, Far-sighted, Fey, Insight, Lucidity, Prophet, Psiphenomena, Psychic, Second sight, Taisch, Taish, Telegnosis, Telepathic, Tel(a)esthesia

**Clam** Bivalve, Chowder, Cohog, Geoduck, Giant, Gweduc, Hardshell, Littleneck, Mollusc, Mya, Quahang, Quahog, Razor(-shell), Round, Soft-shell, Steamer, Tridacna, Venus, Vongole

**Clamant** Vociferous

**Clamber** Climb, Crawl, Scramble, Spra(i)ckle, Sprauchle

**Clammy** Algid, Damp, Dank, Humid, Moist, Sticky, Sweaty

**Clamour(ing), Clamorous** Blatant, Brouhaha, Din, Forensis strepitus, Hubbub, Hue, Katzenjammer, Noise, Outcry, Racket, Raird, Reird, Rout, Shout, Strepitant, Uproar, Utis, Vociferate

**Clamp(er)** Beartrap, Chuck, Clinch, Coupler, Denver boot, Fasten, Grip, Haemostat, Holdfast, Jumar, Pinchcock, Potato-pit, Serrefine, Stirrup, Tread, Vice, Wheel

**Clan(sman)** Brood, Cameron, Campbell, Clique, Gens, Gentile, Group, Horde, Kiltie, Kindred, Name, Ngati, Nomen, Phratry, Phyle, Sect, Sept, Society, Stewart, Stuart, Tribe

**Clandestine** Covert, Furtive, Hedge marriage, Samizdat, Secret, Sneaky, Surreptitious, Underhand

**Clang(er), Clanging, Clank** Bell, Belleter, Boob, Boo-boo, Chime, Clash, Gong, Jangle, Plangent, Ring

**Clap(per), Clapping** Applaud, Blow, Castanet, Chop, Crotal, Dose, Jinglet, Noisemaker, Peal, Plaudit(e), Stroke hands, Thunder, Tonant

**Claptrap** Bilge, Blab, Blah, Bombast, Bunkum, Eyewash, Hokum, Jibberish, Mumbo-jumbo, Rot, Tripe, Twaddle

**Claque(ur)** Fans, Hat, Laudator, Sycophant

**Clara** Bow, Butt

**Clare** Nun, Sister

**Claret** Blood, Loll-shraub, Loll-shrob, Vin

**Clarify, Clarified, Clarifier** Clear, Define, Despumate, Dilucidate, Elucidate, Explain, Explicate, Fine, Finings, Ghee, Illuminate, Purge, Refine, Render, Simplify, Tease out

**Clarinet** Chalumeau, Reed

**Clarion** Brassy, Call, Clear, Trumpet

**Clarity** Cogency, Lucidity, Perspicuity

**Clary** Orval, Sage

**Clash(ing)** Bang, Clangour, Clank, Claver, Coincide, Collide, Conflict, Contretemps, Cymbal, Disharmony, Dissonant, Friction, Gossip, → IMPACT, Incident, Irreconcilable, Jangle, Jar, Lock horns, Loud, Missuit, Riot, Scream, Shock, Showdown, Skirmish, Strike, Swash, Tilt

**Clasp(ing)** Adpress, Agraffe, Amplexus, Barrette, Brooch, Buckle, Button, Catch, Chape, Clip, Embrace, Fibula, Grasp, Hasp, Hesp, Hook, Hug, Inarm, Interdigitate, Link, Morse, Netsuke, Ochreate, Ouch, Peace, Press, Slide, Tach(e), Tie, Unite

**Class(ification), Classify, Classified, Classy** Acorn, Ad(vert), Arrange, Assort, Bourgeois(ie), Bracket, Brand, Breed, Business, Cabin, Canaille, Caste, → CATEGORY, Cattle, Chattering, Cheder, Cl, Cladistics, Clan, Clerisy, Clinic, Club, Coach, Composite, Continuation, Course, Criminal, Dalit, Decimal, Dewey, Digest, Division, Economy, Establishment, Estate, Evening, Faction, First, Folksonomy, Form, Genera, Genre, Gentry, Genus, → GRADE, Group, Harvard, Haryan, Heder, Hubble, Ilk, Keep-fit, Kidney, Kohanga reo, League, Lesson, Life, Linn(a)ean, List, Lower, Mammal, Master, Meritocracy, Middle, Night, Number, Nursery, Order, Peasantry, Pentandrian, Petit bourgeois, Phenetics, Phylum, Pigeon-hole, Pleb(eian), Posh, Proletariat, Proper, Race, Radiate, Range, Rank, Rate, Rating, Raypoot, Raypout, Reception, Remove, Ruling, Salariat, Second, Secret, Seminar, Shell, Siege, Social, Sort(ation), Sort(ment), Spectral, Sphere, Standard, Steerage, Stratum, Stream, Swish, Syntax, Taxonomy, Teach-in, Third, Tony, Tourist, Tribe, Tutorial, → TYPE, U, Universal, Upper, Varna, Water, Working, World, Year

**Classic(al), Classics, Classicist** Ageless, Ancient, Basic, Delphin, Derby, Elzevir, Epic, Flat race, Golden oldie, Grecian, Greek, Humane, Le Grand Siecle, Literature, Oldie, Pliny, Purist, Roman, Standard, St Leger, Traditional, Vintage

**Classmate** Condisciple

**Clatch** Blunk, Smear, Spoil

**Clatter** Bicker, Charivari, Clack, Din, Noise, Rattle

**Clause** Acceleration, Adjunct, Apodosis, Article, Basket, Complement, Condition, Conscience, Coordinate, Dependent, Disability, Endorsement, Escalation, Escalator, Escape, Exclusion, Exemption, Filioque, Four, Golden parachute, Grandfather, Independent, Loophole, Main, Member, Noun, Novodamus, Object, Omnibus, Option, Poison-pill, Predicator, Principal, Protasis, Proviso, Reddendum, Relative, Reopener, Reopening, Reported, Reservation, Reserve, Rider, Salvo, Saving, Sentence, Subject, Subordinate, Sunset, Tenendum, Testatum, Testing, Warrandice

**Clavicle** Collarbone

**Claw** Chela, Claut, Cloye, Crab, Dewclaw, Edate, Falcula, Grapple, Griff(e), Hook, Insessorial, Lark-heel, Nail, Nipper, Pincer, Pounce, Scrab, Scramb, Sere, Talent, → TALON, Tear, Telson, Tokay, Unguis

**Clay** Ali, Allophane, Argil, Argillite, Ball, Barbotine, B(e)auxite, Bentonite, Blaes, Blaise, Blaize, Blunge, Bole, Boulder, Calm, Cam, Cassius, Caum, Ceramic, Charoset(h), China, Cimolite, Cloam, Clunch, Cob, Cornish, Earth, Engobe, Fango, Figuline, Fire, Fuller's earth, Gault, Glei, Gley, Gumbotil, Hardpan, Haroset(h), Illite, Kaolin, Kokowai, Laterite, Lithomarge, Loam, London, Lute, Malm, Marl, Meerschaum, Mire, Mortal, Mud, Oxford, Papa, Pipeclay, Pipestone, Pise, Plastic, Plastilina, Porcelain, Potter's, Pottery, Puddle, Pug, Saggar(d), Sagger, Scroddle(d), Seggar, Sepiolite, Slip, Slurry, Smectite, Terra sigillata, Thill, Till(ite), Tumphy, Varve, Warrant, Warren, Wax

**Clean(er), Cleaning, Cleanse** Abrasive, Absterge, Ammonia, Antiseptic, Aseptic, Bathbrick, Besom, Bidet, Blanco, Bleach, Blue flag, Boots, Bottlebrush, Bream, Breast, Broom, Careen, Catharise, Catharsis, Chambermaid, Chamois leather, Char(e), Chaste, Clear, Cottonbud, Daily, Debride, Decontaminate, Defrost, Dentifrice, Depurate, Descale, Deterge(nt), Detox(ify), Dhobi, Dialysis, Dicht, Dishrag, Disinfect, Do, Douche, Dredge, Dry, Dust(er), Dyson®, Eluant, Emunge, Enema, Epurate, Erase, Ethnic, Evacuant, Evacuate, Expurgate, Fay, Fettle, Fey, Floorcloth, Floss, Flush, Full, Grave, Groom, Gut, Heels, Home help, Hoover®, House-trained, Hygienic, Immaculate, Innocent, J-cloth, Kosher, Launder, Lave, Linish, Loofah, Lustrum, Lye, Mouthwash, Mrs Mop(p), Mundify, Nailbrush, Net, Nipter, Overhaul, Pipem Preen, Porge, Prophylaxis, Pull-through, Pumice, Pure, Purgative, Purge, Q-tip, Ramrod, Rebite, Repay, Rub, Rump, Sandblast, Sanitize, Scaffie, Scavenge,

Scour, Screenwash, Scrub, Shampoo, Shot-blast, Sluice, Snow-white, Soap, Soogee, Soogie, Soojey, Sponge, Spotless, Spring, Square, Squeaky, Squeegee, Squilgee, Sterile, Sujee, Swab, Sweep, Syringe, Tidy, Tissue, Toothpaste, Toothpick, Tooth powder, Totally, Turpentine, Ultrasonic, Uproot, Vac(uum), Valet, → WASH, Whistle, Whiter, Wipe, Zamboni

**Clear(ance), Cleared, Clearer, Clearly, Clear up** Absolve, Acquit, Allow, Aloof, Apparent, Articulate, Assart, Bald, Bell, Berth, Bold, Bore, Brighten, Bus, Candid, Categorical, Clarify, Clean-cut, Cloudless, Cogent, Comprehensive, Concise, Consomme, Crystal, Daylight, Decode, Decongest, Definite, De-ice, Delouse, Demist, Demystify, Diaphanous, Disafforest, Dispel, Distinct, Downright, Drain, Dredge, Earn, Eidetic, Evacuate, Evident, Exculpate, Exonerate, Explicit, Express, Fair, Five-by-five, Flagrant, Gain, Get over, Hawk, Headroom, Highland, Hyaline, Incisive, In focus, Intelligible, Iron, Laund, Leap, Leapfrog, Legible, Limpid, Lucid, Luculent, Manifest, Mop, Neat, Negotiate, Net(t), No brainer, → NOT CLEAR, Observable, Obvious, Ope(n), Outright, Overleap, Overt, Palpable, Patent, Pay, Pellucid, Perspicuous, Plain, Play, Pratique, Predy, Pure, Purge, Quit, Rack, Realise, Reap, Refine, Remble, Rid, Ripple, Serene, Sheer, Shere, Shovel, Silvery, Slash-burn, Slum, Snowplough, Solve, Specific, Stark, Straight, Strip, Succinct, Sweep, Swidden, Terse, Thro(ugh), Thwaite, Transire, Translucent, Transparent, Unambiguous, Unblock, Unclog, Uncork(ed), Unequivocal, Unstop, Vault, Vindicate, Vivid, Void, Well, Whiten, Windage, Wipe

**Clearing** Assart, Glade, Opening, Shire, Slash

**Cleat** Bitt, Wedge

**Cleave, Cleavage, Cleft** Adhere, Bisulcate, Builder's bottom, Builder's bum, Chimney, Chine, Chink, Cling, Cloff, Cohere, Cut, Divide, Division, Divorce(ment), Fissure, Gap, Ghaut, Goose-grass, Grike, Gryke, Harelip, Meroblastic, Notch, Pharynx, Rift, Riva, Scissure, Severance, Slack, Slate, Space, Spathose, Split, Sulcus

**Cleaver** Meat-axe

**Clef** Soprano, Treble

**Cleft** Crevice, Fissirostral, Notch

**Clematis** Montana, Old man's beard, Traveller's joy, Virgin's-bower

**Clemenceau** Tiger

**Clemency, Clement** Ahimsa, Attlee, Balmy, Grace, Lenience, Lenity, Mercy, Mildness, Quarter, Temperate

**Clench(ed)** Close, Double, Fist, Grip, Grit, Squeeze, Stiffen, Tense

**Cleopatra** Needle

**Clergy(man), Cleric(al)** Abbé, Abbot, Archdeacon, Ayatollah, Black, Canon, Cantor, Cardinal, Chancellor, Chaplain, Chapter, Circuit rider, Cleric, Clerk, Cloth, Curate, Curé, Deacon, Dean, Ecclesiast(ic), God-botherer, Goliard, Holy Joe, Incumbent, Josser, Legate, Levite, Ministerial, Ministry, Minor canon, Non-juror, Non-usager, Notarial, Padre, Paperwork, Parson, Pastor, Pontifex, Pontiff, Preacher, Prebendary, Precentor, Prelate, Presbyter, Presenter, Priest, Primate, Prior, Proctor, Rabbi, Rector, Red-hat, Revelationist, Reverend, Rome-runner, Scribal, Secretarial, Secular, Shaveling, Shepherd, Simoniac, Sky pilot, Slope, Spin-text, Spirituality, Squarson, Subdeacon, Theologian, Usager, Vartabed, Vicar

**Clergy-hater** Misoclere

**Clerk(s)** Actuary, Articled, Baboo, Babu, Basoche, Circar, Cleric, Cratchit, Cursitor, Disk jockey, Enumerator, Filing, Heep, Lay, Limb, Notary, Paper-pusher, Parish, Pen-driver, Penman, Penpusher, Petty Bag, Poster, Protocolist, Prot(h)onotary, Quill-driver, Recorder, St Nicholas's, Salaryman, Scribe, Secretariat, Sheriff, Shipping, Sircar, Sirkar, Tally, Teller, Town, Vestry, Vicar, Writer

**Clever(ness)** Able, Accomplished, Adroit, Arch, Astute, Brainbox, Brainy, Bright, Canny, Cool, Cunning, Cute, Daedal(e), Deep-browed, Deft, Genius, Gleg, Habile, Handy, Ingenious, Intellectual, Jackeen, Know-all, Natty, Nifty, Nimblewit, Resourceful, Sage(ness), Shrewd, Skeeley, Skilful, Smart(y), Smarty-pants, Souple, Subtle, Wise, Wiseacre

**Clevis** Becket

**Cliché** Banality, Boilerplate, Commonplace, Corn, Journalese, Platitude, Saying, Stereotype, Tag

**Click(er), Clicking** Castanet, Catch, Forge, Implosive, Pawl, Rale, Ratch(et), Snick, Succeed, Tchick, Ticktack

**Client(ele)** Account, Customer, End-user, Fat, Gonk, John, Patron, Punter, Thin, Trade, Trick

**Cliff(s)** Beachy Head, Bluff, Cleve, Corniche, Crag, Craig, Escarp, Lorelei, Palisade(s), Precipice, Promontory, Sca(u)r

**Cliffhanger** Mountaineer, Samphire, Serial, Thriller

**Climate** Ambience, Atmosphere, Attitude, Continental, Humid, Mood, Saharan, Subhumid, Sun, Temperament, Temperature, Weather

**Climax** Apex, Apogee, Catastasis, Come, Crescendo, Crest, Crisis, Culminate, Edaphic, End, Head, Height, Heyday, Moment of truth, Orgasm, Payoff, Peak, Selling, Top, Zenith

**Climb(er), Climbing** Aid, Alpinist, Aralia, Aristolochia, Artificial, Ascend, Bignonian, Bougainvillaea, Breast, Briony, Bryony, Clamber, Clematis, Clusia, Cowage, Cowhage, Cowitch, Crampon, Creeper, Cubeb, Cucumber, Dodder, Eglatere, Ers, Heart-pea, Hedera, Honeysuckle, Ibex, Ivy, Jamming, Kie-kie, Kudzu, Ladder, Lawyer, Layback, Liana, Liane, → MOUNT, Munro-bagger, Pareira, Parvenu, Pea, Peg, Poison oak, Prusik, Rat(t)an, Rhoicissus, Rise, Root, Rope, Scale, Scan, Scandent, Scansores, Sclim, Scramble, Shin, Shinny, Sklim, Smilax, Soar, Social, Speel, Steeplejack, Stegophilist, Sty(e), Swarm, Sweetpea, Timbo, Tuft-hunter, Udo, Up(hill), Uprun, Upstart, Vetch, Vine, Vitaceae, Wistaria, Wisteria, With(y)wind, Woodbine, Zoom

**Clinch** Attach, Carriwitchet, Determine, Ensure, Fix, Ice, Quibble, Rivet, Secure, Settle, Smooch

**Cling(er), Clinging** Adhere, Barnacle, Bur(r), Cherish, Cleave, Embrace, Hold, Hug, Limpet, Ring, Stick, Suctorial, Tendril

**Clinic** Abortuary, Antenatal, Dental, Dispensary, Health centre, Hospital, Hospitium, Mayo, Well-woman

**Clink** Gingle, Jail, Jingle, Lock up, Nick, Prison, Stir, Ting, Tinkle

**Clinker** Ash, Slag

**Clint** Limestone

**Clip(ped), Clipper, Clipping** Alberta, Banana, Barrette, Bicycle, Brash, Bulldog, Butterfly, Cartridge, Chelsea, Clasp, Crocodile, Crop-ear, Crutch, Curt, Curtail, Cut, Cutty Sark, Dag, Dock, Dod, Excerpt, Film, Fleece, Hairslide, Jubilee, Jumar, Krab, Lop, Money, Mow, Nail, Outtake, Pace, Paper, Pare, Pedicure, Peg, Prerupt, Prune, Roach, Scissel, Secateur, Shear, Ship, Shore, Shorn, Shorten, Slide, Snip, Spring, Staccato, Staple, Terse, Tie, Tie-tack, Tinsnips, Toe, Tonsure, Topiarist, Trim, Trot

**Clippy** Cad, Conductor

**Clique** Cabal, Clan, Club, Coterie, Elite, Faction, Four Hundred, Gang, Incrowd, Junta, Ring, Sect, Set, Tribe

**Clive** Arcot

**Cloak(room), Cloaks** Aba, Abaya, Abba, Abolla, Amice, Anonymity, Bathroom, Buffalo-robe, Burnous, Capa, Cape, Capote, Caracalla, Cardinal, Cassock, Chasuble, Chimer(e), Chlamydes, Chlamys, Chuddah, Chuddar, Cocoon, Conceal, Cope, Cover, Disguise, Dissemble, Djellaba(h), Domino, Gabardine, Gaberdine, Gal(l)abea(h), Gal(l)abi(y)a(h), Gal(l)abi(y)eh, Gentlemen, Gents, Grego, Hall-robe, Heal, Hele, Himation, Hood, Inverness, Jelab, Jellaba, Joseph, Kaross, Korowai, Ladies, Manta, Manteau, Manteel, Mantle, Mant(e)let, → MASK, Mourning, Mousquetaire, Mozetta, Obscure, Opera, Paenula, Paletot, Pallium, Paludamentum, Pelisse, Pilch, Poncho, Powder-room, Rail, Revestry, Rocklay, Rokelay, Roquelaure, Sagum, Sarafan, Scapular, → SCREEN, Shroud, Swathe, Talma, Toga, Tunic, Vestiary, Vestry, Visite

**Clobber** Anoint, Apparel, Attire, Clothing, Do, Dress, Garb, Garment, Gear, Habiliments, Lam, Tack, Thump

**Clock** Alarm, Ammonia, Analogue, Astronomical, Atomic, Beetle, Big Ben, Biological, Blowball, Body, Bracket, Bundy, Caesium, Carriage, Cartel, Clepsydra, Cuckoo, Dandelion, Digital, Doomsday, Dutch, Floral, Grandfather, Grandmother, Hit, Hydroscope, Knock, Long case, Master, Meter, Paenula, Parliament, Puss, Quartz, Repeater, Sandglass, Settler's, Solarium, Speaking, Speedo, Strike, Sundial, Taximeter, Tell-tale, Time(r), Timekeeper, Travelling, Turret, Twelve-hour, Wag at the wa', Water

**Clockmaker** Fromanteel, Graham, Harrison, Knibb, Mudge, Tompion
**Clockwise** Deasil, Deasiul, Deasoil, Deiseal, Deisheal
**Clockwork** Orange, Precision, Regular
**Clod** Clumsy, Divot, Glebe, Lump, Mool, Mould, Mug, Put(t), Scraw, Sod, Stupid, Turf
**Clog(gy)** Accloy, Ball, Block, Choke, Clam, Congest, Crowd, Dance, Fur, Galosh, Golosh, Gum up, Hamper, Jam, Lump, Mire, Obstruct, Overshoe, Patten, Sabot, Sandal, Silt, Stickjaw
**Cloisonné** Shippo
**Cloister** Arcade, Confine, Cortile, Immure, Monastery, Mure, Refuge, Seclude
**Clone, Cloning** Mini-me, Ramet, Replicant, Reproduce, Therapeutic
**Cloots** Worricow
**Close(d), Closing, Closure** Adjacent, Adjourn, Agree, Airless, Alongside, Anigh, Atresia, Block, Boon, By, Cadence, Cap, Cheek by jowl, Clammy, Clap, Clench, Coda, Collapse, Compact, Complete, Concentration, Cone off, Confidante, Court, Crown cap, Curtain, Dear, Debar, Dense, Dissolve, → END, Epilogue, Ewest, Eye to eye, Fasten, Finale, Fingertips, Forby, Gare, Grapple, Handy, Hard, Hard by, Hermetic, Hot, Humid, Imminent, Inbye, Infibulate, Intent, Intimate, Local, Lock, Lucken, Marginal, Mean, Miserly, Muggy, Mure, Narre, Narrow, Near, Nearhand, Neck and neck, Neist, Next, Nie, Niggardly, Nigh, Nip and tuck, Obturate, Occlude, Occlusion, Oppressive, Pally, Parochial, Penny-pinching, Photo-finish, Placket, Point blank, Precinct, Recess, Reserved, Reticent, Seal, Secret, Serre, Serried, Serry, Shet, Shut(ter), Shutdown, Silly, Slam, Snug, Stap, Sticky, Stifling, Stuffy, Sultry, Tailgate, Temenos, Terminate, Tight(knit), Uproll, Velcro®, Wafer, Wanr, Warm, Yard
**Close-cropped** Crewcut, Not-pated
**Close-fitting** Skintight, Slinky, Tight
**Closet** Cabinet, Confine, Cubicle, Cupboard, Dooket, Earth, Linen, Locker, Safe, Wardrobe, WC, Zeta
**Close-up** Detail, Fill, Shut, Stop, Zoom
**Closing-time** Eleven, End
**Clot(ting)** Agglutinate, Ass, Bozo, Clag, Clump, Coagulate, Congeal, Crassamentum, Cruor, Curdle, Dag, Duffer, Embolism, Embolus, Gel, Globule, Gob, Gout, Grume, Heparin, Incrassate, Incrust, Jell, Lapper, Lopper, → LUMP, Mass, Moron, Prothrombin, Splatch, Stupid, Thicken, Thrombosis, Thrombus
**Clotbuster** Heparin
**Cloth** Aba, Abaya, Abba, Antependium, Bandanna, Bearing, Bib, Bribe, Carmelite, Clergy, Cloot, Clout, Communion, Corporal(e), Dishrag, Duster, → FABRIC, → FELT, Focus(ing), Frocking, Frontal, Gremial, G-string, Habit-cloth, Interfacing, Jharan, Kerchief, Loin, Lungi, Manta, → MATERIAL, Mercerise, Mercery, Meshing, Mortcloth, Nap, Napery, Napje, Napkin, Nappie, Neckerchief, Needlework, Netting, Pack, Packsheet, Pad, Painted, Pall, Pane, Pilch, Priesthood, Pull-through, Purificator, Puttee, Putty, Rag, Raiment, Roll, Roon, Runner, Sail, Sashing, Scarlet, Serviette, Sheet, Sheeting, Shirting, Shoddy, Shroud, Stock, Stripe, Stuff, Stupe, Sudarium, Supper, Sweatband, Tapestry, Tea, → TEXTILE, Throw, Tissue, Toilet, Vernicle, Veronica, Washrag, Whole

---

## CLOTH

*1 letter:*
J®
T

*3 letters:*
Abb
Box
Lap®
Rep
Say
Web

*4 letters:*
Aida
Amis
Baft
Bark
Ciré
Doek
Drab
Duck
Felt
Fent
Flax
Gair
Gold
Haik
Harn
Hyke
Ikat
Jean
Kelt
Knit
Lace
Lamé
Lawn
Leno
Line
Lint
Mull
Nude
Pina
Puke
Repp
Rund
Shag
Slop
Sulu
Tapa
Tick
Wire
Wool

*5 letters:*
Atlas
Baize
Beige
Binca
Budge
Chino

Crape
Crash
Crepe
Denim
Dobby
Drill
Duroy
Fanon
Foulé
Frisé
Gauze
Gazar
Grass
Gunny
Haick
Honan
Jaspe
Kanga
Kente
Khadi
Khaki
Kikoi
Linen
Lisle
Llama
Loden
Lurex®
Lycra®
Moiré
Mongo
Monk's
Mummy
Mungo
Ninon
Nylon
Ombre
Orlon®
Panel
Panne
Paper
Perse
Pilot
Piqué
Plaid
Plush
Poult
Print
Rayon
Satin
Scrim
Serge
Slops
Surah
Surat
Surge
Tabby
Tamin
Tammy
Tappa
Terry
Tibet
Toile
Towel
Tulle
Tweed
Tweel
Twill
Union
Voile
Wigan

***6 letters:***
Aertex®
Alpaca
Angora
Armure
Barège
Beaver
Bouclé
Broche
Burlap
Burnet
Burrel
Byssus
Caddis
Calico
Camlet
Camlot
Canvas
Catgut
Chintz
Cilice
Cloqué
Coburg
Cotton
Coutil
Covert
Crepon
Cubica
Cyprus
Dacron®
Damask
Dévoré
Dimity
Domett
Dossal
Dossel
Dowlas
Dralon®
Drapet
Duffel
Duffle
Dupion
Durrie
Etamin
Faille
Fannel
Frieze
Gloria
Greige
Gurrah
Haique
Harden
Herden
Hodden
Hoddin
Humhum
Hurden
Jersey
Kersey
Khanga
Kincob
Lampas
Madras
Medley
Melton
Merino
Mohair
Mongoe
Moreen
Muleta
Mulmul
Muslin
Mutton
Nankin
Nettle
Oxford
Pongee
Poplin
Rateen
Ratine
Russel
Samite
Satara
Sateen
Saxony
Sendal
Shalli
Sherpa
Sindon
Soneri
Stroud
Tactel®
Tamine
Tamise
Tartan
Tencel®
Thibet
Tricot
Vellet
Velour
Velure
Velvet
Vicuna
Wadmal
Wincey
Winsey

***7 letters:***
Abattre
Acrylic
Alamode
Alepine
Baracan
Batiste
Bolting
Brocade
Cabbage
Cambric
Camelot
Challie
Challis
Chamois
Cheviot
Chiffon
Crombie
Cypress
Delaine
Dhurrie
Doeskin
Domette
Dorneck
Dornick
Drabbet
Drapery
Droguet
Drugget
Duvetyn
Etamine
Faconné
Fannell
Fishnet
Flannel
Foulard
Fustian
Galatea
Genappe
Gingham
Gore-tex®
Grogram
Hessian
Holland
Hopsack
Jaconet
Jamdani
Khaddar
Kitenge
Leather
Lockram
Mockado
Nacarat
Nankeen
Oil-silk
Oilskin
Organza
Orleans
Ottoman
Paisley
Percale
Printer
Rabanna
Raploch
Raschel
Ratteen
Rattine
Ripstop
Sacking
Sagathy
Satinet
Schappe
Silesia
Sinamay
Spandex®
Stammel
Supplex®
Tabaret
Tabinet
Taffeta
Ticking
Tiffany
Trolley
Tussore
Viscose
Viyella®
Wadmaal
Webbing
Woolsey
Worsted
Zanella

***8 letters:***
Aircraft
Algerine
American
Armozeen
Armozine
Arresine
Bagheera
Barathea
Barracan

Bayadere
Bearskin
Bobbinet
Boulting
Brocatel
Cameline
Casement
Cashmere
Casimere
Celanese
Chambray
Chamelot
Chenille
Ciclaton
Corduroy
Coteline
Coutille
Cretonne
Damassin
Drabette
Duchesse
Dungaree
Duvetine
Duvetyne
Eolienne
Florence
Gambroon
Gossamer
Homespun
Jacquard
Jeanette
Lambskin
Lava-lava
Lustrine
Lustring
Mackinaw
Mantling
Marcella
Marocain
Mazarine
Moleskin
Moquette
Nainsook
Oilcloth
Organdie
Osnaburg
Pashmina
Plaiding
Pleather
Prunella
Rodevore
Sarcenet
Sarsenet
Sealskin
Shabrack
Shalloon
Shantung
Sicilian
Suedette
Swanskin
Tabbinet
Tarlatan
Toilinet
Velveret
Whipcord
Wild silk
Zibeline

***9 letters:***
Aeroplane
Alcantara
Astrakhan
Baldachin
Balzarine
Bengaline
Bombasine
Calamanco
Camel-hair
Cassimere
Cerecloth
Charmeuse®
Ciclatoun
Cottonade
Courtelle®
Crepoline
Crimplene®
Crinoline
Evenweave
Fabrikoid®
Farandine
Filoselle
Folk-weave
Gaberdine
Georgette
Grenadine
Grosgrain
Haircloth
Horsehair
Indiennes
Interlock
Kalamkari
Levantine
Longcloth
Mandilion
Mandylion
Marseille
Matelassé
Messaline
Moygashel
Nitro-silk
Open-weave
Organzine
Overcheck
Paramatta
Penistone
Percaline
Persienne
Petersham
Pinstripe
Polyester
Ravenduck
Sackcloth
Sailcloth
Satin jean
Sharkskin
Silkalene
Silkaline
Stockinet
Strouding
Swansdown
Tarpaulin
Tricotine
Veloutine
Velveteen
Wire gauze
Worcester
Zibelline

***10 letters:***
Balbriggan
Baldachino
Book muslin
Broadcloth
Brocatelle
Camel's-hair
Candlewick
Farrandine
Fearnought
Ferrandine
Florentine
Geotextile
Kerseymere
Lutestring
Matellasse
Mousseline
Needlecord
Parramatta
Polycotton
Ravensduck
Russel-cord
Seersucker
Shabracque
Shiveshive
Sicilienne
Tattersall
Toilinette
Tuftaffeta
Tuftaffety
Winceyette

***11 letters:***
Abercrombie
Bedford cord
Canton crepe
Cheesecloth
Cloth of gold
Dotted Swiss
Drap-de-berry
Dreadnought
Flannelette
Hammercloth
Harris Tweed®
Kendal green
Marquisette
Nun's veiling
Sempiternum
Stockinette
Stretch knit
Swiss muslin

***12 letters:***
Brilliantine
Cavalry twill
Crepe de chine
Elephant cord
Leather-cloth

***13 letters:***
Gros de Londres
Linsey-woolsey

---

**Cloth-designing** Batik
**Clothe(s), Clothing, Clothed** Accoutrements, Ao dai, Apparel, Array, Attire, Baggies, Basque, Battledress, Beachwear, Bedjacket, Besee, Bib and tucker, Boiler suit, Cape, Casuals, Chasuble, Chino, Chiton, Choli, Cits, Civvies, Clad, Claes, Clericals, Clobber, Coat, Combinations, Confection, Coordinates, Costume, Cour, Cover, Croptop, Cruisewear, Culottes, Deck, Diffusion line, Dight, Don, Drag, → DRESS, Duds, Dungarees, Emboss, Endue, Fig leaf, Finery, Foot muff, Frippery, Garb, Garments, Gear, Gere, Get-up, Glad rags, Grave, Gymslip, Gyves, Habit, Haute couture, Hejab, Hot pants, Hug-me-tight, Ihram Khimar, Innerwear, Judogi, Jump (suit), Kimono, Knitwear, Layette, Leathers, Lederhosen, Leisurewear, Long-togs, Maternity, Menswear, Mitumba, Mocker, Muff, Mufti, Nebris, Nightdress, Nike®, Outfit, Overalls, Pannicle, Pantsuit, Pareu, Pea-coat, Pea-jacket, Pin-striped, Plain, Playsuit, Plus fours, Raggery, Rag trade, Raiment, Rami, Rigout, Robes, Rompers, Samfoo, Samfu, Sayon, Scapulary, Schmutter, Scrubs, Scungies, Shell suit, Shirtwaister, Shmatte, Shorts, Slacks, Slops, Smock, Spacesuit, Stomacher, Strip, Sunday best, Sundress, Sunsuit, Swaddling, Swathe, Sweatshirt, Swothling, Tackle, Tankini, Tank

top, Things, Toga, Toggery, Togs, Tracksuit, Trappings, Trews, Trousseau, Tube top, Tweeds, Two-piece, Unitard, Veiling, Vernicle, Vestiary, Vestiture, Vestment, Wardrobe, Watteau, Wear, Weeds, Wetsuit, Widow's weeds, Workwear, Yclad, Ycled, Y-fronts

**Clothes basket, Clothes horse** Airer, Model, Petara, Winterhedge

**Clothier** Dresser, Dressmaker, Tailor

**Cloud(ing), Clouded, Cloudiness, Cloudy** Altocumulus, Altostratus, Banner, Benight, Blear, C, Cataract, Cirrocumulus, Cirrostratus, Cirrus, Coalsack, Coma, Contrail, Crab Nebula, Cumulonimbus, Cumulus, Dim, Dull, Emission nebula, Fog, Fractocumulus, Fractostratus, Funnel, Goat's hair, Haze, Horsehead Nebula, Infuscate, Magellanic, Mammatus, Mare's tail, Milky, Mist, Molecular, Mushroom, Nacreous, Nebular, Nephele, Nephelometer, Nepho-, Nimbostratus, Nimbus, Nubecula, Nubilous, Nuée ardente, Obnubilation, Obscure, Octa, Okta, Oort, Opaque, Overcast, Pall, Pother, Protostar, Rack, Roily, Smoor, Stain, Storm, Stratocumulus, Strat(o)us, Swarm, Thunder(head), Turbid, Unclear, Virga, War, Water-dog, Weft, Woolpack, Zero-zero

**Cloudberry** Mountain bramble

**Cloudless** Serene

**Clough** Dale, Gorge, Ravine

**Clout** Belt, Cloth, Crown, Hit, Influence, Lap(pie), Lapje, Muscle, Power, Pull, Raddle, Thump

**Clove** Chive, Eugenia, Garlic, Rose-apple, Split, Yrent

**Cloven** Bisulcate, Fissilingual

**Clover** Alfalfa, Alsike, Berseem, Calvary, Cinque, Cow-grass, Dutch, Four-leaf, Hare's-foot, Hop, Hop-trefoil, Japan, Ladino, Lespedeza, Medic(k), Melilot, Owl's, Pin, Rabbit-foot, Red, Serradella, Serradilla, Shamrock, Souple, Sucklers, Suckling, Sweet, Trefoil, Trilobe, Truelove, White

**Clown(ish)** Airhead, Antic, Antick, August(e), Boor, Bor(r)el, Buffoon, Carl, Chough, Chuff, Clout-shoe, Coco, → COMEDIAN, Comic, Costard, Daff, Feste, Froth, Girner, Gobbo, Goon, Gracioso, Grimaldi, Harlequin, Hob, Idiot, Jack-pudding, Jester, Joey, Joker, Joskin, Leno, Merry Andrew, Mountebank, Nedda, Nervo, Owl spiegle, Patch(c)ocke, Peasant, Pickle-herring, Pierrot, Put, Rustic, Slouch, Thalian, Touchstone, Trinculo, Wag, Zany

**Cloy(ing)** Choke, Clog, Glut, Pall, Satiate, Surfeit, Sweet

**Club(s), Club-like** Adelphi, Airn, Alloa, Almack's, Alpeen, Apex, Army and Navy, Arsenal, Artel, Association, Athen(a)eum, Baffy, Band(y), Basto, Bat, Bath, Beefsteak, Blackjack, Blaster, Bludgeon, Boodles, Bourdon, Brassie, Breakfast, Brook's, Bulger, C, Caman, Card, Carlton, Casino, Caterpillar, Cavalry, Chapter, Chartered, Chigiriki, Clavate, Cleek, Clip-joint, Combine, Compassion, Conservative, Constitutional, Cordeliers, Cosh, Coterie, Cotton, Country, Crockford's, Cudgel, Devonshire, Disco(theque), Dive, Driver, Driving iron, Drones, Fan, Farm team, Fascio, Fellowship, Feuillant, Field, Fleshpot, Fustigate, Garrick, Glee, Golf, Guards, Guild, Hampden, Health, Hell-fire, Hercules', Hetairia, Honky-tonk, Indian, Investment, Iron, Jacobin, Jigger, Job, Jockey, Junior Carlton, Kennel, Kierie, Kiri, Kitcat, Kiwanis, Knobkerrie, Landsdowne, Lathi, Laughter, League, Leander, Lions, Lofter, Long iron, Luncheon, Mace, Mallet, Mashie, Maul, Mell, Mere, Meri, Mess, Midiron, Minor suit, Monday, National Liberal, Niblick, Night(stick), Nightspot, Niterie, Nitery, Nulla(-nulla), Oddfellows, Paris, Patu, Pitching wedge, Polt, Pregnant, Priest, Provident, Pudding, Putter, Putting-cleek, Quarterstaff, RAC, R & A, Reform, Ring, Rota, Rotarian, Rotary, Round Table, Sand wedge, Sap, Savage, Savile, Shillelagh, Slate, Society, Soroptimist, Sorority, Sorosis, Spoon, Spot, Spurs, Strike, Strip, Stunner, Suicide, Supper, Texas wedge, Thatched House, Tong, Travellers, Trefoil, Truncheon, Trunnion, Union, United Services, Variety, Waddy, Warehouse, Wedge, White's, Wood, Yacht, Youth

**Club-foot** Kyllosis, Po(u)lt-foot, Talipes, Varus

**Clubhouse** Ch

**Clubman** Golfer, Member

**Club-rush** Deer-hair, Scirpus, Sedge

**Cluck** Cackle, Cherup, Chirrup, Dent

**Clue** 1ac, Across, Acrostic, Anagram, Aradne, Ball, Charade, Clavis, Dabs, Down, → HINT, Indication, Inkling, Key, Lead, Light, Rebus, Scent, Scooby(doo), Signpost, Thread, Tip

**Clueless** Ignorant

**Clump** Cluster, Finial, Knot, Mass, Mot(te), Patch, Plump, Sock, Tread, Tuft, Tump, Tussock

▷**Clumsily** *may indicate* an anagram

**Clumsy** All thumbs, Artless, Awkward, Bauchle, Blunderbuss, Bodger, Buffoon, Bungling, Butterfingers, Cack-handed, Calf, Chuckle, Clatch, Clodhopper, Cumbersome, Dub, Dutch, Fumbling, Galoot, Galumphing, Gauche, Gimp, Gink, Ham(-fisted), Heavy-handed, Horse-godmother, Hulk, Inapt, Inelegant, Inept, Inexpert, Klutz, Lob, Loutish, Lubbard, Lubber, Lumbering, Lummox, Lumpish, Maladdress, Maladroit, Mauther, Mawr, Mawther, Messy, Mor, Nerd, Nurd, Oafish, Off-ox, Overhasty, Palooka, Plonking, Rough, Schlemihl, S(c)hlemiel, Shlep, Squab, Stot, Stumbledom, Swab, Swob, Taupie, Tawpie, Two-fisted, Unco, Ungain, Unskilful, Unsubtle, Unwieldy, Wooden

**Clunk** Thud

**Cluster** Acervate, Agglomeration, Ament, Assemble, Asterism, Bunch, Catkin, Clump, Collection, Concentre, Constellate, Conurbation, Corymb, Cyme, Galactic, Gather, Gear, Globular, Glomeration, Group, Knot, Nodule, Oakleaf, Packet, Plump, Raceme, Rhipidium, Sheaf, Sorus, Strap, Telium, Thyrse, Tone, Truss, Tuffe, Tuft, Umbel, Verticillaster

**Clutch(es)** Battery, Brood, Chickens, Clasp, Cling, Eggs, Friction, Glaum, Grab, → **GRASP**, Gripe, Hold, Nest, Net, Seize, Sitting, Squeeze

**Clutter** Confusion, Impedimenta, Litter, Mess, Rummage, Spam, Untidy

**Coach(es)** Autodidact, Battlebus, Berlin, Bogie, Bus, Car, Carriage, Chara(banc), Clerestory, Crammer, Diligence, Dilly, Double-decker, Drag, Edifier, Fiacre, Fly, Four-in-hand, Gig, Griddle car, Groom, Hackney, Handler, Landau(let), Life, Mail, Microbus, Mourning, Phaeton, Post chaise, Prime, Pullman, Railcar, Rattler, Repetiteur, Rolling stock, Saloon, Shay, Sleeper, Slip, Sobriety, Stage, Surrey, Tally(-ho), Teach(er), Thoroughbrace, Train(er), Transport, Tutor, Voiture

**Coach-horse** Rove-beetle

**Coachmaker** Pumpkin

**Coachman** Automedon, Bunene, Coachy, Dragsman, Jarvey, Jehu, John

**Coagulant, Coagulate, Coagulation** Cautery, Clot, Congeal, Curdle, Curds, Gel, Jell, Rennet, Run, Runnet, Set, Solidify, Thicken

**Coal** Anthracite, Bituminous, Black diamonds, Blind, Block, Brown, Burgee, Caking, Candle, Cannel, Char, Cherry, Clinker, Coking, Coom, Crow, Culm, Day, Dice, Edge, Eldin, Ember, Fusain, Gas, Gathering, Hard, Indene, Jud, Knob, Lignite, Maceral, Mineral, Nut, Open-cast, Paper, Parrot, Pea, Purse, Sapropelite, Score, Sea, Seam, Slack, Soft, Splint, Steam, Stone, Surtarbrand, Surturbrand, Vitrain, Wallsend, White, Wood

**Coalesce(nce)** Accrete, Amalgamate, Blend, Concrescence, Concrete, Fuse, Gel, Merge, Sintery, Synaloepha, Unite

**Coalfish** Saith

**Coalition** Alliance, Bloc, Confederacy, Fusion, Janata, League, Merger, Rainbow, Tie, Union

**Coal-tar** Aniline, Cresol, Indene

**Coal-tub** Corf, Dan, Scuttle

**Coarse(ness)** Barbaric, Base, Bawdy, Blowzy, Blue, Boorish, Bran, Broad, Chav, Common, Crude, Dowlas, Earthy, Fisherman, Foul, Gneissose, Grained, Grobian, Gross, Grossièreté, Gruff, Haggery, Ham, Illbred, Indelicate, Low-bred, Plebeian, Rabelaisian, Rank, Rappee, Raunchy, Ribald, Rough, Rudas, Rude, Russet, Sackcloth, Schlub, Semple, Shaggy, Slob, Sotadic, Uncouth, Unrefined, Vulgar, Yahoo

**Coast(al)** Barbary, Beach, Bight, Caird, Cape, Causeway, Corniche, Coromandel, Costa, Dalmatian, Declutch, Drift, Freewheel, Glide, Gold, Hard, Heritage, Inshore, Ivory, Littoral, Longshore, Malabar, Maritime, Med, Murman(sk), Onshore, Orarian, Riviera, Scrieve, Seaboard, Seafront, Seashore, Seaside, → **SHORE**, Slave, Sledge, Strand, Sunshine, Surf, Toboggan, Trucial

**Coaster** Beermat, Drog(h)er, Mat, Roller, Ship, Smack

**Coastguard** CG, Gobby

**Coastline** Shoreline, Watermark

**Coast-road** Corniche

**Coat(ed), Coating** Ab(b)a, Abaya, Achkan, Acton, Admiral, Afghan, Anarak, Anodise, Anorak, Aril, Balmacaan, Barathea, Basan, Bathrobe, Belton, Benjamin, Blazer, Bloomed,

Bolero, Box, British warm, Buff, Buff-jerkin, Calcimine, Cape, Car, Chesterfield, Cladding, Claw-hammer, Clearcole, Cloak, Clutch, Cocoon, Coolie, Cover, Covert, Creosote, Crombie, Crust(a), Cutaway, Dip, Doggett's, Drape, Dress, Duffel, Duster, Electroplate, Enamel, Encrust, Envelope, Ermelin, Ermine, Exine, Extine, Fearnought, Film, Finish, Fleece, Frock, Fur, Gabardine, Galvanise, Gambeson, Ganoin, Gild, Glaze, Grego, Ground, Hair, Happi, Ha(c)queton, Icing, Impasto, Integument, Inverness, Iridise, Jack(et), Jemmy, Jerkin, Jodhpuri, Joseph, Jump, Jupon, Lacquer, Lammie, Lammy, Lanugo, Layer, Laying, Lerp, Limewash, Loden, Lounge, Mac, Mackinaw, Matinee, Metallise, Mink, Morning, Newmarket, → **OVERCOAT**, Paint, Paletot, Palla, Paper, Parka, Parkee, Passivate, Patina(te), Peajacket, Pebbledash, Pelage, Pelisse, Perfuse, Peridium, Petersham, Phosphor, Pitch, Pla(i)ster, Plate, Plumage, Polo, Pos(h)teen, Primer, Primine, Prince Albert, PVC, Raglan, Redingote, Resin, Resist, Riding, Robe, Roquelaure, Rust, Sable, Sack, Salband, Saque, Sclera, Sclerotic, Scratch, Seal, Sheepskin, Shellac, Sherardise, Sherwani, Silver, Skinwork, Smear, Spencer, Sports, Stadium, Surtout, Swagger, Swallowtail(ed), Tabard, Taglioni, Tail, Tar, Teflon, Tent, Testa, Top, Trench, Truss, Trusty, Tunic, Tuxedo, Ulster(ette), Underseal, Varnish, Veneer, Verdigris, Warm, Wash, Weasel, Whitewash, Windjammer, Wool, Wrap-rascal, Zamarra, Zamarro, Zinc

**Coat of arms** Crest, Hatchment

**Coat-tail** Flap

**Coax** Blandish, Blarney, Cajole, Carn(e)y, Collogue, Cuittle, Entice, Flatter, Lure, Persuade, Tempt, Wheedle, Whillywha(w)

**Cob** Hazel(nut), Horse, Loaf

**Cobalt** Co, Zaffer, Zaffre

**Cobber** Mate

**Cobble(s), Cobbled, Cobbler(s), Cobblestone** Bunkum, Claptrap, Clicker, Coggle, Cosier, Cozier, Dessert, Guff, Mend, Pants, Patch, Pie, Rot, Snob, Soutar, Souter, Sowter, Stone, Sutor, Tripe, Twaddle, Vamp

**Cobra** King, Spitting

**Cobweb(by)** Arachnoid, Araneous, Gossamer, Snare, Trap

**Cocaine** Basuco, C, Charlie, Coke, Crystal, Flake, Freebase, Moonrock, Nose candy, Number, Ready-wash, Snow(ball)

**Coccid** Wax-insect

**Cochlear** Scala

**Cock(y), Cockerel** Alectryon, Ball, Brash, Capon, Chanticleer, Chaparral, Confident, Erect, Escape, Fighting, Flip, Fowl, France, Fugie, Half, Hay, Heath, Henny, Jack-the-lad, Jaunty, Midden, Penis, Perk, Roadrunner, Robin, Rooster, Shake-bag, Shy, Snook, Strut, Sunshine, Swaggering, Tap, Tilt, Turkey, Twaddle, Vain, Valve, Vane, Weather-vane

**Cock-a-hoop** Crowing, Elated, Gleeful, Jubilant

**Cockaigne** Paradise

**Cockatoo** Bird, Corella, Galah, Leadbeater's, Major Mitchell, Parrot

**Cockboat** Cog

**Cockchafer** Dor-bug, Humbuzz, May beetle, Maybug

**Cock crow** Dawn, Skreigh of the day

**Cocker** Blenheim, Cuiter, Spaniel

**Cockeyed** Agee, Askew, Skewwhiff

**Cockfight(ing)** By(e), Main

**Cockle(s)** Bulge, Crease, Heart, Wrinkle

▷**Cockle(s)** *may indicate* an anagram

**Cockney** 'Arriet, 'Arry, Bow, Eastender, Londoner, Londonese

▷**Cockney** *may indicate* a missing h

**Cockpit** Glass, Greenhouse, Office, Well

**Cockroach** Archy, Beetle, Black beetle, Croton bug, German, Oriental, Orthoptera

▶**Cockscomb** *see* **COXCOMB**

**Cocktail** Alexander, Aperitif, Atomic, Bellini, Between the sheets, Black Russian, Black Velvet, Bloody Mary, Brandy Alexander, Buck's fizz, Bullshot, Bumbo, Caipirinha, Champagne cocktail, Cobbler, Cold duck, Crusta, Daiquiri, → **DRINK**, Egg-flip, Fruit, Fustian,

Gibson, Gimlet, Grasshopper, Harvey Wallbanger, Highball, → **HORSE**, Horse's neck, Julep, Kir Royale, Mai-Tai, Manhattan, Margarita, Martini®, Melange, Mix, Molotov, Moscow mule, Negroni, Old-fashioned, Piña colada, Pink lady, Pisco Sour, Planter's punch, Prairie oyster, Prawn, Punch, Rickey, Rusty nail, Sangaree, Sangria, Sazerac®, Screwdriver, Sea Breeze, Sherry cobbler, Side-car, Singapore sling, Slammer, Snakebite, Snowball, Sour, Spritzer, Stengah, Stinger, Swizzle, Tequila sunrise, Tom Collins, Twist, Whiskey Sour, White-lady, White Russian

---

**COCKTAILS**

***4 letters:***
Sour

***5 letters:***
Bumbo
Fruit
Julep
Punch
Twist

***6 letters:***
Atomic
Crusta
Gibson
Gimlet
Mai-Tai
Mimosa
Mojito
Rickey
Rob Roy

***7 letters:***
Bellini
Cobbler
Egg-flip
Fustian
Martini®
Molotov
Negroni
Sangria
Sazerac®
Side-car
Slammer
Stengah
Stinger
Swizzle

***8 letters:***
Aperitif
Bullshot
Cold duck
Daiquiri
Highball
Pink lady
Sangaree
Snowball
Spritzer

***9 letters:***
Alexander
Buck's fizz
Flatliner
Kir Royale
Manhattan
Margarita
Pisco Sour
Rusty nail
Sea Breeze
Snakebite
White-lady

***10 letters:***
Bloody Mary
Calpirinha
Dry Martini
Horse's neck
Moscow mule
Piña colada
Tom Collins

***11 letters:***
Black Velvet
Grasshopper
Screwdriver
Whiskey Sour

***12 letters:***
Black Russian
Cosmopolitan
Old-fashioned
White Russian

***13 letters:***
Planter's punch
Prairie oyster

***14 letters:***
Sherry cobbler
Singapore sling
Tequila sunrise

***15 letters:***
Brandy Alexander

***16 letters:***
Between the sheets
Harvey Wallbanger

***17 letters:***
Champagne cocktail

---

**Cocoa** Carob, Criollo, Nib(s)
**Coconut** Coco-de-mer, Coir, Copra, Head, Madafu, Poonac, Toddy-palm
**Cocoon** Dupion, Mother, Pod, Swathe, Trehala
**Cocotte** Strumpet
**Cod** Bag, Cape, Coalfish, Fish, Gade, Gadus, Haberdine, Hoax, Keeling, Kid, Ling, Lob, Man, Morrhua, Murray, Red, Saith, Saltfish, Spoof, Stockfish, Take in, Tease, Torsk, Tusk, Whiting
**Coda** End(ing), Epilogue, Rondo, Tail(piece)
**Coddle** Cosset, Molly, Pamper, Pet, Poach, Wet-nurse
**Code, Coding, Codification** Access, Alphanumeric, Amalfitan, Answer back, Area, Bar, Barred, Binary, Brevity, Bushido, Canon law, Character, Cheat, Cipher, City, Civil, Clarendon, Codex, Colour, Computing, Condition, Cookie, Country, Cryptogram, Cryptograph, Da Vinci, Dialling, Disciplinary, DNA, Dogma, Dress, DX, Easter egg, EBCDIC, Encipher, Enigma, Error, Escape, Ethics, Etiquette, Fuero, Genetic, Gray, Green Cross, Hammurabic, Highway, Hollerith, Iddy-umpty, Justinian, MAC, Machine, Morse, Napoleon(ic), National, Netiquette, Notation, Object, Omerta, Opcode, Password, Penal, PGP, PIN, Pindaric, Postal, Price, Protocol, QR, Reflective binary, Rulebook, Scytale, Sharia, Shulchan Aruch, Signal, Sort, Source, STD, Talmud, Tax, Time, Toc(k), Twelve Tables, Zip
**Code-breaker, Code-breaking** Bletchley Park, Linear B, Malpractitioner, Turing
**Codger** Buffer, Cove, Fellow
**Codicil** Addendum, Addition, Label, PS, Rider, Supp(lement)

**Codon** Initiator
**Co-driver** Navigator
**Coefficient** Absorption, Correlation, Differential, Diffusion, Distribution, Modulus, Partition, Pearson's correlation, Permeability, Saturation, Spearman's rank-order, Temperature, Transmission, Young's modulus
**Coelacanth** Latimeria
**Coerce, Coercion** Big stick, Brainwash, Bully, Compel, Dragoon, Duress, Extort, Force, Gherao, Impress, Pressure, Railroad, Restrain, Strong-arm, Threaten, Wring
**Coffee, Coffee beans, Coffee pot** Americano, Arabica, Bean, Beverage, Black, Brazil, Cafetiere, Cappuccino, Decaff, Demi-tasse, Espresso, Expresso, Filter, Frappuccino, Gaelic, Gloria, Granules, Grounds, Hag®, Instant, Irish, Java, Latte, Macchiato, Mocha, Nescafé®, Peaberry, Percolator, Robusta, Rye, Skinny latte, Tan, Triage, Turkish, White
**Coffee-house** Café, Costa®, Lloyd's
**Coffer** Ark, Box, Casket, Cassone, Chest, Lacunar, Locker
**Coffin** Bier, Box, Casket, Hearse, Kist, Larnax, Pall, Sarcophagus, Shell, Wooden kimono, Wooden overcoat
**Cog(ged)** Contrate, Gear, Hunting, Mitre-wheel, Nog, Pinion, Tooth, Wheel
**Cogent** Compelling, Forceful, Good, Sound, Telling
**Cogitate** Deliberate, Mull, Muse, Ponder
**Cognate** Akin, Paronym
**Cohabit(ant), Cohabiting** Bed, Indwell, Inquiline, Room-mate, Share, SOP
**Co-heir** Parcener
**Cohere(nt), Coherence** Agglutinate, Clear, Cleave, Cling, Consistency, Logical, Lucid, Stick
**Cohort** Colleague, Crony, Soldier
**Coif** Calotte, Cap, Hood
**Coiffeur** Hair-stylist
**Coiffure** Haircut, Hairdo, Pompadour, Tête
**Coil(s), Coiled** Armature, Bight, Bought, Choke, Choking, Circinate, Clew, Clue, Convolute(d), Convolve, Curl, Current, Element, Fake, Fank, Field, Flemish, Furl, Hank, Helix, Ignition, Induction, Link, Loading, Loop, Mortal, Mosquito, Moving, Primary, Repeating, Resistance, Rouleau, Scorpioid, Skein, Solenoid, Spark, Spiral, Spiraster, Spire, Tesla, Tickler, Toroid, Twine, Twirl, → **WIND**, Wound, Wreath, Writhe, Yoke
**Coin(er)** Base, Bean, Bit, Broad(piece), Cash, Change, Coign(e), Contomiate, Copper, Create, Doctor, Dosh, Double-header, Dump(s), Fiddler's money, Fiver, Han(d)sel, Imperial, Invent, Lucky piece, Make, Mill, Mint, Mintage, → **MONEY**, Neologist, Neoterise, Numismatic, Nummary, Obverse, Piece, Plate, Pocket-piece, Proof, Reverse, Shiner, Slip, Specie, Stamp, Sterling, Strike, Subsidiary, Tenner, Thin'un, Token, Touchpiece, Unity

---

**COINS**

*1 letter:*
D

*2 letters:*
As
DM
Kr
Rd
Xu

*3 letters:*
Avo
Ban
Bar
Bob
Cob
Dam
Ecu
Fen
Fil
Fin
Flu
Hao
Jun
Kip
Lat
Lei
Lek
Leu
Lev
Lew
Mil
Mna
Moy
Ore
Pul
Pya
Rap
Red
Sen
Sol
Som
Sou
Sum
Won
Yen
Zuz

*4 letters:*
Anna
Aora
Baht
Bani
Birr
Buck
Cedi
Cent
Chon
Dibs
Dime
Doit
Dong
Dram
Duro
Euro
Fiat
Fils
Inti
Jack
Jane
Jiao
Kina
Kobo
Kuna
Kyat
Lari
Lion
Lipa
Lira
Loti

Luma
Lwei
Maik
Mark
Merk
Mina
Mite
Mule
Obol
Para
Paul
Peag
Peni
Peso
Pice
Posh
Pula
Puli
Punt
Rand
Real
Reis
Rial
Riel
Rock
Ryal
Sene
Sent
Slog
Sumy
Tael
Taka
Tala
Tein
Toea
Tray
Trey
Vatu
Yuan
Zack

***5 letters:***
Agora
Angel
Asper
Aurar
Baiza
Bekah
Belga
Bodle
Brown
Butat
Butut
Chiao
Colon
Conto
Crore
Cross
Crown
Daric
Dibbs
Dinar
Diram
Dobra
Ducat
Eagle
Eyrir
Franc
Fugio
Gazet
Gerah
Gopik
Groat
Grosz
Haler
Hauer
Khoum
Krona
Krone
Kroon
Kurus
Laari
Laree
Leone
Liang
Liard
Litai
Litas
Livre
Louis
Lumma
Lyart
Maile
Manat
Maneh
Marka
Mohur
Mongo
Mopus
Naira
Nakfa
Ngwee
Noble
Obang
Oscar
Paisa
Paolo
Pence
Pengo
Penie
Penni
Penny
Plack
Pound
Qursh
Razoo
Rider
Riyal
Royal
Rubel
Ruble
Rupee
Sceat
Scudo
Scute
Semis
Sente
Shand
Smelt
Soldo
Souon
Sucre
Sycee
Tenge
Tetri
Thebe
Tical
Ticky
Tiyin
Tolar
Toman
Tyiyn
Unite
Zaire
Zimbi
Zloty

***6 letters:***
Agorol
Ariary
Aureus
Balboa
Bawbee
Bender
Bezant
Billon
Boddle
Byzant
Canary
Centas
Colone
Copeck
Couter
Dalasi
Danace
Deaner
Décime
Denier
Derham
Dirham
Dirhem
Dodkin
Dollar
Double
Drachm
Ekuele
Escudo
Filler
Florin
Forint
Gilder
Gourde
Guinea
Gulden
Halala
Haleru
Heller
Hryvna
Jitney
Kobang
Koruna
Kroner
Kroona
Kruger
Kwacha
Kwanza
Lepton
Likuta
Loonie
Makuta
Mancus
Markka
Mawpus
Mongoe
Nickel
Pa'anga
Paduan
Pagoda
Pataca
Pennia
Peseta
Pesewa
Poisha
Qindar
Qintar
Rappen
Rouble
Rupiah
Santim
Satang
Sceatt
Seniti
Sequin
Shekel
Sickle
Siglos
Somoni
Stater
Stiver
Stotin
Talent
Tanner
Tester
Teston
Thaler
Tickey
Toonie
Tugrik
Turner
Vellon
Wakiki

***7 letters:***
Afghani
Austral
Bolivar
Cardecu
Carolus
Centavo
Centime
Chetrum
Cordoba
Crusado
Drachma
Ekpwele
Guarani
Guilder
Hryvnia
Hryvnya
Jacobus
Joannes
Kopiyka
Kreuzer
Lempira
Lisente
Metical
Millime
Milreis
Moidore
Ostmark
Ouguiya
Patrick
Pfennig
Piastre
Piefort
Pistole
Pollard
Quarter
Quetzal
Ringgit

Ruddock
Rufiyaa
Sextans
Solidus
Spanker
Tambala
Testoon
Testril
Thick'un
Thrimsa
Thrymsa
Tughrik
Unicorn
Xerafin

*8 letters:*
Brockage
Cardecue
Cruzeiro
Denarius
Doubloon
Ducatoon
Emalengi
Farthing
Groschen
Johannes
Kreutzer
Louis d'or
Maravedi
Millieme
Napoleon
Ngultrum
Nuevo sol
Picayune
Pistolet
Planchet
Portague
Portigue
Quadrans
Renminbi
Rigmarie
Semuncia
Sesterce
Shilling
Skilling
Solidare
Spur-rial
Spur-ryal
Stotinka
Twopence
Xeraphin
Zecchino

*9 letters:*
Boliviano
Britannia
Centesimo
Dandiprat
Dandyprat
Didrachma
Dupondius
Fourpence
Half-eagle
Half-tiger
Lilangeni
Luckpenny
Maple leaf
Ninepence
Pistareen
Rix-dollar
Rose noble
Schilling
Sou marque
Sovereign
Spur-royal
Yellowboy
Zwanziger

*10 letters:*
Chervonets
Krugerrand
Portcullis
Reichsmark
Siege-piece

*11 letters:*
Bonnet-piece
Deutschmark
Double eagle
Sword-dollar
Tetradrachm

*12 letters:*
Antoninianus
Iraimbilanja
Renminbi yuan

*13 letters:*
Half-sovereign

*14 letters:*
Three-farthings

*18 letters:*
Maria Theresa dollar

---

**Coinage** Currency, Invention, Nonce-word, Symmetallism
**Coincide(nt), Coincidence** Accident, Agree, Chance, Concur, Consilience, Conterminous, Fit, Fluke, Homotaxis, Overlap, Overlie, Rabat(to), Simultaneous, Synastry, Synchronise, Tally
**Coke** Chark, Coal, Cocaine, Kola
**Col** Nek, Pass, Poort, Saddle
**Colander** Sieve, Strainer
**Cold(-blooded), Cold(ness)** Ague, Algid, Aloof, Apathetic, Arctic, Asocial, Asperity, Austere, Baltic, Biting, Bitter, Bleak, Blue, Brr(r), C, Catarrh, Cauld(rife), Charity, Chill(y), Clinical, Colubrine, Common, Coryza, Coy, Crisp, Dead, Distant, Ectotherm, Emotionless, Fish, Frappé, Frem(d), Fremit, Frigid, Frost(y), Gelid, Glacial, Hiemal, Icy, Impersonal, Jeel, Nippy, Nirlit, Parky, Passionless, Perishing, Piercing, Poikilotherm(ic), Polar, Psychro-, Remote, Reptile, Rheumy, Rigor, Rume, Shivery, Siberia, Snap, Snell, Sniffles, Sour, Standoffish, Starving, Stone, Streamer, Subtemperate, Subzero, Taters, Unmoved, Weed, Wintry
**Cold sore** Herpes, Shiver
**Coldstream** Borderer, Guard
**Cole** Colza, King, Nat, Porter
**Colic** Batts, Bots, Botts, Gripe, Lead, Mulligrubs, Painter's, Sand, Upset, Zinc
**Collaborate, Collaborator, Collaboration** Ally, Assist, Combine, Comply, Concert, → COOPERATE, Joint, Keiretsu, Liaise, Milice, Quisling, Synergy, Team spirit, Vichy, Vichyite, Vichyssois(e)
**Collage** Cut up, Paste up
**Collapse, Collapsing** Apoplexy, Breakdown, Buckle, Burn out, Cave, Conk, Crash, Crumble, Crumple, Debacle, Deflate, Disintegrate, Downfall, Fail(ure), Fall (in), Flake out, Fold, Founder, Give, Go phut, Implode, Inburst, Landslide, Meltdown, Phut, Purler, Rack, Rickety, Rockfall, Rot, Ruin, Scat(ter), Sink, Slump, Snap, Stroke, Subside, Sunstroke, Swoon, Telescope, Topple, Tumble, Tumbledown, Wilt, Wrack, Zonk
▷**Collapsing** *may indicate* an anagram

**Collar(ed)** Arrest, Astrakhan, Band, Bermuda, Bertha, Berthe, Bib, Bishop, Blue, Brecham, Buster, Butterfly, Button-down, Buttonhole, Capture, Carcanet, Chevesaile, Choke(r), Clerical, Collet, Dog, Esses, Eton, Falling-band, Flange, Flea, Gorget, Grandad, Green, Hame, Head(stall), Holderbat, Horse, Jabot, Jampot, Karenni, Lapel, Mandarin, Moran, Mousquetaire, Nab, Nail, Neckband, Necklet, Ox-bow, Peter Pan, Piccadell, Piccadillo, Piccadilly, Pikadell, Pinch, Pink, Polo, Puritan, Rabatine, Rabato, Rebater, Rebato, Revers, Roll, Rollneck, Roman, Romance, Ruff, Sailor, Scoop neck, Seize, Shawl, Steel, Storm, Tackle, Tappet, Tie-neck, Torque, Turndown, Turtleneck, Vandyke, Whisk, White, Wing, Yoke

**Collarbone** Clavicle

**Collateral** Mortgage

**Collation** Comparison, Meal, Repast

**Colleague(s)** Accomplice, Ally, Associate, Bedfellow, Co-host, Confrère, Fellow, Mate, Mentor, Oppo, Partner, Sociate, Team mate, Workmate

**Collect(ion), Collectable, Collected, Collective(ly), Collectivism, Collector** Accrue, Agglomerate, Aggregate, Album, Alms, Amass, Amildar, Ana, Anthology, Arcana, Array, Artel, Assemble, Aumil, Bank, Batch, Bow, Budget, Bunch, Bundle, Burrell, Bygones, Caboodle, Calm, Cancionero, Cap, Cete, Clan, Clowder, Compendium, Compile, Composed, Congeries, Conglobe, Conglomerate, Cool-headed, Covey, Cull, Dossier, Dustman, Earn, Egger, Exaltation, Exordial, Eyrie, Farrago, Fest, (Fest)schrift, Fetch, Fleet, Florilegium, Gaggle, Garbo, Garner, Gather, Get, Gilbert, Glean, Glossary, Grice, Harvest, Heap, Herd, Hive, Idant, In all, Jingbang, Job lot, Kit, Kitty, Levy, Library, Loan, Magpie, Meal, Meet, Meinie, Mein(e)y, Menagerie, Menyie, Miscellany, Mish-mash, Montem, Munro-bagger, Murmuration, Museum, Muster, Nerveless, Nide, Offertory, Olio, Omnibus, Omnium-gatherum, Pack, Paddling, Pharmacopoeia, Pile, Plate, Pod, Poor box, Post, Poste restante, Prayer, Quest, Raft, Ragbag, Raise, Rake, Rammle, Reap, Recheat, Rhapsody, Rouleau, Sangfroid, Scramble, Sedge, Self-possessed, Serene, Set, Shoe, Siege, Skein, Smytrie, Sord, Sottisier, Sounder, Spring, Stand, Stockpile, Tahsildar, Team, Tithe proctor, Together, Toolkit, Tronc, Troop, Ujamaa, Unkindness, Uplift, Watch, Wernher, Whipround, Wisp

▷**Collection** *may indicate* an anagram

**Collection-box** Brod, Ladle, Rammle

**Collectorate** Taluk

**College(s)** Academy, All Souls, Alma mater, Ampleforth, Balliol, Brasenose, Bryn Mawr, Business, C, Caius, Campus, CAT, Cheltenham, Clare, Classical, Coed, Commercial, Community, Conservatoire, Corpus (Christi), Cow, Cranwell, Downing, Dulwich, Electoral, Emmanuel, Eton, Exeter, Foundation, Freshwater, Girton, Grande école, Hall, Heralds', Institute, Institution, Ivy League, Jail, Junior, Keble, King's, Lancing, Linacre, Lincoln, LSE, Lycée, Lyceum, Madras(s)a(h), Madressah, Magdalen(e), Marlborough, Medrese, Medresseh, Merton, Newnham, Nuffield, Open, Oriel, Pembroke, Poly, Polytechnic, Pontifical, Protonotariat, Queen's, Ruskin, Sacred, St Johns, Saliens, Sandhurst, Selwyn, Seminary, Sixth-form, Somerville, Sorbonne, Staff, Tech(nical), Technikon, Tertiary, Theologate, Training, Trinity, Tug, UMIST, Up, Village, Wadham, Winchester, Yeshiva(h)

**Collide(r), Collision** Afoul, Barge, Bird-strike, Bump, Cannon, Carom(bole), Clash, Conflict, Crash, Dash, Elastic, Fender-bender, Foul, Hadron, Head-on, Hurtle, Impact, Inelastic, Into, Kiss, Meet, Pile-up, Prang, Ram, Rencounter, Smash-up, Strike, Thwack

**Collie** Bearded, Border, Dog, Kelpie, Kelpy, Rough, Sheepdog

**Collier** Geordie, Hoastman, Miner, Necklace, Patience, Ship

**Colloid** Aerogel, Emulsoid, Gel, Lyophil(e), Sol, Suspensoid

**Collops** Scotch

**Colloquial** Slang

**Collude, Collusion, Collusive** Abet, Cahoots, Connivance, Connive, Conspire, Deceive

**Colon** Aspinwall, C(a)ecum, Sigmoid, Spastic, Transverse

**Colonel** Bird, Blimp, Bogey, Chinstrap, Col, Everard, Goldstick, Newcome, Nissen, Pride

**Colonial(ist), Colonist** Ant, Antenatal, Bee, Boer, Creole, Emigré, Goan, Oecist, Oikist, Overseas, Phoenician, Pioneer, Planter, Polyp(e), Settler, Sicel(iot), Sikel(ian), Sikeliot, Stuyvesant, Swarm, Territorial, Voter, Wasp

**Colonnade** Ar(a)eostyle, Eustyle, File, Gallery, Peristyle, Porch, Portico, Stoa

**Colony** Acadia, Aden, Barbados, Bermuda, Burkina Faso, Cape, Charter, Cleruchy, Crown, Dependency, Elea, Gibraltar, Halicarnassian, Heronry, Hive, Hongkong, Kaffraria, Macao, Monster, Nest, Nudist, Penal, Plymouth, Presidio, Proprietary, Rookery, Senegal, Settlement, Swarm, Taos, Termitarium, Warren, Zambia, Zimbabwe

**Colophony** Roset, Rosin

**Colossal** → ENORMOUS, Epochal, Gigantic, Huge, Mammoth, Titanic, Vast

**Colosseum** Amphitheatre

**Colossus** Eten, Ettin, Giant

**Colour(ed), Colouring, Colours** Achromatic, Bedye, Blanco, Blee, Blush, Body, C, Cap, Chromatic, Chrome, Complementary, Complexion, Crayon, Criant, Cross, Distort, Dye, False, Field, Film, Flag, Florid, Flying, Garble, Gouache, Haem, → HUE, Imbue, Ink, Irised, Kalamkari, Leer, Livor, Local, Lutein, Metif, Nankeen, Opalescence, Orpiment, Paint, Palette, Pantone®, Pastel, Pied, Pigment, Pochoir, Polychrome, Primary, Prism, Prismatic, Process, Queen's, Raddle, Reddle, Regimental, Rinse, Riot, Ruddle, Secondary, Sematic, Shade, Shot, Slant, Solid, Spectrum, Stain, Standard, Startle, Tertiary, Tie-dye, Tinc(ture), Tinctorial, Tinge, Tint, Tone, Uvea, Wash

---

## COLOURS

***2 letters:***
Or

***3 letters:***
Bay
Dun
Jet
Red
Tan

***4 letters:***
Anil
Aqua
Bice
Blue
Buff
Cyan
Ecru
Fawn
Gold
Grey
Jade
Lake
Lime
Navy
Pink
Plum
Puce
Puke
Roan
Rose
Ruby
Sand
Sloe
Teal
Vert
Woad

***5 letters:***
Amber
Beige
Camel
Chica
Coral
Cream
Eosin
Flame
Green
Gules
Ivory
Khaki
Lemon
Lilac
Liver
Lovat
Mauve
Ocher
Ochre
Olive
Peach
Pearl
Rouge
Sepia
Slate
Taupe
Tenné
Tenny
Umber

***6 letters:***
Anatta
Anatto
Auburn
Bisque
Bister
Bistre
Cerise
Cherry
Day-Glo®
Isabel
Madder
Maroon
Orange
Oyster
Reseda
Roucou
Sienna
Sludge
Titian
Tusser

***7 letters:***
Annatta
Annatto
Apricot
Arnotto
Caramel
Corbeau
Crimson
Emerald
Filemot
Gamboge
Indulin
Magenta
Melanin
Mustard
Oatmeal
Old gold
Old rose
Oxblood
Saffron
Scarlet
Umbrage
Vermeil
Xanthin

***8 letters:***
Alizarin
Burgundy
Cardinal
Chestnut
Cinnamon
Eau de nil
Gunmetal
Isabella
Lavender
Navy blue
Off-white
Pea-green
Philamot
Philomot
Raw umber
Santalin

***9 letters:***
Alizarine
Anthocyan
Carnation
Chocolate
Indigotin
Olive drab
Royal blue
Solferino
Turquoise
Vermilion

***10 letters:***
Aquamarine
Burnt umber
French navy
Tartrazine
Vermillion

***11 letters:***
Burnt sienna
Ultramarine

***12 letters:***
Cappagh-brown
Dragon's blood

***19 letters:***
Thunder and Lightning

---

**Colour blindness** Daltonism, Deuteranopia, Dichrom(at)ism, Monochromatic, Protanomaly, Protanopia, Protanopic, Tritanopia

▷**Coloured** *may indicate* an anagram
**Colourful** Abloom, Brave, Exotic, Flamboyant, Flowery, Gay, Iridescent, Kaleidoscope, Opalescent, Picturesque, Showy, Splashy, Vivid
**Colourless** Albino, Bleak, Drab, Dull, Faded, Flat, Hyalite, Pallid, Pallor, Wan, White
**Colour-spot** Gutta
**Colt** C, Cade, Foal, Gun, Hogget, Sta(i)g, Teenager, Two-year-old, Yearling
**Columbine** Aquilegia
**Column(s), Column foot** Agony, Anta, Architrave, Atlantes, Clustered, Commentary, Control, Corinthian, Correspondence, Cylinder, Decastyle, Diastyle, Distillation, Doric, Editorial, Eustyle, Fifth, File, Flying, Fractionating, Geological, Gossip, Hypostyle, Impost, Lat, Lonelyhearts, Monolith, Nelson's, Newel, Notochord, Obelisk, Pedestal, Pericycle, Peripteral, Peristyle, Persian, Personal, Pilaster, → **PILLAR**, Pilotis, Plume, Prostyle, Pycnostyle, Rachis, Rouleau, Row, Sheet pile, Short, Spina, Spinal, Spine, Stalactite, Stalagmite, Steering, Stylobate, Systyle, Tabulate, Telamone, Thermal, Third, Tige, Tore, Torus, Tower, Trajan's, Vertebral
**Columnist** Advertiser, Agony aunt, Caryatid, Newsman, Stylite, Telamon, Writer
**Coma(tose)** Apoplexy, Crown, Sedated, Sleep, Torpor, Trance
**Comb(er), Combed, Combing** Afro, Alveolate, Beehive, Breaker, Card, Copple, Crest, Ctenoid, Curry, Dredge, Fine-tooth, Hackle, Heckle, Hot, Kaim, Kame, Kangha, Kemb, Noils, Parter, Pecten, Pectinal, Rake, Rat-tail, Red(d), Ripple(r), Rose, Scribble, Search, Side, Small tooth, Smooth, Tease(l), Toaze, Tooth, Tose, Toze, Trawl, Tuft, Wave
**Combat(ant), Combative** Adversarial, Aerial, Agonistic, Argument, Batteilant, → **BATTLE**, Bolshie, Bolshy, Bullfight, Bullring, Competitor, Conflict, Contest, Dispute, Dogfight, Duel, → **FIGHT**, Fisticuffs, Gladiator, Joust, Judicial, Jujitsu, Just, Karate, Kendo, Krav maga, List, Mêlée, Militant, Naval, Oppose, Paintball, Protagonist, Spear-running, Taekwondo, Unarmed, Veteran, War, Warrior
**Combe** Hope
**Combination, Combine(d), Combining** Accrete, Aggregate, Alligate, Ally, Altogether, Amalgam, Associate, Axis, Blend, Bloc, Cartel, Cleave, Clique, Coalesce, Coalition, Composite, Concert, Concoction, Conflated, Conform, Conglomerate, Consolidate, Consortium, Coordinate, Crasis, Fuse, Group, Harvester, Hybrid, Incorporate, Integration, Interfile, Interjoin, Join, Junta, Kartell, League, Meld, Merge(r), Mingle, Mixture, Monogram, Motor cycle, One, Perm(utation), Piece, Pool, Quill, Reaper, Ring, Solvate, Splice, Syncretize, Synthesis, Terrace, Trivalent, Trona, Unify, Unite, Valency, Wed, Zaibatsu
**Comb-like** Ctenoid, Pecten
**Combustible, Combustion** Air-gas, Ardent, Burning, Fiery, Inflammable, Kerosene, Phlogistic, Phlogiston, Spontaneous, Tinder, Wildfire
▷**Combustible** *may indicate* an anagram
**Come (out), Coming (back), Coming out** Accrue, Advent, Anear, Anon, Appear, Approach, Ar(r), Arise, Arrive, Attend, Debouch, Derive, Egress, Emanate, Emerge, Future, Happen, Iceman, In store, Issue, Millenarian, Orgasm, Parousia, Pass, Pop, Reach, Respond, Second, Via
**Come again** Eh
**Comeback** Boomerang, Bounce, Echo, Homer, Quip, Rally, Rearise, Rebound, Recovery, Repartee, Reply, Reprisal, Response, Resurrection, Retort, Retour, Return, Reversion, Riposte
**Come by** Obtain
**Comedian** Benny, Buffo, Buffoon, Chaplin, → **CLOWN**, Comic, Durante, Emery, Farceur, Fields, Gagman, Goon, Groucho, Hardy, Harpo, Hope, Joe Miller, Joker, Jokesmith, Karno, Keaton, Laurel, Leno, Milligan, Punster, Quipster, Riot, Robey, Scream, Screwball, Stand-up, Starr, Tate, Tati, Tummler, Wag, Wise(cracker), Witcracker, Yell
**Comedo** Blackhead
**Comedown** Avale, Bathetic, Bathos, Crash landing, Disappointment, Drop, Letdown, Shower
**Comedy** Alternative, Black, Blackadder, Com, Custard-pie, Drama, Ealing, Errors, Farce, High, Humour, Improv(ised), Keystone, Knockabout, Lazzo, Low, Millamant, Musical, Romantic, Romcom, Screwball, Sitcom, Situation, Slapstick, Stand-up, Thalia, Travesty

**Comely, Comeliness** Beseen, Bonny, Fair, Goodly, Graceful, Jolly, Likely, Looks, Pleasing, Pretty, Proper

**Comestible(s)** Cate, Eats, Fare, Foodstuff

**Comet** Chiron, Geminid, Halley's, Kohoutek, Meteor, Oort cloud, Reindeer, Shoemaker-Levy 9, Vomet, Xiphias

**Come through** Weather

**Come to** Cost, Wake(n)

**Come-uppance** Downfall

**Comfit** Kissing

**Comfort(able), Comforter, Comforting, Comfy** Affluent, Amenity, Analeptic, Armchair, Balm, Bed of roses, Bein, Bildad, Calm, Canny, Cheer, Cherish, Cherry, Clover, Cocoon, Cold, Consolation, Console, Convenience, Cose, Cosh, Cosy, Couthie, Couthy, Creature, Crumb, Cushy, Dummy, Dutch, Ease, Easy (street), Eliphaz, Featherbed, Gemutlich, Heeled, Homely, Homy, Hottie, Job's, Legroom, Luxury, Mumsy, Noah, Plum, Plushy, Reassure, Relaxed, Relief, Relieve, Restful, Rosewater, Rug, Scarf, Sinecure, Snug, Soft, Solace, Soothe, Stay, Succour, There, Tosh, Trig, Warm, Wealthy, Well, Well-to-do, Zofar, Zophar

**Comfortless** Spartan

**Comic(al)** Beano, Buff, Buffo(on), Bumpkin, Buster, Chaplin, Clown, → COMEDIAN, Dandy, Drag, Droll, Eagle, Emery, Facetious, Fields, → FUNNY, Gagster, Hardy, Horror, Humorist, Jester, Knock-about, Laurel, Leno, Mag, Manga, Merryman, Quizzical, Rich, Robey, Stand up, Strip, Tati, Trial, Wag, Zany

**Comma** Inverted, Oxford

**Command(eer), Commanding, Commandment(s)** About face, Attention, Behest, Bid, Categorical imperative, Charge, Coerce, Control, Decalogue, Declare, Dictum, Direct, Direction, Dominate, Domineer, Easy, Edict, Enjoin, Expertise, Fiat, Fiaunt, Fighter, Firman, Grip, Haw, Hest, High, Hijack, Imperious, Impress, Injunction, Instruction, Jussive, Lead, Magisterial, Mandate, Maritime, Mastery, Mitzvah, Mobile, Mush, Obtest, → ORDER, Peremptory, Precept, Press, Query language, Requisition, Rule, Seize, Shun, Ukase, Warn, Warrant, Will, Wish, Writ

**Commander** Admiral, Ag(h)a, Agamemnon, Ameer, Barleycorn, Bey, Bloke, Blucher, Boss, Brennus, Brig, Caliph, Centurion, Cid, Colonel, Decurion, Dreyfus, Emir, Emperor, Encomendero, Exon, Field cornet, Garibaldi, Generalissimo, Haig, Hetman, Hipparch, Imperator, Killadar, Kitchener, Leader, Manager, Marshal, Master, Meer, Mir, Montgomery, Moore, Mr Big, Officer, Overlord, Pendragon, Polemarch, Pr(a)efect, Raglan, Seraskier, Shogun, Sirdar, Supreme, Taxiarch, Trierarch, Turcopolier, Vaivode, Voivode, Waivode, Warlord, Wing

**Commando** Chindit(s), Fedayee(n), Green Beret, Raider, Ranger, SAS

**Commemorate, Commemoration** Celebrate, Encaenia, Epitaph, Eulogy, Immortalise, Keep, Memorial, Month's mind, Monument, Plaque, Remember, Saint's day, Tisha B(e)Ab, Trophy, Year's mind

**Commence** Begin, Initiate, Open, Start

**Commend(ation), Commendable** Applaud, Approval, Approve, Belaud, Bestow, Citation, Cite, Encomium, Entrust, Epitaph, Ingratiate, Laud, Mooi, Panegyric, → PRAISE, Roose, Tribute, Worthy

**Commensal** Epizoon, Messmate

**Commensurate** Adequate, Enough, Equivalent, Proportional, Pro rata, Relevant

**Comment(ary), Commentator, Commenter** Analyst, Animadvert, Annotate, Apercu, Arnott, Barb, Comm, Coryphaeus, Coverage, Critic, Critique, Descant, Discuss, Editorial, Endnote, Essay, Exegete, Explain, Exposition, Expound, Fair, Footnote, Gemara, Gibe, Gloss(ographer), Glossator, Glosser, Hakam, Kibitz, Margin, Marginalia, Midrash(im), Narration, Noise, Note, Obiter dictum, Observation, Par, Platitude, Play-by-play, Postil, Remark, Rider, Running, Scholiast, Scholion, Scholium, Sidenote, Troll, Tweet, Voice-over, Zohar

**Commerce, Commercial** Ad, Adland, Barter, Business, Cabotage, Jingle, Marketable, Mercantile, Mercenary, Merchant, Retail, Shoppy, Simony, Tele-ad, Trade, Traffic, Wholesale

**Commercial traveller** Drummer, Rep

**Commiserate, Commiseration** Compassion, Pity, Sympathise

**Commissar** People's, Political

**Commission(er), Commissioned** Accredit, Agio, Audit, Authorise, Bonus, Boundary, Brevet, Brokage, Brokerage, Charge, Charity, Church, Competition, Contango, Contract, Countryside, Delegation, Depute, ECE, Employ, Engage, Envoy, Errand, European, Factor, Gosplan, High, Husbandage, Interpol, Job, Kickback, Law, Magistrate, Mandate, Office(r), Official, Ombudsman, Order, Oyer and terminer, Percentage, Perpetration, Place, Poundage, Price, Rake-off, Resident, Roskill, Roving, Royal, Shroffage, Task, Task force, Trust, Wreck

**Commit(tal), Committed, Commitment** Allegiance, Aret(t), Behoven, Consign, Contract, Decision, Dedication, Delegate, Devotion, Devout, Do, Engage, Entrust, Enure, Impeachment, Paid up, Perpetrate, Pledge, Plunge, Position, Promise, Rubicon, Staunch, Toe, Undertake

**Committee** ACRE, Audit, Board, Body, Brains trust, Cabinet, COBR(A), Collegium, Commission, Commune, Council, Delegacy, Group, Hanging, Joint, Junta, Politburo, Presidium, Propaganda, Review body, Riding, Samiti, School, Select, Standing, Steering, Syndicate, Table, Think tank, Vigilance, Watch, Ways and means, Works

**Commode, Commodious** Ample, Closestool, Roomy, Spacious

**Commodities, Commodity** Article, Futures, Gapeseed, Goods, Item, Physicals, Product, Soft, Staple, Stock in trade, Ware

**Common(ly), Commoner, Commons** Alike, As per usual, Average, Cad, Cheap, Clapham, Coarse, Conventional, Customary, Diet, Dirt, Doctor's, Ealing, Eatables, Enclosure, Endemic, Epicene, Everyday, Familiar, Fare, Folk, Frequent, General, Green, Greenham, Gutterblood, Hoi polloi, House, Kindred, Law, Lay, Low, Lower House, Mark, Mere, MP, Mutual, Naff, Non-U, Normal, Often, People, Pleb, Plebe(i)an, Prevalent, Prole, Public, Ragtag, Related, Rife, Roturier, Ryfe, Scran, Sense, Shared, Stock, Stray, Tarty, The mob, Tie, Tiers d'état, Trite, Tritical, Tuft, Two-a-penny, Tye, Use, → **USUAL**, Vile, Vul(gar), Vulgo, Vulgus, Widespread, Wimbledon, Working-class

**Common gender** Epicene

**Commonplace** Adversarian, Banal, Copybook, Dime-a-dozen, Dreary, Everyday, Hackneyed, Homely, Humdrum, Idée reçue, Mot, Ordinary, Pedestrian, Philistine, Plain, Platitude, Prosaic, Quotidian, Trite, Truism, Usual, Workaday

**Commonsense** Gumption, Mother wit, Nous, Savoir-faire, Smeddum, Wit

**Commonwealth** Protectorate, Puerto Rico, Res publica

**Commotion** Babel, Bluster, Brouhaha, Bustle, Carfuffle, Civil, Clangour, Clatter, Curfuffle, Dirdam, Dirdum, Do, Dust, Ferment, Flap, Flurry, Fraise, Furore, Fuss, Hell, Hoo-ha(h), Hullabaloo, Hurly-burly, Hurry, Kerfuffle, Pother, Pudder, Racket, Rattlebags, Romage, Rort, Ruckus, Ruction, Rumpus, Shemozzle, Shindig, Shindy, Shivaree, Steer(y), Stir, Stirabout, Storm, Stushie, Tirrivee, Tirrivie, To-do, Toss, Tumult, Turmoil, Upheaval, Uproar, Whirl, Wroth

**Communal, Commune** Agapemone, Collective, Com, Meditate, Menage, Mir, Paris, Phalanstery, Public, Talk, Township

**Communicate, Communication** Ampex, Anastomosis, Announce, Appui, Aviso, Baud, Bluetooth, Boyau, Braille, Cable, Cellnet, Channelling, Citizen's band, Contact, Conversation, Convey, Cybernetic, Dispatch, E-mail, ESP, Expansive, Express, Exude, Impart, Infobahn, Inform, Infrastructure, Intelpost, Intelsat, Interaction, Internet, Liaison, Lifeline, Memoranda, Message, Mime, Multichannel, Multimedia, Nonverbal, Note, Open letter, Oracy, Oralism, Paralanguage, Prayer, Prestel®, Proxemics, Put across, Radio, Reach, Reportage, Revelation, Road, Semaphore, Semiotics, Signal, Sitrep, Syncom, Talkback, Tannoy®, Telecom, Telepathy, Telephony, Teletex, Teletype, Telex, Telstar, Tieline, Transmit, Utraquist, Viewdata, Webmail, Wire, Word of mouth

**Communion** Creed, Fellowship, Host, Housel, Intinction, Lord's Supper, Species, Viaticum

**Communiqué** Announcement, Statement

**Communism, Communist** Apparat(chik), Aspheterism, Bolshevist, Brook Farm, Cadre, Castroism, Com, Comecon, Cominform, Comintern, Commo, Comsomol, Deviationist, Engels, Essene, Fourier, Fraction, Khmer Rouge, Komsomol, Leninite, Maoist, Marxist,

Menshevist, Nomenklatura, Ossi, Perfectionist, Pinko, Politburo, Populist, Red (Guard), Revisionism, Second World, Soviet, Spartacist, Stalinism, Tanky, Titoist, Trot, Trotskyism, Vietcong, Vietminh

**Communities, Community** Agapemone, Alterne, Ashram, Association, Biome, Body, Bourg, Brook Farm, Brotherhood, Clachan, Climax, Closed, Coenobitism, Coenobium, Colonia, Colony, Consocies, Constituency, District, EC, Ecological, Ecosystem, EEC, Enclave, Etat, Ethnic, European, Faith, Formation, Frat(e)ry, Gated, Global, Hamlet, Kahal, Kibbutz, Kraal, Mesarch, Mir, Neighbourhood, Pantisocracy, Parish, People, Phalanx, Phyle, Preceptory, Public, Pueblo, Republic, Sarvodaya, Seral, Sere, Settlement, Shtetl, Sisterhood, Sociation, Society, Speech, Street, Synecology, Toon, Town, Tribe, Ujamaa, Ummah, Village, Virtual, Volost, Zupa

**Commute(r), Commuters** Change, Convert, Reduce, Shuttle, Standee, Straphanger, Train-load, Travel

**Como** Lake, Perry

**Compact** Accord, Agreement, Bargain, Cement, Centralise, Concise, Conglobe, Consolidate, Covenant, Covin, Coyne, Dense, Entente, Fast, Firm, Flapjack, Hard, Knit, League, Match, Neat, Pledge, Powder, Solid, Squat, Tamp, Terse, Tight, Treaty, Well-knit

**Companion(able)** Achates, Arm candy, Associate, Attender, Barnacle, Bedfellow, Bonhomie, Brolga, Bud(dy), Butty, CH, China, Comate, Compadre, Compeer, Compotator, Comrade, Consort, Contubernal, Crony, Cupman, Duenna, Ephesian, Escort, Feare, Felibre, → FELLOW, Fere, Franion, Furked, Handbook, Helpmate, Man Friday, Marrow, Mate, Moll, Native, Oliver, Pal, Pard, Partner, Pheer(e), Playmate, Pot, Roland, Shadow, Sidekick, Skaines mate, Soulmate, Stable, Stablemate, Thane, Thegn, Trojan, Vade-mecum, Wag, Walker

**Company, Companies** Actors, Along, Artel, Ass, Assembly, Band, Bank, Battalion, Bevy, Brigade, → BUSINESS, Bv, Cahoot, Cartel, Cast, Cavalcade, Chartered, Chirm, CIA, Circle, City, Close, Club, Co, Community, Conger, Consort, Cordwainers, Core, Corporation, Corps, Coy, Crew, Crowd, Crue, Decury, Dotcom, East India, Enterprise, Entourage, Express, Faction, Finance, Fire, → FIRM, Flock, Free, Gang, Garrison, Ging, Guarantee, Guild, Haberdashers, Heap, Holding, House party, Hudson's Bay, ICI, Inc, Indie, In-house, Intercourse, Investment, Jingbang, Joint-stock, Keiretsu, Limited, Line, Listed, Livery, Management, Maniple, Manufacturer, Muster, Order, Organisation, Parent, Plc, Present, Pride, Private (equity), Public, Public limited, Push, Quoted, Rep(ertory), Room, SA, Sedge, Set, Set out, Shell, Siege, Sort, SpA, Stationers', Stock, Studio, Subsidiary, Syndicate, Table, Team, Thiasus, Touring, Troop, Troupe, Trust, Twa, Two(some), UPS, Visitor, White, Yfere

**Compare(d), Comparable, Comparison** Analogy, Balance, Beside, Bracket, Collate, Confront, Contrast, Correspond, Cp, Equate, Liken, Match, Odious, Parabole, Parallel, Relation, Resemble, Similar, Simile, Synonymous, Weigh

**Compartment** Alcove, Ballonet, Bay, Booth, Box, Cab, Carriage, Casemate, Cell, Chamber, Cockpit, Cofferdam, Cubbyhole, Cubicle, Dog box, Drawer, Glove, Locellate, Locker, Loculament, Loculus, Pane, Panel, Partition, Pigeonhole, Pocket, Pod, Room(ette), Severy, Sleeper, Smoker, Stall, Till, Trunk, Watertight, Wind chest

**Compass** Ambit, Area, Astro, Beam, Binnacle, Bounds, Bow, Dividers, Extent, Gamut, Goniometer, Gyro, Gyromagnetic, Gyroscope, Infold, Magnetic, Mariner's, Needle, Orbit, Pelorus, Pencil, Perimeter, Prismatic, Radio, → RANGE, Reach, Rhumb, Room, Scale, Spread, Sweep, Tessitura, Trammel, Width

**Compassion(ate)** Aroha, Bleed(ing), Clemency, Commiseration, Empathy, Goodwill, Heart, Humane, Kindliness, Kuan Yin, Kwan Yin, Loving kindness, Mercy, Pity, Remorse, Samaritan, Sympathy, Tender, Ubuntu

**Compatible, Compatibility** Accord, Consistent, Fit, Harmonious

**Compatriot** National

**Compel(ling), Compelled, Compulsion, Compulsive, Compulsory** Addiction, Coact, Coerce, Cogent, Command, Constrain, Dragoon, Driving, Duress, Efforce, Enforce, Exact, Extort, Fain, → FORCE, Force majeure, Gar, Habit-forming, Hypnotic, Insistent, Make, Mandatory, Mania, Obligate, Oblige, Page-turner, Pathological, Required, Steamroller, Strongarm, Tyrannise, Urge, Walk Spanish

**Compendious** Terse

**Compendium** Breviate

**Compensate, Compensation** Amend(s), Balance, Bass, Boot, Bote, Comp, Consideration, Counterbalance, Counterpoise, Damages, Demurrage, Guerdon, Indemnity, Offset, Payment, Recoup, Redeem, Redress, Reparation, Reprisal, Requital, Restitution, Restore, Retaliation, Salvage, Satisfaction, Solatium, Wergild, X-factor

**Compère** Disc jockey, Emcee, Host, MC, Presenter, Toastmaster

**Compete** Contend, Dog eat dog, Emulate, Enter, Match, Outvie, Play, Rival, Run, Vie, Warsle, Wrestle

**Competence, Competent** Ability, Able, Adequate, Aptitude, Can, Capable, Capacity, Dab, Dow, Efficient, Fit, Proficient, Responsible, Sui juris, Worthy

**Competition, Competitive, Competitor** Agonist, Antitrust, Arch rival, Autotest, Backmarker, Battle, Bee, Biathlon, Buckjumping, Candidate, Checks and balances, Comper, Concours, Contender, Contention, Contest, Contestant, Cook off, Corrival, Cup, Dog eat dog, Drive, Emulous, Entrant, Entry, Event, Field, Finals, Freestyle, Gala, Gamesman, Grand Prix, Gymkhana, Head over heels, Head-to-head, Heptathlon, Imperfect, Iron woman, Judoka, Jump off, Jungle, Karateka, Keen, Knockout, League, Match, Match-play, Monopolistic, Olympiad, Open, Opponent, Outsider, Pairs, Panellist, Pentathlon, Perfect, Player, Pools, Premiership, Pro-am, Puissance, Race, Rally, Rat race, Regatta, Repechage, Rival(ise), Rodeo, Run, Runner-up, Seed, Show-jumping, Slam, Spelldown, Sporty, Stableford, Starter, Super G, Tenson, Test, Three-day event, Tiger, Tournament, Tourney, Track meet, Trial, Triallist, Wap(p)enshaw, Wild card

**Compile(r), Compilation** Amass, Anthology, Arrange, Collect, Cross, Doxographer, Edit, Prepare, Segue, Setter, Synthesis, Zadkiel

**Complacent** Babbitt, Fatuous, Joco, Pleasant, Self-satisfied, Smug

**Complain(t), Complainer** Ache, Acne, Adenoids, Affection, Affliction, Alas, Alastrim, Alopecia, Anaemia, Angashore, Angina, Anorexia, Arraign, Arthritis, Asthma, Athlete's foot, Barrack, Beef, Bellyache, Bewail, Bitch, Bleat, Bronchitis, BSE, Carp, Cavil, Charge, Child-crowing, Chorea, Colic, Crab, Cramp, Criticise, Croup, Diatribe, Disorder, Distemper, Dropsy, E-coli, Eczema, Epidemic, Ergot, Exanthema, Fever, Flak, Gastritis, Girn, Gout, Gravamen, Grievance, Gripe, Groan, Grouch, Grouse, Growl, Grudge, Grumble, Grutch, Harangue, Hives, Hone, Hypochondria, Ileitis, → **ILLNESS**, Jeremiad, King's evil, Kvetch, Lament, Lumbago, Lupus, Malady, Mange, Mean(e), Mein, Mene, Moan, Morphew, Mump(s), Murmur, Nag, Natter, Nephritis, Neuralgia, Niggle, Ologoan, Orchitis, Peeve, Peritonitis, Pertussis, Plica, Poor-mouth, Protest, Pule, Pyelitis, Querimony, Quibble, Rail, Remonstrate, Repine, Report, Rhinitis, Rickets, Ringworm, Sapego, Sciatica, Scold, Scream, Sequacious, Sigh, Silicosis, Snivel, Squawk, Squeal, Staggers, Tennis Elbow, Tetanus, Thrush, Tic, Tinea, Upset, Wheenge, Whimper, Whine, Whinge, Yammer, Yaup, Yawp

**Complaisant** Agreeable, Flexible, Suave, Supple

**Complement(ary)** Alexin, Amount, Balance, Biota, Esteemed, Finish, Freebie, Gang, Glowing, Lot, Obverse, Reciprocate

▷**Complement** *may indicate* a hidden word

**Complete(d), Completely, Completion** Absolute, Accomplish, Achieve, All, All-found, Altogether, Arrant, Attain, Clean, Congenital, Consummate, Crashing, Crown, Dead, Do, Downright, End, Entire, Finalise, Finish, Flat, Follow through, Foregone, Fruition, Fulfil, Full, Full-blown, Fully-fledged, Head over heels, Hollow, Incept, Integral, In toto, Neck and crop, One, Ouroboros, Out, Out and out, Perfect, Plenary, Plum, Prolative, Pure, Quite, Radical, Rank, Ready, Root and branch, Rounded, Self-contained, Sew-up, Sheer, Spang, Sum, Teetotal, Thorough(going), Total, Unabridged, Unadulterated, Unanimous, Unbroken, Uncensored, Uncut, Unequivocal, Unmitigated, Up, Uroborus, Utter, Whole (hog), Wrap

**Complex(ity)** Abstruse, Advanced, Arcane, Castration, Compound, Daedal, Developed, Difficult, Elaborate, Electra, Fancy, Golgi, Hard, Heath Robinson, Immune, Inferiority, Intricate, Intrince, Involute, Knot, Major histocompatibility, Manifold, Megalopolis, MHC, Military-industrial, Mixed, Multinucleate, Nest, Network, Obsession, Oedipus, Overwrought, Paranoid, Persecution, Phaedra, Plexiform, Ramification, Subtle, Superiority, Syndrome, System, Tangle, Thick, Web

**Complexion** Aspect, Blee, Hue, Leer, Peaches and cream, Permatan, Temper, Tint, View

**Compliance, Compliant, Comply** Abet, Acquiescent, Agree, Amenable, Assent, Aye-aye, Conform, Deference, Docile, Follow, Hand-in-glove, Meek, Obedience, Obey, Observe, Obtemper, Orchitis, Passive, Plastic, Sequacious, Surrender, Wilco, Yield

**Complicate(d), Complication** Bewilder, Byzantine, Complex, Deep, Elaborate, Embroil, Entangle, Imbroglio, Implex, Intricate, Involution, Involve, Inweave, Knot, Node, Nodus, Perplex, Ramification, Rigmarole, Sequela, Snarl, Tangle, Tirlie-wirlie, Tricky

▷**Complicated** *may indicate* an anagram

**Compliment(s), Complimentary** Backhanded, Baisemain, Bouquet, Congratulate, Devoirs, Douceur, Encomium, Esteemed, Flatter, Flummery, Freebie, Glowing, Gratis, Greetings, Left-handed, Plaudit, Praise, Soap, Trade-last, Tribute

**Component(s)** Base, Capacitor, Cat's whisker, Coherer, Con-rod, Constituent, Contact, CRT, Cytoplasm, Daisy-wheel, Element, Escapement, Factor, Formant, Guidance, Hardware, Hygristor, Impedor, Inductor, Ingredient, Integrand, Integrant, Item, Longeron, Member, Module, Norgate, → **PART**, Partial, Piece, Pixel, Pre-amp, Profile, Pushrod, Reactance, Resistor, Ribosome, Subunit, Tape drive, Tensor, Touchstone, Unit

**Comportment** Behaviour

**Compose(d), Composure** Aplomb, Appeased, Arrange, Calm, Choreograph, Collected, Compile, Consist, Cool, → **CREATE**, Equable, Equanimity, Equilibrium, Even, Face, Improvise, Indite, Level-headed, Lull, Nonchalance, Nonchalant, Notate, Orchestrate, Patience, Pen, Phlegm, Placid, Poise, Produce, Reconcile, Sangfroid, Score, Sedate, Serenity, Settle, Soothe, Thorough, Tranquil, Unruffled, Write

**Composer** Contrapunt(al)ist, Hymnist, Inditer, Inventor, Maker, Melodist, Minimalist, Musician, Musicker, → **POET**, Psalmist, Serialist, Six, Songsmith, Songwriter, Symphonist, Triadist, Troubadour, Tunesmith, Writer

---

**COMPOSERS**

*3 letters:*
Bax

*4 letters:*
Adam
Arne
Bach
Bart
Berg
Blow
Brel
Bull
Byrd
Cage
Dima
Graf
Ives
Kern
Lalo
Monk
Nono
Orff
Peri
Raff
Rota
Wolf

*5 letters:*
Alwyn
Arlen
Auber
Auric
Balfe
Berio
Bizet
Bliss
Bloch
Boito
Boyce
Brian
Bruch
Crumb
D'Indy
Dukas
Dupre
Elgar
Falla
Fauré
Field
Finzi
Glass
Gluck
Grieg
Harty
Haydn
Henze
Holst
Ibert
Lasso
Lehar
Liszt
Loewe
Lully
Nyman
Ogdon
Parry
Prout
Ravel
Reger
Rossi
Satie
Sousa
Spohr
Suppe
Tosti
Verdi
Watts
Weber
Weill
Zappa

*6 letters:*
Alfven
Arnold
Azione
Barber
Bartók
Bennet
Berlin
Boulez
Brahms
Bridge
Burney
Busoni
Chopin
Coates
Czerny
Delius
Duparc
Dvorák
Flotow
Franck
German
Glière
Glinka
Gounod
Handel
Hummel
Joplin
Kodaly
Lassus
Ligeti
Mahler
Martin
Mingus
Morley

Mozart
Ogolon
Parker
Pierne
Porter
Rameau
Rubbra
Schütz
Tallis
Varese
Wagner
Waller
Walton
Webern

*7 letters:*
Albeniz
Alberti
Allegri
Amadeus
Babbitt
Bantock
Bellini
Bennett
Berlioz
Berners
Borodin
Britten
Brubeck
Christy
Copland
Corelli
Debussy
De Falla
Delibes
Dohnany
Dowland
Durufle
Gibbons
Ireland
Janácek
Lambert
Lilburn
Mancini
Martinu
Menotti
Merimee
Milhaud
Nicolai
Nielsen
Novello
Ormandy
Poulenc
Puccini
Purcell
Purnell
Quilter
Rodgers
Rodrigo
Romberg
Rossini
Roussel
Salieri
Smetana
Stainer
Strauss
Tartini
Tavener
Tippett
Vivaldi
Warlock
Xenakis
Youmans

*8 letters:*
Alaleona
Albinoni
Anderson
Boughton
Bruckner
Chabrier
Chausson
Cimarosa
Clementi
Coltrane
Couperin
Gabrieli
Gershwin
Gesualdo
Glazunov
Grainger
Granados
Honegger
Korngold
Kreutzer
Marcello
Mascagni
Massenet
Messager
Messiaen
Paganini
Respighi
Schnabel
Schubert
Schumann
Scriabin
Sessions
Sibelius
Sondheim
Stamford
Stanford
Sullivan
Taverner
Telemann
Vangelis

*9 letters:*
Bacharach
Balakirev
Beethoven
Bernstein
Boulanger
Broughton
Buxtehude
Chaminade
Cherubini
Donizetti
Dunstable
Ellington
Hindemith
Meyerbeer
Offenbach
Pachelbel
Pergolesi
Prokofiev
Scarlatti
Schnittke
Schonberg
Zemlinsky

*10 letters:*
Birtwistle
Boccherini
Canteloube
Carmichael
Cole Porter
Monteverdi
Mussorgsky
Palestrina
Penderecki
Ponchielli
Rawsthorne
Saint-Saëns
Schoenberg
Stravinsky
Villa-Lobos
Waldteufel
Williamson

*11 letters:*
Charpentier
Frescobaldi
Humperdinck
Leoncavallo
Lloyd Webber
Mendelssohn
Niedermeyer
Stockhausen
Tchaikovsky
Theodorakis
Wolf Ferrari

*12 letters:*
Dallapiccola
Khachaturian
Rachmaninoff
Shostakovich

*13 letters:*
Havergal Brian
Maxwell Davies

*14 letters:*
Rimsky-Korsakov

*15 letters:*
Vaughan Williams

---

▷**Composing** *may indicate* an anagram

**Composite** Aster, Cosmea, Costmary, Daisy, Foalfoot, Gerbera, Groundsel, Hawkweed, Hemp agrimony, Hybrid, Integral, Metal, Motley, Opinicus, Racercar, Rag(weed), Sphinx, Synthesized, Tarweed, Thistle

**Composition, Compositor** Albumblatt, Aleatory, Azione, Bagatelle, Beaumontage, Beaumontague, Canon, Capriccio, Caprice, Cob, Concerto, Concertstuck, Concetto, Creation, Dite, Essay, Etude, Exaration, Fantasia, Fugue, Impromptu, Inditement, Ingredient, Line, Literature, Loam, Met, Montage, Morceau, Motet, Nocturne, Nonet(te), Nonetto, Octet,

Opus, Oratorio, Organum, Part-writing, Passacaglia, Pastiche, Piece, Pieta, Poem, Polyphony, Polyrhythm, Port, Printer, Quartette, Raga, Repoussage, Rhapsody, Rondoletto, Round, Setting, Ship, Sing, Smoot, Smout, Sonata, Sonatina, Structure, Study, Suite, Symphony, Synthesis, Terracotta, Texture, Toccata, Treatise, Trio, Typesetter, Verismo, Voluntary, Work

**Compost** Digestate, Dressing, Fertilizer, Humus, Potting, Vraic, Zoo doo

**Compound (stop), Compound word** Addition, Admixture, Aggravate, Amalgam, Analogue, Anti-inflammatory, Anti-knock, Antimutagen, Blend, → CAMP, Composite, Constitute, Coordination, Cpd, Cutting, Decomplex, Decomposition, Derivative, Dibasic, Ethiops, Inorganic, Mix, Mixture, Multiply, Organic, Oxidant, Parathesis, Pot pourri, Ring, Rooting, Sodaic, Synthesise, Tatpurusha, Type, Ureic

---

## COMPOUNDS

***3 letters:***
Azo
Hex
TBT

***4 letters:***
Alum
Calx
Clay
Deet
Dopa
EDTA
Enol
Haem
Heme
Tepa
TEPP
Urea

***5 letters:***
Aldol
Algin
Allyl
Aloin
Amide
Amino
Azide
Azine
Azole
Caria
Diazo
Diene
Dimer
Diode
Erbia
Ester
Furan
Halon
Imide
Imine
Indol
Lipid
Nitro
Olein
Oxide
Oxime
Potin
Pyran
Salol
Sarin
Soman
Tabun
Thiol
Trona
Vinyl

***6 letters:***
Acetal
Alkane
Alkene
Alkyne
Ammine
Arsine
Baryta
Borane
Calque
Cetane
Chrome
Cresol
Diazin
Diquat
Epimer
Fluate
Glycol
Haemin
Halide
Haloid
Hexene
Iodine
Isatin
Isomer
Ketone
Kinone
Lichen
Lithia
Malate
Methyl
Niello
Octane
Phenol
Pinene
Potash
Purine
Pyrene
Rennet
Retene
Silane
Speiss
Tannin
Tartar
Tetryl
Thymol
Triene
Trimer
Uranyl

***7 letters:***
Acetone
Acridin
Adenine
Aglycon
Ammonia
Argyrol®
Aspirin
Barilla
Bauxite
Benzene
Betaine
Borazon
Bromide
Caliche
Calomel
Camphor
Caprate
Carbide
Cellose
Chelate
Choline
Cinerin
Creatin
Creosol
Cumarin
Cyanide
Cystine
Diamine
Diazine
Diazole
Dioxide
Dvandva
Epoxide
Erinite
Ethanol
Eugenol
Excimer
Fenuron
Ferrite
Flavone
Hormone
Hydrate
Hydride
Hylenex®
Indican
Indoxyl
Inosine
Lactate
Lactone
Menthol
Metamer
Monomer
Niobite
Nitride
Nitrile
Nitrite
Orcinol
Oxazine
Oxonium
Pentane
Peptide

Peptone
Polyene
Polymer
Prodrug
Protein
Quassia
Quinoid
Quinone
Realgar
Skatole
Steroid
Sulfide
Syncarp
Taurine
Terpene
Toluene
Tritide
Urethan
Uridine
Vanadic
Vitamin
Wolfram
Zymogen

***8 letters:***
Acridine
Aglycone
Aldehyde
Alizarin
Arginine
Asbestos
Astatide
Butyrate
Caffeine
Carbaryl
Catenane
Cephalin
Ceramide
Chloride
Chromene
Coenzyme
Coumarin
Creatine
Cyanogen
Datolite
Dieldrin
Dopamine
Ethoxide
Farnesol
Fluoride
Furfuran
Glycogen
Haloform
Hydroxyl
Iodoform
Isologue
Ketoxime
Lecithin
Luteolin
Massicot
Melamine
Monoxide
Oligomer
Pentosan
Peroxide
Phthalin
Piperine
Psilocin
Ptomaine
Purpurin
Pyrazole
Pyruvate
Racemate
Retinoid
Rock-alum
Rotenone
Selenate
Silicide
Silicone
Siloxane
Sodamide
Stannate
Stilbene
Sulphide
Sulphone
Tautomer
Tetroxid
Thiazide
Thiazine
Thiazole
Thiophen
Thiotepa
Thiourea
Thyroxin
Titanate
Tolidine
Triazine
Triazole
Trilling
Trioxide
Tyramine
Urethane
Xanthate
Xanthine
Ytterbia
Zirconia

***9 letters:***
Aflatoxin
Alicyclic
Aliphatic
Anhydride
Auranofin
Bahuvrihi
Biguanide
Capsaicin
Carbazole
Carnitine
Caseinate
Celloidin
Cellulose
Cementite
Cetrimide
Chromogen
Copolymer
Cortisone
Deuteride
Dibromide
Dipeptide
Diplotene
Disulfram
Endorshin
Ferrocene
Flavanone
Fool's gold
Fulleride
Glycoside
Greek fire
Guanosine
Haematein
Histamine
Hydantoin
Hydrazide
Hydroxide
Hypericin
Imidazole
Impsonite
Ionophore
Isoniazid
Jasmonate
Limestone
Menadione
Mepacrine
Merbromin
Methoxide
Methylene
Monoamine
Organotin
Pentoxide
Perborate
Phenazine
Phenoxide
Pheromone
Phosphide
Phthalate
Piperonal
Polyamine
Porphyrin
Prussiate
Pyrethrin
Qinghaosu
Quercetus
Quercitin
Quinidine
Quinoline
Saltpetre
Salvarsan
Sapogenin
Serotonin
Sidenafil
Telluride
Tetroxide
Thiophene
Thyroxine
Valproate
Verapamil
Veratrine

***10 letters:***
Adrenaline
Agglutinin
Amphoteric
Argyrodite
Azobenzene
Bradykinin
Cellosolve®
Cytochroma
Dichloride
Dimethoate
Disulphide
Endosulfan
Enkephalin
Ethambutol
Halocarbon
Indophenon
Isocyanate
Jamesonite
Lumisterol
Mercaptide
Nitrazepam
Nucleoside
Nucleotide
Phenacaine
Phenformin
Picrotoxin
Piperazine
Piperidine
Propionate
Putrescine
Pyrethroid
Pyrimidine
Pyrogallol
Sildenafil
Sulphonium

Tetracaine
Thimerosal
Tocopherol

*11 letters:*
Acetanilide
Amphetamine
Coprosterol
Dimercaprol
Diphosphate
Electrolyte
Fluorescein
Galantamine
Ghitathione
Hydrocarbon
Hydroxyurea
Neostigmine
Nitrosamine
Resveratrol
Sesquioxide

Sphingosine
Tributyltin
Trichlorfon
Trichloride

*12 letters:*
Arsphenamine
Carbohydrate
Fluorocarbon
Formaldehyde
Haematoxylin
Hydrastinine
Hydroquinone
Mifepristone
Permanganate
Phenanthrine
Polyurethane
Quinalizarin
Sulphonamide
Testosterone

Thiosinamine
Triglyceride
Trimethadine

*13 letters:*
Catecholamine
Cycloheximide
Diphenylamine
Hydrochloride
Hydrosulphide
Isoproterenol
Mercurochrome
Metronidazole
Nitroglycerin
Nortriptyline
Phenothiazine
Physostigmine
Plastoquinone
Sulphonylurea
Trinucleotide

*14 letters:*
Cyanocobalamin
Oxyhaemoglobin
Phenolphthalin
Polycarboxylic
Polyunsaturate
Sulphonmethane
Trihalomethane

*15 letters:*
Perfluorocarbon
Succinylcholine
Tribromoethanol

*17 letters:*
Pentachlorophenol

---

▹**Compound(ed)** *may indicate* an anagram

**Comprehend, Comprehensive** All-found, All-in, All-round, Broad-brush, Catch-all, Catholic, Compass, Compendious, Contain, Encyclopaedic, Exhaustive, Fathom, Follow, Full-scale, General, Global, Grand, Grasp, Include, In depth, Ken, Large, Omnibus, Overall, Panoptic, Panoramic, Perceive, School, Sweeping, Thoroughgoing, Tumble, → UNDERSTAND, Universal, Wide

**Compress(ed), Compression, Compressor** Astrict, Astringe, Axial-flow, Bale, Coarctate, Contract, Crush, Pack, Pump, Shoehorn, Solidify, Squeeze, Stupe, Thlipsis, Tourniquet, Turbocharger

**Comprise** Contain, Embody, Embrace, Include

**Compromise, Compromising** Arrangement, Avoision, Brule, Commit, Concession, Endanger, Fudge, Give and take, Golden mean, Halfway house, Happy medium, Honeytrap, Involve, Middleground, Middle of the road, Modus vivendi, Negotiate, Settlement, Time-server, Trade off, Via media

▸**Compulsion** *see* COMPEL(LING)

**Compunction** Hesitation, Regret, Remorse, Scruple, Sorrow

**Computation, Compute(r), Computerise, Computing** Analog(ue), Animatronics, Apple (Mac)®, Automate, Botnet, Calcular, Cast, Desknote, Desktop, Digital, Eniac, Fifth generation, Front-end, Host, IALI, iPad®, iPod®, Laptop, Mainframe, Micro, Multiuser, Network, Notebook, Notepad, Number-cruncher, Optical, Palmtop, PC, Personal, Proxy server, Reckon, TALISMAN, Turing machine, Voice response, WIMP

**Computer hardware, Computer memory** Busbar, Chip, Dataglove®, Docking station, DRAM, EAROM, EPROM, Floptical, IDE, Modem, Neurochip, Pentium®, Platform, Plug'n'play, Processor, PROM, RAM, ROM, Router, Tower, Track(er)ball

**Computer language** Acrobat®, ADA, ALGOL, APL, ASCII, Assembly, AWK, Basic, C, COBOL, COL, Computerese, CORAL, Fortran, High-level, ICL, Java®, Java script®, LISP, LOGO, Low-level, OCCAM, PASCAL, Perl, PL, PROLOG, Python, Scratchpad, Scripting, Small-talk, SNOBOL, SQL, Visual Basic, Weblish

**Computer network, Computer system(s)** Arpa, ARPANET, BIOS, Cambridge ring, Darknet, ERNIE, Ethernet, Evernet, Executive, Extranet, Fileserver, Freenet, HOLMES, Hypermedia, Internet, Intranet, JANET, LAN, Linux, Manager, MARC, MIDI, Multipoint, Neural, NOR, Peer-to-peer, Real time, Stand-alone, TALISMAN, Tally, TAURUS, Telnet, Token ring, Unix, Usenet, VAN, WAN, Web, Wide-area, WIMP

**Computer program(s), Computer programmer, Computer programming, Computer software** Abandonware, Acrobat, ActiveX, Address harvester, Adware, Agent,

Antivirus, App(let), Application, Assembler, Auto-responder, Autotune, Bloatware, Bootstrap, Bot, Browse, CADMAT, Cancelbot, Captcha, Careware, Case, Casemix, Chatbot, Checksum, Choiceboard, Client, Closed-loop, Code, Columbus, Co-routine, Courseware, Crawler, Crippleware, CU See Me, Datel®, Debugger, Demo, Device-driver, Diagnostic, Dictionary, Disassembler, Emacs, Enterprise, ERP, Est, E-wallet, EXCEL, Extreme, Facemail, Firewall, Firmware, Flash, Formatter, Free-to-air, Freeware, Groupware, HAL, Hard card, Heuristic, Hypermedia, Input, ITunes®, Linear, Linker, Loader, Logic bomb, Macro, Mail-merge, Malware, Middleware, Mmorpg, Module, Neural net, Object, OCR, Parser, Payware, PERL, Plug-in, Powerpoint, PROM, Relocator, Ripper, RISC, Rootkit, Satnav, Screensaver, Servlet, Shareware, Shell, Shopping agent, Shovelware, Spam killer, Spellchecker, Spider, Spreadsheet, Spyware, Stiffware, Systems, TELNET, Text editor, Translator, Trialware, Trojan, Uninstaller, Utility, Vaccine, Vaporware, Virus, Warez, Web browser, Webcast, Web crawler, Wiki, Windows®, Word processor, Worm

**Computer term(s)** Address bus, Alert box, Algorism, Authoring, Autosave, Backslash, Bank-switching, Bitmap, Bit-slice, Blog(ging), Blogroll, Bookmark, Boot, Boot-virus, Bot army, Breakpoint, Broadband, Calculate, Calculus, Cascade, Chatroom, Choke route, Clickstream, Client-server, Clipboard, Cobweb site, Coder, Cold boot, Conf, Core(dump), Counter, Cron, Cuspy, Cyber(netics), Cybercafe, Cyberslacking, Dataglove, Daughterboard, Defrag(ment), Descriptor, Dial-up, DIF, Disk drive, Domain name, Dotcom, Dot matrix, DRAM, Dynamic routing, Earcon, Enqueue, Estimate, Execute, FAT, Fatfinger, Favicon, FIFO, Figure, Flame war, Flash ROM, Floptical, Forum, GIGO, Gopher, Greybarland, Half-adder, Hardwire, Hashing, Hashtag, High-end, Hot-key, Hotlist, Hybrid, Hypertext, Inbox, Inputter, Integrator, Interface, IT, Joypad, Kludge, Linear, List serv, Liveware, Logic, Loop, Mail merge, Measure, Meatspace, Megaflop, Memory stick, Moblog, Morphing, Motherboard, Mouseover, Mouse potato, Mung, Network, Neural, Non-volatile, Notwork, Numlock, Nybble, Nyetwork, Object, On-line, Outbox, Package, Packet sniffer, Pageview, Patch, Path name, Peer-to-peer, Pel, Permalink, Pharming, Phishing, Phreak, Ping, Pixel, Platform, Plug and play, Podcast, Podcatcher, Point and click, Poke, Popunder, Pop-up, Pseudocode, Pseudorandom, Public-key, Pushdown, Reader farm, README file, Read-out, Realtime, Reboot, Reckoner, Report program, Rogue dialler, Rogue site, Rootserver, Router, Screensaver, Screen turtle, Scriptkiddie, Search engine, Serial port, Server, Server farm, Shared logic, Shell, Shovelware, Sim, Smart, Smurfing, Soft copy, Soft return, Source, Spam, Spigot, Splog, Spreadsheet, Sprite, String, Style sheet, Subroutine, Superserver, Swap file, Systems, Tape streamer, Telecottage, Thick client, Thin client, Time slice, Toggle, Token ring, Triple, Turnkey, Turtle graphics, ULA, Unicode, Username, Utility program, Vaccine, Virus, Vlog, Vodcast, Voice response, Voxel, Wave file, Webbie, WebBoard, Webfarm, Wideband, Wi-fi, Wiki, WIMAX, Wordwrap, WORM, Wysiwyg, Yottabyte, Zettabyte, Zmodem

**Computer user(s)** Alpha geek, Anorak, Brain, Browser, Cast(er), Chiphead, Cybernaut, Cyberpunk, Cybersurfer, Digerati, Hacker, Liveware, Luser, Mouse potato, Nerd, Nethead, Netizen, Nettie, Onliner, Otaku, Pumpking, Surfer, Tiger team, Troll, Webhead, White hat

**Comrade** Achates, Ally, Amigo, Buddy, Bully-rook, Butty, China, Fellow, Frater, Friend, Kamerad, Mate, Oliver, Pal, Pard, Roland, Tovarich, Tovaris(c)h

**Con(man)** Against, Anti, Bunco, Defraudment, Diddle, Dupe, Enveigle, Fleece, Fraudster, Grifter, Gyp, Hornswoggle, Inveigle, Jacob, Lag, Learn, Peruse, Pretence, Ramp, Read, Scam, Scan, Screw, Shark, Steer, Sucker, Swindle, Trickster, Tweedler, Twister

**Concave** Cupola, Dished, Invexed

**Conceal(ed), Concealment** Airbrush, Blanket, Blind, Clandestine, Cloak, Closet, Clothe, Cover, Covert, Curtain, Disguise, Dissemble, Doggo, Drown, Esoteric, Feal, Harbour, Heal, Heel, Hele, → HIDE, Inner, Latent, Latescent, Misprision, Occult, Overgreen, Palm, Paper over, Perdu(e), Recondite, Screen, Scriene, Secrete, Shroud, Sleeve, Smokescreen, Smother, Snow job, Stash, Subreption, Ulterior, Veil, Whitewash, Wrap

**Concede, Concession** Acknowledge, Admit, Allow, Appeasement, Budge, Carta, Charter, Compromise, Confess, Favour, Forfeit, Franchise, Grant, Munich, Ou, Ow, Owe, Own, Pension, Privilege, Ship, Sop, Synchoresis, Yield

**Conceit(ed)** Arrogant, Bumptious, Caprice, Carriwitchet, Cat-witted, Cocky, Concetto, Crank, Crotchet, Device, Dicty, Egoist, Egomania, Fancy, Fastuous, Figjam, Flory, Fop, Fume,

Hauteur, Idea, Mugwump, Notion, Podsnappery, Popinjay, Pretentious, Prig, Princock, Princox, Puppyism, Quiblin, Self-assumption, Self-regard, Side, Snotty, Stuck-up, Swellhead, Swollenhead, Toad, Toffee-nose, Vain(glory), Wind

**Conceive, Conceivable** Beget, Create, Credible, Devise, Imagine, Possible, Surmise

**Concensus** Unanimity

**Concentrate(d), Concentration** Abridge, Address, Aim, Apozem, Application, Attend, Attention, Bunch, Cathexis, Centre, Collect, Compress, Condense, Dephlegmate, Distil, Elliptical, Essence, Extract, Focalise, Focus, Geographical, Intense, Kurtosis, Listen, Major, Mantra, Mass, Molality, Molarity, Navel-gazing, Pithy, Pore, Potted, Reduce, Rivet, Samadhi, Strong, Thick, Titrate, Titre, Undiluted, Undivided

**Concept(ion)** Alethic, Brain, Going concern, Hent, Ideal, Ideation, Image, Immaculate, K(h)arma, Mooncalf, Motif, Myth, Notion, Onomascology, Oogamous, Sortal, Stereotype, Theurgy, Weltanschauung

**Concern(ed), Concerning** About, Affair, After, Agitation, Ail, Alarm, Altruism, Anent, As to, Bother, Business, Care, Cerne, Company, Disquietude, Disturb, Dot com, Firm, Going, Heed, Hereof, House, Humanitarian, In re, Intéressé, Interest, Into, Involve, Lookout, → MATTER, Mell, Mind, Misease, Moment, Over, Part, Pidgin, Pigeon, Priority, Re, Reck, Regard, Reke, Relate, Relevant, Respect, Retch, Shake, Solicitous, Solicitude, Subject, Touch, Trouble, Versant, Wirra, Worry

▷**Concerned** *may indicate* an anagram

**Concert (place)** Agreement, Ballad, Barbicon, Benefit, Chamber, Charivari, Cooperation, Device, Dutch, Gig, Hootanannie, Hootananny, Hootenanny, Hootnannie, Hootnanny, League, Musicale, Odeon, Odeum, Open-air, Pop, Prom(enade), Recital, Singsong, Smoker, Smoking, Subscription, Symphony, The Proms, Together, Unison, Unity, Wit

**Concertgoer** Audience, Promenader

**Concertina** Bandoneon, Pleat, Squeezebox, Squiffer

**Concerto** Brandenburg, Emperor, Grosso

▶**Concession** *see* CONCEDE

**Conch** Seashell, Shell, Strombus

**Conchie** CO

**Concierge** Housekeeper, Porter

**Conciliate, Conciliator** Allay, Appease, Bridge builder, Calm, Disarm, Dove, Ease, Mollify, Pacify, Placate, Reconcile

**Concise** Brief, Compact, Curt, Encapsulated, Epigrammatic, Laconic, Nutshell, Pithy, Short, Snappy, Succinct, Telegraphic, Terse, Tight

**Conclave** Assembly, Caucus, Confab, Meeting

**Conclude(d), Conclusion, Conclusive** Achieve, A fortiori, Afterword, Amen, Binding, Button-up, Cease, Clinch, Close, Coda, Complete, Consectary, Dead, Decide, Deduce, Demise, Diagnosis, → END, End-all, Endwise, Envoi, Epilogue, Explicit, Finale, Finality, Finding, Fine, Finis, → FINISH, Foregone, Gather, Hang up, Illation, Infer, Lastly, Limit, Non sequitur, Omega, Outro, Over, Peroration, Point, Postlude, Punchline, Realise, Reason, Resolve, Settle, Showdown, Summary, Terminate, Upshot, Uptie, Verdict, Wind up

**Conclusive** Cogent, Convincing, Estoppel, Final

**Concoct(ion)** Brew, Compound, Cook, Creation, Hydromal, Plan, Tisane, Trump (up)

**Concomitant** Stablemate

**Concord(ance)** Concent, Consonance, Cruden, Harmony, Peace, Plane, Sympathy, Treaty, Unity

**Concorde** SST

**Concourse** Assembly, Confluence, Esplanade, Throng

**Concrete, Concretion** Actual, Aggregate, Beton, Bezoar, Breeze, Cake, Calculus, Caprolite, Clot, Dogger, Gallstone, Gunite, Hairball, Hard, Laitance, Lean, Mass, Minkstone, No-fines, Otolith, Pile-cap, Positive, Precast, Prestressed, Readimix, Real, Reify, Reinforced, Siporex, Solid, Tangible, Tremie, Vacuum

**Concubine** Apple-squire, Campaspe, Harem, Hetaera, Hetaira, Madam, Mistress, Odalisk, Sultana

**Concur(rence)** Accord, Agree, Assent, Coincide, Comply, → CONSENT, Gree, Syndrome

**Concurrent(ly)** Meantime
**Concuss(ion)** Clash, Shock, Stun
**Condemn(ation)** Abominate, Accuse, Beknave, Berate, Blame, Blast, Cast, Censor, Censure, Convict, Damn, Decry, Denounce, Deprecate, Doom, Judge, Kest, Lambast(e), Obelise, Obloquy, Prejudge, Proscribe, Reprove, Revile, Sentence, Stigmatise, Theta, Upbraid
**Condensation** Dew, Dewdrop
**Condense(d), Condenser** Abbe, Abbreviate, Abridge, Brief, Capacitator, Compress, Contract, Distil, Encapsulate, Epitomise, Jet, Liebig, Précis, Rectifier, Reduce, Shorten, Shrink, Summarise, Surface, Synopsis, Vernier, Vinificator
**Condescend(ing)** De haut en bas, Deign, Patronise, Snobbish, Stoop, Superior, Vouchsafe
**Condiment(s)** Caraway, Catsup, Cayenne, Chutney, Cruet, Cum(m)in, Five-spice, Flavour, Horseradish, Kava, Ketchup, Mustard, Paprika, Pepper, Relish, Salt, Sambal, Sauce, Seasoning, Spice, Tracklement, Turmeric, Vinegar, Wasabi, Zedoary
**Condition(al), Conditioning** Acathisia, Adenoma, Akathisia, Autism, Blindsight, Boundary, Calvities, Case, Cense, Chordee, Cinchonism, Circ(s), Circumstance, Classical, Climate, Congenital, Connote, Contingent, Disease, Disomy, Dropsy, Eclampsia, Enantiostyly, Experimental, Feather, Fettle, Finite, Going, Hammertoe, Health, Hood, Hunk, If, Indoctrinate, → **IN GOOD CONDITION**, Kelter, Kernicterus, Kilter, Latah, Mettle, Mint, Necessary, Nick, Order, Parole, Pass, Pavlovian, Plight, Pliskie, Ply, Point, Position, Predicament, Premise, Premiss, Prepare, Prerequisite, Presupposition, Protasis, Proviso, Provisory, Repair, Reservation, Reserve, Rider, Ropes, Sine qua non, Sis, Spina bifida, Stable, Standing, State (of play), Status quo, Sted, Stipulation, String, Sufficient, Term, Tid, Tone, Tox(a)emia, Trim, Trisomy, Understanding, Unless, Vir(a)emia, Weal, White finger
**Condom(s)** Blob, Cap, Franger, French letter, Gumboot, Johnny, Letter, Prophylactic, Rubber, Rubber goods, Safe, Scumbag, Sheath
**Condone** Absolve, Connive, Excuse, Forgive, Overlook
**Conduct(or), Conductance, Conductress** Abbado, Accompany, Administer, Anode, Ansermet, Antipode, Arm, Arrester, Barbirolli, Barenboim, Bearing, Beecham, Behaviour, Bernstein, Bohm, Boult, Bulow, Bus-bar, Cad, Capellmeister, Chair, Chobdar, Clippie, Clippy, Coil, Comport, Demean(our), Deportment, Direct, Disorderly, Drive, Editor, Electrode, Escort, Feedthrough, Fetch, G, Goings-on, Guide, Haitink, Hallé, Ignitron, Kappellmeister, Karajan, Kempe, Klemperer, Lark, Lead, LED, Liber, Lightning, Mackerras, Maestro, Manners, Mantovani, Mho, Microchip, Nerve, N-type, Officiate, Ormandy, Outer, Ozawa, Parts, Photodiode, → **PILOT**, Previn, Probe, Prosecute, Protocol, Psychagogue, Psychopomp, P-type, Rattle, Safe, Sargent, Scudaller, Scudler, Shunt, Silicon, Skudler, Solicit, Solti, Stokowski, Strauss, Szell, Tao, Thermal, Thermistor, Thyristor, Toscanini, Transact, → **USHER**, Varactor, Varistor, Von Karajan, Walter, Wave guide, Wire, Wood, Zener diode
▷**Conducting** *may indicate* an '-ic' ending
**Conduit** Aqueduct, Canal, Carrier, Channel, Culvert, Duct, Main, Penstock, Pipe, Sewer, Tube, Utilidor, Wireway
**Cone(s), Cone-shaped, Conic, Conical** Alluvial, Cappie, Central, Cinder, Circular, Conoidal, Egmont, Ellipse, Female, Fir, Fusion, Ice-cream, Monticule, Moxa, Nose, Pastille, Peeoy, Pineal, Pingo, Pioy(e), Pottle, Puy, Pyramid, Pyrometric, Retinal, Seger, Shatter, Spire, Storm, Strobilus, Taper, Tee, Traffic, Volcanic, Wind, Windsock
**Coney** Daman, Doe, Hyrax
**Confabulate** Chat, Talk
**Confection(er), Confectionery** Bonbon, Candy, Candyfloss, Caramel, Chocolate, Concoction, Confiserie, Conserve, Countline, Halva, Ice, Kiss, Marshmallow, Marzipan, Meringue, Noisette, Nonpareil, Nougat, Quiddery, Rock, Snow-cone, Sweet, Sweetmeat, Tablet
**Confederal, Confederacy, Confederate, Confederation** Accessory, Alliance, Ally, Association, Body, Bund, Bunkosteerer, Collaborator, Cover, Creek, Dixie, F(o)edarie, Gueux, Illinois, League, Partner, Senegambia, Union, Zupa
**Confer(ence)** Bestow, Bretton Woods, Cf, Collogue, Colloqium, Colloquy, Congress, Convention, Council, Diet, Do, Dub, Endow, Fest, Forum, Grant, Huddle, Hui, Imparlance, Imperial, Indaba, Intercommune, Lambeth, Meeting, Munich, Negotiate, News, Palaver,

Parley, Pawaw, Pear, Potsdam, Pourparler, Powwow, Press, Pugwash, Quadrant, Seminar, Settle, Summit, Symposium, Synod, → TALK, Teach-in, Tete-a-tete, Tutorial, Video, Vouchsafe, Webinar, Yalta

**Confess(ion), Confessor** Acknowledge, Admit, Agnise, Auricular, Avowal, Concede, Confiteor, Cough up, Declare, Disclose, Edward, Helvetic, Own up, Peccavi, Recant, Shema, Shrift, Shriver, Sing, Tetrapolitan, Verbal, Whittle

**Confide(nce), Confident(ial), Confidant** Aplomb, Aside, Assertive, Assured, Authoritative, Bedpost, Belief, Bottle, Bouncy, Brash, Bravado, Can do, Certitude, Chutzpah, Cocksure, Cocky, Cred, Crouse, Dutch courage, Egoistical, Entre nous, Entrust, Extravert, Extrovert, Faith, Favourite, Fearless, Feisty, Gatepost, Hardy, Hope, Hubris, Hush-hush, Inside, Intimate, Morale, Nerve, Nerveless, Pack, Panache, Positive, Presumptuous, Private, Privy, QT, Reliance, Sanguine, Secret, Secure, Self-assured, Self-esteem, Self-possessed, Self-trust, Smug, Suavity, Sub rosa, Sure(ness), Sure-footed, Tell, Together, Top secret, Trust, Unabashed, Unbosom, Under the rose, Unselfconscious, Upbeat, Vaulting

**Confine(d), Confines, Confinement** Ambit, Bail, Bale, Bed rest, Cage, CB, Chain, Closet, Constrain, Contain, Coop, Cramp, Crib, Detain, Down-lying, Emmew, Encase, Enclose, Endemic, Enmew, Ensheath, Gaol, Gate, Gender-moon, Hem in, House arrest, Housebound, Immanacle, Immew, Immure, Impound, → IMPRISON, Incage, Incarcerate, Incommunicado, Inertial, Inhoop, Intern, Kettle, Laid up, Limit, Local, Lying in, Magnetic, Mail, March, Mew, Mure, Narrow, Pen, Pent, Pinion, Poky, Quarantine, Restrict, Rule 43, Rules, Section, Solitary, Tether, Thirl, Trammel, Trap

**Confirm(ed), Confirmation** Addict, Approve, Ascertain, Assure, Attest, Authenticate, Aver, Bear (out), Certify, Check, Chris(o)m, Christen, Chronic, Clinch, Corroborate, Double-check, Dyed-in-the-wool, Endorse, Evidence, Homologate, Ink in, Obsign, Official, OK, Proof, Qualify, Ratify, Reassure, Sacrament, Sanction, Seal, Strengthen, Substantiate, Ten-four, Tie, True, Validate, Vouch

**Confiscate, Confiscation** Attainder, Deprive, Dispossess, Distrain, Escheat, Expropriate, Garnishee, Impound, Infangenethef, Raupatu, Seize, Sequestrate

**Conflagration** Blaze, Holocaust, Inferno, Wildfire

**Conflict(ing)** Agon, Ambivalence, Antinomy, Armageddon, At odds, Battle(ground), Boilover, Camp, Casus belli, Clash, Close, Contend, Contravene, Controversy, Disharmony, Diverge, Encounter, Feud, Fray, Inconsistent, Internecine, Jar, Lists, Mêlée, Muss, Off-key, Oppose, Psychomachia, Rift, Scrape, Shoot-out, Strife, → STRUGGLE, Tension, Tergiversate, War

**Conform(ist), Conforming, Conformity** Accord, Adjust, Agreement, Comply, Conservative, Consistence, Correspond, Ethical, Hellenise, Hew to, Keep step, Normalise, Obey, Observe, Occasional, Procrustean, Propriety, Quadrate, Standardise, Stereotype(d), Suit, Time-server, Toe, Trimmer, Yield

**Confound(ed)** Abash, Amaze, Astound, Awhape, Baffle, Bewilder, Blamed, Blasted, Blest, Blinking, Bumbaze, Contradict, Darn, Dash, Deuce, Devastate, Dismay, Drat, Dumbfound, Elude, Floor, Jigger, Mate, Murrain, Nonplus, Perishing, Perplex, Rabbit, Spif(f)licate, Stump, Throw

▷**Confound** *may indicate* an anagram

**Confrère** Ally

**Confront(ation)** Address, Appose, Beard, Breast, Brush, Challenge, Clash, Cross, Defy, Duel, Eyeball, Face (off), Face down, Hansardise, Head on, Head-to-head, Impasse, Incident, Loggerheads, Mau-Mau, Meet, Militance, Nose, Oppose, Outface, Showdown, Smackdown, Stand, Tackle, Toe-to-toe, War

**Confuse(d), Confusedly, Confusing, Confusion** Addle(-brained), Adrift, Anarchy, Astonishment, At sea, Babel, Baffle, Bamboozle, Bazodee, Bedevil, Befog, Befuddle, Bemuse, Bewilder, Blur, Bobby-die, Burble, Bustle, Callaloo, Chaos, Cloud, Club, Clutter, Cobweb, Complicate, Consternation, Debacle, Deranged, Désorienté, Didder, Disarray, Discombobulate, Disconcert, Disorder, Disorient, Distract, Dither, Dizzy, Doublespeak, Doubting, Dudder, Dust, Dwaal, Egarement, Embrangle, Embroglio, Embroil, Entanglement, Farrago, Flap, Flat spin, Flummox, Flurry, Fluster, Fog, Fox, Fubar, Fuddle, Gaggle, Galley-west, Garble, Guddle, Hash, Havoc, Hazy, Hectic, Helter-skelter, Hirdy-girdy,

Hubble-bubble, Huddle, Hugger-mugger, Hurly-burly, Hurry-scurry, Hurry-skurry, Imbrangle, Imbroglio, Inchoate, Incoherent, → IN CONFUSION, Indistinct, Litter, Lost, Lurry, Maelstrom, Maffled, Mare's nest, Maving, Mayhem, Maze, Melange, Melee, Mess, Mingle, Mish-mash, Misorder, Mither, Mixter-maxter, Mixtie-maxtie, Mix-up, Mizzle, Mizzy maze, Moider, Moither, Moonstruck, Morass, → MUDDLE, Muddle-brained, Mudge, Muss(e), Muzzy, Mystify, Obfuscate, Overset, Pellmell, Perplex, Pi(e), Pig's ear, Pose, Puzzle head, Raddle, Ravel, Razzle-dazzle, Razzmatazz, Rout, Rummage, Rumpus, Scramble, S(c)hemozzle, Skimble-skamble, Snafu, Spaced out, Spin, Stump, Stupefy, Surprise, Swivet, Synchysis, Tangle, Tapsalteerie, Throw, Tizzy, Topsy-turvy, Toss, Turbulence, Turmoil, Tzimmes, Unclear, Upside down, Welter, Whemmle, Whomble, Whommle, Whummle, Woolly, Woozy

▷**Confuse(d)** *may indicate* an anagram

**Confute** Confound, Contradict, Deny, Disprove, Infringe, Redargue, Refel

**Congeal** Coagulate, Freeze, Gel, Gunge, Pectise, Set, Solidify

**Congenial** Affable, Agreeable, Amiable, Compatible, Connate, Couthie, Couthy, Happy, Kindred, Simpatico, Sympathique

**Congenital** Connate, Inborn, Innate, Intrinsic, Inveterate

**Conger** Sea-eel

**Congest(ed), Congestion** Choke, Coryza, Cram, Crowd, Engorge, Impact, Jam, Logjam, Nasal, (O)edema, Snarl up, Turgid

**Conglomerate, Conglomeration** Aggregate, Banket, Chaebois, Chaebol, Empire, Gather, Heap, Mass, Pudding-stone

**Congo(u)** DRC, Shaba, Tea

**Congratulate, Congratulation** Applaud, Compliment, Felicitate, Laud, Mazeltov, Preen, Salute

**Congregate, Congregation(alist)** Assembly, Barnabite, Body, Brownist, Class, Community, Conclave, Ecclesia, Flock, Fold, For(e)gather, Gathering, Group, Host, Laity, Meet, Oratory, Propaganda, Synagogue

**Congress(man)** ANC, Assembly, At it, Capitol, Conclave, Continental, Council, Eisteddfod, Intercourse, Legislature, Pan-Africanist, Rally, Senator, Sex, Solon, Synod, Vienna

**Congruous** Harmonious

**Conifer(ous)** Araucaria, Berg-cedar, Cedar, Cypress, Cyrus, Day cypress, Evergreen, Larch, Macrocarpa, Metasequoia, Picea, Pine, Redwood, Retinispora, Rimu, Spruce, Taiga, Taxus, Thuja, Yew

**Conject(ure)** Augur, Fancy, Gesse, Goldbach's, Guess, Guesswork, Infer, Speculate, Surmise, Theory, View

**Conjoin** Alligate, Ally, Connect, Knit

**Conjugate, Conjugation** Couple, Hermitian, Join, Nuptial, Synopsis, Typto, Zygosis

**Conjunction** Alligation, Ampersand, And, Combination, Consort, Coordinating, Inferior, Nor, Polysyndeton, Subordinating, Superior, Synod, Syzygy, Together, Union, Unition, Unless

**Conjure(r), Conjuror** Angekkok, Charm, Contrive, Cooper, Heypass, Heypresto, Hocus-pocus, Illusionist, Imagine, Invoke, Mage, Magic, Mystery-man, Palmer, Prestidigitator, Prestigiator, Thaumaturgus

**Conk** Nose

**Connect(ed), Connection, Connector** About, Accolade, Adaptor, Adjoin, Affiliate, Affinity, Agnate, Ally, Anastomosis, And, Associate, Attach, Band, Big end, Bind, Bridge, Bridle, Cable, Chiasm, Clientele, Close-knit, Cognate, Coherent, Colligate, Conjugate, Correlate, Couple, Cross-link, Delta, Dial up, DIN, Dovetail, Downlink, Drawbar, Earth, Enlink, Fasten, Fishplate, Fistula, Fuse, Hook-up, Hydrant, → IN CONNECTION WITH, Interlink, Interlock, Interrelation, Isthmus, Join, Jumper, Kinship, Liaison, Lifeline, Link(age), Linkup, Marry, Merge, Mesh, Modem, Neck, Network, Nexus, Nose, On, Online, Patch, Permalink, Pons, Raphe, Rapport, Relate, Relative, Relevant, Respect, Scart, Sentence, Shank, Socket, Splice, S-R, Star, Synapse, Syntenosis, Syssarcosis, Tendon, Through, Tie, Tie-in, Tie up, Twin, Unction, Union, Wire, Y, Yoke, Zygon

**Connecticut** Ct

**Connive, Connivance** Abet, Cahoots, Collude, Condone, Conspire, Lenocinium, Plot, Scheme

**Connoisseur** Aesthete, Barista, Cognoscente, Epicure, Expert, Fancier, Gastronome, Gourmet, Judge, Maven, Mavin, Oenophil(e)

**Connotate, Connotation** Imply, Infer, Intent, Meaning, Overtone

**Conquer(or), Conquering, Conquest** Alexander, Beat, Caesar, Conquistador, Cortes, Crush, Debel, Defeat, Genghis Khan, Hereward, → MASTER, Moor, Norman, Ostrogoth, Overcome, Overpower, Overrun, Pizarro, Saladin, Subdue, Subjugate, Tame, Tamerlane, Vanquish, Victor, Vincent, Win

**Conquistador** Cortes, Cortez, Pizarro

**Conscience, Conscientious** Casuistic, Diligent, Duteous, Dutiful, Guilty, Heart, Inwit, Morals, Painstaking, Pang, Remorse, Scruple(s), Scrupulous, Sense, Superego, Syneidesis, Synteresis, Thorough, Twinge

**Conscious(ness)** Apperception, Awake, Aware, Black, Chit, Deliberate, Ego, Limen, Mindful, On to, Persona, Sensible, Sensitivity, Sentient, Witting

**Conscript(ion)** Blood-tax, Choco, Commandeer, Draft(ee), Impress, Inductee, Landsturm, Levy, Nasho, National Service, → RECRUIT, Register

**Consecrate(d), Consecration** Anoint, Bless, Enoch, Hallow, Noint, Oint, Sacring, Sanctify, Venerate

**Consecutive** Sequential, Successive

**Consensus** Agreement, Harmony, Unanimity

**Consent** Accept, Accord, Acquiesce, Affo(o)rd, Agree, Approbate, Assent, Comply, Concur, Grant, Homologate, Informed, Permit, Ratify, Submit, Una voce, Volens, Yes-but, Yield

**Consequence(s), Consequent(ial), Consequently** After effect, Aftermath, Consectaneous, Corollary, Effect, End, Entail, Ergo, Evolution, Implication, Importance, Issue, Karma, Knock-on, Logical, Matter, Moment, Outcome, Out-turn, Party game, Ramification, Repercussion, → RESULT, Sequel, Spillover, Thence, Thereat, Thus, Upshot, Weight

**Conservative** Blimpish, Blue, Bourgeois, C, Cautious, Diehard, Disraeli, Fabian, Hard-hat, Hidebound, Hunker, Misoneist, Neanderthal, New Right, Old guard, Old-line, Old School, Preppy, Progressive, Reactionary, Rearguard, Redneck, Right(-wing), Safe, Square, Thatcherite, Thrifty, Tory, True blue, Unionist, Verkramp, Verkrampte, Young Fogey

**Conservatory** Hothouse, Lean-to, Orangery, Solarium

**Conserve, Conservation(ist)** Can, Comfiture, Game warden, Greenpeace, Husband(ry), Jam, Jelly, Maintain, Maintenance, Noah, NT, Protect, Save

**Consider(able), Considerate, Consideration, Considering** Adjudge, Ad referendum, Animadvert, Attention, Avizandum, By-end, Caring, Case, Cerebrate, Chew over, Cogitate, Contemplate, Count, Courtesy, Debate, Deem, Deliberate, Entertain, Envisage, Eye up, Factor, Fair, Feel, Forethought, Gay, Gey, Hear, Heed, Importance, Inasmuch, Judge, Kind, Many, Materially, Measure, Meditate, Much, Mull, Muse, Noteworthy, Pay, Perpend, Poise, Ponder, Premeditate, Pretty, Priority, Pro and con, Rate, Reck, Reckon, Reflect, Regard, Respect, Scruple, See, Sensitive, Several, Shortlist, Since, Solicitous, Song, Speculate, Steem, Study, Substantial, Think, Tidy, Vast, View, Ween, Weigh

**Consign(ment)** Allot, Award, Batch, Bequeath, Delegate, Deliver, Doom, Drop shipment, Entrust, Freight, Lading, Ship, Shipment, Transfer

**Consist(ent), Consistency** Agree, Changeless, Coherent, Comprise, Concordant, Enduring, Even, Liaison, Regular, Rely, Seamless, Sound, Steady, Texture, Uniform

**Consolation, Console** Ancon, Appease, Balm, Cheer, Comfort, Games, Keypad, Panel, Play, Prize, Reassure, Relief, Solace, Sop, Station, Terminal

**Consolidate** Coalesce, Combine, Compact, Gel, Merge, Pun, Unify

**Consommé** Julienne, Soup

**Consonant(s)** Affricate, Agma, Agreeing, Alveolar, Cacuminal, Cerebral, Explosive, Fortis, Fricative, Harmonious, Implosive, Labial, Lateral, Lenis, Media, Mouillé, Plosive, Sonorant, Spirant, Surd, Tenuis, Velar

**Consort** Ally, Associate, Fraternise, Maik, Mate, Moop, Moup, Other half, Partner, Spouse

**Consortium** Coalition, Combine, Ring

**Conspectus** Precis

**Conspicuous** Arresting, Blatant, Bold, Clear, Eminent, Eye-catching, Glaring, Kenspeck(le), Landmark, Light, Manifest, Patent, Radiant, Salient, Shining, Showy, Signal, Striking

**Conspiracy, Conspirator, Conspire, Conspiring** Brutus, Cabal, Cartel, Casca, Cassius, Catiline, Cato St, Champerty, Cinna, Collaborate, Colleague, Collogue, Collude, Complot, Connive, Covin, Covyne, Decembrist, Guy Fawkes, Highbinder, In cahoots, Intrigue, Oates, Omerta, →**PLOT**, Practisant, Ring, Scheme

**Constable** Beck, Catchpole, Cop, Dogberry, Dull, Elbow, Harman(-beck), Headborough, High, Hog, Jawan, John, Lord High, Officer, Painter, Petty, Pointsman, →**POLICEMAN**, Posse, Special, Thirdborough, Tipstaff, Uniformed, Verges

**Constancy, Constant** Abiding, Boltzmann, C, Changeless, Chronic, Coefficient, Continual, Cosmic, Cosmological, Decay, Devotion, Dielectric, Diffusion, Dilys, Dirac, Eccentricity, Endless, Enduring, Equilibrium, Eternal, Faith, Firm, Fixed, Frequent, Fundamental, G, Gas, Gravitational, H, Honesty, Hubble's, Incessant, K, Lambert, Leal(ty), Logical, Loyal, Magnetic, Nonstop, Often, Parameter, →**PERPETUAL**, Pi, Planck's, Pole star, Rate, Regular, Relentless, Resolute, Sad, Solar, Stability, Stable, Static, Staunch, Steadfast, Steady, Time, True, Unceasing, Unfailing, Uniform, Usual

**Constellation** Andromeda, Antlia, Apus, Aquarius, Aquila, Ara, Argo, Aries, Auriga, Bootes, Caelum, Camelopardalis, Camelopardus, Canes Venatici, Canis Major, Canis Minor, Carina, Cassiopeia, Centaurus, Cepheus, Cetus, Cham(a)eleon, Circinus, Columba, Coma Berenices, Coma Cluster, Corona australis, Corvus, Crater, Cygnus, Cynosure, Delphinus, Delta, Dolphin, Dorado, Draco, Equuleus, Eridanus, Fornax, Galaxy, Gemini, Great Bear, Gru(i)s, Hercules, Horologium, Hydra, Hydrus, Indus, Lacerta, Leo, Leo Minor, Lepus, Libra, Little Bear, Little Dipper, Lupus, Lynx, Lyra, Mensa, Microscopium, Monoceros, Musca, Norma, Octans, Ophiuchus, Orion, Pavo, Pegasus, Perseus, Phoenix, Pictor, Piscis Austrinus, →**PLANET**, Puppis, Pyxis, Reticulum, Sagitta, Sagittarius, Scorpius, Sculptor, Scutum, Serpens, Sextans, Southern Cross, Spica, →**STAR**, Telescopium, The Rule, Triangulum (Australe), Tucana, Twins, Unicorn, Vela, Vilpecula, Virgin, Virgo, Volans, Vulpecula, Wag(g)oner, Whale, Zodiacal

**Consternation** Alarm, Dismay, Doodah, Fear, Horror, Panic

**Constipate(d), Constipation** Astrict, Bind, Block, Coprolith, Costive, Fardel-bound, Mawbound, Obstipation, Stegnotic, Stenosis

**Constituency, Constituent** Agglutinogen, Borough, Component, Content, Element, Immediate, Ingredient, Marginal, Part, Principle, Seat, Staple, Sub unit, Ultimate, Voter

▷**Constituents** *may indicate* an anagram

**Constitute, Constitution(al)** Appoint, Character, Charter, Clarendon, Compose, Comprise, Congenital, Creature, Establishment, Form, Fuero, Health, Innate, Physique, Policy, Polity, Seat, State, Stroll, Synthesis, Trek, Upmake, Walk

**Constrain(ed), Constraint** Bind, Bondage, Boundary, Coerce, Confine, Coop, Curb, Dragoon, Duress(e), Force, Hard, Impel, Limit, Localise, Oblige, Perstringe, Pressure, Repress, Stenosis, Taboo, Tie, Tighten, Trammel

**Constrict(ed), Constriction** Bottleneck, Cage, Choke, Coarctate, Contract, Cramp, Hour-glass, Impede, Isthmus, Limit, Narrow, Paraphimosis, Phimosis, Squeeze, Stegnosis, Stenosis, Stifle, Strangle, Strangulate, Thlipsis, Tighten, Venturi

**Construct(ion), Constructor, Constructive** Architect, Assemble, Build, Cast, Compile, Dry, Engineer, Erect, Fabricate, Facture, Fashion, Form, Frame, Idolum, Make, Manufacture, Meccano, Partners, Sandwich, Seabee, Stressed-skin, Structure, Tectonic, Weave

**Construe** Deduce, Explain, Expound, Infer

**Consul** Ambassador, Attaché, Cicero, Horse, Lucullus, Praetor

**Consult(ant), Consultation** Avisement, Confer, Deliberate, Discuss, Emparl, Holmes, Imparl, Joint, Peritus, See, Sexpert, Shark watcher, Surgery, Vide

**Consume(r), Consumption, Consumptive** Bolt, Burn, Caterpillar®, Conspicuous, Decay, Devour, Diner, Eat, End-user, Engross, Exhaust, Expend, Feed, Glutton, Hectic, Intake, Mainline, Nash, Preoccupy, Scoff, Spend, Swallow, TB, Use, Waste, Wear

**Consummate, Consummation** Achieve, Crown, Keystone, Seal, Thorough

**Contact** Abut, Adjoin, Adpress, Contingence, Electrode, Eye, Fax, Hit, Hook-up, Lens, Liaise, Liaison, Meet, Outreach, Radio, Reach, Shoe, Taction, Telephone, Text, →**TOUCH**, Touchy-feely, Wiper

**Contagious, Contagion** Infection, Noxious, Plague, Poison, Psora, Taint, Variola, Viral

**Contain(er)** Amphora, Ampoule, Ampulla, Aquafer, Aquifer, Ashcan, Bag, Barrel, Basket, Bass, Beaker, Bidon, Billy(-can), Bin, Boat, Bottle, Bowl, Box, Brazier, Bucket, Buddle, Bunker, Butt, Butter-boat, Cachepot, Caddy, Can, Canakin, Canikin, Canister, Cannikin, Cantharus, Capsule, Carafe, Carboy, Carry, Carton, Cartridge, Case, Cask, Cassette, Censer, Chase, Chest, Chilly bin, Churn, Clip, Coffer, Coffin, Coffret, Comprise, Coolamon, Crate, Crater, Crib, Crucible, Cruse, Cup, Cupel, Cuvette, Cylinder, Decanter, Demitasse, Dracone, Drawer, Dredger, Drum, Encircle, Enclose, Encompass, Enseam, Envelope, Esky®, Feretory, Flagon, Flask, Flat, Gabion, Gallipot, Gourd, Growler, Handbag, Hatbox, → **HOLD**, House, Humidor, Igloo, Include, Incubator, Inkwell, Inseam, Intray, Jar, Jeroboam, Jerrican, Jerrycan, Jug, Keg, Kettle, Kirbeh, Leaguer, Lekythos, Locker, Magnox, Melting-pot, Monkey, Monstrance, Mould, Muffineer, Nosebag, Olpe, Ostensorium, Out-tray, Package, Packet, Pail, Percolator, Pinata, Piscina, Pitcher, Pithos, Pocket, Pod, Poke, Pot, Pottle, Punnet, Pyxis, Receptacle, Reliquary, Repository, Restrain, Sac(k), Sachet, Safe, Saggar, Saltcellar, Scrip, Scuttle, Scyphus, Shaker, Sheath, Silo, Situla, Skin, Skip, Snaptin, Solander, Spittoon, Stamnos, Stillage, Tank, Tantalus, Tea kettle, Terrarium, Tinaja, Trough, Trug, Tub, Tun, Tupperware®, Urn, Valise, Vase, Vat, Vessel, Vinaigrette, Wardian case, Washbag, Wineskin, Woolpack, Workbag

**Contaminate(d), Contaminant, Contamination** Adulterate, Corrupt, Defile, Denature, Flyblown, Impure, Infect, Moit, Mysophobia, Pollute, Salmonella, Soil, Spike, Stain, Sully, Taint, Tarnish, Toxic

**Contemplate, Contemplation** Brood, Consider, Debate, Ecce, Envisage, Hesychasm, Intend, Meditate, Muse, Navel gaze, Ponder, Reflect, Retrospection, Rue, Samadhi, Spell, Study, Think, Watch

**Contemporary** AD, Coetaneous, Coeval, Concomitant, Current, Equal, Fellow, Modern, Modish, Present, Recent, Topical, Verism

**Contempt(ible), Contemptuous** Abject, Ageism, Aha, Arsehole, Bah, Base, BEF, Blithering, Cheap, Contumely, Crud, Crumb, Crummy, Cullion, Cur, Cynical, Derision, Despisal, Diddy, Dis(s), Disdain, Dismissive, Disparaging, Disrespect, Dog-bolt, Douchebag, Dusty, Fico, Fig, Figo, Flouting, Foh, Git, Hangdog, Ignominious, Insect, Irreverence, Jive-ass, Lousy, Low, Mean, Measly, Misbegotten, Misprision, Och, Odious, Paltry, Pelting, Pfui, Pho(h), Phooey, Pipsqueak, Pish, Poof, Poxy, Pshaw, Ratfink, Rats, Razoo, Scabby, Scarab, Schlub, Scofflaw, → **SCORN**, Scumbag, Scurvy, Sdeign, Sexism, Shabby, Sis, Slimeball, Sneer, Sneeze, Sniffy, Snook, Snooty, Snot, Snotty, Soldier, Sorry, Sprat, Squirt, Squit, Supercilious, Swinish, Toad, Toerag, Tossy, Turd, Tush, Vilipend, Weed, Whipster, Wretched

**Contend(er)** Allege, Argue, Aspirant, Athlete, Candidate, Claim, Clash, Compete, Cope, Debate, Dispute, Fight, Grapple, Oppose, Rival, Stickle, → **STRIVE**, Struggle, Submit, Tussle, → **VIE**, Wrestle

**Content(ed), Contentment** Apaid, Apay, Appay, Arcadia, Blissful, Calm, Closure, Glad, Happy, Hog heaven, Inside, Matter, Please, Raza, Reza, Satiate, Satisfy, Subject matter, Volume, Wellbeing

▷**Content** *may indicate* a hidden word

**Contention, Contentious** Argument, Bellicose, Cantankerous, Case, Challenge, Combat, Competitive, Debatable, Discord, Disputatious, Eristic, Hot potato, Issue, Logomachy, Match, Perverse, Polemical, Rivalry, Strife, Struggle, Sturt, Tangle

**Contest(ant)** Agon, Battle (royal), Beauty, Beetle drive, Biathlon, Bout, Catchweight, Challenge, Championship, Charioteer, Combat, Competition, Concours, Darraign, Decathlon, Defend, Deraign, Dogfight, Duathlon, Duel(lo), Entrant, Eurovision, Event, Examinee, Finalist, Free-for-all, Fronde, Game, Handicap, Heptathlon, Joust, Kemp, Kriegspiel, Lampadephoria, Match, Matchplay, Olympiad, Outsider, Pancratium, Panel-beater, Par, Paralympics, Pentathlon, Pingle, Play-off, Prizer, Race (meeting), Rat race, Rival, Roadeo, Rodeo, Scrap, Scrum, Set-to, Skirmish, Slam, Slugfest, Strife, Struggle, Tenson, Tetrathlon, Tournament, Triathlon, Tug-of-war, Tussle, Vie, War, With

**Context** Intentional, Opaque, Transparent

**Continent(al)** Abstinent, Asia, Atlantis, Austere, Chaste, Dark, Epeirogeny, Euro, European, Gallic, Gondwanaland, Greek, Landmass, Laurasia, Lemuria, Mainland, Moderate, NA, Oceania, Pang(a)ea, Shelf, Teetotal, Temperate, Walloon

**Contingency, Contingent** Accident, Arm, Brigade, Casual, Chance, Conditional, Dependent, Event, Fluke, Group, Possibility, Prospect

**Continual(ly), Continuous** Adjoining, Anend, At a stretch, Away, Ceaseless, Chronic, Connected, Durational, Eer, Endlong, Eternal, Eterne, Ever, Forever, Frequent, Incessant, Non-stop, On(going), Perpetual, Unbroken, Unceasing

**Continue, Continuation, Continuing, Continuity** Abye, Drag on, Duration, Dure, During, Enduring, Enjamb(e)ment, Follow-on, Go on, Hold, Keep, Last, Link, Maintain, Ongoing, On the trot, Onward, Perpetuate, Persevere, Persist, Proceed, Prolong, Push on, Remain, Resume, Sequel, Sequence, Soldier on, Stand, Subsist, Survive, Sustain, Synaphe(i)a, Tenor

▹**Continuously** *may indicate* previous words to be linked

**Contort(ion)** Deform, Gnarl, Jib, Twist, Warp, Wreathe, Wry

**Contour** Curve, Graph, Isallobar, Isobase, Isobath, Isobront, Isochasm, Isocheim, Isochime, Isocryme, Isogeothermal, Isohel, Isohyet, Isopach(yte), Isopycnic, Isothere, Isotherm, Line, Profile, Silhouette, Streamline, Tournure

**Contraband** Gun-running, Hot, Illicit, Prohibited, Smuggled

**Contraception, Contraceptive** Billings method, Birth-pill, Cap, Coil, Condom, Depo-Provera®, Diaphragm, Dutch cap, Etonogestrol, IU(C)D, Legonorgestrel, Lippes loop, Loop, Minipill, Oral, Pessary, Pill, Precautions, Prophylactic, Rubber(s), Sheath, Spermicide, Vimule®

**Contract(ion), Contractor** Abbreviate, Abrege, Abridge, Affreightment, Agreement, Appalto, Astringency, Bargain, Betrothal, Biceps, Binding, Bond, Bottomry, Braxton-Hicks, Bridge, Builder, Catch, Champerty, Charter (party), Clench, Clonus, Committal, Compress, Concordat, Condense, Consensual, Constringe, Contrahent, Convulsion, Covenant, Cramp, Crasis, Curtail(ment), Deal, Debt, Develop, Diastalsis, Dupuytren's, Dwindle, Engage, Entrepreneur, Escrow, Extrasystole, Fibrillation, Fitzgerald-Lorentz, Flex, Forward, Gainsay, Gooseflesh, Grand slam, Guarantee, Hand-promise, Hedge, Hire, Incur, Indenture, Jerk, Ketubah, Knit, Labour, Lease, Lessen, Levator, Lorentz-Fitzgerald, Make, Mandate, Miosis, Myosis, Narrow, Obligee, Outsource, Party, Peristalsis, Policy, Pre-nup(tial), Privilege, Promise, Pucker, Purse, Restriction, Risus (sardonicus), Service, Shrink, Shrivel, Sign, Slam, Slim, Social, Spasm, Specialty, Squinch, Steelbow, Stenosis, Stipulation, Straddle, Supplier, Swap, Sweetheart, Synaloepha, Syngraph, Systole, Taper off, Telescope, Tender, Tense, Tetanise, Tetanus, Tic, Tighten, Time bargain, Tittle, Tonicity, Tontine, Treaty, Triceps, Trigger-finger, Trismus cynicus, Undertaker, Wrinkle, Yellow-dog, Z

▹**Contract** *may indicate* a bridge call, e.g. 1S, 1C, 1D

**Contradict(ion), Contradictory** Ambivalent, Antilogy, Antinomy, Belie, Bull, Contrary, Counter, Dementi, Deny, Disaffirm, Disprove, Dissent, → GAINSAY, Negate, Oxymoron, Paradox, Perverse, Refute, Sot, Stultify, Sublate, Threap, Threep, Traverse

**Contralto** Clara Butt

**Contraption** Contrivance, Device, Doodah, Gadget, Scorpion

**Contrapuntal** Fugue

**Contrarily, Contrary** Adverse, A rebours, Arsy-versy, But, Cantankerous, Captious, Converse, Counter, Counterfleury, Crosscurrent, Cross-grained, Cross-purpose, Froward, Heretic, Hostile, Inverse, Mary, Obsequent, Opposite, Oppugnant, Ornery, Perverse, Rebuttal, Retrograde, Wayward, Withershins

**Contrast** Chiaroscuro, Chiasmus, Clash, Colour, Compare, Differ, Foil, Relief

**Contravene** Break, Infringe, Oppose, Thwart, Violate

**Contribute, Contribution** Abet, Add, Assist, Chip in, Conduce, Donate, Dub, Furnish, Go, Help, Input, Kick in, Mite, Offering, Render, Share, Sub, Subscribe, Whack, Widow's mite

▹**Contributing to** *may indicate* a hidden word

**Contrite, Contrition** Apologetic, Penance, Penitent, Remorse, Repentant, Rue, Sackcloth, → SORRY

**Contrivance, Contrive(r), Contrived** Art, Artificial, Cam, Chicaner, Contraption, Cook, Deckle, Deus ex machina, Device, Devise, Die-stock, Dodge, Engine, Engineer, Fictitious, Finesse, Frame, Gadget, Gimmick, Gin, Hatch, Hokey, Humidor, Intrigue, Invention,

Machinate, Manage, Manoeuvre, Page, Plan, Plot, Procure, Rest, Rowlock, Scheme, Secure, Shift, Stage, Trump, Wangle, Weave

**Control(ler), Controllable, Controlled** Ada, Administer, Aircon, Appestat, Arms, Atorvastatin, Autopilot, Ballcock, Bias, Big Brother, Birth, Boss, Boundary layer, Brain, Bridle, Budgetary, Cabotage, Cache, Camshaft, Chair, Check, Choke(hold), Christmas tree, Command, Contain, Corner, Correct(ion), Corset, Cruise, Curb, Cybernetics, Damage, Descendeur, Dirigible, Dirigism(e), Dominate, Dominion, Drive, Driving seat, Duopsony, Dynamic, Elevon, Etatiste, Exchange, Fader, Fast-forward, Fet(ch), Fief, Finger, Flood, Fly-by-wire, Gain, Gar, George, Gerent, Govern, Ground, Gubernation, Hae, Handle, Harness, Have, Heck, Helm, Hog, Influence, Influx, Inhibitor, Interchange, Joystick, Keypad, Knee-swell, Lead, Lever, Limit, Line, → MANAGE, Manipulate, Martinet, Master-switch, Mastery, Moderate, Mouse, Nipple, Noise, Nozzled, Numerical, Operate, Organise, Override, Pacemaker, Pedal, Pilot, Placebo, Police, Population, Possess, Power, Preside, Price, Process, Puppeteer, Quality, Radio, Referee, Regime(nt), Regulate, Regulo®, Reign, Rein, Remote, Rent, Repress, Restrain, Restrict, Rheostat, Ride, Ripple, Rule, Run, School, Servo, Slide(r), Snail, Solion, Spoiler, Stabilise, Stage-manage, Steady, Steer, Stem, Stop, Stopcock, Stranglehold, Stringent, Subdue, Subject, Subjugate, Supervise, Suzerain, Svengali, Sway, Switch, Syndicate, Takeover, Tame, Tap, Temperate, Thermostat, Throttle, Tie, Tiller, Timer, Tone, Traction, Umpire, Upper hand, Valve, Weld, Whiphand, Wield, Zapper

**Controversial, Controversy** Argument, Cause célèbre, Contention, Debate, Dispute, Emotive, Eristic(al), Furore, Heretical, Hot mutton, Hot potato, Moot point, Offensive, Polemic(al), Quarrel, Tendentious, Troll

▷**Contuse** *may indicate* an anagram

**Conundrum** Acrostic, Egma, Enigma, Guess, Puzzle, Riddle, Teaser

**Convalesce(nt), Convalescence** Anastasis, Anastatic, Mend, Rally, Recover, Recuperate, Rest-cure

▶**Convene** *see* CONVOKE(R)

**Convenience, Convenient** Behoof, Commode, Cosy, Easy, Eft, Ethe, Expedient, Facility, Gain, Gents, Handsome, → HANDY, Hend, Latrine, Lav, Leisure, Men's room, Near, On tap, Opportune, Pat, Privy, Public, Suitable, Toilet, Use, Washroom, Well

**Convent** Abbatial, Cloister, Fratry, Friary, House, → MONASTERY, Motherhouse, Nunnery, Port-royal, Priory, Retreat

**Convention(al)** Academic, Accepted, Babbitt, Blackwood, Bourgeois, Caucus, Code, Conclave, Conformity, → CUSTOMARY, Decorous, Diet, Done, Etiquette, Formal, Formulaic, Geneva, Habitude, Hidebound, Iconic, Lame, Lingua franca, Mainstream, Meeting, Middlebrow, Middle-of-the-road, More, National, Nomic, Normal, Ordinary, Orthodox, Ossified, Pompier, Pooterish, Proper, Propriety, Rally, Readymade, Schengen, Square, Staid, Standard, Starchy, Stereotyped, Stock, Straight, Stylebook, Synod, The thing, Treaty, Uptight, Usage, Vanilla, Warsaw

**Converge(nce)** Approach, Focus, Inrush, Meet, Overlap, Toe-in

**Conversation(al), Conversationalist, Converse, Conversant** Abreast, Antithesis, Antitype, Aware, Board, Buck, Cackle, Causerie, Chat, Chinwag, Chitchat, Colloquy, Commune, Confab, Convo, Crack, Craic, Crossfire, Crosstalk, Deipnosophist, Dialogue, Discourse, Discussion, Eutrapelia, Eutrapely, Exchange, Facemail, Hobnob, Interlocution, In tune with, Jaw-jaw, Natter, Opposite, Palaver, Parley, Persiflage, Rap, Rhubarb, Shop, Shoptalk, Sidebar, Small talk, Socialise, Sprechgesang, → TALK, Transpose, Trialogue, Wongi, Word

**Conversion, Converter, Convert(ible)** Adapt, Alter, Assimilate, Azotobacter, Bessemer, Cabriolet, Cash, Catalytic, Catechumen, Change, Commutate, Commute, Cyanise, Damascene, Decipher, Diagenesis, Disciple, Distil, Encash, Etherify, Evangelize, Exchange, Expropriate, Fixation, Goal kick, Gummosis, Hodja, Image, Ismalise, Kho(d)ja, Landau, L-D, Liquid(ate), Low-noise, Marrano, Metamorphosis, Metanoia, Missionary, Neophyte, Noviciate, Novitiate, Persuade, Prill, Proselyte, Put, Ragtop, Realise, Rebirth, Reclamation, Recruit, Recycle, Revamp, Romanise, Sheik(h), Soft-top, Souper, Spam, Tablet, Taw, Torque, Transduce, Transform, Translate, Transmute, Try, Vert

▷**Conversion, Converted** *may indicate* an anagram

**Convex(ity)** Arched, Bombe, Bowed, Camber, Curved, Entasis, Extrados, Gibbous, Lenticle, Nowy

**Convey(ance), Conveyor** Assembly line, Assign, BS, Carousel, Carriage, Carry, Carrycot, Cart, Chaise, Charter, Coach, Conduct, Cycle, Deed, Deliver, Dispone, Eloi(g)n, Enfeoffment, Esloyne, Exeme, Giggit, Grant, Guide, Lease, Litter, Lorry, Mailcar(t), Mortgage, Pirogue, Pneumatic, Put across, Re-lease, Sac, Screw, Ski-tow, Sled, Soc, T-bar, Tip, Title deed, Tote, Tram, Transfer, Transit, Transmit, Transport, Trolley, Vehicle

**Convict(ion), Convicts** Attaint, Belief, Botany Bay, Bushranger, Canary, Certitude, Chain gang, Cockatoo, Cogence, Crawler, Credo, Creed, Crime, Criminal, Demon, Dogma, Emancipist, Faith, Felon, Forçat, Gaolbird, Government man, Jailbird, Lag, Magwitch, Mindset, Old chum, → **PERSUASION**, Plerophory, Previous, Prisoner, Record, Ring, Tenet, Trusty, Vehemence, Yardbird

**Convince(d), Convincing** Assure, Certain, Cogent, Conclusive, Credible, Doubtless, Luculent, Persuade, Plausible, Put across, Satisfy, Sold, Sure

**Convivial(ity)** Bonhomie, Boon, Bowl, Cameraderie, Festive, Gay, Genial, Jovial, Merriment, Social

**Convocation** Assembly

**Convoke(r)** Assemble, Call, Chairman, Convene, Summon

**Convolute(d), Convolution** Coiled, Complex, Contort, Gyrus, Helical, Intricate, Maze, Spiral, Tortuous, Twisty, Whorl, Writhen

**Convolvulus** Bindweed, Dodder

**Convoy** Caravan, Column, Conduct, Escort, Fur brigade, Pilot, Train, Wagon-train

**Convulse, Convulsion(s), Convulsive** Agitate, Clonic, Clonus, Commotion, Disturb, DT, Eclampsia, → **FIT**, Galvanic, Grand mal, Paroxysm, Petit mal, Seizure, Shudder, Sob, Spasm, Throe, Tic

**Cook(s), Cooker(y), Cooking** Aga®, Au gratin, Babbler, Babbling brook, Bain marie, Bake, Balti, Barbecue, Beeton, Benghazi, Bhindi, Bouche, Braise, Broil, Cacciatore, Calabash, Captain, Casserole, Charbroil, Chargrill, Chef, Chillada, Coction, Coddle, Concoct, Cordon bleu, Costard, Creole, Cuisine, Cuisinier, Deep-fry, Delia, Devil, Do, Doctor, Dumple, Easy over, Edit, En papillote, Escoffier, Explorer, Fake, Falsify, Fan oven, Fiddle, Fireless, Fix, Flambé, Forge, Fricassee, Fry, Fudge, Fusion, Gastronomy, Gratinate, Gratine(e), Greasy, Griddle, Grill, Hatch, Haute cuisine, Haybox, Hibachi, Hot plate, Jackaroo, Kiln, Lyonnaise, Marengo, Marinière, Meunière, Microwave, Mount, Mrs Beeton, Nouvelle cuisine, Parboil, Plain, Poach, Prepare, Pressure, Provencale, Range, Ribroast, Rig, Ring, Roast, Roger, Sauté, Short-order, Silver, Simmer, Slow, Sous-chef, Spit, Steam, Stew, Stir-fry, Stove, Tandoori, Teriyaki, Tikka, Tire, Toast

▷**Cook** *may indicate* an anagram

**Cookhouse** Caboose

**Cookie** Biscuit, Fortune, Rye-roll

**Cool(er), Coolant, Cooling, Coolness** Ace, Aloof, Aplomb, Calm, Can, Chill, Chokey, Collected, Composed, Cryogen, Cryostat, Defervescence, Desert, Dignified, Dispassionate, Distant, Esky®, Fan, Fraicheur, Frappé, Fridge, Frigid, Frosty, Gaol, Goglet, Heat sink, Hep, Hip, Ice(box), Impersonal, Imperturbable, In, Jail, Jug, Keel, La Nina, Lubricating oil, Maraging, Nervy, Nonchalant, Offhand, Offish, Phlegm, Poise, Prison, Quad, Quod, Radiator, Reefer, Refresh, Regenerative, Reserved, Sangfroid, Serene, Shady, Skeigh, Splat, Stir, Super-duper, Sweat, Temper(ate), Tepid, Thou(sand), Trendy, Unruffled, Wint(e)ry

**Coon** Maine

**Coop** Cage, Cavie, Confine, Gaol, Hutch, Mew, Pen, Rip

**Cooper** Gary, Henry, Tubman

**Cooperate, Cooperation, Cooperative** Accommodate, Ally, Artel, Bipartisan, Coadjutant, Collaborate, Combine, Conspire, Contribute, Coop, Credit union, Give and take, Liaise, Pitch in, Play (ball), Synergy, Tame, Teamwork, Together, Worker's

**Coordinate(s), Coordinated, Coordination** Abscissa, Abscisse, Agile, Arrange, Cartesian, Del, Dyspraxia, Ensemble, Harmony, Liaise, Mesh, Nabla, Orchestrate, Ordonnance, Organise, Peer, Polar, Right ascension, Spherical, Synergy, Teamwork, Tie-in, Tight, Twistor, Waypoint, X, Y, Z

**Coot** Stupid, Sultan
**Cop(s)** Bag, Bull, Catch, Copper, Dick, Flic, Keystone, Peeler, Peon, → POLICEMAN, Silent
**Copal** Dammar, Resin
**Cope** Bear up, Chlamys, Deal, Face, Fare, Handle, Hood, Make do, → MANAGE, Mantle, Meet, Negotiate, Pallium, Poncho, Scrat(ch), Stand
**Coping (stone)** Balustrade, Capstone, Skew
**Copious** Abundant, Affluent, Ample, Fecund, Fluent, Fruitful, Fulsome, Plentiful, Profuse
**Copper(s)** As, Atacamite, Beast, Blister, Bluebottle, Bobby, Bornite, Busy, Cash, Cent, Chessylite, → COIN, Cu, D, Dam, Double, Enargite, Erinite, Flatfoot, Lawman, Lota(h), Malachite, Mountain-blue, Ormolu, Peacock, Pence, Penny, Pfennig, Pie, Pig, Plack, Policeman, Red, Rosser, Rozzer, S, Sen(s), Sheet, Slop, Small change, Special, Traybit, Venus, Verdet, Verditer, Washer, Washtub, Wire bar
**Coppice, Copse** Thicket, Underwood
**Copulate, Copulation** Intercourse, Line, Mate, Rut, Serve, Tread, Tup
**Copy(ing), Copier, Copyist, Copywriter** Adman, Aemule, Ape, Apograph, Association, Autotype, Back-up, Blurb, Calk, Calque, Camera-ready, Carbon, Clerk, Clone, Counterpart, Crib, Cyclostyle, Dead ringer, Diazo, Ditto, Double, Download, Draft, Duplicate, Dyeline, Echo, Echopraxia, Ectype, Edition, Eidograph, Electro, Emulate, Engross, Estreat, Example, Facsimile, Fair, Fax, Flimsy, Forge, Hard, Hectograph, → IMITATE, Issue, Jellygraph, Knocking, Knockoff, Look-alike, Manifold, Manuscript, Match, Me-tooer, Microdot, Milline, Mimeograph®, Mimic, Mirror, Model, MS, Offprint, Ozalid, Pantograph, Parrot, Photostat®, Pirate, Plagiarism, Polygraph, Read-out, Repeat, Replica, Reprint, Repro, Reproduce, Review, Rip, Roneo®, Scanner, Scribe, Script, Scrivener, Sedulous, Show, Simulate, Skim, Soft, Spit, Stat, Stencil, Stuff, Tall, Telautograph®, Telefax, Tenor, Tenure, Trace, Transcribe, Transume, Transumpt, Typescript, Vidimus, Xerox®
**Copyright** C, Landgrab, Patent
**Coquette, Coquettish** Agacerie, Flirt, Girlish, Rosina, Tease, Vamp
**Cor** Bath, Crumbs, Ephah, Gosh, Homer
**Coracle** Currach, Curragh
**Coral (reef)** Alcyonaria, Aldabra, Atoll, Brain, Coenosteum, Cup, Deadmen's fingers, Gorgonia(n), Laccadives, Madrepore, Millepore, Organ-pipe, Pennatula, Pink, Precious, Red, Reef, Sea fan, Sea ginger, Sea-pen, Sea whip, Seed, Staghorn, Stony, Zoothome
**Cord, Cord-like** Achilles tendon, Aiguillette, Band, Bedford, Bind, Boondoggle, Cat-gut, Chenille, Clew, Communication, Creance, Cybernaculum, Drawstring, Elephant, Flex, Fourragère, Funicle, Gasket, Heddle, Lace, Laniard, Lanyard, Ligature, Line, Moreen, Myelon, Nerve, Net, Ocnus, Picture, Piping, Quipo, Quipu, Rep(s), Restiform, Rip, Rope, Sash, Sennit, Service, Shroudline, Sinew, Sinnet, Spermatic, Spinal, Static line, → STRING, Tassel, Tendon, Tether, Tie, Tieback, Torsade, Twine, Twitch, Umbilical, Vocal, Wick
**Cordial(ity)** Amicable, Anise(ed), Anisette, Benedictine, Cassis, Drink, Elderflower, Gracious, Grenadine, Hearty, Hippocras, Kind, Neighbourly, Open-hearted, Oporice, Orangeade, Persico(t), Pleasant, Rapprochement, Ratafia, Rosa-solis, Roso(g)lio, Shrub, Sweets, Tar-water, Tonic, Warm
**Cordierite** Saphir d'eau
**Cordon** Band, Beltcourse, Picket, Police, Ring, Sanitaire, Sanitary, Surround
**Corduroy** Rep(p)
**Cordyline** Ti-tree
**Core** Barysphere, Cadre, Calandria, Campana, Centre, Chog, Essence, Filament, Hard, Heart, Hub, Kernel, Magnetic, Nife, Nitty-gritty, Nub, Nuclear, Plerome, Quintessence, Runt, Slug
**Co-religionist** Brother
**Corfu** Corfiot(e)
**Coriander** Cilantro
**Corinthian(s)** Casuals, Caulis, Epistolaters
**Cork(ed), Corker** Balsa, Bouché, Bung, Crown, Float(er), Humdinger, Mountain, Oner, Periderm, Phellem, Phellogen, Plug, Seal, Shive, Stopper, Suber(ate), Suberin
**Corkscrew** Bore, Opening, Spiral, Twine
**Corm** Bulb

**Cormorant** Duiker, Duyker, Scart(h), Shag, Skart(h)

**Corn(y)** Bajr(a), Banal, Blé, Callus, Cereal, Cob, Dolly, Durra, Emmer, Epha, Farina, Flint, Gait, Graddan, Grain, Green, Grist, Guinea, Hokey, Icker, Indian, Kanga pirau, Mabela, Maize, Mealie, Muid, Negro, Nubbin, Pickle, Pinole, Posho, Rabi, Rye, Schmaltz, Seed, Shock, Stitch, Straw, Sugar, Sweet, Tail ends, Thrave, Trite, Zea

**Corncrake** Landrail

**Cornel** Dogberry, Tree

**Corner** Amen, Angle, Bend, Buy up, Canthus, Cantle, Canton, Chamfer, Chimney(nook), Cranny, Dangerous, Dièdre, Dominate, Elbow, Entrap, Hog, Hole, Hospital, Inglenook, Long, Lug, Monopoly, NE, Neuk, Niche, Nook, NW, Penalty, Predicament, Quoin, SE, Short, Speakers', Spot, SW, Tack, Tattenham, Tight, Trap, Tree, Vertex

**Cornerstone** Basis, Coi(g)n, Encoignure, Skew-corbel, Skew-put, Skew-table

**Cornet** Cone, Cornopean, Field, Horn

**Cornice** Surbase

**Cornish(man)** Cousin Jack

**Cornstalks** Strammel, Straw, Strummel, Stubble

**Cornucopia** Amalthea, Horn

**Cornwall** SW

**Corollary** Conclusion, Dogma, Porism, Rider, Theory, Truism

**Corona** Aureole, Cigar, Halo, Larmier, Nimbus, Wreath

**Coronation** Enthronement

**Coroner** Procurator fiscal

**Coronet** Diadem

**Corporal** Bardolph, Bodily, Bombardier, Brig(adier), Lance-pesade, Lance-prisade, Lance-prisado, Lance-speisade, Master, Naik, NCO, Nym, Pall, Physical, Trim

**Corporation** Alvine, Beer gut, Belly, Body, Breadbasket, Closed, Commune, Company, Conglomerate, Guild, Kite, Kyte, Paunch, Pot(-belly), Public, Public service, Stomach, Swag-belly, Tum, Wame, Wem

**Corps** Body, C, Cadet, Crew, Diplomatic, Marine, Peace, RAC, RE, REME, Rifle, Salvage, Unit

**Corpse(s)** Blob, Body, Cadaver, Carcass, Carrion, Deader, Dust, Goner, Like, Mort, Mummy, Quarry, Relic, Remains, Stiff, Zombi(e)

**Corpulence, Corpulent** Adipose, Fat, Fleshy, Gross, Obese, Plump, Poddy, Rotund, Stout, Thickset, Tubby

**Corpuscle(s)** Blood(-count), Cell, Erythrocyte, Malpighian, Meissner's, Microcyte, Neutrophil, Pacinian, Phagocyte, Porkilocyte, Tactile

**Corral** Kraal, OK

**Correct(ive), Correcting, Correctly, Correctness, Correction, Corrector** About east, Accepted, Accurate, Alexander, Align, Amend, Aright, Blue-pencil, Bodkin, Castigate, Chasten, Chastise, Check, Cheese, Comme il faut, Corrigendum, Corrigent, Corrigible, Debug, Decorous, Diorthortic, Discipline, Edit, Emend, Epanorthosis, Ethical, Exact, Fair, Fix, Grammatical, Kosher, Legit, Letter perfect, Mark, Mend, Orthopaedic, Politically, Precise, Preterition, Probity, Proofread, Proper, Propriety, Punctilious, Punish, Purism, Rebuke, Rectify, Rectitude, Red pencil, Redress, Reform, Remedial, Reprove, Respectable, Revise, Right(en), Scold, Spinning-house, Spot-on, Straighten, Sumpsimus, Tickety-boo, Tippex®, Trew, True, Twink, U, Yep, Yes

▷**Corrected** *may indicate* an anagram

**Correlation** Ratio

**Correspond(ence), Correspondent, Corresponding** Accord, Agree, Analogy, Antimere, Assonance, Coincident, Commensurate, Communicate, Congruence, Correlate, Counterpart, Cynghanedd, Epistolist, Equality, Equate, Equivalence, Eye-rhyme, Fit, Foreign, Hate mail, Homolog(ue), Identical, Isomorph, Lobby, Match, On all fours, One-one, One to one, Par, Parallel, Parity, Pen-friend, Penpal, Post(bag), Pro rata, Relate, Rhyme, Snail mail, Special, Symmetry, Sync, Tally, Veridical, War, Write

**Corridor** Air, Aisle, Berlin, Entry, Gallery, Greenway, Lobby, Passage(-way), Penthouse, Polish, Re-entry

**Corroborate** Bear out, Confirm, Support, Underpin, Validate, Verify

**Corrode(d), Corrosion, Corrosive** Acid, Acid rain, Brinelling, Burn, Canker, Caustic, Decay, Eat, Erode, Etch, Fret, Gnaw, Hydrazine, Mordant, Oxyacid, → ROT, Rubiginous, Rust, Waste

**Corrugate** Gimp, Ridge

**Corrupt(er), Corruptible, Corrupting, Corruption** Abuse, Addle, Adulterate, Bastardise, Bent, Bobol, Bribable, Canker, Cesspit, Contaminated, Debase, Debauch, Debosh, Decadent, Defile, Degenerate, Depravity, Dishonest, Dissolute, Dry rot, Emancipate, Embrace(o)r, Embrasor, Empoison, Enseam, Etch, Evil, Faustean, Fester, Gangrene, Graft(er), Immoral, Impaired, Impure, Infect, Inquinate, Jobbery, Leprosy, Malversation, Mar, Nefarious, Obelus, Payola, Perverse, Poison, Pollute, Power, Putrefaction, Putrid, Rakery, Ret(t), Rigged, Rot, Scrofulous, Seduce, Sepsis, Septic, Sleaze, Sodom, Sophisticate, Spoil, Stench, Suborn, Taint, Tammany, Twist, Ulcered, Venal, Vice, Vitiate

**Corsage** Buttonhole, Pompadour, Posy, Spray

**Corsair** Barbary, Picaroon, Pirate, Privateer, Robber, Rover

**Corset, Corslet** Belt, Bodice, Busk, Featherbone, Girdle, Hourglass, Lorica, Roll-on, Stays, Thorax, Waspie, Whalebone

**Corsican** Napoleon

**Cortege** Parade, Retinue, Train

**Cortex** Cerebral, Renal

**Cortisone** Hecogenin

**Corundum** Emery, Sapphire

**Coruscate** Flash

**Corvo** Rolfe

**Corybant** Roisterer

**Cosh** Billy, Bludgeon, Chemical, Life preserver, Mug, Sap

**Cosmetic** Aloe vera, Beautifier, Blusher, Bronzer, Chapstick, Conditioner, Detangler, Exfoliant, Eye-black, Eyeliner, Eye-shadow, Face cream, Face-lift, Face-pack, Foundation, Fucus, Highlighter, Kohl, Lightener, Liner, Lip gloss, Lip liner, Lippie, Lipstick, Lotion, Mahua butter, Make-up, Maquillage, Mascara, Moisturizer, Mousse, Mudpack, Nail polish, Paint, Panstick, Pearl-powder, Pearl-white, Perfume, Powder, Q-tip, Reface, Rouge, Talcum, Toiletry, Toner, Warpaint

▸**Cosmic** *see* COSMOS

**Cosmonaut** Gagarin, Spaceman, Tereshkova

**Cosmopolitan** International, Urban

**Cosmos, Cosmic** Globe, Heaven, Infinite, Mundane, Nature, Space, Universe, World

**Cossack** Ataman, Hetman, Kazak(h), Mazeppa, Russian, Tartar, Zaporogian

**Cosset** Caress, Coddle, Fondle, Indulge, Nanny, Pamper

**Cost(s), Costly** Be, Bomb, Carriage, Charge, Current, Damage, Dear, Direct, Disadvantage, Earth, Escuage, Estimate, Exes, → EXPENSE, Factor, Fare, Fetched, Fixed, High-priced, Hire, Historic(al), Indirect, Legal, Loss, Marginal, Opportunity, Outlay, Overhead, Precious, Price, Prime, Quotation, Rate, Rent, Running, Sacrifice, Standard, Storage, Sumptuous, Tab, Toll, Unit, Upkeep, Usurious, Variable

**Costa Rica(n)** Tico

**Costermonger** Barrow-boy, Kerb-merchant, Pearly, Pearly king, Pearly queen

**Costume(s)** Apparel, Attire, Bikini, Camagnole, Cossie, Crinoline, Disguise, Drag, Dress, Ensemble, Garb, Get-up, Gi(e), Guise, Habit, Judogi, Livery, Maillot, Monokini, Motley, National, Nebris, Polonaise, Rig, Ruana, Surcoat, Tanga, Togs, Trollopee, Tutu, Uniform, Wardrobe, Wear

**Cosy** Cosh, Gemutlich, Homely, Intime, Snug

**Cot** Bassinet, Bed(stead), Carry, Cotangent, Dovehouse, Moses basket, Travel

**Coterie** Camarilla, Cell, Cenacle, Circle, Clan, Clique, Club, Faction, Ring, Set, Society

**Cottage(r)** Bach, Batch, Bordar, Bothie, Bothy, Bower, Box, Bungalow, Cabin, Cape Cod, Chalet, Cot, Crib, Da(t)cha, Dove, Gite, Home-croft, Hut, Lodge, Mailer, Thatched, Tied

**Cotton** Absorbent, Agree, AL, Alabama, Balbriggan, Batiste, Batting, Bengal, Calico, Candlewick, Ceiba, Chambray, Cheesecloth, Chino, Chintz, Collodion, Coutil(le), Cretonne, Denim, Dho(o)ti, Dimity, Ducks, Fustian, Galatea, Gingham, Gossypine, Gossypium,

Humhum, Ihram, Jaconet, Kapok, Lavender, Lawn, Lea, Lille, Lint, Lisle, Longcloth, Madras, Manchester, Marcella, Muslin, Nainsook, Nankeen, Nankin, Nap, Osnaburg, Percale, Pique, Pongee, Sateen, Sea-island, Seersucker, Silesia, Stranded, Surat, T-cloth, Thread, Twig, Upland, Velveret, Velveteen

**Cotton soil** Regar, Regur

**Cotyledon** Seed-leaf

**Couch** Bed, Casting, Davenport, Daybed, → DIVAN, Express, Grass, Lurk, Palanquin, Palkee, Palki, Quick, Recamier, Sedan, Settee, Sofa, Studio, Triclinium, Vis-à-vis, Winnipeg, Word

**Coué** Auto-suggestion

**Cougar** Cat, Painter, Puma

**Cough(ing)** Bark, Chin, Croup, Expectorate, Hack, Harrumph, Hawk, Hem, Hoast, Hooping, Kink, Pertussis, Phthisis, Rale, Tisick, Tussis, Ugh, Whooping

**Could** Couth, Mought

**Council (meeting), Councillor, Counsel(lor), Counselling** Achitophel, Admonish, Admonitor, Advice, Advocate, Ahithophel, Alderman, Alfred, Amphictryon, Anziani, Aread, Ar(r)e(e)de, Arts, Assembly, Attorney, Aulic, Aunt, Ayuntamiento, Bar, Board, Body, Boule, Bundesrat, Burgess, Cabal, Cabinet, Casemate, City father, Committee, Community, Consistory, Corporation, County, Cr, Decurion, Defending, Dergue, Devil, Dietine, Divan, Douma, Duma, Ecofin, Ecumenical, Egeria, Europe, European, Executive, Exhort, General, Great, Greenbag, Hebdomadal, Indaba, Induna, Industrial, Info, Islands, Jirga, Junta, Kabele, Kebele, King's, Kite, Landst(h)ing, Lateran, Latrocinium, Leader, Legislative, Loan, Lord Provost, Majlis, Mentor, Nestor, Nicaean, Nicene, Panchayat, Paraclete, Parish, Powwow, Press, Privy, Prosecuting, Provincial, Queen's, Rede, Regional, Reichsrat, Relate, Robber, Runanga, Samaritan, Sanhedrim, Sanhedrin, Security, Senate, Shoora, Shura, Sobranje, Sobranye, Soviet, States, Syndicate, Synedrion, Synod, Therapist, Thing, Town, Tradeboard, Trades, Trent, Tridentine, Trullan, Unitary, Vatican, Vizier, Volost, Wages, Whitley, Witan, Witenagemot, Works, Zemstvo, Zila, Zila parishad, Zillah

**Count(ed), Counter(balance), Counting** Abacus, Add, Algoriam, Anti, Aristo, Balance, Bank, Bar, Basie, Bean, Blood, Body, Buck, Buffet, Calculate, Calorie, Cash desk, Cashier, Cavour, Census, Check, Chip, Compute, Coost, Crystal, Cuisenaire rods, Deem, Depend, Desk, Disc, Dracula, Dump, Earl, Enumerate, Fish, Geiger, Geiger-Muller, Graf(in), Grave, Head, Itemise, Jet(t)on, Landgrave, Margrave, Marker, Matter, Meet, Merel(l), Meril, Milton work, Nobleman, Number, Numerate, Obviate, Olivia, Oppose, Outtell, Palatine, Palsgrave, Paris, Pat desk, Pollen, Presume, Proportional, Rebut, → RECKON, Refute, Rejoinder, Rely, Resist, Respond, Retaliate, Retort, Rhinegrave, Riposte, Scaler, Scintillation, Score, Shopboard, Sperm, Squail, Statistician, Stop, Sum, Table, Tally, Tell, Tiddleywink, Tolstoy, Ugolino, Walk, Weigh, Worktop, Zeppelin, Zinc

**Countdown** Blast off

**Countenance** Approve, Aspect, Brow, Endorse, Face, Favour, Mug, Sanction, Support, Visage

**Counteract(ing), Counteraction** Ant-, Antidote, Backlash, Cancel, Correct, Frustrate, Neutralise, Offset, Talion

**Counterbalance** Bascule, Offset, Undo, Weigh

**Counter-charge** Recrimination

**Counterclockwise** L(a)evorotatory

**Counterfeit(er)** Bastard, Belie, Bogus, Boodle, Brum, Coiner, Doctor, Dud, Duffer, Dummy, Fain, Fake, Fantasm, Fayne, Feign, Flash, Forge, Fraudster, Imitant, Paperhanger, Phantasm, Phoney, Pinchbeck, Postiche, Pseudo, Queer, Rap, Schlenter, Sham, Shan(d), Simular, Simulate, Skim, Slang, Slip, Smasher, Snide, Spurious, Stumer

**Counterfoil** Stub

**Counterglow** Gegenschein

**Counter-irritant** Seton

**Countermand** Abrogate, Annul, Cancel, Override, Overrule, Repeal, Rescind, Retract, Revoke, Unorder

**Counterpart** Copy, Double, Obverse, Oppo(site), Parallel, Shadow, Similar, Spit(ting), Tally, Twin

**Counterpoint** Contrapuntal, Contrast, Descant
**Countersign** Endorse, Password
**Counterthrust** Riposte
**Counterweight** Balance, Ballast
**Counties, County** Co, Comital, Comitatus, District, Hundred, Metropolitan, Palatine, Parish, Seat, Shire, Six

---

**COUNTIES**

***2 letters:***
NI
Sy

***3 letters:***
Ely
Som

***4 letters:***
Avon
Beds
Cork
Down
Fife
Kent
Mayo
Ross

***5 letters:***
Angus
Cavan
Clare
Clwyd
Derry
Devon
Dyfed
Essex
Flint
Gwent
Herts
Hunts
Kerry
Laois
Louth
Meath
Moray
Notts
Omagh
Perth
Powys
Salop
Sligo
Wilts
Worcs

***6 letters:***
Antrim
Armagh
Barset
Carlow
Dorset
Dublin
Durham
Galway
Glamis
Offaly
Surrey
Sussex
Tyrone

***7 letters:***
Cumbria
Donegal
Gwynedd
Kildare
Leitrim
Norfolk
Rutland
Suffolk
Torfaen
Wexford
Wicklow

***8 letters:***
Cheshire
Cornwall
Finnmark
Kesteven
Kilkenny
Limerick
Longford
Lothians
Monaghan
Somerset

***9 letters:***
Berkshire
Buteshire
Caithness
Champagne
Cleveland
Fermanagh
Hampshire
Loamshire
Roscommon
The Mearns
Tipperary
Waterford
Westmeath
Yorkshire

***10 letters:***
Banffshire
Ceredigion
Derbyshire
Devonshire
Humberside
Lancashire
Merseyside
Midlothian
Nairnshire
Perthshire
Shropshire
Sutherland
West Sussex

***11 letters:***
Breconshire
East Lothian
Lanarkshire
Londonderry
Oxfordshire
Radnorshire
Tyne and Wear
West Lothian

***12 letters:***
Berwickshire
Denbighshire
Kinrossshire
Lincolnshire
Mid-Glamorgan
Peeblesshire
Renfrewshire
Selkirkshire
Warwickshire
West Midlands
Westmoreland
Wigtownshire

***13 letters:***
Dumfriesshire
Herefordshire
Monmouthshire
Pembrokeshire
Roxburghshire
Staffordshire
Stirlingshire
West Glamorgan
West Yorkshire

***14 letters:***
Brecknockshire
Dumbartonshire
Glamorganshire
Invernessshire
Leicestershire
Merionethshire
Northumberland
North Yorkshire
South Glamorgan
South Yorkshire

***15 letters:***
Caernarvonshire
Carmarthenshire
Gloucestershire
Kincardineshire
Montgomeryshire
Neath Port Talbot
Ross and Cromarty
Vale of Glamorgan

***16 letters:***
Clackmannanshire
Northamptonshire

***18 letters:***
Kirkcudbrightshire

---

**Countless** Infinite, Innumerable, Myriad, Umpteen, Unending, Untold

**Country(side), Countries, Countrified** Agrest(i)al, Annam, Arcadia, Bangladesh, Bolivia, Boondocks, Bucolic, Champaign, Clime, Colchis, Dahomey, Edom, Enchorial, Farmland, Fatherland, Georgic, Greenwood, High, Homeland, Inland, Jordan, Karoo, Karroo, Kingdom, → **LAND**, Lea, Lee, Low, Macedonia, Mongolia, Motherland, Music, Nation, Nature, Nippon, Oman, Outback, Parish, Paysage, People, Province, Rangeland, Realm, Region, Republic, Rural, Rustic, Satellite, Scenery, Scythia, Soil, Statal, State, Sultanate, Terrain, The sticks, Thrace, Tundra, Tweedy, Veld, Venezuela, Weald, Wold, Yemen

**Country girl** Amaryllis

**Country house** Hall, Manor, Quinta

**Countryman** Arcadian, Bacon, Boor, Cottager, Culchie, Hayseed, Hick, Hillbilly, Hodge, National, Native, Peasant, Ruralist, Un, Yokel

**Countrywide** National

**Coup** Blow, Deal, Grand, Keystroke, KO, Masterstroke, Move, Putsch, Scoop, Stroke, Treason

**Coup d'etat** Putsch

**Coupé** Cabriolet, Drophead, Landaulet

**Couple(r), Coupling** Acoustic, Ally, Attach, Band, Brace, Bracket, Connect, Direct, Duet, Duo, Dyad, Enlink, Fishplate, Flange, Galvanic, Gemini, Geminy, Hitch, Interlock, Item, → **JOIN**, Marrow, Marry, Mate, Meng(e), Ment, Ming, Octave, Pair, Pr, Relate, Shackle, Tenace, Tie, Tirasse, Turnbuckle, Twain, Tway, Twosome, Union, Unite, Universal, Voltaic, Wed, Yoke

**Couple of ducks** Spectacles

**Couplet** Distich, Heroic, Hudibrastic, Riding-rhyme

**Coupon(s)** Ration, Ticket, Voucher

**Courage(ous)** Backbone, Balls, Ballsy, Bottle, Bravado, Bravery, Bulldog, Cojones, Daredevil, Daring, Derring-do, Doughty, Dutch, Fortitude, Gallantry, Game, Gimp, Grit, Gumption, Guts, Hardihood, Hardy, Heart, Heroism, Indomitable, Lion-heart, Macho, Manful, Mettle, Moral, Moxie, Nerve, Pluck, Prowess, Resolve, Rum, Spirit, Spirited, Spunk, Stalwart, Steel, Stomach, Valiant, Valour, Wight

**Courgette** Zucchini

**Courier** Carrier pigeon, Deliveryman, Estafette, Fed-EX, Guide, Harbinger, Herald, → **MESSENGER**, Postillion, Postman

**Course(s)** Access, Afters, Aim, Aintree, Airway, Antipasto, Appetiser, Arroyo, Ascot, Assault, Atlantic, Back straight, Barge, Bearing, Beat, Beeline, Belt, Campaign, Canal, Career, Channel, Chantilly, Chase, Circuit, Civics, Collision, Consommé, Conversation, Conversion, Correspondence, Crash, Current, Curriculum, Cursus, Daltonism, Damp(-proof), Dessert, Diadrom, Direction, Dish, Dromic, Easting, Entrée, Epsom, Fish, → **FOOD**, Foundation, Furrow, Gleneagles, Going, Golf, Goodwood, Greats, Gut, Heat, Hippodrome, Hors d'oeuvres, Induction, Isodomon, Lacing, Lane, Lap, Layer, Leat, Leet, Line, Lingfield, Links, Longchamp, Magnetic, Main, Meal, Meat, Mess, Mizzen, Newbury, Newmarket, Nine-hole, Northing, Nulla, Obstacle, → **OF COURSE**, Orbit, Orientation, Orthodromic, Period, Policy, PPE, Practicum, Procedure, Process, Prognosis, Programme, Progress, Pursue, Quadrivium, Race, → **RACETRACK**, Raik, Ravioli, Refresher, Regimen, Rhumb, Ride, Ring, Rink, Road, Rota, Route, Routine, Run, Rut, Sandown, Sandwich, Semester, Seminar, Series, Slalom, Sorbet, Soup, Southing, Span, Stadium, Starter, Stearage, Steerage, Step(s), Straight, Stratum, Streak, Stream, Stretch, Stretching, String, Subject, Succession, Syllabus, Tack, Tanride, Tenor, Track, Trade, Trail, Trajectory, Trend, Troon, Vector, Via media, Water table, Way, Wearing, Wentworth, Westing

**Court(ier), Courtship, Courtyard** Ad(vantage), Address, Admiralty, Appeal, Appellate, Arbitration, Arches, Areopagus, Atrium, Attention, Audience, Audiencia, Aula, Banc, Bar, Basecourt, Bench, Beth Din, Bishop's, Boondock, Borough, Caerleon, Camelot, Canoodle, Caravanserai, Cassation, Centre, Chancery, Chase, Church, Clay, Cloister-garth, Commercial, Commissary, Commission, Conscience, Conservancy, Consistory, County, Criminal, Crown, CS, Ct, Curia, Curia Regis, Curtilage, Cutcher(r)y, Damocles, Date, Dedans, Deuce, Dicastery, Diplock, District, Divisional, Doctor's Commons, Domestic, Duchy, Durbar, Dusty Feet, En tout cas, Evora, Eyre, Faculties, Federal, Fehm(gericht), Fehmgerichte, Fiars, Fifteen, Forensic, Forest, Forum, Fronton, Galleria, Garth, General Assembly, Go steady, Grass, Guildenstern,

Halimot(e), Hampton, Hard, High, High Commission, Hof, Holy See, Hustings, Hypaethron, Inferior, Innyadr, Intermediate, Invite, Jack, Judicatory, Justice, Juvenile, Kachahri, Kacheri, Kangaroo, Keys, King, King's Bench, Kirk Session, Knave, Law, Law Lords, Leet, Lobby, Lyon, Magistrate's, Majlis, Marshalsea, Mash, Moot, Old Bailey, Open, Osric, Palace, Parvis, Patio, Peristyle, Petty Sessions, Philander, Piepowder, Police, Porte, Praetorium, Prerogative, Presbytery, Prize, Probate, Provincial, Provost, Quad, Quarter Sessions, Queen, Queen's Bench, Racket, Request, Retinue, Romance, Rosenkrantz, Royal, St James's, Sanhedrim, Sanhedrin, Scottishland, See, Seek, Service, Session, Sheriff, Shire-moot, Shoe, Small-claims, Spoon, Stannary, Star Chamber, Sudder, Sue, Suitor, Superior, Supreme, Swanimote, Sweetheart, Synod, Tennis, Thane, Thegn, Traffic, Trial, Tribunal, Vehm, Vehmgericht(e), Vestibulum, Walk out, Ward, Wardmote, Wench, Woo, World, Wow, Yard, Youth

**Courteous, Courtesy** Affable, Agreement, Bow, Chivalry, Civil, Comity, Debonair, Devoir, Etiquette, Fair, Genteel, Gentilesse, Gentility, Gracious, Hend, Obliging, Polite, Politesse, Refined, Strain, Urbanity, Well-mannered

**Courtesan** Anonyma, Aspasia, Bianca, Bona-roba, Delilah, Demi-monde, Demi-rep, Geisha, Hetaera, Lais, Lampadion, Lorette, Madam, Phryne, Plover, Pornocracy, Prostitute, Stallion, Thais

**Courtly** Aulic, Chivalrous, Cringing, Dignified, Flattering, Refined

**Court-martial** Drumhead

**Courtyard** Area, Atrium, Close, Cortile, Enceinte, Garth, Marae, Patio, Quad(rangle)

**Cousin(s)** Bette, Cater, Country, Coz, Cross, First, German, Kin, Kissing, Parallel, Robin, Second, Skater

**Couthy** Bien, Nice

**Couturier** Amies, Chanel, Designer, Dior, Dressmaker, Hartnell

**Cove** Abraham's, Arm, Bay, Bight, Buffer, Creek, Cure, Gink, Grot, Guy, Hithe, Hythe, Inlet, Lulworth, Nook

**Covenant(er)** Abrahamic, Alliance, Appurtenant, Bond, Contract, Hillmen, Pledge, Restrictive, Testament, Warranty, Whiggamore

**Coventry** Isolation, Ostracism

**Cover(ed), Coverage, Covering** Adventitia, Air, A l'abri, Amnion, Antependium, Antimacassar, Apron, Aril, Armour, Attire, Awning, Bandage, Barb, Bard, Bark, Bathrobe, Bed linen, Bedspread, Bestrew, Bind, Blanket, Blindfold, Bodice, Bonnet, Breadcrumbs, Brood, Bubblewrap, Burka, Bury, Cache-sex, Camouflage, Canopy, Cap, Caparison, Cape, Capsule, Carpet, Cartonnage, Casing, Casque, Catch-all, Caul, Caulk, Ceil, Cementum, Ciborium, Ciel, Cladding, Clapboard, Cleithral, Cling film, Clithral, Cloak, Cloche, Coat, Cocoon, Coleorhiza, Conceal, Cope, Copyright, Cosy, Cot, Counterpane, Cour, Covert, Cowl, Crust, Curtain, Deadlight, Debruised, Deck, Deputise, Disguise, Dividend, Dome, Drape(t), Dripstone, Duchesse, Dusting, Dust jacket, Dust-sheet, Duvet, Egg-cosy, Eiderdown, Encase, Endue, Enguard, Enlace, Ensheathe, Enshroud, Envelop(e), Enwrap, Exoderm(is), Exoskeleton, Exposure, Extra, Eyelid, Eye patch, Face, Falx, Fanfare, Fascia, Felting, Fielder, Figleaf, Fingerstall, First-day, Flap, Flashing, Flown, Fother, Front, Frontal, Gaiter, Gambado, Gift wrap, Gild, Gilt, Glove, Gobo, Grolier, Ground, Groundsheet, G-string, Guarantee, Hap, Harl, Hat, Hatch, Havelock, Heal, Heather, Heel, Hejab, Hele, Hell, Helmet, Hide, Hijab, Hood, Housing, Hubcap, Husk, Ice, Immerse, Incase, Include, Indument, Indusium, Inmask, Insulate, Insurance, Insure, Integument, Jacket, Lag, Lambrequin, Laminate, Lampshade, Lay, Leap, Leep, Legging, Legwarmer, Lid, Ligger, Liner, Loincloth, Loose, Manche, Manhole, Mantle, Mask, Mat, Membrane, Metal, Mort-cloth, Mount, Muffle, Mulch, Notum, Numnah, Obliterate, Obscure, OC, Occlude, On, Oose, Operculum, Orillion, Orlop, Overgrown, Overlap, Overlay, Overnet, Overwrap, Pad, Palampore, Palempore, Pall, Pand, Panoply, Parcel, Partlet, Pasties, Patch, Patent, Pave, Pavilion, Pebbledash, Pelmet, Pent, Periderm, Perigone, Pillow sham, Pinny, Plaster, Plate, Pleura, Plumage, Pod, Point, Pseudonym, Pullover, Quilt, Radome, Redingote, Regolith, Render, Report, Riza, Robe, Roof, Roughcast, Rug, Run, Saddlecloth, Sally, Sarafan, Scabbard, Screen, Serviette, Setting, Shagpile, Shawl, Sheath, Sheet, Shell, Shelter, Shield, Shower, Shrink-wrap, Shroud, Shuck, Shutter, Skin, Sleeve, Slipcase, Smokescreen, Solleret, Span, Spat, Splashback, Spread, Stand-by, Stand-in, Stifle, Stomacher, Strew, Strow, Superfrontal, Superimpose, Surplice, Swathe, Tampian, Tampion,

Tapadera, Tapis, Tarmac, Tarp(aulin), Teacosy, Tectorial, Tectum, Tegmen, Tegument, Tent, Terne, Test(a), Tester, Thatch, Thimble, Thong, Throw, Thumbstall, Tick(ing), Tidy, Tile, Tilt, Tinfoil, Toecap, Tonneau, Top, Topsoil, Trapper, Trench, Trip, Turtleback, Twill, Twilt, Umbrella, Underlay, Up, Upholster, Valance, Veale, Veil, Vele, Veneer, Ventail, Vert, Vesperal, Vest, Vestiture, Visor, Volva, Wainscot, Warrant, Waterdeck, Weeper, Whelm, Whemmle, Whitewash, Whomble, Whommle, Whummle, Wrap, Wrappage, Wrapper, Wreathe, Yapp, Yashmak

**Covert(ly)** Clandestine, Copse, Privy, → **SECRET**, Shy, Sidelong, Stealthy, Sub rosa, Surreptitious, Tectrix, Ulterior

**Covet(ed), Covetous** Avaricious, Crave, Desiderata, Desire, Eager, Envy, Greedy, Hanker, Jealous, Yearn

**Cow(s)** Adaw, Alderney, Amate, Appal, Awe, Ayrshire, Belted Galloway, Boss(y), Bovine, Brahmin, Browbeat, Cash, Cattle, Charolais, Colly, Crummy, Dant(on), Daunt, Dexter, Dsomo, Dun, Friesian, Frighten, Galloway, Gally, Goujal, Guernsey, Hawkey, Hawkie, Heifer, Hereford, Humlie, Intimidate, Jersey, Kouprey, Kyloe, Lea(h), Limousin, Mart, Milch, Milker, Mog(gie), Moggy, Mooly, Muley, Mulley, Neat, Oppress, Overawe, Ox-eyed, Redpoll, Red Sindhi, Rother(-beast), Runt, Sacred, Santa Gertrudis, Scare, Simmental, Slattern, Springing, Steer, Step on, Stirk, Subact, Subjugate, Teeswater, Threaten, Unnerve, Vaccine, Zebu, Z(h)o

**Coward(ice), Cowardly** Bessus, Cat, Chicken, Cocoa, Craven, Cuthbert, Dastard, Dingo, Dunghill, Faint-heart, Fraidy-cat, Fugie, Funk, Gutless, Hen, Hilding, Jessie, Lily-livered, Mangy, Meacock, Milk-livered, Nesh, Niddering, Nidderling, Nidering, Niderling, Niding, Nithing, Noel, Panty-waist, Poltroon, Pusillanimous, Recreant, Scaramouch(e), Scaredy cat, Sganarelle, Sissy, Slag, Sook, Spineless, Squib, Viliaco, Viliago, Villagio, Villiago, Weak-spirited, White feather, Yellow, Yellow-belly, Yellowstreak

**Cowboy, Cowgirl** Broncobuster, Buckaroo, Buckayro, Buckeroo, Cowpoke, Cowpuncher, Gaucho, Gunslinger, Herdboy, Incompetent, Inexpert, Io, Jerrybuilder, Leger, Llanero, Neatherd, Puncher, Ranchero, Ritter, Roper, Shoddy, Vaquero, Waddie, Waddy, Wrangler

**Cow-catcher** Fender, Reata

**Cower** Cringe, Croodle, Crouch, Fawn, Quail, Recoil, Ruck, Skulk, Wince

**Cowhide** Leather

**Cowl** Bonnet, Capuchin, Friar's, Granny, Hood, Kilmarnock

**Cowpat** Dung, Tath

**Cowpox** Vaccinia

**Cowshed, Cowstall** Byre, Crib, Loaning, Shippen, Shippon, Stable, Stall, Staw

**Cowslip** Culver-key, Herb Peter, Pa(i)gle

**Cox** Helmsman, Steerer

**Coxcomb** Aril, Caruncle, Copple, Crest, Dandy, Dude, Fop, Jackanapes, Popinjay, Yellow-rattle

**Coy** Arch, Coquettish, Demure, Laithfu', Mim, Modest, Nice, Shamefast, → **SHY**, Skeigh, Skittish

**Coyote** Prairie-wolf, SD

**CPRS** Think tank

**Crab(by), Crablike, Crabwise** Apple, Attercop, Blue swimmer, Boston, Calling, Cancer, Cancroid, Cantankerous, Capernoity, Cock, Coconut, Crusty, Daddy, Decapoda, Diogenes, Dog, Ethercap, Ettercap, Fiddler, Ghost, Glass, Grouch, Hard-shell, Hermit, Horse-foot, Horseman, Horseshoe, Keavie, King, Land, Limulus, Mantis, Mitten, Mud, Nebula, Ochidore, Oyster, Pagurian, Partan, Pea, Perverse, Podite, Roast, Robber, Rock, Sand, Saucepan-fish, Scrawl, Scrog, Sentinel, Sidewards, Sidle, Soft-shell, Soldier, Spectre, Spider, Std, Stone, Velvet, Velvet-fiddler, Woolly-hand, Xiphosura, Zoea

▷**Crab** *may indicate* an anagram

**Crab-apple** Scrog-bush, Scrog-buss

**Crab-eater** Urva

**Crabs-eye** Abrus

**Crack(ed), Cracker(s), Cracking** A1, Ace, Ad-lib, Admirable, Attempt, Bananas, Beaut, Biscuit, Bonbon, Break, Cat, Catalytic, Chap, Chasm, Chat, Chink, Chip, Chop, Clap, Cleave, Cleft, Cloff, Confab, Cranny, Craquelure, Craqueture, Craze, Cream, Crepitate, Crevasse,

Crevice, Crispbread, Dawn, Decipher, Decode, Def, Doom, Dunt, Eggshell, Elite, Excellent, Expert, Fab, Fatiscent, Fent, Firework, First-rate, Fisgig, Fissure, Fizgig, Flake, Flaw, Flip-flop, Fracture, Gap, Gem, Gibe, Go, Graham, Grike, Gryke, Gully, Gunshot, Hairline, Hit, Insane, Jest, Jibe, Joint, Joke, Knacker, Leak, Liar, Little-endian, Lulu, Matzo, Mot, Moulin, One-liner, Oner, Perlite, Petard, Peterman, Pleasantry, Pore, Praise, Prawn, Quarter, Quip, Rap, Rent, Report, Rhagades, Rictus, Rift, Rille, Rima, Rime, Rimous, Rive, Rock, Saltine, Sand, Seam, Shake, Shatter, Snap, Soda, Solve, Splinter, Split, Spring, Squib, Star, Sulcus, Sun, Super, Toe, Top, Try, Waterloo, Whipcord, Wind shake, Witticism, Yegg

**Crackerjack** Ace, Nailer, Trump

**Crackle, Crackling** Craze, Crepitation, Crepitus, Crinkle, Decrepitate, Fizz, Glaze, Rale, Rustle, Skin, Static

**Crackpot** Headbanger, Nutter, Raver

**Cracksman** Burglar, Peterman, Raffles

**Cradle** Bassinet, Berceau, Book rest, Cat's, Cot, Crib, Cunabula, Hammock, Knife, Nestle, Newton's, Rocker

**Craft(y), Craftwork** Adroitness, Aerostat, Arch, Art, Aviette, Barbola, Batik, Boat, Canal boat, Canny, Cautel, Coracle, Crochet, Cunning, Designing, Devious, Disingenuous, Expertise, Finesse, Flotilla, Fly, Foxy, Guile, Hydroplane, Ice-breaker, Insidious, Knack, Kontiki, Landing, Lifeboat, Loopy, Machiavellian, Marquetry, Mister, Mystery, Oomiack, Pedalo, Pirogue, Powerboat, Reynard, Saic, Shallop, Ship, Shrewd, Shuttle, →**SKILL**, Slee, Sleeveen, Slim, Slippy, Sly, Slyboots, Sneaky, Speedboat, State, Subdolous, Subtil(e), Subtle, Surface, Suttle, Tender, Trade, Triphibian, Umiak, Underhand, Versute, →**VESSEL**, Wicker, Wile, Workmanship

▹**Craft** *may indicate* an anagram

**Craftsman, Craftsmen** AB, Artificer, Artisan, Artist, Blue Blanket, Cabinet maker, Chippy, Coppersmith, Cutler, Ebonist, Enameller, Fabergé, Finisher, Glass-blower, Glass-cutter, Glazier, Gondolier, Guild, Hand, Joiner, Journeyman, Mason, Mechanic, Morris, Opificer, Potter, Saddler, Stonemason, Tinsmith, Wainwright, Wright

**Crag(gy)** Coralline, Eyrie, Gnarled, Height, Heuch, Heugh, Krantz, Noup, Rock, Rugged

**Craig** Ailsa

**Cram(mer), Crammed** Bag, Bone up, Candle-waster, Chock-a-block, Cluster, Craig, Fill, Gag, Gavage, Mug up, Neck, Pang, Prime, Revise, Rugged, Scar(p), Shoehorn, Spur, Stap, Stodge, Stow, Swat, Tuck

**Cramp(ed)** Agraffe, Charleyhorse, Claudication, Confine, Constrict, Crick, Hamper, Hamstring, Incommodious, Musician's, Myalgia, Narrow, Pinch, Poky, Potbound, Restrict, Rigor, Sardines, Scrivener's palsy, Spasm, Squeeze, Stunt, Tenesmus, Tetany, Tight, Writer's

**Cranberry** Fen-berry

**Crane, Crane-driver** Adjutant-bird, Australian, Brolga, Cherry picker, Container, Davit, Deck, Demoiselle, Derrick, Dogman, Dragline, Floating, Gantry, Gooseneck, Grabbing, Herd, Heron, Hooper, Ichabod, Jenny, Jib, Jigger, Kenworthy, Luffing-jib, Native companion, Numidian, Rail, Sandhill, Sarus, Sedge, Seriema, Shears, Sheer, Siege, Stork, Stretch, Tower, Tulip, Whooper, Whooping, Winch

**Crane-fly** Daddy-long-legs, Leatherjacket, Spinning-jenny, Tipulidae

**Cranium** Harnpan

**Crank(y)** Bell, Eccentric, Grouch, Handle, Lever, Mot, Oddball, Perverse, Start, Weirdo, Whim, Wince, Winch, Wind

**Crap** Feculence

**Crapulous** Hungover

**Crash** Accident, Bingle, Collapse, Disk, Ditch, Dush, Fail, Fall, Fragor, Frush, Intrude, Linen, Meltdown, Nosedive, Pile up, Plough into, Prang, Rack, Ram, Rhino, Rote, Shock, Shunt, Slam, Smash, South Sea Bubble, Thud, Thunderclap, Topple, Wall Street, Wham, Wrap

▹**Crashes** *may indicate* an anagram

**Crass** Boor, Coarse, Crude, Gross, Naff, Rough, Rude

**Crate** Banger, Biplane, Box, Case, Ceroon, Crib, Hamper, Heap, Jalopy, Langrenus, Petavius, Purbach, Rustbucket, Sero(o)n, Soapbox, Tea chest, Tube

**Crater** Aldrin, Alphonsus, Aniakchak, Aristarchus, Aristotle, Askja, Autolycus, Bail(l)y,

Blowhole, Caldera, Cavity, Cissing, Clavius, Copernicus, Dent, Fra Mauro, Grimaldi, Hipparchus, Hole, Hollow, Impact, Kepler, Kilauea, Maar, Meteor, Newton, Pit, Plato, Ptolemaeus, Pythagoras, Schickard, Sinus iridum, Theophilus, Tycho

**Cravat** Ascot, Neckatee, Neck-cloth, Oerlay, Overlay, Scarf, Soubise, Steenkirk, Steinkirk, Tie

**Crave, Craving** Appetent, Appetite, Aspire, Beg, Beseech, Covet, Desire, Entreat, Gasp, Greed, Hanker, Hunger, Itch, Libido, Long, Lust, Malacia, Methomania, Munchies, Opsomania, Orexis, Passion, Pica, Polyphagia, Sitomania, The munchies, Thirst, Yearn, Yen

**Craven** Abject, Artless, Coward, Dastard, Hen, Non-hero, Recreant

**Crawl(er)** All fours, Aswarm, Australian, Back, Booze up, Clamber, Creep, Cringe, Drag, Emmet, Escargot, Front, Grovel, Inchworm, Isopod, Jenkins, Lag, Lickspittle, Louse, Low gear, Pub, Reptile, Scramble, Scrome, Side, Skulk, Slither, Smarm, Snail, Swim, Sycophant, Tantony, Termite, Trail, Truckle, Trudge(o)n, Yes-man

**Crayfish** Astacology, Gilgie, Jilgie, Marron, Yabbie, Yabby

**Crayon** Chalk, Colour, Conté®, Pastel, Pencil, Sauce

**Craze(d), Crazy** Absurd, Ape, Apeshit, Avid, Barking, Barmy, Bats, Batty, Berserk, Bonkers, Break, Bug, Cornflake, Crack(ers), Crackpot, Cult, Daffy, Dement, Derange, Dingbats, Dippy, Distraught, Doiled, Doilt, Doolally, Doolally tap, Dottle, Dotty, Fad, Flaky, Flaw, Folie, Frantic, Furious, Furore, Furshlugginer, Gaga, Geld, Gonzo, Gyte, Haywire, Headbanger, Headcase, Insane, Kooky, Loco, Loony, Loopy, Lunatic, Madden, Maenad(ic), Mania, Manic, Mattoid, Melomania, Meshug(g)a, Moonstruck, Nuts, Odd, Out to lunch, Porangi, Potty, Psycho(path), Rage, Ramp, Rave, Round the bend, Round the twist, Scatty, Screwball, Screwy, Skivie, Slatey, Stir, Stunt, Thing, Troppo, Typomania, Unhinge, Up the wall, Wacko, W(h)acky, Wet, Whim, Wowf, Zany

▷**Crazy** *may indicate* an anagram

**Creak(y)** Cry, Grate, Grind, Rheumatic, Scraich, Scraigh, Scroop, Seam, Squeak

**Cream(y)** Balm, Barrier, Bavarian, Best, Chantilly, Cherry-pick, Cleansing, Clotted, Cold, Cornish, Crème fraîche, Devonshire, Double, Elite, Flower, Foundation, Frangipane, Ganache, Glacier, Hand, Heavy, Ivory, Jollop, Lanolin, Liniment, Lotion, Mousse, Off-white, Ointment, Opal, Paragon, Pastry, Peppermint, Pick, Ream, Rich, Salad, Salve, Shaving, Sillabub, Single, Skim, Smitane, Sour, Sun(screen), Syllabub, Unguent, Vanishing, Whipped, Whipping

**Creamery** Dairy

**Crease(d)** Bowling, Crinkle, Crumple, → **FOLD**, Goal, Lined, Lirk, Pitch, Pleat, Ply, Popping, Return, Ridge, Ruck(le), Ruga, Rugose, Rumple, Wreathe, Wrinkle

**Create, Creation, Creative** Artificer, Art(s)y, Brahma, Brainstorm, Build, Cause, Coin, Compose, Continuous, Cosmos, Craft, Devise, Dreamtime, Engender, Establish, Fabricate, Forgetive, Form, Found, Frankenstein, Generate, Genesis, Godhead, Hexa(h)emeron, Ideate, Imaginative, Inspire, Intellectual, → **INVENT**, Kittle, Knit, Nature, Omnific, Oratorio, Originate, Produce, Promethean, Shape, Stylist, Synthesis, Universe

**Creator** Ahura Mazda, Author, Demiurge, Demiurgus, God, Inventor, Maker, Ormazd, Ormuzd

**Creature** Animal, Ankole, Basilisk, Beast, Being, Bigfoot, Catfish, Chevrotain, Chocolate, Cratur, Critter, Crittur, Indri, Krill, Leviathan, Mammal, Man, Moner(on), Nekton, Organism, Reptile, Saprobe, Sasquatch, Seahorse, Sphinx, Whiskey, Wight, Zoon

**Creche** Day care, Nursery

**Credence, Credential(s)** Certificate, Document, ID, Papers, Qualifications, Shelf, Testimonial

**Credibility, Credible, Credit(or), Credits** Ascribe, Attribute, Belief, Billboard, Brownie points, Byline, Carbon, Catholic, Crawl, Easy terms, Esteem, Extended, Family, Ghetto, Honour, HP, Kite, Kudos, LC, Lender, Mense, Never-never, On the nod, Overdraft, Post-war, Probable, Reliable, Renown, Repute, Revolving, Shylock, Social, Strap, Street, Surmisable, Tab, Tally, Tax, Tick, Title, Trust, Wash, Weight, Youth

**Credulous** Charlie, Gobe-mouches, Green, Gullible, Naive, Simple, Superstitious, Trusting

**Creed** Apostles', Athanasian, Belief, Doctrine, Faith, Ideology, Islam, Ism, Nicene, Ophism, Outworn, Persuasion, Sect, Tenet

**Creek** Antietam, Bay, Breaches, Cooper, Cove, Crick, Dawson, Estuary, Fleet, Geo, Gio, Goe, Indian, Inlet, Josephine, Kill, Pow, Slough, Vae, Voe, Wick

**Creel** Basket, Hask, Scull, Skull
**Creep(er), Creeping, Creeps, Creepy** Ai, Ampelopsis, Arbutus, Aseismic, Asp, Bog-pimpernel, Boston ivy, Cleavers, Crawl, Eery, Function, Grew, Grovel, Grue, Heebie-jeebies, Heeby-jeebies, Herpetic, Honey, Inch, Insect, Ivy, Mission, Nerd, Nuthatch, Periwinkle, Pussyfoot, Repent, Reptant, Sarmentous, Sidle, Silverweed, Sinister, Sittine, Skulk, Slink, Snake, Sneak(sby), Sobole(s), Soil, Speedwell, Steal, Toad, Tropaeolum, Truckle, Uncanny, Vinca, Vine, Virginia, Wickthing, Willies
**Creeping Jenny** Moneywort
**Creepy-crawly** Bug
**Cremate, Cremation, Crematorium** Burn, Char, Cinerarium, Ghat, Ghaut, Incinerate, Pyre, Sati, Suttee, Ustrinium
**Creole** Gullah, Haitian, Kriol, Papiamento, Tok Pisin
**Crepe** Blini, Blintz(e), Canton, Pancake
**Crescendo** Swell
**Crescent** Barchan(e), Bark(h)an, Fertile, Growing, Lune(tte), Lunulate, Lunule, Meniscus, Moon, Red, Sickle, Waxing
**Cresol** Lysol®
**Cress** Cardamine, Garden, Hoary, Indian, Isatis, Pepperwort, St Barbara's, Spanish, Swine's, Thale, Wart, Water, Yellow
**Crest(ed)** Acme, Brow, Chine, Cimier, Cockscomb, Comb, Copple, Cornice, Crista, Height, Hilltop, Kirimon, Knap, Mon, Peak, Pileate, Pinnacle, Plume, Ridge, Rig, Summit, Tappit, Tee, →TOP, Topknot, Tufty, Wreath
**Crestfallen** Sad
**Cretaceous** Chalky, Senonian, The Chalk
**Cretan** Candiot(e), Minoan, Teucer
**Crevasse** Bergschrund, Chasm, Gorge, Rimaye
**Crevice** Chine, Cleft, Cranny, Fissure, Interstice, Ravine, Vallecula
**Crew** Boasted, Cabin, Company, Complement, Co-pilot, Core, Deckhand, Eight, Eightsmen, Equipage, Four, Gang, Ground, Lot, Manners, Men, Oars, Prize, Roadie, Sailors, Salts, Seamen, Ship men, Team, Teme, Torpid
**Crew-cut** Not(t)
**Crib** Aid, Cheat, Cot, Cowhouse, Cradle, Cratch, Filch, Horse, →KEY, Manger, Pony, Purloin, Putz, Shack, Stall, Steal, Trot, Trough
**Crick** Cramp, Kink, Spasm
**Cricket(er), Cricket term** All-rounder, Balm, Bat, Benaud, Blockhole, Bosanquet, Botham, Bowler, Bradman, CC, Cicada, Dry-bob, Edrich, Extra cover, Fly slip, French, Gentleman, Gower, Grace, Grasshopper, Grig, Hobbs, Hopper, Hutton, Jerusalem, Katydid, Keeper, Knott, Lara, Larwood, Leg, Lloyd, Long-leg, Long-off, Long-on, Longstop, March, May, Mid-on, Mole, Muggleton, Nightwatchman, Nurdle, Offbreak, Off-spinner, Opener, Orthoptera, Overs, Pace bowler, Packer, Player, Plumb, Point, Pyjama, Shield, Single-wicket, Slip, Sobers, Spin bowler, Stool, Stridulate, Tate, Test, Tettix, Tip and run, Twenty-twenty, Vigoro, Warner, Wart-biter, Windball, Windies, Wisden, XI (gent), Yahoo
**Cricket ground** Edgbaston, Lord's, The Oval
**Crier** Bellman, Herald, Muezzin, Niobe, Outrooper
**Crikey** Argh, Gosh, I say, Strewth
**Crime** ABH, Attentat, Barratry, Bias, Caper, Car jack, Chantage, Chaud-mellé, Computer, Corpus delicti, Ecocide, Embracery, Enormity, Fact, Felony, Filicide, Fraud, GBH, Graft, Hate, Heist, Infraction, Iniquity, Inside job, Insider trading, Malefaction, Malfeasance, Mayhem, Misdeed, Misdemeanour, →OFFENCE, Organised, Ovicide, Peccadillo, Perjury, Pilferage, Public wrong, Racket, Ram raid, Rap, Rape, Rebellion, →SIN, Snaffling-lay, Stranger, Theft, Thievery, Tort, Transgression, Treason, Victimless, Villa(i)ny, War, White-collar, Wrong
**Crimea** Balaclava
**Crime-fighter** Vigilante
**Criminal** Accessory, Arsonist, Baddie, Bandit, Bent, Bigamist, Bushranger, Capone, Chain gang, Chummy, Con, Cosa Nostra, Counterfeiter, Crack-rope, →CROOK, Culpable, Culprit, Delinquent, Desperado, Escroc, Evildoer, Fagin, Felon, Flagitious, Forensic, Fraudster,

Fraudulent, Gangster, Goombah, Gunslinger, Hard men, Heavy, Heinous, Highbinder, Highwayman, Hitman, Hood(lum), Illegal, Jailbird, Ladrone, Lag, Larcener, Lifer, Looter, Lowlife, Maf(f)ia, Malefactor, Maleficent, Malfeasant, Mens rea, Miscreant, Mob(ster), Molester, Ndrangheta, Nefarious, Nefast, Offender, Outlaw, Peculator, Pentito, Perp(etrator), Peterman, Prohibited, Racketeer, Ram raider, Receiver, Recidivist, Reprehensible, Reprobate, Ripper, Rogue, Rustler, Safe blower, Safe-cracker, Sinner, Snakehead, Terrorist, Thief, Thug, Transgressor, Triad, Triggerman, Underworld, Villain, Wicked, Wire, Yakuza, Yardie, Yegg

▷**Criminal** *may indicate* an anagram

**Criminologist** Lombroso

**Crimp, Crimper** Hairdresser, Pleat, Quill

**Crimson** Carmine, Cramesy, Cramoisy, Incarnadine, Modena, Red, Scarlet

**Cringe, Cringing** Cower, Creep, Crouch, Cultural, Dread, Fawn, Grovel, Recoil, Shrink, Sneaksby, Sycophantic, Truckle, Wince

**Crinkle, Crinkly** Corrugated, Rugate, Rugose

**Crinoline** Farthingale, Hoop

**Cripple(d)** Damage, Debilitate, Disable, Game, Hamstring, Hamstrung, Handicap, Injure, →LAME, Lameter, Lamiter, Maim, Paralyse, Polio, Scotch, Spoil

**Crisis** Acme, Craunch, Crunch, Drama, Emergency, Exigency, Fastigium, Fit, Flap, Head, Identity, Make or break, Midlife, Panic, Pass, Pinch, Quarterlife, Shake-out, Showdown, Solution, Suez, Test, Turn, Turning-point

**Crisp(ness)** Brisk, Clear, Crimp, Crunchy, Fire-edge, Fresh, Potato, Sharp, Short, Succinct, Terse

**Crispin** Sutor(ial)

**Criss-cross** Alternate, Fret, Interchange, Intersect, Lattice, Vein

**Criteria, Criterion** Benchmark, Gauge, Koch's postulates, Measure, Precedent, Proof, Rayleigh, Rule, Shibboleth, →STANDARD, Test, Touchstone

**Critic(al), Criticise, Criticism** Acute, Agate, Agee, Animadversion, Archer, Aristarch, Armchair, Arnold, Attack, Backbite, Badmouth, Bagehot, Barrack, Belabour, Bellettrist, Berate, Bird, Bitch, Blame, Boileau, Boo, Bottom line, Brickbat, Bucket, Captious, Carp, Castigate, Cavil, Censor(ious), →CENSURE, Climacteric, Clobber, Comment, Condemn, Connoisseur, Crab, Criticaster, Crossroads, →CRUCIAL, Crunch, Dangle, Decisive, Denigrate, Denounce, Deprecate, Desperate, Detractor, Diatribe, Dig, Disapprobation, Diss, Do down, Dress down, Dutch uncle, Earful, Etain, Exacting, Excoriate, Exegesis, Fastidious, Fateful, Fault-finder, Feuilleton, Flak, Flay, Fulminous, Gosse, Hammer, Harrumph, Hatchet job, Higher, Iconoclast, Ideal, Important, Impugn, Inge, Inveigh, Judge, Judgemental, Judicial, Juncture, Knife-edge, Knock(er), Lambast, Lash, Leavis, Lecture, Life and death, Literary, Lower, Masora(h), Mas(s)orete, Monster, Mordacious, Nag, Nasute, Negative, Nibble, Nice, Niggle, Nitpicker, Obloquy, Overseer, Pan, Pater, Peck, Pillory, Pivotal, Poetics, Potshot, Puff, Pundit, Quibble, Rap, Rebuke, Reprehend, Reproach, Review(er), Rip, Roast, Ruskin, Savage, Scalp, Scarify, Scathe, Scorn, Second guess, Serious, Severe, Sharp-tongued, Shaw, Sideswipe, Slag, Slam, Slashing, Slate, Slaughter, Sneer, Snipe, Spray, Stick, Stricture, Strop, Swipe, Tense, Textual, Thersitic, Threap, Tipping-point, Touch and go, Trash, Turning-point, Ultracrepidate, Upbraid, Urgent, Vet, Vital, Vitriol, Vituperation, Vivisect, Watershed, Zoilean, Zoilism

**Croak(er), Croaky** Caw, Creak, Crow, Die, Grumble, Gutturalise, Hoarse, Perish, Rasp, Sciaena

**Croatia(n)** Cravates, Glagolitic, HR, Serb, Slavonian

**Crochet** Lace, Weave

**Crock** Chorrie, Crate, Jar, Mug, Olla, Pig, Pitcher, Pot, Potshard, Potshare, Potsherd, Stean(e)

**Crockery** Ceramics, China, Dishes, Earthenware, Oddment, Service, Sunbeam, Ware

**Crockett** Davy, Frontiersman

▷**Crocks** *may indicate* an anagram

**Crocodile** Bask, Cayman, Dundee, File, Flat dog, Garial, Gavial, Gharial, Gotcha lizard, Line, Mud gecko, Mugger, River-dragon, Saltie, Saltwater, Sebek, Teleosaur(ian)

**Crocus** Autumn, Meadow saffron, Naked boys, Naked lady, Prairie, Quack doctor, Saffron

**Croesus** Lydia

**Croft** Bareland, Goodman's, Pightle, Smallholding
**Cromwell** Antimonarchist, Ironside, Lord Protector, Noll, Oliver, Protector, Richard, Roundhead
**Crone(s)** Beldam(e), Ewe, Graeae, Hag, Mawkin, Ribibe, Rudas, Sibyl, Sybil, Trot, Trout, → WITCH
**Crony** Anile, Chum, Intimate, Mate, Pal, Sidekick
**Crook(ed), Crookedness** Adunc, Ajee, Angle, Aslant, Asymmetric, Awry, Bad, Bend, Bow, Cam, Camsheugh, Camsho(ch), Cock-eyed, Criminal, Cromb, Crome, Crosier, Crummack, Crummock, Crump, Curve, Dishonest, Elbow, Flex, Fraud, Heister, Hook, Ill, Indirect, Kam(me), Kebbie, Lituus, Lowlife, Mackenzie, Malpractitioner, Obliquity, Operator, Shank, Sheep-hook, Shepherd's, Shyster, Sick, Skew(whiff), Slick(er), Squint, Staff, Swindler, Thraward, Thrawart, Thrawn, Twister, Wonky, Wrong'un, Wry, Yeggman
▹**Crooked** *may indicate* an anagram
**Croon(er), Crooning** Balladeer, Bing, Como, Lament, Lull, Monody, Murmur, Sing
**Crop(ped), Cropping, Crops, Crop up** Abridge, Barley, Basset, Befall, Break, Browse, Bumper, Cash, Catch, Cereal, Clip, Corn, Cover, Craw, Culture, Cut, Distress, Dock, Emblements, Emerge, Energy, Epilate, Eton, Foison, Forage, Grain, Graze, → HAIRCUT, Harvest, Hog, Ingluvies, Kharif, Ladino, Lop, Milo, Not(t), Oats, Oilseed, Plant, Poll, Prison, Produce, Prune, Rabi, Rawn, Reap, Riding, Rod, Root, Rye, Scythe, Shave, Shear, Shingle, Silage, Sithe, Snip, Standing, Stow, Strip, Subsistence, Succession, Top, Trim, Truncate, → VEGETABLE, Wheat, White
**Cropper** Downfall, Header, Purler
**Croquet (term)** Pall Mall, Peel, Rover, Wire
**Croquette** Kromesky, Quenelle, Rissole
**Cross(ing), Crossbred, Crossbreed, Crossed** Angry, Ankh, Ansate, Archiepiscopal, Bad-tempered, Banbury, Bandog, Basta(a)rd, Baster, Beefalo, Belisha, Bestride, Bois-brule, Boton(n)e, Brent, Bridge, Bristling, Buddhist, Burden, Calvary, Cancel, Cantankerous, Canterbury, Capital, Capuchin, Cat(t)alo, Cattabu, Celtic, Channel, Charing, Chi, Chiasm(a), Choleric, Cleche, Clover-leaf, Cockapoo, Cocktail, Compital, Constantine, Crisp, Crosslet, Crosswalk, Crotchety, Cruciate, Crucifix, Crux, Cut, Decussate, Demi-wolf, Dihybrid, Double, Dso(mo), Dzobo, Eleanor, Encolpion, Faun, Fiery, Fitché, Fleury, Foil, Footbridge, Ford, Frabbit, Fractious, Frampold, Franzy, Funnel, Fylfot, Geep, Geneva, George, Grade, Greek, High, Hinny, Holy rood, Humette, Hybrid, Ill, Imp, Incensed, Indignant, Interbreed, Intersect, Intervein, Iona, Iracund, Irascible, Irate, Irked, Iron, Jersian, Jerusalem, Jomo, Jumart, King's, Kiss, Krest, Labradoodle, Ladino, Latin, Level, Liger, Lorraine, Lurcher, Maltese, Mameluco, Market, Mermaid, Miffed, Military, Misfortune, Mix, Moline, Mongrel, Monhybrid, Mule, Narky, Nattery, Node, Norman, Northern, Nuisance, Oblique, Obverse, Ordinary, Orthodox, Overpass, Overthwart, Papal, Pass, Patonce, Patriarchal, Pattée, Pectoral, Pedestrian, Pelican, Percolin, Perverse, Plumcot, Plus, Pommé, Potence, Potent, Preaching, Puffin, Quadrate, Quarrelsome, Railway, Ratty, Reciprocal, Red, Riled, Roman, Rood, Rose, Rosy, Rouen, Rouge, Rubicon, Ruthwell, Sain, St Andrew's, St Anthony's, St George's, St Patrick's, St Peter's, Saltier, Saltire, Satyr, Shirty, Sign, Snappy, Southern, Span, Splenetic, Star, Strid, Svastika, Swastika, T, Tangelo, Tau, Tayberry, Ten, Testy, Thraw, Thwart, Tiglon, Tigon, Times, Toucan, Traject, Transit, Transom, Transverse, Traverse, Tree, Unknown, Urdé, Vexed, Vext, Victoria, → VOTE, Weeping, Whippet, Wholphin, Wry, X, Yakow, Zebra(ss), Zebrinny, Zebroid, Zebrula, Zebrule, Zedonk, Zhomo, Z(h)o, Zobu
▹**Cross** *may indicate* an anagram
▸**Cross-bar** *see* CROSSPIECE
▸**Crossbeam** *see* CROSSPIECE
**Cross-bearer** Crucifer
**Cross-bill** Metagnathous
**Cross-bones** Marrowbones
**Cross-bow** Arbalest, Bal(l)ista
**Cross-country** Langlauf, Overland
**Cross-dress(er), Cross-dressing** Drag, En travesti, Eonism, Gender-bender, Transvestite
**Cross-examination, Cross-examine** Elenctic, Grill, Interrogate, Question, Targe

**Cross-eyed** Skelly(-eyed), Squint
**Crossfertilisation** Allogamy, Heterosis, Hybrid vigour, Xenogamy
**Cross-grained** Ill-haired, Mashlam, Mashlim, Mashlock, Mashlum, Mas(h)lin, Stubborn
**Crosspiece, Cross-bar, Crossbeam, Cross-timber** Bail, Bar, Cancelli, Crutch, Fingerground, Footrail, Inter-tie, Lierne, Phillipsite, Putlock, Putlog, Quillon, Rung, Serif, Seriph, Stempel, Stemple, Stretcher, Stull, Swingle-tree, Toggle, Transom, Trave, Whiffle-tree, Whipple-tree, Yoke
**Crossroads** Carfax, Carfox, Carrefour, Compital, Junction, Soap
**Crossword** Cruciverbal, Cryptic, Grid, Puzzle, Quickie
**Crotchet(y)** Eccentric, Fad, Fancy, Grouch, Kink, Liverish, Petulant, Quarter-note, Toy
**Crouch** Bend, Cower, Cringe, Falcade, Fancy, Hunker, Lordosis, Ruck, Set, Squat, Squinch, Stoop
**Croup** Angina, Cough, Kink, Rump
**Crow** Big-note, Bluster, Boast, Brag, Carrion, Chewet, Chough, Corbie, Corvus, Crake, Currawong, Daw, Exult, Flute-bird, Gab, Gloat, Gorcrow, Hooded, Hoodie, Huia, Jackdaw, Jim(my), Ka(e), Murder, Piping, Raven, Rook, Saddleback, Scald, Skite, Squawk, Swagger, Vaunt
**Crowbar** Gavelock, James, Jemmy, Lever
**Crowd(ed)** Abound, Army, Bike, Boodle, Bumper, Bunch, Busy, Byke, Caboodle, Clutter, Compress, Concourse, Congest(ed), Cram, Cramp, Crush, Crwth, Dedans, Dense, Doughnut, Drove, Fill, Flock, Galere, Gang, Gate, Gathering, Heaving, Herd, Horde, → HOST, Huddle, Hustle, Jam, Jam-packed, Lot, Many, Meinie, Mein(e)y, Melee, Menyie, Mob, Mong, Multitude, Ochlo-, Pack, Pang, Populace, Prease, Press, Rabble, Raft, Ragtag, Ram, Ratpack, Ring, Roll-up, Rout, Ruck, Scrooge, Scrouge, Scrowdge, Scrum, Serr(é), Shoal, Shove, Slew, Slue, Squash, Squeeze, Stuff, Swarm, Swell, Teem, Thick, Thrang, Three, Throng, Trinity, Varletry
**Crowfoot** Gilcup, Reate
**Crown** Acme, Apex, Apogee, Bays, Bull, Camp, Cantle, Cap, Capernoity, Cidaris, Civic, Coma, Corona, Cr, Diadem, Ecu, Engarland, Enthrone, Fillet, Garland, Gloria, Haku, Head, Headdress, Honour, Instal, Iron, Ivy, Koruma, Krans, Krantz, Laurel, Monarch, Mural, Naval, Nole, Noll, Northern, Noul(e), Nowl, Olive, Optical, Ore, Ovation, Pate, Peak, Pediment, Pschent, Sconce, Stephen's, Summit, Taj, Thick'un, Tiar(a), → TOP, Treetop, Triple, Triumphal, Trophy, Vallary, Vertex
**Cru** Grand
**Crucial** Acute, All-important, Bottom line, Critical, Decider, Essential, Indispensable, Key, Kingpin, Linchpin, Momentous, Paramount, Pivotal, Quintessential, Significant, Vital, Watershed
**Crucible** Cruset, Melting-pot, Vessel
**Crucifix(ion), Crucify** Calvary, Cross, Golgotha, Mortify, Rood, Torment, Torture
**Crud** Red snow
**Crude(ness)** Bald, Basic, Brash, Brute, Coarse, Earthy, Gross, Halfbaked, Homespun, Ill-bred, Immature, Incondite, Indecent, Lewd, Loutish, No tech, Oil, Primitive, Rabelaisian, Raunch, Raw, Rough, Rough and ready, Rough-hewn, Rough-wrought, Tutty, Uncouth, Unrefined, Vulgar, Yahoo
**Cruel(ty)** Atrocity, Barbarous, Bloody, Brutal, Cold-blooded, Cut-throat, Dastardly, De Sade, Draconian, Fell, Fiendish, Flinty, Hard, Heartless, Immane, Inhuman(e), Machiavellian, Mental, Merciless, Neronic, Persistent, Pitiless, Raw, Remorseless, Sadistic, Stern, Tiger, Tormentor, Tyranny, Unmerciful, Vicious, Violence, Wanton
▷**Cruel** *may indicate* an anagram
**Cruet** Ampulla, Condiments, Decanter
**Cruise(r)** Booze, Busk, Cabin, Coast, Nuke, Orientation, Prowl, Rove, Sail, Sashay, Search, Ship, Tom, Travel, Trip, Voyager
**Crumb(le), Crumbling, Crumbly, Crumbs** Apple, Bread, Coo, Cor, Decay, Derelict, Disintegrate, Ee, Fragment, Friable, Fritter, Golly, Law, Leavings, Moribund, Moulder, Mull, Murl, Nesh, Nirl, Ort, Panko, Particle, Ped, Pulverise, Raspings, Rhubarb, Rot, Rotter, Tumbledown

**Crumpet** Dish, Girl, Muffin, Nooky, Pash, Pikelet
**Crumple** Buckle, Collapse, Crease, Crunkle, Crush, Raffle, Ruck, Scrunch, Wrinkle
**Crunch(y), Crunching** Abdominal, Acid test, Chew, Craunch, Credit, Crisis, Crisp, Gnash, Graunch, Grind, Munch, Number, Nutty, Occlude, Scranch, Shoot-out, Sit-up
**Crusade(r)** Baldwin, Campaign, Caped, Cause, Evangelist, Jihad, Lionheart, Pilgrim, Quest, Tancred, Templar
**Crush(ed), Crusher, Crushing** Acis, Anaconda, Annihilate, Beetle, Bow, Breakback, Careworn, Champ, Comminute, Conquer, Contuse, Cram(p), Cranch, Crumple, Crunch, Defeat, Demoralise, Destroy, Graunch, Grind, Hug, Humble, Jam, Knapper, Levigate, Liquidise, Litholapaxy, Mangle, Mash, Masticate, Mill, Molar, Mortify, Nib, Oppress, Overcome, Overpower, Overrun, Overwhelm, Pash, Policeman, Pound, Press, Pulp, Pulverise, Quash, Quell, Ruin, Schwarmerei, Scotch, Scrum, Scrumple, Scrunch, Smash, Squabash, Squash, Squeeze, Squelch, Squidger, Squish, Stamp, Stave, Steam-roll, Step on, Stove, Stramp, Suppress, Swot, Telescope, Trample, Tread, Vanquish
**Crusoe** Robinson, Selkirk
**Crust(y)** Argol, Beeswing, Cake, Caliche, Coating, Coffin, Continental, Cover, Crabby, Craton, Croustade, Fur, Geogeny, Geosphere, Gratin, Heel, Horst, Ice fern, Kissing, Kraton, Lithosphere, Oceanic, Orogen, Osteocolla, Pie, Reh, Rind, Rine, Sal, Salband, Scab, Scale, Shell, Sial, Sima, Sinter, Sordes, Surly, Tartar, Teachie, Tectonics, Terrane, Tetchy, Upper, Wine-stone
**Crustacea(n)** Acorn-shell, Amphipod, Barnacle, Brachyuran, Branchiopoda, Camaron, Cirriped, Cirripede, Cirripid, Cladoceran, Copepod, Crab, Crawdad, Crayfish, Cumacean, Cyclops, Cyprid, Cypris, Daphnia, Decapod(a), Entomostraca, Euphausia, Fishlouse, Foot-jaw, Gribble, Isopod, Krill, Langoustine, Limpet, Limulus, Lobster, Macrura, Malacostracan, Marine borer, Maron, Nauplius, Nephrops, Oniscus, Ostracoda, Pagurian, Phyllopod, Prawn, Red seed, Rhizocephalan, Sand flea, Sand-hopper, Sand-skipper, Scampi, Scampo, Schizopod, Sea slater, Shellfish, Shrimp, Slater, Squilla, Stomatopod, Woodlouse, Yabbie, Yabby
**Crutch** Morton's, Potent
**Crux** Essence, Gist, Nub
**Cry(ing)** Aha, Alalagmus, Alew, Baa, Banzai, Bark, Battle, Bawl, Bay, Bell, Bemoan, Bill, Bingo, Blat, Bleat, Bleb, Blub(ber), Boo, Boohoo, Boom, Bray, Bump, Caramba, Caw, Chant, Cheer, Chevy, Chirm, Chivy, Clang, Cooee, Crake, Croak, Crow, Dire, Entreaty, Euoi, Eureka, Evoe, Evoke, Exclaim, Eye-water, Fall, Field-holler, Gardyloo, Gathering, Geronimo, Gowl, Greet, Halloo, Harambee, Haro, Harrow, Havoc, Heave-ho, Heigh, Hemitrope, Herald, Hey presto, Hinny, Hoicks, Holler, Honk, Hoo, Hoop, Hosanna, Hout(s)-tout(s), Howl, Howzat, Humph, Hunt's up, Hup, Hurra(h), Io, Kaw, Looning, Low, Mewl, Miaou, Miau(l), Miserere, Mourn, Night-shriek, Nix, O(c)hone, Oi, Olé, Ow, Pugh, Rabbito(h), Rallying, Rivo, Sab, Scape, Scream, Screech, Sell, Sese(y), Sessa, → **SHOUT**, Shriek, Slogan, Snivel, Snotter, Sob, Soho, Sola, Squall, Squawk, Squeak, Street, Sursum corda, Tally-ho, Tantivy, Umph, Vagitus, View-halloo, Vivat, Vociferate, Wail, War, War whoop, Watchword, Waterworks, Waul, Wawl, Weep, Westward ho, Whammo, Whee(ple), Whimper, Whine, Whinny, Whoa, Whoop, Winge, Wolf, Yammer, Yawl, Yelp, Yicker, Yikker, Yip, Yippee, Yodel, Yo-heave-ho, Yo-ho-ho, Yoick, Yoop, Yowl
**Crybaby** Mardy, Prima donna
**Crypt(ic)** Ambiguous, Cabalistic, Catacomb, Cavern, Chamber, Crowde, Encoded, Enigmatic, Esoteric, Favissa, Grotto, Hidden, Mysterious, Mystic, Obscure, Occult, Secret, Sepulchre, Short, Steganographic, Tomb, Unclear, Undercroft, Vault
**Cryptaesthesia** ESP
**Cryptogam** Acotyledon, Acrogen, Fern(-ally), Moss, Pteridophyte, Steganograph
**Cryptogram, Cryptographer, Cryptography** Decoder, Public-key, Steganograph, Ventris
**Crystal(s), Crystal-gazer, Crystalite, Crystalline, Crystallise** Allotriomorphic, Anthraquinone, Axinite, Baccara(t), Beryl, Candy, Citrine, Clathrate, Clear, Cleveite, Copperas, Coumarin, Cumarin, Cut-glass, Dendrite, Druse, Effloresce, Elaterin, Enantiomorph, Epitaxy, Erionite, Form, Fuchsin(e), Geode, Glass, Globulite, Hemihedron, Hemimorphic, Hemitrope,

Ice-stone, Ideal, Imazadole, Jarosite, Lase, Lead, Liquid, Lithium, Love-arrow, Macle, Macro-axis, Melamine, Mixed, Needle, Nematic, Niacin, Nicol, Orthogonal, Orthorhombic, Palace, Pellucid, Penninite, Pericline, Phenocryst, Piezo, Piezoelectric, Pinacoid, Pinakoid, Prism, Pseudomorph, Purin(e), Quartz, R(h)aphide, R(h)aphis, Rhinestone, Rock, Rotenone, Rubicelle, Scawtite, Scryer, Shoot, Silica, Skatole, Skryer, Smectic, Snowflake, Sorbitol, Spar, Spherulite, Spicule, Subhedral, Table, Tina, Tolan(e), Trichite, Triclinic, Trilling, Twin(ned), Wafer, Watch-glass, Xanthene, Xenocryst, Yag

**Cub(s)** Baby, Kit, Lionet, Novice, Pup, Sic, Whelp, Wolf, Youth

**Cuba(n)** C, Castro

**Cube, Cubic, Cubist** Bath, Braque, Crouton, Cu, Dice, Die, Flash, Ice, Magic, Necker, Nosean, Polyhedron, Quadrate, Rubik's®, Serac, Smalto, Snub, Solid, Stere, Stock, Tesseract

**Cubicle** Alcove, Booth, Carrel(l), Compartment, Shower, Stall

**Cuckold** Actaeon, Cornute, Graft, Homer, Lenocinium, Mari complaisant, Two-time, Vulcan's badge, Wittol

**Cuckoo** Ament, Ani, April fool, Bird, Brain-fever bird, Chaparral cock, Dotty, Gouk, Gowk, Inquiline, Insane, Koekoea, Koel, → MAD, Mental, Piet-my-vrou, Rabid, Stupid, Zany

▷**Cuckoo** *may indicate* an anagram

**Cuckoopint** Arum

**Cucumber** Bitter-apple, Choko, Colocynth, Coloquintida, Dill, Elaterium, Gherkin, Pickle, Sea-slug, Squirting, Trepang, Wolly

**Cuddle, Cuddly** Canoodle, Caress, Clinch, Embrace, Fondle, Hug, Inarm, Nooky, Pet, Smooch, Smuggle, Snog, Snuggle, Spoon, Zaftig

**Cudgel** Alpeen, Ballow, Bludgeon, Brain, Club, Cosh, Drub, Fustigate, Oaken towel, Plant, Rack, Rung, Shillelagh, Souple, Stick, Swipple, Tan, Towel, Truncheon

**Cue** Billiard, Cannonade, Catchword, Feed, Feed-line, Half-butt, Hint, Mace, Nudge, Pool, → PROMPT, Reminder, Rod, Sign, Signal, Wink

**Cuff** Box, Buffet, Clout, French, Gauntlet, Iron, Muffettee, Rotator, Slap, Storm, Strike, Swat

**Cuirass** Armour, Corselet, Lorica

**Cuisine** Balti, Bourgeoise, Cajun, Cookery, En croute, Food, Lean, Menu, Minceur, Nouvelle, Tex-Mex

**Cul-de-sac** Blind (alley), Dead-end, Impasse, Loke

**Cull** Gather, Pick, Purge, Reap, Select, Thin, Weed

**Culminate, Culmination** Acme, Apogean, Apogee, Climax, Conclusion, Crest, End, Head, Orgasm

**Culpable** Blameworthy, Faulty, Guilty

**Culprit** Offender, Suspect

**Cult** Aum Shinrikyo, Cabiri, Candomble, Cargo, Creed, Fertility, Flower power, Macumba, Moony, New Age, Personality, Rastafarian, Sect, Shango, Shinto, Snake, Sun, Voodoo, Wicca, Worship

**Cultivate(d), Cultivation, Cultivator** Agronomy, Arty, Breed, Civilise, Contour, Developed, Dig, Dress, Ear, Ere, Farm, Garden, Genteel, Grow, Hoe, Hydroponics, Improve, Labour, Nurture, Plough(man), Polytunnel, Pursue, Raise, Reclaim, Refine, Sative, Sophisticated, Tame, Tasteful, Till, Tilth, Wainage, Woo, Work

**Culture(d), Cultural** Abbevillean, Acheulean, Acheulian, Agar, Art(y), Aurignacian, Azilian, Bacterian, Bel esprit, Brahmin, Broth, Canteen, Capsian, Chilean, Civil(isation), Clactonian, Club, Compensation, Corporate, Cosmopolitan, Dependency, Enterprise, Ethnic, Experiment, Explant, Fine arts, Folsom, Gel, Gravettian, Grecian, Halafian, Hallstatt, Hip-hop, Humanism, Intelligentsia, Kultur(kreis), La Tène, Learning, Levallois, Madelenian, Magdalenian, Maglemosean, Maglemosian, Meristem, Minimalism, Minoan, Monolayer, Mousterian, New Age, Organisational, Perigordian, Polish, Polite, Punk, Pure, Refinement, Solutrean, Sophisticated, Starter, Strepyan, Suspension, Tardenoisian, Tissue, Urbane, Villanovan, Water, Well-read

**Culvert** Ponceau

**Cumbersome** Awkward, Clumsy, Fardel, Heavy, Lumbering, → UNWIELDY

**Cunctator** Dilatory

**Cuneiform** Wedge(d)

**Cunning** Arch, Art, Artifice, Astute, Cautel, Craft(y), Deceit, Deep, Devious, Down, Finesse, Foxy, Guile, Insidious, Knacky, Knowing, Leary, Leery, Machiavellian, Quaint, Ruse, Scheming, Skill, Slee(kit), Sleight, Slim, Sly(boots), Smart, Sneaky, Stratagem, Subtle, Vulpine, Wheeze, Wile, Wily

**Cup(s), Cupped, Cupping** Aecidium, America's, Beaker, Bledisloe, Bra(ssiere), Calcutta, Calix, Calyculus, Cantharus, Ca(u)p, Caudle, Chalice, Claret, Coffee, Communion, Cotyle, Cruse, Cupule, Cyathus, Cylix, Davis, Demitasse, Deoch-an-doruis, Deuch-an-doris, Dish, Doch-an-dorach, Dop, Dry, Egg, European, Eyebath, FA, Fairs, Final, Fingan, Finjan, Fruit, Gemma, Glenoid, Goblet, Grace, Grease, Gripe's egg, Hanap, Horn, Kylix, Loving, Measuring, Melbourne, Merry, Monstrance, Moustache, Mug, Noggin, Nut, Optic, Pannikin, Paper, Parting, Planchet, Plate, Poley, Posset, Pot, Procoelous, Quaff, Quaich, Quaigh, Race, Rhyton, Rider, Ryder, Sangrado, Scyphus, Sippy, Stem, Stirrup, Suction, Tantalus, Tass(ie), Tastevin, Tazza, Tea-dish, Tig, Tot, → **TROPHY**, Tyg, UEFA, Volva, Waterloo, World

▷**Cup** *may indicate* a bra size

**Cup-bearer** Ganymede, Hebe

**Cupboard** Airing, Almery, Almirah, A(u)mbry, Armoire, Beauf(f)et, Cabinet, Chiffonier, Chiff(o)robe, Closet, Coolgardie safe, Court, Credenza, Dresser, Encoignure, Fume, Glory hole, Livery, Locker, Meat-safe, Press, Unit, Walk-in, Wardrobe

**Cup-holder** Bra, Hanaper, Hebe, Plinth, Saucer, Zarf, Zurf

**Cupid** Amoretto, Amorino, Archer, Blind, Bow-boy, Cherub, Dan, Eros, Love, Putto

**Cupola** Belfry, Dome, Tholos

**Cup-shaped** Glenoid, Poculiform

**Cur** Caitiff, Cowardice, Dog, Hound, Messan, Mongrel, Mutt, Pi-dog, Scab, Scoundrel, Whelp, Wretch, Yap

**Curare, Curari** Ourali, Poison, Wourali

**Curassow** Crax

**Curate** Barman, Minister, Nathaniel, Padré, Perpetual, Priest

**Curator** Aquarist

**Curb** Arrest, Bit, Brake, Bridle, Check, Clamp, Coaming, Constraint, Dam, Edge, Puteal, Rein, Restrain, Restringe, Rim, Snub, Stifle, Well

**Curd(s)** Bean, Cheese, Junket, Lapper(ed)-milk, Lemon, Orange, Skyr, Tofu

**Curdle** Clot, Congeal, Earn, Erne, Grue, Lapper, Lopper, Posset, Ren, Rennet, Run, Set, Sour, → **TURN**, Whig, Yearn

**Cure(d), Curative** Ameliorate, Amend, Antidote, Antirachitic, Bloater, Cold turkey, Dry, Dry-salt, Dun, Elixir, Euphrasy, Faith, Fix, Flue, Ginseng, Heal, Heal-all, Heat treatment, Hobday, Hydropathy, Jadeite, Jerk, Kipper, Laetrile, Magic bullet, Medicinal, Nature, Nostrum, Panacea, Park-leaves, Pickle, Posset, Prairie oyster, → **PRESERVE**, Reast, Reck, Recover, Recower, Reest, Relief, Remede, Remedy, Re(i)st, Restore, Salt, Salve, Save, Serum, Smoke, Smoke-dry, Snakeroot, Specific, Tan, Therapy, → **TREATMENT**, Tutsan, Water

▷**Cure** *may indicate* an anagram

**Curfew** Bell, Gate, Prohibit, Proscribe

**Curie** Ci

**Curio, Curiosity, Curious** Agog, Bibelot, Bric a brac, Collector's item, Esoteric, Ferly, Freak, Inquisitive, Interesting, Into, Intriguing, Meddlesome, Nos(e)y, Objet d'art, Objet de vertu, Oddbeat, Oddity, Peculiar, Prurience, Quaint, Rarity, Rum, Spectacle, → **STRANGE**, Wondering

▷**Curious(ly)** *may indicate* an anagram

**Curium** Cm

**Curl(s), Curler, Curling, Curly** Ailes de pigeon, Bev, Bonspiel, Cirrus, Cockle, Coil, Crimp, Crimple, Crinkle, Crisp, Crocket, Dildo, Earlock, Eddy, Favourite, Frisette, Friz(z), Frizzle, Heart-breaker, Hog, Inwick, Kink, Kiss, Leaf, Loop, Love-lock, Outwick, Perm, Pigeon's wing, Pin, Quiff, Repenter, Ringlet, Roaring game, Roll, Roulette, Scroll, Shaving, Spiral, Spit, Tong, Tress, Trunk, Twiddle, → **TWIST**, Ulotrichous, Undée, Wave, Wind

**Curlew** Bird, Thick knee, Whaup, Whimbrel

**Curmudgeon** Boor, Churl, Crab, Crosspatch, Grouch, Hunks, Route, Runt, Skinflint

**Currant** Berry, Flowering, Raisin, Rizard, Rizzar(t), Rizzer

**Currency** Cash, Circulation, → COIN, Coinage, Decimal, Dosh, Euro(sterling), Finance, Fractional, Hard, Jiao, Kip, Koruna, Legal tender, Managed, Monetary, → MONEY, Petrodollar, Prevalence, Reserve, Soft, Tender

▷**Currency** *may indicate* a river

**Current, Currently** Abroad, AC, Actual, Airstream, Alternating, Amp(ere), Amperage, Breeze, California, Canary, Contemporaneous, Cromwell, Dark, DC, Direct, Draught, Drift, Dynamo, Ebbtide, Eddy, Electric, El Nino, Emission, Equatorial, Euripus, Existent, Faradic, Flow, Foucault, Galvanic(al), Going, Gyre, Headstream, Hot button, Humboldt, Hummock, I, Immediate, Inst, Intermittent, In vogue, Japan, Jet stream, Kuroshio, Labrador, Live, Maelstrom, Millrace, Modern, Newsy, North Atlantic, Now, Nowadays, Ongoing, Output, Peru, Present, Present day, Prevalent, Pulsating, Race, Rapid, Recent, Rife, Rip, Roost, Running, Ryfe, Stream, Thames, Thermal, Thermionic, Tide, Tideway, Topical, Torrent, Turbidity, Underset, Undertow, Updraught, Up-to-date

**Curriculum** Core, Cursal, National, Programme, Syllabus

**Curry** Balti, Bhuna, Biriani, Brush, Comb, Cuittle, Dhansak, Dress, Favour, Fawn, Groom, Ingratiate, Korma, Madras, Ruby (Murray), Skater, Spice, Tan, Tandoori, Turmeric, Vindaloo

**Curse(d)** Abuse, Anathema, Badmouth, Ban, Bane, Berate, Beshrew, → BLASPHEME, Blast, Bless, Chide, Dam(me), Damn, Dee, Drat, Ecod, Egad, Evil, Excommunicate, Execrate, Heck, Hex, Hoodoo, Imprecate, Jinx, Malediction, Malgre, Malison, Maranatha, Mau(l)gré, Mockers, Moz(z), Mozzle, Nine (of diamonds), Oath, Paterson's, Pize, Plague, Rant, Rats, Scourge, 'Snails, Spell, Star-crossed, Swear, Tarnation, Upbraid, Vengeance, Vituperate, Wanion, Weary, Winze, Wo(e)

**Cursive** Estrang(h)elo, Run

**Cursor** Mouse, Turtle

**Cursorily, Cursory** Casual, Hasty, Lax, Obiter, Passing, Perfunctory, Sketchy, Speedy, Superficial

**Curt** Abrupt, Blunt, Crusty, Gruff, Laconic, Monosyllabic, Offhand, Short, Snappy, Stern, Terse, Uncivil

**Curtail(ment)** Abate, Abbreviate, Abridge, Apocope, Aposiopesis, Crop, Cut, Reduce, Shorten, Truncate

**Curtain(s), Curtain raiser, Curtain-rod** Air, Arras, Backdrop, Bamboo, Café, Canopy, Casement, Caudle, Cloth, Cyclorama, Death, Demise, Drape, Drop, Dropcloth, Dropscene, Fatal, Hanging, Iron, Lever de rideau, Louvre, Net, Overture, Pall, Portière, Purdah, Rag, Safety, Scene, Screen, Scrim, Shower, Swag, Tab, Tableau, Tormentor, Tringle, Upholstery, Vail, Valance, Veil, Vitrage, Window

**Curtsey** Bob, Bow, Dip, Dop, Honour

**Curve(d), Curvaceous, Curvature, Curving, Curvy** Adiabatic, Aduncate, Anticlastic, Apophyge, Arc, Arch, Archivolt, Assurgent, Axoid, Bandy, Bend, Bezier, Bight, Bow, Brachistochrone, Bulbous, Camber, Campylotropous, Cardioid, Catacaustic, Catenary, Caustic, Characteristic, Chordee, Cissoid, Concave, Conchoid, Conic, Contrapposto, Convex, Crescent, Cycloid, Demand, Diacaustic, Dogleg, Dowager's hump, Ellipse, Entasis, Epicycloid, Epinastic, Epitrochoid, Ess, Evolute, Exponential, Extrados, Felloe, Felly, Folium, Freezing point, French, Gaussian, Geodesic, Gooseneck, Growth, Hance, Harmonogram, Helix, Hodograph, Hollow-back, Hook, Hyperbola, Hypocycloid, Inswing, Intrados, Invected, Isochor, Isochore, Isoseismal, J, Jordan, Kyphosis, Laffer, Learning, Lemniscate, Limacon, Linkage, Liquidus, Lissajous figure, Lituus, Loop, Lordosis, Loxodrome, Magnetic, Meniscus, Normal, Nowy, Ogee, Oxbow, Parabola, Phillips, Pothook, Pott's disease, Pulvinate, Reclinate, Record, Rhumb, RIAA, Roach, Rondure, Rotundate, Scolioma, Scoliosis, Sheer, Sigmoid flexure, Sinuate, Sinusoid, Slice, Sonsie, Spiral, Spiric, Strophoid, Supply, Survival, Swayback, Synclastic, Tautochrone, Tie, Tractrix, Trajectory, Trisectrix, Trochoid, Tumble-home, Twist, Undulose, Upswept, U-turn, Volute, Witch (of Agnesi)

**Cushion(s), Cushioned** Air, Allege, Bank, Beanbag, Bolster, Buffer, Bustle, Cod, Frog, Ham, Hassock, King's, Kneeler, → PAD, Pillow, Pin, Pouf(fe), Pulvinus, Sandbag, Scatter, Soften, Sponge, Spongy, Squab, Tyre, Upholster, Whoopee

**Cushy** Bed of roses, Easy, Sinecure

**Cusp** Horn, Spinode, Tine

**Cuss, Cussed** Stubborn
**Custard (apple)** Crème brulee, Crème caramel, Egg, Flam(m), Flan, Flaune, Flawn, Flummery, Pa(w)paw, Pastry, Zabaglione
**Custodial, Custodian, Custody** Arrest, Care(taker), Claviger, Curator, Guard, Hold, Incarceration, Janitor, Keeping, Protective, Remand, Retention, Sacrist, Steward, Trust, Ward, Wardship
**Custom(ised), Custom-made, Customs (officer), Customs house, Customary** Agriology, Bespoke, Chophouse, Coast-waiters, Cocket, Consuetude, Conventional, Couvade, Culture, Dedicated, De règle, Dhamma, Dharma, Douane, Exciseman, Familiar, Fashion, Folklore, → **HABIT**, Land-waiter, Lore, Manner, Monogyny, Montem, Mores, Nomic, Obsequy, Octroi, Ordinary, Perfunctory, Practice, Praxis, Protocol, Regular, Relic, Rite, Routine, Rule, Set, Sororate, Spanish, Sunna, Tax, Thew, Tidesman, Tide-waiter, Tikanga, Time-honoured, Tradition, Trait, Unwritten, Usance, Used, Usual, Won, Wont, Woon, Zollverein
**Customer(s)** Client, Cove, End user, Fish, Footfall, Gate, Patron, Prospect, Punter, Purchaser, Shillaber, Shopper, Smooth, Stiff, Trade, Trick, Ugly, User, Vendee
**Cut(ter), Cutdown, Cutting** Abate, Abbreviate, Abjoint, Ablate, Abridge, Abscission, Abscond, Acute, Adeem, Adze, Aftermath, Ali Baba, Amputate, Apocopate, Apocope, Axe, Bang, Baron, Bevel, Bisect, Bit, Bitchy, Bite, Bowdlerise, Box, Boycott, Brilliant, Broach, Caesarean, Caique, Canal, Cantle, Caper, Carver, Castrate, Caustic, Censor, Chamler, Chap, Cheese, Chisel, Chopper, Chynd, Circumscribe, Cleaver, Clinker-built, Clip, Clod, Colter, Commission, Concise, Coppice, Coulter, Coupé, Crew, Crop, Cruel, Cube, Culebra, Curtail, Deadhead, Decrease, Dedekind, Diamond, Dicer, Die, Diminish, Director's, Discide, Discount, Disengage, Dismember, Dissect, Division, Divorce, Dock, Dod, Edge, Edit, Elision, Emarginate, Embankment, Engraver, Entail, Entayle, Entrecote, Epistolary, Epitomise, Escalope, Eschew, Estramazone, Estrepe, Etch, Excalibur, Excide, Excise, Exscind, Exsect, Exude, Fashion, Feather, Fell, Filet mignon, Fillet, Flench, Flense, Flinch, Flymo®, Form, Framp, Froe, Frow, Gaillard, Garb, Gash, Go-down, Grater, Graven, Gride, Groove, Gryde, Hack, Hairdo, Handsaw, Harvest, Hew(er), Ignore, Incision, Incisor, Indent, Insult, Intersect, Jigsaw, Joint, Junk, Kerf, Kern, Kerve, Kirn, Knife, Lacerate, Lance, Lapidary, Lase(r), Leat, Lesion, Limit, Loin, Lop, Math, Medaillon, Medallion, Microtome, Milling, Minimise, Minish, Mohel, Mordant, Mortice, Mortise, Mower, Nache, Naval, Nick, Not, Notch, Nott, Occlude, Omit, Open, Operate, Osteotome, Outage, Oxyacetylene, Padsaw, Pare, Pink, Plant, Pliers, Ploughshare, Poll, Pollard, Pone, Power, Precisive, Press, Proin, Quota, Race, Rake off, Rase, Razee, Razor, Reap, Rebate, Reduction, Re-enter, Resect, Retrench, Revenue, Ring, Ripsaw, Roach, Rose, Rout, Saddle, Sarcastic, Sarky, Saw(n), Saw-tooth, Scaloppine, Scarf, Scarify, Scathing, Scion, Scission, Scissor, Score, Scrap, Sculpt, Scye, Scythe, Secant, Secateurs, Sect, Section, Set, Sever, Sey, Share (out), Shaver, Shears, Shin, Shingle, Ship, Shive, Shorn, Short, Shred, Shun, Sickle, Side, Silverside, Sirloin, Skin, Skip, Slane, Slash, Slice(r), Slight, Slip, Slit, Sloop, Sned, Snee, Snib, Snick, Snip, Snippet, Snub, Spade, Speedy, Spin, Spud, Stall, Steak, Stencil, Stereotomy, Stir, Stramac, Stramazon, Strim, Strimmer®, Style, Sunder, Surgeon, Swath(e), Tailor(ess), Tap, Tart, Tenderloin, Tenotomy, Tomial, Tomium, Tonsure, Tooth, Topside, Tournedo, Transect, Trash, Trench, Trenchant, Trepan, Trim, Truant, Truncate, Type, Undersell, Urchin, Vivisection, Whang, Whittle, Winey
▹**Cut** *may indicate* an anagram
▹**Cutback** *may indicate* a reversed word
**Cute** Ankle, Canny, Dinky, Endearing, Perspicacious, Pert, Pretty, Taking, Twee
**Cuticle** Epidermis, Eponychium, Periplast, Pleuron, Skin
**Cut in** Interpose, Interrupt
**Cutlass** Curtalax(e), Machete, Sword
**Cutlery** Canteen, Eating irons, Flatware, Fork, Knife, Service, Setting, Silver, Spoon, Spork, Sunbeam, Tableware, Trifid
**Cutlet** Chop, Nut, (Wiener) Schnitzel
**Cut off** Elide, Enisle, Estrange, Inisle, Insulate, Intercept, → **ISOLATE**, Lop, Ostracise, Prune
**Cut out** Stencil
**Cut-throat** Razor, Ruinous, Sweeney Todd

**Cuttlebone, Cuttlefish** Octopus, Pen, Polyp(e)s, Polypus, Sea-grape, Sea-sleeve, Sepia, Sepiost(aire), Sepium, Squid
**CV** Biodata, Resume
**Cyanide** Acrylonitrile, Hydrogen, Nitrile, Potassium, Prussiate
**Cyberbully** Troll
**Cyberspace** Avatar, Online
**Cyborg** Replicant
**Cycad** Coontie, Coonty
**Cyclades** Thera
**Cyclamen** Sow-bread
**Cycle, Cyclist, Cycling** Anicca, Arthurian, Bike, Biorhythm, Biospheric, Born-Haber, Business, Cal(l)ippic, Calvin, Carbon, Carnot, Cell, Circadian, Citric acid, Closed, Daisy, Diesel, Eon, Era, Fairy, Four-stroke, Freewheel, Frequency, Geological, Gigahertz, Heterogony, Hinault, Hydrologic, Indiction, Keirin, Ko, Krebs, Life, Light-year, Lunar, Lytic, Madison, Metonic, Minibike, Moped, Natural, Nitrogen, Oestrus, Operating, Orb(it), Otto, Pedal, Pedicab, Peloton, Period, Product life, Rankine, Repulp, Revolution, Ride, Roadman, Roadster, Rock, Rota, Round, Samsara, Saros, Scorch, Series, Sheng, Solar, Song, Sonnet, Sothic, Spin, Sunspot, TCA, Trade, Trick, Trike, Turn, UCI, Urea, Vicious, Water, Wheeler, Wheelman, Wu
**Cyclone** Cockeye(d) bob, Storm, Tornado, Tropical, Typhoon, Willy-willy
**Cyclops** Arges, Arimasp(i), Brontes, Polyphemus, Steropes
**Cylinder, Cylindrical** Air, Capstan, Clave, Column, Dandy-roll, Drum, Licker-in, Magic, Master, Nanotube, Pipe, Pitch, Roll, Rotor, Scroll, Siphonostele, Slave, Spool, Steal, Stele, Swift, Terete, Torose, Treadmill, Tube, Type, Vascular
**Cymbal(s)** Gong, High-hat, Hi-hat, Zel, Zill
**Cynic(al)** Crab, Diogenes, Doubter, Hard-bitten, Hard-boiled, Menippus, Mephistophelean, Misanthropist, Pessimist, Sardonic, Sceptic, Snide, Thersites, Timon, Worldly-wise, World-weary
**Cynosure** Centre, Focus
**Cynthia** Artemis, Moon
**Cypress** Bald, Lawson's, Leyland(ii), Monterey, Retinospora, Summer, Swamp, Tree
**Cypriot** Enosis, Eoka
**Cyst** Atheroma, Bag, Blister, Chalazion, Dermoid, Ganglion, Hydatid, Impost(h)ume, Meibomian, Ranula, Sac, Sebaceous, Vesicle, Wen
**Cytogenesis** Amoebic
**Czar** Despot, Nicholas
**Czech(oslovakia), Czechoslovakian** CZ, Moravian, Ruthenian, Sudetenland

# Dd

**D** Daughter, Delta, Died, Edh, Eth, Penny
**Dab(s)** Bit, Blob, Daub, Fingerprint, Fish, Flounder, Lemon, Pat, Print, Ringer, Sand, Smear, Smooth, Smudgeon, Spot, Stupe, Whorl
**Dabble(r)** Amateur, Clatch, Dally, Dilettante, Plouter, Plowter, Potter, Smatter, Splash, Stipple, Trifle
**Dachshund** Badger-dog, Sausage-dog, Teckel
**Dactyl** Anapaest
**Dad(dy)** Blow, Dev(v)el, Father, Generator, Hit, Male, Pa(pa), Pater, Polt, Pop, Slam, Sugar, Thump
**Dada** Surrealist
**Daddy-longlegs** Crane-fly, Jennyspinner, Leather-jacket, Spinning-jenny, Tipula
**Daffodil** Asphodel, Jonquil, Lent-lily, Narcissus
**Daft** Absurd, Crazy, Potty, Ridiculous, Silly, Simple, Stupid
**Dag** Jag, Pierce, Pistol, Prick, Stab, Tag, Wool
**Dagga** Cape, Red, True
**Dagger(s)** An(e)lace, Ataghan, Baselard, Bayonet, Bodkin, Crease, Creese, Da(h), Diesis, Dirk, Double, Dudgeon, Hanger, Han(d)jar, Jambiya(h), Katar, Khanjar, Kindjahl, Kirpan, Kreese, Kris, Lath, Misericord(e), Obelisk, Obelus, Poi(g)nado, Poniard, Pugio, Puncheon, Pusser's, Quillon, Rondel, Sgian-dubh, Shank, Skean, Skene(-occle), Spanish, Stiletto, Swordbreaker, Whiniard, Whinyard, W(h)inger, Yatag(h)an, Yuc(c)a
**Dahlia** Cactus, Cosmea, Pompom
**Daily** Adays, Broadsheet, Char(lady), Circadian, Cleaner, Diurnal, Domestic, Guardian, Help, Journal, Le Monde, Mail, Mirror, Mrs Mopp, → **NEWSPAPER**, Paper, Per diem, Quotidian, Rag, Regular, Scotsman, Sun, Tabloid, Times
**Dainty, Daintiness** Cate(s), Cute, Delicacy, Dinky, Elegant, Elfin, Entremesse, Entremets, Exquisite, Genty, Junket, Lickerish, Liquorish, Mignon(ne), Minikin, → **MORSEL**, Neat, Nice, Particular, Petite, Precious, Prettyism, Pussy, Sunket, Titbit, Twee
**Dairy** Creamery, Days' house, Loan, Milk, Parlour, Springhouse
**Dairymaid, Dairyman** Cowfeeder, Dey, Patience
**Dais** Estrade, Machan, Platform, Podium, Pulpit, Rostrum, Stage, Tribune
**Daisy** African, Aster, Barberton, Bell, Boneset, Cineraria, Composite, Felicia, Gerbera, Gowan, Groundsel, Hardheads, Hen and chickens, Livingstone, Marguerite, Marigold, Michaelmas, Moon, Ox-eye, Ragweed, Saw-wort, Shasta, Transvaal, Vegetable sheep
**Dale(s)** Dell, Dene, Diarist, Dingle, Glen, Lowland, Nidder, Ribbles, Swale, Vale, Valley, Wensley, Wharfe, Yorkshire
**Dally** Coquet(te), Dawdle, Dilatory, Finger, Flirt, Linger, Philander, Play, Spoon, Sport, Tarry, Tick and toy, Toy, Trifle, Wait
**Dalmatian** Spotted dog
**Dam** An(n)icut, Arch, Aswan, Aswan High, Bar, Barrage, Barrier, Block, Boulder, Bund, Cabora Bassa, Cauld, Check, Dental, Grand Coulee, Grande Dixence, Gravity, Hoover, Kariba, Kielder, Ma, Mangla, Mater, Nile, Obstacle, Obstruct, Pen, Sennar, Stank, → **STEM**, Sudd, Tank, Three Gorges, Turkey nest, Volta River, Weir, Yangtze
**Damage(d), Damages, Damaging** Abuse, Accidental, Appair, Bane, Banjax, Besmirch, Blight, Bloody, Blunk, Brain, Breakage, Bruise, Buckle, Burn, Charge, Chip, Clonic, Collateral, Contuse, Corrupt, Cost, Cripple, Defame, Dent, Desecrate, Detriment, Devastate, Devastavit, Discredit, Distress, Estrepe, Exemplary, Expense, Fault, Flea-bite, Foobar, Fubar, Harm,

Havoc, Hedonic, Hit, Hole, Hurt, Impair, Injury, Insidious, Lacerate, Lesion, Loss, Mar, Mayhem, Moth-eaten, Mutilate, Nobble, Opgefok, Pair(e), Prang, Price, Punitive, Ratten, Ravage, Reparation, Retree, Ruin, Sabotage, Scaith, Scath(e), Scotch, Scratch, Shop-soiled, Skaith, Smirch, Solatium, → **SPOIL**, Tangle, Tear, Tigger, Toll, Toxic, Traumatic, Unsound, Value, Vandalise, Violate, Wear and tear, Wing, Wound, Wreak, Wreck, Write off

▷**Damage(d)** *may indicate* an anagram

**Dambuster** Ondatra

**Dame** Crone, Dowager, Edna (Everage), Gammer, Lady, Matron, Nature, Naunt, Pantomime, Partlet, Peacherino, Sis, Title(d), Trot, Woman

**Damn(ation), Damnable, Damned** Accurst, Attack, Blame, Blast, Blinking, Censure, Condemn, Cotton-picking, Curse, Cuss, D, Darn, Dee, Doggone, Drat, Execrate, Faust, Fire and brimstone, Heck, Hell, Hoot, Jigger, Malgre, Perdition, Pocky, Predoom, Ruddy, Sink, Swear, Tarnal, Tarnation, Tinker's, Very

**Damp(en), Damping, Dampness** Aslake, Bedew, Black, Blight, Blunt, Check, Choke, Clam(my), Dank, Dewy, Fousty, Fusty, Humid(ity), Hydric, Mesarch, Moch, Moist(ure), Muggy, Raw, Retund, Rheumy, Rising, Roric, Soggy, Sordo, Sultry, Unaired, Viscous, → **WET**, White

**Damper** Barrier, Check, Dashpot, Killjoy, Mute, Register-plate, Sordino, Sourdine

**Damsel** Girl, Lass, Maiden, Wench

**Damson** Plumdamas

**Dan** Box, Cupid, Dare, Leno, Martial artist, Olivetan, Scuttle, Tribe

**Dance(r), Dancing** Alma(in), Astaire, Avignon, Baladin(e), Balanchine, Ballabile, Ballant, Ballerina, Ballroom, Baryshnikov, Bayadère, Bob, Body-popping, Bump and grind, Caper, Ceili(dh), Choreography, Chorus-girl, Comprimario, Contredanse, Corp de ballet, Corybant, Coryphee, Dervish, De Valois, Diaghilev, Dinner, Disco(theque), Dolin, Egg, Exotic, Figurant, Figure, Fooling, Foot, Foot-it, Gandy, Gigolo, Groove, Hetaera, Hetaira, Hoofer, Isadora Duncan, Kick-up, Knees-up, Leap, Lope, Maenad, Majorette, Markova, Matachina, Mata Hari, Modern, Mosh, Nautch-girl, Night, Nijinsky, Nod, Number, Nureyev, Oberek, Old-time, Orchesis, Orchestic, Partner, Pavlova, Peeler, Petipa, Pierette, Prom(enade), Pyrrhic, Rambert, Raver, Reindeer, Ring, Romp, St Vitus, St Vitus's, Salome, Saltant, Saltatorious, Shearer, Skank, Skipper, Slammer, Spring, Step(per), Strut, Table, Tea, Terpsichore, Thé dansant, Tread, Trip(pant), Vogue(ing), Whirl, Wire-walker

---

## DANCES

*3 letters:*
Bop
Fan
Gig
Hay
Hey
Hop
Ice
Jig
Lap
Pas
Poi
Sun
Tap
Toe
War

*4 letters:*
Ball
Barn
Bull
Clog
Dump
Fado
Folk
Fris
Frug
Giga
Go-go
Haka
Hora
Hula
Jive
Jota
Juba
Juke
Kolo
Line
Lion
Loup
Nach
Pogo
Polo
Punk
Rain
Reel
Rope
Sand
Shag
Slam
Spin
Spot
Stag
Taxi
Wire

*5 letters:*
Bamba
B and S
Belly
Bogle
Brawl
Break
Carol
Ceroc®
Conga
Disco
Fling
Furry
Galop
Ghost
Gigue
Glide
Gopak
Horah
Limbo
Loure
Mambo
Mooch
Natch
Paspy
Pavan
Paven
Pavin
Polka
Ragga
Robot
Round
Rueda
Rumba
Salsa
Samba
Shake
Skirt
Snake
Stomp
Sword
Tango
Torch
Truck
Twist
Valse
Volta
Waltz

*6 letters:*
Apache
Ballet
Bolero
Boogie

Boston
Branle
Bubble
Canary
Can-can
Cha-cha
Fading
Floral
Friska
German
Hustle
Jump-up
Kathak
Lavolt
Maxixe
Minuet
Morris
Pavane
Redowa
Shadow
Shimmy
Smooch
Square
Trophe
Valeta
Veleta
Waggle
Watusi

*7 letters:*
Bambuca
Beguine
Bourrée
Bransle
Brantle
Cantico
Capuera
Carioca
Coranto
Cossack
Country
Courant
Csardas
Farruca
Forlana
Foxtrot
Furlana
Gavotte
Halling
Hoe-down
Lambada
Lancers
Landler
Lavolta
Macabre
Maypole
Mazurka
Measure
Moresco
Morisco
Morrice
Moshing
Musette
One-step
Pericon
Planxty
Polacca
Ridotto
Ringlet
Romaika
Roundel
Roundle
Routine
Sardana
Sashaya
Shuffle
Tanagra
Tordion
Toyi-toy
Trenise
Trip-hop
Two-step
Watutsi
Ziganka

*8 letters:*
Alegrias
Boogaloo
Bunnyhop
Bunnyhug
Cachucha
Cakewalk
Canticoy
Capoeira
Chaconne
Cotillon
Courante
Egg-dance
Excuse-me
Fandango
Flamenco
Flip-flop
Galliard
Guimbard
Habanera
Hay-de-guy
Haymaker
Headbang
Hey-de-guy
Heythrop
Hoolican
Hornpipe
Hula-hula
Irish jig
Joncanoe
Junkanoo
Kantikoy
Kapa haka
Kazachok
Kazatzka
Krumping
Lindy hop
Macarena
Marinera
Matachin
Matelote
Medicine
Merengue
Moonwalk
Murciana
Rigadoon
Robotics
Ronggeng
Saraband
Snowball
Soft-shoe
Taglioni
Toyi-toyi
Trucking

*9 letters:*
Allemande
Bergamask
Bergomask
Bossanova
Caballero
Cha-cha-cha
Chipaneca
Cotillion
Ecossaise
Eightsome
Farandole
Formation
Gallopade
Hoolachan
Jitterbug
Kathakali
Malaguena
Pas de deux
Paso doble
Passepied
Paul Jones
Polonaise
Poussette
Quadrille
Quickstep
Ring-shout
Roundelay
Sarabande
Siciliana
Siciliano
Sink-a-pace
Sugarfoot
Tambourin
Tripudium
Variation
Zapateado

*10 letters:*
Antimasque
Breakdance
Carmagnole
Charleston
Cinderella
Cinque-pace
Corroboree
Gay Gordon's
Hay-de-guise
Hay-de-guyes
Hey-de-guise
Hey-de-guyes
Hokey-cokey
Passamezzo
Petronella
Rug-cutting
Saltarello
Seguidilla
Sicilienne
Sinke-a-pace
Strathspey
Tarantella
Tripudiate
Turkey trot
Tyrolienne
Walk-around

*11 letters:*
Antistrophe
Black bottom
Buck and wing
Cracovienne
Eurhythmics
Lambeth walk
Palais glide
Passacaglia
Pastourelle
Progressive
Schottische
Shimmy-shake
Varsovienne

*12 letters:*
Bharat Natyam
Boogie-woogie
Labanotation
Passemeasure
Passy-measure
Virginia reel

*13 letters:*
Highland fling
Virginian reel

*14 letters:*
Divertissement
Jack-in-the-green

*15 letters:*
Roger de Coverley
Soft shoe shuffle

*16 letters:*
Circassian circle

*18 letters:*
Sir Roger de Coverley

---

**Dance hall** Disco, Juke-joint, Palais

**Dance movement** Arabesque, Balancé, Battement, Batterie, Benesh, Bourree, Brisé, Cabriole, Chaine, Chassé, Dos-à-dos, Dosido, Entrechat, Fishtail, Fouetté, Glissade, Jeté, Lassu, Pantalon, Pas de basque, Pas de chat, Pas seul, Pigeonwing, Pirouette, Plastique, Plié, Poule, Poussette, Promenade, Routine, Sauté, Step, Telemark, Twinkle

**Dance tune** Toy
▷**Dancing** *may indicate* an anagram
**Dancing party** Ball, Ridotto
**Dandelion** Cat's ear, Hawkbit, Kok-saghyz, Piss-a-bed, Scorzonera, Taraxacum
**Dander** Anger, Gee, Passion, Saunter, Temper
**Dandle** Dance, Doodle, Fondle, Pet
**Dandruff** Furfur, Scurf
**Dandy** Adonis, Beau, Beau Brummell, Blood, Boulevardier, Buck(een), Cat, Cockscomb, Coxcomb, Dapper, →**DUDE**, Dundreary, Exquisite, Fancy, Fantastico, Fop, Gem, Jay, Jessamy, Johnny, Kiddy, Knut, Lair, Macaroni, Masher, Modist, Monarcho, Muscadin, Nash, Nut, Onegin, Posh, Puss-gentleman, Roy, Smart, Spark, Spiff, Swell, Ted, Toff, U, Yankee-doodle
**Dandy-horse** Draisene, Draisine
**Dane(s), Danish** Clemence, Dansker, Ogier, Ostmen, Pastry
**Danger(ous)** Alarming, Apperil, Black spot, Breakneck, Ca'canny, Chancy, Crisis, Critical, Dic(e)y, Dire, Dodgy, Emprise, Fear, Firetrap, Hairy, Hazard, Hearie, Hero, High-risk, Hot, Hotspot, Icy, Insecure, Jeopardy, Lethal, Menace, Mine, Minefield, Nettle, Nocuous, Objective, Parlous, Periculous, →**PERIL**, Pitfall, Plight, Precarious, Quicksand, Risk, Rock, Serious, Severe, Sicko, Snag, Snare, Threat, Tight, Tight spot, Trap, Treacherous, Ugly, Unsafe, Wonchancy
**Dangle** A(i)glet, Aiguillette, Critic, Droop, Flourish, Hang, Loll, Swing
**Daniel** Boon, Dan, Defoe, Deronda, Lion-tamer, Portia, Quilp
**Dank** Clammy, Damp, Humid, Moist, Wet, Wormy
**Daphne** Agalloch, Agila, Eaglewood, Lace-bark, Laura, Laurel, Mezereon
**Dapper** Dressy, Natty, Neat, Smart, Spiff, Sprauncy, Spruce, Sprush, Spry, →**TRIM**
**Dapple(d)** Marbled, Motley, Piebald, Speckle(d)
**Darbies** Cuffs, Irons, Snaps
**Dardanian** Aeneas
**Dare, Dare-devil, Daring** Adventure, Audacious, Aweless, Bold, Brave, Bravura, Challenge, Courage, Dan, Da(u)nton, Defy, Dreadless, Durst, Emprise, Face, Fearless, Foolhardy, Gallant, Gallus, Groundbreaking, Hardihood, Hazard, Hen, Heroic, Intrepid, Moxie, Neck, Prowess, Racy, Risk, Stuntman, Swashbuckler, Taunt, Venture
**Dark(en), Darkness** Aphelia, Aphotic, Apophis, Black(out), Blind, Byronic, Caliginous, Cimmerian, Cloud, Colly, Crepuscular, Depth, Dim, Dingy, Dirk(e), Dismal, Dour, Dusky, Eclipse, Embrown, Erebus, Evil, Gloom, Glum, Grim, Inky, Inumbrate, Jet, Kieran, Low-key, Mare, Maria, Melanous, Midnight, Mirk, Murk(y), Night(time), Obfuscate, Obnubilation, Obscure, Obsidian, Ominous, Ousel, Ouzel, Overcast, Pall, Phaeic, Pitch-black, Pit-mirk, Rooky, Sable, Sad, Saturnine, Secret, Shades, Shadowy, Shady, Shuttered, Sinister, Solein, Sombre, Sooty, Sphacelate, Starless, Stygian, Sullen, Sunless, Swarthy, Tar, Tenebrose, Tenebr(i)ous, Unfair, Unlit, Woosell
**Darling** Acushla, Alannah, Angel, Asthore, Beloved, Charlie, Cher, Chéri(e), Chick-a-biddy, Chick-a-diddle, Chuck-a-diddle, Dear, Dilling, Do(a)ting-piece, Duck(s), Favourite, Grace, Hinny, Honey, Idol, Jarta, Jo(e), Lal, Love, Luv, Mavourneen, Mavournin, Minikin, Minion, Oarswoman, Own, Peat, Pet, Poppet, Precious, Squeeze, Sugar, Sweetheart, Sweeting, Yarta, Yarto
**Darn** Begorra, Blow, Doggone, Hang, Mend, Plain, Repair, Sew
**Dart(s), Darter, Darts player** Abaris, Arrow, Banderilla, Beetle, Dace, Dash, Deadener, Dodge, Fleat, Fléchette, Flirt, Flit, Harpoon, Javelin, Launch, Leap, Lunger, Pheon, Race, Scoot, Shanghai, Skrim, Speck, Spiculum, Sprint, Strike, Taylor, Thrust, Wheech
**Darwin** Charles, Evolutionist
**Dash(ing), Dashed** Backhander, Bally, Blade, Blight, Blow, Bribe, Buck, Career, Charge, Collide, Cut, Dad, Dah, Damn, Dapper, Dart(le), Daud, Dawd, Debonair, Ding, Dod, Doggy, Elan, Em (rule), En (rule), Fa(s)cia, Flair, Fly, Gallop, Go-ahead, Hang, Hurl, →**HURRY**, Hurtle, Hustle, Hyphen, Impetuous, Jabble, Jaw, Jigger, Lace, Leg it, Line, Minus, Modicum, Morse, Natty, Nip, Panache, Pebble, Race, Raffish, Rakish, Ramp, Rash, Rule, Run, Rush, Sally, Scamp(er), Scapa, Scarper, Scart, Scoot, Scrattle, Scurry, Scuttle, Shatter, Showy, Skitter,

Skuttle, Soupçon, Souse, Spang, Speed, Spirit, Splash, Splatter, Sprint, Strack, Streak, Strike, Stroke, → STYLE, Swashbuckling, Swung, Throw, Tinge, Touch, Treacherous, Ugly, Viretot

**Dashboard** Fascia, Panel

**Dashwood** Hell-fire club

**Dastard(ly)** Base, Coward, Craven, Nid(d)erling, Poltroon

**Data(base), Datum** Archie, Blueray®, Circumstantial, Computerised, Cyberspace, Donné(e), Evidence, Factoid, Facts, Fiche, File, Floating-point, Garbage, Gen, Griff, Hard copy, HOLMES, Info, Input, IT, Knowledge, List, Material, Matrix, Newlyn, News, Ordnance, Read-out, Recreational, Soft copy, Statistic, Table, Triple

**Date(d), Dates, Dating** AD, Age, AH, Almanac, Appointment, Archaic, Best before, Blind, Boyfriend, Calendar, Carbon, Carbon-14, Closing, Computer, Court(ship), Deadline, Engagement, Epoch, Equinox, Era, Escort, Exergue, Expiry, Fission-track, Fixture, Gig, Girlfriend, Gregorian, Hot, Ides, Julian, Meet, Obsolescent, Outmoded, → OUT OF DATE, Passé, Past, Radioactive, Radio-carbon, Radiometric, Rubidium-strontium, See, Speed, System, Target, → TRYST, Ult(imo), Uranium-lead, Value

**Daub** Begrime, Blob, Dab, Gaum, Mess, Moil, Noint, Plaister, Plaster, Slaister, → SMEAR, Smudge, Splodge, Teer, Wattle

**Daughter (in law)** Child, D, Elect, Girl, Imogen, Jephthah's, Niece, Offspring, Skevington's

**Daunt** Adaw, Amate, Awe, Consternate, Deter, Dishearten, Intimidate, Overawe, Quail, Stun, Stupefy, Subdue, Unnerve

**Dauphin** Delphin

**David** Camp, Dai, Psalmist

**Davit** Crane, Derrick, Hoist

**Davite** Ethic(al)

**Davy** Crockett, Jones

**Daw** Bird, Kae, Magpie, Margery

**Dawdle(r)** Dally, Draggle, Drawl, Idle, Lag(gard), → LOITER, Malinger, Potter, Shirk, Slowcoach, Snail, Tarry, Troke, Truck

**Dawn(ing)** Aurora, Cockcrow, Daw, Daybreak, Daylight, Day-peep, Dayspring, Early, Enlightenment, Eoan, Eos, False, First light, French, Half-light, Light, Morning, Morrow, Occur, Prime, Register, Roxane, Sparrowfart, Spring, Start, Sunrise, Sun up, Ushas

**Day(s)** Account, Ahemeral, All Fools', All Hallows', All Saints', All Souls', Anniversary, Annunciation, Anzac, April Fool's, Arbor, Armistice, Ascension, Australia, Bad hair, Baker, Banian, Banyan, Barnaby, Bastille, Borrowing, Box, Boxing, Broad, Calendar, Calends, Calpa, Canada, Canicular, Childermas, Civil, Columbus, Commonwealth, Contango, Continental, Continuation, D, Daft, Date, Decoration, Degree, Derby, Der Tag, Dismal, Distaff, Dog, Dominion, Double, Dress down, Dressed, Duvet, Early, Easter, Ember, Empire, Epact, Fast, Fasti, Father's, Feast, Ferial, Field, Fiesta, Flag, Fri, Gang, Gaudy, Glory, Groundhog, Guy Fawkes', Halcyon, Hey, High, Hogmanay, Holocaust, Holy, Holy Innocents', Holy-rood, Hundred, Ides, Inauguration, Independence, Intercalary, Jour, J'ouvert, Judgment, Juridical, Kalends, Kalpa, Labo(u)r, Lady, Laetare, Lammas, Last, Law(ful), Lay, Leap, Mardi, Market, May, Memorial, Michaelmas, Midsummer, Mon, Morrow, Mother's, Muck-up, Mufti, Mumping, Name, Ne'erday, New Year's, Nones, Nychthemeron, Oak-apple, Octave, Off, Open, Orangeman's, Palmy, Pancake, Paper, Pay, Poppy, Post, Pound, Present, Press(ed), Primrose, Pulvering, Quarter, Rag, Rainy, Red-letter, Remembrance, Rent, Rest, Robin, Rock, Rogation, Rood(-mas), Rosh Chodesh, Sabbath, St Crispin's, St John's, St Patrick's, Saint's, St Stephen's, St Swithin's, St Thomas's, St Valentine's, Salad, Sansculotterie, Sat, Scambling, Settling, Sexagesima, Shick-shack, Show, Sidereal, Singles, Snow, Solar, Solstice, Speech, Sports, Station, Sun, Supply, Tag, Term, Thanksgiving, Thurs, Ticket, Time, Transfer, Trial, Triduum, Tues, Twelfth, Utas, Valentine's, Varnishing, VE, Vernissage, Veterans', Victoria, Visiting, VJ, Waitangi, Wash, Wed, Wedding, Working

**Day-blindness** Hemeralopia

**Daybreak** Cockcrow, Cockleert, First light, Skreigh of day

**Daydream(er), Daydreaming** Brown study, Castle(s) in the air, Dwam, Dwaum, Escapism, Fancy, Fantasist, Imagine, Lose oneself, Muse, Reverie, Rêveur, Star-gaze, Walter Mitty, Woolgathering

**Daylight** Artificial, Dawn, Living, Robbery, Space, Sun
**Daze(d)** Amaze, Bemuse, Confuse, Dwaal, Gally, Muddle, Muzzy, Petrify, Punch drunk, Reeling, Spaced out, →STUN, Stupefy, Stupor, Trance
**Dazzle(d), Dazzler, Dazzling** Bewilder, Blend, Blind, Bobby, Eclipse, Foudroyant, Glare, Larking glass, Meteoric, Outshine, Psychedelic, Radiance, Resplendent, Splendour, Yblent
**Deacon** Cleric, Doctor, Minister, Permanent
**Deactivate** Unarm
**Dead(en)** Abrupt, Accurate, Alamort, Asgard, Asleep, Bang, Blunt, Brown bread, Bung, Cert, Cold, Complete, D, Damp, Deceased, Defunct, Dodo, Doggo, Expired, Extinct, Flatliner, Gone(r), Inanimate, Inert, Infarct, Late, Lifeless, Morkin, Muffle, Mute, Napoo, Niflheim, Numb, Obsolete, Obtund, Ringer, Sequestrum, She'ol, Slain, Smother, Stillborn, True, Under hatches, Utter, Waned
**Deadbeat** Idler
**Dead end, Deadlock** Blind alley, Cut-off, Dilemma, Impasse, Logjam, Stalemate, Stoppage
**Dead-leaf colour** Filemot, Philamot, Philomot
**Deadline** Closing date, Date, Epitaph, Limit, Lisus, Rebuff, Sell-by date, Worsen
**Deadlock** Impasse, Log-jam, Stalemate, Stand-off, Sticking-point
**Deadly** Baleful, Dull, Exact, Fell, Funest, Internecine, →LETHAL, Malign, Monkshood, Mortal, Mortific, Nightshade, No more, Pestilent, Stone, Thanatoid, Unerring, Venomous
**Deadly nightshade** Atropa, Belladonna, Dwale
**Deadpan** Dry, Expressionless
**Dead reckoning** Dr
**Dead tree** Rampick, Rampike
**Deaf(en), Deafening, Deafness** Adder, Asonia, Deave, Deeve, Dunny, Heedless, Paracusis, Presbyac(o)usis, Presbyc(o)usis, Surd(ity)
**Deal(er), Dealership, Dealing(s), Deal with** Act, Address, Agent, Agreement, Allocate, Allot(ment), Arb, Arbitrageur, Bargain, Biz, Bottle-o, Breadhead, Brinjarry, Broker, Bulk, Business, Cambist, Candyman, Chandler, Chapman, Clocker, Commerce, Connection, Contract, Cope, Coup, Cover, Croupier, Dispense, Distributor, Do, Dole, Done, East, Eggler, Exchange, Fir, Franchise, Fripper, Front-running, General, Goulash, Hack, Hand(le), Help, Horse trading, Inflict, Insider, Interbroker, Intercourse, Jiggery-pokery, Jobber, Lashing, Lay on, Lay out, Loads, Lot, Manage, Mercer, Merchandise, Merchant, Mickle, Middleman, Monger, Mort, Negotiate, New, North, Operator, Package, Pedlar, Pine, Plain, Post, Productivity, Pusher, Racketeer, Raft, Rag and bone man, Raw, Red, Regrate, Relation, Relations, Sale, Scrap merchant, See to, Serve, Side, Sight, Simoniac, Slanger, Sort, South, Spicer, Spiv, Square, Stapler, Stockbroker, Stockist, Stockjobber, Takeover, Tape, Timber, Totter, Tout(er), →TRADE, Trade in, Trade off, Tradesman, Traffic, Traffick, Transaction, Treat, Treaty, Truck, West, Wheeler, White, Wholesaler, Wield, Wood, Woolstapler, Yarborough, Yardie
**Dean** Acheson, Arabin, Chapter-head, Colet, Dale, Decani, Den, Doyen, Forest, Head, Inge, Nellie, Provost, RD, Rural, Rusk, Skater, Slade, Spooner, Swift, Vale, Vicar-forane, V rev
**Dear(er), Dearest, Dear me** Ay, Bach, Beloved, Cara, Caro, Cher(e), Cherie, Chou, Chuckie, Costly, Darling, Duck(s), Expensive, Extortionate, High, Honey(bun), Joy, Lamb, Leve, Lief, Lieve, Loor, Love, Machree, Mouse, My, Pet, Pigsney, Pigsnie, Pigsny, Precious, Soote, Steep, Sugar, Sweet, Sweetheart, Sweetie, Sweeting, Toots(ie), Unreasonable, Up
**Dearth** Famine, Lack, Paucity, Scantity, Scarcity, →SHORTAGE
**Deaspiration** Psilosis
**Death(ly)** Abraham's bosom, Auto-da-fe, Bane, Bargaist, Barg(h)est, Biolysis, Black, Carnage, Cataplexis, Charnel, Civil, Clinical, Commorientes, Cot, Crib, Curtains, Cypress, Demise, Deodand, Departure, Dissolution, Dormition, End, Eschatology, Euthanasia, Exit, Expiry, Extinction, Fatality, Fey, Funeral, Fusillation, Gangrene, Grim Reaper, Hallal, Heat, Hereafter, Infarction, Jordan, Karoshi, King of Terrors, Lead colic, Lethee, Leveller, Living, Loss, Mors, Mortality, Napoo, Natural, Necrosis, Nemesis, Night, Obit, Passing, Quietus, Reaper, Sati, Sergeant, SIDS, Small-back, Sorry end, Strae, Sudden, Suttee, Terminal, Thanatism, Thanatology, Thanatopsis, Thanatos, Yama
**Death-flood** Styx

**Deathless(ness)** Athanasy, Eternal, Eterne, Immortal, Struldberg, Timeless, Undying
**Debacle** Cataclysm, Collapse, Disaster, Fiasco
**Debag** Dack, Unbreech
**Debar** Black, Deny, Deprive, Exclude, Forbid, Preclude, → PREVENT, Prohibit
**Debark** Excorticate
**Debase(d)** Adulterate, Allay, Bemean, Cheapen, Corrupt, Demean, Depreciate, Dialectician, Dirty, Grotesque, Hedge, Lower, Pervert, Traduce, Vitiate
**Debate(r), Debatable** Adjournment, Air, Argue, Casuist, Combat, Consider, Contention, Contentious, Contest, Controversy, Deliberate, Dialectic, Discept, Discourse, Discuss(ion), → DISPUTE, Flyte, Forensics, Forum, Full-dress, Issue, Moot, Paving, Polemics, Powwow, Reason, Teach-in, Warsle, Wrangle, Wrestle
**Debauch(ed), Debauchee, Debauchery** Caligulism, Corrupt, Decadent, Defile, Degenerate, Dissipate, Dissolute, Heliogabalus, Hellbender, Hell-raising, Immoral, Libertine, Licence, Orgy, Profligate, Raddled, Rake-hell, Riot, Roist, Roué, Royst, Seduce, Spree, Stuprate, Wet, Whore
**Debenture** Bond, Security
**Debilitate(d), Debilitation, Debility** Asthenia, Atonic, Cachexia, Enfeeble, Feeble, Languid, Neurasthenia, Weak
**Debit** Charge, Debt, Direct
**Debonair** Cavalier, Chipper, Gallant, Gay, Gracious, Jaunty, Suave
**Debrief** Wash up, Wind up
**Debris** Bahada, Bajada, Detritus, Eluvium, Flotsam, Jetsam, Moraine, Moslings, Pyroclastics, Refuse, → RUBBLE, Ruins, Sawdust, Shrapnel, Tel, Tephra, Waste, Wreckage
▷**Debris** *may indicate* an anagram
**Debt(or)** Abbey-laird, Alsatia, Arrears, Arrestee, Bad, Bankrupt, Bonded, Dr, Due, Floating, Funded, Insolvent, IOU, Liability, Moratoria, National, Obligation, Obligor, Outstanding, Oxygen, Poultice, Public, Queer Street, Red, Score, Senior, Subordinated, Tick, Tie, Unfunded
**Debt-collector** Bailiff, Forfaiter, Remembrancer
**Debut** Launch, Opening, Outset, Premiere, Presentation
**Debutante** Bud, Deb
**Decade** Rosary, Ten
**Decadence, Decadent** Babylonian, Decaying, Degeneration, Dissolute, Effete, Fin-de-siècle, Libertine
**Decamp** Abscond, Absquatulate, Bolt, Bunk, Depart, Flee, Guy, Levant, Make off, Mizzle, Slide, Slope, Vamoose, Welch
**Decant(er)** Carafe, Pour, Unload
**Decapitate, Decapitation** Aphesis, → BEHEAD, Guillotine, Obtruncate
▷**Decapitated** *may indicate* first letter removed
**Decay(ed), Decaying** Alpha, Appair, Beta, Biodegrade, Blet, Canker, Caries, Caseation, Consenescence, Crumble, Decadent, Declension, Decline, Decompose, Decrepit, Detritus, Dieback, Disintegrate, Dissolution, Doat, Doddard, Doddered, Dote, Dricksie, Druxy, Dry rot, Ebb, Effluvium, Fail, F(o)etid, Forfair, Gamma, Gangrene, Heart-rot, Impair, Moulder, Pair(e), Perish, Plaque, Ptomaine, Putrefy, Radioactive, Ret, Rot, Rust, Saprogenic, Sap-rot, Seedy, Senility, Sepsis, Spoil, Tabes, Thoron, Time-worn, Wet-rot
**Decease(d)** Death, Decedent, Demise, Die, Stiff
**Deceit(ful), Deceive(r), Deception** Abuse, Ananias, Artifice, Bamboozle, Barrat, Befool, Bitten, Blag, Blind, Bluff, Braide, Catch, → CHEAT, Chicane, Chouse, Con, Cozen, Cuckold, Decoy, Defraud, Deke (out), Delude, Diddle, Dishonest, Dissemble, Do brown, Double-cross, Double-dealing, Double-tongued, Dupe, Duplicity, False(r), Fastie, Fast-talk, Fiddle, Fineer, Flam, Fool, Four-flusher, Fox, Fraud, Gag, Gerrymander, Gloze, Guile, Gull, Hoax, Hoodwink, Hornswoggle, Humbug, Hype, Hypocritical, Illusion, Imposition, Inveigle, Invention, Jacob, Jiggery-pokery, Kid, Lead on, Liar, Malengine, Mamaguy, Mata Hari, Mendacious, Misinform, Mislead, Mislippen, Patter, Perfidy, Phenakism, Poop, Poupe, Pretence, Prevaricate, Punic, Rig, Ruse, Sell, Sham, Shifty, Sinon, Skulduggery, Sleekit, Snow job, Spruce, Stall, Stratagem, String along, Subreption, Swindle, Swizzle, Take in, Tregetour, Trick, Trump, Trumped up, Two-faced, Two-time, Weasel, Wile

**Decency, Decent** Chaste, Decorum, Ethical, Fitting, Godly, Healsome, Honest, Honourable, Kind, Mensch, Modest, Moral, Passable, Presentable, Proper, Respectable, Salubrious, Seemly, Sporting, Straight, Tolerable, Wholesome, Wise-like

**Decentralise** Disperse

**Deception, Deceptive** Abusion, Artifice, Bluff, Catchpenny, Catchy, Cheat, Chicanery, Codology, → DECEIT, Decoy, Disguise, Dupe, Duplicity, Elusive, Eyewash, Fallacious, False, Feigned, Fineer, Flam, Fraud, Fubbery, Gag, Gammon, Guile, Gullery, Have-on, Hocus-pocus, Hokey-pokey, Hum, Hunt-the-gowks, Hype, Ignes-fatui, Ignis-fatuus, Illusion, Insidious, Jiggery-pokery, Kidology, Legerdemain, Lie, Mamaguy, Moodies, Phantasmal, Runaround, Ruse, Scam, Sciolism, Sell, Sleight, Smoke and mirrors, Specious, Sting, The moodies, Thimblerig, → TRICK, Trompe l'oeil, Two-timing, Underhand

**Decide(r), Decided, Decisive** Addeem, Adjudge, Adjudicate, Agree, Arbitrate, Ar(r)e(e)de, Ballot, Barrage, Bottom-line, Call, Cast, Clinch, Commit, Conclude, Conclusive, → DECISION, Deem, Definite, Determine, Distinct, Draw lots, Effectual, Engrenage, Fatal, Firm, Fix, Foregone, Jump-off, Mediate, Opt, Parti, Play off, Predestination, Pronounced, Rescript, Resolute, → RESOLVE, Result, Rule, Run-off, Seal, See, Settle, Split, Sudden death, Sure, Tiebreaker, Try

**Deciduous** Teeth

**Decimal** Mantissa, Metric, Recurring, Repeating, Terminating

**Decimate** Destroy, Lessen, Tithe, Weaken

**Decipher(ing)** Cryptanalysis, Decode, Decrypt, Descramble, Discover, Disentangle, Explain, Interpret, Solve

▷**Decipher(ed)** *may indicate* an 'o' removed

**Decision** Arbitrium, Arrêt, Bottom line, Call, Crossroads, Crunch, Crux, Decree, Engrenage, Fatwa, Fetwa, Firman, Judg(e)ment, Parti, Placit(um), Referendum, Resolution, Resolve, Responsa, Ruling, Sentence, Split, Sudden death, Verdict

**Decisive** Climactic, Clincher, Crisis, Critical, Crux, Definite, Fateful, Final, Pivotal

**Deck** Adonise, Adorn, Angled, Array, Attrap, Bejewel, Boat, Canted, Cards, Cassette, Clad, Clothe, Daiker, Daub, Decorate, Dizen, Embellish, Equip, Flight, Focsle, Forecastle, Garland, Hang, Helideck, Hurricane, Lower, Main, Mess, Monkey poop, Orlop, Ornament, Pack, Pedestrian, Platform, Poop, Prim, Promenade, Quarter, Saloon, Spar, Sun, Tape, Tarok, Tarot, Upper, Void, Weather, Well

**Declare, Declaration, Declaim, Declamation, Decree** Absolute, A(r)e(e)de, Affidavit, Affirm, Air, Allege, Announce, Annunciate, Aread, Assert, Asseverate, Aver, Avow, Balfour, Bann(s), Bayyan, Breda, Call, Canon, Dictum, Diktat, Doom, Dying, Edict, Elocute, Emit, Enact, Fatwa(h), Fiat, Firman, Go, Grace, Harangue, Hatti-sherif, Improbation, Independence, Indiction, Indulgence, Insist, Interlocutory, Irade, Law, Mandate, Manifesto, Mecklenburg, Meld, Motu proprio, Mou(th), Nisi, Noncupate, Novel(la), Nullity, Nuncupate, Opine, Orate, Ordain, Order, Ordinance, Parlando, Petition of Right, Pontificate, Predicate, Present, Proclaim, Profess, Promulgate, Pronounce, Protest, Psephism, Publish, Rant, Read, Recite, Remark, Rescript, Resolve, Restatement, Rights, Rule, Ruling, Saw, Say-so, SC, Sed, Senatus consultum, Senecan, Shahada, Signify, Speak, Spout, Statement, Statutory, Swear, Testament-dative, Testify, Testimony, Tirade, UDI, Ukase, Ultimatum, Unilateral, Utter, Vie, Voice, Vouch, Will, Word

▷**Declaring** *may indicate* a word beginning 'Im'

**Decline, Declination, Declining** Abate, Abstain, Age, Ail, Atrophy, Catabasis, Comedown, Decadent, Degeneration, Degringoler, Deny, Descend, Deteriorate, Devall, Die, Diminish, Dip, Dissent, Downhill, Downtrend, Downturn, Droop, Drop, Dwindle, Ebb, Elapse, Escarpment, Fade, Fall, Flag, Forbear, Lapse, Magnetic, Opt out, Paracme, Pejoration, Peter, Plummet, Quail, Recede, Recession, Reflow, Refuse, Relapse, Retrogression, Rot, Ruin, Rust, Sag, Senile, Set, Sink, Slide, Slump, Slumpflation, Stoop, Subside, Sunset, Tumble, Twilight, Wane, Welke, → WILT, Withdraw, Wither

**Decoct(ion)** Apozem, Cook, Devise, Ptisan, Tisane

**Decode(d)** Analyse, En clair, Translate

**Decolleté** Low, Neckline

**Decommission(ed)** Ex

**Decompose, Decomposition** Biodegradable, Crumble, Decay, Degrade, Disintegrate, Electrolysis, Fermentation, Hydrolysis, Mor, Pyrolysis, Rot, Wither

**Decompression** Bends

**Decongestant** Inhalant, Menthol

**Deconstruct(ion)** Iconoclasm

**Deconstruction(ist)** Derrida

**Decontaminate** Disinfect, Purify

**Decor** Background, Scenery

**Decorate(d), Decorating, Decoration, Decorative** Adorn, Aiguilette, Angelica, Aogai, Applique, Arpillera, Attrap, Award, Bard, Bargeboard, Baroque, Bauble, Bead, Beaux-arts, Bedeck, Bedizen, Bells and whistles, Biedermeier, Bordure, Braid, Brattishing, Braze, Breastpin, Brooch, Cartouche, Centrepiece, Chain, Chambranle, Champlevé, Chinoiserie, Christingle, Cinquefoil, Cloisonné, Coachline, Coffer, Corn dollie, Cresting, Crocket, Croix de guerre, Cul-de-lampe, Daiker, Decoupage, Dentelle, Dentil, Diamante, Distemper, Doodad, Doodah, Do over, Do up, Dragée, Dragging, Emblazon, Emboss, Embrave, Encrust, Engrail, Enrich, Epaulet, Epergne, Etch, Fancy, Fangle, Festoon, Filigree, Fillet, Finery, Finial, Fleuret(te), Fleuron, Floriated, Florid, Flushwork, Fluting, Fob, Fourragère, Frieze, Frill, Frog, Frost, Furbish, Gadroon, Gammadion, Garnish, Garniture, Gaud, Gild, Gilt, Glitter, Godroon, Goffer, Gold leaf, Gradino, Grecque key, Grotesque, Guilloche, Historiated, Hundreds and thousands, Ice, Illuminate, Impearl, Inlay, Intarsia, Intarsio, Interior, Jabot, Jari, Kalambari, Knotwork, Leglet, Linen-fold, Linen-scroll, Marquetry, MC, Medal(lion), Mola, Motif, Moulding, Oath, OBE, Ogee, Openwork, Order, → **ORNAMENT**, Ornate, Orphrey, Overglaze, Ovolo, Paint, Paper, Paper-stainer, Parament, Passement(erie), Pâté-sur-pâté, Pattern, Photomural, Pinata, Pipe, Pokerwork, Polychromy, Pompom, Prettify, Prink, Purfle, Purple heart, Quilling, Rag-rolling, Rangoli, Repoussé, Ribbon, Rich, Ric(k)-rac(k), Rosemaling, Ruche, Scallop, Schwarzlot, Scrimshander, Scrimshaw, Serif, Set-off, Sgraffito, Skeuomorph, Smocking, Soutache, Spangle, Sprig, Staffage, Stipple, Stomacher, Storiated, Strapwork, Stucco, Studwork, Tailpiece, Tart up, Tassel, Tattoo, TD, Tessellate, Tilak, Titivate, Tool, Topiary, Topping, Tracery, Trim, Trinket, Veneer, Vergeboard, Wallpaper, Well-dressing, Wirework, Zari

**Decorous, Decorum** Becoming, Demure, Dignity, Etiquette, Fitness, Modest, Parliamentary, Prim, → **PROPER**, Propriety, Sedate, Seemlihe(a)d, → **SEEMLY**, Staid, Tasteful

**Decouple** Unhook

**Decoy** Allure, Attract, Bait, Bonnet, Button, Call-bird, Coach, Crimp, Entice, Lure, Piper, Q-ship, Roper, Ruse, Shill, Stale, Stalking-horse, Stall, Stoolie, Stool-pigeon, Tame cheater, Tice, Tole, Toll, Trap, Trepan

**Decrease** Cut back, Decrement, Decrew, Diminish, Dwindle, Fall, Iron, Lessen, Press, Ramp down, Reduce, Rollback, Slim, Step-down, Subside, Tail off, Wane, Wanze

**Decree** → **DECLARE**, Dictate, Preordain

**Decrepit** Crock, Dilapidated, Doddery, Doitit, Failing, Feeble, Frail, Moth-eaten, Spavined, Time-worn, Tumbledown, Warby, Weak

**Decriminalise** Launder

**Decry** Condemn, Crab, Denounce, Derogate, Detract, Downgrade, Traduce

**Dedicate(d), Dedication** Allot, Corban, Determination, Devote, Dinah, Endoss, Hallow, Inscribe, Oblate, Patriotism, Pious, Sacred, Single-minded, Votive, Work ethic

**Deduce, Deduction, Deductive** Allowance, A priori, Assume, Conclude, Consectary, Corollary, Derive, Discount, Dockage, Draw, Gather, Illation, Infer(ence), Natural, Obvert, Off-reckoning, Reason, Rebate, Recoup, Reprise, Stoppage, Surmise, Syllogism, Tax

**Deed(s)** Achievement, Act(ion), Atweel, Backbond, Back letter, Bill of sale, Charta, Charter, Defeasance, Derring-do, Disposition, Escrol(l), Escrow, Exploit, Fact(um), Feat, Indeed, Indenture, Manoeuvre, Mitzvah, Muniments, Premises, Quitclaim, Settlement, Specialty, Starr, → **TITLE**, Trust, Work

**Deem** Consider, Judge, Opine, Ordain, Proclaim, Repute, Think

**Deep(en), Deeply** Absorbed, Abstruse, Abysmal, Bass(o), Brine, Briny, Enhance, Excavate, Grum, Gulf, Hadal, Intense, Low, Mindanao, Mysterious, → **OCEAN**, Outfield, Profound, Re-enter, Rich, Sea, Sonorous, Sunk(en), Throaty, Upsee, Ups(e)y

**Deep-rooted** Hypabyssal, Inveterate

**Deer(-like)** Axis, Bambi, Barasing(h)a, Barking, Blacktail, Brocket, Buck, Cariacou, Caribou, Carjacou, Cervine, Chevrotain, Chital, Doe, Elaphine, Elk, Fallow, Gazelle, Hart, Hog, Irish elk, Jumping, Moose, Mouse, Mule, Muntjac, Muntjak, Musk, Père David's, Pricket, Pudu, Pygarg, Red, Rein, Roe, Rusa, Sambar, Sambur, Selenodont, Sika, Sorel(l), Spade, Spay(d), Spayad, Spitter, Spottie, Stag(gard), Tragule, Ungulate, Virginia, Wapiti, Water, White-tailed

**Deer-hunter** Tinchel

**Deface** Disfigure, Spoil

▷**Defaced** *may indicate* first letter missing

**Defame, Defamatory, Defamation** Abase, Bad mouth, Blacken, Calumny, Cloud, Denigrate, Detract, Dishonour, Impugn, In rixa, Libel, Malign, Mud, Mudslinging, Obloquy, Scandalum magnatum, Sclaunder, Scurrilous, Slander, Smear, Stigmatise, Traduce, Vilify

**Default(er)** Absentee, Bilk, Dando, Delinquent, Flit, Levant, Neglect, Omission, Renegue, Waddle, Welsh

**Defeat(ed), Defeatist** Beat, Best, Bowed, Caning, Capot, Cast, Checkmate, Clobber, Codille, Conquer, Counteract, Cream, Crushing, Debel, Defeasance, Demolish, Destroy, Discomfit, Dish, Ditch, Donkey-lick, Downfall, Drub, Eliminate, Fatalist, Floor, Foil, Foyle, Gub, Hammer, Hiding, Kippered, Laipse, Lick, Loss, Lurch, Marmelize, Master, Mate, Moral, Negative, Out, Outclass, Outdo, Outfight, Outfox, Outgeneral, Outgun, Outplay, Outvote, Outwit, → OVERCOME, Overmarch, Overpower, Overreach, Overthrow, Overwhelm, Pip, Plaster, Pulverise, Quitter, Rebuff, Repulse, Reverse, Rout, Rubicon, Scupper, Set, Shellacking, Sisera, Skunk, Squabash, Stump, Tank, Thrash, Thwart, Toast, Tonk, Trounce, Undo, Vanquish, War, Waterloo, Whap, Whip, Whitewash, Whop, Whup, Wipe-out, Worst

**Defecate, Defecation** Encopresis, Horse, Mute, Poop, Scumber, Skummer, Tenesmus

**Defect(ion), Defective, Defector** Abandon, Amateur, Apostasy, Blemish, Breakaway, Bug, Coma, Crack, Crawling, Deficient, Dement, Desert, Dud, Failing, Faulty, Flaw, → FORSAKE, Frenkel, Glitch, Gotterdammerung, Halt, Hamartia, Hiatus, Impairment, Kink, Lemon, Low, Manky, Mass, Mote, Natural, Paralexia, Point, Psellism, Rachischisis, Renegade, Renegate, Ridgel, Ridgil, Rig, Ring-shake, Rogue, Runagate, Schottky, Shortcoming, Spina bifida, Stammer, Substandard, Terrace, Treason, Trick, Want, Wanting, Weakness, Wreath

**Defence, Defended, Defend(er), Defensible, Defensive** Abat(t)is, Advocate, Alexander, Alibi, Antibody, Antidote, Antigenic, Antihistamine, Anti-predator, Apologia, Apologist, Arm, Back, Back four, Bailey, Barbican, Barmkin, Barricade, Bastion, Battery, Battlement, Berm, Bestride, Bodyguard, Bridgehead, Bulwark, Calt(h)rop, Castling, Catenaccio, CD, Champion, Chapparal, Civil, Counter-measure, Curtain, Demibastion, Ditch, Drawbridge, Embrasure, Enguard, Estacade, Firewall, Goalie, Guard, Hedgehog, Herisson, Hold, Immunity, J(i)u-jitsu, Justify, Kaim, Keeper, Kraal, Laager, Laer, Last-ditch, Libero, Linebacker, Maginot-minded, Mail, Maintain, Martello tower, MIDAS, Miniment, Moat, Motte and bailey, Muniment, Munition, Outwork, Palisade, Parapet, Pentagon, Perceptual, Possessive, Promachos, Propugnation, Protect, Quinte, Rampart, Rearguard, Redan, Redoubt, Refute, Resist, Ringwall, Roman wall, Sandbag, Sangar, Scarecrow, Seawall, → SHELTER, Shield(wall), Sicilian, Stonewall, Strategic, Support, Sweeper, Tenable, Tenail(le), Territorial, Testudo, Tower, Trench, Trou-de-loup, Uphold, Vallation, Vallum, Vindicate, Wall, Warran(t), Zonal

**Defenceless** Helpless, Inerm, Insecure, Naked, Sitting duck, Vulnerable

**Defendant** Accused, Apologist, Respondent, Richard Roe, Suspect

**Defer(ence), Deferential, Deferring** Bow, Complaisance, Curtsey, Delay, Dutiful, Homage, Meek, Moratory, Morigerous, Obeisant, Pace, Polite, Postpone, Procrastinate, Protocol, Reschedule, Respect, Roll over, Shelve, Spaniel, Stay, Submit, Suspend, Waive, Yield

**Defiance, Defiant, Defy** Acock, Bite the thumb, Bold, Brave, Brazen, Cock a snook, Contumacy, Dare, Daring, Disregard, Do or die, Flaunt, Flout, Insubordinate, Kembo, Kimbo, Outbrave, Outdare, Rebellion, Recalcitrant, Recusant, Resist, Scab, Stubborn, Titanism, Truculent, Unruly, Yahboo

**Deficiency, Deficient** Absence, Acapnia, ADA, Anaemia, Anoxia, Aplasia, Beriberi,

Dearth, Defect, Devoid, Failing, Hypinosis, Inadequate, Incomplete, Kwashiorkor, Lack, Osteomalacia, Scant, Scarcity, SCID, Shortage, Shortfall, Spanaemia, Want

▷**Deficient** *may indicate* an anagram

**Deficit** Anaplerotic, Arrears, Defective, Gap, Ischemia, Loss, Overdraft, Poor, Shortfall, Trade

**Defile(ment)** Abuse, Array, Barranca, Barranco, Besmear, Col, Conspurcation, Desecrate, Dishonour, Donga, Enseam, → FOUL, Gate, Gorge, Gully, Inquinate, Inseem, Kloof, Moil, Pass, Pollute, Poort, Ravine, Ray, Roncesvalles, Smear, Spoil, → SULLY, Taint

**Define(d), Definition, Definitive** Clarify, Classic, Clear-cut, Decide, Demarcate, Determine, Diorism, Distinct, Explain, Fix, Limit, Parameter, Pinpoint, Set, Sharp, Specific, Tangible, Term

**Definite(ly)** Categorically, Cert(ainty), Classic, Clear (cut), Concrete, Deffo, Emphatic, Firm, Hard, Indeed, Pos, Positive, Precise, Sans-appel, Specific, Sure, Tangible, Unquestionably, Yes

**Deflate** Burst, Collapse, Flatten, Lower, Prick, Puncture, Squeeze

**Deflect(or), Deflection** Avert, Back-scatter, Bend, Detour, Diverge, Divert, Glance, Head off, Holophote, Otter, Paravane, Parry, Refract, Snick, Swerve, Throw, Trochotron, Veer, Windage

**Deform(ed), Deformity** Anamorphosis, Blemish, Boutonniere, Claw-foot, Contracture, Crooked, Disfigure, Distort, Freemartin, Gammy, Gargoylism, Hammer-toe, Harelip, Misborn, Miscreated, Misfeature, Mishapt, Mooncalf, Mutilate, Phocomelia, Phocomely, Polt-foot, Saddle-nose, Splay feet, Stenosed, Talipes, Valgus, Varus, Warp

▷**Deformed** *may indicate* an anagram

**Defraud** Bilk, Cheat, Cozen, Gull, Gyp, Lurch, Mulct, Shoulder, Skin, Sting, Swindle, Trick

**Defray** Bear, Cover, Meet

**Defrost** Thaw

**Deft** Adept, Agile, Dab, Dexterous, Elegant, Handy, Nimble, Slick

**Defunct** Deceased, Extinct, Obsolete, Write-off

**Defuse** Disarm

▶**Defy** *see* DEFIANCE

**Degauss** Demagnetise

**Degenerate, Degeneration, Degenerative** Acorn-shell, Ascidian, Atrophy, Backslide, Balanus, Base, Cirrhipedea, Cirrhipedia, Cirrhopod(a), Cirripedea, Cirripedia, Decadent, Deprave, Descend, Deteriorate, Eburnation, Effete, Fatty, Hyaline, Kaliyuga, Lapse, Necrobiosis, Pejorate, Pervert, Rakehell, Regress, Relapse, Retrogress, Rot, Salp, Steatosis, Tunicate, Worsen

**Degrade(d), Degradation, Degrading** Abase, Brutalise, Cheapen, Culvertage, Debase, Declass, Demission, Demote, Depose, Diminish, Disennoble, Embase, Embrute, Humble, Imbase, Imbrute, Lessen, Lower, Menial, → SHAME, Sink, Sleazy, Waterloo

**Degree(s)** Aegrotat, As, Attila (the Hun), Azimuthal, BA, Baccalaureate, BCom, BD, Bearing, B ès S, C, Calibre, Carat, Celsius, Class, D, Desmond (Tutu), Doctoral, Doctorate, Double first, Douglas (Hurd), Engler, Extent, External, F, Fahrenheit, First, Forbidden, Foundation, Geoff (Hurst), German, Gradation, Grade, Gradual, Grece, Gree(s), Greece, Gre(e)se, Grice, Griece, Grize, Honours, → IN A HIGH DEGREE, Incept, Incidence, K, Kelvin, Lambeth, Latitude, Letters, Level, Levitical, Licentiate, Longitude, MA, Master's, MBA, Measure, Mediant, Nth, Nuance, Order, Ordinary, Pass, Peg, PhD, Pin, Poll, Quality, Rate, Reaumur, Remove, Second, Stage, Status, Step, Subdominant, Submediant, Subtonic, Supertonic, Temperature, Third, Trevor (Nunn), Water

**Dehiscence** Suture

**Dehydrate(d)** Exsiccate, Shrivel, Thirsty

**Deification, Deify** Apotheosis

**Deign** Condescend, Stoop

**Deity** Alpha and omega, Avatar, Cabiri, Demogorgon, Divine, Faun, → GOD, → GODDESS, Idolise, Immortalise, Krishna, Lar, Numen, Pan, Satyr, Zombi(e)

**Déjà vu** Flashback

**Deject(ed), Dejection** Abase, Abattu, Alamort, Amort, Blue, Cast down, Chap-fallen, Chopfallen, Crab, Crestfallen, Despondent, Discouraged, Dismay, Dispirited, Down, Downcast, Gloomy, Hangdog, Humble, Low, Melancholy, Spiritless, Wae

**Delaware** DE(L)

**Delay(ed), Delaying** Adjourn(ment), After-effect, Ambage, Avizandum, Await, Backlog, Behindhand, Belated, Bottleneck, Check, Cunctator, Dawdle, Defer, Demurrage, Detention, Dilatory, Fabian, Filibuster, Forsloe, For(e)slow, Frist, Hangfire, Hesitate, Hinder, Hitch, Hold up, Hysteresis, Impede, Laches, Lag, Late, Laten, Let, Linger, Loiter, Mora(torium), Obstruct, Pause, Procrastinate, Prolong, Prorogue, Remanet, Reprieve, Respite, Retard, Rollover, Setback, Slippage, Sloth, Slow, → STALL, Stand-over, Stay, Stonewall, Suspend, Tarry, Temporise, Time-lag, Wait

**Delectable** Delicious, Luscious, Tasty

**Delegate, Delegation** Agent, Allocate, Amphictyon, Apostolic, Appoint, Assign, Commissary, Commission, Decentralise, Depute, Devolution, Emissary, Mission, Nuncio, Offload, Outsource, Representative, Secondary, Transfer, Vicarial, Walking

**Delete, Deletion** Adeem, Annul, Axe, Cancel, Clonal, Cut, Erase, Excise, Expunge, Purge, Rase, Scratch, Scrub, Strike, Twink out

**Deliberate(ly), Deliberation** Adagio, Calculated, Conscious, Consider, Debate, Intentional, Measured, Meditate, Moderate, Muse, On purpose, Overt, Plonking, Pointedly, Ponder, Premeditate, Prepensely, Purposely, Ruminate, Studied, Thought, Voulu, Weigh, Witting

**Delicacy, Delicate** Airy-fairy, Beccafico, Blini, Canape, Cate, Caviare, Dainty, Difficult, Discreet, Dorty, Ectomorph, Eggshell, Elfin, Escargot, Ethereal, Exquisite, Fairy, Fastidious, Filigree, Fine, Finespun, Finesse, Flimsy, Foie-gras, Fragile, → FRAIL, Friand, Gentle, Goody, Gossamer, Guga, Hothouse, Inconie, Incony, Kickshaw, Kidglove, Lac(e)y, Ladylike, Light(weight), Lobster, Morbidezza, Nesh, Nicety, Niminy-piminy, Ortolan, Oyster, Pastel, Reedy, Roe, Sensitive, Slight, Soft(ly-softly), Subtle(ty), Sunket, Sweetmeat, Tactful, Taste, Tender, Tenuous, Thorny, Ticklish, Tidbit, Titbit, Trotter, Truffle, Wispy

**Delicatessen** Charcuterie

**Delicious** Ambrosia, Delectable, Exquisite, Fragrant, Goloptious, Goluptious, Gorgeous, Lekker, Lip-smacking, Mor(e)ish, Mouthwatering, Savoury, Scrummy, Scrumptious, Tasty, Toothsome, Yummo, Yummy, Yum-yum

**Delight(ed), Delightful** Ambrosia, Bewitch, Bliss, Charm, Chuff, Coo, Delice, Dreamy, Ecstasy, Edna, Elated, Elysian, Enamour, Enchant, Enjoyable, Enrapture, Exhilarate, Exuberant, Exultation, Felicity, Fetching, Frabjous, Gas, Glad, Glee, Glorious, Gorgeous, Gratify, Honey, Idyllic, Joy, Lap up, Love, Nice, Overjoy, Over the moon, Please, Pleasure, Precious, → RAPTURE, Regale, Rejoice, Revel, Scrummy, Scrumptious, Super, Sweet, Taking, Tickle, Turkish, Whacko, Whee, Whoopee, Wizard, Yippee, Yum-yum

▷**Delight** *may indicate* 'darken'

**Delilah** Temptress

**Delineate** Draft, Outline, Prosciutto, Sketch, Trace

**Delinquent** Bodgie, Criminal, Halbstarker, Hoody, Juvenile, Law-breaker, Negligent, Offender, Remiss, Ted

**Delirious, Delirium** Deranged, DT, Fever, Frenetic, Frenzy, Insanity, Jimjams, Mania, Phrenetic, Phrenitis, Rambling, Spaced out, Wild

**Deliver(ance), Delivered, Deliverer, Delivery(man)** Accouchement, Air-drop, Air-lift, Bailment, Ball, Birth, Born, Bowl, Breech, Caesarean, Consign, Convey, Courier, Deal, Doosra, Drop, Elocution, Escape, Exorcise, Express, Extradition, Fastball, Forward, Free, Gaol, Give, Googly, Jail, Lead, Leg-spin, Liberate, Lob, Long hop, Mail drop, Messiah, Midwifery, Milk round, Obstetrics, Orate, Over, Paper round, Pronounce, Punch-line, Ransom, Receipt, Recorded, Redeem, Refer, Release, Relieve, Render, Rendition, → RESCUE, Rid, Round(sman), Salvation, Santa, Save, Say, Screwball, Seamer, Sell, Service, Shipment, Soliloquy, Speak, Special, Speech, Spell, Tice, Transfer, Underarm, Underhand, UPS, Utter, Ventouse extraction, Wide, Yorker

**Dell** Dale, Dargle, Dene, Dimble, Dingle, Dingl(e)y, Glen, Vale, Valley

**Delphic** Pythian

**Delphinium** Larkspur

**Delta** Camargue, D, Del, Flood-plain, Kronecker, Nabla, Nile, Oil Rivers, Triangle

**Delude, Delusion** Bilk, Cheat, Deceive, Dupe, Fallacy, Fool, Grandeur, Hoax, Kid, Megalomania, → **MISLEAD**, Myth, Paranoia, Schizothymia, Trick, Zoanthropy
**Deluge** Avalanche, Cascade, Flood, Ogygian, Saturate, Submerge, → **SWAMP**
**De luxe** Extra, Plush, Special
**Delve** Burrow, Dig, Excavate, Exhume, Explore, Mine, Probe, Rummage, Search
**Demagogue** Agitator, Fanariot, Leader, Mobsman, Phanariot, Speaker, Tribune
**Demand(ing), Demanded** Appetite, Ball-buster, Call, Choosy, Claim, Cry, De rigueur, Derived, Dictatorial, Difficult, Dun, Exact, Excess, Exigent, Extort, Fastidious, Final, Finicky, Gruelling, Heavy, Herculean, Hest, → **INSIST**, Mandate, Market, Necessitate, Need, Onerous, Order, Perfectionist, Postulate, Pressure, Pushy, Ransom, Request, Requisition, Rigorous, Rush, Sale, Severe, Stern, Stiff, Stipulate, Stringent, Summon, Tax, Ultimatum, Want
**Demean(ing)** Belittle, Comport, Debase, Degrade, Humble, Infra dig, Lower, Maltreat, Stoop
**Demeanour** Air, Bearing, Carriage, Conduct, Expression, Front, Gravitas, Mien, Port, Presence
**Dement(ed)** Crazy, Frenetic, Hysterical, Insane, Mad, Possessed, Wacko
**Demi-god** Aitu, Daemon, Garuda, Hero
**Demi-mondaine** Cocotte, → **LOOSE WOMAN**, Prostitute
**Demise** Death(-damp), Decease, Finish
**Demo** March, Parade, Protest, Rally, Sit-in
**Democracy, Democrat, Democratic** D, Hunker, Industrial, Liberal, Locofoco, Menshevik, Montagnard, People's, Popular, Populist, Republic, Sansculotte, Social, Tammany
**Demoiselle** Crane, Damselfish, Odonata
**Demolish, Demolition** Bulldoze, Devastate, Devour, Dismantle, Floor, KO, Level, Rack, Rase, → **RAZE**, Smash, Tear down, Wreck
▸**Demon** *see* **DEVIL(ISH)**
**Demoness** Lilith
**Demonstrate, Demonstration, Demonstrative, Demonstrator** Agitate, Barrack, Dharma, Display, Emotional, Endeictic, Évènement, Evince, Explain, Gesture, Hunger march, Maffick, Manifest, March, Morcha, Ostensive, Peterloo, Portray, Present, Proof, Protest, Prove, Provo, Send-off, → **SHOW**, Sit-in, Touchy-feely, Verify, Vigil
**Demoralise, Demoralisation** Bewilder, Corrupt, Depths, Destroy, Discourage, Dishearten, Shatter, Unman, Weaken
**Demos, Demotic** Enchorial, Greek
**Demote, Demotion** Comedown, Degrade, Disbench, Disrate, Downgrade, Embace, Embase, Reduce, Relegate, Stellenbosch
**Demotic** Enchorial
**Demur** Hesitate, Jib, Object
**Demure** Coy, Mim, Modest, Prenzie, Primsie, Prudish, Sedate, Shy
**Den** Dive, Domdaniel, Earth, Gambling, Hell, Hide-away, Holt, Home, Lair, Lie, Lodge, Opium, Padding-ken, Room, Shebeen, Spieler, Study, Sty, Wurley
**Denial, Deny, Denier** Abnegate, Antinomian, Aspheterism, Bar, Belie, Contradict, Controvert, Démenti, Denigration, Disavow, Disclaim, Disenfranchise, Disown, Disprove, Forswear, → **GAINSAY**, Nay, Negate, Nick, Nihilism, Protest, Recant, Refuse, Refute, Renague, Renay, Reneg(e), Renegue, Reney, Renig, Renounce, Reny, Repudiate, Sublate, Traverse, Withhold
**Denigrate** Besmirch, Blacken, Defame, Disparage, Libel, Slander, Tar
**Denim** Jeans, Stone-washed
**Denizen** Diehard, Inhabitant, Resident
**Denomination** Category, Cult, Sect, Variety
**Denote** Import, Indicate, Mean, Signify
**Denouement** Anagnorisis, Catastrophe, Climax, Coda, Exposure, Outcome, Showdown
**Denounce, Denunciation** Ban, Commination, Condemn, Criticise, Decry, Delate, Diatribe, Execrate, Fulminate, Hatchet job, Hereticate, Proclaim, Proscribe, Rail, Shop, Stigmatise, Thunder, Tirade, Upbraid

**Denry** Card
**Dense, Density** B, Bovine, Buoyant, Charge, Compact, Critical, Current, D, Double, Firm, Flux, Gauss, High, Intense, Magnetic flux, Neutral, Opaque, Optical, Packing, Rank, Reflection, Relative, Single, Solid, Spissitude, Stolid, Tesla, Thick, Transmission, Vapour, Woofy
**Dent(ed)** Batter, Concave, Dancette, Depress, Dimple, Dinge, Dint, Nock, Punctate, Punt, Stove in, V
**Dental (problem), Dentist(ry)** Crown work, DDS, Entodontics, Extractor, Kindhart, LDS, Malocclusion, Odontic, Paedodontics, Periodontic, Toothy
**Dentures** Biteplate, Bridge, Bridgework, False teeth, Plate, Prosthodontia, Store teeth, Wallies
**Denude** Erode, Strip
▸**Deny** *see* DENIAL
**Deodorant** Anti-perspirant, Cachou, Roll-on
**Deoxidise** Outgas, Reduce
**Depart(ed), Departing, Departure** Abscond, Absquatulate, Apage, Branch, Bunk, D, Dead, Death, Decamp, Decession, Defunct, Demise, Die, Digress, Divergence, Egress, Exception, Exit, Exodus, Expire, Flight, French leave, → GO, Imshi, Late, Leave, Lucky, Moonlight flit, Obiter dicta, Outbound, Rack off, Remue, Scat, Send-off, Skedaddle, Swan off, Vacate, Vade, Vamoose, Walkout
**Department** Achaea, Ain, Aisne, Allier, Alpes de Provence, Alpes-Maritimes, Angers, Arcadia, Ardeche, Ardennes, Argo, Argolis, Ariege, Arrondissement, Arta, Attica, Aube, Aude, Aveyron, Bas-Rhin, Belfort, Bell-chamber, Beziers, Bouches-du-Rhône, Branch, Bureau, Calvados, Cantal, Casualty, Charente, Charente-Maritime, Cher, Cleansing, Commissariat, Corrèze, Cote d'Or, Cotes d'Armor, Cotes du Nord, Creuse, DEFRA, Deme, Deuxième Bureau, Deux-Sevres, Division, Domain, Dordogne, Doubs, Drôme, El(e)ia, Essonne, Eure, Eure-et-Loir, Extramural, Faculty, Finistere, Fire, FO, Foggy Bottom, Gard, Gers, Gironde, Greencloth, Guadeloupe, Gulag, Haberdashery, Hanaper, Haute-Garonne, Haute-Loire, Haute-Marne, Haute-Normandie, Hautes-Alpes, Haute-Saône, Haute Savoie, Hautes-Pyrenees, Haute-Vienne, Haut-Rhin, Hauts-de-Seine, Helpdesk, Herault, Home, Ille-et-Vilaine, Indre, Indre-et-Loire, Inspectorate, Isere, Jura, Landes, Loire, Loiret, Loir-et-Cher, Lot, Lot-et-Garonne, Lozere, Maine-et-Loire, Manche, Marne, Martinique, Mayenne, Menswear, Meurthe-et-Moselle, Meuse, Ministry, Morbihan, Moselle, Nièvre, Nome, Nomos, Nord, Office, OFSTED, Oise, Ordnance, Orne, Pas-de-Calais, Portfolio, Province, Puy de Dôme, Pyrénées(-Atlantique), Pyrénées-Orientales, Region, Rehabilitation, Reunion, Rhône, Sanjak, Saône-et-Loire, Sarthe, Savoie, Secretariat(e), Section, Seine-et-Marne, Seine Maritime, Seine St Denis, Somme, Sphere, State, Tarn(-et-Garonne), Treasury, Tuscany, Unit, Val de Marne, Val d'Oise, Var, Vaucluse, Vendée, Vienne, Voiotia, War, Wardrobe, Yonne, Yvelines
**Depend(ant), Dependence, Dependency, Dependent** Addicted, Anaclitic, Child, Client, Colony, Conditional, Contingent, Count, Dangle, E, Fief, French Guiana, Habit, Hang, Hanger-on, Hinge, Icicle, Lean, Lie, Lippen, Minion, Need, Outpost, Pensioner, Poor relation, Relier, Rely, Retainer, Ross, Sponge, Stalactite, Statistical, Subject, Subordinate, Trust, Turn on, Vassal, Virgin Islands, Ward
**Dependable** Empirical, Reliable, Reliant, Rock, Safe, Secure, Sheet-anchor, Solid, Sound, Stalwart, Staunch, Stolid, Sure, → TRUSTWORTHY
**Depict, Depicted** Bepoint, Delineate, Delineavit, Describe, Display, Draw, Limn, Paint, Portray, Present, Represent
**Depilate, Depilation, Depilatory** Electrolysis, Grain, Rusma, Slate
**Deplete, Depletion** Depauperate, Diminish, Drain, Exhaust, Ozone, Reduce, Sap
**Deplorable, Deplore** Base, Bemoan, Chronic, Complain, Criminal, Deprecate, Dolorous, Execrate, Grieve, Lament, Mourn, Pathetic, Piteous, Regret, Rue, Sad, Shameful, Shocking, Woeful
**Deploy(ment)** Extend, Field, Herse, Invest, Unfold, Use
▹**Deploy(ment)** *may indicate* an anagram
**Depopulate** Deracinate

**Deport(ation), Deportment** Address, Air, Banish, →BEARING, Carriage, Demeanour, Dressage, Exile, Extradite, Gate, Mien, Renvoi, Renvoy, Repatriation

**Depose, Deposition** Affirm, Banish, Dethrone(ment), Displace, Dispossess, Hoard, Inqueen, Oust, Overthrow, Pieta, Testify

**Deposit(s), Depository** Aeolian, Alluvial, Alluvium, Aquifer, Archive, Arcus, Argol, Arles, Atheroma, Bank, Bathybius, Bergmehl, Calc-sinter, Calc-tuff, Caliche, Cave-earth, Coral, Crag, Crystolith, Delta, Depone, Diatomite, Diluvium, Down payment, Drift, Dust, Evaporite, Fan, File, Firn, Fort Knox, Fur, Glacial, Gyttja, Hoard, Icing, Illuvium, Kieselguhr, Land, Laterite, Lava, Lay, Lay away, Lay-by, Laydown, Lead tree, Limescale, Limonite, Lode, Lodge(ment), Loess, Löss, Marl, Measure, Moraine, Mould, Museum, Natron, Outwatch, Park, Pay dirt, Pay in, Phosphorite, Placer, Plank, Plaque, Precipitate, Put, Repose, Residuum, Saave, Saburra, Salamander, Sandbank, Saprolite, Saturn's tree, Scale, Sea dust, →SEDIMENT, Shell-marl, Silt, Sinter, Sludge, Soot, Speleothem, Stake, Stalagmite, Stockwork, Storeroom, Stratum, Surety, Tartar, Terramara, Terramare, Till, Time, Tophus, Tripoli, Turbidite, Warehouse

**Depot** Barracoon, Base, Camp, Coach station, Depository, Etape, Station, Terminus, Treasure-city, Warehouse

**Deprave(d), Depravity** Bestial, Cachexia, Cachexy, Caligulism, →CORRUPT, Dissolute, Evil, Immoral, Licentious, Low, Outrage, Reprobate, Rotten, Sodom, Subhuman, Total, Turpitude, Ugly, Unholy, Vice, Vicious, Vile

**Deprecate** Censure, Deplore, Disparage, Expostulate, Reproach

**Depreciate** Abase, Belittle, Derogate, Detract, Discount, Marginalise

**Depredate, Depredation** Pillage, Plunder, Rob

**Depress(ed), Depressing, Depression** Accablé, Agitated, Alamort, Alveolus, Amort, Astrobleme, Attrist, Basin, Black dog, Blight, Blue devils, Blues, Cafard, Caldron, Canada, Canyon, Cheerless, Chill, Col, Combe, Couch, Crab, Crush, Cyclone, Dampen, Deject, Dell, Demission, Dene, Dent, Despair, Dimble, →DIMPLE, Dip, Dismal, Dispirit, Ditch, Doldrums, Dolina, Doline, Doomy, Downcast, Downlifting, Drear, Drere, Dumpish, Endogenous, Exanimate, Flatten, Fonticulus, Footprint, Foss(ula), Fossa, Fovea, Frog, Geosyncline, Ghilgai, Gilgai, Gilgie, Glen, Gloom, Graben, Grinch, Ha-ha, Hammer, Heart-spoon, Hilar, Hilum, Hilus, Hollow, Hoofprint, Howe, Hump, Hyp, Hypothymia, Indentation, Joes, Kettle, Kick(-up), Lacuna, Leaden, Low(ness), Low-spirited, Megrims, Melancholy, Mood, Moping, Morose, Neck, Ocean basin, Pan, Pit, Polje, Postnatal, Postpartum, Pothole, Prostrate, Punt, Qattara, Recession, Re-entrant, Retuse, Sad, Saddle, Sag, Salt-cellar, Salt-pan, Scrobicule, Sink, Sinkhole, Sinus, Sitzmark, Slot, Slough, →SLUMP, Slumpflation, Soakaway, Spiritless, Stomodaeum, Sump, Sunken, Swag, Swale, Swallowhole, The blues, Trench, Trough, Umbilication, Vale, Vallecula, Valley, Wallow, Weigh down, Wet blanket

**Deprivation, Deprive(d)** Amerce, Bereft, Defibrinate, Deny, Disenfranchise, Disfrock, Dispossess, Disseise, Disseize, Divest, Excommunicate, Expropriate, Famine, Foreclose, Geld, Ghetto, Have-not, Hunger, Needy, Parch, Reduce, Remove, Rob, Sensory, Starve, Strip, Withhold

**Depth** Draught, Draw, F, Fathom, Gravity, Intensity, Isobath, Pit, Profundity

**Deputise, Deputy** Act, Agent, Aide, Assistant, Commis(sary), Delegate, Fill in, In loco parentis, Legate, Lieutenant, Locum, Loot, Mate, Nawab, Number two, Prior, Pro-chancellor, Proxy, Relief, Represent, Secondary, Sidekick, Standby, Stand-in, Sub, Subchanter, Substitute, Succentor, Surmistress, Surrogate, Tanaiste, Vicar, Vice, Viceregent, Vidame

**Derange(d), Derangement** Craze, Détraqué, Disturb, Flipped, Insane, Loopy, Manic, Moonstruck, Skivie, Trophesy, Troppo, Unhinge, Unsettle

**Derby** Boot, Crown, Demolition, Donkey, Eponym, Hat, Kentucky, Kiplingcotes, Local, Race, Roller

**Derek** Bo

**Derelict** Abandoned, Broken-down, →DECREPIT, Deserted, Disused, Negligent, Outcast, Ramshackle, Ruin, Tramp

**Deride, Derision, Derisive, Derisory** Catcall, Contempt, Gup, Guy, Hiss, Ho-ho, Hoot, Ironic, Jeer, Jibe, Mock, Nominal, Pigs, Raspberry, →RIDICULE, Sardonic, Scoff, Scorn, Slag, Sneer, Snifty, Snort, Ya(h)boo (sucks), Yah

**Derive, Derivation, Derivative** Amine, Ancestry, Apiol, Creosote, Deduce, Descend, Elicit, Extract, Get, Kinone, Lewisite, Of, Offshoot, Origin, Pedigree, Picoline, Saponin, Secondary, Taurine, Tyramine

▸**Dermatitis** *see* SKIN DISEASE

**Derogate, Derogatory** Aspersion, Belittle, Critical, Decry, Defamatory, Demeaning, Detract, Diatribe, Discredit, Libellous, Pejorative, Personal, Slanderous, Slighting, Snide, Tushing

**Deronda** Daniel

**Derrick** Crane, Davit, Hoist, Jib, Oil rig, Spar, Steeve

**Derv** Diesel

**Dervish** Calender, Doseh, Mawlawi, Mevlevi, Revolver, Santon, Sufi, Whirling

**Descant** Comment, Discourse, Faburden, Melody, Song

**Descartes** René

**Descend(ant), Descent** Abseil, Ancestry, Avail, Avale, Bathos, Blood, Cadency, Catabasis, Chute, Cion, Decline, Degenerate, Dégringoler, Derive, Dismount, Dive, Drop, Epigon, Extraction, Heir, Heraclid, → LINEAGE, Offspring, Pedigree, Posterity, Progeny, Prone, Purler, Rappel, Said, Say(y)id, Scarp, Scion, Seed, Shelve, Sien(t), Sink, Spearside, Stock, Stoop, Swoop, Syen, Tailspin, Vest, Volplane

**Describe, Describing, Description, Descriptive** Account, Blazon, Blurb, Caption, Define, Delineate, Depict, Designate, Draw, Ekphrasis, Encapsulate, Epithet, Explain, Exposition, Expound, Express, Graphic, Job, Label, Liken, Narrate, Outline, Paint, Portray, Rapportage, Recount, Relate, Report, Sea-letter, Semantic, Signalment, Sketch, Specification, Sum up, Synopsis, Term, Thumbnail, Trace, Vignette, Write-up

▹**Describing** *may indicate* 'around'

**Descry** Behold, Discern, Get, Notice, Perceive

**Desecrate, Desecration** Abuse, Defile, Dishallow, Profane, Sacrilege, Unhallow

▹**Desecrated** *may indicate* an anagram

**Desensitise** Inure

**Desert(er), Deserted, Deserts** Abandon, Absquatulate, Apostasy, Arabian, Areg, Arid, Ar Rimal, Arunta, Atacama, AWOL, Badland, Barren, Bledowska, Bug out, Bunk, Colorado, Come-uppance, D, Dahna, Defect, Desolate, Dissident, Ditch, Drop, Due, Empty, Eremic, Erg, Etosha Pan, Factious, Fail, Fezzan, Foresay, Forhoo, Forhow, Forlorn, Forsake, Forsay, Frondeur, Garagum, Gibson, Gila, Gobi, Great Basin, Great Indian, Great Sandy, Great Victoria, Heretic, Heterodox, Indian, Jump ship, Kalahari, Kara Kum, Karma, Kavir, Kyzyl Kum, Libyan, Lurch, Meeds, Merit, Mohave, Mojave, Nafud, Namib, Negev, Nubian, Ogaden, Painted, Patagonian, Pindan, Quit, Rat, Refus(e)nik, Reg, → RENEGADE, Reward, Rub'al-Khali, Run, Runaway, Sahara(n), Sahel, Sands, Secede, Sertao, Shamo, Simpson, Sinai, Solitude, Sonoran, Sturt, Syrian, Tacna-Arica, Tergiversate, Thar, Turncoat, Ust(y)urt, Victoria, Void, Wadi, Waste(land), Western Sahara, Wild, Wilderness, Worthiness

**Deserve(d)** Condign, Earn, → MERIT, Rate, Well-earned, Worthy

**Desiccate(d)** Arid, Dry, Sere

**Design(er)** Adam, Aim, Amies, Arabesque, Architect(ure), Argyle, Armani, Articulation, Ashley, Banks, Batik, Between-subjects, Broider, Cable stitch, Calligram(me), Cameo, Cardin, Cartoon, Castrametation, Cavo-relievo, Chequer, Chippendale, Choo, Cloisonné, Conran, Courreges, Couturier, Create, Cul de lampe, Damascene, Decal(comania), Decor, Deep, De Havilland, Depict, Device, Devise, Dévoré, Dior, Draft, Dyson, Eiffel, Embroidery, End, Engender, Engine(r), Engineer, Erté, Etch, Fashion, Feng-shui, Flanch, Format, Former, Fretwork, Galliano, Givenchy, Grand, Graphics, Gucci, Hamnett, Hepplewhite, Hitech, Iconic, Imagineer, Impresa, Imprese, Industrial, Inlay, Intaglio, Intelligent, Intend(ment), Intent(ion), Interior, Invent, Issigonis, Klein, Layout, Le Corbusier, Limit-state, Linocut, Logical, Logo, Marquetry, Mascle, Matched pairs, McCartney, McQueen, Mean, Meander, Mehndi, Millefleurs, Model, Modiste, Monogram, Morris, Mosaic, Motif, Muir, Multifoil, Nailhead, Nissen, Paisley, Pattern, → PLAN, Plot, Prada, Propose, Prostyle, Pyrography, Quant, Retro, Rhodes, Roji, Roundel, Ruse, St Laurent, Schema, Scheme, Schiaparelli, Seal, Sheraton, Sketch, Sopwith, Spatterwork, Specification, Sprig, Stencil, Stubble, Stylist, Sunburst, Tatow, Tattoo, Tattow, Tatu, Think, Tiffany, Tooling, Townscape, Trigram, Tupelov, Valentino,

Versace, Vignette, Wang, Watermark, Weiner, Werkstalte, Whittle, Willow pattern, Within-subjects

**Designate** Appoint, Destine, Earmark, List, Mark, Name, Note, Roji, Specify, Title

**Desirable, Desire, Desiring, Desirous** Ambition, Aphrodisia, Appetite, Aspire, Avid, Best, Cama, Conation, Concupiscence, Covet, Crave, Cupidity, Des, Dreamboat, Earn, Eligible, Envy, Epithymetic, Eroticism, Esurience, Fancy, Gasp, Greed, Hanker, Hope, Hots, Hunger, Impulse, Itch, Kama(deva), Le(t)ch, Libido, List, Long, Luscious, Lust, Mania, Month's mind, Motivation, Notion, Nymphomania, Optative, Orectic, Owlcar, Paedophilia, Pica, Pleasure, Plum, Provocative, Reak, Reck, Request, Residence, Rut, Salt, Sexy, Slaver, Spiffing, Streetcar, Thirst, Urge, Velleity, Vote, Wanderlust, Want, Whim, Will, Wish, Yearn, Yen

**Desist** Abandon, Cease, Curb, Pretermit, Quit, Stop

**Desk** Almemar, Ambo, Bonheur-du-jour, Bureau, Carrel(l), Cash, Check-in, Cheveret, City, Copy, Davenport, Desse, Devonport, Dropleaf, E(s)critoire, Enquiry, Faldstool, Lectern, Lettern, Litany, Pay, Pedestal, Prie-dieu, Pulpit, Reading, Roll-top, Scrutoire, Secretaire, Vargueno, Writing

**Desman** Pyrenean

**Desolate, Desolation** Bare, Barren, Bereaved, Bleak, Desert, Devastate, Disconsolate, Emptiness, Forlorn, Gaunt, Godforsaken, Gousty, Heartbreak, Lonesome, Moonscape, Stark, Waste, Woebegone, Wretched

**Despair, Desperate, Desperation** Acharne, Anomy, Crisis, Dan, De profundis, Despond, Dire, Dismay, Drastic, Extreme, Forlorn hope, Frantic, Gagging, Giant, Gloom, Hairless, Headlong, Hopelessness, Last-ditch, Last-gasp, Life and death, Reckless, Unhopeful, Urgent, Wanhope

▸**Despatch** *see* DISPATCH

**Desperado** Bandit, Bravo, Brigand, Outlaw, Ruffian, Terrorist

**Despicable** Abject, Base, Bleeder, Caitiff, Cheap, Churl, Contemptible, Heel, Heinous, Ignoble, Ignominious, Louse, Low-down, Mean, Moer, Poep(ol), Puke, Ratbag, Ratfink, Scumbag, Shabby, Snip, Snot, Toerag, Vermin(ous), Vile, Worm, Wretched, Yellow dog

**Despise(d)** Condemn, Conspire, Contemn, Forhow, Futz, Hate, Ignore, Scorn, Scrote, Spurn, Vilify, Vilipend

**Despite** For, Malgré, Nevertheless, Notwithstanding, Pace, Though, Venom

**Despoil** Bezzle, Mar, Rape, Ravage, Vandalise

**Despondent** Dejected, Downcast, Forlorn, Gloomy, Lacklustre, Sad

**Despot(ism)** Autarchy, Autocrat, Bonaparte, Caesar, Darius, Dictator, Little Hitler, Martinet, Monocrat, Napoleon, Nero, Satrap, Soldan, Stratocrat, Tsar, Tyrant, Tzar

**Dessert** Afters, Apple charlotte, Apple Crumb, Baba, Baclava, Baked Alaska, Baklava, Banana split, Bavarian cream, Bavarois, Blancmange, Bombe, Cannoli, Charlotte, Charlotte russe, Cheesecake, Clafoutis, Cobbler, Compote, Coupe, Cranachan, Cream, Crème brulée, Crème caramel, Crepe Suzette, Dulce de leche, Entremets, Eton mess, Eve's pudding, Flan, Floating Island, Flummery, Fool, Gelato, Granita, Jello, Jelly, Junket, Kissel, Knickerbocker glory, Kulfi, Marquise, Melba, Mousse, Mud pie, Nesselrode, Pannacotta, Parfait, Pashka, Pavlova, Peach Melba, Plum duff, → PUDDING, Rasmalai, Roulade, Rum baba, Sabayon, Sawine, Semifreddo, Shoofly pie, Sorbet, Split, Spumone, Strudel, Sundae, Syllabub, Tapioca, Tart, Tarte tatin, Tartufo, Tiramisu, Torte, Tortoni, Trifle, Vacherin, Whip, Zabaglione

**Destabilise** Unbalance

**Destine(d), Destination** Born, Design, End, Fate, Foredoom, Goal, Gole, Home, Intend, Joss, Meant, Port, Purpose, Vector, Weird

**Destiny** Doom, → FATE, Karma, Kismet, Lachesis, Lot, Manifest, Menesis, Moira, Portion, Yang, Yin

**Destitute, Destitution** Bankrupt, Bare, Beggar, Bereft, Breadline, Broke, Devoid, Dirt-poor, Down and out, Helpless, Impoverished, Indigent, Necessitous, Needy, Pauper, Penniless, Penury, Poor, Poverty, Sterile, Stony broke, Void, Waif and stray

**Destress** Anneal

**Destroy(er)** Annihilate, Antineutrino, Antineutron, Antiparticle, Apollyon, Atomise, Banjax, Blight, Bulldoze, Can, Canker, Corrode, Crush, D, Decimate, Deep-six, Deface, Delete,

Demolish, Demyelinate, Denature, Destruct, Devastate, Dish, Dismember, Dissolve, Eat, Efface, End, Eradicate, Erase, Estrepe, Exterminate, Extirpate, Flivver, Fordo, Graunch, Gut, Harry, Iconoclast, Incinerate, Invalidate, → KILL, KO, Lay waste, Locust, Murder, Obliterate, Overkill, Perish, Predator, Pulverize, Q-ship, Ravage, Raze, Ruin, Saboteur, Sack, Scuttle, Shiva, Shred, Siva, Slash, Smash, Spif(f)licate, Spoil, Sterilize, Stew-can, Stonker, Stultify, Subvert, Trash, Undo, Unlace, Uproot, Vandal, Vitiate, Waste, Whelm, Wildfire, Wreck, Zap

**Destruction, Destructive** Adverse, Apocalypse, Apostosis, Autolysis, Bane, Can, Catabolism, Collapse, Deathblow, Deleterious, Desecration, Devastation, Doom, Downfall, Ecocide, End, Götterdämmerung, Grave, Havoc, Holocaust, Hunnish, Iconoclasm, Insidious, Internecine, Kali, Lethal, Loss, Maelstrom, Maleficent, Malignant, Moorburn, Nihilistic, Pernicious, Pestilential, Pogrom, Quelea, Rack, Ragnarok, Ravage, Ruination, Sabotage, Speciocide, Stroy, Wrack, Wreckage

**Desultory** Aimless, Cursory, Fitful, Idle

**Detach(ed), Detachment** Abeigh, Abstract, Alienate, Aloof, Apart, Body, Break off, Calve, Clinical, Cut, Detail, Discrete, Disengage, Disinterested, Dispassionate, Distinct, Garrison, Insular, Isle, Isolate, Loose, Objective, Outlying, Outpost, Patrol, Picket, Picquet, Separate, Sever, Staccato, Stoic, Uncouple, Unfasten, Unhinge, Unit, Unpick, Withdrawn

**Detached work** Ravelin

**Detail(s), Detailed** Analysis, Annotate, Assign, Blow-by-blow, Brass tacks, Circumstances, Close-up, Depict, Dock, Elaborate, Embroider, Expatiate, Explicit, Exploded, Expound, Instance, Intricate, → ITEM, Itemise, Logistice, Minutiae, Narrate, Nicety, Nitty-gritty, Nuts and bolts, Particular(ise), Pedantry, Point, Recite, Recount, Relate, Respect, Send, Spec, Special, Specific, Specification, Technicality, Thorough, Touch

▷**Detailed** *may indicate* last letter missing

**Detain(ee), Detention (centre)** Apprehend, Arrest, Buttonhole, Captive, Collar, Custody, Delay, Demurrage, Detinue, Gate, Glasshouse, Hinder, Imprison, Intern, Juvie, Keep, POW, Preventive, Remand, Retard, Sin bin, Stay, → WITHHOLD

**Detect(or), Detectable, Detective** Agent, Armchair, Arsène, Asdic, Bergerac, Bloodhound, Brown, Bucket, Busy, Catch, Chan, Chlorometer, CIB, CID, Columbo, Cuff, Det, DI, Dick, Discern, Discover, Divine, Doodlebug, Dupin, Enquiry agent, Espy, Eye, Father Brown, Fed, Find, Flambeau, Flic, Fortune, French, Galvanoscope, Geigercounter, Geophone, G-man, Gumshoe, Hanaud, Hercule, Holmes, Interpol, Investigator, Jack, Lecoq, Lewis, Locate, Lupin, Maigret, Metal, Methanometer, Microwave, Mine, Minitrack®, Morse, Nail, Nose, Peeper, Perceive, PI, Pinkerton, Plant, Poirot, Private, Private eye, Prodnose, Radar, Reagent, Rebus, Retinula, Rumble, Scent, Scerne, Sense, Sensillum, Sensor, Shadow, Shamus, Sherlock, → SLEUTH, Sleuth-hound, Smell out, Smoke, Snooper, Sofar, Solver, Sonar, Sonobuoy, Spot, Store, Tabaret, Take, Tec, Thorndyke, Toff, Trace, Trent, Vance, Visible, Wimsey, Yard(man)

**Detent** Pawl, Trigger

**Deter(rent)** ASBO, Block, Check, Daunt, Dehort, Delay, Disincentive, Dissuade, Faze, Prevent, Restrain, Scare, Scarecrow, Trident, Turn-off, Ultimate

**Detergent** Cationic, Clean(s)er, Non-ionizing, Shampoo, Solvent, Sujee, Surfactant, Syndet, Tepol, Whitener

**Deteriorate, Deterioration** Decadence, Degenerate, Degrade, Degringolade, Dementia, Derogate, Entropy, Go downhill, Go to pot, Lapse, Pejoration, Perish, Regress, Relapse, Retrograde, Rust, Senesce, Worsen

▷**Deterioration** *may indicate* an anagram

▷**Determination** *may indicate* 'last letter'

**Determine(d), Determination** Adamant, All-out, Appoint, Arbitrament, Ardent, Ascertain, Assign, Assoil, Bent, Bound, Causal, Choose, Condition, Dead-set, → DECIDE, Dedicated, Define, Deliminate, Diagnose, Dictate, Doctrinaire, Dogged, Do-or-die, Dour, Drive, Earnest, Fix, Govern, Granite, Grim, Grit(ty), Headstrong, Hell-bent, Indomitable, Influence, Intent, Ironclad, Judgement, Law, Liquidate, Orient, Out, Persistence, Pertinacious, Point, Pre-ordain, Purpose, Quantify, → RESOLUTE, Resolve, Rigwiddie, Rigwoodie, Self-will, Set, Settle, Set upon, Shape, Single-minded, Soum, Sowm, Stalwart, Steely, Stout, Strong(-minded), Tenacious, Thrust, Type, Valiant, Weigh, Willpower

**Detest(able), Detested** Abhor, Abominate, Accursed, Anathema, Bete-noire, Despise, Execrable, Execrate, Hate, Loathsome, Odium, Pestful, Ugh, Vile

**Detonate, Detonator** Blast, Explode, Fire, Fuse, Fuze, Ignite, Kindle, Plunger, Primer, Saucisse, Saucisson, Spring, Tetryl, Trip-wire

**Detour** Bypass, Deviate, Divert

**Detox** Rehab

**Detract** Belittle, Decry, Diminish, Discount, Disparage

**Detriment(al)** Adverse, Bad, Damage, Harm, Injury, Loss, Mischief, Prejudicial

**Detroit** Motown

**Deuce** Dickens, Old Harry, Twoer

**Deuteron** Diplon

**Devalue** Cheapen, Debase, Impair, Reduce, Undermine

**Devastate, Devastation** Demolish, Destroy, Ground zero, Gut, Lay waste, Nuke, Overwhelm, Ravage, Ruin, Sack, Shatter, Traumatise, Waste, Wrack, Wreck

**Develop(er), Developed, Developing, Development** Advance, Age, Agile, Amidol®, Aplasia, Apotheosis, Arise, Breakthrough, Breed, Bud, Build, Burgeon, Catechol, Creep, Cutting edge, Dark room, Educe, Elaborate, Emerge, Enlarge, Epigenetic, Escalate, Estate, Euphonics, Evolue, Evolution, Evolve, Expand, Expatriate, Fixer, Flourish, Foetus, Formulate, Full-blown, Full-fledged, Fulminant, Genesis, Germinate, Gestate, Greenfield, Grow, Hatch, Hothouse, Hydroquinone, Hypo, Imago, Immature, Improve, Incipient, Incubate, Lamarckism, Larva, Mature, Metamorphose, Metol, Morphogenesis, Morphosis, Mushroom, Nascent, Nurture, Offshoot, Oidium, Ongoing, Ontogenesis, Pathogeny, Progress, Pullulate, Pupa, Pyro, Pyrogallol, Quinol, Ribbon, Ripe(n), Sarvodaya, Sensorimetor, Separate, Shape, Soup, Speciation, Sprawl, Subtopia, Technography, Teens, Tone, Twist, Unfold, Upgrow

▷**Develop** *may indicate* an anagram

**Deviant, Deviate, Deviation** Aberrance, Abnormal, Anomaly, Average, Blip, Brisure, Decline, Deflect, Deflexure, Depart, Derogate, Detour, Digress, Discrepant, Diverge, Divert, Drift, Error, Fade, Inflexion, Kinky, Kurtosis, List, Masochist, Mean, Outlier, Pervert, Quartile, Sadist, Sheer, Solecism, Sport, Standard, Stray, Swerve, → **TURN**, Vagary, Valgus, Varus, Veer, Wander, Wend, Yaw

**Device** Allegory, → **APPARATUS**, Appliance, Artifice, Bush, Contraption, Contrivance, Deus ex machina, Dodge, Emblem, Expedient, Gadget, Gimmick, Gismo, Gizmo, Gubbins, Instrument, Logo, Mechanism, Mnemonic, Motto, Plan, Pointing, Ruse, Safeguard, → **STRATAGEM**, Subterfuge, Tactic, Tag, Thing, Tool, Trademark, Trick, Wile

---

## DEVICES

*3 letters:*
Bug
FET
LED
Mux
Pad
Pig
POP
Set
Van
Zip

*4 letters:*
Bulb
Capo
Drag
Fret
Fuse
Gobo
Grab
Head
Hook
Ipod®
Orle
Plug
Rest
Shoe
Skid
Spur
Stop
Tram
Trap

*5 letters:*
Audio
Balun
Brace
CD-ROM
Chaff
Choke
Chuck
Clamp
Cleat
Codec
Combi
Conch
Corer
Cramp
Crank
Crest
Diode
E-nose
Flare
Frame
Gatso®
Gland
Input
Laser
Lidar
Maser
Meter
Mixer
Modem
Mouli
Mouse
Optic®
Otter
Pager
Petar
Prism
Probe
Quipu
Relay
Rotor
Saser
Scale
Scart
Servo
Sewel
Shear
Sieve
Siren
Snare
Sonde
Spool
Sprag
SQUID
Stent
Taser®
Timer
Tromp
Truss
Turbo
Valve
V-chip

Waldo
Winch

***6 letters:***
Airbag
Analog
Atlatl
Balise
Beeper
Biodot
Blower
Bungee
Buzzer
Charge
Chowri
Chowry
Clevis
Cotter
Cursor
Cut-off
Cut-out
Dasher
Deckle
De-icer
Detent
Dimmer
Dongle
Elevon
Engine
Etalon
Euouae
Evovae
Faller
Feeder
Filter
Friend®
Grater
Heddle
Imager
Inhole
Jigger
Joypad
Keeper
Kludge
Logger
Masker
Nanite
Navaid
Packer
Peeler
Petard
Pick-up
Pinger®
Piston
Possum
Pre-amp
Preset
Quippu
Rabble
Reheat
Remote
Reverb
Rocker
Roller
Router
Selsyn
Sensor
Server
Shaker
Shewel
Shower
Socket
Spigot
Stocks
Stoner
Switch
Swivel
Tablet
Tamper
Tardis
Temple
Tipple
Tracer
Tremie
Triode
Trompe
Turtle
Tympan
Viewer
Wafter
Walker
Webcam
Widget
Zapper

***7 letters:***
Adaptor
Aileron
Air-trap
Alidade
Bearing
Bendlet
Bleeper
Blender
Booster
Charger
Chopper
Clapper
Cleaver
Clicker
Coherer
Compass
Counter
Coupler
Crampon
Dashpot
Denture
Digibox®
Dingbat
Divider
Doubler
E-reader
Flip-top
Flyswat
Fuzzbox
Gas mask
Genlock
Gimbals
Grapnel
Hacksaw
Hushkit
Imprese
Inhaler
Ioniser
Isotron
Jetpack
Krytron
Lighter
Limiter
Machine
Minicom
Monitor
Netsuke
Padlock
Pelorus
Pessary
Pickoff
Pillory
Plunger
Ratchet
Reactor
Roll-bar
Rotator
Rowlock
Scanner
Shopbot
Shut-off
Shutter
Shuttle
Simcard
Slipper
Sniffer
Snorkel
Snubber
Snuffer
Sordino
Sounder
Spoiler
Stapler
Starter
Stinger
Storage
Sundial
Swatter
Synchro
Tirasse
Toaster
Tokamak
Tonepad
Trefoil
Vernier
Vocoder

***8 letters:***
Airscoop
Alcolock
Analogue
Anti-icer
Atomiser
Autodial
Ballcock
Ballista
Barostat
Betatron
Bootjack
Calutron
Commutor
Conveyor
Coupling
Cryostat
Cyberpet
Demister
Detector
Diagraph
Diestock
Earphone
Ecraseur
Eggtimer
Enlarger
Eolipile
Episcope
Episemon
Expander
Fairlead
Firework
Flashgun
Flywheel
Forklift
Geophone
Gunsight
Heat pump
Holdback
Hotplate
Ignitron
Intercom
Keyboard
Launcher
Lifebuoy
Lift-gate
Light-pen
Monogram
Nailhead
Occluder
Odograph
Odometer
Orthosis
Ozoniser
Paravane
Playback
Plectrum
Pullback
Pulsator
Pushback
Push-pull
Pyrostat
Radar gun
Radiator
Repeater
Resister
Rheostat
Robotics
Shoehorn
Shredder
Silencer
Slip ring
Snow-eyes
Snowshoe
Solenoid
Speculum
Splitter
Spray gun
Spreader
Squeegee
Sweatbox
Swellbox
Teleport
Terminal
Thin-film
Touch pad
Trembler
Varactor
Varistor
Vibrator
Windlass
Windmill

***9 letters:***
Amplifier
Aspirator
Autometer

Autopilot
Autotimer
Capacitor
Compasses
Condenser
Convector
Converter
Corkscrew
Decoherer
Deflector
Defroster
Delayline
Detonator
Dispenser
Dynamotor
Eccentric
Equalizer
Excelsior
Exerciser
Extractor
Fetoscope
Flowmeter
Gear-lever
Gear-shift
Gearstick
Generator
Gyroscope
Headstock
Heliscoop
Hendiadys
Hodoscope
Hydrofoil
Hydrostat
Hygrostat
Indicator
Insulator
Jack screw
Keylogger
Konimeter
Kymograph
Megaphone
Mekometer
Metronome
Milometer
Modulator
Nebuliser
Obterator
Octophone
Optophone
Overdrive
Pacemaker
Parachute
Patent log
Pedometer
Periscope
Phonopore
Photocell
Pitchbend
Polariser
Polygraph
Powerpack
Precursor
Propeller
Rectifier
Regulator
Remontoir
Resonator
Responsor
Retractor
Rheotrope
Rotachute
Rotameter®
Satellite
Scrambler
Separator
Sequencer
Simulator
Smokejack
Sonograph
Spaceband
Spindryer
Spinhaler
Sprinkler
Stairlift
Standpipe
Steadicam
Stretcher
Tabulator
Tape drive
Tape punch
Tasimeter
Telegraph
Telemeter
Telepoint
Thermette
Thyristor
Tonometer
Tormentor
Trackball
Tremulant
Well sweep

***10 letters:***
Acetometer
Anemoscope
Applicator
Attenuator
Autowinder
Blackberry®
Calculator
Ceilometer
Centrifuge
Chaingrate
Chronotron
Clapometer
Commutator
Comparator
Compressor
Copyholder
Cyclometer
Cyclostyle
Daisy-wheel
Databogger
Derailleur
Descendeur
Eprouvette
Fairleader
Foetoscope
Groundprox
Humidistat
Hygroscope
Hypervisor
Integrator
Jawbreaker
Jaws of Life
Jellygraph
Kicksorter
Lactometer
Mason's mark
Metrostyle
Microphone
Microprobe
Microscope
Mileometer
Moulinette
Nephograph
Nightscope
Noisemaker
Otter-board
Peripheral
Phonoscope
Planometer
Radiometer
Remontoire
Respirator
Self-feeder
Siderostat
Snowplough
Solid state
Spirograph
Stabiliser
Stimpmeter
Suppressor
Switchgear
Tachograph
Tachometer
Tape reader
Telewriter
Theodolite
Thermistor
Thermopile
Thermostat
Tourniquet
Transducer
Transistor
Turbulator
Turnbuckle
Ventilator
Vertoscope®
Videophone
Viewfinder
Viscometer
Water-wheel
Zener diode

***11 letters:***
Afterburner
Annunciator
Answerphone
Autochanger
Baffle-plate
Carburettor
Collet chuck
Compass rose
Conformator
Dendrometer
Distributor
Echo-sounder
Epidiascope
Floor turtle
Fluoroscope
Helping hand
Immobiliser
Immobilizer
Insufflator
Intoximeter
Lie detector
Link trainer
Manipulator
Microfitter
Microreader
Microwriter
Morton's fork
Moving-coils
Multiplexer
Paper cutter
Party popper
Recuperator
Self-starter
Shelftalker
Smokerlyzer
Snickometer
Solarimeter
Space heater

Spectograph
Speedometer
Stuffing-box
Swingometer
Telestrator
Thermoscope
Trackerball
Transceiver
Transformer
Transmitter
Transponder
Weather vane

***12 letters:***
Beamsplitter
Breathalyser
Camera lucida
Concentrator
Crimping iron
Desert cooler
Ebulliometer
Effusiometer
Electrometer
Evaporograph
Extensometer
Extinguisher
Galvanometer
Intrauterine
Kaleidoscope
Lithotripter
Magnetometer
Make and break
Micro-circuit
Mine-detector
Object finder
Oscillograph
Oscilloscope
Picturephone
Sensitometer
Snooperscope
Speaking tube
Spectrometer
Spectroscope
Supercharger
Tape streamer
Telautograph
Teleprompter
Tellurometer
Theatrophone
Thermocouple
Turbidimeter
Viscosimeter

***13 letters:***
Accelerometer
Aetherioscope
Baton-sinister
Contraceptive
Dead man's pedal
Defibrillator
Electromagnet
Electrophorus
Metal detector
Morton's crutch
Octave coupler
Phonendoscope
Potentiometer
Rack and pinion
Read-write head
Scintiscanner
Shock-absorber
Smoke detector

***14 letters:***
Anamorphoscope
Block and tackle
Dead man's handle
Interferometer
Intervalometer
Peltier element
Plethysmograph
Radio telephone
Retroreflector
Scintillometer
Spinthariscope
Surge protector
Trickle charger

***15 letters:***
Radiogoniometer

***18 letters:***
Direction-indicator

---

**Devil(ish), Demon** Abaddon, Afreet, Afrit, Ahriman, Amaimon, Apollyon, Archfiend, Asmodeus, Atua, Auld Hornie, Azazel, Barbason, Beelzebub, Belial, Blue®, Buckra, Cacodemon, Cartesian, Clootie, Cloots, Dasyure, Davy Jones, Deev, Deil, Demogorgon, Demon, Deuce, Devling, Diable, Diabolic, Dickens, Div, Drudge, Duende, Dust, Eblis, Falin, Familiar, Fend, Fiend, Fient, Ghoul, Goodman, Goodwife, Goodyear, Grill, Hangie, Hornie, Iblis, Imp, Incubus, Infernal, Knave, Lamia, Legion, Lilith, Lord of the Flies, Lori, Lucifer, Mahoun(d), Man of Sin, Manta, Mara, Maxwell's, Mazikeen, Mephisto(pheles), Mischief, Mountain, Nick, Nickie-ben, Old Bendy, Old Nick, Old One, Old Pandemonium, Old Poker, Old Roger, Old Split-foot, Old Toast, Printer's, Ragamuffin, Ragman, Rahu, Ralph, Satan, Satan(h)as, Satyr, Scour, Scratch, Screwtape, Season, Setebos, Shaitan, Shedeem, Snow, Sorra, Succubine, Succubus, Tailard, Tasmanian, Tempter, Titivil, Tutivillus, Unholy, Wendigo, Wicked, Wicked One, Wirricow, Worricow, Worrycow, Zernebock

**Devil-child** Changeling

**Devil-may-care** Rakish

**Devious** Artful, Braide, Cunning, Cute hoor, Deep, Eel(y), Erroneous, Evasive, Heel, Implex, Indirect, Insincere, Meandering, Scheming, Shady, Shifty, Sly, Sneaky, Stealthy, Subtle, Swindling, Tortuous, Tricky, Twisting, Two-faced

**Devise(d)** Arrange, Coin, Comment, Concoct, Contrive, Cook up, Create, Decoct, Hatch, Hit-on, Imagine, Invenit, Invent, Plan, Plot, Thermette

**Devitrified** Ambitty

**Devoid** Barren, Destitute, Empty, Vacant, Wanting

**Devolution** West Lothian question

**Devolve** Occur, Result, Transmit

**Devote(e), Devotion(al), Devoted** Acolyte, Addiction, Adherent, Aficionado, Âme damnée, Angelus, Attached, Bhakti, Buff, Bunny, Commitment, Consecrate, Consign, Corban, Dedicate, Disciple, Duteous, Employ, Enthusiast, Fan, Fervid, Fetishism, Fidelity, Fiend, Gallantry, Grebo, Gyniolatry, Holy, Hound, Lapdog, Loyalty, Mariolate, Novena, Nut, Oblate, Ophism, Partisan, Passion, Piety, Pious, Puja, Rasta, Religioso, Sacred, Saivite, S(h)akta, Sanctity, Savoyard, Sea-green incorruptible, Sivaite, Solemn, Sworn, True, Uxorious, Voteen, Zealous

**Devour(ing)** Consume, Eat, Engorge, Engulf, Gorge, Manducate, Moth-eat, Scarf, Scoff, Snarf, → SWALLOW, Vorant, Wolf

▹**Devour** *may indicate* one word inside another
**Devout** God-fearing, Holy, Pia, Pious, Religiose, Reverent, Sant, Sincere, Solemn
**Dew(y)** Bloom, Field, Gory, Moist, Mountain, Rime, Roral, Roric, Rorid, Roscid, Serein, Serene, Tranter
**Dexterity, Dexterous** Adept, Adroit, Aptitude, Cleverness, Craft, Deft, Feat(e)ous, Featuous, → **HANDY**, Knack, Shrewd, Sleight, Slick
**Diablerie** Sorcery
**Diabolic(al)** Cruel, → **DEVILISH**, Infernal, Inhuman, Satanic, Ungodly
**Diacritic (mark)** Acute, Angstrom, Cedilla, Circumflex, Diaresis, Eth, Grave, Háček, Thorn, Tilde, Umlaut
**Diadem** Coronet, Fillet, Garland, Tiara
**Diagnose, Diagnosis, Diagnostic** Amniocentesis, Fetal, Findings, Identify, Iridology, Pulse, Radionics, Scan, Scintigraphy, X-ray
**Diagonal(ly)** Bend(wise), Bias, Cater(-corner), Catty-cornered, Counter, Oblique, Principal, Slant, Solidus, Speed, Twill
**Diagram** Argand, Bar chart, Bar graph, Block, Butterfly, Chart, Chromaticity, Cladogram, Compass rose, Decision tree, Dendrogram, Drawing, Fault-tree, Feynman, Figure, Floral, Flow, Graph, Graphics, Grid, Hertzsprung-Russell, Histogram, Indicator, Logic, Map, Phase, Pie, Plan, Plat, Run-chart, Scatter, Schema, Schematic, Scintigram, Stem-and-leaf, Stemma, Stereogram, Tephigram, Topo, Tree, Venn, Wind rose
**Dial(ling)** Card, Face, Mug, Phiz, Phone, Pulse, Ring, Speed, STD, Tone, Visage
**Dialect** Acadian, Accent, Aeolic, Alemannic, Amoy, Anglican, Arcadic, Attic, Basuto, Burr, Castilian, Damara, Doric, Eldin, Eolic, Epic, Erse, Eye, Franconian, Friulian, Galician, Gallo-Romance, Gascon, Geechee, Geordie, Greenlander, Hassaniya, Hegelian, Idiom, Ionic, Isogloss, Jargon, Jockney, Joual, Kazak(h), Khalka, Khalkha, Koine, Konkani, Ladin, Lallans, Landsmaal, Langobardic, Langue d'oc, Langue d'oil, Langue d'oui, Ledden, Lingo, Low German, Mackem, Min, Norman, Norn, Occitan, Old Icelandic, Old North French, Parsee, Parsi, Patavinity, Patois, Pedi, Picard, Prakrit, Rhaeto-Romance, Rhotic, Riffian, Rock English, Romans(c)h, Ruthenian, Salish, Savoyard, Scouse, Sesotho, Syriac, Taal, Tadzhik, Ta(d)jik, Talkee-talkee, Talky-talky, Tongue, Tshi, Tuscan, Twi, Tyrolese, Umbrian, Vaudois, Vernacular, Walloon, West Saxon, Wu, Yealdon, Yenglish, Yinglish
**Dialogue** Colloquy, Conversation, Critias, Discussion, Exchange, Imparl, Interlocution, Lazzo, Lines, Pastourelle, Repartee, Speech, Stichomythia, Talk, Upspeak
**Dialysis** Kidney, Peritoneal
**Diameter** Bore, Breadth, Calibre, Gauge, Systyle, Tactical, Width
**Diamond(s), Diamond-shaped** Adamant, Black, Blood, Boart, Brilliant, Bristol, Carbon, Carbonado, Cullinan, D, DE, Delaware, Eustace, False, Florentine, Hope, Ice, Industrial, Isomer, Jewel, Jim, Koh-i-Noor, Lasque, Lattice, Lozenge, Minor suit, Off-colour(ed), Paragon, Pick, Pitch, Pitt, Quarry, Reef, Rhinestone, Rhomb, Rock, Rose-cut, Rosser, Rough, Rustre, Sancy, Sixtieth, Solitaire, Spark, Sparklers, Squarial, Suit
**Diana** Artemis, Di, Dors
**Diapason** Normal, Open, Ottava, Stopped
**Diaphanous** Clear, Filmy, Sheer, Translucent
**Diaphoretic** Sweater
**Diaphragm** Cap, Iris, Mid-riff, Phrenic, Stop
**Diapir** Salt dome
**Diaresis** Trema
▸**Diarist** *see* **DIARY**
**Diarrhoea** Aztec two-step, Collywobbles, Delhi belly, Gippy tummy, Lientery, Montezuma's revenge, Runs, Scours, Squitters, Trots, Verbal, Weaning-brash, Wood-evil
**Diary, Diarist** Adrian Mole, Blogger, Bridget Jones, Burney, Chronicle, Crossman, Dale, Day-book, Evelyn, Frank, Hickey, Journal, Journal intime, Kilvert, Log, Mole, Mrs Dale, Nobody, Noctuary, Pepys, Personal organiser, Planner, Pooter, Record, Video
**Diaspora** Exodus, Galuth
**Diatomite** Tripoli
**Diatribe** Harangue, Invective, Philippic, Polemic, Rant, Tirade

**Dibble(r)** Marsupial, Theria
**Dice(r), Dicey** Aleatory, Astragals, Bale, Bones, Chop, Craps, Cube, Doctor, Dodgy, Fulham, Fullams, Fullans, Gamble, Gourd(s), Hash, Highman, Jeff, Mandoline, Mince, Novum, Poker, Shoot, Smalto, Snake-eyes, Tallmen
**Dichotomy** Split
**Dick(y), Dickey** Clever, Deadeye, Front, Ill, Laid up, Moby, OED, Policeman, Private eye, Rumble, Shaky, Shirt, Spotted, Tec, Tonneau, Tucker, Tumbledown, Unstable, Wankle, Weak, Whittington
▷**Dick** *may indicate* a dictionary
**Dickens** Boz, Deuce, Devil, Mephistopheles
**Dicker** Bargain, Barter, Haggle, Trade
▷**Dicky** *may indicate* an anagram
**Dicotyledon** Exogen
**Dictate, Dictator(ial)** Amin, Authoritarian, Autocrat, Big Brother, Bonaparte, Caesar, Castro, Cham, Command, Czar, Decree, Demagogue, Despot, Duce, Franco, Fu(e)hrer, Gaddafi, Gauleiter, Hitler, Idi, Impose, Indite, Junta, Lenin, Mussolini, Ordain, Overbearing, Peremptory, Peron, Pol Pot, Saddam, Salazar, Shogun, Stalin, Tell, Tito, Totalitarian, Trujillo, Tsar, Tyrant, Tzar, Usurper
**Diction** Language, Lexis, Palavinity, Speech, Style
**Dictionary** Alveary, Calepin, Chambers, Data, Etymologicon, Fowler, Gazetteer, Glossary, Gradus, Hobson-Jobson, Idioticon, Johnson's, Larousse, Lexicon, Lexis, OED, Onomasticon, Thesaurus, Vocabulary, Webster, Wordbook
**Dictum** Maxim, Obiter, Saw, Say-so
**Did** Began, Couth, Fec(it), Gan
**Didactic** Sermonical
**Diddle** Cheat, Con, Hoax, Swizz
**Dido** Antic, Caper, Carthaginian, Elissa
**Die(d), Dying** Ache, Buy the farm, Calando, Cark, Choke, Conk out, Crater, Croak, Cube, D, Decadent, Desire, End, Evanish, Exit, Expire, Fade, Fail, Flatline, Forfair, Fulham, Fulhan, Fullam, Go, Go west, Hallmark, Hang, Highman, Hop, Hop the twig, Infarct, Kark, Long, Morendo, Moribund, Ob(iit), Orb, Pass, Peg out, Perdendosi, Perish, Peter, Pop off, Pop one's clogs, Slip the cable, Snuff, Snuff it, Solidum, Sphacelation, Stagheaded, Stamp, Sterve, Succumb, Suffer, Swage, Swelt, Terminal, Tessera, Tine, Touch, Wane
**Diehard** Blimp, Fanatic, Intransigent, Reactionary, Standpatter, Zealot
**Diesel** Red
**Diet(er), Dietary, Dieting** Assembly, Atkins, Augsburg, Balanced, Bant(ing), Cacotrophy, Congress, Council, Crash, Dail, Eat, Fare, Fast, Feed, Halal, Hay, Intake, Kashrus, Kashrut(h), Ketogenic, Knesset, Kosher, Landtag, Lent, Low-fat, Low-salt, Macrobiotic, Nutriment, Nutrition, Parliament, Pleading, Reduce, Regimen, Reichstag, Short commons, Slim, Solid, Sprat, Staple, Strict, Tynwald, Vegan, Vegetarian, Weightwatcher, Worms, Yo-yo
**Dietetics** Sit(i)ology
**Differ(ence), Differing, Different(ly)** Afresh, Allo, Alterity, Anew, Balance, Barney, Change, Cline, Contrast, Contretemps, Deviant, Diacritic, Diesis, Disagree, Discord, Discrepant, Disparate, Dispute, Dissent, Dissimilar, Dissimilitude, Distinct, Diverge, Diverse, Else, Elsewise, Epact, Exotic, Gap, Gulf, Heterodox, Loggerheads, New, Nonconformist, Novel, Nuance, Omnifarious, Other, Othergates, Otherguess, Otherness, Otherwise, Poles apart, Potential, Quantum, Separate, Several, Spat, Special, Symmetric, Tiff, Unlike, Variform, Various, Vary
**Differential, Differentiate, Differentiation** Calculus, Del, Discriminate, Distinguish, Gap, Nabla, Product, Secern, Segregate, Separate, Taxeme, Wage
**Difficult(y), Difficult person** Abstruseness, Ado, Adversity, Aggro, Aporia, Arduous, Augean, Badass, Balky, Ballbuster, Bitter, Block, Bolshie, Bother, Cantankerous, Catch, Challenging, Choosy, Complex, Complication, Contretemps, Corner, Cough drop, Crisis, Crotchety, Crux, Deep, Delphic, Depth, Dysphagia, Embarrassment, Enigma, Extreme, Fiddly, Formidable, Gnomic, Gordian, Handful, → **HARD**, Hassle, Hazard, Hiccough, Hiccup, Hitch, Hobble, Hole, Hoor, Hump, Ill, Impasse, Inconvenient, Incubus, Indocile, Inscrutable,

Intractable, Intransigent, Jam, Jawbreaker, Kink, Kittle, Knot, Lob's pound, Lurch, Matter, Mulish, Net, Nodus, Obdurate, Obstacle, Ordeal, Parlous, Paruresis, Perverse, Pig, Pitfall, Plight, Predicament, Pressure, Pretty pass, Problem(atic), Quandary, Queer St, Recalcitrant, Recondite, Rough, Rub, Scabrous, Scrape, Scrub, Scruple, Setaceous, Shlep, Snag, Soup, Steep, Stey, Stick, Sticky, Stiff, Stinker, Strait, Strenuous, Stretch, Stroppy, Stubborn, Stymie, Swine, Tall order, Testing, Thorny, Ticklish, Tight spot, Tough, Trial, Tricky, Troublous, Trying, Une(a)th, Unwieldy, Uphill, Uppity, Via dolorosa, Woe, Wrinkle

**Diffident** Bashful, Hesitant, Meek, Modest, Reserved, Reticent, Retiring, Shy, Tentative, Timid

**Diffuse, Diffusion** Barophoresis, Disperse, Disseminate, Endosmosis, Exude, Osmosis, Permeate, Pervade, Radiate, Run, Sperse, Spread, Thermal, Winnow

**Dig(s), Digger, Digging, Dig up** Admire, Antipodean, Anzac, Australian, Backhoe, Barb, Beadle, Bed(e)ral, Bedsit, Billet, Bore, Bot, Burrow, Costean, Delve, Deracinate, Enjoy, Excavate, Flea-bag, Flophouse, Fork, Fossorial, Gaulter, Get, Gibe, Gird, Graft, Graip, Grub, Hoe, Howk, Into, Jab, Jibe, Kip, Lair, Like, Lodgings, Luxor, Mine, Navvy, Nervy, Nudge, Pad, Pioneer, Probe, Prod, Prospect(ing), Raddleman, Resurrect, Root(le), Ruddleman, Sap, See, Sneer, Spade, Spit, Spud, Star-nose, Taunt, Till, Tonnell, Trench, Tunnel, Undermine, Unearth

**Digest(ible), Digestion, Digestive** Abridgement, Absorb, Abstract, Aperçu, Archenteron, Assimilate, Beeda, Bile, Bradypeptic, Brief, Codify, Concoct, Endue, Epitome, Eupepsia, Eupepsy, Fletcherism, Gastric, Indew, Indue, Insalivate, Light, Pandect, Pem(m)ican, Pepsin(e), Peptic, Précis, Salt-cat, Steatolysis, → SUMMARY

**Digit(s)** Binary, Bit, Byte, Check, Dactyl, Figure, Finger, Hallux, Mantissa, Number, Pollex, Prehallux, Significant, Thumb, Toe

**Digitiser** Scanner

**Diglot** Bilingual

**Dignified, Dignify** August, Eastdom, Elevate, Ennoble, Exalt, Grace, Handsome, Honour, Imposing, Lordly, Maestoso, Majestic, Manly, Proud, Sober, Solemn, Stately, Statuesque

**Dignitary** Alderman, Big cheese, Bigwig, Dean, Eminence, Mayor, Monsignor, Name, Personage, Provost, → VIP

**Dignity** Aplomb, Bearing, Cathedra, Decorum, Face, Glory, Grandeur, Gravitas, High horse, Maestoso, Majesty, Nobility, Poise, Pontificate, Presence, Scarf, Tiara

**Digraph** Ash, Eng, Ng

**Digress(ion)** Apostrophe, Aside, Deviate, Diverge, Ecbole, Episode, Excurse, Excursus, Maunder, Sidetrack, Vagary, Veer, Wander

**Dike** Bank, Channel, Cludgie, Dam, Ditch, → DYKE, Embank(ment), Estacade, Lav(atory), Levee, Wall

**Dilapidated, Dilapidation** Beat-up, Clapped out, Clunker, Decrepit, Derelict, Desolate, Disrepair, Eroded, Flea-bitten, Rickle, Ruined, Rust bucket, Seedy, Shoddy, Tumbledown

**Dilate, Dilation, Dilatation, Dilator** Amplify, Develop, Diastole, Ecstasis, Enlarge, Expand, Increase, Mydriasis, Nitro, Sinus, Swell, Telangiectasia, Tent, Time, Varix

**Dilatory, Dilatoriness** Procrastination, Protracting, Slow, Sluggish, Tardy

**Dilemma** Casuistry, Choice, Cleft(stick), Double-bind, Dulcarnon, Fix, Horn, Jam, Predicament, Quandary, Stymie, Teaser, Why-not

**Dilettante** Aesthete, Amateur, Butterfly, Dabbler, Playboy

**Diligence, Diligent** Active, Application, Assiduous, Coach, Conscience, Eident, Hard-working, Industry, Intent, Painstaking, Sedulous, Studious, Tireless

**Dill** Anise, Pickle

**Dilute(d), Dilution** Adulterate, Allay, Attenuate, Cut, Deglaze, Delay, Diluent, Lavage, Qualify, Simpson, Thin, Water, Weaken, Wishy-washy

**Dim(ness), Dimming, Dimwit(ted)** Becloud, Blear, Blur, Brownout, Caligo, Cloud, Clueless, Crepuscular, Darken, Dense, Dumbo, Dusk, Eclipse, Fade, Faint, Feint, Fozy, Gormless, Ill-lit, Indefinable, Indistinct, Low, Mist, Nebulous, Ninny, Obliterate, Obscure, Overcast, Owl, Pale, Purblind, Shadow, Stupid, Twilit, Unclear, Unsmart, Wane

**Dimension(s), Dimensional** Area, Breadth, Extent, Fourth, Height, Length, Linear, Measure, New, One, Scantling, Size, Space, Third, Three, Two, Volume, Width

**Dimer** Cystine

**Diminish(ed), Diminishing, Diminuendo, Diminution, Diminutive** Abatement, Allay, Assuage, Attenuate, Baby, Bate, Calando, Contract, Cot(t)ise, Deactivate, Decline, Decrease, Détente, Detract, Disparage, Dissipate, Dwarf, Dwindle, Ebb, Erode, Fourth, Hypocorism(a), Impair, Lessen, Lilliputian, Little, Minify, Minus, Mitigate, Pater, Petite, Pigmy, Ritardando, Scarp, Small, Stultify, Subside, Taper, Toy, Trangle, Wane, Whittle

**Dimple(d)** Dent, Depression, Hollow, Orange-peel

**Din** Babel, Charivary, Chirm, Commotion, Deen, Discord, Gunga, Hubbub, → NOISE, Racket, Raird, Randan, Reel, Reird, Uproar, Utis

**Dine(r), Dining** Aristology, Bistro, Café, Eat, Feast, Mess, Refect, Sup, Trat(toria)

**Dingbat** Doodad, Weirdo

**Dingle** Dimble

**Dingo** Warrigal

**Ding(h)y** Cott, Inflatable, Pram, Shallop, Ship, Skiff

**Dingy** Crummy, Dark, Dirty, Drab, Drear, Dun, Fleapit, Fusc(ous), Grimy, Isabel(la), Isabelline, Lurid, Oorie, Ourie, Owrie, Shabby, Smoky

**Dining-room** Cafeteria, Carvery, Cenacle, Commons, Frater, Hall, Langar, Mess hall, Noshery, Refectory, Restaurant, Triclinium

**Dinky** Cute, Twee

**Dinmont** Ram, Sheep

**Dinner** Banquet, Collation, Dog's, Feast, Hall, Kail, Kale, Meal, Prandial, Progressive, Repast, Spread, TV

**Dinner jacket** Penguin suit

**Dinosaur** Aepyornis, Allosaurus, Ankylosaur, Apatosaurus, Archosaur, Atlantosaurus, Baryonyx, Brachiosaurus, Brontosaurus, Ceratopsian, Ceratosaurus, Ceteosaurus, Chalicothere, Coelurosaur, Compsognathus, Cotylosaur, Cynodont, Dinothere, Diplodocus, Dolichosaurus, Duck-billed, Elasmosaur, Galeopithecus, Glyptodon, Hadrosaur, Has-been, Ichthyosaur(us), Iguanodon, Megalosaur, Microraptor, Mosasaur, Odontornithes, Ornithischian, Ornithopod, Ornithosaur, Oviraptor, Pachycephalosaur, Pelycosaur, Perissodactyl, Placoderm, Plesiosaur, Pliosaur, Prehistoric, Prosauropod, Pteranodon, Pterodactyl, Pterosaur, Pythonomorpha, Raptor, Rhynchocephalian, Saurischian, Sauropod, Sauropterygian, Smilodon, Square, Stegodon(t), Stegosaur, Teleosaurus, Theropod, Titanosaurus, Titanothere, T-rex, Triceratops, Tyrannosaurus, Uintothere, Velociraptor

**Dint** Brunt, Dent, Depression, Force, Means, Power

**Diocese** Archbishopric, Bishopric, District, Eparchate, Eparchy, See

**Diode** Esaki, Tunnel, Zener

**Diogenes** Cynic

**Dionysian** Boozy

**Dioxide** Cassiterite, Needle-tin

**Dip(per), Dippy** Bagna cauda, Baptise, Basin, Bathe, Bob, Brantub, Dabble, Dap, Dean, Dib, Diver, Dop, Double, Douse, Dowse, Duck, Dunk, Fatuous, Foveola, Geosyncline, Guacamole, Houmous, H(o)ummus, Humus, Immerge, Immerse, Intinction, Ladle, Lucky, Magnetic, Ousel, Ouzel, Paddle, Plough, Rinse, Rollercoaster, Sag, Salute, Sheep-wash, Star, Submerge, Tapenade, Taramasalata, Tzatziki, Ursa

**Diphthong** Crasis, Synaeresis, Synaloepha, Synizesis

**Diploma** Bac, Cert(ificate), Charter, Parchment, Qualification, Scroll, Sheepskin

**Diplomacy, Diplomat(ic)** Alternat, Ambassador, Attaché, Career, CD, Chargé d'affaires, Chateaubriand, Cheque-book, Consul, DA, Dean, Discretion, Dollar, Doyen, El(t)chi, Emissary, Envoy, Fanariot, Fetial, Finesse, Gunboat, Legation, Lei(d)ger, Megaphone, Metternich, Negotiator, Phanariot, Plenipotentiary, Politic(s), Shuttle, Suave, → TACT

▷**Dippy** *may indicate* a bather

**Dipsomania** Lush, Oenomania

**Dipstick** Dunce, → STUPID PERSON

**Dire** Dreadful, Fatal, Fell, Grim, Hateful, In extremis, Ominous, Urgent

**Direct(or), Directed, Directly** Address, Ad hominem, Administer, Advert, Agonothetes, Aim, Airt, Air-to-air, Auteur, Aventre, Beeline, Board, Boss, Cann, Cast, Chairperson, Channel, Charge, Choirmaster, Chorus-master, Command, Compere, Con(n), Conduct,

Control, Cox, Dead, Due, Dunstable road, Enjoin, Executive, Explicit, Face to face, Fair, Fast-track, First-hand, Forthright, Frontal, Full, Guide, Helm, Immediate, Impresario, Instruct, Intendant, Kapellmeister, Lead, Manager, Mastermind, Musical, Navigate, Nonexecutive, Outright, Oversee, Person to person, Pilot, Plain-spoken, Play, Point-blank, Ready, Refer, Régisseur, Regulate, Rudder, Send, Set, Signpost, Skipper, Slap-bang, Spotlight, Stear, → **STEER**, Straight, Superintend, Supervise, Teach, Telic, Tell, Train, Unvarnished, Usher, Vector

---

## DIRECTORS

*3 letters:*
Dee
Lee
Ray

*4 letters:*
Coen
Ford
Hall
Lang
Lean
Meno
Nunn
Reed
Roeg
Tati
Weir

*5 letters:*
Boyle
Brook
Capra
Clair
Fosse
Hawks
Joffe
Kazan
Korda
Leone
Loach
Losey
Lucas
Lumet
Lynch
Mamet
Noyce
Orson
Parer
Vidor
Wajda

*6 letters:*
Brooks
Bunuel
Burton
Carlei
Curtiz
De Sica
De Vito
Dreyer
Godard
Herzog
Huston
Jarman
Mendes
Ophuls
Pagnol
Powell
Renoir
Welles
Wilder
Winner

*7 letters:*
Bergman
Berkoff
Bresson
Campion
Chabrol
Coppola
De Mille
Fellini
Guthrie
Kaufman
Kubrick
Reitman
Rivette
Russell
Sennett

*8 letters:*
Cousteau
Griffith
Kurosawa
Merchant
Pasolini
Scorsese
Truffaut
Visconti

*9 letters:*
Antonioni
Hitchcock
Peckinpah
Preminger
Spielberg
Tarantino
Tarkovsky
Wanamaker

*10 letters:*
Bertolucci
Eisenstein
Littlewood
Passbinder
Rossellini
Woody Allen
Zeffirelli

*11 letters:*
Orson Welles
Pressburger
Riefenstahl
Von Stroheim

*12 letters:*
Stanislavski
Van Sternberg

---

**Direction, Directive** Address, Aim, Airt, Arrow, Astern, Bearings, Course, Cross-reference, E, End-on, Guidance, Guide, Heading, Keblah, L, Line, N, Orders, Orientation, Passim, Point, Quarter, R, Recipe, Route, Rubric, S, Sanction, Send, Sense, Side, Slap, Sub-heading, Tacet, Tack, Tenor, Thataway, Tre corde, Trend, W, Way, Wedelns

**Direction-finder** Asdic, Compass, Decca, Quadrant, Radar, Sextant, Sonar

**Directory** Address book, Crockford, Data, Debrett, Encyclop(a)edia, Folder, French, Herbal, Kelly, List, Red book, Register, Roll, Root, Search, Web, Yellow Pages®

**Dirge** Ballant, Coronach, Dirige, Epicedium, Knell, Monody, Requiem, Song, Threnody

**Dirigible** Airship, Balloon, Blimp, Zeppelin

**Dirk** Anelace, Dagger, Skean, Whinger, Whiniard, Whinyard

**Dirt(y)** Augean, Bed(r)aggled, Begrime, Bemoil, Besmear, Cacky, Chatty, Clag, Clarty, Colly, Contaminate, Coom, Crock, Crud, Defile, Distain, Draggle, Dung, Dust, Earth, Festy, Filth, Foul, Gen, Gore, Grime, Grubby, Grufted, Grungy, Impure, Manky, Moit, Mote, Muck, Obscene, Ordure, Pay, Pick, Pollute, Ray, Ribald, Scandal, Scody, Sculdudd(e)ry, Scum, Scungy, Scuttlebutt, Scuzzy, Shop-soiled, Skanky, Skulduddery, Slattery, Smirch, Smut(ch), Soil, Sooty, Sordes, Sordid, Sordor, Squalid, Squalor, Stain, Stuff, Substrata, Sully, Tidemark, Trash, Unclean, Unsatisfactory, Unwashed, Warb, Yucky, Yukky

**Dis** Hades, Hell

**Disability, Disable(d)** Cripple, Crock, Gimp, Handicapped, Hors de combat, Immobilise, Incapacitate, Invalid, Kayo, Lame, Lamiger, Maim, Paralyse, Scissor-leg, Scotch, Scupper, Supercrip, Wreck

**Disabuse** Unteach

**Disadvantage(d)** Detriment, Disamenity, Downside, Drawback, Flipside, Handicap, Liability, Loser, Mischief, Out, Own goal, Penalise, Penalty, Prejudice, Shortcoming, Snag, Supercherie, Upstage, Wrongfoot, Zugswang

**Disaffected, Disaffection** Ennui, Estrange(ment), Malcontent, Rebellious

**Disagree(ing), Disagreeable, Disagreement** Altercation, Argue, Argy-bargy, At odds, Bad, Clash, Conflict, Contest, Contradict, Contretemps, Controversy, Debate, Demur, Differ, Discrepant, Dispute, Dissent, Dissonant, Evil, Fiddlesticks, Flak, Friction, Heterodoxy, Inharmonious, Object, Odds, Onkus, Pace, Plagu(e)y, Rank, Rift, Split, Testy, Tiff, Troll, Uh-uh, Uncongenial, Unpleasing, Vary

**Disallow(ed)** Forbid, No ball, Overrule, Surcharge

**Disappear(ing)** Cook, Dispel, Evanesce, Evanish, Evaporate, Fade, Fizzle out, Ghost, Kook, Latescent, Melt, Occult, Pass, Skedaddle, Slope, → **VANISH**

**Disappoint(ment), Disappointed, Disappointing** Anticlimax, Balk, Baulk, Blow, Bombshell, Bummer, Chagrin, Choked, Comedown, Crestfallen, Delude, Disgruntle, Fizzer, Frustrate, Gutted, Heartsick, Lemon, Letdown, Mislippen, Mistryst, Off, Regret, Sell, Setback, Shucks, Sick, Suck-in, Sucks, Swiz(zle), Thwart, Tsk, Underwhelm

**Disapproval, Disapprove(d), Disapprobation** Ach, Animadvert, Askance, Boo, Catcall, Censure, Condemn, Deplore, Deprecate, Discountenance, Execration, Expostulate, Fie, Flak, Frown, Harrumph, Hiss, Mal vu, Napoo, Object, Pejorative, Po-faced, Protest, Pshaw, Raspberry, Razz, Reject, Reproach, Reprobate, Slow handclap, Squint, Tush, Tut, Tut-tut, Umph, Veto, Whiss

**Disarm(ament), Disarming** Bluff, Defuse, Demobilise, Mutilate, Nuclear, Winsome

**Disarrange** Disturb, Muddle, Ruffle, Tousle, Unsettle

**Disarray(ing)** Confusion, Disorder, Mess, Rifle, Tash, Tousle, Undress

**Disaster, Disastrous** Accident, Adversity, Apocalypse, Bale, Calamity, Cataclysm(ic), Catastrophe, Chernobyl, Crash, Crisis, Debacle, Dire, Doom, Evil, Fatal, Fiasco, Flop, Hardship, Impostor, Meltdown, Mishap, Pandemic, Pitfall, Providence, Quake, Rout, Ruin, Screw-up, Seism, Shipwreck, Titanic, Tragedy, Train wreck, Turkey, Wipeout

**Disavow** Abjure, Deny, Disclaim, Recant, Retract

**Disband** Demob(ilise)

**Disbelief, Disbelieve(r)** Acosmism, Agnosticism, Anythingarian, Apostate, Atheism, Cor, Cynic, Doubt, Fiddle-de-dee, Gawp, Huh, Incredulity, Mistrust, Nothingarianism, Occamist, Pfui, Phew, Phooey, Puh-lease, Puh-leeze, Question, Sceptic, Shoot, Stroll on, Voetsak

**Disburse** Distribute, Expend, Outlay, Spend

**Disc, Disk** Accretion, Brake, Bursting, Button, CD, Chart-buster, Cheese, Clay pigeon, Compact, Coulter, Counter, Diaphragm, Dogtag, DVD, EP, Epiphragm, Fla(w)n, Flexible, Floppy, Frisbee®, Gold, Gong, Granum, Grindstone, Hard, Hard card, Harrow, Impeller, Intervertebral, Laser, LP, Magnetic, Microfloppy, Minifloppy, Mono, O, Optic(al), Parking, Paten, Patin, Planchet, Plate, Platinum, Platter, Puck, RAID, RAM, Rayleigh, Record, Reflector, Rosette, Roundel, Roundlet, Rowel, Rundle, Scanning, Sealed unit, Silver, Slipped, Slug, Stereo, Stylopodium, Sun, Swash plate, System, Tax, Thylacoid, Tiddl(e)ywink, Token, Video, Wafer, Wharve, Whorl, Winchester, Wink, WORM, Zip®

**Discard(ed)** Abandon, Burn, Crib, Defy, Dele, Fag-end, Jettison, Jilt, Kill, Leave, Minimise, Obsolete, Off, Offload, Oust, Outtake, Redundant, → **REJECT**, Scrap, Shed, Shuck, Slough, Sluff, Supersede, Throw over, Trash

**Discern(ing), Discernment** Acumen, Acute, Astute, Clear-eyed, Descry, Detect, Discrimination, Eagle-eyed, Flair, Insight, Intuition, Literati, Penetrate, Perceive, Percipient, Perspicacity, Quick-sighted, Realise, Recognise, Sapient, Scry, See, Sensitivity, Skry, → **TASTE**, Tell, Wate, Wise

**Discharge** Abreact, Absolve, Acquit, Anasarca, Arc, Assoil, Blennorrhoea, Blow off, Boot, Brush, Cashier, Catamenia, Catarrh, Clear, Conditional, Conge, Corona, Corposant, Dejecta, Deliver, Demob, Depose, Disembogue, Disgorge, Dishono(u)rable, Dismiss, Disruptive, Drain(age), Dump, Efflux, Effusion, Egest, Ejaculate, Eject, Embogue, Emission, Emit, Encopresis, Enfilade, Evacuate, Excrete, Execute, Exemption, Expectorate, Expel, Expulsion, Exude, Fire, Flashover, Flower, Flux, Frass, Free, Fusillade, Gleet, Glow, Gunfire, Honourable,

Issue, Jaculatory, Lava, Lay off, Leak, Let off, Leucorrhoea, Liberate, Lochia, Loose, Maturate, Menses, Mitimus, Muster out, Mute, Offload, Otorrhoea, Oust, Outfall, Outflow, Ozaena, Pass, Pay, Perform, Period, Planuria, Pour, Purulence, Pus, Pyorrhoea, Quietus, Redeem, Release, Rheum, Rhinorrhoeal, Run, Sack, Salt rheum, Salvo, Sanies, Secretion, Seepage, Show, Shrive, Smegma, Snarler, Spark, Spill(age), Static, Suppurate, Teem, Unload, Unloose, Vacuate, Vent, Void, Water, Whites

**Disciple(s)** Adherent, Apostle, Babi, Baruch, Catechumen, Chela, Dorcas, Follower, John, Judas, Luke, Mark, Matthew, Peter, Simon, Son, Student, The Seventy, Thomist, Timothy, Votary

**Disciplinarian, Disciplinary, Discipline(d)** Apollonian, Ascesis, Chasten, Chastise, Constrain, Correct, Despot, Dressage, Drill, Exercise, Feng shui, Inure, Judo, Martinet, Mathesis, Orderly, Penal, Philosophy, Phonetics, Punish, Punitive, Ramrod, Regimentation, Regulate, Sadhana, School, Science, Self-control, Sergeant major, Spartan, Spit and polish, Stickler, Subject, Taskmaster, Train, Tutor, Yoga

▸**Disc jockey** *see* **DJ**

**Disclaim(er)** Deny, Disavow, Disown, No(t)chel, Recant, Renounce, → **REPUDIATE**, Voetstoots

**Disclose, Disclosure** Air, Announce, Apocalypse, Confess, Divulge, Expose, Impart, Leak, Manifest, Open, Propale, → **PUBLISH**, Report, Reveal, Revelation, Showdown, Spill, Tell, Unearth, Unheal, Unhele, Unrip, Unveil

**Disco** Nightclub

**Discoloration, Discolour(ed)** Acrocyanosis, Black and blue, Bloodstain, Blotchy, Bruise, Cyanosis, Dyschroa, Ecchymosis, Fox, Livedo, Livid, Livor, Stain, Streak, Tarnish, Tinge, Weather, Yellow

**Discombobulate** Unsettle

**Discomfit(ure)** Abash, Chagrin, Confuse, Disconcert, Disturb, Frustrate, Lurch, Shend

**Discomfort(ed), Discompose** Ache, All-overish, Angst, Dysphoria, Dysthesia, Gyp, Heartburn, Malaise, Pain, Purgatory, Ravel, Torture, Twinge, Unease, Wedgie

**Disconcert(ing), Disconcerted** Abash, Astound, Bemused, Confuse, Disturb, Embarrass, Faze, Feeze, Flummox, Flurry, Fluster, Nonplus, Off-putting, Phase, Pheese, Pheeze, Phese, Put off, → **RATTLE**, Red-faced, Shatter, Startle, Tease, Throw, Unnerve, Upset, Wrong-foot

▹**Disconcert(ed)** *may indicate* an anagram

**Disconnect(ed)** Asynartete, Decouple, Desultory, Detach, Disassociate, Disjointed, Off-line, Segregate, Sever, Staccato, Trip, Uncouple, Undo, Ungear, Unplug

**Disconsolate** Desolate, Doleful, Downcast, → **GLOOMY**

**Discontent(ed)** Disquiet, Dissatisfied, Hotbed, Humph, Repined, Sour, Umph, Unrest

**Discontinue, Discontinuance, Discontinuity** Abandon, Axe, Break off, Cancel, Cease, Desist, Desuetude, Drop, (K)nickpoint, Moho, Prorogue, Stop, Terminate

**Discord(ant), Discordance** Absonant, Ajar, Atonal, Charivari, Conflict, Din, Dispute, Division, Eris, Faction, Hoarse, Inharmonious, Jangle, Jar(ring), Raucous, Ruction, Sharawadgi, Sharawaggi, Strife

▹**Discord(ant)** *may indicate* an anagram

**Discount** Agio, Bulk, Cashback, Cut-rate, Deduct, Disregard, Forfaiting, Invalidate, Leave, Quantity, → **REBATE**, Trade

**Discountenance** Disfavour, Efface, Embarrass

**Discouple** Unconnect

**Discourage(ment)** Caution, Chill, Dampen, Dash, Daunt, Deject, Demoralise, Deter, Dishearten, Disincentive, Dismay, Dispirit, Dissuade, Enervate, Frustrate, Inhibit, Intimidate, Opposition, Oppress, Stifle, Unman

**Discourse** Address, Argument, Colloquy, Conversation, Descant, Diatribe, Direct, Dissertate, Eulogy, Exercitation, Expound, Homily, Lecture, Lucubrate, Orate, Philippic, Preach, Recount, Relate, Rigmarole, Sermon, Wash

**Discourteous, Discourtesy** Disrespect, Impolite, Insult, Rude, Slight, Uncivil, Unmannerly

**Discover(y), Discoverer** Amundsen, Anagnorisis, Ascertain, Betray, Breakthrough,

Columbus, Cook, Descry, Detect, Determine, Discern, Discure, Divine, Esery, Espy, Eureka, Expiscate, → **FIND**, Heureka, Heuristic, Hit on, Learn, Locate, Manifest, Moresby, Protegé, Rumble, Serendip, Serendipity, Spy, Sus, Tasman, Trace, Treasure trove, Trouvaille, Unearth, Unhale, Unmask, Unveil

▷**Discovered in** *may indicate* an anagram or a hidden word

**Discredit(able)** Debunk, Decry, Disbelieve, Disgrace, Explode, Infamy, Negate, Obloquy, Scandal, Slur, Smear, Stigmatise, Unworthy

**Discreet, Discretion** Cautious, Circumspect, Finesse, Freedom, Judicious, Option, Polite, Politic, Prudence, Prudent, Tact, Tactful, Trait, Unobtrusive, Wise

**Discrepancy** Difference, Gap, Inconsistency, Lack, Mismatch, Shortfall, Variance

**Discrete** Distinct, Entity, Separate, Unrelated

**Discriminate, Discriminating, Discrimination** Ag(e)ism, Colour bar, Diacritic, Differentiate, Discern, Distinguish, Elitism, Fastidious, Fattism, Handism, Invidious, Lookism, Nasute, Positive, Racism, Rankism, Reverse, Secern, Segregate, Select, Sexism, Siz(e)ism, Speciesism, Subtle, Taste

**Disc-thrower** Discobolus

**Discursive** Roving

**Discuss(ed), Discussion** Agitate, Air, Bandy, Bat around, Canvass, Commune, Conf(ab), Confer(ence), Consult, Corridor work, Debate, Deliberate, Dialectic, Dialog(ue), Dicker, Disquisition, Emparl, En l'air, Examine, Excursus, Expatiate, Gabfest, Handle, Heart-to-heart, Hob and nob, Imparl, Interlocution, Interplead, Issue, Kick-about, Korero, Moot, Negotiation, Number-crunching, Over, Palaver, Parley, Pourparler, Powwow, Prolegomenon, Quodlibet, Rap, Re, Reason, Round table, Seminar, Symposium, Talk, Talkathon, Talkboard, Talk shop, Tapis, Treatment, Trialogue, Ventilate, Vex, Words

**Disdain(ful)** Belittle, Contempt, Coy, Deride, Despise, Geck, Poof, Pooh-pooh, Pugh, Puh, Rats, Sassy, Scoffer, → **SCORN**, Scout, Sdei(g)n, Sneering, Sniffy, Snub, Sour grapes, Spurn, Stuffy, Supercilious, Ugh

**Disease(d)** Affection, Ailment, Bacteriology, Bug, Communicable, Comorbid, Complaint, Deficiency, Defluxion, Dunt, Ecdemic, E-coli, Epidemic, Epidemiology, Fever, Functional, Industrial, Infection, Malady, Noso-, Nosocomial, Notifiable, Occupational, Organic, Pathogenic, Pest(ilence), Rot, Scourge, Sickness, Virus, Wildfire

---

**DISEASES**

*2 letters:*
CD
MD
ME
MS
TB
VD

*3 letters:*
ALS
BSE
Flu
Haw
MND
Pip
Pox
Sod
→ **STD**
TSE

*4 letters:*
Aids
Boba
Bunt
Clap
Conk
Gout
Keel
Kuru
Loco
Lues
Lyme
Roup
Scab
Wind
Yaws

*5 letters:*
Bang's
Black
Borna
Brand
Dread
Dutch
Ebola
Edema
Ergot
Farcy
Favus
Fifth
Frush
Gapes
Grape
Hoove
Kwok's
Lupus
Lurgi
Lurgy
Mange
Mesel
Mumps
Ngana
Palsy
Pearl
Pinta
Polio
Pott's
Rabid
Scall
Sprue
Surra
Tinea
Weil's
Worms

*6 letters:*
Anbury
Angine
Aphtha
Blight
Blotch
Border
Cancer
Canker
Chagas'
Chorea
Coffee
Cowpox
Crohn's
Cruels
Dartre
Dengue
Eczema
Farcin
Graves'
Herpes
Income
Johne's
Mad cow
Marek's
Meazel
Mildew
Morbus
Mosaic
Nagana
Oedema
Paget's
Parrot
Rabies
Salmon

Sapego
Scurvy
Social
Still's
Thrush
Tunnel
Typhus
Ulitis
Urosis
Yuppie
Zoster

***7 letters:***
Anthrax
Ascites
Batten's
Bird flu
Blue-ear
Bright's
British
Caisson
Cholera
Coeliac
Crewels
Crinkle
Dieback
Dourine
Endemic
English
Eyespot
Frogeye
Frounce
Gum rash
Hansen's
Hardpad
Hydatid
Icterus
Kissing
Leprosy
Lockjaw
Maidism
Malaria
Marburg
Miller's
Mimesis
Mooneye
Moor-ill
Murrain
Mycosis
Myiasis
Pébrine
Podagra
Porrigo
Purples
Pyaemia
Quittor
Redfoot
Rickets
Ring rot
Rosacea
Rosette
Rubella
Scabies
Scrapie
Sequela
Serpigo
Tetanus
Tetters
Typhoid
Variola
Wilson's
Zymosis

***8 letters:***
Addison's
Alastrim
Aujesky's
Basedow's
Beri-beri
Blackleg
Black-rot
Bornholm
Bullnose
Club root
Crown rot
Curly top
Cushing's
Cynanche
Diabetes
Dutch elm
Economo's
Epilepsy
Filander
Fishskin
Fowl pest
Gape-worm
Gaucher's
Gaucher's
Glanders
Glaucoma
Goujeers
Gummosis
Hip-joint
Hodgkin's
Hookworm
Impetigo
Jaundice
Kala-azar
Kawasaki
Leaf-roll
Leaf-spot
Listeria
Liver-rot
Loose-cut
Menière's
Minamata
Mycetoma
Myopathy
Myxedema
Nosology
Pandemic
Pathogen
Pellagra
Phthisis
Phytosis
Progeria
Pullorum
Rachitis
Raynaud's
Red water
Ringworm
Rose-rash
Scaly leg
Scrofula
Shingles
Slimmers'
Smallpox
Soft sore
Suppeago
Swayback
Swinepox
Syphilis
Tay-Sachs
The bends
Time-zone
Trembles
Uteritis
Venereal
Vincent's
Zoonosis

***9 letters:***
Arthrosis
Bilharzia
Blackhead
Black knot
Black-lung
Brown lung
Chancroid
Chloracne
Chlorosis
Christmas
Cirrhosis
Contagion
Cytopathy
Diathesis
Distemper
Drum-belly
Dysentery
Ear-cockle
Enteritis
Exanthema
Filanders
Gonorrhea
Hepatitis
Idiopathy
Influenza
Ixodiasis
Kawasaki's
King's evil
Lathyrism
Leucaemia
Leukaemia
Loose smut
Myxoedema
Navicular
Nephritis
Nephrosis
Newcastle
New Forest
Pellagrin
Pemphigus
Phossy-jaw
Porphyria
Scaldhead
Seborrhea
Siderosis
Silicosis
St Hubert's
Toxicosis
Trichosis
Tularemia
Tulip root
Yuppie flu

***10 letters:***
Acromegaly
Alzheimer's
Amoebiasis
Asbestosis
Autoimmune
Babesiosis
Bagassosis
Black death
Bluetongue
Byssinosis
Chickenpox
Damping off
Dandy-fever
Diphtheria
Erysipelas
Filariasis
Fire-blight
Fowl plague

Framboesia
Giardiasis
Gonorrhoea
Heartwater
Hemophilia
Iatrogenic
Ichthyosis
Impaludism
Lassa fever
Leuchaemia
Limber-neck
Lou Gehrig's
Louping ill
Moniliasis
Muscardine
Myasthenia
Neuropathy
Nosography
Nosophobia
Ornithosis
Parkinson's
Quarter-ill
Rinderpest
Sallenders
Scarlatina
Seborrhoea
Texas fever
Topagnosia
Trenchfoot
Tularaemia
Wind dropsy

*11 letters:*
Anthracosis
Arthropathy
Berylliosis
Brittle-bone
Cardiopathy
Coccidiosis
Consumption
Farmer's lung
Green monkey
Haemophilia
Hebephrenia
Huntington's
Isle of Wight
Kwashiorkor
Listeriosis
Myxomatosis
Parasitosis
Paratyphoid
Psittacosis
Rickettsial
Sarcoidosis
Scleroderma
Scrub typhus
Septicaemia
Thalassemia
Tonsillitis
Trench mouth
Trichinosis
Waldsterben
Woolsorter's
Yellow-fever

*12 letters:*
Alkaptonuria
Athlete's foot
Avitaminosis
Black quarter
Cor Pulmonate
Diacontiasis
Ehrlichiosis
Enterobiasis
Fascioliasis
Finger and toe
Foot and mouth
Furunculosis
Hoof and mouth
Legionnaires'
Molybdenosis
Motor neurone
Osteomalacia
Osteoporosis
Peachy-yellow
Scheuermann's
Shaking palsy
Slapped cheek
Thalassaemia
Tuberculosis
Uncinariasis

*13 letters:*
Elephantiasis
Leichmaniasis
Leptospirosis
Osteomyelitis
Panleucopenia
Poliomyelitis
Salmonellosis
Sclerodermata
Syringomyelia
Toxoplasmosis
Tsutsugamushi
Whooping cough

*14 letters:*
Coalminer's lung
Cystic fibrosis
Histoplasmosis
Leucodystrophy
Onchocerciasis
Pasteurellosis
Pneumoconiosis
Psillid yellows
River blindness
Sporotrichosis
St Anthony's Fire
Trichomoniasis
Trichophytosis
Vincent's angina

*15 letters:*
Graft-versus-host
Hyaline membrane
Myasthema graves
Schistosomiasis
Sydenham's chorea
Trypanosomiasis

*16 letters:*
Pneumonoconiosis
Sleeping sickness
Strongyloidiasis
Sweating sickness

*17 letters:*
Contagious aphthae
Friedreich's ataxia
Huntington's chorea
Montezuma's revenge
Multiple sclerosis
Muscular dystrophy
Pulmonary Fibrosis

---

▹**Diseased** *may indicate* an anagram
**Disembark** Alight, Deplane, Detrain, Land
**Disembarrass** Extricate, Rid, Unthread
**Disembodied** Discarnete
**Disembowel** Eviscerate, Exenterate, Gralloch, Gut, Resect, Viscerate
**Disenchant(ed)** Disabuse, Disillusion, Dismay, Embitter, Jaundiced
**Disencumber** Free, Relieve, Rid, Unburden
**Disengage(d), Disengagement** Breach of promise, Clear, Detach, Divorce, Liberate, Loosen, Neutral, Release, Unclasp, Undo, Untie
**Disentangle** Debarrass, Extricate, Red(d), Simplify, Solve, Uncoil, Unravel, Unsnarl
**Disestablishmentarian** Cosmist
**Disfavour** Doghouse, Maugre
**Disfigure(ment), Disfigured** Agrise, Agryze, Camsho, Club-foot, Deface, Deform, Goitre, Mangle, Mar, Mutilate, Scar, Spoil, Tash, Ugly
▹**Disfigured** *may indicate* an anagram
**Disfunction** Kernicterus
**Disgorge** Discharge, Eject, Regurgitate, Spew, Spill, Vent, Void
**Disgrace, Disgraceful** Atimy, Attaint, Baffle, Blot, Contempt, Contumely, Debasement,

Degrade, Deplorable, Diabolical, Discredit, Dishonour, Dog-house, Embace, Embase, Fie, For shame, Ignoble, Ignominious, Ignominy, Ill-fame, Indign, Indignity, Infamous, Infamy, Mean, Notorious, Obloquy, Opprobrium, Pity, Reprehensible, Scandal, Scandalous, Shame, Shameful, Shend, Slur, Soil, Stain, Stigma, Turpitude, Yshend

**Disgruntled** Brassed off, Hacked off, Malcontent, Narked, Resentful, Sore

▷**Disgruntled** *may indicate* an anagram

**Disguise(d)** Alias, Belie, Blessing, Camouflage, Chameleon, Cloak, Colour, Conceal, Cover, Covert, Dissemble, Hide, Hood, Incog(nito), Mantle, Mask, Masquerade, Obscure, Peruke, Pretence, Pseudonym, Ring, Shades, Stalking-horse, Travesty, Veil, Vele, Veneer, Visagiste, Visor, Vizard

▷**Disguised** *may indicate* an anagram

**Disgust(ing)** Ach-y-fi, Ad nauseam, Aversion, Aw, Bah, Blah, Cloy, Crude, Discomfort, Execrable, Faugh, Fie, Foh, Fulsome, Grisly, Grody, Icky, Irk, Loathsome, Manky, Mawkish, Minging, Nauseous, Noisome, Obscene, Odium, Offensive, Offputting, Oughly, Ouglie, Pah, Pho(h), Pip, Pish, Pshaw, Pugh, Repel, Repugnant, Repulse, → **REVOLT**, Revulsion, Scomfish, Scumfish, Scunner, Scuzz, → **SICKEN**, Sir-reverence, Si(e)s, Slimeball, Slimy, Squalid, The creeps, Turn off, Tush, Ugh, Ugly, Ugsome, Vile, Yech, Yucko, Yucky, Yu(c)k, Yukky

**Dish(y), Dish out** Adonis, Allot, Antenna, Apollo, Ashet, Basin, Belle, Bowl, Butterboat, Chafing, Charger, China, Cocotte, Compotier, Concoction, Cook-up, Crockery, Cutie, Dent, Diable, Dole, Dreamboat, Epergne, Flasket, Flatware, Grail, Kitchen, Laggen, Laggin, Lanx, Looker, Luggie, Menu, Muffineer, Ovenware, Pan, Pannikin, Paten, Patera, Patin(e), Pay, Petri, Plate, Platter, Popsy, Porringer, Ramekin, Ramequin, Receptacle, Rechauffé, Remove, Rout, Sangraal, Sangrail, Sangreal, Satellite, Saucer, Scorifier, Scupper, Scuttle, Serve, Service, Sexpot, Side (order), Smasher, Special(ty), Stunner, Toll, Watchglass, Woodenware

---

**DISHES**

*3 letters:*
Poi

*4 letters:*
Flan
Fool
Giro
Gyro
Hash
Hova
Idli
Kiev
Melt
Mess
Meze
Milt
Okra
Olla
Puri
Sate
Soss
Taco
Tian

*5 letters:*
Adobo
Aspic
Balti
Bhaji
Bhuna
Bitok
Boxty
Brose
Champ
Clack
Crepe
Crout
Curry
Daube
Dolma
Gomer
Gruel
Kasha
Kebab
Keema
Kibbe
Kofta
Korma
Laksa
Maror
Perog
Pilaf
Pilau
Pilow
Pizza
Poori
Raita
Ramen
Rosti
Sabji
Salad
Salmi
Satay
Split
Sushi
Tamal
Tikka
Tripe

*6 letters:*
Bhagee
Bharta
Bhoona
Bridie
Chilli
Confit
Cou-cou
Cuscus
Entrée
Fajita
Fondue
Gratin
Haggis
Hotpot
Junket
Kimchi
Kishke
Kissel
Masale
Mornay
Mousse
Muesli
Nachos
Paella
Pakora
Panada
Pirogi
Quiche
Ragout
Regale
Roesti
Salmis
Sea-pie
Sowans
Sowens
Subgum
Surimi
Tamale
Tsamba

*7 letters:*
Alfredo
Biriani
Bobotie
Burrito
Calzone
Cannoli
Cassava
Ceviche
Chowder
Comport
Compote
Crowdie
Crubeen
Crumble
Custard
Cuvette
Dariole
Dhansak
Dopiaza
Egg roll
Fajitas
Fal-a-fel
Fel-a-fel
Foo yung
Friture
Gravlax
Haroset
Marengo
Mousaka

Padella
Pad thai
Pavlova
Piccata
Pierogi
Polenta
Poutine
Rarebit
Ravioli
Risotto
Roulade
Sasatie
Sashimi
Scallop
Seviche
Sosatie
Soufflé
Spag bol
Stir-fry
Stovies
Supreme
Tartare
Tempura
Terrine
Timbale
Tostada
Zampone

***8 letters:***
Bhelpuri
Biriyani
Brandade
Bresaola
Calabash
Caponata
Chasseur
Chop suey
Chow mein
Coolamon
Coq au vin
Coquille
Couscous
Crostini
Dog's-body
Dolmades
Entremes
Feijoada
Flummery
Frittata
Furmenty
Gado-gado
Grillade
Halloumi
Handroll
Haroseth
Jalfrezi
Kedgeree
Keftedes
Kickshaw
Kouskous
Kreplach
Linguini
Mahi-mahi
Matelote
Mazarine
McCallum
Meat loaf
Meunière
Moussaka
Osso buco
Pandowdy
Pastrami
Poor John
Porridge
Pot-au-feu
Pot-roast
Raclette
Scrapple
Shashlik
Sillabub
Souvlaki
Squarial
Sukiyaki
Syllabub
Teriyaki
Tzatziki
Vindaloo
White-pot
Yakimono
Yakitori

***9 letters:***
Antipasto
Carbonara
Carpaccio
Cevapcici
Clafoutis
Colcannon
Egg-fo-yang
Enchilada
Entremets
Escabeche
Fricassee
Galantine
Gravad lax
Guacamole
Howtowdie
Jambalaya
Lobscouse
Lyonnaise
Manicotti
Marinière
Matelotte
Nut cutlet
Pastitsio
Pepper-pot
Reistafel
Rijstafel
Rillettes
Rogan josh
Scotch egg
Shashlick
Souvlakia
Succotash
Surf 'n' turf
Thermidor
Turducken

***10 letters:***
Blanquette
Bombay duck
Cacciatore
Cottage pie
Coulibiaca
Couscousou
Doner kebab
Egg custard
Egg-foo-yung
Jugged hare
Koulibiaca
Mixed grill
Mousseline
Nasi goreng
Parmigiana
Pease brose
Plat du jour
Provençale
Quesadilla
Rijsttafel
Salmagundi
Sauerkraut
Scaloppine
Shish kebab
Spankopita
Spatchcock
Spitchcock
Spring roll
Steak diane
Stroganoff
Teppan-yaki
Zabaglione

***11 letters:***
Banana split
Buck-rarebit
Chicken Kiev
Chimichanga
Crappit-head
Crème brulee
Dauphinoise
French toast
Fritto misto
Garam masala
Hog's pudding
Ratatouille
Saltimbocca
Sauerbraten
Smorgasbord
Spanakopita
Surf and turf
Welsh rabbit

***12 letters:***
Buffalo wings
Chitterlings
Eggs Benedict
Parmigianino
Plum Porridge
Shepherd's pie
Solomon Gundy
Steak tartare
Sweet and sour
Taramasalata
Welsh rarebit

***13 letters:***
Fish and brewis
Rumbledethump
Salade nicoise
Skirl in the pan
Toad-in-the-hole

***14 letters:***
Beef stroganoff
Beef Wellington
Chilli con carne
Rumbledethumps
Scotch woodcock

***15 letters:***
Bubble and squeak
Chicken Maryland
Eggs in moonshine
Weiner schnitzel

***16 letters:***
Moules marinieres
Potatoes and point

***17 letters:***
Cauliflower cheese

**Dishabille** Disarray, Négligé, Undress
**Disharmony** Distune
**Dishearten(ed)** Appal, Core(r), Cow, Crestfallen, Daunt, Depress, Deter, Discourage, Dispirit, Ettle
**Dishevel(led)** Bedraggled, Blowsy, Blowzy, Daggy, Mess, Rumpled, Scraggly, Touse, Tousle, Touzle, Towse, Tumble, Uncombed, Unkempt, Untidy, Windblown, Windswept
**Dishonest(y)** Bent, Cheat, Crooked, Cross, Dodgy, False, Fraud, Graft, Hooky, Hot, Ill-gotten, Improbity, Jiggery-pokery, Knavery, Light-fingered, Malpractice, Malversation, Maverick, Ringer, Rort, Shonky, Sleazy, Snide, Stink, Twister, Underhand, Venal, Wrong'un
**Dishonour(able)** Abatement, Caddish, Defile, Disgrace, Disparage, Ignoble, Ignom(in)y, Indignity, Infame, Notoriety, Scandal, Seduce, →SHAME, Violate, Wrong
**Disillusion(ment), Disillusioned** Awakening, Cynical, Disenchant, Sour
**Disincline(d), Disinclination** Apathy, Averse, Loth, Off, Reluctant
**Disinfect(ant)** Acriflavin(e), Bleach, Carbolic, Carvacrol, Cineol(e), Cleanse, Cresol, Dip, Eucalyptole, Formalin, Formol, Fuchsine, Fumigate, Lysol®, Orcein, Phenol, Purify, Sheep-dip, Sheep-wash, TCP®, Terebene
**Disinformation** Agitprop
**Disingenuous** Insincere, Mask, Oblique, Two-faced
**Disinherit** Deprive, Dispossess, Exheredate
**Disintegrate(d), Disintegration** Break, Collapse, Crumble, Decay, Dialysis, Erode, Fragment, Lyse, Lysis, Moulder, Osteoclasis, Rd, Rutherford, Tumbledown
**Disinter** Exhume, Unearth
**Disinterested** Apathetic, Impartial, Incurious, Listless, Mugwump, Unbiased, Yawning
**Disjoin** Disannex
**Disjoint(ed)** Bitty, Dismember, Incoherent, Rambling, Scrappy
**Disjunction** Exclusive, Inclusive
▸**Disk** *see* DISC
**Dislike(d)** Abhor, Allergy, Animosity, Animus, Antipathy, Aversion, Bete noire, Derry, Detest, Disesteem, Displeasure, Distaste, Fad, Gross out, Hate, Lump, Mind, Needle, Odium, Prejudice, Resent, Scunner, Ug(h), Warling
**Dislocate, Dislocation** Break, Diastasis, Displace, Fault, Luxate, Slip, Subluxate
**Dislodge** Budge, Displace, Evict, Expel, Luxate, Oust, Rear, Shift, Tuft, Unsaddle, Unseat, Unship, Untenant, Uproot
**Disloyal(ty)** Blue, False, Proditorious, Recreant, Renegade, Treacherous, Treason, Turncoat, Unfaithful, Untrue
**Dismal** Black, Bleak, Blue, Cheerless, Dark, Dowie, Dowly, Drack, Dreary, Dreich, Funereal, →GLOOMY, Grey, Grim, Long-faced, Morne, Obital, Sepulchral, Sombre, Sullen, Trist(e), Unpromising, Wae, Woebegone, Wormy
**Dismantle(d), Dismantling** Break, Decommission, Derig, Divest, Get-out, Sheer-hulk, Strike, Strip, Unpin, Unrig
**Dismast** Unstep
**Dismay(ed)** Aargh, Aghast, Alarm, Amate, Appal, Caramba, Confound, Consternation, Coo, Criv(v)ens, Daunt, Discourage, Dispirit, Dread, Fear, Fie, Ha, Hah, Horrify, Lordy, Lumme, Nonplus, Qualms, Strewth, Uh-oh
**Dismember** Quarter
**Dismiss(al), Dismissive** Airy, Annul, Ax, Banish, Boot, Bounce, Bowl(er), Brush off, Bum's rush, Can, Cancel, Cashier, Catch, Chuck, Congé, Constructive, Daff, Depose, Discard, Discharge, Dooce(d), Eject, Expulsion, Fire, Forget, Golden bowler, Golden duck, Golden handshake, Heave-ho, Kiss-off, Lay off, Let go, License, Marching orders, Mitten, Och, Oust, Pink-slip, Pooh-pooh, Prorogue, Puh, Push, Recall, Red card, Reform, Reject, Remove, R.O., Road, Sack, Scorn, Scout, Send, Shoo, Shrug off, Skittle out, Spit, Spurn, Stump, Suka wena, Turn out, Via, Voetsak, Walking papers, Walking ticket, Wicket, York
**Dismount** Alight, Hecht
**Disney, Disneyland** Anaheim, Walt
**Disobedience, Disobedient, Disobey** Breach, Civil, Contumacy, Defy, Flout, Insubordination, Rebel, Sit-in, Unruly, Wayward

**Disobliging** Unaccommodating

**Disorder(ly), Disordered** Acidosis, Affective, Agraphia, Ague, Ailment, Anarchy, Apnoea, Ariot, Asthma, Ataxia, Attention deficit, Bear garden, Betumbler, Catatonia, Chaos, Chlorosis, Clutter, Collywobbles, Conduct, Confuse, Consumption, Contracture, Conversion, Defuse, Derange, Deray, Diabetes, Dishevel, Dissociative, DT's, Dyscrasia, Dyslexia, Dysthymic, Dystrophy, Echolalia, Entropy, Epilepsy, Farrago, Folie a deux, Greensickness, Grippe, Haemophilia, Hallucinosis, Heartburn, Helter-skelter, Hugger-mugger, Huntingdon's chorea, Hypallage, Inordinate, Irregular, Mange, Mare's nest, Mayhem, ME, Mental, Mess, Misrule, Mistemper, → **MUDDLE**, Muss(y), Neurasthenia, Neurosis, Oncus, Onkus, Overset, Pandemonium, Panic, Para-, Paraphrenia, Parathrian, Pell-mell, Pentonitis, Personality, Pestilence, Phenylketonuria, Phobia, Porphyria, Priapus, Psychomatic, Psychoneurosis, Psychopathic, Psychosis, Raggle-taggle, Ragmatical, Rile, Roughhouse, Rowdy, Rumple, SAD, St Vitus' Dance, Schizophrenia, Schizothymia, Seborrh(o)ea, Shambolic, Shell-shock, Sickness, Slovenly, Snafu, Sydenham's chorea, Tarantism, Tetanus, Thalass(a)emia, Thought, Tobacco-heart, Tousle, Turbulence, Turmoil, Ulcer, Unhinge, Unrest, Unruly, Upheaval, Uproar, Upset, Virilism

▷**Disorder(ed)** *may indicate* an anagram

**Disorganise(d)** At sea, Chaotic, Deranged, Disarray, Disorderly, Haphazard, Haywire, Higgledy-piggledy, Ragtag, Ramshackle, Scatterbrain, Scatty, Scrappy, Shambolic, Structureless

**Disorientation** Jet lag

**Disown(ed)** Abnegate, Deny, Disacknowledge, Disclaim, Disinherit, Renig, Renounce, Reprobate, Repudiate, Unget

**Disparage, Disparaging, Disparagement** Abuse, Belittle, Decry, Defame, Denigrate, Deprecate, Depreciate, Derogate, Detract, Discredit, Do-down, Lessen, Pejorative, Poor mouth, Racist, Run down, Sell short, → **SLANDER**, Slur, Snide, Sour grapes, Traduce, Vilify

**Disparate** Motley

**Disparity** Gap

**Dispassionate** Calm, Clinical, Composed, Cool, Impartial, Objective, Serene

**Dispatch** Bowl, Celerity, Consign, Destroy, Dismiss, Epistle, Expede, Expedite, Export, Express, Gazette, Kibosh, Kill, Letter, Message, Missive, Note, Post, Pronto, Rapidity, Relegate, Remit, Report, → **SEND**, Shank, Ship, Slaughter, Slay, Special, Zip

**Dispel** Disperse, Scatter

**Dispensation, Dispense(r), Dispense with, Dispensary** Absolve, Administer, Aerosol, Apothecary, ATM, Automat, Ax(e), Bin, Cashpoint, Chemist, Chop, Container, Distribute, Dose, Dropper, Exempt, Fountain, Handout, Hole in the wall, Indult, Inhaler, MPS, Optic, Pharmacy, Pour, Scoop, Scrap, Siphon, Soda fountain, Spinneret, Vendor, Visitation

**Disperse, Dispersible, Dispersion** Deflocculate, Diaspora, Diffract, Diffuse, Disband, Dissolve, Distribute, Evaporate, Lyophil(e), Mode, Scail, Scale, → **SCATTER**, Skail, Sow, Spread, Strew

**Dispirit(ed), Dispiriting** Amort, Chapfallen, Crestfallen, Dampen, Dash, Daunt, Demoralise, Depress, Discourage, Dishearten, Exorcism, Gloomy, Listless, Sackless

**Displace(ment), Displaced** Antevert, Blueshift, Chandler's wobble, Depose, Dethrone, Dislodge, Disturb, Ectopia, Ectopy, Evacuee, Fault, Heave, Hernia, Heterotopia, Lateroversion, Load, Luxate, Move, Oust, Proptosis, Ptosis, Reffo, Refugee, Shift, Stir, Subluxation, Unseat, Unsettle, Uproot, Upthrow, Valgus, Varus, Volumetric

**Display, Display ground** Air, Array, Blaze, Blazon, Brandish, Bravura, College, Dangle, Depict, Eclat, Epideictic, Etagere, Etalage, Evidence, Evince, Exhibition, Exposition, Express, Extend, Extravaganza, Exude, Fanfare, Fireworks, Flannelboard, Flannelgraph, Flash, Flaunt, Float, Fly-by, Flypast, Gala, Glitz, Gondola, Hang, Head-down, Head-up, Heroics, HUD, Iconic, Lay out, LCD, LED, Lek, Liquid crystal, Manifest, Motorcade, Mount, Muster, Ostentation, Outlay, Overdress, Pageant, Parade, Paraf(f)le, Peepshow, Pixel, Pomp, Post, Present(ation), Propale, Pyrotechnics, Rode, Rodeo, Roll-out, Ruffle, Scene, Screensaver, Scroll, Set piece, Setting, Shaw, → **SHOW**, Showcase, Sideshow, Sight, Spectacle, Splash, Splatter, Splendour, Splurge, Sport, Spree, State, Stunt, Swank, Tableau, Tattoo, Tournament, Turn out, Up, Vaunt, Wear, Window dressing

**Displease(d), Displeasing, Displeasure** Anger, Dischuffed, Humph, Irritate, Offensive, Provoke, Umbrage, Unwelcome

**Disport** Amuse, Divert, Play

**Dispose(d), Disposal, Disposition** Apt, Arrange, Bestow, Bin, Bomb, Cast, Despatch, Dump, Eighty-six, Ethos, Fly-tip, Incline, Kibosh, Kybosh, Lay(-out), Mood, Ordonnance, Prone, Riddance, Sale, Sell, Service, Settle, Spirit, Stagger, Throwaway, Will

▷**Disposed, Disposition** *may indicate* an anagram

**Disposition** Affectation, Attitude, Bent, Bias, Humour, Inclination, Kidney, Lie, Nature, Penchant, Propensity, Talent, Temper(ament), Trim

**Dispossess(ed)** Abate, Attaint, Bereft, Depose, Deprive, Disseise, Evict, Lumpen, Oust

**Disproportion(ate)** Asymmetric, Excessive, Extreme, Imbalance, Incommensurate, Undue, Unequal

**Disprove, Disproof, Disproval** Debunk, Discredit, Invalidate, Negate, Rebut, Rebuttal, Redargue, Reductio ad absurdum, Refel, Refute

**Dispute(d), Disputant** Altercation, Argue, Argy-bargy, At odds, Barney, Brangle, Brawl, Bust-up, Cangle, Case, Chaffer, Challenge, Chorizont(ist), Contend, Contest, Contravene, Contretemps, Controversy, Debate, Demarcation, Deny, Differ, Discept, Discuss, Eristic, Feud, Fracas, Fray, Gainsay, Haggle, Issue, Kilfud-yoking, Lock-out, Loggerheads, Militate, Moot, Niggle, Ob and soller, Odds, Oppugn, Plea, Polemic, Pro-and-con, Quarrel, Query, → QUESTION, Quibble, Rag, Resist, Run in, Skirmish, Slanging-match, Spar, Spat, Stickle, Stoush, Threap(it), Threep(it), Tiff, Tissue, Tug-of-love, Variance, Vendetta, Wrangle

**Disqualify** Debar, Dishabilitate, Incapacitate, Recuse, Reject, Unfit

**Disquiet(ed), Disquieting** Agitate, Concern, Discomboberate, Discombobulate, → DISTURB, Pain, Perturb(ation), Sinister, Solicit, Tension, Turmoil, Ugly, Uneasy, Unnerve, Unrest, Vex

**Disraeli** Dizzy, Tancred

**Disregard(ed)** Anomie, Anomy, Contempt, Defy, Disfavour, Flout, Forget, Go by, Heedlessness, Ignore, Neglect, Oblivion, Omit, Overlook, Override, Oversee, Pass, Pretermit, Slight, Spare, Violate, Waive

**Disrepair** Decay, Decrepitude, Dilapidation, Fritz, Ruin

**Disreputable, Disrepute** Base, Black sheep, Bowsie, Disgrace, Grubby, Ill fame, Ken, Louche, Low, Lowlife, Notorious, Raffish, Ragamuffin, Ratbag, Reprobate, Riff-raff, Rip, Scuzz(ball), Scuzzbag, Scuzzbucket, Seamy, Seamy side, Seedy, Shady, Shakerag, Shameful, Shy, Shyster, Sleazy, Unsavoury

**Disrespect(ful)** Affront, Contempt, Derogatory, Discourtesy, Flip(pant), Impiety, Impolite, Insolent, Insult, Irreverent, Levity, Naughty, Profane, Sacrilege, Slight, Uncivil, Violate

**Disrupt(ion), Disruptive** Antisocial, Breach, Catabolism, Cataclasm, Dislocate, Disorder, Distract, Hamper, Hiatus, Interrupt, Jetlag, Mayhem, Perturb, Quonk, Ruffle, Sabotage, Screw, Shake-up, Upheaval

▷**Disruption** *may indicate* an anagram

**Dissatisfaction** Displeasure, Distaste, Ennui, Humph, Umph

**Dissect(ion)** Analyse, Dismember, Examine, Necrotomy, Parse, Zootomy

**Dissemble(r)** Conceal, Feign, Fox, Hypocrite, Impostor, Misinform, Pecksniff

**Disseminate** Radiate, Spread

**Dissent(er), Dissension, Dissenting** Altercation, Contend, Demur, Differ, Disagree, Discord, Dissident, Disunion, Divisiveness, Faction, Flak, Friction, Heretic, Holmes, Jain, Leveller, Lollard, Maverick, Methodist, Naysayer, Negation, Noes, Non-CE, Non-con(formist), Occasional conformist, Old Believer, Pantile, Protest, Raskolnik, Recusant, Remonstrant, Sectary, Separat(ion)ist, Splinter group, → STRIFE, Vary, Wesleyan

**Dissertation** Essay, Excursus, Lecture, Paper, Thesis, Treatise

**Dissidence** → DESERTER, Schism

**Dissident** → DESERTER, Heretic, Objector

**Dissimilar** Different, Diverse, Heterogeneous, Unlike

**Dissipate(d)** Debauch, Decadent, Diffuse, Dispell, Disperse, Dissolute, Gay, Revel, Roue, Scatter, Shatter, Squander, Waste

▷**Dissipated** *may indicate* an anagram

**Dissociate** Separate, Sever, Withdraw
**Dissolute** Decadent, Degenerate, Demirep, Falstaffian, Hell, Immoral, Lax, Libertine, Licentious, Loose, Rake-helly, Rakish, Reprobate, Rip, Roué, Wanton
▷**Dissolute** *may indicate* an anagram
**Dissolution** Debauchery, Dismissal, Divorce, End, Karyolysis, Repeal, Separation
**Dissolve(d)** Deliquesce, Digest, Disband, Discandie, Discandy, Disunite, Lap, Liquesce, Melt, Repeal, Solute, Terminate, Thaw
**Dissonance** Cacophony, Wolf
**Dissuade** Dehort, Deter, Discourage
**Distaff** Clotho, Female, Lady, Rock, Stick
**Distance** Absciss(a), Afield, Apothem, Apse, Apsos, Breadth, Centimorgan, Coss, Declination, Earshot, Eloi(g)n, Elongation, Farness, Focal, Foot, Gap, Headreach, Height, Hyperfocal, Ice, Intercalumniation, Interval, Klick, Kos(s), Latitude, League, Length, Light year, Long-haul, Maintenance, Mean, Mean free path, Middle, Mileage, Northing, Ordinate, Outland, Parasang, Parsec, Range, Reserve, Rod, Skip, Span, Spitting, Stade, Step, Stopping, Striking, Thickness, Way, Wheelbase, Yardage, Yojan, Zenith
**Distant** Aloof, Apart, Chilly, Cold, Far, Frosty, Hyperfocal, Icy, Long (view), Northing, Offish, Outland, Outlying, Outremer, Polar, Remote, Standoffish, Subconscious, Tele-, Timbuctoo, Timbuktu, Unfriendly, Yonder
**Distaste(ful)** Dégoût, Gory, Grimace, Gross-out, Repellent, Repugnant, Ropy, Scunner, Sour, Unpalatable, Unpleasant, Unsavoury, Yuck
**Distemper** Ailment, Canine, Colourwash, Emulsion, Equine, Hard-pad, Paint, Panleucopenia, Pip, Tempera
**Distend(ed), Distension** Bloat, Dilate, Ectasia, Emphysema, Expand, Hoove, Inflate, Meteorism, Puffy, → **STRETCH**, Swell, Turgid, Tympanites, Varicocele, Varicose
**Distil(late), Distillation, Distiller, Distillery, Distilling** Alcohol, Alembic, Anthracine, Azeotrope, Bootlegger, Brew, Cohobate, Condense, Destructive, Drip, Dry, Essence, Ethanol, Extract, Fractional, Mashtun, Naphtha, Paraffin wax, Pelican, Pyrene, Pyroligneous, Rosin, Turps, Vacuum, Vapour
▷**Distillation** *may indicate* an anagram
**Distinct(ive)** Apparent, Beside, Characteristic, Chiselled, Clear, Determinate, Different, Discrete, Evident, Grand, Idiosyncratic, Individual, Peculiar, Plain, Separate, Several, Signal, → **SPECIAL**, Stylistic, Trenchant, Vivid
**Distinction** Beaut(y), Blue, Cachet, Class, Credit, Diacritic, Difference, Dignity, Diorism, Disparity, Division, Double-first, Eclat, Eminence, Entelechy, Hair-splitting, Honour, Laureate, Laurels, Lustre, Mark, Mystique, Nicety, Note, Nuance, OM, Prominence, Punctilio, Quiddity, Rank, Renown, Speciality, Style, Title
**Distinguish(ed), Distinguishable, Distinguishing** Classify, Contrast, Demarcate, Denote, Diacritic, Different(iate), Discern, Discriminate, Distinct, Divide, Elevate, Eminent, Ennoble, Especial, Eximious, Grand, Mark, Nameworthy, Notable, Perceive, Pick out, Prestigious, Prominent, Rare, Renowned, Scerne, Secern, Signal, Special, Stamp, Tell, VIP
**Distort(ion), Distorted** Anamorphosis, Astigmatism, Asymmetry, Bend, Bias, Caricature, Colour, Contort, Deface, Deform, Dent, Foreshorten, Fudge, Garble, Grimace, Harmonic, Helium speech, Jaundiced, Mangle, Misshapen, Pervert, Rubato, Skew, Stretch, Thraw, Time-warp, Travesty, Twist, → **WARP**, Wow, Wrest, Wring, Writhe, Wry
▷**Distort(ed)** *may indicate* an anagram
**Distract(ed), Distraction** Absent, Agitate, Amuse, Avocation, Beguile, Bewilder, Divert, Embroil, Éperdu, Forhaile, Frenetic, Loon, Lost, Madden, Mental, Nepenthe, Perplex, Red herring, Scatty, Sidetrack, Sledge, Upstage
▷**Distract(ed)** *may indicate* an anagram
**Distrain(t)** Na(a)m, Poind, Sequestrate, Stress
**Distraught** Deranged, Desperate, Elfish, Elvan, Frantic, Mad, Troubled, Unstrung
**Distress(ed), Distressing** Acerbate, Afflict, Aggrieve, Agony, Ail, Alack, Alopecia, Anger, Anguish, Antique, Crise, Cut up, Desperation, Distraint, Dolour, Exigence, Extremity, Fraught, Fret, Gnaw, Grief, Grieve, Harass, Hardship, Harrow, Heartbreak, Hurt, Ill, → **IN DISTRESS**, Irk, Misease, Misfortune, Need, Oppress, Pain, Poignant, Prey, Privation, Sad,

Shorn, Sore, SOS, Straiten, Straits, Suffering, Tole, Torment, Tragic, Traumatic, Tribulation, → TROUBLE, Une(a)th, Unnerve, Unstrung, Upset, Wound

▷**Distress** *may indicate* a haircut

**Distribute(d), Distribution, Distributor** Allocate, Allot, Apportion, Binomial, Busbar, Carve, Chi-square, Chorology, Circulate, Colportage, Deal, Deliver(y), Deploy, Dish, Dispense, Dispose, Dissemination, Exponential, F, Frequency, Gamma, Gaussian, Geographical, Geometric, Intersperse, Issue, Ladle out, Lie, Lot, Mete, Normal, Out(let), Pattern, Poisson, Prorate, Renter, Repartition, Send out, Serve, Share, Shuffle, Strew

▷**Distributed** *may indicate* an anagram

**District** Alsatia, Amhara, Arcadia, Ards, Area, Arrondissement, Attica, Bail(l)iwick, Banat, Banate, Bannat, Barrio, Belt, Broadway, Bronx, Canton, Cantred, Circar, Classis, Community, Congressional, Diocese, Encomienda, End, English pale, Exurb, Falernian, Federal, Fitzrovia, Gaeltacht, Gau, Ghetto, Hood, Hundred, Jewish pale, Khet, Lake, Land, Lathe, Liberty, Locality, Loin, Manor, Metropolitan, Nasik, → NEIGHBOURHOOD, Oblast, Olympia, Pachalic, Pale, Pargana, Parish(en), Paroch, Pashalik, Patch, Peak, Pergunnah, Phocis, Precinct, Province, Quarter, Quartier, Rape, → REGION, Reserve, Ride, Riding, Ruhr, Rural, Sancerre, Sanjak, Savoy, Section, Sector, Sheading, Shire, Sircar, Sirkar, Soc, Soke(n), Stake, Stannary, Suburb, Sucken, Talooka, Taluk, Tenderloin, Township, Urban, Venue, Vicinage, Visne, Walk, Wapentake, Ward, Way, Wealden, Zila, Zillah, Zone

**Distrust(ful)** Caution, Doubt, Leery, Misanthropic, Misfaith, Suspect, Wariness

**Disturb(ance), Disturbed, Disturbing** Ado, Aerate, Affray, Aggrieve, Agitate, Alarm, Atmospherics, Autism, Betoss, Brabble, Brainstorm, Brash, Brawl, Broil, Carfuffle, Chagrin, Choppy, Clatter, Collieshangie, Concuss, Delirium, Dementia, Derange, Desecrate, Disconcert, Disquiet, Disrupt, Dust, Dysfunction, Eat, Feeze, Firestorm, Fracas, Fray, Fret, Harass, Hoopla, Incident, Incommode, Infest, Interference, Interrupt, Intrude, Jee, Kerfuffle, Kick-up, Kurfuffle, Macabre, Molest, Muss, Neurosis, Outbreak, Perturb(ation), Prabble, Racket, Rammy, Ramp, Riot, Ripple, Rock, Roil, Romage, Roughhouse, Rouse, Ruckus, Ruction, Ruffle, Rumpus, Shake, Shellshock, Shindig, Shindy, Shook-up, Sociopath, Stashie, Static, Steer, Stir, Stress, Sturt, Tremor, Troppo, Trouble, Turbulent, Turmoil, Unnerve, Unquiet, Unrest, Unsettle, Upheaval, Uproot, → UPSET, Upturn, Vex, Whistler

▷**Disturb(ed)** *may indicate* an anagram

**Disunite, Disunity** Alienate, Dissever, Divide, Divorce, Schism, Split

**Disuse** Abandon, Abeyance, Atrophy, Desuetude, Discard, Lapse

**Ditch** Abandon, Abolish, Barathron, Barathrum, Can, Cast aside, Channel, Chuck, Crash land, Cunette, Delf, Delph, Dike, Discard, Donga, Drainage, Drop, Dyke, Eliminate, Euripus, Foss(e), Graft, Grip, Gripe, Gully, Ha(w)-ha(w), Jettison, Khor, Last, Level, Lode, Moat, Nal(l)a(h), Nulla(h), Rean, Reen, Rhine, Rid, Sea, Sheuch, Sheugh, Sike, Sloot, Sluit, Spruit, Stank, Sunk-fence, Syke, Tenail(le), Trench, Trough

**Dither(ing)** Agitato, Bother, Dally, Dicker, Faff, Flap, Flat spin, Haver, Haw, Hesitate, Hum, Indecisive, Irresolute, Pusillanimous, Pussyfoot, Twitter, Vacillate

**Dittany** Gas-plant

**Ditty, Ditties** Air, Arietta, Canzonet, Departmental, Jingle, Lay, Song

**Diuretic** Frusemide, Furosemide, Pareira brava, Pipsissewa, Spironolactone, Thazide, Theobromine, Zea

**Diva** Callas, Melba, Patti, Singer

**Divan** Compilement, Congress, Couch, Council, Ottoman, Settee, Sofa

**Dive, Diver(s), Diving** Aquanaut, Armstand, Backflip, Belly-flop, Cousteau, Crash, Dart, Den, Didapper, Duck, Embergoose, File, Flop, Free-fall, Frogman, Full-gainer, Gainer, Grebe, Guillemot, Half-gainer, Header, Honkytonk, Jackknife, Joint, Ken, Loom, Loon, Lungie, Merganser, Night club, Nitery, Nose, Pass, Pearl, Pickpocket, Pike, Plong(e), Plummet, Plunge, Plutocrat, Pochard, Poker, Power, Puffin, Saturation, Sawbill, Scoter, Scuba, Shebeen, Skin, Sky, Snake-bird, Sound, Speakeasy, Springboard, Stage, Step-to, Stoop, Submerge, Swallow, Swan, Swoop, Tailspin, Urinant, Urinator, Zoom

**Diverge(nce), Divergent** Branch, Deviate, Divaricate, Heterochrony, Spread, Swerve, Variant, Veer

**Divers(e), Diversify** Alter, Branch out, Chequer, Dapple, Different, Eclectic, Interlard,

Intersperse, Manifold, Many, Miscellaneous, Mixed, Motley, Multifarious, Separate, Some, Sundry, Variegate, Various, Vary

**Diversion, Divert(ing)** Amuse, Avocation, Beguile, Cone, Crossword, Deflect, Detour, Disport, Dissuade, Distract, Droll, Entertain, Game, Hare, Hijack, Hive off, Hobby, Interest, Interlude, Pastime, Pleasure, Prolepsis, Ramp, Red-herring, Reflect, Refract, Reroute, Ruse, Shunt, Sideline, Sideshow, Sidetrack, Siphon, Smokescreen, Sport, Stalking-horse, Steer, Stratagem, Sublimation, Sway, Switch, Syphon, Tickle, Upstage, Yaw, Zany

▷**Diverting** *may indicate* an anagram

**Divest** Denude, Rid, Strip, Undeck, Undress

**Divide(d), Divider, Dividing, Division** Abkhazia, Adzharia, Apart, Apportion, Balk, Balkanise, Band, Bifurcate, Bipartite, Bisect, Branch, Cantle, Chancery, Cleave, Cleft, Coal measure, Comminute, Commot(e), Continental, Counter-pale, Cusp, Cut, Deal, Decussate, Demerge, Digital, Dimidiate, Discide, Dismember, Dissever, Estrange, Fork, Fraction, Furcate, Great, Gulf, Indent, Isere, Lot, Montgomery, Parcel, Part, Partite, Partition, Partitive, Party wall, Pentomic, Plebs, Polarise, Potential, Precisive, Quotient, Ramify, Rend, Riding, Rift, Sectionalise, Separate, Sever, Share, → **SPLIT**, Stanza, Sunder, Tierce, Transect, Tribalism, Tribe, Trisect, Twixt, Utgard, Voltage, Watershed, Zone

**Dividend** Bonus, Contango, Div, Interim, Into, Numerator, Peace, Share

**Divination, Divine(r)** Anthroposcopy, Arithmancy, Augurm, Augury, Auspices, Axinomancy, Belomancy, Bibliomancy, Botanomancy, Capnomancy, Cartomancy, Ceromancy, Chiromancy, Clairvoyant, Cleromancy, Coscinomancy, Crithomancy, Crystal-gazing, Crystallomancy, Doodlebug, Dowser, Elysian, Empyromancy, Gastromancy, Geloscopy, Geomancy, Gyromancy, Hariolation, Haruspex, Hepatoscopy, Hieromancy, Hieroscopy, Hydromancy, I Ching, Intuition, Lampadomancy, Leconomancy, Lithomancy, Magic, Mantic, Myomancy, Omphalomancy, Oneiromancy, Onoplatoscopy, Onphalomancy, Onychomancy, Ornithomancy, Ornithoscopy, Osteomancy, Palmistry, Pegomancy, Pessomancy, Pyromancy, Radiesthesia, Rhabdomancy, Scapulimancy, Scapulomancy, Sciomancy, Seer, Sibyl, Sideromancy, Soothsay, Sortes, Sortilege, Spae(man), Spodomancy, Taghairm, Tais(c)h, Tephromancy, Theomancy, Tripudiary, Vaticanator, Xylomancy, Zoomancy

**Divine, Divine presence, Divinity** Acoemeti, Aitu, Ambrose, Atman, Avatar, Beatific, Blessed, Celestial, Chaplain, Clergyman, Conjecture, Curate, DD, Deduce, Deific, Deity, Douse, Dowse, Ecclesiastic, Empyreal, Forecast, Foretell, Fuller, → **GOD**, → **GODDESS**, Godhead, Godlike, Guess, Hallowed, Hariolate, Heavenly, Holy, Hulse, Immortal, Inge, Isiac, Kami, Mantic, Numen, Numinous, Olympian, Pontiff, Predestinate, Predict, Presage, Priest, Prophesy, RE, Rector, RI, Rimmon, Scry, Sense, Seraphic, Shechinah, Shekinah, Spae, Superhuman, Supernal, Theandric, Theanthropic, Theologise, Theology, Triune

**Division, Divisible** Amitosis, Angiosperm, Arcana, Arm, Arrondissement, Bajocian, Banat(e), Bannet, Bar, Bizone, Branch, Brome, Caesura, Canto, Canton, Cantred, Cantref, Cassini's, Caste, Category, Cell, Champart, Chapter, Chulla, Classification, Cleft, Cloison, Clove, Comitatus, Commot(e), Commune, Compartment, Coralline Crag, Corps, County, Crevasse, Curia, Department, Dichotomy, Disagreement, Disunity, Div, Duan, Eyalet, Family, Farren, Fissile, Fork, Fragmentation, Glires, Grisons, Guberniya, Gulf, Gulph, Hapu, Harmonic, Hedge, Hide, Holland, Hotchpot, Hundred, Inning, Isogloss, Keuper, Kim(m)eridgian, Lathe, Leet, Legion, Lindsey, List, Lobe, Long, Mannion, Maturation, M(e)iosis, Mitosis, Mofussil, Nome, Oblast, Over, Pachytene, Parazoa, Pargana, Part, Partition, Passus, Pergunnah, Period, Phratry, Phyle, Phylum, Pipe, Pitaka, Platoon, Polarisation, Precinct, Presidency, Province, Quartering, Queen's Bench, Quotition, Rape, Red Crag, Reduction, Region, Replum, Reservation, Riding, Sanjak, Schism, Section, Sector, Segment, Semeion, Sept(ate), Sever, Share, Sheading, Shed, Shire, Short, Squadron, Stage, Stake, Subgenre, Subheading, Suborder, Tahsil, Tanach, Taxis, Tehsil, Telophase, Tepal, Thanet, Theme, Trichotomy, Trio, Trivium, Troop, Tuath, Unit, Vilayet, Volost, Wapentake, Ward, Watershed

**Divisor** Aliquant, Aliquot, Denominator

**Divorce(d)** Alienate, Apart, Diffarreation, Disaffiliate, Dissolution, Dissolve, Disunion, Div, Estrange, Get(t), Isolate, Part, Put away, Reno, Separate, Sequester, → **SUNDER**, Talak, Talaq, Unhitch

**Divot** Clod, Sod, Turf

**Divulge** Confess, Disclose, Expose, Publish, Reveal, Split, Tell, Unveil, Utter

**DIY** Flatpack

**Dizziness, Dizzy** Beaconsfield, Ben, Blonde, Capricious, Dinic, Disraeli, Giddy, Giglot, Lightheaded, Mazey, Megrim, Mirligoes, Scotodinia, Scotomania, Swimming, Vertiginous, → VERTIGO, Woozy

**DJ** Deejay, Jock, Mixmaster, Monkey-suit, Penguin suit, Presenter, Selecta, Shockjock, Tuxedo, Veejay

**DNA** Adenine, Antisense, Centromere, Chromatin, Chromosome, Cistron, Codon, Complementary, Cytosine, Double helix, Exon, Gene, Heteroduplex, Homopolymer, Intron, Junk, Microsatellite, Mitochondrial, Muton, Nucleosome, Nucleotide, Operator, Palindrome, Papovavirus, Plasmid, Polyoma, Poxvirus, Procaryote, Profiling, Prokaryote, Pseudogene, Purine, Recombinant, Replication fork, Replicon, Retrotransposon, Ribosome, RNA, Satellite, Selfish, Southern blot, Synthetic, Telomere, Thymidine, Transcript(ion), Transfection, Transfer, Translation, Transposon, Vector, Watson-Crick model

**Do(es), Doing** Accomplish, Achieve, Act, Anent, Banquet, Barbecue, Bash, Beano, Begin, Blow-out, Char, Cheat, Chisel, Cod, Con, Cozen, Deed, Defraud, Dich, Diddle, Dish, Div, Doobrie, Doth, Dupe, Effectuate, Enact, Event, Execute, Fare, Fleece, Function, Fuss, Gull, Handiwork, Hoax, Imitate, Jamboree, Measure up, Mill, Occasion, Perform, Perpetrate, Provide, Rip off, Rook, Same, Serve, Settle, Shindig, Soiree, Spif(f)licate, Suffice, Swindle, Thrash, Thrive, Tonic, Up to, Ut, Welsh

▹**Do** *may indicate* an anagram

**Do away** Abolish, Banish, Demolish, Kill

**Dobbie** Elf, Fairy

**Doc** Dwarf

**Docile** Agreeable, Amenable, Biddable, Dutiful, Facile, Manageable, Meek, Obedient, Placid, Submissive, Tame, Timid, Tractable, Yielding

**Dock(er), Docked, Docks** Abridge, Albert, Barber, Basin, Bistort, Bob, Camber, Canaigre, Clip, Crop, Curta(i)l, Cut, Deduct, De-tail, Dry, Fitting out, Floating, Grapetree, Graving, Hoverport, Knotweed, Lay-up, Longshoreman, Lop, Lumper, Marina, Monk's rhubarb, Moor, Off-end, Pare, Patience, Pen, Pier, Quay, Rhubarb, Rumex, Rump, Scene, Seagull, Shorten, Snakeweed, Sorrel, Sourock, Stevedore, Tilbury, Trimmer, Watersider, Wet, Wharf, Wharfie, Yard

**Docket** Bordereau, Invoice, Label, Tag

**Dockyard** Arsenal, Chatham, Naval, Rosyth, Sheerness

**Doctor(s)** Adulterate, Allopath, Alter, Arnold, Asclepiad, Barefoot, Barnardo, Bleeder, BMA, Bones, Bonesetter, Breeze, Bright, Brighton, Brown, Caius, Cape, Castrate, Chapitalize, Clinician, Company, Cook, Crocus, Cup(per), Cure(r), Dale, Death, Diagnose, Dolittle, Dr, Dryasdust, Erasmus, Extern(e), Fake, Falsify, Family, Faustus, Feldsher, Fell, Fiddle, Finlay, Flying, Foster, Fu manchu, Fundholder, Galen, Geriatrician, Geropiga, GP, Guillotin(e), Hakeem, Hakim, Healer, Homeopath, Houseman, Hyde, Imhotep, Intern, Internist, Jekyll, Jenner, Johnson, Juris utriusque, Kildare, Lace, Leach, Leech, Linacre, Load, Locum, Luke, Manette, Manipulate, Massage, MB, MD, Medicate, Medico, Mganga, Middleton, Mindererus, Minister, Misrepresent, MO, MOH, Molla(h), Moreau, Mulla(h), Myologist, Neuter, No, Ollamh, Ollav, Paean, Paediatrician, Panel, Pangloss, Paracelsus, Paramedic, Pedro, PhD, Physician, Pill(s), Practitioner, Quack, Quacksalver, Rabbi, RAMC, Registrar, Resident, Rhinologist, Rig, Rorschach, Salk, Sangrado, Saw, Sawbones, School, Script, Seraphic, Seuss, Shaman, Slammer, Slop, Spay, Spin, Spock, Stum, Surgeon, Syn, Syntax, Therapist, Thorne, Treat, Vaidya, Vet, Water, Watson, Who, Wind, Witch

▹**Doctor(ed)** *may indicate* an anagram

**Doctrine, Doctrinaire, Doctrinate** Adamitism, Adoptianism, Adoptionism, Antinomian, Apollinarian, Archology, Arianism, Averr(h)oism, Blairism, Bonism, Brezhnev, Cab(b)ala, Cacodoxy, Calvinism, Catabasis, Catastrophism, Chiliasm, Consubstantiation, Credo, Creed, Determinism, Diabology, Ditheism, Ditheletism, Divine right, Docetism, Dogma, Doxie, Doxy, Dualism, Dysteleology, Encratism, Eschatology, Esotery, Eutychian, Evangel, Febronianism, Federalism, Fideism, Finalism, Functionalism, Gnosticism, Gospel,

Henotheism, Hesychasm, Holism, Idealism, Ideologise, Illuminism, Immaterialism, Immersionism, Indeterminism, Infralapsarianism, Islam, Ism, Jansenism, Krypsis, Laches, Lore, Machtpolitik, Malthusian, Manich(a)eism, Materialism, Metempsychosis, Modalism, Molinism, Monadism, Monergism, Monism, Monothel(et)ism, Monroe, Neo-Malthusianism, Neonomianism, Nestorianism, Neutral monism, Nihilism, Occamism, Ockhamism, Panentheism, Pantheism, Pelagianism, Personalism, Physiocracy, Pluralism, Ponerology, Pragmatism, Predestination, Premillennialism, Preterition, Probabilism, Psilanthropism, Pythagorean(ism), Pythagorism, Quietism, Real presence, Redaction, Reformism, Relativism, Relativity, Satyagrahi, Scotism, Sectarianism, Secularism, Sharia, Sheria, Shibboleth, Solidism, Soteriology, Strong meat, Subjectivism, Sublapsarianism, Subpanation, Substantialism, Swedenborgianism, Syndicalism, Synergism, System, Teleology, →**TENET**, Terminism, Theory, Theravada, Thomism, Transubstantiation, Trialism, Tridentine, Tutiorism, Universalism, Utilitarianism, Voluntarism, Wasm, Weismannism, Whiteboyism, Zoism, Zwinglian

**Document(s), Documentary** Archive, Blog, Brevet, Brief, Bumf, Bumph, Carta, Certificate, Charge sheet, Charter, Chop, Contract, Conveyance, Copy, Covenant, Daftar, Deed, Diazo, Diploma, Docket, Doco, Dompass, Dossier, E-journal, Elegit, Escrol(l), Escrow, Fiat, Fieri Facias, Fly-on-the-wall, Form, Grand Remonstrance, Green paper, Holograph, Impeachment, Indenture, Latitat, Licence, Logbook, Mandamus, Manifesto, Offer, Organogram, Papers, Permit, Policy, Precept, Production, Pro forma, Public, Ragman, Ragment, Record, Resort, Roll, Roul(e), Screed, Scroll, Sea brief, Source, Spreadsheet, Stamp note, State, Statute, Voucher, Warrant, Waybill, Weblog, Webpage, White paper, Writ, Write up

**Dod** Pet, Poll

**Dodder(y)** Infirm, Old, Shake, Stagger, Strangleweed, Totter, Tremble

**Doddle** Easy(-peasy)

**Dodge(r), Dodgy** Artful, Avert, Avoid, Bell-ringing, Black sheep, Column, Duck, Elude, Evade, Evasion, Evite, Idler, Iffy, Jink, Jook, Jouk, Malinger, Racket, Ruse, Scam, Shirk, Sidestep, Skip, Skive, Slalom, Slinter, Suspect, Suspicious, Swerve, Tip, Trick, Truant, Twist, Urchin, Weave, Welsh, Wheeze, Wire, Wrinkle

**Dodgem** Bumper car

**Doe(s)** Deer, Faun, Hind, John

**Doff** Avail(e), Avale, Remove, Rouse, Shed, Tip

**Dog(s), Doglike** Assistance, Attack, Bowwow, Canes, Canidae, Canine, Cynic, Dirty, Dropper, Feet, Fire, Fog, Gay, Hearing, Hot, Huntaway, Hunter, Isle, Kennel, Leading, Native, Night, Nodding, Pursue, Ranger, Ratter, Running, Sea, Search, Seeing-eye, Shadow, Sleeve, Sleuthhound, Sniffer, Snoopy, Spotted, Stalk, Stray, Strong-eye, Sun, Tag, Tail, Therapy, Toby, Top, Toto, Toy, Tracker, Trail, Truffle, Tumbler, Wammul, Water, Water dog, Working, Yellow

---

**DOGS**

*3 letters:*
Cur
Eye
Gun
Pig
Pom
Pug
Rab
Yap

*4 letters:*
Barb
Bird
Brak
Bran
Bush
Cant
Chow
Dane
Fido
Heel
Iron
Kuri
Kuta
Kuti
Leam
Lyam
Mutt
Oath
Peke
Puli
Rach
Sled
Stag
Tike
Tosa
Tray
Tyke
Wolf

*5 letters:*
Akita
Alans
Apsos
Argos
Boots
Boxer
Brach
Cairn
Coach
Corgi
Dhole
Dingo
Guard
Guide
Haunt

Hound
Husky
Hyena
Kurre
Laika
Lorel
Luath
Merle
Moera
Pidog
Pluto
Pooch
Rache
Ratch
Rover
Shock
Spitz
Spoor
Whelp
Zorro

***6 letters:***
Afghan
Bandog
Barbet
Barker
Basset
Beagle
Bitser
Blanch
Borzoi
Bounce
Bowler
Briard
Caesar
Canaan
Chenet
Cocker
Collie
Coyote
Dangle
Eskimo
Gelert
Goorie
Heeler
Jackal
Katmir
Kelpie
Kennet
Ketmir
Kratim
Lassie
Mauthe
Messan
Moppet
Pariah
Piedog
Police
Poodle
Pye-dog
Saluki
Setter
Shaggy
Shough
Sirius
Sothic
Talbot
Teckel
Touser
Towser
Vizsla
Westie
Yapper
Yorkie

***7 letters:***
Andiron
Basenji
Bobbery
Boerbul
Bouvier
Brachet
Bulldog
Coondog
Courser
Griffon
Harrier
Iceland
Kuvaszi
Lowchen
Lurcher
Maltese
Maremma
Mastiff
Mongrel
Orthrus
Pointer
Prairie
Raccoon
Reynard
Samoyed
Sapling
Sausage
Shar-Pei
Sheltie
Shih tzu
Showghe
Sloughi
Spaniel
Starter
→ **TERRIER**
Volpino
Whiffet
Whippet
Yapster

***8 letters:***
Aardwolf
Aberdeen
Airedale
Alsatian
Blenheim
Bouvrier
Bratchet
Brittany
Carriage
Cerberus
Chow-chow
Doberman
Elkhound
Hovawart
Kangaroo
Keeshond
Komondor
Labrador
Landseer
Malamute
Malemute
Papillon
Pekinese
Pembroke
Pinscher
Samoyede
Sealyham
Sheepdog
Springer
Turnspit
Warragal
Warrigal

***9 letters:***
Blue merle
Boarhound
Buckhound
Chihuahua
Coonhound
Dachshund
Dalmatian
Deerhound
Dobermann
Draghound
Gazehound
Great Dane
Greyhound
Harlequin
Kerry blue
Lhasa apso
Molossian
Pekingese
Red setter
Retriever
Ridgeback
Rin-tin-tin
Schnauzer
Staghound
Wolfhound

***10 letters:***
Bedlington
Bloodhound
Blueheeler
Fox terrier
Otterhound
Pomeranian
Rottweiler
Schipperke
Shin-barker
Tripehound
Weimaraner

***11 letters:***
Bichon frise
Bull mastiff
Irish setter
Jack Russell
Labradoodle
Montmorency
Rough collie
Skye terrier
Tibetan apso
Trendle-tail
Trindle-tail
Trundle-tail
Wishtonwish

***12 letters:***
Border collie
Gazelle hound
Japanese chin
Newfoundland
Saint Bernard
Water spaniel
Welsh terrier
West Highland

***13 letters:***
Affenpinscher
Bearded collie
Boston Terrier
Cocker spaniel
Dandie Dinmont
English setter
Scotch terrier
Sussex spaniel

*14 letters:*
Clumber spaniel
German shepherd
Italian spinone
Norwich terrier
Pit bull terrier
Tibetan mastiff
Tibetan spaniel
Tibetan terrier

*15 letters:*
Alaskan malamute
Bernese mountain
Brussels griffon
Estreia mountain
Golden retriever
Hamilton stovare
Mexican hairless
Norwegian buhund
Portuguese water
Springer spaniel
Swedish vallhund

*16 letters:*
Australian cattle
Doberman-pinscher
Lancashire heeler
Pyrenean mountain
Russian wolfhound
Shetland sheepdog
Yorkshire terrier

*17 letters:*
Anatolian Shepherd
Dobermann-pinscher
Labrador retriever

*18 letters:*
Large Munsterlander
Old English sheepdog
Rhodesian ridgeback

*20 letters:*
Landseer Newfoundland

*21 letters:*
Polish Lowland sheepdog

---

**Dog-bane** Apocynum
**Doge** Dandolo
**Dog-end** Stub, Tail
**Dogfish** Huss, Nurse (hound), Rigg, Rock salmon
**Dogged** Determined, Die-hard, Dour, Indefatigable, Persistent, Pertinacious, Relentless, Stubborn, Sullen, Tenacious
**Doggerel** Cramboclink, Crambo-jingle, Laisse, Rat-rhyme
**Doghouse** Disgrace, Kennel
**Dog letter** R
**Dogma(tic), Dogmatist** Assertive, Belief, Bigot, Bigotry, Central, Conviction, Creed, Doctrinal, En tête, Ewe, Fundamental, Ideology, Ipse dixit, Literal, Opinionative, Pedagogic, Peremptory, Pontifical, Positive, → **TENET**
**Do-gooder** Dorcas, Lady Bountiful, Piarist, Reformer, Salvationist, Samaritan, Scout
**Dogsbody** Bottle-washer, Drudge, Gofer, Menial, Skivvy
**Dogshow** Cruft's
**Dog star** Canicula, Lassie, Sirius, Sothic
**Do it** Dich
**Dolce** Stop, Sweet
**Dole** Alms, Batta, B(u)roo, Give, Grief, Maundy, Mete, Payment, Pittance, Pog(e)y, Ration, → **SHARE**, Tichborne, UB, Vail, Vales
**Doleful** Sombre
**Doll(y)** Baby, Barbie®, Bimbo, Bobblehead, Common, Corn, Creeper, Crumpet, Dress, Dutch, Ewe, Girly, Kachina, Kewpie®, Living, Maiden, Marionette, Matryoshka, Maumet, Mommet, Moppet, Mummet, Ookpik®, Ornament, Paris, Parton, Pean, Peen, Peggy, Pein, Pene, Poppet, Puppet, Ragdoll, Russian, Sindy®, Sis(ter), Sitter, Tearsheet, Toy, Trolley, Varden, Voodoo, Washboard, Washtub, Wax
**Dollar(s)** Balboa, Boliviano, Buck, Cob, Cob money, Euro, Fin, Greenback, Iron man, Peso, Petrol, Piastre, Pink, S, Sand, Sawbuck, Sawhorse, Scrip, Smacker, Spin, Sword, Top, Wheel
**Dollop** Glob, Helping, Share
▷**Dolly** *may indicate* an anagram
**Dolly-bird** Dish
**Dolly Varden** Hat
**Dolour, Dolorous** Anguished, Grief, Pain, Sorrow
**Dolphin** Amazon, Arion, Beluga, Bottlenose, Cetacean, Coryphene, Delphinus, Grampus, Lampuka, Lampuki, Mahi-mahi, Meer-swine, Porpess(e), Porpoise, Risso's, River, Sea-pig
**Dolt** Ass, Blockhead, Clodhopper, Mooncalf, Noodle, Oaf, Ouph(e), Owl, Simpleton, → **STUPID**
**DOM** Lewdsby
**Domain** Archaea, Archduchy, Area, Bacteria, Bourn(e), Demain, Demesne, Duchy, Eminent, Emirate, Empire, Estate, Eukarya, Kingdom, Manor, Net, Predicant, Public, Rain, Realm, Region, Reign, Starosty
**Dome(-shaped)** Al-Aqsa, Bubble, Cap, Cupola, Cupula, Dagoba, Geodesic, Head, Imperial,

Louvre, Millennium, Onion, Periclinal, Pleasure, Rotunda, Salt, Stupa, Tee, Tholobate, Tholos, Tholus, Tope, Vault, Xanadu

**Domestic(ate), Domesticated** Char, Cinderella, Cleaner, Dom, Esne, Familiar, Fireside, Homebody, Home help, Home-keeping, Homely, House, House-broken, Housekeeper, Housetrain, Housewife, Humanise, In-service, Interior, Internal, Intestine, Maid, Menial, Pet, →**SERVANT**, Swadeshi, Tame, Woman

**Domicile** Abode, Dwelling, Hearth, Home, Ménage

**Dominate, Dominance, Dominant, Domination** Alpha, Ascendancy, Assertive, Baasskap, Ballbreaker, Bestride, Bethrall, Boss, Clou, Coerce, Control, Enslave, Hegemony, Henpeck, Maisterdome, Master, Mesmerise, Momism, Monopolise, O(v)ergang, Overarch, Overmaster, Override, Overshadow, Power, Preponderant, Preside, Rule, Soh, →**SUBDUE**, Subjugate, Terrorise, Top dog, Tower

**Domineer(ing)** Authoritarian, Autocratic, Battleaxe, Boss, Henpeck, Imperious, Lord, Officious, Overbear, Possessive, Pushy, Ride, Swagger, Tyrannize, Virago

**Dominica(n)** Blackfriar, Jacobite, Monk, OP, Preaching friar, Predicant, Savonarola, WD

**Dominie** Maister, Master, Pastor, Sampson, Schoolmaster

**Dominion** Canada, Dom, Empire, Khanate, NZ, Realm, Reame, Reign, →**RULE**, Supremacy, Sway, Territory

**Domino(es)** Card, Fats, Mask, Matador

**Don(s)** Academic, Address, Assume, Caballero, Camorrist, Capo, Endue, Faculty, Fellow, Garb, Giovanni, Grandee, Indew, Juan, Lecturer, Mafia, Prof, Quixote, Reader, Señor, Spaniard, Tutor, Wear

**Dona(h)** Duckie, Love

**Donate, Donation** Aid, Alms, Bestow, Contribution, Dole, Gift, Give, Offertory, Peter's pence, Present, Tribute, Wakf, Waqf

**Done** Achieved, Complete, Crisp, Ended, Executed, Had, Over, Spitcher, Through, Tired, Weary

**Donjon** Dungeon, Keep

**Donkey** Ass, Burro, Cardophagus, Cuddie, Cuddy, Dapple, Democrat, Dick(e)y, Dunce, Eeyore, Engine, Funnel, Fussock, Genet(te), Hinny, Ignoramus, Jackass, Jacket, Jennet, Jenny, Jerusalem pony, Kulan, Modestine, Moke, Mule, Neddy, Nodding, Onager, Stupid, Years

**Donor** Benefactor, Bestower, Blood, Organ, Settlor, Universal

**Doo** Dove

**Doodle(r)** Scribble, Yankee

**Doodlebug** Antlion, Larva, V1

**Doofer** Thingumabob

**Doom(ed)** Condemned, Damnation, Date, Destine, Destiny, →**FATE**, Fay, Fey, Fie, Goner, Ill-fated, Ill-omened, Ill-starred, Lot, Predestine, Preordain, Ragnarok, Ruined, Sentence, Spitcher, Star-crossed, Weird

**Doone** Carver, Lorna

**Door(s), Doorstep, Doorway** Aperture, Barn, Cat-flap, Communicating, Damnation, Drecksill, Dutch, Early, Elephant, Entry, Exit, Fire, Folding, French, Front, Gull-wing, Haik, Hake, Hatch, Heck, Ingress, Jib, Lintel, Louver, Louvre, Muntin, Oak, Open, Overhead, Patio, Portal, Postern, Prison, Revolving, Rory, Screen, Side, Sliding, Stable, Stage, Storm, Street, Swing, Tailgate, Tome, Trap, Up and over, Vomitory, Wedge, Wicket, Yett

**Doorkeeper, Doorman** Bouncer, Commissionaire, Concierge, Dvornik, Guardian, Janitor, Nab, Ostiary, Porter, Tiler, Tyler, Usher

**Doormat** Subservient, Weakling, Wuss

**Doorpost** Architrave, Dern, Durn, Jamb, Yate, Yett

**Dope** Acid, Amulet, Bang, Coke, Crack, Datum, →**DRUG**, Dunderhead, Facts, Fuss, Gen, Goose, Info, Joe Soap, Latest, Lowdown, Narcotic, Nitwit, Nobble, Rutin, Sedate, Soup, →**STUPID PERSON**, Tea

**Doppelganger** Double, Look-alike, Ringer

**Dorcas** Gazelle, Needle, Shepherdess

**Dorian, Doric** Metope, Mutule

**Doris** Day, Lessing, Mollusc

**Dormant** Abed, Aestivate, Comatose, Hibernating, Idle, Inactive, Inert, Joist, Latent, Latitant, Quiescent, Resting, → SLEEPING, Torpescent
**Dormer** Luthern
**Dormitory** Barrack, Bunkhouse, Dorter, Dortour, Hall, Hostel, Quarters
**Dormouse** Loir
**Dorothy** Bag, Dot, Sayers
**Dorsal** Back, Neural, Notal
**Dory** Fish, John
**Dosage, Dose** Absorbed, Acute, Administer, Aperient, Booster, Cascara, Cumulative, Drachm, Draught, Drench, Drug, Fix, Hit, Kilogray, Lethal, Mean lethal, → MEASURE, Permissible, Physic, Posology, Potion, Powder, Rem, Standing off, Threshold, Tolerance
**Doss (house), Dosser** Derelict, Dharmsala, Dharmshala, Kip, Layabout, Padding-ken, Spike
**Dossier** File, Record
**Dot(s), Dotted, Dotty** Absurd, Bind(h)i, Blip, Bullet (point), Centred, Criblé, Dieresis, Dit, Dower, Dowry, Drop, Ellipsis, Engrailed, Intersperse, Leader, Lentiginous, Limp, Micro, Morse, Occult, Or, Particle, Pinpoint, Pixel, → POINT, Pointillé, Polka, Precise, Punctuate, Punctulate, Punctum, Schwa, Semé(e), Set, Speck, Spot, Sprinkle, Stigme, Stipple, Stud, Tap, Tittle, Tocher, Trema, Umlaut
**Dote, Dotage, Doting, Dotard** Adore, Anile, Anility, Cocker, Decrepitude, Dobbie, Idolise, Imbecile, Pet, Prize, Senile, Spoon(e)y, Tendre, Twichild
**Double(s)** Alter-ego, Amphibious, Ancipital, Bi-, Bifold, Binate, Body, Clone, Counterpart, Crease, Dimeric, Doppel-ganger, Doppio, Dual, Duo, Duple(x), Duplicate, Equivocal, Fetch, Fold, Foursome, Geminate, Gimp, Image, Ingeminate, Ka, Look-alike, Loop, Martingale, Mixed, Pair, Parlay, Polyseme, Reflex, Replica, Ringer, Run, Similitude, Spit, Stuntman, Trot, Turnback, Twae, Twice, → TWIN, Two(fold), Two-ply
**Double-barrelled** Hyphenated, Tautonym
**Double-cross, Double dealer, Double dealing** Ambidext(e)rous, Knavish, Traitor, Two-time
**Double Dutch** Gibberish
**Double-entendre** Polyseme, Polysemy
**Doublet** Peascod, Pourpoint, TT
**Doubt(s), Doubter, Doubtful** Agnostic, Ambiguous, Aporia, Askance, But, Cynic, Cynical, Debatable, Discredit, Distrust, Dubiety, Dubitate, Erm, Hesitate, Hum, Iffy, Incertitude, Insecure, Misgiving, Mistrust, → NO DOUBT, Or, Precarious, Qualm, Query, → QUESTION, Rack, Reservation, Scepsis, Sceptic, Scruple, Second thoughts, Shady, Shy, Sic, Skepsis, Sus, Suspect, Suspicious, Suss, Thomas, Thos, Umph, Uncertain, Unclear, Unsure, Waver
**Doubtless** Certain, Iwis, Probably, Sure, Truly, Undisputed, Ywis
**Douceur** Bonus, Sop, Sweetener
**Douche** Bath, Ecossaise, Gush, Rinse, Shower, Wash
**Dough(y)** Akkas, Boodle, Cake, Calzone, Cash, Duff, Dumpling, Gnocchi, Hush-puppy, Kachori, Knish, Loot, Magma, Masa, Money, Pasta, Paste, Polenta, Pop(p)adum, Ready, Sad, Sour, Spondulicks, Strudel
**Doughboy** Dumpling, Soldier
**Doughnut** Bagel, Beavertail®, Cruller, Fried cake, Knish, Koeksister, Olycook, Olykoek, Sinker, Torus
**Doughty** Brave, Intrepid, Resolute, Stalwart, Valiant
**Dour** Glum, Hard, Mirthless, Morose, Reest, Reist, Sinister, Sullen, Taciturn
**Douse** Dip, Drench, Extinguish, Snuff, Splash
**Dove** Collared, Columbine, Culver, Cushat, Diamond, Doo, Ground, Ice-bird, Mourning, Pacifist, → PIGEON, Piteousness, Queest, Quoist, Ring, Rock, Stock, Turtle
**Dove-cot(e)** Columbarium, Columbary, Louver, Louvre, Lover
**Dovetail** Fit, Interosculate, Join, Lewis(son), Mortise, Tally, Tenon
**Dowager** Elder, Matron, Widow
**Dowdy** Frumpish, Mopsy, Mums(e)y, Plain Jane, Shabby, Sloppy, Slovenly

**Dowel** Peg, Pin
**Down(s), Downbeat, Downer, Downsize, Downward(s), Downy** A bas, Abase, Abattu, Alow, Amort, Bank, Below, Berkshire, Blue, Cast, Catabasis, Chapfallen, Comous, Cottony, Crouch, Darling, Dejected, Demoralised, Depth, Descent, Disconsolate, Dowl(e), Drink, Duck, Epsom, Feather, Fledge, Floccus, Flue, Fluff, Fly, Fuzz, Glum, Goonhilly, Ground, Hair, Hangdog, Hill, Humble, Humiliate, Jeff, Kennet, Lanate, Lanugo, Latitant, Losing, Low, Lower, Miserable, Mopy, Morose, Moxa, Nap, Neck, North Wessex, Oose, Ooze, Owing, Pappus, Pennae, Pile, Plumage, Powder, Quark, Quash, Repress, Scuttle, Sebum, Sedative, Slim, Sussex, Swallow, Thesis, Thistle, Tomentum, Under, Unserviceable, Urinant, Vail, Watership, Wold, Wretched
**Down and out** Skid row
**Downcast** Abject, Chapfallen, Dejected, Despondent, Disconsolate, Dumpish, Glum, Hangdog, Hopeless, Melancholy, Woebegone
**Downfall, Downpour** Banana skin, Brash, Cataract, Collapse, Deluge, Doom, Fate, Flood, Hail, Onding, Overthrow, Plash, Rain, Rainstorm, Ruin, Shower, Soak, Squall, Thunder-plump, Torrent, Undoing, Waterspout
**Downgrade(d)** Déclassé, Delegate, Deskill, Disrate, Relegate
**Downhearted** Sad
**Download** App
**Downmarket** Naff
**Downright** Absolute, Arrant, Bluff, Candid, Clear, Complete, Flat, Plumb, Plump, Pure, Rank, Sheer, Stark, Utter
**Downstairs** Below
**Downstream** Tail
**Down-trodden** Oppressed, Underfoot
**Downturn** Decrease, Recession, Slump
**Downwind** Leeward
**Dowry** Dot, Dower, Lobola, Lobolo, Merchet, Portion, Settlement, Tocher
**Dowse(r), Dowsing** Divine, Enew, Fireman, Radionics, Rhabdomancy, Water-witch
**Doxology** Gloria, Glory
**Doxy** Harlot, Loose woman, Opinion, Wench
**Doyen** Dean, Elder statesman, Senior
**Doze, Dozy** Ca(u)lk, Catnap, Dove(r), Nap, Nod, Semi-coma, Sleep, Sleepyhead, Slip, Slumber
**Dozen(s)** Baker's, Daily, Devil's, Dz, Long, Round, Thr(e)ave, Twal, Twelve
**Dr** Debtor, Doctor, Dram
**Drab** Ash-grey, Cloth, Dell, Dingy, Dowdy, Dreary, Dull, Dun, Ecru, Hussy, Isabel(line), Lifeless, Livor, Mumsy, Olive, Prosaic, Pussel, Quaker-colour, Rig, Road, Scarlet woman, Slattern, Sloven, Strumpet, Subfusc, Tart, Taupe, Trull, Wanton, Whore
**Drabble** Bemoil, Draggle
**Draconian** Harsh
**Dracula** Bat, Count, Undead, Vampire
**Draft** Bank, Bill, Cheque, Conscript, Draw, Ebauche, Essay, Landsturm, Manuscript, Minute, MS, Outline, Paste up, Plan, Press, Project, Protocol, Recruit, Rough, Scheme, Scroll, Scrowle, → SKETCH
**Drag** Car, Cigarette, Clothing, Drail, Dredge, Drogue, Elicit, Eonism, Epicene, Extort, Fiscal, Form, Gender-bender, Hale, Hang, Harl, → HAUL, Impediment, Induced, Keelhaul, La Rue, Liability, Lug, Nuisance, Parasite, Pressure, Profile, Puff, Pull, Rash, Sag, Schlep, Shockstall, Shoe, Skidpan, Sled, Snake, Snig, Sweep, Toke, Tote, Tow, Trail, Trailing vortex, Train, Travail, Travois, Trawl, Treck, Trek, Tug, Tump, Vortex
**Draggle** Drail, Lag, Straggle
**Dragon** Aroid, Basilisk, Bearded, Bel, Bellemère, Chaperon(e), Chindit, Draco, Drake, Fafnir, Fire-drake, Gargouille, Komodo, Kung-kung, Ladon, Lindworm, Opinicus, Peist, Puk, Python, Rouge, Safat, Serpent, Shrew, Typhoeus, Wantley, Wivern, Worm, Wyvern, Yacht
**Dragonfly** Aeschna, Darter, Demoiselle, Devil's darning needle, Nymph, Odonata
**Dragon's teeth** Cadmus, Spartae, Sparti

**Dragoon** Coerce, Force, Press, Rope-in, Trooper

**Drain(ed), Drainage, Drainer, Draining, Drainpipe** Bleed, Brain, Buzz, Can(n)ula, Catchment, Catchwater, Channel, Cloaca, Colander, Condie, Culvert, Cundy, Cunette, Delf, Delph, Dewater, Ditch, Dry, Ea(u), →EMPTY, Emulge(nt), Enervate, Exhaust, Field, Fleet, Gargoyle, Grating, Grip, Gully, Gutter, Ketavothron, Kotabothron, Lade, Leach, Leech, Lickpenny, Limber, Lose, Lymphatic, Milk, Mole, Nala, Nalla(h), Nip, Nulla(h), Outfall, Outflow, Penrose, Platerack, Pump, Rack, Rone, Sanitation, Sap, Scalpins, Scupper, Seton, Sew(er), Sheuch, Sheugh, Shore, Silver, Sink, Siver, Sluice, Sluse, Small-trap, Soakaway, Soilpipe, Sough, Spend, Spunge, Stank, Storm, Suck, Sump, Sure, Syver, Tile, Trench, Trocar, Unwater, Ureter, U-trap, Weary, Well

**Drainpipe(s)** Downspout, →TROUSERS

**Dram** Drink, Drop, Nipperkin, Nobbler, Portion, Snifter, Tickler, Tiff, Tot, Wet

**Drama(tic), Drama school** Auto, Azione, Catastasis, Charade, Cliffhanger, Closet, Comedy, Costume, Curtain-raiser, Drastic, Epic, ER, Eumenides, Farce, Heroic, Histrionic, Kabuki, Kathakali, Kitchen sink, Legit, Legitimate, Mask, Masque, Mime, Moralities, Music, No, Nogaku, Noh, Oresteia, Piece, Play, RADA, Sangeet, Scenic, Screenplay, Sensational, Serial, Serio-comic, Singspiel, Soap, Spinto, Stagy, Striking, Sudser, Tetralogy, Theatric, The Birds, Thespian, Tragedy, Unities, Wagnerian, Wild

**Dramatist** Adamov, Aeschylus, Albee, Anouilh, Aristophanes, Arrabal, Barrie, Beaumarchais, Beaumont, Beckett, Beddoes, Bleasdale, Brecht, Bridie, Calderon, Centlivre, Chapman, Congreve, Corneille, Coward, Dekker, Drinkwater, Ennius, Euripides, Farquhar, Feydeau, Fletcher, Frisch, Fry, Gay, Genet, Gogol, Goldoni, Havel, Heywood, Ibsen, Ionesco, Jarry, Kaiser, Kyd, Lorca, Lyly, Mamet, Marlowe, Massinger, Menander, Middleton, Molière, Odets, O'Neill, Orton, Osborne, Otway, Pinero, Pinter, Pirandello, Plautus, →PLAYWRIGHT, Racine, Rostand, Rowe, Rowley, Royle, Russell, Schiller, Seneca, Shadwell, Shaffer, Sherriff, Sophocles, Stoppard, Strindberg, Synge, Terence, Thespis, Udall, Vanbrugh, Voltaire, Von Klinger, Webster, Wedekind, Wesker, Wilde, Wilder, Will, →WRITER, Yeats

**Dram-shop** Bar, Boozingken, Bousingken

**Drape(ry)** Adorn, Coverlet, Coverlid, Curtain, Festoon, Fold, Hang, Lambrequin, Mantling, Suspend, Swag, Swathe, Valance, Veil, Vest

**Draper** Clothier, Gilpin, Haberdasher, Hosier, Mercer, Outfitter, Ruth, Scotch cuddy, Tailor

**Drastic** Dire, Dramatic, Extreme, Harsh, Purge, Radical, Senna, →SEVERE, Swingeing, Violent

**Drat** Bother, Dang, Darn

**Draught(s), Draughtsman(ship)** Aloetic, Apozem, Aver, Breeze, Checkers, Chequer, Dam, Dams, Design, Dose, Drench, Drink, Fish, Gulp, Gust, Haal, Hippocrene, King, Line, Men, Nightcap, Outline, Plan, Potation, Potion, Puff, Pull, Quaff, Sketch, Sleeping, Slug, Swig, Tracer, Up-current, Veronal, Waft, Waucht, Waught, Williewaught, Wind

▷**Draught** *may refer to* fishing

**Draught-board** Dam-board, Dambrod

**Dravidian** Tamil

**Draw (off), Drawer(s), Drawing, Drawn** Adduct, Allure, Appeal, Attract, Attrahent, Bleed, Blueprint, Bottom, Cartoon, Charcoal, Cityscape, Cock, Compass, Crayon, Dead-heat, Delineate, Dentistry, Derivation, Describe, Detail, Diagram, Dis(em)bowel, Doodle, Dr, Draft, Drag, Dress, Educe, Elevation, Elicit, Elongate, Entice, Equalise, Escribe, Evaginate, Even-steven, Eviscerate, Extract, Fet(ch), Freehand, Fusain, Gather, Gaunt, Glorybox, Goalless, Graffiti, Graphics, Gravitate, Gunfighter, Gut, Haggard, Hale, Halve, Haul, Heald, Identikit, Indraft, Induce, Indue, Inhale, Isometric, Lead, Lengthen, Limn, Line, Longbow, Lots, Lottery, Lure, Magnet, Mechanical, Monotint, No-score, Orthograph, Pantalet(te)s, Panty, Pastel(list), Pen and ink, Perpetual check, Petroglyph, Profile, Protract, Pull, RA, Rack, Raffle, Realize, Reel, Remark, Scenography, Scent, Score, Seductive, Sepia, Sesquipedalian, Shottle, Shuttle, Silverpoint, Siphon, Sketch, Slub, Snig, Spin, Stalemate, Straws, Stretch, Study, Stumps, Sweepstake, Syphon, Tap, Taut, Technical, Tempera, Tempt, Tenniel, Tie, Till, Toke, Tole, Tombola, Top, Tose, Tow(age), Toze, Trace, Traction, Trice, Troll, Tug, Unsheathe, Uplift, Visual, Wash, Working

▷**Draw** *may indicate* something to smoke

**Drawback** Catch, Downside, Ebb, Handicap, Impediment, → OBSTACLE, Rebate, Retraction, Shortcoming, Shrink, Snag

**Drawbridge** Bascule, Pontlevis

**Drawl** Dra(u)nt, Haw, Slur, Twang

▷**Drawn** *may indicate* an anagram

**Drawn up** Atrip, Drafted

**Dray** Cart, Lorry, Wagon

**Dread(ed), Dreadful** Angst, Anxiety, Atrocious, Awe, Awful, Chronic, Dearn, Dern, Dire, Fear, Formidable, Funk, Gastnesse, Ghastly, Horrendous, Horrific, → HORROR, Nightmare, Nosophobia, Penny, Rasta, Redoubt, Shocking, Sorry, Terrible, Thing, Tragic, Unholy, Willies

**Dreadnought** Battleship

**Dream(er), Dream home, Dreamland, Dreamlike, Dream state, Dreamy** Absent, Aisling, Alchera, Alcheringa, Ambitious, American, Aspire, Castle, Desire, Drowsy, Dwalm, Dwa(u)m, Escapist, Fancy, Fantasist, Fantast, Fantasy, Faraway, Fugue, Gerontius, Idealise, Illusion, Imagine, Joseph, Languor, Long, Mare, Mirth, Moon, Morpheus, Muse, Nightmare, On(e)iric, Pensive, Phantasmagoria, Phantom, Pipe, → REVERIE, Rêveur, Romantic, Somniate, Spac(e)y, Stargazer, Surreal, Sweven, Trance, Trauma, Utopia, Vague, Vision, Walter Mitty, Wannabe, Wet, Wish, Wool-gathering

**Dreamboat** Heart-throb

**Dreary** Arid, Bleak, Desolate, Dismal, Doleful, Drab, Dreich, Dull, Gloom, Gousty, Gray, Grey, Oorie, Ourie, Owrie, Sad

**Dredge(r)** Aspersoir, Caster, Deepen, Scoop, Unearth

**Dreg(s)** Bottom, Draff, Dross, Dunder, F(a)eces, Fecula, Gr(e)aves, Grounds, Lag(s), Lees, Legge, Mother, Mud, Residue, Riffraff, Scaff, Sediment, Settlings, Silt, Snuff, Ullage

**Dreikanter** Ventifact

**Drench(ed)** Dowse, Drown, Saturate, Sluice, Sluse, Soak, Soggy, Souse, Spray, Steep, Submerge, Swamp

**Dress(ing), Dressed, Dressy** Accoutre, Adjust, Adorn, Aguise, Align, Apparel, Array, Attire, Attrap, Bandage, Bandoline, Bedizen, Boast, Boun, Bowne, Brilliantine, Busk, Cataplasm, Charpie, Clad, → CLOTHING, Comb, Compost, Compress, Curry, Dandify, Decent, Deck, Deshabille, Dight, Dink, Dizen, Doll, Don, Dub, Dubbin, Elastoplast®, Endue, Enrobe, Fertiliser, French, Frou-frou, Full, Gamgee tissue, Garnish, Gauze, Get-up, Girt, Graith, Guise, Gussy up, → HABIT, Immantle, Italian, Jaconet, Ketchup, Line, Lint, Livery, Marie Rose, Mayonnaise, Mineral, Mulch, Oil, Ore, Pad, Party, Patch, Plaster, Pledget, Pomade, Potash, Poultice, Prank, Preen, Prepare, Ranch, Rational, Ray, Rehearsal, Rémoulade, Rig, Russian, Rybat, Salad, Salad cream, Sartorial, Sauce, Scutch, Seloso, Smart, Sterile, Stupe, Tap, Tartare, Taw, Tenue, Tew, Thousand Island, Tiff, Tire, Toilet, Tonic, Treat, Trick, Trim, Vinaigrette, Wear, Well, Wig, Window, Yclad, Ycled

---

## DRESSES

*3 letters:*
Fig
Mob
Rag
Tog
Top

*4 letters:*
Coat
Drag
Garb
Gown
Kilt
Maxi
Midi
Robe
Sack
Sari
Suit
Tent
Toga
Tuck
Vest

*5 letters:*
Ao dai
Brale
Cimar
Court
Cymar
Fancy
Frock
Ihram
Kanga
Lungi
Mufti
Power
Samfu
Shift
Shirt
Simar
Smock
Stole
Symar
Talar
Tasar
Tunic

*6 letters:*
Bodice
Caftan
Chimer
Corset
Dirndl
Dolman
Empire
Finery
Kaftan
Khanga
Kimono

Kirtle
Muu-muu
Peplos
Russet
Sacque
Samfoo
Sarong
Sheath
Tartan
Tussah
Tusser
Tuxedo

*7 letters:*
Bloomer
Blouson
Corsage
Costume
Dashiki
Evening
Gymslip
Kitenge
Lounger
Morning
Plumage
Raiment
Simarre
Subfusc
Subfusk
Tea-gown
Tussore
Uniform
Wedding

*8 letters:*
Academic
Black-tie
Cocktail
Djellaba
Fatigues
Flamenco
Highland
National
Pantsuit
Pinafore
Princess
Sundress
White-tie

*9 letters:*
Cheongsam
Clericals
Farandine
Polonaise
Separates
Trollopee

*10 letters:*
Farrandine
Ferrandine
Shirtwaist

*11 letters:*
Dolly Varden
Farthingale

*12 letters:*
Merveilleuse
Princess line
Shirtwaister

*13 letters:*
Mother Hubbard

---

**Dressage** Caracol(e), Demivolt(e), Manège, Passade, Passage, Pesade, Piaffe

▷**Dressed up, Dressing** *may indicate* an anagram

**Dresser** Adze, Almery, Bureau, Chest, Costumier, Couturier, Deuddarn, Dior, Lady's maid, Lair, Lowboy, Sideboard, Transvestite, Tridarn, Welsh

**Dressing-down** Reproof

**Dressing-gown** Bathrobe, Negligée, Peignoir

**Dressing-room** Apodyterium, Tiring-room, Vestiary, Vestry

**Dressing-table** Lowboy

**Dressmaker** Costumier, Dorcas, Midinette, Modiste, Seamstress, Tailor

**Drew** Steeld, Stelled

**Dribble** Drip, Drivel, Drop, Seep, Slaver, Slobber, Slop, Trickle

**Dried fish** Bum(m)alo, Bummaloti, Haberdine, Speld(r)in(g), Stockfish

▶**Dried fruit** *see* DRY FRUIT

**Drift(ing), Drifter** Aimless, Becalmed, Continental, Crab, Cruise, Current, Digress, Diluvium, Drumlin, Float, Floe, Flow, Genetic, Heap, Impulse, Longshore, Maunder, Natant, Nomad, North Atlantic, Plankton, Purport, Rorke, Sail, Sense, Slide, Swan, Tendence, Tendency, → TENOR, Tramp, Trend, Vagrant, Waft, Wander, Zooplankton

**Drill(ing)** Appraisal, Archimedean, Auger, Bore, Brace, Burr, Churn, Close order, Directional, Drop, Educate, Electric, Exercise, Fire, Form, Hammer, Inculcate, Jackhammer, Jerks, Kelly, Kerb, Monkey, Pack, PE, Pierce, Pneumatic, Power, PT, Radial, Reamer, Ridge, Rig, Rimer, Rock, Rope, Seeder, Sow, Square-bashing, Teach, Train, Twill, Twist, Usage, Wildcat

**Drink(er), Drinking, Drunk(enness)** AA, Absorb, Adrian Quist, Alkie, Alky, A pip out, Babalas, Bacchian, Barfly, Bat, Beer up, Bender, Beverage, Bev(v)y, Bezzle, Bib(ite), Bibber, Binge, Birl(e), Bladdered, Bland, Blatted, Blind, Blitzed, Bloat, Blootered, Blotto, Bombed, Boose, Booze, Borachio, Bosky, Bottled, Bouse, Bowl, Bowsey, Bowsie, Bracer, Brahms and Liszt, Brandy, Brew, Bucket, Bumper, Burst, CAMRA, Capernoitie, Cap(p)ernoity, Carafe, Carousal, Cat-lap, Chaser, Chota peg, Compotation, → CORDIAL, Corked, Cot case, Crapulent, Crapulous, Cratur, Crocked, Cuppa, Cut, Demitasse, Diet, Digestif, Dionysian, Dipsomaniac, Discombobulated, Double, Down, Drain, Draught, Drop, Ebriate, Ebriose, Elixir, Energy, Entire, Eye-opener, Feni, Feny, Finger, Fleein', Flush, Flying, Fou, Fuddle-cap, Fuddled, Full, Glass, Glug, Gnat's piss, Grog, Gulp, Half-cut, Half-seas-over, Happy, Heart-starter, Heavy wet, High, Hobnob, Hogshead, Honkers, Hooker, Hophead, Imbibe, In-cups, Indulge, Inebriated, Infusion, Inhaust, Inked, In liquor, Insulse, Intemperate, Irrigate, Ivresse, Jag, Jakey, Jar, Juice, Juicehead, Kaylied, Knock back, Lager lout, Langered, Lap, Legless, Lethean, Libation, → LIQUOR, Lit, Loaded, Lord, Lower, Lush(y), Maggoty,

Mallemaroking, Maltworm, Maudlin, Mellow, Merry, Methomania, Methysis, Mixer, Moon-eyed, Moony, Mops and brooms, Mortal, Mug, Mullered, Neck, Nog(gin), Obfuscated, Ocean, Oenomania, Oiled, On, One, Oppignorate, Overshot, Paid, Paint, Paralytic, Partake, Particular, Peg, Pickled, Pick-me-up, Pie-eyed, Pint(a), Piss-artist, Pissed, Pisshead, Pisspot, Piss-up, Pixil(l)ated, Pledge, Plonk(o), Potation, Poteen, Potion, Primed, Quaff, Quencher, Quickie, Rat-arsed, Ratted, Refreshment, Roaring, Rolling, Rotten, Round, Rouse, Rumfustian, Rummer, St Martin's evil, Screamer, Screwed, Sea, Shebeen, Shicker, Shotover, Silenus, Sink, Sip(ple), Skinned, Slake, Slewed, Sloshed, Slued, Slug, Slurp, Smashed, Smoothie, Snort, Soak, Soused, Sozzled, Sponge, Spongy, Spunge, Squiffy, Steaming, Stewed, Stimulant, Stinko, Stocious, Stoned, Stonkered, Stotious, Stukkend, Stuporous, Sucker, Suckle, Suiplap, Sup, Swacked, Swallow, Swig, Swill, Tank, Tanked up, Tape, Temulence, Tiddl(e)y, Tiff, Tift, Tight, Tincture, Tipper, Tipple, Tipsy, Tope, Toss, Tossicated, Tost, Tot, Two-pot, Two-pot screamer, Under the weather, Upsey Dutch, Upsy, Up the pole, Usual, Wash, Wat, Wauch, Waught, Well away, Well-oiled, Wet, Whiffled, Williewaught, Winebag, Wine bibber, Wino, Wish-wash, Woozy, Wrecked, Zonked

---

## DRINKS

***2 letters:***
It

***3 letters:***
Ale
Ava
Bub
Cha
Cup
Dop
Fap
Gin
G&T
Hom
Kir
L&P
Mum
Pop
Red
Rum
Rye
Sec
Tea
Vin

***4 letters:***
Arak
Asti
Beer
Bock
Bull
Cava
Chai
Chug
Coke®
Flip
Half
Hock
Homa
Kava
Kola
Lilt®
Malt
Marc
Mate
Mead
Mild
Nipa
Ouzo
Port
Purl
Rack
Raki
Rosé
Sack
Sake
Saki
Soda
Soft
Soma
Sour
Sura
Tass
Tent
Wine
Yill

***5 letters:***
Assai
Bingo
Bombo
Bumbo
Cider
Cocoa
Copus
Crush
Doris
Float
Glogg
Haoma
Hogan
Hooch
Joram
Jorum
Julep
Kefir
Kelty
Kvass
Lager
Lassi
Latte
Mâcon
Malwa
Mauby
Meath
Medoc
Meths
Mobby
Mocha
Moppy
Morat
Mosel
Mulse
Nappy
Negus
Pekoe
Pepsi®
Perry
Pimms
Polly
Pombe
Punch
Rakee
Rakia
Rumbo
Rummy
Sarsa
Sarza
Shake
Short
Shrub
Skink
Sling
Smile
Stout
Toddy
Tonic
Totty
Turps
Twist
Vimto®
Vodka
White
Xeres

***6 letters:***
Amrita
Apozem
Arrack
Bishop
Bitter
Bovril®
Bubbly
Burton
Busera
Cassis
Caudle
Cauker
Chasse
Claret
Coffee
Cognac
Cooler
Cooper
Doctor
Eggnog
Enzian
Frappe
Geneva
Gimlet
Grappa
Graves
Gutrot
Hootch
Kalied
Keltie
Kephir
Kirsch
Kumiss
Kümmel
Maotai
Meathe
Mescal
Mickey
Mobbie
Muscat
Nectar
Obarni
Old Tom
Oolong
Orgeat
Oulong
Oxymel
Pastis
Pernod®
Plotty
Porter
Posset
Pulque
Red-eye

Rickey
Rotgut
Saloop
Samshu
Scoosh
Shandy
Sherry
Skoosh
Smiler
Squash
Stingo
Strega
Strunt
Taffia
Tisane
Waragi
Whisky
Yaqona
Zythum

*7 letters:*
Absinth
Akvavit
Alcopop
Amoroso
Aniseed
Aquavit
Bacardi®
Bastard
Bitters
Cachaca
Campari®
Caribou
Catawba
Chablis
Chianti
Cobbler
Curaçao
Curaçoa
Daquiri
Eggflip
Fairish
Fustian
Gin fizz
Guarana
Instant
Italian
Koumiss
Limeade
Madeira
Malmsey
Marsala
Martini
Mineral
Nobbler
Oenomel
Oloroso
Orvieto
Persico
Philter
Philtre
Pilsner
Pink gin
Plottie
Quetsch
Ratafia
Reviver
Rosiner
Rosolio
Samshoo
Sangria
Sazerac
Screech
Scrumpy
Seltzer
Sherbet
Sherris
Sloe gin
Snifter
Soda pop
Stengah
Swizzle
Tequila
Tio Pepe®
Wassail
Whiskey

*8 letters:*
Absinthe
Aleberry
Ambrosia
Anisette
Aperitif
Armagnac
Babbelas
Bordeaux
Brown cow
Burgundy
Calvados
Champers
Charneco
Ciderkin
Club soda
Coca-cola®
Cocktail
Cold duck
Daiquiri
Dog's nose
Dubonnet®
Eau de vie
Geropiga
Gin sling
Gluhwein
Green tea
Highball
Hollands
Homebrew
Horlicks®
Hydromel
Lemonade
Light ale
Log juice
Mahogany
Nepenthe
Nightcap
Persicot
Pilsener
Pinotage
Ragmaker
Red biddy
Regmaker
Resinata
Resinate
Rice beer
Riesling
Root beer
Rosie Lee
Rosoglio
Saketini
Sangaree
Schnapps
Skokiaan
Snowball
Spritzer
Spumante
Switchel
Tequilla
Vermouth
Witblits

*9 letters:*
Applejack
Aqua libra®
Aqua vitae
Ayahuasca
Ayahuasco
Badminton
Buck's fizz
Burnt sack
Calabogus
Cappucino
Champagne
Chocolate
Claret cup
Cream soda
Cuba libre
Eccoccino
Febrifuge
Firewater
Ginger ale
Ginger pop
Grenadine
Hippocras
Lambswool
Manhattan
Metheglin
Milk punch
Milkshake
Mint julep
Mirabelle
Moonshine
Moose milk
Nipperkin
Orangeade
Pinot noir
Refresher
Rosa-solis
Sauternes
Slivovica
Slivovitz
Snakebite
Soda water
Stiffener
Sundowner
The cratur
Whisky mac

*10 letters:*
Blackstone
Bloody Mary
Buttermilk
Café-au-lait
Chartreuse®
Dry Martini
Ginger beer
Ginger wine
Hippomanes
Hop bitters
Lolly water
Maraschino
Mickey Finn
Mochaccino
Piña colada
Poppy water
Pousse-café
Shandygaff
Tanglefoot
Tom Collins

*11 letters:*
Aguardiente
Amontillado
Athole Brose
Barley water
Benedictine
Bitter lemon
Black and tan
Black velvet
Boiler-maker
Doch-an-doris
Frappuccino
Half-and-half
Niersteiner
Screwdriver
Soapolallie
Tom and Jerry
Whiskey sour
Whisky toddy

*12 letters:*
Bloody Caesar
Brandy pawnee
Cherry bounce
Deoch-an-doris
Doch-an-dorach
Doch-an-doruis
Humpty-dumpty
Jimmy Woodser
Marcobrunner
Old-fashioned
Sarsaparilla

*13 letters:*
Cobbler's punch
Deoch-an-doruis
Ginger cordial
Liebfraumilch
Mild and bitter
Planter's punch
Prairie oyster
Sherry cobbler

*14 letters:*
John Barleycorn

*19 letters:*
Dandelion and burdock

---

**Drink store** Cellar, Grog shop

**Drip, Dripping** Bore, Dew-drop, Dribble, Drop, Flop, Gloop, Gutter, IV, Leak, Milksop, Post-nasal, Saline, Saturated, Seep, Splatter, Stillicide, Trickle, Wimp

**Dripstone** Label, Larmier

**Drive(r), Driving, Drive out** AA, Acquired, Actuate, Amber gambler, Ambition, Aroint, Automatic, Backseat, Banish, Battue, Beetle, Belt, Boy racer, Bullocky, Ca', Cabby, Campaign, Carman, Carriage, CD-ROM, Chain, Charioteer, Chauffeur, Coachee, Coachy, Coact, Coerce, Countershaft, Crankshaft, Crew, Crowd, Designated, Disk, Dislodge, Dr, Dragsman, Drayman, Drover, Drum, Drunk, Dynamic, Economy, Eject, Emboss, Energy, Enew, Enforce, Engine, Exorcise, Expatriate, Fairway, Fangio, Faze, Feeze, Ferret, Fire, Firk, Flash, Flexible, Fluid, Force, Four-stroke, Four-wheel, Front-wheel, Fuel, Gadsman, Goad, Goadster, Golfer, Hack, Hammer, Hard, Haste, Heard, Helmsman, Herd, Hie, Hill, Hish, Hiss, Hoon, Hoosh, Hot-rod, Hoy, Hunt, Hurl, Hydrostatic, Impact, Impel, Impetus, Impinge, Impulse, Instinct, Jarvey, Jehu, Jockey, Juggernaut, Key(ring), Lash, Lauda, Learner, Left-hand, Libido, Locoman, L-plater, Lunge, Mahout, Make, Mall, M(a)cGuffin, Micro, Miz(z)en, Moss, Motor, Motorman, Muleteer, Offensive, Oomph, Overland, Peg, Penetrate, Phase, Piston, Pocket, Power, Powertrain, P-plater, Propel, Puncher, Push, Put, Quill, RAC, Rack, Rally(e), Ram, Rear-wheel, Rebut, Reinsman, Ride, Right-hand, Road, Roadhog, Roadsman, Run, Sales, Scorch, Screw, Scud, Senna, Sex, Shepherd, Shoo, Shover, Spank, Spin, Spur, Start, Steer, Stroke, Sumpter-horse, Sunday, Sweep, Swift, Tape, Task-master, Taximan, Teamster, Tee, Test, Testosterone, Thrust, Thumb, Toad, Toe and heel, Tool, Tootle, Torrential, Trot, Trucker, Truckie, Truckman, Tup, Turn, Twoccer, Two-stroke, Urge, Urgence, USB, Vetturino, Villeneuve, Wagoner, Warp, Whist, Wood, Wreak, Zest, Zip

**Drivel** Balderdash, Blather, Blether(skate), Drip, Drool, Humbug, Maunder, Nonsense, Pabulum, Pap, Rot, Salivate, Slabber, Slaver, Trash

**Driving club** AA, Iron, RAC

**Drizzle** Dew, Drow, Haze, Mist, Mizzle, Roke, Scotch mist, Scouther, Scowther, Serein, Skiffle, Smir(r), Smur, Spit, Sprinkle

**Droll** Amusing, Bizarre, Comic, Funny, Humorous, Jocular, Queer, Waggish

**Drone** Air strike, Bagpipe, Bee, Bombilate, Buzz, Dog-bee, Doodle, Dor(r), Drant, Draunt, Drawl, Grind, Hanger-on, Hooray Henry, Hum, Idler, Parasite, Reedy, Tamboura, Thrum, Windbag, Wooster

**Drool** Dribble, Drivel, Gibber, Salivate, Slaver, Slobber, Spawl

**Droop(y), Drooping** Cernuous, Decline, Epinasty, Flabby, Flaccid, Flag, Jowled, Languish, Lill, Limp, Lob, Loll, Lop, Nutate, Oorie, Ourie, Owrie, Peak, Pendulous, Ptosis, → **SAG**, Slink, Slouch, Slump, Weeping, Welk(e), Wilt, Wither

**Drop(s), Dropper, Dropping** Acid, Airlift, Apraxia, Asperge, Bag, Bead, Beres, Blob, Butter, Cadence, Calve, Cascade, Cast, Chocolate, Cough, Cowpat, Dap, Decline, Decrease, Delayed, Descent, Deselect, Dew, Dink, Dip, Ditch, Dolly, Downturn, Drappie, Drib(let), Dung, Ean, Ease, Ebb, Escarp(ment), Fall, Floor, Flop, Fly-speck, Free-fall, Fruit, Fumet, Gallows, Glob(ule), Gout(te), Guano, Gutta, Guttate, Ha-ha, Heel-tap, Instil, June, Knockout, Land, Lapse, Medicine, Minim, Modicum, Moult, Muff, Mute, Nosedive, Omit, Peppermint, Pilot, Plap, Plonk, Plop, Plummet, Plump, Plunge, Plunk, Precepit, Precipice, (Prince) Rupert's, Rain, Relegate, Scat, Scrap, Scrub, Shed, Sip, Skat, Slurry, Spat, Spill, Splash, Spraint, Stilliform, Swoop, Tass, Taste, Tear, Thud, Trapdoor, Turd, Virga, Wrist

**Drop-out** Beatnik, Hippie, Hippy, Parachutist

**Drop-shot** Dink

**Dropsy** Anasarca, Ascites, Edema, Oedema

**Dross** Chaff, Dirt, Dregs, Recrement, Scoria, Scorious, Scum, Sinter, Slack, Slag, Waste

**Drought** Dearth, Drouth, Lack, Thirst

**Drove(r)** Band, Crowd, Flock, Herd, Host, Masses, Mob, Overlander, Puncher

**Drown(ed), Drowning, Drown out** Deafen, Drench, Drent, Drook, Drouk, Engulf, Howl down, Inundate, Noyade, Overcome, Sorrows, Submerge

**Drowse, Drowsiness, Drowsy** Bleary, Blet, Comatose, Doze, Hypnagogic, Hypnopompic, Lethargic, Nap, Narcolepsy, Narcosis, Nod, Snooze, Somnolent

**Drub, Drubbing** Anoint, Rout, Thrash, Trounce

**Drudge(ry)** Boswell, Cinderella, Devil, Dogsbody, Donkey-work, Fag, Grind, Hack,

Hackwork, Hireling, Jackal, Johnson, Menial, Plod, Scrub, Slave(y), Snake, Spadework, Stooge, Sweat, Swink, Thraldom, Toil, Trauchle, Treadmill, Work load

**Drug(ged)** Acaricide, ACE inhibitor, Acid head, Anorectic, Antarthritic, Anti-depressant, Antihypersensitive, Antinephatic, Antipsychotic, Antipyrine, Antiviral, Bag, Barbiturate, Base, Blow, Blue devil, Bolus, Bomber, Boo, Botanical, Cathartic, Chalybeate, Cholagogue, Clofibrate, Clot buster, Contraceptive, Controlled, Corrigent, Custom, Dadah, Deck, Depot, Depressant, Designer, DET, Diuretic, Dope, Dose, Downer, E, Ecbolic, Ecphractic, Elixir, Emmenagogue, Errhine, Euphoriant, Fantasy, Fertility, Fig, Galenical, Gateway, Gear, Generic, Hallucinogen, Hard, Head, High, Hocus, Homeopathy, Hypnotic, Immunosuppressant, Indinavir, Joint, Knockout drops, Largactic, Lifestyle, Line, Load, Loop diuretic, Mainline, Medicine, Mercurial, Mind-expanding, Miracle, Modified release, Monged, Nervine, Nobble, Nootropic, Obstruent, OD, Off-label, Opiate, Orphan, Painkiller, Paregoric, Parenteral, Peace, Pharmaceutics, Pharmacology, Pharmacopoeia, Poison, Popper, Pot, Prophylactic, Proprietary, Psychedelic, Psychoactive, Psychodelic, Purgative, Recreational, Scag, Sedate, Sedative, Shot, Sialogogue, Skin-pop, Smart, Snort, Soft, Soporific, Sorbefacient, Specific, Speedball, Spermicide, Spike, Stash, Stimulant, Stone(d), Street name, Stupefacient, Stupefy, Styptic, Substance, Sudorific, Suppressant, Synthetic, Tincture, Toot, Tout, Tranquiliser, Truth, Upper, Vasoconstrictor, Vasodilator, Vermicide, Vermifuge, Weed, White stuff, Wonder, Wrap, Zeolitic, Zonked

---

## DRUGS

***1 letter:***
H
Q

***3 letters:***
AZT
Dex
EPO
Eve
GHB
Hop
Ice
INH
Kat
Kif
LSD
PCP®
Qat
STP
Tab
Tea

***4 letters:***
Acid
Adam
Aloe
Ara-A
Bang
Bute
Coca
Dopa
Hash
Hemp
Junk
Khat
Leaf
Sida
Snow
Soma
SSRI
Tina
Trip
Whiz

***5 letters:***
Aloes
Benny
Bhang
Botox
Candy
Coxib
Crank
Dagga
Dexie
Ganja
Grass
Hop-up
Horse
Intal®
L-dopa
Meths
Mummy
Opium
Picra
Quina
Rutin
Salep
Salop
Senna
Smack
Soman
Speed
Splay
Sugar
Sulfa
Taxol
Whizz
Zyban®

***6 letters:***
Amulet
Amytal®
Ativan®
Basuco
Bindle
Charas
Curare
Dragée
Heroin
Inulin
Joypop
Lariam®
Mescla
Mummia
Nubain®
Peyote
Pituri
Prozac®
Roofie
Saloop
Statin
Sulpha
Valium®
Viagra®
Zantac®

***7 letters:***
Alcohol
Aricept®
Aspirin
Atabrin
Atebrin®
Botanic
Cascara
Charlie
Churrus
Cocaine
Codeine
Cumbrin
Damiana
Dapsone
Diasone
Diconal®
Ecstasy
Eserine
Eucaine
Guarana
Hashish
Henbane
Hypnone
Insulin
Jellies
Librium®
Metopon
Miltown®
Mogadon®
Morphia
Nurofen®
Pareira
Patulin
Quinine
Relenza®
Ritalin®
Seconal®
Septrin®
Seroxat®
Steroid
Suramin
Tacrine
Tamiflu
Trional
Triptan
Turpeth
Veronal®
Xenical®

***8 letters:***
Adjuvant
Antabuse®
Ataraxic
Atenolol
Banthine
Benadryl®
Coumbrin
Curarine
Diazepam
Doxapram
Fentanyl
Goofball
Hasheesh

Hyoscine
Ibogaine
Ketamine
Laetrile
Laudanum
Mersalyl
Mescalin
Methadon
Miticide
Moonrock
Morphine
Naloxone
Naproxen
Narcotic
Nembutal
Nepenthe
Nystatin
Orlistat
Oxytocic
Procaine
Psilocin
Quaalude®
Reductil®
Retrovir®
Rifampin
Roborant
Rohypnol®
Scopolia
Serevent®
Snowball
Special K
Tetronal
Thiazide
Varidase®
Veratrin
Viricide
Warfarin
Zerumbet
Zolpidem

***9 letters:***
Acyclovir
Analeptic
Angel-dust
Anovulant
Antrycide
Augmentin
Barbitone
Biguanide
Bupropion
Busulphan
Captopril
Carbachol
Celecoxib
Cisplatin
Clonidine
Clozapine
Compound Q
Corticoid
Cortisone
Cyclizine
Cytotoxin
Dexedrine®
Digitalis
Digytoxin
Donepezil
Dramamine®
Electuary
Ephedrine
Foscarnet
Frusemide
Herceptin®
Ibuprofen
Iprindole
Isoniazid
Jaborandi
Largactil®
Lidocaine
Lorazepam
Marijuana
Meloxicam
Mepacrine
Methadone
Minoxidil
Modafinil
Mydriasis
Naltrexol
Novocaine
Nux vomica
Oxycodone
Oxycontin®
Paludrine®
Pethidine
Phenytoin
Practolol
Quinidine
Quinquina
Reserpine
Ritonavir
Synergist
Tamoxifen
Temazepam
Teniacide
Totaquine
Tretinoin
Trinitrum
Verapamil
Veratrine
Wobbly egg
Zanamivir

***10 letters:***
Acedapsone
Amantadine
Ampicillin
Antagonist
Anxiolytic
Atracurium
Belladonna
Benzedrine
Benzocaine
Bufotenine
Cimetidine
Clomiphene
Clonazepam
Colestipol
Disulfiram
Endostatin®
Ergotamine
Etanercept
Ethambutol
Fluoxetine
Formestane
Furosemide
Gabapentim
Hiera-picra
Hydragogue
Imipramine
Indapamide
Iproniazid
Irinotecan
Isoaminile
Isoniazide
Ivermectin
Ketoprofen
Lofexidine
Mandragora
Mefloquine
Methidrine
Methyldopa
Mickey Finn
Nalbuphine
Natorphine
Nifedipine
Nitrazepam
Olanzapine
Omeprazole®
Papaverine
Paroxetine
Penicillin
Pentaquine
Phenacetin
Prednisone
Primaquine
Probenecid
Psilocybin
Quinacrine
Raloxifene
Rifampicin
Salbutamol
Saquinavir
Selegiline
Stramonium
Sucralfate
Tacrolimus
Taeniacide
Taeniafuge
Vagotropic
Vancomycin
Worm-powder
Zidovudine

***11 letters:***
Acamprosate
Aldesleukin
Alendronate
Allopurinol
Aminobutene
Amoxycillin
Amphetamine
Anastrozole
Beta-blocker
Butazolidin®
Carbimazole
Carminative
Chloroquine
Ciclosporin
Cinnarizine
Clenbuterol
Clindamycin
Clopidogrel
Crystal meth
Cyclosporin
Deserpidine
Distalgesic
Finasteride
Fluconazole
Fluvoxamine
Galantamine
Ganciclovir
Gemcitabene
Gemcitabine
Gemfibrozil
Haloperidol
Hydralazine
Idoxuridine
Indometacin
Ipratropium
Isoxsuprine
Magic bullet
Meprobamate
Methicillin
Methoxamine

Neostigmine
Nikethamide
Ondansetron
Oseltamivir
Paracetamol
Pentamidine
Pentazocine
Phentermine
Pravastatin
Propranolol
Purple heart
Risperidone
Simvastatin
Succedaneum
Sulfadoxine
Terfenadine
Thalidomide
Theobromine
Tolbutamide
Tous-les-mois
Tropomyosin
Tumorigenic
Varenicline
Varicomycin
Vinblastine
Vincristine

***12 letters:***
Alpha-blocker
Anistreplace
Anthelmintic
Antiperiodic
Arsphenamine
Atorvastatin
Azathioprine
Capecitabine
Chlorambucil
Clomipramine
Clotrimazole
Cyclandelate
Dipyridamole
Eflornithine
Fenfluramine
Fluorouracil
Fluphenazine
Glanciclover
Gonadotropin
Guanethidine
Indomethacin
Isoprenaline
Isotretinoin
Lansoprazole
Mecamylamine
Methaqualone
Methotrexate
Mifepristone
Noradrenalin
Perphenazine
Physotigmine
Prednisolone
Promethazine
Rivastigmine
Salicylamide
Streptomycin
Sulfadiazine
Temozolomide
Trimethoprim

***13 letters:***
Amitriptyline
Anthelminthic
Antihistamine
Carbamazepine
Depressometer
Flunitrazepam
Materia medica
Metronidazole
Nitroglycerin
Nortriptyline
Penicillamine
Phencyclidine
Pyrimethamine
Spectinomycin
Sulfadimidine
Sulfathiazole
Sulphadiazine
Suxamethonium
Thiabendazole
Triamcinolone

***14 letters:***
Antimetabolite
Bendrofluozide
Benzodiazepine
Bisphosphonate
Butyrhophenone
Combretastatin
Corticosterone
Cyclobarbitone
Cyclopentolate
Cyproheptadine
Discodermolide
Flucloxacillin
Norethisterone
Pentobarbitone
Phenacyclidine
Phenobarbitone
Phenylbutazone
Spironolactone
Sulphanilamide

***15 letters:***
Sympathomimetic

***17 letters:***
Sildenafil citrate

***19 letters:***
Bovine somatotrophin

---

**Druid** Gorsedd

**Drum(mer), Drumming, Drumbeat** Arête, Atabal, Barrel, Bass, Beatbox, Blakey, Bodhran, Bongo, Brake, Carousel, Chamade, Conga, Cylinder, Cymograph, Daiko, Dash-wheel, Devil's tattoo, Dhol, Djembe, Dr, Droome, Drub, Ear, Flam, Gran cassa, Kettle, Kymograph, Lambeg, Magnetic, Mridamgam, Mridang(a), Mridangam, Myringa, Naker, Ngoma, Oil, Pan, Paradiddle, Percussion, Rappel, Rataplan, Reel, Rep, Ridge, Rigger, Rim-shot, Ringo, Roll, Ruff, Ruffle, Salesman, Side, Skin, Snare, Steel, Tabla, Tabour, Tabrere, Tabret, Taiko, Tambour, Tambourin(e), Tam-tam, Tap, Tattoo, Tenor, Thrum, Timbal, Timp(ano), Tom-tom, Touk, Traps, Traveller, Tuck, Tymbal, Tympanist, Tympano, Whim, Winding, Work

**Drum-belly** Hoven

**Drumstick** Attorney, Leg, Rute, Tampon

▸**Drunk(ard)** *see* DRINK(ER)

▹**Drunken** *may indicate* an anagram

**Drupe(l)** Etaerio, Tryma

**Druse** Crystal

**Dry(ing), Drier, Dryness** Abstinent, Air, Anhydrous, Arefaction, Arefy, Arid, Blot, Bone, Brut, Clot, Clothesline, Corpse, Crine, Cure, Dehydrate, Demist, Desiccate, Detox, Drain, Drip, Droll, Dull, Eild, Ensear, Evaporate, Exsiccator, Firlot, Fork, Harmattan, Hasky, Hi(r)stie, Humidor, Husky, Hydrate, Jejune, Jerk, Juiceless, Khor, Kiln, Mummify, Oast, → PARCH, Plate rack, Prosaic, Reast, Rehab, Reist, Rizzar, Rizzer, Rizzor, Sardonic, Scarious, Sciroc, Scorch, Sear, Season, Sec(co), Seco, Sere, Shrivel, Siccative, Silical gel, Siroc(co), Sober, Spin, Sponge, Squeegee, Squeeze, Steme, Sterile, Stove, Ted, Teetotal, Thirsty, Thristy, Toasted, Torrefy, Torrid, Towel, Tribble, Trocken, TT, Tumbler, Turgid, Unsod, Unwatery, Watertight, Welt, Wilt, Win(n), Windrow, Wipe, Wither, Wizened, Wring, Wry, Xeransis, Xerasia, Xero(sis), Xeroderma, Xerophthalmia, Xerostomia

**Dryad** Eurydice, Nymph
**Dry fruit, Dried fruit** Achene, Akene, Cubeb, Currant, Mebos, Prune, Raisin, Samara, Silicula, Siliqua, Silique, Sultana
**Dry mouth** Xerostoma
**DT's** Dingbats, Hallucinations, Jimjams, Zooscopic
**Dual** Double, Twin, Twofold
**Dub** Array, → CALL, Ennoble, Entitle, Hete, Knight, Name
**Dubious** Arguable, Backscratching, Doubtful, Elliptic, Equivocal, Fishy, Fly-by-night, Hesitant, Iffy, Implausible, Improbable, Left-handed, Questionable, Scepsis, Sceptical, Sesey, Sessa, → SHADY, Shifty, Shonky, Suspect, Touch and go, Trumped up, Unclear, Unlikely, Unsure
▷**Dubious** *may indicate* an anagram
**Dubliner** Jackeen
**Duce** Leader, Musso(lini)
**Duchess** Anastasia, Camilla, Her Grace, Malfi, Peeress, Titled, Wife
**Duchy** Anhalt, Brabant, Brunswick, Cornwall, Dukedom, Franconia, Grand, Hesse, Holstein, Limburg, Lorraine, Luxembourg, Nassu, Normandy, Omnium, Realm, Savoy, Swabia, Valois, Westphalian
**Duck(ling), Ducked** Amphibian, Avoid, Aylesbury, Bald-pate, Bargander, Bathe, Bergander, Blob, Blue, Bluebill, Bob, Bombay, Broadbill, Bufflehead, Bum(m)alo, Burrow, Butterball, Canard, Canvasback, → COUPLE OF DUCKS, Crouch, Dead, Dearie, Decoy, Dip, Diving, Dodge, Dodo, Douse, Drook, Drouk, Dunk(er), Eider, Elude, Enew, Escape, Evade, Ferruginous, Flapper, Gadwall, Garganey, Garrot, Golden, Golden-eye, Goosander, Greenhead, Hareld, Harlequin, Heads, Herald, Immerse, Indian runner, Jook, Jouk, King-pair, Lame, Long-tailed, Mallard, Mandarin, Muscovy, Musk, Nil, Nodding, Nun, O, Oldsquaw, Old Tom, Old wife, Orpington, Paddling, Pair of spectacles, Palmated, Paradise, Parry, Pekin(g), Pintail, Plunge, Pochard, Poker, Putangitangi, Redhead, Ring-bill, Ruddy, Runner, Rush, St Cuthbert's, Scaup, Scoter, Sheld, Sheld(d)uck, Shell, Shieldrake, Shirk, Shovel(l)er, Shun, Sitting, Smeath, Smee(th), Smew, Sord, Souse, Sowse, Spatula, Spirit, Sprigtail, Steamer, Surf(scoter), Teal, Team, Tufted, Tunker, Ugly, Velvet scoter, Whio, Whistling, Whitewing, Widgeon, Wigeon, Wild, Wood, Zero
**Duckbill** Ornithorhynchus, Platypus
**Duckwalk** Waddle
**Duckweed** Lemna
**Ducky** Sweet, Twee
**Duct** Bile, Canal(iculus), Channel, Conduit, Diffuser, Diffusor, Emunctory, Epididymus, Fistula, Flue, Gland, Lachrymal, Lacrimal, Laticifer, Lumen, Mesonephric, Pancreatic, Parotid, Passage, Pipe, Tear, Thoracic, Tube, Ureter, Vas deferens, Wolffian
**Dud** Bouncer, Failure, Flop, Non-starter, Shan(d), Stumer
**Dude** Cat, Clothes horse, Coxcomb, Dandy, Fop, Lair, Macaroni, Popinjay, Roy, Swell
**Dudgeon** Anger, Hilt, Huff, Pique
**Due(s)** Accrued, Adequate, Annates, Arrearage, Attributable, Claim, Debt, Deserts, Easter, Entitlement, Expected, Fit(ment), Forinsec, Geld, Heriot, Inheritance, Just, Lot, Mature, Needful, Offerings, Offload, Owing, Prerogative, Reddendo, Rent, Right, Sub, → SUITABLE, Thereanent, Thorough, Toll, Tribute, Worthy
**Duel(list)** Delope, Mensur, Monomachy, Principal, Tilt
**Duenna** Chaperone, Dragon, Governess
**Duettist** Primo
**Duff** Bum, Bungle, Dough, Nelly, NG, Plum, Pudding, Rustle
**Duffer** Bungler, Rabbit, Shmo, Useless
**Dug** Pap, Ploughed, Teat, Titty, Udder
**Dugong** Halicore, Sea-cow, Sea-pig, Sirenian
**Dug-out** Abri, Canoe, Foxhole, Piragua, Pirogue, Shelter, Trench, Trough
**Duke(dom)** Albany, Alva, Chandos, Clarence, D, Duc, Ellington, Fist, Grand, Iron, Milan, Orsino, Peer, Prospero, Rohan, Wellington
**Dulcet** Mellifluous, Sweet
**Dulcify** Sweeten

**Dulcimer** Cembalo, Citole, Cymbalo, Santir, Sant(o)ur

**Dull(ard), Dullness, Dull-witted** Anodyne, Anorak, Bald, Banal, Barren, Beef-witted, Besot, Blah, Bland, Blear, Blockish, Blunt, Boeotian, Boring, Cabbage, Clod, Cloudy, Colourless, Commonplace, Dead (and alive), Deadhead, Dense, Dim, Dinge, Dingy, Ditchwater, Doldrums, Dowf, Dowie, Drab, Drear, Dreich, Dry, Dunce, Faded, Fadeur, Flat, Fozy, Gray, Grey, Heavy, Hebetate, Hebetude, Himbo, Ho-hum, Humdrum, Illustrious, Insipid, Insulse, Jejune, Lacklustre, Languid, Lifeless, Literal, Log(y), Lowlight, Mat(t), Matte, Monochrome, Monotonous, Mopish, Mull, Mundane, Nondescript, Oafish, Obtund, Obtuse, Opacity, Opiate, Ordinary, Overcast, Owlish, Pall, Pedestrian, Perstringe, Plodder, Podunk, Prosaic, Prose, Prosy, Rebate, Rust, Saddo, Slow, Solein, Sopite, Staid, Stick, Stodger, Stodgy, Stolid, Stuffy, Stultify, → STUPID, Stupor, Sunless, Tame, Tarnish, Tedious, Ticky-tacky, Toneless, Torpor, Treadmill, Trite, Tubby, Unimaginative, Unresponsive, Vapid, Witless, Wonk, Wooden, Zoid

**Dumb(ness)** Alalia, Aphonic, Blonde, Crambo, Hobbididance, Inarticulate, Mute, Mutism, Shtum, Silent, Speechless, Stumm, Stupid, Thunderstruck

**Dumbfound(ed), Dumbstruck** Amaze, Astound, Flabbergast, Floor, Goggle-eyed, Stun, Stupefy, Stupent

**Dumb ox** Aquinas

**Dummy** Clot, Comforter, Copy, Effigy, Fathead, Flathead, Jackass, Lummox, Mannequin, Mannikin, Meatball, Mock-up, Model, Pacifier, Placebo, Quintain, Soother, Table, Tailor's, Teat, Waxwork

**Dump(ing), Dumps** Abandon, Ammunition, Blue, Core, Dejection, Dispirited, Ditch, Doldrums, Empty, Eyesore, Fly-tipping, Granny, Hole, Jettison, Jilt, Junk, Landfill, Laystall, Mine, Offload, Pigsty, Scrap, Scrapyard, Screen, Shed, Shoot, Store(house), Thud, Tip, Toom, Unlade, Unload

**Dumpling(s)** Clootie, Dim sum, Dough(boy), Gnocchi, Gyoza, Knaidel, Knaidloch, Kneidlach, Knish, Kreplach, Matzoball, Norfolk, Perogi, Pi(e)rogi, Quenelle, Ribaude, Suet, Won ton

**Dumpy** Pudgy, Squat

**Dun** Annoy, Cow, Importune, Pester, → SUE, Tan

**Duncan** Isadora

**Dunce** Analphabet, Booby, Clod, Dolt, Donkey, Dullard, Fathead, Schmo, Schmuck, Schnook, Stupid

**Dunderhead** Clot

**Dune** Areg, Bar, Barchan(e), Bark(h)an, Erg, Sandbank, Sandhill, Seif, Star, Whaleback

**Dung(hill)** Album Graecum, Argol, Buffalo chips, Buttons, Chip, Cock, Coprolite, Coprozoic, Cowpat, Droppings, Fewmet, Fumet, Fumiculous, Guano, Hing, Manure, Midden, Mixen, Muckheap, Mute, Night soil, Ordure, Puer, Pure, Scat, Scumber, Shairn, Shard, Sharn, Siege, Skat, Skummer, Sombrerite, Sombrero, Spawn brick, Spraint, Stercoraceous, Tath, Turd

**Dungarees** Overalls

**Dung-eating** Merdiverous

**Dungeon** Bastille, Cell, Confine, Donjon, Durance, Keep, Oubliette, Souterrain

**Dunk** Immerse, Sop, Steep, Submerge

**Dunnock** Accentor

**Duo** Couple, Dynamic, Pair, Twosome

**Dupe** Catspaw, Chiaus, Chouse, Con, Cony, Cull(y), Delude, Easy game, Easy mark, Easy meat, Fall guy, Geck, Gull, Hoax, Hoodwink, Mug, Pawn, Pigeon, Plover, Sitter, Soft mark, Sucker, Swindle, → TRICK, Victim

**Duplex** Dual, Twofold

**Duplicate, Duplication, Duplicator** Clone, Copy, Counterpart, Cyclostyle, Ditto, Double, Echo, Facsimile, Match, Ozalid®, Paginal, Replica, Reproduce, Roneo®, Spare, Spit(ting)

**Duplicitous** Two-faced

**Durable, Durability** Enduring, Eternal, Eterne, Hardy, Lasting, Permanent, Stamina, Stout, Tough

**Duralumin®** Y-alloy

**Duration** Extent, Lifetime, Limit, Period, Run(ning) time, Span, Timescale
**Duress** Coercion, Hardship, Pressure, Restraint
**Durham** Palatine
**During** Amid, Dia-, For, In, Live, Over, Throughout, While, Whilst
**Durra** Negro corn
**Dusk(y)** Dark, Dewfall, Dun, Eve, Eventide, Gloaming, Gloom, Half-light, Owl-light, Phaeic, Puliginous, Twilight, Umbrose
**Dust(y)** Angel, Arid, Asbestos, Ash, Blood, Bo(a)rt, Calima, Clean, Coom, Cosmic, Culm, Derris, Detritus, Devil, Dicht, Duff, Earth, Fluff, Fuss, Gold, Khak(i), Lemel, Limail, Limit, Lo(e)ss, Miller, Nebula, Pellum, Pollen, Pother, Pouder, Poudre, Powder, Pozz(u)olana, Pudder, Rag, Rouge, Sea, Seed, Shaitan, Slack, Springfield, Stour, Talc, Timescale, Volcanic, Wipe
▷**Dusted** *may indicate* an anagram
**Duster** Cloth, Feather, Red, Talcum, Torchon
**Dustman** Doolittle, Garbo(logist), Refuse collector, Scaffie, Trashman
**Dust measure** Konimeter, Koniscope
**Dust-up** Fracas, Run-in, Scrimmage
**Dutch(man), Dutchwoman** Batavian, Boor, Butterbox, Cape, Courage, D(u), Double, Elm, Erasmus, Flying, Fri(e)sian, Frow, German, High, Kitchen, Knickerbocker, Meneer, Middle, Missis, Missus, Mynheer, Parnell shout, Patron, Pennsylvania, Sooterkin, Taal, Vrouw, Wife
**Dutiful, Duty** Active, Ahimsa, Allegiance, Attentive, Average, Blench, Bond, Charge, Civic, Corvee, Countervailing, Customs, Death, Debt, Deontology, Detail, Devoir, Docile, Dog-watch, Drow, Due, Duplicand, End, Estate, Excise, Export, Fatigue, Feu, Filial, Function, Heavy, Heriot, Homage, Import, Imposition, Impost, Incumbent, Jury, Lastage, Legacy, Likin, Mintage, Mission, Mistery, Mystery, Night, Obedient, Obligation, Octroi, Office, Onus, Pia, Picket, Pious, Point, Preferential, Prisage, Probate, Rota, Sentry-go, Service, Shift, Stamp, Stillicide, Stint, Succession, Tariff, →**TASK**, Tax, Toll, Transit, Trap, Trow, Vehicle excise, Watch, Zabeta
**Duvet** Bedcover, Doona, Downie®, Quilt, Tog
**Dwarf(ism)** Achondroplasia, Agate, Alberich, Andvari, Ateleiosis, Bashful, Belittle, Bes, Black, Bonsai, Brown, Doc, Dopey, Droich, Drow, Durgan, Elf, Gnome, Grumpy, Happy, Hobbit, Homuncule, Hop o' my thumb, Knurl, Laurin, Leetle, Little man, Man(n)ikin, →**MIDGET**, Mime, Minikin, Minim, Nanism, Nectabanus, Ni(e)belung, Nurl, Outshine, Overshadow, Pacolet, Pigmy, Pipsqueak, Pygmy, Red, Regin, Ront, Rumpelstiltskin, Runt, Skrimp, Sleepy, Sneezy, →**STUNT**, Tiddler, Titch, Tokoloshe, Tom Thumb, Toy, Troll, Trow, White
**Dweeb** Nerd
**Dwell(er), Dwelling** Abide, Abode, Antiscian, Aweto, Be, Bungalow, Cabin, Casa, Cell, Cot(tage), Descant, Discourse, Domicile, Habitation, Harp, Heteroscian, Hogan, House, Hovel, Hut, Ice colours, Igloo, Laura, Lavra, Live, Lodge, Longhouse, Maison(n)ette, Mansion, Messuage, Midgard, Midgarth, Mithgarthr, Pad, Palafitte, Pied-à-terre, Place, Pueblo, Reside, Roof, Shanty, Single-end, Stress, Sty, Tenement, Tepee, Terramara, Tipi, Two-by-four, Weem, Wigwam, Won(ing), Wonning, Woon
**Dwindle** Decline, Diminish, Fade, Fail, Lessen, Peter, Shrink, Wane
**Dye(ing), Dyestuff, Dye-seller** Acid, Alkanet, Amaranth, Aniline, Anthracene, Anthraquinone, Archil, Arnotto, Aweto, Azo(benzine), Azurine, Bat(t)ik, Benzidine, Brazil(e)in, Burnt umber, Camwood, Canthaxanthin, Carthamine, Catechin, Chay(a), Chica, Chicha, Chico, Choy, Cinnabar, Cobalt, Cochineal, Colour, Congo, Coomassie blue, Corkir, Crocein, Crotal, Crottle, Cudbear, Dinitrobenzene, Direct, Embrue, Engrain, Envermeil, Eosin, Flavin(e), Fluoxene, Fuchsin(e), Fustet, Fustic, Fustoc, Gambi(e)r, Gentian violet, Grain, Haematoxylin, Henna, Hue, Hypercolour, Ice colours, Ikat, Imbrue, Imbue, Incarnadine, Indamine, Indican, Indigo, Indigocarmine, Indigotin, Indirubin, Indoxyl, Indulin(e), Ingrain, Kalamkari, Kamala, Kermes, Kohl, Korkir, Lightfast, Madder, Magenta, Mauvein(e), Mauvin(e), Methyl violet, Murex, Myrobalan, Nigrosin(e), Orcein, Orchel(la), Orchil, Orseille, Para-red, Phenolphthalein, Phthalein, →**PIGMENT**, Ponceau, Primuline, Puccoon, Purple,

Purpurin, Pyronine, Quercitron, Quinoline, Raddle, Resorcinol, Rhodamine, Rosanilin(e), Saffron, Safranin(e), Salter, Shaya, → **STAIN**, Stilbene, Stone-rag, Stone-raw, Sumac(h), Sunfast, Tannin, Tartrazine, Tie-dye, Tinct, Tint, Tropaeolin, Trypan blue, Turmeric, Turnsole, Ultramarine, Valonia, Vat, Wald, Weld, Woad, Woald, Wold, Xanthium, Xylidine

▸**Dying** *see* **DIE(D)**

**Dyke** Aboideau, Aboiteau, Bund, Devil's, → **DIKE**, Ditch, Dry-stane, Gall, Offa's, Ring, Sea-wall

**Dynamic(s)** Active, Ballistics, Ball of fire, Driving, Energetic, Forceful, Go-ahead, Gogo, High-powered, Kinetics, Potent, Punchy, Vibrant, Whizz kid

**Dynamite** Blast, Explode, Gelignite, Giant powder, TNT, Trotyl

**Dynamo** Alternator, Armature, Human, Magneto, Tiger

**Dynasty** Abbasid(e), Angevin, Bourbon, Capetian, Carolingian, Chen, Chin(g), Ch'ing, Chou, Era, Fatimid, Frankish, Gupta, Habsburg, Han, Hanoverian, Hapsburg, Holkar, Honan, House(hold), Hyksos, Khan, Manchu, Maurya, Merovingian, Ming, Omayyad, Osman, Pahlavi, Plantagenet, Ptolemy, Qajar, Q'in(g), Rameses, Romanov, Rule, Safavid, Saga, Sassanid, Seleucid, Seljuk, Shang, Song, Sui, Sung, Tai-ping, Tang, Tudor, Umayyad, Wei, Yi, Yuan, Zhou

**Dysentery** Amoebic, Bloody flux, Shigellosis

**Dysfunction** Kernicterus

**Dyslexia** Strephosymbolia

**Dyspepsia** Heartburn

**Dyspeptic** Cacogastric

**Dysprosium** Dy

**Dystrophy** Duchenne's, Muscular

# Ee

**E** Boat, East, Echo, Energy, English, Spain

**Each** All, Apiece, A pop, Ea, → EVERY, Ilka, Per (capita), Respective, Severally

**Eager(ly)** Agog, Animated, Antsy, Ardent, Avid, Beaver, Bloodthirsty, Bore, Bright-eyed, Dying, Earnest, Enthusiastic, Fain, Fervent, Fervid, Fidge, Frack, Game, Greedy, Gung-ho, Hot, Intent, → KEEN, Motivated, Perfervid, Prone, Race, Raring, Rath(e), Ready, Roost, Sharp-set, Sore, Spoiling, Thirsty, Toey, Wishing, Yare, Zealous

**Eagle(s)** Al(l)erion, Altair, American, Aquila, Bald, Bateleur, Berghaan, Bird, Black, Convocation, Double, Eddy, Ensign, Erne, Ethon, Fish, Gier, Golden, Harpy, Hawk, Legal, Lettern, Nisus, Ossifrage, Red, Sea, Spread, Tawny, Wedge-tailed, White

**Ear(drum), Ear problem** Ant(i)helix, Attention, Audience, Auricle, Barotitis, Cauliflower, Cochlea, Concha, Conchitis, Corncob, Deafness, Dionysius, Dolichotus, External, Glue, Hearing, Helix, Icker, Incus, Inner, Internal, Jenkins, Kieselguhr, Labyrinth, Labyrinthitis, Listen, Locusta, Lop, Lug, Lughole, Malleus, Middle, Modiolus, Myringa, Myringitis, Nubbin, Otalgia, Otalgy, Otic, Otocyst, Paracusis, Paramastoid, Parotic, Pavilion, Periotic, Petrosal, Phonic, Pinna, Presby(a)c(o)usis, Prootic, Shell-like, Souse, Spike, Spikelet, Stapes, Thick, Tin, Tragus, Tympanitis, Tympanum, Utricle

**Ear-kiss** Whisper

**Earl(dom)** Belted, Haigh, Leofric, Mar, Peer, Sandwich

**Earlier, Early** Above, Ago, Ahead, Alsoon, AM, Antelucan, Auld, Betimes, Cockcrow, Daybreak, Ere-now, Ex, Foretaste, Germinal, In advance, Incipient, Matin, Matutinal, Onset, Or, Preceding, Precocious, Precursor, Prehistoric, Premature, Premie, Prevernal, Previous, Primeur, Primeval, Primordial, Prior, Rath(e), Rath(e)ripe, Rear, Rough, Rudimentary, Small hours, Soon, Timely, Tim(e)ous

▷**Early** *may indicate* belonging to an earl

**Early man** Eoanthropus, Flat-earther

▷**Early stages of** *may indicate* first one or two letters of the words following

**Earmark** Allocate, Allot, Bag, Book, Characteristic, Designate, Flag, → RESERVE, Tag, Target, Ticket

**Earn(er), Earning(s)** Achieve, Addle, Breadwinner, Cash cow, Curdle, Deserts, Deserve, Digerati, Ern, Gain, Income, Invisible, Make, Merit, O.T.E., Pay packet, Reap, Rennet, Runnet, Win, Yearn

**Earnest(ly)** Agood, Ardent, Arle(s)(-penny), Deadly, Deposit, Devout, Eager, Ex animo, Fervent, Imprest, Intent, Press-money, Promise, Serious, Sincere, Token, Wistly, Zealous

**Ear-phones** Ear-bud, Headset

**Earring** Drop, Ear bob, Hoop, Keeper, Pendant, Sleeper, Snap, Stud

**Earshot** Hail, Hearing

**Earth(y), Earthling** Alkaline, Antichthon, Art, Asthenosphere, Barbados, Brown, Bury, Capricorn, Carnal, Cave, Clay, Cloam, Clod, Coarse, Cologne, Craton, Den, Diatomite, Dirt, Drey, Dust, E, Eard, Edaphic, Epigene, Foxhole, Friable, Fuller's, Gaea, Gaia, Gault, Ge, Globe, Green, Ground, Heavy, Horst, Infusiorial, Kadi, Lair, Leaf-mould, Lemnian, Lithosphere, Loam, Malm, Mankind, Mantle, Marl, Mools, Mould, Mouls, Papa, Pise, Planet, Podsol, Rabelaisian, Racy, Rare, Raunchy, Red, Samian, Seat, Sett, Sod, → SOIL, Subsoil, Surcharge, Taurus, Tectonic, Telluric, Tellus, Terra, Terra firma, Terrain, Terramara, Terran, Terra rossa, Terrene, Tilth, Topsoil, Tripoli, Virgo, Wad, World, Yellow, Ye(a)rd, Yird

**Earth-bound** Chthonian, Mundane

**Earthenware** Arretine, Biscuit, Ceramic, Creamware, Crock(ery), Delf(t), Della-robbia,

Delph, Faience, Figuline, Graniteware, Ironstone, Maiolica, Majolica, Pig, Pot, Queen's ware, Raku, Samian, Sanitary, Terracotta, Terra sigillata

**Earthman** Terran

**Earth-moving** Seismic

**Earthquake** Aftershock, Aseismic, Bradyseism, Foreshock, Mercalli, Richter, Seism, Shake, Shock, Temblor, Trembler, Tremor

**Earth's surface** Sal, Sial

**Earthwork** Agger, Bank, Breastwork, Cursus, Gazon, Parados, Rampart, Remblai, Vallum

**Earthworm** Angledug, Angletwitch, Angleworm, Annelid, Bait, Night-crawler

**Earwig** Clipshear(s), Eavesdrop, Forkit-tail, Forky-tail, Listen

**Ease, Easing, Easygoing** Alleviate, Assuage, Carefree, Clear, Clover, Comfort, Content, Defuse, Deregulate, Détente, Easy-osy, Facility, Genial, Hands down, Informal, Laid back, Lax, Lenify, Mellow, Mid(dy), Mitigate, Otiosity, Palliate, Peace, Pococurante, Quiet, Relaxation, Relent, Relieve, Reposal, Repose, Resilient, Soothe

**East(erly), Eastward** Anglia, Asia, Chevet, E, Eassel, Eassil, Eothen, Eurus, Far, Levant, Middle, Morning-land, Near, Orient, Ost, Sunrise

**Easter** Festival, Island, Pace, Pasch(al), Pasque

**Easter Island** Rapa Nui

**Eastern(er), Eastern language** ASEAN, Asian, Kolarian, Oriental, Ostman, Virginian

**East European** Lettic, Slovene

**East German** Ossi

**Easy, Easily** ABC, Amenable, Approachable, Berth, Breeze, By far, Cakewalk, Carefree, Child's play, Cinch, Comfortable, Comfy, Crispy, Cushy, Degage, Docile, Doddle, Doss, Duck soup, Eath(e), Effortless, Ethe, Facile, Fluent, Free, Gift, Glib, Gravy train, Hands down, Independent, Jammy, Kid's stuff, Lax, Light, Midshipman, Natural, Nimps, No-brainer, Oldster, Painless, Picnic, Pie, Plain sailing, Pushover, Romp, Scoosh, Simple, Sitter, Skoosh, Snap, Snotty, Soft, Spoon fed, Straightforward, Tolerant, Tractable, Turkey shoot, User-friendly, Walk-over, Well, Yare

▷**Easy** *may indicate* an anagram

**Easy-care** Non-iron

**Eat(able), Eater, Eating** Bite, Bolt, Break bread, Champ, Chomp, Chop, Commensal, Consume, Corrode, Cram, Crunch, Devour, Dig in, Dine, Edible, Edite, Endew, Endue, Erode, Esculent, Etch, Fare, Feast, → FEED, Fret, Gastronome, Gnaw, Go, Gobble, Gourmand, Gourmet, Graze, Grub, Guts, Guttle, Guzzle, Have, Hoe into, Hog, Hyperorexia, Hyperphagia, Ingest, Manducate, Mess, Muckamuck, Munch, Nosh, Nutritive, Omnivore, Partake, Peck, Phagomania, Phagophobia, Predate, Refect, Scoff, Slurp, Snack, Stuff, Sup, Swallow, Syssitia, Take, Taste, Trencherman, Trophesy, Tuck away, Tuck into, Twist, Whale

**Eatery** Bistro, Café, Diner, Gastropub, Restaurant

**Eating problem** Anorexia, Aphagia, Bulimia, Cachexia

**Eavesdrop(per)** Bug, Cowan, Detectophone, Earwig, Icicle, Listen, Overhear, Pry, Snoop, Spy, Stillicide, Tab-hang, Tap, Wiretap

**Ebb(ing)** Abate, Decline, Recede, Refluent, Sink, → WANE

**Ebonite** Hard rubber

**Ebony** Black, Cocus-wood, Coromandel, Hebenon, Jamaican

**Ebullient** Brash, Effervescent, Effusive, Enthusiastic, Exuberant, Fervid, Gushing

**Eccentric** Abnormal, Antic, Atypical, Batty, Cam, Card, Character, Crackpot, Crank, Curious, Daffy, Dag, Deviant, Dingbat, Ditsy, Ditzy, E, Farouche, Fay, Fey, Fie, Fifish, Flaky, Freak, Fruitcake, Geek, Gonzo, Goofy, Iffish, Irregular, Kinky, Kook(y), Loon, Madcap, Mattoid, Misfit, Monstre sacré, Nutcase, Nutter, Odd(ball), Offbeat, Off-centre, Off the rails, Off the wall, Original, Outré, → PECULIAR, Phantasime, Pixil(l)ated, Queer, Quirky, Quiz, Rake, Raky, Recondite, Rum, Scatty, Screwball, Screwy, Spac(e)y, Squirrelly, Wack(y), W(h)acko, Wag, Way-out, Weird(o), Weirdie, Zany

▷**Eccentric** *may indicate* an anagram

**Ecclesiast(es), Ecclesiasticus, Ecclesiastical** Abbé, Clergyman, Clerical, Lector, Secular, Sir(ach), Theologian, The Preacher, Vatican

**Echelon** Formation

**Echinoderm** Asteroidea, Basket-star, Brittle-star, Comatulid, Crinoid, Heart-urchin, Ophiurid, Sea-egg, Sea-lily, Sea-urchin, Starfish

**Echo, Echoing, Echo-sounder** Angel, Answer, ASDIC, Ditto, E, Fathometer®, Imitate, Iterate, Mirror, Phonocamptic, Rebound, Recreate, Repeat, Repercussion, Reply, Resemble, Resonant, → RESOUND, Respeak, Reverb(erate), Revoice, Ring, Rote, Sonar, Tape

**Eclat** Flourish, Glory, Prestige, Renown

**Eclectic** Babist, Broad, Complex, Diverse, Liberal

**Eclipse** Annular, Block, Cloud, Deliquium, Excel, Hide, Lunar, Obscure, Occultation, Outclass, Outdo, Outjump, Outmatch, Outshine, Outweigh, Overshadow, Partial, Penumbra, Rahu, Solar, Total, Transcend, Upstage

**Eclogue** Bucolic, Idyll, Pastoral

**Eco-community** Seral

**Eco-friendly** Biodegradable

**Ecology, Ecological** Bionomics, Seral

**Economise** Budget, Conserve, Eke, Entrench, Finance, Husband, Intrench, Pinch, Retrench, Scrimp, Skimp, Spare, → STINT, Whip the cat

**Economist** Angell, Bentham, Chrematist, Cole, Coombs, Friedman, Galbraith, Giffen, Keynes, Laffer, Malthus, Marginalist, Marx, Meade, Mill, Monetarist, Nugget, Pareto, Physiocrat, Rathenau, Ricardo, Schumacher, Schumpeter, Singh, Smith, Tinbergen, Tobin, Toynbee, Veblen, Webb, Weber

**Economy, Economic(al), Economics** Agflation, Agronomy, Autarky, Black, Brevity, Careful, Cheap rate, Chrematistics, Cliometrics, Command, Conversation, Cut, Dismal science, Domestic, False, Frugal, Grey, Hidden, Home, Husband(ry), Informal, Knowledge, Lean-burn, LSE, Market, Mitumba, Mixed, Neat, New, Oligopsony, Parsimony, Phitonamy, Planned, Political, Provident, Pusser's logic, Retrenchment, Shadow, Shoestring, Siege, Sparing, Stagflation, Stakeholder, Stumpflation, Supply-side, Thrift, Tiger, Token, Welfare

**Ecstasy, Ecstatic** Bliss, Delight, Delirious, Dove, E, Enrapt, Exultant, Happy as Larry, Joy, Liquid, Lyrical, Nympholepsy, Paradise, Pythic, Rapture, Rhapsodic, Sent, Trance, Transport, Utopia

**Ecuador** EC

**Ecumenical** Catholic, Lateran

**Eczema** Pompholyx, Salt rheum, Tetter

**Edda** Elder, Legend, Prose, Younger

**Eddo** Taro

**Eddy** Backset, Curl, Duane, Gurge, Maelstrom, Nelson, Pirl, Purl, Rotor, Sousehole, Swelchie, Swirl, Vortex, Weel, Well, Whirlpool, Wiel

**Eden** Bliss, Fall, Heaven, Paradise, PM, Utopia

**Edentate** Ant-eater, Armadillo, Peba, Sloth, Tatou, Xenarthra

**Edge, Edging, Edgy** Advantage, Arris, Bleeding, Border, Bordure, Brim, Brink, Brittle, Brow, Burr, Chamfer, Chimb, Chime, Chine, Coaming, Coast, Costa, Creep, Creston, Cutting, Dag, Deckle, Ease, End, Feather, Flange, Flounce, Frill, Fringe, Frontier, Furbelow, Gunnel, Gunwale, Hem, Hone, Inch, Inside, Kerb, Knife, Leading, Leech, Limb(ate), Limbus, Limit, Lip, List, Lute, Marge(nt), Margin, Neckline, Nosing, Orle, Outside, Parapet, Periphery, Picot, Pikadell, Piping, Rand, Reeding, Restive, Rim, Rund, Rymme, Selvage, Selvedge, Side, Sidle, Skirt, Strand, Surbed, Tense, Tomium, Trailing, Trim, Twitchy, Tyre, Uneasy, Uptight, Verge, Wear, Welt, Whet, Working

▸**Edible** *see* EAT(ABLE)

**Edict(s)** Ban, Bull, Clementines, Commandment, Decree, Decretal, Extravagantes, Fatwa, Firman, Golden bull, Interim, Irade, Nantes, Notice, Order, Pragmatic, Proclamation, Pronouncement, Pronunciamento, Rescript, Sext, Ukase

**Edifice** Booth, Building, Lighthouse, Pyramid, Structure, Stupa, Superstructure

**Edify(ing), Edification** Didactic, Enlighten(ment), Instruct, Teach

**Edinburgh** Auld Reekie

**Edit(or), Editorial** Abridge, Amend, Article, Censor, City, Copy (read), Cut, Dele, Desk, Dramaturg(e), Ed, Emend, Expurgate, Footsteps, Garble, Leader, Manipulate, Overseer, Prepare, Recense, Redact, Revise, Reword, Rewrite, Seaman, Splice, Tweak

▷**Edited** *may indicate* an anagram
**Edith** Sitwell
**Edition** Aldine, Bulldog, Bullpup, Cabinet, Dead-tree, Ed, Extra, Facsimile, Ghost, Hexapla(r), Impression, Issue, Library, Limited, Number, Omnibus, Re-issue, Special, Trade, Variorum, Version
**Edmond, Edmund** Burke, Gosse, Ironside(s), Rostand, Spenser
**Educate(d)** Academic, Baboo, Babu, Civilise, Cultured, Enlighten, Evolué, Informed, Instruct, Intelligent, Learned, Lettered, Literati, Nourish, Noursle, Nousell, Nousle, Nurture, Nuzzle, Polymath, Preppy, Progressive, Scholarly, School, → **TEACH**, Train, Yuppie
**Education(alist)** Adult, Basic, B.Ed, Classical, Conductive, D.Ed, Didactics, Estyn, Froebel, Further, Heurism, Higher, Instruction, Intelligentsia, Learning, Literate, Mainstream, Montessori, Oxbridge, Paedotrophy, Pedagogue, Pestalozzi, Physical, Piarist, Primary, Schooling, Special, Steiner, Teacher, Tertiary, Tutelage, Upbringing
**Educe** Elicit, Evoke, Extract, Infer
**Edward** Confessor, Ed, Elder, Lear, Longshanks, Martyr, Ned, Ted
**Eel** Anguilla, Conger, Congo, Electric, Elver, Grass, Grig, Gulper, Gunnel, Hagfish, Jellied, Kingklip, Lamper, Lamprey, Lant, Launce, Leptocephalus, Moray, Murray, Murr(e)y, Olm, Paste, Salt, Sand(ling), Silver belly, Snake, Snig, Spitchcock, Tuna, Vinegar, Wheat, Wolf
**Eerie** Creepy, Spooky, Uncanny, Unked, Weird
**Efface** Cancel, Delete, Dislimn, → **ERASE**, Expunge, Obliterate
**Effect(s), Effective(ness), Effectual** Able, Achieve, Acid trip, Acting, Alienation, Auger, Babinski, Bags, Barkhausen, Barnstorming, Belongings, Binaural, Bit, Bite, Bohr, Border, Border edge, Bricolage, Bring about, Butterfly, Bystander, Cast, Causal, C(h)erenkov, Chromakey, Coanda, Coastline, Competent, Compton, Consequence, Coriolis, De facto, Do, Domino, Doppler, Dr(y)ice, Eclat, Edge, Efficacious, Electro-optical, Enact, End, Enforce, Ensemble, Estate, Execute, Experimenter, Fet, Foley, Fringe, Functional, Fungibles, Furnishing(s), Fx, Gangbuster, Gear, General, Goods, Greenhouse, Ground, Gunn, Hall, Halo, Hangover, Hawthorne, Home, Horns and halo, Hysteresis, Impact, Impinge, Implement(al), Impression, Influence, Introgenic, Josephson, Joule(-Thomson), Kerr, Keystone, Knock-on, Magneto-optical, Magnus, Meissner, Militate, Moire, Mossbauer, Mutual, Neat, Net, Nifty, Nisi, Notch, Operant, Optical, Outcome, Ovshinsky, Oxygen, Parallax, Peltier, Perficient, Perlocution, Personal, Phi, Photoelectric, Photovoltaic, Piezoelectric, Piezomagnetic, Pinch, Placebo, Pogo, Position, Potent, Practical, Prevailing, Primary, Promulgate, Punchy, Raman, Ratchet, Reaction, Recency, Redound, Repercussion, → **RESULT**, Ripple, Schottky, Seebeck, Shadow, Shore, Side, Sizzler, Skin, Slash-dot, Sound, Sovereign, Special, Spectrum, Spin-off, Stage, Stark, Striking, Stroop, Submarine, Subsidiary, Tableau, Teeth, Telling, Therapeutic, Thermoelectric, Thomson, Toxic, Trenchant, Tunnel, Tyndall, Upshot, Valid, Viable, Virtual, Well, Whammy, Win, Withdrawal, Work, Zeeman
**Effeminate** Airtsy-mairtsy, Camp, Carpet-knight, Carpet-monger, Cissy, Coddle, Cookie-pusher, Epicene, Female, Gussie, Jessie, Meacock, Milksop, Molly(coddle), Nellie, Nelly, Panty-waist, Pretty, Prissy, Sissy, Tender, Tenderling, Unman, Wuss(y)
**Effervescence, Effervescent** Bubbling, Ebullient, Fizz, Frizzante, Gassy, Pétillant, Soda
▷**Effervescent** *may indicate* an anagram
**Effete** Camp, Epicene, Epigon(e)
**Efficacious, Efficacy** Effective, Operative, Potent, Sovereign, Valid, Value
**Efficiency, Efficient** Able, Businesslike, Capable, Competent, Current, Despatch, Ecological, Electrode, Ergonomics, Expeditious, High-powered, Lean, Luminous, Productivity, Quantum, Smart, Spectral luminous, Streamlined, Strong, Thermal, Volumetric
**Effigy** Buddha, Figure, Guy, Idol, Image, Statua, Statue
**Efflorescence** Bloom, Blossom, Reh
**Effluence, Effluent, Effluvia, Effluvium** Air, Aura, Billabong, Discharge, Fume, Gas, Halitus, Miasma, Odour, Outflow, Outrush, Reek
**Effort** Achievement, All-out, Attempt, Best, Conatus, Concentration, Concerted, Damnedest, Drive, Endeavour, Essay, Exertion, Fit, Frame, Hardscrabble, Herculean, Joint, Labour, Legwork, Molimen, Nisus, Offensive, Pains, Pull, Push, Rally, Shy, Spurt, Stab, Strain, Struggle, Team, Travail, → **TRY**, Work, Yo

**Effortless** Cushy, Lenis, Low-impact, Low maintenance, Plain sailing, Spoonfed
**Effrontery** Audacity, Backchat, Brass, Cheek, Face, Gall, Neck, Nerve, Temerity
**Effulgent** Bright, Radiant, Shining
**Effuse, Effusion, Effusive** Emanate, Exuberant, Exude, Gush, Lyric, Ode, Outburst, Prattle, Rhapsody, Sanies, Screed, Spill
**Eft** After
**Eg** As, Example, Zb
**Egalitarian** Democratic, Equaliser
**Egest** Eliminate, Evacuate, Excrete, Void
**Egg(s), Egg on** Abet, Addled, Benedict, Berry, Blow, Bomb, Buttered, Caviar(e), Cavier, Chalaza, Cheer, Cleidoic, Clutch, Cockney, Collop, Coral, Curate's, Custard, Darning, Easter, Edge, Encourage, Fabergé, Fetus, Flyblow, Foetus, Free-range, Frogspawn, Glair(e), Goad, Goog, Graine, Hoy, Incite, Instigate, Isolecithal, Layings, Mine, Nest, Nidamentum, Nit, Oocyte, Oophoron, Ostrich, Ova, Ovum, Pace, Pasch, Plover's, Prairie oyster, Press, Prod, Raun, Roe, Rumble-tumble, Sand saucer, Scotch, Scrambled, Seed, Setting, Spat, Spawn, Spur(ne), Tar(re), Tempt, Thunder, Tooth, Tread(le), Urge, Whore's, Wind, Yelk, Yolk, Zygote
**Egg-case** Eggshell, Pod
**Egghead** Brainbox, Don, Highbrow, Intellectual, Mensa, Pedant
**Eggnog** Flip
**Egg-plant** Aubergine, Brinjal
**Egg-producer** Gametophyte, Hen, Ovipositor
**Egg-shaped** Obovate, Oval, Ovate, Oviform
**Eggshell** China, Doup, Fragile
**Egg-white** Albumen, Glair
**Ego(ism), Egoist, Egotist(ic), Egotistical** Che, Conceit, I, Narcissism, Not-I, Pride, Self, Self-centred, Self-seeker, Solipsism, Tin god, Ubu, Vanity
**Egocentric** Solipsistic
**Egregious** Eminent, Flagrant, Glaring, Shocking
**Egret** Snowy
**Egypt(ian), Egyptologist** Arab, Cairene, Carter, Cheops, Chephren, Cleopatra, Copt(ic), ET, Goshen, Imhotep, Nasser, Nefertiti, Nilote, Nitrian, Old Kingdom, Osiris, Potiphar, Ptolemy, Rameses, Syene, Theban, UAR, Wafd
**Eiderdown** Bedspread, Duvet, Quilt
**Eight(h), Eighth day** Acht, Byte, Crew, Cube, Isis, Middle, Nundine, Oars, Octa, Octad, Octal, Octant, Octastrophic, Octave, Octet, Octonary, Octuor, Ogdoad, Okta, Ottava, Ure, Utas
**Eighteen** Majority
**Eighty** Fourscore, R
**Einsteinium** Es
**Either** Also, Both, O(u)ther, Such
**Ejaculate** Blurt, Discharge, Emit, Exclaim
**Eject** Belch, Bounce, Defenestrate, Disgorge, Dismiss, Emit, Erupt, Evict, Expel, Expulse, Oust, Propel, Spew, Spit, Spue, Turf out, Vent, Void
**Eke** Augment, Eche, Enlarge, Husband, Supplement
**Elaborate** Aureate, Baroque, Creation, Detail, Develop, Dressy, Embroider, Enlarge, Evolve, Expand, Extravagant, Fancy, Flesh out, Florid, Imago, Improve, Intricate, Magnificent, Opulent, Ornate, Rich, Spectacular, Stretch
**Elan** Dash, Drive, Esprit, → **FLAIR**, Gusto, Lotus, Panache, Spirit, Style, Vigour
**Elapse** Glide, Intervene, Overpass, Pass
**Elastic(ity)** Adaptable, Bungee, Buoyant, Dopplerite, Elater, Flexible, Give, Lithe(some), Resilient, Rubber, Scrunchie, Scrunchy, Spandex®, Springy, Stretchy, Tone, Tonus
**Elastomer** Adiprene®
**Elate(d), Elation** Cheer, Cock-a-hoop, Euphoric, Exalt, Exhilarate, Gladden, Hault, High, Lift, Rapture, Ruff(e), Uplift
**Elbow, Elbow tip** Akimbo, Ancon, Angle, Bender, Cubital, Hustle, Joint, Jolt, Jostle, Justle, Kimbo, Noop, Nudge, Olecranon, Tennis
**Elbow room** Leeway

**El Cid** Diaz
**Elder(ly), Eldest** Ainé(e), Ancestor, Ancient, Bourtree, Chief, Classis, Coffin dodger, Eigne, Geriatric, Greying, Guru, Imam, Kaumatua, Kuia, OAP, Presbyter, → SENIOR, Sire, Susanna, Wallwort
**Eldorado** Ophir
**Eleanor(a)** Bron, Duse, Nora(h)
**Elect(ed), Election(eer), Elective, Elector(al)** Ballot, Choice, Choose, Chosen, Constituent, Co-opt, Eatanswill, Elite, General, Gerrymander, Hustings, In, Israelite, Khaki, Member, Off-year, Opt, Optional, Pick, PR, Predetermine, Primary, Psephology, Rectorial, Return, Select, Stump, Vote in
**Electric** Live
**Electrical discharge** Corposant, Ion, Zwitterion
**Electrical instrument** Battery, Charger, Galvaniser, Magneto, Mains, Resistor, Rheostat, Shoe
**Electrical unit** Amp(ere), Coulomb, Farad, Kilowatt, Ohm, Volt, Watt
**Electric eye** Pec
**Electrician** Gaffer, Lineman, Ohm, Siemens, Sparks, Tesla
**Electricity** Current, Galvanism, Grid, HT, Inductance, Juice, Mains, Negative, Positive, Power, Static, Utility, Vitreous
**Electrify** Astonish, Charge, Fire, Galvanise, Startle, Stir, Thrill, Transport
**Electrode** Anode, Cathode, Dynode, Element, Emitter, Photocathode
**Electrolyte** Ampholyte
**Electromagnet(ic)** Abampere, Armature, Oersted, Solenoid, Weber
**Electron(ic), Electronics, Electronic device** Cooper pairs, E-book, Exciton, FET, Fly-by-wire, Hydrated, Linac, Lone pair, Martenot, Mole(cular), Polaron, Possum®, Quantum, Smart, Tetrode, Thermionics, Valence, Valency
**Elegance, Elegant** Artistic, Bijou, Chic, Chichi, Classy, Concinnity, Dainty, Daynt, Debonair, Dressy, Fancy, Feat, Finesse, Flair, Gainly, Galant, Genteel, Grace, Jimp, Luxurious, Natty, Neat, Poise, Polished, Posh, Recherché, Refined, Ritzy, → SMART, Soigné(e), Style, Suave, Svelte, Swish, Tall, Tasteful, Urbane
**Elegy, Elegist** Dirge, Gray, Lament, Poem
**Element(s), Elementary** Abcee, Abecedarian, Absey, Barebones, Chromosome, → COMPONENT, Detail, → ESSENCE, Essential, Ether, Factor, Feature, Fuel, Heating, Hot-plate, Ideal, Identity, Ingredient, Insertion, Logical, M(a)cGuffin, Milieu, Non-metal, Peltier, Pixel, Primary, Principle, Radio, Rare earth, Rudimental, Sieve, Simple, Simplex, Stabial, Straightforward, Strand, Superheavy, Trace(r), Tramp, Transition, Transuranic, Weather

---

## ELEMENTS

*3 letters:*
Air
Tin (Sn)

*4 letters:*
Atom
Fire
Gold (Au)
Iron (Fe)
Lead (Pb)
Neon (Ne)
Ylem
Zinc (Zn)

*5 letters:*
Alloy
Argon (Ar)
Boron (B)
Earth
Morph(eme)
Muton
Niton
Radon (Rn)
Terra
Water
Xenon (Xe)

*6 letters:*
Barium (Ba)
Carbon (C)
Cerium (Ce)
Cesium
Chrome
Cobalt (Co)
Copper (Cu)
Curium (Cm)
Erbium (Er)
Helium (He)
Indium (In)
Iodine (I)
Nickel (Ni)
Osmium (Os)
Oxygen (O)
Radium (Ra)
Silver (Ag)
Sodium (Na)

*7 letters:*
Arsenic (As)
Bismuth (Bi)
Bohrium (Bh)
Bromine (Br)
Cadmium (Cd)
Caesium (Cs)
Calcium (Ca)
Dubnium (Db)
Fermium (Fm)
Gallium (Ga)
Hafnium (Hf)
Hahnium (Hn)
Halogen
Hassium (Hs)
Holmium (Ho)

Iridium (Ir)
Isotope
Krypton (Kr)
Lithium (Li)
Mercury (Hg)
Natrium
Niobium (Nb)
Rhenium (Re)
Rhodium (Rh)
Silicon (Si)
Sulphur (S)
Terbium (Tb)
Thorium (Th)
Thulium (Tm)
Uranide
Uranium (U)
Wolfram
Yttrium (Y)

***8 letters:***
Actinide
Actinium (Ac)
Antimony (Sb)
Astatine (At)
Chlorine (Cl)
Chromium (Cr)
Columbic
Coronium
Didymium
Europium (Eu)
Fluorine (F)
Francium (Fr)
Glucinum
Hydrogen (H)
Illinium
Inchoate
Lutetium (Lu)
Masurium
Nebulium
Nitrogen (N)
Nobelium (No)
Platinum (Pt)
Polonium (Po)
Rubidium (Rb)
Samarium (Sm)
Scandium (Sc)
Selenium (Se)
Tantalum (Ta)
Thallium (Tl)
Titanium (Ti)
Tungsten (W)
Vanadium (V)

***9 letters:***
Alabamine
Aluminium (Al)
Americium (Am)
Berkelium (Bk)
Beryllium (Be)
Brimstone
Columbium (Cb)
Flerovium (Fl)
Germanium (Ge)
Glucinium
Joliotium
Lanthanum (La)
Magnesium (Mg)
Manganese (Mn)
Metalloid
Neodymium (Nd)
Neptunium (Np)
Palladium (Pd)
Plutonium (Pu)
Potassium (K)
Ruthenium (Ru)
Strontian
Strontium (Sr)
Tellurium (Te)
Virginium
Ytterbium (Yb)
Zirconium (Zr)

***10 letters:***
Dysprosium (D)
Gadolinium (Gd)
Lanthanide
Lawrencium (Lr)
Meitnerium (Mt)
Molybdenum (Mo)
Ommatidium
Phlogiston
Phosphorus (P)
Promethium (Pm)
Seaborgium (Sg)
Technetium (Tc)

***11 letters:***
Californium (Cf)
Copernicium (Cn)
Einsteinium (Es)
Livermorium (Lv)
Mendelevium (Md)
Quicksilver
Roentgenium (Rg)
Unnilennium (Une)
Unnilhexium (Unh)
Unniloctium (Uno)
Ununquadium (Uuq)

***12 letters:***
Darmstadtium
Kurchatovium
Nielsbohrium
Praseodymium (Pr)
Protactinium (Pa)
Unnilpentium (Unp)
Unnilquadium (Unq)
Unnilseptium (Uns)

***13 letters:***
Rutherfordium (Rf)
Transactinide

---

**Elephant(ine)** African, Babar, Bull, Calf, Cow, Hathi, Indian, Jumbo, Kheda, Mammoth, Mastodon, Oliphant, Pachyderm, Pad, Pink, Proboscidean, Rogue, Stegodon, Subungulata, Trumpeter, Tusker, White

**Elephant-headed** Ganesa

**Elephant's ears** Begonia

**Elevate(d), Elevation, Elevator** Aerial, Agger, Aggrandise, Attitude, Aweight, Bank, Cheer, Colliculus, El, Eminence, Ennoble, Euphuism, Foothill, Glabella, Grain, Haute, Heighten, Hoist, Jack, Lift, Lob, Lofty, Machan, Montic(u)le, Monticulus, Pitch, Promote, → RAISE, Random, Relievo, Ridge, Rise, Steeve, Sublimate, Sur-, Umbo, Up(lift), Uplying, Upraise, Wallclimber

**Eleven** Elf, Hendeca-, Legs, O, Side, Tail-ender, Team, XI

**Elf(in), Elves** Alfar, Chiricaune, Dobbie, Dobby, Fairy, Fey, Fie, Goblin, Imp, Kobold, Ouph, Pigwiggen, Pixie, Ribhus, Sprite, Troll, Urchin

**Elicit** Evoke, Extract, Provoke, Toase, Toaze, Tose, Toze

**Eligible** Available, Catch, Entitled, Fit, Nubile, Parti, Qualified, Worthy

**Eliminate, Elimination** Abolish, Cull, Cure, Deep-six, Delete, Discard, Egest, Exclude, Execute, Extirpate, Heat, Knock out, Liquidate, Omit, Preclude, Purge, Red-line, Rid, Separate, Slay, Void, Weed out, Zap

**Elision** Apocope, Synal(o)epha, Syncope

**Elite, Elitist** Best, Choice, Crachach, Crack, → CREAM, Crème (de la crème), Egalitarian, Elect, Finest, Flower, Gentry, Jet set, Liberal, Meritocracy, Plutocracy, Snob, Ton, Top drawer, Twelve pitch, U, Upper crust, Zaibatsu

**Elixir** Amrita, Arcanum, Bufo, Cordial, Cure-all, Daffy, Essence, Medicine, Panacea, Philosopher's stone, Quintessence, Tinct

**Elizabeth** Bess(ie), Gloriana, Oriano
**Elk** Deer, Gang, Irish, Moose
**Elkoshite** Nahum
**Ellipse, Elliptic** Conic, Oblong, Oval, Ovolo
**Elm** Dutch, Nettle-tree, Rock, Slippery, Wahoo, Weeping, Wich, Winged, Wych
**Elmer** Gantry
**Elongate** Extend, Lengthen, Protract, Stretch
**Elope** Abscond, Decamp
**Eloquence, Eloquent** Articulate, Blarney stone, Demosthenic, Facundity, Fluent, Honey-tongued, Oracy, Oratory, Rhetoric, Silver-tongued, Speaking, Vocal
**Else(where)** Absent, Alibi, Aliunde, Et al, Other
**Elucidate** Demystify, Explain, Expose, Expound, Interpret, Simplify
**Elude, Elusion, Elusive** Avoid, Dodge, Eel, Escape, → **EVADE**, Evasive, Foil, Intangible, Jink, Pimpernel, Sliddery, Slippy, Subt(i)le, Will o' the wisp
▸**Elves** *see* **ELF(IN)**
**Elysium** Tir-nan-Og
**Em** Mut(ton), Pica
**Emaciate(d), Emaciation** Atrophy, Erasmus, Gaunt, Haggard, Lean, Meagre, Skeleton, Skinny, Sweeny, Tabid, Thin, Wanthriven, Wasted
**Email** Flame, Online, Spam, Spim
**Emanate, Emanation** Arise, Aura, Derive, Discharge, Ectoplasm, Exude, Halo, Issue, Miasma, Radiate, Spring
**Emancipate(d), Emancipation** Catholic, Deliver, Forisfamiliate, Free, → **LIBERATE**, Manumission, Uhuru
**Emasculate** Bobbitt, Castrate, Debilitate, Evirate, Geld, Unsex
**Embalm** Anele, Anoint, Cere, Mummify, Preserve
**Embankment** Berm, Bund, Causeway, Dam, Dyke, Earthwork, Levee, Mattress, Mound, Rampart, Remblai, Sconce, Side-cutting, Staith(e), Stopbank, Terreplein
**Embargo** → **BAN**, Blockade, Boycott, Edict, Restraint
**Embark** Begin, Board, Enter, Inship, Launch, Sail
**Embarrass(ed), Embarrassing, Embarrassment** Abash, Ablush, Ashamed, Awkward, Barro, Besti, Blush, Buttock-clenching, Chagrin, Cheap, Colour, Crimson, Cringe-making, Cringe-worthy, Discomfort, Disconcert, Discountenance, Encumber, Flush, Gêne, Haw, Mess, Mortify, Plethora, Pose, Predicament, Scundered, Scunnered, Shame, Sheepish, Squirming, Straitened, Toe-curling, Tongue-tied, Upset, Whoopsie, Writhing
▹**Embarrassed** *may indicate* an anagram
**Embassy** Chancery, Consulate, Embassade, Legation, Mission
**Embed(ded)** Deep-set, Fix, Immerse, Implant, Inlaid, Inset, Set
**Embellish(ed), Embellishment** Adorn, Beautify, Bedeck, Curlicue, Deck, Decór(ate), Dress, Embroider, Enrich, Fioritura, Frill, Frippery, Garnish, Garniture, Gild, Grace note, Melisma(ta), Mordent, → **ORNAMENT**, Ornate, Overlay, Overwrought, Prank, Prettify, Rel(l)ish, Roulade, Story, Turn, Twist
**Ember(s)** Ash, Cinder, Clinker, Gleed
**Embezzle(ment)** Defalcate, Malversation, Misappropriate, Peculate, Purloin, Shoulder, → **STEAL**
**Embitter(ed)** Acerbate, Aggravate, Enfested, Exacerbate, Fester, Malevolent, Rankle, Sour
**Emblem(atic)** Badge, Bear, Colophon, Daffodil, Device, Eagle, Figure, Fleur-de-lis, Golp(e), Hammer and sickle, Ichthys, Impresa, Insignia, Kikumon, Leek, Lis, Logo, Maple leaf, Mon, Oak, Pip, Rose, Roundel, Shamrock, Sign, Spear-thistle, → **SYMBOL**, Tau-cross, Thistle, Token, Totem(ic), Triskelion, Wattle, Wheel
**Embody, Embodied, Embodiment** Corporify, Epitome, Fuse, Impanation, Incarnation, Incorporate, Personify, Quintessence, Typify, Version
**Embolden** Encourage
**Embolism** Clot, Infarct
**Embosom(ed)** In gremio
**Emboss(ed)** Adorn, Chase, Cloqué, Engrave, Matelassé, Pounce, Raise, Repoussé, Toreutic

**Embrace(d)** Abrazo, Accolade, Amidst, Arm, Bear hug, Canoodle, Caress, Clasp, Clinch, Clip, Coll, Complect, Comprise, Cuddle, Embosom, Encircle, Enclasp, Enclose, Enfold, Enlacement, Envelop, Espouse, Fold, Grab, Grip, Halse, Haulst, Hause, Hesp, Hug, Imbrast, Inarm, Inclasp, Inclip, Include, Inlace, Kiss, Lasso, Neck, Overarch, Press, Snog, Snug(gle), Stemme, Twine, Welcome, Wrap

▷**Embraces, Embracing** *may indicate* a hidden word

**Embrocate, Embrocation** Anoint, Arnica, Liniment, Lotion

**Embroider(y)** Add, Appliqué, Arpillera, Arrasene, Assisi, Battalia-pie, Braid, Brede, Canvas-work, Colour, Couching, Crewellery, Crewel-work, Cross-stitch, Cutwork, Drawn threadwork, Embellish, Exaggerate, Eyelet, Fag(g)oting, Fancywork, Featherstitch, Filet, Framework, Gros point, Handiwork, Knotting, Lace(t), Laid work, Mola, Needlecraft, Needlepoint, Needlework, Open-work, Opus anglicanum, Orfray, Ornament, Orphrey, Orris, Petit point, Pinwork, Pulled threadwork, Purl, Queen-stitch, Sampler, Sew, Smocking, Spider-wheel, Stitch, Stitchery, Stumpwork, Tambour, Tent, Wrap, Zari

**Embroideress** Mimi

**Embroil** Confuse, Entangle, Involve, Trouble

**Embryo(nic), Embryologist** Anlage, Archenteron, Blastocyst, Blastospore, Blastula, Conceptus, Egg, Epicotyl, Fo(e)tus, Gastrula, Germ, Mesoblast, Morula, Nepionic, Neurula, Origin, Rudiment, Seed, Undeveloped, Wolff

**Emend** Adjust, Alter, Blue-pencil, Edit, Reform

**Emerald** Beryl, Gem, Green, Oriental, Smaragd, Uralian

**Emerge(ncy), Emerging** Anadyomene, Arise, Crash-landing, Craunch, Crise, Crisis, Crunch, Debouch, Eclose, Emanate, Enation, Erupt, Exigency, Flashpoint, Forced, Hard-shoulder, Hotline, Issue, Lash-up, Last-ditch, Loom, Need, Originate, Outcrop, Pinch, SOS, Spare, Spring, Stand-by, Stand-in, Strait, Surface

▷**Emerge from** *may indicate* an anagram or a hidden word

**Emeritus** Retired

**Emerson** Waldo

**Emetic** Apomorphine, Cacoon, Evacuant, Ipecac(uanha), Puke, Sanguinaria, Stavesacre, Tartar, Vomitory

**Emigrant, Emigration, Émigré** Chozrim, Colonist, Exile, Italiot, Jordim, Redemptioner, Settler, When-we, Yordim

**Emile** Zola

**Emily** Ellis

**Eminence, Eminent** Alp, Altitude, Cardinal, Celebrity, Distinguished, Eximious, Fame, Grand, Greatness, Grise, Height, Hill, Hywel, Illustrious, Inselberg, Knoll, Light, Lion, Lofty, Luminary, Noble, → **NOTABLE**, Note, Palatine, Prominence, Quality, Red hat, Renown, Repute, Stardom, Stature, Tor, Trochanter, → **VIP**, Wallah

**Emirate** Abu Dhabi, Dubai, Qatar, Sharjah

**Emissary** Agent, Envoy, Legate, Marco Polo

**Emission, Emit** Coronal, Discharge, Emanate, Extrusion, Field, Give, Issue, Radiate, Secrete, Spallation, Spew, Thermionic, Utter, Vent

**Emmer** Amelcorn, Wheat

**Emollient** Paregoric

**Emolument** Income, Perk, Remuneration, Salary, Stipend, Tip, Wages

**Emotion(s), Emotional** Affection, Anger, Anoesis, Atmosphere, Breast, Cathartic, Chord, Cut up, Ecstasy, Empathy, Excitable, Feeling, Flare up, Freak-out, Gushing, Gusty, Gut-wrenching, Hate, Heartstrings, Hippocampus, Histrionics, Hoo, Hysteria, Impassioned, Intense, Joy, Limbic, Maenad, Nostalgia, Nympholepsy, Overcome, Pang, Passion, Poignant, Reins, Rhapsodic, Roar, Sappy, Sensibility, Sensitive, Sentiment, Soulful, Spirit, Stormy, Susceptible, Teary, Theopathy, Torrid, Transport, Weepy, Wigged out

**Emotionless** Bland, Deadpan, Glassy

**Empathy, Empathise** Identifying, Rapport, Rapprochement, Relate, Sympathy

**Emperor** Agramant(e), Akbar, Akihito, Antoninus, Augustus, Aurelian, Babur, Bao Dai, Barbarossa, Bonaparte, Caesar, Caligula, Caracalla, Charlemagne, Claudius, Commodus, Concerto, Constantine, Diocletian, Domitian, Ferdinand, Flavian, Gaius, Galba, Genghis

Khan, Gratian, Great Mogul, Hadrian, Haile Selassie, Heraclius, Hirohito, HRE, Imp, Imperator, Inca, Jimmu, Justinian, Kaiser, Keasar, Kesar, King, Kubla(h) Khan, Manuel I Comnenus, Maximilian, Meiji, Menelik, Mikado, Ming, Mogul, Montezuma, Mpret, Napoleon, Negus, Nero, Nerva, Otho, Otto, Penguin, Peter the Great, Purple, Pu-yi, Rastafari, Rex, Romanov, Rosco, Ruler, Severus, Shah Jahan, Shang, Sovereign, Sultan, Tenno, Theodore, Theodosius, Tiberius, Titus, Trajan, Tsar, Valens, Valentinian, Valerian, Vespasian, Vitellius, Wenceslaus

**Emphasis(e), Emphasize, Emphatic(ally)** Accent, Birr, Bold, Dramatise, Ek se, Forcible, Foreground, Forzando, Forzato, Gesticulate, Hendiadys, Highlight, Insist, In spades, In style, Italic, Marcato, Marked, Point up, Positive, Resounding, Risoluto, Sforzando, Sforzato, Spotlight, → STRESS, Sublineate, Underline, Underscore, Vehement

**Empire** All-red, Assyria, Aztec, British, Byzantine, Celestial, Chain, Chinese, Domain, Empery, First, French, Georgia, Holy Roman, Incan, Indian, Kingdom, Latin, NY, Osmanli, Ottoman, Parthia, Persian, Principate, Realm, Reich, Roman, Russian, Second, Turkish, Western

**Empiricism** Positivism

**Emplacement** Battery, Platform

**Employ(ment), Employed** Appoint, Bestow, Business, Busy, Calling, Designated, Engage, Exercitation, Hire, Occupy, Pay, Place, Portfolio, Post, Practice, Pursuit, Retain, Service, Shiftwork, Task, Trade, Usage, Use, Using, Utilise, Vocation

**Employee(s)** Barista, Casual, Clock-watcher, Earner, Factotum, Full-timer, Hand, Help, Hireling, Intrapreneur, Minion, Munchkin, Networker, Part-timer, Payroll, Pennyboy, Personnel, Rainmaker, Salariat, Servant, Staff, Staffer, Valet, Walla(h), Worker, Workforce, Workpeople

**Employer** Baas, Boss, Governor, Guv, Malik, Master, Melik, Padrone, Taskmaster, User

▷**Employs** *may indicate* an anagram

**Emporium** Bazaar, Market, Megastore, Shop, Store

**Empower** Authorise, Enable, Endue, Entitle, License, Permit

**Empress** Eugenie, Josephine, Matilda, Messalina, Queen, Sultana, Tsarina, VIR

**Empty** Addle, Bare, Barren, Blank, Boss, Buzz, Claptrap, Clear, Dead man, Deflate, Deplete, Deserted, Devoid, Disembowel, Drain, Evacuate, Exhaust, Expel, Forsaken, Futile, Gousty, Gut, Hent, Hollow, Inane, Jejune, Lade, Lave, Meaningless, Null, Phrasy, Pump, Shallow, Space, Strip, Teem, Toom, Tum(e), Unfurnished, Uninhabited, Unlade, Unoccupied, Unpeople, Vacant, Vacate, Vacuous, Vain, Viduous, → VOID

▷**Empty** *may indicate* an 'o' in the word or an anagram

**Empty-headed** Vain

**Emulate** Ape, Copy, Envy, Equal, Imitate, Match

**Emulsion** Nuclear, Pseudosolution, Tempera

**Enable** Authorise, Capacitate, Empower, Facilitate, Permit, Potentiate, Qualify, Sanction

**Enact** Adopt, Effect, Ordain, Personate, Portray

**Enamel(led), Enamel work** Aumail, Champlevé, Cloisonné, Della-robbia, Dentine, Fabergé, Ganoin(e), Lacquer, Mottled, Nail, Polish, Porcelain, Schwarzlot, Shippo, Smalto, Stoved, Vitreous

**Encampment** Bivouac, Castrametation, Douar, Dowar, Duar, Laager, Laer, Settlement

**Encase(d), Encasement** Box, Crate, Emboîtement, Encapsulate, Enclose, Obtect, Sheathe

**Enchant(ing), Enchanted, Enchantment** Bewitch, Captivate, Charm, Delight, Fascinate, Gramary(e), Heaven, Incantation, Magic, Necromancy, Orphean, Rapt, Ravish, Sirenize, Sorcery, Spellbind, Thrill

**Enchanter, Enchantress** Archimage, Archimago, Armida, Circe, Comus, Faerie, Fairy, Houri, Lorelei, Magician, Medea, Mermaid, Prospero, Reim-kennar, Sorcerer, Vivien, Witch

**Encircle(d), Encirclement** Belt, Besiege, Enclose, Encompass, Enlace, Entrold, Gird, Hoop (la), Inorb, Introld, Orbit, Pale, Ring, Siege, Stemme, → SURROUND, Wreathe

**Enclave** Andorra, Cabinda, Ceuta, → ENCLOSURE, Ghetto, Melilla, Pocket, San Marino, Vatican

**Enclose(d), Enclosing, Enclosure** Aviary, Bawn, Beset, Boma, Bower, Box, Bullring, Cage, Carol, Carrel, Case, Circumscribe, Cockpit, Common, Compound, Coop, Cordon,

Corral, Court, Cubicle, Dock, Embale, Embowel, Embower, Embrace, Emure, Encage, Enceinte, Enchase, Encircle, Enclave, Engirt, Enhearse, Enlock, Enshrine, Exclave, Fence, Fold, Forecourt, Garth, Gird, Haggard, Haining, Haw, Hem, Hen-court, Henge, Hope, Immure, Impound, In, Incapsulate, Inchase, Include, Infibulate, Inhoop, Inlock, Insert, Interclude, Interlude, In with, Lairage, Obvolute, Paddock, Pale, Parrock, Peel, Pele, Pen(t), Petavius, Pightle, Pin, Pinfold, Pit, Playpen, Plenum, Pocket, Radome, Rail, Rath, Recluse, Ree(d), Ring, Run, Saddling, Saleyard, Seal, Sekos, Sept, Seraglio, Serail, Several, Sheepcote, Sin bin, Steeld, Stell, Stive, Stockade, Sty, → SURROUND, Tatt(ersall)s, Terrarium, Tine, Unsaddling, Vibarium, Ward, Winner's, Wrap, Yard, Zareba

**Encode** Cipher, Scramble

**Encomium** Eulogy, Praise, Sanction, Tribute

**Encompass** Bathe, Begird, Beset, Cover, Environ, Include, Span, Surround

**Encore** Again, Agen, Ancora, Bis, Ditto, Do, Iterum, Leitmotiv, Recall, Repeat, Reprise

**Encounter** Battle, Brush, Close, Combat, Contend, Cope, Dogfight, Experience, Face, Hit, Incur, Intersect, Interview, → MEET, One-one, Rencontre, Ruffle, Skirmish, Tilt

**Encourage(ment), Encouraging** Abet, Acco(u)rage, Alley-oop, Animate, Attaboy, Attagirl, Barrack, Bolster, Boost, Brighten, Buck, Cheer, Chivy, Clap, Coax, Cohortative, Come-on, Comfort, Commend, Countenance, Dangle, Egg, Elate, Embolden, Empatron, Exhort, Fillip, Fire, Fortify, Foster, Fuel, Gee, Hearten, Heigh, Help, Heuristic, Hope, Hortatory, Incite, Induce, Inspire, Inspirit, Invite, Lift, Motivate, Nourish, Nudge, Nurture, Ole, Pat, Patronise, Pep talk, Proceleusmatic, Prod, Promote, Protreptic, Push, Reassure, Root, Seed, Spur, Steel, Stimulate, Stoke, Support, Sustain, Tally-ho, Train, Up(s)-a-daisy, Upcheer, Uplift, Urge, Wean, Yay, Yo, Yoicks

**Encroach(ment)** Eat out, Impinge, Infringe, Inroad, Intrude, Invade, Overlap, Overstep, Poach, Purpresture, Trample, Trespass, Usurp

**Encrusted** Barnacled

**Encrypt(ion)** Coding, Public key

**Encumber, Encumbrance** Accloy, Ball and chain, Burden, Charge, Clog, Dead weight, Deadwood, Debt, Dependent, Embarrass, → HANDICAP, Impede, Liability, Lien, Load, Obstruct, Onus, Saddle

**Encyclopaedia, Encyclopaedic** Compendium, Comprehensive, Diderot, Extensive, Universal, Vast

**End(ing)** Abolish, Abort, Abrogate, Abut, Aim, Ambition, Amen, Anus, Arse, Big, Bitter, Bourn(e), Business, Butt, Cease, Cessation, Cesser, Climax, Close, Closure, Cloture, Coda, Conclude, Consequence, Crust, Culminate, Curtain, Curtains, Cut off, Dead, Death, Decease, Deep, Demise, Denouement, Design, Desinence, Desistance, Destination, Destroy, Determine, Dissolve, Domino, Effect, Envoi, Envoy, Epilogue, Exigent, Expire, Explicit, Extremity, Fade, Fatal, Fattrels, Feminine, Ferrule, Fin, Final(e), Fine, Finis, → FINISH, Finite, Full-time, Gable, Game, Grave, Halt, Heel, Ice, Ish, Izzard, Izzet, Kill, Knell, Kybosh, Lapse, Last, Let up, Limit, Little, Log off, Loose, Masculine, Mill, Nape, Nirvana, No side, Ort, Out, Outrance, Outro, Period, Peter, Pine, Point, Pole, Purpose, Quench, Receiving, Remnant, Rescind, Result, Roach, Round off, Runback, Scotch, Scrag, Settle, Shallow, Shank, Slaughter, Sopite, Split, Sticky, Stifle, Stub, Supernaculum, Surcease, Swansong, Tag, Tail, Tailpiece, Telesis, Telic, Telos, Term, Terminal, Terminate, Terminus, Thrum, Tight, Tip, Toe, Top, Ultimate, Up, Upshot, Utterance, West, Z

**Endanger** Hazard, Imperil, Periclitate, Risk, Threaten

**Endear(ing), Endearment** Adorable, Affection, Alannah, Asthore, Bach, Caress, Cariad, Chuck, Cute, Darling, Dear, Ducks, Ducky, Enamour, Hinny, Honey(-bunch), Honey-chile, Ingratiate, Jarta, Lovey, Luv, Machree, Mavourneen, Peat, Pet, Pigsnie, Pigsn(e)y, Sweetie, Sweet nothings

**Endeavour** Aim, Attempt, Effort, Enterprise, Essay, Morse, Strain, Strive, Struggle, Try, Venture

**Endemic** Local, Prevalent

**Endive** Escarole

**Endless** Ad infinitum, Aeonian, Continuous, Cornucopia, Ecaudate, Eternal, Eterne, Infinite, Interminable, Perpetual, Undated

▷**Endlessly** *may indicate* a last letter missing
**End of the world** Doomsday, Ragnarok
**Endorse(ment)** Adopt, Aegism, Affirm, Allonge, Approve, Assurance, Back, Certify, Confirmation, Docket, Initial, Okay, Oke, Ratify, Rubber stamp, Sanction, Second, Sign, Signature, Subscript, →**SUPPORT**, Underwrite, Visa
**Endow(ment)** Assign, Bequeath, Bestow, Bless, Cha(u)ntry, Dot, Dotation, Enrich, Foundation, Gift, Leave, Patrimony, Scholarship, State, Vest, Wakf, Waqf
**Endurance, Endure(d), Enduring** Abide, Abought, Aby(e), Ageless, Age-long, Bear, Bide, Brook, Dree, Dure, Face, Fortitude, Granite, Have, Hold, →**LAST**, Livelong, Long-term, Lump, Marathon, Patience, Perseverance, Persist, Pluck, Ride, Stamina, Stand, Stay, Stomach, Stout, Substantial, Suffer, Support, Sustain, Swallow, Tether, Thole, Timeless, Tolerance, Undergo, Wear, Weather
**Endymion** Bluebell
**Enema** Barium, Catharsis, Clyster, Purge
**Enemy** Adversary, Antagonist, Axis, Boer, Devil, Fifth column, Foe(n), Fone, Opponent, Public, Time
**Energetic, Energise, Energy** Active, Alternative, Amp, Animation, Arduous, Atomic, Barnstorming, Battery, Binding, Bond, Brisk, Calories, Cathexis, Chakra, Chi, Dark, Dash, Demon, Doer, Drive, Dynamic, Dynamo, E, Eager beaver, Enthalpy, Entropy, EV, Feng shui, Fermi, Fireball, Firebrand, Firecracker, Force, Fossil, Free, Fructan, Fuel, Fusion, Geothermal, Ginger, Gism, Go, Go ahead, Goer, Graviton, Hartree, H.D.R., Hearty, Horme, Hustle, Hyper, Input, Instress, Internal, Invigorate, Isotonic, →**JET**, Jism, Jissom, Joie de vivre, Joule, Kerma, Kinetic, Kundalini, Lattice, Libido, Life, Live wire, Lossy, Luminous, Magnon, Moxie, Nuclear, Octane, Oomph, Orgone, Pep, Phonon, Pithy, Pizzazz, Potency, Potential, →**POWER**, Powerhouse, Prana, QI, Quantum, Quasar, Rad, Radiant, Radiatory, Refresh, Renewable, Roton, Rydberg, S(h)akti, Sappy, Second-wind, Solar, Stamina, Steam, Sthenic, Stingo, Thermodynamics, Tidal, Trans-uranic, Vehement, Verve, Vibrancy, Vibrational, Vigour, Vim, Vital, Vivo, Wave, Whammo, Whirlwind, Wind(-farm), Zappy, Zealous, Zero point, Zestful, Zing, Zip
**Enervate** Exhaust
**Enfold** Clasp, Embrace, Envelop, Hug, Sheathe, Stemme, Swaddle, Swathe, Wrap
**Enforce(ment), Enforcer** Administer, Coerce, Control, Exact, Implement, Impose, Vigilante
**Eng** Agma
**Engage(d), Engagement, Engaging** Absorb, Accept, Adorable, Appointment, At, Attach, Battle, Bespoken, Betrothal, Bind, Book, Busy, Charter, Contract, Courtship, Date, Embark, Employ, Engross, Enlist, Enmesh, Ensure, Enter, Fascinate, Fiance(e), Fight, Gear, Genial, Gig, Grappple, Hire, Hold, In gear, Interest, Interlock, Involve, Lock, Mesh, Met, Occupy, Partake, Pledge, Promise, Prosecute, Rapt, Reserve, Residency, Rope in, Sapid, Skirmish, Sponsal, Sponsion, Spousal, Sprocket, Trip, Wage, Winsome
▷**Engagement** *may indicate* a battle
**Engender** Beget, Breed, Cause, Occasion, Produce, Spawn
**Engine, Engine part** Air, Analytical, Appliance, Athodyd, Atmospheric, Banker, Banking, Beam, Bogie, Booster, Bricole, Bypass, Carburettor, Catapult, Compound, Crankshaft, Dashpot, Diesel, Dividing, Donkey, Draught, Dynamo, Fan-jet, Fire, Four-cycle, Four-stroke, Gas, Gin, Goods, Green Goddess, Heat, Hemi, Humdinger, ICE, Internal combustion, Ion, Iron horse, Ivor, Jet, Lean-burn, Light, Little-end, Loco(motive), Machine, Mangonel, Manifold, Mogul, →**MOTOR**, Nacelle, Oil, Onager, Orbital, Otto, Outboard, Overhead valve, Petard, Petrary, Petrol, Petter, Pilot, Piston, Plasma, Podded, Pony, Puffer, Pug, Pulp, Pulsejet, Push-pull, Put-put, Radial, Ramjet, Reaction, Reciprocating, Retrorocket, Rocket, Rose, Rotary, RR, Scorpion, Scramjet, Search, Side-valve, Sleeve valve, Stationary, Steam, Stirling, Sustainer, Tank, Terebra, Testudo, Thermometer, Thruster, Top-end, Traction, Trompe, Turbine, Turbofan, Turbojet, Turboprop, Turbo-ram-jet, Two-handed, Two-stroke, V, Vernier, V-type, Wankel, Warwolf, Water, Wildcat, Winch, Winding
**Engineer(ing), Engineer(s)** Aeronautical, AEU, Arrange, Badge, BE, CE, Chartered, Civil, Concurrent, Contrive, Control, Electrical, Genetic, Greaser, Ground, Human, Interactive,

Knowledge, Liability, Manhattan District, Manoeuvre, Marine, Mastermind, Mechanical, Mechatronics, Military, Mime, Operator, Organise, Paper, Planner, Process, RE, Repairman, Reverse, Rig, Sales, Sanitary, Sapper, Scheme, Social, Software, Sound, Stage, Structural, Systems, Tissue, Traffic, Usability, Wangle

---

**ENGINEERS**

***4 letters:***
Ader
Arup
Benz
Otto
Watt

***5 letters:***
Baird
Royce
Tesla

***6 letters:***
Austin
Brunel
Diesel
Eiffel
Fokker
Henley
Karman
McAdam
Savery
Wankel

***7 letters:***
Brinell
Heinkel
Junkers
Marconi
Parsons
Porsche
Rankine
Rogallo
Siemens
Smeaton
Strauss
Telford
Whittle

***8 letters:***
Bessemer
Brindley
Ferranti
Kennelly
Samarski
Sikorsky
Sinclair
Stirling
Von Braun

***9 letters:***
Armstrong
Cockerell
De Lessops
Whitworth

***10 letters:***
Stephenson
Trevithick

***12 letters:***
Barnes Wallis

---

▷**Engineer** *may indicate* an anagram

**England** Albany, Albion, Blighty, Demi-paradise, Eden, John Bull, Merrie, Merry, Middle, The Old Dart

**English(man)** Ang(le), Anglican, Anglice, Anglo-Saxon, Baboo, Babu, Basic, Brit, Bro talk, Canajan, Choom, E, Early, Ebonics, Eng, Estuary, Gringo, Hawaiian, Hiberno, Hong Kong, Indian, Irish, Jackeroo, John Bull, King's, Kipper, Limey, Middle, Mister, Modern, Morningside, Newspeak, New Zealand, Nigerian, Norman, Officialese, Old, Oxford, Philippine, Pidgin, Plain, Pock-pudding, Pom(my), Pommie, Pongo, Queen's, Qui-hi, Qui-hye, Rock, Rooinek, Rosbif, Sassenach, Saxon, Scotic, Scottish, Seaspeak, Shopkeeper, Side, Singapore, Singlish, South African, South Asian, Southron, Southroun, Spanglish, Standard, Strine, Wardour Street, Whingeing Pom, Woodbine, World, Yanqui, Yinglish

**Engorge** Devour, Glut, Swallow

**Engraft** Inset

**Engrave(r), Engraving** Aquatint, Blake, Bury, Carve, Cerography, Cerotype, Chalcography, Character, Chase, Cut, Die-sinker, Dry-point, Durer, Enchase, Eng, Etch, Glyptic, Glyptograph, Heliogravure, Hogarth, Impress, Inchase, Inciser, Inscribe, Insculp, Intagliate, Inter, Lapidary, Line, Lithograph, Mezzotint, Niello, Photoglyphic, Photogravure, Plate, Scalp, Scrimshander, Scrimshandy, Scrimshaw, Steel, Stillet, Stipple, Stylet, Stylography, Superscribe, Toreutics, Turn, Wood, Xylographer

**Engross(ed)** Absorb, Engage, Enwrap, Immerse, Inwrap, Monopolise, → OCCUPY, Preoccupy, Prepossess, Rapt, Rivet, Sink, Thrill, Transfix, Writ large

**Engulf** Overwhelm, Swamp, Whelm

**Enhance(r)** Add, Augment, Better, Catalyst, Elevate, Embellish, Exalt, Heighten, Improve, Intensify, Supplement

**Enigma(tic)** Bewildering, Charade, Conundrum, Cryptic, Dilemma, Gioconda, Gnomic, Mystery, Oracle, Poser, Problem, → PUZZLE, Quandary, Question, Rebus, Recondite, Riddle, Secret, Sphinxlike, Teaser

**Enjoin** Command, Direct, Impose, Prohibit, Require

**Enjoy(able), Enjoyment** Apolaustic, Appetite, Appreciate, Ball, Brook, Delectation, Delight, Fruition, Glee, Groove, Gusto, Have, High jinks, Lap up, Lekker, Like, Own, Palate, Pleasance, Pleasing, Possess, Relish, Ripping, Sair, Savour, Stonking, Taste, Wallow

**Enlarge(ment), Enlarger** Accrue, Acromegaly, Add, Aneurism, Aneurysm, Augment, Blow-up, Bouton, Diagraph, Dilate, Exostosis, Expand, Expatiate, Explain, Extend, Hypertrophy, Increase, Jumboise, → MAGNIFY, Pan, Piece, Ream, Rebore, Sensationalize, Spavin, Stretch, Swell, Telescope, Tumefy, Upbuild, Varicosity, Zoom

**Enlighten(ed), Enlightenment** Aha, Aufklarung, Awareness, Bodhisattva, Dewali, Disabuse, Divali, Edify, Educate, Explain, Haskalah, Illumine, Insight, Instruct, Liberal, Luce, Nirvana, Rebirth, Relume, Revelation, Satori, Verlig(te)

**Enlist(ment)** Attest, Ban, Conscript, Draft, Engage, Enrol, Induct, Join, Levy, Muster, Prest, Recruit, Rope in, Roster, Sign on, Sign up, Volunteer

**Enliven(ed)** Animate, Arouse, Brighten, Cheer, Comfort, Exhilarate, Ginger, Invigorate, Jazz, Juice, Merry, Pep, Refresh, Warm

**Enmity** Animosity, Aversion, Bad blood, Feud, Hatred, Malice, Nee(d)le, Rancour, Spite

**Ennoble(ment)** Dub, Elevate, Ermine, Exalt, Honour, Raise

**Ennui** Boredom, Tedium

**Enormous** Colossal, Exorbitant, Gargantuan, Giant, Gigantic, Googol, Gross, Hellacious, Huge, Humongous, Humungous, → IMMENSE, Jumbo, Mammoth, Mega, Plonking, Princely, Untold, Vast, Walloper, Walloping

**Enough** Adequate, → AMPLE, Anow, Appreciable, Basta, Belay, Do(eth), Enow, Fill, Geyan, Nuff, Pax, Plenty, Qs, Sate, Satis, Sese, Sessa, Suffice, Sufficient, Via, When

**Enounce** Affirm, Declare, State

**Enquire, Enquiring, Enquiry** Ask, Case, Check, Curious, Directory, Eh, Examine, FAQ, Inquest, Inquire, Investigate, Organon, Probe, Public, Request, Research, Scan, Seek, Steward's, Trial

**Enrage(d)** Bemad, Emboss, Enfelon, Imboss, → INCENSE, Inflame, Infuriate, Irate, Livid, Madden, Wild

**Enrapture(d)** Enchant, Eprise, Ravish, Sent, Spellbound, Transport

**Enrich** Adorn, Endow, Enhance, Fortify, Fructify, Oxygenate

**Enrol(ment)** Attest, Conscribe, Conscript, Empanel, Enlist, Enter, Incept, → JOIN, List, Matriculate, Muster, Recruit, Register

**Ensconce(d)** Establish, Niche, Settle, Shelter, Snug

**Ensemble** Band, Gamelan, Octet(te), Orchestra, Outfit, Ripieno, Set, Tout, Whole

**Enshrine** Cherish, Sanctify

**Ensign** Ancient, Badge, Banner, Duster, Ens, → FLAG, Gonfalon, Officer, Pennon, Pistol, Red, White

**Enslave(ment)** Addiction, Bondage, Captivate, Chain, Enthral, Thrall, Yoke

**Ensnare** Illaqueate, Net, → TRAP

**Ensue, Ensuing** Et sequens, Follow, Result, Succeed, Supervene, Transpire

**Ensure** Check, Guarantee

**Entablature** Trabeation

**Entail** Fee-tail, Involve, Necessitate, Require

**Entangle(ment)** Amour, Ball, Cot, Elf, Embrangle, Embroil, Encumber, Ensnarl, Entrail, Fankle, Hank, Implicate, → KNOT, Liaison, Mat, Ravel, Retiarius, Taigle, Trammel

**Entente** Triple

**Enter, Entry** Admit, Board, Broach, Come, Enrol, Field, Infiltrate, Ingo, Inscribe, Insert, Intromit, Invade, Item, Key in, Lodge, Log, Penetrate, Pierce, Post, Record, Run, Slate, Submit, Table, Wild card

**Enterprise, Enterprising** Adventure, Ambition, Aunter, Cash cow, Dash, Emprise, Forlorn hope, Free, Go ahead, Goey, Go-getter, Gumption, Indie, Industry, Initiative, Minefield, Operation, Plan, Private, Project, Public, Push, Spirit, Starship, Stunt, Up and coming, Venture

**Entertain(er), Entertaining, Entertainment** Accourt, Acrobat, Admit, Afterpiece, All-dayer, All-nighter, Amphitryon, Amuse, Apres ski, Balladeer, Ballet, Barnum, Beguile, Belly dancer, Boff, Bread and circuses, Bright lights, Burlesque, Busk, Cabaret, Carnival, Cater, Charade, Cheer, Cher, Chout, Circus, Comedian, Comic, Concert (party), Conjure, Consider, Cottabus, Crack, Craic, Cuddy, Diseur, Diseuse, Distract, Divert, Divertissement, ENSA, Envisage, Extravaganza, Fairground, Fete (champetre), Fleshpots, Floorshow, Foy,

Friendly lead, Fun, Funambulator, Funfair, Gaff, Gala, Gas, Gaudy, Geisha, Gig, Harbour, Harlequin, Have, Hospitality, Host(ess), Hotspot, Houdini, Impresario, Impressionist, In car, Infotainment, Interest, Interlude, Intermezzo, Jester, Juggler, Karaoke, Kidult, Kursaal, Lap-dancer, Lauder, Leg-show, Levee, Liberace, Light, Masque, Melodrama, Mind candy, Minstrel, Movieoke, Musical, Music hall, Nightlife, Niterie, Olio, Opera, Pageant, Palladium, Panto, Pap, Party, Peepshow, Performer, Piece, Pierrot, Play, Pop singer, Puppet show, Raree-show, Reception, Recreation, Redcoat, Regale, Review, Revue, Rice, Ridotto, Rinky-dink, Roadshow, Rodeo, Roman holiday, Rush, Serenade, Showbiz, Showgirl, Showman, Sideshow, Simulcast, Singer, Sitcom, Slapstick, Snake-charmer, Soirée, Son et lumière, Stand-up, Street theatre, Striptease, Table, Tamasha, Tattoo, Treat, Tumbler, Tummler, Variety, Vaudeville, Ventriloquist, Wattle, Wine and dine

**Enthral(l)** Agog, Bewitch, Bond (servant), Charm, Enchant, Enslave, Grip, Rivet, Send, Spellbind, Transport

**Enthuse, Enthusiasm, Enthusiast(ic)** Acclamatory, Addict, Aficionado, Amateur, Ardent, Ardour, Avid, Boy, Buff, Bug, Buzz, Cat, Cheerleader, Crazy, Crusader, Delirium, Demon, Devotee, Eager, Ebullience, Ecstatic, Effusive, Empresse, Energy, Estro, Excited, Extremist, Exuberant, Faddist, Fanatic, Fancier, Fandom, Fashionista, Fervid, Fiend, Fire, Flame, Freak, Furor(e), Geek, Get-up-and-go, Glowing, Gung-ho, Gusto, Hacker, Hearty, Hype, Infomania, Into, Keen, Live wire, Lyrical, Mad, Mane, Mania, Motivated, Muso, Nethead, Nut, Nympholept, Oomph, Outpour, Overboard, Passion, Perfervid, Petrolhead, Preoccupation, Rah-rah, Raring, Rave, Relish, Rhapsodise, Schwärmerei, Sold, Spirit, Teeny-bopper, Thing, Turfite, Verve, Vim, Warmth, Whacko, Whole-hearted, Wonk, Young gun, Zealot, Zest, Zing

**Entice(ment), Enticing** Allure, Angle, Attract, Bait, Cajole, Carrot, Dangle, Decoy, Draw, Inveigle, Lure, Persuade, Seductive, → TEMPT, Tole, Toll, Trap, Trepan

**Entire(ly), Entirety** Absolute, All, Bag and baggage, Clean, Complete, Full Monty, Genuine, Holistic, Inly, Intact, Integral, In toto, Jingbang, Livelong, Lot, Purely, Root and branch, Systemic, Thorough, Total, Tout, Undivided, → WHOLE

**Entitle(ment)** Birthright, Claim, Credentials, Designate, Empower, Enable, Folk-right, Legitim, Name, Peerage, Quota, Right, Surname

**Entity** Being, Body, Existence, Holon, Monad, Tao, Tensor, Thing, Transfinite, Virino

**Entomb** Inter

**Entomologist** Fabré

**Entourage** Cortège, Retinue

**Entrail(s)** Bowels, Chawdron, Giblets, Gralloch, Guts, Ha(r)slet, Humbles, Innards, Lights, Numbles, Offal, Quarry, Tripe, Umbles, Viscera

**Entrance(d), Entrant, Entry** Access, Adit, Admission, Airlock, Anteroom, Arch, Arrival, Atrium, Attract, Avernus, Bewitch, Cat flap, Charm, Closehead, Contestant, Credit, Door, Doorstop, Double, Dromos, Enamour, Eye, Fascinate, Foyer, Frawbridge, Gate(way), Ghat, Hypnotise, Illegal, In-door, Infare, Inflow, Influx, Ingate, Ingress, Inlet, Input, Introitus, Item, Jawhole, Jaws, Jib-door, Lobby, Manhole, Mesmerise, Mineshaft, Mouth, Narthex, Pend, Porch, Porogamy, Portal, Porte-cochère, Portico, Postern, Propylaeum, Propylon, Ravish, Reception, Record, Regest, Registration, Shaft, Single, Spellbound, Starter, Stem, Stoa, Stoma, Stulm, Throat, Torii, Vestibule

**Entrap** Decoy

**Entreat(y)** Appeal, Ask, Beg, Beseech, Flagitate, Impetrate, → IMPLORE, Orison, Petition, Plead, Pray, Precatory, Prevail, Prig, Rogation, Solicit, Sue, Supplicate, Urge

**Entrée** Access, Dish, Entry, Ingate

**Entrench(ment)** Coupure, Encroach, Fortify, Trespass

**Entrepreneur** Branson, Businessman, E-tailer, Executor, Go-getter, Impresario, Salt, Sugar, Wheeler-dealer, Yettie

**Entropy** S

**Entrust** Aret(t), Charge, Commit, Confide, Consign, Delegate, Give

▸**Entry** *see* ENTRANCE(D)

**Entwine** Complect, Impleach, Intervolve, Lace, Twist, Weave

**E-number** Additive

**Enumerate, Enumeration** Catalogue, Count, Detail, Fansi, List, Tell

**Enunciate, Enunciation** Articulate, Declare, Deliver, Diction, Elocution, Proclaim
**Envelop(e), Enveloping** Ambient, Arachnoid, Bangtail, Banker's, Buff, Chorion, Cocoon, Corolla, Corona, Cover(ing), Cuma, Enclose, Enshroud, Entire, First day cover, Flight, Floral, Flown cover, Invest, Involucre, Jiffy(bag)®, Muffle, Mulready, Nuclear, Pay, Perianth, Round, Sachet, Sae, Serosa, Shroud, Skin, Smother, Surround, Swathe, Window, Wrap
**Environment(s), Environmental(ist)** ACRE, Ambience, Cyberspace, Druid, Ecofreak, Ecology, Econut, Eco-warrior, Element, Entourage, Ergonomics, F of E, Green(ie), Greenpeace, Habitat, Hotbed, Hothouse, Milieu, Realo, SEPA, Setting, Sphere, Surroundings, Umwelt, Vicinity
**Envisage** Conceive, Contemplate, Imagine, Intend, Suppose
**Envoi** Farewell, RIP
**Envoy** Agent, Diplomat, Elchee, El(t)chi, Emissary, Hermes, Legate, Missioner, Plenipo(tentiary)
**Envy, Enviable, Envious** Begrudge, Covet, Deadly sin, Jaundiced, Jealousy, Penis, Plum, Resentful
**Enzyme** Biological, Induced

---

**ENZYMES**

*3 letters:*
ACE
PSA

*5 letters:*
DNase
ELISA
Lyase
Lysin
Renin
RNase

*6 letters:*
Cytase
DNAase
Kinase
Ligase
Lipase
Mutase
Papain
Pepsin
Rennin
Zymase

*7 letters:*
Amylase
Apyrase
Caspase
Cyclase
Emulsin
Enolase
Erepsin
Guanase
Hydrase
Inulase
Lactase
Maltase
Oxidase
Pectase
Pepsine
Plasmin
Ptyalin
Sirtuin
Sucrase
Trypsin
Uricase

*8 letters:*
Aldolase
Allozyme
Arginase
Bromelin
Catalase
Diastase
Elastase
Esterase
Lysozyme
Nuclease
Permease
Protease
Steapsin
Synthase
Thrombin

*9 letters:*
Amylopsin
Autolysin
Bromelain
Cathepsin
Cellulase
Coagulase
Deaminase
DNAligase
Hydrolase
Inducible
Invertase
Isomerase
Oxygenase
Peptidase
Reductase
Sulfatase
Synaptase
Trehalase
Urokinase

*10 letters:*
Allosteric
Hexokinase
Kallikrein
Luciferase
Peroxidase
Peroxisome
Polymerase
Proteinase
Rancreatin
Saccharase
Subtilisin
Sulphatase
Telomerase
Tyrosinase

*11 letters:*
Calcineurin
Carboxylase
Chymopapain
Collagenase
Dipeptidase
Exonuclease
Glucosidase
Histaminase
Lecithinase
Nitrogenase
Phosphatase
Restriction
Transferase
Transposase

*12 letters:*
Asparaginase
Carbohydrase
Chymotrypsin
Constitutive
Enterokinase
Fibrinolysin
Flavoprotein
Ribonuclease
Transaminase

*13 letters:*
Decarboxylase
Dehydrogenase
DNApolymerase
Galactosidase
Hyaluronidase
Neuraminidase
Oxdoreductase
Penicillinase
Phosphorylase
Streptokinase
Thrombokinase
Topoisomerase
Transcriptase

*14 letters:*
Cholinesterase
Creatine kinase
Pectinesterase
Streptodornase
Thromboplastin

*17 letters:*
Carbonic anhydrase

---

**Eon** Arch(a)ean, Cenozoic, Epoch, Mesozoic, Phanerozoic, Proterozoic
**Epaminondas** Theban
**Epaulette** Swab
**Ephemera(l)** Brief, Day, Drake, Fungous, Impermanent, Mayfly, Momentary, Passing, Transient, Transitory, Trappings
**Epic** Aeneid, Ben Hur, Beowulf, Blockbuster, Calliope, Colossal, Colubriad, Dunciad, Edda, Epopee, Epyllion, Eyeliad, Gilgamesh, Heroic, Homeric, Iliad, Kalevala, Lusiad(s), Mahabharata, Mock-heroic, Nibelungenlied, Odyssey, Ramayana, Rhapsody, Saga
**Epicene** Hermaphrodite
**Epicure(an)** Apicius, Apolaustic, Connoisseur, Friand(e), Gastronome, Gastrosopher, Glutton, → **GOURMAND**, Gourmet, Hedonist, Sensuous, Sybarite
**Epidemic** Asian flu, Enzootic, Outbreak, Pandemic, Pestilence, Plague, Prevalent, Rampant, Rash, Rife
**Epigram** Adage, Apophthegm, Gnomic, Mot, Proverb
**Epigraph** Citation, Inscription, RIP
**Epilepsy, Epileptic** Clonic, Eclampsia, Falling evil, Falling sickness, Fit, Grand mal, Petit mal, Turn
**Epilogue** Appendix, Coda, End, Postlude, Postscript
**Epiphany** Insight, Twelfthtide
**Epiphenomenon** ESP
**Epiphyte** Air-plant
**Episcopalian** PE, Prelatic
**Episode(s), Episodic** Bipolar, Chapter, Incident, Instalment, Microsleep, Page, Picaresque, Scene, Serial
**Epistle(s)** Catholic, Dispatch, General, Lesson, Letter, Missive, Pastoral, Titus
**Epitaph** Ci-git, Hic jacet, Inscription, RIP
**Epithelium** Pavement
**Epithet** Adj(ective), Antonomasia, Apathaton, Byword, Curse, Expletive, Panomphaean, → **TERM**, Title
**Epitome, Epitomise** Abridge, Abstract, Avowal, Byword, Digest, Embody, Essence, Exemplar, Image, Incarnation, Model, Paragon, Summary, Typify
**Epoch** Age, Eocene, Era, Holocene, Magnetic, Miocene, Neogene, Oligocene, Palaeocene, Palaeolithic, Perigordian, Period, Pleistocene, Pl(e)iocene
**Epsom salts** Kieserite
**Equable, Equably** Calm, Just, Pari passu, Placid, Smooth, Tranquil
**Equal(ly), Equaliser, Equality, Equal quantities** A(n)a, Across the board, Alike, All square, As, Balanced, Commensurate, Compeer, Co-partner, Egal(ity), Emulate, Equinox, Equiparate, Equity, Even, Even-steven, Ex aequo, Fair, Feer, Fe(a)re, Fiere, Fifty-fifty, For, Graphic, Identical, Identity, Is, Iso-, Isocracy, Isonomy, Level, Level-pegging, Maik, Make, Match, Mate, Owelty, Par, Parage, Parallel, Parametric, Pari passu, Parity, → **PEER**, Peregal, Pheer(e), Redress, Rise, Rival, → **SO**, Square, Upsides, Wyoming, Ylike
**Equanimity** Aplomb, Balance, Poise, Serenity
**Equate, Equation(s)** Arrhenius, Balance, Chemical, Cubic, Defective, Differential, Diophantine, Dirac, Exponential, Formula, Gas, Identity, Linear, Logistic, Maxwell, Nernst, Parametric, Personal, Polar, Quadratic, Reduce, Relate, Rhizic, Schrödinger, Simultaneous, Van der Waals', Wave
**Equator(ial)** Celestial, Galactic, Line, Magnetic, Thermal, Tropical
**Equerry** Courtier, Officer, Page
**Equestrian** Dressage, Eventer, Hickstead, Turfite
**Equidistant** Midway
**Equilibrium** Balance, Composure, Homeostasis, Instable, Isostasy, Poise, Punctuated, Stable, Stasis, Steady state, Tautomerism, Thermodynamic
**Equine** Hinny
**Equinox** Autumnal, Vernal
**Equip(ment), Equipage, Equipped** Accoutrement, Accustrement, Adorn, Aguise, Aguize, Apparatus, Apparel, Appliance, Arm, Armament, Array, Attire, Blender, Camcorder,

Carriage, Chequerboard, Clobber, Clothe, Codec, Compass, Deadstock, Deck, Dight, Expertise, Fitment, Fortify, → FURNISH, Gear, Gere, Get-up, Graith, Habilitate, Hamper, Hand-me-up, Hardware, Headset, Hi-tech, Impedimenta, Implement, Incubator, iPod®, Kit, Lie-detector, Log-reel, Material, Matériel, Mechanise, Monitor, Muniments, Outfit, Paraphernalia, Pile-driver, Pipette, Plant, Projector, Receiver, Refit, Retinue, Rig, Scrambler, Sonar, Sonobuoy, Spikes, Stapler, Stereo, Stock, Stuff, Tabulator, Tack(le), Tenderiser, Tool, Trampet(te), Trampoline, Transformer, Trivet, Turn-out, Vision-mixer, Wakeboard, Webcam, Well-appointed, Y-level

**Equitable** Even-handed, Fair, Just

**Equity** Actors, Egalitarian, Equality, Justice, Law, Negative, Owner's, Union

**Equivalence, Equivalent** Akin, Amounting to, Correspondent, Counterpart, Dose, Equal, Equipollent, Ewe, Formal, In-kind, Parity, Same, Tantamount, Version

**Equivocal** Ambiguous, Dubious, Evasive, Fishy, Oracular, Vague

**Equivocate** Flannel, Lie, Palter, Prevaricate, Quibble, Tergiversate, Waffle, Weasel

**Er** Um

**Era** Age, Archaean, C(a)enozoic, Christian, Common, Cretaceous, Cryptozoic, Decade, Dynasty, Ediocaron, Eozoic, Epoch, Hadean, Hegira, Hej(i)ra, Hijra, Jurassic, Lias, Mesozoic, Oligocene, Palaeozoic, Period, Precambrian, Proterozoic, Republican, Torridonian, Vulgar

**Eradicate, Erase** Abolish, Delete, Demolish, Destroy, Dislimn, Efface, Expunge, Exterminate, Extirp, Obliterate, Purge, Rid, Root, Scrat, Scratch, Stamp-out, Strike off, Strike out, Uproot, Uptear, Wipe

**Erasmus** Humanist

**Eratosthenes** Sieve

**Erbium** Er

**Ere** Coram

**Erect(ion), Erector** Attolent, Boner, Build, Construct(ion), Elevate, Exalt, Hard-on, Henge, Horn, Perpendicular, Priapism, Prick, Put up, Rear, Rigger, Stiffy, Straight-pight, Tentigo, Upend, Upright, Vertical, Wall

**Ergo** Argal, Hence, Therefore

**Erica** Heath, Heather, Ling

**Ermine** Fur, Minever, Miniver, Stoat

**Ernie** Bondsman

**Erode, Erosion** Ablate, Abrade, Appair, Corrasion, Degrade, Denude, Destroy, Deteriorate, Detrition, Etch, Fret, Hush, Peneplain, Planation, Spark, Wash, Wear, Yardang

**Eros, Erotic(a)** Amatory, Amorino, Amorous, Aphrodisiac, Carnal, Cupid, Curiosa, Erogenic, Lascivious, Philtre, Prurient, Salacious, Steamy

**Err(or), Errant** Aliasing, Anachronism, Bish, Blip, Blooper, Blunder, Boner, Boob(oo), Botch, Bug, Clanger, Clerical, Comedy, Corrigendum, EE, Execution, Fatal, Fat-finger, Fault, Flaw, Fluff, Gaffe, Glaring, Glitch, Hash, Heresy, Hickey, Howler, Human, Inaccuracy, Inherited, Jeofail, K'thibh, Lapse, Lapsus, Literal, Mackle, Mesprise, Mesprize, Misgo, Misprint, Misprise, Misprize, Misstep, → MISTAKE, Mumpsimus, Out, Paladin, Parachronism, Probable, Recoverable, Rounding, Rove, Runtime, Sampling, Semantic, Sin, Slip, Slip-up, Solecism, Standard, Stray, Trip, Truncation, Type I, Type II, Typo, Typographical, Unforced, Wander

**Errand** Ance, Chore, Commission, Fool's, Message, Mission, Once, Sleeveless, Task, Yince

**Errand-boy** Cad, Galopin, Page

**Erratic** Haywire, Irregular, Planetary, Spasmodic, Temperamental, Unstable, Vagary, Vagrant, Wayward, Whimsical

**Erroneous** False, Inaccurate, Mistaken, Non-sequitur, Untrue

**Ersatz** Artificial, Pseudo, Synthetic

**Erstwhile** One time, Quondam

**Erudite, Erudition** Academic, Didactic, Learned, Literosity, Savant, Scholar, Well-bred, Well-read, Wisdom

**Erupt(ion), Erupture** Belch, Brash, Burst, Creeping, Ecthyma, Eject, Emit, Emphlysis, Exanthem(a), Exanthemata, → EXPLODE, Fissure, Flare, Fumarole, Hives, Hornito, Lichen, Mal(l)ander, Mallender, Morphew, Outbreak, Outburst, Papilla, Paroxysm, Plinian, Pompholyx, Pustule, Quat, Rash, Rose-drop, Scissure, Sneeze, Spew

**Escalate, Escalator** Accrescence, Expand, Granary, Grow, Lift, Snowball, Soar, Travolator
**Escalope** Scaloppine
**Escape(e), Escapade, Escapist** Abscond, Adventure, Antic, Atride, Avoid, Bale out, Bolt, Bolthole, Breakout, Caper, Cheat, Close call, Decamp, Eject, Elope, Elude, Elusion, Esc, Eschewal, Evade, Exit, Fire, Flee, Flight, Fredaine, Frolic, Fugacity, Fugative, Gaolbreak, Gas, Get-out, Hole, Hoot, Houdini, Houdini act, Hout, Lam, Lark, Leakage, Leg-it, Let-off, Levant, Lifeline, Loop(-hole), Meuse, Mews, Miss, Muse, Narrow, Near thing, Outlet, Prank, Refuge, Rollick, Runaway, Sauve qui peut, Scapa, Scarper, Scrape, Seep(age), Shave, Slip, Splore, Squeak, Stunt, Vent, Walter Mitty, Wilding, Wriggle
**Escapement** Anchor, Dead-beat, Foliot, Recoil
**Eschew** Abandon, Avoid, For(e)go, Ignore, → SHUN
**Escort** Accompany, Arm candy, Attend, Beard, Beau, Bodyguard, Bring, Chaperone, Comitatus, Company, Conduct, Convoy, Cortège, Corvette, Date, Destroyer, Entourage, Frigate, Gallant, Gigolo, Guard, Guide, Lead, Outrider, Protector, Retinue, See, Send, Set, Squire, Take, Tend, Usher, Walker
**Esculent** Edible
**Escutcheon** Achievement, Crest, Keyplate, Shield
**Esker** OS
**Eskimo** Aleut, Caribou, Husky, In(n)uit, Inuk, Inukitut, Thule, Yupik
**Esoteric** Abstruse, Acroamatic, Arcane, Hermetic, Inner, Mystic, Occult, Orphic, Private, Rarefied, Recondite, Secret
**ESP** Psi, Retrocognition
**Especial(ly)** Chiefly, Esp, Espec, Outstanding, Particular
**Esperanto** Ido, Zamenhof
**Espionage** Industrial, Secret Service, Spying, Surveillance
**Esplanade** Promenade, Walk
**Espouse** Adopt
**Esprit** Cameraderie, Insight, Spirit, Understanding, Wit
**Espy** Decry
**Esquire** Armiger(o), Esq, Gent
**Essay(s)** Article, Attempt, Causerie, Critique, Dabble, Discourse, Disquisition, Dissertation, Endeavour, Festschrift, Go, Paper, Prolusion, Sketch, Stab, Study, Theme, Thesis, Tractate, Treatise, Try
**Essayist** Addison, Bacon, Carlyle, Columnist, De Quincey, Elia, Ellis, Emerson, Hazlitt, Holmes, Hunt, Huxley, Lamb, Locke, Montaigne, Pater, Prolusion, Ruskin, Scribe, Steele, Temple, Tzara, → WRITER
**Essence** Alma, Atman, Attar, Aura, Being, Bergamot, Coffee, Core, Crux, Element, Entia, Esse, Ester, Extract, Fizzen, Flavouring, Flower, Foison, Gist, Heart, Hom(e)ousian, Inbeing, Inscape, Kernel, Marrow, Mauri, Mirbane, Myrbane, Nature, Nub, Nutshell, Oil, Ottar, Otto, Pearl, Perfume, Per-se, Petrol, Pith, Quiddity, Ratafia, Saul, Soul, Substance, Sum, Ylang-ylang
**Essential(ly), Essentials** Arabin, At heart, Bare, Bare bones, Basic, Central, Crucial, Crux, Distillate, Entia, Formal, Fundamental, Imperative, In, Inbred, Indispensable, Inherent, Innate, In se, Integral, Intrinsic, Kernel, Key, Lifeblood, Linch-pin, Main, Marrow, Material, Mun, Must, Necessary, Need, Nitty-gritty, Nub, Nuts and bolts, Obbligato, Part-parcel, Per-se, Pith, Prana, Prerequisite, Quintessence, Radical, Requisite, Sine qua non, Skeleton, Soul, Staple, Vital, Whatness
**Essex** Roseland
**Establish(ed)** Abide, Anchor, Appoint, Ascertain, Base, Bred-in-the-bone, Build, Chronic, Confirm, Conform, Conventional, Create, Customary, Decide, Deep-seated, Deploy, Embed, Enact, Endemic, Engrain, Ensconce, Entrench, Erect, Evidence, Evince, Fix, → FOUND, Haft, Honoured, Imbed, Ingrain, Initiate, Instal(l), Instate, Instil, Institute, Inveterate, Legislate, Long-standing, Ordain, Orthodox, Pitch, Pre-set, Prove, Radicate, Raise, Redintegrate, Root(ed), Secure, Set, Stable, Standing, State, Stell, Substantiate, Trad(itional), Trite, Valorise, Verify
**Establishment** Building, Business, CE, Church, Co, Concern, Conformation, Creation,

Hacienda, Household, Inception, Instauration, Institution, Lodge, Proving ground, Salon, School, Seat, Succursal, System, Traditional

**Estate(s), Estate-holder** Acres, Allod(ium), Alod, Assets, Campus, Car, Chateau, Commons, Council, Dais, Demesne, Domain, Dominant, Dowry, Est, Estancia, Fazenda, Fee-simple, Fee-tail, Fen, First, Fourth, General, Hacienda, Hagh, Haugh, Having, Hay, Housing, Industrial, Jointure, Land-living, Latifundium, Legitim, Life, Longleat, Manor, Man's, Messuage, Odal, Patrimony, Pen, Personal(ity), Plantation, Press, Princedom, → **PROPERTY**, Real, Runrig, Second, Situation, Spiritual, Standing, Talooka, Taluk(a), Temporal, Termer, Termor, Thanage, Third, Three, Trading, Trust, Udal, Zamindari, Zemindari

**Estate agent** Realtor

**Esteem(ed), Estimable** Account, Admiration, Adoration, Appreciation, Count, Credited, Have, Honour, Izzat, Los, Precious, Prestige, Price, Pride, Prize, Rate, → **REGARD**, Reputation, Respect, Revere, Store, Value, Venerate, Wonder, Worthy

**Ester** Benzocaine, C(o)umarin, Depside, Glyceride, Lactone, Olein, Palmitin, Phthalate, Psilocybin, Succinate, Triglyceride, Urethan(e)

▸**Estimable** *see* **ESTEEM(ED)**

**Estimate, Estimation** Appraise, Approximation, Assess, Calculate, Carat, Conceit, Cost, Esteem, Extrapolation, Figure, Forecast, Gauge, Guess(timate), Idea, Inexact, Interval, Judge, Measure, Opinion, Point, Projection, Quotation, Rate, Rating, Reckon, Regard, Rule-of-thumb, Sight, Value, Weigh

**Estrange** Alienate, Disunite, Wean

**Estuary** Bay, Clyde, Creek, Dee, Delta, Firth, Gironde, Humber, Inlet, Mouth, Orwell, Ostial, Para, Rio de la Plata, Severn, Tay, Thames

**Esurient** Arid, Insatiable

**Etc(etera)** Et al(ia), So on

**Etch(ing)** Aquafortis, Aquatint(a), Bite, → **ENGRAVE**, Erode, Incise, Inscribe, Instil, Lithograph

**Eternal(ly), Eternity** Aeonian, Ageless, All-time, Amarantine, Ceaseless, Endless, Everlasting, Evermore, Eviternal, Ewigkeit, Forever, Immortal, Infinity, Never-ending, Perdurable, Perennial, Perpetual, Sempiternal, Tarnal, Timeless, Triangle, Unending, Yonks

**Ethanol** Alcohol

**Ethelred** Unready

**Ether** Air, Atmosphere, Ch'i, Crown, Diethyl, Ethyl, Gas, Petroleum, Sky, Yang, Yin

**Ethereal** Airy, Angelic, Delicate, Fragile, Heavenly, Nymph, Wraithlike

**Ethic(al), Ethics** Code, Deontics, Deontology, Eud(a)ermonism, Ideals, Marcionite, Moral, Principles, Situation, Work

**Ethiopia(n)** African, Amharic, Asmara, Cushitic, Falasha, Galla, Geez, Kabele, Kebele, Ogaden

**Ethnic** Racial, Roots

**Ethyl** ET

**Etiquette** Code, Conduct, De Brett, Decorum, Kawa, → **MANNERS**, Politesse, Propriety, Protocol, Ps and Qs, Punctilious, Table manners

**Etna** Empedocles, Vessel, Volcano

**Etonian** Oppidan, Victim

**Etrier** Rope ladder

**Etruscan** Tyrrhenian

**Etui** Tweezer case

**Etymologist, Etymology** Hobson-Jobson, Isodore

**Eucalyptus** Blackbutt, Bloodwood, Blue gum, Cadaga, Cadagi, Coolabah, Gum-tree, Ironbark, Jarrah, Mallee, Marri, Morrell, Red gum, Sallee, Sally, Stringybark, Sugar gum, Tallow wood, Tewart, Tooart, Tuart, Wandoo, White gum, Woolly butt, Yate

**Eucharist** Anaphora, Azymite, Communion, Housel, Mass, Prozymite, Supper, Viaticum

**Euchre** Jambone

**Euclid** Geometer

**Eugene** Aram, Onegin

**Eugenia** Jambal, Jambolan(a), Jambu(l)
**Eulogise** Rhapsodise
**Eulogistic, Eulogy** Encomium, Epaenetic, Epainetic, Laudatory, Panegyric, Praise, Tribute
**Eumenides** Furies
**Eunuch** Ridg(e)ling, Rig
**Euphausia** Krill, Shrimp
**Euphemism** Fib, Gosh, Gracious, Heck, Hypocorism, Sir-reverence
**Euphonic** Tuneful
**Euphoria, Euphoric** Buzz, Cock-a-hoop, Ecstasy, Elation, High, Jubilation, Mindfuck, Nirvana, Rapture, Rush
**Euphrasia** Eyebright
**Eurasian** Chee-chee, Chi-chi
**Euro** Wallaroo
**Europe(an)** Andorran, Aryan, Balt, Basque, Bohunk, Bosnian, Catalan, Community, Continent, Croat, Dane, E, Esth, Estonian, Faringee, Faringhi, Feringhee, Fleming, Hungarian, Icelander, Japhetic, Lapp, Lett, Lithuanian, Magyar, Maltese, Monagesque, Palagi, Ruthene, Ruthenian, Serb, Slavonian, Slovak, Slovene, Topi-wallah, Transleithan, Tyrolean, Ugrian, Vlach, Wessi, Yugoslav
**Europium** Eu
**Eustace** Diamonds
**Euthanasia** Exit
**Evacuate, Evacuation** Clearance, Dunkirk, Escape, Excrete, Expel, Getter, Medevac, Movement, Planuria, Planury, Retreat, Scramble, Stercorate, Stool, Vent, Void, Withdraw
**Evade, Evasion, Evasive** Abscond, Ambages, Avoid, Circumvent, Cop-out, Coy, Dodge, Duck, Elude, Equivocate, Escape, Fence, Fend off, Fudge, Hedge, Jink, Loophole, Lose, Mealymouthed, Parry, Prevaricate, Quibble, Quillet, Quirk, Salvo, Scrimshank, Shack, Shifty, Shirk, Shuffling, Sidestep, Skirt, Skive, Skrimshank, Slippy, Stall, Stonewall, Subterfuge, Tergiversate, Waive, Weasel, Weasel out, Whiffler
**Evaluate, Evaluation** Appraise, Assess, Estimate, Gauge, Job, Measure, Ponder, Rate, Review, Try, Waid(e), Weigh
**Evanesce, Evanescent** Cursory, Fade, Fleeting, Fugacious
**Evangelical, Evangelist(ical)** Bible-thumper, Buchman, Clappy-doo, Converter, Crusader, Fisher, Godsquad, Gospeller, Graham, Happy-clappy, Hot gospeller, Jansen, Jesus freak, John, Luke, Marist, Mark, Matthew, Missioner, Moody, Morisonian, Peculiar, Preacher, Propagandist, Revivalist, Salvationist, Salvo, Sankcy, Sim(conite), Stundist, Wild
**Evaporate, Evaporation** Angel's share, Condense, Dehydrate, Desorb, Disappear, Dry, Exhale, Steam, Steme, Ullage, Vaporise
**Eve(ning)** All Hallow's, First lady, First mate, Nightfall, Postmeridian, St Agnes's, St Tib(b)s, Soirée, Subfusk, Sunset, Twilight, Vesperal, Vespertinal, Vigil, Watch night, Yester
**Evelyn** Diarist, Hope
**Even(ly), Evenness** Aid, Albe(e), Albeit, All, All-square, Average, Balanced, Clean, Constant, Drawn, Dusk, Een, Ene, Equable, Equal, Erev, Fair, Fair play, Flush, Forenight, Gradual, Iron, J'ouvert, Level, Level-pegging, Meet, Nay, Pair, Par, Parallel, Plain, Plane, Plateau, Quits, Regular, Rib, Smooth, Square, Standardise, Still, Temperate, Tie(d), Toss-up, Uniform, Well-balanced, Yet
**Even-handed** Ambidextrous, Impartial
**Evening flight** Ro(a)ding
**Evensong** Vespers
**Event(ing)** All-nighter, Athletic, Bash, Break, Case, Ceremony, Circumstance, Classic, Contingency, Control, Cross-country, Discus, Dressage, Encaenia, Encierro, Episode, Fest, Field, Fiesta, Function, Fund-raiser, Grand Prix, Gymkhana, Happening, Happy, Heat, Incident, Iron man, Landmark, Leg, Liquidity, Media, Meeting, Milestone, Occasion, Occurrence, Ongoing, Open-mike, Outcome, Pass, Pentathlon, Pro-am, Rag-day, Regatta, Result, Scramble, Shot put, Show-jumping, Soirée, Stable, Stick-on, Telethon, Three-day, Three-ring circus, Time trial, Tour de France, Track, Triple, Watershed
**Even-tempered** Equanimous

**Eventful** Action-packed
**Even-toed** Artiodactyl
**Eventual(ity), Eventually** Case, Contingent, Finally, Future, In time, Later, Nd, Sooner or later, Ultimate
**Ever** Always, Ay(e), Constantly, Eternal, Eviternity
**Everglade** Vlei
**Evergreen** Abies, Ageless, Araucaria, Arbutus, Cembra, Cypress, Fir, Gaultheria, Golden lie, Holly, Ivy, Macadamia, Mistletoe, Myrtle, Oleander, Olearia, Periwinkle, Pinaster, Pine, Privet, Thuja, Thuya, Washington, Winterberry, Yacca, Yew
**Everlasting** Cat's ear, Changeless, Enduring, Eternal, Immortal, Immortelle, Perdurable, Perennial, Perpetual, Recurrent, Sempiternal, Tarnal, Undying
**Every(one), Everything** All, Apiece, A'thing, Catch-all, Complete, Each, Et al, Existence, Full Monty, Ilk(a), In toto, Monty, Sub chiz, Sum, The full monty, The works, To a man, Tout, Tout le monde, Universal, Varsal
**Everyday** Banal, Informal, Mundane, Natural, Ordinary, Plain, Routine, Verism, Year round
**Everywhere** Ambient, Galore, Omnipresent, Passim, Rife, Throughout, Thru, Ubique, Ubiquity, World
**Evict(ion), Evict(or)** Clearance, Dislodge, Disnest, Disseisor, Eject, Expel, Oust
**Evidence, Evident(ly)** Adminicle, Apparent, Argument, Axiomatic, Circumstantial, Clear, Compurgation, Confessed, Credentials, Deposition, Direct, Distinct, DNA, Document, Empirical, Exemplar, Fact, Flagrant, Forensic, Hearsay, Indicate, Internal, King's, Manifest, Marked, Material, Naked, Obvious, Ostensibly, Overt, → **PATENT**, Perceptible, Plain, Premise, Prima facie, Probable, Proof, Queen's, Record, Sign, Smoking gun, State's, Surrebuttal, Tangible, Testimony, Understandable
**Evil** Ahriman, Alastor, Amiss, Bad, Badmash, Bale, Bane, Beelzebub, Budmash, Corrupt, Curse, Depraved, Eale, Falling, Guilty, Harm, Heinous, Hydra, Ill, Immoral, Iniquity, King's, Loki, Malefic, Malign, Mare, Mischief, Monstrous, Nasty, Necessary, Nefarious, Night, Perfidious, Pestilence, Rakshas(a), St Martin's, Satanic, Shrewd, Sin, → **SINISTER**, Theodicy, Turpitude, Vice, Villainy, Wicked
**Evil eye** Jettatura
**Evince** Disclose, Exhibit, Indicate, → **MANIFEST**, Show
**Eviscerate(d)** Debilitate, Disembowel, Drawn, Gralloch
**Evoke, Evocative** Arouse, Awaken, Educe, Elicit, Haunting, Move, Redolent, Resonant, Retro, Stir
**Evolution(ary), Evolutionist** Bergsonian, Clade, Convergent, Countermarch, Darwin, Development, Emergent, Growth, Holism, Lamarck, Lysenkoism, Moner(on), Neo-Lamarckism, Orthogenesis, Phylogeny, Social, Spencerman, Stellar, Transformism, Turning
▷**Evolution** *may indicate* an anagram
**Evolve** Develop, Speciate
**Ewe** Crone, Gimmer, Keb, Rachel, Sheep, Teg, Theave
**Ewer** Aquamanale, Aquamanile, → **JUG**
**Ex** Former, Late, Old flame, Quondam, Ten
**Exacerbate** Aggravate, Embitter, Exasperate, Inflame, Irritate, Needle
**Exact(ing), Exactitude, Exactly** Accurate, Authentic, Bang on, Careful, Dead, Definite, Due, Elicit, Estreat, Even, Exigent, Extort, Fine, Formal, It, Jump, Literal, Literatim, Mathematical, Meticulous, Minute, Nice(ty), On cue, On the dot, On the nail, On the nose, Pat, Plumb, Point-device, → **PRECISE**, Require, Slap-bang, Spang, Specific, Spot-on, Strict, Stringent, Sweat, T, To a 't', Verbatim
**Exaction** Blackmail, Extortion, Impost, Montem, Sorelion, Tax
**Exaggerate(d), Exaggeration** Aggrandise, Agonistic, Amplify, Ballyhoo, Boast, Brag, Camp, Caricature, Colour, Couleur de rose, Distend, Dramatise, Embellish, → **EMBROIDER**, Exalted, Goliathise, Hoke, Hype, Hyperbole, Inflate, Lie, Line-shoot, Magnify, Munch(h)ausen, Mythomania, Overact, Overdo, Overdraw, Overegg, Overpaint, Overpitch, Overplay, Overrate, Oversell, Overstate, Overstretch, Over-the-top, Play up, Romance, Rose-coloured, Shoot a line, Steep, Stretch, Tall, Theatrical, Writ large

**Exalt(ed), Exaltation** Attitudes, Deify, Dignify, Elation, Enhance, Ennoble, Ensky, Enthrone, Erect, Extol, Glorify, High, Jubilance, Larks, Laud, Lofty, Magnific, → PRAISE, Raise, Rapture, Ruff(e), Sama, Sublime, Supernal, Throne, Upraise

**Exam(ination), Examine, Examinee, Examiner** Agrégé, A-level, Alnage, Analyse, Analyst, Anatomise, Appose, Arthroscopy, Assess, Audit, Audition, Auscultation, Autopsy, Baccalauréat, Biopsy, Case, Check-out, Check-up, Coate, Cognosce, Collate, Comb, Common Entrance, Concours, Consideration, Coroner, Cross-question, CSE, Deposal, Depose, Disquisition, Dissect, Docimasy, Edexcel, Eleven plus, Endoscopy, Entrance, Expiscate, Explore, Eyeball, Finals, GCE, GCSE, Going-over, Grade(s), Great-go, Greats, Gulf, Haruspex, Hearing, Higher, Inspect, Inter, Interrogate, Interview, Introspection, Jerque, Jury, Laparoscopy, Little-go, Local, Look, Mark, Matriculation, Medical, Mocks, Mod(erations), Moderator, Mods, Mug, Multiple choice, O-level, Once-over, Oral, Ordalian, Ordeal, Overhaul, Palp(ate), Paper, Peruse, Physical, Post-mortem, Practical, Prelims, Probe, Process, Professional, Pry, Psychoanalyse, Pump, → QUESTION, Quiz, Ransack, Recce, Reconnaissance, Reconnoitre, Resit, Responsions, Review, Sayer, Scan, Schools, Scope, Screen, Scrutator, Scrutineer, Scrutinise, Search, Seek, Shroff, Sift, Sit, Smalls, Strip search, Study, Survey, Sus(s), Test, Trial, Tripos, Try, Unseen, Vet, View, Viva, Vivisection, Voir dire, X-ray

**Example** Apotheosis, Assay-piece, Byword, Embodiment, Epitome, Erotema, Foretaste, → FOR EXAMPLE, Illustration, Instance, Lead, Lesson, Model, Monument, Paradigm, Paragon, → PATTERN, Praxis, Precedent, Prototype, Quintessence, Role model, Say, Shining, Show home, Show house, Showpiece, Specimen, Standard, Stormer, Such as, Touchstone, Type, Typify

**Exasperate, Exasperating, Exasperation** Aggravate, Anger, Bait, Brass off, Embitter, Exulcerate, Galling, Irk, Irritate, Madden, Nettle, Provoke

**Excavate, Excavation, Excavator** Armadillo, Bore, Burrow, Catacomb, Crater, Cutting, Delf, Delph, → DIG, Dike, Disinter, Ditch(er), Dragline, Dredge, Drift, Drive, Earthwork, Gaulter, Glory hole, Graft, Heuch, Heugh, Hollow, JCB, Mine, Moat, Pichiciago, Pioneer, Pioner, Power shovel, Pyoner, Quarry, Roadheader, Shaft, Sink, Sondage, Spade, Steam-shovel, Stope, Well

**Exceed, Exceeding(ly)** Amain, Not half, Outdo, Outnumber, Outstrip, Overshoot, Overstep, Preponderate, Surpass, Transcend, Very

**Excel(lence), Excellency, Excellent** A1, Ace, Admirable (Crichton), A-per-se, Assay-piece, Awesome, Bangin(g), Bang on, Beat, Beaut, Beezer, Better, Bitchin', Blinder, Bodacious, Boffo, Bonzer, Booshit, Boss, Bottler, Bravo, Brill, Bully, Capital, Castor, Champion, Cheese, Choice, Class(y), Classical, Cool, Copacetic, Copesettic, Copybook, Corking, Crack, Crackajack, Crackerjack, Crucial, Cushty, Daisy, Def, Dic(k)ty, Dilly, Divine, Dominate, Doozy, Dope, Elegant, Excelsior, Exemplary, Eximious, Exo, Exquisite, Extraordinaire, Fab, Fabulous, Fantastic, First-class, First rate, Five-star, Goodly, Goodness, Great, Grit, Grouse, HE, Hellacious, High, Humdinger, Hunky(-dory), Inimitable, Jake, Jammy, Jim-dandy, Kiff, Knockout, Lal(l)a palooza, Laudable, Lollapalooza, Lummy, Matchless, Mean, Mega-, Merit, Neat, Noble, Nonesuch, Olé, Out and outer, Outbrag, Outclass, Outdo, Outgeneral, Outpeer, Outrank, Outstanding, Outstrip, Outtop, Overdo, Overpeer, Overtop, Paragon, Peachy, Peerless, Perfection, Phat, Prime, Pure, Purler, Quality, Rad, Rare, Rattling, Ring, Rinsin', Ripping, Ripsnorter, Say-piece, Scorcher, Shagtastic, → SHINE, Shit-hot, Sick-dog, Sik, Slammin(g), Socko, Sound, Spanking, Spiffing, Stellar, Stonking, Stupendous, Sublime, Superb, Super-duper, Superior, Supernal, Supreme, Surpass, Swell, Terrific, Tip-top, Top flight, Top-hole, Topnotch, Topping, Tops, Transcend, Transcendent, Triff, Virtue, Virtuoso, Wal(l)y, War, Way-out, Whizzo, Whizzy, Wicked, Worth

**Except(ion)** Bar, But, Else, Exc, Nobbut, Omit, Only, Save, Than, Then, Unless

**Exception(al)** Abnormal, Anomaly, Cracker(jack), Doozy, Egregious, Especial, Ever so, Extraordinary, Extreme, Gas, Humdinger, Inimitable, Odd, Rara avis, Rare, Ripsnorter, Scarce, Select, Singular, Spanking, Special, Stellar, Super(normal), Unco(mmon), Unusual, Zinger

**Excerpt(s)** Clip, Digest, Extract, Passage, Scrap

**Excess(ive), Excessively** Ad nauseam, All-fired, Almighty, Basinful, Binge, De trop, Epact, Exaggeration, Exorbitant, Extortionate, Extravagant, Flab, Flood, Fulsome, Glut, Hard, Immoderate, Indulgence, Inordinate, Intemperance, Intense, Lake, → **LAVISH**, Mountain, Needless, Nimiety, OD, Old, OTT, Outrage, Over, Overabundance, Overage, Overblown, Overcome, Overdose, Overflow, Over-indulgence, Overkill, Overly, Overmuch, Overspill, Oversupply, Over-the-top, Owercome, Plethora, Preponderance, Profuse, Remainder, Salt, Satiety, Spate, Spilth, Staw, Steep, Superabundant, Superfluity, Superplus, Surfeit, Surplus, Terrific, Thundering, Too, Troppo, Ultra, Undue, Unequal, Unnecessary, Woundily

**Exchange** Baltic, Bandy, Banter, Barter, Bourse, Cambist, Cash, Catallactic, Change, Chop, Commodity, Commute, Confab, Contango, Convert, Cope, Corn, Crossfire, Cut and thrust, Ding-dong, Discourse, Employment, Enallage, Excambion, Foreign, Gematria, Global, Inosculate, Intercooler, Interplay, Ion, Job centre, Labour, Logroll, → **MARKET**, Mart, Needle, Niffer, Paraphrase, Part, PBX, Post, Quid pro quo, Rally, Rate, RE, Recourse, Redeem, Rialto, Royal, Scorse, Scourse, Sister-chromated, Spoonerism, Stock (market), Swap, Switch, Switchboard, Swop (shop), Telephone, Tolsel, Tolsey, Tolzey, → **TRADE**, Trade in, Traffic, Transfusion, Transpose, Trophallaxis, Truck

**Exchequer** Remembrancer, Treasury

**Excise(man), Excise district** Ablate, Bobbitt, Crop, Expunge, Gauger, Resect, Ride, Tax

**Excite(ment), Excitable, Excitability, Excited, Exciting** Ablaze, Aboil, Abuzz, Action-packed, Adventure, Aerate, Aflutter, Agitate, Agog, Amove, Amp, Animate, Apeshit, Aphrodisiac, Arouse, Athrill, Atwitter, Awaken, Blast, Breathless, Brouhaha, Bubbly, Buck-fever, Buzzing, Climactic, Combustible, Commotion, Crunk, Delirium, Dionysian, Dither, Electrify, Emove, Enthuse, Erethism, Eventful, Febrile, Feisty, Fever (pitch), Fire, Flap, Flat spin, Frantic, Frenetic, Frenzy, Frisson, Furore, Fuss, Galvanise, Gas, Grip, Gusto, Headiness, Heat, Hectic, Het, Hey-go-mad, Highly-strung, Hilarity, Hobson-Jobson, Hoopla, Hothead, Hyped, Hyper, Hypomania, Hysterical, Impel, Incite, Inebriate, Inflame, Intoxicate, Jimjams, Kick, Kindle, Krunk, Liven, Maenad, Mania, Metastable, Must, Nappy, Nervous, Neurotic, Oestrus, On fire, On tenterhooks, Orgasm, Overheat, Overwrought, Page turner, Panic, Passion, Pride, Prime, Provoke, Psyched up, Racy, Radge, Razzle-dazzle, Red-hot, Rile, Roil, → **ROUSE**, Rousement, Ruff(e), Rut, Salutation, Send, Sexy, Shivering, Skittish, Spin, Splash, Spur, Startle, Stimulate, Stir(e), Suscitate, Suspense, Swashbuckling, Temperamental, Tense, Tetanoid, Tetany, Tew, Thrill, Tickle, Titillate, Turn-on, Twitter, Upraise, Va-va-voom, Waken, Whee, Whet, Whoopee, Work up, Yahoo, Yerk, Yippee, Yirk, Yoicks, Zest

▷**Excite(d)** *may indicate* an anagram

**Exclaim, Exclamation (mark)** Ahem, Arrah, Aue, Begorra, Bliksem, Blurt, Bo, By Jove, Ceas(e), Crikey, Criv(v)ens, Dammit, Ecphonesis, Eina, Eish, Ejaculate, Epiphonema, Eureka, Expletive, Fen(s), Good-now, Hadaway, Haith, Halleluiah, Hallelujah, Heigh-ho, Hem, Hip, Hookey Walker, Hosanna, Inshallah, Interjection, Moryah, Omigod, Oof, Oops, Phew, Pish, Pling, Pow, Protest, Pshaw, Push, Sasa, Screamer, Sese(y), Sessa, Sko(a)l, Strewth, Uh-oh, Uh-uh, Unberufen, Vociferate, Voila, Walker, Whau, Whee, Whoopee, Whoops, Wirra, Wow, Yay, Yeehaw, Yippee, Yo-ho-ho, Yummy, Zounds

**Exclave** Cabinda

**Exclude(d), Excluding, Exclusion** Aside, Ban, Banish, Bar, Barring-out, Berufsverbot, Block, Clanish, Competitive, Corner, Debar, Deforcement, Disbar, Drop, Eliminate, Ex, Except, Excommunicate, Freeze out, Gate, Ice out, No-go, Omit, Ostracise, Outbar, Outwith, Pauli, Proscribe, Repress, Rule out, Shut out, Social, Suspend, Upmarket

**Exclusive** Cliquish, Closed-shop, Complete, Debarment, Elect, Elite, Esoteric, In-group, Monopoly, Narrow, Particular, Posh, Pure, Rare, Scoop, Select, Single, Sole, Unique

**Excommunicate** Curse

**Excoriate** Flay, Slam

**Excrement, Excrete, Excretion, Excretory** Cystinuria, Dirt, Doo-doo, Dung, Emunctory, Faeces, Fecula, Flyspeck, Frass, Jobbie, Keech, Ketonuria, Meconium, Oliguria, Ordure, Pat, Poo(p), Poo-poo, Puer, Pure, Refuse, Scatology, Sir-reverence, Stercoraceous, Stool, Strangury, Turd, Urea, Waste, Whoopsie

**Excrescence** Aril, Carnosity, Caruncle, Enate, Gall, Growth, Knob, Knurl, Lump, Nurl, Pimple, Pin, Spavin(e), Strophiole, Talpa, Twitter(-bone), Wart

**Excruciate, Excruciating** Acute, Agonising, Diabolical, Rack, Torment, Torture
**Exculpate** Acquit, Clear, Forgive
**Excursion** Airing, Alarum, Cruise, Dart, Day tour, Day trip, Digression, Jaunt, Junket, LEM, Outing, Pleasure-trip, Railtour, Road, Sally, Sashay, Sortie, Tour, Trip, Vagary
**Excuse, Excusable** Absolve, Alibi, Amnesty, Bunbury, Condone, Cop-out, Essoin, Essoyne, Evasion, Exempt, Exonerate, Explain, Faik, Forgive, Gold brick, Hook, Justify, Let off, Mitigate, Occasion, Off come, Out, Overlook, Palliate, → **PARDON**, Penelopise, Plea, Pretext, Release, Reprieve, Salvo, Venial, Viable, Whitewash
**Execrate, Execration** Abhor, Ban, Boo, Curse, Odium
**Execute(d), Execution(er), Executive, Executor** Abhorson, Accomplish, Account, Administrate, Behead, Carnifex, Deathsman, Despatch, Discharge, Dispatch, Exor, Finish, Fry, Gan, Gar(r)otte, Gin, Guardian, Hang, Headsman, High p, Implement, Ketch, Kill, Koko, Literary, Lynch, Management, Martyr, Monsieur de Paris, Noyade, Official, Perform, Perpetrate, Pierrepoint, Politburo, Rope, Scaffold, Scamp, Top, Tower Hill, Trustee, Tyburn
**Exemplar(y)** Byword, Classic, Ideal, Impeccable, Laudable, Model, Paragon, Perfect, Role model, St, Standard, Warning
**Exemplify** Cite, Epitomise, Illustrate, Instantiate, Satisfy
**Exempt(ion)** Aegrotat, Dispensation, Exclude, Exeem, Fainites, Fains, Free, Immune, Impunity, Indemnity, Indulgence, Overslaugh, Privilege, Quarter, Spare, Tyburn ticket, Vains
**Exercise(s)** Aerobics, Air, Angelus, Antic, Apply, Aquaplaning, Aquarobics, Athletics, Bench press, Boxercise®, Burpee, Buteyko method, Cal(l)isthenics, Callanetics®, Cardio, Chi kung, Chin-up, Circuit training, Cloze, Constitutional, Daily dozen, Dancercise, Drill, Employ, Enure, Etude, Eurhythmics, Examen, Exert, Falun dafa, Falun gong, Fartlek, Feldenkrais method, Five-finger, Floor, Gradus, Gymnastics, Hatha yoga, Inure, Isometrics, Kata, Keep fit, Keepy-uppy, Kegel, Knee drill, Krav Maga, Lat spread, Lesson, Limber, Manual, Medau, Op, Operation, PE, Physical jerks, Pilates, Ply, Plyometrics, Popmobility, Practice, Practise, Preacher curl, Press-up, Problem, Prolusion, PT, Pull-up, Pump iron, Push-up, Qigong, Sadhana, Scales, Shintaido, Sit-up, Solfege, Solfeggi(o), Step (aerobics), Stretch, Tae-Bo®, Tai chi (ch'uan), Task, Thema, Theme, Thesis, Train, Trampoline, Treadmill, Trunk curl, Use, Vocalism, Warm-down, Warm-up, Wield, Work, Work-out, Xyst(us), Yogalates, Yomp, Zumba®
▷**Exercise(d)** *may indicate* an anagram
**Exert(ion)** Conatus, → **EFFORT**, Exercise, Labour, Operate, Strain, Strive, Struggle, Trouble, Wield
**Ex-European** Japhetic
**Exhalation, Exhale** Breath, Fume, Miasma, Reek, Sigh, Smell, Sneeze, Steam, Transpire, Vapour
**Exhaust(ed), Exhausting, Exhaustion, Exhaustive** All-in, Backbreaking, Beaten, Beggar, Bleary, Bore, Bugger(ed), Burn, Burn-out, Bushed, Clapped out, Collapse, Consume, Deadbeat, Debility, Deplete, Detailed, Dissipate, Do, Dog-tired, Done, Drain, Eduction, Effete, Emission, Empty, End, Enervate, Euchred, Fatigue, Finish, Flue, Fordo, Forfeuchen, Forfochen, Forfoughen, Forfoughten, Forjaskit, Forjeskit, Forspent, Forswink, Frazzle, Gruelling, Hackneyed, Haggard, Heat, Heatstroke, Inanition, Jade, Jet-lagged, Jet-stream, Jiggered, Knacker, Mate, Milk, Out, Outspent, Outwear, Overtax, Peter, Play out, Poop, Powfagged, Prostrate, Puckerood, Puggled, Rag, Ramfeezle, Rundown, Sap, Sell out, Shatter, Shot, Shotten, Spend, Spent, Stonkered, Tailpipe, Tax, Tedious, Tire, Trauchled, Up, Use (up), Used up, Wabbit, Wappend, Warby, Washed-up, Wasted, Waygone, Weak, → **WEARY**, Wind, Worn, Zonked
**Exhibition (centre), Exhibit(ing), Exhibitioner, Exhibitionism, Exhibitionist** Aquashow, Bench, Circus, Concours, Demo, Demonstrate, Demy, Diorama, Discover, Display, Earls Court, ENC, Endeictic, Evince, Expo, Expose, Extrovert, Fair, Flaunt, Flower show, Hang, Indicate, Installation, Lady Godiva, → **MANIFEST**, NEC, Olympia, Pageant, Panopticon, Parade, Poseur, Present, Retrospective, Rodeo, Salon, Scene, Set forth, Show(piece), Showcase, Showman, Show-off, Showplace, Showroom, Sideshow, Sight, Spectacle, Sport, Stand, Streaker, Trade fair, Viewing, Waxworks, Wear, Zoo
**Exhilarate(d), Exhilarating** Bubble, Cheer, Elate, Enliven, Heady

**Exhort(ation)** Admonish, Allocution, Caution, Counsel, Harangue, Incite, Injunction, Lecture, Par(a)enesis, Persuade, Protreptic, Urge
**Exhume** Delve, Disinter, Resurrect, Unearth
**Exigency, Exigent** Demanding, Emergency, Pressing, Taxing, Urgent, Vital
**Exile** Adam, Babylon, Ban, Banish, Deport, Deportee, Eject, Elba, Emigré, Eve, Expatriate, Exul, Galut(h), Ostracise, Outlaw, Refugee, Relegate, St Helena, Siberia, Tax, Wretch
**Exist(ence), Existing** Be(ing), Corporeity, Dwell, Enhypostasia, Entelechy, Esse, Extant, Haeccity, Identity, Inbeing, In esse, Inherent, Life, Lifespan, Lifestyle, Live, Ontology, Perseity, Solipsism, Status quo, Subsist, Substantial, Ubiety
**Existentialist** Camus, Sartre
**Exit** Débouché, Door, Egress, Emergency, Exhaust, Gate, Leave, Log off, Log out, Outgate, Outlet, Swansong, Trapdoor, Vent, Vomitory
**Exodus** Book, Departure, Flight, Hegira, Hejira, Hijrah, Passover
**Ex-official** Outler
**Exogamous** Outbred
**Exonerate(d)** Absolve, Acquit, Clear, Discharge, Excuse, Exempt, Shriven
**Exorbitant** Excessive, Expensive, Nimiety, Rip-off, Slug, Steep, Tall, Undue
**Exorcise, Exorcism, Exorcist** Benet, Dispirit, Exsufflation, Lay
**Exordium** Opening, Preface, Prelude
**Exotic** Alien, Chinoiserie, Ethnic, Fancy, Foreign, Free, Outlandish, Recherche, Strange
**Expand(able), Expanse, Expansion** Acreage, Amplify, Arena, Balloon, Boom, Branch out, Bulking, Develop, Diastole, Dilate, Distend, Ectasis, Elaborate, → **ENLARGE**, Escalate, Flesh out, Grow, Increase, Inflate, Magnify, Ocean, Outspread, Outstretch, Sheet, Skyrocket, Snowball, Sprawl, Spread, Stretch, Swell, Tensile, Vastitude, Wax, Wire-draw
**Expatiate** Amplify, Descant, Dwell, Enlarge, Perorate
**Expatriate** Banish, Colonial, Emigrate, Émigré, Exile, Outcast
**Expect(ant), Expectation, Expected, Expecting** Agog, Anticipate, Ask, Await, Due, En l'air, Foresee, Gravid, Hope, Imminent, Intend, In the club, Life, Likely, Lippen, Look, Natural, Offing, On cue, Par, Pip, Predict, Pregnant, Presume, Prim, Probable, Prognosis, Prospect, Require, → **SUPPOSE**, Tendance, Think, Thought, Up the duff, Usual, Ween
**Expectorant, Expectorate** Expel, Guaiacol, Hawk, Spit
**Expedient** Advisable, Artifice, Contrivance, Dodge, Fend, Make-do, Makeshift, Measure, Politic, Resort, Resource, Salvo, Shift, Stopgap, Suitable, Wise
**Expedite, Expedition(ary), Expeditious** Advance, Alacrity, Anabasis, Celerity, Crusade, Dispatch, Excursion, Fastness, Field trip, Hasten, Hurry, Kon-Tiki, Mission, Old Contemptibles, Pilgrimage, Post-haste, Prompt, Quest, Rapidity, Safari, Short cut, Speed, Trek, Trip, Turn out, Voyage, Warpath
**Expel** Amove, Banish, Belch, Blow, Deport, Disbar, Disgorge, Dispossess, Drum out, Egest, Evacuate, Evict, Excommunicate, Excrete, Exile, Exorcize, Hoof, Oust, Out(cast), Read out, Spew, Spit, Suspend, Turn forth, Void
**Expend(iture)** Budget, Consume, Cost, Dues, Gavel, Goings-out, Mise, Occupy, Oncost, Outgo(ing), Outlay, Poll, Squander, Tithe, Toll, Use, Waste
**Expendable** Cannon-fodder
**Expense(s)** Boodle, Charge, Cost, Cost of living, Current, Exes, Fee, Housekeeping, Law, Oncost, Outgoing, Outlay, Overhead, Price, Rent, Sumptuary
**Expensive** Chargeful, Costly, Dear, Executive, High, Precious, Pricey, Ruinous, Salt, Steep, Top dollar, Upmarket, Valuable
**Experience(d)** Accomplished, Adventure, A posteriori, Assay, Blasé, Capture, Come up, Dab (hand), Discovery, Dree, Ego-trip, Empiric, Encounter, Expert, → **FEEL**, Felt, Find, Foretaste, Freak-out, Gust, Hands-on, Hard way, Have, Hindsight, Incur, Know, Learn, Lesson, Level, Live, Mature, Meet, Mneme, Near-death, Occlude, Old bird, Old hand, Old-stager, Old-timer, Ordeal, Out-of-body, Pass, Plumb, Recapture, Seasoned, See, Senior, Sense, Sensory, Sophisticated, Spin, Stager, Stand, Street-smart, Streetwise, Taste, Tirocinium, Transference, Trial, Trip, Try, Undergo, Versed, Veteran, Work, Worldly wise
**Experiment(al)** Attempt, Aufgabe, Avant-garde, Ballon d'assai, Control, Corpus vile, Double blind, Empirical, Essay, Gedanken, → **JET**, Michelson-Morley, Peirastic, Pilot,

Probationary, Research, Sample, Shy, Single-blind, Taste, Tentative, → TRIAL, Trial and error, Trial balloon, Try, Untried, Venture, Vivisection

**Expert(ise), Experts** Able, Accomplished, Ace, Adept, Adroit, Antiquarian, Arch, Artistry, Astacologist, Au fait, Authority, Boffin, Buff, Cambist, Cocker, Cognoscente, Competent, Connoisseur, Crack, Craft, Dab(ster), Dab hand, Dan, Deft, Demon, Diagnostician, Digerati, Don, Egghead, Fancier, Finesse, Fundi, Gourmet, Grand master, Gun, Guru, Hack, Hotshot, Hoyle, Idiot savant, Judoka, Karateka, Know-all, Know-how, Learned, Luminary, Maestro, Masterly, Mastery, Maven, Mavin, Meister, Myth, Nark, Nerd, Nohow, Nutritionalist, Old hand, Old stager, Oner, Oneyer, Oneyre, Oracle, Panel, Past master, Peritus, Practised, Pro, Proficient, Pundit, Ringer, Rubrician, Savant, Savvy, Science, Shroff, Skilful, Skill(y), Sly, Specialist, Techie, Technique, Technocrat, Technofreak, Technophile, Think tank, Tipster, Troubleshooter, Ulema, Used, Whizz, Wireman, Wisard, W(h)iz, Wizard, Wonk

**Expiate, Expiation, Expiatory** Amends, Atone, Penance, Piacular, Purge

**Expire(d), Expiry** Blow, Collapse, Croak, → DIE, End, Exhale, Exhaust(ed), Go, Invalid, Ish, Lapse, Neese, Pant, → PERISH, Sneeze, Terminate

**Explain(able), Explanation, Explanatory** Account, Annotate, Aperçu, Apology, Appendix, Aread, Arede, Arreede, Clarify, Clear up, Commentary, Conster, Construe, Decline, Define, Definition, Describe, Eclaircissement, Elucidate, Epexegesis, Exegesis, Exegetic, Explicate, Exponible, Expose, Exposition, Expound, Extenuate, Farse, Gloss, Glossary, Gloze, Hypothesis, Interpret, Justify, Key, Note, Outline, Parabolize, Preface, Rationale, Rationalise, Reading, Rigmarole, Salve, Solution, Solve, Tell, Theory, Translate, Upknit, Why

**Expletive** Arrah, Darn, Exclamation, Oath, Ruddy, Sapperment, Swear word

**Explicit** Clean-cut, Clear(-cut), Definite, Express, Frank, Full-on, Graphic, Open, Outspoken, → PRECISE, Specific, Unequivocal

**Explode, Explosion, Explosive** Aerobomb, Agene, Airburst, Amatol, Ammonal, ANFO, Antimatter, Aquafortis, Atishoo, Backfire, Ballistic, Bang(er), Bangalore torpedo, Big bang, Blast, Blockbuster, Blow-out, Booby-trap, Boom, Burst, C4, Cap, Charge, Cheddite, Chug, Clap, Controlled, Cordite, Cramp, Crump, Cyclonite, Debunk, Demolitions, Depth bomb, Detonate, Dualin, Dunnite, Dust, Egg, Erupt, Euchloric, Euchlorine, Fiery, Fireball, Firecracker, Firedamp, Firework, Flip, Fulminant, Fulminate, Gasohol, Gelatine, Gelignite, Giant powder, Glottal stop, Grenade, Guncotton, Gunpaper, Gunpowder, Hand grenade, HE, High, Initiator, Iracund, Jelly, Landmine, Low, Lyddite, Megaton, Melinite, Mine, Nail-bomb, Napalm, Nitre, Nitro(glycerine), Nitrobenzene, Nitrocotton, Outburst, Ozonide, Paravane, Payload, Petar(d), Petre, Phreatic, Phut, Plastic, Plastique, Pluff, Pop, Population, Pow, Powderkeg, Priming, Propellant, Ptarmic, Pustular, Report, Roburite, SAM, Saucisse, Semtex®, Sheet, Shrapnel, Snake, Sneeze, Soup, Squib, Supernova, TATP, Tetryl, Thermite, Thunderflash, Tinderbox, TNT, Tonite, Trident, Trinitrobenzene, Trotyl, Volatile, Volcanic, Warhead, Xyloidin(e)

**Exploit(ation), Exploited, Exploiter, Exploiting, Exploits** Abuse, Act, Adventure, Arbitrage, Blaxploitation, Coup, Coyote, Daylight robbery, Deed, Develop, Downtrodden, Escapade, Feat, Freeloader, Gest, Geste, Harness, Ill-use, Impose, Kulak, Manoeuvre, Milk, Mine, Mission, Misuse, Opportunism, Parlay, Play on, Predatory, Profit, Rachmanism, Ramp, Res gestae, Rip-off, Shark, Stunt, Sweat, Tap, Use, Utilise, Venture

**Explore(r), Exploration, Exploratory, Exploring** Bandeirante, Caver, Chart, Discover, Dredge, Examine, Feel, Field trip, Heuristic, Investigate, Map, Navigator, Oceanaut, Pathfinder, Pioneer, Potholer, Probe, Prospect, Research, Scout, Search, Spaceship, Voyageur, Wildcat

---

**EXPLORERS**

*3 letters:*
Fox

*4 letters:*
Byrd
Cook
Dias
Diaz
Eric
Eyre
Grey
Park
Polo
Ross

*5 letters:*
Baker
Banks
Boone
Burke
Cabot
Clark
David
Drake
Fuchs
Giles
Oates
Parry
Peary
Ponce

Scott
Speke
Sturt
Wills

*6 letters:*
Baffin
Balboa
Bering
Burton
Cabral
Cortes
Da Gama
Darwin
De Soto
Lawson
Nansen
Ralegh
Rhodes
Sabine
Stuart
Tasman

*7 letters:*
Amerigo
Barents
Cartier
Cordoba
Dampier
Fiennes
Hillary
Raleigh
Stanley

*8 letters:*
Amundsen
Columbus
Cousteau
Eriksson
Flinders
Franklin
Hargrave
Humboldt
Magellan
Mitchell
Vespucci

*9 letters:*
Champlain
Frobisher
Mackenzie
Marco Polo
Mungo Park
Vancouver
Wentworth

*10 letters:*
Przewalski
Shackleton

*11 letters:*
Leif Ericson
Livingstone
Vasco da Gama

*14 letters:*
Bellingshausen

---

▷**Explosive** *may indicate* an anagram

**Exponent** Advocate, Example, Index, Interpreter, Logarithm

**Export(s)** Despatch, Émigré, Frustrated, Invisible, Klondike, Klondyke, Ship, Visible

**Expose(d), Exposure** Adamic, Air, Anagogic, Apparent, Bare, Bleak, Blot, Blow, Burn, Crucify, Debag, Debunk, Denounce, Denude, Desert, Disclose, Double, Endanger, En prise, Exhibit, Flashing, Gazing-stock, Glareal, Imperil, Indecent, Insolate, In the buff, Liable, Moon, Nail, Naked, Notoriety, Nude, Object, Open, Out, Over, Paramo, Propale, Public, Reveal, Showdown, Snapshot, Starkers, Streak, Strip, Subject, Sun, Time, Unclothe, Uncover, Unmask, Unrip, Unshroud, Vulnerable, Whistle-blow, Windburn, Windswept

**Exposition** Aperçu, Enarration

**Expostulate, Expostulation** Argue, Arrah, Protest, Remonstrate

**Expound(er)** Discourse, Discuss, Disseminate, Exegete, Explain, Open, Prelict, Red, Scribe, Ulema

**Express(ed), Expression, Expressionism, Expressive** Abstract, Air, Alas, APT, Arrah, Articulate, Aspect, Boolean, Breathe, Cacophemism, Circumbendimus, Cliché, Colloquialism, Conceive, Concetto, Couch, Countenance, Crumbs, Declare, Denote, Desorb, Diction, Eloquent, Embodiment, Epithet, Estafette, Evince, Explicit, Face, Fargo, Flying Scotsman, Formulate, Frown, Function, Gesticulate(d), Godspeed, Good-luck, Gotcha, Graphic, Grimace, Gup, Hang-dog, Hech, Heck, Hell's bells, Idiom, Isit, Limited, Locution, Look, Lyrical, Manifest, Metonym, Mien, Mot (juste), Mumpsimus, Neologism, Non-stop, Ole, Orient, Oxymoron, Paraphrase, Phrase, Pleonasm, Pony, Precise, Pronouncement, Pronto, Put, Quep, Rapid, Register, Rhetoric, Rictus, Say(ne), Saying, Shade, Show, Sigh, Soulful, →**SPEAK**, State, Strain, Succus, Sumpsimus, Taxeme, Term, Token, Tone, Topos, Tribute, Trope, Utterance, Vent, →**VOICE**, V-sign

**Expressionless** Aphasia, Blank, Boot-faced, Deadpan, Glassy, Impassive, Inscrutable, Po(ker)-faced, Vacant, Wooden

**Expressman** Fargo

**Expropriate** Dispossess, Pirate, Seize, Usurp

**Expulsion** Abjection, Discharge, Eccrisis, Ejection, Eviction, Exile, Pride's Purge, Removal, Sacking, Synaeresis

**Expunge** Cancel, Delete, Efface, Erase, Obliterate

**Expurgate** Bowdlerize, Castrate, Censor, Purge

**Exquisite** Beautiful, Choice, Ethereal, Fine, Fop, Intense, Lair, Macaroni, Pink, Princox, Refined, Soigné(e), Too-too

**Ex-serviceman** Vet

**Extempore, Extemporise(d)** Ad lib, Autoschediasm, Improvise, Pong

**Extend(ed), Extension** Add, Aggrandise, Annexe, Aspread, Augment, Conservative, Cremaster, Deepen, Dendrite, Draw, Drop-leaf, Ecarté, Eke, Elapse, Ell, Elongate, Enlarge, Escalate, Expand, Exsert, Extrapolation, Fermata, Grow, Increase, Jumboise, Lanai, Leaf, Length, Long, Long-range, Long-stay, Long-term, Offer, Outgrowth, Outspread, Overbite, Overlap, Pong, Porrect, Proffer, Prolong, Propagate, Protract, Reach, Renew,

Retrochoir, Span, Spin out, Spread, Spur, Steso, Stilt, → STRETCH, Substantial, Vert, Widen, Widespread, Yonks

**Extensive, Extent** Acre, Ambit, Area, Capacious, Catch-all, Compass, Comprehensive, Degree, Distance, Duration, Enormity, Far-reaching, Large(-scale), Latitude, Length, Limit, Long, → MAGNITUDE, Measure, Outspread, Panoramic, Range, Reach, Scale, Scope, Size, Spacious, Span, Spread-eagle, Sweeping, Wholesale, Wide, Widespread

**Extenuate** Diminish, Lessen, Mitigate, Palliate

**Exterior** Aspect, Crust, Derm, Exoteric, Facade, Outer, → OUTSIDE, Shell, Surface, Veneer

**Exterminate, Extermination** Abolish, Annihilate, Destroy, Eradicate, Ethnocide, Genocide, Holocaust, The final solution, Uproot

**External** Exoteric, Exterior, Extraneous, Foreign, Outer, Outward

**Extinct(ion)** Archaeopteryx, Bucardo, Bygone, Chalicothere, Creodont, Dead, Death, Defunct, D(e)inothere, Dodo, Glyptodon, Mastodon, Oblivion, Obsolete, Ostracoderm, Placoderm, Quagga, Quietus, Rasure, Rhytina, Saururae, Theodont, Ulmin

**Extinguish(er)** Douse, Dout, Dowse, Dowt, Extirpate, Fire, Obscure, Quash, Quell, Quench, Slake, Slo(c)ken, Smother, Snuff, Sprinkler, Stamp out, Stifle, Suppress

**Extirpate** Abolish, End, Erase, Excise, Obliterate, Root, Uproot

**Extol** Commend, Enhance, Eulogise, Exalt, Laud, Praise, Puff

**Extort(ion), Extortionate, Extortioner** Barathrum, Blackmail, Bleed, Bloodsucker, Chantage, Chout, Churn, Compel, Exact, Force, Gombeen, Malversation, Montem, Outwrest, Prohibitive, Rachman, Rack, Racketeer, Ransom, Rapacious, Screw, Shank, Sokaiya, Squeeze, Sweat, Urge, Usurious, Vampire, Wrest, Wring

**Extra** Accessory, Addendum, Additament, Addition(al), Additive, Adjunct, And, Annexe, Appendix, Attachment, Bisque, Bit player, Bonus, By(e), Codicil, Debauchery, Else, Encore, Etcetera, Frill, Further, Gash, Gooseberry, Lagniappe, Left-over, Leg bye, Make-weight, Mo, More, Nimiety, No ball, Odd, Optional, Out, Over, Overtime, Perk, Plus, Plusage, Reserve, Ripieno, → SPARE, Spilth, Staffage, Sub, Sundry, Super, Superadd, Supernumerary, Supplementary, Suppletive, Surcharge, Surplus, Top up, Trop, Undue, Walking-gentleman, Walking-lady, Wide, Woundy

**Extract(ion), Extractor** Apozem, Bleed, Breeding, Catechu, Clip, Corkscrew, Decoction, Derive, Descent, Distil, Draw, Educe, Elicit, Emulsin, Enfleurage, Enucleate, Episode, Essence, Estreat, Excerpt, Exodontics, Extort, Forceps, Formyl, Gist, Gobbet, Gossypol, Insulin, Ionone, Kino, Liebig, Liver, Malt, Milk, Mine, Mulct, Oust, Page, Parentage, Passage, Pericope, Pick, Piece, Pituitary, Prize, Pry, Pump, Pyrene, Pyrethrin, Quintessence, Quotation, Render, Retour, Retrieve, Smelt, Snippet, Soundbite, Squeeze, Stope, Succus, Suck, Summary, Tap, Tincture, Trie, Try, Vanilla, Vegemite®, Ventouse, Winkle, Withdraw, Worm, Wrest, Wring, Yohimbine

**Extradition** Renvoi

**Extraneous** Extrinsic, Foreign, Inessential, Irrelevant, Outlying, Spurious

**Extraordinary** Abnormal, Amazing, By-ordinar, Case, Curious, Egregious, Fabulous, Humdinger, Important, Marvellous, Non(e)such, Phenomenal, Preternatural, Rare, Remarkable, Signal, Singular, Sorter, Startling, Stellar, Strange, Tremendous, Unusual

**Extrasensory** Clairaudience, Clairvoyance, ESP

**Extraterrestrial** Alien

**Extra time** Lean

**Extravagance, Extravagant, Extravaganza** Bizarre, Bombastic, Dissipation, Elaborate, Enthusiasm, Excessive, Fancy, Feerie, Flamboyant, Fulsome, Glitzy, Grotesque, Heroic, High-flown, High roller, Hyperbole, Immoderate, Lavish, Lush, Luxury, OTT, Outré, Prodigal, Profligate, Profuse, Rampant, Reckless, Riotise, Romantic, Showy, Spectacle, Splash, Splurge, Squander, Sumptuous, Superfluous, Swish, Undue, Waste, Wasterfulness

**Extreme(s), Extremely, Extremist, Extremity** Acute, All-fired, Almighty, Bourn(e), Butt, Crisis, Deep-dyed, Desperate, Die-hard, Digit, Drastic, Edge, Ending, Enormously, Exceptional, Fanatic(al), Farthermost, Fascist, Finger(-tip), Gross, Hard-liner, Hellish, In spades, → INTENSE, Jacobin, Last cast, Leveller, Limb, Loony left, Major, Maximum, Mega-, Merveilleux, Militant, Minimum, Mondo, Much, National Front, Nazi, Not half, Opposite, OTT, Outrance, Overboard, Over the top, Parlous, Pole, Pretty, Radical, Remote, Root and branch, So, Solstice, Sorely, Steep, Sublime, Tendency, Terminal, Terrorist, The last cast, Thule, Tip, Toe, Toe-curling, Too, Tremendous, Ultimate, Ultima thule, Ultra, Unco, Utmost, Utter(ance), →VERY, Violent, Vitally, Wing

▷**Extreme** *may indicate* a first or last letter

**Extricate** Liberate, Loose, Outwind, Rescue, Untangle

**Extrinsic** Aliunde, External, Irrelevant, Outward

**Extrovert** Lad, Outgoing

**Extrude** Debar, Eject, Project

**Exuberance, Exuberant** Abundant, Boisterous, Brio, Bushy, Copious, Ebullient, Effusive, Feisty, Flamboyant, Gleeful, Gusto, Hearty, Joie de vivre, Lavish, Mad, Overflowing, Profuse, Rambunctious, Rumbustious, Skippy, Streamered

**Exudation, Exude** Bleed, Ectoplasm, Emit, Extravasate, Guttate, Ooze, Perspire, Radiate, Secrete, Still, Sweat, Swelter, Ulmin, Weep

**Exult(ant), Exultation** Cock-a-hoop, Crow, Elated, →GLOAT, Glorify, Glory be, Joy, Jubilant, Paeonic, Rejoice, Tripudiate, Triumphant, Whoop

**Eye(d), Eyes, Eye-ball, Eyeful, Eyelike, Eye movement, Eyepiece** Aperture, Apheroid, Armed, Beady, Blinker, Canthus, Compound, Cornea, Cringle, Deepset, Detective, Eagle, Ee, Eine, Electric, Electronic, Emmetropia, Evil, Glad, Glass, Glim, Glom, Goggles, Hurricane, Huygen's, Iridal, Iris, Jack, Keek, Klieg, Lamp, Lazy, Leer, Lens, London, Magic, Many, Mincepie, Mind's, Mongoloid, Naked, Nystagmus, →OBSERVE, Ocellar, Ocular, Ogle, Ommateum, Ommatidium, Optic, Orb, Pedicel, Peeper, Periscope, PI, Pigsnie, Pigsn(e)y, Pineal, Private, Public, Pupil, Regard, Retina, Rhabdom, Roving, Saccade, Saucer, Sclera, Screw, Seeing, Sheep's, Shufti, Shufty, Sight, Spy, Stemma, Storm-centre, Tec, Third, Tiger, Uvea, Watch, Water-pump, Weather, Whally, Windows, Winker

**Eyebright** Euphrasy

**Eyebrow** Bree, Brent-hill, Glib, Penthouse, Superciliary

**Eyeglass** Loupe

**Eyelash** Cilium, Winker

**Eyelet** Cringle, Grommet, Hole

**Eyelid** Canthus, Ectropion, Haw, Palpebral, Winker

**Eye-opener, Eye-opening** Alarm, Revelatory

**Eye-rod** Rhabdom

**Eye-shadow** Kohl

**Eyesore** Blot, Carbuncle, Disfigurement, Sty(e)

**Eye specialist** Optician, Optometrist

**Eye-stalk** Ommatophore, Stipes

**Eye trouble, Eye-problem** Albugo, Amblyopia, Ametropia, Aniridia, Aniseikonia, Anisomatropia, Aphakia, Arcus, Asthenopia, Astigmatism, Caligo, Cataract, Ceratitis, Coloboma, Comae, Conjunctivitis, Cycloplegia, Detached retina, Diplopia, Ectropion, Ectropium, Entropion, Erythropsia, Exophthalmus, Glaucoma, Gravel-blind, Hemeralopia, Hemi(an)op(s)ia, Heterotropia, Hypermetropia, Hyperopia, Iritis, Keratitis, Lazy eye, Leucoma, Lippitude, Micropsia, Miosis, Monoblepsis, Muscae volitantes, Mydriasis, Myosis, Nebula, Nyctalopia, Nystagmus, Ommateum, Palinop(s)ia, Pearl eye, Photophobia, Photopsia, Pin and web, Pink-eye, Presbyopia, Proptosis, Protanopia, Ptosis, Retinitis, Retinoblastoma, Sandy blight, Scotoma(ta), Shiner, Speccy, Stigmatism, Strabismus, Strephosymbolia, Strong, Stye, Synechia, Teichopsia, Thylose, Thylosis, Trachoma, Trichiasis, Tritanopia, Tylosis, Wall-eye, Web and pin, Xeroma, Xerophthalmia

**Eye-wash** Collyrium

**Eye-witness** Passer-by

**Eyrie** Nest

**Ezra** Pound

# Ff

**F** Fahrenheit, Fellow, Feminine, Fluorine, Following, Force, Foxtrot
**Fab** Super
**Fabian, Fabius** Dilatory, Washington, Webb
**Fable(s)** Aesop, Allegory, Apologue, Beast, Exemplum, Fiction, Hitopadesa, La Fontaine, Legend, Lie, Marchen, Milesian, Myth, Panchatantra, Parable, Romance, Tale, Tarand
**Fabric** Acetate, Cheesecloth, → CLOTH, Contexture, Dévoré, Evenweave, Felt, Framework, Fur, Gossamer, Hessian, Interfacing, Interlining, Interlock, Lurex®, Lycra, Neoprene, Orlon®, Plissé, PVC, Ratteen, Ripstop, Scrim, Spandex, Stretch-knit, Tartan, Textile, Velour, Webbing
**Fabricate, Fabrication** Artefact, Concoct, Confabulate, Construct, Contrive, Cook, Fake, Fangle, Figment, Forge, → INVENT, Lie, Make up, Myth, Porky, Trump, Weave, Web
**Fabulous (beast), Fabulous place** Ace, Apocryphal, Apologue, Atlantis, Chichevache, Chimera, Cockatrice, Eldorado, Fictitious, Fung, Gear, Griffin, Hippogriff, Hippogryph, Huma, Incredible, Jabberwock(y), Kylin, Legendary, Magic, Manticora, Manticore, Merman, Monoceros, Mythical, Opinicus, Orc, Phoenix, Roc, Romantic, Simorg, Simurg(h), Snark, Sphinx, Storybook, Tarand, Tragelaph, Unicorn, Unreal, Utopia, Wivern, Wyvern, Yale
**Facade** Front(age), Frontal, Mask, Persona, Pretence, Surface
**Face, Facing** Abide, Affront, Ashlar, Ashler, Aspect, Audacity, Beard, Bide, Bold, Brave, Brazen, Caboched, Caboshed, Cheek, Chiv(v)y, Cliff, Coal, Confront, Countenance, Culet, Dalle, Dare, Dartle, Daur, Deadpan, Dial, Eek, Elevation, Encounter, Expression, Facade, Fat, Favour, Features, Fineer, Fortune, → FRONT, Gardant, Girn, Gonium, Grid, Groof, Groue, Grouf, Grufe, Gurn, Hatchet, Head-on, Hippocratic, Jib, Kisser, Light, Lining, Look, Lore, Map, Mascaron, Meet, Metope, Moe, Mug, Mush, Obverse, Oppose, Opposite, Outstare, Outward, Pan, Paper tiger, Pavilion, Phisnomy, Phiz(og), Physiognomy, Poker, Puss, Revet, Revetment, Roughcast, Rud, Rybat, Side, Snoot, Socle, Stand, Straight, Stucco, Tallow, Three-quarter, Times Roman, Topsoil, Type, Veneer, Vis(age), Visnomy, Wall, Withstand, Zocco(lo)
**Face-ache** Noli-me-tangere
**Faceless** Anonymous
**Face-lift** Rhytidectomy, Transformation
**Face-saving** Redeeming, Salvo
**Facet(ed)** Angle, Aspect, Bezel, Culet, Face, Pavilion, Polyhedron
**Facetious** Frivolous, Jocose, Jocular, Waggish, Witty
**Facile** Able, Adept, Complaisant, Ductile, Easy, Fluent, Glib, Trite
**Facilitate, Facilities, Facility** Agrement, Amenity, App, Assist, Benefit, Bent, Capability, Committed, Datel®, → EASE, Enable, Expedite, Fastext, Fluency, Gift, ISO, Knack, Lavatory, Loo, Provision, Skill
**Facsimile** Copy, Electro, Electrotype, Photostat®, Replica, Repro
**Fact(s), Factual** Actual, Brass tacks, Case, Circumstance, Clue, Corpus delicti, Correct, Data, Datum, Detail, Eo ipso, Evidence, French, Gospel, Griff, Hard, In esse, Info, Information, Input, Literal, Mainor, Material, Nay, Poop, Proof, Reality, Really, Stat, Statistics, Truism, Truth, Veridical, Yes
**Faction** Bloc, Cabal, Camp, Caucus, Clique, Contingent, Gang of four, Ghibelline, Group(let), Guelph, Junta, Junto, Party, Red Army, Schism, Sect, Tendency, Wing
**Factor(s)** Agent, Aliquot, Amildar, Broker, Cause, Chill, Clotting, Coagulation, Co-efficient, Common, → COMPONENT, Consideration, Dealbreaker, Divisor, Edaphic, Element, F,

Feedback, Feel-bad, Feel-good, Fertility, Growth, House, Imponderabilia, Institorial, Intrinsic, Judicial, Load, Modulus, Moment, Multiple, Power, Pull, Q, Quality, Reflection, Representative, Rh, Rhesus, Risk, Safety, Sex, Steward, Transfer, Unit, Utilization, Wind chill, X

**Factory** Ashery, Bakery, Brickworks, Cannery, Condensery, Creamery, Etruria, Gasworks, Glassworks, Hacienda, Ironworks, Maquiladora, Mill, Mint, Plant, Refinery, Sawmill, Shop, Shot tower, Steelworks, Sugarhouse, Sweatshop, Tanyard, Tinworks, Wireworks, Works, Workshop

**Factory-owner** Industrialist

**Factotum** Bottle-washer, Circar, Do-all, Handyman, Servant, Sircar, Sirkar

**Faculty** Aptitude, Arts, Capacity, Department, Ear, Ease, Flair, Hearing, Indult, Knack, Lavatory, Loo, Moral, Power, Psyche, School, Sense, Speech, → **TALENT**, Teachers, Uni(versity), Wits

**Fad(dish), Faddy** Crank, Craze, Cult, Fashion, Foible, Ismy, Newfangled, Picky, Thing, Vogue, Whim

**Fade(d), Fading** Abate, Blanch, Bleach, Decline, Decrescendo, Die, Diminuendo, Dinge, Disperse, Dwindle, Elapsion, Etiolate, Evanescent, Fall, Filemot, Fizzle, Lessen, Mancando, Miffy, Pale, Passé, Perdendo(si), Peter, Pine, Smorzando, Smorzato, Stonewashed, Vade, Vanish, Wallow, Wilt, Wither

**Faeces** Cesspit, Dingleberry, Dung, Kak, Meconium, Motion, Mute, Number two, Scat, Scybalum, Skatole, Stercoraceous, Stools

**Faff** Bother

**Fag(ging)** Brain, Chore, Cigarette, Drag, Drudge, Fatigue, Gasper, Inconvenience, Menial, Pennalism, Reefer, Snout, Tire, Toil, Weary

**Fag-end** Ash, Butt, Dout, Lag, Snipe, Stub

**Fag(g)ot(s)** Bavin, Bundle, Fascine, Firewood, Kid, Knitch, Twigs

**Faience** Trema

**Fail(ing), Failure** Achalasia, Ademption, Anile, Anuria, Awry, Backfire, Bankruptcy, Blemish, Blow, Bomb, Breakdown, Bummer, Burst-up, Cark, Chicken, → **COLLAPSE**, Common-mode, Conk, Crack up, Crash, Cropper, Damp squib, Debacle, Decline, Defalcation, Default, Defeat, Defect, Demerit, Demise, Die, Disaster, Dog, Downfall, Down the tubes, Dry, Dud, Fatigue, Fault, Feal, Fiasco, Fink out, Flame out, Flivver, Flop, Flow, Flunk, Fold, Footfault, Founder, Frost, Fruitless, Futility, Glitch, Go belly up, Goner, Go phut, Gutser, Impotent, Infraction, Isn't, Lapse, Lemon, Lose, Lossage, Malfunction, Manqué, Meltdown, Mis-, Miscarry, Misfire, Misprision, Miss, Muff, Nearly-man, Nerd, No dice, No-hoper, No-no, No-show, Omission, Omit, Outage, Oversight, Peccadillo, Pip, Plough, Plow, Pluck, Pratfall, Reciprocity, Refer, Refusal, Relapse, Remiss, Respiratory, Shambles, Short(coming), Short circuit, Shortfall, Sink, Slippage, Smash, Spin, Stumer, Tank, Turkey, Vice, Wash-out, Waterloo, Weakness, White elephant, Wilt, Wipeout, Write off

**Fain** Lief

**Faineant** Gallio

**Faint(ness)** Black-out, Conk, Darkle, Dim, Dizzy, Dwalm, Fade, Giddy, Keel over, Lassitude, Pale, Slender, Stanck, Subtle, Swarf, Swarve, Swelt, Swerf, Swerve, Swoon, Swound, Syncope, Unclear, Wan, Whitish, Wispy

**Faint-heart, Fainthearted** Boneless, Coward, Craven, Eery, Hen, Squeamish, Timid, Wet

**Fair, Fairground** Adequate, Aefauld, Aefwld, A(e)fald, Barnet, Bartholomew, Bazaar, Beauteous, Beautiful, Belle, Big dipper, Blond, Bon(n)ie, Bonny, Brigg, Carnival, Clean, Clement, Decent, Dinkum, Dishy, Donnybrook, Do's, Eirian, Equal, Equitable, Evenhanded, Even Stevens, Exhibition, Expo(sition), Fancy, Feeing-market, → **FESTIVAL**, Fête, Fine, Fiona, Funfair, Gaff, Gala, Game, Gay, Gey, Goose, Gwyn, Handsome, Hiring, Honest, Hopping, Isle, Isold(e), → **JUST**, Kermess, Kermis, Kirmess, Light, Market, Mart, Mediocre, Mela, Mop, Mousy, Nundinal, Objective, OK, Paddington, Passable, Play, Pro rata, Rag, Rosamond, Sabrina, Second rate, So-so, Sporting, Sportsmanlike, Square, Statute, Steeple, Straight, Tavistock, Tidy, Tolerable, Tow-headed, Trade, Tryst, Unbias(s)ed, Vanity, Wake, Widdicombe, Xanthe

**Fair-buttocked** Callipygean

**Fairing** Ornament, Spat

**Fairly** Clearly, Enough, Evenly, Midway, Moderately, Pari passu, Pretty, Properly, Quite, Ratherish, So-so

**Fairway** Dog-leg, Pretties

**Fairy, Fairies** Banshee, Befana, Brownie, Cobweb, Dobbie, Dobby, Elf(in), Fay, Gloriana, Good neighbour, Good people, Hob, Hop o' my thumb, Leprechaun, Lilian, Little people, Mab, Morgane(tta), Morgan le Fay, Moth, Mustardseed, Nis, Oberon, Peri, Pigwidgin, Pigwiggen, Pisky, Pixie, Puck, Queen Mab, Sandman, Seelie, Sidhe, Spirit, Sprite, Sugar-plum, Tink(erbell), Titania, Tooth, Unseelie, Urchin-shows

**Faith(ful)** Accurate, Achates, Adam, Belief, Constant, Creed, Cupboard, Devoted, Doctrine, Exact, Faix, Fay, Feal, Fegs, Fideism, Fiducial, Good, Haith, Honesty, Implicit, Islam, Lay, Liege, Loyal, Pantheism, Plerophory, Punic, Puritanism, Quaker, Reliance, Religion, Shahada, Shema, Solifidian, Staunch, Strict, Troth, →**TRUE**, True-blue, Trust, Truth, Umma(h), Vera

**Faithless** Atheist, Disloyal, False, Giaour, Hollow, Infidel, Nullifidian, Perfidious, Punic

**Fake(d), Faker, Faking** Bodgie, Bogus, Charlatan, Cod, Copy, Counterfeit, Duff(er), Ersatz, False, Feign, Fold, Forgery, Fraud, Fudge, Imitation, Imposter, Impostor, Inauthentic, Paste, Phoney, Pirate(d), Placebo, Postiche, Pretend, Pseudo, Quack, Scam, Sham, Simulated, Spurious, Straw man, Toy, Trucage, Trumped up, Truquage, Truqueur, Unreal, Untrue

**Falcon** Cast, Gentle, Hawk, Hobby, Iceland, Kestrel, Lanner(et), Merlin, Nankeen kestrel, Nyas, Peregrine, Prairie, Saker, Sakeret, Spar-hawk, Sparrow-hawk, Stallion, Staniel, Stannel, Stanyel, Stone, Tassel-gentle, Tassell-gent, Tercel-gentle, Tercel-jerkin

**Falklander** Kelper

**Fall(s), Fallen, Falling, Fall out** Abate, Accrue, Alopecia, Angel, Anticlimax, Arches, Astart, Autumn, Boyoma, Cadence, Caducous, Cascade, Cataract, Churchill, Chute, Collapse, Crash, Cropper, Cross press, Declasse, Declension, Decline, Decrease, Degenerate, Deluge, Depreciate, Descent, Dip, Domino effect, Douse, Downpour, Downswing, Dowse, →**DROP**, Ebb, End, Firn, Flag, Flop, Flump, Folding press, Free, Grabble, Grand, Gutser, Gutzer, Horseshoe, Idaho, Iguaçu, Incidence, Kabalega, Kaieteur, Keel over, Lag, Landslide, Landslip, Lapse, Lin(n), Montmorency, Mtarazi, Niagara, Oct(ober), Onding, Overbalance, Owen, Perish, Plonk, Plummet, Plump, Plunge, Prat, Precipitance, Prolapse, Ptosis, Purl(er), Rain, Reaction, Relapse, Ruin, Season, Sheet, Sin, Sleet, Slide, Slip, Snow, Soss, Spill, Stanley, Sutherland, Swallow, Tailor, Takakkau, Teem, Topple, Toss, Trip, Tugela, Tumble, Victoria, Voluntary, Wipeout, Yellowstone, Yosemite

**Fallacious, Fallacy** Elench(us), Error, Gamblers', Idolon, Idolum, Ignoratio elenchi, Illogical, Illusion, Material, Naturalistic, Pathetic, Sophism, Specious, Unsound

**Fall guy** Mug

**Fallible** Human, Imperfect

▷**Falling** *may indicate* an anagram or a word backwards

**Fallow** Barren, Lea, Tan, Uncared, Uncultivated, Untilled

**False, Falsify, Falsification, Falsehood** Adulterate, Assumed, Bastard, Bodgie, Bogus, Braide, Bricking, Bum, Calumny, Canard, Cavil, Charlatan, Cook, Counterfeit, Deceitful, Delusion, Disloyal, Dissemble, Doctor, Façade, Fake, Faux, Feigned, Fiddle, Fit-up, Forge, Fudge, Illusory, Inaccurate, Inexact, Insincere, Knave, Leasing, Lying, Masquerade, Mendacious, Meretricious, Misconception, Misrepresented, Misstatement, Mock, Mooncalf, Mooncall, Myth, Obreption, Perjury, Phoney, Pinchbeck, Postiche, Pretence, Prosthesis, Pseudo, Rap, Refute, Roorback, Sham, Specious, Spoof, Spurious, Strumpet, Suspect, Synthetic, Treacherous, Trumped-up, Two-faced, Untrue, Veneer

**False notions** Idola

**False teeth** Dentures

**Falter** Dither, Hesitate, Hobble, Limp, Lurch, Stoiter, Totter, Waver

**Fame, Famous** A-list, All-star, Big, Bruit, Cause célèbre, Celebrity, Distinguished, Eminent, Five, Glitterati, Gloire, Glory, Greatness, History, Humour, Iconic, Illustrious, Immortality, Known, Kudos, Legendary, Luminary, Luminous, Lustre, Megastar, Mononym, Name, Noted, Notorious, Prestige, Reclamé, Renown, Repute, Robert, Rumour, Splendent, Spotlight, Spur, Stardom, Word

**Familiar(ise), Familiarity** Accustom, Acquaint, Assuefaction, Attune, Au fait, Auld, Chummy, Comrade, Consuetude, Conversant, Couth, Crony, Dear, Demon, Easy, Free, Fresh, Friend, Habitual, Hailfellow, Homely, Homey, Incubus, Intimate, Known, Liberty, Maty, Near, Old, Old-hat, Privy, Public, Python, Streetwise, Used, Versant, Versed, Warhorse

**Family** Ainga, Ancestry, Bairn-team, Blood, Breed, Brood, Clan, Class, Close-knit, Cognate, Consanguine, County, Descent, Dynasty, Extended, Eye, Hapsburg, Holy, House(hold), Issue, Kin, Kind, Kindred, Line, Litter, Mafia, Medici, Name, Nuclear, One-parent, Orange, Pedigree, People, Phratry, Progeny, Quiverful, Race, Roots, Sept, Sib(b), Sibship, Single-parent, Stem, Stirps, Storge, Strain, Sub-order, Syndyasmian, Taffy, Talbot, Totem, Tribe, Whanau

**Family tree** Pedigree, Stemma

**Famine** Dearth, Lack, Scarcity

**Famish(ed)** Esurient, Hungry, Ravenous, Starving

▹**Famished** *may indicate* an 'o' in the middle of a word

**Fan(s), Fan-like** Addict, Adherent, Admirer, Adorer, Aficionado, Alligator, Alluvial, Arouse, Bajada, Barmy-army, B-boy, Blow, Buff, Cat, Cheer-leader, Clapper, Claque, Colmar, Cone, Cool, Cuscus, Devotee, Diadrom, Disciple, Dryer, Ducted, Enthusiast, Extractor, Fiend, Film, Flabellum, Following, Goth, Grebo, Groupie, Groupy, Headbanger, Hepcat, Khuskhus, Muso, Nut, Obsessed, Outspread, Partisan, Popette, Propellor, Public, Punka(h), Radiate, Rhipidate, Ringsider, Rooter, Rotary, Sail, Slamdancer, Spectator, Splay, Spread, Supporter, Tail, Tartan army, Teenybopper, Tifosi, Trekkie, Ventilate, Votary, Voteen, Washingtonia, Wind machine, Wing, Winnow, Zealot, Zelant

▹**Fan** *may indicate* an anagram

**Fanatic(al)** Bigot, Boatie, Buff, Devotee, Energumen, Enthusiastic, Extremist, Fiend, Frenetic, Glutton, Idolater, Mad, Maniac, Nut, Partisan, Phrenetic, Picard, Rabid, Santon, Ultra, Workaholic, Wowser, Zealot

**Fancy, Fancies, Fanciful** Admire, Adore, Caprice, Chim(a)era, Conceit, Concetto, Crotchet, Daydream, Dream, Dudish, Elaborate, Embellishment, Fangle, Fantasy, Fit, Flam, Flash, Florid, Flowery, Frilly, Frothy, Guess, Hallo, Idea(te), Idolon, → IMAGINE, Inclination, Intricate, I say, Itch, Lacy, Liking, Maggot, Maya, Metaphysical, Mind, Mind's eye, Mirage, Moonshine, My, Nap, Notion, Opine, Ornamental, Ornate, Passing, Petit four, Phantastry, Picture, Pipe dream, Predilection, Preference, Reverie, Rococo, Romanticise, Suppose, Suspect, Thought, Unreal, Urge, Vagary, Visionary, Ween, Whigmaleerie, Whigmaleery, Whim(sy), Woolgather

▹**Fancy** *may indicate* an anagram

**Fane** Banner, Pronaos

**Fanfare** Flourish, Sennet, Show, Tantara, Trump, Tucket

**Fang** Tooth, Tusk

**Fanny** Adams, Bottom, Gas-lit, Price

**Fantasist, Fantasise, Fantastic, Fantasy** Absurd, Amazing, Antic, Bizarre, Brilliant, Caprice, Centaur, Chimera, Cloud-cuckoo land, Cockaigne, Cockayne, Daydream, Dream world, Escapism, Fab, Fanciful, First class, Grotesque, Hallucination, Idol, Idola, Illusion, Kickshaw(s), Lucio, Make believe, Mega, Myth, Outré, Phantasmagoria, Pipe-dream, Queer, Reverie, Romance, Schizoid, Star-gaze, Surreal, Transcendent, Unreal, Untrue, Walter Mitty, Wannabe(e), → WHIM, Whimsical, Wild, Wishful thinking, Wonderland, Wuxia

**Far** Apogean, Away, Distal, Distant, Eloi(g)n, Extreme, Outlying, Remote, Thether, Thither

**Farce(ur), Farcical** Burletta, Charade, Comedy, Exode, Feydeau, Lazzo, Mime, Mockery, Nonsense, Pantomime, Risible, Rix, Screaming, Sham, Travesty

**Fare** Apex, Charge, Cheer, Commons, Do, Eat, Excess, Excursion, → FOOD, Go, Passage, Passage money, Passenger, Rate, Saver, Table, Traveller

**Farewell** Adieu, Adios, Aloha, Apopemptic, Bye, Cheerio, Departure, Godspeed, → GOODBYE, Leave, Prosper, Sayonara, Send off, So long, Toodle-oo, Toodle-pip, Totsiens, Vale, Valediction

**Far-fetched** Fanciful, Improbable, Recherché

**Farm(ing), Farmhouse, Farm out** Agronomy, Animal, Arable, Bender, Bocage, Bowery, City, Cold Comfort, Collective, Cooperative, Croft, Cultivate, Dairy, Deep-litter,

Dry, Emmerdale, Estancia, Extensive, Factory, Fat, Fieldwork, Fish(ery), Funny, Geoponical, Gite, Grange, Grow, Hacienda, Health, Home, Homestead, Husbandry, Intensive, Kibbutz, Kolkhoz, Land, Ley, Loaf, Location, Mailing, Mains, Mas, Mixed, No-tillage, Onstead, Orley, Oyster, Pen, Plaas, Plough, Poultry, Ranch, Render, Rent, Set-aside, Sewage, Shamba, Sheep run, Sheep station, Smallholding, Sovkhoz, Station, Stead(ing), Sted(d), Stedde, Steed, Stock, Store, Stud, Stump, Subcontract, Subsistence, Tank, Till, Toon, Toun, Town, Trash, Tree, Trout, Truck, Wick, Wind

**Farmer** Blockie, Boer, Campesino, Carl, Cockatoo, Cocklaird, Cocky, Collins Street, Colon, Cow cocky, Crofter, Cropper, Dairy, Dirt, Estanciero, Gebur, Gentleman, George, Giles, Hick, Hobby, Husbandman, Macdonald, Metayer, Nester, NFU, Peasant, Pitt Street, Publican, Queen St, Rancher(o), Reaper, Ryot, Share-cropper, Smallholder, Sodbuster, Squatter, Stubble-jumper, Tax, Tenant, Tiller, Whiteboy, Yeoman, Zeminda(r)

**Farmhand** Byreman, Cadet, Churl, Cottar, Cotter, Cottier, Cowman, Ditcher, Goat herd, Hand, Harvester, He(a)rdsman, Hind, Land girl, Neat herd, Orraman, Peon, Ploughman, Ranchero, Redneck, Rouseabout, Roustabout, Shearer, Sheepo, Stockman, Swineherd, Thresher, Vaquero

▸**Farmhouse** *see* FARM(ING)

**Farmyard, Farm buildings** Barton, Henhouse, Hennery, Homestall, Villatic

**Faroe Islands** FO

**Farouche** Awkward, Blate, Shy, Sullen

**Farrago** Hotch-potch, Jumble, Medley, Mélange

**Farrier** Marshal, Saddler, Smith

**Farrow** Litter, Mia, Sow

**Far-sighted** Clairvoyant, Presbyte, Provident

**Fart** Break wind, Let off, Poep, Trump

**Farthing** Brass, F, Fadge, Har(r)ington, Mite, Q, Quadragesimal, Rag

**Fascia** Band, Fillet, Platband

**Fascinate(d), Fascinating, Fascinator** Allure, Attract, Bewitch, → CHARM, Dare, Enchant, Engross, Enrapt, Ensorcell, Enthral(l), Fetching, Hypnotise, Inthral, Into, Intrigue, Jolie laide, Kill, Mesmeric, Rapt, Rivet, Sexy, Siren, Sirenic, Spellbounding, Witch

**Fascist** Blackshirt, Blue shirt, Body, Brownshirt, Dictator, Falange, Falangist, Iron Guard, Lictor, National Front, Nazi, Neo-Nazi, NF, Phalangist, Rexist, Sinarchist, Sinarquist

**Fashion(able), Fashioned, Fashion house** Adapt, Aguise, À la (mode), Alta moda, Armani, Beau monde, Bon ton, Bristol, Build, Carve, Chic, Construct, Convention, Cool, Corinthian, Craft, Craze, Create, Cult, Custom, Cut, Dernier cri, Design, Directoire, Draft, Du jour, Elegant, Entail, Fabricate, Fad, Fantoosh, Feat, Feign, Fly, Forge, Form, Garb, Genteel, Go, Heroin chic, Hew, High, Hip, Hipster, Hot, In, Invent, Kick, Kitsch, Latest, Look, → MAKE, Man-about-town, Manière, Manners, Manufacture, Method, Mode, Mondain(e), Mould, Newgate, New Look, Parrot, Pink, Posh, Prada, Predominant, Preppy, Rage, Rag trade, Ramil(l)ie(s), Rate, Red-hot, Roy, Sc, Shape, Sloane, Smart, Smith, Snappy, Snazzy, Soigne, Sophisticated, Stile, Stylar, Style, Swish, Tailor, Ton, Tonish, Ton(e)y, → TREND(Y), Trendsetter, Turn, Twig, U, Vogue, Waif, Way, Wear, Wise, With-it, Work, Wrought

**Fast(ing), Faster** Abstain, Apace, Ashura, Bastille, Breakneck, Brisk, Celerity, Citigrade, Clappers, Clem, Clinging, Cracking, Daring, Dharna, Dhurna, Double-quick, Elaphine, Express, Fizzer, Fleet, Hunger strike, Hypersonic, Icebound, Immobile, Lane, Lent, Lightning, Loyal, Maigre, Meteoric, Moharram, Muharram, Muharrem, Nippy, Pac(e)y, Posthaste, Presto, Promiscuous, Pronto, Quadragesimal, Quick, Raffish, Raking, Ramadan, Ramadhan, Rash, Rathe, Relay, Sehri, Siyam, Smart, Spanking, Speedy, Stretta, Stretto, Stuck, Supersonic, Sure, Swift, Tachyon, Thick, Tied, Tight, Tisha b'Av, TishaBov, Tishah-Baav, Tishah-b(e)Ab, Tishah-b(e)Av, Ventre-à-terre, Whistle-stop, Xerophagy, Yarer, Yom Kippur, Zippy

**Fast and loose** Fickle, Prick-the-garter, Strap-game

**Fasten(er), Fastening** Anchor, Attach, Bar, Batten, Belay, Belt, Bind, Bolt, Buckle, Button, Catch, Chain, Clamp, Clasp, Click, Clinch, Clip, Cramp, Cufflink, Dead-eye, Diamond-hitch, Dome, Dowel, Espagnolette, Eye-bolt, Fly-front, Frog, Gammon, Grommet, Hasp, Hesp, Hitch, Hook, Infibulation, Lace, Lash, Latch, Lock, Moor, Morse, Nail, Netsuke, Nip, Nut,

Padlock, Paper-clip, Parral, Patent, Pectoral, Peg, Pin, Preen, Press stud, Reeve, Rivet, Rope, Rove, Safety pin, Screw, Seal, →SECURE, Sew up, Shut, Slide, Spar, Sprig, Staple, Steek, Stitch, Strap, Stud, Suspender, Swift(er), Tach(e), Tag, Tape, Tassel, Tether, Thong, Tintack, Toggle, Twist-tie, U-bolt, Velcro®, Wedge, Zip

**Fastidious** Chary, Choosy, Critical, Dainty, Delicate, Exquisite, Fusspot, Fussy, Neat, Nice, Overnice, Particular, Picky, Precieuse, Precious, Prim, Purism, Quaint, Queasy, Quiddler, Rosewater, Squeamish

**Fat(s), Fatted, Fatten(ing), Fatty** Adipic, Adipocere, Adipose, Aldermanly, Aliphatic, Arcus, Atheroma, Bard, Batten, Battle, Beefy, Blowsy, Blubber, Brown, Bulge, Bunter, Butter, Calf, Calipash, Calipee, Cellulite, Cholesterol, Chubbed, Chubby, Cocoa, Corpulent, Creesh, Curd, Degras, Deutoplasm, Dika-oil, Dosh, Dripping, Embonpoint, Enarm, Endomorph, Ester, Flab, Flesh, Flick, Fozy, Frank, Fubsy, Galam-butter, Ghee, Gor-belly, Grease, Gross, Keech, Kitchen-fee, Lanolin, Lard, Lard-ass, Leaf, Lipaemia, Lipid, Lipoma, Love handles, Marbling, Margarine, Marge, Marrow, Mart, Moti, Motu, Muffin top, Obese, Oil, Olein, Oleomargarine, Olestra, OS, Palmitin, Pinguid, Plump, Poddy, Podgy, Polyunsaturated, Portly, Pudgy, Puppy, Pursy, Rich, Rolypoly, Rotund, Saddlebags, Saginate, Saim, Saturated, Schmal(t)z, Seam(e), Sebacic, Sebum, Shortening, Soil, Spare tyre, Spe(c)k, Squab, Stearic, Steatopygia, Steatorrhea, Steatosis, Suberin, Suet, Tallow, Tin, Tomalley, Trans, Triglyceride, Tub, Unsaturated, Vanaspati, Waller, Well-padded, Well-upholstered, Wool

**Fatal(ism), Fatality, Fate(s), Fated, Fateful** Apnoea, Atropos, Cavel, Chance, Clotho, Comeuppance, Deadly, Death (blow), Decuma, Destiny, Doom, End, Fay, Feedlot, Fell, Hara-kiri, Joss, Karma, Kismet, Lachesis, Lethal, Lethiferous, Loss, Lot, Meant, Moera(e), Moira, Momentous, Morta, Mortal, Mortiferous, Nemesis, Nona, Norn(a), Parca, Pernicious, Portion, Predestination, Pre-ordain, Skuld, Urd, Verdande, Waterloo, Weird, Weird sisters

**Father(s), Fatherly** Abba, Abbot, Abuna, Adopt, Agnation, Apostolic, Bapu, Begetter, Breadwinner, Brown, Chaplain, City, Conscript, Curé, Da, Dad, Engender, Foster, Founding, Fr, Generator, Genitor, Getter, Gov, Governor, Guv, Male, NASCAR dad, Pa, Padre, Papa, Pappy, Parent, Pater(nal), Paterfamilias, Patriarch, Patroclinic, Père, Pilgrim, Pop(pa), Popper, Priest, Rev, Seraphic, Sire, Start, Stud, Thames, Tiber, William

**Father-lasher** Sea-scorpion

**Fathom** Delve, Depth, Dig, F, Plumb, Plummet, Understand

**Fatigue(d)** Battle, Bonk, Chore, Combat, Compassion, Exhaust, Fag, Jade, Jet lag, ME, Metal, Myalgic encephalomyelitis, Neurasthenia, Overdo, Overwatch, Spent, Swinked, Time-zone, Tire, Weariness, Weary

**Fat man** A-bomb

**Fatuous** Gaga, Goop, Idiotic, Inane, Silly, Stupid, Wet

**Faucet** Cock, Spigot, Tap

**Fault(y), Fault-finding** Arraign, Bad, Beam, Blame(worthy), Blunder, Bug, Cacology, Captious, Carp, Compound, Criticise, Culpa, Culpable, Defect, Demerit, Dip, Dip-slip, Down to, Drop-out, Dud, Duff, →ERROR, Expostulate, Failing, Flaw, Foot, Frailty, Gall, Glitch, Gravity, Henpeck, Hitch, Idiot light, Impeach, Imperfect, Kaput, Knock, Literal, Massif, →MISTAKE, Mortal sin, Nag, Nibble, Niggle, Nit-pick, Oblique, Oblique-slip, Out, Outcrop, Overthrust, Pan, Para, Peccadillo, Pre-echo, Quibble, Rate, Red eye, Reprehend, Rift, Rupes Recta, San Andreas, Sclaff, Set-off, Short, Slip, Snag, Step, Strike, Strike-slip, Structional, Technical, Thrust, Trap, Trough, Underthrust, Upbraid, Vice

**Faultless** Immaculate, Impeccable, Lily-white, Perfect, Pure

**Fauna** Benthos, Mesobenthos, Wild life

**Fauvist** Matisse

**Faux pas** Blunder, Boner, Conversation stopper, Gaffe, Leglen-girth, Solecism

**Favour(able), Favoured, Favourite, Favouritism** Advance, Advantage(ous), Advocate, Aggrace, Agraste, Alder-liefest, Anne, Approbation, Approval, Auspicious, Aye, Back, Befriend, Behalf, Benefit, Benign, Bias, Bless, Blue-eyed, Boon, Box seat, Bribe, Cert, Chosen, Cockade, Condescend, Conducive, Countenance, Curry, Darling, Elitist, Endorse, Ewe lamb, Ex gratia, Fancy, Favonian, Firm, Form horse, Front runner, Good turn, Grace, Gracioso, Graste, Gratify, Gree, Hackle, Hot, In, Indulge, Intend, Kickback, Lean, Minion, Mitzvah, Nepotism, Nod, Oblige, Odour, Optimal, Particular, Peat, Persona grata, Pet, Pettle,

Popular, → **PREFER**, Promising, Propitious, Resemble, Rib(b)and, Roseate, Rose-knot, Rosette, Side, Smile, Successful, Toast, Token, White boy, White-headed, Win-win

**Fawn(er), Fawning** Adulate, Bambi, Beige, Blandish, Brown-nose, Camel, Crawl, Creep, Cringe, Deer, Ecru, Elaine, Flatter, Fleech, Footlick, Grovel, Ko(w)tow, Lickspittle, Obsequious, Servile, Slavish, Smarm, Smoo(d)ge, Subservient, Sycophant, Tasar, Toady, Truckle, Tussah, Tusseh, Tusser, Tussore

**Fax** Replica

**Fay** Fairy, Korrigan, Peri

**Faze** Daunt, Unman, Unnerve

**FBI** G-men

**Fear** Aichmophobia, Angst, Apprehension, Astra(po)phobia, Awe, Bathophobia, Bête noire, Bugbear, Claustrophobia, Cold sweat, Crap, Creeps, Cyberphobia, Dismay, Doubt, Drad, Dread, Dromophobia, Dysmorphophobia, Ecophobia, Foreboding, → **FOR FEAR**, Fright, Funk, Genophobia, Hang-up, Hierophobia, Horripilation, Horror, Hypsophobia, Kenophobia, Monophobia, Mysophobia, Nostopathy, Nyctophobia, Ochlophobia, Panic, Phagophobia, → **PHOBIA**, Photophobia, Primal, Redoubt, Revere, Taphephobia, Taphophobia, Technophobia, Terror, Thalassophobia, Trepidation, Willies

**Fearful** Afraid, Cowardly, Cowering, Dire, Horrific, Nervous, Pavid, Rad, Redoubtable, Sinister, Timorous, Tremulous, Windy

**Fearless** Bold, Brave, Courageous, Daring, Gallant, Impavid, Intrepid, Proud, Unafraid, Undaunted, Valiant

**Fearsome** Alarming, Dire, Formidable, Redoubtable

**Feasible** Goer, Likely, On, Possible, Practical, Probable, Viable

**Feast(s)** Adonia, Agape, Asses, Assumption, Banquet, Barmecide, Beano, Belshazzar's, Blow-out, Candlemas, Carousal, Celebration, Convive, Dedication, Dine, Do, Double, Easter, Eat, Encaenia, Epiphany, Epulation, Festival, Fleshpots, Folly, Fool's, Gaudeamus, Gaudy, Hakari, Halloween, Hallowmas, Harvest, Heortology, Hockey, Hogmanay, Holy Innocents, Id-al-Adha, Id-al-Fitr, Immaculate Conception, Ingathering, Isodia, Junket, Kai-kai, Lady Day, Lamb-ale, Lammas, Lots, Love, Luau, Lucullus, Martinmas, Michaelmas, Midnight, Movable, Name days, Noel, Passover, Pentecost, Pesach, Pig, Potlatch, Purim, Regale, Repast, Revel, Roodmas, Seder, Shavuot(h), Shindig, Spread, Succoth, Sukkot(h), Tabernacles, Trumpets, Tuck-in, Wake, Wayzgoose, Weeks, Yule, Zagmuk

**Feast-day** Mass

**Feat** Achievement, Deed, Effort, Exploit, Gambado, Handspring, Heroic, Stunt, Tour de force, Trick

**Feather(s), Feathered, Feather-star** Aigrette, Alula, Barbicel, Boa, Braccate, Brail, Cock, Contour, Covert, Crinoid, Crissum, Down, Duster, Egret, Eiderdown, Filoplume, Flags, Fledged, Fletch, Flight, Gemmule, Goose quill, Hackle, Harl, Hatchel, Herl, Lei, Lure, Macaroni, Manual, Oar, Ostrich, Pen(na), Pin, Pinna, Pith, Plumage, Plume, Plumule, Prince's, Pteryla, Ptilosis, → **QUILL**, Rectrix, Remex, Remiges, Rocket-tail, Rotate, Saddle-hackle, Scapular, Scapus, Secondary, Semiplume, Shaft, Shag, Sickle, Standard, Stipa, Swansdown, Tail covert, Tectrix, Tertial, Tippet, Tuft, Vibrissa, White, Wing covert, Wisp

**Feather-pate** Man-milliner

**Featherweight** Junior, Super

**Feather-worker** Plumassier

**Feature(s)** Acoustic, Amenity, Appurtenance, Article, Aspect, Attribute, Brow, Character, Chin, Contour, Depict, Dimple, Double, Eye, Eyebrow, Face, Facet, Figure, Fronton, Gable(t), Hallmark, Highlight, Item, Jizz, Landmark, Lineament, Neotery, Nose, Nucleus, Overfold, Phiz(og), Physiognomy, Signature, Snoot, Spandrel, Spire, Star, Symptom, Temple, Topline, Topography, Touch, Trait, Underlip

**Featureless** Flat, Nondescript

**Febrifuge** Atabrin, Atebrin®, Mepacrine, Quina

**February** Fill-dyke

**Feckless** Deadbeat

**Fecund(ity)** Fertile, Fruitful, Prolific, Uberty

**Fed** Agent, G-man

**Federal, Federation** Alliance, Axis, Bund, Commonwealth, Interstate, League, Russian, Solidarity, Statal, Tribe, Union

**Fed up** Brassed off

**Fee(s)** Appearance money, Base, Bench, Break, Capitation, Charge, Chummage, Commitment, Common, Conditional, Consideration, Consultation, Contingency, Corkage, Corporation, Drop-dead, Dues, Duty, Emolument, Entrance, Entry, Express, Faldage, Fine, Great, Groundage, Hir(e)age, Hire, Honorarium, Interchange, Kill, Kitchen, Mortuary, Mouter, Multure, Obvention, Pay, Pierage, Pilotage, Premium, Ransom, Refresher, Registration, Retainer, Search, Sub, Subscription, Toll, Transfer, Tribute

**Feeble(ness)** Banal, Characterless, Daidling, Debile, Decrepit, Dotage, Droob, Effete, Faint, Feckless, Fizzenless, Flabby, Flaccid, Foisonless, Footling, Fragile, Fus(h)ionless, Geld, Ineffective, Infirm, Jessie, Lame, Limp, Milk and water, Mimsy, Namby-pamby, Nerveless, Pale, Pathetic, Puny, Rickety, Sackless, Sassy, Sickly, Silly, Sissy, Slender, Slight, Soppy, Tailor, Tame, Thin, Tootle, Unmanly, Wallydrag, Wallydraigle, Wan, Washy, Wastrel, Weak, Weak-kneed, Weak-minded, Weed, Weedy, Wersh, Wet, Wimpish, Worn

**Feed(er), Feeding** Battle, Bib, Bottle, Break, Browse, Cake, Cater, Chicken, Cibation, Clover, Cowfeteria, Cram, Cue, Demand, Diet, Dine, Dressing, Drip, → EAT, Fatten, Filter, Fire, Fishmeal, Flushing, Fodder, Food, Forage, Force, Formula, Gavage, Graze, Hay, Hopper, Input, Intravenous, Line, Lunch, Meal, Munch, Nourish, Nurse, Paid, Pecten, Picnic, Provender, Refect, Repast, Sate, Silage, Soil, Spam, Stoke, Stooge, Storer, Stover, Stuff, Suckle, Sustain, Swill, Tire, Tractor, Wean, Wet nurse

**Feedback** Negative, Positive

**Feel(ingly), Feeling(s)** Aesthesia, Affetuoso, Afterglow, Algesis, Angst, Animus, Ardour, Artificial, À tâtons, Atmosphere, Bad, Ballottement, Compassion, Conscience, Darshan, Déjà vu, → EMOTION, Empathy, Empfindung, Euphoria, Excitement, → EXPERIENCE, Fava, Fellow, Finger, Flavour, Flaw, Frisk, Fumble, Good, Grope, Groundswell, Handle, Hard, Heart, Heartstrings, Hunch, Intuit, Knock, Know, Mondayish, Mood, Morale, Palp(ate), Passible, Passion, Phatic, Pity, Premonition, Presentiment, Probe, Realise, Sensate, Sensation, → SENSE, Sensible, Sensitive, Sentiency, Sentiment, Somesthesis, Spirit, Sprachgefühl, Sympathy, Tactual, Texture, Tingle, Toe-curling, Touch, Turn, Undercurrent, Vehemence, Vibes, Vibrations, Zeal

**Feeler** Antenna, Ballon d'essai, Barbel, Exploratory, Fingertip, Overture, Palp, Sensillum, Tentacle, Trial balloon

▸**Feet** *see* FOOT(ING)

**Feign** Act, Affect, Assume, Colour, Fake, Malinger, Mime, Mock, → PRETEND, Sham, Simulate

**Feint** Deke, Disguise, Dodge, Faint, Fake, False move, Spoof, Trick

**Feisty** Game, Tigerish

**Felicity** Bliss, Happiness, Joy, Relevance

▸**Feline** *see* CAT

**Fell(er)** Axe, Chain saw, Chop, Cruel, Cut down, Deadly, Dire, Dread, Fen, Fierce, Floor, Heath, Hew, Hide, Hill, Inhuman, Knock-down, KO, Lethal, Lit, Log, Malign, Moor, Pelt, Poleaxe, Ruthless, Sca, Shap, Skittle

**Fellow(s), Fellowship** Academic, Associate, Bawcock, Birkie, Blighter, Bloke, Bo, Bod, Bro, Buck(o), Buffer, Buster, Callan(t), Carlot, Cat, Chal, Chap(pie), Chi, China, Chum, Co, Cock, Cod(ger), Collaborator, Colleague, Co-mate, Communion, Companion, Compatriot, Comrade, Confrère, Cove, Cully, Cuss, Dandy, Dean, Dog, Don, Dude, Equal, F, Fogey, Fop, Gadgie, Gadje, Gaudgie, Gauje, Gent, Gink, Guy, Housemate, Joe (Soap), Joker, Josser, Kerel, Lad, Like, M, Mall, Man, Masonry, Match, Mate, Member, Mister, Mun, Odd, Partner, Peare, Peer, Professor, Rival, Seniority, Sister, Skate, Sociate, Society, Sodality, Stablemate, Swab, Teaching, Twin, Waghalter, Wallah, Workmate

**Felon(y)** Baddy, Bandit, Convict, Crime, Gangster, Offence, Villain

**Fel(d)spar** Adularia, Albite, Amazon-stone, Andesine, Anorthite, Bytownite, Gneiss, Hyalophane, Labradorite, Microcline, Moonstone, Oligoclase, Orthoclase, Peristerite, Petuntse, Petuntze, Plagioclase, Sanidine, Saussurite, Sun-stone

**Felt** Baize, Bat(t), Drugget, Knew, Met, Numdah, Numnah, Pannose, Roofing, Sensed, Tactile, Underlay, Velour

**Female (bodies), Feminine, Feminist** Anima, Bit, Dame, Distaff, Doe, F, Fair sex, Filly, Friedan, Girl(y), Greer, Harem, Hen, Her, Kermes, Lady(like), Libber, Maiden, Moll, Muliebrity, Pen, Petticoated, Pistillate, Riot girl, Sakti, Shakti, She, Sheila, Shidder, Soft, Spindle, The eternal, Thelytoky, -trix, → **WOMAN**, Womens' libber, Yin

▷**Female, Feminine** *may indicate* an -ess ending

**Fen** Bog, Carr, Chiao, Coin, Ea, Jiao, Marsh, Morass, Silicon, Swamp, Wash, Yuan

**Fence(r), Fencing (position)** Appel, Balestra, Bar, Barrier, Botte, Carte, Criminal, Croisé, Cyclone®, Deer, Derobement, Dogleg, Electric, Encase, Enclose, Épée, Evade, Feint, Fight, Flanconade, Flèche, Foils, Fraise, Froissement, Haha, Hay, Hedge, Hot, Hurdle, Iaido, Imbroccata, Inquartata, Jump, Kendo, Kittle, Line, Link, Mensur, Molinello, Montant, Netting, Obstacle, Ox, Oxer, Pale, Paling, Palisade, Palisado, Parapet, Parry, Passado, Pen, Picket, Post and rail, Quart(e), Quinte, Rabbit-fence, Rabbit-proof, Raddle, Rail, Rasper, Receiver, Reset, Ring, Scrimure, Seconde, Sepiment, Sept(um), Septime, Singlestick, Sixte, Snake, Snow, Stacket, Stockade, Stramaçon, Stramazon, Sunk, Swordplay, Tac-au-tac, Tierce, Touché, Trellis, Virginia, Wattle, Wear, Weir, Weldmesh®, Wire, Worm, Zigzag

**Fend(er), Fend off** Buffer, Bumper, Cowcatcher, Curb, Mudguard, Parry, Provide, Resist, Skid, Stiff-arm, Ward, Wing

**Fennel** Dwarf, Finnochio, Finoc(c)hio, Florence, French, Giant, Herb, Love-in-a-mist, Narthex, Ragged lady, Sweet

**Fent** Offcut, Remnant, Slit

**Feral** Brutal, Fierce, Savage, Wild

**Ferdinand** Archduke, Bull, Rio

**Ferment(ation), Fermented** Barm, Brew, Enzym(e), Leaven, Mowburn, Must, Protease, Ptyalin, Seethe, Solera, Storm, Stum, Trypsin, Turn, Vinify, Working, Yaourt, Ye(a)st, Zyme, Zymo-, Zymology, Zymolysis, Zymosis, Zymotic, Zymurgy

**Fermium** Fm

**Fern** Acrogenous, Adder's-tongue, Adiantum, Archegonial, Asparagus, Aspidium, Asplenium, Azolla, Barometz, Beech, Bird's nest, Bladder, Bracken, Brake, Bristle, Buckler, Bungwall, Ceterach, Cinnamon, Coral, Cryptogam, Cyathea, Cycad, Dicksonia, Door, Elkhorn, Fairy moss, Filicales, Filices, Filmy, Fishbone, Grape, Hard, Hart's-tongue, Holly, Ice, Isoetes, Lacy, Lady, Lunary, Maidenhair, Male, Man, Mangemange, Marattia, Marsh, Marsilea, Marsilia, Meadow, Miha, Moonwort, Mosquito, Mulewort, Nardoo, Nephrolepis, Northern, Oak, Ophioglossum, Osmunda, Para, Parsley, Peppergrass, Pepperwort, Pig, Pillwort, Polypody, Polystichum, Ponga, Pteridology, Pteris, Punga, Rachilla, Rhizocarp, Rockbrake, Royal, Rusty-back, Salvinia, Scale, Schizaea, Scolopendrium, Seed, Shield, Silver, Snowbrake, Soft tree, Spleenwort, Staghorn, Sweet, Sword, Tara, Tree, Venus's hair, Walking, Wall rue, Water, Whisk, Woodsia

**Ferocious** Brutal, Cruel, Fell, Predatory, Rambunctious, Savage, Tartar, Tiger, Violent, Wild

**Ferret** Albin, Black-footed, Busyness, Fesnyng, Gill, Hob, Jill, Kit, Nose, Polecat, Ribbon, Rootle, Snoop, Trace, Unearth

**Ferry(man)** Channel steamer, Charon, Convey, Flying bridge, Harper's, Hovercraft, Passage, Plier, Ply, Pont, Roll-on, RORO, Sea-cat, Sealink, Shuttle, Soyuz, Train, Traject, Tranect

**Fertile, Fertility (symbol), Fertilisation** Arable, Ashtoreth, Battle, Cleistogamy, Fat, Fecund, Fruitful, Green, Linga, Oasis, Priapus, Productive, Prolific, Rhiannon, Rich, Uberous

**Fertilise(r), Fertilisation** Ammonia, Auxin, Bee, Bone-ash, Bone dust, Bone-earth, Bone-meal, Caliche, Caprify, Compost, Cross, Dress, Fishmeal, Guano, Heterosis, Humogen, Humus, In-vitro, IVF, Kainite, Krilium®, Lime, Manure, Marl, Mulch, Night soil, Nitrate, Nitre, Nitro-chalk, Pearl-ash, Phallus, Phosphate, Pollen, Pollinator, Potash, Potassa, Seaware, Self, Sham, Side dressing, Stamen, Superfetation, Superphosphate, Tankage, Top dressing, Treat, Urea

**Fervent, Fervid, Fervour** Ardent, Avid, Burning, Eagerness, Earnest, Gusto, Heartfelt, Heat, Hot, Hwyl, Intense, Into, Keen, Messianic, Passionate, Vehement, White-hot, Zeal, Zeloso

**Festal** Celebratory

**Fester** Beal, Putrefy, Rankle, Rot, Suppurate

**Festival, Festive, Festivity** Anniversary, Basant, Beano, Cannes, Carnival, Celebration,

Commemoration, Convivial, Eid-al-Adha, Eid-al-Fitr, En fête, → **FAIR**, Feast, Feis, Fête, Fête-champêtre, Gaff, → **GALA**, Gaudy, High day, → **HOLIDAY**, Invention of the Cross, Joyance, Lemural, Let-off, Lupercal, Party, Play, Potlatch, Revel, Rush-bearing, Semi-double, Wake, Wassail, Whit(sun)

---

**FESTIVALS**

***3 letters:***
Ale
Bon
Mod
Pop
Tet

***4 letters:***
Holi
Lent
Mela
Noel
Obon
Puja
Tide
Utas
Yule

***5 letters:***
Doseh
Druid
Hosay
Miraj
Pasch
Pesah
Pooja
Purim
Seder
Vesak
Wesak

***6 letters:***
Adonia
Ashura
Bairam
Dewali
Divali
Diwali
Easter
Fiesta
Fleadh
Fringe
Hosein
Judica
Lammas
Mawlid
Mayday
Moomba
Pardon
Pesach
Pongal
Poojah
Shrove
Yom Tob
Yomtov

***7 letters:***
Al Hijra
Baisaki
Beltane
Greater
Harvest
Holy-ale
J'ouvert
Kermess
Kermiss
Kirmess
Kwanzaa
Lady-Day
Lemuria
Matsuri
Palilia
Potlach
Samhain
Vinalia
Yuan Tan

***8 letters:***
Al Hijrah
Baisakhi
Bayreuth
Biennale
Cerealia
Chanukah
Dassehra
Day of awe
Dionysia
Encaenia
Epiphany
Fête-Dieu
Hanukkah
Hock-tide
Hogmanay
Id-al-fitr
Lag b'Omer
Passover
Salzburg
Shabuath
Shavuath
Slugfest
Tanabata
Yuletide

***9 letters:***
Aldeburgh
Candlemas
Chanukkah
Christmas
Church-ale
Crouchmas
Hallowmas
Kumbh Mela
Martinmas
Navaratra
Navaratri
Pentecost
Thargelia
Up-Helly-Aa
Woodstock
Yom Arafat

***10 letters:***
Ambarvalia
Assumption
Childermas
Corroboree
Eisteddfod
Lughnasadh
Lupercalia
Merry-night
Michaelmas
Quirinalia
Saturnalia
Shrovetide
Terminalia
Visitation
Vulcanalia

***11 letters:***
Anthesteria
Fête-galante
Glastonbury
Harvest home

***12 letters:***
All Saints' Day
Circumcision
Feast of weeks
Glyndebourne
Lailat-ul-Qadr
Lesser Bairam
Panathenaean
Plough Monday
Rosh Hashanah
Simchas Torah
Simchat Torah
Thesmophoria

***13 letters:***
Corpus Christi
Greater Bairam
Laylat-al-Miraj
Simchath Torah

***14 letters:***
Shemini Atseres

***15 letters:***
Transfiguration

---

**Festoon** Deck, Decorate, Encarpus, Garland, Swag, Wreathe
**Fetch(ing), Fetch up** Arrive, Attract, Bonny, Bring, Charming, Fet(t), Get, Gofer, Net, Prepossessing, Realise, Recover, Retrieve, Spew, Winsome
**Fête** Bazaar, Champêtre, Entertain, → **FESTIVITY**, Gala, Honour, Mela, Tattoo
**F(o)etid** Stagnant

▸**Fetid** *see* **F(O)ETID**

**Fetish(ist)** Charm, Compulsion, Gimp, Idol, Ju-ju, Obeah, Obi(a), Talisman, Totem, Voodoo

**Fetter** Anklet, Basil, Bilboes, Chain, Gyve, Hamshackle, Hobble, Hopple, Iron, Leg-iron, Manacle, Shackle

**Fettle** Arrange, Condition, Frig, Potter, Repair

**F(o)etus** Embryo

▸**Fetus** *see* **F(O)ETUS**

**Feu** Tenure

**Feud** Affray, Blood, Clash, Dissidence, Feoff, Fief, Quarrel, Strife, → **VENDETTA**

**Feudal (service), Feudalism** Arriage, Auld-farrant, Fief, Forinsec, Medieval, Old, Vassalage

**Fever(ish)** African coast, Ague, Beaver, Biliary, Blackwater, Brain, Breakbone, Buck, Cabin, Calenture, Camp, Cat-scratch, Cerebrospinal, Childbed, Dandy, Dengue, East coast, Enteric, Equine infections, Febrile, Ferment, Fog, Frenetic, Gaol, Gastric, Gate, Glandular, Gold, Haemorrhagic, Hay, Heatstroke, Hectic, Hyperpyretic, Insolation, Intense, Intermittent, Jail, Japanese river, Jungle, Kala-azar, Kissing disease, Lassa, Malaria, Malta, Marsh, Mediterranean, Miliary, Milk, Mono, Mud, Paratyphoid, Parrot, Parturient, Passion, Phrenitis, Puerperal, Putrid, Pyretic, Pyrexia, Pyrogenic, Q, Quartan, Quintan, Quotidian, Rabbit, Ratbite, Recurrent, Relapsing, Remittent, Rheumatic, Rift Valley, Rock, Rocky Mountain spotted, Roseola, Sandfly, Scarlatina, Scarlet, Sextan, Ship, Splenic, Spotted, Spring, Stage, Sunstroke, Swamp, Swine, Tap, Temperature, Tertian, Texas, Tick, Trench, Typhoid, Typhus, Undulant, Valley, Verruga, Vomito, Weed, West Nile, Whot, Worm, Yellow(jack)

**Few(er)** Handful, Infrequent, → **LESS**, Limited, One or two, RAF, Scarce, Several, Some, Three, Two, Wheen

**Few words** Pocas palabras

**Fey** Clairvoyant, Eccentric, Elfin, Weird

**Fez** Tarboosh, Tarboush, Tarbush

**Fiancé(e)** Betrothed, Intended, Promised

**Fiasco** Bomb, Debacle, Disaster, Failure, Flask, Flop, Lash-up, Turkey, Wash-out

**Fiat** Command, Decree, Dictum, Edict, Order, Ukase

**Fib** Gag, → **LIE**, Prevaricate, Story, Taradiddle, Untruth

**Fibre, Fibrous** Abaca, Abroma, Acrilan®, Acrylic, Aramid, Arghan, Backbone, Bass, Bast, Beaver-board, Beta, Bran, Buaze, Bwazi, Cantala, Carbon, Cellulose, Coir, Constitution, Corpus Callosum, Cotton, Courtelle®, Crimple, Cuscus, Desmosome, Dietary, Dralon®, Elastane, Elastin, Filament, Filasse, Flax, Funicle, Giant, Glass, Gore-Tex®, Graded-index, Guncotton, Hair, Harl, Hemp, Henequen, Henequin, Herl, Hypha, Ispaghula, Istle, Ixtle, Jipyapa, Jute, Kapok, Kenaf, Kevlar®, Kittul, Laps, Lemniscus, Ligament, Maguey, Manilla, Monkey-grass, Monofil, Monomode, Moorva, Moral, Multimode, Mungo, Murva, Muscle, Myotube, Nap, Natural, Nerve, Noil(s), Nub, Nylon, Oakum, Olefin(e), Optic(al), Orlon®, Peduncle, Piassaba, Piassava, Pina, Pine-wool, Pita, Polyarch, Polyester, Pons, Pontine, Pulu, Raffia, Ramee, Rami, Ramie, Rayon, Rhea, Rock-cork, Roughage, Rove, Shoddy, Sida, Silk, Sinew, Sisal, Slagwool, Sleave, Slub(b), Spandex, Spherulite, Splenium, Staple, Stepped-index, Sterculia, Strand, Strick, Sunn-hemp, Tampico, Tencel®, Toquilla, Tow, Towy, Uralite, Viver, Vulcanized, Wallboard, Watap, Whisker, Wood pulp

**Fibula** Bone, Brooch, Perone

**Fickle(ness)** Capricious, Chameleon, Change, Erratic, False, Flibbertigibbet, Inconsistent, Inconstant, Kittle, Light, Mutable, Protean, Shifty, Varying, Volage, Volatile, Wind-changing

**Fiction(al), Fictitious** Airport, Bogus, Chick-lit, Cyberpunk, Fable, Fabrication, Fan, Legal, Myth, Pap, Phoney, Picaresque, Pseudonym, Pulp, Romance, Science, Sci-fi, Sex and shopping, Slash, Speculative, Splatterpunk, Steampunk, → **STORY**, Sword and sorcery, Transgressive, Whole cloth

**Fiddle(r), Fiddlesticks, Fiddlestring, Fiddling** Amati, Bass, Bow, Bull, Calling-crab, Cello, Cheat, Con, Crab, Cremona, Croud, Crouth, Crowd, Crwth, Do, Eyewash, Fidget, Fix, Gju, Ground, Gu(e), Gut-scraper, Jerrymander, Kit, Launder, Nero, Peculate, Petty, Potter, Racket, Rebec(k), Rig, Rote, Sarangi, Saw, Sawah, Scam, Scotch, Scrape, Scrapegut, Second,

Sharp practice, Short change, Spiel, Strad, Sultana, → TAMPER, Thimblerig, Tinker, Toy, Trifle, Tweedle(-dee), Twiddle, Viola, → VIOLIN, Wangle

**Fiddle-faddle** Nipperty-tipperty

**Fidelity** Accuracy, Faith, Fealty, High, Loyalty, Troth, Trust

**Fidget(y)** Fantad, Fanteeg, Fantigue, Fantod, Fike, Fuss, Fyke, Hirsle, Hotch, Impatient, Jimjams, Jittery, Niggle, Restive, Restless, Squirm, Trifle, Twiddle, Twitch, Uneasy

**Fiduciary** Trustee

**Fief** Benefice, Fee

**Field(er), Fielding, Fields(man)** Aalu, Aaru, Abroad, Aceldama, Aerodrome, Agrestic, Airstrip, Area, Arena, Arish, Arpent, Arrish, Aura, Bailiwick, Baseman, Battleground, Bleach, Bocage, Campestral, Campestrian, Catch, Champ(s), Chief, Close, Colour, Coulomb, Cover, Cover-point, Diamond, Discipline, Domain, Electric, Electromagnetic, Electrostatic, Elysian, Entry, Extent, Extra cover, Fid, Fine leg, Flodden, Floe, Flying, Force, Forte, Fylde, Glebe, Gracie, Gravitational, Grid(iron), Gull(e)y, Hop-yard, Ice, Keep wicket, Killing, Land, Landing, Lare, Lay, Lea(-rig), Leg slip, Ley, Line, Long leg, Long-off, Long-on, Longstop, Lord's, Magnetic, Mead(ow), Mid-off, Mid-on, Mid-wicket, Mine, Oil, Padang, Paddock, Paddy, Parrock, Pasture, Peloton, Pitch, Playing, Point, Potter's, Province, Quintessence, Realm, Reame, Runners, Salting, Sawah, Scarecrow, Scope, Scout, Shamba, Short leg, Short stop, Silly, Slip, Sphere, Square leg, Stage, Stray, Stubble, Territory, Third man, Tract, Unified, Vector, Visual, W.C., World

▷**Field** *may indicate* cricket

**Field marshal** Allenby, Bulow, French, Haig, Ironside, Kesselring, Kitchener, Montgomery, Roberts, Robertson, Rommel, Slim, Wavell

**Fieldwork** Lunette, Ravelin, Redan, Redoubt, Tenaillon

**Fiend** Addict, Barbason, Buff, Demon(ic), → DEVIL, Drug, Enthusiast, Flibbertigibbet, Frateretto, Fresh air, Hellhound, Hellion, Hobbididance, Incubus, Mahn, Modo, Obidicut, Smulkin, Succubus

**Fierce(ly)** Amain, Billyo, Breem, Breme, Cruel, Draconic, Dragon, Fell, Grim, Hard-fought, Harpy, Intense, Lorcan, Ogreish, Rampant, Renfierst, → SAVAGE, Severe, Tigerish, Tigrish, Tranchant, Violent, Wild, Wood, Wrathy, Wud

**Fiery** Abednego, Ardent, Argand, Aries, Con fuoco, Dry, Eithna, Etnaean, Fervent, Flambeau, High-mettled, Hot, Hotspur, Idris, Igneous, Impassioned, Leo, Mettlesome, Phlogiston, Piri-piri, Sagittarius, Salamander, Torrid, Zealous

**Fiesta** Carnival, Festival, Fête, Gala, Holiday

**Fife** Piffero

**Fifteen(th)** Crystal

▷**Fifteen** *may indicate* a rugby team

**Fifth** Column, Diapente, Hemiol(i)a, Nones, Perfect, Quentin, Quint(ile), Sesquialtera, Sextans

**Fifth columnist** Infiltrator, Traitor

**Fifty** Bull, Demi-c, Jubilee, L, Quinquagesimal

**Fig** Bania, Banyan, Benjamin-tree, Caprifig, Fico, Figo, Footra, Fouter, Foutra, Foutre, Goat, Hottentot, Indian, Moreton Bay, Mouldy, Sycamore, Sycomium, Sycomore, Trifle

**Fight(er), Fighting** Achilles, Action, Affray, Aggressive, Agonistics, Aikido, Alpino, Altercate, Arms, Bandy, Bare-knuckle, Barney, → BATTLE, Battle royal, Bicker, Biffo, Blue, Bout, Box, Brave, Brawl, Bruiser, Bundeswehr, Bush-whack, Camp, Campaign, Chaud-mellé, Chetnik, Chindit, Clash, Combat, Compete, Conflict, Contest, Contra, Crusader, Cuirassier, Defender, Digladiation, Ding-dong, Dog, Donnybrook, Dreadnought, Duel, Ecowarrior, Encounter, Engagement, Extremes, F, Faction, Fecht, Fence, Fisticuffs, Flyting, Fray, Freedom, Free-for-all, Fund, Gamecock, Garibaldi, Ghazi, Gladiator, Grap(p)le, Green beret, Grudge, Guerilla, Gunslinger, Gurkha, Handicuffs, Hand-to-hand, Hurricane, J(o)ust, Karate, Kendo, Kite, Kumite, Lapith, Lock horns, Maquis, Marine, Matador, Med(d)le, Medley, Mêlée, Mercenary, MIG, Militate, Mill, Mujahed(d)in, Mujahideen, Mujahidin, Naumachy, Night, Ninja, Partisan, Pellmell, Pillow, PLO, Prawle, Press, Psywar, Pugilist, Pugnacity, Punch up, Rammy, Rapparee, Rejoneo, Repugn, Resist, Ring, Rough and tumble, Ruck, Ruction, Rumble, Run-in, Running, Savate, Sciamachy, Scold, Scrap, Scrape, Scrimmage, Scuffle,

Set-to, Shadow, Shine, Shoot-out, Skiamachy, Skirmish, Slam, Slugger, Soldado, Soldier, Spar, Spat, Spitfire, Squabble, Stealth, Stormtrooper, Stoush, Straight, Strife, Struggle, Sumo, Swordsman, Tar, Tatar, Terrier, Thersites, Tilt, Toreador, Torero, Tornado, Tuilyie, Tuilzie, Tussle, Ultimate, Umbrella, War(-dog), War-horse, War-man, Warplane, Warrior, Wrangle, Wraxle, Wrestle, Yike, Zero

**Figment** Delusion, Fiction, Invention, Myth

**Figure(d), Figures, Figurine, Figurative** Action, Allegoric, Arabic, Aumail, Bas-relief, Body, Build, Caganer, Canephorus, Cartouche, Caryatid, Cast, Chladni, Cinque, Cipher, Cone, Cube, Cypher, Data, Decahedron, Diagram, Digit, Dummy, Ecorché, Effigy, Eight, Ellipse, Enneagon, Enneahedron, Epanadiplosis, Equiangular, Escher, Father, Flatback, →FORM, Fret, Full, Fusil, Gammadion, Giosphinx, Girth, Glyph, Gnomon, Graph, Heptagon, Hexagon, Hexagram, Hour-glass, Icon, Icosahedron, Idol, Ikon, Image, Impossible, Insect, Intaglio, Integer, Interference, Lay, Lissajous, Magot, Manaia, Mandala, Matchstick, Mean, Metaphor, Moai, Monogram, Motif, Nonagon, Number, Numeracy, Numeral, Numerator, Numeric, Octagon, Octahedron, Orant, Ornate, Outline, Ovoid, Parallelepiped, Parallelogram, Pentacle, Pentalpha, Plane, Polygon, Polyhedron, Poussette, Prism, Puppet, Pyramid, Reckon, Repetend, Repoussoir, Rhomboid, Rhombus, Sector, See, →SHAPE, Sheela-na-gig, Significant, Simplex, Solid, Sonorous, Staffage, Stat(istic)s, Statue(tte), Stick, String, Suss, Table, Tableau, Tanagra, Telamon, Tetragon, Tetrahedron, Topical, Torus, Triangle, Trigon, Trihedron, Triskele, Triskelion, Trisoctahedron, Tropology, Undecagon, Ushabti, Waxwork

**Figure of speech** Abscission, Allegory, Alliteration, Analogy, Antimask, Antimasque, Antimetabole, Antithesis, Antithet, Antonomasia, Assonance, Asyndeton, Catachresis, Cataphora, Chiasmus, Deixis, Diallage, Ellipsis, Euphemism, Hendiadys, Hypallage, Hyperbaton, Hyperbole, Hysteron proteron, Irony, Litotes, Meiosis, Metalepsis, Metaphor, Metonymy, Onomatopoeia, Oxymoron, Paral(e)ipsis, Prolepsis, Prosopopoeia, Siddhuism, Simile, Solecism, Syllepsis, Synecdoche, Taxeme, Tmesis, Trope, Tropology, Zeugma

**Figure study** Arithmetic, Mathematics, Numeration

**Figure-weaver** Draw-boy

**Filament** Barbule, Byssus, Cirrus, Fibre, Fibrilla, Fimbria, Floss, Gonimoblast, Gossamer, Hair, Hormogonium, Hypha, Mycelium, Mycor(r)hiza, Myofibril, Paraphysis, Protonema, Sleave, Strand, →THREAD, Whisker, Wreath

**Filbert** Hazelnut

**Filch** Appropriate, Drib, Pilfer, Pinch, Prig, Purloin, Smouch, →STEAL, Swipe

**File(s), Filing(s)** Abrade, Archive, Back up, Bastard, Batch, Binary, Binder, Box, Burr, Circular, Clyfaker, Coffle, Croc(odile), Crosscut, Database, Data set, Dead-smooth, Directory, Disc, Disk, Dossier, Download, Emery (board), Enter, Flat, Floatcut, Folder, Generation, Half-round, In-box, Index, Indian, Ini, Lemel, Lever-arch, Limail, Limation, Line, Lodge, Nail, Out-box, Packed, Pickpocket, Pigeon-hole, Pin-dust, Podcast, Pollute, Quannet, Rank, Rasp, Rat-tail, README, Riffler, Risp, Rolodex®, Row, Scalprum, Scratch, Serafile, Serrefile, Signature, Single, Single-cut, String, Swap, Swarf, Text, Tickler, TIF(F)

**Filial generation** F1

**Filibuster** Freebooter, Hinder, Obstruct, Pirate, Run on, Stonewall

**Filigree** Delicate, Fretwork, Sheer

**Filipino** Igorot, Moro, →PHILIPPINE(S), Tagalog

**Fill(ing), Filler** Amalgam, Anaplerosis, Balaam, Banoffee, Banoffi, Beaumontag(u)e, Beaumontique, Billow, Bishop, Bloat, BLT, Brick-nog, Brim, Bump, Caulk, Centre, Charge, Chemisette, Cram, Cream, Debone, Fat-lute, Frangipane, Ganache, Gather, Gorge, Grout, Heart, Imbue, Implete, Impregn(ate), Inlay, Inspirit, Instill, Jampack, Line, Load, Magma, Mastic, Mincemeat, Nagging, Occupy, Pabulous, Packing, Permeate, Plug, Replenish, Repletive, Salpicon, Sate, Satisfy, Sealant, Shim, Slush, Stack, Stock, Stocking, Stopgap, Stopping, →STUFF, Tales, Tampon, Tank-up, Teem, Top up, Ullage

**Fillet(s)** Anadem, Annulet, Band, Bandeau, Bandelet, Bone, Cloisonné, Flaunching, Fret, Goujons, Grenadine, Headband, Infula, Label, Lemniscus, List(el), Mitre, Moulding, Reglet, Regula, Ribbon, Rollmop, Slice, Snood, Sphendone, Stria, Striga, Taeniate, Tape, Teniate, Tilting, Tournedos, Vitta

**Fillip** Bonus, Boost, Kick, Lift, Snap, Stimulus, Tonic

**Filly** Colt, Foal, She, Yearling

**Film(s), Film crew, Filmmaker, Filmy, Filming** Acetate, Actioner, Amnion, Animatronics, Anime, Biopic, Blaxploitation, Blockbuster, Bollywood, Bubble, Buddy, Carry On, Cartoon, Casablanca, Caul, Cel, Chick-flick, Chiller, Chopsocky, Cine, Cinemascope, Cinéma vérité, Cinerama®, Circlorama®, Cliffhanger, Cling, Clip, Coat, Colour, Compilation, Conjunctiva, Cover, Creature feature, Deepie, Dew, Diorama, Docudrama, Documentary, Dogme, Dramedy, Dust, Epic, ET, Exposure, Fantasia, Feature, Featurette, Fiche, Flick, Floaty, Footage, Freeze frame, Gauze, Genevieve, Gigi, Goldwyn, Gossamer, Grip, Hammer, Haze, Hollywood, Horror, Horse opera, Ident, Imax, Infomercial, Jaws, Kell, Kidult, Lacquer, Lamella, Landis, Layer, Limelight, Loid, Machinima, Mask, Medium, Membrane, Merchant, MGM, Microfiche, Mist, Molecular, Monochrome, Montage, Movie, Mylar®, Neo-noir, Newsreel, Noddy, Noir, Non-flam, Oater, Omnimax®, Outtake, Ozacling®, Panchromatic, Pathé, Patina, Pellicle, Photo, Pilot, Plaque, Prequel, Producer, Projection, Psycho, Quickie, Quota-quickie, Record, Reel, Release, Reversal, Rockumentary, Roll, Romcom, Rush, Safety, Scale, Scenario, Scent-scale, Screen, Scum, Sepmag, Sheet, Shoot-'em-up, Short, Shot, Silent, Skin, Skin flick, Slasher-movie, Slashfest, Slick, Slo-mo, Snuff, Spaghetti western, Splatter, Stannotype, Star Wars, Studio, Super 8, Suspensor, Sword and sandal, Take, Talkie, Tarantino, Tati, Tear-jerker, Technicolor, Technothriller, Titanic, Toon, Trailer, Travelogue, Trippy, Two-shot, Ultrafiche, Ultra-rapid, Varnish, Vertigo, Vicenzi, Video, Videogram, Video-nasty, Vitaphone®, Wardour St, Web, Weepie, Weepy, Weft, Western, Wuxia, Zaffirelli

**Filmgoer** Cineaste

**Film star** Extra, Gable, Monroe, Valentino, Vedette

**Filter(ing)** Band-pass, Bo(u)lt, Clarify, Colour, Dialysis, Dichroic, High-pass, Leach, Low-pass, Luxiviation, Percolate, Perk, Polarizing, Purify, Refine, Roach, Seep, Sieve, → SIFT, Sile, Skylight, Strain, Sunscreen, Trickle

**Filth(y)** Addle, Augean, Bilge, Bogging, Colluvies, Crock, Crud, Defile, Dirt, Dung, Feculent, Foul, Grime, Hard core, Litter, Lucre, Mire, Muck, Nasty, Obscene, Ordure, Pythogenic, Refuse, Sewage, Slime, Smut(ch), Soil, Squalor, Stercoral, Sullage, Unwashed, Yuck

**Fin** Adipose, Anal, Caudal, Crack, Ctene, Dollars, Dorsal, Fiver, Flipper, Fluke, Pectoral, Pelvic, Pinna, Pinnule, Rib, Skeg, Skegg, Stabiliser, Ventral

**Final(e), Finalise, Finally** Absolute, Apogee, At last, Climax, Closing, Closure, Coda, Conclusive, Cup, Decider, Denouement, Dying, End, End-all, Epilogue, Eventual, Exam, Extreme, Grand, Last, Last ditch, Last gap, Last hurrah, Last resort, Net(t), Outcome, Peremptory, Sew up, Swansong, Tailpiece, Terminal, Ultimate, Utter

**Finance, Financial, Financier** Ad crumenam, Angel, Arbitrage, Back, Banian, Banker, Bankroll, Banyan, Bay Street, Bottomry, Cambism, Chrematistic, City (man), Economy, Entrepreneur, Equity, Exchequer, Fiscal, Forfaiting, Gnome, Gresham, Grubstake, Invest, Mezzanine, Monetary, Moneyman, Patronise, Purse strings, Revenue, Sponsor, Subsidise, Treasurer, Underwrite, Wall Street

**Finback** Sei, Whale

**Finch** Bird, Brambling, Bunting, Canary, Cardinal bird, Charm, Chewink, Conirostral, Crossbill, Darwin's, Fringillid, Gouldian, Grosbeak, Linnet, Marsh-robin, Peter, Redpoll, Rosy, Serin, Siskin, Spink, Twite, Weaver-bird, Zebra

**Find(er), Finding** Ascertain, Come across, Detect, Dig up, Direction, Discover(y), Get, Gobind, Govind, Hit, Inquest, → LOCATE, Meet, Minitrack®, Provide, Rake up, Rarity, Rumble, Trace, Track down, Trouvaille, Unearth, Verdict

**Fine, Fine words** A1, Admirable, Amende, Amerce(ment), Amerciament, Arts, Assess, Bawcock, Beau(t), Bender, Blood-wit(e), Bonny, Boshta, Boshter, Boss, Brandy, Brave, Braw, Bully, Buttock-mail, Capital, Champion, Clear, Clement, Cloudless, Cobweb(by), Dainty, Dandy, Dick, Donzie, Dry, End, Eriach, Eric(k), Estreat, Excellent, F, Fair, Famous, Forfeit, Gate, Godly, Good(ly), Gossamer, Gradely, Graithly, Grand, Grassum, Hair, Hairline, Handsome, Heriot, Hunkydory, Ideal, Idle, Immense, Impalpable, Inconie, Incony, Infangthief, Issue, Jake, Keen, Leirwite, Log, Maritage, Merchet, Mooi, Mulct, Narrow, Nice, Nifty, Niminy-piminy, Noble, OK, Okay, Oke, Okey-doke(y), Outfangthief, Penalise, → PENALTY, Perfect, Phat, Pleasant, Precise, Pretty, Pure, Rare, Relief, Righto, Safe, Sconce, Scratch, Set fair, Sheer, Sicker, Slender, Smart, Spanking, Subtle, Summery, Super, Sure,

Take, Tax, Terrific, Thin, Ticket(t)y-boo, Tiptop, Topping, Transmission, Triff, Unlaw, Wally, Waly, Well, Wer(e)gild, Wispy

**Fine-collector** Cheater

**Finery** Braws, Caparison, Fallal, Frills, Frippery, Gaudery, Glad rags, Ornament, Regalia, Trinket, Wally, Warpaint

**Finesse** Adroitness, Artifice, Artistry, Delicacy, Savoir faire, Skill, Strategy

**Fine tune** Tweak

**Fine-weather** All-hallond, All-hallow(e)n, All-hollown

**Finger(s), Fingernail** Annular, Dactyl, Digit, Fork, Green, Handle, Idle worms, Index, Litte, Lunula, Medius, Middle, Name, Nip, Piggy, Pinky, Pointer, Potato, Prepollex, Pusher, Ring(man), Shop, Sponge, Sticky, Talaunt, Talon, Tot, Touch, Trigger, Twiddle, White

**Finger-hole** Lill, Ring

**Fingerprint(ing)** Arch, Dabs, Dactylogram, DNA, Genetic, Loop, Whorl

**Fingerstall** Hutkin

**Finial** Bunch, Knob, Ornament, Tee

**Finical, Finicky** Faddy, Fastidious, Fussy, Particular, Pernickety, Precise

**Finish(ed), Finishing (touch), Finish off** Accomplish, Arch, Blanket, Break up, Cadenza, Calendar, Chrome, Close, Coating, Coda, Complete, →**CONCLUDE**, Crown, Defunct, Dénouement, Die, Dish, Do, Dope, Dress, Eat, Eggshell, →**END**, Epilog(ue), Epiphenomena, Eradicate, Exact, Fine, Full, Gloss, Grandstand, Ice, Intonaco, Kibosh, Lacquer, Log off, Mat(t), Mirror, Napoo, Neat, Outgo, Outwork, Pebbledash, Peg out, Perfect, Photo, Picking, Plaster, Polish off, Refine, Ripe, Round, Satin, Settle, Shellac, Shot, Spitcher, Surface, Tail, Tape, Terminate, Through, Top out, Up (tie), Varnish, Veneer, Washed-up, Wau(l)k, Wind-up, Wrap (up)

**Finite** Bounded, Limited

**Finland, Finn(ish)** Esth, Esthonian, Huck(leberry), Karelian, Lapp, Mickey, Mordvin, Suomic, Udmurt, Votyak

**Finn** Huckleberry

**Fiord** Bay, Hardanger, Inlet, Oslo, Randers, Trondheim

**Fir** Abies, Balsam, Douglas, Larch, Oregon, Scotch, Scots, Silver, Spruce, Umbrella

**Fire(side), Firing** Accend, Agni, Aidan, Aiden, Animate, Anneal, Ardour, Arouse, Arson, Atar, Awaken, Axe, Bake, Bale, Barbecue, Barrage, Beacon, Behram, Belting, Biscuit, Blaze, Boot, Brand, Brazier, Brush, Burn, Bush, Cashier, Central, Chassé, Conflagration, Corposant, Counterbattery, Covering, Cremate, Delope, Discharge, Dismiss, Élan, Electric, Element, Embolden, Ena, Energy, Enfilade, Enkindle, Enthuse, Excite, Flak, Flame, Flash, Friendly, Furnace, Glost, Greek, Gun, Hearth, Heater, Hob, Ignite, Indian, Inferno, Ingle, Inspire, Kentish, Kiln, Kindle, Launch, Let go, Let off, Light, Liquid, Log, Lowe, Night, Oust, Pop, Prime, Prometheus, Pull, Pyre, Pyromancy, Quick, Radiator, Rake, Rapid, Red, Red cock, Sack, St Anthony's, St Elmo's, Salvo, Scorch, Shell, Shoot, Shot, Smudge, Spark, Spirit, Spunk, Stoke, Stove, Strafe, Torch, Tracer, Trial, Trigger, Wake, Watch, Wisp, Zeal, Zip

▸**Firearm** *see* **GUN(FIRE)**

**Fireback** Reredos

**Fireball** Bolide

**Firebird** Phoenix

**Fire-break** Epaulement, Greenstrip

**Firedamp** Blower, Methane

**Fire-dog** Andiron

**Fire engine** Green Goddess

**Fire-extinguisher** Halon, Hell-bender, Salamander

**Firefly** Glow-worm, Lightning-bug, Luciferin, Pyrophorus

**Fire-guard** Fender

**Firelighter** Arsonist, Spill

**Fireman** Abednego, Adair, Brigade, Deputy, Prometheus, Stoker, Visiting

**Fire-opal** Girasol

**Fireplace** Camboose, Chiminea, Chimney, Grate, Hearth, Hob, Ingle, Loop-hole, Range

**Fireplug** H, Hydrant

**Fireproof** Abednego, Asbestos, Incombustible, Inflammable, Meshach, Salamander, Shadrach, Uralite

**Firewalker** Abednego, Salamander

**Firewood** Billet, Faggot, Kindling, Knitch, Tinder

**Firework(s)** Banger, Bengal-light, Bunger, Catherine wheel, Cherry bomb, Cracker, Devil, Feu d'artifice, Firedrake, Fisgig, Fizgig, Flip-flop, Fountain, Gerbe, Girandole, Golden rain, Indian fire, Iron sand, Jumping jack, Maroon, Pastille, Peeoy, Petard, Pharaoh's serpent, Pinwheel, Pioy(e), Pyrotechnics, Realgar, Rocket, Roman candle, Serpent, Set piece, Skyrocket, Slap-bang, Sparkler, Squib, Tantrum, Throwdown, Tourbill(i)on, Volcano, Waterloo cracker, Wheel, Whizzbang

**Fire-worshipper** Parsee

**Firing** Baking, Counterbattery, Fusillade, Mitten, Salvo, Touchpaper, Trigger

**Firm, Firmness** Adamant, Agency, Al dente, Binding, Business, Collected, Compact, Company, Concern, Concrete, Conglomerate, Consistency, Constant, Convinced, Crisp, Decided, Definite, Determined, Duro, Establishment, Faithful, Fast, Fixed, Hard, House, Inc, Inelastic, Insistent, Loyal, Marginal, Oaky, Obdurate, Obstinate, Partnership, Persistent, → RESOLUTE, Robust, Sclerotal, Secure, Set, Siccar, Sicker, → SOLID, Sound, Stable, Stalwart, Staunch, Steady, Ste(a)dfast, Steely, Steeve, Stern, Stieve, Stiff, Strict, Sturdy, Sure, Tenacious, Tight, Tough, Unflinching, Unshakeable, Well-knit

**Firmament** Canopy, Empyrean, Heaven, Sky

**First** 1st, Ab initio, Alpha, Arch, Archetype, Best, Calends, Champion, Chief, Curtain raiser, Earliest, Eldest, E(a)rst, Foremost, Former, Front, Head, I, Ideal, Imprimis, Inaugural, Initial, Kalends, Led, Maiden, Major, No 1, One, Opener, Or, Ordinal, Original, Pilot, Pioneer, Pole, Pole position, Premier, Première, Prima, Primal, Prime, Primo, Primordial, Principal, Priority, Prototype, Rudimentary, Scoop, Senior, Starters, Top, Uppermost, Victor, Yama

**First-aid(ers)** Ice pack, Zambu(c)k

**First born** Ariki, Cain, Eigne, Eldest, Heir, Major, Primogeniture, Senior

**First class, First rate** A1, Capital, Crack, Five-star, Plump, Prime, Pukka, Slap up, Super-duper, Supreme, Tiptop, Top(notch)

**First day** Calends

**First fruits** Annat, Arles, Primitiae, Windfalls

**First man** Adam, Ask, Gayomart, Premier, President, Yama, Ymer, Ymir

**First offender** Eve, Probationer

▸**First rate** *see* FIRST CLASS

**First woman** Embla, Eve, Pandora, Premier

**Firth** Dornoch, Estuary, Forth, Inlet, Moray, Pentland, Solway, Tay

**Fiscal** Economic, Monetary

**Fish(ing)** Angle, Bob, Bottom, Cast, Catch, Chowder, Coarse, Counter, Cran, Creel, Deep-sea, Dib, Dredge, Dry, Dry-fly, Episcate, Fighting, Fly, Flying, Frozen, Fry, Game, Gefilte, Gefulte, Goujons, Guddle, Halieutics, Haul, Hen, Inshore, Ledger, Mess, Net, Odd, Offshore, Oily, Otterboard, Overnet, Piscary, Piscine, Poisson, Queer, Roe, Rough, Runner, Sacred, Sashimi, Shoal, Skitter, Sleeper, Snigger, Sniggle, Spin, Spot, Surfcasting, Surimi, Trawl, Troll, Trotline, Tub, Walking, Wet, White

---

**FISH**

*2 letters:*
Ai
Id

*3 letters:*
Ahi
Aua
Ayu
Bar
Bib
But
Cat
Cod
Cow
Dab
Dap
Dog
Eel
Gar
Ged
Hag
Ide
Koi
Lax
Lob
Mud
Par
Pod
Ray
Rig
Sar
Tai
Top

*4 letters:*
Barb
Bass
Blay
Bley
Brit
Butt
Carp
Cave
Cero
Chad
Char
Chub
Chum
Coho
Cray

Cusk
Dace
Dare
Dart
Dory
Drum
Fugu
Gade
Goby
Gump
Hake
Harl
Hoka
Hoki
Huso
Huss
Ikan
Jack
Kelt
Keta
Kill
Lant
Leaf
Ling
Luce
Lump
Lung
Maid
Masu
Maze
Moki
Mola
Mort
Opah
Orfe
Parr
Peal
Peel
Penk
Pike
Pink
Poll
Pope
Pout
Raun
Rawn
Rigg
Rudd
Ruff
Salt
Scad
Scar
Scat
Scup
Seer
Seir
Shad
Sild
Slip
Snig
Sole
Star
Tope
Trot
Tuna
Tusk
Wels
Woof

***5 letters:***
Ablet
Ahuru
Allis
Angel
Apode
Aspro-
Basse
Belta
Blain
Bleak
Bream
Brill
Bully
Capon
Charr
Cisco
Clown
Cobia
Cohoe
Coley
Coral
Cuddy
Danio
Dorad
Doras
Doree
Dorse
Elops
Elver
Fluke
Gadus
Gibel
Grunt
Jewie
Jurel
Koura
Laker
Lance
Loach
Loose
Lythe
Maise
Maize
Manta
Masus
Mease
Molly
Murre
Murry
Nerka
Nurse
Padle
Perai
Perca
Perch
Pilot
Piper
Pirai
Platy
Pogge
Porgy
Powan
Prawn
Roach
Roker
Royal
Ruffe
Saith
Salmo
Sargo
Saury
Scale
Scold
Scrod
Sewen
Sewin
Shark
Sheat
Skate
Slope
Smelt
Smolt
Snoek
Snook
Solen
Speck
Sprat
Sprod
Squid
Tench
Tetra
Tiger
Togue
Torsk
Trout
Tunny
Umber
Wahoo
Whiff
Wirra
Witch
Yabby
Zebra

***6 letters:***
Alevin
Allice
Anabas
Angler
Archer
Ballan
Barbel
Belone
Beluga
Bichir
Big-eye
Blenny
Bonito
Bounce
Bowfin
Braise
Braize
Bumalo
Burbot
Callop
Caplin
Caranx
Caribe
Cheven
Clupea
Cockle
Comber
Conger
Conner
Cottus
Cudden
Cuddie
Cuddin
Cunner
Cuttle
Darter
Dentex
Diodon
Dipnoi
Discus
Doctor
Dorado
Dun-cow
Ellops
Espada
Finnac
Finnan
Fogash
Fumado
Gadoid
Garvie
Gilgie
Goboid
Goramy
Grilse
Groper
Gulper
Gunnel
Gurami
Gurnet
Haddie
Hapuka
Hassar
Inanga
Jerker
Jilgie
Kipper
Kokiri
Labrus
Lancet
Launce
Lizard
Louvar
Lunker
Mad Tom
Mahsir
Maigre
Marari
Marlin
Marron
Matjes
Meagre
Medaka
Medusa
Megrim
Milter
Minnow
Morgay
Mudcat
Mullet
Murena
Nerite
Oyster
Paddle
Paidle
Pakoko
Parore
Parrot
Patiki
Pholas
Piraya
Plaice
Podley
Pollan
Porgie

Puffer
Redfin
Remora
Rewaru
Rizzar
Rizzer
Rizzor
Robalo
Roughy
Saithe
Salmon
Samlet
Sander
Sardel
Sargos
Sargus
Sauger
Saurel
Scampi
Scarus
Sea-bat
Sea-owl
Seeder
Serran
Shanny
Sheath
Shiner
Skelly
Sparid
Splake
Sucker
Tailor
Tarpon
Tautog
Tinker
Toitoi
Tomcod
Trygon
Turbot
Twaite
Ulicon
Ulikon
Vendis
Weever
Wirrah
Wrasse
Yabbie
Zander
Zingel

***7 letters:***

Ale-wife
Anchovy
Anemone
Anhinga
Asterid
Azurine
Batfish
Bellows
Bergylt
Birchir
Bloater
Bluecap
Boxfish
Brassie
Buffalo
Bumallo
Bummalo
Cabezon
Candiru
Capelin
Catfish
Cavalla
Cavally
Ceviche
Cichlid
Clupeud
Codfish
Copepod
Corvina
Cottoid
Crappie
Croaker
Crucian
Crusian
Cutlass
Dipnoan
Dogfish
Drummer
Dunfish
Eelfare
Eel-pout
Escolar
Fantail
Findram
Finnack
Finnock
Flattie
Garfish
Garoupa
Garpike
Garvock
Geelbek
Gemfish
Goldeye
Gourami
Grouper
Growler
Grunion
Gudgeon
Gurnard
Gwiniad
Gwyniad
Haddock
Hagdown
Hagfish
Halibut
Herling
Herring
Hirling
Hogfish
Homelyn
Houting
Icefish
Ichthys
Inconnu
Jewfish
Kahawai
Keeling
Koi carp
Kokanee
Lampern
Lamprey
Lampuki
Lantern
Lingcod
Lobster
Lubfish
Lyomeri
Maatjes
Mahseer
Matelot
Medacca
Merling
Mojarra
Moon-eye
Morwong
Mudfish
Muraena
Oarfish
Old-wife
Oolakan
Opaleye
Osseter
Oulakan
Oulicon
Panchax
Pandora
Peacock
Pegasus
Pelican
Pigfish
Pinfish
Piranha
Pollack
Pollock
Pomfret
Pompano
Pupfish
Ragfish
Rasbora
Ratfish
Rat-tail
Redfish
Rorqual
Roughie
Sand dab
Sand-eel
Sardine
Sawfish
Scalare
Scallop
Schelly
Sculpin
Sea-bass
Sea-cock
Sea-dace
Sea-moth
Sea-pike
Sea-star
Sea-wife
Sevruga
Sillock
Silurid
Skegger
Skipper
Snapper
Sock-eye
Sparoid
Speldin
Sterlet
Sunfish
Sunstar
Surgeon
Teleost
Tiddler
Tilapia
Titling
Torgoch
Torpedo
Tubfish
Ulichon
Vendace
Vendiss
Wall-eye
Whipray
Whistle
Whiting
Wide-gab

***8 letters:***

Albacore
Albicore
Anableps
Arapaima
Asteroid
Atherine
Bandfish
Billfish
Blennius
Bloodfin
Blowfish
Blueback
Bluefish
Bluegill
Boarfish
Bonefish
Bony pike
Brisling
Bullhead
Bullhorn
Bummallo
Cabezone
Cabrilla
Carangid
Cardinal
Cavefish
Characid
Characin
Chimaera
Coalfish
Corkwing
Cow-pilot
Cucumber
Cyprinid
Dealfish
Dragonet
Drumfish
Eagle-ray
Elephant
Escallop
Eulachon
Fallfish
Filefish
Flathead
Flounder
Four-eyes
Frogfish
Gambusia
Ganoidei
Gillaroo
Gilthead
Goatfish
Gobiidae
Graining
Grayling
Greeneye
Hackbolt
Hair-tail
Half-beak

Hard-head
Holostei
Hornbeak
Hornpout
Ichthyic
Jackfish
John Dory
Kabeljou
Killfish
Kingfish
Kingklip
Kukukuma
Lemon dab
Lionfish
Luderick
Lumpfish
Lungfish
Mackerel
Mahi-mahi
Mata Hari
Menhaden
Milkfish
Millions
Monkfish
Moonfish
Moray eel
Mosquito
Mulloway
Nannygai
Nennigai
Nine-eyes
Oulachon
Paradise
Patutuki
Pickerel
Pilchard
Pipefish
Pirarucu
Poor-john
Rascasse
Redbelly
Red roman
Reperepe
Rock-cook
Rockfish
Rockling
Roncador
Rosefish
Saibling
Sailfish
Salmonet
Saltfish
Sardelle
Scabbard
Scaridae
Sciaenid
Scorpion
Scuppaug
Sea-bream
Sea-devil
Seahorse
Sea-lemon
Sea-raven
Sea-robin
Sea trout
Sergeant
Serranid
Serranus
Skipjack
Smear-dab
Snake-eel
Sparidae
Sparling
Spelding
Speldrin
Starfish
Stenlock
Sting-ray
Stonecat
St Peter's
Sturgeon
Surffish
Tarakihi
Tarwhine
Teraglin
Terakihi
Tile-fish
Toadfish
Trevally
Tropical
Tubenose
Tullibee
Weakfish
Whitling
Wolffish

***9 letters:***
Ahuruhuru
Amberjack
Anabantid
Anchoveta
Argentine
Barracuda
Blackfish
Blindfish
Bummaloti
Butterfly
Carangoid
Cascadura
Ceratodus
Chaetodon
Chavender
Clingfish
Clownfish
Clupeidae
Coregonus
Coryphene
Crossfish
Cyprinoid
Devilfish
Gaspereau
Glassfish
Globefish
Golden eye
Goldfinny
Goldsinny
Golomynka
Goosefish
Grass carp
Greenbone
Greenling
Grenadier
Haberdine
Hornyhead
Hottentot
Houndfish
Ichthyoid
Jacksmelt
Jewelfish
Kabeljouw
Killifish
Labyrinth
Latimeria
Matelotte
Menominee
Mudhopper
Mudminnow
Neon tetra
Pikeperch
Porbeagle
Porcupine
Queenfish
Quillback
Red mullet
Roussette
Salmonoid
Scaldfish
Scalefish
Schnapper
Scorpaena
Selachian
Sheatfish
Shubunkin
Siluridae
Slickhead
Snailfish
Snakefish
Snakehead
Snipefish
Solenette
Spadefish
Spearfish
Speldring
Spikefish
Stargazer
Steenbras
Stingaree
Stockfish
Stonefish
Surfperch
Surmullet
Sweetfish
Sweetlips
Swellfish
Swinefish
Swordfish
Sword-tail
Thornback
Threadfin
Tittlebat
Tommy ruff
Toothfish
Topminnow
Trachinus
Troutfish
Troutling
Trumpeter
Trunkfish
Whitebait
White-bass
Wreckfish
Yellowfin

***10 letters:***
Amblyopsis
Archerfish
Arctic char
Barracoota
Barracouta
Barramundi
Bitterling
Bombay duck
Bottlehead
Butterfish
Candlefish
Cockabully
Cofferfish
Cornetfish
Cyclostome
Damselfish
Demoiselle
Dollarfish
Etheostoma
Fingerling

Flutemouth
Groundling
Guitarfish
Horned pout
Lake-lawyer
Largemouth
Lumpsucker
Maskalonge
Maskanonge
Maskinonge
Midshipman
Mossbunker
Mudskipper
Needlefish
Nurse-hound
Ocean perch
Paddlefish
Pakirikiri
Rabbitfish
Red emperor
Red-snapper
Ribbonfish
Roughhound
Rudderfish
Sandsucker
Scopelidae
Sea-poacher
Sea-surgeon
Serrasalmo
Sheepshead
Ship-holder
Shovelnose
Silverside
Small mouth
Springfish
Squeteague
Teleostome
Titarakura
Tommy rough
Trailperch
Tripletail
White cloud
White perch
Yellowtail

***11 letters:***
Blue whiting
Cephalis pie
Chondrostei
Cyprinodont
Dolly Varden
Istiophorus
Lapidosteus
Lepidosiren
Lophobranch
Maskallonge
Moorish idol
Muskellunge
Ostracoderm
Oxyrhynchus
Plagiostome
Plectognath
Pumpkinseed
Scolopendra
Seventy-four
Sharksucker
Snail darter
Soldierfish
Stickleback
Stoneroller
Surgeonfish
Triggerfish
Trumpetfish
Uranoscopus
Water souchy
White martin
Yellowbelly

***12 letters:***
Ballan-wrasse
Elasmobranch
Father-lasher
Heterosomata
Histiophorus
Jack crevalle
Mangrove Jack
Miller's thumb
Mouthbreeder
Mouthbrooder
Neoceratodus
Orange roughy
Plectognathi
Rainbow-trout
Silver dollar
Squirrelfish
Trachypterus

***13 letters:***
Burnett salmon
Horse mackerel
Leatherjacket
Musselcracker
Perennibranch
Rainbow runner
Sailor's choice
Sergeant Baker

***14 letters:***
Arbroath smokie
Corkwing wrasse
Malacopterygil
Smallmouth-bass
Snaggle-toothed
Walking catfish
Winter flounder

***15 letters:***
Crossopterygian

---

**Fish and chips** Greasies
**Fish-basket** Creel, Hask, Kipe
**Fish disease** Argulus
**Fisher(man)** Ahab, Andrew, Angler, Black cat, Caper, Codder, Dragman, Drifter, Heron, Herringer, High-liner, Liner, Pedro, Peter (Grimes), Piscator, Rodster, Sharesman, Walton
▸**Fisherwoman** *see* FISH-SELLER
**Fish-hawk** Osprey
**Fishing-boat** Drifter, Purse seiner, Trawler
**Fishing-ground** Haaf
**Fishing-line** G(u)imp, Gymp, Paternoster
**Fishpond** Ocean, Stew, Vivarium
**Fish-seller, Fisherwoman** Fishwife, Molly Malone, Ripp(i)er, Shawley, Shawlie
**Fishy** Botargo, Dodgy, Suspicious, Vacant
**Fission** Multiple, Nuclear
**Fissure** Chasm, Cleft, Crack, Cranny, Crevasse, Crevice, Gap, Grike, Gryke, Lode, Rent, Rift, Rille, Rolando, Sand-crack, Scam, Spli, Swallet, Swallow hole, Sylvian, Sylvius, Vallecula, Vein, Zygon
**Fist** Bunch of fives, Clench, Dukes, Hand(writing), Iron, Join-hand, Mailed, Neaf(f)e, Neif, Neive, Nief, Nieve, Pud, Punch, Thump, Writing
**Fit(s), Fitful, Fitter, Fitting(s), Fitness** Able(-bodied), Access, Adapt, Adequate, Ague, Align, Aline, Apoplexy, Appointment, Apposite, Appropriate, Apropos, Apt(itude), A salti, Athletic, Attack, Babbitt, Bayonet, Becoming, Belong, Beseemly, Bout, Canto, Capable, Cataleptic, Cataplexy, Click, Competent, Concinnous, Condign, Congruous, Conniption, Convulsion, Culver-tail, Darwinian, Decent, Decorous, Desultory, Dod, Dove-tail, Due, Eclampsia, Egal, Eligible, Ensconce, Epilepsy, Equip, Exies, Expedient, Fairing, Fay,

Fiddle, Form, Furniment, Furnishing, Fytte, Gee, Germane, Glove, Gusty, Habile, Hale, Handsome, Hang, Health, Hinge, Hissy, Huff, Hug, Hysterics, Ictus, Inclusive, In-form, Install, Interference, Interlock, Intermittent, In trim, Jactitation, Jag, Just, Kashrut(h), Like, Lune, Marry, Mate, Meet, Mood, Nest, Opportune, Paroxysm, Passus, Pertinent, Pet, Pipe, Prepared, Press, →PROPER, Queme, Ready, Relevant, Restless, Rig, Rightful, Rind, Ripe, Roadworthy, Rynd, Seemly, Seizure, Serving, Set, Shrink, Sit, Sliding, Slot, Snit, Snotter, Snug, Sort, Sound, Spasm, Spell, Start, Stroke, Suit(able), Syncope, Tailor, Tantrum, Tenoner, Throe, Tide, To prepon, Tref(a), Treif, Trim, Turn, Unit, Up to, Well, Wobbler, Wobbly, Worthy, Wrath

▷**Fit(ting)** *may indicate* a 't'

**Fitment** Adaptor, Ratchet, Unit

**Fitzgerald** Edward, Ella, Scott

**Fitzwilliam** Darcy

**Five(s), Fiver** Cinque, Flim, Mashie, Pallone, Pedro, Pentad, Quinary, Quincunx, Quintet, Sextan, Towns, V

**Five hundred** D, Monkey

**Five years** Lustre, Lustrum

**Fix(ation), Fixed, Fixer, Fixative** Adhere, Affeer, Anchor, Appoint, Appraise, →ARRANGE, Assess, Assign, Attach, Bed, Bind, Brand, Cement, Clamp, Clew, Clue, Confirm, Constant, Corking-pin, Cure, Decide, Destinate, Destine, Determine, Do, Dyed in the wool, Embed, Empight, Encastré, Engrain, Establish, Fast, Fasten, Fetish, Fiddle, Firm, Fit, Freeze, Gammon, Hard and fast, Hold, Hypo(sulphite), Immutable, Impaction, Impasse, Implant, Imprint, Inculcate, Inextensible, Ingrain, Install, Iron on, Jag, Jam, Learn, Locate, Lodge, Mend, Mount, Nail, Name, Narcotic, Nitrogen, Nobble, Odd-job man, Orientate, Patch, Peen, Peg, Permanent, Persistent, Pin, Pithy, Place, Plant, Point, Putty, Quantify, Rectify, Repair, Resolute, Restore, Rig, Righten, Rigid, Rivet, Rove, Rut, Scrape, Screw, Seat, Secure, Seize, Set, Settle, Ship, Shoo, Skatole, Skewer, Solution, Splice, Square, Stable, Stage, Staple, Static, Steadfast, Steady, Stell, Step, Stereotype, Stew, Stuck, Swig, Swing, Technological, Tie, To, Toe, Trouble-shooter, Unchangeable, Valorize, Weld

**Fixture** Attachment, Away (game), Event, Home, Match, Permanence, Rawlplug®, Unit

**Fizz(ed), Fizzy** Bubbles, Buck's, Effervesce, Gas, Hiss, Pop, Sherbet, Sod, Soda

**Fizzle** Failure, Flop, Hiss, Washout

▶**Fjord** *see* FIORD

**Flab(by)** Flaccid, Lank, Lax, Limp, Love-handles, Pendulous, Saggy, Tubby

**Flabbergast(ed)** Amaze, Astound, Floor, Thunderstruck

**Flaccid** Flabby, Lank, Lax, Limp, Soft

**Flag(gy), Flagging, Flags** Acorus, Ancient, Ashlar, Banderol, Banner, Black, Blackjack, Blue (Ensign), Blue Peter, Bunting, Burgee, Calamus, Chequered, Cobblestone, Colour(s), Dan(n)ebrog, Decline, Droop, Duster, Ensign, Fail, Faint, Falter, Fane, Fanion, Field colours, Gladdon, Gonfalon, Green, Guidon, Hail, Hoist, House, Irideal, Iris, Jack, Jade, Jolly Roger, Kerbstone, Languish, Lis, Maple leaf, Old Glory, Orris, Pave(ment), Pavilion, Paviour, Pencel, Pennant, Pennon, Penoncel(le), Pensel, Pensil, Peter, Pilot, Pin, Prayer, Quarantine, Rag, Rainbow, Red, Red Duster, Red Ensign, Repeater, Royal standard, Sag, Sedge, Semaphore, Sett, Sick, Sink, Slab(stone), Slack, Stand, Standard, Stars and Bars, Stars and Stripes, Streamer, Substitute, Sweet, Tire, Tricolour, Union (Jack), Vane, Vexillology, Waft, Wasting, Weaken, Whiff, Whift, White (ensign), Wilt, Wither, Yellow (Jack)

**Flagday** Tagday

**Flagellate** Beat, Euglena, Flog, Mastigophora, Scourge, Trypanosome, Whip

**Flageolet** Penny whistle

**Flagon** Bottle, Carafe, Ewer, Jug, Pitcher, Stoop, Stoup, Vessel

**Flagpole** Pin, Staff

**Flagrant** Blatant, Egregious, Glaring, Gross, Heinous, Patent, Rank, Shameless, Wanton

**Flagship** Admiral, Barge, Victory

**Flag-waving, Flag-waver** Jingoism, Linesman

**Flail** Beat, Drub, Swingle, Swip(p)le, Threshel

**Flair** Art, Artistic, Bent, Élan, Gift, Instinct, Knack, Nose, Panache, Style, →TALENT

**Flak** AA, Attack, Barrage, Criticism

**Flake** Chip, Flame, Flaught, Flaw, Floccule, Flocculus, Fragment, Peel, Scale, Smut, Snow, Spark

**Flam** Impose

**Flamboyant** Baroque, Brilliant, Flame-tree, Florid, Garish, Grandiose, Jazzy, Loud, Ornate, Ostentatious, Panache, Paz(z)azz, Piz(z)azz, Pzazz, Showoff, Swash-buckler

**Flame, Flaming** Ablaze, Ardent, Blaze, Fire, Firelighter, Flake, Flambé, Flammule, Flareback, Glow, Kindle, Leman, Lover, Lowe, Musical, Naked, Olympic, Oxyacetylene, Reducing, Sensitive, Sweetheart

**Flan** Pastry, Quiche, Tart

**Flanders** Mare, Moll

**Flange** Border, Collar, Collet, Lip, Rim

**Flank(s)** Accompany, Anta, Flange, Flitch, Haunch, Ilia, Lisk, Loin, Side, Spur, Wing

**Flannel** Blather, Canton, Cloth, Cotton, Face, Flatter, Outing, Soft-soap, Waffle, Washrag, Zephyr

**Flap(ped), Flapper, Flapping** Ado, Agnail, Aileron, Alar, Alarm(ist), Aventail(e), Bate, Beat, Bird, Blinker, Bobbysoxer, Bustle, Cat (door), Chit, Deerstalker, Dither, Earcap, Elevon, Epiglottis, Epiploon, Eyelid, Fipple, Flacker, Flaff, Flag, Flaught, Flutter, Fly, Fuss, Giglet, Giglot, Hover, → **IN A FLAP**, Labium, Labrum, Lapel, Loma, Loppet, Louvre, Luff, Lug, Omentum, Operculum, Panic, Peak, Shirt-tail, Spin, Spoiler, State, Tab, Tag, Tailboard, Tailgate, Tiswas, To-do, Tongue, TRAM, Volucrine, Wave, Whisk

**Flare(d), Flares, Flare up** Bell, Bell-bottoms, Erupt, Fishtail, Flame, Flanch, Flaunch, Godet, Magnesium, Scene, Signal, Skymarker, Solar, Spread, Spunk, Ver(e)y (light), Widen

**Flash(y), Flasher, Flashpoint** Bling, Bluette, Bolt, Brainstorm, Brash, Bulletin, Coruscate, Cursor, Electronic, Emicant, Epaulette, Essex Man, Exposure, Fire-flag, Flare, Flaught, Fulgid, Fulgural, Garish, Gaudy, Glaik, Gleam, Glent, Glint, Glisten, Glitter, Glitzy, Green, Green ray, Helium, Indicate, Instant, Jay, Lairy, Levin, Lightning, Loud, Lurex, Magnesium, Meretricious, Mo, Moment, Nanosecond, News, Ostentatious, Photopsy, Pyrotechnic, Raffish, Rakish, Ribbon, Ring, Roary, Scintillation, Sec(ond), Sequin, Showboater, Showy, Sluice, Snazzy, Spark, Sparkle, Sport, Streak, Strobe, Swank(e)y, Tawdry, Thunderbolt, Tick, Tigrish, Trice, Tulip, Twinkle, Vivid, Wink, Wire

▷**Flashing** *may indicate* an anagram

**Flask(-shaped)** Ampulla, Aryballos, Bottle, Canteen, Carafe, Cask, Coffin, Conceptacle, Costrel, Cucurbit, Decanter, Dewar, Erlenmeyer, Fiasco, Flacket, Flacon, Florence, Goatskin, Hip, Lekythos, Livery pot, Matrass, Mick(e)(y), Moon, Pocket-pistol, Powder, Pycnidium, Reform, Retort, Thermos®, Vacuum, Vial

**Flat(s), Flatness, Flatten(ed), Flattener** Adobe, Alkali, Amaze, Ancipital, Apartment, Bachelor, Bald, Banal, Beat, Bed-sit, Bland, Block, Blow-out, Bulldoze, Callow, Cape, Complanate, Compress, Condominium, Corymb(ose), Cottage, Coulisse, Court, Dead, Demolish, Diageotropic, Dorsiventral, Double, Dress, Dry, Dull, Even, Feeble, Flew, Floor, Flue, Fool, Gaff, Garden, Granny, Guyot, Haugh, High-rise, Homaloid, Home-unit, Horizontal, Insipid, Ironed, Jacent, Key, KO, Law, Lay, Level, Lifeless, Llano, Lodge, Lowland, Maderised, Maison(n)ette, Marsh, Monotonous, Mud, Nitwit, Norfolk, Obcompressed, Oblate, Ownership, Pad, Pancake, Pedestrian, Peneplain, Peneplane, Penthouse, Pentice, Pied-à-terre, Plain, Planar, Plane, Planish, Plap, Plat, Plateau, Platitude, Point blank, Press, Prone, Prostrate, Puncture, Race, Raze, Recumbent, Rooms, Salt, Scenery, Service, Smooth, Splayfoot, Spread-edged, Squash, Stale, Studio, Tableland, Tabular, Tame, Tasteless, Tedious, Tenement, Time-share, Trample, True, Uniform, Unimaginative, Unsensational, Unvarying, Vapid, Walk-up

**Flat-chested** Cithara

**Flat-faced** Socle

**Flat-foot(ed)** Heelless, Policeman, Splay

**Flat-nosed** Camus

**Flatter(er), Flattering, Flattery** Adulate, Becoming, Beslaver, Blandish, Blarney, Bootlick, Butter, Cajole, Candied, Carn(e)y, Claw(back), Complimentary, Comprabatio, Court-dresser, Court holy water, Crawl, Damocles, Earwiggy, En beau, Eyewash, Fawn,

Fillibrush, Flannel, Flannen, Fleech, Flummery, Foot-licker, Fulsome, Gloze, Gnathonic(al), Grease, Honey, Imitation, Lip-salve, Moody, Oil, Palaver, Palp, Phrase, Poodle-faker, Proneur, Puffery, Sawder, Smarm, Smoothie, Snow job, Soap, Soft soap, Soother, Souk, Spaniel, Stroke, Sugar, Sweet talk, Sycophant, Taffy, Toady, Treacle, Unction, Wheedle, Word

**Flatulence, Flatulent** Belch, Borborygmus, Burp, Carminative, Colic, Gas, Tympanites, Ventose, Wind, Wind dropsy

**Flaunt(ing)** Brandish, Flourish, Gibe, Ostantation, Parade, Show, Skyre, Sport, Strout, Strut, Wave

**Flavour(ed), Flavouring, Flavoursome** Absinth(e), Aftertaste, Alecost, Amaracus, Anethole, Angostura, Anise, Aniseed, Aroma, Benne, Bergamot, Body, Bold, Borage, Bouquet garni, Caramel, Chil(l)i, Clove, Coriander, Cumin, Dill, Essence, Eucalyptol, Fenugreek, Flor, Garlic, Garni, Gingili, Lace, Marinate, Menthol, Mint, Orgeat, Pepper, Piperonal, Potherb, Quark, Race, Ratafia, Relish, Rocambole, Sair, Salt, Sapor, Sassafras, Season, Sesame, Spearmint, Spice, Tack, Tang, Tarragon, → **TASTE**, Til, Tincture, Twang, Umami, Vanilla, Yummy

**Flavourless** Bland

**Flaw(ed)** Achilles' heel, Blemish, Brack, Bug, Chip, Crack, Defect, Fallacy, → **FAULT**, Gall, Hamartia, Hole, Imperfection, Inaccuracy, Infirmity, Kink, Knar, Knothole, Lophole, Misspent, Nick, Red-eye, Rima, Spot, Stain, Taint, Tear, Thief, Tragic, Weakness, Weak spot, Windshake

**Flawless** Impeccable, Intact, Perfect

**Flax(en)** Allseed, Blonde, Codilla, Harakeke, Harden, Hards, Herden, Herl, Hurden, Line, Linseed, Lint, Lint-white, Linum, Mill-mountain, Mountain, Poi, Tow

**Flay** Excoriate, Fleece, Flense, Lash, Scourge, Skin, Strip, Uncase, Whip

**Flea** Aphaniptera, Chigger, Chigoe, Chigre, Daphnid, Hopper, Itch-mite, Jigger, Lop, Pulex, Sand, Turnip, Water

**Flea-bane** Erigeron

**Fleabite** Denier

**Fleck** Dash, Dot, Freak, Spot, Streak

**Fledgling** Aerie, Eyas, Sorage, Stripling

**Flee(ing)** Abscond, Bolt, Decamp, Escape, Eschew, Fly, Fugacity, Lam, Loup, Run, Scapa, Scarper, Scram

**Fleece(d), Fleecy** Atrakhan, Basani, Bilk, Bleed, Coat, Con, Despoil, Flocculent, Golden, Jib, Lambskin, Lambswool, Lanose, Nubia, Overcharge, Pash(i)m, Pashmina, Plo(a)t, Pluck, Rifte, Ring, Rip off, Rob, Rook, Shave, Shear, Sheepskin, Shorn, Skin, Skirtings, Sting, → **SWINDLE**, Toison, Vicuna, Wool

**Fleer** Ogle

**Fleet(ing)** Armada, Brief, Camilla, Caravan, Convoy, Ephemeral, Evanescent, Fast, First, Flit, Flota, Flotilla, Force, Fugacious, Fugitive, Glimpse, Hasty, Hollow, Lightfoot, Momentary, Navy, Pacy, Passing, Prison, Spry, Squadron, Street, Swift, Transient, Velocipede, Volatile

**Flemish** Flamingant

**Flesh(y), Flesh out** Beefy, Body, Carnal, Carneous, Carrion, Corporeal, Corpulent, Creatic, Dead-meat, Digastric, Elaborate, Finish, Flab, Goose, Gum, Hypersarcoma, Joint, Jowl, Ket, Lamb, Long pig, Love handles, Lush, Meat, Mole, Mons, Muffin top, Mummy, Muscle, Mutton, Pork, Proud, Pulp, Quick, Sarcous, Spare tyre, Succulent, Tissue, Venison, Wattle

**Flesh-eating** Cannibalism, Carnassial, Creophagus, Omophagic

**Fleshless** Dry, Maigre, Pem(m)ican

**Flex(ible), Flexibility** Adaptable, Agile, Bend(y), Compliant, Double-jointed, Elastic, Genu, Leeway, Limber, Lissom(e), Lithe, Pliant, → **RESILIENT**, Rubato, Rubbery, Springy, Squeezy, Stretchy, Supple, Tensile, Tolerant, Tonus, Tractile, Versatile, Wieldy, Willing, Willowy, Wiry, Withy

▷**Flexible, Flexuous** *may indicate* an anagram

**Flick(er), Flicks** Bioscope, Cinema, Fillip, Film, Flip, Flirt, Flutter, Glimmer, Gutter, Kinema, Leaf, Movie, Movy, Riffle, Snap, Snow, Spang-cockle, Spark, Switch, Talkie, Twinkle, Waver, Wink, Zap

**Flickertail** ND

**Flier(s)** Aerostat, Airman, Alcock, Amy, Aviator, Biplane, → **BIRD**, Bleriot, Blimp, Brown, Crow, Daedalus, Erk, Fur, George, Gotha, Handout, Hang-glider, High, Icarus, Insert, Leaflet, Lindbergh, Luftwaffe, Montgolfier, Pegasus, Pilot, RAF, Scotsman, Spec, Speedy

**Flight(y), Flight path** Aeronautical, Aerospace, Air corridor, Arrow, Backfisch, Birdbrain, Bird-witted, Bolt, Bubble-headed, Capricious, Charter, Contact, Dart, Dash, Departure, Escalate, Escalier, Escape, Exaltation, Exodus, Fast, Fickle, Flapper, Flaught, Flibbertigibbet, Flip, Flock, Flyby, Fly-past, Free, Fugue, Getaway, Giddy, Grece, Grese, Gris(e), Guy, Hegira, Hejira, Hejra, Hellicat, Hijra, Lam, Loup-the-dyke, Mercy, Milk-run, Mission, Moonshot, Open-jaw, Pair, Parabola, Proving, Redeye, R(a)iser, Rode, Ro(a)ding, Rout, Runaway, Skein, Sortie, Stairs, → **STAMPEDE**, Stayre, Steps, Swarm, Test, Top, Tower, Trajectory, Trap, Vol(age), Volageous, Volatile, Volley, Whisky-frisky, Wing

**Flightless** Kakapo, Nandoo, Ostrich, Penguin, Rhea, Struthious

▷**Flighty** *may indicate* an anagram

**Flim-flam** Nonsense, Trick

**Flimsy** Airy-fairy, Delicate, Finespun, Fragile, Gimcrack, Gossamer, Insubstantial, Jimcrack, Lacy, Paper thin, Shoddy, Sleazy, Sleezy, Tenuous, Thin, Weak, Wispy

**Flinch** Blench, Cringe, Funk, Quail, Recoil, Shrink, Shudder, Start, Wince

**Fling** Affair, Amour, Dance, Flounce, Heave, Highland, Hurl, Lance, Lob, Pitch, Shy, Slat, Slug, Slump, Spanghew, Spree, Taunt, Throw, → **TOSS**

**Flint** Chert, Eolite, Firestone, Granite, Hag-stone, Hornstone, Microlith, Mischmetal, Optical, Pirate, Rock, Silex, Silica, Stone, Touchstone, Tranchet

**Flip(pant), Flippancy, Flipping** Airy, Bally, Brash, Cocky, Facetious, Flick, Frivolous, Glib, Go postal, Impudent, Jerk, Nog, Overturn, Persiflage, Pert, Purl, Ruddy, Sassy, Saucy, Toss, Turn, Upend

**Flipper(s)** Fin-toed, Paddle, Pinniped(e)

**Flirt(ation), Flirtatious, Flirting** Bill, Buaya, Carve, Chippy, Cockteaser, Come-hither, Come-on, Coquet(te), Dalliance, Demivierge, Fizgig, Footsie, Gallivant, Heart-breaker, Kittenish, Lumber, Mash, Minx, Neck, Philander(er), Pickeer, Prick-teaser, Prink, Rig, Sex kitten, Smasher, Soubrette, Spark, Toy, Trifle, Vamp, Wow

**Flit** Dart, Decamp, Flicker, Flutter, Gad, Moonlight, Scoot

**Float(er), Floatability, Floating, Flotation** Ark, Balsa, Bidarka, Bob, Bobber, Bubble, Buoy(ant), Caisson, Camel, Carley, Clanger, Drift, Fleet, Flotsam, Flutterboard, Froth, Fucus, Hover, Inherent, Jetsam, Jetson, Launch, Levitate, Lifebuoy, Milk, Natant, Neuston, Oropesa, Outrigger, Paddle, Planula, Pontoon, Pram, Quill, Raft, Ride, Sail, Skim, Sponson, Stick, Trimmer, Vacillate, Waft, Waggler, Waterwings, Weightless

**Floating garden** Chinampa

**Flock(s)** Assemble, Bevy, Charm, Chirm, Company, Congregation, Dopping, Drove, Flight, Fold, Forgather, Gaggle, Gather, Gregatim, Herd, Mob, Paddling, Parishioners, Rally, Rout, School, Sedge, Sord, Spring, Trip, Troop, Tuft, Vulgar, Walk, Wing, Wisp, Wool

**Flog(ger), Flogging** Baculine, Beat, Birch, Breech, Cane, Cat, Clobber, Exert, Flay, Hawk, Hide, Horsewhip, Knout, Lace, Lambast, Larrup, Lash, Lather, Lick, Orbilius, Retail, Rope's end, Scourge, Sell, Sjambok, Strap, Tan, Tat, Taw, → **THRASH**, Thwack, Tout, Vapulate, Welt, Whip, Whipping-cheer

**Flood(ed)** Avalanche, Awash, Bore, Cataclysm, Deluge, Deucalion's, Diffuse, Diluvium, Drown, Dump, Eger, Engulf, Flash, Freshet, Gush, Inundate, Irrigate, Land, Noachic, Ogygian deluge, Outpouring, Overflow, Overswell, Overwhelm, Plethora, Pour, Rage, Saturate, Smurf, Spate, Speat, Suffuse, Swamp, Tide, → **TORRENT**, Undam, Washland, Waterlog

**Floodbank** Levee

**Floodgate** St(a)unch

**Floodlight** Ashcan, Blond(e), One-key

**Floor(ing)** Area, Astonish, Astound, Baffle, Barbecue, Beat, Bemuse, Benthos, Chess, Confound, Culch, Deck(ing), Dev(v)el, Down, Entresol, Étage, Faze, Fell, Flags(tone), Flatten, Flight, Gravel, Ground, Kayo, KO, Mezzanine, Mould loft, Ocean, Orlop, Paralimnion, Parquet, Pelvic, Piano nobile, Pit, Planch, Platform, Puncheon, Screed, Shop, Siege, Sole, Stage, Stagger, Story, Stump, Terrazzo, Tessella, Tessera, Thill, Thrashing, Threshing, Throw, Trading, Vinyl, Withering, Woodblock

**Floor show** Caberet
**Floozie** Broad, Scarlet woman
**Flop(py)** Belly-landing, Bomb(shell), Collapse, Disaster, Doss, Dud, Failure, Fiasco, Fizzer, Fosbury, Limp, Lollop, Mare's-nest, Misgo, Phut, Plump, Purler, Turkey, Washout, Whap, Whitewash
**Flora** Benthos, Biota, Cybele, Flowers, Intestinal
**Florence, Florentine** Medici, Tuscan
**Florid** Asian, Baroque, Coloratura, Cultism, Flamboyant, Fresh, Gongorism, High, Red, Rococo, Roseate, Rubicund, Ruddy, Taffeta
**Florida** Fa
**Florin** Scotchman
**Florist** Spry
**Floss(y)** Candy, Clean, Dental, Flashy, Florence, Ornate, Silk
▸**Flotation** *see* FLOAT(ER)
**Flotilla** Armada, Escadrille
**Flotsam** Detritus, Driftwood, Flotage, Waift, Waveson, Weft, Wreckage
**Flounce** Falbala, Frill, Furbelow, Huff, Prance, Ruffle, Sashay, Toss
**Flounder** Blunder, Flail, Fluke, Pitch, Reel, Sandsucker, Slosh, Struggle, Stumble, Tolter, Toss, Wallop, Wallow
**Flour** Buckwheat, Cassava, Corn meal, Couscous(ou), Cribble, Crible, Farina, Graham, Gram, Kouskous, Meal, Middlings, Pinole, Plain, Powder, Red-dog, Rice, Rock, Rye, Salep, Self-raising, Soy(a), Strong, Wheatmeal, White, Wholegrain, Wholemeal, Wholewheat, Wood
**Flourish(ed), Flourishing** Abound, Blague, Bless, Bloom, Blossom, Boast, Boom, Brandish, Bravura, Burgeon, Cadenza, Dow well, Epiphonema, Fanfare, Fiorita, Fl, Flare, Floreat, Florescent, Going strong, Green, Grow, Kicking, Lick, Lush, Melisma, Mort, Omar, Palmy, Paraph, Pert, Prosper, Rubric, Ruderal, Scroll, Serif, Swash, Tantara, Thrive, Tucket, Veronica, Vigorous, Wampish, Wave, Welfare
**Flout(er), Flouting** Defy, Disdain, Disobey, Insult, Malign, Mock, Profane, Scofflaw, Scorn, Scout
**Flow(ing)** Abound, Afflux, Cadence, Cantabile, Cantilena, Cash, Circumfluence, Current, Cursive, Cusec, Data, Distil, Drift, Ebb, Emanate, Estrang(h)elo, Fleet, Fluent, Fluid, Flush, Flux, Freeform, Gene, Gush, Indraft, Issue, Knickpoint, Lahar, Laminar, Lava, Legato, Liquid, Loose-bodied, Mane, Nappe, Nickpoint, Obsequent, Onrush, Ooze, Popple, Pour, Purl, Race, Rail(e), Rayle, Rill, Rin, Run, Rush, Scapa, Seamless, Seep, Seton, Setter, Slip, Slur, Spate, Spurt, Stream, Streamline, Teem, Tidal, Torrent, Trickle, Turbulent, Viscous, Wash, Well
**Flower (part), Flowering, Flowers, Flower bed** Best, Bloom, Bloosme, Blossom, Bouquet, Composite, Corsage, Cream, Develop, Disc, Ecblastesis, Efflorescence, Elite, Fiori, Imperfect, Inflorescence, Night, Parterre, Paschal, Passion, Pick, Plant, Pre-vernal, Prime, Quatrefeuille, Quatrefoil, Remontant, → RIVER, Rogation, Serotine, Spray, Square, Stalked, Stream, Thyrse, Trefoil, Trumpet, Verdoy, Vernal, Wreath

---

## FLOWERS

*3 letters:*
May
Mum
Rue

*4 letters:*
Aloe
Arum
Cyme
Disa
Flag
Gold
Gool
Gule
Irid
Iris
Knot
Lily
Pink
Rose
Wald
Weld

*5 letters:*
Agave
Aster
Brook
Bugle
Camas
Canna
Coral
Daisy
Enemy
Erica
Hosta
Lotus
Lupin
Orris
Oxlip
Padma
Pance
Pansy
Phlox
Poppy
Spink
Stock
Tansy

Toran
Tulip
Tyrse
Umbel
Viola
Yulan

*6 letters:*
Adonis
Annona
Arabis
Camash
Camass
Catkin
Corymb
Cosmos
Crants
Dahlia
Gollan
Henbit
Lupine
Madder
Maguey
Mallow
Mimosa
Nuphar
Onagra
Orchid
Oxslip
Paeony
Pompom
Pompon
Protea
Scilla
Sesame
Silene
Smilax
Spadix
Tassel
Thrift
Torana
Wasabi
Yarrow

*7 letters:*
Aconite
Alyssum
Amarant
Anemone
Astilbe
Bugloss
Campion
Cowslip
Freesia
Fuchsia
Fumaria
Gentian
Gilt-cup
Glacier
Gladdon
Godetia
Golland
Gowland
Hawkbit
Heather
Ipomoea
Jonquil
Kikumon
Lobelia
Melilot
Mimulus
Nosegay
Peacock
Pelican
Petunia
Picotee
Primula
Quamash
Rampion
Statice
Sulphur
Tea-rose
Tellima
Verbena

*8 letters:*
Abutilon
Amaranth
Argemone
Asphodel
Bindi-eye
Bluebell
Bullhoof
Carolina
Clematis
Cyclamen
Daffodil
Floscule
Foxglove
Gardenia
Geranium
Gillyvor
Gladioli
Glory-pea
Hepatica
Hesperis
Hibiscus
Hyacinth
Kok-sagyz
Larkspur
Leucojum
Magnolia
Marigold
Myosotis
Oleander
Oncidium
Primrose
Samphire
Scabious
Stapelia
Trollius
Tuberose
Turnsole
Valerian

*9 letters:*
Bald-money
Bee-orchid
Belamoure
Buttercup
Cineraria
Columbine
Edelweiss
Eglantine
Galingale
Gessamine
Golden rod
Hellebore
Hollyhock
Hydrangea
Jessamine
Melampode
Pimpernel
Pyrethrum
Rudbeckia
Santonica
Saxifrage
Speedwell
Strobilus
Tiger lily

*10 letters:*
Bellamoure
Buttonhole
Coronation
Fraxinella
Granadilla
Heliotrope
Immortelle
Lady's smock
Nasturtium
Pentstemon
Poached egg
Poinsettia
Polyanthus
Pulsatilla
Quinsy-wort
Ragged lady
Sidesaddle
Snapdragon
Stavesacre
Tibouchine
Touch-me-not

*11 letters:*
Boutonniere
Bur-marigold
Gillyflower
Loose-strife
Meadow-sweet
Ragged robin
Red hot poker
Saintpaulia
Sweet sultan

*12 letters:*
Hortus siccus
Iceland poppy
None-so-pretty
Pasqueflower
Pheasant's eye
Tradescantia

*13 letters:*
Flannelflower
Marsh-marigold
Orange-blossom

*14 letters:*
Transvaal daisy

*15 letters:*
Star of Bethlehem

---

▷**Flower** *may indicate* a river
**Flower arrangement, Flower work** Barbola, Ikebana, Lei
**Flowery** Anthea, Anthemia, Damassin, Orchideous, →ORNATE, Pseudocarp, Verbose
**Flu** Asian, Bird, Fujian, Gas(tric), →INFLUENZA, ME, Yuppie

**Fluctuate(r), Fluctuating, Fluctuation** Ambivalence, Balance, Dip, Irregular, Seasonal, Seiche, Sway, Trimmer, Unsteady, Vacillate, Vary, Waver, Yo-yo
**Flue** Chimney, Duct, Funnel, Pipe, Recuperator, Tewel, Uptake, Vent
**Fluent(ly)** Eloquent, Facile, Flowing, Glib, Liquid, Oracy, Verbose, Voluble
**Fluff(y)** Blow, Bungle, Candyfloss, Dowl(e), Down, Dust, Dust bunny, Feathery, Fleecy, Flocculent, Floss, Flue, Fug, Fuzz, Girl, Lint, Mess-up, Muff, Noil, Oose, Ooze, Plot, Thistledown
**Fluid** Acid, Aldehyde, Amniotic, Anasarca, Ascites, Bile, Brake, Broo, Chyle, Cisterna, Colostrum, Condy's, Coolant, Correcting, Dewdrop, Edema, Enema, Erf, Fixative, Fl, Glycerin, Humoral, Humour, Joint-oil, Juice, Latex, → LIQUID, Lymph, Movable, Mucus, Oedema, Perfect, Perilymph, Plasma, Pus, Saliva, Sap, Seminal, Serous, Serum, Shifting, Spermatic, Spittle, Streamlined, Succus, Synovia, Transudate, Vitreum, Vril, Water, Wiper
▷**Fluid** *may indicate* an anagram
**Fluke** Accident, Anchor, Chance, Fan, Flounder, Ga(u)nch, Grapnel, Killock, Liver, Lobe, Redia, Schistosome, Scratch, Spud, Trematoid, Upcast
**Flume** Chute
**Flummery** BS, Pudding
**Flummox** Baffle, Bamboozle, Floor, Nonplus, Perplex
**Flunk** Fail
**Flunk(e)y** Chasseur, Clawback, Haiduck, Heyduck, Jeames, Lackey, Minion, Servant, Toady
**Fluorescence, Fluorescent** Bloom, Day-glo, Epipolism, Glow, Neon, Phosphorescence, Uranin
**Fluorine, Fluoride** F, Hexene
**Fluorspar** Blue john
**Flurry** Bustle, Fluster, Haste, Hoo-ha, Shower
**Flush(ed)** Affluent, Beat, Bloom, Busted, Crimson, Even, Ferret, Fever, Florid, Flow, Gild, Hectic, Heyday, Hot, Irrigate, Lavage, Level, Red, Rolling, Rosy, Royal, Rud, Scour, Sluice, Spaniel, Start, Straight, Sypher, Thrill, Tierce, Vigour, Wash, Wealthy, Well-heeled
**Fluster(ed)** Befuddle, Confuse, Disconcert, Faze, Flap, Jittery, Mither, Panic, Pother, Pudder, Rattle, Shake
**Flute (player)** Bellows-mender, Bohm, Channel, Claribel(la), Crimp, English, Fife, Fipple, Flageolet, German, Glass, Glyph, Groove, Kaval, Magic, Marsyas, Nose, Ocarina, Octave, Piccolo, Pipe, Poogye(e), Quena, Recorder, Shakuhachi, Sulcus, Thisbe, Tibia, Toot, Transverse, Whistle, Wineglass, Zuf(f)olo
**Flutter** Bat, Bet, Fan, Fibrillate, Flacker, Flaffer, Flap, Flaught, Flichter, Flicker, Flitter, Fly, → GAMBLE, Hover, Palpitate, Pitapat, Play, Pulse, Sensation, Speculation, Twitter, Waft, Wave, Winnow
**Flux** B, D, Electric, Flow, Fusion, Luminous, Magnetic, Maxwell, Melt, Neutron, Panta rhei, Radiant, Tesla, Weber
**Fly(ing), Flies** Abscond, Agaric, Airborne, Alder, Alert, Antlion, Arch, Assassin, Astute, Aviation, Awake, Aware, A-wing, Baker, Bedstead, Bee, Black, Blister, Blowfly, Blue-arsed, Bluebottle, Bolt, Bot, Breese, Breeze, Brize, Brommer, Buffalo gnat, Bulb, Bush, Buzzer, Cab, Caddis, Canny, Cantharide, Carriage, Carrot, Cecidomyia, Chalcid, Cheesehopper, Cheese skipper, Cleg, Cluster, Cock-a-bondy, Crane, Cuckoo, → CUNNING, Damsel, Dash, Decamp, Deer, Diptera, Dobson, Doctor, Dolphin, Doodlebug, Dragon, Drake, Drone, Drosophila, Dry, Dung, Dutchman, Escape, Face, Fiacre, Flee, Flesh, Flit, Fox, Frit, Fruit, Gad, Glide, Glossina, Gnat, Goutfly, Grannom, Greenbottle, Green drake, Greenhead, Hackle, Hairy Mary, Harl, Harvest, Hedge-hop, Herl, Hessian, Homoptera, Hop, Horn, Horse, Hover, Hurtle, Ichneumon, Instrument, Jenny-spinner, Jock Scott, Ked, Lace-wing, Lamp, Lantern, Laputan, March brown, Meat, Mediterranean fruit, Midge, Mosquito, Mossie, Moth, Motuca, Murragh, Musca, Mutuca, Namu, Needle, New Forest, Night, Nymph, Onion, Opening, Ox-warble, Palmer, Para, Pilot, Pium, Plecopteran, Pomace, Race, Rapid, Robber, Sacrifice, Saucer, Sciaridae, Sciurus, Scorpion, Scotsman, Screwworm, Scud, Sedge, Sharp, Sheep ked, Silverhorn, Simulium, Smart, Smother, Snake, Snipe, Soar, Spanish, Speed, Spinner, Stable, Stone, Stream, Streetwise, Syrphidae, Tabanid, Tachina, Tag, Tail, Tear, Thrips, Tipula, Trichopteran, Tsetse, Tube, Turkey brown, Turnip, Vamoose, Vinegar, Volatic, Volitate,

Warble, Watchet, Water, Welshman's button, Wet, Wheat, Wide-awake, Willow, Wily, Wing (over), Yellow Sally, Yogic, Zebub, Zimb, Zipper, Zoom

**Fly-by-night** Moth, Owl

**Fly-catcher** Attercop, Clamatorial, Cobweb, Darlingtonia, Dionaea, King-bird, Paradise, Phoebe, Spider, Tanrec, Tentacle, Tyrant, Yellowhead

**Flying-fox** Fruit-bat, Kalong

**Flying saucer** UFO

**Fly-killer** Chowri, Chowry, DDT, Empusa, Swat

**Flyover** Overpass

**Foam(ing)** Aerogel, Barm, Bubble, Froth, Head, Lather, Memory, Mousse, Oasis®, Polystyrene, Ream, Scum, Seethe, Spindrift, Spooming, Spume, Sud(s), Surf, Wake, Wild water, Yeast, Yest

**Fob** Chain, Defer, Fub, Pocket, Slang

**Focal, Focus(sed)** Anal, Centre, Centrepiece, Clou, Concentrate, Converge, Dedicated, Epicentre, Fix, Hinge, Hub, Limelight, Narrow, Nub, Pinpoint, Pivot, Point, Pressure point, Prime, Principal, Real, Rivet, Spotlight, Train, Zoom

**Fodder** Alfalfa, Browsing, Buckwheat, Cannon, Clover, Eatage, Emmer, Ensilage, Ers, Fescue, Foon, Forage, Gama-grass, Grama, Guar, Hay, Lucerne, Maize, Mangle, Mangold, Oats, Oilcake, Pasture, Provender, Rye-grass, Sainfoin, Silage, Soilage, Stover, Straw, Ti-tree, Vetch, Yarran

**Foe** Anti, Arch, Contender, → ENEMY, Opponent, Rival

**Fog** Aerosol, Blur, Brume, Cloud, Damp, Fret, Haar, (London) Particular, Miasm(a), Mist, Murk, Obscure, Pea-soup(er), Roke, Sea-fret, Sea-haar, Smog, Smoke, Soup, Thick, Vapour, Yorkshire

**Fogg** Phileas, Solicitor

**Fog(e)y, Fogie** Die-hard, Dinosaur, Dodo, Dotard, Duffer, Fossil, Graybeard, Old guard, Square

**Foible** Failing, Flaw, Idiosyncrasy, Quirk, Weakness

**Foil(ed)** Ba(u)lk, Chaff, Counterpoint, Cross, Dupe, Epée, Fleuret(te), Frustrate, Gold, Gold leaf, Lametta, Leaf, Offset, Paillon, Pip, Scotch, Scupper, Silver, Stime, Stooge, Stump, Stymie, Sword, Tain, Thwart, Tinsel, Touché

**Foist** Fob, Insert, Insinuate, Suborn, Wish

**Fold(er), Folding, Folded, Folds** Accordion, Anticline, Bend, Binder, Camp bed, Close, Collapse, Concertina, Conduplicate, Convolution, Corrugate, Cote, Crash, Crease, Crimp, Crinkle, Cristate, Crunkle, Diapir, Diptych, Dog-ear, Double, Downturn, Duo-tang®, Epicanthus, Epiploon, Fake, Fan, File, Fourchette, Fr(a)enum, Frill, Furl, Gather, Geanticline, Groin, Gyrus, In-box, Inflexure, Intussuscept, Jacket, Jack-knife, Lap, Lapel, Lap(p)et, Lirk, Loose-leaf, Mantle, Mesentery, Mitre, Monocline, Nappe, Nympha, Obvolute, Octuple, Omentum, Origami, Pastigium, Pen, Pericline, Pintuck, Pleach, → PLEAT, Plica, Plunging, Ply, Pound, Prancke, Pran(c)k, Ptyxis, Quiare, Recumbent, Replicate, Ruck(le), Ruga, Sheep-pen, Syncline, Triptych, Tuck, Vocal, Wrap

**Foliage** Canopy, Coma, Finial, Frond, Frondescence, Greenery, Leafage, Leaves

**Folio(s)** Crown, Elephant, F(f), File, Foolscap, Imperial, Music, Percy, Royal

**Folk(sy)** Beaker, Homespun, Kin, Nation, People, Public

**Folklore** Mythology

**Follicle** Graafian

**Follow(er), Following** Acolyte, Acolyth, Adhere, Admirer, After, Agree, Amoret, And, Anthony, Apostle, Attend(ant), Believer, Chase, Clientele, Consequence, Copy, Dangle, Disciple, Dog, Echo, Ensew, Ensue, Entourage, Epigon(e), Equipage, F, Fan, Footfall, Grasp, Grassite, Groupie, Hanger-on, Heel(er), Henchman, Hereon, Hound, Hunt, Imitate, Jacob, Man, Merry men, Mimic, Minion, Muggletonian, Myrmidon, Neist, Next, Obey, Pan, Post, Prosecute, Pursue, Pursuivant, Rake, Retinue, Road, Run, Satellite, School, Sectary, Secundum, Seewing, Segue, Sequel, Sequential, Seriation, Servitor, Shadow, Sheep, Sidekick, S(h)ivaite, So, Stag, Stalk, Stear, Steer, Subsequent, Succeed, Sue, Suivez, Supervene, Tag, Tail, Tantony, Trace, Track, Trail, Train, Twig, Use, Vocation, Votary, Yesman

▷**Follower** *may indicate* B

**Folly** Absurd, Antic, Bêtise, Idiocy, Idiotcy, Imprudence, Inanity, Lunacy, Madness, Mistake, Moria, Niaiserie, Silliness, Stupidity, Unwisdom, Vanity

**Foment(ation)** Agitation, Arouse, Brew, Embrocation, Excite, Incite, Poultice, Stupe
**Fond(ness)** Amatory, Amorous, Ardour, Attachment, Dote, Keen, Loving, Partial, Penchant, Tender, Tendre
**Fondant** Ice, Praline, Sweet
**Fondle** Canoodle, Caress, Dandle, Grope, Hug, Nurse, Pat, Paw, Pet, Snuggle, Spoon, Stroke
**Font** Aspersorium, Bénitier, Bitmap, Caxton, Delubrum, Ennage, Outline, Print, Proportional, Raster, Scalable, Source, True-type, Typeface, Vector
**Food, Foodstuff** Aliment, Ambrosia, Arrowroot, Bait, Bakemeat, Balti, Batten, Battill, Battle, Beefburger, Bellytimber, Bento, Bird's Eye®, Board, Bolus, Bord, Broth, Browse, Bully, Burger, Bush-tucker, Canape, Carry-out, Cate, Cereal, Chametz, Cheer, Cheese, Cheeseburger, Chometz, Chop, Chorizo, Chow (mein), Chowder, Chuck, Chyme, Clio, Cocoyam, Collation, Comestible, Comfort, Commons, Convenience, Cook-chill, Cordon bleu, Course, Couscous, Crab, Cud, Curd, Deutoplasm, Dietetics, → DISH, Dodger, Dog's body, Doner kebab, Dunderfunk, Eatage, Eats, Esculents, Eutrophy, Falafel, Famine, Fare, Fast, Fast casual, Felafel, Fodder, Forage, Formula, Franken(stein), Freedom, Fritter, Fuel, Functional, Giffengood, Gobi, Grillade, Grub, Gruel, Halal, Hamburger, Hangi, Hometz, Incaparina, Ingesta, Jootha, Jorts, Junk, Kai, Keep, Kromesky, Langar, Lasagne, Leben, Lerp, Long-pig, Maigre, Makan, Maki, Manna, Mato(o)ke, Matzoon, Meal, Meat (loaf), Muckamuck, Muesli, Nacho, Nardoo, Nosebag, Nosh, Nourishment, Nourriture, Nutriment, Oats, Obento, Okra, Opsonium, Ort, Oven-ready, Pabulum, Pannage, Pap, Parev(e), Parve, Pasta, Pasture, Peck, Pemmican, Pilaf, Pilau, Pizza, Polenta, Prog, Provand, Provender, Provision, Pu(l)ture, Ration(s), Real, Refreshment, Risotto, Rollmops, Roughage, Royal jelly, Rysttafel, Sambal, Samosa, Sandwich, Sap, Sashimi, Scaff, Schri, Scoff, Scran, Scroggin, Sitology, Sizings, Skin, Skran, Slop, Slow, Snack, Soft meat, Soil, Soul, Spaghetti, Square meal, Staple, Stir fry, Stodge, Sushi, Sustenance, Swill, Table, Tack, Takeaway, Tamale, Taro, Tempeh, Tempura, Teriyake, Tex-Mex, Tofu, Trimmings, Tripe, Trophallaxis, Tsamba, Tuck(er), Vegeburger, Veggie-burger, Viand, Victuals, Vivers, Vivres, Waffle, Wheatgerm, Yantia, Yittles, Yog(h)urt
**Food fad** Locavore
**Foodie** Epicure, Gourmet
**Food-plant** Laser, Silphium
**Food poisoning** Ciguatera
**Foodstore** Delicatessen, Grocery, Larder, Pantry, Silo
**Fool(hardy), Fooling, Foolish(ness)** Air-head, Anserine, April, Asinico, Asinine, Assot, Baloney, Beef-witted, Berk, BF, Blithering, Bob, Booby, Bottom, Brainless, Brash, Buffoon, Cake, Capocchia, Chump, Clot, Clown, Cockeyed, Cockscomb, Cod, Con, Coney, Coof, Coxcomb, Cuif, Cully, Daffy, Daft, Dagonet, Daw, Delude, Desipience, Dessert, Dilly, Dipstick, Divvy, Doat, Doilt, Dote, Dummy, Dunce, Dweeb, Empty, Etourdi, Fatuous, Feste, Flannel(led), Folly, Fon, Fond, Fox, Gaby, Gaga, Galah, Git, Glaikit, Goat, Gobbo, Goon, Goose, Gooseberry, Gormless, Groserts, Gubbins, Gull, Gullible, Halfwit, Hanky-panky, Hare-brained, Have, Haverel, Highland, Hoax, Horseplay, Huntiegowk, Hunt-the-gowk, Idiotic, Imbecile, Inane, Ineptitude, Injudicious, Insensate, Jest, Jester, Joke, Kid, Kissel, Lark, Loon, Madcap, Maffin, Mamba, Misguide, Mislead, Mome, Moron, Muggins, Nelly, Nerk, Niaiserie, Ni(n)compoop, Nigmenog, Ninny, Nong, Noodle, Nose-led, Nut, Nutmeg, Oanshagh, Omadhaun, Outwit, Patch, Pea-brained, Poop, Poupe, Prat, Preposterous, Punk, Rash, Rhubarb, Sawney, Scogan, Scoggin, Senseless, Shallow, S(c)hmo, Silly billy, Simpleton, Snipe, Soft, Sot, Spoony, Stultify, → STUPID, Sucker, Sweet, Thicko, Tom (noddy), Trifle, Turkey, Unredy, Unwise, Unwitty, Vacuous, Vice, Wantwit, Yap, Yorick, Yoyo, Zany
**Foolproof** Fail-safe
**Fool's gold** Mundic, Pyrites
**Foot(ing), Footwork, Feet** Amphibrach, Amphimacer, Anap(a)est, Antibacchius, Antispast, Athlete's, Bacchius, Ball, Base, Board, Choliamb, Choree, Choreus, Choriamb, Club, Cold, Cretic, Dactyl, Dance, Dipody, Dochmii, Dochmius, Epitrite, F, Flat, Ft, Hephthemimer, Hoof, Hoppus (cubic), Iamb(us), Immersion, Infantry, Ionic, Molossus, Ockodols, One-two, Pad, Paeon, Palama, Pastern, Paw, Pay, Pedal, Pedate, Pedicure, Penthemimer, Pes, Pettitoes, Plates, Podiatry, Podium, Proceleusmatic, Pyrrhic, Roothold,

Scazon, Semeia, Serif, Shanks's mare, Shanks's pony, Socle, Spade, Splay, Spondee, Standing, Syzygy, Tarsus, Terms, Tootsie, Tootsy, Tootsy-wootsy, Tread, Trench, Tribrach, Trilbies, Triseme, Trochee, Trotter, Tube, Ungula, Verse, Web(bed), Wrong, Zocco(le)

**Football(er), Football club** Aerial pingpong, American, Association, Attacker, Australian Rules, Back, Banyana-banyana, Barbarian, Ba'spiel, Best, Bladder, Camp, Canadian, Centre, Defender, Double header, Dynamo, Eusebio, Fantasy, FIFA, Five-a-side, Flanker(back), Fly-half, Futsal, Gaelic, Gazza, Goalie, Gridder, Gridiron, Half, Hooker, Juventus, Keeper, Kicker, League, Libero, Linebacker, Lineman, Lock, Loose forward, Loose head, Midfield, Moore, National code, Nickelback, Pack, Pele, Pigskin, Quarterback, Ranger, Redskins, RU, Rugby, Rugger, Rules, Safety, Seven-a-side, Sevens, Soccer(oos), Sport, Stand-off, Striker, Subbuteo®, Superbowl, Sweeper, Table, Tight-end, Togger, Total, Touch(back), Wallgame, Wing, Wingman

**Footboard** Stretcher

**Foot-fault** Bunion, Corn, Hammer-toe, Talipes, Verruca

**Foothills** Submontane

**Foothold** Lodgement, Purchase, Stirrup

**Footlights** Floats

**Footling** Trivial

**Footloose** Fancy-free, Peripatetic

**Footman** Attendant, Flunkey, Hiker, Lackey, Ped(estrian), Pompey, Valet de chambre, Yellowplush

**Footnote** Addendum, Cross-reference, Passim, PS

**Footpad** Land-rat, Mugger, Robber

**Footpath, Footway** Banquette, Catwalk, Causeway, Clapper, Track

**Footplate** Horseshoe

**Footprint** Carbon, Ecological, Electronic, Ichnite, Ichnolite, Ornithichnite, Pad, Prick, Pug, Seal, Slot, Trace, Track, Tread, Vestige

**Footrest, Footstool** Coaster, Cricket, Hassock, Pouffe, Stirrup, Stool, Tramp

**Footrot, Footsore** Blister, Bunion, Corn, Halt, Surbate, Surbet, Weary, Wire-heel

**Footslog(ger)** Infantryman, Trek

**Footwashing** Maundy, Nipter

**Footwear** Bobbysock, Boot(ee), Espadrille, Gumboot, Jackboot, Sandshoe, → **SHOE**, Slipper, Slip-slop, Sock, Spats, Stocking

**Fop(pish)** Apery, Barbermonger, Beau, Buck, Cat, Coxcomb, Dandy, Dude, Exquisite, Fallal, Fangled, Fantastico, Finical, La-di-da, Macaroni, Monarcho, Muscadin, Petit maître, Popinjay, Skipjack, Swell, Toff

**For** Ayes, Because, Concerning, Cos, Pro, Since, To

**Forage** Alfalfa, Etape, Fodder, Graze, Greenfeed, Ladino, Lucern(e), Pickeer, Prog, Raid, Rummage, Sainfoin, Scavenge, Search

**Foray** Attack, Creach, Creagh, Raid, Sortie, Spreagh

**Forbear(ance), Forbearing** Abstain, Clement, Endure, Indulgent, Lenience, Lineage, Longanimity, Mercy, Overgo, Pardon, Parent, Patient, Quarter, → **REFRAIN**, Stoic, Suffer, Tolerant, Withhold

**Forbid(den), Forbidding** Aversive, Ban, Bar, City, Contraband, Denied, Disallow, Don't, Dour, Enjoin, For(e)speak, For(e)warn, Gaunt, Grim, Haram, Hostile, Illicit, Loury, NL, No go, Prohibit, Proscribe, Sinister, Stern, Taboo, Tabu, Tapu, Tref(a), Verboten, Veto

**Force(d), Forceful(ly), Forces, Forcible, Forcing** Activist, Agency, Air-arm, Armada, Army, Assertive, Back emf, Barge, Bind, Birr, Bludgeon, Body, Bounce, Brigade, Bring, Brunt, Brute, Bulldoze, Cadre, Capillary, Cascade, Cataract, Central, Centrifugal, Centripetal, Chi, Coerce, Coercive, Cogency, Commando, Compel, Con brio, Conscript, Constabulary, Constrain, Contingent, Cops, Coriolis, Cram, Delta, Detachment, Dint, Domineer, Downflow, Drag, Dragoon, Drive, Duress(e), Dynamic, Dyne, E, Edge, Electromotive, Emphatic, Energetic, Equilibrant, Erdgeist, Erg, Exact, Exchange, Expeditionary, Extort, Extrude, F, Farci, Feisty, Fifth, Fire brigade, Foot-pound, Foot-ton, Foss, Frogmarch, Full-line, G, Gar, Garrison, Gendarmerie, Geostrophic, Gilbert, Gism, Gouge, Gravitational, Great Attractor, Hale, High-powered, Host, Hunter-killer, Hurricane, Impel, Impetus, Impose, Impress,

Impulsion, Inertial, Insistent, Instress, Intense, Interpol, Irgun, Irrupt, Jism, Juggernaut, Kinetic, Kundalini, Labour, Land, Landsturm, Landwehr, Lashkar, Legion, Leverage, Life, Lift, Lin(n), Live load, Lorentz, Luftwaffe, Magnetomotive, Magnus, Make, Mana, Manpower, Market, Met, Might, Militia, Moment, Momentum, Muscle, Nature-god, Navy, Newton, Numen, Oblige, Od, Odyl(e), OGPU, Old Contemptibles, Orgone, Orotund, Personnel, Peshmerga, Phrenism, Physical, Pierce, Pigs, Pion, Pithy, Plastic, Police, Polis, Posse, Potent, Pound, Poundal, Power, Prana, Press(gang), Pressure, Prise, Procrustean, Propel, Psyche, Psychic, Pull, Pump, Punchy, Pushy, Put, Qi, Railroad, Ram, Rape, Ravish, Reave, Red Army, Regular, Require, Restem, Robust, Route, Rush, SAS, Sforzando, Shear, Shoehorn, Snorting, Spent, Spetsnaz, Squad, Squeeze, Squirt, Stasi, Steam(roller), Steem, Stick, Stiction, Sting and ling, Strained, Strength, → **STRESS**, Strong-arm, Subject, Suction, Sword, TA, Task, Teeth, Telergy, Telling, Territorial, The Bill, The Great Attractor, Thrust, Tiger team, Torque, Tractive, Trenchant, Troops, Upthrust, Van der Waals', Vehement, Vigorous, Vim, Violence, Vires, Vis, Vis major, Vis visa, Vital, Vively, Vociferous, Vril, Weak, Wedge, Wrench, Wrest, Wring, Yeomanry, Zap

▹**Force(d)** *may indicate* an anagram

**Forced labour** Begar

**Force-feeding** Gavage

**Forceps** Bulldog, Capsule, Crow(s)bill, Hemostatic, Mosquito, Obstetrical, Pedicellaria, Pincers, Rongeur, Tenaculum, Thumb, Vulsella

**Ford** Anglia, Anna, Capri, Car, Cortina, Crossing, Drift, Escort, Fiesta, Industrialist, Irish bridge, Sierra, Strid, Tin Lizzy, Wade, Zephyr

**Fore** Prow

**Forearm** Cubital, Radius, Ulna

▸**Forebear** *see* **FORBEAR(ANCE)**

**Foreboding** Anxiety, Augury, Cloudage, Croak, Feeling, Freet, Hoodoo, → **OMEN**, Ominous, Premonition, Presage, Presentient, Presentiment, Sinister, Zoomantic

**Forecast(er), Forecasting** Aeromancy, Augury, Auspice, Cassandra, Demand, Divine, Estimate, Extrapolation, Glass, Horoscope, Long-range, Metcast, Metman, Numerical, Omen, Perm, Portend, Precurse, Predicate, Predict, Presage, Prescience, Prevision, Prognosis, Prognosticate, Projection, Prophesy, Quant, Rainbird, Scry, Shipping, Skry, Soothsay, Spae, Tip, Weather

**Foreclose** Bar, Block, Obstruct, Preclude

**Forefather(s)** Ancestor, Elder, Forebear, Parent, Rude

**Forefront** Van, Vaward

**Foreground** Repoussage, Repoussoir

**Forehead** Brow, Front(let), Frontal, Glabella(r), Metopic, Nasion, Sincipitum, Temple

▹**Foreign** *may indicate* an anagram

**Foreign(er)** Adventitious, Alien, Arab, Auslander, Barbarian, Easterling, Ecdemic, Eleanor, Ethnic, Étranger, Exclave, Exotic, External, Extraneous, Extrinsic, Forane, Forinsecal, Forren, Fraim, Fremit, Gaijin, German, Gringo, Gweilo, Malihini, Metic, Moit, Mote, Outlander, Outlandish, Outside, Oversea, Peregrine, Remote, → **STRANGE**, Stranger, Taipan, Tramontane, Uitlander, Unfamiliar

**Foreign Office** FO, Quai d'Orsay

**Foreknowledge** Prescience

**Foreleg** Metacarpel

**Foreman** Baas, Boss, Bosun, Chancellor, Clicker, Gaffer, Ganger, Manager, Overseer, Steward, Straw boss, Superintendent, Supervisor, Tool pusher, Topsman, Walla(h)

**Foremost** Alpha, First, Front, Leading, Number one, Primary, Prime, Salient, Supreme, Upfront, Van

▹**Foremost** *may indicate* first letters of words following

**Forenoon** Undern

**Forepart** Cutwater, Front

**Forerunner** Augury, Harbinger, Herald, Messenger, Omen, Pioneer, Precurrer, Precursor, Prequel, Trailer, Vaunt-courier

**Foresee** Anticipate, Divine, Envisage, Preview, Prophesy, Scry

**Foreshadow** Adumbrate, Augur, Bode, Forebode, Hint, Portend, Pre-echo, Prefigure, Presage, Threaten, Type

**Foreshow** Betoken, Bode, Signify

**Foresight** Ganesa, Prescience, Prophecy, Prospect, Providence, Prudence, Taish, Vision

**Foreskin** Prepuce

**Forest(ry), Forested** Arboreal, Arden, Ardennes, Argonne, Ashdown, Black, Bohemian, Bracknell, Brush, Bush, Caatinga, Charnwood, Chase, Cloud, Cranborne Chase, Dean, Deer, Elfin, Epping, Firth, Fontainebleau, Gallery, Gapo, Glade, Greenwood, Igapo, Jungle, Katyn, Managed, Monte, Nandi, Nemoral, New, Nottingham, Petrified, Rain, Savernake, Selva, Sherwood, Silviculture, Taiga, Teutoburg, Thuringian, Urman, Virgin, Waltham, Wealden, → WOOD, Woodcraft, Woodland

**Forestall** Anticipate, Head-off, Obviate, Pip, Pre-empt, Prevent, Queer, Scoop

**Forester** Foster, Kangaroo, Lumberjack, Verderer, Waldgrave, Walker, Woodman, Woodward

**Foretaste** Antepast, Antipasto, Appetiser, Avant-goût, Pregustation, Prelibation, Preview, Sample, Trailer

**Foretell(ing), Forewarn** Alert, Augur, Bode, Caution, Divine, Fatidic, Forecast, Portend, Predict, Premonish, Presage, Previse, Prognosticate, Prophecy, Soothsay, Spae, Weird

**Forethought** Anticipation, Caution, Prometheus, Provision, Prudence

**Forever** All-time, Always, Amber, Ay(e), Constant, Eternal, Evergreen, Evermore, Keeps, Permanent

▸**Forewarn** *see* FORETELL(ING)

**Foreword** Introduction, Preamble, Preface, Proem, Prologue

**For example** Eg, Say, Vg, ZB

**For fear** Lest

**Forfeit(ed), Forfeiture** Confiscated, Decheance, Deodand, Fine, Forgo, → PENALTY, Phillepina, Phillepine, Philop(o)ena, Relinquish, Rue-bargain, Sconce

**Forge(d), Forger(y)** Blacksmith, Bloomery, Copy, Counterfeisance, Counterfeit, Drop(-hammer), Dud, Excudit, Fabricate, Fake, False crumen, Falsify, Fashion, Foundry, Hammer, Heater, Horseshoe, Ireland, Ironsmith, Lauder, Metalwork, Mint, Nailery, Paper-hanger, Pigott, Proceed, Progress, Rivet head, Rivet-hearth, Smith(y), Smithery, Spurious, Stiddie, Stiff, Stithy, Stumer, Tilt, Trucage, Truquage, Utter, Valley, Vermeer, Vulcan, Weld

**Forget(ful), Forget-me-not, Forgetting** Amnesia, Dry, Fluff, Infonesia, Lethe, Lotus, Myosotis, Neglect, Oblivious, Omit, Overlook, Scatty, Senior moment, Unlearn, Wipe, Write off

**Forgive(ness), Forgiving** Absolution, Amnesty, Clement, Condone, Divine, Excuse, Lenient, Lenity, Merciful, Overlook, Pardon, Permissive, Placable, Remission, Remittal, Reprieve, Tolerant

**Forgo(ne)** Abstain, Cede, Cut and dried, Expected, Refrain, Renounce, Waive

**Forgotten** Bygone, Lost, Missed, Sad

**For instance** As

**Forjeskit** Overscutched

**Fork(ed), Fork out** Angle, Bifurcate, Biramous, Branch, Caudine, Cleft, Crotch, Crutch, Divaricate, Forficate, Fourchette, Grain, Graip, Morton's, Osmeterium, Oyster, Pastry, Pay, Pickle, Prong, Replication, Runcible, Slave, Split, Sucket, Tine, Toaster, Toasting, Tormenter, Tormentor, Trident, Trifid, Trisulcate, Tuner, Tuning, Y

**Forlorn(ness)** Abject, Aidless, Desolate, Destitute, Drearisome, Godforsaken, Lonely, Miserable, Moping, Nightingale, Sad, Woebegone

**Form(s)** Allotropic, Alumni, Archetypal, Bench, Body, Bumf, Cast, Ceremonial, Charterparty, Class(room), Clipped, Constitute, Contour, Coupon, Create, Document, Draw up, Dress, Eidos, Etiquette, Experience, Fashion, Feature, Fig, → FIGURE, Formula, Frame, Free, Game, Generate, Gestalt, Group, Hare, Idea, Image, Incorporate, Inscape, Keto, Lexicalise, Life, Logical, Mode, Mood, Morph(ic), Morphology, Mould, Nucleate, Order, Originate, → OUT OF FORM, P45, Penitent, Physique, Polyhedron, Protocol, Questionnaire, Redia, Remove, Rite, Ritual, Schedule, Sculpt, Shape, Shell, Sonata, Song, Sound, Stage, Stamp, State, Stem, Stereotype, Structure, Style, Symmetry, Talon, Ternary, Version

▷**Form** *may indicate* a hare's bed

**Formal, Formality** Amylum, Black tie, Ceremonious, Ceremony, Conventional, Dignified, Dressy, Dry, Exact, Fit, Ice, Literal, Mannered, Methodic, Official, Pedantic, Pedantry, Perfunctory, Pomp, Precise, Prim, Protocol, Punctilio, Representation, Reserved, Routine, Set, Solemn, Spit and polish, Starch, Starched, Starchy, Stiff, Stiff-necked, Stilted, Stodgy, Stuffed shirt, Tails, Uptight, White tie

**Formation, Formative** Arete, Battalion, Brown, Catenaccio, Configuration, Diapyesis, Echelon, Eocene, Fours, Growth, Layout, Line (out), Manufacture, Maul, Onomatopoeia, Origin, Pattern, Phalanx, Potence, Prophase, Reaction, Regiment, Reticular, Riss, Scrum, Series, Serried, Shotgun, Square dance, Testudo, Upbringing, Wedge

**Former(ly)** Ance, Auld, Before, Bygone, Ci-devant, Earlier, Ere-now, Erst(while), Ex, Late, Maker, Matrix, Old(en), Once, One-time, Passe, Past, Previous, Prior, Pristine, Quondam, Sometime, Then, Umquhile, Umwhile, Whilere, Whilom, Yesterday

▷**Former** *may indicate* something that forms

**Formidable** Alarming, Armipotent, Battleaxe, Fearful, Forbidding, Gorgon, Grande dame, Powerful, Redoubtable, Shrewd, Stoor, Stour, Stowre, Sture, Tall order, Terrible, Tiger

**Formless** Amorphous, Invertebrate, Nebulous, Shapeless

▷**Form of, Forming** *may indicate* an anagram

**Formosan** Tai

**Formula(te)** Conceive, Define, Dental, Devise, Doctrine, Empirical, Equation, Frame, Graphic, Incantation, Invent, Kekule, Lurry, Molecular, Paternoster, Prescription, Protocol, Prunes and prisms, → **RECIPE**, Reduction, Rite, Ritual, Spell, Stirling's, Structural

**For now** Interim, Meanwhile

**Forsake, Forsaken** Abandon, Desert, Lorn, Quit, Renounce

**Forsooth** Certes, Certy, Even, Marry, Quotha

**For sure** Pukka

**Forswear** Abandon, Abjure, Disavow, Renounce, Reny

**Forsyte** Fleur, Saga, Soames

**Fort(ification), Fortress** Abatis, Acropolis, Alamo, Alhambra, Balclutha, Bastel-house, Bastide, Bastille, Bastion, Battlement, Bawn, Beachhead, Berchtesgaden, Blockhouse, Bonnet, Breastwork, Bridgehead, Burg, Casbah, Castellated, Castellum, Castle, Citadel, Contravallation, Counterscarp, Crémaillère, Defilade, Demilune, Deva, Dun, Earthwork, Edinburgh, Enceinte, Epaule, Escarpment, Fastness, Fieldwork, Flanker, Flèche, Fortalice, Fortilage, Fortlet, Fraise, Ft, Gabion(ade), Garrison, Gatehouse, Golconda, Grenada, Hadrian's Wall, Haven, Hedgehog, Hill, Hornwork, Kaim, Kame, Kasba(h), Keep, Knox, La(a)ger, Lauderdale, Legnaga, Line, Louisbourg, Maiden, Malakoff, Mantua, Martello tower, Masada, Merlon, Mile-castle, Moat, Moineau, Motte and bailey, Orillion, Pa(h), Palisade, Peel, Pele, Pentagon, Peschiera, Place, Przernysl, Rampart, Rath, Ravelin, Redan, Redoubt, Reduit, Ring, Salient, Sallyport, Sangar, Sconce, Stavropol, Stockade, Stronghold, Sumter, Talus, Tenail(le), Terreplein, Tête-de-pont, Ticonderoga, Tower, Tower of London, Trench, Vallation, Vallum, Verona, Vitrified, William, Worth

**Forte** F, Métier, Specialty, Strength, Strong point

**Forth** Away, From, Hence, Out

**Forthright(ness)** Blunt, Candid, Direct, Four-square, Frank, Glasnost, Outspoken, Prompt, Unsubtle, Vocal

**Forthwith** Anon, Directly, Eft(soons), Immediately

**Fortify** Arm, Augment, Brace, Casemate, Defend, Embattle, Lace, Munify, Soup up, Steel, → **STRENGTHEN**

**Fortitude** Endurance, Grit, Guts, Mettle, Patience, Pluck, → **STAMINA**

**Fortune, Fortunate, Fortuitous** Auspicious, Blessed, Blest, Bomb, Bonanza, Chance, Coincident, Dame, Fate, Felicitous, Godsend, Gold, Happy, Killing, → **LUCKY**, Madoc, Opportune, Pile, Providential, Sonce, Tyche, Up, Well, Well off

**Fortune teller, Fortune-telling** Auspicious, Bonanza, Bumby, Cartomancy, Chaldee, Cha(u)nce, Chiromancy, Destiny, Diviner, Dukkeripen, Fame, Fate, Felicity, Forecast, Genethliac, Geomancy, Hap, Hydromancy, I Ching, Lot, Luck, Mint, Motser, Motza, Oracle,

Packet, Palmist, Peripety, Pile, Prescience, Pyromancy, Sibyl, Soothsayer, Sortilege, Spaewife, Success, Taroc, Tarok, Tarot, Tyche, Wealth, Windfall

**Forty, Forties** Capot, F, Hungry, Kemple, Roaring

**Forty-ninth** Parallel

**Forum** Agora, Arena, Assembly, Debate, Platform, Synod, Tribunal

**Forward (looking), Forward(s)** Accede, Advanced, Ahead, Along, Anterior, Antrorse, Arch, Assertive, Assuming, Avanti, Brash, Bright, Cheeky, Early, Flanker, Forrad, Forrit, Forth, Fresh, Front-row, Future, Hasten, Hooker, Immodest, Impudent, Insolent, Lock, Malapert, Minx, Number eight, On(wards), Pack, Pert, Petulant, Porrect, Precocious, Prescient, Prograde, → **PROGRESS**, Promote, Prop, Readdress, Redirect, Sassy, Saucy, Scrum, Send, Stem, Striker, To(ward), Van, Wing

**Fossil(ised), Fossils** Amber, Ammonite, Archaeopteryx, Archaeornithes, Baculite, Baluchitherium, Belemnite, Blastoid(ea), Calamite, Ceratodus, Chondrite, Conodont, Corallian, Corallite, Cordaites, Creodont, Crinite, Derived, Dinoceras, Diplodocus, Dolichosauria, Encrinite, Eohippus, Eozoon, Eurypterus, Exuviae, Fairy stone, Florula, Florule, Fogy, Goniatite, Graptolite, Hadrosaur, Hipparion, Hippurite, Hominid, Ichnite, Ichnolite, Ichnology, Ichthyodurolite, Ichthyolite, Index, Kenyapithecus, Lepidostrobus, Lingulella, Living, Mosasauros, Nummulite, Odontolite, Olenellus, Olenus, Oligocene, Orthoceras, Osteolepis, Ostracoderm, Oxfordian, Pal(a)eo-, Peking man, Pentacrinus, Petrifaction, Phytolite, Plesiosaur, Pliohippus, Pliosaur, Psilophyton, Pteridosperm, Pterodactyl(e), Pterygotus, Pythonomorph, Relics, Reliquiae, Remanié, Reworked, Sigillaria, Sinanthropus, Sivatherium, Snakestone, Stigmaria, Stromatolite, Taphonomy, Teleosaurus, Tentaculite, Thunderegg, Thunderstone, Titanotherium, Trace, Trilobite, Uintatherium, Wood-opal, Zinganthropus, Zone, Zoolite

**Foster (child, mother), Fostering** Adopt, Cherish, Cultivate, Da(u)lt, Develop, Encourage, Farm out, Feed, Fornent, Further, Harbour, Incubation, Metapelet, Metaplot, Nourish, Nourse(l), Noursle, Nousell, Nurse, Nurture, Nuzzle, → **REAR**, Spoonfeed

**Foul, Foul-smelling** Base, Bastardise, Bedung, Beray, Besmirch, Besmutch, Bewray, Bungle, Contaminate, → **DEFILE**, Dirty, Dreggy, Drevill, Dunghole, Enseam, Evil, Feculent, F(o)etid, Funky, Gross, Hassle, Hing, In-off, Mephitic, Miasmic, Mud, Noisome, Noxious, Olid, Osmeterium, Paw(paw), Personal, Professional, Putid, Putrid, → **RANK**, Reekie, Reeky, Rotten, Sewage, Soiled, Squalid, Stagnant, Stain, Stapelia, Technical, Unclean, Unfair, Vilde, Vile, Violation, Virose

▷**Foul** *may indicate* an anagram

**Found (in)** Among, Base, Bed, Bottom, Build, Cast, Caught, Constitute, Create, Emong, Endow, → **ESTABLISH**, Eureka, Fund, Institute, Introduce, Met, Occur, Plant, Predicate, Recovered, Rest, Stablish, Start, Table

**Found(ation), Foundations** Base, Basis, Bedrock, Cast, Corset, Cribwork, Establishment, Fond, Footing, Fund, Girdle, Grillage, Ground, Grounding, Groundwork, Hard-core, Hypostasis, Inception, Infrastructure, Initiate, Institution, Matrix, Mattress, Panty girdle, Pile, Pitching, Roadbed, Rockefeller, Root, Scholarship, Stays, Stereobate, Subjacent, Substrata, Substructure, Trackbed, Underlie, Underlinen

▷**Foundations** *may indicate* last letters

**Founder** Author, Beginner, Bell, Collapse, Crumple, Fail, Inventor, Iron-master, Miscarry, Oecist, Oekist, Patriarch, Perish, Progenitor, Settle, Sink, Steelman, Stumble, Type

**Foundry** Iron, Steelworks

**Fount** Aonian, Digital, Source, Springlet, Wrong

**Fountain, Fountainhead** Acadine, Aganippe, Arethusa, Bubbler, Castalian, Cause, Conduit, Drinking, Fauwara, Forts, Gerbe, Head, Hippocrene, Jet, Origin, Pant, Pirene, Salmacis, Scuttlebutt, Soda, Spring, Trevi, Well-head, Well-spring, Youth

**Fountain basin** Laver

**Four(times), Foursome, Four-yearly** Boundary, Cater, Georges, Horsemen, IV, Mess, Mournival, Penteteric, Qid, Quartet, Quaternary, Quaternion, Reel, Tessara, Tessera, Tetrad, Tetralogy, Tiddy, Warp

**Four-hundred** G

**Fourpence** Groat

**Fourteenth** Bastille, Trecento, Valentine

**Fourth** Deltaic, Estate, Fardel, Farl(e), Firlot, Forpet, Forpit, July, Martlet, Perfect, Quarter, Quartet, Quaternary, Quintan, Sesquitertia, Tritone

**Fowl** Barnyard, Biddy, Boiler, Brahma, Brissle-cock, Burrow-duck, Capon, Chicken, Chittagong, Cob, Cock, Coot, Domestic, Dorking, Duck, Ember, Gallinaceous, Gallinule, Game, Gleenie, Guinea, Hamburg(h), Heather-bleat(er), → **HEN**, Houdan, Jungle, Knob, Kora, Leghorn, Mallee, Moorhen, Orpington, Papageno, Partridge, Pheasant, Pintado, Plymouth Rock, Poultry, Prairie, Pullet, Quail, Rooster, Rumkin, Rumpy, Scrub, Solan, Spanish, Spatchcock, Spitchcock, Sultan, Sussex, Teal, Turkey, Wyandotte

**Fox(y)** Alopecoid, Arctic, Baffle, Bamboozle, Bat-eared, Bemuse, Bewilder, Blue, Canid, Charley, Charlie, Corsac, Crafty, Cunning, Desert, Discolour, Fennec, Floor, Flying, Fool, Friend, Fur, Grey, Kit, Lowrie(-tod), Outwit, Pug, Puzzle, Quaker, Red, Reynard, Rommel, Russel, Silver, Skulk, → **SLY**, Spot, Stimy, Stump, Swift, Tod, Uffa, Uneatable, Vixen, White, Zerda, Zoril(le), Zorro

**Foxglove** Cowflop, Deadmen's bells, Digitalis, Witches'-thimble

**Foxhole** Earth

**Foxtrot** Dance, F

**Foyer** Hall, Lobby, Reception

**Fracas** Brawl, Dispute, Fight, Mêlée, Prawle, Riot, Rumpus, Scrum, Shindig, Uproar

**Fraction(al)** Common, Complex, Compound, Continued, Decimal, Half, Improper, Ligroin, Mantissa, Mixed, Mole, Numerator, Packing, Part, Partial, Piece, Proper, Quarter, Scrap, Simple, Some, Tiny, Tithe, Vulgar

**Fractious** Schismatic

**Fracture** Break, Colles, Comminuted, Complicated, Compound, Crack, Fatigue, Fault, Fissure, Gap, Greenstick, Hairline, Impacted, Incomplete, Oblique, Pathological, Platy, Pott's, Rupture, Shear, Simple, Spiral, Splintery, Split, Stress, Transverse

**Fragile** Brittle, Crisp, Delicate, Eggshell, Flimsy, Frail, Frangible, Nesh, Slender, Tender, Vulnerable, Weak

**Fragment(s), Fragmented** Agglomerate, Atom, Bit, Bla(u)d, Brash, Breccia, Brockage, Brockram, Cantlet, Clastic, Crumb, Disjecta membra, End, Flinder, Flitter, Fritter, Frust, Graile, Lapilli, Mammock, Mite, Morceau, Morsel, Mosaic, Ort, → **PARTICLE**, Piece, Piecemeal, Potshard, Potsherd, Relic, Restriction, Rift, Rubble, Scrap, Scree, Segment, Shard, Shatter, Sheave, Shiver, Shrapnel, Shred, Skerrick, Sliver, Smithereens, Smithers, Snatch, Snippet, Splinter

▷**Fragment of** *may indicate* a hidden word

**Fragrance, Fragrant** Aromatic, Attar, Balsam, Bouquet, Conima, Lavender, Nosy, Odiferous, Odour, Olent, Otto, → **PERFUME**, Pot-pourri, Redolent, → **SCENT**, Sent, Spicy, Suaveolent

**Frail** Brittle, Creaky, Delicate, Feeble, Flimsy, → **FRAGILE**, Nice, Puny, Rushen, Slight, Slimsy, Tottery, Unsound, Weak

**Framboesia** Morula, Yaws

**Frame(work)** A, Abacus, Adjust, Airer, Angle, Armature, Babywalker, Bail, Bayle, Bier, Body, Bow, Box, Brickbat, Build, Bullbars, Bustle, Cadge, Cadre, Cage, Carcass, Cartouche, Case, Casement, Casing, Cel, Centreing, Cent(e)ring, Chase, Chassis, Clamper, Climbing, Cloche, Coaming, Cold, Compages, Companion, Console, Counting, Cowcatcher, Cradle, Cratch, Cribwork, Crinoline, Deckel, Deckle, Drawing, Dutchwife, Easel, Entablature, Espalier, Everest pack, Fabric, Falsework, Fender, Fiddley, Fit-up, Flake, Form, Freeze, Frisket, Gallows, Gambrel, Gantry, Garden, Gate, Gauntry, Griddle, Grid-iron, Haik, Hake, Heck, Hem, Horse, Hovel, Hull, Husk, Incriminate, Jungle gym, Lattice, Limit, Louvre, Mantel, Mixte, Monture, Mood, Mount, Mullion, Muntin(g), Newsreel, Ossature, Outrigger, Oxford, Pack, Pad tree, Pannier, Pantograph, Parameter, Partners, Passe-partout, Pergola, Physique, Picture, Pillory, Plant, Plot, Plummer-block, Poppet head, Portal, Pumphead, Punchboard, Puncheon, Quilting, Rack, Rave, Reading, Redact, Retable, Rib(bing), Rim, Roof rack, Sampling, Sash, Saw, Scaffold, Screen, Scuncheon, Sect(ion), Set, Setting, Skeleton, Spider, Spring-box, Stanchion, Stand, Stern, Still(age), Stitch up, Stocking, Stocks, Straddle, Stretcher, Stretching, Stroma, → **STRUCTURE**, Studwork, Substructure, Surround, Swift,

Tabernacle, Taboret, Tabouret, Tambour, Tent(er), Tepee, Time, Timeline, Trave, Trellis, Tress, Tressel, Trestle, Tribble, Trussing, Tympan, Undercarriage, Vacuum, Victimize, Walking, Wattle, Ways, Window, Yoke, Zarf, Zimmer®

**Framley** Parsonage

**Franc** Fr, Leu, Lev, Lew

**France** Anatole, Marianne, RF, Thibault

**Franchise** Charter, Concession, Contract, Liberty, Pot-wall(op)er, Privilege, Right, Suffrage, Vote, Warrant

**Franciscan** Conventional, Custos, Greyfriars, Minorite, Observant, Salesian, Scotist, Tertiaries

**Francium** Fr

**Franck** Cesar

**Frangipani** Red jasmine

**Frank(ish), Frankly** Artless, Austrasia, Bluff, Blunt, Cancel, → CANDID, Date stamp, Diarist, Direct, Downright, Easy, Eye-to-eye, Forthcoming, Four square, Free, Free-spoken, Guileless, Honest, Ingenuous, Man-to-man, Merovingian, Natural, Open, Outspoken, Overt, Plain-spoken, Postage, Postmark, Raw, Ripuarian, Salian, Sinatra, Sincere, Squareshooter, Stamp, Straight, Straightforward, Sty, Transparent, Upfront, Vocal

**Frankincense** Laser, Olibanum, Thus

**Frans, Franz** Hals, Lehar

**Frantic** Demoniac, Deranged, Desperate, Distraught, Drissy, Frenzied, Hectic, Mad, Overwrought, Phrenetic, Rabid, Violent, Whirl(ing)

▷**Frantic** *may indicate* an anagram

**Frappé** Iced

**Fraternise, Fraternity** Affiliate, Brotherhood, Burschenschaft, Consort, Dervish, Elk, Fellowship, League, Lodge, Mingle, Moose, Order, Shriner, Sodality

**Fratricide** Cain

**Fraud(ulent)** Barratry, Blue sky, Bobol, Bogus, Bubble, Chain-letter, Charlatan, Cheat, Chisel, Collusion, Covin, Cronk, Deceit, Diddle, Dishonesty, Do, Fake, Fiddle, Fineer, Fraus pia, Grift, Gyp, Humbug, Hypocrite, → IMPOSTOR, Imposture, Jiggery-pokery, Jobbery, Kite, Kite-flying, Knavery, Liar, Peculator, Phishing, Phon(e)y, Piltdown, Pious, Pseud(o), Put-up, Quack, Ringer, Rip-off, Roguery, Rort, Salami technique, Scam, Shoulder surfing, South Sea Bubble, Stellionate, Sting, Stumer, Supercherie, Swindle, Swiz(z), Swizzle, Tartuffe, Trick, Vishing, Wire

**Fraught** Perilous

**Fray(ed), Frayer** Bagarre, Brawl, Chafe, Contest, Feaze, Frazzle, Fret, Fridge, Ravel, Raw, Riot, Scrimmage, Wear, Wigs on the green

**Frazzle** Wear down

**Freak(ish)** Bizarre, Cantrip, Caprice, Chimera, Control, Deviant, Geek, Jesus, Lusus naturae, Mooncalf, Mutant, Oddity, Sport, Teras, Vagary, Weirdo, Whim, Whimsy

**Freckle** Dot, Ephelis, Fern(i)tickle, Fern(i)ticle, Heatspot, Lentigines, Lentigo, Spot, Sunspot

**Frederick** Barbarossa, Carno, Great

**Free(d), Freely** Absolve, Abstrict, Acquit, Assoil, At large, Blank, Buckshee, Candid, Canny, Church, Clear, Complimentary, Cuffo, Dead-head, Deliver, Deregulate, Detach, Devoid, Disburden, Disburthen, Disembarrass, Disembroil, Disengage, Disentangle, Eleutherian, Emancipate, Enfranchise, Enlarge, Exculpate, Excuse, Exeem, Exeme, Exempt, Exonerate, Extricate, Familiar, Footloose, Frank, French, Generous, Gratis, Hand, House, Idle, Immune, Indemnify, Independent, Kick, Large, Lavish, Lax, Leisure, Let, Liberal, Liberate, Liege, Loose, Manumit, Open, Parole, Pro bono, Pure, Quit(e), Range, Ransom, Redeem, → RELEASE, Relieve, Requiteless, Rescue, Reskew, Rick, Rid, Save, Sciolto, Scot, Solute, Spare, Spring, Stald, Stall, Trade, Unbowed, Unhampered, Unhitch, Uninhibited, Unlace, Unleash, Unlock, Unloosen, Unmew, Unmuzzle, Unpen, Unshackle, Unsnarl, Unstick, Untangle, Untie, Untwine, Untwist, Vacant, Verse, Voluntary

▷**Free** *may indicate* an anagram

**Freebooter** Cateran, Corsair, Franklin, Marauder, Moss-trooper, Pad, Pindaree, Pindari, Pirate, Rapparee, Rider, Snapha(u)nce, Snaphaunch, Thief, Viking

**Freedom** Abandon, Autonomy, Breadth, Carte blanche, Eleutherian, Exemption, Fear, Fling, Four, Immunity, Impunity, Independence, Laisser aller, Laisser faire, Laissez aller, Laissez faire, Latitude, Leeway, Leisure, Liberty, Licence, Magna Carta, Manumit, Moksha, Play, Range, Recourse, Releasement, Speech, Uhuru, UNITA, Want, Wiggle room, Worship

**Freefall** Sky dive

**Free gift** Bonus, Charism, Perk

**Freehold(er)** Enfeoff, Franklin, Frank tenement, Odal(l)er, Owner, Seisin, Udal(ler), Yeoman

**Freelance** Eclectic, Independent, Mercenary, Stringer, Temp

**Freeload(er)** Cadge, Scambler, Scrounge, Sponge

▹**Freely** *may indicate* an anagram

**Freeman** Burgess, Ceorl, Churl, Franklin, Liveryman, Thegn, Thete, Villein

**Freemason(ry), Freemason's son** Craft, Grand Master, Lewis, Lodge, Moose, Templar

**Free-range** Eggs, Outler

**Free State** Orange

**Freethinker** Agnostic, Bradlaugh, Cynic, Dissenter, Libertine, Sceptic

**Free-trade(r)** Cobdenism, Wright

**Free-wheel** Coast, Idle

**Free-will** Spontaneity

**Freeze(s), Freezer, Freezing** Alcarrazo, Arctic, Benumb, Congeal, Cool, Cryogenic, Cryonics, Crystallise, Deep, Eutectic, Flash, Freon®, Frost, Geal, Harden, Ice, Icebox, Ice cold, Lyophilize, Moratoria, Nip, Numb, Paralyse, Pause, Peg, Regelate, Riss, Stiffen, Subpolar, Sub-zero, Tense, Wage, Zero

**Freight(liner)** Cargo, Carriage, Fraught, Goods, Goods train, Lading, Load

**French(man), Frenchwoman** Alain, Alsatian, Anton, Aristo, Basque, Breton, Cajun, Canadian, Crapaud, Creole, Dawn, Dreyfus, Emil(e), Gallic(e), Gascon, Gaston, Gaul, Gombo, Grisette, Gumbo, Homme, Huguenot, Joual, Jules, M, Mamselle, Marianne, Midi, Monsieur, Mounseer, Neo-Latin, Norman, Parleyvoo, Pierre, René, Rhemish, Richelieu, Savoyard, Yves

**Frenetic** Deranged, Frantic, Manic, Overwrought

**Frenzied, Frenzy** Agitato, Amok, Amuck, Berserk, Corybantic, Deliration, Delirium, Demoniac, Dionysiac, Enrage, Enrapt, Euhoe, Euoi, Evoe, Feeding, Fever, Fit, Frenetic, Fury, Hectic, Hysteric, Lune, Maenad, Mania, Must, Nympholepsy, Oestrus, Phrenetic, Rage, Tantrum, Vehement

**Frequency, Frequent(er), Frequently** Angular, Attend, Audio, Bandwidth, Channel, Common, Constant, Expected, Familiar, Forcing, Formant, FR, Fresnel, Gene, Habitué, Hang-out, Haunt, Hertz, High, Incidence, Intermediate, Kilocycle, L-band, Low, Medium, Megahertz, Mode, Natural, Often, Oft-times, Passband, Patronise, Penetrance, Pulsatance, Radio, Recurrent, Regular, Relative, Repeatedly, Resort, Spatial, Spectrum, Superhigh, Terahertz, Thick, Ultrahigh, Video, Waveband, White noise

**Fresco** Intonaco, Sinopia, Tempera

**Fresh(en), Freshness** Airy, Anew, Aurorean, Brash, Caller, Chilly, Clean, Cool, Crisp, Deodorise, Dewy, Entire, Evergreen, Fire-new, Forward, Green, Hot, Insolent, Live(ly), Maiden, Mint, Nas(s)eem, New, New-laid, Novel, Quick, Rebite, Recent, Rejuvenate, Roral, Roric, Rorid, Rub up, Smart, Span-new, Spic(k), Sweet, Tangy, Uncured, Update, Verdure, Vernal, Virent, Virescent

**Freshman, Fresher** Bajan, Beginner, Bejan(t), Fresher, Frosh, Newcomer, Pennal, Plebe, Recruit, Student

**Fret(ful)** Chafe, Filigree, Fractious, Fray, Gnaw, Grate, Grecque, Haze, Impatient, Irritate, Key, Mist, Ornament, Peevish, Repine, Rile, Ripple, Roil, Rub, Stop, Tetchy, Tracery, Whittle, Worry

**Fretwork** Lattice

**Friable** Crisp, Crumbling, Powdery

**Friar(s)** Augustinian, Austin, Bacon, Barefoot, Black, Bonaventura, Bonaventure, Brother, Bungay, Capuchin, Carmelite, Conventual, Cordelier, Crutched, Curtal, Dervish, Dominican, Fra(ter), Franciscan, Frate, Frere, Grey, Jacobin, Laurence, Limiter, Lymiter, Minim, Minor, Minorite, →**MONK**, Observant, Observantine, Preaching, Predicant, Recollect, Recollet, Redemptionist, Rush, Tuck, White

**Fricative** Rill
**Friction** Attrition, Conflict, Detrition, Discord, Dissent, Drag, Massage, Rift, Rub, Skin, Sliding, Stiction, Stridulation, Tribology, Tripsis, Wear, Windblast, Xerotripsis
**Friday** Black, Casual, Girl, Golden, Good, Holy, Man, Person, Savage
**Fridge** Esky®, Freezer, Icebox, Minibar, Rub
**Fried cake** Croquette, Cruller
**Friend(ly), Friends** Achates, Affable, Ally, Alter ego, Ami(cable), Amie, Amigo, Approachable, Associate, Avuncular, Bach, Belamy, Benign, Boet(ie), Bosom, Bra, Bro, Bru, Bud(dy), Buster, Butty, Cackermander, Cater-cousin, China, Choma, Chommie, Chum, Circle, Cobber, Cock, Cohort, Compadre, Companion, Companionable, Comrade, Confidant, Cordial, Cotton, Couthie, Couthy, Crony, Cully, Damon, Dog, Downhome, Easygoing, Edwin, Ehoa, En ami, Fairweather, False, Familiar, Feare, Feathered, Feer, Fere, Fiere, Folksy, Gemütlich, Genial, Goombah, Gossib, Gossip, Green, Gregarious, Hail-fellow-well-met, Homeboy, Informal, Ingle, Intimate, Inward, Jong, Kidgie, Kith, Litigation, Lover, Marrow, Mate, McKenzie, Mentor, Mucker, Mutual, Near, Next, Oppo, Outgoing, Paisano, Pal, Paranymph, Pard(ner), Pen, Penn, Pheere, Platonic, Playmate, Privado, Prochain ami, Prochein ami, Pythias, Quaker, Sidekick, Sociable, Societal, Sport, Steady, Thawing, Thick, Tillicum, Tonga, Tosh, Type B, User, Wack(er), Warm, Well-disposed, Well-wisher, Wus(s), Yaar
**Friendless** Unpopular
**Friendliness, Friendship** Amity, Bonhomie, Camaraderie, Contesseration, Entente, Goodwill, Platonic, Rapprochement, Sodality
**Frieze** Dado, Metope, Penistone, Zoophorus
**Fright(en), Frightened, Frightening, Frightful** Afear, Affear(e), Agrise, Agrize, Agryze, Alarm, Aroint, Aroynt, Ashake, Bugaboo, Chilling, Cow, Da(u)nt, Dare, Deter, Eek, Eerie, Eery, Faceache, Fear(some), Flay, Fleg, Fleme, Fley, Flush, Gallow, Gally, Ghast, Gliff, Glift, Grim, Grisly, Hair-raising, Hairy, Horrid, Horrific, Intimidate, Menace, Nightmare, Ordeal, Panic, Pants, Petrify, Scar, → SCARE, Scarre, Scaur, Schrecklich, Shocking, Sight, Skear, Skeer, Skrik, Spine-chilling, Spook, Stage, Startle, Terrible, Terrify, Terror, Tirrit, Ugly, Unco, Unease, Unman, White-knuckle, Windy, Yitten
**Frightener** Sasquatch
**Frigid** Bleak, Cold, Dry, Frory, Frosty, Ice, Indifferent, Serac, Stiff
**Frill(y)** Armil, Armilla, Bavolet, Chidlings, Chitlings, Edging, Falbala, Flounce, Furbelow, Jabot, Lacy, Lingerie, Newgate, Oriental, Ornament, Papillote, Ruche, Ruff(le), Shirt, Trimming, Tucker, Valance
▹**Frilly** *may indicate* an anagram
**Fringe(s), Fringed** Bang, Border, Bullion, Celtic, Ciliated, Ciliolate, Edge, Fall, Fimbria, Frisette, Furbelow, Interference, Laciniate, Loma, Lunatic, Macramé, Macrami, Newgate, Pelmet, Peripheral, Peristome, Robin, Ruche, Ruff, Run, Side, Tassel, Thrum, Toupee, Toupit, Tsitsith, Tzitzit(h), Valance, Verge, Zizith
**Frippery** Small beer
**Frisian** Holstein
**Frisk(y)** Buckish, Caper, Cavort, Curvet, Fisk, Flimp, Frolic, Gambol, Search, Skip, Skittish, Wanton
**Frisson** Shiver
**Fritillary** Snake's-head
**Fritter** Batter, Beignet, Dissipate, Dribble, Dwindle, Fragment, Fribble, Pakora, Piddle, Potter, Puf(f)taloon, Samosa, Squander, Waste, Wonder
**Frivolity, Frivolous** Butterfly, Empty(-headed), Etourdi(e), Facetious, Featherbrain, Flighty, Flippant, Footling, Frippet, Frothy, Futile, Giddy, Idle, Inane, Levity, Light, Light-minded, Lightness, Lightweight, Moth, Persiflage, Playboy, Shallow, Skittish, Trifling, Trivial
**Frizz(le), Frizzly** Afro, Crape, Crimp, Crinkle, Curly, Fry, Fuzz, Hiss
**Frock** Dress, Gown, Ordain, Robe, Smock
**Frog** Amphibian, Anoura, Anura, Arrow poison, Batrachia(n), Braid, Breton, Bullfrog, Cape nightingale, Clawed, Crapaud, Depression, Flying, Fourchette, Frush, Goliath, Hairy, Hyla, Kermit, Leopard, Marsupial, Mounseer, Nic, Nototrema, Paddock, Paradoxical, Peeper, Pelobatid, Platanna, Puddock, Puttock, Rana, Ranidae, Spring peeper, Tree, Wood, Xenopus

**Frogman** Diver
**Frogmouth** Mo(re)poke, Podargus
**Frog spawn** Redd, Tadpole
**Frolic(some)** Barnsbreaking, Bender, Bust(er), Cabriole, Caper, Cavort, Curvet, Disport, Escapade, →**FRISK(Y)**, Fun, Galravage, Galravitch, Gambol, Gammock, Gil(l)ravage, Horseplay, How's your father, Jink, Kittenish, Lark, Play, Pollick, Prank, Rag, Rand, Rant, Rig, Romp, Scamper, Skippy, Skylark, Slap and tickle, Splore, Sport, Spree, Stooshie, Tittup, Wanton
**From** A, Against, Ex, For, Frae, Of, Off, Thrae
**Frond** Fern, Leaf, Tendril
**Front(al), Frontman** Antependium, Anterior, Bib, Bow, Brass, Brow, Cold, Cover, Dead, Dickey, Dicky, Esplanade, Facade, Face, Fore(head), Forecourt, Fore end, Foreground, Foreland, Groof, Grouf, Grufe, Head, Home, Insolence, Metope, National, Newscaster, Nose, Occluded, Paravant, People's, Plastron, Polar, Popular, Pose, Preface, Presenter, Pro, Prom, Prow, Rhodesian, Sector, Sinciput, Spearhead, Stationary, Tabula, Temerity, Van, Vaward, Ventral, Warhead, Warm, Western
**Frontier(sman)** Afghan, Barrier, Boone, Border, Boundary, Calamity Jane, Checkpoint, Crockett, Earp, Limit, Limitrophe, List, March, North-west, Outpost, Pathan, Perimeter, Wild West
**Front page** P1
**Front-ranker** Pawn
**Frost(ing), Frosty, Frostbite** Air, Alcorza, Black, Chill, Cranreuch, Cryo-, Freon®, Frigid, Frore(n), Frorne, Glacé, Ground, Hoar, Hore, Ice, Icing, Jack, Mat, Nip, Rime, Silver, Trench foot, White
**Froth(y)** Barm, Bleb, Bubble, Chiffon, Cuckoospit(tle), Despumate, Fizz, Foam, Frogspit, Gas, Head, Lather, Mantle, Nappy, Off-scum, Ream, Saponin, Scum, Seethe, Shallow, Spittle, Spoom, Spoon, Spume, Sud, Toadspit, Yeasty, Yest, Zephir
**Frown(ing)** Glower, Knit, Lour, Lower, Scowl, Stern
**Froze(n)** Arctic, Congealed, Froren, Frorn(e), Frory, Gealed, Gelid, Glacé, Graupel, Ice-bound, Rigid, Spellbound, Static, Stockstill, Tundra
**Fructification, Fructify, Fructose** Aeci(di)um, Basidium, Fertilise, Flower, Fruit, Inulin
**Frugal** Economical, Meagre, Parsimonious, Provident, Prudent, Scant, Skimpy, Spare, Spartan, Thrifty
**Fruit(ing), Fruit tree, Fruity** Accessory, Achaenocarp, Achene, Acinus, Akene, Allocarpy, Apothecium, Autocarp, Bacciform, Catapult, Cedrate, Coccus, Compot(e), Confect, Conserve, Cremocarp, Crop, Dessert, Drupe, Eater, Encarpus, Etaerio, First, Follicle, Forbidden, Fritter, Harvest, Issue, Multiple, Orchard, Output, Pericarp, Primeur, Primitiae, Product(ion), Pseudocarp, Regma(ta), Replum, Result, Return, Rich, Ripe, Schizocarp, Seed, Silicle, Siliqua, Silique, Soft, Sorosis, Stoneless, Succade, Sweetie, Sweety, Syconium, Syncarp, Utricle, Valve, Wall, Xylocarp, Yield

---

**FRUITS**

*3 letters:*
Fig
Haw
Hep
Hip
Hop
Jak
Key
Nut

*4 letters:*
Acai
Akee
Bael
Bito
Cone
Date
Gage
Gean
Jack
Kaki
Kiwi
Lime
Mast
Noni
Pear
Pepo
Plum
Pome
Sloe
Sorb
Star
Tuna
Ugli®
Yuzu

*5 letters:*
Ackee
Acorn
Anana
Anona
Apple
Assai
Berry
Bread
Carob
Choko
Genip
Gourd
Grape
Guava
Jaffa
Lemon
Lichi
Lotus
Mamee
Mamey
Mango
Melon
Nancy
Naras
Nashi
Nelis
Olive
Papaw
Prune
Rowan
Whort

***6 letters:***
Almond
Ananas
Babaco
Banana
Banian
Banyan
Carica
Casaba
Cherry
Chocho
Citron
Citrus
Comice
Damson
Durian
Durion
Emblic
Feijoa
Lichee
Litchi
Longan
Lychee
Mammee
Medlar
Narras
Nelies
Oilnut
Orange
Papaya
Pawpaw
Pepino
Pomace
Pomelo
Pruine
Punica
Quince
Raisin
Rennet
Russet
Samara
Sapota
Seckel
Sharon
Squash
Tomato
Wampee

***7 letters:***
Amygdal
Apricot
Avocado
Bullace
Cassaba
Chayote
Crab-nut
Currant
Cypsela
Geebung
Genipap
Gherkin
Kumquat
Leechee
Litchee
Manjack
Morello
Passion
Pimento
Pinguin
Poperin
Pumpkin
Pupunha
Rosehip
Ruddock
Satsuma
Soursop
Tangelo
Winesap

***8 letters:***
Abricock
Aguacate
Apricock
Bergamot
Bilberry
Blimbing
Calabash
Caprifig
Dewberry
Fraughan
Goosegog
Hagberry
Hastings
Hedgehog
Inkberry
Kalumpit
Minneola
Mirliton
Mulberry
Pearmain
Physalis
Plantain
Prunello
Rambutan
Rathripe
Sebesten
Shaddock
Silicula
Sunberry
Sweeting
Sweetsop
Tamarind
Tayberry
Teaberry
Waxberry

***9 letters:***
Algarroba
Apple-john
Aubergine
Bakeapple
Blueberry
Butternut
Candlenut
Cantaloup
Carambola
Caryopsis
Cherimoya
Colocynth
Crab apple
Cranberry
Deerberry
Freestone
Haanepoot
Hackberry
Juneberry
Love apple
Manzanita
Melon-pear
Mirabelle
Musk melon
Myrobalan
Naseberry
Nectarine
Neesberry
Ortanique
Persimmon
Pineapple
Pinot noir
Plumdamas
Poppering
Raspberry
Ratheripe
Sapodilla
Saskatoon
Shadberry
Sorb-apple
Star-apple
Tamarillo
Tangerine
Tomatillo
Victorine
Whimberry
Whinberry

***10 letters:***
Blackberry
Calamondin
Cantaloupe
Cherimoyer
Chinaberry
Chokeberry
Clementine
Clingstone
Elderberry
Granadilla
Grenadilla
Jargonelle
Loganberry
Mangosteen
Paddymelon
Pick-cheese
Punicaceae
Redcurrant
Scaldberry
Strawberry
Watermelon
Youngberry

***11 letters:***
Blood orange
Boysenberry
Chokecherry
Goldenberry
Granny Smith
Hesperidium
Huckleberry
Lingonberry
Marionberry
Pampelmoose
Pampelmouse
Pomegranate
Pompelmoose
Pompelmouse
Salmonberry

***12 letters:***
Blackcurrant
Checkerberry
Custard-apple
Service-berry
Thimbleberry
Victoria plum
Whortleberry

***13 letters:***
Bullock's heart
Sapodilla plum

***14 letters:***
Worcesterberry

**Fruitcake** Dundee, Madman, Nutter

**Fruitful(ness)** Calathus, Ephraim, Fat, Fecund, Feracious, Fertile, Productive, Prolific, Teeming, Uberty, Worthwhile

**Fruitless** Bare, Fool's errand, Futile, Sisyphean, Sooterkin, Sterile, Useless, Vain

**Fruit machine** One-armed bandit

**Fruit-picker** Eve

**Frump(ish)** Dowdy, Judy, Shabby, Unkempt

**Frustrate(d), Frustration** Baffle, Ba(u)lk, Beat, Blight, Bugger, Check, Cheesed off, Confound, Countermine, Cross, Dash, Defeat, Disappoint, Discomfit, Disconcert, Dish, Disillusionment, Foil, Forestall, Hamper, Hogtie, Outwit, Scotch, Snooker, Spike, Stymie, Tantalise, Thwart

**Fry, Fried, Fries** Blot, Brit, Christopher, Elizabeth, French, Fricassee, Fritter, Frizzle, Parr, Sauté, Sizzle, Skirl-in-the-pan, Small, Spawn, Whippersnapper, Whitebait

**Fuddle(d)** Drunk, Fluster, Fuzzle, Maudlin, Ta(i)vert, Tosticated, Woozy

▷**Fuddle(d)** *may indicate* an anagram

**Fuddy-duddy** Fogey

**Fudge** Cook, Doctor, Dodge, Drivel, Evade, Fiddlesticks, Nonsense, Rot, Stop-press, Sweet(meat)

**Fuel(led)** Alternative, Anthracite, Argol, Astatki, Atomic, Autogas, Avgas, Benzene, Benzine, Benzol, Biodiesel, Biogas, Borane, Briquet(te), Brown coal, Bunker, Butane, Candle-coal, Cannel, Carbonette, Charcoal, Coal, Coalite®, Coke, Derv, Diesel, Eilding, Eldin(g), Esso®, Ethane, Faggot, Feed, Fire(wood), Fossil, Gasahol, Gasohol, Gasoline, Go-juice, Hexamine, Hydrazine, Hydyne, Ignite, Inspirit, Jud, Kerosene, Kerosine, Kindling, Knitch, Lead-free, Lignite, Lox, Meths, Mox, Multigrade, Napalm, Naphtha, Nuclear, Oilgas, Orimulsion, Outage, Paraffin, Peat, Propane, Propellant, Protein, Shell®, Smokeless, Smudge, Solid, Sterno®, Stoke, SURF, Synfuel, Tan balls, Tanked up, Triptane, Unleaded, Yealdon

**Fug** Frowst

**Fugitive** Absconder, Defector, Ephemeral, Escapee, Fleeting, Hideaway, Lot, Outlaw, Refugee, Runagate, Runaway, Runner, Transient, Vagabond

**Fugue** Ricercar(e), Ricercata, Stretto

**Fulcrum** Key-pin, Pivot

**Fulfil(ment), Fulfilled** Accomplish, Come true, Complete, Consummate, Enacture, Fruition, Honour, Implementation, Meet, Pass, Realise, →SATISFY, Serve, Steed, Subrogation

**Fulgent** Bright, Shining

**Full(est), Fullness, Fully** Abrim, Ample, Arrant, Bouffant, Capacity, Chock-a-block, Chocker, Complete, Copious, Embonpoint, Engorged, Entire, Fairly, Fat, Fed, Flush, Fou, Frontal, German, High, Hoatching, Hotch, Jam-packed, Mill, Orotund, Plein, Plenary, Plenitude, Pleroma, Plethora, Plump, Replete, Rich, Rotund, Sated, Satiated, Thorough, Thronged, Torose, Torous, Toss, Turgid, Turgor, Ullage, Uncut, Up, Wau(l)k, Whole hog, Wholly

**Full-bodied** Amoroso

**Full-faced** Caboched, Caboshed

**Full-flavoured** Rich

**Full-grown** Seeded

**Full-throated** Goitred

**Full-time** Twenty-four seven

**Fulminate, Fulminating, Fulmination** Chastise, Curse, Detonate, Explode, Levin, Lightning, Rail, Renounce, Thunder, Tonant

**Fumarole** Hornito, Mofette

**Fumble** Blunder, Bobble, Faff, Grope, Misfield, Muff

**Fume(s)** Bluster, Gas, Halitus, Incense, Nidor, Rage, Reech, Reek, Settle, Simmer, Smoke, Steam, Stum, Vapours

**Fumigate, Fumigator** Disinfect, Pastil(le), Smoke, Smudge

**Fun(ny), Funny bone** Amusing, Antic, Boat, Buffo, Caper, Clownery, Comedy, Comic(al), Crack, Craic, Delight, Droll, Fling, Frolic, Gammock, Gas, Gig, Giocoso, Glaik, Guy, Hilarity,

Hoot, Horseplay, Humerus, Humorous, Hysterical, Ill, Ironic, Jest, Jokey, Jouisance, Jouysaunce, Kicks, Killing, Kinky, Lark, Music, Play, Pleasure, Priceless, Rag, Recreation, Rib-tickling, Rich, Risible, Rummy, Scream, Sidesplitting, Skylark, Slap and tickle, Sport, Strange, Suspect, Unwell, Uproarious, Weird(o), Whoopee, Wisecrack, Wit, Yell

**Funambulist** Blondin, Equilibrist, Tight-rope

**Function(al), Functioning, Functions** Act, Algebraic, Antilog, Apparatchik, Arccos, Arcsin(e), Arctan, Articulate, Assignment, Behave, Bodily, Bunfight, Business, Ceremony, Characteristic, Circular, Cog, Cosec, Cosecant, Cosh, Cosine, Cot(h), Cotangent, Dance, Density, Discriminant, Distribution, Do, Dynamic, Eigen, Exponential, Gamma, Gibbs, Hamilton(ian), Helmholtz, Hyperbolic, Integral, Integrand, Inverse, Jacobian, Job, Klats(c)h, Logarithm, Map(ping), Neutraceutical, Occasion, →**OPERATE**, Periodic, Polymorphic, Practicable, Probability, Propositional, Purpose, Quadric, Quantical, Quartic, Reception, Recursive, Role, Run, Sec(h), Secant, Sensation, Sentential, Service, Sin(e), Sinh, State, Ste(a)d, Stedde, Step, Surjection, Tan(h), Tangent, Tick, Tool bar, Transcendental, Trigonometric, Truth, Up and running, Usage, Use, Utensil, Utility, Versin(e), Vital, Wave, Wingding, →**WORK**

**Functionary** Notary, Official

**Functionless** Otiose

**Fund(ing), Fund raiser, Fundraising, Funds** -athon, Backing, Bank, Bankroll, Barrel, Capital, Chest, Coffers, Consolidated, Emendals, Endow, Evergreen, Exchequer, Fighting, Finance, Fisc, Fisk, Focus, Gap, Gild, Green, Hedge, Imprest, Index, Jackpot, Kail, Kale, Kitty, Lend, Maestro®, Managed, Means, Mutual, Nest-egg, Offshore, Onlend, Pension, Pool, Pork-barrel, Pot, Prebend, Private, Public, Purse, Radiothon, Rest, Revolving, Roll-up, Sinking, Slush, Social, Sou-sou, Stabilisation, Stock, Store, Subsidise, Sustentation, Susu, Telethon, -thon, Tontine, Tracker, Treasury, Trust, Vulture, Wage(s), War chest, Wherewithal

**Fundamental(ist)** Basic(s), Bedrock, Bottom (line), Cardinal, Cornerstone, Essence, Grass-roots, Hamas, Integral, Intrinsic, Missing, Nitty-gritty, Organic, Prime, Principle, Radical, Rudimentary, Taleban, Taliba(a)n, Ultimate

**Fund-holder** Rentier

**Funeral, Funereal** Charnel, Cortege, Dismal, Exequy, Feral, Hearse, Interment, Obit, Obital, Obsequy, Sad-coloured, Solemn, Sombre, Tangi

**Fungicide** Benomyl, Biphenyl, Bordeaux mixture, Burgundy mixture, Captan, Diphenyl, Ferbam, Menadione, PCP, Pentachlorophenol, Resveratrol, Thiram, Zineb

**Fungoid, Fungal, Fungus** Dry rot, Endophyte, Enoki, Flor, Pest, Wet rot

---

**FUNGI**

*3 letters:*
Cup
Ray

*4 letters:*
Asci
Barm
Bunt
Ceps
Conk
Gall
Gill
Pore
Rust
Scab
Smut

*5 letters:*
Black
Brand
Ergot
Favus
Honey
Hypha
Jelly
Morel
Mould
Mucor
Shelf
Slime
Spunk
Stipe
Tinea
Tuber
Yeast

*6 letters:*
Aecium
Agaric
Amadou
Ascius
Elf-cup
Empusa
Ink-cap
Lichen
Mildew
Oidium
Peziza
Pileum
Torula
Wax cap
Xyloma

*7 letters:*
Amanita
Blewits
Blue-rot
Boletus
Bracket
Candida
Chytrid
Fission
Milk cap
Monilia
Mycetes
Oak-wilt
Phallus
Porcino
Pythium
Russula
Tarspot

Truffle
Uredine
Yellows

*8 letters:*
Ambrosia
Basidium
Bootlace
Botrytis
Clubroot
Corn smut
Death-cap
Death-cup
Dutch elm
Erumpent
Fusarium
Fuss-ball
Fuzz-ball
Merulius
Mushroom
Mycelium
Mycology
Noble rot
Oomycete
Puccinia
Puckfist
Puffball
Rhizopus
Rhytisma
Ringworm
Sariodes
Stromata
Thalline

Tremella
Tuckahoe
Ustilago

*9 letters:*
Beefsteak
Bird's nest
Blackknot
Blackspot
Blue-mould
Coral spot
Cramp-ball
Earth-star
Eumycetes
Funnel-cap
Horsehair
Imperfect
Mucorales
Polyporus
Shaggy cap
Stinkhorn
Toadstool
Wheat rust
Zygospore

*10 letters:*
Anthersmut
Apothecium
Armillaria
Ascomycete
Bootstring
Bread-mould
Death angel
Gibberella
Lawyer's wig
Liberty cap
Oak-leather
Orange-peel
Prototroph
Rhizomorph
Saprophyte
Shaggy mane
Shoestring
Sooty mould
Water mould
Yellow rust
Zygomycete

*11 letters:*
Anthracnose
Aspergillus
Chantarelle
Chanterelle
Condiophore
Craterellus
Fairy butter
Ithyphallus
Penicillium
Phycomycete
Saprolegnia
Sulphur tuft
Thallophyte
Velvet shank
Witches' meat
Yellow brain

*12 letters:*
Athlete's foot
Cladosporium
Cryptococcus
Dermatophyte
Discomycetes
Flowers of tan
Hypersarcoma
Shaggy ink cap
Trichophyton
Verticillium
Wood hedgehog

*13 letters:*
Jupiter's beard
Magic mushroom
Plica polonica
Powdery mildew
Saccharomyces
Witches' butter

*14 letters:*
Wood woollyfoot

*15 letters:*
Dermatophytosis
Destroying angel

*19 letters:*
Fairy ring champignon

---

**Fungus-eater** Mycophagist
**Funicular** Cable-car
**Funk(y)** Blue, Dodge, Dread, Fear, Phobia, Scared, Spark, Stylish
**Funnel** Buchner, Chimney, Choana, Cross, Drogue, Flue, Hopper, Infundibulum, Separating, Smokestack, Stack, Stovepipe, Tun-dish, Tunnel, Wine
**Fur(ry)** Astrakhan, Astrex, Atoc, Beaver(skin), Boa, Broadtail, Budge, Calabre, Caracul, Castor, Chinchilla, Civet, Coat, Coati, Cony-wool, Coonskin, Crimmer, Deposit, Ermelin, Ermine, Fake, Fitchew, Flix, Flue, Fun, Galyac, Galyak, Genet, Genette, Gris(e), Kolinsky, Krimmer, Lettice, Marten, Minever, Miniver, Mink, Mohair, Mouton, Muskrat, Musquash, Neckpiece, Nutria, Ocelot, Otter, Palatine, Pane, Pashm, Pean, Pekan, Ponyskin, Rac(c)oon, Roskyn, Sable, Sealskin, Sea-otter, Stole, Stone-marten, Tincture, Tippet, Vair(e), Victorine, Wolverine, Zibeline, Zorino
**Furbish** Polish, Renovate, Spruce, Vamp
**Furcula** Wishbone
**Furl** Clew up, Fold, Roll, Stow, Wrap
**Furlough** Congé, Leave
**Furnace** Arc, Athanor, Blast, Bloomery, Bosh, Breeze, Calcar, Cockle, Cremator, Cupola, Destructor, Devil, Electric, Finery, Firebox, Forge, Gas, Glory-hole, Incinerator, Kiln, Lear, Lehr, Lime-kiln, Oast, Oon, Open-hearth, Oven, Pot, Producer, Reverberatory, Scaldino, Smelter, Solar, Stokehold, Stokehole, Tank, Wind
**Furnish(ing)** Appoint, Array, Battle, Deck, Decorate, Endow, Endue, Equip, Feed, Fledge, Gird, Lend, Nourish, Produce, Provision, Purvey, Soft, Stock, Suit, Supply, Tabaret, Upholster

**Furniture, Furniture designer** Armoire, Bahut, Biedermeier, Bombe, Cabinet, Chattels, Chippendale, Couch, Dresser, Drop-leaf, Duncan Phyfe, Empire, Encoignure, Escritoire, Etagère, Fitment, Flatpack, Fyfe, Hallstand, Hatstand, Hepplewhite, Highboy, IKEA, Insight, Kitchen, Lowboy, Lumber, Moveable, Queen Anne, Screen, Sheraton, Sideboard, Sticks, Stoutherie, Street, Tire, Unit, Washstand, Whatnot

**Furore** Brouhaha, Commotion, Outburst, Outcry, Stink, Storm, Tempest, Uproar

**Furrier** Trapper

**Furrow(ed)** Channel, Corrugate, Crease, Feer, Feerin(g), Frown, Furr, Groove, Gutter, Knit, Plough, Pucker, Rabbet, Ridge, Rill(e), Rugose, Rut, Stria, Sulcus, Trench, Vallecula, Wrinkle

**Fur-seal** Seecatch(ie)

**Further, Furthermore, Furthest** Additional, Advance, Again, Aid, Also, Apolune, Besides, Beyond, Deeper, Else, Enable, Expedite, Extend, Extra, Extreme, Fresh, Infra, Longer, Mo(e), Mow, Onwards, Other, Outermost, Promote, Serve, Speed, Subserve, Then, To boot, Too, Yet

**Furtive(ly)** Clandestine, Covert, Cunning, Hangdog, Hole and corner, Secret, Shifty, Sly, Sneaky, Stealthy, Stowlins, Stownlins, Weaselly

**Fury, Furies, Furious** Acharné, Agitato, Alecto, → ANGER, Apoplexy, Atropos, Avenger, Ballistic, Battleaxe, Demonic, Dragon, Eriny(e)s, Eumenides, Exasperation, Frantic, Frenzied, Furor, Hairless, Hectic, Hot, Incandescent, Incensed, → IRE, Livid, Maenad, Manic, Megaera, Paddy, Rabid, Rage, Red, Ripsnorter, Savage, Seething, Spitting, Tisiphone, Virago, Wood, Wrath, Yond

**Furze** Gorse, Ulex, Whin

**Fuse(d), Fusion** Anchylosis, Ankylosis, Arthrodesis, Blend, Bond, Coalesce, Cohere, Colliquate, Conflate, Consolidate, Converge, Dystectic, Encaustic, Endosmosis, Flow, Flux, Igniter, Integrate, Karyogamy, Knit, Match, Melt, Merge, Merit, Nuclear, Percussion, Plasmogamy, Portfire, Proximity, Rigelation, Run, Sacralization, Safety, Saucisse, Saucisson, Short, Slow-match, Solder, Symphytic, Syncretism, Syngamy, Time, Tokamak, Union, Unite, Weld

**Fuselage** Body, Monocoque, Structure

**Fuss(y)** Ado, Agitation, Anal, Anile, Ballyhoo, Bobsie-die, Bother, Br(o)uhaha, Bustle, Carfuffle, Carry on, Chichi, Coil, Commotion, Complain, Cosset, Create, Cu(r)fuffle, Dust, Elaborate, Faddy, Faff, Fantad, Fantod, Fastidious, Fiddle-faddle, Fike, Finical, Finicky, Finikin, Folderol, Fret, Futz, Hairsplitter, Hoohah, Hoopla, Hullabaloo, Mither, Mother, Niggle, Nit-pick, Noise, Old-womanish, Ornate, Ostentation, Overexact, Overnice, Overwrought, Palaver, Particular, Pedantic, Perjink, Pernickety, Picky, Pother, Precise, Prejink, Primp, Prissy, Pudder, Puristical, Racket, Raise cain, Razzmatazz, Rout, Song, Song and dance, Spoffish, Spoffy, Spruce, Stashie, Stickler, Stink, → STIR, Stishie, Stooshie, Stushie, Tamasha, To-do, Tracasserie

**Fusspot** Fogy, Old woman

**Fustian** Bombast, Gas, Pompous, Rant

**Futile** Empty, Feckless, Hopeless, Idle, Ineffectual, Inept, Meaningless, No-go, Nugatory, Null, Otiose, Pointless, Sleeveless, Stultified, Trivial, Useless, → VAIN, Valueless, Wild-goose chase

**Future(s), Futurist** Again, Avenir, Be-all, By and by, Coming, Demain, Financial, Hence, Hereafter, Horoscope, Index, Interest-rate, Later, Long-range, Offing, Ovist, Paragogic, Paulo-post, Posterity, Prospect, Space age, To-be, To come, Tomorrow, Vista

**Fuzz(y)** Blur, Crepe, Down, Fluff, Foggy, Lint, Nap, Pig, Policeman

# Gg

**G** George, Golf, Gravity
**Gab(ble), Gabbler** Chatter, Dovercourt, Jabber, Pie, Prattle, Talkative, Yabber
**Gable** Bay, Clark, Corbie, Jerkinhead, Pediment, Pine end
**Gabler** Hedda
**Gabriel** Angel, Walter
**Gad(about), Gadzooks** Fisk, Gallivant, Lud, Rover, Sbuddikins, Sdeath, Traipse, Trape(s), Viretot
**Gadfly** Breese, Breeze, Brize, Cleg
**Gadget** Adaptor, Appliance, Artifice, Device, Dingbat, Dingus, Doodad, Doodah, Doofer, Doohickey, Gismo, Gizmo, Gubbins, Hickey, Hopper, Inhaler, Ipad®, Jigamaree, Jiggumbob, Jimjam, Navaid, Notion, Possum, Processor, Tool, Toy, Utility, Waldo, Widget
**Gadolinium** Gd
**Gadzooks** Odsbobs
**Gaekwar** Baroda
**Gael(ic)** Celt, Erse, Goidel, Irish, Scottish, Teague
**Gaff(e), Gaffer** Bêtise, Blague, Bloomer, Blunder, Error, Floater, Flub, Foreman, Gamble, Game, Old man, Overseer, Solecism, Spar, Throat, Trysail, Yokel
**Gag** Brank, Chestnut, Choke, Estoppel, Joke, Pong, Prank, Retch, Running, Scold's bridle, Silence(r), Smother, Wheeze, Wisecrack
**Gage** Challenge, Pawn, Pledge, Plum
▸**Gaiety** *see* **GAY**
**Gain(s), Gained** Acquire, Appreciate, Attain, Avail, Boodle, Boot, Bunce, Capital, Carry, Catch, Chevisance, Clean-up, Derive, Earn, Edge, Fruit, → **GET**, Good, Gravy, Ill-gotten, Land, Lucre, Net, Obtain, Paper, Payment, Plus, Profit, Purchase, Rake-off, Reap, Thrift, Unremittable, Use, Velvet, Wan, Win, Windfall, Winnings
**Gainsay** Contradict, Deny
**Gait** Bearing, Canter, → **CHILD**, Gallop, Pace, Piaffer, Rack, Step, Trot, Volt(e), Waddle
**Gaiter(s)** Cootikin, Cu(i)tikin, Gambado, Hogger, Legging(s), Puttee, Spat(s), Spattee, Spatterdash, Vamp
**Gala** Banquet, Festival, Regatta
**Galaxy, Galaxies** Active, Andromeda, Blazar, Elliptical, Great Attractor, Heaven, Irregular, Local group, Magellanic cloud, Milky Way, Nebula, Radio, Regular, Seyfert, Spiral, Stars, Universe
**Galbanum** Ferula
**Gale(s)** Backfielder, Equinoctial, Fresh, Moderate, Near, Peal, Ripsnorter, Sea turn, Snorter, Squall, Storm, Strong, Tempest, Whole, Winder
**Gall, Gall bladder** Aleppo, Bedeguar, Bile, Bitterness, Brass, Canker, Cholecyst, Crown, Ellagic, Enrage, Fell, Fungus, Irk, Irritate, Mad-apple, Malice, Maugre, Maulgre, Oak(nut), Oak apple, Saddle, Sage-apple, Sandiver, → **SAUCE**, Tacahout, Vine
**Gallant(ry)** Admirer, Amorist, Beau, Blade, Buck, Cavalier, Cavaliere servente, Chevalier, Chivalrous, Cicisbeo, Courtliness, Gentleman(ly), Lover, Prow, Romeo, Sigisbeo, Spark, Valiance
**Galleon** Galloon, Ghostly, Ship
**Gallery** Accademia, Alure, Amphitheatre, Arcade, Assommoir, Balcony, Belvedere, Blind-story, Brattice, Bretasche, Bretesse, Brettice, Brow, Burrell (Collection), Catacomb, Celestials, Cupola, Dedans, Earth-house, Fly, Gods, Hayward, Hermitage, ICA, Jube,

Ladies', Loft, Loggia, Louvre, Machicolation, Mine, Minstrel, National, Organ, Pawn, Picture, Pinacotheca, Pinakothek, Pitti, Portrait, Prado, Press, Public, Rogues', Scaffolding, Serpentine, Shooting, Singing, Strangers', Tate, Tate Modern, Terrace, Traverse, Tribune, Triforium, Uffizi, Veranda(h), Whispering, Whitechapel, Winning

**Galley** Bireme, Birlinn, Bucentaur, Caboose, Drake, Galliot, Kitchen, Lymphad, Penteconter, Proof, Trireme

**Gallimaufry** Duke's mixture, Macedoine, Mishmash, Stew

**Gallium** Ga

**Gallon(s)** Bushel, Cong(ius), Cran, Hin, Imperial, Pottle, Rundlet, Tierce

**Galloon** Lace, Orris

**Gallop(er)** Aide, Canter, Canterbury, Career, Lope, Trot, Wallop

**Gallows** Bough, Cheat, Drop, Dule-tree, Forks, Gibbet, Nub, Nubbing-cheat, Patibulary, Stifler, Three-legged mare, Tree, Tyburn, Tyburn-tree, Widow, Woodie

**Gallows-bird** Crack-halter, Crack-hemp, Crack-rope

**Gall-stone** Cholelith

**Galore** Abundance, À gogo, Plenty, Whisky

**Galosh** Overshoe, Rubber

**Galumph** Stride

**Galvanise** Activate, Buck up, Electrify, Ginger, Rouse, Zinc

**Galvanometer** Tangent

**Gam** Pod

**Gambia** WAG

**Gambit** Manoeuvre, Overture, Ploy, Stratagem

**Gamble(r), Gambling(-house), Gambling place** Adventure, Amber, Ante, Back, Bet, Bouillotte, Casino, Chance, Craps, Dice(-play), Double or quits, Flutter, Football pools, Gaff, Hell, High-roller, Irish sweep, Jeff, Las Vegas, Lotto, Martingale, Mise, Numbers game, Pari-mutuel, Parlay, Partingale, Piker, Plunge, Policy, Punt(er), Raffle, Reno, Risk, Roulette, School, Scratch card, Spec, Speculate, Speculator, Sweep(stake), Throw(ster), Tinhorn, Tombola, Tontine, Toss-up, Treble chance, Two-up, → **WAGER**, Wheeze

**Gambol** Frisk, Frolic, Prance

**Game (birds)** Bag, Colin, Covey, Fowl, Grouse, Guan, Hare, Meat, Partridge, Pheasant, Prairie chicken, Preserve, Prey, Ptarmigan, Quail, → **QUARRY**, Rype(r), Snipe, Spatchcock, Venery, Venison, Wildfowl, Woodcock

**Game(s)** Antic, Away, Board, Caper, Circensian, Closed, Commonwealth, Computer, Console, Decider, Deck, Easy, Electronic, Elis, Exhibition, Fair, Final, Frame, Gallant, Gammy, God, Ground, Gutsy, High-jinks, Highland, Home, International, Intrepid, Invictus, Isthmian, Jeu, → **LAME**, Lark, Match, Middle, Mind, MUD, Needle, Nemean, Net, Numbers, Olympic, On, Open, Panel, Paralympic, Parlour, Perfect, Platform, Play, Plaything, Ploy, Plucky, Preference, Preserve, Pythian, Raffle, Ready, Road, Role-playing, Round, Rubber, Saving, Scholar's, Secular, Sport, Square, Strategy, String, Table, Test, Tie-break, Tournament, TV, Up for, Video, Vie, Waiting, Willing

---

## GAMES

*2 letters:*
Eo
Go
PE
RU

*3 letters:*
Cat
Hob
Loo
Maw
Nap
Nim
Pam
Pit
Put
Sim
Swy
Tag
Tig
Top
War

*4 letters:*
Ball
Base
Brag
Bull
Crap
Dibs
Fa-fi
Faro
Goff
Golf
Grab
I-spy
Keno
Kino
Laik
Loto
Ludo
Main
Mora
Palm
Polo
Pool
Putt
Ruff
Scat
Skat
Slam
Snap
Solo
Taws
Vint
Wall
Word

***5 letters:***
Bingo
Bocce
Bowls
Cards
Cardy
Catch
Chess
Cinch
Cloak
Craps
Darts
Fives
Gleek
Goose
Halma
House
Jacks
Keeno
Lotto
Lurch
Manty
Merel
Meril
Monte
Morra
Noddy
Novum
Omber
Ombre
Pairs
Pareo
Pareu
Poker
Prime
Quino
Roque
Rummy
Shell
Shogi
Spoof
Stops
Tarok
Tarot
Touch
Trugo
Trump
Two-up
Ulama
Whisk
Whist

***6 letters:***
Ballon
Basset
Beetle
Boccia
Bo-peep
Boston
Boules
Bounce
Bridge
Casino
Chemmy
Cluedo
Clumps
Cobnut
Crambo
Ecarté
Euchre
Fantan
Footer
Gammon
Gobang
Gomoku
Hazard
Hearts
Hockey
Hoopla
Hurley
Kaluki
Kho-kho
Kitcat
Merell
Peepbo
Pelota
Piquet
Quinze
Quoits
Shinny
Shinty
Sindon
Soccer
Socker
Squail
Squash
Sudoku
Tenpin
Tipcat
Trunks
T-shirt
Uckers
Vigoro

***7 letters:***
Balloon
Ba'spiel
Bezique
Braemar
Bunting
Camogie
Canasta
Cassino
Charade
Chicken
Codille
Conkers
Coon-can
Croquet
Curling
Diabolo
Doubles
Frisbee
Fusball
God game
Hangman
Hurling
Iceball
In-and-in
Jai alai
Jukskei
Kabaddi
Kalooki
Lottery
Mahjong
Mancala
Marbles
Matador
Muggins
Murphy's
Netball
Old maid
Othello
Pachisi
Paddler
Pallone
Passage
Patball
Peekabo
Peevers
Pharaoh
Pinball
Plafond
Pontoon
Primero
Push-pin
Pyramid
Rackets
Reversi
Ring-taw
Seven-up
Singles
Snooker
Squails
Tag ends
Tenpins
Tombola
Vingt-un
Wet suit
Zero-sum

***8 letters:***
All-fives
All-fours
Baccarat
Baseball
Beat 'em up
Bob-apple
Bumpball
Buzkashi
Canfield
Cardigan
Cat-stick
Charades
Chequers
Chouette
Conquian
Cottabus
Coverall
Cribbage
Dominoes
Draughts
Fivepins
Foosball
Football
Forfeits
Four-ball
Foursome
Fussball
Gallabea
Gin rummy
Goalball
Handball
Handicap
Hardball
Honeypot
Kalookie
Kickball
Klondike
Klondyke
Korfball
Lacrosse
Leapfrog
Mahjongg
Michigan
Monopoly®
Napoleon
Ninepins
Nintendo®
Octopush
Pachinko
Pall-mall
Parchesi
Pastance
Patience
Peekaboo
Pegboard
Penneech
Penneeck
Penuchle
Petanque
Ping-pong
Pinochle
Pintable
Pope Joan
Push-ball
Pyramids
Reversis
Rolypoly
Roulette
Rounders
Sardines
Scrabble®
Scroller
Septleva
Showdown
Skittles
Slapjack
Softball
Sphairee
Subbuteo®
Teetotum
Trap-ball
Tray-trip
Tredille
Tric-trac
Verquera
Verquere
Verquire

***9 letters:***
Acey-deucy
Aunt Sally
Badminton
Bagatelle
Bandyball
Billiards
Black-cock
Black-jack
Bob-cherry
Broomball
Cherry-bob
Crazy golf
Crokinole
Cutthroat
Dodgeball
Duplicate
Fillipeen
Hacky Sack®
Hopscotch

Jackstraw
Jingo-ring
Lanterloo
Level-coil
Long-whist
Matrimony
Minidress
Mistigris
Mournival
Mumchance
Newmarket
Nineholes
Paintball
Parcheesi®
Pelmanism
Punchball
Quadrille
Quidditch®
Shell game
Shoot'em-up
Simon says
Solitaire
Solo whist
Speedball
Spoilfive
Stoolball
Strap-game
Stud poker
Superbowl
Test match
Tip-and-run
Tredrille
Trick-trac
Tric-track
Twenty-one
Vingt-et-un
Water polo

*10 letters:*
Angel-beast
Backgammon
Basketball
Battledore
Boiler suit
Bouillotte
Candlepins
Cat's cradle
Criss-cross
Cup and ball
Deck tennis
Dumb crambo
Five-stones
Flapdragon
Geocaching
Handy-dandy
Horseshoes
Hot cockles
Jackstones
Jackstraws
Knurr-spell
Kriegspiel
Lansquenet
Paddleball
Paper chase
Phillipina
Phillipine
Philopoena
Pooh sticks
Punto-banco
Put and take
Seven-a-side
Short whist
Shuffle-cap
Snapdragon
Spillikins
Strip poker
Tablanette
Tchoukball
Thimblerig
Trick-track
Troll-madam
Trou-madame
Volley-ball

*11 letters:*
Barley-brake
Barley-break
Blind hookey
Bumble-puppy
Catch-the-ten
Chemin de fer
Family coach
Fox and geese
General post
Gerrymander
Hide and seek
Knucklebone
Kriegsspiel
Mumbletypeg
PlayStation®
Post and pair
Puncto-banco
Racquetball
Rouge et noir
Sancho-pedro
Shovelboard
Shuttlecock
Span-counter
Speculation
Table-tennis
Tick-tack-toe
Tiddlywinks
Troll-my-dame

*12 letters:*
Bar billiards
Consequences
Fast and loose
Hoodman-blind
Housey-housey
Knucklebones
Knur and spell
Minister's cat
One-and-thirty
Pitch and putt
Pitch and toss
Shuffleboard
Span-farthing
Squash-tennis
Tiddleywinks
Troll-my-dames

*13 letters:*
Blind man's buff
Chicken-hazard
Chuck-farthing
Double or quits
French cricket
Happy Families
Jingling match
Kiss-in-the-ring
Musical chairs
Pass the parcel
Pitch-farthing
Postman's knock
Prisoner's base
Scavenger hunt
Space Invaders®
Spin-the-bottle
Squash rackets
Table football
Table-skittles
Tenpin bowling
Tickly-benders

*14 letters:*
British bulldog
Cops and robbers
Crown and anchor
Ducks and drakes
Fives and threes
Follow-my-leader
Hunt-the-slipper
Nievie-nick-nack
Nine men's morris
Pig-in-the-middle
Prick-the-garter
Shove-halfpenny
Snip-snap-snorum
Tenpins bowling
Three-card monte

*15 letters:*
Beach volleyball
Chinese checkers
Chinese whispers
Duplicate bridge
Fivepenny morris
King-of-the-castle
Laugh and lay down
Laugh and lie down
Ninepenny morris
Puss-in-the-corner
Russian roulette

*16 letters:*
Piggy-in-the-middle
Scotch and English
Snakes and ladders
Trente-et-quarante

*17 letters:*
Noughts and crosses
Tom Tiddler's ground

*20 letters:*
Kiss-me-quick-in-the-ring
Nievie-nievie-nick-nack

---

**Gamekeeper** Mellors, Velveteen, Venerer, Warrener
**Gamete** Ootid, Ovum
**Gamin(e)** Elfin, Hoyden, Waif
**Gaming place** Bucket-shop, Casino, Saloon, Table

**Gammerstang** Taupie, Tawpie
**Gammon** Baloney, Bilge, Hokum, Tosh
**Gamut** Compass, Range
**Gander** Airport, Glimpse, Look-see, Shufti
**Gandhi** Mahatma
**Gang** Baader-Meinhof, Band(itti), Bevy, Bikers, Bing, Breakdown, Bunch, Cadre, Canaille, Chain, Coffle, Core, Crew, Crue, Droog, Elk, Go, Group, Hell's Angels, Horde, Massive, Mob, Mods, Nest, Outfit, Pack, Posse, Press, Push, Ratpack, Rent-a-mob, Ring, Rockers, Shearing, Tong, Triad, Tribulation, Troop, Tsotsi, Yardie
**Gangle, Gangling** Lanky
**Ganglia** Basal
**Gangrene** Canker, Gas, Mortified, Necrose, Noma, Phaged(a)ena, Sphacelate, Thanatosis
**Gangster** Al, Bandit, Bonnie, Capone, Clyde, Crook, Dacoit, Dakoit, Goodfella, Hatchet-man, Highbinder, Home boy, Homey, Homie, Hood, Mafioso, Mobster, Ochlocrat, Scarface, Skinhead, Skollie, Skolly, Tsotsi, Yakuza, Yardie
**Gangway** Brow, Catwalk, Road
**Gannet** Alcatras, Booby, Guga, Pig, Solan(d)
**Gantry** Elmer
**Ganymede** Cupper
▸**Gaol(er)** *see* JAIL(ER)
**Gap** Aisle, Aperture, Belfort, Breach, Chasm, Chink, Cleavage, Credibility, Crenel, Cumberland, Day, Deflationary, Diastema, Distance, Dollar, Embrasure, Energy, F-hole, Financing, Flaw, Fontanel(le), Gender, Generation, Gulf, Gulph, Hair-space, Hiatus, Hole, Inflationary, Interlude, Interregnum, Interstice, Kirkwood, Lacunae, Leaf, Leap, Lin(n), Loophole, Mews, M(e)use, Muset, Musit, Node of Ranvier, Opening, Ostiole, Outage, Pass, Rest, Rift, Rima, Shard, Sherd, Skills, Slap, → SPACE, Spark, Spread, Street, Synapse, Time lag, Trade, Truth-value, Vacancy, Vent, Water, Wind, Window
**Gape(r), Gaping** Comber, Dehisce, Fatiscent, Gant, Ga(u)p, Gerne, Hiant, Mya, Ogle, Outstare, Rictal, Rictus, Ringent, Rubberneck, Stare, Yawn, Yawp
**Garage** Barn, Carport, Chopshop, Depot, Hangar, Lock-up, Muffler shop
**Garb** Apparel, Burqa, Costume, Gear, Gere, Guise, Ihram, Invest, Leotard, Raiment, Toilet, Uniform
**Garbage** Bunkum, Junk, Refuse, Rubbish, Trash, Waste
**Garble** Edit, Jumble, Muddle
▹**Garble** *may indicate* an anagram
**Garcon** Waiter
**Garden(ing), Gardens** Allotment, Arboretum, Arbour, Area, Babylon(ian), Bagh, Bear, Beer, Botanic, Chinampa, Colegarth, Container, Cottage, Covent, Cremorne, Dig, Eden, Erf, Floriculture, Garth, Gethsemane, Hanging, Heligan, Herb(ar), Hesperides, Hidcote, Hoe, Hop, Horticulture, Italian, Japanese, Kailyard, Kent, Kew, Kitchen, Knot, Landscape, Lyceum, Market, Monastery, NJ, Nursery, Olitory, Orchard, Orchat, Ornamental, Paradise, Parterre, Physic, Plantie-cruive, Pleasance, Plot, Potager, Ranelagh, Rockery, Roji, Roof, Rosarium, Rosary, Rosery, Stourhead, Tea, Tilth, Topiary, Truck-farm, Tuileries, Vauxhall, Vegetable, Walled, Welwyn, Window, Winter, Yard, Zoological
**Gardener** Adam, Capability Brown, Eve, Fuchs, Hoer, Hoy, Jekyll, Landscape, Mali, Mallee, Mary, Nurseryman, RHS, Seedsman, Topiarist, Tradescant, Trucker
**Gargantuan** Enormous, Huge, Pantagruel, Vast
**Gargle** Gargarism, Mouthwash
**Gargoyle** Magot, Waterspout
**Garibaldi** Biscuit, Blouse, Red Shirt
**Garish** Brassy, Criant, Flashy, Gaudy, Glitzy, Jazzy, Kitsch, Painty, Roary, Rorie, Rory, Technicolour
**Garland** Anadem, Anthology, Chaplet, Coronal, Crants, Festoon, Lei, Stemma, Toran(a), Vallar(y), Wreath
**Garlic** Cepaceous, Clove, Elephant, Hedge, Rams(on), Rocambole
**Garment** All-in-one, → DRESS, Habit, Vestment, Vesture

## GARMENTS

*3 letters:*
Aba
Alb
Top

*4 letters:*
Abba
Bubu
Cope
Gown
Izar
Kilt
Rail
Rami
Sari
Slop
Sulu
Toga
Togs
Weed
Wrap

*5 letters:*
Abaya
Ao dai
Boubu
Bubou
Burka
Burqa
Cardy
Cimar
Cloak
Clout
Cotta
Ephod
Fanon
Gilet
Gipon
G-suit
Hoody
Ihram
Jupon
Kanga
Kanzu
Levis
Lungi
Manty
Pareo
Pareu
Parka
Pilch
Ramée
Ramie
Ruana
Shift
Shrug
Skirt
Smock
Stola
Stole
Tanga
Thong
Tunic

*6 letters:*
Anorak
Blouse
Bodice
Bolero
Boubou
Bourka
Breeks
Burkha
Caftan
Chador
Chimer
Cilice
Corset
Dirndl
Exomis
Fleece
Jacket
Jersey
Jibbah
Jilbab
Jubbah
Jumper
Kaftan
Kaross
Khanga
Kimono
Kittel
Mantle
Mantua
Nebris
Nighty
Onesie
Peplos
Polony
Poncho
Reefer
Rochet
Sarong
Shroud
Sindon
Skivvy
Step-in
Sweats
Tabard
Tights
Trunks
T-shirt
Woolly
Yukata
Zephyr

*7 letters:*
Babygro®
Blouson
Bourkha
Burnous
Busuuti
Catsuit
Crop top
Dashiki
Djibbah
Doublet
Exomion
Gymslip
Jilabib
Leotard
Nightie
Paddler
Pallium
Partlet
Pelisse
Polonie
Popover
Rompers
Singlet
Soutane
Spencer
Surcoat
Tankini
Tank-top
Tunicle
Unitard
Wet suit
Woollen
Wrapper

*8 letters:*
Body suit
Cardigan
Chasuble
Chausses
Coverall
Dalmatic
Dishdash
Gallabea
Gambeson
Himation
Jumpsuit
Leggings
Lingerie
Monokini
Negligée
One-piece
Pannicle
Pelerine
Poloneck
Scapular
Slipover
Surplice
Swimsuit
Tailcoat
Two-piece

*9 letters:*
Brassière
Calamanco
Cerements
Cothurnis
Cover-slut
Dishdasha
Dungarees
Housecoat
Mandilion
Mandylion
Minidress
Nightgown
Nightrobe
Nightwear
Outerwear
Pantihose
Pantyhose
Polonaise
Sackcloth
Sanbenito
Sweatsuit
Waistcoat

*10 letters:*
Body warmer
Boiler suit
Cote-hardie
Flying suit
Foundation
Habiliment
Hand-me-down
Hug-me-tight
Jeistiecor
Legwarmers
Nightdress
Salopettes
Sticharion
Sweatpants
Sweatshirt

*11 letters:*
Dreadnought
Panty-girdle
Penitential
Reach-me-down
Windcheater

*12 letters:*
Bodystocking

*13 letters:*
Shalwar kameez

**Garnet** Alabandine, Almandine, Andradite, Carbuncle, Demantoid, Essonite, Grossular(ite), Hessonite, Melanite, Pyrenite, Pyrope, Rhodolite, Spessartite, Topazine, Topazolite, Uvarovite

**Garnish** Adorn, Attach, Cress, Crouton, Decorate, Enarm, Engild, Gremolata, Lard, Parsley, Sippet, Staffage

**Garotte(r)** Thug(gee), Ugly man

**Garret** Attic, Loft, Sol(l)ar, Sol(l)er
**Garrison** Fort, Man, Presidial, Presidiary
**Garrulity, Garrulous** Babbling, Gas, Gushy, Sweetiewife, Windbag
**Garter** Bowyang, Crewel, Flash, G(r)amash, Gramosh, Nicky-tam
**Gary** Glitter, Player
**Gas(sy)** Blah(-blah), Blather, Blether, Blow off, Bottle(d), Chat, Conversation, Emanation, Exhaust, Fizz, Flatulence, Gabnash, Jaw, Meteorism, Prate, Stun, →TALK, Utility, Waffle, →WIND, Yackety-yak

---

**GASES**

*1 letter:*
H
O

*2 letters:*
BZ
CN
CS
He
Kr
Ne
Rn
VX

*3 letters:*
Air
NOx
Oil
War

*4 letters:*
Coal
Damp
Flue
Mace®
Neon
Rare
Sour
Tear
Town

*5 letters:*
Argon
Azote
Bloat
Calor®
Ether
Ideal
Inert
Lurgi
Marsh
Nerve
Niton
Noble
Ozone
Radon
Sarin
Sewer
Soman
Swamp
Sweet
Tabun
Therm
Water
Xenon

*6 letters:*
Allene
Arsine
Butane
Butene
Ethane
Ethene
Ethine
Ethyne
Flatus
Helium
Hot-air
Ketene
Napalm
Olefin
Oxygen
Petrol
Plasma
Poison
Sewage
Silane
Thoron
V-agent
Vapour

*7 letters:*
Ammonia
Argonon
Carrier
Coal-oil
Crypton
Fluorin
Halitus
Krypton
Methane
Mofette
Mustard
Natural
Olefine
Perfect
Propane
Propene
Stibine

*8 letters:*
Chlorine
Cyanogen
Etherion
Ethylene
Firedamp
Fluorine
Fugacity
Hydrogen
Laughing
Lewisite
Nitrogen
North Sea
Phosgene
Producer

*9 letters:*
Acetylene
Afterdamp
Blue water
Butadiene
Chokedamp
Flocculus
Phosphine
Propylene
Protostar
Semiwater
Solfatara
Synthesis
Whitedamp

*10 letters:*
Crab nebula
Diphosgene
Dispersant
Euchlorine
Greenhouse
Propellant

*11 letters:*
Carburetted
Methylamine
Nitric oxide
Non-metallic
Protogalaxy

*12 letters:*
Carbonic acid
Chromosphere
Cyclopropane
Electrolytic
Formaldehyde
Nitrous oxide
Oxyacetylene
Taraniki wind

*14 letters:*
Chromatosphere
Sulphur dioxide

*17 letters:*
Tetrafluoroethene

*19 letters:*
Tetrafluoroethylene

---

**Gasbag** Airship, Blimp, Envelope, Prattler
**Gascon(ade)** Boast, Braggart, Skite

**Gash** Incise, Rift, Rip, Score, Scotch, → SLASH
**Gasket** O-ring, Seal
**Gas-mask** Inhaler
**Gasp(ing)** Anhelation, Apn(o)ea, Breath, Chink, Exhale, Heave, Kink, Last, Oh, Pant, Puff, Singult, Sob, Wheeze
**Gast(e)ropod** Ataata, Augur-shell, Conch, Cowrie, Cowry, Dog-whelk, Dorididae, Doris, Euthyneura, Fusus, Glaucus, Haliotis, Harp-shell, Helmet-shell, Limpet, Mitre, Mollusc, Money cowry, Murex, Nerita, Nerite, Nudibranch, Opisthobranch, Ormer, Pelican's foot, Pennywinkle, Periwinkle, Pteropod, Purpura, Sea-ear, Sea-hare, Slug, Snail, Spindle-shell, Streptoneura, Stromb, Top, Top shell, Triton, Turbo, Turritella, Unicorn, Wentletrap, Whelk, Winkle
**Gate(s), Gateway** Alley, Arch, Attendance, Bill, Brandenburg, Caisson, Cilician, Corpse, Crowd, Decuman, Entry, Erpingham, Five-barred, Golden, Head, Horn, Iron, Ivory, Kissing, Lock, Lodge, Lych, Mallee, Menin, Moon, Moravian, NOR, Payment, Pearly, Port, Portal, Portcullis, Postern, Praetorian, Propylaeum, Propylon, Pylon, Sallyport, Silver, Sluice, Starting, Tail, Taranaki, Toll, Toran(a), Torii, Traitor's, Turnout, Turnstile, Vimana, Waste, Water, Wicket, Yate, Yet(t)
**Gateau** Black Forest, Cupcake
**Gatecrash(er)** Interloper, Intrude, Ligger, Sorn, Unasked
**Gatehouse** Lodge
**Gatepost** Sconcheon, Scontion, Scuncheon
▷**Gateshead** *may indicate* 'g'
**Gather(ed), Gatherer, Gathering** Accrue, Aggregate, AGM, Amass, Army, Assemble, Bee, Boil, Braemar, Ceilidh, Clambake, Cluster, Collate, → COLLECT, Colloquium, Concede, Concentration, Concourse, Conglomerate, Congregate, Convene, Conventicle, Converge, Conversazione, Corral, Corroboree, Coterie, Crop, Crowd, Cull, Cut, Derive, Eve, Fester, Frill, Function, Gabfest, Galaxy, Garner, Get together, Glean, Glomerate, Hangi, Harvest, Hear, Hive, Hoard, Hootenanny, Hotchpot, Hui, Hunter, Husking, In, Infer, Jamboree, Kaffeeklatsch, Kommers, Learn, Lek, Lirk, Log-rolling, Love-in, Mass, Meinie, Menyie, Multitude, Pleat, Plica, Plissé, Pluck, Pucker, Purse, Raft, Raising-bee, Rake, Rally, Rave, Reap, Reef, Reunion, Round-up, Rout, Ruche, Ruck, Ruff(le), Salon, Scavenger, Scrump, Send-off, Sheave, Shindig, Shir(r), Shoal, Shovel, Singsong, Social, Spree, Stockpile, Suppurate, Swapmeet, Take, Throng, Tuck, Vindemiate, Vintage, Wappensc(h)aw, Witches' sabbath
**Gauche** Awkward, Clumsy, Farouche, Graceless, Tactless
**Gaudy, Gaudily** Bedizen, Classy, Criant, Fantoosh, Flash, Garish, Glitz(y), Meretricious, Tacky, Tawdry, Tinsel
**Gauge** Absolute, Alidad(e), Anemometer, Assay, → ASSESS, Barometer, Block, Bourdon, Broad, Calibre, Denier, Depth, Dial, Estimate, Etalon, Evaluate, Feeler, Hydrometer, Indicator, Judge, Lee, Limit, Loading, Manometer, Marigraph, Marking, Measure, Meter, Narrow, Nilometer, Oil, Ombrometer, Oncometer, Paper, Perforation, Plug, Pressure, Rain, Rate, Ring, Scantle, Size, Slip, Standard, Steam, Strain, Tach(ometer), Tape, Template, Thermometer, Tonometer, Tram, Tread, Tyre, Udometer, Vacuum, Water, Weather, Wind, Wire, Yardstick
**Gauguin** Paul
**Gaul** Asterix, Cisalpine, Transalpine, Vercingetorix
**Gaunt** Angular, Bony, Cadaverous, Drawn, Haggard, Lancaster, Lean, Peaked, Randletree, Ranneltree, Rannletree, Rantletree, Rawbone, → THIN, Wasted
**Gauntlet** C(a)estus, Gantlope
**Gauss** G
**Gautama** Buddha
**Gauze, Gauzy** Dandy-roll, Gas mantle, Gossamer, Illusion, Muslin, Sheer, Tiffany, Wire
**Gavel** Hammer
**Gawk(y)** Clumsy, Cow, Gammerstang, Goggle, Sloucher
**Gawp** Rubberneck
**Gay, Gaiety** Blithe, Bonny, Boon, Buxom, Camp, Canty, Daffing, Debonair, Enola, Fem,

Festal, Frolic, Gallant, Gaudy, Gladsome, Glee, Gordon, Grisette, Hilarity, Inverted, Jolly, Lightsome, May, Merry, Nitid, Out, Rackety, Riant, Rorty, Tit(t)upy, Volatile

**Gaze** Crystal, Moon, Pore, Regard, Stare

**Gazebo** Belvedere

**Gazelle** Ariel, Gerenuk, Goa, Mhorr, Mohr, Tabitha, Thomson's

**Gazette** London, Paper

**Gear(ing), Gearbox** Alighting, Angel, Apparatus, Apparel, Arrester, Attire, Bags, Bevel, Capital, Clobber, Dérailleur, Designer, Differential, Draw, Duds, Eccentric, Engrenage, Epicyclic, Fab, Finery, Granny, G-suit, Harness, Helical, Herringbone, High, Hypoid, Idle wheel, Involute, Kit, Landing, Laughing, Lay-shaft, Low, Mesh, Mess, Mitre, Multiplying, Neutral, Notchy, Overdrive, Paraphernalia, Planetary, Ratio, Reduction, Reverse, Rig, Riot, Rudder, Running, Sprocket, Spur, Steering, Stickshift, Straight, Sun and planet, Switch, Synchromesh, →TACKLE, Three-speed, Timing, Tiptronic®, Top, Trim, Tumbler, Valve, Variable, Worm(-wheel)

**Gecko** Tokay

**Gee** Horse, Hump, My, Reist, Sulk, Tout, Towt, Urge

**Geek** Creep, Nerd, Nurd, Uncool

**Geiger-counter** Scintillator

**Geisha** Maiko

**Gel** Agar, Aloe vera, Cohere, Hair, Pectin, Pectise, Shower, Silica, Teething

**Gelatin(e), Gelatinous** Agar-agar, Blasting, Calipash, Coenenchyma, Collagen, Glutinous, Isinglass, Size, Tunicin

**Geld(ing)** Castrate, Desex, Lib, Neuter, Sort, Spado

**Gelignite** Jelly

**Geller** Uri

**Gem** Intaglio, →JEWEL, Stone, Valuable

---

## GEMS

*2 letters:*
ID

*4 letters:*
Jade
Onyx
Opal
Pear
Ruby
Sard

*5 letters:*
Agate
Beryl
Boule
Idaho
Pearl
Prase
Rubin

*6 letters:*
Iolite
Jargon
Jasper
Jaspis
Ligure
Morion
Plasma
Pyrope
Rubine
Scarab
Zircon

*7 letters:*
Abraxas
Asteria
Callais
Cat's eye
Diamond
Emerald
Girasol
Girosol
Jacinth
Jargoon
Kunzite
Peridot
Rose-cut
Sardius
Smaragd

*8 letters:*
Baguette
Cabochon
Diamante
Emeraude
Girasole
Hawk's eye
Heliodor
Hyacinth
Marquise
Melanite
Menilite
Peridote
Pleonast
Sapphire
Sardonyx
Sparkler
Sunstone
Wood opal

*9 letters:*
Almandine
Amazonite
Andradite
Brilliant
Briolette
Cacholong
Cairngorm
Carbuncle
Carnelian
Cornelian
Cymophane
Demantoid
Grossular
Hessonite
Hiddenite
Hornstone
Marcasite
Moonstone
Morganite
Moss agate
Pleonaste
Rhodolite
Rubellite
Rubicelle
Solitaire
Starstone
Tiger's eye
Turquoise
Uvarovite

*10 letters:*
Alabandine
Birthstone
Bloodstone
Chalcedony
Chrysolite
Draconites
Heliotrope
Indicolite
Lherzolite
Mocha stone
Rhinestone
Topazolite
Tourmaline

*11 letters:*
Alexandrite
Amazon stone
Chrysoberyl
Chrysoprase
Lapis lazuli
Rose-diamond
Scarabaeoid
Spessartite
Spleenstone
Verd-antique
Vesuvianite

*12 letters:*
Dumortierite
Grossularite

---

**Gemination, Gemini** Diplogenesis, Twins
**Gemma** Bud, Knosp
**Gen** Info
**Gendarme** Flic
**Gender** Form, Natural, Sex
**Gene(tics), Genetic, Geneticist** Allel(e), Allelomorph, Anticodon, Codominant, Codon, Complementary, Control, Creation, Designer, Disomic, DNA, Dysbindin, Episome, Exon, Factor, Gay, Genome, Hereditary, Heterogamy, Holandric, Hologynic, Homeobox, Homeotic, Intron, Jumping, Lysenko, Lysenkoism, Mendel, Michurinism, Molecular, Muton, Oncogene, Operon, Orthologue, Paralogue, Plasmon, Promoter, Proteome, Recessive, Regulatory, Reporter, Reverse, Selfish, STR, Structural, Suppressor, Synteny, Telegony, Terminator, Testcross, Transposon, Weismannism
**Genealogist, Genealogy** Armory, Cadency, Family, Heraldry, Line, Pedigree, Seannachie, Seannachy, Sennachie, Whakapapa
**General(ly)** At large, Attorney, Average, Broad, Common, Communal, Current, Eclectic, Ecumenical, Election, Endemic, Five-star, Gen, Hoi polloi, Inspector, In the main, In the mass, Main, National, Omnify, On average, Ordinary, Overall, Overhead, Prevailing, Public, Registrar, Rife, Rough, Strategist, Structural, Sweeping, Tactician, → UNIVERSAL, Usual, Vague, Wide(spread)

---

**GENERALS**

***3 letters:***
GOC
Ike
Lee

***4 letters:***
Cato
C in C
Slim
Wade

***5 letters:***
Barca
Booth
Botha
Cleon
Clive
De Wet
Grant
Monty
Smuts
Sulla
Wolfe

***6 letters:***
Antony
Ataman
Banquo
Brutus
Caesar
Custer
Franco
Gordon
Joffre
Joshua
Leslie
Marius
Napier
Patton
Petain
Pompey
Powell
Raglan
Rommel
Scipio

***7 letters:***
Agrippa
Allenby
Blucher
Cassius
Crassus
Fairfax
Gamelin
Hadrian
Massena
Othello
Ptolemy
Sherman
Turenne

***8 letters:***
Agricola
Belgrano
Burgoyne
De Gaulle
Diadochi
Galtieri
Hannibal
Lysander
Marshall
Montcalm
Napoleon
Pershing
Shrapnel
Stilwell
Tom Thumb
Xenophon

***9 letters:***
Agamemnon
Antigonus
Antipater
Boulanger
Kitchener
Lafayette
Macarthur
Marcellus

***10 letters:***
Alcibiades
Clausewitz
Coriolanus
Cornwallis
Eisenhower
Holofernes
Montgomery
Washington

***16 letters:***
Stonewall Jackson

---

**Generate, Generation, Generator** Abiogenetic, Age, Alternator, Beat, Beget, Boomerang, Breeder, Charger, Cottonwool, Create, Dynamo, Electrostatic, Epigon, Father, Fifth, Fuel-cell, House, Kipp, Loin, Lost, Magneto, Me, Motor, Noise, Olds, Parent, Powerhouse, Reactor, Signal, Sire, Spawn, Spontaneous, Stallion, Stonewall, Tesla coil, Turbine, Van de Graaff, Wind farm, Windmill, X, Yield
**Generosity, Generous** Ample, Benevolence, Benevolent, Benign, Bounteous, Bounty, Charitable, Copious, Expansive, Free-handed, Free-hearted, Handsome, Kind, Large, Largess(e), → LAVISH, Liberal, Magnanimous, Munificent, Noble(-minded), Open, Open-handed, Open-hearted, Philanthropic, Plump, Profuse, Public-spirited, Round, Selfless, Spacious, Sporting, Tidy, Unselfish, Unstinting
**Genesis** Cause, Episome, Seed
▸**Genetic** *see* GENE(TICS)

**Geneva(n)** Calvinist, Gin, Hollands
**Genial(ity)** Affable, Amiable, Benign, Bluff, Bonhomie, Cheery, Chin, Convivial, Cordial, Expansive, Hearty, Human, Kindly, Mellow
**Genie** Djinn, Marid, Mazikeen, Shedeem
**Genipap** Lana
**Genital(s)** Ballocks, Bol(l)ix, Bollocks, Crotch, Fourchette, Front bottom, Labia, Lunchbox, Nympha, Private parts, Privates, Pubes, Pudendum, Secrets, Snatch, Tackle, Tail, Vagina, Vulva, Wedding tackle, Yoni
**Genitive** Ethical
**Genius** Agathodaimon, Bel esprit, Brain, D(a)emon, Einstein, Engine, Flash, Ingine, Inspiration, Ka, Maestro, Mastermind, Michaelangelo, Numen, Prodigy, Spirit
**Genome** Prophage
**Genre** Sci-fi, Splatterpunk, Tragedy, Variety
**Gent(leman), Gentlemanly, Gentlemen** Amateur, Baboo, Babu, Beau, Caballero, Cavalier, Cocktail, Dandy, Duni(e)wassal, Dunniewassal, Effendi, Esq(uire), Gemman, Gemmen, Herr, Hidalgo, Ja(u)nty, Knight, M, Messrs, Milord, Mister, Mr, Nob, Proteus, Ritter, Runner, Rye, Sahib, Senor, Signor, Sir, Sirra(h), Smuggler, Squire, Sri, Stalko, Stir(rah), Swell, Tea, Toff, Tuan, Valet, Von, Well-bred, Yeoman, Younker
**Genteel** Conish, Dainty, Ladylike, Polite, Proper, Refined
**Gentian** European, Felwort, Violet, Yellow
**Gentile(s)** Aryan, Ethnic, Goy, Nations, Shi(c)ksa, Uncircumcised
**Gentle(ness)** Amenable, Amenage, Assuage, Bland, Clement, Delicate, Gradual, Grub, Kid glove, Kind, Lamb, Light, Linda, Lynda, Maggot, Mansuete, Mansuetude, Mild, Soft, Sordamente, Tame, Tender
**Gentry** County, Landed, Quality, Squir(e)age
**Gents** Bog, John, Lav, Loo, WC
**Genuflexion** Bend, Curts(e)y, Knee, Kowtow, Salaam
**Genuine** Actual, Artless, Authentic, Bona-fide, Dinkum, Dinky-di, Earnest, Echt, Entire, Fair dinkum, Frank, Heartfelt, Honest, Intrinsic, Jannock, Jonnock, Kosher, Legit(imate), McCoy, Nain, Pass current, Proper, Pucka, Pukka, Pure, Pusser, → REAL, Real McCoy, Right, Simon-pure, Sincere, Square, Sterling, True, Unfeigned, Unsophisticated, Veritable
**Genus** Class, Form, -ia, Mustela, Type
**Geode** Druse
**Geographer, Geography** Chorography, Dialect, Economic, Hakluyt, Linguistic, Mercator, Pausanias, Physical, Political, Strabo
**Geological, Geologist, Geology** Buckland, Dynamic(al), Economic, Erathem, Field, Geodynamics, Geomagnetism, Hard-rock, Historical, Huronian, Hutton, Isotope, Mineralogy, Phanerozoic, Sedgwick, Seismology, Self-rock, Structural, Tectonics, Werner
**Geometry, Geometric, Geometrician, Geometer** Affine, Analytical, Conics, Coordinate, Descriptive, Differential, Elliptic, Euclid(ean), Fractal, Hyperbolic, Moth, Non-Euclidean, Parabolic, Plane, Porism, Projective, Quadrivium, Riemannian, Solid, Space, Spherics, Topologist
**Geordie** Guinea, Tynesider
**George(s)** Autopilot, Best, Borrow, Eliot, Farmer, Lloyd, Orwell, Pilot, Sand
**Georgia(n)** Abkhaz, Ga, Ge, Hanover, Iberian, Mingrel(ian)
**Geraint** Knight
**Geranium** Dove's foot, Lemon, Rose, Scarlet, Stork's bill, Yellow
**Gerbil** Jird
**Germ(s)** Bacteria, Bug, Culture, Klebsiella, Ovule, Salmonella, Seed, Sperm, Spirilla, Staph(ylococcus), Strep, Swarm-cell, Swarm-spore, Virus, Wheat, Zyme
**German(y), Germanic** Alemannic, Al(e)main(e), Angle, Anglo-Saxon, Bavarian, Berliner, Bismarck, Blood-brother, Cimbri, Composer, Cousin, Denglish, Franconian, Frank, G, Goth, Habsburg, Hans, Hapsburg, Herr, Hessian, High, Junker, Jute, Kaiser, Landgrave, Low, Ludwig, Lusatian, Neanderthal, Ossi, Ostrogoth, Otto, Palsgrave, Pennsylvania, Plattdeutsch, Pruce, Prussian, Rolf, Salic, Saxon, Tedesco, Teuton(ic), Vandal, Visigoth, Volsungs, Wessi, Wolfgang

**Germane** Apt, →PERTINENT, Relevant
**Germanium** Ge
**Germ-free** Aseptic
**Germicide** Disinfectant
**Germinal** Embryonic
**Germinate** Grow, Pullulate, Sprout
**Gerrymander** Rig
**Gesticulate, Gesticulation, Gesture(s)** Action, Air-kiss, Air quotes, Ameslan, Backslap, Beck(on), Chirology, Ch(e)ironomy, Fico, Fig, Gest(e), Goodwill, Harvey Smith, Mannerism, Mime, Motion, Mudra, Nod, Pass, Raspberry, Salaam, Salute, →SIGN, Signal, Snook, Token, V-sign, Wave, Wink
**Get(ting), Get back, Get off, Get(ting) by, Get(ting) on, Get out** Acquire, Advance, Aggravate, Annoy, Attain, Bag, Become, Becoming, Brat, Bring, Buy, Capture, Catch on, Click, Come by, Compare, Cop, Cope, Debark, Derive, Draw, Escape, Fathom, Fet(ch), Fette, Gain, Gee, Land, Learn, Make, Manage, Milk, Net, Niggle, Noy, →OBTAIN, Pass, Peeve, Procure, Progress, Reach, Realise, Receive, Recure, Rile, Roil, Secure, See, Shift, Sire, Twig, Understand, Win
**Getaway** Disappearance, Escape, Flight, Vamoose
▷**Getting** *may indicate* an anagram
**Getting better** Convalescing, Improving, Lysis
**Get-up** Tog(s)
**Geum** Avens
**Gewgaw** Bagatelle, Bauble, Doit, Tat, Trifle
**Geyser** Soffioni, Therm
**Ghana** .gh
**Ghanaian** Ashanti, Fantee, Fanti, Tshi, Twi
**Ghastly** Charnel, Gash, Grim, Grisly, Gruesome, Hideous, Lurid, Macabre, Pallid, Spectral, Ugsome, Welladay, White
**Gherkin** Cornichon
**Ghetto** Barrio, Slum
**Ghost(ly)** Acheri, Apparition, Apport, Banquo, Caddy, Chthonic, Duende, Duppy, Eerie, Eery, Fantasm, Fetch, Gytrash, Haunt, Hint, Holy, Jumbie, Jumby, Larva(e), Lemur, Malmag, Manifestation, Marley, Masca, No'canny, Paraclete, Pepper's, Phantasm(agoria), Phantom, Poe, Poltergeist, Revenant, Sampford, Shade, Shadow, Spectre, Spectrology, →SPIRIT, Spook, Trace, Truepenny, Umbra, Unearthly, Vision, Visitant, Waff, Wraith
**Ghoul(ish)** Fiend, Macabre
**GI** Joe, Yankee
**Giant(ess)** Alcyoneus, Alifanfaron, Anak, Antaeus, Archiloro, Argus, Ascapart, Atlas, Balan, Balor, Bellerus, Blunderbore, Bran, Briareus, Brobdingnagian, Cacus, Colbrand, Colbronde, Colossus, Coltys, Cormoran, Cottus, Cyclop(e)s, Despair, Drow, Enceladus, Ephialtes, Eten, Ettin, Ferragus, Gabbara, Galligantus, Gargantua, Géant, Gefion, Geirred, Gentle, Gigantic, Gog, Goliath, Great, Grim, Harapha, Heimdal(l), Hercules, Hrungnir, Hymir, Idris, Irus, Jotun(n), Jumbo, Krasir, Large, Lestrigon, Leviathan, Magog, Mammoth, Mimir, Monster, Oak, Og, Ogre, Orion, Otus, Pallas, Pantagruel, Patagonian, Polyphemus, Pope, Red, Redwood, Rounceval, Skrymir, Slaygood, Talos, Talus, Thrym, Titan, Tityus, Tregeagle, Triton, Troll, Tryphoeus, Typhon, Urizen, Utgard, Ymir, Yowie
**Giant-killer** Jack
**Gibberish** Claptrap, Double Dutch, Double-talk, Drivel, Greek, Jargon, Mumbo-jumbo, Scat, Twaddle
**Gibbet** Gallows, Patibulary, Potence, Ravenstone, Swingle-tree, Tree
**Gibbon(s)** Hoolock, Hylobate, Orlando, Siamang, Stanley, Wou-wou, Wow-wow
**Gibe** Barb, Brocard, Chaff, Fleer, Glike, Jeer, Jibe, Outfling, Quip, Shy, Slant, Wisecrack
**Gibraltar** Calpe, The Rock
**Giddy (girl), Giddiness** Capernoitie, Cap(p)ernoity, Dinic, Dizzy, Fisgig, Fishgig, Fizgig, Giglet, Giglot, Glaikit, Glaky, Haverel, Heeling, Hellicat, Hoity-toity, Jillet, Light, Light-headed, Skipping, Staggers, Sturdy, Turn, Vertigo, Volage(ous), Wheel, Woozy

**Gift(s), Gifted** Ability, Alms, Aptitude, Bef(f)ana, Bent, Bequest, Blessing, Blest, Bonbon, Bonsel(l)a, Bonus, Boon, Bounty, Cadeau, Charism(a), Congiary, Corban, Covermount, Cumshaw, Dash, Deodate, → DONATION, Dowry, Endow, Etrenne, Fairing, Fidecommissum, Flair, Foy, Frankincense, Free, Freebie, Frumentation, Gab, Garnish, Genius, Give, Godsend, Gold, Goody-bag, Grant, Gratuity, Greek, Handout, Han(d)sel, Hogmanay, Idiot savant, Indian, Knack, Koha, Kula, Lagniappe, Largesse, Legacy, Manna, Morning, Myrrh, Mystique, Ne'erday, Nuzzer, Oblation, Offering, Parting, Peace-offering, PET, Potlatch, → PRESENT, Presentation, Prezzie, Prodigy, Propine, Reward, Sop, Stocking-filler, Talent, Theosophy, Tip, Token, Tongues, Treat, Tribute, Wakf, Waqf, Windfall, Xenium

**Gig** Cart, Dennet, Flapper, Hurly-hacket, Moze, Whisk(e)y

**Gigantic** Atlantean, Briarean, Colossal, Goliath, → HUGE, Immense, Mammoth, Monster, Patagonian, Rounceval, Titan, Vast

**Giggle, Giggling** Cackle, Chortle, Chuckle, Fou rire, Ha, Ha-ha, He-he, Keckle, Simper, Snicker, Snigger, Tehee, Titter

**Gigolo** Gallant, Ladykiller, Pimp, Romeo

**Gilbert** Bab, Gb, White, WS

**Gild(ed), Gilding** Checklaton, Embellish, Enhance, Inaurate, Ormolu, S(c)hecklaton, Vermeil

**Gill(s)** Beard, Branchia, Breather, Cart, Ctenidium, Dibranchiate, Jill, Noggin, Spiracle, Trematic

**Gillman's** Aqualung

**Gilpin** Draper, John, Renowned

**Gilt** Elt, Glamour, Ormolu, Parcel, Sow

**Gimcrack** Gewgaw, Tawdry, Trangam

**Gimlet** Auger

**Gimmick** Doodad, Doodah, Hype, Novelty, Ploy, Ruse, Stunt

**Gin** Bathtub, Blue ruin, Geneva, Genever, Hollands, Illaqueable, Juniper, Max, Mother's ruin, Noose, Old Tom, Pink, Ruin, Schiedam, Schnapp(s), Sling, Sloe, Snare, Springe, Square-face, Toil, Trap, Trepan, Twankay

**Ginger, Ginger beer** Activist, Amomum, Asarum, Californian bees, Cassumunar, Costus, Curcuma, Enliven, Galanga(l), Galengale, Galingale, Gari, Malaguetta, Nut, Pachak, Pep, Pop, Putchock, Putchuk, Race, Rase, Red(head), Root, Spice, Stem, Turmeric, Wild, Zedoary, Zingiber

**Gingerbread** D(o)um-palm, Lebkuchen, Parkin, Parliament(-cake), Pepper-cake

**Gingivitis** Ulitis

▸**Gipsy** *see* GYPSY

**Giraffe** Browser, Camelopard, Okapi

**Gird** Accinge, Belt, Equip, Gibe, Jibe, Quip

**Girder** Beam, Binder, Box, H-beam, I-beam, Lattice, Loincloth, Spar

**Girdle** Baldric, Bodice, Center, Cestus, Chastity, Cincture, Cingulum, Corset, Enzone, Equator, Hip, Hippolyte, Hoop, Mitre, Panty, Pectoral, Pelvic, Ring, Sash, Shoulder, Surcingle, Surround, Zona, Zone, Zonulet

**Girl(s), Girly** Backfisch, Ball, Bimbo, Bird, Bit, Bluebell, Blushet, Bobby-dazzler, Bobby-soxer, Bohemian, Bondmaid, Broad, Burd, Calendar, Call, Career, Charlie, Chick, Chit, Chorus, Coed, Colleen, Continuity, Cover, Crumpet, Cummer, Cutey, Cutie, Cutty, Dam(o)sel, Deb, Dell, Demoiselle, Dish, Doll, Dollybird, Essex, Filly, Fisgig, Fizgig, Flapper, Flower, Fluff, Fraulein, Frippet, Gaiety, Gal, Gammerstang, Geisha, Gibson, Gill(et), Gilp(e)y, Giselle, Good-time, Gouge, Gretel, Grisette, Hen, Hoiden, Hoyden, Hussy, It, Italian, Judy, Kimmer, Kinchinmort, Kogal, Kumari, Ladette, Land, Lass(ock), Lorette, Maid(en), Mauther, Mawr, Mawther, May, Midinette, Miss(y), Moll, Moppet, Mor, Mot, Mousmé, Mousmee, Muchacha, Mystery, Nautch, Niece, Number, Nymph(et), Nymphette, Oanshagh, Peach, Peacherino, Petticoat, Piece, Pigeon, Popsy, Poster, Principal, Puss, Quean, Queyn, Quin(i)e, Randy, Riot, Señorita, Sheila, Shi(c)ksa, Shi(c)kse, Sis(s), Smock, Spice, Sweater, Tabby, Taupie, Tawpie, Teddy, Teenybopper, Tiller, Tit, Tootsie, Totty, Trull, Vi, Weeny-bopper, Wench, Widgie, Wimp, Wuss

▹**Girl** *may indicate* a female name

**Girlfriend** Baby, Chérie, Confidante, Date, Flame, Hinny, Lady, Leman, Moll, Peat, Squeeze, Steady, Wag
**Girth** Cinch, Compass, Diameter, Exploitable, Size, Surcingle
**Gismo** Diameter, Gadget
**Gist** Drift, Essence, Kernel, → **NUB**, Pith, Substance
**Give(r), Give up, Giving** Abandon, Abstain, Accede, Accord, Administer, Afford, Award, Bend, Bestow, Buckle, Cede, Confiscate, Consign, Contribute, Dative, Dispense, Dole, → **DONATE**, Drop, Duck, Elasticity, Enable, Endow, Enfeoff, Forswear, Gie, Grant, Hand, Impart, Indian, Jack, Largition, Present, Provide, Render, Resign, Reward, Sacrifice, Sag, Sent, Spring, Stop, Tip, Tolerance, Vacate, Vouchsafe, Yeve, Yield
**Give-away** Freebie, Gift-horse, Present, Spoiler
**Given** If, Wont
**Give out** Assign, Belch, Bestow, Dispense, Emit, Exude, Peter, Utter
**Give over** Cease, Lin
**Glace** Candied
**Glacial, Glaciation** Gunz, Mindel, Riss, Wurm
**Glacier** Aletsch, Crevasse, Drumlin, Fox, Franz-Josef, Hanging, Iceberg, Ice-cap, Icefall, Moraine, Moulin, Muir, Rhône, Riss, Serac, Stadial, Stoss, Stoss and lee, Tasman
**Glad(ly), Gladden, Gladness** Cheer, Fain, → **HAPPY**, Lettice, Lief, Willing
**Glade** Bottom, La(u)nd
**Gladiator** Retiarius, Samnite, Spartacus
**Glamour, Glamorise, Glamorous** Charm, Enhalo, Glitter(ati), Glitz, Halo, It, Prestige, Ritz, SA, Sex up, Sexy, Spell, Swanky, Tinseltown
**Glamour girl** Cheesecake, Odalisk, Odalisque, Pin-up
**Glance** Allusion, Amoret, Argentite, Blink, Browse, Carom(bole), Copper-head, Coup d'oeil, Deflect, Dekko, Draw, Eld, Eliad, Eye-beam, Eye-wink, Galena, Glad eye, Glimpse, Illiad, Inwick, Lustre, Oeillade, Once-over, Peek, → **PEEP**, Ray, Redruthite, Ricochet, Scan, Sheep's eyes, Shufti, Shufty, Side, Sideswipe, Silver, Skellie, Skelly, Slant, Snick, Squint, Squiz, Tip, Twire, Vision, Waff
**Gland(s)** Acinus, Adenoid, Adenoma, Adrenal, Apocrine, Bartholin's, Bulbourethral, Clitellum, Colleterial, Conarium, Cowper's, Craniopharyngioma, Crypt, Dart-sac, Digestive, Ductless, Duodenal, Eccrine, Endocrine, Epiphysis, Exocrine, Follicle, Goitre, Green, Holocrine, Hormone, Hypophysis, Hypothalamus, Ink-sac, Lachrymal, Lacrimal, Liver, Lymph, Mammary, Melbomian, Musk-sac, Nectary, Oil, Osmeterium, Ovary, Pancreas, Paranephros, Parathyroid, Parotid, Parotis, Parotoid, Perineal, Pineal, Pituitary, Pope's eye, Preen, Prostate, Prothoracic, Racemose, Salivary, Salt, Scent, Sebaceous, Sericterium, Shell, Silk, Spermary, Sublingual, Submaxillary, Suprarenal, Sweat, Sweetbread, Tarsel, Tear, Testicle, Testis, Third eye, Thymus, Thyroid, Tonsil, Udder, Uropygial, Vesicle, Vulvovaginal, Zeiss
**Glanders** Farcy
**Glandular (trouble)** Adenitis
**Glare, Glaring** Astare, Blare, Blaze, Dazzle, Egregious, Flagrant, Garish, Gleam, Glower, Gross, Holophotal, Iceblink, Lour, Low(e), Lurid, Naked, Notorious, Shine, Stare, Vivid, Whally
**Glass(es), Glassware, Glassy** Amen, Ampul(la), Aneroid, Avanturine, Aventurine, Aviator, Baccara(t), Balloon, Barometer, Beaker, Bell, Bifocals, Bin(ocular)s, Bock, Borosilicate, Bottle, Brimmer, Bumper, Burmese, Burning, Calcedonio, Case, Cheval, Claude Lorraine, Cloche, Cocktail, Cooler, Copita, Cordial, Coupe, Cover, Crookes, Crown, Crystal, Cullet, Cupping, Cut, Dark, Delmonico, Dildo, Diminishing, Eden, Euphon, Favrile, Fibre, Field, Flint, Float, Flute, Foam, Frigger, Frit, Frosted, Fulgurite, Gauge, Glare, Goblet, Goggles, Granny, Green, Ground, Hand, Handblown, Highball, Horn-rims, Humpen, Hyaline, Iceland agate, Jar, Jena, Jigger, Keltie, Kelty, Lace, Lacy, Lalique, Laminated, Lamp, Lanthanum, Larking, Latticinio, Lead, Lead crystal, Lens, Liqueur, Liquid, Log, Looking, Lorgnette, Loupe, Lozen(ge), Lunette, Magma, Magnifying, Metal, Mica, Middy, Milk, Millefiori, Minimizing, Mirror, Moldavite, Monocle, Mousseline, Multiplying, Murr(h)ine, Muscovy, Musical, Night, Nitreous, Object, Obsidian, One-way, OO, Opal(ine), Opera, Optical, Ovonic, Pane, Parison,

Paste, Pearlite, Pebble, Peeper, Pele, Pele's hair, Perlite, Perspective, Pier, Pince-nez, Pinhole, Pinta, Pitchstone, Plate, Pocket, Pon(e)y, Pressed, Prince Rupert's drops, Prism, Prospective, Prunt, Psyche, Pyrex®, Quarrel-pane, Quarry, Quartz, Reducing, Roemer, Ruby, Rummer, Safety, Schmelz, Schooner, Seam, Seidel, Shard, Sheet, Silex, Silica, Sleever, Slide, Sliver, Smalt(o), Snifter, Soluble, Specs, → **SPECTACLES**, Spun, Spyhole, Stained, Stein, Stem, Stemware, Stone, Storm, Strass, Straw, Sun, Supernaculum, Tachilite, Tachylite, Tachylyte, Tektite, Telescope, Tiffany, Tiring, Toilet, Trifocals, Triplex®, Tumbler, Uranium, Varifocals, Venetian, Venice, Vernal, Vita, Vitrail, Vitreous, Vitreous silica, Vitrescent, Vitro-di-trina, Volcanic, Watch, Water, Waterford, Weather, Window (pane), Wine, Wire, Yard of ale

**Glass-gall** Sandiver

**Glass-house** Conservatory, Orangery

**Glassite** Sandemania

**Glass-maker** Annealer, Blower, Glazier, Lalique, Pontie, Pontil, Ponty, Puntee, Punty

**Glaze(d), Glazing** Aspic, Ciré, Clair de lune, Coat, Crackle, Double, Eggwash, Enamel, Film, Flambé, Frit, Glost, Ice, Majolica, Peach-blow, Salt, Sancai, Slip, Tammy, Temmoku, Triple, Varnish, Velatura, Vitreous

**Gleam(ing)** Aglow, Blink, Flash, Glint, Glisten, Glitter, Gloss, Leme, Light, Lustre, Ray, Relucent, Sheen, Shimmer, → **SHINE**, Spotless, Weather

**Glean(er), Gleaned** Gather, Harvest, Lease, Ruth, Stibbler

**Glee** Delight, Exuberance, Hysterics, Joy, Madrigal, Mirth, Song

**Glen** Affric, Ghyll, Gill, Rushy, Silicon, Strath, Vale

**Glib** Facile, Flip, Pat, Slick, Smooth

**Glide(r), Glideaway, Gliding** Aquaplane, Aviette, Chassé, Coast, Elapse, Float, Illapse, Lapse, Luge, Microlight, Monoplane, Off, On, Parasail, Parascend, Portamento, Rogallo, Sail, Sailplane, Sashay, Scorrendo, Scrieve, Skate, Ski, Skim, Skite, Skyte, Sleek, Slide, Slip, Slur, Swim, Swish, Volplane

**Glimmer(ing)** Gleam, Glent, Glint, Glow, Inkling, Light, Stime, Styme, Twinkle, Wink

**Glimpse** Aperçu, Flash, Fleeting, Glance, Gledge, Glisk, Peep, Stime, Styme, Waff, Whiff

**Glint** Flash, Shimmer, → **SPARKLE**, Trace, Twinkle

**Glisten(ing)** Ganoid, Glint, Sheen, Shimmer, → **SHINE**, Sparkle

**Glitch** Blip, Bug, Misprint, Snafu

**Glitter(ing)** Asterism, Brilliant, Clinquant, Diamante, Garish, Gemmeous, Glee, Iridescence, Paillon, Scintillate, Sequin, Spang(le), Sparkle, Tinsel

**Glitz** Bling, Razzle-dazzle

**Gloaming** Twilight

**Gloat(ing)** Crow, Drool, Enjoy, Exult, Schadenfreude

**Globe, Global, Globule** Artichoke, Ball, Bead, Bubble, Celestial, Drop, Earth, Orb, Pandemic, Pearl, Planet, Shot, Sphear, Sphere, Tectonic, Terrestrial, Theatre, Ubiquitous, Universal, World

**Globetrotter** Jet-set, Travel, Voyager

**Globulin** Gamma, Legumin, Protein

**Gloom(y)** Atrabilious, Benight, Blues, Cheerless, Cimmerian, Cloud, Crepuscular, Crestfallen, Damp, Dark, → **DESPAIR**, Dingy, Dire, Disconsolate, Dismal, Dool(e), Dour, Downbeat, Drab, Drear, Drumly, Dump(s), Dyspeptic, Erebus, Feral, Funereal, Glum, Grey, Grim, Half light, Louring, Lowery, Mausoleum, Mirk, Misery, Mopish, Morbid, Morne, Morose, Mumps, Murk(y), Night(fall), Obscurity, Overcast, Pessimism, Portentous, Sable, Sad, Saturnine, Sepulchral, Shadow, Solein, Solemn, → **SOMBRE**, Sourpuss, Stygian, Subfusc, Sullen, Surly, Tenebrious, Tenebrose, Tenebrous, Unlit, Wan

**Gloriana** Faerie queene

**Glorification, Glorify** Aggrandise, Apotheosis, Avatar, Bless, → **EXALT**, Extol, Glamorise, Halo, Laud, Lionise, Praise, Radiance, Roose, Splendour

**Glorious, Gloria, Glory** Chorale, Crow, Crowning, Grand, Halo, Hosanna, Ichabod, Kentish, Knickerbocker, Kudos, Lustre, Magnificent, Nimbus, Resplendent, Signal, Strut, Sublime, Twelfth

**Glory-pea** Kaka-beak, Kaka-bill, Kowhai

**Gloss(y)** Annotate, Ciré, Enamel, Gild, Glacé, Interpret, Japan, Lacquer, Lip, Lustre, Mag,

Patina, → POLISH, Postillate, Sheen, Shiny, Sleek, Sleekit, Slick, Slide, Slur, Smooth, Supercalendered, Veneer, Wetlook, Whitewash

**Glossary** Catalogue, Clavis, Index, K'thibh

**Gloucester** Cheese

**Glove** Baseball, Boxing, Cestus, Chevron, Dannock, Gage, Gauntlet, Kid, Mermaid's, Mitten, Mousquetaire, Muffle, Oven, Puppet, Rubber, Velvet

**Glow(er), Glowing, Glowworm** Aflame, Ashine, Aura, Bloom, Burn, Calescence, Candent, Candescence, Candlelight, Corona, Emanate, Fire, Firefly, Flush, Foxfire, Gegenschein, Girasol, Glare, Gleam, Glimmer, Glisten, Halation, Iceblink, Incandescence, Lambent, Lamp-fly, Leam, LED, Leme, Luculent, Luminesce, Lustre, Noctilucent, Perspire, Phosphorescence, Radiant, Radiate, Reflet, Ruddy, Rushlight, Rutilant, Scowl, Shine, Snowblink, Sullen, Translucent, → WARMTH

**Glucin(i)um** Gl

**Glucose, Glucoside** Aesculin, Amygdalin, Dextrose, Digitalin, Indican, Maltose, Salicin(e), Saponin, Solanine

**Glue(y)** Affix, Alkyd, Araldite®, Bee, Cement, Colloidal, Epoxy, Fish, Gelatin(e), Gunk, Hot-melt, Ichthyocolla, Isinglass, Marine, Paste, Propolis, PVA, Resin, Rice, Size, Solvent, Spetch, Uhu®

**Glug** Swig

**Glum** Dour, Downhearted, Livery, Lugubrious, Moody, Morose, Ron, Solemn, Sombre

**Glut** Choke, Gorge, Plethora, Sate, Satiate, Saturate, Surfeit, Surplus

**Gluten, Glutinous** Goo, Ropy, Seiten, Sticky, Tar, Viscid, Zymome

**Glutton(ous), Gluttony** Bellygod, Carcajou, Cormorant, Edacity, Esurience, Feaster, Free-liver, Gannet, Gorb, Gourmand, Greedyguts, Gulosity, Gutser, Gutsy, Gutzer, Hog, Lurcher, Pig, Ratel, Scoffer, Sin, Trencherman, Trimalchio, Wolverine

**Glyceride, Glycerine** Ester, Olein, Palmitin

**Glycol** Anti-freeze

**Glycoside** Hesperidin

**Gnarl(ed)** Knot, Knuckly, Knur, Nob, Wizened

**Gnash(ing)** Bruxism, Champ, Grate

**Gnat** Culex, Culicidae, Midge, Mosquito

**Gnaw(ing)** Corrode, Erode, Fret, Lagomorph, Rodent

**Gnome** Adage, Bank-man, Chad, Cobalt, Epigram, Europe, Financier, Garden, Hobbit, Kobold, Maxim, Motto, Proverb, Saw, Sprite, Zurich

**Gnostic(ism)** (A)eon, Archontic, Cainite, Mand(a)ean, Marcionism, Ophite, Sabian, Tsabian, Zabian

**Gnu** Brindled, Horned horse, Implausibility, White-tailed, Wildebeest

**Go, Going (after, ahead, away, back, for, off, on, through, up, etc)** Advance, Afoot, Anabasis, Animation, Apage, Ascent, Assail, Attempt, Attend, Bash, Begone, Betake, Bing, Bout, Brio, Choof, Chunter, Clamber, Comb, Continuance, Crack, Deal, Depart, Die, Do, Effort, Energy, Experience, Fare, Function, Gae, Gang, Gaun, Gee, Gee up, Gonna, Green (light), Hamba, Hark, Heavy, Hence, Hie, Hup, Imshi, Imshy, Ish, Kick, → LEAVE, March, Match, Mosey, Move, Off, OK, Path, Pee, Pep, Perpetual, Ply, Quit, Raik, Repair, Resort, Resume, Run, Satanas, Scat, Scram, Segue, Shoo, Shot, Skedaddle, Snick-up, Sour, Spank, Spell, Spirit, Square, Stab, Success, Swan off, Tag along, Traipse, Transitory, Travel, Trine, Try, Turn, Vamo(o)se, Vanish, Verve, Via, Viable, Vim, Wend, Work, Yead, Yede, Yeed, Zap, Zest, Zing, Zip

**Goad** Ankus, Brod, Gad, Impel, Incite, → NEEDLE, Prod, Provoke, Rowel, Spur, Stimulate, Stimulus, Sting, Taunt

**Goal(posts)** Aim, Ambition, Basket, Bourn(e), Cage, Decider, Destination, Dool, Dream, Drop, Dule, End, Ettle, Field, Golden, Grail, Hail, Home, Horme, Hunk, Intent, Limit, Mark, Mission, Moksha, Net, Own, Penalty, Score, Silver, Tap-in, Target, Tip-in, Touch-in, Ultima Thule, Uprights

**Goalless** Idle

**Goat(-like)** Alpine, Amalthea, Angora, Antelope, Antilope, Billy, Bok, Bucardo, Buck, Caprine, Cashmere, Chamois, Cilician, Gait, Gate, Giddy, Goral, Hircine, Ibex, Izard, Kashmir,

Kid, Libido, Markhor, Mountain, Nan(ny), Nubian, Rocky Mountain, Roue, Ruminant, Saanen, Sassaby, Serow, Serpent-eater, Steenbok, Steinbock, Tahr, Takin, Tehr, Thar, Toggenburg

**Goat's beard** John-go-to-bed-at-noon

**Goatsucker** Fern-owl, Nightjar

**Gob(bet)** Bespit, Clot, Dollop, Mouth, Sailor, Spit, Tar, Yap

**Gobble** Bolt, Devour, Gorge, Gulch, Gulp, Hoover, Scarf, Scoff, Slubber, Wolf

**Gobbledegook** Officialese

**Gobelin** Tapestry

**Go-between** Agency, Broker, Factor, Intermediate, Interpolate(r), Interpret(er), Link, Mediate, Middleman, Pandarus, Pander, Shuttle

**Goblet** Chalice, Grail, Hanap

**Goblin** Banshee, Bargaist, Barg(h)est, Bodach, Bogey, Bogle, Bogy, Brownie, Bucca, Bull-beggar, Croquemitaine, Empusa, Erl-king, Esprit follet, Genie, Gnome, Gremlin, Knocker, Kobold, Lob-lie-by-the-fire, Lubberfiend, Lutin, Nis(se), Phooka, Phynnodderree, Pooka, Pouke, Puca, Puck, Pug, Red-cap, Red-cowl, Shellycoat, →**SPRITE**, Troll, Trow

**Gobstopper** Everlasting, Lollipop

**Goby** Dragonet

**God(s)** All-seer, Amen, Ancient of Days, Creator, →**DEITY**, Deus, Di, Divine, First Cause, Gallery, Gracious, Holy One, Household, Immortals, Inner Light, Light, Maker, Od(d), Olympian, Prime Mover, Principle, Providence, Serpent, Shechina, Soul, Supreme Being, The Creator, Tin, Trinity, Truth, Unknown, Vanir, War, Water

---

**GODS**

*1 letter:*
D

*2 letters:*
An
As
Ra
Re

*3 letters:*
Anu
Bel
Bes
Dis
Gad
Geb
Jah
Keb
Lar
Lir
Lug
Mab
Mot
Pan
Seb
Set
Sol
Tiu
Tiw
Tum
Tyr

*4 letters:*
Abba
Agni
Aitu
Amun
Apis
Ares
Asur
Aten
Atum
Baal
Brag
Bran
Cama
Deva
Dieu
Eros
Faun
Frey
Joss
Kama
Kami
Kane
Llyr
Loki
Lugh
Mars
Mors
Nebo
Odin
Ptah
Rama
Seth
Siva
Soma
Thor
Tyrr
Yama
Zeus

*5 letters:*
Aegir
Aesir
Allah
Ammon
Brage
Bragi
Comus
Cupid
Dagan
Dagon
Donar
Freyr
Haoma
Horus
Hymen
Indra
Janus
Khnum
Liber
Lludd
Mimir
Momus
Njord
Numen
Orcus
Orixa
Pales
Picus
Pluto
Rudra
Satyr
Sebek
Shiva
Silen
Sinis
Surya
Thoth
Titan
Wodan
Woden
Wotan
Yahve
Yahwe

*6 letters:*
Adonai
Adonis
Aeolus
Amen-ra
Amon-ra
Anubis
Apollo

Ashtar
Asshur
Avatar
Balder
Boreas
Brahma
Cabiri
Chemos
Clotho
Cronus
Delian
Elohim
Faunus
Ganesa
Ganesh
Garuda
HaShem
Helios
Hermes
Hughie
Hypnos
Kronos
Mahoun
Mammon
Marduk
Mexitl
Mextli
Mithra
Moerae
Molech
Moloch
Nereus
Njorth
Oannes
Orisha
Ormazd
Ormuzd
Osiris
Panisc
Panisk
Plutus
Rimmon
Saturn
Somnus
Tammuz
Teraph
Teshup
Thamiz
Thunor
Triton
Uranus
Varuna
Vishnu
Vulcan
Yahweh
Zephyr
Zombie

*7 letters:*
Alastor
Alpheus
Angus Og
Anteros
Bacchus
Bhagwan
Chemosh
Daikoku
Ganesha
Goddess
Hanuman
Heimdal
Jehovah
Jupiter
Krishna
Kuan Yin
Kwan Yin
Mahound
Mercury
Mithras
Neptune
Nisroch
Oceanus
Penates
Phoebus
Priapus
Proteus
Rameses
Sarapis
Sat Guru
Serapis
Setebos
Shamash
Silenus
Thammuz
Zagreus

*8 letters:*
Achelous
Dionysus
Heimdall
Hyperion
Kamadeva
Mahadeva
Morpheus
Mulciber
Nataraja
Pantheon
Poseidon
Quirinus
Silvanus
Sylvanus
Terminus
Thanatos
Trimurti
Wahiguru
Zephyrus

*9 letters:*
All-father
Asclepius
Fabulinus
Heimdallr
Jagganath
Promachos
Tetragram
Thunderer
Vertumnus
Zernebock

*10 letters:*
Ahura Mazda
Demogorgon
Elegabalus
Hephaestus
Hephaistos
Juggernaut
Karttikaya
Mumbo-jumbo
Prometheus
Trophonius

*11 letters:*
Adrammelech
Aesculapius
Bodhisattva

*12 letters:*
Quetzalcoati
Trismegistus

*14 letters:*
Tetragrammaton

---

**God-bearing** Deiparous
**Goddess(es)** Bitch, Divine, Domestic, Greek, Green, Muse, Sea nymph

---

**GODDESSES**

*2 letters:*
Ge

*3 letters:*
Ate
Eos
Hel
Mut
Nox
Nut
Nyx
Ops
Pax

*4 letters:*
Dian
Eris
Gaea
Gaia
Hera
Idun
Iris
Isis
Juno
Kali
Leda
Leto
Luna
Maat
Maut
Nike
Norn
Pele
Rhea
Sita
Thea

*5 letters:*
Aruru
Ceres
Diana
Dione
Durga
Erato
Flora
Freya
Grace
Horae
Houri

Hulda
Iduna
Irene
Kotys
Moera
Moira
Pales
Parca
Sakti
Tanit
Terra
Tyche
Ushas
Venus
Vesta

*6 letters:*
Aglaia
Ashnan
Athene
Aurora
Bastet
Cybele
Cyrene
Eastre
Freyja
Frigga
Graeae
Graiae
Hathor
Hecate
Hertha
Hestia
Huldar
Hyaeia
Idalia
Ishtar
Ithunn
Lucina
Pallas
Parcae
Phoebe
Pomona
Satyra
Selene
Semele
Shakti
Tellus
Tethys
Thalia
Themis
Thetis

*7 letters:*
Artemis
Astarte
Astraea
Bellona
Cotytto
Cynthia
Demeter
Fortuna
Kotytto
Lakshmi
Megaera
Minerva
Nemesis
Nepthys
Parvati
Sabrina
Strenia
Victory

*8 letters:*
Cloacina
Cytherea
Libitina
Rhiannon
Valkyrie
Victoria
Walkyrie

*9 letters:*
Aphrodite
Ashtaroth
Ashtoreth
Eumenides
Mnemosyne
Sarasvati

*10 letters:*
Amphitrite
Proserpina
Proserpine

---

**Godfather, Godmother** Capo, Consigliere, Cummer, Don, Fairy, Gossip, Kimmer, Rama, Sponsor, Woden
**God-fearing** Pious
**Godless** Agnostic, Atheistic, Atheous, Impious, Profane, Unholy
**Godly, Godliness** Deist, Devine, Devout, Holy, Pious, Sanctity
**Godown** Hong
**God-willing** Deo volente, DV, Inshallah, Mashallah
**Go-getter** Achiever, Arriviste, Hopeful, Hustler, Yuppie
**Goggle(s)** Bee, Gape, Gaze, Snow-eyes, Stare
**Go-go** Alert
**Goings-on** Hanky-panky
**Going wrong** Aglee, Agley, Misfiring
▷**Going wrong** *may indicate* an anagram
**Goitre** Derbyshire neck, Exophthalmic, Graves' disease, Struma
**Gold(en)** Age, Amber, Apple, Ass, Au, Aureate, Auriel, Auriferous, Auriol, Aurum, Bendigo, Bough, Bull, Bullion, Bull's eye, California, Chryselephantine, Doubloon, Dutch, Eagle, Electron, Electrum, Emerods, Fairy, Fiftieth, Filigree, Filled, First, Fleece, Fool's, Free, Fulminating, Gate, Gilden, Gule, Handshake, Hind, Horde, Horn, Ingot, King of metals, Kolar, Leaf, Lingot, Moidore, Mosaic, Muck, Nugget, Oaker, Obang, Ochre, Ophir, Or, Oreide, Ormolu, Oroide, Pistole, Placer, Pyrites, Red, Reef, Rolled, Silence, Silver-gilt, Sol, Soneri, Standard, Stream, Stubborn, Taelbar, Talent, Talmi, Thrimsa, Tolosa, Treasury, Venice, Virgin, Wash-up, White, Witwatersrand, Xanthe, Yellow
**Gold-digger** Forty-niner, Prospector
**Golden fleece** Phrixus
**Goldfield** Rand
**Goldfinch** Charm, Chirm, Redcap
**Goldfish** Glint, Shubunken
**Gold leaf** Ormolu
**Gold rush** Kalgoorlie, Klondike
**Goldsmith** Cellini, Fabergé, Hilliard, Oliver
**Golf (ball), Golf match** Best ball, Better-ball, Clock, Crazy, Four-ball, Foursome, G, Gutta,

Matchplay, Medal play, Miniature, Pro, Pro-am, Repaint, Round, Stableford, Stroke play, Texas scramble

**Golf course** Augusta, Birkdale, Links, Murrayfield, St Andrew's, St Anne's, Troon

**Golfer** Alliss, Braid, Cotton, Els, Faldo, Hogan, Lyle, Pivoter, Rees, Roundsman, Seve, Snead, Teer, Texas scramble, Tiger Woods, Trevino, Watson, Wolstenholme, Woosnam, Yipper

**Goliath** Giant

**Golly** Cor, Crumbs, Gosh, Lummy

**Gondola** Cable-car

**Gondolier** Balloonist, Bargee, Marco

**Gone** Ago, Dead, Defunct, Deid, Extinct, Napoo, Out, Past, Ygo(e), Yod

▷**Gone off** *may indicate* an anagram

**Gone west** Had it

**Gong** Bell, Clanger, DSO, → MEDAL, Tam-tam, VC

**Gonorrhoea** Clap

**Goo(ey)** Gleet, Gloop, Glop, Gum, Gunge, Mire, Poise, Squidgy, Treacle, Ulmin

**Goober** Monkey nut

**Good(ness), Goods, Goody(-goody)** Agatha, Agathodaimon, Altruism, Angelic, Ascertained, Bad, Bailee, Banner, Behoof, Bein, Benefit, Blesses, Blinder, Bon(ism), Bonzer, Bosker, Bounty, Braw, Brod, Budgeree, By George, Canny, Castor, Civil, Classy, Clinker, Common, Coo, Cool, Corker, Crack(ing), Credit, Crikey, Dab, Dandy, Def, Divine, Doozy, Dow, Dress, Dry, Effects, Enid, Estimable, Fancy that, Fantabulous, Favourable, Finger lickin', First-class, Furnishing, Furniture, G, Gear, Gee, Giffen, Glenda, Gold, Gosh, Guid, Holy cow, Hooray, Humdinger, Law abiding, Lekker, Lois, Lor, Ma foi, Measurement, Mega, Merchandise, Merit, Moral, Neat, Nobility, → NO GOOD, Pi, Plum, Plunder, Prime, Proper, Pucka, Pukka, Purler, Rattling, Rectitude, Riddance, Right(eous), Rum, St, Sake, Salutary, Samaritan, Sanctity, Silver lining, Slap-up, Smashing, Sound, Spiffing, Splendid, Suitable, Super, Superb, Taut, Teacher's pet, Tollol, Topping, Valid, Virtue, Virtuous, Weal, Welfare, Whacko, Wholesome, Worthy, Wrong'un

**Goodbye** Addio, Adieu, Adios, Aloha, Apopemptic, Arrivederci, Au revoir, Cheerio, Cheers, Ciao, Congé, Farewell, Golden, Haere ra, Hamba kahle, Hooray, Hooroo, Later, Sayonara, See-you, So long, Tata, Toodle-oo, Toodle-pip, Vale

**Good evening** Den

**Goodfellow** Brick, Puck, Robin, Samaritan, Sport, Worthy

**Good-for-nothing** Bum, Donnat, Donnot, Dud, Idler, Layabout, Lorel, Lorrell, Losel, Napoo, Naught, Scal(l)awag, Scallywag, Scant o'grace, Sculpin, Shot-clog, Stiff, Useless, Vaurien, Waff, Waster, Wastrel

**Good Friday** Parasceve, Pasch of the Cross

**Good-humour(ed), Good-natured** Amiable, Bonhomie, Clever, Gruntled, Kind, Mellow

**Good life, Good liver** Bon viveur

**Good-looking** Bon(n)ie, Bonny, Bonwie, Comely, Fair, Handsome, Personable, Pretty, Telegenic, Wally, Weel-fa(u)st

**Good news** Evangel

**Good number** Thr(e)ave

**Good order** Eutaxy, Shipshape

**Goods** Bona, Brown, Cargo, Commodities, Consumer, Disposable, Durable, Durables, Fancy, Flotsam, Freight, Futures, Gear, Hardware, Insight, Ironware, Lagan, Lay-away, Line, Luxury, Merchandise, Piece, Products, Property, Schlock, Soft, Sparterie, Stock, Truck, Wares, White

**Good time** Craic

**Goodwill** Affection, Amity, Bonhom(m)ie, Favour, Gree

**Goof** Gaffe

**Goofy** Simple-minded

**Google** Search

**Googly** Bosie

**Goon** Ape, Bentine, Bluebottle, Eccles, Milligan, Secombe, Sellers

**Goop** Ooze

**Goosander** Dun-diver

**Goose, Geese** Anserine, Bargoose, Barnacle, Bernicle, Blue, Brent, Canada, Cape Barren, Colonial, Daftie, Ember, Gaggle, Gander, Gannet, Golden, Grey, Greylag, Grope, Harvest, Hawaiian, Idiot, Iron, Juggins, MacFarlane's, Magpie, Michaelmas, Mother, Nana, Nene, Pink-footed, Pygmy, Quink, Roger, Saddleback, Silly, Simpleton, Skein, Snow, Solan, Strasbourg, Stubble, →STUPID PERSON, Swan, Team, Wav(e)y, Wawa, Wedge, Whitehead

**Gooseberry** Barbados, Cape, Chaperon(e), Chinese, Coromandel, Detrop, Fool, Gog, Goosegob, Goosegog, Groser(t), Groset, Grossart, Grozer, Honey blob, Kiwi, Physalis, Tomato

**Gooseflesh** Goose bumps, Horripilation

**Goosefoot** Allgood, Amarantaceae, Beet, Blite, Fat-hen, Mercury, Orache, Quinoa, Saltbush

**Goosegrass** Catchweed

**Gooseherd** Quill-driver

**Gopher** Camass-rat, Minnesota, Pocket

**Gordian** Knot

**Gordon** Chinese, Flash, Rioter

**Gore, Gory** Blood, Cloy, Danse macabre, Gair, Horn, Inset, Toss

**Gorge(s)** Abyss, Arroyo, Barranca, Barranco, Canyon, Carnarvon, Chasm, Cheddar, Cleft, Couloir, Cram, Defile, Donga, Flume, Gap, Ghyll, Glut, Grand Canyon, Grike, Gulch, Guzzle, Ironbridge, Iron Gate, Katherine, Khor, Kloof, Lin(n), Nala, Nalla(h), Nulla(h), Olduvai, Overeat, Overfeed, Pass, Pig, Ravine, Scarf, Snarf, Staw, →STUFF, Throat, Tire, Tums, Valley, Valley of the Kings, Yosemite

**Gorgeous** Delectable, Dishy, Dreamboat, Eye-candy, Grand, Ravishing, Sexy, Splendid, Superb

**Gorgon** Euryale, Medusa, Ogress, Stheno

**Gorilla** Heavy, →MONKEY, Silverback, Whoop

**Gorse** Broom, Furze, Gosse, Ulex, Whin

**Gosh** Begad, Begorra, Blimey, Coo, Cor, Crumbs, Ecod, Fancy, Gadzooks, Gee, Golly, Gracious, Gum, Heavens, Lor, My, Och, Odsbobs, Odso, Phew, Really, Shucks, Wow, Yikes

**Go-slow** Work-to-rule

**Gospel(s), Gospeller** Apocryphal, Creed, Diatessaron, Evangel, Fact, John, Kerygma, Luke, Mark, Matthew, Nicodemus, Prosperity, Protevangelium, Synoptic, Televangelist, Truth, Waldensian

**Gossamer(y)** Araneous, Byssoid, Cobwebby, Gauzy

**Gossip** Ana(s), Aunt, Backbite, Blah, Blether, Cackle, Cat, Causerie, Chat, Chatterer, Chin-wag, Chitchat, Clash, Clash-me-clavers, Claver, Cleck, Clish-clash, Clishmaclaver, Clype, Confab, Cosher, Coze, Crack, Cummer, Dirt, Flibbertigibbet, Furphy, Gab(nash), Gabfest, Gas, Gash, Goster, Grapevine, Gup, Hearsay, Hen, Jaw, Loose-tongued, Maundrel, Moccasin telegraph, Nashgab, Natter, Newsmonger, Noise, On dit, Pal, Personalist, Prate, Prattle, Prose, Quidnunc, Reportage, Rumour(monger), Scandal(monger), Scandal-bearer, Schmooze, Scuttlebutt, Shmoose, Shmooze, Sweetie-wife, Tabby(cat), Talk(er), Tattle, Tattletale, Tibby, Tittle(-tattle), Twattle, Whisper, Yak, Yatter, Yenta

**Got** Gat, Obtained, Won

**Goth(ic)** Alaric, American, International, Lurid, Moesia

**Gothamite** Abderian, New Yorker

**Gouge** Chisel, Groove, Scoop

**Goulash** Stew

**Gourd** Bottle, Calabash, Courgette, Dishcloth, Guiro, Hercules' club, Loofa, Maraca, Marrow, Melon, Monkeybread, Pumpkin, Squash, Zucchini

**Gourmand, Gourmet** Aesthete, Apicius, Chowhound, →EPICURE, Free-liver, Gastronome, Gastrosopher, Lickerish, Table, Trencherman, Ventripotent

**Gout(y)** Chalkstone, Chiragra, Hamarthritis, Podagra, Taste, Tophus

**Govern(or), Government** Adelantado, Administer, Ag(h)a, Agricola, Alderman, Amban, Amman, Amtman, ANC, Andocracy, Archology, Aristocracy, Autarchy, Autocrat, Autonomy, Bahram, Ban, Bashaw, Beehive, Beg, Beglerbeg, Bencher, Bey, Board, Bridler, Bureaucracy, Burgrave, Cabinet, Caciquism, Caimac(an), Caliphate, Caretaker, Cassio, Castellan, Catapan, Central, Cham, Circar, Classis, Clive, Coalition, Command, Commonwealth, Condominium, Congress, Consistorian, Constable, Constitution, Consulate, Cybernetic,

Darogha, Democracy, Dergue, Despotism, Despotocracy, Dey, Diarchy, Dictatorship, Dinarchy, Directoire, Directory, Domain, Dominate, Dominion, Downing St, Duarchy, D(o)ulocracy, Duumvirate, Dyarchy, Dynast, Earl, Ecclesiarchy, Eminent domain, Empery, Eparch, Ergatocracy, Escapement, Ethnarch, Exarch, Fascism, Federal, Flywheel, G, Gauleiter, Gerontocracy, Gov, Grieve, Gubernator, Guv, Gynarchy, Hagiarchy, Hagiocracy, Hague, Hajjaz, Hakim, Harmost, HE, Helm, Heptarchy, Hexarchy, Hierocracy, Home rule, Honcho, Hospodar, Imperialism, Ins, Inspector, Isocracy, Junta, Kaimakam, Kakistocracy, Kawanatanga, Kebele, Kemalism, Khalifate, Khan, Kleptocracy, Kremlin, Legate, Local, Majlis, Majorism, Matriarchy, Monarchy, Monocracy, Mudir, Nabob, Naik, Nanny state, Nawab, Nomarch, Nomocracy, Ochlocracy, Oireachtas, Oligarchy, Oppress, Optic®, Pa, Pacha, Padishah, Panjandrum, Party, Pasha, Pater, Patriarchism, Pentarch, Père, Petticoat, Physiocracy, Placemen, Plutocracy, Podesta, Politics, Polity, Polyarchy, Pontius Pilate, Porte, Power, Priest-king, Prison, Proconsul, Propraetor, Proveditor, Provedor(e), Providor, Ptochocracy, Quadrumvirate, Quirinal, Raj, Realpolitik, Rection, Rector, Rectrix, Regency, Regié, Regime(n), Regulator, Reign, Rein, Republican, Ride, → RULE, Satrap, Senate, Serkali, Shogun, Signoria, Sircar, Sirkar, Soviet, Stad(t)holder, Stakhanovism, Statecraft, Steam, Stear, Steer, Stratocracy, Subadar, Subah(dar), Sway, Technocracy, Tetrarchy, Thalassocracy, Thalattocracy, Thatcherism, Thearchy, Theocracy, Theonomy, Third Republic, Timocracy, Totalitarianism, Triarchy, Triumvirate, Tuchun, Tyranny, Vaivode, Vali, Viceregal, Viceroy, Vichy, Vichyssois(e), Voivode, Wali, Warden, Wealsman, Whitehall, White House, Witan, Woiwode, Zupan

**Governess** Duenna, Eyre, Fraulein, Griffin, Mademoiselle, Nursery, Prism, Vicereine

**Government revenue** Jaghir(e), Jagir

**Gown** Banian, Banyan, Djellaba(h), Dressing, Empire, Geneva, Green, Housecoat, Jellaba(h), Johnny, Kimono, Kirtle, Manteau, Manto, Mantua, Manty, Mazarine, Morning, Mother Hubbard, Negligee, Peignoir, Polonaise, Robe, Sack, Silk, Slammakin, Slammerkin, Slop, Stola, Stuff, Surplice, Tea, Tunic, Vestment, Wrap(per)

**Grab** Accost, Annexe, Areach, Bag, Clutch, Cly, Collar, Glaum, Grapnel, Hold, Holt, Nab, Rap, Reach, Seise, Seize, Snaffle, → SNATCH, Steal, Swipe, Usurp, Wrest

**Gracchi** Jewels

**Grace(s), Graceful** Aglaia, Airy, Amazing, Amenity, Amnesty, Anna, Bad, Beauty, Become, Benediction, Ben(t)sh, Bethankit, Blessing, Charis(ma), Charites, Charity, Cooperating, Cricketer, Darling, Dr, Elegance, Eloquent, Euphrosyne, Fluent, Gainly, Genteel, Genty, Godliness, Grazioso, Handsome, Honour, Light, Lithe, Mense, Mercy, Molinism, Mordent, Omnium, Ornament, Plastique, Poise, Polish, Pralltriller, Prayer, Sacrament, Sanctity, Saving, Spirituelle, Streamlined, Style, Svelte, Thalia, Thanks, Thanksgiving, Tuesday, WG, Willowy

**Graceless** Gauche, Inelegant

**Grace note** Nachschlag

**Gracious** Benign, By George, Charismatic, Gee, Generous, Good, Handsome, Hend, Lord, Mamma mia, Merciful, Polite

**Grackle** Boattail

**Gradation** Ablaut, Cline, Degree, Nuance, Stage

**Grade, Gradient** Alpha, Analyse, Angle, Assort, Beta, Bubs, Class(ify), Conservation, Dan, Degree, Delta, Echelon, Etat, Gamma, Geothermal, Gon, Gride, Hierarchy, Inclination, Kyu, Lapse, Level, Measure, Order, Ordinary, Pressure, Rank, Reserve, Score, Seed, Slope, Stage, Standard, Status, Temperature, Thermocline, Tier

**Gradual** Gentle, Grail, Imperceptible, Inchmeal, Piecemeal, Slow

**Graduate, Graduation** Alumnus, BA, Bachelor, Calibrate, Capping, Classman, Incept, Laureateship, Licentiate, LlB, MA, Master, Nuance, Optime, Ovate

**Graffiti** Bomb, Doodle, Tag, Tagger

**Graft(ing)** Anaplasty, Autoplasty, Bone-marrow, Boodle, Bribery, Bud, Bypass, Cion, Cluster, Corneal, Coronary bypass, Crown, Dermatoplasty, Dishonesty, Ditch, Dub, Enarch, Enrace, Flap, Hard, Heterogony, Heteroplasty, Imp, Implant, Inarch, Inoculate, Payola, Pomato, Racket, Scion, Shoot, Sien(t), Skin, Slip, Syen, Transplant, Whip, Ympe

**Grail** Chalice, Cup, Sangraal, Sangrail, Sangreal

**Grain(y), Grains** Bajra, Bajree, Bajri, Barley(corn), Bear, Bere, Boll, Bran, Cereal, Corn, Couscous, Crop, Curn, Curn(e)y, Cuscus, Distillers', D(o)urra, Dye, Extine, Floor, Frumentation, Gr, Graddan, Granule, Grit(s), Groats, Grout, Grumose, Intine, Kaoliang, Knaveship, Malaguetta, Malt, Mashlam, Mashlin, Mashloch, Mashlum, Maslin, Meal, Mealie, Millet, Milo, Minim, Mongcorn, Oats, Orzo, Panic(k), Pannick, Paste, Pickle, Pinole, Pollen, Polynology, Popcorn, Proso, Psyllium, Puckle, Quarter, Quinoa, Rabi, Raggee, Raggy, Ragi, Rhy, Rye, Sand, Scruple, Seed, Semolina, Semsem, Sorghum, Spelt, Statolith, Tef(f), Thirlage, Tola, Touch, Wheat, Wheatcorn, Wholemeal

▷**Grain** *may indicate* wood

**Grain-eater** Granivore

**Gram** Black, Chich, Chick-pea, Green, Teen, Tene, Urd

**Grammar(ian), Grammatical** Ablative absolute, Accidence, Amphibology, Anacoluthia, Anacoluthon, Anaphora, Anastrophe, Case, Cataphora, Categorical, Causative, Deixis, Donat, Donet, Generative, Gr, Inessive, Linguistics, Montague, Paradigm, Parataxis, Paucal, Pivot, Primer, Priscianist, Priscianus, Protasis, Relational, Scholiast, Stratificational, Syndetic, Syndeton, Synectics, Synesis, Syntax, Systemics, Tagmeme, Transformational, Trivium, Typto, Universal, Valency

**Gramophone** Record player, Victrolla®

**Grampus** Orc(a), Risso's dolphin, Thresher-whale, Whale

**Granary** Barn, Girnel, Silo

**Grand(eur), Grandiose** Big, Canyon, Concert, Epical, Flugel, G, Gorgeous, Guignol, High-faluting, Homeric, Hotel, Imposing, K, La(h)-di-da(h), Long, Lordly, Magnificent, Majestic, Megalomania, National, Noble, Overblown, Palatial, Piano(forte), Pompous, Regal, Spectacular, Splendid, Stately, Stoor, Stour, Stowre, Sture, Sublime, Superb, Swell, Tour

**Grandchild** Mokopuna, Niece, Oe, Oy(e)

**Grand Duchess** Anastasia

**Grandee** Adelantado, Aristo, Don, Magnifico

**Grandfather** Ancient, Avital, Clock, Goodsire, Gramps, Gudesire, Gutcher, Luckie-dad, Oldster, Old-timer, Oupa

**Grandmother** Babushka, Beldam, Gran(nie), Granny, Gude dame, Luckie, Moses, Nan(a), Nokomis, Ouma

**Grandparent(al)** Aval, Avital

**Grand Prix** Race(-cup)

**Grandsire** Peal

**Grange** Moated

**Granite** Aberdeen, Adamant, Chinastone, Graphic, Greisen, Luxul(l)ianite, Luxulyanite, NH, Pegmatite, Protogine

**Grannie, Granny** Cowl, Forebear, Knot, Nan(a), Trot

**Grant(ed)** Accord, Agree, Aid, Allot, Allow, Assign, Authorise, Award, Benefaction, Bestow, Beteem(e), Block, Bounty, Bursary, Carta, Cary, Cede, Charta, Charter, Concession, → **CONFER**, Cy, Datum, Endow, Enfranchise, Exhibition, Feoff, General, Give, Hugh, Infeudation, Land, Lend, Let, License, Munich, Obreption, Patent, President, Regium donum, Scholarship, Send, Shapps, Sop, Subsidy, Subvention, Supply, Teene, Ulysses, Ure, Vouchsafe, Yeven, Yield

**Granule, Granulate(d)** Chondrule, Grit, Kern, Otolith, Pearl, Plastid, Pound, Prill, Saburra, Statolith, Volutin

**Grape(s)** Aligoté, Aubun, Botros, Botryoid, Bullace, Cabernet, Cabernet Sauvignon, Carmenère, Catawba, Cépage, Chardonnay, Chenin blanc, Colombard, Concord, Cot, Delaware, Diamond, Fox, Gamay, Garnacha, Gewurztraminer, Grenache, Haanepoot, Hamburg(h), Hanepoot, Honeypot, Hyacinth, Lambrusco, Malbec, Malmsey, Malvasia, Malvesie, Malvoisie, Marsanne, Merlot, Montepulciano, Muscadel, Muscadine, Muscat(el), Nebbiolo, Noble rot, Oregon, Petite Syrah, Pinot, Pinotage, Pinot blanc, Pinot Chardonnay, Primitivo, Ptisan, Racemose, Raisin, Rape, Riesling, Sangiovese, Sauvignon, Scuppernong, Sea, Sémillon, Sercial, Shiraz, Sour, Staphyline, Steen, Sultana, Sweet-water, Sylvaner, Syrah, Tokay, Uva, Verdelho, Véronique, Vino, Vognier, Wineberry, Zinfandel

**Grapefruit** Pampelmoose, Pomelo, Pompelmouse, Pompelo, Pumple-nose, Shaddock, Ugli®

**Grape-grower** Vigneron, Vine-dresser
**Grapeshot** Mitraille
**Grape-sugar** Glucose
**Grapevine** Gossip, Hearsay, Mocassin telegraph, Moccasin telegraph
**Graph, Graphic(s)** Avatar, Bar, Chart, Clip art, Computer, Contour, Diagram, Histogram, Learning curve, Nomograph, Ogive, Picturesque, Pie (chart), Plot, Profile, Raster, Sine curve, Sonogram, Table, Turtle, Vivid, Waveform, Waveshape
**Graphite** Kish, Pencil-lead, Plumbago
**Grapple(r)** Clinch, Close, Hook, Lock, Struggle, Tentacle, Tussle, Wrestle
**Grasp(ing)** Apprehend, Catch, Clat, Claut, Claw, Clench, Clinch, → CLUTCH, Compass, Comprehend, Fathom, Get, Go-getting, Grab, Grapple, Greedy, Grip(e), Have, Hend, Hold, Hug, Knowledge, Prehend, Prehensile, Purchase, Raptorial, Reach, Realise, Rumble, Seize, Sense, Snap, Snatch, Squeeze, Twig, Uptak(e)
**Grass(land), Grass roots, Grassy** Agrostology, Alang, Alfa(lfa), Arrow, Avena, Bahia, Bamboo, Bang, Barbed wire, Barley, Barnyard, Beard, Bennet, Bent, Bermuda, Betray, Bhang, Blade, Blady, Blue(-eyed), Blue moor, Bog cotton, Bottom, Bristle, Brome-grass, Bromus, Buffalo, Buffel, Bunch, Bush, Campo, Canary, Cane, Canna, Cannach, Carpet, Cat's tail, Cheat, Chess, China, Citronella, Cleavers, Clivers, Clover, Cochlearia, Cocksfoot, Cockspur, Cogon, Cord, Cortaderia, Cotton, Couch, Cow, Crab, Creeping bent, Culm, Cuscus, Cutty, Dactylis, Danthonia, Dari, Darnel, Deergrass, Dhur(r)a, Diss, Divot, Dogstail, Dog's tooth, Dogwheat, Doob, Doura, Dura, Durra, Eatage, Eddish, Eel, Eelwrack, Elephant, Emmer, Ers, Esparto, Feather, Fescue, Finger, Fiorin, Flag, Flinders, Floating, Flote, Fog, Foggage, Foxtail, Gage, Gama-grass, Ganja, Gardener's garters, Glume, Glumella, Goose, Grama, Gramineae, Green(sward), Guinea, Hair, Halfa, Hard, Harestail, Hashish, Hassock, Haulm, Hay, Haycock, Heath(er), Hemp, Herbage, Herd, High veld, Holy, Indian corn, → INFORM, Jawar(i), Job's tears, Johnson, Jowar(i), Kangaroo, Kans, Kentucky blue, Khuskhus, Kikuyu, Knoll, Knot, Lalang, Laund, Lawn, Lay, Lea, Lee, Lemon, Llano, Locusta, Lolium, Lop, Lucern(e), Lyme, Mabela, Machair, Maize, Manna, Marram, Marrum, Mary Jane, Mat, Materass, Matweed, Mead, Meadow(-fescue), Meadow foxtail, Mealies, Melic, Melick, Millet, Milo, Miscanthus, Monkey, Moor, Moss-crop, Nark, Nassella tussock, Nature strip, Negro-corn, Nit, Nose, Nut, Oat, Orange, Orchard, Oryza, Painted, Palet, Pamir, Pampas, Panic, Paspalum, Pasturage, Peach, Pennisetum, Pepper, Persicaria, Phleum, Pilcorn, Plume, Poa, Porcupine, Pot, Purple moor, Puszta, Quack, Quaking, Quick, Quitch, Ramee, Rami(e), Rat, Rat on, Redtop, Reed, Rescue, Rhodes, Rib, Ribbon, Rice, Rips, Roosa, Rotgrass, Rough, Rumble(r), Rusa, Rush, Rye(-brome), Sacaton, Saccharum, Sago, Salt, Sand, Savanna(h), Saw, Scorpion, Scraw, Scurvy, Scutch, Sea-reed, Sedge, Seg, Sesame, Shave, Sheep's fescue, Shop, Sing, Sinsemilla, Sisal, Sneak(er), Snitch, Snout, Snow, Sorghum, Sour-gourd, Sourveld, Spanish, Sparrow, Spear, Spelt, Spike, Spinifex, Splay, Split, Squeal, Squirrel-tail, Squitch, Stag, Star(r), Stipa, Stool-pigeon, Storm, Sudan, Sugar, Sward, Swath(e), Sword, Tape, Taramea, Tare, Tath, Tea, Tef(f), Tell, Teosinte, Timothy, Toad, Toetoe, Toitoi, Triticale, Triticum, True-love, Tuffet, Turf, Tussac, Tussock, Twitch, Veld(t), Vernal, Vetiver, Viper's, Whangee, Wheat, Wheatgrass, Whistleblower, Whitlow, Wild oat, Windlestraw, Wire, Witch, Wood melick, Worm, Yard, Yellow-eyed, Yorkshire fog, Zizania, Zostera, Zoysia
**Grasshopper** Cicada, Cricket, Grig, Katydid, Locust, Long-horned, Meadow, Reeler, Short-horned, Tettix, Wart-biter, Weta
**Grate(r), Grating** Abrade, Burr, Cancelli, Chafe, Chain, Chirk, Creak, Crepitus, Diffraction, Erosure, → FRET, Graticule, Gravelly, Grid, Grill, Grille, Guichet, Guttural, Hack, Haik, Hake, Harsh, Hearth, Heck, Hoarse, Ingle, Interior, Iron, Jar, Lattice, Mort-safe, Nag, Pare, Portcullis, Rasp, Risp, Rub, Ruling, Scrannel, → SCRAPE, Scrat, Scratchy, Scroop, Shred, Siver, Strident, Syver
**Grateful** Beholden, Cinders, Indebted, Obliged
**Gratification, Gratify(ing)** Aggrate, Delight, Hedonism, Indulge, Kick, Masochism, Narcissism, Oblige, Pander, Pleasure, Regale, Reward, Sadism, Satiate, Satisfaction, Sensuous, Venery, Yummy
**Gratin** Tian
**Gratitude** Appreciation, Debt, God 'a mercy, Obligation, Ta, Thanks

**Gratuitous, Gratuity** Baksheesh, Beer-money, Bonsella, Bonus, Bounty, Cumshaw, Dash, Free, Glove-money, Gratis, Lagn(i)appe, Mag(g)s, Needless, Tip

**Grave(yard)** Accent, Arlington, Austere, Barrow, Bass, Bed of honour, Bier, Burial, Carve, Charnel, Chase, Count, Critical, Darga, Demure, Dignified, Drear, Dust, Eorl, God's acre, Heavy, Heinous, Important, Ingroove, Kistvaen, Kurgan, Lair, Long home, Mool, Mould, Mound, Passage, Pit, Sad, Saturnine, Serious, Sober, Solemn, Sombre, Speos, Staid, Stern, Tomb, Watery

**Grave-digger** Bederal, Fossor, Inhumer, Sexton

**Gravel(ly)** Calculus, Channel, Chesil, Chisel, Eskar, Esker, Glareous, Grail(e), Grayle, Grit, Hard, Hoggin(g), Murram, Nonplus, Pay, Pea, Pingo, Scree, Shingle

**Gravitate** Lean

**Gravity** Barycentric, Downforce, G, Geotaxis, Geotropism, Great Attraction, Magnitude, Mascon, Quantum, Sobriety, Specific, Weight(iness), Zero

**Gravy** Baster, Bisto®, Browning, Coin, Jus, Milk, Money, Sauce

**Gravy-boat** Argyle, Argyll

▸**Gray** *see* GREY(ING)

**Grayling** Umber

**Graze, Grazing, Grazier** Abrade, Abrasion, Agist, Bark, Brush, Crease, Crop, Feed, Glance, Gride, Gryde, Heft, Herdwick, Leasow(e), Machair, Moorburn, Muirburn, Pascual, Pastoralist, Pasture, Rake, Rangeland, Scrape, Scrawn, Scuff, Shave, Sheepwalk, Shieling, Transhumance, Zero

**Grease, Greasy** Axle, Baste, Bribe, Creesh, Dope, Dubbing, Elaeolite, Elbow, Enlard, Enseam, Fat, Glit, Lanolin, Lard, Lubricate, Oil, Ointment, Pinguid, Pomade, Rich, Saim, Seam(e), Shearer, Sheep-shearer, Smarm, Smear, Suint, Unctuous

**Great Bear** Arctic

**Great deal** Mort

**Greater, Greatest, Great(ly), Greats** Alfred, Ali, A majori, Astronomical, Brilliant, Bully, Capital, Classical, Colossus, Considerable, Cosmic, Elephantine, Enorm(ous), Ever so, Excellent, Extreme, Fantastic, Gargantuan, Gatsby, Gay, Gey, Gran(d), Grit, Gt, Guns, Hellova, Helluva, Humdinger, Immense, Immortal, Important, Intense, Jumbo, Large, Limit, Lion, Macro, Magic, Magnus, Main, Major, Massive, Mega, Mickle, Mochell, Modern, Monumental, Much, Muchel(l), Muckle, No end, OS, Preponderant, Profound, Proliferation, Rousing, Smashing, Splendiferous, Stoor, Stour, Stupendous, Sture, Sublime, Super, Superb, Superduper, Swingeing, Synergy, Tall, Thrice, Titan(ic), Top notch, Tremendous, Unco, Untold, Utmost, Vast, Voluminous, Wide, Zenith

**Greave** Jamb

**Grebe** Cargoose

**Grecian** Bend, Nose

**Greed(y)** Avarice, Avid, Bulimia, Bulimy, Cupidity, Edacious, Esurient, Gannet, Gare, Grabby, Grip(ple), Gulosity, Guts(e)y, Harpy, Hungry, Insatiable, Itchy-palmed, Killcrop, Lickerish, Liquorish, Mercenary, Money-grubbing, Piggery, Pleonexia, Rapacity, Selfish, Shark's manners, Solan, Voracity, Wolfish

**Greek(s)** Achaean, Achaian, Achilles, Aeolic, Agamemnon, Ajax, Ancient, Aonian, Arcadia, Archimedes, Argive, Aristides, Athenian, Attic, Boeotian, Byzantine, Cadmean, Cleruch, Corinthian, Cretan, Cumae, Cyzicus, Delphian, Demotic, Demotike, Diomedes, Dorian, Doric, Elea, Eoka, Eolic, Epaminondas, Ephebe, Epirus, Euclid, Evzone, Fanariot, Gr, Helladic, Hellene, Hellenic, Hesychast, Homer, Hoplite, Ionian, Isocrates, Italiot(e), Javan, Katharev(o)usa, Klepht, Koine, Laconian, Lapith, Late, Leonidas, Linear B, Locrian, Lucian, Lysander, Macedonia, Medieval, Middle, Milesian, Modern, Molossian, Momus, Nestor, Nike, Nostos, Orestes, Paestum, Patroclus, Pelasgic, Pelopid, Perseus, Phanariot, Pythagoras, Romaic, Samiot, Seminole, Spartacus, Spartan, Stagirite, Strabo, Sybarite, Tean, Teian, Theban, Thersites, Theseus, Thessal(on)ian, Thracian, Timon, Typto, Uniat, Xenophon, Zorba

**Green(ery)** Almond, Apple, Aqua, Avocado, Baggy, Bice, Biliverdin, Bleaching, Bottle, Bowling, Caesious, Callow, Celadon, Cerulein, Chard, Chartreuse, Chlorophyll, Chrome, Citron, Cole, Collard, Common, Copper, Corbeau, Crown, Cyan, Dioptase, Eau de nil, Eco-,

Ecofreak, Ecofriendly, Ecologic, Econut, Emerald, Emerande, Envious, Environmentalist, Erin, Fingers, Foliage, Forest, Fuchsin, Fundie, Fundy, Gaudy, Glaucous, Go, Goddess, Grass, Gretna, Gull, Herbage, Immature, Inexpert, Jade, Jungle, Kendal, Kensal, Khaki, L, Lawn, Lead-free, Leafage, Lime, Lincoln, Loden, Lovat, Mead, Monastral®, Moss, Moulding, Naive, Neonate, New, Nile, Oasis, Olive, Organic, Paris, Pea, Peridot, Pistachio, Porraceous, Putting, Raw, Realo, Reseda, Rifle, Rink, Rookie, Sage, Sap, Scheele's, Sea, Seasick, Shaw, Sludge, Smaragdine, Sward, Teal, Tender, Terre-vert, Tiro, Turacoverdin, Tyro, Unfledged, Uninitiated, Unripe, Unsophisticated, Untrained, Uranite, Verdant, Verd antique, Verdigris, Verdure, Vert, Village, Virent, Vir(id)escent, Virid, Viridian, Wide-eyed, Yearn, Young

**Greenback** Dollar

**Greenheart** Bebeeru

**Greenhorn** Baby, Dupe, Ingenue, Johnny-raw, Naif, Novice, Put(t), Rookie, Sucker, Tenderfoot

**Greenhouse** Conservatory, Coolhouse, Orangery, Phytotron, Polytunnel

**Greenland(er)** Inuit

**Greens** Broccoli, Cabbage, Calabrese, Cash, Castor, Mangetout, Sprout, Vegetable(s)

**Greet, Greeting(s)** Abrazo, Accost, Air-kiss, All hail, Aloha, Arvo, Banzai, Benedicite, Bid, Blubber, Bonsoir, Card, Chimo, Ciao, Curtsey, Den, G'day, Glad hand, Golden hello, Gorillagram, Hail, Hallo, Halse, Handclasp, Handshake, Haway, Heil, Heita, Hello, Herald, Hi, High-five, Hiya, Hongi, How, How d'ye do, Howsit, Jai Hind, Jambo, Kia ora, Kiss, Kissagram, Mihi, Mwah, Namaskar, Namaste, Respects, Salaam, Salam alaikum, Salue, Salute, Salve, Save you, Sd, Shalom, Shalom aleichem, Sorry, Strippagram, Strippergram, Tena koe, Tena korua, Tena koutou, Wave, Weep, → **WELCOME**, Wellmet, Wotcha, Wotcher, Yo

**Gregarious** Extrovert, Outgoing, Social

**Gregorian** Chant, NS, Plagal

▸**Gremlin** *see* **GOBLIN**

**Grenade, Grenadier** Bomb, Egg, Fragmentation, Hand, Mills, Pineapple, Rat-tail, Rifle, Stun

**Grenadine(s)** Bequia, Canounan, Mustique, Union Island

**Greta** Garbo

**Grey(ing), Gray, Greybeard** Age, Agnes, Argent, Ashen, Ashy, Battleship, Beige, Bloncket, C(a)esius, Charcoal, Cinereous, Clair de lune, Dapple, Dorian, Dove, Drab, Earl, Ecru, Elegist, Feldgrau, Field, Glaucous, Gloomy, Gr, Gridelin, Griesie, Gries(l)y, Grise, Grisy, Grizzled, Gunmetal, Gy, Hoary, Hodden, Hore, Inn, Iron, Leaden, Liard, Lipizzaner, Livid, Lloyd, Lucia, Lyart, Mouse-coloured, Neutral, Oldster, Olive drab, Oyster, Pearl, Pepper and salt, Perse, Pewter, Poliosis, Putty, Sclate, Slaty, Steel, Taupe, Zane

**Greyfriars** Bunter, Magnet

**Greyhound** Grew, Italian, Lapdog, Longtail, Ocean, Persian, Saluki, Sapling, Whippet

**Grey matter** Cinerea

**Gricer** Trainspotter

**Grid(dle), Gridiron** Bar, Barbecue, Brandreth, Cattle, Control, Dot matrix, Grate, Graticule, Grating, Grill, Lattice, National, Network, Reseau, Reticle, Roo-bar, Schema, Screen, Starting, Suppressor, Tava(h), Tawa, Windscale

**Gride** Creak, Grate

**Gridlock** Stalemate

**Grief, Grievance, Grieve, Grievous** Anguish, Axe, Bemoan, Bitter, Complaint, Condole, Cry, Dear(e), Deere, Distress, Dole, Dolour, Eyedrop, Gram(e), Gravamen, Grudge, Heartbreak, Hone, Illy, Io, Lamentation, → **MISERY**, Monody, Mourn, Noyous, O(c)hone, Overset, Pain, Pathetic, Peeve, Pity, Plaint, Plangent, Rue, Score, Sore, Sorrow, Tears, Teen, Tene, Tragic, Wayment, Weeping, Woe, Wrong

**Griffin** Gripe, Grype, Novice, Pony

**Grill(er), Grilling** Barbecue, Braai, Brander, Broil, Carbonado, Crisp, Cross-examine, Devil, Gridiron, Inquisition, Interrogate, Kebab, Mixed, Pump, Question, Rack, Radiator, Reja, Siver, Yakimona

**Grim** Austere, Dire, Dour, Forbidding, Gaunt, Glum, Grave, Grysie, Gurly, Hard, Hideous, Macabre, Reaper, Stern

▷**Grim** *may indicate* an anagram

**Grimace** Face, Girn, Moe, Mop, Moue, Mouth, Mow, Murgeon, Pout, Wince

**Grime(s), Grimy** Colly, Coom, Dirt, Filth, Grubby, Grunge, Peter, Rechie, Reechie, Reechy, Smoke, Soil, Soot, Sweep, Tash

**Grin** Cheesy, Fleer, Girn, Leer, Risus, Simper, Smile, Smirk, Sneer

**Grind(er), Grinding** Angle, Bray, Bruxism, Chew, Coffee, Crunch, →CRUSH, Daily, Droil, Drudgery, Gnash, Grate, Graunch, Grit, Home, Kern, Kibble, Labour, Levigate, Mano, Metate, Mill, Mince, Molar, Muller, Offhand, Pestle, Powder, Premolar, Pug, Pulpstone, Pulverise, Rat-race, Slog, Stamp, Triturate

**Grip(ping), Gripper** Absorb, Adhesion, Arm lock, Ascendeur, Bite, Chuck, Clam, Clamp, Cleat, Clench, Clip, Clutch, Craple, Dog, Duffelbag, Embrace, Engrasp, Enthral, Foothold, Friction, Get, Grapple, →GRASP, Haft, Hair, Hairpin, Hand(fast), Handbag, Handhold, Headlock, Hend, Hold, Hug, Interesting, Jaw, Key, Kirby®, Lewis, Non-slip, Obsess, Pincer, Pinion, Pistol, Prehensile, Purchase, Raven, Rhine, Roadholding, Sally, Setscrew, Sipe, Strain, Streigne, Stud, Thrill, Tongs, Traction, Tread, Twist, Valise, Vice, Walise, Wrestle

**Gripe(s)** Beef, Colic, Complain, Ditch, Grasp, Grievance, Griffin, Grouse, Ileus, Pain, Tormina, Whine

**Grisly** Gory, Macabre

**Grist** Burden

**Gristle, Gristly** Cartilage, Chondroid, Epiglottis, Lytta, Proteoglycan, Raven's bone

**Grit(s), Gritty** Blinding, Clench, Fibre, Gnash, Granular, Grate, Guts, Hominy, Mattress, Millstone, Nerve, Pennant, Pluck, Resolution, Sabulose, Sand, Shingle, Swarf, Tenacity, Toughness, Valour, Yorkshire

**Gritty** Tacky, Ugly

**Grizzle(d)** Grey

**Groan(er), Groaning** Bewail, Bing, Creak, Moan, Overladen, Sigh, Titus

**Grocer(y)** Dairy, Epicier, Grasshopper, Jorrocks, Pepperer, Symbol

**Grog(gy)** Dazed, Queasy, Shaky

**Groin** Gnarr, Inguinal, Lisk

**Groom(ed)** Brush, Coistrel, Coistril, Comb, Curry, Dress, Fettler, Husband, Kempt, Neaten, Ostler, Palfrenier, Paranymph, Preen, Primp, Prink, Rub down, S(a)ice, Smarten, Soigne, Spouse, Spruce up, Strapper, Syce, Tiger, Tracer, Train, Valet, Wrangler

▷**Groom** *may indicate* an anagram

**Groove(d), Grooves, Groovy** Bezel, Canal, Cannelure, Chamfer, Channel, Chase, Clevis, Cool, Coulisse, Croze, Dièdre, Exarate, Fire-plough, Fissure, Flute, Fuller, Furr, Furrow, Glyph, Gouge, Hill and dale, Kerf, Key-seat, Keyway, Lead-in, Lead-out, Nock, Notch, Oche, Pod, Quirk, Rabbet, Race(way), Raggle, Raphe, Rare, Rebate, Rif(f)le, Rifling, Rigol(l), Rout, →RUT, Scrobe, Scrobiculate, Sipe, Slot, Striate, Sulcus, Thread, Throat, Track, Trough, Vallecula

**Grope(r)** À tâtons, Feel, Fumble, Grabble, Hapuka, Ripe, Scrabble

**Gross** All-up, Coarse, Coarse-grained, Complete, Crass, Dense, Earn, Earthy, Flagrant, Frankish, Fustilugs, Giant, Gr, Loathsome, Material, Obese, Obscene, Outsize, Overweight, Pre-tax, Rank, Ribald, Rough, Stupid, Sum, Whole

▷**Gross** *may indicate* an anagram

**Grotesque** Antic, Bizarre, Fantastic, Fright, Gargoyle, Macaroni, Magot, Mascaron, Outlandish, Rabelaisian, Risible, Rococo, Teras

**Grotto** Antre, Cave, Lupercal

**Grotty** Tacky, Ugly

**Grouch** Crosspatch

**Grouchy** Irascible

**Ground(ed), Grounds** Abthane, Acreage, Arena, Astroturf, A terre, Basis, Bottom, Breeding, Campus, Cause, Chewed, Clod, Coffee, Common, Criterion, Crushed, Deck, Dregs, Eard, Earth, Edgbaston, Epig(a)eal, Epig(a)ean, Epigene, Epig(a)eous, Estate, Etching, Floor, Footing, Forbidden, Gathering, Grated, Grist, Grouts, Happy hunting, Headingley, High, Holding, Home, Hunting, Justification, Lees, Leeway, Lek, Lord's, Lot, Marl, Meadow, Mealed, Middle, Motive, Neutral, Occasion, Organ, Oval, Parade, Piste, Pitch, Plat, Pleasure,

Plot, Policy, Proving, Quad, → REASON, Rec(reation), Réseau, Ring, Sandlot, Sediment, Skittle, Slade, Soil, Solum, Sports, Stadium, Stamping, Strand, Terra, Terrain, Tiltyard, Tom Tiddler's, Touch, Tract, Training, Turf, Udal, Vantage, Venue, Waste(land), Yard, Yird

▷**Ground** *may indicate* an anagram

**Groundbait** Chum

**Ground-breaker** Pioneer, Van(guard)

**Ground-crew** Erk

**Grounding(s)** Rabble

**Ground-rent** Crevasse

**Groundsheet** Hutchie

**Groundsman** Greenkeeper

**Groundwork** Research

**Group(ie), Grouping** ABBA, Abelian, Acyl, Affinity, Age, Al Fatah, Align, 'A' list, Apparat, Bananarama, Band, Batch, Battle, Beatles, Bee, Bevy, Bloc(k), Blood, Bloomsbury, Board, Body, Boyband, Bracket, Bratpack, Break-out, Bruges, Bunch, Cabal, Caboodle, Cadre, Camarilla, Camp, Cartel, Category, Caucus, Cave, Cell, Cenacle, Chain, Choir, Chordata, Circle, Clade, Clan, Class(is), Clique, Clump, Cluster, Clutch, Coachload, Cohort, Colony, Combo, Committee, Commune, Community, Company, Complex, Concertino, Confraternity, Conglomerate, Congregation, Consort(ium), Constellation, Contact, Contingent, Control, Convoy, Coterie, Covey, Crew, Decile, Dectet, Delegation, Deme, Demi-monde, Denomination, Department, Detachment, Detail, Division, Draft, Drove, En bloc, Enclave, Encounter, Ensemble, Faction, Family, Fascio, Fauna, Federation, Fleet, Flora, Focus, Fold, Follower, Fraternity, Front, Functional, Gaggle, Galère, Gang, Gathering, Gemeinschaft, Gender, Generation, Genotype, Genus, Gesellschaft, Ginger, Globe, Guild, Hapu, Hardcore, Heading, Herd, Hexad, Hirsel, House, Household, Huddle, Income, In-crowd, Intake, Interest, Internecine, Junction, Keiretsu, Ketone, Kit, Knob, Knot, Komsomol, League, Led Zeppelin, Lichfield, Linkage, Lobby, Local, Lot, Lumpenproletariat, Machine, Mafia, Majority, Marathon, Marshal, Minority, Minyan, Movement, Nest, Network, Nexus, Oasis, Octuor, Opus Dei, Order, Outfit, Oxford, Pack(et), Panel, Parti, Party, Passel, Peer, Phalange, Phalanx, Phratry, Phylum, Platoon, Pleiad, PLO, Plump, Pocket, Pod, Point, Pool, Pop, Portlandian, Posse, Powerbase, Pressure, Prosthetic, Push, Quartet, Quincunx, Race, Raceme, Racemose, Rap, Reading, Retinue, Ring, Rush, Salon, School, Sector, Seminar, Senate, Septet, Series, Set, Several, Sex, Shoal, Shower, Social, Society, Sorority, Sort, Sorus, Species, Splinter, Squad(ron), Stand, Status Quo, Stick, Strain, Stream, String, Study, Subclass, Subculture, Subfamily, Sub-general, Sub-order, Subphylum, Subset, Subspecies, Support, Swarm, Symbol, Syndicate, Synectics, Syntagm, System, T, Tableau, Tales, Task force, Taxon, Team, Tetrad, The few, Tithing, Topological, Trainband, T-Rex, Triad, Tribe, Tribune, Trilogy, Trio, Troika, Troop, Troupe, TU, Umbrella, Undecimole, Union, Unit, Usenet®, User, Vertical, Vigilante, Wing, Workshop, Zaibatsu, Zupa

**Grouse** Bellyache, Black, Blackcock, Bleat, Blue, Caper(caillie), Capercailzie, Covey, Game, Gorcock, Greyhen, Gripe, Growl, Grumble, Hazel-hen, Heath-cock, Heathfowl, Heath-hen, Jeremiad, Kvetch, Moan, Moorcock, Moorfowl, Moor-pout, Muir-poot, Muir-pout, Mutter, Natter, Peeve, Pintail, Prairie chicken, Prairie-hen, Ptarmigan, Rail, Red, Red game, Resent, Ruffed, Rype(r), Sage, Sand, Sharp-tailed, Snarl, Spruce, Squawk, Twelfth, Wheenge, Willow, W(h)inge

**Grout** Cement, Lees

**Grove** Academy, Arboretum, Bosk, Bosquet, Copse, Glade, Hurst, Lyceum, Motte, Nemoral, Orchard, Orchat, Silva, Tope

**Grovel** Cheese, Crawl, Creep, Fawn, Ko(w)tow, Worm

**Grow(ing), Grow out, Growth** Accrete, Accrue, Acromegaly, Adenoma, Aggrandisement, Angioma, Apophysis, Arborescence, Auxesis, Bedeguar, Birthrate, Boom, Braird, Breer, Budding, Build out, Bunion, Burgeon, Bushiness, Carcinoma, Car(b)uncle, Chancre, Cheloid, Chickweed, Cholelith, Chondroma, Compensatory, Condyloma, Corn, Crescendo, Crescent, Crop, Culture, Cyst, Down, Dysplasia, Ectopia, Edema, Ellagic, Enate, Enchondroma, Enlarge, Epiboly, Epinasty, Epitaxy, Excrescence, Exostosis, Expansion, Exponential, Fibroid, Fibrosis, Flor, Flourish, Flush, Gain, Gall, Germinate, Get, Glareal,

Goitre, Groundswell, Hair, Hepatocele, Hummie, Hyperostosis, Hypertrophy, Hyponasty, Increase, Involucrum, Keloidal, Keratosis, Knee, Knur(r), Lichen, Lipoma, Mole, Monopodial, Moss, Mould, Mushroom, Myoma, Neoplasia, Neoplasm, Nur(r), Oak-nut, Oasis, Oedema, Oncology, Osselet, Osteoma, Osteophyte, Pharming, Polyp, Polypus, Proleg, Proliferate, Rampant, Rank, Scirrhus, Scopa, Septal, Shoot, Snowball, Spavin, →**SPROUT**, Stalagmite, Stand, Stipule, Swelling, Sympodial, Tariff, Thigmotropism, Thrive, Trichome, →**TUMOUR**, Tylosis, Upsurge, Vegetable, Vegetate, Wart, Wax, Weed, Witches'-broom, Wox, Zeatin

▷**Grow(n)** *may indicate* an anagram

**Growl(er), Growling** Fremescent, Gnar, Groin, Grr, Gurl, Iceberg, Knar, Roar(e), Roin, Royne, Snar(l)

**Grown up** Adult, Mature, Risen

**Groyne** Breakwater, Mole

**Grub(by)** Assart, Aweto, Bardie, Bardy, Bookworm, Caddis, Caterpillar, Cheer, Chow, Chrysalis, Deracinate, Dig, Eats, Fare, Fodder, →**FOOD**, Gentle, Groo-groo, Gru-gru, Inchworm, Larva, Leatherjacket, Maggot, Mawk, Mess, Nosh, Palmerworm, Peck, Pupa, Root(le), Rout, Rowt, Sap, Shopsoiled, Slave, Stub, Tired, Wireworm, Witchetty, Worm, Wroot

**Grudge, Grudging** Chip, Derry, Envy, Grievance, Grutch, Resent, Score, Sparse, Spite, Spleen, Sting

**Gruel** Brochan, Bross, Kasha, Loblolly, Skilligalee, Skilligolee, Skilly

**Gruesome** Ghastly, Gory, Grisly, Grooly, Horror, Livid, Macaberesque, Macabre, →**MORBID**, Sick

**Gruff** Guttural, Hoarse, Husky, Surly

**Grumble** Beef, Bellyache, Bitch, Bleat, Chunter, Crab, Croak, Girn, Gripe, Grizzle, Groin, Growl, Kvetch, Moan, Mump, Murmur, Mutter, Nark, Natter, Repine, Rumble, Whinge, Yammer

**Grump(y)** Attercop, Bearish, Crabby, Cross, Curmudgeon, Ettercap, Grouchy, Moody, Ogre(ish), Sore-headed, Sourpuss, Surly, Testy

**Grunt** Groin, Grumph, Humph, Oink, Pigfish, Spanish, Ugh, Wheugh

**Guacamole** Avocado

**Guano** Dung, Sombrerite

**Guanoco** Llama

**Guarantee(d)** Accredit, Assure, Attest, Avouch, Barclaycard®, Certify, Cheque card, Collateral, Ensure, Fail-safe, Gage, Hallmark, Insure, Mainprise, Money-back, Pignerate, Pignorate, →**PLEDGE**, Plight, Promise, Ring fence, Seal, Secure, Sponsion, Surety, Underwrite, →**VOUCHSAFE**, Warn, Warrandice, Warrant(y)

**Guard(ed), Guards** Acolouthos, Advance, Apron, Armed, Beefeaters, Blues, Bostangi, Bouncer, Bracer, Cabiri, Cage, Cag(e)y, Cattle, Centinel(l), Centry, Cerberus, Chamfrain, Chaperon(e), Chary, Cheesemongers, Cherry-pickers, Coast, Coldstream, Colour, Conductor, Cordon, Crinoline, Curator, Custodian, Custos, Defend, Diehards, Dragoons, Dress, Duenna, Ensure, Equerry, Escort, Eunuch, Excubant, Exon, Fence, Fender, Gaoler, Gateman, Gauntlet, Grenadiers, Greys, Hedge, Home, Horse, Immunise, INS, Insure, Irish, Iron, Jaga, Jailer, Keep, Knuckle-bow, Lancers, Life, Lilywhites, Look out, Mask, Militia, Mort-safe, Mudflap, Muzzle, National, Nightwatch(man), Noncommital, Nutcrackers, Old, →**ON GUARD**, Out-rider, Out-sentry, Pad, Palace, Patrol, Picket, Point, Policeman, Praetorian, Preserve, →**PROTECT**, Provost, Quillon, Rail, Red, Ride, Roof, Scots, Screw, Secure, Security, Sentinel, Sentry, Shadow, Shelter, Shield, Shin, Shopping, Shotgun, Sky marshal, Splashback, Splashboard, Splasher, SS, Strelitz, Streltzi, Swiss, Switzer, Tapadera, Tapadero, Tile, Toecap, Tsuba, Turnkey, Vambrace, Vamplate, Varangian, Vigilante, Visor, Wage, Wait(e), Ward, Warder, Wary, Watch (and ward), Watchdog, Watchman, Wear, Weir, Welsh, Wire, Yeoman

**Guardian(ship)** Agathodaimon, Altair, Angel, Argus, Caretaker, Chaperone, Curator, Custodian, Custos, Daily, Dragon, Gemini, Granthi, Griffin, Griffon, Gryfon, Gryphon, Hafiz, Janus, Julius, Legal, Miminger, Patron, Protector, Templar, Trustee, Tutelage, Tutelar(y), Tutor, Warder, Watchdog, Xerxes

**Guatemala(n)** Mam

**Gudgeon** Fish, Pin, Trunnion

**Guenon** Grivet, Vervet
**Guerdon** Reward
**Guer(r)illa** Bushwhacker, Chetnik, Comitadji, Contra, ETA, Fedayee, Franc-tireur, Gook, Haiduk, Heyduck, Irregular, Khmer Rouge, Komitaji, Maquis, Mujahadeen, Mujahedeen, Mujahed(d)in, Mujahideen, Partisan, Phalanx, Red Brigade, Tamil Tiger, Terrorist, Tupamaro, Urban, Viet Cong, Zapata, Zapatista
**Guernsey** Sweater
**Guess** Aim, Aread, Arede, Arreede, Assume, Augur, Conjecture, Divine, Educated, Estimate, Harp, Hazard, Hunch, Imagine, Infer, Inspired, Level, Long shot, Mor(r)a, Mull, Potshot, Predict, Psych out, Reckon, Shot, Speculate, Stab, Suppose, Surmise, Theorise, Venture
**Guessing game** Handy-dandy, Mor(r)a, Quiz
**Guess-work** Extrapolation, Idea
**Guest(s)** Caller, Company, House-party, Inquiline, Invitee, Parasite, Paying, PG, Resident, Symbion(t), Symphile, Synoecete, Umbra, Visitant, → VISITOR, Xenial
**Guesthouse** B & B, Minshuku, Taverna, Xenodochium
**Guff** Bosh, Gas
**Guffaw** Belly laugh
**Guianian** S(a)ouari
**Guidance, Guide, Guiding, Guideline** Advice, Antibarbus, A to Z, Aunt, Auspice, AZ, Baedeker, Befriend, Bradshaw, Cicerone, Clue, Code, Command, Concordance, Conduct, Control, Counsel, Courier, Cox, Curb, Cursor, Cybrary, Director(y), Docent, Dragoman, Drive, Engineer, → ESCORT, Field, Form, Gillie, Graticule, Helm, Heuristic, Homing, Index, Inertial, Inspire, Itinerary, Jig, Key, Lad, Landmark, Lead, Lodestar, Mahatma, Manoeuvre, Map, Mark, Marriage, Mentor, Michelin, Missile, Mitre box, Model, Navaid, Navigate, Nose, Pelorus, Pilot, Pointer, Postil(l)ion, Prescript, Principle, Providence, Queen's, Rainbow, Range, Ranger, Reference, Rein, Relate, Road-book, Rudder, Rule of thumb, Sabot, Satnav, Sea Ranger, Shepherd, Sherpa, Shikaree, Shikari, Sight, Sign, Sixer, Standard, Stear, Steer, Stire, Target, Template, Templet, Terminal, Terrestrial, Tiller, Train, Travelogue, Tutelage, Usher(ette), Vocational, Voyageur, Waymark, Weise, Weize, Wise
**Guild** Artel, Basoche, Company, Freemason, Gyeld, Hanse(atic), Hoastman, League, Mistery, Mystery, Society, Tong, Union
**Guilder** Florin
**Guile** Art, Cunning, Deceit, Dole, Malengine
**Guillotine** Closure, Decapitate, Louisiette, Maiden, Marianne
**Guilt(y)** Affluenza, Albatross, Angst, Blame, Cognovit, Contrite, Culpable, Culprit, Flagitious, Hangdog, Liable, Mea culpa, Nocent, Peccavi, Proven, Redhanded, Remorse, Wicked
**Guinea(s)** Canary, Geordie, Gns, Job, Ls, Meg, Spade
**Guinea-fowl** Pintado
**Guinea-pig** Abyssinian, Agoute, Agouti, Cavie, Cavy, Paca, Subject
**Guinea-worm** Dracunculus
**Guinness** Alec
**Guise** Form, Manner, Semblance, Shape
**Guitar(ist)** Acoustic, Axe(man), Bass, Beck, Bottleneck, Bream, Cithern, Cittern, Dobro®, Electric, Fender®, Fretman, Gittarone, Gittern, Guthrie, Hawaiian, Hendrix, Humbucker, Lute, Lyre, May, Page, Pedal steel, Plankspanker, Samisen, Sancho, Sanko, Segovia, Shamisen, Sitar, Slide, Spanish, Steel, Uke, Ukulele
**Gulf** Aden, Anadyr, Aqaba, Bay, Bothnia, California, Cambay, Campeche, Carpentaria, Chasm, Chihli, Corinth, Cutch, Darien, Dvina, Exmouth, Finland, Fonseca, G, Genoa, Gonaives, Hauraki, Honduras, Iskenderun, Isthmus, Izmit, Joseph Bonaparte, Kutch, Lepanto, Leyte, Lingayen, Lions, Mannar, Martaban, Maw, Mexico, Ob, Oman, Patras, Persian, Pozzuoli, Queen Maud, Rapallo, Riga, St Lawrence, St Vincent, Salerno, Salonika, Saronic, Saros, Siam, Sidra, Sinai, Spencer, Taganrog, Taranto, Thailand, Tongking, Tonkin, Trieste, Tunis, Van Diemen, Venice, Vorago
**Gull(s)** Bamboozle, Black-backed, Bonxie, Cat's paw, Cheat, Cob(b), Cod, Cony, Cozen, Cull(y), Dupe, Easy game, Fool, Geck, Glaucous, Haglet, Have, Hoodwink, Hum, Ivory, Kittiwake, Laridae, Larus, Lie to, Maw, Mew, Mollyhawk, Noodle, Pickmaw, Pigeon, Queer,

Ring-billed, Rook, Sabine's, Saddleback, Scaury, Scourie, Scowrie, Sea-cob, Sea-mew, Sell, Simp, Skua, Sucker, Swart-back, Tern, Tystie, Xema

**Gullet** Crop, Enterate, Maw, Oesophagus, Throat, Weasand-pipe

**Gullible** Credulous, Green, Mug punter, Naive, Starry-eyed, Sucker

**Gulliver** Lemuel

**Gully** Arroyo, Couloir, Donga, Fielder, Geo, Gio, Goe, Grough, Gulch, Infielder, Pit, Rake, Ravine, Sloot, Sluit, Trough, Wadi

**Gulp** Bolt, Draught, Gollop, Quaff, Slug, Sob, → **SWALLOW**, Swig, Swipe, Wolf

**Gum (tree)** Acacia, Acajou, Acaroid, Agar, Algin, Angico, Arabic, Arabin, Arar, Arctic, Asafoetida, Bablah, Balata, Balm, Bandoline, Bdellium, Benjamin, Benzoin, Bloodwood, Blue, Boot, British, Bubble, Cerasin, Chewing, Chicle, Chuddy, Chutty, Coolabah, Courbaril, Cow®, Dextrin(e), Dragon's-blood, Ee-by, Eucalyptus, Euphorbium, Flooded, Frankincense, Galbanum, Gamboge, Ghost, Gingival, → **GLUE**, Goat's-thorn, Gosh, Grey, Guar, Ironbark, Juniper, Karri, Kauri, Lac, La(b)danum, Lentisk, Mastic(h), Mucilage, Myrrh, Nicotine, Olibanum, Opopanax, Oshac, Paste, Red, Resin, River red, Sagapenum, Sarcocolla, Scribbly, Size, Sleep, Snow, Spearmint, Spirit, Starch, Sterculia, Stringybark, Sugar, Sweet, Tacamahac, Tragacanth, Tupelo, Ulmin, Water, White, Xanthan

**Gumbo** Okra

**Gumboil** Parulis

**Gumption** Nous, Spirit

**Gun(fire), Guns, Gunfight** Amusette, Archibald, Archie, Arquebus, Automatic, Barker, Baton, Bazooka, Beanbag, Beretta, Big Bertha, Biscayan, Blunderbuss, Bofors, Bombard, Boortree, Bourtree, Breech(-loader), Bren, Broadside, Brown Bess, Browning, Bulldog, Bullpup, Bundook, Burp, Caliver, Cannonade, Carbine, Carronade, Cement, Chokebore, Chopper, Coehorn, Colt®, Dag, Derringer, Elder, Electron, Elephant, Escopette, Falcon(et), Field, Fieldpiece, Firearm, Fire lock, Flame, Flash, Flintlock, Four-pounder, Fowler, Fowlingpiece, Full-bore, Fusil, Garand, Gas, Gat(ling), Gingal(l), Grease, HA, Hackbut, Half-cock, Harpoon, Harquebus, Heater, Hired, Howitzer, Jezail, Jingal, Kalashnikov, Lewis, Long Tom, Luger®, Machine, Magazine, Magnum, Maroon, Martini-Henry®, Matchlock, Mauser®, Maxim, Metal, Minnie, Minute, Mitrailleuse, Mons Meg, Mortar, Musket(oon), Muzzle-loader, Nail, Needle, Neutron, Noonday, Oerlikon, Ordnance, Over and under, Owen, Paderero, Paterero, Ped(e)rero, Pelican, Perrier, Persuader, Petronel, Piece, Pistol(et), Pompom, Pump (action), Punt, Purdey®, Quaker, Radar, Ray, Repeater, Rev, Revolver, Riot, Rod, Roscoe, Saker, Sarbacane, Saturday night special, Scatter, Self-cocker, Shooter, Shooting iron, Shoot-out, Sidearm, Siege, Smoothbore, Snapha(u)nce, Spear, Speed, Spray, Squirt, Staple, Starting, Sten, Sterculia, Sterling, Stern-cannon, Stern-chaser, Stun, Swivel, Taser®, Tea, Thirty eight, Thompson, Three-pounder, Tier, Time, Tire, Tommy, Tool, Tupelo, Turret, Uzi, Walther, Wesson, Wheel-lock, Young, Zip

**Gunge** Goo, Gowl, Paste

**Gunman** Ace, Assassin, Bandit, Earp, Greaser, Hood, Pistoleer, Sharpshooter, Sniper, Starter

**Gunner, Gunner's assistant** Arquebusier, Arsenal, Artillerist, Cannoneer, Cannonier, Culverineer, Gr, Matross, RA

**Gunpowder** Charcoal, Pebble-powder, Saltpetre, Saucisse, Saucisson

**Gunshot** Bullet, Pellet

**Gunwale** Gunnel, Portland, Portlast, Portoise

**Guppy** Million

**Gurgle** Burble, Clunk, Glug, Gobble, Gollar, Goller, Guggle, Ruckle, Squelch

**Gurnard** Tubfish

**Guru** Bhagwan, Gok Wan, Lifestyle, Pundit, Sadhu, Teacher, Technocrat

**Gush(er), Gushing** Blether, Effusive, → **FLOOD**, Flow, Fountain, Jet, Oil well, Outpour, Rail, Raile, Regurgitate, Rhapsodize, Scaturient, Spew, Spirt, Spout, Spurt, Surge, Too-too

**Gusset** Godet, Gore, Insert, Inset, Mitre

**Gust** Blast, Blore, Flaught, Flaw, Flurry, Puff, Sar, Scud, Squall, Waff

**Gusto** Élan, Enjoyment, Enthusiasm, Relish, Verve, Zest

**Gut(s), Gutty** Abdomen, Archenteron, Balls, Beer, Blind, Bowel(s), Caecum, Chitterlings,

Cloaca, Colon, Disembowel, Draw, Duodenum, Enteral, Enteron, Entrails, Eviscerate, Fore, Gill, Hind, Ileum, Innards, Insides, Kishka, Kyle, Mesaraic, Mesenteron, Mid, Minikin, Moxie, Offal, Omental, Omentum, Purtenance, Remake, Sack, Sand, Snell, Stamina, Staying-power, Strip, Thairm, Tripe, Ventriculus, Viscera

**Gutta-percha** Jelutong, Pontianac, Pontianak

**Gutter(ing)** Arris, Channel, Conduit, Coulisse, Cullis, Grip, Gully, Kennel, Rhone, Rigol(l), Roan, Rone, Runlet, Runnel, Sough, Spout, Strand, Swale, Swayl, Sweal, Sweel

**Guttersnipe** Arab, Gamin, Thief

**Guttural** Faucal, Throaty

**Guy** Backstay, Bo, Burgess, Buster, Cat, Chaff, Clewline, Decamp, Deride, Dude, Effigy, Fall, Fawkes, Fellow, Gibson, Gink, Josh, Mainstay, Mannering, Pan, Parody, Rag, Rib, Ridicule, Rope, Scarecrow, Send up, Stay, Taunt, Tease, Vang, Wise

**Guzzle(d)** Gannet, Gorge, Go(u)rmandize, Overeat, Snarf

**Gwyn** Nell

**Gym(nasium), Gymnast(ic)** Acrobat, Akhara, Arena, Contortionist, Dojo, Exercise, Jungle, Korbut, Lyceum, Palaestra, PE, PT, Real, Rhythmic, Sokol, Trampolinist, Tumbler, Turner, Work out

**Gymnosophist** Yogi

**Gynaecologist** Steptoe

**Gyp** Con

**Gypsum** Alabaster, Gesso, Plaster, Satin spar, Satin-stone, Selenite, Terra alba

**Gypsy, Gipsy** Bohemian, Cagot, Caird, Caqueux, Chai, Chal, Chi, Collibert, Egyptian, Esmeralda, Faw, Gipsen, Gitana, Gitano, Hayraddin, Lavengro, Meg, Rom(any), Rye, Scholar, Tinker, Traveller, Travelling folk, Tsigane, Tzigane, Tzigany, Vagabond, Vlach, Walach, Wanderer, Zigan, Zigeuner, Zincala, Zincalo, Zingaro

**Gyrate** Revolve, Rotate, → **SPIN**, Swirl, Swivel, Twirl

# Hh

**H** Ache, Aitch, Aspirate, Height, Hospital, Hotel, Hydrant, Hydrogen, Zygal
**Haberdasher(y)** Clothier, Dry goods, Ferret, Hosier, Notions
**Habit(s), Habitual, Habituate, Habitué** Accustom, Addiction, Apparel, Assuefaction, Assuetude, Attire, Automatic, Bent, Cacoethes, Chronic, Clothes, Coat, Consuetude, Cowl, Crystal, Custom, Dependency, Diathesis, Dress, Ephod, Frequenter, Garb, Garment, Hand-me-down, Inure, Inveterate, Motley, Mufti, Nature, Outfit, Pathological, Practice, Quirk, Raiment, Regular, Riding, Robe, Rochet, Rote, Routine, Scapular, Schema, Season, Second nature, Set, Soutane, Suit, Surplice, Toge, Trait, Trick, Tway, Usual, Way, Won, Wont, Xerotes
**Habitable, Habitat(ion)** Ecad, Element, Environment, Haunt, Home, Locality, Niche, Pueblo, Refugium, Station, Tel
**Hacienda** Ranch
**Hack(er), Hacking** Blackhat, Chip, Chop, Cough, Cut, Cypherpunk, Drudge, Garble, Gash, Ghost, Grub-Street, Hag, Hash, Hedge-writer, Heel, Hew, Horse, Ink-slinger, Jade, Journo, Mangle, Mutilate, Nag, Nerd, Notch, Nuthatch, Pad, Paper-strainer, Penny-a-liner, Phreak, Pick, Plater, Pot-boiler, Rosinante, Scribble, Script kiddie, Slash, Spurn, Steed, Tadpole, Taper, Tap into, Tiger team, Tussis, Unseam, Warchalking, White hat
**Hackle(s)** Comb, Rough
**Hackney(ed)** Banal, Cab, Cliché, Copybook, Corny, Overuse, Percoct, Platitude, Stale, Threadbare, Tired, Trite, Twice-told, Worn
**Had (to)** Ate, Moten, Must, Obliged, Threw
**Haddock** Arbroath smokie, Findram, Finnan, Fish, Norway, Rizzered, Smoky, Speldin(g), Speldrin(g), Whitefish
**Hades** Dis, Hell, Orcus, Pit, Tartarus
**Haematite** Oligist
**Haemoglobin** Chelate, Hb
**Haemorrhoids** Farmer Giles, Piles
**Hafnium** Hf
**Hag(-like)** Anile, Beldame, Besom, Carlin(e), Crone, Harpy, Harridan, Hell-cat, Hex, Moss, Nickneven, Occasion, Rudas, Runnion, Sibyl, Trot, Underwood, Witch
**Haggard** Drawn, → GAUNT, Pale, Rider, Worn
**Haggis** Kishke
**Haggle** Argue, Badger, → BARGAIN, Barter, Chaffer, Dicker, Horse-trade, Huckster, Niffer, Palter, Prig
**Ha-ha** Dike, So there, Sunk-fence
**Hahnium** Hn
**Hail(er)** Acclaim, Acco(a)st, Ahoy, Ave, Bull-horn, Cheer, Fusillade, Graupel, Greet, Gunfire, Hi, Ho, Megaphone, Salue, Salute, Shower, Signal, Skoal, Skol, Sola, Stentor, Storm, Trumpet, What ho, Whoa-ho-ho
**Hair(y), Haircut, Hairlike, Hair problem/condition, Hair style** Afro, Ailes de pigeon, Ainu, Alopecia, Angora, Backcomb, Baldy, Bang, Barnet, Beard, Beehive, Bingle, Bob, Bouffant, Braid, Brede, Bristle, Brutus, Bumfluff, Bun, Bunches, Bush, Butch, Buzz cut, Cadogan, Camel, Capillary, Catogan, Chignon, Cilia, Cleopatra, Coat, Cockernony, Coif, Coiffure, Comal, Comate, Combings, Comb-over, Comose, Cornrow, Corymbus, Cowlick, Crepe, Crew-cut, Crinal, Crinigerous, Cronet, Crop, Crunch, Cue, Curlicue, DA, Dangerous, Dicey, Dreadlocks, Dubbing, Duck's arse, Ducktail, Ear-lock, Earmuffs, Elf locks, En brosse,

Esau, Excrement, Eyebrow, Eyelash, Feather, Feather-cut, Fetlock, Fibril, Filament, Flat-top, Floccus, Follicle, Forelock, French pleat, French roll, Frenulum, Fringe, Fur, Garconne, Glib(s), Glochidium, Goatee, Guard, Hackles, Heare, Heer(i)e, Highlights, Hippy, Hispid, Hog, Indumentum, Kemp, Kesh, Lanate, Lanugo, Lash, List, Lock, Lovelock, Lowlights, Madarosis, Mane, Marcel, Mohawk, Mohican, Mop, Mophead, Mullet, Muttonchops, Not(t), Number two, Pageboy, Pappus, Pashm, Peekabo(o), Pele's, Pelt, Peppercorn, Perm(anent), Pigtail, Pika, Pile, Pilus, Pincurl, Plait, Plica, Plica Polonica, Pompadour, Ponytail, Poodle cut, Porcupine, Pouf(fe), Pow, Precarious, Prison crop, Psilosis, Puberulent, Pubescent, Pudding basin, Punk, Queue, Quiff, Radicle, Rat-tail, Red mullet, Rhizoid, Risky, Roach, Root, Rug, Rush, Scaldhead, Scalp lock, Scopate, Scopula, Sericeous, Set, Shag, Shingle, Shock, Sideburns, Sidelock, Side-whiskers, Snell, Spikes, Stinging, Strammel, Strand, Strigose, Strummel, Switch, Sycosis, Tache, Tarantual, Tête, Thatch, Tomentose, Tonsure, Toorie, Topknot, Tour(ie), Tragus, Tress, Trichoid, Trichology, Trichome, Trichosis, Trim, Ulotrichous, Updo, Vellus, Velutinous, Vibrissi, Villi, Villosity, Villus, Wedge, Whisker, Widow's peak, Wig, Wiglet, Wisp, → **WOOL**, Xerasia

**Hair-cream, Hair-oil, Hairspray** Conditioner, Lacquer, Pomade

**Hairdresser** Barber, Coiffeur, Comb, Crimper, Friseur, Marcel, Salon, Stylist, Trichologist

**Hairless** Bald, Callow, Glabrate, Glabrescent, Glabrous, Irate

**Hairline** Brow, Nape

**Hairnet** Kell, Snood

**Hairpiece** Frisette, Merkin, Periwig, Postiche, Strand, Toupee, → **WIG**

**Hairpin** Barrette, Bobbypin, Bodkin, Clip, Grip, Slide, U, U-turn

**Hair-shirt** Ab(b)a, Cilice

**Hair-splitter** Pedant

**Haiti** RH

**Hal** Prince

**Halberd** Spontoon

**Halcyon** Calm, Kingfisher, Mild

**Hale(r)** Drag, Healthy, Koruna, Raucle, Robust, Well

**Half, Halve(d)** A demi, Bifid, Bisect, Demi, Dimidiate, Dirempt, Divide, Hemi, Moiety, Outside, Semi, Share, Split, Stand-off, Term

**Half-a-dozen** Six, VI

**Half-asleep, Half-conscious** Dove, Dozy

**Half-baked** Foolish, Mediocre, Samel, Slack-bake

**Half-dead** Alamort

**Half-guinea** Smelt

**Half-hearted** Reluctant, Tepid

**Half-hour** Bell

**Half-pence, Half-penny** Bawbee, Mag, Magpie, Maik, Mail(e), Make, Meg, Obolus, Patrick, Portcullis, Posh, Rap, Wood's

**Half-time** Midhour

**Half-turn** Caracol(e), Demivolt

**Half-wit** Changeling, Mome, Numbskull, Simpleton, → **STUPID**

**Hall** Albert, Anteroom, Apadana, Aske, Assembly, Atrium, Auditorium, Aula, Bachelor's, Ballroom, Banqueting, Basilica, Beer, Bingo, Carnegie, Casino, Chamber, Citadel, City, Concert, Concourse, Corridor, Crosby, Dance, Divinity, Dojo, Domdaniel, Dome, Dotheboys, Ex(h)edra, Festival, Foyer, Free Trade, Gallen, Guild, Haddon, Hardwick, Holkham, Hostel, Ivied, Judgement, Kedleston, Liberty, Lobby, Locksley, Lyme, Megaron, Mess, Moot, Music, Narthex, Newby, Odeon, Palais, Palais de danse, Passage, Prytaneum, Rathaus, Rideau, Salle, Saloon, Speke, Stationer's, Study, Tammany, Tara, Tolsel, Town, Trullen, Valhalla, Vestibule, Village, Walhall(a), Wildfell

**Hallmark(ed)** Brand, Contrôlé, Logo, Platemark, Seal, Stamp

**Hallow(ed)** Consecrate, Revere, Sacred, Worship

**Halloween** Guiser

**Hallucinate, Hallucinating, Hallucination, Hallucinatory, Hallucinogen** Autoscopy, DT's, Fantasy, Formication, Freak, Freak out, Illusion, Image, LSD, Mandrake,

Mescalin, Mirage, Negative, Peyote, Photism, Psilocin, Psilocybin, Psychedelic, Psychotic, Trip

**Halo** Antheolion, Areola, Aura, Aureola, Corona, Galactic, Gloria, Gloriole, Mandorla, Nimbus, Rim, Vesica, Vesica piscis

**Halogen** Iodine

**Halt(er), Halting** Abort, Arrest, Avast, Block, Brake, Bridle, Cavesson, Cease, Cessation, Cesse, Check, Deactivate, End, Full stop, Game, Hackamore, Heave-to, Hilch, Inarticulate, Lame(d), Limp, Moratorium, Noose, Paralyse, Prorogue, Rope, Stall, Standstill, Staw, → STOP, Stopover, Suspend, Toho, Tyburn-tippet, Whistle-stop, Whoa, Widdy

**Ham(s)** Amateur, Barnstormer, Beef, Emote, Flitch, Gammon, Haunch, Hock, Hoke, Hough, Hunker, Jambon, Jamon serrano, Jay, Mutton, Nates, Overact, Overplay, Parma, Pigmeat, Prat, Prosciutto, Radio, Serrano, Spe(c)k, Tiro, Westphalian, York

**Hamburger** Big Mac®, Sloppy joe, Vegeburger

**Hamfisted** Maladroit, Unheppen

**Hamite** Berber, Nilot(e)

**Hamlet(s)** Aldea, Auburn, Cigar, Clachan, Dane, Dorp, Hero, Kraal, Settlement, Stead, Thorp(e), Tower, Vill(age), Wick

**Hammer(ed), Hammerhead, Hammering** About-sledge, Atmospheric, Ballpeen, Ballpein, Beetle, Bone, Bully, Bush, Celt, Claw, Dent, Dolly, Drop, Excudit, Flatten, Fore, Fuller, Gavel, Hack, Incuse, Jack, Kevel, Knap, Knapping, Kusarigama, Lump, Madge, Mall(et), Malleate, Martel(late), Martellato, Maul, Mjol(l)nir, Monkey, Nevel, Oliver, Ossicle, Pane, Pean, Peen, Pein, Pene, Percussion, Percussor, Piledriver, Planish, Plessor, Plexor, Pneumatic, Rawhide, Repoussé, Rip, Rout, Sheep's-foot, Shingle, Sledge, Steam, Stone, Strike, Tack, Tenderizer, Tendon, Tilt, Trip, Trounce, Umbre, Water, Wippen

▷**Hammered** *may indicate* an anagram

**Hammerthrower** Thor

**Hammock** Cott

▷**Hammy** *may indicate* an anagram

**Hamper** Basket, Cabin, Ceroon, Cramp, Cumber, Delay, Encumber, Entrammel, Hamstring, Handicap, Hobble, Hog-tie, Impede, Obstruct, Pad, Pannier, Ped, Pinch, Restrict, Rub, Sero(o)n, Shackle, Stultify, Tangle, Top, Trammel, Tuck

**Hampstead Heath** Teeth

**Hamster** Cricetus, Idea

**Hamstring, Hamstrung** Cramp, Hock, Hox, Lame, Popliteal, Powerless, Thwart

**Hand(s), Hand over, Hand down, Hand-like, Handwriting** Applause, Assist(ance), Bananas, Bequeath, Cacography, Calligraphy, Charge, Chicane, Chirography, Clap(ping), Claque, Club, Clutch, Copperplate, Court, Crabbed, Crew, Cursive, Dab, Daddle, Danny, Dawk, Dead, Deal, Deck, Deliver, Devolve, Donny, Dukes, Dummy, Elder, Extradition, Famble, Fin, Fist, Flipper, Flush, Free, Full (house), Glad, Graphology, Half-text, Help, Helping, Hidden, Hond, Hour, Impart, Iron, Israel, Italian, Jambone, Jamboree, Jemmy, Kana, L, Laydown, Lone, Loof, Man, Maniform, Manual, Manus, Maulers, Medieval, Minute, Mitt(en), Mutton-fist, Nap, Nesk(h)i, Niggle, Operative, Orthography, Ovation, Pad, Palaeography, Palm(atifid), Part, Pass, Paw, Podium, Post, Present, Pud, R, Referral, Rein (arm), Round, Royal flush, Running, Script, Second, Secretary, Signature, Span, Spencerian, Stage, Station, Straight, Sweep, Text, Tiger, Transfer, Uncial, Upper, Whip, Widow, Worker, Yarborough

**Handbag** Caba(s), Grip, Indispensable, Pochette, Purse, Reticule, Valise

**Handbook** Baedeker, Companion, Enchiridion, Guide, Manual, Vade-mecum

**Handcart** Barrow, Wheelbarrow

**Handcuff(s)** Bracelet, Darbies, Golden, Irons, Manacle, Mittens, Nippers, Shackle, Snaps, Wristlet

**Handful** Few, Gowpen, Grip, Hank, Problem, Pugil, Rip(p), V

**Handicap** Bisque, Burden, Cambridgeshire, Disable, Ebor, Encumber, Half-one, Hamper, Hamstring, Hunchback, Impede, Impost, Lame, Liability, Lincolnshire, Mental, → OBSTACLE, Off, Penaliser, Physical, Restrict, Scratch, Weigh(t), Welter-race

**Handicraft** Marquetry

**Handkerchief, Hanky** Bandan(n)a, Belcher, Billy, Buffon, Clout, Curch, Fogle, Foulard, Kleenex®, Madam, Madras, Monteith, Mouchoir, Muckender, Napkin, Nose-rag, Orarium, Romal, Rumal, Sudary, Tissue, Wipe(r)

**Handle(d), Handler, Handling** Ansate, Bail, Bale, Behave, Bitstock, Brake, Broomstick, Cope, Crank, Dead man's, Deal, Doorknob, Dudgeon, Ear, Feel, Field, Finger, Forename, Gaum, Gorm, Grab, Grip, Gunstock, Haft, Helve, Hilt, Hold, Knob, Knub, Logistics, Lug, → MANAGE, Manipulate, Manubrium, Maul, Moniker, Name, Nib, Palp, Paw, Pistol-grip, Pommel, Port-crayon, Process, Roadie, Rounce, Shaft, Snath(e), Snead, Sneath, Sned, Sort out, Staff, Staghorn, Stale, Starting, Steal(e), Steel, Steer, Steil, Stele, Stilt, Stock, Sweep, Tiller, Title, To-name, Touch, Transact, Treat, Twiddle, Use, Whipstock, Wield, Winder, With(e)

**Handmade** Crafted

**Handmaid(en)** Iras, Manicurist, Valkyrie

**Hand-out** Alms, Charity, Dole, Gift, Issue, Release, Sample, Treat

**Handshake** Flesh press, Golden, Press flesh

**Hand-signal** Beck(on), Point, Wave

**Handsome** Adonis, Apollo, Attractive, Beefcake, Bonny, Brave, Comely, Dashing, Dishy, Featuous, Fine, Gracious, Hunky, Kenneth, Liberal, Lush, Resplendent, Rugged, Seemly, Shapely, Tidy

**Handspring, Handstand** Cartwheel, Diamodov

**Hand-to-hand** Mano-a-mano

**Hand-warmer** Muff, Pome

**Hand-washer** Pilate

▸**Handwriting** *see* HAND(S)

**Handy(man)** Accessible, Close, Convenient, Deft, Dext(e)rous, Digit, Factotum, Gemmy, Get-at-able, Jack(-of-all-trades), Jemmy, Near, Nigh, Of use, On site, Palmate, Palmist, Ready, Skilful, Spartan, Useful

**Hang(er), Hanging(s), Hang up** Abeyant, Append, Arras, Aweigh, Chick, Chik, Coat, Curtain, Damn, Dangle, Darn, Depend, Dewitt, Dorser, Dossal, Dossel, Dosser, Drape, Droop, Execute, Exhibit, Filipendulous, Frontal, Gobelin, Hinge, Hoove, Hove(r), Icicle, Kakemono, Kilt, Lime, Lobed, Loll, Lop, Lynch, Mooch, Noose, Nub, Obsession, Oudenarde, Overarch, Peg-out, Pend(ant), Pendulous, Pothook, Preoccupation, Sag, Scenery, Scrag, Set, Sit, Sling, String up, Suspend, Suspercollate, Swag, Swing, Tapestry, Tapet, Tapis, The rope, Toran(a)

**Hangdog** Sheepish

**Hanger-on** Bur(r), Camp-follower, Dewdrop, Lackey, Lappet, Leech, Limpet, Liripoop, Parasite, Satellite, Sponge(r), Sycophant, Tassel, Toady

**Hangman, Hangmen** Bull, Calcraft, Dennis, Derrick, Executor, Gregory, Ketch, Lockman, Marwood, Nubbing-cove, Pierrepoint, Topsman, Word game

**Hangnail** Agnail

**Hangover** Canopy, Cornice, Crapulence, Drape, DT's, Eaves, Executer, Head, Hot coppers, Katzenjammer, Mistletoe, Relic, Remnant, Tester, Valance

**Hank** Bobbin, Coil, Fake, Lock, Skein

**Hanker(ing)** Aspire, Desire, Envy, Hunger, Itch, Long, Thirst, Yearn, Yen

**Hanky-panky** Funny business, Nooky, Skulduggery

**Hannibal** Carthaginian, Lecter, Punic

**Hansard** Minutes

**Hanukkah** Feast of Dedication

**Haphazard** Aimless, Anyhow, Casual, Chance, Desultory, Helter-skelter, Higgledy-piggledy, Hit and miss, Hitty-missy, Irregular, Promiscuous, → RANDOM, Rough and tumble, Scattershot, Slapdash, Willy-nilly

**Hapless** Unlucky

**Happen(ing), Happen to** Afoot, Are, Be, Befall, Befortune, Betide, Chance, Come (about), Crop up, Episode, Evenement, Event(uate), Fall-out, Incident, Materialise, → OCCUR, Pan, Pass, Phenomenon, Prove, Subvene, Thing, Tide, Transpire, Turn up, Ultimate, Worth

**Happiness, Happy** Apposite, Ave, Beatific, Beatitude, Blessed, Bliss, Blithe, Bluebird, Bonny, Carefree, Cheery, Chirpy, Chuffed, Cloud nine, Cock-a-hoop, Content, Dwarf, Ecstatic,

Elated, Eud(a)emony, Euphoric, Exhilarated, Exultant, Felicity, Felix, Fool's paradise, Fortunate, Gaiety, Glad(some), Gleeful, Golden, Goshen, Gruntled, Halcyon, Half-cut, Heaven, Hedonism, High-feather, Inebriated, Jovial, Joy, Jubilant, Kvell, Larry, Light-hearted, Mellow, Merry, Nirvana, OK, Opportune, Radiant, Rapture, Sandboy, Seal, Seel, Sele, Serendipity, Serene, Slap, Squiffy, Starry-eyed, Sunny, Thrilled, Tiddl(e)y, Tipsy, Trigger, Warrior

**Happy medium** Juste milieu

**Hara-kiri** Eventration, Seppuku, Suicide

**Harangue** Declaim, Diatribe, Earwigging, Laisse, Lecture, Oration, Perorate, Philippic, Rant, Sermon, Speech, Spruik, Tirade

**Harass(ed)** Afflict, Annoy, Badger, Bait, Bedevil, Bego, Beleaguer, Beset, Bother, Chivvy, Distract, Dun, Gall, Grill, Grind, Grounden, Hassle, Haze, Heckle, Hector, Henpeck, Hound, Importune, Irritate, Molest, Needle, Nettle, Overdo, Persecute, Pester, Pingle, Plague, Press, Sekuhara, Stalk, Tailgate, Thwart, Torment, Trash, Troll, Vex

**Harbinger** Herald, Omen, Precursor, Usher

**Harbour(ed)** Alee, Anchorage, Basin, Brest, Cherish, Deep water, Dock, Entertain, Foster, Gosport, Haven, Heard, Herd, Hide, Hythe, Incubate, Kaipara, Lodge, Macquarie, Manukau, Marina, Mole, Mulberry, Nurse, Pearl, PLA, Poole, Port, Quay, Reset, Scapa Flow, Seaport, → SHELTER, Waitemata, Waterfront, Wellington, Wharf

**Hard(en), Hardened, Hardening, Hardness** Abstruse, Adamant(ine), Adularia, Arduous, Armour-plated, Augean, Austere, Awkward, Bake, Billy-o, Bony, Brindell, Brinell, Brittle, Bronze, Cake, Calcify, Callous, Callus, Caramel, Cast-iron, Chitin, Compact, Concrete, Cornute, Crusty, Demanding, Dentin(e), Diamond, Difficult, Dour, Draconian, Ebonite, Emery, Endure, Enure, Exacting, Fiery, Firm, Flint(y), Geal, Granite, Gruelling, H, Hawkish, Hellish, Herculean, HH, Horny, Indurate, Inure, Inveterate, Iron(y), Jasper, Knotty, Liparite, Lithoid, Metallic, Metally, Mohs, Mohs' scale, Murder, Nails, Obdurate, Obdure, Onerous, Osseous, Ossify, Permafrost, Permanent, Petrify, Picrite, Raw, Rugged, Ruthless, Schist, Scirrhus, Scleral, Sclerosis, Set, Severe, Solid, Sore, Steel(y), Steep, Stereo, Stern, Sticky, Stiff, Stoic, Stony, Strict, Strongly, Tangible, Teak, Temper, Temporary, Tough, Trying, Uneasy, Unsentimental, Unyielding, Wooden

**Hardback** Case-bound

**Hardboard** Masonite®

**Hard-boiled** Cynical

**Hard-core** Riprap, Scalpins

**Hard-headed** Obdurate, Stegocephalian

**Harding** Warden

**Hardliner** Diehard, Hawk, Idealogue, Militant

**Hardly** Borderline, Ill, Just, Scarcely, Uneath(es), Unnethes

**Hard-pressed** Strait, Taxed

**Hardship** Adversity, Affliction, Austerity, Grief, Mill, Mishap, Need, Ordeal, Penance, Poverty, Privation, Rigour, Rigueur, Trial, Trouble

**Hard-top** Carapace, Shell

**Hardware** → COMPUTER HARDWARE, Gear, Ironmongery

**Hard-working** Studious

**Hardy** Brave, Dour, Durable, Gritty, Manful, Oliver, Ollie, Robust, Rugged, Spartan, Sturdy, Thomas

**Hare** Arctic, Baud(rons), Bawd, Belgian, Blue, Body-snatcher, Buck, Dash, Doe, Dolicholis, Down, Electric, Husk, Jack-rabbit, Jugged, Jumping, Lam, Leporine, Malkin, Mara, March, Mawkin, Mountain, Mouse, Ochotona, Pika, Piping, Puss, Scut, Snowshoe, Spring, Wat

**Harebell** Blawort

**Hare-brained** Giddy, Madcap, Scatty

**Harem, Harem lady** Gynaeceum, Gynoecium, Odalisque, Seraglio, Serai(l), Zenana

**Hark(en)** Ear, Hear, List(en)

**Harlequin** Chequered, Columbine, Pantaloon

**Harlot** Blue gown, Drab, Hussy, Loon, Loose, Lown, Paramour, Plover, Pusle, Pussel, Quail, Rahab, Strumpet, Whore

**Harm(ed), Harmful** Adverse, Aggrieve, Bane, Blight, Damage, Deleterious, Dere, Detriment, Discredit, Disfigure, E-coli, Endamage, Evil, Hip, Hurt, Hyp, Inimical, Injury, Insidious, Maim, Maleficent, Malignant, Maltreat, Menace, Mischief, Nocuous, Noisome, Noxious, Pernicious, Scathe, Sinister, Spoil, Toxic, Unsafe, Unwholesome, Wroken, Wrong

**Harmless** Benign, Canny, Drudge, Gentle, Informidable, Innocent, Innocuous, Innoxious, Inoffensive, Safe

**Harmonica** Glass, Harp, Orpheus

**Harmonious, Harmonise, Harmonist, Harmony** Accord, Agree(ment), Alan, Allan, Allen, Alternation, Amicability, Assort, Atone, Attune, Balanced, Barbershop, Blend, Chord, Close, Community, Concent, Concentus, Concert, Concinnity, Concord, Congruous, Consistence, Consonant, Consort, Coordinate, Correspondence, Counterpoint, Descant, Détente, Diapason, Diatessaron, Doo-wop, Euphony, Eur(h)ythmy, Faburden, Feng-shui, Go, In step, In sync, Integrate, Jibe, Keeping, Key, Match, Melody, Mesh, Musical, Overblow, Overtone, Rappist, Rappite, Rapport, Reconcile, Salve, Solidarity, Suit, Symmetry, Sympathy, Symphonious, Sync, Thorough-bass, Tone, Tune, Unanimity, Union, Unison, Unity

**Harmonium** Organ

**Harmotome** Cross-stone

**Harness(maker)** Barnacle, Breeching, Bricole, Bridle, Cinch, D-ring, Equipage, Frenum, Gear, Gere, Girth, Halter, Hitch, Inspan, Lorimer, Loriner, Pad-tree, Partnership, Seat belt, Swingletree, Tack(le), Team, Teme, Throat-stop, Tie, Trace, Trappings, Tug, Utilise, Whippletree, Yoke

**Harp(sichord)** Aeolian, Cembalo, Clairschach, Clarsach, Clavier, Drone, Dwell, Irish, Jew's, Kora, Lyre, Nebel, Spinet, Trigon, Triple, Virginal, Welsh, Wind, Zither

**Harpagon** L'avare, Miser

**Harpoon(er)** Bart, Fis(h)gig, Fizgig, Grain, Iron, Lily iron, Peg, Spear, Specktioneer, Toggle iron, Toggler, Tow-iron, Trident

**Harpy** Aello, Celeno, Eagle, Ocypete

**Harridan** Ball-buster, Hag, Harpy, Shrew, Termagant, Xantippe, Zantippe, Zentippe

**Harrier** Hen, Jet, Montagu's, Plane

**Harriet** Hetty, Martineau

**Harris** Boatman, Cloth, Island, Isle, Rolf

**Harrow(ing)** Alas, Appal, Brake, Disc, Distress, Drag, Frighten, Heart-rending, Herse, Lacerant, Pitch-pole, Plough, Rake, Rend, Shock, Welaway, Welladay, Wellanear, Wellaway, Wring

**Harry** Aggravate, Badger, Bother, Champion, Chase, Chivvy, Coppernose, Dog, Dragoon, Flash, Fret, Hal, Harass, Hassle, Hector, Herry, Houdini, Hound, Lauder, Lime, Maraud, Molest, Nag, Pester, Plague, Rag, Ravage, Reave, Reive, Rieve, Rile, Tate, Tchick, Torment

▷**Harry** *may indicate* an anagram

**Harsh(ness)** Abrasive, Acerbic, Arduous, Asperity, Austere, Barbaric, Biting, Brassy, Cacophonous, Caustic, Coarse, Cruel, Desolate, Discordant, Dissonant, Draconian, Extreme, Glary, Grating, Gravelly, Grim, Gruff, Guttural, Hard, Hoarse, Inclement, Inexorable, Inhospitable, Jarring, Oppressive, Pitiless, Raspy, Raucid, Raucle, Raucous, Raw, Rigour, Risp, Rude, Ruthless, Scabrid, Scrannel, Screechy, →**SEVERE**, Sharp, Spartan, Stark, Stern, Stoor, Stour, Stowre, Strict, Strident, Unkind, Vitriol

**Hart** Deer, Spade, Spay, Spay(a)d, Venison

**Harte** Bret

**Hartebeest** Bubal, Kaama, Kongoni, Sassaby, Tsessebe

**Harum-scarum** Bayard, Chaotic, Madcap, Rantipole

**Harvest(er), Harvest home** Combine, Crop, Cull, Fruit, →**GATHER**, Glean, Hairst, Hawkey, Hay(sel), Hockey, Horkey, In(ning), Ingather, Kern, Kirn, Lease, Nutting, Pick, Produce, Rabi, Random, Reap, Seed-time, Shock, Spatlese, Spider, Tattie-howking, Thresh, Vendage, Vendange, Vintage

**Has** Habet, Hath, Owns, 's

**Has-been** Effete, Ex, Outmoded

**Hash(ish)** Benj, Bodge, Bungle, Charas, Discuss, Garble, Garboil, Hachis, Lobscouse, Mess, Mince, Pi(e), Ragout

▷**Hashed** *may indicate* an anagram
**Hasn't** Hant, Nas
**Hassle** Aggro, Bother, Harry, Incommode, M(o)ither, Moider, Rile, Strife, Upset
**Hassock** Kneeler, Pouf(fe), Stool, Tuffet
**Haste(n), Hastening, Hastily, Hasty** Amain, Bustle, Cursory, Despatch, Elan, Expedite, Express, Extemporary, Festinately, Fly, Gee up, Hare, Headlong, Helter-skelter, Hie, Hotfoot, → HURRY, Hurry-scurry, Impetuous, Precipitant, Race, Ramstam, Rash, Run, Rush, Scuttle, Speed, Spur, Stringendo, Subitaneous, Subito, Sudden, Tear, Tilt, Unwary, Urge, Whistle-stop
**Hastings** Banda, Bustles, Senlac, Warren
**Hat** Bad, Broad-brim, → CAP, Cocked, → HEADDRESS, Head-rig, Lid, Lum, Nab, Red, Scarlet, Tit(fer)

---

**HATS**

*3 letters:*
Fez
Pot
Tam
Tin
Top

*4 letters:*
Chip
Hard
Kepi
Pith
Plug
Poke
Silk
Sola
Tall
Tile
Topi
Ugly

*5 letters:*
Ascot
Beany
Beret
Brass
Bronx
Busby
Chaco
Crush
Derby
Gibus
Gimme
Mitre
Opera
Pagri
Paper
Pixie
Shako
Solah
Straw
Terai
Topee
Toque

*6 letters:*
Akubra®
Basher
Beanie
Beaver
Bicorn
Boater
Bobble
Bonnet
Bowler
Breton
Castor
Claque
Cloche
Coolie
Cowboy
Fedora
Gaucho
Helmet
Hennin
Mob-cap
Panama
Safari
Sailor
Shacko
Shovel
Slouch
Sunhat
Toorie
Topper
Trilby
Turban
Witch's

*7 letters:*
Biretta
Chapeau
Christy
Cossack
Flat-cap
Hattock
Homburg
Leghorn
Matador
Petasus
Picture
Pill-box
Plateau
Pork-pie
Puritan
Skimmer
Stetson®
Sundown
Tarbush
Tricorn

*8 letters:*
Balmoral
Bearskin
Bongrace
Capotain
Christie
Mountie's
Mushroom
Planter's
Puggaree
Ramilies
Runcible
Skull-cap
Snap-brim
Sola-topi
Sombrero
Tarboosh
Tarboush
Thrummed
Tricorne
Tyrolean
Watch cap

*9 letters:*
Astrakhan
Balaclava
Billycock
Cartwheel
Cockle-hat
Dunstable
Glengarry
Lamington
Ramillies
Souwester
Stovepipe
Sugarloaf
Sunbonnet
Tarpaulin
Ten-gallon
Wide-awake

*10 letters:*
Balibuntal
Bluebonnet
Chimneypot
Poke-bonnet
Sola-helmet

*11 letters:*
Cabbage tree
Deerstalker
Dolly Varden
Kamelaukion
Mortarboard
Tam o'Shanter

*12 letters:*
Cheese-cutter
Fore-and-after
Steeple-crown

---

**Hat-band** Weeper
**Hatch(ment), Hatching** Achievement, Altricial, Booby, Breed, Brew, Brood, Buttery, Cleck, Clutch, Companion, Concoct, Conspire, Cover, Devise, Eclosion, Emerge, Escape, Incubate, Serving, Set, Trap-door
**Hatchet(-shaped)** Axe, Bill, Chopper, Claw, Cleaver, Dolabriform, Tomahawk
▷**Hatching** *may indicate* an anagram
**Hatchway (surround)** Companionway, Fiddley, Guichet, Porthole, Scuttle, Service
**Hate(d), Hateful, Hater, Hatred** Abhor, Abominable, Abominate, Animus, Antipathetic, Anti-Semite, Aversion, Bugbear, Cursed, Despise, Detest, Enmity, Execrate, Haterent, Loathe, Malevolent, Misogyny, Odium, Pet, Phobia, Racism, Resent, Sacred, Spite, Toad, Ug(h), Vitriol
**Hatless** Bareheaded, Unbeavered
**Hat-plant** S(h)ola
**Hatter** Mad, Milliner
**Hat-trick** Threepeat
**Hatty** Etta
**Haughty, Haughtiness** Aloof, Aristocratic, Arrogant, Bashaw, Cavalier, Disdainful, Dorty, Fastuous, High, Hogen-mogen, Hoity-toity, Hye, Imperious, Lofty, Lordly, Morgue, Orgillous, Orgulous, Paughty, → PROUD, Scornful, Sdeignful, Sniffy, Snobbery, Stiff-necked, Toffee-nosed, Toplofty, Upstage
**Haul(age), Haulier** Bag, Bouse, Bowse, Brail, Capstan, Carry, Cart, Catch, Drag, Heave, Hove, Kedge, Long, Loot, Plunder, Pull, Rug, Sally, Scoop, Snake, Snig, Swag, TIR, Tote, Touse, Touze, Tow(se), Towze, Transporter, Trice, Truck driver, Winch, Windlass, Yank
**Haunch** Hance, Hip, Huckle, Hunkers, Quarter
**Haunt(s), Haunting** Catchy, Den, Dive, Evocative, Frequent, Ghost, Hang-out, Honky-tonk, Houf(f), Howf(f), Infest, Obsess, Possession, Purlieu, Resort, Spot, Spright, Stamping-ground
**Hauteur** Bashawism, Height, Morgue, Vanity
**Havana** Cigar
**Have, Having** Bear, Ha(e), Han, Hoax, Hold, Hoodwink, Know, Of, → OWN, Possess, Sell, With
**Haven** Asylum, Harbour, Hithe, Hythe, Nature reserve, Oasis, Port, Refuge, Refugium, Retreat, Safe, Sekos, Shelter, Tax
**Haver(s)** Blether, Clanjamfray, Dither, Gibber, Nigel, Owner
▶**Haversack** *see* RUCKSACK
**Havoc** Desolation, Devastation, Hell, Mayhem, Ravage, Waste
▷**Havoc** *may indicate* an anagram
**Haw** Drawl, Hip, Sloe
**Hawaiian** Kanaka
**Hawk(er), Hawkish** Accipitrine, Auceps, Austringer, Badger, Bastard, Buzzard, Cadger, Camelot, Caracara, Cast, Cheapjack, Cooper's, Cry, Duck, Eagle, Elanet, Eyas, Falcon, Fish, Gerfalcon, Goshawk, Haggard, Hardliner, Harrier, Harrumph, Hobby, Honey-buzzard, Keelie, Kestrel, Kight, Kite, Lammergeier, Lanner(et), Marsh, Merlin, Molla(h), Monger, Moolah, Mosquito, Mullah, Musket, Night, Nyas, Osprey, Ossifrage, Passage(r), Pearlie, Pearly, Peddle, Pedlar, Peregrine, Pigeon, Privet, Ringtail, Sacre(t), Sell, Slab, Slanger, Soar(e), Sorage, Sore(-eagle), Sparrow, Spiv, Staniel, Stone, Sutler, Tallyman, Tarsal, Tarsel(l), Tassel(l), Tercel(et), Tiercel, Tote, Tout, Trant(er), Trucker, Warlike, Warmonger
**Hawkeye** IA, Iowa
**Hawk-keeper** Austringer, Ostreger
**Hawser** Cable, Line, Rope
**Hawthorn** Albespine, Albespyne, May(flower), Quickset, Quickthorn
**Hay(cock), Hey, Haybox** Antic, Bale, Cock, Contra-dance, Fodder, Goaf, Hi, Kemple, Math, Mow, Norwegian nest, Norwegian oven, Pleach, Pook, Salt, Stack, Straw, Truss, Windrow
**Hayfever** Pollenosis, Pollinosis
**Haymaker** Blow, Slog
**Hayseed** Chaw-bacon, Hodge, Joskin, Rube, Rustic
**Haywire** Amiss

**Hazard(ous)** Asbestos, Bet, Blind spot, Booby trap, Breakneck, Bunker, Chance, Danger, Dare, Die, Dye, Estimate, Game, Gremlin, Guess, Hero, Hornet's nest, Ice, Iceberg, Imperil, In-off, Jeopardy, Losing, Main, Minefield, Mist, Moral, Nice, Niffer, Occupational, Perdu(e), Peril, Pitfall, Play, Pothole, Queasy, Rash, Razor-edge, Reef, → RISK, Risque, Stake, Thread, Trap, Venture, Vigia, Wage, Winning

**Haze, Hazy** Blear, Blur, Cloud, Filmy, Fog, → MIST, Mock, Muzzy, Nebulous, Pea-souper, Smaze, Smog, Tease, Unclear

▷**Haze** *may indicate* an anagram

**Hazel(wort)** Amenta, Asarabacca, Catkin, Cob, Corylus, Filbert, Lambs' tails

**HC** Encomia, Encomium

**He, HE** A, Cestui, Helium, Tag, Tig, → TNT, Tom

**Head(s), Head for, Heading, Headman, Head-shaped, Heady** Abuna, Aim, Apex, Ard-ri(gh), Beachy, Bean, Behead, Bill, Block, Bonce, Boss, Bound, Brain, Brainpan, Bregma, Brow, But(t), Byline, Cabbage, Caboceer, Can, Cape, Capitani, Capitate, Capitulum, Capo, Captain, Caption, Caput, Caudillo, Cauliflower, Cephalic, Chaton, Chief, Chump, Coarb, Coconut, Coma, Comarb, Commander, Conk, Cop, Coppin, Costard, Cranium, Crest, Crisis, Crown(ed), Crumpet, Crust, Cylinder, Dateline, Dean, Director, Dome, Dummy, Each, Ear, Exarch, Figure, Flamborough, Foam, Foreland, Froth, General, Glomerate, Governor, Grand Master, Grand Mufti, Hegumen(os), Herm(a), Hoe, Hogh, Huff-cap, Inion, Jowl, Karmapa, Keyword, Knob, Knowledge-box, Lead(er), Lemma, Lid, Lizard, Loaf, Loave, Loo, Lore, Malik, Manager, Masthead, Mayor, Maz(z)ard, Melik, Mocuddum, Mogul, Mokaddam, Morne, Mr Big, Mull, Muqaddam, Mutessarif, Nab, Nana, Napper, Nappy, Ness, Nob, Noddle, Noggin, Noll, Noup, Nowl, Nut, Obelion, Obverse, Occiput, Onion, Panicle, Panorama, Parietal, Pash, Pate, Pater(familias), Patriarch, Pick-up, Point, Poll, Pow, Prefect, President, Pressure, Principal, Promontory, Provost, Ras, Read-write, Ream, Rector, Repair, Ringleader, Rubric, Sarpanch, Scalp, Scaup, Scaw, Scholarch, Scolex, Sconce, Short, Sinciput, Skaw, Skull, Sound, Source, Spume, Squeers, Stad(t)holder, Starosta, Strapline, Subject, Superior, Supervisor, Taipan, Talking, Tanadar, Temple, Tete, Thanadar, Throne, Tight, Tintagel, Tip, Title, Toilet, Top, Topic, Tsantsa, Twopenny, Upperworks, Vaivode, Velocity, Voivode, Yorick, Zero in, Zupan

▷**Head** *may indicate* the first letter of a word

**Headache** Cephalalgia, Encephalalgia, Hangover, Hemicrania, Megrim, Migraine, Neuralgia, Red out, Scotodinia, Splitter

**Headband** Blindfold, Diadem, Fillet, Garland, Infula, Sphendone, T(a)enia

**Headbanger** Grebo, Nutcase

**Head cover, Headdress, Head gear, Headwear** Aigrette, Alice band, Ampyx, Balaclava, Bandanna, Bandeau, Bas(i)net, Bearskin, Bonnet, Bridle, Burnous(e), Busby, Calotte, Caul, Chaplet, Circlet, Coif, Comb, Commode, Cor(o)net, Cowl, Coxcomb, Crownet, Curch, Diadem, Doek, Dopatta, Dupatta, Fascinator, Feather bonnet, Flat cap, Fontange, Fool's cap, Frontlet, Hat(tock), Head-hugger, Helm(et), Hijab, Joncanoe, Juliet cap, Kaffiyeh, Kell, Kepi, Kerchief, Kuffiyeh, Kufiah, Kufiya(h), Madras, Mantilla, Mitre, Mobcap, Modius, Mortarboard, Nubia, Periwig, Pill-box, Plug-hat, Porrenger, Porringer, Quoif, Romal, Rumal, Sakkos, Ship-tire, Silly-how, Skid lid, Skullcap, Sphendone, Stephane, Taj, Tarbush, Tiara, Tire-valiant, Topi, Tower, Tricorn(e), Tulban, Turban, War bonnet, Wig, Wimple, Wreath

**Header** Bonder, Brick, Dive, Fall, Rowlock

**Headhunter** Naga

**Headland** Beachy Head, Bill, Cape, Cape Horn, Dungeness, Finisterre, Foreland, Head-rig, Hoe, Hogh, Land's End, Morro, Naze, Ness, Noup, Peninsula, Point, → PROMONTORY, Ras, Ross, St Vincent, Scaw, Skaw

**Headless** Acephalous

**Headlight(s)** Beam, Brights, Dip, Halo, Sealed-beam

**Headline, Headliner** Banner, Caption, Drophead, Frown, Kicker, Lead, Majuscular, Meninx, Ribbon, Scare-head, Screamer, Splash, Strapline, Streamer, Title

**Headlock** Chancery

**Headlong** Breakneck, Helter-skelter, Pell-mell, Plummet, Precipitate, Ramstam, Reckless, Steep, Sudden, Tantivy, Tearaway

▶**Headman** *see* HEAD(S)

**Headmaster** Arnold, Principal, Squeers
**Headphone(s)** Cans, Earpiece, Walkman®
**Headquarters** Base, Command, Command post, Depot, Guardhouse, Guildhall, Pentagon, Praetorium, SHAEF, SHAPE, Station, Torshavn, Valley Forge
▷**Heads** *may indicate* a lavatory
**Headset** Can
**Headsman** Executioner
**Headstrong** Obstinate, Rash, Stubborn, Unruly, Wayward, Wilful
**Head-to-tail** Tête-bêche
**Headway** Advancement, Headroom, Progress
**Head-word** Lemma
**Heal(ing)** Absent, Aesculapian, Ayurveda, Balsam, Chiropractic, Cicatrise, Cleanse, Crystal, Curative, Cure, Distant, Esculapian, G(u)arish, Hele, Hippocratise, Intention, Knit, Medicinal, Mend, Mental, Naturopathy, New Thought, Olosis, Osteopathy, Recuperation, Restore, Sain, Salve, Sanative, Sanitary, Spiritual, Styptic, Therapeutic, Time, Vulnerary
**Healer** Althea, Asa, Doctor, Homeopath, Medicine man, Naturopath, Osteopath, Sangoma, Shaman, Time
**Health(y)** Able-bodied, Aglow, Aseptic, Bottoms up, Bouncing, Bracing, Cheerio, Chin-chin, Community, Constitution, Cosy, Doer, Environmental, Fat-free, Fit(ness), Flourishing, Gesundheit, Hail, Hale, Hartie-hale, Heart, Holism, Hygeian, Kia-ora, L'chaim, Lustique, Lusty, Medicaid, Medicare, Nourishing, Piert, Pink, Prosit, Public, Robust, Rosy, Ruddy, Salubrious, Salutiferous, Sane, Sanitory, Slainte, Sound, Strong, Toast, Tope, Valentine, Valetudinarian, Vigour, Welfare, Well, Wellbeing, WHO, Wholesome
**Heap(ed), Heaps** Acervate, Agglomerate, Amass, Bing, Boneshaker, Bulk, Car, Clamp, Coacervate, Cock, Compost, Congeries, Cumulus, Drift, Hog, Jalopy, Lot, Molehill, Mound, Pile, Plenty, Pyre, Raff, Raft, Rattletrap, Rick(le), Ruck, Scads, Scrap, Shell, Slag, Stash, Tass, Toorie, Up-piled
**Hear(ing), Hearing problem** Acoustic, Attend, Audience, Audile, Avizandum, Captain's mast, Catch, Clairaudience, Colour, Dirdum, Ear, Glue ear, Harken, Learn, List(en), Oyer, Oyez, Panel, Paracusis, Perceive, Pick up, Session, Subpoena, Tin ear, Tinnitus, Try
▷**Hear(say)** *may indicate* a word sounding like one given
**Hearsay** Account, Anecdotal, Gossip, Report, Rumour, Second-hand, Surmise
**Hearse** Beare, Bier, Catafalco, Catafalque, Meat wagon, Shillibeer
**Heart(en), Heartily, Hearty, Heart-shaped** AB, Agood, Auricle, Backslapping, Beater, Bleeding, Bluff, Bosom, Bradycardia, Buoy, Cant, Cardiac, Center, Centre, Cheer, Cockles, Columella, Cordate, Cordial, Core, Courage, Crossed, Daddock, Embolden, Encourage, Essence, Fatty, Floating, Focus, Gist, H, Hale, Herz, Hub, Inmost, Inspire, Jarta, Kernel, Lepid, Lonely, Lusty, Memoriter, Mesial, Mid(st), Middle, Nub, Nucleus, Obcordate, Pericardium, Pith, Purple, Reassure, Robust, Root, Sacred, Sailor, Seafarer, Seaman, Sinoatrial, Staunch, Tachycardia, Tar, Ticker, Tweedy, Yarta, Yarto
**Heartache, Heart-break** Anguish, Crève-coeur, Grief, Sorrow
**Heartbeat** Pulse
**Heartfelt** Deep, Genuine, Real, Sincere, Soulful, Triste
**Hearth** Cupel, Finery, Fireplace, Fireside, Home, Ingle, Killogie, Rivet
**Heartless** Callous, Cored, Cruel, Inhumane, Three-suited
**Heart's ease** Pansy
**Heart-throb** Idol, Ladies' man, Valentino
**Heart trouble, Heartburn** Bradycardia, Brash, Cardialgia, Fallot's tetralogy, Fibrillation, Murmur, Pyrosis, Tachycardia
**Heat(ed), Heater, Heating** Angry, Animus, Anneal, Ardour, Arousal, Atomic, Background, Bainite, Barrage, Beath, Bedwarmer, Blood, Boiler, Brazier, Burner, Calcine, Calescence, Califont, Caloric, Calorifier, Central, Chafe, Chip, Convector, Dead, Decay, Dielectric, Dudgeon, Eccaleobion, Element, Eliminator, Emotion, Endothermic, Enthalpy, Estrus, Etna, Excite, Exothermic, Fan, Favour, Ferment, Fever, Fire, Fluster, Fug, Furnace, Gas, Gat, Gleed, Gun, Het, Hibachi, Hyperthermia, Hypocaust, Immersion, Incalescence, Induction, Ire, J, Kettle, Kindle, Latent, Liquate, Lust, Marrow, Microwave, Mowburn,

Moxibustion, Normalise, Oestrus, Panel, Passion, Prelim, Pre-warm, Prickly, Pyrolysis, Q, Quartz, Radiant, Radiator, Rankine, Recalescence, Red, Render, Repechage, Rut, Salamandrian, Salt, Scald, Sinter, Sizzle, Smelt, Solar, Space, Specific, Spice, Stew, Storage, Stove, Swelter, Teend, Temperature, Thermotics, Tind, Tine, Tog, Torrefy, Total, Tynd(e), Underfloor, Verve, Warming-pan, Warmth, White, Zip®

**Heath(land)** Bearberry, Bent, Briar, Brier, Egdon, Epacrid, Erica, Geest, Lande, Manoao, Manzanita, Moor, Muir, Stead, Ted

**Heathen(s)** Ethnic, Gentile, Godless, Idolator, Infidel, Litholatrous, Nations, Pagan, Pa(i)nim, Paynim, Philistine, Primitive, Profane, Proselyte of the gate, Ungodly

**Heather(y)** Bell, Broom, Calluna, Epacrid, Erica, Ericoid, Foxberry, Ling, Rhodora, Sprig

▷**Heating** *may indicate* an anagram

**Heat stroke** Calenture

**Heave(d), Heaving** Cast, Emesis, Fling, Frost, Heeze, Hoise, Hoist, Hump, Hurl, Lug, Popple, Retch, Shy, Sigh, Vomit

▷**Heave** *may indicate* 'discard'

**Heaven(s), Heavenly** Air, Aloft, Ama, Ambrosial, Arcady, Asgard, Bliss, Celestial, Celia, Divine, Ecstasy, Elysian, Elysium, Empyrean, Ethereal, Euphoria, Fiddler's Green, Firmament, Hereafter, Himmel, Hog, Holy, Hookey Walker, Land o' the Leal, Lift, Mackerel, New Jerusalem, Olympus, On high, Paradise, Pole, Rapture, Seventh, Shangri-la, Sion, Sky, Sublime, Supermundane, Supernal, Svarga, Swarga, Swerga, Tir na n'Og, Upper region, Uranian, Utopia, Welkin, Zion

**Heavy(weight), Heavily, Heaviness** Ali, Biased, Bodyguard, Bouncer, Close, Clumpy, Dutch, Elephantine, Embonpoint, Endomorph, Gorilla, Gothic, Grave, Hefty, Last, Leaden, Lumpish, Muscleman, Onerous, Osmium, Pesante, Ponderous, Roughneck, Sad, Scelerate, Stodgy, Stout, Top, Torrential, Upsee, Ups(e)y, Weighty, Wicked

**Hebe** Barmaid

**Hebrew** Aramaic, Eli, Heb, Israelite, Jesse, Karaism, Levi, Mishnayoth, Modern, Rabbinical

**Hebrides, Hebridean** Harris, Western Isles

**Heck** Doggone

**Heckle(r)** Badger, Boo-boy, Catcall, Gibe, Harass, Hatchel, Jeer, Needle, Ride, Spruik

**Hectic** Ding-dong, Feverish, Frenetic, Rat race

**Hector** Badger, Belabour, Bluster, Browbeat, Bully, Domineer, → HARASS, Nag

**Hedge, Hedging** Box, Bullfinch, Enclosure, Equivocate, Evade, Haw(thorn), Hay, Lay off, Meuse, Mews, Muse, Ox-fence, Pleach, Prevaricate, Privet, Pussyfoot, Quickset, Raddle, Sepiment, Shield, Stall, Stonewall, Temporise, Texas, Thicket, Waffle

**Hedgehog** Erinaceous, Gymnure, Hérisson, Prickle, Tenrec, Tiggywinkle, Urchin

**Hedge-hop** Fly low

**Hedge-parson** Bucklebeggar, Patercove

**Hedge-sparrow** Accentor

**Hedonist** Cyreniac, Epicurean, Playboy, Sybarite

**Heed(ed), Heedful** Attend, Cavendo tutus, Gaum, Gorm, Listen, → MIND, Notice, Obey, Observe, Rear, Reck, Regard(ant), Reke, Respect, Rought, Tent, Tinker's cuss

**Heedless** Blithe, Careless, Inattentive, Incautious, Rash, Scapegrace, Scatterbrain, Unaware

**Heehaw** Bray

**Heel** Achilles, Cad, Calcaneum, Cant, Careen, Cuban, Dogbolt, Foot, French, Incline, Kitten, List, Louse, Parliament, Rat, Rogue, Seel, Spike, Stacked, Stiletto, Tilt, Wedge, Wedgie

**Heel-tap** Snuff

**Hefty** Beefy, Brawny, Heavy, Solid, Weighty

**Heifer** Freemartin, Io, Quey, Stirk

**Height(en), Heights** Abraham, Acme, Altitude, Cairngorm, Ceiling, Dimension, Elevation, Embroider, Eminence, Enhance, Eye-level, Fill-swing, Giddy, Golan, H, Hem, Heyday, Hill, Ht, Hypsometry, Level, Might, Mount, Peak, Procerity, Roof, Shap, Spot, Stature, Stud, Sum, → SUMMIT, Tallness, Tor, X, Zenith

**Heinous** Abominable, Atrocious, Flagrant

**Heir** Alienee, Atheling, Claimant, Coparcener, Dauphin, Devisee, Distributee, Eigne, H(a)eres, Institute, Intitule, Legatee, Parcener, Scion, Sprig, Successor, Tanist

**Heirless** Escheat, Intestate
**Heirloom** Legacy, Relic
**Held** Captive, Hostage, Sostenuto, Ten(uto)
▹**Held by** *may indicate* a hidden word
**Helen** Elaine, Nell(y)
**Helicopter (crew), Heliport** Airstop, Chopper, Egg-beater, Gunship, Hover, Iroquois, Medevac, Rotodyne, Sea Cobra, Sea King, Sea Knight, Sea Sprite, Sea Stallion, Sikorsky, Sky-hook, Whirlybird, Winchman
**Helios** Hyperion
**Heliotrope** Cherry-pie
**Helium** He
**Helix** Alpha, Coil, Double, Parastichy, Spiral
**Hell(ish)** Abaddon, Abyss, Ades, Agony, Amenthes, Annw(yf)n, Avernus, Below, Blazes, Bottomless pit, Chthonic, Dis, Erebus, Furnace, Gehenna, Hades, Heck, Inferno, Jahannam, Lower regions, Malebolge, Naraka, Netherworld, Orcus, Pandemonium, Perditious, Pit, Ruin, Sheol, Stygian, Tartar(ean), Tartaric, Tartarus, Tophet, Torment
**Hellbender** Menopome, Mud-puppy
**Hellebore** Bear's foot, Itchweed, Melampode, Setterwort
**Hellenic** Dorian
**Hellespont** Dardanelles
**Hello, Hallo, Hullo** Aloha, Chin-chin, Ciao, Dumela, G'day, Golden, Hi, Ho(a), Hoh, Howdy, Howzit, Wotcha, Wotcher, Yoo-hoo
**Helm(sman)** Cox, Navigator, Pilot, Steer, Tiller, Timon(eer)
**Helmet** Armet, Balaclava, Basinet, Bearskin, Beaver, Brain bucket, Burganet, Burgonet, Busby, Cask, Casque, Comb, Crash, Galea, Gas, Hard hat, Heaume, Knapscal, Knapscull, Knapskull, Montero, Mor(r)ion, Murren, Murrin, Murrion, Nasal, Pickelhaube, Pith, Plumed, Pot, Pressure, Salade, Sal(l)et, Shako, Skid-lid, Smoke, Sun, Tin hat, Topee, Topi
**Helot** Esne, Slave
**Help(er), Helping, Helpful** Abet, Accommodate, Accomplice, Adjuvant, Advantage, Aid(ance), Aidant, Aide, Alexis, Alleviate, Ally, Asset, → ASSIST, Auxiliary, Avail, Back, Beet-master, Beet-mister, Befriend, Benefit, Bestead, Boon, Brownie, Carer, Char(woman), Charity, Coadjutor, Collaborate, Complice, Conducive, Daily, Dobbie, Dobby, Dollop, Dose, Ezra, First aid, Forward, Further(some), Go, Godsend, Guidance, Hand, Handyman, Henchman, Hint, Home, Hyphen, Instrumental, Intercede, Kind, Leg-up, Life-saver, Maid, Mayday, Medicinal, Minister, Monitor, Obliging, Ophelia, Order, Patronage, Pitch in, Promote, Prompt, Quantity, Ration, Recourse, Relieve, Samaritan, Servant, Serve, Service, Slice, SOS, Stead, Sted, Subserve, Subvention, Succour, Taste, Therapeutic, Tide over, Use
**Helpless(ness)** Adynamia, Anomie, Downa-do, Feeble, High and dry, Impotent, Incapable, Incapacity, Paralytic, Prostrate, Useless
**Helpmate** Consort
**Hem** Border, False, Fringe, Hoop, List
**He-man** Adonis, Hunk, Jock, Macho
**Hemisphere, Hemispherical** Antichthon, Cupular, Dominant, Eastern, Magdeburg, Northern, Rose-cut, Southern, Western
**Hemlock** Conia, Cowbane, Insane root, Tsuga
**Hemp** Abaca, Bhang, Boneset, Bowstring, Carl(ot), Choke-weed, Codilla, Crotalaria, Dagga, Fimble, Ganja, Hards, Henequen, Hiniquin, Indian, Kef, K(a)if, Love-drug, Manil(l)a, Mauritius, Moorva, Murva, Neckweed, Pita, Sida, Sisal, Sunn, Tat, Tow
**Hen(s)** Ancona, Andalusian, Australorp, Biddy, Buff Orpington, Chock, Clocker, Cochin (China), Deep litter, Dorking, Eirack, Fowl, Grig, Houdan, Langshan, Layer, Leghorn, Maori, Marsh, Mother, Mud, Orpington, Partlet, Pertelote, Plymouth Rock, Poulard, Poultry, Prairie, Pullet, Ree(ve), Rhode Island red, Sitter, Spanish fowl, Speckled, Sultan, Tappit, Welsummer, Wyandotte
**Hence, Henceforth** Apage, Avaunt, Ergo, Evermore, Go, Hinc, Scram, So, Therefore, Thus
**Henchman** Abetter, Aide, Attendant, Crony, Follower, Led captain, Myrmidon, Satellite
**Hen-house** Battery, Eggery

**Henna** Camphire
**Hennery** Run
**Hen-party** Kitchen tea
**Hen-pecked** Pussy-whipped, Spineless, Woman-tired
**Henry** Eighth, H, Hal, Hank, Hooray, Hy, James, Navigator, O
**Hep** Bacca, Berry, Hip, Wise
**Hepatic** Scale-moss
**Hepatitis** Favism, Jaundice
**Herald(ic), Heraldry** Annunciate, Crier, Earl Marshal, Harbinger, Hermes, Messenger, Prelude

---

**HERALDRIES**

***2 letters:***
Or

***3 letters:***
Lis
Vol

***4 letters:***
Bars
Bend
Coue
Fess
File
Golp
Lyon
Nowy
Pale
Paly
Pile
Posé
Vair
Vert
Yale

***5 letters:***
Azure
Cabré
Chief
Crest
Fesse
Flory
Golpe
Gules
Morné
Nowed
Pheon
Sable
Scarp
Scrog
Tenné
Trick
Usher
Vairé

***6 letters:***
Albany
Argent
Armory
Bagwyn
Billet
Checky
Cleché
Cotise
Coupee
Erased
Fecial
Fetial
Flanch
Garter
Lionel
Lodged
Moline
Mullet
Naiant
Nebulé
Nebuly
Norroy
Pallet
Potent
Sea dog
Sejant
Verdoy
Verrey
Voided
Volant
Vorant
Wivern
Wreath
Wyvern

***7 letters:***
Alerion
Armiger
Bearing
Bordure
Chevron
Compone
Compony
Cottise
Dormant
Endorse
Enfiled
Fracted
Gardant
Gironny
Gyronny
Herissé
Issuant
Manchet
Martlet
Nascent
Nombril
Passant
Portate
Portend
Purpure
Rampant
Red Hand
Roundel
Roundle
Rousant
Salient
Sea lion
Sejeant
Statant
Stentor
Trangle
Trundle
Urinant

***8 letters:***
Allerion
Bendwise
Blazonry
Caboched
Cicerone
Couchant
Dancette
Degraded
Dragonné
Emblazon
Hauriant
Herisson
Mantling
Naissant
Opinicus
Ordinary
Proclaim
Sanglier
Segreant
Tressure
Trippant
Umbrated
Woodwose

***9 letters:***
Abatement
Debruised
Dimidiate
Displayed
Eightfoil
Enveloped
Precursor
Regardant
Supporter
Woodhouse

***10 letters:***
Bloody Hand
Blue Mantle
Cinquefoil
Clarenceux
Cockatrice
Difference
Fetterlock
Forerunner
King-of-arms
Portcullis
Pursuivant
Quartering
Rouge Croix
Sans nombre

*11 letters:*
Clarencieux
Honour-point
Rouge Dragon
Subordinary

*12 letters:*
Bend sinister
Counter-paled
Interfretted
Vaunt-courier

*13 letters:*
Baton sinister
Calygreyhound
Counter-fleury
Undifferenced

*14 letters:*
Counter-passant
Counter-salient
Lyon King of Arms

---

**Herb(aceous), Herbs** Bouquet garni, Garnish, Maror, Oleraceous, Pot, Salad, Seasoning, Simple, Suffruticose, Weed

---

**HERBS**

*3 letters:*
Bay
Oca
Pia
Rue

*4 letters:*
Aloe
Balm
Cive
Dill
Forb
Mint
Moly
Sage
Wort

*5 letters:*
Anise
Avens
Basil
Chive
Clary
Cumin
Eruca
Fitch
Inula
Medic
Orval
Senna
Tansy
Thyme
Typha
Vetch
Yerba

*6 letters:*
Ajowan
Bennet
Betony
Borage
Capers
Cicely
Cohosh
Cummin
Endive
Fennel
Ferula
Garlic
Hyssop
Lovage
Madder
Orache
Origan
Purpie
Saloop
Salvia
Savory
Sesame
Sorrel
Willow
Yarrow
Za'atar

*7 letters:*
Aconite
Alecost
Aniseed
Arugula
Bayleaf
Boneset
Caraway
Catmint
Chervil
Chicory
Comfrey
Dittany
Felicia
Fuller's
Gentian
Ginseng
Gunnera
Hemlock
Lewisia
Madwort
Monarda
Mustard
Oregano
Origane
Paprika
Parsley
Phlomis
Saffron
Salsify
Vervain
Zabrina

*8 letters:*
Agrimony
Allspice
Amaracus
Angelica
Bergamot
Camomile
Cardamom
Centaury
Cilantro
Costmary
Estragon
Feverfew
Fireweed
Fluellin
Knapweed
Mandrake
Marjoram
Origanum
Plantain
Purslane
Reed-mace
Rosemary
Soapwort
Staragen
Tarragon
Turmeric
Valerian
Veronica
Wormwood

*9 letters:*
Archangel
Chamomile
Colic root
Coriander
Echinacea
Eyebright
Fenugreek
Germander
Haworthia
Kalanchoe
Lamb's ears
Laserwort
Parakelia
Pussytoes
Rhizocarp
Rodgersia
Spearmint
Tormentil

*10 letters:*
Lemon grass
Lemon thyme
Parakeelya
Pennyroyal
Pipsissewa
Rest-harrow

*11 letters:*
Laserpicium
Rupturewort
Sweet cicely

*12 letters:*
Aristolochia
Mountain flax
Ornithogalum
Skunk cabbage
Southernwood

*13 letters:*
Good-King-Henry

*14 letters:*
Paterson's curse

**Herbalist** Simplist
**Herbarium** Hortus siccus
**Herbert** Alan, AP(H), Lom, Spencer
**Herbicide** Agent Orange, Atrazine, Defoliant, Diquat, Glufosinate, Glyphosate, Picloram, Simazine, Spray drift
**Herbivore** Behemoth, Iguanodon, Rhino, Sauropod
**Hercules** Alcides, Huge, Rustam, Rustem
**Herd(er), Herding, Herdsman** Band, Buffalo, Byreman, Corral, Cowpuncher, Drive, Drover, Flock, Gang, Lowing, Marshal, Meinie, Mein(e)y, Menyie, Mob, Pod, Rabble, Raggle-taggle, Round-up, Shepherd, Tail, Tinchel, Vaquero, Wrangling
**Here** Adsum, Hi, Hic, Hither, Kilroy, Local, Now, Oy, Present
**Hereafter** Eternity, Other world
**Hereditary, Heredity** Ancestry, Blood, Breeding, Codon, DNA, Dynastic, Eugenics, Exon, Genetics, Id(ant), Idioplasm, Inborn, Innate, Mendelism, Panagenesis
▷**Herein** *may indicate* a hidden word
**Here is laid** HS
**Heresiarch** Nestor
**Heresy, Heretic(al)** Agnoitae, Albi, Albigensian, Apollinaris, Apostasy, Arian, Arius, Bab, Bogomil, Bugger, Cathar, Cerinthus, Docete, Donatist, Dulcinist, Encratite, Errant, Eudoxian, Giaour, Gnosticism, Heresearch, Heterodoxy, Lollard, Manichaean, Montanism, Nestorian, Non-believer, Nonconformist, Origen, Patarin(e), Pelagius, Phrygian, Racovian, Rebel, Revisionist, Unitarian, Zendik
**Heritage** Birthright, Due, NT, Odette, Ottilie, Patrimony
**Hermaphrodite** Androgynous, Bi-, Gynandromorph, Monochinous, Monoecious, Prot(er)andry, Protogyny
**Hermes (rod)** Caduceus, Mercury
**Hermetic** Airtight, Alchemist, Sealed
**Hermit(age), Hermit-like** Anchoret, Anchorite, Ascetic, Ashram(a), Augustinian, Austin, Cell, Cloister, Crab, Eremite, Grandmontine, Hieronymite, Loner, Marabout, Monk, Museum, Nitrian, Pagurid, Peter, Recluse, Retreat, Robber-crab, Sannyasi, Soldier-crab, Solitary, Troglodyte
**Hernia** Bubonocele, Cystocoele, Diverticulum, Enterocele, Eventration, Hiatal, Hiatus, Inguinal, Rectocele, Rupture
**Hero(es), Heroic** Asgard, Brave, Champ(ion), Couplet, Derring-do, Eidola, Epic, Eponym, Folk, God, Goody, Great, Heart-throb, Icon, Ideal, Idol, Lion, Noble, Olitory, Priestess, Principal, Resolute, Swashbuckler, Tragic, Unsung, Valiant, VC, White knight

---

## HEROES

*3 letters:*
Cid

*4 letters:*
Aitu
Ajax
Eric
Finn
Kami
Tell

*5 letters:*
Bader
Clive
Drake
El Cid
Faust
Jason
Orfeo
Orion
Rambo
Raven
Sheik
Zorro

*6 letters:*
Aeneas
Amadis
Batman
Bunyan
Cyrano
Fingal
Gideon
Hector
Kaleva
Nelson
Nestor
Oliver
Onegin
Orsino
Ossian
Revere
Roland
Rustem
Rustum
Samson
Shandy
Sigurd
Tarzan
Virago

*7 letters:*
Alcides
Asterix
Beowulf
Dan Dare
Demigod
Gluscap
Gluskap
Ivanhoe
Lothair
Marmion
Oedipus
Paladin
Perseus
Rinaldo
Saladin
Tancred

Theseus
Tristam
Tristan
Ulysses
Volsung
Wallace
Werther

*8 letters:*
Achilles
Argonaut
Balarama
Cisco Kid
Crockett
Everyman
Glooscap
Heracles
Hercules
Hiawatha
Leonidas
Meleager
Odysseus
Owlglass
Parsifal
Pericles
Roderego
Roderick
Superman
Tristram

*9 letters:*
Agamemnon
Cuchulain
Dambuster
Garibaldi
John Henry
Lochinvar
Lord Byron
Owleglass
Owspiegle
Siegfried
Spiderman

*10 letters:*
Cuchullain
Howleglass
Owlspiegle

*11 letters:*
Bellerophon
Finn MacCool
Hudibrastic
Philoctetes
Ramachandra
Tam o' Shanter

*13 letters:*
Vercingetorix

---

**Herod** Agrippa, Antipas, Antipater
**Heroin** Chase-the-dragon, Diamorphine, Dogfood, Doojie, Dynamite, Gumball, H, Harry, Henry, Horse, Jack, Junk, Scag, Schmeck, Skag, Smack, Snow, Snowball, Speedball, Sugar, White stuff
**Heroine** Andromeda, Ariadne, Candida, Cleopatra, Darling, Demigoddess, Electra, Eurydice, Hedda, Heidi, Imogen, Isolde, Judith, Juliet, Leading lady, Leda, Leonora, Lulu, Manon, Mimi, Nana, Norma, Pamela, Star, Tess, Tosca, Una
**Heron(s)** Ardea, Bird, Bittern, Boat-billed, Butter-bump, Egret, Green, Handsaw, Kotuko, Screamer, Sedge, Siege, Squacco, Winnard
**Herpes** Cold sore, Dartre, Shingles, Shiver
**Herring** Bismarck, Bloater, Brisling, Brit, Buckling, Caller, Cisco, Clupea, Digby chick(en), Gaspereau, Glasgow magistrate, Kipper, Lake, Maise, Maize, Ma(a)tjes, Mattie, Maze, Mease, Menhaden, Norfolk capon, Ox eye, Rabbitfish, Red, Rollmop, Sea-stick, Shotten, Sild, Silt, Sparling, Teleost, Whitebait
**Herringbone** Sloping
**Hesitant, Hesitate, Hesitation** Balance, Boggle, Cunctation, Delay, Demur, Dicker, Dither, Doubtful, Dubitate, Dwell, Er, Erm, Falter, Halting, Haver, Haw, Irresolute, Mammer, Mealy-mouthed, → PAUSE, Qualm, Scruple, Shillyshally, Shrink, Stagger, Stammer, Stutter, Swither, Tarrow, Teeter, Tentative, Think twice, Um, Um and ah, Ur, Vacillate, Wait, Waver
**Hesperus** Vesper
**Hessian** Burlap, Hireling
**Heterodoxy** Heresy
**Heterogeneous** Diverse, Motley, Piebald
**Heterosexual** Hasbian, Straight
**Hew(er)** Ax, Chop, Cut, Gideon, Hack, Sever
**Hex** Bewitch, Jinx, Voodoo
**Hexameter** Dolichurus, Miurus
▶**Hey** *see* HAY(COCK)
**Heyday** Prime, Summer
**Hi** Cooee, Hello, Howdie
**Hiatus** Caesura, Entr'acte, Gap, Hernia, Interact, Interlude, Interregnum, Interval, Lacuna, Lull, Respite
**Hibernal, Hibernate(r), Hibernating** Dormouse, Estivate, Hiemal, Hole up, Latitant, Sleep, Winter
**Hibernian** Irish
**Hibiscus** China rose, Okra, Roselle, Rozelle
**Hiccup** Blip, Glitch, Hitch, Singultus, Snag, Spasm, Yex
**Hick** Jake, Oaf, Podunk, Rube, Yokel
**Hickory** Black, Jackson, Mockernut, Pecan, Scaly-bark, Shagbark, Shellbark
**Hidden** Buried, Cabalistic, Covert, Cryptic, Delitescent, De(a)rn, Doggo, Eclipsed, Healed,

Hooded, Inner, Inward, Latent, Obscure, Occult, Pentimento, Recondite, Screened, Secret, Shuttered, Sly, Subterranean, Ulterior, Unseen, Veiled, Wrapped

▷**Hidden** *may indicate* a concealed word

**Hide, Hidey hole, Hiding (place)** Abscond, Babiche, Basan, Befog, Bield(y), Blind, Bolthole, Box-calf, Burrow, Bury, Butt, Cache, Camouflage, Cane, Ceroon, Coat, → **CONCEAL**, Coonskin, Cootch, Cordwain, Couch, Cour, Cover (up), Crop, Curtain, Cwtch, Dea(r)n, Deerskin, Derm, Dissemble, Doggo, Earth, Eclipse, Encave, Ensconce, Enshroud, Envelop, Epidermis, Fell, Flaught, Flay, Fur, Gloss over, Harbour, Heal, Heel, Hele, Hell, Hibernate, Hole-up, Hoodwink, Incave, Inter, Kip, Kipskin, Lair, Leather, Lie doggo, Mai-mai, Mask, Mew, Mobble, Morocco, Nebris, Nook, → **OBSCURE**, Paper over, Parfleche, Pell, Pelt, Plank, Plant, Priest's hole, Repress, Robe, Saffian, Screen, Secrete, Sequester, Shadow, Shellac(k), Shroud, Skin, Skulk, Smuggle, Spetch, Squirrel, Stash, Strap-oil, Tappice, Thong, Thrashing, Trove, Veil, Wallop, Whang, Wrap

**Hidebound** Narrow

**Hideous(ness)** Deform(ed), Enormity, Gash, Ghastly, Grotesque, Horrible, Monstrous, Odious, Ugly, Ugsome

**Hie** Dash

**Hierarchic, Hierarchy** Byzantine, Echelon, Elite, Pecking order, Theocracy

**Hierocratic** Priest-ridden

**Hieroglyph, Hieroglyphics** Cipher, Egyptian, Pictogram

**Hi-fi, High-fidelity** Ambisonics®, Ghetto blaster, Stereo

**Higgledy-piggledy** Mixtie-maxtie

**High(er), Highly, Highness** Advanced, Alt(a), Altesse, Alteza, Altissimo, Altitudinous, Apogee, Atop, Brent, Climax, Culminant, Doped, Drugged, E-la, Elation, Elevated, Eminent, Euphoria, Exalted, Excelsior, Exhilarated, Five, Frequency, Gamy, Half seas over, Haut(e), Intoxicated, Jinks, Lofty, Maggotty, Merry, Mind-blowing, Orthian, Prime, Rancid, Ripe, School, Senior, Sent, Shrill, So, Spaced out, Steep, Stenchy, Stoned, Stratospheric, String-out, Strong, Superior, Swollen, Tall, Tension, Tipsy, Tiptop, Top-lofty, Topmost, Top notch, Treble, Turned on, Ultrasonic, Up(per), Upstairs, Upward, Very, Wired, Zonked

▷**High** *may indicate* an anagram

**High and mighty, High-handed** Arrogant, Haughty, Hogen-mogen, Imperious, Lordly

**Highball** Drink, Lob, Loft, Skier, Skyer, Sling

**Highbrow** Brain, Egghead, Intelligentsia, Learned, Long-hair, Third programme

**High church** Spikery, Spiky

**High-class** Best, Pedigree, Superior, U

**High-crowned** Copataine

**Highest** Apotheosis, Best, Cacumen, Climax, Culminant, Maximum, Mostwhat, Ne plus ultra, Progressive, Supreme

**Highest note** E-la

**High-flier, High-flown** Astronaut, Bombastic, Euphuism, Icarus, Jet set, Purple patch

**Highland(er), Highlands** Black Forest, Blue-bonnet, Blue-cap, Cameron, Cat(h)eran, Down, Dun(n)i(e)wassal, Gael, Gaelic, Hielan(d), Hielant, Irish Scot, Karoo, Kiltie, Masai, Nainsel(l), Nepalese, Plaid(man), Redshank, Riff, Scot, Seaforth, Shire, Teuchter

**Highlight** Accent, Beacon, Chandelier, Emphasise, Feature, Focus, Heighten, Spotlight, Streak, Stress

▶**High-pitched** *see* **HIGH(ER)**

**High-spirited** Extravert, Extrovert, Exuberant

**High tension** HT

**Highway** Alaska, Alcan, Autobahn, Autopista, Autostrada, Bus, Camino Real, Divided, Flyover, Freeway, Information, Interstate, King's, Motorway, Overpass, Parkway, Pass, Queen's, Road, Rode, Tarseal, Thoroughfare, Tightrope, Tollway, Trunk road, Watling St

**Highwayman, Highway robber(y)** Bandit, Bandolero, Duval, Footpad, Fraternity, Gilderoy, Jack Sheppard, Land-pirate, Land-rat, Latrocinium, MacHeath, Motorist, Rank-rider, Road-agent, Scamp, Skyjacker, Toby, Tobyman, Turpin, Twitcher, Wheel

**Hijack(er)** Abduct, Mutiny, Pirate

**Hike(r)** Backpack, Bushbash, Bushwalk, Raise, Rambler, Ramp, Rise, Traipse, Tramp, Trape(s), Trek, Up(raise), Walkathon

**Hilarious, Hilarity** Comical, Gaiety, Hoot, Hysterical, Jollity, Laughter, Mirth, Riot, Side-splitting

**Hilary** Term

**Hill(ock), Hills, Hillside, Hilly** Ant, Antidine, Arafar, Areopagus, Aventine, Barrow, Beacon, Ben, Bent, Berg, Beverly, Black, Blackdown, Bluff, Bombay, Brae, Bredon, Breed's, Brew, Broken, Bunker, Butte, Caelian, Calvary, Capitol(ine), Cheviots, Chiltern, Chin, Cleve, Coast, Cone, Coolin, Coteau, Cotswolds, Crag-and-tail, Crest, Cuillin, Damon, Djebel, Drumlin, Dun(e), Dunsinane, Eminence, Esquiline, Fell, Flodden, Gebel, Golan Heights, Golgotha, Gradient, Grampians, Hammock, Height, Helvellyn, Highgate, Holt, Horst, How, Howe, Hummock, Incline, Inselberg, Janiculum, Jebel, Kip(p), Knap, Knoll, Knot, Kop(je), Koppie, Lammermuir, Lavender, Law, Loma, Low, Ludgate, Majubar, Malvern, Mamelon, Man, Marilyn, Matopo, Mendip, Merrick, Mesa, Monadnock, Monte Cassino, Monticule, Morro, Mound, Mount Lofty Ranges, Nab, Naga, Nanatak, Nilgiri(s), North Downs, Otway Ranges, Palatine, Pap, Pennines, Pike, Pingo, Pnyx, Quantocks, Quirinal, Rand, Range, Saddleback, Savoy, Scaur, Seven, Silbury, Sion, Steep, Stoss, Strawberry, Switchback, Tara, Tel(l), Toft, Toot, Tor, Toss, Tump, Tweedsmuir, Upland, Valdai, Vatican, Viminal, Wolds, Wrekin, Zion

**Hillbilly** Yap

**Hill-dweller** Ant

**Hillman** Areopagite, Nepalese

**Hilltop** Crest, Knoll, Nab

**Hilt** Basket, Coquille, Haft, Handle, Hasp, Shaft

**Him(self)** He, Ipse, Un

**Himalaya(n)** Nepali, Panda, Sherpa, Tibetan

**Hind(er), Hindering, Hindrance, Hindsight** Back, Bar, Block, Bog down, Check, Counteract, Cramp, Crimp, Cumber, Debar, → DELAY, Deter, Encumber, Estop, Hamper, Handicap, Harass, Hitch, Holdback, Imbar, Impeach, Impede, Inconvenience, Inhibit, Liability, Obstacle, Obstruct, Overslaugh, Porlock, Posterior, Preclusion, Prevent, Pull-back, Rear, Rein, Remora, Retard, Retral, Retrospect, Rump, Rumple, Set back, Shackle, Slow, Stonewall, Stop, Stunt, Stymie, Taigle, Thwart, Trammel

**Hind(most)** Back, Deer, Lag, Rear, Starn, Stern

**Hindi, Hindu(ism)** Arya Samaj, Babu, Bania(n), Banyan, Brahman, Brahmin, Dalit, Gentoo, Gurkha, Harijan, Jain(a), Kshatriya, Maharishi, Nagari, Pundit, Rajpoot, Rajput, Rama, Sad(d)hu, Saiva, S(h)akta, Saktas, Sanatana Dharma, Sankhya, Shaiva, Sheik(h), Shiv Sena, Shudra, Sivaite, Smriti, Sudra, Swami, Swinger, Trimurti, Untouchable, Urdu, Vaishnava, Vais(h)ya, Varna, Vedanta, Vedism

**Hindquarters** Backside, Crupper, Haunches

**Hinge(d)** Axis, Butt, Cardinal, Cross-garnet, Depend, Drop-leaf, Garnet, Gemel, Gimmer, Ginglymus, Gullwing, Joint, Knee, Mount, Parliament, Piano, Pivot, Stamp, Strap

▷**Hinge(s)** *may indicate* a word reversal

**Hingeless** Ecardinate

**Hinny** Ass, Donkey, Joe

**Hint** Allude, Bit, Clew, Clue, Cue, Echo, Element, Gleam, Hunch, Idea, Imply, Inkle, Inkling, Innuendo, Insinuate, Intimate, Key, Mint, Nod, Nuance, Office, Overtone, Pointer, Preview, Prompt, Ray, Reminder, Scintilla, Shadow, Soupçon, → SUGGEST, Tang, Tinge, Tip(-off), Touch, Trace, Trick, Wind, Wink, Wisp, Word, Wrinkle

▷**Hint** *may indicate* a first letter

**Hip(pie), Hippy, Hips** Beatnik, Cafard, Cheer, Coxa(l), Drop-out, Flower-power, Huck(le), Hucklebone, Hunkers, Ilium, In, Informed, Ischium, Pubis, Sciatic, Tonish, Trendy

**Hip-hop** Rap

**Hippopotamus** Behemoth, Bloat, River-horse, Sea-cow, Sea horse

**Hire(d), Hiring** Affreightment, Charter, Employ, Engage, Fee, Freightage, Job, Lease, Merc(enary), Never-never, Pensionary, Rent, Shape-up, Ticca, Wage

**Hirsute** Hairy, Pilose, Shaggy

▷**His** *may indicate* greetings

**Hispanic** Latino

**Hiss(ing)** Boo, Fizzle, Goose, Hish, Sibilant, Siffle, Sizzle, Static, Swish

**Historian** Acton, Adams, Antiquary, Archivist, Arrian, Asellio, Bede, Biographer, Bryant, Buckle, Camden, Carlyle, Centuriator, Chronicler, Chronographer, Du Bois, Etain, Eusebius, Froude, Genealogist, Gibbon, Gildas, Green, Griot, Herodotus, Knickerbocker, Livy, Macaulay, Oman, Paris, Pliny, Plutarch, Ponsonby, Procopius, Read, Renan, Roper, Rowse, Sallust, Spengler, Starkey, Strabo, Strachey, Suetonius, Tacitus, Taylor, Thiers, Thucydides, Toynbee, Trevelyan, Wells, Xenophon

**History, Historic(al)** Account, Age, Anamnesis, Ancient, Annal, Bunk, Case, Chronicle, Clio, Dark ages, Diachronic, Epoch(a), Epoch-making, Ere-now, Ever, Heredity, Heritage, Legend, Life, Living, Meiji, Memorable, Mesolithic, Modern, Momentous, Natural, Ontogency, Oral, Past, Record, Relie, Renaissance, Retroactive, Saga, Story, Track record, Yesterday

**Histrionic(s)** Melodrama, Operatic, Theatrical

**Hit** Attain, Backhand, Bang, Bash, Baste, Bat, Batter, Bean, Belt, Bepat, Best seller, Blip, Blockbuster, Bloop, Blow, Bludgeon, Boast, Bolo, Bonk, Boot, Brain, Bump, Bunt, Catch, Chartbuster, Chip, Clip, Clobber, Clock, Clout, Club, Collide, Crown, Cuff, Dot, Flail, Flick, Flip, Forehand, Foul, Fourpenny-one, Fungo, Fustigate, Get, Hay, Head-butt, Home(-thrust), Homer, Ice-man, Impact, Inner, Knock, Lam, Lob, Magpie, Mug, Number one, Outer, Pandy, Paste, Pepper, Pinch, Pistol-whip, Polt, Prang, Punto dritto, Ram, Roundhouse, Sacrifice, Score, Sensation, Six, Skier, Sky, Slam, Slap, Slog, Slosh, Slub, Smash(eroo), Smit(e), Sock, Spank, Spike, Stoush, Strack, Straik, Stricken, Strike, Strook, Struck, → **SUCCESS**, Swat, Switch, Tee off, Thwack, Time-thrust, Tip, Tonk, Touché, Undercut, Venewe, Venue, Volley, Wallop, Whack, Wham, Wing, Ythundered, Zap, Zonk

**Hitch(ed)** Catch, Cat's paw, Clove, Contretemps, Edge, Espouse, Harness, Hike, Hirsle, Hoi(c)k, Hotch, Jerk, Kink, Knot, Lorry-hop, Rope, Rub, Setback, Sheepshank, Sheet bend, Shrug, Snag, Technical, Thumb, Timber, Wed

**Hitherto** Before, Yet

**Hitman** Assassin, Eliminator, Gun

**Hittite** Uriah

**HIV** Viral load

**Hive(s)** Colony, Nettlerash, Skep, Spread, Swarm, Wheal

**Hoar(y)** Ashen(-grey), Canescent, Froren, Frost, Gaudy-day, Grizzled, Rime

**Hoard(ing)** Accumulate, Amass, Bill, Billboard, Cache, Coffer, Eke, Heap, Hog, Hoord, Husband, Hutch, Mucker, Plant, Pose, Salt away, Save, Sciurine, Snudge, Squirrel, Stash, Stock, Stockpile, Store, Stow, Treasure

**Hoarse(ness)** Croupy, Frog, Grating, Gruff, Husky, Rasping, Raucous, Roar(er), Roopit, Roopy, Roup, Throaty

**Hoax** April-fish, Bam, Canard, Cod, Do, Doff, Fub, Fun, Gag, Gammon, Gowk, Gull, Have on, Hum, Huntie-gowk, Josh, Kid, Leg-pull, Piltdown, Put-on, Quiz, Scam, Sell, Sham, Skit, Spoof, String, Stuff, Supercherie, → **TRICK**

**Hob** Ceramic, Cooktop, Ferret, Goblin, Lout

**Hobble, Hobbling** Enfetter, Game, Hamshackle, Hilch, Hitch, Impair, Lame, Limp, Pastern, Picket, Shackle, Spancel, Stagger, Tether

**Hobby** Avocation, Eleanora's falcon, Fad, Falcon, Interest, Pastance, → **PASTIME**, Predator, Pursuit, Recreation, Scrimshaw

**Hobby-horse** Dada, Obsession, Play-mare

**Hobbyist** Amateur

**Hobgoblin** Bog(e)y, Buggan(e), Bull-beggar, Puck, Worriecow

**Hobnail** Clinker, Tacket

**Hobnob** Associate, Chat, Fraternise, Mingle, Socialise

**Hobo** Bum, Drifter, → **TRAMP**, Vagrant

**Hock** Cambrel, Dip, Gambrel, Gambril, Gammon, Ham, Heel, Hough, Hypothecate, Pawn, Pledge, Rhenish, Wine

**Hockey, Hockey player** Field, Goal, Grass, Hurling, Ice, Oiler, Pond, Shinny, Shinty, Street, Tonsil

**Hod** Carrier, Tray

**Hodge** Peasant, Rustic, Yokel

**Hoe** Claut, Draw, Dutch, Grub, Grubbing, Jembe, Nab, Pecker, Plymouth, Prong, Rake, Scuffle, Thrust, Weed

**Hoedown** Square dance

**Hog** Babiroussa, Babirussa, Boar, Glutton, Guttle, Mexican, Peccary, Pig, Porker, Puck, Red river, Road, Shoat, Shott, Whole

**Hogmanay** Ne'erday

**Hog-rat** Hutia

**Hogshead** Butt, Cask, Muid

**Hogwash** Bull, Nonsense, Swill, Twaddle

**Hoi-polloi** Oik, Prole(tariat), Rabble

**Hoist(ing)** Boom, Bouse, Bunk-up, Crane, Davit, Derrick, Garnet, Gin, Heave, Heft, Hills, Jack, Lewis, Lift, Raise, Shearlegs, Shears, Sheerlegs, Sheers, Stay-tackle, Sway, Teagle, Trice, Whip-and-derry, Wince, Winch, Windas, Windlass

**Hold(er), Holding, Hold back, out, up, etc** Absorb, Adhere, Airlock, Allege, Alow, Anchor, Apply, Argue, Armlock, Asset, Backbreaker, Bear hug, Belay, Believe, Binder, Boston crab, Cachepot, Caesura, Canister, Cease, Cement, Cinch, Clamp, Clasp, Cling, Clip, Clutch, Contain, Corral, Cotland, Cradle, Cresset, Deem, Defer, Delay, Detain, Display, Document, Dog, Drainer, Eggcup, Embrace, Encompass, Engage, Engross, Er, Facebar, Farm, Fast, Fief, Fistful, Frog, Full nelson, Garter, → GRASP, Grip, Grovet, Half-nelson, Hammerlock, Handle, Haud, Have, Headlock, Heft, Heist, Hiccup, Hinder, Hitch, Ho(a), Hod, Hoh, Hoy, Hug, Impedance, Impede, Impediment, Impound, In chancery, Incumbent, Inhibit, Intern, Intray, Japanese stranglehold, Keep, Keepnet, Lease, Lifebelt, Maintain, Manure, Music, Nef, Nelson, Nurse, Oasis, Obstacle, Occupant, Own, Paperweight, Port, Proffer, Punnet, Purchase, Rack, Reach, Reckon, Reluct, Reserve, Restrain, Retain, Rivet, Rob, Rundale, Runrig, Rush, Save, Scissors, Secure, Shelve, Shoebox, Shore, Sleeve, Sostenuto, Spool, Stand, Stock, Suplex, Suspend, Take, Tenancy, Tenement, Tenure, Territory, Toehold, Toft, Trap, Tray, Tripod, Trivet, Tub, Wait, Wallet, → WRESTLING, Wristlock, Zarf, Zurf

**Holdall** Tote(-bag)

**Hole(s), Holed, Holey** Ace, Agloo, Aglu, Albatross, Antrum, Aperture, Aubrey, Beam, Birdie, Black, Bogey, Bolt, Borrow, Breach, Breathing, Bullet, Burrow, Cat, Cave, Cavern, Cavity, Cenote, Cissing, Coal, Coalsack, Collapsar, Cove, Crater, Cubby, Cup, Dell, Den, Dene, Dog-leg, Dolina, Doline, Dormie, Dormy, Dreamhole, Dry, Dugout, Eagle, Earth, Ethmoid, Eye(let), Faveolate, Finger, Foramen, Funk, Gap, Geat, Glory, Gnamma, Gore, Gutta, Hag(g), Hawse, Hideout, Kettle, Knot, Lenticel, Lill, Limber, Loop, Loup, Lubber's, Lumina, Maar, Mortise, Moulin, Namma, Nineteenth, Oillet, → OPENING, Orifex, Orifice, Ozone, Perforate, Pierce, Pigeon, Pinprick, Pit, Plight, Pocket, Pore, Port, Pot, Potato, Priest's, Punctuate, Punctum, Puncture, Rabbit, Rivet, Rove, Rowport, Sallyport, Scupper, Scuttle, Scye, Sinus, Situation, Slot, Snag, Snow, Soakaway, Socket, Sound, Spandrel, Spider, Spiraculum, Starting, Stead, Stew, Stop, Stove, Swallow, Tear, Thirl, Thumb, Tight spot, Touch, Trema, Vent, Ventage, Ventige, Voided, Vug, Watering, Weep(er), Well, White, Wookey

**Holiday(s), Holiday maker** Away, Bank, Benjo, Break, Busman's, Camper, Caravan(n)er, Carnival, Childermas, Cruise, Days of Awe, Easter, Ecotour, Ferial, Festa(l), → FESTIVAL, Fête, Fiesta, Fly-drive, French leave, Furlough, Gala, Half(term), High, Honeymoon, Kwanzaa, Lag b'Omer, Laik, Lake, Leasure, Leave, Legal, Leisure, Long, Minibreak, Off-day, Off-time, Outing, Pace, Packaged, Pink-eye, Play-day, Playtime, Public, Purim, Recess, Repose, Rest, Roman, Schoolie, Seaside, Shabuoth, Shavuot, Sojourn, Statutory, Stay, Staycation, Sunday, Tax, Time off, Trip, → VACATION, Villeggiatura, Wake(s), Weekend, Whitsun, Xmas

**Holinshed** Chronicler

**Holland(s)** Batavia, Genevese, Gin, Hogen-mogen, Netherlands, NL

**Hollow(ed)** Acetabulum, Aeolipile, Alveary, Antar, Antre, Antrum, Armpit, Axilla, Blastula, Boss, Bowl, Cave(rn), Cavity, Chasm, Chott, Cirque, Cleché, Comb(e), Concave, Coomb, Corrie, Crater, Cup(mark), Cwm, Deaf, Dean, Dell, Delve, Den(e), Dent, Dewpond, Dimple, Dingle, Dip, Dish(ing), Dolina, Doline, Empty, Fossette, Frost, Gilgai, Glenoid, Gnamma-hole, Gowpen, Groove, Grot(to), Hole, How, Howe, Igloo, Incavo, Insincere, Intaglio, Keck(sy),

Kettle(hole), Kex, Khud, Lap, Lip-deep, Mortise, Namma-hole, Niche, Omphaloid, Orbita, Pan, Philtrum, Pit, Playa, Punchbowl, Punt, Recess, Redd, Rout, Rut, Scoop, Shott, Sinus, Slade, Sleepy, Slot, Slough, Socket, Swire, Thank-you-ma'am, Trematic, Trough, Vacuous, Ventricle, Vesicle, Vlei, Vola, Wame, Wem

**Hollow-horned** Cavicorn

**Holly** Aquifoliaceae, Eryngo, Holm, Ilex, Mate, Winterberry, Yaupon

**Hollyhock** Althaea, Malva, Rose mallow

**Hollywood** Bowl, Tinseltown

**Holm** Isle

**Holmes** Sherlock, Wendell

**Holmium** Ho

**Holocaust** Churban, Fire, Shoah

**Holocene** Recency

**Hologram, Holograph** Laser, MS

**Holothurian** Trepang

**Holster** Sheath

**Holy(man), Holiness** Adytum, Alliance, Ariadne, Blessed, → DIVINE, Godly, Grail, Halidom, Hallowed, Helga, Hery, Inner sanctum, Khalif, Loch, Mahatma, Mountain, Olga, Orders, Pan(h)agia, Piety, Pious, Sacred, Sacrosanct, Sad(d)hu, Saintdom, Saintly, Sanctitude, Sannayasi(n), Santon, Sekos, Sepulchre, Shrine, Starets, Staretz, SV, Tirthankara, War

**Holy books, Holy writing** Adigranth, Atharvaveda, Bible, Gemara, Granth, Hadith, Hagiographa, Koran, Mishnah, NT, OT, Pia, Purana, Rigveda, Sama-Veda, → SCRIPTURE, Shaster, Shastra, Smriti, Sura(h), Tanach, Writ, Yajur-Veda

**Holy building, Holy city, Holy place** Caaba, Chapel, Church, Kaaba, Kirk, Mashhad, Mecca, Medina, Meshed, Najaf, Penetralia, Sanctum, Station, Synagogue, Temenos, Temple

**Holy Ghost** Paraclete

**Holy of holies** Sanctum

**Holy water** Amrit

**Holy woman** Magdalene

**Homage** Bow, Cense, Honour, Kneel, Manred, Obeisance, Tribute, Vail

**Home(land), Homeward** Abode, Ancestral, Apartment, Base, Blighty, Bro, Broken, Burrow, Cheshire, Chez, Clinic, Community, Convalescent, Crib, Des res, Domal, Domestic, Domicile, Dwelling, Earth, Eventide, Family, Fireside, Flat, Form, Funeral, Gaff, Goal, Habitat, Harvest, Heame, Hearth, Heme, Hospice, House, Ideal, In, Lair, Libken, Lockwood, Lodge, Love-nest, Maisonette, Mental, Mobile, Montacute, Motor, Nest, Nursing, Old sod, Orphanage, Pad, Penny-gaff, Pied à terre, Pile, Pit dwelling, Plas Newydd, Remand, Res(idence), Rest, Semi, Starter, Stately, Tepee, Turangawaewae, Up-along, Villa, Warren

**Homecoming** Nostos

**Home counties** SE

**Homeless** Arab, Bag lady, Dosser, Evicted, Gangrel, Nomadic, Outler, Rootless, Skell, Stray, Waif

**Homely** Cosy

**Homer(ic)** Comatose, Cor, Epic(ist), Maeonides, Nod, Pigeon, Simpson, Somnolent

**Home-rule** Parnellism, Swaraj

**Homesick(ness)** Heimweh, Mal du pays

**Homespun** Cracker-barrel, Folksy, Plain, Raploch, Russet, Simple

**Homestead** Ranch, Toft

**Homework** → DIY, Prep, Preparation

**Homicidal, Homicide** Chance-medley, Culpable, Justifiable, Killing, Manslaughter

**Homily** Lecture, Midrash, Pi, Postil, Prone, Sermon, Tract

▷**Homing** *may indicate* coming back

**Hominid** Oreopitheous

**Homogeneous** Indiscrete

**Homogram, Homograph** Abac, Heteronym

**Homosexual(ity)** Bardash, Camp, Cat, Catamite, Friend of Dorothy, Gay, Gaydar, Ginger, Homophile, Invert, Lesbian, Minty, Muscle Mary, Pederast, Queer, Queercore, Rough trade, Slash, Tribade, Uranism, Urning

**Hone** Grind, → SHARPEN, Whet

**Honest(y), Honestly** Abe, Aboveboard, Afauld, Afawld, Amin, Candour, Clean, Ethical, Fair dinkum, Faith, Four square, Frank, Genuine, Incorruptible, Injun, Integrity, Jake, Jannock, Jonnock, Legitimate, Lunaria, Lunary, Mensch, Open-faced, Penny, Probity, Realtie, Rectitude, Reputable, Righteous, Round, Sincere, Soothfast, Square, Squareshooter, Straight, Straight-arrow, Straightforward, Straight-out, Trojan, → TRUE, Truepenny, Upfront, Upright, Upstanding

**Honey(ed)** Comb, Flattery, Hybla(ean), Hymettus, Mel, Melliferous, Mellifluous, Nectar, Oenomel, Oxymel, Palm, Peach, Popsy-wopsy, Sis, Sugar, Sweetheart, Sweetie (pie), Virgin, Wild, Wood

**Honeycomb(ed)** Cellular, Faveolate, Favose, Favous, Smock, Waxwork

**Honeydew** Marina lichen, Mildew

**Honey-eater** Bear, Blue-eye, Pooh

**Honeypot** Haanepoot

**Honeysuckle** Abelia, Anthemion, Caprifoil, Caprifole, Lonicera, Rewa rewa, Suckling, Twinflower, Woodbind, Woodbine

**Hong Kong** .hk

**Honk** Blare, Hoot, Puke, Toot

**Honour(able), Honorary, Honoured, Honorific, Honours** A, Acclaim, Accolade, Ace, Adore, Adward, Birthday, Blue, Bow, CBE, Commemorate, Credit, Crown, Curtsey, Dan, Decorate, Doctorate, Elate, Emeritus, Ennoble, → ESTEEM, Ethic, Excellency, Face-card, Fame, Fête, Garland, Gloire, Glorify, Glory, Grace, Greats, Homage, Insignia, Invest, Izzat, J, Jack, K, King, Knave, Knight, Kudos, Last, Laudation, Laureate, Laurels, MBE, Mensch, Mention, Merit, Military, OBE, Obelion, Optime, Order, Peerage, Privilege, Pundonor, Q, Queen, Regius, Remember, Repute, Respect, Revere, Reward, Salute, Straight, Ten, Tenace, Titular, Tribute, Tripos, Venerate, Virtuous, White, Worship, Wranglers

**Honourable companion** CH

**Honourless** Yarborough

**Hooch** Hogan, Hogen, Moonshine

**Hood(ed)** Almuce, Amaut, Amice, Amowt, Apache, Balaclava, Bashlik, Biggin, Blindfold, Calash, Calèche, Calyptra, Capeline, Capouch, Capuccio, Capuche, Chaperon(e), Coif, Cope, Cowl, Cucullate(d), Faldetta, Fume, Gangster, Headdress, Jacobin, Kennel, Lens, Liripipe, Liripoop, Mantle, Mazarine, Mudguard, Nithsdale, Pixie, Robin, Rowdy, Snood, Trot-cosey, Trot-cozy, Visor

**Hoodlum** Gangster, Lowlife, Mobster, Roughneck, Thug, Wanksta, Yob

**Hoodoo** Jonah, Moz(z)

**Hoodwink(ed)** Blear, Bluff, Cheat, → DECEIVE, Delude, Dupe, Gull, Hoax, Kid, Mislead, Nose-led, Seel

**Hoof(ed)** Artiodactyla, Cloot, Coffin, Frog, Tap dance, Trotter, Ungula

**Hooha(h)** Carry on, Fracas, Furore, Humdudgeon

**Hook(ed), Hooker, Hooks** Addict, Adunc, Aduncous, Anchor, Aquiline, Arrester, Barb(icel), Barbule, Becket, Boat, Butcher's, Button, Cant(dog), Catch, Chape, Claw, Cleek, Clip, Clove, Cocotte, Corvus, Crampon, Cromb, Crome, Crook, Crotchet, Cup, Drail, Draught, Duck, Fifi, Fish, Flesh, Floozy, Fluke, Fly, Gab, Gaff, Gig, Grap(p)le, Grapnel, Grappling, Gripple, Hamate, Hamose, Hamulus, Hanger, Heel, Hitch, Inveigle, Kype, Meat, Picture, Pot, Prostitute, Pruning, Punch, Retinaculum, Sickle, Sister, Sky, Snare, Snell, Sniggle, Solicit, Swivel, Tala(u)nt, Tart, Tenaculum, Tenter, Tie, Trip, Uncus, Wanton, Welsh

**Hookah** Bong, Chillum, Hubble-bubble, Kalian, Narghil(l)y, Narg(h)ile, Nargileh, Nargil(l)y, Pipe

**Hookey** Malingering

**Hooligan** Apache, Bogan, Casual, Desperado, Droog, Goonda, Hobbledehoy, Hoon, Keelie, Larrikin, Lout, Ned, Rough(neck), Rowdy, Ruffian, Skollie, Skolly, Tearaway, Ted, Tityre-tu, Tough, Tsotsi, Vandal, Yahoo, Yob(bo)

**Hoop(s), Hooped** Bail, Band, Circle, Crinoline, Farthingale, Garth, Gird, Girr, Hula®, O, Pannier, → RING, Sleeper, Tire, Trochus, Trundle

**Hooray** Whoopee, Yippee

**Hoot(er)** Boo, Conk, Deride, Foghorn, Honk, Madge, Nasal, Nose, Owl, Riot, Screech-owl, Siren, Ululate

**Hoover** Consume, Dam, Vacuum

**Hop(per)** An(o)ura, Ball, Bin, Caper, Cuscus, Dance, Flight, Jeté, Jump, Kangaroo, Leap, Lilt, Long, Opium, Pogo, Roo, Saltate, Scotch, Skip, Spring, Tremié, Vine

**Hope(ful)** Anticipate, Aspirant, Auspicious, Bob, Chance, Combe, Comer, Contender, Daydream, Desire, Dream, Elated, Esperance, Evelyn, Expectancy, Forlorn, Gleam, Good, Great white, Idealistic, Inshallah, Offchance, Pipe-dream, Pray, Promising, Prospect, Ray, Roseate, Rosy, Sanguine, Trust, Upbeat, Valley, Wannabe, White, Wish

**Hopeless(ness), Hopeless quest** Abattu, Anomie, Anomy, Basket case, Black, Buckley's chance, Dead duck, Despair, Despondent, Forlorn, Gloom, Goner, Lost cause, Non-starter, No win, Perdu, Pessimist

**Hophead** Drinker, Lush, Sot

**Hopscotch** Peevers

**Horace** Flaccus, Ode, Satirist

**Horatio** Nelson

**Horatius** Cocles

**Horde** Crowd, Golden, Many, Mass, Mob, Swarm

**Horizon** A, Apparent, Artificial, B, C, Celestial, Event, Gyro, Rational, Scope, Sea-line, Sensible, Skyline, Visible

**Horizontal** Advection, Flat, Level, Prone, Prostrate, Supine, Tabular

**Hormone** Growth, Indoleacetic, Plant, Sex

---

**HORMONES**

***3 letters:***
FSH
IAA
TSH

***4 letters:***
ACTH

***5 letters:***
Auxin
Kinin

***7 letters:***
Gastrin
Ghrelin
Inhibin
Insulin
Relaxin
Steroid
Thyroid

***8 letters:***
Abscisin
Androgen
Autacoid
Bursicon
Ecdysone
Estrogen
Florigen
Glucagon
Juvenile
Oestriol
Oestrone
Oxytocin
Resistin
Secretin
Thymosin

***9 letters:***
Adrenalin®
Corticoid
Cortisone
Cytokinin
Endocrine
Melatonin
Oestrogen
Pituitrin
Progestin
Prolactin
Secretion
Serotonin
Thyroxine

***10 letters:***
Adrenaline
Calcitonin
Folliculin
Intermedin
Lipotropin
Oestradiol

***11 letters:***
Aldosterone
Angiotensin
Gibberellin
Luteinizing
Parathyroid
Progestogen
Somatomedin
Thyrotropin
Vasopressin

***12 letters:***
Androsterone
Antidiuretic
Biosynthesis
Gonadotropin
Luteotrophic
Noradrenalin
Pancreozymin
Progesterone
Secretagogue
Somatostatin
Somatotropin
Stilboestrol
Testosterone
Thyrotrophin

***13 letters:***
Catecholamine
Gonadotrophic
Gonadotrophin
Melanotropine
Noradrenaline
Prostaglandin
Somatotrophin

***14 letters:***
Corticosteroid
Corticosterone
Erythropoietin
Glucocorticoid
Hydrocortisone
Levonorgestrel
Norepinephrine

***15 letters:***
Cholecystokinin

***16 letters:***
Triiodothyronine

***17 letters:***
Mineralocorticoid

**Horn(s), Horny** Acoustic, Advancer, Amalthea, Antenna(e), Antler, Baleen, Bass, Basset, Beeper, Bez, Brass, Buck, Bugle, Bur(r), Cape, Ceratoid, Coach, Cor, Cornet, Cornett, Cornopean, Cornu(a), Cornucopia, Cream, Cromorna, Cromorne, Cusp, Dilemma, English, Exponential, Flugel-horn, French, Frog, Gemshorn, Golden, Gore, Hooter, → HORNBLOWER, Hunting, Ivory, Keratin, Klaxon, Lur, Morsing, Mot, Oliphant, Parp, Periostracum, Plenty, Post, Powder, Pryse, Ram's, Saddle, Scur, Shoe, Shofar, Shophor, Spongin, Tenderling, Trey, Trez, Trumpet, Tusk, Vulcan's badge, Waldhorn

**Hornblende** Syntagmatite

**Hornblower** Brain, Horatio, Peel, Triton, Trumpeter

**Hornbook** Battledoor, Battledore

**Horned (sheep)** Cabrié, Cabrit, Cornute, Hamate, Lunate, Mouflon, Muflon

**Hornet** Stinger

**Hornless** Doddy, Humbel, Humble, Humlie, Hummel, Mooly, Mul(l)ey, Poley, Polled

**Hornpipe** Matelote

**Horoscope** Figure, Future, Prophecy, Star-map

**Horrendous** Fearsome

**Horrible, Horror** Appalling, Aw(e)some, Beastly, Brat, Creepy, Dire, Distaste, Dread(ful), Execrable, Frightful, Gashful, Ghastly, Grand Guignol, Grisly, Grooly, Gruesome, Grysie, Hammer, Hideous, Imp, Loathsome, Minging, Nightmare, Obnoxious, Odious, Panic, Rascal, Shock, Shudder, Stupefaction, Terror, The creeps, Ugh, Vile

**Horrid, Horrific, Horrified, Horrify(ing)** Aghast, Agrise, Appal, Blood-curdling, Chill, Dire, Dismay, Dreadful, Frightful, Ghastly, Gothic, Grim, Grisly, H, Loathy, Lurid, Odious, Scandalise, Shock, Spine-chilling, Spiteful, Ugly

**Hors d'oeuvres** Antipasto, Canapé, Carpaccio, Ceviche, Crudites, Hoummos, Houmus, Hummus, Mez(z)e, Pâté, Smor(re)brod, Smorgasbord, Starter, Tapas, Zak(o)uski

**Horse(s)** Abasta, Airer, Bidet, Bloodstock, Carriage, Clothes, Coach, Cut, Cutting, Dark, Doer, Dray, Drier, Drug, Equine, Eye-necked, Fill, Form, H, → HEROIN, High, Hobby, Horned, Iron, Knight, Kt, Light, Lot, Maiden, Malt, Non-starter, Outsider, Pack, Pantomime, P(h)ilhorse, Plug, Race, Ride, Rocking, Sawbuck, Scag, Screen, Selling-plater, Sense, Stable, Stalking, Standard-bred, Starter, Stayer, Steeplechaser, Stiff, Stock, Teaser, Timber-mare, Trestle, Unicorn, Vanner, Vaulting, White, Willing, Wooden

---

## HORSES

*2 letters:*
GG

*3 letters:*
Ass
Bay
Cob
Dun
Gee
Nag
Pad
Pot
Rip
Tit

*4 letters:*
Arab
Aver
Barb
Buck
Cert
Colt
Crib
Dale
Fell
Foal
Grey
Hack
Jade
Mare
Pole
Pony
Post
Prad
Roan
Snow
Span
Stud
Taki
Trot
Yale
Yaud

*5 letters:*
Arion
Arkle
Bevis
Borer
Caple
Capul
Favel
Filly
Genet
Morel
Mount
Neddy
Pacer
Paint
Pinto
Poler
Punch
Rogue
Screw
Seian
Shire
Stage
Steed
Tacky
Takhi
Trace
Troop
Waler
Wheel
Zebra

*6 letters:*
Alfana
Ambler
Bayard
Bronco
Brumby
Calico
Canuck
Cayuse
Chaser
Cooser
Crollo

Curtal
Cusser
Dobbin
Entire
Exmoor
Favell
Ganger
Garran
Garron
Gennet
Hogget
Hunter
Jennet
Kanuck
Keffel
Lampos
Livery
Morgan
Mudder
Novice
Pad-nag
Plater
Pommel
Poster
Quagga
Randem
Remuda
Roarer
Rouncy
Runner
Sabino
Saddle
Shoo-in
Silver
Sorrel
String
Stumer
Summer
Tandem
Tarpan
Tracer
Trojan

*7 letters:*
Bobtail
Breaker
Caballo
Cavalry
Centaur
Charger
Clipper
Coacher
Courser
Cuisser
Dappled
Draught
Eclipse
Eventer
Gelding
Hackney
Hobbler
Liberty
Marengo
Marocco
Morocco
Mustang
Palfrey
Pegasus
Piebald
Pointer
Quarter
Remount
Saddler
Sheltie
Spanker
Sumpter
Swallow
Swinger
Trigger
Trooper
Trotter
Walking
Wheeler
Xanthos
Xanthus

*8 letters:*
Aquiline
Bangtail
Bathorse
Boerperd
Buckskin
Camargue
Champion
Chestnut
Clay-bank
Cocktail
Dartmoor
Destrier
Eohippus
Friesian
Galloway
Highland
Holstein
Hyperion
Kochlani
Lusitano
Palomino
Schimmel
Shetland
Skewbald
Sleipnir
Springer
Stallion
Stibbler
Trippler
Warragal
Warragle
Warragul
Warrigal
Welsh cob
Whistler
Yarraman
Yearling

*9 letters:*
Appaloosa
Black Bess
Caballine
Clavileno
Coldblood
Connemara
Dapple bay
Foxhunter
Gringolet
Houyhnhnm
Icelandic
Incitatus
Knabstrup
Percheron
Rosinante
Rozinante
Warmblood

*10 letters:*
Andalusian
Bucephalus
Buckjumper
Buttermilk
Clydesdale
Copenhagen
Dapple-grey
Lipizzaner
Lippizaner
Pliohippus
Przewalski
Showjumper
Stagecoach
Svadilfari
Wheelhorse

*11 letters:*
Black Beauty
Daisy-cutter
High-stepper
Przewalski's

*12 letters:*
Cleveland Bay
Hambletonian
Suffolk Punch
Thoroughbred

*13 letters:*
Perissodactyl

*14 letters:*
Strawberry roan

*16 letters:*
Tennessee Walking

---

**Horseback** Croup, En caballo
**Horse-box** Stable, Stall
**Horse-chestnut** Aesculus, Conker
**Horse collar** Brecham, Hame
**Horse complaint, Horse disease, Horse problem, Horse trouble** Blind staggers, Blood spavin, Bogspavin, Bot(t)s, Broken wind, Canker, Capel(l)et, Cracked heels, Cratches, Curb, Deer-neck, Dourine, Drepance, Equinia, Eweneck, Farcin, Farcy, Fives, Founder, Frush, Glanders, Gourdy, Grape, Grass-sickness, Head staggers, Heaves, Hippiatric, Hoof rot, Knee spavin, Laminitis, Lampas, Lampers, Malander, Mallander, Mallender, Megrims,

Miller's disease, Moon blindness, Mooneye, Mud fever, N(a)gana, Parrot mouth, Poll-evil, Quartercrack, Quitter, Quittor, Ringbone, Roaring, Sallenders, Sand crack, Scratches, Seedy-toe, Shaft, Spavie, Spavin, Springhalt, Staggers, Strangles, Stringhalt, Summer sores, Surra, Sway-back, Sween(e)y, Thorough-pin, Thrush, Toe-crack, Tread, Vives, Weed, Weid, Whistling, Windgall, Wind-sucking, Wire-heel, Yellows

**Horse-dealer** Buster, Coper

**Horsefly** Cleg, Tabanid

**Horse-lover** Philip

**Horseman** Ataman, Caballero, Cavalry, Centaur, Conquest, Cossack, Cowboy, Death, Dragman, Famine, Farrier, Hobbler, Hussar, Knight, Lancer, Nessus, Ostler, Parthian, Pestilence, Picador, Pricker, Quadrille, Revere, →RIDER, Slaughter, Spahi, Stradiot, Tracer, War, Wrangler

**Horsemanship** Manège

**Horse opera** Western

**Horseplay** Caper, Chukka, Knockabout, Polo, Rag, Rant, Romp

**Horsepower** Brake, Hp, Indicated, Metric, Ps

**Horseradish** Ben, Moringa

**Horseshoe(-shaped)** Henge, Hippocrepian, King-crab, Lophophorate, Lunette, Manilla, Oxbow, Plate

**Horsetail** Equisetum

**Horse thief** Blanco, Rustler

**Horticultural, Horticulture, Horticulturist** Grower, Pomology, RHS

**Hose** Chausses, Fire, Fishnet, Galligaskins, Gaskins, Hydrant, Lisle, Netherstock(ing), Nylons, Panty, Sock, Sox, Sprinkler, Stockings, Support, Tabi, Tights, Trunk, Tube, Undergarment, Wet

**Hospice, Hospital** Almshouse, Ambulance, Asylum, Barts, Base, Bedlam, Booby hatch, Bughouse, Clinic, Cottage, Day, Dressing station, ENT, Field, Foundation, General, Guest-house, Guys, H, Home, Hôtel dieu, Imaret, Infirmary, Isolation, Karitane, Lambarene, Lazaretto, Leprosarium, Leproserie, Leprosery, Lock, Loony bin, Lying-in, MASH, Mental, Nosocomial, Nuthouse, Nuttery, Ozzie, Pest-house, Polyclinic, Rathouse, San, Scutari, Sick bay, Snake-pit, Special, Spital, Spittle, Teaching, Trauma centre, Trust, UCH

**Hospitable, Hospitality** Cadgy, Convivial, Corporate, Entertainment, Euxine, Kidgie, Lucullan, Open house, Philoxenia, Social, Xenial

**Host(s), Hostess** Air, Alternate, Amphitryon, Anchorman, Army, Barmecide, Brigade, Bunny girl, Chatelaine, Commerce, Compere, Crowd, Definitive, Drove, Emcee, Entertainer, Eucharist, Geisha, Heavenly, Hirsel, Hotelier, Innkeeper, Intermediate, Inviter, Laban, Landlady, Landlord, Legend, Legion, Licensee, Lion-hunter, Lot, Maitre d', Mass, Mavin, MC, Number, Parasite, Presenter, Publican, Quickly, Quizmaster, Sabaoth, Speakerine, Stratonic, Swarm, Taverner, Throng, Torrent, Trimalchio, Wafer, Winfrey

**Hostage** Gherao, Pawn, Pledge, POW

**Hostel(ry)** Asylum, Auberge, Brew pub, Dharms(h)ala, Dorm, Dormitory, Entry, Halfway house, Inn, Y(MCA), YHA, Youth

**Hostile, Hostility** Adverse, Aggressive, Alien, Anger, Animus, Anti, Arms, Aversion, Bad blood, Bellicose, Bitter, Chilly, Currish, Detestation, Diatribe, Enemy, Feud, Forbidding, Hating, Ho, Icy, Ill, Ill-will, Inimical, Inveterate, Needle, Opposed, Oppugnant, Pugnacity, Tension, Unfriendly, Virulent, Vitriolic, War, Wasp's nest

**Hot(spot), Hot (tempered)** Aboil, Aetnean, Aflame, Ardent, Baking, Big, Blistering, Breem, Breme, Cajun, Calid, Candent, Cayenne, Chilli, Dog days, Enthusiastic, Erotic(al), Etnaen, Facula, Febrile, Fervid, Feverish, Fiery, Fuggy, Gospeller, Het, In, Incandescent, Indignant, Irascible, Ireful, Jalfrezi, Latest, Lava, Lewd, Live, Mafted, Mirchi, Mustard, Nightclub, Pepper, Piping, Potato, Quick, Randy, Red, Roaster, Scalding, Scorcher, Sexpot, Sexy, Sizzling, Spicy, Spitfire, Steamy, Stewy, Stifling, Stolen, Sultry, Sweaty, Sweltering, Sweltry, Tabasco®, Thermal, Thermidor, Torrid, Toustie, Tropical, Zealful

**Hotchpotch** Bricolage, Farrago, Hash, Mish-mash, Pot pourri, Powsowdy, Welter

**Hotel, Hotelkeeper** Astor, Astoria, Bo(a)tel, Boutique, Commercial, Fleabag, Flophouse, Gasthaus, Gasthof, H, Hilton, Host, Hydro(pathic), Inn, Internet, Khan, Military, Motel, Parador, Patron(ne), Pension, Posada, Private, Ritz, Roadhouse, Savoy, Tavern, Telco, Temperance, Trust, Waldorf, Watergate

**Hothead(ed)** Cacafago, Impetuous, Madcap, Rash, Spitfire, Volcano
**Hot-house** Conservatory, Forcing-house, Nursery, Orangery, Vinery
**Hot plate** Griddle, Salamander
**Hotpot** Stew
**Hot rod** Dragster
**Hotshot** Gunslinger, Whiz
**Hotspot** Bricolage, Farrago, Mish-mash, Powsowdy, Suntrap, Welter
**Hotspur** Harry, Hothead, Percy, Rantipole
**Hot water** Soup, Therm
**Hound(s)** Afghan, Badger, Basset, Beagle, Bellman, Brach, Buck, Cad, Canine, Cry, → DOG, Entry, Gabriel's, Gaze, Hamiltonstovare, Harass, Harrier, Hen-harrier, Ibizan, Importune, Javel, Kennet, Lurcher, Lyam, Lym(e), Mute, Otter, Pack, Persecute, Pharaoh, Pursue, Rache, Ranter, Reporter, Saluki, Scoundrel, Talbot, True, Tufter
**Hound's bane** Palay
**Hour(s)** Business, Canonical, Complin(e), Daylight, Elders', Eleventh, Flexitime, Golden, H, Happy, Holy, Hr, Laud, Literacy, Little, Lunch, None(s), O'clock, Office, Orthros, Peak, Prime, Rush, Sext, Sidereal, Small, Staggered, Terce, Tide, Time, Undern, Unearthly, Unsocial, Vespers, Visiting, Watt, Witching, Working, Zero
**Hourglass** Meniscoid
**House(s), Housing, Household(er)** Abode, Accepting, Adobe, Aerie, Aery, Astrology, Audience, Auditorium, B, Bach, Bastide, Beehive, Beth, Bhavan, Bhawan, Biggin, Billet, Bingo, Black, Blimp, Block, Boarding, Bondage, Bottom, Brick veneer, Broadcasting, Broiler, Brownstone, Bundestag, Casa, Chalet, Chamber, Chapter, Charnel, Château, Chattel, Chez, Chop, Cinema, Clan, Clapboard, Clearing, Co, Coach, Coffee, Commercial, Concern, Conditioning, Convent, Cote, Cottage (orné), Council, Counting, Country, Crankcase, Crib, Custom(s), Dacha, Dail, Death, Demain, Demesne, Derry, Des res, Discount, Disorderly, Domal, Domestic, Domicile, Donga, Door, Dower, Draught, Drostdy, Drum, Duplex, Dwelling, Dynasty, Edifice, Entertain, Establishment, Estate, Este, Eyrie, Familial, Farm, Fashion, Fibro(cement), Finance, Firm, Forcing, Frame, Fraternity, Free, Frontager, Full, Gaff, Gambling, Gaming, Garage, Gazebo, Gemini, Gite, Government, Grace and favour, Guest, Guise, Habitat, Habitation, Hacienda, Halfway, Hall, Harbour, Hearth, HK, Ho, Home, Homestead, Hutch, Ice, Igloo, Infill, Inn, Inner, Insula, Issuing, Joss, Ken, Lanai, Libken, Lodge, Lofted, Loose, Lot(t)o, Lower, Maison(ette), Malting, Manor, Manse, Mansion, Mas, Meeting, Meiney, Meinie, Meiny, Ménage, Menyie, Messuage, Mobility, Monastery, Montagne, Music, Nacelle, Necessary, Node, Open(-plan), Opera, Outer, Pad, Parliament, Pent, Picts, Picture, Pilot, Play, Pleasure, Pole, Pondokkie, Porter, Post, Prefab, Printing, Prison, Private, Public, Pueblo, Put up, Quinta, Radome, Ranch, Ratepayer, Register, Residence, Rooming, Root, Rough, Sacrament, Safe, Saltbox, Satis, Schloss, School, Seat, Semi, Shanty, Sheltered, Show, Sign, Silo, Social, Software, Spec-built, Sporting, Stable, State, Station, Steeple, Storey, Subtopia, Succession, Tavern, Tea, Tenement, Terrace, Theatre, Third, Tied, Toft, Toll, Tombola, Tool, Tower, Town, Tract, Treasure, Tree, Trust, Try, Upby, Vaulting, Vicarage, Villa(-home), Wash, Watch, Weather, Weatherboard, Weigh, Wendy, Whare, Wheel, Work, Zero, Zodiac

---

**HOUSES**

*3 letters:*
Leo

*4 letters:*
Bush
Keys
Riad
Syon
York

*5 letters:*
Lords
Scala
Tudor
Upper
Usher
White

*6 letters:*
Erddig
Grange
Hurley
Orange
Queen's
Seanad
Stuart
Wilton

*7 letters:*
Althing
Althorp
Bourbon
Commons
Hanover
Kenwood
Knesset
Lodging
Osborne
Stewart
Trinity
Windsor

*8 letters:*
Burghley
Chequers
Cliveden
Hapsburg
Harewood
Hatfield
Holyrood

Lagthing
Longleat
Packwood
Petworth
Somerset

*9 letters:*
Admiralty
Chartwell
Knebworth
Lancaster
Number Ten
Odelsting

*10 letters:*
Banqueting
Chatsworth
Heartbreak
Kirribilli
Odelsthing

*11 letters:*
Plantagenet
Russborough
Sandringham

*12 letters:*
Lockwood Home

*13 letters:*
Seanad Eireann

*15 letters:*
Representatives

---

**House-boat** Wan(i)gan, Wangun
**House-builder** Jack
**House-keeper** Chatelaine, Go(u)vernante, Matron, Publican
**House-leek** Sengreen
**Housemaid's knee** Bursa
**Houseman** Betty, Doctor, Intern, Peer
**Housemate** Co-tenant
**Houses of Parliament** St Stephen's
**House-warming** Infare
**Housewife** Etui, Frau, Needlecase, WI
**Housework** Chore, DIY
**Housing** Case, Crankcase, Shabrack, Shelter, Slum, Tenement
**Hova** Malagash
**Hove** Plim, Swell
**Hovel** Cru(i)ve, Den, Pigsty, Shack, Shanty
**Hover** Hang, Levitate, Lurk, Poise
**Hovercraft** Air-car
**How** Hello, Hill, Hollow, What
**How'dyedo, How d'ye do** Hallo, Pass, Salve
**However** Although, As, But, Ergates, Even-so, Leastwise, Sed, Still, Though, Yet
**Howitzer** Gun
**Howl(er)** Banshee, Bawl, Bay, Bloop, Caterwaul, Clanger, Crybaby, Hue, Mycetes, Sandstorm, Slip up, Squawk, Tornado, Ululate, War whoop, Wow, Yawl, Yell, Yowl
**How much** The
**Hoy** Bilander, Ship
**HP** Never-never
**HQ** Centre, Headquarters, Horse Guards, SHAPE
**Hub** Boss, Boston, Centre, Focus, Hob, Nave, Nerve centre, Nucleus, Pivot, Tee
**Hubbub** Charivari, Chirm, Coil, Din, Level-coil, Palaver, Racket, Row, Stir, Uproar
**Hubris** Pride
**Huckster** Hawker, Kidd(i)er, Pedlar
**Huddle** Cringe, Crowd, Gather, Hunch, Nestle, Ruck, Scrum, Shrink
**Hudson** River, Rock
**Hue** Chroma, Colour, Dye, Outcry, Pastel, Proscription, Steven, Tincture, Tinge, Umbrage, Utis
**Huff** Dudgeon, Hector, Pant, Pet, Pique, Snuff, Strunt, Tiff, Umbrage, Vex
**Hug** Bear, Caress, Clasp, Coll, Cuddle, Embosom, → EMBRACE, Snuggle, Squeeze
**Huge (number)** Astronomical, Brobdingnag, Colossal, Elephantine, Enorm(ous), Epic, Gargantuan, Giant, Gigantian, → GIGANTIC, Gillion, Ginormous, Humongous, Humungous, Immane, Immense, Leviathan, Lulu, Mega-, Milliard, Monolithic, Monster, Monumental, Octillion, Prodigious, Socking, Stupendous, Tall, Terrific, Thumping, Titanian, Tremendous, Vast, Voluminous, Whacking, Whopping
**Hugo** Victor
**Huguenot** Camisard
**Hulk** Lout, Ruin, Shale, Shell, Ship
**Hull** Bottom, Framework, Husk, Inboard, Keel, Monocoque, Pod, Sheal, Sheel, Shell, Shiel, Shill, Shiplap, Stern
**Hullabaloo** Outcry, Raz(z)mataz(z), Razzamatazz

▸**Hullo** *see* HELLO

**Hum(ming)** Abuzz, BO, Bombilate, Bombinate, Bum, Buzz, Chirm, Chirr, Drone, Eident, Lilt, Moan, Murmur, Nos(e)y, Odorate, Odorous, Pong, Ponk, Rank, Reek, Sough, Sowf(f), Sowth, Stench, Stink, Stir, Whir(r), Zing

**Human(e), Humanist, Humanitarian, Humanity, Humanoid** Anthropoid, Anthropology, Bang, Colet, Earthling, Earthman, Erasmus, Hominid, Homunculi, Incarnate, Kindness, Mandom, Mankind, Meatbot, Merciful, More, Mortal, Person, Philanthropic, Species, Sympathy, Ubuntu, Unpaid, Virtual, Wight

**Humble** Abase, Abash, Afflict, Baseborn, Belittle, Chasten, Conquer, Cow, Degrade, Demean, Demiss(ly), Depress, Grovel, Low-born, Lower, Lowly, Mean, Mean-born, → MEEK, Menial, Modest, Morigerate, Obscure, Poor, Rude, Small, Snub, Submissive, Truckle

**Humbug** Baloney, Berley, Blague, Blarney, Buncombe, Bunk(um), Burley, Cant, Claptrap, Con, Delude, Eyewash, Flam, Flummery, Fraud, Fudge, Gaff, Gammon, Gas, Guff, Gum, Hoax, Hoodwink, Hookey-walker, Kibosh, Liar, Maw-worm, Nonsense, Prig, Shenanigan, Tosh, Wind

**Humdinger** Cracker, Lulu

**Humdrum** Banal, Boredom, Bourgeois, Dull, Monotonous, Mundane, Ordinary, Prosaic, Routine, Rut, Tedious, Uninspiring

**Humid(ity)** Clammy, Close, Damp, Dank, Hydrometry, Machie, Machy, Moch, Moist, Muggy, Relative, Saturation, Steam, Sticky, Sultry, Tropical

**Humiliate(d), Humiliation, Humility** Abase(ment), Abash, Baseness, Comedown, Debag, Degrade, Demean, Disbench, Eating crow, Fast, Gall, Ignominious, Indignity, Laughing stock, Lose face, Lowlihead, Mortify, Put-down, Sadism, → SHAME, Skeleton, Take-down, Wither

**Humming-bird** Colibri, Hermit, Racket-tail, Rainbow, Rubythroat, Sabre-wing, Sapphire-wing, Sappho, Sawbill, Sylph, Thornbill, Topaz, Trochilus

**Hummock** Tump

**Hummus** Tahini

**Humorist** Cartoonist, Comedian, Jester, Leacock, Lear, Punster, Thurber, Twain, Wodehouse

**Humour, Humorous** Affability, Aqueous, Bile, Blood, Bonhomie, Caprice, Cardinal, Chaff, Choler, Coax, Cocker, Coddle, Comedy, Cosher, Cuiter, Cuittle, Custard-pie, Daut, Dawt, Droll, Dry, En badinant, Facetious, Fun, Gallows, Ichor, Indulge, Irony, Jest, Jocose, Jocular, Juice, Kidney, Lavatorial, Levity, Light, Melancholy, → MOOD, Observe, One-liner, Pamper, Phlegm, Pun, Pythonesque, Ribaldry, Salt, Satire, Serum, Sick, Temper, Trim, Vein, Vitreous, Vitreum, Wetness, Whim, Whimsy, Wit, Wry

**Humourless** Dry, Po(-faced)

**Hump(ed), Humping** Boy, Bulge, Dorts, Dowager's, Gibbose, Gibbous, Hog, Huff, Humf, Hummock, Humph, Hunch, Middelmannetjie, Pip, Protrusion, Ramp, Road, Sex, Sleeping policeman, Speed bump, Tussock

▸**Humpback** *see* HUNCH(ED)

**Humphrey** Bogart

**Humus** Compost, Leafmould, Moder, Mor, Mull

**Hun** Alaric, Atli, Attila

**Hunch(ed), Hunchback** Camel, Chum, Crookback, Gobbo, Hump, Instinct, Intuition, Kyphosis, Premonition, Presentiment, Quasimodo, Roundback, Sense, Squat, Stoop, Urchin

**Hundred(s), Hundredfold, Hundredth** Burnham, C, Cantred, Cantref, Cent, Centesimal, Centum, Centuple, Century, Chiltern, Commot, Days, Desborough, Great, Host, → IN A HUNDRED, Long, Northstead, Old, Percentage, Shire, Stoke, Tiyin, Ton, Tyiyn, Wapentake

**Hundred and fifty** CL, Y

**Hundred and sixty** T

**Hundred thousand** C

**Hundredweight** Centner, Long, Metric, Quintal, Short

**Hung** Displayed, Executed, Framed, High

**Hungarian, Hungary** Bohunk, Cheremis(s), Csardas, Magyar, Nagy, Szekely, Tzigane, Ugric, Vogul

**Hunger (strike), Hungry** Appestat, Appetite, Bulimia (nervosa), Bulimy, Clem, → CRAVE, Desire, Edacity, Emaciated, Empty, Esurient, Famine, Famish, Fast, Hanker, Hunter, Insatiate, Itch, Orectic, Pang, Pant, Peckish, Pine, Pyne, Rapacious, Raven, Ravin, Sharp-set, Starve, Unfed, Unfuelled, Yaup, Yearn

▷**Hungry** *may indicate* an 'o' in another word

**Hunk(s)** Beefcake, Chunk, Dry-fist, He-man, Miser(ly), Slab, Wedge

**Hunker** Squat

**Hunt(er), Hunting, Huntress, Huntsman** Actaeon, Alew, Archer, Artemis, Atalanta, Battue, Beachcomb, Beagle, Bellman, Blood sport, Bounty, Bushman, Calydon, Chace, Chase(r), Chasseur, Chevy, Chiv(vy), Comb, Cool, Corner, Coursing, Crockett, Cynegetic, Dog, Drag(net), Esau, Ferret, Fox, Free-shot, Gun, Halloo, Herne, Horse, Hound, Jager, Kennet, Lamping, Leigh, Letterbox, Lurcher, Montero, Mouser, National, Nimrod, Orion, Paperchase, Peel, Pig-sticking, Poacher, Poot, Posse, Pout, Predator, Prey, Prowl, Pursue, Quest, Quorn, Rabbit, Rach(e), Rake, Ran, Rancel, Ranzel, Ride, Rummage, Run, Safari, San, Scavenge(r), Scorse, Scout, Sealer, → SEARCH, Seek, Septembrizer, Shikar(ee), Shikari, Skirter, Slave, Slipper, Stag, Stalk, Sticker, Still, Swiler, Terrier, Thimble, Ticker, Tinchel, Tower, Trail, Trap, Treasure, Venatic, Venator, Venerer, Venery, → WATCH, Whale, Whip, Whipper-in, Witch, Wolfer, Woodman, Woodsman, Yager

**Hunting-call** Rechate, Recheat, Tally-ho, View-halloo

**Hunting-ground** Forestation, Walk

**Hurdle(r)** Barrier, Doll, Fence, Flake, Gate, Hemery, High, Jump, Moses, Obstacle, Raddle, Snag, Sticks, Wattle

**Hurdy (gurdy)** Barrel-organ, Hainch, Haunch, Vielle

**Hurl(ing)** Camogie, Cast, Dash, → FLING, Heave, Pitch, Precipitate, Put(t), Sling, Throw, → TOSS

**Hurly-burly** Furore, Noise

**Hurrah** Bravo, Cheers, Huzza, Io, Last, Whee, Yippee

**Hurricane** Baguio, Cyclone, Tornade, Tornado, Typhoon, → WIND

**Hurry, Hurried** Belt, Bustle, Chivvy, Chop-chop, Dart, Dash, Drive, Expedite, Festinate, Fisk, Frisk, Gad, Gallop, Giddap, Giddup, Giddy-up, Hadaway, Hare, Haste, Hie, Hightail, Induce, Mosey, Pop, Post-haste, Press (on), Push, Race, Railroad, → RUSH, Scamper, Scoot, Scramble, Scur(ry), Scutter, Scuttle, Skelter, Skurry, Spank, Speed, Streak, Sudden, Tear, Whirr, Zip

**Hurt(ful)** Abuse, Ache, Adverse, Afflict, Aggrieve, Ake, Bruise, Cutting, Damage, De(a)re, Detriment, Dishearten, Disservice, Harm, Harrow, Hit, → INJURE, Lesion, Maim, Nocent, Nocuous, Noisome, Noxious, Noyous, Offend, Pain, Pang, Prick(le), Resentful, Scaith, Spite, Sting, Trauma, Wound, Wring

**Hurtle** Career, Rush, Spin, Streak, Streek

**Husband(ry), Husbands** Add, Animal, Baron, Betty, Breadwinner, Conserve, Consort, Darby, Ear, Eche, Economy, Eke, Ere, Farm, Gander(-mooner), Georgic, Goodman, Groom, H, Hain, Hoddy-doddy, Hodmandod, Hubby, Ideal, Lord and master, Man, Manage, Mate, Partner, Polyandry, Reserve, Retrench, Save, Scrape, Scrimp, Spouse, Squirrel, → STORE, Tillage

**Hush(-hush)** Bestill, Gag, St, Sh, Silent, Smug, Subdue, Tace, Top secret, Wheesh(t), Whisht

**Husk(s), Husky** Acerose, Bran, Chaff, Draff, Eskimo, Gruff, Hoarse, Hull, Malemute, Seed, Sheal, Shiel, Shuck, Throaty

**Hussar** Cherry-picker, Cherubim

**Hussite** Calixtin(e), Taborite

**Hussy** Besom, Hen, Jezebel, Limmer, Loose, Minx, Vamp, Wench

**Hustle(r)** Fast talk, Frogmarch, Hasten, Jostle, Pro, Push, Railroad, Shoulder, Shove, Skelp

**Hut(s)** Banda, Booth, Bothie, Bothy, Bustee, Cabin, Caboose, Chalet, Choltry, Gazebo, Gunyah, Hogan, Humpy, Igloo, Mia-mia, Nissen, Pondok(kie), Quonset®, Rancheria, Rancho, Rondavel, Shack, Shanty, Sheal(ing), Shebang, Shed, Shiel(ing), Skeo, Skio, Succah,

Sukkah, Tilt, Tolsel, Tolsey, Tolzey, Tramping, Wan(n)igan, Whare, Wigwam, Wi(c)kiup, Wil(t)ja, Woodshed, Wurley, Wurlie

**Hutch** Bo(u)lting, Buddle, Crate, Pen, Rabbit

**Hyacinth** Bluebell, Cape, Grape, Starch, Wild

**Hybrid** Amerasian, Beefalo, Bigener, Bois-brûlé, Cama, Catalo, Centaur, Chamois, Chichi, Chimera, Citrange, Cockatrice, Cross, Dso, Funnel, Geep, Graft, Hippogriff, Hircocervus, Incross, Interbred, Jersian, Jomo, Jumart, Lurcher, Mameluco, Mermaid, Merman, Metif, Métis, Mongrel, Mule, Mutation, Noisette, Onocentaur, Opinicus, Ortanique, Ox(s)lip, Percolin, Plumcot, Pomato, Ringed, Single-cross, Tangelo, Tiglon, Tigon, Topaz, Ugli, Werewolf, Zedonk, Zho(mo)

▷**Hybrid** *may indicate* an anagram

**Hydra** Polyp

**Hydrant** Fireplug, H

**Hydrocarbon** Acetylene, Aldrin, Alkane, Alkene, Alkyl, Alkyne, Amylene, Arene, Asphaltite, Benzene, Benzpyrene, Bisphenol, Butadiene, Butane, Butene, Camphane, Camphene, Carotene, Cetane, Cubane, Cumene, Cycloalkane, Cyclohexane, Cyclopropane, Cymogene, Decane, Diene, Dioxin, Diphenyl, Ethane, Ethylene, Gutta, Halon, Hatchettite, Heavy oil, Hemiterpene, Heptane, Hexane, Hexene, Hexyl(ene), Indene, Isobutane, Isoprene, Ligroin, Limonene, Mesitylene, Methane, Naphtha, Naphthalene, Naphthalin(e), Nonane, Octane, Olefin(e), Paraffin, Pentane, Pentene, Pentylene, Phenanthrene, Phene, Picene, Pinene, Polyene, Propane, Pyrene, Pyridine, Pyrimidine, Retene, Squalene, Stilbene, Styrene, Terpene, Toluene, Triptane, Wax, Xylene, Xylol

**Hydrogen** Deut(er)on, Diplogen, Diplon, Ethene, H, Heavy, Muonium, Protium, Replaceable, Tritium

**Hydroid** Sea-fir

**Hydrolysis** Saponification

**Hydrometer** Salinometer

**Hydrophobia, Hydrophobic** Rabid, St Hubert's disease

**Hydroplane** Skid

**Hydroponic** Soil

**Hydroxide** Gibbsite

**Hydrozoa(n)** Campanularia, Graptolite, Medusoid, Millepore, Physalia, Portuguese man-of-war, Siphonophore

**Hyena** Aard-wolf, Cackle, Earthwolf, Laughing, Nandi bear, Spotted, Strand-wolf, Tiger-wolf

**Hygiene, Hygienic** Aseptic, Clean, Dental, Godly, Oral, Sanitary, Sepsis, Sleep

**Hymen** Maidenhead

**Hymn(s)** Amazing Grace, Anthem, Benedictine, Bhajan, Canticle, Carol, Cathisma, Choral(e), Coronach, Dies Irae, Dithyramb, Doxology, Epithalamia, Gloria, Hallel, Hundredth, Hymeneal, Introit(us), Ithyphallic, Lay, Magnificat, Mantra, Marseillaise, Nunc Dimittis, Ode, P(a)ean, Praise, Processional, Psalm, Psalmody, Recessional, Rigveda, Sanctus, Secular, Sequence, Stabat Mater, Sticheron, Tantum Ergo, Te Deum, Trisagion, Troparion, Veda

**Hymnographer, Hymnologist** Cowper, David, Faber, Heber, Moody, Neale, Parry, Sankey, Watts

**Hype(d)** Aflutter, Ballyhoo, Blurb

**Hyperactive** Frenetic

**Hyperbola** Rectangular

**Hyperbole, Hyperbolic** Auxesis, Exaggeration, Sech

**Hypercritical** Fastidious

**Hyperion** Titan

**Hypermetric** Long-sighted

**Hypersensitive, Hypersensitivity** Allergic, Atopy, Idiosyncratic

**Hypha(e)** Conidiophore, Stroma

**Hyphen(ated)** Dash, Parasyntheton, Soft

**Hypnosis, Hypnotise, Hypnotic, Hypnotism, Hypnotist** Autosuggestion, Braidism, Chloral, Codeine, Enthral, Entrance, Fluence, Hypotonia, Magnetic, Magnetise, Meprobamate, Mesmerism, Psychognosis, Spellbind, Svengali, Trance

**Hypochondria(c)** Atrabilious, Hyp, Nosophobia, Phrenesiac, Valetudinarian

**Hypocrisy, Hypocrite, Hypocritical** Archimago, Bigot, Byends, Cant, Carper, Chadband, Creeping Jesus, Deceit, Dissembler, Dissimulating, Double standards, False-faced, Heep, Holy Willie, Humbug, Insincere, Janus-faced, Lip service, Mucker, Nitouche, Pecksniff, Pharisaic, Pharisee, Phoney, Piety, Plaster saint, Prig, Sanctimony, Self-pious, Self-righteous, Sepulchre, Tartuf(f)e, Two-faced, Whited sepulchre

**Hypothesis, Hypothesize, Hypothetic, Hypothetical** Avogadro, Biophor, Conditional, Continuum, Gaia, Gluon, Graviton, Micella, Nebular, Nostratic, Notional, Null, Opine, Planetesimal, Postulation, Premise, Sapir-Whorf, Suppose, Suppositious, Theory, Virtual, Whorf, Working

**Hyrax** Cony, Daman, Dassie, Klipdas, Rock rabbit

**Hysteria, Hysteric(al)** Achiria, Astasia, Conniption, Crazy, Delirium, Frenzy, Meemie, Mother, Panic, Wobbly

# Ii

**I** A, Ch, Cham, Che, Dotted, Ego, Element, First person, Ich, Indeed, India, Iodine, Italy, J, Je, Me, Muggins, Myself, One, Self, Yours truly
**Iambus** Scazon
**Ian** Scot
**Iberian** Celtiberian
**Ibex** Izard
**Ibis** Hadedah, Sacred, Waldrapp
**Ice(d), Ice-cream, Icing, Icy** A la mode, Alcorza, Anchor, Arctic, Ballicatter, Banana split, Berg, Black, Bombe, Brainstorm, Brash, Butter, Camphor, Cassata, Choc, Coconut, Cone, Cool, Cornet, Coupe, Cream, Crystal, Diamonds, Drift, Dry, Field, Floe, Fondant, Frappé, Frazil, Freeze, Frigid, Frore, Frosting, Frosty, Gelato, Gelid, Gems, Glacé, Glacial, Glacier, Glare, Glaze, Glib, Granita, Graupel, Ground, Growler, Hailstone, Hok(e)y-pok(e)y, Hommock, Hummock, Intention, Kitty-benders, Knickerbocker glory, Kulfi, Lolly, Macallum, Marzipan, Moraine, Neapolitan, Neve, Oaky, Pack, Pancake, Pingo, Pipe, Polar, Popsicle®, Rime, Rink, Ripple, Rivière, Ross, Royal, Sconce, Serac, Shelf, Shell, Sherbet, Slay, Slider, Slob, Sludge, Slush, Sorbet, Spumone, Spumoni, Stream, Sugar, Sundae, Theme, Tickly-benders, Topping, Tortoni, Tutti-frutti, Verglas, Virga, Wafer, Water, Wintry
**Ice-axe** Piolet
**Iceberg** Calf, Floe, Growler, Lettuce
**Ice-box** Cooler, Freezer, Fridge, Frig, Yakhdan
**Ice-breaker** Opener
▸**Ice-cream** *see* ICE(D)
**Icefloe** Pan
**Iceland** IS
**Ice-skating** Choctaw, Figure, Glide
**Ichneumon** Herpestes
**Icicle** Tangle
**Icon, Iconic** Avatar, Emoticon, Fashion, Idol, Image, Madonna, Shrine, Sprite, Toolbar, Totemic
**Icterus** Jaundice
**ID** Dog-tag, Microchip, PIN
**Id(e)** Ego, Fish, Orfe
**Idea(s)** Archetype, Brainchild, Brainstorm, Brainwave, Bright, Clou, Clue, Conceit, Concept, Fancy, Figment, Fixed, Forum, Germ, Gist, Hunch, Idée fixe, Idolum, Image, Impression, Inkling, Innovation, Inspiration, Intention, Interpretation, Keynote, Light, Meme, Motif, → NOTION, Obsession, Plan, Plank, Rationale, Recept, Rough, Theme, Theory, Thought, Whimsy, Zeitgeist
**Ideal(ise)** A1, Abstract, Apotheosis, At best, Bee's knees, Best, Cat's pyjamas, Cat's whiskers, Dream, Eden, Ego, Erewhon, Goal, Halo, Hero, Model, Monist, Mr Right, Nirvana, Notional, Paragon, Pattern, → PERFECT, Perfet, Prince Charming, Role-model, Romantic, Rose, Siddhi, Sidha, Sublimate, Transcendental, Utopian, Vision
**Idealism, Idealist(ic)** Dreamer, Martyr, More, Perfectionist, Quixotic, Romantic, Rose-tinted, Storybook, Subjective, Transcendental, Utopian, Visionary
**Identical** Alike, Carbon copy, Clone, Congruent, Double, Equal, Homogenous, Indistinguishable, Matching, Menechmian, One, Same, Selfsame, Verbatim, Very
**Identification, Identify** Armband, Avatar, Bertillonage, Codeword, Cookie, Credentials,

Designate, Detect, Diagnosis, Differentiate, Discern, Document, Dog-tag, Earmark, E-fit, Empathy, Espy, Ethnicity, Finger(print), ID, Identikit®, Know, Label, Mark, Monomark, Name, Nameplate, Name-tape, Password, Photofit®, Pin, Pinpoint, Place, Point up, Recognise, Registration, Reg(g)o, Secern, Specify, Spot, Swan-hopping, Swan-upping, Title, User, Verify

**Identikit®** E-fit, Videokit

**Identity** Alias, Appearance, Corporate, Credentials, Ego, Equalness, Likeness, Mistaken, Numerical, Oneness, Personal, Qualitative, Seity, Self, Selfhood

**Ideology, Ideologue** Credo, Hard-liner, Ism, Justicialism, Stalinism

**Idiom** Americanism, Argot, Britishism, Cant, Dialect, Expression, Figure of speech, Gallicism, Idioticon, Jargon, Language, Pahlavi, Parlance, Pehlevi, Persism, Scotticism, Slavism, Syri(a)cism, Syrism

**Idiosyncrasy, Idiosyncratic** Eccentricity, Fad, Foible, Mannerism, Nature, Quirk, Trait, Way, Zany

**Idiot(ic), Idiocy** Airhead, Congenital, Dingbat, Dipstick, Dolt, Dotard, Dumbo, Eejit, Fatuity, Fool, Git, Goose, Half-wit, Headbanger, Imbecile, Inane, Klutz, Maniac, Moron, Nana, Natural, Nerk, Nidget, Noncom, Numpty, Oaf, Ouph(e), Stupe, → STUPID, Tony, Twit, Village, Whacko, Zany

**Idle(ness), Idler** Beachcomber, Bludger, Boondoggle, Bum, Bumble, Bummle, Cockaigne, Couch potato, Dally, Deadbeat, Diddle, Dilly-dally, Dole-bludger, Donnat, Donnot, Do-nothingism, Drone, Eric, Fainéant, Fallow, Farnarkel, Fester, Flaneur, Flim-flam, Footle, Frivolous, Gold brick, Groundless, Hawm, Inaction, Indolent, Inert, Lackadaisical, Laesie, Lallygag, Layabout, Laze, Lazy, Lead-swinger, Lie, Lig, Light, Limer, Linger, Loaf, Loiter, Loll, Lollard, Lollop, Lollygag, Lotophagus, Lounge, Lusk, Micawber, Mike, Mollusc, Mooch, Mouch, Neet, Otiose, Otium, Patagonian, Piddle, Potato, Ride, Scapegrace, Shiftless, Skive, Slack(er), Slob, Sloth, Sluggard, Spiv, Stagnate, Stalko, Stock-still, Stooge, Stroam, Sweirt, Tarry, Tick over, Transcendental, Trifle, Trock, Troke, Truant, Truck, Twiddle, Unbusy, Unemployed, Unoccupied, Vacuity, Vain, Vegetate, Veg out, Wait, Waste, Whip the cat, Workshy

**Idol(ise)** Adore, Adulate, Baal(im), Baphomet, Bel, Crush, Eikon, E(i)luned, Fetich(e), Fetish, God, Graven image, Heartthrob, Hero, Icon, Image, Joss, Juggernaut, Lion, Mammet, Manito, Manitou, Matinee, Maumet, Mawmet, Molech, Moloch, Mommet, Moorish, Mumbo-jumbo, Pagoda, Stotter, Swami, Teraph(im), Termagant, Vision, Wood, Worship

**Idyll(ic)** Arcady, Eclogue, Eden, Paradise, Pastoral, Peneian, Xanadu

**Ie** Sc

**If, If it** Albeit, All-be, An('t), Condition, Gif, Gin, In case, Kipling, Pot, Provided, Sobeit, Whether

**Igloo** Snowden

**Igneous** Pyrogenic

**Ignis-fatuus** Elf-fire, Fire-dragon, Fire-drake, Friar's lanthorn, Wildfire

**Ignite, Ignitable, Ignition** Coil, Electronic, Flammable, Flare, Flash-point, Glow plug, Kindle, Lightning, Spark, Spontaneous, Starter, Torch

**Ignoble** Base, Inferior, Mean, Vile

**Ignominious, Ignominy** Base, Dishonour, Fiasco, Humiliation, Infamous, Scandal, → SHAME

**Ignorance, Ignorant** 404, Agnoiology, Analphabet, Anan, Artless, Benighted, Blind, Bliss, Clueless, Darkness, Green, Hick, Illiterate, Inerudite, Ingram, Ingrum, Inscient, Irony, Know-nothing, Lewd, Lumpen, Misken, Nescience, Night, Oblivious, Oik, Philistine, Pig, Purblind, Red-neck, Unaware, Uneducated, Unlessoned, Unlettered, Unread, Unschooled, Untold, Unversed, Unwist

**Ignore(d)** Alienate, Ba(u)lk, Blink, Boycott, Bypass, Cold-shoulder, Connive, Cut, Discount, Disregard, Drop, Exclude, Forget, Leave, Neglect, Omit, Overlook, Override, Overslaugh, Pass, Pass up, Resist, Rump, Scrub round, Skip, Slight, Snub, Tune out, Unheeded

**Igor** Prince

**Iguana** Chuckwalla

**I know** Iwis, Ywis

**Iliad** Homeric

**Ill(ness)** Access, Adverse, All-overish, Awrong, Bad, Bilious, Bird flu, Cronk, Crook, Disorder, Distemper, Evil, German measles, Gout, Grippe, Grotty, Inauspicious, Income, Indisposed, Infection, Labyrinthitis, Laid up, Lovesick, Malady, Misorder, Off-colour, Pneumonia, Poorly, Pox, Queer, Ropy, Rough, Rubella, SARS, Schistosomiasis, Scrofula, Scurvy, Sea-sick, → **SICK**, Strongylosis, Strung out, Terminal, Unpropitious, Unweal, Unwell, Valetudinarian, Vomito, Wrong, Yuppie flu

▷**Ill** *may indicate* an anagram

**Ill-adjusted** Sad sack

**Ill-advised** Foolish, Imprudent, Redeless

**Ill-balanced** Lop-sided

**Ill-bred** Carl, Churlish, Plebeian, Uncouth, Unmannerly

▷**Ill-composed** *may indicate* an anagram

**Ill-considered** Mindless, Rash

**Ill-defined** Blurred, Diagnosis, Grey (area), Hazy, Mongrel, Unclear, Vague

**Ill-disposed** Antagonistic, Baleful, Malevolent

**Ill-dressed** Frumpish

**Illegal, Illicit** Adulterine, Black, Bootleg, Breach, Contraband, Furtive, Ill-gotten, Malfeasance, Misbegotten, Pirated, Racket, Shonky, Unlawful, Wrong(ous)

**Illegitimate** Baseborn, Bastard, By-blow, Come-o'-will, Fitz, Irregular, Love-child, Lucky-piece, Mamzer, Misbegotten, Misborn, Misfortunate, Momzer, Natural, Scarp, Slink, Spurious, Unlawful, Unlineal

**Ill-fated** Inauspicious, Star-crossed, Unlucky

**Ill-favoured** Lean, Offensive, Thin, Ugly

**Ill-feeling, Ill-humour, Ill-will** Acrimony, Animosity, Animus, Bad blood, Bile, Complaint, Curt, Dudgeon, Enmity, Gall, Glum, Grudge, Hate, Hostility, Malice, Maltalent, Mau(l)gre, Miff, Peevish, Pique, Rheum(atic), Sick joke, Spite, Spleen, Tantrum

**Ill-founded** Untenable

**Illiberal** Insular, Intolerant, Redneck, Skinflint, Strict

▶**Illicit** *see* **ILLEGAL**

**Illiterate** Analphabet, Ignoramus, Letterless, Unlettered, Unread

**Ill-judged** Hare-brained

**Ill-looking** Peaky, Poorly

**Ill-luck** Ambs-ace, Ames-ace, Bad trot, Deuce-ace, Fate, Misfortune

**Ill-mannered, Ill-natured, Ill-tempered** Acid, Attercop, Bitchy, Cad, Churl, Coarse, Crabby, Crotchety, Curst, Ethercap, Ettercap, Gnarly, Goop, Grump(y), Gurrier, Guttersnipe, Huffy, Lout, Mean, Splenetic, Stingy, Stroppy, Sullen, Surly, Ugly, Uncouth, Unkind

**Illness** Aids, Ailment, Attack, Autism, Brucellosis, Chill, Complaint, Croup, Death-bed, Diabetes, Disease, DS, Dwalm, Dwaum, Dyscrasia, Eale, Eclampsia, Grippe, Hangover, Hypochondria, Lockjaw, Malady, ME, SAD, Scarlatina, Sickness, Terminal, Toxaemia, Urosis, Weed, Weid

**Ill-nourished** Emaciated

**Illogical** Absurd, Disconnected, Inconsequent, Non-sequitur

**Ill repute** Discredit, Infamy

**Ill-sighted** Owl, Purblind

**Ill-smelling** F(o)etid, High, Hing, Miasmic, Stinking

**Ill-starred** Unlucky

▶**Ill-tempered** *see* **ILL-MANNERED**

**Ill-timed** Inopportune, Unseasonable

**Ill-treat** Harm, Hurt, Shaft

**Illuminate(d), Illumination, Illuminating** Ambient, Aperçu, Brighten, Bright-field, Candlelight, Clarify, Cul-de-lampe, Daylight, Decorate, Educative, Enlighten, Floodlit, Lamplight, Langley, Lantern, Light, Limbourg, Limelight, Limn, Miniate, Moonlight, Nernst, Phot, Pixel, Radiate, Rushlight, Spotlight, Starlight, Sunburst

**Illusion(ary), Illusionist, Illusory, Illusive** Air, Apparition, Barmecide, Blaine, Chimera, Deception, Déjà vu, Escher, Fallacy, Fancy, Fantasy, Fata morgana, Geller,

Hallucination, Ignis-fatuus, Imagining, Indian rope trick, Mare's-nest, Maya, Mirage, Muller-Lyer, Optical, Phantasmal, Phantom, Phi-phenomenon, Size-weight, Specious, Transcendental, Trick, Trompe l'oeil, Unreality, Will o'the wisp

**Illustrate(d), Illustration, Illustrator** Artwork, Attwell, Bleed, Case, Centrefold, Collotype, Demonstrate, Dore, Drawing, Eg, Elucidate, Epitomise, Exemplify, Explain, Figure, Frontispiece, Grangerize, Graphic, Half-tone, Heath Robinson, Hors texte, Illume, Illumin(at)e, Instance, Instantiate, Keyline, Limner, Line-engraver, Lithograph, Pictorial, Plate, Rackham, Rockwell, Show, Sidelight, Spotlight, Symbol, Tenniel, Vignette, Visual, Woodcut

**Illustrious** Bright, Celebrated, Distinguished, Famous, Legendary, Noble, Noted, Prestigious, Renowned, Roshan

▸**Ill-will** *see* ILL-FEELING

**I'm** I'se

**Image(s), Imagery, Imaging** Atman, Blip, Body, Brand, CGI, Corporate, Dead ringer, Discus, Effigy, E-fit, Ego, Eidetic, Eidolon, Eikon, Eiluned, Emoji, Emoticon, Emotion, Enantiomorph, Favicon, Fine-grain, Gift, Graphic, Graven, Hologram, Hypnagogic, Icon, Iconograph, Ident(ikit), Idol, Invultuation, Joss, Latent, Likeness, Litho, Matte, Mirror, Morph, Mouseover, Murti, Paranthelium, Paraselene, Pentimento, Persona, Phantasmagoria, Photogram, Photograph, Pic(ture), Pieta, Pixel(l)ated, Pixil(l)ated, Poetic, Print, Profile, Public, Radionuclide, Real, Recept, Reflectogram, Reflectograph, Representation, Rollover, Scintigram, Search, Shadowgraph, Shrine, Simulacrum, Sonogram, Species, Spectrum, Spitting, Split, Stereotype, Symbol, Teraph(im), Thermal, Thermogram, Thumbnail, Tiki, Tomogram, Totem, Vectograph, Venogram, Video, Virtual, Waxwork, Xoanon

**Image-maker** Scanner

**Imagine(d), Imaginary (land), Imagination, Imaginative** Assume, Bandywallop, Barmecide, Believe, Boojum, Bullamakanka, Cloud-cuckoo-land, Cockaigne, Cockayne, Conceive, Conjure, Create, Cyborg, Dystopia, Envisage, Erewhon, Esemplasy, Faery, Faine, Fancy, Fantasise, Feign, Fictional, Fictitious, Fictor, Figment, Figure, Hallucinate, Hobbit, Ideate, Invent, Mind's eye, Moral, Mythical, Narnia, Never-never-land, Non-existent, Notional, Otherworldly, Oz, Picture, Poetical, Prefigure, Pretend, Propose, Recapture, Replicant, Scotch mist, Snark, Straw, → SUPPOSE, Surmise, Think, Tricorn, Tulpa, Unreal, Vicarious, Vision, Visualise, Whangam, Wonderland

**Imam** Ismail

**Imbalance(d)** Asymmetry, Unequal

**Imbecile** Anile, Fool, Idiot, → STUPID

▹**Imbecile** *may indicate* an anagram

**Imbibe** Absorb, Drink, Lap, Quaff, Suck, Swallow, Tope

**Imbricate** Overlie

**Imbroglio** Complication, Maze

**Imbrue, Imbue** Colour, Impregnate, Indoctrinate, Infuse, Inoculate, Permeate, Revitalise, Soak, Steep

**Imitate, Imitation, Imitator** Act, Ape, Burlesque, Caricature, Clone, Copy(cat), Counterfeit, Crib, Decoy, Dud, Dummy, Echo, Echopraxia, Emulate, Epigon(e), Ersatz, Facsimile, Fake, False, Faux, Follow, Hit off, Marinist, Me-too, Mime, Mimesis, Mimetic, Mimic(ry), Mini-me, Mockery, Monkey, Onomatopoeia, Parody, Parrot, Paste, Paste grain, Pastiche, Pinchbeck, Potichomania, Recreate, Repro, Retro, Rhinestone, Rip-off, Sham, Simulate, Skeuomorphism, Stumer, Take-off, Travesty, Unreal

**Immaculate** Conception, Flawless, Impeccable, Lily-white, Perfect, Pristine, Spotless, Undefiled, Virgin

**Immanentist** Pantheist

**Immaterial** Academic, Insignificant, Spiritual, Trifling

**Immature(ly), Immaturity** Adolescent, Babyish, Beardless, Blast, Callow, Childish, Crude, Embryo, Ergate(s), Green, Imago, Inchoate, Juvenile, Laddish, Larval, Neotenic, Non-age, Nymph, Peter Pan, Puberal, Puberulent, Pupa, Raw, Rudimentary, Sophomoric, Tender, Unbaked, Underage, Unformed, Unripe, Unseasoned, Young

▹**Immature** *may indicate* a word not completed

**Immediate(ly)** Alsoon, Anon, At once, B(e)live, Direct, Eftsoons, Ekdum, First-time, Forthwith, Go on, Imminent, Incontinent, Instantaneous, Instanter, Lickety-split, Near, Next, → NOW, Now-now, On the knocker, Outright, Posthaste, Present, Prompt, Pronto, Proximate, Ready, Right away, Right-off, Short-term, Slapbang, Spontaneous, Stat, Statim, Straight, Straight off, Sudden, Then, Thereupon, Tout de suite, Urgent

**Immense** Astronomical, Brobdingnag, Cosmic, Enormous, → GIGANTIC, Huge, Myriad, Unlimited, Vast, Wide

**Immerse** Baptise, Demerge, Demerse, Drench, Duck, Dunk, Embathe, Emplonge, Enew, Engage, Imbathe, Plunge, Soak, Steep, Submerge

**Immigrant, Immigration, Immigrate** Alien, Aliya(h), Aussledler, Brain gain, Carpet-bagger, Cayun, Chalutz, Choom, Freshie, Gastarbeiter, Greener, Greenhorn, Halutz, Illegal, Incomer, Issei, Jimmy Grant, Latino, Merino, Metic, New chum, Nisei, Non-quota, Olim, Outsider, Overstayer, Pilgrim, Pommy, Quota, Redemption(er), Reffo, Sanei, Sansei, Settler, Wetback, Whenwe

**Imminent** Approaching, Close, Forthcoming, Immediate, Nigh, Pending

**Immobility, Immobile, Immobilise(r)** Akinesia, Cataplexy, Catatonia, Clamp, Ecstasis, Hamstring, Hog-tie, Inactive, Inertia, Paralyse, Pinion, Rigidity, Static, Taser®, Tether

**Immoderate** Excessive, Extreme, Inordinate, Intemperate, Lavish, Undue, Unreasonable, Violent

**Immodest(y)** Brash, Brazen, Conceited, Forward, Impudicity, Indelicate, Unchaste

**Immolation** Sacrifice, Sati, Suttee

**Immoral(ity)** Corrupt, Decadent, Degenerate, Dissolute, Dyke-louper, Evil, Harlot, Lax, Libertine, Licentious, Loose, Misconduct, Nefarious, Peccable, Reprobate, Scarlet, Sleazebag, Sleazeball, Sleazy, Turpitude, Unchaste, Unclean, Unholy, Unprincipled, Unsavoury, Unscrupulous, Vice, Vicious, Wanton

**Immortal(ity)** Agelong, Amarant(h), Amarantin, Amritattva, Athanasy, Deathless, → DIVINE, Endless, Enoch, Eternal, Eternist, Ever-living, Famous, Godlike, Hera, Legendary, Memory, Sin, Struldbrug, Timeless, Undying

**Immovable** Fast, Firm, Gomphosis, Obdurate, Rigid, Rock solid, Stable, Stolid, Stubborn

**Immune, Immunisation, Immunise(r), Immunity** Acquired, Active, Amboceptor, Anamnestic, Anergy, Antiserum, Bar, Cree, Diplomatic, Dispensation, Exempt, Free, Humoral, Inoculate, Klendusic, Natural, Non-specific, Passive, Pasteurism, Pax, Premunition, Properdin, Serum, Tachyphylaxis, Vaccine

**Immure** Confine, Encloister, Imprison

**Imp(ish)** Bottle, Devilet, Elf, Flibbertigibbet, Gamin(e), Gremlin, Hobgoblin, Leprechaun, Limb, Lincoln, Litherly, Monkey, Nickum, Nis(se), Puck, Ralph, Rascal, Spright, Sprite, Troll

**Impact** Affect, Astrobleme, Bearing, Brunt, Bump, Chase, Clash, Collision, Feeze, Glance, Head-on, High, Impinge, Impress, Impression, Imprint, Jar, Jolt, Pack, Percuss, Pow, Slam, Souse, Strike home, Tell, Weight, Wham, Whammo

**Impair(ed), Impairment** Appair, Cripple, Damage, Disease, Dysarthria, Dyskinesia, Emperish, Enfeeble, → HARM, Injure, Lame, Mar, Mental, Odd, Pair(e), Paralogia, Stale, Vitiate

**Impala** Pallah

**Impale** Elance, Ga(u)nch, Gore, Skewer, Spike, Transfix

**Impart** Bestow, Convey, Divulge, Give, Impute, Infect, Inform, Shed, Tell

**Impartial(ity)** Candid, Detached, Disinterest, Dispassionate, Equitable, Equity, Even-handed, Fair, Just, Neutral, Unbiased

**Impasse, Impassable** Deadlock, Dilemma, Invious, Jam, Log jam, Mexican standoff, Snooker, Stalemate, Stand off, Zugzwang

**Impassioned** Earnest, Emotional, Fervid, Fiery, Heated, Hot, Zealous

**Impassive** Apathetic, Bland, Deadpan, Poker-faced, Stoical, Stolid, Unemotional

**Impatience, Impatient** Agog, Chafing, Champ, Chut, Dysphoria, Dysthesia, Eager, Expectant, Fiddle-de-dee, Fiddlesticks, Fidgety, Fretful, Hasty, Hoot(s), Irritable, Itchy, Och, Peevish, Peremptory, Petulant, Pish, Pshaw, Restless, Tilly-fally, Till(e)y-vall(e)y, Tooting, Tut, Twitchy

**Impeach** Accuse, Arraign, Challenge, Charge, Delate, Indict
**Impeccable** Faultless, Novice
**Impecunious** Broke, Land-poor, Penniless, Poor, Short, Skint
**Impedance, Impede, Impediment** Block, Burr, Clog, Dam, Diriment, Encumber, Halt, Hamper, Hamstring, Handicap, → HINDER, Hog-tie, Let, Log, Obstacle, Obstruct, Reactance, Rub, Shackle, Slur, Snag, Speed bump, Stammer, Stutter, Stymie, Tongue-tie, Trammel, Veto, Z
**Impel(led), Impelling** Actuate, Coerce, Drave, Drive, Drove, Goad, Inspire, Projectile, → URGE
**Impend(ing)** Imminent, Looming, Toward
**Impenetrable** Adamantine, Air-tight, Dense, Hard, Impervious, Proof, Watertight
**Imperative** Categorical, Dire, Hypothetical, Jussive, Mood, Need-be, Obligatory, Pressing, Urgent, Vital
**Imperceptible, Imperceptive** Blind Freddie, Intangible, Invisible, Latent, Minimal, Subtle
**Imperfect(ion)** Aplasia, Aplastic, Blotch, Defect, Deficient, Faulty, Feathering, Flawed, Half-pie, Incomplete, Kink, Kinkle, Knothole, Lame, Poor, Reject, Rough, Second, Unideal
**Imperial(ist), Imperious** Adroit, Archduchess, Archduke, Beard, C(a)esarian, Colonialist, Commanding, Dictatorial, Flag-waver, Haughty, Lordly, Majestic, Masterful, Mint, Peremptory, Regal, Rhodes, Royal, Tuft
**Imperil** Endanger, Risk
**Imperishable** Eternal, Immarcescible, Immortal, Indestructible
**Impermeable** Airtight, Athermanous, Greaseproof, Proof, Resistant
**Impermissible** Taboo
**Impersonal** Abstract, Cold, Dehumanised, Detached, Inhuman, Institutional
**Impersonate(d), Impersonation, Impersonator** Amphitryon, Ape, As, Double, Drag queen, Echo, Imitate, Imposter, Impostor, Impression, Mimic, Pose, Spoof
**Impertinence, Impertinent** Backchat, Crust, Disrespect, Effrontery, Flip(pant), Fresh, Impudent, Irrelevant, Nos(e)y, Presumptuous, Rude, Sass, Sauce
**Imperturbable** Cool, Placid, Stoic, Tranquil, Unruffable
**Impervious(ness)** Athermancy, Callous, Hardened, Obdurate, Opaque, Proof, Resistant, Tight
**Impetigo** Scrumpox
**Impetuous, Impetuosity** Birr, Brash, Bullheaded, Careless, Élan, Fiery, Harum-scarum, → HASTY, Headstrong, Heady, Hothead, Impulsive, Rash, Rees, Rhys, Tearaway, Vehement, Violent, Young Turk
**Impetus** Birr, Drift, Drive, Incentive, MacGuffin, Momentum, Propulsion, Slancio, Steam, Swing
**Impious** Blasphemous, Godless, Irreverent, Unholy
**Implacable** Deadly
**Implant(ation)** AID, Cochlear, Embed, Engraft, Enrace, Enroot, Graft, Insert, Inset, Instil, Microchip, Nidation, Silicone, Sow, Stent
**Implausible** Far-fetched, Lame, Off-the-wall
**Implement** Agent, Apply, Backscratcher, Biffer, Brace, Breast plough, Caman, Celt, Chopstick, Cultivator, Curette, Dicer, Disgorger, Do, Enforce, Eolith, Execute, Fire-iron, Fish slice, Flail, Follow out, Fork, Fulfil, Grater, Grubber, Hacksaw, Harrow, Hayfork, Knife, Mezzaluna, Mop, Muller, Neolith, Pin, Pitchfork, Plectrum, Plough, Pruning-bill, Pusher, Razor, Rest, Ricker, Ripple, Scarifier, Scissors, Scuffler, Scythe, Seed drill, Shoehorn, Sickle, Snuffer, Spatula, Spit, Splayd®, Spork, Squeegee, Straw-cutter, Strickle, Sucket fork, Sucket spoon, Tongs, → TOOL, Toothpick, Tribrach, Utensil, Wheelbrace
**Implicate, Implication** Accuse, Concern, Connotation, Drift, Embroil, Entangle, Incriminate, Innuendo, Insinuation, → INVOLVE, Material, Overtone, Subintelligitur
**Implore** Beg, Beseech, Crave, → ENTREAT, Obsecrate, Petition, Plead, Pray
**Imply, Implied** Connote, Hint, Insinuate, Intimate, Involve, Predicate, Signify, Subtle, → SUGGEST, Tacit, Unstated, Unwritten
**Impolite** Abrupt, Ill-bred, Offhand, Ripe, Rude, Uncivil

**Import(s)** Convey, Denote, Drift, Invisible, Mean, Moment, Parallel, Sense, Signify, Spell, Visible

**Importance, Important (person)** Account, Acute, A-list, Big, Big cheese, Big pot, Big-time, Big wheel, Billing, Calibre, Capital, Cardinal, Central, Cheese, Chief, Cob, Coming, Consequence, Considerable, Core, Cornerstone, Count, Critical, Crucial, Crux, Earth-shaking, Earth-shattering, Ego-trip, Eminent, Epochal, Essential, Fateful, Flagship, Focal, Formative, Grandeur, Grave, Gravitas, Gravity, Greatness, Heavy, High, High-muck-a-muck, High-profile, His nibs, Historic, Honcho, Hotshot, Huzoor, Indispensable, Instrumental, Key, Keystone, Kingpin, Large, Leading, Life and death, Macher, Magnitude, Main, Major, Material, Matters, Meaningful, Megastar, Mighty, Milestone, Moment(ous), Much, Nabob, Nawab, Nib, Note, Numero uno, Obbligato, Outbalance, Overriding, Paramount, Personage, Pivotal, Pot, Preponderate, Pressing, Primal, Prime, Principal, Red-carpet, Red-letter, Right-hand, Salient, Seismic, Seminal, Senior, Serious, Signal, Significant, Something, Special, Stature, Status, Stress, Substantive, Supreme, Tuft, Urgent, VIP, Visiting fireman, Vital, Weight, Weighty, Worth

**Importune, Importunate** Beg, Coax, Flagitate, Pester, Press(ing), Pressgang, Prig, Solicit, Urgent

**Impose(r), Imposing, Imposition** Allocate, Assess, August, Burden, Charge, Cheat, Diktat, Dread, Encroach, Enforce, Enjoin, Epic, Fine, Flam, Foist, Fraud, Grand(iose), Handsome, Hidage, Homeric, Hum, Impot, Inflict, Kid, Lay, Levy, Lofty, Lumber, Majestic, Muscle in, Noble, Obtrude, Penance, Pensum, Pole, Scot, Sponge, Stately, Statuesque, Stonehand, Sublime, Titan, Try-on, Whillywhaw

**Impossible** Can't, Hopeless, Inconceivable, Incorrigible, Insoluble, Insuperable, Insurmountable, Irreparable, No can do, No-go, No-no, Unacceptable, Unachievable, Unendurable

**Impost** Excise, Levy, Tax, Toll

**Imposter, Impostor** Bunyip, Charlatan, Disaster, Faitor, Faitour, → **FAKE**, Fraud, Idol, Phantasm, Pretender, Ringer, Sham, Triumph, Warbeck

**Impotent** Barren, Helpless, Powerless, Spado, Sterile, Weak

**Impound(er)** Appropriate, Bond, Confiscate, Incarcerate, Intern, Pen, Pinder, Poind, Seize

**Impoverish(ed)** Bankrupt, Bare, Beggar, Destitute, Exhaust, Hardscrabble, Indigent, Mendicant, Needy, Poor, Reduce, Skint, Straiten

**Impractical** Abstract, Absurd, Academic, Blue-sky, Chim(a)era, Cloud-cuckoo-land, Crackpot, Dreamer, Idealist, Inoperable, Laputan, Non-starter, Not on, Other-worldly, Quixotic, Theoretic, Useless

**Imprecation** Drat, Oath, Pize, Rat(s), 'Slife

**Imprecise** Approximate, Inaccurate, Indeterminate, Inexact, Intangible, Loose, Nebulous, Rough, Sloppy, Vague

**Impregnable, Impregnate** Conceive, Embalm, Enwomb, Imbue, Inexpugnable, Inseminate, Iron-clad, Knock up, Milt, Permeate, Resinate, Virtue-proof, Watertight

**Impresario** D'Oyly Carte, Entrepreneur, Maestro, Manager, Producer, Showman

**Impress(ive), Impression(able)** Affect, Aftertaste, Air, Appearance, Astonish, August, Awe(struck), Blur, Blurb, Bowl over, Brand, Cat's whiskers, Charm, Class act, Cliché, Commanding, Conscript, Crimp, Deboss, Dent, Description, Draft, Dramatic, Edition, Effect, Enforce, Engrain, Engram(ma), Engrave, Enstamp, Epic, Etch, Eye-catching, Feel(ing), Fingerprint, Footmark, Footprint, Fossil, Frank, Gas, Glorious, Grab, Grandiose, Grandstand, Greeking, Heroic, Homeric, Idea, Idée, Imitation, Impact, Impinge, Imposing, Imprint, Incuse, Indent, Ingrain, Insoire, Inspirational, Instil, Intaglio, Kick ass, Knock, Let, Lulu, Magnificent, Majestic, Mould, Name-drop, Niello, Noble, Note, Palimpsest, Pit, Plastic, Plate, Pliable, Powerful, Prent, Presence, Press(gang), Print, Prodigious, Proof, Recruit, Register, Repute, Resplendent, Responsive, Ripsnorter, Rotund, Seal, Seize, Sense, Shanghai, Signet, Simulacrum, Slay, Smite, Soft, Spectacular, Stamp, Stately, Stereotype, Stonker, Strike, Stunning, Stupendous, Susceptible, Sway, Tableau, Take, Touch, Type, Vibrant, Watermark, Wax, Weal, Weighty, Whale, Woodcut, Wow

**Impressionist(ic)** Abstract, Caxton, Cézanne, Impersonator, Liebermann, Lumin(ar)ist, Manet, Matisse, Mimic, Monet, Morisot, Renoir

**Imprint** Edition, Engrave, Etch, Stamp
**Imprison(ment)** Cage, Cape, Committal, Confine, Constrain, Custody, Durance, Embar, Emmew, False, Gherao, Hitch, Immure, Incarcerate, Inside, Intern, Jail, Lock-up, Penal servitude, Quad, Quod, Stretch, Time
**Improbable** Buckley's chance, Buckley's hope, Dubious, Far-fetched, Pie-in-the-sky, Unlikely
**Impromptu** Ad lib(itum), Extempore, Improvised, Offhand, Pong, Spontaneous, Sudden, Unrehearsed
**Improper, Impropriety** Abnormal, Blue, Demirep, False, Illegitimate, Indecent, Indecorum, Naughty, Outré, Prurient, Solecism, Undue, Unmeet, Unseemly, Untoward
▹**Improperly** *may indicate* an anagram
**Improve(ment), Improver, Improving** Advance, Airbrush, Ameliorate, Amend, Beat, Benefit, Bete, Better, Boost, Break, Buck, Cap, Chasten, Conditioner, Convalesce, Cultivate, Defrag, Détente, Didactic, DIY, Ease, Edify, Edutainment, Embellish, Embroider, Emend, Enhance, Enrich, Eugenic, Euthenics, File, Gentrify, J-curve, Kaizen, Lift, Meliorate, Mend, Modernise, Pick up, Polish, Potentiate, Progress, Promote, Rally, Recovery, Refine, Reform, Resipiscence, Retouch, Revamp, Sarvodaya, Slim, Streamline, Surpass, Tart, Tatt, Thrive, Titivate, Top, Touch-up, Turn round, Tweak, Upgrade, Upswing, Uptrend, Upturn, Vernissage
**Improvident** Feckless, Micawber, Poor-white, Wasteful
**Improvise(d), Improvisation** Ad hoc, Adlib, Break, Busk it, Contrive, Devise, Drumhead, Extemporise, Gorgia, Invent, Jury-rig, Knock-up, Lash-up, Noodle, Off-the-cuff, On the fly, Play by ear, Pong, Ride, Scat, Scratch, Sodain, Stopgap, Sudden, Tweedle, Unscripted, Vamp, Wing it
**Imprudent** Foolhardy, Foolish, Impetuous, Impolitic, Indiscreet, Inexpedient, Injudicious, Rash, Reckless, Unadvised, Unguarded, Unwary, Unwise
**Impudence, Impudent** Audacious, Backchat, Bardy, Barefaced, Bold, Brash, Brassy, Brazen, Cheeky, Chit, Chutzpah, Cool, Crass, Crust, Effrontery, Forward, Front, Gall, Gallus, Gobby, Hussy, Impertinent, Insolent, Jackanapes, Jack-sauce, Lip, Malapert, Neck, → **NERVE**, Pert, Sass(y), Sauce, Saucebox, Saucy, Skipjack, Slack-jaw, Temerity, Tongue-in-cheek, Whippersnapper, Yankie
**Impugn** Censure, Challenge, Defame, Impeach, Malign
**Impulse, Impulsive** Acte gratuit, Beat, Caprice, Compelling, Conatus, Dictate, Drive, Efferent, Flighty, Foolhardy, Headlong, Headstrong, Horme, Ideopraxist, Impetus, Instigation, → **INSTINCT**, Libido, Madcap, Nerve, Nisus, Precipitant, Premature, Premotion, Send, Signal, Snap, Specific, Spontaneous, Stimulus, Synapse, Tearaway, Tendency, Thrust, Tic, Urge, Whim
**Impure, Impurity** Adulterated, Contaminated, Donor, Dregs, Dross, Faints, Feints, Indecent, Lees, Lewd, Regulus, Scum, Unchaste, Unclean
**Imputation, Impute** Ascribe, Attribute, Charge, Scandal, Slander, Slur
**In** A, Amid, Amidst, Amongst, At, At home, Batting, Chic, Current, Fashionable, Hip, Home, Hostel, I', Indium, Inn, Intil, Occupying, On, Pop(ular), Pub, Trendy, Within
**Inability** Agnosia, Anosmia, Aphagia, Aphasia, Apraxia, Ataxy, Paraphraxia, Prosopagnosia
**Inaccessible** Abaton, Eyrie, Impervious, Remote, Unattainable, Uncom(e)atable
**Inaccurate** Distorted, Erroneous, Faulty, Imprecise, Inexact, Loose, Misquote, Out, Overestimate, Rough, Slipshod, Unfaithful, Untrue
**Inactive, Inaction, Inactivity** Acedia, Anestrum, Anoestrus, Cabbage, Canicular day, Comatose, Dead, Dog days, Dormant, Extinct, Fallow, Hibernate, Idle, Inert, Languor, Lotus-eater, Masterly, Moratorium, Non-term, Passive, Quiescent, Racemic, Recess, Rusty, Sedentary, Sitzkrieg, Sluggish, Stagnation, Stasis, Static, Torpid, Vacancy, Veg(etate)
**In addition** Eke, Else, Further, Moreover, Plus, Thereto, To boot, Too, Yet
**Inadequate, Inadequacy** Derisory, Feeble, Hopeless, Inapt, Inferior, Joke, Lacking, Lean, Meagre, Measly, Pathetic, Poor, Ropy, Scanty, Slender, Slight, Thin, Unable, Unequal, Unsatisfactory, Want
**Inadvertent(ly)** Accidental, Careless, Chance, Unintentional, Unwitting
▹**In a flap** *may indicate* an anagram

**In a high degree** So
**In a hundred** Percent
**Inane** Drippy, Empty, Fatuous, Foolish, Imbecile, Silly, Vacant
**Inanimate** Abiotic, Lifeless
**Inappropriate** Amiss, Foreign, Ill-timed, Incongrous, Infelicitous, Malapropos, Misplaced, Off-key, Out of place, Pretentious, Tasteless, Unapt, Unbecoming, Undue, Unmeet, Unsuitable, Untoward
**Inapt** Maladroit, Unsuitable
**Inarticulate(ness)** Indistinct, Mumbling, Psellism
**Inartistic** Artless, Crude
**Inattentive, Inattention** Absent, Abstracted, Asleep, Careless, Cloth-eared, Deaf, Distrait, Dwaal, Dwa(l)m, Dwaum, Heedless, Listless, Loose, Remiss, Slack, Unheeding, Unobservant
**Inaudible** Infrasonic, Silent, Superhet
**Inaugural** Maiden
**Inaugurate** Dedicate, Han(d)sel, Initiate, Install, Introduce, Swear in
**Inauspicious** Adverse, Ominous, Sinister
▷**In a whirl** *may indicate* an anagram
▷**In a word** *may indicate* two clue words linked to form one
**Inborn, Inbred** Connate, Homogamy, Inherent, Innate, Native, Selfed, Sib
**Inbox** Email
**Inca** Quechua, Quichua
**Incalculable** Endless, Unpredictable, Untold
**Incandescent** Alight, Bright, Brilliant, Excited, Radiant
**Incantation** Chant, Charm, Magic, Mantra, Spell
**Incapable** Blotto, Can't, Downa-do, Powerless, Unable, Useless
**Incapacitate(d)** Can't, Disable, Paralyse
**Incarcerate** Detain, Intern
**Incarnation** Advent, Avatar, Embodiment, Fleshing, Hyperion, Krishna, Rama, Ramachandra, Ramayana
**In case** Lest, So
**Incautious** Cavalier, Foolhardy, Heedless, Rash, Reckless, Unwary
**Incendiary** Arsonist, Combustible, Firebug, Fire-lighter, Fireship, Flame-thrower, Greek fire, Napalm, Thermite
**Incense(d), Incenser** Anger, Aroma, Elemi, Enfelon, Enrage, Homage, Hot, → INFLAME, Infuriate, Irate, Irk, Joss-stick, Mosquito coil, Navicula, Onycha, Outrage, Pastil(le), Provoke, Stacte, Thurible, Thus, Vex, Wrathful
**Incentive** Bribe, Carrot, Carrot and stick, Cashback, Encouragement, Feather-bed, Fillip, Impetus, Inducement, Motive, Premium, Spur, Stakhanovism, Stimulus, Wage
**Inception** Outset
**Incessant** Constant, Endless, Non-stop, Unabated, Unremitting
**Incest** Backcross, Spiritual
**Inch(es)** Ait, Column, Edge, Isle(t), Mil, Miner's, Sidle, Tenpenny, Uncial
**Inchoate** Formless, Immature, Incipient
**Incident(al), Incidentally** Affair, A propos, Baur, Bawr, Byplay, By the by, Carry-on, Case, Cause célèbre, Chance, Circumstance, Episode, Event, Facultative, Handbags, Negligible, Occasion, Occurrent, Page, Peripheral, Scandal, Scene, Throwaway
**Incinerate, Incinerator** Burn, Combust, Cremate, Destructor
**Incipient** Beginning, Germinal, Inchoate, Nascent
**Incise(d), Incision, Incisive(ness)** Bite, Cut, Discussion, Edge, Engrave, Enterotomy, Episiotomy, Incavo, Intaglio, Lobotomy, McBurney's, Mordant, Notch, Oncotomy, Phlebotomy, Pleurotomy, Punchy, Pungent, Rhizotamy, Scarf, Sclerotomy, Scribe, Slit, Surgical, Tart, Thoracotomy, Tracheotomy, Trenchant
**Incisor** Foretooth
**Incite(ment)** Abet, Agitate, Drive, Egg, Enrage, Fillip, Goad, Hortative, Hoy, Impassion, Inflame, Instigate, Kindle, Motivate, Onsetting, Prod, Prompt, Provoke, Put, Rabble-rouse,

Rouse, Sa sa, Sedition, Set, Sic(k), Sool, → SPUR, Stimulus, Sting, Stir, Suborn, Suggest, Tar, Urge

**Incline(d), Inclination** Acclivity, Angle, Apt, Aslant, Aslope, Atilt, Bank, Batter, Bent, Bevel, Bias, Bow, Camber, Cant, Clinamen, Cock, Crossfall, Declivity, Dip, Disposed, Drift, Enclitic, Escarpment, Glacis, → GRADIENT, Grain, Habitus, Hade, Heel, Hill, Italic, Kant, Kip, Lean, Liable, Liking, List, Maw, Minded, Nod, On, Partial, Partisan, Peck, Penchant, Predisposition, Proclivity, Prone, Propensity, Rake, Ramp, Ready, Rollway, Set, Sheer, Shelve, Slant, → SLOPE, Steep, Steeve, Stomach, Supine, Sway, Tempted, Tend, Tilt, Tip, Trend, Upgrade, Uptilt, Urge, Velleity, Verge, Weathering, Will

**Include(d), Inclusion, Inclusive** Add, All-told, Bracket, Catch-all, Compass, Comprise, Connotate, Contain, Cover, Embody, Embrace, Enclose, Encompass, Generic, Involve, Short-list, Social, Subsume, Therein

**Incognito** Anonymous, Disguised, Faceless, Secret, Unnamed, Unobserved, Unrecognised

**Incoherent** Confused, Delirious, Disconnected, Disjointed, Gabbling, Garbled, Inarticulate, Rambling, Skimble-skamble, Spluttering

**Incombustible** Clinker

**Income** Annates, Annuity, Benefice, Discretionary, Disposable, Dividend, Earned, Entry, Fixed, Franked, Livelihood, Living, Meal-ticket, Milch cow, National, Notional, OTE, Penny-rent, Prebend, Primitiae, Private, Proceeds, Rent(al), Rente, Rent-roll, Returns, Revenue, Salary, Stipend, Take, Unearned, Unfranked, Wages

**Incomeless** E

**Incommunicado** Isolated, Silent

**Incomparable** Disparate, Par excellence, Supreme, Unequalled, Unique, Unlike, Unmatched

**Incompatible, Incompatibility** Clashing, Contradictory, Dyspathy, Incongruous, Inconsistent, Mismatched, Unsuited

**Incompetent(ly)** Blind Freddie, Bungler, Deadhead, Feckless, Helpless, Hopeless, Ill, Inefficient, Inept, Maladroit, Nebbich, Not for nuts, Palooka, Rabbit, Shlepper, Shower, Slouch, Unable, Unfit, Useless

**Incomplete** Broadbrush, Cagmag, Catalectic, Deficient, Inchoate, Lacking, Loose end, Partial, Pendent, Rough, Sketchy, Unfinished

**Incomprehensible, Incomprehension** Acatalepsy, Acatamathesia, Double Dutch, Hard, Obscure, Recondite, Unbelievable

**Inconceivable** Impossible, Incredible, Undreamt

▷**In confusion** *may indicate* an anagram

**Incongruous, Incongruity** Absurd, Discordant, Heterogenous, Ironic, Sharawadgi, Sharawaggi, Solecism

**In connection with** Re

**Inconsequential** Light, Minor

**Inconsiderable** Light, Mere, Slight

**Inconsiderate** Asocial, High-handed, Hog, Lairy, Light-minded, Petty, Presumptuous, Roughshod, Tactless, Thoughtless, Unkind, Unthinking

**Inconsistency, Inconsistent** Alien, Anacoluthon, Anomaly, Arbitrary, Clashing, Contradictory, Disconformable, Discrepant, Double think, Erratic, Fitful, Illogical, Jar(ring), Motley-minded, Mutable, Oxymoronic, Paradoxical, Patchy, Unequal, Unsteady, Variance

**Inconsolable** Heartbroken, Niobe

**Inconspicuous** Background, Obscure, Small, Unobtrusive

**Inconstant** Chameleon, Desultory, Fickle, Light, Mercurial, Moony, Mutable, → VARIABLE

**Incontrovertible** Demonstrable, Evident, Irrefutable

**Inconvenience, Inconvenient** Awkward, Bother(some), Disaccommodate, Disadvantageous, Discommode, Fleabite, Incommodious, Inopportune, Put out, → TROUBLE, Ungain(ly), Unseemly, Untoward

**Incorporate(d), Incorporation** Absorb, Embody, Engraft, Hard wire, Inc(lude), Inorb, Integrate, Introgression, Introject, Join, Merge, Subsume

**Incorporeal** Aery, Airy, Insubstantial, Spiritual

**Incorrect** Catachresis, Erroneous, False, Improper, Invalid, Misconception, Naughty, Wrong

**Incorrigible** Hopeless, Obstinate
**Incorruptible** Copper-bottomed, Honest, Immortal, Pure, Robespierre, Sea-green
**Increase(s), Increasing** Accelerando, Accelerate, Accession, Accretion, Accrew, Accrue, Add, Additur, Advance, Aggrandise, Amplify, Amp up, Appreciate, Approve, Augment, Auxetic, Bolster, Boost, Build up, Bulge, Burgeon, Charge, Crank up, Crescendo, Crescent, Crescive, Cumulate, Deepen, Dilate, Double, Ech(e), Eech, Eik, Eke, Enhance, Enlarge, Enliven, Escalate, → EXPAND, Explosion, Exponential, Extend, Gain, Gather, Greaten, → GROW, Heighten, Hike, Ich, Increment, Inflation, Interbreed, Irrupt, Jack, Jack up, Joseph, Lengthen, Lift, Magnify, Mark up, Mount, Multiply, Plus, Proliferate, Prolong, Propagate, Ramp up, Redshift, Reflation, Regrate, Resurgence, Rise, Rocket, Snowball, Speed up, Spike, Supercharger, Surge, Swell, Thrive, Up, Upload, Upsize, Upswell, Upswing, Up the ante, Wax, Write up
**Incredible** Amazing, Astonishing, Awesome, Cockamamie, Extraordinary, Fantastic, Phenomenal, Preposterous, Staggering, Steep, Stey, Tall, Theeing, Unbelievable, Unreal
**Incredulity, Incredulous** As if, Disbelief, Distrust, Infidel, Sceptic, Suspicion, Thunderstruck, Unbelief
**Increment** Accrual, Augment, Growth, Increase, Unearned
**Incriminate** Accuse, Frame, Implicate, Inculpate, Stitch up
**Incrustation** Sordes, Zaratite
**Incubate, Incubator** Brooder, Develop, Eccaleobion, Hatch, Ovisac
**Incubus** Demon, Load, Nightmare
**Inculcate** Imbue, Implant, Infuse, Instil
**Incumbent** Lying, Obligatory, Occupier, Official, Resident
**Incur** Assume, Earn, Involve, Run up
**Incursion** Foray, Inroad, Invasion, Raid, Razzia
**Indecent** Bare, Blue, Fescennine, Free, Immodest, Immoral, Improper, Indelicate, Lewd, Obscene, Rabelaisian, Racy, Scurril(e), Smut, Sotadic, Spicy, Sultry, Unbecoming, Uncomely, Unnatural, Unproper, Unseem(ly), Vulgar, X-rated
**Indecision, Indecisive** Demur, Dithery, Doubt, Hamlet, Havering, Hesitation, Hum and haw, Hung jury, Inconclusive, Irresolute, Shilly-shally, Suspense, Swither, Unemphatic, Vacillation, Weak-kneed, Wishy-washy
**Indeclinable** Aptote
**Indecorous** Graceless, High-kilted, Immodest, Outré, Unbecoming, Unseemly
**Indeed** Absolutely, And how, Atweel, Ay, Aye, Begorra(h), Da, Een, Even, Faith, Haith, I, Insooth, Ja wohl, La, Marry, Quotha, Soothly, Truly, Verily, Yah, Yea
**Indefensible** Implausible, Inexcusable, Untenable, Vincible
**Indefinable** Je ne sais quoi
**Indefinite(ly)** A, An, Any, Evermore, Hazy, Nth, Sine die, Some, Uncertain, Undecided, Vague
**Indelible** Fast, Permanent
**Indelicate** Broad, Coarse, Crass, Improper, Sultry, Vulgar, Warm
**Indemnify, Indemnification, Indemnity** Assythement, Compensation, Double, Insurance, Repay, Surety, Voetstoots
**Indent(ed), Indentation** Apprentice, Cleft, Contract, Crenellate, Dancetty, Dimple, Impress, Imprint, Niche, Notch, Order, Philtrum, Prophet's thumbmarks, Set in, Subentire
**Independence, Independent** Apart, Autocephalous, Autogenous, Autonomy, Crossbencher, Detached, Extraneous, Free(dom), Free-lance, Free spirit, Freethinker, I, Individual, Liberty, Mana motuhake, Maverick, Mugwump, Perseity, Self-contained, Self-sufficient, Separate, Separatist, Sui juris, Swaraj, Udal, UDI, Uhuru, Viscosity
**Indescribable** Incredible, Ineffable, Je ne sais quoi
**Indestructible** Enduring, Impenetrable, Inextirpable, Permanent
**Indeterminate** Borderline, Formless, Incalculable, Open-ended, Unknown
**Index** Alidad(e), All-Ordinaries, Catalogue, Cephalic, Colour, Concordance, Cranial, Cross, DAX, Dial, Dow Jones, Exponent, Facial, Finger, Fist, Fog, Footsie, Forefinger, FTSE, Gazetteer, Glycaemic, Hang Seng, Kwic, Librorum Prohibitorum, Margin, Misery, Mitotic,

Nasal, Nikkei, Opsonic, Power, Price, Refractive, → **REGISTER**, Rolodex®, Rotary, Share, Stroke, Table, Therapeutic, Thumb, TPI, UV, Verborum, Zonal

**India(n)** Adivisi, Apache, Asian, Assamese, Ayah, Baboo, Babu, Bharat(i), Bihari, Canarese, Carib, Chin, Crazy Horse, Dard, Dravidian, East, File, Gandhi, Goanese, Gond(wanaland), Gujarati, Harijan, Harsha, Hindu, .in, Indic, Ink, Jain, Jat, Jemadar, Jewel in the crown, Kanarese, Kannada, Khalsa, Kisan, Kolarian, Kshatriyas, Lepcha, Mahatma, Maratha, Ma(h)ratta, Maya, Mazhbi, → **MEXICAN**, Mishmi, Mission, Mofussil, Mogul, Mulki, Munda, Munshi, Naga, Nagari, Nair, Nasik, Nation, Nayar, → **NORTH AMERICAN**, Nuri, Ocean, Oriya, Pali, Panjabi, Pargana, Parsee, Parsi, Pathan, Peshwa, Plains, Poppadom, Prakrit, Punja(u)bee, Punjabi, Ravi, Red, Sanskrit, Sepoy, Shri, Sikh, Sind(h), → **SOUTH AMERICAN**, Sowar, Subcontinent, Summer, Swadeshi, Taino, Tamil, Telegu, Treaty, Vakeel, Vakil, West, Ynd

**Indiaman** Clive, Trader

**Indiana, Indianian** Hoosier

**Indicate, Indication, Indicative, Indicator** Adumbrate, Allude, Altimeter, Argue, Arrow, Barcode, Bespeak, Betoken, Blinker, Bode, Buoy, Cite, Clue, Convey, Coordinate, Cursor, → **DENOTE**, Design, Designate, Desine, Dial, Dial gauge, Endeixis, Evidence, Evince, Extort, Finger, Fluorescein, Foreshadow, Gesture, Gnomon, Guideline, Hint, Imply, Litmus, Manifest, Mark, Mean, Mood, Motion, Nod, Notation, Performance, Pinpoint, Plan-position, Point, Portend, Proof, Ray, Register, Remarque, Representative, Reveal, Show, → **SIGN**, Signal, Signboard, Signify, Specify, Speedo, Spell, Symptom, Tip, Token, Trace, Trafficator, Trait, Winker

**Indictment** Accusation, Arraign, Caption, Charge, Dittay, Reproach, Trounce

**Indifference, Indifferent** Adiaphoron, Aloof, Anyhow, Apathetic, Apathy, Blasé, Blithe, Callous, Cauld, Cavalier, Cold, Cool(th), Dead, Deaf, Detached, Disdain, Disinterest, Easy-osy, Empty, Fico, Incurious, Insouciant, Jack easy, Lax, Lukewarm, Mediocre, Meh, Neutral, Nonchalant, Perfunctory, Phlegm, Pococurante, Sangfroid, Shrug, So-so, Stoical, Supercilious, Supine, Tepid, Thick-skinned, Third-rate, Unconcerned

**Indigence, Indigent** Need, Pauper, Penury, Poverty, Want

**Indigenous** Aboriginal, Endemic, Lapp, Native

▷**Indi-gent** *may indicate* Baboo or Babu

**Indigestible** Stodgy

**Indigestion** Apepsia, Apepsy, Dyspepsia, Heartburn, Stomach-ache

**Indignant, Indignation** Anger, Annoyed, Bridling, Incensed, Irate, Outrage, Pique, Resentful, Steamed up, Umbrage, Up in arms, Wrathful

**Indignity** Affront, Outrage

**Indigo** Anil, Blue, Bunting, Carmine, Indole, Isatin(e), Wild

**Indirect** Aside, Back-handed, By(e), Bypath, Circuitous, Circumlocution, Circumstantial, Devious, Evasive, Implicit, Mediate, Oblique, Remote, Roundabout, Second-hand, Sidelong, Sly, Subtle, Third-hand, Vicarious, Zig-zag

**Indiscreet, Indiscretion** Blabbermouth, Folly, Gaffe, Imprudence, Indelicate, Injudicious, Lapse, Loose cannon, Rash, Tactless, Unguarded, Wild oats

**Indiscriminate** Haphazard, Random, Scattershot, Sweeping, Wholesale

**Indispensable** Basic, Essential, King-pin, Linch-pin, Necessary, Requisite, Sine qua non, Vital

**Indispose(d), Indisposition** Adverse, Disincline, Ill, Incapacitate, Loth, Reluctant, Sick, Unwell

**Indisputable** Evident, Watertight

**Indistinct** Ambiguous, Bleary, Blobby, Blur, Bumble, Bummle, Faint, Filmy, Fuzzy, Grainy, Hazy, Misty, Muffled, Mumbling, Mush-mouthed, Nebulous, Neutral, Nondescript, Pale, Sfumato, S(c)hwa, Slurred, Smudged, Unincorporate, → **VAGUE**

**Indistinguishable** Nondescript

▷**In distress** *may indicate* an anagram

**Indite** Compose, Pen, Write

**Indium** In

**Individual(ist), Individuality** Apiece, Being, Discrete, Exclusive, Free spirit, Gemma,

Haecceity, Hand-crafted, Identity, Ka, Libertarian, Loner, Man, Man-jack, Morph, One-to-one, Original, Own, Particular, Person(al), Poll, Respective, Seity, Self, Separate, Single, Singular, Solo, Soul, Special, Unique, Unit, Zoon

**Indivisible** Intrenchant

**Indoctrinate** Brainwash, Discipline, Instruct

**Indo-European** Aryan, Jat(s)

**Indolence, Indolent** Bone idle, Fainéance, Inactive, Languid, Lazy, Lentor, Lotus-eater, Otiose, Purposeless, Shiftless, Sloth, Sluggish, Supine

**Indomitable** Brave, Dauntless, Invincible

**Indonesia(n)** Batavian, .id, Javanese, Nesiot, RI

**Indoor(s)** Within

**Indubitably** Certainly, Certes, Manifestly, Surely

**Induce(ment)** Backhander, Bribe, Carrot, Cause, Coax, Draw, Encourage, Entice, Evoke, Get, Incentive, Inveigle, Invite, Lead, Motivate, → **PERSUADE**, Prevail, Sop, Stimulus, Suasion, Suborn, Tempt, Urge

**Induct(ion), Inductance** Epagoge, Henry, Inaugurate, Initiate, Install, L, Logic, Magnetic, Mutual, Ordain, Prelude, Remanence

**Indulge(nce), Indulgent** Absolution, Aristippus, Binge, Coddle, Cosset, Debauchery, Dissipation, Drink, Favour, Fond, Gentle, Gratify, Humour, Jag, Law, Lie-in, Luxuriate, Oblige, Orgy, Pamper, Pander, Pardon, Partake, Permissive, Pet, Pettle, Pig-out, Please, Plenary, → **SATISFY**, Splurge, Spoil, Spoonfeed, Spree, Surfeit, Sybarite, Tolerant, Treat, Venery, Voluptuous, Wallow

**Industrial, Industrious, Industry** Appliance, Application, Basic, Black Country, Business, Busy, Commerce, Cottage, Deedy, Diligence, Eident, Energetic, Growth, Heavy, Heritage, Key, Labour, Legwork, Millicent, Ocnus, Operose, Process, Ruhr, Service, Smokestack, Sunrise, Technical, Technics, Tertiary, Tourism, Zaibatsu

▸**Inebriate** *see* **INTOXICATE(D)**

**Inedible** Inesculent, Noisome, Rotten

**In effect** Actual

**Ineffective, Ineffectual** Chinless wonder, Clumsy, Deadhead, Drippy, Droob, Dud, Empty, Eunuch, Fainéant, Feeble, Fruitless, Futile, Idle, Ill, Impotent, Invalid, Lame, Lightweight, Mickey Mouse, Milksop, Neuter, Neutralised, Null, Otiose, Paper tiger, Passenger, Powerless, Resty, Sterile, Stumbledown, Toothless, Unable, → **USELESS**, Void, Weak, Weenie, Wet, Wimp, Wishy-washy

**Inefficient** Clumsy, Incompetent, Lame, Shiftless, Slack, Slouch

**Inelegant** Awkward, Inconcinnity, Stiff, Turgid, Unneat

**Ineligible** Unqualified

**Inept** Absurd, Amateurish, Anorak, Bungling, Cack-handed, Farouche, Flaky, Fumbler, Galoot, Loser, Maladjusted, Nerd, Otaku, Plonker, Sad sack, Schlimazel, Schmo, Unskilled, Wet

**Inequality** Anomaly, Chebyshev's, Disparity, Evection, Imparity, Injustice, Odds, Tchebyshev's

**Inert(ia)** Catatonia, Comatose, Dead, Dull, Excipient, Inactive, Krypton, Languid, Leaden, Listless, Mollusc, Motionless, Neon, Oblomovism, Potato, Rigor, Sluggish, Stagnant, Stagnation, Supine, Thowless, Torpid, Turgid

**Inescapable** Act of God

**Inestimable** Incalculable, Invaluable, Priceless

**Inevitable, Inevitably** Always, Automatic, Certain, Fateful, Inescapable, Inexorable, Infallible, Necessary, Needs, Perforce, TINA, Unavoidable

**Inexact(itude)** Cretism, Imprecise, Incorrect, Terminological, Wrong

**Inexcusable** Reprehensible, Untenable

**Inexhaustible** Infinite, Tireless

**Inexorable** Relentless

**Inexpedient** Impolitic, Imprudent, Unwise

**Inexpensive** Bargain, Cheap, Dirt-cheap, Economic

**Inexperience(d), Inexpert** Amateur, Armchair, Awkward, Callow, Colt, Crude, Fledgling,

Fresh, →**GREEN**, Greenhorn, Ham, Ignorance, Ingénue, Jejune, Naïve, Newbie, Noob, Put(t), Raw, Rookie, Rude, Tender, Tyro, Unconversant, Unseasoned, Unseen, Untried, Unversed, Waister, Wide-eyed, Yardbird, Youthful

**Inexplicable** Magical, Mysterious, Paranormal, Supernatural, Unaccountable

**Inexpressible** Mystique

**In fact** Insooth, Truly

**Infallible** Foolproof, Oracle, Right, Sure-fire, Unerring

**Infamous, Infamy** Base, Defame, Ignominious, Notorious, Opprobrium, Shameful, Villainy

**Infant, Infancy** Babe, Baby, Innocent, Lamb, Minor, Newborn, Nonage, Nurs(e)ling, Oral, Rug rat, The cradle

**Infantry(man)** Buff, Foot, Fusilier, Grunt, Jaeger, Phalanx, Pultan, Pulto(o)n, Pultun, →**SOLDIER**, Tercio, Turco, Twenty, Voetganger, Zouave

▷**Infantry** *may refer to* babies

**Infarction** Myocardial

**Infatuate(d), Infatuating, Infatuation** Assot, Besot, Calf love, Circean, Crush, Enamoured, Engou(e)ment, Entêté, Epris, Fanatic, Foolish, Lovesick, Mash, →**OBSESSION**, Pash, Rave, Turn

**Infect(ed), Infecting, Infection, Infectious** Adenoviral, Angina, Anthrax, Babesiasis, Babesiosis, Bacterial, Candidiasis, Canker, Carrier, Catching, Catchy, Cholera, Communicable, Contagious, Contaminate, Corrupt, Cowpox, Croup, Cryptococcosis, Cryptosporidiosis, Dermatophytosis, Diseased, Dysentery, E-coli, Fascioliasis, Fester, Focal, Fomes, Giardiasis, Gonorrhoea, Herpes, Hysteria, Impetigo, Leishmaniasis, Listeria, Lockjaw, Mycetoma, NSU, Opportunistic, Orf, Overrun, Pneumonia, Poison, Polio(myelitis), →**POLLUTE**, Py(a)emia, Pyoderma, Quittor, Rabid, Rife, Ringworm, Roseola, Roup, Salmonella, Sarcoid, SARS, Scabies, Secondary, Sepsis, Septic, Shingles, Smit(tle), Strep throat, Strongyloidiasis, Strongylosis, Taint, Taking, Tetanus, Thrush, Tinea, Toxocariasis, Toxoplasmosis, Transfection, Trichuriasis, Tryp, Tuberculosis, Typhoid, Typhus, Varroa, Vincent's angina, Viral pneumonia, Virion, Virulent, Whitlow, Yersiniosis, Zoonosis, Zymosis

**Infeftment** Sasine, Seisin

**Infer(ence), Inferred** Conclude, Conjecture, Construe, Deduce, Divine, Educe, Extrapolate, Generalise, Guess, Illation, Imply, Judge, Obversion, Putative, Surmise, Syllogism

▷**Infer** *may indicate* 'fer' around another word

**Inferior** Base, Bodgier, Cheap-jack, Cheesy, Coarse, Crummy, Degenerate, Dog, Epigon, Ersatz, Gimcrack, Grody, Grub-Street, Impair, Indifferent, Infra, Jerkwater, Kitsch, Less, Lo-fi, Lousy, Lower, Low-grade, Mediocre, Minor, Naff, Neckbeef, Nether, One-horse, Ornery, Paravail, Petty, Poor, Rop(e)y, Schlock, Second, Second-best, Second-class, Shilpit, Shlock, Shoddy, Shonky, Slopwork, Sprew, Sprue, Subjacent, Subordinate, Substandard, Surat, Tatty, Third-rate, Tinpot, Trashy, Under(man), Underdog, Underneath, Understrapper, Untermensch, Waste, Worse

**Infernal** All-fired, Cotton-picking, Demogorgon, Diabolic, Hellish, Phitonian, Tartarean, Unholy

**Inferno** Hellfire

**Infertile, Infertility** Barren, Farrow, GIFT, Sterile

**Infest(ed), Infestation** Acariasis, Acrawl, Beset, Blight, Dog, Filaria, Giardiasis, Hoatching, Overrun, Pediculosis, Phthiriasis, →**PLAGUE**, Stylopised, Swamp, Swarm, Taeniasis, Torment, Trombiculiasis, Trombidiasis, Trypanosomiasis, Uncinariasis

**Infidel, Infidelity** Adultery, Atheist, Giaour, Heathen, Heretic, Miscreant, Pagan, Paynim, Saracen

**Infield** Intown

**Infiltrate(d), Infiltration, Infiltrator** Encroach, Enter, Entryist, Fifth columnist, Gatecrash, Instil, Intrude, Mole, Pervade, Trojan horse

**Infinite, Infinity** Cosmic, Endless, Eternal, N, Untold

**Infinitive** Split

**Infirm(ity)** Decrepit, Doddery, Feeble, Frail, Frailness, Lame, Shaky, Sick
▷**Infirm** *may indicate* 'co' around another word
**Infirmary** Hospital, Sick bay
**Inflame(d), Inflammable, Inflammation** Afire, Anger, → AROUSE, Bloodshot, Enamoured, Enchafe, Enfire, Enkindle, Fever, Fire, Founder, Gleet, Ignite, Impassion, Incense, Infection, Ire, Kindle, Methane, Napalm, Naphtha, Piceous, Raw, → RED, Rouse, Stimulate, Swelling, Touchwood, Tynd

---

**INFLAMMATIONS**

*3 letters:*
Sty

*4 letters:*
Acne
Gout
Noma
Stye

*5 letters:*
Croup
Felon
Mange

*6 letters:*
Ancome
Angina
Bunion
Canker
Coryza
Eczema
Garget
Iritis
Otitis
Quinsy
Thrush
Ulitis

*7 letters:*
Bubonic
Catarrh
Cecitis
Colitis
Ecthyma
Ignatis
Ileitis
Onychia
Pinkeye
Prurigo
Rosacea
Sunburn
Sycosis
Tylosis
Uveitis
Whitlow

*8 letters:*
Adenitis
Aortisis
Bursitis
Carditis
Colpitis
Cystisis
Fibrosis
Hyalitis
Mastitis
Metritis
Mycetoma
Myelitis
Myositis
Neuritis
Orchitis
Osteitis
Ovaritis
Phlegmon
Pleurisy
Pyelitis
Rachitis
Rectitis
Rhinitis
Thylosis
Uvulitis
Vulvitis
Windburn

*9 letters:*
Arteritis
Arthritis
Balanitis
Barotitis
Carbuncle
Cheilitis
Chilblain
Cloacitis
Dysentery
Enteritis
Fasciitis
Frostbite
Gastritis
Glossitis
Keratitis
Laminitis
Nephritis
Onychitis
Parotitis
Phlebitis
Phrenitis
Pneumonia
Proctitis
Pyorrhoea
Retinitis
Scleritis
Sinusitis
Splenitis
Strumitis
Synovitis
Typhlitis
Vaginitis
Vent gleet

*10 letters:*
Asbestosis
Bronchitis
Cellulitis
Cephalitis
Cerebritis
Cervicitis
Chondritis
Dermatitis
Duodenitis
Erysipelas
Fibrositis
Gingivitis
Hepatitis A
Hepatitis B
Hysteritis
Intertrigo
Laryngitis
Meningitis
Myringitis
Oophoritis
Ophthalmia
Papillitis
Paronychia
Phlegmasia
Phlogistic
Stomatitis
Tendinitis
Tendonitis
Thrombosis
Tracheitis
Tympanitis
Urethritis
Valvulitis
Vasculitis

*11 letters:*
Blepharitis
Farmer's lung
Mad staggers
Mastoiditis
Myocarditis
Parotiditis
Peritonitis
Pharyngitis
Pneumonitis
Prostatitis
Salpingitis
Sandy blight
Sclerotitis
Shin splints
Spondylitis
Staphylitis
Tennis elbow
Thoroughpin
Thyroiditis
Tonsillitis
Trenchmouth
Utriculitis
Woody-tongue

*12 letters:*
Appendicitis
Crystallitis
Encephalitis
Endocarditis
Endometritis
Folliculitis
Golfer's elbow
Lymphangitis
Lympodenitis
Mesenteritis
Ophthalmitis
Osteoporosis

Panarthritis
Pancreatitis
Pericarditis
Polymyositis
Polyneuritis
Sacroillitis
Swimmer's itch
Vestibulitis

*13 letters:*
Cholecystitis
Enterocolitis
Epicondylitis
Jogger's nipple
Labyrinthitis
Lymphadenitis
Osteomyelitis
Perihepatitis
Perinephritis
Periodontisis
Perityphlitis
Tenosynovitis
Tenovaginitis
Thrombophilia

*14 letters:*
Clergyman's knee
Conjunctivitis
Diverticulitis
Osteoarthritis
Pyelonephritis
Sleepy staggers
Tendovaginitis
Trichomoniasis
Vincent's angina

*15 letters:*
Gastroenteritis
Pachymeningitis
Panophthalmitis

*16 letters:*
Bronchopneumonia
Rhinopharyngitis
Thrombophlebitis

*17 letters:*
Encephalomyelitis
Meningocephalitis

*19 letters:*
St Louis encephalitis

---

**Inflate(d), Inflatable, Inflation** Aerate, Aggrandise, Balloon, Bloat, Bombastic, Bracket-creep, Cost-push, Demand-pull, Dilate, Distend, Distent, Exaggerate, Galloping, Grade, Increase, Mae West, Pneumatic, Pompous, Pump, Raise, Remonetise, RPI, Spiral, Stagflation, Stagnation, Swell, Turgid, Wage-push

**Inflect(ion)** Accidence, Cadence, Conjugation, Lilt, Tone, Twang

**Inflexible, Inflexibility** Adamant(ine), Authoritarian, Byzantine, Doctrinaire, Hard-ass, Hard-liner, Hell-bent, Iron, Obstinate, Ossified, Ramrod, Relentless, Resolute, Rigid, Rigour, Set, Staid, Steely, Stiff, Stringent, Stubborn, Unbending

**Inflict(ion)** Deal, Force, Give, Impose, Incur, Subject, Trouble, Visit, Wreak

**Inflorescence** Bostryx, Catkin, Ci(n)cinnus, Drepanium, Glomerule, Monochasium, Panicle, Pleiochasium, Polychasium, Raceme, R(h)achis, Umbel, Verticillaster

**Inflow** Affluence, Influx

**Influence(d), Influential** Act, Affect, After, Amenable, Backstairs, Bias, Brainwash, Catalyse, Charm, Clamour, Clout, Colour, Credit, Decisive, Determine, Dominant, Drag, Earwig, Eclectic, Embrace(o)r, Embracery, Embrasor, Éminence grise, Factor, Fat-cat, Force, Get at, Govern, Guide, Hegemony, Hold, Hypnotise, Impact, Impinge, Impress, Incubus, Inspire, Interfere, Jinx, Lead, Leverage, Lobby, Macher, Manipulate, Market force, Mastery, Militate, Mogul, Mould, Nabob, Nobble, Octopus, Oligarch, Operation, Outreach, Outweigh, Panjandrum, Power, Preponderant, Pressure, Prestige, → PULL, Push, Reach, Rust, Say, Securocrat, Seminal, Significant, Star, Star-blasting, Stimulus, String-pulling, Suggest, Svengali, Sway, Swing, Telegony, Thrall, Undue, Weigh with, Will, Work, Wull

**Influenza** Asian, Equine, Flu, Gastric, Grippe, Lurgi, Spanish, Yuppie

**Influx** Inbreak

**Infold(ing)** Invagination

**Inform(ation), Informant, Informed, Informer** Acquaint, Advise, Agitprop, Apprise, Arise, Au fait, Aware, Beagle, Bit, Blow, Briefing, Burst, Callboard, Canary, Ceefax®, Clype, Contact, Cookie, Database, Datum, Debriefing, Deep throat, Delate, Diane, Dicker, Dob(ber), Dobber-in, Dog, Dope, Download, Education, Exposition, Facts, Fact sheet, FAQs, Feedback, Fink, Fisgig, Fiz(z)gig, Gen, Genome, Good oil, Grapevine, Grass, Griff, Gunsel, Hep, Hip, Immersive, Input, Inside, Instruct, Izvesti(y)a, Light, Literate, Little bird, Lowdown, Mass media, Media, Message, Metadata, Microdot, Moiser, Nark, Nepit, News, Newscast, Nit, Nose, Notes, Notice board, Notify, Occasion, Oracle®, Output, Peach, Pem(m)ican, Pentito, Pimp, Pointer, Poop, Post, Prestel®, Prime, Printout, Promoter, Propaganda, Prospectus, Rat, Read-out, Relator, Report, Revelation, Rheme, Rumble, Shelf, Shop, Sidelight, Sing, Sneak, Snitch, Snout, SP, Squeak, Squeal, Stag, Stoolie, Stool-pigeon, Supergrass, Sycophant, Teletext®, Tell, Throughput, Tidings, Tip-off, Tooltip, Up, Up to speed, Videotext®, Viewdata®, Whistle(-blower), Wire, Witting, Word-wise

**Informal** Bat, Casual, Colloquial, Cosy, Free and easy, Go-as-you-please, Intimate, Irregular, Outgoing, Rough and ready, Sans-ceremonie, Unofficial

**Infra** Under

**Infra dig** Ignominious

**Infrequent** Casual, Occasional, Rare, Scant, Seldom, Sparse
**Infringe(ment)** Contravene, Encroach, Foul, Infraction, Offside, Piracy, Transgression, Violate
**Infuriate(d)** Anger, Apoplectic, Bemad, Bepester, Enrage, Exasperate, Gall, Incense, Livid, Madden, Pester, Provoke
**Infuse(r), Infusion** Brew, Distill, Gallise, Imbue, Instil, Mash, Ooze, Saloop, Saturate, Steep, Tea, Tea-ball, Tea-egg, Tisane, Toddy, Uva-ursi
**Ingenious, Ingenuity** Acumen, Adept, Adroit, Art, Artificial, Clever, Cunning, Cute, Dexterous, Inventive, Natty, Neat, Resourceful, Smart, Subtle, Trick(s)y, Wit
**Ingenuous** Artless, Candid, Green, Innocent, Naive, Open, Transparent
**Ingest, Ingestion** Consume, Eat, Endue, Incept, Indue, Pinocytosis, Swallow
**Ingle** Bardash, Hearth, Nook
**In good condition** Fit, Shipshape, Taut, Trim
**Ingot** Bar, Billet, Bullion, Lingot, Sycee, Wedge
**Ingrain(ed)** Deep-seated, Fix, Impregnate, Inbred, Train
**Ingrate** Thankless, Viper
**Ingratiate, Ingratiating** Bootlick, Butter, Court, Flatter, Greasy, Obsequious, Oily, Pick-thank, Silken, Smarm(y)
**Ingredient(s)** Additive, Admixture, Asafoetida, Basis, Component, Content, Element, Factor, Formula, Makings, Mincemeat, Staple
**Ingrowing, Ingrowth** Onychocryptosis, T(h)ylosis
**Inhabit(ant), Inhabitants** Affect, Ascian, Children, Citizen, Denizen, Dweller, Indweller, Inholder, Inmate, Live, National, Native, Occupant, People, Populate, Population, Populous, Resident, Towny
**Inhale(r), Inhalation** Aspirate, Breath(e), Draw, Gas, Inbreathe, Inspire, Intal, Sniff, Snort, Snuff, Take, Toot, Tout
**Inharmonious** Out, Patchy
**Inherent** Characteristic, Essential, Immanent, Inbred, Innate, Native, Quiddity
**Inherit(ance), Inherited, Inheritor** Accede, Ancestral, Birthright, Borough-English, Congenital, Esnecy, Feoffee, Gene, Genom, Heirloom, Heritage, Inborn, Legacy, Legitim, Meek, Mendelism, Particulate, Patrimony, Per stirpes, Portion, Reversion, Succeed, Tichborne, Ultimogenitive
**Inhibit(ing), Inhibition, Inhibitor** ACE, Antibiotic, Antihistamine, Antisepsis, Anuria, Captopril, Chalone, Chalonic, Deter, Donepezil, Enalapril, Etanercept, Feedback, Finasteride, Forbid, Frustrate, Hang-up, Indinavir, Overawe, Protease, Repress, Restrain, Retard, Retroactive, Ritonavir, Saquinavir, Stunt, Suppress, Thiourea, Tightass
**In-house** Resident
**Inhuman(e)** Abusive, Barbarous, Brutal, Merciless, Robotic
**Inimical** Adverse, Harmful, Hostile
**Inimitable** Unique
**Iniquity, Iniquitous** Damnable, Diabolical, Evil, Offence, Sin, Vice
**Initial** Acronym, First, Inaugural, Letter, Monogram, Paraph, Prelim(inary), Primary, Rubric
▷**Initially** *may indicate* first letters
**Initiate(d), Initiating, Initiation, Initiative** Baptism, Begin, Bejesuit, Blood, Bora, Bring, Ceremony, Debut, Démarche, Enter, Enterprise, Epopt, Esoteric, Gumption, Induct, Instigate, Instruct, Introduce, → LAUNCH, Leadership, Neophyte, Nous, Onset, Open, Proactive, Spark, → START, Telestic, Tyro
**Inject(or), Injection** Antiserum, Bang, Blast, Bolus, Booster, Collagen, Direct, Enema, Epidural, Epipen®, Fuel, Hypo, Immit, Implant, Innerve, Inoculation, Instil, Introduce, Jab, Jack up, Jag, Lidocaine, Mainline, Pop, Reheat, Serum, Shoot, Shoot up, Skin-pop, Solid, Spike, Syringe, Transfuse, Vaccine, Venepuncture, Venipuncture
**Injudicious** Misguided
**Injun** Honest
**Injunction** Command, Embargo, Freezing, Mandate, Mareva, Quia timet, Swear, Writ
**Injure(d), Injury, Injurious, Injustice** ABH, Abuse, Accloy, Aggrieve, Bale, Barotrauma, Bled, Blue-on-blue, Bruise, Casualty, Concuss, Contrecoup, Contuse, Crick,

Damage, De(a)re, Disservice, Forslack, Frostbite, Gammy, Gash, GBH, Harm, → **HURT**, Ill-turn, Impair, Industrial, Iniquity, Lesion, Maieutic, Malign, Mar, Maul, Mayhem, Mistreat, Mutilate, NAI, Needlestick, Nobble, Nocuous, Non-accidental, Noxal, Nuisance, Occupational, Oppression, Outrage, Packet, Paire, Pernicious, Prejudice, Repetitive, Rifle, RSI, Scaith, Scald, Scath(e), Scotch, Scratch, Shend, Shiner, Sore, Sprain, Surbet, Teen(e), Tene, Tort, Trauma, Umbrage, Whiplash, Wound, Wrong

▶**Injury** *see* **AFTER INJURY**

**Ink(y), Inker** Atramental, Black, Blot, Bray, China, Chinese, Copying, Cyan, Gall, Gold, Indian, Invisible, Magnetic, Marking, Monk, Printer's, Printing, Sepia, Stained, Sympathetic, Tattooist, Toner, Tusche

**Inkling** Clue, Glimpse, Hint, Idea, Suspicion

**Inkpot** Standish

**Inlaid, Inlay(er)** Boulle, Buhl, Clear, Compurgation, Crustae, Damascene, Emblemata, Empaestic, Enamel, Enchase, Incrust, Intarsia, Intarsio, Koftgar(i), Koftwork, Marquetrie, Marquetry, Pietra-dura, Piqué, Set, Tarsia, Unsuspecting, Veneer

**Inland** Hinterland, Interior, Up, Upcountry

**Inlet** Arm, Bay, Bohai, Cook, Cove, Creek, Entry, Estuary, Fiord, Firth, Fjord, Fleet, Flow, Geo, Gio, Golden Horn, Gulf, Gusset, Hope, Infall, Ingate, Jervis Bay, Loch, McMurdo Sound, Moray Firth, Pamlico Sound, Pearl Harbor, Plymouth Sound, Pohai, Port Jackson, Port Phillip Bay, Puget Sound, Ria, Rio de la Plata, Sogne Fjord, Solway Firth, Strait, Sullom Voe, Table Bay, The Wash, Torbay, Zuyder Zee

▷**Inlet** *may indicate* 'let' around another word

**Inmate** Intern(e), Lodger, Patient, Prisoner, Resident

**Inn(s), Innkeeper** Albergo, Alehouse, Auberge, Barnard's, Boniface, Caravanserai, Chancery, Change-house, Coaching, Court, Gastropub, Gray's, Halfway-house, Host(ry), Hostelry, Hotel(ier), House, Imaret, In, Inner Temple, Jamaica, Khan, Kneipe, Ladin(ity), Law, Licensee, Lincoln's, Lodging, Luckie, Lucky, Maypole, Middle Temple, Motel, Padrone, Parador, Patron, Porterhouse, Posada, Posthouse, Pothouse, Publican, Roadhouse, Ryokan, Serai, Stabler, Tabard, Taphouse, Tavern(er), Victualler

▷**Inn** *may refer to* the law

**Innards** Entrails, Giblets, Gizzard, Guts, Harigals, Harslet, Haslet, Omasa, Rein, Viscera

**Innate** Congenital, Essential, Inborn, Inbred, Inbuilt, Ingenerate, Ingrown, Instinctive, Natural, Original

**Inner(most)** Bencher, Esoteric, Home, Internal, Intima, Intimate, Lining, Man, Marrow, Medulla, Private, Red, Woman

**Innings** Chance, Knock, Turn

▶**Innkeeper** *see* **INN(S)**

**Innocent** Absolved, Angelic, Arcadian, Artless, Babe, Blameless, Canny, Chaste, Cherub, Childlike, Clean, Clear, Compurgation, Dewy-eyed, Doddypoll, Dodipoll, Dove, Encyclical, Green, Guileless, Idyllic, Inadvertent, Ingenue, Lamb, Lily-white, Maiden, Naive, Opsimath, Pope, Prelapsarian, → **PURE**, Sackless, St, Seely, Simple, Unsuspecting, Unwitting, White

**Innocuous** Harmless, Innocent

**Innovate, Innovative, Innovation, Innovator** Alteration, Avant garde, Cutting edge, Departure, Ground-breaking, Modernise, Newell, Newness, Novelty, Novity, Pioneer, Promethean, Radical, Trendsetter, Wrinkle

**Inn-sign** Bush

**Inns of Court** Gray's Inn, Inner Temple, Lincoln's Inn, Middle Temple

**Innu** Naskapi

**Innuendo** Hint, Insinuation, Overtone, Slur

**Innumerable** Countless, Infinite, Myriad, N

**Inoculate, Inoculation** Engraft, Immunise, Inject, Jab, Pasteurism, Protect, Serum, Vaccine, Variolate

**Inoffensive** Anodyne, Decent, Harmless, Mild, Neutral, Pleasant

**Inoperative** Futile, Nugatory, Silent, Void

**Inopportune** Disadvantageous, Inconvenient, Intempestive, Mistimed, Untimely

**Inordinate** Excessive, Irregular, Undue

▷**Inordinately** *may indicate* an anagram
**Inorganic** Mineral
**In place of** For, Qua, Vice, Vise, With
**Input** Contribution, Data, Direct, OCR
**Inquest** Debriefing, Hearing, Inquiry, Investigation
**Inquire, Inquiring, Inquiry** Ask, Demand, Investigation, Maieutic, Nose, Organon, Post mortem, Probe, Public, Query, Question, See, Seek, Speer, Speir
**Inquisition, Inquisitive, Inquisitor** Curious, Interrogation, Meddlesome, Nosy, Prying, Rubberneck, Snooper, Spanish, Stickybeak, Torquemada
▷**In revolt, In revolution** *may indicate* an anagram
**Inroad(s)** Breach, Encroachment, Honeycomb, Infall, Invasion
**Insane, Insanity** Absurd, Batty, Berserk, Crack-brained, Crazy, Dementia, Deranged, Headcase, Hebephrenia, Loco, Looniness, Lune, Mad, Manic, Mattoid, Mental, Meshuga, Nutso, Paranoia, Pellagra, Psycho, Schizo, Troppo, Yarra
**Insatiable** Barathrum, Greedy, Ravenous, Voracious
**Insatiate child** Killcrop
**Inscribe(d), Inscription** Chisel, Chronogram, Colophon, Dedicate, Emblazon, Endoss, Engrave, Enter, Epigraph, Epitaph, Exergue, Graffiti, Hic jacet, Hierograph, Lapidary, Legend, Lettering, Neum(e), Ogham, Pen, Posy, Writ
**Inscrutable** Deadpan, Enigmatic, Esoteric, Mysterious, Poker-faced, Sphinx
**Insect(s)** Entomic, Nonentity, Non-person, Stridulator, Wax

---

**INSECTS**

***3 letters:***
Ant
Bee
Bot
Bug
Fly
Ked
Lac
Nit

***4 letters:***
Flea
Gnat
Grig
Lice
Luna
Mite
Moth
Pium
Pupa
Tick
Wasp
Weta
Zimb

***5 letters:***
Aphis
Borer
Brise
Cimex
Culex
Emmet
Gogga
Imago
Louse
Midge
Nymph
Ox-bot
Roach
Scale
Stick
Zebub

***6 letters:***
Acarid
Bedbug
Botfly
Breese
Breeze
Capsid
Chigoe
Cicada
Cicala
Coccid
Day-fly
Earwig
Elater
Gadfly
Hopper
Hornet
Instar
Locust
Maelid
Maggot
Mantid
Mantis
Mayfly
Medfly
Noctua
Phasma
Podura
Psocid
Psylla
Punkie
Redbug
Sawfly
Scarab
Slater
Spider
Tettix
Thrips
Vespid
Walker
Weevil

***7 letters:***
Aeschna
Antlion
Bee moth
Bristle
Bushfly
Buzzard
Carabid
Chalcid
Chigger
Corixid
Cornfly
Cricket
Culicid
Cutworm
Daphnid
Ergates
Firefly
Gallfly
Girdler
Gordius
Goutfly
Grayfly
Hexapod
Hive-bee
Humbuzz
Katydid
Lace bug
Ladybug
Ladycow
Ladyfly
Odonata
Oestrus
Oniscus
Phasmid
Pill-bug
Pyralis
Sandfly
Spectre
Spittle
Stylops
Tabanus
Termite

***8 letters:***
Alderfly
Blackfly
Bookworm
Cercopid
Circutio
Coccidae
Crane-fly
Dipteras
Dust mite
Ephemera
Firebrat
Fruit fly
Gall-wasp
Glossina
Goatmoth
Greenfly
Horntail
Horse-bot
Horsefly
Isoptera
Itchmite
Lacewing
Ladybird
Lygus bug
Mealybug
Metabola
Milliped
Mosquito
Myriapod
Oak-egged
Onion-fly
Pauropod
Pillworm
Puss-moth
Reduviid
Ruby-tail
Scarabee
Silkworm
Snowflea
Stinkbug
Stonefly
Symphile
Waterbug
Wheelbug
Whitefly
Wireworm
Woodworm

***9 letters:***
Ametabola
Bird louse
Booklouse
Butterfly
Caddis-fly
Campodeid
Centipede
Cochineal
Cockroach
Damselfly
Dobsonfly
Dor-beetle
Dragonfly
Ephemerid
Ergataner
Gall midge
Grass moth
Hawstreak
Hemiptera
Homoptera
Leaf-miner
May beetle
Mecoptera
Millepede
Millipede
Notonecta
Nut weevil
Oil beetle
Rearhorse
Robber-fly
Songololo
Squash bug
Synoekete
Tabanidae
Thysanura
Tiger-moth
Woodlouse
Xylophage

***10 letters:***
Apterygota
Bark mantis
Bluebottle
Casebearer
Cecidomyia
Chironomid
Cicadellid
Cockchafer
Coleoptera
Collembola
Corn thrips
Fan-cricket
Fen-cricket
Flea-beetle
Froghopper
Greendrake
Harvestman
Leaf-cutter
Leafhopper
Mallophaga
Orthoptera
Phylloxera
Plant-louse
Plecoptera
Pond-skater
Psocoptera
Rhipiptera
Rice weevil
Silverfish
Spider-mite
Spittlebug
Springtail
Thysanuran
Treehopper
Waterstick
Web spinner
Wheat midge

***11 letters:***
Bristletail
Collembolan
Dermapteran
Grasshopper
Greenbottle
Heteroptera
Hymenoptera
Lepidoptera
Mole-cricket
Neuropteran
Plectoptera
Rhopalocera
Tiger-beetle
Trichoptera
Vine-fretter

***12 letters:***
Bishop's mitre
Creepy-crawly
Dictyopteran
Groundhopper
Heteropteran
Neuropterous
Notonectidae
Orthopterous
Rhipidoptera
San Jose scale
Strepsiptera
Thousand-legs
Thysanoptera
Water boatman

***13 letters:***
Cotton stainer
Daddy-long-legs
Jenny-longlegs
Leatherjacket
Pine-leaf scale
Praying mantis
Staphylinidae
Water scorpion

***14 letters:***
Strepsipterous

***19 letters:***
Cottony-cushion scale

---

**Insecticide** Aldrin, Allethrin, Aphicide, Bordeaux mixture, Carbamate, Carbaryl, Carbofuran, Chlordan(e), Chromene, Cube, DDT, Deet, Derris, Diazinon, Dieldrin, Endosulfan, Endrin, Flycatcher, Gammexane®, Ivermectin, Lindane®, Malathion®, Menazon, Methoxychlor, Miticide, Naphthalene, Parathion, Paris green, Piperazine, Pulicide, Pyrethrin, Pyrethrum, Repellent, Rotenone, Spray, Systemic, Timbo, Toxaphene, Zineb

**Insectivore** Aardvark, Agouta, Desman, Donaea, Drongo, Drosera, Golden mole, Hedgehog, Jacamar, Nepenthaceae, Otter-shrew, Sarracenia, Shrew, Tanrec, Tenrec(idae), Tupaia, Venus flytrap, Zalambdodont

**Insecure** Infirm, →LOOSE, Needy, Precarious, Shaky, Unsafe, Unsettled, Unstable, Unsteady, Vulnerable

**Insemination** Artificial, Donor

**Insensible** Iron-witted
**Insensitive, Insensitivity** Analgesia, Blunt, Callous, Crass, Dead, Indurate, Log, Numb, Obtuse, Pachyderm, Stolid, Tactless, Thick-skinned
**Inseparable** Indiscrete, Indivisible, One, Shadow, Simultaneous, United
**Insert(ed), Insertion, Inset** Anaptyxis, Caret, Cue, Embed, Empiecement, Enchase, Enter, Entry, Epenthesis, Foist, Fudge, Godet, Gore, Graft, Gusset, Immit, Imp, Implant, Inchase, Inject, Inlay, Input, Intercalar, Intercalate, Interject, Interleaf, Interpolate, Interpose, Intersperse, Introduce, Intromit, Intubate, Lexical, Mitre, Pin, Plant, Punctuate, Sandwich
**Inshallah** God willing
**Inside(r)** Content, Core, Entrails, Gaol, Giblets, Heart, Indoors, Interior, Internal, Interne, Inward, Inwith, Mole, Prison, Tum, → WITHIN
**Insidious** Artful, Crafty, Sly, Subtle
**Insight** Acumen, Anagoge, Aperçu, Cognition, Discernment, Enlightenment, Hunch, Inkling, Intuition, Parascience, → PERCEPTION, Profundity, Tais(c)h
**Insignia** Armour, Arms, Badger, Charge, Chevron, Club tie, Coat of arms, Crest, Eagle, Emblem, Mark, Order, Regalia, Ribbon, Roundel, Tab
**Insignificant (person)** Bobkes, Bubkis, Bupkes, Bupkis, Chickenfeed, Cog, Dandiprat, Fico, Fiddling, Flea-bite, Fractional, Gnat, Hole-in-the-wall, Inconsiderable, Insect, Jerkwater, Mickey Mouse, Minimus, Miniscule, Minnow, Nebbich, Nickel and dime, Nobody, Nominal, Nondescript, Nonentity, Non-event, Non-person, No one, One-eyed, One-horse, Paltry, Pawn, Peanuts, Petit, Petty, Piddling, Pipsqueak, Pissant, Puny, Quat, Rabbit, Scoot, Scout, Scrub, Shrimp, Slight, Small beer, Small potatoes, Small-time, Squirt, Squit, Teeny, Tenuous, Trifling, Trivial, Two-bit, Unimportant, Venial, Warb, Whiffet, Whippersnapper, Wind
**Insincere, Insincerity** Affected, Artificial, Barmecide, Cant, Crocodile tears, Cupboard love, Disingenuous, Double, Double-faced, Duplicity, Empty, Factitious, Faithless, False, Forced, Glib, Greenwash, Hollow, Janus-faced, Lip service, Mealy-mouthed, Meretricious, Mouth-made, Pseudo, Shallow, Superficial, Synthetic, Tongue-in-cheek, Two-faced, Unction, Unnatural
**Insinuate, Insinuating, Insinuation** Allude, Foist, Hint, Imply, Innuendo, Intimate, Sleek, Slur, Sneck-draw
**Insipid** Banal, Blah, Bland, Drippy, Fade, Flat, Insulse, Jejune, Lash, Mawkish, Milk and water, Shilpit, Spiritless, Tame, Tasteless, Vapid, Weak, Wearish, Wersh
**Insist(ent)** Adamant, Assert, Clamant, Demand, Dogmatic, Emphatic, Enforce, Exact, Maintain, Press, Require, Stickler, → STIPULATE, Stress, Swear, Threap, Threep, Urge
**Insolence, Insolent** Attitude, Audacity, Bardy, Brassy, Cheek, Contumely, Cub, Effrontery, Gum, Hectoring, Hubris, Hybris, Impudence, Lairy, Lip, Mouth, Rude, Sauce, Snash, Snide, Stroppy, Wanton
**Insoluble** Cerasin, Hard, Irresolvable, Mysterious
**Insolvent** Bankrupt, Broke, Destitute, Penniless
**Insomnia** Agrypnotic, Sleeplessness, Wakefulness, White night
**Insouciant** Carefree, Careless, Cavalier, Untroubled
**Inspect(ion), Inspector** Ale-conner, Alnage(r), Auditor, Browse, Case, Censor, Check(er), Comb, Conner, Cook's tour, Counter-round, Darogha, Examine, Exarch, Eyeball, Go-over, Government, Investigator, Jerque, Keeker, Lestrade, Look over, Look round, Look-see, Maigret, Morse, Muster, Once-over, Peep, Perlustrate, Proveditor, Rag-fair, Recce, Review, Sanitary, School, Scrutinise, Searcher, Shufti, Spot check, Supervisor, Survey, Test, Vet, Vidimus, View, Visitation
**Inspire(d), Inspiration, Inspiring** Actuate, Aerate, Afflatus, Aganippe, Animate, Brainstorm, Brainwave, Breath(e), Castalian, Draw, Duende, Elate, Encourage, Erato, Estro, Exalt, Excite, Fire, Flash, Geist, Hearten, Hunch, Hwyl, Idea, Illuminate, Imbue, Impress, Impulse, Indrawn, Induce, Inflatus, Infuse, Inhale, Invention, Kindle, Messianic, Motivate, Move, Muse, Nostril, Passionate, Pegasus, Pig's whisper, Plenary, Prompt, Prophetic, Reassurance, Satori, Sniff(le), Stimulus, Stoke, Taghairm, Theopnautic, Theopneust(y), Uplift, Vatic, Verbal
**In spite of** Malgrado, Malgré, Maugre, Maulgre

**Instability** Anomie, Anomy

**Install(ation)** Elect, Enchase, Ensconce, Enthrone, Fit, Inaugurate, Induction, Infrastructure, Insert, Invest, Put (in)

**Instalment** Call, Deposit, Episode, Fascicle, Fascicule, Heft, Insert, Livraison, Never-never, Part, Piecemeal, Serial, Tranche

**Instance, Instant(aneous)** As, Case, Chronon, Example, Exemplar, Flash, Jiffy, Moment, Present, Say, Shake, Snappy, Split second, Spur, Tick, Time, Trice, Twinkling, Unconsidered, Urgent, Yocto-second

**Instead (of)** Deputy, For, Lieu, Locum, Vice

**Instigate, Instigating, Instigator** Arouse, Foment, Impel, Incite, Proactive, Prompt, Ringleader, Spur

**Instil(l)** Implant, Inculcate, Infuse, Inspire, Teach, Transfuse

**Instinct(ive)** Automatic, Conation, Flair, Gut, Herd, Hunch, Id, Impulse, Inbred, Ingenerate, Innate, Intuition, Knee-jerk, Life, Nature, Nose, Pleasure principle, Prim(a)eval, Reflex, Second nature, Sense, Talent, Tendency, Urge, Visceral

**Institute, Institution** Academy, Activate, Asylum, Athenaeum, Bank, Begin, Bring, Broadmoor, Centre, Charity, City and Guilds, College, Collegiate, Courtauld, Create, Enforce, Erect, Found(ation), Halls of ivy, Hospital, I, Impose, Inaugurate, Inhalatorium, Mechanical, Mechanics, MORI, Organise, Orphanage, Penitentiary, Poorhouse, Protectory, Raise, Redbrick, Reformatory, Retraict, Retrait(e), Retreat, Royal, Smithsonian, Start, Technical, University, Varsity, WI, Women's, Workhouse

**Instruct(ed), Instruction, Instructor** ADI, Advice, Algorithm, Apprenticeship, Brief, CAI, Catechism, Chautauquan, Cheder, Clinic, Coach, Course, Didactic, Direct(ive), Document, Drill, Edify, Educate, Enjoin, Ground(ing), Guide, Heder, How-to, Inform, Lesson, Loop, Macro, Maharishi, Mandate, Manual, Master class, Mentor, MIPS, Mystagogue, Mystagogus, Notify, Order, Patch, Pedagogue, Precept, Prescription, Program, RE, Recipe, RI, Rubric, Rule, Say so, School, Script, Sensei, Statement, Stet, Swami, → **TEACH**, Train, Tuition, Tutelage, Tutorial, Up

**Instrument(al)** Ablative, Act, Agency, Agent, Blunt, Dash(board), Equipment, Helpful, Kit, Mean(s), Measure, Mechanical, → **MUSICAL INSTRUMENT**, Negotiable, → **RESPONSIBLE**, → **TOOL**, Transit, Transposing, → **UTENSIL**, Weapon

---

## INSTRUMENTS

*3 letters:*
Fan
Gad

*4 letters:*
Bell
Celt
Clam
Dupe
Fork
Mike
Prog
Rasp
Rote
Tram

*5 letters:*
Brace
Brake
Chuck
Curet
Fleam
Float
Gadge
Groma
Lance
Meter
Miser
Organ
Probe
Siren
Sonde
Tongs
Wecht

*6 letters:*
Bougie
Broach
Etalon
Grater
Megger®
Octant
Opener
Pallet
Peeler
Pestle
Reamer
Ripple
Scythe
Sector
Seeker
Speedo
Spline
Strobe
Trocar
Wimble
Xyster

*7 letters:*
Alidade
Cadrans
Caliper
Caltrop
Cautery
Compass
Corn van
Curette
Dilator
Diopter
Flesher
Forceps
Grapple
Monitor
Organic
Pelican
Plogger
Plotter
Pointel
Pricker
Probang
Scalpel
Scanner
Scriber
Scummer
Sextant
Shuttle
Snuffer
Sounder

Spatula
Stapler
Strigil
Swatter
Swazzle
Swingle
Swozzle
Syringe
Trammel
Trimmer
Vocoder
Walkman

***8 letters:***
Barnacle
Boothook
Burdizzo
Calutron
Diagraph
Dividers
Ecraseur
Enlarger
Geophone
Iriscope
Luxmeter
Myograph
Nailfile
Odometer
Ohmmeter
Otoscope
Oximeter
Picklock
Quadrant
Repeater
Rheostat
Scalprum
Scissors
Snuffler
Speculum
Stiletto
Strickle
Trephine
Tweezers
Viameter
Vuvuzela
Waywiser

***9 letters:***
Algometer
Alphonsin
Arcograph
Areometer
Astrolabe
Atmometer
Audiphone
Auriscope
Auxometer
Barograph
Barometer
Baroscope
Baryscope
Bolometer
Cauterant
Coelostat
Cork borer
Crows-bill
Cryoprobe
Cryoscope
Cymograph
Depressor
Dermatome
Dip-circle
Dosemeter
Dosimeter
Dropsonde
Eidograph
Endoscope
Ergograph
Ergometer
Eriometer
Extractor
Fadometer
Fetoscope
Flowmeter
Fluxmeter
Focimeter
Graduator
Gyroscope
Haemostat
Heliostat
Hodometer
Hourglass
Konimeter
Koniscope
Kymograph
Lysimeter
Machmeter
Manometer
Marigraph
Megaphone
Megascope
Metronome
Microlith
Microtome
Milometer
Monochord
Nocturnal
Nut-wrench
Oedometer
Oncometer
Ondograph
Optometer
Optophone
Osmometer
Osteotome
Pedometer
Periscope
Pintadera
Polygraph
Potometer
Pyrometer
Pyroscope
Rain gauge
Raspatory
Refractor
Repositor
Retractor
Rheometer
Salometer
Scalprium
Set square
Skiascope
Somascope
Sonograph
Tasimeter
Telemeter
Telescope
Tellurian
Tellurion
Tenaculum
Tonometer
Toothpick
Tripmeter
Try square
Voltmeter
Volumeter
Wattmeter
Wavemeter
Xylometer
Zymometer

***10 letters:***
Acidimeter
Almacantar
Almucantar
Altazimuth
Anemograph
Anemometer
Araeometer
Audiometer
Binoculars
Buttonhook
Ceilometer
Clinometer
Colposcope
Comparator
Cross-staff
Cryophorus
Cultivator
Cyanometer
Cyclograph
Cystoscope
Declinator
Densimeter
Dictograph
Drosometer
Ear trumpet
Eudiometer
Fathometer
Fibrescope
Gaussmeter
Geodimeter®
Goniometer
Gonioscope
Gradienter
Gravimeter
Heliograph
Heliometer
Hydrometer
Hydroscope
Hygrograph
Hygrometer
Hygroscope
Hypsometer
Iconometer
Integrator
Lactometer
Lactoscope
Light organ
Lithoclast
Micrograph
Micrometer
Microphone
Microscope
Mileometer
Milliprobe
Multimeter
Nephograph
Nephoscope
Nitrometer
Opisometer
Orthoscope
Oscillator
Osteoclast
Pachymeter
Pantograph
Photometer
Piezometer
Pilliwinks
Plane table
Planigraph
Planimeter
Protractor
Pulsimeter

Pulsometer
Pycnometer
Radiometer
Radiophone
Radioscope
Radiosonde
Rhinoscope
Scotometer
Siderostat
Spirograph®
Spirometer
Tachograph
Tachometer
Tascometer
Telewriter
Tensimeter
Theodolite
Thermopile
Thermostat
Tintometer
Transputer
Tromometer
Tuning fork
Urinometer
Variometer
Viscometer
Voltameter

***11 letters:***
Actinometer
Auxanometer
Cardiograph
Chronograph
Chronometer
Chronoscope
Coercimeter
Colonoscope
Colorimeter
Coronagraph
Craniometer
Crescograph
Dendrometer
Dilatometer
Dynamometer
Fluorimeter
Fluorometer
Fluoroscope
Fugitometer
Gastroscope
Gradiometer
Helicograph
Intoximeter
Jacob's staff
Keratometer
Laparoscope
Nephroscope
Odontograph
Opeidoscope
Pinnywinkle
Pitchometer
Planetarium
Plastometer
Plessimeter
Polarimeter
Polariscope
Proctoscope
Psychograph
Pyranometer
Pyrgeometer
Quantometer
Ragman Rolls
Rangefinder
Retinoscope
Rocketsonde
Salinometer
Sclerometer
Screwdriver
Seismograph
Seismometer
Seismoscope
Solarimeter
Spherometer
Stactometer
Stadiometer
Stauroscope
Stereometer
Stereoscope
Stethoscope
Stroboscope
Synthesizer
Tacheometer
Tensiometer
Thermograph
Thermometer
Thermoscope
Torsiograph
Trochometer
Vaporimeter
Vectorscope
Velocimeter
Voltammeter
Volumometer

***12 letters:***
Aethrioscope
Astrocompass
Averruncator
Bronchoscope
Camera lucide
Cathetometer
Cephalometer
Declinometer
Densitometer
Electrometer
Electroscope
Ellipsograph
Extensimeter
Extensometer
Galactometer
Galvanometer
Galvanoscope
Gravitometer
Harmonograph
Harmonometer
Inclinometer
Isoteniscope
Kaleidoscope
Katharometer
Keraunograph
Laryngoscope
Magnetograph
Magnetometer
Meteorograph
Methanometer
Monkey wrench
Myringoscope
Nephelometer
Oscilloscope
Penetrometer
Pinniewinkle
Psychrometer
Resectoscope
Respirometer
Scarificator
Scintillator
Sensitometer
Snooperscope
Spectrometer
Spectroscope
Sphygmograph
Sphygmometer
Sphygmophone
Sphygmoscope
Synchroscope
Tape recorder
Tellurometer
Thoracoscope
Turbidimeter
Urethroscope
Zenith-sector

***13 letters:***
Accelerometer
Alcoholometer
Backscratcher
Diaphanometer
Dipleidoscope
Electrophorus
Inclinatorium
Opthalmometer
Perpendicular
Pharyngoscope
Phonendoscope
Pneumatograph
Pneumatometer
Potentiometer
Pyrheliometer
Reflectometer
Refractometer
Saccharometer
Scatterometer
Sigmoidoscope
Stalagmometer
Tachistoscope
Weatherometer

***14 letters:***
Circumferentor
Diffractometer
Dividing engine
Geothermometer
Glove-stretcher
Interferometer
Kinetheodolite
Oesophagoscope
Ophthalmometer
Ophthalmoscope
Phosphoroscope
Pyrophotometer
Scintillascope
Scintillometer
Scintilloscope
Spinthariscope
Synchronoscope
Tobacco stopper

***15 letters:***
Electromyograph
Phenakestoscope
Radiogoniometer
Telestereoscope

***16 letters:***
Photopolarimeter
Sphygmomanometer
Telespectroscope

***17 letters:***
Spectrohelioscope
Spectrophotometer
Transit theodolite

**Insubordinate** Contumacious, Faction, Mutinous, Rebel, Refractory

**Insubstantial** Airy, Brief, Ethereal, Flimsy, Frail, Frothy, Illusory, Intangible, Jackstraw, Light, Scotch mist, Skimpy, Slender, Slight, Spectre, Syllabub, Tenuous, Thin, Unreal, Wispy, Ye(a)sty

**Insufferable** Egregious

**Insufficient** Exiguous, Inadequate, Poor, Scant, Shortfall, Slender, Too few

**Insular** Isolated, Little Englander, Moated, Narrow, Sectarian, Xenophobe

**Insulate, Insulation, Insulator** Biotite, Bushing, Corkboard, Dielectric, Electret, Enwind, Fibrefill, Grommet, Haybox, Inwind, Lagging, Mica, Muscovite, Non-conductor, Padding, Pugging, Sleeving, Standoff, Tea cosy, Tog

**Insulin** Hormone

**Insult(ing)** Abuse, Affront, Aspersion, Barb, Becall, Charientism, Contumely, Cut, Derisory, Derogatory, Diatribe, Dyslogistic, Effrontery, Embarrass, Facer, Fig, Gibe, Injurious, Lese-majesty, Mud, Mud-pie, Offend, Opprobrious, Outrage, Revile, Rip on, Ronyion, Runnion, Scurrilous, Skit, Slagging, Sledge, Slight, Slur, Snub, Trample, Trauma, Uncomplimentary, Verbal, Wazzock, Yenta, Yente

**Insure(r), Insurance** Abandonee, Accident, Actuarial, Comprehensive, Convertible term, Cover, Coverage, Credit, Death futures, Endowment, Fidelity, Fire, Group, Guarantee, Hedge, Indemnity, Knock-for-knock, Life, Lloyds, Marine, Medibank, Medicaid, Medicare, Mutual, Name, National, Participating, Pluvius, Policy, Public liability, Reversion, Safety net, Security, Social, Term, Third party, Tontine, Travel, Underwrite, Whole-life

**Insurgent, Insurrect(ion)** Cade, Jacquerie, Mutiny, Outbreak, Pandy, Rebel, Revolt, Riot, Rising, Sedition, Terrorist, Uprising, Whisky

▷**Insurgent** *may indicate* 'reversed'

**Intact** Complete, Entire, Inviolate, Unused, Vestal, Whole

**Intaglio, Intagliate** Diaglyph, Incavo

**Intake** Absorption, Catchment, Entry, Fuel

**Intangible** Abstract, Unreal

**Integer, Integral** Component, Definite, Entire, Improper, Inbuilt, Indefinite, Needful, Number, Organic, Strategic, Unital, Unitary

**Integrate(d), Integration** Amalgamate, Assimilate, Combine, Coordinate, Fuse, Harmonious, Holistic, Large-scale, Mainstream, Merge, Postural, Synergism, Tightknit, Vertical

**Integrity** Credibility, Honesty, Honour, Principle, Probity, Rectitude, Strength, Uprightness, Whole, Worth

**Integument** Coat, Primine, Secundine, Sheath, Skin, Velum

**Intellect, Intellectual(s)** Academic, Aptitude, Belligerati, Bluestocking, Brain (box), Cerebral, Chattering class, Cultural, Deep-browed, Dianoetic, Egghead, Eggmass, Erudite, Far-out, Genius, Grey matter, Highbrow, Intelligent, Intelligentsia, -ist, Learned, Literati, Luminary, Mastermind, Mental(ity), Mind, Noesis, Noetic, Noology, Nous, Pointy-headed, Profound, Reason, Sublime, Titan

**Intelligence, Intelligent** Acuity, Advice, Artificial, Astute, Boss, Brainiac, Brain-power, Brains, Bright, Cerebral, CIA, Deuxieme Bureau, Discerning, Dope, Eggmass, Emotional, Esprit, G, Gifted, Grey matter, GRU, Guile, Horse sense, Humint, Info, Information, Ingenious, IQ, Knowledgeable, Literati, Lowdown, Machiavellian, Machine, MI, Mossad, Mother wit, News, Pate, Perspicacity, Pointy-headed, Rational, Sconce, Sense, Sharp(-witted), Shrewd, SIS, Smart, Spetsnaz, Spetznaz, Tidings, Wit

**Intelligible** Exoteric, Ungarbled

**Intemperance** Acrasia, Crapulent, Excess, Gluttony, Immoderation

**Intend(ed), Intending** Aim, Allot, Betrothed, Contemplate, Deliberate, Design, Destine, Ettle, Fiancé(e), Going, → **MEAN**, Meditate, Mind, Planned, Propose, Purpose, Think

**Intense, Intensify, Intensity, Intensive** Acute, Aggravate, Ardent, Compound, Concentrated, Crash, Crescendo, Deep, Depth, Earnest, Earthquake, Edgy, Emotional, Enhance, Escalate, Estro, Excess, Extreme, Fervent, Fully, Hot up, Keen, Luminous, Might, Profound, Radiant, Redouble, Saturation, Sharpen, Strong, Towering, Vehement, Vivid, Warmth

**Intent, Intention(al)** À dessein, Agenda, Aim, Animus, Criminal, Deliberate, Design, Dole, Earmark, Earnest, Ettle, Heat, Hellbent, Manifesto, Mens rea, Mind, Paradoxical, Prepense, Purpose, Rapt, Resolute, Set, Special, Studious, Systematic, Thought, Tire, Wilful, Witting, Yrapt

**Inter** Amid, Bury, Earth, Entomb

**Interaction** Chemistry, Enantiodromia, Solvation, Symbiosis, Synergy

**Interbreed(ing)** Cross, Miscegenation, Syngamy

**Intercalation** Embolism

**Intercede, Intercession, Intercessor** Liaise, Mediate, Negotiate, Paraclete, Plead, Prayer

**Intercept** Absciss(a), Abscisse, Check, Hack, Meet, Tackle, Tap, Waylay

**Interchange(d)** Altercation, Alternate, Clover-leaf, Crossing, Equivalent, Junction, Mutual, Permute, Reciprocate, Reshuffle, Substitute, Transpose

**Intercom** Entryphone®

**Intercourse** Bed, Bonk, Buggery, Coition, Coitus, Commerce, Commixture, Congress, Connection, Consummation, Converse, Copulation, Coupling, Cover, Cunnilingus, Deflowering, Enjoy, Fluff, Fornication, Green gown, Greens, Hochmagandy, Houghmagandie, How's your father, Hump, Incest, Jass, Jazz, Jiggy, Jiggy-jiggy, Jig(-a)-jig, Jump, Knee-trembler, Knock, Know(ledge), Koap, Laying, Leg-over, Lie with, Make, Marriage bed, Mell, Mix, Naughty, Necrophilia, Nookie, Nooky, Nooner, Oats, One-night-stand, On the job, Plough, Quickie, Roger, Roll, Root, Rump, Rumpy(-pumpy), Satyriasis, Sexual, Sixty-nine, Sociality, Sodomy, Soixante-neuf, Swive, Teledildonics, The other, Tie, Trade, Tribadism, Trock, Troilism, Truck, Tumble, Venereal, Whoredom

**Interdict** Ban, Forbid, Prohibit, Taboo, Veto

**Interest(ed), Interesting** Amusive, APR, Attention, Behalf, Benefit, Care, Clou, Compound, Concern, Contango, Controlling, Coupon, Curious, Dividend, Double-bubble, Ear-grabbing, Engage, Engross, Enthusiasm, Fad, Fascinate, Fee-simple, Fee-tail, Grab, Hot, Human, Import, Income, Insurable, Int(o), Intrigue, Juicy, Landed, Life, Line, Meaty, Negative, Newsworthy, Nibble, Occupy, Part, Partisan, Percentage, Public, Readable, Rente, Respect, Return, Revenue, Reversion, Riba, Riding, Scene, Sepid, Share, Side, Sideline, Simple, Special, Spice, Stake, Tasty, Tickle, Titillate, Topical, Usage, Usance, Use, Usure, Usury, Vested, Vig(orish), Warm

**Interface** Centronics, Modium, Spigot

**Interfere(r), Interference** Atmospherics, Busybody, Clutter, Crackle, Disrupt, Disturb, Doctor, Hamper, Hinder, Hiss, Inhibit, Intrude, Mar, → MEDDLE, Molest, Noise, Nose, Officious, Pry, Radio, Shash, Shot noise, Snoop, Snow, Static, Tamper, Teratogen

**Interferometer** Etalon

**Intergrowth** Perthite

**Interim** Between times, Break, Meantime, Meanwhile, Temporary

**Interior** Backblocks, Cyclorama, Domestic, Innards, Innate, Inner, Inside, Outback, Plain, Up-country, Vitals

**Interject(ion)** Ahem, Begorra(h), Chime-in, Doh, Duh, Gertcha, Haith, Hoo-oo, Interpolate, Lackaday, Lumme, Nation, Sese(y), Sessa, 'Sheart, 'Slid, Tarnation, Tush

**Interlace** Mesh, Mingle, Pleach, Weave, Wreathe

**Interlink** Clover-leaf, Entangle

**Interlock** Dovetail, Engage, Knit, Mesh, Tangle

**Interlocutor** Elihu, MC, Questioner

**Interloper** Cowan, Gate-crasher, Intruder, Parvenu, Trespasser

**Interlude** Antimask, Antimasque, Divertimento, Entr'acte, Interruption, Kyogen, Lunch-hour, Meantime, Pause, Verset

**Intermediary, Intermediate, Intermediatory** Agent, Bardo, Between, Bytownite, Cat's paw, Comprador(e), Contact man, Go-between, Hypabyssal, In-between, Instar, Liaison, Mean, Medial, Mesne, Mezzanine, Middleman, Middle-of-the-road, Negotiant, Thirdsman, Transitional

**Interminable** Endless, Infinite, Unending

**Intermission** Apyrexia, Break, Interval, Lull, Pause, Recess

**Intermittent** Broken, Episodic, Fitful, Off-on, Periodic, Random, Spasmic, Spasmodic, Sporadic

**Intermix, Intermingle** Lace, Melting pot

**Intern(e)** Confine, Doctor, Impound, Restrict, Trainee

**Internal** Domestic, Inner, Internecine, Inward, Within

**International** Cap, Cosmopolitan, Fourth, I, Lion, Second, Test, Trotskyist, UN, Universal, World-wide

**Internee** POW

**Internet** Blogosphere, Broadband, Dotco(m), e, Infobahn, Online, Skype®, URL, Web(site), Wi-fi, WWW

**Internet language** HTML

**Interplay** Counterpoint

**Interpolate(r), Interpolation** Diaskeuast, Insert, Intercalate, Interrupt, Spatchcock, Tmesis

**Interpose** Butt in, Horn in, Interject, Interlay, Interprone, Intervene, Spatchcock, Stickle

**Interpret(er)** Aread, Ar(r)e(e)de, Conster, Construe, Decipher, Decode, Dobhash, Dragoman, Exegete, Explain, Exponent, Expositor, Expound, Glossator, Hermeneutist, Hierophant, Jehovist, Latiner, Lingster, Linguistic, Linkster, Lipreader, Medium, Moonshee, Moonshi, Moralise, Munshi, Oneirocritic, Oneiroscopist, Origenist, Polyglot, Prophet, Rabbi, Rationalise, Read, Rede, Reed(e), Render, Represent, Spokesman, Subjectivity, Textualist, → **TRANSLATE**, Truchman, Ulema, Unravel

**Interpretation** Anagoge, Anagogy, Analysis, Cabbala(h), Construction, Copenhagen, Diagnosis, Dittology, Eisegesis, Euhemerism, Exegesis, Exegete, Gematria, Gloss(ary), Gospel, Halacha(h), Halakah, Hermeneutics, Kabbala(h), Midrash, Oneirocriticism, Portray, Reading, Rede, Rendition, Spin, Targum, Translation, Tropology, Zohar

**Interrogate, Interrogation, Interrogator** Catechism, Corkscrew, Cross-question, Debrief(ing), Enhanced, Enquire, Examine, Grill, Inquisitor, Maieutic, Pump, → **QUESTION**, Quiz, Quiz-master, Third degree

**Interrupt(ion), Interrupter** Ahem, Aposiopesis, Barge in, Blip, Break, Butt in, Chequer, Chime in, Chip in, Cut in, Disturb, Entr'acte, Heckle, Hiatus, Intercept, Interfere, Interject, Interlard, Interpellate, Interpolate, Interpose, Interregnum, Intrusion, Overtalk, Pause, Portage, Punctuate, Rheotome, Stop, Suspend, Time-out, Tmesis, Waylay

**Intersect(ion), Intersecting** Carfax, Carfox, Carrefour, Chiasm(a), Clover-leaf, Compital, Cross, Crunode, Cut, Decussate, Divide, Groin, Metacentre, Node, Orthocentre, Quadrivium, Trace, Vertex

**Intersperse** Dot, Interlard, Interpose, Punctuate, Scatter, Sprinkle

**Interstice** Areole, Interlude, Pore, Space

**Intertwine** Braid, Impleach, Knit, Lace, Plait, Splice, Twist, Wreathe, Writhe

**Interval** Between, Break, Breather, Class, Closed, Comma, Confidence, Contour, Diapente, Diastaltic, Diatesseron, Diesis, Distance, Ditone, Duodecimo, Entr'acte, Episodic, Fifth, Gap, Half-step, Half-time, Harmonic, Hiatus, Hourly, Imperfect, Interim, Interlude, Intermission, Interregnum, Interruption, Interspace, Interstice, Leap, Limma, Lucid, Lull, Lunitidal, Meantime, Meantone, Meanwhile, Melodic, Microtone, Minor third, Ninth, Octave, Open, Ottava, Parenthesis, Perfect, Period, Pycnon, QT, Recess, Regular, Respite, Rest, Schisma, Semitone, Seventh, Sixth, Space, Span, Spell, Step, Third, Thirteenth, Time lag, Tritone, Twelfth, Unison, Wait

**Intervene, Intervening, Intervention** Agency, Arbitrate, Expromission, Hypothetical, Interfere, Interjacent, Interrupt, Intromit, Mediate, Mesne, Reprieve, Step in, Theurgy, Up

**Interview** Audience, Audition, Beeper, Conference, Debriefing, Doorstep, Examine, Hearing, Oral, Press conference, See, Vox pop

**Interweave, Interwoven, Interwove** Complect, Entwine, Interlace, Knit, Monogram, Pirnit, Plait, Plash, Pleach, Raddle, Splice, Wreathed

**Intestate** Heirless, Unwilling

**Intestinal, Intestine(s)** Bowel, Chit(ter)lings, Derma, Duodenum, Enteric, Entrails, Gastric, Guts, Harigals, Ileum, Innards, Jejunum, Kishke, Large, Mesenteron, Omenta, Rectum, Small, Splanchnic, Thairm, Tripes, Viscera

**In the club** Gravid, Pregnant, Up the spout
**In this year** HA
**Intimacy, Intimate(ly)** Achates, À deux, Arm-in-arm, Boon, Bosom, Cater-cousin, Close, Communion, Confidante, Connote, Cosiness, Familiar, Far ben, Friend, Heart-to-heart, Hint, Imply, Inmost, Innuendo, Intrigue, Nearness, Opine, Pack, Private, Signal, Special, Thick, Throng, Warm, Well
**Intimation** Clue, Hint, Implication, Inkling, Innuendo, Notice, Signal, Si quis
**Intimidate, Intimidating** Awe, Browbeat, Bulldoze, Bully, Cow, Daunt, Dragon, Extort, Harass, Hector, Menace, Niramiai, Overawe, Psych, Scare, Threaten, Tyrannise, Unnerve
**Into** At, Intil, Within
**Intolerant, Intolerable** Allergic, Bigotry, Egregious, Excessive, Illiberal, Impatient, Impossible, Insupportable, Ombrophobe, Redneck, Restrictive, Self-righteous
**Intone, Intonation** Cadence, Chant, Just, Twang
**In touch** Au fait
**Intoxicate(d), Intoxicant, Intoxicating, Intoxication** Alcoholic, Areca-nut, Benj, Bhang, Blasted, Coca, Coked up, Corn, Crink, Cup, Disguise, Ethanol, Fuddle, Ganja, Half-cut, Heady, → HIGH, Hocus, Hou high, Incite, Inebriate, Ivresse, Jag, Krunk, La-la land, Merry, Mescal, Methystic, Narcotise, Nitrogen narcosis, Peyote, Pixil(l)ated, Potent, Rapture of the deep, Rumbullion, Shroom, Slewed, Soma, Sozzle, Spirituous, Swacked, Temulent, The narks, Tight, Tipsy, Trolleyed, Whiskeyfied, Whiskified, Zonked
**Intractable** Disobedient, Kittle, Mulish, Obdurate, Perverse, Surly, Unruly, Wilful
**Intransigent** Adamant, Inflexible, Rigid, Uncompromising
**Intransitive** Neuter, Objectless
**Intravenous** IV
**Intrepid(ity)** Aweless, Bold, Bottle, Brave, Daredevil, Dauntless, Doughty, Fearless, Firm, Gallant, Plucky, → RESOLUTE, Stout, Unafraid, Undaunted, Valiant
**Intricate** Complex, Complicated, Crinkum-crankum, Daedal(ian), Daedale, Dedal, Entangled, Gordian, Intrince, Involute, Knotty, Parquetry, Pernickety, Sinuous, Tirlie-wirlie, Tortuous, Tricky, Vitruvian
**Intrigue(r), Intriguing** Affaire, Artifice, Brigue, Cabal, Camarilla, Cloak and dagger, Collogue, Conspiracy, Fascinate, Hotbed, Ignatian, Interest, Jesuit, Jobbery, Liaison, Machinate, Plot, Politic, Rat, → SCHEME, Stairwork, Strategy, Traffic, Trinketer, Web
**Intrinsic(ally)** Basically, Essential, Genuine, Inherent, Innate, Inner, Per se
▷**Intrinsically** *may indicate* something within a word
**Introduce(r), Introduction, Introductory** Acquaint, Alap, Anacrusis, Cataphoresis, Code name, Curtain-raiser, Debut, Emcee, Enseam, Entrée, Exordial, Foreword, Immit, Import, Induct, Initiate, Inject, Insert, Instil(l), Institutes, Intercalate, Interpolate, Intrada, Introit, Isagogic, Launch, Lead-in, Lead up, Matchmake, Opening, Overture, Phase in, Plant, Preamble, Precede, Preface, Preliminary, Prelude, Prelusory, Preparatory, Present, Presentment, Primer, Proem, Prolegomena, Prolegomenon, Prolocution, Prolog, Prologue, Prooemium, Proponent, Raise, Referral, Standfirst, Start, Usher
▷**Introduction** *may indicate* a first letter
**Intromission** Vicious
**Introspective, Introspection** Indrawn, Musing, Navel-gazing, Reflex, Ruminant, Thoughtful
▷**In trouble** *may indicate* an anagram
**Introvert(ed)** Cerebrotonic, Ingrow, In-toed, Invaginate, Reserved, Shy, Withdrawn
**Intrude(r), Intrusion, Intrusive** Abate, Aggress, Annoy, Barge in, Bother, Burglar, Derby dog, Disturb, → ENCROACH, Gatecrash, Hacker, Impinge, Infiltrate, Inroad, Interfere, Interloper, Invade, Lopolith, Meddle, Nosey, Personal, Porlocking, Presume, Raid, Sorn, Trespass, Unwelcome
**In truth** En verite
**Intuition, Intuitive** Apercu, Belief, ESP, Hunch, Insight, Instinct, Inwit, Noumenon, Premonition, Presentiment, Seat-of-the-pants, Sense, Sixth sense, Telepathy, Theosophy, Visceral
**Inturn(ing)** Trichiasis

▷**In two words** *may indicate* a word to be split
**Inuit** Caribou, Eskimo, Inuk, Inupiat, Yupik
**Inundate(d), Inundation** Awash, Engulf, Flood, Overflow, Overwhelm, Submerge, Swamp
**Inure** Acclimatise, Accustom, Harden, Season, Steel
**Invade(r), Invasion** Aggressor, Angle, Attack, Attila, Cortes, Dane, D-day, Descent, Encroach, Goth, Hacker, Hengist, Horsa, Hun, Incursion, Infest, Inroad, Intruder, Irrupt, Jute, Lombard, Martian, Norman, Norsemen, Occupation, Ostrogoth, Overlord, Overrun, Permeate, Pict, Raid, Trespass, Vandal, Viking, Visigoth
**In vain** No go
**Invalid(ate), Invalidation** Annul(led), Bad, Bogus, Bunbury, Cancel, Chronic, Clinic, Defunct, Diriment, Discredit, Erroneous, Expired, False, Inauthentic, Inform, Inoperative, Irritate, Lapsed, Negate, Nugatory, Null, Nullify, Overturn, Quash, Refute, Rescind, Shut-in, Terminate, Valetudinarian, Vitiate, Void
**Invaluable** Essential, Excellent, Precious, Priceless, Useful
**Invariable, Invariably** Always, Consistent, Constant, Eternal, Habitual, Perpetual, Steady, Uniform
**Invective** Abuse, Billingsgate, Diatribe, Philippic, Reproach, Ribaldry, Tirade
**Inveigh** Declaim, Denounce, Marprelate, Protest, Rail
**Inveigle** Charm, Coax, Dupe, Entice, Persuade, Seduce, Subtrude
**Invent(ion), Inventive** Adroit, Babe, Baby, Brainchild, Chimera, Coin, Concept, Confabulate, Contrive, Cook up, → **CREATE**, Creed, Daedal, Design, Device, Dream up, Embroider, Excogitate, Fabricate, Fain, Fantasia, Feign, Fiction, Figment, Imaginary, Improvise, Independent, Ingenuity, Make up, Mint, Myth, Originate, Patent, Phon(e)y, Plateau, Pretence, Resourceful, Synectics, Trump up, Whittle, Wit
**Inventor** Artificer, Author, Coiner, Creator, Designer, Engineer, Idea-hamster, Mint-master, Patentee

---

**INVENTORS**

*3 letters:*
Kay
Sax

*4 letters:*
Bell
Biro
Boys
Brix
Hero
Land
Moon
Otis
Tull
Watt

*5 letters:*
Baird
Clegg
Dyson
Jubal
Maxim
Mills
Minié
Morse
Nobel
Rubik
Tesla

*6 letters:*
Bramah
Dunlop
Duryea
Edison
Geiger
Hansom
McAdam
Nernst
Pearse
Savery
Singer
Solvay
Sutton
Wright

*7 letters:*
Babbage
Celsius
Daimler
Eastman
Galileo
Hartley
Marconi
Pullman
Schmidt
Siemens
Unaipon
Whitney
Whittle

*8 letters:*
Bessemer
Crompton
Daedalus
Goodyear
Martenot
Mercator
Newcomen
Sinclair
Zworykin

*9 letters:*
Arkwright
Cockerell
Macintosh

*10 letters:*
Archimedes
Cartwright
Hargreaves
Lilienthal
Torricelli
Trevithick
Wheatstone

*11 letters:*
Montgolfier

*12 letters:*
Barnes Wallis
Frankenstein
Prince Rupert

---

**Inventory** Account, Index, Itemise, List, Perpetual, Personality, Record, Register, Scroll, Steelbow, Stock, Terrier

**Inverse, Inversion, Invert(ed)** Anastrophe, Antimetabole, Antimetathesis, Arch, Back to front, Capsize, Chiasmus, Entropion, Entropium, First, Homosexuality, Lid, Opposite, Overset, Reciprocal, Resupinate, Retrograde, Reverse, Second, Tête-bêche, Turn, Upset, Upside down

**Invertebrate** Acanthocephalan, Annelida, Anthozoan, Arrowworm, Arthropod, Brachiopod, Chaetognath, Cnidarian, Coelenterate, Crinoid, Ctenophore, Decapod, Echinoderm, Echinoid, Echiura, Entoprocta, Euripterid, Feather star, Gast(e)ropod, Globigerina, Holothurian, Hydrozoan, Lobopod, Mollusc, Nacre, Onychophoran, Parazoan, Pauropod, Peritrich, Platyhelminth, Polyp, Poriferan, Protostome, Rotifer, Roundworm, Scyphozoan, Sea-cucumber, Sea-lily, → **SHELLFISH**, Slug, Spineless, Sponge, Spoonworm, Starfish, Tardigrade, Trepang, Trochelminth, Trochophore, Unio, Water bear, Worm, Zoophyte

**Invest(or), Investment** Agamemnon, Ambient, Angel, Assiege, Bate, Beleaguer, Beset, Besiege, Bet, Blockade, Blue-chip, Bond, Bottom-fisher, Capitalist, Clothe, Collins Street farmer, Contrarian, Debenture, Dignify, Dub, Embark, Empanoply, Enclothe, Endow, Endue, Enfeoff, Enrobe, Escalado, Ethical, Financier, Flutter, Gilt, Girt, Gross, Hedge fund, Holding, Infeft, Install, Inward, On, Ordain, Pannicle, Panniculus, Parlay, Place, Portfolio, Put, Retiracy, Ring, Robe, Saver, Share(holder), Siege, Sink, Smart money, Spec, Speculation, Stag, Stake, Stock(holder), Surround, Tessa, Tie up, Timeshare, Trochophore, Trojan War, Trust, Trustee, Venture (capital), With profits, Zaitech

▷**Invest** *may indicate* one word surrounding another

**Investigate, Investigation, Investigative, Investigator** Actuary, Analyse, Audit, Canvass, Case, Chart, Chase up, Check, CID, Delve, DI, Enquire, Examine, Explore, Fact-find, Fed, Ferret, Fieldwork, G-man, Going over, Go into, Gumshoe, Hearing, Heuristic, Hunt, Inquest, Inquirendo, Inquiry, Inquisition, Kinsey, McCarthyism, Nose, Ombudsman, Organon, Organum, Private, Probe, Prodnose, Pry, Quester, Rapporteur, Recce, Research, Scan, Scout, Screen, Scrutinise, Search, Sleuth, Snoop, Study, Suss, Tec, Test, T-man, Track, Try, Zetetic

**Investiture** Award, Inauguration

**Inveterate** Chronic, Double-dyed, Dyed-in-the-wool, Engrained, Habitual, Hardened, Long-standing

**Invidious** Harmful, Hostile, Malign

**Invigilator** Proctor

**Invigorate, Invigorating, Invigoration** Analeptic, Animate, Brace, Brisk, Cheer, Crispy, Elixir, Energise, Enliven, Exhilarate, Fortify, Insinew, Inspirit, Pep, Refresh, Renew, Stimulate, Tonic, Vital

**Invincible** Almighty, Brave, Stalwart, Valiant

**Inviolatable, Inviolate, Inviolable** Intemerate, Sacred (cow), Sacrosanct

**Invisible** Blind, Hidden, Imageless, Imperceptible, Infra-red, Secret, Tusche, Unseen

**Invite, Invitation, Inviting** Ask, Attract, Bid, Call, Card, Challenge, Overture, → **REQUEST**, RSVP, Solicit, Stiffie, Summons, Tempt, Toothsome, Woo

**Invocation, Invoke** Appeal, Begorra, Call, Conjure, Curse, Entreat, Epiclesis, Imprecate, Litany, Solicit, White rabbits

**Invoice** Account, Bill, Docket, Itemise, Manifest, Pro forma

**Involuntary** Automatic, Instinctive, Reflex, Unwitting

**Involve(d), Involvement** Active, Close knit, Commitment, Complicate, Complicit, Concern, Deep, Embroil, Engage, Enlace, Entail, Entangle, Envelop, Hands on, Imbroglio, Immerse, → **IMPLICATE**, Include, Intervene, Into, Intricate, Knee-deep, Meet, Necessitate, Partake, Participate, Party to, Tangle, Tortuous, Tricksy

▷**Involved** *may indicate* an anagram

**Inward(s)** Afferent, Centripuntal, Homefelt, Introrse, Mental, Private, Varus, Visceral, Within

**Iodine** I, Kelp, Thyroxin(e)

**Iolanthe** Peri

**Ion** Ammonium, Anion, Carbanion, Carborium, Cation, Hydrated, Hydrogen, Hydronium, Hydroxyl, Isomer, Kation, Onium, Zwitterion

**Ionian** Iastic, Te(i)an

**Ionic** Electrovalent
**Iota** Atom, Jot, Subscript, Whit
**IOU** Cedula, Market, PN, Shinplaster, Vowels
**IOW** Vectis
**Ipecac** Emetine
**IQ** Mensa
**IRA** Provisional, Provo
**Iran(ian)** Babist, Kurd, Mede, Osset, Pahlavi, Parsee, Pehlevi, Persic, Tadzhik, Ta(d)jik
**Irascible, Irascibility** Choleric, Crusty, Fiery, Grouchy, Peevish, Quick-tempered, Short fuse, Short-tempered, Snappy, Testy, Tetchy, Toustie
**Irate** Angry, Cross, Infuriated, Wrathful
**Ire** Anger, Bait, Cholera, Fury, Rage, Wrath
**Ireland** Blarney-land, Composer, Deirdre, Gaeltacht, Hibernia, .ie, Innisfail, Irena, IRL, Iverna, Ould Sod, ROI, Twenty-six counties
**Irenic** Peaceful
**Iridescence, Iridescent** Chatoyant, Flambé, Opaline, Reflet, Shimmering, Shot, Water-gall
**Iridium** Ir
**Iris** Areola, Eye, Flag, Fleur-de-lis, Florence, Flower-delice, Gladdon, Gladioli, Ixia, Lily, Lis, Orris, Rainbow, Roast-beef plant, Sedge, Seg, Stinking, Sunbow, Triandria, Uvea, Water flag
**Irish(man)** Bark, Boy, Bucko, Celt(ic), Clan-na-gael, Declan, Defender, Dermot, Dubliner, Eamon(n), Eirann, Eoin, Erse, Feargal, Fenian, Fionn, Gael, Gaeltacht, Goidel, Greek, Hibernian, Jackeen, Keltic, Kern(e), Middle, Milesian, Mulligan, Neil, Ogamic, Orange(man), Ostmen, Paddy(-whack), Partholon, Pat(rick), Rapparee, Redshank, Reilly, Riley, Rory, Ryan, Sean, Shoneen, Teague, Temper, UDA, Ultonian, Whiteboy, Wildgeese
**Irk(some)** Annoy, Bother, Fardel, Gall, Irritate, Needle, Tedious
**Iron(s), Ironstone, Ironwork(s)** Airn, Alpha, Angle, Barking, Beak, Beta, Bick, Bloom, Boom, Box, Branding, Carron, Cast, Caulking, Cautery, Chains, Chalybeate, Chancellor, Channel, Climbing, Coquimbite, Corrugated, Cramp(on), Crimp, Cross, Curling, Curtain, Delta, Derringer, Dogger, Dogs, Driving, Eagle-stone, Eating, Even, Fayalite, Fe, Ferredoxin, Ferric, Ferrite, Fetter, Fiddley, Flatten, Flip-dog, Foundry, Galvanised, Gamma, Gem, Golfclub, Goose, Grappling, Grim, Grozing, → **GUN**, Gyve, Haematite, Horse, Ingot, Italian, Jagging, Kamacite, Kentledge, Laterite, Lily, Lofty, Long, Magnetite, Maiden, Malleable, Marcasite, Mars, Martensite, Mashie, Mashy, Merchant, Meteoric, Mitis (metal), Pea, Pig, Pinking, → **PRESS**, Pro-metal, Rabble, Rations, Rod, Sad, Scrap, Shackles, Shooting, Short, Smoother, Soft, Soldering, Spathic, Specular, Speeler, Spiegeleisen, Steam, Stirrup, Stretching, Strong, Taconite, Taggers, Terne, Tin terne, Toasting, Toggle, Tow, Turfing, Wafer, Waffle, Wear, Wedge, White, Wrought
**Iron age** Latene, Villanovan
**Ironic, Irony** Antiphrasis, Asteism, Dramatic, Ferrous, Meiosis, Metal, Ribald, Ridicule, Sarcasm, Satire, Socratic, Tongue-in-cheek, Tragic, Trope, Wry
**Ironside** Edmund
**Ironwood** Pyengadu
▸**Ironwork(s)** *see* **IRON(S)**
**Irrational** Absurd, Brute, Delirious, Doolally, Foolish, Illogical, Neurotic, Number, Paranoid, Pi, Squirrelly, Superstitious, Surd, Wild, Zany
**Irreconcilable** Poles apart
**Irrefutable** Cast-iron, Certain, Evident, Positive, Undeniable
**Irregular(ity)** Abnormal, Alloiostrophus, Amorphous, Anomaly, Aperiodic, A salti, Asymmetric, Atypical, Bashi-bazouk, Blotchy, Carlylean, Casual, Crazy, Eccentric, Ectopic, Episodic, Erratic, Evection, Fitful, Flawed, Formless, Free-form, Glitch, Guerilla, Heteroclitic, Higgledy-piggledy, Incondite, Inordinate, Intermittent, Jitter, Kink, Occasional, Orthotone, Para-military, Partisan, Patchy, Rambling, Random, Rough, Scalene, Scraggy, Scrawl, Sebundy, Sharawadgi, Sharawaggi, Snatchy, Solecism, Spasmodic, Sporadic, Strange, TA, Turbulence, Uneven, Unorthodox, Unsteady, Unwonted, Variable, Wayward, Zigzag
▹**Irregular** *may indicate* an anagram

**Irrelevant** Academic, Digression, Extraneous, Gratuitous, Immaterial, Inapplicable, Inconsequent, Inept, Insignificant, Non sequitur, Pointless, Ungermane, Unrelated
**Irreligious** Antinomian, Heathen, Impious, Infidel, Pagan, Profane, Secular
**Irremedial** Hopeless, Incurable, Laches
**Irrepressible** Resilient
**Irreproachable** Blameless, Spotless, Stainless
**Irresistible** Almighty, Endearing, Femme fatale, Inevitable, Mesmeric, Overwhelming
**Irresolute, Irresolution** Aboulia, Cliffhanger, Doubtful, Faltering, Fickle, Hesitant, Timid, Unsure, Wavery, Weak-willed, Wishy-washy
**Irresponsible** Capricious, Feckless, Flighty, Fly-by-night, Free spirit, Gallio, Reckless, Skittish, Slap-happy, Strawen, Trigger-happy, Wanton, Wildcat
**Irretrievable** Black hole
**Irreverent, Irreverence** Blasphemous, Disrespectful, Godless, Impious, Profane, Sacrilege
**Irrigate, Irrigation** Canalise, Colonic, Douche, Drip, Enema, Flood, Get, Water
**Irritable, Irritability, Irritant, Irritate(d), Irritation** Abrasive, Acerbate, Aggravate, Anger, Annoy, Antagonise, Bête noire, Bile, Bitchy, Blister, Bother, Bug, Bugbear, Chafe, Chauff, Chippy, Chocker, Choleric, Crabbit, Crabby, Cross-grained, Crosspatch, Crotchety, Crusty, Dod, Dyspeptic, Eat, Eczema, Edgy, Emboil, Enchafe, Erethism, Ewk, Exasperate, Eyestrain, Fantod, Feisty, Feverish, Fiery, Fleabite, Frabbit, Fractious, Fraught, Fretful, Gall, Get (to), Gnat, Goad, Grate, Gravel, Grumpy, Hasty, Hay fever, Heck, Hoots, Huffy, Humpy, Impatience, Intertrigo, Irk, Itch, Jangle, Jar, Livery, Mardy, Miff, Molest, Narky, Needle, Nerk, Nettle, Niggly, Nudnik, On edge, Ornery, Peckish, Peevish, Peppery, Pesky, Pestilent(ial), Pet, Petulance, Pinprick, Pique, Prickly, Provoke, Rag'd, Ragde, Rankle, Rash, Rasp, Rattle, Ratty, Rile, Riley, Roil, Rub, Ruffle, Savin(e), Scratchy, Shirty, Smart, Snappy, Snit, Snitchy, Sore, Spiky, Splenetic, Sting, Tear gas, Tease, Techy, Testy, Tetchy, Thorn, Tickle, Tiff, Tift, Tingle, Tiresome, Toey, Touchy, Uptight, → **VEX**, Waspish, Waxy, Windburn, Wind-up, Yuke
▷**Irritated** *may indicate* an anagram
**Irving** Actor, Berlin
**Is** Est, Exists, Ist
**Isaiah** Is
**Isinglass** Carlock, Fish-glue, Mica, Sturgeon
**Islam(ic)** Al Q(u)aeda, Crescent, Druse, Druz(e), Hamas, Kurd(ish), Muezzing, Pillars, Salafism, Sanusi, Senus(si), Sheriat, Shia(h), Shiite, Sufism, Sunni(te), Taleban, Taliban, Wah(h)abi, Yemeni
**Island, Isle(t)** Ait, Archipelago, Atoll, Cay, Char, Desert, Eyot, Floating, Heat, Holm, I, Inch, Is, Key, Lagoon, Motu, Refuge, Traffic

---

## ISLANDS

*2 letters:*
TT

*3 letters:*
Aru
Cos
Diu
Fyn
Hoy
Kos
Man
May
Rat
Rum
Sea
Yap

*4 letters:*
Amoy
Aran
Arru
Attu
Bali
Biak
Bute
Calf
Cebu
Coll
Cook
Cuba
Dogs
Dunk
Eigg
Elba
Erin
Fair
Fiji
Goat
Gozo
Guam
Herm
Holy
Hova
Idse
Iona
Java
Jolo
Jura
Keos
King
Line
Long
Mahe
Maui
Mazu
Mona
Muck
Mull
Niue
Oahu
Rona
Ross
Saba
Sark
Skye

Soay
Spud
Thas
Truk
Uist
Unst
Wake
Yell

***5 letters:***
Aland
Apple
Arran
Aruba
Banka
Banks
Barra
Batan
Belle
Bioko
Blest
Bohol
Bonin
Canna
Capri
Ceram
Cheju
Chios
Clare
Cocos
Coney
Coral
Corfu
Crete
Delos
Disko
Ellis
Faial
Farne
Faroe
Fayal
Funen
Haiti
Hondo
Ibiza
Islay
Isola
Iviza
Jerba
Kauai
Kiska
Koror
Kuril
Kyoto
Lanai
Lewis
Leyte
Lundy
Luzon
Maewo
Malta
Matsu
Melos
Nauru
Naxos
Nevis
North
Ocean
Oland
Ormuz
Palau
Panay
Papua
Paros
Pelew
Pemba
Pines
Qeshm
Qishm
Reil's
Rhode
Samar
Samoa
Samos
Saria
Sepoc
Seram
South
Spice
Sumba
Sunda
Thass
Thera
Thule
Timor
Tiree
Tonga
Union
Upolu
Whale
White
Wight
Youth
Zante

***6 letters:***
Achill
Aegean
Aegina
Amager
Andros
Aurora
Avalon
Azores
Baffin
Banaba
Bangka
Barrow
Bedloe
Bequia
Bikini
Borneo
Bounty
Bryher
Butung
Caicos
Caldey
Cancun
Canvey
Cayman
Ceylon
Chiloe
Cyprus
Devil's
Diomed
Djerba
Easter
Eelpie
Ellice
Euboea
Flores
Fraser
Hainan
Harris
Hawaii
Hobart
Honshu
Hormuz
Icaria
Imbros
Indies
Insula
Ionian
Ischia
Ithaca
Jersey
Kodiak
Kurile
Kvaley
Kyushu
Labuan
Laputa
Lemnos
Lesbos
Leucas
Leukas
Levkas
Lipari
Lizard
Lombok
Madura
Majuro
Marajo
Mercer
Midway
Negros
Ogygia
Orkney
Paphos
Patmos
Penang
Pharos
Philae
Phuket
Pladdy
Quemoy
Ramsey
Rhodes
Rialto
Robben
Royale
Ryukyu
Safety
Saipan
Samian
Savage
Savaii
Scilly
Sicily
Skerry
Skomer
Skyros
Snares
Soemba
Soenda
Staffa
Staten
St Mary
Tahiti
Taiwan
Thanet
Thasos
Tobago
Tresco
Tubuai
Tuvalu
Unimak
Ushant
Veneti
Virgin

***7 letters:***
Aeolian
Aldabra

Amboina
Andaman
Antigua
Ashmore
Austral
Bahamas
Baranof
Barbuda
Basilan
Batavia
Battery
Bedloe's
Bermuda
Blessed
Bonaire
Cartier
Celebes
Channel
Chatham
Cipango
Corsica
Crannog
Curacao
Cythera
Diomede
Eivissa
Emerald
Eriskay
Faeroes
Falster
Frisian
Fur Seal
Gambier
Gilbert
Gotland
Grenada
Hawaiki
Howland
Ireland
Iwo Jima
Jamaica
Keeling
Laaland
Ladrone
La Palma
Leeward
Liberty
Lofoten
Lolland
Madeira
Majorca
Mariana
Masbate
Mayotte
Mindoro
Minicoy
Minorca
Molokai
Moreton
Mykonos
Nicobar
Norfolk
Oceania
Okinawa
Orcades
Orkneys
Pacific
Palawan
Palmyra
Paracel
Phoenix
Purbeck
Rathlin
Reunion
Roanoke
Rockall
Salamis
San Juan
Sheppey
Shikoku
Society
Socotra
Sokotra
Solomon
Spratly
St Agnes
St Croix
Stewart
St Kilda
St Kitts
St Lucia
Sumatra
Sumbawa
Suqutra
Surtsey
Tenedos
Tokelau
Tortola
Tortuga
Tutuila
Vanuatu
Visayan
Volcano
Waihake
Watling
Western
Wrangel
Zealand
Zetland

***8 letters:***
Alcatraz
Alderney
Aleutian
Amindiva
Anglesey
Anguilla
Antilles
Atlantis
Auckland
Balearic
Barbados
Bass Rock
Bathurst
Billiton
Blefuscu
Bora-Bora
Bornholm
Brownsea
Campbell
Canaries
Canounan
Caroline
Catalina
Choiseul
Colonsay
Cyclades
Dominica
Falkland
Farquhar
Flinders
Foulness
Friendly
Gothland
Gottland
Guernsey
Hamilton
Hatteras
Hebrides
Hokkaido
Holyhead
Hong Kong
Jan Mayen
Kangaroo
Kermadec
Key Largo
Kiribati
Krakatoa
Ladrones
Lilliput
Lord Howe
Luggnagg
Mackinac
Mainland
Maldives
Mallorca
Malvinas
Marianas
Marquesa
Marshall
Mauna Loa
Melville
Mindanao
Miquelon
Moluccas
Mustique
Njazidja
Northern
Pelagian
Pitcairn
Pleasant
Portland
Pribilof
Principe
Sakhalin
Sandwich
Sardinia
Schouten
Shetland
Soembawa
Somerset
South Sea
Sporades
Sri Lanka
St Helena
St Helier
St Martin
St Thomas
Sulawesi
Svalbard
Sverdrup
Tasmania
Tenerife
Terceira
Thousand
Thursday
Treasure
Trinidad
Tsushima
Unalaska
Venetian
Victoria
Viti Levu
Windward
Zanzibar

***9 letters:***
Admiralty
Alexander
Andreanof
Anticosti
Antipodes
Ascension
Barataria

Belle Isle
Benbecula
Cape Sable
Chichagof
Christmas
Elephanta
Ellesmere
Falklands
Fortunate
Galapagos
Governors
Greenland
Guadalupe
Hainan Tao
Halmahera
Innisfree
Jamestown
Kerguelen
Laccadive
Lampedusa
Lanzarote
Macquarie
Manhattan
Margarita
Marquesas
Mascarene
Mauritius
Melanesia
Nantucket
New Guinea
Polynesia
Rangitoto
Rarotonga
Runnymede
Saghalien
Santorini
Sao Miguel
Shetlands
Sjaelland
St Martin's
Stromboli
St Vincent
Teneriffe
Three Mile
Tongatapu
Trobriand
Vancouver
Vanua Levu
Walcheren
Zakinthos

*10 letters:*
Ailsa Craig
Basse-Terre
Bermoothes
Campobello
Cape Barren
Cape Breton
Cephalonia
Corregidor
Dirk Hartog
Dodecanese
Formentera
Grand Manan
Grenadines
Heligoland
Hispaniola
Isle Royale
Kiritimati
Langerhans
Madagascar
Manitoulin
Marinduque
Martinique
Micronesia
Montserrat
Mornington
New Britain
New Georgia
New Ireland
Pescadores
Puerto Rico
Sahghalien
Samothrace
Sandalwood
Seychelles
Three Kings
Vesteralen
West Indies
Whitsunday

*11 letters:*
Austronesia
Dry Tortugas
Florida Keys
Glubdubdrib
Gran Canaria
Grand Bahama
Grand Canary
Grande-Terre
Guadalcanal
Lakshadweep
Lesser Sunda
Lindisfarne
Mount Desert
New Siberian
Pantelleria
Philippines
Poor Knights
San Salvador
Southampton
South Orkney
Spitsbergen

*12 letters:*
Bougainville
Cassiterides
Ellef Ringnes
Glubbdubdrib
Greater Sunda
Hinchinbrook
Marie Galante
New Caledonia
Newfoundland
Nusa Tenggara
Prince Edward
San Cristobal
Santa Barbara
Seringapatam
South Georgia
Torres Strait

*13 letters:*
Espiritu Santo
Fuerteventura
Furneaux Group
Groote Eylandt
Juan Fernandez
Little Barrier
New Providence
Outer Hebrides
Prince Charles
Prince of Wales
Santa Catalina
South Shetland

*14 letters:*
Amboina oceanic
D'Entrecasteaux
Lesser Antilles
Papua New Guinea
Queen Charlotte
Queen Elizabeth
Tristan da Cunha
Turks and Caicos
Vestmannaeyjar

*15 letters:*
Greater Antilles
Martha's Vineyard
Mont-Saint-Michel
Northern Mariana
North Stradbroke
Wallis and Futuna

*16 letters:*
Heard and McDonald

*17 letters:*
British West Indies
Fernando de Noronha

*19 letters:*
Netherlands Antilles

---

**Islander** Bermudan, Chian, Cretan, D(a)yak, Filipino, Kanaka, Kelper, Laputan, Madeiran, Maltese, Mauritian, Minoan, Native, Nesiot, Newfie, Orcadian, Parian, Rhodian, Samiot, Scillonian, Sican, Singalese, Taiwanese

**Isle of Wight** Vectian, Vectis

**Isn't** Aint, Nis, Nys

**Isogram** Isopleth

**Isolate(d), Isolation** Alienate, Ancress, Apart, Backwater, Cleidoic, Cone off, Cut off, Desolate, Dissociate, Enclave, Enisle, Exclude, Incommunicado, Inisle, In vacuo, Island, Lone, Lonely, Maroon, Outlying, Pocket, Purdah, Quarantine, Sea-girt, Seal off, Seclude, Secret, Segregate, Separate, Sequester, Sequestration, Set apart, Siege, Six-finger country, Solitary, Sporadic, Stray

**Isomer(ic)** Carotene, Carotin, Carvacrol, Geranial, Neral, Octane, Pinene, Pyran, Theophylline, Tolidine

**Isopod** Gribble

**Isosceles** Triangle

**Isotope** Actinon, Cobalt-60, Deuterium, Iodine-131, Muonium, Protium, Radiocarbon, Radiothorium, Strontium-90, Thoron, Tritium

**Israel(i), Israelite** Beulah, Chosen people, IL, Meir, Sabra, Zion

**Issue(s)** Army, Bonus, Capitalization, Children, Come, Crux, Daughter, Debouch, Denouement, Derive, Develop, Disclose, Dispense, Edition, Effluence, Egress, →EMANATE, Embryo, Emerge, Emission, Emit, Escape, Exit, Exodus, Family, Feigned, Fiduciary, Flotation, Fungible, General, Government, Gush, Handout, Hiccup, Immaterial, Ish, Litter, Major, Material, Matter, Mise, Number, Offspring, Outcome, Outflow, Part, Point, Print, Privatization, Progeny, Proof, Publish, Release, Result, Rights, Sally, Scion, Scrip, Seed, Share, Side, Son, Spawn, Special, Spring, Stream, Subject, Tap, Topic, Turn, Utter, Yearbook, Young

**Istanbul** Byzantium, Constantinople

**Isthmus** Darien, Karelian, Kra, Neck, Panama, San Blas, Suez, Tehuantepec

**It** A, Chic, Hep, Hip, Id, Italian, Oomph, SA, Same, Sex appeal, 't, Thing, Vermouth

**Italian, Italy** Alpini, Ausonian, Bolognese, Calabrian, Chian, Este, Etnean, Etrurian, Etruscan, Faliscan, Florentine, Garibaldi, Genoese, Ghibelline, Guelf, Guelph, Hesperia, Irredentist, It, Latian, Latin, Lombard, Marconi, Medici, Mezzogiorno, Milanese, Moro, Neapolitan, Oscan, Paduan, Patarin(e), Rocco, Roman, Sabine, Samnite, Sicel, Sienese, Signor(i), Sikel, Tuscan, Umbrian, Venetian, Vermouth, Volscian

**Italic** Swash

**Itch(ing), Itchiness, Itchy** Acariasis, Annoy, Burn, Cacoethes, Dhobi, Euk, Ewk, Hanker, Heat rash, Hives, Jock, Miliaria, Photopsy, Prickle, Prickly heat, Prurience, Prurigo, Pruritis, Psora, Restless, Scabies, Scrapie, Seven-year, Swimmer's, Tickle, Tingle, →URGE, Urtication, Yen, Yeuk, Youk, Yuck, Yuke

**Item(ise), Items** Also, Article, Bulletin, Couple, Data, Detail, Entry, Equipment, Exhibit, Fitting, Flash, Line, List, Lot, Note, Number, One, Pair, Particular, Piece, Point, Product, Snippet, Spot, Talking point, Titbit, Too, Topic, Twosome, Unit

**Iterate** Repeat

**Itinerant, Itinerary** Ambulant, Chapman, Didakai, Didakei, Did(d)icoy, Dusty Feet, Gipsy, Gypsy, Hobo, Journey, Log, On tour, Pedlar, Peripatetic, Pie-powder, Roadman, Roamer, Romany, Rootless, Route, Schedule, Stroller, Traveller, Vagrom, Waybill, Wayfarer

**Itself** Aseity, In se, Ipso, Per se, Sui

**Ivan** Russian, Terrible

**Ivory (tower)** Black, Bone, Chryselephantine, Dentine, Distant, Eburnean, Impractical, Incisor, Key, Molar, Solitude, Teeth, Tower, Tusk, Vegetable, Whale's bone

**Ivy** Ale-hoof, Angelica-tree, Aralia, Boston, Bush, Cat's-foot, Climber, Creeper, Evergreen, Gill, Grape, Ground, Hedera, Helix, Japanese, Panax, Poison, Rhoicissus, Shield, Sumac, Sweetheart, Udo, Weeping

**Izzard** Z

# Jj

**J** Curve, Juliet, Pen

**Jab(ber)** Chatter, Flu, Foin, Gabble, Immunise, Immunologist, Inject, Inoculate, Jaw, Jook, Lunge, Nudge, One-two, Peck, Poke, Prattle, Prod, Proke, Punch, Puncture, Sook, Sputter, Stab, Stick, Thrust, Venepuncture, Yak

**Jack(s)** AB, Apple, Artocarpus, Ass, Ball, Boot, Bottle, Bower, Bowl(s), Boy, Cade, Card, Cheap, Coatcard, Crevalle, Deckhand, Dibs(tones), Five stones, Flag, Frost, Giant-killer, Hoist, Honour, Hopper, Horner, Hydraulic, Idle, J, Jock, Jumping, Ketch, Kitty, Knave, Knucklebones, Lazy, London, Loord, Lout, Lumber, Maker, Mark, Matlow, Mistress, Nob, Noddy, Pilot, Point, Pot, Pur, Rabbit, Raise, Rating, Ripper, Roasting, Robinson, Russell, Sailor, Salt, Screw, Sea-dog, Seafarer, Seaman, Shaun, Sprat, Spring-heeled, Springtail, Steeple, Sticker, Straw, Tar, Tee, Tradesman, Turnspit, Union, Uplift, Wood, Yellow

**Jackal** Anubis, Dieb, Hack, Lion's provider, Stooge

**Jackass** Aliboron, Goburra, Kookaburra, Laughing, Stupid

**Jackdaw** Bird, Chawk, Chough, Daw, Kae, Raven, Rheims, Thief

**Jacket** Acton, Afghanistan, Air, Amauti(k), Anorak, Atigi, Bainin, Baju, Bania(n), Banyan, Barbour®, Basque, Battle, Bawneen, Bed, Bellhop, Biker, Blazer, Blouse, Blouson, Blurb, Body-warmer, Bolero, Bomber, Brigandine, Bullet-proof, Bumfreezer, Bush, Cagoul(e), Camisole, Can, Caraco, Cardigan, Carmagnole, Casing, → **COAT**, Combat, Cosy, Cover, Dinner, Dolman, Donkey, Doublet, Drape, Dressing, Dressing-sack, Duffel coat, Duffle coat, Dust-cover, Dustwrapper, Duvet, Fearnought, Flak, Fleece, Gambeson, Gendarme, Gilet, Grego, Habergeon, Hacking, Half-kirtle, Ha(c)queton, Hoodie, Hug-me-tight, Jerkin, Jupon, Kagool, Kaross, Life, Life preserver, Lumber, Mackinaw, Mae West, Mandarin, Mandilion, Mao, Matinée, Mess, Monkey, Nehru, Newmarket, Norfolk, Parka, Pea, Petenlair, Pierrot, Pilot, Polka, Potato, Pyjama, Railly, Reefer, Roundabout, Sackcoat, Safari, Sayon, Shearling, Shell, Shooting, Shortgown, Simar(re), Sleeve, Slip-cover, Smoking, Spencer, Sports, Steam, Strait, Sweatshirt, Tabard, Tailcoat, Toreador, Tunic, Tux(edo), Tweed, Vareuse, Waistcoat, Wampus, Wam(m)us, Water, Waxed, Windbreaker®, Windcheater, Windjammer, Wrapper, Zouave

**Jackknife** Dive, Fold, Jockteleg, Pike

**Jackpot** Cornucopia, Kitty, Pool

**Jackson** Old Hickory, Stonewall

**Jackstraw** Spellican, Spil(l)ikin

**Jacob** Epstein, Ladder, Sheep

**Jacobin** Robespierre

**Jacobite(s)** Non-compounder, Non juror, Wild Geese

**Jacquard** Matelasse

**Jacuzzi** Hot tub

**Jade(d)** Axe-stone, Bidet, Blasé, Cayuse, Cloy, Crock, Disjaskit, Exhaust, Fatigue, Greenstone, Hack, Hag, Horse, Hussy, Limmer, Minx, Nag, Nephrite, Passe, Pounamu, Rip, Rosinante, Sate, Screw, Spleenstone, Stale, Tired, Trite, Weary, Yaud, Yu(-stone)

**Jaeger** Skua

**Jag(ged)** Barbed, Cart, Drinking, Erose, Gimp, Hackly, Injection, Laciniate, Ragde, Ragged, Sawtooth, Serrate, Snag, Spree, Spur, Tooth

**Jagger** Huckster, Mick, Pedlar

**Jaguar** American tiger, Car, Caracal, Cat, E-type, Ounce, Tiger

**Jail(er)** Adam, Alcaide, Alcatraz, Bastille, Bedford, Bin, Bridewell, Can, Captor, Clink,

Commit, Cooler, Gaol, Hoosegow, Imprison, Incarcerate, Jug, Keeper, Kitty, Limbo, Lockup, Marshalsea, Newgate, Nick, Pen, Pokey, Porridge, → PRISON, Screw, Shop, Slammer, Spandau, Stir, Strangeways, Tronk, Turnkey, Warder

**Jailbird** Con, Lag, Lifer, Life server, Time-server, Trusty

**Jain(ism)** Mahavira

**Jakarta** Batavia

**Jake** Honest, Hunkydory, OK, Rube

**Jalopy** Banger, Boneshaker, Buggy, Car, Crate, Heap, Shandry(dan), Stock-car

**Jam(my)** Apple butter, Block, Bottleneck, Choke, Clog, Confiture, Crowd, Crush, Cushy, Damson, Dilemma, Extra, Fix, Gridlock, Hold-up, Hole, How d'ye do, Imbroglio, Improvise, Jeelie, Jeely, Lock, Log, Pack, Paper, Pickle, Plight, → PREDICAMENT, Preserve, Press, Quince, Rat run, Rush hour, Scrape, Seize, Snarl-up, Spot, Squeeze, Stall, Standstill, Stick, Tailback, Tangle, Traffic, Vice, Vise, Wedge

**Jamaica(n)** Inn, Rasta(farian), Rastaman, Yardie

**Jamb** Doorpost, Durn, Sconcheon, Scontion, Scuncheon, Upright

**Jamboree** Camporee, Gala

**James** Agee, Bond, Bothwell, Henry, Jacobite, Jemmy, Jesse, Jim, Joyce, Pretender, Screw, Seamus, Seumas, Sid, Watt

**Jane** Austen, Calamity, Eyre, Seymour, Shore, Sian

**Jangle** Clank, Clapperclaw, Clash, Rattle, Wrangle

**Janitor** Caretaker, Concierge, Doorman, Porter, Servitor, Sweeper, Tiler

**Jankers** KP

**Jansky** Jy

**Janus** Two-faced

**Japan(ese), Japanese drama** Ainu, Burakumin, Daimio, Eta, Finish, Geisha, Genro, Gloss, Gook, Haiku, Heian, Hondo, Honshu, Issei, Japlish, Kabuki, Kami, Kana, Kirimon, Lacquer, Mandarin, Meiji, Mikado, Mousmé, Mousmee, Nihon, Nip, Nippon, Nisei, No(h), Resin, Romaji, Samurai, Sansei, Satsuma, Shinto, Shogun, Taisho, Togo, Tycoon, Yamato, Yellow peril

**Jape** Jeer, Joke, Prank, Trick

**Ja(c)ques** Melancholy, Tati

**Jar(ring)** Albarello, Amphora, Bell, Canopus, Churr, Clash, Crock, Cruet, Din, Dissonant, Distune, Dolium, Enrough, Gallipot, Gas, Grate, Greybeard, Gride, Grind, Gryde, Humidor, Hydria, Jam, → JOLT, Kalpis, Kang, Kilner®, Leyden, Mason, Monkey, Off-key, Olla, Pint, Pithos, Pot(iche), Quarrel, Rasp, Rock, Screwtop, Shake, Shelta, Shock, Stamnos, Start, Stave, Stean, Steen, Stein, Tankard, Terrarium, Tinaja, Turn, Untune, Vessel, Water-monkey

**Jargon** Argot, Babble, Baragouin, Beach-la-mar, Buzzword, Cant, Chinese, Chinook, Cyberspeak, Eurobabble, Eurospeak, Geekspeak, Gobbledegook, Gobbledygook, Greenspeak, Jive, Kennick, Legalese, Lingo, Lingoa geral, Lingua franca, Mumbo-jumbo, Netspeak, Newspeak, Officialese, Parlance, Patois, Patter, Patter-flash, Pig Latin, Psychobabble, Shelta, Shoptalk, → SLANG, Sociologese, Technobabble, Technospeak, Telegraphese, Terminology, Vernacular

**Jargoon** Chinook

**Jasmine** Cape, Frangipani, Gelsemine, Gelsemium, Gessamine, Jessamy, Madagascar, Olea, Red

**Jason** Argonaut

**Jasper** Basanite, Bloodstone, Egyptian, Porcelain, Touchstone

**Jaundice(d)** Cholestasis, Cynical, Icterus, Prejudiced, Sallow, Yellow

**Jaunt** Excursion, Journey, Outing, Sally, Spree, Stroll, Swan, Trip

**Jaunty** Airy, Akimbo, Cavalier, Chipper, Debonair, Perky, Pert, Rakish, Sprightly

▷**Jaunty** *may indicate* an anagram

**Java(man)** Pithecanthropus, Sundanese

**Javelin** Dart, Gavelock, Harpoon, Jereed, Jerid, Pile, Pilum, Spear

**Jaw(s), Jawbone** Blab, Chaft, Chap, Chat, Chaw, Cheek, Chide, Chin, Confab, Entry, Gills, Glass, Gnathic, Gnathite, Gonion, Hypognathous, Imparl, Jabber, Jobe, Kype, Lantern, Lumpy, Mandible, Masseter, Maw, Maxilla, Mesial, Muzzle, Mylohyoid, Natter,

Opisthognathous, Overbite, Overshot, Phossy, Pi, Premaxillary, Prognathous, Ramus, Rubber, Shark, Stylet, Underhung, Undershot, Vice, Wapper-jaw, Ya(c)kety-Ya(c)k

**Jay** Bird, Grey, J, Sirgang, Whisky-jack, Whisky-john

**Jazz(er), Jazzman** Acid, Afro-Cuban, Barber, Barrelhouse, Basie, Bebop, Blues, Boogie, Boogie-woogie, Bop, Brubeck, Cat, Coleman, Cool, Count Basie, Dixieland, Enliven, Free, Funky, Gig, Gillespie, Gutbucket, Hardbop, High life, Hipster, Jam, Jive, Kansas City, Kwela, Latin, Lick, Mainstream, Modern, New Orleans, New Wave, Nouvelle Vague, Ory, Progressive, Ragtime, Riff, Scat, Skiffle, Slap base, Stomp, Stride, Swinger, Tailgate, Trad, Traditional, Waller, West Coast

**Jealous(y)** Envious, Green(-eyed), Green-eyed monster, Grudging, Zelotypia

**Jean(s)** Chinos, Denims, Levis®, Pants, Trousers, Wranglers®

**Jeer(ing)** Ballyrag, Barrack, Belittle, Birl, Boo, Burl, Deride, Digs, Fleer, Flout, Frump, Gird, Heckle, Hoot, Jape, Jibe, → MOCK, Rail, Razz, Ridicule, Scoff, Sling off, Sneer, Taunt, Twit, Yah

**Jeeves** Valet

**Jehovah** God, Lord, Yahve(h), Yahwe(h)

**Jehovah's Witness** Russellite

**Jehu** Charioteer, Driver

**Jejune** Arid, Barren, Dry, Insipid, Juvenile

**Jell(y)** Acaleph(a), Acalephe, Agar(-agar), Aspic, Brawn, Calf's foot, Chaudfroid, Comb, Cow-heel, Cranberry, → EXPLOSIVE, Flummery, Gel, Isinglass, Jam, Kanten, K-Y®, Liquid paraffin, Macedoine, Meat, Medusa, Mineral, Mould, Napalm, Neat's foot, Petrolatum, Petroleum, Quiddany, Royal, Set, Shape, Sterno®, Tunicin, Vaseline®, Vitreous humour

▷**Jelly** *may indicate* an anagram

**Jellyfish** Acaleph(a), Acalephe, Aurelia, Blubber, Box, Cnidaria, Discomedusae, Discophora, Hydromedusa, Hydrozoa, Irukandji, Medusa, Mesogloea, Nettlefish, Physalia, Planoblast, Portuguese man-of-war, Quarl, Scyphistoma, Scyphozoan, Sea-blubber, Sea-nettle, Sea-wasp, Strobila, Thread-cell

**Jemmy** Betty, Crowbar, Lever, Prise

**Jenkins** Ear, Roy, Up

**Jenny** Ass, Lind, Long, Mule, Short, Spinner, Spinning, Spinster, Wren

**Jeopardise, Jeopardy** Danger, Double, Endanger, Expose, Hazard, Imperil, Peril, Risk

**Jerboa** Desert rat

**Jeremiad** Lament, Tragedy, Woe

**Jeremy** Fisher, Irons, Jerry

**Jerk(y), Jerkily, Jerking, Jerks** Aerobics, A salti, Bob, Braid, Bump, Cant, Diddle, Ebrillade, Flirt, Flounce, Gym(nastics), Half-wit, Hike, Hitch, Hoi(c)k, Idiot, Jigger, Jolt, Judder, Juggle, Jut, Kant, Knee, PE, Peck, Physical, Saccade, Shove, Shrug, Spasm, Staccato, Start, Stop-go, Strobe, Surge, Switch, Sydenham's chorea, Tic, Toss(en), Tweak, → TWITCH, Wiggle, Wrench, Yank

**Jerkin** Body warmer, Jacket, Tabard

**Jerome** Hieronymic, Kern, Vulgate

**Jerry, Jerry-built** Flimsy, Lego, Mouse, Po(t), Slop-built

**Jersey(s)** Bailiwick, CI, Cow, Football, Frock, Gansey, Guernsey, Kine, Lily, Maillot, Polo, Potato, Roll-neck, Rugby, Singlet, → SWEATER, Sweatshirt, V-neck, Yellow, Zephyr

**Jerusalem** Ariel, Hierosolymitan, Sion, Zion

**Jess(e)** James, Strap

**Jest(er), Jesting** Badinage, Barm, Baur, Bawr, Bourd(er), Buffoon, Clown, Cod, Comic, Droll, Feste, Gleek, Goliard, Humorist, Inficete, Jack-pudding, Jape, Jig, Joculator, Joe Miller, Joker, Josh, Merryman, Miller, Mot, Motley, Patch, Quip, Raillery, Ribaldry, Ribaudry, Rigoletto, Scogan, Scoggin, Sport, Toy, Trinculo, Wag, Waggery, Wit, Yorick

**Jesuit** Bollandist, De Molina, Ignatius, Loyola, Sanchez, Scholastic, SJ

**Jesus** → CHRIST, Emmanuel, IHS, Immanuel, INRI, Isa, Jabers, Lord

**Jet, Jet lag** Airbus®, Aircraft, Beadblast, Black, Bubble, Burner, Chirt, Douche, Executive, Fountain, Geat, Harrier, Ink, Jumbo, Lear, Nigritude, Plane, Pump, Sable, Sandblast, Sloe, Soffione, Spew, Spirt, Spout, Spray, Spurt, Squirt, Stream, Time-zone disease, Time-zone fatigue, Turbine, Turbo, Vapour, Water

**Jettison** Discard, Ditch, Dump, Flotsam, Jetsam, Lagan, Ligan, Offload
**Jetty** Groin, Mole, Pier, Wharf
**Jew(ish), Jews** Ashkenazi, Chas(s)id, Diaspora, Essene, Falasha, Grecian, Greek, Has(s)id, Haskala(h), Hebraic, Hebrew, Hellenist, Hemerobaptist, Kahal, Karaite, Ladino, Landsman, Levite, Lubavitch, Maccabee, Marrano, Misnaged, Mitnag(g)ed, Nazarite, Neturei Karta, Nicodemus, Peculiar People, Pharisee, Refusenik, Sabra, Sadducee, Semite, Sephardim, Shemite, Shtetl, Tobit, Wandering, Yiddish, Zealot, Zion
**Jeweller(y), Jewel(s)** Agate, Aigrette, Almandine, Artwear, Beryl, Bijou(terie), Bling(-bling), Brilliant, Cameo, Cartier, Chrysoprase, Cloisonné, Coral, Cornelian, Costume, Crown, Diamante, Diamond, Earbob, Ear-drop, Emerald, Ewe-lamb, Fabergé, Fashion, Ferron(n)ière, Finery, Garnet, →GEM, Girandole, Gracchi, Jade, Jet, Junk, Lherzolite, Locket, Marcasite, Medallion, Navette, Olivine, Opal, Parure, Paste, Pavé, Pearl, Pendant, Peridot, Rivière, Rock, Rubin(e), Ruby, Sapphire, Sard, Scarab, Showpiece, Smaragd, Solitaire, Stone, Stud, Sunburst, Taonga, Tiara, Tiffany, Tom, Tomfoolery, Topaz, Torc, Treasure, Trinket, Zircon
**Jezebel** Harlot, Loose, Whore
**Jib** Ba(u)lk, Boggle, Boom, →DEMUR, Face, Flying, Foresail, Genoa, Milk, Reest, Reist, Sideswipe, Stay-sail, Storm
**Jibe** Barb, Bob, Correspond, Crack, Dig, Fling, Gleek, →JEER, Mock, Quip, Sarcasm, Slant, Taunt
**Jiffy** Mo, Pronto, Twinkling, Whiff
**Jig(gle)** Bob, Bounce, Dance, Fling, Frisk, Hornpipe, Jog, Juggle, Morris, Shake
**Jigger(ed)** Beat, Chigoe, Jolley, Ruin, Sand flea
**Jill** Ferret
**Jilt(ed)** Abandon, Discard, Ditch, Lorn, Reject, Shed, Throw-over
**Jim(my)** Crow, Diamond, Dismal, Jas, Lucky, Pee, Piddle, Riddle
**Jingle(r)** Clerihew, Clink, Ditty, Doggerel, Rhyme, Slogan, Tambourine, Tinkle, Verse
**Jingo(ism), Jingoist** Chauvin, Flag waver, Gung-ho, Odzooks, Patriot, Sabre-rattling, Warmonger, War-rant
**Jink(s)** Elude, High, Horseplay
**Jinn(i)** Afreet, Eblis, Genie, Jann, Marid, Spirit
**Jinx(ed)** Bogeyman, Curse, Hex, Hoodoo, Jonah, Kibosh, Moz(z), Spoil, Unlucky, Voodoo, Whammy
**Jitter(s), Jittery** Coggly, DT, Fidgets, Funk, Jumpy, Nervous, Panic, Willies
▷**Jitter(s)** *may indicate* an anagram
**Jo** →LOVER, Sweetheart
**Job(bing), Jobs** Agiotage, Appointment, Assignment, Berth, Calling, Career, Chore, Comforter, Crib, Darg, Desk, Duty, Earner, Errand, Gig, Gut, Hatchet, Heist, Homer, Inside, Line, Métier, Mission, Nixer, Occupation, Opening, Oratorio, Paint, Parergon, Patient, Pensum, Place(ment), Plum, Position, Post, Problem, Pursuit, Put-up, Role, Sinecure, Situation, Snow, Spot, Steady, →TASK, Ticket, Trade, Trotter, Truck, Undertaking, Work
▷**Job** *may indicate* the biblical character
**Jobless** Unwaged
**Jock** Deejay, DJ, Mac, Sawn(e)y, Scot
**Jockey** Carr, Cheat, Dettori, Diddle, Disc, Dunwoody, Eddery, Horseman, Jostle, Jump, Lester, Manoeuvre, Mouse, Piggott, Rider, Steve, Suicide, Swindle, Trick, Video, Vie, Winter
▷**Jockey** *may indicate* an anagram
**Jocose, Jocular(ity), Jocund** Badinage, Cheerful, Debonair, Facete, Facetious, Jesting, Lepid, Merry, Scurril(e), Waggish, Wit
**Joe(y), Joseph** Addison, Dogsbody, GI, Kangaroo, Pal, Public, Roo, Sixpack, Sloppy, Stalin, Surface, Trey
**Jog(ger), Joggle, Jog-trot** Arouse, Canter, Dog-trot, Dunch, Dunsh, Heich-how, Heigh-ho, Hod, Jiggle, Jolt, Jostle, Memo, Mnemonic, Mosey, Nudge, Piaffe, Prompt, Ranke, Refresh, Remind, Road-runner, Run, Shake, Shog, Tickle, Trot, Whig
**Johannesburg** Jozi
**John(ny)** Ajax, Augustus, Barleycorn, Beatle, Bog, Bright, Brown, Bull, Bunyan, Can, Cloaca, Collins, Dee, Doe, Doree, Dory, Dunny, Elsan®, Elton, Evan, Gaunt, Gents, Gilpin, Groats,

Halifax, Ia(i)n, Ivan, Lackland, Lat(rine), Latecomer, Lav, Lennon, Little, Loo, Peel, Po(t), Prester, Privy, Stage-door, Throne, Toot, Tout, WC

**Johnny-come-lately** Upstart

**Johnson** Cham, Doctor, Idler

**Join(er), Joined, Joining** Abut, Accede, Accompany, Add, Affix, Alligate, Ally, Amalgamate, And, Annex, Associate, Attach, Bond, Brad, Braze, Butt-end, Cabinet-maker, Carpentry, Cement, Cleave, Club, Cold-well, Combine, Conflate, Confluent, Conglutinate, Conjugate, Conjunct, Connect, Converge, Cope, →COUPLE, Dovetail, Engraft, Enlist, Enrol, Enter, Entrant, Entrist, Fay, Federate, Fuse, Glue, Graft, Hasp, Hitch, Hyphen, Include, Inosculate, Interconnect, Jugate, Juncture, Knit, Link, Marry, Meet, Member, Menuisier, Merge, Mix, Mortar, Mortise, Oop, Oup, Overlaunch, Piece, Piecen, Pin, Push fit, Rabbet, Rebate, Regelation, Rivet, Scarf, Seam, Se-tenant, Sew, Siamize, Snug, Solder, Splice, Spot-weld, Squirrel, Staple, Stick, Stitch, Stylolite, Tack-weld, Tenon, Tie, Toenail, Together, Unite, Wed, Weld, Wire, Yoke

**Joint(ed)** Ancon, Ankle, Arthrosis, Articular, Ball and socket, Bar, Baron, Bayonet, Brisket, Butt, Capillary, Cardan, Carpus, Chine, Clip, Co, Cogging, Collaborative, Collar, Colonial goose, Commissure, Compression, Conjunction, Coursing, Cuit, Cup and ball, Cut, Dive, Dovetail, Dowel, Drumstick, Elbow, Enarthrosis, Entrecôte, Expansion, False, Fetlock, First, Fish, Flitch, Gambrel, Genu, Gigot, Gimmal, Gimmer, Ginglymus, Hainch, Haunch, Heel, Hinge, Hip, Hough, Housing, Huck, Hunker, Inseam, J, Joggle, Jolly, Junction, Knee, Knuckle, Lap(ped), Lith, Loin, Marijuana, Master, Meat, Mitre, Mortise, Mouse (buttock), Mouse-piece, Mutton, Mutual, Node, Phalange, Phalanx, Pin, Popliteal, Psoas, Push-fit, Rabbet, Rack, Raphe, Reducer, Reefer, Rhaphe, Ribroast, Roast, Saddle, Scarf, Scarph, Schindylesis, Seam, Second, Shoulder, Silverside, Sirloin, Soaker, Splice, Spliff, Stifle, Straight, Strip, Symphysis, Synchondrosis, Syndesmosis, T, Tarsus, T-bone, Teamwork, Temperomandibular, Tenon, Together, Toggle, Tongue and groove, Topside, Trochanter, Trochite, Undercut, Union, Universal, Vertebra, Water, Wedging, Weld, Wrist

**Joist** Accouplement, Bar, Beam, Dormant, Ground plate, Groundsill, H-beam, I-beam, Rib, Rolled-steel, Sleeper, Solive, String, Trimmer

**Joke(r), Joke-book, Joking** Banter, Bar, Baur, Bawr, Boff, Booby-trap, Bourdon, Card, Chaff, Chestnut, →CLOWN, Cod, Comedian, Comic, Corn, Crack, Cut-up, Facete, Facetious, Farceur, Farceuse, Fool, Fun, Funster, Gab, Gag(ster), Gamester, Gleek, Glike, Guy, Have-on, Hazer, Hoax, Hum, Humorist, In, In fun, Jape, Jest, Jig, Jocular, Josh, Kid, Knock-knock, Lark, Legpull, Merry-andrew, Merryman, Mistigris, One, One-liner, Pleasantry, Practical, Prank(ster), Pun, Punchline, Pundigrion, Quip, Rag, Raillery, Rib-tickler, Rot, Sally, Scherzo, Scogan, Scoggin, Scream, Sick, Skylark, Sottisier, Squib, Standing, Throwaway, Tongue-in-cheek, Trick, Wag, Wheeze, Wild, Wind up, Wisecrack, Wit

**Jollity, Jolly, Jollification** 'Arryish, Bally, Beano, Boat, Bright, Cheerful, Convivial, Cordial, Dashed, Deeply, Do, Festive, Galoot, Gaucie, Gaucy, Gawcy, Gawsy, Gay, High jinks, Hilarious, Jack Tar, Jocose, Jovial, Marine, Mirth, Playful, Rag, Revel, RM, Roger, Sandboy, Sight, Tar, Trip, Very

**Jolly Roger** Death's head, Flag

**Jolt(ing)** Bump, Jar, Jig-a jig, Jog(gle), Jostle, Jounce, Jumble, Shake, Shog, Start

**Jonah** Hoodoo, Jinx, Moz(z)

**Jones** Davy, Dow, Emperor, Inigo

**Jordan(ian)** Moabite, Pot, Urinal

**Joris** Horseman

▸**Joseph** *see* JOE(Y)

**Josh** Chaff, Kid, Rib, Tease

**Josiah** Stamp, Wedgwood

**Joss** Incense, Luck, Stick

**Jostle** Barge, Bump, Compete, Elbow, Hog-shouther, Hustle, Jockey, Mousle, Push, Shoulder, →SHOVE, Throng, Vie

**Jot(ter), Jotting(s)** Ace, Fig, Hoot, Iota, Memo, Mite, Note, Notebook, Notelet, Pad, Stime, Styme, Tittle, Whit

**Journal** Band(e), Blog, Chronicle, Daily, Daybook, Diary, Ephemeris, E-zine, Gazette,

Hansard, Lancet, Lloyd's List, Log, Mag, Noctuary, Organ, Paper, Periodical, Pictorial, Punch, Rag, Record, Reuter, TES, TLS, Trade, V-log, Waste book, Weblog, Webzine

**Journalism, Journalist** Anchorman, Cheque-book, Columnist, Commentariat, Contributor, Diarist, Diurnalist, Ed, Fleet St, Freelance, (GA) Sala, Gazetteer, Gonzo, Gossip writer, Grub Street, Hack, Hackery, Hackette, Hatchetman, Inkslinger, Interviewer, Investigative, Keyhole, Leader-writer, Lobby, Marat, Muckraker, Newshound, Newsman, Northcliffe, NUJ, Penny-a-liner, Pepys, Press(man), Reporter, Reviewer, Scribe, Sob sister, Stead, Stringer, Wireman, → **WRITER**, Yellow

**Journey** Bummel, Circuit, Cruise, Errand, Expedition, Eyre, Flight, Foray, Grand Tour, Hadj, Hop, Jaunce, Jaunse, Jaunt, Lift, Long haul, Mush, Nestos, Odyssey, Orbit, Passage, Peregrination, Periegesis, Pilgrimage, Ply, Raik, Rake, Red-eye, Ride, Round trip, Route, Run, Sabbath's-day, Sentimental, Soup run, Step, Swag, Tour, Travel, Trek, Trip, Viatical, Voyage, Walkabout, Wend

**Journeyman** Artisan, Commuter, Craftsman, Pilgrim, Sterne, Trekker, Yeoman

**Joust** Giust, Pas d'armes, Tilt, Tiltyard, Tournament, Tourney

**Jove** Egad, Gad, Igad, Jupiter, Thunderbearer, Thunderer

**Jovial** Bacchic, Bon vivant, Boon, Convivial, Cordial, Festive, Genial, Hearty, Jolly, Merry, Playful

**Jowl(s)** Cheek, Chollers, Chops, Jaw

**Joy(ful), Joyous** Ah, Beatific, Bliss, Blithe, Charmian, Cheer, Cock-a-hoop, → **DELIGHT**, Dream, Ecstasy, Elation, Exhilaration, Exulting, Fain, Felicity, Festal, Frabjous, Glad, Glee, Gloat, Groove, Hah, Happy, Hey, Joie de vivre, Jubilant, Nirvana, Rapture, Schadenfreude, Sele, Sprightly, Tra-la, Transport, Treat, Yahoo, Yay, Yippee

**Joyce** Haw Haw, Traitor

**Joyrider** Twoccer

**JP** Beak, Queer cuffin, Quorum

**Jubilant, Jubilation, Jubilee** Celebration, Cock-a-hoop, Diamond, Ecstatic, Elated, Euphoric, Exultant, Golden, Holiday, Joy, Silver, Triumphant

**Judaism** Semitism

**Judas** Double-crosser, Iscariot, Traitor, Tree

**Judder** Put-put, Shake, Vibrate

**Jude** Obscure

**Judge(ment), Judges** Absolute, Acumen, Addoom, Adjudicator, Agonothetes, Alacus, Alcalde, Appraise, Arbiter, Arbitrate, Areopagite, Aret(t), Arrêt, Assess, Assize, Auto-da-fé, Avizandum, Award, Banc, Believe, Bench, Brehon, Cadi, Calculate, Censure, Centumvirus, Chancellor, Chief Justice, Circuit(eer), Cognosce, Commonsense, Common Serjeant, Comparative, Connoisseur, Consider, Coroner, Court, Criterion, Critic(ise), Daniel, Dayan, Daysman, Deborah, Decern(e), Decide, Decision, Decreet, Deem(ster), Dempster, Depth, Determine, Dicast, Dies irae, Dies non, Differential, Dikast, Discern(ment), District, Doom(ster), Ephor, Ermined, Esteem, Estimate, Evaluate, Faisal, Faysal, Gauge, Gesse, Gideon, Good-sense, Guess, Hakeem, Hakim, Hearing, High Court, Hold, Honour, Inky-smudge, Interlocutor, J, Jeffreys, Jephthah, Justice, Justiciar, Kadi, Last, Line, Lord Chief Justice, Lord Justice-General, Lord President, Lords Ordinary, Lud, Lynch, Minos, Mufti, Non prosequitur, Nonsuit, Official Referee, Old Fury, Opine, Opinion, Ordinary, Outfangthief, Panel, Paris, Podesta, Private, Providence, Provisional, Puisne, Puny, Ragnarok, Rate, Reckon(ing), Recorder, Ref(eree), Regard, Rhadamanthus, Ruler, Sagacity, Samson, Samuel, Sapience, Scan, Second guess, See, Sentence, Sentiment, Set down, Shallow, Sheriff, Sizer, Sober, Solomon, Sound, Stipendiary, Suppose, Surrogate, Syndic, Tact, Think, Timing, Touch, Tribunal, Trior, Try, Umpire, Value, Verdict, Ween, Weigh up, Wig, Wik, Wine-taster, Wisdom, Worship

**Judicious** Critical, Diplomatic, Discreet, Politic, Rational, Sage, Sensible, Shrewd, Sound

**Judo, Judo costume** Dan, Dojo, Gi(e), Kyu, Shiai, Waza-ari

**Jug(s)** Amphora, Aquamanale, Aquamanile, Bellarmine, Bird, Blackjack, Bombard, Breasts, Can, Cooler, Cream(er), Crock, Enghalskrug, Ewer, Flagon, Gaol, Gotch, Greybeard, Growler, Jar, John Roberts, Malling, Measuring, Milk, Olpe, Pitcher, Pound, Pourer, Pourie, → **PRISON**, Quad, Quod, Sauceboat, Shop, Slammer, Stir, Tits, Toby, Urceolus

**Juggernaut** Artic, HGV

**Juggle(r), Jugglery, Juggling** Conjuror, Cook, Diabolo, Escamotage, Fake, Fire-eater, Hocus-pocus

**Juice, Juicy** Aloe vera, Bacca, Cassareep, Cassaripe, Cremor, Current, Fluid, Fruity, Gastric, Hypocist, Ichor, Jungle, La(b)danum, Laser, Latex, Lush, Moist, Must, Nectar, Oil, Pancreatic, Perry, Petrol, Ptisan, Rare, Sap, Snake, Soma, Spanish, Stum, Succulent, Succ(o)us, Tarantula, Thridace, Vril, Walnut, Zest

**Juju** Charm, Fetish

**Jujube** Christ's thorn, Lotus, Nabk, Padma, Sweet

**Jukebox** Nickelodeon

**Julian** Apostate

**Juliet** J

**July** Dogdays

**Jumble** Cast offs, Chaos, Conglomeration, Farrago, Gallimawfry, Garble, Hodge-podge, Huddle, Jabble, Lumber, Mass, Medley, Mingle-mangle, Mish-mash, Mixter-maxter, Mixtie-maxtie, Mixture, Mix(t)y-max(t)y, Pasticcio, Pastiche, Praiseach, Printer's pie, Raffle, Ragbag, Randomise, Scramble, Shuffle, Wuzzle

▷**Jumbled** *may indicate* an anagram

**Jumbo** Aircraft, Colossal, Elephant, Huge, Jet, Large-scale, Mammoth, OS, Plane, Vast

**Jump(er), Jumping, Jumpy** Ambush, Antelope, Aran, Assemble, Axel, Barfly, Base, Batterie, Bean, Becher's Brook, Boomer, Bound, Broad, Bungee, Bungy, Bunny-hop, Caper, Capriole, Cicada, Cicata, Crew-neck, Cricket, Croupade, Daffy, Desultory, Entrechat, Euro, Eventer, Flea, Fosbury flop, Frog, Gansey, Gazump, Gelande(sprung), Grasshopper, Guernsey, Halma, Handspring, Helicopter, High, Hurdle, Impala, Itchy, Jersey, Joey, Jolly, Kangaroo, Katydid, Kickflip, Knight, Lammie, Lammy, Leap(frog), Lep, Long, Loop, Lope, Lutz, Nervous, Nervy, Ollie, Pallah, Para, Parachute(r), Pig, Pogo, Pole vault, Polo-neck, Pounce, Prance, Prank, Pronking, Puissance, Pullover, Quantum, Quersprung, Rap, Roo, Salchow, Saltatory, Saltigrade, Saltus, Sand flea, Scissors, Scoup, Scowp, Shy, Skip, Skipjack, Skittish, Skydiver, → **SPRING**, Star, Start, Steeplechaser, Straddle, Sweater, Tanktop, Toe(-loop), Trampoline, Triple, Turtle-neck, Vau(l)t, V-neck, Volatile, Water, Western roll

**Jumping jack** Pantine

**Junction, Juncture** Abutment, Alloyed, Angle, Box, Bregma, Carfax, Circus, Clapham, Close, Clover-leaf, Connection, Crewe, Crossroads, Diffused, Gap, Intersection, Joint, Josephson, Knitting, Meeting, Node, P-n, Point, Raphe, Rhaphe, Roundabout, Spaghetti, Stage, Suture, Synapse, T, Tight, Turning, Turn off, Union, Watershed

**Juneberry** Saskatoon, Shadbush

**Jungle** Asphalt, Blackboard, Boondocks, Bush, Concrete, Forest, Maze, Shola, Tangle

**Junior** Cadet, Chota, Cion, Dogsbody, Filius, Fils, Gofer, Minor, Name-son, Office, Petty, Puisne, Scion, Second fiddle, Sub(ordinate), Underling, Understrapper, Younger

**Juniper** Cade, Pencil-cedar, Red-cedar, Savin(e)

**Junk(ie), Junkshop** Addict, Bric-à-brac, Chuck in, Fiddle-de-dee, Glory hole, Glue-sniffer, Horse, Jettison, Litter, Lorcha, Lumber, Refuse, Scag, Schmeck, Scrap, Ship, Shmek, Spam, Tagareen, Tatt, Trash, Tripe, User

▷**Junk** *may indicate* an anagram

**Junker** Aristo, Prussian

**Junket(ing)** Beano, Celebration, Creel, Custard, Feast, Picnic, Rennet, Spree, Trip

**Juno** Lucina, Moneta

**Junta** Cabal, Council

**Jupiter** Jove, Newspaper, Pluvius, Zeus

**Jurassic** Bajocian, Lias, R(h)aetic

**Jurisdiction** Authority, Bailiwick, Domain, Pashalic, Pashalik, Province, Soke(n), Sucken, Verge

**Jurisprudence** Medical

**Juror(s), Jurist, Jury** Array, Assize, Blue-ribbon, Dicast, Grand, Hung, Inquest, Judges, Man, Mickleton, Old Fury, Pais, Panel, Panellist, Party, Petit, Petty, Sail, Savigny, Special, Strike, Tales, Talesman, Tribunal, Venire, Venireman, Venue

**Just(ice)** Adeel, Adil, Alcalde, All, Aristides, Astraea, Balanced, Barely, By a nose, Condign, Cupar, Deserved, E(v)en, Equal, Equity, Ethical, Even-handed, Exactly, Fair, Fair dinkum, Fair-minded, Forensic, Hardly, Honest, Honourable, Impartial, Incorruptible, J, Jasper, Jeddart, Jethart, Jurat, Kangaroo, Legitimate, Mere(ly), Moral, Natural, Nemesis, Newly, Nice, Only, Palm-tree, Piso, Poetic, Precisely, Provost, Puisne, Pure and simple, Quorum, Reasonable, Recent, Restorative, Right(ful), Righteous, Rightness, Rough, Shallow, Silence, Simply, Solely, Sommer, Street, Themis, Tilt, Unbiased, Upright

**Justifiable, Justification, Justify** Apology, Autotelic, Avenge, Aver, Avowry, Clear, Darraign(e), Darrain(e), Darrayn, Defend, Deraign, Deserve, Excusable, Explain, Grounds, Legitimate, Merit, Pay off, Raison d'être, Rationale, Reason, Sanction, Vindicate, Warrant

**Just so** Exactly, Sic, Stories

**Jut(ting)** Beetle, Bulge, Condyle, Overhang, Project, Protrude, Sail

**Jute** Burlap, China, Corchorus, Gunny, Hengist, Hessian, Horsa, Jew's mallow, Urena, Wool bale

**Juvenile** Childish, Pupa, Teenage(r), Under-age, Yonkers, Young, Younkers, Youth

**Juxtaposition** Parataxis

**K** Kappa, Kelvin, Kilo, King, Kirkpatrick
**K2** Dapsang, Godwin Austen
**Kail, Kale** Borecole, Cabbage, Cole, Curly-greens, Ninepins
**Kaiser** Doorn, Wilhelm
**Kaleidoscope** Dappled, Motley, Myrioscope, Various
**Kangaroo** Bettong, Boodie-rat, Boomer, Boongary, Bounder, Brush, Cus-cus, Diprotodont, Euro, Forester, Hopper, Joey, Macropodidae, Nototherium, Old man, Potoroo, Rat, Red, Steamer, Tree, Troop, Wallaby, Wallaroo
**Kansas** Sunflower
**Kaolin** Lithomarge
**Karate (costume)** Gi(e), Kung Fu, Shotokan, Wushu
**Karma** Destiny, Fate, Predestination
**Kate** Greenaway, Shrew
**Kava** Yaqona
**Kayak** Bidarka
**Kebab** Cevapcici, Doner, Gyro, Impale, Satay, Sate, Shashli(c)k, Shish, Sosatie, Souvlakia
**Keel** Bilge, Bottom, Carina, Centreboard, Cheesecutter, Daggerboard, Even, Faint, False, Fin, List, Overturn, Skeg(g), Sliding
**Keen(ness), Keener** Acid, Acuity, Acute, Agog, Ambitious, Ardent, Argute, Aspiring, Astute, Athirst, Avid, Aygre, Bemoan, Bewail, Breem, Breme, Cheap, Coronach, Cutting, Dash, Devotee, Dirge, Eager, Edge, Elegy, Enthusiastic, Fanatical, Fell, Game, Gleg, Greet, Grieve, Hone, Hot, Howl, Into, Itching, Lament, Mourn, Mustard, Mute, Narrow, Nuts, Ochone, Ohone, Overfond, Partial, Peachy, Penetrating, Perceant, Persant, Pie, Raring, Razor, Ready, Red-hot, Rhapsodic, Saulie, Sharp, Shrewd, Shrill, Slavering, Snell, Thirsting, Threnodic, Thrillant, Trenchant, Ululate, Wail, Whet, Zeal(ous)
**Keep(er), Keeping, Keeps, Kept** Ames, Armature, Austringer, Bastion, Bearward, Caretaker, Castellan, Castle, Celebrate, Chatelain(e), Citadel, Conceal, Conserve, Curator, Custodian, Custody, Custos, Depositary, Depository, Detain, Donjon, Door, Escot, Fastness, Finder, Fort, Gaoler, Goalie, Guard(ian), Harbour, Have, Hoard, → **HOLD**, Inn, Lock, Mahout, Maintain, Nab, Net, Observe, On ice, Ostreger, Own, Park, Permanent, Perpetuate, Pickle, Pocket, Preserve, Retain, Safe, Safeguard, Save, Stay, Stet, Stock, Store, Stow, Stronghold, Stumper, Support, Sustain, Tower (of London), Treasure, Uphold, Warden, Withhold, Zoo
**Keep back** Detain, Recoup, Reserve, Retard, Stave
**Keepsake** Memento, Relic, Souvenir, Token
**Keep under** Cow, Subdue, Submerge
**Keep up** Float
**Keg(s)** Barrel, Cask, Ks, Powder, Tub, Tun, Vat
**Kelly('s)** Eye, Gene, Ned
**Kelp** Varec
**Kelvin** Absolute, K
**Ken** Eyeshot, Grasp, Know(ledge), Purview, Range
**Kennel(s)** Guard, Home, House, Shelter
**Kent** Clark, Lathe, SE, Superman
**Kentuckian, Kentucky** Chicken, Corn-cracker, Derby, KY
**Kenya(n)** EAK, .ke, Luo, Masai, Mau Mau
**Kerala** Nair, Nayar

**Kerb** Edge, Gutter, Roadside
**Kerchief** Babushka, Bandan(n)a, Headcloth, Romal, Scarf
**Kernel** Copra, Core, Corn, Grain, Nucleus, Peanut, Pine, Pistachio, Praline, Prawlin
**Kestrel** Bird, Hawk, Keelie, Stallion, Staniel, Stannel, Stanyel, Windhover
**Ket** Carrion, Wool
**Ketch** Jack
**Ketchup** Relish, Sauce, Tomato
**Ketone** Hypnone, Muscone
**Kettle** Boiler, Caldron, Cauldron, Dixie, Dixy, Drum, Fanny, Pot, Tea, Turpin, War, Whistling
**Kettledrum** Tassa
**Keuper** Trias
**Key(s), Keyhole** A, Ait, Allen, Alt, Answer, Ash, Atoll, B, Backspace, Basic, Black, C, Cardinal, Cay, Central, Chief, Chip, Church, Cipher, Claver, Clavis, Clew, Clink, Clue, Command, Control, Cornerstone, Crib, Cryptographer, D, Del(ete), Dichotomous, Digital, Dital, Dominant, E, Enter, Esc(ape), Essential, F, Flat, Florida, Fruit, Function, G, Grecque, Greek, High, Holm, Hot, Ignition, Important, Inch, Index, INS, Insert, Instrumental, Isle(t), Ivory, Kaie, King-pin, Largo, Latch, Legend, Linchpin, Locker, Low, Main, Major, Master, Minor, Natural, Note, Nut, Octachord, Opener, Open sesame, Oustiti, Outsiders, Pass(word), Passe-partout, Piano, Pipe, Pivot, Pony, Prime, Prong, Reef, Return, Semibreve, Shift, Signature, Skeleton, Space bar, Spanner, Spline, Stimulate, Subdominant, Supertonic, Swipecard, Tab, Table, Tipsy, Tonal, Tuning-hammer, Turning, Type, USB, Vital, Watch, Water, Wedge, West, White, Woodruff, Yale®
**Keyboard, Keypad** Azerty, Calliope, Clavier, Console, Digitorium, Dvorak, Electronic, Manual, Martenot, Numeric(al), Piano, Pianola®, Qwerty, Spinet
**Keyholder** Chatelaine, Occupant, Resident, Tenant, Warder
**Key man** Islander, Kingpin
**Keynote** Line, Mese, Theme, Tonic
**Keystone** Cops, Crux, PA, Pennsylvania, Quoin, Sagitta, Voussoir
**Keyword** KWIC, Sesame
**Khan** Aga, Chagan, Cham, Serai, Shere
**Kibbutz** Collective
**Kick(ing)** Abandon, Back-heel, Banana, Bicycle, Boot, Buck, Buzz, Corner, Dribble, Drop, Fling, Flutter, Fly, Free, Frog, Garryowen, Goal, Grub, Hack, Heel, High, Hitch, Hoof, Hook, Lash, Nutmeg, Pause, Penalty, Pile, Place, Punce, Punt, Recalcitrate, Recoil, Recoyle, Renounce, Savate, Scissors, Shin, Side-foot, Sixpence, Speculator, Spice, Spot, Spur, Spurn, Squib, Stab, Tanner, Tap, Thrill, Toe, Up and under, Vigour, Volley, Wince, Yerk, Zip
**Kid(s)** Bamboozle, Befool, Billy, Brood, Chaff, Cheverel, Cheveril, Chevrette, Child, Chit, Cisco, Cod, Con, Delude, Doeskin, Dupe, Fox, Get, Giles, Goat, Guy, Hircosity, Hoax, Hocus, Hoodwink, Hum, Illude, Jest, Joke, Josh, Leather, Mag, Minor, Misguide, Nappe, Nipper, Offspring, Outwit, Pretend, Rag, Rib, Small fry, Spoof, Sprig, Suede, Sundance, →TEASE, Tot, Trick, Whiz(z), Wiz, Yearling
**Kidnap(per), Kidnapped** Abduct, Captor, Enleve, Hijack, Nobble, Plagium, Shanghai, Snatch, Spirit, Steal
**Kidney(-shaped), Kidney problem** Artificial, Character, Floating, Loop of Henle, Mettle, Nature, Nephron, Pronephros, Reins, Renal, Reniform, Sort, Type
**Kildare** Dr
**Kill(ed), Killer, Killing** Asp, Assassin, Attrit, Axeman, Bag, Battue, Behead, Biocidal, Boojum, Booth, Bump off, Butcher, Carnage, Carnifex, Category, Chance-medley, Choke, Comical, Coup de grâce, Croak, Crucify, Cull, Curiosity, Cut-throat, Deep six, Despatch, Destroy, Do in, Electrocute, Eradicate, Euthanasia, Execute, Exhibition, Exterminate, Extirpate, Fallen, For(e)do, Frag, Garotte, Germicide, Gun(man), Handsel, Hara kiri, Harpoon, Hatchet man, Hilarious, Hitman, Homicide, Honour, Howitzer, Humane, Ice, Immolate, Infanticide, Insecticide, Jugulate, K, Kaput, Knacker, Knock off, Liquidate, Lynch, Mactation, Matador(e), Mercy, Misadventure, Misdo, Mortify, Murder, Napoo, Necklace, Ninja, NK, Off, Orc(a), Penalty, Pesticide, -phage, Pick off, Pip, Pogrom, Predator, Prolicide, Put down, Quell, Quietus, Regrate, Road, Sacrifice, Serial, Settle, Shochet, Shoot up, Slaughter, Slay(er), Slew,

Smite, Snuff, Spike, Stifle, Stonker, Strangle, Swat, Tailor, Take out, Thagi, Thug(gee), Top, Toreador, Total, Vandal, Vaticide, Veto, Waste, Written off, Zap

**Killjoy** Crab, Dampener, Puritan, Sourpuss, Spoilsport, Trouble-mirth, Wowser

**Kiln** Lime, Oast, Oven, Queen's tobacco pipe

**Kilometre** K, Km, Verst

**Kilt** Drape, Filabeg, Fil(l)ibeg, Fustanella, Phil(l)abeg, Phil(l)ibeg, Plaid, Tartan

**Kimono** Yukata

**Kin(ship), Kin(sman)** Ally, Family, Kith, Like, Nearest, Phratry, Relation, Sib(b), Sybbe

**Kind(ly), Kindliness** Akin, Amiable, Avuncular, Benefic, Benevolent, Benign, Boon, Breed, Brood, Brotherly, Category, Charitable, Class, Clement, Compassionate, Congenial, Considerate, Doucely, Favourable, Gender, Generic, Generous, Genre, Gentle, Genus, Good, Good-natured, Goodwill, Gracious, Human, Humane, Ilk, Indulgent, Kidney, Kin, Lenient, Manner, Merciful, Modal, Mode, Nature, Nice, Sisterly, → SORT, Species, Strain, Strene, Such, Thoughtful, Trine, Type, Understanding, Variety, Well-disposed, Ylke

**Kindle, Kindling** Accend, Arouse, Fire, Ignite, Incense, Incite, Inflame, Kitten, → LIGHT, Litter, Lunt, Spark, Stimulate, Stir up, Teend, Tind, Tinderbox, Tine, Touchwood, Tynd(e)

**Kindness** Aloha, Beau geste, Benevolence, Clemency, Favour, Humanity, Mitzvah, Ubuntu

**Kindred** Allied, Blood, Germane, Like, Related

**King(s), Kingly** Ard-ri(gh), Butcher, Card, Catholic, Coatcard, Cobra, Csar, English, ER, Evil, Face card, Highness, Kong, Ksar, Majesty, Monarch, Negus, Pearly, Peishwa(h), Penguin, Peshwa, Pharaoh, Philosopher, Potentate, R, Raja, Ransom, Reigner, Rex, Rial, Roi, Royalet, Ruler, Ryal, Sailor, Seven, Shah, Shepherd, Shilling, Sophy, Sovereign, Stork, Tsar, Tzar

---

**KINGS**

***2 letters:***
GR
Og
Re

***3 letters:***
Asa
Erl
Ine
Lir
Log
Lud
Tut
Zog

***4 letters:***
Agag
Agis
Ahab
Atli
Bean
Brut
Ceyx
Cnut
Cole
Edwy
Fahd
Inca
Jehu
Knut
Lear
Loki
Nudd
Numa
Offa
Olaf
Olav
Otto
Rama
Saul
Zeus

***5 letters:***
Apple
Asoka
Balak
Basil
Brute
Creon
Cyrus
David
Edgar
Edwin
Elvis
Etzel
Gwern
Gyges
Herod
Hiram
Idris
Ixion
James
Laius
Lludd
Louis
Mesha
Midas
Minos
Mpret
Ninus
Oscar
Osric
Penda
Prial
Priam
Rufus
Uther

***6 letters:***
Acetes
Aegeus
Alaric
Alfred
Alonso
Amasis
Arthur
Atreus
Attila
Baliol
Brutus
Canute
Casper
Cheops
Clovis
Daneus
Darius
Duncan
Edmund
Egbert
Faisal
Farouk
Felipe
Fergus
Harold
Hassan
Hellen
Hyksos
Josiah
Lucomo
Ludwig
Lycaon
Memnon
Miledh
Nestor
Oberon
Ogyges
Oswald
Paphos
Peleus
Philip

Ramses
Rhesus
Robert
Rudolf
Utgard
Xerxes

*7 letters:*
Acestes
Admetus
Athamas
Baldwin
Balliol
Beowulf
Busiris
Caradoc
Casimir
Cecrops
Cepheus
Croesus
Danaiis
Diomede
Elidure
Evander
Gentius
Gordius
Gunther
Jupiter
Kenneth
Macbeth
Malcolm
Oedipus
Porsena
Presley
Ptolemy
Pyrrhus
Rameses
Regulus
Servius
Sigmund
Solomon
Stephen
Tarquin
Telamon
Theseus
Umberto

*8 letters:*
Abdullah
Adrastus
Aegyptus
Alberich
Alcinous
Alphonso
Cambyses
Cophetua
Diomedes
Endymion
Ethelred
Hezekiah
Jereboam
Jonathan
Leonidas
Melchior
Menander
Menelaus
Milesius
Nehemiah
Odysseus
Pentheus
Porsenna
Rehoboam
Sarpedon
Siegmund
Sisyphus
Tantalus
Thutmose
Thyestes
Tigranes
Waldener
Zedekiah

*9 letters:*
Agamemnon
Ahasuerus
Alexander
Atahualpa
Athelstan
Balthazar
Bretwalda
Brian Boru
Conchobar
Cunobelin
Cymbeline
Ethelbert
Ferdinand
Florestan
Frederick
Gambrinus
Gargantua
Gilgamesh
Idomeneus
Lionheart
Lobengula
Nabonidus
Pygmalion
Ras Tafari
Rodomonte
Sigismund
Theodoric
Tyndareus
Vortigern
Wenceslas

*10 letters:*
Artaxerxes
Belshazzar
Cadwaladar
Caractacus
Erechtheus
Maximilian
Ozymandias
Tarquinius
Wenceslaus

*11 letters:*
Charlemagne
Constantine
Hardicanute
Jehoshaphat
John Balliol
Melchizedek
Mithridates
Prester John
Sennacherib
Tutenkhamun

*12 letters:*
Ashurbanipal
Wayland Smith

*13 letters:*
Chulalongkorn

*14 letters:*
Harold Harefoot
Nebuchadnezzar
Servius Tullius
Sweyn Forkbeard
Tigrath-pileser
Uther Pendragon

---

**Kingdom, Kingship** An(n)am, Animal, Aragon, Arles, Armenia, Ashanti, Assyria, Austrasia, Babylonia, Barataria, Bavaria, Belgium, Bhutan, Bohemia, Brandenburg, Brunel, Buganda, Burgundy, Cambodia, Castile, Cilicia, Connacht, Connaught, Dahomey, Dalriada, Darfur, Denmark, Domain, Dominion, Edom, Elam, Fes, Fez, Fife, Galicia, Granada, Gwynedd, He(d)jaz, Heptarchy, Hijaz, Jordan, Kongo, Latin, Leon, Lesotho, Lydia, Lyonnesse, Macedon(ia), Media, Mercia, Meroe, Middle, Mineral, Moab, Morocco, Murcia, Naples, Navarre, Nepal, Netherlands, Neustria, Noricum, Northumbria, Norway, Nubia, Numidia, Parthia, Phyla, Plant, Pontic, Protista, Pruce, Prussia, Rayne, Realm, Reame, Reich, Reign, Royalty, Ruritania, Saba, Samaria, Sardinia, Saudi Arabia, Saul, Sennar, Sheba, Siam, Spain, Sphere, Swaziland, Sweden, Sweyn, Thailand, Throne, Tonga, Two Sicilies, UK, Ulster, Vegetable, Wessex, Westphalia, World

**Kingfisher** Alcyone, Halcyon, Kookaburra, Laughing jackass

**Kingmaker** Neville, Warwick

**King-of-arms** Clarenc(i)eux, Garter, Lyon, Norroy (and Ulster)

**Kingpin** Bigwig

**King's evil** Crewels, Cruels, Scrofula

**Kingsley** Amis, Charles

**King's son** Dauphin, Delphin, P, Prince

**Kink(y)** Bent, Buckle, Crapy, Curl, Enmeshed, Flaw, Gasp, Knurl, Null, Nurl, Odd, Perm, Perverted, Quirk, SM, Twist, Wavy

▷**Kink(y)** *may indicate* an anagram

**Kinkajou** Honey-bear, Potto

**Kiosk** Booth, Call-box, Stall, Tollbooth

**Kip(per)** At, Cure, Dosser, Doze, Limey, Nap, Nod, → SLEEPER, Sleepyhead, Smoke, → TIE

**Kipling** Beetle

**Kirkpatrick** K

**Kish** Rubbish, Scum, Tat

**Kismet** Destiny, Fate, Karma, Predestination

**Kiss(er), Kissing** Air, Baisemain, Buss, Butterfly, Caress, Contrecoup, Cross, Deep, Eskimo, French, Graze, Judas, Lip, Mouth, Mwah, Neck, Osculate, Pash, Pax(-board), Pax-brede, Peck, Pet, Plonker, Pree, Salue, Salute, Smack(er), Smooch, Smouch, Snog, Spoon, Suck face, Thimble, Tonsil hockey, Tonsil tennis, Trap, X, Yap

**Kit** Accoutrement, Amenity, Apparatus, Apparel, Christopher, Clobber, Clothes, Cub, Dress, Drum, Equip, Graith, Housewife, Hush, Hussif, Jack, Layette, Marlowe, Mess, → OUTFIT, Press, Rig, Set, Slops, Sportswear, Strip, Tackle, Toolbag, Uniform

**Kitchen** Caboose, Chuck-wagon, Cookhouse, Cookroom, Cuisine, Culinary, Dinette, Galley, Percussion, Scullery, Soup, Thieves

**Kite** Belly, Bird, Box, Chil, Crate, Dragon, Elanet, Forktail, Gled(e), Hawk, Milvus, Paunch, Puttock, Rokkaku

**Kitsch(y)** Cheesy, Corny, Naff

**Kitten(ish)** Cute, Kindle, Sallow, Sexy

**Kittiwake** Bird, Gull, Hacklet, Haglet

**Kitty** Ante, Cat, Fisher, Float, Fund, Jackpot, Pool, Pot, Purse, Puss, Tronc

**Kiwi** Apteryx, Chinese gooseberry, Enzed, Erk, NZ, Ratitae

**Knack** Art, Facility, Faculty, Flair, Forte, Gift, Hang, Instinct, Nose, → TALENT, Technique, Trick

**Knacker** Castanet, Exhaust

**Knapsack** Kitbag, Musette

**Knapweed** Matfelon

**Knave(ry)** Bezonian, Bounder, Bower, Boy, Cad, Card, Coatcard, Coistril, Coystril, Custrel, Dog, Drôle, Fripon, Jack(-a-napes), Jock, Loon, Makar, Maker, Nob, Noddy, One for his nob, Pam, Pur, Rapscallion, → RASCAL, Recreant, Ropery, Scoundrel, Skelm, Taroc, Tarot, Tom, Treachery, Two for his heels, Varlet, Villain

**Knead** Conche, Malax(ate), Massage, Mould, Pug, Pummel, Work

**Knee(s), Knee-cap, Knee-pan** Biscuit, Clergyman's, Genicular, Genu, Hock, Housemaid's, Lap, Marrowbones, Patella, Poleyn, Popliteal, Punch, Rotula, Stifle, Whirl bone

**Knee-jerk** Unthinking

**Kneel(er)** Defer, Genuflect, Hassock, Kowtow, Prie-dieu, Truckle

**Knell** Bell, Clang, Curfew, Death, Dirge, Peal, Ring, Toll

**Knicker(bockers), Knickers** Bloomers, Culottes, Directoire, Drawers, French, Irving, Panties, Plus-fours, Plus-twos, Rational dress, Shorts, Trousers

**Knick-knack** Bagatelle, Bauble, Bibelot, Bric-à-brac, Gewgaw, Pretty(-pretty), Quip, Smytrie, Toy, Trangam, Trifle, Trinket, Victoriana

**Knife, Knife edge** Anelace, Athame, Barlow, Barong, Bistoury, Blade, Boline, Bolo, Bolster, Bowie, Box-cutter, Bread, Bush, Butterfly, Canelle, Carver, Carving, Case, Catling, Chakra, Chiv, Clasp, Cleaver, Couteau, Cradle, Cuttle, Cutto(e), Da(h), Dagger, Dirk, Drawing, Fleam, Flick, Fruit, Gamma, Gulley, Gully, Hay, Hunting, Jockteleg, Kard, Keratome, Kukri, Lance(t), Machete, Matchet, Moon, Near thing, Oyster, Palette, Panga, Paper, Parang, Paring, Peeler, Pen, Pigsticker, Pocket, Putty, Scalpel, Scalping, Sgian-dhu, Sgian-dubh, Sheath, Shiv, Simi, Skean-dhu, Slash, Snee, Snickersnee, Spade, Spring-blade, Stab, Stanley, Steak, Sticker, Stiletto, Swiss army, Switchblade, Table, Toothpick, Tranchet, Trench

**Knight(hood)** Accolade, Accolon, Aguecheek, Alphagus, Amfortas, Artegal, Bachelor,

Balan, Banneret, Bayard, Bedivere, Black, Bliant, Bors, Britomart, Caballero, Calidore, Cambel, Caradoc, Carpet, Cavalier, Chevalier, Chivalry, Companion, Crusader, Douceper, Douzeper, Dub, Equites, Errant, Galahad, Gallant, Gareth, Garter, Gawain, Geraint, Giltspurs, Gladys, Grey, Guyon, Hospitaller, Jedi, Kay, KB, KBE, Kemper, KG, King's, Lamorack, La(u)ncelot, Launfal, Lionel, Lochinvar, Lohengrin, Maecenas, Malta, Mark, Medjidie, Melius, Modred, Mordred, N, Noble, Orlando, Paladin, Palmerin, Palomides, Papal, Paper, Parfit, Parsifal, Perceforest, Perceval, Percival, Pharamond, Pinel, Precaptory, Preux chevalier, Queen's, Red Cross, Ritter, Round Table, St Columba, Samurai, Sir, Tannhauser, Templar, Teutonic, Tor, Trencher, Tristan, Tristram, Valvassor, Vavasour, White

**Knightsbridge** Sloane

**Knit(ting), Knitter, Knitwear** Aran, Cardie, Cardigan, Contract, Crochet, Double, Entwine, Fair Isle, Hosiery, Intarsia, Interlock, Intertwine, Jersey, Jumper, K, Marry, Mesh, Porosis, Pullover, Purl, Seam, Set, Stockinet, Sweater, Tricoteuse, Unite, Weave, Woolly, Wrinkle

**Knob(by)** Berry, Boll, Boss, Botoné, Bottony, Bouton, Bur(r), Cam, Caput, Cascabel, Croche, Dial, Gear, Handle, Heel, Hill, Inion, Knub, Knur(r), Mouse, Mousing, Node, Noop, Pellet, Pommel, Protuberance, Pulvinar, Push-button, Snib, Snub, Snuff, Stud, Torose, Trochanter, Tuber, Tuner, Wildfowl

**Knobless** Enodal

**Knock(er), Knockabout, Knocked, Knock(ed) down, (off, out), Knockout** Aunt Sally, Bang, Beaut, Biff, Blow, Bonk, Bump, Ca(a), Chap, Chloroform, Clash, Clour, Collide, Con, Criticise, Dad, Daud, Dawd, Degrade, Denigrate, Dent, Deride, Dev(v)el, Ding, Dinnyhauser, Dod, Elimination, Etherise, Eyeful, Floor, Grace-stroke, → HIT, Innings, KD, King-hit, Knap, Knobble, Knubble, KO, Lowse, Lowsit, Manhandle, Mickey Finn, Mud-slinger, Nubble, Opportunity, Pan, Pink, Quietus, Rap, Rat-tat, Semi-final, Six, Skittle, Socko, Spat, Steal, Stop, Stoun, Strike, Stun(ner), Sucker punch, Tap, Technical, Thump, Tit(s), Wow

**Knock-kneed** In-kneed, Valgus

**Knot(ted), Knotty** Apollo, Baff, Band, Bend, Bind, Blackwall hitch, Bow, Bowline, Breast, Bur(r), Burl, Carrick-bend, Cat's paw, Clinch, Clove hitch, Cluster, Crochet, Diamond hitch, Englishman's, Entangle, Figure of eight, Fisherman's (bend), Flat, French, Geniculate, Gnar, → GNARL, Gordian, Granny, Half-hitch, Harness hitch, Hawser-bend, Herculean, Hitch, Interlace, Knag, Knap, Knar, Knob, Knur(r), Loop, Love(r's), Macramé, Macrami, Magnus hitch, Marriage-favour, Matthew Walker, Mouse, Nirl, Node, Nowed, Nub, Nur(r), Overhand, Peppercorn, Picot, Porter's, Problem, Prusik, Quipu, Reef, Rolling hitch, Root, Rosette, Running, Seizing, Sheepshank, Sheetbend, Shoulder, Shroud, Sleave, Slip, Slub, Spurr(e)y, Square, Stevedore's, Surgeon's, Sword, Tangle, Tat, Thumb, Tie, Timberhitch, Torose, Truelove, True lover's, Tubercle, Turk's head, Virgin, Wale, Wall, Weaver's (hitch), Windsor, Witch

**Know(how), Knowing(ly), Knowledge(able), Known** Acquaintance, Aptitude, Au fait, Autodidactic, Aware, Canny, Carnal, Cognition, Common, Compleat, Comprehend, Cred, Cum-savvy, Epistemics, Erudite, Experience, Expertise, Famous, Fly, Geognosy, Gnosis, Gnostic, Have, Hep, Hindsight, Hip, Info, Information, Insight, Intentional, Intuition, Jnana, Ken(t), Kith, Kydst, Lare, Light, Lore, Mindful, Omniscience, On, On to, Pansophy, Paragnosis, Party, Polymath, Positivism, Privity, Realise, Recherché, → RECOGNISE, Resound, Sapient, Savvy, Science, Scienter, Scilicet, Sciolism, Sciosophy, Shrewd, Smartarse, Smattering, Suss, Technology, Telegnosis, Understand(ing), Up, Versed, Wat(e), Weet(e), Well-informed, Well-read, Wis(dom), Wise(acre), Wist, Wit, Wonk, Worldly-wise, Wost, Wot

**Know-all** Arrogant, Besserwisser, Bumptious, Clever Dick, Cognoscenti, Pansophist, Polymath, Poseur, Smart alec(k), Smart-arse, Smart-ass, Wiseacre

**Knuckle (bone)** Apply, Dolos, Fist, Hock, Joint, Ossein, Submit

**Koala** Native bear

**Koko** List

**Kookaburra** Laughing jackass, Settler's clock

**Kop** Berg, Spion

**Koran** Scripture, Sura(h)
**Korea(n)** Chosen, ROK
**Kosher** Approved, Genuine, Legitimate, Real
**Kowtow** Kneel
**Kremlin** Citadel, Fortress
**Kri** Masora
**Krypton** Kr
**Kudos** Cachet, Credit, Glory, Praise, Prestige
**Ku Klux Klan** Nightrider
**Kurd** Yezidi
**Kyanite** Disthene

# Ll

**L** Latitude, League, Learner, Left, Length, Liberal, Lima, Litre, Long, Luxembourg, Pound
**La** Indeed, My
**Label** Agnomen, Badge, Band, Book-plate, Brand, Care, Crowner, Designer, Docket, File, Hashtag, Identifier, Indie, Mark, Name tag, Own, Seal, Sticker, Style, Tab, Tag, Tally, Ticket, Trace, Trademark
**Labiate** Catmint, Hoarhound, Horehound
**Laboratory** Dark room, Elaboratory, Lab, Language, Skunkworks, Skylab, Space-lab, Studio, Workshop
**Labour(er), Laboured, Laborious** Aesthetic, Agonise, Apronman, Arduous, Begar, Birth, Bohunk, Carl, Casual, Child, Childbirth, Chore, Churl, Confinement, Coolie, Cooly, Corvée, Cottager, Cottar, Culchie, Dataller, Day, Direct, Docker, Donkey work, Drudgery, Dwell, Dystocia, Effort, Elbow grease, Emotional, Farmhand, Forced, Free, Gandy-dancer, Ganger, Gibeonite, Graft, Grecian, Grind, Grunt, Hard, Hercules, Hod carrier, Hodge, Hodman, Ida, Indirect, Job, Journeyman, Kanaka, Katorga, Leaden, Manpower, Militant tendency, Moil, Navvy, Nemean, New, Okie, Operative, Operose, Opposition, Pain, Peon, Pioneer, Prole, Redneck, Roll, Rouseabout, Roustabout, Rouster, Seagull, Serf, Sisyphean, Slave, Slog, Spalpeen, Statute, Stertorous, Stilted, Stint, Strive, Struggle, Sudra, Swagman, Sweated, Task, Tedious, The grip, The lump, Tiresome, → **TOIL(S)**, Toss, Travail, Uphill, Vineyard, Wetback, → **WORK(ER)**, Workforce, Workmen, Yakka
**Labour-saving** Short cut
**Labrador** Innu, Retriever, Tea
**Laburnum** Golden chain
**Labyrinth** Daedalus, Maze, Mizmaze, Warren, Web
▷**Labyrinthine** *may indicate* an anagram
**Lac** Lacquer, Lakh, Resin, Shellac, Tomans
**Lace, Lacy** Alençon, Babiche, Beat, Blonde, Bobbin, Bone, Bourdon, Brussels, Chantilly, Cluny, Colbertine, Dash, Dentelle, Drug, Duchesse, Embraid, Entwine, Filet, Galloon, Gold, Guipure, Honiton, Inweave, Irish, Jabot, Lash, Macramé, Malines, Mechlin, Mignonette, Mode, Net, Orris, Pearlin, Picot, Pillow, Point, Queen Anne's, Reseau, Reticella, Ricrac, Rosaline, Seaming, Shoestring, Shoe-tie, Spiderwork, Spike, Stay, Tat(ting), Tawdry, Thrash, Thread, Tie, Torchon, Trim, Troll(e)y, Truss, Tucker, Valenciennes, Venise, Weave, Welt, Window-bar
**Lacerate(d)** Ganch, Gash, Gaunch, Maul, Rent, Rip, Slash, Tear
**Lachrymose** Maudlin, Niobe, Tearful, Water-standing, → **WEEPY**
**Lack(ing), Lacks** Absence, Ab(o)ulia, Aplasia, Bereft, Catalexis, Dearth, Decadent, Devoid, Famine, Gap, Ha'n't, Insufficiency, Manqué, Meagre, Minus, → **NEED**, Paucity, Poor, Poverty, Privation, Remiss, Sans, Shortage, Shortfall, Shy, Sterile, Void, Want
**Lackadaisical** Languid, Listless, Torpid
**Lackaday** Haro
**Lackey** Boots, Doormat, Flunkey, Footman, Lapdog, Moth, Page, Poodle, Satellite, Skip-kennel, Stooge, Underling
**Lacklustre** Dull, Insipid, Matt
**Lack of confidence** Doubt, Scepsis
**Laconic** Blunt, Close-mouthed, Curt, Dry, Spartan, Succinct, Terse
**Lacquer** Coromandel, Enamel, Hair(spray), Japan, Shellac, → **VARNISH**
**Lad** Bloke, Boy(o), Bucko, Callan(t), Chap, Chiel(d), Child, Geit, Gossoon, Gyte, Knight, Loonie, Master, Nipper, Shaver, Stableman, Stripling, Tad, Whipper-snapper

**Ladder(y)** Accommodation, Aerial, Bucket, Companion, Companionway, Etrier, Extension, Fish, Jack, Jacob's, Pompier, Potence, Rank, Ratline, Rope, Run, Salmon, Scalado, Scalar, Scaling, Sea, Squash, Step, Stie, Sty, Stye, Trap, Turntable

▸**Lade** *see* LOAD(ED)

**Ladle** Bail, Dipper, Divider, Punch, Scoop, Shank, Spoon, Toddy

**Lady, Ladies** Baroness, Bevy, Bountiful, Burd, Chatelaine, Dame, Dark, Dinner, Don(n)a, Duenna, Female, First, Frau, Frow, Gemma, Godiva, Harvest, Hen, John, Khanum, Lavatory, Leading, Loo, Luck, Maam, Madam(e), Martha, Memsahib, Muck, Nicotine, Palsgravina, Peeress, Powder room, Señ(h)ora, Shopping bag, Signora, Slate, Tea, WC, White, Windermere

▹**Lady** *may indicate* an '-ess' ending

**Ladybird** Cushcow, Hen, Vedalia

▹**Ladybird** *may indicate* a female of a bird family

**Ladykiller, Ladies' man** Bluebeard, Lothario, Masher, Poodle-faker, Wolf

**Lady of the Lake** Vivian

**Lady's fingers** Gumbo, Okra

**Lady's maid** Abigail, Soubrette

**Lady's tresses** Orchid

**Laevorotatory** L, Left

**Lag(gard), Lagging** Culture, Dawdle, Delay, Drag, Flag, Hysteresis, Inmate, Jailbird, Jet, Late(comer), Leng, → LINGER, Loiter, Prisoner, Retard, Slowcoach, Slowpoke, Straggle, Time, Tortoise, Trail

**Lager** Pils(e)ner

**Lagoon** Alexandrina, Aveiro, Barachois, Coorong, Haff, Pontchartrain, Pool, Salina, Saline, Vistula

▸**Laic, Laid** *see* LAY(ING)

**Lair** Couch, Den, Earth, Haunt, Hideaway, Hide-out, Holt, Kennel, Lodge, Sett, Spiv, Warren

**Lake(s)** Alkali, Basin, Bayou, Carmine, Cirque, Cowal, Crater, Crimson, Cut off, Epilimnion, L, Lacustrine, Lagoon, Lagune, Limnology, → LOCH, Lochan, Lode, Lough, Madder, Meer, Mere, Natron, Nyanza, Ox-bow, Poets, Pond, Pool, Pothole, Red, Reservoir, Salina, Salt, Shott, Soda, Tank, Tarn, Turlough, Vlei, Wine, Zee

---

**LAKES**

***2 letters:***
No

***3 letters:***
Ewe
Van

***4 letters:***
Amin
Bala
Biel
Bled
Chad
Como
Erie
Erne
Eyre
Kivu
Nyos
Pink
Taal
Tana
Thun

***5 letters:***
Atlin
Chott
Chuck
Cowan
Frome
Garda
Gatun
Great
Huron
Ilmen
Leman
Leven
Lherz
Lower
Malar
Morar
Mungo
Mweru
Myall
Nam Co
Neagh
Nyasa
Omagh
Onega
Pitch
Playa
Poopo
Pskov
Sevan
Tahoe
Taupo
Tsana
Urmia
Volta

***6 letters:***
Albert
Argyle
Averno
Baikal
Barlee
Bienne
Bitter
Broads
Cayuga
Corrib
Edward
Geneva
George
Itasca
Kariba
Kittle
Ladoga
Lugano
Malawi
Miveru
Mobutu
Monona
Nakuru
Nam Tso
Nasser
Nyassa
Oneida
Peipus
Placid
Poyang
Rudolf
Saimaa

St John
Te Anau
Tekapo
Vanern
Varese
Wanaka
Zurich

*7 letters:*
Amadeus
Aral Sea
Avernus
Axolotl
Balaton
Balqash
Bizerte
Dead Sea
Iliamna
Kara Kul
Katrine
Koko Nor
Lucerne
Managua
Mendota
Nipigon
Ontario
Red Deer
Rotorua
Sempach
Shkoder
St Clair
Toronto
Torrens
Turkana
Vattern

*8 letters:*
Balkhash
Bodensee
Carnegie
Dongting
Gairdner
Grasmere
Issyk-kul
Kinneret
Maggiore
Manitoba
Masurian
Menindee
Michigan
Naumachy
Okanagan
Onondaga
Regillus
Reindeer
Rosebery
Schwerin
Superior
Tiberias
Titicaca
Tonle Sap
Tungting
Veronica
Victoria
Wakatipu
Wanawaka
Winnipeg

*9 letters:*
Athabasca
Bangweulu
Champlain
Constance
Ennerdale
Everglade
Genfersee
Great Bear
Great Salt
Innisfree
Killarney
Macquarie
Manapouri
Maracaibo
Naumachia
Neuchatel
Nicaragua
Nipissing
Qinghai Hu
Serbonian
Thirlmere
Trasimeno
Ullswater
Wairarapa
Wast Water
Winnebago
Ysselmeer

*10 letters:*
Buttermere
Caspian Sea
Chautawqua
Clearwater
Great Slave
Hawes Water
Ijsselmeer
Malabo Pool
Miraflores
Mistassini
Of the Woods
Okeechobee
Okefenokee
Serpentine
Tanganyika
Washington
Windermere

*11 letters:*
Lesser Slave
Paralimnion
Stanley Pool

*12 letters:*
Derwentwater
Memphremagog
Waikaremoana
Winnipegosis

*13 letters:*
Bassenthwaite
Coniston Water
Crummock Water
Pontchartrain

*14 letters:*
Chiputneticook
Disappointment
Ennerdale Water

---

**Lake-dwelling** Crannog
**Lakeland** Cumbria
**Lam** Flee, Scram
**Lama** Dalai, Karmapa, Panchen, Tashi
**Lamb(skin)** Baa, Barometz, Beaver, Budge, Bummer, Cade, Canterbury, Caracul, Cosset, Ean(ling), Elia, Fat, Fell, Grit, Innocent, Keb, Larry, Noisette, Paschal, Persian, Poddy, Rack, Sacrificial, Shank, Shearling, Target, Yean(ling)
**Lambent** Flickering, Glowing, Licking
**Lambert** Constant, L
**Lame(ness)** Accloy, Claude, Cripple, Crock, Game, Gammy, Gimp(y), Halt, Hamstring, Hirple, Hors de combat, Maim, Main, Spavined, Springhalt, Stringhalt, Useless, Weak
**Lament(able), Lamentation, Lamenter, Lamenting** Ay, Bemoan, Bewail, Beweep, Boo-hoo, Complain, Croon, Cry, Deplore, Dire, Dirge, Dumka, Dump, Elegy, Funest, Jeremiad, Jeremiah, Keen, Meane, Mein, Mene, Moon, Mourn, Ochone, Paltry, Piteous, Plain(t), Plangent, Regret, Repine, Rue, Sigh, Sorry, Threne, Threnody, Ululate, → WAIL, Weep, Wel(l)away, Welladay, Yammer
**Lamia** Deadnettle
**Lamina(te), Laminated** Film, Flake, Folium, Formica®, Lamella, Layer, Plate, Scale, Table, Tabular, Veneer
**Lamp(s)** Aladdin's, Aldis, Anglepoise, Arc-light, Argand, Blow, Bowat, Bowet, Buat, Cru(i)sie,

Crusy, Cru(i)zie, Davy, Daylight, Discharge, Diya, Eye, Eyne, Flame, Floor, Fluorescent, Fog, Gas, Geordie, Girandole, Glow, Head, Hurricane, Incandescent, Induction, Kudlik, Lampion, Lantern, Lava, Lucigen, Mercury vapour, Miner's, Moderator, Neon, Nernst, Nightlight, Oil, Padella, Pendant, Photoflood, Pilot, Platinum, Quartz, Reading, Riding, Safety, Sanctuary, Scamper, Searchlight, Signal, Sodium, Sodium-vapour, Spirit, Standard, Street, Stride, Striplight, Strobe, Stroboscope, Sun, Table, Tail, Tantalum, Tiffany, Tilley, Torch, Torchier(e), Tungsten, Uplight(er), Veilleuse, Xenon

**Lampblack** Soot

**Lamplighter** Leerie, Spill

**Lampoon** Caricature, Gollard(y), Parody, Pasquil, Pasquin(ade), Satire, Send-up, Skit, Spoof, Squib

**Lamprey** Hag, Lampern, Sandpride

**Lampshade** Eyelid

**Lancaster** Burt, Osbert, Red rose, War plane

**Lance** Dart, Harpoon, Impale, Morne, Pesade, Pike, Prisade, Prisado, Rejôn, Sand-eel, Spear, Speisade, Thermic, White arm

**Lancelet** Amphioxus

**Lancer** Bengal, Picador, Spearman, Uhlan

**Lancet** Fleam

**Land(s), Landed, Lander** Acreage, Aina, Alight, Alluvion, Arpent, Bag, Beach, Bigha, Bovate, Brownfield, Byrd, Cape, Carse, Carucate, Cavel, Coastline, Common, Conacre, Corridor, Country, Croft, Crown, Curtilage, Debatable, Demain, Demesne, Disbark, Disembark, Ditch, Doab, Dock, Eagle, Earth, Edom, Enderby, Estate, Fairy, Fallow, Fantasy, Farren, Farthingland, Fee, Feod, Feoff, Fern, Feud, Fief, Freeboard, Gair, Gapsite, Glebe, Gondwanaland, Gore, Graham, Green belt, Greenfield, Ground, Heath, Hide, Holding, Holm, Holy, Horst, Ind, Infield, Innings, Interfluve, Isle, Isthmus, Kingdom, La-la, Lathe, Laurasia, Lea, Leal, Ley, Light, Link, Machair, Maidan, Manor, Marginal, Marie Byrd, Mesnalty, Métairie, Moose pasture, Morgen, Mortmain, Nation, Native, Net, Never-never, Nod, No man's, Odal, Onshore, Oxgang, Oxgate, Pakahi, Palmer, Pangaea, Panhandle, Parcel, Pasture, Peneplain, Peneplane, Peninsula, Piste, Plateau, Plot, Ploughgate, Point, Polder, Pr(a)edial, Premises, Private, Promised, Property, Public, Purlieu, Queen Maud, Real estate, Realm, Realty, Reservation, River flat, Roman candle, Run, Rundale, Runrig, Rupert's, Ruritania, Saddle, Savanna(h), Seigniory, Set-aside, Settle, Several, Site, Smallholding, Soil, Spit, Splash down, Swidden, Tack, Taluk, Tenement, Terra(e), Terra-firma, Terrain, Terrestrial, Territory, Thwaite, Tie, Tir na n'Og, Touchdown, Tract, Turbary, Tye, Udal, Unship, Ure, Van Diemen's, Veld(t), Victoria, Wainage, Waste, Whenua, Wilkes, Win, Within, Yird

▸**Landfall** *see* LANDSLIDE

**Landing (craft, gear, pad, stair, system)** Autoflare, Crash, Duck, Forced, Gallipoli, Gha(u)t, Half, Halfpace, Hard, Helipad, Instrument, LEM, Module, Oleo, Omaha, Pancake, Pier, Quay, Quayside, Roman candle, Soft, Solar, Sol(l)er, Sollar, Splashdown, Three-point, Three-pricker, Touchdown, Undercarriage

**Landless** Dispossessed

**Landlock** Embay

**Landlord, Landlady, Land owner** Absentee, Ale-draper, Balt, Boniface, Bonnet laird, Copyholder, Eupatrid, Fiar, Franklin, Herself, Host, Innkeeper, Junker, Laird, Lessor, Letter, Licensee, Lucky, Owner, Patron, Patroon, Proprietor, Publican, Rachman, Rentier, Squatter, Squattocracy, Squire, Squirearchy, Squireen, Taverner, Thane, Thegn, Yeoman, Zamindar(i), Zemindar

**Landmark** Big Ben, Cairn, Historic, Meith, Uluru, Watershed

**Landmass** Angaraland, Laurasia, Subcontinent

**Land right** Emphyteusis

**Landscape** Karst, Paysage, Picture, Saikei, Scene, Stoss and lee, Tundra, Vista

**Landslide, Landfall** Avalanche, Earthfall, Éboulement, Lahar, Scree, Slip

**Landsman** Lubber

**Land tenure** Frankalmoign, Raiyatwari, Rundale, Runrig, Ryotwari

**Lane(s)** Alley, Bikeway, Boreen, Bus, Byroad, Carriageway, Corridor, Crawler, Drangway, Drury, Express, Fast, Fetter, Gut, Inside, La, Loan, Lois, Loke, Lovers', Memory, Middle, Mincing, Nearside, Offside, Outside, Overtaking, Passage, Passing, Petticoat, Pudding, Ruelle, Sea-road, Slow, Twitten, Twitting, Vennel, Wynd

**Langerhans** Insulin, Islets

**Language(s)** Analytical, Argot, Armoric, Artificial, Assembly, Auxiliary, Backslang, Basic, Body, Cant, Centum, Clinic, Command, Community, Comparative, Computer, → **COMPUTER LANGUAGE**, Dead, Demotic, Descriptive, Dialect, Estem, Formal, Georgian, Gothic, Grammar, Heritage, High-level, Hobson-Jobson, Humanities, Idioglossia, Idiolect, Idiom, Inclusive, Jargon, Langue, Ledden, Legalese, Lingo, Lingua franca, Macaronic, Machine code, Median, Mellowspeak, Meta-, Mixed, Mobspeak, Modern, Mother tongue, Native, Natural, Neutral, Newspeak, Novelese, Object, Officialese, Page description, Parlance, Patois, Penutian, PERL, Philology, Pidgin, Plain, Polysynthetic, Pragmatics, Private, Procedural, Programming, Prose, Query, Rabbinic, Register, Relay, Rhetoric, Satem, Scripting, Sea-speak, Second, Semitic, Sign, Slanguage, Sociolect, → **SPEECH**, Strong, Style, Symbolic, Synthetic, Target, Technobabble, Telegraphese, Terms, Tone, → **TONGUE**, Tropology, Tushery, Union, Vedic, Verbiage, Vernacular, Vocabulary, Wawa, Words, World

---

## LANGUAGES

***3 letters:***
Ada
Bat
Edo
Fur
Giz
Gur
Ibo
Ido
Kwa
Lao
Mam
Mon
Neo
San
Tai
Tiv
Twi

***4 letters:***
Ainu
Avar
Cham
Dani
Efik
Erse
Geez
Hopi
Igbo
Inca
Innu
Komi
Krio
Lozi
Manx
Mari
Maya
Motu
Naga
Nakh
Nord
Norn
Nuba
Nupe
Pali
Pedi
Pict
Shan
Shri
Sulu
Susu
Taal
Thai
Tshi
Tupi
Urdu
Veps
Xosa
Zulu
Zuni

***5 letters:***
Aleut
Aryan
Azeri
Balti
Bantu
Batak
Cajun
Carib
Chewa
Cobol
Dogon
Doric
Dutch
Dyula
Fanti
Farsi
Galla
Ganda
Gondi
Greek
Gumbo
Hausa
Hindi
Hokan
Incan
Indic
Irish
Joual
Kafri
Khmer
Koine
Kriol
Kuo-yu
Kwadi
Ladin
Lamba
Lamut
Latin
Lubon
Lunda
Lyele
Makah
Malay
Mande
Maori
Masai
Mayan
Munda
Ngoni
Nguni
Norse
Oriya
Oscan
Palau
Papua
Parsi
P-Celt
Ponca
Ponka
Punic
Sakai
Sango
Saxon
Shona
Shono
Shuar
Sindi
Sinha
Sintu
Sioux
Sotho
Suomi
Swazi
Taino
Tajik
Tamil
Temne
Te reo
Tigre
Tonga
Turki
Ugric

Uzbeg
Uzbek
Venda
Vogul
Welsh
Wolof
Xhosa
Yakut
Yuman
Yupik

***6 letters:***
Adyahe
Adygei
Adyghe
Altaic
Apache
Arabic
Aranda
Asante
Aymara
Bahasa
Baltic
Baluch
Basque
Basutu
Berber
Bihari
Bokmal
Brahui
Breton
Buryat
Celtic
Chadic
Coptic
Creole
Cymric
Danish
Dardic
Divehi
Eskimo
Evenki
Fantee
Fijian
Finnic
French
Fulani
Gaelic
Gagauz
Galibi
German
Gullah
Hebrew
Herero
Inupik
Italic
Jivaro
Kafiri
Kanaka
Ladino
Lahnda
Lakota
Lepcha
Lu-wian
Lycian
Lydian
Macush
Macusi
Manchu
Micmac
Mishmi
Mixtec
Na-Dene
Nepali
Novial
Nubian
Nyanja
Ostyak
Pahari
Paiute
Pakhti
Panoan
Papuan
Parsee
Pashto
Pashtu
Polish
Pushto
Pushtu
Quapaw
Romany
Rwanda
Salish
Samoan
Shelta
Sherpa
Sindhi
Siouan
Slovak
Somali
Strine
Svanan
Syriac
Tanoan
Tartar
Telegu
Telugu
Tigray
Tongan
Tsonga
Tswana
Tuareg
Tungus
Turkic
Udmurt
Ugrian
Uralic
Yakama
Yoruba
Zyrian

***7 letters:***
Adamawa
Amboina
Amerind
Amharic
Aramaic
Ashanti
Austric
Avestan
Baluchi
Bengali
Bislama
Cabiric
Caddoan
Catalan
Chaldee
Chechen
Chinook
Chuvash
Cornish
Cushite
Dhivehi
Dzongka
Elamite
Euskara
Faroese
Flemish
Frisian
Gagauzi
Gaulish
Guajiro
Guarani
Hamitic
Hittite
Hokkien
Ingrian
Inupiaq
Italian
Janlish
Japlish
Judezmo
Kannada
Khoisan
Kikapoo
Kirghiz
Kirundi
Klingon
Kurdish
Kushite
Lallans
Laotian
Lingala
Luganda
Malayan
Maleate
Malinke
Maltese
Marathi
Mashona
Miao-Yao
Mingrel
Miskito
Mordvin
Moriori
Nahuatl
Nauruan
Ndebele
Nilotic
Nynorsk
Nyungar
Occitan
Oceanic
Ossetic
Ottoman
Pahlavi
P-Celtic
Pehlevi
Persian
Pictish
Prakrit
Punjabi
Pushtoo
Quechua
Riksmal
Romance
Romanes
Romansh
Saharan
Sahrawi
Samnite
Samoyed
Serbian
Servian
Sesotho
Shawnee
Sinhala
Sinitic
Slovene
Sogdian
Sorbian
Spanish
Sudanic
Swahili

Swedish
Tagalog
Tahitan
Tibetan
Tlingit
Turkish
Turkmen
Umbrian
Uralian
Venetic
Volapuk
Voltaic
Walloon
Wendish
Wergaia
Yerkish
Yiddish

***8 letters:***
Akkadian
Albanian
Arawakan
Assamese
Balinese
Bulgaric
Cheremis
Cherkess
Chibchan
Chichewa
Creolian
Croatian
Cushitic
Dzongkha
Ethiopic
Etrurian
Etruscan
Faliscan
Fanagalo
Filipino
Frankish
Friesian
Goidelic
Gujarati
Gujerati
Gurkhali
Hinglish
Hiri-Motu
Illyrian
Japanese
Japhetic
Javanese
Judezono
Jugoslav
Kashmiri
Khoikhoi
Kickapoo
Kingwana
Kirgyzad
Kolarian
Kwakiutl
Landsmal
Lusatian
Makyalam
Malagasy
Mampruli
Mandarin
Matabele
Mikasuki
Moldovan
Mongolic
Mon-Khmer
Mordvine
Netspeak
Nez Perce
Old Dutch
Ossetian
Phrygian
Pilipino
Polabian
Rhaetian
Romanian
Romansch
Rumansch
Rumonsch
Salishan
Sanscrit
Sanskrit
Scythian
Setswana
Shemitic
Shoshone
Slavonic
Sumatran
Sumerian
Tahitian
Teutonic
Thracian
Tigrinya
Tshiluba
Tucanoan
Tungusic
Turanian
Turkoman
Tuvaluan
Ugaritic
Volscian
Wakashan
Warlpiri
Yanomani
Yugoslav

***9 letters:***
Abkhazian
Afrikaans
Algonkian
Algonquin
Anatolian
Balto-slav
Brittonic
Brythonic
Cantonese
Cape Dutch
Chari-Nile
Cheremiss
Cingalese
Diglossia
Dravidian
Esperanto
Esthonian
Euro-speak
Euskarian
Franglais
Goidhelic
Gujarathi
Gujerathi
Hottentot
Hungarian
Inuktitut
Iroquoian
Kabardian
Kamilaroi
Kiswahili
Landsmaal
Langue d'oc
Leizghian
Makyaalam
Malayalam
Marquesan
Messapian
Mongolian
Muskogean
Nostratic
Old French
Onondagan
Provençal
Putonghua
Roumanian
Roumansch
Sabellian
Sardinian
Semi-Bantu
Sinhalese
Spanglish
Tocharian
Tokharian
Tokharish
Tungurian
Ukrainian
Ursprache
Varangian
Winnebago

***10 letters:***
Algonquian
Araucanian
Athabascan
Athabaskan
Athapaskan
Azerbayani
Beach-la-Mar
Bêche-la-Mar
Caprolalia
Circassian
Diachronic
Eteocretan
Finno-Ugric
Gallo-Roman
Halkomelom
Himyaritic
Hindustani
Indonesian
Kartvelian
Langue d'oil
Langue d'oui
Lithuanian
Macedonian
Malayalaam
Melanesian
Mingrelian
Montagnais
Muskhogean
Niger-Congo
Papiamento
Phoenician
Pima-pipogo
Police Motu
Portuguese
Proto-Norse
Rajasthani
Serbo-Croat
Singhalese
Synchronic
Ugro-Finnic
Union Shona
Ural-Altaic
Uto-Aztecan
Vietnamese
Wemba-Wemba

***11 letters:***
Azerbaijani
Belarussian
Celtiberean

Dagestanian
Finno-Ugrian
Hokan-Siouan
Indo-pacific
Interglossa
Interlingua
Kordofanian
Langobardic
Micronesian
Moeso-gothic
Nilo-Saharan
Old Prussian
Osco-Umbrian
Oto-Manquean
Pama-Nyungan
Potawatomic
Sino-Tibetan
Sranantongo
Tessaraglot
Tupi-Guarani
Yuwaalaraay

***12 letters:***
Billingsgate
Gallo-Romance
Idiom neutral
Indo-European
Norman French
Platt-deutsch
Proto-Romance
Sprachgefuhl
Tibeto-Burman
Volga-Baltaic

***13 letters:***
Neo-Melanesian
Semito-Hamitic
Serbo-Croatian

***14 letters:***
Church-Slavonic
Palaeo-Siberian
Thraco-Phrygian

***15 letters:***
Sahaptin-Chinook

***16 letters:***
Malayo-Polynesian

---

**Languid, Languish** Die, Divine, Droop, Feeble, Flagging, Listless, Lukewarm, Lydia, Melancholy, Mope, Quail, Torpid, Wilt, Wither
**Languor** Fatigue, Lassitude
**Langur** Simpai, Wanderoo
**Lanky** Beanpole, Gangly, Gawky, Lean(y), Spindleshanks, Spindly, Windlestraw
**Lanolin** Woolfat, Wool oil, Yolk
**Lantern** Aristotle's, Bowat, Bowet, Buat, Bull's eye, Chinese, Dark(e)y, Epidiascope, Episcope, Friar's, Glim, Japanese, Jaw, Lanthorn, Magic, Sconce, Stereopticon, Storm, Turnip
**Lanthanum** La
**Laodicean** Lukewarm
**Lap** Circuit, Drink, Gremial, Leg, Lick, Lip, Luxury, Override, Pace, Sypher
**Lapdog** Messan, Shough, Showghe, Yesman
▷**Lapdog** *may indicate* 'greyhound'
**Lapel** Revers
**Laplander, Lapp** Saam(e), Sabme, Sabmi, Sami
**Lappet** Infula, Jardiniere
**Lapse** Aberration, Backslide, Drop, Error, Expire, Fa', Failure, Fall, Nod, Sliding, Time, Trip
**Lapwing** Hornywink, Peewee, Peewit, Teru-tero
**Larceny** Compound, Grand, Petty, Simple
**Larch** Hackmatack, Tamarack
**Lard** Enarm, Fat, Leaf, Saim, Seam(e)
**Larder** Buttery, Pantry, Spence, Springhouse
**Large(ness), Largest** Ample, Astronomical, Big, Boomer, Bulky, Bumper, Buster, Capacious, Colossus, Commodious, Considerable, Decuman, Double, Elephantine, Enormous, Epical, Extensive, Gargantuan, → GIGANTIC, Ginormous, Gog, Great, Grit, Gross, Handsome, Hefty, Helluva, Huge, Hulking, Humdinger, Humongous, Humungous, Kingsize, L, Labour intensive, Lg, Life-size, Lunker, Macho, Macro, Macrocephaly, Magog, Man-sized, Massive, Maximin, Maximum, Mega, Outsize, Plethora, Prodigious, Rotund, Rounceval, Rouncival, Scrouger, Skookum, Slew, Slue, Snorter, Sollicker, Spacious, Spanking, Stonker, Stout, Swingeing, Tidy, Titanic, Vast, Voluminous, Well-endowed, Whopping
**Large number** Centillion, Fermi, Gazillion, Giga, Gillion, Googol, Googolplex, Grillion, Infinitude, Jillion, Lac, Lakh, Legion, Mille, Myriad, Nation, Nonillion, Nth, Octillion, Quadrillion, Quintillion, Raft, Regiment, Ruck, Scads, Sea, Septillion, Sextillion, Shitload, Slather, Slew, Slue, Squillion, Toman, Trillion, Zillion
**Largess** Alms, Charity, Frumentation, Generosity
**Lariat** Lasso, Reata, Riata
**Lark** Adventure, Aunter, Caper, Dido, Dunstable, Exaltation, Excapade, Fool, Gammock, Giggle, Guy, Laverock, Magpie, Meadow, Mud, Pipit, Prank, Spree
**Larkspur** Delphinium, Stavesacre
**Larva** Ammacoete, Amphibiotic, Amphiblastule, Aphid lion, Apteral, Army-worm, Augerworm, Axolotl, Bagworm, Bipinnaria, Bloodworm, Bookworm, Bot(t), Budworm, Cabbage worm, Caddice, Caddis(-worm), Cankerworm, Caterpillar, Cercaria, Chigger, Chigoe,

Coenurus, Corn borer, Corn earworm, Cysticercoid, Doodlebug, Frogspit, Glass-crab, Grub, Hellgram(m)ite, Hydatid, Indusium, Instar, Jigger, Jointworm, Leather-jacket, Leptocephalus, Maggot, Mealworm, Measle, Microfilaria, Miracidium, Muckworm, Mudeye, Naiad, Nauplius, Neoteny, Nymph, Ox-bot, Planula, Pluteus, Polypod, Porina, Redia, Screwworm, Shade, Silkworm, Spat, Strawworm, Tadpole, Trochophore, Trochosphere, Veliger, Warble, Water penny, Wireworm, Witchetty, Witchetty grub, Woodworm, Xylophage, Zoea

**Larynx, Laryngitis** Cricoid, Croup, Hives, Voice box

**Lascar** Seacunny, Tindal

**Lascivious(ness)** Crude, Drooling, Goaty, Horny, Lewd, Lubric, Paphian, Raunch(y), Satyric, Sotadic, Tentigo, Wanton

**Laser** Argon, Zap

**Lash(ed), Lashing(s)** Cat, Cilium, Firk, Flagellum, Flay, Flog, Frap, Gammon, Gripe, Knout, Mastigophora, Mousing, No end, Oodles, Oup, Quirt, Riem, Rope's end, Scourge, Secure, Sjambok, Strap, Stripe, Swinge, Tether, Thong, Trice, Whang, → **WHIP**, Wire

**Lass(ie)** Colleen, Damsel, Maid, Quean, Queyn, Quin(i)e, Wench

**Lassitude** Accidie, Acedie, Inanition, Languor, Lethargy

**Lasso** Lariat, Lazo, Reata, Rope

**Last(ing)** Abide, Abye, Aft(er)most, Anchorman, → **AT LAST**, Boot-tree, Bottom, Cargo, Chronic, Coda, Dernier, Dure, Dying, Eleventh, Endmost, Endurance, Endure, Epilogue, Exist, Extend, Extreme, → **FINAL**, Finale, Hinder, Hindmost, Hold out, In extremis, Keep, Latest, Latter, Linger, Live, Load, Long-life, Model, Nightcap, Omega, Outstay, Outwear, Perdure, Permanent, Perpetuate, Persist, Rearmost, Rites, Spin, Stable, Stamina, Stand, Stay, Supper, Survive, Swan-song, Tag end, Tail-ender, Thiller, Thule, Tree, Trump, Ult(imate), Ultima, Ultimo, Umpteenth, Utmost, Uttermost, Wear, Weight, Whipper-in, Yester, Z

**Last drop** Supernaculum

**Last minute** Eleventh hour

**Last resort** Pis aller

**Last syllable** Ultima

**Last word(s)** Amen, Envoi, Farewell, L'envoy, Ultimatum, Zythum

**Latch, Latch on** Bar, Clicket, Clink, Espagnolette, Lock, Night, Realise, Sneck, Thumb, Tirling-pin

**Late(r), Latest** After(wards), Afterthought, Anon, Behindhand, Brand-new, Chit-chat, Dead, Deid, Delayed, Dernier cri, Eventual, Ex, Former, Gen, In arrears, Infra, Lag, Lamented, Manana, New(s), No more, Overdue, Overrunning, Owl-car, Past, PM, PS, Recent, Serotine, Sine, Slow, State-of-the-art, Stop-press, Syne, Tardive, Tardy, Top shelf, Trendy, Umquhile, Update

**Late-learner** Opsimath

**Latent** Concealed, Delitescent, Dormant, Maieutic, Potential

**Lateral** Askant, Edgeways, Sideways

**Latex** Antiar, Dental dam, Gutta-percha, Jelutong, Ule

**Lath** Lag, Splat, Sway

**Lathe** Capstan, Mandrel, Mandril, Turret

**Lather** Flap, Foam, Froth, Sapples, Soap(y), Suds, Tan

**Latin(ist)** Albigenses, Biblical, Classical, Clausula, Criollo, Dog, Erasmus, High, Humanity, Italiot, L, Late, Law, Low, Medieval, Mexican, Middle, Modern, Neapolitan, New, Pig, Quarter, Rogues', Romanic, Romish, Scattermouch, Silver, Thieves', Uruguayan, Vulgar

**Latin-American** Criollo, Tico

**Latitude** Breadth, Celestial, Ecliptic, Free hand, Horse, L, Leeway, Liberty, Licence, Meridian, Parallel, Play, Roaring forties, Scope, Tropic, Width, Wiggle room

**Latrine** Ablutions, Benchhole, Bog, Cloaca, Furphy, Garderobe, Loo, Privy, Rear

**Latter** Last, Previous

**Latter-day** Recent, Saints, Young

**Lattice** Bravais, Cancelli, Clathrate, Crystal, Espalier, Grille, Matrix, Mesh, Pergola, Red, Space, Treillage, Treille, Trellis

**Lattice-leaf** Ouvirandra

**Latvian** Lett

**Laud(able), Laudation, Lauder** Commend, Encomium, Eulogist, Extol, Harry, Hery, Praise, Worthily

**Lauderdale** Caballer

**Laugh(ing), Laughable, Laughter** Belly, Boff, Cachinnate, Cackle, Canned, Chortle, Chuckle, Cod, Corpse, Democritus, Deride, Derision, Farcical, Fit, Fou rire, Gas, Gelastic, Giggle, Goster, Guffaw, Ha, He-he, Ho-ho, Homeric, Hoot, Horse, Hout, Howl, Irrision, Isaac, Jackass, Jocular, Kookaburra, Last, Lauch, Leuch, Levity, Ludicrous, → MIRTH, Mock, Nicker, Peal, Present, Riancy, Riant, Rich, Rident, Ridicule, Risus, Scream, Snigger, Snirt(le), Snort, Stitches, Tehee, Titter, Yo(c)k

**Laughing-stock** Outspeckle, Sport

**Launcelot** Gobbo

**Launch(ing), Launcher, Launch pad** Bazooka, Begin, Blast-off, Catapult, Chuck, Cosmodrome, Countdown, Debut, ELV, Fire, Float, Hurl, Initiate, Introduce, Lift-off, Moonshot, Motoscalp, Opening, Pioneer, Presentation, Release, Rolling, Roll out, Send, Shipway, Shot, Slipway, Spaceport, Start, Steam, → TOSS, Unstock, Upsend, VTO

**Launder, Laund(e)rette, Laundress, Laundry** Bagwash, Blanchisseuse, Clean, Clear starcher, Coin-op, Lav, Linen, Steamie, Tramp, Transfer, Wash(ery), Washhouse, Whites

**Laurel(s)** Aucuba, Bay, Camphor, Cherry, Daphne, Japan, Kalmia, Kudos, Mountain, Pichurim, Rose (bay), Sassafras, Spicebush, Spotted, Spurge, Stan, Sweet-bay, True

**Laurence** Sterne

**Lava** Aa, Block, Bomb, Coulée, Cysticercus, Dacite, Flood basalt, Igneous, Lahar, Lapilli, Magma, Mud, Nuée ardente, Pahoehoe, Palagonite, Pillow, Pitchstone, Plug, Pumice, Pyroclast, Scoria, Tephra, Toadstone

**Lavatory** Ajax, Bogger, Brasco, Can, Carsey, Carzey, Cludgie, Comfort station, Convenience, Cottage, Dike, Draught, Dunnakin, Dunny, Dyke, Earth closet, Elsan®, Facilities, Forica, Furphey, Gents, Heads, Jakes, Jane, John, Kars(e)y, Karzy, K(h)azi, Kleinhuisie, Kybo, Ladies, Lat(rine), Loo, Necessary, Netty, Office, Outhouse, Pissoir, Portaloo®, Privy, Rear(s), Reredorter, Shouse, Siege, Smallest room, Superloo, Throne, Thunderbox, Toilet, Toot, Tout, Urinal, Washroom, WC

**Lave** Lip, Wash

**Lavender** Aspic, Plumbago, Sea, Spike

**Lavengro** Borrow

**Laver** Alga, Moabite, Nori, Ore-weed

**Lavish** Barmecidal, Copious, Excessive, Expensive, Extravagant, Exuberant, Flush, Free, Fulsome, Generous, Liberal, Lordly, Lucullan, Lush, Opulent, Palatial, Prodigal, Profuse, Regal, Shower, Slap-up, Sumptuous, Unsparing, Wanton, Waste

**Law(ful), Laws** Abingdon, Act, Agrarian, Ahimsa, Anti-trust, Ass, Association, Avogadro's, Babo's, Bar, Barratry, Bernoulli's, → BILL, Biogenetic, Blue-sky, Bode's, Bonar, Bourlaw, Boyle's, Bragg's, Brehon, Brewster's, Brocard, Buys Ballot's, Byelaw, Byrlaw, Cain, Canon, Capitulary, Case, Chancery, Charles's, Civil, Club, Code, Combination, Common, Constitution, Corn, Coulomb's, Criminal, Cupar, Curie's, Curie-Weiss, Cy pres, Dalton's, Dead-letter, Decree, Decretals, Decretum, De Morgan's, Deodand, Dharma, Dictate, Digest, Din, Distributive, Dry, Edict, Einstein's, Enact, Excise, Fiqh, Forensic, Forest, Fuero, Fundamental, Fuzz, Game, Gas, Gay-Lussac's, Graham's, Gresham's, Grimm's, Grotian, Haeckel's, Halal, Halifax, Hardy-Weinberg, Henry's, Hess's, Homestead, Hooke's, Hubble's, Hudud, Hume's, International, Irade, Iure, Joule's, Jura, Jure, Jus, Kain, Karma, Kashrut(h), Kepler's, Kirchhoff's, Labour, Land, Lay, Legal, Leibniz's, Lemon, Lenz's, Licit, Lien, Liquor, Lor(d), Losh, Lydford, Lynch, Magdeburg, Mariotte's, Martial, May, Megan's, Mendel's, Mercantile, Military, Mishna(h), Mishnic, Moore's, Moral, Mosaic, Murphy's, Natural, Newton's, Noahide, Nomistic, Nomology, Nomothetic, Octave, Ohm's, Oral, Ordinance, Pandect, Parity, Parkinson's, Pass, Penal, Periodic, Planck's, Plebiscite, Plod, Poor, Principle, Private, Public, Rape shield, Regulation, Rhodian, Roman, Rubric, Rule, Salic, Salique, Scout, Sharia(h), Sheria(t), Shield, Shulchan Aruch, Snell's, Sod's, → STATUTE, Statute book, Stefan's, Stokes, Sumptuary, Sunna, Sus(s), Sword, Table, Talmud, Tenet, The (long) robe, Thorah, Thorndike's, Torah, Tort, Tradition, Twelve Tables, Ulema, Unwritten, Use, Valid, Verner's, Vigilante, Written

**Lawbreaker, Lawless(ness)** Anarchy, Anomie, Anomy, Antinomian, Bushranger, Desperado, Offender, Piratical, Rowdy, Ruffian, Wild and woolly, Wrongdoer

**Lawmaker, Lawman, Lawyer** Alfaqui, Ambulance chaser, Att(orney), AV, Avocat, Avvogadore, Barrack room, Barrister, Bencher, BL, Bluebottle, Bramble, Brief, Bush, Cadi, Canon, Coke, Counsel, Crown, DA, Decemvir, Deemster, Defence, Dempster, Doge, Draco, Eagle(t), Earp, Enactor, Fiscal, Greenbag, Grotius, Hammurabi, Jurisconsult, Jurist, Juvenal, Legal eagle, Legist, Mooktar, Moses, MP, Mufti, Mukhtar, Nomothete, Notary, Penang, Pettifoggers, Philadelphia, Proctor, Procurator fiscal, Prosecutor, Rabbi, Sea, Sheriff, Shirra, Shyster, Silk, Solicitor, Spenlow, Stratopause, Talmudist, Templar, Thesmothete, Vakil, Writer, WS

**Lawn** Cambric, Cloth, Grass, Green, Linen, Ruche, Sward, Turf

**Lawrence** DH, Ross, Shaw, TE

**Lawrencium** Lr

**Lawsuit** Action, Case, Cause, Plea, Trover

▸**Lawyer(s), Lawman** *see* LAWMAKER

**Lax(ity)** Freedom, Inexact, Laissez-aller, Latitude, Lenience, Loose, Remiss, → SLACK, Wide, Wide-open

▹**Lax** *may indicate* an anagram

**Laxative** Aloin, Aperient, Aperitive, Cascara, Cassia, Cathartic, Eccoprotic, Elaterin, Elaterium, Glauber's salt, Gregory (powder), Hydragogue, Ispaghula, Loosener, Magnesia, Physic, Purgative, → PURGE, Saline, Senna-pod, Taraxacum

**Lay(ing), Layman, Laic, Laid, Laity** Air, Amateur, Antepost, Aria, Ballad, Bed, Bet, Blow, Chant, Christian Brothers, Civil, Ditty, Drop, Earthly, Egg, Embed, Exhorter, Fit, Impose, Impropriator, Lied, Lodge, Man, Minstrel, Oat, Oblate, Ode, Ordinary, Outsider, Oviparous, Oviposit, Parabolanus, Pose, Secular, Set, Sirvente, → SONG, Songsmith, Sypher, Temporalty, Tertiary, Tribal, Untrained, Wager, Warp

**Layabout** Corner boy, Deadbeat, Idler, Lazybones, Loafer, Lotophagus, Ne'er-do-well, Oaf, Slob, Wastrel

**Lay-by** Rest stop

**Layer(s)** Abscission, Aeuron(e), Ancona, Appleton, Barrier, Battery, Bed, Bedrock, Boundary, Cake, Caliche, Cambium, Canopy, Chromosphere, Cladding, Coating, Crust, D, Depletion, E, Ectoplasm, Ectosarc, Ekman, Epiblast, Epilimnion, Epitaxial, Epitheca, Epithelium, Erathem, E-region, Exine, Exocarp, F, Film, Flake, Friction, Ganoin, Germ, Gossan, Gozzan, Granum, Ground, Heaviside, → HEN, Herb, Hypotheca, Intima, Inversion, Iron-pan, Kennelly(-Heaviside), Kerf, Lamella, Lamina, Lap, Leghorn, Lenticle, Lie, Malpighian, Media, Mesoblast, Miocene, Ozone, Palisade, Pan, Patina, Paviour, Photosphere, Ply, Retina, Reversing, Rind, Scale, Scattering, Sclerite, Screed, Shrub, Skim, Skin, Skiver, Sliver, Spathic, Stratify, Stratopause, Stratum, Substratum, Tabular, Tapetum, Tier, Topcoat, Tremie, Trophoblast, Trophoderm, Uvea, Varve, Vein, Velamen, Veneer

**Lay-off** Dismiss, Hedge, Redundance, Suspend

**Lay-out** Ante, Design, Expend, Fell, Floor plan, Format, Map, Mise, Pattern, Spend, Spreadsheet, Straucht, Straught, Streak, Streek, Stretch, Topography

**Laze, Laziness, Lazy (person), Lazybones** Bed-presser, Bone idle, Bummer, Cabbage, Couch potato, Do naught, Doss, Faineant, Grunge, Hallian, Hallion, Hallyon, Inactive, Indolent, Inert, Lackadaisical, Laesie, Languid, Layabout, Lie-abed, Lig(ger), Lime, Lither, Loaf, Lotus-eater, Lusk, Mollusc, Ne'er-do-well, Oblomovism, Resty, Shiftless, Sleepyhead, Slob, Sloth, Slouch, Slowback, Slug(-a-bed), Sluggard, Susan, Sweer, Sweir, Timeserver, Underactive, Veg, Workshy

▹**Lazily** *may indicate* an anagram

**Lea** Grass, Meadow

**Leach(ing)** Cheluviation, Lixivial, Ooze

**Lead(er), Leading, Leadership** Ag(h)a, Ahead, Akela, Amakosi, Anglesite, Arch, Article, Atabeg, Atabek, Attila, Ayatollah, Bab, Bear away the bell, Bellwether, Black, Bluey, Bodhisattva, Bonaparte, Brand, Brown Owl, Cable, Cade, Calif, Caliph, Came, Capitano, Capo, Captain, Castro, Caudillo, Causal, Centre, Ceruse, Chair, Cheer, Chief, Chieftain, Chiliarch, Chin, China white, Choragus, Choregus, Churchill, Clue, CO, Codder, Commandant,

Concert-master, Condottiere, Conducive, Conduct, Corporal, Coryphaeus, Coryphee, Czar, Dalai Lama, De Gaulle, Demagogue, Den mother, Dictator, Director, Dominant, Drail, Drum-majorette, Duce, Dux, Editorial, Elder, Element, Escort, Ethnarch, Extension, Figurehead, First, Flagship, Flake-white, Floor, Foreman, Foremost, Franco, Friendly, Front man, Frontrunner, Fugleman, Fu(e)hrer, Gaffer, Galena, Gandhi, Garibaldi, General, Gerent, Go, Graphite, Guide(r), Guru, Halter, Hand, Head, Headman, Headmost, Headnote, Heavy metal, Hegemony, Heresiarch, Hero, Heroine, Hetman, Hiawatha, Hierarch, Honcho, Idi, Imam, Imaum, Induna, Ink(h)osi, Inveigle, Jason, Jefe, Jeune premier(e), Jump, Juve(nile), Kabir, Kame, King, Ksar, Leam, Leash, Litharge, Livid, Loss, Lost, Lyam, Lym(e), Mahatma, Mahdi, Main, Market, Marshal, Masjid, Massicot, Masticot, Mayor, Meer, Mehdi, Messiah, Minium, Mir, Mussolini, Nanak, Napoleon, No 1, Nomarch, Nose, Numero uno, Omrah, Open, Pace car, Pacemaker, Pacesetter, Padishah, Panchen Lama, Patriarch, Pb, Petain, Pig, Pilot, Pioneer, Pit, Plumb(um), Plummet, PM, Pointer, Precede, Precentor, Premier(e), President, Price, Primo, Rangitara, Ratoo, Rebbe, Rebecca, Red, Role, Ruler, Sachem, Sagamore, Saturn, Saturn's tree, Scotlandite, Scout, Scuddaler, Scudler, Senior, Shaper, Sharif, Sheet, Sheik(h), Sixer, Skipper, Skudler, Soaker, Soul, Sounding, Spearhead, Stalin, Staple, Star, Start, Sultan, Supremo, Taoiseach, Tecumseh, Tenno, Tetraethyl, Top banana, Top dog, Torch-bearer, Trail(blazer), Trendsetter, Tribune, Tsaddik, Tsaddiq, Tsar, Tzaddik, Up, Usher, Vaivode, Van(guard), Vanadinite, Va(u)nt, Vaunt-courier, Voivode, Vozhd, Waivode, Wali, Warlord, Whip, White, Whitechapel, Wulfenite, Yellow jersey, Yeltsin, Youth, Zaddik, Zia

▷**Lead(s), Leaders** *may indicate* first letters of words

**Leaden** Flat, Pesante, Plumbeous, Saturnine

**Lead-glance** Galena

**Leading lady** Eve

**Leading to** Pre

**Leaf(y), Leaf-shaped, Leaves** Acanthus, Acrospire, Amphigastrium, Amplexicaul, Ascidia, At(t)ap, Baccy, Bay, Betel, Blade, Bract, Bud-scale, Carpel, Cataphyll, Cladode, Coca, Compound, Consent, Corolla, Costate, Cotyledon, Crocket, Dock, Dolma, Drop, Duff, Dutch, Fig, Finial, Foil, Foliage, Foliar, Folio(se), Folium, Frond, Frondose, Glume, Gold, Green, Holiday, Induviae, Jugum, K(h)at, Lanceolate, Lattice, Lilypad, Lobe, Lobulus, Maple, Megaphyll, Microphyll, Needle, Nervate, Obovate, Out, P, Pad, Page, Pan, Paper, Phyllid, Phyllode, Phyllome, Pot, Qat, Recto, Repair, Riffle, Rosula, Runcinate, Salad, Scale, Sclerophyll, Secede, Sepal, Sheet, Siri(h), Skim, Skip, Spathe, Sporophyll, Stipule, Subentire, Succubus, Tea, Ternate, Title, Tobacco, TTL, Unicostate, Valve, Verso, Vert, Vine, Withdraw

**Leafhopper** Thrip

**Leafless** Ebracteate, Nudicaul, Scape

**Leaflet** At(t)ap, Bill, Bracteole, Circular, Dodger, Flier, Fly-sheet, Foliolose, Handbill, Hand-out, Pinna, Pinnula, Prophyll, Stipel, → **TRACT**

**League** Achaean, Alliance, Amphictyony, Arab, Band, Bund, Compact, Decapolis, Delian, Denominal, Entente, Federation, Gueux, Guild, Hanse(atic), Holy, Holy Alliance, Ivy, L, Land, Little, Major, Minor, Muslim, Nations, Parasang, Primrose, Redheaded, Rugby, Solemn, Super, Union, Ypres, Zollverein, Zupa

**Leak(y)** Bilge, Disclosure, Drip, Escape, Extravasate, Gas, Gizzen, Holed, Holey, Ooze, Pee, Porous, Run, Seepage, Sype, Transude, Trickle, Urinate, Wee, Weep, Wee-wee

**Leak-proof** Airtight

**Leamington** Spa

**Lean(ing)** Abut, Angular, Aslope, Atilt, Barren, Batter, Bend, Cant, Careen, Carneous, Carnose, Gaunt, Griskin, Heel, Hike out, → **INCLINE**, Lie, Lig(ge), List, Meagre, Minceur, Partiality, Prop, Propend, Rake, Rawboned, Rely, Rest, Scraggy, Scrawny, Skinny, Slant, Spare, Stoop, Taste, Tend, Thin, Tilt, Tip, Walty, Wiry

**Leander** Abydos

**Lean-to** Skillion

**Leap(ing), Leapt** Assemblé, Bound, Brisé, Cabriole, Caper, Capriole, Cavort, Clear, Croupade, Curvet, Echappé, Entrechat, Falcade, Fishdive, Flying, Frisk, Galumph, Gambade, Gambado, Gambol, Jeté, Jump, Loup, Luppen, Ollie, Over, Pigeon-wing, Pounce, Pronk,

Quantum, Sally, Salmon, Salto, Somersa(u)lt, Somerset, → **SPRING**, Stag, Transilient, Vault, Volte

**Leap year** Bissextile, Penteteric

**Lear** Edward, King, Nonsense

**Learn(ed), Learner, Learning** Associative, Beginner, Blended, Blue, Bluestocking, Chela, Classical, Con, Cram, Culture, Discipline, Discover, Discrimination, Distance, Doctor, Don, Erudite, Erudition, Extra-mural, Gather, Get, Glean, Greenhorn, Hear, Index, Insight, Instrumental, Intern, Knowledge, Kond, L, Latent, Lear(e), Leir, Lere, Letters, Lifelong, Literate, Literati, Literato, Lore, L-plater, Lucubrate, Machine, Master, Memorise, Mirza, Mug up, New, → **NOVICE**, Open, Opsimath(y), Pandit, Polymath, Programmed, Pundit, Pupil, Rep, Rookie, Savant, Scan, Scholar(ship), Scient, See, Sleep, Starter, Student, → **STUDY**, Tiro, Trainee, Tutee, Tyro, Visile, Wise, Wit

**Lease(-holder)** Charter, Farm, Feu, Gavel, Hire, Let, Long, Novated, → **RENT**, Set(t), Sublet, Subtack, Tack, Tacksman

**Leash** Lead, Lune, Lyam, Lym(e), Slip, Tether, Three, Trash, Triplet

**Least** Barest, Minimum, No less, Rap

**Leather(s), Leather-worker, Leathery** Aqualeather, Artificial, Bouilli, Bouilly, Box-calf, Brail, Buckskin, Buff, Cabretta, Calf, Capeskin, Chammy, Chamois, Chaps, Checklaton, Cheverel, Chevrette, Chrome, Cordovan, Cordwain, Corium, Counter, Cowhide, Crispin, Crocodile, Cuir(-bouilli), Cuirass, Currier, Deacon, Deerskin, Diphthera, Doeskin, Dogskin, Durant, Fair, Foxing, Goatskin, Grain, Hide, Hog-skin, Horsehide, Japanned, Kid, Kip(-skin), Labretta, Lacquered, Lamp, Levant, Marocain, Maroquin, Mocha, Morocco, Mountain, Nap(p)a, Neat's, Nubuck®, Oak, Ooze, Oxhide, Paste-grain, Patent, Pigskin, Plate, Rand, Rawhide, Rexine®, Riem(pie), Roan, Rock, Rough-out, Russet, Russia, Saffian, Shagreen, Shammy, Sharkskin, Shecklaton, Sheepskin, Shoe, Skiver, Slinkskin, Snakeskin, Spetch, Split, Spruce, Spur, Spur-whang, Stirrup, Strand, Strap, Strop, Suede, Tan, Taw, Thong, Upper, Wallop, Wash, Waxed, Welt, White, Whitleather, Yuft

**Leatherneck** Marine, RM

**Leave(r), Leaving(s), Leave off** Abandon, Abiturient, Abscond, Absit, Absquatulate, Acquittal, Adieu, Annual, Avoid, Bequeath, Betake, Blessing, Blow, Broken meats, Bug, Compassionate, Congé, Congee, Days off, Debris, Decamp, Depart, Desert, Desist, Devisal, Devise, Ditch, Evacuate, Except, Exeat, Exit, Exodus, Extrude, Flit, Forego, Forget, Forgo, Forsake, French, Furlough, Gardening, Garlandage, Get out, → **GO**, Hit the road, Holiday, Hop it, Inspan, Ish, Legate, Liberty, Licence, Log off, Maroon, Mass, Maternity, Mizzle, Nick, Omit, Orts, Pace, Parental, Park, Part, Paternity, → **PERMISSION**, Permit, → **QUIT**, Repair, Residue, Resign, Retire, Sabbatical, Scapa, Scat, Scram, Set forth, Shore, Sick(ie), Skedaddle, Skidoo®, Split, Stet, Stick, Strand, Vacate, Vade, Vamo(o)se, Will, Withdraw

**Leaven** Barm, Ferment, Yeast

**Lebanese, Lebanon** Druse, RL

**Lecher(ous), Lechery** Gate, Goaty, Lascivious, Libertine, Lickerish, Lustful, Profligate, Rake, Randy, Roué, Salaciousness, Satirisk, Satyr, Silen, Whoremonger, Wolf

**Lectern** Ambo, Bookstand, Desk, Eagle, Oratory, Pulpit

**Lecture(r), Lectures, Lecturing** Academic, Address, Aristotelian, Chalktalk, Course, Creed, Curtain, Dissert(ator), Docent, Don, Earful, Erasmus, Expound, Harangue, Homily, Hulsean, Jaw, Jawbation, Jobe, L, Lantern, Lector, Lesson, Moralise, Orate, Pi-jaw, Preach, Prelect, Privatdocent, Prone, Rate, Read(er), Rebuke, Rede, Reith, Reprimand, Roasting, Rubber chicken circuit, Scold, Sententious, → **SERMON**, Spout, Take to task, Talk, Teacher, Teach-in, Tirade, Tongue-lashing, Wigging, Yaff

**Ledge** Altar, Berm, Buttery-bar, Channel, Fillet, Gradin(e), Linch, Miserere, Misericord(e), Nut, Rake, Scarcement, Settle, → **SHELF**, Sill, Subsellium, Window (sill)

**Ledger** Book, Cash book, General, Purchase, Register

**Lee(s)** Dregs, Dunder, Grout, Heeltaps, Sediment, Shelter, Ullage

**Leech** Annelid, Bleeder, Gnathobdellida, Hirudinea, Horse, Medicinal, Moocher, Parasite, Rhynchobdellida

**Leek** Allium, Fouat, Fouet, House, Porraceous, Rocambole, Scallion, Sengreen

**Leer(y)** Eliad, Fleer, Mistrustful, Oeillade, Ogle, Perv, Twire

**Leeway** Allowance, Drift, Elbow-room, Flexibility, Latitude

**Left (hand), Left-handed, Left-hander, Left-wing(er)** Abandoned, Adrift, Avoided, Balance, Bolshy, Commie, Corrie-fisted, Dolly-push, Extant, Fellow traveller, Forsaken, Gallock, Haw, Hie, High, Inherited, L, Laeotropic, Laevorotation, Larboard, Links, Loony, Lorn, Marxist, Militant, Near(side), New, Other, Over, Pink, Pinko, Port, Portsider, Prompt side, Quit, Rad, Red (Brigade), Red Shirt, Relic, Residuum, Resigned, Secondo, Set out, Sinister, Soc(ialist), Southpaw, Split, Stage right, Thin, Titoism, Trot, Unused, Verso, Vo, Went, West, Wind, Yet

**Left-over** Astatki, Dregs, End, Gone, Heeltap, Lave, Oddment, Offcut, Orra, Ort, Remains, Remanet, → REMNANT, Residue, Rest, Spare, Uneaten, Unsold, Untouched, Waste

**Leg(s), Leggings, Leggy, Leg-wear** Antigropelo(e)s, Bandy, Barbados, Barley-sugar, Bow, Breeches, Cabriole, Cannon, Chaparajos, Chaparejos, Chaps, Crural, Crus, Cuisse, Cush, Dib, Drumstick, Eleven, Fine, Fly-sail, Gaiter, Galligaskins, Gam(b), Gamash, Gambado, Garter, Garters, Gaskin, Giambeux, Gigot, Gramash, Gramoche, Gramosh, Ham, Haunch, Hest, Hexapod, Hock, Jamb, Jambeau, Jambeaux, Knock-knee(d), Limb, Long, Member, Milk, Myriapod, Oleo, On(side), Peg, Peraeopod, Periopod, Peroneal, Pestle, Pin, Podite, Proleg, Puttees, Putties, Pylon, Relay, Scissor, Sea, Section, Shanks, Shanks's pony, Shaps, Shin, Short, Spats, Spatterdash, Spider, Spindleshanks, Square, Stage, Start up, Stifle, Stump, Thigh, Tights, White

**Legacy** Bequest, Cumulative, Demonstrative, Dowry, Endowment, Entail, General, Heirloom, Heritage, Inheritance, Residuary, Specific, Substitutional

**Legal(ism), Legally, Legitimate** Above board, Bencher, Decriminalised, De regle, Forensic, Halacha, Halaka(h), Halakha, Lawful, Licit, Nomism, Scienter, Statutory, Void

**Legal book** Halacha, Halaka(h), Halakha, Talmud

**Leg-armour, Leg-covering** Cootikin, Cu(i)tikin, Gambado, Jamb(e), Pad

**Legate, Legator** A latere, Ambassador, Consul, Devisor, Emissary, Envoy, Nuncio

**Legatee** Heir

**Legato** Slur

**Legend(ary)** Arthurian, Caption, Edda, Fable, Folklore, Golden, Hadith, Motto, Myth, Saga, Story, Urban, Yowie

▷**Legend** *may indicate* leg-end, e.g. foot, talus

**Leger** Swindler

**Leghorn** Livorno

**Legible** Clear, Lucid, Plain

**Legion(ary), Legionnaire** Alauda, American, Army, Brigade, British, Cohort, Countless, Deserter, Force, Foreign, Geste, Honour, → HOST, Maniple, Many, Throng, Thundering, Zillions

**Legislate, Legislation, Legislator, Legislature** Assemblyman, Backbencher, Congress, Decemvir, Decree, Delegated, Diet, MP, Nomothete, Oireachtas, → PARLIAMENT, Persian, Senator, Solon, Supreme soviet, Thesmothete, Zemstvo

**Legitimate, Legitimise** Above board, Fair game, Kosher, Launder, Loyal, Proper, Rightful, Valid

**Legless** Amelia, Blotto, Boozy, Caecilia, Drunk, Mermaid, Paralytic, Psyche

**Leg-pull** Chaff, Joke, Rise, Rot

**Legume, Leguminous** Bean, Guar, Lentil, Lomentum, Pea, Peanut, Pipi, Pod, Pousse, Pulse, Vetch

**Leibniz** Monadism

**Leicester** Sheep

**Leigh** Amyas

**Leisure(ly)** Adagio, Andantino, Bytime, Ease, Lento, Liberty, Moderato, Off day, Otium, Pastime, Respite, Rest, Unhurried, Vacation

**Leitmotif** Theme

**Lemming** Morkin

**Lemon** Answer, Cedrate, Citron, Citrus, Dud, Smear-dab, Sole, Twist, Yellow

**Lemonade** Pop

**Lemur** Angwantibo, Aye-aye, Babacoote, Bush-baby, Colugo, Cynocephalus, Galago,

Half-ape, Indri(s), Loris, Macaco, Malmag, Mongoose, → MONKEY, Nagapie, Potto, Ringtail, Sifaka, Spectre, Tana, Tarsier

**Lend(er)** Accommodate, Advance, Library, Loan, Prest, Sub, Swap line, Usurer, Vaunce

**Length(y), Lengthen(ing), Lengthwise** Archine, Arsheen, Arshin(e), Aune, Barleycorn, Braccio, Cable, Chain, Cubit, Distance, Duration, Eke, Ell, → ELONGATE, Endways, Ennage, Epenthetic, Expand, Extensive, Feature, Focal, Foot, Footage, Furlong, Inch, Ley, Longitudinal, Mile, Nail, Parsec, Passus, Perch, Piece, Plethron, Pole, Prolate, Prolix, Prolong, Protract, Reach, Remen, Rigmarole, Rod, Rope, Slow, Span, Stadium, Three-quarter, Toise, Vara, Verbose, Yard

**Lenient, Lenience, Leniency** Clement, Exurable, Fiddious, Lax, Mercy, Mild, Permissive, Quarter, Soft, Soft line, Tolerant

**Lens** Achromatic, Acoustic, Anamorphic, Anastigmat, Aplanatic, Apochromat(ic), Bifocal, Bull's eye, Compound, Condenser, Contact, Corneal, Crookes, Crown, Crystalline, Dielectric, Diopter, Dioptre, Diverging, Electron, Electrostatic, Eye, Eyeglass, Eye-piece, Facet, Field, Fish-eye, Fresnel, Gas-permeable, Gravitational, Hard, Immersion, Lentil, Macro, Magnetic, Metallic, Mirror, Object(ive), Object-glass, Optic, Pantoscope, Phacoid, Piano-concave, Piano-convex, Soft, Soft-focus, Stanhope, Sunglass, Teleconverter, Telephoto, Toric, Trifocal, Varifocal, Water, Wide-angle, Zoom

**Lent** Carême, Fast, Laetare, Out, Quadragesimal, Term

**Lentigo** Ephelides

**Lentil(s)** D(h)al, Dholl, Ervalenta, Lens, Phacoid, Pulse, Puy, Revalenta

**Leo** Lion, Sign

**Leonora** Overture

**Leopard** Catamountain, Clouded, Cougar, Hunting, Jaguar, Leap, Libbard, Oceloid, Ocelot, Ounce, Panther, Pard, Snow, Spots, Tiger

**Leopold** Bloom

**Leotard** Maillot

**Leper, Leprosy, Leprous** Gehazi, Hansen's disease, Lazar, Leontiasis, Lionism, Meazel, Mesel, Outcast, Pariah

**Lepidopterist** Aurelian, Moth-er, Pendleton, Treacler

**Leprechaun** Elf, Gremlin, Imp

**Lepton** Muon

**Lesbian** Boi, Homophile, Lipstick, Sapphist, Tribade

**Lese-majesty** Treason

**Lesion** Blister, Cut, Gash, Pannus, Scar, Serpiginous, Sore, Ulcer, Wheal, Whelk

**Less(en), Lessened, Lessening, Lesser** Abate, Alaiment, Attenuate, Bate, Below, Beneath, Comedown, Contract, Deaden, Decline, Deplete, Derogate, Dilute, Diminish, → DWINDLE, Extenuate, Fewer, Imminute, Junior, Littler, Meno, Minus, Play down, Reduce, Relax, Relieve, Remission, Scant, Sen, Shrink, Subordinate, Subsidiary, Tail, Under

**Lesson** Class, Example, Lear(e), Lection, Leir, Lere, Life, Liripipe, Masterclass, Moral, Object, Parashah, Period, Sermon, Shiur, Tutorial

**Let (go, off, out), Letting** Allow, Cap, Charter, Conacre, Displode, Divulge, Enable, Entitle, Explode, Hire, Impediment, Indulge, Leak, Lease, Litten, Loot(en), Luit(en), Lutten, Net, Obstacle, Obstruct, → PERMIT, Rent, Reprieve, Sett, Tenancy, Unhand, Warrant

**Let down** Abseil, Betray, Lower, Sell, Vail

**Let-down** Disappointment, Non-event

**Lethal** Deadly, Fatal, Fell, Mortal

**Lethargic, Lethargy** Accidie, Apathy, Coma, Comatose, Drowsy, Ennui, Hebetude, Inactive, Inertia, Lackadaisical, Lassitude, Limp, Listless, Logy, Passive, Sleepy, Sluggish, Stagnant, Stupor, Supine, Torpid, Torpor, Turgid, Weariness

**Letter(s)** Ache, Aerogram, Aesc, A(y)in, Airgraph, Aleph, Alif, Alpha, Ascender, Aspirate, Bayer, Begging, Beta, Beth, Billet doux, Block, Breve, Cadmean, Canine, Caph, Capital, Capon, Casket, Chain, Cheth, Chi, Chitty, Circular, Col, Collins, Consonant, Covering, Credentials, Cue, Cuneiform, Da(w)k, Daled, Daleth, Dead, Dear John, Delta, Digamma, Digraph, Dispatch, Dog, Dominical, Drop, Edh, Ef(f), E-mail, Emma, Encyclical, Ep(isemon), Epistle, Epistolet, Epsilon, Eta, Eth, Express, Fan, Favour, Form, Fraktur, French, Gamma,

Gimel, Grapheme, He, Heth, Hieratic, Initial, Iota, Izzard, Jerusalem, Jot, Juliet, Kaph, Kappa, Koppa, Kufic, Labda, Lambda, Lamed(h), Landlady, Landlord, Lessee, Lessor, Literal, Love, Mail, Mail-shot, Majuscule, Mem, Memo, Message, Miniscule, Minuscule, Missive, Monogram, Mu, Nasal, Night, Note, Notelet, Nu, Nun, Og(h)am, Omega, Omicron, Open, Ou, Pacifical, Pahlavi, Paragoge, Paston, Pastoral, Patent, Pe(h), Pehlevi, Phi, Philem(on), Pi, Plosive, Poison-pen, Polyphone, Postbag, Psi, Pythagorean, Qof, Qoph, Realtor, Resh, Rho, Rhyme, Rom, Romeo, Runestave, Sad(h)e, Samekh, Samian, Sampi, San, Scarlet, Screed, Screeve, Screwtape, Script, See, Shin, Ship, Sick-note, Siglum, Sigma, Sign, Signal, Sin, Sort, Stiff, Swash, Tau, Tav, Taw, Teth, Theta, Thorn, Toc, Tsade, Typo, Uncial, Upsilon, Vau, Vav, Versal, Vowel, Waw, Wen, Wyn, Wynn, Xi, Yod(h), Yogh, Ypsilon, Zayin, Zed, Zeta

**Lettering** Cufic, Kufic

**Lettuce** Batavia, Butterhead, Cabbage, Chicon, Corn-salad, Cos, Frog's, Iceberg, Lactuca, Lamb's, Little gem, Lollo rosso, Mache, Mizuna, Radicchio, Romaine, Salad, Sea, Thridace

**Leucoma** Albugo

**Levant(ine)** Abscond, Coptic, Go, Israelite, Jew, Ottamite, Ottomite

**Levee** Bank, Durbar, Dyke, Embankment, Party

**Level(ler)** A, Abney, Abreast, Aclinic, Ad eundum, Aim, Awash, Bargaining, Base, Best, Break even, Bulldoze, Champaign, Class, Confidence, Countersink, Dead-heat, Degree, Dumpy, Echelon, Energy, Equal, → **EVEN**, Extent, Eye, Flat, Flight, Flush, Fog, Grade, Ground, High, Horizontal, Impurity, Infill, Logic, Low, Meet, Neck and neck, O, Occupation, Ordinary, Par, Plain, Planation, Plane, Plat(eau), Point, Price, Race, Rank, Rase, Raze, Reduced, Savanna, Sea, Spirit, Split, Springing, → **SQUARE**, Stage, Status, Step, Stor(e)y, Stratum, Street, Strew, Strickle, Subsistence, Summit, Support, Surveyor's, Tear-down, Tier, Top, Trophic, True, Water, Wye, Y

**Lever(age)** Backfall, Bell-crank, Brake, Catch, Cock, Control, Crampon, Crowbar, Dues, Gear, Handspike, Jaw, Jemmy, Joystick, Key, Knee-stop, Landsturm, Pawl, Peav(e)y, Pedal, Pinch, Prise, Prize, Pry, Purchase, Stick, Sweep, Swipe, Tappet, Throttle, Tiller, Treadle, Treddle, Tremolo arm, Trigger, Tumbler, Typebar, Whipstaff

**Leveret** Hare

**Leviathan** Titan, Whale

**Levitate, Levitation** Float, Hover, Magnetic, Rise, Yogic flying

**Levity** Flippancy, Glee, Humour, Jollity

**Levy** Capital, Estreat, Impose, Imposition, Leave, Militia, Octroi, Raise, Scutage, Stent, Talliate, Tax, Tithe, Toll

**Lewd(ness)** Bawd(r)y, Blue, Cyprian, Debauchee, Impure, Libidinous, Lubricity, Obscene, Priapism, Prurient, Raunchy, Silen(us), Tentigo, Unclean

**Lewis** Carroll, Tenon

**Lexicographer, Lexicon** Compiler, Craigie, Drudge, Etymologist, Florio, Fowler, Glossarist, Grove, Johnson(ian), Larousse, Liddell, Mental, Murray, OED, Thesaurus, Vocabulist, Webster, Words-man

**Liability, Liable** Anme, Apt, Chance, Current, Debt, Employer's, Incur, Limited, Onus, Open, Product, Prone, Public, Subject, Susceptible, White elephant

**Liaison** Affair, Amour, Contact, Entanglement, Link

**Liana** Guarana

**Libel(lous)** Blasphemous, Defamatory, Malign, Sclaunder, Slander, Smear, Sully, Vilify

**Liberal(ity)** Abundant, Adullamites, Ample, Besant, Bounteous, Bountiful, Breadth, Bright, Broad(minded), Catholic, Charitable, Classical, Enlightened, Free(hander), Free-hearted, → **GENEROUS**, Giver, Grey, Grimond, Grit, Handsome, Indulgent, L, Laissez-faire, Largesse, Latitudinarian, Lavish, Limousine, Munificent, Octobrist, Open, Permissive, → **PROFUSE**, Rad(ical), Right on, Samuelite, Simonite, Soft, Spender, Steel, Tolerant, Trivium, Unstinted, Verlig, Verligte, Whig, Widespread

**Liberate(d), Liberation, Liberationist, Liberator** Animal, Bolivar, Deliver, Dissimure, Emancipate, Fatah, → **FREE**, Gay, Inkatha, Intolerant, Messiah, Nick, PLO, Redeem, Release, Rescue, Risorgimento, Save, Steal, Sucre, Unchain, Unfetter, UNITA, Women's

**Liberian** Kroo, Kru

**Libertarian, Libertine** Chartered, Corinthian, Debauchee, Don Juan, Gay deceiver, Laxist, Lecher, Lothario, Lovelace, Orgiast, Palliard, Playboy, Rake, Rip, Roué, Wencher, Wolf

**Liberty** Bail, Civil, Discretion, Franchise, Freedom, Hall, Ish, Latitude, Licence, Mill, Presumption, Sauce, Statue

**Libido, Libidinous** Lust, Prurient, Satyric

**Libra** L

**Library, Librarian** Bibliothecary, BL, Bodleian, Bookmobile, British, Chartered, Circulating, Copyright, Cottonian, Dewey, Dynamic link, Film, Gene, Genomic, Harleian, Laurentian, Lending, Mazarin, Mobile, Morgue, PL, Public, Radcliffe, Reference, Rental, Subscription, Tauchnitz

**Librettist** Boito, Da Ponte, Gilbert, Hammerstein, Lerner, Lyricist

▸**Lice** *see* **LOUSE (UP)**

**Licence, License, Licensing** Abandon, Allow, Authorisation, Carnet, Charter, Copyleft, Dispensation, Driving, Enable, Entitle, Exequatur, Export, Fling, Franchise, Free(dom), Gale, Game, Import, Imprimatur, Indult, → **LATITUDE**, Let, Liberty, Marriage, Occasional, Passport, Patent, → **PERMIT**, Poetic, Pratique, Provisional, Road-fund, Rope, Slang, Special, Table, Ticket of leave, Warrant

**Licentious** Artistic, Corinthian, Debauchee, Depraved, Hot, Immoral, Large, Lax, Liberal, Loose, Orgiastic, Prurient, Ribald, Sensual, Wanton

**Lichen** Apothecia, Archil, Corkir, Crotal, Crottle, Cup, Epiphyte, Epiphytic, Graphis, Korkir, Lecanora, Litmus, Moss, Oakmoss, Orcein, Orchel, Orchil(la), Orcine, Orseille, Parella, Parelle, Roccella, Rock tripe, Sea-ivory, Soredium, Stone-rag, Stone-raw, Tree-moss, Usnea, Wartwort

**Lick(ing)** Bat, Beat, Deer, Felch, Lambent, Lap, Leather, Rate, Salt, Slake, Speed, Tongue, Trounce, Whip

▸**Licorice** *see* **LIQUORICE**

**Lid(ded)** Cloche, Cover, Crust, Hat, Kid, Maximum, Opercula, Screwtop, Stegocarpus, Twist-off

**Liddell** Alice

**Lido** Beach, Pool

**Lie(s), Liar, Lying** Abed, Accubation, Accumbent, Ananias, Bam, Bare-faced, Bask, Billy, Bounce(r), Braide, Calumny, Cau(l)ker, Cellier, Clipe, Clype, Concoction, Consist, Contour, Couch(ant), Cracker, Cram(mer), Cretism, Cumbent, Deception, Decubitous, Decumbent, Direct, Doggo, Fable, Fairytale, False(r), Falsehood, Falsify, Falsity, Fib, Fiction, Figment, Flam, Gag, Gonk, Hori, Incumbent, Invention, Inveracity, Kip, Lair, Leasing, Lee(ar), Lig(ge), Lurk, Matilda, Mythomania, Nestle, Obreption, Oner, Perjury, Plumper, Porky (pie), Procumbent, Prone, Prostrate, Pseudologia, Recline, Recumbent, Repent, Repose, Reptant, Ride, Romance(r), Sham, Sit, Sleep, Strapper, Stretcher, Supine, Swinger, Tale, Tappice, Tar(r)adiddle, Thumper, Tissue, Try, Untruth, Whacker, Whid, White, Whopper, Yanker

**Lied** Art-song, Serenade, Song

**Lie-detector** Polygraph

**Lien** Mortgage, Title

**Lieu** Locus, Place, Stead

**Lieutenant** Cassio, Flag, Loot, Lord, Lt, No 1, Sub(altern)

**Life** Age, Animation, Artificial, Being, Bio, Biog(raphy), Biota, Breath, Brian, Brio, Career, C'est la vie, Chaim, Clerihew, CV, Energy, Esse, Eva, Eve, Existence, Good, Heart, High, Innings, Low, Mean, Memoir, Mortal coil, Nellie, Nelly, Night, Nomogeny, Non-fiction, Pep, Plasma, Private, Public, Quick, Real, Riley, Shelf, Span, Spirit, Still, Subsistence, Time, True, Useful, Vita, Vitality, Zing, Zoe

**Life-blood** Essence, Lethee

**Lifeboat(man)** Ark, Noah

**Life-cell** Energid

**Life-cycle** Redia

**Life-force, Life-style** Chi, Mana, Od, Orgone, Port, Qi

**Lifeless(ness)** Abiosis, Algidity, Amort, Arid, Azoic, Barren, Catatonic, Cauldrife, → **DEAD**, Dull, Dusty, Exanimate, Flat, Inanimate, Inert, Key-cold, Lank, Log, Mineral, Possum, Stagnant, Sterile, Stonen, Vapid, Wooden

**Lifelike** Android, Breathing, Natural, Realistic, Speaking
**Lifeline** Umbilicus
**Life-rent** Usufruct
**Life-saver** Cheesemonger, Coastguard, Lineman, Mae West, Preserver, Raft, Reelman
**Lift(ed), Lifter, Lifting** Antidepressant, Araise, Arayse, Arsis, Attollent, Bone, Cable-car, Camel, Chair, Clean and jerk, Cly, Copy, Crane, Davit, Dead, Drag, Dumb waiter, Elate, Elevator, Enhance, Exalt, Extol, Filch, Fillip, Fireman's, Greaten, Heave, Heeze, Heezie, Heft(e), Heighten, Heist, Hitch, Hoise, Hoist, Hove, Jack, Jigger, Kleptomania, Leaven, Lefte, Lever, Lewis, Nab, Nap, Nim, Otis®, Paternoster, Pickaback, Piggyback, Pilfer, Press, Pulley, → RAISE, Ride, Rotor, Scoop, Service, Shearlegs, Shop, Ski, Sky, Snatch, Sneak, Spout, Stair, Steal, Surface, T-bar, Teagle, Theft, Thumb, Topping, Up, Weight, Winch, Windlass
**Lig** Mooch
**Ligament** Annular, Cruciate, Fr(a)enum, Paxwax, Peacock-stone, Spring, Suspensory, Tendon, Urachus
**Ligation, Ligature** Ae(sc), Ash, Bandage, Bind, Funicle, Knot, Tubal
**Light(en), Lighter, Light holder, Lighting, Lights** Aerate, Afterglow, Airglow, Airy, Albedo, Ale, Alleviate, Alow, Alpenglow, Amber, Ancient, Ans(wer), Arc, Arson, Aurora, Back-up, Barge, Batement, Batswing, Beacon, Beam, Belisha beacon, Bengal, Beshine, Bezel, Birlinn, Black, Bleach, Blond(e), Brake, Breezy, Bright, Bude, Bulb, Bull's eye, Buoyant, Calcium, Candelabra, Candle, Cannel, Canstick, Casco, Casement, Chandelier, Chiaroscuro, Cierge, Clue, Courtesy, Day(time), Dewali, Dewbow, Diffused, Direct, Diwali, Dormer, Dream-hole, Drop, Drummond, Earth, Earth-shine, Ease, Eddystone, Electrolier, Ethereal, Eulachon, Fair, Fairy, Fall, Fan, Fantastic, Fastnet, Feathery, Fetch-candle, Fidibus, Fill, Filter, Fire, First, Fixed, Flambeau, Flame, Flare, Flash, Flax(y), Flicker, Flimsy, Flippant, Flit(t), Floating, Flood, Fluffy, Fluorescent, Fog (lamp), Frothy, Fuffy, Gas, Gas-poker, Gegenschein, Glare, Gleam, Glim(mer), Glow, Gossamer, Green, Guiding, Gurney, Haggis, Halation, Halogen, Harbour, Hazard, Head, House, Idiot, Ignite, Illum(in)e, Incandescence, Indirect, Induction, Inner, Irradiate, Junior, Keel, Key, Kindle, Kiran, Klieg, Lamp, Lampadary, Lampion, Land, Lantern, Lanthorn, Laser, Leading, LED, Leerie, Leggiero, Lenient, Levigate, Lime, Link, Linstock, Loadstar, Lobuli, Lodestar, Loop, Lozen, Lucarne, Lucigen, Luminaire, Lumine, Luminescence, Luminous, Lungs, Lunt, Lustre, Lux, Mandorla, Match, Menorah, Mercurial, Merry-dancers, Mithra(s), Moon, Naphtha, Navigate, Navigation, Neon, New, Night, Nit, Northern, Obstruction, Od(yl), Offal, Offload, Optics, Owl, Oxycalcium, Pale, Pane, Parhelion, Pavement, Pennyweight, Phosphene, Phosphorescence, Phot(ic), Photon, Photosphere, Pilot, Pipe, Polar, Pontoon, Portable, Porthole, Pra(a)m, Producer-gas, Rainbow, Range, Rear, Red, Reflex, Relax, Relieve, Relume, Rembrandt, Reversing, Riding, Robot, Rocket, Running, Rush, Safe(ty), St Elmo's fire, Satori, Scoop, Scow, Sea-dog, Sea fire, Search, Shine, Shy, Side, Signal, Solid-state, Southern, Southern-vigil, Sparse, Spill, Spot, Spry, Star, Steaming, Strip, Strobe, Stroboscope, Subtle, Sun (lamp), Sunshine, Suttle, Svelte, Tail, Tally, Taper, Taps, Tead, Thistledown, Threshold, Tind, Tine, Torch, Torchère, Torchiere, Touchpaper, Track, Traffic, Trivial, Ultraviolet, Unchaste, Unoppressive, UV, Ver(e)y, Vesica, Vesta, Vigil, Watch, Wax, Welsbach burner, White, Windock, → WINDOW, Winker, Winnock, Zippo, Zodiacal
▹**Light** *may indicate* an anagram
**Lighterman** Bargee
**Light-headed** Captious, Dizzy, Giddy, Kicksin
**Light-hearted** Carefree, Flippant, Gay
**Lighthouse** Beacon, Caisson, Eddystone, Fanal, Fastnet, Needles, Phare, Pharos, Sea-mark, Signal, Spurn
**Lightless** Aphotic, Dark, Obscure, Unlit
**Lightness** Buoyancy, Galant, Levity, Pallor
**Lightning** Ball, Bolt, Catequil, Chain, Dry, Éclair, Enfouldered, Fireball, Fire flag, Forked, Fulmination, Heat, Levin, Sheet, Summer, Thunderbolt, Wildfire, Zigzag
**Lightship** Floating beacon, Nore
**Lightweight** Jack straw, Nobody, Oz, Trivial
**Lignite** Jet, Surtarbrand, Surturbrand

**Like(ness), Liken, Liking** Affinity, À la, Analogon, Anon, Appetite, As, Assimilate, Attachment, Broo, Care, Corpse, Dead spit, Depict, Dig, Duplicate, Effigy, Eg, Egal(ly), Enjoy, Equal, Fancy, Fellow, Fondness, Guise, Isogeny, Lap up, Lich, Palate, Parallel, Peas, Penchant, -philus, Please, Portrait, Predilection, Prefer, Resemblance, Semblant, Shine, Similar, Simile, Similitude, Simulacrum, Smaak, Sort, Speaking, Taste, Tiki, Uniformity

**Likely, Likelihood** Apt, Chance, Evens, Fair, Liable, Maximum, Odds-on, Offchance, On, Plausible, Possible, Probable, Probit, Prone, Prospective

**Likewise** Also, Ditto, Do, Egally, Eke, Item, Similarly, So, Too, Tu quoque

**Lilac** French, Laylock, Mauve, Pipe-tree, Syringa

**Lilliputian** Minute

**Lilt** Burr, Swing

**Lily** African, Agapanthus, Allium, Aloe, Amaryllis, Annunciation, Arum, Asphodel, Aspidistra, Belladonna, Blackberry, Calla, Camas(h), Camass, Canada, Candock, Chincherinchee, Colchicum, Colocasia, Convallaria, Corn, Crinum, Daffodil, Dale, Day, Easter, Elaine, Endogen, Fawn, Fleur de lys, Fritillary, Funkia, Galtonia, Guernsey, Haemanthus, Hellebore, Hemerocallis, Herb-Paris, Jacobean, Jacob's, Jersey, Kniphofia, Laguna, Lent, Leopard, Lote, Lotos, Lotus, Madonna, Mariposa, Martagon, Meadow, Moorva, Mount Cook, Nelumbo, Nenuphar, Nerine, Nuphar, Nymphaea, Orange, Padma, Phormium, Pig, Plantain, Pond, Quamash, Regal, Richardia, Sabadilla, Sansevieria, Sarsa, Scilla, Sego, Skunk cabbage, Smilax, Solomon's seal, Spider, Star of Bethlehem, Stone, Sword, Tiger, Trillium, Tritoma, Tuberose, Turk's cap, Vellozia, Victoria, Water, Water maize, Yucca, Zephyr

**Lily-maid** Elaine

**Lima** L, Sugar bean

**Limb** Arm, Bough, Branch, Crural, Exapod, Flipper, Forearm, Hindleg, Imp, Leg, Leg-end, Member, Phantom, Proleg, Pterygium, Ramus, Scion, Shin, Spald, Spall, Spaul(d), Wing

**Limbless** Amelia

**Limbo** Bardo, Isolation, Oblivion

**Lime** Bass(wood), Beton, Bird, Calc, Calcicolous, Caustic, Lind(en), Malm, Mortar, Shell, Slaked, Soda, Teil, Tilia, Trap, Unslaked, Viscum, Whitewash

**Limerick** Doggerel, Twiner, Verse

**Limestone** Burren, Calcil, Calc-sinter, Calm, Calp, Ca(u)m, Clint, Coquina, Coral Rag, Cornbrash, Cornstone, Dolostone, Forest Marble, Grike, Karst, Kentish rag, Kunkar, Kunkur, Landscape marble, Magnesian, Malm, Marble, Muschelkalk, Nero-antico, Oolite, Pisolite, Rottenstone, Sarcophagus, Scaglia, Stalagma, Stinkstone, Stylolitic, Travertin(e), Tufa

**Limey** Rooinek, Seafarer

**Limit(ation), Limited, Limiting** Ambit, Apolune, Asymptote, Basebound, Bind, Border, Borné, Bound, Boundary, Bourn(e), Brief, Brink, Cap, Cash, Ceiling, Chandrasekhar, Circumscribe, Climax, Compass, Confine, Constrain, Constrict, Credit, Curb, Cut-off, Deadline, Define, Demarcate, Demark, Determine, Earshot, Eddington, Edge, Edition, Elastic, End, Entail, Esoteric, Exclusive, Exhaustible, → EXTENT, Extreme, Finite, Fraenum, Frontier, Gate, Goal, Gole, Height, Horizon, Hourlong, Impound, Induciae, Inhibit, Insular, Limes, Line, Lite, Lynchet, March, Margin, Maximum, Meare, Mete, Minimum, Mortal, Narrow, Nth, Outedge, Pale, Parameter, Partial, Peg, Perimeter, Periphery, Predetermine, Prescribe, Qualify, Range, Rate-cap, Ration, Reservation, Restrict, Rim, Roche, Roof, Saturation point, Scant, Scrimp, Shoestring, Shortcoming, Short-term, Sky, Somedeal, Somedele, Speed, Stint, String, Sumptuary, Tail(lie), Tailye, Tailzie, Term(inus), Tether, Three-mile, Threshold, Thule, Tie, Time, Tramline, Tropic, Twelve-mile, Ultimate, Utmost, Utter, Verge

▷**Limit** *may indicate* 'surrounding'

**Limner** RA

**Limousine** Daimler, Rolls, Stretch, Zil

**Limp** Claudication, Dot, Droopy, Flabby, Flaccid, Flaggy, Flimsy, Floppy, Gimp, Hamble, Hilch, Hirple, Hitch, Hobble, Hop, Lank, Lifeless, Spancel, Tangle, Wilting

**Limpet** Keyhole, Patella, Slipper, Streptoneura

**Limpid** Clear, Lucid, Pure

**Linch** Terrace

**Lincoln(shire)** Abe, Poacher, Yellow-belly
**Linden** Baucis, Lime, Tilia
**Line(d), Lines, Lining** Abreast, Aclinic, Agate, Agonic, Allan, Anacreontic, → ANCESTRY, Anent, Angle, Apothem, Arew, Asclepiadean, Assembly, Asymptote, Attention, Axis, Babbitt, Bakerloo, Bar, Barcode, Baton, Battle, Baulk, Becket, Bikini, Bluebell, Bob, Body, Bombast, Bottom, Boundary, BR, Brail, Brake, Branch, Brand, Bread, Building, Bush, By, Cable, Canal, Caravan, Carolingian, Carriage, Casing, Cathetus, Ceil, Cento, Central, Ceriph, Chord, Ciel, Circle, Clew, Clothes, Club, Coach, Coffle, Colour, Column, Command, Conga, Contour, Cord(on), Coseismal, Course, Crease, Credit, Crib, Crocodile, Crosshatch, Crowfoot, Crow's feet, Cunard, Curve, Cushion, Dancette, Danger, Date, Datum, Dead-ball, Decidua, Delay, Descent, DEW, Diagonal, Diameter, Diffusion, Directrix, Distaff, District, Dochmiachal, Doggerel, Dotted, Doublure, Downhaul, Downrigger, Dress, Dynasty, Earing, El, E-la-mi, Encase, End, Equator, Equinoctial, Equinox, Faint, Fall(s), Fathom, Fault, Feint, Fess(e), Fettle, File, Finishing, Firing, Firn, Fixed, Flex, Flight, Frame, Fraunhofer, Front, Frontier, Frost, Furr(ow), Geodesic, Geotherm, Germ, Gimp, Girdle of Venus, Giron, Goal, Graph, Grass, Green, Gridiron, Gymp, Gyron, Hachure, Hairstroke, Halyard, Hard, Hatching, Hawser, Header, Hemistich, Heptameter, Hexameter, Hexapody, High-watermark, Hindenburg, Hockey, Hogscore, Hot, House, Impot, Inbounds, Inbred, Incase, Inhaul(er), Insole, Interfluve, Intima, Isallobar, Isentrope, Isobar, Isobath, Isobront, Isocheim, Isochime, Isochron(e), Isoclinic, Isoclude, Isocryme, Isogloss, Isogonal, Isogonic, Isogram, Isohel, Isohyet, Isolex, Isomagnetic, Isometric, Isonome, Isopach(yte), Isophone, Isophote, Isopiestic, Isopleth, Isopycnic, Isopyenal, Isotach, Isothere, Isotherm, Jubilee, Kill, Knittle, L, Land, Lane, Lansker, Lap, Lariat, Lasso, Lateral, Latitude, Lead, Leash, Le(d)ger, Length, Ley, Lie, Ling, LMS, Load, Log, Longitude, Lossy, Loxodrome, Lubber, Lugger, Lye, Macron, Maginot, Main, Mainsheet, Mark, Marriage, Mason-Dixon, Median, Meridian, Mesal, Metropolitan, Miurus, Monofilament, Monorail, Multiplet, Nacre, Naman, Nazca, Nidation, Night, Noose, Norsel, Northern, Number, Oche, Octastichon, Ode, Oder-Neisse, Og(h)am, Omentum, Onedin, Ordinate, Orphan, Orthostichy, Painter, Panty, Parallel, Parameter, Parastichy, Party, Paternoster, Path, Penalty, Pencil, Phalanx, Piccadilly, Picket, Pinstripe, Pipe, Plasterboard, Pleuron, Plimsoll, Plumb, Poetastery, Polar, Police, Policy, Popping-crease, Potichomania, Poverty, Power, Princess, Procession, Product(ion), Profession, Punch, Pure, Queue, Race, Radial, Radius, Rail, Rank, Raster, Ratlin(e), Ratling, Rattlin, Ray, Receiving, Red, Reticle, Retinue, Rew, Rhumb, Ridge, Ripcord, Rope, Route, Row, Rubicon, Rugose, Rugous, Rule, Ry, Sarking, Scazon, Score, Scotch, Scratch, Scrimmage, Script, Seam, Secant, Seperatrix, Serif, Seriph, Service, Set, Shielded, Shore, Shout, Shroud, Side, Siding, Siegfried, Sield, Sight, Silver, Six-yard, Slur, Snood, Snow, Soft, Solidus, Sounding, Specialty, Spectral, Spider, Spilling, Spring, Spunyarn, Squall, SR, Staff, Stance, Stanza, Starting, Static, Stave, Stean, Steen, Stein, Stem, Stich(os), Stock, Story, Strain, Strap, Streak, Strene, Stretch mark, Striate, String, Stripe, Stuff, Subject, Subtense, Swap, Swifter, Symphysis, Syzygy, Tag, Tailback, Talweg, Tangent, Teagle, Tea lead, Terminator, Tetrameter, Thalweg, Thin blue, Thin red, Thread, Throwaway, Tidemark, Tie, Tier, Tiercet, Tightrope, Timber, Touch, Tow, Trade, Transmission, Transoceanic, Transversal, Tree, Trimeter, Tropic, Trot, Trunk, Try, Tudor, Twenty-five, Twenty-two, Twiddling, Upstroke, Variety, Verse, Victoria, Vinculum, Virgule, Wad, Wainscot, Waistcoat, Wallace's, Washing, Water(shed), Waterloo, White, Widow, Windrow, Wire, World, Wrinkle, Yellow, Z, Zag, Zip, Zollner's
**Lineage** Ancestry, Descent, Extraction, Filiation, Parage, Pedigree
**Linear** Straight
**Linen** Amice, Amis, Barb, Bed, Byssus, Cambric, Crash, Damask, Dirty, Dornick, Dowlas, Duck, Ecru, Flax, Harn, Huckaback, Inkle, Lawn, Line, Lint, Lockram, Moygashel, Napery, Osnaburg, Percale, Seersucker, Sendal, Silesia, Snow, Table, Toile, Undies
**Liner** Artist, Bin-bag, Eye, Ocean greyhound, RMS, Rule(r), Ship, Sleeve, Steamer, Steen, Titanic
**Linesman** Beeching, Parodist, → POET, Rhymer, Touch-judge, Versifier
**Ling** Heather
**Linger(ing)** Chronic, Dally, Dawdle, Dwell, Hang, Hove(r), Lag, Loaf, → LOITER, Straggle, Taigle, Tarry, Tie

**Lingerie** Bra, Drawers, Teddy, Undies
**Lingo** Argot, Bat, Cant, Jargon, Patter, Polglish, Speech
**Linguist(ic), Linguistics** Chomskey, Clitic, Comparative, Descriptive, Glottic, Historical, Onomastics, Philological, Phonemics, Polyglot, Pragmatics, Semantics, Structural, Stylistics, Syntax, Tagmemics, Taxeme
**Liniment** Balm, Camphor, Carron-oil, Embrocation, Ointment, Opodeldoc, Salve
**Link(ed), Linking, Links** Adaptor, Associate, Between, Bond, Bracket, Bridge, Cause, Chain, Cleek, Close knit, Colligate, Concatenation, Conjunction, Connect, Copula, Couple, Course, Cross-reference, Cuff, Desmid, Drag, Draw-gear, Ess, Flambeau, Golf (course), Hookup, Hot, Hotline, Hyphen, Incatenation, Index, Interconnect, Interface, Internet, Interrelation, Intertwine, Join, Karabiner, Key, Krab, Ley-line, Liaise, Machair, Missing, Modem, Network, Nexus, On-line, Pons, Preposition, Reciprocal, Relate, Ring, Segue, Tead(e), Terrestrial, → **TIE**, Tie-in, Tie-line, Torch, Twin, Unite, Weakest, Wormhole, Yoke
**Linkman** Lamplighter, Mediator
**Linnet** Finch, Lintie, Lintwhite, Twite
**Linoleum** Waxcloth
**Lint** Charpie, Dossil
**Lintel** Summer, Transom
**Lion(ess)** Androcles, Aphid, Aslan, Chindit, Cotswold, Elsa, Glitterati, Hero, Leo, Leopard, Literary, Maned, Mountain, Nemean, Opinicus, Personage, Pride, Puma, Simba
**Lionel** Trilling
**Lion-tamer** Androcles, Dan(iel)
**Lip(py), Lips** Backchat, Beestung, Cheek, Cupid's bow, Fat, Fipple, Flews, Hare, Helmet, Insolence, Jib, Labellum, Labial, Labiate, Labret, Labrum, Ligula, Muffle, Philtrum, → **RIM**, Rubies, Sass, Sauce, Slack-jaw, Spout, Submentum
**Lipase** Steapsin
**Lipid** Ganglioside, Inositol, Sphingarine
**Lipstick** Chapstick
**Liquefy** Deliquesce, Dissolve, Fuse, Melt
**Liqueur, Liquor** Bree, Brew, Broo, Broth, Creature, Elixir, Fumet, Hard stuff, Hooch, Lap, Mother, Ooze, Pot, Potation, Stock, Stuff, Vat

---

## LIQUEURS

*3 letters:*
Ale
Kir
Rum

*4 letters:*
Apry
Feni
Malt
Ouzo
Raki
Rose
Tape
Tiff
Tift
Wine
Wort

*5 letters:*
Anise
Crème
Fenny
Hogan
Hogen
Kirsh
Lager
Mobby
Noyau
Pasha
Rakee
Sabra
Skink
Stout
Toddy

*6 letters:*
Cassis
Cerise
Chasse
Chicha
Eggnog
Enzian
Kahlua®
Kirsch
Kummel
Mastic
Midori®
Mobbie
Pastis
Pernod®
Porter
Rakija
Roiano
Rotgut
Shypoo
Stingo
Strega®
Strunt

*7 letters:*
Chococo
Curaçao
Fraises
Fustian
Persico
Ratafia
Roncoco
Sambuca
Samshoo
Sloe gin
Taplash
Tequila

*8 letters:*
Abisante
Absinthe
Advokaat
Amaretto
Anisette
Calvados
Choclair
Cocoribe
Drambuie®
Galliano
Geropiga
Kaoliang
Prunelle
Rum shrub
Schnapps
Sciarada
Tia Maria®
Witblits

*9 letters:*
Cointreau®
Framboise
Irish Mist
Metheglin
Mirabelle
Triple sec
Van der Hum®

*10 letters:*
Almondrado
Chartreuse

Cher-suisse
Hogan-mogen
Limoncello
Maraschino
Mickey Finn
Pousse-café

***11 letters:***
Aguardiente
Benedictine
Jungle juice
Kirshwasser
Tickle-brain

***12 letters:***
Cherry brandy
Crème de cacao
Grand Marnier®
Kirschwasser
Supernaculum

***13 letters:***
Cherry Marnier®
Crème de menthe
Eau des creoles
Parfait d'amour

***14 letters:***
John Barleycorn
White lightning

---

**Liquid(ate), Liquidise(r), Liquidity, Liquids, Liquefaction** Acetal, Amortise, Annihilate, Apprize, Aqua-regia, Azeotrope, Bittern, Blash, Blend, Bouillon, Bromine, Butanal, Butanol, Butyraldehide, Butyrin, Cacodyl, Cadaverine, Cash, Cash flow, Chloramine, Cinerin, Clyster, Condenser, Coumarone, Court-bouillon, Creosol, Creosote, Decoction, Dispersant, Dope, Eluate, Erase, Ethanal, Ethanol, Ether, Eucalyptol, Eugenol, Flow, Fluid, Fural, Furfural, Furol, Guaiacol, Halothene, Hydraulic, Indisputable, Ink, Isoprene, Jaw, Juice, Kakodyl, Lewisite, Limonene, Linalool, Log, Lye, Massacre, Mess, Minim, Mouillé, Nebula, Picamar, Pipe, Potion, Protoplasm, PSL, Ptisan, Purge, Pyrrole, Pyrrolidine, Quinoline, Raffinate, Rhigolene, Safrole, Sap, Semen, Serum, Smectic, Solution, Solvent, Syrup, Terebene, Thinner, Thixotropy, Titer, Titre, Triptane, Tuberculin, Tusche, Ullage, Unset, Verjuice, Washing-up, Whey, Wind up, Wort

**Liquorice** Aniseed, Indian, Jequirity, Nail, Nail-rod, Pomfret, Pontefract-cake, Spanish juice, Sugarallie, Sugarally, Wild

**Lis** Iris, Lily

**Lisa** Mona

**Lisp(er)** Ephraimite, Sibilance

**Lissom(e)** Agile, Lithe, Nimble, Supple, Svelte

**List(s), Listed, Listing** A, Active, Agenda, Antibarbarus, Appendix, Arena, Army, Atilt, B, Barocco, Barrace, Bead-roll, Bibliography, Bill, Border, British, Bullet point, Calendar, Canon, Cant, Catalog(ue), Categorise, Catelog, Cause, Check, Choice, Chronicle, Civil, Class, Clinamen, Compile, Credits, Danger, Debrett, Detail, Docket, Empanel, Entry, Enumerate, Free, Front, Glossary, Hark, Hearken, Heel, Hit, Hit-parade, Honours, Incline, Index, Indian, Interdiction, Inventory, Itemise, Laundry, Lean, Leet, Line-up, Linked, Litany, Lloyds, Mailing, Manifest, Menu, Navy, Notitia, Official, Panel, Paradigm, Party, Payroll, Portfolio, Price, Prize, Register, Repertoire, Reserved, Retired, Roin, Roll, Roon, Roster, Rota, Rund, Schedule, Script, Scroll, Short, Sick, Slate, Slope, Statement, Strip, Summer Roll, Syllabary, Syllabus (of Errors), Table, Tariff, Tick, Ticket, Tilt, Timetable, Tip, To-do, Transfer, Union, Waiting, Waybill, White, Wine, Wish

▷**List** *may indicate* 'listen'

**Listen(er)** Attend, Auditor, Auscultate, Bug, Ear, Earwig, Eavesdropper, Gobemouche, Hark, → HEED, List, Lithe, Lug, Monitor, Oyez, Simon, Sithee, Stethoscope, Tune-in, Wire-tap, Yo-ho(-ho)

▷**Listen to** *may indicate* a word sounding like another

**Lister** Plough, Surgeon

**Listless(ness)** Abulia, Accidie, Acedia, Apathetic, Atony, Dawney, Draggy, Ennui, Ex-directory, Inanition, Indolent, Lackadaisical, Languor, Mooning, Mope, Mopus, Sloth, Thowless, Torpor, Upsitting, Waff

**Lit** Alight, English, Flambe, Floodlight, Landed

▷**Lit** *may indicate* an anagram

**Litany** Eirenicon, Lesser, Procession, Synapte

**Lite** Fat-free

**Literacy** Emotional

**Literal(ly), Literal sense** Etymon, Misprint, Simply, Typo, Verbatim, Word for word

**Literary** Academic, Bas bleu, Booksie, Erudite, Lettered

**Literary girls** Althea, Jenny, Maud, Pippa

**Literature** Agitprop, Belles lettres, Comparative, Corpus, Edda, Fiction, Gongorism, Grey,

Hagiology, Midrash, Musar, Page, Picaresque, Poesy, Polite, Prose, Responsa, Samizdat, Sci-fi, Splatterpunk, Sturm und Drang, Wisdom

**Lithe** Flexible, Limber, Pliant, Sinuous, Souple, → SUPPLE, Svelte, Willowy

**Lithium** Li

**Litigant** Barrator, John-a-Nokes, John-a-Stiles, John Doe, Party, Richard Roe, Suer, Suitor

**Litmus** Indicator, Lacmus, Lichen, Turnsole

**Litre** L

**Litter** Bed, Brancard, Brood, Cacolet, Cat, Cot, Cubs, Debris, Deep, Doolie, Duff, Emu-bob, Farrow, Jampan, Kago, Kajawah, Kindle, Lumber, Mahmal, Mor, Nest, Norimon, Palankeen, Palanquin, Palkee, Palki, Pup, → REFUSE, Scrap, Sedan, Stretcher, Sweepings, Team, Whelp, Young

**Little** Bagatelle, Beans, Bijou, Billee, Brief, Chicken feed, Chota, Crumb, Curn, Degree, Diddy, Dorrit, Drib, Drop, Dwarf, Fewtrils, Fraction, Haet, Hait, Hate, Ickle, Inconsiderable, Insect, Iota, John, Jot, Leet, Lilliputian, Limited, Lite, Lyte, Manikin, Means, Mini, Miniscule, Minnow, Minuscule, → MINUTE, Modicum, Morceau, Nell, Paltry, Paucity, Paul, Petite, Pink, Pittance, Ronte, Runt, Scant, Scut, Shade, Shoestring, Short, Shred, Shrimp, Slight, Sliver, Sma', → SMALL, Smattering, Smidge(o)n, Smidgin, Smout, Smowt, Some, Soupçon, Spot, Tad, Teensy(-weensy), Tich, Tiddly, Tine, Titch, Touch, Tyne, Unimportant, Vestige, Wee, Weedy, Whit, Women

**Littoral** Coast(al), Strand

**Liturgical, Liturgy** Divine, Doxology, Hallel, Rite, Shacharis, Versicle

**Live(d), Livelihood, Living, Liveliness, Lively, Lives** Abide, Active, Advowson, Agile, Alert, Allegretto, Allegro, Am, Animated, Animation, Animato, Are, AV, Awake, Be, Benefice, Biont, Birkie, Board, Boisterous, Bouncy, Bread, Breezy, Brio, Brisk, Canonry, Cant(y), Capriccio(so), Cheery, Chipper, Chirpy, Cohabit, Con brio, Con moto, Con spirito, Crouse, Crown, Crust, Daily bread, Dash, Durante vita, → DWELL, Dynamic, Ebullient, Energetic, Entrain, Esprit, Euthenics, Exist, Extant, Exuberant, Feisty, Frisky, Galliard, Gamy, Gay, Giocoso, Glebe, Gracious, Grig, Hang-out, Hard, High, High jinks, Hijinks, Hot, Indwell, Inquiline, Is, Jazz, Kedge, Lad, Lead, Lodging, Mercurial, Merry, Mouvementé, Organic, Outgo, Pacey, Peart, Pep, Perky, Piert, Plenarty, Quick, Quicksilver, Rackety, Racy, Reside, Resident, Rousing, Salt, Sassy, Saut, Scherzo, Simony, Skittish, Smacking, Spanking, Sparky, Spiritoso, Spirituel(le), Sprack, Sprightly, Springy, Spry, Spunky, Subsist, Subsistence, Sustenance, Swinging, Symbiotic, Thrive, Unrecorded, Up tempo, Vibrant, Vicarage, Vigoroso, Vital(ity), Vivace, Vive, Vivo, → VOLATILE, Vyvyan, Wick, Zappy, Zingy, Zippy, Zoe

▸**Livelihood** *see* LIVE(D)

**Liver(ish)** Foie gras, Hepar, Hepatic(al), Pate, Porta, Puce, Resident, Tomalley

**Liverpool, Liverpudlian** Scouse(r)

**Liverwort** Gemma-cup, Hepatica, Riccia

**Livery(man)** Costume, Ermine, Flunkeydom, Goldsmith, Skinner, Tiger, Uniform

**Livid** Blae, Bruised, Cross, → FURIOUS, Pale

▸**Living** *see* LIVE(D)

**Living-room** Lanai

**Livingstone** Doctor, Ken

**Liza, Lizzie** Bess, Betty, Flivver, Hexam, Tin

**Lizard** Abas, Agama, American chameleon, Amphisbaena, Anguis, Anole, Basilisk, Bearded, Bearded-dragon, Blindworm, Blue-tongued, Brontosaurus, Chameleon, Chuckwalla, Dinosaur, Draco, Dragon, Eft, Evet, Fence, Flying, Frilled, Frill-necked, Galliwasp, Gecko(ne), Gila, Gila monster, Glass snake, Goanna, Gotcha, Guana, Hatteria, Hellbender, Horned, Iguana, Jew, Kabaragoya, Komodo (dragon), Lacerta, Legua(a)n, Lounge, Malayan monitor, Mastigure, Menopome, Mokomoko, Moloch, Monitor, Mosasaur(us), Mountain devil, Newt, Ngarara, Perentie, Perenty, Reptile, Rock, Sand, Sauria, Scincoid, Seps, Serpent, Skink, Slow-worm, Snake, Sphenodon, Stellio(n), Sungazer, Swift, Tegu(exin), Teiid, Thorny devil, Tokay, Tuatara, Tuatera, Varan, Wall, Whiptail, Worm, Worral, Worrel, Zandoli, Zonure

**Llama** Alpaca, Alpaco, Cria, Guanaco, Huanaco, Paco, Vicuña

**Load(ed), Loader, Loading, Loads** Accommodation, Affluent, Amass, Back-end, Backfill, Ballast, Base, Biased, Boot-strap, Boozy, Burden, Cargo, Charge, Cobblers, Dead weight, Disc, Dope, Drunk, Dummy, Encumber, Fardel, Fill, Fork-lift, Fother, Frau(gh)tage, Freight, Front-end, Fulham, Full, Gestant, Glyc(a)emic, Hampered, Heap, Input, Install, Jag, Lade, Lard, Last, Lay-day, Live, Onus, Opulent, Pack, Packet, Pay, Peak, Power, Prime, Raft, Rich, Scads, Seam, Shipment, Shoal, Some, Span, Stow, Super, Surcharge, →TIGHT, Tipsy, Tod, Traction, Ultimate, Useful, Wealthy, Weight, Wharfinger, Wing

**Loaf(er), Loaves** Baguette, Bannock, Barmbrack, Batch, Baton, Beachbum, Beachcomber, Bloomer, Bludge, Bonce, Boule, Bread, Brick, Bum, Bu(r)ster, Cad, Cob, Coburg, Cottage, Currant, Danish, Farmhouse, French stick, Hawm, Head, Hoe-cake, Idle, Layabout, →LAZE, Lazybones, Long tin, Lusk, Malt, Manchet, Meat, Miche, Milk, Mooch, Mouch, Nut, Pan, Pan(h)agia, Penny, Plain, Plait, Quartern, Roll, Roti, Shewbread, Shirker, Shoe, Showbread, Sliced, Slipper, Slosh, Split tin, Square tin, Stollen, Stotty, Sugar, Tin, Vantage, Vienna, Yob

**Loam** Clay, Loess, Loss, Malm

**Loan(s)** Advance, Balloon, Bank, Benevolence, Bottomry, Bridging, Call, Consolidation, Debenture, Demand, Droplock, Imprest, Lane, Mortgage, Mutuum, Omnium, Out, Prest, Respondentia, Roll-over, Soft, Start-up, Student, Sub, Time, Top-up, War

**Loathe, Loathing, Loathsome** Abhor(rent), Abominate, Carrion, Despise, Detest, Execrate, Hate, Keck, Nauseate, Odious, Reptilian, Repugnant, Scunner, Toad, Ug(h)

**Lob** Fungo, Loft, Sky, Underarm

**Lobby** Antechamber, Box, Concourse, Demo, Division, Entry, Foyer, Gun, Hall, Porch, Press, Pressure group, Urge

**Lobe(d)** Anisocercal, Fluke, Frontal, Glossa, Insula, Jugum, Lacinia, Lap, Occipital, Optic, Palmate, Paraglossate, Parietal, Pinnule, Prostomium, Runcinate, Segment, Temporal, Uvula, Vermis

**Lobster** Cock, Crawfish, Crayfish, Crustacean, Decapoda, Langouste, Macrura, Newburg, Norway, Pereion, Pot, Rock, Scampo, Spiny, Squat, Thermidor, Tomalley

**Local(ity)** Area, Boor, Bro, Close, Des(h)i, Endemic, Home, Inhouse, Inn, Insider, Landlord, Native, Near, Nearby, Neighbourhood, Number, Parochial, Provincial, Pub, Regional, Resident, Swadishi, Tavern, Topical, Type, Vernacular, Vicinal

▹**Local** *may indicate* a dialect word

**Locale** Area, Scene, Site

**Locate(d), Location, Locator** Address, Connect, Echo, Emplacement, Find, Fix, Hide-out, Lay, Milieu, Node, Pinpoint, Pitch, Place, Placement, Plant, Post, Pulsor, Put, Recess, Sat, Scene, Set-up, Site, Situate, Situation, Sofar, Spot, Theatre, Trace, Ubiety, Venue, Website, Where(abouts), Workplace, Zone

**Loch, Lough** Allen, Ashie, Awe, Derg, Earn, Eil, Erne, Etive, Fine, Gare, Garten, Glen Lyon, Holy, Hourn, Katrine, →LAKE, Larne, Leven, Linnhe, Lomond, Long, Moidart, Morar, More, Na Keal, Neagh, Ness, Rannoch, Ryan, Sea, Shiel, Strangford, Tay, Torridon

**Lock(ing), Locker, Locks, Lock up** Bar, Barnet, Bolt, Canal, Central, Chain, Child, Chubb®, Clap-sill, Clinch, Combination, Cowlick, Curlicue, Davy Jones, Deadbolt, Detent, Drop, Fastener, Fermentation, Foretop, Gate, Haffet, Haffit, Handcuff, Hasp, Hold, Intern, Key, Kiss curl, Latch, Lazaretto, Man, Mane, Mortise, Percussion, Prison, Quiff, Ragbolt, Rim, Ringlet, Safety, Sasse, Scalp, Scissors, →SECURE, Sluice, Snap, Spring, Staircase, Sta(u)nch, Stock, Strand, Tag, Talon, Tetanus, Time, Trap, Tress, Tuft, Tumbler, Vapour, Villus, Ward, Watergate, Wet dock, Wheel, Wrestle, Yale®

**Locket** Lucy

**Lockjaw** Tetanus, Trismus

▹**Lockkeeper** *may indicate* a hairnet

**Locksmith** Garret-master, Hairdresser

**Locomotive** Banker, Bogie, Bul(l)gine, Diesel, Engine, Iron horse, Mobile, Mogul, Rocket, Steam, Steamer, Train

**Locum** Deputy, Relief, Stand-in, Stopgap

**Locus** Centrode, Horopter, Lemniscate, Place, Spot

**Locust, Locust tree** Acacia, Anime, Carob, Cicada, Hopper, Nymph, Robinia, Seventeen-year, Voetganger

**Lode** Comstock, Lodge, Mother, Reef, Vein

**Lodestone** Magnes, Magnet

**Lodge(r)** Bestow, Billet, Board(er), Box, Chalet, Cosher, Deposit, Dig, Doss, Encamp, Entertain, Freemason, Grange, Grove, Guest, Harbour, Host, Housemate, Hunting, Inmate, Inquiline, Instal, Layer, Lie, Masonic, Nest, Orange, Parasite, PG, Porter's, Put up, Quarter, Rancho, Resident, Room(er), Roomie, Roommate, Stay, Storehouse, Stow, Sweat, Tenant, Tepee, Up-put, Wigwam

**Lodging(s)** Abode, B and B, Billet, Camp, Chummage, Dharms(h)ala, Diggings, Digs, Dosshouse, Ferm, Grange, Grove, Hospitium, Hostel, Inquiline, Keep, Kip, Minshuku, Pad, Padding-ken, Pension, Pied-à-terre, Quarters, Resiant, Rooms, Singleen, Sponging-house, Spunging-house, Squat, YHA

**Loft(iness), Lofty** Aerial, Airy, Arrogant, Attic, Celsitude, Chip, Choir, Condescending, Cote, Exalted, Garret, Garryowen, Grand, Haymow, High, Hoity-toity, Imposing, Jube, Lordly, Magniloquent, Noble, Olympian, Organ, Pulpitum, Rarefied, Rigging, Rood, Roost, Sail, Sky(ish), Steep, Sublime, Tallat, Tallet, Tallot

**Log(ging), Logs** Billet, Black box, Caber, Cabin, Chip, Chock, Deadhead, Diarise, Diary, Enter, Hack, Key(stroke), Ln, Lumber, Mantissa, Minutes, Nap(i)erian, Neper, Patent, Poling, Raft, → RECORD, Splog, Stock, Tachograph, Yule

**Logarithm** Common, Hyperbolic, Lod, Mantissa, Nap(i)erian, Natural

**Logger** Data

**Logic(al)** Alethic, Analytical, Aristotelian, Boolean, Chop, Cogent, Coherent, Deontic, Dialectic(s), Digital, Distributed, Doxastic, Elench(us), Epistemics, Formal, Fuzzy, Hardhead(ed), Heuristics, Iff, Mathematical, Modal, Organon, Philosophical, Premise, Pusser's, Ramism, Ratiocinate, Rational(e), Reason, Sane, Sequacious, Shared, Sorites, Syllogism, Symbolic, Tense, Trivium, Vienna circle

**Logician** Spock, Venn

**Logo** Brand, Colophon, Monogram, Motif, Trademark

**Loin(s)** Flank, Inguinal, Lisk, Lungie, Lunyie, Reins

**Loincloth** Cache sexe, Dhoti, Lungi, Pareu, Waist-cloth

**Loiter(ing)** Dally, Dare, Dawdle, Dilatory, Dilly-dally, Idle, Lag, Lallygag, Leng, Lime, → LINGER, Loaf, Lollygag, Mike, Mooch, Mouch, Potter, Saunter, Scamp, Suss, Taigle, Tarry

**Lola** Dolores

**Loll** Hawm, Lounge, Slouch, Sprawl

**Lollipop, Lolly** Ice pole, Lulibub, Popsicle®, Sucker, Sweetmeat

**Lolly** Dosh, Dough, Money

**London(er)** 'Arry, Big Smoke, Cockaigne, Cockney, Co(c)kayne, East-ender, Flat-cap, Jack, Metropolis, Port, Roseland, Smoke, Town, Troynovant, Wen

**London pride** None-so-pretty

**Lone(r), Lonely** Anchoret, Bereft, Eremite, Grass widow, Hermit, Isolated, Recluse, Remote, Rogue, Saddo, Secluded, Sole, Solitary, Unked, Unket, Unkid

**Long(er), Longing, Longs** Ache, Aitch, Ake, Appetent, Appetite, Aspire, Brame, Chronic, Covet, Crave, Desire, Die, Earn, Erne, Eternal, Far, Gasp, Greed, Green, Grein, → HANKER, Huey, Hunger, Inveterate, Island, Itch, L, Lanky, Large, Lengthy, Longa, Lust, Macron, Marathon, Miss, More, → NO LONGER, Nostalgia, Option, Pant, Parsec, → PINE, Prolix, Sesquipedalian, Side, Sigh, Tall, Thirst, Trews, Wearisome, Weary, Wish, Wist, Yearn, Yen

**Long-eared** Spicate

**Longitude** Celestial, Ecliptic, Meridian

**Long-lashed** Mastigophora(n)

**Long live(d), Long-life, Long-term** Banzai, Longevity, Macrobian, Permanent, Viva, Vive, Zindabad

**Long-serving** Old-timer

**Longshoreman** Hobbler, Hoveller, Wharfinger

**Long-sighted(ness)** Hypermetropia

**Long-suffering** Job, Patient, Stoical

**Long-tailed** Macrural

**Long time** Ages, Years, Yonks

**Long-winded** Prolix, Rambling, Verbose, Wordy

**Loo** Ajax, Bog, Can, Chapel, Dike, Game, Gents, Jakes, John, Latrine, Privy, Toilet

**Loofah** Towel gourd

**Look(s), Look at, Looking** After-eye, Air, Aspect, Await, Behold, Belgard, Blink, Bonne-mine, Browse, Busk, Butcher's, Butcher's hook, Case, Clock, Close-up, Countenance, Crane, Daggers, Decko, Deek, Dekko, Demeanour, Dirty, Ecce, Ecco, Expression, Eye, Eyeball, Eye-glance, Face, Facies, Forage, Forward, Gander, Gawp, Gaze, Geek, Glad-eye, Glance, Glare, Gleam, Gledge, Glimpse, Glom, Glower, Goggle, Good, Grin, Hallo, Hangdog, Hey, Hippocratic, Iliad, Inspect, Keek, La, Leer, Lo, Mien, New, Ogle, Old-fashioned, Peek, Peep, Peruse, Prospect, Ray, Recce, Refer, → **REGARD**, Scan, Scowl, Scrutinise, Search, See, Seek, Seem, Shade, Sheep's eyes, Shufti, Shufty, Spy, Squint, Squiz, Stare, Survey, Toot, V, Vista, Wet

**Look-out (man)** Achtung, Cockatoo, Crow's nest, Dixie, Huer, Mirador, Nit, Pas op, Picket, Prospect, Sangar, Scout, Sentinel, Sentry, Spotter, Sungar, Tentie, Toot(er), Watch, Watchtower

▷**Look silly** *may indicate* an anagram

**Loom** Beamer, Dobby, Emerge, Impend, Jacquard, Lathe, Lease-rod, Menace, Overhang, Picker, Tappet, Temple, Threaten, Tower

**Loon(y)** Airhead, Diver, Nutter

**Loop(ed), Loophole, Loopy** Articulatory, Becket, Bight, Billabong, Bouclé, Carriage, Chink, Closed, Coil, Eyelet, Eyesplice, Fake, Feedback, Frog, Frontlet, Grom(m)et, Ground, Grummet, Hank, Heddle-eye, Henle's, Hysteresis, Infinite, Kink, Knop, Lasket, Latchet, Lippes, Local, Lug, Noose, Oillet, Parral, Parrel, Pearl(-edge), Picot, Prusik, Purl, Riata, Scrunchie, Squiggle, Staple, Stirrup, Swag, Tab, Tape, Terry, Toe, Twist

**Loos** Anita

**Loose(n), Loose woman** Absolve, Abstrict, Adrift, Afloat, Anonyma, Baggage, Baggy, Bail, Besom, Bunter, Chippie, Chippy, Clatch, Cocotte, Cutty, Demi-mondaine, Demirep, Demivierge, Desultory, Dissolute, Dissolve, Doxy, Draggletail, Dratchell, Drazel, Ease, Emit, Flabby, Flaccid, Flipperty-flopperty, Flirt-gill, Floosie, Floozie, Floozy, Floppy, Franion, Free, Gangling, Gay, Geisha, Hussy, Inexact, Insecure, Jade, Jay, Jezebel, Lax, Light-heeled, Limp, Loast, Loon, Loste, Mob, Mort, Naughty pack, Painted, Pinnace, Profligate, Promiscuous, Quail, Ramp, → **RELAX**, Sandy, Shaky, Slack, Slipshod, Streel, Strumpet, Tart, Tramp, Trull, Unclasp, Ungyve, Unhasp, Unhitch, Unknit, Unknot, Unlace, Unlash, Unleash, Unpin, Unreined, Unscrew, Unstuck, Unthread, Untie, Vague, Waistcoateer, Wappend, Whore

**Loot** Berob, Boodle, Booty, Cragh, Creach, Foray, Haul, Mainour, Oof, Peel, Pillage, Pluck, → **PLUNDER**, Ransack, Rape, Reave, Reif, Rieve, Rob, Sack, Smug, Spoils, Spoliate, Stouth(e)rie, Swag, Treasure, Waif

**Lop** Behead, Clip, Clop, Curtail, Detruncate, Droop, Shroud, Sned, Snee, Trash

**Lope** Stride

**Lop-sided** Asymmetrical, Awry, Badger-legged, Uneven

**Loquacious** Chatty, Communicative, Gabby, Garrulous, Rambling, Wordy

**Lord(s), Lordship, Lordly** Adonai, Ahura Mazda, Anaxandron, Arrogant, Boss, Byron, Cardigan, Chatelain, Cripes, Cyril, Dieu, Dominate, Domineer, Dominical, Drug, Duc, Earl, Elgin, Gad, Gilded Chamber, God, Haw-haw, Herr, HL, Idris, Imperious, Jim, Justice, Kami, Kitchener, Land, Landgrave, Law, Ld, Liege, Lonsdale, Losh, Lud, MCC, Meneer, Mesne, Misrule, Mynheer, Naik, Oda Nobunaga, Omrah, Ordinary, Ormazd, Ormuzd, Palsgrave, Peer, Sea, Second chamber, Seigneur, Seignior, Shaftesbury, Sire, Spiritual, Taverner, Temporal, Tuan, Ullin

**Lords and ladies** Wake-robin

**Lore** Cab(b)ala, Edda, Lair, Lare, Riem, Upanis(h)ad

**Lorelei** Siren

**Lorgnette** Starers

**Loris** Potto

**Lorna** Doone

**Lorry, Lorries** Artic(ulated), Camion, Carrier, Crummy, Double-bottom, Drag, Drawbar outfit, Dropsided, Flatbed, HGV, Juggernaut, Low-loader, Rig, Road train, Tipper, Tonner, Transporter, → **TRUCK**, Wagon

**Los Angeles** La-la-land

**Lose(r)** Also-ran, Decrease, Drop, Elude, Fail, Forfeit, Hesitater, Leese, Misère, Mislay, Misplace, Miss, No-hoper, No-no, Nowhere, Saddo, Spread, Stiff, Tank, Throw, Tine(r), Tyne, Underdog, Unsuccessful, Waste, Weeper

**Loss, Lost** Angel's share, Anosmia, Aphesis, Aphonia, Apocope, Apraxia, Astray, At sea, Attainder, Boohai, Chord, Cost, Dead, Decrease, Decrement, Defeat, Depreciation, Detriment, Disadvantage, Elision, Extinction, Foredamned, Forfeited, Forgotten, Forlorn, Gone, Hurtful, Lore, Lorn, Lurch, Missing, Omission, Outage, Paralysis, Pentimento, Perdition, Perdu, Perished, Preoccupied, Privation, Psilosis, Reliance, Shrinkage, Stray, Tine, Tinsel, Tint, Toll, Traik, Tribes, Tyne(d), Ullage, Unredeemed, Wastage, Wasted, Will, Write-off, Wull

**Loss of memory** Amnesia, Black-out, Fugue, Infonesia, Paramnesia

▷**Lost** *may indicate* an anagram or an obsolete word

**Lot(s)** Abundant, Amount, Aret(t), Badly, Bags, Batch, Boatload, Bomb, Caboodle, Cavel, Chance, Deal, Destiny, Dole, Doom, Drove, Due, → FATE, Fortune, Fowth, Group, Hantle, Hap, Heaps, Horde, Host, Item, Job, Kevel, Kismet, Lank, Lashings, Legion, Loads, Loadsa, Luck, Manifold, Many, Mass, Moh, Moira, Mony, Mort, Much, Myriad, Oceans, Often, Omnibus, Oodles, Oodlins, Pack, Parcel, Parking, Patriarch, Plenitude, Plenty, Plethora, Portion, Power, Purim, Raft, Rich, Scads, Set, Shedload, Sight, Slather, Slew, Slue, Sortilege, Sortition, Stack, Sum, Tall order, The works, Tons, Tranch, Vole, Wagonload, Weird

**Loth** Averse, Circumspect, Sweer(t), Sweir(t), Unwilling

**Lothario** Lady-killer, Libertine, Poodle-faker, Rake, Womaniser

**Lotion** After-shave, After-sun, Blackwash, Calamine, Cleanser, Collyrium, Conditioner, Cream, Emollient, Eye-wash, Humectant, Ointment, Setting, Suntan, Toner, Unguent, Wash, Yellow wash

**Lottery, Lotto** Art union, Ballot, Bingo, Cavel, Draw, El Gordo, Gamble, National, Pakapoo, Pools, Postcode, Punchboard, Raffle, Rollover, Scratchcard, Sweepstake, Tattersall's, Tombola

**Lotus (eater), Lotus land** Asana, Djerba, Lotophagus, Padmasana, White

**Louche** Debauched, Rak(e)ish, Rip

**Loud(ness), Loudly** Bel, Big, Blaring, Booming, Brassy, Clarion, Decibel, Ear-piercing, Ear-splitting, F, FF, Flashy, Forte, Fracas, Full-mouthed, Garish, Gaudy, Glaring, Hammerklavier, High(pitched), Jazzy, Lumpkin, Lurid, Noisy, Orotund, Plangent, Raucous, Roarie, Showy, Siren, Sone, Stentor(ian), Strident, Tarty, Vocal, Vociferous, Volume, Vulgar

**Loudspeaker** Action, Boanerges, Bullhorn, Hailer, Megaphone, PA, Squawk box, Stentor, Subwoofer, Tannoy®, Tweeter, Woofer

▶**Lough** *see* LOCH

**Louis** Armstrong, Baker, Roi, Satchmo

**Louisianian** Cajun

**Lounge(r)** Bar, Cocktail, Couch potato, Daiker, Da(c)ker, Departure, Doze, Executive, Hawm, Idle, Laze, Lie, Lizard, Loaf, Loll, Lollop, Parlour, Paul's man, Recline, Settee, Sitkamer, Slouch, Sprawl, Sun, Sunbed, Transit, Transitive

**Louse (up), Lousy, Lice** Acrawl, Argulus, Biting, Bolix, Bollocks, Chat, Chicken, Cootie, Crab, Crawling, Crummy, Fish, Head, Isopod(a), Kutu, Mallophaga, Nit, Oniscus, Pedicular, Phthiriasis, Plant, Psocid, Psocoptera, Psylla, Pubic, Slater, Snot, Sowbug, Sucking, Vermin, Whale

**Lout(ish)** Auf, Clod(hopper), Coof, Cuif, Galere, Hallian, Hallion, Hallyon, Hick, Hob, Hobbledehoy, Hooligan, Hoon, Jack, Jake, Keelie, Lager, Larrikin, Litter, Lob(lolly), Loord, Lubber, Lumpkin, Lycra, Oaf, Oik, Rube, Swad, Tout, Tripper, Ungallant, Yahoo, Yob(bo)

**Louvre** Shutter, Slat

**Love(d), Lovable, Lover, Loving** Abelard, Admire, Adore, Adulator, Affection, Agape, Alma, Amabel, Amanda, Amant, Amateur, Ami(e), Amoret, Amoroso, Amour, Angharad, Antony, Ardour, Ariadne, Aroha, Aucassin, Beau, Bedfellow, Besotted, Bidie-in, Blob, Brotherly, Calf, Care, Casanova, Chamberer, Chloe, Cicisbeo, Concubine, Coquet, Court, Courtly, Cupboard, Cupid, Daphnis, Dear, Dona(h), Dotard, Dote, Doxy, Duck(s), Ducky, Dulcinea, Eloise, Eloper, Emotion, Enamorado, Enthusiast, Eros, Esme, Fan(boy), Fancy man, Flame, Frauendienst, Free, Gal(l)ant, Goose-egg, Greek, Hon(ey), Idolise, Inamorata,

Inamorato, Iseult, Isolde, Item, Jo, Juliet, Kama, Lad, Lancelot, Leander, Leman, Like, Lochinvar, Loe, Loo, Lurve, Man, Mistress, Nada, Nihility, Nil, Nookie, Nothing, Nought, Nut, O, Old flame, Pairs, Paramour, Pash, Passion, Pet, Phaedra, Philander, -phile, Philtre, Platonic, Precious, Protestant, Psychodelic, Puppy, Revere, Rhanja, Romance, Romeo, Sapphism, Sigisbeo, Smitten, Spark, Spooner, Stale, Storge, Suitor, Swain, Thisbe, Tough, Toyboy, Treasure, Tristan, Troilus, True, Turtle(-dove), Valentine, Venus, Virtu, Woman, Worship, Zap, Zeal, Zero, Zip

**Love-apple** Tomato, Wolf's-peach

**Love-bite** Hickey

**Love-child** By-blow, Come-by-chance

**Love-in-a-mist** Nigella

**Love letter** Capon

**Lovely** Adorable, Beauty, Belle, Cute, Dishy, Dreamy, Exquisite, Fair, Gorgeous, Looker, Nasty, Picturesque, Super

**Love-making** → INTERCOURSE, Kama Sutra, Sex, Slap and tickle, Snog

**Love-sick** Smit(ten), Strephon

**Loving(ly)** Amoroso, Amorous, Fond, Tender

**Low(est), Low-born, Low-cut, Lower(ing), Low-key** Abase, Abate, Abysmal, Amort, Area, Avail(e), Avale, B, Basal, Base(-born), Bass(o), Beneath, Blue, Caddish, Calf, Canaille, Cartoonist, Cheap, Church, Cocktail, Condescend, Contralto, Couch, Cow, Crestfallen, Croon, Crude, Darken, Debase, Decadent, Declass, Décolleté, Deepen, Deepmost, Degrade, Deign, Dejected, Demean, Demit, Demote, Depress, Despicable, Devalue, Dim, Dip, Dishonourable, Dispirited, Doldrums, Downbeat, Downmarket, Downstairs, Drawdown, Drop, Early, Embase, Flat, Foot, Frown, Gazunder, Glare, Glum, Guernsey, Gurly, Gutterblood, Hedge(-hopping), Hidalgo, Humble, Ignoble, Imbase, Inferior, Jersey, Junior, L, Laigh, Lallan, Law, Lessen, Light, Lite, Mass, Mean(born), Menial, Moo, Mopus, Morose, Nadir, Net, Nether, Nett, Nominal, Non-U, Offpeak, Ornery, Ostinato, Paravail, Piss-poor, Plebeianise, Profound, Prole, Reduce, Relegate, Ribald, Rock-bottom, Run down, Sad, Scoundrel, Scowl, Secondo, Settle, Shabby, Short, Soft, Stoop, Subaltern, Subordinate, Subscript, Sudra, Sunken, Undermost, Undertone, Unnoble, Unobtrusive, Vail, Vulgar, Weak, Wretched

**Lowbrow** Essex man, Philistine

**Low country** Flanders

**Lowdown** Dirt, Gen, Info, Stats

▷**Lower** *may refer to* cattle

**Lowland(er)** Carse, Fen, Gallovidian, Glen, Laigh, Lallans, Merse, Mudflat, Plain, Polder, Sassenach, Vlei

**Low-lying** Callow, Epigeous, Fens, Inferior, Sump

**Low maintenance** Easy care

**Low person** Boor, Bunter, Cad, Caitiff, Cocktail, Demirep, Ratfink, Snot

**Lowry** LS

**Loyal(ty)** Adherence, Allegiant, Brand, Brick, Clanship, Dependable, Diehard, Dutiful, Esprit de corps, Faithful, Fast, Fealty, Fidelity, Firm, Gungho, Leal, Liegedom, Liegeman, Patriotic, Pia, Stalwart, Staunch, Sure, Tribalism, Troth, → TRUE, True blue, Trusty

**Loyalist** Hard core, Paisley, Patriot, Tory

**Lozenge** Cachou, Catechu, Coughdrop, Fusil, Jujube, Mascle, Pastille, Pill, Rhomb, Rustre, Tablet, Troche, Voided

**LSD** Acid, Money

**Lubber(ly), Lubbers** Booby, Clod, Clumsy, Gawky, Hulk, Landsman, Lob, Looby, Oaf, Slowback, Swab, Swads

**Lubricant, Lubricate, Lubrication** Carap-oil, Coolant, Derv, Dope, Fluid, Force-feed, Grease, Oil, Petrolatum, Sebum, Synovia, Unguent, Vaseline®, Wool-oil

**Luce** Ged

**Lucerne** Alfalfa, Fodder, Medick, Nonsuch

**Lucia** Mimi

**Lucid** Bright, Clear, Perspicuous, Sane

**Lucifer** Devil, Match, Proud, Satan, Venus

**Luck(y), Lucky moment** Amulet, Auspicious, Beginner's, Blessed, Bonanza, Break, Caduac, Canny, Cess, Chance, Charmed, Chaunce, Daikoku, Dextrotempore, Dip, Enviable, Fat, Fate, Fluke, → FORTUNE, Godsend, Hap, Happy, Heather, Hit, Jam(my), Jim, Joss, Lady, Lot, Mascot, Mercy, Mozzle, Pot, Prosit, Providential, Pudding-bag, Purple passage, Purple patch, Rub of the green, Seal, Seel, Sele, Serendipity, Sess, Sonsie, Sonsy, Spawny, Star(s), Streak, Success, Talisman, Tinny, Tough, Turn-up, White rabbits, Windfall, Wishbone, Worse

**Luckless** Hapless, Ill-fated, Wight

**Lucrative** Cash cow, Earner, Money-spinner

**Lucre** Filthy, Money, Pelf, Tin

**Lucy** Locket

**Lud** Gad

**Luddite** Rioter, Saboteur, Wrecker

**Ludicrous** Absurd, Bathetic, Bathos, Crackpot, Farcical, Fiasco, Inane, Jest, Laughable, Pathetic, Risible

**Ludo** Uckers

**Luff** Derrick

**Lug** Ear, Earflap, Haul, Sea-worm, Sowle, Tote, Tow

**Luggage** Bags, Carryon, Cases, Dunnage, Excess, Grip, Hand, Kit, Petara, Samsonite®, Suiter, Traps, Trunk, Valise

**Luggage-carrier** Grid

**Lugubrious** Dismal, Drear

**Luke-warm** Half-hearted, Laodicean, Lew, Tepid

**Lull, Lullaby** Berceuse, Calm, Cradlesong, Hushaby, Inaction, Respite, Rock, Sitzkreig, Soothe, Sopite

**Lulu** Honey, Stunner

**Lumbar** Hip

**Lumber(ing)** Clump, Galumph, Jumble, Pawn, Plod, Ponderous, Raffle, Saddle, Scamble, Timber

**Lumberjack** Bushwhacker, Feller, Logger, Logman, Rafter

**Luminance, Luminary, Luminous, Luminosity, Luminescence** Aglow, Arc, Candela, Dayglo, Foxfire, Glow, Hero, Ignis-fatuus, L, Light, Meteor, Nit, Phosphorescent, Scintillon, Sea-dog, Star, Wildfire, Will o' the wisp

**Lumme** Coo, Lor

**Lummox** Galoot, Oaf

**Lump(ectomy), Lump(s), Lump(y)** Adam's apple, Aggregate, Blob, Bolus, Bubo, Bud, Bulge, Bur(r), Caruncle, Chuck, Chunk, Clat, Claut, Clod, Clot, Cob, Combine, Da(u)d, Dallop, Dollop, Enhydros, Epulis, Flocculate, Ganglion, Geode, Gnarl, Gob(bet), Goiter, Goitre, Goop, Grape, Grip, Grumose, Hunch, Hunk, Inium, Knarl, Knob, Knub, Knur(r), Knurl, Lob, Lunch, Malleolus, Mass, Mastoid, Moss-litter, Mote, Mott, Myxoma, Neuroma, Nibble, Nirl, Node, Nodule, Nodulus, Nub(bin), Nubble, Nugget, Nur(r), Nurl, Osteophyte, Pat, Plook, Plouk, Quinsy, Raguly, Sarcoma, Scybalum, Sitfast, Slub, Splint, Splodge, Strophiole, Tragus, Tuber(cle), Tumour, Tylectomy, Wart, Wodge

**Lumpsucker** Pad(d)le, Paidle, Sea-owl

**Lunacy, Lunatic** Bedlam, Dementia, Demonomania, Folly, Insanity, Mad(ness), Madman, Maniac, Moonstruck, Nutter, Psychosis

**Lunar** Evection, Mascon, Selenological

▷**Lunatic** *may indicate* an anagram

**Lunch(time)** Bait, Bar, Box, Crib, Dejeune, Déjeuner, Fork, Free, L, Liquid, Nacket, Nocket, Nuncheon, Packed, Piece, Ploughman, Pm, Power, Tiff(in), Working

**Lung(s)** Alveoli, Bellows, Book, Breather, Coalminer's, Farmer's, Green, Iron, Lights, Pleural, Pulmo, Pulmonary, Soul

**Lung disease, Lung problem** Anthracosis, Atelectasis, Barotrauma, Byssinosis, Emphysema, Farmer's lung, Pneumoconiosis, Pneumothorax, Siderosis, Silicosis, Tuberculosis

**Lunge** Breenge, Breinge, Dive, Stab, Thrust, Venue
**Lungfish** Dipnoi(an)
**Lupin** Arsene
**Lurch** Reel, Slew, Stagger, Stoit, Stumble, Swee, Toss
**Lure** Bait, Bribe, Carrot, Decoy, Devon minnow, Entice, Horn, Inveigle, Jig, Judas, Loss leader, Plug, Roper, Spinner, Spoon, Spoonbait, Spoonhook, Squid, Stale, Temptation, Tice, Tole, Toll, Train, Trepan, Trolling bait, Trolling spoon, Wormfly
**Lurgi** Illness
**Lurid** Gaudy, Gothic, Graphic, Gruesome, Purple, Sensational
**Lurk(ing)** Dare, Latitant, Skulk, Slink, Snoke, Snook, Snowk
**Lusatia(n)** Wend(ic), Wendish
**Luscious** Succulent, Sweet
**Lush** Alcoholic, Alkie, Alky, Dipso(maniac), Drunk, Fertile, Green, Juicy, Leafy, Lydian, Soak, Sot, Succulent, Toper, Tosspot, Verdant
**Lust(ful), Lusting, Lusty** Ardent, Cama, Concupiscence, Corflambo, Desire, Eros, Frack, Goatish, Greed, Kama, Lech(ery), Lewd, Libertine, Libido, Megalomania, Obidicut, Prurience, Radge, Randy, Rank, Raunchy, Salacious, Steamy, Venereous
**Lustre, Lustrous** Adamantine, Brilliance, Census, Chatoyant, Galena, Gaum, Gilt, Glare, Gloss, Gorm, Inaurate, Lead-glance, Lovelight, Pearlescent, Pearly, Pentad, Reflet, Satiny, Schiller, → **SHEEN**, Shellac, Water
**Lute, Lutist** Amphion, Chitarrone, Cither, Dichord, Orpharion, Pandora, Pandore, Pipa, Theorbo, Vielle
**Lutetium** Lu
**Lutheran** Adiaphorist, Calixtin(e), Pietist, Protestant, Ubiquitarian
**Luvvie** Theatrical
**Lux** Lx
**Luxemburg** L
**Luxuriant, Luxuriate, Luxurious, Luxury (lover)** Apician, Bask, Clover, Cockaigne, Cockayne, Comfort, Copious, Delicate, Deluxe, Dolce vita, Extravagant, Exuberant, Five-star, Fleshpots, High-end, Lap, Lavish, Lotus-eating, Lucullan, Lush, Milk and honey, Mollitious, Opulence, Ornate, Palatial, Pie, Plush(y), Posh, Rank, Revel, → **RICH**, Ritzy, Sumptuous, Sybarite, Wallow
**Lycanthropist** Werewolf
**Lydia** Languish
**Lye** Buck, Caustic soda
▸**Lying** *see* **LIE(S)**
**Lymph** Chyle
**Lymphoma, Lymphocyte** Burkett's, T-cell
**Lynch(ing), Lyncher** Dewitt, Hang, Necktie party, Nightrider, String up
**Lynx** Bay, Bobcat, Caracal, Cougar, Desert, Rooikat
**Lyre** Box, Cithern, Harp, Psaltery, Testudo, Trigon
**Lyric(s), Lyrical, Lyricist, Lyrist** Awdl, Cavalier, Dit(t), Egan, Epode, Gilbert, Hammerstein, Melic, Melodic, Ode, Orphean, Paean, Pean, Poem, Poetic, Rhapsodic, Song, Spinto, Taupin, Wax, Words

# Mm

**M** Married, Member, Metre, Mike, Mile, Thousand
**MA** Magister Artum
**Mac** Bo, Mino, Scot, Waterproof
**Macabre** Ghoulish, Gothic, Grotesque, Gruesome, Morbid, Sick
**Macaque** Rhesus, Wanderoo
**Macaroni** Beau, Blood, Cat, Dandy, Elbow, Exquisite, Fop, Jack-a-dandy, Olio, Pasta, Petitmaitre
**Macaroon** Biscuit, Signal
**Macaulay** Layman
**Macbeth** Thane
**Mace** Club, Nutmeg, Sceptre, Spice
**Mace-bearer** Beadle, Bedel(l), Poker
**Macedonian** Alexander, Philip, Stagirite, Stagyrite
**Machete** Bolo
**Machiavellian** Savvy
**Machine(ry)** Adding, Apparat(us), Appliance, Automat, Bathing, Cash, → **DEVICE**, Dispenser, Facsimile, Fax, Flourbolt, Fruit, Ice, Infernal, Instrument, Karaoke, Life-support, Mailing, Party, Pinball, Plane, Plant, Printing, Propaganda, Rowing, Sausage, Screwing, Sewing, Slot, Spin, Stapling, Tape, Teaching, Threshing, Time, Tomograph, Vending, Virtual, War, Washing, Weighing

---

**MACHINES**

*3 letters:*
Gin

*4 letters:*
Drum
Haik
Heck
Loom
Mule
Wind

*5 letters:*
Churn
Crane
Cycle
Lathe
Mower
Poker
Pokie
Press
Robot
Rover
Stamp

*6 letters:*
Dredge
Engine
Enigma
Grader
Hopper
Linter
Ludlow
Planer
Pulper
Reaper
Seeder
Slicer
Tardis
Tedder
Turing
Willow

*7 letters:*
Burster
Capstan
Dredger
Hawk-Eye®
Jukebox
Milling
Moviola®
Potcher
Scanner
Slasher
Tumbler
Turbine
Twin tub
Wringer
Zamboni®

*8 letters:*
Calender
Dialyser
Enginery
Filatory
Hot-press
Linotype®
Moulinet
Nintendo®
Pea-viner
Pulsator
Shredder
Spreader
Symatron
Thresher
Throstle
Transfer
Windlass
Windmill

*9 letters:*
Air-engine
Answering
Automaton
Bulldozer
Dynamotor
Excavator
Hummeller
Osmometer
Perfector
Processor
Rotavator®
Separator
Stamp-mill

Stenotype®
Treadmill
Wimshurst

*10 letters:*
Beam-engine
Centrifuge
Clobbering
Earth-mover
Emi-scanner®
Jawbreaker
Liquidiser
Passimeter
Pile-driver
Roadroller
Rototiller
Typewriter
Watersnail

*11 letters:*
Comptometer®
Fourdrinier
Weighbridge

*12 letters:*
Lithotripter
Muckspreader

*13 letters:*
Defibrillator
Slipform paver
Spinning jenny
Supercalender

*14 letters:*
One-armed bandit

*16 letters:*
Archimedean screw
Combine harvester

---

**Machinist** Seamstress
**Macho** Defiant, Hunk, Jock, Laddish, Male, Manly, Rambo, Virile
**Mackerel** Albacore, Amber-fish, Brack, Dory, Fish, Horse, Pacific, Pimp, Scad, Scomber, Shiner, Sky, Spanish, Spotted, Tinker, Trevally
**Mackintosh** Burberry®, Mac, Mino, Oilskin, Slicker, Waterproof
**Macron** Longmark
**Macropus** Euro, Wallaroo
**Mad(den), Madman, Madness** Angry, Apoplectic, Balmy, Bananas, Barking, Barmy, Bedlam(ite), Berserk, Besotted, Bonkers, Crackbrained, Crackpot, Crazy, Cuckoo, Cupcake, Daffy, Delirious, Dement, Deranged, Détraqué, Distract, Dotty, Enrage, Exasperate, Fay, Fey, Fie, Folie, Folly, Frantic, Frenetic(al), Fruitcake, Furioso, Fury, Gelt, Gyte, Harpic, Hatter, Hothead, Idiotic, Incense, Insane, Insanie, Insanity, Into, Irate, Ireful, Irritate, Kook, Livid, Loco, Lunatic, Lycanthropy, Madbrained, Maenad, Mango, Mania, Mattoid, Mental, Meshug(g)a, Metric, Midsummer, Moonstruck, Motorway, Mullah, Nuts, Nutter, Porangi, Provoke, Psycho, Rabid, Rasputin, Raving, Redwood, Redwud, Scatty, Screwy, Short-witted, Starkers, Tonto, Touched, Troppo, Unhinged, Wacko, Wood, Wowf, Wrath, Wud, Xenomania, Yond, Zany
▷**Mad(den)** *may indicate* an anagram
**Madagascan, Madagascar** Aye-aye, Hova, Indri, Lemur, Malagash, Malagasy, RM
**Madam(e)** Baggage, Bawd, Lady, M, Memsahib, Proprietress
**Madcap** Cake, Impulsive, Tearaway
**Madder** Alizari, Alyari, Chay(a), Gardenia, Genipap, Rose, Rubia, Shaya
**Made (it)** Built, Did, Fec(it), Ff, Gart, Invented
**Made (up)** Apocryphal, Synthesized
**Madeira** Cake
**Madge** Pie
▷**Madly** *may indicate* an anagram
**Madonna** Lady, Lily, Mary, Pietà, Sistine, Virgin
**Madras** Chennai
**Madrigal** Ballet, Fala, Song
**Maelstrom** Voraginous, Vortex, Whirlpool
**Maenad** Devotee, Fan
**Maestro** Artist, Toscanini, Virtuoso
**Mafia, Mafioso** Camorra, Capo, Cosa Nostra, Don, Godfather, Goombah, Mob, Ndrangheta, Omerta, Padrone, Pentito, Sicilian, The Mob, Triad
**Mag** Mail
**Magazine** Arsenal, Clip, Colliers, Contact, Cornhill, Cosmopolitan, Digizine, Economist, Elle, E-zine, Field, Girlie, Glossy, Granta, House organ, Jazz mag, Journal, Ladmag, Lady, Lancet, Life, Listener, Little, Magnet, New Yorker, Organ, Paper, Part work, Periodical, Pictorial, Playboy, Powder, Private Eye, Pulp, Punch, Quarterly, She, Skin, Slick, Spectator, Store, Strand, Tatler, Time, Vogue, Warehouse, Weekly, Yoof, Zine
**Magdalene** St Mary
**Maggie** Rita
**Maggot** Bot, Flyblow, Gentiles, Gentle, Grub, Larva, Mawk, Myiasis, Weevil, Whim, Worm

**Magi** Balthazar, Caspar, Gaspar, Melchior

**Magic(al), Magician, Magic square** Abracadabra, Alchemy, Archimage, Art, Baetyl, Black, Black art, Charm, Circle, Conjury, Crowley, Diablerie, Diablery, Druid, Enchanting, Fabulous, Faust, Faustus, Fetish, Genie, Goetic, Goety, Gramary(e), Grimoire, Hermetic, Hey presto, Houdini, Illusionist, Incantation, Makuto, Math, Medea, Medicine man, Merlin, Mojo, Moly, Morgan le Fay, Myal, Nasik, Natural, Necromancer, Obeah, Occult, Pawaw, Powwow, Prospero, Reim-kenner, Rhombus, Shamanism, Sorcery, Sortilege, Spell, Speller, Stardust, Supernatural, Sympathetic, Talisman, Thaumaturgics, Theurgy, Voodoo, Warlock, White, Witch-doctor, Wizard, Zendik

**Magic mushrooms** Philocybin

**Magistracy, Magistrate** Aedile, Alcalde, Amman, Amtman, Archon, Avoyer, Bailie, Bailiff, Bailli(e), Baron bailie, Beak, Bench, Boma, Burgess, Burgomaster, Cadi, Censor, Consul, Corregidor, Curule, Decemvirate, Demiurge, Dictator, Doge(ate), Draco, Edile, Effendi, Ephor, Field cornet, Finer, Foud, Gonfalonier, JP, Judiciary, Jurat, Justice, Kotwal, Landamman(n), Landdrost, Lord Provost, Maire, Mayor, Mittimus, Novus homo, Pilate, Podesta, Portreeve, Pr(a)efect, Pr(a)etor, Prior, Proconsul, Propraetor, Provost, Qadi, Quaestor, Recorder, Reeve, Shereef, Sherif, Stad(t)holder, Stipendiary, Syndic, Tribune, Trier, Worship

**Magnanimity, Magnanimous** Altruistic, Big, Charitable, →GENEROUS, Largeness, Lofty, Noble

**Magnate** Baron, Beaverbrook, Bigwig, Industrialist, Mogul, Onassis, Randlord, Tycoon, Vanderbilt, VIP, Zillionaire

**Magnesia, Magnesium** Bitter-earth, Epsomite, Humite, Kainite, Mg, Periclase

**Magnet(ic), Magnetism** Animal, Artificial, Attraction, Bar, Charisma, Field, Gauss, Horseshoe, Induction, It, Loadstone, Lodestone, Maxwell, Natural, Od, Oersted, Oomph, Permanent, Personal, Polar, Pole, Pole piece, Poloidal, Pull, Remanence, Retentivity, Slug, Solenoid, Terrella, Terrestrial, Tesla, Tole, Weber

**Magnificence, Magnificent** Epic, Fine, Glory, Gorgeous, Grandeur, Imperial, Laurentian, Lordly, Noble, Pride, Regal, Royal, Splendid, Splendo(u)r, State, Sumptuous, Superb

**Magnifier, Magnify(ing)** Aggrandise, Augment, Binocle, →ENLARGE, Exaggerate, Extol, Increase, Loupe, Megaphone, Microscope, Praise, Teinoscope, Telescope

**Magniloquent** Bombastic, Orotund

**Magnitude** Absolute, Abundance, Amplitude, Apparent, Earthquake, Extent, First, Modulus, Muchness, Photoelectric, Photographic, Scalar, Size, Space, Visual

**Magnolia** An(n)ona, Beaver-tree, Champac, Champak, Mississippi, Sweet bay, Umbrella-tree, Yulan

**Magpie** Bell, Bird, Bishop, Chatterer, Hoarder, Madge, Mag, Margaret, Outer, Pica, Piet, Pyat, Pyet, Pyot

**Magus** Artist

**Magyar** Hungarian, Szekei, Szekel(y), Szekler, Ugrian, Ugric

**Mahogany** Acajou, African, Carapa, Cedrela, Philippine, Toon, Wood

**Mahommedan** Dervish, Shiah

**Maid(en), Maidenly** Abigail, Aia, Amah, Biddy, Bonibell, Bonne, Bonnibell, Bowerwoman, Burd, Chamber, Chaste, Chloe, Clothes-horse, Damoisel, Dam(o)sel, Debut, Dell, Dey, Dresser, Femme de chambre, First, Girl, Guillotine, Ignis-fatuus, Imago, Inaugural, Io, Iras, Iron, Kitchen-wench, Lorelei, M, Marian, May, Miss, Nerissa, Nursery, Nymph, Opening, Over, Parlour, Pucelle, Racehourse, Rhian, Rhine, Scullion, Skivvy, Soubrette, Stillroom, Suivante, Tabby, Table, Thestylis, Tirewoman, Tweeny, Valkyrie, Virgin, Walkyrie, Wench, Wicket

**Maidenhair** Fern, Ginkgo

**Mail** Air, →ARMOUR, Byrnie, Cataphract, Chain, Cuirass, Da(w)k, Direct, E(lectronic), Epistle, Express, Fan, Gusset, Habergeon, Hate, Hauberk, Helm, Junk, Letter, Media, Metered, Panoply, Penny, Pony express, Post, Ring, Royal, Send, Snail, Spam, Surface, Tuille(tte), Voice

**Mailbag** Pouch

**Mailboat** Packet

**Maim** Cripple, Impair, Lame, Main, Mayhem, Mutilate, Vuln, Wound

**Main(s)** Atlantic, Brine, Briny, Bulk, →CENTRAL, Chief, Cockfight, Conduit, Essential,

Foremost, Gala, Gas, Generally, Grid, Gross, Head, → KEY, Lead(ing), Major, Ocean, Pacific, Palmary, Predominant, Prime, Principal, Ring, → SEA, Sheer, Spanish, Staple, Star, Water

**Mainland** Continent, Pomona, Udal

**Mainstay** Backbone, Bastion, Cornerstone, Pillar, Support

**Maintain(er), Maintenance** Alimony, Allege, Ap(p)anage, Argue, Assert, Aver, Avouch, Avoure, Avow, Caretake, Claim, Conserve, Contend, Continue, Defend, Escot, High, Hold, Insist, Keep (up), Lengthman, Preserve, Retention, Run, Separate, Serve, Service, Sustain, Top up, Upbear, Uphold, Upkeep

**Maize** Corn, Hominy, Indian, Indian corn, Mealie, Mealy, Milo, Polenta, Popcorn, Samp, Silk, Stamp, Sweetcorn, Water, Zea

**Majestic, Majesty** August, Britannic, Dignity, Eagle, Grandeur, Imperial, Maestoso, Olympian, Regal, Royal, SM, Sovereign, Stately, Sublime, Tuanku

**Major (domo)** Barbara, Drum, Great, → IMPORTANT, Lulu, Momentous, Pipe, PM, Read, Seneschal, Senior, Sergeant, Signal, Star, Trumpet, Wig

**Majority** Absolute, Age, Body, Eighteen, Landslide, Latchkey, Maturity, Moral, Most, Preponderance, Relative, Silent, Working

**Make(r), Make do, Making** Amass, Assemble, Brand, Build, Cause, Clear, Coerce, Coin, Compel, Compulse, Concoct, Creant, Create, Devise, Earn, Execute, Fabricate, Factive, Fashion, Faute de mieux, Fet(t), Force, Forge, Form, Gar(re), God, Halfpenny, Increate, Mail(e), Manage, Marque, Meg, Name, Nett, Prepare, Production, Reach, Render, Shape, Sort, Temporise, Turn, Wright

▷**Make** *may indicate* an anagram

**Make believe** Fantasy, Fictitious, Pretend, Pseudo

**Make good** Abet, Compensate, Remedy, Succeed, Ulling

**Make hay** Ted

**Make off** Bolt, Leg it, Mosey, Run, Scarper

**Makeover** Rebirth, Redo, Restyle, Revamp

**Makeshift** Bandaid, Crude, Cutcha, Expedient, Jury, Jury-rigged, Kacha, Kachcha, Kludge, Kutcha, Lash-up, Mackle, Pis-aller, Rude, Stopgap, Timenoguy

**Make up, Make-up artist** Ad lib, Blusher, Compensate, Compose, Concealer, Constitute, Constitution, Cosmetics, Eye-liner, Fard, Fucus, Gaud, Gawd, Gene, Genome, Genotype, Greasepaint, Identikit®, Kohl, Liner, Lipstick, Maquillage, Mascara, Metabolism, Moistener, Orchel, Paint, Pancake, Panstick, Powder, Prime, Reconcile, Rouge, Slap(stick), Tidivate, Titivate, Toiletry, Visagiste, War paint, White-face

**Maladroit** Awkward, Clumsy, Gauche, Graceless, Inapt, Inelegant, Inexpert, Unperfect

**Malady** Disease, Illness, Sickness

**Malagas(e)y** Hova, RM

**Malaise** Affluenza

**Malamute** Alaskan

**Malapropism** Catachresis, Slipslop

**Malaria** Ague, Falciparum, Marsh-fever, Paludism, Tap, Vivax

**Malawi(an)** Chichewa, Nyanja, Nyasa

**Malay(an), Malaysia(n)** Austronesian, Bahasa, Bajou, Brunei, Datin, Datuk, D(a)yak, Jawi, Madurese, Moro, .my, Sabahan, Sakai, Sulu, Tagalog, Tokay, Tuan

**Mal-de-mer** Seasickness

**Maldives** Dhivehi

**Male** Alpha, Androgenous, Arrhenotoky, Buck, Bull, Butch, Dog, Ephebe, Ephebus, Gent, Hob, John Doe, Macho, Mansize, Masculine, Patriarchal, Patroclinous, Ram, Rogue, Spear(side), Stag, Stamened, Telamon, Tom, Worthiest of the blood

**Malediction** Curse, Cuss, Oath, Slander

**Malefactor** Criminal, Felon, Villain

**Malevolent, Malevolence** Evil, Fell, Malign, Peri, Pernicious, Sinister, Venomous

**Malformation** Parrot-mouth, Teratogenesis

**Malfunction** Act up, Glitch, Hiccup

**Mali** RMM

**Malice, Malicious** Acid, Animosity, Bitchy, Catty, Cruel, Despiteous, Envy, Fell, Grudge,

Hatchet job, Hatred, Ill-will, Malevolent, Malign, Mudslinger, Narquois, Prepense, Schadenfreude, Serpent, Sneering, Snide, Spite, Spleen, Venom, Viperish, Virulent, Vitriol

**Malign(ant), Malignity** Asperse, Backbite, Badmouth, Baleful, Bespatter, Defame, Denigrate, Detract, Evil, Gall, Harm, Hate-rent, Hatred, Libel, Poor-mouth, Sinister, Slander, Spiteful, Swart(h)y, Toxin, Traduce, Vicious, Vilify, Vilipend, Viperous, Virulent

**Malinger(er)** Absentee, Dodge, Leadswinger, Scrimshank, Shirk, Skrimshank, Truant

**Mall** Arcade, Outlet, Parade, Plaza, Strip

**Mallard** Duck, Sord

**Malleable** Clay, Ductile, Fictile, Plastic, Pliable, Soft

▷**Malleable** *may indicate* an anagram

**Mallet** Beetle, Club, Gavel, Hammer, Mace, Maul, Serving, Stick, Tenderizer

**Mallow** Abutilon, Dwarf, Gossyplum, Indian, Musk, Sida, Urena

**Malnourished** Bag of bones

**Malodorous** Mephitic, Stenchy

**Malpractice(s)** Sculduggery, Simony, Skulduggery

**Malt** Brewer's grain, Diastase, Grains, Grist, Single, Stingo, Straik, Wort

**Maltese (cross)** Falcon, GC

**Maltreat** Abuse, Harm, Maul, Mishandle, Misuse

**Mammal(s)** Animal, Marsupial, Primate

---

**MAMMALS**

***3 letters:***
Bat

***4 letters:***
Anta
Arna
Bear
Hare
Lynx
Peba
Pika
Pudu
Seal
Tahr
Titi
Vole

***5 letters:***
Coati
Dhole
Hyrax
Indri
Lemur
Loris
Okapi
Otter
Pekan
Rasse
Ratel
Sable
Saola
Shrew
Skunk
Sloth
Takin
Tapir
Tayra
Whale

***6 letters:***
Alpaca
Badger
Bobcat
Cervid
Colugo
Cuscus
Dassie
Dugong
Fisher
Glires
Grison
Hydrax
Margay
Marten
Numbat
Olingo
Rabbit
Sea-ape
Sealch
Sealgh
Serval
Taguan
Tanrec
Tee-tee
Teledu
Tenrec
Theria
Vicuña
Weasel
Wombat

***7 letters:***
Caracal
Dolphin
Echidna
Fur seal
Giraffe
Glutton
Guanaco
Leporid
Linsang
Manatee
Meerkat
Peccary
Polecat
Raccoon
Rhytina
Sea-lung
Tamandu
Therian
Tylopod
Zorilla

***8 letters:***
Aardvark
Ant-eater
Cetacean
Creodont
Eutheria
Kinkajou
Mongoose
Pangolin
Pinniped
Platypus
Porpoise
Sirenian
Stegodon
Tamandua
Viverrid

***9 letters:***
Armadillo
Binturong
Cacomixle
Charronia
Dinothere
Glyptodon
Lagomorph
Monotreme
Musteline
Pachyderm
Pronghorn
Solenodon
Stegodont
Water vole
Wolverine

***10 letters:***
Cacomistle
Chevrotain
Dermoptera
Jaguarondi
Jaguarundi
Pine marten
Springhaas
Uintathere

*11 letters:*
Artiodactyl
Chiropteran
Metatherian
Monodelphia
Pipistrelle
Titanothere

*12 letters:*
Chalicothere
Prototherian

*13 letters:*
Notocingulate
Perissodactyl

---

**Mammon** Money, Riches, Wealth
**Mammoth** Epic, Gigantic, Huge, Jumbo, Mastodon, Whopping, Woolly
**Man(kind), Manly, Manliness** Adam, Advance, Andrew, Ask(r), Belt, Best, Betty, Bimana(l), Biped, Bloke, Bo, Boxgrove, Boy, Boyo, Bozo, Butler, Cad, Cairn, Calf, Castle, Cat, Chal, Chap, Checker, Chequer, Chiel, Chordate, Cockey, Cod, Contact, Continuity, Cove, Crew, Cro-Magnon, Cuffin, Cully, Dog, Don, Draught, Dude, Emmanuel, Enlisted, Essex, Everyman, Family, Fancy, Fella, Feller, Fellow, Folsom, Friday, Front, G, Gayomart, Geezer, Gent, Gingerbread, Grimaldi, Guy, He, Heidelberg, Himbo, Hombre, Hominid, Homme, Homo, Homo sapiens, Inner, IOM, Iron, Isle, It, Jack, Java, Joe (Bloggs), Joe Blow, Joe Public, Joe Sixpack, Joe Soap, John(nie), John Doe, Josser, Leading, Limit, Link, Lollipop, M, Mac, Male, Medicine, Microcosm, Mister, Mon, Mondeo, Mr, Muffin, Mun, Neanderthal, Numbers, Nutcracker, Oreopithecus, Organisation, Ou, Paleolithic, Party, Pawn, Peking, Person, Piece, Piltdown, Pin, Pithecanthropus, Property, Raff, Ray, Remittance, Renaissance, Resurrection, Rhodesian, Right-hand, Rook, Sandwich, Servant, Servitor, Ship, Sinanthropus, Sir, Sodor, Soldier, Solo, Spear, Staff, Stag, Standover, Straw, Terran, Third, Thursday, Trinil, Twelfth, Tyke, Type, Utility, Valet, Vir(ile), Vitality, White van, Wight
**Man-about-town** Boulevardier
**Manacle** Fetter, Handcuff, Iron, Shackle
**Manage(r), Manageable, Management, Managing** Accomplish, Achieve, Adhocracy, Administer, Agent, Amildar, Anger, Attain, Aumil, Bank, Behave, Board, Boss, Bring off, Chamberlain, Chief, City, Clubmaster, Come by, Conduct, Contrive, Control, Cope, Crisis, Darogha, Direct, Docile, Eke, Exec(utive), Fare, Fend, Find, Floor, Fund, Gerent, Get by, Govern, Grieve, Handle, Head bummer, Honcho, Husband(ry), IC, Impresario, Intendant, Lead, Line, Local, Logistical, MacReady, Maître d'hotel), Make do, Manipulate, Manoeuvre, Middle, Nomenklatura, Operate, Organise, Oversee, Plastic, Proctor, Procurator, Régisseur, Rig, Road(ie), → **RUN**, Scrape, Shift, Stage, Steward, Strategy, Subjugate, Subsist, Succeed, Suit, Superintend, Supervisor, Swing, Sysop, Tawie, Top, Tractable, Transact, Treatment, Trustee, Wangle, Webmaster, Wield(y), Yare
**Manatee** Lamantin, Mermaid, Sea-ape, Sea-cow, Sirenian
**Manchu** Fu
**Mandala** Kalachakra
**Mandarin** Bureaucrat, Chinaman, Kuo-Yu, Nodding, Satsuma, Tangerine, Yamen
**Mandate, Mandatory** Authority, Decree, De rigueur, Fiat, Incumbent, Order, Unavoidable
**Mandela** Madiba, Nelson
**Mandrake** Springwort
**Mandrel** Triblet
**Mane(d), Manes** Crest, Encolure, Jubate, Larva(e), Shades
**Manège** Horseplay, Train
**Manganese** Diagolite, Mn, Synadelphite, Wadd
**Mange, Mangy** Sarcoptic, Scabby
**Manger** Cratch, Crib, Hack, Stall, Trough
**Mangle** Agrise, Butcher, Distort, Garble, Hack, Hackle, Haggle, Mammock, Wring(er)
▷**Mangle** *may indicate* an anagram
**Mango** Dika
**Manhandle** Frogmarch, Maul, Mousle, Paw, Rough
**Manhater** Misanthrope
**Manhattan** Bowery
**Mania(c)** Cacoethes, Craze, Frenzy, Lunacy, Paranoia, Passion, Psychopath, Rage, Tarentism
**Manic** Hectic
**Manichaean** Albi
**Manicurist** Handmaid

**Manifest(ation), Manifestly** Apparent, Arising, Attest, Avatar, Epiphany, Evident, Evince, Exhibit, Extravert, Extrovert, Feat, List, Marked, Mode, Notably, Obvious, Open, Overt, Schizothymia, Show, Sign, Undisguised, Wrath

**Manifesto** Communist, Plank, Platform, Policy, Pronunciamento

**Manifold(ness)** Many, Multeity, Multiple

**Manila** Abaca, Cheroot

**Manioc** Cassava

**Maniple** Fannel, Fanon

**Manipulate, Manipulative, Manipulator, Manipulation** Bend, Card-sharp, Chiropractor, Cog, Control, Cook, Demagogic, Diddle, Exploit, Fashion, Finagle, Finesse, Gerrymander, Handle, Hellerwork, Hot wire, Jerrymander, Juggle, Legerdemain, Logodaedalus, Massage, Masseuse, Master-slave, McTimoney chiropractic, Milk, Osteopath, Physiotherapist, Play off, Ply, Rig, Spin, Svengali, Swing, Tong, Tweeze, Use, Wangle, → WIELD

▷**Manipulate** *may indicate* an anagram

**Manna** Alhagi, Briancon, Food, Godsend, Trehala, Turkish

**Manner(ism), Mannerly, Manners** Accent, Airs, À la, Appearance, Attitude, Bedside, Behaved, Behaviour, Bon ton, Breeding, Carriage, Comedy, Comportment, Conduct, Couth, Crew, Custom, Delivery, Demeanour, Deportment, Ethos, Etiquette, Farand, Farrand, Farrant, Guise, Habit, How, Method, Mien, Mister, Mode, Mood, Morality, Mores, Of, Ostent, Panache, Politesse, Presence, Presentation, P's & Q's, Quirk, Rate, Rhetoric, Side, Sort, Style, Table, Thew(s), Thewe(s), Trick, Upsee, Upsey, Upsy, Urbanity, Vein, Way, Wise

**Manoeuvre(s)** Alley-oop, Box clever, Campaign, Castle, Christie, Christy, Démarche, Deployment, Ebrillade, Engineer, Exercise, Faena, Fianchetto, Finesse, Fork, Gambit, Grey mail, Half-board, Heimlich, Hot-dog, Jink(s), Jockey, Loop, Manipulate, Op(eration), Pendule, Pesade, Ploy, Pull out, Renversement, Ruse, Short cut, Skewer, Steer, Stickhandle, Tactic, Takeover, Telemark, Three-point-turn, Use, U-turn, Valsalva, Wear, Wheel(ie), Whipstall, Wile, Wingover, Zigzag

▷**Manoeuvre** *may indicate* an anagram

**Man-of-war** Armada, Bluebottle, Destroyer, Ironclad, Portuguese

**Manor (house)** Area, Demain, Demesne, Estate, Hall, Kelmscott, Schloss, Snowshill, Township, Vill(a), Waddesdon

**Manse** Glebe-house, Parsonage

**Mansion** Broadlands, Burghley House, Casa, Castle Howard, Chateau, Chatworth House, Chevening, Cliveden, Knole, Luton Hoo, Mentmore, Palace, Palazzo, Penshurst Place, Pile, Queen's House, Seat, Stourhead, Stowe, Waddesdon Manor, Woburn Abbey

**Manslaughter** Culpable homicide

**Mantis** Praying

**Mantle** Asthenosphere, Authority, Blanket, Burnous(e), Capote, Caracalla, Chlamydate, Cloak, Dolman, Elijah, Gas, Lithosphere, Pall, Pallium, Paludament, Pelisse, Rochet, Shawl, Sima, Toga, Tunic, Vakas, Veil

**Mantra** Incantation

**Mantuan** Maro, Virgil

**Manual** Blue collar, Bradshaw, Cambist, Console, Enchiridion, Great (organ), Guide, Hand, Handbook, How-to, Portolan(o), Positif, Sign

**Manufacture(r), Manufacturing** Assemble, Brew, Create, Fabricate, Forger, Industrial(ist), Kanban, Make, Produce, Wainwright

**Manure** Compost, Dressing, Dung, → FERTILISER, Green, Guano, Hen-pen, Lime, Mould, Muck, Sha(i)rn, Tath

**Manuscript(s)** Book of Kells, Codex, Codicology, Folio, Hand, Holograph, Longhand, Miniscule, MS, Opisthograph, Palimpsest, Papyrus, Parchment, Script, Scroll, Scrowl(e), Slush-pile, Uncial, Vellum

**Manx(man)** Cat, Gael, IOM, Kelly, Kelt

▷**Manx** *may indicate* a last letter missing

**Many** Bags, Bevy, C, CD, Countless, Crew(e), D, Galore, Hantle, Herd, Horde, Host, L, Legion, Lot, M, Manifold, Mony, Multi(tude), Multiple, Myriad, Numerous, Oodles, Power, Scad, Scores, Sight, Slew, Stacks, Tons, Umpteen, Untold

▷**Many** *may indicate* the use of a Roman numeral letter
**Many-sided** Versatile
**Maoist** Naxalite, Red Guard
**Maori (house)** Hapu, Hauhau, Hori, Iwi, Jikanga, Kaumatua, Mallowpuff, Moa hunter, Tangata whenua, Te reo, Wahine, Whare
**Map(s), Mapping** Atlas, A-Z, Bijection, Card, Cartogram, Chart, Chorography, Choropleth, Chromosome, Cognitive, Contour, Digital, Face, Genetic, Horoscope, Image, Inset, Key, Linguistic, Loxodromic, Mappemond, Mental, Mosaic, Moving, Mud, OS, Perceptual, Plan(isphere), Plat, Plot, Portolano, Relief, Road, Satnav, Sea-card, Sea-chart, Site, Sketch, Star, Strip, Topography, Weather
**Maple** Acer, Bird's-eye, Box elder, Flowering, Japanese, Manitoba, Mazer, Norway, Plane, Silver, Sugar, Sycamore, Syrup
**Map-maker** Cartographer, OS, Speed
**Maquis** Queach, Underground
**Mar** Blight, Blot, Damage, Denature, Dere, Despoil, Disfigure, Impair, Poison, Soil, Spoil, Taint
**Marabout** Sofi, Sufi
**Marathon** Comrades, Fun run, Huge, London, Long, Race, Run, Two Oceans
**Maraud(er)** Amalekite, Attacker, Bandit, Hun, Pillager, Pirate, Predator, Prowler, Raid, Viking
**Marble(s), Marbling** Aeginetan, Agate, All(e)y, Arch, Arundelian, Bonce, Bonduc, Bool, Boondoggle, Bowl, Calcite, Carrara, Chequer, Cipollino, Commoney, Devil's, Dump, Elgin, Forest, Humite, Hymettus, Knicker, Landscape, Languedoc, Lucullite, Marl, Marmarosis, Marmoreal, Marver, Mind, Mosaic, Mottle, Nero-antico, Nickar, Nicker, Onychite, Onyx, Ophicalcite, Paragon, Parian, Pavonazzo, Pentelic(an), Petworth, Phigalian, Plonker, Plunker, Purbeck, Rance, Ringer, Ring-taw, Ruin, Sanity, Scagliola, Spangcockle, Taw, Tolley, Variegate, Verd antique, Wits, Xanthian
**Marcel** Proust
**March(ing), Marcher** Abut, Adjoin, Advance, Alla marcia, Anabasis, Border(er), Borderland, Boundary, Colonel Bogey, Dead, Defile, Demo(nstration), Étape, File, Footslog, Forced, Freedom, Fringe, Galumph, Go, Goosestep, Grand, Hikoi, Hunger, Ides, Jarrow, Lide, Limes, Lockstep, Long, Lord, Majorette, Meare, Music, → PARADE, Paso doble, Procession, Progress, Protest, Quick, Regimental, Rogue's, Route, Saint, Slow time, Step, Strunt, Strut, Tramp, Trek, Trio, Tromp, Troop, Wedding, Yomp
▷**March** *may indicate* 'Little Women' character, Amy, Beth, Jo, Meg
**Marco** Il Milione, Polo
**Marco Polo** Airport, Explorer
**Mardi Gras** J'ouvert
**Mare** Dam, Flanders, Grey, Horse, M, MacCurdle's, Shanks's, Spanish, Timber, Yaud
**Margaret** Anjou, Meg, Peg, Rita
**Margarine** Oleo
**Marge, Margin(al)** Andean, Annotate, Bank, Border, Borderline, Brim, Brink, Constructive, Convergent, Curb, Edge, Fimbria, Gross, Hair's breadth, Kerb, Lean, Leeway, Limit, Lip, Littoral, Neck, Nose, Periphery, Peristome, Profit, Rand, Repand, → RIM, Selvedge, Sideline, Spread, Tail, Term
**Marginal note** Apostil(le), K'ri, Postil
**Margosa** Melia, Nim
**Maria(nne)** France, Tia
**Marie** Dressler, Tempest
**Marigold** Calendula, Gool, Gule, Kingcup, Tagetes
**Marijuana** Alfalfa, Bhang, Camberwell carrot, Dagga, Gage, Ganja, Grass, Greens, Gungeon, Ha-ha, Hay, Hemp, Herb, J, Jimson weed, Jive, Joint, Kaif, Kef, Kif, Leaf, Lid, Locoweed, Mary-Jane, Pot, Roach, Rope, Sinsemilla, Splay, Spliff, Tea, Toke, Weed
**Marina** Wharf
**Marinade, Marinate** Chermoula, Escabeche, Jerk, Steep
**Marine (animal)** Aquatic, Bootie, Bootneck, Briny, Cephalopod, Chaetognath, Cnidarian,

Coelenterate, Comatulid, Ctenophora, Cunjevoi, Enteropneusta, Flustra, Foram(inifer), Galoot, Graptolite, Harumfrodite, Hemichorda, Holothurian, Horse, Hydrocoral, Hydroid, Hydromedusa, Jarhead, Jolly, Lancelet, Leatherneck, Lobster, Mercantile, Mere-swine, Mistress Roper, Oceanic, Otarine, Physalia, Pogonophoron, Pollywag, Pollywog, Rat-tail, Salpa, Sea(-soldier), Seston, Thalassian, Ultra, Venus's girdle

**Mariner** AB, Ancient, Master, Matelot, MN, Noah, RM, Sailor, Salt, Seafarer, Shellback, Spacecraft, Tar

**Marionette(s)** Fantoccini, Puppet

**Marital** Conjugal

**Marjoram** Amaracus, Origan, Pot, Sweet, Wild, Winter-sweet

**Mark(ing), Marked, Marker, Mark out, Marks** Accent, Aesc, Annotate, Anoint, Antony, Apostrophe, Asterisk, Astrobleme, Badge, Banker, Barcode, Bethumb, Bind(h)i, Biological, Birth, Blaze, Blot, Blotch, Bollard, Brand, Bruise, Buck, Bull, Buoy, Butt, Cachet, Cairn, Calibrate, Caract, Caret, Caste, CE, Cedilla, Celebrate, Characteristic, Chatter, Chequer, Cicatrix, Class, Clout, Colon, Comma, Cone, Control, Coronis, Crease, Criss-cross, Cross(let), Cup (and ring), Cursor, Dash, Define, Denote, Dent, Designate, Diacritic, Diaeresis, Dieresis, Distinction, Ditto, DM, Dot, Duckfoot quote, Dupe, Emblem, Endorsement, Enseam, Ensign, Enstamp, Etch, Exclamation, Expression, Fanion, Feer, Field, Finger, Flag, Flash, Fleck, Fox(ing), Freckle, Genetic, Glyph, Gnomon, Gospel, Grade, Guillemet, Gybe, Hacek, Haemangioma, Hair-line, Hash, Hatch, Heed, Hickey, High water, Hoofprint, Hyphen, Impress(ion), Imprint, Indicium, Infinitive, Ink, Inscribe, Insignia, Interrogation, Inukshuk, Keel, Kite, Kumkum, Label, Lentigo, Line, Ling, Livedo, Logo, Lovebite, Low water, M, Macron, Magic, Matchmark, Mate, MB, Medical, Merk, Mint, Minute, Mottle, NB, Nectar-guide, Nick, Nota bene, Notal, Notch, Note, Notice, Obelisk, Obelus, Observe, Oche, Paginate, Paragraph, Paraph, Peg, Period, Piece together, Pilcrow, Pin, Pinpoint, Pit, Plage, Plimsoll, Pling, Pock, Point(ille), Pointer, Popinjay, Port wine, Post, Presa, Printer's, Pronounced, Proof, Punctuation, Question, Quotation, Record, Reference, Regard, Register, Regulo, Remarque, Rillmark, Ring, Ripple, Roundel, Rune, Sanction, Scar, Scorch, Score(r), Scratch, Scribe, Scuff, Section, See, Senora, Service, Shadow, Shelf, Shilling, Shoal, Sigil, Sign(ature), Singe, Smit, Smut, Smutch, Soft touch, Sordes, Speck, Splodge, Splotch, Spot, Spousage, Stain, Stamp, Stencil, Stigma(ta), Strawberry, Streak, Stress, Stretch, Stripe, Stroke, Sucker, Swan-upping, Swastika, Symbol, Tag, Target, Tarnish, Tatow, Tattoo, Tee, Theta, Thread, Thumb, Tick, Tide, Tie, Tika, Tikka, Tilak, Tilde, Tittle, Token, Touchmark, Trace, Track, Trade, Trema, Trout, Tug(h)ra, Twain, Umlaut, Ure, Utility, Victim, Wand, Warchalking, Watch, Weal, Welt, Whelk

**Market(ing), Market day, Marketeer, Market place** Advergaming, Agora, Alcaiceria, Arbitrageur, Available, Baltic, Bazaar, Bear, Billingsgate, Black, Black stump, Borgo, Bull, Buyers', Capital, Captive, Car boot sale, Cattle, Change, Chowk, Cinema, Circular, Cluster, Commodity, Common, Covent Garden, Demo, Denet, Direct, Discount, Dragon, eBay®, EC, Emergency, Emerging, Emporium, Errand, Exchange, Exhibition, Fair, Farmers', Feeing, Flea, Forum, Forward, Free, Grey, Growth, Insert, Internal, Kerb, Lloyds, Main, Mandi, Mart, Mass, Meat, Mercat, Money, Niche, Nundine, Obigosony, Oligopoly, Open (air), Order-driven, Outlet, Overt, Pamphlet, Perfect, Piazza, Poster, Press, Promote, Publicity, Radio, Rag fair, Reach, Relationship, Rialto, Sale, Sell, Sellers', Servqual, Share, Shop, Single, Social, Societal, Sook, Souk, Spam, Spot, Stance, Staple, Stock, Stock Exchange, Suq, Tattersall's, TECHMARK®, Telesales, Terminal, Test, Third, Tiger, Trade, Tron, Tryst, USP, Vent, Viral, Wall Street, Yard sale

**Market garden** Truck-farm

**Marksman** Archer, Crack shot, Sharpshooter, Shootist, Shot, Sniper, Tell

**Marlborough** Blenheim, Churchill

**Marlene** Lilli

**Marlin** Spearfish

**Marmalade** Cat, Mammee-sapota, Preserve, Squish

**Marmoset** Jacchus, Mico, Midas, Monkey, Wistiti

**Marmot** Bobac, Bobak, Dassie, Groundhog, Hoary, Hyrax, Klipdas, Rodent, Whistler, Woodchuck

**Maroon** Abandon, Brown, Castaway, Enisle, Firework, Inisle, Isolate, Strand
**Marquee** Pavilion, Tent, Top
**Marquess, Marquis** De Sade, Granby, Lorne, Queensberry
**Marquetry** Boul(l)e, Buhl, Inlay
**Marriage, Marry, Married (woman)** → ALLIANCE, Ally, Amate, Arranged, Bed, Beenah, Bigamy, Bridal, Buckle, Buckle-beggar, Civil, Cleek(it), Coemption, Combine, Common law, Commuter, Companionate, Confarreation, Conjoin, Conjugal, Connubial, Couple, Coverture, Digamy, Endogamy, Espousal, Espouse, Exogamy, Feme covert, Forsooth, Fuse, Gandharva, Genial, Goody, Group, Hedge, Hetaerism, Hetairism, Hitch, Hymen(eal), Indeed, Join, Jugal, Ketubah, Knit, Knot, Lavender, Levirate, M, Match, Mating, Matrilocal, Matrimony, Matron, Memsahib, Mésalliance, Ming, Missis, Missus, Mixed, Monandry, Monogamy, Morganatic, Nikah, Noose, Nuptial, Open, Pair, Pantagamy, Pardie, Patrilocal, Polygamy, Punalua, Putative, Quotha, Sacrament, Sannup, Shidduch, Shotgun, Splice, Tie, Tie the knot, Trial, Troggs, Troth, Umfazi, → UNION, Unite, W, Wed, Wedding, Wedlock, Wive
**Marriageable** Marrow, Nubile, Parti
**Marriage-broker** Shadchan
**Marron** Chestnut
**Marrow** Bone, Courgette, Friend, Gist, Kamokamo, Medulla, Mountain, Myeloid, Pith, Pumpkin, Spinal, Squash, Vegetable, Zucchini
**Mars** Areography, Ares, Red (planet), Syrtis major, Tharsis, Tyr
**Marsh(y)** Bayou, Bog, Camargue, Chott, Corcass, Emys, Everglades, Fen(land), Hackney, Maremma, Merse, Mire, Morass, Ngaio, Paludal, Palustrine, Plashy, Pontine, Pripet, Quagmire, Rann of Kutch, Romney, Salina, Salt, Shott, Slade, Slough, Sog, Spew, Spue, Swale, Swamp, Taiga, Terai, Vlei, Wetlands
**Marshal** Air, Arrange, Array, Assemble, Commander, Earl, Earp, Field, Foch, French, Hickok, MacMahon, Muster, Neil, Ney, Order, Pétain, Provost, Shepherd, Sky, Steward, Tedder, Tito, Usher, Vauban, Yardman
**Marshmallow** Althaea, Mallowpuff
**Marsupial** Bandicoot, Bilby, Cuscus, Dasyure, Dibbler, Didelphia, Diprotodon(t), Dunnart, Euro, Honey mouse, Honey possum, Kangaroo, Koala, Macropod, Metatheria, Notoryctes, Nototherium, Numbat, Opossum, Pademelon, Pad(d)ymelon, Petaurist, Phalanger, Pig-rat, Polyprodont, Possum, Potoroo, Pouched mouse, Pygmy glider, Quokka, Quoll, Roo, Tammar, Tasmanian devil, Theria, Thylacine, Tuan, Wallaby, Wambenger, Wombat, Yapo(c)k
**Marten** Fisher, Mustela, Pekan, Pine, Sable, Woodshock
**Martensite** Sorbite
**Martha** Vineyard
**Martial (arts)** Aikido, Bellicose, Budo, Capoeira, Capuera, Chopsocky, Dojo, Iai-do, Judo, Ju-jitsu, Karate, Kata, Kendo, Kick boxing, Krav Maga, Kumite, Kung fu, Militant, Muay thai, Ninjitsu, Ninjutsu, Sensei, Shintaido, Tae Bo®, Tae kwon do, T'ai chi (chuan), Warlike, Wushu
**Martin** Bird, Dean, Luther, Swallow
**Martinet** Captious, Ramrod, Stickler, Tyrant
**Martini®** Cocktail, Henry
**Martyr(dom), Martyrs** Alban, Alphege, Campion, Colosseum, Cranmer, Donatist, Justin, Lara, Latimer, Metric, MM, Passional, Persecute, Ridley, Sebastian, Shaheed, Shahid, Stephen, Suffer, Tolpuddle, Wishart
**Marvel(lous)** Blinder, Bodacious, Brilliant, Bully, Épatant, Fab(ulous), Fantabulous, Lulu, Magic, Marl, Miracle, Mirific, Peachy, Phenomenon, Prodigious, Selcouth, Superb, Super-duper, Swell, Terrific, Wonder
**Marx(ism), Marxist** Aspheterism, Chico, Comintern, Commie, Groucho, Gummo, Harpo, Karl, Lenin, Mao, Menshevik, Revisionism, Tanky, Tipamaro, Zeppo
**Mary** Bloody, Celeste, Contrary, Madonna, Magdalene, Moll, Morison, Our Lady, Tum(my), Typhoid, Virgin
**Marylebone** Station
**Marzipan** Frangipani, Marchpane
**Mascara** Eye-black
**Mascot** Charm, Four-leaf clover, → TALISMAN, Telesm, Token

**Masculine, Masculinity** Butch, He, He-man, Linga(m), M, Machismo, Macho, Male, Manly, Virile, Yang

**Maser** Laser, Optical

**Mash(er)** Beat, Beau, Beetle, Brew, Flirt, Lady-killer, Pap, Pestle, Pound, Puree, Sour, Squash, Squidge

**Mask(ed)** Bird cage, Camouflage, Cloak, Cokuloris, Conceal, Death, Disguise, Dissemble, Domino, Face pack, False face, Front, Gas, Gorgoneion, Guise, Hide, Larvated, Life, Loo, Loup, Mascaron, Matte, Oxygen, Persona, Respirator, Screen, Semblance, Shadow, Ski, Stalking-horse, Stocking, Stop out, Template, Veil, Visor, Vizard

**Mason(ry)** Ashlar, Ashler, Brother, Builder, Chiseller, Corbel, Cowan, Emplecton, Free, Isodoma, Isodomon, Isodomum, Jude, Lodge, Master, Moellon, Monumental, Nogging, Opus, Perry, Random, Rubblework, Rusticwork, Squinch, Stone dresser, Stylobate

**Masque(rade), Masquerader** Comus, Disguise, Domino, Guisard, Mum(m), Mummery, Pose, Pretend

**Mass(es)** Aggregate, Agnus Dei, Anniversary, Atomic, Banket, Bezoar, Bike, Black Dollop, Blob, Body, Bulk, Cake, Canon, Chaos, Clot, Compound, Congeries, Conglomeration, Consecration, Core, Crith, Critical, Crowd, Demos, Density, Dona nobis, Dozens, Flake, Flock, Flysch, Folk, Geepound, Glob, Gradual, Gramme, Gravitational, Great, Heap, Herd, High, Horde, Huddle, Hulk, Inertial, Isobare, Jud, Kermesse, Kermis, Kilo(gram), Kirmess, Lenticle, Low, Lump, M, Magma, Majority, Midnight, Missa, Missa solemnis, Mob, Molar, Month's mind, Mop, Nelson, Nest, Phalanx, Pile, Plebs, Plumb, Pontifical, Populace, Proper, Raft, Ragtag, Red, Requiem, Rest, Ruck, Salamon, Salmon, Sanctus, Scrum, Sea, Serac, Service, Shock, Sicilian, Size, Slub, Slug, Solar, Solemn, Solid, Stack, Stroma, Sursum Corda, Swarm, Tangle, Te Igitur, Tektite, Trental, Vesper, Vigil, Volume, Wad, Weight, Welter

**Massachusetts** Bay State

**Massacre** Alamo, Amritsar, Battue, Beziers, Blood-bath, Butcher, Carnage, Glencoe, Havock, Kanpur, Lidice, Manchester, Peterloo, Pogrom, Purge, St Bartholomew's Day, Scullabogue, Scupper, September, Sicilian vespers, Slaughter, Slay, Trounce, Wounded Knee

**Massage, Masseur** An mo, Cardiac, Chafer, Chavutti thirumal, Do-in, Effleurage, Facial, Hellerwork, Indian head, →KNEAD, Malax, Manipulate, Osteopathy, Palp, Petrissage, Physio, Reiki, Rolf(ing), Rubber, Shampoo, Shiatsu, Stone, Stroke, Swedish, Tapotement, Thai, Tripsis, Tui na

**Massif** Makalu

**Massive** Big, Bull, Colossal, Cyclopean, Gang, Gargantuan, Heavy, Herculean, Huge, Monolithic, Monumental, Ponderous, Seismic, Strong, Titan

**Mast(ed), Masthead** Acorn, Aerial, Banner, Beech, Captain's, Crosstree, Flag, Foretop, Foreyard, High top, Hounds, Jigger, Jury, M, Mizzen, Mooring, Pannage, Pole, Racahout, Royal, Ship-rigged, Spar, Top-gallant, Truck, Venetian

**Master(ly), Mastery** Ace, Adept, Artful, Artisan, Baalebos, Baas, Beak, Beat, Boss, Buddha, Bwana, Captain, Careers, Checkmate, Choir, Chorus, Conquer, Control, Dan, Dominate, Dominie, Drawing, Employer, Enslave, Exarch, Expert, Genius, Gov, Grand, Grip, Harbour, Herr, Himself, International, Learn, Lord, MA, Maestro, Magistral, Mas(s), Massa, Maulana, Mes(s), Nail, Nkosi, Old, Ollamh, Ollav, Oner, Oppress, Original, Overcome, Overlord, Overpower, Overseer, Padrone, Passed, Past, Pedant, Question, Rabboni, Riding, Ring, Schoolman, Seed, Seigneur, Seignior, Signorino, Sir(e), Skipper, →SUBDUE, Subjugate, Superate, Surmount, Swami, Tame, Task, Teach, Thakin, Towkay, Tuan, Usher, Vanquish, Virtuoso

**Mastermind** Brain, Conceive, Direct, Engineer, Genius, Orchestrate, Oversee, Scheme

**Masterpiece** Chef d'oeuvre, Classic, Creation, Magnum opus

**Mastersinger** Sachs

**Master-stroke** Coup, Triumph

**Mastic** Sealant

**Masturbate, Masturbation** Abuse, Blow, Frig, Gratify, Jerk off, Jock, Onanism, Self-pollution, Toss off, Tribady, Wank, Whack off

**Mat(ted), Matting** Bast, Bath, Beer, Capillary, Carpet, Coaster, Coir, Cork, Crash, Doily, Dojo, Door, Doyl(e)y, Dutch mattress, Felt, Floor, Inlace, Mouse, Pad, Paunch, Place, Plat,

Prayer, Rug, Rush, Surf, Table, Taggy, → TANGLE, Tat(ami), Tatty, Taut, Tautit, Tawt, Tomentose, Web, Welcome, Zarf

**Matador** Card, Espada, Ordonez, Theseus, Torero

**Match(ed), Matching** Agree, Alliance, Amate, Balance, Benefit, Besort, Bonspiel, Bout, Carousel, Coincide, Compare, Compeer, Congreve, Consolation, Contest, Cope, Correlate, Correspond, Counterpart, Cup tie, Derby, Doubles, Emulate, Engagement, Equal(ise), Equate, Even, Even Stevens, Event, Exhibition, Fellow, Fit, Fixture, Four-ball, Foursome, Friction, Friendly, Fusee, Fuzee, Game, Go, Greensome, Grudge, International, Joust, Light, Locofoco, Love, Lucifer, Main, Marriage, Marrow, Marry, Meet, Mouse, Needle, ODI, Pair(s), Paragon, Parallel, Parti, Peer, Pit, Play-off, Port-fire, Prizefight, Promethean, Quick, Replica, Reproduce, Return, Rival, Road game, Roland, Rubber, Safety, Semifinal, Sevens, Shield, Shoo-in, Shooting, Shouting, Singles, Slanging, Slow, Slugfest, Spunk, Striker, Suit, Sync(h), → TALLY, Team, Test, Testimonial, Texas scramble, Tie, Tone, To scale, Twin, Twosome, Union, Venue, Vesta, Vesuvian, Wedding

**Matchbox label (collecting)** Phillumeny

**Match girl** Bride

**Match-holder** Lin(t)stock

**Matchless** Nonpareil, Non(e)such, Orinda, Superlative, Unique

**Matchmaker** Blackfoot, Broker, Pairer, Promoter, Shadchan

**Mate, Mating** Achates, Adam, Amigo, Amplexus, Assistant, Assortative, Bedfellow, Bo, Boatswain, Breed, Buddy, Buffer, Butty, Check, Chess, China, Chum, Cobber, Cock, Comrade, Consort, Crony, Cully, Digger, Eve, Feare, Feer, Fellow, Fere, Fiere, First, Fool's, Helper, Husband, Ilex, Inbreed, Maik, Make, Marrow, Marry, Match, Mister, Mucker, Nick, Nickar, Oldster, Oppo, → PAIR, Pal, Pangamy, Panmixia, Panmixis, Paragon, Partner, Pheer(e), Pirrauru, Playfellow, Running, Scholar's, Scouse, Second, Serve, Sex, Skaines, Smothered, Soul, Sport, → SPOUSE, Tea, Tup, Wack, Wacker, Wag, Wed, Wife, Wus(s)

**Material(ism)** Agitprop, Apparatus, Appropriate, Apt, Bakelite, → CLOTH, Compo, Composite, Copy, Corporeal, Data, Dialectical, Documentation, Earthling, Earthly, → FABRIC, Factual, Fallout, Fertile, Fuel, Germane, Glass, Greensand, Historical, Hylic, Illusion, Infill, Kindling, Leading, Magnox®, Matter, Murr(h)a, Padding, Pertinent, Physical, Positive, Raw, Real, Reify, Relevant, Repertoire, Sharkskin, Substance, Tangible, Thingy, Tissue (equivalent), Underfelt, Worldly

---

**MATERIALS**

*3 letters:*
Cob
Pug

*4 letters:*
Bole
Frit
Gang
Moxa
Oils
Tape
Ylem

*5 letters:*
Fibro
Fines
Flong
Fomes
Fritt
Metal
Oasis®
Staff
Stuff

*6 letters:*
Armure
Borsic
Byssus
Cermet
Corfam®
Fablon®
Gangue
Gypsum
Raffia
Sporex®
Tartan®
Tusser

*7 letters:*
Ballast
Ceramic
Matting
Oilskin
Phantom
Protore
Pugging
Sagathy
Textile
Tinfoil

*8 letters:*
Blastema
Concrete
Fettling
Graphite
Illuvium
Lambskin
Oilcloth
Regolith
Silicone
Skirting

*9 letters:*
Aggregate
Austenite
Celluloid
Cellulose
Elastomer
Fibrefill
Macintosh
Micromesh
Pina-cloth
Polythene
Sackcloth
Samsonite®
Towelling

*10 letters:*
Fibreboard
Fibreglass
Protoplasm
Thermolite®

*11 letters:*
Fibrocement
Gutta percha
Interfacing
Papier-maché
Polystyrene

*12 letters:*
Agalmatolite
Plasterboard
Plasterstone

*13 letters:*
Wattle and daub

---

**Materialise** Appear, Apport, Arise, Click, Reify
**Materialist(ic)** Banausian, Earthling, Hylist, Hyloist, Philistine, Somatist
**Mathematician** Babbage, Geometer, Optime, Statistician, Wrangler

---

**MATHEMATICIANS**

***4 letters:***
Hero
Zeno

***5 letters:***
Bayes
Boole
Euler
Frege
Gauss
Godel
Julia
Klein
Pitts

***6 letters:***
Agnesi
Bessel
Briggs
Cantor
Cocker
Euclid
Fermat
Gunter
Jacobi
Jevons
Kaluza
Mobius
Napier
Newton
Pascal
Turing
Walker
Wiener

***7 letters:***
Fourier
Hawking
Hilbert
Laplace
Leibniz
Neumann
Penrose
Poisson
Ptolemy
Pytheas
Riemann
Russell

***8 letters:***
Archytas
Bourbaki
De Morgan
Goldbach
Hamilton
Lagrange
Mercator
Playfair
Poincare

***9 letters:***
Bernoulli
Descartes
Dunstable
Fibonacci
Friedmann
Minkowski
Whitehead

***10 letters:***
Apollonius
Archimedes
Diophantos
Mandelbrot
Pythagoras
Torricelli
Von Neumann

***11 letters:***
Von Leibnitz

***12 letters:***
Eratosthenes

---

**Mathematics, Mathematical, Maths** Algebra, Applied, Arithmetic, Arsmetrick, Calculus, Combinatorics, Exact science, Geometry, Haversine, Higher, Logarithms, Mechanics, New, Numbers, Porism, Pure, Topology, Trig, Trigonometry
**Matilda** Liar, Swag, Untruthful, Waltzing
**Matinee** Coat, Idol, Show
**Mating** Pangamy
**Matins** Nocturn
**Matricide** Orestes
**Matrimony, Matrimonial** Bed, Conjugal, Marriage, Nuptial, Sacrament, Spousal, Wedlock
**Matrix** Active, Array, Boston, Hermitian, Jacobian, Mould, Orthogonal, Pattern, Scattering, SI, Square, Symmetric, Transpose, Uterus
**Matron** Dame, Hausfrau, Lucretia, Nurse, Warden
**Matt(e), Matted** Dense, Dingy, Dull, Taggy
**Matter** Affair, Alluvium, Bioblast, Biogen, Body, Business, Concern, Condensed, Consequence, Content, Count, Dark, Degenerate, Ejecta, Empyema, Epithelium, Evidence, Flux, Front, Gear, Gluon, Go, Grey, Hanging, Humus, Hyle, Ichor, Impost(h)ume, Issue, Mass, Material, Molecule, Multiverse, Neutrino, Phlegm, Pith, Plasma, Point, Positron, Premise, Protoplasm, Pulp, Pus, Quark, Reading, Reck, Reke, Scum, Sediment, Shebang, Signify, Solid, Sputum, Stereome, Stuff, Subject, → SUBSTANCE, Symptom, Theme, Thing, Tissue, Topic, Tousle, Touzle, Vinyl, White, Ylem
**Matter of fact** Pragmatic
**Matthew** Arnold, Levi
**Mattress** Air bed, Bed(ding), Biscuit, Dutch, Featherbed, Foam, Futon, Lilo®, Pallet, Pa(i)lliasse, Spring, Tick, Waterbed
**Mature, Maturity** Adult, Age, Auld, Blossom, Bold, Concoct, Develop, Fully-fledged, Gestate, Grow (up), Mellow, Metaplasis, Old, Puberty, Ripe(n), Rounded, Seasoned, Upgrow(n)

**Maudlin** Fuddled, Mawkish, Sentimental, Slip-slop, Sloppy, Soppy, Too-too
**Maul** Claw, Hammer, Manhandle, Paw, Rough, Savage, Tear
**Maundy** Money, Nipter, Thursday
**Mauretanian, Mauritania(n)** Moor, RIM
**Mauritius** MS
**Mausoleum** Agra, Halicarnassus, Mole, Sepulchre, Taj Mahal, Tomb
**Mauve** Lavender, Lilac, Mallow, Perkin's
**Maverick** Free agent, Loner, Misfit, Nonconformist, Rebel, Rogue, Unconventional
**Mavis** Throstle
**Mavourneen** Asthore, Darling
**Maw** Crop, Gorge, Gull(et), Mouth, Oesophagus
**Mawkish** Dippy, Maudlin, Mushy, Sentimental, Sickly
**Max** Ernst
**Maxim** Adage, Aphorism, Apo(ph)thegm, Axiom, Byword, Dictum, Gnome, Gorki, Gun, Hiram, Moral, Motto, Precept, Proverb, Restaurateur, →RULE, Saw, Saying, Sentence, Sentiment, Watchword
**Maximum** All-out, Full, Highest, Limit, Most, Peak, The full Monty, Utmost
**May** Blossom, Can, Hawthorn, Merry, Might, Month, Mote(n), Quickthorn, Shall, Spring, Whitethorn
**Maybe** Happen, Mebbe, Peradventure, Percase, Perchance, Perhaps, Possibly
▹**May become** *may indicate* an anagram
**May day** Beltane, SOS
**Mayfair** WI
**Mayfly** Ephemera, Ephemeroptera, Green-drake, Sedge, Turkey brown
**Mayhem** Chaos, Crime, Damage, Havoc, Pandemonium, Riotry
**Mayonnaise** Aioli, Rémoulade
**Mayor** Alcaide, Burgomaster, Casterbridge, Charter, Councilman, Portreeve, Provost, Syndic, Whittington, Worship, Worthy
**Maze** Honeycomb, Labyrinth, Meander, Network, Theseus, Warren, Wilderness
**MC** Announcer, Compere, Host, Ringmaster
**MD** Doctor, Healer
**ME** Yuppie flu
**Me** First person, I, Mi, Moi, One, Sel(f), Us
**Mead(ow)** Field, Flood, Grass(land), Haugh, Hayfield, Hydromel, Inch, Ing, Lea(se), Ley, Meath(e), Metheglin, →PASTURE, Runnymede, Saeter, Salting, Water
**Meadowsweet** Dropwort
**Meagre** Arid, Bar, Bare, Exiguity, Exiguous, Insubstantial, Measly, Mingy, Paltry, Pittance, Scant, Scrannel, Scranny, Scrawny, Skimpy, Skinny, Slender, Spare, Sparse, Stingy, Thin
**Meal(s), Mealie, Mealy** Allseed, Banquet, Barbecue, Barium, Beanfeast, Blow-out, Board, Bone, Breakfast, Brunch, Buffet, Carry out, Cassava, Cereal, Chilled, Cholent, Chota-hazri, Collation, Corn, Cornflour, Cottoncake, Cottonseed, Cou-cou, Couscous, Crib(ble), Dejeune(r), Deskfast, Dinner, Dish, Donor kebab, Drammock, Ear, Ervalenta, Fare, Farina, Feast, Feed, Flour, Food, Glacier, Grits, Grout, Hangi, Hearty, High tea, Iftar, Indian, Italian, Kai, Lock, Lunch, Mandioc, Mandioc(c)a, Mani(h)oc, Matzo, Melder, Meltith, Mensal, Mess, Morning, Mush, No-cake, Nosh, Nuncheon, Ordinary, Picnic, Piece, Pizza, Plate, Ploughman's lunch, Poi, Polenta, Porridge, Prandial, Prix fixe, Rac(c)ahout, Refection, Reistafel, Repast, Rere-supper, Revalenta, Rijst(t)afel, Salep, Scambling, Scoff, Seder, Sehri, Slap-up, Smorgasbord, Snack, Sohur, Spread, Square, Stir-fry, Suhur, Supper, Table d'hôte, Takeaway, Take-out, Tamale, Tea, Thali, Tiffin, Tightener, Tousy tea, Twalhours, Undern, Yum cha
**Meal-ticket** LV
**Mean(ing), Meant** Aim, Ariston metron, Arithmetic(al), Average, Base, Betoken, Bowsie, Caitiff, Cheap, Cheeseparing, Close, Connotation, Curmudgeon, Definition, Denotate, Denote, Design, Destined, Dirty, Dog-in-the-manger, Drift, Essence, Ettle, Etymology, Feck, Footy, Foul, Geometric(al), Gist, Golden, Grammatical, Hang, Harmonic, Humble, Hunks, Ignoble, Illiberal, Imply, Import, Inferior, Insect, Intend, Intermediate, Kunjoos,

Lexical, Low(down), Mang(e)y, Marrow, Measly, Medium, Mesquin, Message, Method, Mid, Miserly, Narrow, Nasty, Near, Niggardly, Nirlie, Norm, Nothing, One-horse, Ornery, Paltry, Par, Pedantic, Penny-pinching, Penurious, Petty, Piker, Pinch-penny, Pith, Point, Purport, → PURPOSE, Quadratic, Ratfink, Revenue, Ribald, Roinish, Roynish, Scall, Scrub, Scurvy, Semanteme, Semantic(s), Sememe, Sense, Shabby, Signify, Slight, Slink, Small, Sneaky, Snoep, Snot, Sordid, Sparing, Spell, Squalid, Stingy, Stink(ard), Stinty, Subject, Substance, Symbol, Thin, Threepenny, Tight-arse, Tight-ass, Tight-lipped, Tightwad, Two-bit, Value, Vile, Whoreson

**Meander** Fret, Ring, Sinuate, Stray, Wander, Weave, Wind

**Meaningless** Ducdame, Empty, Flummery, Hollow, Hot air, Insignificant, Nonny, Rumbelow

**Means** Agency, Ample, Dint, Income, Instrumental, Media, Method, Mode, Opulence, Organ, Private, Recourse, Resources, Staple, Substance, Tactics, Tool, Visible, Ways, Wherewithal

**Meantime, Meanwhile** Among, Emong, Greenwich, Interim, Whilst

**Measles** German, Morbilli, Roseola, Rose-rash, Rubella, Rubeola, Sheep

**Measure(d), Measurable, Measuring, Measure(ment)** Accelerometer, Ammeter, Apothecaries', By(e)law, Calibre, Centile, Chronometer, Circular, Corn Law, Crackdown, Customise, → DANCE, Démarche, → DIMENSION, Dipstick, Distance, Doggerel, Dose, Dry, Egg-timer, Ellwand, Forpet, Forpit, → GAUGE, Gavotte, Gross, Imperial, → INSTRUMENT, IQ, Limit, Linear, Liter, Litre, Meed, Metage, Moratorium, Of, Offset, Pipette, Plumb, Precaution, Prophylactic, Protractor, Quantifiable, Quickstep, Ration, Remen, Rhythm, Ruler, Salinometer, Sanction, Sandglass, Sea-level, Share, Short, → SIZE, Sound, Spoonful, Spring balance, Standard, Statute, Step, Stichometry, Strike, Struck, Survey, Tachometer, Tachymetry, Timbre, Time, Token, Tranche, Triangulate, → UNIT, Weigh, Wine

---

## MEASUREMENTS

***2 letters:***
As
Em
En
Mu

***3 letters:***
Are
Bel
Cab
Cor
DIN
Ell
Erg
Fat
Hin
Lay
Lea
Ley
Log
Lug
Mil
Rod
Tot
Tsp
Wey

***4 letters:***
Acre
Aune
Bath
Boll
Bolt
Comb
Cord
Coss
Cran
Culm
Dram
Epha
Foot
Gage
Gill
Hank
Hide
Inch
Koss
Last
Line
Link
Maze
Mete
Mile
Mole
Mott
Muid
Nail
Octa
Okta
Omer
Pace
Peck
Pint
Pipe
Pole
Pond
Pood
Ream
Reau
Rood
Rope
Rotl
Shot
Span
Tape
Thou
Unit
Vara
Volt
Warp
Yard

***5 letters:***
Anker
Ardeb
Barye
Bekah
Bigha
Caneh
Carat
Chain
Clove
Combe
Coomb
Crore
Cubit
Cumec
Cusec
Depth
Ephah
Fermi
Float
Gauge
Grain
Groma
Hanap
Homer
Joule
Kaneh
Lento
Liang
Ligne
Lippy
Loure
Mease
Meter
Metre
Middy
Noddy
Optic®
Perch
Quart
Romer
Scale
Skein
Stade
Stere
Stone
Tesla
Therm
Toise
Verst
Wecht
Yojan

***6 letters:***
Albedo
Alnage
Arpent
Arshin
Barrel
Barren
Beegah

Bovate
Bushel
Chenix
Chopin
Cicero
Cubage
Degree
Denier
Double
Drachm
Etalon
Exergy
Fathom
Firkin
Firlot
Gallon
Height
Hemina
Jigger
Kelvin
Kilerg
League
Lippie
Liquid
Modius
Morgan
Mutton
Noggin
Oxgang
Parsec
Pascal
Pottle
Radius
Rotolo
Runlet
Sazhen
Second
Stadia
Thread
Tierce
Yojana

***7 letters:***
Aneroid
Arshine
Braccio
Breadth
Burette
Caliper
Candela
Chalder
Choenix
Conguis
Coulomb
Cyathus
Decibel
Drastic
Entropy
Furlong
Geodesy
Lambert
Leaguer
Pelorus
Quarter
Refract
Rundlet
Sievert
Sleever
Spindle
Spondee
Venturi
Virgate

***8 letters:***
Angstrom
Calipers
Calliper
Carucate
Chaldron
Crannock
Desyatin
Diameter
Exitance
Fistmele
Foot rule
Hogshead
Kilogray
Luxmeter
Mutchkin
Odometer
Oximeter
Parasang
Poulter's
Puncheon
Quadrant
Tape-line
Teraflop
Viameter
Waywiser

***9 letters:***
Astrolabe
Atmometer
Barometer
Bolometer
Callipers
Cryometer
Decalitre
Decastere
Dosimeter
Ergometer
Eriometer
Flowmeter
Hodometer
Kilojoule
Kilometre
Konimeter
Lysimeter
Machmeter
Manometer
Mekometer
Nipperkin
Octameter
Oenometer
Pedometer
Pentapody
Potometer
Salimeter
Steradian
Tappet-hen
Tasimeter
Telemeter
Titration
Tonometer
Yardstick

***10 letters:***
Acidometer
Amphimacer
Anemometer
Barleycorn
Bathometer
Bathymeter
Centimetre
Chronotron
Coulometer
Cyclometer
Densimeter
Dessiatine
Dessyatine
Drosometer
Eudiometer
Geodimeter
Goniometer
Gravimeter
Humidistat
Hydrometer
Hygrometer
Lactometer
Lactoscope
Micrometer
Mileometer
Millimetre
Opsiometer
Photometer
Piezometer
Pychometer
Resistance
Touchstone
Tromometer
Winchester

***11 letters:***
Actinometer
Auxanometer
Calorimeter
Conformator
Dioptometer
Dynamometer
Gradiometer
Intoximeter
Jacob's staff
Long Hundred
Rangefinder
Stereometer
Tacheometry
Venturi tube
Weighbridge

***12 letters:***
Breathalyzer
Cathetometer
Coulombmeter
Densitometer
Electrometer
Electronvolt
Extensimeter
Extensometer
Galactometer
Gravitometer
Katharometer
Nephelometer
Permittivity
Tellurometer
Thermocouple
Viscosimeter

***13 letters:***
Saccharometer

***15 letters:***
Katathermometer

---

**Meat(s)** Aitchbone, Bacon, Bard, Beef, Beefsteak, Beef Wellington, Biltong, Brawn, Brisket, Brown, Burger, Cabob, Carbonado, Carpaccio, Carrion, Charcuterie, Chop, Collop, Confit,

Croquette, Cut, Cutlet, Dark, Devon, Dog-roll, Doner kebab, Easy, Edgebone, Entrecôte, Escalope, Essence, Fanny Adams, Fatback, Fillet, Fleishig, Fleishik, Flesh, Flitch, Force, Galantine, Game, Gigot, Gobbet, Gosht, Griskin, Halal, Ham, Haslet, Haunch, Jerky, Joint, Junk, Kabab, Kabob, Kebab, Kebob, Lamb, Loin, Luncheon, Mart, Medaillon, Medallion, Mince, Mutton, Noisette, Offal, Olive, Oyster, Pastrami, Paupiette, Pem(m)ican, Piccata, Pith, Pope's eye, Pork, Processed, Prosciutto, Rack, Red, Rillettes, Roast, Saddle, Sasatie, Satay, Scaloppino, Schnitzel, Scran, Scrapple, Sey, Shank, Shashlik, Shishkebab, Short ribs, Side, Sirloin, Soft, Sosatie, Spam®, Spare rib, Spatchcock, Spaul(d), Steak, Strong, Tenderloin, Tiring, Tongue, Variety, Veal, Venison, Vifda, Virgate, Vivda, White, Wiener schnitzel, Wurst

**Meatball(s)** Cecils, Croquette, Faggot, Falafel, Felafel, Fricadel, Frikkadell, Goujon, Knish, Kofta, Kromesky, Quenelle, Rissole

**Meat extract** Brawn, Gravy, Juice, Stock

**Meatless** Banian, Lent, Maigre, Vegetarian

**Mecca** Centre, Honeypot, Kaaba, Keblah, Kibla(h), Mak(k)ah, Omayyad, Qibla, Umayyad

**Mechanic(s)** Apron-man, Artificer, Artisan, Banausic, Barodynamics, Bottom, Card, Celestial, Classical, Dynamics, Engineer, Fitter, Fluid, Fundi, Garageman, Garagist, Grease monkey, Greaser, Hand, Journeyman, Kinematics, Kinesiology, Kinetics, Newtonian, Operative, Quantum, Rock, Soil, Statics, Statistical, Technician, Wave

▷**Mechanic(al)** *may indicate* characters from 'A Midsummer Night's Dream'

**Mechanical, Mechanise, Mechanism** Action, Actuator, Apparatus, Auto, Autodestruct, Automate, Automatic, Banausic, Bottom, Chargehand, Clockwork, Defence, Dérailleur, Escape, Escapement, Foul-safe, Gimmal, Gust-lock, Instrument, Machinery, Movement, Organical, Pulley, Pushback, Rackwork, Ratchet, Regulator, Rigger, Robotic, Rote, Servo, Synchroflash, Synchromesh, Timer, Traveller, Trippet, Works

**Medal(lion)** Award, Bar, Bronze, Cameo, Congressional, Croix de guerre, Decoration, Dickin, DSM, GC, George, Gold, Gong, Gorget, Military, MM, Numismatic, Pan(h)agia, Purple Heart, Putty, Roundel, Silver, Tony, Touchpiece, VC, Vernicle

**Meddle(r), Meddlesome, Meddling** Busybody, Dabble, Finger, Hen-hussy, → **INTERFERE**, Interloper, Intrude, Kibitz, Marplot, Mell, Monkey, Officious, Pantopragmatic, Potter, Pragmatic, Pry, Snooper, Spoilsport, Tamper, Tinker, Trifle

**Media** Fibre, Intelsat, Magnetic, Mass, Mixed, New, PR, Social

**Mediate, Mediation, Mediator** ACAS, Arbitrate, Conciliate, Good offices, Intercede, Interpose, Intervene, Liaison, Muti, Peacekeeper, Peacemaker, Referee, Stickler, Thirdsman, Trouble-shooter

**Medic(k)** Lucern(e), Nonesuch, Snail

**Medic(o), Medicine man** Albergist, Bone-setter, Corpsman, Dentist, Extern, Feldsher, Houseman, Koradji, Oculist

**Medical, Medicine (chest), Medicament, Medication, Medicinal** Adaptogen, Aesculapian, Algology, Allopathy, Aloetic, Aloe vera, Alternative, Amulet, Analgesic, Andrology, Anodyne, Antacid, Antibiotic, Antidote, Antiphlogostic, Antisepsis, Antiseptic, Anti-serum, Arnica, Arrowroot, Asafetida, Aurum potabile, Aviation, Ayurveda, Bariatrics, Bi, Bismuth, Blister, Brunonian, Buchu, Bucku, Calumba, Carminative, Charm, Check-up, Chinese, Chiropody, Chlorodyne, Chrysarobin, Clinician, Community, Complementary, Cordial, Corpsman, Cubeb, Curative, Defensive, Demulcent, Diapente, Diascordium, Diatessaron, Discutient, Doctor's stuff, Dosage, Dose, Draught, Drops, → **DRUG**, Dutch drops, Eardrop, Electuary, Elixir, Emetic, Emmenagogue, Empirics, Enema, Epulotic, Excipient, Expectorant, Eye-drop, Fall-trank, Febrifuge, Feldsher, Folk, Forensic, Fringe, Functional, Galen, Galenism, Gelcap, Genitourinary, Gripe water®, Gutta, Haematinic, Haematology, Herb, Herbal, Hesperidin, Holistic, Hom(o)eopathy, Horse-drench, Hyssop, Iatric(al), Ibuprofen®, Imhotep, Indian, Industrial, Inhalant, Inro, Internal, Iodine, Ipecac(uanha), Iron, Ko cycle, Lariam®, Laxative, L-dopa, Leechcraft, Legal, Lime-water, Linctus, Loblolly, Lotion, Magnesia, Maqui, Menthol, Microbubbles, Mishmi, Mixture, Moxar, Muti, Natural, Naturopathy, Nephritic, Nephrology, Nervine, Neurology, Nosology, Nostrum, Nuclear, Nux vomica, Ob-gyn, Occupational, Officinal, Oncology, Oporice, Orthopoedics, Osteopath, Palliative, Panacea, Paregoric, Patent, Pathology, Pectoral, P(a)ediatrics, Pharmacy, Phlegmagogue, Physic, Physical, Pill, Placebo, Polychrest, Polypill,

Posology, Potion, Poultice, Preparation, Preventive, Proctology, Prosthetics, Prozac®, Psionic, Psychiatry, Ptisan, Purgative, Qinghaosu, Quin(quin)a, Quinacrine, Quinine, Radiology, Reborant, Red Crescent, Red Cross, Relaxative, → REMEDY, Salts, Salve, Sanative, Sanguinaria, Sebesten, Senna, Serology, Sheng cycle, Simple, Snake-oil, Space, Specific, Sports, Steel, Stomachic, Stomatology, Stramonium, Stupe, Suppository, Surgery, Synergast, Syrup, Tabasheer, Tabashir, Tablet, Tar-water, Tetracycline, Therapeutics, Thimerosal, TIM, Tincture, Tisane, Tocology, Tonic, Totaquine, Trade, Traditional Chinese, Traumatology, Treatment, Trichology, Troche, Valerian, Veronal, Veterinary, Virology, Witchhazel, Wychhazel

**Medieval** Archaic, Feudal, Gothic, Med, Old, Trecento

**Mediocre** Average, Bland, Fair, Indifferent, Middle-of-the-road, Middling, Ordinary, Pap, Poor, Respectable, Run-of-the-mill, Second-class, So-So, Third rate, Undistinguished, Unsatisfactory

**Meditate, Meditation, Meditator, Meditative** Brood, Chew, Cogitate, Contemplate, Dhyana, Falun gong, Fifteen o's, Gymnosophy, Hesychast, Insight, Muse, Mystic, Nirvana, Pensive, Ponder, Reflect, Reverie, Revery, Ruminate, Samadhi, Tantric, Thanatopsis, Transcendental, Vipassana, Weigh, Yoga, Yogic flying, Zazen

**Mediterranean** Great Sea, Levant, Med, Midi, Scattermouch

**Medium** (A)ether, Agency, Air, Average, Channel, Clairvoyant, Contrast, Culture, Dispersive, Earth, Element, Ether, Even, Fire, Happy, Home, Intermediary, Interstellar, M, Magilp, Mean, Megilp, Midi, Midsize, Midway, Milieu, Oils, Organ, Ouija, Planchette, Press, Radio, Regular, Shaman, Spiritist, Spiritualist, Television, Telly, TV, Twitter, Vehicle, Water

**Medley** Charivari, Collection, Gallimaufry, Individual, Jumble, Macedoine, Melange, Mishmash, Mix, Pastiche, Patchwork, Pi(e), Pot-pourri, Quodlibet, Ragbag, Salad, Salmagundi, Series, Tat

▷**Medley** *may indicate* an anagram

**Medusa** Gorgon, Jellyfish, Petrifying, Planoblast

**Meek** Docile, Griselda, Humble, Milquetoast, Patient, Sheepy, Tame

**Meerkat** Suricate

**Meerschaum** Sepiolite

**Meet(ing), Meeting place** Abide, Abutment, Achieve, AGM, Appointment, Apposite, Appropriate, Apropos, Apt, Ascot, Assemblage, Assemble, Assembly, Assignation, Audience, Baraza, Board, Bosberaad, Briefing, Cabinet, Camp, Camporee, Caucus, Chapterhouse, Chautauqua, Clash, Commissure, Conclave, Concourse, Concur, Confluence, Confrontation, Congress, Connivance, Conseil d'etat, Consistory, Consult(ation), Contact, Conterminous, Convene, Convent(icle), Convention, Converge, Conversazione, Convocation, Correspond, Cortex, Crossroads, Cybercafé, Date, Defray, Demo, EGM, Encounter, Ends, Experience, Face, Field, Find, Fit, For(e)gather, Forum, Fulfil, Gala, Gemot, General, Giron, Gorsedd, Greeting, Guild, Gyeld, Gymkhana, Gyron, Hall, Howf(f), Hunt, Hustings, Imbizo, Impact, Indaba, Infall, Interface, Interview, Jamboree, Join, Junction, Kgotla, Korero, Lekgotla, Liaise, Marae, Match, Moot, Mother's, Obviate, Occlusion, Occur, Oppose, Overflow, Partenariat, Pay, Plenary, Plenum, Pnyx, Pow-wow, Prayer, Prosper, PTA, Quadrivial, Quaker, Quorate, Quorum, Race, Races, Rally(ing point), Rencontre, Rencounter, Rendezvous, Replay, Reunion, Round Table, Sabbat(h), Satisfy, Séance, See, Seminar, Serve, Session, Sit, Social, Sports, Star Chamber, Suitable, Summit, Swap, Symposium, Synastry, Synaxis, Synod, Tackle, Talkfest, Talk-in, Talking-shop, Think-in, Town, Track, Tryst, Venery, Venue, Vestry, Wapinshaw, Wardmote, Wharenui, Wharepuni, Workshop

**Megalith(ic)** Sarsen, Skara Brae, Stonehenge

**Megalomaniac** Monarcho

**Megaphone** Bull-horn, Loudhailer

**Megapode** Mound-bird, Talegalla

**Meiosis** Understatement

**Meistersinger** Sachs

**Melancholy, Melancholic** Adust, Allicholy, Allycholly, Anatomy, Atrabilious, Blue, Cafard, Chap-fallen, Despond(ency), Dole, Dreary, Dump(s), Gloom, Heart-sore, Hipped, Hump, Hyp, Hypochondria, Jaques, Lienal, Lugubrious, Moper, Panophobia, Pensieroso, Pensive, Saturnine, Sombre, Spleen, Splenetic, Triste, Tristesse, Weltschmerz

**Melanese, Melanesian** Kanak, Motu
**Mêlée** Brawl, Commotion, Dogfight, Fracas, Free-for-all, Rally, Salmagundi, Scrum
**Melia** Margosa, Neem, Nim
**Mellifluent, Mellifluous** Cantabile, Dulcet, Melodic
**Mellow** Age, Fruity, Genial, Mature, Ripe, Smooth
**Melodrama(tic)** Bathos, Histrionic, Lurid, Sensation, Soap, Transpontine
**Melody, Melodious** Air, Arioso, Cabaletta, Canorous, Cantabile, Cantilena, Canto (fermo), Cantus, Cavatina, Chant, Chopsticks, Conductus, Counterpoint, Descant, Dulcet, Euphonic, Fading, Musical, Orphean, Part-song, Plainsong, Ranz-des-vaches, Refrain, Songful, Strain, Sweet, Theme, Tunable, →TUNE(S)
**Melon(like)** Cantaloup(e), Cas(s)aba, Charentais, Galia, Gourd, Honeydew, Mango, Musk, Nar(r)as, Ogen, Pepo, Persian, Rock, Spanspek, Winter
**Melt(ed), Melting** Ablate, Colliquate, →DISSOLVE, Eutectic, Eutexia, Flux, Found, Fuse, Fusil(e), Liquescent, Liquid, Peritectic, Run, Smectic, Syntexis, Thaw, Touch
**Member** Adherent, Arm, Beam, Branch, Bro(ther), Charter, Chin, Confrère, Cornice, Corresponding, Coulisse, Crossbeam, Crypto, Direction, Felibre, Fellow, Finger, Forearm, Forelimb, Founder, Girder, Gremial, Harpin(g)s, Insider, Keel, Leg, Limb, Lintel, Lobby, Longeron, M, Majoritaire, MBE, Montant, MP, Organ, Part, Partisan, Peer, Politicaster, Politician, Private, Rood-beam, Soroptomist, Stile, Stringer, Strut, Syndic, Tie, Toe, Upright
**Membership** Subscription
**Membrane, Membranous** Amnion, Arachnoid, Axilemma, Bilayer, Caul, Cell, Chorioallantois, Chorion, Choroid (plexus), Chromoplast, Conjunctiva, Cornea, Cyst, Decidua, Dissepiment, Dura (mater), Eardrum, Endocardium, Endometrium, Endosteum, Ependyma, Exine, Extine, Fell, Film, Foetal, Frenulum, Fr(a)enum, Haw, Head, Hyaloid, Hymen, Indusium, Intima, Intine, Involucre, Iris, Kell, Mater, Mediastinum, Meninx, Mesentery, Mucosa, Mucous, Neurolemma, Nictitating, Nuclear, Parchment, Patagium, Pellicle, Pericardium, Pericarp, Perichondrium, Pericranium, Periost(eum), Periton(a)eum, Pia mater, Plasma, Plasmalemma, Pleura, Putamen, Retina, Rim, Sarcolemma, Scarious, Schneiderian, Sclera, Serosa, Serous, Skin, Synovial, Tectorial, Tela, Third eyelid, Tissue, Tonoplast, Trophoblast, Tunic, Tympan(ic), Vacuolar, Velamen, Velum, Vitelline, Web, Yolk-sac
**Memento, Memoir** Keepsake, Locket, Relic, Remembrancer, Souvenir, Token, Trophy
**Memo(randum)** Bordereau, Cahier, Chit, IOU, Jot, Jurat, Minute, Note, Notepad, →REMINDER, Slip
**Memoir(ist)** Casanova, Kiss and tell
**Memorable, Memorise(d), Memory** Associative, ATLAS, Bubble, By heart, Byte, Cache, Catchy, Collective, →COMPUTER MEMORY, Con, Core, DIMM, Distant, DRAM, Dynamic, Echoic, Elephantine, Engram(ma), Extended, Flash (bulb), Flashback, Folk, Get, Highlight, High point, Historic, Hypermnesia, Iconic, Immortal, Immunological, Keepsake, Kilobyte, Learn, Living, Long-term, Magnetic bubble, Main, Mainstore, Memoriter, Mind, Mind's eye, Mneme, Mnemonic, Mnemosyne, Non-volatile, Noosphere, Notable, Off-pat, Pelmanism, Photographic, Race, RAM, Read-write, Recall, Recollection, Recovered, Red-letter day, →REMEMBER, Retention, Retrospection, ROM, Ro(a)te, Samskara, Screen, Semantic, Short-term, SIMM, Souvenir, Sovenance, Special, Static, Storage, Study, Video, Virtual, Volatile, Word, Working
**Memorial** Albert, Altar tomb, Brass, Cenotaph, Cromlech, Ebenezer, Gravestone, Hatchment, Headstone, Marker, Martyr's, Mausoleum, Monument, Mount Rushmore, Obelisk, Pantheon, Plaque, Relic, Relique, Remembrance, Statue, Tablet, Tomb(stone), Trophy, War, Wreath
▸**Memory loss** *see* LOSS OF MEMORY
**Men(folk)** Amadoda, Androcentric, Chaps, Chess, Cuffins, Enlisted, Male, Messrs, Mortals, OR, People, Race, Troops
**Menace, Menacing** Danger, Dennis, Endanger, Foreboding, Intimidate, Jeopardise, Minatory, Ominous, Peril, Pest, Scourge, Scowl, Sinister, Threat(en)
**Menagerie** Ark, Circus, Zoo

**Mend(er)** Beet, Bete, Bushel, Cobble, Correct, Cure, Darn, Fix, Heal, Improved, Mackle, Patch, Piece, Recover, Remedy, → REPAIR, Restore, Set, Sew, Solder, Tinker, Trouble-shoot
**Mendelevium** Md
**Mendicant** Beggar, Calender, Fakir, Franciscan, Frater, Friar, Pauper, Servite
**Menhir** Standing stone
**Menial** Bottlewasher, Dogsbody, Drudge, Drug, Eta, Fag, Flunkey, Lackey, Lowly, Scullion, Servile, Skivvy, Toady, Underling, Wood-and-water joey
**Meninx** (D)jerba
**Meniscus** Dome
**Menopause** Andropause, Change, Climacteric
**Menstruation** Curse, Flower, Menarche, Menorrh(o)ea, Menses, Monthly, Period
**Mental (condition), Mental disorder, Mentality, Mentally** Alienism, Barking, Bunker, Cognitive, Doolally, Eject, Hallucinosis, Insane, Noetic, Nut job, Nutty, Paranoia, Psychic, Psychotic, Siege, Upstairs
▷**Mental** *may indicate* the chin
**Menthol** Mint(y)
**Mention(ed)** Advert, Allusion, Bename, Benempt, Bring up, Broach, Bynempt, Citation, Drag up, Hint, Honourable, Hote, Instance, Name(-check), Notice, Obiter dicta, Quote, Refer, Same, Specify, Speech, State, Suggest, Touch
**Mentor** Advisor, Father figure, Guru, Rebbe, Tutor
**Menu** Agenda, Card, Carte, Carte du jour, Cascading, Cuisine, Drop-down, Fare, List, Option, Prix fixe, Table d'hôte, Tariff
**Mercantile** Commercial, Trade
**Mercaptan** Thiol
**Mercator** Cartographer
**Mercenary** Arnaout, Condottiere, Freelance, Gallo(w)glass, Greedy, Hack, Hessian, Hired gun, Hireling, Landsknecht, Legionnaire, Mean, Money-grubbing, Pindaree, Pindari, Rutter, Sordid, Spoilsman, Swiss Guard, Switzer, Venal, Warmonger, Wildgeese
**Merchandise** Cargo, Goods, Line, Produce, Stock, Ware(s)
**Merchant(man)** Abbas, Abudah, Antonio, Argosy, Broker, Bun(n)ia, Burgher, Chandler, Chap, Commission, Crare, Crayer, Dealer, Doom, Factor, Flota, Gossip, Hoastman, Importer, Jobber, Law, Magnate, Marcantant, Mercer, Monger, Nathan, Négociant, Peddler, Pedlar, Polo, Provision, Retailer, Scrap (metal), Seller, Shipper, Speed, Squeegee, Stapler, Sutler, Trader, Tradesman, Vintner, Wholesaler
**Mercia** Offa
**Merciful, Mercy** Amnesty, Charity, Clement, Compassionate, Corporal, Egad, Forgiveness, Grace, Humane, Kind, Kyrie, Lenient, Lenity, Miserere, Misericord(e), Pacable, Pity, Quarter, Ruth, Sparing, Spiritual
**Merciless** Cruel, Hard, Hard-hearted, Inclement, Pitiless, Violent, Wanton
**Mercurial, Mercuric sulphide, Mercury** Azoth, Cyllenius, Dog's, Freddie, Fulminating, Herald, Hermes, Hg, Horn, Hydrargyrum, Messenger, Planet, Proteus, Queen's yellow, Quicksilver, Red, Red-man, Spurge, Thimerosal, Tiemannite, Torr, Volatile
**Mere(ly)** Allenarly, Bare, Common, Lake, Only, Pond, Pool, Poor, Pure, Sheer, Tarn, Ullswater, Very
**Merganser** Sawbill
**Merge(r), Merging** Amalgamate, Blend, Coalesce, Coalise, Composite, Conflate, Consolidate, Die, Elide, Fusion, Incorporate, Integrate, Interflow, Interpenetrate, Liquesce, Meld, Melt, Mingle, Symphysis, Syncretism, Synergy, Unify, Unite
**Meridian** Magnetic, Noonday, Prime
**Meringue** Pavlova
**Meristem** Cambium
**Merit(ed)** CL, Condign, Deserve, Due, Earn, Found, Lustre, Meed, Rate, Virtue, Worth(iness)
**Mermaid** Dugong, Halicore, Merrow, Siren, Tavern, Undine
**Merriment, Merry** Andrew, Blithe(some), Bonny, Boon, Cant, Cherry, Chirpy, Crank, Cricket, Elated, Full, Gaudy, Gay, Gean, Glad, Gleesome, Greek, Hilarity, Jocose, Jocular,

Jocund, Jolly, Joyous, L'allegro, Lively, Mirth, Nitid, On, Page, Revelry, Riant, Sportive, Sunny, Tipsy, Vogie, Waggery, Wassail

**Merry-andrew** Clown, Jack-pudding, Pickle-herring

**Merry-go-round** Carousel, Galloper, Whirligig

**Merry-making** Beano, Cakes and ale, Carnival, Festivity, Gaiety, Gaud, Gawd, Mardi Gras, Revel, Saturnalia, Wassail

**Merrythought** Clavicle, Collarbone, Wishbone

**Mesh** Cancellate, Chain, Cobweb, Entangle, Gauze, Grid, Knit, Mantle, Net, Reseau, Screen, Splice

**Mesmer(ise)** Hypnotise

**Mesomorphic** Nematic

**Meson** X-particle

**Mess(y), Mess up** Anteroom, Balls-up, Bedraggled, Blotch, Bodge, Boob, Boss, Botch, Bungle, Canteen, Caudle, Chaos, Clamper, Clutter, Cock-up, Colcannon, Dining-room, Disorganise, Dog's dinner, Failure, Farrago, Fiasco, Flub, Garboil, Glop, G(l)oop, Gory, Guddle, Gunge, Gunk, Gun-room, Hash, Horlicks, Hotch-potch, Hugger-mugger, Imbroglio, Lash-up, Louse, Mash, Meal, Mire, Misdo, Mismanage, Mix, Mixter-maxter, Modge, Muck, Muddle, Muff, Mullock, Muss, Mux, Pi(e), Pig's ear, Piss-up, Plight, Pollute, Pottage, Praiseach, Screw-up, Scungy, Shambles, Shambolic, Shemozzle, Sight, Slaister, Sloppy, Smudge, Snafu, Soss, Sty, Sully, Tamper, Tinker, Tousle, Trifle, Untidy, Wardroom, Whoopsie, Yuck(y)

**Message(s), Messaging** Aerogram, Bull, Bulletin, Cable(gram), Caption, Contraplex, Dépêche, Despatch, Dispatch, Email, Epistle, Errand, Error, Fax, Flame, Import, Inscription, Kissagram, Kissogram, Letter, Marconigram, Missive, News, Note, Notification, Pager, Ping, Posting, Postscript, Propaganda, PTO, Radiogram, Radio telegraph, Read-out, Rumour, Signal, Slogan, SMS, SOS, Spam, Stripagram, Strippergram, Subtext, Telco, Telegram, Telepheme, Telephone, Teletype®, Telex, Text, Theme, Tidings, Toothing, Tweet, Valentine, Voice mail, Wire, → **WORD**

**Messenger** Angel, Angela, Apostle, Azrael, Beadle, Caddie, Caddy, Carrier pigeon, Chaprassi, Chuprassy, Corbie, Courier, Culver, Despatch-rider, Emissary, Envoy, Errand boy, Express, Forerunner, Gaga, Gillie-wetfoot, Gillie whitefoot, Hatta, Herald, Hermes, Internuncio, Iris, King's, Ladas, Mercury, Nuncio, Page, Peon, Post, Pursuivant, Queen's, Runner, Send, Seraph, Shellycoat, Valet de place, Valkyrie

**Messiah** Christ, Emmanuel, Immanuel, Mahdi, Mashiach, Prince of Peace, Redeemer, Saviour, Shiloh, Son of Man, Southcott

**Met** Constabulary, Faced, Old Bill, Opera, Weather, Weatherman

**Metabolism** Basal, Cryptobiotic

**Metal(s), Metallic, Metalware, Metalwork** Aeneous, Antifriction, Base, Bush, Cannon, Coarse, Death, Expanded, Filler, Fine, Fusible, Heavy, Hot, Jangling, Leaf, Mercuric, Mineral, Noble, Nonferrous, Ore, Perfect, Planchet, Pot, Precious, Prince's, Road, Scrap, Sheet(-iron), Shrapnel, Sprue, Stannic, Thrash, Torque, Tramp, Transition, Type, White, Yellow

---

**METALS**

*2 letters:*
Ag
Al
Er
Sm
Sn

*3 letters:*
Gib
Tin

*4 letters:*
Bell
Foil
Gold
Iron
Munz
Slug
Tole
Zinc

*5 letters:*
Aglet
Brass
Ingot
Invar®
Misch
Monel
Muntz
Steel
Terne

*6 letters:*
Aiglet
Alkali
Billon
Cerium
Chrome
Cobalt
Copper
Erbium
Indium
Monell
Nickel
Niello
Ormolu
Osmium

Pewter
Silver
Sodium
Speiss
Terbic

*7 letters:*
Bismuth
Cadmium
Gallium
Iridium
Lithium
Natrium
Protore
Regulus
Rhenium
Taggers
Terbium
Thorium
Tutania
Tutenag
Wolfram
Zorgite

*8 letters:*
Actinium
Antimony
Babbitt's
Chromium
Europium
Filagree
Filigree
Gold leaf
Kamacite
Platinum
Samarium
Scandium
Speculum
Tantalum
Thallium
Tinplate
Titanium
Tungsten

*9 letters:*
Aluminium
Beryllium
Britannia
Germanium
Manganese
Ruthenium
Strontium
Toreutics

*10 letters:*
Dysprosium
Promethium

*11 letters:*
Aiguillette

*12 letters:*
Vernis martin

---

**Metallurgy** Powder
**Metal-worker** Blacksmith, Founder, Goldsmith, Lorimer, Robot, Silversmith, Smith, Spurrier, Tinsmith, Tubal Cain, Welder, Whitesmith
**Metamorphose, Metamorphosis, Metamorphic, Metamorphism** Imago, Regional, Transfiguration, Transmogrify
▹**Metamorphosing** *may indicate* an anagram
**Metaphor** Conceit, Figure, Image(ry), Kenning, Malonym, Mixed, Symbol, Trope, Tropical
**Metaphysics** Ontology, Scotism
**Mete** Inflict, Measure
**Meteor(ic), Meteorite** Achondrite, Aerolite, Aerolith, Aerosiderite, Bolide, Chondrite, Comet, Drake, Falling star, Fireball, Geminid, Iron, Leonid, Perseid, Quadrantid, Siderite, Siderolite, Star(dust), Stony(-iron), Tektite
**Meteorologist, Meteorology** Aeromancy, Barometry, Weather prophet
**Meter** Alidad(e), Electric, Exposure, Flow, Gas, Light, Orifice, Parking, Postage, Postal, Torque, Torsion, Water, White
**Methamphetamine** Chalk, Ice
**Methane, Methanol** Alkane, Marsh gas, Synthesis gas, Wood Naphtha
**Methedrine®** Speed
**Method(ology), Methodical** Art, Barrier, Billings, Buteyko, Direct, Feldenkrais, Formal, Formula, Gram's, Historical, Hi-tec(h), How, Kenny, Kumon, Line, Manner, Mode, Modus, Modus operandi, Monte Carlo, Montessori, Neat, Orderly, Organised, Organon, Organum, Ovulation, Painstaking, Phonic, Plan, Ploy, Procedure, Process, Q, Rhythm, Schafer's, Scientific, Socratic, Stanislavski, Systematic, Tactics, Technique, Way, Withdrawal
**Methodism, Methodist** Huntingdonian, Itinerant, Jumper, Methody, Primitive, Ranter, Scientism, Sim, Soper, Southcottian, Swaddler, Wesley
**Meths** White Lady
**Methuselah** Bottle, Macrobiote
**Meticulous** Careful, Diligent, → EXACT, Finicky, Minute, Painstaking, Precise, Punctilious, Quiddler, Scrupulous, Thorough
**Métier** Line, Trade, Vocation
**Metonymy** Metalepsis
**Metre, Metrical** Alexandrine, Amphibrach, Amphimacer, Anapaest, Antispast, Arsis, Ballad, Cadence, Choliamb, Choree, Choriamb, Common, Dipody, Galliambic, Iambic, Ithyphallic, Long, M, Penthemimer, Prosody, Pyrrhic, Rhythm, Sapphic, Scansion, Scazon, Semeion, Service, Short, Spondee, Strophe, Tribrach, Tripody, Trochee
**Metric (system)** MKS
**Metroland** Subtopia
**Metropolis, Metropolitan** Big Apple, Capital, City, Eparch
**Metrosexual** Epicene

**Mettle** Ardour, Bravery, Courage, Ginger, Guts, Pith, → PLUCK, Pride, Smeddum, Spirit, Spunk, Steel
**Mew** Caterwaul, Cry, Miaou, Miaow, Pen, Purr, Seagull, Shed, Waul, Wrawl
**Mews** Meuse, Muse(t), Musit, Stables, Yard
**Mexican (Indian)** Atlalt, Aztec, Carib, Chicano, Chichibec, Cuna, Diaz, Gringo, Hairless, Hispanic, Kuna, Latino, Maya, Mixe-Zoque, Mixtec, Montezuma, Nahuatl, Norténo, Olmec, Otomi, Pachuco, Pedro, Ranchero, Taino, Tewa, Toltec, Yucatan, Zapotec, Zuni
**Mezzanine** Entresol
**Mezzo-soprano** Tessa
**MG** TD
**Miasma** Fug
**Mica** Biotite, Cat-silver, Daze, Fuchsite, Glimmer, Isinglass, Lepidolite, Lepidomelane, Muscovite, Paragonite, Phlogopite, Rubellan, Sericite, Talc, Verdite, Vermiculite
**Micawber** Wilkins
**Mice** Mischief
**Michael** Mick(e)y
**Mick(ey)** Greek, Mouse
**Micro** Mu
**Microbe, Microorganism** Extremophile, Germ, Lactobacillus, Nanobe, Organism, Plankton
**Microbiologist** Fleming, Sabine, Salk
**Microchip** ULA
**Micro-organism** Amoeba
**Microphone** Boom, Bug, Carbon, Crystal, Directional, Lavaliere, Lip, Mike, Phonic Ear®, Radio, Ribbon, Throat
**Microscope** Acoustic, Compound, Confocal, Darkfield, Dissecting, Electron, Engyscope, Field-emission, Field-ion, Lens, Optical, Phase-contrast, Phase-difference, Polarizing, Proton, Reading, Reflecting, Scanning electron, SEM, Simple, Solar, TEM, Ultraviolet
**Microsoft** Windows
**Microwave** Nuke
**Mid(st)** Amongst, Mongst
**Midas** Goldinger, Tamarin
**Mid-Atlantic** Anglo-American
**Midday** Meridian, N, Noon, Noon-tide, Noon-time
**Midden** Kitchen
**Middle(way), Middling, Midpoint** Active, Ariston metron, Basion, Centre, Compromise, Core, Crown, Enteron, Epicentre, Epitasis, Equidistant, Excluded, Eye, Girth, Heart, Innermost, Internal, Loins, Meat, Median, Mediocre, Medium, Meridian, Meseraic, Mesial, Mesne, Meso, Midriff, Moderate, Nasion, Noon, Passive, So-so, Turn, Twixt, Undistributed, Via media, Wa(i)st
**Middle age(d)** Forty, Grey, Menopause
**Middle-Cambrian** Menevian
**Middle class** Bourgeois, Hova, Mondeo Man
**Middle East(ern), Middle-Easterner** Arab, Iraqi, Kurdish, Mede, Omani, Persic
**Middle European** Magyar
**Middleman** Agent, Broker, Centre, Comprador(e), Diaphragm, Interlocutor, Intermediary, Jobber, Median, Navel, Regrater, Regrator
**Middlesex** Hermaphrodite
**Midge** Biting, Chironomid, Gall, Gnat
**Midget** Dwarf, Homunculus, Lilliputian, Pygmy, Shrimp
**Midianite** Prowler
**Midlander** Brummie
**Midlands** Mercia
**Midnight** G, O Am, Witching hour
▸**Midnight** *see* PAST MIDNIGHT
**Midriff** Phrenic, Skirt, Waist

**Midshipman** Brass-bounder, Easy, Middy, Oldster, Reefer, Snottie, Snotty
▸**Midst** *see* MID(ST)
**Midsummer** Solstice
**Mid-Westerner** Indianan
**Midwife** Accoucheur, Doula, Gran(nie), Granny, Howdie, Howdy, Lucina, Mab, Maieutic, Obstetric
**Midwinter** Solstice
**Mien** Air, Bearing, Demean, Manner
**Miff(ed)** Indignant
**Might(iness), Mighty** Could, Force, Main, Maud, Mote, Muscle, Nibs, Oak, Potence, →POWER, Prowess, Puissant, Should, Strength
**Mignon(ette)** Dyer's rocket, Fillet, Reseda, Wald, Weld
**Migraine** Megrim, Scotodinia, Teichopsia
**Migrant** Economic, Externe, Gastarbeiter, Lemming, Refugee, Snowbird, Swallow, Traveller
**Migrate, Migration, Migratory** Colonise, Diapedesis, Diaspora, Drift, Eelfare, Exodus, Fleet, Great Trek, Run, Tre(c)k, Volk(er)wanderung
**Mikado** Emperor, Kami, Teno
**Mike** Bug, Idle, M, Stentorphone
**Milanese** Patarine
**Mild(ly), Mildness** Balmy, Benign, Bland, Clement, Euphemism, Genial, Gentle, Lamb, Lenient, Lenity, Litotes, Mansuete, Meek, →MODERATE, Pacific, Patient, Pigeon-livered, Pussycat, Restrained, Sarcenet, Sars(e)net, Temperate
**Mildew** Downy, Foxing, Fungus, Mould, Oidium, Powdery, Vine, Wheat
**Mile(r), Miles** Admiralty, Air, Coss, Coverdale, Food, Geographical, Hour, Irish, Knot, Kos, League, Li, Mi, Milliary, Nautical, Passenger, Roman, Royal, Scots, Sea, Soldier, Square, Standish, Statute, Swedish, Train
**Milesian** Teague
**Milestone** Birthday, Milliary, MS
**Milfoil** Yarrow
**Militancy, Militant, Militarism, Militarist, Military** Activist, Aggressive, Battailous, Belligerent, Black Panther, Black Power, Church, Commando, Fascism, Fortinbras, Hawkish, Hezbollah, Hizbollah, Hizbullah, Hostile, Ireton, Janjaweed, Janjawid, Jihadi, Junta, Kshatriya, Landforce, Landsturm, Landwehr, Leftist, Logistics, Lumper, Mameluke, Martial, Nahal, Naxalite, Presidio, Provisional, Provo, Soldatesque, Stratocracy, Tactical, War machine, Warmonger, War paint, West Point, Zealous
**Militia(-man)** Band, Fyrd, Guard, Haganah, Janjaweed, Janjawid, Milice, Minuteman, Peshmerga, Reserve, Tanzim, Timariot, Trainband, Yeomanry
**Milk(er), Milky** Acidophilus, Beestings, Bland, Bleed, Bonny-clabber, Bristol, Butter, Casein, Certified, Churn, Colostrum, Condensed, Creamer, Crud, Curd, Dairy, Emulge, Evaporated, Exact, Exploit, Extract, Full cream, Galactic, Glacier, Goat's, Homogenised, Jib, Kefir, Kephir, K(o)umiss, Lactation, Lacteal, Latex, Long-life, Maas, Madafu, Madzoon, Magnesia, Malted, Mamma, Matzoon, Mess, Moo-juice, Opaline, Pasteurised, Pigeon's, Pinta, Posset, Raw, Rice, Sap, Semi-skimmed, Shedder, Skim(med), Soya, Squeeze, Strip(pings), Stroke, Suckle, Tap, Town, UHT, Use, Whey, Whig, Whole, Yaourt, Yogh(o)urt
**Milking-machine, Milking parlour** Loan, Tapper
**Milking-pail** Leglan, Leglen, Leglin
**Milkless** Agalactic, Dry, Eild
**Milkmaid, Milkman** Chalker, Dey, Emulge, Kefir, Kephir, Radha, Rounder, Roundsman, Skimmed
**Milksop** Coward, Meacock, Namby-pamby, Pance, Weakling, Wimp
**Milk-vetch** Loco
**Milkweed** Asclepias
**Milkwort** Senega
**Milky Way** Via Lactea
**Mill(ing), Mills** Aswarm, Ball, Barker's, Blag, Boxing, Cane, Clay, Coffee, Crazing, Economist, Flatford, Flour, Gang, Gastric, Gig, Grind(er), Hayley, Horse, Kibble, Knurl, Lumber, Malt, Mano, Melder, Molar, Nurl, Oil, Paper, Pepper, Plunge-cut, Post, Powder, Press, Pug, Pulp,

Quartz, Quern, Reave, Rob, Rolling, Rumour, Satanic, Scutcher, Smock, Spinning, Stamp, Stamping, Strip, Sucken, Sugar, Surge, Thou, Tide, Tower, Tuck, Water, Wool(len), Works

**Millenarian** Chiliast

**Miller** Dusty, Glen, Grinder, Jester, Joe, Molendinar, Multurer

**Millet** Bajra, Bajree, Bajrii, Couscous, Dari, Dhurra, Doura, Dur(r)a, Grain, Indian, Miliary, Negro-corn, Pearl, Proso, Ragee, Raggee, Ragi, Whisk

**Milliner** Hatter, Modiste

**Millionaire** Astor, Carnegie, Gatsby, MOP, Rockefeller, Rothschild, Vanderbilt

**Millions, Millionth** Crore, Femto-, Milliard, Muckle, Pico-

**Millipede** Chilognatha, Diplopod, Myriapod, Songololo

**Millstone** Ligger, Rind, Rynd

**Millstream** Lade

**Mim** Perjink

**Mime, Mimic(ry)** Ape, Batesian, Charade, Copycat, Echo, Farce, Imitate, Impersonate, Lipsync, Marceau, Mina, Mock, Mullerian, Mummer, Myna, Parody, Resemble, Simulate, Starling, Sturnine, Take-off

**Mimosa** Cacoon, Raintree, Saman

**Mince, Mincing** Cecils, Chop, Dice, Grate, Grind, Keema, Nipperty-tipperty, Prance, Rice

**Mind(er)** Agent, Aide, Baby-sitter, Beware, Bodyguard, Brain, Care, Gaum, Genius, Grasshopper, Grey matter, Handler, Head, → **HEED**, Herd, Id, Ideo-, Intellect, Mentality, Month's, Mood, Noology, Noosphere, Nous, One-track, Open, Phrenic, Psyche, Psychogenic, Resent, Sensorium, Split, Tabula rasa, Temper, Tend, Thinker, View, Wit, Woundwort, Year's

**Mindful** Conscious

**Mindset** Ethos

**Mine, Mining** Acoustic, Antenna, Appalachia, Biomining, Bomb, Bonanza, Bord and pillar, Bottom, Bouquet, Burrow, Camouflet, Chemical, Claymore, Coalfield, Colliery, Contact, Creeping, Dane-hole, Data, Dig(gings), Drifting, Egg, Eldorado, Excavate, Explosive, Fiery, Floating, Flooder, Fougade, Fougasse, Fracking, Gallery, Gob, Golconda, Gold, Gopher, Grass, Homing, Land, Limpet, Magnetic, Microbiological, Naked-light, Nostromo, Open-cast, Open-cut, Ophir, Pit, Placer, Pressure, Prospect, Rising, Salt, Sap, Set(t), Show, Silver, Sonic, Stannary, Stope, Strike, Strip, Undercut, Wheal, Win, Workings

**Mine-deflector** Otter, Paravane

**Mine-owner** Operator

**Miner, Mine-worker, Mine-working** Bevin boy, Butty-gang, Buttyman, Collier, Continuous, Corporal, Cutter, Digger, Faceworker, Forty-niner, Geordie, Leaf, Molly Maguire, Noisy, NUM, Oncost(man), Pitman, Sapper, Shot-firer, Stall, Tippler, Tributer, Tunneler, UDM, Undersawyer

▷**Miner** *may indicate* one of the Seven Dwarfs

**Mineral(s)** Accessory, Essential, Illuvium, Index, Ore, Owre, Salic

---

**MINERALS**

*3 letters:*
YAG

*4 letters:*
Clay
Foid
Gang
Mica
Sard
Spar
Talc
Trap
Urao

*5 letters:*
Balas
Borax
Chert
Emery
Flint
Fluor
Macle
Mafic
Nitre
Prase
Topaz
Trona
Umber

*6 letters:*
Acmite
Albite
Augite
Blende
Cerite
Copper
Galena
Gangue
Garnet
Glance
Gypsum
Hauyne
Illite
Iolite
Jargon
Kermes
Lithia
Natron
Nosean
Pinite
Pyrite
Quartz
Rutile
Schorl
Silica
Sphene
Spinel
Tincal
Zircon

*7 letters:*
Alunite
Amosite
Anatase
Apatite
Axinite
Azurite
Barytes
Biotite
Bornite
Brucite

Calcite
Calcium
Calomel
Catseye
Crystal
Cuprite
Cyanite
Diamond
Dysodil
Epidote
Erinite
Euclase
Eucrite
Fahlore
Felspar
Gahnite
Göthite
Gummite
Hessite
Ice spar
Jadeite
Jargoon
Kainite
Kernite
Kyanite
Leucite
Mellite
Mullite
Nacrite
Niobite
Olivine
Pennine
Peridot
Pyrites
Realgar
Rosaker
Sylvine
Sylvite
Thorite
Thulite
Tripoli
Turgite
Ulexite
Uralite
Uranite
Uranium
Zeolite
Zeuxite
Zincite
Zoisite
Zorgite

***8 letters:***

Adularia
Allanite
Analcime
Analcite
Andesine
Ankerite
Antimony
Aphanite
Asbestos
Autunite
Blue john
Boehmite
Boracite
Braunite
Bronzite
Brookite
Calamine
Cerusite
Chlorite
Chromite
Cinnabar
Cleveite
Corundum
Crocoite
Cryolite
Datolite
Dendrite
Diallage
Diaspore
Diopside
Disthene
Dolomite
Dysodile
Dysodyle
Enargite
Epsomite
Erionite
Euxenite
Fayalite
Feldspar
Flinkite
Fluorite
Galenite
Gibbsite
Goethite
Graphite
Gyrolite
Hematite
Idocrase
Ilmenite
Iodyrite
Jarosite
Lazulite
Lazurite
Lewisite
Limonite
Liparite
Massicot
Meionite
Melilite
Mimetite
Monazite
Nephrite
Noselite
Orpiment
Petuntse
Picotite
Plumbago
Prehnite
Pyroxene
Resalgar
Rock-salt
Sanidine
Saponite
Sardonyx
Siderite
Smaltite
Smectite
Sodalite
Stannite
Stibnite
Stilbite
Sunstone
Taconite
Tenorite
Tinstone
Titanite
Troilite
Vesuvian
Xenotime
Zaratite

***9 letters:***

Alabaster
Allophane
Amazonite
Amphibole
Anglesite
Anhydrite
Anorthite
Aragonite
Argentite
Atacamite
Blackjack
Blacklead
Carnelian
Carnotite
Celestine
Celestite
Cerussite
Chabazite
Chalybite
Cheralite
Chondrule
Cobaltine
Cobaltite
Coccolite
Columbate
Columbite
Covellite
Cystolith
Dolomitic
Elaeolite
Endomorph
Enhydrite
Enstatite
Erythrite
Fibrolite®
Flowstone
Fluorspar
Fool's gold
Gehlenite
Germanite
Geyserite
Gmelinite
Goslarite
Haematite
Harmotome
Hercynite
Hiddenite
Hornstone
Kaolinite
Kermesite
Kieserite
Limestone
Magnesite
Magnetite
Malachite
Manganite
Marcasite
Margarite
Marialite
Microlite
Microlith
Millerite
Mispickel
Mizzonite
Moonstone
Muscovite
Natrolite
Nepheline
Nephelite
Niccolite
Nitratine
Olivenite
Ottrelite
Paramorph
Pargasite
Pectolite
Penninite
Periclase

Pericline
Perimorph
Phenacite
Pigeonite
Pleonaste
Polianite
Pollucite
Powellite
Proustite
Rhodonite
Rubellite
Scapolite
Scheelite
Scolecite
Sepiolite
Septarium
Spodumene
Sylvanite
Tantalite
Tremolite
Troostite
Tungstite
Turquoise
Uraninite
Uvarovite
Variscite
Vulpinite
Wavellite
Wernerite
Willemite
Witherite
Wulfenite
Zinkenite

***10 letters:***
Actinolite
Alabandine
Alabandite
Andalusite
Bastnasite
Calaverite
Carnallite
Chalcocite
Chessylite
Chrysolite
Colemanite
Cordierite
Crocoisite
Dyscrasite
Forsterite
Gadolinite
Garnierite
Glauberite
Glauconite
Halloysite
Heulandite
Honey-stone
Hornblende
Indicolite
Indigolite
Jamesonite
Laurdalite
Lead-glance
Lherzolite
Meerschaum
Microcline
Mirabilite
Oligoclase
Oomphacite
Orthoclase
Paragonite
Perovskite
Phosgenite
Piemontite
Polybasite
Polyhalite
Pyrolusite
Pyrrhotine
Pyrrhotite
Redruthite
Riebeckite
Ripidolite
Samarskite
Saphir d'eau
Sapphirine
Saussurite
Serpentine
Smaragdite
Sperrylite
Sphalerite
Staurolite
Tennantite
Thaumasite
Thenardite
Thorianite
Tiemannite
Torbernite
Tourmaline
Triphylite
Vanadinite
Wolframite

***11 letters:***
Alexandrite
Amblygonite
Annabergite
Apophyllite
Baddeleyite
Bastnaesite
Cassiterite
Chiastolite
Chloanthite
Chrysoberyl
Clinochlore
Crocidolite
Dendrachate
Franklinite
Greenockite
Hypersthene
Idiomorphic
Iron pyrites
Josephinite
Labradorite
Melanterite
Molybdenite
Pentlandite
Philogopite
Phosphorite
Piedmontite
Pitchblende
Plagioclase
Pseudomorph
Psilomelane
Pyrargyrite
Pyrrhotiner
Sal ammoniac
Sillimanite
Smithsonite
Tabular spar
Tetradymite
Vermiculite
Vesuvianite
Ythro-cerite

***12 letters:***
Adularescent
Arfvedsonite
Arsenopyrite
Babingtonite
Chalcanthite
Chalcopyrite
Copper-glance
Copper-nickel
Cristobalite
Dumortierite
Feldspathoid
Fluorapatite
Hemimorphite
Lepidomelane
Pyromorphite
Pyrophyllite
Senarmontite
Silver-glance
Skutterudite
Strontianite
Synadelphite
Tetrahedrite
Wollastonite

***13 letters:***
Cummingtonite
Rhodochrosite

***14 letters:***
Yttro-tantalite

***15 letters:***
Gooseberry-stone
Montmorillonite

---

**Mineralogy, Mineralogist** Haüy, Heuland, Miller-Smithson, Oryctology
**Mineral water** Apollinaris, Tonic
**Minesweeper** Oropesa, Unity
**Mingle, Mingling** Assort, Blend, Circulate, Commix, Consort, Interfuse, Intermarry, Intermix, Mell, Merge, → MIX, Participate, Socialise, Theocrasy, Unite
**Mini** Cab, Car, Skirt, Teen(s)y, Teeny-weeny
**Miniature, Miniaturist** Cosway, Dwarf, Lilliputian, Microcosm, Midget, Model, Pygmy, Toy, Young
**Minimise, Minimum (range)** Bare, Downplay, Fewest, Floor, Gloze, Least, Neap, Pittance, Quorum, Scant, Shoestring, Stime, Styme, Threshold, Undervalue

▷**Minimum of** *may indicate* the first letter
**Minion** Flunkey, Lackey, Pet, Subordinate, Tool, Vassal
**Minister** Ambassador, Attend, Buckle-beggar, Cabinet, Chancellor, Chaplain, Cleric, Clerk, Coarb, Commissar, Curate, Deacon, Dewan, Diplomat, Divine, Dominee, Dominie, D(i)wan, Envoy, First, Foreign, Front Bench, Holy Joe, Home Secretary, Mas(s)john, Mes(s)john, Moderator, Nurse, Officiant, Ordinand, Ordinee, Padre, Parson, Pastor, Peshwa, Preacher, Predikant, Prelate, Presbyter, Priest, Prime, Rector, Richelieu, Secretary, Seraskier, → SERVE, Stick, Stickit, Subdeacon, Tanaiste, Tend, Visier, Vizier, Wazir, Wizier
**Ministry** Cabinet, Cloth, Defence, Defra, Department, Dept, DoE, MOD, MOT, Orders, Service, Treasury
▷**Ministry** *may indicate* some government department
**Mink** Kolinsky, Mutation, Vison
**Minnow** Devon, Penk, Pink, Tiddler
**Minoan** Knossus
**Minor(ity)** Child(hood), Comprimario, Ethnic, Faction, Few, Fractional, Harmonic, Incidental, Infant, Junior, Less(er), Marginal, Minutia, Negligible, Nominal, Nonage, One-horse, Peripheral, Petty, Piffling, Pre-teen, Pupillage, Signed, Slight, Small-time, Sub(sidiary), Subordinate, Trivial, Ward, Weeny
**Minotaur** Bull-headed, Cretan
**Minster** York
**Minstrel** Allan-a-Dale, Ballad-monger, Bard, Blondel, Bones, Busker, Cantabank, Christy, Cornerman, Glee maiden, Gleeman, Hamfatter, Joculator, Jongleur, Minnesinger, Pierrot, Scop, Singer, Taillefer, Tannhauser
**Mint** Aim, Bugle-weed, Bull's eye, Catnip, Coin, Ettle, Fortune, Herb, Horse, Humbug, Labiate, Monarda, Monetise, Nep, New, Penny-royal, Pepper, Pile, Polo®, Poly, Rock, Royal, Selfheal, Spear, Stamp, Stone, Strike, Trebor®, Unused, Utter, Water
**Minus** Less, Negative, Nonplus, Sign
**Minute(s), Minutiae** Acta, Alto, Bijou, Degree, Detailed, Diatom, Entry, Infinitesimal, Last, Lilliputian, Little, Memoranda, Mere, Micron, Mo, Mu, Nano-, New York, Pinpoint, Resume, Small, Smidgeon, Teen(t)sy, Teeny, Tine, Tiny, Trivia, Tyne, Wee
**Minx** Hellion
**Miracle(s), Miraculous, Miracle worker** Cana, Lourdes, Marvel, Merel(l), Meril, Morris, Mystery, Mythism, Phenomenon, Saluter, Supernatural, Thaumatology, Thaumaturgic, Theurgy, Wirtschaftswunder, Wonder, Wonderwork
**Mirage** Delusion, Fata morgana, Illusion, Loom, Northern lights
**Mire** Blanket, Bog, Glaur, Lair(y), Latch, Lerna, Lerne, Loblolly, Marsh, Mud, Mudge, Quag, Sludge, Soil
**Mirky** Dark, Dirk(e)
**Mirror(s), Mirrored** Alasnam, Antidazzle, Busybody, Cambuscan, Catoptric, Cheval, Claude Lorraine glass, Coelostat, Conde, Conjugate, Dare, Driving, Enantiomorph, Glass, Handglass, Heliostat, Image, Imitate, Keeking-glass, Lao, Magnetic, Merlin, One-way, Pierglass, Primary, Psyche, Rearview, → REFLECT, Reynard, Shisha, Siderostat, Sign, Specular, Speculum, Stone, Tiring-glass, Two-way, Vulcan, Wing
**Mirror-image** Enantiomorph, Perversion
**Mirth(ful)** Cheer, Dream, Festive, Glee, Hilarity, Joy, Laughter, Spleen
**Misadventure** Calamity
**Misaligned** Askew
▷**Misalliance** *may indicate* an anagram
**Misanthrope** Cynic, Timon
**Misapplication** Catachresis, Misuse
**Misappropriate, Misappropriation** Asport, Detinue, Embezzle, Pocket, Purloin, Steal
**Misbehave, Misbehaviour** Act up, Laddishness
**Miscarry** Abort, Backfire, Fail, Slink, Warp
**Miscegenation** Allocarpy
**Miscellaneous, Miscellany** Ana, Assortment, Chow, Collectanea, Diverse, Etceteras, Gallimaufry, Job lot, Misc, Motley, Odds and ends, Odds and sods, Olio, Omniana,

Omnium-gatherum, Paraphernalia, Pie, Potpourri, Raft, Ragbag, Sundry, Varia, Variety, Various

**Mischance** Misfare

**Mischief(-maker), Mischievous** Arch, Ate, Bale, Bane, Cantrip, Cloots, Devilment, Diablerie, Dido, Disservice, Evil, Gallus, Goings on, Gremlin, Hanky-panky, Harm, Hellery, Hellion, Hob, Imp, Injury, Jiggery-pokery, Jinks, Larky, Larrikin, Limb, Litherly, Loki, Make-bate, Malicho, Mallecho, Monkeyshines, Monkey-tricks, Nickum, Owl-spiegle, Perisher, Pestilent, Pickle, Prank, Puckish, Rascal, Rogue, Scally(wag), Scamp, Scapegrace, Shenanigans, Spalpeen, Spriteful, Tricksy, Varmint, Wag, Wicked, Widgie

**Misconception** Delusion, Fallacy, Idol(on), Idolum, Illusion, Mirage, Misunderstanding, Myth

**Misconduct** Impropriety, Incivism, Malfeasance, Malversation

**Miscreant** Bad lot, Blackguard, Reprobate, Sinner, Tortfeasor

**Misdeed** Crime, Offence, Peccadillo, Trespass, Wrong

▷**Misdelivered** *may indicate* an anagram

**Misdemeanour** Delict, Offence, Peccadillo, Tort, Wrongdoing

**Miser(ly)** Candle-paring, Carl, Cheapskate, Cheese-parer, Close, Curmudgeon, Flay-flint, Gare, Grasping, Harpagon, Hunks, Marner, Meanie, Mingy, Muckworm, Niggard, Nipcheese, Nipcurn, Nipfarthing, Pennyfather, Penny-pincher, Pinch-commons, Puckfist, Runt, Save-all, Scrape-good, Scrape-penny, Screw, Scrimping, Scrooge, Shylock, Skinflint, Snudge, Storer, Tight-fisted, Tightwad, Timon

**Miserable, Misery, Miserably** Abject, Angashore, Bale, Bane, Cat-lap, Crummy, Cut up, Desperation, Distress, Dog's-life, Dole, Face-ache, Forlorn, Gloom, Grief, Grouch, Heartache, Hell, Joyless, Killjoy, Lousy, Mean, Measly, Perdition, Pittance, Punk, Sad, Saturnist, Scungy, Sorry, Sourpuss, Spoilsport, Torture, Tragic, Triste, → UNHAPPY, Wet blanket, Woe(begone), Wretched

**Misfire** Dud, Pink

**Misfit** Black sheep, Drop-out, Geek, Loner, Maverick, Sad sack

**Misfortune** Accident, Adversity, Affliction, Bale, Calamity, Catastrophe, Curse, Disaster, Distress, Dole, Harm, Hex, Ill, Ill-luck, Kicker, Mis(c)hanter, Reverse, Rewth, Ruth, Wroath

**Misgiving(s)** Anxiety, Doubt, Dubiety, Qualms, Scruples

**Misguide(d)** Impolitic, Off-beam

▷**Misguided** *may indicate* an anagram

**Mishandle** Abuse, Fumble, Ill-treat, Muff

**Mishap** Accident, Contretemps, Drere, Glitch, Misaunter, Misfortune, Pile-up, Wroath

**Misheard** Mondegreen

**Mishit, Misstroke** Crab, Draw, Duff, Edge, Fluff, Foozle, Muff, Sclaff, Shank, Slice, Thin, Toe, Top

**Misinformation** Bum steer

**Misinterpret(ation)** Mondegreen, Warp, Wrest

**Misjudge(ment)** Blunder, Goof, Misween, Overestimate, Overrate, Underestimate

**Mislay** Leese, Lose

**Mislead(ing)** Blind, Bum steer, Con, Cover-up, Deceive, Delude, Dupe, Equivocate, Fallacious, False, Gag, Half-truth, Hoodwink, Nutmeg, Red herring, Runaround, Smoke and mirrors, Snow job

▷**Misled** *may indicate* an anagram

**Mismanage** Blunder, Bungle, Muddle

**Mismatch(ed)** Kludge, Odd, Unequal

**Misplace(ment)** Anachorism, Ectopia, Lose, Loss

**Misplay** Fluff, Whitechapel

**Misprint** Error, Literal, Literal error, Slip, Typo

**Mispronunciation, Mispronounce** Cacoepy, Lallation, Lambdacism, Lisp

**Misrepresent(ation)** Abuse, Belie, Calumny, Caricature, Colour, Distort, Falsify, Fudge, Garble, Lie, Slander, Subreption, Traduce, Travesty

**Miss(ing), Missed** Abord, Absent, Airshot, Astray, Avoid, AWOL, Bungle, Colleen, Desiderate, Dodge, Drib, Err(or), Eschew, Fail, Forego, Gal, → GIRL, Kumari, Lack, Lass,

Link, Lose, Mademoiselle, Maid, Maiden, Mile, Mourned, Muff(et), Near, Need, Neglect, Negligence, Omit, Otis, Overlook, Señorita, Shy, Skip, Spinster, Stoke, Unmeet, Wanting, Whiff

▷**Miss** *may refer to* Missouri

**Missal** Breviary, Te igitur, Triodion

**Misshapen** Crooked, Deformed, Dysmelia, Gnarled, Malformed

**Missile** ABM, Air-to-air, ALCM, Ammo, Anti-ballistic, Arrow, Artillery, Atlas, Ball, Ballistic, Beam Rider, Blue streak, Bolas, Bolt, Bomb, Boomerang, Brickbat, Buckshot, Bullet, Condor, Cruise, Dart, Death star, Dingbat, Doodlebug, Dum-dum, Exocet®, Falcon, Firepot, Fléchette, Genie, Grenade, Guided, HARM, Harpoon, Hawk, Hellfire, Hound Dog, ICBM, Interceptor, Jired, Kiley, Kyley, Kylie, Lance, Mace, MARV, Maverick, Minuteman, MIRV, Missive, Mx, Onion, Patriot, Pellet, Pershing, Phoenix, Polaris, Poseidon, Qual, Quarrel, Rocket, SAM, Scud, Sea Skimmer, Seeker, Sergeant, Shell, Shillelagh, Shot, Shrike, Side-winder, Smart bomb, Snowball, Sparrow, Spartan, Spear, Sprint, SSM, Standard Arm, Standoff, Styx, Subroc, Surface to air, Surface to surface, Talos, Tartar, Terrier, Thor, Titan, Tomahawk, Torpedo, Tracer, Trident, UAM, Warhead

**Mission(ary)** Aidan, Alamo, Antioch, Apostle, Assignment, Augustine, Barnabas, Bethel, Boniface, Caravan, Charge, City, Columba, Crusade, Cuthbert, Cyril, Delegation, Embassage, Embassy, Errand, Evangelist, Foreign, Function, Happy-clappy, Iona, Legation, Livingstone, LMS, Message, Missiology, NASA, Neurolab, Ninian, Op, Paul, Pr(a)efect, Quest, Reclaimer, Redemptorist, Schweitzer, Silas, Sortie, Task, Vocation, Xavier

**Missis, Missus, Mrs** Devi, Dutch, Maam, Mrs, Wife

**Missive** Dispatch, Epistle, Letter, Message, Note

**Missouri** Mo

▶**Misstroke** *see* **MISHIT**

**Mist(y)** Aerosol, Australian, Blur, Brume, Cloud, Damp, Dew, Drow, Dry-ice, Film, Fog, Fret, Haar, Haze, Hoar, Miasma, Moch, Nebular, Niflheim, Nimbus, Rack, Red, Roke, Scotch, Sea-fret, Sfumato, Smir(r), Smog, Smur, Spotted, Spray, Steam, Vapour, Veil

**Mistake(n)** Aberration, Barry (Crocker), Bish, Blip, Bloomer, Blooper, Blue, Blunder, Boner, Boob, Booboo, Boss, Botch, Bull, Bungle, Category, Clanger, Clinker, Confound, Deluded, Domino, Erratum, Erroneous, Error, Fallacy, Fault, Flaw, Floater, Flub, Fluff, Folly, Gaffe, Goof, Hash, Horlicks, Howler, Identity, Incorrect, Lapse, Malapropism, Misprision, Miss, Muff, Mutual, Nod, Off-beam, Oops, Oversight, Own goal, Plonker, Pratfall, Ricket, Screw-up, → **SLIP**, Slip-up, Solecism, Stumer, Trip, Typo, Wrongdoing

▷**Mistake(n)** *may indicate* an anagram

**Mister** Aerosol, Atomiser, Babu, Deodorant, Effendi, Lala, Mr, Reb, Sahib, Señor, Shri, Sir, Sri, U

**Mistletoe** Album, Hemiparasite, Missel, Parasite, Sinker, Viscum

**Mistreat** Abuse, Attrite, Manhandle, Violate

**Mistress** Amie, Aspasia, Canary-bird, Chatelaine, Concubine, Courtesan, Delilah, Demimondaine, Devi, Doxy, Goodwife, Herself, Hussif, Inamorata, Instructress, Kept woman, Lady, Leman, Maintenon, Martha, Montespan, Mrs, Natural, Paramour, Querida, Stepney, Teacher, Wardrobe, Wife

**Mistrust(ful)** Askant, Doubt, Gaingiving, Scepticism, Suspect, Suspicion

**Misunderstand(ing)** Cross-purpose(s), Disagreement, Discord, Generation gap, Mistake

**Misuse** Abuse, Catachresis, Defalcate, Exploit, Malappropriate, Malapropism, Maltreat, Peculate, Perversion, Sacrilege, Torment

**Mite** Acaridian, Acarus, Arachnid, Berry bug, Bit, Bulb, Cheese, Child, Dust, Flour, Forage, Fowl, Gall, Harvest, Itch, Lepton, Little, (Red) spider, Rust, Sarcoptes, Speck, Spider, Sugar, Trombiculid, Tyroglyphid, Varroa, Widow's

**Mither** Nag

**Mitigate, Mitigating** Abate, Allay, Allegge, Allieve, Ameliorate, Assuage, Excuse, Extenuating, Lenitive, Lessen, Mease, Palliate, Quell, Relief, Relieve, Soften

**Mitosis** Anaphase

**Mitre** Hat, Tiar(a)

**Mitt(en), Mittens** Fist, Glove, Hand, Paw, Pockies

**Mix(ed), Mixer, Mixture, Mix-up** Adulterate, Allay, Alloy, Allsorts, Amalgam, Ambivalent, Associate, Assortment, Attemper, Balderdash, Bigener, Bittersweet, Bland, Blend, Blunge, Bombay, Bordeaux, Brew, Carburet, Card, Caudle, Cement, Chequered, Chichi, Chow, Coalesce, Cocktail, Combination, Co-meddle, Compo, Compound, Conché, Concrete, Conglomerate, Consort, Cross, Cut, Disperse, Diversity, Dolly, Drammock, Dukkah, Embroil, Emulsion, Eutectic, Farrago, Fold-in, Freezing, Friar's balsam, Garble, Grill, Griqua, Half-breed, Heather, Hobnob, Hodge-podge, Hotchpotch, Hybrid, Imbroglio, Immingle, Interlace, Intermingle, Isomorphous, Jumble, Lace, Lard, Lignin, Linctus, Load, Macedoine, Marketing, Mash, Matissé, Meddle, Medley, Meiny, Melange, Mell, Meng(e), Ment, Mess, Mestizo, Métis, Ming(le), Miscellaneous, Miscellany, Mishmash, Mongrel, Motley, Muddle, Muss(e), Neapolitan, Octaroon, Octoroon, Olio, Olla, Oxymel, Pastiche, Pi(e), Potin, Potion, Pot pourri, Pousowdie, Powsowdy, Praiseach, Preparation, Promiscuous, Raggle-taggle, Ragtag, Salad, Scramble, Shuffle, Snaf, Soda, Solution, Sound, Spatula, Stew, Stir, Swizzlestick, Temper, Through-other, Tonic, Trail, Vision, Whisk, Witches' brew, Yblent

▷**Mixed** *may indicate* an anagram

**Mixed marriage** Miscegenation

**Mizzle** Decamp, Scapa, Scarper

**Mnemonic(s)** Fleming's rules, Mafic, Memoria technica, Quipo, Quipu, Reminder

**Moab(ite)** Balak, Ruth, Wash-pot

**Moan(ing), Moaner** Beef, Bewail, Bleat, Carp, Complain, Groan, Grouse, Grumble, Hone, Keen, →**LAMENT**, Meane, Niggle, Plangent, Sigh, Snivel, Sough, Wail, Whine, W(h)inge

**Moat** Dike, Ditch, Foss(e)

**Mob(ster)** Army, Assail, Canaille, Crew, Crowd, Doggery, Drove, Faex populi, Flash, Gaggle, Gang, Herd, Hoi-polloi, Hoodlum, Horde, Lynch, Many-headed beast, Mobocrat, Ochlocrat, Press, Rabble, Rabble rout, Raft, Ragtag, Ribble-rabble, Riff-raff, Rout, Scar-face, Throng

**Mobile, Mobilise, Mobility** Agile, Cellphone, Donna, Downward, Fluid, Horizontal, Intergenerational, Movable, Plastic, Rally, Social, Thin, Upward(ly), Vagile, Vertical

**Mob-rule** Ochlocracy

**Mocassin** Larrigan, Shoe, Snake

**Mock(ery), Mocking** Ape, Banter, Catcall, Chaff, Charade, Chyack, Cod, Cynical, Deride, Derisory, Dor, Ersatz, False, Farce, Feint, Fleer, Flout, Gab, Geck, Gibe, Gird, Guy, Imitation, Ironise, Irony, Irrisory, Jape, →**JEER**, Jibe, Lampoon, Laugh, Mimic, Narquois, Paraselene, Parody, Paste, Pillorise, Piss-taking, Rag, Rail(lery), Rally, Ridicule, Sacrilege, Sardonic, Satirise, Scoff, Scorn, Scout, Send up, Serve, Sham, Simulate, Slag, Sneer, Snide, Sport, Tease, Travesty, Twit, Wry

**Mocking-bird** Mimus, Sage-thrasher

**Mode, Modish** Aeolian, Authentic, Chic, Church, Convention, Dorian, Ecclesiastical, Fashion, Form, Formal, Greek, Gregorian, Hyperdorian, Hypo(dorian), Hypolydian, Iastic, Insert, Ionian, Locrian, Lydian, Major, Manner, Material, Medieval, Minor, Mixolydian, Phrygian, Plagal, Raga, Rate, Real-time, Sleep, Step, Style, Technique, Ton

**Model(ler), Modelling** Archetype, Bozzetto, Cast, Ceroplastic, Clothes horse, Copy, Cover girl, Cutaway, Demo, Demonstration, Diorama, Doll, Dress-form, Dummy, Ecorché, Effigy, Epitome, Example, Exemplar, Exemplary, Fashionist, Fictor, Figure, Figurine, Icon, Ideal, Image, Instar, Jig, Last, Lay-figure, Layman, Madame Tussaud, Manakin, Man(n)ikin, Mannequin, Maquette, Mark, Matchstick, Mirror, Mock-up, Moulage, →**MOULD**, Norm, Original, Orrery, Papier-mâché, Parade, Paradigm, Paragon, Pattern, Phelloplastic, Pilot, Plasticine, Plastilina, Play-Doh®, Pose(r), Poster bot, Posture-maker, Precedent, Prototype, Replica, Role, Sample, Scale, Schema, Sedulous, Sitter, Specimen, Standard, Stereotype, Superwaif, Swatch, T, Tellurion, Template, Templet, Terrella, Toy, Trilby, Try on, Twiggy, Type, Typify, Version, Waif, Waxwork, Working

▷**Model(s)** *may indicate* an anagram

**Modem** Subset

**Moderate(ly), Moderation** Abate, Abbreviate, Allay, Alleviate, Assuage, Attemper, Average, Ca'canny, Centre, Chair, Chasten, Continent, Decent, Diminish, Discretion, Ease, Gentle, Girondist, Ho(a), Lessen, Lukewarm, Measure, Mediocre, Medium, Menshevik, Mezzo, Middling, Mild, Mitigate, Muscadin, OK, Politique, Pretty, Realo, Reason(able),

Relent, Restraint, RR, Slake, So-so, Sparing, Subdue, Sumptuary, Temper(ate), Temperance, Tolerant, Tone (down), Via media, Wet

**Modern(ise)** AD, Aggiornamento, Contemporary, Fresh, Latter(-day), Millie, Neonomian, Neoterical, → **NEW**, New-fangled, Present-day, Progressive, Recent, Refit, Renovate, Retrofit, Revamp, Space age, State-of-the-art, Streamline, Swinger, Trendy, Update, Upgrade, Up-to-date

**Modest(y)** Aidos, Blaise, Chaste, Coy, Decent, Demure, Discreet, Fair, Homely, Humble, Humility, Ladylike, Low-key, Lowly, Maidenly, Mim, Mussorgsky, Propriety, Prudish, Pudency, Pudicity, Pure, Reserved, Reticent, Shame, Shamefaced, Shy, Simple, Slender, Slight, Unaffected, Unassuming, Unpretending, Unpretentious, Verecund

**Modicum** Dash, Tad

**Modifiable, Modification, Modified, Modifier, Modify** Adapt, Adjust, Adverb, Alter, Attemper, Backpedal, Change, Enhance, Extenuate, Genetically, H, Hotrod, Leaven, Misplaced, Plastic, Qualify, Restyle, Retrofit, Sandhi, Scumble, Soup, Streamline, Sublimate, Temper, Top, Transmute, Trim, Vary

**Modulation, Modulate(d), Module, Modulus** Accent, Amplitude, Bulk, Cadence, Command, Distance, Element, Enharmonic, Excursion, Frequency, Habitat, Inflexion, Lem, Lunar, Mitigate, Phase, Pulse, Service, Shear, Subcarrier, Tune, Unit, Vary, Velocity, Young's

**Mogul** Bigwig, Magnate, Nawab, Padishah, Plutocrat, Potentate, Skiing, Taipan, Tycoon, VIP

**Mohair** Angora, Moire

**Mohammed, Mohammedan (era)** Hadith, Hegira, Hejira, Hejra, Hijra, Islamite, Mahdi, Mahoun(d), Moslem, Muezzin, Mussulman, Prophet, Said, Shiite, Sunna(h)

**Mohican** Haircut

**Moist(en), Moisture** Baste, Bedew, Dab, Damp, Dank, De(a)w, Dewy, Humect, Humidify, Humidity, Humify, Imbue, Latch, Love-in-a-mist, Madefy, Mesarch, Mesic, Moil, Nigella, Oozy, Precipitation, Sap, Slake, Slocken, Soggy, Sponge, Wet

**Moisturiser** Skin care

▷**Moither** *may indicate* an anagram

**Molar** Cheek tooth, Grinder, Mill-tooth, Secodont, Tooth, Wang, Wisdom tooth

**Molasses** Blackstrap, Sorghum, Treacle

**Moldova** MD

**Mole(hill)** Beauty spot, Breakwater, Burrower, Espionage, Fen-cricket, Golden, Groyne, Hydatidiform, Insider, Jetty, Labour, Marsupial, Miner, Mo(u)diewart, Moldwarp, Moudi(e)wart, Mould(i)warp, Naeve, Notoryctes, Orology, Pier, Plant, Sea-wall, Shrew, Sleeper, Spot, Spy, Star-nose(d), Talpa, Want(hill), Want knap, Warp

**Molecule(s), Molecular** Acceptor, Achiral, Aptameter, Atom, Buckyball, Carbene, Cavitand, Chimera, Chiral, Chromophore, Closed chain, Cobalamin, Codon, Coenzyme, Cofactor, Dimer, DNA, Electrogen, Enantiomorph, Footballene, Fullerene, Gram, Hapten, Iota, Isomer, Kinin, Kisspeptin, Ligand, Long-chain, Metabolite, Metameric, Monomer, Nanotube, Nitryl, Oligomer, Peptide, Polymer, Polysaccharide, Quark, Replicon, Ribozyme, Semantide, Stereoisomer, Synthon, Triatonic, Trimer, Uridine, Vector

**Molendinar** Mill

**Molest(er)** Annoy, Bother, Disturb, Harass, Interfere, Nonce, Scour, Touch up

**Moll(y), Mollie** Bloom, Bonnie, Carousal, Cutpurse, Flanders, Girl, Maguire, Malone, May, Sissy, Trollop

**Mollify** Alleviate, Appease, Assuage, Fob, Mease, Mitigate, Pacify, Placate, Relax, Soften, Temper

**Mollusc(s)** Bivalve, Malacology, Opisthobranch, → **SHELLFISH**, Tectibranch, Univalve

---

## MOLLUSCS

*3 letters:*
Mya

*4 letters:*
Arca
Clam
Slug
Spat
Unio

*5 letters:*
Bulla
Capiz
Chank
Conch
Cowry
Doris
Gaper
Helix
Idler
Murex
Olive
Pinna
Polyp
Sepia
Snail
Solen
Spoot

Squid
Turbo
Venus
Whelk

*6 letters:*
Chiton
Cockle
Cowrie
Cuttle
Limpet
Loligo
Mussel
Nerita
Oyster
Pecten
Pholas
Poulpe
Quahog
Tellen
Tellin
Teredo
Triton
Winkle

*7 letters:*
Abalone
Octopod
Octopus
Pandore
Piddock
Quahaug
Scallop
Scollop
Sea-hare
Sea-slug
Spirula
Toheroa
Trochus
Veliger
Vitrina

*8 letters:*
Ammonite
Argonaut
Ark-shell
Auricula
Nautilus
Pteropod
Saxicava
Sea-lemon
Shipworm
Strombus
Top-shell

*9 letters:*
Belemnite
Cone-shell
Dentalium
Gastropod
Goniatite
Nautiloid
Neopilina
Razor-clam
Razor-fish
Rock borer
Scaphopod
Trochidae
Tusk-shell
Wing-shell
Wood-borer

*10 letters:*
Amphineura
Cephalopod
Cuttlefish
Duck mussel
Gasteropod
Heart-shell
Money cowry
Pelecypoda
Periwinkle
Protostome
Razorshell
Scaphopoda
Venus shell
Wentletrap

*11 letters:*
Horse mussel
Marine boxer
Paper-sailor
Trochophore
Trough-shell

*12 letters:*
Heart-cockler
Pelican's-foot

*13 letters:*
Lamellibranch
Paper nautilus
Slipper limpet

*14 letters:*
Monoplacophora
Pearly nautilus
Polyplacophora

---

**Mollycoddle** Indulge, Nanny, Pamper, Spoil
**Moloch** Thorn-devil
**Molten** Dissolved, Fusil, Igneous, Magma, Melted
**Molybdenum** Mo
**Moment(s), Momentous** Aha, Bending, Bit, Blonde, Brief, Dipole, Electromagnetic, Eureka, Eventful, Flash(point), Gliffing, Glift, Hogging, Import, Instant, Jiffy, Light bulb, Magnetic, → MINUTE, Mo, Nonce, Point, Psychological, Pun(c)to, Sagging, Sands, Sec, Senior, Shake, Signal, Split second, Stound, Stownd, Tick, Time, Trice, Twinkling, Two-ticks, Weighty, Wink
**Momentum** Angular, Impetus, L, Speed, Steam, Thrust
**Mona(s)** I, IOM
**Monaco** Grimaldi
**Mona Lisa** La Gioconda
**Monarch(y)** Absolute, Autocrat, Belgium, Britain, Butterfly, Caesar, Cole, Constitutional, Crown, Crowned head, Dual, Emperor, HM, K, Karling, King, Kuwait, Limited, Losotho, Merry, Netherlands, Norway, Oman, Potentate, Q, Queen, R, Raine, Realm, Realty, Reign, Ruler, Saudi Arabia, Sovereign, Swaziland, Sweden, Tonga, Tsar
**Monarchist** Cavalier
**Monastery, Monastic** Abbey, Abthane, Anselm, Beghard, Celibate, Charterhouse, Chartreuse, Cloister, Community, Gompa, Holy, Hospice, Iona, Lamaserai, Lamasery, La Trappe, Laura, Monkish, Oblate, Priory, Retreat, Sangha, Secluded, Tashi, Vihara, Wat
**Monday** Black, Collop, Easter, Handsel, Hock, J'ouvert, Meal, Oatmeal, Plough, Whit
**Mondrian** Piet
**Money, Moneyed, Monetary** Ackers, Akkas, Allowance, Alms, Annat, Ante, Appearance, Archer, Assignat, Banco, Batta, Beer, Blood, Blue, Blunt, Boodle, Bottle, Brass, Bread, Bread and honey, Broad, Bucks, Bull's eye, Bunce, Cabbage, Capital, Cash, Caution, Century, Change, Chink, Circulating medium, Cob, Cock, → COIN, Collateral, Confetti, Conscience, Crackle, Cranborne, Crinkle, Crinkly, Crust, Currency, Danger, Dib(s), Dingbat, Dirty, Dollar,

Dosh, Dough, Dump, Dust, Earnest, Easy, Escrow, Even, Expenditure, Fat, Fee, Fiat, Finance, Fiscal, Float, Folding, Fonds, Found, Fund, Funny, Gate, Gelt, Gilt, Godiva, Gold, Grand, Grant, Gravy, Greens, Gross, Hard, Head, Heavy sugar, Hello, Hoot, Hot, Housekeeping, Hush, Idle, Ingots, Investment, Jack(pot), Kail, Kale, Kembla, Key, King's ransom, Knife, L, Legal tender, Lolly, Loot, Lucre, M, Mammon, Maundy, Mazuma, Means, Megabucks, Mint, Monkey, Monopoly, Moola(h), Narrow, Near, Necessary, Needful, Nest-egg, Note, Nugger, Numismatic, Nummary, Oaker, Ocher, Ochre, Offertory, Oof, Option, Outlay, P, Packet, Paper, Passage, Pavarotti, Payroll, Peanuts, Pecuniary, Pelf, Petrodollar, Pin, Pine-tree, Pink, Pittance, Plastic, Plum, Pocket, Pony, Posh, Premium, Press, Prize, Proceeds, Profit, Protection, Purse, Push, Quid, Rag, Ransom, Ration, Ready, Reap silver, Rebate, Remuneration, Resources, Revenue, Rhino, Ring, Risk, Rogue, Rowdy, Salt(s), Score, Scratch, Scrip, Seed, Settlement, Shekels, Shell, Shin-plaster, Ship, Short, Siller, Silly, Silver, Sinews of war, Slush (fund), Smackers, Smart, Soap, Soft, Solvent, Spending, Spondulicks, Stake, Sterling, Stipend, Stuff, Subsidy, Subsistence, Sugar, Sum, Surety, Table, Take, Takings, Talent, Tea, Tender, Tin, Toea, Token, Tranche, Treaty, Tribute, Turnover, Viaticum, Wad, Wampum, Wealth, Windfall, Wonga

**Money-box** Penny-pig, Piggy bank, Till

**Moneylender** Gombeen, Loan shark, Scrivener, Shroff, Shylock, Usurer

**Moneymaking, Money-spinning** Cash cow, Earner, Lucrative, Profitable, Quaestuary

**Mongol(ian)** Bashkir, Buriat, Buryat, Calmuck, Chuvash, Epicanthic, Evenski, Genghis Khan, Golden Horde, Kalmuck, Kalmyk, Kara-Kalpak, Kazak(h), Khalifa(h), Khalkha, Kubla(i) Khan, Kyrgyz, Lapp, Lepcha, Manchoo, Manchu, Mishmi, Mogul, Pareoean, Samoyed, Shan, Sherpa, Tamerlane, Ta(r)tar, Tungus(ic), Uig(h)ur, Ural-altaic, Uzbek

**Mongoose** Herpestes, Ichneumon, Mangouste, Meerkat, Suricate, Urva

**Mongrel** Bitser, Cross(bred), → DOG, Goorie, Goory, Hybrid, Kuri, Lurcher, Mutt, Tyke, Underbred, Zo

**Monitor(ing)** Dataveillance, Desktop, Detect, ECG, Goanna, Iguana, Komodo dragon, Lizard, Observe, Offer, Ofgas, Ofgem, Oflot, Ofsted, Oftel, Ofwat, Oversee, Prefect, Preview, Record, Regulator, Screen, Server, Ship, Sniffer, Speed trap, Sphygmophone, Surveillance, Tabs, Tag, Track, UDU, Warship, Watchdog, Whole-body, Worral, Worrel

**Monk(s)** Anchorite, Bodhidharma, Bro, Brother, Frere, General, Mechitherast, Mekhiterist, Order, Provincial, Religieux, Thelonious, Votary

---

## MONKS

*3 letters:*
Dan
Dom
Fra

*4 letters:*
Bede
Lama

*5 letters:*
Abbot
Aidan
Black
Bonze
Bruno
Frati
Friar
Minor
Prior
Roshi

*6 letters:*
Austin
Bhikhu
Culdee
Hermit
Jerome
Oblate
Palmer
Sangha

*7 letters:*
Beghard
Caedmon
Caloyer
Cluniac
Dervish
Félibre
Hegumen
Jacobin
Maurist
Recluse

*8 letters:*
Acoemeti
Angelico
Basilian
Cenobite
Jacobite
Minorite
Olivetan
Pelagian
Rakehell
Rasputin
Salesian
Sub-prior
Talapoin
Theatine
Trappist

*9 letters:*
Celestine
Cellarist
Coenobite
Dominican
Feuillant
Gyrovague
Hesychast
Recollect
Thelemite

*10 letters:*
Bernardine
Carthusian
Cistercian
Fraticelli
Hildebrand
Norbertine
Savonarola

*11 letters:*
Abbey-lubber
Augustinian
Benedictine
Bonaventura

Camaldolite
Ignorantine
Mekhitarist
Tironensian

*12 letters:*
Bethlehemite
Mechitharist
Obedientiary

*13 letters:*
Archimandrite
Crutched Friar
Possessionate
Thomas à Kempis

*14 letters:*
Simeon Stylites

---

**Monkey** Anger, Ape, Aye-aye, Baboon, Bandar, Benobo, Bobbejaan, Bonnet, Brass, Bushbaby, Capuchin, Catar(r)hine, Cebidae, Cebus, Chacma, Coaita, Colobus, Cynomolgus, Diana, Douc, Douroucouli, Drill, Durukuli, Entellus, Galago, Gelada, Gibbon, Gorilla, Grease, Green, Grison, Grivet, Guenon, Guereza, Hanuman, Hoolock, Howler, Hylobates, Imp, Indri, Jacchus, Jackey, Jocko, Kippage, Kipunji, Langur, Leaf, Lemur, Loris, Macaco, Macaque, Magot, Malmag, Mandrill, Mangabey, Marmoset, Meddle, Meerkat, Mico, Midas, Mona, Mycetes, Nala, Nasalis, New World, Old World, Orang-utang, Ouakari, Ouistiti, Phalanger, Platyrrhine, Pongo, Powder, → PRIMATE, Proboscis, Pug, Puzzle, Rage, Ram, Rapscallion, Rascal, Rhesus, Sago(u)in, Saguin, Sai(miri), Sajou, Saki, Sapajou, Satan, Scamp, Semnopithecus, Siamang, Sifaka, Silen(us), Silverback, Simian, Simpai, Slender loris, Spider, Squirrel, Talapoin, Tamarin, Tamper, Tana, Tarsier, Tee-tee, Titi, Toque, Trip-hammer, Troop, Tup, Uakari, Urchin, Vervet, Wanderoo, White-eyelid, Wilderness, Wistiti, Wou-wou, Wow-wow, Wrath, Zati

**Monkey-nut** Earth-pea

**Monkey-puzzle** Araucaria, Bunya-bunya, Chilean pine

**Monkshood** Aconite

**Monocle** Eye-glass, Gig-lamp, Lens, Lorgnon, Quiz(zing-glass)

**Monocot(yledon)** Araceae, Distyogen, Endogen, Tradescantia, Typha

**Monodon** Narwhal

**Monogram, Monograph** Chi-rho, Cipher, Initials, Study, Treatise, Tug(h)ra

**Monolith** Ayers Rock, Cenotaph, Chambers Pillar, Uluru

**Monologue** Dramatic, Interior, Patter, Rap, Recitation, Soliloquy, Speech

**Monopolise, Monopoly** Absolute, Appalto, Bloc, Bogart, Cartel, Coemption, Corner, Engross, Hog, Octroi, Patent, Régie, Trust

**Monorail** Aerobus, Gyroca

**Monosyllable** Proclitic

**Monotheist** Parsee

**Monotone, Monotonous, Monotony** Boring, Drear, Dull, → FLAT, Grey, Humdrum, Repetitive, Same(y), Sing-song, Soul-destroying, Tedious, Thrum

**Monoxide** Baryta

**Monsoon** Dry, Hurricane, Typhoon, Wet, → WIND

▷**Monsoon** *may indicate* weekend: Mon soon

**Monster, Monstrosity, Monstrous** Alecto, Apollyon, Asmodeus, Bandersnatch, Behemoth, Bogeyman, Brute, Bugaboo, Bunyip, Caliban, Cerberus, Cete, Charybdis, Chichevache, Chim(a)era, Cockatrice, Colossal, Cyclops, Dabbat, Dalek, Deform, Dinoceras, Dismayd, Div, Dragon, Echidna, Enormous, Erebus, Erinys, Erl-king, Eten, Ettin, Evil-one, Eyesore, Fiend, Fire-drake, Frankenstein, Freak, Geryon, Ghost, Giant, Gila, Goblin, Godzilla, Golem, Gorgon, Green-eyed, Grendel, Harpy, Hippocampus, Hippogriff, Hippogryph, Huge, Hydra, Jabberwock, Kraken, Lamia, Leviathan, Lilith, Lusus naturae, Mastodon, Medusa, Minotaur, Misbegotten, Moloch, Mooncalf, Mylodont, Nessie, Nicker, Nightmare, Ogopogo, Ogre, Ogr(e)ish, Opinicus, Orc, Outrageous, Pongo, Prodigy, Sasquatch, Satyral, Scylla, Serra, Shadow, Simorg, Simurg(h), Siren, Skull, Snark, Spectre, Sphinx, Spook, Stegodon, Stegosaur, Succubus, Taniwha, Teras, Teratism, Teratoid, Triceratops, Triffid, Troll, Typhoeus, Typhon, Unnatural, Vampire, Vast, Wasserman, Wendego, Wendigo, Wer(e)wolf, Whale, Wivern, Wyvern, Xiphopagus, Yowie, Ziffius

**Monstrance** Ostensory

**Monteith** Bandanna

**Montezuma** Aztec

**Month(ly)** Ab, Abib, Adar, Anomalistic, April, Asadha, Asvina, August, Bhadrapada, Brumaire, Bul, Caitra, Calendar, Cheshvan, Chislev, December, Dhu-al-Hijjah,

Dhu-al-Qadah, Draconic, Elul, February, Fence, Floréal, Frimaire, Fructidor, Gander, Germinal, Hes(h)van, Iy(y)ar, January, July, Jumada, June, Jyaistha, Karttika, Kisleu, Kislev, Lide, Lunar, Lunation, Magha, March, Margasirsa, May, Messidor, Mo, Moharram, Moon, Muharram, Muharrem, Nisan, Nivôse, Nodical, November, October, Ovulation, Periodical, Phalguna, Pluviôse, Prairial, Rabi(a), Rajab, Ramadan, Ramazon, Rhamadhan, Safar, Saphar, S(h)ebat, September, Sha(a)ban, Shawwal, Sidereal, Sivan, Solar, Stellar, Synodic, Tammuz, Tebeth, Thermidor, Tishri, Tisri, Tropical, Vaisakha, Veadar, Vendémiaire, Ventôse

**Monument** Ancient, Arch, Archive, Cairn, Cenotaph, Charminar, Column, Cromlech, Cross, Dolmen, Eugubine, Henge, Immortelle, Landmark, Megalith, Memorial, Menhir, Monolith, National, Pantheon, Pyramid, Sacellum, Sphinx, Stele(ne), Stone circle, Stonehenge, Stupa, Talayot, Tombstone, Trilith, Trilithon, Urn

**Mood(y)** Active, Air, Anger, Atmosphere, Attitude, Aura, Bathos, Bipolar, Capricious, Conditional, Conjunctive, Dudgeon, Emoticon, Enallage, Feeling, Fettle, Fit, Foulie, Glum, Grammar, Huff, Humour, Hump, Imperative, Indicative, Infinitive, Mercurial, Miff, Morale, Optative, Passive, Peat, Pet, Revivalist, Sankey, Spleen, Strop, Subjunctive, Sulky, Temper, Temperamental, Tid, Tone, Tune, Vein, Vinegar, Whim

**Moon(light), Moony** Aah, Adrastea, Alignak, Amalthea, Aningan, Apogee, Artemis, Astarte, Blue, Callisto, Calypso, Chandra, Cheese, Crescent, Cynthia, Diana, Epact, Europa, Eye, Flit, Full, Gander, Ganymede, Gibbous, Glimmer, Grimaldi, Harvest, Hecate, Hunter's, Hyperion, Iapetus, Inconstant, Io, Juliet, Leda, Lucina, Luna(r), Mani, Mascon, McFarlane's Buat, Midsummer, Mock, Month, Mooch, Mope, New, Nimbus, Nocturne, Octant, Oliver, Orb, Paddy's lantern, Paraselene, Paschal, Pasiphaë, Phobos, Phoebe, Plenilune, Proteus, Raker, Rear-view, Satellite, Selene, Set, Shepherd, Shot, Sickle, Sideline, Silvery, Sion, Sonata, Stargaze, Stone, Syzygy, Thebe, Thoth, Titan, Triton, Umbriel, Wander

**Moon god** Thoth, Trismegistus

**Moonraker** Astrogeologist, Gothamite

**Moonshine(r)** Balderdash, Distillation, Gibberish, Guff, Hootch, Poteen, Rot, Shebeener, Starveling, Tosh

**Moor(ing), Moored, Moorish, Moorland** Anchor, Berth, Bodmin, Culloden, Dock, Fell, Fen, Fern land, Flow country, Girt, Grouse, Heath, Iago, Ilkley, Makefast, Marina, Marston, Moresque, Moroccan, Mudéjar, Othello, Otter, Palustrine, Roadstead, Ry(e)peck, Saracen, Secure, Sternfast, Tether, → **TIE**, Wharf, Wold

**Moorhen** Gallinule

**Moot** Debatable

**Mop(ping)** Dwile, Flibbertigibbet, Girn, Glib, Malkin, Shag, Squeegee, Squilgee, Swab, Swob, Thatch, → **WIPE**

**Mope, Moping** Boody, Brood, Lovelorn, Moon, Peak, Sulk

**Mopoke** Ruru

**Mor** Humus

**Moral(ity), Morals** Apologue, Austere, Conscience, Deontic, Ethic(al), Ethos, Everyman, Exemplary, Fable, Gnomic, High-minded, Integrity, Laxity, Message, Parable, Precept, Principled, Probity, Puritanic, Righteous, Sententious, Sittlichkeit, Tag, Upright, Virtuous, Well-thewed, Wholesome

**Morale** Ego, Mood, Spirit, Zeal

**Moralise, Moralising** Preach, Sententious

**Moralist** Aesop, Pharisee, Prig, Prude, Puritan, Whitecap

**Morass** Bog, Fen, Flow, Marsh, Moss, Quagmire, Slough

**Moravian** Herrnhuter

**Morbid(ity)** Anasarca, Ascites, Cachaemia, Dropsy, Ectopia, Ghoul(ish), Gruesome, Hypersthenia, Pathological, Peccant, Plethora, Prurient, Religiose, Sick, Sombre, Unhealthy

**Mordant** Base, Biting, Caustic, Critic(al), Sarcastic, Tooth

**Mordent** Inverted, Lower, Pralltriller, Upper

**More** Added, Additional, Else, Excess, Extra, Idealist, Increase, Intense, Less, Mae, Merrier, Mo(e), → **NO MORE**, Over, Piu, Plus, Rather, Seconds, Stump, Surfeit, To spare, Utopia

**Moreover** Again, Also, Besides, Eft, Either, Eke, Further, Too, Withal, Yet

**Mores** Etiquette

**Morgan** Buccaneer, Pirate
**Moribund** Dying, Stagnant, Withered
**Mormon** Apostle, Danite, Jack, Latter-day Saint, Salt Lake City, Utah, Young
**Morning** Ack-emma, Am, Antemeridian, Coffee, Dawn, Daybreak, Early, Forenoon, Levée, Matin(al), Matutinal, Morrow, Sparrowfart
**Morning-glory** Bindweed, Ipomoea, Turbith, Turpeth
**Morning-star** Morgenstern, Phosphor(us), Threshel, Venus
**Moroccan, Morocco** Agadir, Ale, French, Leather, Levant, MA, Mo(o)r, Persian, Riff, Tangerine, Venus
**Moron** Fool, Idiot, Imbecile, Schmuck, → STUPID
**Morose** Acid, Boody, Churlish, Crabby, Cynical, Disgruntled, Gloomy, Glum, Grum, Moody, Sour-eyed, Sulky, Sullen, Surly
**Morph** Phase
**Morphine** Heroin
**Morris** Car, Dance, Fivepenny, Merel(l), Meril, Nine Men's, Ninepenny
**Morrow** Future
**Morse** Code, Dah, Dit, Endeavour, Iddy-umpty, Inventor, Tusker, Walrus
**Morsel** Bit, Bite, Bouche, Canape, Crumb, Dainty, Morceau, Ort, Scrap, Sippet, Sop, Tidbit, Titbit
**Mortal(ity)** Averr(h)oism, Being, Deathly, → FATAL, Grave, Human, Lethal, Yama
**Mortar, Mortar-board** Bowl, Cannon, Cement, Co(e)horn, Compo, Grout, Gunite, Hawk, Howitzer, Life, Metate, Mine-thrower, Minnie, Moaning (Minnie), Parget, Plaster, Pot gun, Screed, Square, Squid, Toc emma, Trench(er)
**Mortgage(e)** Balloon, Bond, Cap and collar, Cedula, Chattel, Debt, Dip, Encumbrance, Endowment, First, Home loan, Hypothecator, Loan, Pension, Pledge, Repayment, Reverse, Wadset(t)
**Mortification, Mortified, Mortify** Abase, Abash, Ashame, Chagrin, Crucify, Crush, Gangrene, Humble, Humiliate, Infarct, Necrose, Penance, Sick, Sphacelus, Wormwood
**Mortuary** Deadhouse, Morgue
**Mosaic** Buhl, Cosmati, Felsic, Impave, Inlay, Intarsia, Musive, Opus musivum, Pietra dura, Screen, Smalto, Tarsia, Terrazzo, Tessella(te), Tessera, Tobacco, Venetian
**Moscow** Dynamo
**Moses** Grandma
▸**Moslem** *see* MUSLIM (RITUAL)
**Mosque** Dome of the Rock, El Aqsa, Jami, Masjid, Medina, Musjid
**Mosquito** Aedes, Anopheles, Bloodsucker, Culex, Culicine, Gnat, Parasite, Skeeter, Stegomyia
**Moss(y)** Acrogen, Agate, Bryology, Bur(r), Carrag(h)een, Ceylon, Club, Fairy, Fog, Fontinalis, Hag(g), Hypnum, Iceland, Irish, Lecanoram, Lichen, Litmus, Liverwort, Long, Lycopod, Marsh, Musci, Muscoid, Parella, Peat, Polytrichum, Protonema, Reindeer, Rose, Scale, Selaginella, Spanish, Sphagnum, Staghorn, Stitch, Tree, Usnea, Wall, Wolf's claw
**Mosstrooper** Freebooter, Raider
**Most(ly)** Basically, Largest, Major, Maxi(mum), Optimum
**Mot** Quip, Saying
**Mote** Atom, Particle, Speck
**Motel** Motor lodge
**Moth(s)** Sand-dart

---

**MOTHS**

*2 letters:*
Io

*3 letters:*
Bag
Bee
Fox
Nun
Owl
Wax

*4 letters:*
Arch
Bell
Corn
Dart
Goat
Hawk
Luna
Meal
Puss
Wave

*5 letters:*
Atlas
Eggar
Egger
Flour
Ghost
Gipsy
Grass
Gypsy
House
Imago
Owlet
Plane
Plume
Snout
Swift

Thorn
Tiger
Tinea
Umber
Wheat
Y-moth
Yucca

*6 letters:*
Antler
Bogong
Bugong
Burnet
Carpet
Codlin
Dagger
Ermine
Herald
Kitten
Lackey
Lappet
Lichen
Magpie
Muslin
Noctua
Psyche
Sphinx
Turnip
Tusser
Veneer
Winter

*7 letters:*
Abraxas
Buff-tip
Cabbage
Clothes
Codling
Emerald
Emperor
Hook-tip
Leopard
Lobster
Noctuid
Old-lady
Pug-moth
Silver-Y
Tortrix
Tussock
Tussore
Unicorn
Zygaena

*8 letters:*
Bobowler
Bombycid
Cecropia
Cinnabar
Dart-moth
Drepanid
Geometer
Goldtail
Night-fly
Oak-egger
Peppered
Saturnia
Silkworm
Sphingid
Tapestry
Tineidae
Vapourer
Wainscot

*9 letters:*
Arctiidae
Brown-tail
Carpenter
Clearwing
Corn -borer
Geometrid
Honeycomb
Notodonta
Pyralidae
Saturniid
Scavenger
Underwing
Woodborer

*10 letters:*
Death's head
Gooseberry
Leafroller
Peach-bloom
Peppercorn
Pine-beauty
Pine-carpet
Polyphemus
Privet hawk

*11 letters:*
Diamondback
Hummingbird
Lepidoptera

*12 letters:*
Cactoblastis
Giant peacock
Kentish glory
Large emerald
Lymantriidae
Red underwing
Sallow-kitten

*13 letters:*
Lasiocampidae
Mother of pearl
Mother Shipton
Processionary
Purple emperor

*15 letters:*
Yellow underwing

*16 letters:*
Clifden nonpareil
Macrolepidoptera
Microlepidoptera

---

**Mothball(s)** Abeyance, Camphor, Naphtha, Preserver
**Moth-eaten** Flea-bitten, Tatty
**Mother** Abbess, Ana, Bearer, Birth, Church, Cognate, Cosset, Courage, Dam(e), Den, Dregs, Ean, Earth, Eoan, Eve, Fecula, Foster, Generatrix, Genetrix, Genitrix, Goose, Hubbard, Lees, Ma, Machree, Madre, Mam(a), Mamma, Mater, Matroclinic, Maya, Minnie, Mollycoddle, Mom, Multipara, Mum, Mummy, Native, Nature, Nourish, Nursing, Parent, Parity, Pourer, Prim(o), Primipara, Progenitress, Reverend, Shipton, Slime, Superior, Surrogate, Teresa, Theotokos, Venter, Wit
▷**Mother** *may indicate* a lepidopterist; moth-er
**Mother-in-law** Naomi
**Motherless** Adam, Orphan
**Motif** Anthemion, Design, Gist, Idée, Pattern, Theme
**Motion** Angular, Blocking, Composite, Contrary, Differential, Direct, Diurnal, Drift, Early day, Fast, Free-fall, Gesture, Harmonic, Impulse, Kepler, Kinematics, Kinetic, Kipp, Link, Move, Oblique, Offer, Parallactic, Parallel, Peculiar, Perpetual, PL, Precession, Proper, Proposal, Rack and pinion, Rider, Sewel, Similar, Slow, Spasm, Tide, Velocity, Wave
**Motionless** Doggo, Frozen, Immobile, Inert, Quiescent, Stagnant, Standstill, Stasis, Static, Still, Stock-still
**Motive, Motivate, Motivation** Actuate, Angle, Arouse, Cause, Drive, Ideal, Impel, Impetus, Incentive, Inspire, Intention, Mainspring, Mobile, Object, Pretext, → PURPOSE, Raison d'être, Rationale, Reason, Spur, Ulterior, Urge
**Motiveless** Wanton
**Motley** Jaspé, Medley, Piebald, Pied, Variegated

**Motor(boat)** Auto, Benz, Booster, Car, Dynamo, Electric, Engine, Hot rod, Hydroplane, Inboard, Induction, Jato, Launch, Linear, Mini, Motoscafo, Outboard, Paint job, Rocket, Scooter, Series-wound, Servo, Shunt-winding, Starter, Stator, Supermini, Sustainer, Synchronous, Thruster, Turbine, Turbo, Universal, Vaporetto, Water

**Motorcade** Procession

**Motorcycle, Motorcyclist** Bambi, Beemer, Bikie, Chookchaser, Chopper, Combination, Dirt bike, Farm-bike, Greaser, Hardtail, Harley Davidson, Hell's Angel, Minimoto, Moped, Pipsqueak, Quad bike, Scooter, Scramble, Tourist Trophy, Trail bike, TT, Yamaha®

**Motorist(s)** AA, Driver, Petrolhead, RAC, Road hog, Tripper

**Motorman** Austin, Benz, Ford, Morris

**Motor race, Motor sport** F1, Formula One, McLaren, Rally, Scramble, TT

**Motorway** Autobahn, Autopista, Autoput, Autoroute, Autostrada, Expressway, Interstate, M(1), Orbital, Superhighway, Throughway, Thruway

**Mottle(d)** Brindled, Chiné, Dapple, Jaspé, Marbled, Marly, Mirly, Pinto, Poikilitic, Tabby

**Motto** Device, Epigraph, Excelsior, Gnome, Ich dien, Impresa, Imprese, Impress(e), Legend, Maxim, Mot, Poesy, Posy, Saw, Slogan

**Mou(e)** Grimace, Mim

**Moufflon** Mus(i)mon

**Mould(ed), Moulder, Mouldable, Moulding, Mouldy** Accolade, Architrave, Archivolt, Astragal, Baguette, Balection, Bandelet, Beading, Bend, Black, Blow, Blue, Bolection, Botrytis, Bread, Briquet(te), Cabling, Casement, Cast(ing), Cavetto, Chain, Chessel, Chill, Cold, Cornice, Cosmoplastic, Coving, Cyma (recta), Cymatium, Dancette, Dariole, Die, Die-cast, Dogtooth, Doucine, Dripstone, Ductile, Echinus, Egg and anchor, Egg and dart, Emboss, Fictile, Flong, Forge, → **FORM**, Foughty, Fousty, Fungose, Fungus, Fusarol(e), Fust, Gadroon, Geat, Godroon, Gorgerin, Green, Hood-mould, Hore, Humus, Ingot, Injection, Iron, Jelly, Leaf, Machine, Matrix, Mildew, Model, Mool, Moulage, Mucedinous, Mucid, Mucor, Must(y), Mycetozoan, Myxomycete, Nebule, Necking, Noble rot, Ogee, Ovolo, Palmette, Papier-mâché, Pelmet, Penicillin, Phycomycete, Picture, Pig, Plasm(a), Plaster, Plastic, Plastisol, Plat, Platband, Plate, Prototype, Prunt, Quarter-round, Reeding, Reglet, Rhizopus, Rib, Rot, Rust, Sandbox, Scotia, Shape, Slime, Smut, Soil, Soot(y), Spindle, Storiated, Stringcourse, Stucco, Surbase, Tailor, Talon, Template, Templet, Timbale, Tondino, Torus, Trochilus, Vegetable, Vinew, Water table

**Moult(ing)** Cast, Metecdysis, Mew, Shed

**Mound** Agger, Bank, Barp, Barrow, Berm, Cahokia, Cone, Dike, Dun, Embankment, Heap, Hillock, Hog, Hump, Knoll, Kurgan, Mogul, Molehill, Monticule, Mote, Motte, Orb, Pile, Pingo, Pome, Rampart, Rampire, Remblai, Tel(l), Teocalli, Teopan, Tuffet, Tump, Tumulus, Tussock

**Mound-bird** Leipoa, Megapode

**Mount(ed), Mounting, Mountain (peak), Mountains, Mountainside** Air, → **ALPINE**, Ascend, Back, Barp, Ben, Berg, Board, Breast, Butter, Chain, Charger, Chassis, Cliff, Clift, → **CLIMB**, Colt, Cordillera, Cradle, Dew, Display, Djebel, Dolly, Eminence, Escalade, Folded, Frame, Hinge, Horse, Inselberg, Jebel, Joss-block, Massif, Monture, Mt, Nunatak, Orography, Orology, Passe-partout, Peak, Pike, Pile, Pin, Plinth, Pownie, Quad, → **RANGE**, Ride, Rosinante, Saddlehorse, Saddle up, Scalado, Scale, Sclim, Set, Soar, Stage, → **STEED**, Stie, Strideways, Tel, Tier, Topo, Tor, Turret, Upgo, Volcano, Yaud

---

## MOUNTAINS

*2 letters:*
K2

*3 letters:*
Apo
Ida
Kaf
Ore

*4 letters:*
Alai
Blue
Bona
Cook
Etna
Fuji
Harz
Hoss
Jaya
Jura
Meru
Nebo
Oeta
Ossa
Rigi
Ubac
Zeil

*5 letters:*
Abora
Adams
Aldan
Altai
Amara
Andes
Aneto
Athos

Atlas
Badon
Black
Blanc
Coast
Djaja
Eiger
Ellis
Er Rif
Evans
Ghats
Green
Guyot
Hekla
Horeb
Idris
Kamet
Kenya
Logan
Munro
Ozark
Pelée
Rocky
Rydal
Sayan
Serra
Sinai
Siple
Smoky
Snowy
Table
Tabor
Tatra
Tirol
Tyree
Tyrol
Uinta
Urals
Welsh
White

***6 letters:***
Ala Dag
Alaska
Amhara
Anadyr
Arafat
Ararat
Averno
Balkan
Bogong
Carmel
Cho Oyu
Dragon
Egmont
Elbert
Elberz
Elbrus
Erebus
Gilead
Gimbal
Hermon
Hoggar
Hoosac
Katmai
Kazbek
Kunlun
Lhotse
Makalu
Mourne
Olives
Ortles
Pamirs
Pelion
Pindus
Pisgah
Pocono
Robson
Scopus
Sintra
Sorata
Steele
Tasman
Taunus
Taurus
Umbria
Vernon
Vosges
Zagros

***7 letters:***
Aetolia
Ala Dagh
Aorangi
Aragats
Arcadia
Bernina
Brocken
Buffalo
Calvary
Cariboo
Cascade
Chianti
Corbett
Dapsang
Estreia
Everest
Helicon
Kaufman
Kennedy
Khingan
Kuenlun
Lebanon
Lucania
Manaslu
Markham
Nan Shan
Olympic
Olympus
Orontes
Palomar
Perdido
Pilatus
Rainier
Rhodope
San Juan
Scafell
Selkirk
Skiddaw
Snowdon
Sperrin
Stanley
St Elias
Sudeten
Tibesti
Travers
Troglav
Whitney
Wicklow

***8 letters:***
Anapurna
Arcadian
Aspiring
Ben Nevis
Cambrian
Carstenz
Catskill
Caucasus
Cevennes
Cotopaxi
Cumbrian
Damavand
Demavend
Fujiyama
Grampian
Guerrero
Hymettus
Illimani
Jungfrau
Katahdin
Kinabalu
King Peak
Leibnitz
McKinley
Mulhacen
Ngaliema
Ouachita
Pennines
Pinatubo
Pyrenees
Rushmore
Seamount
St Helen's
Taraniki
Tian Shan
Tien Shan
Vesuvius
Victoria
Wrangell

***9 letters:***
Aconcagua
Allegheny
Annapurna
Apennines
Ben Lomond
Blackburn
Blue Ridge
Cairngorm
Carstensz
Catskills
Caucasian
Connemara
Corbieres
Demavrand
Dhaulagir
Dolomites
El Capitan
Grampians
Guadalupe
Helvellyn
Hercynian
Highlands
High Tatra
Himalayas
Hindu Kush
Jebel Musa
Karakoram
Lenin Peak
Longs Peak
Marmolada
Mont Blanc
Monte Rosa
Nanda Devi
Parnassus
Pikes Peak
Ruwenzori
Shivering
Sugar Loaf
Tirich Mir
Tongariro
Trans Alai
Trossachs

Tupungato
Vancouver
Venusberg
Voralberg
Weisshorn
Woodroffe
Yablonovy
Zugspitze

*10 letters:*
Altazimuth
Arakan Yoma
Armageddon
Black Hills
Cader Idris
Cantabrian
Carpathian
Delectable
Dhaulagiri
Equatorial
Erymanthus
Erzgebirge
Great Gable
Great Smoky
Harney Peak
Horselberg
Kongur Shan
Kosciuszko
Laurentian
Masharbrum
Masherbrum
Matterhorn
Monte Corno
Montserrat
Pentelicus
Pentelikon
Puncak Jaya
Puy de Sancy
Qomolangma
Sagarmatha
St Michael's
Tengri Khan
Teton Range
Vorarlberg
Washington
Waziristan
Wellington
Wetterhorn

*11 letters:*
Adirondacks
Alaska Range
Anti-Lebanon
Appalachian
Bartle Frere
Bimberi Peak
Brooks Range
Coast Ranges
Drakensberg
Fairweather
Gerlachovka
Kilimanjaro
Kinder Scout
Kirkpatrick
Kolyma Range
Machu Picchu
Nanga Parbat
Pico de Aneto
Pico de Teide
Salmon River
Scafell Pike
Sierra Madre

*12 letters:*
Albert Edward
Cascade Range
Eastern Ghats
Godwin Austen
Gran Paradiso
Ingleborough
Kanchenjunga
Monte Perdido
Ruahine Range
Sierra Morena
Sierra Nevada
Slieve Donard
Southern Alps
Tararua Range
Victoria Peak
Vindhya Range
Vinson Massif
Wasatch Range
Western Ghats

*13 letters:*
Brecon Beacons
Carrantuohill
Croagh Patrick
Flinders Range
Frenchman's Cap
Great Dividing
Grossglockner
Humphrey's Peak
Kangchenjunga
Massif Central
Mount Klinovec
Petermann Peak
San Bernardino
Stanovoi Range
Tibesti Massif

*14 letters:*
Admiralty Range
Bohemian Forest
Carnarvon Range
Finsteraarhorn
Hamersley Range
Kaikoura Ranges
Kommunizma Peak
Liverpool Range
Musgrove Ranges
Queen Maud Range
Ruwenzori Range
Sangre de Cristo
Stirling Ranges
Stzelecki Range
Thadentsonyane
Wind River Range

*15 letters:*
New England Range
Teutoburger Wald

*16 letters:*
Emperor Seamounts
Macdonnell Ranges
Owen Stanley Range
Thabana-Ntlenyana

*17 letters:*
Continental Divide
Transylvanian Alps
Warrumbungle Range

*18 letters:*
Great Dividing Range

*19 letters:*
Macgillicuddy's Reeks

*20 letters:*
Salmon River Mountains

---

**Mountain-building** Orogenesis
**Mountaineer(ing)** Aaron, Abseil, Alpinist, Arnaut, Climber, Hunt, Sherpa, Smythe, Upleader
**Mountebank** Antic(ke), Baladin(e), Charlatan, Jongleur, Quack, Saltimbanco
**Mourn(er), Mournful(ly), Mourning** Adonia, Alack, Black, Con dolore, Cypress, Dirge, Dole, Elegiac, Engrieve, Grieve, Grone, Half-mast, Hatchment, Jamie Duff, Keen, Lament, Mute, Niobe, Omer, Ovel, Plaintive, Plangent, Saulie, Shibah, Shivah, Shloshim, Sorrow, Tangi, Threnetic, Threnodial, Tragic, Weeds, Weep, Willow
**Mouse(like), Mousy** Black eye, Bus, Church, Deer, Dormouse, Dun(nart), Fat, Field, Flitter, Harvest, Honey, House, Icon, Jerry, Jumping, Kangaroo, Marsupial, Meadow, Mechanical, Mickey, Minnie, Mischief, Muridae, Murine, Optical, Pocket, Pouched, Rodent, Shiner, Shrew, Vermin, Waltzer, White-footed
**Mousetrap** Samson's post
**Moussaka** Aubergine
**Mousse** Styling
**Moustache(d)** Algernon, Boxcar, Burnside, Charley, Charlie, Chevron, Excrement, Fu

Manchu, Handlebar, Hindenburg, Horseshoe, Kaiser, Mistletoe, Pencil, Pyramid, Regent, Roman T, Ronnie, Soupstrainer, Toothbrush, Walrus, Waxed, Wings, Zapata

**Mouth(piece)** Aboral, Bazoo, Bocca, Brag, Buccal, Cakehole, Chapper, Check, Crater, Debouchure, Delta, Embouchure, Estuary, Fauces, Fipple, Gab, Gam, Geggie, Gills, Gob, Gub, Gum, Hard, Horn, Kisser, Labret, Laughing gear, Lawyer, Lip, Manubrium, Maw, Neb, Orifex, Orifice, Os, Oscule, Ostium, Outfall, Outlet, Peristome, Port, Potato trap, Potty, Rattle-trap, Speaker, Spokesman, Spout, Stoma, Swazzle, Swozzle, Teat, Trap, Trench, Uvula, Yap

**Mouthful** Bite, Canape, Chewie, Gob, Gobbet, Inlet, Mealy, Morceau, Morsel, Sip, Sup, Taste

**Mouthless** Astomatous

**Mouth-organ** Harmonica, Harp, Palp, Sang

**Mouth-watering** Sialogogue

**Move(d), Mover, Movable, Moving** Act, Actuate, Affect, Agent, Andante, Astir, Aswarm, Budge, Career, Carry, Castle, Catapult, Chattel, Choreic, Circle, Circulate, Claw off, Coast, Counter-measure, Coup, Decant, Démarche, Deploy, Displace, Disturb, Drift, Ease, Eddy, Edge, Eloign, Evoke, Extrapose, False, Fidget, Flap, Flit, Flounce, Flow, Fluctuate, Forge, Fork, Forklift, Frogmarch, Galvanise, Gambit, Gee, Give and go, Glide, Go, Gravitate, Haulier, Hobble, Hustle, Impress, Inch, Inspire, Instigate, Jee, Jink, Jump, Kedge, Kickstart, Kinetic, Knight's progress, Link, Locomotion, Lumber, Lunge, March, Mill, Mobile, Mosey, Motivate, Motor, Mouse, Nip, Opening, Outwin, Overcome, Pan, People, Poignant, Prime, Proceed, Progress, Progressional, Prompt, Propel, Propose, Prowl, Push, Qui(t)ch, Quicken, Quinche, Rearrange, Redeploy, Relocate, Remuage, Retrocede, Roll, Rollaway, Roller-skate, Rouse, Roust, Sashay, Scamper, Scissorhold, Scoot, Scramble, Scroll, Scurry, Scuttle, Sealed, Segue, Sell, Send, Shift, Shimmy, Shog, Shoo, Shunt, Sidle, Skelp, Skitter, Slide, Slither, Soulful, Spank, Steal, Steer, Step, Stir, Styre, Surf, Swarm, Sway, Swish, Tack, Tactic, Taxi, Teleport, Touch, Traipse, Transfer, Translate, Translocate, Transplant, Transport, Transpose, Travel, Troll, Trundle, Turn, Undulate, Unstep, Up, Upgrade, Up sticks, Urge, Vacillate, Vagile, Veronica, Vire, Volt(e), Wade, Waft, Wag(gle), Wapper, Whirry, Whish, Whisk, Whiz, Whoosh, Wuther, Yank, Zap, Zoom, Zwischenzug

**Movement(s)** Action, Advection, Aerotaxis, Akathisia, Al Fatah, Allegro, Allemande, Almain, Andantino, Antic, Antistrophe, Apport, Art autre, Arts and crafts, Azapo, Badinerie, Bandwagon, Bowel, Brisé, Brownian, Buchmanism, Cadence, Capoeira, Cause, Cell, Charismatic, Chartism, Chemonasty, Constructivism, Course, Crusade, Dadaism, Diapirism, Diaspora, Diastole, Earth, Ecumenical, Enlightenment, Eoka, Epeirogeny, Eurhythmics, Expressionism, Faction, Falange, Feint, Fianchetto, Flicker, Flow, Fris(ka), Gait, Gallicanism, Geneva, Gesture, Gold rush, Groundswell, Headway, Heliotaxis, Hip-hop, Honde, Imagism, Indraught, Inkatha, Intermezzo, Jhala, Jor, Kata, Keplarian, Kinematics, Kinesis, Kin(a)esthetic, Kinetic, Kipp, Larghetto, Largo, Lassu, Ligne, Locomotion, Logistics, Maltese cross, Manoeuvre, Men's, Migration, Motion, Mudra, Nastic, Naturalism, Naziism, Neofascism, Neorealism, New Age, New Urbanism, New Wave, Nihilism, Official, Operation, Orchesis, Overspill, Oxford, Oxford Group, Panislamism, Pan-Slavism, Pantalon, Parallax, Pase, Passade, Passage, Pedesis, Photokinesis, Photonasty, Piaffer, Pincer, Plastique, Play, Populist, Port de bras, Poule, Poulette, Procession, Progress, Provisional, Punk, Puseyism, Reconstructionism, Reformation, Regression, REM, Renaissance, Resistance, Revivalism, Ribbonism, Ripple, Risorgimento, Romantic, Rondo, Saccade, Salafism, Scherzo, Scientology, Scissors, Scout's pace, Seiche, Seismic, Sinn Fein, Solifluction, Solifluxion, Spasm, Splafism, Spuddle, Stir(e), Strophe, Sturm und Drang, Subsidence, Swadeshi, Swing, Symbolist, Tachism, Tamil Tigers, Tantrism, Taphrogenesis, Taxis, Tectonic, Telekinesis, Thermotaxis, Thigmotaxis, Tic, Tide, Tractarianism, Transhumance, Transit, Trend, Trenise, Ultramontanism, UNITA, Verismo, Veronica, Wave, Wheel, White flight, Women's, Zionism

**Movie** Bioscope, Buddy, Cine(ma), Disaster, Film, Flick, Newsreel, Nudie, Popcorn, Road, Slasher, Snuff, Splatter, Star Wars, Talkie

**Mow(er), Mowing** Aftermath, Cut, Grimace, Lattermath, Lawn, Math, Rawing, Rawn, Reap, Rowan, Rowen, Rowing, Scytheman, Shear, Sickle, Strimmer®, Tass, Trim

**MP** Backbencher, Commoner, Deputy, Gendarme, Knight of the Shire, Member, Oncer, Politico, Provost, Redcap, Retread, Snowdrop, Stannator, Statist, TD

▸**Mr** *see* **MISTER**

▸**Mrs** *see* MISSIS
**Mrs Brown** VR
**Mrs Copperfield** Agnes, Dora
**Mrs Siddons** Tragic muse
**Mrs Simpson** Marge, Wallis
**Much** Abundant, Considerable, Ever so, Far, Glut, Great, Lots, Mickle, Mochell, Rotten, Scad, Sore, Viel
**Mucilage** Gum, → MUC(O)US, Putty, Resin
**Muck (up), Mucky** Bungle, Dirt, Dung, Grime, Grubby, Island, Lady, Leep, Manure, Midden, Mire, Rot, Sludge, Slush, Soil, Sordid, Spoil, Stercoral
**Mucker** Fall, Pal, Purler
**Muc(o)us** Apophlegmatic, Blennorrhoea, Booger, Catarrh, Gleet, Operculum, Phlegm, Pituate, Pituita, Salt rheum, Sleep, Snivel, Snot, Snotter, Sputum
**Mud(dy)** Adobe, Clabber, Clart, Clay, Cutcha, Dirt, Drilling, Dubs, Fango, Glaur, Glob, Gutter, Kacha, Lahar, Lairy, Limous, Lumicolous, → MIRE, Moya, Mudge, Obfuscate, Ooze, Peloid, Pise, Poach, Red, Riley, Roily, Salse, Silt, Slab, Slake, Sleech, Slime, Slob, Slobland, Slough, Sludge, Slur(ry), Slush, Slutch, Tocky, Trouble, Turbid, Volcanic
**Muddle(d)** Addle, Befog, Bemuse, Botch, Chaos, Cock up, Confuse, Disorder, Disorient, Embrangle, Fluster, Gump, Higgledy-piggledy, Jumble, Mare's nest, Mash, Mêlée, Mess, Mess up, Mix, Morass, Mull, Pickle, Puddle, Screw up, Shambles, Shemozzle, Snarl-up, Stupefy, Tangle, Ta(i)vert, Tiert
▹**Muddled** *may indicate* an anagram
**Mudfish** Lepidosiren
**Mudguard** Fender, Mudflap, Splashboard, Wing
**Mudlark** Guttersnipe, Ragamuffin, Urchin
**Muesli** Granola
**Muff** Blunder, Boob, Botch, Bungle, Drop, Snoskyn
**Muffin** Bun, Chaperon(e), Cupcake, Mule, Popover
**Muffle(d), Muffler** Baffle, Damp, Deaden, Earplug, Envelop, Hollow, Low, Mob(b)le, Mute, Scarf, Silencer, Sourdine, Stifle
**Mufti** Civvies
**Mug(ger), Muggy** Assault, Attack, Bash, Beaker, Bock, Can, Close, Club, Con, Cosh boy, Croc(odile), Cup, Dial, Do over, Dupe, Enghalskrug, Face, Fool, Footpad, Gob, Humid, Idiot, Latron, Learn, Mou, Noggin, Noodle, Pan, Pot, Pushover, Puss, Rob, Roll, Sandbag, Sap, Sconce, Simpleton, Steamer, Stein, Sucker, Swot, Tankard, Tax, Thief, Thug(gee), Tinnie, Tinny, Toby, Trap, Twerp, Ugly, Visage, Yap
**Mulberry** Artocarpus, Breadfruit, Cecropia, Contrayerva, Cow-tree, Indian, Jack, Morat, Morus, Murrey, Osage orange, Overlord, Paper, Sycamine
**Mulch** Compost, Nourish
**Mulct** Fine
**Mule, Mulish** Ass, Bab(o)uche, Barren, Donkey, Fadda, Funnel, Hemionus, Hybrid, Mocassin, Moccasin, Moyl(e), Muffin, Muil, Obdurate, Pack, Rake, Shoe, Slipper, Spinning, Sumpter
**Muleteer** Arriero
**Mull** Brood, Chew, Galloway, Kintyre, Ponder, Promontory, Reflect, Study
**Mullein** Aaron's rod, Adam's flannel
**Mullet** Goatfish, Hairpiece, Wig
**Mullion** Monial, Trumeau
**Multi-coloured** Kaleidoscopic, Scroddled
**Multi-ethnic** Rainbow
**Multiform** Allotropic, Diverse, Manifold
**Multiple, Multiplication, Multiplied, Multiplier, Multiply** Augment, Breed, Chorisis, Common, Double, Elixir, Export, → INCREASE, Manifold, Modulus, Populate, Product, Proliferate, Propagate, Raise, Scalar, Severalfold, Square, Triple
**Multi-purpose** Polychrest
**Multitude** Army, Crowd, Hirsel, Horde, Host, Legion, Mass, Populace, Shoal, Sight, Swarm, Throng, Zillion

**Mum(my), Mummify** Boutonné, Carton(n)age, Corpse, Egyptian, Embalm, Mamma, Mine, Mute, Peace(ful), Pharaoh, Quiet, Reticent, Sh, Shtum, Silent, Speechless, Tacit, Whisht, Wordless

**Mumble** Grumble, Moop, Moup, Mouth, Mump, Murmur, Mushmouth, Mutter, Royne, Slur

**Mumbo jumbo** Hocus pocus, Mammet, Maumet, Mawmet, Mommet

**Mummer(y)** Actor, Guising, Mime, Scuddaler, Scudler, Skudler

**Mumps** Parotitis

**Munch** Champ, Chew, Chomp, Expressionist, Moop, Moup, Scranch

**Mundane** Banal, Common, Earthly, Nondescript, Ordinary, Prosaic, Quotidian, Routine, Secular, Subcelestial, Trite, Trivial, Workaday, Worldly

**Mungo** Park

**Municipal(ity)** Civic, Nasik

**Munificent, Munificence** Bounteous, Generous, Largesse, Liberal, Profuse

**Munition(s)** Arms, Arsenal, Artillery, Matériel, Ordnance

**Munro** Saki

**Mural(s)** Fresco, Graffiti, Stereochrome

**Murder(er), Murderess, Murderous** Abort, Aram, Assassin, Blood guilty, Blue, Bluebeard, Bravo, Burke, Butcher, Butler, Cain, Capital, Cathedral, Crackhalter, Crippen, Crows, Cutthroat, Danaid(e)s, Dispatch, Do in, Eliminate, End, Filicide, First degree, Fratricide, Genocide, Hare, Hatchet man, Hit, Hitman, Homicide, Hyde, Internecine, Judicial, → KILL, Liquidate, Locusta, Made man, Man-queller, Massacre, Matricide, Modo, Mullah, Muller, Parricide, Patricide, Petty treason, Poison, Red, Regicide, Removal, Ripper, Ritual, Ritz, Rub out, Second degree, Sikes, Slaughter, Slay, Stiff, Strangle(r), Sweeney Todd, Take out, Thagi, Throttle, Thug(gee), Tyrannicide, Ugly man, Vaticide, Whodun(n)it

**Murk(y)** Ambiguous, Black, Dark, Dirk(e), Gloom, Obscure, Rookish, Shadowy, Stygian

**Murmur(ing)** Babble, Breath, Brool, Bruit, Bur(r), Burble, Coo, Croodle, Croon, Grudge, Heart, Hum, → MUTTER, Purr, Repine, Rhubarb, Rumble, Rumour, Souffle, Sough, Sowf(f), Sowth, Sturnoid, Syllable, Undertone, Whisper

**Murphy** Chat, Potato, Pratie, Spud, Tater

**Muscle, Muscleman, Muscular** Abductor, Abs, Accelerator, Accessorius, Adductor, Agonist, Anconeus, Aristotle's lantern, Aryepiglottic, Arytaenoid, Athletic, Attollens, Azygous, Beef(y), Beefcake, Biceps, Bodybuilder, Bowr, Brachialus, Brawn, Buccinator, Buff, Cardiac, Ciliary, Clout, Complexus, Corrugator, Creature, Cremaster, Delt(oid), Depressor, Diaphragm, Digastric, Dilat(at)or, Dimyarian, Duvaricator, Dystonia, Écorché, Effector, Elevator, Erecter, Erector, Evertor, Extensor, Eye-string, Flexor, Force, Gastrocnemius, Gemellus, Glute, Glut(a)eus, Gluteus maximus, Gracilis, Hamstring, Heavy, Hiacus, Hunky, Ideomotor, Iliacus, Intrinsic, Involuntary, Kreatine, Lat, Latissimus dorsi, Laxator, Levator, Lumbricalis, Masseter, Mesomorph, Might, Motor, Mouse, Myalgia, Mylohyoid, Myology, Myotome, Myotonia, Nasalis, Obicularis, Oblique, Occlusor, Omohyoid, Opponent, Orbicularis, Pathos, Pec(s), Pectoral, Perforans, Perforatus, Peroneus, Plantaris, Platysma, Popliteus, → POWER, Pronator, Protractor, Psoas, Pylorus, Quad(riceps), Quadratus, Rambo, Rectus, Retractor, Rhomboid, Rhomboideus, Ripped, Risorius, Rotator cuff, Sarcolemma, Sarcous, Sartorius, Scalene, Scalenus, Serratus, Sinew, Six-pack, Smooth, Solar plexus, Soleus, Sphincter, Spinalis, Splenial, Sthenic, Striated, Striped, Strong, Supinator, Suspensory, Temporal, Tenaculum, Tendon, Tensor, Teres, Thenar, Thew, Tibialis, Toned, Tonus, Trapezius, Triceps, Vastus, Voluntary, Xiphihumeralis, Zygomatic

**Muscovite** Mica, Talc

**Muse(s), Muse's home, Musing** Aglaia, Aonia(n), Attic, Calliope, Clio, Cogitate, Consider, Dream, Dwell, Erato, Euphrosyne, Euterpe, Goddess, Helicon, Inspiration, IX, Laura, Meditate, Melpomene, Mull, Nine, Nonet, Pensée, Pierides, Poly(hy)mnia, Ponder, Porer, → REFLECT, Ruminate, Study, Teian, Terpsichore, Thalia, Tragic, Urania, Wonder

**Museum** Aircraft, Alte-Pinakothek, Ashmolean, BM, British, Fitzwilliam, Gallery, Getty, Guggenheim, Heritage centre, Hermitage, Hunterian, Kelvingrove, Louvre, Metropolitan, National Gallery, Parnassus, Prado, Railway, Repository, Rijksmuseum, Science, Smithsonian, Tate, Te papa Tongarewa, Uffizi, VA, V and A, Waxworks

**Mush** Cree, Glo(o)p, Goo, Mess, Pop, Porridge, Puree, Puss, Schmaltz, Slop

**Mushroom** Aecidium, Aedium, Agaric, Ascomycetes, Blewits, Boletus, Burgeon, Button, Cep, Champignon, Chanterelle, Darning, Destroying angel, Enoki, Escalate, Expand, Explode, Field, Fly agaric, →FUNGUS, Girolle, Grisette, Gyromitra, Honey fungus, Horse, Hypha(l), Ink-cap, Liberty cap, Magic, Matsutake, Meadow, Morel, Oyster, Parasol, Penny-bun, Pixy-stool, Porcino, Proliferate, Reishi, Russula, Sacred, St George's, Scotch bonnet, Shaggy cap, Shaggymane, Shiitake, Shroom, Sickener, Snowball, Spread, Start-up, Straw, Truffle, Upstart, Velvet shank, Waxcap

**Music** Absolute, A-side, Beat, B-side, Choral, Classical, Colour, Conductive, Indeterminate, Lesson, Light, Minstrelsy, Mood, Morceau, →MUSICAL INSTRUMENTS, Passage work, Phase, Piece, Popular, Programme, Quotation, Recital, Score, Sound, Table, Tremolando

---

## MUSIC

***2 letters:***
Oi

***3 letters:***
Air
AOR
Art
Dub
EMI
Emo
Gat
Jor
Mas
MOR
Pop
Rag
Rai
Rap
Rug
Ska
Son

***4 letters:***
Alap
Chin
Coda
Duet
Folk
Funk
Go-go
Jass
Jazz
Kalo
Loco
Meno
Note
Opus
Prom
Raga
Rave
Riff
Rock
Romo
Roxy
Soca
Soul
Surf
Tala
Trad
Trio
Tune
Zouk

***5 letters:***
Alaap
Alapa
Bebop
Benga
Blues
Cajun
Canon
Chant
Cliff
Conga
Crunk
Cu-bop
Disco
Dream
Dumka
Early
Etude
Fugue
Funky
Gabba
House
Indie
Jhala
Krunk
Kwela
Largo
March
Motet
Muzak®
Neume
Nonet
Outro
Piped
Ragga
Rondo
Roots
Rough
Salon
Salsa
Salve
Sheet
Sokah
Staff
Suite
Swing
Thema
Tonal
Tra-la
Trash
Truth
Vocal
World
Zoppo

***6 letters:***
Anthem
Arioso
Aubade
Bebung
Bouree
Decani
Doo-wop
Enigma
Equali
Façade
Fugato
Fusion
Gagaku
Galant
Garage
Gospel
Gothic
Grunge
Hip-hop
Jungle
Khayal
Kirtan
Kwaito
Lounge
Lydian
Mantra
Marabi
Mashup
Medley
Melody
Motown®
New Age
Organa
Plagal
Popera
Pycnon
Ragini
Redowa
Reggae
Rhythm
Rootsy
Sextet
Skronk
Sonata
Strain
Techno
Tenuto
Thrash
Trance
Verset
Zydeco

***7 letters:***
Afropop
Allegro
Andante
Ars nova
Ballade
Baroque
Bhangra
Bluette
Bourree
Britpop
Cadenza
Calypso
Cantata
Ceilidh
Chamber
Chorale
Country
Dad rock
Electro
Europop
Euterpe
Fanfare
Gangsta
Hardbag
Introit
Klezmer
Landler
Marcato
Melisma
Messiah
Mordent
New Wave
Numbers
Nu-metal
Organum
Orphean
Partita
Passion
Pecking
Pibroch
Prelude
Qawwali
Quartet

Quintet
Ragtime
Rastrum
Requiem
Reverse
Romanza
Rondeau
Rondino
Rosalia
Roulade
Sanctus
Scherzo
Secondo
Setting
Skiffle
Soukous
Stretto
Toccata
Trip hop
Ziganka

***8 letters:***
Acid rock
Afrojazz
Afrorock
Agitprop
Aleatory
Bel canto
Berceuse
Blue beat
Blue-eyed
Canticle
Chaconne
Cock rock
Concerto
Concrete
Continuo
Coranach
Coronach
Elevator
Entracte
Fantasia
Flamenco
Folk rock
Glam rock
Hard core
Hard rock
High life
In nomine
Isodicon
Janizary
Karnatak
Lollipop
Madrigal
Maggiore
Mariachi
Mbaqanga
Medieval
Modality
Nocturne
Notation
Old-skool
Oratorio
Overture
Parlando
Partitur
Pastiche
Postlude
Post-rock
Preludio
Psalmody
Punk rock
Rhapsody
Ricercar
Romantic
Saraband
Serenade
Serenata
Sinfonia
Symphony
Synth-pop
Waltzian
Warhorse

***9 letters:***
Acid-house
Allemande
Americana
Antiphony
Arabesque
Bagatelle
Bluegrass
Breakbeat
Cantilena
Capriccio
Crossover
Dancehall
Dixieland
Drum'n'bass
Finlandia
Fioritura
Goa trance
Grandioso
Hardhouse
Hillbilly
Honky-tonk
Interlude
Klezmorim
Obbligato
Partitura
Pastorale
Pastorali
Pitchbend
Plainsong
Polonaise
Polyphony
Portabeul
Prick-song
Queercore
Quodlibet
Reggaeton
Ricercare
Rock'n'roll
Septimole
Serialist
Slow march
Spiritual
Swingbeat
Tambourin
Technopop
Toccatina
Voluntary
Wallpaper
Warehouse

***10 letters:***
Albumblatt
Anacrustic
Barbershop
Chopsticks
Coloratura
Death metal
Desert rock
Electronic
Gangsta rap
Gothic rock
Heavy metal
Hindustani
Humoresque
Incidental
Intermezzo
Jam session
Lovers' rock
Martellato
Mersey beat
Minimalist
New Country
Orchestral
Percussion
Polyhymnia
Polyrhythm
Portamento
Quadrivium
Ragamuffin
Rare groove
Ritornello
Rockabilly
Rocksteady
Seguidilla
Shoegazing
Tarantella
Toccatella
Twelve-tone
Urban blues

***11 letters:***
Boeremusiek
Concertante
Country rock
Mersey sound
Motor rhythm
Passacaglia
Psychobilly
Raggamuffin
Renaissance
Rogues' march
Sinfonietta
Solmisation
Stadium rock
Third stream
Thrash metal
Tin Pan Alley

***12 letters:***
Blue-eyed soul
Boogie-woogie
Concertstück
Contrapuntal
Divertimento
Electroclash
Late medieval
Moto perpetuo
Neo-classical
Nunc Dimittis
Pralltriller
Western swing

***13 letters:***
Choral prelude
Detroit techno
Early medieval
Progressional

***14 letters:***
Durchkomponirt
Hypomixolydian
Rhythm and blues

***15 letters:***
Durchkomponiert
Musique concrete
Progressive rock

**Musical** Annie, Arcadian, Azione, Brigadoon, Canorous, Carousel, Cats, Chess, Chicago, Euphonic, Evergreen, Evita, Gigi, Grease, Gypsy, Hair, Half a Sixpence, Harmonious, Kabuki, Kismet, Kiss Me Kate, Les Miserables, Lyric, Mame, Melodic, Miss Saigon, My Fair Lady, Oklahoma, Oliver, → OPERA, Operetta, Oratorio, Orphean, Revue, Showboat, South Pacific, Tommy, Top Hat, Trial by Jury, West Side Story
**Musical box** Juke-box, Polyphon(e), Stereo
**Musical chairs** Level-coil
**Musical instrument(s)**

---

## MUSICAL INSTRUMENTS

*2 letters:*
Ax
Gu

*3 letters:*
Axe
Gue
Kit
Oud
Qin
Saz
Uke
Zel

*4 letters:*
Buva
Chyn
Crwd
Drum
Erhu
Fife
Gong
Harp
Horn
Kora
Koto
Lure
Lute
Lyre
Moog®
Oboe
Pipa
Rate
Reed
Rote
Sang
Tuba
Vina
Viol
Whip
Zeze

*5 letters:*
Aulos
Banjo
Bugle
Cello
Clave
Cobza
Corno
Crowd
Crwth
Dobro®
Esraj
Flute
Gaita
Gazog
Guiro
Guqin
Gusla
Gusle
Gusli
Kaval
Kazoo
Labia
Mbira
Naker
Nebel
Organ
Piano
Quena
Rebec
Regal
Sanko
Sansa
Sarod
Shalm
Shawm
Sitar
Stick
Synth
Tabla
Tabor
Tenor
Tibia
Veena
Viola
Zanze
Zinke

*6 letters:*
Antara
Atabal
Biniou
Bisser
Bongos
Citole
Cornet
Cymbal
Euphon
Flugel
Guitar
Kanoon
Maraca
Poogye
Racket
Rebeck
Relish
Ribibe
Sancho
Santir
Santur
Shalme
Shofar
Sittar
Spinet
Syrinx
Tom-tom
Trigon
Vielle
Violin
Yidaki
Zither
Zufolo

*7 letters:*
Alphorn
Anklong
Anklung
Bagpipe
Bandore
Bandura
Baryton
Bassoon
Bazooka
Celesta
Celeste
Cembalo
Ceol mor
Chikara
Cithara
Cithern
Cittern
Clarino
Clarion
Clavier
Clogbox
Console
Cornett
Dichord
Dulcian
Fagotto
Flutina
Gamelan
Gazogka
Gittern
Hautboy
Helicon
High-hat
Kalimba
Kantela
Kantele
Kithara
Klavier
Lyricon
Mandola
Marimba
Musette
Ocarina
Pandora
Pandore
Pandura
Pianino
Pianola®
Piccolo
Piffero
Poogyee
Posaune
Rackett
Rellish

Ribible
Sackbut
Sambuca
Samisen
Santour
Sarangi
Saxhorn
Saxtuba
Serpent
Symbole
Tambour
Tambura
Theorbo
Timbrel
Timpano
Trumpet
Tympany
Ukelele
Ukulele
Vihuela
Violone
Whistle
Zuffolo

***8 letters:***
Angklung
Archlute
Autoharp®
Barytone
Bass-drum
Berimbau
Bombarde
Bouzouki
Calliope
Canorous
Carillon
Charango
Cimbalom
Clarinet
Clarsach
Clavecin
Cornetto
Cornpipe
Cromorna
Cromorne
Crumhorn
Dulcimer
Gemshorn
Guarneri
Guimbard
Handbell
Hautbois
Humstrum
Jew's harp
Keyboard
Key-bugle
Langspel
Lyra-viol
Mandolin
Manzello
Martenot
Melodeon
Melodica
Melodion
Mirliton
Oliphant
Ottavino
Pan pipes
Phorminx
Pianette
Polyphon
Psaltery
Recorder
Reco-reco
Side drum
Slughorn
Sourdine
Spinette
Squiffer
Sticcado
Sticcato
Surbahar
Tamboura
Tamburin
Tenoroon
Theremin
Triangle
Trichord
Trombone
Virginal
Vocalion
Zambomba
Zampogna

***9 letters:***
Accordion
Aerophone
Alpenhorn
Baby grand
Balalaika
Bandoneon
Bandurria
Banjulele
Bombardon
Bugle-horn
Castanets
Chalumeau
Clarionet
Cornemuse
Decachord
Dulcitone®
Euphonium
Flageolet
Flexatone
Flute-à-bec
Gittarone
Gutbucket
Harmonica
Harmonium
Humbucker
Idiophone
Kent-bugle
Krummhorn
Langspiel
Mandoline
Mellotron®
Monochord
Mouth-harp
Nose flute
Orpharion
Pantaleon
Pastorale
Polyphone
Reed organ
Saxophone
Seraphine
Slughorne
Snare-drum
Sonometer
Sopranino
Steel drum
Stockhorn
Trompette
Vibraharp
Washboard
Welsh harp
Xylophone
Xylorimba

***10 letters:***
Arpeggione
Basset-horn
Bull-fiddle
Bullroarer
Chitarrone
Clavichord
Colascione
Concertina
Contrabass
Cor anglais
Cornettini
Didgeridoo
Flugelhorn
Fortepiano
French horn
Gramophone
Hurdy-gurdy
Kettledrum
Lagerphone
Light organ
Mellophone
Mouth organ
Nun's fiddle
Ophicleide
Orpheoreon
Pentachord
Phonograph
Shakuhachi
Small pipes
Sousaphone
Squeeze-box
Stylophone®
Symphonium
Tambourine
Thumb piano
Tin whistle
Vibraphone
Wokka board

***11 letters:***
Aeolian harp
Chordophone
Clairschach
Contrabasso
Harmoniphon
Harpsichord
Heckelphone
Nickelodeon
Octave flute
Orchestrina
Orchestrion
Phonofiddle
Player piano
Stock-in-horn
Straduarius
Synthesizer
Trump-marine
Viola d'amore
Violoncello
Wobble-board

***12 letters:***
Chapman stick®
Chinese block
Clavicembalo
Glockenspiel
Harmonichord
Harmoniphone
Metallophone
Penny-whistle
Sarrusophone
Stock and horn
Stradivarius
Tromba-marina

Tubular bells
Viola da gamba

*13 letters:*
American organ
Contrabassoon
Contrafagotto
Cornet-a-piston
Ondes Martenot
Panharmonicon
Physharmonica
Slide trombone
Swanee whistle

*14 letters:*
Clavicytherium
Cornet-a-pistons
Glass harmonica
Hawaiian guitar
Jingling Johnny
Musical glasses
Ondes musicales
Piano accordion
Swannee whistle
Viola da braccio

*15 letters:*
Moog synthesiser

*18 letters:*
Chinese temple block

---

**Music fan** Grebo
**Music-hall** Alhambra, Disco, Empire, Folies Bergere, Odeon
**Musician(s), Musicologist** Accompanist, Adler, Arion, Arist, Armstrong, Ashkenazi, Bassist, Beiderbecke, Boy band, Brain, Buononcini, Busker, Carmichael, Casals, Cellist, Chanter, Clapton, Combo, →COMPOSER, Conductor, Consort, Crowder, Dankworth, Duet, Ellington, Ensemble, Executant, Flautist, Gate, Group, Grove, Guido d'Arezzo, Guslar, Handel, Hornist, Jazzer, Jazzman, Joplin, Keyboardist, Klezmer, Labelmate, Luter, Lyrist, Maestro, Mahler, Mariachi, Meistersinger, Menuhin, Minstrel, Moke, Muso, Noisenik, Nonet, Octet, Organ-grinder, Orphean, Percussionist, Peterson, Pianist, Pied Piper, Quartet, Quintet, Rapper, Reed(s)man, Répétiteur, Ripienist, Rubinstein, Satchmo, Schonberg, Septet, Serenader, Session, Sextet, Sideman, Soloist, Spohr, Sting, String, Strummer, Techno, Tortelier, Troubador, Trouvère, Trumpeter, Vibist, Violinist, Waits
**Music-lover** Promenader
**Musk** Civet, Mimulus, Must
**Musket** Brown Bess, Caliver, Carabine, Eyas, Flintlock, Fusil, Gingal(l), Hawk, Jezail, Jingal, Matchlock, Nyas, Queen's-arm, Weapon
**Musketeer** Aramis, Athos, D'Artagnan, Fusilier, Ja(e)ger, Porthos, Rifleman, Sam
**Muslim (ritual), Moslem** Alaouite, Alawite, Ali, Almohad(e), Ayatollah, Balochi, Baluchi, Berber, Black, Caliph, Dato, Dervish, Druse, Fatimid, Ghazi, Hadji, Hafiz, Hajji, Hamas, Hezbollah, Hizbollah, Hizbullah, Iranian, Islamic, Ismaili, Karmathian, Khotbah, Khotbeh, Khutbah, Mawlawi, Meivievi, Mog(h)ul, Moor, Morisco, Moro, Muezzin, Mufti, Mughal, Mus(s)ulman, Mutazilite, Nawab, Panislam, Paynim, Pomak, Said, Saladin, Saracen, Say(y)id, Senus(s)i, Shafiite, Shia(h), Shiite, Sofi, Sonnite, Sufi, Sulu, Sunna, Sunni(te), Tajik, The Faithful, Turk, Umma(h), Wahabee, Wahabi(te), Wahhabi, Whirling Dervish
**Muslin** Buttercloth, Coteline, Gurrah, Jamdani, Leno, Mousseline, Mull, Nainsook, Organdie, Organza, Paper, Persienne, Swiss, Tarlatan, Tiffany
**Musquash** Ondatra
**Muss** Tousle
**Mussel(s)** Bearded, Bivalve, Clabby-doo, Clam, Clappy-doo, Deerhorn, Duck, Edible, Horse, Modiolus, Moules marinières, Mytilus, Naiad, Pearl, River, Scalp, Scaup, Swan, Unio, Unionidae, Zebra
**Mussolini** Benito, Il Duce
**Mussorgsky** Modest
**Must(y)** Amok, Essential, Foughty, Fousty, Froughy, Frowsty, Frowy, Funky, Fust, Gotta, Man, Maun(na), Mote, Mould, Mucid, Mun, Necessary, Need(s)-be, Obbligato, Shall, Should, Stale, Stum, Vinew, Wine
▷**Must** *may indicate* an anagram
**Mustard** Black, Brown, Charlock, Colonel, Cress, Dijon, English, Erysimum, French, Garlic, Gas, German, Hedge, Nitrogen, Praiseach, Quinacrine, Runch, Sarepta, Sauce-alone, Senvy, Treacle, Wall, White, Wild, Wintercress, Yellow
**Mustard plaster** Sinapism
**Musteline** Atoc, Atok, Skunk
**Muster** Array, Assemble, Bangtail, Call up, Enrol, Herd, Marshal, Mass, Peacock, Raise, Rally, Really, Recruit, Round-up, Turn out, Wappenshaw
**Mutability, Mutable** Facile, Wheel

**Mutate, Mutant, Mutation** Auxotroph(ic), Change, Heterogenesis, Polybasic, Saltation, Somatic, Sport, Suppressor, Terata, Transform, Vowel

▷**Mutation** *may indicate* an anagram

**Mute(d), Muteness** Aphasia, Consordino, Deaden, Dumb, Harpo, Mourner, Noiseless, Saulie, Silent, Soften, Sorda, Sordino, Sordo, Sourdine, Stifle, Stop

**Mutilate(d), Mutilation** Castrate, Concise, Deface, Dismember, Distort, Garble, Hack, Hamble, Injure, Maim, Mangle, Mayhem, Obtruncate, Riglin, Tear

▷**Mutilate(d)** *may indicate* an anagram

**Mutineer, Mutiny** Bounty, Caine, Christian, Curragh, Indian, Insurrection, Jhansi, Meerut, Nore, Pandy, Rebel, → REVOLT, Rising, Sepoy, Treason

**Mutter(ing)** Chunter, Drone, Fremescent, Grumble, Maunder, Mumble, Mump, Murmur, Mussitate, Rhubarb, Roin, Royne, Rumble, Sotto voce, Whittie-whattie, Witter

**Mutton** Braxy, Chump, Colonial goose, Em, Ewes, Fanny Adams, Gigot, Hoggerel, Macon, Rack, Saddle, Scrag, Sheep, Theave, Traik

**Mutual (aid)** Common, Complementary, Frank-pledge, Interplay, Log-roll, Reciprocal, Symbiosis

**Muzzle** Decorticate, Gag, Gunpoint, Jaw, Mouth, Mute, Restrain, Snout

**My** Begorra, Blimey, By Jove, Christ, Coo, Crikey, Gad, Gee, Gemini, Golly, Gorblimey, Gosh, Gracious, Great Scott, Ha, Jeepers, Lor, Lumme, M, Musha, Odso, Oh, Our, Tush

**Myna(h)** Hill, Stare, Starling

**Mynheer** Stadholder

**Myopia, Myopic** Hidebound, Mouse-sight, Narrow, Short-sighted, Thick-eyed

**Myriad** Host, Zillion

**Myriapod** Centipede

**Myristic** Nutmeg

**Myrrh** Stacte

**Myrtle** Bog, Callistemon, Crape, Creeping, Crepe, Eucalyptus, Gale, Jambolana, Tasmanian, Tooart, Trailing, Tuart

**Mysterious, Mystery** Abdabs, Abdals, Acroamatic, Arcane, Arcanum, Cabbala, Closed book, Craft, Creepy, Cryptic, Dark (horse), Deep, Delphic, Eleusinian, Enigma(tic), Esoteric, G(u)ild, Grocer, Incarnation, Inscrutable, Marie Celeste, Mary Celeste, Miracle, Mumbo-jumbo, Mystagogue, Numinous, Occult, Original sin, Orphic, Penetralia, Recondite, Riddle, Sacrament, → SECRET, Shadowy, Shady, Spooky, Suspense, Telestic, Thriller, Trinity, UFO, Uncanny, Unearthly, Unexplained, Unknown, Whodunit

▷**Mysterious(ly)** *may indicate* an anagram

**Mystic (word), Mystical, Mysticism** Abraxas, Agnostic, Cabbala, Cab(e)iri, Eckhart, Epopt, Fakir, Familist, Gnostic, Guru, Hesychast, Mahatma, Meg, New Age, Occultist, Quietism, Rasputin, Rosicrucian, Secret, Seer, Sofi, Sufi, Swami, Swedenberg, Tantric, Tantrist, Theosophy, Transcendental, Zohar

**Mystify** Baffle, Bamboozle, Bewilder, Metagrabolise, Metagrobolise, Perplex, Puzzle

**Myth(ology), Mythological, Mythical (beast)** Allegory, Anecdote, Atlantis, Behemoth, Bunyip, Centaur, Cockatrice, Cosmogony, Dragon, Dreamtime, Elf, Euhemerism, Fable, Fantasy, Faun, Fictitious, Folklore, Garuda, Genie, Geryon, Gorgon, Griffin, Hippocampus, Hircocervus, Impundulu, Kelpie, Kylin, Legend, Leviathan, Lore, Lorelei, Lyonnesse, Medusa, Minotaur, Ogre, Orc, Otnit, Pantheon, Pegasus, Phoenix, Sasquatch, Sea horse, Sea serpent, Selkie, Siren, Solar, Speewah, Sphinx, Succubus, Sun, Tarand, Therianthropic, Thunderbird, Tokoloshe, Tragelaph, Troll, Unicorn, Urban, Wivern, Wyvern, Yale, Yeti

# Nn

**N** Name, Nitrogen, Noon, North, November
**Nab** Arrest, Capture, Collar, Confiscate, Grab, Seize
**Nabob** Deputy, Nawab, Wealthy
**Nadir** Bottom, Depths, Dregs, Minimum
**Naff** Kitsch
**Nag(ging)** Badger, Bidet, Brimstone, Callet, Cap, Captious, Chivvy, Complain, Fret, Fuss, Harangue, Harp, Harridan, Henpeck, Horse, Jade, Jaw, Keffel, Pad, Peck, Pester, Pick on, Plague, Rosinante, Rouncy, →SCOLD, Tit, Xant(h)ippe, Yaff
**Nail(ed)** Brad, Brod, Catch, Clinker, Clout, Coffin, Fasten, Frost, Hob, Horse, Keratin, Onyx, Pin, Rivet, Screw, Secure, Seize, Shoe, Sisera, Sixpenny, Sparable, Sparrow-bill, Spick, Spike, Sprig, Staple, Stub, Stud, Tack(et), Talon, Tenpenny, Tenterhook, Thumb, Tingle, Tintack, Toe, Unguis, Wire
**Naive(té)** Artless, Dewy-eyed, Green(horn), Guileless, Gullible, Ingenuous, Innocence, Open, Pollyanna, Simpliste, Simplistic, Starry-eyed, Trusting, Unsophisticated, Wide-eyed
**Naked(ness)** Adamical, Artless, Au naturel, Bare, Blunt, Buck, Buff, Clear, Cuerpo, Defenceless, Encuerpo, Exposed, Gymno-, Jaybird, Kaal gat, Nature, Nuddy, Nude, Querpo, Raw, Scud, Simple, Skyclad, Stark(ers), Uncovered
**Namby-pamby** Milksop, Sissy, Weak, Weakling, White-shoe, Wimp
**Name(d), Names** Agnomen, Alias, Allonym, Anonym, Appellation, Appoint, Attribute, Badge, Baptise, Behight, Brand, Byline, Call, Celeb(rity), Christen, Cite, Cleep, Clepe, Cognomen, Day, Designate, Dinges, Dingus, Dit, Domain, Dub, Entitle, Epithet, Eponym, Exonym, Family, First, Font, Generic, Given, Handle, Hete, Hight, Hypocorism, Identify, Identity, Ilk, Label, Maiden, Marque, Masthead, Mention, Metronymic, Middle, Moni(c)ker, Mud, N, Nap, Nemn, Nempt, Nom, Nomen(clature), Noun, Onomastics, Onymous, Patronymic, Pennant, Personage, Pet, Place, Praenomen, Proper, Proprietary, Pseudonym, Quote, Red(d), Repute, Scilicet, Sign, Signature, Sir, Specify, Stage, Street, Subdomain, Substantive, Tag, Tautonym, Teknonymy, Term, →TITLE, Titular, Titule, Toponymy, Trade, Trivial, User
**Name-dropper** Eponym
**Nameless** Anon, Unchrisom
**Namely** Ie, Sc, Scilicet, To-wit, Videlicet, Viz
**Namesake** Homonym
**Name unknown** Anon, A N Other, NU
**Namibian** Herero
**Nanny** Ayah, Cosset, Foster, Goat, Nurse, Wet-nurse
**Naos** Cell(a)
**Nap(py)** Ale, Bonaparte, Diaper, Doze, Drowse, Fleece, Fluff, Forty winks, Frieze(d), Fuzz, Game, Happen, Hippin(g), Kip, Moze, Nod, Oose, Ooze, Oozy, Power, Put(t), Shag, Shuteye, Siesta, →SLEEP, Slumber, Snooze, Tease, Teasel, Teaze, Terry, Tipsy, Tuft, Zizz
**Nape** Niddick, Noddle, Nucha, Scrag, Scruff, Scuff, Scuft
**Napier** Logarithm
**Napkin** Cloth, Diaper, Doily, Doyley, Linen, Muckender, Paper, Sanitary, Serviette, Table
**Napless** Threadbare
**Napoleon** Badinguet, Bonaparte, Boustrapa, Brandy, Cognac, Coin, Consul, Corporal Violet, Corsican, December, Little Corporal, Nantz, Nap, Pig, Rantipole, Solo

▹**Napoleon** *may indicate* a pig
**Napper** Bonce, Shearman
**Narcissus, Narcissism** Echo, Egocentric, Egomania, Egotism, Jonquil, Vanity
**Narcotic** Ava, B(h)ang, Benj, Cannabin, Cannabis, Charas, Churrus, Coca, Codeine, Dagga, Datura, Dope, → DRUG, Heroin, Hop, Kava, Laudanum, Mandragon, Mandrake, Marijuana, Meconium, Methadone, Morphia, Narceen, Narceine, Nicotine, Opiate, Opium, Pituri, Sedative, Tea, Tobacco, Trional
**Nark** Grass, Inform, Irritate, Nose, Pique, Roil, Squealer, Stag
**Narrate, Narration, Narrative, Narrator** Allegory, Anecdote, Cantata, Describe, Diegesis, Epic, Fable, History, Ishmael, Oblique, Periplus, Plot, Raconteur, Récit, Recital, Recite, Recount, Saga, Sagaman, Scheherazade, Splatterpunk, Story, Tell, Thanatography, Voice-over
**Narrow(ing), Narrowly, Narrow-minded** Alf, Babbitt, Bigoted, Blinkered, Borné, Bottleneck, Close(-run), Constrict, Constringe, Cramp, Ensiform, Grundy(ism), Hairline, Hidebound, Illiberal, Insular, Knife edge, Kyle, Limited, Meagre, Nary, One-idead, Parochial, Phimosis, Pinch, Pinch-point, Po(-faced), Provincial, Prudish, Puritan, Scant, Sectarian, Shrink, Slender, Slit, Specialise, Squeak, Stenosed, Strait, Straiten, Strait-laced, Strict, Suburban, Taper, Verkramp, Wafer-thin, Waist, Whisker
**Narwhal** Monodon
**Nasal** Adenoidal, Rhinolalia, Sonorant, Twang
**Nash** Beau
**Nashville** Bath
**Nastiness, Nasty** Disagreeable, Drevill, Filth, Fink, Ghastly, Lemon, Lo(a)th, Malign(ant), Noisome, Noxious, Obscene, Odious, Offensive, Ogreish, Poxy, Ribby, Scummy, Sif, Sinister, Sordid, Tit, Unholy, Vile, Virose
**Nat(haniel)** Hawthorne, Winkle
**Natal** Inborn, Native, Patrial
**Natant** Afloat, Swimming
**Nation(s), National(ist), Nationalism** Anthem, Baathist, Broederbond, Casement, Chetnik, Citizen, Country, Cuban, Debt, De Valera, El Salvador, Eta, Federal, Five, Folk, Gandhi, Grand, Hindutva, Indian, INLA, IRA, Israeli, Jingoist, Kuomintang, Land, Malcolm X, Mexican, Oman, Pamyat, Parnell, Patriot, → PEOPLE, Plaid Cymru, Polonia, Race, Rainbow, Risorgimento, Scottish, Shiv Sena, Six, SNP, Subject, Swadeshi, Timor-Leste, Togo, Tonga, Tribespeople, Turk, United, Vanuatu, Vatican City, Verkrampte, Vietminh, Wafd, Xenophobe, Yemini, Young Ireland, Young Turk, Zionist
**Nationwide** Coast to coast
**Native(s)** Aborigin, Aborigine, African, Amerind, Annamese, Arab, Ascian, Australian, Autochthon, Aztec, Basuto, Belonging, Bengali, Boy, Bushman, Cairene, Carib, Carioca, Chaldean, Citizen, Colchester, Conch, Congenital, Creole, Criollo, Domestic, Dyak, Edo, Enchorial, Endemic, Eskimo, Fleming, Genuine, Habitual, Home-bred, Inborn, Inbuilt, Inca, Indigene, Indigenous, Inhabitant, Intuitive, Kloo(t)chman, Libyan, Local, Malay, Maori, Micronesian, Moroccan, Norwegian, Oyster, Portuguese, Scythian, Son, Spaniard, Te(i)an, Thai, Tibetan, Tribesman, Uzbeg, Uzbek, Whitstable, Yugoslav
**Nativity** Birth, Jataka, Putz
**Natron** Urao
**Natter** Chat, Gossip, Jack, Prate
**Natty** Bumppo, Chic, Dapper, Leatherstocking, Raffish, Smart, Spruce
**Natural(ly), Naturalise(d), Naturalism** Altogether, Artless, Ass, Denizen, Easy, Endenizen, Genuine, Green, Gut, Homely, Home-made, Idiot, Illegitimate, Inborn, Inbred, Indigenous, Ingenerate, Inherent, Innate, Instinctive, Moron, Native, Necessary, Nidget, Nitwit, Nude, Ordinary, Organic, Prat, Raw, Real, Simpleton, Simpliciter, Sincere, True, Undyed, Untaught, Verism
**Naturalist** Banks, Bates, Buffon, Darwin, De Lamarck, Durrell, Field, Wallace, White
**Nature** Adam, Akin, Character, Disposition, Esse(nce), Ethos, Haecceity, Human, Humanity, Hypostasis, Inbeing, Inscape, Manhood, Mould, Personality, Quiddity, Quintessence, Root, Second, SN, Temperament

**Naught** Cypher, Failure, Nil, Nothing, Zero
**Naughty, Naughtiness** Bad, Disobedient, Girly, Improper, Indecorous, Light, Marietta, Misbehave, Nineties, Nonny, Offender, Peccancy, Rascal, Remiss, Rudery, Saucy, Spright, Sprite, Wayward
**Nausea, Nauseate(d), Nauseous** Car-sickness, Cloy, Disgust, Dwa(l)m, Dwaum, Fulsome, Malaise, Queasy, Repulse, Sea-sickness, Sickness, Squeamish, Travel sickness, Wamble, Wambly
**Nave** Aisle, Apse, Centre, Hub, Modiolus, Nef
**Navel** Belly-button, Jaffa, Naff, Nave, Omphalos, Orange, Tummy button, Umbilicus
**Navigate, Navigator** Albuquerque, Baffin, Bering, Bougainville, Cabot, Cartier, Columbus, Control, Cook, Da Gama, Davis, Dias, Direct, Drake, Eric the Red, Franklin, Frobisher, Gilbert, Hartog, Haul, Henry, Hudson, Keel, Magellan, Navvy, Neighbour, Orienteer, Pilot, Raleigh, Sail, Star-read, →STEER, Tasman, Traverse, Vancouver, Vespucci, Weddell
**Navigation (aid, system)** Asdic, Cabotage, Celestial, Decca, Dectra, Echosounder, Fido, Gee, GPS, Inertial, Inland, Loran, Loxodromics, Navarho, Omnirange, Portolan(o), Portulan, Radar, Satnav, Seamark, Shoran, Tacan, Teleran®, Vor
**Navvy** Workhorse
**Navy, Naval** AB, Armada, Blue, Fleet, French, Maritime, Merchant, N, Red, RN, Seal, Senior Service, Wavy, White squadron, Wren
**Nawab** Huzoor, Nabob, Viceroy
**Nazi** Brownshirt, Gauleiter, Hess, Hitler, Jackboot, SS, Stormtrooper, Third Reich, Wer(e)wolf
**NB** Niobium, Nota bene
**NCO** Bombardier, Corp(oral), Havildar, Noncom, Orderly, Pipe-major, Sergeant, SM
**Neanderthal** Mousterian
**Neap** Low, Tide
**Neapolitan** Ice
**Near(er), Nearest, Nearby, Nearly, Nearness** About, Adjacent, All-but, Almost, Anigh, Approach, Approximate, Beside, By, Close, Cy pres, Degree, Even, Ewest, Feckly, Forby, Gain, Handy, Hither, Imminent, Inby(e), Mean, Miserly, Most, Narre, Neist, Next, Nie, Niggardly, Nigh, Nr, Oncoming, Outby, Propinquity, Proximity, Short-range, Stingy, Stone's throw, Thereabout(s), To, Towards, Upon, Virtually, Warm, Well-nigh
**Neat(ly), Neaten, Neatness** Bandbox, Cattle, Clean-cut, Clever, Dainty, Dapper, Deft, Dink(y), Doddy, Donsie, Elegant, Featly, Feat(e)ous, Featuous, Gayal, Genty, Gyal, Intact, Jemmy, Jimpy, Kempt, Lower, Nett, Nifty, Ninepence, Orderly, Ox(en), Perjink, Preppy, Pretty, Primp, Rother, Saola, Shipshape, Short(horn), Smug, Snod, Spick and span, Spruce, Straight, →TIDY, Trig, Trim, Uncluttered, Unwatered, Well-groomed
**Neb** Beak, Bill, Nose, Snout
**Nebula, Nebulous** Aeriform, Andromeda, Celestial, Cloudy, Dark, Emission, Gum, Hazy, Horsehead, Obscure, Planetary, Reflection, Shadowy, Vague
**Necessary, Necessarily** Bog, Cash, De rigueur, →ESSENTIAL, Estovers, Imperative, Important, Indispensable, Intrinsic, Loo, Money, Moolah, Needful, Ought, Perforce, Prerequisite, Requisite, Vital, Wherewithal
**Necessitate, Necessity** Ananke, Compel, Constrain, Cost, Emergency, Entail, Essential, Exigent, Fate, Indigence, Logical, Mathematical, Moral, Must, Natural, Need, Need-be, Oblige, Perforce, Require, Requisite, Staple
**Neck(ed)** Bottle, Brass, Canoodle, Cervical, Cervix, Channel, Col, Collar, Crag, Craig, Crew, Crop, Cuff, Derbyshire, Embrace, Ewe, Gall, Gorgerin, Halse, Hause, Hawse, Inarm, Inclip, Isthmus, Kiss, Mandarin, Mash, Nape, Nuzzle, Pet, Polo, Rack, Rubber, Scoop, Scrag, Scruff, Smooch, Snog, Stiff, Strait, Surgical, Swan, Swire, Theorbo, Torticollis, Trachelate, Turtle, Vee, Volcanic
▷**Necking** *may indicate* one word around another
**Necklace** Afro-chain, Anodyne, Bib, Brisingamen, Chain, Choker, Collar, Corals, Hei-tiki, Laval(l)ière, Lunula, Mangalsutra, Medallion, Negligee, Pearls, Rope, Sautoir, String, Torc, Torque
**Neckline** Boat, Collar, Cowl, Crew, Décolletage, Lanyard, Palter, Plunging, Scoop, Sweetheart, Turtle, Vee

**Neck problem** Torticollis
**Neck-warmer** Scarf, Snood
**Neckwear** Ascot, Barcelona, Boa, Bow, Collar, Cravat, Fur, Rail, Steenkirk, Stock, Tie
**Necromancer** Goetic, Magician, Ormandine, Osmand, Warlock, Witch, Wizard
**Necropolis** Cemetery
**Necrosis** Gangrene, Infarct, Sphacelus
**Nectar** Ambrosia, Amrita, Honey, Mead
**Ned(dy)** Donkey, Kelly, Ludd
**Need(ed), Needful, Needy** Absence, Ananke, Beggarly, Besoin, Call, Demand, Desiderata, Desperate, Egence, Egency, Essential, Exigency, Gap, Gerundive, Impecunious, Indigent, → LACK, Mister, Necessary, Prerequisite, Pressing, PRN, Rainy day, Require, Special, Strait, Strapped, Thirst, Urgency, Want
**Needle(s)** Acerose, Acicular, Aciform, Acupuncture, Anger, Antagonise, Between, Bodkin, Cleopatra's, Darner, Darning, Dip, Dipping, Dry-point, Electric, Etching, Goad, Gramophone, Hagedorn, Hype, Hypodermic, Ice, Icicle, Inoculate, Knitting, Leucotome, Magnetic, Mainline, Miff, Monolith, Neeld, Neele, Netting, Obelisk, Packing, Pine, Pinnacle, Pique, Pointer, Prick, R(h)aphis, Sew, Sharp, Spanish, Spicule, Spike, Spine, Spud, Stylus, Tattoo, Tease, Thorn, Wire
**Needless** Undue
**Needlewoman** Cleopatra, Seamstress
**Needlework** Acupuncture, Applique, Baste, Crewel, Drawn(-thread), Embroidery, Fag(g)oting, Fancy work, Gros point, Lacet, Mola, Overhand, Patchwork, Petit point, Piqué, Plainwork, Rivière, Sampler, Smocking, Spanish, Tapestry, Tattoo, White-seam, Woolwork, Worsted-work
**Ne'er-do-well** Badmash, Budmash, Bum, Good-for-nothing, Scallywag, Scullion, Shiftless, Skellum, Waster, Wastrel
**Negation, Negative, Negativity** Adverse, Ambrotype, Anion, Apophatic, Cathode, Defeatist, Denial, Double, Downside, Enantiosis, False, Infinitant, Ne, No, Non, Nope, Nullify, Pejorative, Pessimism, Photograph, Privative, Rebuttal, Refusal, Resinous, Unresponsive, Veto, Yin
**Neglect(ed), Neglectful, Negligence, Negligent** Careless, Casual, Cinderella, Contributory, Cuff, Culpa lata, Culpa levis, Default, Delapidated, Dereliction, Disregard, Disuse, Failure, Forget, Forlorn, For(e)slack, G-devant, Heedless, Inadvertence, Inattention, Incivism, Laches, Lax, Malpractice, Misprision, Omission, Oversight, Pass, Pass-up, Rack and ruin, → REMISS, Scamp, Shirk, Slight, Slipshod, Undone, Unilateral, Unnoticed, Waif, Wanton
▷**Neglected** *may indicate* an anagram
**Negligee** Déshabillé, Manteau, Mob, Nightgown, Peignoir, Robe
**Negligible** Fig, Minimal, Slight
**Negotiate, Negotiator** Arbitrate, Arrange, Bargain, Barter, Broker, Clear, Confer, Deal, Diplomat, Haggle, Intercede, Interdeal, Intermediary, Liaise, Manoeuvre, Mediator, Parley, Petition, Shop steward, Talk, Trade, Transact, Treat(y), Tret, Weather
**Negro(id)** → AFRICAN, Baganda, Bambara, Barotse, Bemba, Bergdama, Bini, Black, Buck, Chewa, Creole, Cuffee, Cuffy, Damara, Dinge, Duala, Dyula, Ebon(y), Edo, Efik, Ethiop, Ewe, Fang, Ga, Ganda, Gullah, Hausa, Hutu, Ibibio, Ibo, Igbo, Igorot, Jim Crow, Kikuyu, Kongo, Luba, Luganda, Malinke, Maninke, Moor, Mossi, Ndebele, Nilote, Nupe, Nyanja, Nyoro, Ovambo, Pondo, Sotho, Susu, Temne, Tiv, Tonga, Tsonga, Tswana, Twi, Uncle Tom, Venda, Watu(t)si, Wolof, Xhosa, Yoruba, Zulu
**Negus** Emperor, Rumfruction, Selassie
**Nehru** Pandit
**Neigh** Bray, Hinny, Nicker, Whicker, Whinny
**Neighbour(ly), Neighbouring, Neighbours** Abut(ter), Adjoin, Alongside, Amicable, Beside, Bor, Border, But, Friendly, Joneses, Nearby, Next-door, Tête-bêche, Vicinal
**Neighbourhood(s)** Acorn®, Area, Community, Convicinity, District, Environs, Locality, Precinct, Propinquity, Region, Vicinage, Vicinity
**Neither** Nor

**Nell(ie), Nelly** Bly, Dean, Trent
**Nelson** Columnist, Eddy, Horatio
**Nematode** Eelworm, Roundworm
**Nemesis** Alastor, Avenger, Deserts, Downfall, Fate, Retribution, Revenge
**Neodymium** Nd
**Neolithic** Avebury, Halafian, Skara Brae, Stonehenge
**Neon** Ne
**Nepalese** Gurkha
**Neper** N
**Nephrite** Yu
**Nepotism** Favouritism, Kin, Partisan, Patronage
**Neptune** God, Planet, Poseidon
**Neptunium** Np
**Nerd** Anorak, Dork, Dweeb, Geek, Otaku
**Nereid** Cymodoce, Nymph, Panope, Thetis
**Nerve(s), Nervous(ness), Nervure, Nerve centre, Nervy** Abdabs, Abducens, Accessory, Acoustic, Afferent, Aflutter, Afraid, Alveolar, Antsy, Appestat, Auditory, Autonomic, Axon, Baroreceptor, Bottle, Bouton, Brass neck, Buccal, Butterflies, Chord, Chorea, Chutzpah, Collywobbles, Column, Commissure, Cones, Courage, Cranial, Cyton, Dendron, Depressor, Edgy, Effector, Efferent, Electrotonus, Epicritic, Excitor, Facial, Fearful, Fidgety, Flappy, Gall, Ganglion, Glossopharyngeal, Grit, Guts, Habdabs, Heart-string, High, Highly-strung, Hyp, Hypoglossal, Impudence, Jitters, Jittery, Jumpy, Median, Mid-rib, Motor, Moxie, Myelon, Nappy, Neck, Neurological, Nidus, Oculomotor, Olfactory, On edge, Optic, Pavid, Perikaryon, Pons, Proprioceptor, Protopathic, Rad, Radial, Receptor, Restiform, Restless, Sacral, Sangfroid, Sass, Sauce, Scared, Sciatic, Screaming abdabs, Screaming meemies, Sensory, Shaky, Shpilkes, Solar plexus, Somatic, Splanchnic, Spunk, Squirrel(l)y, Stage fright, Steel, Strung-up, Sympathetic, Synapse, Tense, Timid, Timorous, Tizzy, Toey, Tongue-tied, Trembler, Tremulous, Trigeminal, Trochlear, Twitchy, Ulnar, Uptight, Vagus, Vapours, Vasodilator, Vestibular, Vestibulocochlear, Wandering, Willies, Windy, Wired (up), Wittery, Yips
**Nervous disease, Nervous disorder** Chorea, Epilepsy, Neuritis, Tarantism, Tetany
▷**Nervously** *may indicate* an anagram
**Ness** Cape, Headland, Ras
**Nessus** Centaur
**Nest** Aerie, Aery, Aiery, Anthill, Ayrie, Bike, Bink, Brood, Byke, Cabinet, Cage, Caliology, Clutch, Dray, Drey, Eyrie, Eyry, Guns, Hive, Lodge, Love, Nid, Nide, Nidify, Nidus, Norwegian, Sett, Termitarium, Turkey, Wasp's, Wurley
**Nestle** Burrow, Coorie, Cose, Courie, Cuddle, Nuzzle, Rest, Snug(gle)
**Nestor** Counsellor, Kea, King, Parrot, Sage
**Net(ting), Nets, Network(ing), Networker** Anastomosis, Bamboo, BR, Bunt, Bus, Butterfly, Cast, Casting, Catch, Caul, Clap, Clathrate, Clear, Co-ax(ial), Cobweb, →COMPUTER NETWORK, Craquelure, Crinoline, Criss-cross, Crossover, Diane, Drag, Draught, Draw, Drift, Drop, Earn, Eel-set, Enmesh, Equaliser, Fetch, File server, Filet, Final, Fish, Fisherman, Flew, Flue, Fret, Fyke, Gain, Gate, Gill, →GRID, Hammock, Heliscoop, Honeycomb, Hose, Insect, Kiddle, Labyrinth, Lace, LAN, Land, Landing, Lattice, Leap, Line, Linin, Mains, Malines, Mattress, Maze, →MESH, Mist, Mosquito, Mycelium, Nerve, Neural, Neuropil, Old boys', PCN, Plexus, Portal system, Pound, Pout, Purse-seine, Quadripole, Reseau, Rete, Retiary, Reticle, Reticulate, Reticulum, Ring, Safety, Sagene, Scoop, Screen, Sean, Seine, Senior, Set(t), Shark, Shrimp, Skype®, Snood, Speed, Stake, Sweep-seine, Symplast, System, Tangle, Tela, Telex, Tissue, Toil, Torpedo, Trammel, Trap, Trawl, Trepan, Tulle, Tunnel, Twitter, Wire
**Netball** Let
**Nether** Below, Inferior, Infernal, Lower, Under
**Netherlands** Zeeland
**Nettle(rash)** Anger, Annoy, Day, Dead, Hemp, Hives, Horse, Irritate, Labiate, Nark, Ongaonga, Pellitory, Pique, Ramee, Rami, Ramie, Rhea, Rile, Roman, Ruffle, Sting, Urtica(ceae), Urticaria

**Nettlesome** Testy
**Neuralgia, Neuritis** Migraine, Pleurodynia, Sciatica, Tic
**Neurologist** Alzheimer
**Neurosis** Combat, Compulsion, Hang up, Hysteria, Obsession, Obsessive-compulsive, Shellshock, Trichotillomania
**Neuter** Asexual, Castrate, Counteract, Geld, Gib, Impartial, Neutral, Sexless, Spay
**Neutral(ise), Neutraliser** Alkalify, Angel gear, Antidote, Buffer zone, Counteract, Degauss, Grey, Impartial, Inactive, Schwa, Sheva, Shiva, Unbiased
**Neutron(s)** Delayed, Fast, Nucleon, Prompt, Slow, Thermal, Virgin
**Never(more)** As if, Nary, Nathemo(re), No more, Nowise, St Tibb's Eve
**Never-ending** Age-long
**Never mind** Nix my dolly
**Nevertheless** Algate, All the same, Anyhow, But, Even, Howbeit, However, Quand même, Still, Tout de même, Yet
**New(s), Newborn, News agency** Avant garde, Bulletin, Communique, Copy, Coranto, Dope, Euphobia, Evangel, Feuilleton, Flash, Forest, Fresh, Fudge, Gen, Green, Griff, Info(rmation), Initiate, Innovation, Intake, Intelligence, Itar Tass, Item, Job's, Kerygma, Latest, Mint, Modern, N, Novel, Oil(s), Original, PA, Paragraph, Pastures, Pristine, Propaganda, Raw, Reborn, Recent, Report, Reuter, Scoop, Sidebar, Snippet, Span, Splash, Split, Stop press, Stranger, Tass, Teletext®, Tidings, Ultramodern, Unco, Update, Usenet, Wire service, Word, Young
▷**New** *may indicate* an anagram
**New boy** Gyte
**Newcomer, Newbie** Dog, Freshman, Griffin, Immigrant, Jackaroo, Jackeroo, Jillaroo, Johnny-come-lately, L, Learner, Newbie, Novice, Parvenu, Pilgrim, Recruit, Rookie, Settler, Tenderfoot, Upstart
**New Englander** Down-easter
**Newfoundland** Dog, Nana, Vinland
**Newgate** Calendar
**Newly wed** Benedick, Benedict, Bride, Groom, Honeymooner, Neogamist
**Newman** Cardinal, Noggs, Paul
**New moon** Rosh Chodesh
**New Orleans** Big easy
**Newsman, News-reader** Announcer, Editor, Journalist, Legman, Press, Reporter, Sub, Sysop
**Newsmonger, News-vendor** Butcher, Gossip, Quidnunc
**Newspaper** Beast, Big Issue, Blat(t), Broadsheet, Compact, Courier, Daily, Express, Fanzine, Feuilleton, Figaro, Freesheet, Gazette, Guardian, Heavy, Herald, Intelligencer, Izvestia, Journal, Jupiter, Le Monde, Mercury, National, Organ, Patent inside, Patent outside, Post, Pravda, Press, Print, Rag, Red-top, Scandal sheet, Scotsman, Sheet, Spoiler, Squeak, Sun, Tabloid, Today, Yellow Press
**Newsreel** Actualities
**Newsworthy** Topical
**Newt(s)** Ask(er), Eft, Evet, Swift, Triton, Urodela
**Newton** N
**New World** USA
**New Year** Hogmanay, Ne'er-day, Rosh Hashana(h), Tet
**New York(er)** Big Apple, Bronx, Coney Island, Gotham, Knickerbocker, Manhattan, Queens, Rose
**New Zealand(er)** Aotearoa, Diggers, Enzed, Jafa, Kiwi, Maori, Mooloo, Moriori, .nz, Pakeha, Pig Island, Ronz(er), Shagroon, Zelanian
**Next** Adjacent, Adjoining, After, Alongside, Beside, By, Following, Immediate, Later, Nearest, Neighbour, Neist, Proximate, Proximo, Sine, Subsequent, Syne, Then, Thereafter
**Nib(s)** Cocoa, J, Pen, Point, Tip
**Nibble** Bite, Brouse, Browse, Byte, Canapé, Cheese straw, Crop, Eat, Gnaw, Knap(ple), Moop, Moup, Munch, Nag, Nepit, Nosh, Peck, Pick, Snack

**Niblick** Wedge
**Nice(ly), Nicety** Accurate, Amene, Appealing, Cool, Dainty, Fastidious, Fine, Finical, Genteel, Lepid, Mooi, Ninepence, Pat, Peachy, Pleasant, Precise, Quaint, Rare, Refined, Subtil(e), Subtle, Sweet, T, To a t, Toothsome
**Niche** Alcove, Almehrahb, Almery, Ambry, Apse, Aumbry, Awmrie, Awmry, Columbarium, Cranny, Ecological, Exedra, Fenestella, Mihrab, Recess, Slot
**Nicholas** Santa
**Nick(ed)** Appropriate, Arrest, Bin, Blag, Can, Chip, Cly, Colin, Copshop, Crib, Cut, Denay, Dent, Deny, → DEVIL, Erose, Groove, Hoosegow, Kitty, Knock, Nab, Nap, Nim, Nock, Notch, Pinch, Pocket, Pook, Pouk, Prison, Run in, Scratch, Scrump, Serrate, Sneak, → STEAL, Steek, Swan-upping, Swipe, Thieve, Whip, Wirricow, Worricow, Worrycow
**Nickel (silver)** Coin, Garnierite, Jitney, Millerite, Ni, Packfong, Paktong, Zaratite
**Nicker** Bonduc, Neigh, Whinny
**Nickname** Alias, Byname, Byword, Cognomen, Dub, Epithet, Monicker, So(u)briquet, To-name
**Nicotine** Tobacco, Weed
**Nifty** Smart, Stylish
**Niger** RN
**Nigeria(n)** Biafran, Cross River, Efik, Hausa, Ibibio, Ibo, Igbo, .ng, Nupe, Tiv, WAN, Yoruba
**Niggard(ly)** Dry-fist, Illiberal, Mean, Miser, Near-(be)gaun, Nippy, Nirlie, Nirlit, Parsimonious, Penny wise, Pinchcommons, Pinchgut, Pinchpenny, Scrunt, Skinflint, Tightwad
**Niggle** Carp, Gripe, Irk, Nag, Potter, Trifle
**Night(s), Nightfall** Acronical, Acronychal, Arabian, Burns, Darkling, Darkmans, Darkness, Dusk, Field, First, Gaudy, Guest, Guy Fawkes, Hen, Leila, Nacht, Nicka-nan, Nutcrack, Nyx, Opening, School, Silent, Sleepover, Stag, Twelfth, Twilight, Walpurgis, Watch, White
**Night-blindness** Day-sight, Nyctalopia
**Night-cap** Biggin, Cocoa, Kilmarnock cowl, Nip, Pirnie, Sundowner
**Nightclub** Boite de nuit, Cabaret, Clip joint, Dive, Honkytonk, Hot spot, Stringfellow's
**Night-dew** Serein, Serene
**Nightdress** Baby doll, Wylie-coat
**Nightingale** Bulbul, Cape, Florence, Frog, Jugger, Lind, Philomel, Philomena, Progne, Scutari, Swedish, Watch
**Nightjar** Chuck-will's-widow, Churn-owl, Evejar, Fern-owl, Goatsucker, Night-churr, Poorwill, Potoo
**Night-light** Moonbeam
**Nightmare, Nightmarish** Cacod(a)emon, Cauchemar, Ephialtes, Incubus, Kafkaesque, Oneirodynia, Phantasmagoria
**Night-rider** Revere
**Nightshade** Atropin(e), Belladonna, Bittersweet, Black, Circaea, Deadly, Dwale, Enchanter's, Henbane, Morel, Solanum, Woody
**Nightwatchman** Charley, Charlie, Rug-gown
**Nightwork** Lucubrate
**Nihilist** Anarchist, Red, Sceptic
**Nil** Nothing, Nought, Zero
**Nile** Albert, Blue, Luvironza, Victoria, White
**Nimble(ness), Nimbly** Active, → AGILE, Alert, Deft, Deliver, Fleet, Legerity, Light, Light-footed, Lissom(e), Lithe, Nippy, Quiver, Sciolto, Springe, Spry, Supple, Sure-footed, Swack, Wan(d)le, Wannel, Wight, Ya(u)ld
**Nimbus** Aura, Aureole, Cloud, Gloriole, Halo
**Nimrod** Hunter
**Nincompoop** Ass, Fool, Imbecile, Moron, Ninny, Noodle, Stupid
**Nine, Ninth** Choral, Ennead, Muses, Nonary, Nonet, Novenary, Pins, Sancho, Skittles, Tailors, Worthies
**Nine hundred** Sampi
**Nine of diamonds** Curse of Scotland
**Nineteen(th)** Bar, Decennoval

**Ninetieth, Nineties, Ninety** N, Naughty, Nonagesimal
**Ninevite** Assyrian
**Ninny (hammer)** Fool, Goose, Idiot, Stupid, Tony
**Ninon** Nan
**Niobium** Nb
**Nip(per), Nippers** Bite, Brat, Check, Chela, Chill, Claw, Cutpurse, Dip, Dram, Fang, Foil, Gook, Jack Frost, Jap, Lad, Lop, Nep, Nirl, Outsiders, Peck, Pickpocket, Pincers, Pinch, Pook, Pop, Scotch, Sneap, Susan, Tad, Talon, Taste, Tot, Tweak, Urchin, Vice, Vise
**Nipa** At(t)ap, Palm
**Nipple** Bleed, Dug, Grease, Jogger's, Mastoid, Pap, Teat
**Nis** Brownie, Goblin, Kobold, Sprite
**Nit** Egg, Insect, Louse
**Nit-picking** Carping, Pedantry, Quibble
**Nitre** Saltpetre
**Nitric, Nitrogen** Azote, Azotic, Gas, N, Quinoline
**Nitroglycerine** Glonoin, Soup
**Nitty-gritty** Brass
**Nitwit** Ass, Flat, Fool, Scatterbrain, Simpleton, → STUPID
**No** Aikona, Denial, Na(e), Nah, Naw, Negative, Nix, Nope, Nyet, O, Refusal
**Noah** Arkite, Beery, Utnapishtim
**Nob(by)** Grandee, Parage, Prince, Swell, Toff
**Nobble** Dope, Fiddle, Hilch, Injure, Interfere
▷**Nobbled** *may indicate* an anagram
**Nobelium** No
**Noble(man), Noblewoman, Nobility, Nobly** Adela, Adele, Adeline, Aneurin, Aristocrat, Atheling, Baron(et), Baroness, Baronet(ess), Baronne, Bart, Blue blood, Boyar, Brave, Bt, Burgrave, Childe, Comte, Contessa, Count, County, Cousin, Daimio, Datuk, Dauphine, Dom, Don, Doucepere, Douzeper(s), Duc, Duke, Duniwassal, Earl, Empress, Eorl, Ethel, Eupatrid, Fine, Galahad, Gent, Glorious, Graf, Grandee, Grandeur, Great, Heroic, Hidalgo, Highborn, Illustrious, Infant, Jarl, Junker, King, Landgrave, Lofty, Lord, Maestoso, Magnate, Magnificent, Magnifico, Manly, Margrave, Marquis, Mona, Nair, Nawab, Nayar, Palatine, Patrician, Patrick, Peer, Rank, Ritter, Rose, Seigneur, Seignior, Sheik(h), Stately, Sublime, Thane, Thegn, Titled, Toiseach, Toisech, Top drawer, Vavasour, Vicomte, Vidame, Viscount, Waldgrave
**Noble gas(es)** Argon, Helium, Krypton, Neon, Radon, Xenon
**Nobody** Diarist, Gnatling, Jack-straw, Nebbish, Nemo, None, Nonentity, Nyaff, Pipsqueak, Pooter, Quat, Schlepp, Scoot, Shlep, Upstart, Zero
**Nocturnal (creature)** Bat, Galago, Moth, Night, Owl
**Nod(ding)** Agree, Assent, Beck(on), Bob, Browse, Catnap, Cernuous, Dip, Doze, Drowsy, Headbang, Mandarin, Nutant, Somnolent
**Node, Nodular, Nodule** Ascending, Boss, Descending, Enhydros, Geode, Knot, Lump, Lymph, Manganese, Milium, Pea-iron, Ranvier, Root, Septarium, Swelling, Thorn, Tophus, Tubercle
**No doubt** Iwis, Ywis
**Noel** Christmas, Coward, Yule
**Nog(gin)** Ale, Cup, → DRINK, Nob, Peg
**No go** Anergia
**No good** Dud, NG, Ropy
**No-hoper** Drongo, Gone goose, Goner, Lost cause
**Noise, Noisy** Ambient, Atmospherics, Babble, Babel, Bedlam, Big, Blare, Blat(t), Bleep, Blip, Blue murder, Bobbery, Boing, Boink, Bray, Bruit, Cangle, Charm, Cheep, Chellup, Clam, Clamant, Clamour, Clangour, Clash, Clatter, Clitter, Clutter, Coil, Crackle, Creak, Deafening, Deen, Din, Dirdum, Discord, Euphonia, Euphony, F, Flicker, Fracas, Fuss, Hewgh, Howl, Howlround, Hubbub, Hue, Hullabaloo, Hum, Hurly-burly, Knocking, Loud, Mush, Obstreperous, Phut, Ping, Pink, Plangent, Quonk, Racket, Raucous, Report, Risp, Roar, Roarie, Roary, Robustious, Rorie, Rort, Rory, Row(dow-dow), Rowdedow, Rowdy(dow)(dy),

Rucous, Rumble, Schottky, Schottky-Utis, Scream, Screech, Shindig, Shindy, Shot, Shreek, Shreik, Shriech, Shriek, Slosh, Solar, Sone, Sonorous, Sound, Strepent, Strepitation, Strepitoso, Stridor, Surface, Thermal, Thunder, Tinnitus, Top, Trumpet, Tumult, → UPROAR, VIP, Visual, Vociferous, Whinny, White, Whoomph, Zoom

**Noisome** Fetid, Invidious, Noxious, Offensive, Rank

**No longer** Ex, Past

**Nomad(ic)** Amalekite, Ammonites, Bedawin, Bedu, Bed(o)uin, Berber, Bushman, Chal, Drifter, Edom(ite), Errant, Fula(h), Gypsy, Hun, Hunter-gatherer, Hyksos, Itinerant, Kurd, Kyrgyz, Lapp, Masai, Rom, Rootless, Rover, Saracen, Sarmatian, Strayer, Tigre, Tsigane, Tsigany, Tuareg, Turk(o)man, Unsettled, Vagabond, Vagrant, Wanderer, Zigan

**Noman** Ta(r)tar

**No man's land** Tom Tiddler's ground

**Nom de plume** Aka, Pen-name

**Nome** Province

**Nomenclature** Term

**Nominal** Formal, Onomastic, Soi-disant, Titular, Token, Trifling

**Nominate, Nomination** Appoint, Baptism, Designate, Elect, Postulate, Present, → PROPOSE, Slate, Specify, Term

**Nomogram** Abac

**No more** Gone, Napoo

**Nomothete** Enactor, Legislator

**Non-Aboriginal** Wudjula

**Non-acceptance** Ostrichism

**Non-aligned** Neutral

**Non-attachment** Limbo

**Non-attender** Absentee, Recusant

**Non-attribute** Ens

**Non-believer** Atheist, Cynic, Infidel, Nothingarian, Sceptic

**Non-belligerent** Neutral

**Non-catalyst** Zymogen

**Nonchalance, Nonchalant** Blasé, Carefree, Casual, Cool, Debonair, Insouciant, Jaunty, Poco

**Non-Christian** Gentoo, New-age, Saracen

**Non-combatant** Neutral

**Noncommittal** Guarded, Hedging, Pussyfoot, Trimmer

**Non-communist** West

**Non-conductor** Insulatro

**Non-conformist, Non-conformity** Beatnik, Bohemian, Chapel, Deviant, Dissent(er), Dissident, Drop-out, Ebenezer, Enfant terrible, Heresiarch, Heretic, Maverick, Misfit, Odd-ball, Oddity, Outlaw, Pantile, Patarine, Rebel, Recusant, Renegade, Renegate, Sectarian, Wesleyan

**Non-consulting** Motu proprio

**Non-coordination** Ataxia

**Nondescript** Dull, Formless, Grey, Insipid, Neutral, Nyaff

**Non-directional** Scalar

**Non-drip** Thixotropic

**None** Nada, Nary, Nil, Nought, Zero

**Nonentity** Cipher, Nebbich, Nebbish(er), Nebish, Nobody, Pipsqueak, Quat, Whippersnapper

**Non-essential** Adiaphoron, Disposable, Extrinsic, Incidental

**Nonesuch** Model, Nonpareil, Paradigm, Paragon, Rarity

**Nonetheless** Mind you

▷**Nonetheless** *may indicate* an 'o' to be omitted

**Non-existent, Non-existence** Null, Thin air, Unbeing, Virtual

**Non-finite** Verbid

**Non-Gypsy** Gajo, Gorgio

**Non-interference** Laissez faire

**Non-Jewish** Gentile, Goy, Shegetz, Shi(c)ksa, Shkotzim, Sho(y)getz

**Non-juror** Usager
**Non-Maori** Tangata tiriti, Tauiwi
**Non-Muslim** Dhimmi, Dhimoni, Raia, Rayah
**Non-observance** Breach
**No-nonsense** Hardball, Strict
**Non-orthodox** Progressive
**Non-pairing** Ameiosis
**Nonpareil** Ideal, Nonesuch, Pearl, Peerless, Type, Unequal, Unique
**Nonplus(sed)** Baffle, Bewilder, Blank, Perplex, Stump
**Non-professional** Amateur, Laic
**Non-radiative** Auger
**Non-resident** Extern, Outlier
**Non-runner** Scratched, Solid
**Nonsense** Absurdity, Amphigon, Amphigory, Balderdash, Baloney, Bilge, Bizzo, Blague, Blah, Blarney, Blat(her), Blatherskite, Blether, Bollocks, Boloney, Bombast, Bora(c)k, Borax, Bosh, Bs, Bull, Bulldust, Bullshit, Bull's wool, Buncombe, Bunk, Bunkum, Cack, Chaff, Clamjamfr(a)y, Clamjamphrie, Claptrap, Cobblers, Cock, Cockamamie, Cod, Codswallop, Crap, Crapola, Drivel, Dust, Eyewash, Faddle, Falderal, Fandangle, Farce, Fiddlededee, Fiddle-faddle, Fiddlesticks, Flannel, Flapdoodle, Flim-flam, Folderol, Footling, Fudge, Gaff, Galimatias, Gammon, Gas and gaiters, Get away, Gibberish, Gobbledygook, Guff, Gum, Hanky-panky, Haver, Hogwash, Hokum, Hooey, Hoop-la, Horsefeathers, Hot air, Humbug, Irishism, Jabberwocky, Jazz, Jive, Kibosh, Kidstakes, Malark(e)y, Moonshine, Mouthwash, Mumbo-jumbo, My eye, My foot, Niaiserie, Pants, Phooey, Piffle, Pisheog, Pishogue, Poppycock, Pshaw, Pulp, Ratbaggery, Rats, Rawmaish, Rhubarb, Rigmarole, Rot, Rubbish, Scat, Shenanigans, Squit, Stuff, Taradiddle, Tom(foolery), Tommy-rot, Tosh, Trash, Tripe, Tush, Twaddle, Unreason, Waffle
**Non-sequitur** Anacoluthia, Irish bull, Irrelevant
**Non-sexual** Platonic
**Non-smoker** NS
**Non-specialist** User-friendly
**Non-standard** Anomalous
**Non-starter** No-no
**Non-stick** PTFE, Teflon®, Tusche
**Non-stop** Incessant, Through
**Non-transferable** Adiabatic
**Non-traveller** Gajo
**Non-U** Naff
**Non-Unionist** Freerider
**Non-violence** Ahimsa, Pacificism, Satyagraha
**Non-white** Coloured, Yolk
**Noodle(s)** Capellini, Chow mein, Crispy, Daw, Fool, Head, Laksa, Lokshen, Manicotti, Mee, Moony, Ninny, Noddy, Pasta, Ramen, Sammy, Sap, Simpleton, Soba, Udon
**Nook** Alcove, Angle, Corner, Cranny, Niche, Recess, Rookery
**Noon** Am end, High, M, Midday, N, Narrowdale
**No one** Nemo, None
**Noose** Fank, Halter, Hempen caudle, Lanyard, Lasso, Loop, Necktie, Rebecca, Rope, Rope's end, Snare, Twitch, Widdy
▸**Nor** *see* NOT
**Nordic, Norse(man), Norsemen** Aryan, Icelander, Norn, → NORWEGIAN, Scandian, Scandinavian, Viking, Vikings
**Norm** Canon, Criterion, Rule, Standard
**Normal** Average, Conventional, Customary, Everyday, General, Mainstream, Natural, Norm, Ordinary, Orthodox, Par, Perpendicular, Regular, Standard, Straightforward, Typical, Unexceptional, Usu(al)
**Normal eyes** Emmetropia
**Norman** French, Mailer, Rufus

**North(ern), Northerner** Arctic, Boreal, Cispontine, Copperhead, Dalesman, Doughface, Eskimo, Geographic, Hyperborean, Icelander, Laplander, Magnetic, N, Norland, Runic, Scotia, Scotsman, Sea, Septentrion, True, Up
**North African** Pied noir
**North American (Indian)** Papoose, Red, Totemist, Tribe

## NORTH AMERICAN INDIANS

*3 letters:*
Fox
Sao
Ute

*4 letters:*
Crow
Dene
Erie
Hopi
Innu
Otoe
Pima
Pomo
Sauk
Tewa
Tiwa
Yana
Yuma
Zuni

*5 letters:*
Brave
Cajun
Creek
Haida
Huron
Makah
Miwok
Olmec
Omaha
Osage
Piute
Ponca
Sioux
Taino
Teton

*6 letters:*
Abnaki
Apache
Cayuga
Dakota
Galibi
Klooch
Lakota
Micmac
Mixtec
Mohave
Mohawk
Navaho
Nootka
Oglala
Ojibwa
Oneida
Paiute
Papago
Pawnee
Pequot
Plains
Pueblo
Quapaw
Sachem
Salish
Sannup
Shasta
Yanqui

*7 letters:*
Abenaki
Arapaho
Caddoan
Chibcha
Chinook
Choctaw
Gwich'in
Hidatsa
Kikapoo
Klootch
Kutenai
Mahican
Miskito
Mission
Mohegan
Mohican
Mugwump
Natchez
Norteno
Ojibway
Palouse
Pontiac
Senecan
Serrano
Shawnee
Shuswap
Tahitan
Tlingit
Wichita
Wyandot
Yalkama
Zapotec

*8 letters:*
Algonkin
Angeleno
Cahuilla
Cherokee
Cheyenne
Chippewa
Comanche
Delaware
Flathead
Geronimo
Hiawatha
Iroquois
Kickapoo
Kootenai
Kootenay
Kwakiutl
Menomini
Mikasuki
Mogollon
Muskogee
Nez Percé
Okanagon
Okinagan
Onondaga
Sagamore
Sahaptan
Sahaptin
Seminole
Shoshone

*9 letters:*
Algonkian
Algonquin
Blackfoot
Chichimec
Chickasaw
Chipewyan
Manhattan
Melungeon
Menominee
Mescalero
Muskogean
Sahaptian
Shahaptin
Suquamish
Tsimshian
Tuscarora
Wampanoag
Winnebago
Wyandotte
Yawelmani

*10 letters:*
Algonquian
Crazy Horse
Halkomelem
Hooded Crow
Miniconjou
Montagnais
Montagnard
Muskhogean
Pocahontas
Potawatomi
Six Nations
Tarahumara
Uto-Aztecan

*11 letters:*
Assiniboine
Basket Maker
Five Nations
Kiowa Apache
Massachuset
Minneconjou
Narraganset
Sitting Bull

*12 letters:*
Mound Builder

*13 letters:*
Massachusetts
Northern Piute
Southern Piute
Susquehannock

*14 letters:*
Northern Paiute
Southern Paiute

**Northern Ireland** NI, Six Counties
**North star** Tyrian cynosure
**Northwestern** Aeolis
**Norway, Norwegian** Bokmal, Fortinbras, Landsma(a)l, N, Nordic, Norweyan, Nynorsk, Rollo, Scandinavian
**Nose, Nos(e)y** A(d)jutage, Aquiline, Beak, Bergerac, Boko, Bouquet, Breather, Busy, Button, Catarrhine, Conk, Copper, Cromwell, Curious, Desman, Droop(snoot), Electronic, Fink, Flair, Gnomon, Grass, Grecian, Greek, Grog-blossom, Honker, Hooknose, Hooter, Index, Informer, Instinct, Leptorrhine, Meddle, Muffle, Muzzle, Nark, Neb, Nozzle, Nuzzle, Parker, Paul Pry, Platyrrhine, Proboscis, Prying, Pug, Red, Retrousse, Rhinal, Roman, Scent, Schnozzle, Shove, Smelly, Sneb, Sniff, Snoot, Snout, Snub, Squeal, Stag, Stickybeak, Toffee
**Noseband** Barnacle, Cavesson, Musrol
**Nose-bleed** Epistaxis
**Nose-flute** Poogye(e)
**Nosh** Eat, Food, Nibble, Snack
**Nostalgia** Longing, Memory lane, Oldie, Retrophilia, Wistfulness, Yearning
**Nostril(s)** Blowhole, Cere, Choana, Nare
**Nostrum** Elixir, Medicine, Remede, Remedy
**Not, Nor** Aikona, Dis-, Na(e), Narrow A, Ne, Neither, Never, No, Pas, Polled, Taint
**Notable, Notability** Conspicuous, Dignitary, Distinguished, Eminent, Especial, Landmark, Large, Lion, Memorable, Personage, Signal, Striking, Unco, VIP, Worthy
**Not allowed** NL
▷**Not allowed** *may indicate* a word to be omitted
**Notary** Apostolical, Ecclesiastical, Escribano, Scrivener
**Not at all** Au contraire
**Notation(al)** Benesh, Cantillation, Decimal, Descriptive, Entry, Floating point, Formalism, Hexadecimal, Infix, Memo, Octal, Polish, Positional, Postfix, Romic, Scientific, Staff, Tablature
**Notch(ed)** Crena(l), Crenel, Cut, Dent, Erode, Erose, Gain, Gap, Gimp, Groove, Indent, Insection, Jag, Kerf, Mush, Nick, Nock, Raffle, Score, Serrate, Serrulation, Sinus, Snick, Tally, Vandyke
**Not clear** Blocked, NL, Obscure, Opaque, Pearl
**Note(s), Notebook, Noted** A, Acciaccatura, Accidental, Advance, Adversaria, Advice, Agogic, Apostil(le), Apparatus, Appoggiatura, Arpeggio, Auxiliary, B, Bass-clef, Bill(et), Bradbury, Bread and butter letter, Breve, Buck, C, Cedula, Chit(ty), Chord, Circular, Cob, Comment, Commentary, Conceit, Continental, Cover, Credit, Crotchet, Currency, D, Debit, Delivery, Demand, Dig, Dispatch, Do(h), Dominant, Double-dotted, E, E-la, Eminent, Entry, F, Fa(h), False, Fame, Field, Fiver, Five-spot, Flag up, Flat, Flim, G, Gamut, Gloss(ary), Gold, Grace, Greenback, Greeny, Gruppetto, Harmonic scale, Heed, Hemidemisemiquaver, Hemiole, Hypate, Identic, Index rerum, IOU, Iron man, Item(ise), Jot(tings), Jug(-jug), Key, Kudos, La, Large, Leading, Letter, Lichanos, Line(r), Log, Long, Longa, Lower mordent, Marginalia, Mark, Masora(h), Masoretic, Me, Mediant, Melisma, Melody, Memo(randum), Mese, Message, Mi, Minim, Minute, Missive, → MONEY, Mordent, Music, Muzak®, Nachschlag, Natural, NB, Nete, Neum(e), Oblong, Observe, Octave, Oncer, On record, Open, Ostmark, Outline, Pad, Parhypate, Passing, Personalia, Postal, Post-it®, Pound, Promissory, Prompt, Proslambanomenos, Protocol, PS, Quarter, Quaver, Rag-money, Re, Reciting, Record, Remark, Renown, Request, Right, Root, Sawbuck, Scholion, Scholium, Scotch catch, Scotch snap, Semibreve, Semiquaver, Semitone, Sensible, Septimole, Sextolet, Sharp, Shinplaster, Shoulder, Si, Sick, Side, Sixteenth, Sixty-fourth, Sleeve, Smacker, Snuff-paper, So(h), Sol, Some, Spy, Stem, Strike, Subdominant, Submediant, Subtonic, Supertonic, Te, Ten(ner), Third, Thirty-second, Tierce, Tironian, Tonic, Treasury, Treble, Twenty, Two-spot, Undecimole, Ut, Variorum, Verbal, Wad, Warison, Whole, Wolf, Wood
**Note-case** Pochette, Purse, Wallet
▷**Notes** *may indicate* the use of letters A-G
**Noteworthy** Eminent, Extraordinary, Memorable, Particular, Remarkable, Signal, Significant, Special

**Nothing, Nought** Buckshee, Bugger-all, Chargeless, Cipher, Damn-all, Devoid, Diddlysquat, Emptiness, FA, Gratis, Jack, Love, Nada, Napoo, Naught, Nihil, Niks-nie, Nil, Nix(-nie), Nonentity, Noumenon, Nowt, Nuffin, Nullity, O, Ought, Rap, Rien, Small beer, Sweet FA, Trifle, Void, Z, Zero, Zilch, Zip(po)

**Notice(able)** Ad(vertisement), Advance, Advice, Affiche, Apprise, Attention, Avis(o), Banns, Bill, Blurb, Bold, Bulletin, Caveat, Circular, Clock, Cognisance, Crit, D, DA, Descry, Detect, Discern, Discover, Dismissal, Enforcement, Espy, Evident, Eye catching, Final, Gaum, Get, Gorm, Handbill, →HEED, Intimation, Marked, Mensh, Mention, Message, NB, No(t)chel, Obit(uary), Observe, Obtrusive, Oyez, Perceive, Perceptible, Placard, Plaque, Playbill, Poster, Press, Proclamation, Prominent, Pronounced, →REMARK, Review, See, Short, Sign, Signal, Si quis, Spot, Spy, Sticker, Tent, Warning, Whip

**Notify, Notification** Acquaint, Advise, Apprise, Aviso, Awarn, Bulletin, Inform, Payslip, →TELL, Update, Warn

**Notion(al)** Academic, Chimera, Conceit, →CONCEPT, Crotchet, Fancy, Hunch, Idea, Idée, Idolum, Inkling, Opinion, Reverie, Vagary, Vapour, Whim

**Notoriety, Notorious** Arrant, Byword, Cause célèbre, Crying, Egregious, Esclandre, Fame, Flagrant, Ill-fame, Infamous, Infamy, Legendary, Notour, Proverbial, Réclame, →RENOWN, Repute

**Not pregnant** Farrow

**No trump** Laical, Lay, NT

**Notwithstanding** Albe(e), Although, Despite, Even, For, Howbeit, However, Mau(l)gre, Natheless(e), Nath(e)less, Naythles, Nevertheless, Spite

**Nougat** Montelimar, Sundae

▸**Nought** *see* NOTHING

**Noughts and crosses** Tic(k)-tac(k)-to(e)

**Noumenon** Thing-in-itself

**Noun** Abstract, Agent, Agentive, Aptote, Collective, Common, Concrete, Count, Gerund, Mass, N, Proper, Seg(h)olate, Substantive, Tetraptote, Verbal, Vocative

**Nourish(ing), Nourishment** Aliment, Battill, Cherish, Cultivate, Feed, Grub, Ingesta, Manna, Meat, Nurse, Nurture, Nutrient, Promote, Repast, Replenish, Sustenance, Trophic

**Nous** Commonsense, Intellect, Intelligence, Reason, Sense

**Nova Scotia(n)** Acadia, Blue-nose

**Novel(ty)** Aga-saga, Airport, Bildungsroman, Bodice-ripper, Bonkbuster, Book, Campus, Change, Chick lit, Clarissa, Different, Dime, Dissimilar, E-book, Emma, Epistolary, Erewhon, Fad, Fiction, Fresh, Germinal, Gimmick, Gothic, Graphic, Historical, Horror, Idiot, Innovation, Ivanhoe, Kenilworth, Kidnapped, Kim, Middlemarch, Modern, →NEW, Newfangled, Nouveau roman, Novation, Original, Outside, Page-turner, Pamela, Paperback, Pendennis, Penny dreadful, Persuasion, Picaresque, Pot-boiler, Primeur, Pulp, Rebecca, River, Roman-à-clef, Romance, Roman fleuve, Saga, Scoop, Sex and shopping, She, Shilling-dreadful, Shilling-shocker, Terror, Thesis, Ulysses, Unfamiliar, Unorthodox, Unusual, Weepie, Whodun(n)it, Yellowback

▹**Novel** *may indicate* an anagram

▸**Novelist** *see* WRITE(R)

**November** N, Nov

**Novice** Acolyte, Apprentice, Beginner, Cadet, Chela, Colt, Cub, Green(horn), Griffin, Jackaroo, Jillaroo, Johnny-raw, Kyu, L, Learner, Neophyte, New chum, Noob, Patzer, Postulant, Prentice, Rabbit, Recruit, Rookie, Tenderfoot, Trainee, Tyro(ne), Unweaned

**Now(adays)** AD, Alate, Anymore, Current, Here, Immediate, Instantaneously, Instanter, Interim, Modish, Nonce, Nunc, Present, Pro tem, This

**Nowhere** Limbo

**No-win** Dead heat

**Nowt** Cattle, Cows, Ky(e), Neat, Nothing

**Noxious** Harmful, Miasma, Noisome, Offensive, Poisonous, Toxic, Toxin, Venomous

**Nozzle** Aerospike, A(d)jutage, Fishtail, Nose, Nose-piece, Rose, Spout, Sprayer, Stroup, Syringe, Tewel, Tuyere, Tweer, Twier, Twire, Twyer(e)

**Nuance** Gradation, Nicety, Overtone, Shade

**Nub** Crux, Gist, Knob, Lump, Point
**Nubile** Beddable, Marriageable, Parti
**Nuclear, Nucleoside, Nucl(e)ide, Nucleus** Adenosine, Cadre, Calandria, Centre, Chernobyl, Core, Crux, Daughter, Deuteron, Eukaryon, Euratom, Even-even, Even-odd, Fast-breeder, Heartlet, Hub, Isodiaphere, Isomer, Isotone, Karyon, Kernel, Linin, Mesic, Mesonic, Mox, Mushroom, N, Nub, Nuke, Organelle, Pith, Prokaryon, Recoil, RNA, Sizewell, Synkaryon, Triton
▷**Nucleus** *may indicate* the heart of a word
**Nude, Nudism, Nudist, Nudity** Adamite, Altogether, Aphylly, Au naturel, Bare, Buff, Eve, Exposed, Full-frontal, Godiva, Gymnosophy, → NAKED, Naturism, Nuddy, Scud, Stark(ers), Stripped, Unclad, Undress
**Nudge** Dunch, Dunsh, Elbow, Jab, Jostle, Knee, Poke, Prod
**Nudibranch** Sea-slug
**Nugget** Chunk, Cob, Gold, Lump
**Nuisance** Annoyance, Bore, Bot, Brat, Bugbear, Chiz(z), Drag, Hassle, Impediment, Inconvenience, Irritant, Liability, Mischief, Pain, Pest, Plague, Public, Terror, Trial, Trouble-maker, Varment
**Null(ification), Nullify** Abate, Cancel, Counteract, Defeasance, Destroy, Diriment, Disarm, Invalid(ate), Negate, Neutralise, Overturn, Recant, Terminate, Undo, Veto, Void
**Numb(ness)** Anaesthetise, Analgesia, Asleep, Blunt, Dead(en), Dull, Night-palsy, Stun, Stupor, Torpefy, Torpescent, Torpid, Tranquillise, Unfeeling
**Number(s)** Abscissa, Abundant, Access(ion), Air, Aleph-null, Aleph-zero, Algebraic, Algorithm, Aliquant, Aliquot, Amiable, Amicable, Anaesthetic, Analgesic, Anthem, Antilog, Apocalyptic, Apostrophus, Army, Atomic, Augend, Avogadro, Babylonian, Batch, Binary, Box, Brinell, Calculate, Cardinal, Cetane, Chromosome, Cinque, Class, Cocaine, Coefficient, Cofactor, Complex, Composite, Concrete, Constant, Coordination, Count, Cyclic, Decillion, Decimal, Deficient, Deficit, Diapason, Digit, DIN, Drove, Drug, E, Edition, Epidural, Ether, Eucaine, Ex-directory, F, Feck, Fibonacci, Figurate, Figure, Flock, Folio, Folksong, Fraction, Friendly, Frost(bite), Froude, Gas, Gobar, Golden, Googol, Handful, Hantle, Hash(mark), Hemlock, Host, Hyperreal, Imaginary, Include, Incomposite, Index, Infimum, Integer, Irrational, Isospin, Isotopic, Item, Kochel, Lac, Lakh, Legion(s), Lepton, Lignocaine, Livraison, Local, Mach, Magazine, Magic, Main, Mantissa, Many(fold), Mass, Melodic, Milliard, Minuend, Minyan, Mixed, Mort, Muckle, Multiple, Multiplex, Multiplicity, Multitude, Myriadth, Nasik, Natural, Neutron, No(s), Nonillion, Nth, Nuclear, Nucleon, Num, Numerator, Numerical, Octane, Octillion, Opiate, Opium, Opposite, Opus, Ordinal, OT, Paginate, Par, Paucal, Peck, Perfect, Pile, PIN, Plural, Polygonal, Prime, Procaine, Production, Proton, Quantum, Quarternion, Quorum, Quota, Quotient, Radix, Raft, Random, Rational, Real, Reckon, Registration, Regulo®, Repunit, Reynold's, Root, Sampi, Scads, Serial, Shedload, Show-stopper, Sight, Slew, Slue, Some, Song, Square, Strangeness, Strength, Subtrahend, Summand, Surd, T, Tale, Telephone, Tell, Thr(e)ave, Totient, Totitive, Transcendental, Transfinite, Troop, Turn-out, Umpteen, Umpty, Urethan(e), Verse, Wave, Whole, Wrong, Zeroth
▷**Number** *may indicate* a drug
**Numbskull** Jackass
**Numeral(s)** Arabic, Chapter, Digit, Figure, Ghubar, Gobar, Integer, Number, Roman, Sheep-scoring
**Numerous(ness)** Divers, Galore, Hantle, Legion, Lots, Many, Multeity, Multiple, Myriad, Teeming, Various
**Numskull** Blockhead, Booby, Dunce, Stupid
**Nun(nery)** Basilian, Beguine, Bhikkhuni, Cell, Clare, Cloistress, Cluniac, Conceptionist, Dame, Deaconess, Gilbertine, Minim, Minoress, Mother Superior, Outsister, Pigeon, Poor Clare, Prioress, Religeuse, Retreat, Salesian, Sister, Sister of Mercy, Top, Trappistine, Ursuline, Vestal, Visitant, Vowess, Zelator, Zelatrice, Zelatrix
▷**Nun** *may indicate* a biblical character, father of Joshua
**Nuptial (chamber)** Bridal, Conjugal, Marital, Marriage, Thalamus
**Nurse(ry), Nursing, Nursemaid** Aia, Alice, Amah, Angel, Ant, Au pair, Ayah, Barrier,

Bonne, Caledonia, Candy-striper, Care(r), Cavell, Charge, Cherish, Community, Consultant, Cradle, Crèche, Day, Deborah, District, Dry, EN, Flo(rence), Foster, Gamp, Glasshouse, Glumdalclitch, Greenhouse, Harbour, Health visitor, Karitane, Mammy, Midwife, Minister, Mother, Mrs Gamp, Nan(n)a, Nanny, Night, Nightingale, Norland, Nourice, Nourish, Nursery, Parabolanus, Phytotron, Playroom, Playschool, Plunket, Practical, Pre-school, Probationer, RN, School, Scrub, Seminary, SEN, Sick, Sister, Staff, Suckle, Tend, Therapist, Treat, VAD, Visiting, Wet

**Nursery(man)** Conservatory, Crèche, Garden, Hothouse, Rhyme, Seedsman, Slope

▷**Nursing** *may indicate* one word within another

**Nurture** Breeding, Cherish, Cradle, Cultivate, Educate, Feed, Foster, Rear, Suckle, Tend

**Nut(s), Nutcase, Nutshell, Nutter, Nut tree, Nutty** Acajou, Acorn, Addict, Almond, Amygdalus, Anacardium, Aphorism, Arachis, Areca, Arnut, Babassu, Barcelona, Barking, Barmy, Bats, Beech-mast, Bertholletia, Betel, Bladder, Bonce, Brazil, Briefly, Buffalo, Butterfly, Butternut, Cashew, Castle, Chock, Coal, Cob, Coco-de-mer, Coffee, Cohune, Coke, Cola, Conker, Coquilla, Coquina, Core, Corozo, Cranium, Crankpin, Cream, Cuckoo, Dukka(h), Earth, En, Filberd, Filbert, Freak, Frog, Gelt, Gilbert, Gland, Glans, Goober, Goober-pea, Gum, Hard, Hazel, Head, Helmet, Hickory, Illipe, Ivory, Kachang puteh, Kernel, Kola, Kooky, Lichee, Li(t)chi, Loaf, Lug, Lunatic, Lychee, Macadamia, Macahuba, Macaw-palm, Macoya, Manic, Marking, Mast, Mockernut, Monkey, N, Noisette, Noodle, Nucule, Oak, Oil, Pakan, Palmyra, Para, Pate, Pecan, Pekan, Philippina, Philippine, Philopoena, Physic, Pili, Pine, Pin(y)on, Pistachio, Poison, Praline, Prawlin, Quandang, Quantong, Queensland, Rhus, St Anthony's, Sapucaia, Sassafras, Scaly-bark, Scrotum, Shell, Skull, Slack, Sleeve, Stuffing, Supari, Testicles, Thumb, Tiger, Tough, Wacko, Walnut, Weirdo, Wing, Zany, Zealot

▷**Nut** *may refer to* Egyptian god, father of Osiris

▶**Nutcase, Nutshell** *see* **NUT(S)**

**Nutcracker** Cosh

**Nuthatch** Sitta

**Nutmeg** Calabash, Connecticut, CT, Mace, Myristica

**Nutrient, Nutriment, Nutrition(al)** Betacarotene, Dietary, Dietetics, Eutrophy, Food, Ingesta, Nourishment, Protein, Sitology, Sustenance, Trace element, Trophic, Vitamin

▷**Nuts** *may indicate* an anagram

**Nuzzle** Nose, Snoozle

**Nyasaland** Malawi

**Nymph(et)** Aegina, Aegle, Amalthea, Arethusa, Callisto, Calypso, Camenae, Carme, Clytie, Constant, Cymodoce, Daphne, Doris, Dryad, Echo, Egeria, Eurydice, Galatea, Hamadryad, Hesperides, Houri, Hyades, Ida, Insect, Larva, Liberty, Lolita, Maelid, Maia, Maiden, Mermaid, Naiad, Nereid, Oceanid, Oenone, Oread, Pupa, Rusalka, Sabrina, Satyra, Scylla, Siren, Sprite, Sylph, Syrinx, Tessa, Tethys, Thetis, Water, Wood

**O** Blob, Duck, Nought, Omega, Omicron, Oscar, Oxygen, Round, Spangle, Tan, Zero
**Oaf** Auf, Changeling, Clod, Dolt, Fool, Lout, Mou, Ocker, Ouph(e), Sot, Stupid, Twit, Yahoo
**Oak(s)** Bog, Bur, Cerris, Classic, Cork, Desert, Dumbarton, Durmast, Evergreen, Flittern, Fumed, Gabriel, Herne, Holly, Holm, Honour, Ilex, Jerusalem, Kermes, Live, Major, Native, Parliament, Pedunculate, Philemon, Poison, Quercus, Red, Roble, Royal, Scrub, Sessile, Silky, Swamp, Swilcar, → TREE, Turkey, Valonia, Watch, White
**Oakley** Annie
**Oar(s), Oarsman, Oarsmen** Blade, Bow, Ctene, Eight, Galley slave, Leander, Organ, Paddle, Pair, Palm, Propel, Rower, Scull, Spoon, Stroke, Sweep
**Oasis** Biskra, Buraimi, Haven, Hotan, Hotien, Refuge, Spring, Tafilalet, Tafilelt
**Oat(meal), Oats** Ait, Athole brose, Avena, Brome-grass, Fodder, Grain, Grits, Groats, Gruel, Haver, Loblolly, Parritch, Pilcorn, Pipe, Porridge, Quaker®, Rolled, Wild
**Oatcake** Bannock, Clapbread, Farle, Flapjack, Jannock
**Oath** Affidavit, Bedad, Begorrah, Blast, Blimey, Blood, Bribery, Burgess, Curse, Damn, Dang, Dash, Demme, Doggone, Drat, Ecod, Egad, Expletive, God-so, Gospel, Halidom, Hell, Hippocratic, Igad, Imprecation, Jabers, Jesus, Keech, Lumme, Lummy, Nouns, Oons, Promise, Rats, Sacrament, Sal(a)mon, Sapperment, Saucer, 'Sbodikins, Sbud(dikins), Sdeath, Sfoot, Sheart, Shoot, Slid, 'Slife, 'Slight, Snails, Sonties, Strewth, Stygian, Swear, Tarnation, Tennis-court, Voir dire, Vow, Zbud, Zounds
**Obdurate** Adamant, Cruel, Flinty, Hard(-hearted), Intransigent, Stony, Stubborn, Tenacious
**Obedient, Obedience, Obey** Bent, Biddable, Bridlewise, Canonical, Comply, Dutiful, Follow, Good, Hear, Mindful, Obsequious, Observe, Obtemper, Passive, Perform, Pliant, Servant, Yielding
**Obeisance** → BOW, Salaam
**Obelisk, Obelus** Aguilla, Column, Dagger, Monument, Needle, Pillar
**Oberon** King, Merle
**Obese, Obesity** Bariatrics, Corpulent, Fat, Stout
**Obfuscation** Fudge
**Object(s), Objection(able), Objective(ness), Objector** Ah, Aim, Ambition, Argue, Artefact, Article, Artifact, Bar, Bauble, Beef, But, Case, Cavil, Challenge, Clinical, Cognate, Complain(t), Conchy, Conscientious, Contest, Cow, Demur, Detached, Direct, Dispassionate, Dissent, Doodah, End, Exception, Fetish, Found, Fuss, → GOAL, Grievance, Her, Him, Ifs and buts, Impersonal, Improper, Indifferent, Indirect, Intensional, Intention, It, Item, Jib, Lion, Loathe, Mind, Moral, Near-earth, Niggle, Nimby, Nitpick, Non-ego, Non-partisan, Noumenon, Ob, Obnoxious, Offensive, Oppose, Outness, Percept, Perspective, Pettifog, Plan, Plot, Point, Protest, Proximate, Quasi-stellar, Question, Quibble, Quiddity, Rank, Rebarbative, Recuse, Refuse, Relation, Resent, Resist, Retained, Sake, Scruple, Sex, Subject, Sublime, Target, Thing, Transitive, Tut, Ultimate, Unbiased, Undesirable, Unsavoury, Virtu, Wart
▷**Object** *may indicate* a grammatical variant
**Objectless** Intransitive
**Objet d'art** Curio
**Oblate, Oblation** Gift, Monk, Offering, Offertory, Prothesis, Sacrifice
**Oblige(d), Obliging, Obligate, Obligation, Obligatory** Accommodate, Affable, Amiable, Behold, Binding, Bound, Burden, Charge, Coerce, Compel, Complaisant, Compliant, Constrain, Constraint, Contract, Corvée, Debt, Default, De rigueur, Duty(-bound),

Easy, Easygoing, Encumbent, Force, Giri, Gratify, Impel, Incumbent, IOU, Mandatory, Must, Necessitate, Needed, Novation, Obruk, Obstriction, Onus, Peremptory, Promise, Recognisance, Responsibility, Sonties, Synallagmatic, Tie, Wattle

**Oblique(ly)** Askance, Askew, Asklent, Asquint, Athwart, Awry, Cross, Diagonal, Glance, Glancing, Indirect, Kitty-cornered, Perverse, Plagio-, Separatrix, Sidelong, Skew, Skewwhiff, Slanting, Solidus, Squint, Virgule

▷**Oblique** *may indicate* an anagram

**Obliterate(d)** Annul, Black out, Blot, Dele(te), Destroy, Efface, Eradicate, Expunge, Exterminate, Rase, Rast, Raze, Wash away, Wipe, Zap

**Oblivion, Oblivious** Forgetful, Lethe, Limbo, Nirvana, Obscurity, Silence, Unaware

**Oblong** Rectangular

**Obloquy** Opprobrium

**Obnoxious** Eyesore, Foul, Horrid, Offensive, Pestilent, Repellent, Repugnant, Septic, Sod, Unpleasant, Wart

**Oboe** Piffero

**Obscene(ly), Obscenity** Bawdy, Blue, Coprolalia, Coprology, Fescennine, Filth, Gross, Hard-core, Impure, Indecent, Lewd, Lubricious, Paw(paw), Porn(o), Profane, Raunchy, Ribald, Salacious, Scatology, Smut, Soft-core, Swear word, Vulgar

**Obscure, Obscurity** Abstruse, Anheires, Arcane, Becloud, Bedim, Befog, Black out, Blear, Blend, Blot out, Blur, Break, Cloud, Cobweb, Conceal, Cover, Cryptic, Darken, Deep, Depth, Dim, Disguise, Eclipse, Elliptic, Encrypt, Engloom, Envelop, Esoteric, Filmy, Fog, Hermetic, Hide, Indistinct, Inky, Jude, Mantle, Mist, Murk, Mysterious, Mystic(al), Nebular, Night, Nubecula, Obfuscate, Obnubilate, Opaque, Oracular, Overcloud, Overshade, Overshadow, Recherché, Recondite, Shadowy, Tenebrific, Twilit, Unclear, Unobvious, → **VAGUE**, Veil, Vele, Wrap

▷**Obscure(d)** *may indicate* an anagram

**Obsequious(ness)** Bootlicker, Brown nose, Crawler, Creeping Jesus, Fawn, Fulsome, Grovelling, Heep, Kowtowing, Menial, Oily, Parasitic, Pig, Servile, Slavish, Sleeveen, Slimy, Smarmy, Spaniel, Subservient, Suck-hole, Suck up, Sycophantic, Tantony, Toady

**Observance, Observant, Observation** Adherence, Alert, Aphorism, Attention, Comment, Custom, Earth, Empirical, Espial, Experience, Eyeful, Eyesight, Formality, Hawk-eyed, Holy, Honour, Hour-angle, Inkhorn, Lectisternium, Mass, → **NOTICE**, Obiter dicta, Perceptive, Percipient, Practice, Quip, Ready-eyed, Recce, Remark, Right, Rite, Ritual, Use, Vising

**Observatory** Arecibo, Atalaya, Greenwich, Herstmonceux, Hide, Hurstmonceux, Jodrell Bank, Lookout, Mount Palomar, Tower

**Observe(d), Observer** Behold, Bystander, Celebrate, Commentator, Describe, Detect, Espy, Eye, Eyeball, Fly-on-the-wall, Heed, Keep, Mark, Monitor, NB, Nota bene, Note, Notice, Obey, Onlooker, Optic, Pharisee, Regard(er), Remark, Rite, Scry, See, Seer, Sight, Spectator, Spial, Spie, Spot, Spy, Study, Surveillance, Take, Twig, View, Vigilance, Voyeur, Watch, Witness

**Obsess(ed), Obsession(al), Obsessive** Addict, Anal, Anorak, Besot, Bug, Bugbear, Complex, Craze, Dominate, En tete, Fetish, Fixation, Hang-up, Haunt, Hobbyhorse, Hooked, Idée fixe, Infatuation, Mania, Monomania, Necrophilia, Nerd, Neurotic, One-track, Paranoic, Preoccupy, Smitten, Thing, Wonk

**Obsidian** Pe(a)rlite

**Obsolete, Obsolescence, Obsolescent** Abandoned, Antique, Archaic, Built-in, Dated, Dead, Defunct, Disused, Extinct, Latescent, Obs, Outdated, Outworn, Passé, Planned, Unfashionable

**Obstacle** Barrage, Barricade, Barrier, Boyg, Cheval de frise, Chicane, Clog, Dam, Drag, Dragon's teeth, Drawback, Gate, Handicap, Hazard, Hindrance, Hitch, Hurdle, Node, Oxer, Remora, Rock, Rub, Sandbank, Snag, Stimie, Stumbling-block, Stymie, Tank-trap

**Obstetrics** Gynaecology, Midwifery, Tocology, Tokology

**Obstinacy, Obstinate** Asinine, Bigoted, Bitter-ender, Buckie, Bullheaded, Bullish, Contrarian, Contumacious, Cussed, Die-hard, Dour, Entêté, Froward, Headstrong, Hidebound, High-stomached, Inflexible, Intractable, Intransigent, Mule, Persistent,

Perverse, Pervicacious, Piggish, Pig-headed, Recalcitrant, Refractory, Restive, Rigid, Rusty, Self-will, Stiff(-necked), Stoor, Stour, Strure, Stubborn, Thraward, Thrawart, Wilful, Wrong-headed

**Obstreperous** Defiant, Noisy, Stroppy, Truculent, Undisciplined, Unruly

**Obstruct(ion), Obstructive** Airlock, Bar, Barricade, Barrier, Block, Bottleneck, Caltrop, Chicane, Clog, Congest, Crab, Cross, Cumber, Dam, Delay, Derail, Embolus, Fil(l)ibuster, Gridlock, Hamper, Hand-off, Hedge, Hinder, Hurdle, Ileus, Impede, Intercept, Let, Obstacle, Occlude, Oppose, Resist(ance), Sab(otage), Sandbag, Snarl-up, Snooker, Stall, Stap, Stonewall, Stop, Stymie, Sudd, Thwart, Trammel, Traverse, Trump, Unhelpful

**Obtain** Achieve, Acquire, Borrow, Buy, Cop, Derive, Exist, Gain, Get, Glean, Impetrate, Land, Outsource, Pan, Prevail, Procure, Realise, Reign, Secure, Source, Succeed, Wangle, Win

**Obtrude, Obtruding, Obtrusive** Expel, Impose, King Charles' head, Loud, Prominent, Push, Sorn, Thrust

**Obtuse** Angle, Blunt, Dense, Dull, Purblind, Stolid, Stupid, Thick

**Obverse, Obversion** Complement, Cross, Equipollence, Face, Front, Head, Permutation

**Obviate** Forestall, Preclude, Prevent

**Obvious** Apparent, Axiom, Bald, Blatant, Broad, Brobdingnag, Clear, Conspicuous, Distinct, Evident, Flagrant, Frank, Glaring, Inescapable, Kenspeck(le), Manifest, Marked, Needless, No-brainer, Open(ness), Open and shut, Overt, Palpable, Patent, Pikestaff, Plain, Pronounced, Salient, Self-evident, Staring, Stark, Transparent, Truism, Unsubtle, Visible, Writ large

**Occasion** Call, Cause, Ceremony, Do, Encheason, Engender, Event, Fête, Field day, Nonce, → **OPPORTUNITY**, Reason, Red-letter day, Ride, Sometime, Tide, Time, Treat, Whet

**Occasional(ly)** At times, Black tie, Casual, Cause, Chance, Daimen, Day, Episode, Ever and anon, Instance, Intermittent, Irregular, Lawful, Motive, Odd, Orra, Periodic, Scattered, Seldom, Social, Sometimes, Sporadic, While, White tie

**Occident(al)** West, Western(er)

**Occlude, Occlusion** Absorb, Clog, Coronary, Embolism, Obstruct

**Occult(ist)** Angekkok, Arcane, Art, Esoteric, Gnostic, I-Ching, Magic, Mysterious, Mystic, Paranormal, Psychic, Supernatural

**Occupant, Occupation, Occupy(ing)** Absorb, Acquire, Activity, Amuse, Avocation, Beset, Business, Busy, Career, Denizen, Dwell, Embusy, Employ, Engage, Engross, Fill, Hold, In, Incumbent, Indwell, Inhabitant, Inmate, Invade, Involve, Line, Man, Métier, Obsess, Overrun, People, Possess, Profession, Pursuit, Reserved, Residency, Resident, Runrig, Scrimshandy, Sideline, Sit-in, Squat, Stay, Take, Tenancy, Tenant, Tenure, Thrift, Trade, Upon, Use, Vocation, Walk of life

**Occur(rence)** Arise, Be, Betide, Betime, Case, Contingency, Crop up, Event, Eventuate, Fall, Happen, Incident, Instance, Outbreak, Outcrop, Pass, Phenomenon, Transpire

**Ocean(ic), Oceania** Abundance, Abyssal, Antarctic, Arctic, Atlantic, Blue, Deep, German, Hadal, Herring-pond, High seas, Indian, Melanesia, Micronesia, Millpond, Pacific, Panthalassa, Pelagic, Polynesia, Pond, Sea(way), Southern, Thalassic, Waves, Western

**Och aye** Troggs

**Ochre** Burnt, Keel, Lemnian ruddle, Rubric, Ruddle, Sienna

**Octave** Crown, Diapason, Diminished, Eight, Great, Ottava, Perfect, Small, Utas

**Octopus** Blue-ringed, Cephalopod, Cuero, Devilfish, Paper nautilus, Polyact, Polyp, Poulp(e), Scuttle, Squid

**Od** Energy, Force

**Odd (person), Oddity, Odds** Aberrant, Abnormal, Amiss, Anomaly, Bizarre, Card, Cure, Curio, Curious, Droll, Eccentric, Eery, Erratic, Fishy, Freaky, Gink, Gonzo, Impair, Imparity, Jimjam, Misfit, Offbeat, Original, Orra, Outré, Paradox, Parity, Peculiar, Queer, Quirky, Quiz, Random, Rare, Remote, Rum, Screwball, Singular, Spooky, → **STRANGE**, Unequal, Uneven, Unmatched, Unpaired, Unusual, Weird, Whims(e)y, Zany

▷**Odd(s)** *may indicate* an anagram or the odd letters in words

**Oddball, Oddperson** Ditz, Weirdo

**Oddfellow** OF

**Odd job man** Joey, Loppy, Orraman, Rouster, Smoot, Thronner

**Odds, Oddments** Bits, Carpet, Chance, Fixed, Gubbins, Handicap, Line, Long, Price, Remainder, Short, SP, Tails, Variance

**Ode** Awdl, Dit, Epicede, Epicedium, Epinicion, Epinikion, Genethliacon, Horatian, Hymn, Lay, Lyric, Monody, Paeon, Pindaric, Poem, Sapphic, Song, Stasimon, Strophe, Threne, Threnody, Verse

**Odin** One-eyed, Woden

**Odium, Odious** Comparison, Disestimation, Disgrace, Foul, Hatred, Heinous, Invidious, Ponce, Repellent, Repugnant, Stigma

**Odorous, Odour** Air, Aroma, Bad, BO, Flavour, Funk, Good, Hum, Musk, Opopanax, Perfume, Quality, Redolence, Sanctity, Scent, Smell, Stench, Waff, Waft, Whiff

**Odourless** Silent

**Odysseus** Ulysses

**Odyssey** Epic, Journey, Wandering

**Oedipus, Oedipal** Complex, Laius, Parricide

**Oeillade** Glance, Leer, Ogle, Wink

**Oesophagus** Crop, Gullet

**Oestrogen, Oestrus** Daidzein, Frenzy, Genistein®, Heat, Isoflavone, Mestranol, Must, Rut, Stilb(o)estrol

**Of (me)** About, Among, Aus, By, De, From, In, My, Re

▷**Of** *may indicate* an anagram

**Of course** Certainly, Natch, Yes

**Off** Absent, Agee, Ajee, Away, AWOL, Discount, Distance, Far, From, High, Inexact, Licence, Odd, Putrescent, Rancid, Reasty, Reesty, Relâche, Rotten, Start

▷**Off** *may indicate* an anagram

**Offal** Cagmag, Carrion, Chidlings, Chitterling, Entrails, Fry, Giblets, Gralloch, Gurry, Haggis, Ha(r)slet, Heart, Innards, Kidney, Lamb's fry, Lights, Liver, Numbles, Pig's fry, Pluck, Sweetbread, Tripe, Variety meat

**Off-beat** Zoppo

**Off-colour** Pale, Seedy, Wan

▷**Off-colour** *may indicate* an anagram

**Off-cut** Oddment, Shaving

**Offence** Affront, Attack, Capital, Crime, Delict, Delinquency, Demerit, Distaste, Fault, Huff, Hurt, Indictable, Lapse, Lese-humanity, Lese-liberty, Lese majesty, Malfeasance, Miff, Misdemeanour, Misprision, Odium, Outrage, Peccadillo, Perjury, Pip, Pique, Piracy, Praemunire, Ramp, Regrate, Sedition, → **SIN**, Summary, Traffic, Trespass, Umbrage, Violation

**Offend(ed), Offender** Affront, Anger, Annoy, Boobhead, Bridles, Criminal, Culprit, Default, Delinquent, Disoblige, Displease, Distaste, Felon, Hip, Huff, Hurt, Hyp, Infringe, Inveigh, Lawbreaker, Miffy, Miscreant, Nettle, Nonce, Nuisance, Outrage, Peeve, Perp(etrate), Provoke, Serial, Shock-jock, Sin(ner), Sledge, Sting, Stray, Sus, Touchy, Transgress, Twoccer, Umbrage, Violate, Wrongdoer

**Offensive(ness)** Affront, Aggressive, Alien, Attack, Bombardment, Campaign, Charge, Charm, Cruel, Derisatory, Derogatory, Detestable, Dysphemism, Embracery, Euphemism, Execrable, Eyesore, Forbidding, Foul, Gobby, Halitosis, Hedgehog, Hedgepig, Indecent, Indelicate, Inroad, Insulting, Invidious, Loathsome, Miasmic, Nasty, Noisome, Obnoxious, Obscene, Odious, Peccant, Personal, Pungent, Push, Putrid, Rank, Repugnant, → **RUDE**, Scandalous, Scurrilous, Sortie, Storm, Ugly, Unbecoming, Unsavoury, War

**Offer(ing)** Alms, Altarage, Anaphora, Approach, Bargain, Bid, Bode, Bouchée, Bribe, Cadeau, Corban, Deal, Deodate, Dolly, Donation, Entice, Epanophora, Extend, Ex voto, Gift, Give, Godfather, Heave, Hold, Inferiae, Introduce, Invitation, IPO, Libation, Oblation, Overture, Peace, Peddle, Plead, Pose, Potla(t)ch, Present, Propine, → **PROPOSE**, Propound, Sacrifice, Shewbread, Shore, Special, S(h)raddha, Stamp, Stand, Submit, Suggestion, Tempting, Tender, Utter, Vend, Volunteer, Votive, Wave, Xenium

**Off-guard** Caught napping

**Offhand** Airy, Banana, Blasé, Brevi manu, Brusque, Casual, Cavalier, Currente calamo, Curt, Extempore, Flippant, Impromptu, Indifferent, Snappy

**Office(s)** Abbacy, Agency, Assay, Bedelship, Benefice, Block, Booking, Box, Branch, Broo, Bucket shop, Bureau, Buroo, Caliphate, Chair, Chancellory, Chancery, Circumlocution, Clerical, Colonial, Commonwealth, Complin(e), Consulate, Crown, Cube farm, Cutcher(r)y, Daftar, Dataria, Dead-letter, Deanery, Decemvirate, Den, Desk, Divine, Dogate, Drostdy, Employment, Evensong, Foreign, Front, Function, Grand Penitentiary, Headquarters, Holy, Home, Incumbency, Job, Land, Last, Lav(atory), Left luggage, Lieutenancy, Little, Little hours, Liturgy, Loan, Loo, Lost property, Mayoralty, Met(eorological), Ministry, Missa, Mistery, Mudiria, Mutessarifat, Mystery, Nocturn, Nones, Obit, Oval, Palatinate, Papacy, Paper, Patent, Patriarchate, Penitentiary, Personnel, Petty Bag, Pipe, Place, Plum, Portfolio, Position, Post, Prefecture, Prelacy, Press, Prime, Printing, Priorate, Provosty, Record, Regency, Register, Registry, Rite, Satrapy, Scottish, Secretarial, Secretariat, See, Seraskierate, Sext, Shogunate, Sinecure, Situation, Sorting, Speaker(ship), Stamp, Stationery, Sultanate, Tariff, Tenebrae, Terce, Tiara, Ticket, Tierce, Toilet, Tol(l)booth, Tribunate, Vespers, Vicary, War, Woolsack, Work station, Yamen

**Officer(s)** Branch, Church, Compliance, Counter-round, Customs, Dog's body, Duty, Enforcement, Engineer, Executive, Field, First, Flag, Flying, Gal(l)ant, Gazetted, Group, Incumbent, Liaison, Medical, Non-commissioned, Nursing, Orderly, Peace, Petty, PO, Police, Presiding, Press, Prison, Probation, Radio, Relieving, Returning, Rodent, Safety, Scene-of-crime, Staff, Treasurer, Wardroom, Warrant, Watch

---

## OFFICERS

***2 letters:***
Lt
SL
SM

***3 letters:***
Aga
CEO
Cop
Gen
GOC
NCO
Sub

***4 letters:***
Agha
Aide
Bosn
Capt
CIGS
Exon
Imam
Mate

***5 letters:***
Blimp
Bosun
Druid
Gager
Imaum
Janty
Jonty
Jurat
Macer
Major
Pacha
Pasha
Pilot
Posse
Sewer

***6 letters:***
Acater
Beadle
Beatty
Copper
Cornet
Datary
Deacon
Ensign
Gauger
Guidon
Gunner
Hetman
Jaunty
Lictor
Master
Purser
Pusser
Rector
Rosser
Sbirro
Schout
Serang
Sexton
Tindal
Varlet
Warden
Warder
Yeoman

***7 letters:***
Admiral
Agistor
Bailiff
Blue Rod
Captain
Colonel
Co-pilot
Coroner
Darogha
Dragoon
Equerry
Filacer
Filazer
General
Hayward
Jamadar
Jauntie
Jemadar
Jemidar
Marshal
Pantler
Prefect
Proctor
Provost
Redcoat
Samurai
Sea Lord
Sheriff
Skipper
Speaker
Striper
Subadar
Tribune

***8 letters:***
Adjutant
Alguazil
Bimbashi
Black Rod
Brass-hat
Cursitor
Decurion
Familiar
Gendarme
Havildar
Hog-reeve
Palatine
Phylarch
Subahdar
Tipstaff
Woodward

***9 letters:***
Ale-conner
Apparitor
Brigadier
Catchpole
Catchpoll
Cellarist
Centurion
Commander
Commissar
Commodore
Constable

Exciseman
First mate
Inspector
Messenger
Moderator
Number one
Pipe major
President
Prorector
Select-man
Subaltern
Tahsildar
Tarpaulin
Waldgrave

*10 letters:*
Aide de camp
Air-marshal
Bluebottle
Bombardier
Bumbailiff
Chancellor
Chief Petty
Pursuivant
Second mate
Securocrat
Subchanter
Supercargo
Tidewaiter

*11 letters:*
Beach-master
Chamberlain
Coast-waiter
Earl Marshal
Grand Vizier
Infirmarian
Silver-stick

*12 letters:*
Bound-Bailiff
Commissioned
Commissioner
Field Marshal
Group captain
Hog-constable
Remembrancer

*13 letters:*
Drill-sergeant
Lance-sergeant
Quartermaster
Sailing master
Sergeant-major
Staff-sergeant
Sublieutenant

*14 letters:*
Air vice-marshal
Provost-marshal
Superintendent

*15 letters:*
Attorney General
Lord High Steward

*16 letters:*
Procurator fiscal

*17 letters:*
Official Solicitor

*21 letters:*
Quartermaster-sergeant

---

**Office-worker** Clerk, Peon, Temp, Typist

**Official(s), Officiate, Officious** Administrator, Aga, Agent, Aleconner, Amban, Amtman, Apparatchik, Atabeg, Atabek, Attaché, Authorised, Bailiff, Beadle(dom), Borough-reeve, Bossy, Bumble, Bureaucrat, Catchpole, Censor, Chair, Chamberlain, Chancellor, Chinovnik, Claviger, Commissar, Commissioner, Comptroller, Consul, Convenor, Coroner, Count, Count palatine, Courtier, Curator, Datary, Dean, Dignitary, Diplomat, Dockmaster, Dogberry, Ealdorman, Effendi, Ephor, Equerry, Escheater, Eurocrat, Executive, Executor, Factotum, Fonctionnaire, → FORMAL, Fourth, Functionary, Gauleiter, Governor, Gymnasiarch, Handicapper, Hayward, Hazzan, Incumbent, Inspector, Intendant, Jack-in-office, Jobsworth, Keeper, Landdrost, Lictor, Lifeguard, Line judge, Linesman, Macebearer, Macer, Major domo, Mandarin, Marplot, Marshal, Mayor, MC, Meddlesome, Mirza, Mueddin, Muezzin, Mukhtar, Nazir, Notary, Notary public, Ombudsman, Omlah, Overbusy, Palatine, Panjandrum, Paymaster, Placeman, Pleaseman, Plenipotentiary, Polemarch, Pontificate, Poohbah, Postmaster, Postulator, Praefect, Pragmatic, Prefect, Proconsul, Proctor, Procurator, Proggins, Proveditor, Provedor(e), Providor, Provost, Purveyor, Ranger, Receiver, Recorder, Reeve, Ref(eree), Régisseur, Registrar, Remembrancer, Sachem, Scrutineer, Secretary, Shammash, Shammes, Sherpa, Silentiary, Souldan, Spoffish, Stadtholder, Staff, Standard, Steward, Subdean, Suffete, Suit, Summoner, Superserviceable, Surveyor, Syndic, Timekeeper, Tipstaff, Top Brass, Touch judge, Tribune, Trier, Trior, Triumvir, Turncock, Umpire, Usher, Valid, Valuer General, Veep, Verderer, Verger, Vicar-general, Viscount, Vizier, Walla(h), Whiffler, Whip, Woodward, Yamen, Yeoman

**Offing** Imminent

**Off-key** Flat

**Off-limit(s)** Prohibited

**Off-load** Dump, Shed, Unship

**Offprint** Separate, Separation, Tirage a part

**Off-putting** Deferrable, Dehortative, Discouraging, Mañana, Negative, Procrastination, Rebarbative, Red herring, Repellent, Yips

**Offset** Balance, Cancel, Compensate, Counter(act), Counterbalance, Defray, Neutralise

**Offshoot** Bough, Branch, Cion, Limb, Lye, Member, Outgrowth, Plant, Scion, Sien, Sient, Swarm, Syen

**Offshore** Isle

**Offspring** Boy, Brood, Burd, Chick, Children, Daughter, Descendant, Family, Fruit, Fry, Get, Girl, Heir, Litter, Procreation, Product, Progeny, Seed, Sient, Son, Spawn, Whelp

**Offstage** Wings

**Off-the-cuff** Ad lib, Improv(isation)

**Off-white** Bone, Cream, Ecru
**Often** Frequent, Habitual, Regularly, Repeated
▹**Often** *may indicate* 'of ten'
**Ogee** Cyma, Moulding, Talon
**Ogle** Astare, Drake, Eliad, Eye, Gawk, Glad eye, Glance, Leer, Oeillade, Wodewose
**Ogre(ss)** Baba Yaga, Boyg, Brute, Eten, Etten, Fiend, Giant, Monster, Orc, Shrek
**Ohio** Buckeye
**Oik** Boor
**Oil(s), Oily, Oil producer** Anele, Anoint, Balm, Beech, Bito, Black gold, Bribe, Castrol®, Crab, Crude, Derv, Diesel, Drying, Essence, Essential, Ethereal, Fatty, Fish, Fixed, Frying, Fuel, Good, Grease, Hair, Heavy, Illupi, Joint, Kerogen, Lamp, Landscape, Lanolin, Lipid, Long, Lube, Lubricant, Macaw-tree, Midnight, Mineral, Monkey nut, Monounsaturated, Multigrade, Oint, Oleaginous, Pellitory, Polyunsaturated, Pomade, Residual, Seed, Short, Sleek, Slick, Smalmy, Smarmy, Smeary, Sweet, Topped crude, Turps, Unction, Zest

---

**OIL PRODUCERS**

*2 letters:*
BP®

*3 letters:*
Ben
Emu
Gas
Nim
Nut

*4 letters:*
Baby
Bath
Bone
Cade
Coal
Corn
Musk
Nard
Neem
Nimb
Oleo
Otto
Palm
Poon
Rape
Rock
Rose
Rusa
Slum
Tall
Tolu
Tung
Wood
Wool
Yolk

*5 letters:*
Ajwan
Argan
Attar
Benne
Benni
Clove
Colza
Copra
Fusel
Grass
Maize
Niger
Olein
Olive
Ottar
Poppy
Pulza
Rosin
Savin
Sebum
Shale
Shark
Snake
Sperm
Spike
Stand
Thyme
Train
Ulyie
Ulzie
Whale

*6 letters:*
Ajowan
Almond
Balsam
Banana
Butter
Canola
Carapa
Carron
Castor
Chrism
Cineol
Cloves
Cohune
Croton
Elaeis
Illipe
Jojoba
Magilp
Megilp
Monola®
Neroli
Oleine
Peanut
Ramtil
Savine
Semsem
Seneca
Sesame
Shamoy
Tallow
Virgin
Walnut

*7 letters:*
Aniline
Apiezon®
Arachis
Bittern
Cajeput
Cajuput
Camphor
Cineole
Coconut
Dittany
Eugenol
Gingili
Jinjili
Linalol
Linseed
Lumbang
Menthol
Mirbane
Moringa
Mustard
Myrbane
Myrrhol
Naphtha
Picamar
Pyrrole
Retinol
Ricinus
Rocktar
Saffron
Safrole
Spindle
Verbena
Vitriol
Wallaba

*8 letters:*
Bergamot
Camphire
Cod-liver
Creasote
Creosote
Flaxseed
Gingelli
Gingelly
Hazelnut
Hempseed
Kerosene
Kerosine
Lavender
Linalool
Macassar

North Sea
Oiticica
Pachouli
Paraffin
Photogen
Pristane
Rapeseed
Rosewood
Volatile

*9 letters:*
Aleuritis
Beech-mast
Candlenut
Carvacrol
Eleoptene
Golomynka
Grapeseed
Groundnut
Neat's-foot
Parathion
Patchouli
Patchouly
Petroleum
Photogene
Quinoline
Safflower
Sassafras
Spearmint
Spikenard
Star-anise
Sunflower
Terpineol
Vanaspati
Vegetable

*10 letters:*
Chaulmugra
Citronella
Cotton-seed
Elaeoptene
Eucalyptus
Guttiferae
Juniper tar
Peppermint
Petit grain
Sandalwood
Turpentine
Ylang-ylang

*11 letters:*
Camphorated
Chaulmoogra
Chinese wood
Extra virgin
Stearoptene
Wintergreen

*12 letters:*
Benzaldehyde
Benzonitrile
Brilliantine
Hungary water

*14 letters:*
Glutaraldehyde
Parnassus grass

*15 letters:*
Evening primrose

---

**Oilcake** Poonac
**Oilcan** Pourie
**Oilcloth** American, Lino
**Oilman** Driller, Prospector, Rigger, Texan
**Oil painting** Master, Titian
**Ointment** Arnica, Balm, Basilicon, Boracic, Boric, Cerate, Collyrium, Cream, Liniment, Lipsalve, Lotion, Nard, Pomade, Pomatum, Rub, Salve, Spikenard, Theriac, Tiger balm®, Unction, Unguent, Vaseline®, Zinc
**OK** Agree(d), All right, Appropriate, Approve, Authorise, Clearance, Copacetic, Copesettic, Fine, Go-head, Green light, Hunky-dory, Initial, Kosher, Legitimate, Mooi, No sweat, Not bad, Pass, Permissible, Respectable, Right(o), Roger, Sanction, Sound, U, Vet
**Okra** Bhindi, Gumbo, Lady's fingers
**Old(er), Oldest, Oldie** Ae(t), Aged, Aine(e), Ancient, Antique, Auld, Bean, Bygone, Decrepit, Dutch, Earlier, Elderly, Ex, Fogram, Former, Fossil, Gaffer, Geriatric, Glory, Golden, Gray, Grey, Hills, Hoary, Immemorial, Major, Mature, Methusaleh, Moore, Nestor, Nick, O, OAP, Obsolete, Off, Ogygian, One-time, Original, Outworn, Palae-, Passé, Primeval, Retro, Ripe, Rugose, Sen(escent), Senile, Senior, Shot, Signeur, Stager, Stale, Superannuated, Trite, Venerable, Veteran, Victorian(a), Worn
**Old boy, Old girl** Alumnae, Alumnus, Fossil, OB
**Old days** Once, Past, Yore
**Old English** OE
**Old-fashioned** Aging, Ancient, Antediluvian, Antwackie, Arch(aic), Arriéré, Back number, Bygone, Corn(y), Dated, Dodo, Dowdy, Dusty, Fogey, Fuddy-duddy, Fusty, Hidebound, Medieval, Museum piece, Neanderthal, No tech, Obsolete, Ogygian, Oldfangled, Outdated, Outmoded, Outre, Outworn, Passé, Podunk, Primeval, Quaint, Relic, Retro, Rinky-dink, Schmaltzy, Shot, Square, Square-toes, Staid, Steam, Stick-in-the-mud, Traditional, Uncool, Victorian, Vieux jeu, Vintage, Worm-eaten
**Old-hand** Stager
**Old hat** Clichéd, Outmoded
**Old maid** Biddy, Spinster
**Old man, Old woman** Anile, Aunty, Bodach, Buda, Budi, Burd, Cailleach, Carlin(e), Cicerone, Codger, Coniston, Crinkly, Crone, Crow, Crumbly, Faggot, Fantad, Fantod, Fogey, Fogramite, Fogy, Fussy, Gammer, Geezer, Gramps, Grandam, Grannam, Greybeard, Greyhen, Husband, Kangaroo, Koro, Kuia, Luckie, Lucky, Ma, Matriarch, Methuselah, Mort, Mzee, OAP, Oom, Pa, Pantaloon, Patriarch, Presbyte, Roo, Rudas, Southernwood, Tante, Tripod, Trot, Trout, Whitebeard, Wife, Wight, Woopie, Wrinkly
**Old-timer** Hourglass, Sundial, Veteran

**Oleander** Nerium, Rhododaphne
**Olid** Fetid, Foul, High, Rancid, Rank
**Olio** Hash, Medley, Mess, Potpourri, Stew
**Olive (grove), Olivine** Beef, Calamata, Cerulein, Drupe, Dunite, Elaeagnus, Forsterite, Gethsemane, Green, Kalamata, Lilac, Olea(ster), Peridot, Queen, Russian
**Oliver** Bath, Chef, Cromwell, Goldsmith, Hardy, Noll, Protector, Twist
**Olympian, Olympics, Olympus** Artemis, Asgard, Athlete, Celestial, Coe, Demeter, Elis, Hera, Pantheon, Quadrennium, Summer, Winter, Zeus
**Ombudsman** Trouble shooter, Watchdog
**Omelette** Crêpe, Foo yong, Foo yung, Frittata, Fu yung, Pancake, Spanish, Tortilla
**Omen** Abodement, Absit, Augury, Auspice, Foreboding, Forewarning, Freet, Freit, Portent, Presage, Prodrome, Sign, Token, Warning
**Omentum** Caul, Epiploon
**Ominous** Alarming, Baleful, Bodeful, Dire, Dour, Forbidding, Grim, Inauspicious, Menacing, Oracular, Portentous, Sinister, Threatening, Ugly
**Omission, Omit** Aph(a)eresis, Apocope, Apospory, Apostrophe, Asyndeton, Caret, Disregard, Drop, Elide, Elision, Ellipse, Ellipsis, Exception, Failure, Haplography, Haplology, Lipography, Loophole, Miss, Neglect, Nonfeasance, Non-user, Oversight, Paral(e)ipomenon, Pass, Pretermit, Senza, Skip, Slip
**Omnibus** Anthology, Coach, Collection
**Omnipresent** Ubiquitous
**Omniscient, Omniscience** Aware, Encyclopedia, Pansophy
**Omnivorous** Pantophagous
**On (it)** Aboard, About, Agreed, Alight, An, An't, At, Atop, By, Game, Gaun, Going, Half-cut, In, Leg, O', Of, Oiled, Over, Pon, Re, Running, Tipsy, Up(on), Viable
▷**On** *may indicate* an anagram
**On account of** Over
▷**On board** *may indicate* chess, draughts, or 'SS' around another word
**Once(r)** Ance, As was, → AT ONCE, Bradbury, Earst, Erst(while), Ever, Ex, Fore, Former, Hapax legomenon, Jadis, Oner, Onst, Secular, Sole, Sometime, Whilom
**One(self)** A, Ace, Ae, Alike, An(e), Any, Body, Cardinal, Chosen, Digit, Eeny, Ego, Ein, Formula, I, Individual, Integer, Kelly's eye, Lunchtime, Me, Monad, Per se, Person, Single(ton), Singular, Solo, Tane, Un, Unify, Unit(y), Unitary, United, Us, We, Yin, You
**One-act-er** Playlet
**One-dimensional** Linear
**One-eared** Monaural
**One-eyed** Arimasp(ian), Cyclops
**One-man band** Moke
**One o'clock** 1 am, NNE
**One-off** Ad hoc, Sui generis
**One-rayed** Monact
**Onerous** Arduous, Exacting, Taxing, Tedious, Weighty
**One-sided** Partisan, Unfair
**One-time** Erstwhile
**Ongoing** Continual
**On guard** Excubant
**Onion(s)** Allium, Bengi, Bonce, Bulb, Chibol, Chive, Cibol, Cive, Eschalot, Green, Head, Ingan, Jibbons, Leek, Lyonnaise, Moly, Pate, Pearl, Ramp, Ramson, Rocambole, Ropes, Scallion, Scilla, Shal(l)ot, Soubise, Spanish, Spring, Squill, Sybo(e), Sybow, Tree, Welsh
**Online** Dot com, E, Vlogging
**Onlooker** Beholder, Bottle-holder, Bystander, Kibitzer, Observer, Rubberneck, Spectator, Witness
**Only** Allenarly, Anerly, But, Except, Just, Meer, Merely, Nobbut, One, Seul, Singly, Sole, Sommer, Unique
**Onset** Affret, Attack, Beginning, Charge, Dash, Ending, Rush, → START, Thrust
**Onslaught** Attack, Barrage, Cannonade, Dead-set, Diatribe, Onset, Raid, Spreagh, Storm, Swoop

**On the way** Agate
**On this side** Cis
**On time** Pat, Prompt, Punctual
**Onus** Burden, Charge, → DUTY, Responsibility
**Onward** Advance, Ahead, Away, Forth, Forward, Progress
**Oodles** Heaps, Lashings, Lots, Slather
**Oolite** Peastone, Pisolite, Roestone
**Oomph** Energy, It, SA, Sexiness, Verve
**Ooze, Oozy** Dowl, Drip, Exhale, Exude, Gleet, Globigerena, Ichorous, Mud, Percolate, Pteropod(a), Radiolarian, Seep, Sew, Sipe, Slime, Slob, Spew, Spue, Sweat, Sype, Transude, Uliginose, Uliginous
**Opal(escent)** Black, Cymophanous, Fire, Gem, Girasol, Girosol, Hyalite, Hydrophane, Liver, Menilite, Noble, Potch, Wood
**Opaque, Opacity** Cloudy, Dense, Dull, Intense, Leucoma, Milky, Obscure, Obtuse, Onycha, Onyx, Roil, Thick, Turbid
**Open(er), Opening, Openness** Above board, Adit, Aedicule, Agape, Airhole, Ajar, Anthesis, Anus, Apert(ure), Apparent, Apse, Arch, Armhole, Autopsy, Bald, Bare, Bat, Bay, Begin, Bole, Breach, Break, Broach, Broad, Buttonhole, Candid, Candour, Cardia, Cavity, Champaign, Chance, Chasm, Chink, Circumscissile, Clear, Coamings, Crack, Cranny, Crevasse, Crevice, Crowbar, Curtain-raiser, Dehisce, Deploy, Dilate, Dispark, Door(way), Drawbridge, Dup, Embrasure, Exordium, Expansive, Explicit, Eyelet, Fair, Fenestra, Fissure, Fistula, Flue, Fontanel(le), Foramen, Frank, Free, Free-for-all, Fumarole, Funnel, Gambit, Gap, Gaping, Gash, Gat, Gate, Gateway, Give, Glasnost, Glottis, Guichet, Gullwing, Hagioscope, Hatch, Hatchback, Hatchway, Hiatus, Hilus, → HOLE, Ice-breaker, Inaugural, Initial, Intake, Interstice, Intro, Key, Kisser, Knothole, Lacy, Lamp hole, Lance, Latchkey, Lead, Loid, Loophole, Loose, Machicolation, Manhole, Meatus, Micropyle, Mofette, Moongate, Mouth, Naked, Nare, Natural, Niche, Nook, Obvious, Oillet, Orifice, Os, Oscule, Osculum, Ostiole, Ostium, Ouvert, Overt, Overture, Pandora, Paper knife, Passe partout, Pass key, Patent, Peephole, Persuadable, Pert, Pervious, Pick(lock), Pit, Placket, Plain, Plughole, Pop, Pore, Port(age), Porta, Porthole, Preamble, Preliminary, Premiere, Prise, Pro-am, Public, Pylorus, Receptive, Relaxed, Rent, Ring-pull, Riva, Room, Sallyport, Scuttle, Scye, Sesame, Sicilian, Sincere, Slit, Slot, Spare, Spiracle, Spirant, Squint, Start, Stenopaic, Stokehole, Stoma, Stulm, Suasible, Syrinx, Thereout, Thirl, Touchhole, Transparent, Trapdoor, Trema, Trochlea, Trou, Truthful, Unbar, Unbolt, Unbutton, Uncap, Unclasp, Uncope, Uncork, Undo, Unfold, Unfurl, Unhasp, Unlatch, Unreserved, Unscrew, Unstop, Unsubtle, Untie, Unwrap, Unzip, Upfront, Vacancy, Vent, Vulnerable, Wide, Window, Yawning
**Open air** Alfresco, Sub divo, Sub Jove
**Opera(tic), Opera house, Operetta** Aida, Ariadne, Atalanta, Ballad, Barber of Seville, Boris Godunov, Bouffe, Buffo, Burletta, Carmen, Comic, Comique, Das Rheingold, Der Rosenkavalier, Die Fledermaus, Die Walküre, Don Carlos, Don Giovanni, Dramma giocoso, Electra, ENO, Ernani, Euryanthe, Falstaff, Faust, Fedora, Fidelio, Glyndebourne, Grand, Hansel and Gretel, Horse, Idomeneo, Iolanthe, I Puritani, Kirov, La Bohème, La Donna e Mobile, Lakme, La Scala, Light, Lohengrin, Lulu, Macbeth, Magic Flute, Manon, Merrie England, Met, Musical, Nabucco, Norma, Oater, Oberon, Onegin, Orfeo, Otello, Owen Wingrave, Pag, Parsifal, Pastorale, Patience, Pearlfishers, Peter Grimes, Pinafore, Porgy and Bess, Prince Igor, Princess Ida, Rienzi, Rigoletto, Ring, Ruddigore, Rusalka, Salome, Savoy, Seria, Simon Boccanegra, Singspiel, Soap, Space, Sudsen, Sydney, Tell, Thais, The Met, The Mikado, Threepenny, Tosca, Trial by Jury, Turandot, Verismo, Werther, Work, Zarzuela
**Opera-glasses** Jumelle, Starers
**Opera-lover** Wagnerite
**Opera-singer** Baritone, Bass, Contralto, Diva, Savoyard, Soprano
**Operate, Operating, Operation(s), Operative** Act(ion), Activate, Actuate, Afoot, Agent, Air-lift, Artisan, Attuition, Barbarossa, Bypass, Caesarean, Campaign, Colectomy, Colostomy, Combined, Conduct, Couching, Current, Desert Storm, Detective, Doffer, Exercise, Function, Game, Gastrotomy, Grip, Hobday, Holding, Hysterectomy, In force,

Jejunostomy, Keystroke, Laparotomy, Leucotomy, Liposuction, Lithotomy, Lithotripsy, Lobotomy, Logical, Log roll, Manipulate, Mechanic, Mules, Nip and tuck, Nose job, Oner, Onstream, Overlord, Performance, Plastic, Practice, Proceeding, Rhytidectomy, Run, Sealion, Shirodkar's, Sortie, Splenectomy, Spur, Sting, Strabotomy, Surgery, Ta(g)liacotian, Titration, Transplant, Tummy tuck, Unit, Ure, Use, Valid, Wertheim, Work

**Operator** Agent, Barnard, Camshaft, Conductor, Dealer, Greenmailer, Keycard, Laplace, Manipulator, Nabla, Rigger, Sawbones, Sparks, Surgeon, Sysop, System, Wheeler-dealer

**Opiate, Opium** Buprenorphine, Dope, Drug, Endorphin, Hop, Laudanum, Meconin, Meconite, Meconium, Morphine, Narcotic, Paregoric, Religion, Soporific, Thebaine

**Opinion(ated), Opinionative** Advice, Attitude, Belief, Bet, Bias, Blog, Conjecture, Consensus, Conviction, Cri, Deem, Diagnosis, Dictum, Dogma, Dogmatic, Doxy, Editorial, Entêté, Esteem, Estimation, Fatwa(h), Feeling, Groundswell, Guess, Heresy, Impression, Judgement, Mind, Mumpsimus, Parti pris, Pious, Prejudice, Private, Prognosis, Public, Pulse, Ruling, Say, Second, Sense, Sentence, Sentiment, SO, Stance, Stand, Syndrome, Take, Tenet, Thought, Utterance, View, Viewpoint, Voice, Vote, Vox pop, Vox populi

**Opossum** Lie, Marmose, Phalanger, Tarsipes, Vulpine, Water, Yapo(c)k

**Oppidan** Cit, Townsman, Urban

**Opponent(s)** Adversary, Antagonist, Anti, Antichrist(ian), Anti-establishment, Arch-enemy, Denier, Dissident, E-N, Enemy, E-S, Foe, Gainsayer, Mitnaged, N-E, N-W, Roland, Sab(oteur), S-E, Straw-man, S-W, Them, Tiger, W-N, W-S

**Opportune, Opportunist, Opportunity** Appropriate, Apropos, Break, Buccaneer, Carpetbagger, → CHANCE, Day, El Dorado, Equal, Facility, Favourable, Ganef, Ganev, Ganof, Godsend, Godslot, Go-go, Gold digger, Golden, Gonif, Gonof, Heaven-sent, Lucky, Occasion, Opening, Pat, Photo, Providential, Room, Scope, Seal, Seel, Sele, Snatcher, Sneak thief, Tabula rasa, Tide, Timely, Timous, Toehold, Vantage, Well-timed, Window

**Oppose(d), Opposer, Opposing, Opposite, Opposition** Across, Adversary, Against, Agin, Anti, Anti-marketeer, Antipathy, Antiperistasis, Antipodes, Antiscian, Antithesis, Antithetic, Antitype, Antonym, Argue, At, Athwart, Au contraire, Averse, Battle, Beard, Black, Breast, Buck, Collision, Colluctation, Combat, Conflict, Confront, Contradict, Contrary, Converse, Counter(part), Counterclaim, Countermine, Countermove, Criticise, Diametric, Dis(en)courage, Disfavour, Dissent, Dissident, Distance, E contrario, Face, Foreanent, Fornen(s)t, Freegan, Gainsay, Head on, Hinder, Hostile, Impugn, Inimical, Insurrection, Inverse, Ironic, Meet, Militate, Mugwump, Noes, Object, Obscurant, Obtend, Overthwart, Polar, Reactance, Reaction, Recalcitrate, Reluct, Repugn, Resist, Retroact, Reverse, Rival, Shadow, Subtend, Synoeciosis, Syzygy, Teeth, Terr, Them, Thereagainst, They, Thwart, Toe to toe, Toto caelo, Traverse, V, Versus, Vice versa, Vis-à-vis, Withstand

**Oppress(ion), Oppressive** Airless, Bind, Burden, Close, Crush, Dead hand, Despotic, Heavy, Holy cruel, Incubus, Jackboot, Laden, Onerous, Overbear, Overpower, Pall, Persecute, Ride, Snool, Stifling, Subjugate, Sultry, Tommy, Totalitarian, Tyrannise, Yoke

**Opprobrium, Opprobrious** Disgrace, Dyslogistic, Envy, Odium, Scandal

**Oppugn** Attack, Criticise

**Opt, Option(al)** Alternative, Call, → CHOICE, Choose, Crown-jewel, Decide, Default, Double zero, Elect(ive), Facultative, Fine, Leipzig, Local, Menu, Naked, Omissible, Pick, Plump, Put, Select, Share, Soft, Swap(tion), Trade(d), Traditional, Voluntary, Votive, Wale, Zero(-zero)

**Optic(al), Optics** Active, Adaptive, Dioptrics, Electron, Fibre, Fire, Lens, Photics, Prism, Reticle, Visual

**Optician** Dispensing

**Optimism, Optimist(ic)** Bull, Buoyant, Chiliast, Elated, Expectant, Feelgood, Hopeful, Jam tomorrow, Micawber, Morale, Overplay, Pangloss, Pollyanna, Positive, Rosy, Sanguine, Starry-eyed, Upbeat, Utopiast, Yea-sayer

**Optimum** Technological

**Opulent, Opulence** Abundant, Affluent, Lavish, Lush, Luxury, Moneyed, Rich, Splendour, Wealthy

**Opus** Piece, Study, Work

**Or** Au, Either, Ere, Gold, Ossia, Otherwise, Sol

**Oracle(s), Oracular** Delphi, Dodonian, Mirror, Prophet, Pythian, Pythoness, Sage, Seer, Sibyl(line), Thummim, Trophonius, Urim, Vatic

**Oral** Acroamatic, Noncupative, Sonant, Spoken, Unwritten, Verbal, Viva, Viva voce, Vocal

**Orange** Agent, An(n)atta, An(n)atto, Apricot, Arnotto, Aurora, Bergamot, Bigarade, Bilirubin, Bitter, Blenheim, Blood, Blossom, Calamondin, Chica, Claybank, Clockwork, Croceate, Cumquat, Flame, Flamingo, Fulvous, Genip(ap), Jaffa, Kamala, Kamela, Kamila, Karaka, Kumquat, Mandarin, Methyl, Mock, Naartje, Nacarat, Nartjie, Navel, Ochre, Osage, Petit grain, Pig, Roucou, Ruta, Satsuma, Seville, Shaddock, Sour, Sweet, Tangerine, Tenné, Ugli®, Ulsterman

**Orang-utan** Ape, Monkey, Satyr

**Orate, Oration, Oratory** Address, Chapel, Declaim, Declamation, Eloge, Elogium, Elogy, Eulogy, Harangue, Panegyric, Philippics, Speech

**Oratorio, Orator(y)** Boanerges, Brompton, Brougham, Cantata, Cato, Cicero, Creation, Demagogue, Demosthenes, Diction, Elijah, Hwyl, Isocrates, Lectern, Morin, Nestor, Prevaricator, Proseucha, Proseuche, Rant, Rhetor, Samson, Seneca, Spellbinder, Stump, Tub-thumper, Windbag, Yarra-banker

**Orb** Ball, Eyeball, Firmament, Globe, Mound, Ocellus, Pome, Sphere

**Orbit(al), Orbiter** Adhelion, Apolune, Apse, Apsis, Circuit, Dump, Eccentric, Ellipse, Eye, Graveyard, Lunar, Osculating, Parking, Path, Periastron, Perigee, Perihelion, Perilune, Periselenium, Planet, Polar, Revolution, Satellite, Sputnik, Stationary, Subshell, Synchronous

**Orcadian** Hoy

**Orchard** Arbour, Grove, Holt

**Orchestra(te), Orchestration** Brass, Chamber, Charanga, Concertgebouw, Concerto, ECO, Engineer, Ensemble, Gamelan, Hallé, Instrumentation, LPO, LSO, Musician, Palm Court, Percussion, Pit, Ripieno, Score, Sinfonietta, SNO, Stage-manage, String, Symphony, Woodwind

**Orchid** Adam and Eve, Adder's mouth, Arethusa, Babe-in-a-cradle, Bee, Bee-orchis, Bird's nest, Bog, Burnt-tip, Butterfly, Calanthe, Calypso, Cattleya, Cooktown, Coralroot, Coral wort, Cymbidium, Cypripedium, Disa, Epidendrum, Fly, Fly orchis, Fragrant, Fringed orchis, Frog, Helleborine, Hyacinth, Lady, Lady's slipper, Lady's tresses, Lizard, Man, Marsh, Military, Miltonia, Moccasin-flower, Monkey, Musk, Naked lady, Odontoglossum, Oncidium, Phalaenopsis, Pogonia, Purple-fringed, Puttyroot, Pyramidal, Rattlesnake plantain, Salep, Scented, Slipper, Snakemouth, Soldier, Spider, Spotted, Swamp pink, Swan, Twayblade, Vanda, Vanilla

**Ord** Beginning, Point

**Ordain** Appoint, Arrange, Command, Decree, Destine, Enact, Induct, Japan, Legislate, Predestine, Priest

**Ordeal** Corsned, Disaster, Preeve, Test, → TRIAL, Via Dolorosa

**Order(ed), Orderly, Orders** Acoemeti, Action, Adjust, Administration, Affiliation, Agenda, Alphabetical, Anton Piller, Apollonian, Apple-pie, Arrange, Array, ASBO, Attachment, Attendant, Attention, Attic, Augustine, Avast, Bade, Banker's, Bankruptcy, Bath, Batman, Battalia, Batting, Bed, Behest, Benedictine, Bernardine, Bespoke, Bid, Book, Boss, Brethren, Brotherhood, Buffalo, Call, Camaldolite, Canon, Category, Caveat, CB, Chaprassi, Charter, Cheque, Chit, Chronological, Chuprassy, Class, Cluniac, Coherent, Collate, Command(ment), Committal, Compensation, Composite, Corinthian, Cosmo, Cosmos, Court, Decorum, Decree, Demand, Dictate, Diktat, Direct(ion), Directive, Dispone, Distringas, Dominican, Doric, Draft, DSO, Edict, Embargo, Enclosed, Enjoin, En règle, Errand, Established, Establishment, Eutaxy, Eviction, Exclusion, Feldsher, Fiat, Fiaunt, Firing, Firman, Form(ation), Franciscan, Fraternity, Freemason, Full, Gagging, Garnishee, Garter, Gilbertine, Ginkgo, Good, Grade, Group, Habeas corpus, Heast(e), Hecht, Hest, Holy, Hospitaller, Husbandry, Indent, Injunction, Insectivora, Instruct, Interdict, In turn, Ionic, Irade, Jig, Khalsa, Kilter, Knights Hospitallers, Kosmos, Language, Large, Law, Lexical, Loblolly boy, Loblolly man, Loose, Mail, Major, Mandamus, Mandate, Marching, Marist, Market, Marshal, Masonic, Medjidie, Merit, Methodical, Minor, Mittimus, Monastic, Money, Monitor, Moose, Natural, Neatness, Nunnery, OBE, Oddfellows, Official, OM, Open, Orange, Ord, Ordain, Organic, Organised, Pecking, Plot, Possession, Postal, Precedence, Precept,

Premonstrant, Prepare, Prescribe, Preservation, Prioritise, Provisional, Purchase, Pyragyrite, Rank, Receiving, Reception, Regiment, Règle, Regular, Regulation, Religious, Requisition, Restraining, Return, Right, Rule, Ruly, Sailing, Sarvodaya, Scale, Sealed, Search, Sequence, Seraphic, Series, Settle, Shipshape, Short, Side, Sisterhood, Sort, Standing, Starter's, State, Statutory, Stop(-loss), Straight, Stratify, Subpoena, Summons, Supersedere, Supervision, System, Tabulate, Tall, Taxis, Tell, Templar, Teutonic, Third, Thistle, Tidy, Trim, Tuscan, Ukase, Uniformity, Warison, Warrant, Word, Working, Writ

▷**Ordering** *may indicate* an anagram

**Ordinal** Book, Number, Second, Sequence, Twelfth

**Ordinance** Byelaw, Capitulary, Decree, Edict, Law, Prescript, Rescript, Rite, Statute

**Ordinary** Average, Banal, Bog standard, Canton, Chevron, Comely, Common (or garden), Commonplace, Cot(t)ise, Everyday, Everyman, Exoteric, Fess(e), Flanch, Flange, Folksy, Grassroots, Hackneyed, Humdrum, Mass, Mediocre, Middling, Moderate, Mundane, → **NORMAL**, O, OR, Pedestrian, Plain, Prosy, Pub, Rank and file, Routine, Ruck, Run-of-the-mill, Saltier, Saltire, Scarp, Simple, So-so, Standard, Tressure, Trite, Trivial, Undistinguished, Uneventful, Unexceptional, Uninspired, Unspectacular, Usual, Vanilla, Workaday, Your

**Ordnance** Artillery, Cannon, Guns, Pelican, Supply

**Ordure** Cess, Dung, Fertiliser, Manure

**Ore** Alga, Babingtonite, Bauxite, Beauxite, Bornite, Braunite, Breunnerite, Calamine, Calaverite, Calx, Cerusite, Chalcocite, Chalcopyrite, Chloanthite, Coffinite, Coin, Coltan, Copper, Crocoite, Dry-bone, Element, Enargite, Galenite, Glance, Haematite, Hedyphane, Horseflesh, Ilmenite, Iridosmine, Ironstone, Kidney, Limonite, Magnetite, Mat, Melaconite, Middlings, Millhead, Milling grade, Mineral, Minestone, Morass, Niobite, Oligist, Owre, Peacock, Pencil, Phacolite, Pipe, Pitchblende, Proustite, Psilomelane, Pyrargyrite, Pyromorphite, Realgar, Red-lead, Ruby silver, Schlich, Seaweed, Siderite, Sinoptite, Slime, Slug, Smaltite, Speiss, Sphalerite, Stephanite, Stilpnosiderite, Stockwork, Stream-tin, Taconite, Tailing, Tenorite, Tetrahedrite, Tin, Vein, Wad(d), White-lead, Yellow cake

**Orfe** Ide

**Organ(s), Organic** Adjustor, Adnexa, American, Anlage, Antimere, Apollonicon, Appendix, Archegonium, Barrel, Biogenic, Biotic, Bladder, Brain, Bursa, Calliope, Carbon, Carpel, Carpogonium, Cercus, Chamber, Chemoreceptor, Choir, Chord, Cinema, Claspers, Clave, Colour, Conch(a), Console, Corti's, Cribellum, Ctene, Ear, Echo, Electric, Electronic, Electroreceptor, Emunctory, End, Epinastic, Essential, Exteroceptor, Eyeball, Feeler, Fin, Flabellum, Fundus, Gall bladder, Gametangium, Gill, Glairin, Gland, Gonad, Hammond®, Hand, Hapteron, Harmonica, Harmonium, Haustorium, House, Hydathode, Hydraulos, Imine, Isomere, Kerogen, Kidney, Kist o'whistles, Larynx, Lien, Light, Liver, Lung-book, Lyriform, Mag(azine), Means, Mechanoreceptor, Media, Medulla, Melodion, Ministry, Modiolus, Nasal, Natural, Nectary, Nematocyst, Nephridium, Newspaper, Nose, Olfactory, Oogonia, Ovary, Ovipositor, Ovotestis, Palp, Pancreas, Paper, Parapodium, Part, Pedal, Photogen, Photophore, Photoreceptor, Physharmonics, Pipe, Pipeless, Placenta, Plastid, Portative, Positive, Procarp, Prothallus, Pudenda, Pulmones, Purtenance, Pyrophone, Radula, Receptor, Recit, Reed, Regal, Relict, Retina, Rhizoid, Sang, Saprobe, Scent, Sense, Sensillum, Serinette, Serra, Siphon, Skin, Spermary, Spinneret, Spleen, Sporangium, Sporocarp, Sporophore, Stamen, Statocyst, Steam, Stomach, Swell, Syrinx, Systaltic, Tentacle, Textual, Theatre, Theca, Thymus, Tongue, Tonsil, Tool, Trichocyst, Tympanum, Ureic, Uterus, Vegetative, Velum, Verset, Viscera, Viscus, Vitals, Voice, Voluntary, Wing, Womb, Wurlitzer®

**Organelle** Peroxisome

**Organise(d), Organisation, Organiser** Activate, Administer, Agency, Aggregator, Amnesty, Anatomy, Apparat, → **ARRANGE**, Association, Body, Brigade, Broederbond, Caucus, Charter, CIA, Class(ify), Codify, Collect, Comecon, Company, Compile, Configure, Constitution, Coordinate, Design, Direct, Edifice, Embody, Entrepreneur, Eoka, Fascio, Fatah, Firm, Group, Guild, Hamas, Hierarchy, Impresario, Infrastructure, Institute, Jaycee, Krewe, Ku Klux Klan, Logistics, Machine, Mafia, Marshal, Mastermind, Mobilise, Movement, NATO, Network, Octopus, Opus Dei, Orchestrate, Orderly, Outfit, Personal, PLO, Promotor, Quango,

Rally, Red Crescent, Red Cross, Regiment, Resistance, Rig, Rosicrucian, Run, Schedule, Setup, Sharpbender, Social, Soroptimist, Sort, Stage, Stage manage, Stahlhelm, Steward, Structure, Sysop, System, Tidy, Together, Umbrella, UN, UNESCO, Viet Minh

▷**Organise(d)** *may indicate* an anagram

**Organism(s)** Aerobe, Agamic, Alga, Amoeba, Anaerobe, Archaea, Asymmetron, Auxotroph, Being, Biogenic, Biometric, Biont, Biotic, Cell, Chimeric, Chlamydia, Ciliate, Clade, Coral, Detritivore, Dinoflagellate, Diplont, Ecad, Ecology, Ecotype, Endogenous, Endosymbiont, Entity, Eozoon, Epibenthos, Epizoite, Epizoon, Eucaryote, Euglena, Eukaryote, Eurytherm, Extremophile, Germ, Halobiont, Halophile, Haplont, Hemiparasite, Holophyte, Holoplankton, Homeotherm, Incross, Infauna, Infusoria(n), Lichen, Macrobiote, Medusa, Meiosis, Meroplankton, Metamale, Microaerophile, Microbe, Moneron, Morphology, Mutant, Mycoplasma, Nekton, Neuston, Osmoconformer, Paramecium, Pathogen, Periphyton, Phenetics, Ph(a)enology, Plankter, Plankton, Pleuston, Poikilotherm, Prokaryote, Protist, Protista, Protozoan, Radiolarian, Saprobe, Saprotroph, Schizomycete, Seaslater, Sea spider, Sea squirt, Streptococcus, Symbion(t), Teratogen, Thermophile, Torula, Trypanosome, Virino, Virus, Volvox, Vorticella, Zoarium

**Organ-part, Organ-stop** Bourdon, Clarabella, Diapason, Gamba, Messiaen, Montre, Nasard, Principal, Pyramidon, Quint, Salicet, Stop, Swell

**Organ-tuner** Reed-knife

**Orgasm** Climax, Come

**Orgy** Bacchanalia(n), Binge, Blinder, Bust, Carousal, Dionysian, Feast, Revel, Saturnalia, Spree, Wassail

**Orient(al)** Adjust, Annamite, Attune, Cantonese, Chinoiserie, Dawn, Dayak, E, East(ern), Far-e(ast), Fu Manchu, Hindu, Laotian, Levant, Leyton, Malay, Mongol, Mongolian, Pareoean, Shan, Sunrise, Tatar, Thai, Tibetan, Turk(o)man

**Orientation** Polarity, Satnav, Tropism

**Orifice** Aperture, Blastosphere, Gap, Hole, Micropyle, Nare, Opening, Pore, Spiracle, Trema, Vent

**Origami** Folding

**Origen's work** Tetrapla

**Origin(al), Originate, Originating** Abiogenesis, Adam, Ancestry, Archetype, Arise, As per, Beginning, Big bang, Birth, Breed, Come, Commence, Cradle, Creation, Derive, Designer, Editio princeps, Elemental, Emanate, Epicentre, Etymon, Extraction, First, Firsthand, Focus, Found, Fresh, Generic, Genesis, Genetical, Germ, Grow, Hatch, Imaginative, Incunabula, Ingenious, Initial, Innovate, Invent(ive), Master, Mother, Nascence, Natality, Native, New, Novel, Off the wall, One-off, Ord, Parentage, Precedent, Primal, Primary, Primigenial, Primitive, Primordial, Pristine, Promethean, Protoplast, Prototype, Provenance, Provenience, Radical, Rise, Root, Seed, Seminal, Source, Spring, Start, Unborrowed, Uncut, Ur, Urtext, Ylem, Zoism

**Oriole** Firebird, Hangbird

**Orion** Alnilam, Alnitak, Ballatrix, Betelgeuse, Hatsya, Lambda, Meissa, Mintaka, Rigel, Saiph

**Orison** Blessing, Prayer

**Ormer** Abalone, Haliotis

**Ornament(al), Ornamentation** Acroter(ia), Additament, Adorn, Aglet, Aiguillette, Anaglyph, Antefix, Anthemion, Aplustre, Applique, Arabesque, Bahuti, Ball-flower, Barbola, Baroque, Barrette, Bead, Bedeck, Bez(z)ant, Billet, Blister, Boss, Bracelet, Branchwork, Breloque, Broider, Brooch, Bugle, Bulla, Caparison, Cartouche, Charm, Chase, Clock, Cockade, Conceit, Corbeil(le), Cornice, Coromandel work, Crocket, Cross-quarters, Curin, Curlicue, Deck, Decor, Decorate, Decoration, Dentella, Diamanté, Die-work, Diglyph, Dog's-tooth, Doodad, Dreamcatcher, Egg and anchor, Egg and dart, Egg and tongue, Embellish, Emblem(a), Embroider, Enrich, Epaulet(te), Epergne, Fallal, Fandangle, Festoon, Fiddlehead, Figgery, Figuration, Figurine, Filagree, Filigrain, Filigree, Fillagree, Fleur de lis, Fleuret, Fleurette, Fleuron, Florid, Fret, Fretwork, Frieze, Frill, Frog, Frounce, Furbelow, Furnish, Gadroon, Garnish, Gaud, Gingerbread, Gorget, Griff(e), Guilloche, Gutta, Headwork, Hei-tiki, Helix, Hip-knob, Honeysuckle, Horse-brass, Illustrate, Inlay, Japanaiserie, Jewellery, Knosp, Knotwork, Labret, Lambrequin, Lavalier, Leglet, Loop, Lotus, Lunette,

Lunula, Macramé, Mantling, Medallion, Mense, Millefleurs, Mordent, Moresque, Motif, Nail-head, Necklet, Netsuke, Nicknackery, Niello, Nose-ring, O, Okimono, Ouch, Ovolo, Palmette, Paraphernalia, Parure, Patera, Paternoster, Paua, Pawa, Pectoral, Pendant, Picot, Pipe, Piping, Plume, Pompom, Pompo(o)n, Poppyhead, Pounce, Pralltriller, Prettify, Prunt, Purfle, Quatrefoil, Rel(l)ish, Rocaille, Rococo, Rosette, Running, Scalework, Scrollwork, Shell, Shoulder-knot, Snowdome, Snowglobe, Spangle, Spar, Stomacher, Tassel, Tettix, Tiki, Tool, Torc, Torque, Torsade, Tracery, Trappings, Tremolo, Trill, Trimming, Trinket, Triquetra, Tsuba, Turn, Twiddle, Versal, Wally, Water-leaf, Whigmaleerie, Whigmaleery, Whim-wham

**Ornate** Baroque, Churrigueresque, Dressy, Elaborate, Fancy, Florid, Flowery

▹**Ornate** *may indicate* an anagram

**Ornithologist** Audubon, Birdman

**Orotund** Bombastic, Grandiose, Pompous, Rhetorical, Sonant

**Orphan** Annie, Foundling, Topsy, Twist, Ward

**Orpheus** Lutenist

**Orpiment** Arsenic, Zarnec, Zarnich

**Orpington** Buff, Hen

**Ort** Bit, Crumb, Morsel, Remnant

**Orthodox** Bien-pensant, Cocker, Conventional, Fundamental, Hardshell, Proper, Sound, Standard

**Orthorhombic** Enstatite

**Ortolan** Bird, Bunting, Rail

**Orwell** Blair

**Oscar** Award, O, Statuette, Wilde

**Oscillate, Oscillation, Oscillator** Dynatron, Excitor, Fluctuate, Hunt, Librate, Local, Parasitic, Relaxation, Ripple, Rock, Seesaw, Seiche, Squeg, Surge, Swing(swang), Vibrate, Waver

**Osier** Red, Reed, Sallow, Willow

**Osmium** Os

**Osmosis** Reverse

**Osprey** Fish-hawk, Lammergeier, Ossifrage, Pandion

**Osseous** Bony, Hard, Skeletal, Spiny

**Ossuary** Urn

**Ostensibly** Apparent, External, Seeming

**Ostentation, Ostentatious** Camp, Dash, Display, Dog, Dressy, Éclat, Epideictical, Extravagant, Fantoosh, Fastuous, Flamboyant, Flash(y), Flaunt, Florid, Flourish, Garish, Gaudy, Ghetto fabulous, Highfalutin(g), Kitschy, Large, Parade, Pomp, Ponc(e)y, Pretence, Puff, → SHOW(ING), Showboating, Side, Snobbery, Splash, Swank, Tacky, Tulip

**Osteoporosis** Sudeck's atrophy

**Ostler** Stabler

**Ostracise(d), Ostracism** Banish, Blackball, Blacklist, Boycott, Cut, Exclude, Exile, Outcast, Petalism, Potsherd, Proscribe, Shun, Snub, Taboo, Tabu

**Ostrich** Em(e)u, Estrich, Estridge, Nandoo, Nandu, Ratite, Rhea, Struthio(nes), Tinamou, Titanis

**Othello** Moor, Morisco

**Other(s), Otherwise** Additional, Aka, Alia, Alias, Allo-, Alternative, Besides, Different, Distinct, Else, Et al, Et alli, Etc, Excluding, Former, Further, Hanky-panky, It, Notwithstanding, Othergates, Rest, Significant, Unlike

**Other things** Alia

▹**Otherwise** *may indicate* an anagram

**Other-worldly** Mystic

**Otiose** Idle, Indolent, Ineffective, Lazy, Needless, Superfluous, Useless

**Otis** Bustard

**Otologist** Aurist

**OTT** Ostentatious

**Ottawa** Bytown

**Otter** Edal, Paravane, Sea, Tarka, Waterdog

**Otto** Attar, Chypre, Mahratta
**Ottoman** Osmanli, Porte, Rayah, Rumelia, Turk
**Oubliette** Dungeon, Pit, Prison
**Ouch** Argh, Brooch, Ornament, Ow
**Ought** All, Should
**Ouida** Ramée
**Ouija** Board, Planchette
**Ounce** Cat, Fluid, Liang, Oz, Panther, Snow leopard, Tael, Trace, Uncial
**Our(selves)** Us, We
▸**Ousel** *see* **OUZEL**
**Oust** Depose, Dislodge, Eject, Evict, Expel, Fire, Remove, Supplant, Unnest, Unseat
**Out (of)** Abloom, Absent, Aglee, Agley, Al fresco, Asleep, Aus, Away, Begone, Bowl, Comatose, Dated, En ville, Exposed, External, Extirp, Forth, From, Furth, Haro, Harrow, Hence, Hors, Inaccurate, In bloom, In blossom, Lent, Oust, Passe, Skittle, Spaced, Striking, Stump, Taboo, Uit, Unfashionable, Up, York
▹**Out** *may indicate* an anagram
**Out and out** Absolute, Arrant, Rank, Right down, Sheer, Stark, Teetotal, Thorough, Totally, Utter, Whole hog
**Outback** Backblocks, Bundu, Bush, Never-never, The mulga
**Outbid** Gazump
**Outbreak** Ebullition, Epidemic, Eruption, Explosion, Flare-up, Plague, Putsch, Rash, Recrudescence, Spate
**Outbuilding** Annex(e), Garage, Shed
**Outburst** Access, Blurt, Bluster, Boutade, Brainstorm, Diatribe, Disturbance, Eruption, Evoe, Explosion, Fit, Flaky, Flaw, Furore, Fusillade, Gale, Gush, Gust, Hoo-ha, Paroxysm, Passion, Philippic, Sally, Salvo, Sternutation, Storm, Tantrum, Tirade, Torrent, Tumult, Volley
**Outcast** Cagot, Discard, Eta, Exile, Exul, Ishmael, Leper, Mesel, Pariah, Robinson, Rogue, Untouchable
**Outcome** Aftermath, Consequence, Decision, Dénouement, Effect, Emergence, End, Event, Issue, Reflection, → **RESULT**, Sequel, Upshot, Wash-up
**Outcrop** Basset, Blossom, Crag, Creston, Inlier, Mesa, Rognon, Spur, Tarpit
**Outcry** Alew, Blue murder, Bray, → **CLAMOUR**, Furore, Halloa, Halloo, Howl, Hue, Humdudgeon, Protest, Racket, Shright, Steven, Uproar, Utas
**Outdated, Out of date** Archaic, Corny, Defunct, Dinosaur, Effete, Feudal, Fossil, Horse and buggy, Horse buggy, Obs, Obsolete, Old hat, Outmoded, Passé, Scrap, Square, Worn
**Outdo** Beat, Best, Cap, Picnic, Superate, Surpass, Top, Trump, Worst
**Outdoor(s)** Alfresco, External, Garden, Open air, Outbye, Plein-air, Tweedy
**Outer, Outermost** External, Extreme, Extrogenous, Limit, Magpie, Purlieu, Superficial, Top
**Outfit(ter)** Accoutrement, Arm, Babygro®, Catsuit, Costumier, Drawbar, Dress, Ensemble, Equipage, Fitout, Furnish, Get-up, Haberdasher, Habit, Kit, Layette, Rig, Samfoo, Samfu, Strip, Suit, Tackle, Team, Trousseau, Turnout, Uniform, Weed(s), Whites
**Outflank** Bypass, Overlap
**Outflow** Anticyclone, Discharge, Ebb, Effluence, Eruption, Exodus, Gorge, Issue, Surge
**Outgoing(s)** Egression, Exiting, Expenditure, Extrovert, Migration, Open, Rental, Retiring
**Outgrowth** Ala(te), Appendage, Aril, Bud, Caruncle, Enation, Epiphenomenon, Exostosis, Flagellum, Hair, Ligule, Offshoot, Osteophyte, Propagulum, Root-hair, Sequel, Strophiole, Trichome
**Outhouse** Conservatory, Lean to, Privy, Shed, Skilling, Skillion, Skipper, Stable
**Outing** Excursion, Hike, Jaunt, Junket, Picnic, Sortie, Spin, Spree, Treat, Trip, Wayzgoose
**Outlandish** Alien, Barbarous, Bizarre, Exotic, Foreign, Peregrine, Rum
**Outlaw** Allan-a-Dale, Attaint, Badman, Ban, Bandit(ti), Banish, Broken man, Bushranger, Desperado, Exile, Forbid, Friar Tuck, Fugitive, Hereward, Hood, Horn, Jesse James, Klepht, Maid Marian, Ned Kelly, Proscribe, Put to the horn, Robin Hood, Rob Roy, Ronin, Tory, Waive
**Outlay** Cost, Expense, Mise

**Outlet** Débouché, Drain, Egress, Escape, Estuary, Exit, Femerall, Flue, Hydrant, Market, Opening, Orifice, Outfall, Overflow, Sluice, Socket, Spout, Tuyere, Tweer, Twier, Twire, Twyer(e), Vent

**Outline** Adumbration, Aperçu, Circumscribe, Configuration, Contorno, Contour, Croquis, Delineate, Describe, Digest, → DRAFT, Draught, Esquisse, Footprint, Layout, Limn, Note, Perimeter, Plan, Profile, Projet, Prospectus, Relief, Scenario, Schematic, Shape, Silhouette, Skeletal, Skeleton, Sketch, Stencil, Summary, Syllabus, Synopsis, T(h)alweg, Trace

**Outlook** Aspect, Attitude, Casement, Mindset, Perspective, Prognosis, Prospect, Scenery, View(point), Vista, Weltanschauung

**Outmanoeuvre** Upstage

**Outmoded** Archaic, Old school, Wasm

▷**Out of** *may indicate* an anagram

**Out-of-action** Hors de combat

**Out of date** *see* OUTDATED

**Out of form** Amorphous, Awry

**Out of order** Fritz, Kaput

**Out of sorts** Cachectic, Nohow, Peevish, Poorly

▷**Out of sorts** *may indicate* an anagram

**Out of tune** Discordant, Flat, Scordato, Scordatura

**Outpace** Leave standing

**Outpatient** Externe

**Outpost** Colony, Garrison, Mission, Picquet, Station

**Outpour(ing)** Bavardage, Cascade, Effuse, Flood, Flow, Gush, Libation, Spate, Stream, Torrent

**Output** Data, Emanation, Get, Gross, Print out, Produce, Production, Turnout, Yield

▷**Output** *may indicate* an anagram

**Outrage(ous)** Affront, Apoplectic, Appal, Atrocity, Crime, Desecrate, Diabolical, Disgust, Egregious, Enorm(ity), Flagitious, Flagrant, Flamboyant, Indignation, Infuriate, Insult, OTT, Preposterous, Rich, Sacrilege, Scandal, Shocking, Ungodly, Unholy, Violate

▷**Outrageously** *may indicate* an anagram

**Outrider** Scout

**Outright** Clean, Complete, Entire, Point-blank, Utter

**Outrun** Spreadeagle

**Outset** Ab initio, Beginning, Start

**Outshine** Eclipse, Excel, Overshadow, Surpass, Upstage

**Outside** Ab extra, Crust, Derma, Enthetic, Exterior, External, Extramural, Front, Furth, Hors, Husk, Periphery, Plein-air, Remote, Rim, Rind, Rine, Shell, Surface

**Outsider** Alien, Bolter, Bounder, Cad, Extern, Extremist, Foreigner, Incomer, Lingo, Oustiti, Palagi, Pariah, Ring-in, Roughie, Stranger, Stumer, Unseeded, Upstart

**Outsize** Capacious, Giant, Gigantic, Huge, OS

**Outskirts** Edge, Fringe, Periphery, Purlieu, Suburb(ia)

**Outspoken** Bluff, Blunt, Broad, Candid, Explicit, Forthright, Frank, Plain, Rabelaisian, Round, Vocal, Vociferous

**Outstand(ing)** Ace, Arrears, Beaut(y), Bees' knees, Belter, Billowing, Blinder, Boss, Bulge, Chief, Classic, Crack, Crackerjack, Debt, Egregious, Eminent, Especial, Excellent, Exceptional, Exquisite, Extant, Extraordinaire, First, Fugleman, Highlight, Humdinger, Impasto, Jut, Left, Lulu, Marked, Masterpiece, Masterstroke, Matchless, Oner, Overdue, Owing, Paragon, Paramount, Peerless, Pending, Phenom(enal), Pièce de résistance, Pre-eminent, Prince, Prize, Prominent, Promontory, Prosilient, Protrude, Protuberant, Proud, Purler, Red letter, Relief, Relievo, Salient, Shining light, Signal, Some, Special, Squarrose, Star, Stellar, Strout, Super(b), Top flight, Tour de force, Unmet, Unpaid, Unsettled, Vocal, World-class

**Outstrip** Best, Cap, Cote, Distance, Exceed, Overtake

**Outward** Efferent, Extern(e), External, Extrinsic, Extrorse, Extrovert, Posticous, Postliminary, Superficial

**Outweigh** Preponderate
**Outwit** Baffle, Best, Circumvent, Crossbite, Dish, Euchre, Fox, Outthink, Over-reach, →THWART, Trick
**Outwork** Counterguard, Demilune, Jetty, Moon, Tenail(le), Tenaillon
**Outworn** Decrepit, Obsolete, Used
**Ouzel** Merle, Ring, Water
**Oval(s)** Cartouche, Cassini, Ellipse, Henge, Mandorla, Navette, Obovate, Ooidal
**Ovary** Oophoron, Pistil
**Ovation** Applause, Cheer, Standing
**Oven(-like)** Aga®, Calcar, Camp, Combination, Convection, Cul-de-four, Dutch, Electric, Fan, Furnace, Gas, Hangi, Haybox, Horn(it)o, Kiln, Lear, Leer, Lehr, Lime kiln, Maori, Microwave, Muffle, Norwegian, Oast, Oon, Rotisserie, Stove, Umu
**Over, Overly** Above, Across, Again, Atop, C, Clear, Done, Excess, Finished, Hexad, Left, Maiden, Of, On, Ore, Ort, Owre, Past, Sopra, Spare, Superior, Surplus, Through, Too, Uber, Wicket maiden, Yon
**Over-abundance, Overabundant** Infestation, Rife
**Overact** Burlesque, Emote, Ham, Hell, Hoke
**Overactive** Hyper
**Overall(s)** Boiler suit, Chaps, Denims, Dungarees, Dust-coat, Fatigues, Generally, Jumper, Siren suit, Smicket, Smock, Tablier, Umbrella, Workwear
**Over-anxious** Neurotic
**Overawe** Daunt
**Overbalance** Outweigh, Topple
**Overbear(ing)** Arrogant, Bossy, Dogmatic, Domineering, High-handed, High-muck-a-muck, Imperious, Insolent, Lordly, Macher, Oppressive, Supercilious, Weigh down
**Overbid** Gazump
**Overblown** Grandioso, Turgid
**Overcast** Cloudy, Dull, Lowering, Sew, Sombre
**Over-cautious** Old-maidish
**Overcharge** Clip, Extort, Fleece, Gazump, Gyp, OC, Rack-rent, Rook, Rush, Soak, Sting
**Overcoat** Balmacaan, Benjamin, Benny, British warm, Chesterfield, →COAT, Crombie, Dolman, Grego, Inverness, Jemmy, Joseph, Paletot, Pea-jacket, Petersham, Pos(h)teen, Prince Albert, Raglan, Redingote, Spencer, Surtout, Tabard, Taglioni, Ulster, Warm, Wooden, Wrap-rascal
**Overcome** Beat, Bested, Conquer, Convince, Dead-beat, Defeat, Expugn, Hit for six, Kill, Master, Mither, Moider, Moither, Prevail, Quell, Speechless, Stun, Subdue, Subjugate, Superate, Surmount, Survive, Swampt, Underfong, Vanquish, Weather, Win
**Overconfident, Overconfidence** Besserwisser, Hubris
**Overcritical** Fastidious
**Overcrowd** Congest, Jam, Pack
**Overdo(ne)** Burnt, Exceed, Ham, Hokey, Hokum, OTT, Percoct, Tire
**Overdose** OD, Surfeit
**Overdraft** Loan, Red
▷**Overdrawn** *may indicate* 'red' outside another word
**Overdress(ing)** Dudism, Flossy, Overall
**Overdue** Behindhand, Belated, Excessive, Late, Owing, Tardy, Unpaid
**Overeat(ing)** Binge, Cram, Gorge, Hypertrophy, Pig out, Satiate
**Over-elaborate** Baroque
**Over-emotional** Melodramatic
**Overemphasise** Labour, Rub in, Stress
**Over-excited** Hyper
**Overfeed(ing)** Glut, Gorge, Sate, Stuff
**Overflow(ing)** Abound, Abrim, Cornucopia, Lip, Nappe, Ooze, Outpour, Ream, Redound, Spillage, Surfeit, Teem
**Overfull** Brimming, Hept

**Overground** Subaerial
**Overgrow(n)** Ivy'd, Jungle, Ramp(ant), Rank, Rhinophyma
**Overhang(ing)** Beetle, Bulge, Cornice, →JUT, Loom, Project, Shelvy
**Overhasty** Previous, Rash
**Overhaul** Bump, Catch, Overtake, Recondition, Refit, Revamp, Revision, Service, Strip
**Overhead(s)** Above, Aloft, Ceiling, Cost, Exes, Hair(s), Headgear, Oncost, Rafter, Upkeep, Zenith
**Overhear** Catch, Eavesdrop, Tap
**Overheat** Enrage
**Over here** Psst
**Overindulge(nt), Overindulgence** Binge, Crapulent, Crass, Dissipated, Dissolute, Pig, Surfeit
**Overjoy(ed)** Cock-a-hoop, Elate, Thrill
**Overland** Portage
**Overlap(ping)** Correspond, Equitant, Imbricate, Incubous, Kern(e), Limbous, Obvolute, Stretto, Tace, Tasse
**Overlay** Ceil, Ciel, Smother, Stucco, Superimpose, Too, Veneer
**Overlearned** Pedantic
**Overload** Burden, Plaster, Strain, Surcharge, Tax
**Overlong** Sesquipedalian
**Overlook(ed)** Condone, Disregard, Excuse, Forget, Forgive, Indulge, Miss, Neglect, Omit, Pass, Pretermit, Superintend, Unnoticed, Waive
**Overlord** Edwin, Enslaver, Excess, Invasion, Swoop
**Overlying** Incumbent, Jessant, Pressing
**Overmuch** Excessive, Surplus, Too, Undue
**Overnourishment** Hypertrophy
**Overplay** Ham, Hoke
**Overpower(ing)** Crush, Evince, Irresistible, Mighty, Onerous, Oppress, Outman, Overwhelm, Potent, Profound, Subdue, Surmount, Swelter, Tyrannous, Whelm
**Overpraise** Adulate
**Overprice(d)** Rip off
**Overproduce(d)** Drug
**Overprotect(ive)** Cosset, Nannyish
**Over-refined** Dainty, Nice, Pernickety, Precious
**Override, Overrule** Abrogate, Disallow, Outvote, Outweigh, Paramount, Preponderant, Repeal, Reverse, Talk down, Veto
**Overrun** Exceed, Extra, Infest, Inundate, Invade, Lip, Swarm, Teem
**Overseas** Abroad, Colonial, Foreign, Outremer, Transmarine, Ultramarine
**Oversee(r)** Administer, Baas, Banksman, Boss, Captain, Care, Deputy, Direct, Execute, Eyebrow, Foreman, Forewoman, Grieve, Handle, Induna, Mediate, Moderator, Periscope, Steward, Supercargo, Superintend, Supervise, Survey(or)
**Oversensitive** Allergic
**Oversentimental** Byronic, Slushy
**Oversexed** Satyr
**Overshadow(ed)** Cloud, Dominate, Dwarf, Eclipse, Obscure, Obumbrate, Outclass, Umbraculate
**Overshoe** Arctic, Galosh, Sandal, Snowboot
**Oversight** Blunder, Care, Error, Gaffe, Inadvertence, Lapse, Loophole, Neglect, Parablepsis
**Overskirt** Peplum
**Overstate(ment), Overstated** Dramatise, Embroider, Exaggerate, Hyperbole, Theatral, Theatrical
**Overstep** Transgress
**Overstrained** Epitonic
**Overstrung** Edgy
**Overt** Manifest, Patent, Plain, Public

**Overtake** Catch, For(e)hent, Lap, Leapfrog, Overget, Overhaul, → **PASS**, Supersede, Usurp
**Overthrow** Confound, Dash, Defeat, Demolish, Depose, Dethrone, Down, Labefact(at)ion, Oust, Putsch, Ruin, Smite, Stonker, Subvert, Supplant, Topple, Unhorse, Unseat, Usurp, Vanquish, Whemmle, Whommle, Whummle, Worst
**Overtime** Extension
**Overtone** Harmonic
**Overture** Advance, Approach, Carnival, Concert, Egmont, French, Hebrides, Intro, Italian, Leonora, Offer, → **OPENING**, Prelude, Propose, Serenade, Sinfonia, Toccata, Toccatella, Toccatina
**Overturn(ing)** Capsize, Catastrophe, Coup, Cowp, Engulf, Keel, Quash, Rebut, Rescind, Reverse, Tip, Topple, Up(set), Upend, Whemmle, Whomble, Whommle, Whummle
**Overuse(d)** Hackney(ed), RSI
**Overvalue** Exaggerate, Salt
**Overview** Ethos
**Overweening** Bashaw, Cocky, Excessive, Imperious, Presumptuous
**Overweight** Fat, Heavy, Lardy, Obese, Pursy, Sunk
**Overwhelm(ed), Overwhelming** Accablé, Assail, Avalanche, Banging, Bowl over, Cloy, → **CRUSH**, Dearth, Defeat, Deluge, Devastate, Engulf, Flabbergast, Foudroyant, Inundate, KO, Mind-boggling, Oppress, Overcome, Plough under, Scupper, Smother, Snow, Submerge, Swamp, Whup
**Overwork(ed)** Fag, Forswonck, Hackneyed, Ornament, Slog, Stale, Supererogation, Tax, Tire, Toil, Travail
**Overwritten** Palimpsest
**Overwrought** Excited, Frantic, Hysterical, Ore-rested, Ornate, Rococo
**Overzealous** Rabid
**Ovid** Naso
**Ovule, Ovum** Egg, Oosphere, Seed, Zygote
**Owe(d), Owing** Arrears, Attribute, Due, OD
**Owen** Glendower
**Owl(s)** African, Barn, Barred, Blinker, Boobook, Brown, Bubo, Bunter, Chinese, Church, Eagle, Elegant, English, Fern, Fish, Glimmergowk, Grey, Hawk, Hedwig, Hoo(ter), Horned, Howlet, Jenny, Little, Long-eared, Longhorn, Madge, Moper, Mopoke, Mopus, Night, Ogle, Parliament, Ruru, Saw-whet, Scops, Screech, Sea, Shriek, Snowy, Spotted, Stare, Strich, Striges, Strigiformes, Tawny, Wood
**Own(er), Owning, Ownership** Acknowledge, Admit, Agnise, Ain, Confess, Domain, Dominium, Fess, Have, Hold, Mortmain, Nain, Of, Personal, Possess, Proper, Proprietor, Recognise, Reputed, Shared, Title, Tod, Use
**Own way** More suo
**Ox(en)** Anoa, Aquinas, Aurochs, Banteng, Banting, Bison, Bonas(s)us, Buffalo, Bugle, Bull-beef, Bullock, Cat(t)alo, Draught, Fee, Gaur, Gayal, Gyal, Kouprey, Mart, Musk, Musk-sheep, Neat, Ovibos, Rother, Saola, Sapi-utan, S(e)ladang, Steare, Steer, Stirk, Taurus, Ure, Urus, Vu quang, Water, Water buffalo, Yak, Yoke, Zebu, Z(h)o
**Oxalis** Wood sorrel
**Ox-eye** Daisy, Yellow
**Oxford (group)** Blue, Buchmanism, Circus, OU, Puseyism, Shoe
**Oxgang** Bovate
**Oxhead** Aleph
**Oxidation, Oxide, Oxidise(d)** Alumina, Anatase, Ceria, Eagle-stone, Erbia, Eremacausis, Gothite, Gummite, Holmia, Kernite, Lithia, Magnesia, Nitrous, Ochre, Psilomelane, Quicklime, Rare earth, Red lead, Rust, Rutile, Samarskite, Strontia, Thoria, Tutty, Yttria, Zaffer, Zaffre, Zincite
**Oxlip** Paigle
▷**Oxtail** *may indicate* 'x'
**Oxygen (and lack of)** Aerobe, Anoxia, Epoxy, Liquid, Lox, Loxygen, O, Ozone, Vital air
**Oyer** Hearing, Trial

**Oyster (bed), Oyster disease, Oyster-eater** Avicula, Bivalve, Bonamia, Bush, Cul(t)ch, Kentish, Lay, Mollusc, Native, Ostrea, Ostreophage, Pandore, Pearl, Plant, Prairie, Salsify, Scallop, Scalp, Scaup, Seed(ling), Spat, Spondyl, Stew, Vegetable
**Oyster-catcher** Sea-pie
**Oyster-plant** Gromwell, Salsify
**Oz** Amos, Australia, NSW
**Ozone** Air, Atmosphere, Oxygen

# Pp

**P** Papa, Parking, Penny, Piano, Prince
**PA** Aide, Secretary, Tannoy
**Pabulum** Aliment, Cheer, Food, Fuel, Nourishment
**Pace, Pacemaker, Pacy** Andantine, Canter, Clip, Cracking, Dog-trot, Easter, Footstep, Gait, Geometric, Heel and toe, Jog-trot, Lope, Measure, Military, Pari passu, Pioneer, Prowl, Rack, → RATE, Roman, Scout's, Single-foot, Snail's, Spank, Speed, Step, Stride, Stroll, Tempo, Tramp, Tread, Trot
**Pachyderm** Armadillo, Elephant, Hippo, Mastodon, Rhino
**Pacific, Pacifier, Pacify** Appease, Assuage, Bromide, Calm, Conciliate, Dove, Dummy, Ease, Eirenic, Imperturbable, Irenic, Lull, Mild, Moderate, Ocean, Placate, Placid, Quiet, Serene, Soothe, Subdue, Sweeten, Tranquil
**Pacifist** Anti-war, CO, Conciliator, Dove, D(o)ukhobor, Peacenik
**Pack(age), Packaging, Packed, Packing, Pack in** Back, Bag, Bale, Blister, Bobbery, Box, Bubble(wrap), Bundle, Can, Cards, Carry, Chocker, Cold, Compress, Congest, Cram, Crate, Crowd, Cry, Deck, Dense, Dunnage, Embox, Entity, Everest, Excelsior, Face, Fardel, Flat, Flock, Floe, Forswear, Gasket, Gaskin, Gift-wrap(ped), Glut, Hamper, Hooker, Hunt, Ice, Jam, Kennel, Kitbag, Knapsack, Lies, Load, Matilda, Naughty, Overcrowd, Pair, → PARCEL, Pikau, Power, Presentation, Pun, Ram, Rat, Rout, Ruck, Rucksack, Saddlebag, Serry, Set, Shiralee, Shrink-wrap, Six, Steeve, Stow, Stuff, Suits, Sumpter, Tamp, Team, Tread, Troop, Truss, Wad, Wet, Wolf, Wrap
**Packer** Meat
**Packet** Bindle, Boat, Bomb, Bundle, Cachet, Cookie, Deck, Liner, Mailboat, Mailer, Mint, Parcel, Pay, Red, Roll, Rouleau, Sachet, Steam, Steamboat, Wage
**Pack-horse** Sumpter
**Packman** Chapman, Hawker, Hiker, Pedlar, Tinker
**Pact** Agreement, Alliance, Bargain, Bilateral, Cartel, Contract, Covenant, Entente cordiale, Locarno, Munich, Pactum, Stability, Suicide, → TREATY, Warsaw
**Pad(ding)** Bachelor, Batting, Bombast, Brake, Bustle, Compress, Condo, Crash, Cushion, Dabber, Damper, Dossil, Earmuff, Enswathe, Expand, Falsies, Filler, Flat, Frog, Gumshield, Hard, Hassock, Horse, Ink, Jotter, Knee, Launch, Leg-guard, Lily, Memo, Nag, Note, Numnah, Patch, Paw, Ped, Pillow, Pincushion, Plastron, Pledget, Plumper, Porters' knot, Pouf(fe), Protract, Pudding, Puff, Pulvillus, Pulvinar, Quitting, Scratch, Shin, Shoulder, Skid, Squab, Stamp, Steno, Stuff, Sunk, Swab, Tablet, Thief, Touch, Tournure, Tylopod, Tympan, Velour(s), Velure, Wad, Waffle, Wase, Writing
**Paddington** Bear, Station
**Paddle, Paddle boat, Paddle-foot** Canoe, Dabble, Doggy, Oar, Pinniped, Row, Seal, Side-wheel, Spank, Splash, Stern-wheeler, Wade
**Paddock** Enclosure, Field, Frog, Holding, Meadow, Park, Parrock, Sacrifice
**Paddy, Paddy field** Fury, Ire, Irishman, Pat(rick), Pet, Rag, Rage, Sawah, Strop, Tantrum, Temper, Wax
**Padre** Chaplain, Cleric, Father, Monk, Priest
**Paean** Eulogy, Hymn, Ode, Praise, Psalm
**Paediatrician** Rett
**Paedophile** Nonce
**Pagan(ism)** Animist, Atheist, Baalite, Ethnic, Gentile, Gentoo, Godless, Heathen, Heretic, Idolater, Infidel, Lectisternium, Odinist, Paynim, Saracen, Sun cult, Wicca

**Page(s), Pageboy** Back, Bastard title, Beep, Bellboy, Bellhop, Bleep, Boy, Broadsheet, Buttons, Callboy, Centrefold, Contact, Flyleaf, Fold out, Folio, Foolscap, Front, Gate-fold, Groom, Haircut, Hairdo, Henchman, Home, Hornbook, Leaf, Master, Messenger, Moth, Octavo, Op-ed, P, Pane, PP, Problem, Quarto, Ream, Recto, Ro, Servant, Sheet, Side, Splash, Squire, Tear sheet, Thirty-twomo, Tiger, Title, Varlet, Verso, Web, Yellow

**Pageant** Antic, Anticke, Antique, Cavalcade, Pomp, Spectacle, Tattoo, Triumph

**Pagoda** Anking, Anqing, Temple, To

**Pah** Fy, Pish, Tush, Umph

▶**Paid** *see* PAY(MASTER)

**Pail** Bucket, Kettle, Leglan, Leglen, Leglin, Piggin, Slop

**Pain(ful), Pains** Ache, Aggrieve, Agony, Ake, Algesis, Angina, Anguish, A(a)rgh, Arthralgia, Bad, Bale, Bedsore, Bitter, Bore, Bot(t), Bother, Burn, Causalgia, Colic, Collywobbles, Cramp, Crick, CTS, Distress, Dole, Doleur, Dolour, Dool(e), Dysmenorhoea, Dysury, Eina, Excruciating, Fash, Felon, Fibrositis, Gastralgia, Gip, Grief, Gripe, Growing, Gyp, Harrow, Heartburn, Hemialgia, → HURT, Ill, Kink, Laborious, Lancination, Loaf, Lumbago, Mal, Mastalgia, Mastodynia, Menace, Metralgia, Migraine, Misery, Molimen, Mulligrubs, Myalgia, Neuralgia, Nociceptive, Ordeal, Pang, Persuant, Pest, Phantom, Pleurodynia, Prick, Pungent, Rack, Raw, Referred, Rick, Sair, Sciatica, Smart, Sore, Sorrow, Splitting, Sten(d), Sternalgia, Sting, Stitch, Strangury, Stung, Tarsalgia, Teen(e), Tene, Throe, Topalgia, Torment, Tormina, Torture, Travail, Twinge, Wo(e), Wrench, Wring

▷**Pain** *may indicate* bread (French)

**Painkiller** Aminobutene, Analgesic, Anodyne, Bute, Celecoxib, Cocaine, Coxib, Distalgesic, Endorphin, Enkephalin, Jadeite, Menthol, Meperidine, Metopon, Morphine, Number, Paracetamol, Pethidine

**Painless(ness)** Analgesia, Easy

**Painstaking** Analgesic, Assiduous, Careful, Diligent, Elaborate, Exacting, Meticulous, Sedulous, Studious, Thorough

**Paint(ed), Painting** Abstract, Abstract expressionism, Acrylic, Action, Airbrush, Alla prima, Aquarelle, Arcimboldo, Art autre, Art deco, Artificial, Art nouveau, Ash Can School, Barbizon, Baroque, Battlepiece, Bice, Blottesque, Brushwork, Byzantine, Camaieu, Canvas, Cellulose, Cerograph, Chiaroscuro, Clair-obscure, Clobber, Coat, Colour, Constable, Cubiform, Cubism, Dadaism, Daub, Dayglo, Decorate, Depict, Describe, Diptych, Distemper, Duco, Ecce homo, Eggshell, Emulsion, Enamel, Encaustic, Expressionist, Fard, Fauvism, Finery, Finger, Flatting, Flemish, Fore-edge, Fresco, Fucus, Genre, Gild, Gloss, Gold, Gothic, Gouache, Graining, Gravure, Grease, Grisaille, Guernica, Hard-edge, Historical, Icon, Impasto, Impressionism, Intimism(e), Intonaco, Intumescent, Lead, Lick, Lime, Limn, Lithochromy, Luminous, Magilp, Mannerist, Maquillage, Matt, Megilp, Mehndi, Miniate, Miniature, Modello, Mona Lisa, Monotint, Mural, Naive, Neoclassical, Neo-expressionist, Neo-Impressionism, Neo-Plasticism, Nightpiece, Nihonga, Nocturne, Non-drip, Oaker, Ochre, Oil, Old Master, Oleo(graph), Op art, Orphism, Paysage, Pentimento, Pict, Picture, Pigment, Pinxit, Plein air, Pointillism(e), Polyptych, Pop art, Portray, Poster, Post-Impressionism, Predella, Pre-Raphaelite, Primavera, Primer, Primitive, Quadratura, Raddle, Rag-rolling, Realist, Renaissance, Rococo, Romantic, Rosemaling, Roughstuff, Sand, Sap green, Scenography, Scumble, Secco, Semi-gloss, Sfumato, Sien(n)ese, Skyscape, Smear, Spray, Stencil, Stereochrome, Still life, Stipple, Suprematism, Surrealist, Tablature, Tableau, Tachism(e), Tag, Tall-oil, Tanka, Tempera, Tenebrism, Thangka, Tondo, Townscape, Ukiyo-e, Umber, Umbrian, Undercoat, Underglaze, Vanitas, Veduta, Vorticism, War, Water-based, Wax, Whitewash, Woad

**Painted woman** Courtesan, Harlot, Pict, Tart

**Painter(s)** Animalier, Aquarellist, → ARTIST, Ash Can School, Colourist, Cubist, Decorator, Gilder, Illusionist, Impressionist, Landscape, Lazy, Limner, Little Master, Luminarist, Mannerist, Miniaturist, Modernist, Muralist, Nazarene, Old Master, Paysagist, Plein-airist, Pointillist, Portrait, Primitive, Sien(n)ese, Soutine, Sunday, Vedutista

**Pair(ing)** A deux, Brace, Cooper, Couple(t), Doublet, Duad, Duo, Dyad(ic), Electron, Exciton, Fellows, Geminate, Gemini, Item, Jugate, Jumelle, King, Link, Lone, Match, Mate, Minimal, Ocrea, Pigeon, Pr, Span, Spouses, Synapsis, Syndyasmian, Syzygy, Tandem, Thummim, Twa(e), Tway, Twin, Two(some), Urim, Yoke

**Paisley** Ian, Orange, Shawl
**Pakistan(i)** Jat, Pathan, pk, Punjabi, Sind(h)i
**Pal** Ally, Amigo, Bud(dy), China, Chum, Comrade, Crony, Cully, Friend, Mate, Playmate, Roomie, Wus(s)
**Palace** Alcazar, Alhambra, Basilica, Blenheim, Buckingham, Court, Crystal, Edo, Élysée, Escorial, Escurial, Fontainebleau, Forbidden City, Fulham, Gin, Goslar, Hampton Court, Holyrood, Holyroodhouse, Hotel, Istana, Kensington, Lambeth, Lateran, Linlithgow, Louvre, Mansion, Nonsuch, Palatine, Picture, Pitti, Pushkin, Quirinal, St James's, Sans Souci, Schloss, Scone, Seraglio, Serail, Shushan, Topkapi, Trianon, Tuileries, Valhalla, Vatican, Versailles, Winter
**Paladin** Champion, Charlemagne, Defender, Douzeper, Fièrabras, Ganelon, → KNIGHT, Ogier, Oliver, Orlando, Rinaldo, Roland
**Palanquin** Doolie, Kago, Litter, Palkee, Palki, Sedan
**Palatable, Palatalized, Palate** Cleft, Dainty, Hard, Mouille, Relish, Roof, Sapid, Savoury, Soft, Taste, Toothsome, Uranic, Uraniscus, Uvula, Velum
**Palatial** Alhambresque, Lavish, Ornate, Splendid
**Palatinate, Palatine** Officer, Pfalz
**Palaver** Chatter, Debate, Fuss, Parley, Powwow, → TALK
**Pale, Paling** Albino, Ashen, Blanch, Bleach, Cere, Dim, English, Etiolate(d), Fade, → FAINT, Fence, Ghostly, Grey, Haggard, Insipid, Jewish, Lily (white), Livid, Mealy, Ox-fence, Pallescent, Pastel, Pasty-faced, Peaky, Peelie-wally, Picket, Railing, Sallow, Shilpit, Stang, Verge, Wan, Whey-faced, White, Wishy-washy
**Pal(a)eography** Diplomatics
**Pal(a)eolithic** Acheulean, Acheulian, Aurignacian, Azilian, Capsian, Chellean, Clactonian, Gravettian, Levallois(ian), Lower, Madelenian, Magdalenian, Middle, Neanderthal, Perigordian, Solutrean, Solutrian, Strepyan, Upper
**Pal(a)eozoic** Hercynian, Permian, Silurian
**Palestine, Palestinian** Amorite, Fatah, Gadarene, Galilean, Gaza, Hamas, Holy Land, Intifada, Israel, Pal, Per(a)ea, Philistine, PLO, Samaria
**Palette** Board, Cokuloris, Uraniscus
**Palindrome, Palindromic** Cancrine, Reversal, Sotadic
**Palisade** Barrier, Fence, Fraise, Stacket, Stockade
**Pall** Bore, Cloy, Curtain, Damper, Glut, Hearse-cloth, Mantle, Mortcloth, Satiate, Shroud
**Palladium** Defence, Pd, Safeguard
**Pallas** Athene
**Pallet** Bed, Cot, Couch, Mattress, Tick, Typeholder
**Palliate, Palliative** Alleviate, Anetic, Ease, Extenuate, Lessen, Mitigate, Reduce, Relieve, Sedative
**Pallid** Anaemic, Ashen, Colourless, Insipid, Pale, Wan, Waxy
**Palm** Accolade, Areca, Assai, Atap, Babassu, Bangalow, Betel, Buriti, Burrawang, Bussu, Cabbage, Calamus, Carna(h)uba, Carpentaria, Chamaerops, Chiqui-chiqui, Coco, Cohune, Conceal, Coquito, Corozo, Corypha, Cycad, Date (tree), Doom, Doum, Elaeis, Euterpe, Fan, Feather, Fob, Foist, Gomuti, Gomuto, Groo-groo, Gru-gru, Hand, Hemp, Ita, Itching, Ivory, Jip(p)i-Jap(p)a, Jipyapa, Jupati, Kentia, Kittul, Laurels, Loof, Looves, Macahuba, Macaw, Macoya, Miriti, Moriche, Nikau, Nipa, Oil, Palmyra, Paxiuba, Peach, Pupunha, Raffia, Raphia, Rat(t)an, Royal, Sabal, Sago, Saw palmetto, Sugar, Talipat, Talipot, Thatch, Thenar, Toddy, Triumph, Troelie, Troolie, Trooly, Trophy, Vola, Washingtonia, Wax, Wine, Zamia
**Palmer** Lilli, Pilgrim
**Palmerston** Pam
**Palmistry** Ch(e)irognomy
**Palm-leaf** Frond
**Palm-oil** Bribe, Payola
**Palpable** Evident, Gross, Manifest, Patent, Plain, Tangible
**Palpitate, Palpitation** Flutter, Pitpat, Pulsate, Spasm, Throb, Twitter, Vibrate
**Palsy** Bell's, Cerebral, Paralysis, Scrivener's, Shakes, Shaking, Spastic paralysis

**Paltry** Bald, Cheap, Chickenfeed, Exiguous, Meagre, Mean, Measly, Mere, Peanuts, Pelting, Petty, Pimping, Poor, Puny, Scald, Scalled, Shabby, Shoestring, Sorry, Thingummybob, Tin(-pot), Tinny, Trashy, Trifling, Two-bit, Vile, Waff, Whiffet

**Pamper(ed)** Baby, Cocker, Coddle, Cosher, Cosset, Cuiter, Feather-bed, Gratify, High-fed, →INDULGE, Mollycoddle, Overfeed, Pet, Pompey, Spoil, Spoon-fed

**Pamphlet(eer)** Booklet, Brochure, Catalogue, Chapbook, Defoe, Leaflet, Notice, Sheet, Tract

**Pan** Agree, Auld Hornie, Bainmarie, Balit, Basin, Betel(-pepper), Braincase, Chafer, Chip, Dent, Dial, Drip, Dripping, Drub, Frying, Goat-god, Goblet, God, Hard, Ice-floe, Iron, Jelly, Karahi, Knee, Knock, Ladle, Lavatory, Muffin, Nature-god, Non-stick, Oil, Pancheon, Panchion, Patella, Patina, Peter, Plate, Poacher, Preserving, Prospect, Roast, Salt, Sauce, Search, Siri, Skid, Skillet, Slag, Slate, Spider, Steamer, Steel, Sweep, Tube, Vacuum, Vessel, Warming, Wo(c)k, Work

**Panacea** All-heal, Azoth, Catholicon, Cure(-all), Diacatholicon, Elixir, Ginseng, Heal-all, Parkleaves, Remedy, Tutsan

**Panache** Bravura, Crest, Dash, Elan, Elegance, Flair, Paz(z)azz, Piz(z)azz, Plume, Pzazz, Show, Style, Talent

**Panama** Isthmus

**Pancake** Blin(i), Blintz(e), Burrito, Crêpe (suzette), Crumpet, Drop(ped)-scone, Flam(m), Flapjack, Flaune, Flawn, Fraise, Fritter, Froise, Galette, Latke, Pikelet, Poppadum, Potato, Quesadilla, Ro(e)sti, Scotch, Slapjack, Spring roll, Suzette, Taco, Tortilla, Tostada, Waffle

**Pancreas** Isles of Langerhans, Sweetbread

**Panda** Bear-cat, Car, Chi-chi, Chitwah, Common, Giant, Lesser, Patrol car, Red, Squad car

**Pandarus** Go-between

**Pandemonium** Bedlam, Chaos, Inferno, Mayhem, Tumult, Uproar

**Pander** Broker, Indulge, Minister, Pimp, Procurer, Toady

**Pane** Glass, Light, Panel, Quarrel, Quarry, Sheet

**Panegyric** Encomium, Eulogy, Laudation, P(a)ean, Praise, Tribute

**Panel(ling), Panels** Adoption, Array, Board, Cartouche, Children's, Console, Control, Dado, Dashboard, Display, Faceplate, Fa(s)cia, Fielded, Gore, Hatchment, Inset, Instrument, Jury, Lacunar, Mandorla, Mimic, Mola, Orb, Patch(board), People's, Reredorse, Reredos(se), Rocker, Screen, Skreen, Solar, Stile, Stomacher, Table, Tablet, Tongue and groove, Triptych, Valance, Volet, Wainscot

**Panellist** Juror

**Pang** Achage, Ache, Crick, Qualm, Spasm, Stab, Stound, Travail, Twinge, Wrench

**Pangloss** Optimist

**Pangolin** Ant-eater, Manis

**Panhandle(r)** Beggar, W. Virginia

**Panic** Alar(u)m, Amaze, Blue funk, Consternation, Fear, Flap, Flat-spin, Flip, Fright, Funk, Guinea-grass, Hysteria, Lather, Millet, Raggee, Raggy, Ragi, Sauve qui peut, →SCARE, Scaremonger, Scarre, Stage fright, Stampede, Stampedo, State, Stew, Tailspin, →TERROR

**Panicle** Thyrse

**Panjandrum** Bashaw

**Pannier** Basket, Cacolet, Corbeil, Dosser, Kajawah, Saddlebag, Skip, Whisket

**Panoply** Armour, Array, Pomp

**Panorama, Panoramic** Cyclorama, Range, Scenery, Veduta, View, Vista

**Pan-pipes** Antara

**Pansy** Heart's-ease, Herb-trinity, Kiss-me-quick, Love-in-idleness, Viola

**Pant(s)** Ache, Bags, Boxer shorts, Breeches, Capri, Cargo, Chaps, Chinos, Culottes, Deck, Dhoti, Drawers, Fatigues, Flaff, Gasp, Gaucho, Harem, Hipster, Hot, Knickers, Long johns, Longs, Nonsense, Parachute, Pech, Pedal-pushers, Pegh, Puff, Rot, Ski, Slacks, Smalls, Stirrup, Stovepipe, Sweat, Tap, The pits, Throb, Toreador, Training, Trews, Trousers, Trunks, Wheeze, Yearn

**Pantaloon** Columbine, Dupe, Pants

**Pantheism** Idolatry, Immanency

**Panther** Bagheera, Black, Cat, Cougar, Grey, Jaguar, Leopard, Pink
**Panties** Briefs, Knickers, Scanties, Step-ins, Undies
**Pantomime, Pantomime character** Aladdin, Charade, Cheironomy, Cinderella, Dumb-show, Farce, Galanty, Harlequinade, Pierrot, Play
**Pantry** Butler's, Buttery, Closet, Larder, Spence, Stillroom
**Pantyhose** Tights
**Pap** Dug, Mealie, Mush, Nipple, Teat, Udder
**Papa** Dad, Father, P
**Papal** Catholic, Clementine, Concordat, Encyclic, Guelf, Guelph, Holy See, Legation, Pontifical, RC, Roman, Tiara, Vatican
**Paparazzo** Rat-pack, Snapper
**Paper(s), Paperwork, Papery** Admin, Allonge, Anti-Jacobin, Antiquarian, Art, Atlas, Ballot, Bank, Baryta, Bible, Blat(t), Blotting, Bond, Brief, Broadsheet, Broadside, Bromide, Brown, Building, Bumf, Bumph, Butter, Cap, Carbon, Cartridge, Cellophane®, Chad, Chinese, Chit, Chiyogami, Cigarette, Colombier, Comic, Command, Commercial, Confetti, Corrugated, Cream-laid, Cream-wove, Credentials, Crêpe, Crown, Curl, Cutch, Daily, Deckle-edge, Decorate, Demy, Docket, Document, Dossier, Drawing, Eggshell, Elephant, Emery, Emperor, Essay, Exam, File, Filter, Final, Flash, Flock, Folio, Foolscap, Form(s), Fourdrinier, FT, Funny, Furnish, Galley, Garnet, Gazette, Gem, Gift wrap, Glass(ine), Glumaceous, Government, Grand eagle, Grand Jesus, Graph, Greaseproof, Green, Guardian, Gutter press, Hieratica, ID, Imperial, India, Japanese, Jesus, Journal, Kent cap, Kraft, Kutch, Lace, Laid, Lavatory, Legal cap, Linen, Litmus, Loo-roll, Loose-leaf, Mail, Manifold, Manil(l)a, Marble, Mercantile, Mirror, Monograph, MS, Munimenti, Music(-demy), Needle, News(print), → NEWSPAPER, Note, Notelet, Oil, Onion-skin, Order, Origami, Packet-note, Packing, Pad, Page, Papillote, Papyrus, Parchment, Paste-down, Pickwick, Plotting, Position, Post, Pot(t), Pravda, Press, Print, Printing, Quair, Quarto, Quire, Rag, Ramee, Rami(e), Ream, Red top, Retree, Rhea, Rice, Rolled, Rolling, Royal, Safety, Satin, Saxe, Scent, Scotsman, Scrap, Scrip, Script, Scroll, Scrowl, Sheaf, Sheet, Ship's, Silver, Skin, Slipsheet, Spoilt, Stamp, Starch, State, Steamer, Sugar, Sun, Super-royal, Tabloid, Taffeta, Tap(p)a, Tar, Term, Ternion, TES, Test, Thesis, Thread, Tiger, Tissue, Today, Toilet, Torchon, Touch, Tracing, Tract, Trade, Transfer, Treatise, Treeware, Tri-chad, Turmeric, Two-name, Vellum, Velvet, Voucher, Walking, Wall, Waste, Watch, Wax(ed), Web, Whatman®, White, Willesden, Wirewove, Wood(chip), Woodfree, Worksheet, Wove, Wrapping, Writing, Yellow, Zine
**Paperback** Limp(back)
**Paper-cutting, Paper-folding** Decoupage, Kirigami, Origami, Psaligraphy
**Paperhanger** Billposter, Decorator
**Papier-mâché** Carton-pierre, Flong
**Paprika** Spanish
**Par** Average, Equate, Equivalent, → NORMAL, Scratch
**Parable** Allegory, Fable, Proverb
**Parabola** Arc, Curve, Hyperbola
**Parachute, Parachutist** Aeroshell, Aigrette, Brake, Drag, Drogue, Extraction, Float, Freefall, Golden, Jump, Pack, Pappus, Para, Parabrake, Parapente, Red Devil, Ribbon, Silk, Sky-diving, Skyman, Thistledown, Umbrella
**Parade (ground)** Air, Arcade, Catwalk, Cavalcade, Ceremony, Church, Concours d'élégance, Display, Dress, Drill, Easter, Emu, Esplanade, Flaunt, Fly past, Gala, Ground, Hit, Identification, Identity, Line-up, Maidan, March-past, Monkey-run, Pageantry, Passing-out, Pomp, Prance, Procession, Prom(enade), Sashay, Show, Sick, Sowarry, Stand-to, Strut, Ticker tape, Troop
**Paradigm** Example
**Paradise** Arcadia, Avalon, Bliss, Dream world, Earthly, Eden, Elysium, Fool's, Garden, Goshen, Happy-hunting-ground, Heaven, Idyll(ic), Lost, Malaguetta, Nirvana, Park, Regained, Shangri-la, Sky, Surfer's, Svarga, Swarga, Swerga, → UTOPIA
**Paradox(ical)** Absurdity, Cantor's, Contradiction, Dilemma, Electra, Epimenides, French, Gilbertian, Hydrostatic, Irony, Koan, Liar, Olbers', Puzzle, Russell's, Sorites, Twin, Zeno's
**Paradoxure** Musang

**Paraffin** Earthwax, Kerosene, Kerosine, Liquid, Ozocerite, Ozokerite, Photogen(e), Propane
**Paragon** Model, Non(e)such, Pattern, Pearl, Phoenix, Role model, Rose, Saint
**Paragraph (mark)** Article, Balaam, Causerie, Note, Passage, Piece, Pilcrow
**Paraguay** PY
**Parakeet** Parrot, Popinjay, Rosella
**Parallax** Annual, Daily, Diurnal, Geocentric, Heliocentric
**Parallel** Align, Analog, Analogy, Arctic circle, Collateral, Collimate, Corresponding, Equal, Even, Forty-ninth, Like, Pattern
**Parallelogram** Rhomb(us)
**Paralysis, Paralyse** Akinesia, Apoplexy, Benumb, Cataplexy, Catatonia, Cramp, Curarise, Cycloplegia, Diplegia, Halt, Hemiplegia, Infantile, Lithyrism, Monoplegia, Numbness, Ophthalmoplegia, Palsy, Paraplegia, Paresis, Polio, Quadriplegia, Radial, Scram, Shock, Shut, Spastic, Spina bifida, Stun, Torpefy, Transfix
**Paramedic** Ambulance-man
**Parameter** Definition, Impact
**Paramilitary** Inkatha, Phalangist, SAS, Sena, UDA
**Paramount** Chief, Dominant, Greatest, Overall, Premier, →SUPREME, Topless, Utmost
**Paramour** Beau, Franion, Gallant, Leman, Lover, Mistress, Potemkin, Thais
**Paranoid** Neurotic, Tweak
**Paranormal** Clairvoyant, ESP, Psionics, Psychic, Spiritual, Telekinesis
**Parapet (space)** Balustrade, Barbette, Bartisan, Bartizan, Battlement, Breastwork, Brisure, Bulwark, Crenel, Flèche, Machicolation, Merlon, Rampart, Redan, Surtout, Terreplein, Top, Wall
**Paraphernalia** Armamentarium, Belongings, Equipment, Gear, Trappings
**Parasite, Parasitic** Amoeba, Ascarid, Autoecious, Aweto, Babesiasis, Beech-drops, Bilharzia, Biogenous, Biotroph, Bladder-worm, Bloodsucker, Bonamia, Bot, Candida, Chalcid, Chigoe, Coccus, Conk, Copepod, Cosher, Crab-louse, Cryptosporidium, Cryptozoite, Dodder, Ectogenous, Ectophyte, Endamoeba, Endophyte, Entophyte, Entozoon, Epiphyte, Epizoon, Facultative, Filarium, Flatworm, Flea, Freeloader, Gapeworm, Giaour, Giardia, Gregarinida, Guinea worm, Haematozoon, Hair-eel, Hair-worm, Heartworm, Heteroecious, Hook-worm, Ichneumon, Inquiline, Isopod, Kade, Ked, Lackey, Lamprey, Leech, Leishmania, Licktrencher, Liverfluke, Louse, Lungworm, Macdonald, Mallophagous, Measle, Mistletoe, Mite, Monogenean, Necrotroph, Nematode, Nit, Obligate, Orobanche, Phytosis, Pinworm, Plasmodium, Puccinia, Pulix, Quandong, Rafflesia, Redia, Rhipidoptera, Rickettsia, Root, Roundworm, Schistosoma, Scrounger, Shark, Smut-fungus, Sponge(r), Sporozoa(n), Strangleweed, Strepsiptera, Strongyle, Strongyloid, Stylops, Sucker, Symphile, Tachinid, Tapeworm, Tick, Toady, Toxoplasma, Trematode, Trencher-friend, Trencher-knight, Trichina, Trichomonad, Tryp(anosoma), Vampire, Viscum, Wheatworm, Whipworm, Witchweed, Worms
**Parasol** Awning, Brolly, En tout cas, Marquise, Sunshade, Umbrella
**Paratrooper** Red Devil, Skyman, Stick leader
**Parcel** Allocate, Allot, Aret, Bale, Bundle, Dak, Enwrap, Food, Holding, Inwrap, Lot, Package, Packet, Plot, Sort, Wrap
**Parch(ed), Parching** Arid, Bake, Dehydrate, Dry, Graddan, Hot coppers, Roast, Scorched, Sere, Thirsty, Toast, Torrefied, Torrid, Xerotes
**Parchment** Diploma, Forel, Membrane, Mezuzah, Panel, Papyrus, Pell, Pergameneous, Roll, Roule, Scroll, Scrow, Sheepskin, Vegetable, Vellum, Virgin
**Pard** Leopard, Pal, Partner
**Pardon(able), Pardoner** Absolution, Absolve, Amnesty, Anan, Assoil, Clear, Condone, Eh, Excuse, →FORGIVE, Free, Grace, Mercy, Quaestionary, Quaestuary, Qu(a)estor, Release, Remission, Remit, Reprieve, Venial, What
**Pare** Chip, Flaught, Flay, Peel, Shave, Skive, Sliver, Strip, Whittle
**Parent(al)** Ancestral, Father, Forebear, Foster, Generant, Genitor, Maternal, Mother, Paternal, Rear, Single, Solo, Storge
**Parenthesis** Aside, Brackets, Innuendo
**Parhelion** Sun-dog

**Pariah** Ishmael, Leper, Outcast, Pi(e)dog, Pyedog
**Paris(ian), Parisienne** Abductor, Athene, Elle, Gai, Gay, Grisette, Lutetia (Parisiorum), Lutetian, Maillotin, Midinette, Trojan
**Parish** Charge, District, Flock, Kirkto(w)n, Parischan(e), Parishen, Parochin(e), Peculiar, Province, Title
**Parity** Equalness, Equivalence, Smithsonian
**Park(ing), Parkland** Amusement, Apron, Ball, Business, Car, Caravan, Common, Country, Disc, Domain, Enclosure, Epcot, Forest, Fun, Game, Garage, Gosford, Grounds, Hardstand, Industrial, Longleat, Lung, Motor, National, Off-street, P, Petrified Forest, Pitch, Pleasure ground, Preserve, Rec, Reserve, Safari, Sanctuary, Savanna forest, Science, Sefton, Siding, Skate, Stand, Stop, Technology, Terrain, Theme, Trailer, Valet, Valley, Water, Wildlife, Wind, Yard, Zoo

---

**PARKS**

*4 letters:*
Hyde

*5 letters:*
Dales
Green
Ibrox
Mungo
Tsavo
Upton

*6 letters:*
Etosha
Exmoor
Hwange
Jasper
Kakadu
Katmai
Kruger
Oyster
Tivoli

*7 letters:*
Central
Gardens
Nairobi
Phoenix
Regent's
Sandown

*8 letters:*
Daintree
Dartmoor
Jurassic
Osterley
Paradise
St James's
Yosemite

*9 letters:*
Algonquin
Battersea
Fiordland
Grampians
Green lung
Lamington
Mansfield
Mesa Verde
Serengeti
Snowdonia

*10 letters:*
Disneyland
Everglades
Kejimkujik
Pittie-ward

*11 letters:*
Alton Towers
Death Valley
Grand Canyon
Kobuk Valley
Mammoth Cave
Wood Buffalo
Yellowstone

*12 letters:*
Lake District
Mount Rainier
Peak District
Quttinirpaaq

*13 letters:*
Banff National
Brecon Beacons
Mount Aspiring
Mount McKinley

*14 letters:*
Egmont National
Jasper National
Kruger National
Lassen Volcanic
Northumberland
North York Moors
Riding Mountain
Yorkshire Dales

*15 letters:*
Kalahari Gemsbok
Nahanni National
Sequoia National

*16 letters:*
Gates of the Arctic

*18 letters:*
Mount Kenya National
Prince Edward Island
Shenandoah National

*19 letters:*
Great Smoky Mountains

---

**Parka** Atigi
**Parker** Dorothy, Nos(e)y
**Parkleaves** Tutsan
**Parlance** Idiom
**Parley** Confer, Discourse, Palaver, Speak, Tret
**Parliament** Addled, Althing, Another place, Barebones, Black, Boule, Bundestag, Chamber, Commons, Congress, Cortes, Council, Cross-bench, Dail, Diet, Drunken, D(o)uma, Eduskunta, European, Folketing, Holyrood, House, Hung, Imperial, Knesset, Lack-learning, Lagt(h)ing, Landst(h)ing, Lawless, Legislature, Lok Sabha, Long, Lords, Majlis, Mejlis, Merciless, Mongrel, Odelst(h)ing, Owl, Political, Rajya Sabha, Reichsrat, Reichstag, Riksdag, Rump, St Stephens, Sanhedrin, Seanad, Seanad Éireann, Sejm, Short, Stannary, States-general, Stirthing, Stormont, Stort(h)ing, The Beehive, Thing, Tynwald (Court), Unicameral, Unlearned, Useless, Vidhan Sabha, Volkskammer, Volksraad, Westminster

**Parliamentarian** Cabinet, De Montfort, Fairfax, Ireton, Leveller, Member, MP, Politico, Roundhead, Whip

**Parlour** Beauty, Beer, Funeral, Ice-cream, Keeping-room, Lounge, Massage, Milking, Salon, Sitting-room, Snug, Spence

**Parnassus** Museum, Verse

**Parochial** Insular, Jackeen, Narrow-minded

**Parody** Burlesque, Caricature, Cod, Lampoon, Mock, Piss-take, Satire, Send-up, Skit, Spoof, Travesty

**Parole** Pledge, Promise, Trust, Word

**Paronychia** Agnail, Felon, Whitlow

**Paroxysm** Fit, Frenzy, Rapture, Spasm, Subintrant, Throe

**Parricide** Cenci

**Parrot** Amazon, Ape, Budgerigar, Cockatoo, Conure, Copy, Echo, Emulate, Flint, Green leek, Grey, Imitate, Kaka(po), Kea, Lorikeet, Lory, Lovebird, Macaw, Mimic, Nestor, Owl, Pandemonium, Parakeet, Paroquet, Poll(y), Popinjay, Psittacine, Quarrion, Repeat, Rosella, Rote, Shell, Stri(n)gops, T(o)uraco

**Parrot-bill** Glory-pea

**Parry** Block, Counter, Defend, Dodge, Fend, Forestall, Parade, Repel, Riposte, Septime, Sixte, Tac-au-tac, Thwart, Ward

**Parsee** Zoroastrian

**Parsimonious, Parsimony** Aberdonian, Cheese-paring, Mean, Narrow, Near(ness), Niggardly, Scanty, Scrimping, Stingy, Thrift, Tight

**Parsley** Apiol, Cicely, Cow, Dog, Kecks, Kex, Persillade, Pot-herb

**Parsnip** Buttered, Buttery, Dill, Masterwort, Sium, Skirret

**Parson** Clergyman, Cleric, Fleet, Holy Joe, Minister, Non juror, Pastor, Priest, Rector, Rev, Sky-pilot, Soul-curer, Yorick

**Parsonage** Glebe, Haworth, Manse, Rectory, Vicarage

**Part(s), Parting, Partly** Accession, Aliquot, Among, Antimere, Area, Aspect, Aught, Bad, Behalf, Bit, Bite, Bulk, Bye, Cameo, Character, Chunk, Cog, Compartment, Component, Constituent, Crack, Cue, Department, Detail, Dislink, Diverge, Divide, Divorce, Dole, Element, Episode, Escapement, Farewell, Fascicle, Fork, Fraction, Good, Goodbye, Great, Half, Ill, Imaginary, Ingredient, Inner, Instalment, Integrant, Into, Lathe, Lead, Leave, Leg, Lill, Lilt, Lines, List, Livraison, Member, Meronym, Module, Moiety, Morsel, Organ, Parcel, Passus, Percentage, → **PIECE**, Portion, Primo, Principal, Private, Proportion, Pt, Quit, Quota, Rape, Ratio, Real, Region, Rive, Role, Scena, Scene, Secondo, Section, Sector, Segment, Segregate, Separate, Serial, Sever, Shade, Share, Shed, Sleave, Sle(i)ded, Small, → **SOME**, Spare, Split, Stator, Sunder, Synthon, Tithe, To a degree, Tranche, Twin(e), Unit, Vaunt, Voice, Walking, Walk on, Wrench

**Partake(r)** Allottee, Eat, Figure, Participate, Share

**Parthenogenesis** Deuterotoky, Thelytoky

**Partial(ity), Partially** Biased, Ex-parte, Fan, Favour, Halflins, Imbalance, Incomplete, Nepotism, One-sided, Penchant, Predilection, Prejudiced, Slightly, Unequal, Weakness

**Participate, Participant, Participation** Audience, Engage, Entrant, Field, Join, Member, Muck-in, Panellist, Partake, Pitch in, Play(er), Share, Symposiast, Traceur

**Participle** Dangling, Misrelated, Past, Perfect, Present

**Particle(s)** Accelerator, Alpha, Anion, Antielectron, Antineutron, Antiproton, Atom, Baryon, Beta, Bit, Boson, Charmonium, Corpuscle, Cosmic dust, Curn, Dander, Delta, Deuteron, Dust, Effluvium, Electron, Elementary, Episome, Exchange, Fermion, Fleck, Floccule, Fragment, Fundamental, Gauge boson, Gemmule, Globule, Glueball, Gluon, God, Grain, Granule, Graviton, Grit, Hadron, Heavy, Higgs boson, Hyperon, Ion, J, Jot, J/psi, Kaon, Laitance, Lambda, Lemail, Lemel, Lepton, Lipoplast, Liposome, Macron, Meson, Micelle, Microsome, Mite, Molecule, Monopole, Mote, Muon, Negatron, Neutralino, Neutretto, Neutrino, Neutron, Nibs, Nobiliary, Nucleon, Omega-minus, Parton, Pentaquark, Photon, Pion, Plasmagene, Plastisol, Platelet, Positon, Positron, Preon, Proton, Psi(on), Quark, Radioactivity, Scintilla, Shives, Shower, Sigma, Singlet, Sinter, Smithereen, Spark, Speck, Strange, Subatom, Submicron, Subnuclear, Tachyon, Tardyon, Tau neutrino, Tauon,

Thermion, Tittle, Top quark, Virion, W, Whit, WIMP, X-hyperon, XI, Z

**Parti-coloured** Fancy, Motley, Piebald, Pied, Variegated

**Particular** Choosy, Dainty, → DETAIL, Diligent, Endemic, Especial, Essential, Express, Faddy, Fastidious, Fiky, Fog, Fussy, Item, Itself, London fog, Minute, Nice, Niffy-naffy, Nipperty-tipperty, Nitpicker, Old-maidish, Own, Pea-souper, Peculiar, Pedant, Pernickety, Pet, Point, Prim, Prissy, Proper, → RESPECT, Special, Specific, Stickler, Strict, Stripe

**Partisan** Adherent, Axe, Biased, Carlist, Champion, Devotee, Factional, Fan, Irregular, Partial, Provo, Queenite, Sectarian, Sider, Spear, Stalwart, Supporter, Tendentious, Yorkist, Zealot

**Partition(ed)** Abjoint, Bail, Barrier, Brattice, Bretasche, Bulkhead, Carve up, Cloison, Cubicle, Diaphragm, Dissepiment, Divider, Division, Fence, Hallan, Mediastinum, Parpane, Parpen(d), Parpent, Parpoint, Perpend, Perpent, Replum, → SCREEN, Scriene, Septum, Skreen, Subdivide, Tabula, Wall, With(e)

**Partlet** Hen, Overlaid

**Partner(ship)** Accomplice, Affiliation, Alliance, Ally, Associate, Bidie-in, Butty, Cahoot(s), Civil, Coachfellow, Coalition, Cohab(itee), Cohabitor, Collaborate, Colleague, Comrade, Confederate, Consort, Copemate, Couple, Date, Dutch, Escort, E-W, Firm, Gigolo, Husband, Limited, Mate, Moll, N-S, Offsider, Oppo, Other half, Pair, Pal, Pard, Rival, Sidekick, Significant other, Silent, Sleeping, SOP, Soulmate, Sparring, Spouse, Stablemate, Stand, Steady, Symbiosis, Unite, Wag, Wif(i)e

▷**Part of** *may indicate* a hidden word

**Partridge** Bird, Chik(h)or, Chukar, Chukor, Covey, Flapper, Quail, Red-legged, Tinamou, Ynambu

**Part-timer** Semi-pro

**Party** Acid house, Advance, Aftershow, Alliance, ANC, Apparat, Apres-ski, Assembly, At-home, Ba'ath, Bachelor(ette), Bake, Ball, Band, Barbecue, Bash, Beano, Bee, Binge, Birthday, Bloc, Blowout, Boarding, Body, Bottle, Bridge, Buck's, Bunfight, Bust, Cabal, Caboodle, Camp, Carousal, Carouse, Caucus, Celebration, Centre, Clambake, Coach, Cocktail, Coffeeklat(s)ch, Colour, Commando, Communist, Concert, Congress, Conservative, Contingent, Cookie-shine, Cooperative, Coterie, Crew, Cult, Democratic, Detail, Ding, Dinner, Disco(theque), Do, Drag, Drum, DUP, Faction, Falange, Farewell, Fatigue, Federalist, Fest, Festivity, Fête champêtre, Fête Galante, Fianna Fáil, Fiesta, Fine Gael, Firing, Flying, Foy, Function, Funfest, Gala, Galravage, Gang, Garden, Gathering, Get together, Ghibel(l)ine, GOP, Green, Greenback, Grumbletonian, Guelf, Guelph, Guilty, Hen, High heels, Hoedown, Hooley, Hootenannie, Hootenanny, Hoot(a)nannie, Hoot(a)nanny, House, Housewarming, Hurricane, Inkatha, Irredentist, Jamboree, Jana Sangh, Janata, Jol(lities), Junket, Junto, Kegger, Kettledrum, Kitchen tea, Klat(s)ch, Knees-up, Kuomintang, L, Labour, Landing, Launch, Lawn, Levee, Lib, Lib Dem, Liberal, Lig, Love-in, Low heels, Luau, Mallemaroking, Mollie, Movement, Musicale, National, Necking, Neck-tie, Octobrist, Office, Opposition, Orgy, Peace, People's, Person, Petting, Plaid, Political, Populist, Posse, Progressive, Prohibition, Pyjama, Radical, Rage, Rave, Rave-up, Razzle(-dazzle), Reception, Republican, Reunion, Revel(ry), Ridotto, Roast, Rocking, Roister, Rort, Rout, Scottish Nationalist, SDP, Search, Sect, Send off, Set, Shindig, Shindy, Shine, Shivoo, Shiv Sena, Shooting, Shower, Shower tea, Side, Sinn Fein, Sleepover, Slumber, Small and early, Smoker, SNP, Soc(ialist), Social, Social Credit, Social Democratic, Socialise, Soirée, Spree, Squad(rone), Squadrone volante, Stag, Street, Stretcher, Symposium, Tailgate, Tea, Teafight, Third, Thrash, Toga, Tory, Treat, UKIP, Ultramontane, Unionist, United, Wafd, Wake, Warehouse, Whig, Whoop-de-do(o), Wine, Wingding, Working, Wrap

**Partygoer** Rager, Raver, Reveller, Socialite

**Party-piece** Solo

**Parvenu** Arriviste, Upstart

**Pascal** Blaise, Pa, Pressure

**Pash** Crush, Devotion

**Pasha** Achmed, Bashaw, Dey, Emir, Ismet

**Pass(ed), Passing, Pass on, Past, Pass through** Absit, Aforetime, Ago, Agon, Annie Oakley, Aorist, Approve, Arise, Arlberg, Before, Behind, Bernina, Beyond, Blow over, Boarding, Bolan, Botte, Brenner, Brief, Burgess, Bus, By (the by), Bygone, Carry, Caudine

Forks, Centre, Cerro Gordo, Chal(l)an, Chilkoot, Chine, Chit(ty), Cicilian Gates, Clear, Col, Cote, Cross, Cursory, Death, Dee, Defile, Delate, Demise, Diadrom, Die, Disappear, Double, Dummy, Dunno, Elapse, Emit, Enact, End, Ensue, Ephemeral, Evanescent, Exceed, Excrete, Exeat, Faena, Flashback, Fleeting, Fob, Foist, Forby, Forgone, Former, Forward, Gap, Gate, Gha(u)t, Give, Glencoe, Glide, Go, Go by, Gorge, Great St Bernard, Gulch, Halse, Hand, Happen, Hause, Historic, Horseshoe, Hospital, ID, Impart, Impermanent, Interrail, Interval, In transit, Jark, Jump, Khyber, Killiecrankie, Kloof, La Cumbre, Lap, Late, Lead, Legislate, Live, Long syne, Loss, Mesmerism, Migrate, Momentary, Mont Cenis, Moravian Gate, Needle, Nek, Nine days' wonder, No bid, Nod through, Notch, Nutmeg, Nye, Occur, Oer, Offload, O grade, OK, Okay, Oke, Omit, Once, One-time, One-two, Overhaul, Overshoot, Overslaugh, Overtake, Pa, Palm, Parade, Participle, Perish, Permeate, Permit, Perpetuate, Poll, Poort, Predicament, Preterit(e), Pretty, Proceed, Propagate, Pun(c)to, Qualify, Railcard, Ratify, Reach, Reeve, Refer, Relay, Retro, Retroactive, Retrospect, Reverse, Roncesvalles, Run, Safe conduct, St Bernard, St Gotthard, San Bernardino, Sanitation, Scissors, Sea-letter, Senile, Serve, Shangri-la, Shipka, Simplon, Since, Skim, Skip, Skirt, Slap, Sling, Small and early, Snap, Spend, Stab, State, Swipecard, Temporal, Thermopylae, Thread, Through, Thru, Ticket, Time immemorial, Tip, Train, Transient, Transilient, Transitory, Transmit, Transpire, Transude, Travel, Triptyque, Troop, Uspallata, Veronica, Vet, Visa, Visé, Wall, Wayleave, Weather, While, Wrynose, Yesterday, Yesteryear, Ygoe

**Passable, Passible** Adequate, Fair, Navigable, Tolerable

**Passage(way), Passages** Abature, Adit, Airshaft, Airway, Aisle, Alley(way), Alure, Analects, Apostrophe, Arcade, Archway, Areaway, Arterial, Atresia, Avenue, Bank, Breakthrough, Breezeway, Bridge, Bylane, Cadenza, Canal, Caponier(e), Career, Catwalk, Channel, Choana, Chute, Citation, Clarino, Clause, Close, Coda, Condie, Conduit, Corridor, Creep, Crossing, Crush, Cundy, Dead-end, Deambulatory, Deck, Defile, Drake, Drift, Duct, Eel-fare, Episode, Epitaph, Excerpt, Extract, Fare, Fat, Fauces, Fistula, Flat, Flight, Flue, Fogou, Gallery, Gangway, Gap, Gat, Gate, Ghat, Ginnel, Gorgia, Gully-hole, Gut, Hall, Head, Honeycomb, Inlet, Intestine, Journey, Kyle, Labyrinth, Lane, Lapse, Larynx, Lick, Lientery, Loan, Lobby, Locus, Meatus, Melisma, Meridian, Middle, Mine, Mona, Moto perpetuo, Movement, Northeast, Northwest, Ossia, Para(graph), Parashah, Path, Pend, Pericope, Phrase, Pore, Port, Portion, Prelude, Presto, Progress, Prose, Purple, Race, Retournelle, Ride, Ripieno, Rite, Ritornell(o), Road, Rough, Route, Sailing, Screed, Shaft, Shunt, Sinus, Skybridge, Skywalk, Slap, Slype, Snicket, Solus, Spillway, Sprue, Strait, Street, Stretta, Stretto, Subway, Sump, Text, Thirl, Thorough(fare), Throat, Tour, Trachea, Trance, Transe, Transit(ion), Travel, Tunnel, Tutti, Undercast, Unseen, Ureter, Voyage, Walkway, Way, Windpipe, Windway

▹**Passage of arms** *may indicate* 'sleeve'

**Passé** Corny, Dated, Ex, Obsolete, Old-fashioned

**Passenger(s)** Cabin, Cad, Carload, Commuter, Deck, Fare, Parasite, Pax, Payload, Pigeon, Pillion, Rider, Slacker, Steerage, Straphanger, Transit, Traveller, Voyager, Way, Wayfarer

**Passerine** Crow, Raven

**Passible** Patible

▸**Passible** *see* **BAULK**

**Passion(ate), Passionately** Aflame, Anger, Appetite, Ardent, Ardour, Con calore, Con fuoco, Crush, Dander, Desire, Duende, Emotion, Enthusiastic, Fervour, Fire, Flame, Frampold, Fury, Gust, Gutsy, Hate, Heat, Hot, Hunger, Hwyl, Ileac, Iliac, Infatuation, Intense, Ire, Irish, Kama, Love, Lust, Mania, Messianic, Metromania, Obsession, Oestrus, Polemic, Rage, Reverent, Sizzling, Steamy, Stormy, Strong, Sultry, Torrid, Vehement, Violent, Warm, Wax, Wrath, Yen, Zeal, Zoolatria

**Passion-fruit** Water-lemon

**Passionless** Desiccated, Tepid

**Passion play** Oberammergau

**Passive (stage), Passivity** Apathetic, Dormant, Drifter, Inaction, Inert, Meek, Pathic, Patient, Pupa, Stolid, Supine, Vegetating, Vegetative, Yielding

**Pass out** Faint, Graduate, Swarf, Swarve, Swoon

**Passover** Agadah, Haggada, Omer, Pesach

**Passport** Access, Clearance, Congé(e), E, ID, Key, Laissez-passer, Nansen, Navicert, Sea-letter, Visa, Visitors'

**Password** Code, Countersign, Logon, Nayword, Parole, Sesame, Shibboleth, Sign, Tessera, Watchword

▶**Past** *see* PASS(ED)

**Pasta** Agnolotti, Al burro, Al dente, Anelli, Angel hair, Bucatini, Cannelloni, Cappelletti, Carbonara, Cellentani, Conchiglie, Durum, Eliche, Farfal, Farfalle, Farfel, Fedelini, Fettuc(c)ine, Fusilli, Gnocch(ett)i, Lasagna, Lasagne, Linguini, Macaroni, Maccheroncini, Manicotti, Noodles, Orecchietti, Orzo, Pappardelle, Penne, Perciatelli, Ravioli, Rigatoni, Ruote, Spaghetti, Spaghettina, Tagliarini, Tagliatelle, Tortelli(ni), Vermicelli, Ziti

**Paste, Pasty** Almond, Ashen, Batter, Beancurd, Beat, Berbere, Botargo, Boule, Bridie, Cerate, Clobber, Cornish, Dentifrice, Dough, E, Electuary, Empanada, Fake, Filler, Fish, Fondant, Frangipane, Gentleman's Relish®, Glue, Grout, Guarana, Gum, Hard, Harissa, Knish, Lute, Magma, Marchpane, Marzipan, Masala, Mastic, Meat, Miso, Mountant, Pale, Pallid, Panada, Pâté, Patty, Pearl-essence, Pie, Piroshki, Pirozhki, Poi, Poonac, Pulp, Punch, Putty, Rhinestone, Rillettes, Rout, Sallow, Samosa, Sham, Slip, Slurry, Soft, Spread, Strass, Tahina, Tahini, Tan, Tapenade, Taramasalata, Tooth, Trounce, Wallpaper, Wan, Wasabi, Whey-faced

**Pastern** Hobble, Knee, Tether

**Pastiche** Cento, Collage, Medley, Patchwork, Potpourri

**Pastille** Jujube, Lozenge

**Pastime** Boules, Cat's cradle, Diversion, Game, Hobby, Interest, Pastance, Recreation, Seesaw, Sport, Zeitvertreib

**Past master** Champion, Expert, Historian, Pro

**Past midnight** 1 am

**Pastor(al)** Arcadia, Bucolic, Curé, Eclogue, Endymion, Idyl(l), Minister, Priest, Rector, Rural, Shepherd, Simple

**Pastry** Apfelstrudel, Baclava, Bakemeat, Baklava, Beignet, Bouchée, Bridie, Brik, Calzone, Canape, Cannoli, Chausson, Cheese straw, Choux, Clafoutis, Coquile, Creamhorn, Cream puff, Croissant, Croustade, Cruller, Crust, Danish, Dariole, Dough, Eclair, Empanada, En croute, Feuilleté, Filo, Flaky, Flan, Frangipane, French, Gougère, Hamantasch, Kolacky, Millefeuille, Muffin, Phyllo, Pie, Pie-crust, Pirog, Piroshki, Pirozhki, Profiterole, Puff, Quiche, Raised, Rough-puff, Rug(g)elach, Samosa, Shortcrust, Strudel, Tart, Turnover, Vol-au-vent, Wrap

**Pasture** Alp, Clover, Eadish, Eddish, Feed, Fell, Fodder, Grassland, Graze, Greensward, Herbage, Kar(r)oo, Lair, Lare, Lay, Lea, Lease, Leasow(e), Leaze, Lee, Ley, Machair, Mead(ow), Moose, Outrun, Pannage, Pascual, Potrero, Raik, Rake, Sheal(ing), Shiel(ing), Soum, Sowm, Tie, Transhume, Tye

▶**Pasty** *see* PASTE

**Pat** Apt, Butter, Chuck, Clap, Dab, Dung, Glib, Knob, Letter-perfect, Lump, On cue, Postman, Print, Prompt, Rap, Slap, Stroke, Tap, Touch

**Patch(work)** Cento, Fleck, Miscellany, Mosaic, Motley, Piecing, Pocket, Quilt, Sexton, Speculum, Turf

**Patch(y)** Allotment, Bed, Bit, Blotchy, Cabbage, Chloasma, Clout, Coalsack, Cobble, Cooper, Court plaster, Cover, Friar, Fudge, Knit, Lentigo, Manor, → MEND, Mosaic, Mottled, Nicotine, Pasty, Piebald, Piece, Plage, Plaque, Plaster, Pot, Purple, Repair, Shinplaster, Shoulder, Solder, Sporadic, Sunspot, Tingle, Tinker, Transdermal, Turf, Uneven, Vamp, Variegated

**Pate, Pâté** Crown, Paste, Rillettes, Taramasalata, Terrine

**Patent(ed)** Brevet d'invention, Breveté, Clear, Copyright, Evident, Letters, Licence, License, Obvious, Overt, Plain, Rolls

**Pater(nity)** Father, Filiation, Walter

**Paterfamilias** Coarb, Master

**Path(way)** Aisle, Allée, Alley, Arc, Berm, Berme, Boardwalk, Boreen, Borstal(l), Bridle, Bridleway, Byroad, Career, Catwalk, Causeway, Causey, Cinder, Clickstream, Corridor, Course, Cycleway, Downlink, Eclipse, Ecliptic, Eightfold, Embden-Meyerhof, Finder, Flare, Flight, Gangway, Garden, Gate, Gennel, Ginnel, Glide, Lane, Ley, Lichwake, Lichway, Locus,

Lykewake, Mean-free, Metabolic, Orbit, Packway, Pad, Parabola, Pavement, Peritrack, Primrose, Race, Ride, Ridgeway, Route, Run, Runway, Side, Sidewalk, Slipway, Spurway, Stie, Sty(e), Swath(e), Taxiway, Tow, Track, Trail, Trajectory, Trod, Twitten, Walkway, → WAY, Xystus

**Pathan** Pakhto, Pakhtu, Pashto, Pashtu, Pushto(o), Pushtu

**Pathetic(ally)** Abysmal, Derisory, Doloroso, Drip, Forlorn, Hapless, Hopeless, Piss-poor, Piteous, Pitiful, Plaintive, Poignant, Sad, Saddo, Schlub, Schnook, Sorry, Touching, Wet

**Pathfinder** Compass, Explorer, Guide, Pioneer, Scout

**Pathogen** Virus

**Pathologic(al)** Aphony, Diseased, Gangrene, Morbid, Moria, Septic

**Pathos** Bathos, Pity, Sadness, Sob-stuff

**Patience** Calm, Endurance, Forbearance, Fortitude, Indulgence, Klondike, Klondyke, Longanimity, Monument, Operetta, Solitaire, Stoicism, Suffering, Tolerance, Virtue

**Patient(s)** Calm, Case, Clinic, Cot-case, Forbearing, Grisel(da), Grisilda, Inmate, Invalid, Job, Long-suffering, Passive, Private, Resigned, Stoic, Subject, Unprotesting, Walking case, Ward

**Patio** Terrace

**Patois** Argot, Cant, Creole, Dialect, Gumbo, Jargon, Jive, Lingo, Scouse

**Patriarch** Aaron, Abraham, Abuna, Asher, Catholicos, Ecumenical, Elder, Enoch, Isaac, Jacob, Jesse, Job, Levi, Maron, Methuselah, Nestor, Noah, Pope, Primogenitor, Simeon, Venerable

**Patrician** Aristocrat, Noble, Senator

**Patrick** Paddy, Pat, Spens

**Patrimony** Ancestry, Estate, Heritage

**Patriot(ic), Patriotism** Cavour, Chauvinist, DAR, Emmet, Flag-waving, Flamingant, Garibaldi, Hereward, Irredentist, Jingoism, Loyalist, Maquis, Nationalist, Revere, Tell, Wallace, Zionist

**Patrol** Armilla, Beat, Coastguard, Guard, Highway, Lollipop lady, Lollipop man, Outguard, Picket, Piquet, Prowl-car, Reconnaissance, Round, Scout, Sentinel, Sentry-go, Shark, Shore, Turm

**Patron(age), Patroness, Patronise(d), Patronising** Advowson, Aegis, Athena, Auspices, Backer, Benefactor, Business, Cavalier, Champion, Client, Condescend, Customer, Donator, Egis, Fautor, Favour, Friend, Lady Bountiful, Maecenas, Nepotic, Protector, Protégé, Provider, Shopper, → SPONSOR, Stoop, Stoup

**Patsy** Dupe, Fall guy, Hendren, Scapegoat, Stooge, Sucker

**Patter** Backchat, Cant, Jargon, Lingo, Mag, Pitch, Rap, Sales talk, S(c)htick, Spiel

**Pattern(ed)** Agouti, Agouty, Aguti, Archetype, Argyle, Batik, Bird's eye, Blueprint, Branchwork, Broché, Candy stripe, Check, Chequer, Chiné, Chladni figure, Clock, Crisscross, Design, Dévoré, Diaper, Diffraction, Dog's tooth, Draft, Egg and dart, Epitome, Example, Exemplar, Faconné, Fair-isle, Fiddle, Figuration, Format, Fractal, Fret, Gammadion, Gestalt, Grain, Greek key, Greque, Grid, Herringbone, Holding, Honeycomb, Hound's tooth, Ideal, Imprint, Intarsia, Intonation, Kaleidoscope, Karman vortex street, Koru, Kowhaiwhai, Lace, Life style, Marbled, Matel(l)asse, Matrix, Meander, → MODEL, Moire, Moko, Mosaic, Motif, Norm, Paisley, Paradigm, Paragon, Pinstripe, Plan, Polka-dot, Pompadour, Precedent, Prototype, Queenstitch, Quincunx, Radiation, Raster, Rat-tail, Rhythm, Ribbing, Rosette, Scansion, Sequence, Shawl, Starburst, Stencil, Structure, Symmetry, Syndrome, Tala, Talea, Tangram, Tarsia, Tattersall, Template, Templet, Tessella, Tessera, Test, Tracery, Traffic, Tread, Type, Veneration, Vol, Watermark, Whorl, Willow

**Patty** Bitok, Bouchée, Fishcake, Fritter, Hoecake, Pie

**Paul** Jones, Oom, Pry, Revere, Robeson, S, St

**Pauline** Day-boy, Perils

**Paunch** Beerbelly, Belly, Corporation, Gut, Kite, Kyte, Pod, Potbelly, Rumen, Tripe, Tum

**Pauper** Bankrupt, Beggar, Have-not, Mendicant, Penniless

**Pause** Break, Breakpoint, Breather, Caesura, Cessation, Cesura, Comma, Delay, Desist, Er, Falter, Fermata, Hesitate, Hiatus, Interkinesis, Intermission, Interregnum, Interval, Let up, Limma, Lull, Moratorium, Pitstop, Pregnant, → RESPITE, Rest, Selah, Semi-colon, Stop, Tacet, Time out, Whistle-stop

**Pave(d), Pavement, Paving** Causeway, Causey, Clint, Cobble, Corsey, Crazy, Desert, Diaper, Flagging, Flagstone, Granolith, Limestone, Moving, Path, Plainstanes, Plainstones, Roadside, Set(t), Sidewalk, Tarmac, Tessellate, Travolator, Trottoir

**Pavilion** Chinese, Ear, Gazebo, Jingling Johnny, Kiosk, Marquee, Summerhouse, Tent

**Pavis** Shield

**Paw** Grope, Kangaroo, Maul, Mitt, Pad, Pat, Pud, Pug, Pussyfoot, Touch up

**Pawky** Dry, Humorous, Shrewd, Sly

**Pawn(shop), Pawnbroker, Pawnee** Agent, Betel, Chessman, Counter, Derby, Dip, Fine, Gage, Gallery, Hanging, Hock, Hockshop, Hostage, Isolated, Leaving-shop, Lumber, Lumberer, Moneylender, Mont-de-piété, Monte di pietà, Nunky, Oppignorate, Pan, Passed, Peacock, Piece, Pignerate, Pignorate, Pledge, Pledgee, Pop, Redeemer, Security, Siri, Spout, Stalking-horse, Three balls, Tiddleywink, Tool, Tribulation, Uncle, Usurer, Wadset, Weed

**Pax** Peace, Truce

**Pay(master), Payment, Paid, Pay off, Pay out** Aby, Advance, Advertise, Agterskot, Alimony, Amortise, Annat, Annuity, Ante, Arles, Atone, Backhander, Balloon, Bank draft, Bank roll, Basic, Batta, Benefit, Blench, Bonus, Bukshee, Bukshi, Cain, Cashier, Cens, Charge, Cheque, COD, Commute, Compensate, Consideration, Contactless, Contribute, Damage, Deferred, Defray, Disburse, Discharge, Dividend, Down, Dub, E, Earnest, Emolument, Endow, Equalisation, Eric, Escot, Expiate, Farm, Fee, Feu-duty, Finance, Foot, Fork out, Fund, Gale, Gate, Giro, Give, Golden handshake, Golden parachute, Grassum, Gratuity, Grave, Greenmail, Guarantee, Han(d)sel, Hazard, Hire, Honorarium, Hoot(oo), HP, Imburse, Imprest, Intown multure, Jackpot, Kain, Kickback, Leads and lags, Lin(e)age, Lobola, Lobolo, Lump sum, Mail, MasterCard®, Meet, Merchet, Métayage, Mise, Modus, Mortuary, Outcome, Overtime, Palimony, Part exchange, Payola, Pension, Piece rate, Pittance, Pony, Posho, Prebendal, Premium, Primage, Pro, Pro forma, Progress, Purser, Quarterage, Quit(-rent), Ransom, Rate, Reap-silver, Rebate, Rebuttal, Reckoning, Redundancy, Refresher, Refund, Remittance, Remuneration, Rent, Requite, Residual, Respects, Retainer, Reward, Royalty, Salary, Satisfaction, Scot, Screw, Scutage, Settle, Severance, Shell, Shell out, Shot, Sick, Sink, SO, Sold(e), Soul-scat, Soul-scot, Soul-shot, → SPEND, Sponsor, Square, Stipend, Strike, Stump, Sub, Subscribe, Subsidy, Sweetener, Table, Take-home, Tar, Tender, Tithe, Token, Tommy, Transfer, Treasure, Treat, Tribute, Truck, Unpurse, Usance, Veer, Wage, Wardcorn, X-factor

**PC** Constable, Laptop, Right on

**PE** Aerobics, Gym

**Pea(s)** Asparagus, Black-eyed, Carling, Chaparral, Chickling, D(h)al, Desert, Dholl, Dutch admiral, Egyptian, Garbanzo, Glory, Goober, Hastings, Legume, Mangetout, Marrow, Marrowfat, Mushy, Passiform, Petit pois, Pigeon, Pulse, Rounceval, Snow, Split, String, Sturt's desert, Sugar, Sugar snap, Vetch

**Peace(ful), Peaceable, Peace-keeper, Peace organisation, Peace symbol** Ahimsa, Antiwar, Armistice, Ataraxy, Calm, Ceasefire, Concord, Douce, Ease, Equilibrium, Frieda, Frith, Green, Halcyon, Harmony, Hush, Idyllic, Interceder, Irenic(on), King's, Lee, Lull, Nirvana, Olive, Order, Pacific, Pax, Pbuh, Queen's, Quiet, Repose, Rest, Rose, Roskilde, Salem, Serene, Sh, Shalom, Siegfried, Siesta, Silence, Solomon, Soothing, Still, Tranquil, Truce, UN

**Peacemaker** ACAS, Arbitrator, Conciliator, Mediator, Trouble-shooter, Wilfred

**Peach** Blab, Cling, Clingstone, Dish, Dob, Freestone, Humdinger, Inform, Laetrile, Malakatoone, Melba, Melocoto(o)n, Nectarine, Oner, Quandang, Shop, Sing, Sneak, Split, Squeak, Stunner, Tattle, Tell, Victorine

**Peachum** Polly

**Peacock** Coxcomb, Dandy, Fop, Junonian, Muster, Ostentation, Paiock(e), Pajock(e), Pavo(ne), Pawn, Payock(e), Pown, Sashay

**Peak(y)** Acme, Aiguille, Alp, Ancohuma, Apex, Ben, Cap, Chimborazo, Climax, Comble, Communism, Cone, Cotopaxi, Crag, Crest, Darien, Drawn, Eiger, Flower, Gable, Gannett, Garmo, Harney, Height, Horn, Ismail Samani, Kazbek, Matterhorn, Meridian, Mons, → MOUNTAIN, Nevis, Nib, Nunatak, Optimum, Pale, Petermann, Pikes, Pin, Pinnacle, Piton, Point, Pyramidal, Rainier, Sallow, Snowcap, Snowdon, Spire, Stalin, Sukarno, Top, Tor, Visor, Widow's, Zenith

**Peal** Carillon, Change, Chime, Clap, Toll, Triple
**Peanut(s)** Arnut, Chickenfeed, Goober, Groundnut, Monkey-nut, Pad Thai, Pittance, Satay
**Pear** Aguacate, Alligator, Anchovy, Anjou, Asian, Asparagus, Avocado, Bartlett, Bergamot, Beurré, Blanquet, Carmelite, Catherine, Choke, Colmar, Comice, Conference, Cuisse-madame, Dutch admiral, Jargonelle, Muscadel, Muscatel, Musk, Nashi, Neli(e)s, Perry, Poperin, Poppering, Poprin, Prickly, Pyrus, Queez-maddam, Sabra, Seckel, Seckle, Taylor's Gold, Warden, William
**Pearl(s), Pearly** Barocco, Barock, Baroque, Cultured, False, Gem, Harbo(u)r, Imitated, Jewel, Mabe, Margaret, Margaric, Nacrous, Olivet, Onion, Orient, Prize, Rope, Seed, Simulated, String, Sulphur, Unio(n)
**Pear-shaped** Obconic, Obovate, Pyriform
**Peasant** Bogtrotter, Bonhomme, Boor, Bumpkin, Carlot, Chouan, Churl, Clodhopper, Contadino, Cossack, Cottar, Cott(i)er, Fellah(s), Fellahin, Hick, Jungli, Kern(e), Kisan, Kulak, M(o)ujik, Muzhik, Oik, Prole, Quashi(e), Raiyat, Roturier, Rustic, Ryot, Swain, Tyrolean, Volost, Whiteboy, Yokel
**Pea-shaped** Pisiform
**Peat(y)** Moss-litter, Sharny, Sod, Turbary, Turbinacious, Turf, Yarfa, Yarpha
**Pebble(s), Pebbly** Banket, Bibble, Calculus, Chuck, Cobblestone, Dornick, Dreikanter, Gallet, Gooley, Gravel, Psephism, Pumie, Pumy, Scotch, Scree, Shingle, Ventifact
**Peccadillo** Mischief, Misdemeanour, Offence
**Peccary** Mexican hog, Tayassuid
**Peck** Bill, Bushel, Dab, Forpet, Forpit, Gregory, Job, Kiss, Lip, Lippie, Modius, Nibble, Pickle, Tap
**Pecksniff** Charity
**Peculiar(ity)** Abnormal, Appropriate, Bizarre, Characteristic, Curiosity, Curious, Distinct, Eccentric, Eery, Especial, Exclusive, Ferly, Funny, Idiosyncratic, Kink, Kooky, Loopy, Mannerism, Odd, Original, Own, Personal, Proper, Queer, Quirk, Royal, Rum, Singular, → SPECIAL, Specific, Strange, Unusual
▹**Peculiar** *may indicate* an anagram
**Pedagogue** Academic, B.Ed, Teacher
**Pedal** Accelerator, Bike, Brake, Chorus, Clutch, Cycle, Damper, Lever, P, Rat-trap, Soft, Sostenuto, Sustaining, Treadle, Treddle, Wah-wah
**Pedal-coupler** Tirasse
**Pedant(ic)** Casaubon, Chop logic, Dogmatic, Don, Dryasdust, Elucubrate, Inkhorn, Intellectual, Jobsworth, Logic-chopper, Lucubrate, Nit-picking, Pedagogue, Pernickety, Pompous, Precisian, Purist, Quibbler, Scholastic, Sesquipedalian, Stickler
**Peddle, Pedlar** Bodger, Boxwallah, Camelot, Chapman, Cheapjack, Colporteur, Crier, Deal, Doorstepper, Drummer, Duffer, Hawk, Huckster, Jagger, Packman, Pedder, Pether, Push, Sell, Smouch, Smouse(r), Sutler, Tallyman, Tink(er), Trant, Yagger
▹**Peddling** *may indicate* an anagram
**Pedestal** Acroter(ion), Axle guard, Basis, Dado, Die, Footstall, Pillar, Plinth, Stylobate, Support
**Pedestrian** Banal, Commonplace, Dull, Earth-bound, Ganger, Hack, Hike, Itinerant, Jaywalker, Laborious, Mediocre, Mundane, Ordinary, Ostrich, Trite, Unimaginative, Voetganger, Walker
**Pedigree(s)** Ancestry, Blood(line), Bloodstock, Breeding, Descent, Family tree, Genealogy, House, Lineage, Phylogeny, Pure-bred, Stemma(ta), Stirp(s), Studbook, Thoroughbred, Whakapapa
**Pediment** Fronton
**Peduncle** Scape, Stalk
**Peek** Eye, Glance, Glimpse, Peep
**Peel(er)** Bark, Bobby, Candied, Chemical, Constable, Decorticate, Desquamate, Exfoliate, Flake, Flype, Grilse, Lemon, Orange, Pare, PC, Pill, Potato, Rind, Rine, Rumbler, Scale, Sewen, Shell, Skin, → STRIP, Tirr, Undress, Zest
▹**Peeled** *may indicate* outside letters to be removed from a word
**Peep(er), Peephole** Bo, Cheep, Cook, Crow, Glance, Gledge, Judas, Keek, Kook, Lamp, Nose, Peek, Pink, Pry, Snoop, Spy, Squeak, Squint, Stime, Styme, Voyeur

**Peer(age), Peers** Archduke, Aristocrat, Backwoodsman, Baron(et), Burke, Coequal, Coeval, Counterpart, Daimio, Debrett, Doucepere, Douzeper(s), Duke, Earl, Egal, Elevation, Equal, Eyeball, Gynt, Hereditary, Law Lord, Life, Lord, Lords Temporal, Marquis, Match, Noble, Paladin, Peregal, Pink, Pry, Rank, Representative, Scry, Spiritual, Squint, Stare, Stime, Styme, Temporal, Toot, Tweer, Twire, Viscount

**Peerless** Best, Matchless, Nonpareil, Supreme

**Peevish(ness), Peeve** Capernoited, Captious, Crabby, Cross, Doddy, Frabbit, Frampal, Frampold, Franzy, Fretful, Girner, Girnie, Hipped, Ill, Lienal, Meldrew, Moody, Nattered, Pet, Petulant, Pindling, Protervity, Querulous, Shirty, Sour, Spleen, Teachie, Te(t)chy, Testy, Vex

**Peewit** Lapwing, Peewee

**Peg(gy)** Cheville, Cleat, Clothespin, Cotter-pin, Crawling, Die, Dowel, Drift-pin, Fix, Freeze, Hat, Hook, Jukskei, Kabaddi, Knag, Lee, Leg, Margaret, Nail, Nog, Odontoid, Pin(-leg), Piton, Shoe, Snort, Spigot, Spile, Square, Stengah, Stinger, Support, Tap, Tee, Thole, Tholepin, Thowel, Toggle, Tooth, Tot, Tuning, Vent, Woffington

**Pegboard** Solitaire

**Pegleg** Timber-toes

**Peking man** Pithecanthropus, Sinanthropus

**Pelagic** Deep-sea, Marine, Oceanic

**Pelargonium** Geranium

**Pelf** Lucre, Mammon, Money, Notes, Riches

**Pelican** Alcatras, Bird, Crossing, Golden Hind, LA, Louisiana, Steganopode

**Pellagra** Maidism

**Pellet** Birdshot, Bolus, Buckshot, Bullet, Coprolite, Granule, Grapeshot, Pill, Pilula, Pilule, Pithball, Prill, Shot, Slug, Snow

**Pellucid** Clear

**Pelmet** Valance

**Pelt** Assail, Bearskin, Bombard, Clod, Coonskin, Fleece, Fur, Hail, Hide, Hie, Lam, Pepper, Random, Sealskin, Shower, Skin, Squail, Stone

**Peltast** Soldier, Targeteer

**Pelvis** Groin, Ilium, Pubis, Renal

**Pen** Author, Ballpoint, Bamboo, Bic®, Biro®, Bull, Cage, Calamus, Can, Cartridge, Catching, Confine, Coop, Corral, Crawl, Crib, Croove, Crow-quill, Cru(i)ve, Cub, Cyclostyle, Dabber, Data, Drawing, Enclosure, Epi®, Fank, Farm, Felt(-tipped), Fold, Fountain, Gaol, Gladius, Hen, Highlighter, Hoosegow, J, →**JAIL**, Keddah, Kraal, Lair, Laser, Light, Magic Marker®, Marker, Mew, Mure, Music, Piggery, Poison, Pound, Quill(-nib), Rastrum, Ree, Reed, Ring, Rollerball, Scribe, Sheepfold, Stell, Stie, Stir, Stockade, Sty(e), Stylet, Stylo, Stylograph, Stylus, Submarine, Swan, Sweatbox, Tank, Weir, Write, →**WRITER**

▷**Pen** *may indicate* a writer

**Penal(ize)** Cost, Fine, Gate, Handicap, Huff, Mulct, Punitive, Servitude

**Penalty** Abye, Amende, Card, Cost, Death, Demurrage, Endorsement, Eriach, Eric, Fine, Fixed, Foot-fault, Forfeit, Han(d)sel, Huff, Keltie, Kelty, Levy, Major, Pain, Price, Punishment, Rubicon, Sanction, Tap, Ticket, Wide

**Penance** Atonement, Expiation, Shrift

**Penates** Lares

**Pence** D, P, Peter's

**Penchant** Predilection, Tendency

**Pencil** Beam, Blue, Ca(l)m, Caum, Charcoal, Chinagraph®, Crayon, Draft, Draw, Drawing, Eyebrow, Fusain, Grease, Harmonic, Ink, Keelivine, Keelyvine, Lead, Outline, Propelling, Slate, Stub, Stump, Styptic, Tortillon

**Pend(ing)** Imminent, In fieri, On hold, On ice, Unresolved, Until

**Pendant** Albert, Chandelier, Drop, Eardrop, Earring, Girandole, Laval(l)ière, Locket, Medallion, Necklace, Poffle, Sautoir, Stalactite

**Pendragon** Uther

**Pendule** Poffle

**Pendulous, Pendulum** Compensation, Dewlap, Foucault's, Metronome, Noddy, One-way, Seconds, Swing, Wavering

**Penetrate, Penetrating, Penetration** Acumen, Acuminate, Bite, Bore, Bridgehead, Cut, Enpierce, Enter, Imbue, Impale, Incisive, Indent, Indepth, Infiltrate, Inroad, Insight, Into, Intrant, Lance, Leach, Permeate, Pierce, Probe, Sagacious, Shear, Shrill, Strike, Thrust, Touch, X-ray

**Penguin** Adélie, Aeroplane, Anana, Auk, Blue, Emperor, Fairy, Gentoo, King, Korora, Little, Macaroni, Rock-hopper

**Penicillin** Cloxacillon, Fleming

**Peninsula** Arm, Neck, Promontory, Spit, Spur

---

**PENINSULAS**

*4 letters:*
Alte
Ards
Cape
Eyre
Kola
Oman

*5 letters:*
Banks
Fylde
Gaspé
Gower
Kerch
Korea
Lleyn
Malay
Otago
Sinai
Upper
Yorke

*6 letters:*
Alaska
Arabia
Avalon
Balkan
Bataan
Crimea
Iberia
Istria
Palmer
Seward
Taimyr
Tasman
Taymyr
Wirral

*7 letters:*
Arabian
Boothia
Cape Bon
Cape Cod
Chukchi
Florida
Furness
Iberian
Jutland
Kintyre
Kowloon
Leizhou
Luichow
Olympic
S.W. Malay
Yucatan

*8 letters:*
Brittany
Cape York
Delmarva
East Cape
Galloway
Hispania
Labrador
Liaodong
Liaotung
Malaysia
Melville
Portland
Quiberon
S. Jutland

*9 letters:*
Antarctic
Black Isle
Cape Verde
Freycinet
Gallipoli
Indo-China
Kamchatka
Kathiawar
Northland
The Lizard

*10 letters:*
Cape Blanco
Chalcidice
Chersonese
Coromandel
Dunnet Head
Graham Land
Mornington
Nova Scotia

*11 letters:*
Lindisfarne
Peloponnese

*12 letters:*
Scandinavian

*14 letters:*
Baja California
Cape Finisterre

*16 letters:*
Rhinns of Galloway

*17 letters:*
Wilson's Promontory

---

**Penis** Archie, Chopper, Cock, Cor(e)y, Dick, Dildo(e), Dipstick, Dong, Dork, Ferret, Giggle(stick), Horn, Jack, John Thomas, Knob, Langer, Member, Membrum virile, Mojo, Organ, Pecker, Peezle, Percy, Peter, Phallus, Pillicock, Pintle, Pisser, Pizzle, Plonker, Prick, Putz, Rod, Roger, Schlong, Schmock, Shaft, Shmock, Shmuck, Stiffy, Tallywhacker, Tockley, Todger, Tonk, Tool, W(h)ang, Weenie, Weeny, Willie, Willy, Winkle, Yard, Zeppelin

**Penitent(iary)** Calaboose, Cilice, Clink, Contrite, Gaol, Jail, Jug, Prison, Repenter, Rosary, Rueful, Stir

**Pennant, Pennon** Banner, Broad, Bunting, Fane, Flag, Guidon, Streamer

**Penniless** Bankrupt, Boracic, Broke, Bust, Impecunious, Needy, Poor, Skint, Strapped

**Penny** Arle(s), Bean, Cartwheel, Cent, Copper, D, Dreadful, Gild, Honest, New, P, Pretty, Sen, Sou, Sterling, Stiver, Win(n), Wing

**Penny-farthing** Bicycle, Ordinary

**Penny-pinching** Cheapskate

**Penpusher** Plumassier

**Pension(er)** Allowance, Ann(at), Annuitant, Board, Chelsea, Cod, Cor(r)ody, Full-board, Gasthaus, Gratuity, Guest-house, Half-board, Hostel, Hotel, Non-contributory, Occupational,

Old-age, Oldster, Payment, Personal, Retire(e), Senior citizen, Serps, SIPP, Stakeholder, Stipend, Superannuation

**Pensive** Dreamy, Moody, Musing, Thoughtful, Triste, Wistful

**Pentameter** Elegiac, Iambic

**Pentateuch** Samaritan, T(h)orah

**Pentathlon** Modern

**Pentecost** Whit(sun)

**Penthouse** Apartment, Cat, Lean-to, Roof, Skyhome

**Penultimate** Semifinal, Y

**Penury** Need

**Peon** Peasant, Serf, Slave, Ticca

**Peony** Moutan

**People(s)** Beautiful, Beings, Bods, Body, Chosen, Commonalty, Commons, Demos, Ecology, Electorate, Enchorial, Flower, Folk, Fraim, Gens, Good, Grass roots, Guild, Herd, Homo, Human(kind), Inca, Indigenous, Inhabit, Janata, Kin, Land, Lapith, Lay, Man(kind), Masses, Men, Mob, Mortals, Nair, Nation(s), Nayar, One, Peculiar, Personalities, Phalange, Populace, Proletariat(e), Public, Punters, Quorum, Rabble, Race, Raffle, Room, September, Settle, Society, Souls, They, Throng, Tribe, Tuath, Tungus, Volk

**Pep** Buck, Dash, Enliven, Gism, Go, Jism, Jissom, Stamina, Verve, Vim

**Pepper(y)** Alligator, All-spice, Ancho, Ava, Betel, Bird, Black, Caper, Capsicum, Cayenne, Cherry, Chilli, Chipotle, Condiment, Cubeb, Devil, Dittander, Dittany, Ethiopian, Green, Guinea, Habanero, Jalapeno, Jamaica, Kava, Long, Malaguetta, Matico, Mow down, Negro, Paprika, Pelt, Pim(i)ento, Piper, Piperine, Piquillo, Red, Riddle, Sambal, Scotch bonnet, Spice, Sprinkle, Sweet, Szechuan, Szechwan, Tabasco®, Talapino, Techy, Testy, Wall, Water, White, Yaqona, Yellow

**Peppercorn** Nominal, → **PAYMENT**, → **RENT**

**Peppermint** Bull's Eye, Humbug, Pandrop

**Peptide** Cecropin, Kallidin, Substance P

**Per** By, Each, Through, Thru

**Perambulate, Perambulator** Buggy, Expatiate, Pedestrian, Pram, Stroller, Wagon, Walker

**Perceive, Perceptible, Perception, Perceptive** Acumen, Acute, Alert, Anschauung, Apprehend, Astute, Clairvoyance, Clear-eyed, Cognition, Cryptaesthetic, Descry, Detect, Dianoia, Discern, Divine, ESP, Extrasensory, Fathom, Feel, Image, Insight, Intelligence, Intuit(ion), Keen-eyed, Kinaesthesia, Noesis, Notice, Observe, Pan(a)esthesia, Penetration, Remark, → **SEE**, Sense, Sensitive, Sentience, Shrewd, Sixth sense, Subitize, Subjective, Subliminal, Tact, Tangible, Taste, Telegnosis, Tel(a)esthesia, Understanding, Visual

**Percentage** Agio, Commission, Contango, Cut, Mark-up, Proportion, Rake off, Royalty, Scalage, Share, Vigorish

**Perch(ing)** Aerie, Alight, Anabis, Bass, Comber, Eyrie, Fish, Fogash, Gaper, Insessorial, Lug, Miserere, Ocean, Perca, Pole, Roost, Ruff(e), Seat, Serranid, → **SIT**, Wall-eye, Zingel

**Percolate, Percolation** Filter, Infiltrate, Leach, Lixiviate, Ooze, Osmosis, Permeate, Seep, Sipe, Soak, Strain, Sype

**Percussion (cap)** Amorce, Battery, Chinese temple block, Cowbell, Cymbal, Gamelan, Gong, Idiophone, Impact, Knee, Knock, Spoons, Thump, Timbrel, Traps

**Percy** Harry Hotspur, Shelley

**Perdition** Ades, Hades

**Peremptory** Absolute, Decisive, Haughty, Imperative, Imperious

**Perennial** Aroid, Continual, Enduring, Flower, Livelong, Perpetual, Recurrent

**Perfect(ly), Perfection(ist)** Absolute, Accomplish, Accurate, Acme, Apple-pie, Bloom, Complete, Consummation, Cross-question, Dead, Develop, Edenic, Exemplary, Fare-thee-well, Faultless, Finish, Flawless, Free-lover, Fulfil, Full, Holy, Hone, Ideal(ist), Idyllic, Impeccable, Intact, It, Letter, Lilywhite, Matchless, Mature, Mint, Mr Right, Par, Paradisal, Paragon, Past, Pat, Peace, Pearl, Pedant, Peerless, Point-device, Practice, Present, Pure, Quintessential, Refine, Ripe, Salome, Siddha, Soma, Sound, Spotless, Spot-on, Stainless, Stickler, Sublime, Tense, The nines, Thorough, Three-pricker, To a t(ee), Unblemished, Unflawed, Unqualified, Unspoilt, Utopian, Utter, Very, Whole, Witeless

**Perfidy** Betrayal, Falsehood, Treachery, Treason

**Perforate(d), Perforation, Perforator** Colander, Cribrate, Cribrose, Drill, Eyelet, Fenestration, Hole, Leaky, → PIERCE, Prick, Punch, Puncture, Riddle, Trephine, Trocar

**Perforce** Necessarily, Needs

**Perform(ed), Performer, Performing** Achieve, Acrobat, Act(or), Action, Aerialist, Appear, Artist(e), Barnstorming, Basoche, Busk, Carry out, Chansonnier, Comedian, Contortionist, Discharge, Do, Duo, Effect, Enact, Entertainer, Execute, Exert, Exhibit, Extra, Fancy Dan, Fire-eater, Fulfil, Function, Geek, Hand, Headliner, Hersall, Hot dog, Houdini, Implement, Improvise, Interlocutor, Lion-tamer, Maestro, Majorette, Make, Mime, Minstrel, Moke, Nonet, Octet, Officiate, On, Operant, Patzer, Perpetrate, Player, Praxis, Quartet(te), Quintet, Rap artist, Recite, Render, Represent, Ripieno, Scene-stealer, Septet, Sextet, Showstopper, Soloist, Stand-up, Strongman, Supererogate, Svengali, Sword-swallower, Throw, Transact, Trio, Troupe, Vaudevillian, Virtuoso, Wire-dancer

**Performance** Accomplishment, Achievement, Act(ion), Auto, Benefit, Blinder, Bravura, Broadcast, Chevisance, Command, Concert, Dare, Deed, Demonstration, Discharge, Division, Double act, Enactment, Entr'acte, Execution, Floorshow, Gas, Gig, Hierurgy, Holdover, Hootenanny, House, Karaoke, Masque, Master-class, Masterstroke, Matinee, Mime, Monodrama, Monologue, Nach, Nau(t)ch, One-night stand, Operation, Perpetration, Practice, Première, Preview, Production, Programme, Recital, Rehearsal, Rendering, Rendition, Repeat, Repertoire, Rigmarole, Roadshow, Scene, Second house, Show (stopper), Showing, Simul, Sketch, Sneak preview, Solo, Son et lumière, Specific, Spectacle, Stunt, Synergy, Theatricals, Track record, Turn, Unicycle

**Perfume (box)** Abir, Ambergris, Angel water, Aroma, Attar, Bergamot, Cassolette, Chanel®, Chypre, Civet, Cologne, C(o)umarin, Eau de cologne, Eau de toilette, Enfleurage, Essence, Fragrance, Frangipani, Incense, Ionone, Lavender (water), Linalool, Millefleurs, Muscone, Musk, Muskone, Myrrh, Nose, Opopanax, Orris, Orrisroot, Otto, Patchouli, Patchouly, Pomander, Potpourri, Redolence, Rose water, → SCENT, Smellies, Terpineol, Toilet water, Tonka bean

**Perfunctory** Apathetic, Careless, Cursory, Dismissive, Indifferent, Scamp, Token

**Perhaps** A(i)blins, Belike, Haply, Happen, May(be), Peradventure, Percase, Perchance, Possibly, Relative, Say, Yibbles

▷**Perhaps** *may indicate* an anagram

**Perigee** Apsis, Epigeum

**Peril(ous)** → DANGER, Hazard, Jeopardy, Precarious, Risk, Threat, Yellow

**Perimeter** Boundary, Circuit, Circumference, Coastline, Limits

**Perineum** Grundle

**Period(ic)** Abbevillian, Acheulian, AD, Aenolithic, Age, Alcher(ing)a, Andropause, Annual, Archaean, Aurignacian, Azilian, Base, Bi-weekly, Bout, Cal(l)ippic, Cambrian, Carboniferous, Catamenia, Chalcolithic, Chukka, Chukker, Climacteric, Comanchean, Cooling off, Cretaceous, Critical, Curse, Cycle, Day, Decad(e), Devonian, Diapause, Dot, Down, Dreamtime, → DURATION, Eocene, Eolithic, Epoch, Etesian, Excerpt, Floruit, Full-stop, Gestation, Glacial, Grace, Great schism, Haute époque, Hercynian, Heyday, Holocene, Honeymoon, Horal, Incubation, Indiction, Innings, Interim, Interlude, Interregnum, Jurassic, Kalpa, Latency, Latent, Lesson, Liassic, Limit, Meantime, Meanwhile, Menarche, Menopause, Menses, Mesolithic, Mesozoic, Middle Kingdom, Miocene, Mississippian, Moment, Monthly, Moratorium, Neocomian, Neolithic, Neozoic, Octave, Oestrus, Olde-worlde, Oligocene, Ordovician, Palaeogene, Paleolithic, Patch, Payback, Pennsylvanian, Permian, Phanerozoic, Phase, Phoenix, Pleistocene, Pliocene, Pre-Cambrian, Proterozoic, Protohistory, Puberty, QT, Quarter, Quaternary, Recurrent, Reformation, Refractory, Regency, Rent, Riss, Romantic, Saeculum, Safe, Saros, Season, Sentence, Session, Sidereal, Silurian, Solutrean, Solutrian, Sothic, Span, Spasm, Spell, Stage, Stop, Stretch, Synodic, Teens, Term, Tertiary, Time, Trecento, Triassic, Triduum, Trimester, Tri-weekly, Usance, Weekly, Window

**Periodical** Bi-weekly, Comic, Digest, Economist, Journal, Listener, Mag, New Yorker, Organ, Paper, Publication, Punch, Rambler, Regency, Review, Scandal sheet, Spectator, Strand, Tatter, Tract

**Peripatetic** Ambulatory, Gadabout, Itinerant, Promenader, Travelling

**Periphery, Peripheral** Ambit, Bounds, Disk-drive, Exurb, Fringe, Outer, Outskirts, Surface, Tangential

**Periscope** Eye(-stalk)

**Perish(able), Perished, Perishing** Brittle, → DIE, End, Ephemeral, Expire, Fade, Forfair, Fungibles, Icy, Tine, Tint, Transitory, Tyne, Vanish

**Periwinkle** Apocynum, Blue, Madagascar, Myrtle

**Perjure(d), Perjurer, Perjury** Forswear, Lie, Mansworn, Oates

**Perk(s), Perky, Perk up** Bonus, Brighten, Chipper, Deadhead, Dividend, Enliven, Freebie, Freshen, Fringe benefit, Jaunty, LV, → PERQUISITE, Tronc

**Perm(anent)** Abiding, Durable, Enduring, Eternal, Everlasting, Fixed, For keeps, Full-time, Indelible, → LASTING, Marcel, Stable, Standing, Stative, Timeless, Unending, Wave

**Permeable, Permeability, Permeate** Imbue, Infiltrate, Leaven, Magnetic, Osmosis, Penetrate, Pervade, Poromeric, Porous, Seep, Transfuse

**Permission, Permissive, Permit(ted), Permitivity** Absolute, Allow, Authorise, By-your-leave, Carnet, Chop, Clearance, Congé(e), Consent, Copyright, Easy, Empower, Enable, Entitle, Franchise, Give, Go-ahead, Golden bough, Grant, Green card, Green light, Indult, Lacet, Laissez-passer, Latitude, Leave, Legal, Legitimise, Let, Liberty, Licence, License, Lief, Loan, Luit, Nihil obstat, Ok(e), Optional, Pace, Pass, Permis de sejour, Placet, Planning, Power, Pratique, Privilege, Relative, Remedy, Safe-conduct, Sanction, Stamp-note, Suffer, Ticket, Tolerate, Triptyque, Visa, Vouchsafe, Warrant, Way-leave, Wear

**Pernicious** Adverse, Baneful, Damnable, Evil, Fatal, Harmful, Lethal, Noisome, Noxious, Pestilent, Wicked

**Pernickety** Faddish, Fikish, Fussbudget, Hair-splitting, Niggly, Particular

**Peroration** Pirlicue, Purlicue

**Peroxide** Bleach, Blonde, Colcothar, Hydrogen

**Perpendicular** Aplomb, Apothem, Atrip, Cathetus, Erect, Normal, Orthogonal, Plumb, Sheer, Sine, → UPRIGHT, Vertical

**Perpetrate** Commit, Effect, Execute, Offender, Redo

**Perpetual** Constant, Eternal, Incessant, Never-ending, Non-stop, Sempiternal, Unceasing

**Perplex(ed), Perplexity** Anan, At a loss, Baffle, Bamboozle, Bemuse, Beset, Bewilder, Bother, Buffalo, Bumbaze, Cap, Confound, Confuse, Embarrass, Feague, Floor, Flummox, Fox, Knotty, Meander, Mystify, Nonplus, Obfuscate, Out, Pother, Pudder, Puzzle, Quizzical, Stump, Tangle, Throw, Tickle, Tostication

**Perquisite** Ap(p)anage, Emolument, Extra, Gratuity, → PERK, Tip

**Perrier** Stoner

**Perry** Mason

**Persecute, Persecution** Afflict, Annoy, Badger, Bully, Crucify, Dragon(n)ades, Harass, Haze, Intolerant, McCarthyism, Oppress, Paranoia, Pogrom, Race-baiting, Ride, Torment, Torture, Victimise, Witch hunt

**Persevere, Perseverance** Application, Assiduity, Continue, Endure, Fortitude, Hold on, Insist, Jusqu'auboutisme, Patience, Persist, Plug, Press on, Soldier on, Stamina, Steadfastness, Stick, Stickability, Tenacity, Undeterred

**Persia(n)** Achaemenid, Babee, Babi, Bahai, Cyrus, Dari, Farsi, Iran(ian), Mazdean, Mede, Middle, Pahlavi, Parasang, Parsee, Pehlevi, Pushtu, Samanid, Sassanid, Sohrab, Xerxes, Zoroaster

**Persiflage** Satire

**Persimmon** Kaki, Sharon fruit

**Persist(ence), Persistent** Adhere, Assiduity, Chronic, Constant, Continual, Diligent, Doggedness, Endure, Eternal, Hang-on, Importunate, Incessant, Keep at, Labour, Last, Longeval, Lusting, Nag, Obdurate, Persevere, Press, Relentless, Sedulous, Sneaking, Stamina, Stick, Stubborn, Tenacity, Unabated, Urgent

**Person(s), Personal(ly)** Ad hominem, Alter, Artificial, Aymaran, Being, Bird, Bod(y), Chai, Chal, Character, Chav, Chi, Cookie, Displaced, Entity, Everyman, Figure, First, Fish, Flesh, Ga(u)dgie, Gadje, Gauje, Gut, Head, Human, Individual, Inner, In propria persona, Me, Myself, Nabs, Natural, Nibs, One, Own, Party, Passer-by, People, Pod, Private, Quidam, Second, Selfhood, Skate, Sod, Soul, Specimen, Tales, Third, Type, Walla(h), Wight

**Persona** Image

**Personage, Personality** Alter ego, Anima, Celeb(rity), Character, Charisma, Dignitary, Ego, Godhead, Grandee, Identity, Jekyll and Hyde, Megastar, Multiple, Noble, Notability, Panjandrum, Presence, Psychopath, Sama, Schizoid, Seity, Sel, Self, Sell, Somatotonia, Split, Star, Temperament, Tycoon, Viscerotonia

**Personified, Personification, Personify** Avatar, Embody, Epitome, Incarnate, Prosopop(o)eia, Represent

**Personnel** Employees, Hands, HR, Liveware, Manpower, Staff

**Perspective** Aerial, Astute, Atmospheric, Attitude, Distance, Foreshorten(ed), Linear, Point of view, Proportion, Scenography, Slant, Take, View, Vista

**Perspicacious, Perspicacity** Astute, Clear-sighted, Discerning, Insight, Keen, Shrewd

**Perspiration, Perspire, Perspiring** Aglow, Forswatt, Glow, Hidrosis, Sudor, Suint, Sweat, Swelter

**Persuade(d), Persuasion, Persuasive** Brainwash, Cajole, Carrot and stick, Coax, Coerce, Cogent, Conviction, Convince, Disarm, Eloquent, Exhort, Faith, Feel, Forcible, Geed, Get, Induce, Inveigle, Lead on, Make, Move, Plausible, → **PREVAIL**, Religion, Rhetoric, Seduce, Sell, Silver-tongued, Smooth-talking, Soft sell, Suborn, Sway, Sweet-talk, Tempt, Truckled, Wheedle, Winning

**Pert(ness)** Bold, Brisk, Cocky, Dicacity, Flippant, Forward, Fresh, Impertinent, Insolent, Jackanapes, Minx, Quean, Saucy, Smart, Tossy

**Pertain** Apply, Belong, Concern, Effeir, Effere, Relate, Touch

**Pertinacious** Dogged, Obstinate, Persistent, Stickler, Stubborn

**Pertinent** Ad rem, Apropos, Apt, Fit, Germane, Relevant, Timely

**Perturb(ation)** Aerate, Confuse, Dismay, Disturb, Dither, Faze, Pheese, State, Trouble, Unnerve, Unsettle, Upset, Worry

**Peru(vian)** Inca, PE, Quechua(n), Quichua(n)

**Peruse, Perusal** Examine, Inspect, Read, Scan, Scrutiny, → **STUDY**

**Pervade, Pervasion, Pervasive(ness)** Aroma, Atmosphere, Diffuse, Drench, Fill, Immanence, Infuse, Permeate, Saturate

**Perverse, Perversion, Pervert(ed), Perversity** Aberrant, Abnormal, Algolagnia, Awkward, Awry, Balky, Cam(stairy), Camsteary, Camsteerie, Cantankerous, → **CONTRARY**, Corrupt, Crabbed, Cussed, Decadent, Deform, Deviate, Distort, Donsie, False, Froward, Gee, Ironic, Kam(me), Kinky, Licentious, Misinterpret, Misuse, Nonce, Paraphilia, Protervity, Refractory, Sadist, Sicko, Stubborn, Thrawn, Traduce, Travesty, Twist, Unnatural, Untoward, Uranism, Warp(ed), Wayward, Wilful, Wrest, Wry

▹**Perverted** *may indicate* an anagram

**Pessimism, Pessimist(ic)** Alarmist, Bear, Cassandra, Crapehanger, Crepehanger, Cynic, Defeatist, Dismal Jimmy, Doom merchant, Doomsayer, Doomwatch, Doomy, Doubter, Downbeat, Eeyore, Fatalist, Glumbum, Jeremiah, Killjoy, Negative, Weltschmerz

**Pest(er)** Aggravate, Badger, Bedbug, Beleaguer, Besiege, Blight, Bluebottle, Bombard, Bot, → **BOTHER**, Brat, Breese, Breeze, Brize, Bug, Dim, Disagreeable, Earbash, Fly, Fowl, Fruit fly, Gapeworm, Greenfly, Harass, Harry, Hassle, Importune, Irritate, Maggot, Menace, Microbe, Mither, Molest, Mouse, Nag, Nudnik, Nuisance, Nun, Oestrus, Pize, Plague, Rotter, Scourge, Slug, Snail, Tease, Terror, Thysanoptera, Vermin, Weevil

**Pesticide** Benomyl, Botanic(al), DDT, Derris, Dichlorvos, Endrin, Glucocorticoid, Glucosinolate, Heptachlor, Mouser, Permethrin, Synergist, Warfarin

**Pestilence, Pestilent** Curse, Epidemic, Evil, Lues, Murrain, Murren, Noxious, Outbreak, Pernicious, Plague

**Pet** Aversion, Cade, Canoodle, Caress, Chou, Coax, Coddle, Cosset, Cuddle, Dandle, Darling, Daut(ie), Dawt(ie), Dear, Dod, Dort, Ducky, Favourite, Fondle, Glumps, Hamster, Huff, Hump, Indulge, Ire, Jarta, Jo, Lallygag, Lapdog, Messan, Miff, Mouse, Neck, Pamper, Pique, Poach, Rabbit, Smooch, Snog, Spat, Stroke, Strum, Sulk(s), Tantrum, Teacher's, Temper, Tiff, Tout, Towt, Umbrage, Virtual, Yarta

**Petal(s)** Ala, Corolla, Keels, Labellum, Leaf, Standard, Vexillum

**Petard** Firework, Squib

**Pete(r), Peter out** Aumbry, Bell, Cell, Diminish, Dwindle, End, Fizzle, Grimes, Hermit, Pan,

Pears, Pegleg, Principle, Quince, Quint, Rabbit, Safe, Saint, Sellers, Simon, Simple, Wane, Weaken

**Petite** Dainty, Mignon, Small

**Petition(er)** Appeal, Beg, Boon, Claimant, Crave, Entreaty, Litany, Millenary, Orison, Plaintiff, Postulant, Prayer, Press, Representation, Request, Round robin, Solicit, Sue, Suit(or), Suppli(c)ant, Supplicat, Vesper

**Pet-name** Hypocorisma, Nickname, So(u)briquet

**Petrel** Bird, Mother Carey's chicken, Nelly, Prion, Procellaria, Stormbird, Stormy, Wilton's

**Petrify(ing)** Fossilise, Frighten, Lapidescent, Niobe, Numb, Ossify, Scare, Terrify

**Petrol(eum)** Avgas, Cetane, Cutting, Diesel, Esso®, Ethyl, Fuel, Gas, Green, High-octane, High-test, Leaded, Ligroin, Maz(o)ut, Octane, Oilstone, Olein, Platforming, Refinery, Rock oil, Rock-tar, STP, Styrene, Unleaded, Vaseline®

**Petticoat** Balmoral, Basquine, Crinolette, Crinoline, Female, Filabeg, Fil(l)ibeg, Jupon, Kilt, Kirtle, Phil(l)abeg, Phil(l)ibeg, Placket, Sarong, Shift, Slip, Underskirt, Wylie-coat

**Pettifogger** Lawmonger

**Petty, Pettiness** Baubling, Bumbledom, Childish, Little, Mean, Minor, Narrow, Niggling, Nyaff, One-horse, Parvanimity, Picayunish, Piffling, Pimping, Puisne, Puny, Shoestring, Small, Small-minded, Small-time, Small town, Stingy, Tin, Trivial, Two-bit

**Petty officer** Cox, CPO, PO

**Petulance, Petulant** Cranky, Crass, Flouncing, Fretful, Huff, Mardy, Moody, Peevish, Perverse, Procacity, Querulous, Sullen, Touchy, Toutie, Waspish

**Pew** Box, Carrel, Chair, Perch, Seat, Stall

**Pewter** Trifle, Tutenag

**Phaeton** Spider

**Phalanger** Cus-cus, Honey-mouse, Honey possum, Opossum, Petaurist, Phascogale, Possum, Sugar glider, Tait, Tarsipes, Tuan, Wambenger

**Phalanx** Cohort, Coterie, Legion

**Phalarope** Lobe-foot

**Phallus** Linga(m), Penis, Priapus

**Phantasist, Phantasm** Apparition, Chimera, Spectre, Werewolf

**Phantom** Apparition, Bogey, Bugbear, Eidolon, Feature, Idol, Incubus, Maya, Pepper's ghost, Shade, Spectre, Tut, Wild hunt, Wraith

**Pharaoh** Akhenaton, Amenhotep, Cheops, Egyptian, Ptolemy, Rameses, River-dragon, Theocrat, Thutmose, Tut, Tutankhamen, Tutankhamun, Tyrant

**Pharisee** Formalist, Humbug, Hypocrite, Nicodemus

**Pharmacist, Pharmacologist** Apothecary, → **CHEMIST**, Dispenser, Druggist, Loewi, MPS, Officinal, Preparator

**Phase** Climacteric, Coacervate, Colour, Cycle, Disperse, Form, Nematic, Period, Post-boost, Primary, Quarter, REM, Schizont, Stage, State, Step, Synchronise, Transition

**Pheasant** Argus, Bird, Fireback, Golden Swamp, Junglefowl, Mona(u)l, Nide, Nye, Pea-chick, Peacock, Pea-fowl, Pea-hen, Ring-necked, Silver, Tragopan

**Phenol** Carbolic, Orcine, Orcinol, Resorcinol, Xylenol

**Phenomenon** Autokinetic, Blip, Eclipse, Effect, Event, Figure ground, Flying saucer, Flysch, Geohazard, Heterography, Hormesis, Marvel, Meteor, Miracle, Mirage, Paranormal, Parascience, Phenology, Phi, Psi, Rankshift, Raynaud's, Synergy, UFO

**Phial** Bologna, Bottle, Flask

**Phil, Philip** Fluter, Macedonia, Pip

**Philander(er)** Flirt, Keeper, Libertine, Lothario, Playboy, Seduce(r), Toyer, → **TRIFLE**, Wolf, Womaniser

**Philanthropist, Philanthropy** Altruist, Barnardo, Benefactor, Carnegie, Charity, Chisholm, Coram, Donor, Freemason, Gates, Geldof, Getty, Guggenheim, Hammer, Humanist, Humanitarian, Lever, Mayer, Nobel, Nuffield, Peabody, Rockefeller, Rowntree, Samaritan, Shaftesbury, Tate, Well-wisher, Wilberforce

**Philately** Timbromania

**Phileas** Fogg
▸**Philip** *see* PHIL
**Philippic** Diatribe, Invective, Tirade
**Philippine(s)** Bisayan, Igorot, Moro, Pangasinian, PI, RP, Tagalog, Visayan
**Philistine, Philistinism** Artless, Ashdod, Barbarian, Bigot, Foe, Gath, Gaza, Gigman, Goliath, Goth, Lowbrow, Podsnappery, Vandal
**Philology** Linguistics, Semantics, Speechcraft
**Philosopher, Philosophy** Academist, Activism, Ahimsa, Analytical, Animism, Anthrosophy, Antinomianism, Antiochian, A priorist, Atomic, Atomist, Attitude, Averr(h)oism, Cartesian, Casuist, Comtism, Conceptualism, Conservatism, Cracker-barrel, Critical, Cynic, Deipnosophist, Deontology, Eclectic, Eleatic, Empiricism, Enlightenment, Epistemology, Ethics, Existentialism, Fatalism, Feng shui, Gnostic, Gymnosophist, Hedonism, Hermeneutics, Hobbism, Holist, Humanism, I Ching, Idealism, Ideology, Instrumentalism, Ionic, -ism, Kaizen, Linguistic, Logical atomism, Logicism, Logos, Maieutic, Marxism, Materialism, Mechanism, Megarian, Metaphysician, Metaphysics, Metempiricism, Monism, Moral(ist), Natural, Neo-Kantian, Neoplatonism, Neoteric, New Age, Nihilism, Nominalism, Occamist, Occam's razor, Ockhamist, Opinion, Panhellenism, Peripatetic, Phenomenology, Platonism, Pluralist, Populism, Positivism, Rationalism, Realism, Rosminian, Sage, Sankhya, Sceptic, Schoolman, Scientology, Scotism, Secular-humanism, Sensist, Shankara(-charya), Solipsism, Sophist, Stoic, Synthetic, Taoism, Theism, Theosophy, Thomist, Thought, Transcendentalism, Ultraism, Utilitarianism, Utopianism, Vedanta, Voluntarism, Weltanschauung, Whitehead, Yoga, Yogi

---

## PHILOSOPHERS

*4 letters:*
Ayer
Hume
Jedi
Kant
Mach
Mill
Ryle
Weil
Wolf
Zeno

*5 letters:*
Amiel
Bacon
Bayle
Bruno
Buber
Burke
Comte
Croce
Dewey
Hegel
James
Locke
Moore
Paine
Pater
Plato
Quine
Renan
Smith
Sorel
Taine

*6 letters:*
Agnesi
Arendt
Carnap
Cicero
Cousin
Engels
Farabi
Godwin
Herder
Hobbes
Hutton
Lao-tzu
Ockham
Olbers
Ortega
Pascal
Peirce
Popper
Pyrrho
Sartre
Scotus
Seneca
Tagore
Thales

*7 letters:*
Abelard
Aquinas
Barthes
Bentham
Bergson
Bradley
Buridan
Derrida
Diderot
Eckhart
Emerson
Erasmus
Erigena
Haldane
Herbart
Hypatia
Leibniz
Malthus
Marcion
Marcuse
Mencius
Meng-tse
Ptolemy
Rosmini
Russell
Schlick
Serbati
Sheffer
Spencer
Spinoza
Steiner
Thoreau
Tillich

*8 letters:*
Alembert
Anderson
Avicenna
Berkeley
Boethius
Cyreniac
Diogenes
Epicurus
Foucault
Hamilton
Harrison
Maritain
Menippus
Old Moore
Passmore
Plotinus
Plutarch
Rousseau
Schiller
Socrates
Xenophon

*9 letters:*
Antiochus
Aristotle
Bosanquet

Cleanthes
Confucius
Descartes
Euhemerus
Heidegger
Leucippus
Lucretius
Nietzsche
Santayana
Schelling

***10 letters:***
Anacharsis
Anaxagoras
Anaximenes
Antiochene
Apemanthus
Apollonius
Aristippus
Campanella
Chrysippus
Democritus
Empedocles
Helveticus
Heraclitus
Hutchinson
Maimonides
Paracelsus
Parmenides
Protagoras
Pythagoras
Saint Simon
Swedenborg
Von Leibniz
Xenocrates
Xenophanes

***11 letters:***
Anaximander
Antisthenes
Kierkegaard
Machiavelli
Montesquieu

***12 letters:***
Callisthenes
Merleau-Ponty
Schopenhauer
Theophrastus
Wittgenstein

---

**Philosophic(al)** Calm, Fatalistic, Rational, Resigned, Thoughtful, Tranquil
**Philtre** Aphrodisiac, Charm, Drug, Hippomanes, Potion
**Phlegm(atic)** Calm, Composed, Pituita(ry), Pituite, Placid, Stolid, Unperturbed, Unruffled
**Phloem** Leptome, Liber
**Phobia** Aversion, Dread, Fear, Neurosis, Thing
**Phoebe, Phoebus** Apollo, Artemis, Day-star, Deaconess, Moon, Selene, Sol, Sun
**Phoenician** Tripolitania
**Phoenix** Bird-of-wonder, Fum, Fung, Paragon, Self-begotten
**Phone** App, Bell, Blower, Buzz, Call, Camera, Cellular, Clamshell, Dial, Dual band, Feature, Flip, Handset, Hotline, Intercom, Mob(i)e, Mobile, Moby, Pay, Picture, Ring, Roam, Satellite, Saver, Skype, Smart, Talkback, Tel, → **TELEPHONE**, Text
**Phonetic(s)** Acoustic, Articulatory, Auditory, Interdental, Mouille, Oral, Palaeotype, Palatal, Palato-alveolar, Plosion, Spoken, Symbol, Synaeresis
▷**Phonetically** *may indicate* a word sounding like another
**Phon(e)y** Bogus, Charlatan, Counterfeit, Ersatz, Faitor, Fake, Hokey, Impostor, Poseur, Quack, → **SHAM**, Specious, Spurious
▷**Phony** *may indicate* an anagram
**Phosphate** Apatite, Monazite, Sphaerite, Torbernite, Vivianite, Wavellite, Xenotime
**Phosphor(escent), Phosphorescence, Phosphorus** Bologna, Briming, Cephalin, Foxfire, Friar's lantern, Ignis fatuus, Jack o'lantern, Luminescent, Malathion®, Noctilucent, P, Pyrosome, Sarin, Sea-fire, Tabun, Will o' the wisp
**Photo(copy), Photograph(y), Photographic, Photo finish** Ambrotype, Anaglyph, Angiogram, Beefcake, Black and white, Blow-up, Cabinet, Calotype, Clog, Close-up, Composite, Contre-jour, Daguerrotype, Diazo, Digicam, Duplicate, Dyeline, Eastman, Enlargement, Enprint, Exposure, Ferroprint, Ferrotype, Film, Flash, Half-tone, Headshot, Heliochrome®, Heliotype, Hologram, Infra-red, Kallitype, Karyogram, Kirlian, Kodak®, Microdot, Microfilm, Microgram, Micrograph, Microprint, Monochrome, Montage, Mugshot, Negative, Nephogram, Opaline, Panel, Picture, Pinhole, Platinotype, Polaroid®, Positive, Print, Red-eye, Resorcin, Rotograph, Rotogravure, Schlieren, Selfie, Sepia, Shoot, Shot, Shutterbug, Slide, Snap, Spectrogram, Spirit, Still, Sun-print, Take, Talbotype, Time-lapse, Tintype, Tomography, Topo, Trimetrogon, Vignette, Wire, Woodburytype, Xerography, Xerox, X-ray
**Photographer** Adams, Bailey, Beaton, Brandt, Brassai, Cameraman, Cameron, Capa, Cartier-Bresson, Daguerre, Fox Talbot, Man Ray, Mapplethorpe, Pap(arazzo), Schlierin, Shutterbug, Snapper, Snowdon, Stalkerazzi, Stannotype
**Phrase** Abject, Actant, Asyndeton, Axiom, Buzzword, Cadence, Catch(word), Catchcry, Cliché, Climacteric, Comma, Epithet, Expression, Hapax legomenon, Hashtag, Heroic, Hook, Idiom, Idiophone, Laconism, Leitmotiv, Lemma, Locution, Mantra, Motto, Noun, Phr, Prepositional, Refrain, Riff, Set, Slogan, Soundbite, Tag, Term, Theme, Trope, Verb
**Phrygian** Midas
**Phthisis** Decay, TB
**Phylactery** Amulet, Talisman, Tefillin, Tephillin

**Phyllopod** Brine-shrimp
**Phylum** Craniata
**Physic(s)** Cluster, Cryogenics, Culver's, Cure, Dose, Electronics, Electrostatics, Geostatics, Health, High-energy, Kinematics, Kitchen, Low temperature, Medicine, Nuclear, Nucleonics, Particle, Photometry, Purge, Remedy, Rheology, Science, Solid-state, Sonics, Spintronics, Statistics, Thermodynamics, Ultrasonics
**Physical** Bodily, Body check, Carnal, Corpor(e)al, Material, Medical, Natural, Tangible
**Physician** Addison, Allopath, Bach, Buteyko, Chagas, Culpeper, Curer, Doctor, Erastus, Eustachio, Galen, Gilbert, Graves, Guillotin, Hakim, Hansen, Harvey, Hippocrates, Internist, Jenner, Lamaze, Leech, Linacre, Lister, Medic(o), Menière, Mesmer, Mindererus, Paean, Paian, Paracelsus, Practitioner, Preceptor, Quack, Ranvier, Roget, Russell, Salk, Sézary, Sloane, Spiegel, Stahl, Still, Therapist, Time, Vaidya, Wavell
**Physicist** → SCIENTIST

---

**PHYSICISTS**

*3 letters:*
Ohm

*4 letters:*
Bohr
Born
Bose
Gold
Hahn
Kerv
Lawe
Mach
Rabi
Vafa

*5 letters:*
Adams
Auger
Bondi
Bragg
Curie
Debye
Dicke
Dirac
Fermi
Gamow
Gauss
Henry
Hertz
Hooke
Hoyle
Joule
Lodge
Nambu
Pauli
Penny
Popov
Raman
Stark
Volta
Weber
Young
Zener

*6 letters:*
Alfven
Ampère
Carnot
Dalton
Davies
Geiger
Giorgi
Kelvin
Landau
Morley
Nernst
Newton
Peirce
Penney
Picard
Planck
Powell
Skyrme
Teller
Walton
Wilson

*7 letters:*
Alhazen
Alvarez
Bardeen
Broglie
Charles
Coulomb
Crookes
Doppler
Faraday
Feynman
Fresnel
Galileo
Gilbert
Hawking
Huygens
Laplace
Lorentz
Marconi
Maxwell
Meitner
Moseley
Nielsen
Oersted
Peebles
Penzias
Piccard
Rankine
Reaumur
Richter
Rontgen
Sievert
Tyndall
Wheeler

*8 letters:*
Anderson
Angstrom
Appleton
Avogadro
Blackett
Brattain
Brewster
Bridgman
Cerenkov
Davisson
Einstein
Foucault
Millikan
Oliphant
Rayleigh
Roentgen
Schottky
Susskind
Van Allen

*9 letters:*
Alanasoff
Becquerel
Cockcroft
Friedmann
Heaviside
Josephson
Kirchhoff
Michelson
Ovshinsky
Robertson

*10 letters:*
Archimedes
Bernouilli
Fahrenheit
Heisenberg
Rutherford
Torricelli
Watson-Watt

*11 letters:*
Chamberlain
Joliot-Curie
Oppenheimer
Schrödinger
Van der Waals

---

**Physiognomist, Physiognomy** Face, Features, Lavater

**Physiology, Physiologist** Bernard, Bordet, Dale, Eccles, Einthoven, Gender, Loeb, Malpighi, Pavlov, Purkinje, Schafer, Wagner, Zoonomia

**Physiotherapist** Masseur

**Physique** Anatomy, Body, Build, Figure, Pyknic, Set-up, Somatotype

**Pi, Pious** Breast-beater, Craw-thumper, Devotional, Devout, Fraud, Gallio, God-fearing, Godly, Holy, Holy Willie, Mid-Victorian, Orant, Religiose, Reverent, Saintly, Sanctimonious, Savoury, Smug, Unco guid, Wise, Zaddik

**Piaffe** Spanish-walk

**Pianist** Anda, Arrau, Bernstein, Concert, Hambourg, Hess, Hofmann, Liberace, Liszt, Mingus, Morton, Ogdon, Pachmann, Paderewski, Peterson, Répétiteur, Richter, Schnabel, Tatum, Vamper, Virtuoso, Waller

**Piano** Baby grand, Bechstein, Boudoir grand, Broadwood, Celesta, Celeste, Concert grand, Cottage, Dumb, Electric, Electronic, Flugel, Forte, Grand, Hammerklavier, Honkytonk, Joanna, Keyboard, Mbira, Overstrung, P, Player, Prepared, Semi-grand, Softly, Steinway, Stride, Thumb, Upright, Yamaha

**Piano-maker** Erard

**Picaresque** Roman à tiroirs

**Picaroon** Brigand, Corsair, Pirate, Rogue

**Picasso** Cubist

**Piccadilly** Whist

**Piccolo** Ottavino

**Pick(er), Pickaxe, Picking, Pick out, Pick up** Break, Cherry, Choice, → **CHOOSE**, Contract, Cream, Cull, Draw, Elite, Emu-bob, Evulse, Flower, Gather, Glean, Gurlet, Hack, Hear, Holing, Hopper, Ice, Mattock, Nap, Nibble, Oakum, Option, Plectrum, Pluck, Plum, Select, Single, Sort, Steal, Strum, Tone arm, Tong, Wale

▷**Picked** *may indicate* an anagram

**Picket** Demonstrate, Fence, Flying, Pale, Palisade, Post, Protester, Riata, Stake, Tether, Tie

**Pickings** Harvest, Profits, Scrounging, Slim, Spoils

**Pickle(r)** Achar, Beetroot, Brine, Cabbage, Caper, Chow-chow, Chutney, Corn, Corner, Cucumber, Cure, Dilemma, Dill, Eisel, Esile, Gherkin, Girkin, Imp, Jam, Kimchi, Marinade, Marinate, Mess, Mull, Olive, Onion, Peculate, Peregrine, Piccalilli, → **PLIGHT**, Preserve, Relish, Rod, Salt, Samp(h)ire, Scrape, Souse, Spot, Steep, Trouble, Vinegar, Wolly

**Picklock** Oustiti, Peterman

**Pick-me-up** Bracer, Drink, Restorer, Reviver, Stimulant, Tonic

**Pickpocket(s)** Adept, Bung, Cly-faker, Cutpurse, Dip, Diver, Fagin, File, Nipper, Purse-snatcher, Swell mob, Swellmobsman, Whizzer, Wire

**Pick-up** Arrest, Light o'love, Truck, Ute

**Picky** Fastidious

**Picnic** Alfresco, Braaivleis, Burgoo, Clambake, Fun, Junketing, Outing, Push-over, Spread, Tailgate, Valium, Wase-goose, Wayzgoose

**Picture(s)** After-image, Anaglyph, Arpillera, Art, Bambocciades, Bitmap, B-movie, Cabinet, Canvas, Caricature, Cartoon, Cinema, Cloudscape, Collage, Cutaway, Cyclorama, Decoupage, Depict, Describe, Diptych, Drawing, Dreamscape, Drypoint, Emblem, Envisage, Envision, Epitome, Etching, Fancy, Film, Flick, Fresco, Gouache, Graphic, Histogram, Icon, Iconic, Identikit®, Illusion, Imagery, Imagine, Inset, Kakemono, Landscape, Lenticular, Likeness, Lithograph, Montage, Mosaic, Motion, Movie, Moving, Movy, Mugshot, Myriorama, Oil, Painture, Photo, Photofit®, Photogram, Photomontage, Photomosaic, Photomural, Pieta, Pin-up, Pix, Plate, Polaroid, Polyptych, Portrait, Predella, Prent, Presentment, Print, Programme, Represent, Retraitt, Retrate, Rhyparography, Scene, Semble, Shadowgraph, Shot, Skyscape, Slide, Snapshot, Stereochrome, Stereogram, Stereograph, Stevengraph, Still-life, Table(au), Talkie, Tapestry, Tattoo, Thermogram, Tone, Topo, Transfer, Transparency, Vanitas, Vectograph, Vignette, Vision, Votive, Vraisemblance, Word, X-ray, Zincograph

**Picturesque** Chocolate box, Idyllic, Scenic

**Pidgin** Beach-la-mar, Bislama, Chinook jargon, Creole, Fanagalo, Fanakalo, Hiri Motu, Japlish, Kamtok, Mobilian, New Guinea, Police Motu, Solomon Islands, Tok Pisin

**Pie(s)** Anna, Banoffee, Battalia, Bird, Bridie, Camp, Chewet, Cinch, Cobbler, Cottage, Coulibiac, Curry puff, Custard, Deep-dish, Easy, Eskimo, Flan, Floater, Florentine, Hash, Humble, Key lime, Koulibiaca, Lumber, Madge, Meat, Mess, Mince(meat), Mud, Mystery bag, Pandowdy, Pastry, Pasty, Patty, Pecan, Périgord, Pica, Piet, Pirog, Pizza, Pork, Printer's, Pumpkin, Pyat, Pyet, Pyot, Quiche, Rappe, Resurrection, Shepherd's, Shoofly, Shred, Spoil, Squab, Stargaz(e)y, Star(ry)-gazy, Sugar, Sweetie, Tart, Tarte tatin, Torte, Tourtière, Turnover, Tyropitta, Umble, Vol-au-vent, Warden

▷**Pie** *may indicate* an anagram

**Piebald** Calico, Dappled, Lacuna, Motley, Paint, Pied, Pinto, Skewbald, Tangun

**Piece(s)** Adagio, Add, Arioso, Bagatelle, Bishop, Bit, Blot, Cameo, Cannon, Cent, Charm, → **CHESSMAN**, Chip, Chunk, Clip, Coin, Companion, Component, Composition, Concerto, Conversation, Counter, Crown, Crumb, Domino, End, Entr'acte, Episode, Extract, Firearm, Fit, Flake, Flitters, Fragment, Frust, Gat, Goring, → **GUN**, Gusset, Haet, Hait, Hunk, Item, Join, Lucky, Mammock, Man, Médaillons, Minor, Mite, Money, Morceau, Morsel, Mourning, Museum, Nip, Novelette, Nugget, Oddment, Off-cut, Ort, Part, Party, Pastiche, Patch, Pawn, Pce, Period, Peso, Pin, Pistareen, Pole, → **PORTION**, Recital, Rifle, Rondo, Rook, Scliff, Scrap, Section, Sector, Set, Shard, Sherd, Skliff, Slice, Slip, Sliver, Smithereen, Snatch, Snippet, Soffit, Sonata, Sou, Spare part, Speck, String, Stub, Swatch, Tad, Tait, Tate, Tile, Toccata, Truncheon, → **WEAPON**, Wedge, Wodge

**Pièce de résistance** Star-turn

**Piecemeal, Piecework** Gradually, Intermittent, Jigsaw, Serial, Task, Tut

**Pie-crust** Coffin, Lid, Pastry

**Pied-à-terre** Nest, Pad

**Pieman** Pastrycook, Shepherd

**Pier(s)** Anta, Buttress, Chain, Groyne, Jetty, Jutty, Landing, Mole, Plowman, Quay, Slipway, Swiss roll, Wharf, Wigan

**Pierce(d), Piercer, Piercing** Accloy, Awl, Bore, Broach, Cleave, Cribrose, Dart, Drill, Endart, Enfile, Fenestrate(d), Fulminant, Gimlet, Gore, Gride, Gryde, Grypt, Hull, Impale, Jag, Keen, Labret, Lance, Lancinate, Lobe, Move, Needle, Penetrate, Perforate, Pertusate, Pike, Pink, Poignant, Prick, Prince Albert, Punch, Puncture, Riddle, Rive, Shrill, Skewer, Slap, Sleeper, Spear, Spike, Spit, Stab, Steek, Stilet(to), Sting, Tap, Thirl, Thrill(ant), Transfix

**Piety** Devotion, Godliness, Lowliness, Purity, Saintliness, Sanctity

**Piffle** Bilge, Codswallop, Hogwash, Nonsense, Poppycock, Tommy-rot, Tosh, Twaddle

**Pig(s), Piggy, Pigmeat, Pigskin** Anthony, Babe, Babirusa, Baconer, Barrow, Bartholomew, Bessemer, Bland, Boar, Bonham, British Lop, Bush, Captain Cooker, Cutter, Doll, Duroc, Elt, Farrow, Fastback, Football, Gadarene, Gilt, Gloucester, Gloucester Old Spot, Glutton, Greedy guts, Grice, Grumphie, Gryce, Guffie, Guinea, Gus, Gutzer, Ham, Hampshire, Hog, Ingot, Iron, Javelina, Kentledge, Kintledge, Kunekune, Lacombe, Landrace, Land-shark, Lard, Large Black, Large White, Lingot, Long, Middle White, Napoleon, Old Spot, Peccary, Policeman, Porchetta, Pork(er), Raven, Razorback, Rosser, Runt, Saddleback, Shoat, Shot(e), Shott, Slip, Snowball, Sounder, Sow, Squealer, Sucking, Suid(ae), Tamworth, Tayassuid, Tithe, Toe, Tootsie, Truffle, Vietnamese potbellied, Warthog, Welsh, Yelt

**Pig-disease** Bullnose

**Pigeon** Archangel, Barb, Bird, Bronze-winged, Cape, Capuchin, Carrier, Clay, Cropper, Culver, Cumulet, Danzig, Didunculus, Dove, Fairy Swallow, Fantail, Goura, Ground, Gull, Homer, Homing, Horseman, Jacobin, Kereru, Kuku, Lahore, Manumea, Mourning dove, New Zealand, Nun, Owl, Passenger, Peristeronic, Piwakawaka, Pouter, Ringdove, Rock(er), Roller, Ront(e), Ruff, Runt, Scandaroon, Solitaire, Spot, Squab, Squealer, Stale, Stock-dove, Stool, Stork, Swift, Talkie-talkee, Tippler, Tooth-billed, Trumpeter, Tumbler, Turbit, Wonga(-wonga), Zoozoo

**Pigeonhole** Classify, Compartment, File, Label, Postpone, Shelve, Slot, Stereotype, Typecast

**Pigeon-house** Columbary, Cote, Dovecot(e)

**Pig-food** Mast, Slop, Swill

**Pig-headed** Opinionated, Self-willed

**Pig-iron** Kentledge, Kintledge

**Pigman** Hog-reeve

**Pigment(s), Pigmentation** Accessory, Alizarin, Anthoclore, Anthocyan(in), Argyria, Betacyanin, Bilirubin, Biliverdin, Bister, Bistre, Bronzing, Cappagh-brown, Carmine, Carotene, Carotenoid, Carotin, Carotinoid, Chloasma, Chlorophyll, Chrome, Chromogen, Cobalt, Colcothar, Colour, Crocus, Cryptochrome, Curcumin, Dye, Etiolin, Eumelanin, Flake-white, Flavin(e), Fucoxanthin, Gamboge, Gossypol, Green earth, Haem, Hem(e), H(a)ematin, H(a)emocyanin, H(a)emoglobin, Iodopsin, King's yellow, Lake, Lamp-black, Lipochrome, Lithopone, Liverspot, Lutein, Luteolin, Lycopene, Madder, Madder lake, Melanin, Monastral®, Mummy, Naevus, Naples yellow, Nigrosine, Oaker, Ochre, Opsin, Orpiment, Paris-green, Phthalocyanine, Phycobilin, Phycocyan, Phycoerythrin, Phycophaein, Phycoxanthin, Phytochrome, Porphyrin, Porphyropsin, Pterin, Puccoon, Quercetin, Realgar, Red lead, Respiratory, Retinene, Rhiboflavin, Rhodophane, Rhodopsin, Saffron, Scheele's green, Sepia, Sienna, Sinopia, Sinopsis, Smalt, Tapetum, Tempera, Terre-verte, Tincture, Titanium, Toner, Turacoverdin, Ultramarine, Umber, Urobilin, Urochrome, Verditer, Vermilion, Viridian, Whitewash, Xanthophyll, Xanthopterin(e), Yellow ochre, Zinc white

**Pigsty** Frank

**Pigtail** Braid, Cue, Plait, Queue

**Pi jaw** Cant

**Pike** Assegai, Crag, Dory, Fogash, Gar(fish), Ged, Gisarme, Glaive, Hie, Holostei, Jack(fish), Javelin, Lance, Langdale, Luce, Partisan, Pickerel, Ravensbill, Scafell, Snoek, Spear, Speed, Spontoon, Vouge, Walleyed

**Pikeperch** Zander

▸**Pilaster** *see* PILLAR(ED)

**Pilchard** Sardine

**Pile(d), Piles, Piling** Agger, Amass, Atomic, Big, Bing, Bomb, Bubkes, Camp-sheathing, Camp-shedding, Camp-sheeting, Camp-shot, Clamp, Cock, Column, Crowd, Deal, Dolphin, Down, Emerods, Farmer Giles, Farmers, Fender, Fig, Floccus, Fortune, Galvanic, Hair, Haycock, Heap, Hept, Historic, Hoard, Load, Lot, Mansion, Marleys, Mass, Moquette, Nap, Pier, Post, Pyre, Raft, Reactor, Ream(s), Rick, Rouleau, Screw, Shag, Sheaf, Sheet, Slush, → STACK, Starling, Stately home, Stilt, Toorie, Trichome, Upheap, Velvet, Voltaic, Wad, Wealth, Windrow, Wodge

**Pile-driver** Tup

**Pilfer(ing)** Crib, Filch, Finger, Maraud, Miche, Nick, Peculate, Pickery, Pickle, Pinch, Plagiarise, Plunder, Purloin, Snitch, → STEAL, Swipe

**Pilgrim(age)** Aske, Childe Harold, Expedition, Fatima, Gaya, Hadj(i), Haji, Hajj(i), Karbala, Kerbela, Kum, Loreto, Lourdes, Mathura, Mecca, Nasik, Nikko, Palmer, Pardoner, Qom, Questor, Qum, Reeve, Scallop-shell, Shrine, Umra(h), Voyage, Yatra

**Pill(s)** Abortion, Ball, Beverley, Bitter, Bolus, Cachou, Caplet, Capsule, Chill, Dex, Doll, Dose, Globule, Golfball, Goofball, Lob, Medication, Medicine, Morning after, Number nine, Peace, Peel, Pellet, Pep, Pilula, Pilule, Placebo, Poison, Protoplasmal, Radio, Sleeping, Spansule, Tablet, Troche, Trochisk, Upper

**Pillage** Booty, Devastate, Plunder, Raid, Ransack, Rapine, Ravage, Razzia, Robbery, Sack, Spoil, Spoliation

**Pillar(ed), Pillars** Anta, Apostle, Atlantes, Baluster, Balustrade, Boaz, Canton, Caryatides, Chambers, Cippus, Colonnade, Columel, Column, Earth, Eustyle, Gendarme, Goal, Hercules, Herm, Impost, Islam, Jachin, Lat, Man, Modiolus, Monolith, Newel, Nilometer, Obelisk, Pedestal, Peristyle, Pier, Post, Respond, Saddle, Sandspout, Serac, Stack, Stalactite, Stalagmite, Stanchion, Stoop, Telamon, Tetrastyle, Trumeau

**Pill-box** Hat, Inro

**Pillion** Cushion, Pad, Rear

**Pillory** Cang(ue), Cippus, Crucify, Jougs, Little-ease, Pelt, Satirise, Slam

**Pillow(case)** Bear, Beer, Bere, Bolster, Cod, Cow, Cushion, Headrest, Hop, Lace, Pad, Pulvinar, Throw

**Pilot(s)** Ace, Airman, Auto(matic), Aviator, Bader, Biggles, Branch, Bush, Captain, → CONDUCT, Experimental, Flier, George, Govern, Guide, Hobbler, Hoveller, Kamikaze, Lead, Lindbergh, Lodesman, Lodestar, Navigate, Palinure, Palinurus, Pitt, Prune, Radar, Red Baron, Shipman, Steer, Test, Tiphys, Trial, Trinity House, Usher, Wingman

**Pimento** Allspice
**Pimp** Apple-squire, Bludger, Fancyman, Fleshmonger, Hoon, Lecher, Mack, Pandarus, Pander, Ponce, Procurer, Solicit, Souteneur
**Pimpernel** Bastard, Bog, Poor man's weatherglass, Scarlet, Water, Wincopipe, Wink-a-peep, Yellow
**Pimple, Pimply** Blackhead, Botch, Bubukle, Button, Goosebump, Gooseflesh, Grog-blossom, Hickey, Horripilation, Milium, Papilla, Papula, Papule, Plook, Plouk, Pock, Pustule, Quat, Rumblossom, Rum-bud, Spot, Tetter, Uredinial, Wen, Whelk, Whitehead, Zit
**Pin** Axle, Bayonet, Belaying, Bobby, Bolt, Breast, Brooch, Candle, Cask, Clothes, Corking, Cotter, Curling, Dowel, Drawing, Drift, End, Fasten, Fid, Firing, Fix, Gam, Gnomon, Gudgeon, Hair, Hairgrip, Hob, Hook, Joggle, Kevel, King, Leg, Merry, Nail, Needle, Nog, Panel, Peg, Pintle, Pivot, Preen, Prick, Rivet, Rolling, Saddle, Safety, Scarf, SCART, Scatter, Shear, Shirt, Skewer, Skittle, Skiver, Spike, Spindle, Split, Staple, Stick, Stump, Swivel, Tack, Taper, Tertial, Thole, Thumbtack, Tie, Tietac(k), Tirling, Tre(e)nail, Trunnion, U-bolt, Woolder, Wrest, Wrist
**Pinafore** Apron, Brat, HMS, Overall, Pinny, Save-all, Tire
**Pinball** Pachinko
**Pince-nez** Nose-nippers
**Pincer(s)** Chela, Claw, Forceps, Forfex, Nipper, Nips, Pliers, Tongs, Tweezers
**Pinch(ed)** Arrest, Bit, Bone, Chack, Constrict, Cramp, Crimp, Crisis, Emergency, Gaunt, Half-inch, Misappropriate, Nab, Narrow, Nick, Nim, Nip, Nirlit, Peculate, Peel, Pilfer, Pocket, Pook(it), Pouk, Prig, Pugil, Raft, Raw, Rob, Save, Scrimp, Scrounge, Skimp, Smatch, Snabble, Snaffle, Sneak, Sneap, Sneeshing, Snuff, Squeeze, →**STEAL**, Swipe, Tate, Trace, Tweak, Twinge
**Pine(s), Pining** Ache, Arolla, Bristlecone, Celery, Cembra, Chile, Cluster, Cone, Conifer, Cypress, Deal, Droop, Dwine, Earn, Erne, Evergreen, Fret, Green, Ground, Hone, Hoop, Huon, Jack, Japanese umbrella, Jeffrey, Kauri, Knotty, Languish, Languor, Loblolly, Lodgepole, Long, Longleaf, Lovelorn, Lovesick, Monkey-puzzle, Monterey, Moon, Mope, Norfolk Island, Norway, Nut, Oregon, Parana, Picea, Pinaster, Pitch, Ponderosa, Radiata, Red, Scotch, Scots, Screw, Sehnsucht, Slash, Softwood, Spruce, Starve, Stone, Sugar, Tree, Umbrella, Urman, Waste, White, Wish, Yearn, Yellow
**Pineapple** Anana, Bomb, Bromelia, Grenade, Hand grenade, Piña, Poll, Sorosis, Tillandsia
**Ping** Knock, Whir(r)
**Pinguin** Anana(s)
**Pinion** Fetter, Lantern, Penne, Pinnoed, Secure, Shackle, Wing
**Pink, Pink-eyed** Albino, Blush, Carnation, Carolina, Castory, Cheddar, Clove, Colour, Coral, Cyclamen, Dianthus, Dutch, Emperce, FT, Fuchsia, Gillyflower, Indian, Knock, Kook, Lake, Lily, Lychnis, Maiden, Moss, Mushroom, Old rose, Oyster, Peach-blow, Peak, Perce, Pierce, Pompadour, Pounce, Rose(ate), Rose-hued, Rose madder, Ruddy, Salmon, Scallop, Sea, Shell, Shocking, Shrimp, Spigelia, Spit, Stab, Tiny
**Pinkerton** Detective
**Pinnacle** Acme, Apex, Apogee, Crest, Crown, Gendarme, Height, Hoodoo, Needle, Pinnet, Summit, Zenith
**Pinniped** Seal
**Pin-point** Focus, Highlight, Identify, Isolate, Localise, Locate
**Pint(s)** Cab, Jar, Log, Reputed
**Pintail** Duck, Smeath, Smee(th)
**Pinto** Piebald
**Pin-up** Bimbo, Cheesecake, Dish, Poser, Star, Sweater girl
**Pioneer(ing)** Alcock, Armstrong, Avant garde, Babbage, Baird, Bandeirante, Blaze, Boone, Brown, Caxton, Colonist, Emigrant, Explore, Fargo, Fawkner, Fleming, Frontiersman, Ground-breaking, Harbinger, Herodotus, Innovator, Lead, Lister, Marconi, Oecist, Pathfinder, Penn, Planter, Rochdale, Sandgroper, Settler, Spearhead, Stopes, Trail-blazer, Trekker, Tull, Turing, Voortrekker, Waymaker, Wells, Yeager
▸**Pious** *see* **PI**
**Pip** Ace, Acinus, Beat, Blackball, Bleep, Distemper, Heart, Hip, Hump, Lurgi, Phil, Pyrene, Seed, Star, Time-signal

**Pipe(s), Piper, Pipeline, Piping** Ait, Antara, Aorta, Aulos, Balance, Barrel, Blast, Blub, Boatswain's, Bong, Briar, Briarroot, Bronchus, Broseley, Bubble, Calabash, Call, Calumet, Cask, Chanter, Cheep, Cherrywood, Chibouk, Chibouque, Chillum, Churchwarden, Clay, Cob, Conduit, Corncob, Crane, Cutty, Delivery, Dip, Division, Down, Downcomer, Drain, Drill, Drillstring, Drone, Dry riser, Duct, Dudeen, Dudheen, Ell, Escape, Exhaust, Faucet, Feed, Fistula, Flageolet, Flue, Flute, Gage, Gas main, Gedact, Gedeckt, Goose-neck, Great, Hawse, Hod, Hogger, Hooka(h), Hose, Hubble-bubble, Hydrant, Ice, Indian, Injection string, Irish, Jet, Kalian, Kelly, Kill line, Mains, Manifold, Marsyas, Meerschaum, Mirliton, Montre, Narghile, Nargile(h), Narg(h)il(l)y, Oat(en), Oboe, Oesophagus, Organ, Ottavino, Outlet, Pan, Peace, Pepper, Pibroch, Piccolo, Pied, Pifferaro, Pitch, Poverty, Principal, Pule, Qanat, Quill, Rainwater, Recorder, Ree(d), Rise, Riser, Sack-doudling, Salicional, Sand, Sennit, Serpent, Service, Sewer, Shalm, Shawm, Sheesha, Shisha, Shoe, Shrike, Sing, Siphon, Skirl, Sluice, Snorkel, Soil, Spout, Squeak, Stack, Standpipe, Stopcock, Stummel, Sucker, Syrinx, Tail, Tee, Throttle, Tibia, Tobacco, Tootle, Trachea, Tremie, Tube, Tubule, Tweet, U-bend, Uillean(n), Union, Uptake, U-trap, U-tube, Vent, Ventiduct, Volcanic, Waste, Water(-spout), Watermain, Weasand, Whiss, Whistle, Woodcock's head, Woodnote, Worm

**Pipefish** Sea-adder

**Pipe-laying** Graft

**Pipit** Bird, Skylark, Titlark

**Pippin** Apple, Orange, Ribston

**Pipsqueak** Nobody

**Piquancy, Piquant** Heat, Pungent, Racy, Relish, Salt, Savoury, Sharp, Spicy, Tangy

**Pique** Bah, Dod, Huff, Irritation, Pride, Resentment, Titillate

**Piranha** Caribe, Characinoid, Piraya

**Pirate(s), Pirated, Piratical, Piracy** Algerine, Barbarossa, Blackbeard, Boarder, Bootleg, Brigand, Buccaneer, Buccanier, Cateran, Condottier, Conrad, Corsair, Crib, Dampier, Desperado, Fil(l)ibuster, Flint, Gunn, Hacker, Hijack, Hook, Kidd, Lift, Loot, Morgan, Penzance, Pew, Picaro(on), Pickaroon, Plagiarise, Plunder, Rakish, Rover, Sallee-man, Sallee-rover, Sea-dog, Sea-king, Sea-rat, Sea-robber, Sea-wolf, Silver, Skull and crossbones, Smee, Steal, Teach, Thief, Unauthorised, Viking, Water-rat, Water-thief

**Pirouette** Twirl

**Pistillate** Female

**Pistol** Air, Ancient, Automatic, Barker, Barking-iron, Cap, Captive bolt, Colt®, Dag, Derringer, Gat, → **GUN**, Hackbut, Horse, Iron, Luger®, Pepperbox, Petronel, Pocket, Puffer, Revolver, Rod, Saloon, Shooter, Sidearm, Six-gun, Starter, Starting, Very, Water, Weapon, Zip gun

**Piston** Four-stroke, Plunger, Ram, Trunk

**Pit(ted), Pitting, Pits** Abysm, Abyss, Alveolus, Antrum, Bear, Bed, Bordered, Borrow, Bottomless, Catch, Cave, Cesspool, Chasm, Cissing, Clay, Cloaca, Coalmine, Colliery, Crater, Den, Depression, Depth, Dungmere, Ensile, Fossa, Fougasse, Fovea, Foxhole, Gehenna, Hangi, Heapstead, Heartspoon, Hell, Hillhole, Hole, Hollow, Inferno, Inspection, Khud, Lacunose, Lime, Low, Mark, Marl, Match, Measure, → **MINE**, Mosh, Nadir, Orchestra, Parterre, Pip, Plague, Play, Pock-mark, Potato, Potholer, Punctate, Putamen, Pyrene, Ravine, Rifle, Salt, Sand, Saw, Scrobicule, Silo, Slime, Soakaway, Solar plexus, Stone, Sump, Tan, Tar, Tartarus, Tear, Trap, Trous-de-loup, Underarm

**Pitch(ed)** Absolute, Asphalt, Atilt, Attune, Bitumen, Burgundy, Camp, Careen, Catapult, Clef, Coal-tar, Concert, Crease, Curveball, Diamond, Diesis, Dive, Ela, Elect, Elevator, Encamp, Erect, Establish, Fever, Fling, Fork(ball), French, Ground, Heave, Height, International, Intonation, Key, Knuckleball, Labour, Length, Level, Lurch, Macadam, Maltha, Mineral, Nets, Neume, Outfield, Patter, Peck, Perfect, Philharmonic, Philosophical, Piceous, Pight, Pin, Plong(e), Plunge, Pop, Purl, Relative, Resin, Rock, Ruff(e), Sales, Scend, Sealant, Seel, Send, Shape, Sling, Slope, Soprarino, Spiel, Spitball, Stagger, Stoit, Tar, Tessitura, Tilt, Tone, Tonemic, Tonus, Tremolo, Tune, Unison, Vibrato, Wicket, Wild, Wood

**Pitchblende** Cleveite

**Pitcher(-shaped)** Aryt(a)enoid, Ascidium, Baseballer, Bowler, Cruse, Ewer, Jug, Steen, Tuning-key, Urceolus

**Pitchfork** Hurl, Toss
**Pitchstone** Retinite
**Pitfall** Ambush, Danger, Hazard, Snare, Trap
**Pith(y)** Ambatch, Aphorism, Apo(ph)thegm, Brief, Core, Down, Essence, Gnomic, Hat-plant, Heart, Laconic, Marrow, Meaty, Medulla, Moxa, Nucleus, Rag, Sententious, Succinct, Terse
**Pithead** Broo, Brow, Minehead
**Pithless** Thowless
**Pitiless** Flint-hearted, Hard, Hard-headed, Relentless, Ruthless, Stony
**Piton** Rurp
**Pitt** Brad, Chatham
**Pittance** Peanuts
**Pity, Piteous, Pitiable, Pitiful** Ah, Alack, Alas, Commiseration, → COMPASSION, Hapless, Mercy, Pathetic, Pathos, Pilgarlic, Poor, Quarter, Red-leg, Rue, Ruth(ful), Seely, Shame, Sin, Sympathy, Too bad, Tragic, Waefu(l), Wretched
**Pivot(al)** Axial, Ax(i)le, Central, Focal, Fulcrum, Gooseneck, Gudgeon, Hinge, Kingbolt, Marker, Revolve, Rotate, Slue, → SWIVEL, Trunnion, Turn, Wheel
**Pixel** Pel
**Pixie** Brownie, Elf, Fairy, Gremlin, Sprite
**Pizza** Calzone, Pepperoni
**Pizzazz** Elan, Flair
**Placard** Affiche, Bill, Playbill, Poster, Sign
**Placate** Appease, Calm, Conciliate, Mollify, Pacify, Placate, Propitiate, Soothe
**Place(ment), Places** Ad loc, Aim, Allocate, Appoint, Area, Arena, Assisted, Ballpark, Berth, Bro, Circumpose, Decimal, Deploy, Deposit, Dispose, First, Fix, Habitat, Haunt, High, Hither, Howf, Identify, Impose, → IN PLACE OF, Insert, Install, Job, Joint, Juxtapose, Lay, Lieu, Locality, Locate, Locus, Niche, Parking, Pitch, Plat, Plaza, Point, Posit, → POSITION, Post, Product, Put, Realm, Region, Repose, Resting, Room, Rowme, Scene, Second, Set, Sit, Site, Situate, Situation, Slot, Spot, Station, Stead, Sted(e), Stedd(e), Stratify, Third, Toponym, Town, Vendôme
**Placebo** Snake-oil
**Placid** Cool, Easy, Easy-osy, Even-tempered, Quiet, Serene, Tame, Tranquil, Untroubled
**Plagiarise, Plagiarist** Copy, Crib, Lift, Pirate, Steal
**Plague (spot)** Ailment, Annoy, Bane, Bedevil, Beset, Black death, Blight, Boil, Bubonic, Burden, Cattle, Curse, Death, Dog, Dun, Epidemic, Eyam, Frogs, Gay, Goodyear, Goujeers, Harry, Importune, Infestation, Locusts, Lues, Molest, Murrain, Murran, Murrin, Murrion, Nag, Obsess, Pest, Pester, Pox, Press, Scourge, Tease, Token, Torment, Torture, Try, Vex
**Plaid** Maud, Roon, Shepherd's, Tartan, Wales
**Plain(s)** Abraham, Archimedes, Artless, Ascetic, Au naturel, Bald, Banat, Bare, Blatant, Broad, Campagna, Campo, Campus Martius, Candid, Carse, Ceará, Chryse, Clavius, Clear, Cook, Dowdy, Downright, Dry, Esdraelon, Evident, Explicit, Flat, Flood, Girondist, Gran Chaco, Grassland, Great, Homely, Homespun, Inornate, Jezreel, Kar(r)oo, Lande, Langrenus, Liverpool, Llano, Lombardy, Lowland, Maidan, Manifest, Marathon, Mare, Matter of fact, Monochrome, Nullarbor, Obvious, Ocean of Storms, Oceanus Procellarum, Olympia, → ORDINARY, Outspoken, Overt, Packstaff, Palpable, Pampa(s), Paramo, Patent, Pikestaff, Plateau, Playa, Polje, Prairie, Prose, Ptolemaeus, Purbach, Sabkha(h), Sabkhat, Sailing, Salisbury, Savanna(h), Secco, Serengeti, Severe, Sharon, Simple, Sodom, Spoken, Staked, Steppe, Tableland, Thessaly, Tundra, Unadorned, Uncoloured, Unremarkable, Vanilla, Vega, Veldt, Visible, Walled
**Plainchant** Canto fermo
**Plainsman** Llanero
**Plainsong** Alternatim, Ambrosian, Chant
**Plaint(ive)** Complaint, Dirge, Lacrimoso, Lagrimoso, Lament, Melancholy, Sad, Whiny
**Plaintiff** Doe, Impeacher, Litigant, Suer
**Plait** Braid, Crimp, Cue, Entwine, Frounce, Furbelow, Goffer, Intertwine, Pigtail, Plica, Plight, Queue, Ruche, Sennit, Sinnet, Splice, Tress, Weave
**Plan(s), Planned, Planner, Planning** Afoot, Agenda, Aim, American, Angle, Architect,

Arrange, Atlas, Axonometric, Battle, Blueprint, Brew, Budget, Business, Campaign, Care, Chart, Commission, Complot, Conspire, Contingency, Contrive, Dalton, Dart, Deep-laid, Deliberate, Delors, Design, Desyne, Device, Devise, Diagram, Draft, Drawing, Elevation, Engineer, European, Family, Figure on, Five-Year, Flight, Floor, Forethought, Format, Galveston, Game, Ground, Hang, Ichnography, Idea, Idée, Initiative, Instal(l)ment, Intent, Itinerary, Lay(out), Leicester, Leicestershire, Logistics, Machinate, Manoeuvre, Map, Marshall, Master, Mastermind, Mean, Meditate, Nominal, Open, Outline, Pattern, Pension, Pipe-dream, Plat, Plot, Ploy, Policy, Premeditate, Prepense, Procedure, Programme, Project, Projet, Proposal, Prospectus, Protraction, Rapacki, Relief map, Road map, Ruse, Scenario, Schedule, Scheme, Schlieffen, Shape, Sketch map, Spec(ification), Stratagem, Strategy, Subterfuge, System, Tactician, Theory, Town, Trace, View, Wallchart, Wheeze

**Planck** Quantum theory

**Plane(s)** Aero(dyne), Air, →AIRCRAFT, Airliner, Airship, Axial, Bandit, Basal, Block, Boeing, Bomber, Bus, Buttock, Camel, Canard, Cartesian, Cessna, Chenar, Chinar, Comet, Concorde, Crate, Dakota, Datum, Delta-wing, Ecliptic, Even, Facet, Fault, Fillister, Flat, Float, Focal, Freighter, Galactic, Glider, Gliding, Gotha, Homaloid, Hurricane, Icosahedron, Icosohedra, Inclined, Jack, Jet, Jointer, Jumbo, Level, London, Mail, Main, MIG, Mirage, Mosquito, Moth, Octagon, Perspective, Platan(us), Polygon, Prop-jet, Pursuit, Rocket, Router, Shackleton, Shave, Shuttle, Smooth, Soar, Sole, Spitfire, Spokeshave, Spy, Stealth (bomber), STOL, Surface, Sycamore, Tail, Taube, Thrust, Tow, Trainer, Tree, Trident, Tropopause, Trying, Two-seater, Viscount

**Plane figure** Endecagon, Hendecagon

**Planet(s), Planetary** Alphonsine, Ariel, Asteroid, Body, Cabiri, Ceres, Chiron, Constellation, Dispositor, Dwarf, Earth, Eros, Extrasolar, Gas giant, Georgian, Giant, House, Hyleg, Inferior, Inner, Jovian, Jupiter, Lucifer, Major, Mars, Mercury, Minor, Moon, Neptune, Outer, Pallas, Pluto, Primary, Psyche, Quartile, Red, Satellitium, Saturn, Secondary, Sedna, Significator, Sphere, Starry, Sun, Superior, Terra, Terrestrial, Uranus, Venus, Vista, Vulcan, World, Zog

**Plangent** Mournful

**Plank** Board, Chess, Deal, Duckboard, Garboard, Manifesto, Plonk, Sarking, Skateboard, Slab, Spirketting, Straik, Strake, Stringer, Weatherboard, Wood, Wrest

**Plankton** Nekton, Neuston, Noctiluca, Pelagic, Red tide, Salpa, Seston, Spatfall

**Plant(s), Plant part** Acrogen, Agent, Amphidiploid, Anemochore, Annual, Anther, Aphotoic, Autophyte, Bed, Biennial, Biota, Bloomer, Botanical, Bryophyte, CAM, Catalytic(-cracker), Chamaephyte, Chomophyte, Conspecific, Cotyledon, Creeper, Cropper, Cultigen, Cultivar, Dayflower, Dibble, Diffusion, Ecad, Eccremocarpus, Embed, Endogen, Enemy, Enrace, Epilithic, Epiphyllous, Epiphyte, Establish, Factory, Fix, Flora, Foliage, Forb, Gasworks, Geophyte, G(u)ild, Growth, Gymnosperm, Halophyte, Halosere, Hardy annual, Herbage, Herbarium, House, Humicole, Hydrastus, Hydrophyte, Hygrophyte, Hylophyte, Incross, Insert, Instil, Inter, Labiate, Land, Lathe, Legume, Lithophyte, Livelong, Locate, Longday, Lurgi, Machinery, Medical, Mesophyte, Mill, Mole, Monocotyledon, Ombrophile, Ornamental, Oxygenator, Perennial, Phanerogam, Phloem, Pilot, Pitcher, Pot, Power, Protophyte, Psilophyte, Ramet, Refinery, Resurrection, Root, Rosin, Saprophyte, Schizophyte, Sciophyte, Sclerophyll, Scrambler, Sensitive, Sere, Shortday, Shrub, Simple, Sow, Spermatophyte, Sponge, Spy, Steelworks, Stickseed, Sticktight, Strangler, Streptocarpus, Succulent, Superweed, Thallophyte, Therophyte, Thickleaf, Trailer, →TREE, Trifolium, Trillium, Tropophyte, Twining, Vascular, Vegetal, Vegetation, Washery, Wilding, Works, Zoophyte

---

## PLANTS

*3 letters:*
Dal
Ers
Hom
Hop
Ivy
Kex
Lis
Meu
Nep
Pia
Rue
Set
Soy
Til
Udo
Urd
Yam

*4 letters:*
Alga
Aloe
Anil
Arum

Balm
Beet
Bixa
Chay
Cube
Daal
Dahl
Deme
Dhal
Dill
Fern
Flag
Flax
Geum
Gobo
Grex
Guar
Hebe
Hemp
Herb
Hioi
Homa
Hoya
Ixia
Jute
Kaki
Kali
Kava
Khat
Lily
Ling
Loco
Mate
Mint
More
Moss
Musk
Nard
Noni
Ombu
Pink
Pita
Poke
Poly
Rami
Rape
Reed
Rhus
Rose
Rush
Ruta
Sage
Sego
Shaw
Sida
Silk
Snow
Sola
Soma
Spit
Sunn
Tare
Taro
Thea
Vine
Weld
Woad
Wort
Yarr

***5 letters:***
Abaca
Agave
Ajwan
Anise
Anona
Arnut
Aroid
Aster
Avens
Basil
Benni
Betel
Blite
Bluet
Boree
Broom
Buchu
Bucku
Bugle
Calla
Camas
Canna
Carex
Chara
Chaya
Chufa
Clary
Clote
Cress
Cubeb
Cumin
Daisy
Dwale
Erica
Ficus
Fitch
Fouat
Fouet
Fucus
Gemma
Glaux
Gorse
Guaco
Hosta
Hovea
Inula
Jalap
Kenaf
Knawe
Kudzu
Laser
Ledum
Liana
Linum
Loofa
Lotus
Luffa
Lupin
Medic
Morel
Murva
Musci
Naiad
Orach
Orpin
Orris
Orval
Oshac
Osier
Oxeye
Oxlip
Panax
Pansy
Peony
Phlox
Pilea
Poppy
Ramee
Ramie
Reate
Sedge
Sedum
Senna
Shaya
Sotol
Spart
Spink
Stock
Tansy
Tetra
Timbo
Tulip
Urali
Urari
Urena
Vetch
Vinca
Viola
Vitex
Vitis
Xyris
Yucca
Yulan
Zamia

***6 letters:***
Abelia
Acacia
Acorus
Ajowan
Alisma
Allium
Alpine
Althea
Ambari
Ambary
Amomum
Annona
Arabis
Aralia
Arnica
Aucuba
Azalea
Bablah
Balsam
Bamboo
Banana
Bauera
Betony
Bonsai
Borage
Briony
Bryony
Burnet
Cactus
Caltha
Camash
Camass
Carica
Cassia
Catnep
Catnip
Celery
Cereus
Cicely
Cicuta
Cissus
Cistus
Cleome
Clivia
Clover
Clusia
Cnicus

Cockle
Cohage
Cohosh
Coleus
Conium
Coonty
Cornel
Cosmea
Cosmos
Cotton
Cowpea
Crinum
Crocus
Croton
Cummin
Dahlia
Daphne
Darnel
Datura
Derris
Dodder
Echium
Endive
Eringo
Erinus
Erynga
Exacum
Exogen
Fat hen
Fennel
Ferula
Funcka
Funkia
Garlic
Gnetum
Henbit
Hoodia
Hyssop
Iberis
Indigo
Jojoba
Juncus
Kentia
Kerria
Kie-kie
Kiss-me
Knawel
Kochia
Korari
Kumara
Kumera
Lentil
Lichen
Lolium
Loofah
Lovage
Lunary
Lupine
Luzula
Madder
Maguey
Mallow
Manioc
Manoao
Medick
Mimosa
Moorva
Nerine
Nerium
Nettle
Nuphar
Onagra
Opulus
Orache
Orchid
Orchis
Orpine
Ourali
Ourari
Oxalis
Oxslip
Oyster
Pachak
Paeony
Peanut
Pepino
Pepper
Pieris
Protea
Quinoa
Radish
Ramtil
Rattle
Reseda
Retama
Rubber
Ruscus
Sallow
Salvia
Savory
Scilla
Senega
Sesame
Seseli
Shrimp
Silene
Smilax
Sorbus
Sorrel
Spider
Spirea
Spurge
Spurry
Squill
Styrax
Sundew
Teasel
Teazle
Thrash
Thrift
Tomato
Tulipa
Turnip
Tutsan
Urtica
Violet
Viscum
Wasabi
Yacona
Yarrow
Yautia
Zinnia

*7 letters:*
Absinth
Aconite
Ale-hoof
Alfalfa
Alkanet
All-good
Allheal
Allseed
Alyssum
Anchusa
Anemone
Arachis
Astilbe
Awlwort
Barilla
Bartsia
Bee-balm
Begonia
Bistort
Bogbeam
Boneset
Brinjal
Bugbean
Bugloss
Bugwort
Burdock
Burweed
Calluna
Caltrap
Caltrop
Campion
Caraway
Cardoon
Carduus
Carline
Cascara
Cassava
Catechu
Catmint
Cat's ear
Celosia
Century
Chayote
Chelone
Chervil
Chicory
Clarkia
Clivers
Cocoyam
Comfrey
Compass
Coontie
Cowbane
Cowbird
Cowhage
Cowherb
Cowitch
Cowslip
Cudweed
Cumquat
Curcuma
Cushion
Dasheen
Day lily
Deutzia
Diascia
Digynia
Dioecia
Dittany
Dogbane
Dogwood
Drosera
Epacris
Ephedra
Erodium
Eugenia
Felicia
Felwort
Filaree
Fly-trap
Freesia
Frogbit
Fuchsia
Gazania
Genista
Gentian
Gerbera
Ginseng
Goat-rue
Godetia

Grapple
Gunnera
Haemony
Hawkbit
Heather
Hemlock
Henbane
Hogweed
Ipomoea
Isoetes
Jasmine
Jonquil
Juniper
Kingcup
Kumquat
Lantana
Lettuce
Liatris
Lobelia
Logania
Lucerne
Lychnis
Lythrum
Madwort
Mahonia
Manihot
Maranta
Matweed
Mayweed
Melilot
Mercury
Milfoil
Mimulus
Monarda
Mudwort
Mugwort
Mullein
Mustard
Nelumbo
Nemesia
Nigella
Nonsuch
Olearia
Opuntia
Palmiet
Papyrus
Pareira
Parella
Parelle
Parsley
Parsnip
Penguin
Penthia
Petunia
Pigface
Pinesap
Pinguin
Potherb
Primula
Puccoon
Pumpkin
Ragwort
Rampion
Raoulia
Redroot
Rhatany
Rhodora
Rhubarb
Ribwort
Ricinus
Robinia
Romneya
Rosebay
Ruellia
Saffron
Salfern
Salsify
Salsola
Sampire
Sanicle
Sawwort
Scandix
Seakale
Sea pink
Senecio
Setwall
Skirret
Solanum
Spignel
Spinach
Spiraea
Spurrey
Squilla
Stachys
Stapela
Statice
Syringa
Tagetes
Tellima
Thallus
Tobacco
Trefoil
Triffid
Tritoma
Turbith
Turpeth
Vanilla
Verbena
Vervain
Vetiver
Weigela
Woorali
Woorara
Wourali
Yaquona
Zebrina
Zedoary

***8 letters:***
Abelmosk
Absinthe
Abutilon
Acanthus
Achillea
Ageratum
Agrimony
Agueweed
Alocasia
Aloe vera
Alumroot
Angelica
Apocynum
Arenaria
Argemone
Asphodel
Barbasco
Barberry
Barometz
Bauhinia
Bear's ear
Bedstraw
Beetroot
Bellwort
Bergamot
Bergenia
Bignonia
Bindi-eye
Bindweed
Bird's eye
Bluebell
Bottonia
Boxberry
Brassica
Buckbean
Buddleia
Bull-hoof
Buplever
Caladium
Calamint
Calamite
Calathea
Calomine
Calthrop
Camellia
Camomile
Canaigre
Cannabis
Capsicum
Cardamom
Cardamum
Carl-hemp
Catchfly
Cat's foot
Centaury
Charlock
Chayroot
Chenopod
Chickpea
Cilantro
Cleavers
Clematis
Clubrush
Coltwood
Costmary
Cow-wheat
Crowfoot
Crucifer
Cucurbit
Cumbungi
Cunjevoi
Cyclamen
Daffodil
Damewort
Dentaria
Diandria
Dianthus
Dicentra
Dielytra
Dipsacus
Dogberry
Dog daisy
Dog's bone
Dracaena
Dropwort
Duckweed
Dumbcane
Earthnut
Eelgrass
Erigeron
Eucharis
Euonymus
Feverfew
Fireweed
Flax-lily
Fleabane
Fleawort
Fluellin
Foxglove
Fumitory
Furcraea
Galangol
Galtonia
Gardenia
Geranium

Gesneria
Gladioli
Gloriosa
Glory pea
Gloxinia
Glyceria
Gnetales
Goutweed
Grape ivy
Gromwell
Hag-taper
Harakeke
Hardhack
Hardhead
Harebell
Hare's ear
Hawkweed
Helenium
Henequen
Hepatica
Hesperis
Heuchera
Hibiscus
Hippuris
Honewort
Hornwort
Horokaka
Hyacinth
Hydrilla
Hyperium
Itchweed
Japonica
Jatropha
Khuskhus
Knapweed
Knotweed
Kohlrabi
Krameria
Lad's love
Larkspur
Lathyris
Lavatera
Lavender
Licorice
Locoweed
Lonicera
Lungwort
Macleaya
Malefern
Mandrake
Marigold
Mariposa
Marjoram
Martagon
Milkweed
Milkwort
Miltonia
Monstera
Moonseed
Moonwort
Mosspink
Mouse-ear
Myosotis
Navicula
Nenuphar
Nepenthe
Nymphaea
Oleander
Oleaster
Oncidium
Opopanax
Origanum
Oxtongue
Pandanus
Paspalum
Phacelia
Phormium
Physalis
Pinkroot
Pipewort
Plantain
Plumbago
Pokeroot
Pokeweed
Polygata
Pondweed
Primrose
Prunella
Psilotum
Psoralea
Psyllium
Purslane
Putchock
Queencup
Ratooner
Ratsbane
Redshank
Rock rose
Roly-poly
Rosemary
Sainfoin
Saltbush
Saltwort
Salvinia
Samnitis
Samphire
Sandwort
Scabious
Scammony
Sea-blite
Sea-holly
Self-heal
Sept-foil
Shamrock
Shinleaf
Sidalcea
Silkweed
Silphium
Snowdrop
Soapwort
Solidago
Sowbread
Sparaxis
Spergula
Stapelia
Staragen
Starwort
Suckling
Sunberry
Sundrops
Sweet pea
Tamarisk
Tarragon
Tayberry
Tickseed
Tigridia
Toadflax
Tree-fern
Tree-lily
Trigynia
Tritonia
Trollius
Tuberose
Tuckahoe
Turmeric
Turnsole
Valerian
Venidium
Veratrum
Veronica
Viburnum
Viscaria
Wait-a-bit
Wallwort
Water yam
Wistaria
Wisteria
Withwind
Woodroof
Woodruff
Woodrush
Wormseed
Wormwood
Xanthium

***9 letters:***
Aaron's rod
Achimenes
Adderwort
Alfilaria
Alfileria
Amaryllis
Anacharis
Andromeda
Anthurium
Apple mint
Aquilegia
Archangel
Arracacha
Arrowhead
Arrowroot
Artemisia
Artichoke
Artillery
Asclepias
Asparagus
Astrantia
Astrophel
Aubrietia
Ayabuasca
Bald-money
Baneberry
Bearberry
Bear's foot
Beech fern
Bee-orchid
Birthroot
Birthwort
Bloodroot
Bog myrtle
Breadroot
Bromeliad
Brooklime
Brookweed
Broom-rape
Browallia
Buck's horn
Buckwheat
Buglewood
Burrawang
Butterbur
Buttercup
Calcicole
Calcifuge
Calendula
Calla lily
Campanula
Candytuft
Cardamine
Carnation
Catchweed
Ceanothus
Celandine
Centaurea

Chamomile
Cherry pie
Cineraria
Claytonia
Clianthus
Clintonia
Clove pink
Cocklebur
Cock's comb
Colchicum
Colicroot
Colicweed
Collinsia
Colocasia
Colocynth
Coltsfoot
Columbine
Cordaites
Coreopsis
Coriander
Corydalis
Creamcups
Crocosnia
Crosswort
Crowberry
Crowsfoot
Dandelion
Day nettle
Decagynia
Desert pea
Desmodium
Devil's bit
Didynanua
Digitalis
Dittander
Dock-cress
Dog fennel
Dog violet
Doronicum
Dulcamara
Dutch rush
Dyer's weed
Echeveria
Echinacea
Edelweiss
Eglantine
Epilobium
Equisetum
Erythrina
Euphorbia
Eyebright
Fatshedra
Fenugreek
Feverwort
Flame tree
Forsythia
Fourcroya
Friar's cap
Galingale
Gelsemium
Germander
Gessamino
Gladiolus
Glasswort
Goldenrod
Goosefoot
Grass tree
Greenweed
Grindelia
Groundnut
Groundsel
Gypsywort
Hardheads
Heliconia
Hellebore
Helophyte
Herb-Paris
Herb Peter
Hieracium
Hoarhound
Hollyhock
Horehound
Horsemint
Horse-tail
House leek
Houstonia
Hydrangea
Hypericum
Impatiens
Jacaranda
Job's tears
Judas tree
Juneberry
Kalanchoe
Knee-holly
Kniphofia
Ladysmock
Lamb's ears
Laserwort
Lespedeza
Liquorice
Lithodora
Liver-wort
Lousewort
Manzanita
Mare's-tail
Marijuana
Marshwort
Meadow-rue
Mistletoe
Mitrewort
Monandria
Moneywort
Monkshood
Monogynia
Monotropa
Moon daisy
Moschatel
Moss plant
Mousetail
Muscadine
Myristica
Naked lady
Narcissus
Navelwort
Nemophila
Nicotiana
Oenothera
Ouviranda
Parrot jaw
Patchouli
Pearlwort
Pellitory
Pennywort
Penstemon
Peperomia
Pickaback
Piggyback
Pimpernel
Pineapple
Pokeberry
Polygonum
Portulaca
Pyrethrum
Quillwort
Rafflesia
Rattlebox
Riverweed
Rocambole
Rosinweed
Rudbeckia
Sabadilla
Safflower
Sagebrush
Santolina
Santonica
Saponaria
Saxifrage
Screwpine
Sea-rocket
Shoreweed
Sinningia
Snakeroot
Snakeweed
Spearmint
Spearwort
Speedwell
Spikenard
Spikerush
Sprekalia
Stargrass
Stickweed
Stinkweed
Stone-crop
Strapwort
Sunflower
Sweet flag
Sweet-gale
Taraxacum
Telegraph
Thorow-wax
Tiger lily
Titan arum
Tomatillo
Toothwort
Tormentil
Twinberry
Vaccinium
Verbascum
Vetchling
Wake-robin
Waterleaf
Water vine
Wild thyme
Wincopipe
Witchweed
Withywind
Wolf's bane
Wood avens
Woundwort
Xanthoxyl
Xerophyte

***10 letters:***

Adder's wort
Agapanthus
Alexanders
Ampelopsis
Anacardium
Angiosperm
Artocarpus
Asarabacca
Aspidistra
Astralagus
Barrenwort
Beech-drops
Beggarweed
Biddy-biddy
Bitter-king
Bitterweed
Bladder-nut
Bluebottle
Brugmansia
Busy Lizzie

Butterdock
Butterwort
Buttonbush
Calico-bush
Canada-lily
Candelilla
Catananche
Cat-cracker
China aster
Chionodoxa
Cinquefoil
Cloudberry
Commiphora
Coneflower
Coralberry
Corncockle
Cornflower
Cottonweed
Cow parsley
Cow parsnip
Crakeberry
Cranesbill
Crown vetch
Cuckoopint
Cupid's dart
Day-neutral
Deadnettle
Delphinium
Dog's-fennel
Dog's-tongue
Dragonhead
Dragonroot
Dyer's-broom
Earth-smoke
Easter lily
Elecampane
Escallonia
Eupatorium
Five-finger
Flamboyant
Fleur-de-lis
Foamflower
Four o'clock
Frangipani
Fraxinella
Friar's cowl
Fritillary
Frog's mouth
Gaillardia
Gaultheria
Glycophate
Gnaphalium
Goat-sallow
Goatsbeard
Goat's-thorn
Goat-willow
Goldenseal
Goldilocks
Goldthread
Goose grass
Grass cloth
Gypsophila
Hawksbeard
Heart's-ease
Heathberry
Helianthus
Heliotrope
Herb-bennet
Herb-Robert
Hobble-bush
Hop-trefoil
Hyoscyamus
Icosandria
Illecebrum
Immortelle
Indian pink
Indian pipe
Indian poke
Indian shot
Jew's mallow
Jew's-myrtle
Jimsonweed
Joe-pye weed
Joshua-tree
King's spear
Lemon grass
Loganberry
Maidenhair
Marchantia
Marguerite
Marsh-locks
Masterwort
Meconopsis
Mexican-tea
Mignonette
Mist-flower
Montbretia
Moonflower
Motherwort
Nasturtium
Nightshade
Nipplewort
Orange-root
Ouvirandra
Ox-eye daisy
Painted cup
Parkleaves
Parrot-beak
Parrot-bill
Passiflora
Pennycress
Pennyroyal
Pentagynia
Pentandria
Pentstemon
Peppermint
Pepperwort
Periwinkle
Pimpinella
Pipsissewa
Plume poppy
Poinsettia
Polemonium
Polianthes
Polyanthus
Pontederia
Potentilla
Puschkinia
Ragged lady
Ranunculus
Rest-harrow
Rhoicissus
Rock violet
Rose laurel
Rose mallow
Salicornia
Sarracenia
Sauce-alone
Scindapsus
Scorzonera
Setterwort
Silverweed
Sinsemilla
Snake's-head
Snapdragon
Sneezewort
Spiderwort
Stavesacre
Stitchwort
Stonebreak
Storksbill
Strelitzia
Sweetbriar
Thalictrum
Thunbergia
Tibouchina
Tillandsia
Touch-me-not
Tragacanth
Tree mallow
Tropaeolum
Tropaesium
Tumbleweed
Turtlehead
Twinflower
Venus's comb
Wallflower
Watercress
Water lemon
Windflower
Woodsorrel
Yellowroot
Yellowweed
Yellowwort

***11 letters:***

Aaron's beard
Acidanthera
Adam's needle
Antirrhinum
Baby's breath
Bastard balm
Bear's-breech
Beggar's lice
Biscuit-root
Bishop's weed
Bittercress
Bittersweet
Bitter vetch
Bladderwort
Blazing star
Blood-flower
Bog asphodel
Bottlebrush
Brankursine
Bristle-fern
Bur-marigold
Burning bush
Calceolaria
Callitriche
Camel's thorn
Cheddar pink
Cheese plant
Convallaria
Convolvulus
Corn spurrey
Cotoneaster
Crape-myrtle
Crepe-myrtle
Dame's violet
Dragon's head
Dusty-miller
Dyer's rocket
Erythronium
Field-madder
Fingergrass
Flamboyante
Forget-me-not
Fothergilla
Gentianella
Gillyflower
Globeflower
Gobe-mouches
Gooseflower

Green dragon
Hart's tongue
Helichrysum
Herb of grace
Herb-trinity
Hippeastrum
Honeysuckle
Horseradish
Hurtleberry
Incarvillea
Kangaroo paw
Kidney vetch
Kiss-me-quick
Labrador tea
Lady's finger
Lady's mantle
Lamb's tongue
Lattice-leaf
Lithotripsy
London pride
Long purples
Loosestrife
Love-in-a-mist
Luckengowan
Madonna lily
Maquilodora
Marsh mallow
Meadowsweet
Menispermum
Monadelphia
Mountain tea
Nancy-pretty
Oysterplant
Pachysandra
Paritaniwha
Parma violet
Parrot's bill
Pelargonium
Potamogeton
Proletarian
Ragged robin
Red hot poker
Rupturewort
Saintpaulia
Sanguisorba
Sansevieria
Schizanthus
Scurvy grass
Sea lavender
Sea milkwort
Sea purslane
Selaginella
Sempervivum
Shrimp plant
Slipperwort
Spanish moss
Sparaganium
Steeplebush
Stephanotis
St John's wort
Strawflower
Sulphurwort
Sweet cicely
Sweet sultan
Swiss cheese
Thimbleweed
Thoroughwax
Tiger flower
Tous-les-mois
Trumpetweed
Vallisneria
Water purple
Water violet
Welwitschia
White bryony
Wild mustard
Wintercress
Wintergreen
Xeranthemum

***12 letters:***
Adam's flannel
Adder's tongue
Alstroemeria
American aloe
Aristolochia
Autumn crocus
Bacon and eggs
Beggar's ticks
Brandy bottle
Cactus dahlia
Calico flower
Cape hyacinth
Cape primrose
Carolina pink
Checkerbloom
Cheese-rennet
Christophene
Christ's thorn
Cobblers' pegs
Corn marigold
Cuckoo flower
Cucumber tree
Darlingtonia
Devil-in-a-bush
Dragoon's head
Elephant's ear
Epacridaceae
Eschscholzia
Fennelflower
Flower delice
Flower deluce
Globe-thistle
Grapple-plant
Helianthemum
Hemp-agrimony
Hortus siccus
Hound's tongue
Iceland poppy
Indian turnip
Jacob's ladder
Lady's fingers
Lady's slipper
Lady's thistle
Lady's tresses
Lemon verbena
Leopard's bane
Lithospermum
Mariposa lily
Marvel of Peru
Midsummermen
Monkey flower
Morning glory
Mountain flax
None-so-pretty
Old man's beard
Ornithogalum
Parsley-piert
Pasqueflower
Pheasant's eye
Philadelphus
Philodendron
Phytobenthos
Pickerelweed
Pitcher plant
Plantain lily
Pleurisy root
Prickly poppy
Pteridosperm
Pterydophyte
Rhododendron
Rose geranium
Rose of Sharon
Salpiglossis
Sarsaparilla
Scouring rush
Scrophularia
Sea buckthorn
Service berry
Shepherd's rod
Shirley poppy
Snow-in-summer
Solomon's seal
Southernwood
Spring beauty
Stone bramble
Stone parsley
St Peter's wort
Strophanthus
Sweet alyssum
Sweet William
Tradescantia
Venus flytrap
Virgin's bower
Wandering Jew
Water-soldier
Weatherglass
Wild hyacinth
Wild williams
Zantedeschia

***13 letters:***
African violet
Alligator pear
Asparagus fern
Barbados pride
Black bindweed
Bladder cherry
Bleeding heart
Bougainvillea
Butcher's broom
Butterfly bush
Canary creeper
Carrion-flower
Christmas rose
Cranberry bush
Creeping jenny
Creosote plant
Crown imperial
Dieffenbachia
Dutchman's pipe
Elephant's ears
Elephant's foot
Eschscholtzia
Flannel flower
Grape hyacinth
Greek valerian
Indian tobacco
Jointed cactus
Mariposa tulip
Marsh marigold
Marsh samphire
Meadow saffron
Mountain avens
Mourning bride
Noli-me-tangere
Paschal flower
Passionflower
Rose of Jericho
Savanna flower
Shepherd's club
Slipper orchid
Spathyphyllum
Summer cypress

Sweet woodruff
Swine's succory
Tortoise plant
Townhall clock
Traveller's joy
Venus's flytrap
Viper's bugloss
Virginia stock
Water chestnut
Water dropwort
Water hyacinth
Water plantain
Water-purslane
Winter aconite

***14 letters:***
Alder-buckthorn
Barberton daisy
Belladonna lily
Bird of paradise
Black-eyed Susan
Bladder campion
Bougainvillaea
Canterbury bell
Cape gooseberry
Cardinal flower
Castor-oil plane
Chincherinchee
Chinese cabbage
Chinese lantern
Gold-of-pleasure
Hen and chickens
Lords and ladies
Love-in-idleness
Partridgeberry
Prince's feather
Queen Anne's lace
Shepherd's glass
Shepherd's purse
Spanish bayonet
Star-of-the-earth
Sweet horsemint
Treacle mustard
Vegetable sheep
Witches' thimble

***15 letters:***
Bird's nest orchid
Burnet saxifrage
Christmas cactus
Creeping thistle
Dog's tooth violet
Evening primrose
Golden saxifrage
Jack-in-the-pulpit
Lily-of-the-valley
Marsh-cinquefoil
Meadow saxifrage
Michaelmas daisy
Shepherd's myrtle
Star of Bethlehem
Virginia creeper
Wandering sailor

***16 letters:***
Annunciation lily
Barren strawberry
Bird's foot trefoil
Carolina allspice
Clove gillyflower
Clowgillie-flower
Deadly nightshade
Herb of repentance
Indian paintbrush
Livingstone daisy
Love-lies-bleeding
Mesembrianthemum
Poached-egg flower
Queen-of-the-meadow
Scarlet pimpernel
Swiss cheese plant

***17 letters:***
Devil's bit scabious
Dutchman's breeches
Jack-go-to-bed-at-noon
Mother-of-thousands
Queen of the prairie
Sheep's bit scabious
Snow-on-the-mountain
Squarrose knapweed
St Patrick's cabbage

***18 letters:***
Mother-in-law's tongue
Venus's looking glass

***19 letters:***
Mind-your-own-business
Ploughman's spikenard

***20 letters:***
Chickweed wintergreen
Enchanter's nightshade

---

**Plantagenet** Angevin, Broom
**Plantain** Mato(o)ke, Ribwort, Waybread
**Plantation** Arboretum, Bosket, Bosquet, Estate, Fazenda, Grove, Hacienda, Orangery, Pen, Pinetum, Ranch, Tara, Tope, Veticetum, Vineyard
**Plant disease** Anthracnose, Blight, Bunt, Club-root, Curl, Curlytop, Downy mildew, Ear-cockle, Eyespot, Frogeye, Leaf curl, Leaf-roll, Leaf-spot, Psyllid yellows, Rootknot, Rosette, Shanking, Smut, Sooty mould, Streak
**Planted** In, Under
**Planter** Dibber, Farmer, Pot, Settler, Trowel
**Plant-holder** Pot, Tub
**Plaque** Calculus, Dental, Plateau, Scale, Tablet
**Plasm** Germ
**Plasma** Blood, Dextran, Sigmond
**Plaster(ed), Plaster board** Artex®, Bandage, Bandaid®, Blister, Blotto, Butterfly clip, Cake, Cataplasm, Clam, Clatch, Compo, Court, Daub, Diachylon, Diachylum, Dressing, Drunk, Emplastrum, Fresco, Gesso, Grout, Gyprock®, Gypsum, Intonaco, Laying, Leep, Lit, Mud, Mustard, Oiled, Parge(t), Polyfilla®, Porous, Poultice, Render, Roughcast, Scratch-coat, Screed, Secco, Shellac, Sinapism, Smalm, Smarm, Smear, Sowsed, Staff, Sticking, Stookie, Stucco, Teer, Wattle and daub
**Plastic** Amex®, Bakelite®, Bubblewrap, Cel(luloid), Cling film, Ductile, Fablon®, Fibreglass, Fictile, Flexible, Fluon, Formica®, Ionomer, Laminate, Loid, Lucite®, Melamine, Mylar®, Perspex®, Plexiglass®, Pliant, Polyethylene, Polystyrene, Polythene, Polyvinyl, PVC, Reinforced, Styrene, Styrofoam®, Supple, Teflon®, Urea-formaldehyde, Vinyl, Wet-look, Xylonite, Yielding
▷**Plastic** *may indicate* an anagram
**Plasticine** Morph

**Plastic surgeon** McIndoe
**Plastic surgery** Neoplasty, Nose job, Otoplasty, Rhinoplasty
**Plate(s), Plated, Platelet, Platelike, Plating** Acierage, Ailette, Anchor, Angle, Anode, Armadillo, Armour, Ashet, Baffle, Bakestone, Baleen, Base, Batten, Blood, Brass, British, Butt, Chamfrain, Chape, Charger, Chrome, Clypeus, Coat, Coccolith, Communion, Continental, Copper, Cramper, Cribellum, Ctene, Dasypus, Deadman, Denture, Diaphragm, Dinner, Disc, Dish, Draw, Earth, Echo, Electro, Electrotype, Elytron, Elytrum, Enamel, Entoplastron, Equatorial, Escutcheon, Etching, Face, Fashion, Feet, Fine, Finger, Firemark, Fish, Flatware, Foil, Frog, Frons, Frontispiece, Futtock, Glacis, Gold, Graal, Gravure, Griddle, Ground, Gula, Half, Hasp, Home, Horseshoe, Hot, Hypoplastron, Illustration, Kick, L, Lamboys, Lame, Lamella, Lamina, Lanx, Latten, Lead, Licence, Madreporic, Mascle, Mazarine, Meat, Nail, Nef, Neural, Nickel, Notum, Number, Onycha, Ortho, Osteoderm, P, Palette, Paten, Patin(e), Patina, Pauldron, Peba, Petri, Phototype, Placord, Planometer, Plaque, Plastron, Platter, Pleximeter, Poitrel, Prescutum, Print, Pygal, Quarter, Race, Register, Registration, Riza, Roof, Rove, Salad, Salamander, Scale, Screw, Scrim, Scutcheon, Scute, Scutum, Seg, Selling, Sheffield, Shield, Shoe, Side, Sieve, Silver, Slab, Soup, Spacer, Spoiler, Squama, Stall, Steel, Stencil, Stereo(type), Sternite, Strake, Surface, Swash, T, Tablet, Tace, Tasse(l), Tea, Tectonic, Tergite, Terne, Thali, Theoretical, Tin(ware), Torsel, Touch, Trade, Tramp, Trencher, Trivet, Trophy, Tsuba, Tuill(ett)e, Tymp, Urostegite, Vane, Vanity, Vassail, Vessail, Vessel, Wall, Water, Web, Wet, Whirtle, Whole, Wobble, Workload, Wortle, Wrap(a)round, Zincograph
**Plateau** Altiplano, Anatolian, Barkly Tableland, Barren, Central Karoo, Chota Nagpur, Darling Downs, Dartmoor, Deccan, Durango, Eifel, Ellesworth Land, Field, Fjeld, Fouta Djallon, Had(h)ramaut, Highland, Highveld, Horst, Kalahari, Kar(r)oo, Kimberleys, Kurdestan, Kurdistan, La Mancha, Lamington, Langres, Laurentian, Mat(t)o Grosso, Mesa Verde, Meseta, Najd, Nilgiris, Ozark, Paramo, Piedmont, Puna, Shan, Shillong, Shire Highlands, Tableland, The Kimberleys, Ust Urt, Ustyurt
**Platelayer** Trackman
**Platform** Accommodation, Almemar, Balcony, Bandstand, Barbette, Base, Bay, Bema, Bench, Bier, Bridge, Catafalque, Catwalk, Crane, Crow's nest, Dais, Deck, Dolly, Drilling, Drillship, Emplacement, Entablement, Estrade, Exedra, Exhedra, Fighting top, Flake, Focsle, Footpace, Footplate, Foretop, Gangplank, Gantry, Gauntree, Gauntry, Gravity, Hustings, Kang, Landing stage, Launch-pad, Machan, Maintop, Manifesto, Monkeyboard, Oil, Oil-rig, Pad, Paint-bridge, Pallet, Perron, Plank, Podium, Predella, Production, Programme, Pulpit, Quay, Raft, Rig, Rostrum, Round-top, Scaffold, Shoe, Skidway, Skylab, Soapbox, Space, Sponson, → STAGE, Stand, Station, Stereobate, Stoep, Strandflat, Stylobate, Tee, Terminal, Thrall, Ticket, Top, Traverser, Tribunal, Tribune, Turntable, Wave-cut, Wharf
**Platinum** Pt, Ruthenium, Sperrylite, Spongy
**Platitude** Bromide, Cliché, Commonplace, Phrase, Truism
**Platocephalus** Flat-headed
**Platonic, Platonist** Academician, Ideal, Spiritual
**Platoon** Company, Squad, Team
**Platter** Charger, Dish, EP, Graal, Grail, Lanx, LP, Plate, Record, Salver, Trencher
**Platypus** Duckbill, Duck-mole, Water mole
**Plausible, Plausibility** Cogent, Credence, Credible, Fair, Glib, Likely, Logical, Oil, Probable, Proball, Sleek, Smooth, Specious
**Play(s), Playing** Accompany, Active, Amusement, Antic, Antigone, Assist, At, Brand, Busk, Candida, Caper, Charm, Child's, Chronicle, Clearance, Closet, Coriolanus, Crucible, Curtain-raiser, Dabble, Daff, Dalliance, Dandle, Docudrama, Doodle, Drama, Echo, Endgame, Epitasis, Equus, Escapade, Everyman, Extended, Fair, Finesse, Foul, Freedom, Frisk, Frolic, Fun, Gamble, Gambol, Game, Ghosts, Grand Guignol, Hamlet, Harlequinade, Harp, History, Holiday, Inside, Interlude, Jam, Jape, Jest, Jeu, Kinderspiel, Kitchen-sink, Laik, Lake, Lark, Latitude, Lear, Leeway, Licence, Lilt, Long, Loot, Macbeth, Mask, Masque, Match, May, Medal, Melodrama, Miracle, Monodrama, Morality, Mousetrap, Mummers, Musical, Mysteries, Nativity, Noh, Nurse, Oberammergau, On, One-acter, Orestaia, Othello, Parallel, Passion, Pastorale, Perform, Personate, Peter, Portray, Power, Prank, Pretend, Puppet, Recreation, Represent, Riff, Role, Rollick, Romp, Room, Rope, RUR, Satyr, Saw, Screen,

Shadow, Shoot, Show, Shuffle, Sketch, Sport, Squeeze, Stage, Straight, Strain, Strike up, Stroke, Strum, Summerstock, Thrum, Thumb, Tolerance, Tonguing, Toot, Touchback, Toy, Tragedy, Tragicomedy, Trifle, Triple, Tweedle, Twiddle, Two-hander, Vamp, Vaudeville, Vent, Whitechapel, Word

▷**Play** *may indicate* an anagram

**Playback** Echo, Repeat, Replay

**Playboy** Adulterer, Casanova, Don Juan, Hedonist, Rake, Roué, Seducer

**Player(s)** Accompanist, Actor, Athlete, Back, Backstop, Ball, Black, Brass, Bugler, Busker, Cast, CD, Centre, Centre-back, Centre forward, Centre-half, Clutch, Colt, Contestant, Cornerback, Cover point, Curler, Dealer, Defenceman, Disc, DVD, E, East, ENSA, Equity, Fetcher, Fiddle, Flanker, Fly-half, Flying wing, Fly-slip, Forward, Franchise, Fullback, Gary, Ghetto-blaster, Goalie, Goalkeeper, Goaltender, Gramophone, Grand master, Gridder, Guard, Half, Half-back, Half-forward, Harlequin, Histrio, Hooker, Hoopster, Infielder, iPod®, It, Juke-box, Keg(e)ler, Kest, Kicker, Left-winger, Linebacker, Lineman, Lion, Lock, Long-leg, Longstop, Loose-head, Lutanist, Lutenist, Man, Marquee, Midfield, Mid-on, Mime, Muffin, Musician(er), N, Nero, Nickelback, Nightwatchman, North, Nose guard, Nose tackle, Ombre, Onside, Orpheus, Outfielder, Out(side)-half, Outside-left, Outside-right, Pagliacci, Participant, Pianola®, Pitcher, Pocket, Pone, Pro, Prop, Quarterback, Receiver, Record, Red shirt, Reliever, Reserve, Right-winger, Rover, S, Safetyman, Scrape, Scratch, Scrum half, Seagull, Secondo, Seed, Shamateur, Short-leg, Shortstop, Side, South, Split end, Stand-off, Stand-off half, Stereo, Striker, Strings, Strolling, Substitute, Super, Sweeper, Tabrere, Target man, Team, Thesp(ian), Tight end, Troubador, Troupe, Upright, Utility, Virtuosi, W, Walker-on, Walkman®, West, White, Wide receiver, Wing(back), Winger, Wingman

**Playfair** Code

**Playfellow** Actor, Chum, Companion

**Playful** Arch, Coy, Frisky, Gamesome, Humorous, Impish, Jocose, Kittenish, Ludic, Merry, Piacevole, Scherzo, Skittish, Sportive, Spry, Waggish, Wanton

**Playgirl** Actress, Electra

**Playgoer** Groundling, Savoyard

**Playground** Adventure, Close, Garden, Park, Rec(reational), Rectangle, Theatre, Tot lot, Yard

**Playhouse, Playroom** Amphitheatre, Cinema, Nursery, Red Lion, Theatre, Wendy

**Play off** Decider

**Playsuit** Rompers

**Playtime** Break

**Playwright** →DRAMATIST, Dramaturge, Dramaturgist, Scriptwriter

---

## PLAYWRIGHTS

*3 letters:*
Fry
Hay
Kyd

*4 letters:*
Bolt
Bond
Gems
Hare
Inge
Shaw
Tate

*5 letters:*
Albee
Arden
Barry
Behan
Frayn
Genet
Gorky
Ibsen
Leigh
Odets
Orton
Simon
Synge
Wilde

*6 letters:*
Barrie
Bellow
Besier
Brecht
Coward
Dekker
Dryden
Jonson
Lerner
Mercer
Miller
Morton
O'Casey
O'Neill
Pinero
Pinter
Racine
Sartre
Sherry
Storey
Toller
Wesker
Wilder

*7 letters:*
Anouilh
Beckett
Bennett
Chekhov
Dario Fo
Delaney
Doggett
Feydeau
Garrick
Goldoni
Harwood
Hellman
Ionesco
Kaufman
Marlowe
Marston
Maugham

Mauriac
Molière
Osborne
Plautus
Rostand
Simpson
Terence
Thespis
Travers
Webster

*8 letters:*
Beaumont
Congreve
Etherege
Fletcher
MacNeice
Marivaux
Menander
Mortimer
Rattigan
Sheridan
Stoppard
Vanbrugh
Wedekind
Williams

*9 letters:*
Aeschylus
Ayckbourn
Bleasdale
Corneille
Euripides
Goldsmith
Massinger
Priestley
Sophocles
Wycherley

*10 letters:*
Drinkwater
Pirandello
Strindberg
Williamson

*11 letters:*
Maeterlinck

*12 letters:*
Beaumarchais

---

**Plea(s)** Alford, Appeal, Claim, Common, Cri de coeur, Defence, Entreaty, Essoin, Excuse, Exoration, Fains, Invocation, Nolo contendere, Orison, Petition, Placit(um), Prayer, Rebuttal, Rebutter, Rogation, Suit

**Plead(er), Pleading** Answer, Argue, Beg, Beseech, Entreat, →IMPLORE, Intercede, Litigate, Moot, Placitory, Solicit, Special, Supplicant, Urge, Vakeel, Vakil

**Please(d), Pleasant, Pleasing, Pleasure(-seeker), Pleasurable** Affable, Aggrate, Agreeable, Alcina, Algolagnia, Amenable, Amene, Amiable, Amuse, Apolaustic, Appeal, Aromatic, Arride, Artistic, Be my guest, Beneplacito, Benign, Bitte, Bonne mine, Braw, Charm, Cheerful, Chuffed, Comely, Comfort, Complaisant, Congenial, Content, Cordial, Cute, Delectation, Delice, Delight, Divine, Do, Ecstasy, Euphonic, Eye candy, Fair, Felicitous, Fit, Flatter, Fun, Genial, Glad, Gladness, Glee, Good-o, Goody-goody, Gratify, Gusto, Harmonious, Hedonism, Indulge, Jammy, Jocose, Joy, Kama, Kindly, Lekker, Lepid, List, Naomi, Oblige, Piacevole, Primrose path, Prithee, Prythee, Purr, Queme, Regale, Revel, Sapid, Satisfy, Schadenfreude, Sightly, Suit, Tasty, Thrill, Tickle, Tickle pink, Toothsome, Treat, Vanity, Voluptuary, Wally, Will, Winsome, Wrapped, Xanadu List

**Pleasure-garden, Pleasure-ground** Lung, Oasis, Paradise, Park, Policy, Ranelagh, Tivoli

**Pleasure-seeker** Gadabout, Hedonist, Playboy

**Pleat** Accordion, Box, Crimp, Crystal, Fold, French, Frill, Gauffer, Goffer, Gusset, Inverted, Kick, Kilt, Knife, Plait, Pranck(e), Prank, Ruff(le), Sunburst, Sunray, Tuck

**Pleb(eian)** Common, Essex Man, Hoi-polloi, Homely, Laic, Low-born, Ordinary, Popular, Roturier

**Plebiscite** Vote

**Pledge(r)** Abstainer, Affidavit, Arlene, Arles, Assertion, Band, Betroth, Bond, Borrow, Bottomry, Collateral, Commitment, Dedicate, Deposit, Earnest(-penny), Engage, Fine, Frithborn, Gage, Gilbert, Giselle, Guarantee, Hand, Hock, Hypothecate, Impignorate, Mortgage, Oath, Pass, Pawn, Pignerate, Pignorate, Plight, Pop, Promise, Propine, Sacrament, Security, Sponsorship, Stake, Surety, Teetotal, Toast, Troth, Undertake, Vow, Wad, Wage(r), Wed

**Pleiades** Alcyone, Celaeno, Electra, Maia, Merope, Sterope, Taygete

**Plenitude** Stouth and routh

**Plentiful, Plenty** Abounding, Abundance, Abundant, Ample, Bags, Copious, Copy, Cornucopia, Easy, Excess, Foison, Fouth, Ful(l)ness, Fushion, Galore, Goshen, Lashings, Loads, Lots, Numerous, Oodles, Pleroma, Profusion, Quantity, Riches, Rife, Routh, Rowth, Scouth, Scowth, Slue, Sonce, Sonse, Teeming, Umpteen

**Plenum** Spaceless

**Pliable, Pliant** Amenable, Docile, Flexible, Limber, Limp, Lithe, Malleable, Plastic, Sequacious, Supple, Swack, Swank, Wanle

▸**Pliers** *see* PLY

**Plight** Betrothal, Case, Dilemma, Misdight, Peril, Pickle, Pledge, Predicament, State, Troth

**Plimsoll(s)** Dap, Gutty, Gym-shoe, Line, Mutton-dummies, Pumps, Sandshoe, Sannie, Tacky

**Plinth** Acroter, Base, Block, Pedestal, Socle, Stand, Zocco, Zoccolo

**Plod(der)** Drudge, Ploughman, Stomp, Traipse, Tramp, Trog, Trudge
**Plonk(er)** Bonce, Marble, Rotgut, Wine
**Plop** Cloop, Drop, Fall, Gloop, Plap, Plump
**Plot(s)** Allotment, Area, Babington, Bed, Box (and whisker), Brew, Cabal, Carpet, Chart, Cliché, Collude, Connive, Conspiracy, Conspire, Contrive, Covin, Covyne, Croft, Device, Engineer, Erf, Erven, Frame-up, Garden, Graph(ics), Gunpowder, Honeytrap, Imbroglio, Intrigue, Lair, Locus, Lot, Machination, Map, Meal-tub, Odograph, Orchard, Pack, Parcel, Patch, Plan, Plat, Popish, Rye-house, Scenario, → SCHEME, Sect(ion), Seedbed, Shamba, Shot, Site, Story, Storyline, Taluk, Terf, Turf, Web
**Plotter** Artist, Brutus, Cabal, Camarilla, Casca, Catesby, Conspirator, Device, Digital, Engineer, Incremental, Intrigant, Microfilm, Oates, Rosary, Schemer, Trinketer
**Plough(man), Ploughed, Ploughing** Arable, Ard, Arval, Big Dipper, Breaker, Bull tongue, Chamfer, Charles's Wain, Contour, Dipper, Disc, Drail, Dray, Drill, Ear, Earth-board, Ere, Fail, Fallow, Farmer, Feer, Flunk, Gadsman, Gang, Great Bear, Harrow, Lister, Middlebreaker, Middlebuster, Mouldboard, Piers, Pip, Pleuch, Pleugh, Plodder, Push, Rafter, Rib, Ridger, Rive, Rotary, Rove, Sand, Scooter, Septentrion(e)s, Sill, Sodbuster, Sow, Spin, Stump-jump, Swing, The Wagon, Till(er), Tractor, Trench, Triones, Wheel
**Plough-cleaner** Pattle, Pettle
**Ploughshare** Co(u)lter, Sock
**Ploughwise** Boustrophedon
**Plover** Bud, Congregation, Dott(e)rel, Lapwing, Peewit, Pratincole, Prostitute, Ring-dotterel, Ringed, Stand, Tewit, Wing
**Plowman** Piers
**Ploy** Brinkmanship, Dodge, Feint, Finesse, Gambit, Gimmick, Manoeuvre, M(a)cGuffin, Ruse, Stratagem, Strike, Subterfuge, Tactic, Wile
**Pluck(ing), Plucky** Avulse, Bare, Carphology, Cock, Courage, Deplume, Epilate, Evulse, Floccillation, Gallus, Game, Gather, → GRIT, Guts, Loot, Mettle, Pick, Pinch, Pip, Pizzicato, Plectron, Plectrum, Ploat, Plot, Plumassier, Plunk, Pook(it), Pouk(it), Pull, Race, Scrappy, Snatch, Spin, Spirit, Spunk, Summon, Tug, Twang, Tweak, Tweeze, Vellicate, Yank
**Plug** Access eye, Ad, Adapter, Adaptor, Advocate, Banana, Block, Bung, Caulk, Chaw, Chew, Commercial, Dam, DIN, Dook, Dossil, Dottle, Douk, Fipple, Fother, Gang, Glow, Go-devil, Heater, Hype, Jack, Lam, Operculum, Pessary, Phono, Prod, Promote, Publicity, Ram, Rawlplug®, Recommendation, Safety, Salt, Scart, Sealant, Socket, Spark(ing), Spigot, Spile, Spiling, Stem, Stop(per), Stopple, Strobili, Suppository, Tampion, Tap, Tent, Tobacco, Tompion, Vent, Volcanic, Wage, Wall, Wander, Wedge
**Plum** Beach, Bullace, Cherry, Choice, Damask, Damson, Drupe, French, Gage, Greengage, Ground, Jamaica, Japanese, Java, Kaki, Mammee-sapota, Marmalade, Maroon, Mirabelle, Musk, Mussel, Myrobalan, Naseberry, Neesberry, Peach, Persimmon, Proin(e), Pruin(e), Prune(llo), Quetsch, Raisin, Sapodilla, Sebesten, Victoria, Wodehouse
**Plumage, Plume** Aigrette, Crest, Eclipse, Egret, Feather, Hackle, Mantle, Panache, Preen, Ptilosis, Quill, Topknot
**Plumb(er), Plumbing** Bullet, Dredge, Fathom(eter), Lead(sman), Perpendicular, Plummet, Sheer, Sound, Test, True, U-trap, Vertical
**Plumbago** Graphite, Leadwort, Wad(d), Wadt
**Plummet** Dive, Drop, Lead, Nosedive, → PLUNGE
**Plump(er)** Bold, Bonnie, Bonny, Buxom, Choose, Chopping, Chubbed, Chubby, Cubby, Cuddly, Dumpy, Embonpoint, Endomorph, Fat, Fleshy, Flop, Fubsy, Full, Lie, Matronly, Opt, Pick, Plank, Plonk, Plop, Podgy, Portly, Pudgy, Roll-about, Rolypoly, Rotund, Round(about), Rubenesque, Sonsie, Sonsy, Soss, Souse, Squab, Squat, Stout, Swap, Swop, Tidy, Tubby, Well-covered, Well-fed, Well-padded, Well-upholstered, Zaftig, Zoftig
**Plunder(er)** Berob, Booty, Brigand, Depredate, Despoil, Devastate, Escheat, Fleece, Forage, Freebooter, Gut, Harry, Haul, Herriment, Herryment, Hership, Loot, Maraud, Peel, Pill(age), Predation, Prey, Privateer, Raid, → RANSACK, Rape, Rapparee, Ravage, Raven, Ravin, Ravine, Reave, Reif, Reive, Rieve, Rifle, Rob, Rummage, Sack, Scoff, Shave, Skoff, Spoil(s), Spoliate, Sprechery, Spuilzie, Spuly(i)e, Spulzie, Swag

**Plunge(r)** Dasher, Demerge, Dip, Dive, Douse, Dowse, Duck, Enew, Immerge, Immerse, La(u)nch, Nose-dive, Plummet, Plump, Raker, Send, Sink, Souse, Swoop, Thrust
**Plural** Multiply, Pl
**Plus** Addition, And, Gain, More, Positive, Sign
**Plush(ed)** Die, Luxurious, Opulent, Rich, Smart, Tint, Velour, Velvet
**Pluto(crat), Plutonic** Abyssal, Croesus, Dis, Dog, Hades, Hypogene, Magnate, Nob, Pipeline, Underground
**Plutonium** Pu
**Ply, Plier(s)** Bend, Birl, Cab, Exercise, Exert, Gondoliers, Importune, Layer, Practise, Run, Trade, Wield
▷**Plying** *may indicate* an anagram
**Plymouth Brethren** Darbyite
**PM** Addington, Afternoon, Arvo, Asquith, Attlee, Autopsy, Balfour, Blair, Bute, Cabinet-maker, Callaghan, Cameron, Chamberlain, Chatham, De Valera, Disraeli, Gladstone, Leader, Macmillan, Major, Melbourne, Nehru, Peel, Pitt, Portland, Premier, → PRIME MINISTER, Salisbury, Taoiseach, Walpole
**Pneumonia** Lobar, Lobular, Visna
**Poach** Burn-the-water, Cook, Encroach, Filch, Head-hunt, Lag, Steal, Trespass
**Pochard** Duck, Scaup
**Pocket(s)** Air, Appropriate, Bag, Bin, Breast, Cargo, Cavity, Cly, Cup, Enclave, Fob, Glom, Hideaway, Hip, Jenny, Marsupia, Misappropriate, Patch, Placket, Plaid-neuk, Pot, Pouch, Purloin, Purse, Sac, Sky, Slash, Sling, Slit, Steal, Take, Trouser, Vest, Watch, Whitechapel
**Pocketbook** Reader, Wallet
**Pockmark** Cicatrice
**Pod(s)** Babul, Bean, Belly, Boll, Carob, Chilli, Dividivi, Engine, Gumbo, Hull, Lablab, Legume, Lomentum, Neb-neb, Okra, Pea, Pipi, Pregnant, Pudding-pipe, Seed, Senna, Shell, Siliqua, Tamarind, Vanilla, Vine
**Podgy** Gaucie, Gaucy, Gawcy, Gawsy, Roll-about, Roly-poly
**Podium** Dais
**Poem(s), Poetry** Acmeism, Acrostic, Aeneid, Alcaic, Anthology, Art, A Shropshire Lad, Awdl, Ballad(e), Beowulf, Bestiary, Bucolic, Byliny, Caccia, Canto, Canzone, Cargoes, Cento, Chanson de jeste, Choliamb, Choriamb, Cicada, Cinquain, Complaint, Concrete, Decastich, Dewan, Dit(t), Dithyramb, Divan, Dizain, Doggerel, Duan, Dub, Dunciad, Eclogue, Elegy, Elene, Endymion, Epic(ede), Epigram, Epilogue, Epithalamium, Epode, Epopee, Epopoeia, Epos, Epyllion, Erotic, Fifteener, Finlandia, Gauchesco, Gay Science, Georgic, Ghazal, Graveyard, Haikai, Haiku, Heptastich, Heroic, Hexastich, Hokku, Hull, Hypermeter, Idyl(l), If, Iliad, Imagism, Inferno, Jazz, Kalevala, Kyrielle, Lay, Limerick, Logaoedic, London, Madrigal, Mahabharata(m), Mahabharatum, Meliboean, Melic, Metaphysical, Metre, Mock-heroic, Monostich, Monostrophe, Nostos, Ode, Odyssey, Palinode, Paracrostic, Parnassus, Pastoral, Penill(ion), Pentameter, Pentastich, Performance, Poesy, Prelude, Prose, Prothalamion, Punk, Purana, Qasida, Quatorzain, Quatrain, Quire, Ramayana, Rat-rhyme, Renga, Rhapsody, Rig-Veda, Rime, Rime riche, Rondeau, Rondel(et), Rubai(yat), Rune, Scazon (iambus), Senryu, Sestina, Sijo, Sirvente, Sixain, Song, Sonnet, Sound, Spondee, Stanza, Stornello, Symphonic, Tanka, Tankia, Telestich, Temora, Tercet, Tetrastich, Thebaid, Title, Tone, Triolet, Tristich, Vers(e), Versicle, Villanelle, Völuspá, Voluspe, Waka
**Poet(s), Poetic** Acmeist, Amorist, Bard(ling), Beatnik, Cavalier, Cumberland, Cyclic, Elegist, Georgian, Iambist, Idyllist, Imagist, Lake, Laureate, Layman, Liner, Lyrical, Lyrist, Makar, Maker, Meistersinger, Metaphysical, Metrist, Minnesinger, Minor, Minstrel, Mistral, Monodist, Odist, Parnassian, Performance, PL, Pleiad(e), Poetaster, Rhymer, Rhymester, Rhymist, Rymer, Scald, Scop, Silurist, Skald, Smart, Sonneteer, Sound, Spasmodic, Spasmodic School, Te(i)an, Thespis, Tragic, Trench, Troubadour, Trouvère, Trouveur, Verse-monger, Verse-smith, Versifier, Vers librist(e), Water

## POETS

***2 letters:***
AE

***3 letters:***
Gay
Paz
Poe

***4 letters:***
Abse
Baif
Bemi
Blok
Cory
Dyer
Gray
Gunn
Hogg
Hood
Hope
Hugo
Hunt
Lang
Lear
Omar
Ovid
Owen
Pope
Rowe
Rumi
Tate
Vega

***5 letters:***
Alley
Arion
Auden
Ayres
Basho
Bemia
Blair
Blake
Blunt
Burns
Byron
Cadou
Carew
Cinna
Clare
Crane
Dante
Donne
Duffy
Eliot
Flint
Frost
Gosse
Gower
Griot
Heine
Hesse
Homer
Horne
Hulme
Iqbal
Jarry
Keats
Keyes
Lewis
Logue
Lorca
Lucan
Marot
Meyer
Moore
Nashe
Noyes
Plath
Pound
Prior
Rilke
Rishi
Sachs
Smith
Tasso
Theon
Tzara
Vazor
Wever
Wyatt
Yeats
Young

***6 letters:***
Adamov
Alonso
Arnold
Austin
Barham
Barnes
Belloc
Binyon
Borges
Brecht
Brooke
Butler
Cibber
Clarke
Clough
Cowley
Cowper
Crabbe
Curnow
Daniel
Daurat
Davies
Domett
Dowson
Dryden
Dunbar
Ennius
Fuller
George
Glycon
Goethe
Graves
Harpur
Heaney
Hemans
Hesiod
Horace
Hughes
Jensen
Jonson
Landor
Larkin
Lawman
Lowell
Marini
Milton
Morris
Motion
Neruda
Newman
Ossian
Pindar
Porter
Racine
Sappho
Seaman
Shanks
Sidney
Tagore
Thomas
Valery
Vergil
Villon
Virgil
Waller
Warton
Watson

***7 letters:***
Addison
Alcaeus
Alfieri
Aneirin
Aretino
Ariosto
Beddoes
Belleau
Blunden
Bridges
Bunting
Caedmon
Campion
Chapman
Chaucer
Cocteau
Collins
Corinna
Crashaw
Cynwulf
Doughty
Douglas
Drayton
Emerson
Enright
Flaccus
Flecker
Herbert
Heredia
Herrick
Hopkins
Housman
Juvenal
Khayyam
Layamon
Lydgate
Martial
Marvell
Meynell
Montale
Newbolt
Orpheus
Patmore
Philips
Pushkin
Rimbaud
Ronsard
Russell
Sassoon
Seferis
Service
Shelley
Sitwell

Skelton
Sotades
Southey
Spender
Spenser
Statius
Terence
Thomson
Vaughan
Whitman
Woolner

*8 letters:*
Akenside
Anacreon
Banville
Beranger
Berryman
Betjeman
Brentano
Browning
Campbell
Catullus
Cummings
Cynewulf
Davenant
Day Lewis
De la Mare
De Musset
Drummond
Du Bellay
Ginsberg
Hamilton
Harrison
Hausmann
Kynewulf
Laforgue
Langland
Lawrence
Leopardi
Lovelace
Macaulay
Mallarmé
Menander
Meredith
Petrarch
Rossetti
Sandberg
Schiller
Shadwell
Stephens
Suckling
Taliesin
Tennyson
Thompson
Traherne
Tyrtaeus
Verlaine
Voltaire
Whittier

*9 letters:*
Aeschylus
Alexander
Bunthorne
Coleridge
Deschamps
Dickinson
Euripides
Goldsmith
Henderson
Lamartine
Lucretius
Marinetti
Masefield
Quasimodo
Shenstone
Simonides
Sophocles
Stevenson
Swinburne
Wergeland

*10 letters:*
Baudelaire
Chatterton
Drinkwater
Fitzgerald
La Fontaine
Longfellow
McGonagall
Propertius
Tannhauser
Theocritus
Wordsworth

*11 letters:*
Apollinaire
Archilochus
Asclepiades
Bildermeier
Castiglione
Maeterlinck
Pherecrates

*12 letters:*
Archilochian
Aristophanes

*14 letters:*
Dante Alighieri

*15 letters:*
Ettrick Shepherd

---

**Poetaster** Della-Cruscan
**Poetess** Ingelow, Orinda
**Poet laureate** Bridges, Motion, PL
▸**Poetry** *see* POEM(S)
**Po-faced** Stolid
**Poignant** Acute, Biting, Emotive, Haunting, Keen, Moving, Pungent, Stirring, Touching
**Point(ed), Pointer, Points** Accumulation, Ace, Acerose, Acnode, Acro-, Aculeate, Advice, Aim, Angular, Antinode, Antler, Apex, Aphelion, Apogee, Apolune, Appui, Apse, Apsis, Arrowhead, Ascendant, Asterisk, Bar, Barb, Barrow, Base, Basis, Beachy Head, Bisque, Boiling, Bradawl, Break(ing), Brownie, Bull, Burble, Burbling, Cacumen, Calk, Cape, Cardinal, Caret, Cash, Catch, Centre, Choke, Clou, Clovis, Clue, Colon, Comma, Compass, Compensation, Cone, Conic, Corner, Cover, Crag, Crisis, Critical, Crux, Culmination, Cultrate, Curie, Cursor, Cusp, Cuss, Cutting, Danger, Datum, Dead, Decimal, Deflater, Deflator, Degree, Descendant, Detail, Dew, Diamond, Di(a)eresis, Direct, Dot, Dry, E, Ear, End, Entry, Epanodos, Épée, Equant, Equinoctial, Eutectic, Exclamation, Extremity, Fang, Fastigiate, Feature, Fescue, Fesse, Fielder, Fieldsman, Finger(tip), Firing, Fitch(e), Five, Fixed, Flash, Focal, Focus, Foreland, Fourteen, Freezing, Fulcrum, Gallinas, Game, Germane, Gist, Gnomon, Gold, Hastate, Head, High, Hinge, Hint, Home-thrust, Horn, Hour hand, Ice, Icicle, Ideal, Index, Indicate, Indicator, Intercept, Ippon, Isoelectric, Issue, Jag, Jester, Jog, Juncture, Keblah, Kiblah, Kip(p), Knub, Lace, Lagrangian, Lance, Lanceolar, Lead, Limit, Lizard, Locate, Locus, Low, Mandelbrot set, Mark, Match, Melting, Metacentre, Microdot, Moment, Moot, Mucro, Mull, Muricate, N, Nail, Nasion, Near, Neb, Needle, Neel, Ness, Nib, Nocking, Node, Nodus, Nombril, Now, Nub, Obconic, Obelion, Obelisk, Objective, Opinion, Ord, Organ, Oscillation, Particle, Peak, Pedal, Penalty, Periapsis, Periastron, Perigee, Perihelion, Perilune, Pin, Pinch, Pinnacle, Pixel, Place, Pour, Power, Pressure, Prickle, Promontory, Prong, Prow, Punchline, Punctilio, Punctual, Punctum, Purpose, Radix, Rallying, Ras, Reef,

Relevance, Respect, Rhumb, Rhumbline, S, Sample, Saturation, Scribe, Seg(h)ol, Selling, Set, Setter, Shaft, Sharpener, Sheva, Show, Shy, Silly, Socket, Sore, Spearhead, Specie, Spicate, Spick, Spike, Spinode, Spinulose, Stage, Stagnation, Starting, Stationary, Steam, Sticking, Stigme, Stiletto, Sting, Stipule, Strong, Sum, Suspension, Synapse, Tacnode, Talking, Tang, Taper, Tax, Technicality, Thorn, Tine, → TIP, Tipping, Tippytoe, Tongue, Trafficator, Train, Transition, Trig, Trigger, Triple, Turning, Umlaut, Urde(e), Urdy, Use, Vane, Vanishing, Vantage, Verge, Verse, Vertex, Vowel, Voxel, W, Waggle-dance, Weak, Weight, Yad, Yield, Yuko, Zenith

**Pointless** Blunt, Curtana, Flat, Futile, Idle, Inane, Inutile, Love, Muticous, Otiose, Outlandish, Stupid, Vain

**Point of honour** Pundonor

**Poise** Aplomb, Balance, Composure, Grace, P, Serenity

**Poison(er), Poisoning, Poisonous** Arrow, Bane, Blood, Contact, Contaminate, Deleterious, Envenom, Ergotise, Food, Gossypine, Hydrargyrism, Listeria, Malevolent, Miasma, Mycotoxicosis, Noxious, Plumbism, Rankle, Rat, Rot, Sausage, Systemic, Taint, Toxic, Toxicology, Toxicosis, Toxin, Toxoid, Venom(ous), Viperous, Virose, Virous, Virulent

---

## POISONS

***4 letters:***
Cube
Fugu
Gila
Lead
Loco
Tutu
Upas

***5 letters:***
Abrin
Algae
Aspic
Ricin
Sarin
Soman
Timbo
Urali
Venin

***6 letters:***
Aldrin
Antiar
Borgia
Cicuta
Curara
Curare
Curari
Datura
Dioxin
Durban
Emetin
Endrin
Hebona
Iodism
Obeism
Ourali
Ourari
Phenol
Pyemia
Septic
Uremia
V-agent
Wabain

***7 letters:***
Aconite
Amanita
Arsenic
Atropia
Atropin
Boletus
Bromism
Brucine
Cacodyl
Coniine
Cowbane
Cyanide
Emetine
Flybane
Hebenon
Hemlock
Henbane
Lindane
Mineral
Neurine
Neutron
Ouabain
Oxalate
Phallin
Pyaemia
Safrole
Solpuga
Stibine
Stibium
Surinam
Tanghin
Tropine
Venefic
Woorali
Woorara
Wourali

***8 letters:***
Acrolein
Adamsite
Apocynum
Atropine
Barbasco
Botulism
Cannabin
Cyanuret
Daturine
Dumbcane
Embolism
Exotoxin
Flypaper
Gossypol
Lewisite
Litharge
Lobeline
Locoweed
Mephitic
Methanol
Mezereon
Miticide
Nerve gas
Nicotine
Paraquat®
Ptomaine
Pulicide
Raphania
Ratsbane
Rhodanic
Samnitis
Santonin
Solanine
Thebaine
Toxaemia
Trembles
Urushiol
Veratrin
Warfarin

***9 letters:***
Aflatoxin
Autotoxin
Benzidine
Brominism
Bufotalin
Ciguatera
Coyotillo
Digitalin
Echidnine
Fluorosis
Gelsemine
Monkshood
Muscarine
Mycotoxin
Parathion
Sapraemia
Sassy wood
Saturnism
Saxitoxin
Sparteine
Stonefish
Tanghinin
Toxaphene

Veratrine
Wolfsbane
Yohimbine

***10 letters:***
Aqua-tofana
Belladonna
Bufotenine
Cadaverine
Colchicine
Hydrastine
Jimson weed
Limberneck
Manchineal
Mandragora
Molybdosis
Neurotoxin
Paris green
Phalloidin
Phylotoxin
Picrotoxin
Salicylism
Salmonella
Strychnine
Tetrotoxin
Thorn-apple

***11 letters:***
Calabar-bean
Dog's mercury
Gelseminine
Gila monster
Hyoscyamine
Listeriosis
Phosphorism
Pilocarpine
Scopolamine
Septicaemia
Sugar of lead
Sulphur tuft
Veratridine

***12 letters:***
Fool's parsley
Formaldehyde
Hydrargyrism
Nitromethane
Noogoora burr
Strophanthus
Tetrodotoxin

***13 letters:***
Scheele's green
Silver nitrate

***16 letters:***
Deadly nightshade

---

**Poke, Pokey, Poky** Bonnet, Broddle, Chook, Dig, Garget, Goose, Indian, Itchweed, Jab, Jook, Meddle, Mock, Nousle, Nudge, Nuzzle, Ombu, Peg, Pick, Poach, Pock, Pote, Pouch, Powter, → PRISON, → PROD, Prog, Proke, Punch, Root(le), Rout, Rowt, Rummage, Sporran, Stab, Stir, Thrust

**Poker (work)** Brag, Bugbear, Curate, Draw, Game, Gas, High-low, Lowball, Mistigris, Penny ante, Pyrography, Red-hot, Salamander, Strip, Stud(-horse), Texas hold'em, Tickler, Tine, Toe

**Poland, Polish** Cracovian, PL, Pomeranian, Racovian, Sarmatia, Sejm, Slav, Stefan

**Polar, Pole(s), Poler** Alpenstock, Animal, Anode, Antarctic, Arctic, Barber's, Bean, Boathook, Boom, Bowsprit, Bum(p)kin, Caber, Celestial, Clothes, Copernicus, Cowl-staff, Crossbar, Electret, Extremity, Fishgig, Fizgy, Flagstaff, Flagstick, Furlong, Gaff, Galactic, Gas, Geomagnetic, Greasy, Hop, Icy, Janker, Kent, Liberty, Lodge, Lug, Magnetic, Mast, May, N, Nadir, Negative, Nib, North, Oar, Periscian, Permafrost, Po, Positive, Punt, Quant, Quarterstaff, Range, Ricker, Ridge, Ripeck, Rood, Roost, Ry(e)peck, S, Shaft, South, Spar, Spear, Spindle, Sprit, Staff, Stake, Stanchion, Stang, Starosta, Stilt, Sting, Stobie, Telegraph, Terrestrial, Thyrsos, Thyrsus, Tongue, Topmast, Totem, Utility, Vegetal, Zenith

▷**Polar** *may indicate* with a pole

**Polaris** Lodestar, Rhodanic, Rocket, Star

**Polecat** Ferret, Fitch, Fitchet, Foulmart, Foumart, Quail, Weasel

**Polemic(al)** Argument, Controversy, Debate, Eristic(al)

**Police(man), Policewoman** Askari, Babylon, Bear, Beast, Beria, Bill, Bizzy, Black and Tans, Blue, Bluebottle, Blue heeler, Bobby, Bog(e)y, Boss, Boys in blue, Bull, Busy, Carabinero, Carabiniere, Catchpole, Centenier, Cheka, Chekist, Chief Constable, CID, Commissioner, Constable, Cop(per), Cotwal, Crusher, Darogha, Detective, DI, Dibble, Druzhinnik, Europol, Filth, Flatfoot, Flattie, Flic, Flying Squad, Force, Fuzz, Gangbuster(s), Garda, Garda Siochana, Gendarme, Gestapo, Gill, G-man, Guard, Gumshoe, Harmanbeck, Heat, Hermandad, Inspector, Interpol, Jamadar, Jawan, Jemadar, John Hop, Keystone, KGB, Kitchen, Kotwal, Lawman, Limb, Mata-mata, Met(ropolitan), Military, Mobile, Monitor, Morse, Mountie, MP, Mulligan, Nabman, Nark, Ochrana, Officer, OGPU, Ovra, Patrolman, PC Plod, Peeler, Peon, Pig, Plod, Pointsman, Polis, Polizei, Porn squad, Posse (comitatus), Prefect, Provincial, Provost, Puppy-walker, Ranger, Redbreast, Redcap, Regulate, RIC, Riot, Robert, Rosser, Roundsman, Rozzer, RUC, Sbirro, SC, Scotland Yard, Secret, Securitate, Securocrat, Sepoy, Shamus, Sleeping, Slop, Smokey, Snatch squad, Sowar(ry), Special, Special Branch, Stasi, State Trooper, Super, Superintendent, Sureté, Sweeney, T(h)anadar, Texas Rangers, The Bill, The Law, The Yard, Thin blue line, Thirdborough, Thought, Traffic, Traps, Vice squad, Vigilante, Walloper, Wolly, Woodentop, Yardie squad, Zabtieh, Zaptiah, Zaptieh, Zomo

**Police car** Black Maria, Panda, Patrol, Prowl

**Police station** Copshop, Lock-up, Tana, Tanna(h), Thana(h), Thanna(h), Watchhouse

**Policy** Assurance, Ballon d'essai, Byline, CAP, Comprehensive, Course, Demesne,

Endowment, Expedience, First-loss, Floating, Good neighbour, Gradualism, Hard line, Insurance, Keystone, Knock for knock, Laisser-faire, Lend-lease, Line, Manifesto, Method, Open(-sky), Open door, Ostpolitik, Perestroika, Plank, Platform, Pork-barrel, Practice, Programme, Reaganism, Reaganomics, Revanchism, Scorched earth, Set-aside, Socred, Stance, Stop-go, Tack, Tactics, Thatcherism, Third party, Ticket, Traditional, UDI, Valued, White Australia

**Polish(ed), Polisher** Beeswax, Black(ing), Blacklead, Bob, Brasso®, Bruter, Buff, Bull, Burnish, Chamois, Complaisant, Edit, Elaborate, Elegant, Emend, Emery, Enamel, Finish, French, Furbish, Gentlemanly, Glass, Glaze, Gloss, Heelball, Hone, Inland, Jeweller's rouge, Lap, Lustre, Nail, Perfect, Pewter-mill, Planish, Polite, Polverine, Pumice, Racovian, Refinement, Refurbish, Rottenstone, Rub, Sand, Sandblast, Sandpaper, Scour, Sheen, Shellac, Shine, Sleekstone, Slick, Slickenside, Sophistication, Supercalender, Svelte, Tutty, Urbane, Varnish, Veneer, Wax

**Politburo** Committee

**Polite(ness)** Affable, Cabinet, Civil, Courteous, Genteel, Grandisonian, Mannered, Mannerly, Suave, Urbane, Well-bred, Well-mannered

**Politic(al), Politics** Apparat, Azapo, Body, Chartism, Civic, Diplomacy, Discreet, Dog-whistle, Expedient, Falange, Fascism, Fatah, Gesture, Leftism, Left-winger, Neoliberalism, New Left, Party, Peronism, Poujadism, Power, Practical, Public, Radicalism, Rightism, Right-winger, Sinn Fein, State, Statecraft, Tactful, Wise, Yuppie, Yuppy

**Politician(s), Politico** Back bench, Bright, Cabinet, Carpet-bagger, Catiline, CC, Centrist, Chancellor, Chesterfield, Christian Democrat, Con, Congressman, Coningsby, Delegate, Demagogue, Demo(crat), Diehard, Disraeli, Draco, DUP, Eden, Euro-MP, Eurosceptic, Evita, Federalist, Front bench, Gladstone, Green, Guevara, Hardie, Hardliner, Incumbent, Independent, Ins, Isolationist, Kennedy, Laski, Left, Legislator, Liberal, Log-roller, Loony left, MEP, Merkel, Minister, Moderate, Molotov, Mowlam, MP, Nationalist, Nazi, Obstructionist, Octobrist, Paisley, Parliamentarian, Parnell, Politico, Pollie, Polly, Poujade, Powell, Puppet, Rad, Rep, Republican, Richelieu, Senator, Socialist, Statesman, Statist, Tadpole, Taper, TD, Thatcherite, Tory, Trotsky, Unionist, Veep, Warhorse, Whig, Whip, Wilberforce

**Poll(ing)** Advance, Ballot, Bean, Canvass, Count, Cut, Deed, Dod, Election, Exit, Gallup, Head count, Humlie, Hummel, Lory, MORI, Nestor, Noggin, Not(t), Opinion, Parrot, Pineapple, Pow, Push, Referendum, Scrutiny, Sondage, Straw, Votes

▷**Poll** *may indicate* a first letter

**Pollack** Coalfish, Coley, Fish, Lob, Lythe, Saith(e)

**Pollard** Doddered

**Pollen, Pollinate(d), Pollination** Anemophilous, Beebread, Dust, Entomophilous, Errhine, Ex(t)ine, Farina, Fertilised, Geitonogamy, Intine, Malacophily, My(i)ophily, Palynology, Sternotribe, Witch-meal, Xenia

**Pollenbrush** Scopa

**Pollex** Thumb

**Pollster** Psephologist

**Pollute(d), Pollutant, Pollution** Acid rain, Adulterate, Atmosphere, Besmear, Blend, Contaminate, Defile, Dirty, Feculent, File, Fly ash, Foul, Impure, Infect, Light, Miasma, Noise, Nox, Oil slick, Rainout, Smog, Soil, Soilure, Stain, Sully, Taint, Thermal, Violate, Waldsterben

**Polly** Flinders, Parrot, Peachum

**Polo** Bicycle, Chukka, Chukker, Marco, Mint, Navigator, Rink, Water

**Polonium** Po

**Poltergeist** Apport, Ghost, Spirit, Trouble-house

**Poltroon** Coward, Craven, Dastard, Scald, Scaramouch

**Polyandry** Nair

**Polygon** Isogon, Spherical

**Polygraph** Lie-detector

**Polymath** Knowall, Labruz, Toynbee

**Polymer** Acrylic, Elastomer, Fructans, High, Isotactic, Lignin, Metaldehyde, Oligomer, Paraldehyde, Resin, Seloxane, Silicone, Sporopollenin, Tetramer, Trimer

**Polymorphic** Multiform, Proteus, Variform
**Polynesian** Moriori, Niuean, Tahitian, Tongan
**Polyp(s)** Alcyonaria, Cormidium, Gonophore, Hydra, Hydranth, Nematophore, Obelia, Sea-anemone, Tumour
**Polyphemus** Cyclops
**Polyphony** Counterpoint
**Polysaccharide** Cellulose
**Polystyrene** Expanded
**Polyzoan** Sea-mat
**Pom** Choom
**Pomander** Pounce(t)-box
**Pome** Apple
**Pomegranate** Punica, Punic apple
**Pommel** Beat, Knob, Pound, Pummel
**Pomp(ous)** Aldermanlike, Big, Bloviate, Bombastic, Budge, Ceremonial, Display, Dogberry, Euphuistic, Fustian, Glory, Grandiloquent, Grandiose, Heavy, Highfalutin(g), High-flown, High-muck-a-muck, High-sounding, Hogen-mogen, Holier than thou, Inflated, Magniloquent, Orotund, Ostentatious, Pageantry, Panjandrum, Parade, Pontificating, Pooh-Bah, Pretentious, Self-important, Sententious, Solemn, Splendour, Starchy, State, Stilted, Stuffed shirt, Stuffy, Turgid, Turkey cock
**Pom-pom** Ball, Tassel
**Ponce** Pander, Pimp, Solicit, Souteneur
**Poncho** Ruana
**Pond(s)** Atlantic, Curling, Dew, Dub, Flash, Hampstead, Lakelet, Lentic, Mill, Oceanarium, Pool, Pound, Puddle, Settling, Shield(ing), Slough, Stank, Stew, Tank, Turlough, Vivarium, Viver
**Ponder(ous)** Brood, Cogitate, Contemplate, Deliberate, Heavy, Laboured, Mull, Muse, Perpend, Poise, Pore, Puzzle, Reflect, Ruminate, → **THINK**, Vise, Volve, Weigh, Weight(y), Wonder
**Pondweed** Canadian
**Poniard** Bodkin, → **DAGGER**, Dirk, Stiletto
**Pontiff, Pontifical, Pontificate** Aaron, Aaronic, Antipope, Dogmatise, Papal, Spout
**Pontoon** Blackjack, Bridge, Caisson, Chess, Game, Twenty one, Vingt-et-un
**Pony** Bidet, Canuck, Cayuse, Cow, Dales, Dartmoor, Eriskay, Exmoor, Fell, Garran, Garron, Gen(n)et, GG, Griffin, Griffon, Gryfon, Gryphon, Jennet, Jerusalem, Mustang, New Forest, One-trick, Pit, Polo, Pownie, Sable Island, Shanks', Sheltie, Shetland, Show, Tangun, Tat(too), Timor, Welsh, Welsh Mountain, Western Isles
**Ponytail** Queue
**Pooch** Dog
**Poodle** Barbet, Swan
**Pooh** Bah, Bear, Pish, Pow-pow, Pugh, Tush, Winnie, Yah
**Pool(s)** Backwater, Bank, Bethesda, Billabong, Birthing, Bogey hole, Car, Cenote, Cess, Collect, Combine, Dub, Dump, Flash, Flow, Fund, Gene, Hag, Hot, Infinity, Jackpot, Jacuzzi®, Kitty, Lasher, Lido, Lin(n), Malebo, Meer, Mere, Mickery, Mikvah, Mikveh, Millpond, Moon, Natatorium, Paddling, Piscina, Piscine, Plash, Plesh, Plunge, → **POND**, Puddle, Reserve, Share, Siloam, Snooker, Spa, Stank, Stanley, Sump, Tank, Tarn, Treble chance, Wading, Water(ing) hole, Wave
**Poop** Stern
**Poor(ly)** Abysmal, Adverse, Bad, Bare, Base, Bijwoner, Boracic, Breadline, Buckeen, Bywoner, Catchpenny, Cheapo, Churchmouse, Conch, Cronk, Destitute, Desuetude, Dire, Dirt, Gens de peu, Gritty, Half-pie, Hard-up, Have-nots, Hopeless, Humble, Hungry, Ill(-off), Impecunious, Indigent, Lame, Lazarus, Lean, Lo-fi, Lousy, Low, Low-downer, Low-fi, Low-paid, Lumpen, Meagre, Mean, Mediocre, Naff, Needy, Obolary, One-horse, Pathetic, Patzer, Pauper, Peaky, Poxy, Redleg, Roinish, Rop(e)y, Roynish, Sad, Scrub, Second rate, Shabby, Shoddy, Sober, Sorry, Strapped, Sub, Tacky, Tatty, Tenth rate, Thin, Third-rate, Threadbare, Tinpot, Trashy, Undeserving, Unwell, Useless, Wattle, Wishy-washy, Wretched

▷**Poor** *may indicate* an anagram

**Poorhouse** Union, Workhouse

**Pooter** Nobody, Nonentity

**Pop (off), Popper, Popping** Bang, Brit, Burst, Cloop, Coke®, Cream soda, Crease, Daddy, Die, → DRUG, Each, Father, Fr, Ginger ale, Gingerbeer, Hip-hop, Hock, Iggy, Insert, Lemonade, Lumber, Mineral, Nip, Number, Parent, Party, Pater, Pawn, Pepsi®, Pledge, Population, Press-stud, Punk, Rock'n'roll, Scoosh, Sherbet, Slip, Snap fastener, Soda, Soft drink, Splutter, Sputter, Weasel

▷**Pop** *may indicate* an anagram

**Pope(s)** Adrian, Alexander, Atticus, Benedict, Black, Boniface, Borgia, Clement, Dunciad, Eminence, Fish, Great Schism, Gregory, Hildebrand, Holiness, Innocent, Joan, Leo, Medici, Papa, Pius, Pontiff, Ruff(e), Schism, Sistine, Sixtius, Theocrat, Tiara, Urban, Vatican, Vicar-general of Christ, Vicar of Christ

**Pop-gun** Bourtree-gun

**Popinjay** Barbermonger, Coxcomb, Dandy, Fop, Macaroni, Parrot, Prig, Skipjack

**Poplar** Abele, Aspen, Balsam, Cottonwood, Lombardy, Trembling, Tulip, White, Yellow

**Poppet** Cutie pie, Valve

**Poppy** Argemone, Bloodroot, Blue, California, Chicalote, Coquelicot, Corn, Corydalis, Diacodin, Eschscholtzia, Field, Flanders, Horned, Iceland, Matilija, Mawseed, Opium, Papaver, Plume, Ponceau, Prickly, Puccoon, Rhoeadales, Shirley, Tall, Welsh

**Poppycock** Baloney, Bosh, Nonsense, Piffle, Rubbish

**Popular(ity), Popularly** Best-seller, Catchy, Common, Crowd-pleaser, Cult, Democratic, Demotic, Enchorial, Evergreen, Fashionable, General, Grass roots, Heyday, Hit, Hot ticket, In, Laic, Lay, Mass, Plebeian, Prevalent, Public, Sell-out, Street cred, Successful, Tipped, Trendy, Vogue, Vulgo

**Population, Populace** Catchment, Census, Closed, Deme, Demography, Inhabitants, Joe Public, Malthusian, Mass, Mob, Optimum, → PEOPLE, Public, Universe

**Porcelain** Arita, Artificial, Bamboo, Belleek®, Blanc-de-chine, Celadon, Chantilly, Chelsea, China, Coalport, Crackle(ware), Crouch-ware, Crown Derby, Derby, Dresden, Eggshell, Famille, Famille jaune, Famille noir, Famille rose, Famille verte, Frit, Goss, Hard-paste, Hizen, Imari, Ivory, Jasp, Jasper(ware), Kakiemon, Limoges, Lithophane, Meissen, Ming, Minton, Parian, Petuntse, Petuntze, Sèvres, Softpaste, Spode, Sung, Yuan

**Porch** Galilee, Lanai, Stoa, Stoep, Veranda(h)

**Porcino** Cep

**Porcupine** Hedgehog, Prickle, Urson

**Pore** Browse, Hole, Hydrathode, Lenticel, Muse, Ostiole, Ostium, Outlet, Ponder, Stoma, Study

**Porgy** Braise, Scup(paug)

**Pork(y)** Bacon, Boar, Brawn, Chap, Char sui, Crackling, Cracknel, Fatback, Flitch, Griskin, Ham, Lie, Pancetta, Salt, Scrapple, Scruncheon, Scrunchion, Spare-rib, Spek, Tenderloin

**Porn(ography), Pornographic** Adult, Curiosa, Erotica, Hard, Hard-core, Jazz mag, Rhyparography, Snuff-film, Soft, Soft-core, Video nasty

**Porous** Cancellate, Cellular, Permeable, Pumice, Sponge

**Porpoise** Bucker, Dolphin, Mereswine, Pellach, Pellack, Pellock, Phocaena, Sea pig, Sea swine

**Porridge** Berry, Bird, Brochan, Brose, Burgoo, Busera, Crowdie, Drammach, Drammock, Gaol, Grits, Grouts, Gruel, Hominy, Kasha, Mabela, Mahewu, Mealie pap, Mielie pap, Oaten, Oatmeal, Parritch, Pease-brose, Polenta, Pottage, Praiseach, Sadza, Samp, Sentence, Skilly, Stirabout, Stretch, Sup(p)awn, Time, Ugali

**Porridge stick** Thible, Thivel

**Port(s)** Beeswing, Carry, Cinque, Coaling station, Container (terminal), Entrepot, Free, Gate, Gateway, Geropiga, → HARBOUR, Haven, Hinterland, Hover, Induction, Larboard, Left, Manner, Mien, Outport, Parallel, Raft, Row, Ruby, Serial, Tawn(e)y, Treaty, USB, VSOP, Wine

## PORTS

*3 letters:*
Abo
Ayr
Gao
Hué
Rio
Rye
Tyr

*4 letters:*
Acre
Aden
Akko
Amoy
Apia
Baku
Bari
Boma
Cobh
Cork
Deal
Dill
Doha
Eisk
Elat
Faro
Gary
Gaza
Gyor
Hilo
Hull
Icel
I-pin
Kiel
Kiev
Kobe
Kure
Lima
Linz
Lomé
Luda
Naha
Oban
Omsk
Oran
Oslo
Oulu
Perm
Pori
Pula
Puri
Ruse
Safi
Said
Salé
Sfax
Suez
Susa
Suva
Tang
Tema
Tvev
Tyre
Vigo
Wick
Wuhu

*5 letters:*
Akaba
Anzio
Aqaba
Arhus
Arica
Aulis
Bahia
Bahru
Banff
Barry
Basra
Batum
Beira
Belem
Bharu
Blyth
Brest
Cadiz
Cairo
Canea
Colon
Dakar
Davao
Derry
Dilli
Dover
Duala
Dubai
Eilat
Elath
Emden
Fowey
Gabes
Galle
Gavie
Genoa
Ghent
Gijon
Goole
Haifa
Hania
Hithe
Horta
Hythe
Imari
Izmir
Jaffa
Jambi
Jedda
Jidda
Joppa
Kerch
Kochi
Larne
Leith
Lulea
Mainz
Malmo
Masan
Merca
Miami
Mocha
Mokpo
Narva
Newry
Omaha
Ophir
Osaka
Ostia
Palma
Palos
Pisco
Ponce
Poole
Pusan
Pylos
Rabat
Rouen
Saida
Sakai
Salto
Selby
Sidon
Skien
Split
Surat
Susah
Tajik
Tampa
Tanga
Tunis
Turku
Vaasa
Varna
Visby
Vlore
Volos
Yalta
Yeisk
Yeysk
Yibin

*6 letters:*
Aarhus
Abadan
Agadir
Albany
Alborg
Amalfi
Ancona
Andong
Annaba
Aveiro
Balboa
Bastia
Batumi
Bergen
Bilbao
Bissao
Bissau
Blanca
Bombay
Bootle
Boston
Braila
Bremen
Bukavu
Burgas
Cairns
Calais
Callao
Candia
Cannes
Canton
Cavite
Chania
Chi-lin
Cochin
Cuiaba
Cuyaba
Dalian
Da Nang
Danzig
Darwin
Dieppe
Djambi
Douala
Duluth

Dunbar
Dundee
Durban
Durres
Elblag
Galata
Galati
Gdansk
Gdynia
Harbin
Havana
Hobart
Ichang
Iligan
Iloilo
Inchon
Jaffna
Jarrow
Juneau
Kalmar
Khulna
Kisumu
Lepaya
Lisbon
Lobito
Lubeck
Lushun
Macelo
Mackay
Madras
Malabo
Malaga
Manado
Manama
Manaos
Manaus
Manila
Maputo
Matadi
Melaka
Menado
Mersin
Mobile
Mumbai
Muscat
Nagano
Namibe
Nantes
Napier
Naples
Narvik
Nassau
Nelson
Newark
Ningbo
Ningpo
Nizhni
Oamaru
Odense
Odessa
Oporto
Ostend
Padang
Patras
Peoria
Pesaro
Quebec
Quincy
Rabaul
Ragusa
Recife
Reggio
Rijeka
Rimini
Romney
Roseau
Rostov
Samara
Samsun
Santos
Sarnia
Sasebo
Savona
Skikda
Smyrna
Sousse
Speyer
Spires
St John
St Malo
St Paul
Suakin
Sydney
Syzran
Szeged
Tacoma
Tajiki
Thurso
Timaru
Tobruk
Toledo
Toulon
Tromso
Tyumen
Velsen
Venice
Vyborg
Weihai
Whitby
Wismar
Wonsan
Xiamen
Yangon
Yantai

***7 letters:***
Aalborg
Abidjan
Ajaccio
Alesund
Almeria
Antalya
Antibes
Antwerp
Aracaju
Astoria
Augusta
Averiro
Bamberg
Bangkok
Bayonne
Bengasi
Berbera
Bizerta
Bizerte
Bristol
Buffalo
Bushehr
Bushire
Calabar
Cam Ranh
Canopus
Cantala
Cardiff
Catania
Changde
Changte
Chicago
Chilung
Cologne
Colombo
Conakry
Corinth
Corunna
Cotonou
Derbent
Detroit
Drammen
Dunedin
Dunkirk
El Minya
Ephesus
Esbjerg
Foochow
Fukuoka
Funchal
Gauhati
Geelong
Gosport
Grimsby
Halifax
Hamburg
Hampton
Harwich
Heysham
Hodeida
Horsens
Houston
Hungnam
Incheon
Iquique
Iquitos
Kaolack
Karachi
Karumba
Kavalla
Kenitra
Kherson
Kinsale
Kolding
Konakri
Kowloon
Kuching
La Plata
Latakia
Legaspi
Le Havre
Lepanto
Liepaja
Livorno
Lorient
Makurdi
Marsala
Masbate
Massaua
Massawa
Maulman
Melilla
Memphis
Messina
Milazzo
Mits'twa
Mombasa
Moulman
Munster
Nanjing
Nanking
Nanning
Neusatz
Newport
Niigata
Niteroi
Novi Sad
Oakland

Okayama
Onitsha
Otranto
Pahsien
Palermo
Pelotas
Phocaea
Piraeus
Qingdao
Qiqihar
Randers
Rangoon
Rapallo
Ravenna
Rosario
Rostock
Runcorn
Salerno
San Remo
Sao Luis
Seattle
Sekondi
Setubal
Seville
Shantou
Shantow
Sinuiju
Stettin
St John's
St Louis
Sukhumi
Swansea
Tadzhik
Tallinn
Tampico
Tangier
Taranto
Trabzon
Trapani
Trieste
Tripoli
Ulan-Ude
Ushuaia
Vitebsk
Vitoria
Wanxian
Wenchou
Wenchow
Wenzhou
Whyalla
Yakutsk
Yichang
Yingkou
Yingkow

***8 letters:***

Aalesund
Abeokuta
Aberdeen
Acapulco
Alicante
Alleppey
Arbroath
Auckland
Badalona
Barletta
Batangas
Bathurst
Benghazi
Benguela
Bobruisk
Bobryusk
Bordeaux
Boulogne
Brindisi
Brisbane
Bromberg
Caesarea
Cagliari
Calcutta
Castries
Changsha
Changteh
Chaochow
Cheribon
Chimbote
Chingtao
Chongjin
Cuxhaven
Dortmund
Drogheda
Duisburg
Dunleary
El Ferrol
Elsinore
Falmouth
Flushing
Freetown
Gisborne
Gonaives
Goteborg
Greenock
Haiphong
Hakodate
Halmstad
Hamilton
Hangchow
Hangzhou
Harfleur
Hartford
Hastings
Helsinki
Holyhead
Honolulu
Iraklion
Istanbul
Jayapura
Jinjiang
Kanazawa
Kawasaki
Keflavik
Kingston
Klaipeda
La Coruna
La Guaira
La Guyara
La Spezia
Lattakia
Les Cayes
Limassol
Limerick
Luderitz
Mariupol
Matanzas
Maulmain
Mayaguez
Mazatlan
Monrovia
Montreal
Moulmein
Murmansk
Mytilene
Nagasaki
Nan-ching
Newhaven
Nha Trang
Novgorod
Nykøbing
Pago Pago
Paramibo
Pavlodar
Paysandu
Peiraeus
Penzance
Pevensey
Plymouth
Pnom Penh
Port Said
Pozzuoli
Qui Nhong
Ramsgate
Rio Bravo
Rosslare
Salcombe
Salvador
Samarang
Sanarang
Sandakan
San Diego
Sandwich
Santarem
Santiago
Savannah
Schiedam
Selencia
Semarang
Shanghai
Sorrento
St Helier
Stockton
Surabaja
Surabaya
Syracuse
Szczecin
Tadzhiki
Taganrog
Takoradi
Tangiers
Tarshish
Tauranga
Teresina
Thurrock
Tjirebon
Tsingtao
Valdivia
Valencia
Veracruz
Victoria
Wakayama
Wanganui
Weymouth
Yarmouth
Yokohama
Yokosuka
Zaanstad

***9 letters:***

Anchorage
Angostura
Annapolis
Antserana
Archangel
Balaclava
Balaklava
Baltimore
Barcelona
Bass-Terre
Bhavnagar
Bujumbura
Bydgoszcz
Carnarvon
Cartagena
Cherbourg

Chisimaio
Chongqing
Chungking
Cleveland
Constanta
Dartmouth
Den Helder
Djajapura
Dordrecht
Dubrovnik
Dunkerque
Ellesmere
Epidaurus
Esperance
Esquimalt
Essaouira
Europoort
Famagusta
Fishguard
Fleetwood
Flensburg
Fortaleza
Fremantle
Gallipoli
Gateshead
Geraldton
Gravesend
Guayaquil
Hangchoio
Helsinger
Heraklion
Hiroshima
Immingham
Inhambane
Jasselton
Kagoshima
Kaohsiung
King's Lynn
Kingstown
Kirkcaldy
Kota Bahru
Kozhikode
Krasnodar
Kronstadt
Las Palmas
Lowestoft
Magdeburg
Mahajanga
Mangalore
Maracaibo
Mariehamn
Marseille
Matamoros
Matsuyama
Melbourne
Milwaukee
Morecambe
Newcastle
Nuku'alofa
Palembang
Peterhead
Phnom Penh
Pontianak
Port Blair
Port Louis
Port Sudan
Reykjavik
Rotterdam
Santa Cruz
Santander
Schleswig
Sheerness
Singapore
Soerabaja
Stavanger
St George's
St Nazaire
Stornoway
Stralsund
Stranraer
Sundsvall
Takamatsu
Tarragona
Toamasina
Tobermory
Trebizond
Trondheim
Tynemouth
Volgograd
Walvis Bay
Waterford
Weihaiwei
Whangarei
Zamboanga
Zeebrugge

***10 letters:***
Alexandria
Balikpapan
Belize City
Birkenhead
Bratislava
Bridgeport
Bridgetown
Caernarvon
Cap-Haitien
Casablanca
Charleston
Cheboksary
Chittagong
Cienfuegos
Copenhagen
Corrientes
Dzerzhinsk
East London
Felixstowe
Folkestone
Fray Bentos
Fredericia
Georgetown
Gothenburg
Hammerfest
Hartlepool
Herakleion
Iskenderun
Joao Pessoa
Karlskrona
Khabarovsk
Khota Bharu
Kitakyushu
La Rochelle
Launceston
Libreville
Los Angelos
Louisville
Matozinhos
Montevideo
Mostaganem
New Bedford
New Orleans
Norrkoping
Paramaribo
Pittsburgh
Pontevedra
Port Gentil
Portobello
Portsmouth
Port Talbot
Providence
Queenstown
Sacramento
Santa Marta
Sebastopol
Sevastopol
Strasbourg
Sunderland
Talcahuano
Thunder Bay
Townsville
Valparaiso
Whitstable
Willemstad
Wilmington
Winchelsea

***11 letters:***
Antofagusta
Antseranana
Bahia Blanca
Banjarmasin
Banjermasin
Baranquilla
Bremerhaven
Cheng-chiang
Dares Salaam
Fredrikstad
Grangemouth
Helsingborg
Hermoupolis
Kaliningrad
Makhachkala
Maryborough
New Plymouth
Newport News
Nuevo Laredo
Pointe-Noire
Port Moresby
Porto Alegre
Port of Spain
Punta Arenas
Rockhampton
San Fernando
Scarborough
Shimonoseki
Southampton
Telukbetong
Trincomalee
Vizagapatam
Vlaardingen
Vladivostok

***12 letters:***
Angtofagasta
Bandjarmasin
Bandjermasin
Barranquilla
Buenaventura
Chandemagore
Dun Laoghaire
Ho Chi Min City
Jacksonville
Kota Kinabalu
Kristiansand
Milford Haven
Philadelphia
Pointe-à-Pitre
Ponta Delgada
Port Adelaide
Port-au-Prince
Port Harcourt
Prince Rupert
Rio de Janeiro
San Francisco
San Sebastian

Santo Domingo
South Shields
St Petersburg
Tanjungpriok
Thessaloniki
Ujung Pandang
Usti nad Labem

*13 letters:*
Chandernagore
Charlottetown
Ciudad Bolivar
Corpus Christi
Florianopolis
Great Yarmouth
Ho Chi Minh City
Hook of Holland
Middlesbrough
Port Elizabeth
Tandjungpriok
Teloekbetoeng
Trois Rivières
Visakhapatnam
Wilhelmshaven

*14 letters:*
Burnie-Somerset
Mina Hassen Tani
Nizhni Novgorod
Santiago de Cuba
Vishakhapatnam

*15 letters:*
Alexandroupolis
Angra-de-Heroismo
Blagoveshchensk
Charlotte-Amalie
Forster-Tuncurry
Sault SaintMarie

*16 letters:*
Reggio di Calabria
Sault Sainte Marie

*18 letters:*
Castellon de la Plana

---

**Portable** Cordless, Lapheld, Laptop, Luggable, Mobile, Palmtop
**Portal** Gate
**Portend, Portent(ous)** Augur, Awesome, Bode, Dire, Omen, Ominous, Ostent, Phenomenon, Presage, Sign, Solemn, → WARN(ING)
**Porter** Ale, Bearer, Bellboy, Bellhop, Bummaree, Caddie, Caddy, Carrier, Cole, Concierge, Coolie, Door-keeper, Doorman, Dvornik, Entire, Gatekeeper, Gateman, Ham(m)al, Hamaul, Humper, Janitor, Night, October, Ostiary, Plain, Red-cap, Skycap, Stout, Stretcher-bearer, Ticket
**Portfolio** Briefcase, Holding
**Portico** Colonnade, Decastyle, Distyle, Dodecastyle, Exedra, Loggia, Narthex, Parvis(e), Porch, Propylaeum, Prostyle, Stoa, Veranda(h), Xyst(us)
**Portion** Aliquot, Ann(at), Bit, Deal, Distribute, Dole, Dollop, Dose, Dotation, Endowment, Fraction, Fragment, Helping, Heritage, Hunk, Instalment, Jointure, Lot, Lump, Measure, Meed, Mess, Modicum, Moiety, Nutlet, Ounce, Parcel, → PART, Piece, Quota, Ratio, Sample, Scantle, Scantling, Section, Segment, Serving, Share, Size, Slice, Something, Spoonful, Tait, Taste, Tate, Tittle, Tranche, Wodge
**Portland** Bill, Cement, Stone
**Portly** Ample, Corpulent, Gaucie, Gaucy, Gawcy, Gawsy, Rotund, Stout, Tubby
**Portmanteau, Portmanteau word** Avoision, Bag, Combination, Holdall, Valise
**Portrait(ist)** Carte de visite, Composite, Depiction, Drawing, Eikon, Icon, Identikit®, Ikon, Image, Kit-cat, Lely, Likeness, Painting, Pin-up, Retraitt, Retrate, Self, Sketch, Vignette
**Portray(al)** Caricature, Depict, Describe, Enactment, Feature, Image, Limn, Notate, Paint, Personate, Render, Represent, → SHOW
**Portsmouth** Pompey
**Portugal, Portuguese** Lusitania(n), Luso-, Macanese, Senhor
**Pose(r), Poseur** Aesthete, Affect(ation), Arabesque, Asana, Ask, Contrapposto, Conundrum, Dilemma, Drape, Enigma, Lotus, Man(n)ikin, Mannequin, Masquerade, Model, Place, Plastique, Posture, Pretend, Problem, Propound, Pseud, Puzzle, Sit, Stance, Sticker, Tableau vivant, Tickler
**Poseidon** Earthshaker
**Posh** Chic, Classy, Cut-glass, Grand, Lah-di-dah, Ornate, Ritzy, Sou, Superb, Swanky, Swish, Toff, Top drawer, U, Upper crust
**Posit** Suppose
**Position** Angle, Arrange, Asana, Attitude, Bearing(s), Box seat, Brace, Bridgehead, Case, Close, Codille, Delta, Deploy, Ecarte, Echelon, Emplacement, Enfilade, False, F(o)etal, Fixure, Foothold, Fowler's, Grade, Honour point, Instal, Lay, Lie, Location, Locus, Lodg(e)ment, Lotus, Midfield, Missionary, Mudra, Niche, Office, Open, Pass, Peak, Place, Plant, Point, Pole, Port, Possie, Post, Posture, Pozzy, Put, Rank, Recovery, Recumbent, Root, Seat, Set(ting), Sextile, Sims, Sinecure, Sit, Site, Situ, Situation, Situs, Stance, Standing, Standpoint, Station, Status, Strategic, Syzygy, Tagmeme, Thesis, Tierce, Toehold, Trendelenburg's, Tuck, Viewpoint
**Positive, Positivist** Absolute, Actual, Anode, Assertive, Categorical, → CERTAIN, Comte, Convinced, Definite, Emphatic, False, Plus, Print, Rave, Sure, Thetic, Upbeat, Uplifting, Upside, Utter, Veritable, Yang, Yes

**Posse** Band, Bevy, Gang, Lawmen, Mob, Vigilantes

**Possess(ed), Possession(s), Possessive** Adverse, Apostrophe, Asset, Aver, Bedevil, Belonging(s), Chattel, Demonic, Driven, Energumen, Estate, Ewe lamb, Have, Haveour, Haviour, Heirloom, His, Hogging, Hold, Know, Lares (et) penates, Lawful, Mad, Obsessed, Occupation, →OWN, Proprietorial, Receipt, Sasine, Seisin, Sprechery, Substance, Tenancy, Usucap(t)ion, Vacant, Worth

**Possible, Possibility, Possibly** Able, Attainable, Chance, Contingency, Could, Feasible, Imaginable, Likely, Maybe, Mayhap, Off-chance, On, Option(al), Oyster, Peradventure, Perchance, Perhaps, Posse, Potential, Prospect, Resort, Suspicion, Viable, Well, Will

▷**Possibly** *may indicate* an anagram

**Possum** Burramys, Cataplexy, Opossum, Pygmy, Rigo(u)r, Ringtail, Sugar glider, Sugar squirrel, Tait, Tarsipes

**Post(s), Postage** Affix, After, Airmail, Appointment, Assign, Base, Billet, Bitt, Bollard, Capstan, Carrick bitt, Column, Command, Correspondence, Cossack, Crown, Dak, Dawk, Delivery, Doorjamb, Dragon's teeth, Durn, Emily, Excess, Finger, Finishing, First(-class), Flagpole, Fly, Forebitt, Gate, Goal, Graded, Gradient, Guardhose, Heel, Hitching, Hovel, Hurter, Jamb, Job's, Joggle, Junk, King, Last, Laureate, Listening, Log, Mail, Mast, Newel, Observation, Outstation, Pale, Paling, Parcel, Pendant, Penny, Picket, Pigeon, Pile, Piling, Piquet, Placard, Place, Plant, Plum, Pole, Pony Express, Position, Presidio, Puncheon, Pylon, Queen, Quintain, Quoin, Registered, Remit, Residency, RM, Rubbing, Samson's, Seat, Second-class, Send, Sheriff's, Snail mail, Snubbing, Sound, Spile, Staff, Staging, Stake, Stanchion, Stand, Starting, Station, Stell, Stoop, Stoup, Stud, Studdle, Tana, Tee, Term(inal), Thanna(h), Tom, Tool, Totem pole, Trading, Troll, Upright, Vacancy, Waymark, Whipping, Winning

**Postboy** Messenger

**Postcard(s)** Deltiology, Picture

**Poster** Advertisement, Affiche, Bill, Broadsheet, Mailer, Pin-up, Placard, Playbill, Sender, Showbill, Solus, Sticker, Troll

**Posterior** Behind, Bottom, Jacksie, Jacksy, Later, Lumbar, Pygal, Rear, Tail

**Post-free** Franco

**Posting(s)** Thread

**Postman, Postmaster, Postwoman** Carrier, Courier, Emily, Hill, Messenger, Nasby, Pat, Portionist, Sorter

**Postmark** Frank

**Post-modern** Po-mo

**Post mortem** Autopsy, Dissection, Enquiry, Necropsy

**Postpone(ment), Postponed** Adjourn, Backburner, Carryover, Contango, Defer, Delay, Frist, Hold over, Lay over, Long-finger, Moratorium, Mothball, Offput, On ice, Pigeon-hole, Postdate, Prorogue, Put over, Raincheck, Remanet, Reprieve, Reschedule, Respite, Roll back, Shelve, Spike, Stay, Suspend, Withhold

**Postscript** Addendum, Appendix, Envoi, PS

**Postulant** Candidate, Noumenon, Novice

**Postulate(s)** Assert, Assume, Claim, Koch's, Posit, Propound, Theorise

**Posture(r), Posturing** Affectation, Asana, Attitude, Birkie, Camp, Carriage, Counter-view, Decubitus, Deportment, Gesture, Mudra, Pose, Pretence, Site, Stance, Swank, Vorlage, Yoga

**Post-war** Post-bellum

**Posy** Bouquet, Buttonhole, Corsage, Nosegay, Tussiemussie, Tussle-mussle, Tuzzi-muzzy, Tuzzy-muzzy

**Pot(s), Potting, Potty** Abridge, Aludel, Ante, Bankroll, Basil, Belly, Besotted, Billycan, Cafetière, Ca(u)ldron, Cannabis, Cannikin, Casserole, Cast, Ceramic, Chamber, Chanty, Chatti, Chatty, Chimney, Close-stool, Coal, Cocotte, Coffee, Coil, Commode, Creel, Crewe, Crock(ery), Crucible, Cruse(t), Cupel, Delf(t), Dixie, Doolally, Ewer, Flesh, Gaga, Gage, Gallipot, Ganja, Gazunder, Grass, Hash(ish), Helmet, Hemp, Hooped, In off, Inurn, Jardinière, Jordan, Kaif, Kef, Kettle, Kitchenware, Kitty, Livery, Lobster, Loco, Lota(h), Maiolica, Majolica, Marijuana, Marmite, Melting, Ming, Monkey, Olla, Olpe, Pan, Pat, Pepper, Piñata, Pint, Pipkin, Planter, Po, Pocket, Pool, Poot, Posnet, →POTTERY, Pottle, Pounce, Pout, Prize,

Quart, Samovar, Shoot, Sink, Skeet, Skillet, Smudge, Steamer, Steane, Stomach, Tajine, Tea, Terrine, Test, Throw, Togine, Trivet, Tureen, Urn, Vial, Ware, Wash, Whitechapel, Wok

**Potash** Caustic, Kalinite, Polverine, Potassa, Sylvine, Sylvite

**Potassium** K, Kalium, Pearl ash, Saleratus, Saltpetre

**Potation** Dram, Drink

**Potato(es)** African, Aloo, Alu, Batata, Chat, Clean, Couch, Crisp, Datura, Duchesse, Early, Fluke, Hashbrowns, Hog, Hole, Hot, Irish, Jacket, Jersey, Kidney, Kumara, Lyonnaise, Maris piper, Mash, Mouse, Murphy, Parmentier, Peel-and-eat, Pratie, Praty, Ro(e)sti, Rumbledethump(s), Scallop, Seed, Small, Solanum, Stovies, Sweet, Tater, Tatie, Tattie, Teddy, Tuber, Ware, White, Yam

**Pot-bearer** Trivet

**Pot-bellied** Kedge, Kedgy, Kidge, Paunchy, Portly, Stout

**Potboiler** Hob

**Pot-boy** Basil, Ganymede, Scullion

**Potent(ate)** Cogent, Despot, Dynamic, Emeer, Emir, Emperor, Huzoor, Imaum, Influential, Kinglet, Liege, Mogul, Nawab, Panjandrum, Powerful, Ras, Ruler, Satrap, Squirearch, Sultan, Virile

**Potential(ly)** Action, Capability, Capacity, Chemical, Electric, Electrode, In posse, Ionization, Latent, Making(s), Manqué, Possible, Promise, Resting, Scope, Viable

▷**Potentially** *may indicate* an anagram

**Pothole(r)** Chuckhole, Giant's kettle, Spelunker

**Pot-house** Shebeen, Tavern

**Potion** Dose, Draught, Drink, Dwale, Elixir, Love, Mixture, Philtre, Tincture

**Pot-pourri** Hotchpotch, Medley, Miscellany, Pasticcio, Salmi

**Potsherd** Ostracon, Ostrakon

**Pottage** Berry

**Potter** Amble, Cue, Dabbity, Dabble, Dacker, Daidle, Daiker, Daker, Dibble, Dilly-dally, Dodder, Etruscan, Fettle, Fictor, Fiddle, Footer, Footle, Fouter, Gamesmanship, Harry, Idle, Mess, Minton, Muck, Niggle, One-upmanship, Plouter, Plowter, Poke, Spode, Thrower, Tiddle, Tink(er), Troke, Truck, Wedgwood

▷**Potter** *may indicate* a snooker-player

**Pottery** Agatewear, Bank, Basalt, Bisque, Cameo ware, Celadon, Ceramet, Ceramic, Chelsea, China, Creamware, Crock, Crouch-ware, Dabbity, Delf(t), Dresden, Earthenware, Encaustic, Etruria(n), Faience, Flatback, Gombroon, Granitewear, Hollowware, Ironstone, Jomon, Lustreware, Maiolica, Majolica, Ming, Minton, Pebbleware, Queensware, Raku, Red-figured, Satsuma, Scroddled, Sgraffito, Slab, Slipware, Smalto, Spode, Spongeware, Stoke, Stoneware, Studio, Sung, Terra sigillata, Ware, Wedgwood®, Wemyss, Whieldon, Whiteware

**Pouch(ed)** Bag, Brood, Bum-bag, Bursa, Caecum, Cheek, Cisterna, Codpiece, Cyst, Diverticulum, Fanny pack, Gill, Jockstrap, Marsupial, Marsupium, Ovisac, Papoose, Pocket, Poke, Posing, Purse, Sac, Saddlebag, Scrip, Scrotum, Sheath, Snood, Spleuchan, Sporran, Tobacco

**Pouffe** Humpty

**Poultice** Application, Cataplasm, Embrocation, Emollient, Epithem(a), Lenient, Plaster

**Poultry** Dorking, Fowl, Gallinaceous, Minorca, Plymouth Rock, Poot, Pout, Welsummer

**Poultry disease** Keel, Pip, Scaly-leg, Vent gleet

**Pounce** Claw, Jump, Lunge, Powder, Sere, Souse, Sprinkle, Swoop, Talon

**Pound(er)** Ache, As, Bar, Bash, Batter, Battersea, Beat, Belabour, Bombard, Bradbury, Bray, Broadpiece, Bruise, Catty, Clomp, Contund, Coop, Drub, Embale, Enclosure, Ezra, Fold, Green, Greenie, Greeny, Hammer, Hatter, Imagist, Intern, Iron man, Jail, Jimmy o'goblin, Kiddle, Kidel, Kin, Knevell, L, Lam, Lash, Lb, Lock, Mash, Nevel, Nicker, Oncer, One-er, Oner, Pale, Palpitate, Pen, Penfold, Pestle, Pin, Pindar, Pinfold, Pink, Powder, Pulverise, Pun, Quid, Quop, Rint, Scots, Smacker, Sov(ereign), Squid, Stalag, Stamp, Sterling, Strum, Tenderise, Throb, Thump, Tower, Troy, Weight

**Pour(ing)** Affusion, Be mother, Birl(e), Bucket, Cascade, Circumfuse, Decant, Diffuse, Disgorge, Effuse, Extravasate, Flood, Flow, Jaw, Jirble, Libate, Rain, Seil, Shed, Sile, Skink, Spew, Stream, Teem, Trill, Turn, Vent, Weep, Well

**Pout** Bib, Blain, Brassy, Eel, Fish, Horn(ed), Mope, Mou(e), Scowl, Sulk, Tout, Towt, Whiting

**Poverty** Beggary, Dearth, Deprivation, Destitution, Hardship, Illth, Indigence, → LACK, Locust years, Necessity, Need, Paucity, Pauperism, Penury, Poortith, Puirtith, Squalor, Tobacco Road, Want

**Powder(ed), Powdery** Allantoin, Alumina, Amberite, Araroba, Baking, Ballistite, Bleaching, Boracic, Calamine, Calomel, Chalk, Chilli, Cocoa, Colcothar, Condition, Cosmetic, Crocus, Culm, Curry, Custard, Cuttlefish, Dentifrice, Diamond, Dover's, Dust, Dusting, Emery, Eupad, Explosive, Face, Flea, Floury, Fly, Fulminating, Giant, Glaucous, Goa, Gregory, Grind, Gun, Hair, Insect, Itching, Kohl, Levigate, Lithia, Litmus, Lupulin, Magnesia, Meal, Mepacrine, Mould-facing, Moust, Mu(i)st, Pearl, Pebble, Pemoline, Percussion, Persian, Plaster of Paris, Plate, Polishing, Pollen, Pounce, Pound, Priming, Prismatic, Projecting, Pruinose, Pulver, Pulvil, Putty, Rachel, Rochelle, Rottenstone, Rouge, Saleratus, Sawdust, Seidlitz, Seme(e), Sherbet, Silver iodide, Sitosterol, Smeddum, Smokeless, Snuff, Soap, Spode, Spodium, Talc(um), Talcose, Thimerosal, Toner, Tooth, Triturate, Tutty, Washing, Worm, Zedoary, Zein

**Power(ful), Powers** Ability, Able, Aeon, Aggrandisement, Air, Almighty, Alpha, Amandla, Arm, Arnold, Athletic, Atomic, Attorney, Audrey, Autarchy, Authority, Axis, Beef, Big, Capability, Catworks, Central, Chakra, Cham, Charge, Charisma, Clairaudience, Clairvoyance, Clout, Cogency, Colossus, Command, Conductance, Contol, Corridor, Cube, Danger, Despotic, Diadem, Dieu, Dioptre, Dominion, Effective, Electricity, Eminence, Éminence grise, Empathy, Empery, Energy, Eon, ESP, Exponent, Facility, Faculty, Fire, Flower, Force, Force majeure, Gaddi, Gas, Generator, Geothermal, Government, Greatness, Grey, Grip, Gutty, Hands, Hefty, Hegemony, Herculean, High, Hildebrandic, Horse, Hot, Hp, Hydroelectric, Imperium, Imput, Influence, Juice, Kami, Kick, Kilowatt, King, Leccy, Leverage, Locomotion, Log, Logarithm, Lusty, Mana, Mandarin, Mandate, Mastery, Mechanical, Megalomania, Megawatt, Might, Mogul, Mojo, Motive, Motor, Movers and shakers, Muscle, Natural, Nature, Nth, Nuclear, Od-force, Oligarch, Omnificent, Omnipotent, Option, P, Panjandrum, People, Pester, Photocell, Plenary, Plenipotency, Posse, Potency, Prepollence, Prepotent, Puissant, Punch, Purchasing, Regime, Resolving, Say-so, Sea, Siddhi, Sinew, Solar, Soup, Stamina, Staying, Steam, Steel, Stiff, Stopping, Stranglehold, Strength, → STRONG, Supercharge, Superman, Superwoman, Supreme, Suzerain, Sway, Teeth, Telling, Throne, Tidal, Titan, Turbine, Tycoon, Tyranny, Tyrone, Ulric, Valency, Vertu(e), Vigour, Vis, Volt, Vroom, Water, Watt, Wattage, Wave, Weight, Welly, Wheel and axle, Whiphand, Wind, World, Yeast

**Powerless** Diriment, Downa-do, Failing, Freewheel, Hamstrung, Helpless, Impotent, Impuissant, Incapable, Inert, Numb, Unable, Unarmed, Weak

**Power station** Chernobyl, Dungeness, Sellafield

**Powwow** Confab, Conference, Council, Meeting

**Pox** Chicken, Cow, French, Great, Orf, Pize, Small, Spanish

**Practical, Practicable, Practicalities** Active, Applied, Brass tacks, Doable, Down-to-earth, Easy-care, Feasible, Hands on, Hard-boiled, Joker, Logistics, Nitty-gritty, No-nonsense, Nuts and bolts, On, Pragmatic, Realist(ic), Realpolitik, Rule of thumb, Sensible, Shrewd, Technical, Useful, Utilitarian, Viable, Virtual

**Practice(s), Practise, Practitioner, Practised** Abuse, Acupuncture, Adept, Apply, Bones, Copybook, Custom, De facto, Distributed, Do, Drill, Dry run, Dummy run, Enure, Exercise, Exponent, Fire, General, Graft, Group, Habit, Inure, Ism, Keep, Knock-up, Massed, Medical, Meme, Mock, Nets, Operate, Order, Ordinance, Pipe opener, Ply, Policy, Praxis, Private, Prosecution, Pursuit, Rehearsal, Rehearse, Restrictive, Rite, Rule, Rut, Sadhana, Sharp, Sighter, Spanish, System, Target, Teaching, Test-run, Trade, Tradition, Train, Trial, Try out, Ure, Usage, Use, Wage, Warm up

**Pragmatic, Pragmatist** Ad hoc, Busy, Dogmatic, Humanist, Meddling, Officious, Realist, Trimmer, Unholy

**Prairie** IL, Illinois, Llano, Plain, Savanna, Steppe, Tundra, Veldt

**Prairie dog** Whippoorwill, Wishtonwish

**Praise(worthy)** Acclaim, Accolade, Adulation, Alleluia, Allow, Anthem, Applause, Beatify, Belaud, Bepuff, Bless, Blurb, Bouquet, Bravo, Butter, Carol, Citation, CL, Commend(ation),

Compliment, Congratulate, Crack up, Cry up, Dulia, Ego boost, Encomium, Envy, Eulogise, Eulogium, Eulogy, Exalt, Exemplary, Extol, Flattery, Gloria, Glory, Hail, Hero-worship, Herry, Hery(e), Hosanna, Hymn, Hype, Incense, Kudos, Laud, Laurels, Lip service, Lo(o)s, Meritorious, Paean, Palmary, Palp, Panegyric, Plaudit, Puff(ery), Rap, Rave, Recommend, Roose, Talk-up, Thank, Tout, Tribute, Wrap

**Pram** Buggy

**Prance** Brank, Canary, Caper, Cavort, Frolic, Galumph, Gambol, Jaunce, Jaunse, Prank(le), Swagger, Tittup, Trounce

**Prang** Accident, Crash, Smash, Whale

**Prank(s)** Attrap, Bedeck, Bedizen, Caper, Dido, Escapade, Fredaine, Frolic, Gaud, Jape, Lark, Leg-pull, Mischief, Pliskie, Rag, Reak, Reik, Rex, Rig, Spoof, Trick, Vagary, Wedgie

**Praseodymium** Pr

**Prat** Bottom, → **STUPID PERSON**

**Prate** Babble, Boast, Haver, Jabber, Talk

**Prattle** Babble, Bavardage, Blat(her), Chatter, Gab(nash), Gas, Gibber, Gossip, Gup, Jabber, Lalage, Patter, Smatter, Yabber, Yap

**Prawn** Banana, Crevette, Dublin Bay, King, Scampi, School, Shrimp, Tiger

**Pray(ing)** Appeal, Bed, Beg, Beseech, Bid, Daven, → **ENTREAT**, Impetrate, Intercede, Intone, Invoke, Kneel, Mantis, Patter, Solicit, Suppliance, Worship, Wrestle

**Prayer(s), Prayer book, Prayer wall** Acoemeti, Act, Amidah, Angelus, Ardas, Ave (Maria), Bead, Beadswoman, Bede, Bene, Bidding, Breviary, Carmelite, Collect, Commination, Common, Confiteor, Cry, Cursus, Daven, Deus det, Devotion, Eleison, Embolism, Entreaty, Epiclesis, Euchologion, Evensong, Geullah, Grace, Habdalah, Hail Mary, Hallan-shaker, Imam, Intercession, Introit, Invocation, Kaddish, Karakia, Khotbah, Khotbeh, Khutbah, Kol Nidre, Kyrie, Kyrie eleison, Lauds, Litany, Lord's, Loulat-ul-qadr, Lychnapsia, Ma'ariv, Ma(c)hzor, Maiden's, Mani, Mantis, Mat(t)ins, Mincha(h), Missal, Morning, Musaf, Novena, Opus dei, Orant, Orarium, Orison, Our Father, Paternoster, Patter, Petition, Phylactery, Placebo, Plea, Preces, Priest, Prime, Proseucha, Proseuche, Puja, Requiem, Requiescat, Responses, Rogation, Rosary, Salat, Secret, Shema, Siddur, State, Stations of the Cross, Suffrage, Te igitur, Tenebrae, Terce, Thanksgiving, Triduum, Venite, Vesper, Vigils, Wish, Yajur-Veda, Yizkor

▷**Prayer** *may indicate* one who begs

**Praying mantis** Rear-horse

**Preach(er)** Ainger, Boanerges, Camp, Circuit rider, Dawah, Devil-dodger, Dominican, Donne, Ecclesiastes, Evangelist, Exhort, Field, Gospeller, Graham, Holy Roller, Itinerant, Kerygma, Knox, Lecture, Local, Mar-text, Minister, Missionary, Moody, → **MORALISE**, Patercove, Pontificate, Postillate, Predicant, Predicate, Predikant, Priest, Prophet, Pulpiteer, Rant, Revivalist, Sermonise, Soper, Spintext, Spurgeon, Teach, Televangelist, Wesley

**Preamble** Introduction, Lead-in, Preface, Proem, Prologue

**Prearrange(d)** Book, Stitch up

**Pre-Cambrian** Torridonian

**Precarious** Dangerous, Iffy, Knife edge, Parlous, Perilous, Risky, Touch and go, Trickle, Uncertain, Unsteady, Unsure

**Precaution** Care, Fail-safe, Foresight, Guard, In case, Prophylaxis, Safeguard, Safety net

**Precede(nce), Precedent** Antedate, Example, Forego, Forerun, Head, Herald, Override, Pas, Predate, Preface, Prepotent, Priority, Protocol, Test case, Zeroth

**Precept(s)** Adage, Canon, Commandment, Maxim, Mishna, Motto, Saw

**Precession** Larmor

**Precinct(s)** Ambit, Area, Banlieue, Close, Courtyard, District, Environs, Pedestrian, Peribolos, Region, Shopping, Temenos, Verge, Vihara

**Precious** Adored, Chary, Chichi, Costly, Dear, Dearbought, Ewe-lamb, Few, La-di-da, Murr(h)a, Nice, Owre, Precise, Priceless, Prissy, Rare, Twee, Valuable

**Precipice** Bluff, Cliff, Crag, Krans, Kran(t)z, Sheer

**Precipitate, Precipitation, Precipitous, Precipitator** Abrupt, Accelerate, Bring on, Catalyst, Cause, Deposit, Engender, Flowstone, Hailstone, Hasty, Headlong, Impetuous, Launch, Lees, Pellmell, Pitchfork, Rain, Rash, Sca(u)r, Serein, Serene, Sheer, Shoot, Sleet, Snowfall, Snowflake, Start, → **STEEP**, White

**Précis** Abstract, Aperçu, Epitome, Résumé, Summary
**Precise(ly), Precisian, Precision** Absolute, Accurate, Dry, Exact, Explicit, Fine-drawn, Literal, Meticulous, Minute, Nice(ty), Niminy-piminy, Overnice, Particular, Pedantry, Perfect, Pernickety, Plumb, Point-device, Prig, Prim, Punctilious, Razor, Sharpness, Spang, Specific, Spot on, Starchy, Stickler, Strict, Stringent, Succinct, Surgical, Tight, To the letter, Very
**Preclude** Bar, Debar, Estop, Foreclose, Hinder, Impede, Prevent, Rule out
**Precocious(ness)** Advanced, Bratpack, Enfant terrible, Forward, Madam, Premature, Protogyny
**Precognition** Foresight
**Preconception** Ideating
**Precursor** Avant-courier, Forerunner, Harbinger
**Predator(y)** Carnivore, Condor, Eagle, Elanet, Eyas, Fox, Glede, Harpy-eagle, Honey badger, Hunter, Jackal, Kestrel, Kite, Lycosa, Mantis, Marauder, Nyas, Pike, Predacious, Prey, Puma, Shark, Skua, Tanrec, Tarantula, Tenrec, Trapper, Wolf
**Pre-dawn** Antelucan, Ante lucem
**Predecessor** Ancestor, Forebear, Foregoer
**Predestined** Doomed, Fated, Tramway
**Predetermine(d)** Programme, Set
**Predicament** Box, Dilemma, Embarrassment, Embroglio, Hobble, Hole, In chancery, Jam, Pass, Peril, Pickle, Plight, Quagmire, Quandary, Scrape, Spot
**Predict(ion), Predictable, Predicted, Predictor** Astrologer, Augur, Belomancy, Bet, Clairvoyance, Damn, Divination, Doomsayer, Doomster, Doomwatch, Ex ante, Far-seeing, Forecast, Foreordain, Foreread, Foresay, Foresee, Foreshadow, Foreshow, Forespeak, Foretell, Formulaic, Forsay, Fortune-telling, Futurist, Geomancy, Guess, Horoscope, Jeremiah, Knee-jerk, Nap, Necromancy, Nostradamus, Odds, Omen, Palmistry, Portend, Presage, Previse, Prognosis, Project, Prophecy, Prophesy, Quant, Regular, Second-guess, Soothsayer, Spae, Tip
**Predilection** Fancy, Liking, Prejudice, Taste, Tendency
**Predisposition** Aptitude, Bent, Inclination, Parti-pris, Tendency
**Predominate, Predominance** Abound, Govern, Overshadow, Prepollency, Prevail, Reign, Ruling
**Pre-eminence, Pre-eminent** Arch, Foremost, Monarchic, Palm(ary), Paramount, Primacy, Supreme, Top dog, Topnotch, Unique
**Pre-empt(ive)** Enter
**Preen** Perk, Primp, Prink, Prune, Titivate
**Prefab(ricated)** Quonset, Terrapin®
**Preface** Avant-propos, Foreword, Herald, Intro, Preamble, Precede, Proem, Prolegomenon, Prolepsis, Usher
**Prefect** Grave, Haussmann, Monitor, Pilate, Prepositor, Pr(a)epostor
**Prefecture** Amiens
**Prefer(ence), Preferment, Preferred** Advance, Better, Choose, Discriminate, Druthers, Elect, Elevation, Faard, Faurd, Favour, Imperial, Incline, Lean, Liquidity, Predilect(ion), Prefard, Priority, Proclivity, Promote, Rather, Select, Sooner, Stocks, Taste, Will
**Prefix** Eka, Introduce, Name
**Pregnancy, Pregnant** Big, Clucky, Cyesis, Due (to), Ectopic, Enceinte, Extrauterine, Fertile, F(o)etation, Gestation, Gravid(a), Great, Great-bellied, Heavy, Hysterical, In foal, In pig, In pup, In the club, Knocked-up, Molar, Mother-to-be, Phantom, Pseudocyesis, Pudding-club, Retirement, Significant, Stomack, Teem, Up the duff, Up the pole, Up the spout, Up the stick, With child
**Prehistoric** Ancient, Azilian, Beaker Folk, Boskop, Brontosaurus, Cambrian, Clovis, Cro-Magnon, Eocene, Folsom, Mound Builder, Ogygian, Primeval, Primitive, Pteranodon, Pterodactyl(e), Pterosaur, Saurian, Sinanthropus, Stegosaur, Stonehenge, Titanis, Titanosaurus, Trilith(on)
**Prejudice(d), Prejudicial** Ageism, Bias, Bigotry, Chauvinistic, Derry, Discrimination, Down, Illiberal, Impede, Inequity, Injure, Insular, Intolerance, Partiality, Parti pris, Partisan, Preoccupy, Prepossession, Racism, Sexism, Slant, Unfair

**Prelate** Archiepiscopal, Cardinal, Churchman, Exarch, Monsignor, Odo, Priest
**Preliminary** Build-up, Curtain-raiser, Draft, Exploration, Foretaste, Heat, Initial, Introductory, Opening, Precursory, Preface, Preparatory, Previous, Prodrome, Proem, Prolusion, Propaedeutic, Rough, Title-sheet
**Prelude** Choral, Countdown, Entrée, Forerunner, Intrada, Overture, Proem(ial), Ritornell(e), Ritornello, Verset
**Premature** Early, Precocious, Pre(e)mie, Premy, Pre term, Previous, Slink, Untimely, Untimeous
**Premedication** Atropia
**Premeditate(d)** Anticipate, Foresee, Intentional, Plan
**Premier** Chief, Leader, Lenin, Main, PM, → PRIME MINISTER, Tojo, Top (drawer)
**Premise(s)** Assumption, Basis, Datum, Epicheirema, Ground, Hypothesis, Inference, Lemma, Licensed, Major, Minor, Postulate, Property, Proposition, Reason, Syllogism, Term, Unlicensed
**Premium** Ap, Bond, Bonus, Discount, Grassum, Pm, Reward, Scarce, Share
**Premonition** Hunch, Omen, Presentiment, Prodromal, Specter, Spectre, Warning
**Premonstratensian** Norbertine
**Preoccupation, Preoccupied, Preoccupy** Absent, Absorb, Abstracted, Distrait, Engross, Hang-up, Intent, Obsess, Self-centred, Thing
**Pre-owned** Hand-me-downs, Reach-me-downs
**Prepaid** Pro-forma, Sae
**Prepare(d), Preparation** Address, À la, Anticipate, Arrange, Attire, Boun, Bowne, Brilliantine, Busk, Calver, Cock, Codeine, Concoct, Confect, Cook, Cooper, Countdown, Decoct, Did, Do, Dress, Edit, Extract, Forearm, Format, Foundation, Game, Garnish, Gear (up), Groom, Ground, Groundwork, Inspan, Key, Lay (out), Legwork, Limber (up), Lotion, Make-ready, Measure, Mobilise, Mousse, Organise, Oven-ready, Parasceve, Paste up, Pomade, Poultice, Preliminary, Prime, Procinct, Prothesis, Provide, Psych, Qualified, → READY, Redact, Rehearsal, Revise, Ripe, Run up, Rustle up, Scout, Scrub up, Set, Spadework, Stand-to, Steep, Suborn, Train, Trim, Truss, Tune up, Type, Up to, Warm-up, Whip up, Willing, Yare
▷**Prepare(d)** *may indicate* an anagram
**Preponderance, Preponderant, Preponderate** Important, Majority, Outweigh, Paramount, Prevalence, Sway
**Preposition** Lemma
**Prepossessing, Prepossession** Attractive, Fetching, Predilection, Winsome
**Preposterous** Absurd, Chimeric, Exorbitant, Foolish, Grotesque, Rich, Tall order, Unreasonable
▷**Preposterous** *may indicate* a word reversed
**Pre-Raphaelite** Rossetti, Waterhouse
**Prerequisite** Condition, Essential, Necessity, Sine qua non
**Prerogative** Faculty, Franchise, Liberty, Privilege, Right, Royal
**Presage** Abode, Foresight, Herald, Omen, Portend, Presentiment, Prophesy
**Presbyter(ian)** Berean, Blue, Cameronian, Classic, Classis, Covenanter, Elder, Knox, Macmillanite, Moderator, Sacrarium, Seceder, Secesher, Secession Church, Wee Free, Whig(gamore)
**Prescient** Clairvoyant, Fly
**Prescribe(d), Prescription** Appoint, Assign, Dictate, Enjoin, Impose, Negative, Ordain, Recipe, Rule, Scrip, Set, Statutory
**Prescription** Cipher, Decree, Direction, Formula, Medicine, Placebo, R, Rec, Receipt, Ritual, Specific
**Presence** Aspect, Attendance, Bearing, Closeness, Company, Debut, Face, Hereness, Imminence, Mien, Real, Shechinah, Shekinah, Spirit
**Present(ation), Presented, Presenter, Presently** Ad sum, Advowson, Anchorman, Anon, Assists, Autocutie, Award, Befaba, Bestow, Bonsela, Boon, Bounty, Box, Breech, By, By and by, Cadeau, Co-host, Congiary, Coram, Current, Debut, Dee-jay, Demo, Deodate, DJ, Donate, Dotal, Douceur, Dower, Emcee, Endemic, Endew, Endow, Endue, Enow, Étrenne,

Exhibit, Existent, Exposition, Fairing, Feature, Format, Free-loader, Front-man, Gie, → GIFT, Give, Going, Grant, Gratuity, Hand, Here, Historical, Hodiernal, Holocene, Host(ess), Image, Immediate, Inbuilt, In person, Inst, Introduce, Jock(ey), Largess(e), Linkman, Lodge, MC, Mod, Newsreader, Nonce, Now, Nuzzer, Offering, On hand, Packaging, Porrect, Pose, Potlach, Pr, Prevailing, Produce, Proffer, Pro-tem, Put, Render, Rendition, Serve-up, Show, Slice, Stage, Study, Submit, Tense, The now, There, Tip, Today, Trojan horse, Vee-jay, Window dressing, Xenium, Yeven

**Present day** Christmas, Xmas

**Preserve(d), Preservation, Preservative, Preserver** Additive, Bottle, Burnettize, Can, Chill, Chow-chow, Chutney, Cocoon, Confect, Confiture, Corn, Creosote, Cure, Damson cheese, Dehydrate, Dry, Eisel, Embalm, Enshield, Enshrine, Fixative, Formaldehyde, Formalin, Fossil, Freeze, Game, Guard, Hain, Hesperides, Index link, Jam, Jerk, Keep, Kinin, Kipper, Konfyt, Kyanise, Lay up, Lemon curd, Life, Lifebelt, → MAINTAIN, Marmalade, Mothball, Mummify, National Trust, On ice, Paraben, Pectin, Peculiar, Pentachlorophenol, Piccalilli, Pickle, Pot, Powellise, Quince, Quinoline, Rescue, Salt(petre), Salve, Saut, Season, Sorbic acid, Souse, Store, Stratify, Stuff, Sweetmeat, Tanalith, Tanalized, Tar, Taxidermist, Tin, Unspoilt, Vinegar, Waterglass

**Preshrunk** Sanforized®

**Preside(nt)** Abe, Adams, Allende, Amin, Arafat, Arthur, Ataturk, Banda, Botha, Buchanan, Bush, Carter, Chair, Chief Barker, Childers, Chirac, Cleveland, Clinton, Coolidge, Coty, Dean, De Gaulle, Director, Eisenhower, Fillmore, Ford, Garfield, Grand Pensionary, Grant, Harding, Harrison, Hayes, Hoover, Ike, Jackson, Jefferson, Johnson, Kennedy, Kruger, Lead, Lincoln, Madison, Mandela, Mitterand, Moderator, Monroe, Mugabe, Nasser, Nixon, Obama, Old Hickory, P, Peron, Pinochet, Polk, Pompidou, Pr(a)eses, Prexy, Putin, Reagan, Roosevelt, Sa(a)dat, Speaker, Superintendent, Supervisor, Taft, Taylor, Tito, Truman, Trump, Tyler, Van Buren, Vasquez, Veep, Washington, Wilson, Yeltsin

**Press(ed), Pressing, Pressure** Acute, Aldine, Armoire, Arm-twist, Atmospheric, Bar, Barometer, Bench, Blackmail, Blood, Bramah, Button, Cabinet, Calender, Chivvy, Cider, Clarendon, Click, Closet, Clothes, Coerce, Compact, Compression, Cooker, Copying, Coverage, Cram, Crease, Crimp, Critical, Crowd, Crush, Cupboard, Cylinder, Dragoon, Drill, Drop, Dun, Durable, Duress, Duresse, Enforcement, Enslave, Exhort, Exigent, Filter, Flat-bed, Fleet St, Fluid, Fly, Folding, Force, Fourth estate, Free, Full-court, Goad, Greenmail, Gutter, Harass, Hard sell, Hassle, Hasten, Head, Heat, Herd, Hie, High, Hothouse, Hug, Hurry, Hustle, Hydraulic, Hydrostatic, Hypertension, Hypotension, Impact, Impel, Impinge, Important, Importune, Inarm, Instant, Intense, Iron, Isobar, Jam, Jostle, Knead, Leverage, Lie, Lobby, Low, Make, Mangle, Megabar, Microbar, Mill, Minerva, Newspapers, Obligate, Oil, Onus, Osmotic, PA, Packing, Palpate, Partial, Pascal, Peer, Permanent, Persist, Piezo-, Ply, Prease, Printing, Private, Psi, Pump, → PUSH, Racket, Ram, Ratpack, Record, Recruit, Reportage, Reporter, Ridge, Roll, Root, Rotary, Rounce, Rub, Rush, Samizdat, Sandwich, Screw, Scrooge, Scrouge, Scrowdge, Scrum, Serr(e), Shanghai, Sit, Speed, Spur, Squash, Squeeze, Stanhope, Static, Stop, Strain(t), Stress, Tax, Tension, Thlipsis, Threap, Three-line-whip, Threep, Throng, Throttle, Thrutch, Torr, Tourniquet, Tread, Trouser, Turgor, → URGE, Urgence, Urgency, Vanity, Vapour, Vice, Waid(e), Wardrobe, Weight, Wine, Wring, Yellow

**Press agent** Flack, Spin doctor

**Press-gang** Crimp, Force, Impress, Shanghai

**Pressman** Bramah, Ed, Hack, Journalist, Journo, PRO, Reporter, Twicer

**Pressure group** Greenpeace

**Prestidigitate(r)** Conjure, Juggle, Legerdemain, Magician, Palm

**Prestige, Prestigious** Asma, Cachet, Credit, Distinguished, Fame, Influence, Izzat, Kudos, Mana, Notable, Status, Upmarket

**Presume, Presumably, Presumption, Presumptuous** Allege, Arrogant, Audacity, Believe, Bold, Brass, Cocksure, Cocky, Doubtless, → EXPECT, Familiar, Forward, Free, Gall, Impertinent, Infer, Insolent, Liberty, Nerve, Outrecuidance, Overweening, Pert, Probably, Put upon, Suppose, Uppish, Upstart, Whipper-snapper

**Pretence, Pretend(er), Pretext** Act, Affect(ation), Afflict, Assume, Blind, Bluff, Bogus,

Cant, Charade, Charlatan, Claim, Claimant, Cover, Cram, Dauber(y), Dissemble, Dissimulate, Dive, Excuse, False, Feign, Feint, Gondolier, Guise, Hokum, Humbug, Hypocrisy, Impersonation, Impostor, Jactitation, Kid(stakes), Lambert Simnel, Let-on, Make-believe, Malinger, Masquerade, Obreption, Old, Ostensible, Parolles, Perkin Warbeck, Play act, Plea, Pose, Pretension, Profess, Pseud(o), Quack, Sham, Simulate, Stale, Stalking-horse, Subterfuge, Suppose, Swanking, Two-faced, Warbeck, Would-be, Young

**Pretentious(ness), Pretension** Arty(-farty), Bombast, Chi-chi, Fantoosh, Fustian, Gaudy, Grandiose, High-falutin(g), Kitsch, La-di-da, Lady Muck, Orotund, Ostentatious, Overblown, Paraf(f)le, Pompous, Ponc(e)y, Pseud(o), Sciolism, Show, Showy, Snob, Snobbish, Squirt, Tat, Tattie-peelin, Tinhorn, Toffee-nosed, Uppity, Upstart, Vulgar, Wanky, Whippersnapper

**Pretty** Attractive, Becoming, Belle, Bobby-dazzler, Chi-chi, Chocolate-box, Comely, Cute, Dear, Decorate, Dish, Elegant, Fair(ish), Fairway, Fetching, Inconie, Incony, Keepsaky, Kind of, Looker, Moderately, Nice, Pass, Peach, Personable, Picturesque, Primp, Pulchritudinous, Purty, Quite, Rather, Sitting, Substantial, Sweet, Twee, Winsome

**Pre-Union** Antenati

**Prevail(ing)** Cap, Dominate, Endure, Go, Induce, Mainstream, Outweigh, Persist, Persuade, Predominant, Preponderate, Reign, Ring, Triumph, Victor, Win

**Prevalent, Prevalence** Catholic, Common, Currency, Dominant, Endemic, Epidemic, Obtaining, Rampant, Rife, Set in, Widespread

**Prevaricate, Prevarication** Equivocate, Fib, Hedge, Lie, Runaround, Stall, Whiffle, Whittie-whattie

**Prevent(ion), Prevent(at)ive** Antidote, Avert, Bar, Block, Contraception, Crime, Daidzein, Debar, Deprive, Deter, Disallow, Disenable, Dissuade, Embar, Estop, Foil, Foreclose, Forestall, Forfend, Frustrate, Gag, Hamper, Hamstring, Help, Hinder, Hold back, Impound, Inhibit, Keep, Let, Nobble, Obstruct, Obturation, Obviate, Preclude, Prophylactic, Save, Sideline, Stop, Stymie, Theriac, Thwart, Trammel

**Preview** Foretaste, Sneak, Taster, Trailer, Vernissage

**Previous(ly)** Afore, Already, Antecedent, Backlog, Before, Earlier, Ere(-now), Fore, Foreran, Former, Hitherto, Old, Once, Prior, Whilom

**Prewar** Antebellum

**Prey** Booty, Currie, Curry, Feed, Goshawk, Kill, Pelt, Plunder, Predate, Proul, Prowl, Quarry, Raven, Ravin(e), Soyle, Spreagh, Victim

**Price(d), Pricing, Price-raising, Pricy** Appraise, Asking, Assess, Bride, Charge, Closing, Consequence, Contango, → **COST**, Cost-plus, Dearth, Differential, Due, Evens, Exercise, Expense, Extortionate, Factory-gate, Fare, Farmgate, Fee, Fiars, Hammer, Hire, Intervention, Issue, Limit, List, Lobola, Loco, Market, Mark up, Odds, Offer, Packet, Perverse, Predatory, Prestige, Purchase, Quotation, Quote, Rack, Ransom, Rate, Regrate, Reserve, Sale, Selling, Shadow, Sky high, Song, Spot, Starting, Street value, Striking, Subscription, Toll, Trade, Unit, Upset, Valorise, Value, Vincent, Weregild, Wergeld, Wergild, Worth, Yardage

**Priceless** Comic, Inestimable, Invaluable, Killing, Unique

**Prick(ed), Prickle, Prickly** Acanaceous, Acanthus, Accloy, Argemone, Arrect, Bearded, Brakier, Bramble, Brog, Bunya, Bur(r), Cactus, Cloy, Cnicus, Echinate, Goad, Gore, Gorse, Hedgehog, Hedgepig, Impel, Inject, Jab, Jag, Jaggy, Jook, Juk, Kali, Penis, Perse, Pierce, Prod, Prog, Puncture, Rowel, Rubus, Ruellia, Sea-urchin, Seta, Setose, Smart, Spicula, Spinate, Stab, Star-thistle, Stimulus, Sting, Tattoo, Tatu, Teasel, Thistle, Thorn, Tingle, Urge, Waspish, Whin

**Prickly heat** Miliaria

**Prickly-pear** Opuntia, Tuna

**Pride** Arrogance, Barbados, Bombast, Brag, Conceit, Dignity, Elation, Esprit de corps, Glory, Hauteur, Hubris, Inordinate, Lions, London, Machismo, Plume, Preen, Purge, Triumphalism, Vainglory, Vanity

**Priest(ess), Priests** Aaron, Abaris, Abbess, Abbot, Ananias, Annas, Archimandrite, Bacchae, Bacchantes, Baptes, Becket, Bonze, Brahmin, Caiaphas, Cardinal, Celebrant, Clergyman, Cleric, Club, Cohen, Concelebrant, Confessor, Corybant(es), Curé, Dalai Lama, Druid, Eli, Elisha, Exorcist, Ezra, Father, Fetial, Flamen, Fr, Habacuc, Habakkuk,

Hero, Hierarch, Hieratic, Hierophant, High, H(o)ungan, Io, Jethro, John, Kahuna, Kohen, Lack-Latin, Lama, Laocoon, Lazarist, Levite, Lucumo, Mage, Magus, Mallet, Mambo, Marabout, Mass, Mess, Metropolitan, Minister, Missionary, Monsignor, Mufti, Non-juror, Norma, Oratorian, Ordinand, P, Padre, Papa, Parish, Parson, Pastor, Patercove, Patrico, Pawaw, Père, Pontifex, Pontiff, Pope, Pope's knight, Powwow, Pr, Preacher, Prelate, Presbyter, Prior(ess), Pujari, Pythia, Pythoness, Rabbi, Rebbe, Rector, Rev, Sabellius, Sacerdotal, Salian, Samuel, Savonarola, Seminarian, Shaman, Shaveling, Sir John Lack-Latin, Sky pilot, Spoiled, Tohunga, Turbulent, Usager, Vestal, Vicar, Vivaldi, Worker, Zadok, Zymite

**Prig(gish)** Dandy, Fop, Humbug, Nimmer, Pharisee, Pilfer, Prim, Prude, Puritan

**Prim** Demure, Governessy, Mun, Neat, Old-maidish, Perjink, Preceese, Precise, Prissy, Proper, Schoolma'amish, Starchy

**Primacy, Primate** Angwantibo, Ape, Archiepiscopal, Australopithecus, Aye-aye, Baboon, Bandar, Bigfoot, Biped, Bishop, Bush baby, Cardinal, Catar(r)hine, Chimpanzee, Colobus, Ebor, Gibbon, Hanuman, Hominid, Jackanapes, King Kong, Langur, Lemur, Loris, Macaque, Magot, Mammal, Marmoset, → MONKEY, Orang, Pongid, Potto, Prosimian, Protohuman, Quadruman, Ramapithecus, Rhesus, Sifaka, Simian, Slender loris, Tarsier, Wanderoo, Zinjanthropus

**Prima donna** Diva, Patti, Star

**Prime(r), Primary, Priming** Arm, Basic, Beef, Bloom, Cardinal, Charging, Chief, Choice, Claircolle, Clearcole, Clerecole, Closed, Detonator, Direct, Donat, Donet, Election, Enarm, Fang, First, Flower, Heyday, Mature, Open, Original, Paint, Paramount, Peak, Principal, Radical, Remex, Sell-by-date, Supreme, Thirteen, Tip-top, Totient, Totitive, Valuable, Windac, Windas, Ylem

**Prime Minister** Aberdeen, Ahern, Asquith, Attlee, Baldwin, Balfour, Begin, Blair, Bute, Callaghan, Cameron, Campbell-Bannerman, Canning, Chamberlain, Chatham, Churchill, Dewan, Diefenbaker, Disraeli, Diwan, Eden, Gandhi, Gladstone, Grafton, Grand Vizier, Grey, Heath, Home, Iron Duke, Leaderene, Liverpool, Lloyd George, Macdonald, Macmillan, Major, Melbourne, Nehru, North, Number Ten, Palmerston, Peel, Perceval, Pitt, PM, Premier, Rockingham, Shastri, Tanaiste, Taoiseach, Thatcher, Trudeau, Walpole, Wilson, Winston

**Prim(a)eval** Ancient, Prehistoric, Primitive

**Primitive** Aborigine, Amoeba, Antediluvian, Arabic, Archaic, Atavistic, Barbaric, Basic, Caveman, Crinoid, Crude, Early, Elemental, Eozoon, Evolué, Feather-star, Fundamental, Hunter-gatherer, Medi(a)eval, Naive, Neanderthal, Neolithic, Oidia, Old, Persian, Prim(a)eval, Primordial, Pro, Prothyl(e), Protomorphic, Protyl(e), Radical, Rudimentary, Savage, Subman, Turkish, Uncivilised, Ur, Zygote

**Primogeniture** Majorat

**Primordial** Blastema, Earliest, Fundamental, Original

**Primp** Preen

**Primrose, Primula** Auricula, Bear's ear, Bird's eye, Cape, Cowslip, Creeping Jenny, Evening, League, Oenothera, Onagra, Ox-lip, Pa(i)gle, Rosebery, Vicar, Yellow

**Prince(ly)** Ahmed, Albert, Ameer, Amir, Amphitryon, Anchises, Arjuna, Atheling, Barmecide, Black, Cadmus, Caliph, Chagan, Charming, Crown, Czarevich, Donalbain, Elector, Emir, Equerry, Eugene, Florizel, Fortinbras, Gaekwar, Ganymede, Gospodar, Guicowar, Hal, Hamlet, Highness, Hospodar, Huzoor, Igor, Inca, Infante, Jason, Khan, Ksar, Lavish, Lucumo, Maharaja, Margrave, Meleager, Merchant, Mir, Mirza, Nawab, Nizam, Noble, Orange, Otto, P, Pantagruel, Paris, Pendragon, Pirithous, Porphyrogenite, Potentate, Rainier, Rajah, Rana, Ras, Rasselas, Ratoo, Ratu, Regal, RH, Rudolph, Rupert, Serene, Sharif, Shereef, Sherif, Siegfried, Student, Tengku, Tereus, Troilus, Tsar(evich), Tunku, Upper Roger

**Princess** Anastasia, Andromache, Andromeda, Anne, Ariadne, Begum, Creusa, Czarevna, Czarista, Danae, Di(ana), Electra, Electress, Eudocia, Europa, Grace, Helle, Hermione, Hesione, Ida, Ilse, Imogen, Infanta, Isabella, Iseult, Isolde, Jezebel, Maharanee, Maharani, Medea, Palatine, Philomela, Pocahontas, Procne, Rani, Regan, Sadie, Sara(h), Tou Wan, Tsarevna, Tsarista, Turandot, Yseult

**Principal** Arch, Capital, Cardinal, Central, → CHIEF, Decuman, Especial, First, Foremost, Grand, Head, Headmaster, Leading, Lion's share, Main(stay), Major, Mass, Mistress, Protagonist, Ringleader, Special, Staple, Star, Top banana, Uppermost

**Principality** Andorra, Flanders, Liechtenstein, Moldavia, Moldova, Monaco, Muscovy, Orange, Wal(l)achia, Wales

**Principle(s), Principled** Accelerator, Aesthetic, Animistic, Anthropic, Aphorism, Archimedes, Aufbau, Axiom, Basis, Bernouilli, Brocard, Canon, Carnot, Code, Conscience, Contradiction, Correspondence, Cosmological, Covenant, Credo, Creed, Criterion, Cui bono, Cy pres, D'Alembert's, Doctrine, Dogma, Element, Entelechy, Equivalence, Essential, Estoppel, Ethic, Exclusion, Fermat's, First, Fourier, Gause's, Geist, Generale, Germ, Greatest happiness, Ground rule, Guideline, Hard line, Heisenberg uncertainty, High, Hinge, Honourable, Huygen's, Ideal, Indeterminacy, Jus sanguinis, Jus-soli, Key, Law, Least time, Le Chatelier's, Leninism, Lights, Logos, Methodology, Modus, Morality, Object soul, Occam's razor, Organon, Ormazd, Ormuzd, Pauli-exclusion, Peter, Plank, Platform, Pleasure, Precautionary, Precept, Prescript, Psyche, Purseyism, Rationale, Reality, Reason, Reciprocity, Relativity, Remonstrance, Right-thinking, Rudiment, Rule (of three), Sakti, Sanction, Scruple, Scrupulous, Seed, Shakti, Spirit, Standard, Summum bonum, Tao, Tenet, Theorem, Ticket, Uncertainty, Uti possidetis, Verification, Vital, Weismannism, Word, Yang, Yin

**Prink** Beautify, Bedeck, Dress

**Print(er), Printing** A la poupée, Aldine, Arial, Baskerville, Batik, Benday, Block, Blunker, Bromide, Calotype, Caslon, Caveman, Caxton, Cerograph, Chain, Chapel, Chromo, Cibachrome, Cicero, Collotype, Compositor, Contact, Copperplate, Counter, Courier, Coverage, Creed, Cyclostyle, Dab, Delta Jaeger, Dot matrix, Duotone, Electrostatic, Electrothermal, Electrotint, Electrotype, Elzevir, Engrave, Etching, Ferrotype, Film set, Fine, Finger, Flexography, Font, Futura, Gravure, Gurmukhi, Gutenberg, Half-tone, Hard copy, Hectograph, Heliotype, Helvetica, HMSO, Image, Impact, Impress, Incunabula, India, Ink-jet, Intaglio, Italic, Jobbing, Kabel, Laser, Letterpress, Letterset, Line, Line-engraving, Lino-cut, Lithograph, Logotype, Lower-case, Matrix, Metallographer, Mezzotint, Mimeograph®, Monotype®, Moon, Non-impact, Novarese, Off-line, Offset, Offset litho, Old-face, Oleo, Oleograph, Opaline, Perfector, Perfect proof, Phototype, Plate, Platinotype, Positive, Press, Process, Publish, Quorum, Release, Remarque, Report, Reproduction, Retroussage, Reverse, Rotogravure, Run off, Salon, Samizdat, Screen, Serigraph, Ship, Shout, Silk-screen, Small, Smoot, Splash, Spore, Stamp, Stenochrome, Stereotype, Stonehand, Strike, Thermal, Three-colour, Thumb, Thumb mark, Times New Roman, Trichromatic, Typesetter, Typewriter, Typography, Typothetae, Weiss, Whorl, Woodburytype, Woodcut, Xerography, Xylograph, Zincograph

**Printing-press** Rounce

**Print out** Hard copy

**Prior(ity)** Abbot, Afore, Antecedent, Anterior, Aperture, Earlier, Former, Grand, Hitherto, Monk, Outweigh, Overslaugh, Pre-, Precedence, Prefard, Preference, Previous, Privilege, Shutter, Triage, Until, Urgent

▸**Prise** *see* PRIZE(S)

**Prism(s), Prismatic** Catadioptric, Iriscope, Nicol('s), Periaktos, Quadrilateral, Rhombohedron, Spectrum, Teinoscope, Triangular, Wollaston

**Prison** Albany, Alcatraz, Bagnio, Barracoon, Bastille, Belmarsh, Big house, Bin, Bird, Boob, Bridewell, Brig, Brixton, Bullpen, Cage, Can, Carceral, Cell, Chillon, Chok(e)y, Clink, Club, College, Confine, Cooler, Coop, Counter, Dartmoor, Dispersal, Dungeon, Durance, Encage, Fleet, Fotheringhay, Gaol, Glass-house, Guardhouse, Guardroom, Gulag, Hokey, Holloway, Hoos(e)gow, Hulk(s), Internment, →JAIL, Jug, Kitty, Labour camp, Laogai, Limbo, Little-ease, Lob's pound, Lock-up, Logs, Lumber, Marshalsea, Massymore, Mattamore, Maze, Newgate, Nick, Oflag, On ice, Open, Panopticon, Parkhurst, Pen, Penitentiary, Pentonville, Pit, Pok(e)y, Porridge, Pound, Princetown, Quad, Quod, Rasp-house, Reformatory, Roundhouse, Scrubs, Shop, Sing-Sing, Slammer, Spandau, Stalag, State, Stir, Strangeways, Supermax, The joint, The Leads, Tol(l)booth, Tower, Tronk, Wandsworth, Wormwood Scrubs

**Prisoner** Canary-bird, Captive, Collegian, Collegiate, Con(vict), Detainee, Detenu, Hostage, Inmate, Internee, Jailbird, Lag, Lifer, Parolee, Passman, Political, POW, Rule 43, Trustee, Trusty, Yardbird, Zek

**Pristine** Fire-new, Flawless, Fresh, New, Original, Pure, Unmarked, Unspoiled

**Private(ly), Privacy** Ain, Apart, Aside, Atkins, Auricular, Buccaneer, Byroom, Clandestine,

Close, Closet, Conclave, Confidential, Enisle(d), Entre nous, Esoteric, Homefelt, Hush-hush, In camera, Individual, Inmost, Inner, Intimate, Inward, Non-com, Non-governmental, Own, Personal, Piou-piou, Poilu, Postern, Proprietary, Pte, Rank(er), Retired, Retreat, Sanctum, Sapper, Secluded, Secret, Sequestered, Several, Single soldier, →**SOLDIER**, Squaddie, Sub rosa, Tommy, Under the rose

**Privateer(s)** Buccaneer, Corsair, Freebooter, Marque(s), Pirate

**Privation** Hardship, Penury, Want

**Privilege(d)** Aristocratic, Birthright, Blest, Charter, Chosen (few), Curule, Dead-head, Enviable, Exempt, Favour, Franchise, Freedom, Haves, Indulgence, Insider, Letters patent, Liberty, Mozarab, Nomenklatura, Octroi, Palatine, Parliamentary, Patent, Prerogative, Pryse, Regale, Regalia, Right, Sac, Sloane

**Privy** Apprised, Bathroom, Can, Close-stool, Closet, Draught-house, In on, Intimate, Jakes, John, Loo, Necessary, Reredorter, Secret, Sedge, Siege

**Prix** Grand

**Prize(s), Prizewinner, Prized** Acquest, Acquisitive, Apple, Archibald, Assess, Award, Best, Booby, Booker, Bravie, Bronze, Capture, Champion, Cherish, Coconut, Consolation, Creach, Cup, Dux, Efforce, →**ESTEEM**, Force, Garland, Gold, Goncourt, Grice, Honour, Jackpot, Jemmy, Lever, Loot, Lot, Man Booker, Money, Nobel, Palm, Pay out, Pearl, Pewter, Pie, Plate, Plum, Plunder, Pot, Premium, Prix Goncourt, Pulitzer, Purse, Ram, Reprisal, →**REWARD**, Rollover, Rosette, Russell, Scalp, Ship, Silver, Spreaghery, Sprechery, Stakes, Sweepstake, Taonga, Tern, Treasure, Trophy, Turner, Value, Win, Winnings, Wooden spoon

**Pro** Aye, Coach, Expert, For, Harlot, Moll, Paid, Tramp, Yea, Yes

▸**Pro** *see* **PROSTITUTE**

**Probable, Probability** Apparent, Belike, Classical, Conditional, Enthymeme, Ergodic, Feasible, Likely, Marginal, Mathematical, Odds on, Possible, Posterior, Presumptive, Prior, Proball, Ten-to-one, Verisimilar

**Probation(er)** Cadet, Novice, Novitiate, P-plater, Stibbler, Test, Trainee, Trial

**Probe** Antenna, Bore, Bougie, Canopus, Cassini, Corot, Delve, Dredge, Examine, Explore, Fathom, Feeler, Fish, Fossick, Galileo, Gene(tic), Giotto, Inquire, Investigate, Magellan, Mariner, Mars Surveyor, Otoscope, Palpitate, Pelican, Pioneer, Poke, Pump, Ranger, →**SEARCH**, Seeker, Sonde, Sound, Space, Stardust, Stylet, Tent, Thrust, Tracer, Venera

**Probity** Honour, Integrity, Justice

**Problem(s), Problematic** Acrostic, Aggro, Anuria, Arthritis, Black spot, BO, Boyg, Brainteaser, Bug, Business, Can of worms, Catch, Challenge, Conundrum, Crisis, Crux, Difficulty, Dilemma, Drawback, Egma, Enigma, Facer, Fault, Glitch, Handful, Hang-up, Hassle, Headache, Hiccup, Hitch, Hot potato, How d'ye do, Hurdle, Iffy, Indaba, Issue, Knot(ty), Koan, Mind-body, Miniature, Musive, Mystery, Net, Nuisance, Obstacle, Pons asinorum, Poser, Predicament, Quandary, Question, Re, Rebus, Red tape, Retractor, Riddle, Rider, Setback, Slipped disc, Snag, Snarl-up, Sorites, Stickler, Stimy, Stinker, Sum, Teaser, Teething, Thing, Thorny, Tickler, Tinnitus, Toughie, Trilemma, Trouble, Tsuris, Weed, Yips

**Problem-solving** Synectics

**Proboscis** Haustellum, Promuscis, Snout, Trunk

**Proceed(s), Proceeding, Procedure** Acta, Action, Afoot, Algorithm, Assets, Case, Continue, Course, Derive, Do, Drift, Drill, Emanate, Fand, Firedrill, Flow, Fond, Form, Fundoplication, Goes, Haul, Heimlich, Issue, Machinery, March, Mechanics, Method, Mine, MO, Modal, Move, On (course), Paracentesis, Pass, Point of order, Practice, Praxis, Process, Profit, Protocol, Punctilio, Pursue, Put, Rake, Receipts, Return, Rigmarole, Rite, Ritual, Rope(s), Routine, Sap, Steps, Subroutine, System, Take, Tootle, Tribunal, Use, Yead(s), Yede, Yeed

**Process(ing), Procession, Processor** Acromion, Action, Additive, Ala, Ambarvalia, Anger, Apheresis, Axon, Ben Day, Bessemer, Bosch, Bowel, Calcination, Caravan, Castner, Catalysis, Cavalcade, Central, Cibation, Coction, Concoction, Congelation, Conjunction, Corso, Cortège, Cyanide, DAP, Demo, Dense media, Diagonal, Digest, Dissolution, Double, Enantiodromia, Exaltation, Exequy, Expedite, Fermentation, Frack(ing), Front-end, Fusion, Haber(-Bosch), Handle, Line, Managing, Markov, Metabolism, Method, Moharram, Mond, Motorcade, Muharram, Multiple pounding, Multiplication, Number-crunch, Odontoid,

Olecranon, Open hearth, Operation, -osis, Pageant, Parade, Parallel, Parapophysis, Paseo, Peace, Photosynthesis, Pipeline, Planar, Pomp, Primary, Projection, Pterygoid, Puddling, Pultrusion, Purex, Putrefaction, Recycle, Rigmarole, Ritual, Screen, Secondary, Separation, Series, Silkscreen, Single, Skimmington, Solvay, Speciation, Spinous, Sterygoid, String, Sublimation, Subtractive, System, Thermite, Thought, Three-colour, Tie and dye, Titration, Torchlight, Train, Transaction, Transverse, Treat, Trial, Turn(a)round, Unit, Vermiform, Xephisternum, Xiphoid, Zygomatic

**Proclaim, Proclamation** Announce, Annunciate, Ban, Blaze, Blazon, Boast, Broadsheet, Cry, Decree, Edict, Enounce, Enunciate, Fiat, Herald, Indiction, Kerygma, Manifesto, Oyez, Preconise, Predicate, Profess, Publish, Ring, Shout, Trumpet, Ukase

**Proconsul** Ape, Hominid

**Procrastinate, Procrastinating, Procrastinator** Cunctator, Defer, Delay, Dilatory, Dilly-dally, Hang-fire, Linger, Pettifog, Postpone, Shelve, Temporise, Vacillate

**Procreate** Beget, Engender, Generate, Initiate

**Procrustean** Conformity, Stretcher

**Proctor** Agent, King's, Monitor, Prog, Proggins, Proxy, Queen's

**Procurator, Procure(r)** Achieve, Acquire, Aunt, Crimp, Earn, Get, Induce, Naunt, Obtain, Pander, Pilate, Pimp, Secure, Sort, Suborn

**Prod** Cattle, Egg, Goad, Impel, Jab, Job, Jog, Nudge, Poke, Pote, Powter

**Prodigal** Costly, Extravagant, Free, Lavish, Profligate, Scattergood, Spendall, Unthrift, Wanton, Wasteful, Waster, Wastrel

**Prodigious, Prodigy** Abnormal, Amazing, Huge, Immense, Infant, Little wonder, Monster, Monument, Mozart, Phenomenal, Portentous, Tremendous, Wonder, Wonderwork, Wunderkind

**Produce(r), Producing** Afford, Bear, Beget, Breed, Cause, Churn out, Create, Crop, De Mille, Disney, D'Oyly Carte, Dramaturg, Ean, Edit, Effect, Engender, Entail, Evoke, Exhibit, Extend, Fabricate, Form, Fruit, Generate, Get, Giulini, Godrich, Goldwyn, Grow, Harvest, Home-grown, Impresario, Ingenerate, Issue, Kind, Make, Merchandise, Offspring, Onstream, Originate, Output, Outturn, Propage, Propound, Puttnam, Raise, Realise, Roach, Selznick, Sloganeer, Son, Spawn, Spielberg, Stage, Supply, Teem, Throw, Tree, Trot out, Upcome, Wares, Whelp, Yield, Zeffirelli, Ziegfeld

▷**Produces** *may indicate* an anagram

**Product(ion), Productive(ness), Productivity, Products** Actualities, Addition, Apport, Artefact, Ashtareth, Ashtaroth, Astarte, Autogeny, Bore, Cartesian, Coefficient, Commodity, Cosmeceutical, Creation, Cross, Dairy, Depside, Dot, Drama, Effectual, Efficient, End, Factorial, Farming, Fecund, Fertile, Floruit, Fruit, Genesis, Global, Handiwork, Harvest, Inner, Line, Mass, Net domestic, Net national, Opera, Output, Outturn, Pair, Partial, Pastiche, Pharming, Power(house), Primary, Prolific, Range, Resinoid, Result, Rich, Scalar, Secondary, Set, Show, Speiss, Substitution, Uberous, Uberty, Vector, Waste, Work, Yield

▷**Production** *may indicate* an anagram

**Proem** Foreword, Overture, Pre, Preface

**Profane, Profanation, Profanity** Blaspheming, Coarse, Coprolalia, Desecrate, Impious, Irreverent, Sacrilege, Temporal, Ungodly, Unholy, Violate

**Profess(ed), Professor** Absent-minded, Academic, Acknowledge, Adjoint, Admit, Artist, Aspro, Asset, Assistant, Associate, Avow, Challenger, Claim, Declare, Disney, Emeritus, Full, Higgins, Hodja, Kho(d)ja, Know-all, Ostensible, Own, Practise, Pundit, Regent, Regius, RP, STP, Visiting, Wiseacre

**Profession(al)** Accomplished, Actuary, Admission, Assurance, Avowal, Buppy, Business, Calling, Career, Creed, Expert, Métier, Mister, Practice, Practitioner, Pretence, Pursuit, Regular, Salaried, Skilled, Testimony, Trade, Vocation, Yappie, Yappy, Yuppie

**Proffer** Give, Present, Proposition, Tender

**Proficiency, Proficient** Able, Accomplished, Adept, Alert, Dan, Excellent, Expert, Forte, Master, Past master, Practised, Skill, Technique

**Profile** Analysis, Contour, Cross, Half-cheek, Half-face, High, Long, Loral, Low, Market, Outline, Silhouette, Sketch, Statant, T(h)alweg, Vignette

**Profit(able), Profiteer, Profits** Advantage, Arbitrage, Asset stripper, Avail, Benefit,

Bestead, Boon, Boot, Box, Bunce, Cash cow, Cash in, Cere, Clear, Commercial, Divi(dend), Earn, Economic, Edge, Emblements, Emoluments, Expedient, Exploit, Extortionist, Fast buck, Fat, Fruitful, Gain, Gelt, Graft, Gravy, Grist, Gross, Income, Increase, Increment, In pocket, Interest, Issue, Jobbery, Juicy, Landshark, Leech, Lucrative, Makings, Margin, Melon, Mesne, Milch cow, Mileage, Moneymaker, Money-spinner, Negative, Net, Overcharge, Packet, Paper, Pay(ing), Pay (off), Perk, Pickings, Plummy, Preacquisition, Proceeds, Productive, Quids in, Rake-off, Return, Reward, Royalty, Scalp, Spoils, Tout, Use, Usufruct, Utile, Utility, Vail, Windfall

**Profligate** Corinthian, Corrupt, Degenerate, Dissolute, Don Juan, Extravagant, Lech(er), Libertine, Lorel, Losel(l), Lothario, Oatmeal, Rakehell, Reprobate, Roué, Spend-all, Spender, Spendthrift, Unprincipled, Wasteful, Wastrel

**Profound, Profundity** Abstract, Altum, Bottomless, Complete, Deep(-seated), Depth, Inner, Intense, Pithy, Recondite, Unfathomable

**Profuse, Profusion** Abounding, Abundant, Copious, Excess, Free, Galore, Lavish, Liberal, Lush, Quantity, Rank, Rich, Two-a-penny

**Progenitor, Progenitrix** Ancestor, Ma, Predecessor, Sire, Stock

**Progeny** Burd, Children, Descendants, Fruit, Issue, Offspring, Seed

**Prognosis** Forecast, Prediction

**Prognosticate, Prognostication** Augur, Foretell, Omen, Predict, Presage, Prophesy

▶**Program(ming), Programming language, Programmer** *see* **COMPUTER PROGRAM(S)**

**Programme(s)** Agenda, Blue Peter, Broadcast, Card, Chat show, Code, Community, Corrida, Countdown, Course, Docudrama, Documentary, Docusoap, Docutainment, Double-header, Dramedy, Entitlement, Episode, Est, Event, Faction, Feature, Fly-on-the-wall, Format, Infotainment, Linear, Live show, Mastermind, Medicaid, Miniseries, Minisode, Mockumentary, Neighbours, Neurolinguistic, Newscast, Newsreel, PDL, Phone-in, Pilot, Plan, Playbill, Podcast, Prank, Preset, Race card, Radiothon, RECHAR, Regimen, Report, Satellite, Schedule, Scheme, Sepmag, Serial, Shockumentary, Show, Simulcast, Sitcom, Sked, Soap, Software, Spin-off, Sportscast, Sustaining, Syllabus, System, Talk-show, Telecast, Teleplay, Telethon, Timetable, Twelve step, Webcast, YPO

**Progress(ive), Progression** →**ADVANCE**, Afoot, Arithmetic, Arpeggio, Avant garde, Career, Course, Endosmometric, Evolve, Expedite, Fabian, Flow, Forge, Forward, Forward-looking, Gain, Geometric, Get along, Go (ahead), Growth, Harmonic, Headway, Incede, Inroads, Knight's, Left, Leftist, Liberal, Move, Ongoing, Onwards, Paraphonia, Periegesis, Pilgrim's, Prosper, Rack, Radical, Rake's, Reformer, Roll, Run, Sequence, Series, Step, Stepping stone, Stop-go, Vaunce, Way, Yead, Yede, Yeed

**Prohibit(ed), Prohibition(ist), Prohibitory** Ban, Block, Contraband, Debar, Dry, Embargo, Enjoin, Estop, Fen, Forbid, Hinder, Index, Injunct, Interdict, Noli-me-tangere, Off-limits, Out of bounds, Preclude, Prevent, Pussyfoot, Rahui, Suppress, Taboo, Tabu, Verboten, Veto

**Project(ile), Projecting, Projection, Projector** Adam's apple, Aim, Ammo, Antitragus, Assignment, Astral, Astrut, Axonometric, Azimuthal, Baby, Ball, Ballistic, Beetle, Bullet, Butt, Buttress, Cam, Canopy, Carina, Cast, Catapult, Channel, Cinerama®, Cog, Conceive, Condyle, Conic, Conical, Console, Corbel, Corner, Coving, Cremaster, Crossette, Cutwater, Dendron, Dentel, Denticle, Diascope, Discus, Dripstone, Ear, Eaves, Echinus, Eden, Elance, Enterprise, Epidiascope, Episcope, Excrescence, Exsert, Extrapolate, Extrude, Fet(ter)lock, Flange, Gair, Gore, Grapeshot, Guess, Halter(e), Hangover, Helicity, Hoe, Homolosine, Hood-mould, Housing, Human genome, Hurtle, Inion, Jut, Kern, Kinetoscope, Knob, Launch, Ledge, Lobe, Lug, Lump, Magic lantern, Malleolus, Manhattan, Map, Megascope, Mercator, Mitraille, Mohole, Mollweide, Mucro, Mutule, Nab, Nose, Nunatak(er), Oblique, Olecranon, Opaque, Orillion, Orthogonal, Orthographic, Outcrop, Outjet, Outjut, Outrigger, Outshot, Overhang, Overhead, Oversail, Palmation, Peak, Peters', Pitch, Planetarium, Planisphere, Polyconic, Pork barrel, Prickle, Promontory, Prong, Propel, →**PROTRUDE**, Proud(er), Prow, Pseudopod, Quillon, Raguly, Roach, Rocket, Sail, Salient, Sally, Sanson-Flamsteed, Scaw, Scheme, Scrag, Screen, Shelf, Shot, Shrapnel, Sinusoidal, Skaw, Skeg, Slide, Sling, Snag, Snout, Spline, Sponson, Sprocket, Spur, Squarrose, Stand out, Stereopticon, Stick out, Stud, Tang, Tappet, Tenon, Thorn, Throw, Toe, Tongue, Tracer, Transparency, Trimetric, Trippet, Trunnion, Turnkey, Turtleback, Tusk, Umbo, Underhung, Undertaking, Villiform, Villus, Vitascope, Whizzbang, Zenithal

**Prolapse** Procidence

**Proletarian, Proletariat** Jamahiriya, Jumhouriya, Lumpen, People, Plebeian, Popular

**Proliferate** Expand, Increase, Multiply, Mushroom, Propagate, Snowball, Teem

**Prolific** Abounding, Bumper, Fecund, Fertile, Fruitful, Lavish, Profuse, Teeming

**Prolix(ity)** Lengthy, Longueur, Prosaic, Rambling, Rigmarole, Verbose, Wire-draw, Wordy

**Prologue** Introduce, Preface

**Prolong(ed), Prolongation** Continue, Drag out, Extend, Gonophore, Lengthen, Persistent, Protract, Sostenuto, Spin, Sustain

**Prom(enade)** Alameda, Boulevard, Cakewalk, Catwalk, Concert, Crush-room, Esplanade, Front, Mall, Parade, Paseo, Pier, Sea-front, Stroll, → **WALK**

**Prometheus** Fire

**Promethium** Pm

**Prominence, Prominent** Adam's apple, Antitragus, Blatant, Bold, Bump, Centre stage, Colliculus, Condyle, Conspicuous, Egregious, Emphasis, Featured, Gonion, Headliner, High profile, Important, Insistent, Landmark, Leading light, Luminary, Manifest, Marked, Mastoid, Noted, Obtrusive, Outstanding, Protuberant, Salient, Signal, Solar, Splash, Spotlight, Tall poppy, Teat, Toot, Tragus

**Promiscuous, Promiscuity** Casual, Chippie, Chippy, Demivierge, Fast, Free, Goer, Hornbag, Horny, Indiscriminate, Licentious, Light, Loose, Loslyf, Mixed, Motley, Pell-mell, Tomcat, Trollop, Wanton, Whoredom

**Promise, Promising** Accept, Agree, Assure, Augur, Auspicious, Avoure, Behest, Behight, Behote, Betrothal, Bode, Bright, Coming, Commit, Compact, Covenant, Earnest, Engagement, Foreshadow, Foretaste, Gratuitous, Guarantee, Hecht, Hest, Hete, Hight, Hope, IOU, Likely, Manifest, Oath, Parole, Pledge, Plight, Pollicitation, Potential, Pregnant, Recognisance, Recognizance, Resolution, Rosy, Sign, Sponsor, Swear, Tile, Troth, Undertake, Upbeat, Vow, Warranty, Word

**Promised land** Beulah, Canaan, Israel

**Promissory note** IOU, PN

**Promontory** Bill, Cape Sable, Cliff, Flamborough Head, Foreland, Giant's Causeway, Hatteras, → **HEADLAND**, Hoe, Hogh, Land's End, Mull, Mull of Galloway, Naze, Ness, Nose, Peak, Pillars of Hercules, Ras, Rock, Spit, The Lizard, Tintagel Head

**Promote(r), Promotion** Ad, Adman, Admass, Advance, Advancement, → **ADVERTISE**, Advocate, Aggrandise, Aid, Assist, Back, Ballyhoo, Banner ad, Bill(ing), Blurb, Boost, Breed, Brevet, Buggins' turn, Campaign, Churn, Dog and pony show, Elevate, Encourage, Eulogy, Event, Exponent, Float, Foment, Foster, Further, Help, Hype, Incite, Increase, Kick upstairs, Leaflet, Lord of Misrule, Mailshot, Make, Market, Merchandise, Peddle, Plug, Pracharak, Prefer, Prelation, Promulgate, Provoke, Push, Queen, Raise, Rear, Referment, Remove, Roadshow, Run, Salutary, Sell, Sponsor, Spruik, Stage, Step (up), Subserve, Tendencious, Tendentious, Tout, Upgrade, Uplead, Uprate

**Prompt(er), Promptly, Promptness** Accelerate, Actuate, Alacrity, Autocue®, Believe, Cause, Celerity, Chop-chop, Cue, Early, Egg, Expeditious, Feed, Frack, Idiot-board, Immediate, Incite, Induce, Inspire, Instigate, Motivate, Move, On cue, On-the-nail, Opposite, Pernicious, Post-it note, Premove, Prod, Punctual, Quick, Ready, Reminder, Sharp, Speed(y), Spur, Stage right, Stimulate, Stir, Sudden, Swift, Tight, Tit(e), Titely, Trigger, Tyte, Urge, Urgent

**Promulgate** Preach, Proclaim, Publish, Spread

**Prone** Accident, Apt, Groof, Grouf, Grovel, Laid back, Liable, Lying, Prostrate, Recumbent, Subject, Susceptible

**Prong** Fang, Fork, Grain, Peg, Tang, Tine

**Pronghorn** Cabrie, Cabrit

**Pronoun** Deictic, Impersonal, Itself, Oneself, Personal, Reciprocal, Relative

**Pronounce(d), Pronouncement** Adjudicate, Affirm, Agrapha, Articulate, Assert, Asseveration, Clear, Conspicuous, Declare, Definite, Dictum, Emphatic, Enunciate, Fatwa,

Fiat, Indefinite, Intense, Marked, Opinion, Palatalise, Pass, Philosophise, Pontificate, Predication, Recite, Utter, Velarise, Vocal, Voice, Vote

**Pronto** asap, PDQ

**Pronunciation** Accent, Betacism, Cacoepy, Delivery, Diction, Etacism, Itacism, Labiodental, Labionasal, Labiovelar, Lallation, Localism, Orthoepy, Phonetics, Plateasm, Proclitic, Received, Rhotacism, Sound, Syllabic, Tense

**Proof(s)** Acid test, Apagoge, Argument, Artist's, Assay, Ball, Bead, Bona fides, Confirmation, Corroboration, Credentials, Direct, Evidence, Firm, Foundry, Galley, Godel's, Grease, Impervious, India, Indirect, Justification, Lemma, Page, Positive, Preif(e), Probate, Pull, Quality, Receipt, Refutation, Remarque, Reproduction, Resistant, Revision, Secure, Slip, Smoking gun, Strength, Test, Tight, Token, Trial, Upmake, Validity, Watertight

**Prop(s)** Airscrew, Becket, Bolster, Bookend, Bookrest, Buttress, Clothes, Crutch, Dog-shore, Fulcrum, Leg, Loosehead, Misericord(e), Pit, Point d'appui, Punch(eon), Rance, Rest, Scotch, Set, Shore, Sprag, Spur, Staff, Stay, Stempel, Stemple, Stilt, Stoop, Stoup, Strut, Studdle, Stull, →**SUPPORT**, Tighthead, Trig, Underpin

**Propaganda, Propagandism, Propagandist** Agitprop, Ballyhoo, Black, Brainwashing, Chevalier, Doctrine, Exponent, Goebbels, Grey, Hot gospeller, Promotion, Psyop, Psywar, Publicity, Slogan, Spin doctor, White

**Propagate, Propagator, Propagation** Breed, Clone, Dispread, Generate, Graft, Hatch, Hotbed, Hothouse, Increase, Layering, Populate, Produce, Promulgate, Provine, Spread, Tan-bed

**Propel(ler), Propellor** Airscrew, Ca', Drive, Fin, Flick, Fling, Frogmarch, Launch, Leg, Lox, →**MOVE**, Oar(sman), Paddle, Pedal, Pole, Project, Push, Rotor, Row, Screw, Send, Tail rotor, Throw, Thruster, Tilt-rotor, Tractor, Twin-screw, Vane

**Propensity** Aptness, Bent, Inclination, Penchant, Tendency

**Proper(ly)** Ain, Apt, Convenance, Correct, Courteous, Decent, Decorous, Due, Eigen, En règle, Ethical, →**FIT**, Genteel, Governessy, Journal, Kosher, Legitimate, Maidenish, Nimity-pimity, Noun, Ought, Own, Pakka, Pathan, Priggish, Prim, Prissy, Prudish, Pucka, Pukka, Puritanic, Real, Rightful, Seemly, Staid, Strait-laced, Suitable, Tao, Trew, True, Veritable, Well

**Property, Properties** Acreage, Assets, Attribute, Aver, Belongings, Capacitance, Chattel, Chirality, Chose, Community, Contenement, Dead-hand, Demesne, Des res, Dowry, Effects, Enclave, Enthalpy, Escheat, Escrow, Essence, Estate, Fee, Feu, Flavour, Fonds, Freehold, Goods, Haecceity, Hereditament, Heritable, Holding, Home, Hot, Hotchpot, Immoveable, Inertia, In rem, Intellectual, Jointure, Land, Leasehold, Living, Means, Mortmain, Mystique, Paraphernalia, Peculium, Personal, Personalty, Pertinent, Possessions, Predicate, Premises, Private, Projective, Public, Quale, Quality, Realty, Second home, Settlement, Stock, Stolen, Theft, Thixotropy, Time-share, Timocracy, Trait, Usucapion, Usucaption

**Prophesy, Prophecy, Prophesying, Prophet(s), Prophetess, Prophetic** Amos, Augur, Bab, Balaam, Calchas, Cassandra, Clairvoyant, Daniel, Deborah, Divine, Druid, Eli, Elias, Elijah, Elisha, Ezekiel, Ezra, Fatal, Fateful, Fatidical, Forecast, Foretell, Former, Geomancer, Habakkuk, Haggai, Haruspex, Hosea, Is, Isa, Is(a)iah, Jeremiah, Joel, Jonah, Latter, Mahdi, Mahound, Major, Malachi, Mani, Mantic, Micah, Minor, Mohamet, Mohammed, Mopsus, Mormon, Moses, Mother Shipton, Nahum, Nathan, Necromancy, Nostradamus, Obadiah, Old Mother Shipton, Ominous, Oracle, Portend, Precurse, Predictor, Prognosticate, Pythoness, Samuel, Second sight, Seer, Sibyl, Tipster, Tiresias, Vatic, Vaticinate, Völuspá, Weather, Zachariah, Zarathustra, Zechariah, Zephaniah, Zoroaster, Zwickau

**Prophylactic, Prophylaxis** Inoculation, Preventive, Serum, Vaccine, Variolation

**Propitiate** Appease, Atone, Pacify, Reconcile, Sop

**Propitious** Benign, Favourable, Lucky

**Proponent** Advocate, Backer, Partisan, Statist

**Proportion(ate)** Commensurable, Cotangent, Dimension, Fraction, Harmonic, Inverse, Per cent, Percentage, Portion, Pro rata, Quantity, Quota, Ratio, Reason, Regulate, Relation, Sine, Size, Soum, Sowm, Symmetry, Tenor

**Propose(r), Proposal** Advance, Advocate, Aim at, Approach, Ask, Bid, Bill, Canvass,

Eirenicon, Feeler, Fiancé, Idea, Intend, Irenicon, Mean, Moot, Motion, Move, Nominate, Offer, Overture, Plan, Pop, Posit, Premise, Proffer, Propound, Recommend, Resolution, Scheme, Slate, Submission, → SUGGEST, Table, Tender, Toast, Volunteer, Woot, Would

**Proposition** Asses' bridge, Axiom, Convertend, Corollary, Deal, Disjunction, Ergo, Hypothesis, Identical, Implicature, Lemma, Offer, Overture, Pons asinorum, Porism, Premise, Premiss, Rider, Solicit, Sorites, Spec, Superaltern, Tempt, Theorem, Thesis

**Propound** Advocate, Purpose, State

**Proprietor, Propriety** Bienséance, Convenance, Correctitude, Decorum, Etiquette, Grundy, Keeper, Laird, Lord, Master, Owner, Patron, Peasant, Rectitude

**Prosaic** Common, Drab, Everyday, Flat, Humdrum, Matter of fact, Pedestrian, Tedious, Workaday

**Proscenium** Forestage

**Proscribe(d)** Exile, Forbid, Outlaw, Prohibit, Taboo, Tabu, Verboten

**Prose, Prosy** Essay, Euphuism, Haikai, Polyphonic, Purple, Purple patch, Saga, Stich, Verbose, Version, Writing

**Prosecute, Prosecutor, Prosecution** Allege, Arraign, Avvogadore, Charge, Conviction, Crown, Do, Double jeopardy, Fiscal, Furtherance, Impeach, Indict, Lord Advocate, Plaintiff, Practise, Public, Pursue, Sue, Wage

**Proselytise(r), Proselytism** Convert, Indoctrination, Propagandism, Souper

**Prosody** Logaoedic

**Prospect(or), Prospecting** Bellevue, Costean, Dowser, Explore, Forty-niner, Fossick, Future, Gold miner, Gold rush, Look-out, Mine, Opportunity, → OUTLOOK, Panorama, Perspective, Pleases, Possibility, Reefer, Scenery, Search, Sourdough, Street, Sweep-washer, View, Vista, Visto, Wildcatter

**Prospectus** Brochure, Menu, Pathfinder

**Prosper(ity), Prospering, Prosperous** Aisha, Ay(e)sha, Blessed, Blossom, Boom, Do well, Fair, Fat cat, Flourish, Get ahead, Heyday, Mérimée, Opulent, Palmy, Sleek, → SUCCEED, Thee, Thrift, Thrive, Up, Warison, Wealth, Welfare, Well-heeled, Well-to-do, Well-to-live

**Prosthetic** Fals(i)e

**Prostitute, Prostitution** Bona-roba, Brass, Broad, Bulker, Callet, Catamite, Chippie, Cockatrice, Cocotte, Comfort woman, Convertite, Debase, Dell, Demi-mondaine, Dolly-mop, Doxy, Drab, Fancy woman, Fille de joie, Floozie, Floozy, Grande cocotte, Harlot, Hetaera, Hetaira, Hierodule, Ho, Hooker, Hostess, Hustler, Jailbait, Laced mutton, Lady of the night, Loon, Loose-fish, Loose woman, Lowne, Madam, Magdalen(e), Moll, Mutton, Night-walker, Pict, Plover, Pole-cat, Poule, Pro, Public woman, Pug, Punk, Quail, Quiff, Rent-boy, Road, Rough trade, Scrubber, Shippie, Slap, Social evil, Stale, Stew, Streetwalker, Strumpet, Tart, Tom, Tramp, Trull, Venture, Wench, Whore, Working girl

**Prostrate, Prostration** Collapse, Exhausted, Fell, Flat, Flatling, Ko(w)tow, Laid, Lying, Obeisance, Overcome, Procumbent, Prone, Recumbent, Repent, Throw

**Protactinium** Pa

**Protagonist** Anti-hero, Leading man

**Protean** Amoebic, Fusible, Taro, Variable

**Protect(ed), Protection, Protective, Protector** Adonise, Aegis, Airbag, Aircover, Alexin, Amulet, Antigropelo(e)s, Antiserum, Arm, Armour, Asylum, Auspice, Balustrade, Barbican, Bastion, Bestride, Bield, Bodyguard, Boom, Brolly, Buckler, Bullbar, Bullet-proof, Cathodic, Chaffron, Chain mail, Chamfrain, Chamfron, Charm, Cherish, Cloche, Coat, Cocoon, Coddle, Coleor(r)hiza, Conserve, Contraception, Copyright, Cosset, Cover, Covert, Crash helmet, Cromwell, Curb, Cushion, Danegeld, Data, Defend, Defilade, Degauss, Diaper, Drawbridge, Egis, Enamel, Entrenchment, Escort, Estacade, Eyeshade, Fatherly, Faun, Featherbed, Fence, Fender, Fireguard, Firewall, Flank, Gobo, Goggle, Grill(e), Groundsheet, Guard(ian), Guard rail, Gumshield, Hedge, House, Hurter, Immune, Inalienable, Indemnify, Indemnity, Indusium, Insulate, Insure, Integument, Keckle, Keep, Kickback, Klendusic, Kneepad, Lag, Lee, Levee, Listed, Mac(k)intosh, Mail, Male, Mentor, Mollycoddle, Mother, Mothproof, Mouthpiece, Mudguard, Muniment, Nannyish, Napkin, Nappy, Noddy suit, Noll, Nosey, Oilskin, Oliver, Ombrella, Orillion, Overall, Pad, Palladium, Parados, Parapet, Patent, Paternal, Patron, Pelta, Penthouse, Police, Polytunnel, Pomander, Porch,

Pot-holder, Preserve, Procrypsis, Rabbit's foot, Radome, Rampart, Raymond, Reserve, Revetment, Ride shotgun, Ring-fence, Roo-bar, Sacrosanct, Safeguard, Safe-keeping, Safety net, Sandbag, Save, Schanse, Schan(t)ze, Screen, Scug, Security, Self-defence, Serviette, Shadow, Sheathing, Sheeting, Shelter, →SHIELD, Shinguard, Shinpad, Skug, Souteneur, Splashback, Splashboard, Splasher, Starling, Stockade, Sunblock, Sunglasses, Sunscreen, Sunshade, Supermax, Talisman, Telomere, Testa, Testudo, Thimble, Throw, Thumbstall, Toecap, Tower, Tribune, Tribute, Tutelar, Twilled, Umbrella, Underlay, Underseal, Vaccine, Waist-cloth, Ward(ship), Warhead, Warrant, Weatherboard, Weatherproof, Weatherstrip, Windbreaker, Windshield, Wing, Winterweight, Write

**Protectorate** Qatar

**Protégé** Godson, Pupil, Tutee, Ward, Whiteheaded boy

**Protein** Apolipoprotein, Complement, Conjugated, Keratin, Kisspeptin, Myostatin, Repressor, Simple

---

## PROTEINS

*3 letters:*
PSA
RNA
TSP
TVP

*4 letters:*
CREB
Meat
Soya
Zein

*5 letters:*
Abrin
Actin
Lysin
Mucin
Opsin
Pharm
Porin
Prion
Quorn®
Renin
Ricin

*6 letters:*
Alexin
Avidin
Capsid
Cyclin
Enzyme
Fibrin
Globin
Gluten
Lectin
Leptin
Leucin
Myogen
Myosin
Ossein
Pepsin
Tempeh

*7 letters:*
Adipsin
Alanine
Albumen
Albumin
Aleuron
Elastin
Fibroin
Gelatin
Gliadin
Histone
Hordein
Isozyme
Legumin
Leucine
Nuclein
Opsonin
Pepsine
Peptone
Sarcode
Sericin
Spongin
Tubulin

*8 letters:*
Aleurone
Allergen
Amandine
Analogon
Antibody
Collagen
Copaxone®
Cytokine
Ferritin
Gliadine
Globulin
Glutelin
Integrin
Pellicle
Permease
Prolamin
Proteose
Pyrenoid
Ribosome
Spectrin
Troponin
Vitellin

*9 letters:*
Apoenzyme
Aquaporin
Capsomere
Fibrillin
Filaggrin
Flagellin
Luciferin
Myoglobin
Ovalbumin
Phaseolin
Prolamine
Properdin
Protamine
Sclerotin
Spirulina
Ubiquitin

*10 letters:*
Actomyosin
Bradykinin
Calmodulin
Caseinogen
Conchiolin
Dystrophin
Factor VIII
Ferredoxin
Fibrinogen
Huntingtin
Incaparina
Interferon
Lewy bodies
Lymphokine
Single-cell
Thrombogen
Toxalbumin

*11 letters:*
Angiostatin
Angiotensin
Haemoglobin
Haptoglobin
Interleukin
Lactalbumin
Prothrombin
Transferrin
Tropomyosin

*12 letters:*
Fibronectina
Neurotrophin
Serum albumin

*13 letters:*
Ceruloplasmin
Lactoglobulin
Macroglobulin
Serum globulin

*14 letters:*
Immunoglobulin

---

**Proteron** Hysteron

**Protest(er)** Abhor, Andolan, Anti, Aver, Avouch, Black Bloc(k), Boycott, Clamour, Come, Complaint, Démarche, Demo, Demonstrate, Demur, Deprecate, Dharna, Dhurna, Dissent, Dissident, Expostulate, Fulminate, Gherao, Go-slow, Gripe, Hartal, Hunger march, Inveigh, I say, Lady Godiva, Lock-out, Luddite, March, Moonlighter, Mr Chad, Nimby, Object, Outcry, Peenge, Picket, Plea, Rail, Refus(e)nik, Remonstrate, Representation, Riot, Sit-in, Squawk, Squeak, Squeal, Stand, Suffragette, Work-to-rule

**Protestant** Amish, Anabaptist, Anglo, Arminian, Calvin, Congregationalism, Covenanter, Cranmer, Dissenter, Evangelic, Gospeller, Huguenot, Independent, Lady, Loyalist, Lutheran, Mennonite, Methodist, Moravian, Neo-Orthodoxy, Nonconformist, Oak-boy, Orangeman, Peep o' day Boys, Pentecostal, Pietism, Prod(die), Puritan, Reformed, Religioner, Right-footer, Sacramentarian, Seventh Day Adventist, Stundist, Swaddler, Waldensian, Wasp, Wesleyan

**Protocol** Agreement, Code, Convention, Etiquette, Geneva, Internet, Kyoto, Point-to-Point

**Proton** Nucleon, Quark

**Protoplasm(ic)** Biogen, Coenocyte, Coenosarc, Cytode, Plasmodium, Sarcode, Somatoplasm

**Prototype** Blueprint, Exemplar, Model, Original, Paradigm, Pattern, Pilot

**Protozoa(n)** Am(o)eba, Foraminifer, Giardia, Globigerina, Gregarine, Heliozoan, Infusoria, Leishmania, Mastigophoran, Merozoite, Moner(a), Moneron, Paramecium, Peritricha, Phagocyte, Radiolaria, Rhizopod, Sarcodinian, Sea-mat, Toxoplasm, Trichomonad, Trophozoite, Trypanosome, Volvox, Vorticella

**Protract(ed)** Delay, → EXTEND, Lengthen, Livelong, Long, Prolong

**Protrude, Protrusion** Bulge, Eventration, Exsert, Hernia, Jut, Pop, Pout, Project, Pseudopodium, Rectocele, Strout, Tel

**Protuberance, Protuberant** Apophysis, Bulge, Bump, Burl, Caput, Condyle, Crankle, Ergot, Gibbous, Hump, Inia, Knap, Knob, Limb, Malleolus, Mamelon, Node, Nodule, Papilla, Papillose, Papule, Spadix, Styloid, Swelling, Tragus, Tuber, Tuberosity, Venter

**Proud** Arrogant, Boaster, Cocky, Conceited, Dic(k)ty, Egotistic, Elated, Embossed, Flush, Haughty, Haut, Jutting, Level, Lordly, Orgulous, Outstanding, Protruding, Superb, Vain

**Prove(d), Proving** Apod(e)ictic, Argue, Ascertain, Assay, Attest, Attribution, Authenticate, Aver, Confirm, Convince, Deictic, Establish, Evince, Justify, Probative, → PROOF, Quote, → SHOW, Substantiate, Test, Trie, Try, Turn out

**Proverb** Adage, Axiom, Byword, Gnome, Maxim, Paroemia, Saw

▷**Proverbial** *may refer to* the biblical Proverbs

**Provide(d), Provident(ial)** Afford, Allow, Arrange, Besee, Bring, Cater, Compare, Conditional, Endow, Endue, Equip, Far-seeing, Feed, Fend, Find, Fund, Furnish, Generate, Give, Grubstake, Heaven sent, If, Lay on, Lend, Maintain, Offer, Plenish, Proviso, Purvey, Quote, Render, Serve, So, Sobeit, → SUPPLY, Suttle

**Province, Provincial(ism)** Area, Circar, Countrified, County, District, Eparchy, Exclave, Eyalet, Forte, Insular, Land, Mofussil, Narrow, Nomarchy, Nome, Nomos, Oblast, Palatinate, Pale, Petrographic, Presidial, Realm, Regional, Rural, Sircar, Sirkar, Small-town, Subah, Suburban, Territory, Vilayet

---

**PROVINCES**

*2 letters:*
NI

*4 letters:*
Bari
Gaul
Ifni
Jaen
Jaya
Shoa
Sind

*5 letters:*
Anhui
Anjou
Anwei
Coorg
Gansu
Hebei
Hejaz
Henan
Honan
Hopeh
Hopei
Hubei
Hunan
Irian
Jehol
Jilin
Kansu
Kirin
Liege
Macao
Namur
Natal
Otago
Skane
Tibet
Tigre
Tirol
Tyrol

*6 letters:*
Acadia
Anhwei
Aragon
Artois
Basque

Bengal
Fujian
Fukien
Gansul
Hainan
Kosovo
Marche
Poitou
Pontus
Punjab
Quebec
Raetia
Sanjak
Shansi
Shanxi
Shensi
Sikang
Tabasa
Ulster
Yunnan

*7 letters:*
Alberta
Almeria
Angevin
Antwerp
Bohemia
Brabant
Drenthe
Eritrea
Galilee
Gascony
Gauteng
Granada
Guienne
Guizhou
Guyenne
Hainaut
Jiangsu
Jiangxi
Jiazhou
Kiangsi
Kiangsu
Kwazulu
Lapland
Limburg
Limpopo
Livonia
Munster
Ningsia
Ontario
Picardy
Prairie
Qinghai
Rhaetia
Satrapy
Shaanxi
Sichuan
Suiyuan
Tucuman
Utrecht
Western
Zeeland

*8 letters:*
Atlantic
Chekiang
Chinghai
Connacht
Dauphine
Hainault
Helvetia
Illyrian
Kiaochow
Leinster
Liaoning
Limousin
Lorraine
Lyonnais
Manitoba
Maritime
Ninghsia
Normandy
Northern
Nuristan
Pashalic
Pashalik
Provence
Shandong
Shantung
Szechuan
Szechwan
Telemark
Touraine
Tsinghai
Zhejiang

*9 letters:*
Apeldoorn
Aquitaine
Boondocks
Bubalidar
Connaught
Flevoland
Free State
Friesland
Groningen
Guangdong
Hainan Tao
Illyricum
Kurdistan
Languedoc
Lusitania
Nivernais
North West
Orleanais
Santa Cruz
Sungkiang
Tarragona
Transvaal

*10 letters:*
Gelderland
Mpumalanga
New Castile
Nova Scotia
Overijssel
Patavinity
Roussillon
Wellington
Westphalia

*11 letters:*
Balochistan
Baluchistan
Eastern Cape
Grand Priory
Guelderland
Hesse-Nassau
Kaliningrad
Paphlagonia
Western Cape
West Prussia

*12 letters:*
Heilongjiang
New Brunswick
North Brabant
North Holland
Saskatchewan
South Holland

*13 letters:*
Syrophoenicia

*14 letters:*
Eastern Rumelia
Flemish Brabant
Walloon Brabant

*15 letters:*
British Columbia
Orange Free State

*17 letters:*
North West Frontier

*23 letters:*
Newfoundland and Labrador

---

**Provision(s), Provisional, Provisioner** Acates, Ap(p)anage, Board, Budget, Cellarer, Contingency, Cover(age), Endowment, Entrenched, Fodder, Foresight, Groceries, Insolvency, Interim, Jointure, Larder, Lend-lease, Mart, Proggins, Scran, Skran, Stock, Stuff, Supply, Suttle, Viands, Viaticum, Victuals

**Proviso, Provisional** Caution, Caveat, Clause, Condition, Interim, Interlocutory, IRA, Makeshift, Nisi, On trial, Reservation, Salvo, Stipulation, Temporary, Tentative

**Provocation, Provocative, Provoke** Agacant, Aggro, Alluring, Anger, Annoy, Arouse, Bait, Challenge, Egg, Elicit, Erotic, Exacerbate, Excite, Flirty, Gar, Goad, Harass, Ignite, Impassion, Incense, Incite, Incur, Induce, Inflame, Instigate, Insure, In yer face, Irk, Irritate, Kindle, Needle, Nettle, Occasion, Pique, Prompt, Raise, Raunchy, Red rag, Sedition, Sexy, Sound, Spark, Stimulate, Stir, Sultry, Tantalise, Tar, Tarty, Taunt, Tease, Titillate, Troll, Urge, Vex, Wind up

**Provost** Dean, Keeper, Marshal, Warden
**Prow** Bow, Cutwater, Fore, Nose, Prore, Stem
**Pro-war** Hawk
**Prowess** Ability, Bravery, Forte, Fortitude
**Prowl(er)** Hunt, Lurch, Lurk, Mooch, Pad, Prog, Prole, Rache, Ramble, Ratch, Roam, Rove, Snoke, Snook, Snowk, Tenebrio, Tom
**Proxime accessit** Next best
**Proximity** Handiness
**Proxy** Agent, Attorn, Deputy, Per pro, PP, Regent, Sub, Surrogate, Vicar, Vice
**Prude(nce), Prudent, Prudery, Prudish** Bluenose, Canny, Caution, Circumspect, Comstocker, Conservative, Discreet, Discretion, Economy, Far-sighted, Foresight, Frugal, Grundyism, Judicious, Metis, Mimsy, Mrs Grundy, Politic, Prig, Prissy, Provident, Puritan, Restrained, Safe, Sage, Sensible, Sparing, Strait-laced, Strait-lacer, Thrifty, Tight-laced, Vice-nelly, Victorian, Ware, Wary, Well-advised, Wise
**Prune(r)** Bill-hook, Clip, Deadhead, Dehorn, Lop, Plum, Proign, Proin(e), Reduce, Reform, Secateur, Shred, Slash, Sned, Snip, Thin, Trim
**Prunella** Hedge-sparrow, Self-heal
**Prurient** Avaricious, Itchy, Lewd, Obscene, Salacious
**Prussia(n)** Blue, Junker, Pruce, Spruce, Westphalian
**Pry** Delve, Ferret, Force, Lever, Meddle, Nose, Paul, Peep, Question, Search, Snoop, Stickyback, Toot
**Psalm** Anthem, Cantate, Chant, Chorale, Hallel, Hymn, Introit, Jubilate, Metrical, Miserere, Neck-verse, Paean, Penitential, Proper, Ps, Song, Tone, Tract, Tractus, Venite
**Psalter** Nocturn
**Pseud(o)** Bogus, Mock, Posy, Pretentious, Sham, Spurious
**Pseudonym** Aka, Alias, Allonym, Anonym, Code name, Pen-name, Stage-name
**Pshaw** Chut, Pooh, Tilley-valley, Tilly-fally, Tilly-vally
**Psyche** Anima, Ego, Self, Soul, Spirit, Superego
**Psychiatrist, Psychologist** Adler, Alienist, Asperger, Clare, Coué, Ellis, Freud, Headshrinker, Jung, Kraft-Ebing, Laing, Müller-Lyer, Rat-tamer, Reich, Shrink, Skinner, Trick-cyclist
**Psychic, Psychosis** Clairvoyant, ESP, Fey, Korsakoff's, Lodge, Medium, Mind-reader, Seer, Telekinesis, Telepathic
**Psychoanalyst** Lacan, Therapist
**Psychological, Psychology, Psychologist** Analytical, Behaviourism, Binet, Clinical, Comparative, Constitutional, De Bono, Depth, Development, Dynamic, Educational, Experimental, Eysenck, Freud, Gestalt, Hedonics, Humanistic, Industrial, James, Latah, Occupational, Organisational, Pavlov, Pavlovian, Piaget, Skinner, Social, Structural, Windt
**Psychosis, Psychotic** Korsakoff's, Manic-depressive, Organic, Schizophrenia, Sociopath
**Psychotherapist, Psychotherapy** Analysis, Coué, Laing, Rebirthing, Shen
**Ptarmigan** Rype, Ryper
**Ptolemy** Geographer
**Ptomaine** Neurine
**Puberty, Pubic** Adolescence, Beaver, Bush, Hebetic, Teens
**Pubescence** Tomentum
**Pub(lic) house** Alehouse, Bar, Beerhall, Beverage room, Boozer, Brew, Chequers, Free-house, Gastro, Gin-palace, Groggery, Hostelry, Houf(f), House, Howf(f), Inn, Jerry-shop, Joint, Local, Lush-house, Mughouse, PH, Pothouse, Potshop, Roadhouse, Rubbidy, Rubbity, Shanty, Tavern, Tiddlywink, Tied house, Tippling-house, Watering-hole
**Pubis** Sharebone
**Public** Apert, Audience, Civil(ian), Common, Demos, Estate, General, Great unwashed, Janata, Lay, Limelight, National, Open, Out, Overt, Populace, State, Vulgar, World
**Publican** Ale-keeper, Bartender, Bung, Host, Landlord, Licensee, Saloon-keeper, Tapster, Taverner
**Publication** Announcement, Annual, Bluebook, Book, Booklet, Broadsheet, Edition, Ephemera, Exposé, E-zine, Fanzine, Festschrift, Issue, →JOURNAL, Lady, Mag, Magazine,

Organ, Pamphlet, Part work, Periodical, Pictorial, Red-top, Samizdat, Tabloid, Tatler, Tract, Tribune, Weekly, Yearbook

**Publicise, Publicist, Publicity** Ad(vert), Airing, Announce, Ballyhoo, Billing, Build up, Coverage, Declassify, Exposure, Flack, Glare, Headline, Hoopla, Hype, Leakage, Limelight, Notoriety, Photocall, Plug, PR(O), Print out, Promo(te), Promotion, Promulgate, Propaganda, Réclame, Spin-doctor, Splash, Trailer

**Public school** Eton, Harrow, St Paul's, Winchester

**Publish(er), Published, Publishing, Publicise** Advertise, Air, Baedeker, Blaze, Cape, Copyleft, Delator, Desktop, Disclose, Edit, Electronic, Evulgate, Gollancz, Issue, Larousse, Noise, OUP, Out, Pirate, Plug, Post, Print(er), Proclaim, Propagate, Put about, Release, Ren, Run, Stationer, Vanity, Vent, Ventilate

**Puck** Disc, Elf, Lob (lie by the fire), Sprite, Squid

**Pucker(ed)** Bullate, Cockle, Contract, Crease, Gather, Plissé, Purse, Ruck, Shir(r), Wrinkle

**Pud** Fin, Fist, Neafe, Nief, Nieve, Paw

**Pudding** Afters, Baked Alaska, Bakewell, Black, Blancmange, Blood, Bread (and butter), Brown Betty, Cabinet, Charlotte, Christmas, Clootie dumpling, College, Crumble, Custard, → **DESSERT**, Dog's body, Drisheen, Duff, Dumpling, Eton mess, Eve's, Flummery, Fool, Fritter, Fromenty, Frumenty, Furme(n)ty, Furmity, Haggis, Hasty, Hodge, Hog's, Ice-cream, Kugel, Lokshen, Mealie, Milk, Nesselrode, Panada, Pandowdy, Panna cotta, Parfait, Pease, Plum, Plum-duff, Pockmanky, Pockmantic, Pock-pudding, Popover, Portmanteau, Queen's, Rice, Roly-poly, Sago, Savarin, Semolina, Sowens, Sponge, Spotted dick, Spotted dog, Stickjaw, Stodge, Suet, Summer, Sundae, Sweet, Tansy, Tapioca, Umbles, White, White hass, White hause, White hawse, Yorkshire, Zabaglione

**Puddle** Collect, Dub, Flush, Pant, Plash, Plouter, Plowter, Pool, Sop

**Pueblo** Aldea, Hopi, Zuni

**Puerile** Childish, Immature

**Puff(ed), Puffer, Puffy** Advertise, Bellows, Bloat, Blouse, Blow, Blowfish, Blurb, Bouffant, Breath, Chuff, Chug, Cream, Drag, Encomist, Eulogy, Exsufflicate, Flaff, Flatus, Fluffy, Fuff, Globe-fish, Grampus, Gust, Hype, Lunt, Pech, Pegh, Pluffy, Plug, Powder, Quilt, Recommend, Skiff, Slogan, Smoke, Steam, Swell, Toke, Twilt, Waff, Waft, Waif, Whiff, Whiffle

**Puffin** Fratercula, Manx shearwater, Rockbird, Sea-parrot, Tammie Norie, Tam Noddy

**Pug(ilist), Pugilism** Belcher, Boxer, Bruiser, Carlin, Fancy, Fistic, Monkey, Ring

**Pugnacious, Pugnacity** Aggressive, Aggro, Belligerent, Combative, Feisty, Scrappy

**Puke** Retch, Sick, Vomit

**Pukka** Authentic, Genuine, Real, True, Valid

**Pulchritude** Beauty, Cheese-cake, Grace

**Pull (up), Pull out** Adduce, Attraction, Charm, Crane, Cry off, Demand, Drag, Draw, Earn, Force, Gravity, Haul, Heave, Heeze, Hitch, Hoick, Hoist, Hook, → **INFLUENCE**, Lug, Mousle, Pluck, Pop-top, Rein, Rick, Ring, Rove, Row, Rug, Saccade, Sally, Seduce, Snatch, Sole, Sool(e), Sowl(e), Stop, Suction, Tit, Touse, Touze, Tow, Towse, Towze, Traction, Trice, Tug, Undertow, Uproot, Withdraw, Wrench, Wrest, Yank

**Pulley** Block, Capstan, Fusee, Idle(r), Jack-block, Swig, Trice, Trochlea, Truckle

**Pullover** Jersey, Jumper, Roll-neck, Slip on, Sweater, Sweatshirt, Tank-top, Windcheater

**Pullulate** Teem

**Pulp** Cellulose, Chyme, Chymify, Crush, Flong, Gloop, Kenaf, Marrow, Mash, Mush, Pap, Paste, Pomace, Pound, Puree, Rot, Rubbish, Soursap, Squeeze, Squidge, Tamarind, Wood

**Pulpit** Ambo(nes), Bully, Lectern, Mimbar, Minbar, Pew, Rostrum, Tent, Tub, Wood

**Pulsar** Geminga

**Pulsate, Pulsatory** Beat, Palpitate, Pound, Quiver, Systaltic, Throb, Thump, Vibrate

**Pulse** Adsuki, Adzuki, Alfalfa, → **BEAN**, Beat, Calavance, Caravance, Chickpea, Daal, D(h)al, Dholl, Dicrotic, Fava (bean), Flageolet, Garbanzo, Gram, Groundnut, Heartbeat, Ictus, Lentil, Lucerne, Pea, Rhythm, Sain(t)foin, Snow pea, Soy beans, Sphygmic, Sync, Systaltic, Systole, Throb

**Pulverise(r)** Calcine, Comminute, Contriturate, Demolish, Grind, Pestle, → **POUND**, Powder, Smash

**Puma** Catamount, Cougar, Mountain lion, Panther
**Pummel(ling)** Batter, Beat, Drub, Fib, Knead, Massage, Nevel, Pound, Tapotement, Thump
▷**Pummelled** *may indicate* an anagram
**Pump(ing)** Aerator, Air, Beer, Bellows, Bicycle, Bilge, Bowser, Breast, Centrifugal, Chain, Compressor, Cross-examine, Cross-question, Diaphragm, Donkey, Drive, Electromagnetic, Elicit, Feed, Filter, Foot, Force, Fork, Geissler, Grease-gun, Grill, Heart, Heat, Hydropult, Inflate, Inquisition, Interrogate, Knee-swell, Lift, Monkey, Mud, Nodding-donkey, Optical, Parish, Petrol, Piston, Pulsometer, Question, Quiz, Rotary, Sand, Scavenge, Shoe, Sodium, Stirrup, Stomach, Suction, Turbine, Vacuum, Water, Wind
**Pumpernickel** Rye (bread)
**Pumphandle** Sweep
**Pumpkin** Butternut, Cashaw, Cushaw, Gourd, Pampoen, Pompion, Quash, Queensland blue, Squash
**Pun** Calembour, Clinch, Equivoque, Jeu de mots, Paragram, Paronomasia, Quibble, Quip, Ram, Wordplay
**Punch(ed)** Antic, Bell, Biff, Blow, Boff, Bolo, Box, Bradawl, Bumbo, Card, Centre, Chad, Check, Chin, Chop, Clip, Cobbler's, Conk, Cross, Dong, Dry-beat, Eggnog, Fib, Fid, Fist(ic), Fourpenny one, Gang, Glogg, Haymaker, Hit, Hook, Horse, Jab, Job, Key, Kidney, Knevell, Knobble, Knubble, KO, Lace, Lam, Lander, Mat, Milk, Nail set, Nevel, Nubble, One-er, One-two, Overhand, Perforate, Pertuse, Planter's, Plug, Poke, Polt, Pommel, Posset, Pounce, Prod, Pummel, Puppet, Rabbit, Roundhouse, Rum, Rumbo, Sangria, Slosh, Sock, Steed, Sting(o), Stoush, Stunner, Sucker, Suffolk, Sunday, Swop, Tape, Upper-cut, Wap, Wind, Zest
**Punch-drunk** Slap-happy
**Punctilious** Exact, Formal, Nice, Particular, Picked, Precise, Prim, Stickler
**Punctual(ly), Punctual(ity)** Betimes, Politesse, Prompt, Regular, Sharp
**Punctuate, Punctuation (mark)** Apostrophe, Bracket, Close, Colon, Comma, Duckfoot quote, Em-dash, Emphasize, Em-rule, Guillemet, Hyphen, Interabang, Interrobang, Interrupt, Mark, Semicolon, Tittle
**Puncture(d)** Bore, Centesis, Criblé, Cribrate, Deflate, Drill, Flat, Hole, Lance, Lumbar, Pearse, Perforate, Pierce, Pinhole, Pounce, Prick, Scarify, Thoracocentesis
**Pundit** Egghead, Erudite, Expert, Guru, Maven, Oracle, Sage, Savant, Swami, Teacher, Tipster
**Pungency, Pungent** Acid, Acrid, Acrolein, Alum, Ammonia, Bite, Bitter, Caustic, Garlic, Hot, Incense, Mordant, Nidorous, Piquant, Poignant, Point, Racy, Sair, Salt, Spice, Sting, Tangy, Witty
**Punish(ment), Punished, Punishing** Algates, Amerce, Attainder, Baculine, Baffle, Bastinado, Beat, Belt, Birch, Brasero, Bread and water, Bum rap, Cane, Cang, Capital, Cart, Castigate, Chasten, Chastise, Come-uppance, Commination, Community service, Corporal, Correct, Cucking-stool, Dam(nation), Defrock, Desert(s), Detention, Dirdam, Dirdum, → DISCIPLINE, Durdum, Execution, Fatigue, Fine, Flog, Gantlope, Gate, Gauntlet, Gruel, Hellfire, Hiding, High jump, Horsing, Hot seat, Imposition, Impot, Interdict, Jankers, Jougs, Kang, Keelhaul, Knee-capping, Knout, Laidie, Laidy, Lambast(e), Leathering, Lesson, Lines, Log, Marmalise, Necklace, Nemesis, Pack-drill, Padre Pio, Pandy, Pay out, Peine forte et dure, Penalise, Penance, P(o)enology, Pensum, Perdition, Picket, Pillory, Pine, Piquet, Rap, Red card, Reprisal, Retribution, Riding the stang, Ruler, Rustication, Sanction, Scaffold, Scath, Scourge, Sentence, Serve out, Six of the best, Smack, Smite, Spank, Spif(f)licate, Stick, Stocks, Stoning, Strafe, Straff, Strap, Strappado, Swinge(ing), Talion, Tar and feather, Thick-ear, Timber-mare, Toco, Toko, Tophet, Torture, Treadmill, Trim, Tron(e), Trounce, Tumbrel, Tumbril, Vice anglais, Visit, War(r)ison, What for, Whip, Whirligig, Wild mare, Ywrake, Ywroke
▷**Punish** *may indicate* an anagram
**Punk** Goop, Inferior, Ne'er-do-well, Nobody, Pogo, Touchwood, Worthless
**Punnet** Basket, Pottle, Thug
**Punt(er), Punting** Antepost, Back, Bet, Gamble, Gondolier, Kent, Kick, Pound, Quant, Turfite, Wager

**Puny** Frail, Inferior, Petty, Reckling, Runtish, Scram, Shilpit, Sickly, Small, Weak, Weeny

**Pup(py)** Cub, Hush, Nurseling, Whelp

**Pupa** Chrysalis, Exarate, Neanic, Nymph, Obtect

**Pupil** Abiturient, Academical, Adie's, Apple, Apprentice, Bluecoat, Boarder, Cadet, Catechumen, Dayboy, Daygirl, Disciple, Etonian, Exit, Eyeball, Fag, Follower, Greycoat, Gyte, Head boy, Head girl, Intake, Junior, L, Monitor, Prefect, Preppy, Protégé(e), Scholar, Senior, Sixth-former, Student, Tiro, Trainee, Tutee, Ward, Wykehamist

▷**Pupil** *may refer to* an eye

**Puppet(s), Puppeteer** Bunraku, Creature, Doll, Dummy, Fainéant, Fantoccini, Finger, Galanty show, Glove, Guignol, Jack-a-lent, Judy, Mammet, Marionette, Mawmet, Mommet, Motion(-man), Motion generative, Pageant, Pawn, Petrushka, Pinocchio, Promotion, Punch(inello), Quisling, Rod, Sooty, Sweep, Thunderbird, Tool

**Purchase(r), Purchasing** Acquire, Acquisition, Adhesive, Bargain, Buy, Coff, Compulsory, Earn, Emption, End-user, Gadsden, Get, Grip, Halliard, Halyard, Hold, Layaway, → LEVERAGE, Louisiana, Money, Offshore, Oligopsony, Parbuckle, Perquisitor, Repeat, Score, Secure, Shop, Take, Toehold, Traction

**Pure, Purist, Purity** Absolute, Angelic, Authentic, Cando(u)r, Carat, Cathy, Chaste, Chiarezza, Classified, Clean(ly), Cleanness, Cosher, Fine, Glenys, Good, Holiness, Holy, Immaculate, Incorrupt, Innocent, Intemerate, Inviolate, Kathy, Kosher, Lily, Lilywhite, Maidenhood, Meer, Me(a)re, Net(t), Pedant, Perfectionist, Precisionist, Pristine, Quintessence, Refined, Sanctity, Sheer, Simon, Simple, Sincere, Snow-white, Snowy, Spotless, Stainless, Sterile, Thoroughbred, True, Unalloyed, Unapplied, Undrossy, Vertue, Virgin, Virtue, White

**Puree** Baba ghanoush, Coulis, D(h)al, Fool, Pulp

**Purgative, Purge** Aloes, Aloetic, Araroba, Aryanise, Blood, Cacoon, Calomel, Cascara, Cassia, Castor-oil, Catharise, Catharsis, Cholagogue, Colquintida, Comstockery, Croton, Delete, Detox, Diacatholicon, Diarrh(o)ea, Drastic, Elaterin, Elaterium, Eliminate, Eluant, Emetic, Enos®, Epsom salts, Epurate, Erase, Evacuant, Exonerate, Expiate, Flux, Gleichschaltung, Hiera-picra, Hydragogue, Ipecacuanha, Ipomoea, Jalap, Jalop, Laxative, McCarthyism, Number nine, Physic, Picra, Pride's, Relaxant, Scour, Scur, Senna, Soil, Turbith, Turpeth, Wahoo

**Purgatory** Cacatopia

**Purification, Purifier, Purify(ing)** Absolve, Bowdlerise, Catharsis, Clay, Clean(se), Depurate, Despumate, Dialysis, Distil, Edulcorate, Eluent, Elution, Exalt, Expurgate, Filter, Fine, Gas-lime, Green vitriol, Lustre, Lustrum, Niyama, Osmosis, Purge, Refine, Retort, Reverse osmosis, Samskara, Sanctify, Sanitise, Scorify, Scrub, Smudging, Sublime, Try, Whiten

**Puritan(ical)** Ascetic, Bible belt, Bluenose, Browne, Cromwell, Digger(s), Ireton, Ironsides, Killjoy, Moralist, Pi, Pilgrim, Plymouth Colony, Precisian, Prig, Prude, Prynne, Roundhead, Seeker, Strait-laced, Traskite, Waldenses, Wowser, Zealot

**Purl(er)** Cropper, Eddy, Fall, Knit, Ripple, Stream

**Purloin** Abstract, Annex, Appropriate, Lift, Nab, Pilfer, Snaffle, Sneak, Steal, Thieve

**Purple** Amaranthine, Amarantin(e), Amethyst, Assai, Aubergine, Burgundy, Cassius, Chlamys, Claret, Corkir, Cudbear, Dubonnet, Eminence, Fuchsia, Golp(e), Heather, Heliotrope, Hyacinthine, Imperial, Indigo, Korkir, Lavender, Lilac, Magenta, Mallow, Mauvin(e), Mulberry, Murrey, Orcein, Orcin(e), Orcinol, Pance, Pansy, Plum, Pompadour, Pontiff, Porporate, Proin(e), Prune, Puce, Puke, Punic, Purpure, Rhodopsin, Royal, Solferino, Tyrian, Violet, Visual

**Purport** Bear, Claim, Drift, Feck, Mean, Tenor

**Purpose(ful)** Ad hoc, Advertent, Aim, Avail, Calculated, Cause, Cautel, Cross, Dedication, Design, Earnest, Errand, Ettle, Function, Goal, Here-to, Idea, → INTENT, Marrow, Mean(ing), Meant, Mint, Mission, Motive, Object, Plan, Point, Raison d'être, → REASON, Resolution, Resolve, Role, Sake, Telic, Telos, Tenor, Use, View

**Purposeless** Dysteleology, Futile, Indiscriminate, Otiose

**Purr** Curr, Rumble

**Purse** Ad crumenam, Bag, Billfold, Bung, Caba, Clutch, Contract, Crease, Crumenal, Egg, Embouchure, Exchequer, Fisc, Fisk, Long Melford, Mermaid's, Pocket, Porte-monnaie, Prim, Privy, Prize, Public, Pucker, Shepherd's, Spleuchan, Sporran, Wallet, Whistle, Winnings

▷**Pursed** *may indicate* one word within another

**Purser** Mud-clerk

**Purslane** Sea, Water

**Pursue(r), Pursuing, Pursuit** After, Alecto, Business, Chase, Chivvy, Course, Dog, Follow, Follow up, Harry, Hobby, Hot-trod, Hound, Hue and cry, Hunt, Line, Pastime, Practice, Practise, Proceed, Prosecute, Quest, Scouring, Speciality, Stalk, Trace, Track, Trail, Trivial, Woo

**Pursuivant** Blue Mantle, Rouge Cross, Rouge Dragon

**Purulent** Mattery

**Purvey(or)** Cater, Provide, Provisor, Sell, Supply

**Pus** Empyema, Matter, Purulence, Pyuria, Quitter, Quittor

**Push(er), Push in, Push out, Pushy** Airscrew, Astrut, Barge, Birr, Boost, Brash, Buffet, Bunt, Butt, Ca', Detrude, Drive, Drug, Dunch, Edge, Effort, Elbow, Fire, Horn, Hustle, Hyper, Impulse, Intrusive, Invaginate, Jostle, Motivation, Nose, Nudge, Nurdle, Obtrude, Offensive, Onrush, Peddle, Pitchfork, Plod, Ply, Press, Promote, Propel, Railroad, Ram, Rush, Sell, Shog, Shoulder, →**SHOVE**, Snoozle, Subtrude, Thrust, Urge

**Pushchair** Baby Buggy®, Buggy, Stroller, Trundler

**Pushover** Doddle, Soda

**Pusillanimous** Coward, Timid, Weak, Weak-kneed, Wimp, Yellow

**Puss(y)** Amentum, →**CAT**, Catkins, Face, Feline, Galore, Glamour, Hare, Malkin, Mouth, Rabbit, Septic

**Pussyfoot** Dry, Equivocate, Inch, Paw, Steal, TT

**Pustule** Blotch, Pimple, Pock

**Put (off, on, out, up, upon)** Accommodate, Add, Alienate, Assume, Bet, Board, Cup, Daff, Defer, Dish, Do, Don, Doormat, Douse, Extinguish, Implant, Impose, Include, Incommode, Inn, Lade, Launch, Lay, Locate, Lodge, Lump, Miff, Oust, Pit, Pitch, Place(d), Plant, Plonk, Set, Sheathe, Simulate, Sited, Situate, Smoor, Smore, Snuff, Station, Stow, Temporise

**Put away, Put by** Distance, Save, Sheathe, Store, Stow

**Put down** Abase, Degrade, Demean, Disparage, Floor, Humiliate, Land, Relegate, Repress, Reprime, Snuff, Write

▷**Put off** *may indicate* an anagram

**Putrefaction, Putrefy(ing), Putrid** Addle, Bitter, Corrupt, Decay, Fester, Mephitic, Olid, Rot, Sepsis, Septic

**Putsch** Revolution

**Putt(ing)** Gimme, Gobble, Green, Hash, Pigeon, Sink, →**STUPID PERSON**

**Putter** Chug, Club

**Put together** Assemble, Compile, Synthesize

**Putty** Glaziers', Jewellers', Mastic, Painters', Plasterers', Polishers'

**Puzzle(r), Puzzled** Acrostic, At a loss, Baffle, Bemuse, Bewilder, Brainteaser, Chinese, Confound, Confuse, Conundrum, Crossword, Crux, Crux medicorum, Dingbat, Egma, Elude, Enigma, Feague, Floor, Fox, Get, Glaik, Gravel, Intrigue, Jigsaw, Jumbo, Kakuro, Kittle, Logogriph, Magic pyramid, Maze, Mind-bender, Monkey, Mystery, Mystify, Nonplus, Perplex, Ponder, Pose(r), Rebus, Riddle, Rubik's Cube®, Sorites, Sphinx, Stick(l)er, Stump, Sudoku, Tangram, Teaser, Thematic, Tickler, Wordsearch, Wordsquare

**Pygmalion** Centennial brown

**Pygmy** Atomy, Dwarf, Hop o'my thumb, Negrillo, Negrito, Pyknic, Thumbling

**Pyjamas** Baby-doll, Churidars, Jimjams

**Pyramid(s)** Cheops, Chephren, Egyptology, Frustum, Magic, Population, Stack, Teocalli

**Pyre** Bale(-fire), Bonfire, Brasero, Darga(h), Gha(u)t

**Pyrenean** Basque

**Pyridoxin** Adermin

**Pyrites** Arsenical, Cockscomb, Copper, Fool's gold, Iron, Magnetic, Mispickel, Mundic, Pyrrhotite, Spear, White
**Pyrotechnics** Arson, Fireworks
**Pyroxene** Aegirine, Aegirite, Diopside, Omphacite
**Pyrus** Service-tree
**Pythagoras** Samian
**Pythian (seat)** Delphic, Tripod
**Python** Anaconda, Diamond, IDLE, Kaa, Monty, → SNAKE, Zombi(e)

# Qq

**Q** Koppa, Quebec, Question
**Qatar** Emirate
**Q-boat** Mystery ship
**QC** Silk
**Qua** As
**Quack** Charlatan, Crocus, Dulcamara, Empiric, Fake, Homeopath, →IMPOSTOR, Katerfelto, Mountebank, Pretender, Saltimbanco
**Quad(rangle)** Close, Complete, Compluvium, Court, Em, En, Horse, Oblong, Pane
**Quadrilateral** Lambeth, Tetragon, Trapezium, Trapezoid
**Quadrille** Dance, Lancers, Matador(e), Pantalon
**Quaff** Carouse, Drink, Gulp, Imbibe
**Quagmire** Bog, Fen, Imbroglio, Marsh, Morass, Swamp, Wagmoire
**Quahog** Clam
**Quail** Asteria, Bevy, Bird, Blench, Bob-white, Button, Caille, Colin, Cower, Flinch, Harlot, Hen, Quake, Recoil, Shrink, Tremble, Wince
**Quaint** Cute, Far(r)and, Farrant, Fie, Naive, Odd, Old-world, Picturesque, Strange, Twee, Wham, Whim(sy)
**Quake(r), Quaking** Aminadab, Broad-brim, Didder, Dither, Dodder, Fox, Friend, Fry, Hicksite, Obadiah, Palpitate, Penn, Quail, Seism, Shake(r), Shiver, →TREMBLE, Tremor, Trepid, Wamble
**Qualification, Qualified, Qualify** Able, Adapt, Adverb, Agrege, Alloy, But, Capable, Capacitate, Caveat, Competent, Condition, Credential, Degree, Diplomatic, Doctorate, Eligible, Entitle, Fit, Graduate, Habilitate, Higher Still, Meet, Moderate, Modifier, Nisi, Parenthetical, Pass, Past-master, Proviso, Quantify, Restrict, Rider, Temper, Versed
**Quality** Aroma, Asset, Attribute, Aura, Body, Calibre, Cast, Charisma, De luxe, Esse, Essence, Extra virgin, Fabric, Fame, First water, Five-star, Flavour, Gilt-edged, Grade, High-class, Inscape, Insight, It, Kite-mark, Letter, Long suit, Mystique, Nature, Phat, Pitch, Plus, Premium, Primary, Property, Q, Quale, Reception, Sanctitude, Savour, Shade, Sort, Spirit, Standard, Stand out, Stature, Style, Substance, Suchness, Terroir, Texture, Thew, Thisness, Timbre, Tone, Top drawer, Tophole, Top-notch, Total, Up-market, Vein, Vinosity, Virgin, Virtu(e), Water, Worth
**Qualm** Compunction, Fear, Misgiving, Scruple
**Quandary** Dilemma, Fix, Predicament, Trilemma
**Quantifier, Quantify** Existential measure
**Quantity** →AMOUNT, Analog(ue), Batch, Bundle, Capacity, Deal, Dose, Feck, Fother, Hank, Heaps, Hundredweight, Idempotent, Intake, Jag, Lion's share, Loads, Lock, Lot, Mass, Measure, Melder, Multitude, Myriad, Niblet, Nip, Nonillion, Number, Ocean(s), Omnium, Operand, Output, Parameter, Parcel, Peck, Plenty, Posology, Pottle, Qs, Qt, Quire, Quota, Quotient, Radicand, Raff, Ream, Scalar, Slather, Slew, Slue, Sum, Surd, Tret, Unknown, Vector, Wad, Warp, Whips
**Quantum** Graviton, Isospin, Magnon, Phonon, Photon, Roton
**Quarantine** Isolate, Lazarette
**Quark** Bottom, Charm(ed), Down, Flavo(u)r, Particle, Strange, Top up
**Quarrel(some), Quarreler** Affray, Aggress, Altercate, Argue, Argy-bargy, Arrow, Barney, Barratry, Barretry, Bate, Bicker, Brabble, Brattle, Brawl, Breach, Breeze, Broil, Brulyie, Brulzie, Bust-up, Cagmag, Cantankerous, Carnaptious, Cast out, Cat and dog, Caterwaul, Catfight,

Chance-medley, Chide, Clash, Combative, Contentious, Contretemps, Difference, Disagree, Dispute, Domestic, Dust-up, Eristic, Estrangement, Exchange, Fall out, Feisty, Feud, Fire-eater, Flyte, Fracas, Fractious, Fratch(et)y, Fray, Hassle, Issue, Jar, Loggerheads, Miff, Outcast, Outfall, Pugnacious, Ragbolt, Row, Ruction, Spat, Squabble, Stroppy, Tangle, Tiff, Tile, Tink, Tweedledee, Tweedledum, Vendetta, Vitilitigation, Wap, Whid, Wrangle

**Quarry, Quarry face** Chalkpit, Chase, Currie, Curry, Game, Heuch, Mark, Mine, Pit, Prey, Scabble, Scent, Stone pit, Victim

**Quart** Winchester

**Quarter(ing), Quarters** Airt, Barracks, Barrio, Billet, Camp, Canton(ment), Casbah, Casern(e), Chinatown, Chum, Clemency, Close, Coshery, District, Dorm, E, Empty, Enclave, Fardel, Farl, First, Fo'c'sle, Forecastle, Forpet, Forpit, Fourth, Ghetto, Ham(s), Harbour, Haunch, Last, Latin, Medina, → MERCY, N, Note, Oda, Pity, Point, Principium, Quadrant, Region, S, Season, Sector, Tail, Trimester, Two bits, W, Wardroom, Warp, Winter

**Quarter-day** LD

▷**Quarterdeck** *may indicate* a suit of cards

**Quartermaster** Seacunny

**Quartet** Dissonance, Foursome, Mess, String, Tetrad

**Quarto** Crown, Demy, Foolscap, Imperial, Medium, Royal, Small

**Quartz** Adventurine, Agate, Amethyst, Bristol diamond, Buhrstone, Burrstone, Cacholong, Cairngorm, Chalcedony, Chert, Citrine, Cornelian, Crystal, Flint, Granophyre, Granulite, Itacolumite, Jasp(er), Love-arrow, Morion, Onyx, Plasma, Prase, Rainbow, Rose, Rubasse, Sapphire, Silex, Silica, Smoky, Spanish topaz, Stishovite, Tiger-eye, Tonalite, Whin Sill

**Quash(ing)** Abrogate, Annul, Cassation, Nullify, Oppress, Quell, Rebut, Recant, Repress, Scotch, Subdue, Suppress, Terminate, Void

**Quasimodo** Bellringer, Gibbose, Hunchback

**Quaver(ing)** Shake, Tremble, Tremolo, Tremulous, Trill, Vibrate, Warble

**Quay** Bund, Jetty, Landing, Levee, Staithe, Wharf

**Queasy** Delicate, Nauseous, Squeamish

**Quebec** Q

**Queen(ly)** Adelaide, African, Alcestis, Alexandra, Anna, Anne, Artemesia, Atossa, Balkis, Beatrix, Beauty, Bee, Begum, Bess, Boadicea, Boudicca, Brun(n)hild(e), Camilla, Candace, Card, Caroline, Cat, Chesspiece, Christina, Cleopatra, Closet, Clytemnestra, Coatcard, Dido, Drag, Drama, Eleanor(a), Ellery, Ena, ER, Esther, FD, Gertrude, Guinevere, Harvest, Hatshepset, Hatshepsut, Hecuba, Helen, Henrietta Maria, Hera, Here, Hermione, Hippolyta, HM, Homecoming, Isabel, Isabella, Ishtar, Isolde, Jezebel, Jocasta, Juliana, Juno, King, Leda, Maam, Mab, Maeve, Margaret, Marie Antoinette, Mary (Tudor), Matilda, May, Medb, Mobled, Monarch, Nefertiti, Omphale, Oriana, Parr, Pearly, Penelope, Persephone, Phaedra, Prince, Prom, Proserpina, Qu, R, Ranee, Rani, Regal, Regina(l), Reina, Sara, Semiramis, Sheba, Sultana, Titania, Vashti, Victoria, Virgin, Warrior

**Queen Anne** Mrs Morley

**Queenslander** Banana-bender, Bananalander

**Queer(ness)** Abnormal, Bizarre, Crazy, Cure, Curious, Fey, Fie, Fifish, Fishy, → ODD, Outlandish, Peculiar, Poorly, Quaint, Rum, Spoil

**Quell** Alegge, Allay, Calm, Quiet, Repress, Subdue, Suppress

**Quench** Assuage, Cool, Extinguish, Satisfy, Slake, Slo(c)ken, Sta(u)nch, Yslake

**Querulous** Huffy

▶**Query** *see* QUESTION(ING)

**Quest** Goal, Graal, Grail, Hunt, Mission, Pursuit, Search, Venture, Vision

**Question(ing), Questioner, Questionnaire** Appose, Arraign, Ask, Bi-lateral, Burning, Catechise, Challenge, Chin, Consult, Contest, Conundrum, Cross-examine, Curious, Debrief, Dichotomous, Direct, Dispute, Dorothy Dixer, Doubt, Erotema, Eroteme, Erotesis, Examine, Fiscal, Good, Grill, Heckle, Homeric, Impeach, Impugn, Indirect, Information, Innit, Inquisitor, Interpellation, Interrogate, Interview, Investigate, Issue, Koan, Leading, Loaded, Maieutic, Matter, Open, Oppugn, Peradventure, Point of order, Pop, Pose, Previous, Probe, Problem, Pump, Q, Qu, Quaere, Query, Quiz, Rapid-fire, Refute, Rhetorical, Riddle, Socratic method, Sound, Speer, Speir, Survey, Suspect, Tag, Teaser, Tickler, Tiebreaker, Twenty, Vexed, West Lothian, WH, What, Worksheet

**Questionable** Ambiguous, Dubious, Equivocal, Fishy, Shady, Socratic, Unclear

**Question-master** Interrogator, Socrates, Torquemada, Ximenes

**Queue** Braid, Breadline, Cercus, Crocodile, Cue, Dog, File, Kale, →LINE, Line up, Pigtail, Plait, Plat, Stack, Tail(back), Track

**Quibble(r), Quibbling** Balk, Carp, Carriwitchet, Casuist, Cavil, Chicaner, Dodge, Elenchus, Equivocate, Haggle, Hairsplitting, Nitpick, Pedantry, Pettifoggery, Prevaricate, Pun, Quiddity, Quillet, Quirk, Sophist

**Quiche** Flan, Tart

**Quick(en), Quickening, Quicker, Quickie, Quickly, Quickness, Quick-tempered, Quickwitted** Accelerate, Acumen, Adroit, Agile, Alert, Alive, Allegr(ett)o, Animate, Apace, Apt, Asap, Astute, Breakneck, Breathing, Bright, Brisk, Celerity, Chop-chop, Citigrade, Cito, Con moto, Core, Cracking, Cuticle, Dapper, Deft, Enliven, Existent, Expeditious, Express, Fastness, Festination, Fleet, Foothot, Gleg, Hasten, Hasty, Hie, High-speed, Hotfoot, Hypersonic, Impetuous, Impulsive, Intelligent, Jiffy, Keen, Lickety-split, Living, Mercurial, Meteoric, Mistress, Mosso, Nailbed, Nifty, Nimble, Nippy, Nooner, Pdq, Piercing, Piu mosso, Post-haste, Prestissimo, Presto, Prompt, Pronto, Rapid, Rath(e), Ready, Rough and ready, Schnell, Sharp, Short cut, Skin, Slippy, Smart, Snappy, Snort, Sodain(e), Soon, Spry, Streamline, Stretta, Stretto, Sudden, Swift, Swith, Tout de suite, Trice, Up tempo, Veloce, Vital, Vite, Vivify, Volable, Wikiwiki, Yare

**Quicksand** Flow, Syrtis

**Quicksilver** Mercury

**Quid** Chaw, Chew, L, Nicker, Oner, Plug, Pound, Quo, Sov, Tertium, Tobacco

**Quidnunc** Gasbag

**Quid pro quo** Mutuum, Tit-for-tat

**Quiescence, Quiescent** Calm, Di(o)estrus, Inactive, Inert, Latent, Passive, Still

**Quiet(en), Quieter, Quietly** Accoy, Allay, Appease, Barnacle, Calm, Clam, Compose, Conticent, Decrescendo, Diminuendo, Doggo, Ease, Easeful, Easy, Encalm, Entame, Gag, Grave, Hush, Kail, Laconic, Loun(d), Low, Lown(d), Low-profile, Lull, Meek, Mezzo voce, Millpond, Mouse, Mp, Muffle, Mum(budget), Mute, Off-season, Orderly, P, Pacify, Pastel, Pauciloquent, Pause, Peace, Piano, Pipe down, Plateau, QT, Reserved, Reticent, Sedate, Settle, Sh, Shtoom, Shtum, Silence, Sitzkrieg, Sly, Sober, Somnolent, Soothe, Sotto voce, Still(ness), Stum(m), Subact, Subdued, Tace, Taciturn, Tight-lipped, Tranquil, Wheesht, Whish, Whisht, Whist

**Quill** Barb, Calamus, Feather, Float, Plectre, Plectron, Plectrum, Plume, Remex, Spine

**Quillwort** Isoetes

**Quilt(ed), Quilting** Comfort(er), Continental, Counterpane, Cover, Crazy, Doona®, Duvet, Echo, Eiderdown, Futon, Kantha, Matel(l)asse, Pad, Patch(work), Puff, Trapunto

**Quince** Bael, Bel, Bengal, Bhel, Flowering, Japanese, Japonica

**Quinine** China, Crown-bark, Kina, Quina, Tonic

**Quinsy** Angina, Cynanche, Garget, Squinancy

**Quintessence, Quintessential** Classic, Heart, Pith

**Quintet** Pentad, Trout

**Quip** Carriwitchet, Crack, Epigram, Gibe, Jest, Jibe, Joke, One-liner, Repartee, Taunt, Zinger

**Quirk(y)** Concert, Foible, Idiosyncrasy, Irony, Kink, Mannerism, Oddity, Strange, Twist

**Quisling** Collaborator, Traitor

**Quit(s), Quitter** Abandon, Absolve, Ap(p)ay, Cease, Chuck, Defeatist, Desert, Desist, Drop out, Even(s), Go, Kick, Leave, Meet, Part, Resign, Rid, Stash, →STOP, Stow, Vacate, Yield

**Quite** Actually, All, Altogether, Ap(p)ay, Badly, Clean, Dead, Enough, Enow, Fairly, Fully, Mezzo, Precisely, Pretty, Rather, Real(ly), Right, Sheer, Very, Yes

**Quiver(ing)** Ashake, Aspen, Flicker, Pulsate, Quake, Ripple, Shake, Sheaf, Sheath, The yips, Tingle, Tremble, Tremolo, Tremor, Tremulate, Trepid, Vibrant, Vibrate, Wobble

**Qui vive** Go-go

**Quixote, Quixotic** Don, Errant, Impractical

**Quiz** Bandalore, Banter, Bee, Catechism, Examine, Grill, Hoax, Interrogate, I-spy, Mastermind, Mockery, Oddity, Probe, Pub, Pump, Question, Rebus, Smoke, Third degree, Trail, Yo-yo

**Quizzical** Askance, Curious, Derisive, Odd, Queer, Socratic

**Quod** Can, Clink, Jail, Prison

**Quoit(s)** Deck, Disc(us), Disk, Ring

**Quondam** Erstwhile, Former, Once, Sometime, Whilom

**Quorum** Minyan

**Quota** Numerus clausus, Proportion, Ration, Share

**Quotation, Quote(d)** Adduce, Citation, Cite, Co(a)te, Duckfoot, Epigraph, Estimate, Evens, Excerpt, Extract, Forward, Instance, List, Locus classicus, Name, Price, Recite, Reference, Say, Scare, Soundbite, Stock, Tag, Verbatim, Wordbite

**Quoth** Co, Said

**Quotient** Achievement, Intelligence, Kerma, Quaternion, Ratio, Respiratory

# Rr

**R** Arithmetic, Canine letter, Dog letter, King, Queen, Reading, Recipe, Right, Romeo, Run, Writing
**RA** Academy, Argentina
**Rabbi** Dayan, Mashgiah, Rav, Rebbe
**Rabbit** Angora, Astrex, Blather, Brer, British Lop, Buck, Bun(ny), Bury, Chat, Chitchat, Chunter, Con(e)y, Cottontail, Daman, Dassie, Doe, Duffer, Earbash, Gas, Goon, Harp, Haver, Himalayan, Hyrax, Jabber, Jack, Jaw, Klipdas, Long White, Lop-eared, Marmot, Muff, Natter, Nest, Novice, Oarlap, Palaver, Patzer, Prate, Prattle, Rack, Rattle, Rex, Rock, Sage, Snowshoe, Tail-ender, Tapeti, Terricole, Waffle, Warrener, Welsh, White, Witter, Yak, Yap, Yatter
**Rabble, Rabble-rouser, Rabble-rousing** Canaille, Clamjamphrie, Clanjamfray, Colluvies, Crowd, Demagoguery, Doggery, Galère, Hell-raiser, Herd, Hoi-polloi, Horde, Legge, Meinie, Mein(e)y, Menyie, Mob, Raffle, Rag-tag, Rascaille, Rascal, Riff-raff, Rout, Scaff-raff, Sedition, Shower, Tag, Tagrag
**Rabelaisian** Pantagruel, Panurge
**Rabid, Rabies** Extreme, Frenzied, Hydrophobia, Lyssa, Mad, Raging, Virulent
**Raccoon** Coati(-mondi), Coati-mundi, Olingo, Panda, Procyon
**Race, Racing** Alpine, Ancestry, Arms, Autocross, Autopoint, Aztec, Bathtub, Belt, Boat, Boskop, Breed, Broose, Brouze, Bumping, Career, Car rally, Caucus, Chantilly, Chase, Claiming, Classic, Compete, Comrades, Cone, Consolation, Contest, Corso, Country, Course, Criterium, Cross-country, Current, Cursus, Cyclo-cross, Dash, Dogs, Double sculls, Drag, Egg and spoon, Enduro, Event, F1, Fastnet, Flapping, Flat, Flow, Formula One, Fun-run, Gallop, Generation, Ginger, Gokart, Grand National, Grand Prix, Half-marathon, Handicap, Hare and hounds, Harness, Herrenvolk, Hialeah, High hurdles, Horse, Human(kind), Hurdles, Hurry, Hurtle, Inca, Indy car, Japhetic, Keiren, Keirin, Kentucky Derby, Kermesse, Kind, Lampadedromy, Lampadephoria, Leat, Leet, Lick, Lignage, Line(age), Maiden, Mankind, Marathon, Master, Mediterranean, Meets, Mile, Monza, Motocross, Nascar, Nation, → NATIONAL, National Hunt, Nursery, Nursery stakes, Obstacle, One-horse, Orienteer, Palio, Pancake, Paper chase, Pattern, Picnic, Pigeon, Plate, Pluck, Point-to-point, Potato, Pre-Dravidian, Prep, Pursuit, Rallycross, Rallying, Rapids, Rat, Regatta, Relay, Rev, Rill, Road, Rod, Ronne, Roost, Run-off, Sack, St Leger, Scramble, Scratch, Scud, Scurry, Seed, Selling(-plate), Shan, Sheep, Slalom, Slipstream, Sloot, Slot-car, Sluit, Smock, Speedway, Sprint, Stakes, Steeplechase, Stem, Stirp(s), Stirpes, Stock, Strain, Streak, Strene, Supermoto, Sweepstake, Tail, Taste, Tear, Three-legged, Tide, Torch, Torpids, Tribe, Trotting, TT, Turf, Two-horse, Volsungs, Walking, Walk-over, Waterway, Welter, Wetherby, Whid, White, Zip
**Racehorse, Racer** Arkle, Dragster, Eclipse, Filly, Go-kart, Hare, Kart, Maiden, Mudder, Neddy, Novice, Plater, Red Rum, Shergar, Snake, Steeplechaser, Trotter
**Raceme** Bunch, Corymb, Panicle
**Race meeting, Racecourse, Racetrack** Aintree, Ascot, Ayr, Brands Hatch, Cambridgeshire, Catadrome, Catterick, Cesarewitch, Chepstow, Derby, Doggett's Coat and Badge, Doncaster, Dromical, Dromos, Epsom, Goodwood, Grand National, Grand Prix, Guineas, Hippodrome, Imola, Indy, Kentucky Derby, Leger, Le Mans, Longchamps, Madison, National Hunt, Newmarket, Oaks, Paceway, Racino, Redcar, Regatta, St Leger, Silverstone, Super G, Thousand Guineas, Towcester, Two Thousand Guineas, Velodrome, Wetherby, Wincanton, York
**Racial (area), Racialist** Anti-semite, Apartheid, Colour, Ethnic, Eugenic, Ghetto, National Front, Quarter

**Rack** Agonise, Anguish, Bin, Cloud, Cratch, Creel, Drainer, Drier, Flake, Frame, Hack, Hake, Hat, Heck, Meat, Pipe, Plate, Pulley, Roof, Spider, Stretcher, Toast, Torment, Torture, Touse, Towse

**Racket(eer)** Bassoon, → BAT, Battledore, Bloop, Blue murder, Brattle, Cacophony, Caterwaul, Charivari, Chirm, Clamour, Clatter, Con, Crime, Crosse, Deen, Din, Discord, Earner, → FIDDLE, Fuss, Gyp, Hooha, Hubbub, Hullaballoo, Hustle, → NOISE, Noisiness, Numbers, Protection, Ramp, Rattle, Rort, Ruction, Scam, Sokaiya, Stridor, Swindle, Tirrivee, Tumult, Uproar, Utis

▷**Racketeer** *may indicate* a tennis or squash player

**Racy** Ethnic, Piquant, Pungent, Ribald, Salty, Spicy, Spirited

**Rad** Rem

**Radar** Acronym, Angel, AWACS, Beacon, DEW line, Doppler, Gadget, Gee, Gull, Lidar, Loran, Monopulse, Navar, Rebecca-eureka, Scanner, Shoran, Surveillance, Teleran®, Tracking

**Raddle** Hurdle, Ochre, Red

**Radial** Osteal, Quadrant, Rotula, Spoke, Tire, Tyre

**Radiance, Radiant** Actinic, Aglow, Aura, Aureola, Beamish, Brilliant, Gleam(y), Glisten(ing), Glittery, Glory, Glow, Happy, Luminous, Lustre, Refulgent, Shechina, Sheen, Shekinah

**Radiate, Radiating, Radiation, Radiator** Actinal, Adaptive, Air-colour, Annihilation, Atomic, Beam, Black body, Bremsstrahlung, Cavity, C(h)erenkov, Characteristic, Cosmic (background), Disseminate, Diversion, Dosimetry, Effulgence, Effuse, Emanate, Emit, Exitance, Fluorescence, Gamma, Glow, Hard, Hawking, Heater, Infrared, Insolation, Ionizing, Isohel, Laser, Microwave, Millirem, Non-ionizing, Pentact, Photon, Picowave, Pulsar, Quasar, Rem(s), Rep, Roentgen, → SHINE, Sievert, Soft, Solar, Spherics, Spoke, Stellate, Stray, SU, Sun, Synchrotron, Terrestrial, Ultra violet, UVA, UVB, Van Allen, Visible

**Radical** Acetyl, Alkyl, Allyl, Amide, Ammonium, Amyl, Aryl, Avant garde, Benzil, Benzoquinone, Benzoyl, Bolshevist, Bolshie, Butyl, Calumba, Carbene, Cetyl, Chartist, Dibutyl, Drastic, Dyad, Egalitarian, Elemental, Ester, Ethynyl, Extreme, Free, Fundamental, Fundie, Fundy, Gauchist, Genre-busting, Glyceryl, Glycosyl, Hexyl, Hydroxy, Innate, Isopropyl, Jacobin, Leftist, Left wing, Leveller, Ligand, Maximalist, Methyl, Montagnard, Nitryl, Oxonium, Parsnip, Phenyl, Phosphonium, Pink, Propyl, Red, Revolutionary, Rhizocaul, Root, Rudiment, Sulfone, Sulphone, Taliban, Taproot, Trot(sky), Uranyl, Vinyl, Vinylidene, Whig, Xylyl, Yippie, Yippy, Young Turk

**Radio** Alarm, Beatbox, Blooper, Bluetooth, Boom-box, Broadcasting, Caroline, Cat's whisker, CB, Cellular, Citizen's band, Clock, Cognitive, Community, Crystal set, Digital, Direction-finder, Ether, Gee, Ghetto-blaster, Ham, Local, Long wave, Loudspeaker, Marconigraph, Media, Pirate, Receiver, Receiving-set, Rediffusion®, Reflex, Rig, Set, Short wave, Simplex, Sound, Steam, Talk, Talkback, Tranny, Transceiver, Transistor, Transmitter, Transponder, Tuner, Walkie-talkie, Walkman®, Walky-talky, Wireless

**Radioactive, Radioactivity** Actinide, Americium, Artificial, Astatine, Autinite, Becquerel, Bohrium, Cheralite, Cobalt 60, Curie, Darmstadtium, Emanation, Fall-out, Fermium, Hot, Megacurie, Niton, Nucleonics, Plutonium, Radon, Steam, Thorianite, Thorite, Thorium, Torbernite, Unstable, Uranite, Uranium

**Radiogram, Radiograph(y)** Cable, Telegram, Venography, Ventriculography, Wire

**Radiology** Interventional

**Radish** Charlock, Daikon, Mooli, Runch

**Radium** Ra

**Radius** Bone, Long, Schwarzschild, Short, Turning

**Radon** Rn

**Raffia** Rabanna

**Raffle(s)** Burglar, Draw, Lottery, Sweepstake

**Raft(ing)** Balsa, Carley float, Catamaran, Float, Kon-Tiki, Life, Log, Mohiki, Pontoon, Slew, Whitewater

**Rafter** Barge-couple, Beam, Chevron, Jack, Joist, Principal, Ridge, Spar, Timber

**Rag(ged), Ragged(ness), Rags** Bait, Bate, Clout, Coral, Daily, Deckle, Dishcloth, Dud(s), Duddery, Duddie, Duster, Fent, Figleaf, Glad, Gutter press, Guyed, Haze, Horror, Kid,

Lap(pie), Lapje, Mop, Moth-eaten, → **NEWSPAPER**, Nose, Paper, Red(top), Remnant, Revel, Rivlins, Roast, Rot, Scabrous, Scold, Scrap, S(c)hmatte, → **SHRED**, Slate, Slut, Splore, Tack, Tat(t), Tatter(demalion), Tatty, Taunt, Taver, → **TEASE**, Tiger, Tongue, Uneven

▷**Rag(ged)** *may indicate* an anagram

**Rage, Raging** Amok, → **ANGER**, Ardour, Bait, Bate, Bayt, Boil, Chafe, Conniption, Explode, Fad, Fashion, Fierce, Fit, Fiz(z), Fume, Furibund, Furore, Fury, Gibber, Go, Irate, Ire, Madness, Mania, Mode, Monkey, Paddy(-whack), Passion, Pelt, Pet, Pique, Rabid, Rail, Ramp, Rant, Road, 'roid, See red, Snit, Storm, Tantrum, Tear, Temper, Ton, Trolley, Utis, Wax, Wrath

**Raglan** Sleeve

**Ragout** Blanquette, Compot, Goulash, Haricot, Salami, Stew

**Rag-picker** Bunter

**Ragwort** Yellowseed

**Raid(er)** Ambush, Assail, Assault, Attack, Baedeker, Bear, Bodrag, Bust, Camisado, Chappow, Commando, Corporate, Dawn, Do, Excursion, Forage, For(r)ay, Imburst, Incursion, Inroad, Inrush, Invade, Jameson, Maraud, March-treason, Mosstrooper, Pict, Pillage, Plunder, Ram, Ransel, Razzia, Reive, Rob, Sack, Scrump, Skrimp, Skrump, Smash-and-grab, Sortie, Spreagh, Storm, Swoop, Viking

**Rail(er), Railing** Abuse, Amtrack, Arm(rest), Arris, Balustrade, Ban, Banister, → **BAR**, Barre, Barrier, Bird, Breast, Bullhead, Cloak, Communion, Conductor, Coot, Corncrake, Crake, Criticise, Dado, Edge, Fender, Fiddle, Fife, Flanged, Flat-bottomed, Flite, Flow, Fulminate, Grab, Grinding, Guide, Gush, Insult, Inveigh, Light, Limpkin, Live, Metal, Monkey, Neckerchief, Notornis, Parapet, Parclose, Picture, Pin, Plate, Post, Pulpit, Pushpit, Rack, Rag, Rate, Rave, Rung, Scold, Slang-whang, Slate, Slip, Snash, Sneer, Sora, Soree, Spar, T, Taffrail, Takahe, Taunt, Thersites, Third, Towel, Track, Train, Vituperation, Weka

**Raillery** Badinage, Banter, Chaff, Persiflage, Sport

**Railroad, Railway** Aerial, Amtrak, BR, Branch line, Bulldoze, Cable, Canadian-Pacific, Cash, Coerce, Cog, Crémaillère, Dragoon, El, Elevated, Eurostar, Funicular, Gantlet, GWR, Inclined, L, Light, Lines, LMS, LNER, Loop-line, Maglev, Marine, Metro, Monorail, Mountain, Narrow-gauge, Press, Rack, Rack and pinion, Rly, Road, Rollercoaster, Ropeway, ROSCO, Ry, Scenic, Ship, Siding, SR, Stockton-Darlington, Switchback, Telpher-line, Track, Train, Tramline, Tramway, Trans-Siberian, Tube, Underground

**Railwayman** Driver, Fettler, Footplateman, Gandy dancer, Guard, Length(s)man, Locoman, NUR, Plate layer, Stephenson, Stoker, Tracklayer

**Raiment** Apparel, Clothes, Finery, Garb, Ihram

**Rain(y), Rainstorm** Acid, Blash, Blood, Deluge, Downpour, Drizzle, Flood, Hyad(e)s, Hyetal, Mistle, Mizzle, Monsoon, Oncome, Onding, Onfall, Pelt, Pelter, Piss, Plump, Pluviose, Pluvious, Pour, Precipitation, Right, Roke, Scat, Scotch mist, Seil, Serein, Serene, Shell, Shower, Sile, Silver thaw, Skiffle, Skit, Smir(r), Smur, Soft, Spat, Spet, Spit, Storm, Teem, Thunder-plump, Virga, Water, Weep, Wet, Yellow

**Rainbow(-maker)** Arc, Arc-en-ciel, Bifrost, Bruise, Dew-bow, Iridescence, Iris, Moon-bow, Spectroscope, Sunbow, Sundog, Torrent-bow, Trout, Water-gall, Weather-gall, White

**Raincoat, Rainproof, Rainwear** Anorak, Burberry®, Cagoule, Gaberdine, Mac, Mino, Oils(kins), Slicker, Souwester, Waterproof, Weatherboard

**Raingauge** Ombrometer, Udometer

**Rain-maker** Indra

**Rain tree** Saman

**Raise(d), Raiser, Raising** Advance, Aggrade, Attollent, Aweigh, Boost, Bouse, Bowse, Broach, Build, Buoy up, Cameo, Cat, Coaming, Cock, Collect, Curtain, Elate, → **ELEVATE**, Emboss, Enhance, Ennoble, Erect, Escalate, Exalt, Extol, Fledge, Fund, Grow, Heave, Heezie, Heft, Hell, High(er), Hike, Hoick, Hoist, Increase, Inflate, Jack, Key, Leaven, Levy, Lift, Mention, Overcall, Parent, Perk, Prise, Rear, Regrate, Relievo, Repoussé, Revie, Rouse, Saleratus, Sally, Siege, Sky, Snarl, Step-up, Sublimate, Take up, Up, Upgrade, Uplift, Uprear, Weigh

**Raj** Zila

**Rake, Raker, Rakish** Bag of bones, Bed-hopper, Buckrake, Casanova, Comb, Corinthian, Croupier, Dapper, Dissolute, Don Giovanni, Don Juan, Enfilade, Gay dog, Jaunty, Lecher,

Libertine, Lothario, Raff, Reprobate, Rip, Roam, Roué, Scan, Scour, Scowerer, Scrape, Scratch, Sporty, Strafe, Straff, Stubble, Swash-buckler, Swinge-buckler, Wagons, Wolf, Womaniser

**Rale** Crepitus, Rattle

**Rally, Rallying-point** Assemble, Autocross, Autopoint, Badinage, Banter, Battle cry, Buck up, Demo, Gather, Improve, Jamboree, Meeting, Mobilise, Monte Carlo, Morcha, Muster, Oriflamme, Persiflage, Raise, Recover, Recuperate, Regroup, Rely, Rest, Reunion, Revive, Risorgimento, Roast, Rouse, Scramble, Spirit, Strengthen, Treasure hunt

**Ralph** Imp, Nader, Rackstraw

**Ram** Aries, Battering, Buck, Bunt, Butt, Butter, Corvus, Crash, Drive, Hidder, Hydraulic, Mendes, Pound, Pun, Sheep, Stem, Tamp, Thrust, Tup, Wether

**Ramble(r), Rambling** Aberrant, Aimless, Desultory, Digress, Excursive, Exponential, Fell-walk, Hike, Incoherent, Indirect, Liana, Liane, Maunder, Meander, Phrasy, Rabbit, Rigmarole, Roam, Rose, Rove, Skimble-skamble, Sprawl, Stray, Stroll, Vagabond, Waffle, Wander, Wind

**Rameses** Pharaoh

**Ramp** Bank, Gradient, Helicline, Incline, Linkspan, Runway, Slipway, Slope, Speed, Vert

**Rampage** Fury, Riot, Spree, Storm, Warpath

**Rampant** Lionel, Predominant, Profuse, Rearing, Rife

▷**Rampant** *may indicate* an anagram or a reversed word

**Rampart** Abat(t)is, Brisure, Bulwark, Butt, Defence, Fortification, Parapet, Terreplein, Vallum, Wall

**Ramrod** Gunstick

**Ramshackle** Decrepit, Derelict, Heath Robinson, Rickety, Rickle

**Ranch** Bowery, Corral, Dude, Estancia, Farm, Fazenda, Hacienda, Spread, Stump

**Rancher** Cowpuncher, Fazendeiro

**Rancid** Frowy, Rafty, Rank, Reast(y), Reest(y), Reist(y), Sour, Turned

**Rancour, Rancorous** Acrimony, Bad blood, Gall, Hate, Malgré, Malice, Resentment, Spite, Vitriolic

**Rand** Border, R, Roon

**Random** Accidental, Ad hoc, Aleatoric, Arbitrary, →**AT RANDOM**, Blind, Casual, Desultory, Fitful, →**HAPHAZARD**, Harvest, Hit and miss, Hit-or-miss, Hitty-missy, Hobnob, Indiscriminate, Lot, Lottery, Lucky dip, Pot luck, Pot-shot, Scattershot, Sporadic, Stochastic, Stray, Willy-nilly

▷**Random(ly)** *may indicate* an anagram

**Randy** Lustful

**Range(r), Ranging, Rangy** Admiralty, Aga®, Align, Ambit, Andes, Atlas, AZ, Ballpark, Band, Bowshot, Bushwhack, Capsule, Carry, Cascade, Chain, Cheviot, Compass, Cotswolds, Course, Dandenong, Darling, Diapason, Dispace, Dolomites, Dynamic, Earshot, Eclectic, Err, →**EXTENT**, Eye-shot, Flinders, Forest, Game warden, Gamme, Gamut, Glasgow, Grade, Great Dividing, Gunshot, Hamersley, Harmonic, Helicon, Himalayas, Home, Interquartile, Kaikoura, Karakoram, Ken(ning), Kitchen, Kolyma, Ladakh, Leggy, Limit, Line, Locus, Lone, Long, MacDonnell, Massif, Middleback, →**MOUNT**, Musgrave, New England, Orbit, Otway, Oven, Owen Stanley, Palette, Pennine Hills, Point-blank, Prairie, Prism, Purview, Pyrenees, Radius, Rake, Rayburn®, Reach, Register, Repertoire, Ridge, Rifle, Roam, Rocket, Rove, Ruivenzori, Run, Saga, Scale, Scope, Sc(o)ur, Selection, Serra, Shooting, Short, Sierra, Sloane, Spectrum, Sphere, Stanovoi, Stanovoy, Stove, Strzelecki, Sweep, Tape, Tessitura, Teton, Texas, The Wolds, Tier, Urals, Waldgrave, Wasatch, Waveband, Woomera

**Range-finder** Radar, Telemeter

**Rank(s), Ranker, Ranking** Arrant, Assort, Ayatollah, Barony, Begum, Brevet, Caste, Category, Cense, Class, Classify, Condition, Cornet, Curule, Degree, Dignity, Downright, Earldom, Echelon, Estate, État(s), Family, First Sea Lord, Flag, Flight sergeant, General(issimo), Grade, Graveolent, Gree, Gregarian, Gross, Hierarchy, High, Hojatoleslam, Hojatolislam, Lieutenant, Majority, Malodorous, Olid, Order, Other, Parage, Percentile, Petty Officer, Place, Profuse, Queue, Rammish, Range, Rate, Reist, Rooty, Row, Seed, Seigniorage, Sergeant, Serried, Sheer, Shoulder-strap, Sort, Stance, Stand(ing), →**STATION**, Status, Sublieutenant, Substantive, Table, Taxi, Tier, →**TITLE**, Titule, Top drawer, Utter, Viscount

**Rankle** Chafe, Fester, Gall, Grate, Irritate, Nag, Niggle
**Ransack** Fish, Loot, Pillage, Plunder, Riff, Rifle, Ripe, Rob, Rummage, Tot(ter)
**Ransom** King's, Redeem, Release, Rescue
**Rant(er), Ranting** Bluster, Bombast, Declaim, Diatribe, Fustian, Ham, Harangue, Rail, Rodomontade, Scold, Slang-whang, Sound off, Spout, Spruik, Stump, Thunder, Tirade, Tub-thump
**Rap(ped)** Blame, Censure, Chat, Chinwag, Clour, Gangsta, Halfpenny, Knock, Ratatat, Shand, Strike, Swapt, Tack, Tap
**Rapacious** Accipitrine, Esurient, Exorbitant, Greedy, Harpy, Kite, Predatory, Ravenous, Ravine
**Rape** Abuse, Assault, Belinda, Cole-seed, Colza, Creach, Creagh, Date, Deflower, Despoil, Grass(line), Hundred, Linseed, Lock, Lucretia, Navew, Oilseed, Plunder, Ravish, Statutory, Stuprate, Thack, Tow, Violate, Vitiate
**Rapid(ity), Rapidly** Celerity, Chute, Dalle, Double-quick, Express, Fast, Fleet, Meteoric, Mosso, Presto, Pronto, Quick-fire, Quicksilver, Riffle, Sault, Shoot, Skyrocket, Speedy, Staccato, Stickle, Swift, Tantivy, Veloce, Vibrato, Whiz(zing), Wildfire
**Rapier** Sword, Tuck
**Rappel** Abseil
**Rapport** Accord, Affinity, Agreement, Chemistry, Harmony
**Rapprochement** Détente, Reconciliation
**Rapscallion** Rogue
**Rapt** Engrossed, Riveted
**Raptor** Eagle, Elanet, Kestrel, Osprey, Standgale, Staniel, Stannel, Stanyel, Stooper
**Rapture, Rapturous** Bliss, → DELIGHT, Ecstasy, Elation, Euphoria, Joy, Trance
**Rare, Rarity** Blue moon, Curio, Earth, Few, Geason, Gold dust, Infrequent, Intemerate, Oddity, One-off, Promethium, Rear, Recherché, Scarce, Seeld, Seld(om), Singular, Surpassing, Thin, → UNCOMMON, Uncooked, Underdone, Unusual
**Rare earth** Lu(tetium)
**Rarefied** Thin
**Rascal(ly)** Arrant, Bad hat, Cad, Cullion, Cur, Deer, Devil, Gamin, Hallian, Hallion, Hallyon, Imp, → KNAVE, Limner, Loon, Lorel, Losel(l), Low, Lozel(l), Nointer, Rip, Rogue, Scallywag, Scamp, Scapegrace, Schelm, Skeesicks, Skellum, Skelm, Smaik, Spalpeen, Tinker, Toe-rag, Varlet, Varmint, Villain
**Rash(ness), Rasher** Acne, Ate, Bacon, Barber's, Brash, Collop, Daredevil, Eczema, Eruption, Erysipelas, Exanthem(a), Fast, Foolhardy, Gum, Harum-scarum, → HASTY, Headlong, Heat, Hives, Hotbrain, Hotspur, Ill-advised, Ill-considered, Ill-judged, Impetigo, Impetuous, Imprudent, Impulsive, Indiscreet, Lardo(o)n, Lichen, Madbrain, Madcap, Miliaria, Morphew, Nappy, Nettle, Outbreak, Overhasty, Pox, Precipitate, Purpura, Reckless, Road, Roseola, Rubella, St Anthony's fire, Sapego, Scarlatina, Serpigo, Spots, Temerity, Tetter, Thoughtless, Unadvised, Unheeding, Unthinking, Unwise, Urticaria
**Rasp(er), Rasping** File, Grate, Guttural, Odontophore, Radula, Risp, Rub, Scrape, Scroop, Xyster
**Raspberry** Berate, Black(cap), Boo, Bronx-cheer, Etaerio, Hindberry, Razz, Wineberry
**Rastafarian** Dread
**Rat(s), Ratty** Agouta, Apostate, Bandicoot, Beaver, Betray, Blackleg, Blackneb, Boodie, Brown, Bug-out, Cad, Camass, Cane, Cur, Cutting grass, Defect, Desert, Fink, Footra, Foutra, Geomyoid, Gopher, Gym, Heck, Heel, Hog, Hood, Hutia, Hydromys, Informer, Kangaroo, Malabar, Mall, Maori, Mole, Moon, Musk, Nark, Norway, Pack, Pig, Poppycock, Potoroo, Pouched, Pshaw, Pup(py), Renegade, Renegate, Rice, Rink, Rodent, Roland, Rot(ten), Sandmole, Scab, Sewer, Shirty, Skunk, Squeal, Stinker, Tell, Turncoat, Two-time, Vole, Water, Wharf, Whiskers, White, Wood
**Rat-catcher** Cat, Ichneumon, Mongoose, Pied Piper
**Rate(s), Rating** A, Able, Able-bodied, Apgar, Appraise, Appreciate, Assess, Bank, Base, Basic, Baud, Birth, Bit, Carpet, Castigate, Cess, Cetane, Chide, Classify, Click, Conception, Conversion, Cost, Count, Credit, Death, Deserve, Discount, Dress down, Effective, ELO, Erk, Esteem, Estimate, Evaluate, Exchange, Exempt, Going, Grade, Headline, Hearty,

Horsepower, Hurdle, Incidence, Interest, ISO, Knot, Lapse, Leading, Lick, Mate's, Merit, Michelin, Minimum lending, Mortality, Mortgage, MPH, Mutation, Octane, Ordinary, OS, Pace, Penalty, Percentage, PG, Piece, Poor, Prime (lending), Rag, Rank, Rebuke, Red, Refresh, Reproof, Rocket, Row, Sailor, Scold, Sea-dog, Seed, → **SET**, Slew, → **SPEED**, Stand, Standing, Starting, Steerageway, Surtax, Take-up, TAM, Tariff, Tax, Tempo, Tick off, Tog, U, Upbraid, Value, Water, Wig, World-scale, X, Zero

**Rather** Affirmative, Agreed, Assez, Degree, Fairly, Gay, Gey, Indeed, Instead, Kinda, Lief, Liever, Loor, More, Not half, Prefer, Pretty, Some(what), Somedele, Sooner, Yes

**Ratify** Amen, Approve, Confirm, Homologate, Pass, Sanction, Seal, Validate

**Ratio** Advance, Albedo, Aspect, Bypass, Cash, Compound, Compression, Cosine, Distinctiveness, Duplicate, Focal, Fraction, Gear, Golden, Gyromagnetic, Inverse, Liquidity, Loss, Mark space, Mass, Neper, PE, Pi, Picture, Pogson, Poisson's, Position, Price-dividend, Price-earnings, Proportion, Protection, Quotient, Reserve, Savings, Signal-to-noise, Sin(e), Slip, Space, Tensor, Trigonometric

**Ration(s)** Allocate, Allot, Apportion, Compo, Dole, Étape, Iron, K, Quota, Restrict, Scran, Share, Short commons, Size, Stint, Whack

**Rational(ism), Rationalisation, Rationalist, Rationalize** Animal, A posteriori, Descartes, Dianoetic, Dispassionate, Free-thinker, Humanistic, Level-headed, Logical, Lucid, Matter-of-fact, Pragmatic, Reasonable, Sane, Sapient, Sensible, Sine, Sober, Sound, Tenable, Wice

**Rationale** Motive

**Rattan** Cane

**Ratten** Sabotage

**Rattle (box), Rattling, Rattle on** Alarm, Blather, Chatter, Clack, Clank, Clap, Clatter, Clitter, Conductor, Crescelle, Crotalaria, Death, Demoralise, Discombobulate, Discomfort, Discompose, Disconcert, Gas-bag, Hurtle, Jabber, Jangle, Jar, Maraca, Natter, Nonplus, Rale, Rap, Red, Reel, Rhonchus, Ruckle, Sabre, Shake, Sistrum, Sunn, Tirl, Unnerve, Upset, Vuvuzela, Yellow

**Rattlesnake** Rumba

**Rat-trap** Pedal

**Raucous** Discordant, Guttural, Hoarse, Loud, Strident

**Raunchy** Lecherous

**Ravage(d)** Depredation, Desecrate, Despoil, Havoc, Pillage, Prey, Ruin, Sack, War-torn, Waste

**Rave, Raving** Adulate, Boil, Doiled, Enthuse, Praise, Redwood, Redwud, Storm, Ta(i)ver, Tear

**Ravel** Disentangle, Entrammel, Explain, Fray, Involve, Knot, Snarl, Tangle

**Raven(ous)** Black, Corbel, Corbie, Corvine, Croaker, Daw, Grip, Hugin, Munin, Prey, Unkindness, Wolfish

**Ravine** Arroyo, Barranca, Barranco, Canada, Canyon, Chasm, Chine, Clough, Coulée, Couloir, Dip, Flume, Ghyll, Gorge, Goyle, Grike, Gulch, Gully, Kedron, Khor, Khud, Kidron, Kloof, Lin(n), Nal(l)a, Nallah, Nulla(h), Pit, Purgatory, Wadi

**Ravish(ing)** Abduct, A ravir, Constuperate, Constuprate, Debauch, Defile, Devour, Outrage, Rape, Stuprate, Transport, Violate

**Raw** Brut, Chill, Coarse, Crude, Crudy, Damp, Fresh, Green(horn), Natural, New, Recruit, Rude, Sashimi, Tartare, Uncooked, Wersh

**Raw-boned** Gaunt, Lanky, Lean, Randle-tree

**Ray(s), Rayed** Actinic, Alpha, Beam, Beta, Bivium, Canal, Cathode, Cosmic, Cramp-fish, Death, Delta, Devil, Devilfish, Diactine, Dun-cow, Eagle, Electric, Extraordinary, Fish, Gamma, Grenz, Guitarfish, Homelyn, Laser, Manta, Medullary, Monactine, Numbfish, Ordinary, Polyact, Positive, R, Radioactive, Radius, Re, Roentgen, Roker, Röntgen, Sawfish, Sea-devil, Sea-vampire, Sephen, Shaft, Skate, Starburst, Stick, Sting, Stingaree, Sunbeam, T, Tetract, Thornback, Torpedo, UV, Vascular

**Rayon** Acetate, Faille, Viscose

**Raze** Annihilate, Bulldoze, Demolish, Destroy, Level, Slight

**Razor(-maker)** Cut-throat, Occam, Remington®, Safety, Shaver, Straight

**Razorbill** Murre
**Razor-fish** Solen
**Razz** Raspberry
**RE** Sappers
**Re** About, Rhenium, Touching
**Reach(ed)** Achieve, Ar(rive), Attain, Boak, Boke, Carry, Come, Contact, Extend, Gain, Get at, Get out, Grasp, Hent, Hit, Key-bugle, Lode, Octave, Peak, Raught, Rax, Retch, Ryke, Sease, Seize, Stretch, Touch, Win
**Reach-me-downs** Slop-clothing
**React(or), Reaction(ary)** Addition, Allergy, Anaphylaxis, Answer, Backlash, Backwash, Behave, Blimp, Blowback, Boiling water, Bourbon, Breeder, Bristle, Bummer, Calendria, CANDU, Cannizzaro, Catalysis, Chain, Chemical, Converter, Convertor, Core, Counterblast, Dark, Dibasic, Diehard, Diels-Adler, Dinosaur, Double-take, Dounreay, Dyed-in-the-wool, Emotion, Endergonic, Exergonic, Exoergic, Falange, Fast(-breeder), Feedback, Fission, Flareback, Flehmen, Flinch, Friedel-Crafts, Furnace, Fusion, Gas-cooled, Graphite, Gut, Heavy-water, Hydrolysis, Imine, Incomplete, Initial, Insulin, Interplay, Inulase, Junker, Kickback, Knee-jerk, Light, Lightwater, Magnox, Molten salt, Neanderthal, Nuclear, Old Guard, Outcry, Oxidation, Pebble-bed, Photolysis, Pile, Polymerization, Poujade, Pressure-tube, Pressurized water, Reciprocate, Recoil, Redox, Reflex, Repercussion, Respond, Reversible, Rigid, Sensitive, Solvolysis, Spallation, Sprocket, Stereotaxis, Stimulus, Swing-back, Thermal, Thermonuclear, Tokamak, Topochemistry, Tut, Ultraconservative, Vaccinia, Wassermann, Water
▷**Reactionary** *may indicate* reversed or an anagram
**Read(ing)** Abomasum, Bearing, Browse, Con, Decipher, Decode, Devour, Exegesis, First, Gauge, Grind, Grounden, Haftarah, Haphtarah, Haphtorah, Interpret, Learn, Lection, Lesson, Lu, Maftir, Maw, Paired, Pericope, Peruse, Pore, Rad, Rennet-bag, Say, Scan, Second, See, Sight, Skim, Solve, Speech, Speed, Stomach, → **STUDY**, Third, Uni(versity), Vell, Version, Ycond
**Reader(s)** ABC, Academic, Alidad(e), Bookworm, Document, Editor, Epistoler, Gauge, Gentle, Homeridae, Lay, Lector, Lip, Microfilm, Palm, Phrenologist, Primer, Proof, Silas Wegg, Softa, Tape, Taster
**Readiest, Readily, Readiness, Ready** Alacrity, Alamain, Alert, Amber, Amenability, Apt, Atrip, Available, Boun, Bound, Braced, Brass, Cash, Conditional, Dosh, Dough, Eager, Early, Eftest, En garde, Fettle, Fired up, Fit, Fiver, Forward, Game, Geared-up, Gelt, Go, In the wings, Keyed, Latent, Letter perfect, Lolly, Masterman, Mature, Money, On (call), On hand, On tap, Open, Oven, Pat, Petty cash, Predy, Prepared, Present, Prest, Primed, Procinct, Prompt, Promptitude, Ransom, Reckoner, Ripe, Running costs, Set, Soon, Spot, Standby, Tenner, To hand, Turnkey, Unhesitant, Usable, Wherewithal, Willing, Yare, Yark
**Readjust** Mend, Regulate, Retrue
**Readymade** Bought, Fetch-me-down, Precast, Prepared, Prêt-à-porter, Slops, Stock, Store
**Reagent** Analytical, Benedict's, Grignard, Ninhydrin, Reactor, Schiff's, Titrant, Tollens
**Real, Reality, Realities, Really** Actual, Ah, Augmented, Bona-fide, Brass tacks, Coin, Deed, De facto, Dinkum, Dinky-di(e), Earnest, Echt, Ens, Entia, Entity, Essence, Ever so, Fact(ion), → **GENUINE**, Hard, Honest (to God), Indeed, Mackay, McCoy, McKoy, Naive, Ontic, Positive, Quite, Royal, Simon Pure, Sooth, Sterling, Straight up, Substantial, Tangible, Tennis, The case, Thing(li)ness, True, Verismo, Verity, Very, Virtual
**Realgar** Rosaker, Zarnec, Zarnich
**Realise, Realisation, Realism, Realist(ic)** Achieve, Attain, Attuite, Cash (in), Cinéma vérité, Dirty, Discern, Down-to-earth, Embody, Encash, Entelechy, Fetch, Fruition, Fulfil, Gritty, Hard-edged, Hard-headed, Learn, Lifelike, Magic, Naive, Naturalism, Plato, Practical, Pragmatism, See, Sell, Sense, Social, Socialist, Suss, Understand, Verisimilitude, Verismo, Verité
▶**Realities, Reality** *see* **REAL**
**Realm** Domain, Dominion, Duchy, Field, Kingdom, Land, Notogaea, Region, Special(i)ty, UK
**Realtor** Estate agent
**Ream** Bore, Foam, Froth, Paper, Printer's, Rime, Screed

**Reap(er)** Binder, Crop, Death, Earn, Gather, Glean, Harvest, Scythe, Shear, Sickleman, Solitary, Stibbler

**Reappear(ance)** Atavism, Emersion, Materialise, Recrudesce

**Rear(ing)** Aft, Back(side), Background, Baft, Behind, Bottom, Breeches, Bring-up, Bunt, Butt, Cabré, Catastrophe, Derrière, Empennage, Estrapade, Foster, Haunch, Hind, Hindquarters, Loo, Natch, Nousell, Nurture, Podex, Poop, Prat(t), → RAISE, Rampant, Retral, Rump, Serafile, Serrefile, Stern, Sternward, Tail end, Tonneau, Train

**Rearmament** Moral

**Rearrange(ment)** Adjust, Anagram, Ectopia, Permute, Reorder, Shuffle

**Reason(able), Reasoning** A fortiori, Agenda, Analytical, Apagoge, A priori, Argue, Argument, Basis, Call, Casuistry, Casus belli, Cause, Colour, Consideration, Decent, Deduce, Economical, Expostulate, Fair (do's), Ground(s), Hypophora, Ijtihad, Inductive, Inference, Intellect, Intelligent, Ipso facto, Justification, Logic, Logical, Logistics, Logos, Metamathematics, Mind, Moderate, Motive, Noesis, Petitio principii, Plausible, Point, Practical, Pretext, Pro, Proof, Proportionate, Pure, Purpose, Ratiocinate, Rational(e), Sake, Sane, Sanity, Sense, Sensible, Settler, Somewhy, Sophism, Syllogism, Synthesis, Temperate, Think, Viable, What for, Why, Wit

**Reassure, Reassurance** Comfort, Convince, Solace, There(-there)

**Reave** Despoil, Reif, Rob, Spoil

**Rebate** Diminish, Lessen, Refund, Repayment, Return

**Rebecca** Sharp

**Rebel(s), Rebellion, Rebellious** Aginner, Anarchist, Apostate, Arian, Beatnik, Blouson noir, Bolshy, Bounty, Boxer, Cade, Contra, Croppy, Danton, Defiance, Diehard, Disobedient, Dissident, Drop out, Easter, Emeute, Fifteen, Forty-five, Frondeur, Glendower, Green Mountain Boys, Hampden, Heretic, Hereward the Wake, Hippy, Iconoclast, Insubordinate, Insurgent, Insurrection, IRA, Jacobite, Jacquerie, Kick, Luddite, Maccabee, Malignant, Mutine(er), Mutiny, Oates, Pilgrimage of Grace, Putsch, Rebecca, Recalcitrant, Recusant, Reluct, Renegade, Resist, → REVOLT, Revolutionary, Rise, Rum, Scofflaw, Sedition, Sepoy, Spartacus, Steelboy, Straw, Taiping, Ted, Titanism, Tyler, UDI, Unruly, Venner, Warbeck, Wat Tyler, Whiteboy, Young buck, Young Turk, Zealot

▷**Rebellious** *may indicate* a word reversed

**Rebirth** Palingenesis, Reincarnation, Renaissance, Revival, Samsara

**Rebound** Backfire, Bounce, Cannon, Carom, Echo, Elastic, Recoil, Repercussion, Ricochet, Snapback

**Rebuff** Censure, Check, Cold-shoulder, Earwig, Noser, Quelch, Repulse, Retort, Rubber, Setdown, Slight, Sneb, Snib, Snub

**Rebuild** Haussmannize

**Rebuke** Admonish, Berate, Check, Chide, Diatribe, Earful, Lecture, Neb, Objurgate, Rap, Rate, Razz, Reprimand, Reproof, Reprove, Rollick, Scold, Score, Slap, Slate, Snib, Snub, Strop, Threap, Threep, Tick off, Trim, Tut, Upbraid, Wig

**Rebut** Disprove, Elide, Refute, Repulse, Retreat

**Rebuttal** Counter-claim, Denial

**Recalcitrant** Mulish, Obstinate, Renitent, Unruly, Wilful

**Recall(ing)** Annul, Echo, Eidetic, Encore, Evocative, Flashback, Go over, Memory, Partial, Reclaim, Recollect, Redolent, Remember, Remind, Reminisce, Repeal, Retrace, Revoke, Total, Unsay, Withdraw

**Recant(ation)** Disclaim, Palinode, Retract, Revoke

**Recap(itulate), Recapitulation** Epanodos, Palingenesis, Summarise

**Recapture** Rescue

▷**Recast** *may indicate* an anagram

**Recasting** Rifacimento

▶**Recce** *see* RECONNAISSANCE

**Recede, Receding** Decline, Ebb, Hairline, Lessen, Regress, Retrograde, Shrink, Withdraw

**Receipt(s)** Acknowledge, Chit, Docket, Dock-warrant, Gate, Profit, Quittance, Recipe, Revenue, Take, Ticket, Voucher

**Receive(d), Receiver** Accept, Accoil, Acquire, Admit, Aerial, Antenna, Assignee, Bailee, Bleeper, Cop, Dipole, Dish, Donee, Ear, Earphone, Earpiece, Fence, Get, Grantee, Greet, Harmonic, Headset, Hydrophone, Inherit, Intercom, Official, Pernancy, Phone, Pocket, Radio, Radiopager, Remit, Reset, Responser, Responsor, Roger, Set, Socket, Sounder, Take, Tap, Transistor, Transponder, Tuner, Wide, Wireless

**Recent(ly)** Alate, Current, Fresh, Hot, Just, Late, Low, Modern, New, New-found, Of late, Yesterday, Yestereve, Yesterweek

**Receptacle** Ash-tray, Basket, Bin, Bowl, Box, Catch-all, Chrismatory, Ciborium, Container, Cyst, Dustpan, Hell-box, Hypanthium, Locket, Loom, Monstrance, Muffle, Ossuary, Outtray, Portfolio, Receiver, Reliquary, Relique, Reservatory, Sacculus, Skip, Spermatheca, Spittoon, Tank, Thalamus, Tidy, Tore, Torus, Trash can

**Reception, Receptionist, Receptive** Acceptance, Accoil, Antechamber, At home, Bel-accoyle, Couchée, Court, Durbar, Entertainment, First-class, Foyer, Ghost, Greeting, Helpdesk, Hospitable, Infare, Kursaal, Levée, Open, Ovation, Pervious, Ruelle, Saloon, Sensory, Soirée, Superheterodyne, Teleasthetic, Ticker-tape, Warm, Welcome

**Receptor(s)** Metabotropic, Steroid

**Recess(ion)** Alcove, Antrum, Apse, Apsidal, Apsis, Bay, Bole, Bower, Break, Breaktime, Bunk, Closet, Columbarium, Confessional, Corner, Corrie, Cove, Croze, Dinette, Ebb, Embrasure, Exedra, Fireplace, Grotto, Hitch, Indent, Inglenook, Interval, Loculus, Mortise, → **NICHE**, Nook, Oriel, Outshot, Pigeonhole, Rabbet, Rebate, Respite, Rest, Slump, Toehold, Withdrawal

▷**Recess** *may indicate* 'reversed'

**Rechabite** TT

**Réchauffé** Hachis, Hash, Salmi

**Recidivist** Relapser

▷**Recidivist** *may indicate* 'reversed'

**Recipe** Dish, Formula, Plan, Prescription, R, Receipt, Take

**Recipient** Allottee, Assignee, Beneficiary, Disponee, Donee, End user, Grantee, Heir, Legatee, Receiver, Suscipient

**Reciprocal, Reciprocation, Reciprocate** Corresponding, Counter charge, Elastance, Even the score, Exchange, Inter(act), Mutual, Repay, Return, Two-way

**Recite(r), Recital, Recitation(ist)** Ave, Chant, Concert, Declaim, Diseuse, Enumerate, Incantation, Intone, Litany, Monologue, Mystic, Parlando, Quote, Reading, Reel, Relate, Rendition, Rhapsode, Say, Sing, Tell

**Reckless(ness)** Adventuresome, Bayard, Blindfold, Careless, Catiline, Chicken, Daredevil, Desperado, Desperate, Devil-may-care, Foolhardy, Gadarene, Harum-scarum, Hasty, Headfirst, Headlong, Hell-bent, Improvident, Indiscreet, Irresponsible, Jaywalker, Madcap, Perdu(e), Ramstam, Rantipole, → **RASH**, Slapdash, Tearaway, Temerarious, Temerity, Ton-up, Wanton, Wildcat

▷**Reckless** *may indicate* an anagram

**Reckon(ed), Reckoner, Reckoning** Abacus, Assess, Bet, Calculate, Cast, Census, Computer, Consider, Count, Date, Dead, Deem, Doomsday, Estimate, Exclusive, Fancy, Figure, Guess, Impute, Inclusive, Number, Rate, Reputed, Score, Settlement, Shot, Tab

**Reclaim(ed), Reclamation** Assart, Empolder, Impolder, Innings, Novalia, Polder, Recover, Redeem, Restore, Salvage, Swidden, Tame, Thwaite

**Recline, Reclining** Accubation, Accumbent, Lean, Lie, Lounge, Rest

**Recluse, Reclusive** Anchor(et), Anchorite, Ancress, Eremite, Essene, Hermit, Lone wolf, Low-profile, Monastical, Solitaire

**Recognise(d), Recognisable, Recognition** Accept, Accredit, Acknow(ledge), Admit, Anagnorisis, Appreciate, Apprehend, Ascetic, Character, Cit(ation), Count, Credit, Discern, Exequatur, Formal, Gaydar, Iconic, Identify, Isolated, Ken, → **KNOW**, Kudos, Nod, Notice, Oust, Own, Perception, Resipiscence, Reward, Salute, Scent, Sense, Standard, Sung, Voice, Wate, Weet, Wit, Wot

**Recoil** Backlash, Boomerang, Bounce, Cower, Cringe, Flinch, Kick(back), Quail, Rebound, Redound, Repercussion, Resile, Reverberate, Shrink, Shy, Spring, Start, Whiplash

**Recollect(ion)** Anamnesis, Memory, Pelmanism, Recall, → **REMEMBER**, Reminisce, Retrospect

▷**Recollection** *may indicate* an anagram

**Recommend(ation)** Advise, Advocate, Counsel, Direct, Encourage, Endorse, Exhort, Move, Nap, Plug, Praise, Precatory, Promote, Rider, Suggest, Testimonial, Tip, Tout, Urge

**Recompense** Cognisance, Deodand, Deserts, Eric, Expiate, Fee, Guerdon, Pay, Remunerate, Repayment, Requite, Restitution, Reward

**Reconcile(d), Reconciler, Reconciliation** Accord, Adapt, Adjust, Affrended, Atone, Bridge builder, Harmonise, Henotic, Make up, Mend, Resigned, Square, Syncretism

**Recondite** Difficult, Esoteric, Mystic, Obscure, Occult, Profound

**Recondition** Facelift

**Reconnaissance, Reconnoitre** Case, Investigate, Patrol, Recce, Scout, Survey

**Reconstitute, Reconstitution** Diagenesis

**Reconstruction** Dramatisation, Perestroika, Telophase

**Record(er), Recorded, Recording (company)** Acta, All-time, Ansafone®, Answerphone, Blu-ray®, Book, Camera, Cardiogram, Cassette, Chart, Chronicle, Clock, Coat(e), Counterfoil, Descant, Diarist, Echocardiogram, Enrol, Enter, Entry, Ever, Fact, File, Flipside, Gold, Hard copy, Hi-fi, Imager, Itemise, Log, Mark, Memorise, Mind, Notate, Note, Pedometer, Previous, Quote, Release, Remember, Remix, Seismograph, Set down, Snapshot, Somerset House, Sunshine, Take, Tally, Tallyman, Trace, Trip, Vinyl, Vote, VTR, Weigh, Write

---

## RECORDS

***2 letters:***
CD
EP
LP

***3 letters:***
Can
Cut
EMI
Rec
Vid
Wax

***4 letters:***
Disc
Film
Form
Gram
List
Memo
Mono
Roll
Tape
TiVo®
VERA
Wire

***5 letters:***
Album
Ampex
Annal
A-side
Aulos
B-side
Crash
Decca®
Diary
Eloge
Elpee
Fiche
Flute
Indie
Meter
Notch
Promo
Quipo
Quipu
Score
Track
Video

***6 letters:***
Flight
Ledger
Memoir
Minute
Public
Regest
Single
Wisden

***7 letters:***
Account
Acetate
Archive
Daybook
Digital
Dossier
Epistle
Estreat
Filater
Hansard
History
Journal
Logbook
Memento
Platter
Podcast
Practic
Shellac

***8 letters:***
Analogue
Annalist
Black box
Bookmark
Casebook
Demo-tape
Document
Herstory
Hologram
Lap-chart
Marigram
Memorial
Miniment
Noctuary
Odometer
Open-seel
Pass book
Playback
Practick
Pratique
Pressing
Protocol
Rapsheet
Register
Studbook
Travelog

***9 letters:***
Archivist
Audiotape
Bench-mark
Cartulary
Ephemeris
Forty-five
Score card
Seven-inch
Spirogram
Statement
Stenotype®
Tachogram
Time sheet
Videogram
Videotape
Worksheet

***10 letters:***
Audit trail
Blue Riband
Bookmarker
Dictaphone®
Dictograph®
Gramophone
Maxi-single
Memorandum
Provenance
Quadruplex
Reel-to-reel
Scoreboard

Spectogram
Tachograph
Transcript
Twelve-inch

*11 letters:*
Cardiograph
Case history
Clickstream
Clog-almanac
Electrogram
Endorsement
Helical scan
Hill and dale
Incremental
Oscillogram
Sphygmogram
Thirty-three

*12 letters:*
English flute
Hierogrammat
Remembrancer
Seventy-eight

*13 letters:*
Congressional
Ghetto blaster
Quadrophonics

*14 letters:*
Campbell-Stokes

---

**Record-holder** Champion, Sleeve
**Record-player** DJ, Stereo
**Recount** Describe, Enumerate, →NARRATE, Relate, Tell
**Recoup** Claim, Clawback, Reimburse
**Recourse** Access, Resort
**Recover(y), Recovered** Amend, Better, Bounce back, Catch up, Clawback, Comeback, Common, Convalescence, Cure, Dead cat bounce, Get over, Green shoots, Heal, Lysis, Over, Perk (up), Pull round, Pull through, Rally, Rebound, Recapture, Reclaim, Recoup, Recuperation, Redeem, Regain, Rehab, Repaint, Replevin, Replevy, Repo(ssess), Rescript, Rescue, Resile, Resume, →RETRIEVE, Revanche, Salvage, Salve, Second-wind, Spontaneous, Upswing, Upturn
**Recreant** Apostate
**Recreate, Recreation** Diversion, Hobby, Palingenesia, Pastance, Pastime, Play, Pleasure, R&R, Reinvent, Revive, Sport
**Recriminate, Recrimination** Ruction
**Recruit(s), Recruiter** Attestor, Bezonian, Choco, Conscript, Crimp, Draft, Employ, Engage, Enlist, Enrol, Headhunt, Hire, Intake, Muster, Neophyte, New blood, Novitiate, Nozzer, Press, Rookie, Sprog, Talent scout, Tenderfoot, Volunteer, Wart, Yardbird, Yobbo
**Rectangle, Rectangular** Dimetric, Golden, Matrix, Oblong, Quad, Quadrate, Square
**Rectifier, Rectify** Adjust, Amend, Dephlegmate, Redress, Regulate, →REMEDY, Repair, Right, Silicon
**Rectitude** Probity
**Recto** Ro
**Rector** R
**Rectum** Tewel
**Recumbent** Prone
**Recuperate** Convalesce, Rally, Recover
**Recur(rent), Recurrence, Recurring** Chronic, Ergodic, Flashback, Periodic, Quartan, Quintan, Recrudesce, Repeated, Repetend, Return, Theme
▹**Recurrent** *may indicate* 'reversed'
**Recycle(r), Recycling** Blue box, Freecycle, Freegan, Nephron, Pulp
**Red(den), Redness** Admiral, Alizarin, Anarch(ist), Angry, Archil, Arun, Ashamed, Auburn, Bashful, Beet, Bilirubin, Blood, Bloodshot, Blush, Bolshevik, Brick, Burgundy, C, Cain-coloured, Cardinal, Carmine, Carrot-top, Carroty, Castory, Cent, Cerise, Cherry, Chianti, Chica, Chinese, Choy-root, Chrome, Cinnabar, Claret, Coccineous, Commie, Commo, Communist, Congo, Copper, Coquelicot, Coral, Corallin(e), Corkir, Cramesy, Cremosin, Crimson, Crocoite, Cuprite, Cyanin, Damask, Debit, Deficit, Dubonnet, Duster, Embarrassed, Eosin, Eric, Erik, Erythema, Ffion, Flame, Flaming, Florid, Flush, Foxy, Garnet, Geranium, Ginger, Gory, Grog-blossom, Gule(s), Guly, Hat, Henna, Herring, Incarnadine, Indian, Indigo, Inflamed, Infra, Inner, Intertrigo, Iron, Jacqueminot, Judas-coloured, Keel, Kermes, Korkir, Lac-lake, Lake, Lateritious, Left(y), Lenin, Letter, Magenta, Maoist, Maroon, Marxist, McIntosh, Medoc, Menshevik, Miniate, Minium, Modena, Mulberry, Murrey, Neaten, Orchel, Orchilla-weed, Orseille, Overdraft, Oxblood, Phenol, Pillar-box, Pinko, Plethoric, Plum, Pompeian, Ponceau, Poppy, Pyrrhous, Raddle, Radical, Raspberry, Raw, Realgar, Rhodamine, Rhodopsin, Ridinghood, Roan, Rosaker, Rose, Rot, Rouge, Roy, Rubefaction, Rubefy, Rubella, Rubescent, Rubicund, Rubric, Ruby, Ruddle, Ruddy, Rufescent, Rufus, Russ(e),

Russet, Russian, Russky, Rust(y), Rutilant, Safranin(e), Sang-de-boeuf, Sanguine, Santalin, Sard, Scarlet, Sea, Sericon, Setter, Shame-faced, Solferino, Stammel, Suffuse, Tape, Tidy, Tile, Titian, Trot, Trotsky, Turacin, Turkey, Tyrian, Venetian, Vermeil, Vermilion, Vermily, Vinaceous, Wallflower, Wax, Wine, Zincite

▷**Red** *may indicate* an anagram

**Redact** Censor

**Redcoat** Rust, Soldier

**Redeem(er), Redemption(ist)** Cross, Liberate, Liguorian, Lowse, Mathurin, Messiah, Ransom, Retrieve, Salvation, Save

**Red-faced** Coaita, Florid, Flushed, Rubicund

**Red-handed** Bang to rights

**Redhead** Auburn, Bashful, Blue(y), Carrot-top, Carroty, Commie, Commissar, Ginger, Mao, Medoc, Rufus, Safranin(e), Sea

**Red herring** Norfolk capon, Soldier

▸**Red Indian** *see* NORTH AMERICAN (INDIAN)

**Redirect, Redirection** Pharming, Reset, Sublimate

▷**Rediscovered** *may indicate* an anagram

**Redistil** Cohobate

**Redneck** Hillbilly

**Redolent** Aromatic, Fragrant, Reeking, Suggestive

**Redoubtable** Stalwart

**Redress** Amends, Offset, Recompense, Rectify, Regrate, Remedy, Right

**Redrutherite** Copper-glance

**Redshank** Gambet, Totanus

**Red spot** Tika

**Reduce(d), Reducer, Reduction** Abatement, Allay, Alleviate, Amortize, Asyndeton, Attenuate, Bate, Beggar, Beneficiate, Calcine, Cheapen, Clip, Commutation, Commute, Concession, Condense, Contract, Cull, Curtail, Curtate, Cut, Cutback, Damping, Debase, Decimate, Decrease, Decrement, De-escalate, Degrade, Demote, Deoxidate, Deplete, Depreciation, Detract, Devalue, Dil(ute), Diminish, Diminuendo, Discount, Downgrade, Downscale, Downsize, Draw-down, Drop, Emasculate, Epitomise, Foreshorten, Grate, Grind, Half-price, Hatchet job, Jeff, Kinone, → LESSEN, Lite, Markdown, Miniature, Minimise, Mitigate, Model, Moderate, Offset, Palliate, Pot, Proclitic, Pulp, Pulverise, Put, Quinol, Rarefaction, Razee, Regression, Relegate, Remission, Retrench, Rundown, Scale down, Scant, Shade, Shorten, Shrinkage, Slash, Strain, Streamline, Supersaver, Taper, Telescope, Thicken, Thin, Water down, Weaken, Whittle, Write-off

**Redundancy, Redundant** FIFO, Frill, Futile, Lay-off, Needless, Obsolete, Otiose, Pink slip, Pleonasm, Retrenchment, Superfluous, Surplus

**Redwood** Amboyna, Mahogany, Sanders, Wellingtonia

**Reed** Arundinaceous, Broken, Calamus, Double, Free, Oboe, Osier, Papyrus, Pipe, Quill, Raupo, Rush, Sedge, Seg, Sley, Spear, Sudd, Syrinx, Thatch, Twill, Whistle

**Reef** Atoll, Barrier, Bioherm, Bombora, Bommie, Cay, Coral, Fringing, Great Barrier, Key, Knot, Lido, Motu, Saddle, Sca(u)r, Skerry, Witwatersrand

**Reefer** Cigarette, Grass, Jacket, Joint

**Reek** Emit, Exude, Stench, Stink

**Reel** Bobbin, Dance, Drum, Eightsome, Hoolachan, Hoolican, Inertia, Log, Lurch, Multiplier, News, Pirn, Spin, Spool, Stagger, Strathspey, Sway, Swift, Swim, Teeter, Tirl, Totter, Tulloch, Virginia, Wheel, Whirl, Wince, Wintle

**Re-enlist** Re-up

**Reestablish** Redintegrate, Transplant

**Reeve** Hen

**Refectory** Frater

**Refer** Advert, Allude, Assign, Cite, Direct, Mention, Pertain, Relate, Remit, Renvoi, Renvoy, See, Submit, Touch, Trade

**Referee** Arbiter, Commissaire, Linesman, Mediate, Oddsman, Official, Ref, Umpire, Voucher, Whistler, Zebra

**Reference(s), Reference room** Allusion, Almanac, Apropos, Autocue®, Benchmark, Biaxal, Chapter and verse, Character, Coat, Credentials, Criteria, Cross, Directory, Grid, Guidebook, Index, Innuendo, Lexicon, Mention, Morgue, Passion, Promptuary, Quote, Regard, Renvoi, Respect, Retrospect, Testimonial, Thesaurus, Thumb index, Vide, Who's Who, Yearbook

**Reference mark** Asterisk, Dagger, Double-dagger

**Referendum** Ballot, Mandate, Plebiscite, Vox populi

**Refill** Replenish, Top up

**Refine(d), Refinement, Refiner(y)** Alembicated, Attic, Bleeding, Catcracker, Civilise, Clean, Couth, Cultivate, Culture, Cupellation, Cut-glass, Dainty, Distil, Distinction, Elaborate, Elegance, Ethereal, Exility, Exquisite, Filter, Genteel, Grace, Horsy, Ladify, Nice, Nicety, Polish(ed), Polite, Précieuse, Preciosity, Process, Pure, Rare(fy), Recherché, Saltern, Sieve, Sift, Smelt, Sophisticated, Spiritualize, Spirituel, Style, Sublimate, Subtilise, Subtlety, Tasteful, Try, U, Urbane, Veneer

**Reflect(ing), Reflection, Reflective, Reflector** Albedo, Apotheosis, Aspersion, Blame, Catoptric, Cat's eye®, Chaff, Chew, Cogitate, →CONSIDER, Echo, Glass, Glint, Glisten, Image, Introspection, Luminous, Meditate, Mirror, Muse, Narcissus, Nonspecular, Ponder, Redound, Repercuss, Reverberate, Ricochet, Ruminate, Spectacular, Speculate, Speculum, Symmetrical, Tapetum, Thought

**Reflex(ive)** Achilles, Babinski, Bent, Cancrizans, Conditioned, Diving, In, Involuntary, Knee-jerk, Patellar, Pavlovian, Reciprocal, Re-entrant, Single-lens, Tic, Twin-lens

**Reflux** Acid

**Reform(er), Reformed, Reforming, Reformist** AA, Agrarian, Amend, Apostle, Besant, Better, Beveridge, Bloomer, Calvin, Chartism, Chastise, Convert, Correct, Counter-Reformation, Enrage, Fourier, Fry, Gandhi, Glassite, Gradualism, Howard, Hus, Hussite, Improve, Knox, Lafayette, Land, Lollard, Luther, Meiji, Melanchthon, Mend, Modify, Mucker, New Deal, Owenite, Penn, Perestroika, Pestalozzi, Pietism, PR, Progressionist, Protestant, Proudhon, Puritan, Rad(ical), Really, Recast, Reclaim, Reconstruction, Rectify, Regenerate, Resipiscence, Restyle, Ruskin, Satyagraha, Savonarola, Simons, Stanton, Syncretise, Tariff, Taskmaster, Transmute, Tyndale, Whig, Wilberforce, Wilkes, Worms, Wycliffe, Young Turk, Zinzendorf, Zwingli

▷**Reform(ed)** *may indicate* an anagram

**Reformation** Palingenesis

**Reformatory** Borstal, Magdalen(e), Penitentiary

**Refract(ion), Refractive, Refractor(y)** Anaclastic, Double, Firestone, Obstinate, Perverse, Prism, Recalcitrant, Refringe, Restive, Stubborn, Sullen, Wayward

**Refrain** Abstain, Alay, Avoid, Bob, Burden, Chant, Chorus, Desist, Ditty, Epistrophe, Faburden, Fading, Fa-la, Forbear, Forsake, Haunting, Hemistich, Leave, Mantra, O(v)erword, Owreword, Repetend, Resist, Ritornello, Roundel, Rumbelow, Rum(p)ti-iddity, Rum-ti-tum, Spare, Tag, Tirra-lirra, Tirra-lyra, Tra-la, Turn again, Undersong, Waive, Wheel

**Refresh(ment), Refresher, Refreshing** Air, Bait, Be(a)vers, Buffet, Cheer, Coffee, Elevenses, Enliven, Exhilarate, Food, Four-hours, Milk shake, Nap, New, Nourishment, Purvey, Refection, Reflect, Refocillate, Reinvigorate, Renew, Repast, Restore, Revive, Seltzer, Shire, Slake, Sorbet, Tea, Tonic, Update, Water

**Refrigerator** Chill, Chiller, Cold store, Cooler, Deep freeze, Esky®, Freezer, Freon, Fridge, Ice-box, Minibar, Reefer

**Refuel(ling)** Pit stop

**Refuge** Abri, Adytum, Ark, Asylum, Bolthole, Bothie, Bothy, Burrow, Caravanserai, Dive, Fastness, Foxhole, Funkhole, Girth, Grith, Harbour, Haven, Hideaway, Hole, Holt, Home, Hospice, Oasis, Port, Reefer, Resort, Retreat, Sanctuary, Sheet-anchor, →SHELTER, Soil, Stronghold, Women's

**Refugee(s)** Boat people, DP, Economic, Escapist, Evacuee, Fugitive, Grenzganger, Huguenot, Reffo

**Refund** Clawback, Rebate, Reimburse, Repayment, Restore, Surcharge

**Refurbish** New, Refit, Renew, Renovate

▷**Refurbished** *may indicate* an anagram

**Refusal, Refuse** Attle, Bagasse, Ba(u)lk, Bilge, Bin, Black, Blackball, Boycott, Bran, Brash, Breeze, Brock, Bull, Bunkum, Cane-trash, Chaff, Cinder, Clap-trap, Contumacy, Crane, Crap, Cul(t)ch, Debris, Decline, Denay, Defy, Deny, Disallow, Discountenance, Disown, Draff, Drivel, Dross, Dump, Dunder, Dung, Eighty-six, Fag-end, Fenks, Fiddlesticks, Finks, First, Flat, Flock, Frass, Garbage, Gob, Guff, Hards, Hogwash, Hold-out, Hurds, Husk, Interdict, Jib, Junk, Knickknackery, Knub, Landfill, Lay-stall, Leavings, Litter, Lumber, Mahmal, Marc, Megass(e), Midden, Mother, Mullock, Mush, Nay(-say), Nill, No (dice), No(t)chel, Nope, Noser, Nould(e), Nub, Offal, Off-scum, Orts, Passup, Pellet, Pigswill, Pigwash, Potale, Punk, Radwaste, Raffle, Rags, Rape(cake), Rat(s), Rebuff, Recrement, Recusance, Red(d), Redargue, Redline, Reest, Regret, Reject, Reneg(u)e, Renig, Repudiate, Resist, Rot, Roughage, → **RUBBISH**, Ruderal, Scaff, Scrap, Scree, Screenings, Scum, Sewage, Sewerage, Shant, Shell heap, Slag, Sordes, Spurn, Sullage, Sweepings, Swill, Tailings, Tinpot, Tip, Toom, Tosh, Trade, Trash, Tripe, Trock, Troke, Trumpery, Turndown, Twaddle, Unsay, Utter, Wash, Waste, Waste paper, Wastrel

▷**Re-fused** *may indicate* an anagram

**Refutation, Refute** Deny, Disprove, Elench(us), Rebut, Rebuttal, Redargue, Refel

**Regain** Recoup, Recover, Retrieve, Revanche

**Regal** Maeve, Majestic, Organ

▶**Regal** *see* **ROYAL(TY)**

**Regalia** → **CIGAR**, Crown jewels, Livery, Mound, Orb, Sceptre

**Regard(ing)** Admire, Anent, Apropos, As to, Attention, Care, Consider, Deem, → **ESTEEM**, Eye, Gaum, Look, Observe, Odour, Pace, Rate, Re, Repute, Respect, Revere, Sake, See, Steem, Value, Vis-à-vis

**Regardless** Anyway, Despite, Heedless, In any event, Irrespective, No matter, Notwithstanding, Rash, Though, Uncaring, Unmindful, Willy-nilly

**Regatta** Cowes, Head of the river, Henley

**Regenerate** Restore

**Regent** Interrex, Ruler, Viceroy

**Regent's Park** Zoo

**Reggae** Ska

**Regicide** Ireton, Macbeth

**Regime(n)** Administration, Control, Diet(etics), Method, Nanny state, Raj, Regency, Reich, Tyrannis

**Regiment** Black Watch, Buffs, Colour(s), Discipline, Foot, Greys, Ironsides, Life Guards, Marching, Monstrous, Nutcrackers, Organise, RA, RE, REME, Rifle, Royals, → **SAS**, Scots Greys, Tercio, Tertia

▷**Regiment** *may indicate* an anagram

**Region(s), Regional** → **AREA**, Belt, Canton, Central, Climate, Climature, Clime, Critical, District, Doldrums, Domain, Enclave, End, Endemic, Locality, Offing, Part, Province, Quart(er), Realm, Sector, Side, Sunbelt, Territory, Tract, Variable, Zone

---

**REGIONS**

*1 letter:*
D
E
F

*4 letters:*
Aceh
Ards
Asir
Brie
Midi
Nejd
Oudh
Vaud

*5 letters:*
Attic
Bundu
Caria
Dacia
Ionia
Lazio
Loire
Lycia
Lydia
Macao
Mysia
Negeb
Negev
Nubia
Opher
Sahel
Segou
Sumer
Tagma
Thule
Tibet
Tigré
Troas
Weald

*6 letters:*
Alsace
Amhara
Aoulia
Canaan
Epirus
Guiana
Mallee
Mascon
Mercia
Molise
Murcia
Ogaden
Persis
Punjab
Savoie
Saxony
Sparta
Thrace
Tigray
Tundra
Umbria
Ungava
Valois
Veneto

*7 letters:*
Abruzzi
Algarve
Alsatia

Bavaria
Bohemia
Borders
Cariboo
Chaldea
Chiasma
Cilicia
Elysium
Etruria
Hundred
Illyria
Kashmir
Katanga
Lapland
Lothian
Lusatia
Maghreb
Masuria
Moravia
Navarre
Neogaea
Oceania
Ossetia
Pargana
Riviera
Scythia
Siberia
Silesia
Tayside
Teeside
Tuscany

***8 letters:***
Anatolia
Asturias
Auvergne
Balearic
Brittany
Calabria
Camargue
Carnatic
Carniola
Caucasia
Chaldaea
Dust bowl
Ethiopia
Flanders
Hebrides
La Mancha
Lombardy
Lorraine
Nearctic
Niflheim
Normandy
Nuristan
Oriental
Pannonia
Piedmont
Provence
Refugium
Ruthenia
Sarmatia
Slavonia
Sogdiana
Stannery
Subtopia
Taymiria
Teesside
Thessaly
Walachia
Zululand

***9 letters:***
Andalusia
Aquitaine
Arctogaea
Bantustan
Caithness
Caledonia
Cantabria
Catalonia
Circassia
Cleveland
Ecosphere
Holarctic
Lusitania
Macedonia
Manchuria
Molossian
Mordvinia
New Quebec
Palestine
Patagonia
Pergunnah
Provencal
Rhineland
Turkestan
Turkistan
Val d'Aosta
Vojvodina

***10 letters:***
Appalachia
Bessarabia
Cappadocia
Constantia
Hinterland
Ionosphere
Lacustrine
Mauretania
Micronesia
Midlothian
New Castile
Old Castile
Westphalia

***11 letters:***
Austronesia
Mecklenburg
Mesopotamia
Namaqualand
Rhizosphere
Spanish Main
Strathclyde
Tetrarchate
Ultima Thule
Vuelta Abajo

***12 letters:***
Low Countries
Matabeleland
Thermosphere
The Trossachs
Transylvania

***13 letters:***
Transcaucasia

***14 letters:***
Heaviside layer
Transdniestria

***16 letters:***
Champagne-Ardenne

---

**Register(ing), Registered, Registration, Registry** Actuarial, Almanac, Annal, Cadastral, Cadastre, Calendar, Cartulary, Cash, Census, Check-in, Child abuse, Clock in, Control, Controle, Dawn, Diptych, Docket, Electoral, Enlist, Enrol, Enter, Flag out, Gross, Handicap, Index, Indicate, Inscribe, Inventory, Land, Ledger, List, Lloyd's, Log, Matricula, Menology, NAI, Net, Note, Notitia, Obituary, Parish, Park, Patent, Patent Rolls, Poll, Quotation, Read, Reception, Record, Reg(g)o, Rent-roll, Roll, Rota, Roule, Score, Shift(ing), Ship's, Sign, Sink in, Soprano, Terrier, Till, Voice

**Registrar** Actuary, Greffier, Medical, Protocolist, Recorder, Specialist, Surgical

**Regress(ion)** Backslide, Recidivism, Relapse, Revert

**Regret(ful), Regrettable** Alack, Alas, Apologise, Bemoan, Bewail, Contrite, Deplore, Deprecate, Ewhow, Forthink, Ichabod, If only, Lackaday, Lament, Mourn, Otis, Penitent, Pity, Remorse, Repentance, Repine, Resent, Rew, → RUE, Ruth, Sad, Sigh, Sore, Sorrow, Tragic

**Regular(ity), Regularly, Regulars** By turn, Clientele, Clockwork, Constant, Custom(er), Daily, Episodic, Equilateral, Even, Frequent, Giusto, Goer, Habitual, Habitude, Habitué, Hourly, Insider, Level, Methodic, Nightly, Nine-to-five, Normal, Often, Orderly, Orthodox, Patron, Peloria, Periodic, Punter, Rhythmic, Routine, Set, Smooth, Soldier, → STANDARD, Staple, Stated, Statutory, Steady, Strict, Symmetric, Uniform, Usual, Yearly

**Regulate(d), Regulation, Regulator** Adjust, Align, Appestat, Ballcock, Ballonet, Barostat, Bye-law, Code, Control, Correction, Curfew, Customary, Direct, Dispensation,

Estyn, Gibberellin, Governor, Guide, Hormone, King's, Logistics, Meter, Metrostyle, Modulate, Order, Ordinance, Pacemaker, Police, Prescriptive, Protocol, Queen's, Red tape, Rule, Snail, Square, Standard, Statute, Stickle, Stopcock, Sumptuary, Thermostat, Valve

**Regulus** Matte

**Regurgitation, Regurgitate(d)** Cud, Disgorge, Hairball, Merycism, Trophallaxis

**Rehab(ilitate), Rehabilitation** AA, Cure, Orthotics, Physio(therapy), Repone

**Rehearsal, Rehearse** Band-call, Dress, Drill, Dry-block, Dry-run, Dummy-run, Practice, Practise, Preview, Recite, Repeat, Run through, Technical, Trial, Walk through

**Reichenbach** Falls, Od

**Reign(ed)** Era, Govern, Meiji, Prevail, Raine, Rang, Realm, Restoration, Ring, → RULE, Sway

**Reimburse(ment)** Compensate, Indemnity, Recoup, Redress, Repay

**Rein(s)** Bearing, Caribou, Check, Control, Curb, Deer, Free, Gag, Harness, Leading strings, Long, Lumbar, Restrain, Ribbons, Safety, Stop, Tame, Tight, Walking

**Reincarnation** Palingenesis

**Reindeer** Blitzen, Caribou, Comet, Cupid, Dancer, Dasher, Donner, Moss, Prancer, Red-nosed, Rudolf, Tarand, Vixen

**Reinforce(ment)** Aid, Augment, Beef up, Bolster, Boost, Brace, Buttress, Cleat, Counterfort, Line, Negative, Partial, Patch, Plash, Pleach, Positive, Re-bar, Recruit, Reserve, Ripieno, Stiffen, → STRENGTHEN, Support, Tenaille, Tenaillon, Tetrapod, Underline, Welt

**Reinstate** Repone, Restore

**Reinvigorate** Recruit

**Reiterate(d), Reiteration** Battology, Ding, Emphasize, Ingeminate, Ostinato, Plug, → REPEAT

**Reject(ion), Rejected, Rejecter** Abhor, Abjure, Apostate, Athetise, Bin, Blackball, Brush off, Cast, Castaway, Cast off, Debar, Deny, Deselect, Dice, Disallow, Discard, Disclaim, Discount, Disdain, Disown, Diss, Elbow, Eliminate, Exclude, Export, Flout, Frass, Has-been, Heave-ho, Iconoclasm, Jettison, Jilt, Junk, Kest, Kill, Knock-back, No(t)chel, Ostracise, Oust, Outcast, Outtake, Overrule, Pip, Plough, Quash, Rebuff, Rebut(tal), Recuse, Refuse, Renounce, Reny, Repel, Reprobate, Repudiate, Repulse, Retree, Scout, Scrub, Spet, Spike, Spin, Spit, → SPURN, Sputum, Throw out, Thumbs-down, Trash, Turndown, Veto

**Rejoice, Rejoicing** Celebrate, Exult, Festivity, Gaude, Glory, Joy, Maffick, Sing

**Rejoin(der), Rejoined** Answer, Comeback, Counter, Relide, Reply, Response, Retort, Reunite

**Rejuvenation** Shunamitism

**Rekindle** Relume

**Relapse** Backslide, Deteriorate, Hypostrophe, Recidivism, Regress, Revert, Sink

**Relate(d), Relation(ship), Relations, Relative, Relativity** About, Account, Affair, Affine, Affinity, Agnate, Akin, Allied, Amour, Analogy, Ancestor, Antibiosis, Appertain, Apply, Apposition, Associate, At it, Blood, Blude, Bluid, Brer, Brisure, Causality, Cognate, Commensal, Commune, Community, Concern, Connection, Connexion, Consanguinity, Coosen, Cousin(-german), Coz, Dalliance, Deixis, Dependent, Diplomatic, Dispersion, Einstein, Eme, Enate, Equation, Equivalence, Exogamy, External, False, Formula, German(e), Goodfather, Granny, Guanxi, Heterogeneous, Homologous, How's your father, Impart, Inbreeding, Industrial, In-law, Internal, International, Item, Kin, Kinsman, Labour, Liaison, Link, Love-hate, Mater, Material, Matrix, Mutualism, Nan(n)a, Narrative, Naunt, Nooky, Object, One-to-one, Osculant, Pertain, Phratry, Pi, Platonic, Poor, Predation, Privity, → PROPORTION, Pro rata, Proxemics, Public, Race, Rapport, Rapprochement, Ratio, Reciprocity, Recite, Recount, Rede, Refer(ence), Relevant, Respect(s), Romance, Saga, Sib(b), Sibbe, Sibling, Sine, Special Theory, Sybbe, Symbiosis, Syntax, Tale, Tell, Tie(-in), Truck, Who

**Relating to** Of

**Relax(ation), Relaxant, Relaxed** Abate, Atony, Autogenics, Calm, Carefree, Casual, Chalone, Chill (out), Com(m)odo, Contrapposto, Dégagé, Délassement, Détente, Diversion, Downbeat, Ease, Easy-going, Flaccid, Gallamine, Icebreaker, Informal, Laid-back, Laze, Leisured, Lesh states, Let-up, Lighten, → LOOSEN, Low key, Mellow (out), Mitigate, Outspan, Peace, Recline, Relent, Relief, Remit, Rest, Settle, Sit down, Slacken, Sleep, Slump, Soma, Soothe, Toneless, Tranquil, Unbend, Unbrace, Unclench, Unknit, Unrein, Unstiffen, Untie, Unwind, Veg out, Yoga

▷**Relaxed** *may indicate* an anagram

**Relay(er)** Convey, Medley, OB, Race, Shift, Tell, Telstar, Torch-race, Webcast

▷**Relay(ing)** *may indicate* an anagram

**Release** Abreact, Abrogation, Amnesty, Announcement, Bail, Block, Cable, Catharsis, Clear, Day, Death, Deliver(y), Demob, Desorb, Disburden, Discharge, Disclose, Disengage, Disenthral, Disimprison, Dismiss, Disorb, Emancipate, Enfree, Equity, Exclaustration, Excuse, Exeem, Exeme, Exemption, Exonerate, Extricate, Exude, Free, Handout, Happy, → LIBERATE, Manumit, Merciful, Moksa, Nirvana, Outlet, Outrush, Parole, Press, Quietus, Quitclaim, Quittance, Relieve, Relinquish, Remission, Ripcord, Soft, Spring, Surrender, Time, Tre corde, Trip, Unbitt, Unchain, Unconfine, Uncouple, Undo, Unhand, Unharness, Unleash, Unlock, Unloose, Unpen, Unshackle, Unsnap, Unteam, Untether, Untie

**Relegate, Relegation** Banish, Consign, Demote, Exile, Marginalise, Renvoi, Sideline, Stellenbosch

**Relent** Bend, Mollify, Soften, Weaken, Yield

**Relentless** Cruel, Hard, Hardface, Indefatigable, Inexorable, Pitiless, Remorseless, Rigorous, Stern

**Relevance, Relevant** Ad rem, Appliable, Applicable, Apposite, Apropos, Apt, Bearing, Germane, Material, Pertinent, Point, Real world, Valid

▶**Reliable, Reliance** *see* RELY

**Relic** Antique, Ark, Artefact, Ash, Dinosaur, Fly-in-amber, Fossil, Holdover, Leftover, Memento, Mummy, Neolith, Remains, Sangraal, Sangrail, Sangreal, Souvenir, Survival, Vestige

**Relict** Survivor, Widow

**Relief, Relieve(d)** Aid, Air-lift, Allay, Allegeance, Alleviate, Alms, Anaglyph, Analgesia, Anastatic, Anodyne, Assistance, Assuage, Bas, Beet, Beste(a)d, Bete, Bold, Cameo, Catharsis, Cavo-relievo, Coelanaglyphic, Comfort, Contour, Contrast, Cure, Decongest, Détente, Ease(ment), Emboss, Emollient, Exempt, Free, Godsend, Grisaille, Help, High, Ice-breaker, Indoor, Let-up, Lighten, Linocut, Locum, Low, Lucknow, Mafeking, MIRAS, Mitigation, On the parish, Outdoor, Oxfam, Palliate, Phew, Photo, Pog(e)y, Reassure, Red Crescent, Red Cross, Redress, Refection, Remedy, Remission, Replacement, Repoussé, Reprieve, → RESCUE, Respite, Retirement, Rid, Scratch, Sigh, Soothe, Spare, Spell, Stand-in, Stiacciato, Succour, Taper, Tax, TENS, Thankful, Thermoform, Tondo, Toreutics, Wheugh, Whew, Woodcut

**Religion, Religious (sect)** Augustine, Cleric, Congregant, Creed, Cult, Denomination, Devout, Doctrine, Eremite, Faith, Godfearing, God-slot, God-squad, Hebraism, Hieratic, Hospital(l)er, Messeigneurs, Missionary, Missioner, Monastic, Monseigneur, Nun, Oblate, Opium, Opus Dei, Orthodox, Pagan, Pi, Rasti, Russellite, Sabaism, Salvo, Serious, Spiritual, State, Theology, Voodoo, Votress, Whore, Zealous

---

### RELIGIONS

***3 letters:***
MAM

***4 letters:***
Druz
Jain

***5 letters:***
Baha'i
Druse
Druze
Hasid
Islam
Jaina
Jewry
Moony
Pietà
Spike
Sunna
Wicca

***6 letters:***
Culdee
Gueber
Guebre
Hadith
Hassid
Jesuit
Khalsa
Loyola
Maoism
Sabian
Shaker
Shango
Shiism
Shinto
Taoism
The Way
Yezidi
Zabian

***7 letters:***
Aaronic
Animism
Biblist
Bogomil
Ismaili
Judaism
Lamaism
Macumba
Mahatma
Orphism
Parsism
Piarist
Sikhism
Tsabian

***8 letters:***
Buddhism
Druidism

Familist
Lutheran
Manichee
Mathurin
Mazdaism
Mazdeism
New Light
Revealed
Salesian
Santeria
Sodality
Stundism
Theatine

*9 letters:*
Arya Samaj
Candomble
Cargo cult
Celestine
Coenobite
Falun Gong
Jansenism
Mithraism
Mormonism
New Church
Pantheist
Parseeism
Postulant
Sectarian
Shamanism
Shintoism
Theravada
Utraquist
Voodooism
Zoroaster
Zwinglian

*10 letters:*
Albigenses
Brahmanism
Carthusian
Cistercian
Gilbertine
Gnosticism
Heathenism
Manicheism
Revivalism
Solifidian
Triphysite
Zend-Avesta

*11 letters:*
Camaldolite
Hare Krishna
Ignorantine
Manichaeism
Progressive
Rastafarian
Reformation
Rosicrucian
Ryobu Shinto
Sabbatarian
Scientology®
Trinitarian

*12 letters:*
Christianity
Confucianism
Zarathustric

*13 letters:*
Redemptionist
Sons of Freedom
Swedenborgian
Tractarianism

*14 letters:*
Sacramentarian

*15 letters:*
Christadelphian
Jehovah's Witness
Resurrectionist

*17 letters:*
Premonstratensian

---

**Religious book** Bible, Koran, Missal, NT, OT, Sefer, Sifrei, Tantra, Targum, T(h)orah

**Relinquish** Abdicate, Cede, Demit, Discard, Drop, Forgo, Forlend, Forsake, Remise, Render, Resign, Surrender, Waive(r), Yield

**Reliquary** Chef, Encolpion, Encolpium, Simonious, Tope

**Relish(ing)** Appetite, Aspic, Botargo, Caponata, Catsup, Chakalaka, Chow-chow, Chutney, Condiment, Embellishment, Enjoy, Flavour, Garnish, Gentleman's, Gout, Gust(o), Horseradish, Ketchup, Lap(-up), Lust, Opsonium, Palate, Pesto, Piccalilli, Pickle, Sapid, Sar, Sauce, Savour, Seasoning, Tang, Tooth, Worcester sauce, Zest

**Relocate** Transfer

**Reluctant, Reluctance** Averse, Backward, Camera-shy, Chary, Circumspect, Cockshy, Cold feet, Conchie, Grudging, Half-hearted, Hesitant, Hum, Laith, Lethargy, Loath, Loth, Nolition, Prudish, Renitent, Resistance, Shy, Under protest, Unwilling

**Rely, Reliance, Reliant, Reliable** Addiction, Authentic, Bank, Bread and butter, Brick, Confidence, Constant, Copper-bottomed, →COUNT, Credible, Dependent, Found, Honest, Hope, Inerrant, Jeeves, Leal, Lean, Loyal, Mensch, Predictable, Presume, Pukka, Rest, Roadworthy, Robin, Rock, Safe, Secure, Solid, Sound, Sponge, Stalwart, Stand-by, Staunch, Steady, Straight, Sure, Trade on, True, Trump, Trustworthy, Trusty, Unfailing, Upright

**Remain(s), Remainder, Remaining** Abide, Ash(es), Balance, Bide, Cadaver, Carcass, Clinker, Continue, Corse, Dreg(s), Dwell, Embers, Estate, Extant, Exuviae, Fag-end, Fossils, Heeltap, Kreng, Last, Late, Lave, Leavings, Left, Leftovers, Lie, Locorestive, Manet, Nose, Oddment, Orts, Other, Outstand, Persist, Relic(ts), Reliquae, →REMNANT, Residue, Rest, Ruins, Rump, Scourings, Scraps, See out, Stand, Stay, Stet, Stick, Stub, Stump, Surplus, Survive, Tag-end, Talon, Tarry, To-do, Wait, Wreck(age)

**Remark** Apercu, Aside, Aspersion, Barb, Bisecting, Bon mot, Bromide, Comment(ary), Compliment, Descry, Dig, Epigram, Generalise, Mention, Noise, →NOTE, Notice, Obiter dictum, Observe, Personal, Platitude, Pleasantry, Quip, Reason, Sally, Say, Shot, Snide, State

**Remarkable, Remarkably** A1, Amazing, A one, Arresting, Beauty, Bodacious, Come-on, Conspicuous, Dilly, Egregious, Eminent, Extraordinary, Heliozoan, Hot stuff, Lamentable, Legendary, Lulu, Mirable, Notable, Notandum, Noteworthy, Of note, Personal, Phenomenal, Rattling, →SIGNAL, Singular, Some, Striking, Tall, Unco, Uncommon, Visible

**Remedial, Remedy** Adaptogen, Aid, An mo, Antacid, Antibiotic, Antidote, Antihistamine, Antiodontalgic, Antispasmodic, Arcanum, Arnica, Azoth, Bach®, Bach Flower®, Basilicon, Bicarb, Boneset, Calomel, Catholicon, Corrective, Cortisone, →CURE, Cure-all, Decongestant,

Dinic, Drug, Elixir, Emetic, Febrifuge, Femiter, Feverfew, Fumitory, Ginseng, Hair of the dog, Heal, Hoarhound, Horehound, Ipecac, Leechdom, Medicate, Medicine, Moxa, Nosode, Nostrum, Palliative, Panacea, Panpharmacon, Paregoric, Physic, Poultice, Provisional, Rectify, Redress, Repair, Rescue®, Salutory, Salve, Simillimum, Simple, Solve, Sovereign, Specific, Sucralfate, Taraxacum, Therapeutic, Tonga, Treatment, Tutsan

**Remember(ed), Remembering, Remembrance** Bethink, Catchy, Commemorate, Con, Mem, Memorial, Memorise, Mention, Mneme, Poppy, Recall, Recollect, Remind, Reminisce, Retain, Rosemary, Souvenir

▷**Remember** *may indicate* RE-member, viz. Sapper

**Remind(er)** Aftertaste, Aide-memoire, Autocue®, Bell ringer, Bethought, Bookmark, Cue, Evocatory, Evoke, Jog, Keepsake, Mark, Memento (mori), Memo, Mnemonic, Mnemotechnic, Monition, Nudge, Phylactery, Prod, Prompt, Recap, Scar, Shades of, Souvenir, Spur, Throwback, Token, Twinge, Verbal note

**Reminiscence(s), Reminisce, Reminiscent** Ana, Evocative, Hark back, Memory, Recall, Recollect, Redolent, Remember, Retrospect

**Remiss** Careless, Derelict, Errant, Lax, Lazy, Neglectful, Negligent, Slack-handed, Tardy, Thoughtless

**Remission** Abatement, Absolution, Acceptilation, Amnesty, Indulgence, Pardon, Pause, Spontaneous

**Remit** Excuse, Forgive, Forward, Pardon, Postpone, Send

**Remnant** Butt, End, Fent, Heeltap, Leavings, Left-over, Odd-come-short, Offcut, Relic, Relict, →**REMAINDER**, Rump, Shrapnel, Shred, Stub, Sweepings, Trace, Vestige, Witness

**Remonstrate** Argue, Complain, Expostulate, Protest, Reproach, Reprove

**Remorse(ful)** Angst, Apologetic, Ayenbite, Breast-beating, Compunction, Conscience, Contrition, Guilt, Had-i-wist, Pity, →**REGRET**, Repentance, Rue, Ruing, Ruth, Shame, Sorrow, Worm

**Remote(ness)** Afield, Aloof, Aphelion, Back blocks, Backveld, Backwater, Backwood, Booai, Booay, Boohai, Boondocks, Bullamakanka, Bundu, Bush, →**DISTANT**, Extreme, Far flung, Forane, Foreign, Handset, Inapproachable, Insular, Irrelevant, Jericho, Lonely, Long(inquity), Long shot, Mystique, Nowhere, Off-the-map, Out(part), Outback, Out of the way, Reassert, Scrub, Secluded, Shut-out, Slightest, Surrealistic, Unlikely, Withdrawn, Woop Woop, Wop-wops

**Remould** Retread

**Remount(s)** Remuda

**Removal, Remove(d)** Abduct, Ablation, Abstract, Adenectomy, Airbrush, Air-dress, Airlift, Apocope, Asport, Assuage, Banish, Blot, Borrow, Circumcision, Clear, Couch, Deaccession, Deadhead, Debridement, Declassify, Deduct, Dele(te), Depilate, Depose, Deracinate, Detach, Dethrone, Detract, Dishelm, Dislodge, Disloign, Dismiss, Dispel, Displace, Dispose, Doff, Dredge, Efface, Eject, Eliminate, Eloi(g)n, Emend, Eradicate, Erase, Esloin, Esloyne, Estrange, Evacuate, Evict, Exalt, Excise, Expel, Expunge, Expurgate, Extirpate, Extract, Extradite, Extricate, Far, Fillet, Flit, Gut, Huff, Lift, Nick, Obviation, Ouster, Purge, Raise, Raze, Razee, Recuse, Redline, Remble, Rid(dance), Scratch, Sequester, Shift, Sideline, Spirit, Strip, Sublate, Subtract, Supplant, Swipe, Transfer, Transport, Unbelt, Uninstall, Unload, Unperson, Unseat, Unstep, Uproot, Withdraw, Wrest

**Remuneration, Remunerate** Pay, Return, Reward, Salary, Solde, Stipend, Wage

**Remus** Uncle

**Renaissance** Awakening, Cinquecento, Early, Erasmus, High, Quattrocento, Revival, Risorgimento

**Rend** Cleave, Harrow, Lacerate, Rip, Rive, Rupture, Split, Tear

**Render(ing)** Construe, Deliver, Do, Gie, Give, Interpretation, Make, Melt, Necessitate, Pebble-dash, Plaster, Provide, Recite, Represent, Restore, Roughcast, Setting, Submit, Tallow, Try, Version, Yeve, Yield

**Rendezvous** Date, Meeting, Philippi, Tryst, Venue

**Rendition** Account, Delivery, Interpretation, Translation, Version

**René** Descartes

**Renegade, Reneg(u)e** Apostate, Default, Defector, Deserter, Pike, Rat(ton), Recreant, Traitor, Turncoat, Weasel out

▷**Renegade** *may indicate* a word reversal
**Renew(al)** Instauration, Neogenesis, Palingenesis, Refresh, Regenerate, Replace, Resumption, Retrace, Revival, Update, Urban
**Rennet** Steep, Vell
**Renounce, Renunciation** Abandon, Abdicate, Abjure, Abnegate, Abstain, Disclaim, Disown, Forfeit, For(e)go, Forisfamiliate, Forsake, For(e)say, Forswear, Kenosis, Outclaim, Pass up, Quitclaim, Recede, Recuse, Refuse, Relinquish, Renay, Retract, Sacrifice, Waiver
**Renovate(d), Renovation** Duff, Face-lift, Furbish, Instauration, Makeover, Overhaul, Refurbish, Renew, Repair, Restore, Revamp, Touch up, Translate
**Renown(ed)** Fame, Glory, Illustrious, Kudos, Legendary, Lustre, Notoriety, Prestige, Stardom
**Rent(er), Rented, Renting** Asunder, Attorn, Broken, Charge, Cornage, Cost, Crack, Cranny, Cuddeehih, Cuddy, Division, Economic, Fair, Farm, Fee, Fissure, Gale, Gavel, Ground, → HIRE, Lease, Let, Life, List, Mail, Market, Occupy, Opening, Pendicle, Penny(-mail), Peppercorn, Quit-rent, Rack, Rip, Rived, Riven, Screed, Seat, Slit, Split, Stallage, Subtenant, Tare, Tenant, Tithe, Tore, Torn, Tythe, White
**Reoffend** Backslide
**Reorganise** Rationalise, Realign, Shake up
▷**Reorganised** *may indicate* an anagram
**Reorientate** Rabat
**Repair(s), Repairer, Reparation** Amend(s), Anaplasty, Assythment, Atone, Botch, Cobble, Damages, Darn, DIY, Doctor, Dry dock, Expiation, Fettle, Fitter, Fix, Garage, Go, Haro, Harrow, Heel, Jury rig, Make good, Mechanic, → MEND, Neoplasty, Overhaul, Patch, Piece, Plastic surgery, Point, Recompense, Recover, Redress, Refit, Reheel, Remedy, Renew, Renovate, Repoint, Resort, Restore, Retouch, Revamp, Roadworks, Running, Satisfaction, Save, Service, Steeplejack, Stitch, Stopgap, Tenorrhaphy, Tinker, Ulling, Vamp, Volery, Wright
**Repartee** Backchat, Badinage, Banter, Cross talk, Persiflage, Rejoinder, Retort, Riposte, Wit, Wordplay
**Repast** Bever, Collection, Food, Meal, Tea, Treat
**Repay(ment)** Avenge, Compensate, Perseverate, Quit, Reassert, Refund, Reimburse, Requite, Retaliate, Revenge, Reward, Satisfaction
**Repeal** Abrogate, Annul, Cancel, Rescind, Revoke
**Repeat(ed), Repeatedly, Repetition, Repetitive** Again, Alliteration, Anadiplosis, Anaphora, Ancora, Battology, Belch, Bis, Burden, Burp, Copy, Cycle, Ditto(graphy), Do, Duplicate, → ECHO, Echolalia, Encore, Epanalepsis, Epistrophe, Epizeuxis, Eruct, Facsimile, Habitual, Harp, Image, Imitate, Ingeminate, Iterate, Iterum, Leit-motiv, Litany, Mantra, Merism, Ostinato, Palillogy, Parrot, Parrot-fashion, Passion, Perpetuate, Perseverate, Persistent, Playback, Polysyndeton, Quote, Reassert, Recapitulate, Recite(r), Redo, Refrain, Regurgitate, Reiterate, Rematch, Renew, Rep, Repechage, Repetend, Replay, Reprise, Rerun, Retail, Ritual, Rondo, Rosalia, Rote, Same(y), Screed, Segno, Serial(ly), Symploce, Tautology, Tautophony, Thrum, Trite, Verbigerate
**Repel(lent)** Aversive, Camphor, Deet, Estrange, Harsh, Offensive, Rebarbative, Reject, Repulse, Resist, Revolt, Scare, Shark, Shoo, Spurn, Squalid, Turn-off, Ug(h), Ward
**Repent(ant), Repentance** Cutty-stool, Metanoia, Penitent, Regret, Rue, Sackcloth, Yamim Nora'im
**Repercussion** Backlash, Backwash, Echo, Effect, Impact, Recoil
**Repertoire, Repertory** Company, Depot, Rep, Store
▶**Repetition** *see* REPEAT(ED)
**Replace(ment), Replaceable, Replacing** Arthroplasty, Change, Deputise, Diadochy, Euphorism, For, Instead, Novation, Overwrite, Pinch-hit, Pre-empt, Prosthesis, Raincheck, Refill, Reinstate, Relief, Renew, Replenish, Restore, Spare part, Stand-in, Substitute, Supersede, Supervene, Supplant, Surrogate, Taxis, Transform, Transliterate, Transplant, Understudy, Upgrade, Usurp
**Replay** Action, Instant, Iso(lated), Segno, Slo-mo
**Replenish** Recharge, Refill, Refresh, Renew, Revictual, Stock, Stoke, Supply, Top (up)
**Replete, Repletion** Awash, Full, Gorged, Plenitude, Plethora, Sated, Satiation

**Replica** Clone, Copy, Duplicate, Facsimile, Image, Repetition, Spit

**Reply** Accept, Answer, Churlish, Counter-attack, Duply, Echo, Over, Rejoinder, Replication, Repost, Rescript, Response, Retort, Riposte, Roger, RSVP, Surrebut, Surrebutter, Surrejoinder, Triply

**Report(s), Reporter** Account, Announce, Annual, Auricular, Bang, Beveridge, Blacksmith, Boom, Bruit, Bulletin, Cahier, Clap, Columnist, Comment, Commentator, Compte rendu, Correspondent, Court, Court circular, Cover, Crack, Crump, Cub, Debrief, Describe, Despatch, Disclose, Dispatch, Dissertation, Document, Embedded, Explosion, Fame, Fireman, Grapevine, Gunshot, Hansard, Hearsay, Informant, Item, Jenkins, Journalist, Legman, Libel, Message, Minority, Narrative, News, Newsflash, Newshawk, Newshound, Newsman, Noise, Notify, On dit, Paper, Pop, Powwow, Pressman, Proces verbal, Protocol, Rapporteur, Read-out, Recount, Relate, Relay, Representation, Repute, Return, Roorback, Roundsman, Rumour, Shot, Sitrep, Sound(bite), Staffer, State(ment), Stringer, Survey, Tale, → **TELL**, Thesis, Thunder (clap), Transactions, Transcribe, Tripehound, Troop, Update, Weather, Whang, Whistle-blower, White paper, Wolfenden, Write up

▷**Reported** *may indicate* the sound of a letter or word

**Repose** Ease, Kaif, Kef, Kif, Lie, Lig, Peace, Relax, → **REST**, Serenity, Slumber

**Repository** Archive, Ark, Cabinet, Cinerarium, Container, Genizah, Museum, Reservoir, Salvatory, Sepulchre, Vault

**Repossess(ion)** Distringas

**Reprehend, Reprehensible** Base, Blame, Blameworthy, Censure, Criminal, Criticise, Flagrant, Ill, Paper, Rebuke, Shameful, Warn

**Represent(ation), Representational, Representative, Represented** Agent, Ambassador, Anaconic, Archetypal, Assembly-man, Attorney, Bargraph, Blue, Caricature, Client, Commercial, Commissary, Commissioner, Cross-section, Delegate, Depict, Deputation, Deputy, Describe, Design, Display, Drawing, Drummer, Effigy, Elchee, Eltchi, Emblem, Embody, Emissary, Epitomise, Example, Figurative, Histogram, Icon, Ikon, Image, Instantiate, John Bull, Legate, Limn, Lobby, Mandala, Map, Mime, Mimesis, Model, Mouthpiece, MP, Nuncio, Official, Personate, Personify, Piechart, Portray, Proportional, Quintessence, Rep, Resemble, Salesman, Senator, Shop steward, Simulacrum, Singspiel, Spokesman, Stand-in, Statua, Status, Steward, Symbolic, Syndic, Tableau, Tableau vivant, Tiki, Token, Transcription, Traveller, Typical, Typify, Vakeel, Vakil, Vernicle, Vice-consul, Visitor-general

▷**Represented** *may indicate* an anagram

**Repress(ed), Repressive** Bottle, Check, Contain, Crackdown, Curb, Inhibit, Pent, Quell, Reprime, Sneap, Stifle, Stultify, Subjugate, Withhold

**Reprieve** Delay, Mercy, Postpone, Relief, Respite

**Reprimand** Admonish, Berate, Blast, Bollock, Bounce, Carpet, Castigate, → **CENSURE**, Chastise, Chew out, Chide, Dressing-down, Earful, Jobe, Lace into, Lambast, Lash into, Lecture, Rark up, Rating, Rebuke, Reproof, Rocket, Rollicking, Scold, Slate, Strafe, Targe, Tick off, Tongue-lashing, What for, Wig

**Reprint** Copy, Paperback, Replica

**Reprisal(s)** Backlash, Marque, Recaption, Retaliation, Revenge

**Reproach** Besom, Bisom, Blame, Braid, Byword, Cataian, Catayan, Chide, Discredit, Dispraise, Exprobrate, Gib, Mispraise, Odium, Opprobrium, Rebuke, Ronyon, Runnion, Scold, Shend, Sloan, Stigma, Taunt, Truant, Twit, Upbraid, Upcast, Yshend

**Reprobate** Cur, Degenerate, Libertine, Lost soul, Outcast, Rascal, Scallywag, Scamp

**Reprocess** Re-make

**Reproduce(r), Reproduction, Reproductive (organ)** Ambisonics®, Amphimixis, Ape, Apomixis, Archegonium, Arrhenotoky, Bearing, Carpel, Clone, Copy, Counterfeit, Depict, Duplicate, Ectype, Edition, Egg(s), Etch, Eugenics, Gamogenesis, Gemmate, Generation, Genitalia, Homogenesis, Isospory, Loins, Megaspore, Meristematic, Mono, Monogenesis, Monogony, Multiply, Oogamy, Ozalid®, Parthenogenesis, Phon(e)y, Photocopy, Pirate, Playback, Proliferate, Propagate, Pullulation, Refer, Replica, Roneo®, S(h)akti, Schizogony, Seminal, Simulate, Soredium, Spermatia, Spore, Stereo, Strobilation, Syngamy, Syngenesis, Vegetative, Viviparism

▹**Reproduce** *may indicate* an anagram

**Reproof, Reprove** Admonish, Berate, Brickbat, Censure, Chide, Correction, Correption, Lecture, Rap, Rate, Rebuff, Rebuke, Reprehension, Scold, Sloan, Take to task, Tut, Upbraid

**Reptile, Reptilian** Agamid, Alligarta, Alligator, Base, Basilisk, Caiman, Cayman, Chameleon, Chelonian, Creeper, Crocodile, Cynodont, Diapsid, Dicynodont, Dinosaur, Galliwasp, Gecko, Goanna, Hatteria, Herpetology, Lacertine, Lizard, Mamba, Pelycosaur, Pit viper, Pteranodon, Pterodactyl, Pterosaur, Pythonomorpha, Rhynchocephalian, Sauroid, → SNAKE, Sphenodon, Squamata, Synapsid, Tegu(exin), Terrapin, Thecodont, Therapsid, Theriodontia, Tortoise, Tuatara, Tuatera, Turtle, Worm

**Republic(an)** Antimonarchist, Belarussian, Democrat, East Germany, Esth, Fenian, Fianna Fáil, Ghana, Girondist, GOP, International Brigade, IRA, Iraqi, Leveller, Montagnard, Mugwump, Plato, Presidency, Provisional, Provo, R, Red, Sansculotte, Sansculottic, Sinn Fein, Whig, Young Italy

**Republic(s)** Antimonarchist, Banana, Federal, Fifth, First, Fourth, People's, Second, State, Third

---

## REPUBLICS

***1 letter:***
R

***3 letters:***
RMM
UAR
USA

***4 letters:***
Chad
Cuba
Eire
Fiji
Iran
Iraq
Komi
Laos
Mali
Peru
Togo
Tuva

***5 letters:***
Adhar
Altai
Belau
Benin
Chile
China
Congo
Czech
Egypt
Gabon
Ghana
Haiti
India
Italy
Kenya
Khmer
Libya
Malta
Nauru
Nepal
Niger
Palau
Sakha
Sudan
Syria
Tatar
Yakut
Yemen
Zaire

***6 letters:***
Adygai
Adygei
Angola
Bharat
Biafra
Brazil
Bukavu
Buryat
Cyprus
France
Gambia
Greece
Guinea
Guyana
Ingush
Israel
Kalmyk
Kosovo
Latvia
Malawi
Mari-El
Mexico
Myanma
Panama
Poland
Russia
Rwanda
Serbia
Somali
Turkey
Udmurt
Uganda
Venice
Weimar
Zambia

***7 letters:***
Adharca
Albania
Algeria
Andorra
Armenia
Austria
Bashkir
Belarus
Bolivia
Burkina
Burundi
Chechen
Chuvash
Comoros
Croatia
Ecuador
Estonia
Finland
Georgia
Germany
Hungary
Iceland
Ireland
Jibouti
Kalmuck
Kalmyck
Khakass
Lebanon
Liberia
Moldova
Myanmar
Namibia
Nigeria
Romania
Senegal
Somalia
Surinam
Tunisia
Ukraine
Uruguay
Vanuatu
Vietnam
Yakutia

***8 letters:***
Abkhazid
Botswana
Bulgaria
Buryatia
Cambodia
Cameroon
Chechnya
Colombia
Dagestan
Djibouti
Dominica
Esthonia
Honduras
Karelian
Kiribati
Malagasy

Maldives
Moldavia
Mongolia
Pakistan
Paraguay
Portugal
Roumania
Sinn Fein
Slovakia
Slovenia
Sri Lanka
Suriname
Tanzania
Udmurtia
Zimbabwe

*9 letters:*
Argentina
Badakshan
Cape Verde
Costa Rica
Dominican
Guatemala
Indonesia
Kazakstan
Lithuania
Macedonia
Mauritius
Nicaragua
San Marino
Singapore
Tatarstan
Venezuela

*10 letters:*
Azerbaijan
Bangladesh
Belarussia
El Salvador
Gorno-Altai
Kara-Kalpak
Kazakhstan
Khakhassia
Kyrgyzstan
Madagascar
Mauritania
Montenegro
Mordvinian
Mozambique
North Korea
North Yemen
Seychelles
South Korea
South Yemen
Tajikistan
Ubang-Shari
United Arab
Uzbekistan
Yugoslavia

*11 letters:*
Afghanistan
Burkina-Faso
Byelorussia
Cote d'Ivoire
Nakhichevan
Philippines
Sierra Leone
South Africa
Soviet Union
Switzerland
Tadjikistan
West Germany

*12 letters:*
Guinea-Bissau
South Vietnam
Turkmenistan

*13 letters:*
Bashkortostan
North Ossetian

*14 letters:*
Czechoslovakia

*15 letters:*
Gorno-Badakhshan
Kabardino-Balkar
Marshall Islands
United Provinces

*16 letters:*
Congo-Brazzaville
Equatorial Guinea
Karachai-Cherkess
São Tomé e Príncipe

*17 letters:*
Bosnia-Herzegovina
Mari El-Nakhichevan
Trinidad and Tobago

---

**Repudiate** Abjure, Deny, Disaffirm, Disavow, Discard, Disclaim, Disown, Ignore, Recant, Reject, Renounce, Repel, Retract

**Repugnance, Repugnant** Abhorrent, Alien, Disfavour, Disgust, Distaste, Fulsome, Hatred, Horror, Loathing, Nastiness, Noisome, Obscene, Odious, Revulsion

**Repulsive, Repulse** Abhorrent, Creepy, Evil-favoured, Grooly, Icky, Lo(a)th, Odious, Off-putting, Rebuff, Rebut, Refel, Refuse, Repel, Repugnant, Slimy, Squalid, Ugly, Vile

**Reputable, Reputation, Repute(d)** Bubble, Credit, Dit, Estimate, Fame, Good, Izzat, Loos, Los, Name, Note, Notoriety, Odour, Opinion, Prestige, Putative, Regard, Renown, Said, Sar, → STANDING, Stature, Status, Stink, Stock, Trustworthy

**Request** Adjure, Appeal, Application, Apply, Ask, Beg, Demand, Desire, D-notice, Entreaty, Implore, Invite, Order, Petition, Plea, Prayer, Precatory, Solicit, Supplication, Touch

**Requiem** Agnus Dei, Mass, War

**Require(d), Requirement** Charge, Crave, Demand, De rigueur, Desideratum, Desire, Enjoin, Entail, Essential, Exact, Expect, Formality, Incumbent, Lack, Mandatory, Necessity, Need, Prerequisite, Priority, Proviso, Seek, Sine qua non, Stipulate, Then

**Requisite, Requisition** Capable, Commandeer, Due, Embargo, Essential, Indent, Necessary, Needful, Order, Press, Simplement

**Rerun** Play back

**Reschedule** Postpone, Prepone

**Rescind** Abrogate, Annul, Recant, Remove, Repeal

**Rescue(r)** Aid, Air-sea, Bring off, Deliver, Free, Liberate, Lifeboat, Lifeline, Lifesave, Mountain, Noah, Ransom, Reclaim, Recover, Recower, Redeem, Regain, Relieve, Repatriate, Reprieve, Retrieve, Salvage, Salvation, → SAVE, White knight

**Research(er)** Audience, Boffin, Delve, Dig, Enquiry, Explore, Fieldwork, Indagator, Investigate, Legwork, Market, MORI, Motivation(al), Near-market, Operational, Opposition, Pioneer, Post-doctoral, Psychical, Quest, Res, Scientist, Study, Sus(s), Test, Thesis, Think-tank

**Resell** Scalp

**Resemblance, Resemble, Resembling** Affinity, Apatetic, Ape, Approach, Assimilate,

Assonant, Dead ringer, Homophyly, Likeness, Match, -oid, -opsis, Parallel, Quasi, Replica, Similitude, Simulacrum, Simulate

**Resent(ful), Resentment** Acrimony, Anger, Begrudge, Bitter(ness), Bridle, Chippy, Choler, Cross, Derry, Dudgeon, Embittered, Envy, Grudge, Huff, Indignation, Ire, Jaundiced, Malic, Malign, Miff, Mind, Offence, Outrage, Pique, Rancour, Rankle, Smart, Snarling, Spite, Umbrage

**Reservation, Reserve(d), Reservist(s)** Aloof, Arrière-ban, Arrière-pensée, Aside, Auxiliary, Backlog, Bag, Bank, Bashful, Book, But, By, Cache, Capital, Caveat, Central, Cold, Condition, Coy, Demiss, Detachment, Distant, Earmark, Engage, Ersatz, Except, Fall-back, Federal, Fort Knox, Fund, General, Gold, Hold, Husband, Ice, Indian, In hand, Introvert, Landwehr, Layby, Locum, Masai Mara, Median strip, Mental, Militiaman, Modesty, Nature, Nest-egg, Nineteenth man, Pool, Pound, Proviso, Qualification, Reddendum, Res, Rest, Restraint, Retain, Reticence, Retiring, Rez, Ring-fence, Safari park, Salvo, Sanctuary, Save, Scenic, Scruple, Serengeti, Set aside, Shy, Shyness, Special, Spoken for, Stand-by, Stand-in, Stand-offishness, Starch, Stash, Stock(pile), Store, Sub(stitute), Supply, TA (men), Taciturn, Twelfth man, Uncommunicate, Undemonstrative, Understudy, Warren, Waves, Wetlands, Withhold

**Reservoir** Basin, Cistern, Font, G(h)ilgai, Gilgie, Header tank, Holder, Inkholder, Lake, Oilcup, Repository, Rybinsk, Service, Stock, Sump, Tank, Water tower, Well

**Reset** Taxis

**Reside(nce), Resident(s), Residential** Abode, Address, Amban, Chequers, Commorant, Consulate, Denizen, Domicile, Dwell, Embassy, Establishment, Expatriate, Exurb(anite), Gaff, Gremial, Guest, Home, Hostel, Housemate, In, Indweller, Inholder, Inmate, Intern, Ledger, Lei(d)ger, Lieger, Liveyer(e), Local, Lodgement, Lodger, Masonry, Metic, Native, Occupant, Pad, Parietal, Permanent, Populace, Resiant, Roost, Settle, Settlement, Sojourn, Squat, Stay, Suburban, Tenant, Tenement, Up, Uptown, Vicinage, Villager, Yamen

**Residual, Residue** Ash, Astatki, Boneblack, Calx, Caput, Chaff, Cinders, Clinker, Coke, Crud, Dottle, Draff, Dregs, Expellers, Greaves, Heeltap, Leavings, Mazout, Mortuum, Pitch, Prefecture, Raffinate, Remainder, Remanent, Remnant, Scourings, Sediment, Slag, Slurry, Snuff, Soot, Trace, Vinasse

**Resign(ed), Resignation** Abandon, Abdicate, Demit, Fatalism, Heigh-ho, Leave, Meek, Patience, Philosophical, → QUIT, Reconcile, Step down, Stoic, Submit

**Resilience, Resilient** Bounce, Buoyant, Elastic, Flexible, Recoil, Rugged, Springy, Stamina

**Resin** Acaroid, Acrylic, Agila, Alkyd, Amber, Amine, Amino, Anime, Araldite®, Arar, Asaf(o)etida, Bakelite®, Bal(sa)m of Gilead, Balsam, Bdellium, Benjamin, Benzoin, Burgundy pitch, Bursera, Cachou, Cannabin, Cannabis, Caranna, Carauna, Catechu, Charas, Cholestyramine, Churrus, Colophony, Conima, Copai(ba), Copaiva, Copal(m), Coumarone, Courbaril, Cutch, Cymene, Dam(m)ar, Dammer, Dragon's blood, Elaterite, Elemi, Epoxy, Frankincense, Galbanum, Galipot, Gambi(e)r, Gamboge, Glyptal, Guaiacum, Gum, Hasheesh, Hashish, Hing, Jalapic, Jalapin, Kino, Labdanum, Lac, Ladanum, Lignaloes, Limonene, Lupulin, Mastic, Melamine, Methacrylate, Myrrh, Natural, Olibanum, Opopanax, Perspex®, Phenolic, Phenoxy, Pitch, Plastisol, Podophyl(l)in, Polycarbonate, Polyester, Polymer, Polypropylene, Polysterene, Polyvinyl, Propolis, Retinite, Roset, Rosin, Rosit, Rozet, Rozit, Sagapenum, Sandarac(h), Saran®, Scammony, Shellac, Silicone, Storax, Styrene, Synthetic, Tacamahac, Tacmahack, Takamaka, Taxin, Thus, Urea, Urethane, Vinyl, Xylenol

**Resist, Resistance, Resistant, Resistor** All-weather, Anti, Antibiotic, Barretter, Bleeder, Bristle, Buck, Ceramal, Cermet, Chetnik, Coccidiostat, Combat, Consumer, Contest, Defiance, Defy, Diehard, Drag, Drug, Element, Face, Fend, Friction, Gainstrive, Grapo, Hostile, Immunity, Impede, Impediment, Internal, Intifada, Invar, Klendusic, Klepht, Maquis, Maraging, Market, Megohm, Microhm, Negative, Obstacle, Ohm(age), Omega, Oppose, Partisan, Passive, Pat, Pull, R, Radiation, React, Redound, Reluct, Reluctance, Renitent, Resilient, Rheostat, Sales, Satyagraha, Shockproof, Soul-force, Specific, Stability, Stand (pat), Stonde, Stubborn, Tamil Tiger, Tough, Toughen, Vendean, Voltage divider, → WITHSTAND

**Resolute, Resolution** Adamant, Analysis, Bold, Cast-iron, Casuistry, Closure, Courage, Decided, Decision, Denouement, Determined, Dogged, Doughty, → FIRM, Fortitude,

Granite, Grim, Grit, Hardiness, Insist, Iron, Joint, Manful, Motion, New Year, Pertinacity, Promotion, Rede, Reed(e), Resolve, Settlement, Single-minded, Stable, Stalwart, Staunch, Stiff, Stout(-hearted), Strength, Strong-willed, Sturdy, Telic, Tenacity, Tough, Unbending, Unflinching, Unmoved, Valiant, Willpower

**Resolve(d), Resolver** Aim, Analyse, Calculate, Conation, Conciliate, Decide, Declare, → **DETERMINE**, Deus ex machina, Factorise, Fix, Grit, Hellbent, Intent, Nerve, Pecker, → **PURPOSE**, Right, Settle, Sort out, Steadfast, Tenacity, Vow, Will

▷**Resolved** *may indicate* an anagram

**Resonance, Resonant, Resonator** Canorous, Cavity, Electromer, Morphic, Orotund, Parallel, Rhumbatron, Ringing, Sonorous, Timbre, Vibrant

**Resort** Acapulco, Antibes, Arbroath, Aspen, Benidorm, Biarritz, Blackpool, Bognor, Bournemouth, Brighton, Cancun, Cannes, Centre, Chamonix, Clacton, Copacabana, Davos, Dive, Estoril, Étaples, Expedient, Frame, Frequent, Frinton, Gstaad, Haunt, Health, Herne Bay, Holiday camp, Hove, Hydro, Invoke, Klosters, Lair, Last, Las Vegas, Llandudno, Locarno, Lowestoft, Malaga, Malibu, Margate, Menton, Miami, Minehead, Morecambe, Nassau, Nice, Orlando, Ostend, Paignton, Palm Beach, Pau, Penzance, Pis aller, Poole, Portrush, Ramsgate, Rapallo, Recourse, Redcar, Repair, Rhyl, Rimini, Riviera, St Ives, St Tropez, Seaside, Skegness, Southend, Spa(w), Stand by, Swanage, Tampa, Thredbo, Torquay, Torremolinos, Troon, Use, Utilise, Waikiki, Watering place, Weston-super-Mare, Weymouth, Whitby, Worthing, Yalta, Zermatt

---

## RESORTS

*3 letters:*
Ayr
Goa

*4 letters:*
Bude
Elat
Lobe
Peel
Suva

*5 letters:*
Barry
Eilat
Elath
Tahoe

*6 letters:*
Amalfi
Bangor
Cromer
Selsey
St Malo

*7 letters:*
Exmouth
Key West
Lucerne
Mombasa
Newport
Newquay
Rotorua

*8 letters:*
Aviemore
Hastings
Shanklin
St Moritz

*9 letters:*
Colwyn Bay
Dubrovnik
Lyme Regis
Nantucket
Southport

*10 letters:*
Eastbourne
Ilfracombe
Westward Ho
Whitstable

*11 letters:*
Broadstairs
Scilly Isles

*12 letters:*
Santa Barbara
Saundersfoot

---

▷**Resort(ing)** *may indicate* an anagram

**Resound(ing)** Echo, Plangent, Reboant, Reboation, Reverberate, Ring, Sonorous, Ting, Vibrate

**Resource(s), Resourceful** Assets, Beans, Bottom, Chevisance, Clever, Enterprise, Faculty, Funds, Gumption, Human, Imaginative, Ingenious, Input, Inventive, Manpower, Means, Natural, Renewable, Shared, Sharp, Smeddum, Stock-in-trade, Streetwise, → **VERSATILE**, Ways and means, Wealth, Webliography

**Respect(ed), Respectability, Respectable, Respectful** Admire, Ahimsa, Aspect, Behalf, Bien-séance, Clean cut, Consecrate, Consider, Cred(it), Curtsey, Decent, Deference, Devoir, Douleia, Doyen(ne), Duty, Eminent, Esteem, Fear, Genteel, Genuflection, Gigman, Homage, Honorific, → **HONOUR**, Intent, Kempt, Kowtowing, Latria, Nice, Obeisant, Officious, Pace, Particular, Polite, Preppy, Presentable, Prestige, Proper, Reference, Regard, Relation, Reputable, Revere, Seemly, Sir, S(t)irrah, U, Venerate, Way, Wellborn, Well-thought-of, Wise, Worthy

**Respective** Several

**Respirator, Respiratory, Respire, Respiration** Artificial, Asthma, Blow, Breathe, Exhale, External, Gasmask, Inhale, Iron lung, Mouth-to-mouth, Pant, Snorkel

**Respite** Break, Breather, Frist, Interval, Leisure, Let up, Pause, Reprieve, Rest, Stay, Truce

**Resplendent** Flamboyant

**Respond(ing), Response, Responsive** Amenable, Answer, Antiphon, Autoreply,

Backchat, Backlash, Bi, Comeback, Conditioned, Counteroffer, Duh, Echo, Efficacy, Feedback, Flechman, Geotaxis, Grunt, Immune, Interactive, Kneejerk, Kyrie, Litany, Meow, Nastic, Pavlovian, Photonasty, Plea, Prebuttal, Psychogalvanic, Racket, React(ion), Reagency, Rebutter, Reflex, Reply, Repost, Retaliate, Retort, Rheotaxis, Rheotropism, Rise, Sensitive, Stayman, Surrejoinder, Synapte, Syntonic, Tender, Thigmotropic, Tic, Tropism, Unconditioned, Voice, Warm, Wilco

**Responsibility, Responsible** Accountable, Anchor, Answerable, Baby, Behind, Blame, Buck, Can, Charge, Collective, Culpable, Dependable, Diminished, Duty, Frankpledge, Guilty, Hot seat, Incumbent, Instrumental, Liable, Mantle, Mea culpa, Millstone, Noblesse oblige, Obligation, Onus, Parental, Perpetrate, Pigeon, Remit, Role, Sane, Solid, Stayman, Trust

**Rest(ing), Rest day** Abutment, Alt, Anchor, Avocation, Balance, Bed, Beulah, Break, Breather, Calm, Catnap, Cetera, Comma, Depend, Dormant, Dwell, Ease, Easel, Etc(etera), Fermata, Feutre, Fewter, Gallows, Gite, Half-time, Halt, Inaction, Inter alia, Jigger, Lance, Lave, Layover, Lay to, Lean, Leasure, Leisure, Lie, Lie-in, Light, Lodge, Loll, Lound, Lull, Lyte, Minim, Nap, Noah, Nooning, Oasis, Others, Outspan, Overlie, Pause, Quiescence, Quiet, Recess, Relâche, Relax, Rely, Remainder, Repose, Requiem, Reserve, Residue, Respite, Sabbath, Shut-eye, Sick leave, Siesta, Silence, → SLEEP, Slide, Sloom, Slumber, Spell, Spider, Static, Stopover, Support, Surplus, Teabreak, Time out, Waypoint, Y-level

**Re-start** Da capo, Reboot

**Restate** Reformulate

**Restaurant, Restaurateur** Automat, Beanery, Bistro, Brasserie, British, Buffet, Cabaret, Café, Canteen, Carvery, Chew'n'spew, Chinese, Chippy, Chip-shop, Chophouse, Coffee shop, Commissary, Cook shop, Creperie, Diner, Drive through, Eatery, Eating-house, Estaminet, Gastropub, Greasy spoon, Grill, Grillroom, Grub shop, Indian, Luncheonette, Maxim's, Naafi, Noshery, Padrone, Pizzeria, Porter-house, Rathskeller, Ratskeller, Raw bar, Roadhouse, Rotisserie, Slap-bang, Steakhouse, Takeaway, Taqueria, Taverna, Tea garden, Teahouse, Tearoom, Teashop, Trat(toria)

**Rest-home** Aggie, Hospice

**Resting-place** Bed, Couch, Dharmsala, Gite, Grave, Inn, Khan, Serai, She'ol, Stage

**Restitute, Restitution** Amends, Apocatastasis, Reparation, Restore, Return

**Restive, Restless(ness)** Agitato, Chafing, Chorea, Fantods, Feverish, Fidgety, Fikish, Fitful, Free-arm, Impatient, Itchy, Jactitation, Skittery, Spring fever, Toey, Unsettled, Wanderlust

▷**Restless** *may indicate* an anagram

**Restoration, Restorative, Restore(d)** Beauty sleep, Bring to, Cure, Descramble, Graft, Heal, Instauration, Mend, New, Pentimento, Pick-me-up, Postliminy, Rally, Reawaken, Reclaim, Recondition, Reconstitute, Recuperate, Redeem, Redintegrate, Redress, Redux, Refresh, Refurbish, Regenerate, Rehabilitate, Reinstate, Reintegrate, Rejuvenate, Remedial, Renew, Renovate, Replenish, Replevy, Repone, Reset, Restitute, Resurrect, Resuscitate, Retouch, Revamp, Revive, Righten, Salvage, Stet, Therapeutic, Tonic, Undelete, Whole

**Restrain(ed), Restraint** Abstinence, Ban, Bar, Bate, Bit, Bottle, Branks, Bridle, Cage, Censor, Chain, Chasten, → CHECK, Checks and balances, Chokehold, Coerce, Cohibit, Compesce, Confinement, Contain, Continent, Control, Cramp, Curb, Dam, Decorum, Detent, Dry, Duress, Embargo, Enfetter, Estoppel, Fetter, Freeze, Gag-rein, Gyve, Halt, Hamshackle, Handcuffs, Harness, Heft, Hinder, Hopple, Immanacle, Impound, Inhibit, Jess, Leash, Leg-iron, Lid, Low-key, Manacle, Measure, Mince, Moderation, Muzzle, Patient, Pen, Pinion, Quiet, Rein, Repress, Reserve, Restrict, Ritenuto, Seat belt, Shackle, Sober, Sobriety, Spancel, Squeeze, Stay, Stent, Stint, Straitjacket, Strait-waistcoat, Tabu, Temper(ate), Tether, Tie, Tieback, Trash, Underplay, Withhold

**Restrict(ed), Restriction** Band, Bar, Bind, Bit, Block, Budget, Burden, Cage, Catch, Censorship, Chain, Circumscribe, Closet, Condition, Confinement, Constrain, Cord, Corset, Cramp, Curb, Curfew, DORA, Entail, Fence, Fetter, Fold, Gate, Ground, Guard, Hamper, Hamstring, Handcuff, Hedge, Hidebound, Hobble, Inhibit, Intern, Irons, Kennel, Let, → LIMIT, Localise, Lock, Mere, Narrow, Net, Nick, No-go, Oche, Pale, Parochial, Pen, Pent, Pier, Pin, Poky, Pot-bound, Private, Proscribed, Qualify, Ration, Regulate, Rein, Rent, Repression, Rope, Safety belt, Scant, Seal, Section, Selected, Shackle, Snare, Squeeze, Stenopaic, Stent, Stint, Stop, Straiten, Stunt, Swaddle, Tether, Tie

**Rest-room** Convenience, Loo

**Restructure, Restructuring** Perestroika

**Result(s)** After-effect, Aftermath, Ans(wer), Arise, Bring, Causal, Consequence, Effect, Emanate, End, End-product, Ensue, Entail, Even Stevens, Event, Eventuate, Finding, Fruict, Fruition, Fruits, Issue, Karmic, Knock-on, Lattermath, → OUTCOME, Outturn, Pan, Pay off, Proceeds, Product, Quotient, Score-line, Sequel, Side-effect, Sum, Thereby, Therefore, Upshot, Verdict, Wale, Wysiwyg

**Resume, Résumé, Resumption** Continue, Pirlicue, Purlicue, Reprise, Summary

**Resurrect(ion)** Anabiosis, Anastasia, Rebirth, Revive, Zomb(ie)

**Resuscitate(d), Resuscitation** Mouth-to-mouth, Quicken, Redivivus, Restore, Revive

**Retail(er)** Category killer, Chain store, Chandler, Cheesemonger, Dealer, Emailer, Haberdasher, IKEA®, Jeweller, Middleman, → NARRATE, Regrate, Sell, Shopkeeper, Shopman, Stockist, Superstore, Symbol, Tell

**Retain(er), Retains, Retention, Retentive** Brief, Conserve, Contain, Deposit, Fee, Hold, Hold-all, Keep, Long, Memory, Panter, Pantler, Reserve, Retinue, Servant, Ur(a)emia, Vassal

**Retaliate, Retaliation** Avenge, Carousel, Counter(measure), Lex talionis, Pay back, Pay home, Quid pro quo, Quit(e), Redress, Repay, Reprisal, Requite, Retort, Revenge, Talion, Tit for tat

**Retard(ed), Retardation** Arrest, Belate, Brake, Cretin, Encumber, Hinder, Hysteresis, Inhibit, Slow, Stunt

**Retch** Boak, Bock, Boke, Cowk, Gap, Heave, Keck, Reach, Vomit

**Reticence, Reticent** Boutonne, Clam, Close, Cowardly, Coy, Dark, Guarded, Introvert, Laconic, Reserve, Restraint, Secretive, Shy, Silence, Taciturn

**Reticule, Reticulum** Bag, Carryall, Dragnet, Handbag, Lattice, Net

**Retina** Detached, Fovea, Macula lutea

**Retinue** Comitatus, Company, Cortège, Equipage, Following, Meiney, Meinie, Meiny, Menyie, Sowarry, Suite

**Retire(d), Retiree, Retirement, Retiring** Abed, Aloof, Asocial, Baccare, Backare, Backpedal, Blate, Bowler-hat, Bow out, Cede, Coy, Demob, Demure, Depart, Ebb, Emeritus, Essene, Former, Leave, Lonely, Modest, Mothball, Nun, Outgoing, Pension, Perfing, Private, Put out, Quit, Recede, Recluse, Repair, Reserved, Resign, Retract, Retread, Retreat, Retrocedent, Roost, Rusticate, Scratch, Sequester, Shy, Superannuate, Timid, Unassertive, Unsay, Withdraw

▷**Retirement** *may indicate* 'bed' around another word, or word reversed

**Retort** Alembic, Comeback, Courteous, Floorer, Quip, Repartee, → REPLY, Retaliate, Riposte, Still, Tu quoque

**Retract(ion)** Backpedal, Backtrack, Disavow, Epanorthosis, Palinode, Recall, Recant, Renounce, Revoke

**Retread** Recap

**Retreat** Abbey, About turn, Arbour, Ashram(a), Asylum, Backpedal, Backward step, Backwater, Berchtesgaden, Bower, Bug, Camp David, Cell, Climb down, Cloister, Convent, Crawfish, Dacha, Den, Departure, Donjon, Draw back, Flight, Funkhole, Girth, Grith, Growlery, Hermitage, Hibernaculum, Hideaway, Hide-out, Hole, Interstadial, Ivory-tower, Katabasis, Lair, Lama(sery), Mew, Monastery, Nest, Neuk, Nook, Nunnery, Pullback, Recede, Recoil, Recu(i)le, Redoubt, Reduit, Refuge, Retire, Retraite, Right-about, Rout, Shangri-La, Shelter, Skedaddle, Stronghold, Withdraw

**Retrench(ment)** Lay off

**Retribution** Come-uppance, Deserts, Karma, Nemesis, Revenge, Reward, Utu, Vengeance

**Retrieve(r), Retrieval** Access, Bird-dog, Chesapeake Bay, Fetch, Field, Gundog, Information, Jason, Labrador, Read-out, Recall, Reclaim, Recoup, Recover, Redeem, Rescue, Salvage

**Retroflex** Cacuminal

**Retrograde** Backward, Deasi(u)l, Deasoil, Decadent, Decline, Hindward, Rearward, Regrede

**Retrospect(ive)** Back-dated, Contemplative, Ex post facto, Hindsight, Regardant

**Return(s)** Agen, Answer, Bricole, Census, Comeback, Counter, Day, Derequisition, Diminishing, Dividend, Earnings, Echo, Elect, Er, Exchange, Extradite, Gain, Homecoming, Nil, Pay, Payback, Proceeds, Profit, Rally, Rebate, Rebound, Recur, Redound, Regress, Reject, Rejoin, Render, Rent, Repair, Repay, Replace, Reply, Requital, Respond, Rest, Restitution, Restoration, Restore, Retort, Retour, Revenue, Reverse, Revert, Riposte, Soft, Takings, Tax, Tit for tat, Traffic, Volley, Winnings, →YIELD

**Reuse(d)** Cannibalise, Palimpsest

**Rev(ving)** Gun, Minister, Vroom

**Reveal(ing), Revelation** Acute, Admit, Advertise, Air, Apocalyptic, Bar, Bare, Betray, Bewray, Confess, Declare, Decollete, Descry, Disbosom, Disclose, Discover, Discure, →DIVULGE, Epiphany, Evince, Exhibit, Explain, Expose, Eye-opener, Giveaway, Hierophantic, Impart, Indicate, Indiscreet, Ingo, Kythe, Lay bare, Lay open, Leak, Let on, Low-cut, Manifest, Open, Out, Parade, Peekaboo, Pentimento, Rake up, Satori, Scanty, Scry, →SHOW, Skimpy, Spill, Spring, Strip, Tell-tale, Unclose, Uncover, Unfold, Unheal, Unmask, Unveil

**Reveille** Raise

**Revel(ling), Revelry** Ariot, Bacchanalia, Bask, Bend, Carnival, Carouse, Comus, Dionysian, Disport, Feast, Gloat, Glory, Joy, Luxuriate, Maffick, Merriment, Night-rule, On the tiles, Orgy, Rant, Rejoice, Riot, Roister, Rollicks, Rout, Royst, Saturnalia, Splore, Spree, Swig, Upsee, Ups(e)y, Wallow, Wassail, Whoopee

**Reveller** Bacchant, Birler, Corybant, Guisard, Guiser, Maenad, Merrymaker, Orgiast, Silenus

**Revenant** Fetch, Ghost, Spectre

**Revenge(r), Revengeful** Aftergame, Avenge, Commination, Goel, Grenville, Montezuma's, Nightrider, Payback, Reprise, Requite, Retaliation, Revanche, Settlement, Tit for tat, Ultion, Utu, Vigilante, Vindictive

**Revenue** Capital, Fees, Finance, Fisc(al), Fisk, Income, Inland, Internal, Jaghire, Jag(h)ir, Prebend, Primitiae, Proceeds, Rent, Taille, Take, Tax, Turnover, Zamindar, Zemindar

**Reverberate, Reverberation** Boom, Clang, Echo, Reboant, Recoil, Reflect, Repercuss, Resound

**Revere(nce), Revered** Admire, Adoration, Awe, Bostonian, Dread, Dulia, Esteem, Fear, Hallow, Hero, Hery, Homage, →HONOUR, Hyperdulia, Idolise, Latria, Obeisance, Paul, Prostration, Respect, Salaam, Venerate

**Reverie** Abstraction, Brown study, Daydream, Dream(iness), Fantasy, Memento

**Revers** Lap(p)el

**Reversal, Reverse, Reversing, Reversion, Reversible** Anatropy, Antithesis, Antonym, Arsy-versy, Atavism, Back(slide), Backwards, B-side, Change-over, Chiasmus, Commutate, Counter(mand), Escheat, Evaginate, Exergue, Flip, Flip side, Inversion, Mirror image, Misfortune, →OPPOSITE, Overturn, Palindrome, Pile, Regress, Rein back, Repeal, Retrograde, Revoke, Rheotropic, Setback, Somersault, Switchback, Tails, Throwback, Transit, Turn, Turnabout, Two-faced, Un-, Undo, Upend, U-turn, Verso, Vice versa, Volte-face, Woman

**Revert** Annul, Backslide, Regress, Relapse, Resort, Retrogress, Return

**Review(er)** Appeal, Appraisal, Audit, Censor, Credit, Crit, Critic, Criticaster, Critique, Editor, Encomium, Feuilleton, Footlights, Glimpse, Inspect, Iso-, Judicial, Magazine, March-past, Notice, Pan, Panorama, Peer, Pick over, Pundit, Quarterly, Recapitulate, Regatta, Repeat, Retrospect, Revise, Rundown, Run over, Slate, Spithead, Summary, Summing-up, Survey, Write-up

▹**Review** *may indicate* an anagram or a reversed word

**Revile, Reviling** Abuse, Execrate, Inveigh, Rail, Rayle, Vilify, Vituperate

**Revise(r), Revision(ist)** Alter, Amend, Brush up, Change, Correct, Diaskeuast, Diorthosis, Edit, Emend, Expurgate, Heretic, Mug-up, Peruse, Reappraise, Reassess, Recense, Reform, Rev, Rework, Swot, Update

▹**Revise(d)** *may indicate* an anagram

**Revitalise** Rejuvenate, Resuscitate

**Revive(r), Revival(ist), Revivify, Reviving** Araise, Classical, Enliven, Gothic, Greek, Kiss of life, Neo-classical, Rake up, Rally, Reanimate, Reawake(n), Rebirth, Redintegrate,

Redux, Refresh, Rekindle, Relive, Renaissance, Renascent, Renew, Renovate, Restore, Resurgence, Resurrect, Resuscitate, Risorgimento, Romantic, Romo, Rouse, Sal volatile, Smelling salts, Wake

**Revoke** Abrogate, Cancel, Countermand, Negate, Nullify, → RECALL, Repeal, Rescind

**Revolt(ing), Revolution(ary)** Agitator, Agitprop, American, Anarchist, Apostasy, Appal, Barrel roll, Bloodless, Bolivar, Bolshevik, Bolshevist, Boxer, Bukharin, Bulldog, Cade, Cartwheel, Castro, Chartist, Che, Chinese, Circle, Commune, Coup d'état, Cultural, Cycle, Danton, Defection, Degree, Dervish, Desmoulins, De Valera, Disgust, Durutti, Emeute, Emmet, Engels, Enragé, February, Fenian, Firebrand, Foul, French, Germinal, Girondin, Girondist, Glorious, Green, Grody, Guevara, Gyration, Ho Chi Minh, Icky, Industrial, Inqilab, → IN REVOLT, Insurgent, Insurrection, Intifada, IRA, Jacobin, Jacquerie, Komitaji, Lafayette, Lap, Lenin, Leninist, Mao, Marat, Marti, Marx, Marxist, Maximalist, Maypole, Minimalist, Montagnard, Mutiny, Nauseating, Nihilist, October, Odious, Orbit, Outbreak, Paine, Palace, Paris Commune, Peasants, Pilgrimage of grace, Poujadist, Putsch, Radical, → REBEL, Red, Red Guard, Red Shirt, Reformation, Reign of terror, Repellent, Riot, Rise, Robespierre, Roll, Rotation, Round, Run, Russian, Sandinista, Sansculotte(rie), Savimbi, Sedition, Septembrist, Sicilian Vespers, Spartacist, Spartacus, Spiral, Syndicalism, The Mountain, Thermidor, Titanomachy, Trot(sky), Turnstile, Twist, Ugly, Ultra, Unsavoury, Up(rise), → UPRISING, Upryst, Velvet, Villa, Wat Tyler, Weatherman, Whirl, Wolfe Tone, Young Turk, Yucky, Zapata

▷**Revolutionary** *may indicate* 'reversed'

**Revolve(r), Revolving** Carrier, Catherine wheel, Centrifuge, Colt®, Gat, Girandole, Grindstone, → GUN, Gyrant, Gyrate, Iron, Klinostat, Lathe, Maelstrom, Merry-go-round, Peristrephic, Pistol, Pivot, Planet, Roll, Roller, Rotate, Rotifer, Rotor, Roul, Roundabout, Run, Six-shooter, Spin, Swivel, Tone, Turn(stile), Turntable, Turret, Twiddle, Waterwheel, Wheel, Whirl(igig), Whirlpool

**Revue** Follies

**Revulsion** Abhorrence, Distaste, Goose skin, Horror, Loathing, Repugnance, The creeps, Ugh

**Reward(ing)** Albricias, Bonus, Boon, Bounty, Compensate, Consideration, Desert, Emolument, Fee, Guerdon, Head money, Jackpot, Medal, Meed, Palm, Payment, Premium, Price, Prize, Profit, Purse, Push money, Reap, Recognise, Recompense, Reguerdon, Remuneration, Repay, Requital, Requite, S, Shilling, Spoils, Stipend, Tanti, Tribute, Wage, War(r)ison

**Reword** Edit, Paraphrase

**Reworking** Rifacimento

**Rex** Cornish, Devon, Priam, R

**Reynolds** Joshua, PRA

**Rhapsodic, Rhapsody** Bohemian, Ecstasy, Epic, Music, Unconnected

**Rhea** Em(e)u, Nandoo, Nandu, Nhandu, Ostrich, Ramee, Rami, Ramie

**Rhenium** Re

**Rheostat** Potentiometer

**Rhesus** Bandar, Macaque, Monkey

**Rhetoric(al)** Alliteration, Anaphora, Anastrophe, Antimetabole, Antimetathesis, Antistrophe, Antithesis, Apophasis, Aposiopesis, Assonance, Asteism, Asyndeton, Aureate, Bombast, Brachylogia, Cacophony, Catachresis, Chiasmus, Ecbole, Eloquence, Enantiosis, Epanadiplosis, Epanados, Epanalepsis, Epanorthosis, Epexegesis, Epistrophe, Epizeuxis, Erotema, Eroteme, Erotesis, Euphemism, Hendiadys, Hypallage, Hyperbole, Litotes, Metalepsis, Metonymy, Oratory, Oxymoron, Paradox, Paral(e)ipsis, Periphrasis, Peroration, Platform, Pleonasm, Polysyndeton, Scesisonomaton, Speechcraft, Syllepsis, Synoeciosis, Trivial, Trivium, Zeugma

**Rhino** Blunt, Bread, Cash, Crash, Keitloa, Lolly, Loot, → MONEY, Tin

**Rhinoceros** Baluchitherium, Keitloa, Square-lipped, Sumatran, White

**Rhizome** China-root, Rootstock

**Rhodes, Rhodesia(n)** Cecil, Colossus, Ridgeback, Scholar, Zimbabwe

**Rhodium** Rh

**Rhododendron** Azalea

**Rhomboid** Fusil

**Rhubarb** Cobblers, Eyewash, Fiddlesticks, Forced, Monk's, Pie-plant, Rhapontic, Rheum, Rot, Spat, Tripe

**Rhyme(s), Rhymer, Rhyming** Assonance, Bouts rimes, Clerihew, Closed couplet, Counting out, Couplet, Crambo, Cynghanedd, Doggerel, Double, Eye, Feminine, Head, Identical, Internal, Jingle, Macaronic, Male, Masculine, Measure, Mother Goose, Near, Nursery, Ode, Pararhyme, Perfect, Poetry, Poulter's measure, Rich, Riding, Rime riche, Rondel, Royal, Runic, Sight, Slang, Slant, Tail(ed), Tercet, Terza-rima, Thomas, Triple, → **VERSE**, Virelay, Vowel

**Rhythm(ic)** Agoge, Alpha, Asynartete, Backbeat, Beat, Beta, Bo Diddley beat, Breakbeat, Cadence, Circadian, Clave, Dolichurus, Dotted, Drumbeat, Duple, Euouae, Evovae, Four-four, Hemiol(i)a, Ictic, In-step, Lilt, Meter, Movement, Oompah, Ostinato, Prosody, Pulse, Pyrrhic, Rising, Rove-over, Rubato, Scotch catch, Scotch snap, Sdrucciola, Sesquialtera, Singsong, Sprung, Stride piano, Swing, Syncopation, Tala, Talea, → **TEMPO**, Theta, Three-four, Time, Two-four, Voltinism

**Rialto** Market

**Rib(bed), Ribbing, Rib-joint** Bar, Better half, Chaff, Chiack, Chip, Chyack, Cod, Cord, Costa, Cross-springer, Dutch, Eve, False, Fin, Floating, Futtock, Gill, Groin, Intercostal, Lierne, Nervate, Nervular, Nervure, Ogive, Persiflage, Rack, Rag, Rally, Short, Slat, Spare, Springer, Subcosta, Taunt, Tease, Tendron, Tierceron, Tracery, True, Wife

**Ribald(ry)** Balderdash, Bawdy, Coarse, Earthiness, Scurrilous, Smut, Sotadic, Vulgar

**Ribbon** Band, Bandeau, Blue, Bow, Braid, Caddice, Caddis, Caddyss, Cordon, Fattrels, Ferret, Fillet, Grosgrain, Hatband, Infula, Multistrike, Pad, Petersham, Radina, Red, Rein, Riband, Rosette, Rouleau, St Johnston's, Soutache, Taenia, Tape, Teniate, Tie, Topknot, Torsade, Yellow

**Ribless** Ecostate

**Rice (cake)** Arborio, Basmati, Bir(i)yani, Brown, Canada, Carnaroli, Elmer, Entertainer, Golden, Idli, Indian, Kedgeree, Miracle, Paddy, Patna, Pilaf, Pilau, Pilaw, Pillau, Reis, Risotto, Spanish, Sushi, Twigs, Vialone nano, Water, Wild, Zizania

**Rich(es), Richness** Abounding, Abundant, Affluent, Ample, Amusing, Bonanza, Buttery, Comfortable, Comic, Copious, Croesus, Dives, Edmund, Edwin, Fat, Feast, Fertile, Filthy, Flamboyant, Flush, Fruity, Full, Generous, Golconda, Haves, Heeled, High, Idle, Larney, Loaded, Luscious, Lush, Luxe, Luxurious, Mammon, Moneybags, Moneyed, Nabob, New, Oberous, Oofy, → **OPULENT**, Plenteous, Plush, Plutocrat, Prolific, Resonant, Rolling, Silvertail, Sumptuous, Tallent, Toff, Top hat, Treasure, Upper ten, Vulgarian, → **WEALTHY**, Well-heeled, Well off, Well-to-do, Windfall

**Richard** Angevin, Burbage, Dick(y), Lionheart, Nixon, Rick, Roe

**Richthofen** Red Baron

**Rick (burning)** Goaf, Haymow, Sprain, Swingism, Twist, Wrench

**Rickets, Rickety** Dilapidated, Rachitis, Ramshackle, Rattletrap, Shaky, Unsound, Wobbly

▷**Rickety** *may indicate* an anagram

**Rickshaw** Auto, Bicycle, Pedicab, Tuktuk

**Ricochet** Boomerang, Glance, Rebound

**Rid** Clear, Deliver, Ditch, Eliminate, Eradicate, Expulse, Expunge, Free, Obviate, Offload, Purge, Scrap, Scrub, Shot

**Riddle(r)** Boulter, Charade, Colander, Conundrum, Dilemma, Enigma, Koan, Logogriph, Pepper, Perforate, Permeate, Puzzle, Screen, Searce, Search, Seil, Sieve, Sift, Sile, Siler, Sorites, Sphinx, Strain, Tems(e), Trommel, Winnow

**Ride, Riding** Annoy, Aquaplane, Bareback, Bestride, Big dipper, Bruise, Burn, Canter, Car(r)ousel, Coast, Crog(gy), Cycle, District, Division, Donkey, Draisene, Draisine, Drive, Equitation, Ferris wheel, Field, Free, Freewheel, Galloper, Hack, Harass, Haute école, Helter-skelter, Hitchhike, Joy-wheel, Lift, Merry-go-round, Mount, Pick(-a-)back, Pickpack, Piggyback, Postil(l)ion, Rape, Revere's, Roadstead, Rollercoaster, Rural, Sit, Sleigh, Spin, Stang, Surf, Switchback, Third, Transport, Trot, Waltzer, Weather, Welter, Wheelie, Whip, White-knuckle

**Rider(s)** Addendum, Addition, Adjunct, Afterthought, Appendage, Attachment, Boundary, Bucket, Caballero, Cavalier, Charioteer, Circuit, Clause, Coachman, Codicil, Condition,

Corollary, Dispatch, Equestrian, Eventer, Freedom, Gaucho, Godiva, Guidon, Haggard, Horseman, Jockey, Lochinvar, Messenger, Passenger, Peloton, Postil(l)ion, Proviso, PS, Revere, Scrub, Spurrer, Transport, Walkyrie

**Ridge(pole)** Alveolar, Annapurna, Anthelix, Antihelix, Arête, Arris, As(ar), Aseismic, Balk, Bank, Bar, Baulk, Berm, Brow, Bur(r), Carina, Chine, Clint, Costa, Coteau, Crease, Crest, Crista, Cuesta, Culmen, Darling Range, Drill, Drum(lin), Dune, Eskar, Esker, Fret, Gap, Gonys, Gyrus, Hammock, Hoe, Hogback, Hog's back, Horst, Hummock, Interfluve, Kaim, Kame, Keel, Knur(l), Ledge, Linch, List(er), Lynchet, Mid-Atlantic, Middleback, Mid-ocean, Missionary, Moraine, Nek, Nut, Oceanic, Oche, Offset, Pressure, Promontory, Ramp, Rand, Raphe, Razor-back, Reef, Rib, Riblet, Rig, Rim, Road hump, Roof-tree, Sastruga, Screw-thread, Serac, Serpentine, Shoulder, Sowback, Spit, Torus, Varix, Verumontanum, Vimy, Wale, Weal, Welt, Whelp, Whorl, Windrow, Withers, Witwatersrand, Wrinkle, Yardang, Zastruga

**Ridicule, Ridiculous** Absurd, Badinage, Bathos, Chaff, Charade, Cockamamie, Crackpot, Debunk, Deride, Derisory, Diss, Egregious, Foolish, Gibbet, Gibe, Gird, Goad, Guy, Haze, Jeer, Jibe, Josh, Lampoon, Laughable, Ludicrous, Mimic, Mock, Paradox, Pasquin, Pillory, Pish, Pooh-pooh, Rag, Raillery, Rally, Rib, Rich, Risible, Roast, Satire, Scoff, Scout, Screwy, Send up, Sight, Silly, Skimmington, Sneer, Taunt, Travesty

**Ridinghood** Nithsdale, Red, Trot-cos(e)y

**Riding-master** RM

**Riding-school** Manège

**Rife** Abundant, Epidemic, Manifest, Numerous, Prevalent

**Riffle** Rapid

**Riff-raff** Canaille, Hoi polloi, Mob, Populace, Rag-tag, Rag, tag and bobtail, Scaff, Scum, Trash

**Rifle(man)** Air, Armalite®, Assault, Bone, Browning, Bundook, Burgle, Calic, Carbine, Chassepot, Elephant-gun, Enfield, Enfield musket, Escopette, Express, Ferret, Garand, → GUN, Jaeger, Kalashnikov®, Lee Enfield, Loot, Magazine, Martini®, Martini-Henry, Mauser®, MI, Minié, Pea, Petronel, Pick, Pilfer, Pillage, Raid, Ransack, Reave, Reive, Remington, Repeater, Rieve, Rob, Ruger, Saloon, Shiloh, Springfield, Winchester®

**Rift** Altercation, Breach, Canyon, Chasm, Chink, Cleft, Crevasse, Fault, Fissure, Gap, Gulf, Separation, Split

**Rig(ging), Rigger** Accoutre, Apparel, Attire, Bermuda, Deadeye, Drilling, Equip, Feer, Frolic, Gaff, Get-up, Gunter, Hoax, Jack-up, Jury, Mainbrace, Manipulate, Marconi, Martingale, Oil(man), Oilwell, Outfit, Panoply, Platform, Ratline, Rattlin, Ropes, Roughneck, Running, Schooner, Semisubmersible, Slant, Sport, Stack, Standing, Stay, Strip, Stuns'l, Swindle, Tackle, Togs, Top hamper, Trull, Wanton, Yardarm

▹**Rigged** *may indicate* an anagram

**Right(s), Righten, Rightful, Rightness** Accurate, Advowson, Affirmative, Ancient lights, Angary, Animal, Appropriate, Appurtenance, Axiom, Ay, Bang, Befit, Blue-pencil, BNP, Bote, Bragging, Cabotage, Champart, Civil, Claim, Competence, Conjugal, Conservative, Copyhold, Cor(r)ody, → CORRECT, Coshery, Cuddy, Cure, Curtesy, Customer, Dead on, De jure, Dexter, Direct, Divine, Doctor, Droit, Due, Easement, Emend, Eminent domain, Emphyteusis, Entitlement, Equal, Equity, Esnecy, Estover, Ethical, Exactly, Faldage, Farren, Fascist, Feal and divot, Feu, Fiar, Fire-bote, Fitting, Forestage, Franchise, Free-bench, Freedom, Gay, Germane, Gunter, Haybote, Hedge-bote, House-bote, Human, Inalienable, Infangthief, Interest, Isonomy, Iure, Junior, Jural, Jure, Jus (mariti), Leet, Legal, Legit(imate), Letters patent, Liberty, Lien, Maritage, Maternity, Meet, Merit, Miner's, Miranda, Moral, Naam, Neo-con, New, Ninepence, Ninepins, Off, Offhand, Offside, OK, Okay, Oke, Okey-dokey, Option, Ortho-, Oughtness, Paine, Pannage, Passant, Pasturage, Pat, Patent, Paternity, Performing, Pit and gallows, Ploughbote, Pose, Postliminy, Pre-emption, Prerogative, Primogeniture, Priority, Prisage, Privilege, Proper, Property, Pukka, R, Rain, Reason, Recourse, Rectify, Rectitude, Redress, Remainder, Remedy, Repair, Ripe, Rt, Sac, Sake, Serial, Side, Slap, So, Soc, Spot-on, Squatter's, Stage, Starboard, Stillicide, Substantive, Suo jure, Suo loco, Tao, Tenants', Terce, Ticket, Tickety-boo, Title, Tory, Trivet, Trover, True, Turbary, User, Usucap(t)ion, Usufruct, Venville, Vert, Warren, Water, Women's

**Right-angle(d)** Orthogonal
**Righteous(ness)** Devout, Good, Just, Moral, Pharisee, Prig, Rectitude, Sanctimonious, Tzaddik, Virtuous
**Right-hand** Dexter, E, Far, Recto, RH, Ro
**Right-wing(er)** Bircher, Dry, Falangist, Fascist, Hard hat, Neocon, Neo-fascist, Reactionary, Republican
**Rigid(ity)** Acierated, Cast iron, Catalepsy, Catatonic, Craton, Extreme, Fixed, Formal, Hard and fast, Hard-liner, Hard-set, Hard-shell, Hidebound, Inflexible, Lignin, Ossified, Renitent, Rigor, Set, Slavish, Starch(y), Stern, Stiff, Stretchless, Strict, Stringent, Tense, Turgor
**Rigmarole** Jazz, Nonsense, Palaver, Paraphernalia, Protocol, Ragman, Ragment, Riddlemeree, Screed
**Rigorous, Rigo(u)r** Accurate, Austere, Cruel, Exact, Firm, Hard, Harshness, Inclement, Iron-bound, Severe, Stern, Strait, Strict, Stringent, Thorough
**Rile** Anger, Annoy, Harry, Irritate, Needle, → **NETTLE**, Vex
▷**Rile(y)** *may indicate* an anagram
**Rill** Nal(la), Purl, Sike
**Rim** Atlantic, Border, Chimb, Chime, Edge, Felloe, Felly, Flange, Girdle, Kelyphitic, → **LIP**, Margin, Pacific, Strake, Verge
**Rime** Crust, Frost, Hoar, Rhyme, Rhythm
**Rind** Bark, Crackling, Crust, Peel, Skin
**Ring(ed), Ringer, Ringing, Rings** Anchor, Angelus, Annual, Annulus, Anthelion, Arcus, Arena, Band, Bangle, Base, Bayreuth, Bell, Benzine, Betrothal, Boom-iron, Broch, Brogh, Buzz, Call, Cambridge, Carabiner, Cartel, Cartouche, Change, Chime, Circinate, Circle, Circlet, Circlip, Circus, Claddagh, Clam, Clang, Clink, Coil, Collet, Cordon, Cornice, Corona, Corral, Corrida, Cramp, Crawl, Cricoid, Cringle, Cromlech, Cycle, Cyclic, Dead, Death's head, Dial, Dicyclic, Diffraction, Ding, Disc, Dohyo, Dong, Donut, Doorbell, Double, Draupnir, Dress, D(o)uar, Echo, Encircle, Enclosure, Encompass, Engagement, Engrailment, Enhalo, Enlace, Envelop, Environ, Enzone, Eternity, Extension, Eyelet, Fainne, Fairlead(er), Fairy, Ferrule, Fisherman, Fisti(cuffs), Gas, Gimmal, Gimmer, Gird(le), Girr, Gloriole, Groin, Grom(m)et, Growth, Grummet, Guard, Gyges, Gymmal, Gyre, Halo, Hank, Hob, → **HOOP**, Hoop-la, Hound, Hula-hoop, Ideal, Image, Inner, Inorb, Involucre, Jougs, Jow, Karabiner, Kartell, Keeper, Key, Knell, Knock-out, Kraal, Lactam, Laer, Lifebelt, Link, Loop, Lophophore, Luned, Lute, Magpie, Manacle, Manilla, Marquise, Marriage, Mourning, Napkin, Newton's, Nibelung, Nimbus, Nose, O, Oil-control, Onion, Orb, Outer, Pappus, Parral, Parrel, Peal, Pele, Pen, Phone, Ping, Piston, Potato, Price, Prize, Puteal, Quoit, Re-echo, Resonant, Resound, Retaining, Reverberate, Round, Rove, Rowel, Rundle, Runner, Rush, Sale, Saturn, Scarf, Scraper, Screw eye, Scrunchy, Seal, Signet, Slinger, Slip, Snap-link, Solomon, Sound, Spell, Split, Stemma, Stemme, Stonehenge, Surround, Swivel, Syndicate, Tang, Tattersall, Teething, Terret, Territ, Thimble, Thumb, Timbre, Ting, Tingle, Tink(le), Tinnitus, Tintinnabulate, Toe, Toggle, Token, Toll, Toplady, Tore, Torquate, Torques, Torret, Torus, Travelling, Tree, Trochus, Troth, Turret, Tweed, Varvel, Vervel, Vice, Vortex, Wagnerian, Washer, Wedding, Welkin, Whorl, Withe, Woggle, Wreath, Zero
**Ring-dance** Carol
**Ring-dove** Que(e)st, Qu(o)ist
**Ring-leader** Bell-wether, Fugleman, Instigator
**Ringlet** Curl(icue), Lock, Tendril, Tress
**Ringmaster** Wagner
**Ringworm** Serpigo, Tinea
**Rink** Ice, Roller, Skating
**Rinky-dink** Moss-backed
**Rinse** Bathe, Blue, Cleanse, Douche, Sind, Sine, Sluice, Swill, Synd, Syne, Tint, Wash
**Riot(er), Riotous(ly), Riots** Anarchy, Brawl, Clamour, Demo, Deray, Gordon, Hilarious, Hubbub, Luddite, Medley, Mêlée, Nicker, Orgy, Pandemonium, Peterloo, Petroleur, Porteous, Profusion, Quorum, Race, Rag, Ragmatical, Rampage, Rebecca, Rebel, Roaring, Roister, Rout, Rowdy, Ruction, Ruffianly, Scream, Sedition, Swing, Tumult
▷**Rioters, Riotous** *may indicate* an anagram

**Rip(per), Ripping, Rip off** Avulse, Basket, Buller, Cur, Dilacerate, Fleece, Grand, Handful, Horse, Jack, Lacerate, Rent, Rep, Roué, Scallywag, Splendid, Tear, Tide, Topnotch, To-rend, Unseam

**Ripe, Ripen(ing)** Age, Auspicious, Drop, Full, Geocarpy, Mature, Mellow, Rathe, Ready

**Riposte** Counterblow, Countermove, Repartee, Retaliate, Retort, Sally

**Ripple, Rippling** Bradyseism, Fret, Jabble, Overlap, Popple, Purl, Ruffle, Undulation, Wave, Wavelet, Wimple, Wrinkle

▷**Rippling** *may indicate* an anagram

**Rise(r), Rising** Advance, Appreciate, Ascend, Aspire, Assurgent, Bull, Butte, Cause, Dry, Dutch, Early, Easter, Eger, Elevation, Emanate, Emerge, Emerse, Émeute, Eminence, Erect, Escalate, Get up, Gradient, Hance, Hauriant, Haurient, Heave, Heliacal, Hike, Hill, Hillock, Hummock, Hunt's up, Improve, Increase, Incremental, Insurgent, Intifada, Intumesce, Jibe, Knap, Knoll, Lark, Leap, Levee, Levitate, Lift, Molehill, Motte, Mount, Mutiny, Orient, Origin, Peripety, Point, Prove, Putsch, Rear, Rebel, Resurgent, Resurrection, → **REVOLT**, Riot, Rocket, Saleratus, Scarp, Sklim, Sky-rocket, Soar, Spiral, Stand, Stay, Stie, Sty, Stye, Surface, Surge, Swell, The Fifteen, Tor, Tower, Transcend, Up, Upbrast, Upburst, Upcurl, Upgo, Upland, Uprest, Upshoot, Upspear, Upsurge, Upswarm, Upturn, Well

**Risk(y)** Actuarial, Adventure, Apperil, Back, Calculated, Chance, Compromise, Counterparty, → **DANGER**, Daring, Dice, Dicy, Emprise, Endanger, Fear, Gamble, Game, Hairy, Hazard, High, High-wire, Iffy, Imperil, Impetuous, Incur, Jeopardy, Liability, Low, Morass, Nap, Parlous, Peril(ous), Plight, Precarious, Security, Shoot the works, Spec(ulate), Stake, Throw, Touch and go, Touchy, Unsafe, Venture

**Risorgimento** Renaissance

**Risqué** Blue, Racy, Salty, Saucy, Scabrous, Spicy

**Rissole(s)** Cecils, Chillada, Croquette, Faggot, Falafel, Felafel, Meatball, Patty, Paupiette, Quennelle, Veggieburger

**Rite(s)** Asperges, Bora, Ceremony, Circumcision, Confirmation, Eastern, Exequies, Initiation, Last honours, Last offices, Liturgy, Mystery, Nagmaal, Obsequies, Observance, Powwow, Ritual, Sacral, Sacrament, Sarum use, Solemnity, Superstition, York

**Ritual** Agadah, Arti, Ceremony, Chanoyu, Cultus, Customary, Formality, Haggada, Lavabo, Liturgy, Mumbo-jumbo, Puja, Rite, Sacrament, Sacring, Seder, Social, Tantric, Telestic, Totem, Use

**Rival(ry), Rivals** Absolute, Acres, Aemule, Binocular, Challenge, Compete, Competitor, Contender, Emulate, Emule, Envy, Fo(n)e, → **MATCH**, Needle, Opponent, Retinal, Sibling, Touch, Vie

**River(s)** Bayou, Creek, Dalles, Ea, Eau, Estuary, Flood, Flower, Fluvial, Potamic, Potamology, R, Rapids, Riverain, Runner, Stream, Tide(-way), Tributary, Waterway

---

**RIVERS**

*2 letters:*
Ay
Ob
Po
Si
Xi

*3 letters:*
Aar
Aln
Axe
Ayr
Bug
Cam
Dee
Don
Ems
Esk
Exe
Fal
Fly
Fox
Han
Hsi
Hué
Inn
Lee
Lot
Luo
Lys
Mur
Nar
Oil
Oka
Ord
Red
San
Tay
Tet
Ure
Usk
Wye
Yeo

*4 letters:*
Abus
Abzu
Acis
Adda
Adur
Aire
Alma
Alph
Amur
Aran
Aras
Arno
Aude
Avon
Back
Beni
Bomu
Cher
Culm
Dart
Deva
Doon
Dove
Drin
Earn
East
Ebbw
Ebro
Eden

Eder
Elbe
Emme
Erne
Esla
Eure
Gila
Gota
Huon
Idle
Isar
Iser
Isis
Isla
Ivel
Jiul
Juba
Kama
Kill
Kura
Kwai
Lahn
Lech
Lena
Liao
Luan
Lune
Maas
Main
Meta
Milk
Mino
Mole
Nene
Neva
Nile
Nith
Oder
Ohio
Oise
Ouse
Oxus
Prut
Rock
Ruhr
Saar
Sava
Soar
Spey
Styx
Swan
Swat
Tadi
Taff
Tana
Tarn
Tees
Teme
Test
Tone
Tyne
Uele
Ural
Uvod
Vaal
Waal
Wear
Xero
Yalu
Yare
Yate
Yser
Yuan
Yuen

***5 letters:***
Abana
Acton
Adige
Afton
Agate
Aisne
Aldan
Apure
Argun
Avoca
Benue
Boyne
Broad
Cauca
Chari
Clwyd
Clyde
Clyst
Colne
Congo
Conwy
Cross
Culbá
Dasht
Desna
Doubs
Douro
Drava
Drave
Duero
Dvina
Eblis
Ebola
Firth
Fleet
Forth
Ganga
Gogra
Green
Greta
Havel
Hotan
Indre
Indus
Isere
Ishim
James
Jumna
Juruá
Kasai
Kaven
Kefue
Kenga
Kuban
Lethe
Liard
Limay
Loire
Marne
Mbomu
Meuse
Minho
Mosel
Mulla
Mures
Namoi
Negro
Neman
Niger
Ogowe
Onega
Oreti
Peace
Pearl
Pecos
Pelly
Piave
Pison
Plate
Purus
Rainy
Rance
Rhine
Rhône
Rogue
Roper
Saône
Seine
Shari
Shire
Siang
Siret
Skien
Slave
Snake
Snowy
Somme
Spree
Staff
Stour
Swale
Tagus
Tamar
Tapti
Tarim
Teign
Terek
Tiber
Tisza
Tobol
Trent
Tweed
Volga
Volta
Warta
Weser
Xiang
Xingu
Yaqui
Yarra
Yonne
Yssel
Yukon

***6 letters:***
Allier
Amazon
Anadyr
Angara
Arzina
Atbara
Barcoo
Barrow
Bio-Bio
Broads
Buller
Calder
Canton
Chenab
Clutha
Colima
Croton
Crouch
Cydnus
Danube
Dawson
Donets
Duddon
Durack
Escaut
Finlay
Fraser
Gambia
Ganges
Glomma
Granta
Harlem
Hodder
Hsiang
Hudson
Humber
Iguacu
Ijssel
Irtish
Irtysh
Irwell
Isonzo
Itchen
Japura
Javari
Javary
Jhelum
Jordan
Kaduna
Kagera
Kaveri
Kennet
Kistna
Kolyma
Komati
Liffey
Loiret
Mamoré
Medway
Mekong
Mersey
Mindel
Mohawk
Molopo
Morava
Moskva
Murray
Neckar
Neisse
Nelson
Nyeman
Ogooue
Orange
Orwell
Ottawa
Pahang
Parana
Peneus
Platte

Pripet
Prosna
Rakaia
Ribble
Riffle
Rother
Sabine
Saluda
Sambre
Santee
Seneca
Severn
St John
Struma
Sutlej
Swanee
Tanana
Tarsus
Tevere
Teviot
Thames
Ticino
Tigris
Tugela
Tyburn
Ubangi
Ussuri
Vardar
Vienne
Vltava
Vyatka
Wabash
Wairau
Wensum
Wharfe
Wupper
Yarrow
Yellow

***7 letters:***
Acheron
Aruwimi
Bassein
Berbice
Berezua
Bermejo
Buffalo
Burnett
Caqueta
Cauvery
Chagres
Cocytus
Damodar
Darling
Derwent
Detroit
Dnieper
Dubglas
Durance
Ettrick
Fitzroy
Garonne
Genesee
Gironde
Guapore
Hari Rud
Helmand
Hooghly
Huang He
Hwangho
Iguassu
Irawadi
Kanawha
Klamath
Krishna
Lachlan
Limpopo
Lualaba
Madeira
Manning
Maranon
Maritsa
Mataura
Meander
Moselle
Narbada
Narmada
Neuquén
Niagara
Nipigon
Oceanus
Orinoco
Orontes
Parrett
Pechora
Pharpar
Potomac
Red Deer
Rubicon
Sabrina
Salinas
Salween
Salzach
Sanders
San Juan
Scheldt
Senegal
Shannon
Songhua
Spokane
St Clair
St Croix
St Johns
St Mary's
Stygian
Swannee
Tapajos
Thomson
Tugaloo
Ucayali
Uruguay
Vistula
Waikato
Waitaki
Washita
Wateree
Welland
Xi Jiang
Yangtse
Yenisei
Yenisey
Zambese
Zambezi

***8 letters:***
Amu Darya
Anderson
Apurimac
Araguaia
Araguaya
Arkansas
Berezina
Blue Nile
Burdekin
Canadian
Charente
Cherwell
Cheyenne
Chindwin
Chu Kiang
Clarence
Colorado
Columbia
Congaree
Daintree
Demerara
Dneister
Dordogne
Flinders
Franklin
Gascoyne
Godavari
Granicus
Guadiana
Hamilton
Han Jiang
Illinois
Kennebec
Kentucky
Klondike
Kootenay
Maeander
Mahanadi
Manawatu
Menderes
Missouri
Mitchell
Ob 'Irtysh
Ocmulgee
Okanagan
Okavango
Okovango
Ouachita
Pactolus
Paraguay
Parnaiba
Putumayo
Rio Negro
Safid Rud
Saguenay
Savannah
Suwannee
Syr Darya
Thompson
Tonle Sap
Torridge
Toulouse
Tunguska
Van Hades
Veronezh
Victoria
Volturno
Wanganui
Windrush
Zhu Jiang

***9 letters:***
Allegheny
Ashburton
Athabasca
Billabong
Churchill
Crocodile
Des Moines
Essequibo
Euphrates
Irrawaddy
Kuskokwim
Mackenzie
Magdalena
Murchison
Parnahiba
Perihonca
Pilcomayo

Porcupine
Qu'Appelle
Rangitata
Richelieu
Rio Branco
Rio Grande
Salambria
Santa Cruz
St George's
White Nile
Wisconsin

*10 letters:*
Black Volta
Blackwater
Chao Phraya
Courantyne
Cumberland
Great Slave
Hawkesbury
Housatonic
Kizil Irmak
Phlegethon
Rangitaiki
Rangitikei
Sacramento
San Joaquin
Schuylkill
Shenandoah
St Lawrence
White Volta
Yesil Irmak

*11 letters:*
Aegospotami
Assiniboine
Brahmaputra
Castlereagh
Connecticut
Cooper Creek
Delaguadero
Guadalentin
Lesser Slave
Madre de Dios
Mississauga
Mississippi
Monongahela
Montmorency
Shatt-al-Arab
Susquehanna
Yellowstone

*12 letters:*
Guadalquivir
Murrumbidgee
Saõ Francisco
Saskatchewan
Victoria Nile

*13 letters:*
Little Bighorn

*14 letters:*
Jacques Cartier

*17 letters:*
North Saskatchewan
South Saskatchewan

---

**River-bank, Riverside** Brim, Carse, Riparian
**River-bed** T(h)alweg
**River-mouth** Firth, Frith
**Rivet(ing)** Bolt, Clinch, Clink, Concentrate, Engross, Explosive, Fasten, Fix, Pean, Peen, Stud, Transfix, Unputdownable
**Riviera** Cornish, French, Italian
**Rivulet** Beck, Brook, Burn, Creek, Gill, Rill, Runnel, Strand
**RMA** The Shop
**RNA** Antisense, → DNA, Initiator codon, Messenger, Molecule, M-RNA, Retrotransposon, Ribosomal, Ribosome, Ribozyme, Soluble, Transcribe, Transfer, Uracil, Viroid
**Roach** Arch(ie), Fish, Incurve, Red-eye
**Road(s), Roadside, Road surface** A, A1, Access, Anchorage, Approach, Arterial, Asphalt, Autobahn, Autopista, Autostrada, Ave(nue), B, Beltway, Blacktop, Blind, Boulevard, Broadway, Burma, Bypass, Carriageway, Causeway, Churchway, Clay, Clearway, Close, Cloverleaf, Coach, Concession, Corduroy, Corniche, Course, Crossover, Crown, Cul-de-sac, Dirt, Drift-way, Driveway, Drove, Dunstable, Escape, Exit, Expressway, Fairway, Feeder, Fly-over, Fly-under, Foss(e) Way, Freeway, Frontage, Grid, Hampton, Hard, High, Highway, Horseway, Interstate, Kerb, Lane, Loan, Loke, M1, Macadam, Mall, Metal, Motorway, Off-ramp, Orbital, Overpass, Parkway, Path, Pike, Post, Private, Rat-run, Rd, Relief, Ride, Ridgeway, Ring, → ROUTE, Royal, Service, Shoulder, Shunpike, Side, Silk, Skid, Slip, Speedway, Spur(way), St(reet), Superhighway, Switchback, Tarmac, Tar-seal, Terrace, Thoroughfare, Throughway, Tobacco, Toby, Tollway, Track(way), Trunk, Turning, Turnpike, Unadopted, Underpass, Unmade, Verge, Via, Viaduct, Way
**Roadblock** Barrier, Cone, Jam, Sleeping policeman, Thank-you-ma'am, Toll
**Roadhog** Tailgater
**Road-keeper** Way-warden
**Road-maker** Drunkard, Macadam, Navigator, Telford, Wade
**Roadstead** La Hogue
**Roam** Enrange, Extravagate, Nomadic, Peregrinate, Rake, Ramble, Rove, Stray, Wander, Wheel
**Roan** Barbary, Bay, Horse, Leather, Schimmel, Strawberry
**Roar(ing)** Bant, Bawl, Bell(ow), Blare, Bluster, Boom, Boys, Cry, Forties, Guffaw, Laugh, Leonine, Roin, Rote, Rout, Royne, Thunder, Tumult, Vroom, Wuther, Zoom
**Roast** Attack, Bake, Barbecue, Baste, Birsle, Brent, Cabob, Cook, Crab, Crown, Decrepitate, Dripping, Excoriate, Grill, Kabob, Pan, Parch, Pot, Ridicule, Scald, Scathe, Scorch, Sear, Slate, Spit, Tan, Torrefy, Turnspit
**Rob(bed), Robber(y)** Abactor, Abduct, Bandalero, Bandit, Barabbas, Bereave, Blag,

Bonnie, Brigand, Burgle, Bust, Cabbage, Cacus, Cateran, Clyde, Dacoit, Dakoit, Daylight, Depredation, Deprive, Despoil, Dispossess, Divest, Do, Drawlatch, Fake, Filch, Fleece, Flimp, Footpad, Gilderoy, Haul, Heist, Hership, Highjack, High toby, Highwayman, Hijack, Hold-up, Hustle, Job, Knock off, Kondo, Ladrone, Land-pirate, Larceny, Latrocinium, Latron, Loot, Low toby, Mill, Moskonfyt, Mosstrooper, Mug, Pad, Pandoor, Pandour, Pillage, Pinch, Piracy, Pluck, Plunder, Procrustes, Ramraid, Rapine, Reave, Reft, Reive, Rieve, Rifle, Road agent, Roberdsman, Robertsman, Roll, Rover, Roy, Rubbet, Rustler, Sack, Safe-cracker, Sciron, Score, Screw, Sheppard, Short change, Sinis, Sirup, Skinner, Smash and grab, Snaphaunch, Snatch, Spoiler, Spoliation, Spring-heeled Jack, → STEAL, Steaming, Stick-up, Sting, Strip, Swindle, Syrup, Thief, Thug(gee), Toby, Turn-over, Turpin

**Robe(s)** Alb, Amice, Amis, Attrap, Buffalo, Camis, Camus, Canonicals, Cassock, Chimer, Chrisom(-cloth), Christom, Dalmatic, Djellabi, Dolman, → DRESS, Gown, Habit, Ihram, Jilbab, Kanga, Kanzu, Khalat, Khilat, Kill(a)ut, Kimono, Mantle, Night, Parament, Parliament, Pedro, Peplos, Pontificals, Purple, Regalia, Rochet, Saccos, Sanbenito, Sari, Soutane, Sticharion, Stola, Stole, Talar, Tire, Toga, Vestment, Yukata

**Robert** Bob(by), Bridges, Browning, Burns, Cop, Flic, Peel, Rab, Rob

**Robin** Adair, American, Bird, Cock, Day, Goodfellow, Hob, Hood, Puck(-hairy), Ragged, Redbreast, Reliant, Round, Ruddock, Starveling, Wake

**Robot** Android, Animatronic, Automaton, Cyborg, Dalek, Golem, Nanobot, Puppet, RUR, Telechir

**Robust** Able-bodied, Fit, Hale, Hard-wearing, Hardy, Healthy, Hearty, Iron, Lusty, Muscular, Rude, Sound, Stalwart, Sthenic, Stout, Strapping, Sturdy, Vigorous

**Roc** Bird, Ruc, Rukh

**Rock(s), Rocker, Rocking, Rocky** Acid, Ages, Agitate, Astound, Ayers, Birthstone, Bone-breccia, Brighton, Cairn, Cap, Cock, Country, Cradle, Destabilise, Edinburgh, Elvis, Erratic, Extrusive, Garage, Gem, Gib(raltar), Goth, Heavy metal, Hybrid, Instable, Jounce, Jow, Kimmeridgian, Lithology, Mantle, Marciano, Marlstone, Matrix, Native, Nunatak(kr), Oscillate, Pelitic, Permafrost, Petrology, Petrous, Picrate, Platform, Plymouth, Progressive, Punk, Quake, Reel, Reggae, Reservoir, Rimrock, Rip-rap, Rudaceous, Sally, Sard, Scar, Scare, Scaur, Schorl, Sclate, → SHAKE, Shoogle, Showd, Soft, Sphene, Stonehenge, Stun, Sway, Swee, Swing, Ted, Teeter, Terra, Totter, Traverse, Treadle, Tremble, Ultrabasic, Ultramafic, Uluru, Unstable, Unsteady, Verd-antique, Verde-antico, Wall, Weeping, Whin, Wind, Windsor, Wobble

---

**ROCKS**

***2 letters:***
Aa

***3 letters:***
Ice
Tor

***4 letters:***
Bell
Coal
Crag
Gang
Glam
Jura
Lava
Lias
Noup
Reef
Sill
Sima
Trap
Tufa
Tuff
Zoic

***5 letters:***
Arête
Brash
Calpe
Chair
Chalk
Chert
Cliff
Clint
Craig
Elvan
Emery
Flint
Geode
Glass
Krans
Loess
Mafic
Magma
Nappe
Olgas
Peter
Scalp
Scrae
Scree
Shale
Slate
Solid
Stone
Trass
Wacke

***6 letters:***
Albite
Aplite
Arkose
Banket
Basalt
Dacite
Desert
Diapir
Dogger
Dunite
Felsic
Flaser
Flysch
Fossil
Gabbro
Gangue
Garnet
Gibber
Gneiss
Gossan
Gozzan
Inlier

Kingle
Living
Marble
Masada
Norite
Oolite
Oolith
Ophite
Pelite
Pluton
Pumice
Rognon
Sarsen
Schist
Sinter
Skerry
Sklate
S. Peter
Stonen
Synroc
Tephra

***7 letters:***
Aquifer
Archean
Arenite
Boulder
Breccia
Clastic
Cuprite
Cyanean
Diamond
Diorite
Erathem
Eucrite
Fastnet
Felsite
Geofact
Granite
Greisen
Haplite
Igneous
Lignite
Lorelei
Marlite
Minette
Molasse
Moraine
Needles
Olivine
Ophites
Outcrop
Outlier
Pennant
Peridot
Picrite
Remanie
Rhaetic
Sinking
Spilite
Stadium
Syenite
Terrane
Thulite
Tripoli
Wenlock

***8 letters:***
Adularia
Aegirine
Aiguille
Andesite
Aphanite
Archaean
Asbestos
Basanite
Brockram
Burstone
Calcrete
Calc-tufa
Calc-tuff
Ciminite
Diabasic
Dolerite
Dolomite
Eclogite
Eklogite
Elvanite
Eutaxite
Fahlband
Felstone
Footwall
Ganister
Hepatite
Hornfels
Idocrase
Inchcape
Isocline
Laterite
Lenticle
Liparite
Lopolith
Mesolite
Mudstone
Mylonite
Obsidian
Oil shale
Peperino
Petuntse
Phyllite
Pisolite
Plutonic
Porphyry
Psammite
Psephite
Ragstone
Regolith
Rhyolite
Rocaille
Roe-stone
Saxatile
Saxonite
Scorpion
Sunstone
Taconite
Tarpeian
Tephrite
The Olgas
Tonalite
Trachyte
Trappean
Volcanic
Whin sill
Xenolith

***9 letters:***
Anticline
Argillite
Batholite
Batholith
Bentonite
Bluestone
Buhrstone
Caenstone
Claystone
Cockhorse
Colluvium
Cornstone
Dalradian
Diatomite
Dinantian
Dolostone
Eddystone
Evaporite
Firestone
Flagstone
Flowstone
Gannister
Goslarite
Granulite
Greensand
Greystone
Greywacke
Gritstone
Hornstone
Impactite
Intrusion
Ironstone
Laccolite
Laccolith
Lardalite
Larvikite
Limestone
Meteorite
Mica-slate
Migmatite
Monadnock
Monocline
Monzonite
Mortstone
Mugearite
Natrolite
Neocomian
Ophiolite
Ottrelite
Pegmatite
Phonolite
Phosphate
Pleonaste
Propylite
Protogine
Quartzite
Sandstone
Saprolite
Scablands
Schistose
Siltstone
Soapstone
Tachylyte
Theralite
Tinguaite
Toadstone
Travertin
Underclay
Uriconian
Variolite
Veinstone
Veinstuff
Ventifact
Vulcanite
Whinstone
White Lias
Whunstane
Zechstein

***10 letters:***
Ailsa Craig
Amygdaloid
Camptonite
Epidiorite
Foundation
Granophyre
Greenstone
Grey-wether

Hypabyssal
Ignimbrite
Kersantite
Kimberlite
Laurdalite
Laurvikite
Lherzolite
Limburgite
Mica-schist
Novaculite
Orthophyre
Palagonite
Peridotite
Phenocryst
Pitchstone
Pyroxenite
Rhinestone
Rupestrian
Schalstein
Serpentine
Sparagmite
Stinkstone
Stonebrash
Syntagmata
Teschenite
Touchstone
Travertine
Troctolite

*11 letters:*
Agglomerate
Alexandrite
Amphibolite
Annabergite
Anorthosite
Carbonatite
Geanticline
Halleflinta
Lamprophyre
Metamorphic
Monchiquite
Napoleonite
Nephelinite
Phillipsite
Pyroclastic
Sedimentary
Slickenside
Symplegades

*12 letters:*
Babingtonite
Baltic Shield
Coal Measures
Granodiorite
Grossularite
Serpentinite
Straticulate
Stromatolite
Syntagmatite
Thunderstone

*13 letters:*
Hypersthenite

*14 letters:*
Giant's Causeway
Knotenschiefer
Rhombenporphyr
Roche moutonnée

*18 letters:*
Scandinavian Shield

---

**Rock-boring** Pholas, Saxicavous
**Rock-cress** Arabis
**Rocket** Arugula, Blue, Booster, Capsule, Carpet, Carrier, Congreve, Dame's, Delta, Doodlebug, Drake, Dressing down, Dyer's, Earful, Engine, Eruca, Exocet®, Flare, Ion, Iron horse, Jato, Life, Locomotive, London, Missile, Multistage, Mushroom, Onion, Payload, Posigrade, Reprimand, Reproof, Retro, Rockoon, Rucola, Salad, SAM, Sea, Sky, Skylark, Soar, Sonde, Sounding, Space probe, Step, Stephenson, Take-off, Thruster, Tourbillion, Ullage, Upshoot, V1, Vernier, Von Braun, Wall, Warhead, Weld, Yellow, Zero stage
**Rockface** Headwall
**Rock-living** Rupicoline, Saxatile, Saxicoline, Saxicolous
**Rock-pipit** Sea-lark
▷**Rocky** *may indicate* an anagram
**Rococo** Baroque, Fancy, Ornate, Quaint
**Rod(-shaped), Rodlike, Rods** Aaron's, Angler, Axle, Baculiform, Bar, Barbel(l), Barre, Birch, Bow, Caduceus, Calm, Came, Camshaft, Can, Cane, Centre, Connecting, Control, Cue, Cuisenaire®, Dipstick, Divining, Dopper, Dowel, Dowser, Drain, Ellwand, Emu, Fasces, Filler, Fin-ray, Firearm, Fisher, Fishing, Fly, Fuel, Gauging, Gold stick, Gun, Handspike, Jacob's staff, Kame, King, Laver, Lease, Lightning, Linchpin, Lug, Mapstick, Measure, Measuring, Mopstick, Moses, Napier's bones, Nervure, Newel, Notochord, Perch, Pin, Pistol, Piston, Pitman, Pointer, Poker, Poking-stick, Pole, Pontie, Pontil, Ponty, Probang, Puntee, Punty, Push, Raddle, Range, Regulating, Rhabdoid, Rhabdus, Riding, Rood, Scollop, Shaft, Sounding, Spindle, Spit, Stadia, Stair, Stanchion, Staple, Stave, Stay-bolt, Stick, Sticker, Strickle, Strut, Switch, Swizzle stick, Tensile, Tension, Tie, Track, Triblet, Tringle, Trocar, Twig, Urochord, Ventifact, Verge, Virgate, Virgulate, Wand, Welding, Withe
**Rod-bearer** Lictor
**Rode** Raid
**Rodent** Acouchi, Acouchy, Agouty, Ag(o)uti, Bandicoot, Bangsring, Banxring, Beaver, Biscacha, Bizcacha, Bobac, Bobak, Boomer, Camass-rat, Capybara, Cavy, Chickaree, Chincha, Chinchilla, Chipmunk, Civet, Coypu, Cricetus, Dassie, Deer-mouse, Degu, Delundung, Dormouse, Fieldmouse, Gerbil(le), Gerboa, Glires, Glutton, Gnawer, Gopher, Groundhog, Guinea pig, Ham(p)ster, Hedgehog, Hog-rat, Hutia, Hydromys, Hyrax, Hystricomorph, Jerboa, Jird, Lemming, Loir, Mara, Marmot, Mole rat, Mountain-beaver, Mouse, Murid, Mus, Musk-rat, Musquash, Nutria, Ochotona, Ondatra, Paca, Porcupine, Potoroo, Prairie dog, Rabbit-squirrel, Rat, Ratel, Ratton, Renegade, Runagate, Sciurine, Sewellel, Shrew, Simplicidentate, Spermophile, Springhaas, Springhase, Squirrel, S(o)uslik, Taguan, Taira, Tuco-tuco, Tucu-tuco, Vermin, Viscacha, Vole, Woodchuck, Woodmouse
**Roderick** Random, Usher

**Rodney** Admiral
**Rodomontade** Bluster, Boast, Bombast, Brag, Gas
**Roe** Avruga, Botargo, Bottarga, Caviar(e), Coral, Fry, Hard, Melt, Milt(z), Pea, Raun, Rawn, Richard, Soft
**Roger** Ascham, Bacon, Jolly, OK, Rights
**Rogue, Roguish(ness)** Aberrant, Arch, Bandit, Bounder, Charlatan, Chiseller, City slicker, Crook, Deviant, Drole, Dummerer, Elephant, Espiègle(rie), Ganef, Ganev, Ganof, Gonif, Gonof, Greek, Gypsy, Hedge-creeper, Heel, Hempy, Herries, Imp, Knave, Latin, Limmer, Miscreant, Monkey, Palliard, Panurge, Picaresque, Picaroon, Pollard, Poniard, Rapparee, Ra(p)scal(l)ion, Reprobate, Riderhood, Rotter, Savage, Scallywag, Scamp, Schellum, Schelm, Scoundrel, Skellum, Sleeveen, Slip-string, Sly, Swindler, Terror, Varlet, Villain, Wrong 'un
**Roil** Agitate, Annoy, Churn, Provoke, Vex
**Roin** Roar
**Roister(er), Roisterous** Blister, Carouse, Ephesian, Laddish, Revel, Rollick, Scourer, Scowrer, Skylark, Swashbuckler, Swinge-buckler
**Role** Bit, Cameo, Capacity, Function, Gender, Hat, Lead, Métier, → **PART**, Persona, Prima-donna, Stead, Task, Title, Travesty
**Roll(ed), Roller, Roll-call, Rolling, Rolls** Absence, Bagel, Bap, Barmcake, Barrel, Beigel, Billow, Birmingham, Bolt, Bridge, Brioche, Bun, Butterie, Calender, Cambridge, Chamade, Comber, Convolv(ut)e, Cop, Couch, Court, Croissant, Cylinder, Dandy, Drum, Dutch, Electoral, Enswathe, Enwallow, Eskimo, Even, Fardel, Fardle, Finger, Flatten, Forward, Furl, Go, Goggle, Holy, Hotdog, Inker, Involute, Kitchen, Labour, List, Loaded, Lurch, Makimono, Mangle, Mano, Marver, Matricula, Morning, Motmot, Moving, Music, Muster, Notitia, Opulent, Pain au chocolat, Paradiddle, Patent, Paupiette, Pay, Petit-pain, Piano, Pigeon, Pipe, Platen, Porteous, Rafale, Ragman, Record, Reef, Reel, Register, Ren, Rent, Revolute, Revolve, Rhotacism, Rich, Ring, Road, Rob, Rolag, Roster, Rota, Rotate, Rotifer, Roul(e), Roulade, Rouleau, Row, RR, Rub-a-dub, Rumble, Run, Sausage, Schnecke(n), Skin up, Snap, Somersault, Souter's clod, Spool, Spring, Summar, Surge, Sway, Swell, Swiss, Table, Tandem, Taxi, Temple, Tent, Terrier, Thread, Toilet, Tommy, Toss, Trill, Trindle, Trundle, Tsunami, Tube, Upfurl, Valuation, Victory, Volume, Volutation, Wad, Wallow, Wamble, Waul, Wave, Wawl, Weather, Web, Well-heeled, Welter, Western, Wince, Wrap, Yaw, Zorbing
**Rollerball** Pen
**Rollercoaster** Emotional
**Rollick(ing)** Frolic, Gambol, Riotous, Romp, Sport
▷**Rollicking** *may indicate* an anagram
**Roly-poly** Chubby
**Roman** Agricola, Agrippa, Aurelius, Brutus, Caesar, Calpurnia, Candle, Catholic, Cato, Centurion, Consul, CR, Crassus, Decemviri, Decurion, Empire, Flavian, Galba, Holiday, Italian, Jebusite, Latin, Maecenas, Nero, Patrician, PR, Quirites, Raetic, RC, Retarius, Rhaetia, Road, Scipio, Seneca, Sulla, Tarquin, Tiberius, Trebonius, Type(cast), Uriconian, Veneti, Volsci
**Romance, Romantic (talk)** Affair, Amatory, Amoroso, Amorous, Boon, Byronic, Casanova, Catalan, Chocolate box, Dreamy, Fancy, Fantasise, Fib, Fiction, Gest(e), Gothic, Historical, Idealist, Invention, Ladin(o), Ladinity, Langue d'oc(ian), Langue d'oil, Langue d'oui, Liaison, Lie, Mills, Neo-Latin, New, Novelette, Poetic, Quixotic, Rhapsodic, R(o)uman, Ruritania, Sentimental, Stardust, Starlit, Sweet nothings, Tale, Tear-jerker, Woo
**Ro(u)manian, Rumanian** Ro, RO, R(o)uman, Transylvanian, Vlach, Wal(l)achian
**Romanov** Nicholas
▶**Romany** *see* **GYPSY**
**Romcom** Chick-flick
**Rome** Eternal City, Holy See, Imperial City
**Romeo** Casanova, Montagu, R, Star-crossed, Swain
**Romp(ing)** Carouse, Escapade, Fisgig, Fizgig, Frisk, Frolic, Hoyden, Jaunce, Randy, Rig, Rollick, Skylark, Sport, Spree
**Ron** Glum, Moody

**Rondo** Rota
**Ronnie** Biggs
**Röntgen** R, X-ray
**Roo** Joey
**Roof (edge), Roofing** Asphalt, Belfast, Bell, Broach, Ceil, Cl(e)ithral, Cover, Curb, Divot, Dome, Drip, Eaves, French, Gable, Gambrel, Hardtop, Hip(ped), Home, Housetop, Hypostyle, Imperial, Jerkin-head, Leads, M, Mansard, Monopitch, Onion dome, Palate, Pavilion, Pent, Pitched, Pop-top, Porte-cochère, Rag top, Rigging, Saddle, Saddleback, Shingle, Skillion, Skirt, Span, Sun(shine), Targa top, Tectiform, Tectum, Tegula, Thatch, Thetch, Tiling, Top, Uraniscus, Vaulting, Yealm
**Roof-climber, Roofer** Slater, Stegopholist, Tiler, Tin, Wattle
**Roofless** Hypaethral, Upaithric
**Rook** Bird, Building, Castle, Cheat, Crow, Fleece, Fool, Overcharge, R, Swindle
**Rookie** Beginner, Colt, Galoot, Greenhorn, Learner, Novice, Recruit, Tenderfoot, Tyro
**Room(y), Rooms** Bar-parlour, Barracks, Box, Breakfast, Capacious, Capacity, Cavernous, Ceiling, Clearance, Commodious, Counting, Court, Elbow, Emergency, Harness, Jury, Kitchen, Latitude, Leeway, Locutory, Lodging, Mail, Margin, Morning, Place, Scope, Shelf, Sick, Smoke-filled, → SPACE, Spacious, Standing, Thalamus, Toilet, Tolerance, Wiggle, Zenana

---

**ROOMS**

***2 letters:***
CC
Rm

***3 letters:***
Ben
But
Day
End
Gap
Gun
Lab
Leg
Loo
Oda
Pad
Sun
Tap
Tea

***4 letters:***
Cell
Chat
Dark
Digs
Dojo
Hall
Kiva
Loft
Long
Pump
Rest
Sale
Snug
Tool
Twin
Ward
Wash
Work
Zeta

***5 letters:***
Attic
Berth
Bibby
Bower
Cabin
Cuddy
Divan
Foyer
Green
Grill
Lanai
Laura
Lavra
Lodge
Music
Oriel
Panic
Press
Rangy
Sales
Salle
Salon
Solar
Spare
Staff
Steam
Still
Stock
Study
Suite

***6 letters:***
Boiler
Camera
Cellar
Closet
Common
Durbar
Engine
Exedra
Family
Garret
Hostel
Living
Locker
Lounge
Lumber
Parvis
Powder
Public
Robing
Rubber
Rumpus
School
Serdab
Single
Spence
Street
Strong
Studio
Tardis
Throne
Tiring
Ullage
Vestry

***7 letters:***
Apadana
Boudoir
Cabinet
Cenacle
Chamber
Chaumer
Control
Cubicle
Cutting
Dinette
Drawing
Exhedra
Genizah
Kursaal
Library
Megaron
Oratory
Orderly
Parlour
Pentice
Pentise
Private
Reading
Rotunda
Sanctum
Servery
Service

Shebang
Sitting
Smoking
Stowage
Two-pair
Utility
Waiting

*8 letters:*
Anteroom
Assembly
Casemate
Changing
Cockloft
Conclave
Delivery
Dressing
Incident
Property
Recovery
Sacristy
Scullery
Sitkamer
Solarium
Vestiary

*9 letters:*
Apartment
Boardroom
Camarilla
Composing
Extension
Glory-hole
Herbarium
Mould-loft
Palm Court
Receiving
Reception
Single-end
Voorkamer

*10 letters:*
Commercial
Consulting
Dissecting
Lebensraum
Misericord
Operations
Penetralia
Priesthole
Projection
Recitation
Recreation

*11 letters:*
Antechamber
Calefactory
Chancellery
Combination
Compartment
Misericorde
Scriptorium

*13 letters:*
Spheristerion

---

**Roost(er)** Cock, Nest, Perch, Siskin, Sit

**Root(s), Rooted, Rooting, Rootstock** Aruhe, Aryl, Asarum, Beet, Buttress, Calamus, Calumba, Cassava, Celeriac, Cheer, Cocco, Contrayerva, Costus, Couscous, Cube, Culver's, Cuscus, Dasheen, Delve, Deracinate, Derivation, Derris, Dig, Eddo, Elecampane, Eradicate, Eringo, Eryngo, Etymic, Etymon, Extirpate, Fern, Fibrous, Foundation, Gelseminine, Ginseng, Grass, Grout, Grub, Heritage, Horseradish, Hurrah, Immobile, Implant, Incorrigible, Ingrain, Insane, Ipecac(huana), Irradicate, Jalap, Jicama, Khuskhus, Knee, Lateral, Licorice, Liquorice, Mallee, Mandrake, Mangold, Mishmee, Mishmi, Mooli, More, Myall, Navew, Nousle, Nuzzle, Origins, Orris, Pachak, Pleurisy, Pneumatophore, Poke, Prop, Pry, Putchock, Putchuk, Race, Radical, Radicate, Radicle, Radish, Radix, Repent, Reptant, Rhatany, Rhizic, Rhizoid, Rhizome, Rummage, Rutabaga, Scorzonera, Senega, Sessile, Setwall, Skirret, Snuzzle, Source, Springwort, Spur, Square, Stilt, Stirpes, Stock, Strike, Tap, Taro, Tuber, Tuberous, Tulip, Turbith, Turnip, Turpeth, Ventral, Vetiver, Yam, Zedoary

**Rootless** Psilotum

**Rope(s)** Abaca, Backstay, Ba(u)lk, Becket, Bind, Bobstay, Boltrope, Bracer, Brail, Breeching, Bunt-line, Bush, Cable(-laid), Cablet, Cat's paw, Colt, Cord, Cordage, Cordon, Cringle, Downhaul, Drag, Earing, Fake, Fall, Flake, Flemish coil, Fly, Foot, Fore-brace, Foresheet, Forestay, Funicular, Futtock-shroud, Gantline, Garland, Grass line, Grist, Guest, Guide, Guy, Halliard, Halser, Halter, Halyard, Hawser, Hawser-laid, Headfast, Inhaul, Jack-stay, Jeff, Jib-sheet, Jump, Keckle, Keckling, Kernmantel, Kickling, Knittle, Ladder, Lanyard, Lasher, Lashing, Lasso, Lazo, Leg, Lifeline, Line, Longe, Lunge, Mainbrace, Mainsheet, Manil(l)a, Marlin(e), Match-cord, Messenger, Monkey, Mooring, Nettle, Nip, Noose, Oakum, Outhaul, Painter, Parbuckle, Pastern, Prolonge, Prusik, Pudding, Raft, Rawhide, Reef point, Riata, Ridge, Rigging, Ringstopper, Roband, Robbin, Rode, Runner, St Johnston's ribbon, St Johnston's tippet, Sally, Salt-eel, Seal, Selvagee, Sennit, Sheet, Shroud, Sinnet, Span, Spancel, Spun-yarn, Stay, Sternfast, Stirrup, String, Strop, Sugan, Swifter, Tackle, Tail, Tether, Tie, Tiller, Timenoguy, Tippet, Tow(line), Trace, Trail, Triatic, Triatic stay, Vang, Wanty, Warp, Widdy, Wire, Yarn

**Ropework** Macrame

**Rosalind** Ganymede

**Rosary** Beads, Mala, Paternoster

**Rose(-red), Rosie, Rosy** Albertine, Alexandra, Amelanchier, Aurorean, Avens, Bear's-foot, Blooming, Bourbon, Breare, Briar, Brier, Burnet, Cabbage, Canker, Ceiling, Cherokee, China, Christmas, Circumnavigator, Compass, Corn, Crampbark, Damask, Dog, Eglantine, Eglatère, England, English, Floribunda, G(u)elder, Geum, Golden, Hellebore, Hybrid, Jack, Jacque, Jacqueminot, Lal(age), Lancaster, Lee, Lenten, Monthling, Moss, Multiflora, Musk, Noisette, Opulus, Peace, Petra, Pink, Potentilla, Promising, Provence, Province, Provincial, Provins, Pyrus, Quillaia, Quillaja, Rambler, Red(dish), Remontant,

Rhoda, Rhodo-, Rock, Rugosa, Scotch, Snowball, Sprinkler, Standard, Sweetbrier, Tea, Tokyo, Tudor, White, Whitethorn, York

**Rose-apple** Jamboo, Jambu

**Rose-bay** Oleander

**Roseland** SE

**Rosemary** Rosmarine

**Rosette** Buttonhole, Chou, Cockade, Favour, Patera, Rosula

**Rosin** Colophony, Resin, Roset, Rosit, Rozet, Rozit

**Rosinante** Jade

**Roster** List, Register, Scroll, Table

**Rostrum** Ambo, Bema, Lectern, Podium, Pulpit, Tribune

**Rot(ten), Rotting** Addle, Baloney, Biodegrade, Boo, Bosh, Botrytis, Brown, Bull, Caries, Carious, Carrion, Corrode, Corrupt, Crown, Daddock, Decadent, → DECAY, Decompose, Decrepitude, Degradable, Dotage, Dricksie, Drivel, Druxy, Dry, Eat, Erode, Fester, Foot, Foul, Gangrene, Halt, Kibosh, Lousy, Manky, Mildew, Noble, Nonsense, Off, Perish, Piffle, Poppycock, Poxy, Punk, Putid, Putrefy, Putrescent, Putrid, Rail, Rancid, Rank, Rat, Red, Ret, Rhubarb, Ring, Rust, Sapropel, Septic, Soft, Sour, Squish, Twaddle, Vrot, Wet

**Rotate, Rotating, Rotation, Rotator(y)** Alternate, Axial, Backspin, Crankshaft, Crop, Feather, Gyrate, Job, Laevorotation, Lay-farming, Optical, Peristrephic, Pivot, Pronate, Rabat(te), Reamer, Rebato, Revolve, Roll, Selsyn, Spin, Succession, Sway, Teres, Topspin, Trochilic, Trundle, Turn, Turntable, Twiddle, Twirl, Vortex, Vorticose, Wheel, Windmill

**Rote** Heart, Memory, Recite, Routine

**Rotisserie** Spit

**Rotor** Armature, Auxiliary, Blade, Flywheel, Impeller, Squirrel cage, Tail, Tilt

▸**Rotten** *see* ROT(TEN)

▹**Rotten** *may indicate* an anagram

**Rotter** Bad apple, Cad, Dastard, Heel, Knave, Stinker, Swine

**Rotund** Chubby, Corpulent, Plump, Roly-poly, Round, Stout, Tubby

**Rotunda** Pantheon

**Roué** Debauchee, Decadent, Libertine, Lothario, Philanderer, Profligate, Rake(-shame), Rip

**Rouge** Blush, Gild, Jeweller's, Raddle, Redden, Reddle, Ruddle, Ruddy

**Rough(en), Roughly, Roughness** About, Abrasive, Approximate, Asper(ate), Blunt, Bristly, Broad, Broad brush, Burr, C, Ca, Callus, Chap(ped), Choppy, Circa, Coarse, Craggy, Craig, Crass, Crude, Draft, Drusy, Exasperate, Frampler, Grained, Gravelly, Gross, Gruff, Guestimate, Gurly, Gusty, Hard, Harsh, Hirsute, Hispid, Hoarse, Hoodlum, Hooligan, Ill, Impolite, Imprecise, Incondite, Indecorous, Inexact, Irregular, Jagged, Karst, Keelie, Kokobeh, Lumpy, Muricate, Obstreperous, Of sorts, Or so, Push, Ragged, Ramgunshoch, Raspy, Raucle, Rip, Risp, Robust, Row, Rude, Rugged, Rusticate, Rusty, Sandblast, Scabrid, Scabrous, Scratchy, Sea, Shaggy, Sketchy, Some, Spray, Spreathe, Squarrose, Stab, Strident, Strong-arm, Stubbly, Swab, Tartar, Tearaway, Ted, Textured, Tiger country, Tousy, Touzy, Towsy, Towzy, Uncut, Unfinished, Unkempt, Violent, Yahoo

**Roughage** Ballast, Bran, Fibre, Fodder

**Rough breathing** Asper, Rale, Wheeze

**Roughcast** Harl

▹**Roughly** *may indicate* an anagram

**Roulette** Russian

**Round(ed), Roundness, Round off** About, Ammo, Ball, Beat, Bombe, Bout, Bullet, Cartridge, Catch, Circle, Circular, Complete, Crown, Cycle, Dance, Dome, Doorstep, Egg, Fat, Figure, Full, Geoidal, Global, Globate, Globose, Globous, Hand, Heat, Inorb, Jump-off, Lap, Leg, Milk, O, Oblate, Obtuse, Orb, Orbicular, Orbit, Orby, Orotund, Ought, Paper, Patrol, Peri-, Pirouette, Plump, Pudsy, Qualifying, Quarter, Quarter-final, Rev, Ring, Robin, Roly-poly, Ronde, Rondure, Rota, Rotund, Route, Routine, Rundle, Rung, Salvo, Sandwich, Sarnie, Sellinger's, Semi-final, Shot, Skirt, Slice, Sphaer, Sphere, Spherical, Spiral, Step, Table, Tour, Trick, Tubby, Tune, U-turn, Walk

▹**Round** *may indicate* a word reversed

**Roundabout** Ambages, Approximately, Bypass, Carousel, Circle, Circuit, Circumambient,

Circumbendibus, Circus, Devious, Eddy, → INDIRECT, Merry-go-round, Peripheral, Rotary, Tortuous, Traffic circle, Turntable, Waltzer, Whirligig, Windlass

▷**Roundabout** *may indicate* an anagram

**Round building** Tholos, Tholus

**Rounders** Patball

**Round-mouth** Hag

**Round up** Bang-tail muster, Collate, Corner, Corral, Drag-net, Gather, Herd, Muster, Rodeo, Spiral

**Roup** Auction, Croak, Pip, Roop

**Rouse(r), Rousing** Abrade, Abraid, Abray, Amo(o)ve, Animate, Awaken, Beat, Bestir, Cheerleader, Emotive, Enkindle, Excite, Firk, Flush, Hearten, Heat, Innate, Inspire, Kindle, Knock up, Rear, Send, Shake up, Stimulate, Stir, Suscitate, Switch on, Unbed, Waken, Whip

**Rousseau** Émile

**Rout** Clamour, Debacle, Defeat, Drub, Fleme, Flight, Hubbub, Hurricane, Rabble, Retreat, Rhonchal, Snore, Thiasus, Upsee, Upsey, Upsy, Vanquish, Whoobub

**Route(s)** Arterial, Autobahn, Avenue, Beat, Bypass, Byroad, Camino real, Causeway, Clearway, Corridor, Course, Direction, Escape, Itinerary, I-way, Line, Ling, Motorway, M-way, Path, Red, Road, Round, Sea-lane, Skyway, Stock, Tail, Topo, Track, Trade, Transit, Via, Via Dolorosa, Walk, Waterway, Way

**Routine** Automatic, Bread and butter, Day-to-day, Drill, Everyday, Grind, Groove, Habitual, Heigh-ho, Helch-how, Ho-hum, Input, Jogtrot, Journeywork, Monotony, Mundane, Pattern, Perfunctory, Pipe-clay, Prosaic, Red tape, Regimen, Regular, Rota, Rote, Round, Run-of-the-mill, Rut, Schtik, S(c)htick, SOP, Stand-up, Treadmill, Workaday

**Rove(r), Roving** Car, Discursive, Enra(u)nge, Errant, Freebooter, Gad, Globetrotter, Marauder, Nomad, Prowl(er), Ralph, Range, → ROAM, Slub(b), Stray, Tramp, Vagabond, Varangarian, Viking, Wander

**Row(er)** Align, Altercation, Arew, Argue, Argument, Artillery, Babel, Bank, Barney, Bedlam, Bicker, Bobbery, Bow, Brattle, Brawl, Brulyie, Bru(i)lzie, Cacophony, Cannery, Cat fight, Clatter, Colonnade, Crescent, Death, Debate, Deen, Din, Ding-dong, Dispute, Domestic, Dust-up, Feud, File, Fireworks, Food, Fyle, Hoo-ha, Hullabaloo, Leander, Line(-up), Noise, Note, Oar, Octastich, Orthostichy, Paddle, Parade, Peripteral, Pluriserial, Ply, Pull, Quarrel, Queue, Rammy, Range, Rank, Raunge, Remigate, Reproach, Rew, Rhubarb, Rotten, Ruction, Rumpus, Savile, Scene, Scrap, Scull, Series, Set (to), Shindig, Shindy, Shine, Skid, Spat, Splore, Stern, Stound, Street, Stridor, Stroke, Stushie, Sweep, Terrace, Tier, Tiff, Tone, Torpid, Twelve-tone, Vendetta, Wetbob, Wherryman, Wrangle

**Rowan** Ash, Quicken, Sorb

**Rowdy, Rowdiness** Boisterous, Bovver, Cougan, Hoo, Hooligan, Ladette, Loud, Noisy, Obstreperous, Rorty, Rough, Roughhouse, Ruffian, Rumbustious, Scourer, Scozza, Skinhead, Stroppy, Turbulent, Unruly, Uproarious

**Roy** Rob

**Royal(ty), Royalist** Academy, Angevin, Basilical, Battle, Bourbon, Crowned, Emigré, Exchange, Fee, Hanoverian, HR(H), Imperial, Imposing, Inca, Kingly, King's man, Majestic, Malignant, Palatine, Payment, Pharaoh, Plantagenet, Prince, Princess, Purple, Queenly, Real, Regal, Regis, Regius, Regnal, RH, Sail, Sceptred, Society, Tsarista

**Rub(bing), Rubber(y), Rub out** Abrade, Attrition, Balata, Brass, Bridge, Buff, Buna®, Bungie, Bungy, Bunje(e), Bunjie, Bunjy, Butyl, Calk, Calque, Camelback, Caoutchouc, Chafe, Chloroprene, Cold, Condom, Corrade, Corrode, Cow gum®, Crepe, Cul(t)ch, Delete, Destroy, Dunlop®, Ebonite, Efface, Elastic, Elastomer, Elaterite, Embrocate, Emery, Eradicator, Erase, Factice, Factis, Fawn, Faze, Foam, Foursome, Fray, Fret, Friction, Fridge, Frottage, Frotteur, Fudge, Funtumia, Gall, Galoch, Goodyear®, Grate, Graze, Grind, Guayule, Gum elastic, Gutta-percha, Hale, Hard, Hevea, High-hysteresis, Hule, India, Inunction, Irritate, Isoprene, Jelutong, Johnnie, Lagos, Latex, Leather, Masseur, Negrohead, Neoprene®, Nuzzle, Obstacle, Para, Polish, Pontianac, Pontianak, Root, Safe, Sandpaper, Scour, Scrape, Scrub, Scuff, Seringa, Sheet, Silastic®, Smoked, Sorbo®, Sponge, Stretchy, Stroke, Synthetic, Towel, Trace, Ule, Vulcanite, Wild, Wipe, Xerotripsis

▷**Rubbed** *may indicate* an anagram

**Rubberneck** Gape
**Rubbish** Bad mouth, Balls, Bilge, Brash, Brock, Bull, Bunkum, Cack, Chaff, Chronic, Clap-trap, Cobblers, Codswallop, Culch, Debris, Degenerate, Detritus, Dirt, Discredit, Dre(c)k, Drivel, Dross, Eyewash, Fiddlesticks, Flotsam, Garbage, Grot, Grunge, Gubbins, Guff, Hogwash, Hokum, Kack, Kak, Landfill, Leavings, Litter, Mullock, Mush, Nonsense, Pan, Pants, Phooey, Piffle, Pish, Raff, Raffle, Red(d), → **REFUSE**, Riff-raff, Scrap, Sewage, Slate, Spam, Stuff, Sweepings, Thrash, Tinpot, Tinware, Tip, Tom(fool), Tommy rot, Tosh, Totting, Trade, Tripe, Trouch, Truck, Trumpery, Twaddle, Urethra
**Rubbish heap** Coup, Cowp, Dump, Lay-stall, Sweepings, Toom
**Rubble** Brash, Debris, Detritus, Hard-core, Moellon, Random, Remains, Riprap, Talus
**Rubicund** Red, Ruddy
**Rubidium** Rb
**Ruby** Agate, Balas, Bohemian, Brazilian, Colorado, Cuprite, Oriental, Pigeon's blood, Port, Red, Spinel, Star, Starstone, Type
**Ruche** Frill
**Ruck** Furrow, Scrum, Wrinkle
**Rucksack** Backpack, Bergen, Pickapack, Pikau
**Ruction** Ado, Affray, Fuss, Quarrel
**Rudder** Budget, Helm, Jury, Steerer
**Rudderless** Adrift
**Ruddle** Keel, Lemnian
**Ruddy** Bally, Bloody, Blowsy, Flaming, Flashy, Florid, Raddled, Red, Roseate, Rubicund, Rufous, Sanguine
**Rude(ness)** Abusive, Barbaric, Bear, Bestial, Bumpkin, Callow, Carlish, Churlish, Coarse, Discourteous, Disrespect, Elemental, Goustrous, Green, Gross, Ignorant, Ill-bred, Impolite, Inconsiderate, Indecorous, Indelicate, Inficete, Ingram, Ingrum, Insolent, Ocker, Offensive, Peasant, Profane, Raw, Ribald, Risqué, Rough, Rusticity, Simple, Surly, Unbred, Uncivil, Uncomplimentary, Uncourtly, Unlettered, Unmannered, Vulgar, Yobbish
**Rudiment(ary), Rudiments** ABC, Absey, Anlage, Basidial, Beginning, Element, Embryo, Foundation, Germ(en), Germinal, Inchoate, Primitive, Primordial, Seminal, Vestige
**Rudolph** Hess, Reindeer
**Rue(ful)** Apologetic, Boulevard, Dittany, Goat's, Harmala, Harmel, Herb of grace, Long-visaged, Meadow, Mourn, Poignant, Regret, Repent, Rew, Ruta, Sorry, Wall
**Ruff** Collar, Crest, Fraise, Frill, Mane, Partlet, Pope, Rabato, Rebato, Ree, Ruche, Trump
**Ruffian** Apache, Bashi-bazouk, Brute, Bully, Cut-throat, Desperado, Goon(da), Highbinder, Hoodlum, Hooligan, Keelie, Larrikin, Loord, Lout, Miscreant, Mohock, Myrmidon, Ned, Phansigar, Plug-ugly, Raff, Rowdy, Skinhead, Sweater, Tearaway, Thug, Toe-ragger, Trailbaston, Tumbler
**Ruffle(d), Ruffles** Bait, Crumple, Dishevel, Falbala, Flounce, Fluster, Fret, → **FRILL**, Gather, Irritate, Jabot, Peplum, Ripple, Rouse, Ruche, Rumple, Shirty, Tousle, Windswept
▷**Ruffle** *may indicate* an anagram
**Rug** Afghan, Bearskin, Bergama, Buffalo-robe, Carpet, Drugget, Ensi, Flokati, Gabbeh, Hearth, Herez, Heriz, Hooked, Kelim, K(h)ilim, Kirman, Lap robe, Mat, Maud, Numdah, Oriental, Pilch, Prayer, Rag, Runner, Rya, Scatter, Steamer, Tatami, Throw, Toupee, Travelling, Wig
**Rugby (player)** Back, Fifteen, Fives, Forward, Harlequin, League, Lion, Pack, Quin, RU, Scrum, Sevens, Threequarter, Touch, Union, Wing
**Rugged** Craggy, Gnarled, Hardy, Harsh, Knaggy, Rough, Strong, Uneven
**Ruin(ed), Ruination, Ruins, Ruinous** Annihilate, Banjax, Bankrupt, Blast, Blight, Blue, Butcher, Carcase, Collapse, Corrupt, Crash, Crock, Damn, Decay, Defeat, Demolish, Despoil, Destroy, Devastate, Dilapidation, Disaster, Disfigure, Dish, Disrepair, Dogs, Do in, Doom, Downcome, Downfall, Dry rot, End, Fine, Fordo, Hamstring, Heap, Hell, Insolvent, Inure, Kaput(t), Kibosh, Loss, Mar, Mockers, Mother's, Overthrow, Perdition, Perish, Petra, Pigs and whistles, Pot, Puckerood, Ravage, Reck, Relic, Rust, Scotch, Screw, Scupper, Scuttle, Seduce, Shatter, Sink, Smash, Spill, → **SPOIL**, Stramash, Subvert, Undo, Unmade, Unmake, Ur, Violate, Vitiate, Whelm, Woe, Wrack, Wreck, Write off

▷**Ruined** *may indicate* an anagram

**Rule(r), Rules, Ruling** Advantage, Algorithm, Align, Aristocrat, Arrêt, Article, Australian, Autocracy, Bosman, Bylaw, Calliper, Canon, Chain, Club-law, Code, Commonly, Condominium, Constitution, Control, Criterion, Decree, Divine right, Dominate, Domineer, Dominion, Em, Empire, En, Establishment, Estoppel, Etiquette, Fatwa, Feint, Fetwa, Fleming's, Formation, Formula, Gag, Global, Golden, Govern, Govern-all, Ground, Guideline, Gynocracy, Home, In, Institutes, Jackboot, Junta, Kronos, Law, Leibniz's, Lesbian, Lex, Lindley, Liner, Majority, Markownikoff's, Mastery, Matriarchy, Maxim, McNa(u)ghten, Measure, Mede, Meer, Meteyard, Method, Ministrate, Mistress, Mobocracy, Motto, Naismith's, Netiquette, No-no, Norm(a), Oppress, Orcus, Ordain, Order, Ordinal, Organon, Organum, Pantocrator, Parallel, Parallelogram, Phase, Phrase-structure, Pie, Placitum, Plumb, Precedent, Precept, Predominant, Prescript, Prevail, Principle, Proscribe, Protocol, Ptochocracy, Pye, Rafferty's, Raine, Rayne, Realm, Reciprocity, Rector, Regal, Regnant, Regula, Regulate, Reign, Rewrite, Ring, Routine, Rubric, Scammozzi's, Selection, Setting, Slide, Squirearchy, Standard, Standing, Statute, Straight edge, Stylebook, Sutra, Sway, Syntax, System, Ten-minute, Ten-yard, Theorem, Three, Thumb, Transformation(al), Trapezoid, Triumvir, T-square, Tycoon, Tyrannise, Tyrant, Uti possidetis, Vespasian, Wield, Yao, Yardstick

---

## RULERS

*1 letter:*
K
R

*3 letters:*
Ban
Bey
Dey
Mir
Oba
Raj
Rex

*4 letters:*
Amir
Cham
Czar
Doge
Duce
Emir
Imam
Inca
Khan
King
Nero
Pope
Rana
Ratu
Shah
Tsar
Vali
Wali

*5 letters:*
Ameer
Ardri
Creon
Dewan
Diwan
Henry
Herod
Hoyle
Hyleg
Judge
Mogul
Mpret
Mudir
Nawab
Negus
Nizam
Octet
Pasha
Queen
Rajah
Ratoo
Shaka
Sheik
Sophi
Sophy
Tenno

*6 letters:*
Atabeg
Atabek
Caesar
Caliph
Castro
Chagan
Cheops
Dergue
Despot
Dynast
Exarch
Franco
Führer
Gerent
Harold
Hitler
Judges
Kabaka
Kaiser
Mamluk
Manchu
Mikado
Peshwa
Prince
Rajput
Regent
Ronald
Sachem
Satrap
Sheikh
Sherif
Shogun
Sirdar
Sovran
Squier
Squire
Stalin
Sultan
Swaraj
Walter

*7 letters:*
Abbasid
Ardrigh
Autarch
Bajayet
Bajazet
Bodicea
Catapan
Chogyal
Elector
Emperor
Gaekwar
Gaikwar
Jamshid
Jamshyd
Khedive
Miranda
Monarch
Omayyad
Pharaoh
Podesta
Rajpoot
Richard
Saladin
Serkali
Souldan
Toparch
Umayyad
Viceroy
Zamorin

*8 letters:*
Archduke
Autocrat
Bismarck
Boudicca
Burgrave
Caligula
Caudillo
Cromwell
Dictator

Ethnarch
Frederic
Heptarch
Hespodar
Hierarch
Maharaja
Mamaluke
Mameluke
Napoleon
Oligarch
Overlord
Padishah
Pentarch
Pericles
Reginald
Roderick
Sagamore
Sassanid
Suleiman
Suzerain
Synarchy
Tetrarch
Thearchy
Theocrat

*9 letters:*
Alexander
Amenhotep
Bretwalda
Britannia
Cleopatra
Cosmocrat
Frederick
Montezuma
Ochlocrat
Pendragon
Plutocrat
Potentate
President
Sovereign
Tamerlane

*10 letters:*
Caractacus
Plantocrat
Principate
Rajpramukh
Stratocrat

*11 letters:*
Charlemagne
Genghis Khan
Prester John
Queensberry
Stadtholder
Tutankhamun

*12 letters:*
Chandragupta

*13 letters:*
Haile Selassie

---

**Rule-book** Code, Pie, Pye

**Rum(mer)** Abnormal, Baba, Bacardi, Bay, Cachaca, Curious, Daiquiri, Dark, Demerara, Droll, Eerie, Eery, Freaky, Glass, Grog, Island, Jamaica, Kooky, Odd(er), Peculiar, Quaint, Queer, Screech, Strange, Tafia, Weird

▸**Rumanian** *see* RO(U)MANIAN

**Rumble, Rumbling** Borborygmus, Brool, Curmurring, Drum-roll, Groan, Growl, Guess, Lumber, Mutter, Roll, Rumour, Thunder, Tonneau, Twig

**Ruminant, Ruminate** Antelope, Bongo, Bovid, Cabrie, Camel, Caribou, Cavicornia, Cervid, Champ, Chew, Contemplate, Cow, Deer, Eland, Gemsbok, Gnu, Goat, Ibex, Llama, Meditate, Merycism, Muse, Nilgai, Nyala, Okapi, Oorial, Oryx, Palebuck, Pecora, Pronghorn, Reindeer, Saola, Serow

**Rummage** Delve, Ferret, Fish, Foray, Fossick, Jumble, Powter, Ransack, Rifle, Root, Rootle, Scavenge, Search, Tot

**Rummy** Canasta, Cooncan, Game, Gin, Queer

**Rumour** Breeze, Bruit, Buzz, Canard, Cry, Fama clamoso, Fame, Furphy, → GOSSIP, Grapevine, Hearsay, Kite, Kite-flying, Mail, Noise, On-dit, Pig's-whisper, Report, Repute, Roar, Say-so, Smear, Tale, Talk, Tattle, Underbreath, Unfounded, Vine, Voice, Whisper, Word

**Rump** Arse, Bottom, Buttocks, Croup(e), Croupon, Crupper, Curpel, Derrière, Nates, Parliament, Perineal, Podex, Prat, Pygal, Steak, Uropygium

**Rumple** Corrugate, Crease, Mess, Muss, Touse, Tousle, Touze, Towse, Towze, Wrinkle

**Rumpus** Bagarre, Commotion, Din, Noise, Rhubarb, Riot, Row, Ruction, Shemozzle, Shindig, Shindy, Shine, Storm, Stushie, Tirrivee, Uproar

**Run(ning), Run away, Run into, Run off, Runny, Runs** Abscond, Admin(ister), Arpeggio, Arris-gutter, Black, Bleed, Blue, Bolt, Break, Bunk, Bye, Canter, Career, Chase, Chicken, Clip, Consider, Control, Coop, Corso, Courant, Course, Cresta, Cross-country, Current, Cursive, Cursorial, Cut, Dart, Dash, Decamp, Diarrhoea, Dinger, Direct, Dog-trot, Double, Dribble, Drive, Dry, Dummy, Enclosure, Enter, Escape, Execute, Extra, Fartlek, Flee, Flit, Flow, Fly, Follow, Fun, Fuse, Gad, Gallop, Gauntlet, Glissando, Go, Green, Ground, Hare, Haste(n), Hennery, Hie, Hightail, Home, Hoof, Idle, In service, Jog, Jump bail, Ladder, Lam, Lauf, Leg(work), Leg bye, Lienteric, Liquid, Long, Lope, Manage, Marathon, Melt, Milk, Mizzle, Mole, Molt, Monkey, Neume, Now, Offset, On, On-line, Operate, Orchestration, Organise, Pace, Pacific, Paper chase, Parkour, Pelt, Pilot, Ply, Pour, Print, Purulent, R, Race, Range, Rear end, Red, Renne, Riff, Rin, Roadwork, Romp, Root, Roulade, Rounder, Ruck, Scamper, Scapa, Scarpa, Scarper, School, Schuss, Score, Scud, Scuddle, Scutter, Scuttle, See, Sequence, Shoot, Single, Skate, Skedaddle, Ski, Skid, Skirr, Skitter, Slalom, Slide, Smuggle, Speed, Spew, Split, Spread, Sprint, Sprue, Squitters, Stampede, Steeplechase, Straight, Streak, Stream, Superintend, Taxi, Tear, Tenor, Test drive, Tick over, Tie-breaker, Tirade, Trial, Trickle, Trill, Trot, Watery, Well, Wide

**Runaway** Drain, Easy, Eloper, Escapee, Fugie, Fugitive, Refugee
**Run down** Asperse, Belie, Belittle, Calumniate, Decry, Demonise, Denigrate, Deplete, Derelict, Detract, Dilapidated, Infame, Knock, Low, Obsolesce(nt), Poorly, Rack, Résumé, Scud, Seedy, Short, Synopsis, Tirade, Traduce
**Rune, Runic** Aesc, Ash, Futhark, Futhorc, Futhork, Kri, Ogham, Spell, Thorn, Wen, Wyn(n)
**Rung** Crossbar, Roundel, Rundle, Spoke, Stave, Step, Tolled, Tread
**Runner(s)** Abrahams, Atalanta, Athlete, Bean, Blade, Blockade, Bolt, Bow Street, Candidate, Carpet, Chataway, Cheetah, Coe, Contrabandist, Courser, Dak, Deserter, Drug, Emu, Errand boy, Field, Foot, Geat, Gentleman, Gillie-wetfoot, Harrier, Hatta, Hencourt, Indian, Internuncio, Lampadist, Leg bye, Legman, Messenger, Middle distance, Miler, Milk, Mohr, Monoski, Mousetrap, Nurmi, Oribi, Ovett, Owler, Pacemaker, Pacesetter, Policeman, Racehorse, Radcliffe, Rhea, → **RIVER**, Rug, Rum, → **RUN(NING)**, Sarmentum, Scarlet, Scud, Series, Slipe, Smuggler, Snowshoe, Stolon, Stream, Tailskid, Trial
▷**Running, Runny** *may indicate* an anagram
**Run of the mill** Average, Mediocre
**Runt** Anthony, Dilling, Oobit, Oubit, Reckling, Scalawag, Scrog, Scut, Smallest, Tantony, Titman, Woobut, Woubit
**Run through** Impale, Pierce, Rehearsal
**Runway** Airstrip, Drive, Slipway, Strip, Tarmac®, Trajectory
**Run wild** Lamp, Rampage
**Rupee(s)** Lac, Lakh, Re
**Rupert** Bear
**Rupture** Amniotomy, Breach, Burst, Crack, Enterocele, Hernia, Rend, Rhexis, Rift, Scissure, Split
**Rural** Agrarian, Agrestic, Arcadia, Backwoodsman, Boo(h)ai, Booay, Boondocks, Bucolic, Country(side), Cracker-barrel, Forane, Georgic, Hick, Mofussil, Pastoral, Platteland, Praedial, Predial, Redneck, Rustic, Sticks, The Shires, Ulu, Upland, Wop-wops
**Ruse** Artifice, Decoy, Dodge, Engine, Hoax, Pawk, Stratagem, Subterfuge, → **TRICK**
**Rush(ed)** Accelerate, Barge, Bolt, Bustle, Career, Charge, Dart, Dash, Debacle, Dutch, Eriocaulon, Expedite, Fall, Faze, Feese, Feeze, Feze, Flaw, Flowering, Fly, Forty-nine, Frail, Friar, Gad, Gold, Gust, Hare, Hasten, Hectic, High-tail, Horsetail, → **HURRY**, Hurry and Scurry, Hurtle, Jet, Juncus, Lance, Lash, Leap, Luzula, Moses, Nip, Odd-man, Onset, Palmiet, Pellmell, Phase, Pheese, Pheeze, Phese, Plunge, Pochard, Precipitate, Race, Railroad, Rampa(u)ge, Rash, Rayle, Reed, Rip, Sally, Scamp(er), Scarper, Scirpus, Scoot, Scour(ing), Scramble, Scud, Scurry, Scuttle, Sedge, Shave-grass, Spate, Speed, Spurt, Stampede, Star(r), Streak, Streek, Surge, Swoop, Swoosh, Tantivy, Tear, Thrash, Thresh, Tilt, Toad(grass), Torrent, Tule, Viretot, Whizz, Whoosh, Zap, Zoom
**Rusk** Zwieback
**Russell** AE, Bertrand, Jack
**Russet** Rutile
**Russia(n), Russian headman, Russian villagers** Alexei, Apparatchik, Ataman, Bashkir, Bear, Belorussian, Beria, Bolshevik, Boris, Boyar, Buryat, Byelorussian, Cesarevitch, Chechen, Chukchee, Chukchi, Circassian, Cossack, Dressing, D(o)ukhobor, Esth, Evenki, Ewenki, Igor, Ingush, Ivan, Kabardian, Kalmuk, Kalmyck, Leather, Leonid, Lett, Mari, Menshevik, Mingrel(ian), Minimalist, Mir, Misha, Muscovy, Octobrist, Old Believer, Osset(e), Putin, Red, Rissky, Romanov, Rus, Russ(niak), Russki, Ruthene, Salad, Serge, Sergei, Slav, Stakhanovite, SU, Tatar, The Bear, Thistle, Udmurt, Ukrainian, Uzbeg, Uzbek, Vladimir, Vogul, White, Yakut, Yuri, Zyrian
**Rust(y)** Aeci(di)um, Blister, Brown, Corrode, Cor(ro)sive, Eat, Erode, Etch, Ferrugo, Goethite, Iron oxide, Iron-stick, Laterite, Maderise, Oxidise, Puccinia, Reddish, Rubiginous, Soare, Stem, Teleutospore, Telium, Uredine, Uredo, Verdigris, Wheat, Yellow
**Rust-fungus** Aecidiospore
**Rustic** Arcady, Bacon, Bor(r)el(l), Bucolic, Bumpkin, Carl, Carlot, Chawbacon, Churl, Clodhopper, Clown, Corydon, Countryman, Cracker-barrel, Crackle, Culchie, Damon, Doric, Forest, Georgic, Hayseed, Hick, Hillbilly, Hind, Hob, Hobbinoll, Hodge, Homespun, Idyl(l),

Pastorale, Peasant, Pr(a)edial, Put(t), Rube, Rural, Silk, Strephon, Swain, Sylvan, Uplandish, Villager, Villatic, Yokel

▷**Rustic** *may indicate* an anagram

**Rusticate** Banish, Ruralize, Seclude

**Rustle(r), Rustling** Abactor, Cattle-lifter, Crackle, Crinkle, Duff, Fissle, Frou-frou, Gully-raker, Poach, Silk, Speagh(ery), Sprechery, Steal, Stir, Stocktaking, Susurration, Swish, Thief, Whig

**Rust-proof** Antioxide, Oxidant, Zinced

**Rut** Channel, Furrow, Groove, Heat, Routine, Sulcus, Track

**Rutabaga** Swede

**Ruth** Babe, Compassion, Mercy, Pity, Remorse, Rewth

**Ruthenium** Ru

**Rutherfordium** Rf

**Ruthless** Brutal, Cruel, Dog eat dog, Fell, Fierce, Hard, Hardball, Hard-bitten, Indomitable, Inhuman, Rat race

**Rutile** Sagenite

**Rwanda(n)** Hutu, Tutsi

**Rye** Gentleman, Grain, Grass, Spelt, Whisky

# Ss

**S** Ogee, Saint, Second, Sierra, Society, South, Square
**SA** It, Lure
**Sabbatarian** Wee Free
**Sabbath** Juma, Lord's Day, Rest-day, Shabbat, Sunday, Witches'
**Sabbatical** Gap year, Leave, Year off
**Sabine** Horace, Samnite, Women
**Sable** American, Black, Jet, Pean, Zibel(l)ine
**Sabotage, Saboteur** Cripple, Destroy, Disrupt, Frame-breaker, Hacktivism, Ratten, Sab, Spoil, Subverter, Treachery, Undermine, Vandalise, Worm, Wrecker
**Sabre, Sabre rattler** Jingo, Sword, Tulwar
**Sabrina** Severn
**Sac** Air, Allantois, Amnion, Aneurism, Aneurysm, Bag, Bladder, Bursa, Caecum, Castoreum, Cisterna, Cyst, Diverticulum, Embryo, Follicle, Ink, Pericardium, Peritoneum, Pneumatophore, Pod, Pollen, Scrotum, Spermatheca, Stamen, Tylose, Tylosis, Utricle, Vesica, Vocal, Yolk
**Saccharine** Dulcite, Dulcose
**Sack(cloth), Sacking** Axe, Bag, Bed, Boot, Bounce, Budget, Bulse(r), Burlap, Can, Cashier, Chasse, Chop, Coal, Compression, Congé, Congee, Dash, Day, Depose, Depredate, Despoil, Discharge, Dismissal, Doss, Dressing, Fire, Growbag, Gunny, Havoc, Heave-ho, Hessian, Hop-pocket, Jute, Knap, Lay off, Lay waste, Loot, Mailbag, Maraud, Marching orders, Mat, Mitten, Pillage, Plunder, Poke, Postbag, Push, Raid, Rapine, Ravage, Reave, Replace, Rieve, Rifle, Road, Rob, Sad, Sanbenito, Self-abasement, Sherris, Sherry, Spoliate, Vandalise, Walking papers
▷**Sacks** *may indicate* an anagram
**Sacrament** Baptism, Blessed, Christening, Communion, Confirmation, Eucharist, Extreme unction, Housel, Last rites, Lord's Supper, Matrimony, Nagmaal, Orders, Penance, Promise, Reconciliation, Ritual, Unction, Viaticum
**Sacred (object), Sacred books, Sacred place** Adytum, Antioch, Churinga, Consecrated, Delphi, Divine, Enshrined, Hallowed, Hareem, Harem, Harim, Heart, Hierurgy, →HOLY, Ineffable, Inner sanctum, Manito(u), Nine, Omphalos, Padma, Pietà, Purana, Sacrosanct, Sanctum, Taboo, Tapu, Temenos
**Sacrifice** Alcestic, Blood, Burnt offering, Cenote, Corban, Cost, Forego, Gambit, Gehenna, Hecatomb, Holocaust, Immolate, Iphigenia, Isaac, Lay down, Molech, Moloch, Molochize, Oblation, →OFFERING, Paschal lamb, Peace offering, Relinquish, Sati, Suovetaurilia, Supreme, Surrender, Suttee, Taurobolium, Tophet, Vicarious, Victim
**Sacrilege, Sacrilegious** Blaspheme, Impiety, Profane, Violation
**Sacristan, Sacristy** Diaconicon, Sceuophylax, Sexton
**Sacrosanct** Inviolable
**Sad(den), Sadly, Sadness** Alas, Attrist, Bittersweet, Blue, Con dolore, Dejected, Depressed, Desolate, Disconsolate, Dismal, Doleful, Dolent, Doloroso, Dolour, Downcast, Drear, Dull, Dumpy, Elegiac, Fadeur, Forlorn, Grief, Heartache, Heart-rending, Heavy, Inconsolable, Lamentable, Lovelorn, Low, Lugubrious, Mesto, Mournful, Niobe, Oh, Plaintive, Plangent, Poignancy, Proplastid, Shame, Sorrowful, Sorry, Tabanca, Tearful, Tear-jerker, Threnody, Tragic, Triste, Tristesse, Unhappy, Wan, Weltschmerz, Wo(e)begone
**Saddle (bag, cloth, flap, girth, pad), Saddled** Alforja, Aparejo, Arson, Bicycle, Burden, Cantle, Cinch, Col, Crupper, Demipique, Housing, Kajawah, Lumber, Numnah,

Oppress, Pack, Pad, Panel, Pannier, Pigskin, Pilch, Pillion, Seat, Sell(e), Shabrack, Shabracque, Side, Skirt, Stock, Tree, Unicycle, Western

**Saddle-bow** Arson

**Saddler** Whittaw(er)

**Sadie** Thompson

**Sadism, Sadist(ic)** Algolagnia, Cruel, Dominator

▷**Sadly** *may indicate* an anagram

**Safari** Expedition, Hunt

**Safe(ty)** Active, All right, Almery, Ambry, Awmrie, Blue-chip, Cert, Coolgardie, Copper-bottomed, Deliverance, Delouse, Deposit, Fireproof, GRAS, Harmless, Haven, Hunk, Immunity, Impunity, Inviolate, Keister, Meat, Night, Passive, Peter, Proof, Refuge, Reliable, Roadworthy, Sanctuary, Secure, Sheltered, Sound, Strong-box, Strongroom, Sure, Unadventurous, Vault, Whole-skinned, Worthy

**Safebreaker** Peterman, Yegg, Yeggman

**Safeguard** Air bag, Bulwark, Caution, Ensure, Fail-safe, Frithborh, Fuse, Hedge, Inoculate, Insurance, Palladium, Preserve, Protection, Register, Shield, Ward

**Saffron** Bastard, Crocus, False, Meadow, Mock, Naked lady, Yellow

**Sag(gy), Sagging** Decline, Dip, Droop, Floppy, Hang, Hogged, Lop, Slump, Swayback, Wilt

**Saga** Aga, Chronicle, Edda, Epic, Forsyte, Icelandic, Laxdale, Legend, Odyssey, Volsunga

**Sagacity, Sagacious** Astute, Commonsense, Depth, Elephant, Judgement, Sapience, Wisdom

**Sage(s)** Abaris, Aquinian, Bactrian, Bias, Carlyle, Cheronian, Chilo(n), Clary, Cleobulus, Confucius, Counsellor, Egghead, Elder, Far-sighted, Greybeard, Hakam, Herb, Imhotep, Jerusalem, Maharishi, Mahatma, Malmesbury, Manu, Mirza, Moolvie, Ollav, Orval, Pandit, Periander, Philosopher, Pittacus, Rishi, Sadhu, Salvia, Sartre, Savant, Seer, Seven, Solomon, Solon, Tagore, Thales, Wiseacre, Wood

**Sage-brush** Nevada

**Sago** Pearl, Portland

**Saharan** Hassaniya, Sahrawi

**Sahelian** Chad, Mali, Mauritania, Niger

**Sahib** Burra, Pukka, Tippoo, Tipu

**Said** Above-named, Co, Emir, Port, Quo(th), Related, Reputed, Spoken, Stated

▷**Said** *may indicate* 'sounding like'

**Sail(s), Sailing** Balloon, Bunt, Canvas, Circumnavigate, Clew, Cloth, Coast, Course, Cross-jack, Crowd, Cruise, Drag, Drift, Fan, Fore(course), Fore-and-aft, Full, Gaff(-topsail), Gennaker, Genoa, Goose-wing, Head, Jib, Jigger, Jut, Land, Lateen, Leech, Luff, Lug, Moon, Moonraker, Muslin, Navigate, Orthodromy, Parachute spinnaker, Peak, Plain, Plane, Ply, Rag, Raven(s)-duck, Reef, Rig, Ring-tail, Royal, Seafaring, Sheet, Shoulder-of-mutton, Smoke, Solar, Spanker, Spencer, Spinnaker, Spritsail, Square, Staysail, Steer, Storm-jib, Studding, Stun, Stuns'l, Suit, Top(-gallant), Top-hamper, Up anchor, Van, Vela, Wardrobe, Water, Windsurf, Yard

**Sailable** Seaworthy

**Sailboard** Windsurf

**Sailor(s)** AB, Admiral, Anson, Argonaut, Blue-jacket, Boater, Boatman, Boatswain, Bos'n, Bos(u)n, Budd, Canvas-climber, Circumnavigator, Commodore, Crew, Deckhand, Drake, Evans, First mate, Foremastman, Freshwater, Galiongee, Gob, Greenhand, Grommet, Hand, Hat, Hearties, Helmsman, Hornblower, Hydronaut, Jack, Janty, Jauntie, Jaunty, Jonty, Khalasi, Killick, Killock, Kroo(boy), Krooman, Kru(boy), Kruman, Lascar, Leadsman, Liberty man, Limey, Loblolly (boy), Lt, Lubber, Mariner, Matelot, Matlo(w), Middy, MN, Nelson, Noah, NUS, Oceaner, Oldster, OS, Petty Officer, Pirate, Polliwog, Pollywog, Popeye, Powder monkey, Privateer, Rating, Reefer, RN, Salt, Seabee, Seacunny, Sea-dog, Seafarer, Sea-lord, → SEAMAN, Serang, Shellback, Sin(d)bad, Steward, Stowaway, Submariner, Swabber, Swabby, Tar, Tarp(aulin), Tarry-breeks, Tindal, Topman, Triton, Waister, Wandering, Water-dog, Wave, Wren, Yachtie, Yachtsman

**Sailplane** Glider

**Saint(ly)** Canonise, Canonize, Hagiology, Hallowed, Holy, Latterday, Leger, Patron, Pi, Pillar, Plaster, St, Sunday, Templar, Thaumaturgus

## SAINTS

*1 letter:*
S

*2 letters:*
SS

*3 letters:*
Cyr

*4 letters:*
Bede
Bees
Chad
Elmo
Eloi
Hugh
Ives
John
Jude
Just
Lucy
Luke
Malo
Mark
Odyl
Olaf
Paul
Ride
Roch
Rule

*5 letters:*
Agnes
Aidan
Alban
Alvis
Asaph
Basil
David
Denis
Denys
Diego
Elvis
Enoch
Giles
Hilda
James
Kevin
Kilda
Linus
Lucia
Mungo
Peter
Ronan
Roque
Simon
Vitus

*6 letters:*
Agatha
Alexis
Andrew
Anselm
Audrey
Brigid
Canute
George
Helena
Hilary
Jerome
Joseph
Loyola
Magnus
Martha
Martin
Monica
Ninian
Oswald
Simeon
Teresa
Thecia
Thomas
Tobias
Ursula

*7 letters:*
Alphege
Ambrose
Anthony
Barbara
Bernard
Birinus
Brandan
Brendan
Bridget
Cecilia
Clement
Columba
Crispin
Dominic
Dunstan
Dymphna
Eulalie
Francis
Isidore
Leonard
Matthew
Michael
Pancras
Patrick
Quentin
Regulus
Rosalie
Severus
Stephen
Swithin
Theresa
Vincent
Walstan
Wilfred
William

*8 letters:*
Aloysius
Aurelius
Barnabas
Benedict
Boniface
Columban
Crispian
Cuthbert
Dorothea
Gertrude
Hilarion
Ignatius
Lawrence
Margaret
Nicholas
Paulinus
Polycarp
Veronica
Vladimir
Winifred

*9 letters:*
Augustine
Catharine
Genevieve
Hildegard
Kentigern
Sebastian
Valentine

*10 letters:*
Bernadette
Crispinian
Hieronymus
Stanislaus

*11 letters:*
Bartholomew
Christopher

*12 letters:*
Simon Zelotes

*13 letters:*
Francis Xavier

---

**Sake** Account, Behalf, Cause, Drink, Mirin
**Sal** Nitre, Salt, Volatile
**Salacious, Salacity** Fruity, Lewd, Lust, Obscene, Prurient, Raunchy, Scabrous
**Salad** Beetroot, Burnet, Caesar, Calaloo, Calalu, Capsicum, Celery, Chef's, Chicon, Coleslaw, Corn, Cos, Cress, Cucumber, Days, Endive, Escarole, Fennel, Finnochio, Finoc(c)hio, Frisée, Fruit, Greek, Guacamole, Horiatiki, Kachumber, Lactuca, Lamb's lettuce, Lettuce, Lollo rosso, Lovage, Mache, Mesclum, Mesclun, Miscellany, Mixture, Mizuna, Niçoise, Purslane, Radicchio, Radish, Rampion, Rocket, Rojak, Roquette, Russian, Salmagundi, Salmagundy, Side, Slaw, Tabbouleh, Tabbouli, Tomato, Waldorf, Watercress, Word
▹**Salad** *may indicate* an anagram

**Salamander** Axolotl, Congo eel, Ewt, Hellbender, Lizard, Menopome, Mole, Mudpuppy, Newt, Olm, Proteus, Siren, Snake, Spring-keeper, Tiger

**Salami, Salami technique** Fraud, Peperoni

**Salary** Emolument, Fee, Hire, Pay, Prebend, Screw, Stipend, → WAGE

**Sale(s)** Attic, Auction, Boot, Breeze up, Bring and buy, Cant, Car-boot, Clearance, Clearing, Farm-gate, Fire, Forced, Garage, January, Jumble, Market, Market overt, Outroop, Outrope, Party, Pitch, Raffle, Retail, Roup, Rummage, Subhastation, Trade, Turnover, Upmarket, Venal, Vend, Vendition, Vendue, Vent, Voetstoets, Voetstoots, Warrant, Wash, White, Wholesale, Yard

**Saleable** Pot boiler

**Saleroom** Pantechnicon

**Salesman, Saleswoman** Agent, Assistant, Bagman, Banian, Banyan, Broker, Buccaneer, Bummaree, Cheapjack, Counterhand, Counter jumper, Drummer, Hawker, Huckster, Loman, Pedlar, Rep, Retailer, Scotch draper, Tallyman, Tout, Traveller, Vendeuse, Vendor

**Salient** Coign, Jut, Projection, Prominent, Redan, Spur

**Salisbury** Cecil, Sarum

**Saliva** Dribble, Drool, Parotid, Ptyalism, Sial(oid), Sialagogue, Slobber, Spawl, Spit(tle), Sputum

**Sallow** Adust, Pallid, Pasty, Sale, Sauch, Saugh, Wan

**Sally** Aunt, Boutade, Charge, Dash, Escape, Excursion, Flight, Foray, Incursion, Issue, Jest, Mot, Pleasantry, Quip, Retort, Ride, Riposte, Sarah, Sortie, Wisecrack, Witticism

**Salmagundi** Mess

**Salmon** Alevin, Atlantic, Australian, Baggit, Blueback, Blue-cap, Boaz, Burnett, Char(r), Chinook, Chum, Cock, Coho(e), Dog, Dorado, Golden, Grav(ad)lax, Grayling, Grilse, Humpback, Kelt, Keta, King, Kipper, Kokanee, Lax, Ligger, Lox, Masu, Mort, Nerka, Oncorhynchus, Ouananiche, Par(r), Peal, Pink, Quinnat, Red, Redfish, Rock, Samlet, Shedder, Silver, Skegger, Slat, Smelt, Smolt, Smout, Smowt, Sockeye, Sparling, Spirling, Springer, Sprod, Togue, Umber

**Salon, Saloon** Barrel-house, Beauty, Car, Hair, Hall, Honkytonk, Last chance, Lounge, Nail bar, Pullman, Sedan, Shebang, Tavern

**Salt(s), Salty** AB, Acid, Alginate, Alum, Aluminate, Andalusite, Antimonite, Arseniate, Arsenite, Ascorbate, Aspartite, Attic, Aurate, Azide, Barnacle, Base, Basic, Bath, Benzoate, Bicarbonate, Bichromate, Boiler, Borate, Borax, Borosilicate, Brackish, Brine, Bromate, Bromide, Capr(o)ate, Caprylate, Carbamate, Carbonate, Carboxylate, Celery, Cerusite, Chlorate, Chlorite, Chromate, Citrate, Columbate, Complex, Condiment, Corn, Cream of tartar, Cure(d), Cyanate, Cyclamate, Datolite, Deer lick, Diazonium, Dichromate, Dioptase, Dithionate, Double, Efflorescence, Enos, Eosin, Epsom, Ferrate, Ferricyanide, Formate, Glauber, Glutamate, Halite, Halo-, Health, Hydrochloride, Hygroscopic, Hyponitrite, Hypophosphate, Iodide, Ioduret, Isocyanide, Kosher, Lactate, Lake-basin, Linoleate, Lithate, Liver, Magnesium, Malate, Malonate, Manganate, Manganite, Mariner, Matelot, Mersalyl, Microcosmic, Monohydrate, Mucate, Muriate, NaCl, Niobate, Nitrate, Nitrite, Oleate, Orthoborate, Orthosilicate, Osm(i)ate, Oxalate, Palmitate, Pandermite, Perborate, Perchlorate, Periodate, Permanganate, Phenolate, Phosphate, Phosphite, Phthalate, Picrate, Piquancy, Plumbate, Plumbite, Potash, Potassium, Powder, Propionate, Pyruvate, Rating, Reh, Resinate, Rochelle, Rock, Rosinate, Sailor, Sal ammoniac, Sal atticum, Salicylate, Salify, Salsuginous, Sal volatile, Saut, Saxo®, Sea-dog, Seafarer, Seasoned, Sebate, Selenate, Smelling, Soap, Sodium, Solar, Sorbate, Sorrel, Stannate, Stearate, Suberate, Succinate, Sulfite, Sulphate, Sulphite, Sulphonate, Table, Tannate, Tantalate, Tartrate, Tellurate, Tellurite, Thiocyanate, Thiosulphate, Titanate, Toluate, Trithionate, Tungstate, Uranin, Uranylic, Urao, Urate, Vanadate, Volatile, Water-dog, Whewellite, White, Wit(ty), Xanthate

**Salt meat** Mart

**Saltpetre** Caliche, Chile, Cubic, Nitre, Norway, Sal prunelle

**Salt-water** Sea

**Salubrious** Healthy, Sanitary, Wholesome

**Salutary** Beneficial, Good, Wholesome

**Salutation, Salute** Acclaim, Address, Asalam-wa-leikum, Australian, Ave, Banzai, Barcoo, Bid, Cap, Cheer, Command, Coupé(e), Curtsey, Embrace, Feu de joie, Fly-past, Genuflect,

Greet, Hail, Hallo, Halse, Harvey Smith, Homage, Honour, Jambo, Kiss, Middle finger, Namas kar, Namaste, Present, Salaam, Salvo, Shalom, Sieg Heil, Toast, Tribute, Wassail, Wave

**Salvador** Dali

**Salvage** Cannibalise, Dredge, Lagan, Ligan, Reclaim, Recover, Recycle, Rescue, Retrieve, Tot

**Salvation(ist)** Booth, Redemption, Rescue, Socinian, Soterial, Yeo

**Salve** Anele, Anoint, Assuage, Ave, Lanolin(e), Lip, Lotion, Ointment, Remedy, Saw, Tolu, Unguent, Weapon

**Salver** Dish, Platter, Tray, Waiter

**Salvo** Broadside, Feu de joie, Fusillade, Salute, Volley

**Sal volatile** Hartshorn

**Sam** Browse, Soapy, Uncle, Weller

**Samara** Ash-key

**Samaritan** Good

**Samarium** Sm

**Same(ness)** Ae, Agnatic, Congener(ic), Congruent, Contemporaneous, Coreferential, Do, Egal, Ejusd(en), Equal, Equiparate, Equivalent, Ib(id), Ibidem, Id, Idem, Identical, Identity, Ilk, Iq, Isotropy, Like, One, Rut, Thick(y), Thilk, Uniform, Ylke

**Sami** Lapp

**Samovar** Urn

**Samoyed** Dog, Uralian, Uralic

**Sample, Sampling** Amniocentesis, Biopsy, Blad, Browse, Cross-section, Example, Extract, Fare, Foretaste, Handout, Matched, Muster, Pattern, Pick, Pree, Preview, Prospect, Quadrat, Quota, Random, Representative, Scantling, Scoop, Smear, Snip, Specimen, Spread, Stratified, Swatch, Switch, → **TASTE**, Taster, Test, Toile, Transect, Try

**Samuel** Pepys, Smiles

**Samurai** Ronin

▹**Sam Weller** *may indicate* the use of 'v' for 'w' or vice versa

**San(atorium)** Sickbay

**Sanctify** Bless, Consecrate, Dedicate, Enhalo, Purify, Saint

**Sanctimonious, Sanctimony** Banbury, Creeping Jesus, Devout, Goody-goody, Holy, Pi, Preachy, Prig, Religiose, Righteous, Saintly

**Sanction(s), Sanctioned** Allow, Appro, Approbate, Approof, Approve, Assent, Authorise, Bar, Confirm, Countenance, Economic, Empower, Enable, Endorse, Fatwa(h), Fetwa, Fiat, Green light, Homologate, Imprimatur, Legal, Legitimate, Mandate, OK, Pass, Pragmatic, Ratify, Smart, Sustain, Upstay, Warrant

**Sanctities, Sanctity** Enhab, Halidom, Holiness, Hollidam, Sonties

**Sanctuary, Sanctum** Adytum, Ark, Asylum, By-room, Cella, Ch, Chancel, Church, Delubrum, Frithsoken, Frithstool, Girth, Grith, Haven, Holy, Inner, JCR, Kaaba, Lair, Naos, Oasis, Oracle, Penetralia, Preserve, Refuge, Sacellum, Sacrarium, Salvation, SCR, → **SHELTER**, Shrine, Tabernacle, Temple

**Sand(bank), Sandbar, Sands, Sandy** Alec, Alex, Alexander, Areg, Arena(ceous), Arenose, Arkose, As, Atoll, Bar, Barchan(e), Bark(h)an, Beach, Beige, Caliche, Dene, Desert, Dogger Bank, Down, Dudevant, Dune, Dupin, Ecru, Eremic, Erg, Esker, Foundry, Gat, George, Ginger, Goodwin, Grain, Granulose, Harbour-bar, Hazard, Hurst, Iron, Light, Loess, Machair, Musical, Nore, Oil, Outwash, Overslaugh, Podsol, Podzol, Portlandian, Psammite, Rangoli, Ridge, River, Sabulous, Saburra, Sawney, Seif dune, Shelf, Shoal, Shore, Silica, Singing, Tar, Tee, Time, Tombolo

**Sandal(s)** Alpargata, Buskin, Calceamentum, Chappal, Espadrille, Flip-flop, Ganymede, Geta, Huarache, Jelly, Patten, Peep-toe, Pump, Slip-slop, Talaria, Thong, Zori

**Sandalwood** Algum, Almug, Chypre, Pride, Red, Santal, White

**Sandarac** Arar

**Sand-dwelling, Sand-living** Arenicolous

**Sander** Pike-perch

**Sandgroper** Pioneer

**Sandhopper** Amphipod

**Sandhurst** RMA
**Sand-loving** Ammophilous, Psammophil(e)
**Sandpiper** Bird, Dunlin, Knot, Oxbird, Peetweet, Redshank, Ree, Ruff, Sandpeep, Stint, Terek, Turnstone
**Sandstone** Arkose, Calciferous, Cat's brains, Dogger, Fa(i)kes, Flysch, Greensand, Grey-wether, Grit, Hassock, Holystone, Itacolumite, Kingle, Molasse, New Red, Old Red, Psammite, Quartzite, Red, Sarsen, Silica
**Sandstorm** Haboob, Tebbad
**Sandwich(es), Sandwiched** Between, BLT, Bruschetta, Butty, Club, Clubhouse, Croque-monsieur, Cuban, Doorstep, Earl, Gyro, Hamburger, Hoagie, Island, Jam, Jeely piece, Knuckle, Open, Panini, Piece, Roti, Round, Sanger, Sango, Sarmie, Sarney, Sarnie, Smørbrød, Smörgåsbord, Smørrebrød, Squeeze, Stottie, Sub, Submarine, Tartine, Thumber, Toastie, Toebie, Triple-decker, Twitcher, Victoria, Wad, Western, Zak(o)uski
▷**Sandwich(es)** *may indicate* a hidden word
**Sane, Sanity** Compos mentis, Formal, Healthy, Judgement, Rational, Reason, Right-minded, Sensible, Wice
**Sangfroid** Aplomb, Cool, Poise
**Sanguine** Confident, Haemic, Hopeful, Optimistic, Roseate, Ruddy
**Sanitary, Sanitise** Disinfect, Hygienic, Salubrious, Sterile
**Sanitation** Drainage
**Sans** Sine, Without
**Sanskrit** Bhagavad-Gita, Panchatantra, Purana, Ramayana, Sutra, Upanishad, Vedic
**Santa (Claus)** Abonde, Kriss Kringle, Secret
**Sap** Attenuate, Benzoin, Bleed, Cosh, Cremor, Depress, Drain, Enervate, Entrench, Ichor, Juice, Laser, Latex, Latice, Lymph, Mine, Mug, Nuclear, Pulque, Ratten, Resin, Roset, Rosin, Rozet, Rozit, Secretion, Soma, Sucker, Sura, Swot, Tire, Undermine, Unnerve, Weaken
**Sapid** Flavoursome, Savoury, Tasty
**Sapience, Sapient** Discernment, Sage, Wisdom
**Sapless** Exsuccous
**Sapling** Ash-plant, Flittern, Ground-ash, Plant, Tellar, Teller, Tiller, Youth
**Sapper(s)** Engineer, Miner, RE
**Sapphire** Star, Water, White
**Sappho** Lesbian
**Sapwood** Alburnum
**Saracen** Arab
**Sarah** Battle, Gamp, Sal
**Sarcasm, Sarcastic** Acidity, Antiphrasis, Biting, Caustic, Cutting, Cynical, Derision, Dry, Irony, Mordacious, Mordant, Pungent, Quip, Quotha, Sarky, Satire, Sharp, Sharp-tongued, Smartmouth, Snide, Sting, Wisecrack, Wry
**Sardine** Fish, Sard
**Sardonic** Cutting, Cynical, Dry, Ironical, Scornful, Wry
**Sargasso** Ore, Sea(weed)
**Sark** Chemise, CI, Shirt
**Sarong** Sulu
**SAS** Red Devils
**Sash** Baldric(k), Band, Belt, Burdash, Cummerbund, Fillister, French, Lungi, Obi, Scarf, Turban, Window
**Saskatchewan** .sk
**Sassaby** Tsessebe
**Sassenach** English, Lowlander, Pock-pudding
**Satan(ic)** Adversary, Apollyon, Arch-enemy, Arch-foe, Cram, → DEVIL, Diabolic, Eblis, Evil One, Lucifer, Prince of darkness, Shaitan, Tempter, The old serpent
**Satchel** Bag, Postbag, Scrip
**Sate(d), Satiate** Cloy, Glut, Replete, Sad, Surfeit
**Satellite** Adrastea, Ananke, Ariel, Artificial, Astra, Atlas, Attendant, Aussat, Belinda, Bianca, Bird, Callisto, Calypso, Camenae, Carme, Charon, Communications, Comsat®, Cordelia,

Cosmos, Cressida, Deimos, Desdemona, Despina, Dione, Direct-broadcast, Disciple, Early bird, Earth, Echo, Elara, Enceladus, Europa, Explorer, Fixed, Follower, Galatea, Galilean, Ganymede, Geostationary, Helene, Henchman, Himalia, Hipparchus, Hyperion, Iapetus, Intelsat, Io, Janus, Lackey, Larissa, Leda, Lysithea, Meteorological, Metis, Mimas, Miranda, Moon, Mouse, Naiad, Navigation, Nereid, Oberon, Ophelia, Orbiter, Pan, Pandora, Pasiphae, Phobos, Phoebe, Planet, Portia, Prometheus, Puck, Rhea, Rosalind, Sinope, Smallset, Space probe, Space station, SPOT, Sputnik, Syncom, Telesto, Telstar, Tethys, Thalassa, Thebe, Tiros, Titan, Titania, Triton, Umbriel, Weather

▸**Satin** *see* SILK(Y)

**Satire, Satirical, Satirist** Arbuthnot, Archilochus, Burlesque, Butler, Candide, Chaldee, Dryden, Erewhon, Horace, Iambographer, Juvenal, Lampoon, Lash, Lucian, Mazarinade, Menippean, Menippos, Mockery, Pantagruel, Parody, Pasquil, Pasquin(ade), Pope, Rabelais, Raillery, Sarky, Sotadic, Spoof, Squib, Swift, Travesty, Wasps

**Satisfaction, Satisfactory, Satisfy(ing), Satisfied, Satisfactorily** Adequate, Agree, Ah, Answer, Ap(p)ay, Appease, Assuage, Atone, Change, Compensation, Complacent, → CONTENT, Convince, Copacetic, Defrayment, Enough, Feed, Fill, Fulfil, Glut, Gratify, Happy camper, Hunky-dory, Indulge, Jake, Job, Liking, Meet, Nice, OK, Okey-dokey, Pacation, Palatable, Pay, Please, Pride, Propitiate, Qualify, Redress, Relish, Repay, Replete, Reprisal, Revenge, Sate, Satiate, Sensual, Serve, Settlement, Slake, Smug, Square, Suffice, Supply, Tickety-boo, Topping, Well

**Satnav** GPS

**Saturate(d)** Drench, Flood, Glut, Imbue, Impregnate, Infuse, Permeate, → SOAK, Sodden, Steep, Surcharge, Waterlog

**Saturday** Holy, Sabbatine

**Saturn** God, Kronos, Lead, Planet, Rocket

**Satyr** Faun, Lecher, Leshy, Lesiy, Libertine, Marsyas, Pan, Silen(us), Woodhouse, Woodwose

**Sauce, Saucier, Saucy** Agrodolce, Aioli, Alfredo, Allemanse, Apple, Arch, Avgolemono, Baggage, Barbecue, Béarnaise, Béchamel, Bigarade, Bold(-faced), Bolognese, Bordelaise, Bourguignonne, Bread, Brown, Caper, Carbonara, Catchup, Catsup, Chasseur, Chaudfroid, Cheek, Chef, Chilli, Chutney, Condiment, Coulis, Cranberry, Cream, Creme anglaise, Cumberland, Custard, Dapper, Dip, Dressing, Enchilada, Espagnole, Fenberry, Fondue, Fricassee, Fudge, Fu yong, Fu yung, Gall, Garum, Gravy, Hard, Hoisin, Hollandaise, Horseradish, HP®, Impudence, Jus, Ketchup, Lip, Malapert, Marie Rose, Marinade, Marinara, Matelote, Mayo(nnaise), Melba, Meunière, Mint, Mirepoix, Mole, Monkeygland, Mornay, Mousseline, Mouth, Nam pla, Neck, Nerve, Newburg, Nuoc mam, Orange, Oxymal, Oyster, Panada, Parsley, Passata, Peart, Peking, Perky, Pert, Pesto, Piert, Piri-piri, Pistou, Pizzaiola, Ponzu, Portugaise, Puttanesca, Ragu, Ravigote, Relish, Remoulade, Rouille, Roux, Sabayon, Sal, Salad cream, Salpicon, Salsa, Salsa verde, Sambal, Sass, Satay, Shoyu, Soja, Soubise, Soy(a), Stroganoff, Sue, Sugo, Supreme, Sweet and sour, Tabasco®, Tamari, Tartar(e), Tomato, Topping, Tossy, Trimmings, Velouté, Vinaigrette, Vindaloo, White, Wine, Worcester, Worcestershire, Yakitori

**Sauceboat-shaped** Scaphocephalate

**Saucepan** Chafer, Goblet, Skillet, Steamer, Stockpot

**Saucer, Saucer-shaped** Ashtray, Discobolus, Flying, Lopolith, Pannikin, UFO

**Sauna** Banya, Bath, Steam-bath, Steam room, Sudatorium, Sudorific, Turkish bath

**Saunter** Amble, Dacker, Da(i)ker, Dander, Lag, Mosey, Promenade, Roam, Shool, Stroll, Toddle

**Sausage(s)** Andouille, Andouillette, Banger, Black pudding, Blood, Blutwurst, Boerswors, Bologna, Boudin, Bratwurst, Cervelat, Cheerio, Chipolata, Chorizo, Corn dog, Cumberland, Devon, Drisheen, Frankfurter, Garlic, Hot dog, Kielbasa, Kishke, Knackwurst, Knockwurst, Liver(wurst), Lorne, Luncheon, Mortadella, Mystery bag, Pep(p)eroni, Polony, Pudding, Salami, Sav(eloy), Snag(s), Snarler, Square, String, Vienna, Weenie, Weeny, White pudding, Wiener(wurst), Wienie, Wourst, Wurst, Zampone

**Sausage-shaped** Allantoid

**Sauté** Fry

**Savage, Savagery** Ape, Barbarian, Bestial, Bitter, Boor, Brute, Cannibal, Carnage, Cruel,

Feral, Ferocious, Fierce, Frightful, Grim, Gubbins, Hun, Immane, Inhuman, Maul, Noble, Remorseless, Sadistic, Truculent, Vicious, Violent, Vitriolic, Wild

**Savanna** Cerrado, Plain, Sahel, Treeless

**Savant** Egghead, Expert, Idiot, Mahatma, Sage, Scholar

**Save(r), Saving(s)** Back-up, Bank, Bar, Besides, But, Capital, Collect, Conserve, Cut-rate, Daylight, Deposit, Download, Economy, Except, Goalie, Hain, Hoard, Husband, Investment, ISA, Keep, Layby, Lay up, National, Nest egg, Nirlie, Nirly, Not, PEPS, Post office, Preserve, Put by, Reclaim, Recover, Recycle, Redeem, Relieve, Reprieve, →RESCUE, Reskew, Sa', Salt (away), Salvage, SAYE, Scrape, Scrimp, Shortcut, Slate club, Soak away, Sock away, Sou-sou, Spare, Stint, Stokvel, Succour, Susu, TESSA, Time, Unless

**Saviour** Aslan, Deliverer, Jesu(s), Lifeline, Messiah, Redeemer

**Savour(ed), Savoury** Aigrette, Bouchée, Canapé, Delight, Devils-on-horseback, Enjoy, Essence, Fag(g)ot, Flavour, Odour, Olent, Ramekin, Rarebit, Relish, Resent, Sair, Sapid, Sar, Smack, Starter, Tang, →TASTE, Umami, Vol au vent

**Savoy** Cabbage, Opera

**Savvy** Gumption, Sense

**Saw** Adage, Aphorism, Apothegm, Azebiki, Back, Band, Beheld, Bow, Bucksaw, Buzz, Chain, Circular, Cliché, Commonplace, Compass, Coping, Cross-cut, Crown, Cut, Dictum, Double-ender, Dovetail, Dozuki, Ensured, Flooring, Frame, Fret, Gang, Glimpsed, Gnome, Grooving, Hack, Hand, Jig, Keyhole, Legend, Log, Maxim, Met, Motto, Pad, Panel, Paroemia, Phrase, Pitsaw, Proverb, Pruning, Quarter, Rabbeting, Rack, Ribbon, Rip, Ryoba, Sash, Saying, Scroll, Serra, Skil®, Skip-tooth, Slasher, Slogan, Span, Spied, Stadda, Stone, Sweep, Tenon, Trepan, Trephine, Whip, Witnessed

**Sawbill** Merganser

**Sawbones** Surgeon

**Saw-toothed** Runcinate

**Sawyer** Logger, Tom

**Saxifrage** Astilbe, Bishop's cap, Burnet, Golden, Heuchera, London pride, Mitre-wort, St Patrick's cabbage

**Saxon** Cedric, Hengist, Hereward, Wend

**Saxophone** Axe, Tenor

**Say, Saying(s)** Adage, Agrapha, Allege, Aphorism, Apophthegm, Apostrophise, Articulate, Axiom, Beatitude, Blurt, Bon mot, Bromide, Byword, Cant, Catchphrase, Centos, Cliché, Declare, Dict(um), Eg, Enunciate, Epigram, Expatiate, Express, Facetiae, Fadaise, For example, For instance, Gnome, Impute, Input, Logia, Logion, →MAXIM, Mean, Mention, Mot, Mouth, Observe, Phrase, Platitude, Predicate, Pronounce, Proverb, Put, Quip, Recite, Rede, Relate, Remark, Report, Repute, Rusticism, Saine, Saw, Sc, Sententia, →SPEAK, Suppose, Sutra, Talk, Utter, Voice, Word

▷**Say, Saying(s)** *may indicate* a word sounding like another

**Scab(by)** Blackleg, Crust, Eschar, Leggism, Leprose, Mangy, Rat, Scald, Scall, Sore, Strike-breaker

**Scabbard** Frog, Pitcher, Sheath, Tsuba

**Scabies, Scabious** Devil's bit, Itch, Psora, Scotch fiddle, Sheep's (bit)

**Scabrous** Harsh, Rough, Thersites

**Scaffold(ing), Scaffolder** Gallows, Gantry, Hoarding, Putlock, Putlog, Rig, Spiderman, Stage, Staging

**Scald** Blanch, Burn, Leep, Ploat, Plot

**Scale(s), Scaly** Analemma, API gravity, Ascend, Balance, Baumé, Beaufort, Binet- Simon, Bismar, Brix, Bud, Burnham, Celsius, Centigrade, Ceterach, Chromatic, →CLIMB, Compass, Cottony-cushion, Dander, Dandruff, Desquamate, Diagonal, Diatonic, Dorian mode, Douglas, Elo, Enharmonic(al), Escalade, Fahrenheit, Fish plate, Flake, Fujita, Full, Furfur, Gamme, Gamut, Ganoid, Gapped, Gauge, Gravity, Gray, Gunter's, Heptatonic, Hexachord, Humidex, Indusium, Interval, Kelvin, Krab, Ladder, Lamina, Layer, Leaf, Lepid, Lepidote, Leprose, Libra, Ligule, Likert, Lodicule, Loricate, Magnitude, Major, Mercalli, Mesel, Metric, Minor, Model, Mohs, Munsell, Natural, Nominal, Octad, Ordinal, Oyster shell, Palea, Palet, Patagium, Peel, Pentatonic, Pholidosis, Placoid, Plate, Platform, Proportion, Ramentum,

→ **RANGE**, Rankine, Ratio, Réau(mur), Regulo, Richter, San Jose, Scalade, Scan, Scarious, Scent, Scincoid, Scurf, Scutellate, Shin, Skink, Sliding, Speel, Spring, Squama, Squame(lla), Submediant, Supertonic, Tegmentum, Tegula, Time, Tonal, Tridymite, Tron(e), Unified, Vernier, Wage, Weighbridge, Wentworth, Whole-tone, Wind

▷**Scale(d)** *may indicate* a fish

**Scallion** Leek

**Scallop(ed)** Bivalve, Clam, Coquille, Crenate, Crenulate, Escalop, Frill, Gimp, Mush, Pecten, Queenie, Seashell, Vandyke

**Scallywag** Ne'er-do-well, Rascal, Scamp, Skeesicks, Whippersnapper

**Scalp** Cut, Mussel, Scrape, Skin, Trophy

**Scalpel** Bistoury, Knife

**Scam** Con, Deception, Dodge, Fast and loose, Grift, Ramp, Strap game

**Scamp** Blighter, Fripon, Imp, Limb, Lorel, Lorrell, Losel, Lozell, Neglect, → **RASCAL**, Reprobate, Rip, Rogue, Scallywag, Skeesicks, Toerag

**Scamper** Dart, Gambol, Lamp, Run, Scoot, Scurry, Scutter, Skedaddle, Skelter, Skitter, Trot

**Scampi** Norway lobster

**Scan(ning), Scanner** Barcode, Body, CAT, CT, ECG, EEG, Examine, Flat-bed, Helical, Inspect, Interlaced, Iris, OCR, Optical, Oversee, Peruse, PET, Phish, Rake, Raster, Read, Scintigraph, Scrutinise, Sector, SEM, Sequential, SPET, Study, Survey, Tomography, Ultrasound, Vertical, Vet

**Scandal(ous), Scandalise** Belie, Canard, Commesse, Disgrace, Exposé, Flagrant, Gamy, -gate, Hearsay, Muck-raking, Mud, Notorious, Opprobrium, Outrage, Shame, Slander, Stigma, Stink, Tattle, Watergate

**Scandalmonger** Alarmist, Blabbermouth, Muckraker, Tattler

**Scandinavian** Dane, Finn, Gotland, Icelander, Laplander, Lapp, Nordic, Norman, Norseland, Northman, Olaf, Runic, Swede, Varangian, Viking

**Scandium** Sc

**Scant(y), Scantness** Bare, Brief, Exiguous, Jejune, Jimp, Light, Low, Meagre, Oligotrophy, Parsimonious, Poor, Scrimpy, Short, Shy, Skimpy, Slender, Spare, Sparse, Stingy

**Scapegoat, Scapegrace** Butt, Fall-guy, Hazazel, Joe Soap, Martyr, Patsy, Skainesmate, Stooge, Target, Victim, Whipping-boy

**Scapula** Blade, Omoplate

**Scar(face)** Al, Blemish, Cheloid, Cicatrix, Cliff, Craig, Epulotic, Hilum, Keloid, Leucoma, Leukoma, Mark, Pockmark, Stigma, Ulosis, Weal, Wipe

**Scarab** Beetle, Gem

**Scarce(ly), Scarcity** Barely, Dear, Dearth, Famine, Few, Hardly, Ill, Infrequent, Lack, Paucity, Rare, Scanty, Seldom, Short, Strap, Tight, Uncommon, Want

**Scare(d), Scarify, Scaring, Scaremongering, Scary** Adaw, Afraid, Agrise, Alarmist, Alert, Amaze, Aroint, Etch, Fleg, Fright, Gally, Gliff, Glift, Hair-raising, Hairy, Panic-(stricken), Petrify, Skeer, Spook, Startle, Tattie-bogle, Unnerve, Windy

**Scarecrow** Bogle, Bugaboo, Dudder, Dudsman, Gallibagger, Gallibeggar, Gallicrow, Gallybagger, Gallybeggar, Gallycrow, Malkin, Mawkin, Potato-bogle, Ragman, S(h)ewel, Tattie-bogle

**Scarf** Babushka, Belcher, Boa, Cataract, Comforter, Cravat, Curch, Doek, Dupatta, Fascinator, Fichu, Hai(c)k, Haique, Headsquare, Hijab, Hyke, Lambrequin, Madras, Mantilla, Muffettee, Muffler, Neckatee, Neckcloth, Neckerchief, Neckgear, Neckpiece, Necktie, Neckwear, Nightingale, Orarium, Pagri, Palatine, Pashmina, Patka, Pugg(a)ree, Rail, Rebozo, Sash, Screen, Shash, Stock, Stole, Tallith, Tippet, Trot-cosy, Trot-cozy, Vexillum

**Scarifier** Scuffler

**Scarlet** Cinnabar, Cochineal, Crimson, Lac, Lac-dye, Pimpernel, Pink, Ponceau, Red, Vermilion

**Scarper** Abscond, Absquatulate, Bunk, Hightail, Imshi, Run, Shoo, Welsh

**Scat** Aroint, Dropping, Vamo(o)se

**Scathe, Scathing** Caustic, Mordant, Sarcastic, Savage, Severe, Trenchant, Vitriolic

**Scatter(ed), Scattering** Bestrew, Broadcast, Diaspora, Diffuse, Disgregation, Disject, Dispel, → **DISPERSE**, Dissipate, Dot, Flurr, Inelastic, Intersperse, Litter, Rayleigh, Rout, Scail,

Scale, Scall, Skail, Sow, Sparge, Sparse, Splutter, Sporadic, Sprad, Spread, Sprinkle, Squander, Straw, Strew, Strinkle

**Scatterbrain(ed), Scatty** Dippy, Ditsy, Ditz(y), Dotty, Harum-scarum, Tête folie

**Scavenge(r)** Ant, Dieb, Forage, Gully-hunter, Hunt, Hy(a)ena, Jackal, Rake, Ratton, Rotten, Scaffie, Sweeper, Totter, Vulture

**Scenario** Outline, Plot, Script, Storyboard, Worst case

**Scene(ry), Scenic** Arena, Backcloth, Boscage, Cameo, Coulisse, Crime, Decor, Diorama, Drop, Episode, Flat(s), Landscape, Locale, Outtake, Periaktos, Phantasmagoria, Picturesque, Prop, Prospect, Riverscape, Set, Set piece, Sight, Site, Sketch, Stage, Tableau, Take, Tormenter, Tormentor, Transformation, Venue, View, Vista, Wing

**Scent** Aroma, Attar, Chanel®, Chypre, Civet, Cologne, Eau de cologne, Essence, Fragrance, Frangipani, Fumet(te), Gale, Moschatel, Musk, Nose, Odour, Orris, Ottar, Otto, Perfume, Pomander, Sachet, Smell, Spoor, Vent, Waft, Wind

**Scentless** Anosmia

**Sceptic, Sceptical(ly), Scepticism** Agnostic, Askant, Cynic, Disbeliever, Doubter, Europhobe, Incredulous, Infidel, Jaundiced, Nihilistic, Nullifidian, Pyrrho(nic), Sadducee, Solipsism, Thomas

**Schedule** Agenda, Arrange, Calendar, Checklist, Classification, Form, Itinerary, List, Prioritise, Programme, Register, Slot, Table, Timescale, Time-sheet, Timetable

**Scheme, Schemer, Scheming** Angle, Calculate, CATS, Collude, Colour, Concoct, Connive, Conspire, Crafty, Cunning, Dare, Darien, Dart, Decoct, Décor, Design, Devisal, Diagram, Dodge, Draft, Engineer, Evince, Game plan, Gin, Honeytrap, Housing, Intrigue, Jezebel, Machiavellian, Machinate, Manoeuvre, Master plan, Nostrum, Pension, Pilot, → PLAN, Plat, Plot, Ploy, Ponzi, Project, Proposition, Purpose, Put-up job, Pyramid, Racket, Rhyme, Ruse, Scam, Scenario, Set-aside, Stratagem, System, Table, Tactic, Top-hat, Wangle, Wheeler-dealer, Wheeze

**Schism(atic)** Antiburgher, Break, Disunion, Division, Eastern, Great, Greek, Heterodox, Protestantism, Rent, Secession, Split, Western

**Schizo(phrenia)** Catatonic, Dementia praecox, Hebephrenia, LSD

**Schloss** Castle

**Schmaltz(y)** Goo, Mush, Slush, Tear-jerker

**Schmieder** S

**Schmook** Drip

**Schmuck** Gunsel

**Schnapps** Enzian

**Scholar, Scholiast** Abelard, Academic, Alcuin, Alumni, Atticus, BA, Bookman, Boursier, Cabalist, Catachumen, Classicist, Clergy, Clerisy, Clerk, Commoner, Copernicus, Demy, Disciple, Don, Erasmus, Erudite, Etonian, Exhibitioner, Extern(e), Externat, Faculty, Goliard, Graduate, Grecian, Hafiz, Hebraist, Imam, Inkhorn, Jowett, Literate, Littérateur, MA, Mal(l)am, Masorete, Maulana, Noter, Occam Ulama, Ollamh, Ollav, Pauline, Plutarch, Polymath, Pupil, Rhodes, Sap, Savant, Saxonist, Schoolboy, Sizar, Soph, → STUDENT, Tabardar, Taberdar, Taberder, Tom Brown, Varro

**Scholarship** Bursary, Closed, Education, Erudition, Exhibition, Grant, Grant-in-aid, Learning, Lore, Mass, Rhodes

**School** Brainwash, Discipline, Drill, Educate, Exercise, Feeder, Fish, Peripatetic, Reform, Riding, Sciences, Scul, Scull(e), Teach, → TRAIN, Tutor, Verse

---

**SCHOOLS**

*2 letters:*
GS

*3 letters:*
Day
Gam
LSE
Old
Pod
RAM
Ski

*4 letters:*
Coed
Cool
Cult
Dada
Dame
Dojo
Dual
Eton
Free
High
Home
Kant
Lake
Life
Play

Poly
Prep
RADA
Real
Sect
Sink
Song
Tech

***5 letters:***
Board
Charm
Choir
Drama
Faith
First
Grade
Group
Heder
Hedge
Ionic
Kindy
List D
Lower
Lycée
Night
Perse
Piano
Rydal
Shoal
Slade
State
Stowe
Style
Trade
Upper

***6 letters:***
Ash Can
Beacon
Cheder
Church
Fettes
Harrow
Honour
Hostel
Infant
Junior
Kindie
Lyceum
Magnet
Middle
Normal
Oundle
Public
Ragged
Ramean
Repton
Summer
Sunday
Whales

***7 letters:***
Academy
Alleyn's
Bauhaus
Cockney
Council
Crammer
Driving
Essenes
Flemish
Grammar
Jim Crow
Lancing
Loretto
Madrasa
Nursery
Primary
Private
Rhodian
Roedean
Rossall
Sabbath
Satanic
Special
Writing
Yeshiva

***8 letters:***
Approved
Barbizon
Benenden
Bluecoat
Boarding
Business
Cranwell
Downside
Externat
Graduate
Hospital
Kailyard
Kaleyard
Language
Mahayana
Mannheim
National
Provided
Sadducee
Seminary
Separate
Tenebrum

***9 letters:***
Chartreux
Classical
Community
Composite
Finishing
Frankfurt
Gymnasien
Gymnasium
Institute
Madrassah
Palaestra
Parochial
Porpoises
Sandhurst
Secondary
Single-sex
Spasmodic
Tonbridge
Voluntary

***10 letters:***
Ampleforth
Chautauqua
Elementary
Foundation
Grange Hill
Grant-aided
Greyfriars
Historical
Industrial
Integrated
Maintained
Manchester
Parnassian
Pensionnat
Scandalous
Sole charge
Stonyhurst
St Trinian's
Wellington
Winchester

***11 letters:***
Direct grant
Giggleswick
Gordonstoun
Hypermodern
Independent
Maintaining
Marlborough
Preparatory
Reformatory
Residential

***12 letters:***
Charterhouse
Conservative
Conservatory
Intermediate
Kindergarten
Malory Towers
Progymnasium

***13 letters:***
Comprehensive
Conservatoire
Dotheboys Hall

***14 letters:***
Correspondence
Voluntary-aided

***15 letters:***
Grant-maintained
Secondary-modern

***19 letters:***
Voluntary-controlled

---

**Schoolboy, Schoolgirl** Alumna, Bluecoat, Bunter, Carthusian, Coed, Colleger, East, Etonian, Fag, Gait, Geit, Gyte, Miss, Monitor, Oppidan, Petty, Stalky, Wykehamist

**School-leaver** Abiturient

**Schoolma'am, Schoolman, Schoolmaster, Schoolmistress, Schoolteacher** Aram, Beak, Dominie, Duns, Holofernes, Miss, Occam, Orbilius, Pedagogue, Pedant, Servitor, Sir, Squeers, Teacher, Tutress, Ursuline

**Schooner** Glass, Hesperus, Hispaniola, Prairie, Ship, Tern

**Schubert** D
**Sciatica** Hip-gout
**Science** Aerodynamics, Aeronautics, Alchemy, Anatomy, Anthropology, Applied, Art, Astrodynamics, Astrophysics, Atmology, Avionics, Axiology, Behavioural, Biology, Bionics, Biotech, Botany, Chemistry, Christian, Cognitive, Computer, Cosmography, Cosmology, Creation, Cryogenics, Crystallography, Cybernetics, Dismal, Domestic, Earth, Ekistics, Electrodynamics, Endocrinology, Energetics, Entomology, Eth(n)ology, Eugenics, Euphenics, Exact, Forensic, Gay, Geodesy, Geogeny, Geology, Geopolitics, Hard, Hierology, Hydrodynamics, Hydrometry, Information, Kinetics, Knowledge, Life, Lithology, Logic, Macrobiotics, Magnetics, Materia medica, Mechanics, Metallurgy, Meteorology, Metrology, Military, Mineralogy, Mnemonics, Morphology, Natural history, Noble, Nomology, Noology, Nosology, Occult, Ology, Ontology, Optics, Optometry, Orthotics, Palaeontology, Pedagogy, Penology, Phrenology, Physical, Physics, Planetology, Pneumatics, Policy, Political, Praxis, Psychics, Pure, Rocket, Rural, Semantics, Semiology, Serology, Skill, Social, Soft, Soil, Sonics, Stinks, Stylistics, Tactics, Taphonomy, Technics, Technology, Tectonics, Telematics, Thermodynamics, Thremmatology, Toxicology, Tribology, Trigonometry, Typhlology, Zootechnics
**Science fiction** Cyberpunk
**Scientist** Alchemist, Anatomist, Archimedes, Aston, Astronomer, Atomist, Audiologist, Bacteriologist, Bell, Berners-Lee, → **BIOLOGIST**, Boffin, Bohr, BSc, Cavendish, → **CHEMIST**, Climatologist, Copernicus, Curie, Dalton, Darwin, Davy, Doppler, Eddington, Egghead, Einstein, Euler, Experimenter, Expert, Faraday, Fourier, Frankenstein, FRS, Galileo, Gay-Lussac, Geodesist, Geometer, Harvey, Heaviside, Herschel, Hooke, Hubble, Introchemist, Kennelly, Lamarck, Laplace, Lodge, Lovell, Mach, Magnetist, Medawar, Mendeleev, Metallurgist, Newton, Oersted, Oncologist, Pascal, Pasteur, Pauli, → **PHYSICIST**, Piccard, Potamologist, Priestley, Réaumur, Researcher, Rocket, Seaborg, Technocrat, Tesla, Theremin, Van der Waals, Volta
**Scimitar** Acinaciform, Sword
**Scintillate** Dazzle, Emicate, Gleam, Glitter, → **SPARKLE**
**Scion** Cion, Graft, Imp, Offspring, Sien(t), Slip, Sprig, Sprout, Syen
**Scissors** Clippers, Criss-cross, Cutters, Forfex, Nail, Probe, Shears
**Sclerosis** Disseminated, Multiple
**Scoff(ing)** Belittle, Boo, Chaff, Deride, Devour, Dor, Eat, Feast, Flout, Food, Gall, Geck, Gibe, Gird, Gobble, Irony, → **JEER**, Jest, Mock, Rail, Rib, Ridicule, Roast, Scaff, Scorn, Send up, Sneer, Swallow, Taunt
**Scold(ing)** Admonish, Berate, Callet, Catamaran, Chastise, Chide, Clapperclaw, Cotquean, Do, Dressing down, Earful, Earwig, Flite, Flyte, Fuss, Jaw(bation), Jobation, Lecture, Nag, Objurgate, Philippic, Rag, Rant, Rate, → **REBUKE**, Reprimand, Reprove, Revile, Roast, Rollick, Rollock, Rouse on, Row, Sas(s)arara, Sis(s)erary, Slang, Slate, Termagant, Threap, Threep, Through-going, Tick-off, Tongue-lash, Trimmer, Upbraid, Virago, What for, Wig, Xant(h)ippe, Yaff, Yankie, Yap
**Sconce** Candlestick, Crown, Forfeit, Head, Ice, Nole
**Scone** Drop, Girdle, Griddle cake, Pikelet, Potato, Soda
**Scoop** Bale, Dipper, Dredge, Exclusive, Flash, Gouge, Grab, Hollow, Ladle, Lap, Pale, Rout, Shovel, Spoon, Story, Trowel
**Scoot** Scamper
**Scooter** Vespa®
**Scope** Ambit, Bargaining, Breadth, Compass, Cover(age), Diapason, Domain, Elbow-room, Extent, Freedom, Gamut, Indulgence, Ken, Latitude, Leeway, Play, Purview, Range, Remit, Room, Rope, Scouth, Scowth, Size, Sphere
**Scorch(er)** Adust, Birsle, Blister, Brasero, → **BURN**, Char, Destroy, Frizzle, Fry, Parch, Scathe, Scouther, Scowder, Scowther, Sear, Singe, Sizzle, Soar, Speed, Swale, Swayl, Sweal, Sweel, Torrefy, Torrid, Wither
**Score(s), Scoring** Aggregate, Apgar, Arrange, Behind, Bill, Birdie, Bogey, Bradford, Bye, Capot, Chalk up, Chase, Clock up, Conversion, Count, Credit, Crena, Debt, Dunk, Eagle, Etch, Full, Gash, Goal, Groove, Hail, Honours, Incise, Ingroove, Ippon, Koka, Law, Leaderboard,

Lots, Magpie, Make, Mark, Music, Net, Nick, Notation, Notch, Nurdle, Open, Orchestrate, Partitur(a), Peg(board), Pique, Point, Record, Repique, Result, Rit(t), Rouge, Run, Rut, Scotch, Scrat, Scratch, Scribe, Scrive, Set, Sheet music, Single, Spare, Stableford, Stria, String, Sum, Tablature, → TALLY, TE, Touchdown, Try, Twenty, Vocal, Waza-ari, Win, Yuko

**Score-board, Score-sheet** Card, Telegraph

▹**Scorer** *may indicate* a composer

▹**Scoring** *may indicate* an anagram

**Scorn(ful)** Arrogant, Bah, Contemn, Contempt, Contumely, Deride, Despise, Dis(s), Disdain, Dislike, Disparagement, Flout, Geck, Haughty, Insult, Meprise, Mock, Opprobrium, Phooey, Putdown, Raillery, Rebuff, Ridicule, Sarcastic, Sardonic, Sarky, Scathing, Scoff, Scout, Sdaine, Sdeigne, Sneer, Sniffy, Snort, Spurn, Wither

**Scorpion** Arachnid, Book, Chelifer, False, Father-lasher, Pedipalp(us), Rock, Vinegarroon, Water, Whip

**Scot(sman), Scots(woman), Scottish** Alistair, Angus, Antenati, Berean, Blue-bonnet, Bluecap, Caledonian, Celt, Clansman, Covenanter, Duni(e)wassal, Dunniewassal, Erse, Fingal, Gael, Highland, Ian, Jock, Kelt, Kelvinside, Kiltie, Kitty, Knox, Laird, Lallan(s), Lot, Lowland, Luckie, Lucky, Mac, Mon, Morningside, Pecht, Peght, Pict, Ross, Sandy, Sawn(e)y, Shetlander, Stuart, Tartan, Tax, Teuchter, Torridonian

**Scotch(man)** Censor, Dish, Distiller, Foil, Glenlivet®, Nip in the bud, Notch, Score, Scratch, Stop, Thwart, Usquebaugh, Whisky

**Scot-free** Wreakless

**Scotland** Alban(y), Albion, Caledonia, Gaeltacht, Gaidhealtachd, Lallans, Lothian, NB, Norland, Scotia

**Scoundrel** Cad, Charlatan, Cur, Dog, Donder, Fink, Heel, Hound, Knave, Miscreant, Rat(bag), Reprobate, Scab, Smaik, Swine, Varlet, → VILLAIN, Wretch

**Scour(er)** Beat, Depurate, Full, Holystone, Lant, Purge, Quarter, Scrub

▹**Scour** *may indicate* an anagram

**Scourge** Bane, Bible-thumper, Cat, Disciplinarium, Discipline, Flagellate, Flog, Knout, Lash, Pest, → PLAGUE, Punish, Scorpion, Whip, Wire

**Scouse** Liver bird, Wacker

**Scout** Akela, Baden-Powell, Beaver, Bedmaker, Bird dog, Boy, Colony, Deride, Disdain, Emissary, Explorer, Flout, Guide, King's, Mock, Outrider, Pathfinder, Patrol(ler), Pickeer, Pioneer, Queen's, Ranger, Reconnoitre, Rover, Runner, Scoff, Scorn, Scourer, Scurrier, Scurriour, Sea, Sixer, Spial, Spyal, Talent, Tenderfoot, Tonto, Track, Troop, Vedette, Venture

**Scowl(ing)** Frown, Glare, Glower, Gnar, Lour, Lower, Sullen

**Scrabble** Clamber, Claw, Paw

**Scrag(gy)** Bony, Dewitt, Ewe-necked, Neck, Scrawny

**Scram** Begone, Hence, Scarper, Scat, Shoo

**Scramble** Addle, Clamber, Encipher, Encode, Grubble, Hurry, Maul, Mêlée, Mix, Motocross, Muss(e), Rat race, Ruck, Scamble, Sprattle, Sprawl, Swerve, Texas

**Scrap(s), Scrappy** Abandon, Abolish, Abrogate, Atom, Bin, → BIT, Brock, Cancel, Conflict, Cutting, Discard, Ditch, Dump, End, Erase, → FIGHT, Fisticuffs, Fragment, Fray, Iota, Jot, Junk, Leftover, Mêlée, Mellay, Morceau, Morsel, Nucleon, Odd, Off-cut, Ort, Ounce, Papier collé, Particle, Patch, Piece, Pig's-wash, Pigswill, Quarrel, Rag, Rase, Raze, Relic, Remnant, Rescind, Rew, Row, Ruck, Scarmoge, Scintilla, Scissel, Scissil, Scroddled, Scrub, Set-to, Shard, Sherd, Shred, Skerrick, Skirmish, Snap, Snippet, Spall, Stoush, Tait, Tate, Tatter, Titbit, Trash, Truculent, Tussle, Whit, Wisp

**Scrap book** Album, Grangerism

**Scrap box** Tidy

**Scrape(r)** Abrade, Agar, Bark, Clat, Claw, Comb, Curette, D and C, Erase, Escapade, Grate, Graze, Gride, Harl, Hoe, Hole, Jar, Kowtow, Lesion, Lute, Pick, Predicament, Racloir, Rake, Rasorial, Rasp, Rasure, Raze, Razure, Saw, Scalp, Scart, Scrat(ch), Scroop, Scuff, Shave, Skimp, Skin, Skive, Squeegee, Strake, Stridulate, Strigil, Xyster

**Scraping noise** Curr, Scroop

**Scrap merchant** Didakai, Didakei, Diddicoi, Diddicoy, Didicoi, Didicoy, Gold-end-man, Totter

**Scratch(es), Scratched, Scratching** Annul, Cancel, Cla(u)t, Claw, Cracked heels, Curry, Devil, Efface, Eradicate, Erase, Etch, Grabble, Graze, Hatch, Key, Lucifer, Mar, Nick, Par, Periwig, Pork, Quit, Race, Rase, Rasp, Rast, Ritt, Root, Satan, Scarify, Scart, Score, Scrab(ble), Scram(b), Scrape, Scrattle, Scrawm, Scrawp, Scrooch, Scrorp, Scrub, Scuff, Spag, Streak, Striation, Tease, Teaze, Wig, Withdraw

▷**Scratch(ed)** *may indicate* an anagram

**Scrawl** Doodle, Scratch, Scribble, Squiggle

**Scream(er)** Aargh, Amusing, Bellow, Black-necked, Cariama, Caterwaul, Comedian, Comic, Crested, Cry, Eek, Headline, Hern, Hoot, Kamichi, Laugh, Priceless, Primal, Riot, Scare-line, Screech, Seriema, Shriek, Skirl, Squall, Squawk, Sutch, Yawl, Yell

**Scree** Bahada, Bajada, Eluvium, Talus

**Screech(ing)** Cry, Hoot, Screak, Screich, Screigh, Scriech, Scritch, Skreigh, Skriech, Skriegh, Ululant, Whoot

**Screed** Blaud, Megillah, Ms, Plastered, Rat-rhyme, Tirade

**Screen(s), Screening** Abat-jour, Air, Arras, Back projection, Backstop, Blind(age), Block, Blue, Boss, Breast, Brise-soleil, Camouflage, Cervical, Chancel, Check, Chick, Cinema, Cinerama®, Cloak, Clothes, Comb, Cornea, Coromandel, Cover, Cribble, Curtain, Divider, Dodger, Draught, Eclipse, Eyelid, Festoon-blind, Fight, Fire, Flat, Fluorescent, Glib, Gobo, Grid, Grille, Hallan, Help, Hide, Hoard, Hoarding, Iconostas(is), Intensifying, Jube, Lattice, Long-persistence, Mantelet, Mask, Meat, Monitor, Net, Nintendo®, Nonny, Obscure, Organ, Over-cover, Overhead, Page, Parclose, Partition, Part-off, Pella, Plasma, Pulpitum, Purdah, Radar, Radarscope, Reardos, Reredorse, Reredos(se), Retable, Riddle, Rollerblind, Rood, Scog, Sconce, Scope, Seclude, → **SHADE**, Shelter, Shield, Shoji, Show, Sift, Sight, Silver, Skug, Small, Smoke, Split, Strain, Sunblock, Televise, Tems, Test, Testudo, TFT, Touch, Transenna, Traverse, Umbrella, VDU, Vet, Visor, Wide, Windbreak, Window, Windshield, Winnow

**Screenplay** Script

**Screw** Adam, Allen, Archimedes, Blot, Butterfly, Cap, Cheat, Coach, Coitus, Countersunk, Double-threaded, Dungeoner, Endless, Extort, Eyebolt, Female, Fleece, Grub, Guard, Gyp, Ice, Interrupted, Jack, Jailer, Jailor, Lag, Lead, Levelling, Lug, Machine, Male, Mar, Micrometer, Miser, Monkey-wrench, Niggard, Pay, Perpetual, Phillips®, Prop(ellor), Pucker, Raised head, Robertson, Rotate, Ruin, Salary, Screweye, Scrunch, Skinflint, Spiral, Squinch, Swiz(zle), Thumb(i)kins, Tighten, Turnkey, Twin, Twine, Twist, Vice, Wages, Warder, Whitworth, Worm, Wreck, Wring

**Screwdriver** Cocktail, Phillips®, Pozidriv®, Ratchet, Scrum, Stubby, Tweaker

**Scribble(r)** Doodle, Graffiti, Inkhorn-mate, Note, Pen, Scrawl

**Scribe** Clerk, Ezra, Mallam, Scrivener, Sopherim, Tabellion, Writer, WS

**Scrimmage** Bully, Fracas, Maul, Mêlée, Rouge, Scrap, Skirmish, Struggle

**Scrimp** Economise, Pinch, Save, Scrape, Skimp, Skrimp

**Script (reader)** Arabic, Book, Calligraphy, Demotist, Devanagari, Gurmukhi, Hand, Hieratic, Hiragana, Italic, Jawi, Kana, Kufic, Libretto, Linear A, Linear B, Lines, Lombardic, Longhand, Miniscule, Nagari, Nashki, Nastalik, Nastaliq, Nes(h)ki, Og(h)am, Prompt book, Ronde, Scenario, Screenplay, Shooting, Shorthand, Sumerian, Writing

**Scriptless** Improvised

**Scripture(s), Scriptural version** Adi Granth, Agadah, Alcoran, Antilegomena, Avesta, Bible, Gemara, Gematria, Gospel, Granth (Sahib), Guru Granth, Haggada(h), Hermeneutics, Hexapla, Holy book, Holy writ, Koran, K'thibh, Lectionary, Lesson, Lotus Sutra, Mishna(h), OT, Rig-veda, Smriti, Tantra, Targum, Testament, Torah, Upanishad, Veda, Vedic, Verse, Vulgate

**Scrivener** Tabellion

**Scrofula** Crewels, Cruel(l)s, King's evil, Struma

**Scroll(-work)** Cartouche, Dead Sea, Gohonzon, Makimono, Megillah, Mezuza(h), Monkeytail, Parchment, Pell, Roll, Roul(e), Scrow, Sefer Torah, Stemma, Torah, Turbinate, Upcurl, Vitruvian, Volume, Volute

**Scrooge** Blagueur, Miser, Niggard

**Scrotum** Oscheal

**Scrounge(r)** Beg, Blag, Bludge(r), Borrow, Bot, Cadge, Forage, Freegan, Freeload, Layabout, Ligger, Scunge, Sponge

**Scrub(ber), Scrubland, Scrubs** Abandon, Cancel, Chaparral, Cleanse, Dele(te), Exfoliate, Expunge, Facial, Fynbos, Gar(r)igue, Heath, Hog, Holystone, Horizontal, Loofa(h), Luffa, Mallee, Masseur, Nailbrush, Negate, Pro, Rescind, Rub, Scour, Sticks, Strim, Wormwood

▷**Scrub** *may indicate* 'delete'

**Scruff(y)** Dag(gy), Dog(-eared), Fleabag, Grubby, Mangy, Manky, Moth-eaten, Nape, Nucha, Raddled, Ragamuffin, Ragbag, Raggle-taggle, Scarecrow, Tatterdemalion, Tatty, Uncombed, Untidy

**Scrum(mage)** Bajada, Fracas, Maul, Melée, Mob, Pack, Rouge, Ruck

**Scrummy, Scrumptious** Delectable, Delicious, Toothy, Yum-yum

**Scrumpy** Cider

**Scrunt** Carl

**Scruple(s), Scrupulous** Compunction, Conscience, Doubt, Meticulous, Nicety, Precise, Punctilious, Qualm, Queasy, Righteous, Scr, Stickle, Thorough

**Scrutinise, Scrutiny** Audit, Check, Docimasy, Examine, Inspect, Observe, Peruse, Pore, Pry, → **SCAN**, Size up, Study

**Scud** East, Scoot, Spark, Spindrift, Spoom, Spoon, Spray

**Scuff** Brush, Nape, Shuffle

**Scuffle** Bagarre, Brawl, Melee, Scarmage, Skirmish, Struggle, Tussle

▷**Scuffle** *may indicate* an anagram

**Scull** Oar, Row

**Scullion** Drudge, Kitchen slave

**Sculpt(ure)** Acrolith, Aeginetan, Bas-relief, Boast, Bronze, Bust, Calvary, Canephor(a), Canephore, Canephorus, Carve, Chisel, Chryselephantine, Della-robbia, Figure, Glyptics, High-relief, Kore, Kouros, Marble, Mezzo-relievo, Mezzo-rilievo, Mobile, Nude, Pergamene, Pietà, Relief, Relievo, Sc, Scabble, Scapple, Shape, Stabile, → **STATUARY**, Topiary

**Sculptor** Arp, Artist, Bartholdi, Bernini, Brancusi, Butler, Calder, Canova, Cellini, Daedalus, Della Robbia, Donatello, Dubuffet, Epstein, Flaxman, Giacometti, Gibbons, Gill, Gormley, Hepworth, Klippel, Landseer, Michelangelo, Moore, Myron, Nicholson, Noguchi, Nollekens, Paolozzi, Pevsner, Phidias, Picasso, Pisano, Praxiteles, Pygmalion, Rodin, Scopas, Stevens, Tatlin, Wheeler, Woolner

**Scum, Scumbag** Confervoid, Dregs, Dross, Epistasis, Film, Glass-gall, Kish, Legge, Louse, Mantle, Mother, Pellicle, Pond, Rabble, Rat, Sandiver, Scorious, Scruff, Slag, Slime, Spume, Sullage, Vermin

**Scupper** Drain, Ruin, Scuttle, Sink

**Scurf, Scurvy** Dander, Dandriff, Dandruff, Furfur, Horson, Lepidote, Lepra, Leprose, Scabrous, Scall, Scorbutic, Whoreson, Yaws, Yaw(e)y

**Scurrilous** Cur, Fescennine, Profane, Ribald, Sotadic, Thersites, Vulgar

**Scurry** Beetle, Hurry, Scamper, Scutter, Skedaddle, Skelter, Squirr

**Scut** Fud, Tail

**Scute** Plate

**Scuttle** Abandon, Dan, Dash, Hod, Purdonium, Scamper, Scoop, Scrattle, Scupper, Scurry, Sink, Wreck

**Scythe** Bushwhacker, Cradle, Cut, Hook, Sickle, Sieth, Snath(e), Snead, Sneath, Sned

**Sea(s), Seawards** Beam, Billow, Brine, Briny, Deep, Ditch, Drink, Electron, Epicontinental, Euphotic, Euxine, Foam, Forties, Herring-pond, Lagoon, Main, Mare, Mare clausum, Mare liberum, Maritime, Molten, Narrow, → **OCEAN**, Offing, Offshore, Oggin, Open, Out, Quantity, Strand, Tide, Tide-rip, Water

---

**SEAS**

*3 letters:*
Ler
Med
Red
Zee

*4 letters:*
Aral
Azov
Blue
Dead
Four
Head
High
Java
Kara
Ross
Sulu

*5 letters:*
Banda
Black
Ceram
China
Coral
Cross

Great
Irish
Japan
North
Seven
Short
South
Timor
White

*6 letters:*
Aegean
Aonian
Baltic
Bering
Biscay
Celtic
Cortes
Flores
Inland
Ionian
Laptev
Tasman
Tethys
Yellow

*7 letters:*
Andaman
Arabian
Arafura
Barents
Benthos
Caspian
Celebes
Channel
Chukchi
Euripus
Galilee
Icarian
Marmara
Marmora
Okhotsk
Pelagic
Polynya
Solomon
Weddell

*8 letters:*
Adriatic
Amundsen
Beaufort
Bismarck
Bosporus
Hwang Hai
Kattegat
Labrador
Ligurian
Sargasso
Tiberias

*9 letters:*
Bosphorus
Caribbean
East China
E. Siberian
Greenland
Hudson Bay
Norwegian
Skagerrak
Thalassic
Waddenzee

*10 letters:*
Philippine
South China
Tyrrhenian

*11 letters:*
Spanish Main

*12 letters:*
Nordenskjold

*13 letters:*
Mediterranean

*14 letters:*
Bellingshausen

---

**Sea-anemone** Actinia, Zoantharia
**Sea-bear** Fur-seal, Otary, Seal, Seecatchie
**Sea-beast** Ellops, Lamp-shell, Loriciferan, Manatee
**Sea-bream** Carp, Fish, Porgie, Porgy, Tai
**Sea-cow** Dugong, Lamantin, Manatee, Rhytina, Sirenian
**Sea-cucumber** Bêche-de-mer, Trepang
**Sea-dog** Salt, Seal, Tar
**Sea-eagle** Erne
**Sea-ear** Abalone, Ormer, Paua
**Sea-fight** Naumachy
**Seafood** Abalone, Calamari, Clappy doo, Crab, Crevette, → FISH, King prawn, Langouste, Lobster, Oyster, Pilchard, Plankton, Prawn, Scampi, Shrimp, Squid, Urchin, Whelk, Winkle, Zooplankton
**Seafront, Seashore, Seaside** Beach, Coast(line), Esplanade, Littoral, Orarian, Prom(enade), Seaboard, Waterfront
**Sea-god** Neptune, Nereus, Triton
**Sea-green** Glaucous, Incorruptible, Robespierre
**Sea-horse** Hippocampus, Hippodame, Lophobranchiate, Morse, Pipefish, Tangie
**Seal(ant), Seal box, Sealed, Seals** Airtight, Appose, Atlantic, Bachelor, Bladdernose, Block(ade), Bull(a), Cachet, Cap, Caulk, Chesterfield, Chop, Clinch, Close, Cocket, Common, Consign, Cork, Crab-eater, Cylinder, Eared, Earless, Electric, Elephant, Emblem, Fisherman's ring, Fob, Fur, Gasket, Grave, Great, Greenland, Grey, Hair, Harbour, Harp, Hermetic, Hooded, Hudson, Impress, Jark, Lemnian, Leopard, Lute, Mastic, Monk, Obsign(ate), Operculum, O-ring, Otary, Phoca, Pinnipedia, Pintadera, Plug, Pod, Privy, Proof, Putty, Quarter, Ribbon, Ringed, Ronan, Rookery, Saddleback, Sea-bear, Sealch, Sea-leopard, Sealgh, Seecatch(ie), Selkie, Sigil, Signet, Silkie, Silky, Size, Skippet, Solomon's, Sphragistics, Stamp, SWALK, Tape, Tar, Vacuum-packed, Wafer, Washer, Water, Weddell, Whitecoat, Womb, Zalophus, Ziplock
**Sea-legs** Balance, Pleons
**Sea-level** Geoid, Mean
**Sea-life** Anthozoa
**Sea-lily** Crinoid, Palmatozoa
**Seam, Seamstress** Channel, Commissure, Dorsal suture, Fell, Felled, French, Furrow, Join, Layer, Middle-stitching, Midinette, Monk's, Sew, Stratum, Suture, Thread, Welt, Zawster

**Seaman, Seamen** AB, Argonaut, Circumnavigator, Crew, Jack, Lascar, Lubber, Mariner, OD, Ordinary, OS, PO, Rating, RN, → SAILOR, Salt, Swabby, Tar
**Sea-mat** Flustra, Hornwrack
**Sea-matiness** Gam
**Sea-monster** Hippocampus, Kraken, Merman, Wasserman, Ziffius
**Sea-mouse** Bristle-worm
**Séance** Communication, Levitation, Session, Sitting
**Sea-parrot** Puffin
**Sea-plane** Hydrovane
**Sear** Brand, Burn, Catch, Cauterise, Char, Frizzle, Parch, Scath(e), Scorch, Singe, Wither
**Search(ing), Searcher** Beat, Body, Comb, Delve, Dowse, Dragnet, Examine, Federated, Ferret, Fingertip, Fish, → FORAGE, Fossick, Frisk, Global, Google(-whack), Grope, Home, Hunt, Indagate, Inquire, Jerk, Jerque, Kemb, Manhunt, Mudlark, Perquisition, Perscrutation, Probe, Proll, Prospect, Proul, Prowl, Pursue, Quest, Rake, Rancel, Ransack, Ransel, Ranzel, Ravel, Ripe, Root, Rootle, Rummage, Scan, Scavenge, Scour, Scout, Scur, Sker, Skirr, Snoop, Squirr, Strip, Surf, Sweep, Talent spotting, Thumb, Trace, Trawl, Zotetic
**Sea-rover** Norseman, Viking
**Sea-serpent, Sea-snake** Ellops, Hydrophidae, Phoca
▶**Seaside** *see* SEAFRONT
**Sea-slug** Bêche-de-mer, Trepang
**Sea-snail** Neritidae
**Season(able), Seasonal, Seasoned, Seasoning** Accustom, Age, Aggrace, A propos, Autumn, Betimes, Christmas, Close, Condiment, Devil, Dress, Duxelles, Easter, Enure, Etesian, Fall, Fennel, Festive, Fines herbes, Flavour, Garlic, G(h)omasco, Growing, Heat, Hiems, High, Holiday, In, Inure, Lent, Marjoram, Master, Mature, Noel, Nutmeg, Off, Open, Paprika, Peak, Pepper, Powellise, Practised, Ripen, Salt, Sar, Seal, Seel, Seil, Sele, Silly, Solstice, Spice, Spring, Summer(y), Tahini, Ticket, Tide, Time, Timeous, Weather-beaten, Whit, Winter, Xmas, Yule
**Sea-squirt** Ascidian, Cunjevoi, Salpa(e)
**Seat(ing)** Arthur's, Auditorium, Back, Backside, Balcony, Banc, Banquette, Barstool, Beanbag, Behind, Bench, Bleachers, Booster, Booty, Borne, Bosun's chair, Bottom, Box, Bucket, Bum, Bunker, Buttocks, Canapé, Catbird, Centre, Chair, Chaise longue, Choirstall, Coit, Constituency, Couch, Country, Creepie, Croup(e), Croupon, Cushion, Davenport, Deckchair, Derrière, Dick(e)y, Dicky, Divan, Driving, Duff, Ejection, Ejector, Epicentre, Faldistory, Faldstool, Foundation, Front, Fud, Fundament, Gradin, Hall, Hassock, Home, Hot, Houdah, Howdah, Humpty, Hurdies, Inglenook, Judgement, Jump, Knifeboard, Lap, Love, Marginal, Marquise, Mercy, Miserere, Misericord, Natch, Nates, Ottoman, Palanquin, Palfrey, Passenger, Perch, Pew, Pillion, Pit, Pouffe, Prie-dieu, Rear, Ringside, Rocker, Royal box, Rumble, Rumble-tumble, Rump, Saddle, Safe, Sagbag, Sedes, Sedile, Sedilium, See, Sell, Selle, Settee, Settle, Shooting stick, Sidesaddle, Siege, Siege Perilous, Sliding, Sofa, Squab, Stall, Stand, Stool, Strapontin, Subsellium, Sunk(ie), Sunlounger, Synthronus, Tabo(u)ret, Throne, Thwart, Tip up, Tonneau, Upholstery, Window, Woolsack
**Sea-urchin** Asterias, Cidaris, Echinus, Pluteus, Sphaeridia, Whore's egg
**Sea-vampire** Manta
**Sea-wall** Bulwark, Dyke, Groyne
**Seaweed** Agar, Alga(e), Arame, Badderlock, Bladderwort, Bladderwrack, Carrag(h)een, Ceylon moss, Chondrus, Conferva, Coralline, Cystocarp, Desmid, Devil's apron, Diatom, Driftweed, Dulse, Enteromorpha, Florideae, Fucus, Gulfweed, Heterocontae, Hijiki, Hornwrack, Irish moss, Kale, Karengo, Kelp, Kilp, Kombu, Konbu, Laminaria, Laver, Lemon-weed, Maerl, Nori, Nullipore, Oarweed, Ore, Peacock's tail, Phaeophyceae, Phyco-, Porphyra, Purple laver, Redware, Rockweed, Sargasso, Seabottle, Sea-furbelow, Sea-girdle, Sea-lace, Sea-lettuce, Sea-mat, Sea-moss, Sea-tangle, Seaware, Sea-whistle, Sea-wrack, Tang(le), Tetraspore, Ulva, Varec(h), Vraic, Wakame, Ware, Wrack
**Sea-wolf** Pirate
**Sea-worm** Palolo, Spunculid

**Sea-worthy** Watertight
**Sebastian** Coe
**Sec** Dry, Instant
**Secateurs** Pruners
**Secede(r), Secession(ist)** Adullamite, Antiburgher, Breakaway, Cave, Defy, Desert, Dissident, Flamingant, Separatist, Sever, Splinter, UDI
**Seclude(d), Seclusion** Byway, Cloister, Incommunicado, Isolate, Ivory tower, Maroon, Nook, Pleasance, Poke(y), Privacy, Purdah, Quarantine, Remote, Retiracy, Retreat, Secret, Sequester, Shyness, Solitude
**Second(ary), Seconds** Abet, Alternative, Another (guess), Approve, Appurtenance, Assist, Atomic, Back(er), Beta, Byplay, Chaser, Collateral, Coming, Comprimario, Congener, Cornerman, Deuteragonist, Ephemeris, Fiddle, Flash, Flip, Friend, Handler, Imperfect, Indirect, Inferior, Instant, Jiffy, Latter, Leap, Lesser, Minor, Mo(ment), Nature, Other, Pig's-whisper, Red ribbon, Redwood, Runner-up, Saybolt-Universal, Sec, Shake, Share, Side(r), Sideline, Sight, Silver, Split, Subsidiary, Subtype, Support, Tick, Tone, Trice, Twinkling, Universal, Wind
**Second-best** Worsted
▸**Second-class** *see* SECOND-RATE
**Second coming** Parousia
**Second earth** Antichthon
**Second-hand** Flea market, Hand-me-down, Hearsay, Preloved, Reach-me-down, Re-paint, Trade in, Tralaticious, Unoriginal, Used, Vicarious
**Second-rate, Second-class** B, Inferior, Mediocre, Sub
**Second-sight** Deuteroscopy, Divination, Tais(c)h
**Second tine** Bay, Bez
**Second-year student** Semi(e)(-bajan), Sophomore
**Secrecy, Secret(s), Secretive** Apocrypha, Arcana, Arcane, Arcanum, Back-door, Backstairs, Cabbalistic, Cagey, Clam, Clandestine, Classified, Closet, Code, Conference, Confidence, Conventicle, Corner, Couvert, Covert, Cranny, Cryptadia, Cryptic, Crypto, Dark, Dearn, Deep, Deep-laid, Dern, Devious, Esoteric, Espionage, Furtive, Hidden, Hidling, Hidlin(g)s, Hole and corner, Hugger-mugger, Hush-hush, Hushy, In camera, Inly, Inmost, Inner, In pectore, In petto, Know-nothing, Latent, Mysterious, Mystical, Mystique, Open, Oyster, Password, Penetralia, Petto, → PRIVATE, Privity, Privy, QT, Rune, Scytale, Seal, Sensitive, Shelta, Silent, Slee, Sly, Sneaky, State, Stealth, Sub rosa, Surreptitious, Tight-lipped, Top, Trade, Ulterior, Unbeknown, Underboard, Undercover, Underground, Underhand, Undescried, Unknown, Unre(a)d, Unrevealed, Untold
**Secretary** Aide, Amanuensis, Chancellor, Chronicler, CIS, Company, Desk, Desse, Famulus, Home, Minuteman, Moonshee, Munshi, Notary, Parliamentary, Permanent, Private, Prot(h)onotary, Scrive, Social, Steno(grapher), Stenotyper, Temp
**Secretary-bird** Messenger, Serpent-eater
**Secrete, Secretion** Aequorin, Aldosterone, Allomone, Apocrine, Autacoid, Cache, Castor, Cerumen, Chalone, Colostrum, Cuckoo-spit, Discharge, Earwax, Emanation, Exude, Gland, Hide, Honeydew, Hormone, Insulin, Juice, Lac, Lactate, Lerp, Melatonin, Mucus, Musk, Nectar, Osmidrosis, Phlegm, Prostacyclin, Pruina, Ptyalin, Recrement, Renin, Resin, Rheum, Royal jelly, Saliva, Sebum, Secern, Smegma, Spit(tle), Succus, Trypsin, Wax
**Secret Service** Mossad
**Sect(arian), Secret society** Abelite, Adamite, Adventist, Ahmadiy(y)ah, Albigenses, Amish, Anabaptist, Assassin, Babee, Babi, Bahai, Bigendian, Bigot, Brahmin, Cabal, Cainite, Calixtin(e), Camorra, Campbellite, Cathar, Christadelphian, Clan, Clapham, Covenantes, Crypto, Cult, Cynic, Danite, Darbyite, Disciples of Christ, Dissenter, Docate(s), Donatist, Druse, Druze, D(o)ukhabor, Dunkard, Dunker, Ebionite, Encratite, Essene, Familist, Fifth monarchy, Gabar, Gheber, Ghebre, Giaour, Glassite, Gnostic, Group, Gueber, Guebre, Gymnosophist, Harmonist, Harmonite, Hassid, Hauhau, Hemerobaptist, Hesychast, Hillmen, Holy Roller, Hutterite, Illuminati, Ismaili, Jacobite, Jansenist, Jehovah's Witness, Jodo, Karaite, Karmathian, Little-endian, Lollard, Lubavitch, Macedonian, Macmillanite, Mandaean, Marcionite, Maronite, Mendaites, Monothelite, Montanist, Moonie, Mormon,

Mucker, Muggletonian, Nasorean, Nazarine, Noetian, Ophites, Order, Partisan, Patripassian, Paulician, Perfectation, Perfectionist, Pharisee, Philadelphian, Phrygian, Picard, Pietist, Plymouth Brethren, Plymouthite, Porch, Pure Land, Ranter, Rappist, Rasta, Ribbonism, Russellite, Sabbatian, Sabian, Sadducee, S(h)aiva, Saktas, Sandeman, School, Schwenkfelder, Seekers, Senus(s)i, Seventh Day Adventist, Sex, Shafiite, Shaker, Shembe, Shia(h), Shiite, Soka Gakkai, Sons of Freedom, Taliban, Therapeutae, Tunker, Unitarian, Utraquist, Vaishnava, Valdenses, Vaudois, Wahabee, Wahabi(i)te, Waldenses, Yezdi, Yezidee, Yezidi, Zealot, Zen, Zezidee

**Section(ed), Sector** Appendix, Area, Balkanize, Bit, Caesarian, Chapter, Classify, Compartment, Conic, Cross, Cut, Department, Dermatose, Directorate, Division, Edge, Element, Ellipse, Empennage, Episode, Eyalet, Gan, Golden, Gore, Hyperbola, Length, Lith, Lune, Meridian, Metamere, Microtomic, Mortice, Movement, Octant, Outlier, Panel, Part, Passus, Peraeon, → **PIECE**, Platoon, Private, Public, Pull-out, Quarter, Reach, Rhythm, Rib, S, Segment, Septum, Severy, Sextant, Shard, Sherd, Slice, Stage, Track, Ungula, Unit, Warm, Wing, Zenith, Zone

**Secular(ise), Secularist** Cosmist, Earthly, Laic, Non-CE, Profane, Temporal, Ungod, Worldly

**Secure(d), Security** Affix, Anchor, Assurance, Bag, Bail, Band, Bar, → **BASIC**, Batten, Bearer, Belay, Bellwether, Belt and braces, Bolt, Bond, Bottomry, Buckle, Buck Rogers, Button, Calm, Cash ratio, Catch, CCTV, Cement, Chain, Cheka, Chinstrap, Cinch, Clamp, Clasp, Clench, Clinch, Close, Cocoon, Collateral, Collective, Come by, Confine, Consolidate, Consols, Cosy, Counterseal, Cushy, Debenture, Deposit, Disreputable, Doorman, Dunnage, Earn, Earthwork, Engage, Enlock, Ensure, Equity, Establishment, Fasten, Fastness, Firewall, Firm, Fortify, Frap, Fungibles, Gain, Gamma, Gilt, Gilt-edged, Gird, Grith, Guarantee, Guy, Heritable, Hostage, Hypothec, Immune, Impregnable, Indemnity, Inlock, In the bag, Inurn, Invest(ment), Key, Knot, Lace, Land, Lash, Latch, Lien, Listed, Lock (up), Lockaway, Lockdown, Lockfast, Long-dated, Longs, Medium-dated, Moor, Mortgage, Nail, National, Obtain, Padlock, Password, Patte, Pawn, Pin, Pledge, Pot, Pre-empt, Preference, Procure, Protect, Quad, Rope, Rug, → **SAFE**, Safety, Scrambler, Screw, Seal, Settle, Shutter, Snare, Snell, Snug, Social, Solvency, Sound, Stable, Stanchion, Staple, Staylace, Stick, Stock, Strap, Sure(ty), Tack, Take, Tie, Tight, Trap, Trice, Truss, Tyde, Vest, Warrant, Watertight, Wedge, Win

**Sedan** Battle, Brougham, Chair, Jampan(i), Jampanee, Kago, Litter, Palanquin, Palkee, Palki, Saloon

**Sedate** Calm, Cool, Decorous, Demure, Dope, Douce, Drug, Sad, Serene, Sober(sides), Staid, Stand

**Sedative** Amytal®, Analgesia, Anodyne, Aspirin, Barbitone, Bromal, Bromide, Chloral, Depressant, Deserpidine, Hypnic, Laurel water, Lenitive, Lupulin(e), Meprobamate, Metopryl, Miltown, Morphia, Narcotic, Nembutal®, Opiate, Painkiller, Paraldehyde, Pethidine, Phenobarbitone, Premed(ication), Rohypnol®, Roofie, Scopolamine, Seconal®, Snuff, Soothing, Soporific, Temazepam, Thridace, Valerian, Veronal®

**Sedentary** Inactive, Sessile, Stationary

**Sedge** Carex, Chufa, Cinnamon, Clubrush, Deer hair, Eriophorum, Grey, Sawgrass, Seg, Xyris

**Sediment** Alluvium, Chalk, Deposit, Dregs, F(a)eces, Fecula, Flysch, Foots, Graded, Grounds, Grouts, Incrustation, Lees, Molasse, Placer, Residue, Salt, Sapropel, Silt, Sludge, Terrigenous, Till, Turbidite, Varve, Warp

**Sedition, Seditious** Incitement, Insurrection, Leasing-maker, Revolt, Riot, Treason

**Seduce(r), Seduction, Seductive** Allure, Bed, Beguilement, Betray, Bewitch, Bribe, Come-hither, Courtesan, Cuckold-maker, Debauch, Dishonour, Entice, Femme fatale, Honeyed, Honied, Ixion, Jape, Lothario, Luring, Mislead, Pull, Sexpot, Sexy, Siren, Slinky, Tempt, Titillate, Trepan, Undo, Vamp, Wrong

▷**Seduce** *may indicate* one word inside another

**See(ing), See to** Acknow, Apostolic, Barchester, Bath and Wells, Behold, Believing, Berkeley, Bishopric, C, Carlisle, Consider, Date, Deek, Descry, Diocesan, Discern, Durham, Ebor, Ecce, Ely, Episcopal, Exeter, Eye, Get, Glimpse, Holy, Imagine, In as much as, La, Lincoln, Lo, Meet, Norwich, Notice, Observe, Organise, Papal, Perceive, Realise, Remark,

Ripon, Rochester, Rubberneck, Rumble, St David's, Salisbury, Sight, Since, Sodor and Man, Spae, Spot, Spy, Truro, Twig, Understand, V, Vatican, Vid(e), View, Vision, Visit, Voilà, Witness, York

**Seed(s), Seedbud, Seedy** Achene, Apiol, Argan, Arilli, Arillode, Ash-key, Bean, Ben, Benne, Best, Blue, Bonduc, Bur(r), Cacoon, Canary grass, Caraway, Cardamom, Carvy, Cebadilla, Cedar-nut, Cevadilla, Chickpea, Cocoa, Colza, Coriander, Corn, Crabstone, Cum(m)in, Dragon's teeth, Embryo, Endosperm, Ergot, Eye, Favourite, Fern, Germ, Grain, Gritty, Inseminate, Issue, Ivory-nut, Kernel, Lentil, Lima, Lomentum, Mangy, Mawseed, Miliary, Mote, Nickar, Nicker, Niger, Nucellous, Nut, Oat, Offspring, Origin, Ovule, Pea, Peaky, Pinole, Pinon, Pip, Pomegranate, Poorly, Poppy, Pulse, Pyxis, Rape, Sabadilla, Samariform, Scuzz, Semen, Seminal, Senvy, Sesame, Shabby, Shea-nut, Silique, Sordid, Sorus, Sow, Sperm, Spore, Stane, Stone, Tamarind, Terminator, Thistledown, Urd, Zoosperm

**Seed-case** Aril, Boll, Bur(r), Endopleura, Husk, Pea(s)cod, Pod, Testa, Theca

**Seed-leaf** Cotyledon

**Seedsman** Driller, Nurseryman, Sower

**Seek(er), Seeking** Ask, Aspire, Beg, Busk, Call in, Cap-in-hand, Chase, Court, Endeavour, Ferret out, Fish, Forage, Gun for, Pursue, Quest, Scavenge, Scur, Search, Skirr, Solicit, Suitor, Try

**Seem(ing), Seemingly** Apparent, Appear, As if, Look, Ostensible, Purport, Quasi, Think

**Seemly** Apt, Comely, Decent, Decorous, Fit, Proper, Suitable

**Seep(age)** Angel's share, Bleed, Dribble, Exude, Leak, Ooze, Osmose, Percolate, Permeate

**Seer** Augur, Auspex, Balaam, Eye, Melampus, Nahum, Nostradamus, Observer, Oculiform, Onlooker, Oracle, Prescience, Prophet, Sage, Sibyl, Soothsayer, T(e)iresias, Witness, Zoroaster

**Seesaw** Bascule, Boom and bust, Oscillate, Teeter(-totter), Teeter-board, Tilt, Vacillate, Wild mare

**Seethe(d), Seething** Aboil, Boil, Bubble, Churn, Ferment, Fume, Simmer, Smoulder, Sod

**Segment(ation)** Antimere, Arthromere, Cut, Division, Gironny, Gyronny, Intron, Joint, Lacinate, Leg, Lith, Lobe, Merogenesis, Merome, Merosome, Metamere, Metathorax, Part, Piece, Pig, Proglottis, Propodeon, Prothorax, Quadrant, Scliff, Section, Share, Shie, Skliff, Slice, Somite, Split, Sternite, Syllable, Tagma, Telson, Trochanter, Urite, Uromere

**Segregate, Segregation** Apartheid, Exile, Insulate, Intern, →ISOLATE, Jim Crow, Seclude, Separate

**Seidlitz** Powder, Rochelle

**Seigneur** Grand

**Seismic, Seismography** Richter, Terremotive

**Seismograph** Tromometer

**Seize, Seizing, Seizure** Angary, Apprehend, Appropriate, Areach, Arrest, Assume, Attach(ment), Bag, Bone, Capture, Catch, Claw, Cleek, Clutch, Cly, Collar, Commandeer, Confiscate, Cop, Coup, Distrain, Distress, Extent, Fit, For(e)hent, →GRAB, Grip, Hend, Hi-jack, Ictus, Impound, Impress, Intercept, Maverick, Nab, Na(a)m, Nap, Nim, Pin, Poind, Possess, Pot, Raid, Ravin, Replevy, Rifle, Sease, Sequestrate, Smug, Snag, Snatch, Stroke, Tackle, Trover, Usurp, Wingding, Wrest

**Seldom** Infrequent, Rare, Unoften

**Select(ion), Selected, Selecting, Selector** Adopt, Appoint, Artificial, Assortment, Auslese, Bla(u)d, Cap, Casting, Catalogue, Cherry-pick, Choice, Choose, Classy, Clonal, Compendium, Cream, Cull, Darwinism, Discriminate, Draft, Draw, Eclectic, Edit, Elite, Excerpt, Exclusive, Extract, Favour, Garble, Handpick, Inside, K, Kin, Mix and match, Nap, Natural, Nominate, Opt, Pericope, →PICK, Playlist, Pot-pourri, Prefer, Recherché, Redline, Sample, Seed, Sex, Short list, Single, Sort, Stream, Target, Tipster, Triage, Tuner, UCCA, Vote

**Selenium** Se, Zorgite

**Self** Atman, Auto, Being, Character, Ego, Inner, Person, Psyche, Seity, Sel, Soul

**Self-assertive** Arrogant, Uppish

**Self-concern** Dog-eat-dog

**Self-confident, Self-confidence, Self-willed** Aplomb, Ego, Headstrong, Jaunty

**Self-conscious** Awkward, Guilty, Inhibited

**Self-contained** Absolute, Continent, Reticent, SC, Taciturn
**Self-contradictory** Absurd
**Self-control, Self-discipline** Abstinence, Ascesis, Encraty, Modesty, Patience, Restraint, Stiff upper lip, Temper(ance), Willpower
**Self-criticism** Psychogas
▸**Self-defence** *see* MARTIAL (ARTS)
**Self-destructive** Lemming
**Self-effacing** Meek, Modest
**Self-esteem** Amour-propre, Conceit, Confidence, Egoism, Ego trip, Pride, Vainglory
**Self-evident** Axiom, Ipso facto, Manifest, Obvious, Patent, Truism, Truth
**Self-examination** Soul-searching
**Self-existence** Solipsism
**Self-fertilisation, Self-origination** Aseity, Autogamy
**Self-governing** Autonomy, Idior(r)hythmic, Kabele, Kebel, Puritanism, Swaraj
**Self-guiding** Autonomy
**Self-help** Smiles
**Self-important, Self-importance, Self-indulgence, Self-indulgent, Self-interested, Self-regard(ing)** Aristippus, Arrogant, Bumptious, Chesty, Cocky, Conceited, Coxy, Donnism, Effete, Egocentric, Ego-trip, Hedonist, His Nibs, Immoderate, Jack-in-office, Licentious, Monomania, Mugwump, Narcissistic, Pompous, Pooterish, Pragmatic, Primadonna, Profligate, Solipsist, Stuffed shirt, Sybarite, Tin god, Vainglorious
**Selfish(ness)** Avaricious, Dog eat dog, Dog-in-the-manger, Egocentric, Egoist, Egomaniac, Grabby, Greedy, Hedonist, Hog, Mean, Possessive, Solipsism
**Selfless(ness)** Altruistic, Non-ego, Tuism
**Self-limiting** Kenotic
▸**Self-origination** *see* SELF-FERTILISATION
**Self-pollinating** Cl(e)istogamic
**Self-possession** Aplomb, Assurance, Composure, Cool, Nonchalant, Phlegm
**Self-restraint** Reserve
**Self-righteous** Pharisee
**Self-satisfied, Self-satisfaction** Complacent, Narcissism, Smug, Tranquil
**Self-service** Automat, Buffet, Cafeteria, Supermarket
**Self-styled** Soi-disant
**Self-sufficient, Self-sufficiency** Absolute, Autarky, Complete, Hunter-gatherer
**Self-taught** Autodidact
**Selkirk** Alexander, Castaway
**Sell(er), Selling** Apprize, Auction, Barter, Bear, Betray, Blackmail, Blockbuster, Cant, Catch, Chant, Chaunt, Cold-call, Cope, Costermonger, Direct, Dispose, Divest, Do, Eggler, Fancier, Fellmonger, Flog, Go, Hard, Have, Hawk, Huckster, Hustle, Inertia, Knock down, Market, Marketeer, Ménage, Merchant, Missionary, Oligopoly, Pardoner, Party, Peddle, Peddler, Pick-your-own, Provender, Purvey, Push, Pyramid, Rabbito(h), Realise, Rep, Retail, Ruse, Scalp, Shift, Short, Simony, Soft, Stall-man, Stockist, Sugging, Switch, Tout, → TRADE, Trick, Vend, Vent, Wholesaler
**Sell out** Betray
**Selvage** Border, Edge, Roon, Rund
**Semantics** General, Generative, Interpretive, Notional, Onomasiology, Semasiology, Sematology
**Semaphore** Signal, Tic-tac, Wigwag
**Semblance** Appearance, Aspect, Guise, Likeness, Sign, Verisimilitude
**Semen** Jis(so)m, Milt, Spoof, Spunk
**Semi-circular** D, Hemicycle
**Semi-conductor** Diode, Germanium, LED, Thryristor
**Seminar(y)** Class, → COLLEGE, Colloquium, Group, Theologate, Tutorial, Webinar, Workshop, Yeshiva
**Semi-opaque** Frosted
**Semiotics** Syntactics

**Semi-paralysis** Dyaesthesia
**Semitic** Accadian, Akkadian, Ammonite, Amorite, Arab, Aramaic, Canaanite, Chaldean, Geez, Jewish, Phoenician
**Semitone** Pycnon
**Semolina** Couscous
**Senate** Council, Curia, Seanad (Eireann), Second chamber
**Senator** Antiani, Cicero, Conscript father, Elder, Legislator, Patrician, Shadow, Solon
**Send, Send off, Sent** Consign, → DESPATCH, Disperse, Emanate, Emit, Entrance, Extradite, Issue, Launch, Mail, Order, Post, Rapt, Red card, Refer, Remit, Route, Ship, Transmit, Transport
**Send back** Refer, Remand, Remit, Return
**Send down** Demit, Lower, Refer, Rusticate
**Send up** Chal(l)an, Lampoon, Promote
**Seneca** Stoic
**Senegal** SN
**Senescence** Age
**Senile, Senility** Caducity, Dementia, Disoriented, Doddery, Doited, Doitit, Dotage, E(i)ld, Gaga, Nostology, Twichild
**Senior(ity)** Aîné, Doyen, Elder, Father, Grecian, High-ranker, Major, Majorat, Old(er), Oldie, Oldster, Oubaas, Père, Primus, Superior, Upper
**Senna** Bladder, Cassia
**Señor(a)** Caballero, Don(a), Hidalga, Hidalgo
**Sensation(al)** Acolouthite, Aftershock, Anoesis, Aura, Blood, Blood and thunder, Commotion, Déjà vu, Drop-dead, Emotion, Empfindung, Feeling, Furore, Gamey, Gas, Impression, Lurid, Megastar, Melodrama, Organic, Par(a)esthesia, Phosphene, Photism, Pyrotechnic, Rush, Sensory, Shocker, Shock-horror, Showstopper, Splash, Stir, Styre, Synaesthesia, Thrill, Tingle, Vibes, Wow, Yellow
**Sense, Sensual(ist), Sensing** Acumen, Animalist, Attuite, Aura, Carnal, Clothes, Coherence, Common, Conscience, Dress, Ear, ESP, Faculty, Feel, Gaydar, Gist, Gross, Gumption, Gustation, Hearing, Horse, Idea, Import, Instinct, Intelligence, Intuition, Kinaesthesia, Lewd, Libertine, Loaf, Logic, Marbles, Meaning, Moral, Muscular, Nous, Olfactory, Palate, Perceptual, Proprioceptive, Rational, Receptor, Remote, Road, Rumble-gumption, Rum(m)el-gumption, Rumgumption, Rum(m)le-gumption, Sanity, Satyr, Sight, Sixth, Slinky, Smell, Spirituality, Subaudition, Sybarite, Synesis, Taste, Taste bud, Touch, Voluptuary, Voluptuous, Wisdom, Wit
**Senseless** Absurd, Anosmia, Asinine, Illogical, Inane, Lean-witted, Mad, Numb, Silly, Stunned, Stupefied, Stupid, Stupor, Unconscious, Unwise, Vegetal
**Sensible, Sensibly** Advisedly, Aware, Clear-headed, Dianoetic, Down to earth, Level-headed, Logical, Lucid, No-nonsense, Politic, Pragmatic, Prudent, Raisonné, Rational, Realistic, Sane, Sapient, Solid, Together, Well-advised, Well-balanced
**Sensitive, Sensitivity** Aesthete, Algesia, Alive, Allergic, Atopy, Considerate, Dainty, Delicate, Discreet, Emotive, Erethism, Erogenous, Hot button, Hypaesthesia, Keen, Mimosa, Mystique, Nesh, Niceness, Nociceptive, Orthochromatic, Panchromatic, Passible, Psychic, Quick, Radiesthesia, Sore, Sympathetic, Tactful, Tender, Thermaesthesia, Thin-skinned, Ticklish, Touchy(-feely), Vulnerable
**Sensor(y)** Cercus, Detector, Exteroceptor, Interoceptor, Nerve end, Palpi, Proprioceptor, Remote
**Sentence(s)** Antiphon, Assize, Bird, Carpet, Clause, Closed, Commit, Complex, Compound, Condemn, Custodial, Death, Decree(t), Deferred, Doom, Fatwah, Indeterminate, Jail, Judgement, Life, Matrix, Open, Pangram, Paragraph, Period(ic), Porridge, Predicate, Probation, Punish, Rap, Rheme, Rune, Sanction, Send up, Simple, Stretch, Suspended, Swy, Tagmene, Time, Topic, Verdict, Versicle, Weigh off
**Sententious** Concise, Gnomic, Laconic, Pithy, Pompous, Terse
**Sentience** Awareness
**Sentiment(al), Sentimentality** Byronism, Chocolate box, Corn, Cornball, Drip, Emotive, Feeling, Fluffy, Goo, Govey, Gucky, Gush, Hokey, Icky, Lovey-dovey, Lyrical, Maudlin,

Mawkish, Mind, Mush, Namby-pamby, Nationalism, Nostalgia, Opinion, Posy, Romantic, Rose-pink, Rosewater, Saccharin, Schmaltzy, Sloppy, Slushy, Smoochy, Sob-stuff, Softy, Soppy, Spoony, Sugary, Swoony, Syrupy, Tear-jerker, Too-too, Traveller, Treacly, Twee, View, Weepy, Wertherian, Yucky

**Sentry, Sentinel** Caveman, Cordon sanitaire, Custodian, Guard, Jaga, Look-out, Patrol, Picket, Sentinel, Vedette, Vidette, Watch

**Separate(d), Separately, Separation, Separatist, Separator** Abscise, Abstract, Analyse, Apart, Asunder, Atmolysis, Avulsion, Bulkhead, Bust up, Comma, Compartmentalise, Cull, Curdle, Cut, Decant, Decollate, Decompose, Decouple, Deduct, Deglutinate, Demarcate, Demerge, Detach, Dialyse, Diastasis, Diazeuxis, Diremption, Disaggregate, Disally, Discerp, Disconnect, Discrete, Disespouse, Disintegrate, Disjoin, Disjunction, Dissect, Dissociate, Distance, Distinct, Disunite, Diverse, Divide, Divisim, Division, Divorce, Eloi(g)n, Elute, Elutriate, Esloin, Estrange, ETA, Extricate, Filter, Flaky, Fret, Grade, Gulf, Heckle, Hive, Holocrine, Hyphenate, Insulate, Intervene, Isolate, Judicial, Laminate, Lease, Legal, Liquate, Monosy, Part, Particle, Partition, Partitive, Parturition, Peel off, Piece, Prescind, Prism, Ramify, Red(d), Remove, Rift, Sashing, Scatter, Schism, Screen, Scutch, Secern, Segregate, Sequester, Sever, Several, Shear, Shed, Shore, Shorn, Sift, Sleave, Sle(i)ded, Smelt, Solitary, Sort, → **SPLIT**, Spread, Staccato, Steam-trap, Stream, Sunder, Sundry, Tease, Tems(e), Thresh, Tmesis, Try, Twin(e), Unclasp, Unhitch, Unravel, Winnow, Wrench, Yandy

**Sepia** Cuttle, Ink

**Seppuku** Hara-kiri, Hari-kari

**Septic** Festering, Poisonous, Rotting

**Septimus** Small

**Septum** Cloison, Mediastinum

**Sepulchral, Sepulchre** Bier, Cenotaph, Charnel, Crypt, Easter, Funeral, Monument, Pyramid, Tomb, Vault, Whited

**Sequel** After-clap, Aftermath, Consequence, Effect, Offshoot, Outcome, Suite, Threequel

**Sequence, Sequential** Agoge, Algorithm, Byte, Cadence, Chronological, Consecution, Consensus, Continuity, Continuum, Cycle, Escape, Fibonacci, Gene, Intervening, Intron, Line, Linear, Main, Montage, Order, Peptide, Plot, Polar, Program(me), Progression, Rotation, Routine, Run, Seriatim, Series, Shot, Signal, Sonnet, Storyboard, String, Succession, Suit, Suite, Train, Vector

**Sequester, Sequestrate** Confiscate, Esloin, Esloyne, Impound, Isolate, Retire, Seclude, Separate

**Sequin** Paillette, Zecchino, Zechin

**Sequoia** Redwood, Wellingtonia

**Seraph** Abdiel, → **ANGEL**

**Serb(ian)** Chetnik

**Sere** Arid, → **DRY**, Scorch, Wither

**Serenade(r)** Aubade, Charivari, Horning, Love song, Minstrel, Nocturne, Shivaree, Sing-song, Wait, Wake

**Serene, Serenity** Calm, Composed, Impassive, Placid, Quietude, Repose, Sangfroid, Sedate, Seraphic, Smooth, → **TRANQUIL**

**Serf(dom)** Adscript, Bondage, Bondman, Ceorl, Churl, Helot, Manred, → **SLAVE**, Thete, Thrall, Vassal, Velle(i)nage, Villein

**Serge** Russian, Say

**Sergeant** Buzfuz, Chippy, Chips, Colour, Cuff, Drill, Flight, Halberdier, Havildar, Kite, Lance, Master, → **NCO**, Pepper, Platoon, RSM, Sarge, SL, SM, Staff, Technical, Troy

**Serial(ism)** Episode, Feuilleton, Heft, Livraison, Part, Soap, Total

**Series** Actinide, Actinium, Arithmetical, Balmer, Battery, Catena, Chain, Concatenation, Consecution, Continuum, Course, Cycle, Cyclus, Docusoap, Electromotive, Enfilade, Engrenage, En suite, Episode, Epos, Ethylene, Exponential, Fibonacci, Fourier, Geometric, Gradation, Harmonic, Homologous, Lanthanide, Line, Links, Loop, Maclaurin's, Methane, Molasse, Neptunium, Partwork, Pedigree, Power, Process, → **PROGRESSION**, Radioactive, Rally, Random walk, Ranks, Rest, Rosalia, Rosary, Rounds, Routine, Rubber, Run, Scale,

Sequence, Ser, Set, Sitcom, String, Succession, Suit, Taylor's, Test, Thorium, Time, Tone, Tournament, Train, Uranium, World

**Serious(ly)** Acute, Critical, Earnest, Extreme, For real, Funereal, Grave, Gravitas, Harsh, Heavy, Important, In earnest, Intense, Major, Momentous, Pensive, Po, Profound, Radical, Real, Sad, Serpentine, Sober, Solemn, Sombre, Staid, Stern, Straight(-faced), Unamused, Very, Weighty, Wonk

**Sermon** Address, Discourse, Gatha, Homily, Khutbah, Lecture, Oration, Preachment, Prone, Ser, Speech, Spital

**Serow** Goral, Thar

**Serpent(ine)** Adder, Amphisbaena, Anguine, Apepi, Apophis, Asp, Aspic(k), Basilisk, Bass horn, Boa, Caduceus, Cockatrice, Dipsas, Firedrake, Hydra, Meandering, Midgard, Nagas, Ophiolite, Ouroboros, Peridotite, Pharaoh's, Reptile, Retinalite, Sea-snake, Shesha, →**SNAKE**, Traitor, Uraeus, Uroborus, Verd-antique, Verde-antico, Viper, Wyvern

**Serrate(d), Serration** Diprionidian, Indent, Saw, Scallop, Serried, Tooth

**Serum** Albumin, Antiglobulin, Antilymphocyte, Antitoxin, ATS, Fluid, Globulin, Humoral, Opsonin, Senega, Truth

**Serval** Bush-cat

**Servant, Server** Aid(e), Attendant, Ayah, Bartender, Batman, Bearer, Bedder, Bedmaker, Between-maid, Body, Bond, Boot-catcher, Boots, Boy, Busboy, Butler, Caddie, Chambermaid, Chaprassi, Chokra, Chuprassy, Civil, Columbine, Cook, Cook-general, Daily, Dogsbody, Domestic, Dromio, Drudge, Employee, Esne, Factotum, Famulus, File, Flunkey, Footboy, Footman, Friday, Ganymede, Gehazi, General, G(h)illie, Gip, Gorsoon, Gully, Gyp, Haiduk, Handmaid, Helot, Henchman, Heyduck, Hind, Hireling, Humble, Iras, Jack, Jack-slave, Jeames, Khansama(h), Khidmutgar, Khitmutgar, Kitchen-knave, Kitchen-maid, Knave, Lackey, Ladle, Lady's maid, Lazy Susan, Leroy, Livery, Maid, Major-domo, Man, Man Friday, Menial, Minion, Mixologist, Muchacha, Muchacho, Myrmidon, Nethinim, Obedient, Orderly, Page, Pantler, Parlourmaid, Person, Pistol, Postman, Public, Pug, Redemption, Retainer, Retinue, Scout, Scrub, Scullion, Servitor, Sewer, Skip, Skivvy, Slavey, Soldier, Soubrette, Steward, Tablespoon, Tapsman, Tendance, Theow, Thete, Tiger, Trotter, Turnspit, Tweeny, Underling, Vails, Vales, Valet, Valkyrie, Varlet, Vassal, Waiter, Wash-rag, Weller

**Serve(r), Served, Service(s)** Acas, Ace, Act, Active, Agency, All-up, Altar boy, Amenity, Answer, Armed, Army, Arriage, Asperges, Assist, ATS, Attendance, Avail, Baptism, Barista, Barman, Barperson, Benediction, Breakfast, Campaign, Candlemas, Cannonball, Canteen, Ceefax®, Ceremony, China, Christingle, Church, Civil, Coffee, Communion, Community, Complin(e), Conscription, Corvée, Credo, Deferential, Devotional, Dien, Dinner lady, Dinnerset, Diplomatic, Dish, Divine, Do, Dollop, Dow, Drumhead, Dry, Duty, Ecosystem, Ecphonesis, Emergency, Employ, Evensong, Facility, Fault, Fee, Feudal, Fish, Flower, Foreign, Forensic, Forward, →**FUNCTION**, Funeral, Further, Go, Health, Help, Helpline, Hour, Ibadah, Ibadat, Jury, Ka(e), Kol Nidre, Ladle, Lauds, Let, Line, Ling, Lip, Litany, Liturgy, Ma'ariv, Marriage, Mass, Mat(t)ins, Memorial, Memory, Mincha, Minister, Ministration, Ministry, Missa, National, Navy, Nocturn, Nones, Oblige, Offertory, Office, Oracle, Overarm, Overhaul, Pass, Pay, Personal, Pit stop, Placebo, Possum, Pottery, Pour, Prayer meeting, Prime, Proper, Public, Radio, RAF, Regular, Represent, Requiem, Rite, RN, Room, Sacrament, SAS, Satisfy, SBS, Scoop, Secret, Selective, Senior, Sext, Shacharis, Shaharith, Shuttle, Silent, Silver, Skeleton, Social, Sorb(us), Stead, Sted, Sue, Tableware, Tea, Tenebrae, Tierce, Trental, Uncork, Under-arm, Use, Utility, Vespers, Wait, Waiterage, Waitron, Waitstaff, Watch-night, Wild, Willow pattern, Worship, Yeoman('s)

**Service-book** Hymnal, Hymnary, Missal, Te igitur, Triodion

▹**Serviceman** *may indicate* a churchman

**Servile, Servility** Abasement, Base, Crawling, Creep, Grovelling, Knee, Kowtowing, Lickspittle, Menial, Minion, Obsequious, Slavish, Slimy, Submissive, Suck-hole, Sycophantic, Tintookie, Truckle

**Serving** Helping, Heuristic, Portion, Precursory

**Servitude** Bondage, Domination, Penal, Peonage, Peonism, Slavery, Thirlage, Thrall, Vassalry, Yoke

**Sesame** Beni, Benne, Gingelly, Gingili, Grapple-plant, Jinjilli, Semsem, Tahini, Til

**Session(s)** All-nighter, Bout, Bull, Executive, Galah, Hearing, Jam, Kirk, Meeting, Nightshift, Petty, Poster, Quarter, Rap, Round, Séance, Sederunt, Settle, Sitting, Special, Term

**Set(ting) (about, aside, down, in, off, out, up)** Activate, Adjust, Apply, Appoint, Arrange, Array, Assail, Assiege, Backdrop, Batch, Bent, Bezel, Boun, Box(ed), Brooch, Cabal, Cake, Case, Cast, Chaton, Class, Claw, Clique, Cliveden, Closed, Clot, Coagulate, Cock, Cockshy, Codomain, Collection, Collet, Comp(ositor), Companion, Compose, Congeal, Congelation, Context, Coterie, Couvert, Crew, Crystal, Cyclorama, Data, Dead, Decline, Decor, Detonate, Devote, Diorama, Direct, Dispose, Duchesse, Earmark, Earnest, Earth, Enchase, Ensky, Environment, Establish, Explode, Film, Firm, Fit, Flagstone, Flash, Flat(s), Found, Framed, F-stop, Gang, Garniture, Geal, Gel, Gelatinise, Genome, Group, Habitat, Hairdo, Harden, Heliacal, Ilk, Inchase, Incrowd, Incut, Infinite, Inlay, Jee, Jeel, Jell(y), Jet, Julia, Key, Kit, Knit, Laid, Land, Lay, Layette, Leg, Locale, Locate, Lot, Mandelbrot, Mental, Milieu, Mise en scène, Miserere, Monture, Mournival, Nail, Nest, Occident, Open, Ordain, Ordered, Ordinate, Ossify, Ouch, Pack, Pair, Parure, Pavé, Permanent, Physique, Pitch, Place(ment), Plant, Plaste, Ply, Point, Poised, Posed, Posit, Power, Prepare, Primed, Put, Radio, Rate, Ready, Receiver, Relay, Repertoire, Resolute, Rig, Rigid, Rooted, Rouse, Rubber, Saw, Scenery, Series, Service, Settle(d), Showcase, Sink, Slate, Smart, Solidify, Solution, Squad, Stand, Stationed, Stede, Stell, Stick, Stiffen, Still, Stream, Stud, Subscriber, Suit, Suite, Surround, Synchronize, Tar, Tea, Team, Teeth, Televisor, Telly, The four hundred, Theme, Tiffany, Till, Toilet, Trannie, Transistor, Trey, Trigger, Trip, Truth, Tube, TV, Union, Universal, Venn (diagram), Weather, Wide-screen, Yplast

**Setback** Adversity, Blow, Bodyblow, Checkmate, Downturn, Glitch, Hiccough, Hiccup, Hitch, Jolt, Knock, Relapse, Retard, Retreat, Reversal, Scarcement, Sickener, Tes, Vicissitude, Whammy

**Settee** Sofa bed

**Setter** Adjuster, Cement, Comp, Compiler, Concrete, Dog, English, Gelatin(e), Gordon, Gundog, Hair gel, Hairspray, Irish, Pectin, Plaster of Paris, Red, Smoot, Sphinx, Sun, Trend

**Settle(d), Settlement, Settler** Acadian, Adjust, Agree, Alight, Ante, Appoint, Arbitrate, Arrange, Ascertain, Ausgleich, Avenge, Balance, Bandobast, Beachcomber, Bed, Bench, Boer, Borghetto, Borough, Botany Bay, Bundobust, Bustee, Camp, Clear, Clench, Clinch, Colonial, Colonise, Colony, Compose, Compound, Compromise, Contract, Cough up, Crannog, Cut and dry, Decide, Defray, Determine, Diktat, Discharge, Dispose, Dorp, Dowry, Ekistics, Encamp, Endow, Ensconce, Entail, Establish, Expat, Faze, Feeze, Finalise, Fix, Foot, Foreclose, Gravitate, Gridironer, Guilder, Habitant, Hama, Hyannis, Illegitimate, Informal, Inhabit, Iron out, Jamestown, Jointure, Kibbutz, Land, Ledge, Light, Lull, Lyte, Manyat(t)a, Marriage, Meet, Merino, Mise, Mission, Moreton Bay, Moshav, Nahal, Negotiate, Nest, Nestle, New Amsterdam, Oecist, Oikist, Opt, Ostman, Outpost, Outstation, Over, Pa(h), Pakka, Paleface, Patroon, Pay, Payment, Peise, Penal, People, Perch, Pheazar, Pheese, Pheeze, Phese, Pilgrim, Pioneer, Placate, Planter, Pondicherry, Populate, Port Arthur, Port Nicholson, Presidio, Pucka, Pueblo, Pukka, Rancheria, Rancherie, Readjust, Reckoning, Reconcile, Redditch, Reduction, Reimburse, Remit, Repay, Reside, Resolve, Rest, Roofie, Roost, Sate, Satisfaction, Saxon, Scare, Seal, Seat, Secure, Sedimentary, Set fair, Shagroon, Shanty town, Shtetl, Silt, Smoot, Snuggle, Sofa, Soldier, Solve, Sooth, Soweto, Square, Square up, Squatter, Staid, State, Still, Straits, Subside, Sudden death, Taurus, Tiebreak, Township, Ujamaa, Undertaker, Utu, Vest(ed), Viatical, Visigoth, Voortrekker, Wrap up

▷**Settlement** *may indicate* an anagram

▷**Settler** *may indicate* a coin

**Set upon** Assail, Attack, Sick

**Seven(th), Seven-sided** Ages, Days, Dials, Great Bear, Hebdomad, Hepta-, Hills, Magnificent, Nones, Pleiad(es), S, Sages, Seas, Septenary, Septilateral, Septimal, Sins, Sisters, Sleepers, Stars, Wonders, Zeta

**Seventy** S, Ytterbium

**Seven-week** Omer

**Sever** Amputate, Cut, Detach, Divide, Lop, Sunder

**Several** Divers, Many, Multiple, Plural, Some, Sundry, Various

**Severe(ly), Severity** Acute, Astringent, Austere, Bad, Catonian, Caustic, Chronic, Cruel,

Dour, Draconian, Drastic, Eager, Extreme, Grave, Grievous, Gruel(ling), Hard, → HARSH, Ill, Inclement, Ingravescent, Morose, Penal, Rhadamanthine, Rigo(u)r, Roaming, Roundly, Ruthless, Serious, Sharp, Snell(y), Sore, Spartan, Stark, Stern, Strict, Swingeing

**Sew(ing), Sewer, Sew up** Baste, Clinch, Cope, Darn, Embroider, Fell, Fine-draw, Hemstitch, Machine, Mitre, Overcast, Overlock, Run up, Seam, Seel, Singer®, Stitch, Tack, Whip

**Sewage, Sewer** Bacteria, Cesspool, Cloaca, Culvert, Dorcas, → DRAIN, Effluence, Jaw-box, Jaw-hole, Mimi, Needle, Privy, Seamster, Shore, Soil, Sough, Soughing-tile, Sure, Waste

**Sex(ist), Sexual, Sexy** Bed-hopping, Bonk, Carnal, Congress, Coupling, Cunnilingus, Cybersex, Erogenous, Erotic, Fair, Favours, Fellatio, Female, Foreplay, Fornication, French, Gender, Greek love, Hanky-panky, Heterogametic, Hump, Incest, Intercourse, Intimacy, Jailbait, Kind, Knee-trembler, Koap, Libidinous, Libido, Lingam, Lumber, Male, Mate, Naughty, Non-penetrative, Nookie, Nooky, Nubile, Oats, Oomph, Opposite, Oral, Outercourse, Paedophilia, Paraphilia, Pederasty, Phallocratic, Phat, Phone, Priapean, Prurient, Race, Randy, Raunchy, Rough trade, Rut(ish), Safe, Salacious, Sect, Six, Slinky, SM, Steamy, Stud, Sultry, Tantric, Teledildonics, Troilism, Unprotected, Unsafe, Venereal, Venery, VI, Voluptuous, Weaker

**Sex appeal** It, Oomph, SA

**Sexcentenarian** Shem

**Sexless** Agamogenetic, Atoke, Epicene, N, Neuter, Platonic

**Sextet** Over, Six

**Sexton** Blake, Fossor, Patch, Sacristan, Shammes, Warden

**Seychelles** SY

**Sh** P, Quiet

**Shabby** Base, Buckeen, Dilapidated, Dingy, Dog-eared, Down-at-heel, Flea-bitten, Fleapit, Fusc(ous), Grotty, Grungy, Ill, Low-lived, Mangy, Mean, Moth-eaten, Old hat, Oobit, Oorie, Oubit, Ourie, Outworn, Owrie, Raunch, Rundown, Scaly, Scarecrow, Scruffy, Seedy, Shoddy, Sloven, Slum, Squalid, Tacky, Tatty, Tawdry, Threadbare, Unkempt, Worn, Woubit

**Shack** Fibro, Heap, Hideout, Hovel, Hut, Sheal

**Shackle(s)** Bilboes, Bind, Bracelet, Chain, Constrain, Darbies, Entrammel, Fetter(lock), Gyve, Hamper, Irons, Leg-iron, Manacle, Restrict, Tie, Trammel, Yoke

**Shad** Allice, Allis, Fish, Twait(e)

**Shaddock** Grapefruit, Pomelo

**Shade(d), Shades, Shading, Shadow, Shady** Adumbrate, Arbour, Arcade, Awning, Blear, Blend, Blind, Bongrace, Bowery, Brise-soleil, Brocken spectre, Buff, Cast, Cerise, Chiaroscuro, Chroma, Cloche, Cloud, Colo(u)r, Corrupt, Cross-hatch, Darkness, Degree, Demirep, Dis, Dog, Dubious, Eclipse, Enigma, Eye, Fawn, Five o'clock, Galanty, Gamp, Ghost, Gnomon, Gradate, Gray, Hachure, Hatch, Hell, Herbar, Hint, Hue, Inumbrate, Larva, Lee, Louche, Magnolia, Mark, Melt, Mezzotint, Modena, Nuance, Opaque, Overtone, Parasol, Pastel, Penumbra, Phantom, Presence, Rain, Ray-Bans®, Satellite, Screen, Shroud, Sienna, Silhouette, Silvan, Skia-, Soften, Sound, Spectre, Spirit, Stag, Sunglasses, Swale, Swaly, Tail, Tenebrious, Tinge, Tint, Titian, Tone, Track, Trail, Ugly, Ultramarine, Umbra(tile), Umbrage(ous), Umbrella, Umbrose, Underhand, Underworld, Velamen, Velar(ium), Velum, Vestige, Visitant, Visor, Wraith

**Shadowless** Ascian

**Shaft(ed), Shafting** Arbor, Arrow, Axle tree, Barb, Barrow-train, Beam, Befool, Capstan, Cardan, Chimney, Cloth-yard, Collet, Column, Crank, Cue, Diaphysis, Disselboom, Dolly, Downcast, Drive, Escape, Fil(l), Flue, Fust, Gleam, Hoistway, Idler, Incline, Jack, Journal, Lamphole, Lay, Limber, Loom, Mandrel, Mandril, Manhole, Moon pool, Moulin, Paddle, Parthian, Passage, Pile, Pit, Pitbrow, Pitch, Pithead, Pole, Propeller, Quill (drive), Ray, Rib, Rise, Scape, Scapus, Shank, Snead, Spindle, Staff, Stairwell, Stale, Steal(e), Steel, Steen, Steil, Stele, Stem, Stulm, Sunbeam, Telescopic, Thill, Tige, Tomo, Trave, Truncheon, Upcast, Well, Winning, Winze

**Shag** Cronet, Hair, Nap, Pile, Scart(h), Skart(h), Tire, Tobacco

**Shaggy** Ainu, Beetle-browed, Bushy, Comate, Hairy, Hearie, Hirsute, Horrid, Horror, Maned, Nappy, Ragtag, Rough, Rugged, Shock, Shough, Tatty, Tousy, Touzy, Towsy, Towzy, Untidy

**Shah** Abbas, Pahlavi, Ruler, Sophi, Sophy

**Shake(n), Shake off, Shakes, Shakiest, Shaky** Agitate, Ague(-fit), Astonish, Bebung, Brandish, Cocktail, Coggle, Concuss, Dabble, Dick(e)y, Didder, Diddle, Disconcert, Dither, Dodder, → DT'S, Epicentre, Feeble, Groggy, Hod, Hotch, Ictal, Jar, Jiggle, Jingle, Joggle, Jolt, Jounce, Judder, Jumble, Lose, Milk, Mo, Nid-nod, Oscillate, Press flesh, Quake, Quiver, Quooke, Rattle, Rickety, Rickle, → ROCK, Rouse, Shimmer, Shimmy, Shiver, Shock, Shog, Shoogle, Shudder, Steel, Succuss(ation), Sweat, Swish, Thunderstruck, Tremble, Tremolo, Tremor, Tremulous, Trill(o), Tumbledown, Undulate, Unsteady, Vibrate, Vibrato, Wag, Waggle, Wind, Wobble, Wonky

▷**Shake** *may indicate* an anagram

**Shakedown** Blackmail, Chantage, Pallet

**Shakespeare** Bard, Will, WS

**Shale** Blaes, Fa(i)kes, Kerogen, Kupferschiefer, Oil, Rock, Till, Torbanite

**Shall** Sal

**Shallot** C(h)ibol, Onion, Scallion, Sybo(e), Sybow

**Shallow(s)** Ebb, Flat, Fleet, Flew, Flippant, Flue, Justice, Neritic, Rattlebrain, Riffle, Sandbank, Sandbar, Shoal, Slight, Superficial

**Sham** Apocryphal, Bluff, Bogus, Braide, Charade, Counterfeit, Deceit, Fake, → FALSE, Hoax, Idol, Impostor, Mimic, Mock, Pasteboard, Phony, Pinchbeck, Postiche, Potemkin, Pretence, Pseudo, Repro, Simulated, Snide, Spurious, Straw man, Travesty

**Shaman** Angek(k)ok, Sorcerer

**Shamble(s)** Abattoir, Bauchle, Butchery, Dog's breakfast, Fiasco, Mess, Scamble, Shuffle, Totter, Tripple

**Shame(ful), Shame-faced** Abash, Aidos, Atimy, Aw, Chagrin, Confusion, Contempt, Crying, Degrade, Discredit, Disgrace, Dishonour, Disrepute, Embarrass, False, Fi donc, Fie, Gross, Guilt, Hangdog, Honi, Humiliate, Ignominy, Infamy, Inglorious, Modesty, Mortify, Ohone, Pity, Pudency, Pudor, Pugh, Reprehensible, Sad, Scandal, Sheepishness, Shend, Sin, Slander, Stain, Stigma, Tsk, Tut, Vile, Wanton, Yshend

**Shameless** Audacious, Barefaced, Brash, Brazen, Flagrant, Hussy, Immodest, Impudent, Ithyphallic, Jezebel, Reprobate

**Shampoo(ing)** Massage, Tripsis, Wash

**Shandy** Drink, Sterne, Tristram

**Shanghai** Abduct, Kidnap, Trick

**Shank** Leg, Shaft, Steal(e), Steel, Steil, Stele, Strike

**Shanty, Shanty town** Bidonville, Boatsong, Bothy, Bustee, Cabin, Chant, Ditty, Dog-hole, Favela, Forebitter, Hutment, Lean-to, Pondok, Sea, Seasong, Shack, Shypoo, Song

**Shape(d), Shapely, Shaping** Blancmange, Boast, Bruting, Cast, Chisel, Contour, Cuneiform, Cylinder, Die-cast, Domino, Ellipse, Face, Fashion, Figure, Forge, Form, Format, Fractal, Geoid, Geometrical, Gnomon, Guise, Headquarters, Hew, Holohedron, Jello, Knap, Model, Morph, Morphology, Motif, → MOULD, Navette, Net, Oblong, Octagon(al), Pendentive, Polygon, Polyomine, Quadrant, Ream, Rhomb(us), Roughcast, Scabble, Scalene, Scallop, Scapple, Sculpt, Spheroid, Spile, Step-cut, Style, Trim, Tromino, Turn, Voluptuous, Whittle, Wrought, Zaftig, Zoftig

**Shapeless** Amorphous, Blob, Chaos, Dumpy, Glob, Indigest, Vague

**Shard** Fragment, Sliver, Splinter

**Share(d), Shares, Sharing** Allocation, Allotment, Allottery, Angels' cost, Apportion, Blue-chip, Bovate, Cahoots, Chop, Co, Cohabit, Coho(e), Common, Communal, Contango, Co-portion, Co-tenant, Culter, Cut, Deferred, Distribute, Divi(dend), Divide, Divvy (up), Dole, Double up, Dutch, Equity, Finger, Flatmate, Footsie, Founders, Go Dutch, Golden, Grubstake, Holding, Impart, Interest, Job, Joint, Kangaroo, Law, Lay, Lion's, Market, Moiety, Mutual, Odd lot, OFEX, Ordinary, Oxgang, Oxgate, Oxland, Parcener, → PART, Partake, Participate, Penny, PIBS, Plough, Plough-iron, Portfolio, Portion, Prebend, Pref(erred), Preference, Pro rata, Prorate, Quarter, Quota, Rake off, Ration, Rug, Rundale, Scrip, Security, Shr, Slice, Snack, Snap, Sock, Split, Stock, Taurus, Teene, Time, Tranche, Two-way, Whack

**Shareholder** Plough, Stag

**Shark** Angel, Basking, Beagle, Blue, Bluepointer, Bonnethead, Bottle-nosed, Bronze-whaler, Bull, Carpet, Cestracion, Cow, Demoiselle, Dog(fish), Flake, Fox, Great white, Gummy, Hammerhead, Houndfish, Huss, Lemonfish, Leopard catshark, Loan, Mackerel, Mako, Miller's dog, Monkfish, Noah, Nurse, Operator, Penny-dog, Plagiostomi, Porbeagle, Requiem, Reremai, Rhin(e)odon, Rigg, Rook, Sail-fish, Sand, Saw, School, Sea-ape, Sea-fox, Sea-lawyer, Sevengill, Sharp, Shortfin mako, Shovelhead, Smoothhound, Soupfin, Spotted ragged-tooth, Squaloid, Swindler, Thrasher, Thresher, Tiger, Tope, Usurer, Whale, Whaler, Wobbegong, Zygaena

**Sharkskin** Shagreen

**Sharp(er), Sharpen(er), Sharply, Sharpness** Abrupt, Accidental, Acerose, Acetic, Acidulous, Acrid, Aculeus, Acumen, Acuminate, Acutance, Acute, Alert, Angular, Arris, Astringent, Bateless, Becky, Benchstone, Bitter, Brisk, Cacuminous, Cheat, Clear, Clever, Coticular, Cutting, Dital, Edge(r), Fine, Fly, Focus, Gleg, Grind, Grindstone, Hone, Hot, Keen, Kurtosis, Massé, Mordant, Oilstone, Pencil, Penetrant, Peracute, Piquant, Poignant, Precision, Prompt, Pronto, Pungent, Quick-witted, Razor, Rogue, Rook, Saw doctor, Set, Shrewd, Smart, Snap, Snell, Sour, Spicate, Stark, Steel, Stoccato, Strop, Swindler, Tangy, Tart, Testy, Tomium, Twenty-twenty, Varment, Vivid, Volable, Vorpal, Whet

**Sharpshooter** Bersaglier, Franc-tireur, Sniper, Tirailleur, Voltigeur

**Sharp-sighted** Eagle, Lynx-eyed

**Shatter(ing)** Astone, Astound, Break, Brisance, Bust, Craze, Dash, Explode, Shiver, Smash, Smithereen, Splinter, Traumatic, Unnerve

**Shave(r), Shaving(s)** Barb(er), Close, Depilation, Electric, Excelsior, Filings, Flake, Grain, Lad, Moslings, Pare, Plane, Pogonotomy, Poll, Rasure, Raze, Sawdust, Scrape, Shear, Skive, Sliver, Splinter, Swarf, Todd, Tonsure, Turnings, Whittle

**Shaw** Artie, Green, Spinn(e)y, Wood

**Shawl** Afghan, Buibui, Cashmere, Chuddah, Chuddar, Dopatta, Dupatta, Fichu, India, Kaffiyeh, Kashmir, Manta, Mantilla, Maud, Paisley, Partlet, Pashmina, Prayer, Serape, Sha(h)toosh, Stole, Tallis, Tallit(ot), Tallith, Tippet, Tonnag, Tozie, Tribon, Whittle, Wrap(per), Zephyr

**She** A, Hoo

**Sheaf, Sheave** Aplustre, Bee, Bundle, Clevis, Dorlach, Folder, Gait, Garb(e), Gerbe, Mow, Shock, Thr(e)ave, Wheat

**Shear(er), Shearing, Shears** Clip, Cut, Fleece, Greasy, Jaws of life, Mulesing, Pinking, Poll, Pruning, Ring(er), Secateurs, Shave, Snips, Tarboy, Tinsnips, Trim, Wind

**Sheath(e)** Axolemma, Caddis-case, Capsule, Case, Cocoon, Coleoptile, Coleorhiza, Condom, Cover, Encase, Epineurium, Extine, Fingerstall, Glume, Medullary, Myelin, Neurilemma, Neurolemma, Node of Ranvier, Oc(h)rea, Perineurium, Periosteum, Quiver, Retract, Rhinotheca, Root, Scabbard, Shard, Spathe, Thecal, Thumbstall, Urceolus, Vagina, Volva, Wing

**Shed(ding), Shedder** Autotomy, Barn, Byre, Cast, Cho(u)ltry, Coducity, Cootch, Cwtch, Depot, Discard, Doff, Downsize, Drop, Ecdysis, Effuse, Emit, Exuviate, Hangar, Hovel, Hut, Infuse, Lair, Lean-to, Linhay, Linn(e)y, Mew, Milking, Moult, Outbuilding, Outhouse, Pent, Potting, Salmon, Shearing, Shippen, Shippon, Shuck, Skeo, Skillion, Skio, Slough, Sow, Spend, Spent, Spill, Spit, Tilt, Tool

**Sheen** Glaze, Gloss, Luminance, Lustre, Patina, Schiller, Shine

**Sheep(ish)** Ammon, Ancon(es), Aoudad, Argali, Ashamed, Barbary, Bell(wether), Bharal, Bident, Bighorn, Black, Blackface, Blate, Blue, Border Leicester, Broadtail, Burhel, Burrel(l), Caracul, Charollais, Cheviots, Coopworth, Corriedale, Cotswold, Cotswold lion, Coy, Crone, Dall('s), Dinmont, Domestic, Dorset Down, Dorset Horn, Down, Drysdale, Embarrassed, Ewe, Exmoor, Fank, Fat-tailed, Flock, Fold, Gimmer, Hair, Hampshire, Hampshire Down, Hangdog, Herdwick, Hidder, Hirsel, Hog(g), Hogget, Jacob, Jemmy, Jumbuck, Karakul, Kent, Kerry Hill, Lamb, Lanigerous, Leicester, Lincoln, Lo(a)ghtan, Loghtyn, Long, Lonk, Marco Polo, Masham, Merino, Mor(t)ling, Mouf(f)lon, Mountain, Muflon, Mug, Musk, Mus(i)mon, Mutton, Oorial, Ovine, Oxford Down, Perendale, Portland, Ram, Rambouillet, Romeldale, Romney Marsh, Rosella, Ryeland, Scottish Blackface, Shearling, Shetland, Shidder, Short, Shorthorn, → SHY, Soay, Southdown, Spanish, Stone('s), Suffolk, Sumph, Swaledale,

Teeswater, Teg(g), Texel, Theave, Trip, Tup, Twinter, Two-tooth, Udad, Urial, Vegetable, Welsh Mountain, Wensleydale, Wether, Wiltshire Horn, Woollyback, Yow(e), Yowie

**Sheep disease, Sheep problem** Black, Blue tongue, Braxy, Dunt, Gid, Hoof rot, Hoove, Louping-ill, Orf, Ringwomb, Rubbers, Scabby mouth, Scrapie, Staggers, Sturdy, Swayback, Tweak, Variola, Water-brain, Wildfire, Wind

**Sheepdog** Collie, Huntaway, Maremma, Polish Lowland, Puli

**Sheepfold** Fank, Pen

**Sheepskin** Basan, Caracul, Karakul, Mouton, Parchment, Roan, Wool

**Sheeptrack** Terracette

**Sheer** Absolute, Clear, Main, Mere, Peekaboo, Perpendicular, Plumb, Precipitous, Pure, See-through, Simple, Stark, Steep, Swerve, Thin, Utter

**Sheet(ing), Sheets** Balance, Cel, Cellophane, Cere-cloth, Cerement, Charge, Chart, Clean, Crime, Cutch, Diet, Dope, Draw, Expanse, Film, Flow, Fly, Folio, Foolscap, Heft, Ice, Inset, Intrusive, Lasagne, Leaf, Mane, Membrane, Nappe, Out-hauler, Pack(ing), Page, Pane, Pay, Pot(t), Pour, Proof, Prospectus, Rap, Ream, Rope, Sail, Scandal, Scratch, Shroud, Stern, Stratus, Taggers, Tarpaulin(g), Tear, Tentorium, Terne, Thunder, Time, Tip, Title, Web, White, Winding

**Sheet-anchor** Letter-weight, Paper clip, Paperweight

**Sheet-iron** Taggers, Terne(plate)

**Sheik(dom)** Abu Dhabi, Bahrein, Dubai, Kuwait

**Shekel** Mina, Sickle

**Sheldrake, Shelduck** Bargander, Bergander

**Shelf, Shelve(d), Shelves** Bank, Bar, Bracket, Chimneypiece, Continental, Counter, Credence, Delay, Delete, Dresser, Étagère, Gondola, Grand Banks, Hob, Ice, Lay aside, Ledge, Leeboard, Mantelpiece, Mantle, On ice, Overmantel, Parcel, Postpone, Rack, Retable, Rick, Ross Ice, Shunt, Sidetrack, Sill, Slope, Spinsterhood, Top, Whatnot, Windowsill

**Shell(ed), Shellfish, Shellwork** Abalone, Acorn-shell, Admiral, Ambulacrum, Ammo, Ammonite, Argonaut, Balamnite, Balanus, Balmain bug, Barnacle, Belemnite, Bergmehl, Bivalve, Blitz, Boat, Body, Bodywork, Bombard, Buckie, Camaron, Cameo, Camera, Capiz, Capsid, Carapace, Cartridge, Casing, Chank, Chelonia, Chitin, Clam, Cleidoic, Clio, Coat-of-mail, Cochlea, Cockle, Cohog, Conch, Cone, Copepoda, Cover, Cowrie, Cowry, Crab, Cracked, Crustacea, Cuttlebone, Dariole, Deerhorn, Dentalium, Dop, Drill, Electron, Escallop, Eugarie, Foraminifer, Framework, Frustule, Gas, Geoduck, Globigerina, Haliotis, Hard, Harp, Hull, Husk, Hyoplastron, Isopoda, Kernel, Lamp, Langouste, Limacel, Limpet, Live, Lobster, Lorica, Lyre, Malacostraca, Midas's ear, Mitre, Mollusc, Money, Monocoque, Moon, Moreton Bay bug, Mother-of-pearl, Murex, Music, Mussel, Nacre, Nautilus, Nutcase, Olive, Ormer, Ostracod, Ostrea, Otter, Oyster, Paua, Pawa, Pea(s)cod, Peag, Peak, Pecten, Peel, Pereia, Periostracum, Periwinkle, Pilgrim's, Pipi, Pipsqueak, Plastron, Pod, Prawn, Projectile, Purple fish, Putamen, Quahaug, Quahog, Razor, Rocaille, Sal, Scalarium, Scallop, Scollop, Sea-ear, Sea-pen, Shale, Shard, Sheal, Sheel, Shiel, Shill, Shock, Shot, Shrapnel, Shrimp, Shuck, Sial, Smoke-ball, Snail, Soft, Spat, Spend, Spindle, Star, Stomatopod, Stonk, Straddle, Strafe, Stromb(us), Swan-mussel, Taco, Tear, Tellen, Tellin, Test(a), Thermidor, Toheroa, Tooth, Top, Torpedo, Tracer, Trivalve, Trough, Trumpet, Turbo, Turritella, Tusk, Univalve, Valency, Venus, Wakiki, Wampum, Whelk, Whiz(z)bang, Winkle, Worm tube, Xenophya, Yabbie, Yabby, Zimbi

▷**Shelled** *may indicate* an anagram

**Shell money** Wakiki, Wampum, Zimbi

**Shelter(ed)** Abri, A l'abri, Alee, Anderson, Arbour, Ark, Asylum, Awn, Awning, Barn, Bay, Belee, Bender, Bield, Billet, Bivouac, Blind, Blockhouse, Booth, Bothy, Bower, Bunker, Burladero, Butt, Byre, Cab, Carport, Casemate, Cocoon, Cold harbour, Coop, Cot(e), Cove, Covert, Coverture, Defence, Dodger, Donga, Dovecote, Dripstone, Dug-out, Earth, Embower, Fall-out, Garage, Gunhouse, Gunyah, Harbour, Haven, Hide, Hithe, Hospice, Hostel, House, Hovel, Humpy, Hut, Hutchie, Hwl, Igloo, Imbosom, Kipsie, Lee, Lee-gage, Loun, Lound, Lown, Lownd, Mai mai, Mission, Morrison, Nest, Nissen, Nodehouse, Palapa, Pilothouse, →REFUGE, Rest centre, Retreat, Roadstead, Roof, Roost, Sanctuary, Scog, Sconce, Scoog, Scoug, Screen, Scug, Secluded, Sentry box, Shade, Shed, Shiel(ing), Shroud, Silo, Skug,

Snowhole, Snowshed, Stell, Storm-cellar, Succah, Sukkah, Summerhouse, Suntrap, Tax, Tent, Te(e)pee, Testudo, Tortoise, Tupik, Twigloo, Umbrage, Weather, Wheelhouse, Wickyup, Wi(c)kiup, Wil(t)ja, Windbreak, Windscreen, Windshield, Workhouse

**Shemozzle** Debacle

**Shenanigan(s)** Antic, Goings on, Mischief

**Shepherd(ess)** Abel, Acis, Amaryllis, Amos, Bergère, Bo-peep, Bucolic, Chloe, Clorin, Conduct, Corin, Corydon, Cuddy, Daphnis, Dorcas, Drover, Endymion, Escort, Ettrick, Feeder, Flock-master, German, Good, Grubbinol, Gyges, Herdsman, Hobbinol, Lindor, Marshal, Menalcas, Padre, Pastor(al), Pastorella, Phebe, Pie, Pilot, Sheepo, Strephon, Tar-box, Thenot, Thyrsis, Tityrus, Usher

**Sherbet** Beer, Soda

**S(c)heherezade** Story-teller

**Sheriff** Bailiff, Deputy, Earp, Grieve, High, Land-dros(t), Lawman, Process-server, Shireman, Shire-reeve, Shirra, Shrievalty, Under, Viscount

**Sherry** Amoroso, Bristol milk, Cobbler, Cream, Cyprus, Doctor, Dry, Fino, Gladstone, Jerez, Manzanilla, Oloroso, Palo cortado, Sack, Solera, Sweet, Whitewash, Xeres

**Sherwood** Anderson, Forest

**Shiah** Ismaili

**Shibboleth** Password

**Shield(s), Shield-shaped** Ablator, Achievement, Aegis, Ancile, Armour, Arms, Baltic, Biological, Bodyguard, Box, Brolly, Buckler, Canadian, Carapace, Cartouche, Clypeus, Creosote, Defend, Dress, Escutcheon, Fence, Giron, Glove, Gobo, Guard, Gumshield, Gyron, Hatchment, Heat, Hielaman, Human, Inch, Inescutcheon, Insulate, Laurentian, Lozenge, Mant(e)let, Mask, Pavis(e), Pelta, Plastron, Protect, Randolph, Ranfurly, Riot, Rondache, Scandinavian, Screen, Scutcheon, Scute, Scutum, Sheffield, Splashboard, Sternite, Targe(t), Thyroid, Toecap, Vair, Visor, Water

**Shift(er), Shifting, Shifty** Amove, Astatic, Back, Blue, Budge, Change, Chemise, Core, Cymar, Day, Devious, Displace, Dodger, Dogwatch, Doppler, Dress, Dying, Einstein, Evasive, Expedient, Fend, Fluid, Function, Graveyard, Great Vowel, Hedging, Heel and toe, Jiggle(r), Lamb, Landslide, Lateral, Linen, Louche, Meve, Move, Night, Nightie, Nighty, Oil, Paradigm, Realign, Red, Relay, Remove, Rota, Ruse, Scorch, Sell, Shirt, Shovel, Shuffle, Shunt, Simar(re), Slicker, Slip(pery), Sound, Spell, Split, Stagehand, Steal, Stick, Stint, Swerve, Swing, Switch, Tergiversate, Tour, Transfer, Tunic, Turn, Turnabout, Untrustworthy, Vary, Veer, Warp

▷**Shift(ing)** *may indicate* an anagram

**Shiftless** Drifter

**Shilling** Bob, Deaner, Falkiner, Hog, King's, Queen's, S, Teston, Twalpenny

**Shilly-shally** Hesitate, Whittie-whattie

**Shimmer(ing)** Avanturine, Aventurine, Chatoyant, Flash, Gleam, Glint, Glitter, Haze, Iridescence, Mona(u)l, Opalescence, Shine

▷**Shimmering** *may indicate* an anagram

**Shin, Shinbone** Clamber, Climb, Cnemial, Leg, Shank, Skink, Swarm, Tibia

**Shindig, Shindy** Bobbery, Row, Ruction, Rumpus, Shivoo, Uproar

**Shine(r), Shining, Shiny** Aglitter, Aglow, Beam, Bright, Buff, Burnish, Deneb, Effulge, Excel, Flash, Glaze, Gleam, Glimmer, Glisten, Glitzy, Glory, Gloss, → GLOW, Irradiant, Japan, → LAMP, Leam, Leme, Lucent, Luminous, Lustre, Micate, Mouse, Nitid, Nugget, Phoebe, Phosphoresce, Polish, Radiant, Radiator, Refulgent, Relucent, Resplend, Rutilant, Shellac, Shimmer, Skyre, Sleek, Twinkle, Varnish

**Shingle(s), Shingly** Beach, Chesil, Cut, Dartre, Dartrous, Gravel, Herpes, Herpes Zoster, Herpetic, Loose metal, Shake, Shale, Stone, Tiles, Zona, Zoster

**Shinpad** Greave

**Shinty** Caman, Camanachd

▷**Shiny** *may indicate* a star

**Ship(ping), Shipping area, Ships** Boat, Cabin, Consign, Convoy, → DISPATCH, Embark, Export, Fastnet, Flota, German Bight, Her, Keel, Landing, Lundy, Man, Marine, Nautical, Post, Prize, Prow, Raft, Ram, Sail, She, SS, Tight, Transport, Tub, Vessel, Victualling

## SHIPS

*1 letter:*
Q

*2 letters:*
MV
PT

*3 letters:*
Ark
Cat
Cog
Dow
Fly
Hoy
Kit
Red

*4 letters:*
Argo
Bark
Brig
Buss
Cock
Cott
Dhow
Dory
Duck
Fire
Flat
Grab
Hulk
Isis
Koff
Long
Nina
Pink
Pont
Pram
Prau
Proa
Ro-ro
Saic
Scow
Snow
Tall
Tern
Trow
Yare
Yawl
Zulu

*5 letters:*
Aviso
Barge
Broke
Camel
Canoe
Cargo
Coble
Coper
Crare
Dandy
Dingy
Drake
Ferry
Funny
Guard
Jolly
Ketch
Laker
Liner
Moses
Oiler
Pinky
Pinto
Plate
Praam
Prahu
Prore
Pucan
Q-boat
Razee
Rover
Sabot
Saick
Scoot
Screw
Scull
Shell
Skiff
Slave
Sloop
Smack
Space
Tramp
Troop
U-boat
Umiak
Wager
Whiff
Xebec
Yacht
Zabra
Zebec

*6 letters:*
Argosy
Banker
Barque
Bateau
Bawley
Beagle
Bethel
Bireme
Borley
Bottom
Bounty
Caique
Carack
Carvel
Castle
Coaler
Cobble
Codder
Coffin
Cooper
Crayer
Curagh
Cutter
Decker
Dingey
Dinghy
Dogger
Droger
Dromon
Drover
Dugout
Escort
Flying
Frigot
Galiot
Galley
Gay-you
Goldie
Hooker
Howker
Jigger
Launch
Lorcha
Lugger
Masula
Monkey
Mother
Nuggar
Packet
Pedalo
Pequod
Pinkie
Pirate
Pitpan
Prison
Pulwar
Puteli
Randan
Reefer
Saique
Sampan
Sandal
School
Schuit
Schuyt
Settee
Slaver
Tanker
Tartan
Tender
Tonner
Torpid
Trader
Trek-ox
Triton
Turret
Whaler
Wherry
Zebeck

*7 letters:*
Belfast
Bidarka
Bumboat
Capital
Caravel
Carrack
Carract
Carrect
Catboat
Clipper
Coaster
Collier
Consort
Coracle
Counter
Cruiser
Currach
Curragh
Dredger
Drifter
Drogher
Dromond
Factory
Felucca
Flattop
Flyboat
Frigate
Gabbard
Gabbart

Galleon
Galliot
Galloon
Geordie
Gondola
Gunboat
Jetfoil
Kontiki
Liberty
Lymphad
Masoola
Mistico
Monitor
Mudscow
Mystery
Oomiack
Patamar
Pelican
Pinnace
Piragua
Pirogue
Polacca
Polacre
Pontoon
Repulse
Revenge
Sculler
Shallop
Sharpie
Steamer
Stew-can
Tartane
Titanic
Trawler
Trireme
Tugboat
Vedette
Victory
Vidette
Weather

***8 letters:***
Acapulco
Bilander
Billyboy
Bylander
Cabotage
Corocore
Corocoro
Corvette
Dahabieh
Faldboat
Flagship
Flatboat
Foldboat
Galleass
Galliass
Gallivat
Graf Spee
Hospital
Hoveller
Indiaman
Ironclad
Longboat
Longship
Mackinaw
Mary Rose
Masoolah
Merchant
Monohull
Mosquito
Pinafore
Sallyman
Savannah
Schooner
Shanghai
Showboat
Training

***9 letters:***
Blockship
Bucentaur
Catamaran
Container
Cutty Sark
Dahabeeah
Dahabiyah
Dahabiyeh
Discovery
Dromedary
First-rate
Freighter
Frigatoon
Hollander
Hydrofoil
Klondiker
Klondyker
Lapstrake
Lapstreak
Leviathan
Lightship
Lusitania
Mayflower
Minelayer
Monoxylon
Multihull
Outrigger
Peter-boat
Privateer
Sallee-man
Shear-hulk
Sheer-hulk
Steamboat
Submarine
Temeraire
Twin-screw
Vaporetto
Whale-back
Whaleboat

***10 letters:***
Barkentine
Brigantine
Fourmaster
Golden Hind
Hydroplane
Icebreaker
Knockabout
Mine-hunter
Paddleboat
Quadrireme
Sandsucker
Santa Maria
Tea-clipper
Trekschuit
Triaconter
Windjammer

***11 letters:***
Barquentine
Bellerophon
Berthon-boat
Cockleshell
Dreadnought
Merchantman
Minesweeper
Penteconter
Quinquereme
Side-wheeler
Skidbladnir
Submersible
Supertanker
Three-decker
Three-master
Torpedo boat

***12 letters:***
Deepwaterman
East Indiaman
Fore-and-after
Great Eastern
Marie Celeste
Stern-wheeler
Tangle-netter

***13 letters:***
Battlecruiser
Paddle steamer

***14 letters:***
Flying Dutchman
Ocean greyhound

---

**Shipmate** Crew, Hearty, Sailor
**Shipment** Cargo, Delivery, Load, Transit
**Shipping line** P and O
**Ship's biscuit** Dandyfunk, Dunderfunk
**Shipshape** Apple-pie, Neat, Orderly, Tidy, Trim
**Shipwreck(ed)** Castaway, Logen, Split
**Shire** Carthorse, Comitatus, County
**Shirk(er)** Absentee, Bludge, Cop out, Cuthbert, Dodge, Duck, Elude, Embusqué, Evade, Funk, Gold brick, Malinger, Mike, Pike, Poler, Quitter, Scrimshank, Skive, Skrimshank, Slack, Soldier
**Shirt** Aloha, Black, Boiled, Brown, Bush, Caftan, Calypso, Camese, Camise, Chemise, Choli, Cilice, Coat-style, Dasheki, Dashiki, Dick(e)y, Dress, Fiesta, Garibaldi, Grandad, Guernsey, Hair, Hawaiian, Hoodie, Jacky Howe, Jersey, Kaftan, Kaross, K(h)urta, Muscle, Nessus,

Non-iron, Parka, Partlet, Polo, Rash, Red, Rugby, Safari, Sark, Serk, Set, Shift, Smock, Sports, Stuffed, Subucula, Swan(n)dri®, Sweat, T, Uncle (Bert)

**Shiva** Destroyer

**Shiver(ing), Shivers, Shivery** Aguish, Aquiver, Atingle, Break, Brrr, Chitter, Crumble, Dash, Dither, Fragile, Frisson, Gooseflesh, Grew, Grue, Malaria, Matchwood, Nither, Oorie, Ourie, Owrie, Quake, Quiver, → SHAKE, Shatter, Shrug, Shudder, Smash, Smither, Smithereens, Splinter, Timbers, Tingle, Tremble

▷**Shiver(ed)** *may indicate* an anagram

**Shoal** Bar, Fish, Quantity, Reef, Run, Sand-bar, School, Shallows, Shelf, Tail

**Shock(ed), Shocker, Shocking** Acoustic, Aghast, Agitate, Amaze, Anaphylactic, Appal, Astone, Astony, Astound, Astun, Awful, Awhape, Bombshell, Boo, Brunt, Bunch, Consternate, Criminal, Culture, Daze, Defibrillate, Devastate, Disconcert, Disgust, Dorlach, Dreadful, Drop, Dumbfound, Earthquake, ECT, Egregious, Electric, Electrocute, Epiphenomenon, EST, Eye-opener, Fleg, Floccus, Forelock, Gait, Galvanism, Gobsmack, Hair, Hammer-blow, Haycock, Haystack, Horrify, Horror, Impact, Infamous, Insulin, Isoseismic, Jar, Jolt, Knock cold, Live, Lurid, Mane, Mop, Numb, Obscene, Outrage, Outre, Poleaxe, Putrid, Recoil, Return, Revolt, Rick(er), Rigor, Scandal(ise), Seismic, Sensational, Septic, Shaghaired, Shake, Sheaf, Shell, Shilling, Shog, Shook, Stagger, Start(le), Stitch, Stook, Stound, Stun, Stupefy, Stupor, Surgical, Surprise, Tangle, Taser®, Thermal, Thunderbolt, Thunderstruck, Torpedinidae, Trauma, Tremor, Turn

**Shock-absorber** Buffer, Oleo, Snubber

▷**Shocked** *may indicate* an anagram

**Shod** Calced

**Shoddy** Cagmag, Catchpenny, Cheap, Cheapjack, Cheapo, Cloth, Cowboy, Dog's breakfast, Drecky, Gimcrack, Imitation, Oorie, Ourie, Owrie, Poor, Rag-wool, Ropy, Schlock, → SHABBY, Slapdash, Slopwork, Tatty, Tawdry, Tinny

**Shoe(s)** Accessory, Arctic, Athletic, Ballet, Balmoral, Bauchle, Birkenstock, Blocked, Boat, Boot, Bootee, Brake, Brogan, Brogue, Brothel creepers, Buskin, Calceate, Calk(er), Calkin, Carpet slipper, Casuals, Caulker, Cawker, Charlier, Chaussures, Chopin(e), Clodhopper, Clog, Clout, Co-respondent, Court, Creeper, Dap, Deck, Espadrille, Flattie, Flip-flops, Flipper, → FOOTWEAR, Galage, Galoche, Galosh, Gatty, Geta, Ghillie, Golosh, Gumboot, Gumshoe, Gym, High-low, High tops, Hot, Hush-puppies®, Jandal®, Jellies, Kamik, Kletterschue, Kurdaitcha, Lace up, Launch(ing), Loafer, Mary-Janes®, Mocassin, Moccasin, Muil, Mule, Open-toe, Oxford, Oxonian, Panton, Patten, Peeptoe, Pennyloafer, Pile, Plate, Plimsole, Plimsoll, Poulaine, Pump, Rivlin, Rope-soled, Rubbers, Rullion, Runner, Sabaton, Sabot, Saddle, Safety, Sandal, Sandshoe, Sannie, Scarpetto, Shauchle, Skid, Skimmer, Slingback, Slip-on, Slipper, Slip-slop, Sneaker, Snow, Sock, Soft, Solleret, Spike, Stoga, Stogy, Suede, Tabi, Tackies, Takkies, Tennis, Tie, Topboot, Track, Trainer, T-strap, Upper, Vamp(er), Veld-schoen, Veldskoen, Velskoen, Vibram®, Vibs, Wagon lock, Wedgie, Welt, Winkle-picker, Zori

**Shoeless** Barefoot, Discalced

**Shoemaker** Blacksmith, Choo, Clogger, Cobbler, Cordiner, Cordwainer, Cosier, Cozier, Crispi(a)n, Farrier, Gentle craft, Leprechaun, Sachs, Smith, Snob, Soutar, Souter, Sowter, Sutor

**Shoe-string** Cheap, Lace, Pittance

**Shoe-toe** Poulaine

**Shoo** Away, Begone, Hoosh, Off, Scat(ter), Voetsek

**Shoot(er), Shooting, Shooting up, Shoot out** Ack-ack, Airgun, Arrow, Bamboo, Bean, Bine, Bostryx, Braird, Breer, Bud, Bulbil, Burgeon, Camera, Catapult, Chit, Cion, Crossfire, Cyme, Dart(le), Delope, Discharge, Drib, Elance, Enate, Eradiate, Film, Fire, Firearm, Flagellum, Germ, Germain(e), Germen, Germin(ate), Glorious twelfth, → GUN, Gunsel, Head-reach, Hurl, Imp, In bud, Jet, Lateral, Layer, Lens, Limb, Loose, Marksmanship, Offset, Osier, Outgun, Pepper, Photocall, Photograph, Pip, Plink, Pluff, Plug, Poot, Pop, Pot, Pout, Ramulus, Rapids, Ratoon, Riddle, Rod, Rough, Rove, Runner, Scion, Septembriser, Shell, Showdown, Side, Sien(t), Skeet, Skyrocket, Snap, Snipe, Spire, Spirt, Spout, Spray, Sprout, Spurt, Spyre, Start, Stole, Stolon, Strafe, Sucker, Syen, Tellar, Teller, Tendril, Tendron, Tiller, Trap, Turion, Turkey, Twelfth, Twig, Udo, Vimen, Wand, Weapon, Whiz(z), Wildfowler, Zap

**Shooting star** Meteorite

**Shop(per), Shopping, Shops** Agency, Arcade, Assembly, Atelier, Automat, Bag, Betray, Betting, Body, Bottle, Boutique, Bucket, Buy, Cantina, Centre, Chain, Charcuterie, Charity, Chippy, Chop, Closed, Coffee, Commissary, Cook, Co-op, Cop, Corner, Customer, Cut-price, Dairy, Delicatessen, Denounce, Dobbin, Dolly, Duddery, Duka, Duty-free, Emporium, Factory, Farm, Five and dime, Food court, Galleria, Gift, Grass, In bond, Inform, Junk, Kiosk, Kirana, Luckenbooth, Machine, Mail (order), Mall, Mall crawl, Mall-rat, Market, Megastore, Mercat, Messages, Minimart, Muffler, Mystery, Naafi, Never-never, Office, Officinal, Off-licence, Off-sales, Op(portunity), Open, Outlet, Parlour, Patisserie, Pattern, Pawn, Personal, Pharmacy, Pie, Porn, Precinct, Print, PX, Rat on, Repair, Report, Retail, RMA, Salon, Sex, Shambles, Share, Shebang, Snitch, Spaza, Spree, Squat, → STORE, Strip, Strip mall, Studio, Sundry, Superette, Supermarket, Superstore, Swap, Talking, Tally, Tea (room), Thrift, Tick, Tommy, Trade, Truck, Tuck, Union, Vintry, Warehouse, Whistle-blow, Window, Works

**Shopfront** Façade, Fascia

**Shopkeeper, Shop assistant** Barista, Bookseller, British, Butcher, Chemist, Clothier, Gombeen-man, Greengrocer, Grocer, Haberdasher, Hosier, Ironmonger, Merchant, Midinette, Newsagent, Provisioner, Retailer, Stationer, Tobacconist, Tradesman, Vendor

**Shoplift(er)** Boost, Heist, Hoister

**Shore** Bank, Beach, Buttress, Coast, Coastline, Coste, Eustatic, Foreside, Landfall, Lee, Littoral, Machair, Offing, Prop, Rance, Rivage, Saxon, Seaboard, Strand, Strandline, Support

**Short(en), Shortening, Shortest, Shortly, Shortness** Abbreviate, Abridge, Abrupt, Anon, Apocope, Arc, Beeline, Brevity, Brief, Brusque, Close-in, Commons, Compendious, Concise, Contract, Crisp, Cross, Curt, Curtail, Curtal, Cutty, Digest, Diminish, Drink, Eftsoons, En brosse, Epitomise, Ere-long, Flying, Fubsy, Fuse, Hard up, Impolite, Inadequate, In a while, In brief, Lacking, Laconical, Light, Limited, Low, Mini, Near, Nip, Nirlie, Nutshell, Offing, Opuscule, Pastry, Pithy, Pot, Pudsey, Punch, Pyknic, Ratty, Reduce, Reef, Retrench, Scantle, Scanty, Scarce, Shrift, Shy, Skimpy, Skint, Snatch, Soon, Sparse, Spirit, Squab, Squat(ty), Staccato, Stint, Stocky, Strapped, Stubby, Succinct, Syncopate, Systole, Taciturn, Take up, Teen(s)y, Telescope, Temporal, Temporaneous, Terse, Tight, Tot, Towards, Transient, Under, Wee

**Shortage** Brevity, Dearth, Deficiency, Deficit, Drought, Famine, Lack, Need, Paucity, Scarcity, Sparsity, Ullage, Wantage

**Short circuit** Varistor

**Shortcoming** Defect, Failure, Limitation, Sin, Weakness

**Shortfall** Deficit

**Shorthand** Diphone, Gregg, Outline, Phonographic, Phraseogram, Pitman, Speedwriting®, Stenography, Stenotypy, Tachygraphy, Tironian, Tironian notes, Triphone, Weblish

**Short-headed** Brachycephal

**Short-lived, Short-term** Day to day, Ephemeral, Fad, Flash-in-the-pan, Fragile, Meson, Transitory

**Shorts** Bermuda, Board, Boxer, Briefs, Culottes, Cycling, Hot pants, Kaccha, Lederhosen, Plus-fours, Skort, Stubbies®, Trunks

**Short-sight** Glance, Myopia, Myosis

**Short-winded** Breathless, Concise, Puffed, Purfled, Pursy, Succinct

**Shot(s)** Aim, Air, All-in, Ammo, Angel, Angle, Approach, Attempt, Backhand, Ball, Bank, Barrage, Bash, Bisque, Blank, Blast, Boss, Break, Bricole, Broadside, Buck, Bull, Bullet, Burl, Canister, Canna, Cannon(ball), Cartridge, Case, Catapulted, Chain, Chatoyant, Chip, Close up, Corner, Cover, Crab, Crack, Daisy cutter, Dink, Dolly, Drag, Dram, Draw, Drive, Drop, Duckhook, Dum dum, Dunk, Elt, Enfilade, Essay, Exhausted, Explosion, Flew, Forehand, Fusillade, Gesse, Get, Glance, Go, Grape, Guess, Gun-stone, Hazard, Hook, Indian, In-off, Iridescent, Jab, Jump, Kill, Langrage, Langrel, Langridge, Lay-up, Lob, Long, Longjenny, Magpie, Mail, Marksman, Maroon, Massé, Matte, Mitraille, Money, Moon-ball, Mulligan, Multi-coloured, Musket, Nip, Noddy, Opalescent, Pack, Parthian, Parting, Passing, Pelican, Pellet, Penalty, Photo, Pitch, Plant, Pluff, Pop, Pot, Puff, Push, Rake, Rid, Rifle, Round, Safety, Salvo, Scratch, Shell, Shy, Sighter, Silk, Six, Slam-dunk, Slap, Slice, Slug, Slung, Smash, Snap, Snifter, Sped, Spell, Spent, Square cut, Stab, Still, Streaked, Strike, Tap in, Tee,

Throw, Toe-piece, Toepoke, Tonic, Tot, Tracking, Trial, Try, Turn, Volley, Warning, Wrist, X-ray, Yahoo

**Shotgun** Sawn-off

**Should** Ought

**Shoulder(-blade)** Carry, Cold, Crossette, Epaule, Frozen, Hard, Hump, Joggle, Omohyoid, Omoplate, Pick-a-back, Roadside, Scapula, Shouther, Soft, Spald, Spall, Spaul(d), Speal, Spule, Tote, Withers

**Shoulder-piece** Epaulette

**Shout(er), Shouting** Ahoy, Alley-oop, Barrack, Bawl, Bellock, Bellow, Boanerges, Boo, Boom, Call, Cheer, Claim, Clamour, Conclamation, Cry, Din, Exclaim, Geronimo, Harangue, Heckle, Hey, Hoi(cks), Holla, Holla-ho(a), Holler, Hollo, Holloa, Hooch, Hosanna, Howzat, Hue, Och, Oi, Outcry, Oy, Parnell, Rah, Rant, Rave, Roar, Root, Round, Sa sa, Storm, Treat, Trumpet, Vociferate, Whoop, Yammer, Yell(och), Yicker, Yippee, Yodel, Yoohoo, Yorp

**Shove** Barge, Birr, Elbow, Jostle, Push, Ram, Spoon, Thrust

**Shovel** Backhoe, Dustpan, Fire, Hat, Loy, Main, Peel, Power, Scoop, Shool, Spade, Steam, Trowel, Van

**Show(ing), Shown, Showy** Air, Anonyma, Appearance, Aquacade, Bad, Bench, Betray, Branky, Brash, Broadcast, Brummagem, Burlesque, Cabaret, Cattle, Chat, Circus, Come, Con, Cruft's, Dashing, Define, Demo(nstrate), Depict, Describe, Dime museum, Diorama, Display, Do, Drama, Dramedy, Dressy, Dumb, Eclat, Effeir, Effere, Endeictic, Entertainment, Epideictic, Establish, Evince, →EXHIBIT, Expo, Express, Extravaganza, Exude, Facade, Fair, Fangled, Farce, Fine, Flamboyant, Flash (Harry), Flaunt, Floor, Fly, Folies Bergere, Gala, Galanty, Game, Gang, Garish, Gaudy, Gay, Gig, Girly, Give, Glitter, Glitz(y), Gloss, Good, Horse, Indicate, Jazzy, Kismet, Koni, Lay bare, Les Mis(erables), Light, Lord Mayor's, Loud, Manifest, Matinée, Meretricious, Minstrel, Moon, Musical, Naumachy, One-man, Ostensible, Ostentatious, Pageant, Panel game, Panto(mime), Parade, Patience, Peacock, Peep, Performance, Phen(o), Phone-in, Picture, Point, Pomp, Portray, Presentation, Pretence, Preview, Prevue, Pride, Procession, Prog(ramme), Project, Prominence, Prove, Pseudery, Puff, Puppet, Quiz, Raree, Razzmatazz, Reality, Register, Represent, Reveal, Revue, Road, Rodeo, Roll-out, Ruddigore, Rushes, Screen, Shaw, Side, Sight, Singspiel, Sitcom, Slang, Soap, Son et lumière, Specious, Spectacle, Splash, Splay, Stage, Stunt, Swankpot, Talk, Tamasha, Tattoo, Tawdry, Telecast, Telethon, Theatrical, Three-man, Tinhorn, Tinsel(ly), Tulip, Unbare, Uncover, Unveil, Usher, Vain, Variety, Vaudeville, Veneer, Viewy, Wear, Wild west, Zarzuela

**Showcase** Cabinet

**Showdown** Confrontation, Crunch

**Shower** April, Douche, Downfall, Exhibitor, Flurry, Hail, Indicant, Indicator, Kitchen tea, Lavish, Lot, Meteor, Panoply, Party, Pelt, Pepper, Power, Precipitation, Rain, Regale, Scat, Scouther, Scowther, Scud, Skatt, Skit, Snow, Spat, Spet, Spit, Splatter, Spray, Sprinkle, Squall(y), Thunder-plump, Ticker tape, Volley

▹**Showers** *may indicate* an anagram

**Showgirl** Evita, Nanette

▹**Showing, Shown in** *may indicate* a hidden word

**Showjumping** Puissance

**Showman** Bailey, Barnum, Buffalo Bill, Entertainer, Goon, Houdini, Impresario, Lord Mayor, MC, Ringmaster, Todd

**Show-off** Coxcomb, Exhibitionist, Extrovert, Flash Harry, Jack the lad, Masher, Peacock, Piss artist, Poseur, Sport, Swagger, Swank, Tulip, Wiseacre

**Showpiece** Flagship

**Show-place** Exhibition, Olympia, Pavilion, Theatre

**Show up** Unmask

**Shrapnel** Fragment, Shell, Splinter

**Shred** Clout, Filament, Grate, Julienne, Mammock, Mince, Mummock, Rag, Screed, Swarf, Tag, Tatter, Ta(i)ver, Tear up, Thread, To-tear, Vestige, Wisp

**Shrew** Bangsring, Banxring, Battleaxe, Callet, Catamaran, Common, Elephant, Fury, Hellcat, Kate, Marabunta, Musk, Nag, Otter, Pygmy, Show, Solenodon, Sondeli, Sorex, Spitfire, Squirrel, Tana, Termagant, Tree, Trull, Tupaia, Virago, Vixen, Water, Xant(h)ippe, Yankie, Yenta

**Shrewd(ness)** Acumen, Acute, Arch, Argute, Artful, Astucious, Astute, Callid, Canny, Clued-up, Cute, Discernment, Far-sighted, File, Gnostic, Gumptious, Hard-nosed, Horse-trader, Judicious, Knowing, Pawky, Perspicacious, Politic, Prudent(ial), Sagacious, Sapient(al), Savvy, Sharp-sighted, Tactical, Wide boy, Wily, Wise

**Shriek** Cry, Scream, Scrike, Shright, Shrike, Shrill, Shritch, Skirl, Yell

**Shrift** Attention, Penance, Short

**Shrike** Bird, Boubou, Butcher-bird, Loggerhead

**Shrill** Argute, Ear-piercing, High(-pitched), Keen, Piping, Pipy, Reedy, Scraich, Screech(y), Sharp, Skirl, Squeaky, Treble

**Shrimp(s)** Brine, Crevette, Fairy, Freshwater, Krill, Mantis, Midge, Opossum, Potted, Prawn, Runt, Sand, Skeleton, Small, Spectre, Squill(a), Stomatopod, Tiger

**Shrine** Adytum, Alamo, Altar, Dagaba, Dagoba, Dargah, Delphi, Fatima, Feretory, Harem, Holy, Joss house, Kaaba, Lourdes, Marabout, Martyry, Memorial, Monument, Naos, Oracle, Pagoda, Pilgrimage, Reliquary, Scrine, Scryne, Stupa, Tabernacle, Temple, Tope, Vimana, Walsingham

**Shrink(age), Shrink from, Shrinking, Shrunk** Abhor, Alienist, Analyst, Blanch, Blench, Boggle, Cling, Compress, Constringe, Contract, Cour, Cower, Creep, Crine, Cringe, Dare, Decrew, Depreciate, Dread, Dwindle, Flinch, Funk, Gizzen, Less, Minimise, Nirl, → **PSYCHIATRIST**, Pycnosis, Quail, Recoil, Reduce, Retract, Sanforised, Shrivel, Shrug, Shy, Sphacelate, Timid, Violet, Wane, Waste, Wince, Wither, Wizened

**Shrivel(led)** Cling, Crine, Desiccate, Dry, Dwindle, Gizzen, Nirl, Parch, Scorch, Scrump, Sear, Shrink, Skrimp, Skrump, Tabid, Welk, Wilt, Wither, Wizened, Writhled

**Shropshire** Salop

**Shroud(s)** Cerecloth, Chadri, Chuddah, Chuddar, Cloak, Cloud, Conceal, Cover, Futtock, Grave-cloth, Pall, Rigging, Screen, Sheet, Sindon, Turin, Veil, Winding-sheet, Wrap

**Shrove Tuesday** Fastens, J'ouvert, Pancake

**Shrub(bery)** Arboret, Brush, → **BUSH**, Dead-finish, Horizontal, Plant, Undergrowth

---

**SHRUBS**

*3 letters:*
Kat
Qat
Rue

*4 letters:*
Acer
Aloe
Coca
Cola
Dita
Grex
Hebe
Kava
Nabk
Olea
Rhus
Ruta
Sunn
Titi
Tutu
Ulex

*5 letters:*
Aalii
Bosky
Brere
Briar
Brier
Broom
Buaze
Buazi
Buchu
Bucku
Caper
Elder
Furze
Gorse
Hakea
Hazel
Henna
Holly
Ledum
Maqui
Monte
Mulga
Nebek
Peony
Pyxie
Ramee
Ramie
Salal
Savin
Senna
Sumac
Thyme
Toyon
Wahoo
Yapon
Yupon
Zamia

*6 letters:*
Abelia
Acacia
Alhagi
Ambach
Aucuba
Azalea
Bauera
Cobaea
Correa
Croton
Crowea
Daphne
Fatsia
Feijoa
Frutex
Fustet
Fynbos
Gambir
Garrya
Jojoba
Kalmia
Laurel
Lignum
Manoao
Manuka
Maquis
Matico
Mimosa
Myrica
Myrtle
Nebbuk
Nebeck
Neinei
Paeony
Pituri
Privet
Protea

Prunus
Savine
Smilax
Sorbus
Storax
Styrax
Sumach
Tutsan
Wandoo
Yaupon

***7 letters:***
Acerola
Akiharo
Ambatch
Arbutus
Bauhini
Boronia
Bullace
Cascara
Chamise
Chamiso
Cytisus
Deutzia
Dogwood
Emubush
Epacris
Ephedra
Filbert
Fuchsia
Gambier
Guayule
Hop-tree
Jasmine
Juniper
Lantana
Mahonia
Mesquit
Muntrie
Oleacea
Olearia
Phlomis
Rhatany
Romneya
Rosebay
Savanna
Shallon
Skimmia
Syringa
Tea-tree
Waratah
Weigela

***8 letters:***
Abutilon
Allspice
Balisier
Barberry
Bayberry
Berberis
Bignonia
Bilberry
Bluebush
Buddleia
Camellia
Caragana
Coprosma
Cowberry
Danewort
Euonymus
Gardenia
Hardhack
Heketara
Hibiscus
Horopito
Inkberry
Ink plant
Japonica
Jetbread
Koromiko
Krameria
Lavender
Leadwort
Magnolia
Mairehau
Mesquite
Mezereon
Ninebark
Ocotillo
Oleander
Oleaster
Photinia
Rangiora
Rock rose
Rosemary
Saltbush
Savannah
Shadbush
Snowbush
Sorbaria
Spekboom
Sweetsop
Tamarisk
Viburnum
Waxplant

***9 letters:***
Andromeda
Arrowroot
Beach plum
Bearberry
Buckthorn
Ceanothus
Clianthus
Cordyline
Coreopsis
Coyotillo
Crowberry
Eucryphia
Firethorn
Forsythia
Gelsemium
Grevillia
Hamamelis
Helwingia
Hydrangea
Jaborandi
Jessamine
Kumarahou
Manzanita
Melaleuca
Mistletoe
Patchouli
Petty whin
Pernettya
Perovskia
Phillyria
Rauwolfia
Sagebrush
Saskatoon
Screw bean
Snowberry
Spicebush
Sterculia
Tree peony
Twinberry
Widow wail
Wolfberry

***10 letters:***
Aphelandra
Buttonbush
Callicarpa
Cascarilla
Coralberry
Corylopsis
Crossandra
Embothrium
Eriostemon
Escallonia
Fatshedera
Frangipani
Fringe tree
Gaultheria
Goat's thorn
Gooseberry
Greasewood
Holodiscus
Joshua tree
Laurustine
Marcgravia
Mock orange
Mock privet
Parkleaves
Pilocarpus
Poinsettia
Potentilla
Pyracantha
Schefflera
Supplejack
Twinflower

***11 letters:***
Beautybrush
Bottlebrush
Candleberry
Carpenteria
Chaenomeles
Cheese plant
Cotoneaster
Farkleberry
Honeysuckle
Huckleberry
Japan laurel
Leatherwood
Mustard tree
Pittosporum
Postanthera
Sheep laurel
Silverberry
Staggerbush
Steeplebush
Stephanotis
Wintergreen
Wintersweet
Wortleberry

***12 letters:***
Buffalo-berry
Phanerophyte
Philadelphus
Rhododendron
Serviceberry
Southernwood
St Peter's wort
Streptosolen
Strophanthus

***13 letters:***
Wayfaring tree
Winter jasmine

**Shrug** Discard, Dismiss(ive), Toss
**Shuck** Peel
**Shudder(ing)** Abhor, Ashake, Frisson, Grew, Grise, Grue, Horror, Jerk, Quake, Quiver, Shake, Shiver, Spasm, Tremble, Tremor
**Shuffle(d)** Dodge, Drag, Hedge, Make, Mix, Palter, Permute, Randomise, Rearrange, Redeployment, Riffle, Scuff, Shamble, Shauchle, Soft-shoe, Stack, Waddle
▷**Shuffle(d)** *may indicate* an anagram
**Shun** Attention, Avoid, Boycott, Eschew, Evade, Forbear, Freeze, Ignore, Ostracise, Secede, Snub, →SPURN
**Shunt** Move, Prang, Shelve, Shuttle, Side-track
**Shut (down, in, out, up), Shuts** Bar, Cage, Close, Closet, Confined, Coop, Debar, Embar, Emure, Fasten, Fend, Impale, Impound, Imprison, Latch, Lay-off, Lock, Occlude, Paralysis, Rid, Scram, Seal, Shet, Slam, Spar, Steek, Telescope, Tine, To
**Shutter(s)** Blind, B-setting, Damper, Dead-lights, Douser, Eyelid, Focal-plane, Jalousie, Louver, Louvre, Persiennes, Shade
**Shuttle** Alternate, Challenger, Commute, Drawer, Flute, Go-between, Navette, Orbiter, Shoot, Shunt, Space, Tat(t), Weave
**Shy** Bashful, Blate, Blench, Cagey, Camera, Cast, Catapult, Chary, Clam, Coconut, Coy, Deficient, Demure, Diffident, Farouche, Flinch, Funk, Go, Heave, Introvert, Jerk, Jib, Laithfu', Leery, Lob, Mim, Mims(e)y, Modest, Mousy, Rear, Recoil, Reserved, Reticent, Retiring, Sally, Sheepish, Shrinking violet, Skeigh, Sling, Start, Thraw, Throw, Timid, Tongue-tied, Toss, Try, Verecund, Wallflower, Willyard, Willyart, Withdrawn
**Shyster** Ambulance chaser, Wheeler-dealer
**Siamese, Siamese twins** Chang, Eng, Parabiosis, Seal-point, T(h)ai
**Siberia(n)** Chukchi, Evenki, Frozen, Ostiak, Ostyak, Samo(y)ed, Tungus, Vogul, Yakut, Yupik
**Sibilant** Hissing, Swish, Whistling
**Sibling** Brother, German, Kin, Sister
**Sibyl** Diviner, Oracle, Prophetess, Seer, Seeress, Soothsayer, Voluspa, Witch
**Sicilian** Sicanian, Trinacrian
**Sick(en), Sickener, Sickening, Sickliness, Sickly, Sickness** Aegrotat, Affection, Ague, Ail, Altitude, Anaemic, Bad, Bends, Bilious, Bush, Cat, Chalky, Chunder, Cloying, Colic, Crapulence, Cringeworthy, Crook, Decompression, Delicate, Diseased, Disorder, Donsie, Eclampsia, Emetic, Emetin(e), English, Gag, Grass, Green, Hacked off, Hangover, Icky, Ill, Infection, Infirm, Lazar, Leisure, Loathsome, Maid-pale, Mal, Mawkish, Milk, Morbid, Morning, Motion, Mountain, Nauseous, Off-colour, Pale, Peaky, Peelie-wallie, Peely-wally, Pestilent, Pindling, Plague, Poorly, Puly, Puna, Qualm, Queachy, Queasy, Queechy, Radiation, Regorge, Repulsive, Retch, Serum, Shilpit, Sleeping, Sleepy, Soroche, Space, Spue, Squeamish, Sweating, Travel, Twee, Uncle Dick, Valetudinarian, Virus, Vomit, Wamble-cropped, Wan
**Sick bay, Sickroom** San, Ward
**Sickle(-shaped)** Ba(d)ging-hook, Falcate, Falx, Grasshook, Hook, Scythe, Shear
**Side, Sidepiece** Abeam, Airs, Ally, B, Beam, Blind, Border, Branch, Broad, Camp, Cis-, Distaff, Division, East, Edge, Effect, Elevation, Eleven, English, Epistle, Ex intraque parte, Facet, Flank, Flip, Gospel, Gunnel, Hand, Heavy, Hypotenuse, Iliac, Lateral, Lee(ward), Left, Long, Lore, Obverse, Off, On, OP, Pane, Part, Partisan, Party, Pleura, Port, Pretension, Profile, Prompt, Rave, Reveal, Reverse, Right, Rink, Scratch, Short, Silver, Slip, Snobbery, Spear, Spindle, Starboard, Swank, →TEAM, Tight, Weak, West, Wind, Windward, Wing, XI
**Sideboard(s)** Beauf(f)et, Buffet, Cellaret, Commode, Credence, Credenza, Dinner-wagon, Dresser, Whiskers
**Side by side** Appose(d)
**Side-effect, Side-issue** Fall-out, Logograph, Logogriph, Offshoot, Secondary, Spin-off
**Sidekick** Crony, Right-hand man, Satellite
**Side-line** Bay, Demote, Hobby, Lye, Siding, Spur
**Sidepost** Cheek
**Sideshoot** Offset
**Side-step** Crab, Dodge, Evade, Hedge, Maori, Volt

**Side-track** Distract, Divert, Shunt
**Sidewalk** Crab, Footpath, Pavement
**Sideways** Askance, Crab, End-on, Indirect, Laterally, Laterigrade, Oblique
**Siding** Alliance, Byway, Lie, Lye, Spur, Turnout
**Sidle** Edge, Passage
**Siege (work), Siege engine** Alamo, Antioch, Antwerp, Beleaguer, Beset, Blockade, Bog, Charleston, Gherao, Heron, Investment, Khartoum, Ladysmith, Leaguer, Mafeking, Masada, Metz, Obsidional, Perilous, Pleven, Plevna, Poliorcetic, Ravelin, Sarajevo, Surround, Verdun, Vicksburg, Warsaw, Warwolf
**Sienese** Tuscan
**Sienna** Burnt, Raw
**Sierra** Range, S
**Sierra Leone** Mende
**Siesta** Nap, Noonday, Nooning
**Sieve, Sift(ing)** Analyse, Bolt(er), Boult(er), Bunting, Colander, Coliform, Cribble, Cribrate, Cribrose, Cullender, Eratosthenes, Ethmoid, Filter, Griddle, Molecular, Pan, Rice, Riddle, Screen, Searce, Search, Separate, Siler, Strain, Sye, Tamis, Tammy, Tems(e), Trommel, Try, Winnow
**Sigh** Exhale, Heave, Lackaday, Long, Moan, Sithe, Sough, Suspire, Welladay
**Sight(ed)** Aim, Barleycorn, Bead, Conspectuity, Eye(ful), Eyesore, Glimpse, Ken, Long, Oculated, Panoramic, Peep, Prospect, Range, Rear, Riflescope, Scene, Scotopia, Second, See, Short, Spectacle, Taish, Telescopic, Twenty-twenty, Vane, →VIEW, Visie, Vision, Vista, Vizy, Vizzie
**Sight-screen** Eyelid
**Sightsee(ing), Sightseer** Do, Lionise, Observer, Rubberneck, Tourist, Tripper, Viewer
**Sign(ing), Signpost, Signs** Accidental, Ache, Addition, Air, Ale-pole, Ale-stake, Ampassy, Ampersand, Ankh, Apostrophe, Aquarius, Archer, Aries, Arrow, Auspice, Autograph, Badge, Balance, Beacon, Beck, Beckon, Birth, Board, Brand, Bull, Bush, Call, Cancer, Capricorn, Caract, Caret, Character, Chevron, Clue, Coronis, Crab, Credenda, Cross, Crossbuck, Cue, Dactylology, Dele, Denote, Diacritic, Di(a)eresis, Diphone, Division, Dollar, DS, Earmark, Earth, Emblem, Endeixis, Endorse, Endoss, Enlist, Enrol(l), Equals, Evidence, Exit, Fascia, Fire, Fish, Gemini, Gesture, Goat, Grammalogue, Hallmark, Hamza(h), Harbinger, Harvey Smith, Hash, Hex, Hieroglyphic, High-five, Hint, Ideogram, Indian, Indicate, Indication, Indicium, Initial, Inn, INRI, Inscribe, Ivy-bush, Leo, Lexigram, Libra, Local, Logogram, Milepost, Milestone, Minus, Motion, Mudra, Multiplication, Nameplate, Negative, Neume, Nod, Notice, Obelisk, Obelus, Omen, Peace, Phaseogram, Phraseogram, Pisces, Placard, Plus, Positive, Pound, Presa, Presage, Prodrome, Prodromus, Radical, Ram, Ratify, Red lattice, Register, Rest, Road, Rune, Sacrament, Sagittarius, Sain, Scorpio, Segno, Semeion, Semiotics, Shingle, Shorthand, Show, Sigil, Sigla, Signal, Sky, Star, Subscribe, Subtraction, Superscribe, Symbol, Symptom, Syndrome, Tag, Taurus, Tic(k)tac(k), Tilde, Tironian, Titulus, Token, Trace, Triphone, Twins, Umlaut, V, Vestige, Virgo, Vital, Warison, Warning, Water, Waymark, Word, Zodiac
**Signal(ler), Signalled** Alarm, Aldis lamp, Alert, All clear, Amber, Assemble, Baud, Beacon, Beckon, Bell, Bengal fire, Bengal light, Bleep, Bugle, Busy, Buzz, Call, Chamade, Code, Compander, Compandor, Cone, Cue, Detonator, Diaphone, Distant, Distress, Duplex, Earcon, Emit, Engaged, Flag, Flagman, Flare, Flash, Fog, Gantry, Gesticulate, Gesture, Gong, Griffin, Gun, Hail, Harmonic, Heliograph, Heliostat, Herald, Heterodyne, High sign, Home, Hooter, Horse and hattock, Icon, Important, Indicator, Input, Interrupt, Interval, Knell, Luminance, Marconi, Mark, Mase, Mayday, Megafog, Message, Modem, Morse, Motion, Navar, NICAM, Notation, Noted, Omen, Output, Password, Peter, Pheromone, Pinger, Pip, Pollice verso, Portend, Prod, Pulsar, Radio, Red alert, Renowned, Reveille, Robot, Salient, Semaphore, Semiology, Semiotic, Sign, Simplex, Singular, Smoke, Snook, Sonogram, SOS, Spoiler, Squawk, Storm, Taps, Target, Tattoo, Tchick, Telegraph, Teles(e)me, Thumb, Tic(k)-tac(k), Time, Token, Traffic, Transmit, Troop, Vehicle-actuated, Very, Video, V-sign, Waff, Waft, Wave, Wave-off, Whistle, Wigwag, Wink, Word, Yeoman
**Signal-box** Cabin

**Signature** Alla breve, Allograph, Autograph, By-line, Digital, Electronic, Hand, John Hancock, John Henry, Key, Mark, Moni(c)ker, Onomastic, Per pro, Sculpsit, Sheet, Specimen, Subscription, Tag, Time
**Signet** Ring, Seal, Sigil, Sphragistics
**Significance, Significant** Cardinal, Consequence, Cosmic, Emblem, Epochal, Ethos, Great, Impact, Important, Indicative, Instrumental, Key, Landmark, Magnitude, Major, Material, Matter, M(a)cGuffin, Meaningful, Milestone, Moment(ous), Notable, Noted, Noteworthy, Operative, Other, Paramount, Pith, Pregnant, Red-letter day, Salient, Special, Telling, Totemic, Weight
**Signify** Bemean, Bode, Denote, Imply, Indicate, Intimate, Matter, →**MEAN**, Represent, Symbolise
**Sign language** Ameslan, Finger spelling, Makaton, Semaphore, Shorthand, Tic(k)tac(k)
**Sikh(ism)** Granth, Kaccha, Kangha, Kara, Kesh, Khalsa, Kirpan, Mazhbi, Mechanised, Nanak, (Ranjit) Singh
**Silage** Haylage
**Silas** Uncle, Wegg
**Silence(r), Silent** Amyclaean, Aposiopesis, Choke-pear, Clam, Clamour, Conticent, Creepmouse, Cut short, Dead air, Dolby, Dumbfound, Dumbstruck, Earplug, Gag, Hesychastic, Hist, Hush, Hushkit, Mim(budget), Muffler, Mum(p), Mumchance, Mute, Obmutescent, Omertà, Pauciloquent, Quench, Quiesce, →**QUIET**, Quietude, Reticence, Shtoom, Shtum, Shush, Speechless, Squelch, Still, Sulky, Tace(t), Tacit(urn), Throttle, Tight-lipped, Tongue-tied, Trappist, Unvoiced, Wheesh(t), Whis(h)t
**Silhouette** Contour, Outline, Planform, Profile, Shadow figure, Shadowgraph, Shape, Skyline
**Silica(te)** Albite, Allanite, Analcime, Analcite, Andalusite, Anorthite, Asbestos, Chabazite, Chert, Cristobalite, Datolite, Diopside, Dioptase, Epidote, Euclase, Eudialyte, Fayalite, Float-stone, Gadolinite, Garnierite, Harmotome, Heulandite, Hiddenite, Humite, Iolite, Kieselguhr, Kyanite, Monticellite, Montmorillonite, Natrolite, Olivine, Opal, Pectolite, Penninite, Phillipsite, Pinite, Quartz, Rhodonite, Riebeckite, Saponite, Sard, Sardius, Scapolite, Silex, Spodumene, Staurolite, Stishovite, Tridymite, Tripoli, Ultrabasic, Vermiculite, Vitreosil®, Vitreous, Zeolite
**Silicon** Chip, Moore's law, Si
**Silk(y), Silk screen** Alamode, Artificial, Atlas, Barathea, Blonde-lace, Brocade, Bur(r), Charmeuse®, Chenille, Chiffon, Cocoon, Corn, Crape, Crepe, Duchesse, Dupion, Faille, Fibroin, Filature, Filoselle, Florence, Florentine, Flosh, Floss, Flox, Foulard, Gazar, Gazzatum, Georgette, Gimp, Glossy, Grosgrain, Honan, KC, Kente, Kincob, Lustrine, Lustring, Lutestring, Madras, Makimono, Malines, Marabou(t), Matelasse, Mercery, Milanese, Moiré, Near, Ninon, Oiled, Organza, Ottoman, Paduasoy, Parachute, Peau de soie, Pongee, Prunella, Prunelle, Prunello, Pulu, QC, Raw, Samite, Sars(e)net, Satin, Schappe, Seal(ch), Sendal, Seric, Sericeous, Sericite, Serigraph, Shalli, Shantung, Sien-tsan, Sleave, Sle(i)ded, Sleek, Slipper satin, Smooth, Soft, Spun, Surah, Tabaret, Tabby, Taffeta, Tasar, Thistledown, Thrown, Tiffany, Tram, Tulle, Tussah, Tusseh, Tusser, Tussore, Vegetable, Velvet, Wild
**Silkworm (eggs), Silkworm disease** Bombyx, Eria, Graine, Multivoltine, Muscardine, Sericulture, Tussore
**Sill** Ledge, Straining, Threshold, Whin
**Silly, Silliness** Absurd, Anserine, Apish, Brainless, Buffer, Childish, Clownish, Crass, Cuckoo, Daffy, Daft, Dandy, Ditsy, Divvy, Dotish, Drippy, Dumb(o), Dunce, Dweeb, Fatuous, Feather-brained, Fluffy, Folly, Fool, Foolery, Footling, Frivolous, Goopy, Goosey, Gormless, Hen-witted, Idiotic, Imbecile, Inane, Inept, Infield(er), Liminal, Mid-off, Mid-on, Mopoke, Prune, Puerile, Scatterbrain, Season, Simple, Soft(y), Sot, Spoony, →**STUPID**, Tomfoolery, Tripe, Wacky, Wally
▷**Silly** *may indicate* relating to a sill
**Silo** Granary
**Silt** Alluvium, Deposit, Dregs, Land, Lees, Loess, Residue, Sullage, Varve
**Silver(skin)** Ag, Albata, Alpac(c)a, Arg(ent), Argyria, British plate, Cardecue, Cat, Cerargyrite, Diana's tree, Electroplate, Free, Fulminating, German, Grey, Horn, Long John,

Luna, Nickel, One-legged, Pa(c)kfong, Pakt(h)ong, Parcel-gilt, Pegleg, Piastre, Pine-tree, Pirate, Plate, Plateresque, Ruby, Runners-up, Second, Stephanite, Sterling, Sycee, Talent, Thaler, Twenty-fifth

▷**Silver** *may indicate* a coin

**Silversmith** Demetrius, Lamerie, Plater

**Silver-tongued** Fluent

**Simian** Apelike, Catar(r)hine

**Similar(ity)** Affinity, Akin, Analog(ue), Analogical, Assonance, Comparable, Corresponding, Equivalent, Etc, Homoeoneric, Homogeneous, Homoiousian, Homologous, Homonym, Isomorphism, Kindred, → LIKE, Likeness, Likewise, Metaphor, Parallel, Patristic, Resemblance, Samey, Suchlike

**Simile** Epic, Homeric

**Similitude** Parable

**Simmer** Bubble, Poach, Seethe, Stew

**Simon** Bolivar, Cellarer, Magus, Peter, Pure, Simple, Zealot

**Simper** Bridle, Giggle, Smirk

**Simple(r), Simplicity, Simplify, Simply** ABC, Aefa(u)ld, Afa(w)ld, Arcadian, Artless, Austere, Bada-bing, Bada-boom, Bald, Bare, Basic, Bog-standard, Breeze, Chaste, Child's play, Cinch, Crude, Daw, Disentangle, Doddle, Doric, → EASY, Eath(e), Elegant, Elemental, ESN, Ethe, Eyebright, Facile, Fee, Folksy, Foolproof, Gomeral, Gotham, Green, Gullish, Herb(alist), Herborist, Homespun, Idyllic, Incomposite, Inornate, Jaap, Japie, Light, Mere, Moner(on), Moronic, Naive(té), Naked, Niaiserie, No brainer, Noddy, One-fold, Only, Open and shut, Ordinary, Paraphrase, Pastoral, Peter, Plain, Pleon, Provincial, Pure, Reduce, Renormalise, Rude, Rustic, Saikless, Sapid, Semplice, Sheer, Silly, Simon, Spartan, Straightforward, Streamline, Stupid, Suave, Tout court, Uncluttered, Understated, Unicellular, Unsophisticated, Woollen

**Simpleton** Abderite, Airhead, Cokes, Cuckoo, Daw, Duffer, Flat, Fool, Gaby, Galah, Gomeral, Gomeril, Gothamist, Greenhorn, Johnny, Juggins, Natural, Shot-clog, Spoon, → STUPID PERSON, Wiseacre, Zany

**Simulate(d), Simulating** Affect, Anti, Feign, Mock, Pretend, VR

**Simultaneous** Coincidental, Coinstantaneous, Contemporaneous, Synchronous, Together, Unison

**Sin(ful), Sinfulness** Aberrant, Accidie, Acedia, Actual, Anger, Avarice, Besetting, Bigamy, Capital, Cardinal, Covetousness, Crime, Deadly, Debt, Depravity, Envy, Err, Evil, Folly, Gluttony, Guile, Hamartiology, Harm, Hate, Impious, Impure, Lapse, Lust, Misdeed, Misdoing, Mortal, → OFFENCE, Omission, Original, Peccadillo, Piacular, Pride, Sacrilegious, Scape, Scarlet, Shirk, Sine, Sloth, Transgress, Trespass, Unrighteous, Venial, Vice, Wicked, Wrath, Wrong

**Sinai** Horeb, Mount

**Since** Ago, As, Cos, For, Meantime, Seeing, Sens, Sine, Sinsyne, Sith(en), Syne, Whereas, Ygo(e)

**Sincere(ly), Sincerity** Bona-fide, Candour, Earnest, Entire, Frank, Genuine, Heartfelt, Heartwhole, Honest, Open, Real(ly), Realtie, Simple-hearted, True, Verity, Whole-hearted

**Sinclair** Lewis, Upton

**Sine** Coversed, Versed

**Sinecure** Bludge, Commendam

**Sinew(y)** Fibre, Ligament, Nerve, String, Tendinous, Tendon

▶**Sinful** *see* SIN(FUL)

**Sing(ing)** Antiphony, Barbershop, Bel canto, Belt out, Bhajan, Carol, Chant, Cheep, Chirp, Chorus, Coloratura, Community, Cough, Croon, Crow, Descant, Diaphony, Diddle, Doo-wop, Glee club, Gorgia, Gregorian, Hum, Incant, Inform, Intone, Karaoke, Kirtan, La-la, Lilt, Lyricism, Melic, Parlando, Peach, Pen(n)illion, Pipe, Plainchant, Rand, Rant, Rap, Record, Render, Scat, Second(o), Serenade, Solmization, Spinto, Sprechgesang, Sprechstimme, Squeal, Tell, Thrum, Trill, Troll, Unitary, Vocalese, Warble, Woodshedding, Yodel

**Singapore** .sg

**Singe** Burn, Char, Scorch, Swale, Swayl, Sweal, Sweel

**Singer(s)** A cappella, Alto, Baillie, Baker, Balladeer, Bard, Baritone, Bass, Beatle, Bing, → BIRD, Blondel, Bono, Brel, Buffo, Callas, Canary, Cantabank, Cantatrice, Cantor, Car, Carreras, Caruso, Cash, Castrato, Chaliapin, Chanteur, Chanteuse, Chantor, Chauntress, Chazan, Cher, Chorine, Chorister, Coloratura, Comprimario, Countertenor, Crooner, Dawson, Diva, Dylan, Ella, Elvis, Falsetto, Folk, Gigli, Glee club, Gleemaiden, Gleeman, Gobbi, Grass, Griot, Hammond, Haz(z)an, Heldentenor, Isaac, Kettle, Lark, Lauder, Lay clerk, Lead, Lind, Lorelei, Lulu, Madrigalist, Mathis, Meister, Melba, Melodist, Mezzo(-soprano), Minstrel, Opera, Orbison, Oscine, Patti, Pavarotti, Piaf, Pitti, Precentor, Presley, Prima donna, Qawwal, Rapper, Robeson, Semi-chorus, Session, Shrike, Sinatra, Siren, Snitch, Songman, Songstress, Soprano, Soubrette, Spinto, Stoolie, Succentor, Swan, Syren, Tatiana, Tenor, Tenure, Torch, Treble, Troubador, Vocalist, Voice, Wait, Warbler

**Single, Singly** Ace, Aefa(u)ld, Aefawld, Alone, Azygous, Bachelor, Celibate, Discriminate, EP, Exclusive, Feme sole, Haplo-, Individual, Isolate, Lone, Matchless, Monact, Mono, Odd, Once, One-off, One-shot, One-way, Only, Pick, Run, Seriatim, Sole, Solitary, Solo, Spinster, Unary, Unattached, Uncoupled, Uniparous, Unique, Unwed, Versal, Yin

**Single-cell** Protista

**Single-chambered** Monothalamous

**Singlestick** Sword

**Singlet** Tunic, Vest

**Singleton** Lonely heart, Stag

▷**Singleton** *may indicate* an old recording, e.g. Forty-five, Seventy-eight

**Singular(ity)** Curious, Especial, Exceptional, Extraordinary, Ferly, Legion, Naked, Odd, Once, One, One-off, Peculiar, Queer(er), Rare, S, Strange, → UNIQUE, Unusual

**Singultus** Hiccup

**Sinister** Bend, Dark, Dirke, Evil, L, Left, Lh, Louche, → OMINOUS, Port, Rasputin, Spooky, Svengali

**Sink(ing), Sinker, Sink in, Sunk(en)** Abandon, Atlantis, Basin, Bidet, Bog, Bore, Cadence, Carbon, Cower, Deep-set, Delapse, Depress, Descend, Devall, Dip, Down, Drain, Draught-house, Drink, Drop, Drown, Ebb, Embog, Flag, Founder, Full, Gravitate, Heat, Hole, Immerse, Infiltrate, Invest, Jawbox, Kitchen, Lagan, Laigh, Lapse, Ligan, Merger, Pad, Poach, Pot, Prolapse, Put(t), Relapse, Sag, Scupper, Scuttle, Set, Settle, Shaft, Shipwreck, Slump, Steep-to, Stoop, Sty, Submerge, Subside, Swag, Swamp, Titanic

**Sinner** Evildoer, Malefactor, Offender, Reprobate, Trespasser

**Sinuous** Curvy, Eely, Ogee, Slinky, Snaky, Wavy, Winding

**Sinus** Cavity, Ethmoidal, Frontal, Maxillary, Recess, Sphenoidal

**Sioux** Dakota, Sitting Bull

**Sip(ping)** Delibate, Hap'orth, Libant, Sample, Sowp, Sup, Taste, Tiff(ing), Tift

**Siphon** Draw, Rack, Soda, Suck, Transfer

**Sir** Dan, Dom, K, Knight, Kt, Lord(ing), Milord, Sahib, Signor, Sirrah, Stir, Stirra(h), Towkay, Tuan

**Sire** Ancestor, Beget, Father, Get

**Siren** Alarm, Alert, Charmer, Delilah, Diaphone, Enchanter, Femme fatale, Foghorn, Hooter, Houri, Leucosia, Ligea, Lorelei, Mermaid, Oceanides, Parthenope, Salamander, Shark, Teaser, Temptress, Vamp

**Sirenian** Dugong, Lamantin, Manatee, Manati, Sea-cow

**Sirius** Sothic

**Sirloin** Backsey

**Sirree** Bo

**Sisal** Agave

**Siskin** Aberdevine, Bird, Finch

**Sister(s)** Anne, Beguine, Bronte, Carmelite, Fatal, Lay, Minim, → NUN, Nurse, Out, Pleiades, Religeuse, Sib, Sibling, Sis, Sob, Soul, Swallow, Theatre, Titty, Ugly, Ursuline, Verse, Ward, Weak, Weird

**Sistine** Chapel, Sextus

**Sisyphean** Uphill

**Sit(ter), Sitting** All-night, Bestride, Clutch, Dharna, Duck, Gaper, Gimme, Incubate, Lime,

Lit de justice, Model, MP, Perch, Pose, Reign, Represent, Roost, Séance, Sederunt, Sejeant, Sesh, Session, Slouch, Squat

**Site, Siting** Area, Arpa, Bomb, Brochure, Brownfield, Building, Camp, Caravan, Chat room, Cobweb, Ebay®, Feng shui, Gap, Greenfield, Home-page, Locality, Location, Lot, Mirror, Orphan, Pad, Place, Plot, Ramsar, Rogue, Sacred, Silo, Spot, Stance, Venue, Visie, Vizy, Vizzie, Web, World Heritage

**Sitting-room** Lounge, Parlour

**Situation** Affair, Ballpark, Bearings, Berth, Can of worms, Cart, Case, Catch, Catch-22, Chicken and egg, Cliff-hanger, Contretemps, Corner, Cow, Dilemma, Drama, Galère, Hole, Hornet's nest, Hot seat, Job, Knife-edge, Lie, Location, Lurch, Matrix, Mire, Nail-biter, Niche, Novel, No-win, Office, Outcome, Pickle, Place, Plight, Position, Post, Scenario, Scene, Schmear, Schmeer, Seat, Set-up, Shebang, Showdown, State of play, Status quo, Sticky wicket, Strait, Stringalong, Where, Worst case

**Six(th)** Boundary, Digamma, French, German, Half(-a)dozen, Hexad, Italian, Neapolitan, Prime, Sax, Senary, Sestett(e), Sextet, Sice, Size, Vau, VI

**Six counties** NI

**Six days** Hexa(e)meron

**Six feet, Six-footer** Fathom, Hornet, Insect, Miurus, Termite

**Sixpence** Bender, Kick, Mill, Slipper, Tanner, Tester(n), Testril(l), Tizzy, VID, VIP, Zack

**Sixteen** Hexadecimal, Sweet

**Sixty** Degree, Sexagesimal, Shock, Threescore

**Size(able)** Amplitude, Area, Bulk, Calibre, Clearcole, Countess, Demy, Displacement, → **EXTENT**, Format, Girth, Glair, Glue, Guar, Gum, Imperial, Magnitude, Measure, Particle, Party, Paste, Physique, Plus, Pot(t), Princess, Proportion, Quarto, Tempera, Tidy, Trim

**Sizzle** Fry, Hiss, Scorch

**Skate(r), Skateboard(er), Skateboarding, Skating** Blade, Bob, Cheap, Choctaw, Cousins, Curry, Dean, Fakie, Figure, Fish, Free, Grommet, Half-pipe, Hot dog, In-line, Long-track, Maid, Mohawk, Ollie, Overacid, Rink, Rock(er), Roller, Rollerblade®, Runner, Short-track, Sit spin, Speed, Torvill

**Skedaddle** Beat it, Scarper, Scram, Shoo, Vamoose

**Skein** Hank, Hasp

**Skeleton, Skeletal** Anatomy, Atomy, Axial, Bones, Cadaverous, Cadre, Cage, Coenosteum, Coral, Corallite, Corallum, Emaciated, Family, Framework, Hydrostatic, Key, Ossify, Outline, Scenario, Sclere, Tentorium

**Sketch(y)** Bozzetto, Cameo, Character, Charade, Charcoal, Croquis, Delineate, Describe, Diagram, Doodle, Draft, → **DRAW**, Ébauche, Esquisse, Illustration, Limn, Line, Map out, Maquette, Modello, Outline, Pencilling, Pen portrait, Playlet, Pochade, Précis, Profile, Representation, Rough, Scrappy, Skit, Study, Summary, Tenuous, Thumbnail, Trick, Vague, Vignette, Visual

**Skew, Skew-whiff** Agee, Ajee, Awry, Cock-eyed, Oblique, Sheer, Squint, Swerve, Veer

**Skewer** Brochette, En brochette, Impale, Kebab, Prong, Satay, Souvlaki, Spear, Spit, Transfix

**Ski(er), Skiing** Aquaplane, Carving, Free ride, Glide, Glissade, Hot-dog, Langlauf, Mogul, Nordic, Schuss, Schussboomer, Super G, Telemark, Vorlage, Wedeln

**Skid** Aquaplane, Drift, Fishtail, Jackknife, Side-slip, Slew, Slide, Slip, Slither, Spinout

▷**Skidding** *may indicate* an anagram

**Skiff** Canoe, Dinghy, Outrigger

**Skilful, Skill(ed)** Ability, Able, Accomplished, Ace, Address, Adept, Adroit, Art, Artistic, Bravura, Bushcraft, Canny, Chic, Competence, Craft, Deacon, Deft, Demon, Dextrous, Endowment, Enoch, Etude, Expertise, Exponent, Facility, Feat, Finesse, Flair, Gleg, Habile, Hand, Handicraft, Handy, Hend, Hot, Ingenious, Keepy-uppy, Knack, Know-how, Knowing, Lear(e), Leir, Lere, Marksmanship, Masterly, Masterpiece, Mastery, Mean, Métier, Mistery, Mystery, Mystique, People, Practic(k), Practique, Practised, Proficient, Prowess, Quant, Resource, Savvy, Science, Skeely, Sleight, Soft, Speciality, Strategy, Tactics, Talent, Technic, Technique, Touch, Trade, Transferable, Trick, Versed, Virtuoso, Wise, Workmanship

**Skim** Aquaplane, Cream, Despumate, Flit, Glide, Graze, Plane, Ream, Scan, Scud, Scum, Skiff, Skitter, Thumb

**Skimp(y)** Cut corners, Restrict, Scamp, Scrimp, Short, Stint

**Skin(s)** Ablate, Agnail, Armour, Banana, Bark, Basan, Basil, Bingo wing, Box-calf, Bronzed, Buff, Calf, Callus, Case, Cere, Chevrette, Coat, Corium, Cortex, Crackling, Cutaneous, Cuticle, Cutis, Deacon, Deer, Derm(a), Dermatome, Dermis, Dewlap, Disbark, Ectoderm, Enderon, Envelope, Epicanthus, Epicarp, Epidermis, Eschar, Excoriate, Exterior, Fell, Film, Flaught, Flay, Flench, Flense, Flinch, Forel, Fourchette, Goldbeater's, Hangnail, Hide, Integra®, Jacket, Kip, Kirbeh, Leather, Membrane, Muktuk, Nebris, Nympha, Pachyderm, Parfleche, Patagium, Peau, Peel, Pell, Pellicle, Pelt, Perinychium, Pith, Plew, Plu(e), Prepuce, Pteryla, Rack, Rape, Rind, Scalp, Scarfskin, Scurf, Serosa, Shagreen, Shell, Shoder, Spetch, Strip, Swindle, Tegument, Tulchan, Velvet, Veneer, Water-bouget, Wattle, Woolfell, Zest

**Skin disease, Skin problem, Skin trouble** Boba, Boil, Buba, Causalgia, Chloasma, Chloracne, Cowpox, Cradle cap, Cyanosis, Dartre, Dermatitis, Dermatosis, Dyschroa, EB, Ecdysis, Ecthyma, Eczema, Erysipelas, Exanthem(a), Favus, Flay, Framboesia, Gum rash, Herpes, Hives, Ichthyosis, Impetigo, Leishmaniasis, Leucodermia, Lichen, Livedo, Lupus vulgaris, Maidism, Mal del pinto, Mange, Miliaria, Molluscum, Morphew, Morula, Patagium, Pellagra, Pemphigus, Pinta, Pityriasis, Prurigo, Pseudofolliculitis, Psoriasis, Pyoderma, Rash, Red-gum, Ringworm, Rosacea, Rose-rash, St Anthony's fire, Sapego, Scabies, Sclerodermia, Scurvy, Seborrhoea, Serpigo, Strophulus, Telangiectasia, Tetter, Tinea, Vaccinia, Verruca, Verruga, Vitiligo, Xanthoma, Xerodermia, Xerosis, Yaws, Yawy

**Skinflint** Cheapo, Cheapskate, Dryfist, Freeloader, Miser, Niggard, Pinch-gut, Scrooge, Tightwad

**Skinful** Drunk, Sausage

**Skinhead** Not, Punk, Scalp

**Skink** Scincoid, Seps

**Skinless** Ecorché

**Skinny** Angular, Barebone, Bony, Cutaneous, Dermal, Emaciate, Lean, Scraggy, Thin, Underweight, Weed

**Skint** Boracic (lint), Broke, Ghat, Penniless, Stony

**Skip(ped), Skipper** Boss, Bound, Caper, Captain, Cavort, Drakestone, Dumpster, Elater, Frisk, Hesperian, Jump, Jumping-mouse, Lamb, Luppen, Miss, Omit, Patroon, Ricochet, Roo, Sand, Saury, Scamper, Scombresox, Spring, Tittup, Trip, Trounce(r), Truant

**Skirl** Humdudgeon, Pibroch, Pipe, Screigh

**Skirmish(er)** Brawl, Brush, Dispute, Engagement, Escarmouche, Fray, Pickeer, Spar, Tirailleur, Velitation, Voltigeur

**Skirt(ing)** Bases, Bell, Border, Bouffant, Bypass, Cheongsam, Circle, Coat, Crinoline, Culotte(s), Dado, Dirndl, Divided, Edge, Fil(l)ibeg, Fringe, Fustanella, Fustanelle, Girl, Gore, Grass, Harem, Hobble, Hoop, Hug, Hula, Kilt, Lamboys, Lava-lava, Marge, Margent, Maxi, Micro, Mini, Mopboard, Pareo, Pareu, Pencil, Peplum, Petticoat, Philibeg, Pinafore, Piu-piu, Plinth, Puffball, Ra-ra, Rim, Sarong, Sidestep, Stringboard, Tace, Tail, Taslet, Tasse(t), Tonlet, Tube, Tutu, Valance, Washboard, Wrapover, Wrap(a)round

**Ski-run** Nursery slope

**Ski-suit** Salopettes

**Skit** Lampoon, Parody, Sketch

**Skittish** Coy, Curvetting, Frisky, Restless, Shy, Skeigh

**Skittle(s)** Bayle, Bowl, Cheese, Kail(s), Kayle, Kingpin, Kittle-pins, Ninepin, Pin, Spare

**Skive(r)** Absentee, Laik, Malinger, Scrimshank, Shirk, Skewer, Swing the lead

**Skivvy** Drudge, Potboy, Slave

**Skrimshank** Bludge, Skive

**Skua** Boatswain, Bos'n

**Skulk** Loiter, Lurk, Mooch, Shool, Sneak

**Skull** Brainpan, Bregma(ta), Calvaria, Cranium, Death's head, Fontanel, Harnpan, Head, Head case, Malar, Maz(z)ard, Obelion, Occiput, Pannikell, Phrenology, Scalp, Sinciput, Vault, Yorick

**Skullcap** Kippa, Ya(r)mulka, Yarmulke, Zucchetto

**Skunk** Atoc, Atok, Ferret, Hognosed, Polecat, Pot, Striped, Surfeit, Teledu, Zoril(lo), Zorino

**Sky(-high), Sky-tinctured, Skywards** Aerial, Air, Azure, Blue, Canopy, Carry, Cloud-kissing, El Al, E-layer, Element, Empyrean, Ether, Firmament, Heaven, Lift, Lob, Loft, Mackerel, No-fly zone, Occident, Octa, Okta, Raise, Rangi, Uranus, Welkin

**Sky-diver** Para
**Skylark** Aerobatics, Bird
**Skylight** Abat-jour, Aurora, Comet, Companion, Lunette, Star
**Skyline** Horizon, Rooftops
**Sky-pilot** Chaplain, Vicar
**Skyscraper** Gherkin
**Slab(s)** Briquette, Bunk(er), Cake, Cap(e)stone, Chunk, Dalle, Hawk, Ledger, Marver, Metope, Mihrab, Mud, Paver, Paving-stone, Planch, Plank, Sclate, Sheave, Slate, Slice, Stela, Stelene, Tab, Tablet, Tile, Wood-wool
**Slack(en), Slacker, Slackness** Abate, Baggy, Careless, Clock-watch, Crank, Dilatory, Dross, Ease (off), Easy-going, Ebb, Flaccid, Glen, Idle, Inanition, Languor, Lax(ity), Lazybones, Let-up, Loose, Malinger, Negligent, Nerveless, Off-peak, Off-season, Relax, Release, Remiss, Shirk, Skive, Slatch, Slow, Surge, Unscrew, Unwind, Veer
**Slacks** Pedalpushers
**Slade** Dean
**Slag** Badmouth, Basic, Calx, Cinder, Clinker, Dross, Foamed, Lava, Scoria, Scum, Sinter, Tap cinder
**Slake** Abate, Cool, Quench, Refresh, Satisfy, Slo(c)ken
**Slalom** Super-G
**Slam, Slammer** Cocktail, Crash, Criticise, Dad, Grand, Little, Pan(dy), Poetry, Small, Sock, Swap, Swop, Vole, Wap
**Slander(ous)** Asperse, Backbite, Badmouth, Calumny, Defame, Derogatory, Detraction, Disparage, Infame, Insult, Libel, Malediction, Malign, Mendacity, Missay, Mud, Mudslinging, Obloquy, Sclaunder, Smear, Traduce, Vilify, Vilipend, Vitriol
**Slang** Abuse, Argot, Back, Berate, Blinglish, Cant, Colloquial, Ebonics, Flash, Jargon, Lingo, Nadsat, Parlyaree, Polari, Rhyming, Slate, Tsotsitaal, Verlan, Vernacular, Zowie
**Slant(ed), Slanting** Angle, Asklent, Atilt, Bevel, Bias, Brae, Cant, Careen, Catty-cornered, Chamfer, Clinamen, Diagonal, Escarp, Oblique, Outlook, Prejudice, Rake, Slew, → **SLOPE**, Spin, Splay, Squint, Talus, Tilt, Virgule
**Slap(ping)** Clatch, Clout, Cuff, Daub, Happy, Klep, Make-up, Paddy-whack, Pandy, Piston, Sclaff, Scud, Skelp, Smack, Spat, Swipe, Tape, Twank, Warpaint
**Slapdash** Anyhow, Careless, Hurried, Messy, Random
**Slaphead** Bald pate
**Slash(ed)** Chive, Cut, Diagonal, Gash, Hack, Jag, Lacerate, Laciniate, Leak, Oblique, Rash, Rast, Reduce, Scorch, Scotch, Separatrix, Slice, Slit, Solidus, Stroke, Virgule, Wee
**Slat(s)** Fish, Jalousie, Louvre, Spline, Stave
**Slate, Slaty, Slating** Alum, Berate, Blast, Calm, Cam, Caum, Clay, Clean, Countess, Credit, Criticise, Decry, Diatribe, Double, Duchess, Duchy, Enter, Flak, Greywacke, Griseous, Imperial, Killas, Knotenschiefer, Lady, List, Log, Marchioness, Ottrelite, Pan, Peggy, Polishing, Princess, Queen, Rag(g), Rap, Roof, Run down, Schalstein, Shingle, Slat, Small, Small lady, Tabula, Tomahawk, Viscountess
**Slater** Hellier, Insect
**Slattern** Bag, Besom, Bisom, Drab, Drazel, Frump, Mopsy, Ragbag, Ragdoll, Slammakin, Slammerkin, Sloven, Slummock, Sozzle, Traipse, Trapes, Trollop
**Slaughter(house), Slaughterer** Abattoir, Behead, Bleed, Bloodshed, Butcher, Carnage, Decimate, Genocide, Hal(l)al, Holocaust, Immolation, Jhatka, Kill, Mactation, → **MASSACRE**, Off, Scupper, Shambles, S(c)hechita(h), Shochet, Smite, Trounce
**Slav, Slavonic** Bohunk, Bulgar, Croat, Czech, Czechic, Jack, Kulak, Lusatia, Polabian, Russian, Serb, Sorb, Toil, Wend(ic)
**Slave(ry), Slaves, Slavish** Addict, Aesop, Aida, Androcles, Barracoon, Blackbird, Bond, Bond(s)man, Bondwoman, Bordar, Boy, Caliban, Coffle, Contraband, Dogsbody, Drudge, Drug, Dulocracy, Dulosis, Enthralment, Esne, Galley, Gibeonite, Helot, Hierodule, Jack, Mameluke, Mamluk, Marmaluke, Maroon, Minion, Nativity, Odali(s)que, Odalisk, Peasant, Pr(a)edial, Rhodope, Serf, Servitude, Spartacus, Terence, Theow, Thersites, Thete, Thrall, Toil, Topsy, Vassal, Villein, Wage, Wendic, White, Yoke
**Slave-driver, Slave-owner** Assam, Sweater, Task-master

**Slaver** Bespit, Dribble, Drivel, Drool, Slabber, Slobber, Spawl, Spit
**Slay(er), Slaying** Destroy, Execute, Ghazi, → KILL, Mactation, Murder, Quell, Saul, Slaughter, Transport
**Sleazy, Sleaze** Affair, Flimsy, Red-light, Scuzzy, Seamy, Seedy, Sordid, Squalid, Tack, Thin
**Sled(ge), Sleigh(-ride)** Bob, Bobsleigh, Dog train, Dray, Hurdle, Hurley-hacket, Kibitka, Komatic, Komatik, Lauf, Luge, Mud-boat, Mush, Polack, Pulk(h)(a), Pung, Rocket, Skeleton bob(sleigh), Skidoo®, Slipe, Stoneboat, Tarboggin, Toboggan, Train, Travois
**Sledge-hammer** Maul
**Sleek** Bright, Glossy, Shine, Silky, Smarm, Smooth, Smug, Streamlined
**Sleep, Sleeper(s), Sleepiness, Sleeping, Sleepy** Beauty, Bed, Bivouac, Blet, Bundle, Bye-byes, Car, Catnap, Coma, Couchette, Crash, Cross-sill, Cross-tie, Dormant, Dormient, Dormouse, Doss, Dove, Doze, Drop off, Drowse, Earring, Endymion, Epimenides, Flop, Forty winks, Gowl, Gum, Hibernate, Hypnology, Hypnos, Kip, Land of Nod, Lassitude, Lethargic, Lie, Morpheus, Nap, Narcolepsy, Narcosis, Nod, Oscitation, Over, Paradoxical, Petal, Policeman, Pop off, Psychopannychism, REM, Repast, Repose, Rest, Rip Van Winkle, Roomette, Rough, Sandman, Seven, Shuteye, Siesta, Skipper, Sleepover, Sloom, Slumber, Snooz(l)e, Somnolent, Sopor(ose), Sownd, Spine bashing, Stayover, Swone, Tie, Torpid, Twilight, Wagon-lit, Wink, Zeds, Zizz
**Sleeping place, Sleeping bag** Bed, Bedroll, Cot, Dormitory, Fleabag, Kang, Roost
**Sleeping sickness** Trypanosomiasis
**Sleeping tablet** Wobbly egg
**Sleepless** Wake-rife, Wauk-rife
**Sleep-walking** Noctambulation, Somnambulism
**Sleet** Graupel, Hail, Virga
**Sleeve (opening)** Arm(hole), Balloon, Batwing, Bishop's, Bush, Cap, Collet, Cover, Dolman, Gatefold, Gigot, Gland, Kimono, Lawn, Leg-o'-mutton, Liner, Magyar, Manche, Pagoda, Pudding, Querpo, Raglan, Record, Sabot, Scye, Slashed, Trunk, Turnbuckle, Wind
**Sleeveless** Exomis
▸**Sleigh** *see* SLED(GE)
**Sleight** Artifice, Conjury, Cunning, Dodge, Legerdemain, Trick
**Slender(ness)** Asthenic, Ectomorph, Elongate, Exiguity, Exility, Fine, Flagelliform, Flimsy, Gracile, Jimp, Leptosome, Loris, Narrow, Rangy, Skinny, Slight, Slim, Small, Spindly, Stalky, Styloid, Svelte, Swank, Sylph, Tenuous, Thready, Trim, Waif
**Sleuth** Bloodhound, Detective, Dick, Eye, Holmes, Lime-hound, Lyam(-hound), Lyme(-hound), Poirot, Wimsey
**Slew** Number, Skid, Slide, Twist
**Slice** Cantle, Carve, Chip, Collop, Cut, Doorstep, Fade, Fish, Frustrum, Lop, Piece, Rasure, Round, Runner, Sector, Segment, Share, Shave, Sheave, Shive, Slab, Sliver, Spoon, Tranche, Wafer, Whang
▹**Slice of** *may indicate* a hidden word
**Slick(er)** Adroit, City, Glib, Mealy-mouthed, Oil, Sheen, Sleeveen, Smooth, Suave
**Slide** Aquaplane, Bar, Barrette, Chute, Cursor, Diapositive, Drift, Ease, Fader, Flume, Glissage, Glissando, Hair, Hairpin, Helter-skelter, Hirsle, Hollow-ground, Ice-run, Illapse, Lantern, Mount, Portamento, Pulka, Schuss, Scoop, Ski, Skid, Skite, Slew, Slip, Slippery dip, Slither, Snowboard, Spin, Tailskid, Telescope, Transparency, Volplane
**Slight(ly)** Affront, Belittle, Cold shoulder, Cut, Detract, Disparage, Disregard, Disrespect, Elfin, Facer, Flimsy, Fragile, Gaunt, Halfway, Insult, Mere, Minor, Misprise, Neglect, Nominal, Partial, Pet, Petty, Puny, Rebuff, Remote, Scorn, → SLENDER, Slim, Slimsy, Slur, Small, Smattering, Sneaking, Snub, Sparse, Stent, Subtle, Superficial, Sylphine, Tenuous, Thin, Tiny, Trifling, Trivial, Wee, Wispy
**Slim(mer)** Attenuate, Bant, Cut, Diet, Jimp, Lissome, Macerate, Pickings, Reduce, Slender, Slight, Svelte, Sylph, Tenuous, Thin, Trim, Weight-watcher
**Slime (ball), Slimy** Alga, Glair, Glareous, Glit, Gorydew, Guck, Gunk, Mother, Muc(o)us, Myxomycete, Oily, Ooze, Sapropel, Slabbery, Slake, Sludge, Snot, Uliginous
**Sling** Balista, Catapult, Drink, Fling, Hang, Parbuckle, Prusik, Shy, Singapore, Support, Toss, Trebuchet

**Sling(shot)** Catapult, Gin, Throw
**Slink** Lurk, Proll, Prowl, Skulk, Slope
**Slip(ped), Slipping, Slips** Avalanche, Blunder, Boner, Boob, Come home, Coupon, Cover, Cutting, Deteriorate, Disc, Docket, Drift, EE, Elapse, Elt, Engobe, Error, Escape, Faux pas, Fielder, Form, Freudian, Glide, Glissade, Glitch, Infielder, Label, Landslide, Lapse, Lapsus linguae, Lath, Lauwine, Leash, Lingerie, Lingual, Mistake, Muff, Nod, Overbalance, Oversight, Parapraxis, Pass, Pay, Peccadillo, Petticoat, Pink, Plant, Prolapse, Ptosis, Quickset, Rejection, Relapse, Run, Scape, Sc(h)edule, Scoot, Set, Shim, Side, Sin, Ski, Skid, Skin, Skite, Slade, Slidder, Slide, Slither, Slive, Spellican, Spillican, Stumble, Surge, Ticket, Trip, Tunicle, Underskirt, Unleash, Voucher, Wage(s)
**Slipper(s)** Baboosh, Babouche, Babuche, Baffies, Banana skin, Calceolate, Carpet, Chappal, Eel, Errorist, Japanese, Mocassin, Moccasin, Moyl, Muil, Mule, Pabouche, Pampootie, Pantable, Pantof(f)le, Panton, Pantoufle, Pump, Rullion, Runner, Ski, Sledge, Sneaker, Sock
**Slippery** Eely, Elusive, Errorist, Evasive, Foxy, Glid, Icy, Labile, Lubric, Shady, Shifty, Skidpan, Slick, Slimy
**Slipshod** Careless, Haphazard, Hurried, Jerry, Lax, Slapdash, Slatternly, Sloppy, Slovenly, Toboggan
▹**Slipshod** *may indicate* an anagram
**Slit** Buttonhole, Cranny, Cut, Fent, Fissure, Fitchet, Gash, Gill, Loop, Pertus(at)e, Placket, Placket-hole, Race, Rit, Scissure, Spare, Speld(er), Unseam, Vent
**Slithy** Tove
**Sliver** Flake, Fragment, Moslings, Rove, Shard, Shaving, Slice, Splinter, Trace
**Sloan** Snib, Snub
**Slob(ber)** Couch potato, Drool, Lout, Slaver, Smarm, Wet
**Sloe(thorn)** Blackthorn, Slae
**Slog(ger)** Drag, Grind, Logwork, Strike, Swink, Swot, Thump, Traipse, Tramp, Trape, Trauchle, Trudge, Yacker, Yakka, Yakker
**Slogan** Amandla, Battle-cry, Byword, Catchphrase, Catchword, Chant, Cry, Jai Hind, Jingle, Masakhane, Mot(to), Murdabad, Nayword, Phrase, Rallying-cry, Shibboleth, Slughorn(e), Splash, Street cry, Tagline, Warcry, Watchword
**Sloop** Cutter, Hoy, Ship
**Slop(pily), Slops, Sloppy** Careless, Cop(per), Gardyloo, Jordeloo, Lagrimoso, Lowse, Madid, Muck, Mushy, Policeman, Remiss, Rossers, Rozzers, Schmaltz, Schmaltzy, Shower, Slaister, Slapdash, Slipshod, Sloven, Slushy, Sop, Sozzly, Spill, Swill, Syrupy, Unmethodical, Untidy, Weepie
**Slope(s), Sloping** Acclivity, Angle, Anticline, Bahada, Bajada, Bank, Batter, Bevel, Borrow, Borstal(l), Brae, Breast, Camber, Chamfer, Cle(e)ve, Cuesta, Declivity, Delve, Diagonal, Dip, Dry, Escarp, Escarpment, Fastigiate, Fla(u)nch, Foothill, Geanticline, Glacis, Glide, Grade, Gradient, Heel, Hill, Hipped, Ice-contact, Incline, Isoclinical, Kant, Lean, Natural, Nursery, Oblique, Pediment, Pent, Periclinal, Piste, Pitch, Rake, Ramp, Rollway, Scarp, Schuss, Scrae, Scree, Shelve, Sideling, Skewback, Sklent, Slade, Slant, Slippery, Slipway, Splay, Steep, Stoss, Talus, Tilt, Verge, Versant, Weather
▹**Sloppy** *may indicate* an anagram
**Slosh(y)** Dowse, Fist, Spatter, Splash, Wet
**Slot(ted)** Expansion, God, Graveyard, Groove, Hasp, Hesp, Hole, Key, Keyway, Letterbox, Mortice, Mortise, Niche, Riffle, Seat, Slit, Swanmark, Time
**Sloth(ful)** Accidie, Acedia, Ai, Bradypus, Deadly sin, Edentate, Ground, Idle, Inaction, Indolent, Inertia, Lazy, Lie-abed, Megatherium, Mylodon, Slugabed, Sweer(t), Sweered, Sweir(t), Three-toed, Torpor, Unau
**Slot machine** One-armed bandit, Pokey, Pokie
**Slouch** Loll, Lop, Mooch, Mope, Slump
**Slough(ing)** Cast, Despond, Ecdysis, Eschar, Exfoliate, Exuviae, Lerna, Marish, Marsh, Mire, Morass, Paludine, Shed, Shorten, Shuck, Swamp
**Slovakia** .sk
**Sloven(ly)** Careless, Dag(gy), D(r)aggle-tail, Dishevelled, Down-at-heel, Frowsy, Grobian,

Jack-hasty, Mawkin, Rag-doll, Ratbag, Slaister, Slammakin, Slammerkin, Slattern, Sleazy, Slipshod, Slubberdegullion, Slubberingly, Slummock, Slut, Streel, Untidy

**Slow(er), Slow down, Slowing, Slowly, Slowness, Slow-witted** Adagio, Allargando, Andante, Andantino, Behindhand, Brady, Brake, Broad, Calando, Calf, Crawl, Dawdle, Decelerate, Deliberate, Dilatory, Dim, Doddery, Draggy, Dull, Dumka, ESN, Flag, Gradual, Halting, Hesitant, Inchmeal, Insulse, Lag, Lane, Langsam, Languid, Larghetto, Largo, Lash, Lassu, Late, Lean-witted, Leisurely, Lentamente, Lentando, Lento, Lethargy, Lifeless, Loiter, Losing, Meno mosso, Obtuse, Pedetentous, Rall(entando), Recession, Rein, Reluctant, Retard, Ribattuta, Rit, Ritardando, Ritenuto, Roll-out, Slack, Slug, Sluggish, Snail's pace, Snaily, Solid, Stem, Tardigrade, Tardive, Tardy, Tardy-gaited, Thick

**Slowcoach** Slowpoke, Slug

**Slow-match** Portfire

**Sludge** Activated, Goo, Gunge, Mire, Muck, Sapropel, Slime, Slob

**Slug(s)** Ammo, Bêche-de-mer, Blow, Brain, Bullet, Cosh, Draught, Drink, Gast(e)ropod, Grapeshot, Knuckle sandwich, Lead, Limaces, Limax, Linotype®, Mollusc, Nerita, Pellet, Shot, Snail, Tot, Trepang

**Sluggard** Drone, Laggard, Lazy, Lie-abed, Lounger, Lusk, Unau

**Sluggish** Dilatory, Drumble, Idler, Inactive, Inert, Jacent, Lacklustre, Laesie, Languid, Lazy, Leggy, Lentor, Lethargic, Lug, Phlegmatic, Saturnine, Sleepy, → **SLOW**, Stagnant, Tardy, Torpid, Unalive

**Sluice** Aboideau, Aboiteau, Drain, Floodgate, Gutter, Koker, Penstock, Rinse, Sasse

**Slum** Basti, Bustee, Busti, Cabbagetown, Cardboard city, Favela, Ghetto, Rookery, Shanty, Shantytown, Slurb, Warren

**Slumber** Doze, Drowse, Nap, Nod, Sleep, Sloom, Snooze

**Slump** Decline, Decrease, Depression, Deteriorate, Dip, Flop, Loll, Recession, Sag, Sink, Slouch, Sprawl, Stoop

**Slur(ring)** Defame, Drawl, Innuendo, Libel, Ligature, Opprobrium, Slight, Smear, Synaeresis, Tie

**Slush(y)** Bathos, Boodle, Bribe, Drip, Money, Mush, Pap, Slop, Slurry, Snow-broth, Sposh, Swash, Swashy

**Slut** Candle, Dollymop, Draggle-tail, Dratchell, Drazel, Floosie, Harlot, Pucelle, Puzzle, Slattern, Sow, Tart, Traipse, Trapes, Trollop

**Sly, Slyness** Canny, Christopher, Clandestine, Coon, Covert, Cunning, Devious, Foxy, Furtive, Guile, Leery, Peery, Reynard, Secretive, Shifty, Slee, Sleekit, Sleeveen, Slicker, Sneaky, Snide, Stallone, Stealthy, Subtle, Surreptitious, Tinker, Tod, Tricky, Underhand, Weasel, Wily

▷**Slyly** *may indicate* an anagram

**Smack(er)** Aftertaste, Buss, Cuff, Flavour, Foretaste, Fragrance, Hooker, Kiss, Klap, Lander, Lips, Pra(h)u, Relish, Salt, Saut, Skelp, Slap, Slat, Smatch, Smell, Smouch, Soupçon, Spank, Spice, Splat, Tack, → **TANG**, Taste, Thwack, Tincture, Trace, Twang, X, Yawl

**Small (thing), Smaller, Smallest amount** A minori, Ateleiosis, Atom, Bantam, Beady, Beer, Bijou, Bittie, Bitty, Centesimal, Chickenfeed, Chotta, Collops, Crumb, Curn, Denier, Diddy, Diminutive, Dinky, Dreg, Drib, Driblet, Elfin, Elfish, Endomorphic, Few, Fleabite, Fry, Grain, Haet, Ha'it, Half-pint, Handful, Hint, Hobbit, Holding, Hole-in-the-wall, Hyperosmia, Insect, Ion, Itsy-bitsy, Knurl, Leet, Leetle, Lepton, Lilliputian, Limited, Lite, → **LITTLE**, Lock, Low, Meagre, Mean, Measly, Microscopic, Midget, Mignon, Miniature, Minikin, Minority, Minute, Mite, Modest, Modicum, Neap, Nominal, Nurl, Paltry, Party-size, Peerie, Peewee, Petit(e), Petty, Pickle, Pigmean, Pigmy, Pink(ie), Pinky, Pint-size, Pittance, Pocket, Poco, Poky, Poujadist, Puckle, Puny, Rap, Reduction, Runt, S, Scantling, Scattering, Scintilla, Scrump, Scrunt, Scruple, Scut, Shoebox, Shortarse, Shrimp, Single, Skerrick, Slight, Slim, Smattering, Smidge(o)n, Smidgin, Smithereen, Smout, Snippet, Soupçon, Sprinkling, Spud, Squirt, Stim, Stunted, Subminiature, Suspicion, Tad, Teenty, Thin, Tidd(l)y, Tiny, Titch(y), Tittle, Tot(tie), Totty, Trace, Trivial, Unheroic, Wee, Weedy, Whit

**Smallest** Least, Minimal, Runt

**Small-headed** Microcephalic

**Smallholder, Smallholding** Croft, Nursery, Rundale, Share-cropper, Stead

**Small-minded(ness)** Parvanimity, Petty
**Smallness** Exiguity, Exility, Parvanimity, Paucity
**Smallpox** Alastrim, Variola
**Smarm(y)** Oil, Smoothie, Unctuous
**Smart(en), Smartest, Smartness** Ache, Acute, Alec, Astute, Best, Bite, Burn, Chic, Classy, Clever, Cute, Dandy, Dapper, Dressy, Elegant, Flash, Flip, Fly, Groom, Gussy up, Jemmy, Kookie, Kooky, Larnery, Natty, Neat, New pin, Nifty, Nip, Nobby, Outwit, Pac(e)y, Pacy, Pert, Posh, Preen, Primp, Prink, Pusser, Raffish, Rattling, Ritzy, Saucy, Slick, Sly, Smoke, Smug, Snappy, Snazzy, Soigné(e), Spiff, Sprauncy, Sprightly, Spruce, Sprush, Spry, Sting, Street cred, Stylish, Swagger, Sweat, Swish, Tiddley, Tippy, Titivate, Toff, Trendy, U, Well-groomed, Wiseacre, Zippy
**Smash(ed), Smasher, Smashing** Atom, Bingle, Brain, Break, Cannon, Corker, Crush, Demolish, Devastate, Dish, Drunk, Forearm, High, Jarp, Jaup, Kaput, Kill, Lulu, Plastered, Ram, Shatter, Shiver, Slam, Squabash, Squiffy, Stave, Super, Terrific, Tight, To-brake, → WRECK
▷**Smash(ed)** *may indicate* an anagram
**Smear** Anoint, Assoil, Bedaub, Besmirch, Blur, Borm, Calumniate, Cervical, Clam, Daub, Defile, Denigrate, Discredit, Drabble, Enarm, Gaum, Gild, Gorm, Lick, Mud, Oil, Oint, Pap(anicolaou), Pay, Plaster, Slairg, Slaister, Slake, Slander, Slather, Slime, Slubber, Slur, Smalm, Smarm, Smudge, Splodge, Spredd, Sully, Swipe, Teer, Traduce, Wax
**Smell(ing), Smelly** Anosmia, Aroma, Asafoetida, BO, Cacodyl, Caproate, Effluvium, Empyreuma, Exhale, F(o)etid, Fetor, Fug, Funky, Gale, Gamy, Graveolent, Guff, Hing, Honk, Hum, Ionone, Mephitis, Miasm(a), Ming, Musk, Nidor, Niff, Nose, Odour, Olent, Olfact(ory), Osmatic, Osmeterium, Osmic, Perfume, Pong, Ponk, Pooh, Rank, Redolent, Reech, Reek, Ripe, Sar, Savour, → SCENT, Sensory, Skunk, Smack, Sniff, Snifty, Snoke, Snook, Snuff, Steam, Stench, Stifle, Stink, Tang, Whiff
**Smelling salts** Ammonia, Sal volatile
**Smelt(ing)** Atherinidae, Matte, Melt, Salmon, Scoria, Sparling, Speiss, Sperling, Spirling
**Smidgen** Tad
**Smile(s), Smiling, Smily** Agrin, Beam, Cheese, Emoticon, Favour, Gioconda, Grin, Rictus, Samuel, Self-help, Simper, Smirk, Watch the birdie
**Smirk** Grimace, Simper
**Smite, Smitten** Assail, Bash, Enamoured, Epris(e), Hit, Strike, Strook
**Smith** Adam, Artisan, Farrier, FE, Forger, Hammerman, Mighty, Stan, Vulcan, Wayland
**Smithy** Forge, Smiddy, Stithy, Studdie
**Smock** Blouse, Chemise, Drabbet, Gather, Overall, Shift, Slop, Smicket
**Smog** Electronic, Photochemical
**Smoke(r), Smoking, Smoky** Arbroath, Blast, Bloat, Cape, Censer, Chain, Chillum, Chimera, Chimney, → CIGAR(ETTE), Cure, Drag, Earth, Exhaust, Fog, Fuliginous, Fume, Fumigate, Funk, Gasper, Hemp, Incense, Indian hemp, Inhale, Kipper, Latakia, London ivy, Lum, Lunt, Mainstream, Manil(l)a, Nicotian, Opium, Panatella, Passive, Peat reek, Peaty, Pother, Pudder, Puff, Reech, Reefer, Reek, Reest, Roke, Secondary, Sidestream, Smeech, Smeek, Smirting, Smoor, Smother, Smoulder, Smudge, Snout, Tear, Tobacconalian, Toke, Vape, Vapour, Viper, Water, Whiff, Wreath
**Smoke-hating** Misocapnic
**Smokestack** Funnel
**Smoking-room** Divan
**Smollett** Tobias
▶**Smooch** *see* SMOUCH
**Smooth(er), Smoothly** Alabaster, Bald, Bland, Brent, Buff, Cantabile, Chamfer, Clean, Clockwork, Debonair, Dress, Dub, Easy, Equable, Even, Fettle, File, Flat, Fluent, Fretless, Glabrous, Glare, Glass paper, Glassy, Glib, Glissando, Goose, Hairless, Iron, Legato, Level, Levigate, Linish, Lubricate, Mealy-mouthed, Mellifluous, Mellow, Millpond, Oil, Plane, Planish, Plaster, Polished, Pumice, Rake, Rasp, Roll, Rub, Sad-iron, Sand(er), Satiny, Scrape, Segue, Shiny, Silky, Sleek, Sleeveen, Slick, Slickenslide, Slithery, Slur, Smug, Snod, Sostenuto, Straighten, Streamlined, Suave, Swimmingly, Terete, Terse, Trim, Unwrinkled, Urbane

**Smooth-haired** Lissotrichous
**Smother** Blanket, Burke, Choke, Dampen, Muffle, Oppress, Overlie, Smoor, Smore, Smoulder, Stifle, Suppress
**Smouch** Cheat, Kiss, Lallygag, Lollygag, Neck
**Smoulder** Burn, Seethe
**SMS** Text
**Smudge** Blur, Dab, Offset, Slur, Smear, Smooch, Stain
**Smug** Complacent, Conceited, Gloating, Goody-goody, Goody-two-shoes, Neat, Oily, Pi, Sanctimonious, Self-satisfied, Trim
**Smuggle(d), Smuggler, Smuggling** Body-packer, Bootleg, Contraband, Contrabandist, Coyote, Donkey, Drug-runner, Fair trade, Free trader, Gunrunning, Moonshine, Mule, Owler, Rum-runner, Run, Secrete, Sneak, Steal, Traffic
**Smut(ty)** Bawdy, Black, Blight, Blue, Brand, Burnt-ear, Coom, Crock, Filth, Grime, Racy, Soot, Speck, Stinking
**Smut-fungus** Basidia, Ustilago
**Snack** Bever, Bhaji, Bhelpuri, Bite, Blintz, Bombay mix, Breadstick, Breakfast bar, Brunch, Burger, Butty, Canapé, Chack, Cheeseburger, Choc bar, Churro, Crisps, Croque monsieur, Crostini, Crudités, Doner kebab, Elevenses, Enchilada, Entremets, Falafel, Finger buffet, Four-by-two, Gorp, Goujons, Hoagie, Hors (d'oeuvres), Hot dog, Knish, Meze, Munchies, Nacho, Nacket, Nibble, Nigiri, Nocket, Nooning, Nuncheon, Olive, Padkos, Pasty, Paupiette, Peanuts, Pie, Piece, Ploughman's lunch, Popcorn, Pork scratchings, Rarebit, Refreshment, Samo(o)sa, Sandwich, Sarney, Sarnie, Savoury, Scotch egg, Scroggin, Sloppy joe, Small chop, Smorgasbord, Spring roll, Sushi, Tapa, Taste, Toast(y), Trail mix, Vada, Voidee, Vol-au-vent, Wada, Wrap, Zakuska
**Snaffle** Bit, Bridoon, Grab, Purloin
**Snag** Aggro, Anoint, Catch, Contretemps, Disadvantage, Drawback, Glitch, Hindrance, Hitch, Impediment, Knob, Ladder, Limitation, Nog, Obstacle, Problem, Remora, Rub, Snubbe, Stub, Stumbling block, Tear
**Snail(s)** Brian, Cowrie, Cowry, Dew, Dodman, Escargatoire, Escargot, Garden, Gast(e)ropod, Giant African, Heliculture, Helix, Hodmandod, Limnaea, Lymnaea, Mollusc, Nautilus, Nerite, Planorbis, Pond, Ramshorn, Roman, Slow, Slug, Strombus, Unicorn-shell, Univalve, Wallfish, Whelk, Wing
**Snake, Snaking** Drag, Meander, → SERPENT, Slither, Wind

---

### SNAKES

*3 letters:*
Asp
Boa
Kaa
Rat
Sea

*4 letters:*
Apod
Boma
Bull
Corn
Habu
Hoop
King
Milk
Naga
Naia
Naja
Pine
Pipe
Ring
Rock
Sand
Seps
Tree
Whip
Worm

*5 letters:*
Adder
Apode
Blind
Brown
Cobra
Congo
Coral
Cribo
Elaps
Glass
Grass
Green
Hydra
Krait
Mamba
Mulga
Racer
Tiger
Viper
Water

*6 letters:*
Anguis
Carpet
Clotho
Daboia
Dipsas
Dugite
Elaeis
Ellops
Flying
Garter
Gopher
Indigo
Karait
Python
Ratbag
Rattle
Ribbon
Ringed
Smooth
Taipan
Thread
Uraeus
Vasuki

*7 letters:*
Anguine
Camoodi
Coluber

Diamond
Hognose
Langaha
Rattler
Reptile

*8 letters:*
Anaconda
Cerastes
Jararaca
Jararaka
Joe Blake
Lachesis
Mocassin
Moccasin
Ophidian
Pit-viper
Plumber's
Ringhals
Ringneck
Rinkhals
Slowworm
Spitting
Squamata
Sucurujú
Surucucu
Takshaka

*9 letters:*
Berg-adder
Blue-racer
Boomslang
Coachwhip
Hamadryad
Horsewhip
King cobra
Puff-adder
River jack
Sand viper

*10 letters:*
Bandy-bandy
Blacksnake
Bush-master
Copperhead
Crotalidae
Death-adder
Dendrophis
Fer-de-lance
Homorelaps
Massasauga
Sidewinder

*11 letters:*
Aesculapian
Amphisbaena
Constrictor
Cottonmouth
Diamond-back
Horned viper
Hydrophidae
Massasauger

*13 letters:*
Russell's viper
Water moccasin

*17 letters:*
Timber rattlesnake

---

**Snake-charmer** Lamia
**Snake-in-the-grass** Peacher, Rat, Traitor
**Snake-root** Bistort, Senega, Snakeweed, Virginia, White
**Snap(per), Snappy, Snap up** Abrupt, Alligator, Autolycus, Bite, Break, Brittle, Camera, Click, Cold, Cold wave, Crack, Crocodile, Cross, Curt, Edgy, Fillip, Gator, Girnie, Glitch, Glom, Gnash, Grab, Hanch, Impatient, Knacker, Knap, Lensman, Livery, Mugshot, Photo, Photogene, Retort, Scotch, Snack, Snatch, Spell, Still, Swift, Tetchy, Vigour
**Snare** Bait, Benet, Engine, Enmesh, Entrap, Gin, Grin, Honeytrap, Hook, Illaqueate, Inveigle, Mantrap, Mousetrap, Net, Noose, Rat-trap, Springe, Springle, Toil, → TRAP, Trapen, Trepan, Web, Weel, Wire
**Snarl(ing)** Chide, Complicate, Cynic, Enmesh, Girn, Gnar(l), Gnarr, Growl, Grumble, Knar, Knot, Snap, Tangle, Yirr
**Snatch** Claucht, Claught, Excerpt, Fragment, Glom, Grab, Grasp, Kidnap, Nip, Pluck, Race, Ramp, Rap, Rase, Raunch, Refrain, Snippet, Song, Spell, Steal, Strain, Take, Tweak, Wheech, Whip up, Wrap, Wrest
▷**Snatch** *may indicate* the first letter of a word
**Snazzy** Cat
**Snead** Snath
**Sneak(y)** Area, Blab, Carry-tale, Clipe, Clype, Creep, Deceitful, Furtive, Infiltrate, Inform, Lurk, Mumblenews, Nim, Peak, Scratch, Scunge, Skulk, Slink, Slip, Slither, Slyboots, Snitch, Snoop, Split, Steal, Stoolie, Surreptitious, Tell(-tale), Underhand
**Sneer(ing)** Barb, Critic, Cynical, Deride, Fleer, Gibe, Jeer, Sardonic, Scoff, Smirk, Snide, Twitch
**Sneeze (at), Sneezing** A(t)choo, Atishoo, Errhine, Neese, Neeze, Ptarmic, Scorn, Sternutation
**Sneezewort** Yarrow
**Snick** Click, Cut, Edge, Glance
**Snicker** Snigger, Te-hee, Titter, Whinny
**Snide** Bitchy, Shand
**Sniff, Sniffle** E-nose, Inhale, Nose, Nursle, Nuzzle, Scent, Smell, Snivel, Snort, Snuffle, Vent, Whiff
**Snifter** Noggin
**Snigger** Deride, Giggle, Laugh, Snicker, Snirtle, Titter, Whicker
**Snip(pet)** Bargain, Cert, Clip, Cut, Doddle, Piece, Sartor, Snatch, Snick, Tailor
**Snipe(r)** Backbite, Bird, Bushwhacker, Criticise, Dunlin, Franc-tireur, Gunman, Gutter, Heather-bleat(er), Heather-bluiter, Heather-blutter, Pick off, Potshot, Scape, Shoot, Walk, Wisp

**Snitch** Conk, Grass, Konk, Nose, Rat on
**Snivel** Blubber, Snotter, Snuffle, Weep, Whine
**Snob(bery), Snobbish** Cobbler, Crachach, Crispin, Dic(k)ty, Elitist, Genteel, High-hat, Inverted, La-di-da, Prudish, Pseud, Scab, Side, Sloane, Snooty, Snow, Soutar, Souter, Sowter, Toffee-nose, Vain, Vamp
**Snooker, Snooker player** Crucible, Davis, Frame, Pool, Stimie, Stimy, Stym(i)e, Thwart
**Snoop(er)** Curtain-twitcher, Eavesdrop, Gumshoe, Meddle, Nose, Pry, Tec
**Snooty** Bashaw, Pooh Bah, Sanctimonious, Snob(bish)
**Snooze** Calk, Caulk, Dove, Dover, Doze, Nap, Nod, Siesta, Sleep
**Snore, Snoring** Rhonchus, Rout, Snort, Snuffle, Stertorous, Zz
**Snort(er)** Dram, Drink, Grunt, Nare, Nasal, Roncador, Snore, Toot
**Snot(ty)** Mucoid
**Snout** Bill, Boko, Cigar, Gasper, Gruntie, Informer, Muzzle, Nose, Nozzle, Proboscis, Schnozzle, Tinker, Tobacco, Wall
**Snow(y), Snowdrift, Snowstorm** Brig, Buran, Cocaine, Coke, Corn, Cornice, Crud, Firn, Flake, Flurry, Graupel, Half-pipe, Heroin, Horse, Marine, Mogul, Neve, Nival, Niveous, Nivose, Noise, Nose-candy, Oncome, Onding, Powder, Red, Sastruga, Sleet, Spotless, Stall, Virga, Weather, White-out, Wintry, Wreath, Yellow, Zastruga
**Snowball** Accelerate, Cramp-bark, Cumulative, Escalate, Guelder-rose, Increase, Magnify, Opulus, Pelt, Rose
**Snowdrop** Avalanche, Eirlys, Galenthus
**Snowfall** Flurry
**Snowflake(s)** Graupel, Leucojum, St Agnes' flower
**Snow-goose** Wav(e)y
**Snowman** Abominable, Eskimo, Junkie, Sherpa, Yeti
**Snowmobile** Sno-cat
**Snowshoe** Bear paw, Racket, Racquet, Ski
**Snub** Affront, Brush off, Cut, Diss, Go-by, Lop, Pug, Put-down, Quelch, Rebuff, Reproof, Retroussé, Set-down, Short, Slap, Slight, Sloan, Sneap, Snool, Wither
**Snuff(le)** Asarabacca, Douse, Dout, Errhine, Extinguish, Maccabaw, Maccaboy, Maccoboy, Ptarmic, Pulvil, Rappee, Smother, Snaste, Sneesh(an), Sniff, Snift, Snotter, Snush, Stop, Tobacco, Vent
**Snuffbox** Anatomical, Mill, Mull, Ram's horn
**Snug(gery), Snuggle** Burrow, Comfy, Cose, → **COSY**, Couthie, Couthy, Croodle, Cubby(hole), Cuddle, Embrace, Intime, Lion, Neat, Nestle, Nuzzle, Rug, Smooch, Snod, Tight, Trim
**So** Argal, Ergo, Forthy, Hence, Indeed, Nevertheless, Sae, Sic(h), Sol, Such, Then, Therefore, This, Thus, True, Very, Yes
**Soak(ed)** Absorb, Bate, Bath(e), Beath, Bewet, Bloat, Blot, Buck, Cree, Deluge, Drench, Drent, Drink, Drook, Drouk, Drown, Drunk, Duck, Dunk, Embay, Embrue, Fleece, Grog, Imbrue, Impregnate, Infuse, Inundate, Lush, Macerate, Marinate, Mop, Oncome, Permeate, Plastered, Rait, Rate, Ret(t), Rinse, Rob, Saturate, Seep, Sipe, Sog, Sop, Sorb, Souce, Souse, Sows(s)e, Steep, Sype, Thwaite, Toper, Waterlog, Wet, Wino
**Soap(y), Soap opera** Brookside, Cake, Carbolic, Castile, Cleanser, Coronation St, Dallas, Dynasty, Eluate, Emmerdale, ER, Flake, Flannel, Flattery, Glass, Green, Hard, Hollyoaks, Joe, Lather, Lux®, Marine, Metallic, Moody, Mountain, Pears®, Pinguid, Saddle, Safrole, Saponaceous, Saponin, Sawder, Serial, Shaving(-stick), Slime, Soft, Spanish, Suds, Sudser, Sugar, Syndet, Tablet, Tall-oil, Tallow, The Bill, Toheroa, Toilet(ry), Washball, Windsor, Yellow
**Soapstone** French chalk, Spanish chalk, Steatite, Talc
**Soar(ing)** Ascend, Essorant, Fly, Glide, Hilum, Plane, Rise, Rocket, Tower, Zoom
**Sob (stuff)** Blub(ber), Boohoo, Goo, Gulp, Lament, Singult, Singultus, Snotter, Wail, Weep, Yoop
**Sober(sides), Sobriety** Abstemious, Austere, Calm, Demure, Pensive, Sedate, Staid, Staidness, Steady, Steddy, TT
**Sobriquet** Byname, Cognomen, Epithet, Nickname, To-name

**So-called** Alleged, Nominal, Soi-disant
**Soccer** Footer, Footie
**Sociable, Sociability** Affable, Cameraderie, Chummy, Clubby, Cosy, Couthie, Extravert, Extrovert, Folksy, Friendly, Genial, Gregarious, Mixer, Phatic
**Social(ise)** Apres-ski, Barn dance, Convivial, Formal, Hobnob, Hui, Interact, Mingle, Mix, Musicale, Party, Phatic, Salon, Tea-dance, Thé dansant, Yancha
**Socialism, Socialist** Ba'(a)th, Champagne, Chartist, Dergue, Engels, Fabian, Fourierism, Guild, Hardie, ILP, International, Karmathian, Lansbury, Left(y), Loony left, Marxism, Menchevik, Menchevist, Menshevik, National, Nihilism, Owen(ist), Owenite, Parlour pink, Pasok, Pinko, Red, Revisionist, St Simonist, Sandinista, Second international, Spartacist, Utopian, Webb
**Socialite** Deb, It girl, Jet set, Mingler, Silvertail, Sloane
**Social worker** Almoner
**Society** Affluent, Alternative, Association, Band of Hope, Beau monde, Benefit, Black Hand, Body, Boxer, Brahma, Brahmo, Broederbond, Building, Camorra, Carbonari, Casino, Choral, Class, Club, College, Company, Conger, Consumer, Co-op, Cooperative, Culture, Danite, Debating, Defenders, Dorcas, Duddieweans, Eleutheri, Elite, Elks, Fabian, Fashion, Fellowship, Foresters, Freemans, Freemasons, Friendly, Friends, Glee club, Grand monde, Grotian, Group, Guarantee, Guilds, Haut monde, Hetairia, High, High life, Humane, Illuminati, Institute, Invincibles, John Birch, Ku-Klux-Klan, Kyrle, Law, Linnean, Loan, Lodge, Mafia, Malone, Masonic, Mass, Mau-Mau, Ménage, Mensa, Molly Maguire, Mutual admiration, Mutual improvement, National, Oddfellows, Open, Oral, Orangemen, Oratory, Order, Oxford Union, Permissive, Phi Beta Kappa, Plunket, Plural, Pop, Provident, Repertory, Ribbonism, Risk, Rosicrucian, Rotary, Royal, S, Samaj, School, Secret, Soc, Sodality, Somaj, Soroptomist, Sorority, Stakeholder, Surveillance, Tammany Hall, Technopolis, Theosophical, Toc H, Ton, Tong, Triad, U, Whiteboy, World
**Sociologist** Weber
**Sock(s)** Almond, Ankle, Argyle, Argyll, Biff, Bobby, Bootee, Digital, Dipso, Hose(n), Knee, Lam, Leg warmer, Punch, Rock, Slipper, Slosh, Strike, Tabi, Thwack, Trainer, Walk, Wind
**Socket** Acetabulum, Alveole, Bayonet, Budget, Eyepit, Gudgeon, Hollow, Hosel, Hot shoe, Jack, Keeper, Lampholder, Nave, Nozzle, Orbit, Ouch, Outlet, Plug, Pod, Point, Port, Power-point, Screw, Serial port, Shoe, Strike, Torulus, Whip
**Sock-eye** Nerka, Salmon
**Socle** Tube, Zocco(lo)
**Socrates, Socratic** Ironist, Maieutics, Sage
**Sod** Clump, Delf, Delph, Divot, Fail, Gazo(o)n, Grass, Mool, Mould, Mouls, Scraw, Sward, Turf
**Soda, Sodium** Acmite, Arfvedsonite, Baking, Barilla, Bicarb, Caustic, Club, Cream, Keratophyre, La(u)rvikite, Na, Natrium, Natron, Reh, Saleratus, Seltzer, Splash, Thenardite, Trona, Washing
**Sodden** Soggy, Waterlogged
**Sodomy** Vice anglais
**Sofa** Canapé, Chaise longue, Chesterfield, Couch, Daybed, Divan, Dos-à-dos, Dosi-do, Lounge, Ottoman, Settee, Squab, Tête-à-tête
**So far (as)** As, As yet, Quoad, Until, Yonder
**Soft(en), Softener, Softening, Softly** Abbreviate, Amalgam, Anneal, Assuage, B, BB, Blet, Boodle, Calm, Casefy, Cedilla, Cottony, Cree, Cushion, Dim, Dolcemente, Doughy, Ease, Emolliate, Emollient, Flabby, Fluffy, Furry, Gentle, Hooly, Humanise, Intenerate, Lash, Lax, Lenient, Lenition, Limp, Low, Macerate, Malacia, Malax(ate), Malleable, Mardarse, Mardie, Mease, Mellow, Melt, Mild, Milksop, Mitigate, Modify, Modulate, Mollify, Mollities, Morendo, Mulch, Mush(y), Mute, Neale, Nesh, Option, P, Pad(ded), Palliate, Pastel, Piano, Plastic, Plushy, Porous, Propitiate, Quiet, Rait, Rate, Relent, Scumble, Sentimental, Silly, Slack, Soda, Spongy, Squashy, Squidgy, Squishy, Sumph, Talcose, Temper, → TENDER, Tone, Velvet, Weak, Yielding
**Softness** Lenity
▸**Software** *see* COMPUTER PROGRAM(S)
**Sog(gy)** Goop, Sodden

**Soil(ed), Soily** Acid, Adscript, Agrology, Agronomy, Alkali(ne), Alluvium, Azonal, Backfill, Bedraggle, Begrime, Bemire, Beray, Besmirch, Blacken, Chernozem, Clay, Cohesive, Contaminate, Defile, Desecrate, Desert, Dinge, Dirt(y), Discolour, Duricrust, Eard, Earth, Edaphic, Edaphology, Frictional, Gault, Glebe, Grey, Grimy, Ground, Gumbo, Hotbed, Humus, Illuvium, Intrazonal, Lair, Land, Latosol, Lithosol, Loam, Loess, Lome, Loss, Marl, Mire, Mo(u)ld, Mool, Mud, Mulch, Mull, Night, Ordure, Peat, Ped, Pedalfer, Pedocal, Pedogenic, Pedology, Phreatic, Planosol, Podsol, Podzol, Pollute, Prairie, Pure, Regar, Regolith, Regosol, Regur, Rendzina, Rhizosphere, Root-ball, Sal, Sedentary, Smudge, Smut, Solonchak, Solonetz, Solum, Soot, Stain, Stonebrash, Sub, Sully, Taint, Tarnish, Tash, Terrain, Terricolous, Tilth, Top, Tschernosem, Udal, Umber, Virgin, Yarfa, Yarpha, Zonal

**Soirée** Drum, Levee, Musicale

**Sojourn** Abide, Respite, Stay, Tabernacle, Tarry

**Sol** G, Soh, Sun

**Solace** Cheer, Comfort, Relief

**Solar(ium)** Heliacal, Orrery, Tannery

**Sold** Had

**Solder** Braze, Join, Spelter, Tin, Weld

**Soldier(s)** Ant, Bandsman, Chocolate, Detachment, Fighter, Gyrene, Insect, Lance Corporal, Musquetoon, Old Bill, Persevere, Sharpshooter, Unknown, Warmonger

---

## SOLDIERS

*2 letters:*
GI
OR

*3 letters:*
ATS
Bod
Ded
Inf
Joe
NCO
POW
Reb
SAS
Tin
Toy
Vet

*4 letters:*
Army
Corp
Foot
Fyrd
Impi
Jock
Kern
Levy
Line
Merc
Naik
Peon
Post
Rank
Swad

*5 letters:*
Anzac
Bluff
Botha
Brave
Cadet
Choco
Corps
El Cid
Emmet
Fagot
GI Joe
Grunt
Jawan
Kerne
Miles
Miner
Nahal
Nizam
Pandy
Perdu
Poilu
Pongo
Sabre
Sammy
Sepoy
Soger
Sowar
Sweat
Tommy
Turco
Uhlan
Wagon

*6 letters:*
Alpini
Amazon
Arnaut
Askari
Atkins
Banner
Caimac
Chocko
Cohort
Cornet
Detail
Digger
Dugout
Evzone
Faggot
Galoot
Gurkha
Hussar
Knight
Lancer
Nasute
Non-com
Perdue
Rajput
Ranger
Ranker
Reiter
Rutter
Sodger
Swaddy
Tercio
Troops
Yankee
Yeoman
Zouave

*7 letters:*
Arnaout
Brigade
Bullman
Charlie
Chindit
Colonel
Colours
Cossack
Dog-face
Draftee
Dragoon
Enomoty
Federal
Flanker
General
Goorkha
Grim dig
Guardee
Hobbler
Hoplite
Jackman
Lashkar
Lobster
Maniple
Man o' war
Orderly
Palikar
Pandoor
Pandour
Peltast

Phalanx
Pikeman
Platoon
Private
Rat-tail
Redcoat
Regular
Retread
Saddler
Samurai
Sebundy
Snarler
Soldado
Sowaree
Sowarry
Squaddy
Tarheel
Templar
Terrier
Trooper
Vedette
Velites
Veteran
Warrior

***8 letters:***
Achilles
Bluecoat
Borderer
Buff-coat
Caimacam
Centinel
Centonel
Chasseur
Commando
Crusader
Doughboy
Engineer
Fugleman
Fusilier
Greycoat
Guerilla
Immortal
Infantry
Iron Duke
Ironside
Janizary
Kaimakam
Linesman
Martinet
Palatine
Partisan
Piou-piou
Point man
Regiment
Rifleman
Sentinel
Serafile
Silladar
Spearman
Speisade
Squaddie
Stalhelm
Strelitz
Timariot
Trencher
Warhorse
Woodbind
Woodbine
Yardbird

***9 letters:***
Battalion
Blue beret
Butter-nut
Cannoneer
Carbineer
Carbinier
Centinell
Centonell
Centurion
Desert fox
Desert rat
Fencibles
Field-gray
Field-grey
Gregarian
Grenadier
Guardsman
Irregular
Janissary
Johnny Reb
Kitchener
Legionary
Men-at-arms
Mercenary
Minuteman
Missileer
Musketeer
Paratroop
Pistoleer
Rapparree
Reformado
Reservist
Signaller
Subaltern
Targeteer
Train-band
Turcopole
Voltigeur
Volunteer
Whitecoat
Wild Geese

***10 letters:***
Bersaglier
Bombardier
Buff-jerkin
Cameronian
Campaigner
Carabineer
Carabinier
Cataphract
Contingent
Cuirassier
Foederatus
Fortinbras
Galloglass
Green beret
Hackbuteer
Lansquenet
Militiaman
Serviceman
Stalhelmer

***11 letters:***
Bashi-Bazouk
Bersagliere
Confederate
Continental
Forlorn-hope
Gallowglass
Imperialist
Johnny Rebel
Landsknecht
Leatherneck
Legionnaire
Rank and file
Territorial

***12 letters:***
Cannon-fodder
Old moustache
Stormtrooper

***14 letters:***
Miles gloriosus

***16 letters:***
Old Contemptibles

---

▷**Soldiers** *may indicate* bread for boiled eggs

**Sole, Solitaire, Solitary** Alone, Anchoret, Anchorite, Antisocial, Ascetic, Asocial, Clump, Convex, Corporation, Crepe, Dover, Dropped, Eremite, Fish, Friendless, Incommunicado, Independent, Inner, Lemon, Lonesome, Meered, Megrim, Merl, Meunière, Monastical, Monkish, One, On ice, Only, Pad, Palm, Patience, Pegboard, Pelma, Planta(r), Plantigrade, Platform, Recluse, Sand, Scaldfish, Single(ton), Skate, Slip, Smear-dab, Tap, Thenar, Tread, Unique, Vibram®, Vola

**Solemn** Agelast, Austere, Devout, Earnest, Grave, Gravitas, Impressive, Majestic, Owlish, Po-faced, Sacred, Sedate, Serious, Sober, Sobersides, Sombre, Stodgy

**Solent** Lee

**Solicit** Accost, Approach, Ask, Attract, Bash, → **BEG**, Canvass, Commission, Cottage, Court, Drum up, Importun(at)e, Pimp, Plead, Ply, Proposition, Seek, Speer, Speir, Touch, Tout, Woo

**Solicitor(s)** Advocate, Attorney, Avoué, Beggar, Canvasser, Chugger, Courtier, Crown agent, Hallanshaker, Law-agent, Lawyer, Moll, Notary, Official, Side-bar, SL, Tout, Trull, Writer to the Signet, WS

**Solid(arity), Solidify, Solidity** Burly, Cake, Chunky, Clot, Clunky, Compact, Comradeship, Concrete, Cone, Congeal, Conoid, Consolidate, Cube, Cylinder, Decahedron, Dense, Dilitancy, Enneahedron, Esprit de corps, Ethal, Firm, Foursquare, Freeze, Frustrum, Fuchsin(e), Gel, Hard, Holosteric, Impervious, Kotahitanga, Masakhane, Merbromin, Octahedron, Pakka, Parallelepiped, Petrarchan, Platonic, Polyhedron, Prism, Pucka, Pukka, Purin(e), Robust, Rockhewn, Set, Skatole, Square, Squatly, Stable, Staunch, Stereoscopic, Stilbene, Sturdy, Sublimate, Substantial, Tetrahedron, Thick (set), Trusty, Unanimous

**Solipsism** Egotism, Panegoism

▸**Solitary** *see* **SOLE**

**Solitude** Privacy, Seclusion

**Solo(ist)** Aria, Cadenza, Cavatine, Concertante, Lone, Monodrama, Monody, Ombre, One-man, Recit, Scena, Single-handed, Succentor, Unaccompanied, Unaided, Variation

**Solon** Sage

**So long** Cheerio, Ciao, Goodbye, Tata, Toodle pip

**Solstice** Summer, Tropic, Winter

**Soluble** Alkaline, Consolute, Poristic, Surfactant

**Solution** Acetone, Alkali, Ammonia, Amrit, → **ANSWER**, Austenite, Benedict's, Brine, Collodion, Colloidal, Dakin's, Dobell's, Éclaircissement, Electrolyte, Elixir, Emulsion, Eusol, Fehling's, Final, Fix, Formalin, Hairspray, Key, Leachate, Limewater, Liquid, Lixivium, Lye, Magic bullet, Normal, Oleoresin, Oleum, Rationale, Reducer, Remedy, Ringer's, Rinse, Rubber, Saline, Solid, Solvent, Soup, Standard, Suspensoid, Tincture, Titrate, Tone, Viscose

▹**Solution** *may indicate* an anagram

**Solve(d), Solver** Absolve, Assoil, Calculate, Casuist, Clear, Crack, Decode, Holmes, Loast, Loose, Panacea, Read(er), Suss out, Troubleshoot, Unclew, Undo, Unravel, Unriddle, Work

**Solvent** Above water, Acetaldehyde, Acetone, Afloat, Alcahest, Aldol, Alkahest, Anisole, Aqua-regia, Banana oil, Benzene, Chloroform, Cleanser, Cyclohexane, Cyclopentane, Cymene, Decalin, Denaturant, Diluent, Dioxan(e), Eleunt, Eluant, Ether, Funded, Furan, Heptane, Hexane, Ligroin, Megilp, Menstruum, Methanol, Methylal, Naphtha, Nitromethane, Paraldehyde, Pentane, Picoline, Protomic, Pyridine, Sound, Stripper, Terebene, Terpineol, Terts, Tetrachloromethane, Thinner, Thiophen, Toluene, Toluol, Trike, Trilene, Turpentine, White spirit

**Somalia** .so

**Sombre** Dark, Drab, Drear, Dull, Funereal, Gloomy, Grave, Morne, Morose, Solemn, Subfusc, Subfusk, Sullen, Triste

**Some** Any, Arrow, Ary, Certain, Divers, Few, Many, One, Part, Portion, Quota, Sundry, These, They, Wheen

▹**Some** *may indicate* a hidden word

**Somebody** Dignitary, Name, Notable, One, Person, Quidam, Someone, Tuft, → **VIP**

**Somehow** Somegate

▹**Somehow** *may indicate* an anagram

**Somersault** Back-flip, Barani, Catherine wheel, Deltcher, Flip(-flap), Flip-flop, Handspring, Pitchpole, Pitchpoll

**Somerset** Maugham, Protector

**Something** Aliquid, Article, Chattel, Item, Matter, Object, Summat, What, Whatnot

**Sometime(s)** Erstwhile, Ex, Former, Intermittent, Occasional, Off and on, Otherwhiles, Quondam

**Somewhat** Bit, -ish, Mite, Partially, Partly, Poco, Quasi, Quite, Rather, Relatively, Slightly, Summat, To a degree, Wheen

**Somewhere** Somegate

**Somnolence** Drowsiness

**Son** Boy, Descendant, Disciple, Epigon(e), Fils, Fitz, Lad, Lewis, M(a)c, Native, Offspring, Prodigal, Progeny, Scion

**Sonata** Minuet, Moonlight, Trio, Waldstein

**Song** Air, Amoret, Anthem, Antistrophe, Aria, Ariette, Art, Aubade, Ayre, Ballad, Ballant, Ballata, Barcarol(l)e, Belter, Berceuse, Bhajan, Blues, Brindisi, Burden, Burthen, Cabaletta, Calypso, Cancionero, Cantata, Cante hondo, Cante jondo, Canticle, Canticulum, Canticum,

Cantilena, Cantion, Canto fermo, Canzona, Canzone, Canzonet(ta), Carmagnole, Carol, Catch, Cavatina, Chanson(ette), Cha(u)nt, Chantey, Come-all-ye, Conductus, Corn-kister, Corroboree, Cradle, Cycle, Descant, Dirge, Dithyramb, Ditty, Drinking, Duettino, Dynasty, Elegy, Epithalamion, Epithalamium, Fado, Fit, Fitt, Flamenco, Folk, Forebitter, Gaudeamus, Gita, Glee, Gorgia, Gradual, Hillbilly, Hokey-cokey, Hum, Hunting, Hymeneal, Hymn, Internationale, Jug(-jug), Lament, Lay, Lied(er), Lilt, Lullaby, Lyric, Madrigal, Magnificat, Marseillaise, Matin, Melic, Melisma, Melody, Mento, Minnesang, Negro spiritual, Noel, Number, Nunc dimittis, Oat, Octastichon, Paean, Pane, Part, Patter, Penillion, Plain, Plain chant, Plaint, Plantation, Pop, Prick, Prothalamion, Prothalamium, Psalm, Qawwali, Rap, Recitativo, Red Flag, Relish, Rhapsody, Rispetto, Roulade, Roundelay, Rune, Scat, Scolion, Sea-shanty, Secular, Serenade, Shanty, Shosholoza, Siren, Sirvente, Skolion, Solo, Sososholoza, Speech, Spiritual, Stave, Stomper, Strain, Strophe, Swan, Taps, Tenebrae, Theme, Threnody, Title track, Torch, Trill, Tune, Tyrolienne, Vaudeville, Villanella, Volkslied, Waiata, War, Warble, Wassail, Waulking, Yodel, Yodle

**Songbook** Cancionero, Hymnal, Kommersbuch, Libretto, Psalter

**Songsmith, Songwriter** Balladeer, Carmichael, Dowland, Espla, Foster, Kern, Lennon, Lyricist, Minot, Newman, Porter, Sheeran, Simon, Waits, Zappa

**Sonnet** Amoret, Elizabethan, English, Italian, Miltonic, Petrarch(i)an, Shakespearean, Shakespearian, Spenserian

**Sonometer** Monochord

**Soon(er)** Anon, Betimes, Directly, Early days, Enow, Erelong, Imminent, Lief, Nearly, OK, Oklahoma, Presently, Shortly, Tight, Timely, Tit(ely), Tite, Tyte

**Soot(y)** Colly, Coom, Crock, Fuliginous, Gas black, Grime, Lampblack, Smut, Speck

**Soothe(r), Soothing** Accoy, Allay, Anetic, Anodyne, Appease, Assuage, Bucku, Calm, Compose, Console, Demulcent, Dulcet, Ease, Emollient, Honeyed, Irenic, Lenitive, Lull, Mellifluous, Mollify, Obtundent, Pacific, Paregoric, Placate, Poultice, Quell, Relieve, Rock, Stroke

**Soothsayer** Astrologer, Augur, Calchas, Chaldee, Divine, Forecaster, Haruspex, Melampus, Oracle, Picus, Prophet, Pythoness, → SEER, Shipton, Tiresias

**Sop(py)** Appease, Berry, Douceur, Rait, Ret, Salvo, Sashy, Sponge

**Sophist(ic)** Casuist, Choplogic, Elenchic, Quibbler

**Sophisticate(d)** Blasé, Boulevardier, City slicker, Civilised, Classy, Cogniscento, Cosmopolitan, Couth, Cultured, Doctor, High-end, Hi-tech, Patrician, Polished, Refined, Sative, Slicker, Smooth, Suave, Svelte, Urbane, Worldly

▷**Sophoclean** *may indicate* Greek alphabet, etc.

**Sophomore** Semie

**Soporific** Barbiturate, Bromide, Drowsy, Halothane, Hypnotic, Lullaby, Narcotic, Opiate, Seconal, Sedative, Tedious

**Soppiness, Soppy** Maudlin, Salvo, Sashy, Schwärmerei, Sloppy, Slushy, Wet

**Soprano** Caballé, Callas, Castrato, Crespin, Descant, Lehmann, Lind, Patti, Treble

**Sorb** Wend

**Sorbet** Glacé, Water ice

**Sorcerer, Sorceress, Sorcery** Angek(k)ok, Ashipu, Black art, Circe, Conjury, Diablerie, Diabolist, Genie, Hoodoo, Kadaitcha, Kurdaitcha, Lamia, Mage, Magian, Magic(ian), Magus, Medea, Merlin, Morgan le Fay, Mother Shipton, Necromancer, Obi, Pishogue, Prospero, Shaman, Sortilege, Venefic(ious), Voodoo, Warlock, Witch, Witch knot, Wizard

**Sordid** Base, Low-life, Miserable, Rhyparography, Scungy, Seamy, Seedy, Sleazy, Squalid, Vile

**Sore(ly), Sores** Abrasion, Abscess, Anthrax, Bitter, Blain, Blister, Boil, Canker, Chancre, Chap, Chilblain, Cold, Dearnly, Felon, Gall, Impost(h)ume, Ireful, Kibe, Nasty, Noma, Pressure, Quitter, Quittor, Raw, Running, Rupia(s), Saddle, Sair, Sensitive, Shiver, Sitfast, Soft, Surbate, Tassell, Tercel, Ulcer(s), Whitlow, Wound

**Sore throat** Garget, Prunella, Quinsy, Tonsillitis

**Sorghum** Kaoliang, Mabela, Milo

**Sorrel** Common, French, Hetty, Mountain, Oca, Roman, Sheep, Soar(e), Sore, Sourock

**Sorrow(ful)** Affliction, Attrition, Deplore, Despond, Distress, Dole, Dolente, Doloroso,

Dolour, Emotion, Fee-grief, → GRIEF, Lament, Misery, Nepenthe, Ochone, Penance, Pietà, Plaintive, Remorse, Repentance, Rue, Triste, Wae, Waugh, Wirra, Woe, Yoop

**Sorry** Apologetic, Ashamed, Contrite, Eh, Miserable, Oops, Paltry, Penitent, Pitiful, Poor, Regretful, Relent, Rueful, Simple, Soz, Wan, Wretched

▷**Sorry** *may indicate* an anagram

**Sort(ing)** Arrange, Brand, Breed, Category, Character, Classify, Codify, Collate, Drive, Genre, Good, Grade, Ilk, Kidney, → KIND, Nature, Permutation, Pranck(e), Prank, Settle, Sieve, Sift, Species, Stamp, Straighten, Stratify, Stripe, Systemise, Tidy, Triage, Type, Variety

**Sortie** Attack, Foray, Mission, Outfall, Raid, Sally

▶**Sorts** *see* OUT OF SORTS

**SOS** Mayday

**So-so** Average, Indifferent, Mediocre, Middling

**So to speak** Quasi

▷**So to speak** *may indicate* 'sound of'

**Sotto voce** Murmur, Whisper

▶**Soubriquet** *see* SOBRIQUET

**Sough** Rustle, Sigh

**Soul(ful)** Alma, Ame, Anima, Animist, Atman, Ba, Bardo, Bod(y), Brevity, Deep, Entelechy, Eschatology, Essence, Expressive, Heart, Inscape, Ka, Larvae, Lost, Manes, Motown, Object, Person, Pneuma, Psyche, Saul, Shade, Spirit, Traducian, Universal

**Sound(ed), Sounding, Soundness, Sound system** Accurate, Ach-laut, Acoustic, Affricate, Albemarle, Allophone, All there, Alveolar, Amphoric, Apical, Aspirate, Audio, Bay, Beep, Blare, Bleat, Bleep, Blip, Bloop, Blow, Boing, Bong, Bray, Breathed, Cacophony, Chime, Chirl, Chirr(e), Chord, Chug, Clam, Clang, Clank, Clink, Cloop, Clop, Clunk, Compos, Consistent, Continuant, Copper-bottomed, Crump, Dah, Dental, Diphthong, Dit, Dive, Dolby®, Dream, Dub, Dusky, Echo, Eek, Epenthesis, Euphony, Fast, Fathom, Fere, Fettle, Fit, Flap, Flawless, Flow, Foley, Formant, Glide, Good, Hale, Harmonics, Hayle, Healthy, Hearty, Hiccup, Hi-fi, Hiss, Ich-laut, Inlet, Intact, Islay, Jura, Kalmar, Knell, Kyle, Labiodental, Lene, Lo-fi, Long Island, Low, Lucid, Mach, Madrilene, McMurdo, Mersey, Milford, Monophthong, Mouillé, Murmur, Musak, Music, Muzak®, Narrow, Nasal, Nicam, → NOISE, Off-glide, Onomatopoeia, Oompah, Optical, Orate, Orinasal, Orthodox, Palatal, Palato-alveolar, Pamlico, Paragog(u)e, Peal, Pectoriloquy, Pest, Phone(me), Phonetic, Phonic, Phonology, Phut, Pitter(-patter), Plap, Plink, Plonk, Plop, Plosion, Plosive, Plumb, Plummet, Plunk, Plymouth, Probe, Pronounce, Puget, Put-put, Quadraphonic(s), Quadrophonic(s), Rale, Rational, Rat-tat, Real, Reasonable, Reliable, Resonate, Rhythm, Ring, Roach, Robust, Rong, Rumble, Rustle, Sabin, Safe, Sandhi, Sane, Scoresby, Sensurround®, S(c)hwa, Skirl, Solid, Sonance, Sonar, Sondage, Sone, Souffle, Sough, Sowne, Speech, Splat, Stereo, Stereophony, Strait, Stroke, Surround, Swish, Tamber, Tannoy®, Tchick, Tenable, Thorough, Timbre, Ting, Tone, Toneme, Trig, Trill, Triphthong, Trumpet, Twang, Ultrasonic(s), Unharmed, Unscathed, Uvular, Valid, Viable, Voice, Vowel, Wah-wah, Watertight, Well, Whine, Whinny, Whistle, Whole(some), Whoosh, Whump, Wolf

**Sounder** Ballon d'essai, Echo, Lead(sman)

**Sounding board** Abat-voix

**Soundproof** Deaden

**Sound-track** Dubbing, Movietone®, Stripe, Sync

**Soup** Alphabet, Avgolemono, Bird's nest, Bisk, Bisque, Borsch, Bouillabaisse, Bouillon, Brewis, Broth, Burgoo, Cal(l)aloo, Chowder, Cioppino, Clam chowder, Cock-a-leekie, Cockieleekie, Cockyleeky, Consommé, Crab chowder, Cullen skink, Duck, Garbure, Gazpacho, Gomb(r)o, Gruel, Gumbo, Harira, Hoosh, Julienne, Kail, Kale, Laksa, Lokshen, Madrilene, Marmite, Mess, Minestrone, Miso, Mock turtle, Mulligatawny, Oxtail, Palestine, Pea(se), Pho, Pot(t)age, Pot-au-feu, Primordial, Puree, Ramen, Rice, Rubaboo, Sancoche, Scoosh, Scotch broth, Shchi, Shtchi, Skilligalee, Skilligolee, Skilly, Skink, Stock, Tattie-claw, Toheroa, Turtle, Vichyssoise

▷**Soup** *may indicate* an anagram

**Soupçon** Thought, Touch

**Sour(puss)** Acerb, Acescent, Acid, Acidulate, Aigre-deux, Alegar, Bitter, Citric, Crab, Curdle,

Eager, Embitter, Esile, Ferment, Moody, Stingy, Subacid, → TART, Turn, Unamiable, Verjuice, Vinegarish

**Source** Authority, Basis, Bottom, Centre, Closed, Database, Derivation, Egg, Fons, Font, Fount, Fountain-head, Germ, Head-stream, Leak, Literary, Lode, Mine, Mother, Neutron, Origin, Parent, Pi, Pion, Point, Principle, Prot(h)yle, Provenance, Quarry, Reference, Rise, Riverhead, Root, Seat, Seed, Spa, Spring, Springhead, Stock, Supply, Upriver, Urn, Well, Wellhead, Wellspring, Widow's cruse, Ylem

**Sour milk** Curds, Smetana, Whey, Whig, Yogh(o)urt

**Souse** Beath, Duck, Immerse, Marinate, Pickle, Plunge, Soak, Spree, Steep

**South(ern), Southerner** Austral, Confederacy, Decanal, Decani, Deep, Dixieland, Meridian, Meridional, S, Scal(l)awag, Scallywag

**South Africa(n)** Azania, Bantu, Boer, Caper, Ciskei, Grikwa, Griqua, Lebowa, Qwaqwa, SA, Soutie, Springbok, Swahili, Xhosa, ZA, Zulu

**South American** Araucanian, Arawak, Argentino, Aymara, Bolivian, Carib, Chibcha, Chilean, Galibi, Guarani, Inca, Jivaro, Kechua, Latin, Llanero, Mam, Mapuchi, Mayan, Mixe-Zogue, Mixtac, Mochica, Patagonian, Quechua, SA, Shuar, Tapuyan, Tupi

**South-east** Home Counties, Roseland, SE

**Southpaw** Corrie-fisted

**Southwark** Boro'

**Souvenir** Goss, Keepsake, Memento, Relic, Remembrance, Scalp, Token, Trophy

**Sou'wester** Cornishman

**Sovereign(ty), Sovereign remedy** Anne, Autocrat, Bar, Condominium, Couter, Dominant, Emperor, ER, Goblin, Haemony, Harlequin, Imperial, Imperium, James, King, L, Liege, Monarch, Napoleon, Nizam, Peshwa, Pound, Quid, Rangatiratanga, Reign, Royalty, Ruler, Shiner, Sultan, Supreme, Swaraj, Synarchy, The Raj, Thick 'un, Thin 'un

**Soviet** Circassian, Council, Estonian, Russian, Stalin, Supreme, Volost

**Sow(ing)** Catchcrop, Elt, Foment, Gilt, Inseminate, Plant, Scatter, Seed, Sprue, Strew, Yelt

**Soya** Sitosterol, Tempe(h), Tofu

**Spa** Aachen, Baden, Baden-Baden, Bath, Buxton, Ems, Evian, Fat farm, Godesberg, Harrogate, Hydro, Jacuzzi, Kurhaus, Kursaal, Leamington, Malvern, Pump-room, Vichy, Watering place, Wiesbaden

**Space, Spaced (out), Spaceman, Spacing, Spacious, Spatial** Abyss, Acre, Airy, Alley, Antechoir, Area, Areola, Bay, Bedsit, Bolthole, Bracket, Breathing, Bronchus, Catatonic, Cavern, Cellule, C(o)elom(e), Cislunar, Clearing, Cofferdam, Compluvium, Concourse, Contline, Crawl, Crookes, Cubbyhole, Cyber, Daylight, Deducted, Deep, Diastema, Distal, Distance, E-la-mi, Elbow-room, Elliptic, Em, En, Esplanade, Ether, Exergue, Expanse, Extent, Flies, Footprint, Forecourt, Freeband, Gagarin, Gap, Glade, Glenn, Goaf, Gob, Groggy, Gutter, Hair, Hash(mark), Headroom, Hell, Homaloid, Indention, Inner, Intergalactic, Interim, Interlinear, Interplanetary, Interstellar, Interstice, Invader, Kerning, Killogie, Kneehole, Lacuna, Lair, Leading, Lebensraum, Legroom, Life, Lobby, Logie, Lumen, Lunar, Lung, Machicolation, Maidan, Manifold, Manorial, Meat, Metope, Mihrab, Minkowski, Mosh pit, MUD, Muset, Musit, Orbit, Outer, Palatial, Parking, Parvis(e), Peridrome, Personal, Plenum, Polemics, Pomoerium, Priest hole, Proportional, Proxemics, Quad, Retrochoir, Riemannian, → ROOM, Ruelle, Sample, Sheets, Shelf room, Sinus, Slot, Spandrel, Spandril, Sparse, Step, Steric, Storage, Synapse, Third, Topological, Tweendecks, Tympanum, Ullage, Uncluttered, Vacua, Vacuole, Vacuum, Vast, Vector, Virtual, Void, Volume, Well

**Space age** Hi-tech

**Spacecraft, Space agency, Space object, Spaceship, Space station** Apollo, Capsule, Challenger, Columbia, Columbus, Deep Space, Explorer, Galileo, Gemini, Genesis, Giotto, Impactor, Lander, LEM, Luna, Lunik, Mariner, Mercury, MIR, Module, NASA, Orbiter, Pioneer, Probe, Quasar, Ranger, Rocket ship, Salyut, Shuttle, Skylab, Soyuz, Space lab, Sputnik, Starship, Tardis, UFO, Viking, Voskhod, Vostok, Voyager, Zond

**Spacer (plate)** Bead(s)

**Space walk** EVA

**Spade** Breastplough, Caschrom, Cas crom, Castrato, Detective, Flaughter, Graft, Loy, Mole,

Paddle, Paddle staff, Pattle, Peat, Pettle, Pick, S, Shovel, Slane, Spit, Suit, Turf, Tus(h)kar, Tus(h)ker, Twiscar

**Spaghetti** Bolognese

**Spain** E, Hesperia, Iberia, Wean

**Spalpeen** Sinner

**Span** Age, Arch, Attention, Bestride, Bridge, Chip, Ctesiphon, Extent, Life, Memory, Octave, Range, Timescale

**Spangle(d)** Avanturine, Aventurine, Glitter, Instar, O, Paillette, Sequin

**Spaniard, Spanish** Alguacil, Alguazil, Andalusian, Aragonese, Asturian, Balearic, Barrio, Basque, Cab, Caballero, Carlist, Castilian, Catalan, Chicano, Diego, Don, Fly, Galician, Grandee, Hidalgo, Hispanic, José, Lorca, Madrileno, Main, Mestizo, Mozarab, Pablo, Papiamento, Señor

**Spaniel** Blenheim, Cavalier, Clumber, Cocker, Crawler, Creep, Dog, Fawner, Field, Irish water, King Charles, Maltese, Papillon, Placebo, Skip-kennel, Springer, Sussex, Tibetan, Toad-eater, Toady, Toy, Water, Welsh springer

**Spank(ing)** Cob, Paddywhack, Rapid, Scud, Slap, Slipper, Sprack

**Spanner** Aqueduct, Arc, Box, Bridge, Clapper, Key, Monkey wrench, Ring, Shifter, Shifting, Socket, Spider, Torque, Wrench

**Spar** Barite, Barytes, Birefringent, Blue John, Boom, Bowsprit, Box, Cauk, Cawk, Cryolite, Debate, Derbyshire, Fight, Gaff, Heavy, Iceland, Icestone, Jib-boom, Mainyard, Manganese, Martingale, Mast, Mizzenmast, Nail-head, Outrigger, Pearl, Quarrel, Rafter, Rail, Ricker, Satin, Schiller, Shearleg, Sheerleg, Snotter, Spathic, Sprit, Steeve, Stile, Tabular, Triatic, Whiskerboom, Whiskerpole, Yardarm

**Spare, Sparing(ly)** Angular, Ascetic, Cast-off, Dup(licate), Economical, Fifth wheel, Free, Frugal, Galore, Gash, Gaunt, Hain, Lean, Leftover, Lenten, Meagre, Narrow, Other, Pardon, Relieve, Reprieve, Reserve, Rib, Save, Scant, Skimp, Skinny, Slender, Stint, Subsecive, Tape, Thin, Thrifty

**Spark** Animate, Arc, Beau, Blade, Bluette, Dandy, Flash, Flaught, Flicker, Flint, Funk, Ignescent, Ignite, Kindle, Life, Muriel, Quenched, Scintilla, Smoulder, Spunk, Trigger, Vital, Zest

**Sparkle(r), Sparkling** Aerated, Aventurine, Bling, Burnish, Coruscate, Crémant, Diamanté, Effervesce, Élan, Emicate, Fire, Fizz, Flicker, Frizzante, Gassy, Gem, Glamour, Glint, Glisten, Glister, Glitter, Glitz, Life, Patina, Pétillant, Scintillate, Seltzer, Seltzogene, Shimmer, Spangle, Spirited, Spritzig, Spumante, Tingle, Twinkle, Verve, Witty, Zap

**Sparrow** Bird, Cape, Chipping, Hedge, Isaac, Java, Junco, Mah-jong(g), Mossie, Passerine, Piaf, Prunella, Savanna, Song, Spadger, Speug, Sprug(gy), Titling, Tree, Vesper

**Sparrow-grass** Asparagus, Sprue

**Sparse** Meagre, Rare, Scant, Scattered, Thin

**Spartan(s)** Ascetic, Austere, Basic, Enomoty, Hardy, Helot, Heraclid, Lacedaemonian, Laconian, Lysander, Menelaus, Severe, Valiant

**Spasm(s), Spasmodic** Ataxic, Blepharism, Chorea, Clonus, Contraction, Convulsive, Cramp, Crick, Fit(ful), Hiccup, Hippus, Hyperkinesis, Intermittent, Irregular, →JERK, Kink, Laryngismus, Nystagmus, Pang, Paroxysm, Periodical, Start, Strangury, Tetany, Throe, Tonic, Tonus, Trismus, Twinge, Twitch, Vaginismus, Writer's cramp

▷**Spasmodic** *may indicate* an anagram

**Spastic** Athetoid, Clonic, Jerky

**Spat(s)** Altercation, Bicker, Brattle, Gaiters, Legging, Oyster, Quarrel, Scrap, Set to, Shower, Tiff

**Spate** Flood, Garnish, Gush, Sluice, Torrent, Upsurge

▶**Spatial** *see* SPACE

**Spatter** Disject, Ja(u)p, Scatter, Splash, Splosh, Spot, Spray, Sprinkle

▷**Spattered** *may indicate* an anagram

**Spatula** Applicator, Tongue depressor

**Spawn(ed), Spawning (place)** Anadromous, Beget, Blot, Eelfare, Fry, Progeny, Propagate, Redd, Roud, Seed, Shotten, Spat, Spet, Spit

**Spay** Neuter

**Speak(er), Speaking** Address, Ad lib, Articulate, Bang on, Broach, Chat, Cicero, Collocuter, Communicate, Converse, Coo, Declaim, Diction, Dilate, Discourse, Diseur, Dwell, Earphone, Effable, Elocution, Eloquent, Expatiate, Express, Extemporise, Filibuster, Headphone, Intercom, Intone, Inveigh, Jabber, Jaw, Lip, Loq, Loquitur, Management, Mang, Mention, Mike, Mina, Mouth, Mouthpiece, Mumble, Nark, Native, Open, Orate, Orator, Palaver, Parlance, Parley, Perorate, Plain, Pontificate, Prate, Preach, Prelector, Public, Recite, Rhetor, →SAY, Sayne, Soliloquize, Spout, Spruik, Squawk box, Stump, Talk, Tannoy®, Tongue, Trap, Tub-thumper, Tweeter, Utter, Voice, Waffle, Wibble, Windbag, Witter, Woofer, Word

**Speakeasy** Fluent, Shebeen

**Spear** Ash, Asparagus, Assagai, Assegai, Barry, Boar, Dart, Demi-lance, Engore, Fishgig, Fizgig, Gad, Gavelock, Gig, Glaive, Gleave, Gum digger's, Gungnir, Harpoon, Hastate, Impale, Javelin, Lance(gay), Launcegaye, Leister, Morris-pike, Partisan, Pierce, Pike, Pilum, Prong, Skewer, Spike, Trident, Trisul(a), Waster

**Spear-carrier, Spear-thrower** Atlatl, Extra

**Spear-fish** Marlin

**Spearhead** Lead

**Spear-rest** Feutre, Fewter

**Special(ly)** Ad hoc, Constable, Designer, Disparate, Distinctive, Extra, Important, Imposing, Notable, Notanda, Particular, Peculiar, Red-letter, S, Specific, Strong suit, Vestigial

**Specialise, Specialist(s), Speciality** Allergist, Attaché, Authority, Concentrate, Connoisseur, Consultant, ENT, Esoteric, Expert, Field, Forte, Freelance, Illuminati, Internist, Logistician, Maestro, Major, Optometrist, Pomologist, Quant, Recondite, Technician

**Species** Biotype, Class, Darwin, Ecad, Ecotype, Endangered, Genera, Genre, Genus, Indicator, Infima, Kind, Opportunistic, Pioneer, Strain, Taxa

**Specific(ally), Specifical, Specification, Specified, Specify** Adduce, Ad hoc, As, Ascribe, Assign, Bespoke, Concretize, Cure, Define, Designate, Detail, Exact, Explicit, Express(ly), Formula, Full-blown, Given, Itemise, Lay down, Medicine, Namely, Of, Particular, Precise, Quantify, Remedy, Sp, Special, Spell out, State, Stipulate, Stylesheet, The, To wit, Trivial, Vide licit

**Specimen(s)** Archetype, Assay, Example, Exemplar, Imago, Model, Museum piece, Sample, Showpiece, Slide, Swab, Topotype, Type

**Specious** False, Glib, Hollow, Pageant, Plausible, Seeming, Spurious

**Speck, Speckle(d)** Atom, Bit, Dot, Fleck, Floater, Freckle, Gay, Mealy, Mote, Muscae volitantes, Particle, Peep(e), Pip, Smut, Spot, Spreckle, Stud

**Spectacle(s), Spectacled, Spectacular** Arresting, Barnacles, Bifocals, Blazers, Blinks, Bossers, Cheaters, Colourful, Coup, Epic, Escolar, Giglamps, →GLASSES, Goggles, Half-moon, Horn-rims, Light show, Lorgnette, Lorgnon, Meteoric, Nose-nippers, Oo, Optical, Outspeckle, Pageant, Pebble glasses, Phenomenon, Pince-nez, Pomp, Preserves, Raree-show, Resplendent, Rose-coloured, Scene, Show, Sight, Son et lumière, Staggering, Stunt, Sunglasses, Tableau, Tamasha, Tattoo, Trifocal, Varifocals

**Spectate, Spectator(s)** Audience, Bystander, Dedans, Etagère, Eyer, Gallery, Gate, Groundling, Kibitzer, Observer, Onlooker, Passer-by, Ringsider, Standerby, Terrace, Wallflower, Witness

**Spectral, Spectre** Apparition, Bogle, Bogy, Brocken, Eidolon, Empusa, Ghost, Idola, Iridal, Larva, Malmag, Phantasm, Phantom, Phasma, Spirit, Spook, Tarsier, Walking-straw, Wraith

**Spectrograph, Spectrometer** Aston, Calutron

**Spectrum** Absorption, Action, Band, Continuous, Emission, Fission, Iris, Mass, Optical, Radio, Rainbow, Range, Sunbow, Sundog, Visible, X-ray

**Speculate, Speculative, Speculator, Speculation** Academic, Agiotage, Arb(itrage), Assume, Bear, Better, Boursier, Bull, Conjecture, Entrepreneur, Flier, Flyer, Gamble, Guess, Hearsay, Ideology, If, Imagine, Investor, Land-jobber, Meditate, Notional, Operate, Pinhooker, Presume, Raider, Shark, Stag, Theoretical, Theorise, Theory, Thought, Trade, Transcendent, Wonder

**Speech, Speech element** Accents, Address, Argot, Articulation, Bat, Blah, Bunkum, Burr, Curtain, Declamation, Delivery, Dialect, Diatribe, Diction, Direct, Discourse,

Dithyramb, Drawl, Éloge, Eloquence, English, Epilogue, Eulogy, Farewell, Filibuster, Free, Gab, Glossolalia, Grandiloquence, Guttural, Harangue, Helium, Idiolect, Idiom, Inaugural, Indirect, Intonation, Jargon, Keynote, King's, Lallation, → LANGUAGE, Lingua franca, Litany, Logopaedics, Maiden, Monologue, Morph(eme), Motherese, Musar, Oblique, Occlusive, Oral, Oration, Parabasis, Parle, Peroration, Phasis, Philippic, Phonetics, Prolocution, Prolog(ue), Queen's, Rant, Reported, Rhetoric, RP, Sandhi, Say, Scanning, Screed, Sermon, Set, Side, Slang, Soliloquy, Stemwinder, Stump, Tagmeme, Talk, Taxeme, Tirade, Toneme, Tongue, Uptalk, Vach, Verbal, Visible, Voice, Wawa, Whaikorero, Whistle-stop, Xenoglossia

**Speech defect, Speech disease** Alalia, Alogia, Aposiopesis, Dysarthria, Dysphasia, Dysphoria, Echolalia, Halt, Idioglossia, Lallation, Lisp, Palilalia, Paralalia, Paraphasia, Pararthria, Phonasthenia, Psellism, Rhinolalia, Stammer, Stutter, Word salad

**Speechless** Alogia, Dumb(founded), Dumbstruck, Inarticulate, Mute, Obmutescent, Silent, Taciturn, Tongue-tied

**Speech-writer** Logographer

**Speed(ily), Speedster, Speedy** Accelerate, Alacrity, Amain, Amphetamine, ANSI, Apace, ASA, Average, Barrel, Bat, Baud, Belive, Belt, Benzedrine, Breakneck, Burn, C, Career, Cast, Celerity, Chock, Clip, Cruising, Dart, Despatch, Dictation, DIN, Dispatch, Expedite, Fang, Fast, Film, Fleet, Full-fling, Further, Gait, Gallop, Goer, Group, Gun, Hare, Haste, Hie, Hotfoot, Hot-rodder, Hypersonic, Induce, Instantaneous, Knot, Landing, Lick, Mach, Merchant, MPH, → PACE, Pelt, Phase, Pike, Post-haste, Prompt, Pronto, Race, Rapidity, Rate, Rev, RPS, Rush, Scorch, Scud, Scurr, Skirr, Soon, Spank, Split, Streak, Stringendo, Subsonic, Supersonic, Swift, Tach, Tear, Tempo, Teraflop, Ton up, V, Velocity, Ventre à terre, Vroom, Wave, Whid, Whoosh, Wing, Zoom

**Speedwell** Bird's eye, Brooklime, Fluellin, Germander, Veronica

**Spelaean** Troglodyte

**Spelk** Skelf, Splinter

**Spell(ing), Spellbind** Abracadabra, Bewitch, Bout, Burst, Cantrip, Charm, Conjuration, Do, Elf-shoot, Enchantment, Enthrall, Entrance, Fit, Go, Gri(s)-gri(s), Hex, Incantation, Innings, Interval, Jettatura, Juju, Knock, Knur, → MAGIC, Mesmerise, Mojo, Need-fire, Nomic, Open sesame, Orthography, Period, Phase, Philter, Philtre, Phonetic, Pinyin, Relieve, Ride, Romaji, Run, Rune, Scat, Shift, Shot, Signify, Sitting, Snap, Snatch, Sorcery, Sp, Span, Spasm, Splinter, Stint, Stretch, Tack, Term, Time, Tour, Trick, Turn, Voodoo, Weird, Whammy, Wicca, Witchcraft

**Spelling-book** ABC, Grimoire

**Spencer** Bodice, Topcoat, Tracy, Vest

**Spend(er), Spending** Anticipate, Birl, Blow, Blue, Boondoggling, Consume, Deficit, Deplete, Disburse, Exhaust, Extravagant, Fritter, Lash out, Lay out, Live, Outlay, Pass, Pay, Shopaholic, Splash, Splash out, Splurge, Squander, Squandermania, Ware

**Spendthrift** Essex Man, High-roller, Prodigal, Profligate, Profuser, Scattergood, Wastrel

**Spent** All-in, Consumed, Dead (beat), Done, Exhausted, Expended, Gone, Jaded, Stale, Tired, Used, Weak, Weary, Zonked

**Sperm(atocyte), Spermatophyte** Gonocyte, Gossypol, Phanerogam, Seed, Semen

**Spew** Eject, Emit, Gush, Regurgitate, Spit, Vomit

**Sphagnum** Moss, Peat

**Sphere, Spherical** Arena, Armillary, Attraction, Ball, Benthoscope, Blastula, Celestial, Discipline, Earth, Element, Field, Firmament, Globe, Magic, Mound, Orb(it), Planet, Primum mobile, Prolate, Province, Realm, Rotund, Schwarzschild, Theatre, Wheel

**Sphincter** Pylorus

**Sphinx** Criosphinx, Hawk-moth, Oracle, Riddler

**Spice, Spicy** Amomum, Anise, Aniseed, Aryl, Baby, Baltic, Caraway, Cardamom, Cardamon, Cardamum, Cassareep, Cassaripe, Cayenne, Chili powder, Cinnamon, Clove, Clow, Coriander, Cough drop, Cubeb, Cum(m)in, Dash, Devil, Enliven, Galingale, Garam masala, Ginger, Green ginger, Hot, Jerk, Mace, Malaguetta, Marjoram, Masala, Myrrh, Nutmeg, Oregano, Paprika, Peppercorn, Picante, Pimento, Piperic, Piquant, Posh, Risque, Root ginger, Saffron, Salsa verde, Scurrilous, Season, Sexed up, Stacte, Staragen, Star anise, Tamal(e), Tamara, Tansy, Tarragon, Taste, Turmeric, Vanilla, Variety, Vindaloo, Za'atar

**Spick** Dink, Neat, Spike, Tidy
**Spicule** Sclere, Tetract
**Spider(s)** Anancy, Ananse, Arachnid, Aranea, Araneida, Arthrapodal, Attercop, Bird, Black widow, Bobbejaan, Bolas, Cardinal, Cheesemite, Chelicerate, Citigrade, Diadem, Epeira, Epeirid, Ethercap, Ettercap, Funnel-web, Harvest(er), Harvestman, House, Hunting, Huntsman, Jumping, Katipo, Lycosa, Mite, Money, Monkey, Mygale, Orb-weaver, Pan, Phalangid, Podogona, Program, Pycnogonid, Red, Redback, Rest, Ricinulei, Saltigrade, Scorpion, Solifugae, Solpuga, Spinner, Strap, Tarantula, Telary, Trapdoor, Violin, Water, Wolf, Zebra
**Spiderwort** Tradescantia
**Spiel** Patter, Pitch, Spruik
**Spignel** Baldmoney, Meu
**Spigot** Bung, Plug, Tap
**Spike(d)** Adulterate, Barb, Brod, Calk, Calt(h)rop, Chape, Cleat, Cloy, Crampon, Doctor, Ear, Fid, Filopodium, Foil, Gad, Gadling, Goad, Grama, Herissé, Icicle, Impale, Kebab, Lace, Locusta, Marlin(e), Nail, Needle, → PIERCE, Pin, Piton, Point, Pricket, Prong, Puseyite, Raceme, Rod, Sharp, Shod, Skewer, Spadix, Spear, Spicate, Spick, Spicule, Spire, Strobiloid, Surge, Tang, Thorn, Tine
**Spikenard** Ploughman's
**Spile** Soft
**Spill(age)** Divulge, Drop, Fidibus, Jackstraw, Lamplighter, Leakage, Let, Lighter, Overflow, Overset, Pipe-lighter, Reveal, Scail, Scale, Shed, Skail, Slart, Slop, Stillicide, Swatter, Taper, Tumble, Ullage
**Spin(ner), Spinning (wheel)** Aeroplane, Arabian, Arachne, Aswirl, Bielmann, Birl, Camel, Centrifuge, Chark(h)a, Cribellum, Cut, Dance, Day trip, Dextrorse, DJ, Eddy, Eke, Flat, Flax-wrench, Flip, Gimp, Googly, Gymp, Gyrate, Gyre, Gyroscope, Hurl, Isobaric, Isotopic, Jenny, Lachesis, Misrepresent, Mole, Nun, Peg-top, Piecener, Piecer, Pirouette, Pivot, PR, Precess, Prolong, Propaganda, Purl, Reel, Rev(olve), Ride, Romancer, Rotate, Royal, Screw, Side, Sinistrorse, Slant, Slide, Somersault, Spider, Stator, Strobic, Swirl, Swivel, Throstle, Tirl, Top, Toss, Trill, Trundle, Turntable, Twirl, Twist, Wheel, Whirl, Whirligig, Work
**Spinach** Florentine, Orach(e), Popeye, Sa(a)g
**Spinal (cord), Spine(d), Spiny** Acanthoid, Acerose, Acicular, Acromion, Aculeus, Areole, Arête, Backbone, Barb, Chine, Coccyx, Column, Doorn, Dorsal, Epidural, Lumbar, Muricate, Myelon, Notochord, Ocotillo, Prickle, Quill, Rachial, R(h)achis, Ray, Ridge bone, Sea-urchin, Styloid, Thorn, Torso, Tragacanth
**Spindle(-shanks), Spindly** Arbor, Axis, Axle, Bobbin, Capstan, Fusee, Fusiform, Fusil, Mandrel, Mandril, Pin, Scrag, Staff, Triblet
▸**Spine** *see* SPINAL (CORD)
**Spinel** Balas, Picotite, Pleonaste
**Spineless(ness)** Cowardice, Inerm, Invertebrate, Lily-livered, Muticous, Timid, Weak, Wimp, Wishy-washy
**Spinning-wheel** *see* SPIN(NER)
**Spinn(e)y** Coppice, Shaw, Thicket
**Spin-off** By-product, Derivative, Payola
**Spinster** Discovert, Feme sole, Old maid, Tabby
**Spiral** Archimedes, Caracol, Chalaza, Cochlea, Coil, Corkscrew, Curl, Dexiotropic, Dextrorse, Ekman, Genetic, Gyrate, Gyre, Helical, Helix, Hyperbolic, Inflationary, Logarithmic, Loxodromical, Parastichy, Ringlet, Screw, Scroll, Sinistrorse, Spin, Swirl, Tailspin, Turbinate, Turnpike, Twist, Vibrio, Volute, Vortex, Whorl, Wind
**Spire(-shaped)** Broach, Flèche, Peak, Shaft, Steeple, Thyrsoid
**Spirit(s), Spirited** Afreet, Afrit, Animal, Animation, Animus, Ardent, Blithe, Community, Dash, → DRINK, Dulcified, Dutch courage, Élan, Element(al), Emit, Entrain, Essence, Ethereal, Etheric, Ethos, Euphoric, Feisty, Fettle, Fiend, Fight, Free, Game, Gasoline, Geist, Ginger, Gism, Go, Grit, Gumption, Heart, Holy, Hugh, Kindred, → LIQUOR, Lively, Mettle, Morale, Mystique, Nobody, Oversoul, Panache, Pecker, Pep, Presence, Pride, Racy, Rotgut, Scientology, Sloe gin, Soul, Spunk, Steam, Stomach, Team, Temperament, Ton, Verve, Vigour, Vim, Vital, Zing

## SPIRITS

***2 letters:***
Ka

***3 letters:***
Div
Imp
Nis
Nix
Rum
Rye

***4 letters:***
Arak
Bogy
Brio
Cant
Deev
Deva
Feni
Fury
Gamy
Ginn
Grog
Jann
Jinn
Jism
Loki
Mare
Ouzo
Peri
Puck
Raki
Ruin
Salt
Saul
Wili
Wine
Wood

***5 letters:***
Angel
Ariel
Bogey
Bogie
Bogle
Djinn
Dryad
Duppy
Eblis
Fenny
Genie
→GHOST
Ghoul
Huaca
Jinni
Jumby
Kehua
Kelpy
Larva
Lemur
Manes
Marid
Metal
Meths
Mobby
Numen
Party
Peart
Pluck
Pooka
Proof
Rakee
Satyr
Shade
She'ol
Short
Sylph
Tafia
Turps
Vodka
White

***6 letters:***
Arrack
Astral
Brandy
Buggan
Buggin
Cherub
Cognac
Crouse
Daemon
Djinni
Duende
Dybbuk
Empusa
Esprit
Fachan
Faints
Feints
Fetich
Fetish
Geneva
Genius
Grappa
Jinnee
Jumbie
Kelpie
Kirsch
Kobold
Lemure
Manito
Manitu
Metaxa®
Methyl
Mobbie
Numina
Ondine
Orenda
Pernod®
Petrol
Plucky
Pneuma
Potato
Poteen
Psyche
Python
Samshu
Seraph
Shadow
Sprite
Strunt
Tangie
Undine
Voodoo
Wairua
Wraith
Zephon
Zombie

***7 letters:***
Ahriman
Akvavit
Alcohol
Ammonia
Apsaral
Aquavit
Archeus
Asmoday
Banshee
Bitters
Boggart
Bravura
Buggane
Courage
Eidolon
Erl king
Eudemon
Fetiche
Glastig
Gremlin
Gytrash
Incubus
Indwelt
Kachina
Manitou
Mineral
Neutral
Phantom
Rakshas
Samshoo
Shaitan
Smeddum
Spectre
Spright
Taniwha
Tequila

***8 letters:***
Archaeus
Bogeyman
Creature
Erdgeist
Familiar
Hollands
Rakshasa
Schnapps
Surgical
Witblits

***9 letters:***
Applejack
Aqua vitae
Bottle-imp
Domdaniel
Firewater
Hartshorn
Nain rouge
Paraclete
Rectified
Tokoloshe
Weltgeist
Zeitgeist

***10 letters:***
Brollachan
Glendoveer
Methylated
Mindererus
Rumbullion
Turpentine
Water horse

***11 letters:***
Poltergeist
Rosicrucian

***12 letters:***
Agathodaimon
Distillation

***13 letters:***
Crême de menthe

---

**Spiritless** Craven, Dowf, Inanimate, Insipid, Jaded, Languid, Meek, Milksop, Poor, Tame, Vapid
**Spirit-level** Vial
**Spiritual(ism), Spiritualist, Spirituality** Aerie, Aery, Channelling, Ecclesiastic, Ethereous, Eyrie, Eyry, Fey, Incorporeal, Inwardness, Medium, Mystic, Negro, Planchette, Platonic, Psychic, Sacred, Slate-writing, Swedenborg, Table-rapping, Table-turning, Yogi
**Spirt** Gush, Jet, Rush, →SPURT, Squirt
**Spit(ting), Spittle** Bar, Barbecue, Broach, Brochette, Chersonese, Dead ringer, Dribble,

Drool, Emptysis, Eructate, Expectorate, Frog, Fuff, Gob, Golly, Gooby, Goss, Grill, Hawk, Hockle, Impale, Jack, Lookalike, Peninsula, Phlegm, Ras, Ringer, Rotisserie, Saliva, Sandbar, Shish kebab, Skewer, Slag, Spade(ful), Spawl, Spear, Splutter, Sputter, Sputum, Toad, Tombolo, → TONGUE, Yesk, Yex

**Spite(ful)** Backbite, Bitchy, Catty, Grimalkin, Harridan, Ill-natured, Irrespective, Malevolent, Malgrado, Malgré, Malice, Mau(l)gre, Mean, Mischievous, Nasty, Petty, Pique, Rancour, Spleen, Venom, Viperish, Waspish

**Spitfire** Cacafogo, Cacafuego, Hellcat, Plane, Warplane, Wildcat

**Spittoon** Cuspidor(e)

**Spiv** Flash Harry, Lair, Rorter

**Splash** Befoam, Blash, Blue, Cataract, Dabble, Dash, Dog, Drip, Feature, Flouse, Fl(o)ush, Gardyloo, Jabble, Ja(u)p, Jirble, Paddle, Plap, Plop, Plowter, Sket, Slop, Slosh, Slush, Soda, Soss, Sozzle, Spairge, Spat(ter), Spectacle, Splat(ch), Splatter, Splodge, Splosh, Splotch, Spot, Spray, Spree, Squatter, Swash, Swatter, Water, Wet

▷**Splash** *may indicate* an anagram

**Splay(ed)** Curl, Flew, Flue, Patté(e), Spread

**Spleen** Acrimony, Ague-cake, Bite, Lien, Melt, Milt(z), Pip, Stomach, Vitriol, Wrath

**Splendid, Splendour** Ah, Braw, Brilliant, Bully, Capital, Champion, Clinker, Corking, Dandy, Divine, Éclat, Effulgent, Excellent, Fine, Finery, First class, Fulgor, Gallant, Garish, Glitterand, Glittering, Glorious, Glory, Gorgeous, Grand(eur), Grandiose, Ha, Heroic, Hunky-dory, Lavish, Lustrous, Luxury, Magnificent, Majestic, Mooi, Noble, Palatial, Panache, Pomp, Proud, Radiant, Rich, Ripping, Royal, Stunning, Sumptuous, Super(b), Superduper, Tophole, Wally, Zia

**Splice(d)** Braid, Eye, Join, Knit, Mainbrace, Married, Wed

▷**Spliced** *may indicate* an anagram

**Splint** Air, Airplane, Banjo, Brace, Cal(l)iper, Splenial, Stent, T

**Splinter(s)** Bone-setter, Breakaway, Flake, Flinder, Fragment, Matchwood, Shatter, Shiver, Skelf, Sliver, Spale, Spall, Spalt, Speel, Spelk, Spell, Spicula, Spill

**Split(ting), Splitter** Areolate, Axe, Banana, Bifid, Bifurcate, Bisect, Breach, Break, Broach, Burst, Chasm, Chine, Chop, Chorism, Cleave, Cleft, Clint, Clove(n), Crack, Crevasse, Cut, Decamp, Departmentalise, Disjoin, Distrix, Disunite, → DIVIDE, Division, Divorce, Divvy, End, Estrange, Fissile, Fissure, Flake, Fork(ed), Fragment, Grass, Headache, Lacerate, Left, Leg it, Maul, Optical, Partition, Red(d), Rift(e), Rip, Rive, Rupture, Russian, Ryve, Schism, Scissor, Segment, Segregate, Separate, Septemfid, Sever, Share, Skive, Slit, Sliver, Spall, Spalt, Speld, Spring, Tattle, Tmesis, Told, To-rend, To-tear, Trifurcate, Vamoose, Wedge, Xerochasy

▷**Split** *may indicate* a word to become two; one word inside another; or a connection with Croatia (or the former Yugoslavia)

**Splodge, Splotch** Blob, Blot, Drop, Speckle, Splash

**Splurge** Binge, Indulge, Lavish, Spend, Splash, Spree

**Splutter** Chug, Cough, Expectorate, Fizz, Gutter, Spray, Stammer

**Spode** Roderick

**Spoil(s), Spoiler, Spoilt** Addle, Agrise, Agrize, Agryze, Air dam, Blight, Blunk, Booty, Botch, Bribe, Coddle, Contaminate, Corrupt, Crool, → DAMAGE, Dampen, Deface, Defect, Defile, Deform, Disfigure, Dish, Disrupt, Disturb, Fairing, Feather-bed, Foul, Gum, Hames, Harm, Impair(ed), Impoverish, Indulge, Kibosh, Loot, Maderise, Maim, Maltreat, Mar, Mardy, Mollycoddle, Muck, Mutilate, Mux, Pamper, Party pooper, Pet, Pickings, Pie, Pillage, Plunder, Prejudicate, Prize, Queer, Rait, Rate, Ravage, Reif, Ret, Rot, Ruin, Screw up, Scupper, Spoon-fed, Spuly(i)e, Swag, Taint, Tarnish, Turn, Vitiate, Wanton, Winnings, Wreck

▷**Spoil(ed), Spoilt** *may indicate* an anagram

**Spoilsport** Damper, Killjoy, Marsport, Meddler, Party pooper, Wet blanket, Wowser

**Spoke(s)** Concentric, Radius, Ray, Rung, Said, Sed, Strut

**Spoken** Dixi, Said, Vocal

▷**Spoken** *may indicate* the sound of a word or letter

**Spokesman** Foreman, Mouthpiece, Orator, Prolocutor, Prophet, Representative, Wheelwright

**Spoliation, Spoliative** Devastation, Pillage, Plunder, Predatory, Reif

**Sponge(r), Spongy** Alcoholic, Ambatch, Angel cake, Argentine, Battenburg, Bloodsucker, Bum, Cadge, → CAKE, Cleanse, Diact, Diploe, Fozy, Free-loader, Glass-rope, Hanger-on, Hexact, Hyalonema, Leech, Lig, Lithistid(a), Loofa(h), Madeira, Madeleine, Mermaid's glove, Mooch, Mop, Mouch, Mump, Parasite, Parazoa, Pentact, Platinum, Poachy, Porifera(n), Porous, Quandong, Rhabdus, Rum baba, Sarcenchyme, Scambler, Schnorrer, Scrounge, Shark, Shool(e), Shule, Siphonophora, Smell-feast, Soft, Sooner, Sop, Sucker, Swab, Sweetbriar, Sycophant, Tectratine, Tetract, Tetraxon, Tiramisu, Tylote, Vegetable, Velamen, Venus's flowerbasket, Wangle, Wipe, Zimocca, Zoophyte

**Spongewood** Sola

**Sponsor(ship)** Aegis, Angel, Auspice, Backer, Bankroll, Egis, Finance, Godfather, Godparent, Gossip, Guarantor, Lady Bountiful, Lyceum, Patron, Surety, Undertaker

**Spontaneous** Ad hoc, Ad lib, Aleatoric, Autonomic, Exergonic, Free, Gratuitous, Immediate, Impromptu, Improvised, Impulsive, Instant, Intuitive, Lightning, Natural, Off-the-cuff, Ultroneus, Unasked, Unbidden, Unpremeditated, Unprompted, Unrehearsed, Untaught

**Spoof** Chouse, Cozenage, Deception, Delusion, Fallacy, → HOAX, Imposture, Ramp, Send-up, Swindle, Trick

**Spook(s), Spooky** CIA, Eerie, Fantom, Frightening, Ghost, Haunted, Mysterious, Phantom, Shade, Spectral, Uncanny, Weird

**Spool** Bobbin, Capstan, Pirn, Reel, Spit, Trundle

**Spoon(ful), Spoon-shaped** Apostle, Canoodle, Cochlear, Deflagrating, Dollop, Dose, Egg, Eucharistic, Gibby, Greasy, Horn, Labis, Ladle, Measuring, Mote, Neck, Rat-tail, Runcible, Salt, Scoop, Scud, Server, Snuff, Sowp, Spatula, Stir, Sucket, Trolling, Trout, Woo, Wooden

**Spoonerism** Marrowsky, Metathesis

**Spoor** Trace, Track, Trail

**Sporadic** Episodic, Fitful, Isolated, Occasional, Patchy

**Spore(s), Spore case** Asexual, Conidium, Ex(t)ine, Fern-seed, Fungus, Glomerule, Lenticel, Palynology, Pollen, Resting, Seed, Sexual, Sorus, Spreathed, Telium, Uredinium

**Sporran** Pock

**Sport(ing), Sportive, Sports, Sporty** Amusement, Bet, Blood, Breakaway, Brick, By-form, Contact, Daff, Dalliance, Dally, Demonstration, Deviant, Extreme, Field, Freak, Frisky, Frolic, Fun, → GAME, Gent, Good egg, Hearty, In, Joke, Laik, Lake, Lark, Merimake, Merry, Morph, Mutagen, Nautics, Pal, Pastime, Recreate, Rogue, Rules, Shikar, Spectator, Superbowl, Tournament, Tourney, Toy, Wear, Winter

---

## SPORTS

*2 letters:*
PE
RU

*3 letters:*
Gig

*4 letters:*
Polo
Sumo

*5 letters:*
Basho
Fives
Kendo

*6 letters:*
Aikido
Diving
Hockey
Karate
NASCAR®
Pelota
Shinny
Shinty
Squash
Tennis

*7 letters:*
Angling
Archery
Camogie
Curling
Fencing
Hurling
Netball
Parkour
Putting
Rackets
Rafting
Shot put
Skating
Snooker
Surfing
Tailing

*8 letters:*
Aquatics
Ballgame
Bonspiel
Climbing
Dressage
Eventing
Handball
Korfball
Lacrosse
Langlauf
Natation
Octopush
Ringette
Skipping
Softball
Speedway
Swoffing

*9 letters:*
Abseiling
Athletics
Autocross
Autopoint
Canyoning
Ice hockey

Motocross
Potholing
Skijoring
Ski-kiting
Ski-towing
Skydiving
Speedball
Twitching
Wargaming
Water polo
Wrestling

***10 letters:***
Cyclo-cross
Drag-racing
Flat-racing
Heli-skiing
Kickboxing
Monoskiing
Pace-egging
Pancratium
Parakiting
Paraskiing
Rallycross
Real tennis
Rugby Union
Sky-jumping
Sky-surfing
Street luge
Volleyball

***11 letters:***
Bear-baiting
Bicycle polo
Coasteering
Fell-running
Fell walking
Free running
Hang-gliding
Kite-surfing
Paragliding
Paralympics
Parapenting
Parasailing
Race-walking
Rugby League
Scuba-diving
Showjumping
Snorkelling
Table tennis
Tent-pegging
Tombstoning
Truck racing
Water-skiing
Windsurfing

***12 letters:***
Bar billiards
Boardsailing
Cross country
Eton wall game
Heli-boarding
Kite-boarding
Landboarding
Orienteering
Parascending
River bugging
Sailboarding
Snowboarding
Speed-skating
Steeplechase
Tag-wrestling
Trampolining
Trapshooting
Wakeboarding

***13 letters:***
Bungee-jumping
Prizefighting
Skeet Shooting
Ten-pin bowling
Weightlifting

***15 letters:***
Extreme fighting

***16 letters:***
Ultimate fighting

***17 letters:***
Whitewater rafting

***18 letters:***
White-water canoeing

---

▹**Sport(s)** *may indicate* an anagram

**Sports ground** Anfield, Astrodome, Ballpark, Rec, Stadium, Twickenham

**Sportsman, Sportsmen** All-rounder, Amateur, Athlete, Blue, Corinthian, Decathlete, Defender, Half-blue, Hunter, Nimrod, Pentathlete, Pitcher, Rower, Shamateur, Shikaree, Shikari, Shot putter, Showjumper, Springbok, Varment, Varmint, Wrestler

**Sportswear** Gie, Shell suit, Wet suit

**Spot(s), Spotted, Spotter, Spotting, Spotty** Ace, Acne, Anthelion, Area, Areola, Areole, Baily's beads, Bausond, Bead, Beauty, Befoul, Bespatter, Birthmark, Blackhead, Blain, Blemish, Blind, Blip, Blister, Blob, Blot, Blotch(ed), Blur, Brind(l)ed, Café-au-lait, Carbuncle, Caruncle, Cash, Check, Cicatrice, Cloud, Colon, Comedo, Coral, Corner, Curn, Cyst, Dalmatian, Dance, Dapple(-bay), Defect, Descry, Detect, Dick, Dilemma, Discern, Discover, Dot, Drop, Eruption, Espy, Eye, Facula, Fenestra, Flat, Flaw, Fleck, Floater, Flyspeck, Fogdog, Foxed, Freak, Freckle, Furuncle, G, Gay, Glimpse, Gout, Gräfenberg, Gricer, Guttate, High, Hot, Identify, Iron mole, Iron mould, Jam, Leaf, Lentigo, Leopard, Light, Little, Liver, Locale, Location, Loran, Low, Mackle, Macle, Macul(at)e, Mail, Meal, Measly, Microdot, Milium, Moil, Mole, Morbilli, Mote, Motty, Muscae volitantes, Naevoid, Naevus, Nightclub, Note, Notice, Ocellar, Ocellus, Paca, Papule, Paraselene, Pardal, Parhelion, Patch, Peep(e), Penalty, Perceive, Performance, Petechia, Pied, Pimple, Pin, Pip, Place, Plague, Plight, Plook, Plot, Plouk, Pock, Point, Poxy, Predicament, Punctuate, Pupil, Pustule, Quat, Radar, Rash, Recognise, Red, Rose-drop, Rubella, Scene, Scotoma, Scout, Sight, Situation, Skewbald, Smut, Soft, Soil, Speck(le), Speculum, Splodge, Splotch, Spoil, Spy, Stigma, Sully, Sun, Sweet, Taint, Tar, Tarnish, Tight, Touch, Trace, Trouble, Venue, Weak, Whelk, Whitehead, Witness, Woodpecker, X, Yellow, Zit

**Spotless** Clean, Immaculate, Pristine, Spick and span, Unbruised, Virginal

**Spotlight** Ace, Baby, Bon-bon, Brute, Foreground, Maxi-brute

**Spot on** Exact, To a t

**Spouse** Better half, Companion, Consort, Dutch, Feare, Feer, F(i)ere, Hubby, Husband, Mate, Oppo, Other half, Partner, Pheer, Pirrauru, Significant other, Wife, Xant(h)ippe

**Spout(er)** Adjutage, Downpipe, Drainpipe, Erupt, Gargoyle, Geyser, Grampus, Gush, Impawn, Jet, Mouth, Nozzle, Orate, Parrot, Pawn, Pourer, Raile, Rote, Spurt, Stream, Stroup, Talk, Tap, Vent

**Sprain(ed)** Crick, Rax, Reckan, Rick, Stave, Strain, Wrench, Wrick
**Sprat** Brit, Fish, Garvie, Garvock
**Sprawl** Conurbation, Grabble, Loll, Scamble, Spraddle, Sprangle, Spread, Stretch, Urban
**Spray** Aerosol, Aigrette, Airbrush, Antiperspirant, Atomiser, Bespatter, Blanket, Bouquet, Buttonhole, Chap, Corsage, Cyme, Egret, Fly, Hair, Jet, Mace®, Nasal, Nebuliser, Perse, Pesticide, Posy, Rose, Rosula, Scatter, Shower, Sparge, Spatter, Spindrift, Splash, Spoondrift, Sprent, Sprig, Sprinkle, Spritz, Strinkle, Syringe, Twig, Wet
▷**Spray** *may indicate* an anagram
**Spread(ing), Spreader** Air, Apply, Banquet, Bestrew, Beurre, Bid offer, Blow-out, Branch, Bush, Butter, Carpet, Centre, Circumfuse, Contagious, Couch, Coverlet, Coverlid, Deploy, Diffract, Diffuse, Dilate, Disperse, Dissemination, Dissipate, Distribute, Divulge, Double, Double-page, Drape, Dripping, Effuse, Elongate, Emanate, Engarland, Expand, Extend, Fan, Feast, Flare, Guac(h)amole, Honeycomb, Infect, Jam, Lay, Mantle, Margarine, Marge, Marmalade, Marmite®, Meal, Metastasis, Middle-age(d), Multiply, Mushroom, Nutter, Oleo, Open, Overgrow, Palliate, Paste, Pâté, Patent, Patté, Patulous, Perfuse, Pervade, Picnic, Pour, Proliferate, Propagate, Radiant, Radiate, Rampant, Ran, Ranch, Run, Scale, Scatter, Sea-floor, Set, Sheet, Slather, Smear, Smörgåsbord, Sow, Span, Speld, Spelder, Spillover, Splay, Sprawl, Spray, Straddle, Straw, Stretch, Strew, Strow, Suffuse, Swell, Systemic, Tath, TED, Teer, Unfold, Unfurl, Unguent, Unroll, Vegemite®, Viral, Widen, Wildfire
▷**Spread** *may indicate* an anagram
**Spree** Bat, Batter, Beano, Bender, Binge, Blow-out, Bum, Bust, Buster, Carousal, Frolic, Gilravage, Jag, Jamboree, Juncate, Junket, Lark, Loose, Orgy, Randan, Rantan, Razzle(-dazzle), Revel, Rouse, Skite, Skyte, Splore, Tear, Ups(e)y
**Sprig** Brad, Branch, Cion, Cyme, Floret, Nail, Scion, Shoot, Sien, Sient, Spray, Syen, Twig, Youth
**Sprightly, Sprightliness** Active, Agile, Airy, Chipper, Elfin, Esprit, Gallus, Jaunty, Mercurial, Pip, Sprack
**Spring(s), Springtime, Springy** Aganippe, Air, Alice, Arise, Axel, Black smoker, Bolt, Bounce, Bound, Box, Bunt, Cabriole, Caper, Capriole, Castalian, Cavort, Cee, Coil, Dance, Elastic, Emanate, Eye, Fount(ain), Free, Gambado, Germinate, Geyser, Grass, Hair, Helix, Hippocrene, Hop, Hot, Jeté, Jump, Leaf, Leap, Lent, Lep, Litt, Lollop, Low-water, Main, May, Mineral, Oasis, Originate, Persephone, Pierian, Pounce, Prance, Primavera, Prime, Rebound, Recoil, Resilient, Ribbon, Rise, Saddle, Salt, Season, Skip, Snap, Source, Spa, Spang, Spaw, Start, Stem, Stot, Submarine, Sulphur, Summer, Suspension, Teal, Thermae, Thermal, Trampoline, Valve, Vault, Vaute, Vawte, Vernal, Voar, Ware, Watch, Waterhole, Weeping, Well(-head), Well up, Whip, Winterbourne
▷**Spring(y)** *may indicate* an anagram
**Springbok** Amabokoboko
**Springless** Telega
**Springtail** Apterygota
**Sprinkle(r), Sprinkling** Asperge, Aspergill(um), Bedash, Bedew, Bedrop, Bescatter, Caster, Disponge, Dispunge, Dredge, Dust, Hyssop, Lard, Pepper, Pouncet, Powder, Rose, Scatter, Scouthering, Shower, Sift, Sow, Spa(i)rge, Spatter, Splash, Spray, Spritz, Strinkle
**Sprint(er)** Burst, Dash, Gallop, Race, Rash, Run, Rush, Scurry, Wells
**Sprite** Apsaras, Ariel, Banshee, Croquemitaine, Dobbie, Dobby, Echo, Elf, Fairy, Fiend, Genie, Gnome, Goblin, Gremlin, Hobgoblin, Icon, Kelpie, Kelpy, Nickel, Nis(se), Nymph, Oberon, Ondine, Puck, Pug, Spirit, Troll, Trow, Umbriel, Undine
**Sprocket** Jaded, Whelp
**Sprog** Kid
**Sprout** Bean, Braird, Breer, Brussels, Bud, Burgeon, Chit, Crop, Eye, Germ(inate), Grow, Pullulate, Shoot, Spire, Tendron, Vegetate
**Spruce** Balsam, Bedeck, Dapper, Engelmann, Hemlock, Natty, Neat, Nifty, Norway, Picea, Pitch-tree, Prink, Refresh, Shipshape, Sitka, Smart, Snazzy, Spiff, Tidy, Tree, Trim, Tsuga, White
**Spry** Active, Agile, Constance, Dapper, Nimble, Volable

**Spud** Murphy, Potato, Spade, Tater, Tatie
**Spume** Eject, Foam, Froth, Lather, Spet, Spit
**Spunk** Courage, Grit, Pluck, Spark, Tinder
**Spur(s)** Accourage, Activate, Aphrodisiac, Bone, Calcar(ate), Encourage, Fame, Fire, Fuel, Galvanise, Gee, Gilded, Goad, Groyne, Heel, Impel, Incite, Limb, Lye, Needle, Offset, Prick, Prod, Prong, Rippon, Rowel, Shoot, Spica, Stimulus, Strut, Stud, Tar, Urge
**Spurge (tree)** Candelilla, Croton, Euphorbia, Kamala, Manihot, Poinsettia, Ricinus
**Spurious** Adulterine, All-to, Al-to, Apocryphal, Bogus, Counterfeit, Dog, Ersatz, Fake, False, Phoney, Pseudo, Sciolism, Supposititious, Untrue
▷**Spurious** *may indicate* an anagram
**Spurn** Despise, Disdain, Eschew, Ignore, Jilt, Leper, Rebuff, Reject, Repudiate, Repulse, →SCORN, Sdayn, Shun, Snub
**Spurrey** Yarr
**Spurt** Burst, Forge, Fountain, Geyser, Jet, Outburst, Pump, Spout, Start
**Sputter** Bespit, Fizzle, Spit, Splutter, Stutter
**Spy(ing), Spies** Agent, Beagle, Blunt, Bond, Burgess, Caleb, CIA, Cicero, Curtain-twitcher, Descry, Dicker, Double agent, Eavesdrop, Emissary, Espionage, Fink, Fuchs, Infiltrate, Informer, Keeker, Maclean, Mata Hari, MI, Mole, Mossad, Mouchard, Nark, Ninja, Nose, Operative, Pickeer, Pimp, Plant, Pry, Recce, Scout, See, Setter, Shadow, Sinon, Sleeper, Snoop, Spetsnaz, Spook, Tachometer, Tarpeia, Tout, Voyeur, Wait
**Spyhole** Eyelet, Judas-hole, Oillet, Peephole
**Squab** Chubby, Cushion, Obese
**Squabble** Argue, Bicker, Brabble, Quarrel, Rhubarb, Rift, Row, Scene, Scrap, Spar, Tiff
**Squad(ron)** Awkward, Band, Blue, Bomb, Company, Crew, Death, Decury, Drugs, Escadrille, Fifteen, Firing, Flying, Force, Fraud, Hit, Nahal, Platoon, Porn, Red, Snatch, Vice, White, Wing, Yardie
**Squaddie** Private
**Squalid, Squalor** Abject, Colluvies, Dickensian, Dinge, Dingy, Filth, Frowsy, Grungy, Mean, Poverty, Scuzzy, Seedy, Skid Row, Sleazy, Slum(my), Slurb, Sordid
**Squall** Blast, Blow, Chubasco, Commotion, Cry, Drow, Flaw, Flurry, Gale, Gust, Line, Rainstorm, Sumatra, Wail, White, Williwaw, Yell, Yowl
**Squander** Blow, Blue, Dissipate, Fritter, Frivol, Lamb down, Lash, Misspend, Mucker, Scamble, Slather, Splash, Splurge, Ware, →WASTE
**Square(d), Squares** Agree, Anta, Arrièré, Ashlar, Ashler, Bandanna, Bang, Barrack, Belgrave, Berkeley, Bevel, Block, Boxy, Bribe, Chequer, Compone, Compony, Corny, Cube, Deal, Dinkum, Dodo, Even(s), Fair, Fog(e)y, Forty-nine, Fossil, Four, Gobony, Grey, Grosvenor, Latin, Least, Leicester, Level, Madison, Magic, Market, Meal, Mean, Mitre, Nasik, Neandert(h)aler, Nine, Norma, Old-fashioned, Old school, Old-time, Out, Palm, Passé, Pay, Perfect, Piazza, Place, Platz, Plaza, Quad(rangle), Quadrate, Quarry, Quits, Red, Rhomboid, Rood, S, Set(t), Settle, Sloane, Solid, Squier, Squire, Stick-in-the-mud, Straight, T, Tee, Tiananmen, Times, Traditionalist, Trafalgar, Try, Uncool, Unhip
**Square-rigger** Tall ship
**Squash(y)** Adpress, Butternut, Conglomerate, Crush, Flatten, Gourd, Kia-ora®, Knead, Lemon, Marrow, Mash, Obcompress, Oblate, Orange, Pattypan, Press, Pulp, Pumpkin, Rebut, Shoehorn, Silence, Slay, Slew, Slue, Soft, Squeeze, Squidge, Squidgy, Summer, Suppress, Torpedo, Winter
**Squat(ter), Squatting** Bywoner, Caganer, Crouch, Croup(e), Cubby, Dumpy, Fubby, Fubsy, Hunker, Inquilinism, Occupy, Pudsey, Pyknic, Rook, Ruck, Sawed off, Sit, Spud, Squabby, Stocky, Stubby, Stumpy, Swatter, Thickset, Tubby, Usucaption
**Squawk** Cackle, Complain, Cry, Scrauch, Scraugh
**Squeak(er)** Cheep, Close call, Creak, Narrow, Near, Peep, Pip, Scroop, Shoat, Squeal
**Squeal(er)** Blow, Creak, Eek, Howl, Inform, Peach, Pig, Screech, Sing, Sneak, Tell, Wee, Yelp
**Squeamish(ness)** Delicate, Disgust, Mealy-mouthed, Missish, Nervous, Prudish, Queasy, Reluctant
**Squeeze(r)** Bleed, Chirt, Clench, Coll, Compress, Concertina, Constrict, Cram, Cramp,

Credit, Crowd, Crush, Dispunge, Embrace, Exact, Express, Extort, Extrude, Hug, Jam, Lemon, Mangle, Milk, Nip, Pack, Preace, Press, Reamer, Sandwich, Sap, Scrooge, Scrouge, Scrowdge, Scruze, Shoehorn, Squash, Squish, Strangle, Sweat, Thrutch, Thumbscrew, Vice, Wring

**Squelch** Gurgle, Squash, Squish, Subdue

**Squib** Banger, Damp, Dud, Firework, Lampoon

**Squid** Calamari, Calamary, Cephalopod, Cuttlefish, Flying, Ink-fish, Loligo, Mortar, Nautilus, Octopus, Sleeve fish

**Squiffy** Drunk, Lit, Tiddley, Tipsy

▷**Squiggle** *may indicate* an anagram

**Squill** Sea, Spring

**Squint(ing)** Boss-eyed, Cast, Cock-eye, Cross-eye, Glance, Gledge, Glee, Gley, Hagioscope, Heterophoria, Louche, Opening, Proptosis, Skellie, Skelly, Sken, Squin(n)y, Strabism, Swivel-eye, Vergence, Wall-eye

**Squire** Armiger(o), Beau, Donzel, Escort, Hardcastle, Headlong, Land-owner, Sancho Panza, Scutiger, Swain, Western, White

**Squirm(ing)** Fidget, Reptation, Twist, Wiggle, Worm, Wriggle, Writhe

**Squirrel, Squirrel's nest** Aye-aye, Boomer, Bun, Cage, Chickaree, Chipmuck, Chipmunk, Dray, Drey, Flickertail, Flying (-fox), Gopher, Grey, Ground, Hackee, Hoard(er), Marmot, Meerkat, Petaurist, Phalanger, Prairie dog, Rabbit, Red, Richardson's ground, Sciuroid, Secrete, Sewellel, Skug, Spermophile, S(o)uslik, Taguan, Vair, Zizel

**Squirt(er)** Chirt, Cockalorum, Douche, Jet, Scoosh, Scoot, Skoosh, Spirt, Spout, Spritz, Toerag, Urochorda, Wet, Whiffet, Whippersnapper

**Sri Lanka(n)** Ceylon, Cingalese, CL, .lk, Serendip, Sinhalese, Tamil, Vedda

**St** Saint, Street

**Stab** Bayonet, Chib, Chiv, Crease, Creese, Dag, Effort, Go, Gore, Guess, Jab, Knife, Kreese, Kris, Lancinate, Pang, Pierce, Pink, Poniard, Prick, Prong, Punch, Stick, Stiletto, Turk, Wound

**Stabilise(r), Stability** Aileron, Anchor, Balance, Ballast, Balloonet, Emulsifier, Even, Fin, Fixure, Gyroscope, Maintain, Pax Romana, Peg, Permanence, Plateau, Poise, Steadfastness, Steady, Tail panel

**Stable(s)** Adjusted, Augean, Balanced, Barn, Byre, Certain, Consistent, Constant, Durable, Equerry, Equilibrium, Firm, Livery, Loose box, Manger, Mews, Permanent, Poise, Sane, Secure, Settled, Solid, Sound, Stall, Static(al), Steadfast, Steady, Stud, Sure, Together, Well-adjusted

**Stableman** Groom, Lad, Ostler

**Stachys** Betony

**Stack(s)** Accumulate, À gogo, Chimney, Clamp, Cock, End, Flare, Funnel, Heap, Lum, Nest, → PILE, Reckan, Rick, Ruck, Shock, Sight, Smoke, Staddle

**Stackyard** Rick-barton

**Stadium** All-seater, Anfield, Arena, Astrodome, Ballpark, Bowl, Circus, Circus Maximus, Coliseum, Ground, Headingley, Hippodrome, Maracana, Murrayfield, Shea, Speedway, Trent Bridge, Velodrome, Wembley

**Staff** Aesculapius, Alpenstock, Ash-plant, Bato(o)n, Bouche, Bourdon, Bread, Burden, Caduceus, Cane, Churn, Crew, Crook, Crosier, Cross(e), Crozier, Crutch, Cudgel, Entourage, Equerry, Establishment, État-major, Faculty, Ferula, Ferule, Flagpole, General, Ground, Jack, Jacob's, Jeddart, Linstock, Lituus, Mace, Man, Office, Omlah, Pack, Pastoral, Personnel, Pike, Pole, Ragged, Rod, Rung, Runic, Sceptre, Seniority, Skeleton, Stave, Stick, Supernumerary, Taiaha, Tapsmen, Tau, Thyrsus, Token, Truncheon, Verge, Wand, Workers, Workforce, Wring

**Stag** Actaeon, Brocket, Buck, Deer, For men, Hummel, Imperial, Knobber, Line, Male, Party, Royal, Rutter, Shadow, Ten-pointer, Wapiti

**Stage** Act, Anaphase, Apron, Arena, Ashrama, Bandstand, Bardo, Bema, Boards, Catasta, Catwalk, Centre, Chrysalis, Committee, Dais, Degree, Diligence, Dog-leg, Estrade, Fare, Fargo, Fit-up, Gastrula, Grade, Hop, Imago, Instar, Juncture, Key, Landing, Leg, Levee, Level, Metaphase, Milestone, Moment, Mount, Napron, Oidium, Orbital, Perform, Phase, Phasis,

Pier, Pin, Platform, Podium, Point, Pontoon, Postscenium, Present, Prophase, Proscenium, PS, Puberty, Report, Resting, Rostrum, Round, Scene, Sensorimotor, Sound, Stadium, Step, Stepping stone, Stor(e)y, Subclimax, Subimago, Theatre, Theatrical, Thrust, Transition, Trek, Wells Fargo, Yuga, Zoea

**Stage-coach** Diligence, Fly, Thoroughbrace, Wells Fargo

**Stagecraft** Pinafore

**Stagehand** Flyman, Grip

**Stagger(ed), Staggering** Alternate, Amaze, Astichous, Astonish, Astound, Awhape, Daidle, Dodder, Falter, Floor, Lurch, Recoil, Reel, Rock, Sensational, Shock, Startle, Stoiter, Stot(ter), Stumble, Surprise, Sway, Teeter, Thunderstricken, Thunderstruck, Titubate, Tolter, Totter, Waddle, Wamble, Wintle

▷**Staggered** *may indicate* an anagram

**Stagirite, Stagyrite** Aristotle

**Stagnant, Stagnate, Stagnation** Cholestasis, Ditchwater, F(o)etid, Foul, Inert, Moribund, Ossify, Scummy, Stasis, Static

**Staid** Decorous, Demure, Formal, Grave, Matronly, Prim, Prudish, Sad, Seemly, Sober, Stick-in-the-mud

**Stain(er)** Aniline, Bedye, Begrime, Besmirch, Blemish, Blob, Blot, Blotch, Chica, Discolour, Dishonour, Dye, Embrue, Ensanguine, Eosin, Fox, Gram-negative, Gram-positive, Gram's, Grime, Imbrue, Inkspot, Iodophile, Keel, Maculate, Mail, Mar, Mark, Meal, Mote, Picrocarmine, Portwine, Slur, Smirch, Smit, Soil, Splodge, Splotch, Stigma, Sully, Taint, Tarnish, Tincture, Tinge, Tint, Vital, Woad

**Stair(case), Stairs** Apples, Apples and pears, Caracol(e), Cochlea, Companionway, Escalator, Flight, Moving, Perron, Rung, Scale (and platt), Spiral, Step, Tread, Turnpike, Vice, Wapping, Winding

**Stake(s)** Ante, Bet, Claim, Deposit, Eclipse, Estacade, Extracade, Gage, Go, Holding, Impale, Impone, Interest, Lay, Loggat, Maiden, Mark, Mise, Nursery, Paal, Pale, Paliform, Paling, Palisade, Peel, Peg, Pele, Picket, Pile, Play, Post, Pot, Punt, Put, Rest, Revie, Risk, Septleva, Set, Shareholding, Skewer, Spike, Spile, Stang, Stob, Straddle, Sweep, Tether, Vie, Wager, Weir, Welter

**Stalactite** Dripstone, Dropstone, Helictite, Lansfordite, Soda straw

**Stalagmite** Onyx marble

**Stale** Aged, Banal, Chestnut, Flat, Fozy, Frowsty, Fusty, Hackneyed, Handle, Hoary, Mouldy, Musty, Old, Pretext, Rancid, Stagnant, Urine, Worn

▷**Stale** *may indicate* an obsolete word

**Stalemate** Deadlock, Dilemma, Draw, Hindrance, Impasse, Mexican standoff, Saw-off, Standoff, Tie, Zugswang

**Stalinist** Kirov

**Stalk(er), Stalks** Anthophore, Bennet, Bun, Cane, Caudicle, Chimney, Follow, Funicle, Garb(e), Gynophore, Ha(u)lm, Hunt, Keck(s), Kecksey, Keksye, Kex, Ommatophore, Pedicel, Pedicle, Peduncle, Petiole, Petiolule, Phyllode, Prowler, Pursue, Reed, Rush, Scape, Seta, Shaw, Spear, Spire, Stem, Sterigma, Still-hunter, Stipe(s), Strae, Straw, Stride, Strig, Strut, Stubble, Stump, Track, Trail, Yolk

**Stalking-horse** Stale

**Stall(s)** Arrest, Bay, Booth, Box, Bulk, Coffee, Crame, Crib, →**DELAY**, Floor, Flypitch, Hedge, Horse-box, Kiosk, Loose-box, Market, Orchestra, Pen, Pew, Prebendal, Procrastinate, Seat, Shamble, Sideshow, Stable, Stand, Starting, Stasidion, Sty, Sutlery, Temporise, Trap, Traverse, Travis, Trevis(s), Tribune, Whip, Whipstall

**Stall-holder** Choirboy, Fly-pitcher

**Stallion** Cooser, Cuisser, Cusser, Entire, →**HORSE**, Stag, Staig, Stonehorse, Stud

**Stalwart** Anchor-man, Buirdly, Firm, Hearty, Manful, Partisan, Robust, Sturdy, Trusty, Undeterred, Valiant

**Stamen(ed), Stamens** Androecium, Octandria, Phalanx, Polyandria, Synandrium

**Stamina** Endurance, Fibre, Fortitude, Guts, Last, Stamen, Stay, Steel, Vigour

**Stammer(ing)** Balbutient, Er, Hesitate, Hum, Psellism, Sputter, Stumble, →**STUTTER**, Waffle

**Stamp(s), Stamped, Stamping** Albino, Appel, Blind, Cachet, Cast, Character, Coin, Date(r), Definitive, Die, Dry print, Enface, Enseal, Fiscal, Frank, Gutter-pair, Health, Imperforate, Impress, Imprint, Incuse, Kind, Label, Matchmark, Mint, Mintage, Obsign, Pane, Penny black, Perfin, Philately, Pintadera, Postage, Postmark, Press(ion), Print, Rubber, Seal, Seebeck, Se-tenant, Signet, Spif, Strike, Swage, Tête-bêche, Touch, Touchmark, Trading, Trample, Tread, Tromp, Type, Visa

**Stamp-collecting** Philately, Timbrology, Timbrophily

**Stampede** Debacle, Flight, Onrush, Outrush, Panic, Rampage, → RUSH, Sauve qui peut

**Stamping ground** Haunt

**Stance** Akimbo, Attitude, Deportment, Ecarté, En garde, Pose, Position, Posture, Quinte

**Stand(ing), Stander, Stand for, Stand up** Abide, Apron, Arraign, Attitude, Base, Bay, Be, Bear, Bide, Bier, Binnacle, Bipod, Booth, Bristle, Brook, Candidate, Canterbury, Caste, Cock, Confrontation, Cradle, Crease, Credit, Dais, Degree, Desk, Dock, Dree, Dumb-waiter, Easel, Endure, Epergne, Étagère, Extant, Face, Firedog, Foothold, Freeze, Gantry, Gueridon, Hard, Hat, Hob, Importance, Improv(ised), Insulator, Klinostat, Last, Lazy Susan, Lectern, Leg, Level, Lime, Monopode, Music, Nef, Odour, One-night, Ovation, Pedestal, Place, Plant, Podium, Pose, Position, Pou sto, Predella, Prestige, Promenade, Protest, Qua, Rack, Rampant, Rank, Regent, Remain, Represent, Repute, Rest, Ring, Rise, Rouse, Shout, Soapbox, Stall, Statant, Station, → STATUS, Stay, Stillage, Stock, Stomach, Stool, Straddle, Straphang, Striddle, Stroddle, Strut, Table, Tantalus, Taxi, Teapoy, Terrace, Toastrack, Toe, → TREAT, Tree, Tripod, Trivet, Umbrella, Upright, Whatnot, Witness

**Standard(s)** ANSI, Banner, Base, Baseline, Basic, Benchmark, Bog, Bogey, Bread and butter, British, Canon, CAT, Classic(al), Cocker, Code, Colour(s), Conventional, Copybook, Criterion, Double, Eagle, Ego ideal, English, Epitome, Ethics, Etiquette, Examplar, Example, Exemplar, Fiducial, Flag, Ga(u)ge, Gold, Gonfalon, Grade, Guidon, Horsetail, Ideal, Jolly Roger, Kite-marker, Labarum, Level, Living, Mainstream, Measure, Model, Morals, Netiquette, Norm(a), Normal, Numeraire, Old Glory, Oriflamme, Par, Parker Morris, Pennon, Principle, Proforma, Rate, Regular, Rod, Rose, Routine, Royal, → RULE, Scruples, Silver, Spec(ification), Staple, Stereotype, Sterling, Stock, Time, Touchstone, Tricolour, Troy, Two-power, Uniform, Usual, Valuta, Vexillum, Yardstick

**Standard-bearer** Alferez, Cornet, Ensign, Vexillary

**Stand-by** Adminicle, Reserve, Substitute, Support, Twelfth man, Understudy

**Stand-in** Double, Locum, Place-holder, Prince Regent, Stunt man, Sub(stitute), Surrogate, Temp, Understudy

**Standish** Miles

**Stand-off(ish)** Aloof, Five-eighth, Half-back, Impasse, Number ten, Remote, Reserved, Stalemate, Upstage

**Standpoint** Angle, Slant, View

**Standstill** Deadset, Halt, Jam, Log jam, Stalemate, Stoppage

**Stanley** Baldwin, Knife, Rupert

**Stannic** Tin

**St Anthony's fire** Ergotism, Erysipelas

**Stanza** Antistrophe, Ballad, Couplet, Elegiac, Envoi, Envoy, Heroic, Matoke, Ottava, Ottava rima, Poem, Quatrain, Sixaine, Spasm, Spenserian, Staff, Stave, Tantum ergo, Tetrastich, Troparion, Verse

**Staple** Basic, Bread, Chief, Maize, Matoke, Oats, Pin, Plantain, Potato, Rice, Stock, Tack, Wool

**Star(s)** Adept, Aster(isk), Binary, Blazing, Body, Celeb(rity), Champ, Class act, Coma Berenices, Companion, Constant, Constellation, Cushion, Cynosure, Dark, Death, Double, Earth, Esther, Exploding, Falling, Fate, Feather, Feature, Film, Fixed, Flare, Galactic, Giant, Headline, Hero, Hester, Hexagram, Idol, Late type, Lead, Leading light, Lion, Magen David, Main sequence, Matinee idol, Mogen David, Movie, Mullet, Multiple, Pentacle, Personality, Phad, Pip, Plerion, Pointer, Prima donna, Principal, Pulsating, Red-top, Seven, Shell, Shine, Shooting, Sidereal, Solomon's seal, Spangle, Starn(ie), Stellar, Stern, Swart, (The) Pointers, Top banana, Top-liner, Ultraviolet, Valentine, Variable, Vedette

## STARS

***3 letters:***
Dog
Sol

***4 letters:***
Argo
Beta
Grus
Lode
Lyra
Mira
Nova
Pavo
Pole
Ursa
Vega
Vela
Zeta

***5 letters:***
Acrux
Agena
Algol
Alpha
Ceres
Cetus
Comet
Delta
Deneb
Draco
Dubhe
Dwarf
Gamma
Hyads
Indus
Lupus
Mensa
Merak
Mizar
Norma
North
Polar
Radio
Rigel
Rigil
Saiph
Spica
Theta
Venus
Virgo
Wagon
Whale

***6 letters:***
Alioth
Alkaid
Altair
Aquila
Auriga
Boötes
Carbon
Carina
Castor
Cygnus
Dorado
Étoile
Fornax
Galaxy
Hatsya
Hyades
Lambda
Lizard
Megrez
Meissa
Merope
Meteor
Octans
Phecda
Plough
Pollux
Psyche
Pulsar
Puppis
Quasar
Saturn
Sirius
Sothis
Uranus
Vesper
Volans

***7 letters:***
Alnilam
Alnitak
Antares
Calaeno
Canopus
Capella
Cepheus
Chamber
Columba
Dolphin
Epsilon
Éstoile
Evening
Gemingo
Lucifer
Mintaka
Morning
Neutron
Perseus
Phoenix
Polaris
Procyon
Proxima
Regulus
Sabaism
Serpent
Sterope
Triones
Wagoner

***8 letters:***
Achernar
Arcturus
Barnard's
Circinus
Denebola
Equuleus
Eridanus
Hesperus
Magnetar
Mira Ceti
Pegasean
Phosphor
Pleiades
Praesepe
Red dwarf
Red giant
Scorpius
Synastry
Waggoner

***9 letters:***
Aldebaran
Andromeda
Bellatrix
Big Dipper
Black hole
Centaurus
Collapsar
Delphinus
Fire-drake
Fomalhaut
Hypernova
Meteorite
Ophiuchus
Pentagram
Rigil-Kent
Supernova
Wolf-Rayet

***10 letters:***
Betacrucis
Betelgeuse
Betelgeuze
Brown dwarf
Cassiopeia
Orion's Belt
Phosphorus
Supergiant
White dwarf

***11 letters:***
Circumpolar

***12 letters:***
Little Dipper
Septentrione

***13 letters:***
Alpha Centauri
Grande vedette
Southern Cross

***14 letters:***
Camelopardalis
Tyrian cynosure

***15 letters:***
Proxima Centauri

**Starboard** Right

**Starch(y), Starch producer** Amyloid, Amylum, Animal, Arrowroot, Cassava, Ceremony, Congee, Conjee, Coontie, Coonty, Cycad, Farina, Fecula, Formal, Glycogen, Impersonal, Kuzu, Lichenin, Manioc, Maranta, Pentosan, Pyrene, Pyroid, Sago, Stamina, Statolith, Stiff, Stodgy, Tapioca, Tous-les-mois

**Stare** Eyeball, Fisheye, Gape, Gapeseed, Gawk, Gawp, Gaze, Geek, Glare, Glower, Goggle, Gorp, Look, Ogle, Outface, Peer, Rubberneck, Scowl
**Starfish** Ambulacra, Asterid, Asteroid(ea), Bipinnaria, Brittlestar, Ophiurid, Radiata
**Star-gaze(r), Star-gazing** Astrodome, Astronomy, Copernicus, Magus
**Stark(ers)** Apparent, Austere, Bald, Bare, Bleak, Gaunt, Harsh, Naked, Nude, Sheer, Stiff, Utterly
**Starling** Bird, Gippy, Hill mynah, Murmuration, Pastor, Rosy pastor, Stare, Stuckie, Sturnus
**Star of Bethlehem** Chincherinchee, Chinkerinchee
**Start(ed), Starter, Starting, Starting-point** Ab ovo, Abrade, Abraid, Abray, Activate, Actuate, Baseline, Begin, Bhajee, Boggle, Boot-up, Bot, Broach, Bug, Bully off, Bump, Chance, Commence, Consommé, Course, Crank, Create, Crudités, Curtain up, Dart, Debut, Ean, Embryo, Entrecote, Entrée, Face-off, Fall-to, False, Fire, Flinch, Float, Flotation, Flush, Flying, Found, Gambit, Gan, Generate, Genesis, Getaway, Gun, Handicap, Head, Hors-d'oeuvres, Hot-wire, Impetus, Imprimis, Incept(ion), Initiate, Instigate, Institute, Intro(duce), Jar, Jerk, Judder, Jump, Jump lead, Jump-off, Kick-off, Kindle, L, Lag, Launch, Lead, Lift off, Melon, Nidus, Novice, Off, Offset, Onset, Ope(n), Ord, Origin, Outset, Poppadom, Potage, Preliminary, Prelude, Proband, Push, Put-up, Reboot, Resume, Roll, Roul, Rouse, Scare, Send, Set off, Shy, Slip, Snail, Soup, Source, Spark, Spring, Springboard, Spud, String, Syndicate, Tee-off, Terminus a quo, Toehold, Wince
▷**Start** *may indicate* an anagram or first letters
**Startle(d), Startling** Agape, Alarm, Bewilder, Disturb, Electric, Eye-opener, Flush, Frighten, How d'y(e)do, Lurid, Magical, Rock, Scare
**Starvation, Starve(d), Starving** Anorexia, Anoxic, Bant, Clem, Cold, Deprive, Diet, Famish, Foodless, Inanition, Innutrition, Macerate, Perish, Pine, Undernourished
▷**Starving** *may indicate* an 'o' in the middle of a word
**Stash** Hide, Hoard, Salt, Secrete
**Stasis** Inaction
**State(s), Stated, Stateside** Affirm, Alle(d)ge, Aread, Arrede, Assert, Assever, Attest, Aver, Avow, Buffer, Cacotopia, Case, Circar, Cite, Client, Commonwealth, Condition, Confederate, Construct, Corporate, Country, Critical, Cutch, Declare, Dependency, Dirigisme, Emirate, Empire, État, Explicit, Express, Federal, Fettle, Flap, Formulate, Free, Going, Habitus, Humour, Kingdom, Land, Lesh, Limbo, Maintain, Mess, Metastable, Mode, Mood, Name, Nanny, Nation, Native, Palatinate, Papal, Para, Plateau, Plenarty, Plight, Police, Pomp, Posit, Power, Predicament, Predicate, Premise, Profess, Pronounce, Protectorate, Puppet, Quantum, Realm, Republic, Rogue, Samadhi, Sanctitude, Satellite, Satori, Say, Sircar, Sirkar, Situation, Slave, Sorry, Sovereign, Standard, Standing, Steady, Succession, Sunbelt, Threeness, Thusness, Uncle Sam, Union, United, Welfare, Yap

---

**STATES**

*2 letters:*
Ga
Ia
Md
Me
Mi
NC
NY
Pa
RI
UK
US
Ut
Va

*3 letters:*
Ark
Del
Fla
Goa
NSW
Oyo
USA
Wis

*4 letters:*
Abia
Acre
Chad
Conn
Gulf
Iowa
Kano
Kogi
Laos
Mass
Ogun
Ohio
Oman
Ondo
Osun
Shan
Swat
Togo
Utah

*5 letters:*
Amapa
Assam
Bahia
Benin
Benue
Bihar
Ceará
Dixie
Dubai
Gabon
Ghana
Haiti
Hesse
Idaho
Jammu

Kalat
Kedah
Kutch
Kwara
Libya
Lippe
Lycia
Maine
Malay
Mewar
Nepal
Niger
Oshun
Perak
Piaui
Qatar
Reich
Sabah
Samoa
Texas
Tibet
Tyrol

***6 letters:***
Alaska
Balkan
Baltic
Baroda
Bauchi
Belize
Bremen
Brunei
Cochin
Colima
Dakota
Greece
Hawaii
Indore
Jigawa
Johore
Kaduna
Kansas
Kerala
Khelat
Kosovo
Kuwait
Latvia
Madras
Malawi
Malaya
Mysore
Nevada
Oaxaca
Oregon
Orissa
Pahang
Panama
Parana
Penang
Perlis
Puebla
Punjab
Rivers
Saxony
Serbia
Sikkim
Sokoto
Sonora
Sparta
Styria
Tassie
Tonkin

***7 letters:***
Alabama
Alagoas
Algeria
America
Anambra
Andorra
Arizona
Barbary
Bavaria
Belarus
Benelux
Buffalo
Chiapas
Comoros
Croatia
Durango
Eritrea
Estonia
Etruria
Florida
Georgia
Grenada
Gujarat
Gujerat
Haryana
Hidalgo
Indiana
Ireland
Jalisco
Jamaica
Jodhpur
Kashmir
Lebanon
Lesotho
Malacca
Manipur
Mizoram
Montana
Morelos
Morocco
Nayarit
New York
Nirvana
Paraiba
Pelican
Pradesh
Prussia
Roraima
Sarawak
Sergipe
Sinaloa
Tabasco
Tongkin
Tonking
Tripura
Trucial
Udaipur
Vanuatu
Vatican
Vermont
Vietnam
Wyoming
Yucatan

***8 letters:***
Abu Dhabi
Amazonas
Arkansas
Botswana
Campeche
Carolina
Coahuila
Colombia
Colorado
Delaware
Ethiopia
Honduras
Illinois
Jharkand
Kelantan
Kentucky
Kiribati
Maranhao
Maryland
Michigan
Missouri
Nagaland
Nebraska
Oklahoma
Paraguay
Rondonia
Saarland
Sao Paulo
Selangor
Tanzania
Tasmania
Tiaxcala
Tongking
Transkei
Veracruz
Victoria
Virginia

***9 letters:***
Chihuahua
Costa Rica
Dixieland
Guatemala
Hyderabad
Indonesia
Karnataka
Louisiana
Manchukuo
Meghalaya
Michoacán
Minnesota
Nassarawa
New Jersey
New Mexico
Nuevo Léon
Queretaro
Rajasthan
Rajputana
San Marino
Singapore
St Vincent
Tamil Nadu
Tennessee
Thuringia
Tocantins
Trengganu
Venezuela
Wisconsin
Zacatecas

***10 letters:***
Azerbaijan
California
East Bengal
Guanajuato
Jamahiriya
Jumhouriya
Manchoukuo
Orange Free
Pernambuco
Queensland
South Korea
Tamaulipas
Tanganyika
Terengganu

Travancore
Washington
West Bengal

*11 letters:*
Brandenberg
Connecticut
Jamahouriya
Maharashtra
Mecklenburg
Minas Gerais
Mississippi
North Dakota
Quintana Roo
Rhode Island
South Dakota
Uttaranchal
Vatican City

*12 letters:*
Chhattisgarh
Madhya Bharat
New Hampshire
Pennsylvania
Saxony-Anholt
Uttar Pradesh
West Virginia

*13 letters:*
Andhra Pradesh
Madhya Pradesh
Massachusetts
Negri Sembilan
New South Wales
San Luis Potosi
Santa Catarina
South Carolina

*14 letters:*
Aguascalientes
Rio Grande do Sul
South Australia
Vindhya Pradesh

*15 letters:*
Himachal Pradesh
Schaumburg-Lippe
St Kitts and Nevis

*16 letters:*
Rio Grande do Norte

*17 letters:*
Schleswig-Holstein
Trinidad and Tobago

*19 letters:*
Rhineland-Palatinate

*20 letters:*
North Rhine-Westphalia

---

**Statecraft** Politics
▷**Stated** *may indicate* a similar sounding word
**Stately, Stately home** August, Courtly, Dome, Grand, Imposing, Junoesque, Majestic, Mansion, Mausolean, Noble, Pile, Regal, Solemn
**Statement** Accompt, Account, Affidavit, Aphorism, Assertion, Asseveration, Attestation, Avowal, Axiom, Balance, Bank, Bill, Bulletin, Case, Colophon, Communiqué, Credo, Declaration, Declension, Deposition, Description, Dictum, Diktat, Encyclical, Enigma, Evidence, Expose, Factoid, Generalisation, Grand Remonstrance, Impact, Indictment, Invoice, Jurat, Manifesto, Mission, Motto, Non sequitur, Note, Outline, Paraphrase, Plaint, Pleading, Press release, Profession, Pronouncement, Pronunciamento, Proposition, Protocol, Quotation, Recital, Release, Report, Return, Sentence, Shema, Shout out, Soundbite, Sweeping, Testament, Testimony, Theologoumenon, Truism, Utterance, Verbal
**Stateroom** Bibby, Cabin
**Statesman** American, Attlee, Augustus, Baldwin, Botha, Brandt, Briand, Bright, Canning, Castlereagh, Cato, Chesterfield, Chirac, Churchill, Cicero, Clarendon, Clemenceau, Cosgrave, De Gaulle, De Valera, De Witt, Diefenbaker, Diplomat, Disraeli, Dollfuss, Draco, Dulles, Elder, Flaminius, Franklin, Gambetta, Gandhi, Genro, Georgian, Gladstone, Gracchi, Grotius, Guy, Iron Duke, Kissinger, Kruger, Lafayette, Lie, Lucullus, Metternich, Mitterand, Molotov, More, Nasser, Nehru, Nixon, North, Nyerere, Palmerston, Peel, Perceval, Pericles, Peron, Pitt, Politician, Politico, Pompidou, Potemkin, Pretorius, Pym, Raffles, Rockingham, Seneca, Smuts, Solon, Stein, Talleyrand, Tasmanian, Texan, Thiers, Tito, Verwoerd, Vorster, Walesa, Walpole, Walsingham, Wealsman, Yankee
**Static** Atmospherics, Becalmed, Electricity, Inert, Maginot-minded, Motionless, Sferics, Stagnant, Stationary
**Station(s)** Action, Aid, Air, Base, Berth, Birth, Camp, Caste, CCS, Channel, Charing Cross, Coaling, Comfort, Crewe, Deploy, Depot, Docking, Dressing, Earth, Euston, Filling, Fire, Fort, Garrison, Gas, Generation, Halt, Head, Hill, Hilversum, Ice, King's Cross, Lay, Location, London Bridge, Marylebone, Meridian, Mir, New Street, Nick, Outpost, Paddington, Panic, Pay, Petrol, Pitch, Place, Plant, Point, Police, Polling, Post, Power, Powerhouse, Quarter, Radio, Rank, Relay, Rowme, St Pancras, Seat, Service, Sheep, Sit, Situate, Skylab, Space, Stance, Stand, Star, Status, Stond, Subscriber, Tana, Tanna(h), Terminus, Testing, Thana(h), Thanna(h), Tracking, Transfer, Triangulation, Vauxhall, Victoria, Waterloo, Waverley, Way, Weather, Whistlestop, Wind farm, Wireless, Work
**Stationary** At rest, Fasten, Fixed, Immobile, Parked, Sessile, Stable, Static
**Stationer(y), Stationery-case** Continuous, Multi-part, Papeterie
**Statistic(ian), Statistical, Statistics** Actuary, Bose-Einstein, Cusum, Demography, Descriptive, ERA, Fermi-Dirac, Figure, Gallup, Gradgrind, Graph, Inferential, Isotype, Lod, Nonparametric, Number, Parametric, Percentage, Quant(um), Sampling, Student's t, Vital
**Statuary, Statue(tte)** Acrolith, Bronze, Bust, Colossus (of Rhodes), Discobolus, Effigy,

Eros, Figure, Figurine, Galatea, Idol, Image, Kore, Kouros, Liberty, Marmoreal, Memnon, Monolith, Monument, Oscar, Palladium, Pasquil, Pasquin, Pietà, Sculpture, Sphinx, Stonework, Stookie, Tanagra, Torso, Xoanon

**Stature** Growth, Height, Inches, Rank

**Status** Amateur, Beacon, Cachet, Caste, Class, Curule, Pecking-order, Political, → **POSITION**, Prestige, Professional, Quo, Rank, Standing

**Statute** Act, Capitular, Chapter 11, Chapter 7, Decree, Edict, Law, Limitations, Novels, Provisors, Westminster

**Staunch** Amadou, Leal, Resolute, Steady, Stem, Stout, Styptic, Watertight

**Stave** Break, Dali, Forestall, Lag, Slat, Stanza, Ward

**Stay(ing), Stayer, Stays** Abide, Alt, Appease, Avast, Bide, Blay, Board, Bolster, Cohab(it), Continue, Corselet, Corset, Embar, Endure, Forbear, Fulcrum, Gest, Guest, Guy, Hawser, Hold, Indwell, Jump, Lie, Lig, Linger, Lodge, Manet, Moratorium, Pause, Pernoctate, Piers, Postpone, Prop, → **REMAIN**, Reprieve, Respite, Restrain, Rope, Settle, Shore, Sist, Sleepover, Sojourn, Stamina, Stem, Stop off, Stop-over, Strut, Sustain, Tarry, Triatic, Villeggiatura, Visit

**Stay-at-home** Indoor, Tortoise

**STD** Aids, Herpes, Telephone, VD

**Stead** Lieu

**Steadfast** Abiding, Changeless, Constance, Constant, Dilwyn, Firm, Immutable, Implacable, Perseverant, Resolute, Sad, Stable, Unswerving

**Steadier, Steady** Andantino, Ballast, Beau, Boyfriend, Changeless, Composer, Consistent, Constant, Even, Faithful, Fast, Firm, Girlfriend, Level-headed, Malstick, Measured, Regular, Rock, Rock-solid, Stabilise, Stable, Staid, Sustained, Unswerving

**Steak, Steakhouse** Au poivre, Carpet-bag, Chateaubriand, Chuck, Diane, Entrecote, Fillet, Flitch, Garni, Grill room, Mignon, Minute, Pepper, Pope's eye, Porterhouse, Ribeye, Rump, Slice, Tartare, T-bone, Tenderloin, Tournedos, Vienna

**Steal(ing), Steal away** Abstract, Appropriate, Bag, Bandicoot, Bargain, Blag, Bone, Boost, Cabbage, Cly, Condiddle, Convey, Creep, Crib, Duff, Edge, Elope, Embezzle, Filch, Glom, Grab, Half-inch, Heist, Hijack, Hotting, Joyride, Kidnap, Kleptomania, Knap, Knock down, Knock off, Lag, Liberate, Lift, Loot, Mag(g), Mahu, Mill, Misappropriate, Naam, Nam, Nap, Nick, Nim, Nip, Nobble, Nym, Peculate, Phone-jack, Pilfer, Pillage, Pinch, Piracy, Plagiarise, Plunder, Poach, Pocket, Prig, Proll, Purloin, Purse, Ram-raid, Remove, Rifle, Rip-off, Rob, Rustle, Scrump, Sculk, Shoplift, Skrimp, Skulk, Smug, Snaffle, Snatch, Sneak, Snitch, Souvenir, Swipe, Take, Theft, Thieve, Tiptoe, TWOC, Whip

**Stealth(y)** Art, Catlike, Covert, Cunning, Furtive, Obreption, Sneaky, Stolenwise, Surreptitious, Tiptoe

**Steam(ed), Steaming, Steamy** Boil, Condensation, Cushion, Dry, Exhaust, Fume, Gaseous, Het, Humid, Live, Livid, Mist, Porn, Radio, Roke, Sauna, Snift, Spout, Vapor, Vapour, Wet

**Steamer, Steamboat** Hummum, Kettle, Ocean tramp, Paddle, Screw, Showboat, Side-wheeler, SS, Str, Tramp, Turbine

**Steam-hammer, Steamroller** Crush, Ram

**Steam-organ** Calliope

**Steed** Avenger, Charger, Horse, Mount, Pownie

**Steel(y)** Acierate, Adamant, Bainite, Bethlehem, Blade, Blister, Bloom, Brace, Carbon, Cast, Chrome, Chromium, Cold, Concrete, Crucible, Cutlass, Damascus, Damask, High-carbon, High-speed, Low-carbon, Magnet, Manganese, Maraging, Martensite, Metal, Mild, Nerve, Nickel, Pearlite, Pedal, Ripon, Rolled, Shear, Silver, Sorbite, Spray, Stainless, Structural, Sword, Taggers, Terne plate, Toledo, Tool, Tungsten, Vanadium, Wootz

**Steelyard** Bismar

**Steep(ening)** Abrupt, Arduous, Bold, Brent, Buck, Cliff-face, Costly, Embay, Expensive, High-pitched, Hilly, Immerse, Krans, Krantz, Kranz, Macerate, Marinade, Marinate, Mask, Monocline, Plo(a)t, Precipice, Precipitous, Rait, Rapid, Rate, Ret, Saturate, Scarp, → **SHEER**, Soak, Sog, Sop, Souse, Stey, Stickle, Tan, Towery

**Steeple(jack)** Belfry, Spiderman, Spire, Turret

**Steer(er), Steering** Ackerman, Airt, Buffalo, Bullock, Bum, Cann, Castor, Con(n), Cox,

Coxswain, Direct, → GUIDE, Handlebar, Helm, Navaid, Navigate, Ox, Pilot, Ply, Power, Rudder, Stot, Whipstaff, Zebu

**St Elmo's fire** Corona discharge, Corposant

**Stem** Alexanders, Arrow, Axial, Biller, Bind, Bine, Bole, Cane, Caudex, Caulicle, Caulis, Caulome, Check, Cladode, Cladophyll, Confront, Corm, Culm, Dam, Eddo, Epicotyl, Floricane, Ha(u)lm, Kex, Originate, Pedicle, Peduncle, Pin, Pipe-stopple, Pseudaxis, R(h)achilla, Rachis, Ram, Rhachis, Rhizome, Rise, Rod, Runt, Sarment, Sarmentum, Scapus, Seta, Shaft, Shank, Sobole(s), Spring, Stalk, Staunch, Stipe, Stolon, Stopple, Straw, Sympodium, Tail, Tamp, Terete

**Stench** F(o)etor, Funk, Miasma, Odour, Pong, Reek, Smell, Stink, Whiff

**Stencil** Copy, Duplicate, Mimeograph®, Pochoir

**Stenographer, Stenography** Amanuensis, Secretary, Shorthand, Typist

**Step(s)** Act, Apples and pears, Balancé, Chassé, Choctaw, Companionway, Corbel, Corbie, Curtail, Dance, Degree, Démarche, Echelon, Escalate, False, Firing, Flight, Fouetté, Gain, Gait, Glissade, Goose, Grade, Grapevine, Grecian, Greece, Grees(e), Greesing, Grese, Gressing, Grice, Griece, Grise, Grize, Halfpace, Increment, Lavolt, Lock, Measure, Move, Naughty, Notch, Pace, Pas, Pas de souris, Perron, Phase, Pigeon('s) wing, Quantal, Quick, Raiser, Ratlin(e), Rattlin(e), Rattling, Roundel, Roundle, Rung, Sashay, Shuffle, Side, Slip, Slow march, Stage, Stair, Stalk, Stile, Stoop, Stope, Stride, Sugarfoot, Toddle, Trap, Tread, Trip, Unison, Waddle, Walk, Whole, Winder

**Step by step** Gradation

**Stephen** Martyr, Stainless

**Stepmother** Novercal

**Stepney** Spare

**Steppe** Kyrgyz, Llano, Plain

**Stereo** Ghetto blaster, iPod®, Nicam, Personal, Walkman®

**Stereoscope** Pseudoscope

**Stereotype(d)** Hackney, Ritual, Spammy

**Sterile, Sterilise(r), Sterilisation, Sterilising, Sterility** Acarpous, Aseptic, Atocia, Autoclave, Barren, Clean, Dead, Disinfected, Fruitless, Impotent, Infertile, Neuter, Pasteurise, Spay, Tubal ligation, UHT, Uninfected, Unproductive, Vasectomy

**Sterling** Excellent, Genuine, Pound, Silver, Sound

**Stern** Aft, Austere, Back, Counter, Dour, Flinty, Grim, Hard, Implacable, Iron, Isaac, Nates, Poop, Rear, Relentless, Rugged, Stark, Strict, Tailpiece, Transom

**Steroid** Anabolic, Androsterone, Calciferol, Cortisone, Dexamethasone, Ergosterol, Fusidic, Lipid, Lumisterol, Mifepristone, Nandrolone, Predniso(lo)ne, Spironolactone, Stanozolol, Testosterone, Tetrahydrogestrinone

**Sterol** Stigmasterol

**Stertorous** Snore

**Stet** Restore

**Stethoscope** Pinard

**Stevedore** Coal-whipper, Docker, Dockhand, Lighterman, Loader, Longshoreman, Stower, Wharfinger

**Stevenson** RLS, Tusitala

**Stew(ed), Stews** Bagnio, Bath, Blanquette, Boil, Bordel(lo), Bouillabaisse, Bouilli, Bourguignon, Braise, Bredie, Broth, Brothel, Burgoo, Cacciatora, Cacciatore, Carbonade, Carbonnade, Casserole, Cassoulet, Cholent, Chowder, Coddle, Colcannon, Compot(e), Daube, Feijoada, Flap, Fricassee, Fume, Fuss, Goulash, Grillade, Haricot, Hash, Hell, Hot(ch)pot(ch), Irish, Jug, Lather, Lobscouse, Maconochie, Matapan, Matelote, Mulligan, Navarin, Olla podrida, Osso bucco, Oyster, Paddy, Paella, Pepperpot, Pot-au-feu, Pot-pourri, Ragout, Ratatouille, Rubaboo, Salmi, Sass, Scouse, Seethe, Simmer, Slumgullion, Squiffy, Stie, Stove, Stovies, Sty, Succotash, Sweat, Swelter, Tajine, Tatahash, Tzimmes, Zamzawed, Zarzuela

**Steward(ess)** Attendant, Bailiff, Butler, Cabin crew, Cellarer, Chamberlain, Chiltern Hundreds, Dewan, Factor, Flight attendant, Hind, Keeper, Major domo, Malvolio, Manciple, Maormor, Mormaor, Official, Oswald, Panter, Purser, Redcoat, Reeve, Seneschal, Sewer, Shop, Smallboy, Sommelier, Trolley dolly, Waiter

▹**Stewed** *may indicate* an anagram
**St Francis** Seraphic Father
**Stibnite** Antimony, Kohl
**Stick(ing) (out), Stickiness, Sticks, Stuck, Sticky** Adhere, Adhesive, Affix, Agglutinant, Agglutinogen, Aground, Ash, Ashplant, Atlatl, Attach, Backwater, Baguette, Bamboo, Bastinado, Bat, Baton, Bauble, Bayonet, Beanpole, Birch, Blackthorn, Bludgeon, Bond, Boondocks, Broadside, Caman, Cambrel, Cammock, Cane, Celery, Cement, Chalk, Chapman, Charcoal, Chewy, Clag, Clam(my), Clarty, Clave, Cleave, Cleft, Cling, Clog, Club, Cocktail, Cohere, Coinhere, Composing, Control, Crab, Crayon, Crosier, Cross(e), Crotch, Crozier, Crummack, Crummock, Cudgel, Cue, Digging, Distaff, Divining-rod, Dog, Drum, Dure, Dynamite, Elemi, Endure, Execration, Exsert, Fag(g)ot, Firewood, Fix, Flak, Flypaper, Founder, French, Fuse, Gad(e), Gaid, Gambrel, Gear, Gelatine, Glair, Gliadin, Glit, Gloopy, Glue, Goad, Gold, Gong, Goo, Gore, Ground-ash, Gum, Gunge, Gunk, Harpoon, Hickory, Hob, Hockey, Hold on, Hurley, Immobile, Impale, Inhere, Isinglass, Jab, Jam, Joss, Jut, Kebbie, Kid, Kierie, Kindling, Kip, Kiri, Knife, Knitch, Knobkerrie, Ko, Lance, Lath(i), Lathee, Lentisk, Limy, Lug, Mallet, Message, Minder, Molinet, Muggy, Needle, Orange, Parasitic, Paste, Penang-lawyer, Persist, Phasmid, Piceous, Pierce, Pin, Piolet, Plaster, Pogo, Poise, Pole, Porridge, Posser, Pot, Protrude, Protuberant, Pugil, Q-tip, Quarterstaff, Ramrod, Rapier, Rash, Ratten, Resinous, Rhubarb, Rhythm, Rod, Ropy, Rural, Scouring, Seat, Seize, Shaft, Shillela(g)h, Shooting, Single, Size, Skewer, Ski, Smeary, Smudge, Spanish windlass, Spear, Spillikin, Spurtle, Squail(er), Stab, Staff, Stand, Stang, Stob, Stodgy, Stomach, Stubborn, Supplejack, Swagger, Switch, Swizzle, Swordstick, Tacamahac, Tack(y), Tally, Tar, Thick, Throwing, Toddy, Tokotoko, Truncheon, Trunnion, Twig, Vare, Viscid, Viscose, Viscous, Waddy, Wait, Walking, Wand, Wattle, Waxy, Wedge, White, Woolder, Woomera(ng), Yard, Yardwand
**Sticker** Araldite®, Barnacle, Bumper, Bur, Burr, Decal, Flash, Gaum, Glue, Label, Limpet, Partisan, Pin, Poster, Post-it®, Slogan, Viscose
**Stickler** Fusspot, Legalist, Pedant, Poser, Problem, Purist, Rigid, Rigorist, Tapist
**Stickybeak** Nosy Parker, Paul Pry
**Stiff, Stiffen(er), Stiffening, Stiffness** Anchylosis, Angular, Ankylosis, Baleen, Bandoline, Body, Brace, Buckram, Budge, Cadaver, Corpse, Corpus, Crick, Dead, Defunct, Dilate, Expensive, Fibrositis, Firm, Formal, Frore(n), Frorn(e), Gammy, Goner, Gromet, Grommet, Grummet, Gut, Hard, Inelastic, Inelegant, Interfacing, Lignin, Mort, Muscle-bound, Myotonia, Petrify, Pokerish, Prim, Ramrod, Rheumatic(ky), Rigid, Rigor, Rigor mortis, Robotic, Sad, Scarious, Set, Shank-iron, Size, Solid, Starch, Stark, Stay, Steep, Steeve, Stieve, Stilted, Stoor, Stour, Stowre, Sture, Tarlatan, Tensive, Trubenize®, Unbending, Unyielding, Upper lip, Whalebone, Wigan, Wooden
**Stifle** Choke, Crush, Dampen, Depress, Funk, Gag, Muffle, Mute, Scomfish, Smore, Smother, Stive, Strangle
**Stigma(tise)** Blemish, Brand, Carpel, Discredit, Note, Saffron, Slur, Smear, Spot, → STAIN, Taint, Wound
**Stile** Gate, Slamming, Steps, Sty
**Stiletto** Bodkin, Heel, Knife
**Still** Accoy, Airless, Alembic, Anymore, Assuage, At rest, Becalm, Breathless, Calm, Check, Current, Doggo, Ene, Even(ness), Flat, Freeze-frame, Higher, Howbe, However, Hush, Idle, Illicit, Inactive, Inanimate, Inert, Kill, Languid, Limbec(k), Lull, Motionless, Nevertheless, Nonetheless, Notwithstanding, Patent, Peaceful, Photograph, Placate, Placid, Polaroid, Posé, Pot, Practitioner, Quiescent, Quiet, Resting, Retort, Serene, Shot, Silent, Snapshot, Soothe, Stagnant, Static, Stationary, Stock, Stone, Though, Tranquil, Unmoving, Windless, Yet
**Stilt** Avocet, Bird, Poaka, Prop, Scatch
**Stilted** Formal, Mannered, Pedantic, Stiff, Unruffled, Wooden
**Stimulate, Stimulus, Stimulant, Stimulation** Activate, Adrenaline, Anilingus, Ankus, Antigen, Aperitif, Aphrodisiac, Arak, Arouse, Auxin, Benny, Betel nut, Brace, Caffeine, Cardiac, Cinder, Clomiphene, Coca, Coffee, Conditioned, Coramine, Cue, Dart, Dex(edrine)®, Digitalin, Digoxin, Doxapram, Egg, Energise, Erotogenic, Evoke, Excitant, Fillip, Foreplay, Fuel, Galvanize, Ginger, Goad, Grains of Paradise, G-spot, Guinea grains, Hop up, Hormone,

Hyper, Impetus, Incentive, Incitant, Incite, Innerve, Inspire, Irritate, Jog, K(h)at, Key, Kick, L-dopa, Liven, Mneme, Motivate, Nikethamide, Oestrus, Oxytocin, Pa(a)n, Paraphilia, Paratonic, Pemoline, Pep, Pep pill, Peyote, Philtre, Pick-me-up, Piquant, Pituitrin, Potentiate, Prod, Promote, Provoke, Psych, Qat, Ritalin®, Roborant, → ROUSE, Rowel, Rub, Sassafras, Sensuous, Shot, Smelling salts, Somatosensory, Spark, Spur, Sting, Stir, String, Suggestive, Tannin, Tar, Tea, Theine, Tickle, Tik-tik, Titillate, Tone, Tonic, Tropism, Unconditioned, Upper, Urge, Urolagnia, Whet(stone), Wintergreen, Winter's bark

**Sting(er), Stinging** Aculeate, Barb, Bite, Cheat, Cnida, Con, Fleece, Goad, Jellyfish, Nematocyst, Nettle(tree), Overcharge, Perceant, Piercer, Poignant, Prick, Provoke, Pungent, Rile, Scorcher, Scorpion, Sea anemone, Sephen, Smart, Spice, Stang, Stimulus, Surcharge, Tang, Tingle, Trichocyst, Urent, Urtica, Venom, Wasp

**Sting-ray** Sephen, Trygon

**Stingy** Cheap, Cheeseparing, Chintzy, Close, Costive, Hard, Illiberal, Kunjoos, Mean, Miserly, Narrow, Near, Niggardly, Nipcheese, Nippy, Parsimonious, Save-all, Skimpy, Snippy, Snudge, Tight(wad), Tight-arse

▹**Stingy** *may indicate* something that stings

**Stink(er), Stinking, Stinks** Abroma, Atoc, Atok, Brock, Cacodyl, Cad, Crepitate, Desman, Fetor, Foumart, Frowsty, Guff, Heel, Hellebore, Malodour, Mephitis, Miasma, Ming, Niff, Noisome, Pen, Polecat, Pong, Ponk, Rasse, Reek, Rich, Science, → SMELL, Sondeli, Stench, Teledu

**Stinkbird** Hoa(c)tzin

**Stint** Allot, Bout, Chore, Economise, Kitchen, Limit, Scamp, Scantle, Scrimp, Session, Share, Skimp, Spell

**Stipend** Ann(at), Annexure, Pay, Prebend, Remuneration, Salary, Wages

**Stipple** Dot

**Stipulate, Stipulation** Clause, Condition, Covenant, Insist, Provision, Proviso, Rider, Specify, String, Term

**Stipule** Ocrea

**Stir(red), Stirrer, Stirring** Accite, Admix, Ado, Afoot, Agitate, Amo(o)ve, Animate, Annoy, Araise, Arouse, Awaken, Beat, Bird, Bother, Bustle, Buzz, Can, Churn, Cooler, Egg on, Emotional, Emotive, Evocative, Excite, Foment, Furore, Fuss, Gaol, Goad, Hectic, Impassion, Incense, Incite, Inflame, Inspire, Instigate, Insurrection, Intermix, Jee, Jog, Jug, Kitty, Limbo, Live, Makebate, → MIX, Molinet, Move, Nervous, Newgate, Nick, Noy, Paddle, Penitentiary, Poach, Poss, Pother, → PRISON, Prod, Provoke, Quad, Quatch, Quetch, Qui(t)ch, Quinche, Quod, Rabble(-rouse), Rear, Roil, Rouse, Roust, Rummage, Rustle, Sod, Spirtle, Steer, Styre, Swizzle, To-do, Touch, Undulate, Upset, Upstart, Wake

▹**Stir(red), Stirring** *may indicate* an anagram

**Stirrup (guard)** Bone, Footrest, Footstall, Gambado, Iron, Stapes, Tapadera, Tapadero

**Stitch(ing), Stitch up** Bargello, Bar tack, Basket, Baste, Blanket, Blind, Box, Buttonhole, Cable, Chain, Couching, Crewel, Crochet, Cross, Daisy, Embroider, Fancy, Feather, Fell, Flemish, Florentine, Garter, Gathering, Grospoint, Hem, Herringbone, Honeycomb, Insertion, Kettle, Knit, Lazy daisy, Lock, Machine, Middle, Monk's seam, Moss, Needle, Open, Overcast, Overlock, Pearl, Petit point, Pinwork, Plain, Purl, Queen, Rag, Railway, Rib, Rope, Running, Saddle, Satin, Screw, Sew, Slip, Smocking, Spider, Split, Stab, Stay, Steek, Stem, Stockinette, Stocking, Straight, Sutile, Suture, Tack, Tailor's tack, Tent, Topstitch, Vandyke, Wheat, Wheat-ear, Whip, Whole, Zigzag

**St James** Scallop-shell

**St Jerome** Hieronymic

**St John's bread** Carob

**St Lucia** WL

**Stoat** Kit

**Stock(ed), Stockpile, Stocks, Stocky** Acates, Aerie, Aery, Alpha, Ambulance, Amplosome, Ancestry, Arsenal, Banal, Barometer, Beefy, Blue-chip, Bouillon, Bree, Breech, Brompton, Buffer, But(t), Cache, Capital, Cards, Carry, Cattle, Cellar, Choker, Cippus, Common, Congee, Conjee, Court-bouillon, Cravat, Crop, Cube, Dashi, Debenture, Delta, Die, Endomorph, Equip, Evening, Fill, Fumet, Fund, Gamma, Gear(e), Government, Graft, Gravy,

Growth, Gun, Hackneyed, Handpiece, He(a)rd, Hilt, Hoard, Hoosh, Industrial, Intervention, Inventory, Joint, Just-in-time, Kin, Larder, Laughing, Line, Little-ease, Locuplete, Log, Market, Merchandise, Night-scented, Omnium, Pigeonhole, Pile, Preferred, Pycnic, Race, Ranch, Recovery, Rep(ertory), Replenish, Reserve, Resource, Rolling, Root, Scrip, Seed, Share, Shorts, Soup, Squat, Standard, Staple, Stash, Steale, Steelbow, Stereotype, Stirp(e)s, → STORE, Strain, Stubby, Supply, Surplus, Talon, Tap, Taurus, Team, Thickset, Tie, Trite, Trust(ee), Usual, Utility, Virginian, Water, Yeomanry

**Stockade** Barrier, Eureka, Zare(e)ba, Zereba, Zeriba

**Stock Exchange** Big Board

**Stocking(s)** Bas, Body, Boot-hose, Fishnet, Hogger, Hold ups, Hose, Hosiery, Leather, Legwarmer, Legwear, Moggan, Netherlings, Netherstocking, Nylons, Popsock, Seamless, Sheer, Silk, Sock, Spattee, Support, Surgical, Tights

**Stockman, Stockbroker, Stockholder** Broker, Cattleman, Cowpuncher, Herdsman, Jobber, Neatherd, Ringer, Rustler

**Stocktaking** Rustling

**Stodge, Stodgy** Dull, Filling, Heavy

**Stoic(al)** Impassive, Job, Logos, Patient, Philosophical, Plato, Porch, Seneca(n), Spartan, Stolid, Uncomplaining, Zeno

**Stoke(r), Stokes** Bram, Chain grate, Coal-trimmer, Fire(man), Fuel, S, Shovel

**Stole(n)** Bent, Boa, Epitrachelion, Fichu, Hot, Maino(u)r, Manner, Manor, Nam, Orarion, Orarium, Reft, Scarf, Screen, Soup, Staw, Tippet, Tweedler, Waif, Wrap

**Stolid** Beefy, Deadpan, Dour, Dull, Impassive, Passive, Phlegmatic, Po(-faced), Thickset, Wooden

**Stomach(ic)** Abdomen, Abomasum, Accept, Alvine, Appetite, Belly, Bible, Bingy, Bonnet, Bread-basket, Brook, C(o)eliac, Corporation, Craw, Epigastrium, Epiploon, Face, Fardel-bag, Gaster, Gastric, Gizzard, Gut, Heart, Inner man, Jejunum, King's-hood, Kite, Kyte, Little Mary, Manyplies, Mary, Maw, Mesaraic, Midriff, Omasum, Opisthosoma, Paunch, Potbelly, Propodon, Proventriculus, Psalterium, Puku, Pylorus, Read, Rennet, Reticulum, Rumen, Stand, Stick, Swagbelly, → SWALLOW, Tripe, Tum, Tun-belly, Urite, Uromere, Vell, Venter, Wame, Washboard, Wem, Zingiber

**Stomach-ache, Stomach trouble** Caecitis, Colic, Colitis, Collywobbles, Gastralgia, Giardiasis, Gripe, Gutrot, Mulligrubs

**Stomp** Tread

**Stone(s), Stone age, Stoned, Stony** Blotto, Cast, Coggle, Deseed, Drake, Drunk, Foundation, → GEM, Henge, Imposing, Ink, Inukshuk, Lapideous, Lucky, Lydian, Masonry, Mort, Neolithic, Niobe(an), Obdurate, Ore, Pelt, Petrified, Precious, Putting, Rolling, Roughcast, Seeing, Sermon, Shingle, Standing, Step(ping), Through, Touch, Tusking

---

## STONES

*2 letters:*
St

*3 letters:*
Gem
Hog
Pip
Pit
Rag
Tin
Top

*4 letters:*
Bath
Blue
Bond
Celt
Door
Drop
Flag
Grit
Hone
Horn
Iron
Jade
Jasp
Kerb
Lias
Lime
Lode
Onyx
Opal
Plum
Ragg
Sard
Skew
Slab
Soap
Tile
Toad
Trap

*5 letters:*
Agate
Amber
Balas
Beryl
Black
Chalk
Chert
Coade
Culch
Drupe
Field
Flint
Geode
Gooly
Grape
Grind
Jewel
Kenne
Lapis
Logan
Menah
Metal
Mocha
Paste
Penny
Prase
Pumie
Quern
Quoin
Quoit
Rubin
Rufus
Rybat
Satin
Scone
Scree
Slate

Sleek
Slick
Sneck
Stela
Stele
Topaz
Wacke
Wyman

***6 letters:***
Amazon
Arthur
Ashlar
Ashler
Baetyl
Bezoar
Brinny
Chesil
Chisel
Cobble
Coping
Cultch
Dolmen
Flusch
Fossil
Gibber
Gooley
Goolie
Gravel
Humite
Iolite
Jargon
Jasper
Kernel
Kidney
Kingle
Ligure
Lithic
Marble
Menhir
Metate
Mihrab
Mosaic
Muller
Nutlet
Oamaru
Paving
Pebble
Pencil
Pot-lid
Pumice
Pyrene
Rip-rap
Samian
Sarsen
Scarab
Summer
Tablet
Tanist
Yonnie

***7 letters:***
Asteria
Avebury
Azurite
Blarney
Bologna
Boulder
Breccia
Callais
Cat's eye
Chuckie
Clinker
Curling
Falling
Girasol
Granite
Hyacine
Hyalite
Jacinth
Jargoon
Lia-fail
Lithoid
Moabite
Olivine
Parpane
Parpend
Parpent
Peacock
Pennant
Peridot
Perpend
Perpent
Petrous
Pudding
Purbeck
Putamen
Rocking
Rosetta
Rubbing
Sardine
Sardius
Sarsden
Scaglia
Schanse
Schanze
Smaragd
Staddle
Tambour
Tektite
Telamon
Thunder
Trilith
Tripoli
Urolith
Zauxite

***8 letters:***
Aerolite
Aerolith
Amethyst
Asteroid
Baguette
Cabochon
Calculus
Cinnamon
Corundum
Cromlech
Cryolite
Ebenezer
Elf-arrow
Endocarp
Essonite
Ganister
Girasole
Lapidate
Megalith
Menamber
Meteoric
Monolith
Nephrite
Omphalos
Onychite
Parpoint
Peastone
Petrosal
Phengite
Pisolite
Portland
Potstone
Rollrich
Sapphire
Sardonyx
Scalpins
Schantze
Specular
Tonalite
Traprock
Voussoir

***9 letters:***
Alabaster
Almandine
Asparagus
Cairngorm
Carnelian
Cholelith
Chondrite
Cornelian
Crossette
Dichroite
Firestone
Gannister
Greensand
Hessonite
Hoarstone
Lithiasis
Malachite
Meteorite
Paleolith
Pipestone
Rollright
Rubicelle
Scagliola
Tiger's eye
Trilithon
Turquoise
Ventifact

***10 letters:***
Adamantine
Alectorian
Aragonites
Astragalus
Chalcedony
Draconites
Enhydritic
Fieldstone
Gastrolith
Grey-wether
Kimberlite
Lherzolite
Lithophyte
Pearlstone
Penny-stone
Rhinestone
Sleekstone
Slickstone

***11 letters:***
Alexandrite
Lapis lazuli
Meteorolite
Pencil-stone
Peristalith

***12 letters:***
Carton-pierre
Lithographic
Philosopher's

**Stone-crop** Orpin(e), Rose-root, Sedum, Succulent
**Stone-pusher** Sisyphus
**Stone-thrower** Bal(lista), Catapult, David, Mangonel, Onager, Perrier, Sling, Trebuchet
**Stone-wall(er)** Block, Jackson, Mule, Revet
**Stoneware** Crouch-ware
**Stone-worker** Jeweller, Knapper, Sculptor
**Stooge** Butt, Cat's-paw, Feed, Joe Soap, Pawn, Straight man
**Stook(s)** Sheaf, Stack, Thr(e)ave
**Stool** Bar, Buffet, Camp, Commode, Coppy, Cracket, Creepie, Cricket, Cucking, Curule, Cutty, Ducking, Faeces, Fender, Foot, Footrest, Hassock, Litany, Milking, Music, Piano, Pouf(fe), Repentance, Ruckseat, Seat, Sir-reverence, Step, Stercoral, Sunkie, Taboret, Tripod, Tripos, Turd
**Stoolpigeon** Informer, Nark
**Stoop(ed)** Bend, Condescend, Cower, Cringe, Crouch, C(o)urb, Daine, Deign, Incline, Lout, Lowt, Porch, Round-shouldered, Slouch
**Stop(page), Stopcock, Stopped, Stopper, Stopping** Abate, Abolish, Abort, Adeem, Anchor, An(n)icut, Aperture, Arrest, Aspirate, Avast, Avert, Bait, Ba(u)lk, Ballcock, Belay, Bide, Blin, Block, Bouche, Brake, Buffer, Bung, Can, Canting-coin, Carillon, Cattle, → **CEASE**, Cessation, Chapter, Check, Checkpoint, Cheese, Cholestasis, Clarabella, Clarino, Clarion, Clog, Close, Cog, Colon, Comfort, Comma, Conclude, Conversation, Cork, Coupler, Cremo(r)na, Cremorne, Cromorna, Cut, Cut out, Deactivate, Debar, Demurral, Desist, Deter, Devall, Diapason, Diaphone, Discontinue, Discourage, Dit, Dock, Dolce, Dot, Drop, Dulciana, Echo, Embargo, Emergency, End, Enough, Expression, Extinguish, F, Fagotto, Fare stage, Field, Fifteenth, Flag (down), Flue, Flute, Forbid, Foreclose, Forestall, Foundation, Freeze, Fr(a)enum, Frustrate, Full, Full point, Gag, Gamba, Gemshorn, Glottal, Gong, Halt, Hamza(h), Hang, Hartal, Heave to, Hinder, Hitch, Ho, Hoa, Hoh, Hold, Hoy, Inhibit, Intermit, Ischuria, Jam, Kibosh, Kill, Lay-by, Lay to, Let-up, Lill, Limit, Lin, Lute, Media, Moratoria, Mutation, Nasard, Oboe, Obstruent, Obturate, Occlude, Oppilate, Organ, Outage, Outspan, Pack in, Pause, Period, Piccolo, Pit, Plug, Point, Poop, Preclude, Prevent, Principal, Prop, Prorogue, Pull-in, Pull over, Pull-up, Punctuate, Pyramidon, Quash, Quint, Quit, Racket, Red, Reed, Refrain, Register, Rein, Remain, Request, Rest, Roadblock, Salicet, Salicional, Scotch, Screw-top, Seal, Semi-colon, Sese, Sesquialtera, Sext, Silence, Sist, Sneb, Snub, Snuff out, Sojourn, Solo, Spigot, Stall, Stanch, Standstill, Stap, Stash, Stasis, Station, Staunch, Stay, Stent, Stive, Strike, Subbase, Subbass, Suction, Supersede, Suppress, Surcease, Suspend, T, Tab, Tackle, Tamp(ion), Tap, Tea break, Tenuis, Terminate, Thwart, Toby, Toho, Tremolo, Truck, Trumpet, Tuba, Twelfth, Voix celeste, Vox angelica, Vox humana, Waldflute, Waldhorn, Waylay, Waypoint, When, Whistle, Whoa, Wind up
**Stopgap** Caretaker, Gasket, Gaskin, Interim, Makeshift, Pis aller, Temporary
**Stopover** Motel
**Stopwatch** Chronograph
**Storage, Store(house)** Accumulate, Archive, Armoury, Arsenal, Associative, ATLAS, Backing, Barn, Big box, Bin, Bookshop, Boot, Bottle, Bottom drawer, Boxroom, Buffer, Bunker, Buttery, Byte, Cache, Candy, Capacitance, Catacomb, CD-Rom, Cell, Cellar(et), Chain, Charge, Cheek pouch, Clamp, Clipboard, Coffer, Commissary, Convenience, Co-op(erative), Cootch, Core, Corn-crib, Cupboard, Cutch, Database, Deep freeze, Deli, Dene-hole, Dépanneur, Department(al), Depository, Depot, Digipack, Dime, Discount, Dolia, Dolly-shop, Drawer, Drive, DVD, EAROM, Elevator, Emporium, Ensile, Entrepot, Étape, External, File, Freezer, Fridge, Fund, Galleria, Garner, Gasholder, General, Genizah, Girnal, Glory hole, Go-down, Grain, Granary, Groceteria, Hayloft, Hive, → **HOARD**, Hog, Hold, Honeycomb, Hope chest, Host, House, Houseroom, Humidor, Husband, Hypermarket, IKEA®, Imbarn, Keep, Larder, Lastage, Lazaretto, Left luggage, Liquor, Locker, Lumber room, Magazine, Main, Marine, Mart, Mattamore, Meat safe, Memory, Mine, Minimart, Morgue, Mothball, Mow, Multiple, Nest-egg, Off-licence, One-step, Ottoman, Outlet, Package, Pantechnicon, Pantry, Pithos, Preserve, Provision, Pumped, Rack(ing), RAM, Reel, Repertory, Reposit, ROM, Root house, Salt away, Save, Sector, Shed, Shelving, → **SHOP**, Silage, Silo, Sim card, Speakeasy, Spence, Spooling, Springhouse, Squirrel, Stack, Stash, Stillroom, Stock, Stockpile,

Stockroom, Stow, Sump, Superbaza(a)r, Superette, Supermarket, Supply, Tack-room, Tank, Tea chest, Thesaurus, Tithe-barn, Tommy-shop, Trading post, Uplay, Vestiary, Vestry, Virtual, Volutin, Warehouse, Woodshed, Woodyard, Wool (shed), WORM

▸**Storey** *see* STORY

**Stork** Adjutant, Antigone, Argala, Bird, Jabiru, Marabou(t), Marg, Saddlebill, Shoebill, Wader, Whale-headed, Wood, Wood ibis

**Stork's bill** Erodium

**Storm(y)** Ablow, Adad, Assail, Assault, Attack, Baguio, Blizzard, Bluster, Bourasque, Brain, Brouhaha, Buran, Calima, Charge, Cloudburst, Cockeye(d) bob, Cyclone, Devil, Dirty, Dust (devil), Electric, Enlil, Expugn, Furore, Gale, Gusty, Haboob, Hurricane, Ice, Line, Magnetic, Meteor(ic), Monsoon, Onset, Oragious, Pelter, Rage(ful), Raid, Rain, Rampage, Rant, Rate, Rave, Red spot, Rugged, Rush, Sand, Shaitan, Snorter, Snow, Squall, Sumatra, Tea-cup, Tebbad, Tempest, Thunder, Tornade, Tornado, Tropical, Turmoil, Unruly, Violent, Weather, White squall, Willy-willy, Wroth, Zu

**Stormproof** Unassailable

**Stormtrooper** Brown shirt

▹**Stormy** *may indicate* an anagram

**Story, Storyline, Stories** Account, Actioner, Allegory, Anecdote, Apocrypha, Apologise, Arthuriana, Attic, Bar, Basement, Baur, Bawr, Bedtime, Biog, Blood and thunder, Chapbook, Chestnut, Clearstory, Clerestory, Cock and bull, Conte, Cover, Decameron, Detective, Edda, Epic, Episode, Etage, Exclusive, Exemplum, Fable, Fabliau, Fabrication, Fairy, Falsehood, Feature, Fib, Fiction, Flat, Floor, Folk-lore, Folk-tale, Gag, Geste, Ghost, Glurge, Hair-raiser, Hard-luck, Heptameron, Hitopadesa, Horror, Idyll, Iliad, Item, Jataka, Lee, Legend, Lie, Lore, Mabinogion, Märchen, Mezzanine, Myth(os), Mythus, Narrative, Nouvelle, Novel(la), Oratorio, Parable, Passus, Pentameron, Photo, Picture-play, Plot, Rede, Report, Roman a clef, Romance, Rumour, Saga, Scoop, Script, Serial, SF, Shaggy dog, Shilling shocker, Shocker, Short, Smoke-room, Sob, Spiel, Spine-chiller, Splash, Spoiler, Stage, Storey, Sub-plot, Success, Tale, Tall, Thread, Thriller, Tier, Tragedy, Triforium, Upper, Version, Whodun(n)it, Yarn

**Storyteller** Aesop, Fibber, Grimm, Griot, Liar, Miller, Munchausen, Narrator, Raconteur, Sagaman, Shannachie, Tusitala, Uncle Remus

**Stoup** Benitier, Bucket, Vessel

**Stout(ness)** Ale, Beer, Black velvet, Burly, Chopping, Chubby, Cobby, Corpulent, Doughty, Embonpoint, Endomorph, Entire, Fat, Fubsy, Guinness, Hardy, Heavyset, Humpty-dumpty, Lusty, Manful, Milk, Obese, Overweight, Plump, Porter, Portly, Potbelly, Robust, Rotund, Stalwart, Stalworth, Sta(u)nch, Strong, Stuggy, Sturdy, Substantial, Tall, Tufty, Velvet

**Stove** Aga, Baseburner, Break, Calefactor, Chauf(f)er, Chiminea, Cockle, Cooker, Cooktop, Furnace, Gasfire, Hob, Oven, Potbelly, Primus®, Range, Salamander

**Stovepipe** Hat

**Stow** Cram, Flemish (down), Load, Pack, Rummage, Stack, Stash, Steeve

**St Paul's** Wren-ch

**Strabismus** Squint

**Straddle, Straddling** Bestride, Enjamb(e)ment, Span, Strodle

**Strafe** Bombard, Shell, Shoot

**Straggle(r), Straggly** Estray, Gad, Meander, Ramble, Rat-tail, Spidery, Sprawl, Stray, Wander

**Straight(en), Straightness** Align, Bald, Beeline, Blunt, Boning, Correct, Dead, Die, Direct, Downright, Dress, Frank, Gain, Het(ero), Home, Honest, Lank, Legit, Level, Line, Linear, Narrow, Neat, Normal, Ortho-, Orthotropous, Rectilineal, Rectitude, Righten, Sheer, Slap, Tidy, True, Unbend, Unbowed, Uncoil, Uncurl, Unlay, Unroll, Upright, Veracious, Virgate

**Straight edge** Lute, Ruler

**Straightfaced** Agelast

**Straightforward** Candid, Direct, Downright, Easy, Even, Forthright, Honest, Jannock, Level, Plain sailing, Pointblank, Simple, Unadorned, Uncomplicated

**Straight-haired** Leiotrichous

**Strain(ed), Strainer, Straining** Agonistic, Air, Ancestry, Aria, Breed, Bulk, Carol, Charleyhorse, Clarify, Colander, Crick, Distend, Drawn, Effort, Exert, Filter, Filtrate, Fit,

Fitt(e), Force, Fray, Fytt(e), Intense, Kind, Lineage, Lullaby, Melody, Milsey, Minus, Molimen, Music, Nervy, Note, Overstretch, Overtask, Passus, Percolate, Plus, Pressure, Pull, Purebred, Rack, Raring, Reck(an), Repetitive, Retch, Rick, Riddle, Seep, Seil(e), Set, Shear, Sieve, Sift, Sile, Stape, Start, Stirps, Stock, Streak, Stress, Stretch, Stripe, Sye, Tamis, Tammy, Taut, Tax, Tems(e), Tenesmus, Tense, Tension, Threnody, Torsion, Try, Tune, Unease, Vein, Vice, Work, Wrick

**Strait(s)** Bab el Mandeb, Basilan, Bass, Bering, Bosp(h)orus, Canso, Channel, Condition, Cook, Crisis, Cut, Dardanelles, Davis, Denmark, Desperate, Dire, Dover, Drake Passage, East River, Euripus, Florida, Formosa, Foveaux, Gat, Gibraltar, Golden Gate, Great Belt, Gut, Hainan, Hormuz, Hudson, Johore, Juan de Fuca, Kattegat, Kerch, Korea, Kyle, Little Belt, Lombok, Mackinac, Magellan, Malacca, Menai, Messina, Mona Passage, Narrow, North Channel, Oresund, Otranto, Palk, Predicament, Scapa Flow, Soenda, Solent, Sound, St, Sumba, Sunda, Taiwan, Tatar, Tiran, Torres, Tsugaru, Windward Passage

**Straiten(ed)** Impecunious, Impoverish, Poor, Restrict

**Strait-laced** Blue-nosed, Narrow, Prig, Primsie, Prudish, Puritan, Starchy, Stuffy

**Strand(ed)** Abandon, Aground, Bank, Beach, Castaway, Cord, Desert, Enisle, Fibre, Ground, Haugh, Hexarch, Isolate, Lock, Maroon, Neaped, Ply, Rice, Rope, Shore, Sliver, Thread, Three-ply, Tress, Twist, Wisp

**Strange(ness), Stranger** Abnormal, Alien, Aloof, Amphitryon, Bizarre, Curious, Dougal, Eccentric, Eerie, Exotic, Ferly, Foreign, Fraim, Freaky, Frem(d), Fremit, Frenne, Funny, Guest, Hypercharge, Jimmy, Malihini, New, Novel, Odd(ball), Outlandish, Outré, Outsider, Quare, Quark, Queer, Rum, S, Screwy, Selcouth, Singular, Surreal, Tea-leaf, Uncanny, Unco, Uncommon, Unfamiliar, Unked, Unket, Unkid, Unnatural, Unused, Unusual, Wacky, Weird, Weyard, Wondrous

▷**Strange** *may indicate* an anagram

**Strangle(r)** Anaconda, Bindweed, Boa, Choke, Garotte, Jugulate, Suffocate, Suppress, Throttle, Thug(gee)

**Strap(ping)** Able-bodied, Band, Barber, Beat, Belt, Bowyangs, Braces, Brail, Braw, Breeching, Browband, Cheekpiece, Crownpiece, Crupper, Cuir-bouilli, Curb, Deckle, Garter, Girth, G-string, Halter, Harness, Holdback, Jess, Jock(ey), Kicking, Larrup, Lash, Leather, Ligule, Lorate, Lore, Lusty, Manly, Martingale, Nicky-tam, Octopus, Overcheck, Palmie, Pandy, Rand, Rein, Robust, Sam Browne, Seatbelt, Shoulder, Sling, Spaghetti, Spider, Strop, Surcingle, Suspender, T, Tab, Taws(e), T-bar, Thong, Thoroughbrace, Throatlash, Throatlatch, Trace, Tump-line, Wallop, Watch, Watchband

**Stratagem, Strategist, Strategy** Artifice, Campaign, Clausewitz, Closet, Contrivance, Coup, Deceit, Device, Dodge, Exit, Fetch, Finesse, Fraud, Game plan, Generalship, Guile, Heresthetic, Kaupapa, Lady Macbeth, Malengine, Manoeuvre, Maskirovka, Masterstroke, Maximum, Minimax, Plan, Ploy, Realpolitik, Rope-a-dope, → **RUSE**, Salami, Scam, Scheme, Scorched earth, Sleight, Spin doctor, Subterfuge, Tack, Tactic(s), Tactician, Trick, Wheeze, Wile

**Stratum, Strata** Bed, Coal Measures, Kar(r)oo, Layer, Neogene, Permian, Schlieren, Seam, Syncline, Tier

**Strauss** Levi

**Straw(s), Strawy** Balibuntal, Boater, Buntal, Chaff, Cheese, Crosswort, Halm, Hat, Haulm, Hay, Insubstantial, Kemple, Last, Leghorn, Monkey-pump, Nugae, Oaten, Panama, Parabuntal, Pea(se), Pedal, Rush, Rye, Short, Sipper, Stalk, Strae, Stramineous, Strammel, Strummel, Stubble, Sucker, Trifles, Truss, Wisp, Ye(a)lm

**Strawberry** Alpine, Barren, Birthmark, Fragaria, Fraise, Garden, Hautbois, Hautboy, Potentilla, Wild

**Stray(ing)** Abandoned, Aberrant, Alleycat, Chance, Depart, Deviate, Digress, Err, Excursion, Forwander, Foundling, Gamin, Maverick, Meander, Misgo, Pye-dog, Ramble, Roam, Sin, Straggle, Streel, Street arab, Traik, Unowned, Waff, Waif, Wander, Wilder

**Streak(ed), Streaker, Streaky** Archimedes, Bended, Blue, Brindle, Comet, Flambé, Flaser, Flash, Fleck, Freak, Hawked, Hawkit, Highlights, Lace, Layer, Leonid, Lowlight, Marble, Mark, Merle, Mottle, Primitive, Race, Ra(t)ch, Run, Schlieren, Seam, Shot, Splodge, Striate, Striga, Strip(e), Vein, Venose, Vibex, Waif, Wake, Wale, Yellow

**Stream** Acheron, Anabranch, Arroyo, Beam, Beck, Blast, Bogan, Bourne, Brook, Burn, Consequent, Course, Current, Driblet, Fast, Flow, Flower, Freshet, Ghyll, Gill, Gulf, Gush, Headwater, Influent, Influx, Jet, Kill, Lade, Lane, Leet, Logan, Main, Meteor, Nala, Nalla(h), Nulla(h), Obsequent, Onflow, Pokelogan, Pour, Pow, Riffle, Rill, River, Rivulet, Rubicon, Run, Runlet, Runnel, Side, Sike, Slip, Slough, Spill, Spruit, Squirt, Star, Strand, Streel, Subsequent, Syke, The Fleet, Third, Thrutch, Tide-race, Torrent, Tributary, Trickle, Trout, Watercourse, Water-splash, Winterbourne

**Streamer** Banderol(e), Bandrol, Banner(all), Bannerol, Party popper, Pennon, Pinnet, Ribbon, Tape, Tippet, Vane

**Streamline(d), Streamliner** Clean, Fair, Fairing, Simplify, Sleek, Slim

**Street** Alley, Ave(nue), Bay, Boulevard, Bowery, Broad, Broadway, Carey, Carnaby, Cato, Causey, Champs Elysées, Cheapside, Civvy, Close, Coronation, Corso, Court, Crescent, Downing, Drive, Easy, Ermine, Fleet, Gate, Grub, Harley, High(way), Kármán vortex, Lane, Lombard, Main, Main drag, Meuse, Mews, One-way, Parade, Paseo, Poultry, Queer, Road(way), Sesame, Side, Sinister, St, Strand, Terrace, Thoroughfare, Threadneedle, Throgmorton, Two-way, Vortex, Wall, Wardour, Watling, Way, Whitehall

**Street arab** Mudlark

**Streetcar** Desire, Tram

**Street seller** Hawker, Patterer

**Streetwise** Cynical

**Strength(en), Strengthened, Strengthener, Strengthening** Afforce, Anneal, Arm, Asset, Augment, Ausforming, Bant, Beef, Brace, Brawn, Build, Confirm, Consolidate, Edify, Embattle, Enable, Energy, Fibre, Field, Fish, Foison, Force, Force majeure, Forte, Fortify, Fortitude, Freshen, Fur, Fus(h)ion, Grit, Heart, Herculean, Horn, Integrity, Intensity, Invigorate, Iron, Lace, Line, Main, Man, Might, Munite, Muscle, Neal, Nerve, → POWER, Prepotence, Pre-stress, Proof, Reinforce, Roborant, Shear, Sinew, Spike, Spine, Stability, Stamina, Steel, Sthenia, Stoutness, → STRONG, Sustain, Tenacity, Tensile, Thews, Titration, Ultimate, Unity, Vigour, Vim, Willpower, Yield

**Strenuous** Arduous, Effort, Exhausting, Hard, Laborious, Vehement

**Strephon** Rustic, Wooer

**Stress(ed), Stressful** Accent, Actuate, Angst, Arsis, Birr, Breaking, Brunt, Careworn, Creep, Drive home, Emphasis, Highlight, Ictus, Impress, Insist, Italicise, Marcato, Nerves, Ordeal, Orthotonesis, Oxidative, Oxytone, Paroxytone, Post-traumatic, Press, Primary, Proclitic, Proof, PTSD, Rack, Ram (home), Repetitive, Rhythm, RSI, Secondary, Sentence, Sforzando, Shear, Strain, Taut, Tense, → TENSION, Testing, Thetic, Tonic, Try, Umlaut, Underline, Underscore, Urge, Wind shear, Word, Yield (point)

**Stretch(able), Stretched, Stretcher, Stretching** Acreage, Alength, Amplitude, Belt, Brick, Bungee, Crane, Distend, Doolie, Draw, Ectasis, Eke, Elastic, Elongate, Exaggerate, Expanse, Extend, Extensile, Farthingale, Fib, Frame, Full, Give, Gurney, Home, Lengthen, Lie, Life, Limo, Litter, Narrows, Outreach, Pallet, Pandiculation, Porrect, Procrustes, Prolong, Protend, Pull, Rack, Rax, → REACH, Sentence, Shiner, Span, Spell, Spread, Spreadeagle, Strain, Streak, Taut, Tax, Tend, Tense, Tensile, Tenter, Term, Time, Tract, Tractile, Traction, Tree, Trolley

**Striate** Lineolate, Vein

**Stricken** Beset, Hurt, Overcome, Shattered

**Strict(ly)** Authoritarian, De rigueur, Dour, Exacting, Formal, Fundamentalist, Giusto, Hard and fast, Harsh, Iron hand, Literal, Medic, Narrow, Orthodox, Penal, Precise, Proper, Puritanical, Religious, Rigid, Rigorous, Severe, Spartan, Stern, Strait(-laced), Stringent, To the letter, Tough

**Stricture** Discipline

**Stride(s)** Gal(l)umph, Giant's, Jeans, Leg, Lope, March, Pace, Piano, Stalk, Sten, Stend, Straddle, Stroam, Strut, Stump

**Strident** Brassy, Discordant, Grinding, Harsh, Raucous, Screech, Shrill

**Strife** Bargain, Barrat, Bate(-breeding), Brigue, Colluctation, Conflict, Conteck, Contest, Discord, Disharmony, Dissension, Eris, Feud, Food, Friction, Ignoble, Scrap(ping), Sturt

**Strike(r), Striker, Striking, Strike out** Affect, Affrap, Air, Alight, Annul, Appulse, Arresting, Astonishing, Attitude, Backhander, Baff, Band, Bandh, Bang, Bash, Bat, Baton, Batsman, Batter, Beat, Befall, Belabour, Better, Biff, Bird, Black, Bla(u)d, Bludgeon, Bonanza, Bop, British disease, Buff, Buffet, Bund(h), Butt, Cane, Catch, Chime, Chip, Clap, Clash, Clatch, Clip, Clock, Clout, Club, Cob, Collide, Conk, Constitutional, Coup, Cue, Cuff, Dad, Dele, Dent, Dev(v)el, Ding, Dint, Dismantle, Distingué, Douse, Dowse, Dramatic, Drive, Dush, Éclat, Effective, Emphatic, Especial, Événement, Fat, Fet(ch), Fillip, Firk, Fist, Flail, Flog, Frap, General, Get, Gnash, Go-slow, Gowf, Hail, Handsome, Hartal, Head-butt, →HIT, Horn, Hour, Hunger, Ictus, Illision, Impact, Impinge, Impress, Jarp, Jaup, Jole, Joll, Joule, Jowl, Knock, Lam, Lambast, Laser, Lash, Lay(-off), Lightning, Lucky, Match, Memorable, Middle, Mint, Notable, Noticeable, Official, Out, Pash, Pat(ter), Pat, Pean, Peck, Peen, Pein, Pene, Percuss, Picket, Pize, Plectrum, Pounce, Pound, Pronounced, Pummel, Punch, Quarter-jack, Rag-out, Raid, Ram, Rap, Remarkable, Rolling, Roquet, Salient, Scrub, Scutch, Shank, Sick out, Sideswipe, Signal, Sitdown, Sit-in, Sizzling, Slam, Slap, Slat, Slog, Slosh, Smack, Smash, Smite, Sock, Souse, Sowce, Sowse, Space bar, Spank, Stayaway, Stop(page), Stub, Swap, Swat, Swinge, Swipe, Switch, Swop, Sympathy, Tan, Tangent, Tapotement, Tat, Thump, Thwack, Tip, Token, Tonk, Tripper, Unconstitutional, Unofficial, Vivid, Walk-out, Wallop, Wap, Whack, Whale, Whang, Whap, Wherret, Who does what, Whomp, Whop, Wick, Wildcat, Wipe, Wondrous, Zap

**Strike-breaker** Blackleg, Fink, Rat, Scab

**String(s), Stringy** Anchor, Apron, Band, Bant, Beads, Bootlace, Bow, Bowyang, Catgut, Cello, Chalaza, Chanterelle, Cord, Cosmic, Creance, Cremaster, Drill, Enfilade, Fairy, Fibre, Fiddle, Fillis, First, Floss, G, Glass, Gut, Henequin, Heniquin, Hypate, Idiot, Injection, Keyed, Kill, Kissing, Lace, Lag, Laisse, Leading, Lichanos, Macramé, Mese, Necklace, Nete, Nicky-tam, Oil, Paramese, Paranete, Pledget, Production, Proviso, Purse, Quint, Riempie, Ripcord, Rope, Rosary, Rough, Second, Series, Shoe(-tie), Silly®, Sinewy, Snare, Spit, Stable, Straggle, Strand, Sultana, Sympathetic, Team, Tendon, Thairm, Tie, Tough, Train, Trite, Twiddling-line, Twine, Viola, Violin, Worry-beads, Wreathed

**String-course** Moulding, Table

**Stringent** Exacting, Extreme, Rigid, Severe, Strict, Urgent

**String-pulling** Cat's cradle

**Strip(ped), Stripper, Stripping, Striptease** Acetone, Agent orange, Airfield, Armband, Asset, Band(eau), Bare, Bark, Batten, Belt, Bereave, Bimetallic, Blowtorch, Caprivi, Cartoon, Casparian, Chippendale, Comic, Cote, Defoliate, Denude, Deplume, Deprive, Derobe, Despoil, Devest, Disbark, Dismantle, Dismask, Disrobe, Divest, Doab, Dosing, Drag, Ecdysiast, Ecdysis, Écorché, Excorticate, Fannel(l), Feeler gauge, Fiche, Film, Flashing, Flaught, Flay, Fleece, Flench, Flense, Flight, Flinch, Flounce, Flype, Furring, Gaza, Goujon, Hatband, Infula, Isthmus, Jib, Label, Landing, Lap-dancer, Lardon, Lath, Ledge, Linter, List, Littoral, Loading, Locust, Magnetic, Mail-rod, Maniple, Median, Möbius, Nature, Noodle, Nude, Paint, Panhandle, Parting, Peel, Pillage, Pluck, Pull, Puttee, Puttie, Rand, Raunch, Raw, Reglet, Reservation, Riband, Ribbon, Ridge, Rifle, Ring-bark, Roon, Royne, Rumble, Rund, Runway, Scent, Screed, Scrow, Shear, Shed, Shim, Shorn, Showgirl, Shred, Shuck, Skin, Slat, Slit, Sliver, Spellican, Spilikin, Spill(ikin), Spit, Splat, Splent, Spline, Splint, Splinter, Spoil, Sportswear, Stave, Straik, Strake, Strap, Streak, Strop, Sugar soap, Swath(e), Sweatband, Tack, Tear, Tear-off, Tee, Thong, Tirl, Tirr, Tombolo, Tongue, Trash, Unbark, Uncase, Unclothe, Uncover, Undeck, Undress, Unfrock, Unrig, Unrip, Unrobe, Unvaile, Valance, Weather, Widow, Zona, Zone

**Stripe(d)** Agate, Band, Bar, Bausond, Candy, Chevron, Cingulum, Cove, Endorse, Go-faster, Lance-jack, Lash, Laticlave, Line, List, Magnetic, →NCO, Ombré, Pale, Paly, Pin, Pirnie, Pirnit, Ribbon, Slash, Snip, Straik, Strake, Streak, Striation, Stroke, Tabaret, Tabby, Tiger, Tragelaph(us), Vitta, Weal, Zebroid

**Stripling** Lad

**Strive, Striving** Aim, Aspire, →ATTEMPT, Contend, Emulous, Endeavour, Enter, Kemp, Labour, Nisus, Persevere, Pingle, Press, Strain, Struggle, Toil, Try, Vie

**Stroke** Apoplex(y), Approach, Back, Backhander, Bat, Bisque, Blow, Boast, Breast, Brushwork, Butterfly, Cannon, Caress, Carom, Chip, Chop, Counterbuff, Coup, Coy, Crawl,

Dab, Dash, Dint, Dog(gy)-paddle, Down-bow, Drear(e), Drere, Drive, Dropshot, Effleurage, Estrarnazone, Exhaust, Feat, Flick, Fondle, Foozle, Forehand, Freestyle, Glance, Glide, Ground, Hairline, Hand(er), Hyphen, Ictus, In-off, Inwick, Jenny, Jole, Joll, Joule, Jowl, Knell, Knock, Lash, Lightning, Like, Line, Loft, Long jenny, Loop, Loser, Massé, Master, Oarsman, Oblique, Odd, Off-drive, Outlash, Palp, Paw, Pet, Pile-driver, Pot-hook, Pull, Punto reverso, Put(t), Reverso, Ridding straik, Roquet, Rub, Scart, Scavenge, Sclaff, Scoop, Seizure, Serif, Seriph, Sheffer's, Short Jenny, Sider, Sixte, Slash, Slice, Smash, Smooth, Solidus, Spot, Strike, Stripe, Sweep, Swipe, Tact, Tittle, Touch, Touk, Trait, Trudgen, Trudgeon, Tuck, Upbow, Virgule, Wale, Whang, Wrist shot

**Stroll(er), Strolling** Amble, Ambulate, Bummel, Dander, Daun(d)er, Dawner, Flânerie, Flâneur, Frescade, Idle, Lounge, Perambulate, Ramble, Saunter, Stravaig, Stray, Toddle, Walk, Walkabout, Wander

**Strong(est)** Able, Boofy, Brawny, Buff, Cast-iron, Doughty, Drastic, Durable, F, Fat, Fierce, Firm, Fit, Forceful, Forcible, Forte, Full-blown, Hale, Hardy, Heady, Hercules, High-powered, Humming, Husky, Intense, Ironside, Keen, Marrowy, Mature, Mighty, Muscular, Nappy, Ox, Pithy, Pollent, Potent, Powerful, Predominant, Pronounced, Pungent, Racy, Rank, Robust, Samson, Solid, Sour, Stale, Stalwart, Stark, Steely, Stentorian, Sthenic, Stiff, Stout, Str, Strapping, → STRENGTH, Sturdy, Substantial, Suit, Tarzan, Tenable, Theory, Thesis, Thewy, Thickset, Tough, Trusty, Valid, Vegete, Vehement, Vigorous, Violent, Virile, Well-built, Well-set, Wight, Ya(u)ld

**Strongbox** Safe

**Stronghold** Acropolis, Aerie, Bastion, Castle, Citadel, Eyrie, Eyry, Fastness, Fortalice, Fortress, Holt, Keep, Kremlin, Redoubt, Tower

**Strong point** Forte

**Strongroom** Genizah, Safe

**Strontium** Sr

**Strop(py)** Cantankerous, Leather, Sharpen, Strap

**Struck** Aghast, Raught, Smitten, Smote

**Structural, Structure** Acrosome, Allotrope, Analysis, Anatomy, Arch, Armature, Atomic, Building, Bulk, Catafalque, Centriole, Chromosome, Cold frame, Compage(s), Constitution, Conus, Darga(h), Data, Database, Deep, Edifice, Erection, Fabric, Fairing, Filigree, Flaser, Format(ion), Formwork, Frame, Galea, Ganglion, Gantry, Headframe, Helictite, Heterarchy, Hierarchy, Honeycomb, Hut, Hyperbolic, Hyperfine, Ice-apron, Idant, Kekulé, Lantern, Lattice, Macrocosm, Malpighian, Manubrium, Mole, Organic, Ossature, Pagoda, Palapa, Palisade, Palmation, Parawalker, Pea-trainer, Pediment, Pergola, Phloem, Physique, Pier, Pod, Power, Prophyll, Protein, Pylon, Retinaculum, Scala, Set-up, Shape, Shell, Shoring, Skeleton, Sponson, Sporocarp, Squinch, Staging, Stand, Starling, Stylobate, Surface, Syntax, System, Tectonic, Telomere, Texas, Texture, Thylakoid, Trabecula, Trilithon, Trochlea, Trophic, Undercarriage

**Struggle, Struggling** Agon(ise), Agonistes, Amelia, Battle, Buckle, Camp, Chore, Class, Combat, Conflict, Contend, Contest, Cope, Debatement, Duel, Effort, Encounter, Endeavour, Exertion, Fag, Fight, Flounder, Grabble, Grapple, Hassle, Jockey, Kampf, Labour, Luctation, Maul, Mill, Pingle, Rat-race, Reluct, Resist, Scrabble, Scramble, Scrape, Scrimmage, Scrum, Scrummage, Scuffle, Slugfest, Sprangle, Strain, Strift, → STRIVE, Toil, Tug, Tuilyie, Tussle, Up a tree, Uphill, Vie, War(sle), Warfare, Work, Wraxle, Wrest(le), Writhe

▷**Struggle** *may indicate* an anagram

**Strum** Thrum, Twang, Tweedle, Vamp

**Strumpet** Cocotte, Harlot, Hiren, Lorette, Paramour, Succubus, Waistcoateer, Wench

**Strut(ter), Strutting** Bracket, Brank, Bridging, Cock, Dolphin striker, Flounce, Haught(y), Jet, Kingrod, Longeron, Martingale boom, Member, Nervure, Peacock, Pown, Prance, Pronk, Prop, Scotch, Shore, Spur, Stalk, Stretcher, Strunt, Swagger, Swank, Tail-boom, Tie-beam

**Stuart** Anne, James, Pretender

**Stub(by), Stubs** Butt, Counterfoil, Dout, Dowt, Dumpy, Squat, Stob, Stocky, Tusking

**Stubble** Ar(r)ish, Bristle, Designer, Hair, Ill-shaven, Stump

**Stubborn(ness)** Adamant, Bigoted, Bulldog, Bull-headed, Contumacious, Cross-grained, Cussed, Diehard, Dogged, Entêté, Hard(-nosed), Hidebound, Intransigent, Inveterate,

Moyl(e), Mulish, Mumpsimus, Obdurate, Obstinate, Opinionated, Ornery, Ortus, Pertinacious, Perverse, Pig-headed, Recalcitrant, Reesty, Refractory, Rigwiddie, Rigwoodie, Self-willed, Stiff, Stoor, Stout, Tenacious, Thrawn, Tough, Wrong-headed

**Stubbs** Una

**Stucco** Cement

**Stuck** Aground, Beached, Fast, Glued, Jammed, Lodged, Set, Stopped, Stumped, Trapped, Wedged

**Stuck-up** Chesty, Highty-tighty, Hoity-toity, La(h)-di-da(h), Proud, Sealed, Snooty, Toffee-nosed, Vain

**Stud(ded)** Boss, Cooser, Cripple, Cu(i)sser, Doornail, Encrust, Entire, Farm, Frost, He-man, Knob, Nail, Press, Race, Rivet, Seg, Set, Shear, Shirt, Sire, Stallion, Stop

**Student(s)** Abiturient, Alphabetarian, Alumnus, Apprentice, Bajan, Bejant, Bursar, Bursch(en), Cadet, Candle-waster, Catechumen, Classmate, Coed, Collegian, Commoner, Dan, Dig, Disciple, Dresser, Dux, Exchange, Exhibitioner, Extensionist, External, Fellow, Form, Fresher, Freshman, Goliard, Gownsman, Graduand, Green welly, Grind, Gyte, Hafiz, Ikey, Internal, Junior, Kommers, Kyu, → LEARNER, Lucubrator, Magistrand, Matie, Mature, Medical, Mootman, Nomologist, NUS, Opsimath, Ordinand, Oxonian, Peking duck, Pennal, Plebe, Poll, Postgraduate, Preppy, Pupil, Reader, Rushee, Sap, → SCHOLAR, Self-taught, Semi, Seminar, Seminarian, Senior, Shark, Sixth former, Sizar, Sizer, Smug, Softa, Soph(omore), Sophister, Spod, Subsizar, Swat, Swot, Talibe, Templar, Tiro, Tosher, Trainee, Tuft, Tukkie, Tutee, Underclassman, Undergraduate, Wedge, Welly, Witsie, Wonk, Wooden spoon, Wooden wedge, Wrangler, Year

**Studio(s)** Atelier, Bottega, Ealing, Elstree, Film set, Gallery, Lot, Pinewood, Shepperton, Workshop

**Study, Studies, Studied, Studious, Studying** Analyse, Arch(a)eology, Bionics, Bone up, Brown, Carol, Carrell, Case, Classics, Comparability, Con(ne), Conscious, Consider, Course(work), Cram, Den, Dig, Étude, Examine, Eye, Feasibility, Field, Gen up, Intramural, Isagogics, Lair, Learn, Liberal, Lucubrate, Media, Motion, Mug up, Mull, Muse, Nature, Oceanology, Ology, Perusal, Peruse, Petrochemistry, Pilot, Pore, Portrayal, Post-doctoral, Prep(aration), Probe, Read, Recce, Reconnoitre, Research, Reverie, Revise, Sanctum, Sap, Scan, Science, Scrutinise, Shiur, Sketch, Specialize, Stew, Subject, Swat, Swot, Take, Time and motion, Trade-off, Train, Tutorial, Typto, Voulu, Wonk, Work

**Stuff(iness), Stuffing, Stuffy** Airless, Bloat, Bombast, Canvas, Close, Cloth, Cloy, Codswallop, Cram, Crap, Dimity, Engorge, Equipment, Farce, Feast, Fiddlesticks, Fill, Force, Forcemeat, Formal, Frows(t)y, Frowzy, Fug, Funny, Gear, Glut, Gobble, Gorge, Gubbins, Guff, Hair, Havers, Hooey, Horsehair, Hot, Inlay, Kapok, Lard, Line, Linen, → MATERIAL, Matter, Money, Mourning, Musty, No-meaning, Nonsense, Overeat, Pad, Pang, Panne, Pompous, Ram, Replete, Rot, Salpicon, Sate, Satiate, Sausage meat, Scrap, Sob, Stap, Steeve, Stew, Stifling, Substance, Surfeit, Taxidermy, Trig, Upholster, Wad, Youth

**Stultify** Repress, Ridicule, Smother

**Stumble** Blunder, Bobble, Daddle, Err, Falter, Flounder, Founder, Lurch, Misstep, Peck, Snapper, Stoit, Titubate, Trip

**Stump(ed), Stumps, Stumpy** At sea, Bamboozle, Black, Bobtail, Butt, Clump, Fag-end, Floor, Flummox, More, Nog, Nonplus, Orate, Peg, Runt, Scrag, Snag, Snooker, Spud, Squab, St, Staddle, Stob, Stock, Stool, Stub(ble), Tortillon, Tramp, Truncate, Wicket

**Stun(ned), Stunning** Agape, Astonish, Astound, Awhape, Bewilder, Bludgeon, Concuss, Cosh, Daze, Dazzle, Deafen, Donnard, Donnert, Dove(r), Drop-dead, Dumbfound, Eclectic, Eyecatcher, Fantastic, Faze, Flabbergast, Glam, Gobsmack, KO, Numb, Phenomenal, Poleaxe, Shell-shocked, Shock, Startle, Stoun, Stupefy, Taser®

**Stunner** Belle, Bobby-dazzler, Cheese, Cosh, Doozy, KO, Peach, Plastic bullet, Taser®

**Stunt(ed), Stuntman** Aerobatics, Confine, Daredevil, Droichy, Dwarf, Escapade, Exploit, Feat, Gimmick, Hot-dog, Hype, Jehad, Jihad, Loop, Nirl, Puny, Ront(e), Runt, Ruse, Scroggy, Scrub(by), Scrunt(y), Stub, Trick, Wanthriven, Wheelie

**Stupefaction, Stupefy(ing), Stupefied** Ag(h)ast, Amaze(ment), Assot, Astonishment, Awesome, Bemuse, Benumb, Catatonic, Dopy, Dozen, Dumbfound, Etherise, Fuddle, Hocus, Moider, Moither, Mull, Narcoses, Numb, Stonne, Stun

**Stupendous** Mighty
**Stupid, Stupid person** Anserine, Asinine, Barmy, Beef-witted, Besotted, Bêtise, Blithering, Blockish, Braindead, Clay-brain(ed), Crass, Daft, Datal, Dense, Desipient, Dim(wit), Dip, Dippy, Donner(e)d, Dozy, Dull(ard), Fat-brained, Fatuous, Flat, Foolish, Gaumless, Gross, Half-arsed, Half-baked, Hammerheaded, Hare-brained, Hatter, Hen-witted, Inane, Insensate, Insipient, Lamming, Mindless, Natural, Obtuse, Senseless, Silly, Sodden-witted, Thick, Thick-witted, Torpid, Vacuous, Witless, Wooden(head)

---

## STUPID PERSON

***3 letters:***
Ape
Ass
Auf
Bev
Bob
Cod
Daw
Div
Fon
Git
Jay
Lob
Log
Nit
Oaf
Owl
Put
Sap
Sot
Wof
Yap

***4 letters:***
Berk
Bete
Bobb
Bozo
Burk
Cake
Calf
Clod
Clot
Cony
Coof
Coot
Cuif
Dill
Ditz
Doat
Dodo
Does
Dolt
Dorb
Dork
Dote
Fogy
Fool
Fozy
Gaby
Gaga
Geck
Gelt
Goat
Goof
Goon
Goop
Gorm
Gouk
Gowk
Gull
Gump
Hash
Jaap
Jerk
Lown
Lunk
Meff
Mome
Mook
Mutt
Nana
Nerd
Nerk
Nong
Nurd
Ouph
Poon
Poop
Prat
Putt
Putz
Rook
Simp
Slow
Stot
Tony
Tube
Twit
Warb
Yo-yo
Zany

***5 letters:***
Bevan
Blent
Bobby
Booby
Brute
Bumbo
Chick
Chump
Clunk
Cokes
Cuddy
Cully
Dicky
Diddy
Dilly
Divvy
Dobby
Dorba
Dorky
Dubbo
Dumbo
Dummy
Dunce
Dweeb
Eejit
Fogey
Galah
Golem
Goofy
Goose
Hoser
Idiot
Kerky
Klutz
Looby
Loony
Lowne
Moron
Neddy
Ninny
Nitty
Noddy
Ocker
Ouphe
Patch
Plank
Prune
Quo-he
Schmo
Simon
Snipe
Spoon
Stock
Stupe
Sumph
Tonto
Twerp
Waldo
Wally
Yampy

***6 letters:***
Bampot
Barren
Bauble
Boodle
Buffer
Cretin
Cuckoo
Cuddie
Dawney
Dickey
Dobbie
Dodkin
Donkey
Doofus
Dottle
Drongo
Gander
Gaupus
Gawpus
Gunsel
Ignaro
Ingram
Ingrum
Johnny
Josser
Loonie
Lummox
Lurdan
Lurden

Muppet
Newfie
Nidget
Nincum
Nitwit
Noodle
Nudnik
Numpty
Obfusc
Oxhead
Sawney
Schlep
Schmoe
Scogan
Shmock
Shmuck
Simple
Sucker
Tavert
Thicko
Tosser
Tumphy
Turkey
Turnip
Wigeon
Wommit
Zombie

*7 letters:*
Airhead
Asinico
Barmpot
Becasse
Buffoon
Charlie
Cupcake
Damfool
Dawbake
Dawcock
Dim bulb
Dingbat
Dizzard
Donnard
Donnart
Donnert
Gomeral
Gomeril
Gubbins
Half-wit
Haverel
Insulse
Jackass
Johnnie
Juggins
Jughead
Lurdane
Mafflin
Mampara
Minnock
Muggins
Palooka
Pampven
Pillock
Pinhead
Plonker
Pot-head
Saphead
Schlepp
Schmock
Schmuck
Schnook
Scoggin
Taivert
Thickie
Tosspot
Twinkle
Want-wit
Wazzock

*8 letters:*
Abderian
Abderite
Baeotian
Boeotian
Bonehead
Boofhead
Bullhead
Butthead
Clodpate
Clodpole
Clodpoll
Clotpoll
Clueless
Crackpot
Deadhead
Dipstick
Dodipoll
Dotterel
Dottrell
Dumbbell
Dumpling
Flathead
Goofball
Goose-cap
Gormless
Imbecile
Liripipe
Liripoop
Lunkhead
Maffling
Meathead
Moon-calf
Numskull
Omadhaun
Pea-brain
Shot-clog
Softhead
Tom-noddy
Wiseacre
Woodcock

*9 letters:*
Beccaccia
Birdbrain
Blockhead
Capocchia
Chipochia
Clarthead
Clothhead
Cornflake
Doddipoll
Doddypoll
Dottipoll
Dumb-cluck
Gothamite
Ignoramus
Jobernowl
Lamebrain
Malt-horse
Nicompoop
No brainer
Numbskull
Pigsconce
Schlemiel
Schlemihl
Simpleton
Thickhead
Thick-skin
Woodentop

*10 letters:*
Analphabet
Beetle-head
Changeling
Dummelhead
Dunderhead
Dunderpate
Green goose
Headbanger
Hoddy-doddy
Huntiegowk
Loggerhead
Muttonhead
Nickumpoop
Nincompoop
Sheepshead
Silly-billy
Thickskull
Thimblewit
Touchstone

*11 letters:*
Beetle-brain
Chowderhead
Chucklehead
Featherhead
Feather-pate
Hunt-the-gowk
Knucklehead
Leather-head
Ninny-hammer
Simple Simon
Van der Merwe

*12 letters:*
Apple-knocker
Featherbrain
Scatterbrain
Shatterbrain

---

**Stupidity** Betise, Folly, Goosery, Hebetude, Oscitancy, Thickness, Torpor, Unwisdom
**Stupor** Catatony, Coma, Daze, Dwa(u)m, Fog, Lethargy, Narcosis, Trance
**Sturdy** Burly, Dunt, Gid, Hardy, Hefty, Lubbard, Lubber, Lusty, Robust, Rugged, Solid, Stalwart, Staunch, Steeve, Stieve, Stocky, Strapping, Strong, Stuffy, Substantial, Thickset, Turnsick, Vigorous, Well-set
**Sturgeon** Beluga, Ellops, Fish, Huso, Osseter, Sevruga, Sterlet
**Stutter(ing)** Blaise, Hesitate, Stammer

**St Vincent** WV

**Sty** Frank, Hogpen, Hovel, Pen, Piggery, Pigpen

**Stye** Eyesore, Hordeolum

**Style(s), Stylish, Stylist** Adam, À la, A-line, Anime, Art nouveau, Band, Barocco, Barock, Baroque, Bel canto, Biedermeier, Blocked, Blow-dry, Brachylogy, Burin, Call, Cantilena, Carry-on, Chic, Chi-chi, Chinoiserie, Chippendale, Class, Cultism, Cursive, Cut, Dapper, Dash, Decor, Decorated, Demotic, Diction, Directoire, Dress sense, Dub, Dude, Élan, Elegance, Empire, Entitle, Euphuism, Execution, Face, Fancy Dan, Farand, → **FASHION**, Fetching, Finesse, Flamboyant, Flashy, Flava, Flossy, Fly, Font, Form(at), Free, Friseur, Galant, Genre, Ghetto fabulous, Glamour, Gnomon, Gongorism, Gothic, Grace, Grand, Grande Dame, Grass, Gr(a)ecism, Greek, Groovy, Hair-do, → **HAIR STYLE**, Hand, Hepplewhite, Heroic, Heuristic, Hip, Homeric, House, Iconic, Imagism, International (Gothic), Intitule, Italianate, Katharev(o)usa, Lapidary, Locution, Louis quatorze, Louis quinze, Manner, Marivaudage, Metrosexual, Mock heroic, Mod(e), Modernism, Modish, Natty, Naturalism, New, New Look, Nib, Nifty, Novelese, Old, Panache, Pattern, Pen, Perm, Perpendicular, Personal, Phrase, Picturesque, Pistil, Plateresque, Pointel, Port, Posh, Post-modernism, Preponderant, Probe, Prose, Queen Anne, Rakish, Rank, Regency, Retro, Ritzy, Rococo, Romanesque, Rudie, Russo-Byzantine, Sassoon, Sheraton, Signature, Silk, Slap-up, Smart, Snappy, Snazzy, Soigné, Spiffy, Sporty, Stereotype, Street, Superrealism, Surname, Swish, Taste, Term, Title, Ton, Tone, Tony, Touch, Traditional, Trendsetter, Tuscan, Uncial, Unisex, Vain, Va-va-voom, Verismo, Vogue, Way

**Stylus** Needle

**Stymie** Baulk, Frustrate, Thwart

**Styptic** Alum, Amadou, Matico, Sta(u)nch

**Suave** Bland, Debonair, Oily, Smooth, Soft-spoken, Unctuous, Urbane

**Sub** Advance, Due, Fee, Journalist, Journo, Lieu, Submarine, Subordinate, U-boat, Under

**Subaltern** Loot, Lt

**Subarea** Talooka

**Sub-atomic** Mesic

**Subconscious** Inner, Instinctive, Not-I, Subliminal, Suppressed

**Sub-continent** India(n)

**Subcontract** Farm out, Outsource

**Subculture** Goth

**Subdivision** Arm, Banner, Branch, Cohort, Commot(e), Cotyledon, Oblast, Sanjak, Section, Segment, Senonian, Sheading, Tepal, Wapentake, Zone

**Subdominant** Fah

**Subdue(d)** Abate, Adaw, Allay, Chasten, Conquer, Cow, Crush, Dampen, Dant(on), Daunt(on), Dim, Dominate, Entame, Lick, Low-key, Lull, Master, Mate, Mortify, Mute, Oppress, Overawe, Overbear, Overpower, Quail, → **QUELL**, Quieten, Reduce, Refrain, Repress, Restrain, Slow, Sober, Soft pedal, Subact, Suppress, Tame, Under

**Subfusc, Subfusk** Dim, Dressy, Dusky, Evening, Sombre

**Subheading** Strapline

**Subhuman** Apeman, Bestial

**Subject(ed), Subjection, Subjectivity, Subjects, Subject to** Amenable, Art, Bethrall, Caitive, Case, Citizen, Contingent, Core, Cow, Dedicatee, Dhimmi, Donné(e), Enthrall, Foundation, Gist, Guinea pig, Hobby, Hobby-horse, Inflict, Issue, Liable, Liege(man), Matter, Metic, Motif, National, On, Oppress, Overpower, PE, People, Personalism, Poser, PPE, Rayah, RE, RI, Serf, Servient, Servitude, Sitter, Slavery, Snool, Submit, Suit, Syllabus, → **THEME**, Thirl, Thrall, Topic, Under, Undergo, Vassal, Villein

**Subjoin** Add, Affix

**Subjugate** Enslave, Ensnare, Master, Oppress, Overcome, Overpower, Reduce, Repress, Suppress

**Sublieutenant** Cornet

**Sub-lieutenant** Cornet

**Sublimate(r)** Aludel, Cleanse, Corrosive, Suppress, Transfer

**Sublime** Ali, Alice, August, Empyreal, Exalted, Grand, Great, Holy, Lofty, Majestic, Noble, Outstanding, Perfect, Porte, Splendid

**Submarine(r)** Boomer, Diver, Hydronaut, Innerspace, Nautilus, Pig-boat, Polaris, Silent Service, Sub, U-boat, Undersea, X-craft

▷**Submarine** *may indicate* a fish

**Submerge(d)** Dip, Dive, Drown, Embathe, Engulf, Imbathe, Impinge, Lemuria, Overwhelm, Ria, Sink, Take, Whelm

**Submissive, Submission, Submit** Acquiesce, Arbitration, Bow, Capitulate, Claim, Comply, Cringe, Defer, Docile, File, Folio, Gimp, Knuckle, Lapdog, Lodge, Meek, Obedient, Obtemperate, Passive, Pathetic, Pliant, Propound, Refer, Render, Resign, Servile, Snool, Stepford, Stoop, Succumb, Truckle, Weak, → YIELD

**Subordinate** Adjunct, Below, Dependent, Flunky, Inferior, Junior, Minion, Myrmidon, Nether, Offsider, Postpone, Secondary, Second banana, Servient, Stooge, Subject, Subservient, Subsidiary, Surrender, Under(ling), Underman, Under-strapper, Vassal

**Subpoena** Cite

**Subscribe(r), Subscription** Abonnement, Approve, Assent, Cedilla, Conform, Due, Endorsement, Pay, Pay TV, Sign(atory), Signature, Undersign, Underwrite

**Subsequent(ly)** Anon, Consequential, Future, Later, Next, Postliminary, Since, Then, Thereafter, Ulterior

**Subservient, Subservience** Kneel, Obedient, Obsequious, Slavish, Tame cat, Thraldom

**Subside, Subsidence, Subsidy** Abate, Adaw, Aid, Assuage, Bonus, Cauldron, Diminish, Ebb, Grant, Headage, Lysis, Sink, Sit, Slake, Swag

**Subsidiary, Subsidise** Anglesey, Auxiliar(y), By(e), By-end, Feather-bed, Junior, Secondary, Second banana, Side(-shoot), Sideline, Spin-off, Succursal, Valvassor, Vavasour

**Subsist(ence)** Batta, Bread-line, Dole, Keep, Live, Maintain, Rely, Survive

**Subsoil** Claypan, Permafrost

**Substance, Substantial** Additive, Air, Allergen, Ambergris, Anethole, Antacid, Antibody, Antichlor, Antigen, Anti-icer, Antiknock, Antiodontalgic, Antioxidant, Antithrombin, Antitoxin, Apiol, Axerophthol, Balsam, Blanco, Blocky, Body, Brobdingnagian, Calyx, Castoreum, Cermet, Chalone, Chemzyne, Chitin, Chromatin, Cofactor, Colloid, Considerable, Content, Cosmin(e), Creatine, Cytochalasin, Dense, Diosgenin, Durable, Ectocrine, Ectoplasm, Elaterium, Elemi, Endorphin, Enorm(ous), Enzyme, Essential, Ester, Ethambutol, Ethylamine, Excipient, Extender, Exudate, Fabric, Feck, Fixative, Flavanone, Flesh, Ganoin(e), Getter, Gist, Gluten, Gossypol, Gravamen, Growth, Guanazolo, Guanine, Gutta-percha, Hearty, Hefty, Hirudin, Hyalin, Hylic, Imine, Indol, Inhibitor, Iodoform, Iodophor, Isatin(e), Isomer, Kryptonite, Lase, Lecithin, Lectin, Leucotriene, Linin, Luciferin, Material, Matter, Meaning, Meat(y), Metabolite, Metol, Mineral, Misoprostol, Mitogen, Molal, Mole, Morphactin, Morphogen, Mucigen, Murr(h)ine, Mutagen, Myelin, Nacre, Naloxone, Neotoxin, Neurotoxin, Noselite, Nutrient, Oestrogen, Oligomer, Orgone, P, Papier mâché, Particulate, Pepsinogen, Perforine, Phlogiston, Phosphor, Pith, Plenteous, Polymer, Proinsulin, Promoter, Properdin, Prostaglandin, Protyl(e), Purin(e), Queen (bee), Quid, Reagent, Reality, Resin, Salacin(e), Secretagogue, Sense, Septarium, Sequestrant, Sizeable, Smeclic, Solid, Solvent, Sorbitol, Stramonium, Stuff, Sturdy, Suint, Sum, Sunblock, Surfactant, Sympathin, Synergist, Syntonin, Tabasheer, Tabashir, Taeniafuge, Tangible, Tannin, Terra alba, Thermoplastic, Thiouracil, Thiourea, Tocopherol, Tusche, Vapour, Viricide, Volutin, Weighty, Ylem

**Substandard** Inferior, Infra dig, Off, Poor, Schlo(c)k, Second, Small

▶**Substantial** *see* SUBSTANCE

**Substantiate** Back up, Confirm, Flesh, Prove, Strengthen, Support, Verify

**Substantive** Direct, Noun

**Substitute, Substitution** Acting, Agent, Alternative, Carborundum®, Change, Changeling, Commute, Creamer, Deputy, Dextran, Double, Dub, Emergency, Ersatz, -ette, Euphemism, Eusystolism, Exchange, Fill-in, Imitation, Improvise, In lieu, In situ, Instead, Lieu(tenant), Locum, Makeshift, Metonymy, Mock, Nominee, Novation, Paraphasia, Pinch-hit, Proxy, Regent, Relieve, Replace, Represent, Reserve, Resolution, Ringer, Sentence, Seth, Simulacrum, Soya, Spare, Stalking-horse, Stand-by, Stand-in, Stead, Step in, Stopgap, Subrogate, Succedaneum, Supernumerary, Supply, Surrogate, Switch, Swop, Synthetic, Twelfth man, Twentieth man, Understudy, Vicar(ial), Vicarious, Vice

**Substructure** Base, Foundation, Keelson, Platform, Podium
**Subsume** Include
**Subterfuge** Artifice, Chicane, Creep-hole, Evasion, Hole, Manoeuvre, Off-come, Ruse, Strategy, Trick
**Subterranean** Concealed, Mattamore, Sunken, Underground, Weem
**Subtle(ty)** Abstruse, Alchemist, Crafty, Delicate, Fine(spun), Finesse, Hair-splitting, Ingenious, Innuendo, Nice(ty), Nuance, Overtone, Refinement, Sly, Subdued, Suttle, Tact, Thin, Wily
**Subtle difference** Nuance
**Subtract(ion)** Commission, Deduct, Discount, Remove, Sum, Take, Tithe, Withdraw
**Suburb(s)** Banlieue, Dormitory, Environs, Exurbia, Faubourg, Garden, Metroland, Outskirts, Purlieu, Shoreditch, Soweto, Subtopia, Township, Uptown
**Subverse, Subversion, Subversive, Subvert** Agitprop, Fifth column, Overthrow, Reverse, Sabotage, Sedition, Treasonous, Undermine, Upset
**Subway** Dive, Metro, Passage, Tube, Underground, Underpass
**Succeed, Success(ful), Successfully** Accomplish, Achieve, Answer, Arrive, Big-hitter, Bingo, Blockbuster, Boffo, Breakthrough, Chartbuster, Clean sweep, Coast, Come off, Contrive, Coup, Cut it, Do well, Éclat, Effective, Efficacious, Ensue, Fadge, Fare, Felicity, Flourish, Flying colours, Follow, Fortune, Gangbuster, Get, Go, Heyday, Highflyer, Hit, Hotshot, Inherit, Killing, Landslide, Luck, Made, Make good, Make it, Make out, Manage, Masterstroke, Mega, Midas touch, Offcome, Parlay, Pass, Prevail, Procure, Profitable, Promising, Prosper, Pull off, Purple patch, Pyrrhic, Rags to riches, Reach, Replace, Result, Riot, Roll, Score, Seal, Seel, Sele, Sell out, Sensation, Smash, Soaraway, Socko, Speed, Stardom, Superstar, Sure thing, Take, Tanistry, The bitch goddess, Thrive, Thumbs up, Triumph, Up, Up and coming, Upstart, Vault, Victory, Weather, Well, Win, Winnitude, W(h)iz(z)kid, Wow, Wunderkind
**Succession, Successive** Apostolic, Chain, Cognate, Dead men's shoes, Ecological, Heirdom, Indian file, Line, Mesarch, Neum(e), Order, Parlay, Result, Reversion, Sequence, Serial, Seriatim, Series, String, Suite
**Successor** Co(m)arb, Deluge, Descendant, Ensuite, Epigon(e), Heir, Incomer, Inheritor, Khalifa, Next, Replacement, Syen
**Succinct** Brief, Cereus, Compact, Concise, Encapsulating, Houseleek, Laconic, Pithy, Short
**Succour** Aid, Assist, Help, Minister, Relieve, Rescue, Sustain, Sympathy
**Succulent** Agave, Aloe, Cactus, Echeveria, Hoodia, Ice-plant, Juicy, Lush, Rich, Saguaro, Sappy, Spekboom, Tender, Toothy
**Succumb** Capitulate, Fall, Go under, Surrender, Yield
**Such** Like, Sae, Sike, Similar, So, That
**Suck(er), Sucking** Absorb, Acetabular, Acetabulum, Amphistomous, Antlia, Aphid, Aphis, Aspirator, Ass, Bull's eye, Culicidae, Dracula, Drink, Dupe, Fawn, Felch, Fellatio, Gnat, Gobstopper, Graff, Graft, Greenfly, Gull, Haustellum, Haustorium, Hoove, Lamia, Lamprey, Leech, Liquorice, Lollipop, Mammal, Monotremata, Mouth, Mug, Muggins, Osculum, Patsy, Plunger, Remora, Rook, Scolex, Shoot, Siphon, Slurp, Smarm, Spire, Spyre, Straw, Surculus, Sweetmeat, Swig, Sycophant, Tellar, Teller, Tick, Tiller, Toad-eater, Turion, Vampire
**Suckle, Suckling** Feed, Infant, Mother, Nourish, Nurse, Nurture
**Suction** Adhere, Implosion, Pump, Siphon
**Sud(s)** Foam, Lather, Sapples
**Sudan(ese)** Dinka, Mahdi, Nigritian, Nilot, Nuba
**Sudden(ly)** Abrupt, Astart, Astert, Extempore, Ferly, Flash, Fleeting, Foudroyant, Fulminant, Hasty, Headlong, Impulsive, Overnight, Precipitate, Rapid, Rude, Slap (bang), Sodain, Subitaneous, Subito, Swap, Swop, Unexpected
**Sue** Apply, Ask, Beseech, Claim, Dun, Entreat, Implead, Implore, Litigate, Petition, Pray, Process, Prosecute, Woo
**Suede** Split
**Suet** Mutton
**Suffer(er), Suffering** Abide, Aby(e), Ache, Affliction, Agonise, Ail, Answer for, Auto, Bale, Be, → BEAR, Brook, Calvary, Cop, Die, Distress, Dree, Dukkha, Endurance, Endure, Feel,

Gethsemane, Golgotha, Grief, Hardship, Have, Heartbreak, Hell, Incur, Indolent, Languish, Let, Luit, Mafted, Martyr, Ordeal, Pain, Passible, Passion, Passive, Patible, Patience, Pay, Pellagrin, Permit, Pine, Plague, Punitive, Purgatory, Scrofula, Smart, Stand, Stomach, Stress, Sustain, Thole, Tolerate, Toll, Torment, Torture, Trial, Tribulation, Undergo, Use, Victim

**Suffering remnant** Macmillanite

**Suffice, Sufficiency, Sufficient** Abundance, Adequate, Ample, Basta, Do, Due, Enough, Enow, Experimental, Nuff, Run to, Satisfy, Serve

**Suffix** Enclitic

**Suffocate** Asphyxiate, Choke, Drown, Smoor, Smore, Smother, Stifle, Stive, Strangle, Throttle

**Suffrage(tte)** Ballot, Davison, Feminist, Franchise, Lucy Stoner, Manhood, Pankhurst, Vote

**Suffuse** Bathe, Colour, Glow, Imbue, Saturate, Spread, Tinge

**Sugar(y), Sugar cane** Aldohexose, Aldose, Amygdalin, Arabinose, Barley, Beet, Blood, Brown, Candy, Cane, Caramel, Carn(e), Cassonade, Caster, Cellobiose, Cellose, Chaptalise, Confectioner's, Cube, Daddy, Date, Demerara, Deoxyribose, Dextrose, Disaccharide, Flattery, Fructose, Fucose, Furanose, Galactose, Gallise, Glucosamine, Glucose, Glucosoric, Glycosuria, Goo(r), Granulated, Granulose, Grape, Gur, Heptose, Heroin, Hexose, Honeydew, Hundreds and thousands, Iced, Icing, Inulin, Invert, Jaggary, Jaggery, Jagghery, Ketose, Lactose, Laevulose, Loaf, Lump, Maltose, Manna, Mannose, Maple, Maudlin, Milk, Money, Monosaccharide, Muscovado, Nectar, Nucleoside, Oligosaccharide, Palm, Panocha, Pentose, Penuche, Pyranose, Raffinose, Rhamnose, Ribose, Saccharine, Saccharoid, Simple, Sis, Sorbitol, Sorbose, Sorghum, Sorg(h)o, Sparrow, Spun, Sweet(ener), Syrup, Tetrose, Trehalose, Triose, White, Wood, Xylose

**Sugar-daddy** Lyle, Tate

**Suggest(ion), Suggestive** Advance, Advice, Advise, Auto, Blue, Breath, Broach, Clue, Connote, Counter-proposal, Cue, Float, Foreshadow, Guess, Hint, Hypnotic, Idea, Imply, Inkling, Innuendo, Insinuate, Intimate, Kite, Mention, Modicum, Moot, Move, Nominate, Nuance, Pointer, Posit, Posthypnotic, Postulate, Prompt, Proposal, Propound, Provocative, Racy, Raise, Recommend, Redolent, Reminiscent, Ring, Risqué, Savour, Scenario, Smacks, Soft core, Suspicion, Threat, Tinge, Tip, Touch, Trace, Twang, Undertone, Vestige, Vote, Wind, Wrinkle

**Suicide** Felo-de-se, Hara-kiri, Hari-kari, Kamikaze, Lemming, Lethal, Race, Sati, Seppuku, Shinju, Suttee

**Suit** Action, Adapt, Adjust, Agree, Answer, Anti-G, Apply, Appropriate, Become, Befit, Beho(o)ve, Bequest, Beseem, Besit, Birthday, Boiler, Business, Cards, Case, Cat, Civil, Clubs, Conform, Courtship, Demob, Diamonds, Dinner, Dittos, Diving, Do, Drapes, Dress, Dry, Effeir, Effere, Entreat, Etons, Exec(utive), Fadge, Fashion, Fit, G, Garb, Gee, Get on, Gree, Hearts, Hit, Jump, Lis pendens, Litigation, Long, Lounge, Major, Mao, Match, Menswear, Minor, Monkey, NBC, Noddy, Onesie, Orison, Outcome, Paternity, Penguin, Petition, Pinstripe, Plaint, Play, Plea, Please, Point, Power, Prayer, Pressure, Process, Pyjama, Quarterdeck, Queme, Request, Res judicata, Romper(s), Safari, Sailor, Salopettes, Samfoo, Samfu, Satisfy, Serve, Shell, Siren, Skeleton, Slack, Space, Spades, Strong, Sun, Sunday, Supplicat, Sweat, Swim, Swords, Tailleur, Three-piece, Track, Trial, Trouser, Trumps, Tsotsi, Tweeds, Twin, Two-piece, Uniform, Union, Wet, Wingsuit, Zoot

**Suitable** Apposite, Appropriate, Apropos, Apt, Becoming, Capable, Competent, Congenial, Consonant, Convenance, Convenient, Decorous, Due, Eligible, Expedient, → FIT, Giusto, Habile, In order, Keeping, Meet, Opportune, Pertinent, Relevant, Right, Seasonal, Seemly, Sittlichkeit, Timely, Very, Worthy

**Suitcase** Port, Valise

**Suite** Allemande, Apartment, Chambers, Court, Dolly, Edit, Ensemble, Entourage, Hospitality, Lounge, Nutcracker, Partita, Planets, Retinue, Rooms, Serenade, Set, Skybox, Tail, Three-piece, Train, Two-piece

**Suitor** Beau, Gallant, John Doe, Lover, Petitioner, Pretendant, Pretender, Pursuer, Suppli(c)ant, Swain, Wooer

**Sulk(y), Sulkiness, Sulking** B(r)oody, Bouderie, Carriage, Disgruntled, Dod, Dort, Gee, Glout(s), Glower, Glum, Grouchy, Grouty, Grumps, Gumple-foisted, Huff, Hump, Jinker,

Mardy, Maungy, Moody, Mope, Mulligrubs, Mump, Pet, Petulant, Pique, Pout, Snit, Spider, Strunt, Stuffy, Stunkard, Sullen, Tout(ie), Towt, Umbrage

**Sullen** Black, Brooding, Dorty, Dour, Farouche, Glum(pish), Grim, Grumpy, Moody, Mumpish, Peevish, Po, Pouting, Saturnine, Sourpuss, Stunkard, Sulky, Sumph, Surly, Truculent

**Sully** Assoil, Bedye, Besmirch, Blot, Deface, Defile, Glaur(y), Smear, Smirch, Smutch, Soil(ure), Taint, Tarnish, Tar-wash

**Sulphate, Sulphide** Alum, Alunite, Blende, Bluestone, Bornite, Copper(as), Coquimbite, Enargite, Glance, Green vitriol, Jarosite, Melanterite, Pentlandite, Pyrites, Troilite, Zarnec, Zarnich

**Sulphur** Baregine, Brimstone, Cysteine, Hepar, Oleum, S, Stannite, Thionic

**Sultan(a), Sultanate** Brunei, Caliph, Emir, Grand Seignoir, Grand Turk, Hen, Kalif, Murad, Nejd, Oman, Osman, Padishah, Roxane, Saladin, Soldan, Suleiman, Tippoo, Tipu, Vizier, Wadai

**Sultry** Houri, Humid, Sexy, Smouldering, Steamy, Tropical

**Sum(s), Sum up** Add(end), Aggregate, All (told), Amount, Arsmetric, Bomb, Connumerate, Encapsulate, Foot, Logical, Lump, Number, Packet, Perorate, Plumule, Proceeds, → QUANTITY, Re-cap, Refund, Remittance, Reversion, Slump, Solidum, Tidy, Total, Vector

**Summarize(d), Summary** Abridge, Abstract, Aperçu, Bird's eye, Breviate, Brief, Coda, Compendium, Condense, Conspectus, Digest, Docket, Epanodos, Epitome, Footnote, Gist, Headnote, Instant, Memo, Minute, Offhand, Outline, Overview, Pirlicue, Pot(ted), Précis, Purlicue, Recap(itulate), Resume, Résumé, Round-up, Rundown, Short (shrift), Sitrep, Syllabus, Synopsis, Tabloid, Tabulate, Tabulation, Wrap-up

**Summer(time)** Abacus, Accountant, Adder, Aestival, August, BST, Computer, Estival, Heyday, Indian, Lintel, Luke, Prime, St Luke's, St Martin's, Season, Sigma, Solstice, Totter

**Summerhouse** Belvedere, Chalet, Conservatory, Folly, Gazebo, Pavilion

**Summit** Acme, Acro-, Apex, Blind, Braeheid, Brow, Climax, Conference, → CREST, Crown, Eminence, Height, Hillcrest, Jole, Jungfrau, Mont Blanc, Peak, Pike, Pinnacle, Ridge, Spire, Top, Vertex, Vertical, Yalta

**Summon(s)** Accite, Arraign, Arrière-ban, Azan, Beck(on), Bleep, Call, Call in, Call up, Cist, Cital, Citation, Command, Conjure, Convene, Convent, Drum, Evoke, Garnishment, Gong, Hail, Invocation, Muster, Order, Originating, Page, Post, Preconise, Rechate, Recheat, Reveille, Signal, Sist, Subpoena, Ticket, Warn, Warrant, What-ho, Whoop, Writ

**Sumo (wrestling)** Basho, Makunouchi, Niramial, → WRESTLING, Yokozuna

**Sump** Bilge, Cesspit, Drain, Pool, Sink

**Sumpter** Led horse, Pack-horse

**Sumptuous** De luxe, Expensive, Lavish, Luxurious, Opulent, Palatial, Rich(ly), Slap up, Superb

**Sun(-god), Sunlight, Sunny, Sunshine** Albedo, Amen-Ra, Amon-Ra, Apollo, Artificial, Ashine, Aten, Bright, Cheer, Combust, Daily, Day(star), Dry, Earthshine, Eye of the day, Glory, Heater, Heliacal, Helio(s), Helius, Horus, Mean, Midnight, Mock, New Mexico, Nova, Orb, Paper, Paranthelion, Parhelion, Pet-day, Phoebean, Photosphere, Ra, Radiant, Rays, Re, Rising, Shamash, Sol(ar), Soleil, Sonne, Surya, Svastika, Swastika, Tabloid, Tan, Titan, UV

**Sunbathe** Apricate, Bask, Brown, Tan

**Sunbeam** Car, Ray

**Sunbed** Lounger

**Sunblock** Parasol

**Sunburn** Bronze, Combust, Heliosis, Peeling, Tan

**Sunday** Advent, Best, Cantate, Care, Carle, Carling, Dominical, Easter, Fig, Jubilate, Judica, Laetare, Lord's Day, Lost, Low, Mid-Lent, Mothering, Orthodox, Palm, Passion, Quadragesima, Quasimodo, Quinquagesima, Refection, Refreshment, Remembrance, Rogation, Rose, Rush-bearing, S, Septuagesima, Sexagesima, Stir-up, Tap-up, Trinity, Whit

**Sunday school** SS

**Sunder** Divide, Divorce, Part, Separate, Sever, Split

**Sundew** Drosera, Eyebright

**Sundial** Analemma, Gnomon, Solarium

**Sundry** Divers, Several, Various
**Sunflower** Kansas, KS
**Sunglasses** Ray-Bans®, Shades
▸**Sun-god** *see* **SUN(-GOD)**
▸**Sunken** *see* **SINK(ING)**
**Sunrise, Sun-up** Aurora, Cosmical, Dawn, East
**Sunset** Acronical, Eve(ning), Eventide
**Sunshade** Awning, Bongrace, Brise-soleil, Canopy, Chi(c)k, Cloud, Parasol, Umbrella
**Sunspot** Facula, Freckle, Macula
**Sunstroke** Heliosis, Siriasis
**Sunwise** Deasi(u)l, Deasoil, Deis(h)eal, Eutropic
**Sun-worshipper** Heliolater
**Sup** Dine, Eat, Feast, Sample, Sip, Swallow
**Super** A1, Actor, Arch, Extra, Fab(ulous), Great, Grouse, Ideal, Lulu, Paramount, Superb, Terrific, Tip-top, Top-notch, Tops, Walker-on, Wizard
**Superabundance** Plurisie
**Superadded** Advene
**Superb** A1, Concours, Fine, Gorgeous, Grand, Great, Majestic, Peerless, Phat, Resplendent, Sensational, Splendid, Top-notch
**Supercilious** Aloof, Arrogant, Bashaw, Cavalier, Haughty, Lordly, Snide, Sniffy, Snooty, Snotty, Snouty, Superior, Toffee-nosed, Upstage, Withering
**Supercontinent** Pangaea
**Superficial** Catchpenny, Cosmetic, Cursenary, Cursory, Dilettante, Exterior, Facile, Frivolous, Glib, One-dimensional, Outside, Outward, Overlying, Perfunctory, Shallow, Sketchy, Skindeep, Smattering, Veneer, Window-dressing
▹**Superficial(ly)** *may indicate* a word outside another
**Superfluous, Superfluity** Appendix, Cheville, De trop, Extra, Lake, Mountain, Needless, Otiose, Pleonastic, Plethora, Redundant, Spare, Unnecessary
**Super-giant** Rigel
**Superhuman** Bionic, Demigod, Herculean, Heroic, Supernatural
**Superintend(ent)** Boss, Curator, Director, Foreman, Guide, Janitor, Oversee(r), Preside, Provost, Sewer, Supercargo, Surveillant, Warden, Zanjero
**Superior(ity)** Abbess, Abbot, Abeigh, Above, Advantage, Ahead, Aloof, Ascendant, Atop, Better, Brahmin, Choice, Class act, Classic, Classy, Condescending, Custos, De luxe, Dinger, Disdainful, Elite, Eminent, Excellent, Exceptional, Feuar, Finer, Forinsec, Gaffer, Gree, Herrenvolk, High-class, High-grade, Jethro, Lake, Liege, Master race, Mastery, Morgue, Mother, Nob, Noble, Outgrown, Outstanding, Over, Overlord, Oversee, Paramount, Plum, Pooh-Bah, Posh, Predominance, Premium, Prestige, Pretentious, Prevalent, Prior, Rolls Royce, Senior, Side, Smug, Snooty, Speciesism, Stuck up, Subject, Superordinate, Supremacy, Swell, Toffee-nosed, Top(-loftical), Top-sawyer, Transcendent(al), U, Udal, Upmarket, Upper(most), Upper crust, Uppish, Upstage
**Superlative** Best, Dinger, Exaggerated, Peerless, Smasheroo, Supreme, Utmost
**Superman** Batman, Bionic, Clark, Kent, Spiderman, Titan, Übermensch
**Supermarket** ALDI, ASDA, Co-op, Fund, GUM, Self service, Store
**Supernatural** Divine, Djinn, Eerie, Endemon, Fay, Fey, Fie, Fly, Gothic, Kachina, Mana, Manito(u), Metaphysical, Occult, Paranormal, Selky, Sharp, Siddhi, Tokoloshe, Uncanny, Unearthly, Wargod, Wight
**Supernova** Plerion
**Supernumerary** Additional, Corollary, Extra, Mute, Orra
**Supersede** Outmode, Replace, Stellenbosch, Supplant
**Superstar** VIP
**Superstition** Aberglaube, Abessa, Fable, Folk-lore, Freet, Myth, Pisheog, Pishogue, Uncertainty
**Superstructure** Mastaba(h)
**Supertonic** Ray
**Supervise(d), Supervision, Supervisor** Administer, Chaperone, Check, Direct,

Engineer, Floorwalker, Foreman, Gaffer, Grieve, Handle, Honcho, Invigilate, Key grip, Manager, Marshal, Monitor, Officiate, Organise, Overman, Oversee(r), Probation, Proctor, Regulate, Seneschal, Shopwalker, Stage-manage, Steward, Symposiarch, Targe, Taskmaster, Tool pusher, Under, Walla(h)

**Supine** First, Inactive, Inert, Lying, Passive, Protract, Second

**Supper** Bar, Burns, Dinner, →DRINK(ER), Fork, Hawkey, Hockey, Horkey, Last, Meal, Nagmaal, Repast, Soirée

**Supplant** Displace, Exchange, Oust, Overthrow, Pre-empt, Replace, Substitute, Supersede

**Supple, Suppleness** Agile, Compliant, Leish, Limber, Lissom(e), →LITHE, Loose, Loose-limbed, Lythe, Malleable, Plasticity, Pliable, Sinuous, Souple, Wan(d)le, Wannel, Whippy

**Supplement(ary), Supplementing** Addend(um), Addition, Adjunct, Ancillary, And, Annex(e), Appendage, Appendix, As well as, Augment, Auxiliary, Beres drops, Bolt-on, Codicil, Colour, Eche, Eik, Eke, Extra, Footnote, Glucosamine, Incaparina, Insert(ion), Inset, Mend, Paralipomena, Postscript, Practicum, PS, Relay, Ripienist, Ripieno, Rutin, Sports, TES, Weighting

**Supplicant, Supplicate, Supplication** Beg, Entreat, Importune, Invoke, Petition, Plead, Pray, Request, Rogation, Schnorr, Sue

**Supply, Supplies, Supplier** Accommodate, Advance, Afford, Amount, Cache, Cater, Chandler, Commissariat, Contribute, Crop, Deal, Distribute, Endue, Equip, Excess, Exempt, Feed, Fill, Find, Fit, Foison, Fund, Furnish, Give, Grant, Grist, Grubstake, Heel, Holp(en), Hydrant, Indew, Indue, Issue, Lay on, Lend, Lithely, Mains, Matériel, Merchandise(r), Ordnance, Pipeline, Plenish, Ply, Pool, →PROVIDE, Provision, Purvey, Push, Quartermaster, RASC, Replenishment, Reservoir, Resource, Retailer, Serve, Short, Source, Stake, Stock, →STORE, Viands, Vintner, Water, Widow's cruse, Yield

**Support(er), Supporting** Abacus, Abet, Abutment, Acco(u)rage, Adherent, Adminicle, Advocate, Aegis, Affirm, Aficionado, Aftercare, Aid, Aidance, Aide, Aliment(ative), Ally, Ammunition, Anchor, Anciliary, Andiron, Angle iron, Anta, Appui, Arch, Arm, Assistant, Athletic, Axle, Back(bone), Back-up, Baculum, Baluster, Banister, Bankroll, Barmy army, Barrack, Barre, Base, Basis, Batten, Beam, Bear, Bedpost, Befriend, Behind, Belt, Benefactor, Bibb, Bier, Bolster, Book end, Boom, Bouclée, Bra, Brace, Bracket, Brassiere, Breadwinner, Breast-summer, Bridge, Bridgeboard, Buttress, Cal(l)iper, Carlist, Caryatid, Cavalier, Chair, Champion, Chaptrel, Cheerleader, Chenet, Cherish, Child, Circumstantiate, Clientele, Clipboard, Colonnade, Column, Comfort, Confirm, Console, Corbel, Corbel-table, Cornerstone, Corroborate, Corset, Countenance, Cradle, Cripple, Cross-beam, Crosstie, Cruck, Crutch, C(ee)-spring, Dado, Defend, Diagrid, Disciple, Dog-shore, Doula, Easel, Encourage, Endorse, Endoss, Endow, Engager, Enlist, Enthusiast, Espouse, Evidence, Family, Fan, Favour, Feed, Fid, Finance, Flag-waving, Flying buttress, Fly-rail, Footrest, Footstool, For, Foster, Friend, Fulcrum, Gamb, Gantry, Garter, Girder, Glia, Grapevine, Grass roots, Groundswell, Guy, Handrail, Hanger, Harpin(g)s, Hat-peg, Headrest, Help, Help desk, Henchman, Hold with, Home help, Horse, Hound, I-beam, Idealogue, Impost, Income, Indorse, Instantiate, Ite, Jack, Jackstay, Jockstrap, Joist, Keep, Keystone, Kingpost, Knee, Knife rest, Knighthead, Lath, Learning, Lectern, Leg, Lierne, Lifebelt, Lifebuoy, Lintel, Lobby, Loper, Loyalist, Mahlstick, Mailstick, Mainbrace, Mainstay, Maintain, Makefast, Mill-rind, Miserere, Misericord(e), Monial, Moral, Mortsafe, Mount, Neck, Nervure, Neuroglia, -nik, Nourish, Pack, Pack-frame, Packstaff, Parachute, Paranymph, Parawalker, Partisan, Partizan, Partners, Patronage, Pedestal, Peronist, Pessary, Phalanx, Pier, Pile(-cap), Pillar, Pillow, Pin, Plinth, Poppet, Post, Potent, Price, Promote, Prop, Proponent, Prop-root, PTA, Pull-for, Puncheon, Purlin(e), Purlins, Pylon, Queenite, Raft, Rally round, Rebato, Regular, Reinforce, Relieve, Resource, Respond, Rest, Rind, Rod, Roof-plate, Root, Royalist, Rynd, Samaritan, Sanction, Sarking, Sawhorse, Scaffolding, Sconce, Second, Shoetree, Shore, Side, Skeg, Skeleton, Skewput, Skid, Sleeper, Sling, Snotter, Socle, Solidarity, Spectator, Spider, Splat, Splint, Sponson, Sponsor, Sprag, Spud, Squinch, Staddle, Staddlestone, Staff, Staging, Stake, Stalwart, Stanchion, Stand(-by), Stay, Steady, Stem(pel), Step, Sternpost, Stick, Stirrup, Stool, Stringer, Strut, Stull, Stylobate, Subscribe, Subsidy, Substantiate, Succour, Suffragist, Summer, Suppedaneum, Suspender, Sustain, Sustentacular, Sustentaculum, Sustentation, Sympathise, Tailskid, Tartan army, Technical, Tee, Telamon, Tendril, Third, Tie, Tige, Torsel,

Trabecula, Transom, Trellis, Tress(el), Trestle, Tripod, Trivet, Trotter, Truss, Tumpline, Underlay, Underpin, Understand, Unipod, Uphold, Upkeep, Verify, Vindicate, Viva, Walker, Waterwings, Welfare, Well-wisher, Yardarm, Y-level, Yorkist, Zealot

**Suppose(d), Supposedly, Supposition** An, Assume, Believe, Conjecture, Daresay, Expect, Guess, Hypothetical, Idea, If, Imagine, Imply, Infer, Opine, Postulate, Presume, Putative, Reputedly, Said, Say, Sepad, Theory, What if

**Suppository** Pessary

**Suppress(ion), Suppressed** Abate, Abolish, Adaw, Bottle, Burke, Cancel, Censor, Check, Clampdown, Conditioned, Crackdown, Crush, Cushion, Ecthlipsis, Elide, Elision, Enslave, Epistasis, Gag, Gleichschaltung, Hide, Hush-up, Inhibit, Mob(b)le, Muffle, Quash, Quell, Quench, Restrain, Silence, Sit on, Smother, Squash, Squelch, Stamp out, Stand on, Stifle, Strangle, Subdue, Submerge, Subreption, Throttle, Under

**Suppurate, Suppuration** Diapyesis, Discharge, Exude, Fester, Maturate, Ooze, Pus, Pyorrhoea, Rankle

**Supreme, Supremacy, Supremo** Apical, Baaskap, Best, Caudillo, Consummate, Dominant, Kronos, Leader, Napoleon, Overlord, Paramount, Peerless, Pre-eminent, Regnant, Sovereign, Sublime, Sudder, Superlative, Top, Utmost, White

**Surcharge** Addition, Extra, Tax

**Surd** Voiceless

**Sure(ly)** Assured, Ay, Bound, Cert(ain), Certes, Confident, Definite, Doubtless, Firm, Indeed, Inevitable, Infallible, Know, Pardi(e), Pardy, Perdie, Positive, Poz, Safe, Secure, Self-confident, Shoo-in, Sicker, Stable, Syker, Uh-huh, Unerring, Yeah, Yep, Yes

**Surefire** Dead

**Surety** Bail, Frithborth, Guarantee, Mainprise, Security, Sponsional

**Surf(er), Surfing** Breach, Breaker, Browse, Corndogging, Grommet, Internet, Lurk, Onliner, Rollers, Rote, Sea, Spume, Waxhead

**Surface** Aerofoil, Appear, Apron, Area, Arise, Astroturf®, Bitumen, Brane, Camber, Carpet, Catenoid, Caustic, Ceiling, Control, Crust, Cutis, Day, Dermal, Dermis, Emerge, Epigene, Exterior, External, Extrados, Face, Facet, Finish, Flock, Interface, Linish, Macadam, Meniscus, Nanograss, Notaeum, Out, Outcrop, Outside, Outward, Overglaze, Paintwork, Patina, Pave, Peneplain, Plane, Pop up, Reveal, Rise, Salband, Scarfskin, Side, Skim, Skin, Soffit, Spandrel, Superficial, Superficies, Supracrustal, Tarmac®, Tar-seal, Texture, Top, Topping, Toroid, Veneer, Wearing course, Worktop

**Surf-boat, Surfboard(er), Surfboard(ing)** Goofy-footer, Masoola(h), Masula, Shredder

**Surfeit(ed)** Blasé, Cloy, Excess, Glut, Overcloy, Plethora, Satiate, Stall, Staw

▷**Surfer** *may indicate* programming

**Surge** Billow, Boom, Boost, Burst, Drive, Gush, Leap, Onrush, Seethe, S(c)end, Storm, Sway, Swell, Upgush, Wind

**Surgeon** Abernethy, Barber, Barnard, BCh, Brain, BS, CHB, CM, Dental, Doctor, DS, Dupuytren, House, Hunter, Leech, Lister, Lithotriptist, Medic, Operator, Orthopod, Plastic, Sawblade, Sawbones, Staff, Tang, Tree, Vet(erinary)

**Surgery** Anaplasty, Angioplasty, Boob job, Bypass, Clinic, Cordotomy, Cosmetic, Day, Dental, Dentistry, Facelift, Hobday, Ileostomy, Keyhole, Knife, Laparotomy, Laser, LASIK, Mammoplasty, Medicine, Nip and tuck, Nose job, Op, Open-heart, Orthop(a)edics, Osteoplasty, Otoplasty, Plastic, Prosthetics, Reconstructive, Repair, Section, Spare-part, Stereotaxis, Ta(g)liacotian, Thoracoplasty, Tuboplasty, Zolatrics

**Surly** Bluff, Brusque, Cantankerous, Chough, Chuffy, Churl(ish), Crabby, Crusty, Curmudgeon, Cynic, Glum, Gruff, Grum, Grumpy, Huffy, Ill-tempered, Rough, Snarling, Sullen, Truculent

**Surmise** Assume, Deduce, Extrapolate, Guess, Imagine, Infer, Opine, Presume, Speculate, Suppose

**Surmount** Beat, Climb, Conquer, Crest, Master, Overcome, Scan, Superate, Tide, Transcend

**Surname** Cognomen, Patronymic

**Surpass(ing)** Bang, Beat, Best, Better, Cap, Cote, Ding, Eclipse, Efface, Exceed, Excel, Frabjous, Outclass, Outdo, Outfoot, Outgo, Outgun, Out-Herod, Outlie, Outman, Outmanoeuvre, Outreach, Outshine, Outstrip, Outthink, Overshadow, Overtop, Transcend, Trump

**Surplice** Cotta, Ephod, Rochet, Sark, Serk, Vakass
**Surplus** De trop, Excess, Extra, Gash, Glut, Lake, Mountain, Offcut, Out-over, Over, Overabundance, Overage, Overcome, Remainder, Residue, Rest, Spare, Superplus, Surfeit, Unwanted
**Surprise(d), Surprising** Ag, Alert, Amaze, Ambush, Arrah, Astonish, Astound, Aykhona wena, Bewilder, Blimey, Boilover, Bombshell, By Jove, Caramba, Catch, Confound, Coo, Cor, Crick(e)y, Crikey, Crimíné, Cripes, Criv(v)ens, Crumbs, Dear, Eye-opener, Gadso, Gee, Geewhiz, Gemini, Geminy, Gemony, Gobsmacked, Godsend, Golly, Good grief, Good heavens, Good-lack, Good-now, Gorblimey, Gordon Bennett, Gosh, Gotcha, Great Scott, Ha, Hah, Hallo, Heavens, Hech, Heck, Heh, Hello, Hell's teeth, Hey, Hit for six, Ho, Holy cow, Hullo, Jeepers, Jeepers creepers, Jeez(e), Jinne, Jirre, Kissagram, Law, Lawks, Lor, Lordy, Lumme, Lummy, Man alive, Marry, Musha, My, Nooit, Obreption, Och, Odso, Omigod, Oops, Open-mouthed, Overtake, Phew, Pop-eyed, Really, Sheesh, Shock, Singular, Sjoe, So, Spot, Stagger, Startle, Strewth, Struth, Stun, Sudden, Treat, Turn-up, Twist, Uh, Upset, Whew, Whoops(-a-daisy), Wide-eyed, Wonderment, Wow, Wrongfoot, Yikes, Yipes, Yow, Zart, Zinger, Zowie
**Surrealist** Bizarre, Dali, Ernst, Grotesque, Magritte, Man Ray, Miró
**Surrender** Abandon, Capitulate, Cave-in, Cede, Cessio honorum, Cession, Enfeoff, Extradite, Fall, Forego, Forfeit, Handover, Hulled, Kamerad, Naam, Recreant, Release, Relinquish, Remise, Rendition, Renounce, Resign, Roll over, Strike, Submit, Succumb, Waive, → **YIELD**, Yorktown
**Surreptitious** Clandestine, Covert, Fly, Furtive, Hole and corner, Secret, Slee, Sly, Stealthy, Underhand
**Surrey** Carriage, Sy
**Surrogate, Surrogacy** Agent, Depute, Deputy, Locum, Proxy, Wet nurse, Womb-leasing
**Surround(ed), Surrounding(s)** Ambient, Amid, Amongst, Architrave, Background, Bathe, Begird, Begirt, Bego, Beset, Besiege, Bundwall, Cinct, Circumvallate, Circumvent, Compass, Doughnutting, Ecology, Embail, Encase, → **ENCIRCLE**, Enclave, Enclose, Encompass, Enfold, Entomb, Envelop, Environ, Enwheel, Enwrap, Fence, Fender, Frame, Gherao, Gird, Girt, Hedge, Hem in, Impale, Inorb, Invest, Mid, Moat, Orb, Orle, Outflank, Outside, Perimeter, Periphery, Setting, Trap, Wall
**Surtees** Jorrocks, Sponge
**Surveillance, Survey(ing), Surveyor** Behold, Browse, Cadastre, Case, CCTV, Census, Chartered, Conspectus, Dialler, Domesday, Doomwatch, Espial, Examination, Eye, Geodesy, Geodetic, Geological, Groma, Look-see, Map, Monitor, Once-over, Ordnance, Overeye, Overview, Patrol, Poll, Prospect, Quantity, Recce, Reccy, Reconnaissance, Regard, Review, Rodman, Scan, Scrutiny, Staffman, Stakeout, Straw poll, Supervision, Terrier, Theodolite, Triangulate, Trilateration, View, Vigil, Watch, Y-level
**Survival, Survive, Surviving, Survivor** Abednego, Bushcraft, Castaway, Cope, Die hard, Endure, Exist(ence), Extant, Finalist, Fittest, Hang over, Hibakusha, Last (out), Leftover, Live, Meshach, Outdure, Outlast, Outlive, Outwear, Overlive, Persist, Pull through, Relic(t), Ride (out), Shadrach, Sole, Street-wise, Subsist, Viability, Warhorse, Weather, Withstand
**Susan** Lazy
**Susceptible, Susceptibility** Allergy, Anaphylaxis, Electrical, Impressionable, Liable, Prone, Receptive, Vulnerable
**Suspect, Suspicion, Suspicious** Apprehend, Askance, Assume, Breath, Cagey, Curious, Distrust, Dodgy, Doubt, Dubious, Equivocal, Fishy, Grain, Grey list, Guess, Hinky, Hint, Hunch, Hunky, Iffy, Imagine, Inkling, Jalouse, Jealous, Leery, Misdeem, Misdoubt, Misgiving, Mislippen, Mistrust, Modicum, Notion, Paranoia, Queer, Scent, Sense, Shady, Smatch, Soupçon, Stealthy, Think, Thought, Tinge, Trace, Whiff
▷**Suspect, Suspicious** *may indicate* an anagram
**Suspend(ed), Suspender, Suspense, Suspension** Abate, Abeyance, Adjourn, Anabiosis, Anti-shock, Cliffhanger, Colloid, Dangle, Defer, Delay, Dormant, Freeze, Garter, Ground, → **HANG**, Hang-gliding, Hovering, Hydraulic, Independent, Intermit, Lay off, Limbo, Mist, Moratorium, Mystery, Nailbiter, Pensile, Poise, Prorogue, Put on ice, Reprieve, Respite,

Rub out, Rusticate, Sideline, Sol, Stand off, Stay, String, Swing, Table, Tension, Tenterhooks, Truce, Undercurrent, Underslung, Withhold

▹**Suspended** *may indicate* 'ice' on ice at the end of a down light

**Sussex** Rape

**Sustain(ed), Sustaining, Sustenance** Abide, Afford, Aliment, Bear, Constant, Depend, Endure, Food, Keep, Last, Maintain, Nourish, Nutrient, Nutriment, Nutrition, Pedal, Prolong, Scaffold, Sostenuto, Succour, Support, Ten(uto), Undergo, Upbear, Upstay

**Sutler** Vivandière

**Suture** Button, Catgut, Cobbler, Coronal, Dorsal, Lambda, Pterion, Purse-string, Sagittal, Stitch

**Suzanne, Suzie** Lenglen, Wong

**Svelte** Lithe, Slender, Slim, Trim

**Swab** Dossil, Dry, Mop, Pledget, Scour, Sponge, Squeegee, Stupe, Tampon, Tompon, Wipe

**Swaddle, Swaddling** Bind, Envelop, Incunabula, Swathe, Wrap

**Swag** Booty, Bundle, Encarpus, Festoon, Haul, Loot, Maino(u)r, Manner, Matilda, Shiralee, Toran(a)

**Swagger(er), Swaggering** Birkie, Bluster, Boast, Bobadil, Brag, Bragadisme, Bravado, Bucko, Cock, Cockiness, Crow, Jaunty, Machismo, Matamore, Nounce, Panache, Pra(u)nce, Roist, Roll, Rollick, Roul, Royster, Ruffle, Sashay, Side, Strive, Strut, Swagman, Swank, Swash(-buckler), Tigerism

**Swain** Amoretti, Beau, Churl, Corin, Damon, Hind, Lover, Rustic, Shepherd, Strephon, Wooer

**Swallow(able), Swallowing** Absorb, Accept, Aerophagia, Ariel, Barn, Bird, Bolt, Bredit, Buy, Cliff, Consume, Credit, Deglutition, Devour, Down(flow), Drink, Dysphagia, Eat, Endue, Englut, Engulf, Engulph, Esculent, Glug, Gobble, Gula, Gulch, Gulp, Hirundine, Incept, Ingest, Ingulf, Ingurgitate, Itys, Lap, Martin, Martlet, Neck, Progne, Quaff, Shift, Sip, Sister, Slug, Stomach, Swift, Swig, Take, Take off

**Swamp(y), Swamped** Awash, Bayou, Bog, Bunyip, Cowal, Cypress, Deluge, Dismal, Drown, Engulf, Everglade, Flood, Great Dismal, Inundate, Lentic, Lerna, Lerne, Loblolly, Mar(i)sh, Mire, Morass, Muskeg, Okavango, Okefenokee, Overrun, Overwhelm, Pakihi, Paludal, Poles'ye, Pripet Marshes, Purgatory, Quagmire, Slash, Slough, Sudd, Uliginous, Urman, Vlei, Vly, Wetland

**Swan(s)** Avon, Bewick's, Bird, Black, Cob, Cygnet, Cygnus, Game, Hooper, Leda, Lindor, Mute, Pen, Seven, Seward, Song, Stroll, Trumpeter, Whistling, Whooper, Whooping

**Swank(y)** Boast, De luxe, Grandstand, Lugs, Posh, Pretentious, Side, Style

**Swansong** Finale, Last air, Last hurrah

**Swap, Swop** Alternate, → BARTER, Chop, Commute, Debt, Exchange, Pass, Scorse, Switch, Trade, Transplant, Transpose, Truck

▹**Swap(ped)** *may indicate* an anagram

**Sward** Grass, Green, Lawn, Sod, Turf

**Swarm(ing)** Abound, Alive, Bike, Bink, Byke, Cast, Clamber, Cloud, Crawl, Crowd, Dyke, Flood, Geminid, Hoatching, Host, Hotch, Hotter, Infest, Meteor, Overrun, Pullulate, Rife, Shin, Shoal, Teem, Throng

**Swarthy** Black-à-vised, Dark, Dusky, Melanotic

**Swash** Send, Swig, Swill

**Swashbuckler, Swashbuckling** Adventurer, Boaster, Braggart, Dashing, Gascon, Swordsman

**Swastika** Filfot, Fylfot, Gamma(dion), Gammad, Gammation, Hakenkreuz

▸**Swat** *see* SWOT

**Swath(e)** Bind, Drape, Enfold, Enroll, Envelop, Swaddle, Swipe, Wrap

**Sway(ing)** Careen, Carry, Change, Command, Diadrom, Domain, Dominion, Flap, Fluctuate, Govern, Hegemony, Influence, Lilt, Oscillate, Prevail, Reel, Reign, Rock, Roll, Rule, Sally, Shog, Shoogie, Shoogle, Swag, Swale, Swee, Swing(e), Teeter, Titter, Totter, Vacillate, Wobble

**Swear(ing), Swearer, Swear word** Asseverate, Attest, Avow, Billingsgate, Coprolalia, Curse, Cuss, Darn, Depose, Eff (and blind), Execrate, Expletive, Invective, Jurant, Juratory, Oath, Objure, Pledge, Plight, Rail, Sessa, State, Tarnal, Tarnation, Trooper, Verify, Vouch, Vow

**Sweat(ing), Sweaty** Agonise, Apocrine, Beads, Bloody, Clammy, Cold, Dank, Diaphoresis,

Eccrine, Egest, English, Excrete, Exude, Flop, Forswatt, Glow, Hidrosis, Lather, Muck, Ooze, Osmidrosis, → PERSPIRE, Secretion, Slave, Stew, Sudament, Sudamina, Sudate, Suint, Swelter, Toil

**Sweater** Aran, Argyle, Circassian, Circassienne, Cowichan, Fair Isle, Gansey, Guernsey, Indian, Jersey, Knitwear, Polo, Pullover, Roll-neck, Skinny-rib, Skivvy, Slip-on, Slop-pouch, Sloppy Joe, Turtleneck, V-neck, Woolly

**Swede** Brassica, Inga, Nordic, Olaf, Rutabaga, Scandinavian, Sven, Turnip

**Sweeney** Police, Todd

**Sweep(er), Sweeping(s)** Besom, Breadth, Broad, Broom, Brush, Carpet, Chimney, Chummy, Clean, Curve, Debris, Detritus, Expanse, Extensive, Generalisation, Lash, Libero, Lottery, Net, Oars, Pan, Phasing, Police-manure, Range, Scavenger, Scud, Sling, Snowball, Soop, Sooterkin, Spoom, Street, Stroke, Surge, Swathe, Sway, Vac(k), Vacuum, Vast, Waft, Well, Wholesale, Wide, Widespread

**Sweepstake** Draw, Gamble, Lottery, Raffle, Tattersall's, Tombola

**Sweet(s), Sweeten(er), Sweetmeat, Sweetness** Acesulfame-K, Afters, Aspartame, Boiled, Bonus, Bribe, Bung, Cassata, Chaptalise, Charity, Charming, Cherubic, Cloying, Confect(ion), Confiserie, Conserve, Countline, Crème, Cute, → DESSERT, Douce(t), Dowset, Drop, Dulcet, Dulcie, Dulcitude, Edulcorate, FA, Flan, Flapjack, Flummery, Fool, Fragrant, Fresh, Glucose, Glycerin, Goody, Honey(ed), Icky, Indican, Kiss, Lavender, Liqueur, Luscious, Melodious, Molasses, Money, Nectared, Nonpareil, Nothing, Pea, Pet, Pie, Pinata, Pud(ding), Redolent, Romic, Saccharin(e), Seventeen, Sillabub, Sixteen, Solanine, Soot(e), Sop, Sorbet, Spice, Split, Sucrose, Sugar, Sugary, Syllabub, Syrupy, Tart(let), Thaumatin, Torte, Trifle, Twee, Uses, William, Winsome, Xylitol, Zabaglione

---

## SWEETS

*3 letters:*
Gum
Ice

*4 letters:*
Choc
Jube
Mint
Rock

*5 letters:*
Bombe
Candy
Dolce
Dolly
Fudge
Gundy
Halva
Lolly
Taffy

*6 letters:*
Aldose
Bonbon
Cachou
Choccy
Comfit
Confit
Dragée
Eringo
Eryngo
Halvah
Humbug
Jujube
Mousse
Nougat
Sucker
Tablet
Toffee

*7 letters:*
Adeline
Alcorza
Amabile
Baclava
Baklava
Caramel
Fondant
Gumdrop
Halavah
Lozenge
Pandrop
Praline
Swedger
Truffle
Wine-gum

*8 letters:*
Acid drop
Bull's eye
Confetti
Cracknel
Licorice
Lollipop
Marzipan
Noisette
Pastille
Peardrop
Pick'n'mix
Pomfret
Scroggin
Stickjaw

*9 letters:*
Bubble gum
Chocolate
Cyclamate
Honeycomb
Jelly baby
Jelly bean
Lemon drop
Liquorice
Marchpane
Muscavado
Sugarplum

*10 letters:*
Brandyball
Candyfloss
Coconut ice
Elecampane
Fairy floss
Gob-stopper
Nanaimo Bar

*11 letters:*
Aniseed ball
Banana split
Barley sugar
Marshmallow

*12 letters:*
Burnt-almonds
Butterscotch
Dolly mixture

*14 letters:*
Peppermint drop
Pontefract cake
Turkish delight

*15 letters:*
Peppermint cream

*20 letters:*
Hundreds and thousands

---

**Sweetbread** Bur(r), Inchpin, Pancreas, Thymus
**Sweetcorn** Cob, Maize
**Sweetheart** Amoret, Amour, Beau, Boyfriend, Darling, Dona(h), Dowsabel(l), Doxy, Dulcinea, Flame, Follower, Girlfriend, Honey(bunch), Honeybun, Jarta, Jo(e), Lass, Leman, Lover, Masher, Neaera, Peat, Romeo, Steady, Toots(y), True-love, Valentine, Yarta, Yarto
**Sweet-seller** Butcher, Confectioner
**Sweet talk** Taffy, Wheedle
**Swell(ing)** Adenomata, Ague-cake, Anasarca, Aneurysm, Apophysis, Bag, Balloon, Bellying, Berry, Billow, Blab, Blister, Bloat, Blow, Boil, Boll, Bolster, Botch, Braw, Bubo, Bulb, Bulge, Bump, Bunion, Burgeon, Capellet, Carbuncle, Carnosity, Cat, Chancre, Chilblain, Clour, Cratches, Curb, Cyst, Dandy, Desmoid, Diapason, Dilate, → DISTEND, Dom, Don, Eche, Ectasia, Edema, Eger, Elephantiasis, Encanthis, Enhance, Enlarge, Entasis, Epulis, Excellent, Farcy-bud, Fop, Frog, Gall, Gathering, Gent, Gnarl, Goiter, Goitre, Gout, Grandee, Ground, Head sea, Heave, Heighten, H(a)ematoma, Hove, Hydrocele, Hydroma, Hygroma, Increase, Inflate, Intumesce, Kibe, L, Lampas(se), Lampers, Louden, Lump, Macaroni, Milk leg, Mouse, Node, Nodule, Odontoma, Oedema, OK, Onco-, Ox-warble, Parotitis, Plim, Plump, Podagra, Protrude, Protuberance, Proud, Puff up, Pulvinus, Rise, Roil, Roller, Scirrhus, Scleriasis, Sea, Shinsplints, Splenomegaly, Sprain, Strout, Struma, Stye, Stylopodium, Sudamina, Surge, Teratoma, Toff, Torose, Torulose, Tragus, Tuber(cle), Tumefaction, Tumescence, Tumour, Tympanites, Tympany, Upsurge, Varicocele, Varicose, Venter, Vesicle, Vulvitis, Vulvovaginitis, Wallow, Warble, Wen, Whelk, Whitlow, Windgall, Xanthoma
▷**Swelling** *may indicate* a word reversed
**Swelter(ing)** Perspire, Roast, Stew, Sweat, Torrid, Tropical
**Swerve, Swerving** Bias, Body, Broach, Careen, Deflect, Deviate, Dodge, Inswing, Lean, Sheer, Shy, Snoke, Stray, Sway, Swee, Swing, Veer, Warp, Wheel
**Swift(ly)** Apace, Bird, Dean, Dromond, Fleet, Flock, Hasty, Ironist, Martlet, Newt, Nimble, Presto, Prompt, Pronto, Quick, → RAPID, Reel, Slick, Sodaine, Spanking, Speedy, Sudden, Velocipede, Wight
**Swig** Drink, Gulp, Nip, Pull, Scour, Swill, Tighten
**Swill** Guzzle, Leavings, Pig, Rubbish, Slosh, Swash
▷**Swilling** *may indicate* an anagram
**Swim(ming)** Bathe, Bogey, Bogie, Crawl, Dip, Float, Freestyle, Naiant, Natant, Natatorial, Paddle, Reel, Run, Skinny-dip, Soom, Synchro(nized), Trudgen, Whim, Whirl
▷**Swim** *may indicate* an anagram
**Swimmer** Bather, Cichlid, Copepod(a), Ctene, Duckbill, Duckmole, Dugong, Fin, Frogman, Leander, Mermaid, Nautilus, Pad(d)le, Paidle, Planula, Pleopod, Pobble, Salpa, Spitz, Terrapin, Trochosphere, Trudgen, Webb
▷**Swimmer** *may indicate* a fish
**Swimming costume** Bathers, Bikini, Cossie, Maillot, Monokini, One-piece, Tanga, Tankini, Tog, Trunks
**Swindle(r)** Beat, Bite, Bucket(-shop), Bunco, Bunkosteerer, Cajole, Champerty, → CHEAT, Chiz(z), Chouse, Con, Concoct, Crimp, Defraud, Diddle, Do, Dodge, Dupe, Escroc, Fake, Fiddle, Finagle, Fineer, Flam, Fleece, Fraud, Gazump, Gip, Gold brick, Goose-trap, Graft, Grift(er), Gull, Gyp, Hocus, Hoser, Hustler, Leg, Leger, Long-firm, Magsman, Mountebank, Mulct, Nobble, Peter Funk, Plant, Ponzi scheme, Racket, Ramp, Rig, Rip, Rogue, Scam, Sell, Shaft, Shakedown, Shark, Sharper, Shicer, Shyster, Skelder, Skin, Skin game, Slicker, Sting, Stitch-up, Stumer, Suck, Swiz(z), Take, Trick, Tweedle, Twist, Two-time
**Swine(herd)** Boar, Brute, Cad, Eumaeus, Gadarene, Heel, Hogward, Peccary, Pig, Porcine, Pork, Rat, Rotter, Sounder, Sow, Sybotic
**Swing(er), Swinging** Colt, Dangle, Flail, Gate, Gybe, Hang, Hep, Hip, Kip(p), Lilt, Metronome, Mod, Music, Oscillate, Pendulate, Pendulum, Reverse, Rock, Rope, Shog, Shoogie, Shuggy, Slew, Slue, Swale, Sway, Swee, Sweep, Swerve, Swey, Swipe, Swivel, Trapeze, Veer, Vibratile, Voop, Wave, Western, Wheel, Whirl, Yaw
**Swinge, Swingeing** Severe
**Swipe(s)** Backhander, Beer, Haymaker, Knock, Purloin, Seize, Side, Steal, Strike, Tap-lash
**Swirl** Eddy, Gyrate, Purl, Swoosh, Tourbill(i)on, Twist, Whirl

▷**Swirling** *may indicate* an anagram
**Swish** Cane, Frou-frou, Rustle, Smart, Whir, Whisper
**Swiss** Genevese, Ladin, Roll, Tell, Vaudois
**Switch(ed), Switches, Switching** Birch, Button, Change, Churn, Convert, Crossbar, Cryotron, Dead man's handle, Dimmer, Dip, Dolly, Exchange, Gang, Hairpiece, Isolator, Knife, Legerdemain, Master, Mercury, Mercury tilt, Message, On-off, Packet, Pear, Point, Relay, Replace, Retama, Rocker, Rod, Scutch, Shift, Surf, Swits, Thyristor, Time, Toggle, Transpose, Tress, Trip, Tumbler, Twig, Vary, Wave, Zap
**Switchback** Rollercoaster
▷**Switched** *may indicate* an anagram
**Switzerland** CH, Helvetia
**Swivel** Caster, Pivot, Root, Rotate, Spin, Terret, Territ, Torret, Turret, Twist, Wedein
**Swiz** Chiz(z)
**Swollen** Blown, Bollen, Bombe, Bulbous, Full, Gourdy, Gouty, Incrassate, Nodose, Puffy, Tumid, Turgescent, Turgid, Varicose, Ventricose, Vesiculate
**Swoon** Blackout, Collapse, Deliquium, Dover, Dwa(l)m, Dwaum, Faint, Swarf, Swerf
**Swoop** Canceleer, Cancelier, Descend, Dive(-bomb), Glide, Onrush, Plummet, Pounce, Souse
▶**Swop** *see* **SWAP**
**Sword(-like), Swordplay** Andrew Ferrara, Anelace, Angurvadel, Anlace, Arondight, Assegai, Balisarda, Balmunc, Balmung, Bilbo, Blade, Brand, Brandiron, Broad(sword), Brondyron, Caliburn, Cemitare, Claymore, Colada, Cold steel, Court, Curtal-ax, Curtana, Curtax, Cutlass, Daisho, Damascene, Damaskin, Damocles, Dance, Dirk, Duranda(l), Durindana, Ensate, Ensiform, Epée, Espada, Estoc, Excalibur, Falchion, Faulchi(o)n, Firangi, Foil, Forte, Fox, Gladius, Glaive, Glamdring, Gleave, Glorious, Hanger, Iai-do, Jacob's staff, Joyeuse, Katana, Kendo, Khanda, Kirpan, Kreese, Kris, Kukri, Kusanagi, Machete, Mandau, Merveilleuse, Mimming, Montanto, Morglay, Nothung, Parang, Philippan, Rapier, Reverso, Rosse, Sabre, Samurai, Schiavone, Schläger, Scimitar, Semita(u)r, Shabble, Shamshir, Sharp, Sigh, Simi, Skene-dhu, Slangwhanger, Smallsword, Spadroon, Spirtle, Spit, Spurtle(blade), Steel, Tachi, Toasting-iron, Toledo, Tuck, Tulwar, Two-edged, Waster, Whinger, Whiniard, Whinyard, White-arm, Xiphoid, Yatag(h)an
**Sword-bearer, Swordsman(ship), Swordswoman** Aramis, Athos, Baldric, Blade, Brenda(n), D'Artagnan, Fencer, Frog, Gladiator, Matador, Porthos, Sai-do, Samurai, Selictar, Spadassin, Spadroon, Spartacus, Swashbuckler, Zorro
**Sword-dancer** Matachin
**Swordfish** Espada, Istiophorus, Xiphias
**Sword-swallower** Samite
**Swot** Cram, Dig, Grind, Kill, Mug, Read up, Revise, Smug, Spod, Stew, Strike, Swat, Wonk
**Sybarite, Sybaritic** Aristippus, Decadent, Epicure, Hedonist, Voluptuary
▶**Sybil** *see* **SIBYL**
**Sycamore** Acer, Maple, Mulberry fig, Plane, Tree
**Sycophant(ic)** Apple polisher, Brown-nose, Claqueur, Crawler, Creeper, Damocles, Fawner, Flatterer, Gnathonic, Groveller, Hanger-on, Lackey, Lickspittle, Oily, Oleaginous, Parasite, Pickthank, Placebo, Servile, Slimy, Toad-eater, Toady, Yesman
**Syllabary** Hiragana, Kana, Katakana
**Syllable(s)** Acatalectic, Anacrusis, Aretinian, Closed, Nonsense, Om, Outride, Thesis, Tonic, Ultima
**Syllabus** Program(me), Prospectus, Résumé, Summary, Table, Timetable
**Syllogism** Argument, Conclusion, Deduction, Enthymeme, Epicheirema, Sorites
**Sylph** Ariel, Nymph
**Symbiotic** Adnascent
**Symbol(ic), Symbolise, Symbolism, Symbolist, Symbols** Allegory, Ampussy-and, Character, Charactery, Decadent, Del, Descriptor, Diesis, Embody, Iconography, K, Keynote, Klimt, Logotype, Metaphor, Minus, Moral, Mystical, Nominal, Notation, Operator, Placeholder, Plus, Quantifier, Regalia, Seal, Semicolon, Semiotic, Sex, Shadowy, Shamrock, Slur, Status, Syllabary, Syllabogram, Synthetism, T-cross, Trisul, Type, Typify, Weather

## SYMBOLS

*2 letters:*
Om
Pi

*3 letters:*
Edh
Eng
One
Tag

*4 letters:*
Agma
Ankh
Clef
Hash
Icon
Ikon
Logo
Mark
Neum
Rose
Rune
Sign
Tiki
Yoni

*5 letters:*
Arrow
Badge
Caret
Chord
Colon
Crest
Eagle
Emoji
Equal
Index
Kanji
Motif
Nabla
Neume
Omega
Presa
Redon
Segno
Sigla
Tilde
Token
Totem

*6 letters:*
Cachet
Cipher
Emblem
Em-dash
Filfot
Fylfot
Letter
Obelus
Smiley
Uraeus
Wreath

*7 letters:*
Algebra
Cedilla
Chevron
Dingbat
Heitiki
Ichthus
Ichthys
Mandala
Menorah
Mezuzah
Thistle
Waymark

*8 letters:*
Aniconic
Aramanth
Asterisk
Caduceus
Crucifix
Daffodil
Emoticon
Grapheme
Hashmark
Hiragana
Ideogram
Kitemark
Lexigram
Logogram
Pentacle
Phonetic
Svastika
Swastika
Talisman
Triskele
Wild card

*9 letters:*
Acrophony
Ampersand
Double-axe
Fertility
Hierogram
Horseshoe
Ideograph
Logograph
Ouroborus
Paragraph
Phonogram
Pictogram
Sacrament
Trademark

*10 letters:*
Choropleth
Hieroglyph
Kalachakra
Length mark
Mogen David
Pictograph
Triskelion

*11 letters:*
Apostrophus
Christogram
Grammalogue
Liberty Bell
Phraseogram
Punctuation
Spread eagle
Star of David

*12 letters:*
Metalanguage

*14 letters:*
Tetragrammaton

---

**Symmetric(al), Symmetry** Balance, Bilateral, Digonal, Diphycercal, Even, Harmony, Isobilateral, Mirror, Pseudocubic, Radial, Regular, Skew

**Sympathetic, Sympathise(r), Sympathy** Affinity, Agreeable, Approval, Commiserate, Commiseration, Compassion, Condole(nce), Condone, Congenial, Console, Crypto, Dear-dear, Empathy, Fellow-traveller, Genial, Humane, Kind, Mediagenic, Par, Pathos, Pity, Rapport, Ruth, Side, Supportive, Understanding, Vicarious, Well-disposed

**Symphony** Alpine, Antar, Babi Yar, Bear, Clock, Concert, Drum-roll, Echo, Eroica, Farewell, Feuer, Fifth, Finlandia, Haffner, Horn-signal, Hunt, Ilya Murometz, Jupiter, Laudon, Leningrad, Linz, London, L'Ours, Manfred, Matin, Midi, Miracle, Music, New World, Ninth, Opus, Oxford, Pastoral, Prague, Queen, Resurrection, Rhenish, Sinfonia, Sinfonietta, Surprise, Tragic, Unfinished

**Symposium** Assembly, Conference, Synod

**Symptom(s)** Diagnostic, Epiphenomenon, Feature, Heartburn, Indicia, Ketonuria, Merycism, Mimesis, Prodrome, Semiotic, Sign, Syndrome, Token, Trait, Withdrawal

**Synagogue** Beit Knesset, Beth Knesseth, Schul, Shul, Temple

**Synchronise(r)** Coincide, Genlock, Interlock, Tune

**Synclinal** Basin

**Syncopated, Syncopation, Syncope** Abridged, Breakbeat, Offbeat, Revamp, Vasovagal, Zoppa, Zoppo

**Syndicate** Associate, Cartel, Combine, Mafioso, Mob, Pool, Ring, Stokvel, Trade union

**Syndrome** Adams-Stokes, Alport's, Asperger's, Battered baby, Carpal tunnel, Cerebellar, Characteristic, China, Chinese restaurant, Chronic fatigue, Compartment, Couvade, Cri du chat, Crush, Cushing's, De Clerambault's, Down's, Economy-class, Empty nest, Erotomania, False memory, Fetal alcohol, Fragile X, Goldenhar's, Gorlin, Guillain-Barré, Gulf War, Hughes, Hutchinson-Gilford, Irritable-bowel, Jerusalem, Klinefelter's, Korsakoff's, Locked-in, Long QT, Marfan, ME, Menières, Metabolic, Munch(h)ausen's, Nonne's, Overuse, Parkinson's, Pattern, POS, Postviral, Prader-Willi, Premenstrual, Proteus, Reiter's, Rett's, Revolving door, Reye's, SADS, SARS, Savant, Sezary, Shaken baby, Sick building, SIDS, Sjogren's, Stevens-Johnson, Stockholm, Stokes-Adams, Sturge-Weber, Tall-poppy, Temperomandibular, TMJ, Total allergy, Tourette's, Toxic shock, Turner's, Wag the dog, Wernicke-Korsakoff, Williams, Wobbler, XYY

**Synod** Assembly, Conference, Convocation, General, Robber, Whitby

**Synonym(ous), Synonyms** Comparison, Reciprocal, Thesaurus

**Synopsis** Abrege, Abstract, Blurb, Conspectus, Digest, Outline, Précis, Résumé, Schema, → SUMMARY

**Syntax** Ellipsis, Grammar, Synesis

**Synthesis** Amalgam, Anabolism, Aperture, Fusion, Merger

**Synthesizer** Moog®, Music, Vocoder, Wind

**Synthetic** Android, Dralon, Empirical, Ersatz, Fake, False, Guanazolo, Man-made, Mock, Neoprene, Plastic, Polyamide, Polypropylene, Resin, Silicone, Spencerian, Tow, Unnatural, Urea

**Syphilis** Chancre, French pox, Lues, Pip, Pox, Secondary, Tertiary

**Syrian** Aramaean, Aramaic, Damascene, Druse, Druz(e), Hittite, Hurrian, Levantine, Phoenician

**Syringe(s)** Douche, Flutes, Harpoon, Hypo, Hypodermic, Needle, Reeds, Spray, Squirt, Wash, Works

**Syrphid** Hoverfly

**Syrup(y)** Capillaire, Cassareep, Cassis, Cocky's joy, Coquito, Corn, Diacodion, Diacodium, Flattery, Glycerol, Golden, Goo, Grenadine, Linctus, Maple, Molasses, Moskonfyt, Orgeat, Quiddany, Rob, Rosehip, Sorghum, Starch, Sugar, Treacle, Viscous, Wig

**System(s), Systematic** ABO, Additional member, Add-to, Alpha, An mo, Apartheid, Auditory, BACS, Beam, Bertillon, Binary, Block, Bordereau, Braille, Brunonian, Carboniferous, Ceefax, Centauri, Circulatory, Closed loop, Code, Colloidal, Colonial, Compander, Complexus, Continental, Copernican, Cosmos, Course, Crystal, Cybernetics, Decimal, Decision support, Delsarte, Dewey (Decimal), Dianetics, Distributed, Dolby®, DOS, Early warning, Economy, Eocene, Ergodic, Establishment, Ethic, Expert, Feng Shui, Feudal, Fixed, Folksonomy, Formal, Fourierism, Froebel, Front-end, Giorgi, Grading, Harvard, Haversian, Heliocentric, Hexagonal, HLA, Holist, Honour, Hub and spoke, Iastic, I Ching, Immune, Imperial, Imprest, Imputation, Induction loop, Inertial, Infrastructure, ISA, Ism, Just-in-time, Kalamazoo, Kanban, LAN, Life-support, Limbic, Lobby, Long wall, Loop, Lymphatic, Machinery, Madras, Mercantile, Mereology, Merit, → METHOD, Metric, Microcosm, Midi, Minitel, Minitrack, Miocene, MKSA, Movable, Muschelkalk, Natural, Navigational, Neat, Nervous, Network, Nicam, Notation, Number, Octal, Operating, Order, Organon, Orphism, Orrery, Panel, Periodic, Permian, Pleiocene, Plenum, Points, Portal, Process, Ptolemaic, Public address, Purchase, Quota, Quote-driven, Raisonné, Regime, Regular, Reproductive, Respiratory, Root, Run-time, SARSAT, Satnav, Scheme, Schmitt, Scientific, Sciosophy, Selsyn, Servo, Sexual, SI, Sloid, Sloyd, Sofar, Solar, Solmisation, Sonar, Sound, Spoils, Sprinkler, Squish lip, Stack(ing), Staff, Stakhanovism, Stand-alone, Stanislavski, Star, STOL, Structure, Studio, Support, Sweating, Tactic, Talk-down, Tally, Ternary, Theory, Third-rail, Tommy, Tonic sol-fa, Totalitarianism, Touch, Trias(sic), Truck, Turnkey, Tutorial, Two-party, Universe, Unix®, Urogenital, Vestibular, VOIP, Warehousing, Water, Water vascular, Weapon, Windows

# Tt

**T** Bone, Junction, Potence, Tango, Tau-cross, Tee, Time, Toc(k)
**Tab(s)** Bill, Check, Cig(arette), Decimal, Flap, Fob, → LABEL, Monitor, Ring-pull, Slate, Stay-on, Tally, Trim, Trimming
**Tabby** Blabbermouth, Brindled, → CAT, Gossip, Mottled, Spinster, Striped, Trout
**Tabernacle** Niche
**Tabitha** Gazelle
**Table(-like), Tables** Alphonsine, Altar, Bird, Board, Bradshaw, Breakfast, Calendar, Capstan, → CHART, Coffee, Communion, Console, Contingency, Corbel, Counter, Credence, Credenza, Cricket, Decision, Desk, Diagram, Dinner, Dissecting, Dolmen, Drawing, Draw-leaf, Draw-top, Dressing, Drop-leaf, Drum, Earth, Enter, Ephemeris, Experience, Food, Gateleg, Gate-legged, Glacier, Graph, Green-cloth, Grub, Gueridon, High, Imposing, Index, Inking, Key, Ladder, League, Life, Light, → LIST, Log, Look up, Lord's, Lowboy, Mahogany, Matrix, Mensa(l), Mesa, Monopode, Mortality, Multiplication, Nest, Occasional, Operating, Orientation, Pembroke, Periodic, Piecrust, Pier, Plane, Plateau, Platen, Pool, Prothesis, Pythagoras, Ready-reckoner, Reckoner, Refectory, Roll, Round, Rudolphine, Sand, Schedule, Scheme, Slab, Sofa, Spoon, Stall, Statistical, Stone, Suggest, Taboret, Tabular, Tariff, Tea, Te(a)poy, Throwing, Tide, Times, Toilet, Toning, Top, Tray(mobile), Trestle, Trolley, Truth, Twelve, Washstand, Water, Whirling, Wool, Workbench, Writing
**Tableau** Pageant, Semantic
**Tablecloth** Damask, Linen
**Table-land** Barkly, Kar(r)oo, Mesa, Plateau, Puna
**Table-list** Memo, Menu
**Tablet** Abacus, Album, Aspirin, Brass, Caplet, Cartouche, Disclosing, E, Eugebine, Graphics, Hatch, Hatchment, Ipad®, Medallion, Opisthograph, Osculatory, Ostracon, Ostrakon, → PAD, Painkiller, → PILL, Pilule, Plaque, Rune, Slate, Stela, Stele, Stone, Tabula, Tombstone, Torah, Triglyph, Triptych, Troche, Trochisk, Ugarit, Votive, Wax
**Table-talker** Deipnosophist
**Table-turner** Tartar
**Table-ware** China, Cutlery, Silver
**Tabloid** Rag
**Taboo, Tabu** Ban(ned), Bar, Blackball, Forbidden, Incest, Non dit, No-no, Off-limits, Tapu, Unclean
**Tachograph** Spy-in-the-cab
**Tacit, Taciturn(ity)** Clam, Implicit, Laconic, Mumps, Oyster, Reticent, Silent, Understood, Unheard
**Tack(y)** Adhesive, Bar, Baste, Beat, Boxhaul, Brass, Cheesy, Cinch, Clubhaul, Cobble, Drawing pin, Glutinous, Gybe, Harness, Kitsch, Leg, Martingale, Nail, Noseband, Saddlery, Salt-horse, → SEW, Sprig, Stirrup, Tailor's, Tasteless, Veer, Wear, White-seam, Yaw, Zigzag
**Tackle** Accost, Address, Approach, Attempt, Beard, Bobstay, Buckle down, Burton, Cat, Challenge, Chin, Claucht, Claught, Clevis, Clew-garnet, Collar, Dead-eye, Fishing, Garnet, Gear, Haliard, Halyard, Harness, Jury-rig, Kit, Ledger, Nose, Rig, Rigging, Sack, Scrag, Spear, Stick, Straight-arm, Topping-lift, Undertake, Wedding
**Tact, Tactful** Delicacy, Diplomacy, Diplomatic, Discreet, Discretion, Finesse, Kidglove, Politic, Savoir-faire
**Tactic(s)** Audible, Carrot and stick, Crossruff, Finesse, Hardball, Manoeuvre, Masterstroke,

Plan, Ploy, Ruse, Salami, Scare, Shock, Smear, Spoiling, → **STRATEGY**, Strong-arm, Zwischenzug

**Tactless(ness)** Blundering, Brash, Clanger, Crass, Gaffe, Gauche, Indelicate, Indiscreet, Loud mouth, Maladroit

**Tadpole** Ascidian, Polliwig, Polliwog, Pollywig, Pollywog, Porwiggle, Taddie

**Taffy** Thief, Toffee, Welshman

**Tag** Aglet, Aiguillette, Badge, Bar code, Cliché, Dog, Electronic, End, Epithet, → **FOLLOW**, Kabaddi, Kimball, Label, Meta, Price, Question, Quotation, Quote, Remnant, Tab, Tail end, → **TICKET**, Treasury

**Tahini** Sesame

**Tail, Tailpiece, Tailboard** All-flying, Amentum, Apocopate, → **APPENDAGE**, Bob, Brush, Bun, Caudal, Cercal, Cercus, Coda, Codetta, Colophon, Cue, Dock, Empennage, Endgate, Fan, Fee, Flag, Floccus, → **FOLLOW**, Fud, Liripoop, Parson's nose, Point, Pole, Pope's nose, PS, Queue, Rumple-bane, Scut, Seat, Shirt, Stag, Stern, Telson, → **TIP**, Trail, Train, Uro(some), Uropod, Uropygium

**Tailless** Acaudal, An(o)urous, Fee-simple

**Tail-lobes** Anisocercal

**Tailor(ed)** Adapt, Bespoke, Bushel, Cabbager, Clothier, Couturier, Customise, Cutter, Darzi, Draper, Durzi, Epicene, Feeble, Flint, Form, Merchant, Nine, Orient, Outfitter, Personalise, Pick-the-louse, Pricklouse, Sartor, Seamster, Snip, Starveling, Style, Whipcat, Whipstitch

▷**Tailor** *may indicate* an anagram

**Taint(ed)** Besmirch, Blemish, Fly-blown, Foughty, High, Impure, Infect, Leper, Off, Poison, → **SPOIL**, Stain, Stale, Stigma, Tinge, Trace, Unwholesome

**Taiwan** RC

**Take(n), Take in, Taking(s), Take over, Takeover** Absorb, → **ACCEPT**, Adopt, Annex, Appropriate, Assume, Attract, Bag, Beg, Besotted, Bewitch, Bite, Bone, Borrow, Bottle, Buy out, → **CAPTURE**, Catch, Charming, Claim, Colonise, Consume, Cop, Coup (d'etat), Detract, Dig, Dishy, Distrain, Eat, Entr(y)ism, Epris, Exact, Expropriate, Filch, Film, Get, Grab, Greenmail, Handle, Haul, Hent, Hijack, House, Howe, Huff, Impound, Incept, Ingest, Leveraged buy out, Loot, Mess, Misappropriate, Nationalise, Nick, Occupy, On, Photograph, Pilfer, Pocket, Poison pill, Purloin, Quote, R, Rec, Receipt, Receive, Recipe, Reserved, Reverse, Rob, Seise, Sequester, Ship, Smitten, Snaffle, Snatch, Sneak, Spoken for, → **STEAL**, Stomach, Subsume, Swallow, Sweet, Swipe, Toll, Trump, Turnover, Usher, Usurp, Wan, Winsome, Wrest

**Take away, Take-away, Take back, Take off** Abduct, Annex, Aph(a)eresis, Asport, Assisted, Carry-out, Chippy, Curry, Deduct, Destruct, Dock, Doff, Doggy bag, Dot, Esloin, Exenterate, Expropriate, Indian, Jato, Minus, Parody, Parrot, Press-gang, Recaption, Resume, Scramble, Shanghai, Skit, Spirit, Spoof, Streak, Subtract, Travesty, Vertical, VTO(L)

**Take care** Guard, See, Tend, Watch

**Take down, Take up** Appropriate, Cap, Choose, Osmose, Shot, Snaffle, Unhook

▷**Taken up** *may indicate* reversed

**Take part** Act, Engage, Side

**Taker** Recipient

**Talbot House** Toc H

**Talc** Potstone, Rensselaerite, Soapstone, Steatite, Venice

**Tale(s)** Aga-saga, Allegory, Anecdote, Blood, Boccaccio, Cautionary, Conte, Decameron, Edda, Fable, Fabliau, Fairy, Fairy story, Fiction, Folk, Gag, Geste, Hadith, Hair-raiser, Iliad, Jataka, Jeremiad, Legend, Lie, Mabinogion, Maise, Märchen, Ma(i)ze, Mease, Milesian, Narrative, Odyssey, Old wives', Pentameron, Rede, Saga, Sandabar, Score, Sinbad, Sind(a)bad, Sob-story, Spiel, → **STORY**, Teratology, Toy, Tradition, Traveller's, Weird, Yarn

**Tale-bearer, Tale-teller** Gossip, Grass, Grimm, Informer, Sneak, Tattler, Tusitala

**Talent(ed)** Ability, Able, Accomplishment, Aptitude, Beefcake, Bent, Brilliance, Budding, Dower, Endowment, Faculty, Flair, Forte, Genius, Gift, Idiot savant, Ingenium, Knack, Long suit, Natural, Nous, Obol, Prodigy, Schtick, Strong point, Tottie, Versatile, Virtuoso, Whiz-kid, W(h)iz(z)

**Talion** Reprisal

**Talisman** Amulet, Charm, Luck, Mascot, Saladin, Sampo, Scarab, Telesm

**Talk(ing), Talking point, Talker, Talks** Address, Ana, Articulate, Babble, Bibble-babble, Blab, Blague(er), Blah, Blat, Blather, Blether-skate, Burble, Cant, Causerie, Chalk, Chat, Chew the fat, Chinwag, Chirp, Chitchat, Circumlocution, Colloquy, Commune, Confabulate, Confer, Contact, Converse, Coo, Cross, Descant, Dialog(ue), Diatribe, Dilate, Discourse, Discursion, Discussion, Diseur, Dissert, Double, Dwell on, Earbash, Earful, Expatiate, Express, Fast, Fighting, Filibuster, Froth, Gab, Gabble, Gabnash, Gas, Gibber, Gossip, Grandiloquence, Guff, Harp, Hearsay, High-level, Hobnob, Hot air, Imparl, Jabber, Jargon, Jaw-jaw, Jazz, Korero, Lalage, Lalla, Legalise, Line, Lip, Logorrhoea, Macrology, Malarkey, Mang, Maunder, Mince, Monologue, Motormouth, Nashgab, Natter, Noise, Omniana, Palabra, Palaver, Parlance, Parley, Patter, Pawaw, Pep, Perorate, Phraser, Pidgin, Pillow, Pitch, Potter, Powwow, Prate, Prattle, Presentation, Prittle-prattle, Prose, Proximity, Ramble, Rap, Rattle on, Regale, Rigmarole, Rote, Sales, SALT, Sermon, Shop, Slang(-whang), Small, Soliloquy, → **SPEAK**, Speech, Spiel, Spout, Straight, Summit, Sweet, Table, Tachylogia, Topic, Turkey, Twaddle, Twitter, Unbosom, Up(s), Utter, Vocal, Waffle, Wibble, Witter, Wongi, Wrangle, Yabber, Yack, Yad(d)a-yad(d)a-yad(d)a, Yak, Yalta, Yammer, Yap, Yatter

**Talkative** Chatty, Expansive, Fluent, Gabby, Garrulous, Gash, Glib, Loquacious, Mouthy, Vocular, Voluble, Windbag

**Tall** Beanpole, Etiolated, Exaggerated, Far-fetched, Hie, High, Hye, Lanky, Lathy, Leggy, Lofty, Long, Order, Palatial, Procerity, Randle-tree, Rangy, Rantle-tree, Reedy, Spindly, Tangle, Taunt, Tower, Towery, Unlikely

**Tallboy** Chest, Dresser, Highboy

**Tallow** Greaves, Hatchettite, Lead-arming, Mineral, Mountain, Suet, Vegetable, Wax

**Tally** Accord, → **AGREE**, Census, Correlate, Correspond, Count, Match, Nickstick, Notch, Reckoning, Record, → **SCORE**, Stick, Stock, Tab, Tag

**Talmud** Gemara, Mishna(h)

**Talon** Claw, Ogee, Single

**Talus** Scree

**Tamarind** Assam

**Tamarisk** Myrica

**Tamasha** Fuss, To-do

**Tambourine** Timbrel

**Tame** Amenage, Break (in), Docile, Domesticate, Gentle, Lapdog, Mail, Mansuete, Meek, Mild, Safe, Snool, Subdue

**Tamil** Tiger

**Tammany** Hall, Sachem

**Tamp, Tampon** Plug, Ram

**Tamper(ing)** Bishop, Cook, Doctor, Fake, Fiddle, Interpolate, Meddle, Medicate, Monkey, Nobble, Phreaking

**Tam-tam** Gong

**Tan(ned), Tanned skin, Tanning** Adust, Bablah, Babul, Bark, Basil, Beige, Bisque, Boarding, Bronze, → **BROWN**, Canaigre, Catechu, Furan, Furfuran(e), Insolate, Lambast, Leather, Neb-neb, Paste, Pipi, Puer, Pure, Spank, Spray, Sun, Sunbathe, Tenné, Umber, Valonea, Val(l)onia, Weather-beaten, Ybet

**Tandem** Duo, Randem

**Tang** Relish, Smack, Taste

**Tangent** Ratio, Slope, Touching

**Tangible** Actual, Concrete, Palpable, Plain, Solid, Tactile, Tactual

**Tangle** Alga, Badderlock, Burble, Driftweed, Dulse, Embroil, Enmesh, Entwine, Fank, Fankle, Heap, Hole, Imbroglio, Implication, Ket, → **KNOT**, Labyrinth, Laminaria, Lutin, Mat, Mess, Mix, Nest, Oarweed, Ore, Perplex, Pleach, Raffle, → **RAVEL**, Sea-girdle, Seaweed, Skean, Skein, Snarl, Taigle, Taut(it), Tawt, Thicket, Tousle, Varec

▷**Tangled** *may indicate* an anagram

**Tango** Dance, T

**Tank(ed)** Abrams, Alligator, Amphibian, Aquarium, Back boiler, Belly, Bosh, Casspir, Centurion, Cesspool, Challenger, Chieftain, Cistern, Crusader, Dracone, Drop, Drunk, Fail,

Feedhead, Float, Flotation, Fuel, Gasholder, Gasometer, Header, Keir, Kier, Mouse, Panzer, Pod, Quiescent, → **RESERVOIR**, Ripple, Sedimentation, Septic, Sherman, Shield pond, Silo, Sponson, Sump, Surge, Think, Tiger, Valentine, Vat, Venter, Ventral, Vivarium, Water, Weasel, Whippet

**Tankard** Blackjack, Jug, Peg, Pewter, Pot, Stein, Tappit-hen

**Tanker** Bowser, Crude carrier, Lorry, Oiler, Torrey Canyon, VLCC

**Tanner(y)** Bender, Currier, Kick, Ray, Solarium, Sunbather, Sunlamp, Sunshine, Tawery, Tester(n), 'VId', Zack

**Tannin** Catechu, Cutch, Sumac

**Tantalise** Entice, Tease, Tempt, Torture

**Tantalum** Ta

**Tantivy** Alew, Halloo

**Tantrum** Boutade, Conniption, Hissy fit, Outburst, Paddy, Pet, Rage, Scene, Snit, Strop, Tirrivee, Tirrivie, Wobbly

**Tanzania(n)** EAT, Sandawe

**Tap(ping), Taps** Accolade, Ague, Bibcock, Blip, Bob, Broach, Bug, Cock, Col legno, Dip into, Drum, Eavesdrop, Faucet, Fever, Fillip, Flick, Hack, H and C, Listen, Mag, Milk, Mixer, Monitor, Paracentesis, Pat, Patter, Percuss, Petcock, → **RAP**, Screw, Spigot, Spile, Spinal, Standpipe, Stopcock, Stroup, Tack, Tat, Tit, Touk, Tuck, Water

**Tapas** Meze

**Tape** Adhesive, Cassette, Chrome, DAT, Demo, → **DRINK**, Duct, Ferret, Finish, Friction, Gaffer, Grip, Idiot, Incle, Inkle, Insulating, Magnetic, Masking, Measure, Measuring, Metal, Mix, Narrowcast, Paper, Passe-partout, Perforated, Punched, Record, Red, Reel to reel, Ribbon, Scotch, Sellotape®, Shape, Show reel, Stay, Sticky, Strap, Ticker, Tit, Video, Welding

**Taper(ed), Tapering** Candle, Diminish, Fastigiate, Featheredge, Flagelliform, Fusiform, Lanceolate, Morse, Narrow, Nose, Spill, Subulate, Tail

**Tapestry** Alentous, Arras(ene), Aubusson, Bayeux, Bergamot, Crewel-work, Dosser, Gobelin, Hanging, Mural, Oudenarde, Petit point, Sewing, Tapet, Weaving

**Tapeworm** Coenurus, Echinococcus, Hydatid, Measle, Scolex, Strobila, Taenia, Teniasis

**Tapioca** Cassava, Pearl, Yuca, Yucca

**Tapir** Anta, S(e)ladang

**Tar, Tar product** AB, Aniline, Bitumen, Carbazole, Coal, Creosote, Deckhand, Egg, Furan, Gas, Gladwellise, Gob, Indene, Juniper, Maltha, Matelot, Matlo, Mineral, Naphtha, Needle, OS, Parcel, Pay, Picamar, Picene, Pine, Pitch, Rating, Retene, Sailor, Salt, Uintahite, Uintaite, Wood, Wood pitch, Wren, Xylol

**Tardy** Behindhand, Belated, Dilatory, Late, → **SLOW**

**Tare** T, Tine, Vetch

**Target** Admass, → **AIM**, Ambition, Attainment, Aunt Sally, Barndoor, Blank, Butt, Clay, Clout, Cockshy, Dartboard, Drogue, End, Ettle, Floating stock, Focus, Hit, Home, Hub, Inner, Magpie, Mark, Mark-white, Motty, Nick, → **OBJECT**, Object ball, Outer, Peg, Pelta, Pin, Popinjay, Prey, Prick, Quintain, Sitter, Sitting (duck), Soft, Tee, Victim, Wand, Whipping boy, Zero in, Zero on

**Tariff** Levy, List, Menu, Preferential, Protective, Rate, Revenue, Zabeta

**Tarmac** Runway

**Tarnish(ed)** Asperse, Besmirch, Defile, Discolour, Discredit, Impure, Mar, Soil, Stain, Sully, Taint

**Taro** Arum, Coc(c)o, Dasheen, Eddo

**Tarot** Arcana

**Tarpaulin** Weathercloth

**Tarragon** Staragen

**Tarry** Bide, Bituminous, Dally, Leng, → **LINGER**, Stay, Sticky

**Tarsier** Malmag

**Tarsus** Saul

**Tart** Acetic, Acid, Apple, Bakewell, Call-girl, Charlotte, Cheesecake, Cocotte, Croquante, Cupid, Custard, Dariole, Deck, Doxy, Duff, Flam(m), Flan, Flawn, Frock, Harlot, Ho, Hussy, Jade, Jam, Jay, Lemony, Mirliton, Moll, Mort, Nana, Painted woman, → **PIE**, Pinnace, Piquant,

Pro, Pungent, Quean, Quiche, Quine, Rate, → SHARP, Snappy, Sour, Stew, Strumpet, Tatin, Tom, Tramp, Treacle, Trollop, Trull, Unsweet, Vinegary

**Tartan** Argyle, Argyll, Check, Maud, Plaid, Set(t), Trews

**Tartar** Argal, Argol, Beeswing, Calculus, Crust, Hell, Plaque, Rough, Scale, Tam(b)erlane, Zenocrate

**Tarzan** Greystoke

**Tashkent** Uzbek

**Task** Assignment, Aufgabe, Boondoggle, → CHORE, Clat, Commission, Drudgery, Duty, Emprise, Errand, Exercise, Fag, Imposition, Legwork, Marathon, Mission, Onus, Ordeal, Pensum, Remit, Stint, Thankless, Uphill, Vulgus

**Taskmaster** Hercules, Martinet, Slave driver

**Tasmania** Apple Isle, Van Diemen's Land

**Tassel** Fringe, Pompom, Toorie, Tourie, Tsutsith, Tuft

**Taste(ful), Taster, Tasty** Acquired, Aesthetic, Appetite, Artistic, Assay, Dash, Degust, Delibate, Delicious, Discrimination, Drop, → EAT, Elegant, Esculent, Excerpt, Fad, Fancy, Fashion, Flavour, Form, Gout, Gust, Gustatory, Hint, Lekker, Lick, Liking, Palate, Penchant, Pica, Pree, Refinement, Relish, → SAMPLE, Sapor, Sar, Savour, Scrummy, Seemly, Sensation, Sense, S(c)hme(c)k, Sip, Smack, Smatch, Smattering, Snack, Soupçon, Specimen, Stomach, Succulent, Tang, Titbit, Toothsome, → TRY, Umami, Vertu, Virtu, Waft, Wine, Yummy

**Tasteless** Appal, Bland, Brassy, Coarse, Fade, Flat, Gaudy, Indelicate, Insipid, Insulse, Kitsch, Stale, Tacky, Tawdry, Vapid, Vulgar, Watery, Wearish, Wersh

**Tat, Tatter, Tatty** Flitter, Grot, Moth-eaten, Rag, Ribbon, Roon, Schlock, Scrap, Shabby, Shred, Tag, Tan, Ta(i)ver, Untidy

**Tattie-bogle** Scarecrow

**Tattle(r)** Blab, Chatter, Gash, → GOSSIP, Prate, Rumour, Sneak, Snitch, Totanus, Willet

**Tattoo** Devil's, Drum, Edinburgh, Ink, Moko, Pony, Rataplan, Row-dow, Tat

**Tatum** Art

**Taught** Educated, Up

**Taunt** Bait, Catcall, Deride, Dig, Fling, Gibe, Gird, → JEER, Jest, Jibe, Rag, Razz, Ridicule, Twight, Twit

**Taut** Stiff, Strained, Tense

**Tavern** Bar, Beer parlour, Bodega, Bousing-ken, Bush, Fonda, → INN, Kiddleywink, Kneipe, Mermaid, Mitre, Mughouse, Night-cellar, Night-house, Pothouse, Shebeen, Taphouse

**Taw** Alley, Ally, Marble

**Tawdry** Brash, Catchpenny, → CHEAP, Flashy, Gaudy, Gingerbread, Kitsch, Meretricious, Raffish, Sleazy, Tatty, Tinsey, Vulgar

**Tawny** Brindle, Dusky, Fawn, Fulvous, Port, Tan

**Tawse** Cat, Lash, Thong, Whip

**Tax(ation), Taxing** ACT, Agist, Aid, Alms-fee, Arduous, Assess, Blood, Capital gains, Capitation, Carbon, Carucage, Cense, Cess, → CHARGE, Corporation, Council, CRT, Custom, Danegeld, Death duty, Deferred, Direct, Duty, Energy, EPT, Escot, Escuage, Eurotax, Exact, Excise, Exercise, EZT, Fat, Gabelle, Geld, Gelt, Gift, Green, Head, Head money, Hearth money, Hidage, Hidden, Impose, Imposition, Impost, Impute, Indirect, Inheritance, IR, Jaghir(e), Jagir, Keelage, Land, Levy, Likin, Lot, Murage, Negative, Octroi, Operose, Overtask, Overwork, Pavage, PAYE, Peter's-pence, Poll, Poundage, Precept, Primage, Property, Proportional, PT, Punish, Purchase, Rate, Regressive, Road, Rome-pence, Sales, Scat(t), Scot (and lot), Scutage, Sess, SET, Severe, Ship money, Sin, Single, Skat, Stealth, Stent, Strain, Streetage, Stretch, Stumpage, Super, Taille, Tallage, Talliate, Tall order, Tariff, Tartan, Task, Teind, Tithe, Tobin, Toilsome, Toll, Tonnage, Tribute, Try, Turnover, Tyre, Unitary, Value-added, VAT, Wattle, Wealth, Weary, White rent, Windfall, Window, Withholding, Zakat

**Tax area** Tahsil, Talooka, Taluk(a)

**Tax-collector, Taxman** Amildar, Cheater, Exciseman, Farmer, Gabeller, Ghostbuster, Inspector, IR(S), Publican, Stento(u)r, Tidesman, Tithe-proctor, Tollman, Undertaker, Vatman, Zemindar

**Taxi(s), Taxi driver** Air, Cab, Coast, Gharri, Gharry, Hackie, Hackney carriage, Joe baxi, Minicab, Rank, Samlor, System, Uber, Zola Budd

**Taxidermist** Venus
**Taxiway** Peritrack
▸**Taxman** *see* **TAX-COLLECTOR**
**TB** Scrofula
**TE** Lawrence, Ross, Shaw
**Tea** Afternoon, Assam, Beef, Black, Bohea, Brew, Brew-up, Brick, Bubble, Bush, Cambric, Camomile, Caper, Ceylon, Cha, Chai, Chamomile, Chanoyu, Char, China, Chirping-cup, Congo(u), Cream, Cuppa, Darjeeling, Earl Grey, Grass, Green, Gunfire, Gunpowder, Herb(al), High, Hybrid, Hyson, Ice(d), Indian, Jasmine, K(h)at, Kitchen, Labrador, Lapsang, Lapsang Souchong, Leaves, Ledum, Lemon, Malt, Manuka, Marijuana, Maté, Meat, Mexican, Mint, Morning, Mountain, New Jersey, Oolong, Orange pekoe, Oulong, Paraguay, Pekoe, Post and rail, Pot, Qat, Red-root, Rooibos, Rosie Lee, Russian, Sage, Senna, Souchong, Stroupach, Stroupan, Switchel, Tannin, Tay, Thea, Theophylline, Tousy, Twankay, White, Yapon, Yerba (de Maté)
**Teacake** Sally Lunn
**Teach(er), Teaching (material), Teachings** Academe, Academician, Acharya, Adjoint, Advisory, Agrege, AMMA, Anthroposophy, Apostle, Aristotle, AUT, Barbe, Beale, BEd, Bhagwan, Buddha, Buss, Catechist, Chalk and talk, Chalkface, → **COACH**, Communicate, Con(ne), Confucius, Didactic, Didascalic, Docent, Doctrine, Dogma, Dominie, Dressage, Edify, → **EDUCATE**, Educationalist, Edutainment, EIS, ELT, Explain, Faculty, Froebel, Gerund-grinder, Gooroo, Gospel, Governess, Guru, Head, Heuristic, Hodja, Inculcate, Indoctrinate, Inform, Instil, Instruct, Ism, Kho(d)ja, Kindergart(e)ner, Kumon (Method), Lair, Lancasterian, Larn, Lear(e), Lecturer, Leir, Lere, Maam, Maggid, Magister, Maharishi, Mahavira, Mallam, Marker, Marm, Master, Maulvi, Mentor, Message, Miss, Mistress, Molla(h), Monitor, Montessorian, Moola(h), Moolvi(e), Moralist, Mufti, Mullah, Munshi, Music, Mwalimu, Mystagogue, Nuffield, NUT, Paedotribe, PAT, Pedagogue, Pedant, Peripatatic, Phonic method, Posture-master, Preceptor, Pr(a)efect, Privat-docent, Privat dozent, Proctor, Prof, Prog, PT, Pupil, Rabbetzin, Rabbi, Rav, Realia, Rebbe, Remedial, Rhetor, Scholastic, Schoolie, Schoolman, Scribe, Sensei, Show, Sir, Smriti, Socrates, Sophist, Specialist, Staff, Starets, Staretz, Stinks, Substitute, Sufism, Sunna, Supply, Swami, Tantra, Team, Tonic sol-fa, Train(er), Tuition, Tutelage, Tutor, Tutress, Tutrix, Usher
**Teach-in** Seminar
**Teahouse** Sukiya
**Teak** African, Bastard, White
**Teal** Spring
**Team** All Blacks, Argyll, Bafana Bafana, Colts, Crew, Dream, Écurie, Eleven, Équipe, Farm, Fifteen, Hearts, Line-up, Lions, Man U, Nine, Outfit, Oxen, Panel, Possibles, Probables, Proto, Relay, Scrub, Set, → **SIDE**, Span, Special, Spurs, Squad, Squadron, Staff, Syndicate, Tiger, Troika, Troupe, Turnout, Unicorn, Unit, United, XI
**Team spirit** Solidarity
**Tea-party** Boston, Bunfight, Cookie-shine, Drum, Kettledrum, Shine
**Teapot** Billycan, Cadogan, Samovar
**Tear(s), Tearable, Tearful, Tearing** Beano, Claw, Crocodile, Dismember, Divulsion, Drop(let), Eye-drop, Eye-water, Greeting, Hurry, Lacerate, Lachrymose, Laniary, Mammock, Maudlin, Pelt, Ranch, Rash, Reave, → **REND**, Rheum, Rip, Rive, Rume, Scag, Screed, Shred, Snag, Split, Spree, Sprint, Tire, Vale, Waterworks, Wet, Worry, Wrench, Wrest
**Tearaway** Get, Hothead, Madcap, Ned, Yahoo
**Tear-jerker** Melodrama, Onion, Shallot, Weepie
**Tea-room** Café
**Tear-pit** Crumen, Larmier
**Tease, Teaser, Teasing** Arch, Backcomb, Badinage, Bait, Ballyrag, Banter, Brain, Card, Chaff, Chap, Chiack, Chip, Chyack, Cod, Comb, Coquet, Discredit, Drag, Enigma, Grig, Guy, Hank, Imp, Ironic, Itch, Josh, Kemb, Kid, Mag, Mamaguy, Mock, Nark, Persiflage, → **RAG**, Raillery, Rally, Razz, Rib, Rip on, Rot, Strip, → **TANTALISE**, Titillate, Toaze, Torment(or), Touse, Touze, Towse, Towze, Twilly, Twit, Wind up, Worrit
**Teasel** Dipsacus, Valerian

**Teat** Dug, Dummy, Mamilla, Mastoid, Nipple, Pap, Soother, Tit
**Tea-time** Chat
**Teaze** Gig, Moze
**Technetium** Tc
**Technical, Technician, Technique** Adept, Alexander, Anti-jamming, Art, Artisan, Brushwork, Campimetry, Chief, College, Craftsmanship, Cusum, Delphi, Dental, Double-stopping, Execution, Foley artist, Footsteps editor, Harmolodics, Honey-trap, Junior, Kiwi, Know-how, Lap dissolver, Layback, Manner, Metamorphic, → **METHOD**, Operative, Phasing, Phlebotomist, Pixil(l)ation, Reflectography, Salami, Sandwich, Science, Scientist, Senior, Serial, Slam-dunk, Slo-mo, Split-screen, Stop-motion, System, Toe and heel, Touch, Western blotting, Work around, Zift
**Technology, Technologian, Technological** Aerospace, Alternative, Appropriate, Bluetooth®, Electronics, Engineering, High, Information, Intermediate, IT, Pull, Push, Robotics, Rocketry, State of the art, Stealth, Telescience, Thickfilm, Thinfilm
**Ted(dy)** Bodgie, Dexter, Ducktail, Moult, Roosevelt, Underwear, Widgie, Yob
**Tedium, Tedious** Balls-aching, Boring, Chore, Deadly, Doldrums, Drab, Drag, Dreariness, Dreich, Dull, Ennui, Foozle, Heaviness, Ho-hum, Humdrum, Irksome, Laborious, Langueur, Long, Longspun, Longueur, Long-winded, Mind-numbing, Monotony, Operose, Prosy, Repetitive, Rigmarole, Rut, Snore, Soul-destroying, Tame, Tiresome, → **TIRING**, Twaddle, Wearisome, Yawn
**Tee** Hub, Umbrella, Wind
**Teem(ing)** Abound, Alive, Bustling, Empty, Great, Heaving, Live, Pullulate, Swarm
**Teenage(r)** Adolescent, Bobbysoxer, Junior, Juvenile, Minor, Mod, Pubertal, Rocker, Sharpie, Skinhead, Youth
**Teeter** Wobble
▸**Teeth** *see* **TOOTH(ED)**
**Teething ring** Coral
**Teetotal(ler)** Abdar, Abstainer, Blue Ribbon, Nephalist, Rechabite, Sober, Temperate, TT, Water-drinker, Wowser
**Tegument** Seed coat
**Telecommunications** Cellnet®, Vodafone®
**Telegram, Telegraph** Bush, Cable, Ems, Facsimile, Fax, Grapevine, Greetings, International, Marconi, Message, Moccasin, Mulga wire, Overseas, Quadruplex, Radiogram, Singing, Telautograph®, Telex, Wire
**Telegu** Gentoo
**Telepath(y), Telepathic** Clairvoyance, ESP, Psychic, Seer, Thought-reader
**Telephone, Telephonist** Ameche, ATLAS, Bell, Blackberry, Blower, BT, Call, Cellphone, Centrex, Cordless, DECT, Detectophone, Dial, Dog and bone, Exchange, Extension, Freephone®, GRACE, Handset, Horn, Hotline, Intercom, Line, Lo-call®, Mercury, Mobile, Mob(e)y, Noki, Operator, Patchboard, Payphone, Pay-station, Pdq, → **PHONE**, POTS, Ring, Scrambler, Skype®, Snitch line, Speakerphone, Squawk box, STD, Telebridge, Textphone, Tie line, Touch-tone, Utility, Vodafone®, Wire
**Teleprinter** Creed
**Teleprompter** Autocue®
**Telescope** Altazimuth, Astronomical, Binocle, Cassegrain(ian), Collimator, Comet finder, Coronagraph, Coronograph, Coudé, Electron, Equatorial, Finder, Galilean, Gemini, Glass, Gregorian, Heliometer, Hubble, Interferometer, Intussuscept, Meniscus, Newtonian, Night-glass, Optical, Palomar, Perspective, Prospect(ive)-glass, Radio, Reading, Reflecting, Reflector, Refractor, Schmidt, Sector, Shorten, Sniperscope, Snooperscope, Speculum, Spyglass, Stadia, Terrestrial, Tube, X-ray, Zenith
**Teletext®** Ceefax®, Oracle®
**Television, Telly** Appointment, Box, Breakfast, Cable, Closed-circuit, Confessional, Daytime, Digibox®, Digital, Diorama, Docu-soap, Event, Flatscreen, Goggle box, High-definition, Iconoscope, Image orthicon, Interactive, ITV, MAC, Narrowcast, PAL, Pay, Plumbicon®, Projection, Reality, RTE, Satellite, SECAM, Set, Small screen, Subscription, Terrestrial, Tree and branch, Tube, → **TV**, Video

**Tell(ing), Teller, Telltale** Acquaint, Announce, Apprise, Archer, Beads, Blab, Break, Cashier, Clipe, Clype, Compt, Confess, Direct, → DISCLOSE, Divulge, Effective, Fess, Give, Grass, Impart, Influential, Inform(er), Militate, → NARRATE, Noise, Nose, Notify, Number, Peach, Pointer, Rat, Recite, Recount, Relate, Report, Retail, Rumour, Scunge, Sing, Sneak, Snitch, Spin, Teach, Unbosom, William

**Tellurium** Te

**Temerity** Audacity, Cheek, Gall, Impertinence, Imprudence, Impudence, Incaution, Rashness, Recklessness

**Temper, Temperate** Abstemious, Abstinent, Adjust, Allay, Alloy, Anneal, Assuage, Attune, Balmy, Bate, Bile, Blood, Calm, Cantankerous, Chasten, Choler, Comeddle, Continent, Dander, Delay, Ease, Fireworks, Flaky, Inure, Irish, Leaven, Lines, → MILD, Mince, Mitigate, Moderate, Modify, → MOOD, Neal, Outburst, Paddy, Paddywhack, Pet, Radge, Rage, Season, Short fuse, Snit, Sober, Soften, Spitfire, Spleen, Strop, Swage, Tantrum, Techy, Teen, Teetotal, Tetchy, Tiff, Tone, Trim, Tune, Wax

**Temperament(al)** Artistic, Bent, Blood, Choleric, Crasis, Cyclothymia, Disposition, Equal, Just, Kidney, Mean-tone, Melancholy, Mettle, Moody, → NATURE, Neel, Over-sensitive, Phlegmatic, Prima donna, Sanguine, Unstable, Up and down, Viscerotonia

**Temperance** Good Templar, Moderation, Pledge, Rechabite

**Temperature** Absolute, Black body, Celsius, Centigrade, Chambré, Colour, Core, Critical, Curie, Dew point, Enantiotropy, Eutectic, Fahrenheit, Fever, Flashpoint, Heat, Heterothermal, Hyperthermia, Ignition, Kelvin, Melting, Néel, Permissive, Regulo, Restrictive, Room, Supercritical, T, Thermodynamic, Transition, Weed, Weid

**Tempest(uous)** Bourasque, Euraquilo, Euroclydon, Gale, High, Marie, → STORM(Y), Wrathy

**Template** Prototype, Stencil

**Temple, Temple gate** Abu Simbel, Abydos, Adytum, Amphiprostyle, Amritsar, Artemis, Capitol, Cella, Chapel, Church, Delphi, Delubrum, Ephesus, Erechtheum, Erechthion, Fane, Gompa, Gurdwara, Haffet, Haffit, Heroon, Inner, Josshouse, Karnak, Mandir(a), Masjid, Middle, Mithraeum, Monopteron, Monopteros, Mosque, Museum, Naos, Nymphaeum, Pagod(a), Pantheon, Parthenon, Sacellum, Serapeum, → SHRINE, Shul(n), Synagogue, Teocalli, Teopan, Torii, Vihara, Wat

**Tempo** Agoge, Andantino, Beat, Lento, Rate, → RHYTHM, Rubato

**Temporal** Petrosal, Petrous, Secular

**Temporary, Temporarily** Acting, Awhile, Caretaker, Casual, Cutcha, Ephemeral, Erasable, Fleeting, Freelance(r), Hobjob, Impermanent, Interim, Intermittent, Jury-rigged, Kutcha, Lash-up, Locum, Make do, Makeshift, Pro tem, Provisional, Quick-fix, Scratch, Short-term, Stopgap, Temp, Transient, Transitional

**Temporise(r)** Politique

**Tempt(ation), Tempting, Tempter, Temptress** Allure, Apple, Bait, Beguile, Beset, Circe, Dalilah, Dangle, Decoy, Delilah, Draw, → ENTICE, Eve, Femme fatale, Groundbait, Impulse, Induce, Invite, Irresistible, Lure, Mephistopheles, Peccable, Providence, Satan, Seduce, Serpent, Sexy, Siren, Snare, Tantalise, Test, Tice, Trial, Vamp, Woo

**Ten** 10, Commandments, Count, Decad, Dectet, Decury, Denary, Googol, Iota, Long, Tera-, Tribes, X

**Tenacious, Tenacity** Adhesive, Clayey, Determined, Dogged, Drive, Fast, Grim death, Guts, Hold, Intransigent, Persevering, Persistent, Resolute, Retentive, Sticky, Tough

**Tenancy, Tenant(s)** Boarder, Censuarius, Cosherer, Cottager, Cottar, Cotter, Cottier, Dreng, Feuar, Feudatory, Gavelman, Homage, Ingo, Inhabit, Joint, Kindly, Leaseholder, Lessee, Liege, Life, → LODGER, Mailer, Metayer, Occupant, Occupier, Pendicler, Periodic, Regulated, Rentaller, Renter, Secure, Shorthold, Sitting, Socager, Socman, Sokeman, Suckener, Tacksman, Valvassor, Vassal, Vavasour, Villein, Visit

**Tenant-farmer** Gebur

**Tend(ing)** Aftercare, Apt, Care, Dress, Herd, Incline, Keep, Lean, Liable, Mind, Minister, Nurse, Prone, Run, Shepherd, Stoke, Verge, Volunteer, Watch

**Tendency** Apt, Bent, Bias, Central, Conatus, Disposition, Drift, Genius, Idiosyncrasy, Import, Inclination, Leaning, Militant, Orientation, Penchant, Proclivity, Propensity, Trend

**Tender(iser), Tenderly, Tenderness** Affettuoso, Amoroso, Bid, Bill, Charitable, Coin, Con amore, Crank, Dingey, Ding(h)y, Fond, Frail, Gentle, Green, Humane, Jolly-boat, Legal, Nesh, Nurse(maid), → OFFER, Painful, Papain, Pinnace, Pra(a)m, Prefer, Present, Proffer, Proposal, Quotation, Red Cross, Sair, Shepherd, → SOFT, Sore, SRN, Submit, Sweet, Swineherd, Sympathy, Tendre, Volunteer, Warmth

**Tenderfoot** Babe, Chechacho, Che(e)chako, Cub, Greenhorn, Innocent, Rookie

**Tenderloin** Psoas, Undercut

**Tendon** Achilles, Aponeurosis, Hamstring, Kangaroo, Leader, Ligature, Paxwax, Sinew, String, Vinculum, Whitleather

**Tendril(led)** Capreolate, Cirrose, Cirrus, Tentacle, Wisp

**Tenement(s)** Dominant, Land, Rook, Rookery, Tack

**Tenet** Adiaphoron, Credo, Creed, → DOCTRINE, Dogma

**Tenfold** Decuple

**Tennis** Close, Court, Deck, Doubles, Jeu de paume, Lawn, LTA, Real, Royal, Set, Short, Singles, Sphairistike, Squash, Table, Wimbledon

**Tennis court** En-Tout-Cas®

**Tennis player** Agassi, Ashe, Borg, Edberg, Evert, Graf, Laver, Lendle, Maskell, Nastase, Novak, Seles, Sharapova, Williams

**Tenon** Cog, Dovetail, Lewis, Lewisson, Tusk

**Tenor** Carreras, Caruso, Course, Direction, Domingo, → DRIFT, Effect, Even, Feck, Ferreras, Gigli, Gist, Heldentenor, Heroic, Pavarotti, Purport, Sense, Singer, T, Tide, Timbre, Trial, Vein

**Tense** Agitato, Aor, Aorist, Case, Clench, Cliffhanger, Conditional, Drawn, Edgy, Electric, Essive, Flashpoint, Flex, Fraught, Future perfect, Historic present, Imperfect, Keyed up, Knife-edge, Laconic, Mood(y), Nail-biting, Nervy, On edge, Overstrung, Past, Perfect, Pluperfect, Present perfect, Preterit, Preterite, Rigid, Simple, Stiff, Strained, Stressed(-out), Strict, T, → TAUT, Tighten, Uptight

**Tensing** Sherpa

**Tension** Abdabs, Creative, Dialectic, High, Isometrics, Isotonic, Meniscus, Nail-biting, Nerviness, Premenstrual, → STRAIN, Stress, Stretch, Surface, Suspense, Tone, Tonicity, Tonus, Yips

**Tent** Beer, Bell, Big top, Bivouac, Bivvy, Cabana, Douar, Dowar, Duar, Ger, Gur, Kedar, Kibitka, Marquee, Oxygen, Pavilion, Praetorium, Probe, Pup, Red wine, Ridge, Shamiana(h), Shamiyanah, Shelter, Tabernacle, Teepee, Tepee, Tilt, Tipi, Top, Topek, Trailer, Tupek, Tupik, Wigwam, Wine, Y(o)urt

**Tentacle(d)** Actinal, Cirrate, Feeler, Hectocotylus, Horn, Limb, Lophophore, Octopus, Squid

**Tentative** Cautious, Empirical, Experimental, Feeler, Gingerly, Hesitant, Noncommital, Peirastic

**Tent-dweller, Tent-maker** Camper, Indian, Kedar, Omar, St Paul

**Tenterhooks** Edginess

**Tenth** Cohort, Deciare, Disme, Submerged, Teind, Tithe

**Ten Thousand** Toman

**Tenuous** Frail, Slender, Slight, Thin, Vague

**Tenure** Blench, Burgage, Copyhold, Cottier(ism), Drengage, Fee, Fee-farm, Feu, Frankalmoi(g)n(e), Frank-fee, Gavelkind, Leasehold, Manorial, Occupation, Raiyatwari, Rundale, Runrig, Ryotwari, Serjeantry, Socage, → TERM, Vavasory, Venville, Zemindar

**Tepid** Laodicean, Lew, Lukewarm

**Terbium** Tb

**Terete** Centric(al)

**Term(s), Terminal, Termly** Air, Anode, Boundary, Buffer, Buzzword, Cathode, Coast, Container, Coste, Designate, Desinent(ial), Distal, Distributed, Dub, Dumb, Easy, Electrode, → EPITHET, Euphemism, Expression, Final, Gnomon, Goal, Half, Heathrow, Helipad, Hilary, Inkhorn, Intelligent, Kathode, Law, Lent, Lethal, Major, Michaelmas, Middle, Minor, Misnomer, Negative, Never-never, → PERIOD, Point-of-sale, Positive, Rail(head), Real, Remit, Removal, Sabbatical, School, Semantics, Semester, Session, Smart, Spell, Stint, Stretch, Telson, Tenure, Trimester, Trimestrial, Trinity, Ultimatum, VDU, Verb, Waterloo, → WORD, Work station, Zeroth

**Termagant** Jade, Shrew, Shrow, Spitfire, Virago, Vixen
**Terminate, Termination, Terminus** Abolish, Abort, Axe, Cease, Conclude, Demise, Depot, Desinent, Earth, → END, Euston, Expiry, → FINISH, Goal, King's Cross, Liquidate, Naricorn, Paddington, Railhead, Suffix, Waterloo
**Terminology** Jargon
**Termite** Duck-ant, White ant
**Tern** Arctic, Egg-bird, Noddy, Scray(e), Sooty, Three, Trio
**Terpene** Squalene
**Terrace** Barbette, Beach, Bench, Crescent, Kop, Linch, Lynchet, Offset, Patio, Perron, River, Row house, Shelf, Stoep, Tarras, Tier, Undercliff, Veranda(h)
**Terra-cotta** Della-Robbia, Rustic ware, Tanagra
**Terrain** Area, Hinterland, Landscape, Scablands, Tract
**Terrapin** Diamondback, Emydes, Emys, Slider, Turtle
**Terrible, Terribly** Appalling, Atrocity, Awful, Deadly, Dire, Fearsome, Fell, Fiendish, Frightful, Ghastly, Heinous, Hellacious, Horrible, Humgruffi(a)n, Ivan, Much, Odious, Shocker, Very
**Terrible person** Humgruffi(a)n, Ivan, Ogre
**Terrier** Aberdeen, Airedale, Apsos, Australian, Australian silky, Bedlington, Black and tan, Border, Boston, Bull, Cairn, Catalogue, Cesky, Dandie Dinmont, Fox, Glen of Imaal, Griffon, Irish, Jack Russell, Kerry blue, Lakeland, Maltese, Manchester, Norfolk, Norwich, Pinscher, Pit bull, Ratter, Register, Schauzer, Scotch, Scottie, Scottish, Sealyham, Silky, Skye, Soft-coated wheaten, Staffordshire bull, Sydney silky, TA, Tibetan, Welsh, West Highland, West Highland white, Westie, Wheaten, Wire-haired, Yorkie, Yorkshire
**Terrific, Terrified, Terrify(ing)** Affright, Aghast, Agrise, Agrize, Agryze, Appal, Awe, Blood-curdling, Enorm, Fear, Fine, Fley, Gast, Grise, Helluva, Huge, Mega, Nightmarish, Overawe, → PETRIFY, Scare, Superb, Thumping, Unman, Yippee
**Territory, Territorial(ist)** Abthane, Ap(p)anage, Area, Colony, Coral Sea Islands, Despotate, Doab, Domain, Dominion, Duchy, Emirate, Enclave, Exclave, Goa, Golan Heights, Indian, Irredentist, Kingdom, Latium, Lebensraum, Mandated, Manor, Margravate, No-man's-land, Northern, Northwest, Nunavut, Palatinate, Panhandle, Papua, Patch, Petsamo, Princedom, Principality, Principate, Protectorate, Province, Realm, → REGION, Reserve, Rupert's Land, Scheduled, Sphere, Stamping ground, Sultanate, Swazi, Ter(r), Trieste, Trust, Tuath, Turf, Union, Yukon
**Terror(s), Terrorise** Blue funk, Brat, Bugaboo, Bugbear, Eek, → FEAR, Fright, Holy, Imp, Intimidate, Menace, Night, Panic, Rapscallion, Skrik
**Terrorism, Terrorist** Alarmist, Al Fatah, Anarchist, Black Hand, Bogeyman, Bomber, Bully, Cagoulard, Consumer, Death squad, Desperado, Dynamitard, Eta, Grapo, Hijacker, Ku Klux Klan, Mau-mau, Maximalist, Mountain, Nightrider, Nihilist, OAS, Pirate, Player, PLO, Provo, Red Brigade, Robespierre, Ustashi
**Terry** Ellen, Towel
**Terse** Abrupt, Brief, Brusque, Curt, Laconic, Pithy, Precise, Succinct
**Tertiary** Cainozoic, Eocene, Miocene, Neogene, Oligocene, Palaeogene, Pliocene
**Tessellation** Mosaic
**Test(er), Testing, Tests** Achievement, Acid, Alpha, Ames, Amnio(centesis), Analyse, Apgar, Appro, Aptitude, Ashes, Assay, Assess(ment), Audition, Barany, Bench, Bender, Benedict, Beta, Bioassay, Biopsy, Blood, Breath, Breathalyser®, Brinell, Burn-in, Calorie, Candle, Canopy, Challenge, Check, Chi-square, Cis-trans, Cloze, Conn(er), Coomb's, Corsned, Crash, Criterion, Crosscheck, Cross-match, Crucial, Crucible, Crunch, Dick, Docimastic, Driving, Drop, Dummy-run, Eleven plus, Éprouvette, Esda, Essay, Etudes, Exacting, Examine, Exercise, Experiment, Fehling's, Field, Finals, Flame, Flight, Frog, Hagberg, Ink-blot, Intelligence, International, Iron man, Litmus, Lydian stone, Mann-Whitney, Mantoux, Match, Mazzin, Means, Medical, Mom, MOT, Mug, Neckverse, Needs, Objective, Oral, Ordalian, → ORDEAL, Pale, Pap, Papanicolaou, Paraffin, Patch, Paternity, Performance, Personality, PH, Pilot, Ping, Pons asinorum, Pree, Preeve, Preif, Prelim, Preve, Prieve, Probative, Probe, Projective, Proof, Prove, Proving-ground, PSA, Pyx, Q-sort, Qualification, Quiz, Rally, Reagent, Reliability, Road, Rorschach, SAT, Scalogram, Scan, Schick's, Schilling,

Schutz-Charlton, Scientise, Scratch, Screen, Shadow, Shibboleth, Showdown, Shroff, Sign, Signed-ranks, Significance, Sixpence, Skidpan, Skin, Slump, Smear, Smoke, Snellen, Soap, Sound, Sounding, Spinal, Spot check, Stanford-Binet, Stress, Tanner, Task, Tempt, Tensile, Thematic apperception, Tongue-twister, Touch, Touchstone, Trial, Trier, Trior, Try, Turing, Ultrasonic, Verify, Viva, Wassermann's, Weigh, Wilcoxon, Zack, Zohar

**Testament** Bible, Covenant, Hagographa, Heptateuch, Hexateuch, Hornolog(o)umena, Midrash, New, Old, Pentateuch, Scripture, Septuagint, Tanach, Targum, Will

**Test-drive** Trial run

**Testicle(s)** Ballocks, Balls, Bollix, Bollocks, Bush oyster, Cobblers, Cojones, Cruet, Doucets, Dowsets, Family jewels, Goolie, Gool(e)y, Knackers, Monkey-gland, Monorchid, Nads, Nuts, Orchis, Pills, Prairie oyster, Ridgel, Ridgil, Rig(gald), Rocks, Stone

**Testify(ing), Testimonial, Testimony** Attestation, Character, Chit, Declare, Depone, Deposition, → EVIDENCE, Hard, Rap, Reference, Scroll, Tribute, Viva voce, Vouch, Witness

**Testy, Tetchy** Cross, Examiner, Legal, Narky, Peevish, Ratty, Splenetic

**Tetanus** Lockjaw

**Tête-à-tête** A quattr' occhi, Collogue, Confab, Hobnob, Twosome

**Tether** Chain, Cord, Endurance, Hitch, Knot, Lariat, Leash, Noose, Picket, Seal, Stringhalt, → TIE

**Tetrahedrite** Fahlerz, Fahlore

**Tetrarchy** Iturea

**Tetrasyllabic** Paeon

**Tetrode** Resnatron

**Teuton(ic)** Erl-king, German, Goth, Herren, Vandal

**Texas** Lone Star, Ranger

**Text(s), Textbook, Texting** ABC, Alkoran, Apocrypha, Body, Brahmana, Church, Codex, Copy, Corpus, Donat, Ennage, Greeked, Harmony, Letterpress, Libretto, Lines, Mandaean, Mantra(m), Masoretic, Mezuzah, Minitel, Ms, Nynorsk, Octapla, Op-cit, Panegyricon, Perfect, Philology, Plain, Proof, Purana, Pyramid, Quran, Responsa, Rubric, S(h)astra, Screenplay, Script, Sermon, Set, Shema, SMS, → SUBJECT, Sura, Sutra, Tantric, Tao Te Ching, Tefillin, Tephillin, Tetrapla, Thesis, Topic, Tripitaka, Tweet, Typography, Upanis(h)ad, Urtext, Variorum, Viewdata, Vulgate, Writing, Zohar

**Textile** Cloth, Fabric, Mercy, Tapestry, Twill

**Texture** Complexion, Constitution, Feel, Fiber, Fibre, Floury, Grain, Open, Set(t), Wale, Waxy, Weave, Woof

**Thai(land)** Karen, Lao(s), Mon, Shan, Siam

**Thalamus** Optic

**Thallium** Tl

**Thames** Father, Tamesis

**Than** And

**Thane** Banquo, Ross

**Thank(s), Thankful, Thanksgiving** Appreciate, Collins, Deo gratias, Gloria, Grace, Gramercy, Grateful, Gratitude, Kaddish, Mercy, Roofer

**Thankless** Ingrate, Vain

**That (is), That one** As, By, Cestui, Das heisst, Dh, Exists, How, Id est, Ie, Ille, Namely, Que, Sc, Such, Thence, Thon(der), What, Which, Yon, Yonder, Yt

**Thatch(er), Thatching** At(t)ap, Daych, Hair, Heard, Hear(i)e, Hele, Hell, Lath, Mane, PM, Reed, Straw, Sway, Thack, Theek, Wig, Ye(a)lm

**Thaw** Debacle, Defreeze, Defrost, Detente, Freeze, Fresh, → MELT, Melt-water, Relax, Silver

▹**Thaw** *may indicate* 'ice' to be removed from a word

**The** Der, Die, El, Il, La, Le, Los, T', That, Ye, Ze

**Theatre(s), Theatrical(ity)** Abbey, Absurd, Adelphi, Aldwych, Arena, Auditorium, Balcony, Broadway, Camp, Cinema, Circle, Coliseum, Criterion, Crucible, Drama, Dramaturgy, Drury Lane, Epic, Event, Everyman, Field, Folies Bergere, Footlights, Ford's, Fourth-wall, Fringe, Gaff, Gaiety, Globe, Grand Guignol, Grandiose, Great White Way, Hall, Haymarket, Hippodrome, Histrionic, House, Kabuki, La Scala, Legitimate, Little, Living, Lyceum, Melodramatic, Mermaid, Moulin Rouge, Musical, Music-hall, National, News,

Nickelodeon, Noh, Novello, Odeon, Odeum, Off-Broadway, Off-off-Broadway, Old Vic, Operating, OUDS, Palladium, Panache, Pennygaff, Pit, Playhouse, Political, Rep(ertory), Royal Court, Sadler's Wells, Shaftesbury, Sheldonian, Shop, Stage, Stalls, Stoll, Straw-hat, Street, Studio, Summer stock, Tivoli, Total, Touring, Vic, Windmill, Winter Garden(s), Wyndham's, Zarzuela

**Theatregoer** Circle, Gallery, Gods, Pit, Pittite, Stalls

**Theft, Thieving** Appropriation, Bluesnarfing, Burglary, Haul, Heist, Identity, Kinchinlay, Larceny, Maino(u)r, Manner, Petty larceny, Pilfery, Pillage, Piracy, Plagiarism, Plunder, Pugging, Ram-raid, Rip off, Robbery, Shrinkage, Stealth, Stouth(rief), →THIEF, Touch, TWOC, Walk-in

**Their** Her

**Theist** Believer, Unitarian

**Them** 'Em, Hem, Tho

**Theme** Burden, Crab canon, Donnée, Fugue, Idea, Leitmotiv, Lemma, Lemmata, →MELODY, Motif, Mythos, Mythus, Peg, Question, →SUBJECT, Subtext, Text, Topic, Topos

**Themepark** Alton Towers, Keynote

**Then(ce)** Afterwards, Already, Away, Next, Since, Sine, So, Syne, Thereupon, Tho

▷**The northern** *may indicate* t'

**Theodolite** Diopter, Dioptre, Groma, Tacheometer, Tachymeter, Transit

**Theologian, Theologist, Theology** Abelard, Ambrose, Aquinas, Arminius, Barth, Baur, Calvin, Christology, Colet, DD, Divine, Eckhart, Erastus, Eschatology, Eusebius, Exegetics, Faustus, Federal, Fideism, Genevan, Harnack, Hase, Infralapsarian, Irenics, Isidore, Jansen, Kierkegaard, Knox, Laelius, Liberation, Luther, Moral, Mullah, Natural, Newman, Niebuhr, Origen, Paley, Pastoral, Patristics, Pectoral, Pelagius, Peritus, Pusey, Rabbi, Religious, Sacramentarian, Schoolman, Schwenkfeld, Scotus, Socinus, Softa, STP, Supralapsarian, Swedenborg, Tertullian, Thomas à Kempis, Tirso de Molina, Tutiorism, Ulema, Universalist

**Theory, Theorem, Theoretical, Theorise, Theorist** Abstract, Academic, Atomic, Attachment, Attribution, Auteur, Automata, Band, Bayes(ian), Bernouilli's, Big bang, Binomial, Blue sky, Bohr, Boo-hurrah, Boolean, Calorie, Calorific, Catastrophe, Chaos, Cladistics, Communications, Complexity, Connectionism, Conspiracy, Corpuscular, Cosmogony, Creationism, Darwinian, Decision, Deduction, Dependency, Dictum, Doctrinaire, Domino, Double aspect, Dow, Einstein, Emboîtement, Emission, Empiricism, Epigenesist, Euhemerism, Exponential, Fermat's (last), Fortuitism, Gaia, Galois, Game, Gauge, Germ, Gödel's, Grand Unified, Grotian, Group, Guess, Holism, Hormic, Hypothesis, Ideal, Identity, Ideology, Information, Ism(y), James-Lange, Jordan curve, Kinetic, Kock's, Laingian, Lamarckism, Lemma, Lunar, MAD, Metaphysical, Milankovitch, Model, Monism, Mythical, Nebular, Neo-Lamarckism, Neovitalism, Nernst heat, Notion, Number, Object relations, On paper, Pancosmism, Pantologism, Perturbation, Petrinism, Pluralism, Positivism, Postulate, Poynting, Preposition, Probability, Proof, Pure, Pythagoras, Pythagorean, Quantity, Quantum, Quantum field, Queueing, Random walk, Rational choice, Reception, Relativism, Relativity, Satisfaction, Set, Solipsism, Speculative, Steady state, String, Superdense, Superstring, Supersymmetry, Supposition, System, Tachyon, TOE, Traducianism, Trickle-down, Twistor, Tychism, Unified Field, Utilitarianism, Voluntarism, Vortex, Vulcanist, Wages fund, Wasm, Wave, Wholism, Wolfian

**Therapy, Therapeutic, Therapist** Analyst, Creative, Cure, Family, Fever, Herbalist, Homeopath, Insight, Masseur, Medicinal, Nicotine, Non directive, Past life, Physio, Regimen, Rehab, Remedial, →TREATMENT

---

## THERAPIES

| | | | | |
|---|---|---|---|---|
| ***3 letters:*** | ORT | Germ | ***5 letters:*** | Narco |
| Art | Sex | SHEN | Bowen | Natal |
| CST | | TENS | Drama | Radio |
| ECT | ***4 letters:*** | X-ray | Group | Reiki |
| HRT | Deep | Zone | Light | Serum |
| MLD | Gene | | Music | Shock |

Sound
Touch

*6 letters:*
Colour
Gerson
Larval
Oxygen
Primal
Radium
Retail
Scream
Speech

*7 letters:*
Crystal
Gestalt
Natural
Pattern
Rainbow
Rōlfing
Shiatsu
Shiatzu

*8 letters:*
Aura-Soma
Aversion
Cellular
Curative
Faradism
Gemstone
Germ-line
Hypnosis
Live cell
Magnetic
Movement
Physical
Polarity
Pressure
Reichian
Rogerian
Sanatory
Sitz-bath

*9 letters:*
Auricular
Behaviour
Chelation
Cognitive
Dianetics
Flotation
Implosive
Radiation
Root-canal
Theriacal
Water cure

*10 letters:*
Hellerwork
Logopedics
Looyenwork
Osteopathy
Regression
Relaxation
Supportive

*11 letters:*
Acupressure
Acupuncture
Combination
Gate control
Logopaedics
Psychodrama
Reflexology
Scientology®

*12 letters:*
Chemotherapy
Craniosacral
Curietherapy
Electroshock
Heliotherapy
Narcotherapy
Occupational
Phototherapy
Primal scream

*13 letters:*
Arsenotherapy
Brachytherapy
Client-centred
Electric shock
Immunotherapy
Speleotherapy
Thermotherapy

*14 letters:*
Crystal healing
Electrotherapy

*15 letters:*
Minimal invasive
Oral rehydration
Psychosynthesis
Röntgenotherapy
Thalassotherapy

*16 letters:*
Chavuttithirumal

*17 letters:*
Electroconvulsive

*20 letters:*
Cognitive-behavioural
Metamorphic technique

---

**There(after), Thereby, Thereupon** Attending, Ecco, Holla, Ipso facto, Present, Thither, Thon, Upon, With that, Y, Yonder
**Therefore** Argal, Ergo, Forthy, Hence, So, Thus, Why
**Thermodynamic** Enthalpy, Entropy
**Thermometer** Aethrioscope, Centesimal, Clinical, Cryometer, Differential, Gas, Glass, Katathermometer, Maximum and minimum, Psychrometer, Pyrometer, Resistance, Thermograph, Water, Wet and dry bulb, Wet bulb
**Thermoplastic** Cel(luloid), Resin
**Thermos** Flask
**Thesaurus** Dictionary, Lexicon, Roget, Treasury, Word-finder
**These** Thir
**Theseus** Champion
**Thesis** Argument, Dissertation, Doctorial, Paper, Theme
**Thespian** → ACTOR, Ham, Olivier, Performer, Theatrical
**Thessalian** Aeolus
**Thessalonian** Lapith
**They** A
**Thick(en), Thickening, Thickener, Thickness, Thickset** Abundant, Agar-agar, Algin, Brainless, Burly, Bushy, Callosity, Callus, Clavate, Cloddy, Coagulate, Condense, Cornflour, Cruddle, Curdle, Dense, Dextrin(e), Dumb, Dumose, Engross, Fat, Flour, Grist, Grouty, Grume, Guar, Gum, Hyperostosis, In cahoots, Incrassate, Inspissate, Kuzu, Liaison, Lush, Luxuriant, Nirlie, Nuggety, Pally, Panada, Ply, Reduce, Roux, Sclerosis, → SOLID, Soupy, Spissitude, Squat, Stocky, Stubby, Stumpy, → STUPID, Thieves, This, Thixotropic, Turbid, Viscous, Waulk, Wooden, Xantham
**Thick-coated** Atheromatous

**Thicket** Bosk, Brake, Brush, Cane-brake, Chamisal, Chap(paral), Coppice, Copse, Covert, Dead-finish, Fernshaw, Greve, Grove, Macchia, Maquis, Queach, Reedrand, Reedrond, Salicetum, Shola

**Thick-lipped** Labrose

**Thick-skinned** Armadillo, Call(o)us, Pachyderm, Tough

**Thief, Thieves, Thievish** Abactor, Area sneak, Autolycus, Blood, Bulker, Cat burglar, Chummy, Coon, Corsair, Cracksman, Cutpurse, Dip, Dismas, Dysmas, Embezzler, Filcher, Flood, Footpad, Forty, Freebooter, Furacious, Ganef, Gestas, Gully-raker, Heist, Hotter, Huaquero, Ice-man, Jackdaw, Joyrider, Kiddy, Kleptomaniac, Kondo, Larcener, Lifter, Light-fingered, Limmer, Looter, Mag, Magpie, Montith, Nip(per), Nuthook, Pad, Peculator, Petty, Pickpocket, Pilferer, Pirate, Plagiarist, Poacher, Poddy-dodger, Prig, Raffles, River-rat, → ROBBER, Rustler, Safeblower, Safebreaker, Safecracker, St Nicholas's clerks, Scrump, Shark, Shop-lifter, Sneak, Snowdropper, Sticky fingers, Taffy, Taker, Tarry-fingered, Tea-leaf, Thick, Twoccer

**Thigh** Femoral, Flank, Gaskin, Ham, Haunch, Hock, Meros

**Thimblerig** Shell-game

**Thin(ner), Thinness** Acetone, Atomy, Attenuate, Bald, Beanpole, Bony, Cadaverous, Cornstalk, Cull, Diluent, Dilute, Ectomorph, Emaciated, Enseam, Filmy, Fine, Fine-drawn, Flaky, Flimsy, Gaunt, Hair('s)-breadth, Hairline, Inseem, Lanky, Lathy, Lean, Matchstick, Mawger, Narrow, Paper, Puny, Rackabones, Rail, Rangy, Rare, Rarefied, Reedy, Runny, Scant, Scraggy, Scrannel, Scranny, Scrawny, Sheer, Sieve, Skeletal, Skelf, Skimpy, Skinking, Slender, Slight, Slim, Slimline, Slink, Soigne, → SPARE, Sparse, Spidery, Spindly, Stilty, Stringy, Subtle, Svelte, Taper, Tenuous, Threadbare, Turpentine, Turps, Wafer, Warfarin, Washy, Waste, Watch, Water(y), → WEAK, Wear, Weedy, Whirtle, Wiry, Wispy, Wortle, Wraith

**Thing(s)** Alia, Article, Chattel, Chose, Cratur, Craze, Doodah, Doofer, Entia, Fetish, First, Fixation, It, Item, Jingbang, Job, Last, Material, Matter, Memorabilia, Near, Notanda, Noumenon, → OBJECT, Obsession, Paraphernalia, Phobia, Res, Tool, Vision, Whatnot

**Thingumabob, Thingummy** Dingbat, Dinges, Dingus, Doings, Doobrey, Doobrie, Doodad, Doodah, Doofer, Doohickey, Gubbins, Hootenanny, Hoot(a)nanny, Jigamaree, Oojah, Oojamaflip, Whatsit, Yoke

**Think(er), Thinking** Appraise, Associate, Attitude, Audile, Believe, Brain, Brainstorm, Brood, Casuistry, Cerebrate, Chew over, Cogitate, Cognition, Concentrate, Conjecture, Consider, Contemplant, → CONTEMPLATE, Convergent, Deem, Deliberate, Descartes, Devise, Dianoetic, Divergent, Esteem, Fancy, Fear, Feel, Fogramite, Forward, Ghesse, Gnostic, Guess, Hegel, Hold, Ideology, → IMAGINE, Intelligentsia, Introspection, Judge, Lateral, Meditate, Mentation, Mindset, Mull, Muse, Opine, Pensive, Philosopher, Phrontistery, Ponder, Pore, Presume, Ratiocinate, Rational(e), Reckon, Reflect, Reminisce, Ruminate, Speculate, Suspect, Synectics, Trow, Vertical, Ween, Wishful, Wonder

**Thin-skinned** Sensitive

**Third, Third rate** Bronze, C, Eroica, Gamma, Gooseberry, Interval, Major, Mediant, Minor, Picardy, Quartan, Tertiary, Tertius, Tierce, Trisect

**Third man** Abel, Lime

**Thirst(y)** Adry, → CRAVE, Dives, Drought, Drouth, Dry, Hunger, Hydropic, Nadors, Pant, Parched, Polydipsia, Thrist

**Thirteen** Baker's dozen, Devil's dozen, Long dozen, Riddle, Triskaidekaphobia, Unlucky

**Thirty** Lambda

**Thirty-nine books** All-OT, OT

**This** Hic, Hoc, The, Thick, Thilk, Thir

**Thistle** Canada, Carduus, Carline, Cnicus, Cotton, Creeping, Dayshell, Echinops, Milk, Musk, Rauriki, Russian, Safflower, St Barnaby's, Scotch, Sow, Spear, Star, Thrissel, Thristle

**This year** Ha

**Thomas** Aquinas, Arnold, Christadelphian, De Quincey, Didymus, Doubting, Dylan, Erastus, Hardy, Loco, Parr, Rhymer, Tompion, True, Turbulent

**Thomas Aquinas** Angelic Doctor

**Thong** Babiche, Jandal®, Lash, Latchet, Leather, Lorate, Lore, Riem, Riempie, Shoe-latchet,

→ **STRAP**, Strop, Taws(e), Whang, Whip

**Thor** Thunderer

**Thorax** Chest, Peraeon, Pereion, Scutellum, Throat

**Thorium** Th

**Thorn(y)** Acantha, Aculeus, Bael, Barb, Bel, Bhel, Bramble, Briar, Coyotillo, Doom, Edh, Eth, Irritation, Jerusalem, Jew's, Mahonia, Mayflower, Nabk, Nar(r)as, Nebbuk, Nebe(c)k, → **NEEDLE**, Paloverde, Pricker, Prickle, Slae, Spine, Spinescent, Spinulate, Trial, Wagn'bietjie, Y, Ye, Zare(e)ba, Zariba, Zeriba

**Thorn-apple** Jimpson-weed

**Thornless** Inerm

**Thorough(ly), Thoroughgoing** À fond, Arrant, Complete, Deep, Downright, Even-down, Exhaustive, Firm, Fully, Good, In depth, Ingrained, Inly, Intensive, Not half, Out, Out and out, Painstaking, Pakka, Pucka, Pukka, Radical, Rigorous, Ripe, Root and branch, Searching, Sound, Strict, Total, Tout à fait, Up

**Thoroughbred** Arab, Bloodstock, Full-blooded, Pedigree, Post-vintage, Pursang

**Thoroughfare** Avenue, Broadway, Causeway, Freeway, Highway, Parkway, → **ROAD**, Street

**Those** Thae, Thaim, Them, Tho, Yon

**Thou** M, Mil

**Though** Albe, Albeit, All-be, Ever, Tho, Whenas

**Thought(s), Thoughtful(ness)** Avisandum, Broody, Censed, Cerebration, Charitable, Cogitation, Concept, Conscience, Considerate, Contemplation, Dianoetic, Felt, Idea, Imagination, Indrawn, Innate, Kind, Logic, Maieutic, Mind, Mindset, Musing, Notion, Opinion, Pansy, Pensée, Pensieroso, Pensive, Philosophy, Reason, Reflection, Respect, Rumination, Second, Studious, View

**Thoughtless** Blindfold, Careless, Etourdi(e), Goop, Heedless, Improvident, Incogitant, Inconsiderate, Pillock, → **RASH**, Reckless, Reflexive, Remiss, Scatter-brained, Stupid, Unintentional, Unkind, Vacant, Vain

**Thousand(s)** Chiliad, G, Gorilla, Grand, K, Lac, Lakh, M, Millenary, Millennium, Myriad, Octillion, Plum, Sextillion, Toman

**Thracian** Spartacus

**Thrall** Captive, Esne, Serf, Slave

**Thrash(ing)** → **BEAT**, Belabour, Belt, Bepelt, Binge, Bless, Cane, Dress, Drub, Flail, Flog, Horsewhip, Jole, Joll, Joule, Jowl, Lace, Laidie, Laidy, Lambast, Larrup, Lather, Leather, Lick, Marmelise, Onceover, Paste, Ploat, Punish, Quilt, Raddle, Rout, Slog, Smoke, Strap-oil, Swaddle, Swat, Tan, Tank, Targe, Thraiping, Towel, Trim, Trounce, Wallop, Whale, Whap, Work over, Writhe

**Thread(ed), Threadlike** Acme screw, Addenda, Ariadne, Bar, Bottom, Bride, Buttress, Chalaza, Chromatid, Chromatin, Chromosome, Clew, Clue, Cop(pin), Cord, Coventry blue, Denier, Eel-worm, End, Female, Fibre, Filament, File, Filiform, Filose, Filoselle, Float, Floss, Flourishing, Gist, Gold, Gossamer, Hair, Heddle, Hypha, Ixtle, Lace, Lap, Lingel, Lingle, Link, Lisle, Lurex®, Male, Meander, Microfibre, Mycellum, Needle, Nematode, Nematoid, Organzine, Pack, Pearlin(g), Pick, Plasmodesm, Ravel, Reeve, Roon, Rope-yarn, Rove, Sacred, Screw, Sellers screw, Seton, Shoot, Silver, Single, Spider line, Spireme, Sporangiophore, Stamen, → **STRAND**, String, Stroma, Suture, Tassel, Tendril, Tenor, Theme, Thrid, Thrum, Trace, Tram, Trundle, Tussore, Twine, Twist, Two-start, Warp, Watap, Wax(ed) end, Weft, Whitworth, Whitworth screw, Wick, → **WIND**, Wisp, Worm, Yarn, Zari

**Threadbare** Frayed, Hackneyed, Motheaten, Napless, Shabby, Worn

**Threadworm** Nemathelminth, Strongyl, Vinegar-eel

**Threat(en), Threatened, Threatening** Baleful, Black(en), Blackmail, Bluster, Brew, Brutum fulmen, Bully, Coerce, Comminate, Denounce, Discovered check, Duress, Endanger, Extort, Face, Fatwa, Fraught, Greenmail, Greymail, Hazard, Idle, Impend, Imperil, Intimidate, Jeopardise, Loom, Lower, → **MENACE**, Minacious, Minatory, Mint, Nuclear, Omen, Ominous, Or else, Overcast, Overhang, Parlous, Peril, Portent, Ramp, Sabre-rattling, Shore, Strongarm, Ugly, Veiled, Warning, Yellow peril

**Three, Threefold, Three-wheeler, Thrice** Cheers, Graces, Har, Harpies, Jafenhar, Leash, Muses, Musketeers, Pairial, Pair-royal, Parial, Prial, Ter, Tercet, Tern(ate), Terzetta,

Thridi, Tid, T.i.d, Tierce, Tray, Trey, Triad, Trial, Tricar, Triennial, Trifid, Trigon, Trilogy, Trinal, Trine, Trinity, Trio, Triple, Triptote, Troika

**Three-D(imensional)** Cinerama, Lenticular, Spatial, Stereopsis, Vectograph

**Three-day** Triduan, Triduum

**Threehalfpence** Dandiprat, Dandyprat

**Three-handed** Cutthroat

**Three-headed** Cerberus, Geryon, Triceps

**Three hundred** B, Carpet

**Three-legged** IOM, Triskele, Triskelion

**Threepence, Threepenny bit** Tickey, Tray, Trey, Treybit

**Three-piece** Suite

**Three-quarter** Wing

**Three-year old** Staggard

**Threnody** Dirge, Epicede, → LAMENT

**Thresh(er)** Beat, Flail, Sea-ape, Separate

**Threshold** Absolute, Brink, Cill, Colour, Difference, Doorstep, Limen, Liminal, Nuclear, Sill, Tax, Verge

▸**Thrice** *see* THREE

**Thrift(y)** Economy, Frugal, Husbandry, Oeconomy, Scrimping, Sea-grass, Sea-pink, Skimp, Virtue, Wary

**Thrill(er), Thrilling** Action-packed, Atingle, Buzz, Charge, Delight, Dindle, Dinnle, Dirl, Dread, Dynamite, Electric, Emotive, → ENCHANT, Enliven, Excite, Exhilaration, Film noir, Frisson, Gas, Jag, Kick, Page-turner, Perceant, Plangent, Pulsate, Pulse, Quiver, Sensation, Thirl, Tinglish, Titillate, Tremor, Vibrant, Whee, Whodunit, Wow(-factor), Zing

**Thrive** Batten, Blossom, Boom, Do, Fl, → FLOURISH, Flower, Grow, Mushroom, → PROSPER, Succeed, Thee

**Throat(y)** Craw, Crop, Deep, Dewlap, Fauces, Gorge, Gular, Gullet, Guttural, Hot coppers, Jugular, Laryngeal, Maw, Oropharynx, Pereion, Pharynx, Prunella, Quailpipe, Red lane, Roopit, Roopy, Strep, Swallet, Thrapple, Thropple, Throttle, Weasand, Wesand, Whistle, Windpipe

**Throb(bing)** Beat, Palpitate, Pant, Pit-a-pat, Pound, Pulsate, Quop, Stang, Tingle, Vibrato

▹**Throbbing** *may indicate* an anagram

**Throe(s)** Agony, Pang, Paroxysm

**Thrombosis, Thrombose** Clot, Coronary, Deep-vein

**Throne** Bed-of-justice, Cathedra, Episcopal, Gadi, → LAVATORY, Mercy-seat, Peacock, Rule, Seat, See, Siege, Stone of Scone, Stool, Tribune

**Throng(ing)** Crowd, Flock, Horde, Host, Multitude, Press, Resort, Swarm

**Throttle** → CHOKE, Gar(r)otte, Gun, Mug, Regulator, Scrag, Silence, Stifle, Strangle, Strangulate, Thrapple, We(a)sand

**Through, Throughout** Along, Ana, By, Dia-, During, Everywhere, Over, Passim, Per, Pr, Sempre, Sic passim, To, Trans, Up and down, Via, Yont

**Throw (up), Thrower, Throw-out** Bin, Bounce, Bung, Cast-off, Chunder, Dink, Discobolus, Dump, Egesta, Eject, Emesis, Estrapade, Floor, Flummox, Flying mare, Go, Hound, Jettison, Mangonel, Overarm, Pash, Pick, Pitch, Puke, Reject, Shy, Slam-drunk, Spatter, Spew, Squirt, Squit, → TOSS, Underarm, Unsaddle, Ventriloquism

▸**Throw(n)** *see* TOSS(ING)

**Throwback** Atavism, Echo

**Thrush** Antbird, Aphtha, Bird, Chat, Fieldfare, Hermit, Homescreetch, Mavis, Missel, Mistle, Mocking-bird, Olive-back, Pitta, Prunella, Redwing, Ring-ousel, Sprue, Turdine, Veery

**Thrust(er)** Abdominal, Aventre, Bear, Boost, Botte, Burn, Burpee, Detrude, Dig, Drive, Elbow, Engine, Exert, Extrude, Flanconade, Foin, → FORCE, Gist, Hay, Hustle, Imbroc(c)ata, Impulse, Jet, Job, Lift-off, Lunge, Montant(o), Muscle, Obtrude, Oust, Pass, Passado, Peg, Penetrate, Perk, Pitchfork, Poach, Poke, Potch(e), Pote, Probe, Prog, Propel, Pun, Punto, → PUSH, Put, Ram, Remise, Repost, Riposte, Run, Shoulder, Shove, Single-stock, Sock, Sorn, Squat, Stap, Stick, Stoccado, Stoccata, Stock, Stuck, Thrutch, Tilt, Tuck, Venue

**Thud** Bounce, Drum, Dull, Dump, Flump, Phut, Plod, Thump, Thunk, Whump

**Thug(s)** Brute, Gangster, Goon(da), Gorilla, Gurrier, Heavy, Hood(lum), Hooligan, Keelie, Loord, Ninja, Ockers, Phansigar, Plug-ugly, Rough(neck), Ruffian, SS, Strangler, Ted, Tityre-tu, Tsotsi, Yahoo
**Thule** Ultima
**Thulium** Tm
**Thumb** Bally, Gouge, Green, Hitch, Leaf, Midget, Mount of Venus, Ovolo, Pollex, Scan, Sore, Tom
**Thump(ing)** Blow, Bonk, Clobber, Cob, Crump, Da(u)d, Dawd, Ding, Dod, Drub, Dub, Enormous, Hammer, Knevell, Knock, Lamp, Nevel, Oner, Paik, Percuss, → **POUND**, Pummel, Ribroast, Slam, Slosh, Sock, Souse, Swat, Swingeing, Thud, Trounce, Tund, Wallop, Whud, Whump
**Thunder(ing), Thunderstorm** Astrophobia, Bolt, Boom, Clap, Coup de foudre, Donnerwetter, Foudroyant, Foulder, Fulminate, Intonate, Lei-king, Microburst, Pil(l)an, Raiden, → **ROAR**, Rumble, Summanus, Tempest, Thor, Tonant
**Thunderbolt** Ward
**Thurible** Incense burner
**Thursday** Chare, Holy, Maundy, Sheer, Shere
**Thus** Accordingly, Ergo, Hence, Sic, So, Therefore
**Thwart** Baffle, Balk, → **CROSS**, Dash, Dish, Foil, Forestall, Frustrate, Hamstring, Hogtie, Obstruct, Outwit, Pip, Prevent, Scotch, Scupper, Snooker, Spike, Spite, Stonker, Stymie, Transverse
**Thy** Yourn
**Thyme** Basil, Lemon, Water
**Thymus** Neck, Sweetbread
**Thyroid** Goitre, Myxodema
**Tiara** Cidaris, Crownet, Diadem, Triple crown
**Tiberius** Gracchus
**Tibetan** Ladakhi, Lamaist, Naga, Sherpa, Sitsang
**Tic** Spasm, Synkinesis, Twitch, Vocal
**Tick, Ticking-off, Tick off** Acarida, Acarus, Arachnid, Beat, Bloodsucker, Check, → **CHIDE**, Click, Cr, → **CREDIT**, Deer, HP, Idle, Instant, Jar, Ked, Mattress, Mile, Mo, Moment, Ricinulei, Second, Seed, Sheep, Soft, Strap, Wigging, Worm
**Ticker** Clock, Heart, Metronome, Watch
**Ticket(s)** Billet, Bone, Brief, Carnet, Commutation, Complimentary, Coupon, Day, Docket, Dream, E(lectronic), Excursion, Fare, Hot, Kangaroo, Label, Library, Lottery, Meal, One-day, One-way, Open-jaw, Parking, Pass, Pass-out, Pasteboard, Pawn, Platform, Raffle, Raincheck, Return, Round-trip, Rover, Saver, Scratchcard, Season, Single, Soup, Split, Straight, Stub, Supersaver, → **TAG**, Tempest, Tessera(l), Through, Tix, Transfer, Tyburn, Unity, Voucher, Walking, Zone
**Ticket-seller** Scalper
**Tickle, Ticklish** Amuse, Delicate, Divert, Excite, Fondle, Gratify, Gump, → **ITCH**, Kittle, Queasy, Thrill, Titillate
**Tiddler** Brit, Titch, Tom
**Tiddleywink** Counter
**Tide, Tidal** Current, Drift, Eagre, Easter, Eger, Estuary, Even, Flood, High, High water, Lee, Low, Marigram, Neap, Red, Rising, River, Roost, Sea, Seiche, Slack water, Spring, Surge, Trend, Wave, Whitsun
**Tide-gate** Aboideau, Aboiteau, Weir
**Tidings** Gospel, → **NEWS**, Rumour, Word
**Tidy** Big, Comb, Considerable, Curry, Do, Fair, Fettle, Groom, Kempt, Large, Neat, Neaten, → **ORDER**, Pachyderm, Predy, Preen, Primp, Red(d), Slick, Snug, Sort, Spruce, Trim, Valet
**Tie, Tied, Tying** Ascot, Attach, Barcelona, Berth, Bind, Black, Bolo, → **BOND**, Bootlace, Bow, Bowyang, Cable, Chain, Clip-on, Cope, Copula, Cord, Cravat, Cup, Dead-heat, Dickie, Dick(e)y, Drag, Draw, Dress, Fasten, Fetter, Four-in-hand, Frap, Halter, Halve, Handicap, Harness, Hitch, Holdfast, Kipper, → **KNOT**, Lace, Lash, Leash, Level, Ligament, Ligate, Ligature, Link, Marry, Match, Moor, Neck and neck, Neckcloth, Oblige, Obstriction, Old

School, Oop, Oup, Overlay, Pinion, Raffia, Relation, Restrain, Rod, Rope, Sash, Scarf, School, Score draw, Scrunchie, Semifinal, Shackle, Sheave, Shoelace, Shoestring, Sleeper, Slur, Solitaire, Soubise, Splice, Stake, Standoff, Strap, String, Tawdry-lace, Tether, Together, Trice, Truss, Unite, White, Windsor

**Tie-breaker** Decider, Eliminator

**Tier** Apron, Bank, Bleacher, Gradin(e), Knotter, Layer, Range, Rank, Row, Stage, Storey, Terrace

**Tierce** Leash, Tc

**Tiff** Bicker, Contretemps, Difference, Dispute, Exchange, Feed, Feud, Huff, Miff, Skirmish, Spat, Squabble

**Tiffany** Gauze

**Tiger, Tigress** Ambush, Bengal, →CAT, Clemenceau, Demoiselle, Lily, Machairodont, Machairodus, Man-eater, Margay, Paper, Sabre-tooth, She-cat, Shere Khan, Smilodon, Stripes, Tamil, Tasmanian, Woods

**Tight(en), Tightness, Tights** Bladdered, Boozy, Bosky, Brace, Canny, Cinch, Clingy, Close(-hauled), Close-fisted, Constriction, Cote-hardie, →DRUNK, Figure-hugging, Fishnet, Fleshings, High, Hose, Jam, Leggings, Leotards, Lit, Loaded, Maillot, Mean(-spirited), Merry, Niggardly, Oiled, Pang, Pantihose, Phimosis, Pickled, Pinch(penny), Plastered, Prompt, Proof, Rigour, Snug, Squiffy, Stenosis, →STINGY, Stinko, Strict, Stringent, Support, Swift, Swig, Taut, Tense, Tipsy, Trig, Woozy

**Tight-lipped** Shtum, Taciturn

**Tightrope(-walker)** Aerialist, Blondin, Equilibrist, Funambulist, High wire, Petauriste

**Tightwad** Cheapskate, →MISER, Scrooge

**Tile(s), Tiled** Antefix, Arris, Azulejo, Carpet, Chapeau, Dalle, Derby, Dutch, Encaustic, Field, →HAT, Hung, Imbrex, Imbricate, Lid, Lino, Mahjong(g), Ostracon, Ostrakon, Peever, Quarrel, Quarry, Rag(g), Ridge, Rooftop, Samel, Sclate, Shingle, Slat, →SLATE, Soughing, Tegular, Tessella, Tessera, Titfer, Topper, Wall, Wally

**Till** Cashbox, Cash register, Checkout, Coffer, Ear, Eulenspiegel, Farm, Hasta, Hoe, Husband, Lob, Peter, →PLOUGH, Rotavate, Set, Unto, Up to

**Tiller** Coxswain, Gardener, Helm, Ploughman, Rotavator, Wheel

**Tilt(ed)** Awning, Bank, Camber, Cant, Careen, Cock, Dip, Heel, Hut, Incline, Joust, Just, →LIST, Quintain, Rock, Tip, Trip, Unbalance, Version

**Timber** Apron, Ashlaring, Balk, Batten, Beam, Beechwood, Beefwood, Blackwood, Bolster, Bond, Bowsprit, Bridging, Cant-rail, Carapa, Cedarwood, Chess, Clapboard, Compass, Coulisse, Cross-tree, Cruck, Deadwood, Dogshores, Dogwood, Driftwood, Druxy, Dwang, Elmwood, Flitch, Float, Four-by-two, Futchel, Futtock, Greenheart, Groundsell, Hardwood, Harewood, Intertie, Iroko, Ironwood, Joist, Keel, Knee, Knighthead, Lauan, Ligger, Lignum, Lintel, Log, Loggerhead, Lumber, Nogging, Nothofagus, Plank-sheer, Purlin(e), Putlock, Putlog, Pyengadu, Radiata, Rafter, Ramin, Rib, Ridgepole, Roseweed, Roundwood, Rung, Sandalwood, Sapele, Sapodilla, Satinwood, Scantling, Shook, Shorts, Sissoo, Skeg, Sneezewood, Softwood, Souari, Stemson, Stere, Sternpost, Sternson, Straddle, Stud, Stull, Stumpage, Summer, Swing-stock, Tilting fillet, Towing-bitts, Transom, Trestletree, Two-by-four, Wale, Wall plate, Weatherboard, Whitewood, →WOOD, Yang

**Timbre** Clang, Klang(farbe), Register, →TENOR, Tone, Tone colour

**Time(s), Timer, Timing** Access, African, Agoge, Apparent, Assymetric, Astronomical, Atlantic, Atomic, Autumn, Awhile, Bird, Borrowed, BST, By, Captive, Central, Chronaxy, Chronic, Chronograph, Chronometer, Chronon, Civil, Clock, Closing, Common, Compound, Connect, Core, Counter, Cryptozoic, Date, Day, Daylight-saving, Dead, Decade, Dimension, Double, Duple, Duration, Early, Eastern, Eastern Standard, Egg-glass, Enemy, Eon, Ephemeris, Epoch, Epocha, Epoque, Equinox, Era, EST, Eternity, European, Eve(ning), Extra, Father, Flexitime, Fold, Forelock, Four-four, Fourth dimension, Free, Full, Geological, Gest, Glide, GMT, Godslot, Half, Healer, High, Horologe, Hour, Hourglass, Hr, Idle, Imprisonment, Injury, Innings, Instant, Interim, Interlude, Jiff, Juncture, Kalpa, Killing, Krytron, Latent, Lay-day, Lead, Lean, Leisure, Length, Life, Lighting-up, Lilac, Local, Lowsing, Lustra, Man-day, Man-hour, Mark, Mean (solar), Menopause, Metronome, Moment, Mountain standard, Multiple, Needle, Nonce, Nones, Noon, Normal, Occasion, Oft,

→**ON TIME**, Opening, Pacific, Paralysis, Part, Peak, Period, Phanerozoic, Pinger, Porridge, Post, Precambrian, Prelapsarian, Prime, Proper, Quadruple, Quality, Question, Quick, Reaction, Real, Reaper, Recovery, Released, Response, Responsum, Reverberation, Rhythm, Run(ning), Sandglass, Sands, Schedule, Seal, →**SEASON**, Seel, Seil, Semeion, Sentence, Serial, Session, Shelf-life, Sidereal, Sight, Simple, Sith(e), Slot, Slow, Solar, Solstice, Space, Spacious, Span, Spare, Spell, Spin, Split, Spring, Squeaky-bum, Standard, Stint, Stoppage, Stopwatch, Stound, Stownd, Stretch, Summer, Sundial, Sundown, Sync(h), Sythe, T, Tem, Tempo, Tempore, Tense, Thief, Three-four, Thunderer, Tick, Tid, Tide, Trice, Triple, True, Turnaround, Two-four, Umpteenth, Universal, Usance, Whet, While, Winter, X, Yonks, Yukon, Zero(-hour)

**Timebomb** Demographic

**Timekeeper, Timekeeping, Timepiece** Ben, Chronometer, Clock, Clockwork, Hourglass, Metronome, Ref, Sand-glass, Sundial, Ticker, Tompion, Watch

**Timeless** Eternal, Everlasting, ND, Undying

**Timely** Appropriate, Apropos, Happy, Heaven-sent, Opportune, Pat, Periodical, Prompt, Punctual, Seasonal

**Time-machine** Tardis

**Timescale** Geological

**Time-server** Convict, Fence-sitter, Prisoner, Trimmer, Vicar of Bray

**Timeshare** Box and cox

**Timetable** ABC(ee), Absee, Bradshaw, →**CHART**, Roster, Schedule, Sked

**Time-waster** Filibuster

**Timid, Timorous** Afraid, Aspen, Bashful, Blate, Chicken, Cowardly, Eerie, Eery, Faint-hearted, Fearful, Fibreless, Hare, Hen-hearted, Meticulous, Milksop, Milquetoast, Mouse, Mous(e)y, Pavid, Pigeon-hearted, Pusillanimous, Pussy, Quaking, Schnok, Sheep, Shrinking, →**SHY**, Skeary, Sook, Tremulous, Wuss, Yellow

**Timothy** Cat's-tail, Grass, Phleum

**Tin(ned), Tinfoil, Tinny** Argentine, Block, Britannia metal, Can, Cash, Debe, Dixie, Maconochie, Mess, →**MONEY**, Moola(h), Ochre, Plate, Rhino, Sheet, Sn, Stannary, Stannic, Stream, Tain, Tole, Vasculum

**Tincture** Argent, Arnica, Brown, Bufo, Chroma, Elixir, Fur, Infusion, Iodine, Laudanum, Metal, Or, Sericon, Sol, Spice, Taint, Tenné, Vert

**Tinder** Amadou, Bavin, Faggot, Fuel, Funk, Punk, Spark, Spunk, Touchwood

**Tine** Antler, Bay, Bez, Cusp, Grain, Prong, Snag, Spire, Surroyal, Tray, Trey

**Tinge(d)** Cast, Colour, Dye, Eye, Flavour, Gild, →**HUE**, Imbue, Infuscate, Taint, Tincture, Tone, Touch

**Tingle, Tingling** Dinnle, Dirl, Frisson, Paraesthesia, Pins and needles, Prickle, Thrill, Throb, Tinkle

**Tinker** Adjust, Bell, Caird, Coster, Dabble, Didakai, Didakei, Diddicoy, Didicoy, Didikoi, →**FIDDLE**, Gypsy, Meddle, Mender, Pedlar, Potter, Prig, Putter, Repair, Sly, Smouse, Snout, Tamper, Tramp, Traveller, Tweak

**Tinkle, Tinkling** Pink, Ring, Thin

**Tinsel(ly)** Clinquant, Gaudy, Glitter, O, Spangle, Turkey

**Tint** Blue rinse, Colour, Grey, Henna, Hue, Pigment, Sepia, →**STAIN**, Tinct, Tinge, Tone, Woad

**Tiny** Atto-, Baby, Chickenfeed, Diddy, Dwarf, Fleabite, Ha'it, Infinitesimal, Itsy-bitsy, Leet(le), Lilliputian, Meagre, Microscopic, Midget, Minikin, Minim, Mite, Negligible, Petite, Pint-sized, Pitiful, Pittance, Small, Smidge(o)n, Smidgin, Stime, Teeny, Tiddl(e)y, Tiddy, Tim, Tine, Tittle, Tottie, Totty, Toy, Wee(ny)

**Tip (off), Tipping** Advice, Anteversion, Apex, Arrowhead, Ash-heap, Asparagus, Backshish, Baksheesh, Batta, Beer-money, B(u)onamono, Bonsel(l)a, Bonus, Cant, Capsize, Cert, Chape, Clue, Counsel, Coup, Cowp, Crown, Cue, Cumshaw, Cusp, Doff, Douceur, Dump, Ear, Extremity, Fee, Felt, Ferrule, Filter, Forecast, Glans, Gloryhole, Gratillity, Gratuity, Heel, →**HINT**, Horn, Hunch, Inkle, Iridise, Lagniappe, Largess(e), Lean, List, Mag(g), Mess, Middenstead, Nap, Nib, Noop, Ord, Overbalance, Perk, Perquisite, Point, Pointer, Pour, Pourboire, Previse, Prong, Scrapheap, Slagheap, Straight, Suggestion, Summit, Tag, Tail, Tilt, Toecap, Toom, Touch, Tronc, Upend, Upset, Vail, Vales, Warn, Whisper, Wink, Wrinkle

**Tipper** Ale, Dump truck

**Tippet** Cape, Fur, Scarf, Titbit

**Tipple** Bib, Booze, → DRINK, Paint, Pot, Poteen

**Tipster** Prophet, Tout

**Tipsy** Askew, Bleary, Boozy, Bosky, → DRUNK, Elevated, Merry, Moony, Nappy, Oiled, On, Rocky, Screwed, Slewed, Slued, Squiffy, Stewed, Tight, Wet

▹**Tipsy** *may indicate* an anagram

**Tiptoe** Digitigrade, Pussyfoot, Spanish, Walk

**Tiptop** Pinnacle

**Tirade** Diatribe, Earful, Harangue, Invective, Jobation, Laisse, Philippic, Rand, Rant, Rave, Screed, Slang

**Tire(d), Tiredness, Tiring** All-in, Aweary, Beat, Bejade, Bleary-eyed, Blown, Bore, Brain fag, Bushed, Caparison, Cooked, Deadbeat, Dress, Drowsy, → EXHAUST, Fag, Fagged out, Fatigue, Flag, Footsore, Fordid, Fordod, Forjeskit, Frazzle, Gruel, Hoary, Irk, Jack, Jade, Languor, Lassitude, Limp, ME, Overspent, Pall, Poop, Puggled, → ROBE, Rubber, Sap, Shagged, Sicken, Sleepry, Sleepy, Sloomy, Snoozy, Spent, Stereotyped, Swinkt, Tax, Tedious, Trying, Tucker, Wabbit, Wappend, Wear, Weary, World-weary, Wrecked, Zonked

**Tireless** Inexhaustible

**Tiresome** Boring, Drag, Exhausting, Galling, Humdrum, Pill, Tedious, Trying, Vexing, Wearing

**Tirl** Rattle, Risp, Strip, Turn

▸**Tiro** *see* TYRO

**Tissue** Adenoid, Adhesion, Adipose, Aerenchyma, Aponeurosis, Archesporium, Bast, Callus, Carbon, Cartilage, C(o)elom, Cementum, Chalaza, Cheloid, Chlorenchyma, Coenosarc, Collagen, Collenchyma, Commissure, Conducting, Connective, Corpus luteum, Corpus Striatum, Cortex, Dentine, Diploe, Elastic, Elastin, Endarch, Endosperm, Endosteum, Epigenesis, Epimysium, Epineurium, Epithelium, Eschar, Evocator, Fabric, Fascia, Fibroid, Filament, Flesh, Gamgee, Gauze, Gleba, Glia, Granulation, Granuloma, Gum, Handkerchief, Hankie, Heteroplasia, Histogen, Histoid, Hypoderm(is), Infarct, Interlay, Junk, Keloid, Kleenex®, Lamina, Liber, Lies, Ligament, Ligature, Luteal, Lymphate, Lymphoid, Macroglia, Marrow, Matrix, Mechanical, Medulla, → MEMBRANE, Meristem, Mesenchyme, Mesophyll, Mesothelium, Mestom(e), Mole, Muscle, Myelin(e), Myocardium, Neoplasia, Neoplasm, Neuroglia, Nodal, Nucellus, Olivary, Pack, Palisade, Pannus, Paper, Papilla, Parenchyma, Periblem, Perichylous, Pericycle, Peridesmium, Perimysium, Perinephrium, Perineurium, Perisperm, Phellogen, Phloem, Pith, Placenta, Plerome, Polyarch, Pons, Primordium, Procambium, Prosenchyma, Prothallus, Pterygium, Pulp, Radula, Retina, Sarcenchyme, Sarcenet, Sars(e)net, Scar, Sclerenchyma, Scleroma, Sequestrum, Sinew, Siphonostele, Siphuncle, Slough, Soft, Somatopleure, Stereome, Stroma, Submucosa, Suet, Tarsus, Tela, Tendon, Toilet, Tonsil, Trace, Tunica, Vascular, Velum, Web, Wound, Xylem, Zoograft

**Tit, Tit-bit(s)** Analecta, Bearded, Canapé, Crested, Currie, Curry, Delicacy, Dug, Nag, Nipple, Nun, Pap, Quarry, Sample, Scrap, Snack, Snippet, Teat, Tug, Twitch, Willow, Wren, Zakuska

**Titan(ic), Titaness** Atlas, Colossus, Cronos, Cronus, Drone, Enormous, Giant, Ginormous, Huge, Hyperion, Kronos, Large, Leviathan, Liner, Oceanus, Phoebe, Prometheus, Rhea, Superman, Themis, Vast

**Titanium, Titanite** Rutin, Sagenite, Sphene, Ti

**Tit for tat** Deserts, Reprisal, Revenge, Talion

**Tithe** Disme, Dyzemas, Frankpledge, Teind, Tenth

**Titian** Abram, Auburn

**Titillate(r), Titillating, Titillation** Delight, Excite, Fluffer, Naughty, Racy, Suggestive, Tickle

**Titivate** Preen, Primp

**Title** Abbé, → ADDRESS, Ag(h)a, Aga Khan, Agname, Antonomasia, Appellative, Bab, Bahadur, Baroness, Baronet, Bart, Bastard, Bhai, Bretwalda, Buddha, Burra sahib, Calif, Caliph, Caption, Charta, Chogyal, Claim, Conveyance, Count(ess), Courtesy, Credit, Dan, Datin, Datuk, Dauphin, Dayan, Deeds, Denominative, Devi, Dom, Don, Don(n)a, Dowager,

Dub, Duchess, Duke, Earl, Effendi, Elector, Eminence, Epithet, Esquire, Excellency, Fra, Frau(lein), Ghazi, Gospodin, Grand Master, Great Mogul, Gyani, Hafiz, Handle, Header, Heading, Headline, Hereditary, Highness, Hojatoislam, Hojatoleslam, Hon, Honour, Il Duce, Imperator, Interest, Kabaka, Kalif, Kaliph, Kaur, Khan, King, Kumari, Lady, Lala, Lemma, → **LIEN**, Lord, Madam(e), Mal(l)am, Marchesa, Marchese, Marquess, Marquis, Master, Masthead, Maulana, Memsahib, Meneer, Mevrou, Miladi, Milady, Milord, Mirza, Monsignor, Mr(s), Mynheer, Name, Native, Negus, Nemn, Nickname, Nizam, Nomen, Ownership, Pacha, Padishah, Pasha, Peerage, Pir, Polemarch, Prefix, Prince(ss), Queen, → **RANK**, Reb, Reverence, Reverend, → **RIGHT**, Rubric, Running, Sahib, Said, Sama, San, Sardar, Sayid, Sayyid, Senhor(a), Señor(a), Shri, Singh, Sir, Sirdar, Son, Sowbhagyawati, Sri, Stratum, Tannie, Tanno, Tenno, Titule, Torrens, Tuanku, Tycoon, U, Voivode, Worship

**Title-holder** Cartouche, Champion, Landlord, Noble

**Titmouse** Bird, Hickymal, Mag. Reedling, Tit

**Tito** Gobbi

**Titter** Giggle, Snigger, Tehee

**Tittle** Jot

**Titus** Oates

**Tizz(y)** Discombobulation, Flap, Flat spin, Pother, Spin, State, Tanner, Testril, VId

**TNT** Explosive, Trotyl

**To(wards)** At, Beside, Inby, Intil, Oncoming, Onto, Prone, Shet, Shut, Till, Until

**Toad(y)** Bootlicker, Bufo, Cane, Clawback, Clawed, Crapaud, Crawler, Fawn, Frog, Hanger-on, Horned, Jackal, Jenkins, Knot, Lackey, Lick-platter, Lickspittle, Midwife, Minion, Natterjack, Nototrema, Paddock, Parasite, Pick-thank, Pipa, Placebo, Platanna, Poodle, Pouch, Puddock, Queensland cane, Sook, Spade-foot, Squit, Surinam, Sycophant, Tree, Tuft-hunter, Walking, Warty, Xenopus, Yesman

**Toadstone** Lava

**Toadstool** Amanita, Death-cap, Death-cup, Destroying angel, Fly agaric, → **FUNGUS**, Grisette, Horsehair, Marasmus, Paddock-stool, Parrot, Saffron milk cap, Sickener, Sulphur tuft, Verdigris, Wax cap

**Toast(er)** Bacchus, Bell, Birsle, Brindisi, → **BROWN**, Bruschetta, Bumper, Cheers, Chin-chin, Crostini, Croute, Crouton, Drink-hail, French, Gesundheit, Grace-cup, Grill, Health, Heat, Iechyd da, Immortal memory, Kia-ora, L'chaim, Lechayim, Loyal, Melba, Pledge, Pop up, Propose, Prosit, Round, Salute, Scouther, Scowder, Scowther, Sentiment, Sippet, Skoal, Slainte, Slainte mha(i)th, Soldier, Sunbathe, Wassail, Zwieback

**Toastmaster** MC, Symposiarch

**Tobacco, Tobacco-field** Alfalfa, Bacchi, Baccy, Bird's eye, Broadleaf, Burley, Burn, Canaster, Capa, Caporal, Cavendish, Chew, Cigarette, Dottle, Filler, Honeydew, Indian, Killikinnick, Kinnikinick, Latakia, Mundungus, Nailrod, Navy-cut, Nicotian, Nicotine, Perique, Pigtail, Pipe, Plug, Quid, Rapper, Régie, Returns, Shag, Sheesha, Shisha, Sneesh, Snout, Snuff, Straight cut, Stripleaf, Turkish, Twist, Vega, Virginia, Weed, Wrapper

**To be arranged** TBA

**Toboggan** Skidoo, Sled(ge), Sleigh

**To boot** Furthermore

**Toby** Dog, High, Highwayman, Jug, Low

**Tocsin** Alarm, Siren

**Today** Hodiernal, Now, Present

**Toddle(r)** Baim, Gangrel, Mite, Tot, Totter, Trot, Waddle

**Toddy** Arrack, → **DRINK**, Sura, Whisky

**To-do** Sensation, Stir

**Toe(s), Toed** Dactyl, Digit, Fissiped, Great, Hallux, Hammer, Pigeon, Piggy, Pinky, Pointe, Poulaine, Prehallux, Tootsie

**Toeless** Pobble

**Toff** Gent, Highbrow, Nob, Nut, Snob, Swell

**Toffee** Banket, Butterscotch, Caramel, Chew, Cracknel, Gundy, Hard-bake, Hokey-pokey, Humbug, Tom-trot

**Toga** Palla

**Together** Along, Among, At-one, Atone, Attone, Col, Commensual, Corporate, En bloc, En masse, Gathered, Hand-in-glove, Hand-in-hand, In concert, Infere, In mass, In step, In sync, In tandem, Job lot, →JOINT, Juxtaposed, Pari-passu, Sam, Simultaneous, Tutti, Unison, Wed, Y, Yfere, Ysame

**Toggle** Fastener, Netsuke

**Togs** Clothes, Gear, Rig, Strip

**Toho** Halt

**Toil(s)** Donkey work, Drudge, Fag, Graft, Industry, →LABOUR, Mesh, Net, Seine, Sisyphus, Slog, Sweat, Swink, Tela, Tew, Trap, Trauchle, Travail, Tug, Web, →WORK, Wrest, Yacker, Yakka, Yakker

**Toilet** Can, Chemical, Coiffure, Garderobe, Gents, Head(s), Jacks, John, Ladies, Lat(rine), Lavabo, →LAVATORY, Loo, Necessary house, Necessary place, Pan, Pot, Powder room, Restroom, Thunderbox, Toot, WC

**Token** Abbey-counter, Abbey-piece, Buck, Check, Chip, Counter, Coupon, Disc, Double-axe, Emblem, Favour, Gift, Indication, Mark, →MEMENTO, Monument, Nominal, Omen, Portend, Seal, Sign, Signal, Slug, Symbol, Symptom, Tessella, Tessera, Valentine, Voucher, White flag

**Tokyo** Edo, Kyoto

**Tolbooth** Tolsel, Tolsey, Tolzey

**Tolerable** Acceptable, Bearable, Fair(ish), Mediocre, Passable, So-so, Tol-lol

**Tolerance, Tolerant, Tolerate(d)** Abear, Abide, Accept, Admit, →ALLOW, Bear, Broadminded, Brook, Countenance, Elastic, Endure, Enlightened, Fault, Good-natured, Hack, Had, Immunological, Latitude, →LENIENT, Liberal, Long-suffering, Lump, Mercy, Patient, Permit, Resistant, Stand (for), Stick, Stomach, Studden, Suffer, Support, Thole, Understanding, Wear, Zero

**Toll** Chime, Chok(e)y, Customs, Due, Duty, Excise, Jole, Joll, Joule, Jow, Light-dues, Octroi, Pierage, Pike, Pontage, Rates, →RING, Scat, Scavage, Streetage, Tariff, Tax, Turnpike

**Toll-breaker** Rebecca

**Tom(my)** Atkins, Bell, Bowling, Bread, Brown, →CAT, Chimney sweep, Collins, Edgar, Gib, Grub, Gun, He-cat, Jerry, Jones, Mog(gy), Nosh, Peeping, Private, Pro(stitute), Pte, Puss, Ram-cat, Sawyer, Snout, Soldier, Stout, Thos, Thumb, Tiddler, Tucker

**Tomahawk** Hatchet

**Tomato** Beef(steak), Cherry, Gooseberry, Husk, Love-apple, Plum, Portuguese, Strawberry, Tamarillo, Tree, Wolf's peach

**Tomb(stone)** Burial, Catacomb, Catafalque, Cenotaph, Cist, Coffin, Cromlech, Dargah, Dolman, Durgah, Grave, Hypogeum, Inurn, Kistvaen, Marmoreal, Mastaba, Mausoleum, Megalithic, Monument, Pyramid, Repository, →SEPULCHRE, Sepulture, Serdab, Shrine, Speos, Tell el Amarna, Tholos, Tholus, Through-stane, Through-stone, Treasury, Vault

**Tombola** Draw, Lottery, Raffle

**Tomboy** Gamine, Gilpey, Gilpy, Hoyden, Ladette, Ramp, Romp

**Tome** →BOOK, Omnibus, Volume

**Tomfoolery** Caper, Fandangle, Shenanigan

**Tomorrow** Future, Manana, Morrow, The morn

**Tompion** Watchman

**Tom Snout** Tinker

**Ton(nage)** C, Century, Chic, Displacement, Freight, Gross, Hundred, Long, Measurement, Metric, Net register, Register, Shipping, Short, T

**Tone, Tonality** Aeolian, Brace, Cadence, Colour, Combination, Compound, Dialling, Difference, Differential, Eigen, Engaged, Fifth, Gregorian, Harmonic, Headnote, Hum, Hypate, Inflection, Key, Klang, Mean, Mediant, Minor, Ninth, Partial, Passing, Pure, Qualify, Quarter, Real, Resultant, Ring, Ringing, Side, →SOUND, Strain, Summational, Temper, Tenor, Timbre, Touch, Trite, Twang, Whole

**Tong(s)** Curling, Discharging, Forceps, Lazy, Sugar, Wafer

**Tongue, Tonguing** Brogue, Burr, Chape, Clack, Clapper, Doab, Double, Final, Flutter, Forked, Glossa, Glossolalia, Glottal, Isthmus, Jinglet, →LANGUAGE, Languet(te), Lap, Lick, Ligula, Lill, Lingo, Lingual, Lingulate, Lytta, Mother, Organ, Ox, Radula, Ranine, Rasp, Red rag, Silver, Single, Spit, Tab, Triple, Voice, Vulgar

**Tongue-tied** Inarticulate, Mush-mouthed, See a wolf
**Tongue-twister** Breakjaw, Jaw-breaker, Shibboleth
**Tonic** Booster, Bracer, C(h)amomile, Cascara, Doh, Elixir, Key, Keynote, Mease, Medicinal, Mishmee, Mishmi, Myrica, Oporice, Pareira brava, Pick-me-up, Quassia, Quinine, Refresher, Roborant, Sage tea, Sarsaparilla, Solfa
▷**Tonic** *may indicate* a musical note
**Tonsil, Tonsillitis** Almond, Amygdala, Antiaditis, Pharyngeal, Quinsy
**Tonsure(d)** Epilate, Haircut, Peel, Pield
**Tony** Bête, Chic, Classy, Fool, Smart, U
**Too** Als(o), As well, Besides, Eke, Excessive, Item, Likewise, Moreover, Oer, Over, Overly, Plus, Troppo
**Took** Naam, Nam, Set, Stole, Wan, Won
**Tool(s), Tooling, Tool-maker** Countersink, Flatter, Gadget, →IMPLEMENT, →INSTRUMENT, Knapper, Maker, Palaeolith, Penis, Percussion, Power, Property, Utensil

---

**TOOLS**

*2 letters:*
Ax

*3 letters:*
Awl
Axe
Bit
Bur
Die
Fid
Gad
Hob
Hoe
Saw
Set

*4 letters:*
Adze
Brog
Burr
File
Froe
Frow
Iron
Loom
Lute
Pawn
Pick
Rasp
Rirp
Roll
Rurp
Snap
Tint
Vice

*5 letters:*
Auger
Bevel
Blind
Burin
Croze
Dolly
Drift
Drill
Drove
Edger
Elsin
Facer
Float
Graip
Hardy
Jemmy
Level
Lewis
Miser
Piton
Plane
Prunt
Punch
Snake
Spade
Swage
Tongs

*6 letters:*
Bed-key
Beetle
Bodkin
Broach
Chaser
Chisel
Dibber
Dibble
Eatche
Eolith
Firmer
Former
Fraise
Fuller
Gimlet
Gnomon
Gouger
Graver
Hammer
Harrow
Hopdog
Husker
Jackal
Jumper
Laster
Mallet
Muller
Pattle
Pestle
Pliers
Rabble
Rammer
Reamer
Ripple
Roller
Router
Sander
Saw set
Scutch
Scythe
Shoder
Sickle
Slater
Strike
Switch
Trowel
Wimble
Wrench

*7 letters:*
Bandsaw
Bradawl
Carbide
Catspaw
Chopper
Cleaver
Crampon
Fretsaw
Go-devil
Grapnel
Grinder
Hatchet
Icepick
Insculp
Jim Crow
Jointer
Machine
Nail gun
Nail set
Nippers
Oustiti
Pickaxe
Plunger
Pointer
Pricker
Rocking
Rounder
Scalpel
Scalper
Scauper
Scorper
Scraper
Scriber
Seamset
Slasher
Sleeker
Spanner
Spudder
Swingle
Swipple

Syringe
Terebra
Triblet
T-square
Tweaker
Twibill
Upright
Whipsaw

*8 letters:*
Aiguille
Airbrush
Allen key
Billhook
Calipers
Chainsaw
Clippers
Driftpin
Findings
Frame-saw
Grattoir
Hardware
Picklock
Pitching
Puncheon
Roulette
Scissors
Strickle
Strimmer®
Tjanting
Tranchet
Tweezers
Vibrator
Vulsella

*9 letters:*
Blowtorch
Centre bit
Come-along
Corkscrew
Drawknife
Drawshave
Lazy-tongs
Microlith
Moon-knife
Nail punch
Outsiders
Pitchfork
Secateurs
Staple-gun
Toothpick
Try square
Tyre-gauge

*10 letters:*
Claw-hammer
Float-stone
Fore-hammer
Jackhammer
Loggerhead
Spokeshave
Tenderiser

*11 letters:*
Bagging-hook
Glass-cutter
Hammer-drill
Marlinspike
Mitre square
Oyster tongs
Plough-staff
Sand-thrower
Screwdriver
Spirit-level
Spitsticker
Steam hammer

*12 letters:*
Hedge-trimmer
Marlinespike
Monkey wrench
Sledge-hammer
Spell-checker
Wire-stripper

*13 letters:*
Microkeratome
Packet-sniffer
Shooting stick

---

**Toot(er)** Beep, Blow, Horn, Parp, Trumpet

**Tooth(ed), Toothy, Teeth** Baby, Bicuspid, Bit, Buck, Bunodont, Cadmean, Canine, Carnassial, Chactodon, Cheek tooth, Chewers, Chisel, Choppers, Cog, Colt's, Comb, Comer, Cott's, Crena(te), Ctenoid, Cusp, Deciduous, Denticle, Dentin(e), Dentures, Egg, Eye, False, Fang, Gam, Gap, Gat, Gnashers, Grinder, Heterodont, Impacted, Incisor, Ivory, Joggle, Laniary, Leaf, Milk, Mill, Molar, Nipper, Odontoid, Orthodontics, Overbite, Pawl, Pearly gates, Pearly whites, Pectinate, Periodontics, Peristome, Permanent, Phang, Plate, Poison-fang, Pre-molar, Prong, Radula, Ratch, Ratchet, Saw, Scissor, Secodont, Sectorial, Selenodont, Serration, Set, Snaggle, Sprocket, Stomach, Store, Sweet, Trophi, Tush, Tusk, Uncinus, Upper, Wallies, Wang, Wiper, Wisdom, Wolf, Zalambdodont, Zygodont

**Toothache, Tooth troubles** Caries, Odontalgia, Odontoma, Tartar

**Toothless(ness)** Anodontia, Edentate, Gummy, Pangolin

**Toothpaste** Dentifrice, Gel

**Toothsome** Delectable

**Top (drawer, hole, line, notcher), Topper, Topping, Topmost** 1st, A1, Ace, Acme, Altissimo, Apex, Apical, Ascender, Beezer, Behead, Best, Better, Big, Blouse, Blouson, Boob tube, Brow, Bustier, Cacumen, Camisole, Cap, Capstone, Ceiling, Classic, Coma, Cop, Coping, Corking, Cream, → CREST, Crista, Crop, Crown, Culmen, Decapitate, De capo, Decollate, De luxe, Diabolo, Dog, Dome, Dominant, Double, Drawer, Dreid(e)l, Dux, Elite, Execute, Fighting, Finial, Flip, Foremost, Gentry, Gyroscope, Halterneck, Hard, Hat, → HEAD, Height, Hoodie, Hummer, Humming, Imperial, Impost, Jersey, Jumper, Kaftan, Lead, Lid, Maillot, Management, Marzipan, Mountain, Neck, Nonpareil, Nun, One-er, Optimate, Orb, Parish, → PEAK, Pediment, Peerie, Peery, Peg, Peplos, Peplus, Pileum, Pinnacle, Pitch, Pullover, Quark, Replenish, Ridge, Roof, Sawyer, Screw, Secret, Shaw, Shirt, Skim, Sky, Slay, Slipover, Soft, Spinning, Star, Summit, Superate, Superb, Supernal, Supreme, Supremo, Surface, Sweater, Table, Tambour, Tank, Targa, Teetotum, Texas, Tile, Trash, Trump, T-shirt, Tunic, Turbinate, Unroof, Up(most), Uppermost, V, Vertex, Vest, Whipping, Whirligig, Winner

▹**Top** *may indicate* first letter

**Topaz** Bohemian, Citrine, Colorado, Occidental, Oriental, Pycnite, Rose, Scottish, Spanish

**Topcoat** Finish, Overall, Overcoat, Ulster

**Tope(r)** Boozer, Bouser, Dagaba, Dagoba, → DRUNK, Imbibe, Sot, Tosspot

**Topic(al)** Agenda, Head, Hobbyhorse, Issue, Item, Local, Motion, Place, Shop, Subject, Text, →THEME, Timely, Up to date
**Top-knot** Tuft
**Top man** Wallah
**Topping** Grand, Icing, Meringue, Pepperoni, Piecrust, Streusel
**Topple** Depose, Dethrone, Knock down, Oust, Overbalance, Overturn, Tip, Upend, →UPSET
**Topsy** Parentless
**Topsy-turvy** Careen, Cockeyed, Inverted, Looking-glass, Summerset, Tapsalteerie, Tapsleteerie
**Top to tail** Heads and thraws
**Torah** Maftir
**Torch** Blow, Brand, Cresset, Fire, Flambeau, Flashlight, Hards, Hurds, Lamp, Lampad, Link, Olympic, Penlight, Plasma, Roughie, Tead(e), Weld, Wisp
**Torch-bearer** Link boy, Usherette
**Toreador** Escamillo, Matador, Picador, Torero
**Torment(ed), Tormentor** Agony, Angst, Anguish, Bait, Ballyrag, Bedevil, Butt, Cruciate, Crucify, Curse, Desperation, Distress, Excruciate, Frab, Gehenna, Gibe, Grill, Hag-ridden, Harass, Harry, Haunt, Hell, Intimidate, Martyrdom, Molest, Nag, Nettle, Oppress, Pang, Pine, Plague, →RACK, Sadist, Tantalise, Tease, Wrack
**Torn** Agnail, In two, Ripped
**Tornado** Cyclone, Twister, Waterspout, Whirlwind
**Toronto** Hogtown
**Torpedo** Bangalore, Bomb, Fish, Missile, Ray, Subroc, Tin fish, Weapon
**Torpedo-guard** Crinoline
**Torpid, Torpor** Accidie, Acedia, Apathy, Comatose, Dormant, Gouch, Inertia, Languid, Lethargic, Sluggish, Slumbering, Stupor
**Torquemada** Inquisitor
**Torrent** Deluge, Downpour, Flood, Spate
**Torrid** Amphiscian, Fiery, Hot, Steamy, Sultry, Tropical
**Torsk** Cusk
**Torso** Body, Midriff, Trunk
**Tortilla** Enchilada, Pancake, Quesadilla, Taco, Tostada
**Tortoise** Chelonia, Emydes, Emys, Galapagos, Giant, Hic(c)atee, Kurma, Pancake, Snapping-turtle, Terrapin, Testudo, Timothy, Turtle, Water
**Tortoiseshell** Cat, Epiplastra, Hawksbill, Puss(y), Testudo
**Tortuous** Ambagious, Elaborate, Twisty, Winding
▷**Tortuous** *may indicate* an anagram
**Torture, Torture chamber, Torture instrument** Agonise, Anguish, Auto-da-fé, Bastinade, Bastinado, Boot, Bootikin, Catasta, Chinese burn, Chinese water, Crucify, Devil-on-the-neck, Engine, Excruciate, Flageolet, Fry, Gadge, Gauntlet, Gyp, Hell, Iron maiden, Knee-cap, Naraka, Peine forte et dur, Persecute, Pilliwinks, Pine, Pinniewinkle, Pinnywinkle, →RACK, Sadism, Scaphism, Scarpines, Scavenger, Scavenger's daughter, Scourge, Skeffington's daughter, Skevington's daughter, Strappado, Tantalise, Third degree, Thumb(i)kins, Thumbscrew, Torment, Treadmill, Triphook, Tumbrel, Tumbril, Water, Wheel, Wrack
▷**Tortured** *may indicate* an anagram
**Torturer** Torquemada
**Torus** Disc, Stellarator
**Tory** Abhorrer, Blimp, Blue, C, Catholic, Opposition, Right, Taig, Tantivy, U, Unionist, Wet, Young England
**Tosh** Old bean
**Toss(ing), Throw(n)** Abject, Bandy, Birl, Bounce, Buck, Bung, Buttock, Caber, Cant, Canvass, Cast, Catapult, →CHUCK, Cottabus, Crabs, Crap, Cross-buttock, Dad, Daud, Dawd, Deal, Delivery, Dink, Discomfit, Disconcert, Dod, Elance, Estrapade, Falcade, Faze, →FLING, Flip, Floor, Flump, Flutter, Flying (head)-mare, Free, Full, Gollum, Hanch, Haunch, Heave, Hipt, Hoy, →HURL, Jack, Jact(it)ation, Jaculation, Jeff, Juggle, Jump, Lance, Launch, Lob,

Loft, Nick, Pash, Pick, Pitch, Purl, Put(t), Roll, Round-arm, Salad, Seamer, Shy, Slat, Sling, Squail, Throw, Turf, Unhorse, Unseat, Upcast, Wheech, Yuko

**Toss-up** Cross and pile, Heads or tails

**Tot** Add, Babe, Bairn, →CHILD, Dop, Dram, Infant, Mite, Moppet, Nightcap, Nip(per), Nipperkin, Slug, Snifter, Snort, Tad, Toddler

**Total(ity), Totally, Toto** Absolute, Aggregate, All(-out), All told, Amount, Balance, Be-all, →COMPLETE, Control, Count, Entire, Grand, Gross, In all, Lot, Mass, Ouroborus, Outright, Overall, Slay, Sum(mate), Tale, Tally, Unqualified, Uroborus, Utter, Whole

**Totalitarian** Autocrat, Despot, Étatiste, Fascist

**Tote** Bear, →CARRY, Mutuel, Yomp

**Totem** Fetish, Icon, Image, Pole

**To the point** Ad rem

**Tottenham** Hotspur

**Totter** Abacus, Daddle, Daidle, Didakai, Didakei, Didicoi, Did(d)icoy, Halt, Lurch, Ragman, Reel, Rock, Scavenger, Shamble, →STAGGER, Swag, Sway, Topple, Waver, Wobble

**Toucan** Ariel, Ramphastos

**Touch(ed), Touching, Touch up, Touchy** Abut, Accolade, Adjoin, Affect, Against, Airbrush, Anent, Apropos, Badass, Barmy, Cadge, Captious, Carambole, Caress, Carom, Common, Concern, Connivent, Contact, Contiguous, Dash, Easy, Emove, →FEEL, Feisty, Final, Finger, Finishing, Flick, Fondle, Glance, Handle, Haptic, Heart-warming, Huffish, Huffy, Impinge, →IN TOUCH, Iracund, Irascible, Irritable, J'adoube, Kiss, Liaison, Libant, Loan, Loco, Meet, Midas, Miffy, Near, Neighbour, Nie, Nigh, Nuance, Nudge, Palp, Pathetic, Paw, Poignant, Potty, Re, Reach, Sense, Shade, Skiff, Soft, Sore, Spice, →SPOT, Stroke, Tactile, Tactual, Tag, Tangible, Tap, Taste, Tat, Tetchy, Tickle, Tig, Tinderbox, Tinge, Titivate, Trace, Trait, Trifle, Tuck, Vestige

**Touchdown** Rouge

**Touchline** Tangent

**Touchstone** Basanite, Criterion, Norm, Standard

**Touch wood** Unberufen

**Touchwood** Absit omen, Monk, Punk, Spunk, Tinder

**Tough(en)** Adamantine, Anneal, Apache, Arduous, Ballsy, Bruiser, Burly, Chewy, Dab, Exacting, Fiendish, →HARD, Hardball, Hard-boiled, Hard-nosed, Hard nut, Hardy, Heavy duty, He-man, Hood, Hoodlum, Husky, Indurate, Keelie, Knotty, Leathern, Leathery, Nut, Pesky, Rambo, Rare, Resilient, Rigwiddie, Rigwoodie, Robust, Roughneck, Sinewy, Skinhead, Spartan, Steely, Stiff, Strict, String, Sturdy, Teuch, Thewed, Thug, Tityre-tu, Virile, Wiry, Withy, Yob

**Toupee** Hairpiece, Rug, Tour, →WIG

**Tour(er), Tourism, Tourist** Adventure, Barnstorm, Benefit, Circuit, Coach, Conducted, Cook's, Emmet, Excursion, Gig, Globetrotter, Grand, Grockle, GT, Holiday-maker, Itinerate, →JOURNEY, Lap, Lionise, Mystery, Outing, Package, Parra, Posting, Pub crawl, Reality, Roadie, Road show, Rubberneck, Safari, Sightsee, Spin, Steerage, Swing, Tiki, →TRAVEL, Trip(per), Viator, Weather, Whistle-stop

**Tourmaline** Indicolite, Indigolite, Schorl, Zeuxite

**Tournament** American, Basho, Bonspiel, Bridge drive, Carousel, Drive, Event, Gala, Jereed, Jerid, Joust, Just, Ladder, Open, Plate, Pro-am, Pro-celebrity, Round robin, Royal, Spear-running, Super Twelve, Swiss, Tilt-yard, Tourney, Whist drive, Wimbledon

**Tourniquet** Gar(r)otte, Garrot(e), Throttle, Torcular

**Tousle** Dishevel, Rumple

**Tout** Barker, Laud, Ply, Praise, Runner, Solicit, Spruik, Toot, Work-watcher

**Tow(ing), Towpath** Aquaplane, Button, Fibre, →HAUL, Hobbler, Pull, →ROPE, Ski, Skijoring, Stupe, Track road

▸**Towards** *see* TO(WARDS)

**Towel** Dry, Jack, Nappy, Pantyliner, Roller, Rub, Sanitary, Tea, Tea-cloth, Terry, Turkish

**Tower(ing), Tower over, Towers** AA, Alton, Armada, Aspire, Atalaya, Babel, Barbican, Bastille, Bastion, Belfry, Bell, Blackpool, Bloody, Brattice, Brettice, Brogh, Campanile, Clock, Conning, Control, Cooling, Dominate, Donjon, Dungeon, Dwarf, Edifice, Eiffel, Fly, Fortress, Gantry, Garret, Gate, Giralda, Gopura(m), Guérite, Hawser, Horologium, Husky, Ivory, Keep,

Leaning, Lofty, Loom, Maiden, Martello, Minar(et), Monument, Mooring, Mouse, Nuraghe, Nurhag, Overtop, Peel, Pinnacle, Pisa, Pound, Pylon, Rear, Rise, Rolandseck, Rood, Round, Sail, Sears, Shot, Signal, Sikhara, Silo, Ski-lift, Skyscraper, Space Needle, Specula, Spire, Stealth, Steeple, Swiss Re, Tête-de-pont, Texas, Tractor, Tugboat, → TURRET, Victoria, Watch, Water, Yagura, Ziggurat, Zikkurat

**Town, Township** Boom, Borgo, Borough, Bourg, Burg(h), City, Company, Conurbation, County, Deme, Dormitory, Dorp, Favella, Five, Garrison, Ghost, Ham(let), Intraurban, Market, Municipal, Nasik, One-horse, Open, Place, Podunk, Pueblo, Satellite, Shanty, Shire, Soweto, Spa, Staple, Tinsel, Tp, Twin, Urban, Whistle stop, Wick

**Townee, Townsman** Cad, Cit(izen), Dude, Freeman, Oppidan, Philister, Resident, Snob, Urbanist, Urbanite

**Town hall** Prytaneum

**Toxaemia** Eclampsia

**Toxic(ity), Toxin** Abrin, Aflatoxin, Antigen, Asbestos, Botox®, Botulin, Cadaverine, Cadmium, Chlorin(e), Coumarin, Curare, Deadly, Dioxan, Dioxin, Eclampsia, Endrin, Fluorin(e), Lethal, Melittin, Muscarine, Nicotine, Paraquat, Patulin, Phalloidin, Phenol, Phenothiazine, Pre-eclampsia, Psoralen, Pyrrole, Ricin, Sepsis, Serology, Venin, Venomous, Virulence, Yellow rain, Zootoxin

**Toy** Babyhouse, Bandalore, Bauble, Bottle-imp, Bull-roarer, Cartesian devil, Cockhorse, Coral, Cyberpet, Dally, Dandle, Dinky®, Doll, Doll's house, Dreid(e)l, Executive, Faddle, Fiddle, Finger, Flirt, Frisbee®, Gewgaw, Golly, Gonk, Jack-in-the-box, Jumping-jack, Kaleidoscope, Kickshaw, Kite, Knack, Lego®, Meccano®, Newton's cradle, Noah's ark, Novelty, Paddle, Pantine, Peashooter, Pinwheel, Plaything, Pogo stick, Popgun, Praxinoscope, Quiz, Rag doll, Rattle, Rocking-horse, Russian doll, Scooter, Shoofly, Skipjack, Soft, Stroboscope, Tamagotchi®, Tantalus-cup, Taste, Teddy, Thaumatrope, Top, → TRIFLE, Trinket, Tu(r)ndun, Wheel of life, Whirligig, Windmill, Yoyo, Zoetrope

**Trace, Tracing** Atom, Barogram, Cast, Derive, Describe, Draft, Draw, Dreg, Echo, Footprint, Ghost, Gleam, → HINT, Leaf, Limn, Locate, Mark, Memory, Nuance, Outline, Relic, Relict, Remnant, Scan, Scintilla, Semblance, Sign, Smack, Soupçon, Spark, Strap, Streak, Suspicion, Tinge, → TOUCH, Track, Vestige, Whiff, Whit

**Tracery** Filigree, Frostwork

**Track(s), Tracker, Tracking, Trackman** Aintree, Aisle, Backing, Band, B-road, Caterpillar®, Chase, Cinder, Circuit, Course, Crawler, Cycleway, Dirt, Disrail, Dog, DOVAP, Drag strip, Drift, Ecliptic, El, Fast, Fettler, Flap(ping), Footing, Footprint, Footstep, Gandy dancer, Green road, Greenway, Groove, Hunt, Ichnite, Ichnolite, Icknield Way, Inside, Lane, Ley, Line, Loipe, Loke, Loopline, Mainline, Mommy, Monitor, Monza, Moonglade, Orbit, Pad, → PATH, Persue, Pipe, Piste, Pitlane, Pug, Pursue, Race, Raceway, Rail, Railway, Rake, Ridgeway, Riding, Route, Run, Runway, Rut, SARSAT, Scent, Side, Siding, Sign, Skidway, Sleuth, Slot, Sonar, Speedway, Spoor, Stylus, Tan, Tan-ride, Taxiway, Tenure, Tideway, Title, Towpath, Trace, → TRAIL, Trajectory, Tram, Tramline, Tramroad, Tramway, Tread, Trode, Tug(boat), Twin, Wake, Wallaby, Way, Y

**Tract(able), Tracts** Area, Belt, Bench, Clime, Colporteur, Common, Dene, Digestive, Enclave, Enteral, Farthingland, Flysheet, Lande, Leaflet, Monte, Moor, Olfactory, → PAMPHLET, Park, Prairie, Province, Purlieu, Pusey, Pyramidal, Region, Scabland, Screed, Taluk, Tawie, Terrain, Wold

**Tractarian(ism)** Newman, Oxford movement, Pusey(ism)

**Tractor** Back hoe, Bombardier®, Bulldozer, Cat, Caterpillar®, Chelsea, Fendalton, Pedrail, Remuera, Skidder, Tower

**Tracy** Dick, Spencer

**Trade(r), Tradesman, Trading** Arb(itrageur), Art, Banian, Banyan, Bargain, Barrow boy, Barter, Bear, Bilateral, Bricks and clicks, Bull, Bun(n)ia, Burgher, Business, Cabotage, Calling, Carriage, Chaffer, Chandler, Chapman, Cheapjack, Cheesemonger, Clicks and mortar, Clothier, Coaster, Comanchero, → COMMERCE, Coper, Coster, Costermonger, Coulisse, Crare, Crayer, Custom, Day, Deal(er), Decorator, Dicker, Easterling, Eggler, Electrician, Errand, Exchange, Exporter, Factor, Fair, Floor, Fly-pitcher, Free, Galleon, Glazier, Handle, Higgler, Horse, Hosier, Hot, Importer, Indiaman, Industry, Insider, Ironmonger, Jobber,

Kidder, Line, Logrolling, Marketeer, Matrix, Mercantile, Mercer, Merchant, Mercosur, Métier, Middleman, Milkman, Mister, Monger, Mystery, Occupy, Outfitter, Paralleling, Pargeter, Pitchman, Plasterer, Plumber, Ply, Printer, Program(me), Rag, Retailer, Roaring, Rough, Roundtripping, Salesman, Scalp, Screen, Sell, Shrivijaya, Simony, Slave, Stallenger, Stallholder, Stallinger, Stationer, Sutler, Suttle, → SWAP, Tailor, Traffic, Transit, Trant, Truck, Union, Vaisya, Vend, Wheeler-dealer, Wholesaler, Wind, Worker

**Trademark, Trade name** Brand, Chop, Idiograph, Label, Logo, Tm, TN

**Trade union, Trade group** Amicus, ASLEF, Chapel, COHSE, Community, EFTA, Equity, Local, Samiti, Solidarity, Syndicalism, UNISON, USDAW

**Trading money, Trading post** Cabotage, Fort, Wampum

**Tradition(s), Traditional(ist)** Ancestral, Classical, Convention, Custom(ary), Diehard, Eastern, First-footing, Folksy, Folkway, Hadith, Heritage, Legend, Lore, Mahayana, Misoneist, Old guard, Old-line, Old-school, Orthodox, Pharisee, Pompier, Practice, Purist, Square, Suburban, Time-honoured, Trad, Tralaticious, Tralatitious, Unwritten

**Traduce** Abuse, Asperse, Defame, Impugn, Malign, Smear, Vilify

**Traffic(ker), Traffic pattern** Air, Barter, Broke, Cabotage, Clover-leaf, Commerce, Contraflow, Coyote, Deal, Export, Merchant, Negotiate, Passage, Rolling stock, Run, Sell, Slave trade, Smuggle, Tailback, Through, Trade, Truck, Vehicular, Way

**Tragedian, Tragedy, Tragic** Aeschylus, Antigone, Buskin, Calamity, Catastrophe, Cenci, Corneille, Dire, → DRAMA, Dramatist, Euripides, Lear, Macbeth, Macready, Melpomene, Oedipean, Oresteia, Othello, Otway, Pathetic, Seneca, Sophoclean, Thespian, Thespis

**Trail(er), Trailing** Abature, Advert, Appalachian, Audit, Bedraggle, Caravan, Condensation, Creep, Dissipation, Drag, Draggle, Fire, Follow, Forerunner, Foretaste, Horsebox, Husting, Ipomaea, Ivy, Lag, Liana, Liane, Low-loader, Nature, Oregon, Paper, Path, Persue, Preview, Prevue, Promo(tion), Pursue, Repent, Road train, Runway, Santa Fe, Scent, Shadow, Sickle-cell, Sign, Sleuth, Slot, Slowcoach, Snail, Spoor, Stalk, Straggle, Stream, Streel, Tag, Tow, Trace, → TRACK, Trade, Traipse, Trape, Trauchle, Trayne, Troad, Vapour, Vine, Virga, Wake

**Train(er), Training** Accommodation, Adidas®, Advanced, Aim, Amtrak, Apprenticeship, APT, Autogenic, Baggage, Boat, Boot camp, BR, Break in, Breed, Brighton Belle, Bullet, Callisthenics, Caravan, Cat, Cavalcade, Choo-choo, Circuit, Coach, Commuter, Condition, Corrective, Corridor, Cortège, Day release, Diesel, Direct, Discipline, Dog, Double-header, Dressage, Drill, Drive, Educate, Entourage, Enure, Epicyclic, Eurostar®, Excursion, Exercise, Express, Fartlek, Field, Flier, Flight simulator, Freightliner®, Fuse, Gear, Ghan, Ghost, Gravy, Grounding, GWR, Handle(r), Hover, HST, → INSET, Instruct, Intercity®, Interval, Jerkwater, Journey, Limber up, Liner, Link, LMS, LNER, Loco, Longe, Lunge, Maglev, Mail, Mailcar, Manège, Manrider, Meinie, Mein(e)y, Mentor, Milk, Mixed, Monorail, Multiple unit, Nopo, Nurture, Nuzzle, Off-(the)-job, Omnibus, On-job, Orient Express, Outward Bound®, Owl, Pack, Paddy, Parliamentary, Passenger, Pavlov, PE, Pendolino, Personal, Potty, Power, Practise, → PREPARE, Procession, PT, Puffer, Puff-puff, Push-pull, Q, Qualified, Queue, Railcar, Rattler, Rehearse, Retinue, Road, Roadwork, Rocket, Roughrider, Royal Scot, Ry, Sack, Sacque, → SCHOOL, Series, Shoe, Shuttle service, Siege, Simulator, Sinkansen, Skill centre, Sleeper, Sloid, Sloyd, Sneaker, Sowarree, Sowarry, Special, Square-bashing, SR, Steam, Steer, String, Suite, Tail, Tame, → TEACH, Through, Tilting, Tire, Tirocinium, Toilet, Tone up, Track shoe, Trail, Trellis, Tube, Tutor, Twin bill, Wage, Wagon, Wave, Way, Wean, Whale oil

▹**Train(ed)** *may indicate* an anagram

**Trainee** → APPRENTICE, AT, Cadet, Cub, Fledgling, Intern, Jackaroo, Jackeroo, Learner, Ordinand, Probationer, Pupil, Rookie, Rooky, T

**Train-spotter** Gricer

**Traipse** Gad

**Trait** Characteristic, Feature, Knack, Oddity, Peculiarity, Ph(a)enotype, Sickle-cell, Strain, Thew, Trick, Vein

**Traitor** Benedict Arnold, Betrayer, Casement, Defector, Dobber-in, Dog, Fifth column, Joyce, Judas, Judas Maccabaeus, Mordred, Nid(d)ering, Nid(d)erling, Nithing, Proditor, Quisling, Renegade, Reptile, Snake, Tarpeian, Traditor, Treachetour, Turncoat, Viper, Wallydraigle, Weasel

**Trajectory** Parabola, Track
**Tram, Tramcar** Streetcar, Tip, Trolley
▷**Trammel** *may indicate* an anagram
**Tramp, Trample(d)** Bog-trotter, Bum, Caird, Clochard, Clump, Crush, Deadbeat, Derelict, Derro, Dingbat, Dosser, Down and out, Downtrodden, Drifter, Estragon, Footslog, Freighter, Gadling, Gangrel, Gook, Hike, Hobo, Knight of the road, Lumber, Meff, Override, Overrun, Pad, Piepowder, Piker, Plod, Poach, Potch(e), Prostitute, Rover, Scorn, Ship, Slog, Slop, Splodge, Stomp, Sundowner, Swagman, → **TINKER**, Toe-rag(ger), Tom, Track, Traipse, Tread, Trek, Trog, Tromp, Truant, Trudge, Tub, Vagabond, Vagrant, Weary Willie, Whore
**Trampoline** Trampet(te)
**Trance** Aisling, Catalepsy, Cataplexy, Goa, Hypnotic, Mesmerise, Narcolepsy, Somnambulism
**Tranche** Gold, Reserve
**Tranquil(lity)** Ataraxy, Calm, Compose, Composure, Easy, Halcyon, Lee, Pacific, Peace(ful), Placid, Quietude, Restful, Sedate, → **SERENE**, Still
**Tranquillise(r)** Appease, Ataractic, Ataraxic, → **CALM**, Compose, Diazepam, Downer, Hypnone, Hypnotic, Largactil®, Librium®, Lullaby, Nervine, Nitrazepam, Oxazepam, Paregoric, Placate, Satisfy, Sedative, Soothe, Still, Valium®
**Transact, Transaction(s)** Affair, Agio, Brokerage, Deal, Deed, Escrow, Ex-div, Fasti, Leaseback, Passage, Proceeding, Put through, Retour, Tr
**Transcend(ent), Transcendental(ist), Transcendentalism** Emerson, Excel, Mystic, Overtop, Surpass, Thoreau
**Transcribe, Transcript(ion)** Copy, Inclusive, Pinyin, Rescore, Tenor, → **TRANSLATE**, Transume
**Transfer(ence)** Alien, Alienate, → **ASSIGN**, Attorn, Blit, Bosman, Calk, Calque, Carryover, Cede, Chargeable, Communize, Consign, Convey(ance), Credit, Cross over, Crosstalk, Cutover, Dabbity, Decal(comania), Deed, Demise, Devolution, Devolve, Download, Embryo, Exchange, Explant, Extradite, Ferry, Flit, Gene, Ghost, Handover, Hive off, Incardinate, Iron-on, Launder, Letraset®, Make over, Mancipation, Metathesis, Mortmain, Nuclear, On-lend, Pass, Photomechanical, Print through, Provection, Reassign, Redeploy, Remit, Remove, Render, Repot, Rollover, Second, Settlement, Shunt, Slam, Spool, Telepathy, Thought, Transcribe, Transduction, Transfection, Transhume, Translocation, Transplant, Unload, Uproot, Vire, Virement
▷**Transferred** *may indicate* an anagram
**Transfix** Gore, Impale, Paralyse, Rivet, → **SKEWER**, Spear, Spit
**Transform(ation), Transformer** Affine, Alchemist, Alter, Apotheosis, Balun, Change, Conformal, Fourier, Linear, Lorentz, Makeover, Metamorphism, Metamorphose, Metamorphosis, Metaplasia, Metastasis, Morphallaxis, Morphing, Mutate, Permute, Rectifier, Restyle, Revolutionise, Sea change, Sepalody, Tesla coil, Tinct, Toroid, Toupee, Transfigure, Transmogrify, Turn, Variation, Werewolf, Wig
▷**Transform(ed)** *may indicate* an anagram
**Transfusion** Apheresis, Blood
**Transgender** Unisex
**Transgress(ion)** Encroach, Err, Infraction, Infringe, Offend, Overstep, Peccancy, → **SIN**, Violate
**Transient, Transit(ion), Transitory** Brief, Caducity, Ecotone, Ephemeral, Evanescent, Fleeting, Fly-by-night, Forbidden, Fugacious, Hobo, Impermanent, Metabasis, Passage, Passing, Provisional, Rapid, Segue, Sfumato, T, Temporary
**Transistor** Drift, Emitter, Epitaxial, Field-effect, Junction
**Translate, Translation, Translator** Calque, Construe, Convert, Coverdale, Crib, Decipher, Decode, Decrypt, Encode, Explain, Free, Horse, Interpret, In vitro, Itala, Jerome, Key, Linguist, Loan, Machine, Metaphrase, Nick, Paraphrase, Pinyin, Polyglot, Pony, Reduce, Render, Rendition, Rhemist, Septuagint, Simultaneous, Targum, Tr, Transcribe, Transform, Trot, Tyndale, Unseen, Version(al), Vulgate, Wycliffe
▷**Translate(d)** *may indicate* an anagram
**Translucent** Opaline

**Transmigrate, Transmigration** Exodus, Metempsychosis, Passage, Trek

**Transmit(ter), Transmitted, Transmission** Aerial, Air, Aldis lamp, Allele, Analogue, Automatic, Band, Baseband, Beacon, Broadband, → **BROADCAST**, Cable, Carry, CB, Communicate, Compander, Compandor, Conduct, Consign, Contagion, Convection, Convey, Digital, Diplex, Endoradiosonde, Facsimile, Fax, Filler, Forward, Gearbox, Gene, Heredity, Impart, Intelsat, Localizer, Manual, Mast, Mic(rophone), Modem, Nicol, Permittivity, Pipe, Prism, Propagate, Racon, Radiate, Radio (galaxy), Receiver, Responser, Send, Simplex, Simulcast, Sonabuoy, Spark, Spread, Synchronous, Tappet, Telautograph®, Telecast, Telegony, Telematics, Telemetry, Telepathy, Teleprinter, Teletex, Televise, Telex, Telstar, Tiptronic®, Tiros, Traduce, Traject, Tralaticious, Tralatitious, UART, Ultrawideband, Uplink, Upload, Walkie-talkie, WAP, Webcam, Webcast, Wi-Fi®

**Transmutation** Atomic

**Transom** Reverse, Traverse

**Transparent, Transparency** Acetate, Adularia, Clarity, Clear, Crystal(line), Diaphanous, Dioptric, Glassy, Glazed, Hyaloid, Iolite, Leno, Limpid, Lucid, Luminous, Patent, Pellucid, Porcelain, Sheer, Slide, Tiffany, Transpicuous

**Transpire** Happen, Occur

**Transplant** Allograft, Anaplasty, Graft, Repot, Reset(tle), Shift

**Transport(ed), Transporter, Transportation** Active, Aerotrain, Air-bus, Air-lift, Airline, Ambulance, Ar(a)ba, Argo, Barca, Bathorse, Battlebus, Beachbuggy, Bear, Bike, Black Maria, Boat, Boat-train, Bring, Broomstick, BRS, Buggy, Bus, Cable-car, Cargo, Carract, → **CARRY**, Cart, Casevac, Cat-train, Chairlift, Charabanc, Charm, Coach, Conductor, Convey, Cycle, Cyclo, Delight, Deliver, Dray, Ecstasy, Elation, Electron, Eloin, Enrapt, Enravish, Entrain, Esloin, Estro, Exalt, Fare, Ferriage, Ferry, Fishyback, Freight (train), Haul(age), Hearse, Helicopter, Hydrofoil, Jag, Jerrican, Jet ski, Joy, Kart, Kurvey, Landau, Lift, Loco(motive), Lug, Maglev, Mambrane, Matatu, Medevac, Minicab, Minivan, Monorail, Motor cycle, Overjoy, Ox-cart, Pack animal, Palanquin, Pantechnicon, Park and ride, Patrol wagon, Paytrain, Penny farthing, Pipeline, Plane, Portage, Public, Put, Q-train, Rape, Rapine, Rapture, Ravish, Rickshaw, Roadster, Ropeway, Shanks's pony, Ship, Shorthaul, Shuttle, Sidecar, Skateboard, Sledge, Sleigh, Sno-Cat, Snowmobile, SST, Stagecoach, Supersonic, Supertanker, Tandem, Tanker, Tape, Tardis, Taxi, Tote, Train, Tramcar, Tramway, Transit, Trap, Tricycle, Trolley, Troopship, Tuktuk, Tumbril, Ubiquinone, Unicycle, Waft, Waterbus, Wheelchair, Wheels, Wireway

**Transpose, Transposition** Anagram, Commute, Convert, Invert, Metathesis, Shift, Spoonerism, Switch, Tr

▷**Transposed** *may indicate* an anagram

**Transsexual** Invert

**Transubstantiate, Transubstantiation** Capernaite

**Transverse** Across, Crosscut, Diagonal, Obliquid, Thwart

**Transvest(it)ism, Transvestite** Berdache, Berdash, Cross-dressing, Eonist, Ladyboy

**Tranter** Dolly

**Trap(s), Trapdoor, Trapped, Trappings** Accoutrement, Ambush, → **BAGGAGE**, Bags, Bait, Belongings, Birdlime, Booby, Buckboard, Bunker, Carriage, Catch, Catch-basin, Catch-pit, Clapnet, Cobweb, Corner, Creel, Crevasse, Cru(i)ve, Curricle, Deadfall, Death, Decoy, Dip, Dogcart, Downfall, Drain, Eelset, Emergent, Enmesh, Ensnare, Entoil, Entrain, Fall, Fire, Fit-up, Fly, Flypaper, Frame-up, Fyke, Gas, Geel, Gig, Gin, Gob, Gravel, Grin, Haaf-net, Hatch, Honey, Housings, Ice-bound, Illaqueate, Jinri(c)ksha(w), Keddah, Kettle, Kheda, Kiddle, Kidel, Kipe, Kisser, Knur(r), Light, Lime, Live, Lobster pot, → **LUGGAGE**, Lure, Mesh, Mist-net, Mouth, Net, Nur(r), Oil, Paraphernalia, Pitfall, Plant, Polaron, Police, Pot, Poverty, Putcheon, Putcher, Quicksand, Radar, Regalia, Sand, Scruto, Scuttle, → **SNARE**, Speed, Spell, Spider, Springe, Stake-net, Star, Steam, Stench, Sting, Stink, Sun, Tangle, Tank, Teagle, Toil, Tonga, Tourist, Trapfall, Tripwire, Trojan horse, Trou-de-loup, Two-wheeler, U, U-bend, Vampire, Waterseal, Web, Weel, Weir, Wire

**Trapezist** Leotard

**Trapper** Carson, Voyageur

**Trash(y)** Bosh, Deface, Desecrate, Dre(c)k, Dump, Garbage, Junk, Kitsch, Off-scum, Pap,

Pulp, → **RUBBISH**, Schlock, Scum, Tinpot, Trailer, Trumpery, Vandalise, White, Worthless, Write off

**Trauma, Traumatise** Insult, Scar, Shell-shock, Shock, Stress

**Travel(ler), Travelling** Aeneas, Backpack, Bagman, Bushwhacker, Caird, Chapman, Columbus, Commercial, Commute, Crustie, Crusty, Drifter, Drive, Drummer, Eurostar, Explorer, Fare, Fellow, Fly, Fogg, Geoffrey, Gipsen, Gipsy, Gitano, Globe-trotter, Go, Gulliver, Gypsy, Hike, Hippy, Hitchhiker, Interrail, Itinerant, Jet-setter, Journey, Locomotion, Long-haul, Marco Polo, Meve, Migrant, Motor, Move, Mush, New Age, Nomad, Odysseus, Pardoner, Passenger, Passepartout, Peregrination, Peripatetic, Pilgrim, Ply, Polo, Pootle, Range, Rep, Ride, Road, Roam, Rom(any), Rove, Safari, Sail, Salesman, Samaritan, Sinbad, Sledger, Space, Spaceman, Steerage, Stowaway, Teleport, Tool, → **TOUR**, Tourist, Trek, Tripper, Tsigane, Viator, Voyage, Waft, Waltz Matilda, Wanderjahr, Wayfarer, Wend, Wildfire, Zigan

**Traverse** Cross, Girdle, Measure, Pass, Perlustrate, Quest, Trace

**Travesty** Burlesque, Charade, Distortion, Farce, Parody, Show, Skit

**Trawl** Beam, Drag-net, Hose-net, Net, Otter

**Tray** Antler, Bottle-slide, Carrier, Case, Charger, Coaster, Crumb, Galley, In, Joe, Lazy Susan, Litter, Mould, Out, Pallet, Plateau, Platter, → **SALVER**, Seed, Shower, Tea, Trencher, Typecase, Voider, Waiter

**Treacherous, Treachery** Back-stabbing, Bad faith, Betrayal, Deceit, Delilah, False(-hearted), Fickle, Ganelon, Guile, Insidious, Judas-kiss, Knife, Mala fide, Medism, Perfidious, Punic, Punic faith, Quicksands, Sedition, Serpentine, Sleeky, Snaky, Sneaky, Trahison, Traitor, Trappy, → **TREASON**, Two-faced, Unleal, Viper, Weasel

**Treacle** Black(jack), Butter, Molasses, Syrup, Venice

**Tread** Clamp, Clomp, Clump, Dance, Pad, Step, Stomp, Stramp, Track, Trample

**Treadle** Footboard, Pedal

**Treason** Betrayal, Constructive, High, Insurrection, Lèse-majesté, Lese-majesty, Perduellion, Perfidy, Petty, Sedition, → **TREACHERY**

**Treasure(r), Treasury** Aladdin's cave, Angel, Banker, Bursar, Cache, Camera, Camerlengo, Camerlingo, Cherish, Chest, Cimelia, Coffer, Esteem, Ewe-lamb, Exchequer, Fisc(al), Fisk, Godolphin, Golden, Heirloom, Heritage, Hoard, Hon(ey), Montana, National, Nugget, Palgrave, Pork barrel, → **PRIZE**, Procurator, Purser, Quaestor, Relic, Riches, Steward, Sweetie, Taonga, Thesaurus, Trove

**Treat, Treatment** Actinotherapy, Action, Acupressure, Acupuncture, Address, Aftercare, Allopathy, Antidote, Antiserum, Apitherapy, Archilowe, Arenation, Aromatherapy, Arsphenamine, Attention, Balneotherapy, Bariatric, Beano, Beauty, Beneficiate, Besee, Blanco, Body wrap, Botox®, Capitulate, Care, Chemotherapy, Chiropractic, Condition, Course, Coverage, Crymotherapy, Cryotherapy, Cupping, Cure, Curry, Day care, Deal, Defibrillation, Detox(ification), Dialysis, Discursis, Do, → **DOCTOR**, Dose, Dress, Dutch, ECT, Electrotherapy, Enantiopathy, Entertain, EST, Face-lift, Facial, Faith-healing, Fango, Faradism, Figuration, Finish, Foment, Frawzey, GIFT, Handle, Heat, Heliotherapy, Hellerwork, Holistic, Homeopathy, HRT, Hydrotherapy, Hypnotherapy, Immunotherapy, Insulin, Intermediate, Jin shin do, Kenny, Kinesiatric, Kiss of life, Laser, Liposuction, Luxury, Makeover, Manage, Massage, Massotherapy, Mechanotherapy, Medicament, Medicate, Mercerise, Mesotherapy, Moxibustion, Mudbath, Narcotherapy, Naturopathy, Negotiate, Opotherapy, Organotherapy, Orthoptics, Osteopathy, → **OUTING**, Pamper, Pasteur, Pedicure, Pelotherapy, Phototherapy, Physiatrics, Physic, Physiotherapy, Pie, Podiatry, Poultice, Probiotics, Process, Prophylaxis, Psychoanalysis, Psychodrama, Psychotherapy, Radiotherapy, Regale, Regimen, Rehab(ilitation), Reiki, Rest cure, Root, Sanforize®, Secretage, Serotherapy, Setter, Shiatsu, Shout, Shrift, Sironise, Smile, Softener, Speleotherapy, → **STAND**, Statin, Tablet, Taw, Tebilise®, TENS, Thalassotherapy, → **THERAPY**, Thermotherapy, The works, Titbit, Traction, Turkish bath, Twelve-step, UHT, Usance, Use, Vet

▷**Treated** *may indicate* an anagram

**Treatise** Almagest, Bestiary, Commentary, Cybele, Didache, Discourse, Dissertation, Essay, Monograph, Pandect, Prodrome, Profound, Summa, Tract(ate), Upanishad, Vedanta

**Treaty** Accord, Agreement, Alliance, Assiento, Concordat, Covenant, Entente, GATT, Jay's,

Lateran, Locarno, Lunéville, Maastricht, Nijmegen, North Atlantic, → **PACT**, Paris, Private, Protocol, Rapallo, Rijswijk, Ryswick, San Stefano, Sovetsk, Test-ban, Utrecht, Verdun, Versailles, Westphalia, Yorktown

**Treble** Castrato, Chanterelle, Choirboy, Chorist(er), High-pitched, Pairial, Soprano, → **TRIPLE**, Triune, Voice

**Tree(s)** Actor, → **ANCESTRY**, Axle, Beam, Bluff, Boom, Boot, Bosk, Candelabrum, Chaparral, Clump, Conifer, Coppice, Corner, Covin, Cross, Daddock, Deciduous, Decision, Dendrology, Descent, Dwarfed, Family, Fault, Fringe, Gallows, Genealogical, Greenery, Grove, Hang, Hardwood, Jesse, Nurse, Pedigree, Phanerophyte, Pole, Rood, Roof, Sawyer, Shoe, Silviculture, Softwood, Staddle, Stand, Stemma, Summer, Thicket, Timber, Tragedian, Tyburn, Ulmaceous, Vista, Wicopy, → **WOOD**

---

**TREES**

***2 letters:***
Bo
Ti

***3 letters:***
Ake
Ash
Asp
Bay
Bel
Ben
Box
Cow
Elm
Fig
Fir
Gum
Ita
Jak
Koa
Mot
Nim
Oak
Oil
Sal
Tea
Til
Ule
Wax
Yew

***4 letters:***
Acer
Akee
Aloe
Amla
Arar
Atap
Bael
Bean
Bhel
Bito
Cade
Coco
Cola
Dali
Dhak
Dika
Dita
Eugh
Gean
Hule
Jack
Kaki
Karo
Kiri
Kola
Lead
Lime
Lote
Mako
Meal
Milk
Ming
Mira
Mott
Mowa
Neem
Nipa
Noni
Olea
Ombu
Palm
Pine
Pipe
Pith
Plum
Poon
Puka
Rain
Rata
Rhus
Rimu
Sack
Shea
Silk
Sloe
Soap
Sorb
Tawa
Teak
Teil
Titi
Toon
Tung
Tutu
Upas
Wych
Yang
Yuzu

***5 letters:***
Abele
Abies
Ackee
Afara
Agila
Alamo
Alder
Alnus
Anona
Areca
Argan
Aspen
Babul
Banak
Bania
Beech
Belah
Birch
Bodhi
Boree
Bread
Bunya
Butea
Cacao
Carap
Carob
Cedar
Ceiba
China
Cigar
Clove
Cocoa
Cocus
Coral
Ebony
Elder
Fagus
Fever
Flame
Fruit
Gauze
Genip
Grass
Guava
Hakea
Hazel
Hevea
Holly
Iroko
Ivory
Jambu
Jarul
Judas
Kapok
Karri
Kauri
Khaya
Kiaat
Kokum
Larch
Lemon
Lichi
Lilac
Lotus
Mahoe
Mahua

Mahwa
Maire
Mamey
Mango
Mapau
Maple
Marri
Matai
Melia
Motte
Mowra
Mugga
Mulga
Mvule
Myall
Ngaio
Nikau
Nyssa
Olive
Opepe
Osier
Palas
Palay
Panax
Peach
Pecan
Pinon
Pipal
Pipul
Pitch
Plane
Quina
Ramin
Roble
Rowan
Sabal
Saman
Sassy
Scrog
Silva
Smoke
Sumac
Tawai
Taxus
Thorn
Thuja
Thuya
Tilia
Tsuga
Tuart
Tulip
Vitex
Wahoo
Wenge
Wilga
Withy
Xylem
Yacca
Yulan
Zaman
Zamia

***6 letters:***

Abroma
Acacia
Akeake
Alerce
Angico
Annona
Antiar
Arbute
Arolla
Babaco
Bablah
Balsam
Banyan
Baobab
Beaver
Bilian
Bombax
Bonsai
Bo-tree
Bottle
Buriti
Butter
Cadaga
Cadagi
Candle
Carapa
Carica
Cashew
Cembra
Cercis
Cerris
Chaste
Chenar
Cherry
Chinar
Citron
Coffee
Cordon
Cornel
Cornus
Damson
Deodar
Diana's
Dragon
Durian
Durion
Emblic
Eumong
Eumung
Feijoa
Fustet
Fustic
Gallus
Garjan
Gidgee
Gidjee
Gingko
Ginkgo
Glinap
Gnetum
Gopher
Guango
Gurjun
Gympie
Hupiro
Illipe
Illipi
Illupi
Jambul
Jarool
Jarrah
Joshua
Jujube
Jupati
Kamahi
Kamala
Kamela
Kapuka
Karaka
Karamu
Karite
Kentia
Kowhai
Laurel
Lebbek
Linden
Locust
Longan
Loquat
Lucuma
Lungah
Macoya
Mallee
Manuka
Mastic
Mazard
Medlar
Mimosa
Missel
Mopane
Mopani
Myrtle
Nutmeg
Obeche
Orange
Orihou
Padauk
Padouk
Pagoda
Papaya
Pawpaw
Peepul
Pepper
Platan
Pomelo
Poplar
Popple
Protea
Pumelo
Puriri
Quince
Red-bud
Red gum
Ricker
Roucou
Rubber
Sabicu
Sallow
Samaan
Sandal
Sapele
Sapium
Sapota
Saxaul
She-oak
Sinder
Sissoo
Sorrel
Souari
Spruce
Styrax
Sumach
Sunder
Sundra
Sundri
Tallow
Tamanu
Tawhai
Tewart
Thyine
Titoki
Tooart
Totara
Tupelo
Waboom
Wandoo
Wicken
Willow
Witgat
Yarran
Zamang

*7 letters:*
Ailanto
Ambatch
Amboina
Apricot
Araroba
Arbutus
Avocado
Avodire
Bebeeru
Bilimbi
Bilsted
Bubinga
Buck-eye
Bursera
Cajeput
Cajuput
Calamus
Camphor
Camwood
Canella
Carbeen
Cascara
Cassava
Catalpa
Cedrela
Champac
Champak
Chayote
Chesnut
Coquito
Corylus
Corypha
Cumquat
Cypress
Dagwood
Dogwood
Dryades
Durmast
Geebung
Genipap
Gluinap
Gumtree
Hickory
Hog-plum
Holm-oak
Houhere
Jambool
Jipyapa
Juniper
Kumquat
Lacquer
Lagetto
Lentisk
Live-oak
Logwood
Lumbang
Madrono
Mahaleb
Manjack
Marasca
Margosa
Mastich
Mazzard
Meranti
Mesquit
Moringa
Morrell
Mustard
Papauma
Paxiuba
Pereira
Pilinut
Pimento
Platane
Pollard
Populus
Pukatea
Quassia
Quicken
Quillai
Quinain
Radiata
Rampick
Rampike
Redwood
Rock elm
Saksaul
Sandbox
Saouari
Sapling
Saturn's
Sausage
Sequoia
Seringa
Service
Shittah
Sourgum
Soursop
Spindle
Sundari
Talipat
Talipot
Taraire
Taupata
Tawhiri
Trumpet
Varnish
Wallaba
Wirilda
Witchen
Wych-elm
Xylopia
Zelkova

*8 letters:*
Aguacate
Algaroba
Aquillia
Bangalay
Bangalow
Basswood
Beamtree
Benjamin
Bergamot
Berrigan
Blackboy
Blimbing
Blue pipe
Bountree
Bourtree
Box-elder
Breadnut
Brigalow
Calabash
Chestnut
Cinchona
Cinnamon
Cocoplum
Coolabah
Coolibah
Corkwood
Crabwood
Cucumber
Cudgerie
Dendroid
Doomboom
Dracaena
Espalier
Flittern
Fraxinus
Funtumia
Garcinia
Ghost-gum
Gnetales
Guaiacum
Hagberry
Hawthorn
Hinahina
Hornbeam
Huon-pine
Igdrasil
Inkberry
Ironbark
Ironwood
Jambolan
Jelutong
Kawakawa
Kingwood
Laburnum
Lacebark
Lecythis
Loblolly
Magnolia
Mahogany
Makomako
Mangrove
Manna-ash
Mesquite
Mulberry
Ocotillo
Oiticica
Oleaceae
Oleaster
Pachouli
Palmetto
Pandanus
Parapara
Pichurim
Pinaster
Pithtree
Pyinkado
Quandang
Quandong
Quantong
Quillaia
Quillaja
Raintree
Rambutan
Rangiora
Rewa-rewa
Sago-palm
Sandarac
Santalum
Sapindus
Sapucaia
Sasswood
Sea grape
Shaddock
Shagbark
Simaruba
Snowball
Snowdrop
Soapbark
Sourwood
Standard
Stinging
Sugar gum
Sweet gum
Sweetsop
Sycamine
Sycamore
Sycomore
Tamarack

Tamarind
Tamarisk
Taxodium
Umbrella
Whitegum
Wine-palm
Ygdrasil

***9 letters:***
Agila-wood
Ailantous
Albespine
Angophora
Araucaria
Azedarach
Bilimbing
Bitternut
Blackbutt
Blackjack
Blackwood
Bloodwood
Bolletrie
Boobialla
Broadleaf
Bulletrie
Bully-tree
Bulwaddee
Burrawary
Butternut
Caliatour
Caliature
Candlenut
Canoewood
Carambola
Casuarina
Chempaduk
Cherimoya
Chincapin
Chinkapin
Coachwood
Coco-de-mer
Cordyline
Courbaril
Crab apple
Cupressus
Curryleaf
Eaglewood
Evergreen
Firewheel
Flame-leaf
Grapetree
Greengage
Greenwood
Grevillea
Hackberry
Ivory palm
Jacaranda
Jackfruit
Jambolana
Kahikatea
Krummholz
Kurrajong
Lancewood
Lemonwood
Leylandii
Macadamia
Mangostan
Marmalade
Melaleuca
Mirabelle
Mockernut
Monkeypot
Naseberry
Nectarine
Nux vomica
Paloverde
Paperbark
Patchouli
Patchouly
Paulownia
Persimmon
Pistachio
Pitch-pine
Poinciana
Ponderosa
Pontianac
Prickwood
Pricky ash
Primavera
Quebracho
Rauwolfia
Rose-apple
Sandarach
Sapodilla
Saskatoon
Sassafras
Satinwood
Scots pine
Shellbark
Silver ash
Simarouba
Soapberry
Star-anise
Star-apple
Sterculia
Stinkwood
Stone pine
Sweetwood
Tacamahac
Tamarillo
Terebinth
Toothache
Torchwood
Wagenboom
Wayfaring
Whitebeam
White pipe
Whitewood
Wild mango
Wineberry
Wych-hazel
Yggdrasil
Zebrawood

***10 letters:***
Arbor Vitae
Axe-breaker
Bitterbark
Blackbully
Breadfruit
Bulletwood
Bunya-bunya
Buttonball
Buttonwood
Calamondin
Calliature
Candle-wood
Cannonball
Carico-wood
Chamaerops
Chaulmugra
Cheesewood
Chinaberry
Chinquapin
Cottonwood
Cowrie-pine
Eucalyptus
Fiddlewood
Flamboyant
Flindersia
Frangipani
Ginkgoales
Green-heart
Hackmatack
Hobblebush
Ilang-ilang
Jaboticaba
Jippi-jappa
Kotokutuku
Letter-wood
Lilly-pilly
Macrocarpa
Manchineel
Mangabeira
Mangosteen
Manna-birch
Marblewood
Nithofagus
Palisander
Paper birch
Pepperidge
Pohutukawa
Prickly ash
Quercitron
Ribbonwood
Sandalwood
Sappanwood
Schefflera
Silk-cotton
Silverbell
Sneezewood
Spotted gum
Strawberry
Tawheowheo
Traveller's
Turpentine
Witch-hazel
Witgatboom
Woollybutt
Yellowwood
Ylang-ylang

***11 letters:***
Anchovy-pear
Appleringie
Bladderwort
Bristlecone
Bristlepine
Cabbage-palm
Chaulmoogra
Chokecherry
Copper beech
Crack-willow
Cryptomeria
Dawn redwood
Dipterocarp
Eriodendron
Flamboyante
Fothergilla
Gingerbread
Guttapercha
Honey locust
Horseradish
India rubber
Jesuit's bark
Leatherwood
Lignum vitae
Liquidambar
Loblolly bay
Maceranduba
Metasequoia
Mountain ash
Osage orange
Pomegranate

Purpleheart
Pussy-willow
Retinispora
River red gum
Shittimwood
Silver birch
Sitka spruce
Stringybark

*12 letters:*
African tulip
Haemotoxylon
Hercules' club
Liriodendron
Mammee-sapota
Masseranduba
Monkey-puzzle
Norway spruce
Raspberry jam
Washingtonia
Wellingtonia

*13 letters:*
Barbados pride
Cream of tartar
Paper-mulberry

*14 letters:*
Western hemlock

*15 letters:*
Emblic Myrobalan

---

**Tree-climber, Tree-dweller** Monkey, Opossum, Sciurus, Squirrel, Unau
**Tree disease** Dutch elm, Oak wilt, Waldsterben
**Tree-man** Ent
**Tree-moss** Usnea
**Tree-paeony** Moutan
**Tree-pecker** Picus
**Tree-shrew** Tana
**Treetop** Canopy
**Trefoil** Bird's foot, Clover, Hop, Lotos, Lotus
**Trek(ker)** Afrikaner, Hike, Journey, Leg, Odyssey, Safari, Yomp
**Trellis** Espalier, Lattice, Pergola, Treillage, Treille
**Tremble, Trembling, Tremor** Aftershock, Aquiver, Ashake, Ashiver, Butterfly, Dither, Dodder, Foreshock, Fremitus, Heartquake, Hotter, Intention, Judder, Marsquake, Milk sickness, Moonquake, Palpitate, Quail, Quake, Quaver, Quiver, Seism, Seismal, → SHAKE, Shiver, Shock, Shudder, Stound, Temblor, Thrill, Titubation, Trepid, Twitchy, Vibrant, Vibrate, Vibration, Vibratiuncle, Vibrato, Wobble, Wuther, Yips
**Tremendous** Big, Enormous, Exceeding, Extreme, Gargantuan, Howling, Immense, Marvellous, Thundering
**Tremolo** Bebung, Quaver, Trill(o)
▸**Tremor** *see* TREMBLE
**Tremulous** Cranky, Dithering, Hirrient, Quaking, Quavery, Shaky, Timorous, Vibrato
**Trench(er), Trencherman** Boyau, Cunette, Cuvette, Delf, Delph, Dike(r), → DITCH, Dyke(r), Encroach, Fleet, Foss(e), Foxhole, Fur(r), Furrow, Grip(e), Gullet, Gutter, Knife and fork, Leat, Leet, Line, Mariana, Moat, Oceanic, Outwork, Passage, Rill, Rille, Ring-dyke, Robber, Salient, Sap, Shott, Slidder, Slit, Sod, Sondage
**Trenchant** Acid, Cutting
**Trend(y), Trendsetter** A la mode, Bandwagon, Bellwether, Bent, Bias, Chic, Climate, Cool, Drift, Fad, Fashion, Groovy, Hep, Hip, Hipster, In, Latest, Mainstream, Mode, Modern, New Age(r), Newfangled, Pacemaker, Pop, Poserish, Posey, Rage, Right-on, Smart, Style, Swim, Tendency, Tendenz, Tenor, Tide, Tonnish
**Trepidation** Butterflies, Timidity
**Trespass(er), Trespassing** Aggravated, Encroach, Errant, Hack, Impinge, Infringe, Intrude, Offend, Peccancy, Sin, Trench, Usurp, Wrong(doer)
**Tress(es)** Curl, Elf-locks, Lock, Ringlet, Switch, Tallent
**Trestle** Sawhorse
**Triad** Chord, Harmonic, Ternion, Three, Trey, Trimurti, Trinity
**Trial** Acid test, Adversity, Affliction, Appro, Approbation, Approval, Assize, Attempt, Audition, Bane, Bernoulli, Bout, Burden, Case, Clinical, Compurgation, Corsned, Court-martial, Cow, Cross, Dock, Drumhead, Dry run, Dummy run, Empirical, Essay, → EXPERIMENT, Field, Fitting, Go, Hearing, Horse, Jeddart justice, Jethart justice, Lydford law, Lynch, Nuremberg, Ordeal, Pest, Pilot, Pree, Probation, Proof, Race, Rehearsal, Reliability, Rigour, Road test, Salem, Scramble, Sheepdog, Show, Shy, State, Taste, Test, Test bed, Test drive, Time
**Triangle(d), Triangular** Acute, Bermuda, Circular, Cosec, Deltoid, Equilateral, Eternal, Frame, Gair, Golden, Gore, Gyronny, Isosceles, Obtuse, Pascal's, Pedimental, Pendentive,

Pyramid, Rack, Right-angled, Scalene, Similar, Spherical, Three-cornered, Trigon, Triquetral, Tromino, Warning

**Trias(sic)** Bunter, Keuper, Muschelkalk, Rhaetic

**Triathlon** Iron man

**Tribe(s), Tribal, Tribesman** Amalekite, Ammonites, Angle, Ashanti, Asher, Bedouin, Benjamin, Celt, Cherokee, Cimmerii, Clan(nish), Cree, Creek, Crow, Dan, Dinka, D(a)yak, Dynasty, Edomites, Ephraim, Family, Gad, Gens, Gentes, Gentilic, Gond, Goth, Guarani, Hapu, Helvetii, Hittite, Horde, Hottentot, Ibo, Iceni, Israelite, Issachar, Iwi, Jat, Judah, Kenite, Kurd, Lashkar, Levi, Levite, Longobardi, Lost, Manasseh, Masai, Maya, Moabite, Mongol, Moro, Naga, Nair, Naphtali, Nation, Nayar, Nervii, Ngati, Ordovices, Ostrogoths, Pathan, Phyle, Picts, →**RACE**, Reuben, Riff, Rod, Sakai, Salian, Schedule, Senones, Senussi, Sept, Shawnee, Silures, Simeon, Strandloper, Tasaday, Teuton, Trinobantes, Ute, Vandals, Wolof, Wyandot(te), X(h)osa, Zebulun

**Tribune, Tribunal** Aeropagus, Bema, Bench, →**COURT**, Divan, Employment, Forum, Hague, Industrial, Leader, Platform, Rienzi, Rota, Star-chamber, Waitangi

**Tributary** Affluent, Bogan, Branch, Confluent, Creek, Feeder, Fork

**Tribute** Cain, Capelline, Citation, Commemoration, Compliment, Crants, Danegeld, Dedication, Deodate, →**DUE**, Encomium, Epitaph, Eulogy, Festschrift, Floral, Gavel, Heriot, Homage, Kain, Knee, Memento, Ode, Panegyric, Peter's pence, →**PRAISE**, Rome-penny, Rome-scot, Salute, Scat(t), Tax, Testament, Testimonial, Toast, Toll, Wreath, Wroth

**Trice** Flash, Instant, Wink

**Trichosanthin** Q

**Trick(ed), Trickery, Tricks(ter), Tricky** Antic, Art, Artifice, Attrap, Awkward, Bamboozle, Begunk, Book, Bunco, Bunko, Cantrip, Capot, Catch, Charley pitcher, Cheat, Chicane(ry), Chouse, Claptrap, Cod(-act), Cog, Con(fidence), Coyote, Crook, Davenport, Deceit, Deception, Deck, Decoy, Deke, Delicate, Delude, Device, Dirty, →**DO**, →**DODGE**, Double, Dupe, Elf, Elfin, Elvan, Elven, Entrap, Fard, Feat, Fetch, Fiddle, Find the lady, Finesse, Finicky, Flam, Flim-flam, Fob, Fox, Fraud, Fun, Gambit, Game, Gammon, Gaud, Get, Gimmick, Gleek, Glike, Gowk, Guile, Had, Hanky-panky, Hat, Hey presto, Hoax, Hocus(-pocus), Hoodwink, Hornswoggle, Hot potato, Hum, Hype, Illude, Illusion, Illywhacker, Imposture, Indian rope, Jadery, Jape, Jockey, John, Kid, Kittle, Knack, Knotty, Lark, Lead on, Legerdemain, Leg pull, Magic, Magician, Magsman, Mislead, Monkey, Monkey-shine, Mousetrap, Murphy's game, Nap, Nasruddin, Outfox, Palter, Parlour, Pass, Pawk, Phish, Plant, Pleasantry, Pliskie, Prank, Prestige, Pretty, Put-on, Quick, Ramp, Raven, Reak, Reik, Rex, Rig, Rope, Ropery, Roughie, Ruse, Scam, Sell, Set-up, Shanghai, Shavie, Shenanigan, Shifty, Shill, Skin-game, Skite, Skul(l)duggery, Skylark, Skyte, Slam, Sleight, Slight, Slinter, Sophism, Spoof, Stall, Stealth, Stint, Stunt, Subterfuge, Sug, Swiftie, Take in, Thimble-rig, Three-card, Ticklish, Tip, Trait, Trap, Tregetour, Trump, Turn, Tweedler, Undercraft, Underplot, Vole, Wangle, Wheeze, Wile, Wrinkle

▹**Trick** *may indicate* an anagram

**Trickle** Drib(ble), Driblet, Drip, Dropple, Gutter, Leak, Ooze, Rill, Seep

**Trickless** Misère

**Triclinic** Anorthic

**Tricycle** Pedicab

**Trident** Fork, Plane, Submarine, Trisul(a)

**Trifle(s), Trifling** Bagatelle, Banal, Baubee, Bauble, Bibelot, Birdseed, Bit, Bric-a-brac, Bubkes, Cent, Chickenfeed, Coquette, Dabble, Daidle, Dalliance, →**DALLY**, Denier, Desipient, Dessert, Dilly-dally, Do, Doit, Faddle, Falderal, Falderol, Fallal, Fattrell, Feather, Fewtril, Fiddle, Fiddle-faddle, Fig, Fingle-fangle, Fizgig, Flamfew, Fleabite, Flirt, Folderol, Fool, Footle, Fribble, Frippery, Fritter, Frivol, Gewgaw, Idle, Inconsequential, Insignificant, Iota, Kickshaw, Knick-knack, Luck-penny, Mere, Mess, Mite, Nick-nacket, Niff-naff, Nothing, Nugae, Nugatory, Nyaff, Old song, Palter, Paltry, Peanuts, Peddle, Peppercorn, Petty, Philander, Picayune, Piddle, Piffle, Pin, Pingle, Pittance, Play, Potty, Quelquechose, Quiddity, Quiddle, Sherry, Slight, Small beer, Small wares, Smatter, Song, Sport, Stiver, Strae, Straw, Sundry, Sweet Fanny Adams, Sweet nothing, Tiddle, Tom, Toy, Trinket, Trivia, Whifflery, Whim-wham, Whit

**Trig(onometry)** Neat, Sech, Spherical, Tosh, Trim
**Trigger** Activate, Catalyst, Detent, Detonate, Fuse, Hair, Instigate, Krytron, Pawl, Precipitate, Schmitt, Set off, Spark, Start, Switch on, Touch off, Tripwire
**Trill(ed), Triller, Trilling** Burr, Churr, Hirrient, Quaver, Ribattuta, Roll, Staphyle, Trim, Twitter, Warble, Yodel
**Trilobite** Olenellus, Olenus, Paradoxide
**Trim(med), Trimmer, Trimming** Abridge, Adorn, Adornment, Ballast, Barb, Bleed, Braid, Bray, Chipper, Clip, Dapper, Defat, Dinky, Dress, Edging, Ermine, Face, Falbala, Fettle, File, Froufrou, Galloon, Garni, Garnish, Garniture, Gimp, Guimpe, Haircut, Hog, Macramé, Macrami, Marabou, Neat, Net(t), Order, Ornament, Pare, Passament, Passement(erie), Pipe, Plight, Posh, Preen, Proign, Proyn(e), Pruin(e), Prune, Roach, Robin, Ruche, Sax, Sett, Shear, Shipshape, Sleek, Smirk, Smug, Sned, Snod, Soutache, → **SPRUCE**, Straddle, Stroddle, Strodle, Stylist, Svelte, Tiddley, → **TIDY**, Time-server, Top, Torsade, Trick, Whippersnipper, Wig
**Trinidadian** Carib
**Trinity, Trinitarian** Mathurin(e), Prosopon, Triad, Trimurti, Triune, Word
**Trinket(s)** Amulet, Bauble, Bibelot, Bijou(terie), Charm, Curio, Falderal, Fallal, Folderol, Knickknack, Nicknack, Toy, Trankum, Trumpery
**Trio** Catch, Graces, Magi, Randan, Randem, Skat, Terzetto, Threesome
**Trip(per)** Awayday, Cook's tour, Cruise, Dance, Day, Druggie, Ecotour, Ego, Emmet, Errand, Expedition, → **FALL**, Field, Flight, Flip, Guilt, Head, High, Hop, Jaunt, Joint, Jolly, Journey, Junket, Kilt, Lap, Launch, Link, Outing, Passage, Pleasure, Ply, Power, Ride, Round, Run, Sail, Sally, Sashay, School, Spin, Spurn, → **STUMBLE**, Tootle, Tour, Trek, Trial, Tumble, Voyage
▷**Trip** *may indicate* an anagram
**Tripe** Abracadabra, Bosh, Bull, Caen, Claptrap, Entrails, Honeycomb, Offal, Plain, Rot
**Triple, Triplet** Codon, Hemiol(i)a, Perfect, Sdrucciola, Ternal, Tiercet, Treble, Trifecta, Trilling, Trin(e), Tripling
**Tripod** Cat, Cortina, Highhat, Oracle, Triangle, Trippet, Trivet
**Triptych** Volet
**Trishaw** Cycle
**Trite** Banal, Boilerplate, Cornball, Corny, Hackneyed, Hoary, Laughable, Mickey Mouse, Novelettish, Pabulum, Platitude, Rinky-dink, Stale, Stock, Time-worn, Truism, Well-worn, Worn
**Triton** Eft, Evet, Ewt, Newt, Trumpet-shell
**Triumph(ant)** Church, Cock-a-hoop, Codille, Cowabunga, Crow, Eureka, Exult, Glory, Impostor, Jubilant, Killing, Oho, Olé, Ovation, Palm, Prevail, Succeed, Victorious, → **WIN**
**Triumvir** Caesar, Crassus, Pompey
**Trivet** Brandise, Tripod, Trippet
**Trivia(l), Triviality** Adiaphoron, Bagatelle, Balaam, Bald, → **BANAL**, Bathos, Footling, Frippery, Frothy, Futile, Idle, Inconsequential, Light, Minutiae, Nitpicking, No-brainer, Nonentity, Nothingism, Paltry, Pap, Peppercorn, Pettifoggery, Petty, Picayune, Piddling, Piffling, Puerile, Shallow, Small, Small beer, Small fry, Snippety, Squirt, Squit, Toy(s), Twaddle, Vegie
**Trixie** Bea
**Trochee** Choree
**Troglodyte** Ape, Caveman, Hermit, Spelean, Wren
**Trojan** Aeneas, Agamemnon, Dardan(ian), Iliac, Paris, Priam, Teucrian, Troic
**Troll** → **FISH**, Gnome, Rove, Spoon, Trawl, Warble
**Trolley** Brute, Cart, Crane, Dinner-wagon, Dolly, Gurney, Hostess, Shopping, Tea, Teacart, Traymobile, Truck, Trundler
▸**Trollop** *see* **LOOSE(N)**
**Trombone** Bass, Posaune, Sackbut, Tenor
**Trompe l'oeil** Quadratura, Quadrature
**Troop(s), Trooper** Alpini, Anzac, Band, BEF, Brigade, Camelry, Cavalry, Cohort, Company, Depot, Detachment, Dog-of-war, Garrison, Guard, Horde, Household, Logistics, Midianite,

Milice, Militia, Monkeys, Parachute, Pultan, Pulton, Pultoon, Pultun, SAS, School, Scout, Shock, Sky, → **SOLDIER**, Sowar, State, Storm, Subsidiary, Tp, Turm(e), Velites

**Troopship** Transport

**Trope** Euouae, Evovae

**Trophy** Adward, Ashes, → **AWARD**, Bag, Belt, Brush, Cup, Emmy, Jackpot, Memento, Palm, Palm d'Or, Plate, → **PRIZE**, Scalp, Schneider, Shield, Silverware, Spoils, Tourist, Triple crown, TT

**Tropic(al)** Cancer, Capricorn, Derris, Jungle, Neogaea, Sultry

**Trot(ter), Trot out** Air, Clip, Crib, Crubeen, Hag, Job, Jog, Passage, Pettitoes, Piaffe, Pony, Ranke, Red(-shirt), Rising, Tootsie, Trotskyist

**Troth** Perfay, Troggs

**Trotsky(ist)** Entr(y)ism, Leon, Militant Tendency

**Troubador** Blondel, Griot, Manrico, Minstrel, Singer, Sordello

**Trouble(s), Troubled, Troublemaker, Troublesome** Ache, Ado, Affliction, Aggrieve, Aggro, Agitate, Agitator, Ail, Alarm, Annoy, Assail, Bale, Barrat, Bedevil, Beleaguer, Beset, → **BOTHER**, Bovver, Breakdown, Brickle, Burden, Care, Coil, Concern, Debate, Disaster, Dismay, Disquiet, Distress, Disturb, Dog, Dolour, Double, Eat, Esclandre, Exercise, Fash, Fashious, Finger, Firebrand, Fossick, Fret, Frondeur, Fun and games, Fuss, Gram(e), Gremlin, Grief, Hag-ride, Harass, Hard-pressed, Harry, Hassle, Hatter, Heat, Heist, Hellion, Hot potato, Hot water, Howdyedo, Hydra, Incommode, Inconvenience, Infest, → **IN TROUBLE**, Irk, Jam, Kaugh, Kiaugh, Malcontent, Mayhem, Mess, Mischief, Mixer, Moil, Molest, Noy, Onerous, Perturb, Pester, Pestiferous, Picnic, Plague, Play up, Poke, Reck, Rioter, Rub, Ruffle, Scamp, Scrape, Shake, Shtook, Shtuck, Soup, Spiny, Stir, Stirrer, Storm, Sturt, Tartar, Teen, Teething, Thorny, Tine, Toil, Trial, Tsouris, Tsuris, Turn-up, Tyne, Typhoid Mary, Unpleasant, Unrest, Unsettle, Upsetter, Varmint, Vex, Wife, → **WORRY**

**Trouble-free** Gallio

**Trouble-shooter** Ombudsman

▷**Troublesome** *may indicate* an anagram

**Trough** Back, Backet, Bed, Buddle, Channel, Chute, Culvert, Depression, Dip, Graben, Gutter, Hod, Hopper, Hutch, Langmuir, Launder, Leachtub, Manger, Pneumatic, Puerto Rico, Sand-trap, Sheep-dip, Stock, Straik, Strake, Syncline, Troffer, Tundish, Tye, Vale, Watering

**Trounce** → **BEAT**, Hammer, Thrash, Thump

**Trouser(s)** Bags, Bell-bottoms, Bloomers, Breeches, Breeks, Bumsters, Capri pants, Cargo pants, Chinos, Churidars, Clam-diggers, Combat, Continuations, Cords, Corduroys, Cossacks, Culottes, Cut-offs, Daks, Denims, Drainpipe, Drawers, Ducks, Dungarees, Eel-skins, Flannels, Flares, Galligaskins, Gaskins, Gauchos, Hip-huggers, Hipsters, Indescribables, Inexpressibles, Innominables, Jazzpants, Jeans, Jeggings, Jodhpurs, Jogging bottoms, Jog-pants, Kaccha, Ke(c)ks, Knee cords, Lederhosen, Leggings, Levis, Longs, Loon-pants, Loons, Moleskins, Overalls, Oxford bags, Palazzo (pants), Palazzos, Pantalet(te)s, Pantaloons, Pants, Pedal pushers, Pegtops, Plus-fours, Plus-twos, Pyjamas, Rammies, Reach-me-downs, Salopettes, Shalwar, Ski pants, Slacks, Stirrup pants, Stovepipes, Strides, Strossers, Sweatpants, Thornproofs, Trews, Trouse, Trunk-breeches, Unmentionables, Unutterables, Utterless

**Trout** Aurora, Brook, Brown, Bull, Char(r), Coral, Cutthroat, Finnac(k), Finnock, Fish, Gillaroo, Hag(fish), Herling, Hirling, Kamloops, Peal, Peel, Phinnock, Pogies, Quintet, Rainbow, Salmon, Sewen, Sewin, Speckled, Splake, Steelhead, Togue, Whitling

**Trow** Faith, Meseems

**Trowel** Float, Slicker

**Troy** Ilium, Laomedon, Sergeant, T, Weight

**Truant** Absentee, AWOL, Bunk off, Dodge, Hooky, Idler, Kip, Mich(e), Mitch, Mooch, Mouch, Skive, Wag

**Truce** Armistice, Barley, Ceasefire, Fainites, Fains, Hudna, Interlude, Keys, Pax, Stillstand, Treague, Treaty

**Truck** Bakkie, Bogie, Breakdown, Business, Cabover, Cattle, Cocopan, Dealings, Dolly, Dray, Dumper, Fire, Flatbed, Forklift, Haul, Hopper, Journey(-weight), → **LORRY**, Low-loader, Maatatu, Monster, Pallet, Panel, Pick-up, Road-train, Semi, Skip, Sound, Stacking, Tipper, Tommy, Tow(ie), Traffic, Tram, Trolley, Trundle, Ute, Utility, Van, Wrecker

**Truckdriver** Teamster

**Trudge** Footslog, Jog, Lumber, Pad, Plod, Stodge, Stramp, Taigle, Traipse, Trash, Trauchle, Trog, Vamp, Wade

**True** Accurate, Actual, Apodictic, Axiomatic, Candid, Constant, Correct, Exact, Factual, Faithful, Genuine, Honest, Indubitable, Leal, Literal, Loyal, Platitude, Plumb, Pure, Real, Realistic, Richt, Right, Sooth, Straight, Vera, Very

**Truffle** Tartuffe, Tuber, Tuberaceae

**Trug** Basket, Wisket

**Truly** Certainly, Certes, Fegs, Forsooth, Honestly, Indeed, Insooth, Surely, Verily, Yea

**Trump(s), Trumpet(er)** Agami, Alchemy, Alchymy, Armstrong, Bach, Bass, Blare, Blast, Bray, Buccina, Bugle(r), Call, Card, Carnyx, Clang, Clarion, Conch, Cornet, Corona, Crossruff, Crow, Daffodil, Ear, Elephant, Extol, Fanfare, Hallali, Herald, Honours, → **HORN**, Invent, Jew's, Last, Lituus, Long ten, Lur(e), Lurist, Manille, Marine, Megaphone, → **NO TRUMP**, Overruff, Pedro, Proclaim, Ram's-horn, Rant, Resurrect, Rogue, Ruff, Salpingian, Salpinx, Sancho, Satchmo, Sennet, Shell, Shofar, Shophar, Slug-horn, Speaking, Splash, Surpass, Swan, Tantara, Tantarara, Tar(at)antara, Theodomas, Tiddy, Triton, Triumph, Tuba

**Trumpery** Fattrels, Jimcrack, Paltry, Trashy

**Truncate(d)** Abridge, Abrupt, Cut, Dock, Shorten, Snub

**Truncheon** Baton, Billie, Billy, Blackjack, Cosh, Night-stick, Warder

**Trundle** Hump, Roll, Trill, Troll, Wheel

**Trunk(s)** Aorta(l), A-road, Body, Bole, Box, Bulk, Bus, But(t), Caber, Cabin, Carcase, Chest, Coffer, Hose, Imperial, Log, Nerve, Peduncle, Pollard, Portmanteau, Portmantle, Proboscis, Puncheon, Ricker, Road, Saratoga, Shorts, STD, Steamer, Stock, Stud, Suitcase, Synangium, Togs, Torso, Valise, Wardrobe

**Truss** → **BIND**, Ligate, Oop, Oup, Sheaf, Tie, Upbind

**Trust(y), Trusting, Trustworthy** Active, Affy, Apex, Authentic, Belief, Bet on, Blind, Bona fide, Box, Camaraderie, Care, Carnegie, Cartel, Charge, Charitable, Combine, Confide, Count on, Credit, Dependable, Dewy-eyed, Discretionary, Endowment, Escrow, → **FAITH**, Fidelity, Fiduciary, Foundation, Gullible, Honest, Hope, Hospital, Investment, Leal, Lippen, Loyal, Naif, National, NT, Reliable, Reliance, Rely, Repose, Reputable, Responsible, Sound, Special, Split, Staunch, Tick, Trojan, Trow, True, Trump, Unit

**Trustee** Agent, Executor, Fiduciary, Judicial, Pensioneer, Public, Tr

**Truth(ful), Truism** Accuracy, Alethic, Axiom, Bromide, Cliché, Cold turkey, Dharma, Dialectic, → **FACT**, Facticity, Faction, Forsooth, Gospel, Griff, Home, Honesty, Idea(l), Logical, Maxim, Naked, Necessary, Pravda, Principle, Reality, Sober, Sooth, Soothfast, Strength, Troggs, Veracity, Veridical, Verisimilitude, Verity, Vraisemblance

**Try(ing), Tried** After, Aim, Approof, Arraign, Assay, Attempt, Audition, Bash, Bate, Bid, Birl, Burden, Burl, Conative, Contend, Court martial, Crack, Effort, Empiric(utic), → **ENDEAVOUR**, Essay, Examine, Experiment, Fand, Fish, Fling, Foretaste, Go, Gun for, Harass, Hard, Hear, Highly, Impeach, Importunate, Irk, Noy, Offer, Ordalium, Ordeal, Penalty, Pesky, Pop, Practise, Pree, Prieve, Prove, Push-over, → **SAMPLE**, Seek, Shot, Sip, Stab, Strain, Strive, Struggle, Tackle, Taste, Tax, Tempt, Test, Touchdown, → **TRIAL**, Whirl

**Tryst** Assignation, Date, Rendezvous

**Tsar(ist)** Alexis, Boris, Drug, Emperor, Godunov, Ivan the Terrible, Octobrist, Peter the Great, Romanov, Ruler, Tyrant

**TT** Dry, Race, Rechabite, Soberside

**Tub(by), Tubbiness, Tubman, Tub-thumper** Ash-leach, Back, Bath, Boanerges, Bran, Bucket, Cooper, Corf, Cowl, Dan, Demagogue, Diogenes, Dolly, Endomorph, Firkin, Hip bath, Jacuzzi, Keeve, Kid, Kieve, Kit, Luckydip, Mashing, Meat, Obese, Pin, Podge, Pot-bellied, Powdering, Pudge, Pulpit, Rolypoly, Seasoning, Stand, Swill, Tun, Twin, Vat, Wash, Whey

**Tuba** Bass, Bombardon, Euphonium, Helicon

**Tube, Tubing, Tubular** Acorn, Arteriole, Artery, Barrel, Blowpipe, Bronchus, Buckyball, Buckytube, Burette, Calamus, Camera, Canaliculus, Can(n)ula, Capillary, Cartridge, Casing, Catheter, Cathode-ray, Cave, Conduit, Crookes, Delivery, Diffusion, Digitron, Diode, Discharge, Drain, Draw, Drift, Dropper, Duct, Electron, Endiometer, Epididymis, Eustachian,

Extension, Fallopian, Fire, Fistula, Flash, Fluorescent, Fulgurite, Geissler, Germ, Glowstick, Grommet, Hawsepipe, Hose, Iconoscope, Idiot box, Image (orthicon), Inner, Kenotron, Kinescope, Klystron, Lightning, Macaroni, Malpighian, Matrass, Metro, Morris, Nasogastric, Neural, Nixie, Optic, Orthicon, Oval, Oviduct, Pastille, Peashooter, Pentode, Picture, → **PIPE**, Pipe-stem, Pipette, Piping, Pitot(-static), Pneumatic, Pollen, Postal, Promethean, Salpinx, Saticon®, Saucisse, Saucisson, Schnorkel, Scroll, Shadow-mask, Shock, Sieve, Siphon(al), Siphonet, Siphonostele, Siphuncle, Skelp, Skiatron, Sleeve, Slide, Snorkel, Spaghetti, Speaking, Spout, Staple, Static, Stem, Stent, Stone canal, Storage, Strae, Straw, Strip light, Strobotron, Subway, Sucker, Swallet, Syringe, Tele, Telescope, Teletron, Television, Telly, Terete, Test, Tetrode, Thermionic, Thyratron, Tile, Torpedo, Torricellian, Trachea, Travelling-wave, Triniscope, Trocar, Trochotron, Trunk, Tunnel, Tuppenny, TV, Tyre, U, Underground, Ureter, Urethra, Vacuum, Vas, VDU, Vein, Vena, Venturi, Video, Vidicon®, Worm, X-ray

**Tuber(s)** Arnut, Arracacha, Bulb, Chufa, Coc(c)o, Dahlia, Dasheen, Earth-nut, Eddoes, Ginseng, Jicama, Mashua, Oca, Pignut, Potato, Root, Salep, Taproot, Taro, Tater, Tuckahoe, Yam, Yautia

**Tuberculosis** Consumption, Crewels, Cruel(l)s, Decline, King's evil, Lupus, Lupus vulgaris, Phthisis, Scrofula, White plague

**Tuck** Dart, Food, Friar, Gather, Grub, Hospital corner, Kilt, Pin, Pleat, Rapier, Scran, Truss, Tummy

**Tudor** Stockbrokers'

**Tuesday** Hock, Pancake, Shrove, Super

**Tuff** Peperino, Schalstein

**Tuft(ed)** Aigrette, Amentum, Beard, Candlewick, Catkin, C(a)espitose, Clump, Cluster, Coma, Comb, Cowlick, Crest, Dollop, Ear, Flaught, Floccus, Flock, Goatee, Hank, Hassock, Knop, Knot, Lock, Pappus, Penicillate, Pledget, Quiff, Scopate, Shola, Tait, Tassel, Tate, Toorie, Topknot, Toupee, Tourie, Tussock, Tuzz, Whisk, Wisp

**Tug** Chain, Drag, Haul, Hoick, Jerk, Lug, Pug, → **PULL**, Rive, Rug, Saccade, Ship, Sole, Soole, Sowl(e), Tit, Tow, Towboat, Yank

**Tui** Poebird

**Tuition** Coaching, Grind, Masterclass, Seminal, Sleep-learning

**Tully** Cicero

**Tumble, Tumbler** Acrobat, Cartwheel, Drier, Fall, → **GLASS**, Header, Jack, Jill, Lock, Pitch, Popple, Purl, Realise, Roller-coaster, Spill, Stumble, Tailer, Topple, Touser, Towser, Trip, Twig, Voltigeur, Welter

▷**Tumble** *may indicate* an anagram

**Tumbledown** Decrepit, Dilapidated, Ramshackle, Rickle, Ruinous

**Tumbleweed** Russian

**Tumbril** Caisson

**Tummy** Belly, Colon, Mary, Paunch, Pod

**Tummy-ache** Colic, Gripe, Tormina

**Tumour** Adenoma, Anbury, Angioma, Angiosarcoma, Astroblastoma, Astrocytoma, Burkitt('s) lymphoma, Cancer, Carcinoid, Carcinoma, Carcinosarcoma, Chondroma, Condyloma, Crab(-yaws), Craniopharyngioma, Dermoid, Encanthis, Encephaloma, Enchondroma, Endothelioma, Epulis, Exostosis, Fibroid, Fibroma, Ganglion, Germinoma, Glioblastoma, Glioma, Granuloma, Grape, → **GROWTH**, Gumma, Haemangioma, Haematoma, Hepatoma, Lipoma, Lymphoma, Medulloblastoma, Melanoma, Meningioma, Mesothelioma, Metastasis, Mole, Myeloma, Myoma, Myxoma, Neoplasm, Nephroblastoma, Neuroblastoma, Neurofibroma, Neuroma, Odontoma, -oma, Oncogenesis, Oncology, Osteoclastoma, Osteoma, Osteosarcoma, Papilloma, Polypus, Retinoblastoma, Rhabdomyoma, Rous sarcoma, Sarcoma, Scirrhous, Secondary, Seminoma, Steatoma, Struma, Syphiloma, Talpa, Teratocarcinoma, Teratoma, Thymoma, Wart, Warthin's, Wen, Wilms', Windgall, Wolf, Xanthoma, Yaw

**Tumult, Tumultuous** Brattle, Brawl, Coil, Deray, Disturbance, Ferment, Fracas, Hirdy-girdy, Hubbub, Hurly-burly, Reird, Riot, → **ROAR**, Romage, Rore, Stoor, Stour, Stowre, Stramash, Tew, Tristan, Tristram, Turbulent, → **UPROAR**

**Tumulus** Barrow, How(e), Mote, Motte
**Tun** Cask, Keg, Mash
**Tuna** Ahi, Eel, Pear, Skipjack, Yellowfin
**Tundra** Barren Grounds, Barren Lands
**Tune(s), Tuneful, Tuner, Tuning** Adjust, Air, Aria, Ayre, Canorous, Carillon, Catch, Choral(e), Dial, Dump, Earworm, Étude, Fine, Fork, Gingle, Harmony, Hornpipe, Hunt's up, Jingle, Key, Maggot, Measure, Melisma, → MELODY, Morrice, Morris, Old Hundred, → OUT OF TUNE, Peg, Planxty, Port, Potpourri, Raga, Rant, Ranz-des-vaches, Reel, Scordatura, Signature, Snatch, Song, Spring, Strain, Sweet, Syntonise, Syntony, Temper, Temperament, Theme, Tone, Toy, Tweak
**Tungstate, Tungsten** Scheelite, W, Wolfram
**Tunic** Ao dai, Caftan, Chiton, Choroid, Cote-hardie, Dalmatic, Dashiki, Gymslip, Hauberk, Kabaya, Kaftan, Kameez, Kirtle, K(h)urta, Salwar kameez, → SINGLET, Surcoat, Tabard, Toga
**Tunicate** Pyrosoma, Salpa
**Tunnel(ler)** Blackwall, Bore, Channel, Chunnel, Condie, Countermine, Culvert, Cundy, Earthworm, Euro, Gallery, Head, Mersey, Mine, Mole, Qanat, Railway, Rotherhithe, Sewer, Simplon, Smoke, Stope, Subway, Sure, Syrinx, Transmanche, Tube, Underpass, Warren, Water, Wind, Wormhole
**Tunny** Bonito, Tuna
**Turban** Bandanna, Hat, Mitral, Pagri, Puggaree, Puggery, Puggree, Sash, Scarf, Toque, Tulipant
**Turbid** Cloudy, Dense, Drumly, Roily
**Turbine** Francis, Gas, Impulse, Ram air, Reaction, Steam, Water, Wind
**Turbulence, Turbulent** Agitation, Atmospheric, Becket, Bellicose, Buller, Combustious, Factious, Fierce, Maelstrom, Overfall, Rapids, Roil, Stormy, Unruly
▷**Turbulent, Turbulence** *may indicate* an anagram
**Tureen** Terreen
**Turf** Astro, Caespitose, Clod, Divot, Earth, Fail, Feal, Flaught, Gazo(o)n, → GRASS, Greensward, Kerf, Peat, Racing, Scraw, → SOD, Sward, Territory
**Turk(ic)** Golden Horde, Pasha
**Turk(ish)** Anatolian, Bashaw, Bashkir, Bey, Bimbashi, Bostangi, Byzantine, Caimac(am), Crescent, Effendi, Golden Horde, Grand, Gregory, Horse(tail), Irade, Kaimakam, Kazak(h), Kurd, Mameluke, Mutessarif(at), Omar, Osman(li), Ottamite, Ottoman, Ottomite, Rayah, Scanderbeg, Selim, Seljuk(ian), Seraskier, Spahi, Tartar, Tatar, Timariot, Usak, Uzbeg, Uzbek, Yakut, Young
**Turkey, Turkey-like** Anatolia, Antioch, Bomb, Brush, Brussels, Bubbly(-jock), Cock, Cold, Curassow, Dud, Eyalet, Flop, Gobbler, Lame brain, Lemon, Norfolk, Plain, Poult, Scrub, Stag, Sultanate, Talegalla, Talk, TR, Trabzon, Vulturn
**Turkish delight** Rahat lacoum, Trehala
**Turmeric** Curcumin(e)
**Turmoil** Agitation, Anarchy, Angst, Ariot, Chaos, Confusion, Din, Disruption, Dust, Ferment, Maelstrom, Mess, Pother, Pudder, Stoor, Stour, Tornado, Tracasserie, Tumult, Unrest, Upheaval, → UPROAR, Welter
**Turn(ing), Turn(ed) away, Turn(ed) up, Turns** Acescent, Act, Adapt, Addle, Advert, Alter, Antrorse, Apostrophe, Apotropaic, Avert, Bad, Bank, Become, Bend, Blow in, Buggins, Bump, Canceleer, Cancelier, Caracol(e), Careen, Cartwheel, Cast, Chainé, Chandelle, Change, Char(e), Chore, Christiania, Christie, Christy, Churn, Coarsen, Cock, Coil, Convert, Corotate, Crank(le), Cuff, Curd(le), Curve, Defect, Deflect, Demi-volt(e), Detour, Deviate, Dextrorse, Dig, Digress, Divert, Ear, Earn, Elbow, Evert, Evict, Fadge, Ferment, Flip, Forfend, Go, Good, Gruppetto, Gyrate, Hairpin, Handbrake, Head-off, Hie, High, Hinge, Hup, Immelmann, Influence, Innings, Intussuscept, Invert, Jar, Jink, Jump, Keel, Kick, Laeotropic, Lodging, Lot, Luff, Mohawk, Move, Nip, Number, Obvert, Parallel, Parry, Penchant, Pivot, Plough, Pronate, Prove, PTO, Quarter, Quersprung, Rebut, Recourse, Refer, Refract, Remuage, Retroflex, Retroussé, Retrovert, Rev, Revolt, Ride, Riffle, Rocker, Roll, Root, → ROTATE, Rote, Roulade, Rout, Routine, Screw, Secund, Sheer, → SHOT, Shout, Sicken, Sinistrorse, Skew, Skit, Slew, Slue, Solstice, Sour, → SPELL, Spin, Splay, Spot, Sprain, Star, Start, Stem, Step, Stunt, Swash, Swerve, Swing, Switch, Swivel, Telemark, Thigmotropism, Three-point, Throw, Tiptilt, Tirl,

T-junction, Torque, Transpose, Trend, Trick, Trie, Trochilic, Turtle, Twiddle, Twist, Twizzle, U, Uey, U-ie, Up, Variety, Veer, Versed, Version, Vertigo, Volta, Volte-face, Volutation, Wap, Warp, Wedeln, Wend, Went, → WHEEL, Whelm, Whirl, Whorl, Wimple, Wind, Wrast, Wrest, Wriggle, Zigzag

▷**Turn(ing)** *may indicate* an anagram

**Turn-coat** Apostate, Cato, Defector, Quisling, Rat, Renegade, Rottan, Tergiversate, Traitor

**Turndown** Refusal

**Turner** Axle, Capstan, Centrifuge, Crank, Lana, Lathe, Page, Painter, Pivot, Remueur, Rose-engine, Rotisserie, Spanner, Tina, Worm, Wrench

**Turning point** Crisis, Crossroads, Landmark, Solstice, Watershed

**Turnip(-shaped)** Baggy, Bagie, Hunter, Indian, Jicama, Napiform, Navew, Neep, Prairie, Rutabaga, Shaw, → STUPID PERSON, Swede, Tumshie

▷**Turnip** *may indicate* a watch

**Turnkey** Gaoler, Jailer, Locksman

**Turn on** Boot

**Turn-out, Turn out** Boot, Clothing, Eventuate, Evict, Gathering, Product, Rig, Splay, Style, Team, Transpire, Wear

**Turn over, Turnover** Bridie, Capsize, Careen, Flip, Inversion, Mull, Production, PTO, Samosa, Somersault, TO, Up-end

**Turnpike** Highway, Toll

**Turnstile** Tourniquet

**Turnstone** Tangle-picker

**Turntable** Racer, Rota, Rotator, Round-house

**Turpentine** Galipot, Rosin, Thinner, Turps, Venice

**Turquoise** Aqua, Bone, Cyan, Fossil, Ligure, Occidental, Odontolite, Oriental, Turkey stone

**Turret(ed)** Barmkin, Bartisan, Belvedere, Garret, Gazebo, Louver, Louvre, Mirador, Pepperbox, Pinnacle, Pinnet, Sponson, Tank top, → TOWER, Turriculate

**Turtle, Turtle head** Bale, Box, Calipash, Calipee, Chelone, Cooter, Diamondback, Emys, Floor, Green, Hawk(s)bill, Inverted, Leatherback, Loggerhead, Matamata, Mossback, Mud, Musk, Ninja, Painted, Ridley, Screen, Snapper, Snapping, Soft-shelled, Stinkpot, Terrapin, Thalassian

**Tuscany** Chiantishire

**Tusk** Gam, Horn, Ivory, Tooth, Tush, Walrus

**Tusker** Dicynodont, Elephant, Mastodon

**Tussle** Giust, Grapple, Joust, Mêlée, Scrimmage, Scrum, Scuffle, Skirmish, Touse, Touze, Towse, Towze, Tuilyie, Wrestle

**Tussock** Hassock, Tuft

**Tut(-tut)** Mummy, Och, Pooh

**Tutelary** Guardian, Protector

**Tutor** Abbé, Aristotle, Ascham, Bear, → COACH, Crammer, Don, Edify, Instruct, Leader, Mentor, Preceptor, Répétiteur, Starets, Staretz, Supervisor, Teacher, Train

**Tutorial** Lesson

**Tuxedo** DJ

**TV** Baird, Box, Breakfast, Cable, Car-crash, Closed circuit, Digibox®, Digital, Docudrama, Docusoap, Flat screen, Gogglebox, Idiot-box, Image orthicon, Lime Grove, Medium, Mini-series, Monitor, NICAM, PAL, Pay, Plasma, Reality, SECAM, Sitcom, Sky®, Small screen, Tele, → TELEVISION, Telly, Tie-in, Triniscope, Tube, Video

**Twaddle** Blether, Drivel, Fadaise, Rot, Slipslop, Tripe

**Twang** Drawl, Nasal, Pluck, Plunk, Rhinolalia

**Tweak** Adjust, Fine tune, Modify, Pinch, Pluck, Primp, Twiddle, Twist, Twitch

**Twee** Chocolate box

**Tweed(y)** Donegal, Harris®, Homespun, Lovat, Raploch

**Tweet** Cherup, Chirrup

**Tweezers** Optical

**Twelfth, Twelve** Apostles, Dozen, Epiphany, Glorious, Grouse, Midday, Midnight, N, Night, Noon(tide), Ternion, Twal

**Twenty, Twenty-sided** Icosahedron, Score, Vicenary, Vicennial, Vicesimal, Vigesimal
**Twenty-five, Twentyfifth** Inner, Pony, Quartern, Semi-jubilee
**Twenty-four** Thr(e)ave
**Twenty-one** Blackjack, Pontoon, Vingt-et-un
**Twerp** Pipsqueak
▸**Twice** *see* TWO(SOME)
**Twice-yearly** Biennial, Equinox
**Twiddle** Fidget, Twirl
**Twig(s)** Besom, Birch, Brushwood, Cotton, Cow, Dig, Fathom, Grasp, Kow, Osier, Realise, Reis, Rice, Rod, Rumble, Sarment, See, Sprig, Stick, Sticklac, Switch, Understand, Walking, Wand, Wattle, Whip, Wicker, Withe, Withy
**Twilight** Astronomical, Civil, Cockshut, Crepuscular, Demi-jour, Dimpsy, Dusk, Gloam(ing), Götterdämmerung, Nautical, Ragnarok, Summerdim
**Twill** Cavalry, Chino, Serge
**Twin(s)** Asvins, Castor, Coetaneous, Complementary, Conjoined, Couplet, Didymous, Dioscuri, Ditokous, Dizygotic, Double, Dual, Fraternal, Gemel, Geminate, Gemini, Hemitrope, Identical, Isogeny, Juxtaposition, Kindred, Kray, Look-alike, Macle, Monozygotic, Parabiotic, Pigeon-pair, Pollux, Remus, Romulus, Siamese, Thomas, Tweedledee, Tweedledum
**Twine** Binder, Braid, Coil, Cord, Inosculate, Lace, Packthread, Sisal, Snake, String, Twist, Wreathe
**Twinge** Pang, Scruple, Stab, Twang
**Twinkle, Twinkling** Gleam, Glimmer, Glint, Mo(ment), Shimmer, → SPARKLE, Starnie, Trice
**Twirl** Spin, Swivel, Tirl, Tirlie-wirlie, Trill, Trundle, Twiddle, Twizzle, Whirl
▹**Twirling** *may indicate* an anagram
**Twist(ed), Twister, Twisting, Twisty** Aglee, Agley, Anfractuous, Askant, Askew, Baccy, Back-flip, Becurl, Bought, Braid, Buckle, Card-sharper, Chisel, Coil, Contort, Convolution, Corkscrew, Crinkle, Crinkum-crankum, Crisp, Cue, Curl(icue), Curliewurlie, Cyclone, Deform, Detort, Diddle, Dishonest, Distort, → DODGE, Eddy, Embraid, Entrail, Entwine, Garrot, Gnarl, Helix, Imposture, Kink, Knittle, Lemon peel, Loop, Mangulate, Mat, Meander, Misshapen, Möbius strip, Oliver, Pandanaceous, Perverse, Plait, Quirk, Raddle, Ravel, Rick, Rogue, Rotate, Rove, Serpent, Skew, Slew, Slub(b), Slue, Snake, Snarl, Spin, Spiral, Sprain, Squiggle, Squirm, Strand, Swivel, Tendril, Thraw(n), Torc, Tornado, Torque, Torsade, Torsion, Torticollis, Tortile, Turn, Tweak, Twiddle, Twine, Twirl, Twizzle, Typhoon, Valgus, Volvulus, Wamble, Warp, Welkt, Wigwag, Wind, Wound-wrap, Wrast, Wreathe, Wrench, Wrest, Wrethe, Wrick, Wriggle, Wring, Writhe, Wry, Yaw, Zigzag
▹**Twisted, Twisting** *may indicate* an anagram
**Twit, Twitter** Airhead, Birdbrain, Birdsong, Chaff, Cheep, Cherup, Chirp, Chirrup, Dotterel, Gear(e), Giber, → JEER, Rag, Stupid, Taunt, Tweet, Warble
**Twitch(ing), Twitchy** Athetosis, Birdwatch, Clonic, Edgy, Fibrillation, Fidget, Grass, Jerk, Life-blood, Nervy, Saccadic, Sneer, Spasm, Start, Subsultive, Tic, Tig, Tippet, Tit, Toss, Tweak, Twinge, Vellicate, Yips
**Two(some), Twofold, Twice** Bice, Bis, Bisp, Both, Brace, Company, Couple(t), Deuce, Double, Duad, Dual, Duet, Duo, Duple, Dyad, Item, → PAIR, Snake-eyes, Swy, Tête-à-tête, Twain, Twins, Twister
**Two-coloured** Pied
**Two-edged** Ancipitous
**Two-faced** Dihedral, Dorsiventral, Hypocritical, Janus, Redan
**Two-gallon** Peck
**Two-headed** Amphisbaenic, Dicephalous, Orthos
**Two hundred** H
**Two hundred and fifty** E, K
**Two-master** Brig
**Two-piece** Bikini
**Two-pronged** Bidental

**Two-rayed** Diactinal
**Two-sided** Bilateral, Equivocatory
**Two thousand** Z
**Two-time** Cheat
**Two-tone** Shot, Trillo
**Two-up** Kip, Swy
**Two-way** Contraflow
**Two-wheeler** Bicycle, Scooter
**Tycoon** Baron, Empire-builder, Entrepreneur, Fat cat, Gates, Magnate, Mogul, Murdoch, Nabob, Oligarch, Onassis, Packer, Plutocrat, Shogun
**Tyke** Geit, RC
**Tympany, Tympanum** Castanets, Cymbal, Drum, Eardrum, Kitchen, Triangle, Xylophone
**Tyneside(r)** Geordie, George
**Type(s), Typify, Typing** A, Agate, Aldine, Antimony, Antique, B, Balaam, Baskerville, Bastard, Batter, Beard, Bembo, Black-letter, Block, Blood, Bodoni, Body, Bold face, Bold Roman, Bourgeois, Braille, Brand, Brevier, Brilliant, Canon, Caslon, Category, Character, Chase, Cicero, Clarendon, Class, Columbian, Condensed, Cut, Egyptian, Elite, Elzevir, Em, Emblem, Embody, Emerald, En(nage), English, Epitomise, Exemplar, Face, Font, Footer, Form(e), Founder's, Fount, Fraktur, Fudge, Garamond, Gem, Generic, Genre, Gent, Gothic, Great primer, Gutenberg, Hair, Hobo, Hot metal, Ilk, Image, Kern(e), Key, Keyboard, Kidney, Kind, Late-star, Ligature, Light-faced, Logotype, Longprimer, Ludlow, Make, Mating, Melanochroi, Minion, Modern, Monospaced, Moon, Mould, Mullioned, Non-pareil, Norm, Old English, Old-face, Old Style, Paragon, Pattern, Pearl, Peculiar, Personality, Pi, Pica, Pie, Plantin, Point, Primer, Print, Quad(rat), Roman, Ronde, Ruby, Sanserif, Secretary, Semibold, Serif, Serological, Slug, → **SORT**, Sp, Species, Spectral, Stanhope, Stereo, Style, Talbotype, Times, Times Roman, Tissue, Touch, Variety, Version
▷**Type of** *may indicate* an anagram
**Typesetting** Hot metal
**Typewriter** Golfball, Olivetti®, Portable, Stenograph, Stenotype®, Varityper®
**Typhoid, Typhus** Camp-fever, Murine, Putrid fever, Scrub, Tick-borne
**Typhoon** Cyclone, Hurricane, Monsoon, Tornado, Wind
**Typical** Average, Characteristic, Classic, Echt, Everyman, Natural, Normal, Quintessential, Representative, Standard, Symbolic, True-bred, Usual
**Typist** Audio, Copy, Printer, Steno(grapher), Temp
**Typo** Literal
**Tyrannise(d)** Domineer, Down-trodden, Lord, Under
**Tyrant, Tyranny, Tyrannical** Absolutism, Authoritarian, Autocrat, Caligula, Czar, Despot, Dictator, Domineering, Dominion, Drawcansir, Gelon, Herod, Ivan the Terrible, Lordly, Nero, Oppressor, Pharaoh, Pisistratus, Sardanapalus, Satrap, Stalin, Totalitarian, Tsar, Yoke
**Tyre(s)** Balloon, Cross-ply, Cushion, Earthing, Flab, Flat, Michelin®, Pericles, Pneumatic, Radial(-ply), Recap, Remould, Retread, Shoe, Sidewall, Slick, Snow, Spare, Stepney, Toe in, Tread, Tubeless, Whitewall
**Tyro** Beginner, Ham, Learner, → **NOVICE**, Rabbit, Rookie, Rooky, Starter
**Tyrolese** R(h)aetian

# Uu

**U, U-type** Gent, Unicorn, Universal, Uranium
**U-bend** Airtrap, Drip trap
**Ubiquitous** Everywhere, Inescapable, Omnipresent, Wall-to-wall
**Udder** Bag, Dug
**UFO** Roswell
**Uganda(n)** Obote, .ug
**Ugly** Abhorrent, Butters, Cow, Crow, Customer, Disfigured, Eyesore, Faceache, Foul, Gorgon, Grotesque, Gruesome, Hideous, Homely, Huckery, Ill-favoured, Jolie laide, Loath, Loth, Mean, Monstrosity, Ominous, Plain, Sight, Unsightly
**Ugrian** Ostiak, Ostyak, Samo(y)ed, Vogul
**UK** GB
**Ukase** Decree
**Ukraine, Ukrainian** Russniak, Ruthene, UA
**Ulcer(ous)** Abscess, Aphtha, Bedsore, Canker, Chancre, Chancroid, Decubitus, Duodenal, Enanthema, Fistula, Gastric, Helcoid, Imposthume, Mouth, Noli-me-tangere, Noma, Peptic, Phagedaena, Plague-sore, Pressure sore, Rodent, Rupia, Sore, Varicose, Wolf
**Ulster** NI, Overcoat, Raincoat, Red hand, Ulad
**Ulterior** External, Hidden
**Ultimate(ly)** Absolute, Basic, Deterrent, Endmost, Eventual, Final, Furthest, Last, Maximum, Mostest, Omega, So, Supreme, Thule, Ult
**Ultimatum** Threat
**Ultra** Drastic, Extreme, Mega, Radical
**Ultra-modern** Space age
**Ultra-republican** Leveller
**Ultrasound** Lithotripsy
**Ululate** Wail
**Ulysses** Bloom, Grant, Odysseus
**Umbellifer(ous)** Angelica, Arnut, Car(r)away, Dill, Honewort, Narthex, Pig-nut, Pimpinella, Seseli
**Umber** Burnt, Mottled, Raw, Waved
**Umbilical cord** Navel string
**Umbrage** Offence, Pique, Resentment, Shade
**Umbrella(-shaped)** Brolly, Bubble, Bumbershoot, Chatta, En tout cas, Gamp, Gingham, Gloria, Mush(room), Nuclear, Parasol, Sunshade, Tee
**Umbria** Eugubine, Iguvine
**Umpire** Arb(iter), Byrlawman, Daysman, Decider, Judge, Mediate, Oddjobman, Odd(s)man, Overseer, Oversman, Referee, Rule, Stickler, Thirdsman
**Unabashed** Bare-faced, Brazen, Shameless
**Unable** Can't, Downa-do, Incapable
**Unaccented** Atonic, Proclitic
**Unacceptable** Beyond the pale, Errant, Ineligible, Non-U, Not on, Out, Repugnant, Rude, Stigmatic, Taboo
**Unaccompanied** A cappella, Alone, High-lone, Secco, Single, Solo, Solus
**Unaccustomed** Desuetude, Inusitate, New, Unwonted, Usedn't
**Unacknowledged** Covert
**Unadorned** Au naturel, Austere, Bald, Basic, Naked, Plain, Stark

**Unadulterated** Natural, Pure, Sincere
**Unadventurous** Staid, Stay-at-home
**Unaffected** Artless, Genuine, Homely, Insusceptible, Naif, Naive, Natural, Plain, Sincere, Unattached
**Unaffordable** Prohibitive
**Unaided** Single-handed, Solo
**Unaligned** Neutral
**Unalloyed** Pure
**Unaltered** As is, Constant, Same
**Unambiguous** Categorical, Clear, Direct, Univocal
**Unanimous** Accord, Nem con, Per curiam, Single-minded
**Unanswerable** Erotema, Irrefragable, Irrefutable
**Unappealing** Distasteful, Grim, Offensive, Off-putting, Rank
**Unappeasable** Implacable
**Unappreciated, Unappreciative** Ingrate, Thankless
**Unapproachable** Aloof, Remote
**Unapproved** Black list
**Unarguable** Erotema
**Unarmed** Inerm, → MARTIAL ARTS, Naked, Vulnerable
**Unashamed** Blatant, Brazen, Open
**Unassailable** Cast-iron, Impregnable, Water-tight
**Unassigned** Adespota, Anonymous, Vacant
**Unassisted** Naked eye
**Unassuming** Lowly, Modest
**Unattached** Disengaged, Fancy free, Freelance, Free-standing, Loose
**Unattractive** Demagnetised, Dowdy, Drac(k), Eyesore, Frump(y), Hideous, Lemon, Minger, Munter, Plain, Plug-ugly, Rebarbative, Scungy, Seamy, Skanky, Ugly
**Unattributable** Anon
**Unauthentic, Unauthenticated** Apocryphal, Plagal
▷**Unauthentic** *may indicate* an anagram
**Unavail(able), Unavailing** Bootless, Futile, Ineluctable, Lost, NA, No use, Off, Useless, Vain
**Unavoidable** Enforced, Fatal, Ineluctable, Inevitable, Necessary, Perforce
**Unaware(ness)** Blind-side, Cloistered, Coma, Heedless, Ignorant, Incognisant, Innocent, Insentient, Oblivious, Stupor, Unconscious
**Unbalance(d)** Asymmetric, Deranged, Doolalli, Doolally, Giddy, Loco, Lopsided, Nutty, Out to lunch, Psycho, Skewwhiff, Twisted, Uneven, Wrong-foot
**Unbearable** Bassington, Intolerable, Severe
**Unbeaten, Unbeatable** All-time, Best, Indomitable, Perfect
**Unbecoming, Unbefitting** Improper, Indecent, Infra dig, Shabby, Unfitting, Unseemly, Unsuitable, Unworthy
**Unbelievable, Unbeliever** Agnostic, Atheist, Cassandra, Doubter, Giaour, Heathen, Heretic, Incredible, Infidel, Outlandish, Pagan, Painim, Paynim, Sceptic, Tall, Zendik
**Unbend(ing)** Relax, Relent, Resolute, Steadfast, Stiff, Strict
**Unbent** Relaxed
**Unbiased** Fair, Impartial, Independent, Just, Neutral, Non-partisan, Objective, Open-minded, Unattainted
**Unblemished** Clean, Immaculate, Intact, Spotless, Vestal
**Unblinking** Alert, Astare, Fearless
**Unblock(ing)** Clear, Free, Recanalization
**Unborn** Foetus, Future, Unbred
**Unbounded** Infinite
**Unbowed** In-kneed, Resolute
**Unbranded** Cleanskin, Clear skin, Generic
**Unbreakable, Unbroken** Adamantine, Infrangible, Intact, Inviolate, Nonstop, Sheer
**Unbridled** Fancy free, Footloose, Lawless, Uncurbed, Unrestricted, Unshackled, Untramelled

**Unburden** Confide, Disembosom, Offload, Relieve, Unload
**Uncanny** Eerie, Eldritch, Extraordinary, Geason, Rum, Spooky, Wanchancie, Wanchancy, Weird
**Uncastrated** Stone
**Unceasing** Continuous, Open-ended
**Unceremonious** En famille, Offhand
**Uncertain(ty)** Acatalepsy, Agnostic, Blate, Broken, Chancy, Chary, Confusion, Contingent, Delicate, Dicey, Dither, Dodgy, Doubtful, Dubiety, Equivocal, Grey, Heisenberg, Hesitant, Iffy, Indeterminate, Indistinct, Irresolute, Limbo, Obscure, Parlous, Peradventure, Precarious, Queasy, Questionable, Risky, Shilly-shally, Slippery, Suspense, Tentative, Vagary, Vor, Wide open
▷**Uncertain** *may indicate* an anagram
**Unchallengeable, Unchallenge(d)** Inerrant, Irrecusable, Sackless
**Unchangeable, Unchanged, Unchanging** As is, Enduring, Eternal, Idempotent, Immutable, Intact, Monotonous, Perennial, Pristine, Read only, Semper idem, Stable, Standpat, Timeless
**Uncharacteristic** Atypical
**Uncharged** Neutral, Neutron
**Unchaste** Corrupt, Immodest, Immoral, Impure, Lewd, Light-heeled, Wanton
**Unchecked** Rampant, Raw, Unrestrained
**Unchristian** Islamic, Mean
**Uncivil(ised)** Barbaric, Benighted, Boondocks, Brutish, Discourteous, Disrespectful, Giant-rude, Goth, Heathen, Impolite, Liberty, Lout, Military, Rude, Rudesby, Short, Unmannerly
**Uncle** Abbas, Afrikaner, Arly, Bob, Dutch, Eme, Nunky, Oom, Pawnbroker, Pawnee, Pawnshop, Pledgee, Pop-shop, Remus, Sam, Silas, Tio, Tom, U, Usurer, Vanya
**Unclean** Defiled, Dirty, Impure, Obscene, Ordure, Squalid, Tabu, T(e)refa(h)
**Unclear** Ambitty, Blurred, Cloudy, Foggy, Grey area, Hazy, Inarticulate, Inexplicit, Nebulous, Obscure, Opaque, Overcast, Sketchy, Slurred
**Unclothed** Bald, Nude
**Uncloven** Soliped
**Uncoded** En clair
**Uncomfortable** Awkward, Mean, Spartan, Uneasy
**Uncommitted** Evasive, Free-floating, Laodicean, Neutral
**Uncommon** Aristocratic, Infrequent, Occasional, Rara avis, Rare, Regal, Sparse, Strange, Unusual
▷**Uncommon(ly)** *may indicate* an anagram
**Uncommunicative** Clam, Oyster, Reserved, Taciturn, Tight-lipped
**Uncompanionable** Threesome
**Uncomplaining** Stoic
**Uncomplicated** Naive
**Uncomplimentary** Blunt, Critical
**Uncomprehending** Anan, Ignorant, Obtuse
**Uncompromising** All or nothing, Cutthroat, Hardline, Hard-nosed, Hardshell, Intransigent, Relentless, Rigid, Strict, Ultra, Zero tolerance
**Unconcealed** Open, Overt, Pert
**Unconcerned** Aloof, Amoral, Bland, Careless, Casual, Cold, Impassive, Indifferent, Insouciant, Nonchalant, Strange
**Unconditional** Absolute, Categorical, Free, No strings, Pure
**Unconfident** Diffident, Doubtful
**Unconfirmed** Uncertain
**Uncongenial** Icy
**Uncongested** Roomy
**Unconnected** Asyndetic, Detached, Discrete, Disjointed, Enodal, Off-line
**Unconscionable** Ordinate, Ungodly
**Unconscious(ness)** Asleep, Automatic, Blackout, Catalepsy, Cold, Collective, Collywest,

Comatose, Galleywest, Greyout, Instinctive, Narcosis, Non-ego, Not-I, Oblivious, Racial, Subliminal, Syncope, Trance, Unaware, Under, Zonked out

**Unconsidered** Impetuous, Rash

**Unconstrained** En pantoufles

**Unconsummated** Mariage blanc

**Uncontaminated** Axenic

**Uncontrolled** Adrift, Anarchic, Atactic, Free, Hysterical, Incontinent, Independent, Intemperate, Loose, Loose cannon, Rampant, Skid, Wild

**Uncontroversial** Anodyne

**Unconventional** Anti-hero, Avant garde, Beatnik, Bohemian, Divergent, Drop-out, Eccentric, Far-out, Freakish, Freeform, Gonzo, Heretic, Heterodox, Hippy, Informal, Irregular, Offbeat, Off-the-wall, Original, Outlandish, Outré, Out there, Quirky, Raffish, Rebel, Screwball, Spac(e)y, Swinger, Unorthodox, Way-out, Wild

▷**Unconventional** *may indicate* an anagram

**Unconverted** Neat

**Unconvinced, Unconvincing** Farfet(ched), High-flow, High-flown, Humph, Lame, Thin, Wafer-thin

**Uncooked** Rare, Raw

**Uncooperative** Bolshie, Recalcitrant, Stroppy

**Uncoordinated** Asynergia, Ataxic, Awkward, Clumsy

**Uncorrect** Stet

**Uncorrupted** Innocent, Pure

**Uncouth(ness)** Baboon, Backwoodsman, Bear, Boorish, Churlish, Crass, Crude, Gothic, Inelegant, Rough(-hewn), Rube, Rude, Rugged, Rustic, Slob, Sloven, Uncivil

**Uncover(ed)** Bare, Denude, Disclose, Dismask, Expose, Find, Inoperculate, Naked, Open, Overt, Peel, Reveal, Shave, Shill, Shuck, Uncap, Unhood, Unveil

**Uncritical** Indiscriminate

**Unction, Unctuous(ness)** Anele, Balm, Chrism, Extreme, Greasy, Last rites, Oil(y), Ointment, Oleaginous, Ooze, Smarm, Soapy

**Uncultivated, Uncultured** Artless, Bundu, Fallow, Feral, Ignorant, Incult, Lowbrow, Philistine, Rude, Set aside, Tramontane, Waste, Wild, Wildland, Wildwood

**Undamaged** Intact, Inviolate, Sound, Whole

**Undated** Sine die

**Undecided** Aboulia, Ambivalent, Dithering, Double-minded, Doubtful, Havering, Hung, Moot, Non-committal, Open-ended, Pending, Pendulous, Torn, Uncertain, Wavering

**Undefiled** Chaste, Clean, Pure, Virgin

**Undefined** Imprecise, Open-ended, Vague

**Undeniable** Fact, Incontestable, Irrefutable

**Undependable** Capricious

**Under(neath)** Aneath, Below, Beneath, Hypnotized, Hypo-, Infra, Sotto, Sub-, Unconscious, Unneath

**Underage** Minority

**Underarm** Axilla, Lob

**Underbodice** Camisole, Jump

**Underburnt** Samel

**Under-butler** Bread-chipper

**Undercarriage** Bogie, Chassis, Landing gear

**Undercoat** Base, Primer

**Undercooked** Rare, Raw, Samel

**Undercover** Cloak and dagger, Espionage, Secret, Veiled

**Undercurrent** Acheron, Overtone, Rip(tide), Undertone, Undertow

**Underdeveloped, Underdevelopment** Aplasia, Ateleiosis, Backward, Retarded, Tiny

**Underdog** Cerberus, Loser, Victim

**Underestimate** Play down

**Underfed** Malnourished

▸**Undergarment** *see* UNDERWEAR

**Undergo(ing)** Bear, Dree, Endure, Solvate, Sub judice, Sustain
**Undergraduate** Commoner, Fresher, L, Pup, Questionist, Sizar, Sophomore, Student, Subsizar, Tuft
**Underground (group)** Basement, Catacomb, Cellar, Clandestine, Erebus, Fogou, Hell, Hypogaeous, Infernal, Irgun, Kiva, Macchie, Maquis, Mattamore, Metro, Phreatic, Pict, Plutonia, Pothole, Secret, Souterrain, Subsoil, Subterranean, Subterrene, Subway, Tube, Tunnel, Warren, Weem
**Undergrowth** Brush, Chaparral, Firth, Frith, Scrub
**Underhand** Arch, Backstair, Dirty, Furtive, Haunch, Hole and corner, Insidious, Lob, Oblique, Scullduggery, Secret, Shady, Sinister, Sly, Sneaky, Surreptitious
**Underlease** Subtack
**Underlie, Underlying** Subjacent, Subtend, Ulterior, Undercurrent
**Underline** Emphasise, Insist, Reinforce, Reiterate, Sublineation
**Underling** Bottle-washer, Cog, Inferior, Jack, Menial, Minion, Munchkin, Subordinate
**Undermine** Destabilise, Erode, Fossick, Handbag, Sap, Subvert, Tunnel, Weaken
**Undernourished** Puny, Skinny, Starveling
**Underpaid** Rat
**Underpass** Simplon, Subway
**Underside** Bed, Soffit
**Undersized** Mini, Puny
**Underskirt** Petticoat, Slip
**Understand(able), Understanding, Understood** Accept, Acumen, Agreement, Alliance, Apprehend, Capeesh, Catch on, Clear, Cognisable, Comprehend, Conceive, Concept, Connivance, Consideration, Cotton-on, Deal, Dig, Digest, Empathy, Enlighten, Entente, Exoteric, Fathom, Follow, Gather, Gauge, Gaum, Geddit, Get it, Gorm, Grasp, Grip, Grok, Have, Head, Heels, Hindsight, Implicit, Indulge, Insight, Intelligible, Intuit, Ken, Kind, Knowhow, Latch on, Learn, Light(s), Lucid, OK, Omniscient, Pact, Perspicuous, Plumb, Prajna, Rapport, Rapprochement, Realise, Roger, Savey, Savvy, See, Sense, Sole, Subintelligitur, Substance, Tacit, Take, Tenderness, Tolerance, Treaty, Tumble, Twig, Unspoken, Unstated, Uptak(e), Wisdom, Wit
**Understate(d), Understatement** Litotes, Low-key, Minify, M(e)iosis, Subtle
▸**Understood** *see* UNDERSTAND(ABLE)
**Understudy** Deputy, Double, Stand-in, Sub
**Undersurface** Gastraeum
**Undertake, Undertaking** Adventure, Attempt, Commitment, Contract, Covenant, Emprise, Endeavour, Enterprise, Essay, Feat, Guarantee, Misere, Pledge, Promise, Scheme, Shoulder, Tackle, Task, Venture, Warranty
**Undertaker** Editor, Entrepreneur, Mortician, Obligor, Sponsor, Upholder
**Under-ten** Unit, Yarborough
**Undertone** Murmur, Rhubarb, Sotto voce
**Undervalue** Denigrate, Depreciate
**Underwater** Demersal
**Underwear** Alb, Balbriggan, Balconette, Basque, Bloomers, Bodice, Body, Bodyshaper, Body stocking, Body suit, Boxers, Bra(ssiere), Briefs, Broekies, Butt bra, Camiknickers, Camisole, Camitop, Chemise, Chemisette, Chuddies, Combinations, Combs, Corselet, Corset, Dainties, Drawers, (French) knickers, Frillies, Girdle, Grundies, G-string, Hosiery, Innerwear, Jump, Knick(er)s, Linen, Lingerie, Linings, Long johns, Pantalets, Pantaloons, Panties, Pantihose, Panty girdle, Petticoat, Scanties, Semmit, Shift, Shimmy, Shorts, Singlet, Skivvy, Slip, Smalls, Spencer, Stammel, Stays, Step-ins, Subucula, Suspender-belt, Suspenders, Tanga, Teddy, Thermal, Trunks, Underdaks, Undergarments, Underlinen, Underpants, Underset, Undershirt, Underthings, Undies, Unmentionables, Vest, Wonderbra®, Wyliecoat, Y-fronts®
**Underworld** All-fired, Avernus, Chthonic, Criminal, Gangland, Hades, Hell, Lowlife, Mafia, Pluto, Shades, Tartar(e), Tartarus, Tartary
**Underwrite, Underwriter, Underwritten** Assure, Endorse, Guarantee, Insure, Lloyds, Name, PS

**Undeserving** Immeritous
**Undesirable** Kibitzer, Riff-raff
**Undeveloped** Ament, Backward, Depauperate, Green, Inchoate, Latent, Nubbin, Potential, Ridgel, Ridgil, Ridgling, Rig, Riggald, Riglin(g), Rudimentary, Seminal, Tiny
**Undifferentiated** Thalliform, Thallus
**Undigested** Crude
**Undignified (end)** Demeaning, Disaster, Foot, Improper, Infra dig, Unseemly
**Undiluted** Absolute, Neat, Pure, Sheer, Straight
**Undiminished** Entire, Intact, Whole
**Undiplomatic** Brusque, Tactless
**Undirected** Aimless
**Undisciplined** Bacchanalian, Hothead, Off message, Rule-less, Rulesse, Sloppy, Unruly, Wanton
**Undisclosed** Hidden, In petto, Secret
**Undisguised** Apert, Clear, Overt, Plain
**Undisputed** Authentic
**Undistinguished** Mediocre, Nameless, Plebeian, Run of the mill
**Undisturbed** Halcyon, Serene
**Undivided** Aseptate, Complete, Entire, Indiscrete, One
**Undo(ing)** Annul, Defeat, Destroy, Disconnect, Dismantle, Downfall, Dup, Loosed, Poop, Poupe, Release, Rescind, Ruin, Unravel
**Undoctored** Neat
**Undomesticated** Feral
**Undone** Arrears, Left, Postponed, Ran, Ruined, Unlast
**Undoubted(ly)** Ay, Certes, Clearly, Ipso facto, Outright, Positively, Sure, To be sure
**Undraped** Nude
**Undress(ed)** Bare, Disarray, Disrobe, En cuerpo, Expose, Négligé, Nude, Nue, Peel, Querpo, Raw, Rough, Self-faced, Spar, Strip, Unapparelled
**Undue** Premature
**Undulate, Undulating** Billow, Nebule, Ripple, Roll, Swell, Wave
**Unduly** Inordinately
▷**Unduly** *may indicate* an anagram
**Undyed** Greige
**Undying** Amaranthine, Eternal
**Unearth(ly)** Astral, Dig, Discover, Disentomb, Eldritch, Exhumate, Indagate
**Unease, Uneasiness, Uneasy** Angst, Angular, Anxious, Creeps, Discomfort, Disquiet, Dysphoria, Embarrassment, Inquietude, Itchy, Malaise, Qualm, Queasy, Restive, Restless, Shy, Tense, The willies, Trepidation, Uptight, Windy, Womble-cropped
**Unedifying** Idle
**Unembarrassed** Blasé, Dégagé
**Unemotional** Bland, Bloodless, Clinical, Cool, Frigid, Iceberg, Impassive, Matter-of-fact, Objective, Phlegmatic, Poker-face, Sober, Stoic, Stolid
**Unemployed, Unemployment** Drone, Idle, Jobless, Laik, Lake, Latent, Lay-off, Neet, Redundant, Residual, Stalko, Surfie
**Unending** Chronic, Eternal, Lasting, Sempiternal
**Unenlightened** Feudal, Ignorant, Nighted, Obscure
**Unenthusiastic** Cool, Damp, Desultory, Half-hearted, Lackadaisical, Listless, Tepid
**Unenveloped** Achlamydeous
**Unequal(led)** All-time, Aniso-, Disparate, Matchless, Mismatch, Non(e)such, Scalene, Unjust
**Unequivocal** Direct, Downright
**Unerring** Dead, Exact, Precise
**Unestablished** Free
**Unethical** Amoral, Anomie, Corrupt, Immoral, Sharp, Shyster
**Uneven(ness)** Accident, Blotchy, Bumpy, Erose, Erratic, Irregular, Jaggy, Lopsided, Patchy, Ragged, Rough, Scratchy, Streaky

▷**Unevenly** *may indicate* an anagram
**Unexceptional** Ordinary, Run of the mill, Workaday
**Unexciting** Flat, Mundane, Sedate, Spammy, Staid, Tame, Uneventful
**Unexpected(ly)** Abrupt, Accidental, Adventitious, Bonus, Curveball, Emergency, Ex-improviso, Fortuitous, Infra dig, Inopinate, Ironic, Offbeat, Snap, Sodain(e), Startling, Sudden, Surprise, Turn-up, Twist, Unawares, Unforeseen, Untoward, Unware, Unwary, Windfall
**Unexperienced** Strange
**Unexplained** Mystery, Obscure
**Unexploded** Live
**Unfading** Evergreen, Immarcescible
**Unfailing** Sure
**Unfair** Bias(s)ed, Crook, Dirty, Discriminatory, Inclement, Iniquitous, Invidious, Mean, One-sided, Partial, Raw deal, Thick, Unsportsmanlike
**Unfaithful** Adulterer, Cuckold, Disloyal, Godless, Infidel, Traitor, Two-timing
**Unfamiliar** Alien, Disinure, Foreign, New, Quaint, Strange
**Unfashionable** Cube, Daggy, Dated, Demode, Dowdy, Lame, Mumsy, Obsolescent, Out(moded), Out-of-date, Passé, Square, Vieux jeu
▷**Unfashionable** *may indicate* 'in' to be removed
**Unfasten** Undo, Untie, Untruss
**Unfathomable** Abysmal, Bottomless, Deep
**Unfavourable** Adverse, Disadvantage, Ill, Inimical, Outsider, Poor, Untoward
**Unfeeling** Adamant, Apathetic, Brutish, Callous, Cold, Cruel, Dead, Empty, Frigid, Hard, Inhuman(e), Insensate, Iron-witted, Numb, Robotic, Scared, Stony-hearted
**Unfeigned** Heartfelt, Sincere
**Unfilled** Vacant
**Unfinished, Unfinishable** Backlog, Crude, Inchoate, Incomplete, Incondite, Loose end, Raw, Scabble, Scapple, Sisyphean, Stickit
**Unfit(ting)** Cronk, Disabled, Faulty, Ill, Impair, Improper, Inept, Outré, Seedy, Stiffie, Tre(i)f, Trefa, Unable, Zero-rated
▷**Unfit** *may indicate* an anagram
**Unfixed** Afloat, Indeterminate, Isotropic, Loose
**Unflappable** Stoic
**Unflattering** Dowdy
**Unfledged** Gull
**Unflinching** Fast, Staunch
**Unfluctuating** Even
**Unfocused** Bleary, Glazed, Grasshopper-mind, Vague
**Unfold** Deploy, Develop, Disenvelop, Display, Divulge, Evolve, Interpret, Open, Relate, Spread
**Unforced** Voluntary
**Unforeseen** Accident, Emergency, Sudden, Surprising
**Unfortunate(ly)** Accursed, Alack, Alas, Catastrophic, Devil, Down and out, Hapless, Ill-omened, Ill-starred, Indecorous, Luckless, Peculiar, Shameless, Sorry, Star-crossed, Tragic, Unlucky, Worse luck
**Unfounded** Baseless, Groundless
**Unfrequented** Lonely
**Unfriendly** Aloof, Antagonistic, Asocial, Chill(y), Cold, Cold fish, Crusty, Distant, Fraim, Fremd, Fremit, Frigid, Frosty, Hostile, Icy, Impersonal, Inhospitable, Remote, Standoffish, Surly, Wintry
**Unfruitful** Abortive, Barren, Sterile
**Unfulfilled** Frustrated, Manqué
**Unfurl** Unroll
**Ungainly** Awkward, Gawkish, Lanky, Lumbering, Uncouth, Weedy
**Ungenerous** Cheapskate, Illiberal, Mean, Meanies, Small
**Ungirded** Discinct

**Ungodliness, Ungodly** Impiety, Irreligious, Pagan, Perfidious, Profane, World
**Ungracious** Cold, Meanie, Meany, Mesquin(e), Offhand, Rough, Rude
**Ungrammatical** Anacoluthia
**Ungrateful** Ingrate, Snaky
**Ungrudging** Liberal
**Unguarded** Trusting
**Unguent** Balm, Nard, Pomade, Salve
**Unguis** Nail
**Ungulate** Anta, Antelope, Dinoceras, Eland, Equidae, Hippo, Hoofed, Mesohippus, Moose, Pachydermata, Rhino, Ruminantia, Takin, Tapir, Titanotherium, Tylopoda
**Unhampered** Footloose
**Unhappily, Unhappy, Unhappiness** Blue, Dejected, Depressed, Desolate, Disconsolate, Disgruntled, Dismal, Distress, Doleful, Downcast, Down-hearted, Dysphoria, Glumpish, Ill-fated, Indignant, Love-lorn, Lovesick, Miserable, Sad, Sore, Tearful, Unlief, Upset
▷**Unhappily** *may indicate* an anagram
**Unharmed, Unharmful** Innocuous, Safe, Scatheless, Spared
**Unharness** Outspan
**Unhealthy** Bad, Clinic, Diseased, Epinosic, Insalubrious, Morbid, Noxious, Peaky, Poxy, Prurient, Scrag, Sickly, Twisted
**Unheeding** Oblivious
**Unhelpful** Detrimental, Disadvantageous
**Unhesitating** Decisive
**Unholy** Profane, Wicked
**Unhoused** Outlier
**Unhurried** Deliberate, Gradual, Leisurely, Patient
**Unhurt** Whole-skinned
**Unhygienic** Grubby
**Uniat** Maronite, Melchite
**Unicorn** Ch'i-lin, Coin, Monoceros, Moth, Myth, Narwhal, U
**Unidentified** Anon, Anonym(ous), Incognito, Ligure, Nameless, Unknown
**Unification, Unify(ing)** Esemplastic, Henotic, Integrate, Moonie, Risorgimento, Unite
**Uniform** Abolla, Alike, Apparel, Battledress, Bell-bottoms, Concolor, Consistent, Constant, Doublet, Dress, Equable, Equal, Even, Flat, Forage-cap, Gymslip, Homogeneous, Homomorphic, Identical, Khaki, Kit, Level, Livery, Monkey suit, Regimentals, Regular, Rig, Robe, Same, Sole, Standard, Steady, Strip, Suit, U, Unitary, Unvaried
**Unify** Consolidate, Integrate
**Unilateral** One-sided
**Unimaginative** Banausic, Cabbage, Earthbound, Literalistic, Meagre, Pedestrian, Pooter, Prosaic, Short-sighted, Slavish
**Unimpaired** Entire, Intact, Sound
**Unimportant** Academic, Back-burner, Banal, Cog, Down-the-line, Expendable, Fiddling, Folderol, Footling, Frivolous, Hot air, Idle, Immaterial, Inconsequent, Inconsiderable, Insignificant, Irrelevant, Junior, Light, MacGuffin, Makeweight, Miniscule, Minnow, Minor, Minutiae, Negligible, Nobody, Nonentity, Nugatory, Peddling, Peripheral, Petty, Piddling, Slight, Small beer, Small fry, Small-time, Tinpot, Trifling, Trivia(l)
**Unimpressible, Unimpressed, Unimpressive** Blasé, Cynical, Pale
**Uninformed** Ingram
**Uninhabited** Bundu, Deserted, Desolate, Lonely
**Uninhibited** Abandoned, Bold, Free spirit, Raunchy
**Uninjured** Inviolate
**Uninspired, Uninspiring** Barren, Bored, Flat, Humdrum, Nondescript, Pedestrian, Pompier, Stereotyped, Sterile, Tame
**Unintelligent** Bimbo, Dull, Dumb, Himbo, Obtuse, Quo-he, Stupid, Subnormal, Witless
**Unintelligible** Arcane, Code, Double Dutch, Greek, Inarticulate
**Unintentional** Inadvertent, Unwitting

**Uninterested, Uninteresting** Apathetic, Arid, Bland, Blasé, Drab, Dreary, Dry, Dull, Grey, Incurious, Nondescript, Non-event
**Uninterrupted** Constant, Continuous, Incessant, Running, Steady
**Uninvited** Gatecrasher, Interloper, Intruder, Sorner, Trespasser, Umbra
**Union(ist)** Affiance, African, Agreement, Allegiance, Alliance, Amicus, Anschluss, Art, ASLEF, Association, Bed, Benelux, Bond, Brotherhood, Brussels, Chain, Civil, Close, Coalition, Combination, Company, Concert, Confederacy, Consortium, Covalency, Craft, Credit, Customs, Diphthong, Economic, Enosis, Ensemble, Equity, EU, European, Fasciation, Federal, Federation, French, Frithgild, Fusion, Group, Guild, Heterogamy, Horizontal, Impanation, Industrial, Integration, Isogamy, Junction, Knight of labour, Latin, League, Liaison, Liberal, Link-up, Management, Marriage, Match, Merger, NUM, Nuptials, NUR, NUS, NUT, OILC, Oxford, Pan-American, Parabiosis, Pearl, Postal, Print, RU, Rugby, Samiti, Sex, Sherman, Shop-steward, Solidarity, Soviet, Splice, Sponsal, Student, Symphysis, Syngamy, Synizesis, Synostosis, Synthesis, Syssarcosis, Teamsters, Tenorrhaphy, →**TRADE UNION**, TU, U, UNISON, USDAW, Uxorial, Verein, Vertical, Vienna, Wedding, Wedlock, Western European, Wield, Yoke, ZANU, Zollverein, Zygosis
**Unique(ness)** Alone, A-per-se, Farid, Hacceity, Incomparable, Inimitable, Irreplaceable, Lone, Matchless, Nonesuch, Nonpareil, Nonsuch, One-off, One(-to)-one, Onliest, Only, Peerless, Rare, Singular, Sole, Specific, Sui generis
**Unisex(ual)** Epicene, Hermaphrodite
**Unison** Chorus, Harmony, One, Sync
**Unit(s)** Ampere-hour, Bargaining, Battery, Bel, Board of Trade, Brigade, Cadre, Cell, Cohort, Commando, Commune, Control, Corps, Derived, Detachment, Division, Dyad, Ecosystem, Element, Ensuite, Entity, Feedlot, Flight, Force, Fundamental, Home, Horsepower, Hub, Income, Item, Kiloton, Kitchen, Last, Legion, Measure, Megabit, Message, Modem, Module, Monetary, Panzer, Patrol, Peninsular, Period, Peripheral, Practical, Sealed, Secure, Segment, Shed, Squad(ron), Stock, Syllable, Task force, Team, Terminal, Theme, Timocracy, Tower

---

**UNITS**

***1 letter:***
G
K
X

***2 letters:***
AU
Em
En
RA
SI
TA

***3 letters:***
Ace
Amp
Bar
Bit
BTU
DIN
Dol
EMU
Erg
Fps
Gal
Gee
GeV
Ion
Lux
Mho
Mil
Mol
Nit
Ohm
Ped
Rem
Rep
Tex
Tod
Tog
Var

***4 letters:***
Acre
Barn
Base
Baud
Byte
DALY
Dyne
Gram
Grav
Gray
Hank
Hapu
Hide
Hour
Inch
Mile
Mole
Nest
Octa
Okta
Phon
Phot
Pica
Pint
Pond
Rood
Sink
Slug
Sone
Torr
Vara
Volt
Wall
Watt
Wing
Yard

***5 letters:***
Barye
Cable
Catty
Codon
Crith
Cusec
Daraf
Darcy
Debye
Ephah
Farad
Fermi
Field
Gauss
Henry
Hertz
Holon
Joule
Katal

Litre
Lumen
Metre
Monad
Mongo
Neper
Nepit
Ounce
Pixel
Point
Poise
Pound
Power
Quart
Qubit
Remen
Sabin
Stere
Stilb
Stoke
Stone
Tesla
Therm
Token
Voxel
Weber
Yrneh

***6 letters:***
Biogen
Bushel
Calory
Dalton
Degree
Denier
Dobson
Emdash
Erlang
Gallon
Jansky
Kelvin
Kilerg
League
Lexeme
Megohm
Micron
Minute
Mongoe
Morgan
Morgen
Newton
Pascal
Phyton
Probit
Radian
Reverb
Second
Sememe
Stokes
Vanity

***7 letters:***
Archine
Biophor
Calorie
Candela
Centare
Chronon
Congius
Coulomb
Dioptre
Echelon
Energid
Episome
Foot-ton
Fresnel
Gestalt
Gigabit
Gilbert
Hartree
Hectare
Lambert
Langley
Maceral
Man-hour
Maxwell
Megaton
Micella
Micelle
Milline
Nephron
Oersted
Pangene
Phoneme
Poundal
Rontgen
Semeion
Siemens
Sievert
Syntagm
Tagmeme
Tripody
Tritone

***8 letters:***
Abampere
Absolute
Acre-foot
Angstrom
Bioblast
Biophore
Centiare
Chaldron
Electron
Gigaflop
Gigawatt
Glosseme
Hogshead
Kilowatt
Magneton
Megabyte
Megaflop
Megawatt
Millirem
Morpheme
Mutchkin
Parasang
Petaflop
Roentgen
Syntagma
Terabyte
Teraflop
Therblig
Vanitory
Watt-hour

***9 letters:***
Arcminute
Arcsecond
Becquerel
Degree day
Foot-pound
Gigahertz
Kilderkin
Kilometre
Light-year
Megahertz
Microinch
Microvolt
Organelle
Singleton
Steradian
Strontium
Tetrapody
Yottabyte
Zettabyte

***10 letters:***
Atomic mass
Centimetre
Centipoise
Dessiatine
Foot-candle
Hoppus-foot
Microcurie
Millilitre
Millimetre
Nanosecond
Person-hour
Picosecond
Ploughgate
Protoplast
Rutherford

***11 letters:***
Centimorgan
Foot-lambert
Pennyweight

***12 letters:***
Archiphoneme
Astronomical
Bohr magneton
Electron volt
Millisievert

***13 letters:***
Electrostatic

***15 letters:***
Electromagnetic

---

**Unitarian** Arian, Paulian, Racovian, Socinian

**Unite(d), Uniting** Accrete, Band, Bind, Cement, Close-knit, Coadunate, Coalesce, Combine, Concordant, Concorporate, Conjugate, Connate, Connect, Consolidate, Consubstantiate, Corporate, Covalent, Ecumenical, Fay, Federal, Federalise, Federate, Fuse, Gene, Graft, Harmonise, Injoint, Inosculate, Join, Joinder, Jugum, Kingdom, Knit, Lap, Link, Marry, Meint, Meng, Ment, Merge, Meynt, Ming, Nations, Oneness, Oop, Oup, Piece, Reconcile, Siamese, Solid, Splice, States, Tie, Tightknit, Together, Unify, Utd, →WED, Weld, Yoke

**United Ireland** Fine Gael
**United Kingdom** Old Dart, UK
**Unity** Cohesion, Harmony, One, Solidarity, Sympathy, Togetherness
**Univalent** Monatomic
**Universal, Universe** All, All-embracing, Catholic, Cosmogony, Cosmos, Creation, Ecumenic(al), Emma, Expanding, General, Global, Infinite, Inflationary, Island, Macrocosm, Mandala, Microcosm, Omnify, Oscillating, Rife, Sphere, U, Via Lactea, World(wide)
**University** Academe, Academy, Alma mater, Ames, Aston, Bangor, Bath, Berkeley, Bonn, Brown, Campus, Civic, College, Columbia, Cornell, Dartmouth, Douai, Exeter, Gown, Harvard, Heidelberg, Ivy League, Keele, MIT, Open, OU, Oxbridge, Pennsylvania, Princeton, Reading, Redbrick, St Andrews, Sorbonne, Stamford, Syracuse, Varsity, Whare wanaga, Wittenberg, Witwatersrand, Yale
**Unjust(ified)** Groundless, Inequitable, Inequity, Iniquitous, Invalid, Tyrannical, Undue
**Unkempt** Bedraggled, Bushy, Dishevelled, Greaseball, Greebo, Mal soigné, Raddled, Ragged, Raggle-taggle, Scarecrow, Scody, Scraggy, Scruffy, Scuzzy, Shaggy, Straggly, Tatty, Tousled, Tousy, Touzy, Towsy, Towzy
**Unkind** Harsh
**Unknot** Burl
**Unknown, Unknowable** Acamprosate, Agnostic, Anon, A.N. Other, Dark horse, Hidden, Ign, Ignotum per ignotius, Incog(nito), Inconnu, Indeterminate, John Doe, N, Nameless, Nobody, Noumenon, Occult, Quantity, Recondite, Secret, Soldier, Strange, Symbolic, Tertium quid, Unchartered, Unsourced, Untold, Warrior, X, Y
**Unlawful** Illegal, Non-licit
**Unleash** Wreak
**Unleavened** Azymous
**Unless** Nisi, Save, Without
**Unlevel** Cock-eyed
**Unliable** Exempt
**Unlicensed** Illicit
**Unlike(ly)** As if, Different, Difform, Disparate, Dubious, Far-fetched, Implausible, Improbable, Inauspicious, Last, Long shot, Outsider, Remote, Tall, Unlich
**Unlimited** Almighty, Borderless, Boundless, Indefinite, Inexhaustible, Measureless, Nth, Open-ended, Pure, Universal, Vast
**Unlisted** Ex-directory
**Unload** Disburden, Discharge, Drop, Dump, Jettison, Land, Strip, Unship
**Unlock(ed)** Bald
**Unlucky** Donsie, Hapless, Ill(-starred), Ill-fated, Ill-omened, Inauspicious, Infaust, Jinxed, Jonah, Misadventure, Misfallen, S(c)hlimazel, Sinister, Stiff, Thirteen, Untoward, Wanchancie, Wanchancy, Wanion
**Unman, Unmanned** Castrate, Desex, Gelding
**Unmanageable** Handful, Riotous, Tartarian
**Unmannerly** Crude, Discourteous, Impolite, Low bred, Rude, Solecism
**Unmarried** Bachelor, Celibate, Common-law, Lane, Lone, Single, Spinster, Tallywoman
**Unmask** Expose, Out, Rumble
**Unmatched** Bye, Champion, Oddment, Orra, Unique
**Unmentionable(s)** Bra, Foul, No-no, Secret, → UNDERWEAR, Undies
**Unmethodical** Desultory
**Unmindful** Heedless, Oblivious, Regardless
**Unmissable** Must see
**Unmistakable** Clear, Manifest, Plain
**Unmitigated** Absolute, Arrant, Sheer, Ultra
**Unmixed** Meer, Me(a)re, Neat, Nett, Pure, Raw, Sincere, Straight
**Unmoved, Unmoving** Adamant, Doggo, Dry-eyed, Firm, In situ, Serene, Static, Stolid
**Unmusical** Tin-ear, Tone deaf
**Unnamed** Anon, So-and-so

**Unnatural** Abnormal, Absonant, Affected, Artificial, Cataphysical, Contrived, Eerie, Far-fetched, Flat, Geep, Irregular, Man-made, Strange, Studied, Transuranian
▷**Unnaturally** *may indicate* an anagram
**Unnecessary** De trop, Dispensible, Extra, Gash, Gratuitous, Needless, Otiose, Redundant, Superfluous
**Unnerve(d), Unnerving** Creepy, Discouraging, Eerie, Faze, Rattle, Spooked
**Unobserved, Unobservant** Backstage, Breached, Inattentive, Sly, Unseen
**Unobtainable** Nemesis
**Unobtrusive** Background, Discreet, Low profile, Quiet, Stealthy
**Unoccupied** Désouvré, Empty, Free, Idle, Inactive, Otiose, Vacant, Void
**Unofficial** Black, Disestablish, Fringe, Informal, Wildcat
**Unopened** Sealed
**Unorganised** Amorphous
**Unoriginal** Banal, Copy, Déjà vu, Derivative, Imitation, Plagiarised, Slavish, Trite
**Unorthodox** En passant, Heretic, Heterodox, Irregular, Maverick, Off-beat, Off-the-wall, Outré, Stagyrite, Unconventional
▷**Unorthodox** *may indicate* an anagram
**Unpaid** Amateur, Brevet, Due, Hon(orary), Outstanding, Voluntary
**Unpaired** Azygous, Bye
**Unpalatable** Acid, Bitter, Unsavoury
**Unparalleled** Sublime, Supreme, Unique
**Unpartitioned** Aseptate
**Unpatented** Generic
**Unperturbed** Bland, Calm, Collected, Serene
**Unpigmented** Albino
**Unpinned** Legless
**Unplaced** Also-ran, Legless
**Unplanned** Ad hoc, Ad lib, Disorganised, Happenstance, Impromptu, Improvised, Nameless, Spontaneous
**Unpleasant, Unpleasant person** Cow, Creep, Drastic, Fink, Foul, God-awful, Grim, Grotty, Gruesome, Gunk, Harsh, Hoor, Horrible, Icky, Insalubrious, Invidious, Mucky, Nasty, Obnoxious, Odious, Offensive, Painful, Pejorative, Poxy, Putrid, Rank, Rebarbative, Reptile, Scrote, Shady, Shocker, Skanky, Snarky, Snot, So-and-so, Sour, Sticky, Thorny, Toerag, Unenviable, Wart
**Unploughed** Lea-rig
**Unpolished** Coarse, Inelegant, Rough
**Unpolluted** Sterile
**Unpopular** Abhorred, Avant garde, Detested, Friendless, Hat(e)able
**Unpractical** Academic, Futile, Orra
**Unpredictable** Act of God, Aleatory, Capricious, Dicy, Erratic, Fluid, Loose cannon, Maverick, Mercurial, Moody, Scatty, Vagary, Volatile, Wayward, Wild card
**Unprejudiced** Tolerant
**Unpremeditated** Spontaneous
**Unprepared** Ad lib, Cold, Extempore, Green, Impromptu, Improvised, Last minute, On the hop, Raw, Unready
**Unpretentious** Comely, Down home, Hodden-grey, Hole in the wall, Honest, Modest, Natural, Plain, Quiet
**Unprincipled** Amoral, Dishonest, Godless, Irregular, Opportunist, Reprobate, Sleazeball, Unscrupulous
**Unprocessed** Raw
**Unproductive** Abortive, Arid, Atokal, Atokous, Barren, Dead-head, Desert, Eild, Fallow, Futile, Infertile, Lean, Poor, Shy, Sterile, Yeld, Yell
**Unprofessional** Amateur, Laic, Malpractice
**Unprofitable** Bootless, Fruitless, Lean, Losing, Thankless, Wasted
**Unprogressive** Inert, Square
**Unpronounceable** Clitic

**Unpropitious** Bleak
**Unproportionate** Incommensurate
**Unprotected** Exposed, Nude, Underbelly, Vulnerable
**Unpublished** Inedited
**Unpunctual** Tardy
**Unqualified** Absolute, Arrant, Categoric, Downright, Entire, Flat, Ill-equipped, Outright, Perfect, Profound, Pure, Quack, Sheer, Straight, Thorough, Total, Tout court, Unreservedly, Utter
**Unquestionably, Unquestioning, Unquestioned** Absolute, Axiomatic, Certain, Doubtless, Implicit
**Unravel(ling)** Construe, Denouement, Disentangle, Feaze, Fray, Solve, Undo
**Unreadable** Poker-faced
**Unready** Unripe
**Unreal(istic)** Academic, Alice-in-Wonderland, Cockamamie, Dreamy, Eidetic, En l'air, Escapist, Fake, Fancied, Illusory, Impractical, Insubstantial, La-la-land, Mirage, Mythical, Oneiric, Phantom, Phon(e)y, Pipe dream, Planet Zog, Pseudo, Romantic, Sham, Spurious, Storybook, Virtual
**Unreasonable, Unreasoning** Absurd, Bigot, Exorbitant, Extreme, Illogical, Irrational, Misguided, Perverse, Rabid, Steep, Tall order
**Unreciprocated** One-way
**Unrecognised** Incognito, Inconnu, Invalid, Obscure, Thankless, Unnoticed, Unsung
**Unrefined** Bestial, Coarse, Common, Crude, Earthy, Gauche, Gur, Impudent, Impure, Inelegant, Natural, Rude, Rustic, Slob, Vul(g), Vulgar
**Unreformed** Impenitent
**Unregistered** Flapping
**Unrehearsed** Ad lib, Candid, Extempore, Impromptu, On sight
**Unrelenting** Grim, Implacable, Remorseless, Severe, Stern
**Unreliable** Anecdotal, Broken reed, Chequered, Deceptive, Dishonest, Dodgy, Dubious, Erratic, Fair-weather, Fickle, Flaky, Flibbertigibbet, Flighty, Fly-by-night, Illusive, Insecure, Insincere, Kludge, Misleading, Shonky, Skitter, Unstable, Wankle, Weak sister, Wonky
**Unremarkable** Nondescript
**Unremitting** Dogged, Intensive
**Unreserved** Implicit, Total
**Unresisting** Passive
**Unresolved** Outstanding
**Unresponsive** Aloof, Apathetic, Blank, Catatonic, Cold, Echoless, Frigid, Inert, Nastic, Rigor
**Unrest** Discontent, Disturbance, Ferment, Hot spot, The Troubles
**Unrestrained, Unrestricted** Ariot, At large, Effusive, Extravagant, Free, Freewheeling, Hearty, Homeric, Immoderate, Incontinent, Infinite, Intemperate, Lax, Loose, Lowsit, Open-door, Orgic, Rampage, Rampant, Ultra, Wanton, Wild
**Unreturnable** Ace
**Unrighteousness** Adharma
**Unrivalled** Nonesuch, Nonpareil, Peerless, Supreme
**Unroll** Straighten, Unfurl
**Unromantic** Classic(al), Mundane, Prosaic
**Unruffled** Calm, Placid, Serene, Smooth, Tranquil
**Unruly** Anarchic, Bodgie, Buckie, Camstairy, Camsteary, Camsteerie, Coltish, Disruptive, Exception, Fractious, Insubordinate, Lager lout, Lawless, Obstreperous, Obstropalous, Ragd(e), Raged, Ragged, Rambunctious, Rampageous, Rattlebag, Rebellious, Refractory, Riotous, Rowdy, Rumbustious, Tartar, Torn-down, Turbulent, Turk, Wanton, Wayward, Zoo
▹**Unruly** *may indicate* an anagram
**Unsafe** Deathtrap, Fishy, Insecure, Perilous, Precarious, Rickety, Unsound, Vulnerable
**Unsatisfactory, Unsatisfied, Unsatisfying** Bad, Disappointing, Discontent, Lame, Lemon, Lousy, Meagre, Rocky, Thin, Wanting
**Unsavoury** Epinosic, On the nose, Sordid
**Unsay** Recant

**Unscramble** Decode, Decrypt
**Unscripted** Ad lib
**Unscrupulous** Chancer, Fiddling, Immoral, Rascally, Roguish, Sharp, Shyster, Slippery, Spiv
**Unseasonable, Unseasoned** Green, Hors de saison, Murken, Raw, Untimely
**Unseat** Depose, Dethrone, Oust, Overset, Overthrow, Throw, Topple
**Unseemly** Coarse, Improper, Incivil, Indecent, Indecorous, Indign, Risque, Seedy, Tasteless, Untoward
**Unseen** Exam, Masked
**Unselfish** Altruist, Considerate, Generous
**Unsent** Square
**Unsentimental** Cynical, Gradgrindery, Hard-nosed
**Unserious** Flippant
**Unsettle(d), Unsettling** Creepy, Discombobulated, Disconcert, Faze, Grey area, Homeless, Hunky, Inconclusive, Indecisive, Nervous, Open, Outstanding, Overdue, Owed, Perturb, Queasy, Restive, Restless, Rootless, Tentative, Troublous
▷**Unsettled** *may indicate* an anagram
**Unsexy** N, Neuter
**Unshakeable** Shockproof
**Unshaven** Designer stubble, Setulous
**Unsheltered** Bleak, Exposed, Homeless
**Unshockable** Resilient
**Unsight(ed), Unsightly** Eyeless, Hideous, Monstrosity, Repulsive, Ugly
**Unsinning** Impeccable, Pure
**Unskilled, Unskilful** Awkward, Dilutee, Gauche, Green, Hunky, Inexpert, Menial, Raw, Rude, Stumblebum, Talentless, Whitechapel
**Unsmiling** Agelastic
**Unsociable** Aloof, Anchoretic, Grouchy, Solitary, Stay-at-home
**Unsolicited** Sponte sua
**Unsolved** Cold
**Unsophisticated** Alf, Basic, Boondocks, Boonies, Bushie, Cornball, Corny, Cracker-barrel, Direct, Down-home, Faux-naïf, Green, Hick, Hillbilly, Homebred, Homespun, Ingenu(e), Inurbane, Jaap, Jay, Naive, Natural, Primitive, Provincial, Rough, Rube, Rustic, Verdant, Yokel
**Unsound** Barmy, Infirm, Invalid, Shaky, Specious, Wildcat, Wonky
▷**Unsound** *may indicate* an anagram
**Unsown** Fallow
**Unsparing** Severe
**Unspeakable** Dreadful, Ineffable, Nefandous
**Unspecific, Unspecified** Broad, General, Generic, Somehow, Such, Thingummy(jig), Umpteenth, Vague, Whatever, Whenever, Wherever, Whoever
**Unspoiled, Unspoilt** Idyllic, Innocent, Natural, Perfect, Pristine, Pure, Virgin
**Unspoken** Silent, Tacit
**Unspotted** Innocent
**Unstable, Unsteady** Anomic, Astatic, Bockedy, Casual, Crank(y), Dicky, Doddery, Erratic, Fickle, Fitful, Flexuose, Flexuous, Flit(ting), Fluidal, Giddy, Groggy, Infirm, Insecure, Labile, Lurch, Mattoid, Minute-jack, On-off, Precarious, Quicksand, Rickety, Shaky, Shifty, Skittish, Slippy, Tickle, Top-heavy, Tottery, Totty, Vacillating, Variable, Volatile, Walty, Wambling, Wankle, Warby, Wobbly, Wonky
**Unstated** Concordat, Tacit, Unknown
▶**Unsteady** *see* UNSTABLE
**Unstressed** Enclitic, Schwa
**Unstructured** Loose
▷**Unstuck** *may indicate* an anagram
**Unstudied** Natural
**Unsubstantial** Aeriform, Airy, Flimsy, Paltry, Shadowy, Slight, Thin, Yeasty

**Unsubtle** Blatant, Overt, Sledgehammer
**Unsuccessful** Abortive, Also ran, Disastrous, Duff, Futile, Joyless, Loss-maker, Manqué, Vain
**Unsuitable** Amiss, Ill-timed, Impair, Improper, Inapt, Incongruous, Inexpedient, Malapropos, Misbecoming, Unbecoming, Unfit
**Unsullied** Chaste, Pristine
**Unsupported, Unsupportable** Astylar, Floating, Free-standing, Stroppy, Unfounded
**Unsure** Hesitant, Tentative, Unconvinced, Vacillating
**Unsurpassed** All-time, Best, Nonpareil, State-of-the-art, Supreme
**Unsuspecting** Credulous, Ingenuous, Innocent, Naive
**Unsweetened** Brut, Natural
**Unswerving** True
**Unsymmetrical** Heterauxesis(m), Irregular, Lopsided
**Unsympathetic** Hard, Short shrift
**Unsystematic** Piecemeal, Random
**Untainted** Axenic
**Untamed** Feral
**Untangle** Comb
**Untaught** Intuitive
**Untaxed** Exempt
**Unthinking** Inadvertent, Inconsiderate, Knee jerk, Mechanical, Not-I, Robotic, Slapdash
**Untidy** Daggy, Dishevelled, Dog's breakfast, Dog's dinner, Dowd(y), Frowzy, Frump, Guddle, Litterbug, Ragged, Ragtag, Raunchy, Scarecrow, Scrappy, Scruff(y), Slipshod, Slob, Sloppy, Slovenly, Slut, Straggly, Tatty
▹**Untidy** *may indicate* an anagram
**Untie** Free, Undo, Unlace
**Until** Hasta, Thereto
**Untilled** Fallow
**Untimely** Anachronism, Intempestive, Premature
**Untiring** Assiduous, Indefatigable
**Unto** Intil, Until
**Untold** Secret, Umpteen, Unread, Unred, Vast
**Untouchable** Burakumin, Dalit, Harijan, Immune, Pariah, Sacred, Sacrosanct, Sealed
**Untouched** Chaste, Intact, Inviolate, Pristine, Virgin
▹**Untrained** *may indicate* 'BR' to be removed
**Untreated** Raw
**Untried** New, Potential, Virgin
**Untroubled** Carefree, Insouciant
**Untrue, Untruth** Apocryphal, Eccentric, Fable, Fabrication, Faithless, False(hood), Invalid, Lie, Lopsided, Prefabrication, Sham, Unleal
**Untrustworthy** Dishonest, Disloyal, Eel, Fickle, Fly-by-night, Mamzer, Momzer, Shifty, Sleeky, Slippery, Tricky
**Untypical** Anomalous, Etypic(al), Foreign, Isolated, Unusual
**Unused, Unusable** Impracticable, New, Over, Spare, Wasted
**Unusual(ly)** Aberration, Abnormal, Anomalous, Atypical, Departure, Different, Especial, Exceptional, Exotic, Extra(ordinary), Eye-popping, Freak, Gonzo, Kinky, New, Non-standard, Novel, Odd, Offbeat, Original, Other, Out-of-the-way, Outré, Particular, Peculiar, Phenomenal, Quaint, Queer, Rara avis, Rare (bird), Remarkable, Singular, Special, → STRANGE, Unco, Uncommon, Unique, Untypical, Unwonted, Variant, Wacko
▹**Unusual** *may indicate* an anagram
**Unutterable** Ineffable
**Unvarnished** Bald
**Unvarying** Constant, Eternal, Monotonous, Repetitive, Stable, Static, Uniform
**Unveil** Expose, Honour, Reveal, Roll up
**Unvoiced** Surd
**Unwanted** Black list, De trop, Exile, Gooseberry, Nimby, Outcast, Pidog, Sorn, Troll, Waste

**Unwarranted** Outburst
**Unwashed** Grubby
**Unwatered** Dry, Neat
**Unwavering** Determined, Staunch, Steadfast, Steady, Thick and thin
**Unwed** Celibate, Single
**Unwelcome, Unwelcoming** Bleak, Frosty, Hostile, Icy, Inhospitable, Intruder, Lulu, Obtrusive, (Persona) Non grata, Repugnant
**Unwell** Ailing, Bedridden, Crook, Dicky, Ill, Impure, Indisposed, Off-colour, Out of sorts, Poorly, Quazzy, Queasy, Rop(e)y, Rough, Seedy, Shouse, Toxic
**Unwholesome** Insalutary, Miasmous, Morbid, Noxious, Stagnant, Stinkpot
**Unwieldy** Cumbersome, Elephantine
**Unwilling(ness)** Averse, Disinclined, Grudgingly, Hidebound, Intestate, Laith, Loath, Loth, Nolition, Nolo, Obdurate, Perforce, Reluctant, Shy, Tarrow
**Unwind** Descramble, Relax, Straighten, Unclew, Uncoil, Undo, Unravel, Unreave, Unreeve
▷**Unwind** *may indicate* an anagram
**Unwinnable** Catch 22
**Unwise(ly)** Foolish, Ill-advised, Ill-judged, Impolitic, Imprudent, Inexpedient, Injudicious, Insipient, Rash
**Unwitting** Accidental, Nescient
**Unwonted** Inusitate
**Unworkable** Impossible, Inoperable
**Unworldly** Naif, Naive
**Unworried** Carefree
**Unworthy** Below, Beneath, Golden calf, Ignoble, Indign, Inferior, Infra dig, Substandard, Undeserving
**Unwrap** Unmuffle
**Unwritten** Verbal
**Unyielding** Adamant, Cast-iron, Eild, Firm, Granite, Hardline, Inexorable, Inextensible, Intransigent, Mulish, Obdurate, Obstinate, Relentless, Rigid, Steadfast, Steely, Stern, Stiff, Stolid, Stubborn, Tenacious, Tough, Unalterable
**Unyoke** Outspan
**Up(on), Upturned, Upper, Uppermost, Uppish, Uppity** A, Acockbill, Afoot, Ahead, Aloft, Antidepressant, Apical, Arrogant, Astir, Astray, Astride, Cloud-kissing, Elevated, Erect, Euphoric, Excited, Heavenward, Hep, Horsed, Incitant, In pocket, Off, On, Overhead, Primo, Quark, Range, Ride, Riding, Risen, Senior, Skyward, Speed, Standing, → UPPER CLASS, Vamp, Ventral, Wart
**Up-anchor** Atrip, Weigh
**Upbeat** Anacrusis, Arsis, Cheery, Optimistic
**Upbraid** Abuse, Berate, Rebuke, Reproach, Reprove, Scold, Storm, Tell off, Twit
**Upbringing** Nurture
**Upcoming** Offing
**Upcountry** Anabasis, Inland
**Update** Brief, Newsletter, Refresh, Renew, Report, Sitrep
**Upfront** Open
**Upgrade** Improve, Promote, Renovate
**Upheaval** Cataclysm, Chaos, Eruption, Maelstrom, Rummage, Seismic, Shake out, Stir, Turmoil, Upturn, Volcano
▷**Upheld** *may indicate* 'up' in another word
**Uphill** Arduous, Borstal, Sisyphean
**Uphold** Affirm, Assert, Defend, Maintain, Support, Sustain
**Upholster(ed), Upholstery** Fleshy, Lampas, Moquette, Pad, Tabaret, Trim
**Upkeep** Support
**Upland(s)** Alps, Dartmoor, Downs, Hilly, Moor, Wold
**Uplift(ed)** Boost, Buoyant, Edify, Elate, Elevation, Exalt, Hoist, Levitation, Raise, Sky
**Upmarket** Classy, High-end, Smart
**Upmost** Top

**Upper class, Upper crust** Aristocrat, County, Crachach, Green wellie, Hooray Henry, Nobility, Patrician, Posh, Privileged, Sial, Top-hat, Tweedy, U

**Upright(s), Uprightness** Aclinic, Anend, Apeak, Apeek, Aplomb, Arrect, Atrip, Beanpole, Bedpost, Doorpost, Endways, Endwise, Equity, Erect, Goalpost, Honest, Incorrupt, Integrity, Jamb, Joanna, Merlon, Moral, Mr Clean, Mullion, Orthograde, Perpendicular, Piano, Pilaster(s), Pillar, Post, Prig, Probity, Rectitude, Reputable, Roman, Splat, Stanchion, Standing, Stares, Stile, Stud, Vertical, Virtuous, White

**Uprising** Incline, Insurrection, Intifada, Meerut, Naxalbari, Rebellion, Revolt, Tumulus

**Uproar(ious)** Bagarre, Ballyhoo, Bear-pit, Bedlam, Blatancy, Brouhaha, Charivari, Clamour, Clangour, Collieshangie, Commotion, Cry, Din, Dirdam, Dirdum, Durdum, Emeute, Ferment, Flaw, Fracas, Furore, Garboil, Hell, Hooha, Hoopla, Hubbub(oo), Hullabaloo, Hurly(-burly), Imbroglio, Katzenjammer, Madhouse, Noise, Noyes, Outcry, Pandemonium, Racket, Raird, Randan, Razzmatazz, Reird, Riot, Riotous, Roister, Romage, Rough music, Rowdedow, Rowdydow(dy), Ruckus, Ruction, Rumpus, Shemozzle, Stramash, Tempest, Tumult, Turmoil, Utis, Whoobub

**Uproot** Averruncate, Deracinate, Dislodge, Eradicate, Evict, Outweed, Supplant, Weed

**Upset(ting)** Aerate, Aggrieve, Alarm, Applecart, Arsy-versy, Ate, Bother, Capsize, Catastrophe, Choked, Coup, Cowp, Crank, Derail, Derange, Desolate, Destabilise, Dip, Disarrange, Disarray, Discomboberate, Discombobulate, Discomfit, Discomfort, Discommode, Disconcert, Disgruntled, Dismay, Disorganise, Displease, Disquiet, Distraught, Distress, Disturb, Dod, Eat, Evoke, Fuss, Grieve, Gutted, Heart-rending, Hiccup, Inversion, Keel, Miff, Montezuma's revenge, Nauseative, Nettle, Niggling, Offend, Overbalance, Overthrow, Overtip, Overturn, Peeve, Perturb, Pip, Pother, Purl, Rattle, Renverse, Rile, Rock, Ruffle, Rumple, Sad(den), Seel, Shake, Shatter, Shook up, Sore, Spill, Tapsalteerie, Teary, Tip, Topple, Trauma, Undo, Unsettled

▷**Upset** *may indicate* an anagram; a word upside down; or 'tes'

**Upshot** Consequence, Outcome, Result, Sequel

**Upside down** Inverted, Resupinate, Tapsie-teerie, Topsy-turvy

**Upsilon** Hyoid

**Upstart** Buckeen, Johnny-come-lately, Jumped-up, Mushroom, Parvenu, Vulgarian, Whippersnapper, Wiseacre

▷**Upstart** *may indicate* 'u'

**Upstream** Contranatant, Thermal

**Upsurge** Groundswell, Thrust, Waste

**Uptake** Shrewdness, Understanding, Wit

**Up to** Till, Until

**Up-to-date** Abreast, Advanced, Contemporary, Current, Fashionable, Gear, Hip, Mod, New-fashioned, Rad, Right-on, State-of-the-art, Swinging, Switched on, Topical, Trendy

**Upwards** Acclivious, Aloft, Antrorse, Cabré

**Uranium** Depleted, Pitchblende, U, Yellowcake

**Uranus** Georgian planet

**Urban, Urbanite** Civic, Megalopolis, Municipal, Oppidan, Street, Town, Townsman

**Urbane, Urbanity** Civil, Debonair, Eutrapelia, Refined, Smooth, Suave, Townly, Worldly

**Urchin** Ambulacrum, Arab, Asterias, Brat, Crinoid, Crossfish, Cystoid, Echinoderm, Echinoidea, Echinus, Gamin, Guttersnipe, Gutty, Heart, Hedgehog, Mudlark, Nipper, Pedicellaria, Pluteus, Ragamuffin, Sand-dollar, Sea, Sea-egg, Spatangoidea, Spatangus, Street-arab, Townskip, Waif

**Urge, Urgency, Urgent** Acute, Admonish, Asap, Burning, Ca, Cacoethes, Cajole, Caution, Coax, Coerce, Constrain, Craving, Crying, Desperate, Dire, Drive, Egg, Emergency, Enjoin, Exhort, Exigent, Gee up, Goad, Hard, Haste, Hie, Hoick, Hunger, Hurry, Id, Immediate, Impel, Imperative, Importune, Impulse, Incense, Incite, Insist(ent), Instance, Instigate, Itch, Kick, Libido, Nag, Orexis, Peremptory, Persuade, Press(ing), Prod, Push, Scrub, Set on, Sore, Spur, Stat, Strenuous, Strident, Strong, Threapit, Threepit, Triage, Vehement, Wanderlust, Whig, Whim, Yen

▷**Urgent** *may indicate* 'Ur-gent', viz. Iraqi

**Uriah** Hittite, Humble, Umble

**Urinal** Bog, John, Jordan, → LAVATORY, Loo, Pissoir

**Urinate(d), Urine** Chamber-lye, Emiction, Enuresis, Lant, Leak, Micturition, Number one, Oliguria, Pee, Piddle, Piss, Planuria, Relieve, Slash, Stale, Strangury, Tiddle, Uresis, Werris (Creek), Whiz(z), Widdle

**Urn(s), Urn-shaped** Canopic, Cinerarium, Ewer, Grecian, Lachrymal, Olla, Ossuary, Samovar, Storied, Tea, Urceolate, Vase

**Us** Me, Ourselves, 's, UK, Uns, We

**Usage, Use(r), Used, Utilise** Accustomed, Application, Apply, Avail, Boot, Clientele, Consume, Custom, Deploy, Dow, → EMPLOY, End, Enure, Ex, Exercise, Exert, Expend, Exploit, Flesh, Function, Habit(uate), Hand-me-down, Inured, Loanee, Manner, Milk, Mores, Ply, Practice, Pre-owned, Sarum, Snorter, Spare, Spent, Sport, Stock, Stoner, Take, Tradition, Treat, Try, Ure, Utilisation, Wield, With, Wont

**Useful** Asset, Availing, Commodity, Constructive, Convenient, Dow, Expedient, Invaluable, Plus, Practical, Versatile

**Useless** Appendix, Base, Bung, Cumber, Cumber-ground, Dead duck, Dead loss, Dead-wood, Dud, Empty, Futile, Gewgaw, Grotty, Ground, Idle, Inane, Incapable, Ineffective, Inutile, Lame, Lemon, Ne'er-do-well, Ng, Nonstarter, Nugatory, Otiose, Plug, Pointless, Reject, Sculpin, Sterile, Swap, Unavailing, US, Vain, Void, Washout, Waste, Wet, White elephant

**Usher** Black Rod, Blue Rod, Chobdar, Commissionaire, Conduct(or), Doorman, Escort, Gentleman, Guide, Herald, Huissier, Macer, Marshal, Rod, Show, Steward

**Usual, Usually** Average, Common, Customary, Habit(ual), In general, In the main, Most, Natural, Normal, Ordinary, Prevalent, Routine, Rule, Solito, Standard, Stock, Tipple, Typical, Vanilla, Wont

**Usurer, Usury** Gombeen, Gripe, Lender, Loanshark, Moneylender, Note-shaver, Shark, Uncle

**Usurp(er)** Abator, Arrogate, Assume, Encroach, Invade, Seize

**Ut** As, Doh, Utah

**Utah** Ut

**Utensil(s)** Batterie, Battery, Bedpan, Cafetiere, Ca(u)ldron, Canteen, Chopsticks, Colander, Cookware, Corer, Double boiler, Egg-slice, Egg-timer, Egg-whisk, Fish-kettle, Fish-slice, Fork, Funnel, Gadget, Grater, Griddle, Gridiron, Holloware, Implement, Instrument, Jagger, Kettle, Knife, Mandolin(e), Ricer, Scoop, Sieve, Skillet, Spatula, Spoon, Steamer, Things, Tongs, Tool, Whisk, Zester

▶**Utilise** *see* USAGE

**Utilitarian** Benthamite, Mill, Practical, Useful

**Utility** Elec(tricity), Expected, Gas, Mains, Public, Water

**Utmost** Best, Extreme, Farthest, Maximum, Nth

**Utopia(n)** Adland, Cloud-cuckoo-land, Eden, Ideal, More, Never-never-land, Pantisocracy, Paradise, Perfect, Shangri-la

**Utter(ance), Uttered, Utterly** Absolute, Accent, Agrapha, Agraphon, Aread, Arrant, Aside, Cry, Dead, Deliver, Dictum, Dog, Downright, Ejaculate, Emit, Enunciate, Express, Extreme, Glossolalia, Issue, Judgement, Lenes, Lenis, Locution, Mint, Most, Oracle, Pass, Phonate, Pronounce, Pure, Quo(th), Rank, Rap, Rattle, Remark, Saw, → SAY, Sheer, Sing, Speak, Spout, Stark, State, Syllable, Tell, Thorough, Tongue, Total, Ug, Unmitigated, Vend, Vent, Very, Voice

**Uvula** Staphyle

# Vv

**V** Anti, Bomb, Del, Five, Nabla, See, Sign, Verb, Verse, Versus, Victor(y), Volt, Volume

**Vacancy, Vacant** Blank, Empty, Free, Glassy, Goaf, Hole, Hollow, Inane, Opening, Place, Space, To let, Vacuum, Wooden

**Vacation** Break, Get away, Holiday, Leave, Long, Non-term, Outing, Recess, Trip, Voidance, Volunteer

**Vaccination, Vaccine** Antigen, Antiserum, Attenuated, Bacterin, Booster, Cure, HIB, Jenner, Lymph, MMR, Sabin, Salk, Serum, Subunit

**Vacillate, Vacillating** Chop, Dither, Feeble, Halt, Haver, Hesitate, Shilly-shally, Teeter, Trimmer, Wabble, Wave(r), Whiffle

**Vacuous, Vacuity** Blank, Empty, Inane, Toom, Vacant, Void

**Vacuum, Vacuum cleaner** Blank, Cleaner, Dewar, Dyson®, Eiky, Emptiness, Magnetron, Nothing, Nothingness, Plenum, Suction, Thermos®, Torricellian, Ultra-high, Void

**Vade-mecum** Ench(e)iridion, Notebook

**Vagabond** Bergie, Gadling, → GYPSY, Hobo, Landlo(u)per, Outcast, Palliard, Picaresque, Rapparee, Romany, Rover, Runabout, Runagate, Tramp

**Vagrant** Bag lady, Beachcomber, Bum, Bummer, Caird, Circumforaneous, Crusty, Cursitor, Derro, Dosser, Drifter, Flotsam, Gadabout, Gangrel, Gang-there-out, Goliard, Gypsy, Hobo, Landlo(u)per, Lazzarone, Nomad, Patercove, Rinthereout, Rogue, Romany, Rover, Scatterling, Strag, Straggle, Stroller, Swagman, Tinker, Tinkler, → TRAMP, Truant, Vagabond, Walker

**Vague(ness)** Airy-fairy, Amorphous, Bleary, Blur, Confused, Dim, Dreamy, Equivocal, Evasive, Faint, Free, General, Hazy, Ill-defined, Ill-headed, Imprecise, Indecisive, Indefinite, Indeterminate, Indistinct, Inexact, Loose, Loste, Mist, Nebulous, Obscure, Shadowy, Sketchy, Unclear, Woolly-minded

▷**Vaguely** *may indicate* an anagram

**Vain** Bootless, Conceited, Coquette, Coxcomb, Coxcomical, Dandyish, Egoistic, Empty, Fruitless, → FUTILE, Hollow, Idle, Narcissistic, Peacock, Pompous, Pown, Profitless, Proud, Self-important, Strutting, Toffee-nosed, Unuseful, Useless, Vogie

**Vainglory** Panache

**Valance** Pand, Pelmet

**Vale** Addio, Adieu, Aloha, Cheerio, Coomb, Dean, Dedham, Dene, Ebbw, Enna, Evesham, Glamorgan, Glen, Tara, Ta-ta, Tempé, Valley

**Valediction, Valedictory** Apopemptic, Cheerio, Farewell, Tata

**Valentine** Card, Sweetheart

**Valerian** All-heal, Cetywall, Greek, Red, Setuale, Setwale, Setwall, Spur

**Valet** Aid, Andrew, Batman, Gentleman's gentleman, Jeames, Jeeves, Lacquey, Man, Passepartout, Quint, Servant, Skip-kennel

**Valetudinarian** Hypochondriac, Invalid

**Valiant** Brave, Doughty, Heroic, Redoubtable, Resolute, Stalwart, Stouthearted, Wight

**Valid(ity), Validate** Authentic, Confirm, Establish, Holding, Just, Legal, Legitimate, Probate, Rational, Reasoned, Right, Sound

**Valise** Bag, Case, Dorlach, Satchel

**Valkyrie** Brynhild, Choosers of the slain, Warmonger

**Valley** Ajalon, Aosta, Argolis, Baca, Barossa, Bekaa, Beqaa, Bolson, Cleavage, Cleugh, Clough, Comb(e), Coomb(e), Cwm, Dale, Dargle, Dean, Death, Defile, Dell, Den, Dene, Dingle, Dip, Drowned, Dry, Emmental, Gehenna, Ghyll, Glen, Glencoe, Gleneagles, Glyn, Gorge,

Graben, Great Glen, Great Rift, Griff(e), Grindelwald, Gulch, Hanging, Haugh, Heuch, Hollow, Hope, Humiliation, Hutt, Imperial, Indus, Ladin, Lagan, Lallan, Loire, Lowland, Monument, Napa, Neanderthal, Nemea, Olympia, Ore, Po, Ravine, Rhondda, Ria, Rift, Rille, Ruhr, San Fernando, Seaton, Silicon, Slack, Slade, Sonoma, Strath(spey), Strathmore, Tempe, Tophet, Trossachs, Umbria, U-shaped, Valdarno, Vale, Vallambrosa, Vallis Alpes, Water, Water gap, Yosemite

**Valour** Bravery, Courage, Gallantry, Heroism, Merit, Prowess

**Valuable, Valuation, Value(s)** Absolute, Account, Acid, Appraise, Appreciate, Apprize, Assess(ment), Asset, Attention, Bargain, Blue chip, Book, Break up, Cachet, Calibrate, Calorific, Carbon, Checksum, Cherish, CIF, Cop, Cost, Crossover, Datum, Dear, Denomination, Eigen, Entry, Equity, Esteem, Estimate, Exit, Expected, Face, Feck, Hagberg, Intrinsic, Limit, Market, Merit, Modulus, Money's worth, Museum piece, Net present, Net realizable, Nominal, Nuisance, Number, Omnium, Par, PH, Place, Prairie, Precious, Premium, Present, Price, Prize, Prys, Q, Quartile, Quintile, Rarity, Rate, Rateable, Rating, Regard, Residual, Respect, Rogue, Salt, Scarcity, Sentimental, Set, Snob, Steem, Stent, Store, Street, Surplus, Surrender, Taonga, Time, Treasure, Tristimulus, Truth, Utility, Valuta, →WORTH

**Valueless** Bum, Fig, Mare's nest, Orra, Trivial, Useless, Worthless

**Valve** Acorn, Air, Aortic, Ball(cock), Bicuspid, Bistable, Bleed, Bleed nipple, Blow, Butterfly, Check, Choke, Clack, Cock, Diode, Drawgate, Dynatron, Escape, Eustachian, Exhaust, Flip-flop, Foot, Gate, Induction, Inlet, Magnetron, Mitral, Mixing, Needle, Non-return, Outlet, Pallet, Pentode, Petcock, Piston, Poppet, Pulmonary, Puppet, Radio, Resnatron, Safety, Seacock, Semilunar, Shut-off, Side, Sleeve, Slide, Sluice, Sluicegate, Snifter, Snifting, Stopcock, Suction, Tap, Tetrode, Thermionic, Throttle, Thyratron, Tricuspid, Triode, Turncock, Vacuum, Ventil, Vibrotron

**Vamoose** Abscond, Begone, Decamp, Scarper, Scat, Scram

**Vamp** Adlib, Charm, Improvise, Maneater, Rehash, Seduce, Siren, Strum, Twiddle

**Vampire** Bat, Dracula, False, Ghoul, Lamia, Lilith, Nosferatu, Pontianak, Stringes, Undead

**Van(guard)** Advance, Black Maria, Box, Box-car, Brake, Breakdown, Camper, Cart, Cube, Delivery, Dormobile®, Float, Forefront, Foremost, Freight-car, Front, Furniture, Guard's, Head, Kombi®, Lead, Leader(s), Lorry, Loudspeaker, Luggage, Mail, Meat wagon, Panel, Panel-truck, Pantechnicon, Patrol-wagon, Pick-up, Prison, Removal, Spearhead, Tartana, Transit, Truck, Ute, Wagon

**Vanadium** V

**Vandal(ise), Vandalism** Deface, Desecrate, Freebooter, Hooligan, Hun, Loot, Pillage, Ravage, Rough, Sab(oteur), Sack, Saracen, Skinhead, Slash, Smash, Trash, Wrecker

**Vandyke** Beard, Painter

**Vane(s)** Dog, Fan, Guide, Rudder, Swirl, Telltale, Vexillum, Weather(cock), Web, Wind (tee), Wing

**Vanessa** Butterfly

**Vanguard** Front, Vaward

**Vanilla** Orchid, Pinole

**Vanish(ed), Vanishing** Cease, Depart, Disappear, Disperse, Dissolve, Evanesce(nt), Evaporate, Extinct, Faint(ed), Mizzle, Slope, Transitory, Unbe

**Vanity** Amour-propre, Arrogance, Ego, Ego-trip, Esteem, Fair, Futility, Narcissism, Peacockery, Pomp, Pretension, Pride, Self-conceit, Self-esteem, Self-importance, Self-regard

**Vanquish, Vanquished** Beat, Conquer, Floor, Loser, Master, Overcome, Overwhelm, Rout, Subdue

**Vantage (point)** Ascendancy, Coign(e), Crow's nest, Height

**Vaporise, Vapour** Aerosol, Boil, Cloud, Contrail, Effluent, Effluvium, Fog, Fume, Gas, Halitus, Inhalant, Iodine, Miasma, Mist, Moisture, Reek, Roke, Skywriting, →STEAM, Steme, Water

▸**Variable, Variance, Variant, Variation** *see* VARY(ING)

**Varicose** Haemorrhoids

▸**Varied, Variety** *see* VARY(ING)

▹**Varied** *may indicate* an anagram

**Variegate(d)** Calico, Dappled, Flecked, Fretted, Harlequin, Motley, Mottle, Pied, Rainbow, Skewbald, Tissue

▹**Variety of** *may indicate* an anagram

**Various** Divers(e), Manifold, Multifarious, Separate, Several, Sundry

**Various years** Vy

**Varlet** Cad, Knave, Page, Rascal, Rogue

**Varnish(ing)** Arar, Bee-glue, Copal, Cowdie-gum, Dam(m)ar, Dammer, Desert, Dope, Dragon's-blood, French polish, Glair, Japan, Lacquer, Lentisk, Mastic, Nail, Nibs, Oil, Resin, Sandarac, Shellac, Spirit, Tung-oil, Tung-tree, Vernis martin, Vernissage

**Vary(ing), Variable, Variance, Variant, Variation, Varied, Variety, Various** Ablaut, Aelotropy, Allomorph, Alter, Amphoteric, Antigenic, Assorted, Assortment, Breed, Brew, Cepheid, Change, Chequered, Colour, Contrapuntal, Counterpoint, Daedal(e), Dedal, Dependent, Deviation, Differ, Discrepancy, Dispute, Diverse, Diversity, Dummy, Eclectic, Eclipsing, Enigma, Entropy, Erratic, Farraginous, Fickle, Fluctuating, Form, Goldberg, Grid, Heterodox, Iid, Inconsistent, Inconstant, Independent, Intervening, Isochor, Isopleth, Isotopy, Issue, Kind, Line, Local, Loggerheads, Magnetic, Medley, Mix, Modulate, Morph, Morphosis, Multifarious, Multiplex, Multiplicity, Music hall, Mutable, Nimrod, Nuance, Nutation, Odds and ends, Olio, Omniform, Orthogenesis, Parametric, Partita, Protean, Random, Remedy, Response, Revisal, Selection, Smörgåsbord, Sort, Species, Spice, Sport, Stirps, Stochastic, Strain, String, Timeserver, Tolerance, Twistor, Uneven, Unknown, Var, Varicellar-zoster, Vaudeville, Versatile, Versiform, Version, Vicissitude, Vl, Wane, Wax, X, Y, Z

**Vase** Bronteum, Canopus, Cornucopia, Diota, Hydria, Jardinière, Kalpis, Lachrymal, Lecythus, Lekythos, Lustre, Moon flask, Murr(h)a, Portland, Pot, Potiche, Stamnos, Urn, Vessel

**Vasectomy** Desexing

**Vassal** Client, Daimio, Dependant, Feoffee, Lackey, Liege, Liegeman, Man, Manred, Servant, Vavaso(u)r

**Vast(ness)** Astronomical, Big, Cosmic, Cyclopic, Enormous, Epic, Extensive, Googol, Huge(ous), Immeasurable, Immense, Large(-scale), Mighty, Monumental, Ocean, Prodigious

**Vat** Back, Barrel, Bath, Blunger, Chessel, Copper, Cowl, Cuvée, Fat, Girnel, Keir, Kier, Mash tub, Pressfat, Stand, Tank, Tan-pit, Tub, Tun, Winefat

**Vatican** Enclave, Rome, V

**Vaudeville** Music hall, Zarzuela

**Vaughan** Silurist

**Vault(ed), Vaulting** Arch, Barrel, Cavern, Cellar, Chamber, Charnel house, Clear, Cross, Crypt, Cul-de-four, Cupola, Dome, Dungeon, Fan, Firmament, Fornicate, Groin, Hurdle, Hypogeum, Jump, Kiva, Leap(frog), Lierne, Mausoleum, Ossuary, Overarch, Palm, Pend, Pendentive, Pole, Rib, Safe, Sepulchre, Serdab, Severy, Shade, Souterrain, Tholus, Tomb, Tunnel, Undercroft, Underpitch, Vaut, Wagon, Weem, Wine

▹**Vault** *may indicate* an anagram

**Vaunt** Boast, Brag, Crow, Skite

**VCR** Beta

**Veal** Escalope, Fricandeau, Galantine, Scallop, Schnitzel, Vituline, Wiener schnitzel

**Vector, Vector operator** Del, Dyad, Eigen, Expression, Nabla, Phasor, Polar, Radius

**Veda** Atharvaveda, Yajurveda

**Veer** Bag, Boxhaul, Broach, Clubhaul, Deviate, Draw, Gybe, Splay, Sway, Swerve, Tack, Turn, Wear, Yaw

**Veg(etate), Vegetator, Vegetation** Alga, Biome, Brush, Cover, Flora, Fynbos, Gar(r)igue, Greenery, Herb, Laze, Lemna, Maquis, Quadrat, Scrub, Stagnate, Sudd, Transect

**Vegan** Parev(e), Parve

**Vegetable(s)** Flora, Hastings, Inert, Jardinière, Olitory, Plant, Root, Salad, Sauce, Succade, Truck

**VEGETABLES**

*3 letters:*
Alu
Oca
Pea
Udo
Yam

*4 letters:*
Aloo
Bean
Beet
Cole
Gobi
Guar
Kale
Leek
Neep
Okra
Okro
Sium
Spud
Taro
Wort

*5 letters:*
Beans
Chana
Chard
Chive
Choko
Chufa
Crout
Ingan
Mooli
Navew
Onion
Orach
Pease
Pulse
Sabji
Savoy
Sibol
Swede
Tuber

*6 letters:*
Allium
Batata
Calalu
Camote
Carrot
Catalu
Celery
Coulis
Daikon
Endive
Fennel
Frisée
Garlic
Greens
Jicama
Kumara
Lablab
Legume
Mangel
Marrow
Matoke
Mibuna
Mizuna
Orache
Pepper
Pomato
Potato
Pratie
Quinoa
Radish
Rapini
Sorrel
Squash
Tattie
Tomato
Turnip
Wakame

*7 letters:*
Bok choy
Brinjal
Cabbage
Calaloo
Cardoon
Castock
Cataloo
Chayote
Chicory
Cocoyam
Collard
Custock
Earlies®
Filasse
Gherkin
Legumen
Lettuce
Mangold
Matooke
Pak-choi
Parsnip
Pimento
Pot herb
Pottage
Pumpkin
Rampion
Salsify
Shallot
Skirret
Soybean
Spinach
Spinage
Sprouts
Succory
Triffid
Witloof

*8 letters:*
Beetroot
Borecole
Brassica
Broccoli
Celeriac
Chick pea
Cucumber
Cucurbit
Eggplant
Escarole
Eschalot
Kohlrabi
Leaf-beet
Mirepoix
Mushroom
Rutabaga
Samphire
Scallion
Zucchini

*9 letters:*
Artichoke
Asparagus
Aubergine
Broad bean
Calabrese
Colcannon
Courgette
Finocchio
Macedoine
Mangetout
Primavera
Radicchio
Rocambole
Romanesco
Succotash
Sugar beet
Sweet corn
Tonka-bean
Turnip top

*10 letters:*
Alexanders
Beansprout
Cavalo nero
Chiffonade
Kidney bean
Runner bean
Sauerkraut
Scorzonera
String bean
Swiss chard
Tuscan kale

*11 letters:*
Bamboo shoot
Cauliflower
Chinese leaf
Haricot bean
Ratatouille
Spinach-beet
Spring onion
Sweet potato

*12 letters:*
Cherry tomato
Corn-on-the-cob
Mangel-wurzel
Marrow-squash

*14 letters:*
Globe artichoke

*18 letters:*
Jerusalem artichoke

**Vegetable extract** Solanine

**Vegetarian** Giraffe, Herbivore, Lactarian, Maigre, Meatless, Ovolacto, Parev(e), Parve, Pythagorean, Tofu, Vegan, Veggie

**Vegetation** Algae, Greenery, Herbage, Scrub, Sudd, Verdure
**Vehemence, Vehement(ly)** Amain, Ardent, Emphatic, Fervid, Forcible, Frenzy, Heat, Hot, Intense, Violent
**Vehicle(s)** Agent, Artic, Articulated, Auto, Baby buggy, Base, Commercial, Conveyance, Double-bottom, Fleet, Half-track, Haywain, Highlander, High occupancy, Hybrid, Konaki, Machine, Means, Medium, Multipurpose, Offroad, Oil, PSV, Rattletrap, Recovery, Recreational, Re-entry, Snowcat, Space, Spacecraft, Superload, Tandem, Tempera, Toboggan, Tourer, Tracked, Traffic, Troop carrier, Ute, Utility, Wheels, Wrecker

---

## VEHICLES

*3 letters:*
ATV
Bus
Cab
Car
Fly
LEM
SUV

*4 letters:*
Biga
Cart
Dray
Duck
Jeep®
Kago
Kart
Limo
MIRV
Quad
Rego
Scow
Shay
Sled
Tank
Taxi
Tram
Trap

*5 letters:*
Brake
Buggy
Crate
Cycle
Delta
Float
Go-Ped®
Lorry
Motor
Reggo
Rover
Soyuz
Sulky
Tip-up
Tonga
Truck
Turbo
Vespa®
Wagon

*6 letters:*
Boxcar
Camper
Dennet
Dodgem
Estate
Fiacre
Gharri
Gharry
Go-cart
Go-kart
Hansom
Hearse
Hummer
Humvee®
Jet-Ski
Jingle
Jinker
Jitney
Koneke
Landau
Launch
Limber
Litter
Matatu
Pick-up
Put-put
Samlor
Skibob
Skidoo®
Sledge
Sleigh
Sno-Cat®
Spider
Surrey
Tanker
Tardis
Tricar
Troika
Tuk tuk
Vahana
Weasel

*7 letters:*
Air taxi
Amtrack
Blokart
Capsule
Caravan
Casspir
Channel
Chariot
Crew cab
Dog-cart
Gritter
Growler
Jeepney
Minibus
Minicab
Minivan
Norimon
Pedicab
Phaeton
Rail bus
Ricksha
Shebang
Shuttle
Sidecar
Taxi cab
Tipcart
Tractor
Trailer
Tramcar
Trishaw
Trolley
Tumbril
Volante

*8 letters:*
Brancard
Cable car
Carriage
Carry-all
Curricle
Dragster
Rickshaw
Runabout
Sport ute
Stanhope
Steam-car
Tarantas
Tricycle
Trimotor
Unicycle

*9 letters:*
Ambulance
Autocycle
Battlebus
Buckboard
Dormobile®
Dune buggy
Estate car
Gladstone
Hatchback
Land Rover®
Motorhome
Sand-yacht
Tarantass
Tumble-car
Two-seater
Wagonette
Winnebago

*10 letters:*
All-terrain
Earth-mover
Four-by-four
Four-seater
Gas-guzzler
Hovercraft
Juggernaut
Load-lugger
Mammy wagon
Roadroller
Rust-bucket
Snowmobile
Snowplough
Trolleybus
Tumble-cart

Two-wheeler
Velocipede

*11 letters:*
People-mover
Semitrailer
Transporter
Wheelbarrow

*12 letters:*
Autorickshaw
Double-decker
Micro-scooter
Pantechnicon
Perambulator
Single-decker
Space shuttle
Station wagon
Three-wheeler

*13 letters:*
Paddock-basher
Penny-farthing
People carrier

*14 letters:*
Chelsea tractor

*16 letters:*
Personnel carrier

---

**Veil** Burk(h)a, Calyptra, Chad(d)ar, Chador, Chuddah, Chuddar, Cloud, Cover, Curtain, Envelop, Eucharistic, Hejab, Hide, Hijab, Humeral, Kalyptra, Khimar, Kiss-me, Lambrequin, Mantilla, Mask, Mist, Nikab, Niqab, Obscure, Purdah, Sacramental, Scene, Sudarium, Veale, Volet, Weeper, Wimple, Yashmak

**Vein** Artery, Azygas, Basilic, Brachiocephalic, Coronary, Costa, Diploic, Epithermal, Fahlband, Gate, Hemiazygous, H(a)emorrhoid, Innominate, Jugular, Ledge, Lode, Mainline, Media, Midrib, Mood, Naevus, Nervure, Organic, Outcrop, Percurrent, Pipe, Pipework, Portal, Postcava, Precava, Pulmonary, Radius, Rake, Reef, Rib, Saphena, Seam, Sectorial, Spur, Stockwork, Stringer, Style, Thread, Tone, Varicose, Varix, Vena (cava), Venule, Vorticose

**Vellum** Cutch, Japanese, Kutch, Parchment

**Velocity** Angular, Circular, Escape, Mustard, Muzzle, Orbital, Parabolic, Radial, Rate, Speed, Terminal, V

**Velvet(y)** Bagheera, Chenille, Moleskin, National, Panne, Pile, Three-pile, Velour, Velure, Villose, Villous

**Venal** Corruptible, Mercenary, Sale

**Vend(or), Vending** Auctor, Automat, Emporium, E-tailor, Hawk, Peddle, Pedlar, Purvey, Rep, Sammy, Sell, Sutler

**Vendetta** Feud

**Veneer** Facade, Finish, Gloss, Varnish

**Venerable** Aged, August, Augustus, Bede, Guru, Hoary, Iconic, Sacred, Sage, Vintage

**Venerate, Veneration** Adore, Awe, Douleia, Dulia, Filiopietistic, GOM, Hallow, Homage, Honour, Hyperdulia, Iconise, Idolise, Latria, Respect, Revere, Worship

**Venereal** NSU, VD

**Venery** Chase

**Venetian** Aldine, Blind, Doge, Gobbo, Polo

**Vengeance, Vengeful** Commination, Erinyes, Nemesis, Reprisal, Ultion, Vindictive, Wan(n)ion, Wrack, Wreak

**Venial** Base, Excusable

**Venice** La Serenissima

**Venison** Cervena, Deer

**Venom(ous)** Bitchy, Black widow, Gall, Gila, Jamestown-weed, Jim(p)son-weed, Platypus, Poison, Rancour, Solpuga, Spite, Toxic, Virus, Zootoxin

**Vent** Airway, Aperture, Belch, Chimney, Duct, Emit, Express, Flue, Fumarole, Hornito, Issue, Louver, Louvre, Ostiole, Outlet, Smoker, Solfatara, Spiracle, Undercast, Wreak

**Venter** Uterus

**Ventilate, Ventilator** Air, Air-brick, Air-hole, Discuss, Draught, Express, Louvre, Plenum, Shaft, Voice, Windsail, Windway, Winze

**Venture(d)** Ante, Assay, Bet, Callet, Chance, Dare, Daur, Durst, Enterprise, Flutter, Foray, Handsel, Hazard, Jump, Long shot, Mint, Opine, Presume, Project, Promotion, Prostitute, Risk, Spec, Strive, Throw

**Venue** Arena, Bout, Locale, Outlet, Place, Showground, Stadium, Stateroom, Tryst, Visne

**Venus** Armless, Clam, Cohog, Cytherean, Hesper(us), Love, Lucifer, Morning-star, Phosphorus, Primavera, Quahaug, Quahog, Rokeby, Vesper

**Venus fly-trap** Dionaea

**Veracity, Veracious** Accurate, Factual, Sincere, Truth(ful)

**Veranda(h)** Balcony, Gallery, Lanai, Patio, Piazza, Porch, Sleep-out, Stoep, Stoop, Terrace
**Verb(al), Verbs** Active, Argy-bargy, Auxiliary, Causative, Conative, Copula, Ergative, Factitive, Finite, Infinitive, Intransitive, Irregular, Modal, Passive, Perfective, Performative, Phrasal, Preterite, Stative, Transitive, Vb, Word-of-mouth
**Verbalise** Articulate
**Verbascum** Mullein
**Verbatim** Literally
**Verbena** Lemon, Vervain
**Verbiage** Perissology
**Verbose, Verbosity** Gassy, Padding, Pleonast, Prolix, Talkative, Wordy
**Verboten** No-no
**Verdant** Green, Leafy, Lush
**Verdict** Decision, Epitaph, Fatwah, Formal, Judg(e)ment, Majority, Narrative, Not proven, Open, Opinion, Pronouncement, Resolution, Ruling, Special
**Verdigris** Aeruginous, Patina
**Verge** Border, Brink, → **EDGE**, Hard shoulder, Incline, Limit, Long paddock, Rim, Roadside, Threshold
**Verger** Beadle, Pew-opener
**Verify, Verification** Accredit, Affirm, Ascertain, Check, Confirm, Constatation, Control, Crosscheck, Prove, Validate
**Verily** Yea
**Verisimilitude** Artistic, Authenticity, Credibility, Realism
**Verity** Fact, Sooth, Truth
**Vermicelli** Chocolate, Pasta
**Vermifuge** Cow(h)age, Cowitch
**Vermilion** Cinnabar, Minium, Red
**Vermin(ous)** Carrion, Catawampus, Lice, Mice, Pest, Ratty, → **RODENT**, Scum
**Vermouth** Absinthiated, Cinzano®, French, It(alian), Martini®
**Vernacular** Common, Dearnly, Dialect, Idiom, Jargon, Lingo, Native, Patois, Slang, Vulgate
**Veronica** Hebe, Hen-bit, Speedwell
**Verruca** Plantar wart, Wart
**Versatile** Adaptable, All-rounder, Flexible, Handy, Many-sided, Multipurpose, Octavalent, One man band, Protean, Resourceful
**Verse(s), Versed** Copy, Dactyl, Fluent, Free, Galliambics, Linked, Logaoedic, Passus, Pentastich, Poetry, Political, Reported, Rhophalic, → **RHYME**, Seguidilla, System

---

**VERSES**

*1 letter:*
V

*3 letters:*
Fit

*4 letters:*
Awdl
Blad
Duan
Epic
Epos
Fitt
Hymn
Line
Neck
Poem
Rime
Sijo
Song
Vers

*5 letters:*
Blank
Blaud
Canto
Comus
Epode
Fitte
Fytte
Gazal
Haiku
Hokku
Ionic
Lyric
Meter
Poesy
Renga
Rubai
Spasm
Stave
Tanka
Tract
Triad

*6 letters:*
Adonic
Ballad
Burden
Ghazal
Ghazel
Gnomic
Haikai
Heroic
Jingle
Laisse
Miurus
Octave
Pantun
Rondel
Scazon
Senary
Sonnet
Stanza
Strain
Tenson
Tercet
Vulgus

*7 letters:*
Alcaics
Couplet
Dimeter
Elegiac
Epigram
Fabliau
Huitain
Leonine
Pantoum
Pennill
Prosody
Pythian
Rondeau
Sapphic
Sestina
Sestine

Sixaine
Stiches
Strophe
Tiercet
Triolet
Tripody

***8 letters:***
Cinquain
Clerihew
Doggerel
Glyconic
Hexapody
Kyrielle
Madrigal
Nonsense
Pindaric
Quatrain
Rhopalic
Rove-over
Rubaiyat
Scansion
Senarius
Sing-song
Sirvente
Syllabic
Terzetta
Trimeter
Tristich
Versicle

***9 letters:***
Amphigory
Asclepiad
Beatitude
Dithyramb
Ditrochee
Goliardic
Hexameter
Macaronic
Monometer
Monorhyme
Monostich
Octameter
Octastich
Saturnian
Stornello
Terza rima
Vers libre

***10 letters:***
Asynartete
Catalectic
Cynghanedd
Fescennine
Hypermeter
Mock-heroic
Ottava rima
Pennillion
Pentameter
Rhyme-royal
Serpentine
Tetrameter
Tetrastich
Villanelle

***11 letters:***
Acatalectic
Alexandrine
Hudibrastic
Octastichon
Riding-rhyme
Septenarius

***12 letters:***
Archilochian
Asclepiadean
Hudibrastics
Octosyllabic

***14 letters:***
Longs and shorts

***15 letters:***
Poulter's measure

---

▷**Versed** *may indicate* reversed
**Versed sine** Sagitta
**Versifier, Versification** Lyricist, Poetaster, Prosody, Rhymer, Rhymester
**Version** Account, Adaptation, Authorised, Cephalic, Cover, Draft, Edition, Form, Paraphrase, Rede, Remake, Remix, Rendering, Rendition, Revised, Revision, Rhemish, Standard, Summary, Translation, Urtext, Variorum
**Versus** Against
**Vertebra(e), Vertebrate** Agnathan, Amniote, Amphioxus, Ascidian, Atlas, Axis, Bone, Centrum, Cervical, Chordae, Coccyx, Cyclostome, Dorsal, Foetus, Gnathostome, Ichthyopsida, Lamprey, Lumbar, Placoderm, Reptile, Sacral, Sand pride, Sauropsida, Spondyl, Tetrapod, Tunicata, Vermis
**Vertex** Apex, Crest, Crown, Summit, Zenith
**Vertical** Apeak, Apeek, Apothegm, Atrip, Erect, Lapse, Montant, Muntin(g), Ordinate, Perpendicular, Plumb, Prime, Sheer, Standing, Stemmed, Stile, Upright
**Vertigo** Dinic, Dizziness, Fainting, Giddiness, Megrim, Nausea, Staggers, Whirling
**Vertue** Visne
**Verve** Dash, Energy, Go, Gusto, Panache, Pep, Vigour
**Very (good, well)** A1, Ae, Assai, Awfully, Boffo, Bonzer, Boshta, Boshter, Bosker, Bully, Dashed, Dead, Def, Ever (so), Extreme(ly), Fell, Frightfully, Full, Gey, Grouse, Heap, Hellova, Helluva, Highly, Hugely, Jolly, Keen, Light, Mighty, Molto, Much, OK, Opt, Precious, Precise, Purler, Real(ly), Right, Self same, So, Sore, Stinking, Très, Unco, Utter, V, VG, Way
**Vesicle** Ampul, Bladder, Sudamina
**Vespers** Evensong, Lychnic, Placebo, Sicilian
**Vessel(s)** →**BOAT**, Capillary, Container, Craft, Dish, Lacteal, Logistics, Motor, Pressure, Receptacle, Retia, Seed, →**SHIP**, Tomentum, Utensil, Vascular, Weaker

---

## VESSELS

***3 letters:***
Bin
Cog
Cup
Dow
Fat
Obo
Pan
Pig
Pix
Pyx
Tub
Urn
Vas
Vat

***4 letters:***
Back
Bowl
Brig
Buss
Cask
Cowl
Dhow
Etna
Font
Grab
Horn
Lota
Olla
Olpe
Raft
Skin
Snow
Vase
Vein
Vena
Vial
Zulu

***5 letters:***
Aorta
Aviso
Blood
Cogue
Crare
Crewe
Crock
Cruet
Cruse
Cupel
Dandy
Dixie
Gourd
Grail
Ketch
Laver
Liner
Lotah
Mazer
Oiler
Phial
Pokal
Quart
Round
Scoop
Shell
Sloop
Stean
Steen
Stoop
Stoup
Tazza
Varix
Xebec
Zabra

***6 letters:***
Aludel
Argyle
Argyll
Artery
Banker
Beaker
Bicker
Bouget
Bucket
Carafe
Carboy
Censer
Chatty
Copper
Crayer
Dinghy
Dogger
Dolium
Droger
Elutor
Flagon
Frigot
Galiot
Galley
Goblet
Goglet
Guglet
Humpen
Jam jar
Jet-ski
Kettle
Lorcha
Mortar
Noggin
Pedalo
Retort
Rumkin
Sailer
Sampan
Sconce
Settee
Shippo
Situla
Steane
Tassie
Teacup
Teapot
Trough
Tureen
Urinal
Varice
Venule
Wherry

***7 letters:***
Amphora
Ampoule
Ampulla
Canteen
Carrier
Chalice
Cistern
Coaster
Costrel
Creamer
Cresset
Cuvette
Cyathus
Dredger
Drifter
Drogher
Felucca
Firepan
Four oar
Frigate
Gaff-rig
Galleon
Galliot
Gunboat
Gunship
Gurglet
Jugular
Mash tun
Mudscow
Patamar
Pinnace
Pirogue
Pitcher
Polacca
Precava
Sharpie
Steamer
Stewpot
Tankard
Terreen
Vedette
Washpot

***8 letters:***
Billycan
Calabash
Cauldron
Ciborium
Colander
Coolamon
Crucible
Cucurbit
Decanter
Figuline
Flagship
Flatboat
Galleass
Galliass
Gallipot
Gallivat
Hoveller
Hydroski
Jerrican
Lifeboat
Longboat
Monteith
Pancheon
Panchion
Pannikin
Schooner
Showboat
Sinusoid
Spittoon
Stockpot
Trimaran
Workboat

***9 letters:***
Alcarraza
Autoclave
Bucentaur
Calandria
Casserole
Cullender
Destroyer
Fining-pot
Hydrofoil
Pint-stoup
Powerboat
Privateer
Storeship
Tappit-hen
Whaleback
Whaleboat
Wineglass

***10 letters:***
Advice-boat
Bathyscape
Bathyscaph
Chamberpot
Deep-sinker
Icebreaker
Jardinière
Monstrance
Narrow boat
Triaconter
Windjammer

***11 letters:***
Aspersorium
Bathyscaphe
Side-wheeler

***12 letters:***
Fore-and-after
Lachrymatory
Stern-wheeler
Sternwheeler

---

**Vest** Beset, Bulletproof, Confer, Crop top, Gilet, Modesty, Rash, Semmit, Singlet, Skivvy, Spencer, Sticharion, String, Undercoat, Undershirt, Waistcoat

**Vestibule** Anteroom, Atrium, Entry, Exedra, Foyer, Hall, Lobby, Narthex, Oeil-de-boeuf, Porch, Portico, Pronaos, Tambour

**Vestige** Hint, Mark, Mention, Shadow, Sign, Trace

**Vestment** Alb, Breastplate, Canonicals, Chasuble, Chimar, Chimer(e), Cope, Cotta, Dalmatic, Ephod, Fannel, Fanon, Garb, → GARMENT, Maniple, Mantelletta, Omophorion, Pallium, Parament, Ph(a)elonian, Pontificals, Raiment, Rational, Rochet, Rocquet, Saccos, Sakkos, Sticharion, Stole, Superhumeral, Surplice, Tunic(le)

**Vestry** Common, Sacristy, Select

**Vet(ting), Veterinary, Vets** Censor, Check, Doc(tor), Examine, Ex-serviceman, Farrier, Herriot, Horse-doctor, Inspect, OK, Peruse, Positive, Screen, Spot check, Verify, Veteran, Zoiatria, Zootherapy

**Vetch** Bitter, Ers, Fitch, Kidney, Locoweed, Milk, Tare, Tine

**Veteran** BL, Expert, GAR, Master, Old-stager, Oldster, Old sweat, Old-timer, Old 'un, Retread, Seasoned, Soldier, Stager, Stalwart, Stalworth, Vet, War-horse, Warrior

▷**Veteran** *may indicate* 'obsolete'

**Veto** Ban, Bar, Blackball, Debar, Item, Line-item, Local, Negative, Pocket, Reject, Taboo, Tabu

**Vex(ing), Vexatious, Vexed** Ail, Anger, Annoy, Bepester, Bother, Chagrin, Debate, Exasperate, Exercised, Fret, Gall, Grieve, Harass, Haze, Irritate, Madden, Mortify, Noy, Peeve, Pester, Rankle, Rile, Sore, Spite, Tease, Torment, Trouble(some), Trying, Worrisome

**Vexation(s)** Barrator, Chagrin, Drat, Fashery, Grief, Humph, Irksome, Nuisance, Pique, Spite, Trouble, Try, Umph, Untoward

**Vexillum** Web

**Via** By, Per, Through

**Viable** Economic, Going, Healthy, Possible

**Viaduct** Bridge

**Vial** Spirit-level

**Viand** Cate

**Vibrate, Vibration(s), Vibrant, Vibrato** Active, Atmosphere, Chatter, Diadrom, Dindle, Dinnle, Dirl, Dynamo, Energetic, Flutter, Free, Fremitus, Harmonogram, Hotter, Jar, Judder, Oscillate, Plangent, Pulsate, Pulse, Purr, Quake, Reed, Resonance, Resonant, Rumble, Seiche, Shake, Shimmy, Shudder, Supersound, Thrill, Throb, Tingle, Tremble, Tremolo, Tremor, Trill, Trillo, Twinkle, Uvular, Wag, Whir(r)

**Viburnum** Opulus, Snowball

**Vicar** Apostolic, Bray, Choral, Cleric, Elton, Forane, General, Incumbent, Lay, Pastoral, Plenarty, Primrose, Rector, Rev(erend), Trimmer

**Vicarage** Manse

**Vice** Acting, Clamp, Cramp, Crime, Deputy, Eale, Evil, Foible, Greed, Iniquity, Instead, Jaws, Regent, Second (in command), → SIN, Stair

**Vice-president** Croupier, Veep

**Viceroy** Khedive, Nawab, Provost, Satrap, Willingdon

**Vichy (water)** Eau, Milice

**Vicinity** Area, Environs, Hereabouts, Locality, Neighbourhood, Region, Round about

**Vicious** Brutal, Cruel, Defamatory, Flagitious, Hotbed, Lethal, Savage, Vitriolic

**Vicissitude(s)** Chops and changes, Reverse

**Victim(s), Victimisation, Victimise** Abel, Angel, April fool, Butt, Casualty, Currie, Curry, Dupe, Easy meat, Fall guy, Fashion, Frame, Gay-bashing, Hitlist, Host, Judenhetze, Lay-down, Mark, Martyr, Nebbich, Neb(b)ish, Pathic, Patsy, Persecute, Pigeon, Prey, Quarry, Sacrifice, Scapegoat, Sitting duck, Stooge, Target, Torment

**Victor(y)** Bangster, Banzai, Beater, Cadmean, Cannae, Captor, Champ(ion), Clean sweep, Conqueror, Conquest, Coup, Epinicion, Epinikion, Eunice, Flagship, Fool's mate, Gree, Gris, Hallelujah, Hugo, Jai, Jai Hind, Kobe, Landslide, Lepanto, Ludorum, Mature, Moral, Nike, Palm, Philippi, Prizewinner, Pyrrhic, Romper, Runaway, Scalp, Shut-out, Signal, Squeaker, Success, Sweeping, Triumph, V, VE (day), Vee, Vic, Walk-away, Walkover, Win(ner)

**Victoria(n)** Aussie, Empress, Plum, Prig, Prude(nt), Station, Terminus

**Victualler** Caterer, Grocer, Licensed, Purveyor, Supplier, Vivandière

**Video(-tape)** Betacam®, Camcorder, Cassette, Digital, Full-motion, Interactive, Laser vision, Minitel, Pixelation, Promo, Quadruplex, Reverse, Scratch, Still, Vera, Webcast

**Vie** Compete, Contend, Emulate, Strive

**Vienna** Wien

**Vietcong** Charley, Charlie

**Vietnam(ese)** Annam, Cham, Tonkin, VN

**View(er), Viewing** Aim, Angle, Aspect, Attitude, Behold, Belief, Bird's eye, Butcher's (hook), Cineaste, Consensus, Consider, Cosmorama, Cutaway, Dekko, Dogma, Doxy, Endoscope, Estimation, Exploded, Eye (shot), Facet, Gander, Glimpse, Grandstand, Helicopter, Heresy, Idea, Introspect, Jaundiced, Kaleidoscope, Landscape, Line, Look, Notion, Observe, Opinion, Optic, Outlook, Pan, Panorama, Parallax, Peak, Perception, Perspective, Point, Private, Profile, → PROSPECT, Ringside, Scan, Scape, Scene(ry), Scope, See, Side, Sight, Sightlined, Skyscape, Slant, Snapshot, Spectate, Spectre, Specular, Spyglass, Standpoint, Stereoscope, Strain, Survey, Synop(sis), Tenet, Terrain, Thanatopsis, Theory, Vantage-point, Veduta, Vista, Visto, Watch, Witness, Worm's eye

**Viewpoint** Angle, Attitude, Belvedere, Conspectus, Dogma, Elevation, Eyeshot, Grandstand, Instance, Observatory, Opinion, Perspective, Sight, Sightline, Tendentious, Voxpop, Watch tower

**Vigil(ance), Vigilant(e)** Alert, Argus, Awake, Aware, Baseej, Basij, Deathwatch, Eve, Guardian angel, Hawk-eyed, Lyke-wake, On guard, Open-eyed, Pernoctate, Prudence, Wake, Wake-rife, Wary, Watch, Waukrife, Weather eye, Whitecap

**Vignette** Print, Profile, Sketch

**Vigorous(ly), Vigour** Aggressive, Agitato, Alive, Animation, Athletic, Bant, Bellona, Billy-o, Billy-oh, Birr, Blooming, Bouncing, Brio, Brisk, Con brio, Cracking, Drastic, Dynamic, Élan, Elbow grease, Emphatic, Energetic, Flame, Forceful, Full-blooded, Furioso, Go, Green, Gusto, Heart(y), Heterosis, Hybrid, Intensity, Kick-ass, Lush, Lustihood, Lustique, Lusty, Manful, Moxie, P, Pep, Pith, Potency, Punchy, Pzazz, Racy, Rank, Raucle, Red-blooded, Robust, Round, Rude, Sap, Scherzo, Smeddum, Spirit, Sprack, Sprag, Stamina, Steam, Sthenic, Stingo, Strength, Strenuous, Strong, Thews, Tireless, Tone, Tooth and nail, Trenchant, Two-fisted, Up, Vegete, Verve, Vim, Vinegar, Vitality, Vivid, Vivo, Voema, Zeal, Zip

▷**Vigorously** *may indicate* an anagram

**Viking** Dane, Erik the Red, Leif, Norseman, Raider, Rollo, R(y)urik, Sea king, Sea wolf, Varangian

**Vile(ness)** Base, Corrupt, Depraved, Dregs, Durance, Earthly, Infamy, Infernal, Mean, Offensive, Scurvy, Vicious

**Vilify, Vilification** Denigrate, Slander, Smear

**Villa** Bastide, Chalet, Dacha, House

**Village** Aldea, Auburn, Borghetto, Burg, Clachan, Corporate, Dorp, Endship, Global, Gotham, Gram, Greenwich, Hamlet, Kaik, Kainga, Kampong, Kirkton, Kraal, Legoland, Manyat(t)a, Mir, Outlet, Outport, Pit, Pueblo, Rancheria, Rancherie, Shtetl, Skara Brae, Thorp(e), Ujamaa, Vill, Wick

**Villain(y)** Anti-hero, Baddy, Bluebeard, Bravo, Card-sharp, Crim(inal), Crime, Dalek, Dastard, Dog, Fagin, Heavy, Iago, Knave, Lawbreaker, Macaire, Miscreant, Mohock, Nefarious, Ogre, Reprobate, Rogue, Ruffian, Scab, Scelerat, Scoundrel, Sikes, Skelm, Squeers, Steerforth, Tearaway, Traitor

**Villein** Bordar, Churl, Serf

**Vim** Energy, Go, Vigour, Vitality, Zing

**Vincent** Van Gogh

**Vindicate, Vindication** Absolve, Acquit, Apologia, Avenge, Clear, Compurgation, Darraign(e), Darrain(e), Darrayn, Defend, Deraign, Exculpate, Exonerate, Justify, Redeem

**Vindictive** Bunny-boiler, Hostile, Malevolent, Repay(ing), Spiteful, Vengeful

**Vine(yard)** Akatea, Ampelopsis, Ayahuasco, Balloon, Balsam apple, Bindweed, Bine, Bush rope, Château, Clinging, Clos, Colocynth, Cross, Cru, Cubeb, Cypress, Dodder, Dolina, Domaine, Grapery, Haoma, Hop, Idaean, Ivy, Kangaroo, Kudzu, Lawyer, Liana, Martha's, Matrimony, Muskmelon, Naboth's, Potato, Puncture, Quinta, Russian, Sarsaparilla, Stephanotis, Supplejack, Swallowwort, Trumpet, Turpeth, Vitis, Winery, Wonga-wonga, Yam, Yquem

**Vinegar** Acetic, Acetum, Alegar, Balsam, Balsamic, Eisel(l), Esile, Malt, Oxymel, Tarragon, Wine, Wood

**Vintage** Classic, Crack, Cru, Old, Quality

**Viol(a), Violet** African, Alto, Amethyst, Archil, Bass, Crystal, Dame's, Dog, Dog's tooth, Gamba, Garden, Gentian, Gridelin, Heart's ease, Hesperis, Ianthine, Indole, Iodine, Ionone, Kiss-me, Lilac, Lyra, Mauve, Methyl, Neapolitan, Orchil, Pansy, Parma, Prater, Quint(e), Rock, Saintpaulia, Shrinking, Sweet, Tenor, Visual, Water

**Violate, Violating, Violation** Abuse, Breach, Contravene, Defile, Desecrate, Fract, Infraction, → INFRINGE, Invade, March-treason, Outrage, Peccant, Rape, Ravish, Sacrilege, Solecism, Stuprate, Transgress, Trespass

**Violence, Violent(ly)** Acquaintance, Aggro, Amain, Attentat, Bangster, Battery, Berserk, Bloody, Brutal, Brute force, Cataclysmic, Crude, Drastic, Droog, Extreme, Fierce, Flagrant, Force, Frenzied, Furious, Gridelin, Heady, Het, High, Hooliganism, Hot, Inbreak, Mighty, Onset, Outrage, Rabid, Rage, Rampage, Rampant, Riot, Rogue, Rough, Rough stuff, Rude, Ruffian, Rumbustious, Savage, Severe, Shoot 'em up, Slap, Stormy, Strongarm, Ta(r)tar, Tearaway, Terrorism, Thuggery, Tinderbox, Tub-thumping, Vehement, Vie, Wild, Wrath

**Violet** Anil, Dog's tooth, Gentian, Gridelin, Neapolitan, Parma, Purple, Shrinking, → VIOLA

**Violin(ist), Violin-maker, Violin-shaped** Alto, Amati, Cremona, Fiddle, Griddle, Gu(e), Guarneri(us), Guarnieri, Heifetz, Kennedy, Kit, Kubelik, Leader, Luthier, Menuhin, Nero, Oistrakh, Paganini, Pandurate, Rebec(k), Rote, Stradivarius

**VIP** Bashaw, Bigshot, Bigwig, Brass, Cheese, Cob, Effendi, Envoy, Grandee, Imago, Kingpin, Magnate, Magnifico, Mugwump, Nabob, Nib, Nob, Pot, Snob, Someone, Swell, Top brass, Tuft, Tycoon, Worthy

**Viper** Asp, Berg-adder, Cerastes, Fer-de-lance, Gaboon, Horned, Ingrate, Judas, Pit, Puff adder, Rattlesnake, River-jack, Russell's, Sand, Saw-scaled, → SNAKE, Traitor, Villain

**Virago** Amazon, Battle-axe, Beldam(e), Harpy, Hellcat, Randy, Shrew, Termagant

**Virgil** Maro(nian)

**Virgin(al), Virginity, Virgin Mary** Airline, Blessed, Celibate, Chaste, Cherry, Extra, Intact, Ladykin, Madonna, Maiden, Maidenhead, Maidenhood, Marian, May, New, Our lady, Pan(h)agia, Parthenos, Pietà, Pucel(l)age, Pucelle, Pure, Queen, Snood, Spotless, Tarpeia, Theotokos, Untainted, Vestal, Zodiacal

**Virginia(n)** Creeper, Old Dominion, Tuckahoe, Va, Wade

**Virile, Virility** Energetic, Lusty, Machismo, Macho, Male, Manly, Red-blooded, Stud

**Virtu** Curio

**Virtue(s), Virtuous, Virtual** Angelic, Aret(h)a, Assay-piece, Attribute, Cardinal, Caritas, Charity, Chastity, Continent, Cyber, Dharma, Efficacy, Ethical, Excellent, Faith, Foison, Fortitude, Fus(h)ion, Good, Goody-goody, Grace, Honesty, Hope, Justice, Moral(ity), Natural, Noble, Nominal, Patience, Plaster-saint, Practical, Principal, Prudence, Pure, Qua, Saintly, Say-piece, Squeaky-clean, Straight and narrow, Temperance, Theological, Upright, Worth

**Virtuosity, Virtuoso** Artist, Bravura, Brilliance, Excellence, Executant, Maestro, Menuhin, Paganini, Savant, Whiz

**Virulent** Acrimonious, Deadly, Hostile, Malign, Noxious, Toxic, Vitriolic, Waspish

**Virus** AIDS, Antigen, Arbovirus, Bacteriophage, Boot, Capsid, Chikungunya, Cold sore, Computer, Contagium, Coronavirus, Coxsackie, Defective, DNA, EB, Ebola, ECHO, Enterovirus, Epstein-Barr, Filovirus, Filterable, Fowlpest, Germ, Granulosis, Hantavirus, Hendra, Herpes, HIV, HIV negative, HIV positive, Human immunodeficiency, Lassa, Latent, Leaf-mosaic, Lentivirus, Michelangelo, Microbe, Microorganism, Mumps, Noro, Norwalk, Oncogen, Oncornavirus, Parainfluenza, Parvo(virus), Pathogen, Peach-yellow, Picornavirus, Polyoma, Prophage, Reovirus, Retrovirus, Rhabdovirus, Rhinovirus, Ross River, Rotavirus, SARS, Shingles, Slow, Street, SV40, Swine flu, Tobacco mosaic, Trojan horse, Varicella, Venom, Virino, Virion, West Nile, Zoster

**Visa** Transit

**Viscera** Bowels, Entrails, Giblets, Guts, Harigal(d)s, Haslet, Innards, Omentum, Splanchnic, Umbles, Vitals

**Viscount** Vis

**Viscous (liquid), Viscosity** Absolute, Gel, Glaireous, Gleety, Gluey, Goop, Gummite, Gummy, Kinematic, Slab, Specific, Sticky, Stoke, Tacky, Tar, Thick, Thixotropic
**Visible, Visibility** Clear, Conspicuous, Discernible, Evident, Explicit, Export, Eyeshot, In sight, Obvious, Zero-zero
**Visigoth** Asaric
**Vision(ary)** Abstraction, Aery, Aisling, Apparition, Awareness, Beatific, Binocular, Bourignian, Bourignon, Day-dreamer, Double, Dream(er), Emmetropia, Fancy, Fantast, Fey, Foresight, Fortune teller, Hallucination, Idealist, Ideologist, Illusionist, Image, Kef, Moonshine, Mouse-sight, Mystic, Ocular, Phantasm(a), Phantom, Pholism, Photism, Photopia, Prospect, Rainbow-chaser, Revelation, Romantic, Seeing, Seer, Sight, Sightline, Stereo, Stereopsis, Sweven, Tunnel, Twenty-twenty, Viewy
**Visit(or)** Affliction, Alien, Away, Caller, Day-tripper, Domiciliary, Emmet, ET, Event, First-foot, Flying, Frequent, Gam, Guest, Habitué, Haunt, Health, Hit, House-call, Inflict, Kursaal, Look in, Look up, Manuhiri, Pop in, Prison, See, Sightseer, Sojourn, State, Stay, Stranger, Take, Theatregoer, Tourist, Wait upon, Weekender
**Visor, Vizor** Eyeshade, Face-saver, Mesail, Mezail, Umbrel, Umbr(i)ere, Umbril, Vent(ayle)
**Vista** Enfilade, Outlook, Scene(ry), View
**Visual(ise)** Envisage, Graphical, Imagine, Ocular, Optical, Picture, See, Sketch, Visible
**Vital(ity)** Alive, Bounce, Central, Critical, Crucial, Energy, Esprit, Essential, Evergreen, Existent, Fervour, Foison, Gusto, Indispensable, Juice, Key, Kick, Life-blood, Lifeline, Linchpin, Lung, Mites, Momentous, Necessary, Oomph, Organ, Pizzazz, Pulse, Salvation, Sap, Statistics, Urgent, Verve, Viable, Vigour, Zing, Zoetic
**Vitals** Numbles, Umbles, Viscera
**Vitamin(s)** A, Adermin, Aneurin, Axerophthol, B, Bioflavonoid, Biotin, C, Calciferol, Calcitriol, Citrin, Cobalamin, D, E, Ergocalciferol, Folacin, G, Goji, H, Inositol, K, Linoleic, Menadione, Menaquinone, Niacin, Niacinamide, P, Pan(to)thenol, Phylloquinone, Phytonadione, Pyridoxin(e), Retinene, Retinol, Riboflavin, Ribose, Thiamin(e), Tocopherol, Torulin, Tretinoin
**Vitiate(d)** Flaw(ed)
**Vitreous** Glassy, Hyaline
**Vitriol(ic)** Acid, Acrimonious, Biting, Blue, Caustic, Green, Mordant, White
**Vituperate** Abuse, Berate, Castigate, Censure, Defame, Inveigh, Lash, Rail, Scold
**Viva** Oral
**Vivacity, Vivacious** Animation, Brio, Effervescent, Esprit, Exuberant, Sparkle, Spirit, Sprightly, Verve
**Vivid** Bright, Brilliant, Colourful, Dramatic, Eidetic, Fresh, Graphic, Keen, Live, Lurid, Pictorial, Picturesque, Sharp, Shocking, Violent
**Vivien** Leigh
**Vixen** Catamaran, Harridan, Shrew, Virago
**Viz** Sc, Videlicet
**Vizier** Pheazar, Wazir
▸**Vizor** *see* **VISOR**
**Vocabulary** Active, Glossary, Glottochronology, Idiolect, Idioticon, Jargon, (Kata)kana, Lexicon, Lexis, Meta-language, Nomenclator, Passive, Wordbook
**Vocal(isation), Vocalist** Articulate, Cantilena, Doo-wop, Eloquent, Minstrel, Oral, Phonal, Schwa, Singer, Songster, Sprechgesang
**Vocation** Call, Career, Métier, Mission, Priesthood, Profession, Pursuit, Shop
**Vociferous(ly)** Clamant, Loud, Loud-mouth(ed), Ore rotundo, Strident
**Vodka** Smirnoff®
**Vogue** Chic, Day, →**FASHION**, Groovy, It, Mode, Rage, Style, Ton, Trend
**Vogul** Ugrian, Ugric
**Voice(d)** Active, Air, Alto, Ancestral, Bass, Chest, Contralto, Countertenor, Descant, Edh, Emit, Eth, Express, Falsetto, Glottis, Harp, Head, Inner, Intonate, Lyric, Mastersinger, Meistersinger, Mezzo-soprano, Middle, Mouth, Opinion, Passive, Phonic, Pipe, Presa, Quill, Say, Sonant, Soprano, Speak, Spinto, Sprechstimme, Stentorism, Steven, Syrinx, Tais(c)h, Tenor, Throat, Tone, →**TONGUE**, Treble, Utter, White

**Voiceless** Aphonia, Aphony, Dumb, Edh, Eth, Mute, Silent, Tacit
**Voice over** Narration
**Void** Abrogate, Abyss, Annul, Belch, Blank, Chasm, Counter, Defeasance, Defecate, Diriment, Empty, Erase, Evacuate, Gap, Hollow, Inane, Inoperative, Invalid, Irritate, Lapse, Negate, Nullify, Quash, Space, Vacuum
**Voila** There
**Volatile** Excitable, Explosive, Flashpoint, Inconsistent, Inflammable, Latin, Live(ly), Mercurial, Skittish, Tear gas, Temperamental, Terpene, Tinderbox, Unpredictable, Unstable
**Volcano(es), Volcanic** Agglomerate, Basalt, Black smoker, Burning mountain, Composite, Cone, Conic, Crater, Fumarole, Greystone, Hornito, Ice, Idocrase, Igneous, Ignimbrite, Monticule, Mud, Obsidian, Pele, Pelée, Plinian, Pozz(u)olana, Pumice, Puzzolana, Sandblow, Shield, Soffioni, Solfatara, Stratovolcano, Tephra, Trass, Tuff

---

**VOLCANOES**

***2 letters:***
Aa

***3 letters:***
Aso
Puy

***4 letters:***
Etna
Fuji
Maui
Taal

***5 letters:***
Askja
Hekla
Katla
Kauai
Mayon
Misti
Okmok
Salse
Thera

***6 letters:***
Ararat
Asosan
Azores
Egmont
Erebus
Ischia
Katmai
Kazbek
Lipari
Semeru
Shasta
Tolima

***7 letters:***
Aragats
Comoros
El Misti
Huascan
Iliamna
Iwo Jima
Kilauea
Mofette
Rotorua
Ruapehu
Semeroe
St Kilda
Tambora

***8 letters:***
Amygdale
Andesite
Antisana
Cameroon
Cotopaxi
Jan Mayan
Krakatoa
Mauna Kea
Mauna Loa
St Helena
St Helens
Taranaki
Unalaska
Vesuvius

***9 letters:***
Aniakchak
Corcovado
Haleakala
Helgafell
Huascaran
Mount Fuji
Nevis Peak
Paricutin
Scablands
Stromboli
Tangariro

***10 letters:***
Chimborazo
Lassen Peak
Montserrat
Mount Eigon
Mount Kenya
Mount Pelée
Nyiragongo

***11 letters:***
Erciyas Dagi
Kilimanjaro
Mount Egmont
Mount Erebus
Mount Katmai
Mount Kazbek
Mount Shasta
Nyamuragira
Olympus Mons
Pico de Teide
Pico de Teyde

***12 letters:***
Citlaltépetl
Ixtaccahuatl
Iztaccahuatl
National Park
Popocatepetl

***13 letters:***
Mount Demavend
Mount Pinatubo
Mount St Helens

***14 letters:***
Mount Suribachi
Nevada de Colima
Nevada de Toluca
Soufrière Hills

***17 letters:***
Fernando de Noronha
Warrumbungle Range

***20 letters:***
D'Entrecasteau Islands

---

**Vole** Arvicola, Field, Meadow mouse, Muskrat, Musquash, Ondatra
**Volition** Velleity, Will
**Volley** Barrage, Boom, Broadside, Platoon, Round, Salvo, Tirade, Tire
**Volt(age)** BeV, Bias, Breakdown, Electron, Grid bias, HT
**Voltaire** Arouet
**Volte face** Enantiodromia, U-turn, Zig
**Voluble** Fluent, Garrulous, Glib

**Volume** Atomic, Band, Bande, Barrel, Book, Bushel, Capacity, CC, Code(x), Content, Critical, Cubage, Gallon, Hin, Loudness, Mass, Ml, Molecular, Omnibus, Peck, Pint, Quart(o), Roll, Roul(e), Size, Space, Specific, Stere, Swept, Tidal, Titre, Tom, Tome, Ullage, Vol

**Voluntary, Volunteer** Docent, Enlist, Fencible, Free, Free-will, Honorary, Offer, Optional, Postlude, Reformado, Spontaneous, Tender, Tennessee, Terrier, TN, Ultroneous, Unpaid, Yeoman

**Voluptuary, Voluptuous** Buxom, Carnal, Curvy, Goluptious, Hedonist, Houri, Luscious, Sensuist, Sensuous, Sybarite

**Volute** Helix, Roll

**Vomit(ing)** Anacatharsis, Barf, Black, Boak, Boke, Cascade, Cat, Chuck up, Chunder, Disgorge, Egest, Egurgitate, Emesis, Fetch-up, Haematemesis, Honk, Keck, Kotch, Parbreak, Posset, Puke, Ralph, Regorge, Regurgitate, Retch, Rolf, Spew, Technicolour yawn, Throw up, Upchuck

**Voodoo** Charm, Jettatura, Kurdaitcha, Macumba, Mambo, Obeah, Sorcery, Zombi(e)

**Voracious, Voracity** Bulimia, Edacity, Gluttony, Greed, Man-eater, Ravenous, Serrasalmo

**Vortex** Charybdis, Eddy, Gyre, Trailing, Whirlpool

**Votary** Adherent, Cenobite, Devotee, Disciple, Fan, Nun, Swinger, Zealot

**Vote(r), Votes, Voting** Alternative, Assentor, Aye, Ballot, Ballotee, Block, Card, Casting, Choose, Colonist, Constituent, Coopt, Cross, Crossover, Cumulative, Division, Donkey, Electoral, Fag(g)ot, Floating, Franchise, Free, Grey, Informal, Mandate, Nay, Negative, No, Opt, People, Placet, Plebiscite, Plump, Plural, Poll, Postal, Pot-wabbler, Pot-waller, Pot-walloner, Pot-walloper, Pot-wobbler, PR, Preferential, Proportional representation, Protest, Qualified majority, Referendum, Return, Scrutin de liste, Scrutiny, Show of hands, Side, Single transferable, Straw(-poll), Suffrage, Swinging, Sympathy, Tactical, Ten-pounder, The stump, Theta, Ticket, Token, Transferable, Voice, X, Yea, Yes

**Vote-catcher** Pork

**Vouch(er), Vouchsafe** Accredit, Airmile, Assure, Attest, Beteem(e), Book token, Chit, Coupon, Credit note, Docket, Endorse, Gift, Guarantee, Luncheon, Meal-ticket, Pass, Promise, Receipt, Slip, Ticket, Token, Warrant

**Voussoir** Quoin, Wedge

**Vow** Affirm, Baptismal, Behight, Behot(e), Earnest, Ex voto, Hecht, Hest, I do, Nuncupate, → OATH, Obedience, Pledge, Plight, Promise, Simple, Solemn, Swear, Troth, Vum

**Vowel(s)** Ablaut, Anaptyxis, Aphesis, Breve, Cardinal, Crasis, Diphthong, Gradation, Indeterminate, Monophthong, Murmur, Mutation, Point, Rhyme, Seg(h)ol, S(c)hwa, Svarabhakti, Triphthong

**Voyage(r)** Anson, Columbus, Course, Cruise, Launch, Maiden, Passage, Peregrinate, Salt, Sinbad, Travel

**Voyeur** Peeping Tom, Scopophiliac

**VTOL** Convertiplane

**Vulcan(ite)** Blacksmith, Ebonite, Fire, Mulciber, Spock, Wayland

**Vulgar(ian)** Banausic, Barbaric, Base, Bawdy, Blatant, Blue, Brassy, Buffoon, Canaille, Cheap, Cit, Coarse, Common, Crude, Demotic, Earthy, Filthy, Flash(y), Forward, Gaudy, General, Gent, Gorblim(e)y, Gross, Heel, Hussy, Ignorant, Indecent, Kitsch, Laddish, Lavatorial, Lewd, Low(-life), Naff, Obscene, Ostentatious, Pandemian, Parvenu, Plebby, Plebeian, Popular, Proletarian, Raffish, Ribald, Riff-raff, Rude, Scaff, Scurrilous, Slag, Snob, Tacky, Tarty, Tawdry, Threepenny, Tiger, Tink, Twopenny, Unseemly, Upstart, Vulg

**Vulnerable, Vulnerability** Achilles heel, Defenceless, Endangered, Exposed, Frangible, Helpless, Open, Pregnable, Susceptible, Tender, Unguarded, Weak, Wide-open

**Vulture** Aasvogel, Bearded, Bird, Buzzard, California (condor), Condor, Culture, Falcon, Gallinazo, Gier, Griffon, Gripe, Grype, King, Lammergeier, Lammergeyer, Ossifrage, Predator, Turkey, Urubu, Zopilote

**W** Watt, West, Whisky, Women
**Wacky** Offbeat, Useless
**Wad(ding)** Batt(ing), Lump, Pad, Pledget, Roll, Swab, Wodge
**Waddle** Toddle, Waggle
**Waddy** Club, Cowboy, Stick
**Wade(r), Wading** Antigropelo(e)s, Ardea, Crane, Curlew, Dikkop, Egret, Flamingo, Ford, Godwit, Grallae, Grallatorial, Greenshank, Gumboot, Heron, Ibis, Jacksnipe, Lapwing, Limpkin, Oyster-catcher, Paddle, Phalarope, Plodge, Plover, Pukeko, Ree, Sandpiper, Sarus, Seriema, Shoebill, Snipe, Splodge, Stilt(bird), Stint, Terek, Virginia, Wellington
**Waesucks** Ewhow, O(c)hone
**Wafer** Biscuit, Chip, Cone, Cracker, Crisp, Gaufer, Gaufre, Gofer, Gopher, Host, Papad, Seal
**Waff** Flap, Flutter, Wave
**Waffle** Adlib, Belgian, Blather, Cake, Equivocate, Fudge, Gas, Gaufer, Gaufre, Gofer, Gopher, Hedge, Padding, Poppycock, Prate, Rabbit, Wibble
**Waft(ing)** Airborne, Aura, Blow, Drift, Float
**Wag(gish), Waggle** Arch, Card, Comedian, Facetious, Joker, Lick, Niddle-noddle, Nod, Rogue, Shake, Sway, Swee, Wit(snapper), Wobble
**Wage(s)** Ante, Award, Board, Earnings, Fee, Greengage, Hire, Income, Living, Meed, Minimum, Nominal, Pay, Penny-fee, Portage, Practise, Prosecute, Rate, Salary, Screw, Slave, Subsistence
**Wage-earner** Breadwinner, Employee, Proletariat(e)
**Wager** Ante, Back, → **BET**, Gamble, Lay, Pascal's, Stake, Wed
**Wagon(er)** Ar(a)ba, Aroba, Boötes, Box, Boxcar, Brake, Break, Buck, Buckboard, Buggy, Caisson, Carriage, Cart, Cattle truck, Chuck, Coachman, Cocopan, Conestoga, Corf, Covered, Democrat, Drag, Dray, Flatcar, Fourgon, Freight-car, Gambo, Go-cart, Hopper, Hutch, Low-loader, Luggage-van, Mammy, Meat, Paddy, Palabra, Patrol, Plaustral, Police, Prairie schooner, Rave, Reefer, Rubberneck, Shandry, Stage, Station, Tank, Tartana, Telega, Tender, Trap, Trekker, Truck, Van, Victoria, Wain, Water
**Waif** Arab, Foundling, Gamin, Guttersnipe, Jetsam, Stray, Urchin, Victoria, Wastrel, Water, Weft
**Wail(er)** Banshee, Bawl, Blubber, Howl, Keen, Lament, Moan, Skirl, Threnody, Threnos, Ululate, Vagitus, Wah-wah, Yammer
**Wain** Cart, Dray, Wagon
**Waist(band)** Belt, Cummerbund, Girdlestead, Girth, Hour-glass, Middle, Midship, Obi, Sash, Shash, Wasp, Zoster
**Waistcoat** Bodice, Gilet, Jerkin, Lorica, MB, Pressure, Sayon, Shawl, Sleeve(d), Stabvest, Tuxedo, Vest, Weskit
**Wait(er), Waiting** Abid(e), Ambush, Attend, Barista, Bide, Busboy, Butler, Buttle, Carhop, Commis, Cupbearer, Dally, Delay, Dumb, Estragon, Expect, Flunkey, Frist, Garçon, Hang on, Hesitate, Hover, In limbo, Interval, Khidmutgar, Lead time, Lime, Linger, Loiter, Lurch, Lurk, Maître d', Maître d'hôtel, Minority, Omnibus, Pannier, Pause, Penelope, Pozzo, Queue, Remain, Serve(r), Sommelier, Stacking, Stay, Steward, Suspense, Taihoa, Tarry, Tend(ance), Tray, Vladimir, Wine, Won
**Waitress** Bunny girl, Hebe, Miss, Mousme(e), Nippy, Parlourmaid, Server
**Waive** Abandon, Defer, Forgo, Overlook, Postpone, Relinquish, Renounce, Suspend
**Wake(n)** Abrade, Abraid, Abray, Aftermath, Alert, American, Animate, Arouse, Astern,

Backwash, Deathwatch, Excite, Finnegan's, Hereward, Keen, Knock-up, Lich(wake), Like(wake), Lyke(wake), Prod, Rear, Reveille, Revive, → ROUSE, Surface, Trail, Train, Wash

**Waldo** Emerson

**Wale(r)** Prop, Ridge, Weal

**Wales** Cambria, Cymru, Dyfed, Principality

**Walk(er), Walking, Walkabout, Walkway** Aisle, Alameda, Alley, Alure, Amble, Ambulate, Arcade, Berceau, Birdcage, Charity, Cloister, Clump, Constitutional, Daddle, Dander, Dauner, Emu, Esplanade, EVA, Expatiate, Festination, Flânerie, Forefoot, Frescade, Gait, Gallery, Gangplank, Ghost, Go, Gradient, Gressorial, Heel and toe, Hike, Hookey, Hump, Lambeth, Leg, Loggia, Lumber, Mainstreeting, Mall, March, Mince, Mooch, Mosey, Nordic, Pace, Pad, Paddle, Pasear, Paseo, Passage, Passerby, Path, Pavement, Ped(estrianism), Perambulate, Pergola, Perp, Piaffe, Piazza, Pipe-opener, Platform, Pole, Pound, Power, Prance, Prom(enade), Rack, Ramble, Rampart, Random, Ring, Routemarch, Sashay, Scamble, Schlep, Shamble, Side, Sidle, Slommock, Space, Spanish, Sponsored, Stagger, Stalk, Step, Stoa, Striddle, Stride, Stroll, Strut, Stump, Taligrade, Teeter, Terrace, Toddle, Totter, Traipse, Tramp, Trash, Travolator, Tread, Trog, Truck, Trudge, Turn, Wade, Wander, Wayfare, Wend, Widow's, Xyst

**Walking-stick** Cane, Hickory, Stilt

**Walk-over** Doddle, Pie, Scratch

**Wall** Antonine, Bail, Bailey, Barrier, Battlement, Berlin, Berm, Breast, Bulwark, Cavity, Cell, Chinese, Climbing, Countermure, Crib, Curtain, Dado, Dam, Dike, Dry-stone, Dyke, Enceinte, Epispore, Exine, Fail-dike, Fire, Fourth, Fronton, Frustule, Gable, Great, Groyne, Hadrian's, Hanging, Hangman, Head, Hot, Immure, Intine, Mahjongg, Mani, Merlon, Mutual, Myocardium, Non-bearing, Parapet, Parie(te)s, Parietal, Parpane, Parpen(d), Parpent, Parpoint, Partition, Party, Pay, Peribolos, Pericarp, Perpend, Perpent, Pleuron, Podium, Puteal, Qibla, Rampart, Retaining, Reveal, Revet(ment), Ring, River, Roman, Roughcast, Screen, Sea, Septum, Severus, Side, Somatopleure, Spandrel, Spandril, Stockade, Street, Studding, Tambour, Tariff, Trumeau, Vallation, Vallum, Video, Wa', Wailing, Western, Withe, Zooecia

**Wallaby** Brusher, Dama, Kangaroo, Pademelon, Pad(d)ymelon, Quokka, Tammar, Whiptail

**Wallah** Competition

**Wallaroo** Euro

**Wall-covering, Wallpaper** Anaglypta®, Arras, Burlap, Flock, Lincrusta, Paper, Tapestry, Tapet

**Waller** Fats, Mason

**Wallet** Billfold, Case, Flybook, Folder, Notecase, Pochette, Pocket-book, Purse, Scrip

**Wallflower** Crucifer, Dowd(y), Pariah

**Wall-game** Eton, Mahjongg

**Wallop** Axe, Bash, Baste, Batter, Beat, Biff, Clout, Cob, Dunt, Gigantic, → HIT, Lam, Lounder, Oner, Polt, Pound, Slog, Strap, Swinge, Tan, Tat, Thud, Trounce

**Wallow(ing)** Bask, Flounder, Luxuriate, Revel, Roll, Slubber, Splash, Swelter, Tolter, Volutation, Welter

**Wall-painting** Fresco, Graffiti, Grisaille

**Wallpaper** → WALL-COVERING, Woodchip

**Wall-plate** Tassel, Torsel

**Wall-support** Beam, Foundation, Pier, Rear-arch, Rere-arch

**Wally** Ass, Dipstick, Moron, Nerd, Nincompoop, Prat

**Walnut** Black, Butternut, Hickory, Juglans, Satin, White

**Walrus** Morse, Moustache, Pinniped, Rosmarine, Sea-cow, Sea-horse, Tash, Ugly

**Walter** Bruno, Mitty, Pater, Raleigh, Scott

**Waltz, Waltzing** Anniversary, Blue Danube, Boston, Concert, Dance, Hesitation, Matilda, Minute, Rotate, Valse, Viennese

**Wampum** Peag(e), Shell-money

**Wan** Lurid, Pale, Pallid, Pasty, Sanguine, Sorry

**Wanchancy** Unlucky

**Wand** Baton, Caduceus, Magic, Rod, Runic, Stick, Thyrse, Thyrsus, Vara, Vare

**Wander(er), Wandering** Aberrance, Adrift, Amble, Bedouin, Berber, Bum, Caird, Daiker, Daydream, Delirious, Desultory, Deviate, Digress, Divagate, Diverge, Drift, Errant, Estray, Evagation, Excursive, Expatiate, Extravagate, Gad(about), Grope, Hobo, Itinerant, Jew, Landloper, Maunder, Meander, Meandrian, Mill, Mither, Moider, Moither, Moon, Noctivagant, Nomad(e), Odysseus, Pedder, Peregrine, Peripatetic, Polar, Prodigal, Rache, Ramble, Range, Ratch, Roamer, Romany, Room, Rove, Solivagant, Stooge, Straggle, Stravaig, Stray, Strayve, Streel, Stroam, Stroll, Swan, Ta(i)ver, Traipse, Tramp, Troll, Truant, Tuareg, Vagabond, Vagile, Vagrant, Vague, Waif, Wend, Wheel, Wilder, Wolves

▷**Wandering** *may indicate* an anagram

**Wane** Decline, Decrease, Diminish, Ebb

**Wangle** Arrange, Finagle, Trick

**Wannabe** Aspirant

**Want(ing), Wants** Absence, Conative, Covet, Crave, Cut, Dearth, Defect, Deficient, Derth, Desiderata, → DESIRE, Destitution, Distress, Envy, For, Hardship, Indigent, Itch, Lack, Like, Long, Mental, Moldwarp, Mole, Need, Penury, Require, Scarceness, Scarcity, Shortfall, Shy, Void, Wish, Yen

**Wanton(ness)** Bona-roba, Cadgy, Chamber, Cocotte, Colt's tooth, Deliberate, Demirep, Filly, Flirt-gill, Gammerstang, Giglet, Giglot, Gillflirt, Hussy, Jay, Jezebel, Jillflirt, Lewd, Licentious, Light o' love, Loose, Nice, Protervity, Rig, Roué, Smicker, Sportive, Sybarite, Toyish, Twigger, Unchaste, Wayward

**Wap** Blow, Knock, Strike

**Wapiti** Deer, Elk

**War(fare), Wars** American Civil, American Independence, Ares, Armageddon, Arms, Asymmetrical, Atomic, Attrition, Bacteriological, Barons', Bate, Battle, Biological, Bishop, Blitz(krieg), Chemical, Civil, Clash, Class, Cod, Cold, Combat, Conflict, Crescentade, Crimean, Crusade, Culture, Desert Storm, Dirty, Electronic, Emergency, Feud, → FIGHT, Flagrante bello, Flame, Food, Franco-Prussian, Fray, Germ, Gigantomachy, Great, Guer(r)illa, Gulf, Holy, Hostilities, Hot, Hundred Years', Information, Internecine, Jehad, Jenkins' ear, Jihad, Jugurthine, Korean, Krieg, Limited, Mars, Mexican, Nam, Napoleonic, Nuclear, Opium, Peasants', Peloponnesian, Peninsular, Phon(e)y, Price, Private, Propaganda, Psychological, Punic, Push-button, Queen Anne's, Rebellion, Revolutionary, Roses, Russo-Japanese, Secession, Seven against Thebes, Seven Years', Shooting, Six Day, Social, Spam, Spanish-American, Spanish Civil, Star, Stoush, Sword, Terrapin, Theomachy, Thirty Years', Titanomachy, Total, Trench, Trojan, Turf, Vietnam, Winter, World, Yom Kippur

**Warble(r)** Carol, Cetti's, Chiff-chaff, Chirl, Fauvette, Peggy, Record, Rel(l)ish, Sedge, Singer, Sylvia, Trill, Vibrate, Yodel, Yodle

**War-chant, War-cry** Alalagmos, Haka, Slogan

**Ward (off)** Artemus, Averruncate, Avert, Care, Casual, Casualty, Charge, Defend, Deflect, District, Fend, Guard, Hand-off, Inner, Keyhole, Marginal, Maternity, Minor, Nightingale, Oppose, Orphan, Outer, Parry, Protégé, Pupil, Soc, Soken, Thunderbolt, Vintry, Wear, Weir

**Warden** Beefeater, Caretaker, Church, Concierge, Constable, Crossing, Curator, Custodian, Game, Guardian, Keeper, Lollipop man, Lollipop woman, Maori, Meter maid, Parkie, Pear, Provost, Ranger, Septimus, Sidesman, Spooner, Steward, Traffic, Way

**Warder, Wardress** Beefeater, Gaoler, Guardian, Keeper, Matron, Provost, Screw, Turnkey, Twirl, Yeoman

**Wardrobe** Almirah, Armoire, Breakfront, Capsule, Closet, Clothes, Garderobe, Outfit, Vestuary

**Ware(s)** Alga, Arretine, Basalt, Beware, Biscuit, Cameo, Canton, Chelsea, China, Dresden, Etruria, Fabergé, Faience, Goods, Hollow(w)are, Jasper, Lapis lazuli, Lustre, Merchandise, Palissy, Plate(d), Queen's, Samian, Sanitary, Satsuma, Shippo, Truck, Wemyss

**Warehouse** Bonded, Data, Depository, Entrepôt, Freight-shed, Go-down, Hong, Store

▶**Warfare** *see* WAR(FARE)

**War-game** Kriegs(s)piel

**War-god** Ares, Mars, Tiu, Tiw, Tyr

**Warhead** Atomic, Supremo

**Warhorse** Charger, Destrier, Fighter

**Wariness, Wary** Ca'canny, Cagey, Careful, Cautel, Caution, Chary, Discreet, Distrust, Gingerly, Guarded, Leerie, Leery, Mealy-mouthed, Mindful, Prudent, Pussyfoot, Sceptical, Suspicious, Tentie, Tenty, Vigilant

**Warlike** Battailous, Bellicose, Gung-ho, Lachlan, Martial, Militant

**Warlock** Sorcerer

**Warlord** Haw-haw, Kitchener, Shogun, Tuchun

**Warm(er), Warming, Warmth** Abask, Admonish, Affectionate, Air, Ardour, Atingle, Balmy, Bonhomie, British, Calefacient, Calid(ity), Cardigan, Chambré, Cordial, Cosy, Eager, El Nino, Empressement, Enchafe, Fervour, Flame, Fleecy, Foment, Gemütlich, Genial, Gladden, Global, Glow, → HEAT, Hospitable, Hot, Incalescent, Kang, Kindly, Lew, Logic, Loving, Muff, Muggy, Mull, Nuke, Radiator, Tepid, Thermal, Toast, Toasty, Tog

**Warm-blooded** Endothermic, Homothermal, Homothermic, Homothermous, Idiothermous

**Warmonger** Hawk, Merc(enary)

**Warn(ing)** Admonish, Alar(u)m, Alert, Amber, Aposematic, Apprise, Beacon, Bell, Beware, Bleep, Buoy, Caution, Cave, Caveat, Caveat emptor, Commination, Cone, Counsel, Cowbell, Detector, DEW, Document, Early, En garde, Example, Fire alarm, Foghorn, Fore, Foreshadow, Foretoken, Gardyloo, Garnishment, Griffin, Harbinger, Hazchem, Heads up, Hoot, Horn, Illocution, Klaxon, Knell, Larum, Lesson, Light, Maroon, Minatory, Monition, Nix, Noli-me-tangere, Nota bene, Notice, Notification, Omen, Pi-jaw, Portent, Premonish, Premonitory, Presage, Prodromal, Profit, Protevangelium, Rear light, Red alert, Red flag, Red light, Remind, Riot Act, Rumble strip, Scaldings, Scarborough, Sematic, Shore, Signal, Siren, Smoke alarm, Spindle, Stoplight, Storm, Tattler, Threat, Timber, Tip-off, Token, Toot, Vigla, Vor, Yellow card

**Warner** Alarm, Fore, Griffon, Gryfon, Gryphon, Lighthouse, Official, Plum, Siren

**Warp(ed)** Bent, Bias, Buckle, Cast, Contort, Distort, Hog, Kam, Kedge, Pandation, Spring, Time, Twist, Weft, Zag

**Warpath** Rampage

▷**Warped** *may indicate* an anagram

**Warrant(y), Warrant officer** Able, Authorise, Behight, Behote, Bench, Bosun, Capias, Caption, Certificate, Charter, Death, Deserve, Detainer, Distress, Dividend, Fiat, Fiaunt, Fugle, General, Guarantee, Justify, Merit, Mittimus, Mortgage, Peace, Permit, Precept, Reprieve, Royal, Search, Sepad, Special, Swear, Ticket, Transire, Vouch, Warn, Writ

**Warren** Burrow, Colony, Hastings, Maze, Rabbit

**Warrior** Achilles, Agamemnon, Ajax, Amazon, Anzac, Arimasp, Attila, Berserk(er), Brave, Cold, Cossack, Crusader, Eorl, Fianna, Fighter, Finlay, Finley, Geronimo, Ghazi, Gurkha, Haiduk, Heimdall, Heyduck, Housecarl, Impi, Jihadi, Lewis, Louis, Myrmidon, Nestor, Rainbow, Rajpoot, Rajput, Road, Roger, Saladin, Samurai, Soldier, Tatar, Unknown, Wardog, Warhorse, Warwolf, Zulu

**Warship** Battleship, Blockship, Castle, Cog, Corvette, Cruiser, Destroyer, Drake, Dromon(d), Frigate, Galleass, Galliass, Invincible, Man-o-war, Mine-layer, Monitor, Privateer, Ram, Repulse, Trireme, Wooden Walls

**Wart(y)** Anbury, Angleberry, Blemish, Condyloma, Genital, Keratose, Lump, Muricate, Plantar, Tuberous, Verruca, Wen

**Warthog** Boar

**Warwick** Kingmaker, Neville

▶**Wary** *see* WARINESS

**Was** Erat, Existed, Lived, Past

**Wash(ed), Washer, Washing (up), Wash out** Ablution, Affusion, Alluvion, Bath, Bay(e), Bidet, Bubble-dancing, Buck, Bur(r), Calcimine, Circlip, Clean(se), Cradle, D, Dashwheel, Dele(te), Dip, Edulcorate, Elute, Elutriate, Enema, Erode, Fen, Flush, Freshen, Front-loader, Gargle, Grom(m)et, Grummet, Hose, Hush, Irrigate, Kalsomine, Lap, → LAUNDER, Lavabo, Lave, Leather, Lip, Lotion, Marsh, Maundy, Mop, Nipter, Pan, Pigswill, Poss, Purify, Rinse, Sapple, Scrub, Shampoo, Shim, Sind, Sloosh, Sluice, Soogee, Soojee, Soojey, Squeegie, Stand-up, Stone, Stream, Sujee, Swab, Synd, Syne, Tempera, Tie, Toiletry, Toilette, Top and tail, Twin tub, Tye, Wake, Wudu, Yellow

**Washbasin, Washing machine, Washtub, Washhouse** Copper, Dash-wheel, Lavabo, Scullery, Steamie

**Washerman, Washerwoman** Dhobi, Laundress

**Washington** Dinah, Evergreen, Wa

**Wash-out** Disaster

**Wasn't** Nas, Wasna

**Wasp(ish)** Appledrain, Bembex, Bink, Bite, Chalcid, Cuckoo-fly, Cynipidae, Cynips, Digger, European, Fig, Fretful, Gall(-fly), Gold, Hornet, Horntail, Hoverfly, Irritable, Marabunta, Mason, Miffy, Muddauber, Paper, Peevish, Pompilid, Potter, Ratty, Ruby-tail, Sand, Seed, Solitary, Spider, Syrphus, Velvet ant, Vespa, Wood, Yellow jacket

▹**Wasp** *may indicate* a rugby player

**Wasp's nest** Bike, Bink, Byke

**Wassail** Carouse, Pledge, Scolion, Toast

**Wast** Wert

**Wastage, Waste(d), Wasting, Wasteful, Wasteland, Wastepipe, Waster, Wastrel** All-in, Amyotrophy, Atrophy, Bilge, Blight, Blow, Blue, Bluer, Boondoggle(r), Cesspit, Cirrhosis, Colliquative, Consume, Contabescent, Coom(b), Cotton, Crud, Culm, Decay, Dejecta, Desert, Detritus, Devastate, Dilapidate, Dishwater, Dissipate, Dregs, Dross, Dung, Dwindle, Dwine, Dystrophy, Effluent, Egesta, Electronic, Emaciate, Erode, Estrepe, Excrement, Exhaust, Expend, Exudate, Faeces, Flue, Forpine, Fribble, Fritter, Garbage, Gash, Gob, Grog, Guano, Gunge, Haggard, Half-cut, Havoc, Hazardous, Heck and manger, High, High-level, Hi(r)stie, Husk, Ice-field, Idler, Inefficient, Kill, Knub, Landfill, Lavish, Lean, Loose, Lose, Loss, Low-level, Marasmus, Merino, Misspent, Moor, Moulder, Muir, Mullock, Mungo, Natural, Ne'er-do-well, Novalia, Nub, Nuclear, Offal, Offcut, Off-scouring, Oller, Ordure, Pellagra, Perish, Phthisis, Pigswill, Pine, Prodigalise, Profligate, Rack and manger, Radioactive, Rammel, Ravage, Recrement, Red mud, Red tape, → REFUSE, Reif, Rubble, Ruderal, Ruin, Scant o' grace, Scattergood, Schappe, Scissel, Scoria, Scrap, Scum, Sew(er)age, Skeletal, Slag, Slurry, Spend, Spend-all, Spendthrift, Spill(age), Splurge, Spoil(age), Squander, Stalko, Sullage, Swarf, Syntexis, Tabes, Tailing, Thin, Thwaite, Tight, Toxic, Trash, Tundra, Ureal, Urine, Uropoiesis, U-trap, Vagabond, Vast, Wanze, Wear, Wilderness, Yearn

▹**Wasted** *may indicate* an anagram

**Watch(er), Watchable, Watch out** Accutron®, Analog(ue), Analogon, Argus, Await, Bark, Behold, Big brother, Bird-dog, Black, Case, Cave, Chronograph, Clock, Coastguard, Cock-crow, Digital, Dog, Eryl, Espy, Eyeball, Fob, Glom, Gregory, Guard, Half-hunter, Huer, Hunter, Kettle, Latewake, Lever, Lo, Look, Look-out, Lykewake, Middle, Monitor, Morning, Nark, Neighbourhood, Night, Nit, Note, Nuremberg egg, Observe, Overeye, Patrol, Pernoctation, Posse, Quartz, Regard, Repeater, Rolex®, Rubberneck, Scout, Sentinel, Sentry, Shadow, Snoop, Spectate, Spie, Spotter, Spy, Stake out, Stemwinder, Suicide, Surveillance, Telegenic, Tend, Ticker, Timekeeper, Timepiece, Timer, Tompion, Tout, Turnip, Vedette, View, → VIGIL, Voyeur, Wait, Wake, Ward, Weather eye, Wrist(let)

**Watch-chain** Albert, Slang

**Watch-control** Escapement

**Watchful(ness)** Alert, Aware, Care, Dragon, Ira, Jealous, Vigilant, Wakerife, Wary, Waukrife, Weather eye, Wide awake

**Watchman** Argus, Bellman, Charley, Charlie, Cho(w)kidar, Chok(e)y, Guard, Huer, Patrol, Sentinel, Sentry, Speculator, Tompion, Viewer

**Watch-tower** Atalaya, Barbican, Beacon, Garret, Mirador, Sentry-go, Turret

**Watchword** Cry, Password, Shibboleth, Slogan

**Water(ed), Waters, Watery** Adam's ale, Adam's wine, Aerated, Amrit, Apollinaris, Aq(ua), Aquatic, Aqueous, Ascites, Barley, Bayou, Bedabble, Bilge, Black, Bore, Bound, Branch, Brine, Broads, Brook, Burn, Canal, Cancer, Chlorine, Chresard, Chuck, Cold, Cologne, Compensation, Conductivity, Connate, Dampen, Dead, Deaw, Deg, Demersal, Dew, Dill, Dilute, Distilled, Dribble, Drinking, Eau, Ebb, Echard, Elderflower, Element, Ennerdale, Epilimnion, Euphotic, Evian®, First, Flood, Ford, Fossil, Functional, Gallise, Gallize, Ganga jal, Gas, Grey, Gripe, Ground, Gulf, Hard, Heavy, Hectum, Hellespont, High, Holy, Hose, Hot, Hungary, Hydatoid, Hydration, Hydrogen, Irrigate, Javel(le), Kuroshio, Kyle, Lagoon, Lagune,

Lake, Lant, Laurel, Lavender, Leachate, Lentic, Light, Lime, Limnology, Lithia, Loch(an), Lode, Lotic, Lough, Low, Lubricated, Lymph, Mains, Melt, Meteoric, Mineral, Miner's inch, Moiré, Mother, Nappe, North, Oasis®, Oedema, Orange-flower, Overfall, Oxygen, Pani, Pawnee, Peach, Pee, Perrier®, Phreatic, Pisces, Pluvial, Polly, Polynia, Polynya, Poppy, Potash, Potass, Pump, Purest, Quarry, Quick, Quinine, Rain, Rapids, Rate, Reach, Reservoir, Rheumy, Rice, Rip, Riverine, Rose, Running, Runny, Rydal, Salt, Saltchuck, Scorpio, Sea, Seltzer, Sera, Serous, Serpentine, Serum, Shallows, Shoal, Shower, Simpson, Skinkling, Slack, Slick, Sloshy, Sluice, Soda, Sodden, Soft, Solent, Sound, Souse, Southampton, Spring, Sprinkle, Standpipe, Steam, Stream, Surface, Tabby, Table, Tam, Tap, Tar, Tarn, Temper, Territorial, Thermocline, Thin, Tide, Toilet, Tonic, Urine, Utility, Vadose, Vapour, Vichy, Viscous, Vlei, Vly, Wai, Wake, Wash(y), Weak, Wee, Whey, White, White coal, Wild, Wishy-washy

**Waterbaby** Moses, Tom

**Water-bed** Channel

**Water-boa** Anaconda

**Water-boatman** Notonecta

**Water-brash** Pyrosis

**Waterbuck** Kob

**Water-buckets** Noria

**Waterbug** Boat fly

**Water-carrier** Aqueduct, Bheestie, Bheesty, Bhistee, Bhisti, Bucket, Carafe, Chatty, Drain, Furphy, Hose, Hydra, Hydria, Kirbeh, Pail, Pitcher, Rigol

**Water-chestnut** Saligot

**Water-colour** Aquarelle, Painting, Pastel, RI

**Water-course** Arroyo, Billabong, Canal, Ditch, Dyke, Falaj, Furrow, Gutter, Khor, Lead, Leat, Nala, Nalla(h), Nulla, Nullah, Rean, Rhine, Rill, River(et), Riverway, Serpentine, Shott, Spruit, Wadi, Whelm

**Watercress** Nasturtium

**Water-device** Shadoof, Shaduf

**Water-diviner** Dowser, Hydrostat

**Waterfall** Angel (Falls), Cascade, Cataract, Churchill, Chute, Cuquenan, Espelands, → FALL(S), Force, Foss, Iguaçú, Kahiwa, Kaieteur, Kile, Lasher, Lin(n), Lower Mar Valley, Mardel, Montmorency, Mtarazi, Niagara, Overfall, Rapid, Salmon leap, Sault, Sutherland, Takakkaw, Tugela, Tyssestrengene, Utigord, Victoria, Yellowstone, Yosemite

**Water-fern** Marsilea, Salvinia

**Waterfront** Dockland

**Water-gate** Penstock, Sluice, Sluse

**Water-god** Aleion, Aleyin, Alpheus

**Water-hen** Gallinule

**Water-hole, Watering place** Bore, Gilgai, Mickery, Oasis, Wiesbaden

**Waterless** Arid, Dry, Neat

**Water-lily** Candock, Lotus, Nenuphar, Nuphar, Spatterdock, Victoria

**Waterlog(ged)** Saturate, Sodden

**Waterloo** Rout, Station

**Waterman** Aquarius, Bargee, Ferryman, Oarsman

**Water-monster** Nicker

**Water-nymph** Kelpie, Kelpy, Naiad, Ondine, Rusalka

**Water-parsnip** Sium, Skirret

**Water-plant** Alga, Alisma, Aquatic, Callitriche, Cress, Crowfoot, Elodea, Gulfweed, Lace-leaf, Lattice-leaf, Nelumbo, Nenuphar, Nuphar, Ouvirandra, Pontederia, Quillwort, Reate, Rush, Sea-lace, Sea-mat, Sedge, Seg, Stratiotes, Urtricularia, Vallisneria

**Waterproof, Water-tight** Cagoul(e), Caisson, Camlet, Caulk, Cerecloth, Cofferdam, Corfam®, Curry, Dampcourse, Dubbin(g), Groundsheet, Loden, Mac, Mino, Oilcloth, Oilers, Oilpaper, Oilskin, Pay, Sealant, Sealskin, Seaworthy, Sta(u)nch, Stank, Suberin, Tarp, Tar-paper, Tarpaulin, Waders

**Water pump** Ee, Eye

**Water-rat** Arvicola, Musk-rat, Ratty, Vole
**Watershed** Divide, Height of land, Hilltop
**Water-spout** Gargoyle, Geyser, Hurricano
**Water-sprite** Kelpie, Kelpy, Nix(ie), Nixy, Tangie, Undine, Water-nymph
**Water supply** Dewpond, H, Hydrant, Spring, Tank, Tap
**Waterway** Aqueduct, Billabong, Canal, Channel, Creek, Culvert, Ditch, Dyke, Igarapé, Illinois, Intracoastal, Lode, River, St Lawrence Seaway, Sny(e), Sound, Straight, Strait, Suez
**Water-wheel** Noria, Overshot, Pelton, Sakia, Saki(y)eh, Turbine, Tympanum, Undershot
**Watford** Gap
**Wattle(s)** Acacia, Boobialla, Boree, Dewlap, Gills, Golden, Hurdle, Mimosa, Mulga, Sallow, Savanna, Snot, Snotter
**Wave(s), Waved, Waveform, Wavelength, Waver, Wavy** Alfven, Alpha, Beachcomber, Beam, Beck, Beta, Billow, Bore, Bow, Brain, Brandish, Breaker, Carrier, Circular polarisation, Clapotis, Cold, Comber, Complex, Compression, Continuous, Crenulate, Crest, Crime, Crimp, Crispate, Curly, Curve, Cymotrichous, De Broglie, Decuman, Delta, Dominant, Dumper, Eagre, Elastic, Electromagnetic, Feather, Finger, Flag, Flap, Flaunt, Flicker, Float, Flote, Flourish, Fourier series, Gesticulate, Gesture, Gravitational, Gravity, Graybeard, Ground, Groundswell, Gyrose, Harmonic, Haystack, Head sea, Heat, Hertzian, Impulse, Internal, Ionospheric, Lee, Long, Longitudinal, Marcel, Matter, Medium, Mexican, Nebule, New, Oscillate, Oundy, Peristalsis, Perm(anent), Plunger, Primary, Pulse, Radar, Radiation, Radio, Rayleigh, Repand, Rip, Ripple, Roller, Rooster, Sastrugi, Scrub, Sea, Secondary, Seiche, Seismic, Shake, Shock, Short, Signal, Sine, Sinuate, Sinuous, Skipper's daughter, Sky, Skyrmion, Snaky, Soliton, Sound, Spiller, Square, Squiggle, Standing, Stationary, Stern, Stream, Supersonic, Supplementary, Surf, Surge, Sway, Tabby, Theta, Third, Thought, Tidal, Tidal bore, Tide, Tide rip, Train, Transverse, Travelling, Tsunami, Ultrasonic, Undate, Unde, Undertow, Undulate, Vermicular, Waffle, Waft, Wag, Waive, Wand, Wash, Waw, Wawe, Whelm, Whitecap, White-horse, Wigwag
▷**Wave(s)** *may indicate* an anagram
**Wave-band** Channel, UHF
**Wave-detector** Coherer
**Wavelength** Band, Complementary, De Broglie, Ultrashort
**Waver(ing), Waverer** Dither, Double-minded, Falter, Flag, Gutter, Halt, Hesitate, Indecision, Oscillate, Reel, Stagger, Sway, Swither, Teeter, Trimmer, Vacillate, Waffle, Wet, Wobble, Wow
**Wax(ed), Waxing, Waxworks, Waxy** Adipocere, Ambergris, Appal, Bate, Bees, Bone, Brazilian, Candelilla, Carna(h)uba, Cere, Ceresin, Cerumen, Chinese, Cobbler's, Cutin, Ear, Earth, Effuse, Enseam, Enthuse, Ethal, Fury, Geraldton, Grave, Greaves, Grow, Heelball, Honeycomb, Increase, Increscent, Inseam, Ire, Japan, Kiss, Lecithin, Lipide, Livid, Lost, Lyrical, Mineral, Montan, Mummy, Myrtle, Ozocerite, Ozokerite, Paraffin, Parmacitie, Pela, Petroleum, Propolis, Pruina, Rage, Rise, Seal, Sealing, Spermaceti, Suberin, Tallow, Tantrum, Temper, Toxaphene, Tussaud, Vegetable, White, Yielding
**Waxwing** Cedar-bird, Icarus
**Way(s), Wayside** Access, Agate, Alameda, Appian, Autobahn, Avenue, Boardwalk, Borstal(l), Bridlepath, Budo, Bypass, Companion, Course, Covered, Crescent, Defile, Direction, Door, Draw, E, Each, Entrance, Family, Fashion, Flaminian, Foss(e), Four-foot, Gate, Greek, Habit, Hatch, Hedge, High, Hither, How, Icknield, Lane, Manner, Means, Method, Milky, MO, Mode, Modus (vivendi), N, Pass, Passage, Path, Pennine, Permanent, Pilgrim's, Procedure, Railroad, Regimen, Ridge, → ROAD, Route, S, Sallypost, St(reet), Steerage, Style, System, Taoism, Technique, Third, Thoroughfare, Thus, Trace, Trail, Troade, Turning, Turnpike, Underpass, Untrodden, Via, W, Wise
**Wayfarer** Commuter, Hiker, Passer by, Piepowder, Pilgrim, Traveller, Voyager
**Waylay** Accost, Ambuscade, Ambush, Beset, Bushwhack, Buttonhole, Molest, Obstruct, Stick up
**Way-out** Advanced, Avant garde, Bizarre, Egress, Esoteric, Exit, Exotic, Extreme, Offbeat, Trendy

**Wayward** Capricious, Devious, Disobedient, Errant, Erratic, Loup-the-dyke, Obstreperous, Perverse, Rogue, Scapegrace, Stray, Unruly, Wilful
**WC** Fields, Gents, Ladies, Lav, Loo
**We** I and I, Oo, Royal, Us
**Weak(er), Weaken(ing), Weakest, Weakness** Achilles' heel, Acrasia, Adynamia, Antimnemonic, Aphesis, Appair, Appal, Arsis, Assuage, Asthenia, Attenuate, Blot, Brickle, Brittle, Cachexia, Cataplexy, Chink, Cissy, Cripple(d), Debile, Debilitate, Decimate, Decrease, Delay, Delicate, Deplete, Dilling, Dilute, Disable, Drip, Effete, Emasculate, Embrittle, Enervate, Enfeeble, Entender, Fade, Faible, Failing, Faint, Fallible, Fatigue, Feeble, Fissile, Flag, Flaw, Flimsy, Foible, Fragile, Frail(tee), Frailty, Frontolysis, Give, Glass chin, Gone, Groggy, Gutless, Ham, Hamartia, Helpless, Honeycomb, Impair, Impotence, Infirm, Knock-kneed, Labefaction, Lame, Languishing, Languor, Lassitude, Leptosomatic, Loophole, Low, Low ebb, Malaise, Meagre, Mild, Milk and water, Myasthenia, Namby-pamby, Pale, Pall, Paraparesis, Paresis, Penchant, Powerless, Puny, Push-over, Pusillanimous, Reckling, Reduce, Reedy, Relent, Runt, Sap, Shortcoming, Simp, Slack, Softie, Softling, Soft spot, Spineless, Stagger, Starveling, Tenuous, Thesis, Thin, Thready, Tottery, Unable, Underdog, Undermine, Unman, Unnerve, Unsound, Unstable, Vapid, Velleity, Vessel, Vice, Vincible, Vulnerability, W, Wane, Washy, Water(y), Weed, Weenie, Wimp, Wish(y)-wash(y), Wuss(y)
**Weakling** Dilling, Drip, Milksop, Nerd, Nisgul, Pushover, Reed, Runt, Shrimp, Softie, Wimp, Wuss
**Weal** Ridge, Stripe, Urticant, Wealth, Welfare, Welt, Whelk
**Wealth(y)** Abundance, Affluence, Bonanza, Bullion, Capital, Croesus, Digerati, Dives, Ease, Eldorado, Fat-cat, Fortune, Golconda, Jet-set, Klondike, Klondyke, Load(sa), Loaded, Loadsamoney, Lolly, Long purse, Magnate, Mammon, Means, Megabucks, Mine, Mint, Moneyed, Nabob, Old money, Opulence, Ore, Pelf, Plutocrat, Possessions, Privileged, Prosperous, Reich, Rich, Ritzy, Solid, Substance, Tom Tiddler's ground, Treasure, Trustafarian, Tycoon, Untold, Well-heeled, Well-off, Well-to-do
**Wean** Ablactation, Bairn, Spain, Spane, Spean
**Weapon(s)** Ammo, Antitank, Arm, Armament, Arsenal, Assault, Binary, Cultural, Deterrent, Directed energy, Enhanced radiation, Greek fire, → **GUN**, Hoplology, Long-range, Missile, Munition, Nuclear, Nuke, Ordnance, Piece, → **PISTOL**, Semi-automatic, Small arm, Surface-to-air, → **SWORD**, Theatre, Thermonuclear, Tool, Traditional

---

**WEAPONS**

*2 letters:*
Da
V1

*3 letters:*
Axe
Bow
Dag
Gad
Gat
Rod
SAM
Uzi

*4 letters:*
Beam
Bill
Bolo
Bomb
Club
Cosh
Dart
Foil
Gade
Gaid
Kris
Mace
Mere
Mine
Pike
Spat
Sten
Tank
Tuck

*5 letters:*
Arrow
Baton
Blade
Brand
Estoc
Flail
Knife
Kukri
Lance
Laser
Lathi
Maxim
Orgue
Panga
Pilum
Rifle
Sabre
Saker
Sling
Spear
Staff
Stick
Sting
Taser®
Vouge

*6 letters:*
Airgun
Archie
Cestus
Cohorn
Creese
Cudgel
Dagger
Dragon
Duster
Gingal
Glaive
Jingal
Katana
Lathee
Martel
Mauser®
Mortar
Musket
Napalm
Onager

Popgun
Rapier
Sparke
Sparth
Sumpit
Taiaha
Tomboc
Voulge

*7 letters:*
Arblast
Assagai
Assegai
Ataghan
Bayonet
Bazooka
Blowgun
Bondook
Caliver
Caltrap
Caltrop
Carbine
Chopper
Coehorn
Cutlass
Dragoon
Enfield
Firearm
Fougade
Gingall
Gisarme
Grenade
Halberd
Halbert
Harpoon
Hatchet
Javelin
Longbow
Machete
Matchet
Petrary
Poleaxe
Poniard
Sandbag
Shotgun
Sidearm
Sjambok
Sticker
Swatter
Tear gas
Torpedo
Trident
Warhead

*8 letters:*
Alderman
Arbalest
Armalite®
Arquebus
Ballista
Blowpipe
Bludgeon
Calthrop
Catapult
Crossbow
Culverin
Elf-arrow
Field gun
Fougasse
Gas shell
Howitzer
Mangonel
Nerve gas
Nunchaku
Partisan
Pea-rifle
Petronel
Repeater
Revolver
Scimitar
Scorpion
Shuriken
Skean-dhu
Skene-dhu
Spontoon
Stiletto
Stinkpot
Tomahawk
Tommy gun
Whirl-bat
Whorl-bat
Yataghan

*9 letters:*
Arquebuse
Backsword
Battleaxe
Boomerang
Catchpole
Chainshot
Derringer
Doodlebug
Escopette
Excalibur
Flintlock
Forty-five
Harquebus
Matchlock
Nunchucks
Sarbacane
Slingshot
Slungshot
Swivel gun
Sword cane
Tormentum
Trebuchet
Truncheon
Welsh hook

*10 letters:*
Broadsword
Knobkerrie
Pea-shooter
Shillelagh
Six-shooter
Smallsword
Swordstick
Throw-stick

*11 letters:*
Hand grenade
Morgenstern
Morning star
Singlestick
Snickersnee
Switchblade

*12 letters:*
Dagger of lath
Flamethrower
Jeddart staff
Quarterstaff

*13 letters:*
Knuckleduster
Life-preserver
Manrikigusari

*14 letters:*
Nunchaku sticks

---

**Weapon-carrier** Frog, Holster, Quiver, Rocket-launcher, Sheath

**Wear(ing), Wear Out** Abate, Ablative, Abrade, Air, Attrition, Chafe, Clothing, Corrade, Corrode, Cruise, Deteriorate, Detrition, Efface, Enfeeble, Erode, Erosion, Exhaust, Fashion, Fatigue, For(e)spend, Fray, Frazzle, Fret, Garb, Garni, Impair, In, Mush, Outlast, Pack, Sap, Scuff, Sport, Stand, Tedy, Tolerate, Utility

▷**Wear** *may indicate* the NE, e.g. Sunderland

**Weariness, Wearisome, Weary(ing)** Beat, Bejade, Blethered, Bore, Bother, Cloy, Deave, Dog-tired, Effete, Ennui, Ennuyé, Exhaust, Fag, Fatigate, Fatigue, Flag(ging), Harass, Hech, Heigh-ho, Irk, Jade, Lacklustre, Lassitude, Monotonous, Pall, Puny, Ramfeezle, Sate, Sick, Sleepy, Spent, Tire, Tiresome, Trash, Try, Tucker, Wabbit, World, Worn

**Weasel** Beech-marten, Cane, Delundung, Ermine, Ferret, Foumart, Glutton, Grison, Kolinsky, Marten, Mink, Mustela, Otter, Pekan, Pine-marten, Polecat, Skunk, Sneak, Stoat, Taira, Tayra, Vermin, Whit(t)ret, Whitterick, Whittrick, Wolverine, Woodshock, Zorilla

**Weather(ed), Weather forecast** Atmosphere, Bermuda high, Climate, Cyclone, Discolour, Dreich, Ecoclimate, Elements, El Niño, Endure, Hail, La Nina, Lived-in, Met, Monkey's wedding, Outlive, Rain, Resist, Ride, Sky, Snow, Sprat, Stand, Survive, Synoptic, Tiros, Undergo, Withstand

**Weatherbeaten** Leathery
**Weatherboard** Rusticating
**Weathercock** Barometer, Fane, Vane
**Weatherman** Fish
**Weave(r), Weaves, Weaving** Arachne, Basket, Broché, Cane, Complect, Contexture, Entwine, Finch, Fishnet, Folk, Heald, Heddle, Interlace, Intertwine, Jacquard, Knotwork, Lace, Lease, Leno, Lion, Loom, Marner, Osiery, Penelope, Pick, Plain, Plait, Raddle, Ripstop, Rya, Satin, Shuttle, Sparrow, Spider, Splice, Stevengraph, Taha, Textorial, Texture, Thread, Throstle, Throwster, Tissue, Tweel, Twill, Twine, Wabster, Waggle, Wattle, Webster, Zigzag
**Weaver-bird** Amadavat, Avadavat, Quelea, Rice-bird, Taha, Zebra-finch
**Web(bed), Webbing, Web-footed, Web-site** Ebay®, Facebook®, Fansite, Favourite, Fissipalmate, Food, Forum, Fourchette, Funnel, Hit, Infomediary, Internet, Mat, Maze, Mesh(work), Network, Offset, Palama, Palmate, Palmiped, Patagium, Pinnatiped, Portal, Retiary, Semantic, Skein, Snare, Social media, Spider, Tear, Tela, Tissue, Toil, Totipalmate, Twitter®, Vane, Wiki, World Wide
**Webster** Spider, Weaver
**Wed(ding), Wedlock** Alliance, Bet, Destination, Diamond, Espousal, Golden, Hymen, Join, Knobstick, Liaison, Link, Marriage, Marry, Mate, Matrimony, Meng(e), Me(i)nt, Meynt, Ming, Monkey's, Nuptials, Pair, Penny, Platinum, Ruby, Sacrament, Shotgun, Silver, Spousage, Spousal, → UNION, Unite, Wad, White, Y
**Wedge(d)** Accretionary, Canting-coin, Chock, Chunk, Cleat, Cotter, Cuneal, Doorstop, Dunnage, Feather, Forelock, Gad, Gagger, Gib, Impacted, Jack, Jam, Key, Lofter, Niblick, Pitching, Prop, Quoin, Sand, Scotch, Segment, Shim, Spaceband, Sphenic, Stick, Texas, Trig, Vomerine, Voussoir, Whipstock
**Wedgwood** Benn, China
**Wednesday** Ash, Midweek, Pulver, Spy
**Wee** Leak, Little, Pee, Slash, Sma(ll), Tinkle, Tiny, → URINATE, Widdle
**Weed(y)** Adderwort, Agrestal, Alga, Allseed, Anacharis, Arenaria, Bedstraw, Bell-bind, Bishop's, Blinks, Burdock, Buttercup, Canadian, Carpetweed, Catch, Charlock, Chickweed, Chlorella, Cigar(ette), Cissy, Clotbur, Clover, Cobbler's pegs, Cockle, Cocklebur, Colonist, Coltsfoot, Corncockle, Couch, Daisy, Dallop, Dandelion, Darnel, Dock, Dollop, Dulse, Elder, Elodea, Ers, Fag, Fat hen, Femitar, Fenitar, Figwort, Fluellen, Fluellin, Fork, Fucoid, Fumitory, Furrow, Gangly, Goutweed, Goutwort, Ground elder, Groundsel, Hedge-mustard, Helodea, Hoe, Indian, Joe-pye, Knapweed, Knawel, Knot-grass, Lanky, Lemna, Lemon, Maiden, Mare's-tail, Marijuana, Matfelon, Mayweed, Nard, Nettle, Nipplewort, Nostoc, Onion, Oxygen, Paterson's curse, Pearlwort, Peed, Perique, Pickerel, Pilewort, Pineapple, Piri-piri, Plantain, Potamogeton, Purslane, Ragi, Ragwort, Reate, Rest-harrow, Ribbon, Rib-grass, Ribwort, Ruderal, Runch, Sagittaria, Sargasso, Scal(l)awag, Scallywag, Senecio, Shrimp, Softy, Sorrel, Spanish needles, Speedwell, Spurge, Spurrey, Stink, Sudd, Sun-spurge, Swine's-cress, Tab, Tansy, Tare, Thistle, Tine, Tobacco, Tormentil, Twitch, Ulotrichale, Ulva, Vetch, Viper's bugloss, Wartcress, Widow's, Winnow, Yarr
▹**Weed** *may indicate* 'urinated'
**Weedkiller** Arsenic, Atrazine, Dalapon, Diquat, Diuron, Herbicide, Hoe, Paraquat®, Selective, Simazine
**Week(s), Weekly** Ember, Expectation, Great, Hebdomadary, Holy, Omer, Orientation, Ouk, Oulk, Passion, Periodical, Prophetic, Rag, Rogation, Schoolies, Sennight, Working
**Weekday** Feria
**Weekend** Dirty, K, Sat, Sun
**Weep(er), Weeping, Weepy, Wept** Bawl, Blubber, Cry, Grat, Greet, Lachrymose, Lament, Leak, Loser, Maudlin, Niobe, Ooze, Pipe, Screet, Seep, Sob, Tearful, Wail, Waterworks
**Weevil** Anthonomous, Bean, Boll, Bug, Cornworm, Curculio, Diamond-beetle, Grain, Insect, Nut, Pea, Rice, Seed, Snout beetle
**Weft** Roon, Shot, Texture, Warp, Woof
**Weigh(ing), Weigh down, Weight(y)** All-up, Apothecaries', Atomic, Avoirdupois, Balance, Ballast, Bantam, Barbell, Baric, Bias, Birth, Bob, Bow, Bulk, Burden, Casting,

Centrier, Clout, Consider, Count, Counterpoise, Cruiser, Dead, Deliberate, Denier, Drail, Dumbbell, Emphasis, Equivalent, Feather, Flab, Formula, Grammage, Gravity, Great, Gross, Handicap, Heaviness, Heft, Import, Importance, Impost, Incumbent, Influence, Journey, Kerb, Live, Load, Mark, Massive, Matter, Metage, Metrology, Minimum, Molecular, Moment, Mouse, Nett, Onerous, One-sided, Oppress, Overpoise, Payload, Perpend, Pical, Plumb-bob, Plummet, Poise, Ponderal, Pregnant, Preponderance, Prey, Rate, Sash, Sinker, Slang, Slung-shot, Stress, Tare, Throw, Ton(nage), Tophamper, Tron(e), Troy, Trutinate, Unmoor, Welter, Wey

---

## WEIGHTS

***1 letter:***
G
K

***2 letters:***
As
Ct
Oz
Wt

***3 letters:***
Kat
Kin
Kip
Mna
Oke
Pud
Rod
Ser
Sit
Tod

***4 letters:***
Dram
Gram
Kati
Khat
Last
Mina
Nail
Obol
Peck
Pood
Rotl
Seer
Tael
Tola
Unce

***5 letters:***
Artal
Candy
Carat
Catty
Clove
Gerah
Grain
Kandy
Katti
Liang
Libra
Maund
Ounce
Pease
Peaze
Peise
Peize
Peyse
Pikul
Pound
Pudge
Recul
Stone
Tical
Tonne
Truss

***6 letters:***
Arroba
Candie
Cantar
Cental
Derham
Dirham
Dirhem
Drachm
Firkin
Fother
Kantar
Rotolo
Talent

***7 letters:***
Centner
Drachma
Kiloton
Lispund
Pesante
Quintal
Scruple

***8 letters:***
Decagram
Lispound
Semuncia

***9 letters:***
Micromole
Shippound

***10 letters:***
Decagramme

---

**Weighing machine** Bismar, Scales, Steelyard, Tron(e)
**Weightless** Agravic
**Weight-lifter** Atlas, Crane, Lewis, Windlass
**Weir** Cauld, Dam, Garth, Kiddle, Kidel, Lasher, Pen, Watergate
**Weird** Atypical, Bizarre, Curious, Dree, Eerie, Eery, Eldritch, Far out, Freak, Kookie, Odd, Oddball, Offbeat, Outre, Paranormal, Spectral, Spooky, Strange, Supernatural, Taisch, Uncanny, Unearthly, Zany
**Welch, Welsh** Abscond, Cheat, Default, Embezzle, Levant, Rat, Reneg(u)e, Renig, Skedaddle, Weasel
**Welcome, Welcoming** Acclaim, Aloha, Ave, Bel-accoyle, Ben venuto, Ciao, Embrace, Entertain, Glad-hand, Godsend, Greet, Haeremai, Hail, Hallo, Halse, Handshake, Heil, Hello, Hi, Hospitable, How, Hullo, Karanga, Open-armed, Open house, Ovation, Powhiri, Receive, Reception, Red carpet, Salute, Snug, Ticker-tape, Wotcha, Wotcher, Yellow-ribbon
**Weld(ing), Welder** Arc, Butt, Cold, Explosion, Fillet, Friction, Fuse, Gas, Join, Merge, MIG, Oxyacetylene, Resistance, Seam, Sinter, Spot, Stud, Tack, TIG, Ultrasonic, Unite
**Welfare** Advantage, Alms, Benefit, Benison, Common weal, Ha(y)le, Heal, Health, Sarvodaya, Social, Weal

**Welkin** Firmament, Sky

**Well (done)** Appraisal, Artesian, Atweel, Ave, Aweel, Bien, Bore(hole), Bravo, Carbon, Casinghead, Cenote, Chipper, Development, Discovery, Downhole, Draw, Dropping, Dry hole, Easily, Euge, Famously, Fine, Fit, Foot, Gas, Gasser, Geyser, Good, Gosh, Gusher, Hale, → **HEALTHY**, Hot, Inkpot, Ka pai, Law, Live, Mickery, Mineral, My, Namma hole, Odso, Oh, Oil(er), Phreatic, Potential, Pour, Pump, So, Source, Spa, Spouter, Spring, Sump, Surge, Teek, Tube, Um, Upflow, Wildcat, Wishing, Worthily, Zemzem

**Wellbeing** Atweel, Bien-être, Comfort, Eudemonic, Euphoria, Euphory, Good, Health, Oomph, Welfare

**Well-born** Eugene

**Well-bred** Genteel

**Well-built** Robust, Sturdy, Tight

**Well-covered** Chubby, Padded

**Well-curb** Puteal

**Welles** Orson

**Wellington, Welly** Accelerate, Boot, Green, Gumboot, Iron Duke, Nosey

**Well-known** Famous, Iconic, Illustrious, Infamous, Notorious, Notour, Prominent

**Well-mannered** Civil, Polite

**Well-meaning** Do-gooder

**Well-off** Affluent, Bien, Far, Rich, Wealthy, Woopie

**Well part** Bucket, Shadoof, Shaduf

**Well-read** Erudite

**Wells** Bombardier, Fargo, HG, Llandrindod, Sadler's

**Well-supplied** Locuplete

**Well-tempered** Tuned

**Well-turned** Elegant

**Well-versed** Fluent

**Well-wisher** Friend

**Welsh(man), Welshwoman** Aled, Briton, Brittonic, Brython, Cake, Cambrian, Celtic, Cog, Crachach, Cym(ric), Cymry, Dafydd, Dai, Ebbw, Emlyn, Emrys, Enid, Evan, Fluellen, Gareth, Harp, Idris, Ifor, Ivor, Keltic, Megan, P-Celtic, P-Keltic, Rabbit, Rarebit, Rees, Rhys, Sion, Taff(y), Tudor, W, Walian

▸**Welsh** *see* **WELCH**

**Wen** Cyst, Talpa, Tumour, Wart

**Wench** Blowze, Court, Floozie, Girl, Gouge, Hussy, Maid, Ramp, Rig, Smock, Strumpet

**Wend** Meander, Sorb, Steer

**Wendy** Darling, House

**Went** Left, Peed, Sold, Yode

**Werewolf** Loup-garou, Lycanthrope, Nazi, Turnskin, Vampire

**Wesleyan** Epworth, Methodist

**West(ern), Westerly** Ang mo, Far, Favonian, Film, Hesperian, Mae, Middle, Movie, Oater, Occidental, Ponent, Spaghetti, Sunset, True Grit, W, Westlin, Wild

**West African** Fantee, Fanti, Guinean, Kroo, Mande, Mandingo, Togolese, Wolof

▹**West end** *may indicate* 't' or 'W1'

**West Indian** Carib, Creole, Jamaican, Taino

**Westminster** SW1

**Wet(ting), Wetland** Bedabble, Bedraggled, Clammy, Daggle, Damp, Dank, Dew, Dip, Douse, Dowse, Drench, Drip(ping), Drook, Drouk, Dunk, Embrue, Enuresis, Feeble, Fen, Foppish, Humect, Humid, Hyetal, Imbrue, Imbue, Irrigate, Irriguous, Macerate, Madefy, Madid, Marshy, Moil, Moist(en), Molly, Namby-pamby, Pee, Piddle, Pouring, Rainy, Ramsar site, Ret(t), Rheumy, Roral, Roric, Runny, Saturate, Seepy, Shower, Simp(leton), Sipe, Sissy, Sluice, → **SOAK**, Sodden, Sopping, Sour, Steep, Tiddle, Tipsy, Urinate, Wat, Wee, Widdle, Wimpy, Wringing

**Wetsuit** Steamer

**Whack(ed), Whacking** Astronomic, Belt, Bemaul, Biff, Clobber, Deadbeat, Hefty, Jiggered, Joll, Joule, Jowl, Lambast, Lounder, Share, Swat, Swish, Thump, Tired, Weary

**Whale(meat), Whaling** Baleen, Beaked, Beluga, Black, Blower, Blubber, Blue, Bottlehead, Bottlenose, Bowhead, Bull, Cachalot, Calf, Cetacea(n), Cete, Cetology, Cow, Cowfish, Dolphin, Dorado, Fall, Fin(back), Finner, Gam, Glutton, Grampus, Greenland (right), Grey, Greyback, Humpback, Ishmael, Killer, Kreng, Leviathan, Manatee, Minke, Monodon, Mysticeti, Narwhal, Odontoceti, Orc(a), Paste, Physeter, Pilot, Pod, Porpoise, Right, River dolphin, Rorqual, School, Scrag, Sea-canary, Sea-unicorn, Sei, Social, Sperm, Spouter, Sulphur-bottom, Thrasher, Thresher, Toothed, Toothless, White, Zeuglodon(t), Ziphius

▷**Whale** *may indicate* an anagram

**Whalebone** Busk

**Whaler** Ahab, Harpooner, Ship, Specksioneer, Specktioneer, Waister

**Whales' meat** Clio

**Wham(my)** Bang, Collide, Double, Triple

**Whang** Blow, Flog, Thrash, Whack

**Wharf(inger)** Canary, Coal-whipper, Dock(er), Jetty, Key, Landing, Pier, Quay(side), Roustabout, Rouster, Staith(e)

**What, Whatever** Anan, Any, Come again, Eh, How, Owt, Pardon, Que, Regardless, Siccan, Sorry, Such, That, Which

**Whatnot, What's-its-name** Dinges, Dingus, Doings, Doobrey, Doobrie, Étagère, Gismo, Jigamaree, Jiggumbob, Thingamy, Thingumajig, Thingumbob, Thingummy, Timenoguy

**Wheat** Allergen, Amber, Amelcorn, Bald, Beard(ed), Beardless, Blé, Bulg(h)ur, Cone, Couscous, Cracked, Durum, Einkorn, Emmer, Federation, Fromenty, Frumenty, Furme(n)ty, Furmity, Grain, Hard, Mummy, Red, Rivet, Sarrasin, Sarrazin, Seiten, Semolina, Sharps, Soft, Spelt, Spring, Straw, Summer, Triticum, White, Winter

**Wheatsheaf** Bale, Gerbe, Stook

**Wheedle** Banter, Barney, Blag, Blandish, Butter up, Cajole, Coax, Cog, Cuiter, Cuittle, Flatter, Inveigle, Tweedle, Whilly(whaw)

**Wheel(er)** Balance, Band, Bedel, Bevel, Bicycle, Big, Bogy, Brake, Breast, Bucket, Buff(ing), Caracol(e), Cart's tail, Caster, Castor, Catherine, Chain, Chark(h)a, Circle, Cistern, Coach, Contrate, Count, Crown, Cycle, Daisy, Diamond, Disc, Driving, Emery, Epicycloidal, Escape, Fan, Felloe, Felly, Ferris, Fifth, Fly, Fortune, Gear, Grinding, Gyrate, Helm, Hull, Hurl, Idle(r), Jagger, Jigger, Jockey, Jolley, Joy, Kick, Lantern, Magnate, Master, Measuring, Medicine, Mitre, Monkey, Mortimer, Nabob, Nave, Nose, Paddle, Pattern, Pedal, Pelton, Perambulator, Persian, Pin, Pinion, Pitch, Pivot, Planet, Potter's, Prayer, Pulley, Rag, Ratchet, Rhomb, Roll, Roller, Rotate, Roulette, Rowel, Sheave, Side, Snail, Spare, Spider, Spinning, Sprocket, Spur, Star, Steering, Stepney, Stitch, Swing, Tail, Throwing-table, Training, Tread, Treadmill, Trindle, Trochus, Trolley, Truckle, Trundle, →TURN, Tympan(um), Water, Web, Wharve, Whirling-table, Wire, Worm, Zoetrope

**Wheelbarrow** Ball-barrow, Hurlbarrow, Monotroch

**Wheeler-dealer** Hustler

**Wheelhouse** Caravan, Paddle-box

**Wheel-hub** Axle, Nave

**Wheelman** Croupier, Cyclist, Ixion

**Wheelwright** Spokesman

**Wheeze** Asthma, Breathe, Jape, Joke, Pant, Pech, Ploy, Rale, Reak, Reik, Rhonchus, Ruse, Stridor, Trick, Whaisle, Whaizle

**Whelk** Buccinum, Buckie, Limpet, Shellfish, Stromb, Triton

**Whelm** Nalla(h), Nulla(h)

**Whelp** Bear, Bra(t)chet, Pup

**When(ever)** Although, As, If, Once, Though, Time

**Where(abouts)** Location, Neighbourhood, Place, Site, Vicinity, Whaur, Whither

**Wherefore** Cause, Reason, Why

**Whereupon** So, When

**Wherewithal** Capacity, Finance, Means, Money, Needful, Resources

**Wherry** Barge, Rowboat

**Whet(stone)** Coticular, Excite, Hone, Oilstone, Rubstone, Sharpen, Stimulate, Stroke

**Whether** Conditional, If

**Whey** Plasma, Serum, Whig
**Which(ever), Which is** Anyway, As, QE, Quod, Whatna, Whilk, Who
**Whiff** Breath, Cigarette, Gust, Hum, Puff, Redolence, Smatch, Smell, Sniff, Trace, Waft
**Whig** Adullamite, Jig, Liberal, Rascal, Tory, Whey
**While** Although, As, Interim, Since, Space, Span, Spell, Though, Throw, Time, When, Whenas, Whereas, Yet
**Whim(s), Whimsical, Whimsy** Bizarre, Caprice, Conceit, Crotchet, Droll, Fad, Fancy, Fantastic, Fay, Fey, Fie, Flisk, Impulse, Kicksy-wicksy, Kink, Maggot, Notion, Passing, Quaint, Quirk, Tick, Toy, Vagary
**Whimper** Cry, Grizzle, Mewl, Pule, Snivel, Whine
**Whin** Furze, Gorse, Ulex
**Whine, Whinge(r)** Cant, Carp, Complain, Cry baby, Gripe, Grumble, Kvetch, Mewl, Miaow, Moan, Peenge, Pule, Snivel, Sword, Whimper, Yammer
**Whinny** Neigh, Nicker, Whicker
**Whip(ped), Whip out, Whipping** Beat, Braid, Brede, Bullwhack, Bullwhip, Cat, Cat o' nine tails, Chabouk, Chantilly, Chastise, Chief, Cilium, Coach, Colt, Crop, Drive, Feague, Firk, Five-line, Flagellate, Flagellum, Flay, Gad, Hide, Jambok, Knout, K(o)urbash, Larrup, → **LASH**, Leather, Limber, Lunge, Pistol, Quirt, Rawhide, Riding (crop), Riem, Scourge, Sjambok, Slash, Steal, Stock, Strap-oil, Swinge, Swish, Switch, Taw, Thong, Three-line, Thresh, Trounce, Welt, West Country, Whap, Whop
**Whippersnapper** Dandiprat, Dandyprat, Pup, Squirt
**Whippoorwill** Wishtonwish
**Whirl(er), Whirling** Bullroarer, Circumgyrate, Dervish, Eddy, Gyrate, → **IN A WHIRL**, Maelstrom, Pivot, Reel, Spin, Swing, Swirl, Viennese, Vortex, Vortical, Vorticose, Vortiginous, Whirry
**Whirlpool** Eddy, Gulf, Gurge, Maelstrom, Moulin, Sea purse, Swelchie, Vorago, Vortex, Weel, Wiel
**Whirlwind** Cyclone, Dust devil, Eddy, Sand-devil, Tornado, Tourbillion, Typho(o)n, Vortex, Willy-willy
**Whirr(er)** Birr, Bull-roarer
**Whisk** Balloon, Beat, Chowri, Chowry, Fly, Swish, Switch, Whid, Whip
**Whisker(s)** Beard, Beater, Bristles, Burnsides, Cat's, Dundreary, Eggbeater, Excrement, Face fungus, Hackle, Hair, Moustache, Mutton-chop, Samuel, Satyric tuft, Side(-boards), Side-burns, Sidelevers, Stibble, Stubble, Vibrissa
**Whisk(e)y** Alcohol, Auld Kirk®, Barley-bree, Barley-broo, Barley-broth, Bond, Bourbon, Canadian, Cape smoke, Chain lighting, Corn (brandy), Cratur, Craythér, Creature, Drambuie®, Fife, Fire-water, Grain, Hard stuff, Hard tack, Highball, Hokonui, Hoo(t)ch, Irish, Islay, Malt, Monongahela, Moonshine, Morning, Mountain dew, Nip, Peat-reek, Pot(h)een, Ragwater, Red eye, Rye, Scotch, Sourmash, Southern Comfort®, Spunkie, Stirrup-dram, Tanglefoot, Tarantula juice, Tim, Tun, Usquebaugh, W, Wheech, Whiss
▷**Whisky** *may indicate* an anagram
**Whisper** Aside, Breath(e), Bur(r), Chinese, Hark, Hint, Innuendo, Murmur, Pig's, Round, Rumour, Rustle, Sigh, Stage, Susurrus, Tittle, Undertone, Whittie-whattie
**Whist** Dummy, Hush, Long, Mum, Progressive, Quiet, Sh, Short, Solo, Whisk and swabbers
**Whistle(r)** Blow, Boatswain's, Calliope, Catcall, Feedback, Flageolet, Flute, Hewgh, Hiss, Marmot, Pedro, Penny, Phew, Ping, Pipe, Quail-pipe, Ref, Siffle(ur), Sowf(f), Sowth, Steam, Stop, Stridor, Swab(ber), Swanee, Tin, Toot, Tweedle, Tweet, Warbler, Wheeple, Wheugh, Whew, Whiffle, Wolf
**Whistle-blower** Informer, Nark, Ref
**Whit** Atom, Doit, Figo, Haet, Hait, Hate, Iota, Jot, Particle, Pentecost, Point, Red cent, Snap, Straw
**White(n), Whitener, Whiteness, White-faced** Agene, Agenise, Alabaster, Albedo, Albescent, Albino, Albugineous, Albumen, Argent, Ashen, Au lit, Bakra, Blameless, Blanch, Blanche, Blanco, Bleach, Buckra, Cabbage, Calm, Cam, Camstone, Candid, Candida, Candour, Canescent, Canities, Caucasian, Caum, Chalk(y), Chardonnay, Chaste, China, Chinese, Christmas, Cliffs, Collar, Company, Cream, Cue ball, Dealbate, Egg, Elephant, Ermine,

European, Fang, Fard, Feather, Flag, Flake, French, Glair, Gwen(da), Gwendolen, Gwyn, Hawked, Hoar(y), Hock, Honorary, Hore, House, Innocent, Ivory, Large, Leucoma, Lie, Lily, Livid, Man, Marbled, Mealy, Milky, Muscadet, Niveous, Opal, Oyster, Pakeha, Pale(face), Pallor, Paper, Paris, Pearl(y), Poor, Pure, Redleg, Russian, Sauterne, Sclerotic, Selborne, Sheep, Silver, Small, Snow(y), Spanish, Taw, Vitiligo, Wan, Wedding, Wine, Wyn, Zinc

**Whitefish** Menominee

**Whitefriars** Alsatia

**Whitehall** Ministry

**Whitehead** Milium

**White horse(s)** Skipper's daughters, Wave

**White man** Anglo, Ba(c)kra, Buckra, Caucasian, Corn-cracker, Haole, Kabloona, Larney, Mzungu, Norteno, Occidental, Pakeha, Paleface, Redleg, Redneck, Umlungu, WASP, Wigga, Wigger

**Whitewash** Calcimine, Concealment, Excuse, Grannie, Granny, Kalsomine, Lime, Skunk, Trounce

**Whitlow** Ancome, Felon, Panaritium, Paronychia

**Whitsun** Pentecost, Pinkster, Pinxter

**Whittle** Carve, Pare, Sharpen

**Whizz** Virtuoso, Wheech

**Who** As, Doctor, Qui, Time traveller

**Whodunit** Mystery

**Who knows** Quien sabe

**Whole, Wholehearted, Wholeness, Wholly** All(-out), Cosmos, Eager, Entire(ty), Entity, Every inch, Fully, Hale, Indiscrete, Intact, Integer, Integral, Integrity, In toto, Largely, Lot, Shebang, Sound, Sum, Systemic, Thoroughly, Total, Tout à fait, Unbroken, Uncut

**Wholesale(r)** Cutprice, En bloc, Engrosser, Ingross, Jobber, Root and branch, Stockjobber, Supplier, Sweeping, Trader

**Wholesome** Clean, Good, Healthy, Physical, Pure, Salubrious, Salutary, Sound

**Whoop(er), Whooping cough** Alew, Celebrate, Chincough, Crane, Cry, Excite, Kink(cough), Kink-host, Pertussis, Swan, War

**Whoopee** Carouse, Evoe, Hey-go-mad, Roister

**Whoosh** Birr, Rustle, Swish

**Whopper, Whopping** Barn, Crammer, Goliath, Huge, Immense, Jumbo, Lie, Lig, Oner, Out and outer, Plumper, Scrouger, Slapper, Slockdolager, Soc(k)dalager, Soc(k)dolager, Soc(k)doliger, Soc(k)dologer, Sogdolager, Sogdoliger, Sogdologer, Stonker, Tale, Taradiddle

**Whore** Drab, Harlot, Loose woman, Pinnace, Pro, Prostitute, Quail, Road, Strumpet, Tart

**Whorl** Coil, Corolla, Eucyclic, Spiral, Swirl, Verticil, Volute, Volution

**Why** How come, Raison d'être, Reason, Yogh

**Wicca(n)** Pagan

**Wick** Farm, Rush, Snaste, Snuff, Vill(age)

**Wicked(ness)** Adharma, Atrocity, → BAD, Candle, Criminal, Cru(i)sie, Crusy, Depravity, Devilish, Evil, Fab, Facinorous, Flagitious, Goaty, Godless, Heinous, High-viced, Immoral, Impious, Improbity, Iniquity, Lantern, Malevolent, Miscreant, Naughty, Nefarious, Night-light, Pernicious, Perverse, Ponerology, Pravity, Rush, Satanic, Scelerate, Sin(ful), Splendid, Super, Taper, Turpitude, Unchaste, Unholy, Vile

▷**Wicked** *may indicate* containing a wick

**Wicker(work)** Basketry, Rattan, Sale, Seal, Wattlework

**Wicket** Crease, Gate, Hatch, Infield, Maiden, Pitch, Square, Sticky, Stool, Stump, W, Yate

**Wicket-keeper** Gateman, Stumper

**Wide, Widen(ing), Width** Abroad, Ample, Aspect, Bay, Braid, Broad, Comprehensive, Dilate, Drib, Eclectic, Expand, Extend, Far, Flanch, Flange, Flare, Flaunch, Ga(u)ge, General, Latitude, Miss, Prevalent, Roomy, Scope, Set, Spacious, Span, Spread, Sundry, Sweeping, Vast, Yawning

**Wide-awake** Alert, Fly, Hat, Wary, Watchful

**Widespread** Catholic, Common, Diffuse, Epidemic, Extensive, General, Pandemic, Panoramic, Pervasive, Prevalent, Prolate, Rife, Routh(ie), Sweeping, Universal

**Widow(ed)** Bereft, Black, Dame, Discovert, Dowager, Golf, Grass, Hempen, Jointress, Relict, Sati, Sneerwell, Suttee, Twankey, Vidual, Viduous, Whydah-bird, Widdy

**Wield** Brandish, Cede, Control, Exercise, Exert, Handle, → MANIPULATE, Ply, Sound

**Wife, Wives** Ball and chain, Better half, Bride, Common-law, Concubine, Consort, Devi, Dutch, Enid, Evadne, Feme, Feme covert, Fiere, Frau, Goody, Haram, Harem, Harim, Helpmate, Helpmeet, Hen, Her indoors, Kali, Kickie-wickie, Kicksy-wicksy, Kloo(t)chman, Lakshmi, Little woman, Mate, Memsahib, Missis, Missus, Mrs, Mummer's, Partner, Penelope, Pirrauru, Potiphar's, Rib, Seraglio, Spouse, Stepford, Trophy, Trouble and strife, Umfazi, Ux(or), Vrou, W, Wag

**Wife-beater** (Mr) Punch

**Wig** Adonis, Bagwig, Bob(wig), Brigadier, Brutus, Buzz-wig, Cadogan, Campaign, Carpet, Cauliflower, Caxon, Chastise, Chevelure, Chide, Cockernony, Dalmahoy, Fright, Full-bottomed, Gizz, Gooseberry, Gorgone, Gregorian, Hair(piece), Heare, Jas(e)y, Jazy, Jiz, Macaroni, Major, Periwig, Peruke, Postiche, Ramil(l)ie(s), Rate, Reprimand, Rug, Scold, Scratch, Sheitel, Spencer, Syrup, Targe, Tie, Toupee, Toupet, Tour

**Wiggle, Wiggly** Jiggle, Scoleciform, Wobble, Wriggle

**Wight** Man, Vectis, Wraith

**Wigmaker** Perruquier

**Wigwam** Te(e)pee

**Wild(er), Wildness** Abandoned, Aberrant, Agitato, Agrestal, Amok, Amuck, Angry, Barbarous, Baresark, Berserk, Bundu, Bush, Chimeric, Crazy, Demented, Dionysian, Earl, Enraged, Enthusiastic, Errant, Erratic, Extravagant, Farouche, Feral, Frantic, Frenetic, Frontier, Gene, Gohardery, Haggard, Hectic, Hell-raiser, Hooligan, Lawless, Mad(cap), Maenadic, Manic, Meshugge, Myall, Natural, Outlaw, Rampant, Raver, Riotous, Romantic, Rumbustious, → SAVAGE, Skimble-skamble, Tearaway, Unbroken, Unhinged, Unmanageable, Unruly, Untamed, Violent, Warrigal, West, Woolly

▹**Wild(ly)** *may indicate* an anagram

**Wild beast** Eyra, Sapi-utan, Scrubber

**Wildcat** Civet, Destruction, Eyra, Lion, Manul, Ocelot, Pallas's cat, Strike, Tiger, Zibet

**Wilde** Marty, Oscar

**Wildebeest** Gnu

**Wilderness** Bush, Desert, Negev, Outback, Ruderal, Sinai, Solitude, Waste, Wasteland

**Wild goose** Chase, Greylag

**Wild oats** Haver

**Wile, Wily** Art, Artful, Artifice, Astute, Braide, → CUNNING, Deceit, Devious, Foxy, Peery, Ruse, Shifty, Shrewd, Slee, Slippery, → SLY, Spider, Stratagem, Streetwise, Subtle, Trick, Versute, Wide (boy), Wide girl

**Wilful(ly)** Deliberate, Headstrong, Heady, Obstinate, Recalcitrant, Refractory, Scienter, Wayward

**Will, Willing(ly)** Alsoon, Amenable, Bard, Bequeath, Bewildered, Biddable, Bill(y), Can do, Complaisant, Compliant, Conation, Consensual, Content, Desire, Devise, Fain, Force, Free, Game, General, Glad, Hay, Holographic, Leave, Legator, Leve, Lief, Lieve, Living, Mind, Nerve, Noncupative, Obedient, On, Open, Pacable, Please, Prone, Purpose, Raring, Rather, Ready, Receptive, Resolution, Scarlet, Shakespeare, Soon, Spirit, Swan, Testament, Testate, Thelma, Tolerant, Up for, Velleity, Volens, Volition, Voluntary, Volunteer, Way, Wimble, Woot

▹**Will** *may indicate* an anagram

**William(s)** Bill(y), Conqueror, Occam, Orange, Pear, Rufus, Silent, Sweet, Tell, Tennessee

**Will o' the wisp** Fatuous fire, Fen-fire, Friar's lantern, Ignis-fatuus, Jack o'lantern, Min min, Nightfire, Rush, Spunkie, Wildfire

**Willow(ing), Willowy** Arctic, Crack, Diamond, Lissom(e), Lithe, Osier, Poplar, Port Jackson, Pussy, Sale, Salix, Sallow, Sauch, Saugh, Seal, Slender, Supple, Twilly, Weeping, Withy

**Willpower** Ab(o)uha, Determination, Resolve, Strength

**Willy-nilly** Malgré lui, Nolens volens, Perforce

**Wilt** Decline, Droop, Fade, Flag, Languish, Sag, Shalt, Wither

**Wiltshireman** Moonraker

▸**Wily** *see* WILE

**Wimp(ish)** Chicken, Drip, Milksop, Mouse, Namby-pamby, Pantywaist, Saddo, Sissy, Snool, Weed
**Wimple** Gorget, Meander, Ripple, Turn, Veil
▷**Wimple** *may indicate* an anagram
**Win(ner), Winning** Achieve, Acquire, Adorable, Ahead, Appealing, Attain, Backgammon, Bangster, Banker, → **BEAT**, Capot, Carry off, Cert, Champion, Charismatic, Charm, Checkmate, Conciliate, Conquer, Cup, Cute, Decider, Disarming, Dividend, Dormie, Dormy, Earn, Effect, Endearing, Engaging, Fetching, First, Fool's mate, Gain, Gammon, Grand slam, Hit, Ippon, Jackpot, Knockout, Land(fall), Landslide, Laureate, Lead, Lovesome, Luck out, Medallist, Motser, Motza, Nap hand, Nice, On a roll, Overcome, Pile, Pot, Prepossessing, Prevail, Profit, Purler, Reap, Repique, Result, Rollover, Rubicon, Scoop, Seduce, Shoo-in, Slam, Snip, Success, Sweep, Sweet, Take, Top dog, → **TRIUMPH**, Unbeaten, Up, Vellet, Velvet, Victor(y), Vole, Walk over, Wrest, Yellow jersey, Yokozuna
**Wince** Blench, Cringe, Flinch, Recoil
**Winch** Crab, Crane, Jack, Windlass
**Winchester®** Rifle, Wykehamist
**Wind(er), Winding(s), Windy** Air, Airstream, Anabatic, Anfractuous, Backing, Ball, Bend, Blow, Bottom, Brass, Burp, Capstan, Carminative, Chill, Coil, Colic, Crank, Creeky, Curl, Curve, Cutter, Draught, Draw, Entwine, Entwist, Evagation, Fart, Fearful, Flatulence, Flatus, Flaw, Gas, Gust, Ill, Katabatic, Key, Meander, Nervous, Periodic, Ponent, Poop, Prevailing, Purl, Quarter, Quill, Reeds, Reel, Roaring forties, Roll, Sand, Sandblast(er), Screw, Sea, Second, Series, Serpentine, Serpentize, Sinuous, Slant, Snake, Spiral, Spool, Stellar, Surface, Swirl, Tail, Tendril, Thread, Throw, Tortuous, Trade, Trend, Turn, Twaddle, Twine, Twisty, Veer, Veering, Ventose, Waffle, Weave, Wiggle, Winch, Windle, Winnle, Woold, Wrap, Wreathe, Wrest, Wuthering

---

**WINDS**

*4 letters:*
Berg
Bise
Bora
Firn
Fohn
Gale
Libs
Link
Puna
Vayu

*5 letters:*
Blore
Buran
Chili
Corus
Eurus
Foehn
Gibli
Greco
Noser
Notus
Ostro
Solar
Sough
Zonda

*6 letters:*
Aquilo
Auster
Baguio
Boreas
Breeze
Buster
Ghibli
Haboob
Heaves
Kamsin
Levant
Samiel
Sciroc
Shamal
Simoom
Simoon
Solano
Squall
Typhon
Wester
Zephyr

*7 letters:*
Aeolian
Ambages
Aquilon
Bluster
Chinook
Cyclone
Etesian
Gregale
Kamseen
Khamsin
Maestro
Meltemi
Mistral
Monsoon
Muzzler
Noreast
Norther
Pampero
Shimaal
Sirocco
Snifter
Snorter
Souther
Sumatra
Tornado
Twister
Typhoon

*8 letters:*
Apparent
Argestes
Downwash
Easterly
Favonian
Favonius
Levanter
Libeccio
Scirocco
Taranaki
Westerly
Williwaw
Zephyrus

*9 letters:*
Anti-trade
Bourasque
Cordonazo
Dust devil
Euraquilo
Harmattan
Hurricane
Hurricano
Jet stream
Knee-swell
Libecchio
Norwester
Volturnus

*10 letters:*
Cape doctor

Euroclydon
Rip-snorter
Tourbillon
Tramontana
Whirlblast
Willy-willy

*11 letters:*
Northwester
Norwesterly
White squall

*12 letters:*
Brickfielder

*13 letters:*
Northwesterly
Tehuantepecer

*15 letters:*
Southerly buster

---

**Windbag** Balloon, Bore, Chatterbox, Drogue, Prattler, Whoopee cushion, Zeppelin
**Windfall** Bonanza, Buckshee, Caduac, Fortune, Godsend, Manna
**Windflower** Anemone
**Windlass** Differential, Spanish, Whim, Winch
**Windless** Doldrums
**Windmill** Pinwheel, Post, Smock, Whirligig
**Window(s)** Atmosphere, Bay, Bow, Casement, Catherine-wheel, Companion, Compass, Day, Deadlight, Dormer, Double-hung, Dream-hole, Entry, Eye, Eyelids, Fanlight, Fenestella, Fenestra, French, Gable, Garret, Glaze, Guichet, Jalousie, Jesse, Judas, Jut, Lancet, Lattice, Launch, Light, Loop-light, Louver, Louvre, Lozen, Lucarne, Lunette, Luthern, Lychnoscope, Marigold, Mezzanine, Mirador, Monial, Mullion, Oculus, Oeil-de-boeuf, Ogive, Opportunity, Orb, Oriel, Oval, Ox-eye, Pane, Pede, Picture, Plate glass, Pop-under, Pop-up, Porthole, Program, Quarterlight, Radio, Re-entry, Rosace, Rose, Round, Sash, Sexfoil, Shed dormer, Shop, Shot, Sidelight, Skylight, Spyhole, Storm, Transom, Trellis, Velux, Ventana, Viewfinder, Weather, Wheel, Wicket, Windock, Windore, Winnock
**Window-bar, Window-fastening** Astragal, Espagnolette
**Windpipe** Bronchus, Gular, Throat, Trachea, Weasand
**Windscale** Beaufort
**Windsock** Drogue, Sleeve
**Windsor** Barbara, Castle, Knot
**Windsurf** Sailboard
**Windswept** Scud
**Wind-up** End, Fright, Liquidate, Miff, Needle, Span
**Windward** Ahold, Aloof, A-weather, Laveer, Luff, Up
**Wine** Bin, Blush, Cabinet, Case, Crusty, Cup, Cuvée, Dessert, Doc, Essence, Fortified, Grand cru, House, Libation, Low, Mulled, Must, Piece, Pigment, Premier cru, Prisage, Rotgut, Rouge, Semi-dry, Sparkling, Steen, Tannin, Terroir, The grape, Tirage, Unoaked, Varietal, Vat, Vin blanc, Vin rouge, Vintage, Zymurgy

---

**WINES**

*2 letters:*
It

*3 letters:*
Dao
Kir
Red
Sec
Tun
Vin

*4 letters:*
Asti
Brut
Cava
Hock
Mull
Palm
Pipe
Port
Race
Rosé
Rosy
Sack
Sekt
Stum
Tent
Tutu
Vino

*5 letters:*
Anjou
Anker
Biddy
Blanc
Bombo
Comet
Elder
Gallo
Gamay
Macon
Maqui
Médoc
Mirin
Mosel
Negus
Pinot
Plonk
Rhine
Rioja
Soave
Straw
Syrah
Table
Tavel
Toddy
Tokay
White
Xeres

*6 letters:*
Alsace
Barley
Barolo
Barsac
Beaune
Bishop
Bubbly
Canary
Claret
Ginger
Graves

Lisbon
Malaga
Malbec
Merlot
Muscat
Piment
Plotty
Red Ned
Sherry
Shiraz
Solera

*7 letters:*
Alicant
Amoroso
Auslese
Bastard
Catawba
Chablis
Château
Chianti
Cowslip
Currant
Demi-sec
Eiswein
Fendant
Icewine
Madeira
Malmsey
Margaux
Marsala
Moselle
Oenomel
Orvieto
Pomerol
Pommard
Retsina
Rhenish
Sangria
Sherris
Vouvray

*8 letters:*
Bordeaux
Bucellas
Buckfast®
Burgundy
Cabernet
Champers
Charneco
Dubonnet®
Espumoso
Essencia
Frascati
Gluhwein
Grenache
Jerepigo
Kabinett
Log-juice
Malvasia
Malvesie
Montilla
Mountain
Muscadel
Muscadet
Muscatel
Nebbiolo
Oenology
Pinotage
Pradikat
Prosecco
Red biddy
Resinata
Rheingau
Riesling
Sancerre
Sangaree
Sauterne
Sémillon
Spätlese
Spumante
St Julien
Sylvaner
Verdelho
Vermouth
Vinsanti

*9 letters:*
Bacharach
Bardolino
Carmenère
Champagne
Colombard
Dandelion
En primeur
Falernian
Gladstone
Hermitage
Hippocras
Hoccamore
Inglenook
Lambrusco
Languedoc
Loll-shrob
Malvoisie
Meersault
Minervois
Muscadine
Ordinaire
Pinot noir
Sauvignon
Sauvignon
St Emilion
Tafelwein
Tarragona
Vin-du-pays
Zinfandel

*10 letters:*
Beaujolais
Bull's blood
Chambertin
Chardonnay
Constantia
Elderberry
Genevrette
Gooseberry
Hochheimer
Loll-shraub
Manzanilla
Montrachet
Muscadelle
Napa Valley
Peter-see-me
Piesporter
Sangiovese
Vinho verde

*11 letters:*
Amontillado
Dom Perignon
Niersteiner
Petite Sirah
Pinot Grigio
Pouilly-Fumé
Rudesheimer
Scuppernong
Steinberger
Tempranillo

*12 letters:*
Johannisberg
Marcobrunner
Supernaculum
Valpolicella
Vin ordinaire

*13 letters:*
Beerenauslese
Entre-Deux-Mers
Liebfraumilch
Montepulciano
Pouilly-Fuissé

*14 letters:*
Gewürztraminer
Johannisberger

*15 letters:*
Lachryma Christi
Liebfrauenmilch

*16 letters:*
Chateau cardboard
London particular

*17 letters:*
Cabernet Sauvignon
Nuits Saint Georges

*20 letters:*
Trockenbeeren-auslese

---

**Wine-cellar, Wine-shop** Bistro, Bodega, Vault, Vaut(e)
**Wine-glass** Flute
**Wine-making** Gallising, Remuage
**Wineseller** Bodeguero
**Wing(s), Winged, Winger, Wing-like** Aerofoil, Ala(r), Aliform, Alula, Annexe, Appendage, Arm, Baryo, Bastard, → BIRD, Branch, Buffalo, Canard, Cellar, Corium, Coulisse, Delta, Dipteral, El(l), Elevon, Elytral, Elytriform, Elytron, Elytrum, Fan, Fender, Flank, Flap, Flew, Flex, Flipper, Flying, Forward, Gull, Halteres, Hurt, Left, Limb, Offstage, Parascenia, Parascenium, Patagium, Pegasus, Pennate, Pennon, Pinero, Pinion, Pip, Pterygoid,

Putto, Right, Rogallo, Sail, Samariform, Satyrid, Scent-scale, Segreant, Seraphim, Split, Standard, Sweepback, Sweptback, Sweptwing, Swift, Swingwing, Tailplane, Tectrix, Tegmen, Tormentor, Transept, Van, Vol(et), Water, Wound(ed)

**Winged sandals** Talaria

▷**Winger** *may indicate* a bird

**Wing-footed** Aliped, Fleet, Swift

**Wingless** Apteral, Impennate

**Wink (at)** Atone, Bat, Condone, Connive, Eliad, Eyelid, Flicker, Ignore, Illiad, Instant, Nap, Nictitate, Oeillade, Pink, Twinkle

**Winkle** Gastropod

**Winnie** Pooh

**Winnow** Fan, Riddle, Separate, Sift, Van, Wecht

**Winsome** Bonny, Engaging, Gay, Pleasant

**Winter, Wintry** Blackthorn, Bleak, Brumal, Cold, Dec, Fimbul, Frigid, Frore, Hibernate, Hiemal, Hiems, Hodiernal, Jack Frost, Jasmine, Nuclear, Shrovetide, Snowy, Subniveal, W

**Winter cherry** Chinese lantern

**Wintergreen** Chickweed, Pyrola, Sarcodes

**Winter pear** Nelis

**Winter-sport** Ski

**Wipe (out), Wiping** Abolish, Abrogate, Absterge, Amortise, Annihilate, Cancel, Cleanse, Demolish, Destroy, Deterge, Dicht, Dight, Dust, Efface, Eradicate, Erase, Expunge, Forget, Format, Hanky, Kleenex®, Mop, Nose-rag, Null, Purge, Raze, Retroussage, Rub, Slorm, Sponge, Tersion, Tissue

**Wire(s), Wirework, Wiry** Aerial, Barb(ed), Cable, Cat's whiskers, Cheese, Chicken, Coil, Earth, Element, Fencing, Filament, Filar, File, Filigree, Fuse, Gold (thread), Heald, Heddle, High, In on, Kirschner, Lead, Lean, Lecher, Live, Marconigram, Messenger, Mil, Nichrome®, Nipper, Number eight, Piano, Pickpocket, Picture, Razor, Sevice, Shroud, Sinewy, Snake, Solenoid, Spit, Staple, Stilet, Strand, String, Stylet, Telegram, Telegraph, Thoth, Thread, Tightrope, Trace, Trip

**Wireless (operator), Wireless part** Baffle, Receiver, Set, Sparks, Tranny, Valve

**Wirral** Peninsula

**Wise(acre), Wisdom** Advisedly, Ancient, Anthroposophy, Astute, Athena, Athene, Canny, Conventional, Cracker barrel, Depth, Ernie, Ganesa, Gothamite, Gudrun, Hep, Hindsight, Horse sense, Judgement, Judicious, Knowledge, Learned, Long-headed, Lore, Manner, Mimir, Minerva, Norman, Oracle, Owl, Pearl, Penny, Philosopher, Philosophy, Politic, Polymath, Prajna, Profound, Provident, Prudence, Sagacity, Sage, Salomonic, Sapience, Savvy, Seer, Shrewd, Smartie, Solomon, Solon, Sophia, Tooth, Wice

**Wisecrack** Dig, One-liner, Quip, Sally

**Wise guy** Clever clogs

**Wise man** Balthazar, Caspar, Gaspar, Hakam, Heptad, Melchior, Nestor, Pandit, Sage, Sapient, Seer, Solomon, Swami, Thales, Tohunga, Worldly

**Wish(es), Wishing** Ache, Ake, Aspire, Broody, Covet, Crave, Death, Desiderate, →**DESIRE**, Envy, For, Hope, Itch, List, Long, Nill, Pant, Pleasure, Pray, Precatory, Regards, RIP, Velleity, Want, Yearn

**Wishbone** Furcula, Marriage-bone, Merrythought, Skipjack

**Wishy-washy** Bland, Feeble, Insipid, Irresolute, Milksop, Weak, Wheyey

**Wisp(y)** Cirrate, Cirrose, Frail, Scrap, Shred, Virga, Wase

**Wistful** Elegiac

**Wit(s), Witticism, Witty** Acumen, Attic (salt), Badinage, Banter, Bon mot, Brevity, Card, Commonsense, Concetto, Cunning, Dry, Epigram, Esprit (de l'escalier), Estimation, Eutrapelia, Eutrapely, Facetious, Fantasy, Gnome, Hartford, Horse sense, Humour, Imagination, Intelligence, Irony, Jest, Jeu d'esprit, Joke, Marbles, Marinism, Memory, Mind, Mot, Mother, Native, Nous, One-liner, Oscar Wilde, Pawky, Pun, Quipster, Repartee, Rogue, Sally, Salt, Saut, Sconce, →**SENSE**, Shaft, Smart, Sparkle, Videlicet, Viz, Wag, Weet, Wilde, Wisecrack, Word-play

**Witch(craft)** Beldam(e), Besom-rider, Broomstick, Cantrip, Carline, Circe, Coven, Craigfluke, Crone, Cutty Sark, Diabolism, Enchantress, Ensorcell, Galdragon, Glamour, Goety, Gramary(e), Gyre-carline, Hag, Hecat(e), Hex, Invultuation, Lamia, Magic, Medea, Myal(ism), Necromancy, Night-hag, Obeahism, Obia, Obiism, Pishogue, Pythoness, Salem, Selim, She-devil, Sibyl, Sieve, Sorceress, Speller, Sycorax, Termagant, Trout, Valkyrie, Vaudoo, Vilia, Voodoo, Water, Weird, Wicca, Wise woman

**Witch-doctor** Animist, Boyla, Medicine man, Mganga, Obi, Pawaw, Powwow, Sangoma, Shaman

**Witch-hazel** Fothergilla, Platan(e), Winter-bloom

**Witch-hunter** McCarthy

**Witching hour** Midnight

**With** And, By, Con, Cum, Hereby, In, Mit, Of, Plus, Using, W

**Withdraw(al), Withdrawn** Abdicate, Abstract, Alienate, Aloof, Back out, Backpedal, Breakaway, Climb down, Cloistered, Cold turkey, Cry off, Debit, Decentralise, Deduct, Desertion, Detach, Disengage, Distrait, Enshell, Estrange, Evacuate, Extract, Hive off, Inshell, Introvert, Leave, Offish, Palinode, Phantom, Precede, Preserve, Recant, Recede, Recoil, Renegue, Repair, Rescind, Resile, Reticent, Retire, Retract(ion), Retreat, Revoke, Revulsion, Scratch, Secede, Secesh, Sequester, Shrink, Shy, Stand down, Subduce, Subduct, Subtract, Tap, Unreeve, Unsay

**Wither(ed), Withering, Withers** Arefy, Atrophy, Blast, Blight, Burn, Corky, Decadent, Die, Droop, Dry, Evanish, Fade, Forpine, Gizzen, Googie, Languish, Marcescent, Miff, Nose, Sarcastic, Scram, Sere, Shrink, Shrivel, Welk, Welt

**Withershins** Eastlin(g)s

▷**With gaucherie** *may indicate* an anagram

**Withhold(ing), Withheld** Abstain, Conceal, Curt, Deny, Detain, Detinue, Hide, Keep, → RESERVE, Ritenuto, Trover

**Within** Enclosed, Endo-, Immanent, Indoors, Inside, Interior, Intra

**With it** Hep, Hip, Syn, Trendy, W

**Without** Baht, Bar, Beyond, Empty-handed, Ex, Lack(ing), Less, Minus, Orb, Outdoors, Outside, Sans, Save, Sen, Senza, Sine, X

▷**Without** *may indicate* one word surrounding another

▷**Without restraint** *may indicate* an anagram

**Without stimulus** Nastic

**Withstand** Blight, Brave, Contest, Defy, Endure, Oppose, Resist, Weather

**Witless** Crass, → STUPID PERSON

**Witness** Attend, Attest, Behold, Bystander, Catch, Character, Compurgator, Confirm, Crown, Deponent, Depose, Endorse, Evidence, Experience, Expert, Eye, Glimpse, Hostile, Jehovah's, Mark, Martyr, Material, Muggletonian, Notary, Note, Notice, Observe, Obtest, Onlooker, Passer-by, Perceive, Proof, → SEE, Show, Sight, Sign, Spectator, Spy, Stander-by, Survey, Testament, Teste, Testify, Testimony, View, Vouchee, Watch

**Witness-box** Peter, Stand

**Witter** Prattle, Rabbit

▶**Witticism** *see* WIT(S)

**Wizard (priest)** Archimage, Awesome, Carpathian, Conjuror, Demon, Expert, Financial, Gandalf, Hex, Mage, Magician, Merlin, Obiman, Oz, Prospero, Shaman, Sorcerer, Super, Warlock, → WITCH-DOCTOR

**Wizen(ed)** Dehydrate, Dry, Scrunty, Sere, Shrivel, Sphacelate, Wither

**Woad** Anil, Dye, Indigo, Isatis, Pastel, Pastil

**Wobble, Wobbling, Wobbly** Chandler's, Coggle, Groggy, Hissy fit, Insecure, Precess, Quaver, Reel, Rock, Shimmy, Shoggle, Shoogle, Teeter, Totter, Tremble, Trillo, Unstable, Unsteady, Wag, Waggle, Walty, Waver, Wibble

**Wodehouse** Plum

**Woe(ful), Woebegone, Woeful** Agony, Alack, Alas, Bale, Bane, Distress, Dool(e), Dule, Ewhow, Execrable, Gram, Grief, Hurt, Jeremiad, Lack-a-day, Misery, Misfortune, Pain, Plague, Rueful, → SORROW, Torment, Tribulation, Triste, Unhappy, Wailful, Wednesday's child

**Wolds** Lincoln(shire), Yorkshire

**Wolf(ish), Wolf-like** Akela, Assyrian, Bolt, Cancer, Carcajou, Casanova, Coyote, Cram, Dangler, Dasyure, Dire, Earth, Engorge, Fenrir, Fenris, Gorge, Grey, Ise(n)grim, Lobo, Lone, Lothario, Lupine, Luster, Lycanthrope, MI, Michigan, Pack, Philanderer, Prairie, Rake, Ravenous, Red, Rip, Roué, Rout, Rudolph, Rye, Scoff, Sea, Seducer, Strand, Tasmanian, Thylacine, Tiger, Timber, Wanderer, Were, Whistler

**Wolfram** Tungsten

**Wolf's bane** Aconite, Friar's-cap

**Wolseley** Sir Garnet

**Woman(hood), Women** Aguna(h), Anile, Beldam(e), Bellibone, Besom, Biddy, Bimbo, Bit, Boiler, Broad, Cailleach, Callet, Caryatid, Chai, Chap(p)ess, Chook, Citess, Cotquean, Crone, Crumpet, Cummer, Dame, Daughter, Distaff, Doe, Dona(h), Dorcas, Doris, Doyenne, Drab, Duenna, Eve, F, Fair, Fair sex, → FEMALE, Feme, Femme fatale, Flapper, Floozy, Frail, Frow, Gammer(stang), Gimmer, Girl, Gyno-, -gyny, Harpy, Harridan, Hausfrau, Hen, Her, Ho, Housewife, Inner, It, Jade, Jane, Kloo(t)chman, Lady, Liberated, Lilith, Lorette, Madam(e), Mademoiselle, Maenad, Mary, Miladi, Milady, Millie, Mob, Modicum, Mort, Ms, Muliebrity, Painted, Pandora, Peat, Petticoat, Pict, Piece, Piece of goods, Placket, Point, Popsy, Quean, Queen, Ramp, Rib, Ribibe, Ronyon, Rudas, Runnion, Sabine, Sakti, Scarlet, Shakti, Shawlay, Shawlie, She, Skirt, Sloane Ranger, Sort, Tedesca, Tib, Tiring, Tit, Tottie, Totty, Trot, Umfazi, Vahine, Wahine, Weaker sex, Wifie, Zena

**Womaniser** Casanova, Lady-killer, Poodle-faker, Seducer, Wolf

**Womb** Belly, Matrix, Metritis, Side, Uterus, Ventricle

**Women's club, Women's lib** S(h)akti, Soroptimist

**Won** Chon, W

**Wonder(s)** Admire, Agape, Amazement, AR, Arkansas, Arrah, Awe, Chinless, Colossus, Eye-opener, Ferly, Grape-seed, Hanging Gardens, Humdinger, Marle, → MARVEL, Mausoleum, Meteor, Mirabilia, Miracle, Muse, Nine-day, One-hit, Pharos, Phenomenon, Prodigy, Pyramids, Rarity, Seven, Speculate, Statue of Zeus, Stupor, Suppose, Surprise, Temple of Artemis, Thaumatrope, Theorise, Wheugh, Whew, Wow(ee)

**Wonderful(ly)** Amazing, Bees' knees, Bitchin(g), Chinless, Divine, Épatant, Fantastic, Far-out, Ferly, Geason, Gee-whiz, Glorious, Gramercy, Grand, Great, Heavenly, Keen, Lal(l)apalooza, Magic, Mirable, Must-see, Old, Priceless, Purely, Ripping, Smashing, Stellar, Sublime, Superb, Terrific, Wicked

**Wonder-worker** Fakir, Thaumaturgist, Thaumaturgus

**Wonky** Cockeyed, Lopsided

**Wont(ed)** Accustomed, Apt, Custom, Habit, Shan't, Used, Way, Winna

**Woo(er)** Address, Beau, Carve, Chase, Court, Frog, Pursue, Seduce, Serenade, Suitor, Swain, Wow

**Wood(s), Wooden, Woodland, Woody** Arboretum, Batten, Beam, Birken, Board, Boord(e), Bough, Brake, Cask, Channel, Chipboard, Chuck, Chump, Clapboard, Conductor, Dead, Deadpan, Early, Expressionless, Fardage, Fathom, Fire, Fish, Funk, Furious, Gantry, Gauntree, Guthrie, Hanger, Hard, Hyle, Kindling, Knee, Krummholz, Late, Lath, Loggerhead, Lumber, Mad, Magnetic, Miombo, Nemoral, Nemorous, Offcut, Pallet, Pegboard, Plastic, Pulp(wood), Punk, Silvan, Slat, Spilikin, Spill, Spinney, Splat, Spline, Splint, Stick, Stilted, Stolid, Sylvan, Tenon, Three-ply, Timber, Tinder, Touch, Treen, Trees, Twiggy, Two-by-four, Vert, Xylem, Xyloid

---

**WOODS**

*3 letters:*
Ash
Box
Cam
Elm
Log
Oak
Red

*4 letters:*
Beef
Bent
Bowl
Carr
Cord
Cork
Deal
Eugh
Gapó
Holt
Iron
King
Lana
Lima
Lime
Pine
Rata
Rock
Shaw
Soft
Spar
Teak
Wild
Yang

***5 letters:***
Afara
Agila
Algum
Almug
Balsa
Bavin
Beech
Cedar
Cocoa
Copse
Drive
Ebony
Elfin
Firth
Frith
Green
Grove
Heben
Hurst
Igapó
Iroko
Jarul
Joist
Kauri
Kiaat
Kokra
Lance
Loper
Maple
Mazer
Myall
Opepe
Peach
Plane
Ramin
Rowan
Sapan
Spoon
Stink
Taiga
Thorn
Tiger
Tulip
Wenge
Zante
Zebra

***6 letters:***
Alerce
Bamboo
Beaver
Birnam
Bocage
Brazil
Calico
Canary
Candle
Carapa
Cheese
Citron
Citrus
Deodar
Dingle
Forest
Fustet
Fustic
Fustoc
Gaboon
Gopher
Herman
Jarool
Jarrah
Letter
Lignum
Loggat
Manuka
Muntin
Obeche
Orache
Orange
Paddle
Poplar
Raddle
Sabele
Sabicu
Sandal
Sapele
Sappan
Sissoo
Sponge
Spring
Tallow
Tupelo
Violet
Waboom
Walnut
Wandoo
Yellow

***7 letters:***
Amboina
Barwood
Boscage
Brassie
Cambium
Cerrado®
Coppice
Dudgeon
Dunnage
Duramen
Gambrel
Gumwood
Hadrome
Hickory
Leopard
Meranti
Mesquit
Nutwood
Palmyra
Paranym
Pimento
Sanders
Sapwood
Shawnee
Shittim
Trumpet
Wallaba

***8 letters:***
Agalloch
Alburnum
Basswood
Bushveld
Caatinga
Corkwood
Coulisse
Harewood
Hornbeam
Kingwood
Laburnum
Ligneous
Mahogany
Masonite®
Mesquite
Mountain
Ovenwood
Pyengadu
Pyinkado
Rosewood
Sapucaia
Shagbark
Southern
Tamarack

***9 letters:***
Balsam fir
Briarwood
Butternut
Caliature
Campeachy
Coachwood
Cocuswood
Driftwood
Eaglewood
Fruitwood
Heartwood
Ivorywood
Matchwood
Partridge
Porcupine
Primavera
Quebracho
Satinwood
Snakewood
Torchwood

***10 letters:***
Afrormosia
Blockboard
Bulletwood
Calamander
Candlewood
Cheesewood
Chittagong
Coromandel
Fiddlewood
Greenheart
Hackmatack
Marblewood
Nettle-tree
Orangewood
Palisander
Scaleboard
Sneezewood
Springwood
Summerwood

***11 letters:***
Lignum-vitae
Sanderswood
Slippery elm

***13 letters:***
Savanna-wattle

---

▷**Wood** *may indicate* an anagram in sense of mad
**Wood-carver** Bodger, Gibbons, Whittler
**Woodchuck** Bobac, Groundhog, Marmot

**Woodcock** Becasse, Beccaccia, Snipe
**Woodcutter** Adze, Axe, Saw
**Wood-hyacinth** Bluebell
**Woodlouse** Isopod, Oniscus, Slater
**Woodman** Ali (Baba), Coureur de bois, Feller, Forester, Hewer, Logger, Lumberjack, Sawyer
**Woodpecker** Bird, Descent, Flicker, Hairy, Hickwall, Picalet, Picarian, Pileated, Rainbird, Sapsucker, Saurognathae, Witwall, Woodspite, Woodwale, Woody, Wryneck, Yaffle
**Wood-pigeon** Bird, Cushat, Que(e)st, Qu(o)ist, Torquate
**Wood-sorrel** Oca
**Wood-tar** Furan, Furfuran
**Woodwind** Bassoon, Clarinet, Cornet, Flute, Oboe, Piccolo, Pipe, Recorder, Reed
**Woodwork(er)** Carpentry, Ebonist, Forestry, Intarsia, Joinery, Marquetrie, Marquetry, Sloid, Sloyd, Tarsia, Termite
**Woodworm** Gribble, Termes
**Wookey** Stalactite
**Wool(len), Woolly (haired)** Alpaca, Angora, Aran, Ardil, Bainin, Barège, Beige, Berlin, Botany, Bouclé, Calamanco, Cardi(gan), Cashmere, Cas(s)imere, Clean, Clip, Combings, Cotton, Crutchings, Daglock, Delaine, Doeskin, Dog, Doily, Down, Doyley, Drugget, Duffel, Fadge, Fingering, Fleece, Flock, Fluffy, Frib, Frieze, Fuzz, Glass, Greasy, Guernsey, Hank, Hause-lock, Heather mixture, Hogget, Indumentum, Jaeger, Jersey, Kashmir, Ket, Knitwear, Lamb's, Lanate, Laniferous, Lanigerous, Lanose, Llama, Lock, Loden, Merino, Mineral, Mortling, Moul, Mullein, New, Noil(s), Nun's-veiling, Offsorts, Oo, Paco, Paisley, Pashm, Pelage, Persian, Pine, Qiviut, Rock, Rolag, Sagathy, Saxon, Say, Shahtoosh, Shalloon, Shamina, Shetland, Shoddy, Skein, Skin, Slag, Slipe, Slip-on, Sloppy Joe, Slub, Smart, Spencer, Staple, Steel, Strouding, Stuff, Swansdown, Tamise, Tammy, Tank top, Telltale, Thibet, Three-ply, Tod, Tricot, Tweed, Twin set, Ulotrichous, Vague, Vicuña, Virgin, Wire, Wood, Worcester, Yarn, Zephyr, Zibel(l)ine
**Wool-gather(er), Woolgathering** Abstraction, Argo, Dreamer, Reverie
**Wool-holder, Woolsack** Bale, Distaff
**Woolly-bear** Tiger-moth, Woubit
**Wool-oil** Yolk
**Woopie** Glam
**Wooster** Bertie
**Woozy** Drunk, Faint, Vague, Woolly
**Worcester** Wigorn
**Word(s), Wording, Wordy** Al(l)-to, Appellative, Argument, Aside, Bahuvrihi, Buzz, Cataphor(a), Catch, Cheville, Claptrap, Clipped, Clitic, Code, Coinage, Comment, Content, Dick, Dicky bird, Dirty, Dit(t), Double-speak, Echoic, Effable, Embolalia, Enclitic, Epitaph, Epithet, Epos, Etymon, Faith, Four-letter, Function, Functor, Ghost, Grace, Hapax legomenon, Hard, Heteronym, Hint, Holophrase, Homograph, Homonym, Horseman's, Household, Hyponym, → **IN A WORD**, → **IN TWO WORDS**, Janus, Jonah, Key, Last, Lexeme, Lexicon, Lexis, Loan, Logia, Logos, Long-winded, Lyrics, Mantra, Meronym, Message, Morpheme, Mot, Neologism, News, Nonce, Nonsense, Noun, Oath, Om, Operative, Oracle, Order, Palabra, Paragram, Paranym, Parenthesis, Parlance, Parole, Paronym, Paroxytone, Particle, Perissology, Peristomenon, Phrase, Piano, Pledge, Pleonasm, Polysemen, Portmanteau, Preposition, Prolix, Promise, Pronoun, Reserved, Rhematic, Rhyme, Rumbelow, Rumour, Sapheaded, Saying, Selah, Semantics, Signal, Soundbite, Subtitle, Surtitle, Syntagma, Talkative, Tatpurusha, Term, Tetragram, Text, Tirade, Trigger, Trope, Typewriter, Verb, Verbiage, Verbose, Vocab(ulary), Vogue, Warcry, Weasel, Windbag, Winged, Woodpecker, Wort, Written
**Word-blindness** Alexia, Dyslexia
**Wordless** Tacit
**Word-play** Charade, Paronomasia, Pun
**Wordsmith** Logodaedalus
▷**Work** *may indicate* a book or play, etc.
**Workable** Feasible, Practical

**Workaholic, Work(er), Working(-class), Workman, Workmen, Works, Workman(ship)** Act(ivate), Aga saga, Ant, Application, Appliqué, Apronman, Artefact, Artel, Artifact, Artificer, Artisan, At it, At task, Barbola, Barmaid, Beamer, Beaver, Bee, Blue-collar, Blue-singlet, Bohunk, Boon(er), Boondoggle, Brief, Bull, Business, Busy, Careerist, Caseload, Casual, Char, Chare, Chargehand, Chigga, Chippy, Chore, Claim, Classics, Clock, Colon, Community, Computer, Contingent, Coolie, Cooly, Coromandel, Corpus, Corridor, Corvée, Craftsman, Crew, Cultivate, Darg, Dig, Dimension, Dirty, Diss(ertation), Do, Dog, Dogsbody, Donkey, Draft-mule, Drawn (thread), Droil, Drudge, Drug, Dung, Earn, Effect, Effort, Elbow grease, Em, Enforcement, Erg(ataner), Ergatoid, Erg-nine, Ergon, Ergonomics, Erg-ten, Eta, Everything, Evince, Exercise, Exergy, Exploit, Factotum, Facture, Fast, Fat, Ferment, Fettler, Field, Filter, Fitter, Flat cap, Flex(i)time, Floruit, Fret, Fuller, → FUNCTION, Gae, Gastarbeiter, Gel, Girl Friday, Go, Graft, Grass, Grind, Grisette, Grunt, Guest, Hand, Harness, Hat, Hobo, Horse, Hot-desking, Hunky, Indian, Industry, Innards, Intray, Jackal, Job, Journeyman, Key, Kilojoule, Knead, Knit, Knowledge, Kolhoznik, Labour, Laid, Leave, Luddite, Lump, Machinist, Maid, Man, Manipulate, Manpower, McJob, Mechanic(ian), Meng, Menge, Menial, Midinette, Mine, Ming, MO, Modus, Moider, Moil, Moonlight, Movement, Navvy, Neuter, Nine-to-fiver, Number, Oeuvre, On, On (the) job, Op, Opera(tion), Operative, Operator, Opus, Opusc(u)le, Orderly, Outreach, Outside, Ouvrier, Ox, Panel-beater, Parergon, Part, Partisan, Passage, Peasant, Peg, Pensum, Peon, Perform, Pink-collar, Plasterer, Ply, Poker, Portfolio, Postlude, Potboiler, Practicum, Practise, Print(ing), Production, Project, Prole(tariat), Prud'homme, Public, Pursuit, Red-neck, Reduction, Rep, Ride, Robot, Rotovate, Roughneck, Round, Rouseabout, Roustabout, Run, Salaryman, Samiti, Sandhog, Satisfactory, Scabble, Scapple, Scullion, Secretariat, Sedentary, Servant, Serve, Service, Servile, Seven, Sewage, Shift, Shop (floor), Situation, Skanger, Slogger, Smithy, Social, Soldier, Spiderman, Staff, Stagehand, Stakhanovite, Stevedore, Stint, Strap, Straw, Strive, Support, Surface, Swaggie, Swagman, Sweat, Swink, Take, Tamper, Task, Team, Technician, Telecommuter, Temp, Tenail(le), Tenaillon, Termite, Tew, Text, Tick, Till, Toccata, Toil, Toreutic, Tradesman, Travail, Treatise, Trilogy, Trojan, TU, TUC, Turk, Tut, Tutman, Typto, Uphill, Villein, Wage plug, Walla(h), Wark, Welfare, White-collar, Wobblies, Wright, Yacker, Yakka, Yakker, Yarco

**Work-basket, Workbox** Caba(s), Nécessaire

**Workbench** Banker, Siege

**Workhouse** Casual ward, Spike, Union

▷**Working** *may indicate* an anagram

**Working-party** Bee, Quilting-bee, Sewing-bee, Squad

**Workmate** Yokefellow

**Work out** Deduce, Exercise, Figure, PE, PT

**Works, Workplace, Workshop** Atelier, Engine, Factory, Forge, Foundry, Garage, Hacienda, Hangar, Innards, Lab, Mill, Passage, Plant, Pottery, Public, Shed, Sheltered, Shipyard, Shop, Skylab, Smithy, Studio, Study, Sweatshop, Tannery, Telecottage, Time, Tin, Turnery, Upper

**Workshy** Indolent, Lazy, Skiver, Sweer(ed), Sweert, Sweir(t)

**Workstation** Desk

**World(ly), Worlds, Worldwide** Adland, Carnal, Chthonic, Cosmopolitan, Cosmos, Cyberspace, Dream, Earth, First, Fleshly, Fourth, Free, Ge, Global village, Globe, Jurassic, Kingdom, Lay, Lower, Mappemond, Meatspace, Microcosm, Midgard, Mondaine, Mondial, Mould, Mundane, Natural, Nether, New, Old, Orb, Other, Oyster, Planet, Possible, Second, Secular, Sensual, Small, Society, Sophisticated, Sphere, Spirit, Temporal, Terra, Terrene, Terrestrial, Third, Universe, Vale, Web, Welt, Whole

**Worm(-like), Worms, Wormy** Acorn, Angle, Anguillula, Annelid, Annulata, Apod(e), Apodous, Army, Arrow, Articulata, Ascarid, Bilharzia, Bladder, Blind, Blood, Bob, Bootlace, Brandling, Bristle, Bud, Cabbage, Caddis, Capeworm, Caseworm, Catworm, Cercaria, Cestode, Cestoid, Chaetopod, Clamworm, Clew, Copper, Creep, Dew, Diet, Diplozoon, Dracunculus, Edge, Enteropneust, Fan, Filander, Filaria, Flag, Flat, Flesh, Fluke, Galley, Gape, Gilt-tail, Gordius, Gourd, Gru-gru, Guinea, Hair, Hair-eel, Hairworm, Heartworm, Helminth, Hemichordata, Hookworm, Horsehair, Ice, Idle, Inchworm, Leech, Liver-fluke,

Lob, Lumbricus, Lytta, Maw, Meal, Measuring, Merosome, Miner's, Mopani, Muck, Nemathelminthes, Nematoda, Nematode, Nematodirus, Nematomorpha, Nemertean, Nemertina, Nereid, Night-crawler, Oligochaete, Onychophoran, Paddle, Palmer, Palolo, Paste-eel, Peripatus, Phoronid, Pile, Pin, Piper, Planarian, Platyhelminth, Polychaete, Ragworm, Redia, Ribbon, Rootworm, Roundworm, Sabella, Sand mason, Schistosome, Scoleciform, Scolex, Screw, Seamouse, Serpula, Servile, Ship, Sipunculacea, Sipunculoidea, Spiny-headed, Stomach, Strawworm, Strongyl(e), Taenia, Tag-tail, Taint, Tapeworm, Tenioid, Teredo, Termite, Threadworm, Tiger, Tiger tail, Tongue, Toxocara, Trematode, Trichin(ell)a, Trichinosed, Triclad, Tube, Tubifex, Turbellaria, Vermiform, Vinegar, Vinegar eel, Wheat, Wheat-eel, Wheatworm, Whipworm

**Wormkiller** Anthelmintic, Santonin

**Wormwood** Absinth, Appleringie, Artemisia, Moxa, Mugwort, Santonica, Southernwood

**Worn (out)** Attrite, Banal, Bare, Bauchle, Decrepit, Detrition, Effete, Épuisé, Exhausted, Forfairn, Forfoughten, Forjaskit, Forjeskit, Frayed, Frazzled, Gnawn, Hackneyed, Knackered, Old, On, Passé, Raddled, Rag, Seedy, Shabby, Shopsoiled, Shot, Spent, Stale, Tatty, Threadbare, Tired, Traikit, Trite, Used, Weathered, Whacked

**Worried, Worrier, Worry** Agonise, Ail, Angst(-ridden), Annoy, Anxiety, Badger, Bait, Beset, Bother, Brood, Burden, Care(worn), Cark, Chafe, Concern, Consternate, Deave, Deeve, Distraught, Distress, Disturb, Dog, Eat, Exercise, Faze, Feeze, Frab, Frantic, Fret, Fuss, Gnaw, Harass, Harry, Headache, Hyp, Inquietude, Knag, Nag, Niggle, Obsess, Perturb, Pester, Pheese, Pheeze, Phese, Pingle, Pium, Preoccupy, Rattle, Rile, Savage, Sool, Stew, Tew, Touse, Towse, Trouble, Unease, Unnerve, Unsettle, Vex, Wherrit, Worn

▷**Worried** *may indicate* an anagram

**Worse(n)** Adversely, Aggravate, Compound, Degenerate, Deteriorate, Exacerbate, Impair, Inflame, Pejorate, Regress, Relapse, War(re), Waur, Well away

**Worship(per)** Adore, Adulation, Allostery, Ancestor, Angelolatry, Aniconism, Animist, Autolatry, Bardolatry, Bless, Churchgoer, Congregation, Cosmolatry, Cult, Deify, Devil, Devotion, Dote, Douleia, Doxology, Dulia, Elementalism, Epeolatry, Exalt, Exercise, Fetish, Glorify, Groupie, Gurdwara, Happy-clappy, Henotheism, Hero, Hierolatry, Ibadah, Iconology, Idolatry, Idolise, Latria, Lauds, Lionise, Liturgics, Lordolatry, Mariolatry, Meeting-house, Monolatry, Nature, Odinism, Oncer, Ophiolatry, Orant, Praise, Puja, Revere, Sabaism, Sakta, Service, Shacharis, Shakta, Sun, Synaxis, Thiasus, Vaishnava, Venerate, Votary, Wodenism

**Worst** Beat, Best, Better, Conquer, Defeat, Get, Less, Nadir, Outdo, Overpower, Pessimum, Rock-bottom, Scum, Severest, The pits, Throw, Trounce

**Worsted** Caddis, Caddyss, Challis, Coburg, Crewel, Genappe, Lea, Ley, Prunella, Serge, Shalli, Tamin(e), Whipcord

▷**Worsted** *may indicate* an anagram

**Wort** Hopped, Laser, Parkleaves, Plant, Sweet, Tutsan

**Worth(while), Worthy, Worthies** Admirable, Ad valorem, Asset, Be, Cop, Cost, Cost effective, Deserving, Eligible, Estimable, Face value, Feck, Laudable, → MERIT, Nine, Notable, Rewarding, Significant, Substance, Tanti, Use, Value, Venerable, Vertu, Virtu(e), Virtuous, Wealth

**Worthless (person)** Average, Bad egg, Base, Beggarly, Bilge, Blown, Bodger, Bootless, Bum, Candy floss, Catchpenny, Chaff, Cheapjack, Crumb, Cypher, Damn, Despicable, Docken, Dodkin, Doit, Doitkin, Draffish, Draffy, Dreck, Dross, Duff, Ephemeron, Fallal, Footra, Fouter, Foutre, Frippery, Gimcrack, Gingerbread, Glop, Gubbins, Hilding, Ignoble, Javel, Jimcrack, Junk, Knick-knack, Left, Light, Lorel, Lorrell, Losel, Lozell, Manky, Mare's nest, Mauvais sujet, Mud, Naughty, Nugatory, Nyaff, Obol, Ornery, Orra, Otiose, Pabulum, Paltry, Pin, Poxy, Punk, Raca, Rag, Rap, Razoo, Riffraff, Rubbishy, Rump, Scabby, Scrote, Scum, Shinkin, Shotten, Sixpenny, Sorry, Straw, Tawdry, Tinhorn, Tinpot, Tinsel, Tittle, Toerag, Trangam, Trashy, Tripy, Trumpery, Tuppenny, Two-bit, Twopenny, Useless, Vain, Vile, Waff, Wanworthy, Wauff, Zero

**Wotchermean** Anan

**Would be** Assumed, Pseudo, Soi-disant

**Wouldn't** Nould(e)

**Wound(ed), Wounding** Barb, Battery, Bite, Bless, Blighty, Bloodshed, Bruise, Chagrin, Coiled, Crepance, Cut, Dere, Dunt, Engore, Entry, Exit, Fleabite, Flesh, Ganch, Gash, Gaunch, Gore, Harm, Hurt, Injury, Knee, Lacerate, Lesion, Maim, Maul, Molest, Mortify, Offend, Pip, Sabre-cut, Scab, Scar, Scath, Scotch, Scratch, Shoot, Snaked, Snub, Sore, Stab, Sting, Trauma, Twined, Umbrage, Vuln, Vulnerary, Walking, Wing, Wint

**Woundwort** Clown's, Marsh

**Woven** Faconne, Inwrought, Knitted, Pirnit, Textile, Wattle

**Wow** Amaze, Astound, Gee, Howl, Impress, My, Success

**Wrack** Destroy, Downfall, Kelp, Ore, Sargasso, Torment, Varec(h), Vengeance

**Wraith** Apparition, Fetch, Ghost, Phantom, Shadow, Spectre

**Wrangle(r), Wrangling** Altercate, Argie-bargie, → ARGUE, Bandy, Bicker, Brangle, Broil, Cample, Controvert, Dispute, Haggle, Hassle, Herder, Horse, Mathematical, Rag, Rodeo, Second, Senior, Vitilitigation

**Wrap(per), Wrapped, Wrapping, Wraparound, Wrap up** Amice, Amis, Bag, Bandage, Bathrobe, Bind, Boa, Body, Bubble, Bundle, Carton(age), Cellophane®, Cere, Clingfilm, Cloak, Clothe, Cocoon, Conclude, Cover-up, Drape, Emboss, Encase, Enfold, Enrol(l), Ensheath(e), Envelop(e), Enwind, Foil, Folio, Furl, Gift, Gladwrap®, Hap, Hem, Infold, Kimono, Kraft, Lag, Lap, Mail, Mob, Muffle, Mummy, Negligee, Night-rail, Nori, Obvolute, Outsert, Package, Packet, Parcel, Plastic, Roll, Rug, Sarong, Shawl, Sheath(e), Sheet, Shrink, Shroud, Stole, Swaddle, Swathe, Throw, Tinfoil, Tsutsumu, Velamen, Wap, Wimple

**Wrasse** Conner, Cunner, Parrot-fish, Scar

**Wrath** Anger, Cape, Fury, Ire, Passion, Vengeance

**Wreak** Avenge, Indulge, Inflict

**Wreath(e)** Adorn, Anadem, Bridal, Chaplet, Civic crown, Coronal, Crown, Entwine, Festoon, Garland, Laurel, Lei, Steven, Torse, Tortile, Twist

**Wreathe(d)** Hederated

**Wreck(age), Wrecked, Wrecker** Banjax, Blight, Blotto, Crab, Debris, Demolish, Devastate, Dustbucket, Flotsam, Founder, Goner, Hesperus, Hulk, Lagan, Ligan, Loss, Luddite, Mutilate, Nervous, Ruin(ate), Sabotage, Saboteur, Scotch, Shambles, Shatter, Sink, Smash, Spif(f)licate, Stramash, Subvert, Torpedo, Trash, Vandalise, Wrack

▷**Wrecked** *may indicate* an anagram

**Wren** Architect, Bird, Fairy, Fire-crested, Golden-crested, Hannah, Heath, Jenny, Kinglet, Rifleman-bird, Sailor, Superb blue, Willow

**Wrench** Allen, Bobbejaan, Box, Fit, Jerk, Lug, Mole, Monkey, Nut, Pin, Pipe, Pull, Rick, Screw, Socket, Spanner, Spider, Sprain, Stillson®, Strain, Strap, T-bar, Tear, Torque, Twist, Windlass, Wrest

**Wrestle(r), Wrest, Wrestling** All-in, Antaeus, Arm (lock), Backbreaker, Basho, Bearhug, Bodycheck, Boston crab, Brawl, Catch-as-catch-can, Catchweight, Clinch, Clothes line, Cross buttock, Cross press, Featherweight, Flying mare, Foil, Folding-press, Forearm smash, Freestyle, Full-nelson, Grapple, Gr(a)eco-Roman, Grovet, Half-nelson, Hammerlock, Haystacks, Headlock, Hip-lock, → HOLD, Indian, Judo, Knee-drop, Makunouchi, Milo, Monkey climb, Mud, Nelson, Niramiai, Ozeki, Palaestral, Pancratium, Pinfall, Posting, Rikishi, Sambo, Stable, Straight arm lift, Stranglehold, Struggle, Sumo, Sumotori, Suplex, Tag (team), Toehold, Tussle, Whip, Wraxle, Wristlock, Writhe, Yokozuna

**Wretch(ed)** Abject, Bally, Blackguard, Blighter, Blue, Caitiff, Chap-fallen, Crumb, Cullion, Cur, Darned, Dolent, Donder, Fleabitten, Forlorn, Git, Goddamned, Hapless, Ignoble, Lorn, Low, Measly, Miscreant, Miser, Miserable, Peelgarlic, Pilgarlick, Pipsqueak, Pitiable, Poltroon, Poor, Punk, Rakeshame, Rascal, Rat, Scoundrel, Scroyle, Seely, Snake, Sorry, Toerag, Trist(e), Unblest, Waeful, Wo(e), Woebegone, Woeful

▷**Wretched** *may indicate* an anagram

**Wriggle** Fidget, Hirsle, Shimmy, Squirm, Twine, Wiggle, Worm, Writhe

**Wright** Smith

**Wring(er)** Drain, Extort, Mangle, Screw, Squeeze, Twist

**Wrinkle(d), Wrinkly** Clue, Cockle, Corrugate, Crankle, Crease, Crepy, Crimple, Crimpy, Crinkle, Crow's-foot, Crumple, Fold, Frounce, Frown, Frumple, Furrow, Gen, Groove,

Headline, Hint, Idea, Knit, Line, Lirk, Plissé, Plough, Pucker, Purse, Ridge, Rimple, Rivel, Rop(e)y, Ruck(le), Rugose, Rumple, Runkle, Seamy, Shrivel, Sulcus, Time-worn, Tip, Whelk, Wizened, Wrizled

**Wrist, Wristband** Carpus, Cuff, Radialia, Shackle-bone

**Writ(s)** Attachment, Audita querela, Capias, Certiorari, Cursitor, Dedimus, Devastatit, Distringas, Elegit, Fieri facias, Filacer, Habeas corpus, Holy, Injunction, Jury process, Latitat, Law-burrows, Mandamus, Mise, Mittimus, Noverint, Praemunire, Process, Quare impedit, Quo warranto, Replevin, Scirefacias, Significat, Subpoena, Summons, Supersedeas, Supplicavit, Tolt, Venire, Venire facias, Warrant

**Write(r), Writing** Allograph, Amphigory, Annotator, Apocrypha, → **AUTHOR**, Automatic, Balladist, Ballpoint, Belles lettres, Bellet(t)rist, BIC®, Biographer, Biro®, Blog, Bloomsbury Group, Book-hand, Boustrophedon, Calligraphy, Causerie, Cento, Chalk, Charactery, Clerk, Clinquant, Collectanea, Columnist, Continuity, Copperplate, Creative, Cuneiform, Cursive, Diarist, Dissertation, Dite, Draft, → **DRAMATIST**, Elohist, Endorse, Endoss, Engross, Enrol, Epigrammatise, Epistle, → **ESSAYIST**, Expatiate, Farceur, Festschrift, Feudist, Fine, Fist, Form, Formulary, Freelance, Ghost, Gnomist, Gongorism, Graffiti, Grammatology, Graphite, Graphology, Hack, Hairline, Hand, Haplography, Hieratic, Hieroglyphics, Hierology, Hiragana, Homiletics, Indite, Ink, Inkhorn-mate, Ink-jerker, Inkslinger, Inscribe, Join-hand, Jot(tings), Journalese, Journalist, Journo, Kaleyard School, Kana, Kanji, Katakana, Keelivine, Keelyvine, Leader, Leetspeak, Lexigraphy, Lexis, Linear A, Lipogram, Literary, Literature, Littérateur, Longhand, Lucubrate, Marivaudage, Memoirist, Mimographer, Minoan, Mirror, Miscellany, Monodist, Monograph, Ms(s), Neoteric(al), Nesk(h), Nib, Notary, Notate, Novelese, → **NOVELIST**, Obituarist, Palaeography, Pamphleteer, Paragraphia, Pasigraphy, Pen, Pencil, Penmanship, Penne, Penny-a-liner, Pentel®, Phrasemonger, Picture, Pinyin, Planchette, → **POET**, Polemic, Polygraphy, Pot-hook, Prosaist, Proser, Pseudepigrapha, Psychogram, Psychography, Purana, Purple patch, Quill, Rhymer, Roundhand, Runic, Samizdat, Sanskrit, Sastra, Satirist, Scenarist, Sci-fi, Scissorer, Score, Scratch, Scrawl, Screed, Screeve, Scribble, Scribe, Scrip(t), Scripture, Scrivener, Scrow, Scytale, Secretary, Shaster, Shastra, Sign, Sing, Slate, Sling-ink, Small-hand, Space, Spirit, Stenographer, Stichometry, Style, Stylist, Stylography, Subscript, Superscribe, Sutra, Syllabary, Syllabic, Syllabism, Syngraph, Synoptist, Tantra, Telegraphese, Text, Tractarian, Tragedian, Transcribe, Treatise, Tushery, Type, Uncial, Varityper®, Wisdom, Wordsmith, Zend-Avesta

---

## WRITERS

*3 letters:*
APH
Eco
Lee
Paz
Poe
RLS
Roy

*4 letters:*
Agee
Amis
Asch
Aymé
Bede
Behn
Bolt
Buck
Cary
Dahl
Elia
Gide
Grey
Hope
Hugo
Hunt
King
Lamb
Lang
Lear
Loos
Loti
Lyly
Mahy
Mann
More
Muir
Nash
Opie
Ovid
Pope
Roth
Rudd
Saki
Sand
Seth
Shaw
Snow
Ward
West
Zola

*5 letters:*
Acton
Adams
Aesop
Ahern
Aiken
Albee
Alger
Asher
Auden
Awdry
Ayres
Bacon
Bates
Benet
Blair
Blake
Byatt
Caine
Camus
Capek
Corvo
Crane
Crump
Dante
Defoe
Doyle
Dumas

Duras
Eliot
Ellis
Elton
Genet
Gogol
Gorki
Gorky
Gosse
Grass
Greer
Grimm
Hardy
Harte
Hecht
Hegel
Henry
Henty
Hesse
Heyer
Homer
Hoyle
Ibsen
Innes
James
Joyce
Kafka
Levin
Lewis
Lodge
Lorca
Marsh
Mason
Milne
Munro
Musil
Nashe
Niven
Orczy
Ouida
Paine
Pater
Paton
Pliny
Pound
Powys
Ramée
Reade
Renan
Rilke
Sagan
Scott
Segal
Seuss
Shute
Smith
Spark
Stark
Stead
Steel
Stein
Stowe
Svevo
Swift
Synge
Twain
Verne
Vidal
Walsh
Waugh
Wells
White
Wilde
Woolf
Yates
Yonge

***6 letters:***
Alcott
Ambler
Aragon
Archer
Arnold
Arnott
Artaud
Asimov
Atwood
Austen
Balzac
Baring
Barrie
Belloc
Bellow
Bierce
Binchy
Blyton
Borges
Borrow
Braine
Brontë
Bryson
Buchan
Bunyan
Butler
Capote
Cardus
Cather
Cicero
Clancy
Clarke
Conrad
Cooper
Cowper
Cronin
Darwin
Daudet
De Sade
Dexter
Dryden
Duggan
Engels
Ennius
Forbes
Fowles
France
Frisch
George
Gibbon
Goethe
Graves
Greene
Harris
Heller
Hobbes
Hoberg
Hornby
Hughes
Huxley
Jekyll
Jerome
Jonson
Keller
Le Fanu
Lennon
Le Sage
London
Lowell
Lucian
Ludlum
Lytton
Mailer
Malory
Mannin
Masoch
Mayhew
McEwan
Miller
Milton
Morgan
Morris
Nerval
Nesbit
O'Brien
Onions
Orwell
Powell
Proust
Racine
Rankin
Romaji
Runyon
Ruskin
Sapper
Sappho
Sartre
Sayers
Sendac
Seneca
Sewell
Singer
Smiles
Sontag
Spring
Steele
Sterne
Stoker
Storey
Stubbs
Tagore
Thiele
Thomas
Updike
Virgil
Walker
Walton
Wilder
Wright

***7 letters:***
Addison
Aldrich
Allende
Allston
Angelou
Aretino
Bagehot
Bagnold
Balchin
Baldwin
Ballard
Beckett
Bennett
Bentley
Blunden
Boileau
Boswell
Burgess
Burnett
Carlyle
Chaucer
Chekhov
Claudel
Cobbett
Cocteau

Coetzee
Colette
Collins
Cookson
Coppard
Corelli
Cranmer
Deeping
Dickens
Diderot
Dinesen
Dodgson
Douglas
Drabble
Dreiser
Duhamel
Durrell
Emerson
Fenelon
Feydeau
Fleming
Forster
Forsyth
Fuentes
Gardner
Gaskell
Gissing
Golding
Grahame
Grisham
Haggard
Hammett
Hazlitt
Hazzard
Herbert
Herriot
Hichens
Holberg
Johnson
Kerouac
Kipling
Lardner
Leacock
Le Carre
Lessing
Malamud
Mallory
Marryat
Maugham
Mauriac
Mérimée
Mitford
Molière
Moravia
Murdoch
Nabokov
Naipaul
Narayan
Osborne
Peacock
Pullman
Pushkin
Pynchon
Ransome
Rendell
Richter
Robbins
Rostand
Rowling
Rushdie
Saroyan
Sassoon
Shelley
Simenon
Sitwell
Spender
Surtees
Tennant
Terence
Theroux
Thoreau
Tolkien
Tolstoy
Travers
Tremain
Ustinov
Wallace
Walpole
Walters
Wharton
Whitman
Wyndham

***8 letters:***
Anacreon
Andersen
Beaumont
Beerbohm
Benjamin
Bernanos
Bradbury
Brittain
Brookner
Browning
Caldwell
Cartland
Chandler
Childers
Christie
Congreve
Constant
Cornwell
Crompton
Deighton
De la Mare
Disraeli
Donleavy
Faulkner
Fielding
Flaubert
Forester
Goncourt
Gordimer
Ishiguro
Jhabvala
Kingsley
Koestler
Langland
Lawrence
Lovelace
Mannheim
McCarthy
Melville
Meredith
Mitchell
Ondaatje
Perrault
Plutarch
Proudhon
Rabelais
Rattigan
Remarque
Rossetti
Rousseau
Salinger
Schiller
Shadbolt
Sheridan
Sherriff
Sherwood
Sillitoe
Smollett
Spillane
Stendhal
Strachey
Taffrail
Traherne
Trollope
Turgenev
Voltaire
Vonnegut
Williams
Xenophon

***9 letters:***
Aeschylus
Ainsworth
Aldington
Allingham
Blackmore
Boccaccio
Burroughs
Cervantes
Charteris
Corneille
Courtenay
De Quincey
Descartes
Dos Passos
Du Maurier
Edgeworth
Goldsmith
Hawthorne
Hemingway
Isherwood
La Bruyère
Lampedusa
Lermontov
Linklater
Lovecraft
Mackenzie
Madariaga
Mansfield
Martineau
Monsarrat
Montaigne
O'Flaherty
Oppenheim
Pasternak
Priestley
Santayana
Sholokhov
Sophocles
Steinbeck
Stevenson
Thackeray
Wodehouse

***10 letters:***
Ballantyne
Chesterton
De Beauvoir
Dostoevsky
Fitzgerald
Galsworthy
Mandeville
Maupassant
Pirandello
Richardson
Waterhouse
Williamson

***11 letters:***
Dostoyevsky

Machiavelli
Maeterlinck
Shakespeare

*12 letters:*
Aristophanes
De Maupassant
Quiller-Couch
Robbe-Grillet
Saint-Exupéry
Solzhenitsyn

*13 letters:*
Chateaubriand
Sackville-West

*14 letters:*
Compton-Burnett

*15 letters:*
Somerset Maugham

---

**Write-off** Amortise, Annul, Cancel, Scrap
**Writhe, Writhing** Athetosis, Contort, Curl, Scriggle, Snake, Squirm, Thraw, Twist, Wriggle
▷**Writhing** *may indicate* an anagram
**Writing-case** Kalamdan
**Writing-room** Scriptorium
**Wrong(ful), Wrongdoer, Wrongdoing** Aggrieve, Agley, Amiss, Astray, Awry, Bad, Bum, Chout, Defect, Delict, Disservice, Dysfunctional, Err, Fallacious, False, Falsism, Harm, Ill, Immoral, Improper, Incorrect, Injury, Injustice, Mischief, Misconduct, Misdeed, Misfaring, Misintelligence, Misled, Mistake(n), Misuse, Nocent, Not so, Offbase, Offend, Pear-shaped, Peccadillo, Perpetrator, Perverse, Private, Public, Sin(ful), Sinner, Tort, Tortious, Transgress, Unethical, Unright, Unsuitable, Withershins, Wryly, X
▷**Wrong** *may indicate* an anagram
**Wrong-headed** Perverse
**Wrong opinion** Cacodoxy
**Wrought (up)** Agitated, Beaten, Carved, Created, Excited, Filigree, Freestone, Shaped
**Wrung** Twisted, Withers
**Wry** Askew, Contrary, Devious, Distort, Droll, Grimace, Ironic
**Wryneck** Iynx, Jynx, Torticollis, Yunx
**Wycliffian** Lollard
**Wyoming** Wy

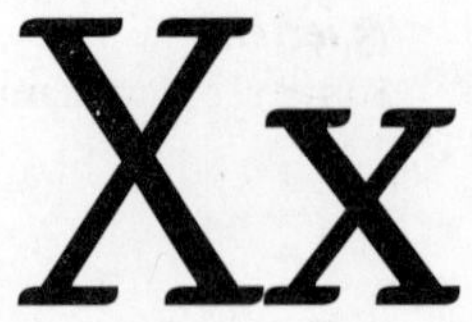

**X(-shaped)** Buss, By, Chi, Christ, Cross, Decussate, Drawn, Generation, Kiss, Ten, Times, Unknown, X-ray
**Xant(h)ippe** Battle-axe, Dragon
**Xenon** Xe
**Xenophobia** Insularism
**Xerophyte, Xerophytic** Cactus, Cereus, Mesquite, Tamaricaceae, Tamarisk
**Ximenes** Cardinal
▸**Xmas** *see* CHRISTMAS(TIME)
**X-ray** Angiogram, Anticathode, Arthrogram, Characteristic, Cholangiography, C(A)T-scanner, Emi-Scanner, Encephalogram, Encephalograph, Fermi, Grenz, Mammogram, Plate, Pyelogram, Radiogram, Radiology, Radioscopy, Rem, Roentgen, Sciagram, Screening, Sigmatron, Skiagram, Skiagraph, Tomography, Venogram, X, Xeroradiography
**Xylophone** Marimba, Semantra, Sticcado, Sticcato

# Yy

**Y** Samian, Unknown, Yankee, Yard, Year, Yen, Yttrium
**Yabber** Convo
**Yacht(s), Yachting** Britannia, Cowes, Dragon, Ice, Keelboat, Ketch, Knockabout, Land, Maxi, Sailboat, Sand, Scow, Yngling
**Yachtsman, Yachtsmen** Chichester, Heath, RYS
**Yak** Gup, Natter, Talk
**Yale®** Key, Lock
**Yam** Adjigo, Batata, Breadroot, Camote, Dioscorea, Diosgenin, Kumara
**Yank(ee)** Bet, Carpetbagger, Hitch, Jerk, Jonathan, Lug, Northerner, Pluck, Pull, Rug, Schlep(p), So(o)le, Sowl(e), → TUG, Tweak, Twitch, Wrench, Wrest, Y
▷**Yank** *may indicate* an anagram
**Yap** Bark, Nyaff, Yelp, Yicker
**Yard(s)** Area, Church, CID, Close, Court, Exercise, Farm-toun, Garden, Hard, Haw, Hof, Junk, Kail, Knacker's, Lay, Lumber, Main, Marshalling, Mast, Measure, Met, Mews, Navy, Patio, Poultry, Prison, Ree(d), Sail, Scotland, Show, Spar, Sprit, Steel, Stick, Stockyard, Stride, Switch, Tilt, Timber, Victualling, Y, Yd, Y-track
**Yardstick** Precedent
**Yarn(s)** Abb, Anecdote, Berlin, Bouclé, Caddice, Caddis, Chenille, Clew, Clue, Cop, Cord, Crewel, Fib, Fibroline, Fingering, Genappe, Gimp, Gingham, Guimp(e), Gymp, Homespun, Jaw, Knittle, Knot, Lay, Lea, Ley, Line, Lisle, Lurex®, Marl, Merino, Mohair, Nylon, Organzine, Orlon®, Ply, Rigmarole, Ripping, Rogue's, Rope, Saxony, Schappe, Sennit, Sinnet, Skein, Small stuff, Spun, Story, Strand, Tale, Taradiddle, Thread, Thrid, Thrum(my), Tram, Twice-laid, Warp, Water twist, Weft, Woof, Wool, Worsted, Zephyr
**Yarrow** Milfoil
**Yashmak** Veil
**Yaw(s)** Boba, Buba, Button-scurvy, Crab, Deviate, Framboesia, Lean, Morula, Tack, Veer
**Yawn(ing)** Agape, Boredom, Chasmy, Fissure, Gant, Gape, Gaunt, Greys, Hiant, Oscitation, Pandiculation, Rictus, Wide open
**Yea** Certainly, Surely, Truly, Verily, Yes
**Year(ly), Years** A, Age, Anno, Annual, Anomalistic, Astronomical, AUC, Autumn, Calendar, Canicular, Civil, Common, Cosmic, Decennium, Donkey's, Dot, Ecclesiastical, Egyptian, Embolismic, Equinoctial, Financial, Fiscal, Gap, Grade, Great, Hebrew, Holy, Indiction, Julian, Leap, Legal, Light, Locust, Lunar, Lunisolar, Man, Natural, PA, Perfect, Platonic, Prophetic week, Riper, Sabbatical, School, Sidereal, Solar, Sothic, Spring, Summer, Sun, Tax, Theban, Thousand, Time, Towmon(d), Towmont, Tropical, Twelvemonth, Vintage, Wander(jahr), Winter, Zodiac
**Yearbook** Almanac, Annual
**Yearling** Colt, Hogget, Stirk, Teg
**Yearn(ing)** Ache, Ake, Aspire, Brame, Burn, Covet, Crave, Curdle, Desire, Erne, Greed, Green, Grein, Hanker, Hone, Itch, → LONG, Lust, Nostalgia, Nympholepsy, Pant, Pine, Sigh, Wistful
▷**Yearning** *may indicate* an anagram
**Year's end** Dec
**Yeast** Barm, Bees, Brewer's, Ferment, Flor, Leaven, Saccharomycete, Torula, Vegemite®
**Yell** Bawl, Cry, Hue, Rant, Rebel, Screech, Shout, Shriek, Skelloch, Squall, Thunder, Tiger, Ululate, Waul, Yoick

**Yellow(ish)** Abram, Amber, Anthoclore, Auburn, Back, Beige, Bisque, Bistre, Buff, Butternut, Cadmium, Canary, Champagne, Chartreuse, Chicken, Chrome, Citrine, Clay-bank, Cowardly, Craven, Curcumin(e), Daffadowndilly, Daffodil, Ecru, Eggshell, Etiolin, Fallow, Fever, Filemot, Flavescent, Flavin(e), Flavon, Flaxen, Fulvous, Gamboge, Gaudy-green, Gold, Icteric, Isabel(le), Isabella, Jack, Jaundiced, King's, Lammer, Lemon(y), Lupulin, Lurid, Lutein, Luteous, Lutescent, Maize, Mustard, Nankeen, Naples, Oaker, Ochery, Ochre(y), Ochroid, Off-white, Or(eide), Oroide, Pages, Peach, Peril, Pink, Primrose, Queen's, River, Saffron, Sallow, Sand, Sear, Sherry, Spineless, Strae, Straw, Sulfur, Sulphur, Tawny, Topaz, Tow, Turmeric, Unheroic, Vitelline, Weld, Xanthous, Yolk
**Yellowhammer** Bunting, Yeldring, Yeldrock, Yite, Yoldring
**Yellow-wood** Gopher
**Yelp** Cry, Squeal, Whee, Ya(w)p
**Yemeni** Adeni, Saba, Sabean, Sheba
**Yen** Desire, Itch, Longing, Urge, Y, Yearn
**Yeoman** Beefeater, Exon, Farmer, Goodman, Goodwife, Salvation
**Yep** OK, Yes
**Yerd** Inter
**Yes** Agreed, Ay(e), Da, I, Indeed, Ja, Jokol, Nod, OK, Oke, Quite, Sure, Truly, Uh-huh, Whoopee, Wilco, Yah, Yea, Yokul, Yup
**Yesman** Crawler
**Yesterday** Démodé, Eve, Hesternal, Pridian
**Yet** But, Even, How-be, Moreover, Nay, Nevertheless, Now, Still, Though
**Yeti** Abominable snowman, Sasquatch
**Yew** Podocarp(us), Taxus, Yvonne
**Yibbles** A(i)blins
**Yield(ing), Yielded** Abandon, Afford, Bear, Bend, Bow, Breed, Capitulate, Catch, Cave in, Cede, Come, Comply, Concede, Crack, Crop, Defer, Dividend, Docile, Ductile, Easy, Elastic, Exert, Facile, Flaccid, Flexible, Foison, Give, Harvest, Interest, Knock under, Knuckle, Knuckle under, Meek, Meltith, Mess, Obedient, Obey, Obtemper, Output, Pan, Passive, Pay, Pliant, Produce, Quantum, Redemption, Relent, Render, Return, Sag, Soft, Spawn, Squashy, →**SUBMIT**, Succumb, Supple, Surrender, Susceptible, Sustained, Temporise, Tolerant, Truckle, Weak-kneed, Yold
**Yob(bo)** Hoon, Lager lout, Lout, Oaf, Oik, Ted
**Yodel** Song, Warble
**Yoga, Yogi** Asana, As(h)tanga (vinyasa), Bear, Bhakti, Bikram, Fakir, Hatha, Hot, Maha, Power, Raja, Sid(d)ha, Sivananda
**Yog(h)urt** Dahi, Madzoon, Matzoon, Raita, Tzatziki
**Yoke** Bow, Cang(ue), Collar, Couple, Harness, Inspan, Jugal, Oxbow, Pair, Span, Square, Tucker
**Yokel** Boor, Bumpkin, Chaw(-bacon), Clumperton, Culchie, Hayseed, Hick, Jake, Jock, Joskin, Peasant, Rube, Rustic
**Yolk(ed)** Azygous, Isolecithal, Meroistic, Parablast, Vitellicle, Vitelline, Vitellus, Yelk, Yellow
**Yon(der)** Distant, Further, O'erby, Thae, There, Thether, Thither
**Yonks** Years
**Yore** Agone, Olden, Past
**Yorick** Sterne
**York(shire), Yorkshireman** Batter, Bowl, Dales, Ebor, Pudding, Ridings, See, Tyke, White rose
**Yorker** Tice
**You** One, Second person, Sie, Thee, Thou, Usted, Wena, Ye
**Young (person), Youngster, Youth(ful)** Adolescent, Ageless, Amorino, Bairn, Bev(an), Bit, Bodgie, Boy, Boyhood, Brigham, Bub, Buckeen, Buckie, Buppie, Calf-time, Ch, Charver, Chick, Chicken, Chiel, Child, Chile, Cion, Cock(erel), Cockle, Colt, Comsomol, Cornstalk, Cub, Damsel, Day-old, Dell, Dilling, DJ, Early, Ephebe, Ephebus, Esquire, Flapper, Fledgling, Foetus, Fox, Fresh, Fry, Ganymede, Gigolo, Gilded, Gillet, Girl, Gunsel, Halfling, Hebe, Hobbledehoy, Immature, Imp, Infant, Issue, Jeunesse d'orée, Junior, Juvenal, Juvenesce,

Juvenile, Keral, Kid, Kiddo, Kiddy, Kipper, Knave-bairn, Komsomol, Lad, Lamb, Latter-day, Leaping-time, Less, Litter, Little, Loretta, Middle, Minor, Misspent, Mod, Mormon, Mot, Muchacha, Nance, Narcissus, Neanic, Ned(ette), Neophyte, Nestling, New, New Romantic, Nipper, Nonage, Nurs(e)ling, Nymph, Plant, Popsy, Poult, (Pre-)pubescent, Pre-teen, Progeny, Protégé(e), Punk, Pup, Rude boy, Salad days, Sapling, Scent, Scion, Screenager, Shaveling, Shaver, Sien(t), Skinhead, Slip, Small, Son, Spark, Spawn, Spide, Sprig, Springal(d), Stripling, Subteen, Swain, Syen, Ted, Teenager, Teens, Teenybopper, Tir na n'Og, Tit, Tot, Toyboy, Tyke, Vernal, Waif, Well-preserved, Whelp, Whippersnapper, Widge, Wigga, Wigger, Wimp, Yippy, Yoof, Yopper, Young gun, Younker, Yukon, Yumpie, Yuppie

**Younger, Youngest** Baby, Benjamin, Cadet, Last born, Less, Minimus, Seneca, Wallydrag, Wallydraigle, Yr

**Your(s)** Thee, Thine, Thy

▸**Youth** *see* YOUNG (PERSON)

**Yo-yo** Bandalore

**Ytterbium** Yb

**Yttrium** Y

**Yucatan** Maya

**Yucca** Adam's needle, Joshua tree

**Yuck(y)** Glairy, Gooey, Grooly, Gross, Sickly, Sticky

**Yugoslav** Croat(ian), Serb, Slovene, Ustashi

**Yukon** YT

**Yuletide** Advent, Dec, Noel, Xmas

**Yummy** Delish, Gorgeous

# Zz

**Z** Izzard, Izzet, Zambia, Zebra
**Zambia** .zm
**Zamenhof** Esperanto
**Zander** Fogash, Sander
**Zany** Barmy, Bor(r)el, Comic, Cuckoo, Idiotic, Mad, Offbeat, Pythonesque, Wacky
**Zanzibar** EAZ, Swahili
**Zap, Zapper** Control, Nuke, Obliterate, Remote (control)
**Zeal(ous)** Ardour, Bigotry, Devotion, Eager, Earnest, Enthusiasm, Evangelic, Fanatical, Fanaticism, Fervour, Fire, Gungho, Gusto, Hamas, Happy-clappy, Heat, Perfervid, Rabid, Study, Zest
**Zealot** Bigot, Crusader, Devotee, Essene, Extremist, Fan(atic), St Simon, Votary
**Zebra** Convict, Quagga, Z, Zeal
**Zebu** Brahmin bull, Brahmin cow
**Zenith** Acme, Apogee, Height, Peak, Pole, Summit, Vertex
**Zeno** Colonnade, Elea, Stoic
**Zeolite** Analcime, Analcite, Gmelinite, Mesolite
**Zephyr** Breeze, Wind
**Zeppelin** Airship, Balloon, Dirigible, Led
**Zero** Absolute, Blob, Cipher, Circle, Donut, Double, Duck, Ground, Nil, Nilpotent, None, Nothing, Nought, O, Ought, Status, Year, Z, Zoom
**Zest** Brio, Condiment, Crave, Élan, Enthusiasm, Esprit, Gusto, Peel, Pep, Piquancy, Relish, Spark, Spice, Tang, Taste, Zap, Zing
**Zeus** Titan
**Ziegfeld** Flo
**Zigzag** Crémaillère, Crinkle-crankle, Criss-cross, Dancette, Feather-stitch, Indent, Major Mitchell, Meander, Pink, Ric-rac, Slalom, Stagger, Switchback, Tack, Traverse, Vandyke, Yaw
**Zillah** Pargana
**Zimbabwe** -.zw
**Zinc** Blende, Gahnite, Mossy, Sherardise, Spelter, Sphalerite, Tutenag, Tutty, Willemite, Wurtzite, Zn
**Zip(per)** Dart, Dash, Energy, Fastener, Fly, Go, Nada, Nil, O, Oomph, Pep, Presto, Slide fastener, Stingo, Verve, Vim, Vivacity, Whirry, Zero, Zilch
**Zircon** Hyacinth, Jacinth, Jargo(o)n
**Zirconium** Baddeleyite, Zr
**Zither** Autoharp, Cithara, Kantela, Kantele, Koto
**Zodiac(al)** Aquarius, Archer, Aries, Bull, Cancer, Capricorn, Counter-glow, Crab, Fish, Gegenschein, Gemini, Goat, Horoscope, Leo, Libra, Lion, Ophiuchus, Pisces, Ram, Sagittarius, Scales, Scorpio(n), Taurus, Trigon, Twins, Virgin, Virgo, Watercarrier
**Zola** Budd, Emile, Nana, Realism
**Zombie** Catatonic, Dolt, Robot, Undead
**Zone(s)** Abyssal, Aerospace, Anacoustic, Area, Arid, Auroral, Band, Bathyal, Belt, Benioff, Buffer, Canal, Climate, Collision, Comfort, Convergence, Crumple, Dead, Demilitarized, District, Drop, Economic, Ecotone, End, Enterprise, Erogenous, Eruv, Euro, Exclusion, Exclusive, F layer, Fracture, Free(-fire), Fresnel, Frigid, Hadal, Home, Hot, Impact, Ionopause, Krumhole, Low velocity, Mix, Neutral, No-fly, Nuclear-free, Precinct, →REGION, Rift, Ring, Russian, Sahel, Saturation, Schlieren, Sector, Shear, Skip, Smokeless, Soviet, Stratopause,

Strike, Subduction, T, Taiga, Temperate, Time, Tolerance, Torrid, Tropic, Tundra, Twilight, Vadose, Z

**Zoo** Bedlam, Circus, Menagerie, Vivarium, Whipsnade

**Zoolite** Harmotome

**Zoologist, Zoology** Biologist, Botanist, Cetology, Leisler, Lorenz, Naturalist, Primatology, Schneider

**Zoom** Close-up, Soar, Speed

**Zoroastrian** Avestan, Fire-worshipper, Gabar, Gheber, Ghebre, Gueber, Guebre, Magus, Mazdaist, Mazdean, Ormazd, Ormuzd, Parsee, Parsi

**Zounds** Egad

**Zucchini** Courgette

**Zulu** Chaka, Impi, Inkatha, Inkisi, Matabele, Niger, Shaka, Warrior, Z

**Zut** Crimini

**Zygote** Oospore